Historical
Information
Science

Historical Information Science

An Emerging Unidiscipline

Lawrence J. McCrank

Information Today, Inc.

Medford, New Jersey

First printing, 2002

Historical Information Science: An Emerging Unidiscipline

Copyright © 2001 by Lawrence J. McCrank

Publisher's Note: The author and publisher have taken care in preparation of this book but make no expressed or implied warranty of any kind and assume no responsibility for errors or omissions. No liability is assumed for incidental or consequential damages in connection with or arising out of the use of the information or programs contained herein.

Many of the designations used by manufacturers and sellers to distinguish their products are claimed as trademarks. Where those designations appear in this book and Information Today, Inc. was aware of a trademark claim, the designations have been printed with initial capital letters.

Library of Congress Cataloging-in-Publication Data

McCrank, Lawrence J.
   Historical information science : an emerging unidiscipline / Lawrence J. McCrank.
     p. cm.
   Includes bibliographical references and index.
   ISBN 1-57387-071-4
     1. History—Research. 2. Historiography—Methodology. 3. Electronic records. 4. History—Computer network resources. 5. Internet (Computer network) 6. Information technology—History. I. Title.

     D16.2+
     020--dc21

                                       00-037008

Printed and bound in the United States of America.

Publisher: Thomas H. Hogan, Sr.
Editor-in-Chief: John B. Bryans
Managing Editor: Deborah R. Poulson
Copy Editor: Diane Zelley
Production Manager: M. Heide Dengler
Cover Designer: Jeremy M. Pellegrin
Book Designers: Jeremy M. Pellegrin and Kara Mia Jalkowski
Subject Indexer: Lawrence J. McCrank
Author Name Indexer: Sharon Hughes

to
Eric H. Boehm,
Ph.D., D. Litt. (h.c.)

———•——

historian, bibliographer, information scientist,
and
entrepreneur;
founder of both the American Bibliographic Center and
Clio Press (ABC-CLIO, Inc.),
publisher of *Historical Abstracts* and *America: History and Life*,
and of the International School of Information Management.

In appreciation for
a half-century of contributions to the bibliography
of historical studies and to information management.

Table of Contents

Preface

This bibliographic essay addresses the merging of once separate subject domains in relation to converging technologies and cross-disciplinary research in History *per se* and history embedded in cognate fields. It argues for:

1. a post-Postmodern historical method which addresses the truth-claim in History with a realistic sense of objectivity that admits to reconstruction and embraces an interaction between past and present, but distinguishes history from fiction; and

2. a vastly enhanced Information Science component and adroit use of modern information technology in History.

It suggests that trends in information retrieval, research, and teaching using modern information technology point toward a unidisciplinary field, Historical Information Science, which potentially can grow out of older quantification and Social Science history, the interplay between History and Information Science, and new methodologies and multimedia technology that merge visual, audio, textual, and data sources in the study of the past.

Major trends are delineated over a little more than a decade from circa 1984, after widespread personal computing began to accelerate change in work habits, by surveying the automated bibliographic control over historiographic literatures and archival control over primary sources; interdisciplinary methodological discussions; research and instructional projects in History that employ databases, image and textual, and use Social Science research methods and linguistic analysis; and those developments that employ computer technology, consider appropriate applications of technology, use telecommunications, and try new multimedia to inform, teach, and advance research. Emphasis has been on developments since the mid-1980s, when the impact of personal computing, frame relays and packet switching for efficient telecommunications and growth in networking, increased retrospective conversion of sources into digital form, production of current documentation electronically, and growth of electronic archives and libraries came into play. Problems posed to History by the new technology, especially regarding the nature of historical evidence, interpretation, and presentation, are discussed. Achieving a super-informed history with methodologies to master the vastness of accumulated information for historical synthesis and interpretation requires a veritable revolution in conceptualization from historiography that mines fragmentary and incomplete sources to one that addresses the richness syndrome of mass of data beyond current capabilities to control, analyze, or comprehend.

Educational reform is called for both in teaching history and in training professional historians in graduate programs. It is recommended that a hybrid field of study be recognized, Historical Information Science, which integrates equally the subject matter of a historical field of investigation, quantified Social Science and linguistic research methodologies, computer science and technology, and information science, which is focused on historical information sources, structures, and communications. An extensive bibliography is supplied as a backdrop to the discussion and for further reading. While not an exhaustive bibliographic survey, the works cited constitute concrete examples of the broad trends discussed, illustrate the rich secondary sources available for curricular innovation, and provide the ingredients for the synthesis attempted.

The Files
(The Sub-editor Speaks)

Files—
     The Files—
Office files!

Oblige me by referring to the Files.
Every question man can raise,
Every phrase of every phase
Of that question is on record in the Files—
(Threshed out threadbare—
    fought and finished in the Files)....

Warn all coming
    Robert Brownings and Caryles,
It will interest them to hunt among the
    Files,
Where unvisited, a-cold,
Lie the crowded years of old
In that Kensall-Green of greatness called
    the Files....
Where the dead men lay them down
Meekly sure of long renown,
And above them, sere and swift,
Packs the daily deepening drift
Of the all-recording, all-effacing Files—
The obliterating, automatic Files.

Count the mighty men who slung
Ink, Evangels, Sword or Tongue
When Reform and you were young—
Made their boasts and spake according in
    the Files—
(Hear the ghosts that wake applauding in
    the Files!)

Trace each all-forgot career
From long primer through brevier
Unto Death, a para minion in the Files
(para minion—solid—bottom of the Files)....
Some successful Kings and Queens adorn
    the Files

They were great, their views were leaded,
And their Deaths were triple-headed,
So they catch the eye in running through
    the Files.
For their "paramours and priests,"
And their gross, jack-booted feasts,
And their "epoch-marking actions" see
    the Files....

Who remembers...?
Only sextons paid to dig among the Files
(Such as I am, born and bred among
    the Files).
You must hack through much deposit
Ere you know for sure who was it
Came to burial with such honour in the
    Files.

...It is good to read a little in the Files;
'Tis a sure and sovereign balm
Unto philosophic calm,
Yea, and philosophic doubt when Life
    beguiles.
When the Conchimarian horns
Of the reboantic Norms
Usher gentlemen and ladies
With new lights on Heaven and Hades,
Guaranteeing to Eternity
All yesterday's modernity;...

Light your pipe and take a look along
    the Files
You've a better change to guess
At the meaning of Success....
When you've seen it in perspective in
    the Files.

Rudyard Kipling,
1903

Introduction

The genesis of this project dates to the very early 1970s, when my initial exploration in computing to create intellectual access to historical sources began. Its seminal notions began to take shape when teaching as a historian in a graduate School of Library and Information Science while the field of Information Science was evolving rapidly. Since then, some ideas emerged or were strengthened by personal observation and experience while reforming information services in libraries and archives, coping with the frustrations of working with unstable information technologies, lack of clear vision at the highest levels about how such changes would affect higher education, and a pervasive need for faculty and staff development to keep abreast of new technology, methodology, and information (increased mass and greater variety of formats and media). Such frustrations were often most heightened by the historians with whom I worked, since most had little liking for or much competence in Information Science (IS) or Information Technology (IT), but I understood some of the disadvantages under which they have worked and could appreciate the differences in organizational and disciplinary cultures. In ways not as common in information technology environments, historians have always seemed to balance any critical reactions with stimulating introspection, thought provocation, and interesting dialogue in addition to friendship and professional support. I had wondered how such interesting, intellectual, and well-meaning academicians could be so removed from the reality of where information technology, modern communications, and the transition to electronic records were taking History with the rest of academe and the world. How could people of such character, intelligence, learning, and positions of influence be so resistant to information technology? Could they not see the opportunities offered by the wonderful technical advances of our own time? Or was it that I was not prone to see the disadvantages, problems, and challenges created by the onslaught of modern information technology, chaotic and poorly managed as so many of these changes have been? Any tendency to become hypercritical of historians and my colleagues in the Arts and Humanities, or Social Sciences where computing spread more rapidly, was counterbalanced by my wondering about the lack of contextual knowledge, historical sensibility, and social or interpersonal skills by those technical wizards with whom I worked. I have always been struck by the cognitive and behavioral differences between the traditional academic disciplines and classroom faculty and the new information and technical professions which work in less confined environments. I learned to appreciate the bridge between the two provided by librarianship and its relations in archives and museums. The ambiguity of the latter positions, an interdisciplinary niche, is a strength.

My views became more sanguine as I advanced to academic administration in the information profession and became responsible and accountable for large, complex organizations with multimillion-dollar budgets, where effectiveness, character, and culture could so pervasively affect the success of the institutions I served. My purview became less concentrated in history and focused more on History and the organizational and programmatic development of the disciplines I served. My understanding of organizational, cultural, and motivational problems in academe provided context for addressing Information Technology (IT), Information Systems and Services (ISS), and Information Resource Management (IRM) in the environments of archives, museums, libraries, and universities. These have evolved as disciplines in my life, in ways I could not have imagined at one time. These disciplines were problematic as well, but could not be confronted *in vacuo* successfully.

My training as a historian had been largely content oriented but had included a broad range of teaching in a variety of situations. For reasons that will become clear in this work, I must acknowledge an indebtedness to an academic pedigree that transferred to me certain attitudes about History, and about medieval history in particular, from my mentor for my doctorate at the University of Virginia, Charles J. Bishko, who in turn was indebted to Charles Homer Haskins during the latter's last years at Harvard. I am unabashedly an intellectual heir thereby to a progressive tradition rooted in scientific historicism at the turn of the century, with its taint of positivism, a certain idealism mixed with rationalism, and the conviction that all history is relevant to the present regardless of its place or time. To paraphrase HASKINS (1923, p. 215), all histories are ultimately but one. In this last idea, a holistic sense of humanity and a world view, lies sublime spirituality encompassed by my Christian faith imbued with Catholic ecumenism. I acknowledge these formative and pervasive influences on my current thought. The limitation of it all is not in its making, reality, or conceptualization, but in its perception, piecemeal viewing, and our incremental understanding—or so I have always supposed.

My training as an archivist was built upon this education as a medievalist and early modern historian, with formal training in diplomatics, paleography, languages, and linguistics. But my American archives and modern records management training at the University of Oregon and National Archives Institute was recent and contemporary in focus, as well as pragmatic, procedural and organizational, which balanced the former exposure to source criticism and concentration on origins, foundations, and remote history. My service orientation from librarianship remains influential; and while my exposure to Information Science (IS) has been largely Information Resources Management (IRM)-oriented, I was immersed at the University of Maryland and the Baltimore-Washington, D.C. corridor in some of the best European, Canadian, and American thinking in the 1970s about information storage and retrieval, systems development, user behavioral, and Information Science at the time of its very formation. I witnessed a dramatic shift toward understanding user perspectives in order to make our information organizations and delivery services more responsive to human behaviors and cognitive abilities. All of these influences have tempered my natural inclination to understand the world about me only through my eyes and direct experience. As a historian, I knew better. I had little practice as a futurologist, although actually a History degree is somewhat of a credential in that arena because it provided perspective on where I had been. I did have a strong reaction to the *status quo*, a distrust of fads but an enthusiasm for change, and I had fortunately been given a disciplined, rigorous education. In keeping with the French historian autobiographic mode of *ego-histoire*, but perhaps more in the spirit of John Henry Cardinal Newman's *Apologia pro vita sua*—not an apology where forgiveness is required, but some explanation in the classic sense of the term—it seems appropriate to divulge the genesis of this current work. Hence this extended introduction. These reflections are prolegomena in the rhetorical tradition as exemplified by Walter J. Ong's *The Presence of the Word*, an essay that left a lasting impression on me. But in contemporary street language, the idea is: Do you know where I am coming from?

From this vantage point of a historian with Information Science in the information profession milieu, with more awareness of what should not be continued than a sure understanding of what needed to be done, I ventured into graduate and professional studies curricular reform in 1976, by implementing the HIstory-Library Science (HILS) joint-graduate program (MA + MLS) at the University of Maryland. This has been judged by my successor there and longtime colleague, Fred Stielow, as "a major event in archival education" (STIELOW, 1993, p. 57). He credits me with some serious innovation in curricular development and redirection of research agenda in archival science in the 1970s and 1980s—one is always thankful for such notice when for the most part such efforts have slow impact on a profession at large. Moreover, credit for an original idea or contribution, once it is diffused to a general population as in a profession, is seldom traced to an originator. At the time, however, course work at UMCP was genuinely innovative and it advanced specialization a full decade ahead of any competing graduate program in the United States. Stielow recalls my early penchant for interdisciplinarity and my advocation in 1979 of fusing historical studies that had a strong component of quantification into a new hybrid with library and information science to create a new kind of archivist different from those before the 1970s (STIELOW, 1993 p. 64, n. 22). Half of these archivists lacked any formal training in the field other than what they were told by historians and picked up by apprenticeship in or as users of archives (EVANS & WARNER, p. 169). He is somewhat misleading in stating I "was not an experienced archivist" nor "originally an automation specialist," although I had not earned my living as a *bona fide* archivist. Few historians have. I had at least completed my internship with modern records and had gained ample archival experience with historical records as a researcher in multiple archives in the United States and in Spain, and I could bring to bear on Archival Science multiple languages and text criticism plus formal training in paleography and diplomatics, codicology and analytic bibliography, and historical research methods. When I reflect upon the matter, these interests can be traced back to several years of state competition in debate and declamation in high school taught by an exemplary teacher, Lenora Johnson or Mrs. "J." as everyone called her. She was a historian and mathematician who saw no conflict between the two, but instead saw logic as a link between them. I recall also my being led into research using microfilmed primary materials as an undergraduate History major at the command of caring, gifted teachers, and especially the influence of Professor John Smurr, a Toynbee enthusiast, who introduced us to global, world history long before it came into vogue.

On the other hand, my exposure to early information technology was largely accidental. My extracurricular work had introduced me to online information systems and office automation. My exposure to online information retrieval working with the pioneering *HOLIDEX* systems as an auditor for a large Holiday Inn franchise, while I put myself through graduate school, was an education then not provided by any History Department or archival education program. As a result, for the time, I was more experienced and better trained than most of my colleagues. When I completed an MLS after my doctorate in History, the Library Science faculties in pre-MARC days were just beginning to explore automation, standardization of electronic records, and the potential of computing. In those days, one had little choice in being self-made if one wanted to engage computing. There were few real mentors, but several experimenters, and all who innovate, experiment, and reform face considerable professional risk. To learn more about the information profession, information technology, and unconventional approaches, I could not turn to most historians for assistance. They were not the change agents I needed when I became convinced that information technology was already altering the world in which we lived in fundamental and lasting ways.

From 1975 on I engaged in computerized cataloging, indexing, and thesaurus work and confronted issues of intellectual access to historical manuscripts and rare books, when few in the field even understood what I was attempting—or even cared. I became acutely aware of how much History depends on information access and retrieval over time, and how historical reconstruction is conditioned by its information search methods, their efficiency and sufficiency, and the documentation assembled for research; the importance of metadata and description in documentation; the critical need to preserve context with text; and the difference between information and evidence which entails authentification, verification, and continual documentation of process and transmission as fundamental to source criticism and interpretation. When text processing technology was so primitive, it was a bold vision to attempt codicological formatting of medieval manuscript descriptions in electronic description buried like hyperlinked tables into catalog entries. The very idea of a "textual database" at the time was novel, as GOLDFARB *ET AL.* (p. 657) now recall, when key-punching machines from the 1970s were uppercase only and newer means of direct data input were less mechanical but not much more sophisticated. The IBM mainframe-based software used, *DPS* (*Document*

Processing System), required that all codes be entered with text. Very little was genuinely automatic in those days.

The published Mt. Angel Abbey pilot project begun in the mid-1970s (MCCRANK, 1982, 1983) was reviewed only from the traditional historical angles, without a single reviewer understanding that the entire work was computerized, including the actual book production which used technologies such as *DPS*, batch processing, and paper-tape communications between the CPU and a photocompositor or Linotron for camera-ready printing—all of which today seems ridiculously primitive. Access to the pilot catalog project was limited because the publisher never arranged for prepublication cataloging of the fiche catalog separately from the text or a separate ISBN identifier, so it still lacks a Library of Congress record even though other library's catalogers (e.g., University of Michigan) cataloged the Mt. Angel catalog in MARC and subsequently entered it into OCLC. The thinking at Scholarly Resources Inc. was still to consider text processing as simply an electronic mode of book production rather than database publishing. In fact, the book and fiche catalog were byproducts of an electronic experiment.

Remember when this work was undertaken. Regarding textbases, J. D. MASON (p. 593) recently referred to anything before 1986 when Standardized General Markup Language (SGML) was being formalized, as being in the computing "dark ages." I did not understand then how cutting edge some of my efforts were, but I can reflect now, with the benefit of hindsight, about why this experimental project was so little understood. The catalog's tag structures adopted were pre-MARC, so few people were then thinking about tagging electronic records components for an overall document architecture that allowed for the manipulation of data elements for information retrieval, report generation, or pre-coordinated indexing. The descriptive cataloging of the rare books was relatively simple, but the codicological layout of medieval manuscripts, as recommended by the art historian L. M. J. Delaissé, was creative data processing and phototypesetting for its day. It brought G. OUY's wishful thinking in the late 1970s about computer access to medieval manuscripts one step closer to reality. The experimental merging of thesauri and rotational indexing was innovative and exploratory. Main author entry normalization invoked standardization that was just coming into vogue but which was not yet common in the Humanities. The modification of early text processing programs for foreign languages was necessarily a *vade mecum* because no off-the-shelf packages existed; the project's costing offered one of the first models for retrospective conversion in rare book cataloging before the latter term even came into widespread use (MCCRANK, 1983), a decade before standards emerged to catalog rare books electronically (H. MAYO), and nearly two decades before Electronic Archival Description (EAD).

Alas, the problem of intradisciplinary reviewing interdisciplinary work is rather typical, as my colleague Richard Cox points out in the example of reviewing documentary editions always as histories rather than as archives. Unfortunately, the Mt. Angel project's implications for the issues of deployment of such information technology for the Humanities in general, and History in particular, were not well understood in such intradisciplinary reviewing, and cross-disciplinary reviews were then, and still are, uncommon. Perceptions then commonly divorced the Humanities from computing and information scientists were then not very interested in the Arts and Humanities: New technological efforts were judged by old standards, historians were paying little attention to computerization except for quantified analyses, and nascent Information Science was antagonistic with any attachment to historical bibliography and History itself. Although this experimental project never had the impact I would have liked, it was overtaken by larger trends in the same direction. I was always thankful to be a participant in early automation efforts, and especially in the important role as educator. However, here too disappointments curbed unbridled enthusiasm. Although I was rewarded immediately from positive impact on my students who provided direct feedback, and on the profession through them, my influence on the larger agenda of reformed curricula, archival research, and electronic access to rare books and manuscripts was unfortunately never so immediate or direct. *C'est la vie.*

Richard Cox, like Fred Stielow at about the same time, recalled that I had argued for inter-disciplinarity, had taught that way, and had introduced information technology, electronic records, etc., into the HILS curriculum and to the profession in a series of essays (MCCRANK, 1979, 1981, 1985, etc.), "but they generally have been overlooked by the American Archival profession, at least as regards any practical implementation" (R. COX, 1994a, p. 3). Elsewhere COX (p. 19) commends me for a "perspective [that] is unique and useful, and he [myself] has often been somewhat ahead of many of us in his ideas and practices." I suspect that some of the ideas expressed in this essay may also be taken the same way, as somewhat ahead of the times. Yet the extensive citations throughout, the bibliography provided, and the commentary itself, show that I am observing contemporary phenomena around me everywhere, not highly theoretical and isolated rarities; my focus is on overriding trends, not the occasionally insight-ful and inspiring breakthrough. I hope that my observations are not really "ahead," because if so, too many are too far behind. Instead, I had envisioned this essay as a synthetic overview, allowing a review of what has been transpiring to act as a preview of more to come.

I was pleased as well when Anne Kenney in her accolade at the 1995 Society of American Archivists conference in Washington, D.C., when I was elected an SAA Fellow, paid special homage to my interdisciplinary writing: my archivist colleagues honored me as having "proven constant in his [that is, my] commitment to advancing our understanding of things archival. As an author and editor he has consistently articulated archival concerns to a wider audience, and conversely, provided information from other communities that helps feed archival understand-ing of the information world ... his interests and activities transcend the professional boundaries that sometimes keep historians, librarians, information professionals, and archivists at odds." I hope that this undertaking will have a useful life and will make an impact on readers more immediately and pervasively than my earlier experiments with terminological control and auto-mated cataloging of historical sources, or interdisciplinary curricular development, and my attempts to guide historians, archivists, and librarians forward in a common cause in the use of modern information technology for the preservation and access to primary sources, their analy-sis, and the creation of new electronic sources. As will be apparent, however, is my continuing advocation for interdisciplinarity and a rich mixture of History, Social Sciences, Information Science, and the applied fields of archival administration, museology, and librarianship—and teaching, through any means and media, form and forum, or arena.

Some of the ideas presented here crystallized only in 1991-1992 while teaching Research Methods and serving as a consultant for the Department of History at Western Michigan University. This experience stirred some of the motivation for this present endeavor. I asked myself, "what would it take to construct a holistic approach to historical information access, retrieval, analysis, and presentation using modern information technology?" Experience with my graduate students and discussions about the focus of the graduate program on methodology with the department chairman, Professor Ronald Davis, left me very aware of the impossibility of introducing computer research methodology when allocated a one-course slot for about forty hours of contact time to prepare beginning graduate students in medieval and early modern European History for their research seminars. The students in my colloquium were bright, capa-ble, and to their credit, willing to learn; nevertheless, nearly half of the material covered was, to my mind, remedial, and should have been learned in undergraduate education (such as biblio-graphic online and manual searching, library and archives use, and conceptualization of search strategies to identify, locate, and retrieve documentation before proceeding into research *per se*). They were introduced not only to practical reference procedures but to bibliographic rigor, and to an intellectual framework exposing them to classification and taxonomies, terminology and applied linguistics, appraisal and rules of evidence, form criticism, critical apparatus construc-tion, and an array of national and international standards as reported in NISO's *Information Standards Quarterly* (1988-) (see also SPIVAK & WINSELL's *Sourcebook on Standards Information*). As the course progressed through modules of formal instruction and exercises that insured such remediation, these students by default became tutors for others in the department who had managed to move along in their programs without similar training. Although computing methods could hardly be introduced as well, given the constraints of single course, the discipline, procedural logic, and sense of technique needed to engage modern information technology were nevertheless inculcated.

During the same time I benefitted from numerous discussions over coffee with my friend and fellow librarian, the late Dr. Edwin Harris, an anthropologist by training whose expertise by education and experience in the Peace Corps and higher education lies in the impact of technology on social change and behavioral modification. I still feel the loss of his friendship and shall always miss his counsel. His untimely passing came in May 1996, only months after he had read a draft of this essay. As always, he had some remarks to share for my benefit. His remarks invariably led to extended conversation. He often made me conscious that I was trying to transform an academic library through modern information technology so it could have even a greater impact on quality higher education. What I attempted in the classroom with my teaching was not all that different from what I attempted through administrative leadership as a dean and university librarian. In both roles I have operated with high expectations but apparently have been, so I have been told, "formidable," "overwhelming," and in both the positive sense of problem solving and in one case the negative sense, "confrontational." Not everyone enjoys being questioned or challenged, put on the spot, or afforded the opportunity to develop and defend an idea or position. Confrontation, it seems, is characteristic of most reformers; they do confront the *status quo*, initiate change, and expect others to join in and adapt. Not everyone is willing or able to do so. All change agents incur some risk in judging the pace of change, but seldom has one the luxury of real change management. Leadership is different from management. It rests less on official authority than on personal character, and it requires not orders so much as persuasion. Like religious conversion, dramatic and thorough attitudinal and behavioral change can be disturbing, confrontational, stressful, until resolution restores balance, harmony, and comfort. Most organizational change is more like angling through troubled waters than making a beeline through it all. More than directing or steering on course, it is more like charting a direction and catching opportunities and avoiding pitfalls. I have been fortunate to have had colleagues who enjoyed a little risk and were not afraid of change. During my tenure as dean, the FSU Library and Instructional Services invested heavily in information technology and networking, and in people as well, transforming itself accordingly. The result was improved education for all.

Like most universities, Western Michigan's Department of History had invested in a computer laboratory for its students, the university library was automated, and the institution had embarked on an aggressive program to computerize its administration and engage Computer-Assisted Instruction and Learning (CAI/CAL) technology in its teaching. Granted that technical problems still exist, funding never allows one to move as fast as one might want, and people adopt various technologies at their own pace in any case. The critical problem was not technology alone, however, but in most cases was one of conceptualization, initiative and self-actualization, or accommodation and acculturation. The tendency is always to computerize what is done manually and traditionally in teaching and in research, without undergoing a transformation of the process and inducing reformed thinking to take advantage of the vast array of options now available. Certainly one could not combine History and computing in a single course and hope that applications would be automatically spread throughout a student's program or the graduate curriculum. However, something more structured was required on the magnitude of a new curriculum, or at least a movement like "writing across the curriculum" for the widespread successful application of modern information technology. Otherwise the tendency is to do with a computer the same as without one, but more quickly in final execution, rather than to alter substantively the very nature of historical research and its presentation.

Having designed award-winning graduate programs before at the University of Maryland, whereby graduate students earned two Masters (MLS and MA) over two to three years of integrated study in History and Information Science, I had some notions of graduate school requirements, general curricular structures, course design, program assessment, etc., but I was still struggling with the very conceptualization of something other than simply a mix of History and Computing which would not guarantee genuine specialization or a demonstrable mastery by recipients of master's degrees. I could identify few model curricula in the United States and Canada. Then an invitation in 1993 to speak before the VIII International Conference on History and Computing at the Karl Franz University of Graz, Austria, provided a unique opportunity to explore similar ventures being undertaken in Europe, with more structure and vigor than in American graduate schools. Another invitation from Professor Benedito Miguel Gil of the Universidade Estadual Paulista at Assis to speak before the IV Encontro Internacional de Historia e Computação in São Paulo, November 3-5, 1994, provided another opportunity to explore internationally the idea of interdisciplinary research, history teaching, computing, and information technology from two vantage points, intra-disciplinary within History, and supra-disciplinary from the overview provided by Information Science. I had the opportunity to interact with computing historians again at the International Association for History and Computing (IAHC) on 1995 when it convened with the International Congress of Historical Sciences (ICHS) at Montreal, and I was pleased to receive an invitation from Leonid Borodkin to convene a session and speak on electronic archives at the 1996 conference to be hosted by the Moscow State University. At Santiago de Compostela in the conference *History Under Debate*, I had the opportunity this past year to reflect with 300 historians from twenty countries on the tremendous strain on History during this last generation and the change modern historiography has undergone. These conferences prompted me to revisit a vast literature that I had been following as best I could. Consulting intermittently as I explored specific problems related to my own projects, but growing aware of overall epistemological and professional rather than purely technical issues, I was forced to synthesize and reconsider what I had been gleaning from this literature and observations in my own work as an academic administrator and educator.

The IAHC had already held a conference and follow-up workshops on training future historians, not simply as computer literate, but as computer historians—meaning much more than word processing, i.e., that they had the technical knowledge to conduct research with sources in electronic form, to use a variety of software and methodologies, and to adjust to changing technology. Slowly, computing historians began discussing their work with non-historians, and the expanded dialogue has proved most interesting. Discussions with historians developing new curricula, establishing computer laboratories for historical research, and struggling to reconceptualize History and its praxis, or how History is done with modern information concepts, standards, operations, and technology, was invigorating. I had rarely encountered such discussion in the United States, except at the Social Science History Association where History was, of course, always done as Social Science; I heard many potentially relevant discussions and papers at the American Society for Information Science, but always ahistorical and the context for such discussion was always inbred and circumscribed by the self-imposed boundaries of information research as interpreted by a relatively small and elite band of researchers. At ASIS gatherings, History is seldom mentioned except as fleeting background and general conversation, and methodological debates and the testing of assumptions and premises such as commonly occur in History, seem rare among information scientists. They appear, and indeed strive to give the appearance, that they know what they are about, are secure in their methods and assumptions, and speak authoritatively on the basis of their scientific research. Most conference papers focused on this or that application, single courses, and one-person projects. Although the American Historical Association (AHA) conferences began to explore Information Technology for History more and more, until recently most presentations and interaction in these forums have been disappointing. Moreover, the very nature of these conferences is to discuss what is going on inside a discipline, rather than to inform those on the inside about what is going on outside. In any case, outsiders often have difficulty communicating with insiders, both in adjusting to organizational cultures and use of sublanguage, and in making their content relevant.

Computing does not necessarily eradicate particularism; sometimes this is reinforced by a certain isolation, social and intellectual, created by personal computing. Yet, while I found European notions of Historical Informatics challenging, they also seemed self-limiting by using the term as synonymous with computer science, and by their attachment to older quantification techniques and the grudge work of data processing. In the early 1990s, European computing historians have been breaking out of that old mold. Some, like my host at Graz and colleague in medieval studies, Professor Ingo Kropač, had come to a more holistic and interdisciplinary concept of historical computing, linguistic and Social Science research methodologies, interactive teaching, and effective information dissemination. His thinking was closer to what I had come to realize from developments in American Information Science circles, which is larger in scope and even more interdisciplinary than as discussed by those who have remained within History *per se* or any one of the Social Sciences. Moreover, I have always thought that true intellectual exchange had to be bilateral, in that History had as much to give Information Science as *vice versa*. This assumption clearly sets me off from not all, but many of my colleagues in the Information Sciences, and creates a similar rift with some historian colleagues. I admit my ignorance about why information scientists are so little interested in such intellectual exchange, except to speculate that an overriding practicality sometimes precludes such speculative discourse. Equally perplexing has been the slow engagement of nonhistorical technical and professional expertise by historians whose endeavor is by nature interdisciplinary and syncretistic. No subject or field seems beyond the historian's reach, except if curtailed by lack of awareness or discomfort with the unfamiliar, limited by a sense of a disciplinary core in History, or confined by some other aspect of the profession such as over specialization, which restricts communication and individualization to a point of loneliness where information transfer is only unilateral.

In all of these academic forums it is difficult to relate generality and theory with specific examples and case studies, so this essay attempts to accomplish just that—trace large trends and provide a comprehensive overview, while providing concrete examples and ample references to standards, work groups, projects, discussions, and research. This essay and bibliographic review, therefore, is not a closing discussion, but an opener to the new millennium.

The interstices of Social Science research methodology, modern information technology, and historical sources and practice of History are where the currents of this essay meander; and the impact of numerical computing on History in the great debates over quantification is the juncture for this essay's departure. It was conceived as a bibliographic essay:

1. to survey trends and place the notion of Historical Informatics into the American intellectual construct of Information Science, i.e., Historical Information Science; and

2. to encourage historians, archivists, and other historically minded information professionals to consider the science in computerization rather than mere utilization of this new technology for an immediate end.

American practicality in technical applications is often shortsighted, i.e., a clear aim is always in sight. The questions of "when? how?" and often "how much?" seem more immediate than "why?" and "what if?" With foresight, one might envision different kinds of research, multiple approaches to sources, cross-checking analyses, and a dynamic interplay between man, machine, and source that hitherto seemed impossible. This essay does not seek so much to define the territory of the historian because subject and scope delimiters seem unwarranted other than the focus on something past, but it attempts to chart a critical orientation, create a mentality, and extol an intellectual ecumenism in subjecting all things to historical review even when using modern information technology.

This bibliographic review extends back to the 1970s for historical perspective to delineate once parallel but largely separate developments of History, which does not see itself as primarily an information profession but as an academic discipline when the two are not really so distinct, and the rise of a history-less Information Science, which is allied with the Social Sciences and yet is professionally independent. A synthesis could lead to a more conscious and formal interplay between historical research and Information Science, i.e., Historical Information Science. Developments forging such a synthesis since the mid-1980s may be associated with a more general commingling, often seen as a converging under the influence of computing and information technology (V. BURTON). Its coverage extends through 1995-96 during the project's initial composition, with selective updating and integration thereafter to the last possible date for insertion in 1998. As such, this is a synopsis of about one and a half decades of multidisciplinary work that may be seen as related corpora carrying into the next millennium.

This essay adopts, with some accommodation to personal preference, the style used by the American Society for Information Science (ASIS) for its *Annual Review of Information Science and Technology (ARIST)*, edited by Martha Williams who unwittingly promoted this project by accepting a proposal to include a highly condensed slice of this survey for *ARIST* (MCCRANK, 1995). Coverage provided by its nearly 6,000 citations is primarily in English but it selectively reaches into Western and Eastern European literatures purposely to broaden its horizon. For background it extends into the 1970s, but its concentration is after the advent and widespread distribution of personal computers in the mid-1980s; it especially searches thesis and dissertation work completed in the United States during the last half-decade to ascertain what is forthcoming from our graduate programs. The scope is deliberately multidisciplinary, going beyond the older confines of History computing in the Social Sciences by embracing computing in the Arts and Humanities. It also attempts to relate Historical Information Science to other varieties, namely Library and Archival Sciences as these interface with a more ecumenical Information Science that is not institution-bound. Finally, I reach out to the field of Business for project management specifically and for organizational culture studies not commonly consulted by historians. Aspects of Computer Science and technology are interwoven from the field of Electrical Engineering, without converting this treatise into a technical manual, and I borrow from my colleagues in Engineering as well because of their attention to quality assurance in technical manufacturing (e.g., ISO 9000 standards for proper documentation and process control), which is quite foreign to historians but is highly applicable to database production, large-scale projects, and serial publication over time. The result, I hope, is not merely a literature survey, but an essay as a working out of ideas, particularly this idea of a Historical Information Science as an intellectual umbrella covering much of what is transpiring already but in a somewhat disjointed manner. With all of the talk about merging technologies, institutions, and disciplines, one might expect a newly emerging synthesis that is particularly historical in orientation and mentality, approach and methodology, and longitudinal perspective. It is this present use of modern technology to study the past for a better understanding in our future that is the essence of Historical Information Science.

Originally I had thought of presenting this essay in my own series, *Primary Sources and Original Works*, because of the profound impact computer, telecommunications, and other information technologies are having on primary sources with the old being converted into new electronic forms, and the contemporary being created in ways that fundamentally alter traditional research approaches to physical documentation. It seemed to follow nicely the previous contribution by Richard COX (1994) about training the future generation of electronic archivists. Unfortunately the scope of the survey and the attempt to place this bibliographic coverage into the form of a critical essay meant that the project outgrew the parameters of the Haworth Press series. So it was logical to turn to Information Today, Inc., the publisher of ARIST, because of a match in subject matter, but also because Tom Hogan's publishing company had previously undertaken thousand-page projects effortlessly, resulting in pleasing presentation and successful marketing. In preparation for publication, the draft underwent peer review by (1) a historian specializing in methodology, (2) a philosopher whose dissertation was on the Philosophy of History, (3) a cultural anthropologist and librarian, (4) a historian and archivist, and (5) an information scientist who has studied the historians' information seeking behaviors and preferences in more depth than have they. Others read separate chapters relating to their own specialization. Each contributed with notes and suggestions from their particular perspectives. More importantly, each reviewer encouraged the book's publication; three pointed out the lack of anything comparable in their fields, and two asked for permission to use the typescript as assigned reading for their graduate students rather than wait for publication. Their comments were helpful, and their reception was encouraging, especially for a project that necessarily includes dense summations, ample but terse references hopefully interspersed in interesting reading without the mesmerization of a litany, intricate dovetailing and interwoven evaluation of works already completed with direction to work yet to be done, and a call to reform based on a wider appreciation for and synthesis of what has been already accomplished. My convoluted style and tendency toward complex writing benefitted from simplification and clarity added by Information Today's book editor, John Bryans; able copy editor, Diane Zelley; managing editors, Dorothy Pike and Janet Spavlik; and production manager, Heide Dengler. Hopefully their efforts have made this work more readable and thereby better understood. I appreciate their sensibility that this extended bibliographic essay deserved publication as a whole, when the trend in publishing today is serial production and ever smaller monographs.

Historical Information Science is not something yet to be invented; it is already here, in myriad shapes, reflected in many works, awaiting definition, integration, and reformation. I believe that the issues of conservation and preservation, accumulated mass and speed of current production for an unheralded quantity, and the relentless marching on of time provide imperatives for accountable and responsible historians to change how they function as academics and professionals, how they teach and perpetuate historical consciousness, and how they interact with each other and with colleagues in other disciplines, particularly the information professions and information industry. To ignore what is happening all around academic History seems to indicate a certain dysfunctional historicism at the least; and in the extreme, debilitating inbreeding. Continued lack of awareness and assimilation simply fosters ignorance and induces intellectual paralysis. Without compromising their intellectual prowess, their sophisticated academic discourse, and dedication to cultural preservation through teaching and research, one hopes that historians will continue to make more use of information technology to further their objectives, to collaborate with each other and colleagues in related disciplines and especially information professions such as archives, and to insert into larger information systems a pervasive historical consciousness that contributes to the quality of long-term information preservation and access.

This essay is offered, then, not only as a survey and thereby a historical reminder of ingredients already assembled for this new mix, but ideally as inspiration to others to take up the idea, develop the concept further, experiment with applications in teaching and research, and to link History as a syncretist discipline and academic profession with the larger world of information technological, scientific, and professional communities. There is admittedly, therefore, a manifesto herein, thinly veiled in a bibliographic review. I necessarily paint with a broad brush and cover a vast canvas in depicting the evolution of a unidisciplinary Historical Information Science; the literature is voluminous, access to it is problematic, and synthesis, when space and time do not allow detailed attention to every contribution, is fraught with the danger of oversimplification. I apologize in advance for errors of omission, misinterpretation, and fact, if that be the case, or for my own limitations in knowing thoroughly all of the fields and technologies I may have superficially explored. Instead, I ask that would-be critics suppress any latent technophobia and open their vision beyond the confines of their own disciplines, to stand back and take in the big picture. Enjoy what can be appreciated. Most importantly, consider the idea; if inviting, embrace it and contribute to the development of Historical Information Science. Use the extensive bibliography provided to explore in further detail. Follow the motto I proposed to my faculty: "Informing to Learn; Learning to Know; Knowing to Act" by letting technology assist us as enthusiastic learners, influential teachers, and productive scholars.

Lawrence J. McCrank

Foundations
and Definitions

The combination of the terms, "Historical Information" and "Information Science," does not constitute an oxymoron. Yet, at the onset a seemingly nouveau concept like Historical Information Science requires some explanation immediately and arrival at a working definition so that the following discussions, chapter by chapter, have an overall coherence. Certain arguments are repeated in each section intentionally to remind the reader how one section is related to the other, since the idea of Historical Information Science is integrative. Altogether the chapters cover the major ingredients of what I perceive to comprise Historical Information Science, but my perception is more ecumenical than most. Many of the assumptions in this treatment rest on the foundations of scientific historicism as this was conceived one century ago in a major paradigm shift that has affected all historical thinking in the West thereafter. Although whether or how History is a science is much debated especially regarding its predictive capability, its descriptive and analytic capacity rests on the very foundations laid a century ago to bolster History as a scientific enterprise rather than a gentleman's antiquarian pursuit or purely recreational reading for general edification. Throughout this century, until relatively recently, History has been regarded as a literary pursuit and communication art, but distinct from fiction and therefore separate from Literature. History has been seen to elicit fact, tell what actually happened, and to interpret events in the past for the present. Its aim was to give the past meaning, and thereby to contribute to enhanced awareness of things present, and to offer some ideas about a probable future or possible futures. History may not predict the future, but in keeping with a certain sense of progress and optimism, historical awareness could guide choice and therefore improve life.

Scientific historicism throughout this century has underpinned the practice and writing of History with a pervasive sense of documentation, proof, and evidence (W. EDGAR). William Forsyth in 1874 made this connection between rules of evidence and the credibility of history (FORSYTH), but others have noted that since the rise of scientific historicism there is a disconnection between Law and History regarding evidential criteria and use (RESCHER & JOYNT; see YAGER, FEDRIZZI & KOSPRYK on evidential reasoning in information systems, e.g., the Dempster-Shafer theory of evidence). The Social Sciences have not escaped the pervasive influence of postmodernism (HOLLINGER), and this has had some impact on the idea of evidence as conditioned by social constructions of knowledge (RETTIG). Such a premise of anchoring argument in indisputable evidence is still held widely, but it seems that very little is ever indisputable, and old concepts of evidence have been tempered somewhat even in Law where whatever is admissible is also contestable in and of itself, or its transmission and interpretation. Nevertheless, the motivation, interpretation, and application aspects of History that are so controversial today ultimately go back to the identification, custody, and retrieval of information as evidence. PHELAN and REYNOLDS tie evidence and argument together as essential for the Social Sciences, but they suggest methods for critical analysis that are definable, identifiable, tested, and respected. The same connection between evidence and explanation in the Social Sciences is made by STUDDERT-KENNEDY. In this regard Historical

Information Science may be seen as the forensics of History, in that more than merely to inform, the goal is to establish a foundation for the acceptability, reliability, and credibility of information and its interpretation in contexts—both the proximate or immediate, and the more remote, larger sense. After calling attention to seminal notions about scientific historicism, this discussion will move on to the contested notion that History is a science, specifically a Social Science, and more ecumenically in European usage, a *Science Humaine* and bridge to the Arts and Humanities. The contention here is that History, even when not seen as a science, nevertheless has a scientific base in its regard for evidential information and documentation, and in its explanation and argumentation.

The neologism "Historical Information Science" is used here as more than simply an interdisciplinary combination of History and Information Science (which is also seen as a Social Science, distinct from Computer Science). The whole, it will be argued, is greater than the sum of its parts in this case. Information Systems (IS) and Information Technology (IT), technological specializations in their own right, are herein subordinated to Science and are therefore subsumed by the holistic term "Historical Information Science." The pervasive influence of information technology is given its due attention immediately and throughout this discussion, but for the most part specific technologies will be discussed as they support the mission and role of Historical Information Science rather than treatment of technology as such.

The argument made throughout this presentation is for an interdisciplinary union, a unidiscipline, that can exist by itself at the intersection of the traditional discipline and information profession, or as a branch of either History or Information Science. Its context might well provide a certain character for the endeavor; for example, toward source criticism in the former, or in the latter more of a systems orientation. After arriving at a working definition of Historical Information Science based on an evolution in methods and actual usage, this discussion will consider the developments of major components of Historical Information Science in earlier quantification movements and related methodology in History specifically and the Social Sciences generally. It will consider the continued debate over the objectivity issues in human affairs research, will suggest the need for collaborative research more common in the Social Sciences and in keeping with the notion of a unifying metadiscipline, and will note trends (professional, social, and technical) that suggest why a new science, namely Historical Information Science, is feasible at the turn of this century and millennium.

CHANGING TIMES AND TERMS

Scientific Historicism, Method, and Technique

When the famous British historian J. B. Bury in 1902 referred to "the science of history," he thought of *science* in the continental and traditional sense of *scientia* or wisdom (BURY). More precisely in the classical tradition of textual criticism to which Bury was heir, science was synthesized knowledge based logically on evidence. Moreover, the aim was more than description, but explanation. This critical approach to objective history, reflected in Leopold von Ranke's dictum of providing a documented past and telling the story as it actually happened ("wie es eigentlich gewesen"), formed the concept of "scientific historicism" which was exported with the idea of the research seminar to American graduate schools. IGGERS (1995) explains that von Ranke's theory was based on "epistemological idealism" (see D. ROSS [1988] for other misunderstandings concerning von Ranke's positions). MULLER & CROMPTON point out, "for many it [scientific historicism] is a negatively charged term of contention, which can[not] be used without cognitive exertion in maneuvers of exclusion and delineation." Today historians would be more prone to retell the story from a variety of perspectives, rather than blending them into a dominant model or single story line that is believed to be actual, correct, and definitive. Nevertheless, each rendition to be admissible must have some basis in sources relevant to the subject, and thus it may be entered into critical debate as something more than mere speculation or contrived fiction. The objectivity lies in the object, something concrete and observable that has form and substance, i.e., a source, in the original or an acceptable surrogate. The "scientific" refers to how sources are examined and preserved, and how history is thus observed—indirectly through its remnants. Today the term "scientific historicism" is not unequivocally defined and is often associated with positivism, which in the extreme is something to which most historians today would object. Such objection to motive, philosophical bent, and interpretation, however, should not be confused with the methodological underpinning of historical research. In this regard one might suggest a distinction between "scientific historicism" as a school of thought building a monolithic ideology, and "scientific history" as a focus on source preservation, criticism, and analysis, and such methodology as modeling. In the broadest sense, in addition to source criticism and forensics, this might well include examining historians as researchers, conveyors of historical information, professional interpreters, and creators of historical consciousness in society at large. The idea of scientific history is large enough to embrace History's metaphysics, objectivism, and positivism, and because of these, relativism especially for the era to which its history is to be related (STEENBLOCK). One may retain the ideal of objectivity and its practice in examining information sources scientifically from an individual perspective, and even by multiple individuals sharing their perspectives and recognizing their relative commonalities and differences. Relativism does not necessarily negate objectivity. It need not be subjective. But that was not the way anti-positivist relativist historians in the inter-war period saw things. Their argument was really over authority between author and audience, i.e., personal and internal authority versus external and the authority lodged with someone else, namely the historian doing the interpretation.

In keeping with the European tradition of seeing History as a science, broadly construed, one may nonetheless also move toward an Americanist view of method as technique, thus combining this European ecumenical notion of science with an American penchant for technology. In this vein, note that a decade earlier than Bury's writings when historical research, writing, and teaching were undergoing initial professionalization, one of the American Historical Association's founders, J. Franklin Jameson, had unabashedly assumed History to be a science (JAMESON, 1891, pp. 132-33). He called for History's development through "the improvement of its technical processes." He inherited this notion from the experiential learning emphasis of von Ranke and other advocates of scientific historicism: the same notion of "historical exercises" and of practice to improve skill in extracting information from documents is apparent in the teaching of Herbert Baxter Adams as well, and it was specifically advocated by Ephraim Emerton at Harvard. The approach was characteristic of philology and document examination from the Maurists and Bollandists through the German school associated with editing the *Monumenta Germaniae Historica,* whose orientation toward textual studies was not unlike modern documentation except that the former lacked modern information technology (W. CLARK). T. PORTER has shown also that the rise of statistical thinking occurred at the same time, 1820-1900, that scientific historicism came into vogue. Document examination and (ac)counting went hand in hand. Although the Von Rankian paradigm suffered a crisis in the very late nineteenth century (IGGERS, 1990; 1997), and in the United States it was buffeted by the skepticism prevalent during the inter-war period. Renewed attacks upon the intellectual program of positivism were directed at scientific history simply because of their previous association. The eminent historians Carl Becker and Charles Beard in 1931 and 1933 respectively espoused a new relativism over old positivism in their presidential addresses before the American Historical Association, the first by democratizing history by declaring "Everyman His Own Historian" (BECKER) and the second by seeing "Written History as an Act of Faith" (BEARD). Objectivity and scientific methodology still had champions like the medievalist MCILWAIN, rooted in philology as he was, who railed against the unbridled relativism of his Americanist historians who would make everyone his or her own authority about anything at anytime, just by having an opinion, or even by having an informed opinion by reading texts in translation or secondary sources in common parlance, and confusing such with real, hard evidence and logical argument.

Although one can dismiss the extreme relativism in popular history as distinct from professional, expert history, the status of History as a science which some sought in their advocacy of scientific historicism was irretrievably lost with the latter's debunking. History developed in the United States as a discipline onto itself with no clear, legitimate home. Caught like an orphan between the Social Sciences and the Humanities and shunted back and forth between these foster homes, it vacillated between these larger divisions, being lured toward each at times and repelled at others. In such a precarious position it is always open to attack from both groups. History's position as a quasi-science at best (pseudo-science at worst) was weakened further after World War II when its political and economic bent allied it with the Social Sciences. The subsequent trend toward empiricism in socioeconomic history leading to the Cliometric movement during the late 1960s and early 1970s, invited another reaction (to be described later) in the mid-1970s. After recovering somewhat, scientific history took another battering with assaults from deconstructionism and the linguistic bent of cultural text-based historians within History and historically oriented scholars in Literature; still another from a feminine critique that sometimes verges on the vicious and really destructive throughout the 1980s and into this decade (reviewed by B. SMITH); and most recently postmodernism from LYOTARD's use of the term in 1979 (or in American historiography, after 1984 when his French treatise on the *Postmodern Condition* was translated into English). These forays are still ongoing.

This is still a precarious time, therefore, to suggest History should be allied with the Social Sciences more than with the Humanities in order to stress its scientific aspects. In fact, this is not necessary; History may retain its relations with both and form another with Information Science which seems like a Social Science, but which, like History, does not fit squarely in either. Such an alliance of two inter-disciplinary fields makes sense. Moreover, the characterization of History as scientific with a quest for objectivity, even if not as empirical and objective as a science, is longstanding and persists (BERLIN). It is still seen commonly as a human science in European terms, or a Social Science in the Anglo-American tradition, while being a bridge to, if not actually one of, the Humanities (H. HUGHES). The most optimistic resolution of this "home" predicament is to see History as having dual citizenship, its pick, and the best of two worlds! It must be at home with itself and hospitable to all others.

If the scientific characterization of History is so in question, it might be difficult to convince skeptics and critics, practitioners and professionals as well as nonhistorians, about the technique of History (i.e., historical methods) in relation to technology, specifically Information Technology (IT), as the way to see scientific history as an ally of Information Science—or as one of the Information Sciences, namely Historical Information Science. However, Jameson's linkage of historical method with technique makes the extension between History and modern information technology less novel than one might suppose, especially when one conceives of technology, as does HAERD, as ideas in action, or, more simply, practice and execution. Technique has always influenced science (S. HALL), and sometimes the two are indistinguishable (NARIN & NOMA; DOEBLER). The turn-of-the-century advocates of scientific historicism might have been puzzled, but I suspect they would have been intrigued by the notion of Historical Information Science, i.e., the application of modern information technology and analytic methodology to historical sources and their interpretation. Contemporary critics of scientific history are a different lot, including information scientists who do not normally care for History, or about history in any form. Regardless of common interests in research methods, technique, or use of information technology, for them history is a thing of the past; Information Science deals with the present and is focused on future developments.

Michel de Certeau also argued that history was linked to practice and technique, but with a different outcome. While advocates of scientific historicism related science and objectivity,

DE CERTEAU (1988) turned the table around and argued objectively how such practice led to subjectivity. "Every 'historical fact' results from a praxis.... It results from procedures which have allowed a mode of comprehension to be articulated as a discourse of facts" (p. 30). While the French intelligentsia since the late eighteenth century have traditionally expunged method from theory because these relate to practice, I will risk the impudence disdained by DE CERTEAU (p. 64) by evoking their importance in bringing History into the realm of science precisely because neither is autonomous, and holding onto the traditional antinomy between theory and practice, or academic versus professional, is duplicitous. Although English does not have the advantage of German in being able to distinguish between *Geschichte* and *Geschichtswissenschaft* or History and Historical Science (as in the translation of G. DUBY's dialogue [1961] between these two perspectives), it has made distinctions between the history, historical method, and the philosophy of history. The dominant *praxis* explored here is what generally is thought of as scientific in Social Science, e.g., Social Science History, but this dichotomy is increasingly invalid if it invokes too strong a contrast between the Social Sciences and the Humanities (as in the more empirical English usage than the French *Science humaine*). As shall be seen, neither persuasion is entirely free from the other, and increasingly methods used in either are pulled from a mixed methodological bag that cannot be seen as strictly this or that, or specifically disciplinary in any case.

The concept of scientific history has changed since the turn of the century, and indeed it must be conceived more broadly in view of modern technology than Von Ranke, Jameson, or others could have imagined. Part of this broadening is a comfort in admitting the science as well as the art in History, just as some philosophers of Science acknowledge that Science is a cultural and historical process (ZVIGLIANICH). Today, the "master narrative" in History, other than for the Bible it seems, is in disrepute; synthesis is difficult to come by; and a tension exists between qualitative and quantitative orientations stemming from the ageless dialectic between art and science. RUSSO discerns some of these aspects of historical study in regard to American History as troubling; he portrays Clio as "confused." PAGE uses stronger language still, accusing History of betrayal in its walk away from philosophical historicism and truth-finding mission. History perceived as a perpetual argument, or a constant rethinking, retelling, and rewriting of the past, lacks a consensus that would seem to provide resolution to the intellectual problems it tackles. Historical reflection has recently turned from simplifying the complex through clarification and explanation to confounding History's natural complexity by deep, abstract thinking, convoluted arguments, and multilayered explanation.

This is unsatisfying for those who want a product, a generalized answer to the problem, and an end to the discussion, so that one might confidently refer to what is understood at any one time as known for all time. Such viewpoints may well identify technique and method with a single production, e.g., this or that monographic treatment to be read as something definitive as opposed to an installment, and to confuse the containment of historical thought in a particular package such as a book, with the science in History which lies in the process rather than any particular product. Moreover, as LANDOW & DELANY (p. 15) point out, in a world of digitized and networked texts, the "containers" of print media are smashed; units of text in any size can be retrieved, manipulated, and merged. Permanent packaging in any container is gone, and with the destruction of containment, so too is identity increasingly problematic. Foci switch from things to processes in this far more nebulous milieu. In any case, the perceived definitive nature of Science (itself a misconception) is problematic for History, which is so integrative or interdisciplinary, with its totally encompassing world view co-existing with a concern for the microcosm of human affairs, that one must understand how the continual process of history is science in thought and action, rather than expect that historical products can be judged as scientific by themselves. The informing process, therefore, is critical for History; and this brings us to the issue of information, information technology, and its use (HEWER; for IT terms see LONGLEY's dictionary [1982, 1989]). In this regard, History as science is an Information Science. Its speciality is informing the present about the past.

Simon Schama recently reminded the American public that *Historia*, "hot-wired [or] unplugged" in its Greek origins simply meant inquiry: "For all the elaborateness of modern scholarship, we [i.e., historians] still do what the Greeks and Romans did: figure out how we got from there to here. Electronic technology is only the latest and most potent tool in that work. With the arrival of the digital archive[s], or the historical hypertext, manipulating alternative eventualities, the record of the past faces a brave new future" (FORBES *ASAP*, p. 55). DOORN (1996) observes that the "intelligence of History" always lies in its accumulation. Indeed, it is this problem of mass accumulation that must link History to Information Science, especially the processes of information storage and retrieval, and which requires an intellectual technology of inventing, adopting, and adapting new tools for the endless inquiry about humankind's journey from there to here. In 1991, FRAWLEY, PIATETSKY-SHAPIRO & MATHEUS estimated that information in the world today is doubling every 20 months! Could anyone have predicted that information in digital form would increase exponentially so rapidly during this generation that estimates for the end of this millenium are as much as a thousand Petabytes (PB) or the equivalent to sixty billion 500-page books! (KEMPSTER, 1997, p. 2; his estimate is also cited by DOLLAR [1999] to make the same point). We are not talking about the minuscule ancient Greek and Latin corpus here; in fact, nobody at any previous time has faced such an enormity of information in such a ethereal environment. Nobody in this world can boast of mastering a field of knowledge anymore—at least not in the traditional sense of knowing the primary sources and keeping abreast with the secondary literature—even when we are narrowing specializations to domains that would have once seemed like trivial matters. Skeptics may feel that we know so much more about much less. This current survey with its bounded foci and massive bibliography, although only a sampling and limited in scope and by period, is itself testimony to the problem of identifying, comprehending, and integrating the vast amounts of relevant information we have available today. In plotting the path from there to here and on to the immediate future, to say nothing of more ambitious goals, historians like everyone else are liable to get lost in a literally amazing mass. Historians may retreat into the pasts they study because they are so much easier to traverse than the present. However, the present is contemporary history, every historian lives at present, and to ignore the present is a disservice to History.

The voice of History must be heard, but this is not easy in a world of information overload, mass communication, and general din. Alan Brinkley of Columbia University in a 1996 Ford Hall televised forum on "Past and Future of Democracy" remarked that historians do not have a broad market for their opinions outside academic history because in the public's perception History lacks "scientific legitimacy" (cf., the essays edited by R. WALTERS on "scientific authority" in twentieth-century America). Brinkley's distinguished fellow panelists, Arthur Schlesinger and John Kenneth Galbraith, pointed out that the range of historical research today is remarkable, both in scope and depth, and because of its richness in methods and techniques ("the things historians do"), that consensus is not necessarily a universal goal. Indeed, such over-generalization would seem to hide the diversity, complexity, and texture of history and lessen the intrinsic allure of History.

The underpinning of History, that is the objectivity of information searching, research including document examination and analysis of the surviving record, and reaching an understanding of the state of the art, before interpretation, exposition, and dissemination, would seem to be very scientific. But communication of historical thought based on such research is most often crafted as a literature. Historians often express themselves in language other than what is expected of formal discourse in science, except when writing dissertations. Such historical writing may not, to adopt the terms of Walters' essayists, use the expected "language of authority" associated with science; or historians relate so much with each other and a specialized readership that they speak only to their own "community of discourse." On the other hand, scientists like the late Carl Sagan also shied away from definitive answers and eschewed scientific jargon.

His wonderment based on his scientific knowledge of astronomy and physics was expressed eloquently and poetically, as he also moved from the objective to the subjective to personalize communications, to inspire, and to teach when reaching a wide audience. Such scientists do so with no loss of "scientific legitimacy" in the public's view. Historians, whose work is based on the record, whose methods conform to accepted standards and enlarge upon them, whose arguments are logical and persuasive, whose writings transcend mere reporting, and whose teaching intrigues and inspires, should not fare worse.

What, then, may be made of the concept Historical Information Science? The idea is not simply the adoption of the language of science; this misses the mark and may not be called for at all. The issue is more methodological. If conceived as simply the scientific study of historical information, the idea is not too far removed from scientific historicism. It is the application of information technology in research and its dissemination, however, that distances today's capabilities from those one century ago. This makes Historical Information Science substantially different than reliance on personal integrity and judgement, traditional disciplinary rigor, ample documentation and close reading, the usual source criticism or reliance on philology, and continued preference for monographic publication. All of these may be important, to be sure, but Historical Information Science would aim at the extraction of information from historical sources and construction of knowledge scientifically, coupled with an objectivity about assumptions and interpretation; tested methods that are repeatable, whose results are verifiable, and where interpretation is accountable; theory-building beyond case study, description, and narration; collaborative, strategic approaches more common in business and engineering than in the traditional arts; and a renewed focus on evidence.

Although History is recognized as a discipline everywhere, it has always existed also as a subdiscipline within other disciplines, as in the case of "the history of..." literally anything, including the discipline itself (Historiography as the history of History; or for example, Art History versus the History of Art, or the historiography of Art History, Music, Religion, Literature, Science, Technology, etc.). In some cases, e.g., Art and Music History, the speciality is easily recognized because it can be so easily juxtaposed to the performance or execution of the art. In Computer Science, and Information Science as well, it is hardly recognized at all even through historical thought and processing are used pervasively. History is less discernible as a separate endeavor in many cases when it is fused into another discipline, conjoined, or made into an adjunct, e.g., Social History, History in Sociology, and the History of Sociology. As COHEN & ROTH's collaborators show, history is alive and well in many environments not strictly seen as the discipline of History. MONKKONEN also relates how the Social Sciences have used History.

Stanley Katz asks "Do disciplines matter?" in regard to the blending of socioeconomic history with the Social Sciences (KATZ, 1995). The same question can be applied to History and Literature or any other combination. Katz sees the relationship of the identifiable disciplines as essential and the maintenance of disciplinary distinctiveness as a challenge in the future. Those working in the Social Sciences sometimes feel the same need to preserve identity by distinguishing their disciplines from History. Consider, for examples, Historical Geography or History in Geography versus Geography in History. ROCCA sees the integration of History and Geography as beneficial, but nevertheless stresses five features that characterize Geography. GUELKE argues that the role of historical geography falls into Collingwood's type of History where the geographer displays the thought of historical agents as these relate to the physical environment. Such distinctions are mighty fine. Although not claiming an autonomous status for Psychology, MUNSTERBERG does this for his discipline by seeing Psychology as the examination of the causal structure of the human mind, while excluding volitional acts (agency) and social interactions which concern History. L. GRIFFIN does the same for Sociology, while explaining how this discipline is informed by History. Even Historical Sociology, he argues, is a distinctive way of approaching problems, namely to exploit the temporality of social life to ask and answer questions of perennial importance (cf., ALEXANDER, BOUDON & CHERKAQUI for their survey of classical Sociology in Europe and America). C. TILLY in 1981 argued the reverse, in how Sociology informed History. MCDONALD likewise distinguishes between Social History and Historical Sociology, even though they may be in constant dialogue with each other. PLATT combines both in her history of sociological research in America. For the nonspecialist, however, these distinctions may appear too subtle for notice. Rather than stressing the case from the vantage point of History's borrowing from the Social Sciences as in Social Science History, S. KATZ sees the problem as being created by a current trend of prominent social scientists adopting historical methodologies in their pursuit of knowledge. However, M. R. HILL's recent attempt to introduce sociologists to archives shows how far the fields are removed from each other. He portrays archives as foreign territory. Either way, the very need for such redefinition and self-assurance of disciplinary identities is evidence of the convergence occurring in contemporary intellectual life.

The resulting increased inter- and multi-, or perhaps even non- or supra-disciplinarity (J. KLEIN), might be expressed better as a "unidisciplinarity" instead of the more common descriptor "interdiscipline" to describe a co-equal mix or a thorough blending which does make the disciplinary identity difficult to maintain and does not aim to do so. This convergence toward a unidiscipline, however, does not require sameness to achieve a sense of unity, and the older proclivity toward a prescriptive methodological program or a ultramonotheistic devotion to one technology or another should be resisted. However, improved information access across disciplinary lines is needed (DAY, WALTON & EDWARDS). A tension will always exist between unifiers and those focusing on commonalities, and those who see uniqueness everywhere and revel in diversity. Integration and segregation in an uneasy balance are likely to continue in the intellectual world as much as in social, economic, and political life. MESSER-DAVIDOW, SHUMWAY, & SYLVAN, eds., in the University of Virginia series *Knowledge, disciplinarity and beyond*, choose to refer to "knowledges" in the plural, in an attempt to retain respect for individual disciplines at least as ways of looking at and thinking about things, and yet they accommodate interdisciplinarity, but as a mixture rather than a solution. WORSLEY likewise uses the plural "knowledges" sociologically to split the comprehensive singular into its culture, counterculture, and subculture aspects. GREETHAM prefers the term "antidiscipline" for what I have labeled a "unidiscipline," because "it has no definable *Fach* or subject matter" (p. 32), but his characterization of textual bibliographic scholarship as "an exemplary postmodernist antidiscipline" is negative compared with my positive approach to Historical Information Science. He sees textual scholarship, for example, as consisting of "co-opted and deformed quotations from other fields... [through] Misappropriating concepts and vocabulary" from them to make "a fragmented pastiche." One need not be a purist or elitist to embrace the idea of a unifying approach to historical knowledge through the use of information technology, as varied as this is, with a wide selection of methods appropriated from multiple fields, to confront the issue of massive data in the study of human affairs. But it does seem imperative to hold onto the notion of evidence and the recorded aspect of information for historical reinterpretation as a basis for objective discernment and critical appraisal of our past (cf., GLYMOUR; PHELAN & REYNOLDS). In this sense, my orientation is not as pliable as the extreme relativism and skepticism in postmodernist tendencies, while one can appreciate postmodernism's contribution to the sociology of knowledge; and it is anything but negative and cynical, but instead may be seen to lean toward positivism because of its innately positive optimism.

Historians have also considered the potential role of a unidiscipline in modern academe. Some have suggested ways to rethink the traditional historiographic paradigm of national histories dissected by chronological periods and such orientations as social, socioeconomic, cultural, intellectual, political, institutional, etc. The FERNAND BRAUDEL CENTER (*Newsletter*, nos. 16-17 [Aug. 1992-1993]) for the Study of Economies, Historical Systems, and Civilizations at

SUNY-Binghamton still supports the Annaliste platform for broad synthesis and ongoing integration from all disciplines. Although Emmanuel Wallerstein's approach (e.g., his focus on "historical agency") has been criticized as very Eurocentric, a globalization of scope and the recent recognition of multiple cores for historical watersheds are correcting such deficiencies. Less easily dealt with is the criticism that a systems approach marginalizes people; this is resurrection of the traditional humanist critique balancing Social Science tendencies in History. It is a concern mentioned throughout this current essay as a tempering influence on ultra-positivist notions of science. In any case, the Center's thrust is so philosophical that not enough attention seems to be paid to the impetus lent to its position by merging information technologies. Backed by the Calouste Gulbenkian Foundation, which also supports a commission "on the Restructuring of the Social Sciences," the Center's current program is entitled "The Historical Social Sciences— Beyond Multidisciplinarity, Towards Unidisciplinarity." The term "unidiscipline" has been adopted in this essay in the same spirit, and as appropriate for both History and Information Science, which already cut across all disciplinary boundaries and borrow freely from the whole human intellectual enterprise.

To illustrate this trend beyond inter- or Unidisciplinarity, this essay uses examples from seminal literature to follow academic discourse in once diverse fields where trends favor a unity in methodology, employment of technology, and common problems that might contribute to Historical Information Science. This is a selective, critical review, therefore, rather than a comprehensive historical overview; and by going beyond the English-language barrier in America to international information, it is a complement to and an extension of such earlier benchmark reviews commissioned by American Society of Information Science (ASIS) as by RABEN & BURTON, or by Helen Tibbo who placed History in the context of information technology, systems, and services for the Humanities (TIBBO, 1991). Tibbo astutely noted the importance of developments in linguistic and literary computing that, with quantified history computing, form the two mainstreams of an emerging Historical Information Science. Rather than simply update such reviews, this essay expands upon them, engaging fields not brought under their purview, and because of their Humanities bias, this survey seeks some counterweight in the Social Sciences, Management, and Technology.

This bibliographic essay attempts to use literature to review trends, rather than simply to review literature. Purely from an historian's viewpoint, it is always risky reviewing ongoing trends or predicting a convergence of developments still unfolding. Rather than merely describe some of these developments, this very pointing to commonalities in shared technology, methodology, and often subject matter as well may further convergence simply by drawing attention to it. John Maeda, a professor of design and computation at MIT's Media Lab, when interviewed by M. J. Zuckerman for *USA Today* (6/29/1998, p. 1-2), predicts such convergence between disciplines because of computing that knows no such boundaries: "People tend to think of the humanities and sciences as two separate boxes,... but someday, not very far in the future, that distinction will be very thin." The review is therefore also a preview what is potentially to come, especially in the combination of historical computing and rapidly developing information technologies with electronic archives. D. ROSS (1991) has outlined the history of American Social Science. The old Social Science methodologies hammered out largely by the Chicago school of social scientists in the 1920s (BULMER, 1981, 1984) and also at Columbia University (CAMIC, 1989; CAMIC & XIE) still dominate historical quantified research, but new methodologies must be forged to handle mass, complexity, and multimedia. MAINZER talks about the added requirements of "thinking in complexity" in the Social Sciences, aided by computing (about which more will be said later). This may require an experimental history to devise and test new methods and techniques as a legitimate aim in itself, and a moderation in criticism, appreciation of the novel, and a tolerance for risk that seems nonexistent in the historical temperament, past or present.

All good futurology seems to be grounded in History because most development is continuous, interspersed with relatively few revolutionary alterations of the intellectual odyssey of mankind. Some of the trends currently noticed are more longstanding than many realize, and contemporary developments and current expectations contain solid indicators of future probabilities. Such review of late twentieth-century developments in source recovery, increased scope and scale of historical study due to information technology, new methods of document analysis with computer-based tools beyond the limitations of older empirical means, and the potential of simulation leading to virtual historical realities, should warrant reform in History education at the undergraduate and graduate levels. Minimally this requires a more formalized approach to the concept of information to clarify thinking and to make explicit fundamental assumptions and selection of appropriate methodologies. If the more technical side of such formalization puts the historian off, then perhaps the behavioral side is more palatable, i.e., as in the field of Speech Communications (M. CHESTER; J. PETERS). In any case, information technology itself, like technique, cannot be ignored. Digitization, telecommuting, new protocols and developing standards, and expanding networks make possible another level of "New History" that requires further development of History's foundations in methodology, epistemology, and technology, which I call Historical Information Science.

Historical and Information Work

The assumption that emerging technologies are merging disciplines and are radically changing how intellectual work is being done, which requires a paradigm shift among historians as much as any other intra-disciplinary focused group, has importance for the relevance of History in the development of the information industry, how historians function as information analysts and providers, and how they teach to prepare students for a lifestyle that is more diverse than ever. They are entering future unchartered careers which will be nothing like well-traveled paths, or focused trajectories where they needed to know the history only for where they had been. A wider and more comparative historical perspective is demanded for such flexibility, but this seems lacking. At stake is the marginalization of History from the mainstream of American, indeed Western, cultural and socioeconomic development.

Without hype from the cyber-crowd, techno-enthusiasts, computer addicted, and the perverse condescension of techno-centrism, or, on the other hand, from the snobbish disdain of classical education for anything applied, one must consider historically with long-range and comprehensive perspectives the implications of rapidly changing information technology for both History and Information Science. How will a historian be able to research business history when 80 percent of the commerce is electronic if he or she is not adept in computing and telecommunications? The economic historian must relate information to competition, when being at the "cutting edge" can mean phenomenal success as in the case of Microsoft, Inc., or sometimes in the case of massive failure, on the "bleeding edge" to paraphrase MEYER & BOONE's *The Information Edge*. So too must the political scientist and historian understand how information is converted to power, or the linkage BOONE makes between computers and leadership. More introspectively, does not most of what is new, innovative, and exciting in History depend on the discovery in little-used sources and the use of unknown information, or the application of new technique borrowed from another field? As all fields move toward use of a greater array of information resources, multi-media (not excluding traditional media, i.e., books), and more integration to operate from a larger information base, so too must historians. The issue is not merely keeping current, but one of greater objectivity because of the larger information base, quality control, and complexity.

As the resources of historians are changing, their work habits must change also. Historians today understand this, as illustrated by the deliberations of the AHA's Committee on Redefining Historical Scholarship. Such discussions within AHA, however, are focused more on activities and products than training, methods, techniques, and technology in practice. Moreover, more and more history is being done outside of academe and professional affiliations, often under guise of another name and embedded into other activities, and this is likely to continue.

History is certainly not alone in this trend to work outside the traditional confines of a discipline or of academe. Nor is it the only discipline to feel bombarded by information from all sides, in all forms, with both beneficial and harmful effects. Many professionals feel the pressures of the Information Age, including anxiety and distrust despite being more (better?) informed. The perceived compression of time in an era of accelerated technological change is a virtual aging process. It can be invigorating at one stage and debilitating at another. A historical timeline can put things into perspective but can also reveal that some of these perceptions are not merely imagined. Consider the Internet, as collapsed by *Hobbe's Internet Timeline* and abbreviated further by the following selected milestones (see Appendix F for a more complete chronology):

- 1957   Advanced Research Projects Agency (ARPA) founded in the U.S. Department of Defense (DOD) in reaction to the USSR's launching of Sputnik Science research emphasis in U.S. aids technology development

- 1962   Packet-switching

- 1965   Networks begin to form using time-sharing computers

- 1969   ARPANET formed in DOD; four hosts

- 1971   Intra-machine e-mail and file transfer

- 1972   TELNET

- 1974   Transmission Control Program (TCP)

- 1975   E-mail spreads

- 1979   NSF focus on computer networking

- 1981   BITNET in IBM systems

- 1984   Domain Name Server (DNS) introduced
  Joint Academic Network (JANET) in the U.K.

- 1986   NSFNET in the U.S.
  First Freenets in America

- 1987   NSF, MERIT, and MCI collaboration

- 1988   OSI preferred over TCP/IP for U.S. Government (GOSIP)

- 1989   Compuserve and Corporation for
  the National Research Initiative (CNRI)
  International spread of NSFNET; growth
  of CERT advisories; 130,000 hosts

- 1990   ARPANET ceases; Miscellaneous developments, e.g., Archie, ISO

- 1991   Wide Area Information Servers (WAIS) invented by B. Kahle Gopher
  released from the University of Minnesota
  National Research and Education Network (NREN)
  formed by the so-called Gore Act
  NSFNET traffic explodes; JANET upgrade

- 1992   Internet Society (ISOC) chartered
         Veronica released; Jean Armour Polly's *Surfing the Internet*

- 1993   U.S. National Information Infrastructure Act
         Mosaic; WWW "explodes" with 130 Web sites!

- 1995   NSFNET reformed
         Sites proliferate; standards movement;
             conventions for citation styles
         Mobile code like JAVA and VRML (Virtual environments)
         Digital libraries

- 1996   Domain registration system developed into
             American Registry for Internet Numbers (ARIN)
         Continued exponential growth of the Internet/WWW: 16,146,000
             hosts, 828,000 domains, 150,000 networks;
             1,117,259 Web sites; 171 countries "Internetted."
         The number of Web sites doubles every six months!
         Internet II

- 2000   The global information supermarket.

What does the future portend? Who knows? But consider these forecasts:

1.   Faster access

2.   More sites and competition

3.   Increased reliance on graphics/audiovisual than text alone

4.   Greater information mass and more redundancy

5.   Increased ambiguity and contradiction with problematic verification

6.   More complex formats, structures, and multilayered presentations
     Possible improvements, but not guaranteed:

     a. Improved quality control, accuracy and accountability

     b. Better information retrieval

     c. Enhanced synthesis or

     d. Greater knowledge.

8.   Continued overproduction of information

9.   Effects of information glut, overload, tuning-out, withdrawal

10. Pressure on time management

11. Inverse ratio between mass production, speed of communication, and availability, with
     human abilities to access information strategically, consume and assimilate it, and lag
     time in application.

This is remarkable history! Disturbing trends? Serious implications. Internet/WWW development is exerting a tremendous pressure on established institutions like libraries, conventions like bibliographic reference, standards for scholarship, and old scholarly ways. The dramatic growth of electronic data and information on the Web in place of hard copy and of new forms of popular culture that are less than a decade old means that traditional forms of communication and formats have decreased not in total number, but in the ratio of total information available. Archives have not kept pace with official electronic records, say nothing of this newborn electronic culture. Few attempt to preserve Web pages, HTML databases, and computer graphics except for their own organizations; even then, many archives with institutional homepages have not treated these new forms as archival. So, the history of one of the most dramatic communications revolutions in history, in an era when massive output has outstripped all capabilities for preservation, may eventually become the largest black hole of historical knowledge yet known. This is not because an external enemy destroys a culture and its institutions, as has happened so often in the past, but it is because modern Western culture has become so self-destructive and mutable. We, contemporary participants, are the problem—and the solution.

A few struggle to preserve this history in the making, so that it is not all lost. Notable among them is Brewster Kahle's Internet Archives, which started as "a quirky history project." It is funded now by his sale for $15 million of his Wide Area Information Service (WAIS) to America Online (AOL), but he hopes to make it self-sufficient by selling advertising once the user base is developed (reported by SELINGO). This MIT graduate hopes that one day "digital anthropologists" will explore these archives, perhaps by using his own free shareware, *Alexa*. This is not a term-matching software, but a user-tracking mapping software that builds guides to the sites contacted most often, down into their separate homepages and even to deleted pages, and then connects paths to related sites. The links and paths are not assigned or precoordinated but are self-designing as Web searches are performed. A half-million people have already downloaded *Alexa* to search his archives (http://www/alexa.com). Based on what *Alexa* tracks, Kahle has taken three snapshops each for 500 sites (texts and images) and continues to trigger downloading for the most popular sites once every two months. So, even if a homepage were edited, redone entirely and overwritten, or if a site disappears altogether, these snapshots may be called from these digital archives. His facility now has a capacity for digital tapes holding twenty terabytes of data, of which half are full coming into 1998 (one terabyte equals 800,000 books) and are being queried at fourteen hits per second. He proudly compares this usage with the busiest public libraries and this capacity to the Library of Congress. The significance of such developments for archives everywhere, for history in the *long durée*, and interdisciplinary research of all kinds, is unprecedented. We have no models from the past to forecast History in the future that can use such resources. If the data are available in such mass and retrieval mechanisms are in order, will methodologies also be available for their analysis?

How does one make sense of this? The call to change is often one of modernization; that is, to keep up with current developments on the assumption that they are worth endorsement, emulation, and participation. The technology imperative is often stated like this, that because the technology exists, surely one must use it. This was captured best as ascribed to the acronym BITNET (Because Its There Network). Technology, by definition, depends on use, application, and adoption, to be successful; conversely, to be successful in today's world one often feels the need to use technology. This is the case for information technology as well, and one may be rationally skeptical of the bandwagon lure, but a circumspect human being at this turn of the millennium, even without developed historical prowess or acute consciousness of history, must acknowledge that change wrought by information technology is pervasive, accelerating, and lasting to produce what forecasters in the early 1970s heralded as "post-industrial society" (TOURAINE; D. BELL). A turn of this phrase has been the "information society." TOFFLER (1981) and NAISBITT (1982) called attention to dramatic changes, which in this decade are still being used to argue for new approaches, skills, techniques, and means to handle information overload which D. SHENK calls "data smog." HAWKES, for example, reminds us about the tremendous increase in mass communication (151 percent between 1960 and 1980) whereby an average American at the eve of personal computing was already being exposed to 61,556 words per day or one per second during each workday. Relying on VON NEUMANN and De Sola Pool (1984), Hawkes notes that the ratio of words consumed to those produced had decreased by half during the same period. Historians, like people at large, cannot consume the amount of information supplied.

Whereas once historians complained about the lack of information about their subjects, now the issue is time management and inability to cover any topic completely. Few academics have studied the overload problem for their disciplines, but its impact on society at large has attracted the attention of several critics who have pointed out information technology's negative aspects, partly to counterweigh the advertising and hype about all of its merits and benefits. SHENK, for example, speaks of such problems as "paralysis by analysis"; the "village of Babel," referring not only to technological Newspeak, but the splintering of culture; the opposing extremes of "dataveillance" and "anecdotage"; and the coarsening of American culture. He advocates that to clean up one's information environment, one should simplify, filter, "denichify" and defend oneself against "data spam" ("spamming" is "the wanton mass transmittal of unsolicited electronic messages," p. 24) in order to return to a more intelligent tranquility. In short, he argues that the information glut has produced too much of a good thing, which overall has had deteriorating consequences for our society. Such critiques balance my own enthusiasm for information technology and access and create a healthy skepticism when subjected to advertising hype, but nevertheless one must recognize the major shift in how work has changed in the United States. and Europe because of modern information technology and the relative state of academic *vis-á-vis* other kinds of work.

Consider scholarship as the work of research, publishing, teaching, and creating in terms of the following data and conclusions drawn by PRITCHETT, a psychologist and organizational change consultant who uses historical benchmarks to impress upon his audiences the degree of change around them, in his wake-up call for *"New Work Habits for a Radically Changing World."*

- 85 percent of American workers were in agriculture at the beginning of this century; now only 3 percent are.

- 73 percent of U.S. employees at midcentury were in manufacturing; now 15 percent are.

- 5-10 percent of an educated elite one generation ago worked in data gathering, processing, and analysis; by the end of this decade 44 percent of all American workers will.

- 50 percent or more workers in industrialized countries made things in the 1960s; by 2000 A.D. no developed country will have more than 16 percent making or moving goods.

- Only 16 of the top 100 U.S. companies in the early 1900s are still in existence; 230 companies (46 percent) of the *Fortune* 500 companies (first compiled in 1956) from the 1980s have disappeared; and among the original *Fortune* 500 companies, only 29 of the "top 100" were still at the top in 1992.

- While 66 percent of American workers are now in service industries, their most important product is knowledge.

- Self-help and team interplay are altering old hierarchical support roles and reporting lines in project management; the number of secretarial jobs in the U.S. has decreased by 521,000 since 1987.

- Predictions are that more and more people will be self-employed, by choice and necessity, with a minority of the workforce in the decades to come in conventional full-time jobs within organizations; adjunct status is increasingly prevalent (HANDY).

- In 1991, one of every three Americans had worked for the same employer for less than a year; and two of three had been with their company less than five years.

• The contingent workforce in the U.S. (self-employed, part-timers, outsourcing agents, or consultants, etc.) has grown 57 percent since 1980 (O'HARA-DEV-EREAUX & JOHANSEN).

• "Workplace" is being replaced by "workspace."

Such data, gathered over a decade, produce a history of technological and accompanying social/labor change, which both creates certain expectations and allows general predictions, such as provided by Bill Gates in *The Road Ahead* (GATES *ET AL.*). Gates does not operate formally as a historian, but he is nevertheless an acute observer of change around him. In making sense out of the Internet and to counter "backward-looking dreamers," he quotes none other than Antoine de Saint-Exupery who lauded technological progress through history. Gates is aware of history and of his own role in it: "we are watching something historic happen" (p. 313). Of course, he is making some of this happen, since his historical sensibilities and visions chart the course of major technological development at Microsoft which will affect all of us. Indicative of this is Gate's reorientation in 1996 of his company around the Internet. In reviewing this 1995 bestseller, the *New York Post* maintained: "If only 10 percent of this book actually happens, our lives will be transformed." Gates and his colleagues speculate about how current information technology and particularly global networking are about to revolutionize life as we have known it over the past century: he predicts a "content revolution" more than simply more technology, business over the Internet leading to a friction-free capitalism, and the merger of the home and workplace. He also sees critical problems arising in policy (public versus private interest), a possible parochialism from "individual over-indulgence" and isolationism ironically resulting from the convenience of unheralded communication capabilities, an altered style of democracy because of instant referendum possibilities, creation of an information-rich and therefore wealthy elite; and the loss of privacy. (Gates finds the prospect of "documented lives" to be "chilling" [p. 304]), and the creation of a new technological dependency on the network.) Given to optimism, Gates views education as "the best investment" and expects the most from it, but he deplores the "PC's mediocre track record in the classroom" and the skepticism in academe which by itself has forestalled progressive adaptation (pp. 209-10). He speculates about the impact on teaching of Web sites, access everywhere, and digital white boards. Overall he sees proper investment in education's technical infrastructure as yielding a profound return in the future. Coincidentally, he has begun to invest heavily in public libraries and digital archives outside the formal structure of higher education.

These trends have already made an impact on academe where conventional History has flourished, but the track record in higher education to which Bill Gates refers, is not very respectable. Trends accompanying increased use of information and instructional technology are not very encouraging because they seem to counter goals for which such technology is being deployed. Consider the downsizing of the Arts and Humanities in many schools and the closures of many liberal arts colleges simultaneously with the growth of community colleges and trade schools; the increased reliance on adjunct faculty for cost-savings and flexibility to glide with under- and overloads; the spread of course offerings over 90 hours workweeks instead of the traditional 8 AM to 5 PM schedule often with dilution of content, diversity in interaction, and free time for independent learning; the decreased campus investments in faculty offices and traditional office suites, more common space, and a move toward distributed campuses and networking; the increased spending on the information infrastructure of universities but at the expense of library acquisitions and resident resources; and shifts in library collection development from monographs to serials and now to electronic media, resulting in greater fragmentation of sources and piecemeal learning. Whereas the basic unit of information conveyed in libraries was once thought to be the single page that could be photocopied, it is now the single paragraph or less—no more than can fit on a monitor's 12-inch screen. The problem is not just the increased mass of information, but its fragmentary nature, i.e., the discrete micro-units of information. The art of synthesis is far more complicated than it ever was; envisioning the "big picture" is a stretch of the imagination rather than simply gathering information. Moreover, information retrieval, the dominant ideal in the last generation's acquisition mentality, is today being compromised by a real need to filter and discard. Complexity is heightened immeasurably by the rate of information processing which is simultaneously data production, acquisition, appraisal, retention, and disposal. Knowledge, something more than mere information, is the result of distillation and synthesis. Thus a new sense of information ecology is evolving out of necessity. More is not necessarily better; it may simply be more. The critical factor is time management, which translates into strategy and technological know-how.

The futurist David Pearce Snyder and his colleagues have forecast broad socioeconomic changes in America for the first decade of the new millennium, based on their sense of history and data supplied from Stanford University's Center for Economic Policy Research (EDWARDS & SNYDER; SNYDER). SNYDER opens his seminars by questioning his audiences if they believe they are passing through a genuine revolution of the type described in History books. Each month as he travels throughout the United States, more and more people raise their hands to affirm that they are living in a whole-scale, thorough socioeconomic revolution wrought by modern information technology. He is fond of saying that life is time travel, with the exception that one cannot go back again, but one assuredly moves forward. Thus it is the future that deserves our scrutiny as we go into it. His futurism is not rampant speculation, but is based on historical hindsight and modeling because these are the only means to know the future, however imperfectly. Moreover, his technique shows that rather than predicting the future, his real contribution is helping people understand what they already know and surmise. Snyder is quoted (RATZ, p. 49):

> "We are, in fact, in the middle of a genuine revolution—the kind they write about
> in history books. Fifty to sixty years from now, whole partitions of history disks
> will be devoted entirely to "High Noon for High Tech: America in the 1990s."

Snyder is talking about the "re-invention of America," in a shift as dramatic as that from steam to electricity, but which has taken time since the 1960s because the system is huge, and established systems resist change. He sees the often tragic and costly change, with its dislocation of fifty million of American laborers between 1981 and 1996 and the investment of one trillion dollars in information technology by American firms between 1984 and 1993 with no real increase in rates of productivity, as having undergone the most difficult transition already. Yet, the "social pain" from massive displacements is likely to continue, sustaining racial and sectarian tension and turbulence. EDWARDS & SNYDER characterize these tumultuous ups and downs as "roller coaster 2000." (Refer to the speculative work of, in chronological order during this decade: ZUBOFF for the changing nature of office work; P. DAVID on the productivity paradox; OSBORNE & GAEBLER on re-inventing government; LEYDEN predicts direct democracy with electronic voting rather than layers of representative government; MCCRAE points to smaller governments by regulation without provision; W. BRIDGES on prosperity without jobs in the traditional sense or "jobshift"; D. HULL on the need for smart workers; H. SMITH on how all of this calls for a *Rethinking America* with a special challenge to education; D. SUCHER's design of the seemingly contradictory "urban village" of the future as new communications decentralize new work; WEISBORD & JANOFF's discussion of interaction between organizations and communities; BRANDS's characterization of the 1890s as "the reckless decade" that parallels the 1990s; and DAVIS & WESSEL's prediction of the coming economic boom and prosperity predicted for the next decade.

David Pearce Snyder thinks that the turnaround in the current revolution can be dated to about 1995 and continued restructuring through 2010 will be more positive in an era of general economic growth and prosperity for America and for Europe as well with a ten-year lag-time and more for the rest of the world, as this investment in information and information technology finally pays off. The hallmarks of this turnaround, as SNYDER sees it include: deregulation; shift from labor to information intensive work; recovery from the decline in performance and real prosperity; growth inter-modal enterprise (mixture of private and public sector contributions) and new forms of collaboration; transfer of decision-making from entrenched management to front-line workers in teams; reestablishment of the extended family and multigenerational households that includes a doubling of self-employment and home-office enterprise; spread of part-time, intermittent jobs and careers that demand greater flexibility; more embedded information content in goods; reshaping organizations from vertical to horizontal architectures; migration to suburbs and rural areas; growing dependence on "I-ways," expert systems, and "conversational computing" or chatting with computers equipped with more microprocessing power and endowed with a colloquial command of natural language.

The aforementioned facts, speculations, and forecasts underlie what must be considered a cliché by now, that "the Industrial Age has given way to the Information Age" (PRITCHETT, p. 5). They attest change all around us, but they do not necessarily provide easy differentiation between good and bad trends. As the proverb goes, modern information technology brings with it mixed blessings, some of which are disguised curses underscoring the folk wisdom that ignorance is bliss. These trends are not necessarily detrimental to History, but History as a discipline and profession has been slow to reconceptualize its potential role in the "Information Age" and to move willingly beyond the conventional walls of academe. Historians are information professionals even if they do not now identify their roles this way. The idea is not to clone historians into stereotypical electronic businessmen, but to enlist them as reflective thinkers, thorough researchers, expert synthesizers and interpreters, and effective teachers, into entrepreneurial endeavors in and outside academe. They too are being affected by the trends SNYDER outlines. The profession will continue to be affected by these overriding developments. So the issue is how to ensure a future with a history, and a socioeconomic milieu that is enriched by historians and a historically conscious citizenry. This does require change in History's professional culture.

Consider historians' work habits with other trends related to information and telecommunication technologies in the American work environment outside academe to which PRITCHETT alludes:

- In 1993, 19,000,000 American workers carried pagers; 12,000,000,000 messages were left in voice mailboxes; 16,000,000 Americans have cellular phones.

- 10,000,000 telefax machines have been added to American homes and offices since 1987, a million each year.

- E-mail addresses have increased since 1987 by over 26,000,000.

- 25,000,000 computers have been added to workplaces in the U.S. since 1983.

The implications for contemporary history and archives are profound. WURMAN maintains that the information supply available to us now is doubling every five years. He attempts to place this into historical perspective by asserting that "There has been more information produced in the last 30 years than during the previous 5,000." Or "A weekday edition of *The New York Times* contains more information than the average person was likely to come across in a lifetime during seventeenth century England." He recalls, as many have on the centennial of the *Times* in 1996, that this information enterprise has been called one of the American "wonders of the world." The newspaper's recent commemoration reminds everyone that the mass of current information production and accumulation is mind-boggling when contrasted with any previous century, making the future task of historians daunting indeed. The problem of historical information preservation, access, and research is formidable, that all historians, regardless of specialty, should be contributing to solutions, accommodating their teaching accordingly, and becoming involved in policy formulation, project development, and organizational efforts to safeguard their own fields and History in general. Again, an approach might be development of a unidisciplinary set of technical skills, domain knowledge, and research methodological expertise, all of which constitute Historical Information Science. The tools for such development are formidable, as they need be, given the magnitude of the current problem and the challenges ahead. Information technology is causing some of these problems but is also providing tools for their resolution.

Consider the order of magnitude of computing power achieved in the last two generations:

- Just after World War II when computing began to take off, the ENIAC computer took up more space than an 18-wheel tractor trailer, consumed 140,000 watts of electricity, to execute 5,000 basic arithmetic operations per second.

- Today the 486 PC, which is now totally eclipsed by Pentium 75 PCS, using a silicon chip the size of a dime and weighing less than a packet of sweetener, uses two watts of electricity, to execute 54,000,000 instructions per second.

- Consumers today wear more computing power in wrist watches and calculators than anyone had access to in 1961.

- A portable home video camera now contains more processing capability than the old IBM 360 PC.

- Sega's game maker which supports computer video games, has more processing capability than the 1976 Cray supercomputer that only physicists could use a generation ago.

- While practical industrial robots were just being introduced in the 1960s, by 1982 32,000 were used in American industry, and today more than 20,000,000 are working around the clock.

- Integrated circuits invented in the 1950s have transformed computing, driving miniaturization during the 1960s when the number of components in microchips doubled each year to more than 1,000 by 1970 and 1,000,000,000 by 1992 (MORRISON & SCHMID).

- The cost of computing power drops roughly 30 percent/year while microchips are doubling in performance capabilities every 18 months.

- This means that computing power today is 8,000 times less expensive that it was 30 years ago.

- NAISBITT in his *Global Paradox* quotes former AT&T vice-chairman Randall Tobias to make this point by using an hypothetical historical comparison: "If we had similar progress in automotive technology, today you could buy a Lexus for about two dollars. It would travel at the speed of sound, and go about 600 miles on a thimble of gas."

Historians can now afford computing. They can only blame themselves for not using computers and related information technology. They can use it traditionally or to its fullest power to redesign research, to explore data never before accumulated in such mass or with such extraordinary tools, and to be genuinely creative. In addition to advancing knowledge of history in a field of study, each historian must also contribute to History in the larger sense by evolving methods, techniques, approaches, and appropriate technology for the future of historical studies. Intra-disciplinary field study with traditional and often idiosyncratic approaches will not suffice for this larger task.

Stanford University's Paul Romer, a leading proponent of the New Growth Theory, recently discussed the economics of new technology development and its success or failure in the marketplace (interviewed in FORBES *ASAP*, 43-44). History itself is not a significant market, but higher education overall is. Within the context of academe, History is being subjected to certain pressures from technology which will induce far-reaching change—if not change in and by History, and then to History, perhaps resulting in further marginalization. Romer proposes directing technological change rather than just letting it happen, and he rejects technological determinism. Although Romer understands that "the vast majority of possible arrangements lead to muck," he reduces the crux of the problem to the following:

> The key to technological change and economic growth is to sort quickly and inexpensively through the possibilities to find valuable formulas. Fundamentally, this search is an information-processing activity.... Most search processes involve some combination of the two [rational design and mass screening].... From the beginning, everyone expected that computers would aid the process of rational design.... Surprisingly, computer-automated systems are also making screening more efficient.... So even if the rate of technological progress in the computer industry itself comes to a stop [i.e., because there is a limit on how small and powerful a chip can become], the digital revolution will leave us with valuable information-processing tools for the future. Because searching will be cheaper, market incentives will cause us to search more. Technological change and economic growth will therefore be more rapid (p. 44).

Some see this growth and development as a revolution leading to a new "civilization" (perhaps "culture" is a better term here), which scares people partially because of the bad connotations of "revolution" instead of something more positive like "renewal" as Harvard University's Jeffrey Eisenach advocates, even though he sees "the indestructible pillars of the industrial world, its ideas as well as its great institutions, have crumbled before the forces of the digital 'revolution' " (FORBES *ASAP*, p. 59). Others see the change about us as something less traumatic. Robert Kaplan, for example, argues that "The record of history is clear: Though technological innovations have changed the way we live, they have not changed man's essential nature" (FORBES *ASAP*, p. 51). Robert Conquest, a specialist on Stalinism, reminded the American public, as a sobering thought for those who enthusiastically foresee a technologically enhanced democracy around the corner: "We seldom remember nowadays that the totalitarianism that emerged early this century was thought to embody, above all, modernity and technology" (FORBES *ASAP*, p. 39). Information technology is not "good" or "bad" except in terms of operational efficiency and effectiveness; the value judgement that includes a moral and ethical dimension should be reserved for its applications and uses.

More agreement is possible when limiting the discussion to how we live, both play and work. Eisenach describes what has already changed in our lives, based on Alvin and Heidi Toffler's 1994 Progress & Freedom Foundation book (TOFFLER & TOFFLER). He sees technological change as overturning the rules of Western civilization set down in the Enlightenment and throwing out the process notions of the Progressive Era, "from Max Weber's 'bureaucracy' to Frederick Taylor's 'one best way'." The Tofflers generalize that such ideas about process governed institutional development during the Industrial Age, which was characterized by standardization, synchronization, specialization, centralization, and "massification". When Eisenach considers the new rules of the Digital Age, he cites Peter Drucker and Peter Senge's emphasis on knowledge production and learning organizations instead of Taylor, and substitutes W. Edward Deming's horizontal flow charts for Arthur Sloan's vertical approach to organization (cf., DRUCKER 1985, 1986; SENGE). Paul Romer's "New Science" of interconnectivity and complexity replaces Adam Smith, just as Albert Einstein and Stephen Hawking replaced Darwin and Descartes for the intellectual framework of this new world. He observes (p. 60):

As for our institutions, every one of the five characteristics the Toffler's identify is being turned on its head. Customization is replacing standardization. Just-in-time production is replacing synchronization. Holism and integration are replacing specialization. Empowerment and telecommunications are replacing centralization. And "small is beautiful " is replacing "big is better." The notion that we are creating a new civilization is neither hyperbolic nor romantic. It is a fact.

Eisenach sees four main challenges confronting us at the turn of the millennium: (1) the task of creating a new civilization (or culture?) by design rather than accident; (2) which requires understanding the nature and magnitude of the change around us (i.e., the implication's of what the Toffler's observe); (3) finding the will to undertake a conscious creation; and (4) delivery on our promises to ourselves. History's role in such change is manifest in the first two challenges, vision and understanding; and those looking for inspiration to meet challenge number three often turn to history for their examples. But historians may be reluctant to engage the fourth challenge, which requires political activism and impact on policy formation.

The argument here for development of a superdisciplinary Historical Information Science obviously falls into line with trends toward holistic intellectual integration while distributing the enterprise itself, and other recommendations following from this, are in line with other trends to be described. For the time, however, historians can serve as critics to force circumspection and reflection of the changes wrought by current information technologies. Mark Helprin, a historical fiction writer, remarks on the situation and chides leaders and followers alike about bringing some discipline to what seems like chaotic change:

> History is in motion, and those moving with it are so caught up that they cannot always see its broad outlines. Like soldiers in battle, they are concerned with objectives rather than principles. They are you....
>
> The revolution that you have made is indeed wonderful, powerful, and great, and it has hardly begun. But you have not brought to it the discipline, the anticipation, or the clarity of vision that it, like any vast argumentation in the potential of humankind, demands. You have been too enthusiastic in your welcome of it, and not wary enough. Some of you have become arrogant and careless, and, quite frankly, too many of you at the forefront of this revolution lack any guiding principles whatsoever or even the urge to seek them out. In this, of course, you are not alone. Nor are you the first. But you must. You must fit this revolution to the needs and limitations of man, with his delicacy, dignity, and mortality always in mind. Having accelerated tranquility, you must now find a way to slow it down (FORBES *ASAP*, pp. 15, 22).

Are historians responding to the aforementioned changes? They are unlikely to be the revolutionaries or makers of history during this era of rapid change, but by virtue of their profession, they ought to be keen observers. One could expect in an era of dramatic change that History be responsive and that in responding, it would change also. Historians have already become more ecumenical in redefining themselves. Most recently the AHA (1995, p. 23) attempted to identify who could have affiliation with the AHA and be considered members of "a community of historians" who are "individuals with formal training in history who practice history through either teaching or research, or both." Three further explanations clarified what these activities included:

1.   Teaching is understood as encompassing a wide range of communication in varied settings—museums and historic sites as well as classrooms—and as involving visual materials and artifacts as well as words.

2. Research is understood as the discovery and exchange of new information and interpretations.

3. The professional communicates with students, other scholars, the general public, and decision makers in memoranda, research reports, articles, reviews, books, monographs, and textbooks; it communicates via print and electronic means, exhibits, films, newsletters, scholarly meetings, public testimony, and historic sites.

These activities are reflected by this essay's coverage, which assumes an equally embrasive concept of History's subject domain as anything past to the present. Research methods are left undefined, but interestingly as a sign of changing times "electronic communications" received specific attention. Neither the teaching or research aspects of the AHA definitions refer to History as a humanity, art, or science; in the spirit of AHA ecumenism, all three may be included but this essay pays more attention to history as science than do most, at least as Social Science, not to slight the art in historical interpretation and presentation or link to the humanities in description, criticism, and ethos, but to stress research as "discovery" and generation of "new information and interpretations." Here the connection between history and information as "historical information" studied scientifically, whatever the source or medium, is central to the discussion. Moreover, the foci are on computer-assisted research, interpretation, presentation, and communication. The original target for its completion at the end of 1996 may also have some commemorative significance, since this year is considered to be the fiftieth anniversary of the computer based on the 1946 dedication of the ENIAC at the University of Pennsylvania.

A definition of Historical Information Science as scientific thought applied to historical information is too encompassing to be very meaningful, since all information soon becomes historical, if not immediately, then in just a matter of years. No chronological definition suffices to define what is or is not historical. How recent must something be to be considered outside the purview of history? Or, does History encompass everything for which the past tense is used? That is the case in our personal lives. The use of computer memory for searches and especially repetitions in an information system to assist a user's or system's improvement is perceived by A. Lee as creating a "history tool." Many computing systems contain such history-based user-support mechanisms that allow recall of past operations to be reused in a current procedure. This is especially true of change management in software engineering and in transaction log analysis and diagnostics (most of which could be adopted and adapted for historical database development and control systems for electronic archives). In such instances, the history is obviously recent; indeed, perhaps a matter of seconds. After all, if processing loops are to be avoided, the modern computer programmer must take seriously George Santayana's dictum, "Those who do not learn from History are doomed to repeat it." Indeed, this philosopher's observation nearly a half-century ago takes on new meaning in this technical context, far more exact, minute, and predictable than he realized.

Although historians have not formalized space-time theory similarly as in the hard sciences (EARMAN, GLYMOUR & STACHEL, eds.), such cardinal elements of historical thought as the relation between an event and its time and place, which provide a locus and context for all historical interpretation, are also essential to Information Storage and Retrieval (ISAR), query processors (i.e., "temporal reasoning" processes) in monitoring and expert systems (e.g., STEPHENS using Inference Corporation's *Automated Reasoning Tool* [*ART*] which can work in realtime or history). MANSAND, LINOFF & WALTZ use memory-based reasoning to classify news stories in a way that seems highly applicable to historical narratives. But information scientists do not commonly associate such techniques as temporal or memory-based reasoning with history because they assume that some longer period of time must have lapsed between the event and its recall for something to be historical. Nor would they relate to the anthropologist's interest in time as a cultural construction of temporal maps, even though such work can be integrated profitably to work in Information Science involving cognitive mapping in information displays and knowledge representation. GELL, for example, maintains that people's awareness of time is culturally conditioned, different cultures deal with temporal problems differently, and such differences reveal themselves in the West's consideration of time, an intangible element over which people have no control, yet it should be considered a "resource" that can be economized. He explores the thoughts of Durkheim, Evans-Pritchard, Levi-Strauss, Geertz, Piaget, Husserl, Bourdieu, and others on the subject—all of whom are underrepresented in Information Science literature or research involving temporal reasoning in computation.

J. A. N. LEE, despite misattributions of clichés about "why study history" and some assumptions that would be anathema to philosophers of history, argues practically about "why I study the history of computing." One of his arguments pertains to the study of history as a series of case studies, successes and failures, to understand context, trends, and positioning of projects and developments into a continuum in which they have some chance of success. To overcome the "stigma" that pertains both to history and the study of educational needs in computer science, namely that any scientist undertaking historical study is under "a suspicion that they are becoming senile" (p. 54), he appeals to the practicality of those drawn into science and technology to justify historical studies. He thus attempts to justify the legitimate place of history in computer science specifically and thereby in all information sciences. Systems people may wonder about the even more radical vision of History in the future provided by A. PENA & TALLABS who consider historians as sense-makers who enable people to adapt to change while simultaneously retaining the resemblance of society and civilization.

Perhaps it is the level of consciousness that demarcates History from history, and the application component of historical data and reasoning in other than purely academic contexts that separates history from History. History, above all particular specializations, is a remembering, informing, interpreting, and teaching endeavor which, when perceived as a science, may always be construed as an Historical Information Science. The purposes of such historical study as delineated by TOSH are to inform, to orient and socialize, to preserve information and provide recall, to encourage discussion and learning. LANDES & TILLY (pp. 5-6), again thinking purely in academic terms, add that History is also to guard against the extremes of indoctrination and self-delusion (notwithstanding H. WHITE [1987] and others who have disputed that History ever presents a neutral, objective forum for debating the great issues of humankind). FERRO (1981/1984) likewise distinguishes between proper use of History in education for broad, comparative perspectives, and abuses in indoctrination or a single contrived perspective that has an ulterior motive, especially in teaching bias, prejudice, and racism to children. These goals or uses of History are not dissimilar from the purposes and uses of history tools or time-sequence reasoning in automated information systems, except outside academic utility, historical data and chronological reasoning can and are being used in a host of applications under a different rubric.

Computer Science has its equivalent in both "temporal reasoning" and "time and event analysis" which can be (but seldom is) related to the "collective action event" history tradition exemplified in recent work by Charles Tilly (TARROW commenting on TILLY, 1984, 1994). In the Social Sciences this may be "longitudinal research" (e.g., HUBER & VAN DE VEN). In educational terms, for example, history is "experiential-based learning." In Information Science, some refer to history as "retrospective research," or less frequently simply as "retrospection" supposedly as distinct from contemporary "inspection." In an ahistorical mind, such processes are more like backward chaining in information retrieval and indexing techniques than they are truly a form of historical thought, but they resemble procedures based on historical reasoning, the sequential ordering of data with the inference that proximity and placement in time (i.e., immediacy) are meaningful attributes (J. D. ANDERSON relates such concerns and indexing through cognitive psychology). On the other hand, both spatial and temporal reasoning, especially when combined, are often historical. In short, information technology and the Social Sciences use history just as History can use technology and Social Science methodology, but awareness of the history outside formal History is often confused, and the placement of historical awareness and interpretation in technical thought and procedure are not as overt and obvious as is the intrusion of technology into History. They should be, and ought to be, explicitly *historical* reasoning in such information processing. One might argue conversely, that there ought to be equally explicit reasoning and procedural documentation in scientifically constructed history.

Historical Information Science

Apart from its contributions to and benefits from an ever-present historiographic criticism, Historical Information Science would seek especially to enlighten historians as information specialists and professionals about (1) the nature of historical information, its formation, structure, initial use, and survival, and how its secondary use for History today is affected by its transposition in time and place; and (2), how modern information technology can be used to process historical information and how to develop it through linkage never before made and analysis not possible without the aid of computing. Conversely, from this broad viewpoint, all Information Science research that is longitudinal or retrospective is historical. Moreover, all organizational memory is history, as is understood in recent debates on the interaction between memory, culture and collective recall (commemoration in NORA's analysis), and history (e.g., discontinuity as a memory crisis, *á la* TERDIMAN). The medievalist Georges Duby reminds us of the cardinal precept of History, that is "history continues" (DUBY, 1994). The issues are as follows: *if* people know it does continue beyond their own brief experience and elsewhere beyond their immediate environment; and then, *how* do they know it? The latter is as much a question of information technologies and organizational continuity than it is a query about intellect. Few historians, however, have interjected key issues in such a debate into the realm of computer technology and interplay between information technologies and cultural history in the same way that the history of writing and printing has made its mark on intellectual thought in publishing and communications. Might a better understanding of history improve the content quality of databases and expand their scope in time, as well as point to directions in operations research for more context-sensitive computing? OUKSEL & NAIMAN take up this issue of coordinating context building with the design of heterogeneous information systems. Likewise, Historical Information Science could contribute to modern Information Science precisely by broadening and lengthening its often narrow trajectory and short-range focus, and thereby assist in the difficult problems of generalization pertaining to all kinds of information and human behavior and experience resulting from interaction with information.

In both cases, scientific History and Information Science, the appellation of "science" might be disclaimed (as it has been often in both cases, but more by historians), as it is when juxtaposed to a field like Physics (WINCHESTER, 1984), but it has a greater chance of acceptance when compared with Economics (MCCLOSKEY, 1994). The degree of favorable comparison between a so-called "soft" and "hard" science depends on one's definition of Science, ranging from what the Latin progenitor *scientia* (i.e., wisdom generally or bodies of wisdom) meant, to something much more narrowly defined. DOEBLER maintains that the largest studies in past decades, *Project Hindsight*, (SHERWIN & ISENSON) and the *Trace* project during the late 1960s when researchers tried to distinguish between pure science and everything else (Impure? As tainted by technology, application, etc.?) failed to provide comprehensive and consistent pictures about Science as separate from other forms of inquiry. The modern debate was framed earlier most influentially by C. P. Snow's two-culture theory, which set up an antithesis between the Sciences and Arts and Humanities that is no longer in vogue. The theorist A. I. MIKHAILOV (primarily, but with colleagues CHERNYI & GILJAREVSKII, 1969) after the post-Sputnik concentration of defining and developing the Sciences and at the initial surge in history computing, argued for the following prerequisites to the formation of a genuine Science (paraphrased also by B. C. BROOKES, 1972, p. 137, and reiterated by BUCKLAND, 1983, p. 17, and others, since this has become a commonly accepted set of criteria):

1. A specifically defined subject-area to be studied

2. Clarification of basic descriptive concepts

3. Fundamental laws, capable of being expressed quantitatively, must be particular to the subject

4. A theory must be developed that can be applied to multiple phenomena

To these may be added Karl Popper's famous falsification test for genuine science. In 1934, he not only attacked the turn-of-the-century notions of objectified history reflecting actual reality with a different sense of theoretical historicism but also introduced to History a justification for discussion of possibilities or alterative histories and, therefore, laid an intellectual groundwork for historical modeling and simulation (POPPER). Popper's lasting contribution may be updated by J. ZIMAN's discussion of the reliability of knowledge, including long-term or historical value and scientific knowledge, which also takes the subject of information to a realm seldom treated in Information Science, but which is very germane to archival science. While so many have sought to distinguish science from non-science, others have taken an ecumenical approach, perhaps best articulated in 1939 in the midst of this debate by NEURATH, CARNAP & MORRIS who pointed to the commonality or foundations for a unity of science.

Of the aforementioned criteria for a "hard" science, MIKHAILOV did not think that more than the first two could be claimed by Information Science. History qualifies for no more, except that in the third area it can employ considerable quantification. However, the once central paradigm of post-World War II historiography, the attempt to embrace "covering laws" in History (HEMPEL, 1942, 1974; critiqued by MANDELBAUM, 1974) has been abandoned since the mid-1960s just before MIKHAILOV promulgated his famous *sine qua non* dictum. Even when granting the first two criteria, there is ample contention in defining or interpreting what is mean by "information." And if one wants something less restricting than mathematically measuring efficiency in signal transmission in a channel as the core of information theory, as early postulated in 1949 by SHANNON & WEAVOR (see D. RITCHIE, 1986b), thankfully one can find inspiration as did BUCKLAND (1992) in their contemporary, Vannevar Bush, who in his influential essay "As We May Think" opened up wider possibilities (BUSH, 1945). This could include "As We May Think Historically." R. A. Fairthorne in this vein thought the chief focus of Information Science was what he called "documentary discourse" (FAIRTHORNE, 1969, p. 79)—as a visionary before his time (i.e., as early as 1961 [pp. 95-96] before the work of BENVENISTE in 1966, but which did not circulate in English until after 1971).

Michael Buckland explains: "By this [i.e., information science], we mean an understanding of the relationships between author and document, between one document and another, and between document and reader" (BUCKLAND, 1983, p. 21). Archivists might refer to the same idea as "appraisal." Others will recognize immediately the possible connection between such thinking in Information Science and textual criticism, and especially New Literary Criticism. Many scholars like Buckland would argue that while Information Science, and hence Historical Information Science, would not qualify as a "hard" science, it may be considered as hard as any of the Social Sciences. The spectrum of science is broad enough to accommodate varieties. More contested, except from the vantage point of historians, would be the view of Buckland's colleague Patrick G. Wilson, namely that all Information Science, not just Historical Information Science, should best be regarded like the Social Sciences as a branch of

History because while certain scientific techniques can be applied, descriptive methods prevail, governing laws are difficult to identify, and there are logical limits to what can be learned rationally through direct observation and methods cloned from the natural sciences (P. G. WILSON, 1980). Most information scientists may have some difficulty accepting a case for Historical Information Science; they assuredly do not share Wilson's view that Information Science is History or is essentially historical in methodology or ethos. Martha Williams in 1995 refused to have my *ARIST* chapter entitled "Historical Information Science" because she thought that most ASIS members would not know on sight what the chapter was about (MCCRANK, 1995). I suspect she was right.

The central regenerative idea of recalling older data for reinterpretation to form new information is obviously appealing for historians, even if they disagree about specific applications or part company with natural science over the issue of predictability (MODIS claims that predictions, like expectations, are made by everyone from society's "telltale signatures" that reveal the past and forecast the future). Having abandoned the so-called "covering laws" notion in contemporary epistemology as well as a simplistic notion of historical facts (VEYNE, pp. 21-22, claims that the old choice between writing history as a "body of laws" or one "of facts" is simply shopworn), historians would seem to be devoted to piecemeal history and niche expertise.

The problematic tension is attempting to work within a closed system, where laws may appear to be intrinsically more predictable, and within the openness of History where this is less feasible. One might see laws more compatible with History if one saw them as in Law rather than hard science, as descriptors of norms rather than absolute dicta. As such, laws become guiding principles, descriptive norms, and sense-making generalizations akin to the dictum in Information Science that people generally retrieve information through the path of least resistance.

In the philosophy of science, however, certain strains of thought still cling to the notion and quest for "proof that everything in our world is organized in terms of a small number of natural laws comprising the principles underlying every branch of learning" including History, according to Pulitzer-prize winner socio-biologist Edward O. Wilson of Harvard University's Museum of Comparative Zoology. This is what he calls "consilience" rather than convergence, when he calls for a return to Enlightenment thinking, an extension of current methods of synthesis, and an appreciation of "the fundamental unity of all knowledge" in exploring consciousness, the relationships between biology and culture, and human nature and affairs (E. WILSON). This is another term for the older idea of syncretism whereby post-Reformation reformers, Lutherans especially, wanted to preserve their identity as distinct from the Reformed Churches. They achieved a new overall identity as Protestants united by their common opposition to the Roman Catholic Church, and ultimately they restored their common identity with the latter as well in their new understanding of Christianity. The distinction between faith and religion, and between organization and denomination, allowed a holistic reconceptualization of an overarching unity encompassing diversity (a concept like string indexing where the syntax starts with the broadest term as the class and works toward the narrowest term). Similarly, scientific and humanistic scholarship in Wilson's thinking are not only compatible, but their compatibility and integration are necessary for the unity of knowledge. He has not shied away in his *On Human Nature* from attempting to explain the complex, namely biodiversity, in terms of simplicity, namely, the unfolding of history as determined by information encased in our genes, common rules of human activities, and certain prerequisites for creations of the mind. Wilson's *Consilience: The Unity of Knowledge* is thought provoking in the same manner.

Just as historians have abandoned belief in and their previous search for underlying principles or "laws," so too have historians left behind the broad comparative approach of Arnold Toynbee (M. PERRY). Very early, Toynbee used the term "postmodern" to demarcate mid-century changes, and is still an unheralded pioneer in classification theory and modeling who remains virtually unknown to the Information Science community (for remedy to this colossal oversight, consider

TOYNBEE [1961], pp. 8-12, 103-135, 158-169, etc.) to overview and reclassify civilizations (which in any case failed to reform library classification schedules in History). Toynbee's influence today is similar to Freud's, pervasive in the general, seldom acknowledged in the specific, and better regarded outside his discipline than from within because he never was confined by the boundaries of disciplinarity. Historians, especially in Europe, may still extol the grand themes of history as they did in the 1990 International Congress of Historical Sciences in Madrid and may pay respect to the ideal of "general history" upheld by Henri-Irenée Marrou, one of its last champions (MARROU, 1961, 1965), but the tendency overall is toward less grandiose ambitions characterized by microscopic analysis, contextualized biographies, families and communities, localities and regions (but nations still), and "bottom-up" History—except that seldom does one see an impressive theoretical architecture, a grand conclusion, a generalized overlay or cover, and closure. And certainly no laws! That would be worse than refutable; it would be passé! Consequently much of History has become a continuing conversation and a cultural practice, much like Literary Criticism *qua* Literature, and less like a problem-oriented Social Science that requires specific conclusions and generally applicable lessons. History's bridge between the Humanities and Social Sciences is ever enriched by the cross-traffic, but such a habitat at any crossroads can and does produce an identity problem because of the constant commotion from outside influences and internal mulching. As is the case for Information Science, where disciplinary identity and synthesis are also problematic (PRENTICE), historians have difficulty extrapolating broader meaning and general interpretation from their many narrowly focused studies (BENDER, 1995, p. 995, refers to the "synthetic aspiration" of History). It is professionally risky to do so, but this goal lies behind the rationale of all scientific inquiry and it is not passé for everyone.

Richard Hofstader, one of the most renowned of historians among Americanists, referred to his discipline as "literary anthropology" as a way of combining the Humanities and Social Sciences in History (HOFSTADER, p. 363). Gordon Leff characterized History very generally as "a field of epistemological inquiry" (LEFF, 1969, p. 1). Michel de Certeau also grappled with this perennial problem of definition and identification of the "science" in History by characterizing the works of historians as "laboratories of epistemological experimentation" (DE CERTEAU, 1988, p. 82). He comments:

> Certainly they (historians) can give an objective form to these investigations only by combining the models with other sectors of their documentation about a society. Whence their paradox: they put scientific formalizations into play in order to test them, using the nonscientific objects with which they practice such testing. History thus continues to maintain no less than ever the function that it has exercised over the centuries in regard to many different "reasons," which are of interest to each of the established sciences: namely, its function as a form of criticism.

A key issue is when or whether foci and activities concentrating on historical information, both source criticism and technique with the related technology for processing information from resources, will evolve into a conscious discipline, either within History *per se*, or equally questionable within Information Science, or as reflecting the mixed backgrounds of both parents in a separate hybrid discipline like American Studies, Medieval Studies, General Humanities, etc. History lacks the establishment outside academe to support a development like Medical Informatics (BLUM & DUNCAN) unless there were to be more financial support and a more rigorous academic component in museums, archives, historical societies, and other culture industries and organizations. Does the evolution of metaknowledge about historical sources and information systems, thinking about them, and analysis of their content and structures, depend on the overall health of the historical profession and vigor of the discipline? History either as a discipline or profession has no monopoly on these activities but does have a concentrated vested interest. What characterizes a particular type or mode of History when the attributes of approach, method, technique, and applied information and instructional technology are emphasized over the traditional framework of period and geographic specialization? Must such technical specialization always be combined with a traditionally defined subject area? History typically has not acknowledged a coherent field within the discipline that is unaligned with a historical field traditionally defined by geography and chronology (as delineated for the 1980s by KAMMEN for the American Historical Association and for the 1990s by the AHA *Guide to Historical Literature*).

Methodologically oriented endeavors that cut across time and space, or which are highly introspective rather than comparative, like oral history, psycho-history, etc., have a difficult time in the establishment because they are often not identifiable in curricula or program articulation, and academic departmentalization mitigates against shared appointments or allocating positions to people who share their specialization outside the department's core or scope. The normal perspective on historical biography or bibliography, for example, would be a historian in a particular area studies field (e.g., American History) who happens to be a biographer or, less respected among historians, a bibliographer. It is no accident that historical bibliographers in history have attempted to find their niche in sociocultural and intellectual history within a traditional field. This same problem of identity and placement plagues historical computing. Moreover, technically competent people have many more career options than teaching history *per se*, but the historical profession as reflected by the American Historical Association and definition of historical studies along lines of curricular definition and departmentalization in higher education both illustrate the current dominant confusion of teaching history with the notion of a historian's practice as a professional. The Public History movement is a noted exception, but it has lacked the engagement of Information Science and information technology that one might have expected. Another exception is the field of Psycho-history which has broken new methodological ground because of its inter-disciplinarity, and the same may be said for history within other disciplines (POMPER; M. ROTH). But historical research outside of History *per se* has problems as well in support, context, acceptability, and respectability, except in areas like music and art history where numerical strength and mutual reinforcement are sufficient to form a parallel discipline to History (COHEN & ROTH, eds.). Developments in these Arts and Humanities are a long way from anything similar in the information field where history as an intellectual pursuit is barely identifiable and in some cases is discouraged because of misconceptions about its relevance. The study of inter-disciplinarity has shown that it is somewhat dangerous for scholars to work on the periphery of any discipline, as it is for all frontiersmen, without stable support groups, identifiable audiences, and clearly established norms for personnel budgeting, position description, promotion, and in teaching securing a defined niche in the overall program (J. KLEIN). Disciplinary identification in the Social Sciences has often been described as a form of ethnocentrism (D. T. CAMPBELL), operating similarly to more general social cohesion and exclusion in society at large (MULLINS).

Will historical information specialists, under this or another name, form a methodological and technical elite corps within History? Academic history departments have not normally had the means to use advanced computer technology very conveniently, but the technology itself has changed this situation so the issue is now more one of sociology and professionalization. Such self-identification and socio-academic cohesion is usually a precondition for professionalization with attendant educational programs for growth and further development (B. KIMBALL). In this regard, SULLIVAN (1995) makes an equation between *Work and Integrity*. These same artificial demarcations exist in perceiving one's collegial affiliation as a learned society versus a professional association, as though such a distinction were still meaningful today or that an information professional would belong to only one professional organization and somehow distinguish this as practice rather than anything learned or scholarly. Yet, if such practice were so diffused and its practitioners are so scattered, how is a professional or disciplinary identity cultivated? This is not merely a terminological problem of definition, but a socioeconomic and political issue that confronts any new field, especially a multidiscipline (PAISLEY, 1990).

This conceptualization problem, combined with the issue of professionalization, is reflected also in Information Science. It seems not altogether different from criticism two decades ago of economic history *qua* Econometrics as having advanced in the application of statistics and quantitative methodology at the expense of conceptualization because, as F. MAURO maintained, positivism and the scientific method destroy formalized ideas on one hand and on the other ideologies crystallized into doctrine rather than theory. That is the intellectual argument; the other is simply lack of funding for a proper incubation period. Is Historical Information Science an idea whose time has finally come? Or is the past too unforgiving to allow a retry in History? It seems doubtful that Information Science as identified with Library Science could become a more supportive partner, but the relationship is worth exploring.

In common parlance Library Science is almost inexorably related to libraries and hence bound codices or books, even though the root for the term "library," *liber*, refers to a different format altogether. The scroll form actually seems more in concert with the serial nature of most modern information. When scientific historicism was congealing, an attempt was made to disentangle content and form on the one hand, and on the other to recombine them in source criticism. To cover all formats the term "documentation" was preferred over the older use of "bibliography" not only to enlarge the idea of embracing archives as well as libraries, but because documentation included everything, the physical and metaphysical, whereas "information" seemed to pertain more to the latter. BUCKLAND (1997, p. 804), following WOLEDGE, argues that from ca. 1920 onward "documentation" came "to encompass bibliography, scholarly information service (*wissenschaftlicthe Aufklärrung [Auskunft]*), records management, and archival work" (citing also M. Godet from 1939; Paul Donker Duyvis from 1942; and Carl Björkbom [1959], etc., all of whom worked from within the documentation-information tradition). Such a claim cannot be made for usage outside the narrow field Buckland studied. Archivists and records managements, for example, never adopted the term in any specific sense, but continued to refer to the record and often to use records and documents interchangeably. A record sometimes carries the connotation of something tedious and arcane, whereas a document seems more upscale. R. Barry (1995) notes that in common parlance in business, managers relish information but are disdainful of records and associate them only with paper form, and they confuse information technology and media with the importance of the content and form in which information is captured. They erroneously separate records from information management based on such common assumptions, no matter how inappropriate. They likewise confuse Information Technology (IT) with Information Management or Information Resource Management (IRM). Historians, like their literary counterparts, often thought of "source" as the general, all-inclusive term as in "source criticism" or "primary source," and used "document" more than "record" as in "documentary editing" to distinguish it from narrative or literary text. They rarely think of these terms with the management additive.

The term "document," of course, from its Latin etymology, *docere* or to teach, retained an authoritative connotation as to instruct, or less formally to advise, rather than merely to inform. In this educational context, a moral lesson was conveyed, i.e., what was right, a precept. Documentation therefore was not perceived as value neutral or accidental; it was purposeful, meaningful, and positive. Above all, documentation had to do with proof, facts, and evidence. As such, its meaning was construed differently in history, archives, and legal and actuarial fields, than in the extension and ultimate replacement it experienced during the 1950s in the transition from documentation to information in the lineage of modern Information Science (LOSEE). Historical Information Science should retain this older evidential notion of formally conveyed information, as distinct from information confused with communication of any sort. The extension of the term seemed necessary to include more kinds of formats and information technology. As Michael Buckland and Boyd Hayward rightly point out, Paul Otlet in his *Traité de Documentation* (1934) thought anything, text or object, was a document if a viewer were informed by it. But Otlet and his contemporaries did not disembody information from form or presentation and means of conveyance as we are more prone to do in telecommunications. They were not materialists alone, but attributed the value of human thought and interpretation to a document. Documentation was interactive and objective, embracing object and thought.

BUCKLAND (1997, p. 805) cites the highly synthetic definition contrived in 1937 by the League of Nation's International Institute for Intellectual Cooperation and the Union Français des Organismes de Documentation (officially promulgated in English, French, and German):

> Any source of information, in material form, capable of being used for reference or study as an authority. Examples: manuscripts, printed matter, illustrations, diagrams, museum specimens, etc.

The French remained closer to the archival idea of documentation, influenced as they were by training in Diplomatics and its pervasive quest for authenticity in documentation as an underlying principle of *archivistique*, and the continued influence of such research centers as the École d'Chartes. Moreover, they have enjoyed a closer union between archives and libraries in organizations than what occurred in the United States where libraries and library organizations developed a half century before archives and have remained largely independent.

Suzanne Duprey-Briet's influential *Qu'est-ce que la documentation?* (1951) declared simply that "Un document est une preuve à la appui d'un fait" [A document is a proof in support of a fact] including any "concrete or symbolic *indice*, conserved or registered, ultimately to represent, reconstitute, or prove a physical or conceptual phenomenon" (Buckland's translation, 1997, p. 806, moves away from the empirical, legal meaning of her original, but he captures the scholasticism in her argument that an antelope in the wild is not a document, simply a creature, but when transported into a zoo and studied as a specimen, the animal becomes documentary). Buckland is correct in pointing to the materiality and intentionality of Briet's determination related to due process. Her thought reflects archival thinking going back to the twelfth century (MCCRANK, 1995). Both her phenomenological position and logic are highly Scholastic. Buckland, relying on a collegial tip for a close reading, focuses on the important term *indice* which he construes rightly to mean indexicality, that is "the quality of having been placed in relationship with other evidence" (p. 806). It is this quality of evidentiality and contextuality which has often been lost in the replacement of the term documentation by information. In the phrase Historical Information Science, I mean to extend the older concept of documentation rather than replace it totally, and in adopting the term "information" to bring the concept into congruence with modern usage and especially to relate the intellectual process of documentation with modern information technology.

Information Science, as distinct from Information Technology [IT], is a mid-century extension from Documentation, but in some cases its usage is narrower, while in others the older comprehensive scope is retained. One might think that it would be fairly easy to define what the history of information would entail and to construe this to be the proper purview of Historical Information Science when approaching the topic historically. This would be a necessary component, but not the entirety when describing the scope of such a hybrid field. One would have to consider the scientific study of information in its historical context and also historical information out of its original context, as conveyed in time and across space, into the contemporary (the individual historian, the historical research project, the organization in which the research is conducted, etc.) as it is being analyzed and used now. The crux of such definition falls on the key word "information" and understanding that many definitions are discipline dependent. RITCHIE (1991) rightly observes that it is a common subject in both the Humanities and Social Sciences. The Latin *informationem* comes from the verb *informare* meaning to place the intangible into something, literally to give it form, i.e., shape, as distinct from changing forms, i.e., *transformation*. Forms (*forma*) pertain to many formats in Latin, all of which offer external appearance as distinguishable from the thing's material composition. Shape and figure are the usual descriptors (sometimes mold), as anything seen, but form need not be static; it pertained, for example, to ceremony and rites, modes, and manner of behavior as well (this usage is still current, as in wearing formal attire when going to a formal, etc.; the importance of this dimension will be seen later when discussing organizational culture). Rules and regulations, social and otherwise, can be forms, producing formation, which is informed. The connotation is, however, good condition, a fitness as in usage pertaining to sports where athletes are in form. In all cases, the transaction is between the metaphysical and physical, as in manifestation of any object to another's senses. In early printing a body of composed type constituted a *forme*. Moreover, information is new, in that the term applies to the first instance of forming something from an impression, thought, idea, and communication.

In its medieval evolution with writing and written law, information was confused with its form, package, i.e., the writing, or in law, a writ of formal declaration as a summons, warrant, etc., which was issued on oath (so the assumption is that information is accurate, true, or accountable in some way). Information is small scale, common, and is embedded into other more formal and elaborate entities. In English criminal law, for example *information* was a substitute for an indictment for minor offenses. The communication when put into form is a piece of intelligence, and the flow of such intelligence is what makes someone knowledgeable. Such usage is with us still in the spy world, as in the Central Intelligence Agency (CIA). This connotation of one form after another or many together rather than a single thing, which produces information as a whole, goes back to the verb and hence the concept of informing as a process rather than something isolated, sporadic, or unreliable. Act and action are inseparable. Unlike mere data, information is organized, deliverable, and understandable.

Although information may lack the attributes associated with the higher dimensions of knowledge (synthesized information for meaning with values added) and wisdom, it supposes some kind of system for systematic delivery, interpretation, and sense making, storage and retrieval, reference and transference. The embrace is necessarily large, since information to be effective must be assimilated and acted upon; this enlargement of scope seems to defy definition, constraint, and disciplinarity. Consider, for example, the observation of T. M. PORTER (1985; 1996, p. 20) reflecting on the study by TEMIN of the use of information in business: "...the history of information is a history of trust and distrust." Or is he confusing information with something more? Something like value-added information? Information accepted, believed, and assimilated is something different from information provided, retrieved, and perused. FUKUYAMA (1995) argues that trust is an essential social virtue in the creation of prosperity. Yet faith and trust, like belief, are absent from most information science research. They should not be so excluded, since as FISHBEIN & AJZEN demonstrated two decades ago, belief, attitude, intention, and behavior are always entwined. When present, it is usually translated into reliability as a characteristic of the information rather than a predilection for acceptance or rejection of information on the part of a recipient or user.

Historians have learned this, that belief in addition to language or anything material must be taken in account when studying human affairs. Cultural historian J. SMITH (p. 1439), for example, when reviewing recent trends in linguistic analysis of texts for cultural studies, concluded:

> How and why, then, do political agents effect discursive changes while acting and thinking always within established linguistic boundaries? For students of political change, this is the question that defines the purpose of cultural analysis. To answer it, I argue, the historian must seek to uncover and explore the realm of experience where language and material existence inevitably converge: *the realm of beliefs.* Language expresses meanings that are determined not only by semiotic context but also by the collective and value-laden assumptions of the people who constitute society.

Although these beliefs and values are themselves expressed through established linguistic conventions, they are not fully determined by them....

Beliefs are not fixed entities, and they never unite all the members of a community. Close contextual analysis of the meanings of key words in the political vocabulary nevertheless discloses what can fairly be called the dominant perspective in
a given political culture.

SMITH (p. 1438) holds to the principle that "all experience is cultural," which underscores
word study and linguistic analysis applied to social and political discourse. "This means, of
course, that the evolution or mutation of discourse cannot be attributed to the force of new
motivations detached from those discourses—such as self-interests, competition, or a will to
power." Might one add new information to his list? Information sought, retrieved, and integrated is pre-conditioned by source, provider, format and access; and judgement of its relevance and receptivity to it are matters of culture, both what occurred before (i.e., history or
inherited assumptions, etc., which are matters of knowledge and belief) and at the moment
(i.e., preparedness or cognitive ability, and context). In short, the process of informing oneself
and others is a complicated phenomenon, difficult to define or to limit to any particular discipline and therefore a supra-disciplinary subject of study.

Information scientists may not be prone to use etymology to convey the meaning of information, but they struggle nevertheless with arriving at an operational definition for the term
(ARTANDI; BAR-HILLEL; BELKIN & ROBERTSON; BRILLOUIN; POLLOCK, etc.).
Devotees struggled longer to define Information Science in such a way as to produce an identity for its practitioners: in 1972 the NATO Advanced Study Institute for Information Science
entitled its conference "Information Science: Search for Identity" (DEBONS, ed.); and in 1975
the INTERNATIONAL FEDERATION OF DOCUMENTATION (FID) had difficulty defining
the scope of Information Science and its "objects of research and problems." Twenty years later,
this is still the case. The problem persists, that a general, holistic definition that invites people
in and fosters collaboration ironically works against professionalization and identity building.
In R. DUNN's view, this would be one of multiple identity crises issuing from postmodernity.

LOSEE (1990) understood that the phenomena common to most definitions of "information" often pertain to a subset of the inclusive phenomenon of information itself. He then
sought a domain-independent definition of information as "the values within the outcome of
any process" where value means a variable's attribute or characteristic. During 1995, LOSEE
(1997) elaborated upon this ideal definition for a common language between disciplines:
"Information is produced by all processes and it is the values of characteristics in the processes' output that are information." This is not a definition that would meet the criteria of lexi-
cologists in definition construction for dictionaries today since he uses the term being defined
for definition, and its purposeful all-inclusiveness will bother many. The concept is somewhat
convoluted, but it suffers no more defect than the common definition of information as "the
process of being informed." He is attempting to capture the concepts associated with the term
in a variety of disciplines. He notes that the common dictionary definitions of information as
"news or facts about something" are what is conveyed to youth by *Sesame Street's* Cookie
Monster (hardly a lexical authority, but influential nonetheless in concept formation). That is,
information is something, and it is new, true, and about something (LOSEE, 1997, p. 255). Its
etymology would also mean that something is taken into something else, and is thereby given
new form; mere data, then, are transformed in the process. Structure is added for meaning.

Human-centered approaches to information stress the meaning and use of messages, and
sometimes meaning and information are seen as the same (e.g., G. L. MILLER; an extension
of MCLUHAN's deliberate confusion in 1962 of medium and message from the communication viewpoint). Others go further to see information as disembodied knowledge assimilated

by another sentient being (PETERS). Cognitive scientists often see information as a creation of the mind, which makes it highly relative (like beauty "in the mind of the beholder" notes LOSEE, p. 257, referencing DRETSKE as an example). In any case, epistemologically what information is can be understood better by pointing to what is informative. Losee claims that measurements of "informativeness" lead to stronger qualitative notions about the nature of information, and he lauds the function-output approach to information because of the ability thereby to describe information of various levels (p. 260), and the use of models to study information communication, transfer, dissemination, diffusion, etc., through physical processes (E. A. CHATMAN; DRETSKE, 1981). In telecommunications, information flow could be measured by counting "things" in channels and their rate of transmission (hence BUCKLAND's 1991 critique of "information as thing" going back to SHANNON & WEAVER). As LOSEE (1997, p. 264) correctly points out, Shannon's definition is domain specific (telecommunications), and has been misapplied too often to other fields. Finally, one must note that information dissemination is not the same as cultural diffusion, where the spread of information, ideas, and practices are interwoven and are evidenced by changed technologies, forms, and products that indicate how information came to be applied. These more complex phenomena in diffusion are often treated, unfortunately, as something beyond information studies *per se* (for diffusion theory see E. MANSFIELD's early work on imitation and technological change, updated by ENGELSMAN & VAN RAAN; GRUBLER, 1991, 1995; NAKICENOVIC & GRUBLER; and MARCHETTI, and TOFFLER, 1974, on forecasting). G. HUBER, at The Institute for Invention and Innovation in Austin, Texas, is one of the few to combine technology and information diffusion studies into a holistic perspective.

If somewhat nebulous, nevertheless such approaches allow for an objectification of an otherwise very subjective topic, which means that information, however complex, can be studied scientifically and the scope, embracing the user, is wider than documentation which has the author or record creator as its chief referent. Information Science, a term which SHAPIRO claims was used first in 1955 in the English-speaking world, has been defined in a variety of ways (LE COADIC). UCLA's Harold Borko defined Information Science as:

> an interdisciplinary science that investigates the properties and behavior of information, the forces that govern the flow and use of information, and the techniques, both manual and mechanical, of processing information for optimal storage, retrieval, and dissemination (BORKO, 1968, p. 5).

Joseph Becker thought of Information Science simply as the study of how people "create, use, and communicate information" (BECKER, 1976, p. 10). These are very broad, and from one perspective, could mean that historians who have studied information sources, structures, and processes in the past are sort of retrospective information scientists without knowing it. The epistemological problem addressed by Columbia University's Jessica Harris by narrowing the definition of Information Science as "the study of the ways in which organisms process information" to "the methods of human learning and information generation" and more specific facets, seems not to be resolved (J. HARRIS, 1982). R. M. Hayes' abstract definition of Information Science as "the theoretical study of properties of recorded symbols and of means by which they are processed" is equally inclusive (R. HAYES, 1994, p. 275). The shorter the definition, the more general it is and this makes its scope seem even larger.

A more practical approach was taken more recently by BUCKLAND & LIU (1995, p. 385) who tried to avoid the trap of including "every field that invokes the word 'information'" and shun any attempt at an epistemological approach. Instead, in surveying the spartan literature for a history of Information Science, they relied on their "perceptions of the principle interests of the membership of the American Society for Information Science (ASIS) since its foundation in 1937 as the American Documentation Institute. In this view, IS [Information Science] is centered on the representation, storage, transmission, selection (retrieval, filtering), and the use of documents and messages, where documents and messages are created for use by humans." History *per se*, or more particularly the History of Information Science, is not included by BUCKLAND & LIU as one of the principal interests of the ASIS membership, but that is something these authors were seeking to change by contributing to *The Annual Review of Information Science and Technology* (*ARIST*). They chide (p. 401) the ASIS membership for having to wait thirty years for such an *ARIST* review. While attempting to confine the scope of Information Science to these stated interests, with expansion to IS history, BUCKLAND & LIU (p. 385) note that these interests "extend outwards in many directions because of the need to understand contextual, institutional, methodological, technological, and theoretical aspects." Their survey is expanded slightly by R. V. WILLIAMS, WHITMIRE, & BRADLEY who took an equally pragmatic approach to the subject and likewise artificially delimited the scope to Information Science as conceived and practiced by the ASIS membership. Both display the problem addressed by DEBONS and his collaborators who in 1974 searched for an identify for Information Science. STIEG (1990, p. 62) likewise stresses: "The adjective *interdisciplinary* is especially important; it reminds us that information science has many intellectual ties." She would be one especially sensitive to its connections with History, and that both are mutually interdisciplinary. When one examines the quantitative methodologies employed by information scientists as prescribed by I. RAO, one of the most cited authorities in the field, with those adopted by quantification historians, one discovers a complementarity and considerable overlap whenever the research tends toward the Social Sciences. As shall be seen, the same convergence is now observable in methods used in Natural Language Processing (NLP) in Information Science and a host of disciplines using computerized text analysis (see MILLER & WALKER's assessment of NLP coming into the 1990s).

The added adjective "historical" does not substantially change this inter-disciplinary focus, but expands its horizon. The practical foci of both are functional: information generation, storage, retrieval, communication, and use. The distinguishing criterion is, therefore, that the information and initial processing are identified as historical, but there is no agreement about how old something must be to qualify. Because Information Science has so concentrated on current applications and perceives itself to be new, or at least modern in the sense of post-World War II, like Social Sciences the dominant focus is on the contemporary and historical perspective that has been sorely wanting. Many recognize the interdisciplinary debt of Information Science to older disciplines (PEMBERTON & PRENTICE), but seldom is there any recognition of intellectual borrowing from History. PAISLEY (1990, p. 12) views Information Science as having borrowed three paradigms that became fundamental for the field: taxonomy, general systems theory, and the communication paradigm of source-channel-receiver. He follows these closely with ZIPF's law and statistical functions of linguistics, cognitive processing from Psychology, change paradigms from Sociology, and the idea of production/distribution from Economics. The Social Science orientation is obvious (which is why HJÖRLAND & ALBRECTSEN and others see Information Science as a Social Science), as is the obscurity of historical consciousness and thought as an important paradigm in Information Science. Only in the 1990s has this begun to change, with the re-addition of historians to Information Science faculties to examine the impact of information technology, systems, and sources on society with long-range perspective and thereby to contribute to debates about current developments and policy. This appears to be in keeping with a recent shift toward historical perspective inside several non-History Humanities and Social Science disciplines as described by T. J. MCDONALD and his collaborators. History operates as an integrator, just as information technology merges developments across disciplines. Information Science is not, it seems now, immune to such influence.

Understandably, therefore, most publications using computing with Social Science research and analytic techniques applied to historical data and inquiry appear in historical journals rather than information science publications (note, for example, the journal recommendations for history and computing of the Organization of American Historians, OAH, 1988). Moreover, if the articles are focused on methodology and technique, rather than appearing throughout core sub-ject-area journals, they appear largely as a subset of historical publications or they gravitate to Social Science history outlets. Few are released through professional association journals. The location of such articles identifies the current locus for such activity in academe and indicates that for the time being those who might identify with Historical Information Science are still aligned with formal academic History and Social Science more than Information Science. Perhaps this is because of the latter's Library Science derivation. In any case, information sci-entists do not seem to cultivate a relationship with the Social Sciences strong enough to create a reciprocal overlap. The irony of this is that in the United States closely related fields like archives administration, as archivists have conceived of an Archival Science mostly as praxis (i.e., practice more than theory), have moved from their former alignment with History toward Library and Information Science. European historians engaged in computing are calling for a coalescence of their interests and skills into an Historical Information Science seemingly with little awareness of movements in allied fields like Library Science, or archives and museum informatics. They are aware of Social Science connections, but not the same kind of profes-sional movements outside academe *per se* that in the United States lend themselves to a more broadly conceived development than simply a subset of History. As such, the European move-ment is transnational but intradisciplinary in ethos and communications, and while being inter-disciplinary in its borrowing, is less sharing across the academic-discipline/profession bound-ary. Awareness, as MARTON & BOOTH demonstrate, is integral to learning: a change in the learner's way of seeing and understanding the world so that knowledge may be constructed dif-ferently, is the underlying motive of this bibliographic approach to the fusion of History and Information Science in the study of historical information.

The evolving usage of Historical Information Science as an extension of BENSON's "sci-entific study of History" (1972) denotes specifically the application of modern information technology (e.g., computing and telecommunications, including both the apparatus or machin-ery and skills or techniques) with a defined methodology or procedure(s) that usually involves classification, discrimination, aggregation, measurement and quantification, and comparison of sets (record linkage, collocation, concordancing, etc.), to historical sources (numeric, tex-tual, and image) for their analysis and interpretation. ANKERSMIT (1989) is one of the few historians who has investigated the relationship between historical analysis and historiograph-ical topology although not specifically relating this to the formal literature of classification the-ory and practice (cf., DOUGLAS & HULL investigation into Social Science classification). The analytic focus on sources and their contents used in a particular history always relies on a body of more general "auxiliary sciences" (so labeled by the Library of Congress classifica-tion schedules) or meta-information about documentary types (Diplomatics or form criticism), genre (text criticism), language and communication (Paleography for writing; Typography for printing; Iconography and Semiotics for symbol in art and Text or Literary Criticism for image or icon, emblem, and metaphor [SASSOON & GAUR]; and a variety of other -graphies for newer electronic media, etc. [EASTERBY & ZWAGA]), in addition to the historical context for understanding a subject. Parallel to the descriptive or analytic history of the source as a physical document is its own history or provenance (its metahistory, *meta* meaning "beyond" from the Greek) and whatever has been brought to bear on it—e.g., the history of the infor-mation and encompassing information or communication technology. An example would be the history of writing (e.g., R. HARRIS' *Origins of Writing* or SENNER's collections of essays under the same title) rather than the history of what has been written.

Historical interpretation always relies on an interplay between multiple histories of people and things. This observation is expressed interestingly by A. Appadurai as "the social life of things" in history (APPADURAI, 1986), which may be related to Information Science by recalling Michael Buckland's construct of "information as thing" (BUCKLAND, 1991). Such thinking is slightly more abstract and advanced than traditional thinking about documents or artifacts alone, out of context, as if they were inanimate objects without influence, when their being acted upon is process and this produces history. Human-information interaction is seldom simply unilateral, however, and keeping track of multiple influences and concurrences defies the powers of observation by historians as much as it does the circumspection of contemporaries, so it is often this complexity factor that invites the assistance of modern information technology. W. REEVES argues that "systematic comprehension" rather than the accumulation of data is the key to dealing with information overload. Achieving this skill to manage complexity requires new tools, teaching methods, and approaches to how research results are disseminated and communicated.

History has always developed by absorbing ideas and methodologies from other fields, most often the social sciences. Various sets of methodologies constitute a historical-technique meta-discipline when applied to a specified time and place other than the contemporary. Technique has often preceded technology in the sense of mechanical or electronic assistance, but even in early computing technology, the majority of applications managed information manually after it was extracted from traditional historical documents. They did not transform documentation into electronic surrogates and employ automatic information processing directly from records. More recently, of course, the very creation of the modern record electronically obviates the necessity of such retroconversion. Such transformations of historical records for manipulation with modern technology gives new meaning to Marshal McLuhan's 30-year-old dictum about the fusion of medium and message (MCLUHAN). Historians have investigated the communications and technologies of past cultures to explore their records and to write their histories, but in addition to this task, now historians must be equally adept in relating modern technology to historical inquiry. Computer technology is another addition to their methodological repertoire rather than a replacement of previous methods, techniques, or skills. Typically, historians inspect a methodology used in another field, analyze it, and justify its application for a specific historical inquiry before proceeding. It is rarer for them to pioneer really new methodologies or techniques.

The same syncretism should be apparent for applied technology and technical information transfer, but this has not been the case. Cross-disciplinary methodological imitation and the transposition of theory between fields has been easier than technical transference (technological diffusion takes longer than technical information exchange). This suggests peculiar problems in higher education that ought to be addressed. The repeated application of methodologies and techniques and use of certain kinds of technology can evolve in time into a parallel specialization through practice, of course, but the issue is whether or how both the practical and theoretical can be inculcated into formal education so a historian would have a traditionally defined subject domain combined with some specialized knowledge of useful technologies. The two specializations, if genuinely symbiotic, should not be split as purely subject versus method or theory versus practice. Likewise, one might suspect that in Historical Information Science a reflexive relationship would exist between History and Information Science inspecting each other simultaneously, one to appropriate methodology and technology, and the other to delineate data according to the pervasive historical paradigm that classifies nearly everything by time and place (ANKERSMIT, 1989; DAHLBERG). This duality or multi-disciplinary reflexive and syncretistic aspect of Historical Information Science, which suggests the maturity of Information Science to the point of having identifiable varieties of specialization as in History, should reveal a mutual relevance and complementarity that have been denied by the "presentism" of many information scientists and the antiquarianism of many historians. Historical Information Science, if it is to achieve its own identity, must coalesce commonalities from these two fields and be aware of differences that may justify separate professional identifies without letting such segregation impede intellectual sharing. Syncretism itself may be an identifying characteristic (MORAZE). Such cross-disciplinary intercourse requires a flexibility, an enlargement of disciplinary scope, and an attitudinal adjustment in both History and Information Science to benefit from each other.

The phrase "Historical Information Science" has not been used much in the United States by either Information Science or History. Instead it has evolved in the 1990s, like such earlier constructions two decades ago as "Social Science History" (SOCIAL SCIENCE HISTORY ASSOCIATION, 1976-), to translate the European term "Informatics" which was common enough in the Soviet Union during the 1960s to create *Informatika* (A. I. MIKHAILOV, ed.) or *Informatics Abstracts* (1963-). One of the earliest organizational developments in France to adopt the term was by Phillipe Drefus and his colleagues in systems and software design when in 1962 they formed the Société pour l'Informatique et Applique (SIA). During the late 1960s, the term in French came to mean "the modern science of electronic information processing" (BAUER, p. 76). In that same year, without any direct and conscious borrowing, BAUER and his associates Richard Hill, Werner Frank, and Frank Wagner formed an American software company to develop online systems, called Informatics. They, as recalled years later, batted about their "informatics vision" which eventually became software engineering, and subsequently manufacturing. Their American pragmaticism showed forth in the dualism of their conceptualization, that Informatics was "the science of information handling" and was therefore science and management at the same time. They moved to this neologism from "Datamatics" by intentionally combining the Greek suffix denoting "science of" to the verb "to inform" (BAUER, p. 76) The newly coined term in English seems to have caught on, since Bauer maintains that the Association for Computing Machinery (ACM) later wanted to change its name to the Society of Informatics. He and his partners were disinclined to let the name, which they though of as a trademark, pass into generalized use as happened in other cases, e.g., company names like Xerox or Cellophane that became household words. Their conservative instincts were to no avail, however, since the term with its classical etymology had been coined simultaneously in more than one place and in more than one language. Before long "informatics" evolved into a generic term in American English for computer applications in any field and was widely adopted in Biomedicine without regard for its origins (BLUM & DUNCAN). WELLISCH has explored the term's usage related to "Information Science."

While its original usage, and continued use in conservative circles, means computer science emphasizing software, processing, and project design rather than hardware, a more refined and specialized usage also evolved. Informatics denoted the formation of broad but structured databases accumulating previous research, and the extrapolation of data relevant to a query or problem to produce meaningful information and assist thereby with a solution. What in History might be thought of as simply as "wrong-headed" questions, are "ill-structured problems" in the more scientific rendering of H. SIMON (1973). The solving of ill-structured problems is still identified with expertise and is therefore a goal of most expert systems. These involve an unknown problem space, uncertain pathways or search procedures for alternative solutions to a problem, inexact connections between the means and an end, and such difficulties as incomplete data. "Problem space" is the domain or sector of a domain in which both the problem and solution are known to lie. Many historians are unwilling to impose structure on such naturally ill-structured issues, e.g., models, and therefore the heuristic methods required are left undeveloped. Herbert Simon, in opening the field of Artificial Intelligence (AI) research, defined "well-structured problems" as those for which one can precisely specify a process of trial and error that will lead to a desired solution in a practical amount of time (H. SIMON, 1973, 1981). This approach is different from mere data processing, for example, or the automation of routine and repetitive processes (i.e., "Complex Information Processing" as the legacy of H. Simon: KLAHR & KOTOVSKY, eds.). Problem definition and structuring are key components of Informatics which precede data collection, processing, and analysis. The sequence is the same in History, but the approach and manner in which these are handled often differ dramatically.

Informatics was applied to History perhaps first in the late 1970s by French medieval Annalistes in their *Informatique et histoire mediéval* (1977), with very broad implications. French computing historians gave the notion organizational definition in 1993 by forming a national chapter of the International Association for History and Computing (IAHC), but usage in French remains very open-ended as reflected in the most recent treatment of history and computing in France by GENET (1995). Such ecumenical usage was transported to French Canada for computerized demographic research (e.g., CHARBONNEAU, 1988, p. 296) where its meaning as in "methodes informatiques" is more or less synonymous with anything computerized. It was used more empirically, however, by such influential contemporaries as Ivan KOVAL'CHENKO (1977, 1982) who in 1985 described historical computing as a "mathematical methodology for historical data processing" meaning statistics and modeling using "electronic machines." In 1986, he also spoke of the "historiography of historical science in the Soviet Union" (*isotrii istoricheskothi nauki v SSSR*: KOVAL'CHENKO & SHIKLO). KOVAL'CHENKO's treatise on historiography in 1987 for the Soviet Academy of Science leaves no doubt about his perception of History as a Science, mainly socioeconomic, and emphasis on quantification as its primary methodology.

The Soviet school of quantitative historians more recently represented by L. BORODKIN adopted the term "Historical Informatics" in 1986 when relating computing and mathematics. Its usage spread among East-West History and Computing conferees in Uzhgorod, Ukraine (June, 1992). The Austrian medievalist I. KROPAČ (1987, pp. 43-45) defines Historical Informatics more broadly as "the science of a formal processing of information out of and about historical source[s] and phenomena." To balance the impact of quantification of numeric data, he stresses the confluence of linguistic computing and text analysis into this development of the "missing link" between Computer Science and History. It is this foundational thinking, a reconsideration of the older emphasis on technique and the mechanics of computation in Historical Informatics and a moving onto the science of historical information processing, analysis, interpretation and presentation while using modern information technology, which is the basis of this current essay.

Because the source for information, its custody, transformation, and delivery, are so important, I retain the connotation of Library and Archival Sciences in, or closely associated with Information Science, to be blended with History. History is naturally emphasized by historians. They would see Historical Information Science as methodological and empirical orientation residing in the History domain, whereas I would envision this orientation, blend of methodologies, and technical utility as fusing into a multi-disciplinary or more correctly, uni-disciplinary specialization which may be applied to many subjects. It is by its nature inclusive, integrative, and collaborative, participating in several subject domains. It is a framework, like a crucible ready to hold many ingredients, and with energy added, to transform the substance into something new. DEBONS, HORNE, & CRONENWETH attempt to describe, more than define, Information Science from an "integrated view" not altogether different from the approach many take to History. Or one can take a discriminating view as when Elsevier Science, publishers of the journal *Information Sciences,* use the plural deliberately to denote different kinds of Information Science, of which one could be Historical Information Science. MCCAIN (1995) uses the term "interstitial" to describe studies that fit poorly in the "home paradigm" but instead sit comfortably in the interstice between two or more disciplines. This is somewhat different from interdisciplinary overlap, because it suggests that the new breed has a place of its own and a growing identity increasing distinct from the cognate disciplines around it. This is the case for "Historical Information Science" even though the term has not been used commonly in the United States, perhaps because the concepts involved have not yet gelled into a unifying discipline or found a proper niche for themselves. Moreover, certain cultural and American historiographic trends in the History profession mitigate against its lodging securely within academic History. It is to assist this development of cross-disciplinary mix, new identity, and strategic position, and proper fit that this bibliographic essay was conceived.

In the 1996 International Association for Computing and History conference in Moscow, a plenary session was devoted to exploring the need for and development of "a theory of historical computing." Two keynote speakers, Peter Doorn of the Netherlands Historical Data Archives (NHDA) and University of Leyden Department of History, and Ingo Kropac of the Karl-Franzens University of Graz's Forschungen für Historische Grundwissenschaften, presented formal papers. There was also a brief rendition of the history of historical computing in the former Soviet Union provided by Leonid Milov, followed by commentaries of Moscow State University's Natalia Selounskaya, and Manfred Thaller in a panel discussion (MILOV; SELOUNSKAYA; THALLER).

This forum deserves comment here because the two papers present positions that both complement each other while presenting differing positions and perspectives representative of current debates, and these illustrate the gradual evolution in the thinking of computing historians about a unifying discipline apart from the subjects studied. DOORN (1996) addresses the issue of modeling in quantitative history and the Social Sciences, to which many historians object, as a continuation of old "misunderstandings." D. BRITT presents a similarly reconciliatory perspective on modeling, with attention to the importance of context as an attempt to construct a bridge between quantitative and qualitative extremes. DOORN particularly refers to a recent essay by THALLER (1995) who contrasts "model-oriented" and "source-oriented" approaches to historical computing and sees the distinction as an extension of older debates pitting science and nonscience (the Humanities) or "hard" versus "soft" sciences, quantification (Cliometrics) and narration (descriptive History), and emphasis on the unique (antiquarian) versus generalization (Social Science), against each other. LAVE & MARCH provide a good overview of models as used in the Social Sciences during the 1970s when debates in historical methodology shifted from the novelty of computer applications in History and quantification to more sophisticated inquiries regarding methodology. Modeling was then, and still is, a point of contention. Doorn, who sees models as similar to Max Weber's "ideal types," relies on the works by Sir Moses Finley, whose approach to ancient history was all-encompassing and multi-disciplinary (FINLEY), and of the paleontologist Stephen Jay Gould who argues for the study of certain aspects of the Natural Sciences (cosmology, geology, evolution, etc.) with historical methods, to show the underlying, unifying nature of most studies (GOULD).

Doorn warns against "crude analogies" comparing Physics to the Social Sciences or to Biology and History. Rather than contrast old Cliometrics with narrativist historiography, he evokes David Harvey's tripartite notion of explanation: i.e., techniques (pragmatics), conceptual content [semantics], and logical structure (syntax), to illustrate how History uses a variety of modes of explanation in complementary fashion (D. HARVEY, who turns back to CARNAP, leader of the Vienna Circle who in 1934 had argued for a "unified science"). The issue is not one or the other as correct, as argued too rigidly as "monothesis versus ideography" in the old Popper-Hempel debates about "covering laws" or a model-based explanation of history, but more one of style, preference, timeliness, and appropriateness. Doorn adopts BOMMELJ's view of History as a "slow science" and sees history as part of the continuum in scientific inquiry even though History cannot boast of precision or predictability as in the physical sciences. Knowing something is a prerequisite; it always entails a certain supposition of predictability. Otherwise, why learn something beforehand, i.e, unrelated to need to know? The most common justification for studying history is its general, future utility (see M. LEVINE about the aftermath of the "informative act"). "Facts and visions" both have their place in Science and in History.

DOORN dismisses Manfred Thaller's argument for source-oriented data processing versus scientific computing that relies on models as a modern rendition of the old determinism versus probabilism debates. Thaller, of course, argues also that the object of historical study is so much more complex than in science, requiring a level of abstraction of much greater magnitude. Doorn hopes that greater computer processing power will overcome the limitations which led to so much disappointment in quantification during the decade of the 1970s and early 1980s. Today, rather than moving toward a methodological canon, Doorn encourages historians to add all methodologies to their toolkit, and to employ whatever statistical methodology seems appropriate for a given study. He sees the extension of inferential statistics based on probabilistic methods as most promising, especially those for handling fuzzy data (KANDEL, 1986). Doorn thus shies away from a particular theory of historical computing in favor of incorporating all computing techniques and capabilities and whatever statistical methods work; his is essentially an ecumenical, all-encompassing embrace. Consequently, he reiterates the great historiographic debates of the past generation resulting from quantification and the advent of computing as a series of great misunderstandings that (pp. 15-16):

1. Models are necessarily mechanistic, deterministic, causal and mathematical.

2. Natural Sciences are "hard" and the Social are "soft."

3. The application of statistics always leads to "hard" statements.

4. Causal models explain everything by themselves.

5. Statistics can explain anything substantial.

6. One set of the Sciences is always oriented to generalization.

7. History is oriented always toward the unique.

8. Data modeling is the only aim of history computing.

9. Only historians study the past.

10. Applying quantitative models means exploration of universal laws.

Perhaps the continuing nature of these "misunderstandings" is revealed poignantly by Simon Schama in a recent interview about digital technology and the future of historical scholarship, in which this historian remarks about historical computing and overly generalized models:

> Liberated [by computing] from these chores [lecturing and teaching, conferencing, using libraries, etc.] the historian can resume his role as Grand Arbitrator between what has been and what is to be. The inexhaustible electronic serf will nail down the database wherever it may be hiding, rummage through its content, flag the significant item, and produce for the analytical scrutiny of his mistress discrete threads of the past, expertly scissored away from the endless ribbon of the time continuum.
>
> So what should we fear? What is there to lose? Nothing but our imagination. The trouble is, though, that history without imagination is just so much data processing about the dead.
>
> For all the things that the computer does brilliantly—the searching, sifting, flagging, storing—constitute the beginning, not the end, of historical wisdom. It gets the historian to the starting line of his real job: the resurrection of a vanished past; its reconstitution into something as real, as vivid, and as important as the fleeting present. And for all the tricky, invaluable business, the electronic archive[s] is still a real collaborator, for it lacks all the properties that trigger the historian's precious intuition of recall: the smell, the feel, the instinct of the past. Bulldozing broad, straight highways through the chaotic tangle of the past carries with it the peril of losing its messy authenticity; of obliterating the accidental nature of so many fateful turns in history. Had Archduke Francis Ferdinand's chauffeur not gotten lost in the streets of Sarajevo... had President Lincoln not been fond of theater... without

a keen sense of these tragic pratfalls with which the past is littered, the historian threatens to turn into the most overdetermined political scientist, addicted to an unrealistically net relationship between cause and effect (FORBES *ASAP*, p. 55).

Schama is echoing the old juxtaposition of objectified Social Science history as being unimaginative and a mere marshaling of facts now abetted by computer technology, as distinct from the historian as mediator, storyteller, and neighbor of poetry and philosophy squarely inside the Humanities. He wants the public to perceive History as "a meditation in time that better helps us to understand the nature of human behavior." Schama concludes: "At its most prosaic, history is supposed to tell us how to avoid the next calamity—recession, revolution, war. It has never done this well, and there is absolutely no reason to suppose that electronically enhanced history will do the job any better." So much for past misunderstandings about the past; they are with us still, and the great divide is thus protected most eloquently.

DOORN, despite his ecumenism and diplomatic attempt to override past controversies with a new understanding of past misunderstandings, is the consummate historian; he views history computing as an auxiliary science of History, and if he were to accede to the notion of Historical Information Science, it too would be subservient to History as if Clio were Queen of the Sciences. Doorn's paper was used as a centerpiece of a post-conference "virtual discussion" in Leonid Borodkin's words, consisting of over 20 commentaries exchanged over the Internet and published in Russian (BORODKIN *ET AL.*, 1996b). My own contribution to this discussion raised the question about whether such "misunderstandings" in History indicate cognitive dissonance in the field, which is basic psychological differences reflected in the preferences, apprehensions, defenses, and strengths that cluster historians into this or that group and persuasion (MCCRANK, 1996b). These intrinsic differences may not have so much to do with methodologies or subject matter as native abilities (e.g., math or language aptitude) and cognitive styles (culturally induced modes of thinking [OLSON & TORRANCE, eds.], e.g., leanings toward narrative description and reliance on language models, or toward quantifiable models relying on measurement; or the degree of tolerance for ambiguity, etc.). This juxtaposition of description versus quantification, or narration versus measurement is a theme which will reappear throughout this current discussion. It is a pervasive concern and an issue which seems beyond resolution since the late-medieval shift in Western Civilization from purely qualitative views to more quantitative analysis of the world around us (A. CROSBY; T. PORTER place this development chiefly in the nineteenth century).

In contrast to DOORN (1997) who would subordinate the history in everything to History and appropriate all techniques, methods, and computing capabilities for History, KROPAČ ([1997]) sees History as an Information Science. He contrasts Informatics as the science about the computer, with Information Science as the science of information; thus he distinguishes immediately Historical Informatics from Historical Information Science. For KROPAČ (1987), who began this intellectual journey in 1980s, this development is that of "a further discipline." He notes that the German *Geschichte* contains two meanings, referring both to real past events, and to their description. The *Quellenkunde* of History are systematically organized sources, whose assessment is the focus of *Quellenkritik*.

Like Doorn, Kropač also sees all of the subdisciplines of History to include theories, methodologies, and techniques, but Kropač sees History itself as a specialized form of communication using historical sources and he is comfortable with a classical interpretation of History in terms of Communications (particularly by J. G. DROYSEN) as this evolved in Information Science after the 1970s because of its compatibility with late nineteenth-century scientific historicism. "Historical research" is defined as "a process of cognition, in which we deduce and process information out of sources to put theory-based knowledge about the human past empirically into a concrete form." He seems to speak here from the vantage point of Diplomatics in tune with Documentation, reflecting his experience and expertise working with official documents. He acknowledges the subjectivity implicit in the term "information" as dependent on its trans-mission; so historical cognition is established by the "diagnostic transmission of information" which on the surface is a series of signals. The communication's successful reception in time depends on the modern historian's ability to receive such information from the time it was cre-ated and times through which it was transmitted, i.e., to understand historical signals (terms, descriptors, symbols, models, and even whole cognitive structures). KROPAČ uses the *Molescher Organismus der Kybiack-Klasse* or Kybiak-Organism in Cybernetics to explain his interpretation of History as communication between past and present in Information Science terms. The Kybiak Organism consists of the preceptor to pull information from a particular environment (which necessitates classification or *begriff* [idea or concept] formation, or an internal model of an external world) into a structure of knowledge; an effector to react to the environment which now includes this information; an operator to structure perception; and a motivator. He outlines the processes that transform information in the course of its transmis-sion and reception (which today would be called metadata), all of which need to be taken into account in the process of historical interpretation. Kropač ultimately comes to the point where he concedes that historians really create virtual worlds from historical sources which are man-ifestations of one or more mini-worlds. Historical views achieve a superior vantage point after time and broader perspective from the synthesis of sources, above and beyond what was pos-sible by a contemporary viewer or actor in the environment being studied historically. A tem-poral view is no match for the historical overview. The role of Historical Information Science is to assist in discernment between such overviews as a legitimate forms of cognition from something purely imaginative or simple illusion.

It was up to the commentators to make sense out of these different yet complementary and reconciliatory views of Doorn and Kropač at the IAHC '96 meeting (BORODKIN, ed., 1996, pp. 61-195). SELOUNSKAYA tried to show how older notions of quantified history had grown to History Computing: (1) in theory the issue was whether such empirical study qualified as a Science, but even if this were not conceded, most agreed that this was "New History"; (2) in methodology, the focus was on statistical method, the difference between qualitative and quan-titative explanation, and the limits of analysis; and (3) in the arena of sources, less attention was paid to criticism than to data recovery and conservation. The contemporary scene, judging from Doorn and Kropac's papers, represented a shift from these older foci to (1) theoretically, a reduction of earlier tensions in a new and ever broader synthesis; (2) in method, new concerns in the identification of facts through the process of transmission, and new tensions created by the transfer of ideas from one discipline to another (Literary Criticism and now Information Science); and (3) in source criticism, the interpretation of signs, codes, and other dimensions of historical information unrecognized in previous eras.

Manfred Thaller stated categorically that some of the older concerns had been superseded by technology, as in the case of limitations in first-generation statistical analysis by the capacity of computing (THALLER, 1997). He likens the situation to manufacturing where a company that produced ball bearings conducted sampling for quality control, but today robotics and scanning make it easier simply to check each and every one rolling off the assembly line. Likewise, he argues, data sampling is needed less when a computer can in fact examine every known instance in a historical data set, regardless of size. POINCARE argued early in this century that one of the best uses of statistics is to compensate for particular errors and resolving the problem of selection of facts for study when one might include them all. Unlike the accommodation of ambiguity in the Arts and Humanities generally, total quality control in technology does not tol-erate an acceptable margin of error. Even a .1 percent tolerance of error in certain applications is unacceptable as, for example, assuming that during two random hours per year one would accept contaminated drinking water; that banks in the United States could post 10,000 checks per hour to the wrong accounts; or more personally, that the human heart skipped 3,000 beats per year. Technology's increased capacity has lessened this tolerance for error and ambiguity and the need for certain kinds of statistical operations, and this is true of information processing as well (W. PERRY, 1983, 1991). These gains, however, are being overshadowed by the awareness of our hitherto lack of massive information integration, so other kinds of problems are coming into clearer focus. History, for example, still consists of histories and collections of historical views, rather than a seamless web. Thaller points also to the problematic evolution of historical studies and computing without the development of essential tools, namely customized software. Little software exists that has been written with any theoretical understanding of what it is supposed to do in historical research. So, past debates have focused too much on transitory and internal perception and interpretation problems, but have delayed really critical developments. He harkens back to the Historical Informatics position, rather than enthusiastically embracing Kropač's theoretical view of Historical Information Science.

While American historians have remained more conservative and subject-bound in their terminology, European historians using computers to accomplish information storage and retrieval, and even analysis, had begun in the mid-1970s referring to "historical informatics" regardless of subject domain. With empirical technique and data processing, they included the more philosophical ideas of hermeneutics and source criticism in their sense of documentation, congruence between sources and methodology or appropriate technique, measurement or quantification, and heuristics or geometrically expandable learning from human experience which means reexamination of prior study (history's history, e.g., what may be thought of as metahistory, as distinct from historiography or the literary history of History; or the aforementioned meta-discipline of comparing and analyzing methodologies to determine how appropriate they might be for a given application) and building upon usable foundations while guarding against duplication and re-invention. Like Information Science versus Computer Science, the term connotes a theoretical dimension, more than just technique, method, or engineering, to place more emphasis on intellectual tasks, application of logic, and conceptualization, interpretation, and synthesis, more than on the computer as tool. Informatics has also been applied to archives, museums, etc., in similar fashion (BEARMAN, 1987-), specifically to archival documentation by O. BUCCI (1990-), and to Philology and historical texts (BUSA, 1990) as well, to encompass more than quantification.

EGGHE & ROUSSEAU and others in Information Science use "Informetrics" as a narrower term than Informatics (see BOOKSTEIN, 1976 and 1990a-c, for a sense of the evolution of this speciality; B. BROOKES). BOOKSTEIN (1997, p. 2) connects this field of inquiry with Scientometrics, the statistical science of measurement (LYDESDORF, 1995; cf., PUGH & WINSLOW for physical measurement), as does the International Society for Scientometrics and Informetrics. Bookstein defines Informetrics:

> Informetrics is the study of quantitative regularities in information related processes. Typically, its techniques use counts of artifacts related to the production and use of information, and its conclusions describe patterns that occur in these data.

> The fundamental question of Informetrics is under what conditions are our measurements able to reflect nature's underlying regularities.

In Information Science circles "Informatics" was often used as by NOVELLI (1983) to be the analytic component of "Documentation" (as developed by the French beyond systematic bibliography: cf., P. FRANK; RAUZIER). In any case, Historical Informatics, if this were taken to mean little more than computer applications to historical sources, should be expanded into a larger concept of Historical Information Science.

I would define Historical Information Science as:

> the scientific study of historical information and of information and communication technologies, and the techniques, methods, and intellectual frameworks by which we extract meaning from these sources. This includes the creation of sources and

their use in original context, historical use, and current use in studying History. This broad, integrative and unifying super-discipline or unidiscipline concerns records of all kinds but especially electronic sources and archives because of the application of modern information technology for their access and analysis; historical information access and retrieval and contemporary access to historical materials; meta-history and metadata in documentation; data-text-image analysis; forensics and computing applications; and information technologies applied in historical research, communication, and instruction.

It is this enlargement of scope and move away from simply using computers for historical data analysis to which some computing historians object. In a panel presentation to the American Social Science History Association at its annual conference in Atlanta (October 14, 1994), a formal delegation of the Association for History and Computing attempted to implant into the American scene the narrower European definition of Historical Informatics as simply Computer Science applied to History, or even more narrowly, computer technology used by historians. The latter is terribly self-limiting. The chief spokesman for IAHC and its then president, Jan Oldervoll of the University of Bergen History Department, attempted to define the topic as something more precise than just talking about computers and History. He did so by juxtaposing the narrow European technical approach to the larger American Social Science or technical-behavioralist approach, and in so doing, greatly maligned Information Science as it has evolved in the United States (OLDERVOLL, 1994, p. 1 [emphases are his]):

> Informatics in many European languages stands for "computer science" (NOT the library-bound information science) of English usage. So the term should be translated as "historical computer science"—as would quite a few companion terms in other European languages like the German Historische Fachinformatik or some parts of the Dutch Historish-Culturele Informatiekunde.

Somewhat in contradiction to his narrowing of the term in accordance with German empiricism and his attempt at linguistic precision, his argument immediately turned to the lament that American discussions of computing in history had become too technical ("methodology by Microsoft" as one panelist quipped), whereas in Europe historians have retained a more proper inclusion of methodological discourse. He then lauded IAHC for providing the most important of these forums.

The 1994 IAHC (p. 2) delegation was supposed to address three questions, each by a different respondent on the panel:

1. If Historical Informatics is a proper specialization, how and how much of its should be taught? What is the role of the computer in teaching history? D. GREENSTEIN (1994) then discusses the considerable difference in European curricular approaches to the topic.

2. Are there software needs of the historical community which are not fulfilled by the industry? OLDERVOLL (1994b) himself takes up the issue of software, with reference to such traditional activities as census analysis

3. How can large amounts of historical data be made available for computer-supported research? THALLER (1994) supposedly addresses this issue, but actually resumed the discussion by OLDERVOLL about software needs. THALLER (1994, p. 30) embraces the term "Historical Computer Science," likening it to "source-oriented data processing."

The framing of these questions, which supposedly illustrates the key issues in the minds of Europeans engaged in historical computing, betrays self-doubt about the propriety of the specialization as currently defined, and displays ambivalence between the technical and theoretical aspects of a still nascent discipline. After this "theoretical" groundwork, T. PARCER, LEV-ERMANN & GROTUM and R. F. COLSON exploited the approach to make their points about the complexity of large databases and how the very characteristic of volume requires special attention in teaching methods and in obtaining appropriate software. P. DOORN then reviewed the European situation regarding networking.

It is nearly impossible to detect from these discussions any precision forthcoming for the term "Historical Informatics" as promised at the onset, but it is possible to discern confusion of such a definition with "Computer Science" when attempting to embrace such issues as the structure of historical data, teaching methods, and theoretical issues of methodology and interpretation. While wanting a narrow technical definition to their term, each respondent in his own way breaks out of the mold and leaves Computer Science for larger issues, or, perhaps, goes back and forth between History and Computer technology in an applied concern without the "science" of the either field. The polarization issue, still reflecting the lack of real hybridization, is captured again by D. GREENSTEIN (1994, p. 3) who returns to the usage of "History and Computing." Thus this IAHC panel most recently endorsed the use of the term "historical Informatics" as Computer Science applied to History, but shunned the notion of an embracing "Historical Information Science" because they stereotypically associate the latter with Library Science. Even then, however, other computing historians on the same panel (e.g., DOORN, 1994, p. 69) who use the Internet, invoked Library Science by calling for a "new Dewey" to make sense out of the chaos online. OCLC in 1993 proposed such to the U.S. Department of Education Office of Education Research and Improvement.

THALLER (p. 42) does not juxtapose such terms or make Historical Informatics quite so exclusionary, although his English usage is typically German in translating Informatics as Computer Science. But he more wisely simply concentrates on what he identifies as "Historical Computer Science" which may or may not be subsumed under a larger, even more theoretical umbrella. For him, Historical Computer Science is a fulfillment of certain roles, namely the computer scientist who specializes in aiding historians by supplying technical solutions for their problems. To do this, this specialist must understand the formal analysis of historical source material, its ambiguity, complexity, and volume, to bring about general solutions not readily available in current software. This is a self-actualized definition, of course, with Thaller himself as the chief prototype. There are few other exemplars (very few) to illustrate his point. I doubt that right now many historical computer scientists are coming out of any American History or Computer Science Departments. Nor can they be identified readily from Information Science. They are, however, coming out of European research centers.

Nevertheless, one may argue for a larger conceptualization of Informatics than Computer Science as a science applied to technology, and the adoption of an embracing term to include the information itself with the technology and methodology. That term, "Historical Information Science," has appeared more frequently since formally proposed by the Soviet quantification historians during the 1980s (KROPAČ, 1987; THALLER & MULLER, 1989, THALLER, 1989; BORODKIN, 1992; MCCRANK, 1994b; BORODKIN, 1996) at History and Computing conferences (1987, 1989-1990, 1992-1993, 1994 with ALLC, and most recently, IAHC at Moscow, 1996). This was the preferred translation into English of Leonid Borodkin's continued advocacy of an *istoricheskaia informatika* which he articulated in 1992, reflecting the post-1968 experience of Moscow's Historical Informatics Laboratory under the USSR's Academy of Sciences (BORODKIN & LEVERMANN, p. 7), and this English-translation as "Historical Information Science" was used most significantly by the Russian hosts for the 1996 IAHC conference in Moscow (BORODKIN *ET AL.*,1997). At the same time, Jean-Philippe Genet is credited with coining the theme of an international conference occurring on November 6-8, 1997 in

Victoria-Gasteiz, Spain, where conferees focused their attention on moving from "des bases de donneés aux systemes d'information historique [databases to historical information systems]" (cited by CHAREILLE, p. 32, n. 1). The whole spectrum includes source criticism to understand the original purpose and structure of historical information; the formalization of documentation; historical data conversion into tagged or coded machine-readable or electronic form; retrospective conversion into digital form and attendant access; computerized sorting, data linking, and counting for statistical analysis; telecommunications for data exchange and conferencing, and computer-assisted History teaching and learning (CAI/CAL). Add to this the information behavior of historians themselves, the information structure of historical science, historiography, and philosophical issues on the one hand; and on the other, the more technical dimension of creation and customization of software, automated technique, new analytical procedures, etc., for History that as THALLER argues, frees the historian from the constraints of current software.

The framework for discussions on such diverse and immense issues is often too narrow, however, and the scientific inspection of contemporary applications, assumptions, attitudes, uses, methods, and results with computer techniques seems sadly lacking. Historians trapped in their mindset, even when using computers, are unwilling to apply to themselves and their current work the same technology they use for historical information. By sticking to the technical as in current European usage of Informatics rather than Information Science, historians exclude themselves from self-study. This is ironic when historians are perhaps more self-evaluating than most professions, or at least they have always engaged in a prolific evaluation of historical literature and in debate, which has developed a prolific historiography (surveyed for the twentieth century by IGGERS, 1997). Their approach to evaluation for research and teaching, however, is very individualistic and often lacks the programmatic character of other disciplines or the kind of benchmarking used in business and some fields to relate productivity to costs or input and output rations (C. WHITE; cf., SPENDOLINI). CHEUMSKY & SHADISH survey such evaluation methods, especially for future developments. What is wanting is a sociology of historical work, a socioeconomic approach to the business of history, and comparative psychoanalytic and cognitive studies about historians.

The gerund form "computing" does not exist in Russian, so hitherto former Soviet quantification researchers have simply combined "historian" and "computer" for their book titles and description of their work. Borodkin wants to switch the emphasis from the man and machine to the intellectual process, and the very paradigm shift requires language invention. As this essay attempts to point out, in English as well, the science needs to be stressed over the technology. It would be a grave mistake to exclude the historian and the critical element in historiographic thought from systems design and evaluation, just as in Information Science it would be irresponsible not to consider the user in any information needs analysis. Rather than exclude library, archival, and information science from this purview, one may incorporate them into it for good advantage. Thus, this essay takes a broader look at Historical Informatics than as confined by the European delegation to the 1994 Social Science History conference, and attempts an eclectic, ecumenical, and inclusive approach so characteristic of Information Science—thus, Historical Information Science.

The author recognizes, however, that in popular opinion the subject of this essay will likely still remain simply "hi-tech History" (as construed by reporters DE LOUGHRY and WILD).

ORIGINS AND DEVELOPMENTS

Debated New Beginnings

History is neither as cohesive nor as coherent a discipline as commonly thought (so D. CARR observes). Instead, as F. STERN maintained, "varieties of History" exist with many foci, specializations, and varying degrees of interest in new technologies and methodologies. Historians are also distributed throughout many disciplines; at any major university as many historians work in other departments as in the Department of History. More work outside academe. Some historians, especially those with a Social Science orientation, are more prone to engage in Historical Information Science than others. Such historians, few in number, began computing late in the 1960s and early 1970s (BOGUE, 1983, referring to the early years; cf., for alterative background views: BERKHOFER; SWIERENGA). Ironically, historians stopped teaching historical methods *per se* in the 1970s about the same time that computing was making some inroads into the profession. Many departments began to replace historical methods courses with units in subject-area tracks within their curricula, resulting in a contextualization of method in keeping with trends toward ever more particularistic study. Although historical computing might have promoted comparative studies because of the capability of computers to parallel process and automatically compare data in disparate files, this did not happen. Instead, computing seemingly spurred specialization, particularism, and emphases on specific technique because so much of it remained highly individualized rather than collaborative, so it did not necessarily promote comparative studies or unify historical methods into systematic methodologies. The relation of microcomputing and micro-conceptualization in historical studies during the 1970s has never been investigated adequately.

The tardiness of historians in adopting the computer as a tool may be explained by many reasons. FOGEL attributes this delay to no fault of historians, but partially to the arcane language of early computer programming and stereotypical judgment of computer center managers who deferred to technology and engineering, then the sciences, and finally business, as a matter of cost-effectiveness, so that the Social Sciences and at long last, the Humanities, finally got to use them. From this viewpoint, historians were deprived not by their own incompetency, but by their institutional context, through policies set by university administrations, and the monopolistic tendencies of Science and Applied Technology to control computer technology development. Certainly the discrepancy in time for adaptation and the difference in prowess and effectiveness in funding are evident when one compares program activities in the National Science Foundation with the National Endowment for the Humanities. The time lag is more than 15 years, and the difference in funding makes the two incomparable. As JENSEN (1983a & b) has shown, historians were finally empowered by the microcomputer revolution and marketing trends in the 1980s, neither of which catered to historians or were very much influenced by them. The result, however, has been revolutionary indeed, even though the goals of technical and methodological revolutionaries may not yet be fulfilled. Changes are noticeable.

Among the soul-searching historians who have reflected on the profession and this delayed entry into the "Information Age" is Chad Gaffield, a historian who engaged the data archives field in the 1980s. He mused:

> ...computerization has proceeded far more slowly than anticipated by optimistic promoters in the 1960s. The cultural cleavage between humanists and scientists remains quite evident in the arts, where many scholars, often harboring grim memories of high school mathematics, still recoil from the binary underpinnings of even logging on. The transition from index cards, foolscap and fountain pens to machine-readable files, printout, and never-as-comparable-or-portable-as-promised equipment has proven to be both emotionally and technically less than smooth.

> While many factors explain the reluctance of historians to enter the Information Age enthusiastically, a rarely discussed phenomenon involves a general misconception about what computers can do for historians. The misconception is that computers can simply help historians do better (or, to a greater extent) what they

already do. In other words, computers are a tool by which historians can handle larger amounts of data, undertake more complex analyses, and write up their reports more efficiently. Computers are, therefore, non- revolutionary. They represent for historians basic continuity rather than substantive change (GAFFIELD, 1988, pp. 312-313).

Here Gaffield is reflecting a use of History as it is so often used, to create a comfort level and thereby to coax change. But he understood how misleading such assurances could be:

...this notion may deny for us the truly exciting future which computerization is bringing to other fields. I am referring here to questions of disciplinary organization, epistemology and, ultimately, creativity. My argument is that computerization is offering historians not only a tool to do better what we have always done, but also the opportunity to redefine and reconstruct the process of historical inquiry....it seems worthwhile to explore the possibility that computerization is fueling a research paradigm shift of truly revolutionary proportions. Significantly, this possibility is far removed from the now outmoded quantitative-qualitative, humanist-social scientist controversies of the 1960s and 1970s. In fact, the current terms of debate do not even allow for such dichotomous conceptualizations (GAFFIELD, 1988, pp. 312-313).

I agree, except that the old paradigm is with us still. The new paradigm of data sharing, teamwork, and group decision-making is currently the subject of intense study for electronic conferencing and groupware to create environments only dreamed about by historians a decade ago (see AXELROD's historical study of the "cooperation" phenomenon; the sociology of group dynamics is presented by J. E. MCGRATH; the problems in and accrued benefits of shared data in research are treated by SIEBER; current perspectives are found in GALEGHER, KRAUT & EGIDO). ORAVEC talks about the human dimensions of networking involving "virtual individuals" and "virtual groups." The vision of the NATIONAL RESEARCH COUNCIL (1993) of the "collaboratory" for multi-institutional research projects by interdisciplinary teams with state-of-the-art information technology and unlimited access to machine-readable data is an extension and formalization of the kind of historical research environment Gaffield and his colleagues attempted. Other examples of "proto-collaboratories" will be mentioned throughout this survey as possible models for continued collaborative projects, but nearly a decade later, such a vision expressed by Gaffield would still be considered new and challenging in History in which most work is self-directed, unaccountable to external management, immune to effectiveness and efficiency evaluation, low-tech, highly individualized, and solitary.

Early enthusiasts (the Cliometricians as they were called since Stanley Reiter coined the term in 1961, hence "Cliometry", CROUZET) in the 1970s reinvented everything as "new"—New Social History (STEARNS), New Political History (at the national level: BOGUE, 1980; or international: GIBBS & SINGER), New Economic History which is often aligned with Econometrics, etc. (IGGERS; BLOW & DICKENSEN; RABB, etc.). Robert Swierenga had dubbed the early practitioners of computerized history as constituting the "New Generation" (SWIERENGA, 1974), which Gertrude Himmelfarb later, more than contrasting the "old" historical school, had to rename the old "new" school to make room for a new "new" generation (HIMMELFARB, 1987). This enthusiasm for new methods and new technology, or "new tools for 'new' history" as BURTON (1989) observed, was invigorating to some. The anticipation of great strides through technology, which some (H. SEGAL, 1988) likened to a wave of History utopianism, was hardly confined to History. It occurred at the same time when Paul Wasserman and other reformers called for the "New Librarianship" (WASSERMAN, 1972) that heralded the impact of Information Science in American library schools. Both fields carried forth with equally strident rhetoric. Ironically, the latter transformation in the United States temporarily mitigated against bibliographic scholarship (MCCRANK, 1980a) and History (e.g., P. WILSON, 1978, pp. 164-165; she voiced a widespread sentiment that History was irrelevant for Information Science) precisely when historical scholarship experienced a parallel reformation which then could have augmented each other. Historians in the United States unfortunately paid little attention to the Information Science movement, or else viewed it with suspicion if not disdain, and subsequently did little to incorporate it into their traditional approach to archives. This did not happen partially because of the alignment of History in Library Science with the Humanities, namely bibliography and literary studies, more than with institutional history, quantified socioeconomic history, or archives. Historians made little sense of what was occurring in the archival profession with recent shifts toward the scientific, and consequently were caught unaware of the separation, indeed actual divorce, between History and the Information Science fields even though they continued to share mutual interests in libraries and archives, common causes, and even intermittent convivial reunions. The Library Information Science field, on the other hand, did not undergo and therefore did not benefit from the intense methodological debate that occurred in History over computing and quantification.

It should not be surprising now, or when debates over quantified methodology and historical computing broke out in the late 1960s, that the experimentation and application of the new information technology to a traditional discipline should be anything but controversial. Studies of learning curves in organizations, which may apply to professions as well, have shown that the most rapid learning occurs immediately after the introduction of anything novel, and then tapers off (TYRE & ORLIKOWSKI). Early pioneers were learning by doing, similar to what happens in production where, it has been argued, normal learning curves are often made to fluctuate whenever change is introduced (VON SICKEL, 1996, p. 327). LEWIN described change as a three-stage process: "unfreezing," "change," and "refreezing." The central point of instability is always uncomfortable and this produces an impetus to restabilize as quickly as possible. When seen as a progression, therefore, change is not a smooth flow but rather a jerky action. Reaction to new techniques and technology, therefore, is to be expected, and it occurred more viciously than ever expected by the pioneers of early history computing. Moreover, ORLIKOWSKI & HOFMAN, who adopt Lewin's change model to suggest improvisation in change management in the case of groupware use, note that "there is a discrepancy between how people think about technological change and how they implement it" (p. 11). Learning in production has been associated more with the changes in production than with the number of units produced. Moreover, as STAUDENMAIER (p. 107) has pointed out: "Whether catastrophe or not, ignorance revealed in normal usage calls attention to a fundamental characteristic of technological knowledge. No technology is ever completely understood, even after it has been introduced into normal practice." This certainly holds true for computing and is well exemplified by the overzealous claims of its first practitioners and in the prognostications and fulminations of its early detractors.

The hostility and emotion of this debate in History was exemplified by Carl Bridenbaugh's infamous attack on pioneer computer historians like Robert W. Fogel and Stanley L. Engermann whose *Time on the Cross* (FOGEL & ENGERMANN) was characterized as a subjective "sermon on the methods of quantification" (MACLEOD). Others referred to the cluster of quantification method books (AYDELOTTE, 1971; BENSON, 1972; DOLLAR and JENSEN, 1971; FLOUD, 1973) in the early 1970s as "Numerophilia" (RIDGEWAY). Bridenbaugh's fears of "runaway technology" and the "Great Mutation" of History resulted in his vilification of quantitative methodology as "the Bitch Goddess Clio" (BRIDENBAUGH). This phrase was subsequently immortalized by A. BOGUE (1983) who waved it like a banner when he later recalled the bumpy origins of the Cliometric movement in American economic and political history and its reactionary opposition. The synchronic onslaught included such noted historians as Jack Hexter who was initially identified with the new methodology, and Arthur Schlesinger who maintained that the really significant questions in History could never be reduced to numbers (cf., HEXTER; SCHLESINGER). The attack was enjoined as well as by the eminent education philosopher Jacques Barzun (BARZUN), whom Konrad Jarausch later dismissed as an "obsurcantist" (JARAUSCH, 1991, p. 204). The late Lawrence Stone, well-respected in the field, was initially more difficult to dismiss because of his early enthusiasm for quantification. Subsequently he became disillusioned when not everything hoped for could be realized in the first generation of computing historians (STONE, 1979, 1993). His objections have also been disreputed by GROSSBART (p. 100) as "the ranting of a frustrated historian." THALLER (1994, p. 31) regards Stone's conversion "from a determined follower of quantification to one of its most outspoken enemies" as "apostasy" and disputes some of Stone's allegations, thought by many of his contemporaries as "shattering," in retrospect to be "absurd." The many reactionary critics of Cliometrics from the 1970s evoked a vigorous defense from FOGEL & ENGERMANN, but nonetheless computing historians were forced into retreat, and everywhere a diminishment in the claims of the counters and empiricists could be sensed. The most *avant garde* historians made claims beyond their limited means; these claims were regarded by many historians as somewhat fantastic, but today seem rather modest given the capabilities information technology now affords historians and everyone else.

The historical debate was in some ways just a skirmish in a larger theater of embattled ideologies, but was triggered in part by a vehement reaction to technocratic "computerese" and related "new" jargon, or the hype associated with the much heralded "information society" (ROSZAK). A veritable industry exploded in writing about societal changes wrought by computers (e.g., POSTMAN's bizarre arguments). The issues raised in the 1970s are debatable still, as SCHAMA (1991) suggests in his comments on the critical role of History, when he also engaged the ageless theme of versions of historical source narratives that "compete for credibility" (SCHAMA, 1991, p. 322) then as today in the modern historian's mind. Although Schama thinks of History as an ally of literary criticism, poetry, and philosophy more than the Social Sciences, it is nevertheless in this same vein that K. WEBB argues for methodological pluralism in Social Science research—History included. So too, descriptive and analytical approaches to historical interpretation often compete for similar credibility; even when they sometimes complement each other, they still vie for attention and assimilation fitting the reader's cognitive style. More may be at issue than the research methodology and means of analysis or the resulting interpretation in terms of being right or wrong, insightful or obtuse, and meaningful or silly; at issue may be the receptivity of a history reader to alternative modes of thought, cognitive styles, and numerate versus literate expression.

The great debate over quantification entailed a further splintering along a division between those who saw History either as an art and or a science (a lasting dichotomy delineated by H. S. HUGHES). Some historians like L. BENSON initially, and BAILYN, CLUBB, and HOBSBAWN subsequently, were more reconciliatory. STONE's entreaty in 1979 for the return to narrative history (which can be one of several types: RUSH, 1987) has been seen later as less hostile to quantification than when he was first enjoined by KOUSSER (1984). The debate was over other issues than just quantification; for example, early quantification studies were technical and addressed technique in such a way that their readership would be limited to professional historians and sometimes, among them, only specialists. Underlying the attack on quantification was a legitimate concern that historians were writing increasingly for themselves, for ever smaller audiences of specialists, and this trend was removing history from the public forum. This increased distance between academic history and the reading public is a concern today as well, but is less related to the initial impact of computing in historical analysis. Nevertheless, FOGEL & ELTON, and others like BERKHOFER, have seen History since the 1970s as permanently divided between two camps or each on the move marching down separate roads into history. KOUSSER's tolerant position (1989), described by JARAUSCH (1991, p. 204) as "lukewarm," reflects much of the sentiment of historians in the 1990s that quantification is a "subordinate, illustrative utility," but KOUSSER (1984) had justified such approaches as modeling because historical relationships could thereby be defined so much more precisely than through narrative description only. But the prejudice, once entrenched, lingers still. In some cases "computer historians" left History for Political and Social Science departments (e.g., HERSBERG) as predicted by CLUBB & BOGUE.

The more vigorously mathematical Econometrics became, the more it moved into Economics *per se* (exemplified in its early years by A. S. GOLDBERGER; see the bibliography on econometric models by ÜBE, HUBER & FISHER). Quantitative Social Science historians once active within AHA as a special task force, formed their own association; and other practitioners entered civil service careers in which they made significant contributions to the National Archives and government information services (e.g., F. BURKE; C. DOLLAR, 1971). More historians, like myself, found their way into the information profession through librarianship, some crossed over through consulting, and fewer still went into the information industry, e.g., WEISSMAN. Their accommodations, however, were usually a matter of individual choice and almost chance opportunities based on a unique combination of experience, training, evolving interest, and circumstance, rather than any conscious career trajectory or impetus provided by History graduate education. They shared one common background experience: sometime in the 1970s, earlier than most, they engaged modern information technology for their work and developed technical skills, broader perspectives, and management experience that took them down nonconventional tracks, different from teaching History or operating solely within the self-imposed confines of the historical profession.

The jargon remains, and so does the skepticism. These debates often confused computerization with quantification, and played into a more generalized fear of automation generally, such as reactions to such developments as Online Public Access Catalogs (OPACs) in libraries, online bibliographic information retrieval, and the "discarding" of the card catalog. Moreover, the argument that modern information technology, like modern technology in general, is dehumanizing and seems to be rooted in personal neurosis and a certain romantization of the past, if one is to believe the case made by D. ROTHENBERG about the historical interplay between technology and man's self-image. A. KEMENY, in her dissertation "S(t)imulating Subjects," confronted the negative aspect of computerization in postmodern fiction where she finds evidence, especially extreme in those mounting a utopian feminist critique where militarism, computer technology, and phallocentrism become confused, of a "cybernetic" and "information" episteme in Western culture as cyborgs and computer simulations "abrogate the body." Such is the "post-modern condition"! A few—hopefully very few—historians may feel that way, and reactionary responses are still easily provoked by blatant intrusions of technique and technology, and especially "technobabble," into historical discourse (J. BARRY). However, the historian's objective sense of History usually includes awareness of technological and ideological synchrony so that some accommodation is always possible in time (awareness as related to learning by MARTON & BOOTH). Despite the terrible recrimination that occurred in the initial debates over quantification and computer-assisted historical analysis, tempers have cooled, the integration of quantitative reasoning into historical analysis is pervasive and ubiquitous (REINITZ); computers today are everywhere including historians' offices and in their studies. Of course, the test is whether electronic workstations are used merely as text processors and an electronic means of communication as an upgrade from typewriters and adjunct to telephones, or if they are being used to change substantially how history is being done and if human thought is being extended by new possibilities created through the interaction of mind and machine when studying historical phenomena. That is an "acid test" in identifying a Historical Information Science specialization.

History in Europe was equally acrimonious in the early years of historical computing. German empiricism was already predisposed to adopt a technical, practical approach (cf., E. JOHNSON; BEST & SCHRADER). IGGERS (1983) identified a national tradition of historical thought that favored an empirical approach, but debates also raged in German about quantification methodology, specific applications, and their role in the research seminar (cf.,

STROETMANN to contrast German pragmatism in defining issues in library services and Information Science). German historians and their counterparts in education greatly influenced American historical studies through the seminar, and simultaneously through the notion of a "course of study" or curricular guides (WINTERS); subsequently, they borrowed heavily from the United States in the postwar decades (DEMM; KOCKA). Now, as shall be seen, certain centers in German higher education are again poised to teach Americans how to proceed along a course of study in Historical Information Science, but detractors (K.-P. BUSCHE) are still critical of history teaching in German universities that seems not to integrate computing into the whole fabric of History. Moreover, the cross-Atlantic influence this time is really more pan-European than national. In the Soviet Union the earliest attempts at quantification in classical history, to ascertain correlations between grain supplies, food shortages, and political upheavals in ancient Greece, met singular opposition as Cliometrics did in the United States. Not only was the methodology attacked, but the fundamental questions probed seemed impertinent, such as in ascribing Greek political developments to hunger and social unrest rather than purely intellectual aspirations. After rebuff and ostracization, the quantifiers there also left History for more congenial fields in Soviet Social Sciences, similar to trans-disciplinary migrations which occurred elsewhere. Quantification studies have had a Renaissance in the last years of the Soviet Union and will survive the current political transition.

The export of brainpower and computing expertise hardly served the technical development of History and the swings back and forth over the past generation have left modern history shaken, diffuse, self-critical, somewhat volatile, and while intellectually stimulating as in any times of trouble, in crisis regarding such practicalities as employment opportunities and professionalization. Historians in Europe have always moved in and out of academe, government and privately patronized think tanks or research centers, the publishing and information industry, and between disciplines, without losing their identity as historians. The nature of the university in Europe often makes for a more fluid exchange; this is perhaps why History in the United States seems especially susceptible to European intellectual influence, but History in Europe does not seem much more in tune with developments outside the academic arena than in America. The most recent debates, therefore, have become highly introspective. They have not been as methodological as those about quantitative history, but have become more philosophical, skeptical, and often negative; and criticism such as that hurled against early experimental quantification has extended itself to all types of history. The criticism of quantifiable modeling, for example, has now been leveled as well at descriptive history as a form of qualitative verbal modeling. Indeed, W. DOISE advocates the quantitative analysis of social representation as a primary method in social psychology, in a field dealing largely with social perceptions, which is usually composed of narratives, descriptions, case studies, etc., that are thought to be basically qualitative and subjective in nature (cf., CRANACH, DOISE, & MUGNY, eds.). The idea, of course, is to objectify the subjective and to build a model of social perception (singular) by counting instances, similarities and differences, attributes, metaphors and other reoccurring expressions. Description and narrative approaches, once juxtaposed against quantification, increasingly are now seen as simply different kinds of modeling subject to the same scrutiny and in some cases even more severe criticism.

The blending of qualitative and quantitative research methods is not unique to History or the Social Sciences. The collection of essays by LAMBERTS & SHANKS shows the shift in Information Science from almost totally empirical and quantitative research to a better balance with qualitative methods. Description, after all, can be quite empirical. Consider the case of descriptive cataloging as portrayed by SVENONIUS and others. In this case, description is primarily of the object, and yet it attempts to reveal content. Such description is not seen as narrative or as a literary form, but there is an art to it. Descriptive cataloging follows a model; it is positivistic in ethos, and empirical in the sense that descriptive catalogs as databases are quantifiable; but in the application of classes, rules, and forms, cataloging can be quite subjective.

While classification battles chaos, it does not resolve all ambiguity; and cataloging does convey qualitative information. Most notably, subject access is a different process than document retrieval by author and title. But these methods of access are complementary, and they operate together for accessibility overall that is improved over that achieved by any one of them alone. The quantitative and qualitative aspects of librarianship's approach to knowledge organization are integrated. The general model and individual identities are simultaneously operational.

In this case as in so many others, when considering quantitative versus qualitative approaches to knowledge, the critical question is not one or the other but the flawed outcome when one is used without the other. The empirical side of Truth is revealed in accuracy and detail when counting what is described, as well as how, when and where something is described. But the "why" of the matter often needs more description for explanation, and describing in narrative form, telling its history, may be considered as a form of explanation. Measurement alone may be accused of presenting half-truth, but the reverse holds true as well, that description without measurement is the other half-truth. In any case, the centrality of most debates over objectivity is still the truth claim of History which is seldom proclaimed now in a fundamentalist way, and seems to be claimed in any fashion less forcibly every day (cf., PAUL RICOEUR, 1965, on *History and Truth*; PAGE on the philosophical basis for History; and B. ALLEN for the idea of Truth in Philosophy as historically expressed; and S. SHAPIN for the "social history of Truth"). Arguments, often grounded in highly abstract language, are often about objectivity versus subjectivity in historical reconstruction. Invariably the real issue is about our imperfect knowledge about the past. Imperfection in any endeavor is something to be acknowledged, embraced even, and compensated for, but it is no excuse for not trying, giving up, or casting doubt on the entire enterprise. An approximation of truth, a blurred vision of it, and even an intelligent guess at it are better than nothing at all. This fundamental assumption and most primal of motivations underlies the social theory of science and knowledge (S. FUCHS). It has also been basic to the epistemology of History. Objectivity in the study of the past or the quest thereof, and the inherent objective of study for both description and explanation, should distinguish History from everything else, i.e., "its other" (NATTER, SCHATZKI, & JONES, eds.). It is indeed a high ideal, and even when not achieved, it remains as NOVICK calls it, ironically, "a noble dream."

Introspection and New Skepticism

English pragmatists were accommodating of new ways of "doing" History in HEXTER's terms, as a matter of fact especially for economic history methodology. This appealed to American sensibilities in narrow fields, but nothing like the general impact of the French penchant for conceptualization. DE CERTEAU (pp. 19-55) as early as 1970 and other Frenchmen immediately afterward (LE GOFF & NORA, 1974), under the earliest influences of linguistics and language critiques of historical method, preferred the term "making history" because they perceived historical reconstruction to be an intellectual artifact. De Certeau's critique is more introspective, however, than the characterization of "superhistorians" as "makers of the past" (BARKER) as shapers of historian opinion and forming school of thought, or "inventors" (CANTOR) as those who reconceptualize traditional periodization and areas of historical study. It goes more to the philosophical heart of the connectivity, accuracy, and relevance of history. While the thrust of such thinking, based on modern notions of language utility and cognition, is philosophical and often highly theoretical, it almost unwittingly lends itself to the justification of data models, simulation, and computer-generated analyzes in using technology to construct a critical apparatus for historical thought. If most historical constructs are intellectual artifices, artificially contrived, then if the means of such construction were computerized, this would seem to be less foreign to historiography than one might first assume or understand from the great furor over quantification.

Methodologically oriented Annaliste French historians (FURET; GLENISSON; CHAUNU; LE ROY LADURIE, etc.), predisposed by the pre-computer influence of the Annales School (the forerunner of the New Social History, e.g., M. BLOCH, BRAUDEL, FEBVRE, etc.) seemed especially inclusive and flexible because of this philosophical bent (DOSSE). In 1989 The Annales school proposed a new alliance between History and the Social Sciences, but this has provoked attacks from those advocating a pluralism in history rather than any movement toward unity, integration, or reliance on common methods and technique (BEDERIDA pulls together essays tracing the formation of schools in French historiography, 1945-1995). The Annaliste influence in Germany may have done the same for German historicism, infusing it with a Social Science perspective, but there too such approaches have come under attack (L. RAPHAEL). Regardless of where their ideas took hold, certainly their thinking was decidedly different than the new wave of anecdotal and literary forms that have more recently dominated narrative history at the exclusion of more empirical approaches.

Regardless of the source of influence, the inevitability of change is one lesson from History on which all historians could agree. But the objectivity claimed in scientific historicism, quantified or not, received its most formidable challenge from which it has not really recovered. In the mid-1980s, Dominick LaCapra and Jacque Derrida, *et al.* differentiated between historicism, i.e., created perception, and history reconstructed with actual congruence to the past, i.e., belief in a past reality that could be retold, if not reenacted later (LACAPRA; DERRIDA; cf., TOEWS; KLOPPENBERG; etc. for historians' response; and DEBOLLA; GEARHART, etc., for reaction from literary critics). Derrida sees the writing of History as substantially different from history; the writing itself is the *différence* since it all has an opaque quality. The current division has been described (M. ROTH, 1994, p. 744) as between "those who think they are talking about real, lived experience, and those who thing they are talking about texts (as if this were a viable contrast …)." This quasi-anthropological interpretation of history *qua* literature sees History as the practice of creating culture in the sense of projecting an image of the past into the present. Such approaches, exemplified by GEERTZ's focus (1983) on the local and description techniques to relate local knowledge to broader genres (BIERSACK; CAMIC, 1995), and the emphasis on language as symbolic and human behavior as something to be read like literature, are in line with the approach to text analysis by CHARTIER. Those who argue that everything communicated through language is so subjective that it is literature have had their detractors. B. PALMER is among their formidable adversaries. R. WALTERS very early criticized such interpretative movements as contributing to the fragmentation of social and cultural history. His critique (1980) is illustrative of the earlier link made between overquantification and a dehumanization of historical studies. The highly theoretical and abstracted becomes too far removed from practical existence, reality in everyday life, and human self-consciousness. Or, as in the case of Hayden White's critique of Michel Foucault (FOUCAULT, 1970), such discourse is severely criticized as "The Rhetoric of Anti-Humanism" (WHITE, 1987; KRAMER). This may be apt if the criticism is about the convergence of disciplines, which S. KATZ (1995) thinks is increasingly problematic today. Moreover, a strand of historical criticism still operates against seeing history merely as literature, either nonfiction as most historians see their writing, or as a form of fiction according to the textual deconstructionists. Simply put, History for historians is history. Not only does contemporary history reject lawgiving as a basic premise for its intellectual contribution, but the mainstream is guarding against the opposite reaction toward history as being viewed purely as narration or literary discourse.

Indeed, some claim History itself no longer achieves a unifying narrative of any sort which can be trusted (NOVICK, pp. 573-629). In some respects History is done piecemeal as histories, like case studies which are never drawn together to support generalization (see R. YIN on the case method). This phenomenon of fragmentation is characterized by some as "historical atomism." TILLY (1984) notes in his *Big Structures, Large Processes, Huge Comparisons* that venturing comprehensive explanations or theories about grand themes or writing about the "grand tides" in H. PIRENNE's famous phrase is more risky than small-step science or historians examining minutia and staking out small claims. The larger the generalization the less sure we are about it (hence more description and less explanation, and more complexity rather than reduction to simplicity), but the big picture is nevertheless desirable to place detail into perspective. The arguments over objectivity reflect this insecurity about complex, holistic scenarios drawn from details no matter how sure we are about the data on which the whole rests. Others have suggested that the modern predicament reflects nineteenth-century efforts by Wilhelm Dilthey and others to argue for a *Geisteswissenschaften* as methodologically and phenomenologically unique from *Naturwissenschaften* which would take a comparative approach and retain a unifying sense of history as an ongoing attempt to understand mankind in its totality (cf., M. SCHULTZ in this regard, especially in reference to Max Weber). Such movements that undermine the older unifying world view or *Geistesgeschichte*, search for cause and order, and a sense of distinctive disciplines and the autonomy of History, and they are perhaps epitomized by FOUCAULT (1970; 1971), but his French penchant for returning to synthesis is atypical of Anglo-American or Germanic empiricism. Moreover, his approach to synthesis is not based on continuity, but on discontinuities as the start of something new. He is antagonistic with tradition, but instead stresses the significance of transformations, i.e., new beginnings. A. MEGILL labeled Foucault and Derrida as "prophets of extremity." If Foucault is antihumanistic in Hayden White's eyes, this does not make him pro-Social Science. Indeed, he seems to defy easy classification, partially because he moves across disciplinary barriers so easily and is so synoptic. Some see Foucault as arguing for an inter-disciplinary approach to knowledge, and ultimately that all approaches would be translated into the language of History (NOIRIEL) The danger, of course, is that if history is all things to all people, then it is so commonplace and amorphous that it means little. If totally ubiquitous, then what is History really? In postmodern times a distinction is made between history and History.

This agonizing controversy, it seems, veils more fundamental debates about the success or failure of philosophical positivism on the one hand, and on the other the reliability of communication that is too imaginative or mostly symbolic. Deconstructionists in their enthusiasm for linguistic analyzes and semiotics have overstated their case similar to the earlier enthusiasts for computing and quantification. The regard by the first generation of positivists for method as monolithic and their system orientation may have undermined their general argument that if History claims to impart knowledge, then it must emulate scientific method. This was seen as formalistic, rigid, and even dictatorial. In this same way, positivists AYER, HEMPEL, and others of their persuasion now appear to have been overly confident in the self-sufficiency of method, much like computer enthusiasts a generation later promoted quantification as a single-method approach to history. Computer technicians like salespeople often take the same position today, to the dismay of those priding themselves on having greater sophistication than to fall for single explanations and simple cause and effect relationships. On the other hand, a healthy reoccurrence of positivist thought acts as a antidote to trendy conceptualism and ambiguous thought. S. TURNER, for example, recently argues against superficial explanations based on vague notions of paradigms, tacit knowledge, and style, or for that matter when historians simply repeat anthropological terms like "culture" and "tradition" without adequate specification for clarity and precision. He accuses many scholars of playing with structural concepts in an unreflective manner and is especially critical of historians who fall back on these superindividual constructs as though they were entities. These are treated, he maintains, in a straightforward style similar to what is regarded as loathsome in other practices. TURNER's work is positivistically deconstructionist, whereas writers like FOUCAULT and to a lesser extent DE CERTEAU, etc., seen as deconstructionists also, seem radically antipositivist. They revel in personal insight, creative interpretation, and continuing discourse. J. SMITH recently called for "no more language games" (a reference to WITTGENSTEIN's analogy) in his review of the "central occupation" of historians of French political culture to analyze language. Such language analyses have often been influenced by linguistics and cognitive psychology and are therefore cloaked in a metalanguage of science, but their methods are usually nonempirical and unscientific in their approaches. Instead they rely on close, personal reading of the texts, which may be informed by science. Is this enough to qualify such research as scientific?

Taken to extremes, the relativism of text studies based on personal inspiration during their reading is certainly antiscience but may also be regarded as nihilistic when novelty in interpretation is the goal for its own sake. Moreover, extreme relativism certainly mitigates against History's use in value judgments, if it does not also play a role in values formation (R. PERRY). It is the thin demarcations between contrived novelty and language games, new insight and interpretation, and creativity that makes judgment calls so difficult when assigning value in the review process or in one's reading History's vast secondary literature. A tension always exists between the objective, impersonal historical analysis and the personal, subjective, and value-related interpretation. Popular reactions regard such valueless history not simply as amoral, but worse, as untruthful (GILLEY). Marc Ferro's historiographic treatise *L'histoire sous surveillance* carries the interesting subtitle "*science et conscience de l'histoire*" to remind us how conscience goes with science, including historical science (FERRO, 1985). Earlier he applied this notion to the teaching of History, especially to children, in order to discern the difference between *The Use and Abuse of History* (FERRO, 1981/1984). Objective historical description may be qualified in one way or another, and even history as literature can be measured by assigning values to interpretation and degrees in judgment, and conversely, quantified data can be described, and indeed must be, to insure understanding as history. But the attempt at objectivity in historical reconstruction, and all quantification, must be linked to an empirical and hence at least an attenuated positivist view of history.

BEVIR proposes that consensus about objectivity versus subjectivity could be approached by modeling; that is, using set criteria to compare and contrast accounts, to calculate the degree of reinforcement in the case of agreement, and in the case of rival interpretations to note dissent and alternatives and what support they garner. One could, thereby, use commonalities for articulating consensus and use variance to point to biases and other perspectives. This is sort of consensus by automated democracy in the acceptance of historical positions, but he argues that it is a form of recognition of cultures within histories. In final analysis, it is an empirical approach that essentially argues that things were so because historians say so in sufficient numbers to warrant acceptance. The truth claim in History would therefore reside not in the facts studied, but in their telling and retelling, somewhat like citation analysis which identifies authorities on the basis of how their work is cited. The more people believe it, the more that make it so. Truth, therefore, is an attributed rather than intrinsic value (PERRY construes values in terms of interests). If so, tradition would always reign supreme with little possibility of revision. It is doubtful that such a recommendation will gain much endorsement from historians. They are commonly and naturally skeptical of such approaches, and more so now under the influence of deconstructionism and linguistic studies of communications; they seldom move comfortably into such a positivist mode of thought as the scientism which pervades Information Science (cf., NOVICK; RORTY). By and large historians tend toward middle ground, with prudent wariness of either extreme.

Meanwhile, the dialectic that results from the tension between objectivity and subjectivity in the philosophy of history or any other discipline always created reoccurring controversy (ANKERSMIT & KELLNER). E. KORNFELD juxtaposes the "politics of objectivity and the promise of Subjectivity" as if the former were not promising and the latter were not political. PORTER's *Trust in Numbers* and the essays edited by M. WISE in *The Values of Precision* recount the ebb and flow of recurrent enthusiasm alternating with aversion to numeric approaches to knowledge, breakthroughs and overkills, and corrections and rehabilitations.

Too often the use of measurement and counting is seen as essential to objective views, while description is seen as purely subjective. The quantitative versus qualitative debates are often framed this way. The most recent version of this old dichotomy in History has been reworded as History versus Metahistory, with chief combatants Arthur Marwick and Hayden White hammering away at each other in this ageless dialectic. SOUTHGATE castigates both protagonists as reflecting a certain paranoia in History today. KANSTEINER views the debate as a concern for the integrity of history. MARWICK juxtaposes the metaphysical and historical approaches to historical studies, in such a way that the former does not constitute the work of "true" historians. Real historians in common parlance "stick to the facts" to establish historical truth. By contrast, metaphysicists under the guise of History are castigated as being ideologically oriented; they apply speculative methods without reference to real sources. Marwick is particularly critical of postmodernism and deconstructionism (but seems to confuse discourse analysis with deconstruction), and the method used by postmodernists that confines itself to single patterns or process in a limited sample. He is commonly seen as a traditional historian who views objectivity as the accurate rendition of events as they happened, free from moral judgment and politics. In this regard he falls into line with RICOEUR's caveats when considering the hermeneutics of textual studies (1974, 1976) about reading too much into something, more than is there, to produce a "surplus of meaning" in interpretation.

Hayden White, of course, wants historians like Marwick to be more aware of the philosophical nature of the historian's work, even when they think they are operating purely in narrative mode (WHITE). Even in a phenomenological approach, there is always more than meets the eye. Objectivity is, after all, a value and a philosophical stance in itself. White is here operating as a critic, but not necessarily as a postmodernist. Although he takes his stance on other grounds, he is well-supported by recent work in cognitive sociopsychology as in BODEN-HAUSEN & WYER who compared information acquisition in the laboratory and real world to highlight the "social reality" that influences cognition in either case. LATOUR, among his several commentaries about science and culture (1976-1996), once subjected Biology to scrutiny from the vantage point of Sociology to argue that scientific facts have a "social construction" peculiar to "laboratory life" (cf., ZVIGLAINICH on science as a cultural or historical process). Historians who have jumped into this debate about the nature of history have expanded its dimensions, but they have not exploited the behavioral literature in the Social Sciences very much and in the medical sciences not at all. G. ROBERTS thinks that structuralists, for example, seldom theorize about what drives their empirical research both in terms of method and what they choose to study. He hits on something that should be pursued further, which could be framed as a research subject fitting comfortably within Information Science. The delineation of the interplay between personal cognition and socialization in topic selection and specialization by historians, for example, would be an interesting inquiry, although it might prove disturbing for the subjects.

Information scientists are not likely to engage such a debate about objective versus subjective nuance in the same way that historians have gone about this business of juxtaposing the two as though they were incompatible and irreconcilable. They would, I suspect, want to be more objective about subjectivity, to analyze its causes and impact and to devise corrections and compensating mechanisms for undesirable effects so that one could engineer more desirable outcomes. They might dissect the problem(s) as analytically as Hayden White, but would not talk the problem to death, and they would search for some form of measurement to assist in this analysis. The problem itself becomes a research topic (bias, skewing, congruence, variability, etc.) and the language discussing the problem is decidedly different. They might go about such analysis in the mode practiced by M. H. DAVID, GROVES, NORMAN, and others who study research from the vantage point of cognitive psychology. The real thrust of such historiographic argument is that subjective influences produce error; or conversely, overconfidence in objectivity produces error.

Consider such diagnostics in contemplating the nature of error, for example, reduced to the following typology by ROBBIN & FROST-KUMPF (1997):

1. Inferential error as in classical statistics and hypothesis testing when an incorrect judgment is "based on an obtained statistical result conditioned on the assumption that the null hypothesis is true. An error occurs when the obtained statistical result produces one of two, mutually exclusive, but incorrect decisions" (p. 107).

2. Residual or model error like "noise" existing in the data, related to multivariate model building, which shows up in the difference between expected and observed scoring. "The implications for producing large but irreducible unexplained variations under any statistical model are significant" (p. 108).

3. Task performance error is a mistake made in operations which produced unwanted outcomes or undesirable consequence, as in processing data from records.

4. Decision-making error is an incorrect selection of a course of action from a set of alternatives, as in a poor choice of queries or sampling design in survey research (GROVES), or a selection of an inappropriate database management system for longitudinal or crosssectional data files.

5. Method error is a mismatch between analytical methods available or used and the researchers' identification of the fundamental underlying structure of organizational problems in the research (e.g., within a range from ill- to well-structured data).

The dissection of error and classification in this manner is to enable accommodation and redesign for communicative and cognitive competence. "Rather than avoid error it must be embraced, especially, when it is realized through breakdowns in data production and use. Embracing error in this fashion allows greater control to be exercised when error does occur but would otherwise remain concealed (which is, of course, the worst error of all)" argue ROBBIN & FROST-KUMPF (p. 114) in the same vein as SEIFERT & HUTCHINS. The same might be said for inherent subjectivity, which needs to be acknowledged as by Hayden White, but objectified in such a way that it can be measured, handled, moderated, altered, compensated for, and neutralized if necessary. The historian's acknowledgment of the problem, without doing much about it, is what might make the difference between Historiography and Historical Information Science.

If such questioning of objective interpretation of data, historical texts (or any documentation, for that matter) has proven so unsettling, how much more does such thinking confront some of the basic suppositions brought to bear on History by Informatics and Knowledge Representation (which never seem to take on the introspection they deserve *à la* H. PITKIN's critique of "descriptive representation") by mere numbers, graphs, and charts, versus terms, strings, and abstracts? Or, will such attacks on History as totally subjective, especially in its narrative form, reinforce the persistent quest for objectivity and revive quantification as a form of empirical research perceived to satisfy objective standards? Information Science, which has always favored empiricism over description and narration, has seemed impervious to the contemporary deconstructionist critique; the latter is simply ignored. References to the critique of historical scientism and the attack upon quantification as false objectivity, which could be readily turned onto operations research in Library and Information Science, simply do not appear in the latter's literature until the 1990s. Then, as ROBBIN & FROST-KUMPF observe, more librarians and information scientists have become dissatisfied with traditional approaches to information systems design.

They argue that professionals must move *away from* an approach that views information or data as objective, and information or data as determined by the expert system designers and system managers as controllers of data resources. They most move *toward* an approach that posits information as a user construct and system design as a user-centered enterprise. Implied by this change in orientation is that our conceptions of users, how they perceive information, and their information needs and uses require a different theoretical basis for information system design and user services ([original emphases] ROBBIN & FROST-KUMPF, p. 97).

The dissatisfaction they refer to may have been influenced by the debates in other fields, notably the Social Sciences and the critique of quantification; if so, the lag time has been more than a decade. But now Information Science too must objectively confront the idea of subversive subjectivity in all information processing as a first step in learning to cope with it and compensate for its negative effects.

History, being more introspective than Information Science, tends not to be so insulated from such philosophical debate, but it does not always confront subjectivity objectively and scientifically. The current challenge may have a debilitating affect on historians embracing a formal Historical Information Science openly; the transition may be more timid and like subversion, unobtrusive and gradual. Or a dissatisfaction with History in its current micro-analytic state, its attributed subjectivity, and an easily perceived fragmentation may propel others to quantify and employ methodologies perceived to be more objective. Such reaction to History as Literature may promote realignment with the Social Sciences, but History's syncretism contributes to its appearance of fragmentation precisely because it relates to all disciplines, some of which are very divergent. Such a dichotomy will insure continued varieties of history in a wide spectrum, and therefore, perhaps, allow for the growth of the technical and methodological specialization conceived here as Historical Information Science. Such a development is bound to be controversial given the history of History, ongoing critical debate, and the fact that methodological assumptions left unarticulated in History are less obvious targets than the kind of rigorous exposition of technique espoused in the sciences and Historical Information Science.

Keith Jenkins categorically claims "History (historiography) is an inter-textual, linguistic construct" in modern thinking (JENKINS, 1991, p.7). While historians may acknowledge generally that historical interpretation reflects current thinking interacting with documentation from the past and that historical narrative is a form of literature (BARTHES, 1981), most balk at seeing history as purely signification (GOSSMAN) or fiction (MINK) even if parallels between literary and historical modes of thought and presentation are granted. Historians are likely to rail at being accused of forming a historical consciousness deliberately for ulterior purposes as in the case of using history to support nationalism even if they concede past uses, especially in the realm of religious myth and history, as abuses. The general socialization value of History is commonly upheld, however, as in the discipline's centrality to General Studies curricula. Arguments for history's relevance on the basis of formation, socialization, and professionalization, can be construed easily into the ideology of history being myth. Historians have themselves questioned whether History is one of "Myths we live by" when considering personal mythologizing revealed in Oral History (SAMUEL & THOMPSON, eds.). Mythologists like HEEHS no longer see history and myth (unverifiable narratives) as mutually exclusive; he suggests that the two should be viewed as a dialectic, but not as the same. The general liberalism among historians that opposes such overt applications of History as conservative is thus juxtaposed to the conservatism often attributed to them. Their altruism is often a distinction of academic history from applied history for socialization or formation, as in nurturing organizational culture for employee loyalty or good public relations and marketing in business, or building an *ésprit de corps* in military and religious organizations or government bureaucracies.

The common disdain of academic historians for such applied history, coupled often with considerable ignorance about it, reflects not only old-style elitism but also the still formidable barriers between academe and the "real" world that stifles an exchange that could benefit both. Moreover, it suggests some problems to be faced by historical information scientists working outside academe in business, government, or industry, where the applicability of History to present problem solving seems too indirect to be relevant immediately and practically. Conversely, the skepticism with which modern Information Science is viewed from within History often relates to its minutia, immediacy, and present-mindedness, as though it were not reflective enough, properly contextual, or long-range in vision. Neither has much patience with the other and this contributes to many misunderstandings, all of which reinforce cognitive groupings by like persuasions and separate organizational cultures.

Peter Doorn's aforementioned rendition of misunderstandings that have plagued historiography since the advent of historical computing does not take into account such cognitive dissonance which could split an already diversified field like History into separate camps (DOORN, 1997). Doorn attributes the past misunderstandings to misinterpretation of the issues by overemphasizing differences rather than common ground. He sees continued debates on a variety of issues, most recently modeling versus source-oriented computing, as a continuation of old arguments in new guises, but he does not explain the underlying reason for the debate's continuation through three decades and two major technological shifts. In short, he begs the question of continuing dissonance, which may pertain to something more than the issues as discussed publicly. Few studies have analyzed historians as personality types, aptitudes, and basic psychology, or correlated backgrounds, training, attitudes, and operational styles with their specializations and preferences for narrative or descriptive versus analytic and explanatory history, or any of the polarized options that are available in a continuum of practice. One might wonder, for example, why so many who attacked historical computing had in fact never done it themselves. Was this because they chose not to, or could not master the technology or could not devote the time needed then for data preparation? How many tried and failed, and then turned against the new technique in righteous self-defense, and self-denial? Suspicion of such underlying, personal motives is perhaps why computing historians felt so betrayed when one of their number, Jack Hexter, became disillusioned and hypercritical. My point is that such study of historians and the historical profession in the mode of Social Science inquiry would produce different kinds of history than traditional historiography (MCCRANK, 1997).

DOORN (p. 2) quotes Sir Moses Finley who in 1985 observed the absence of this kind of self-inspection in the History field (FINLEY, pp. 1-2): "Historians, like members of other disciplines ... are reluctant to analyze themselves and their activity: they leave that to the philosophers, whose efforts they then dismiss as ignorant or irrelevant, or both." This insulatory attitude may also explain why researchers, historians included, have tended not to pay attention or use studies by information scientists, psychological group profiles except of great historical figures (e.g., Psycho-History), or organizational culture studies by behaviorists studying project management and overall administration. History's approach to epistemology and heuristics has tended to be problem- and source-oriented, but not organizational. Critical histories of the major historical associations and organizations, for example, are less available than the self-congratulatory genre of centennial observances. The professional histories of HIGHAM and others tend to be historiographic as if the literature existed apart from its authors. An exception to such glossing at the most general levels was CANTOR's exploration of great medievalists whose histories were, so he argues, profoundly influenced by contemporary socioeconomic and political events. Several French historians, of course, have provided a confessional literature (*Ego-histoire* in NORA's words, 1987) connecting personal lives and individual political and religious persuasions with their historical interpretations (reviewed by POPKIN). Some of these fall into the apologetic tradition (in the classical sense of the term, as explanation). In some cases they reveal influences understood only in retrospect, and in others motivations for exploring quantification are examined; there is a penchant toward empirical investigations and modeling at times and swings to more descriptive approaches which are not entirely dependent on the sources, or operating in this or that school of thought (i.e., an alliance with the Annalistes).

It seems that at times, historians argue for objectivity on very subjective grounds. When attempting a more scientific understanding of the historian mind set collectively, it is necessary to study individual historians; few have left themselves so exposed as these French historians with their autobiographic accounts that seem to imply a certain egotism. Such primary historiographic sources can be supplemented, of course, by subjecting the secondary literature of History to discourse analysis and other empirical approaches (as A. J. GREIMAS did for Social Science literature to study the communications of social scientists; see also NELSON, MEGILL & McCLOSKEY, eds., on the comparative rhetoric of "the human science"). History literature could be studied similarly, but not much survey data exists to put the historians as a scholarly community under the Social Science microscope. The major historical associations have failed History miserably by not providing such data for a longitudinal historical record even from their memberships. Historians by necessity have studied themselves historiographically in literary mode, but at best scientifically they would have to be studied using anthropological approaches using their writings as artifacts with the few remnants of their lifework left in manuscript collections. Few individual archives of historians' personal records exist.

Many of the observations of the classics of historical method and interpretation, such as COLLINGWOOD's ideas of "historical knowing" and critiques of linked data without interpretation (cf., GOTTSCHALK; GARDINER; ELTON; MANDELBAUM, etc.), still seem relevant today for historical computing because the original source material is unchanged (HAWORTH, 1990, p. 93), the purpose of History endures, and so much of historical computing is a technological-assistance in speed and quantity of data processing rather than a substantive change (except for original machine-readable records) in documentation or methodologies employed. The issues of interpretation, however, are more complex than ever partially because of the ability to handle more data, and these debates will certainly affect Historical Information Science. Our technology has progressed as have techniques, but the central issues, such as the congruence between original sources transmogrified into numeric data, abstracts, and electronic records, the transmutation caused by such processing, and appropriateness of certain methods for particular applications, deserve this continued attention. Unfortunately, however, a negative residue of this conflict has been the stereotyping of History as conservative if not reactionary and unaccommodating of modern information technology and processes.

The reputation of History as a scholarly discipline has been impugned by devotees of technology for its own sake, while some historians regard applied technology as somehow unscholarly and have adhered to a far narrower definition of scholarship than espoused, for example, by the CARNEGIE FOUNDATION (1994). Like so many stereotypes, these also break down upon inspection; but these biases still keep sci-tech-engineering and History-oriented Information Sciences separate today. This separation is reinforced by academic departmentalization, tenure and promotion policies that disfavor collaboration and inter-disciplinarity, and geographic distances across sprawling campus that keep potential colleagues from knowing each other or their work. When teaching is not confused with operating as an historian, with everything else being "alternative," other possibilities emerge for research historians to join other information and knowledge industries. This is where by the year 2000, according to Department of Labor projections, 44 percent of American workers will find their employment. This cognitive and real distancing impedes the transfer of technological information and adaptation of technique and information technology to History. This lack in turn limits the ability of historians to teach collaboratively, interactively, and cross-disciplinarily—to train by example and style more than course content the "different kind of workers" DRUCKER in his *Post-Capitalist Society* and others say are required for "different organizations" in the coming millennium when constant training, retraining and self-improvement, job- and career-hopping, and continual social and environmental adaptation will be the norm (O'HARA-DEVERAUX & JOHANSEN).

These same cross-disciplinary methodological debates and communication issues pertain not to History alone, but to all Social Sciences and to Information Science as well. The furor over quantitative techniques in History, which reverberated throughout academe and was related to the same Social Science methodologies, statistical analytics, and computer technologies imported synchronically into Library Science through quantified research in documentation, seems not to have had much cross-disciplinary impact on nascent Information Science (cf., MARTYN & LANCASTER; MEADOW & KRAFT; TAGUE-SUTCLIFFE). It has always remained enthusiastic about technology, and during its academic development was more concerned with differentiation from librarianship and co-opting Library Science than philosophical debate. The latter, however, has since lost its immunity (or at least some of its innocence) from the larger intellectual controversies swirling around it (PEMBERTON & PRENTICE). There is nothing, for example, in Information Science comparable to APPLEBY, HUNT & JACOB's *Telling the Truth About History* which offers a "practical realism" as the compromise between doubters and believers regardless of their methodology and technology. There should be. Perhaps the time lag for the issues in the historical and humanistic critique to infiltrate Information Science is about the same as the reverse, i.e., for information theory to impact History—about one decade. A positive result of the conflagration in History, which has not benefitted Information Science, is a substantial philosophical literature concerning the evaluation of sources and data, documentation and evidence, and the appropriate selection of methodology for interpretation, and the validity of empirical research. NATHAN associates evidence with assurance, which in turn may be associated with the truth-claim of History.

The philosophical debates about objectivity versus subjectivity between historians and literary critics over reconstruction from evidence from the distant past and deconstructionist linguistic theory have obscured the greater threat of modern technology and information practices to what BEARMAN and other archivists (1993, p. 22) call "evidential historicity" for the immediate past, present, and future (i.e., the sum of information about an accountable transaction, for example, data, structural and contextual analyzes of the "whole" record). The lack of an historical record would make such arguments mute. But the archivist's concern for the "recordedness" of information, accountability, and evidence is rooted in practicality and everyday realism, not in the historiographic and philosophical debates as treated by W. EDGAR, but in the world of business, government, courts, lawyers, accountants, and auditors. Historians and information scientists have had little to do in their classrooms with this aspect of current events that controls the operation of history in everyday affairs and dictates the real future of history, both as a discipline, but as a pervasive belief that the past is connected to the present and hence with the future.

Converging Technologies, Ideas, and Disciplines

Much of the research currently undertaken that would qualify as Historical Information Science is either highly individualized and privatized like so much of historical study, or else it exists under the umbrella of research centers and special think tanks. Even then such group effort often centers around a lead professor or researcher. Collaboration in historical research (GAFFIELD, 1988), so typical of the Sciences and increasingly common in the Social Sciences, is still problematic (MCCRANK, 1994), and long-term, group-supported project management is not a highly developed skill in History or the Humanities in general (as a remedy, consult LIENTZ & REA). Social scientists have had more experience with collaborative research and even cross-national research, so their handbooks are more likely to include management issues (HANTAIS & MANGEN). A common theme in recent literature about globalization is its impact on leveling regional and even national preferences and customs, to produce not so much a standardization in the sense of sameness, but a hybrid level of accommodation which impacts theoretical approaches and both limits and enhances possibilities for cross-disciplinary work (KOFMAN & YOUNGS). That may seem to compromise individualism in action if not in thought.

Some great historians, Arnold Toynbee notably, writing about "the ineffectiveness of team-work in intellectual operations," assumed as have so many that "As far as we know at present, only single minds can think thoughts and express them" (TOYNBEE, p. 103). For him, with some foresight since he was writing before the advent of sophisticated groupware, computer technology would serve best as a network linking psyches, or producing a collectivity confronting the problem of quantity of data, but breakthroughs in interpretation are still the product of individual genius (see SIMONTON's work on "who makes history and why"). Such a position, of course, encounters stiff opposition nowadays, especially from the business viewpoint where teamwork, partnerships, etc., are touted as the keys to the competitive edge in a global market (L. OLIVIA).

The typical technological approach to research and development is team based, and hence project management in business and engineering is far more formalized than in History. Why? Historical research is often long-range, multi-site, and equally complicated, but historians are not armed with the same formal tools and training in logistics to accomplish what they do individually as a collective enterprise. What syntheses there are require acceptance after the fact, rather than input in their making. Although this technically based collaborative paradigm has flourished outside of History, inside perspectives have remained steadfast. There, loners work privately on their research, perhaps with assistance from graduate students, while ironically they are expected to be gregarious, open, and interactive in their teaching and cooperative in collegial management within academe. Although H-Net activities are modifying such attitudes, historians continue to view computing largely as an individual operation because of their traditional work habits, and this solitary outlook inhibits even collaboration with the machine. Others, for example, have reflected similar skepticism more recently about computing, such as military historian John Keegan who reminds us that "computers can't replace judgment" and concludes that the computer has little value when dealing with intangibles like courage, willpower, etc., which he must assess personally and apparently as a sole authority (*FORBES*, p. 36). In forum after forum, historians betray a fear that somehow the computer threatens their ability to use their own judgment without the kind of inspection of "judgment under uncertainty" offered by TVERSKY (cf., TVERSKY & KAHNEMAN; SENGUPTA, 1985); or that computer use diminishes rather than enhances the skill of the historian (MALI). They seem to relish what a computer cannot do, rather than appreciate fully what they can provide; the limitations they cite are often based on false premises and insufficient familiarity with the latest in information technology. There are indeed limitations to computers at every stage of their development, which are to be linked to human limitations in comprehension and behavior as much as to the technology itself. But if one wants to explore "the trouble with computers," see LANDAUER's critique of the massive financial outlay since 1973 with unequaled progress in productivity, efficiency, or peace of mind in an increasingly complicated world, one complicated rather than simplified by computers. He provides a real sobering antidote to the technologist running wild. His arguments are not so easily dismissed as are the forebodings of prominent historians who display little understanding of modern information technology, but who nevertheless express their opinions in national forums and presumably their classrooms as well.

If attitudes have not changed, times have. So too has interactive, distributed computing and groupware, and communications that make possible collaboration untested by even the most harmonious committee, and with the automatic polling and weighting of opinion to facilitate an instant computerized democracy in the boardroom, workplace, or increasingly it is speculated, across the country (WASKO & MOSCO, eds.). Intellectual prowess, individual or collective, continues to operate within definite parameters that are set by policy, not by computers, which are the disciplinary enforcers or facilitators and sometimes arbitrators, but not original thinkers or directors. Despite the idea of open-systems, ironically some form of enclosure seems necessary to work with high-end information technology designed to break out of such localization. Anthropologists now point out the benefits of borders and identities, and Esther Dyson, publisher of *Release 1.0* for the high-tech industry, reacted to Bill Gates' notion of friction-free commerce across the Internet and pleaded to keep some friction as a constraint against unthinking action and reaction, and as a stimulus for reflection, thought, and judgment even in the case of free speech (FORBES *ASAP*, p. 99). Likewise, potential criticism tempers historians' pronouncements. To what effect might they be tempered or radicalized in virtual environments or as facilitated by H-Net, where criticism might be immediate, negative or affirming, reactionary and even vociferous? Studies of other less professional electronic discussion forums have revealed a tendency for unbridled rudeness worse than on the telephone, especially when the discourse is asynchronous. Interactive debate may spawn new work and creativity, or can stifle it; in either case, it will change how historians carry on discourse about the past.

Social pressures on historians to compromise their traditional individualism and to become more collaborative, engaging, and market-conscious become more pronounced as one moves History in the continuum from an Art to Humanities, and thence to Social Sciences. Local Area Networks (LANs), improved telecommunications, freer access through the Internet, etc., are creating new "virtual" environments in which historians can now work and will work increasingly in the future, offering a compromise between individual and collaborative historical production. Physical isolation, required for reflective and creative thought, no longer means intellectual loneliness. As so many cartoons depict these days, the scribe in the monk's cell or scholar in his or her carrel can escape electronically and mentally without leaving a safe haven and can socialize without sacrificing privacy. The historian in a home office, library, or den is likewise privileged. Such convenience, however, often mitigates against collaboration and innovation rather than supports these activities. Personal research in isolation may stimulate thought in some cases, but stifle inspiration in others precisely because a safe haven is non-confrontational. Such adaptability, flexibility, and change in the very nature of intellectual intercourse requires technical and navigational expertise that frees one from older limitations and yet entails new dependencies and support needs. Information systems and project management must be coupled in Historical Information Science more like the Social Sciences and Information Science itself than in large-scale business management, but some transition is required from adherence to the old individualism of History and the serialized discourse of the lone historian to interactive thinking, synchronic communication, and parallel processing (MCCRANK, 1993). It also means reciprocal borrowing and building a reflexive relationship between History and technical fields.

> History was *not* [his emphasis] included in relation to algorithms and data structures (computer) architecture, database and information retrieval, human-computer communication, numerical and symbolic computation, and software methodology and engineering. Some of these are quite surprising; the history of computer architecture, for example, has been well researched and could provide a series of case studies which would strongly enhance this module.

> However, the curriculum is not accompanied by guidelines and support materials related to the history of these subjects, and few teachers have the background, training or resources to effectively provide this instruction. Common knowledge of the field is primarily populated with anecdotes and myths. The system of rewards and recognition in our academic institutions does not encourage teachers to develop their own materials in history, and regrettably, there are few comprehensive textbooks to

lead the way. Moreover, there is a stigma that often accompanies the decision of scholars to study history after a career in science—a suspicion that they are becoming senile. This is the same stigma that accompanies the move to the study of the social impact of computing, and concerns for the ethical issues in the field. Yet the study of history is as intense as that of the study of the sciences and many of the techniques of searching and researching, deduction and derivation are applicable to both activities.... The techniques of historical research differ little from the techniques used in quality management reviews. In fact, the number of facts to be sifted through in order to reveal an event and to analyze the consequences is often far greater than in a "pure" science!

Lee's insight, however, does not reflect common attitudes, as he recognizes in defending himself from charges of senility because of his historical interests. Unfortunately, he may have few allies in History who assist in remedying the problem he alludes to, namely the dearth of instructors, teaching materials, and formal curricula. The inter-disciplinary collaboration he calls for requires re-engineering graduate curricula and reforming higher education in both History and the Information Sciences, or the very least, creating new opportunities for cooperation, project management, and use of interactive technology more than simply perpetuating traditional modes of operation through conventional personal computing (observations made also by BASKERVILLE & GAFFIELD; GAFFIELD, 1988; and others). Colloquia in curricula are designed for such interaction, conferencing helps, and listservs, too, if they rise above the character of informal conversations to the level of colloquia, conferences, and the quasi-publication they actually are. In all things, quality control begins with oneself and it takes two to collaborate. Cooperative teaching and research are social activities. Program development is a political process.

The viability of Internet communications enhanced by recent campus-wide networking and computerization projects, albeit often at the expense of library budgets, promises increased greater inter-disciplinary dialogue and cross-national cooperation but ironically also poses the threat of greater insularity, inbreeding in communication circles, and continued overspecialization. European and American historians have taken to the Internet: listservs (as indicated in the directory by STRANGELOVE & KOVAS, the *History List* [University of Illinois at Chicago Circle], and appended lists in GREENSTEIN, 1993, MCCRANK, 1994), the hosting of more than 80 electronic conferences in History, and international collaboration are occurring across the nation's electronic "superhighway" (MCCRANK, 1994b; KROPAČ *ET AL.*, eds., 1994). While such advances in telecommunications allow for cross-disciplinary communication, they have also created new "virtual communities" as subsets of the historical profession in general (as for other associations), each with their own memberships, insider sub-language, and subject preferences (B. LEE, 1993). ABOBA claims there are over 100,000 publicly accessible bulletin boards to watch—if one had the time. Many are related to local publicity and directory services such as calendars of events, tourist services, entertainment guides, weather forecasts, etc. (the postings of which all produce chronologs of a city or region's cultural and social life, which historians will assuredly want transferred to local and regional electronic archives).

Of the growing number of listservs like *Humanist* and *Artswire* that pertain to History, *H-Net* (i.e., originally "History NETwork", then "Humanities OnLine," and now a Humanities and Social Sciences forum) is by far the most influential (cf., H-Net's WWW homepage at http.//h-net.msu.edu). It began in 1992 at the University of Illinois at Chicago (R. JENSEN); in 1993 a $300,000 NEH grant supported development of an official organization with officers and a staff at Michigan State University, and in 1995 H-Net became affiliated with the AHA. It now has more than 43,000 subscribers in more than 70 countries (1996). Its stated goals are

• To enable scholars to communicate easily current research and teaching interests

- To discuss new approaches, methods, and tools of analysis

- To share information on electronic databases

- To test new ideas and share comments on the literature in their fields

With NEH funding, H-Net supports 61 (73 are planned) lists or discussion groups (AHA *Perspectives*, 1995 Feb., 33[2]: 15) moderated or managed by over 150 specialists. Each has its own "personality" (http://h-net2.msu.edu/about). Members engage in friendly chit-chat averaging fifteen to sixty messages each week, but also typically exchange syllabi for course preparation, bibliographic and instructional guides, book and software reviews, job announcements, and data sets. Some think of H-Net as a "perpetual electronic seminar" where like a course, components and sessions are devoted to thematic interests. This is typical of thinking related to the growth of real-time, synchronous communications on a variety of *MUD*s, *MOO*s, and *MUSE*s, where the need to keep company seems to be matched by an enthusiasm for new acronyms, an electronic Newspeak, and a fantasy world (QUITNER). Historians have been more subdued than their Literature counterparts, or sane as the case may be, in evolving systematically an interconnected family of listservs. As H-Net matures, subgroups have appeared, specialization has occurred, and slowly it is adding to its communications functions more and more content, including the creation of resource archives. NEH funding ($190,000) has allowed six multimedia teaching centers to develop, and another $50,000 grant has initiated scanning of historical documents into a text archives for Gopher and Web access. H-Teach, the subgroup focusing on teaching history at the university level, for example, began as a usual discussion forum, but the exchange of syllabi and other teaching materials has created almost spontaneously a clearinghouse and now an accumulating electronic resource repository (accessible at http://h-net.msu.edu). H-Net is currently engaged in the establishment of a major online review effort; it lists jobs worldwide; and it posts reports from the national Coordinating Committee for the Promotion of History, which relates developments in Washington, D.C. that affect the humanities. In 1997 the AHA officially honored H-Net with the James Harvey Robinson Prize, accepted by Jensen and co-networker Mark Kornbluh, for the outstanding contribution H-Net is making to the teaching and learning of history.

Additionally archivists communicate on their listserv, *Archives* (Archives theory and practice: listserv@Miamiu.muohio.edu) and are being drawn increasingly into professional, as somewhat distinct from academic, listservs such as the twenty-six recommended by WALLACE (see also Appendix B). Discussion groups on listservs do not by themselves insure cross-disciplinary dialogue or communications between academic and professional enterprises. Mirroring conferencing and other social mixing, electronic communications follow similar patterns of group self-organization by common interests, reinforcement from meetings, and hierarchies by status and institution ("pecking orders" in classifications according to KIPFER). Although some virtual communities have been studied sociologically, electronically connected historians have yet to be investigated and profiled. Methods borrowed from family history might be applied to non-biological families and these information sharing communities, especially given trends toward family privatization as described by K. A. LYNCH.

H-Net's H-Teach syllabi collection is an electronic equivalent of a manuscript repository rather than a true archives. The archival record should reside at the institution, either in its archives or electronically as part of its electronic records, with proper appraisal, authentification, sanction, and appropriate metadata for retrieval. Indeed, syllabi, as in the case of other courseware for courses which are contractually part of a university curriculum and which are developed with university funding, may not be traded without regard to institutional property rights. In any case, such electronic "archives" are actually retrospectively reproduced electronic facsimiles; that is, they are surrogates rather than originals. Several "digital archives" now accessible lack major components of a genuine archives; most importantly, they may lack legal authority as official records; the chain of custody may have been broken, so ownership and intellectual property rights may be contended; copyright clearances, permissions, and transfer rights for electronic conveyance are frequently left in abeyance; metadata for access and citation may be different from the original mechanisms; and the critical apparatus for appraisal decisions and diplomatic and content analysis may not be sufficient even to ascertain that the whole document is reproduced, to say nothing of its placement in original order and provenance information (all issues to be discussed later). Historians know better, presumably, but their management of some of these electronic resource centers reflects the best and worst of archival and business practices. Because these are so public, they both expose historians to severe criticism about their teaching authority in archival science and project management abilities, but when successful and model projects they also display an entrepreneurial side of History which is commonly thought dormant.

Particularly noteworthy are the efforts by historians to share primary documentation through the World Wide Web (WWW). Digital archives have been tested now for more than a decade, with gigantic projects such as that of the Archivo Histórico de las Indias (AHI) in Sevilla leading the way. The technology has changed considerably from when AHI in 1988 began its manuscripts' conversion to digital archives. Resolution then was 640 x 480 = 16, but by 1991 the 256-bit color was available, and this became the industry standard by 1993. By 1996 1024 x 768 = 256 resolution was widely available, and there seems to be no limit for the dpi threshold. Computing historians have a special interest in digital archives, as well as new scanning technology, ease in electronic facsimile reproduction, and growth of Web sites as the technology makes electronic publication of documents relatively easy. THALLER (1996), noting that the rapid pace of technological change is scaring administrators of projects into indecision, advises emphasis not on the latest or theoretically "best" technology solution but on appropriateness. He suggests that physiological limits on what the human eye can take in will limit screen sizes under 24 inches and this may create a practical solution on the resolution increase at ca. 1600 x 1200 = 16M in the next couple of years. The impact of information technology, therefore, on the availability of historical sources is undeniable. The following discussion, therefore, interweaves technical considerations with historical research and projects, because rather than being separate issues in discreet fields, converging technologies, ideas, and disciplines are beckoning a new era of integration.

Many of the smaller projects are actually libraries misnamed archives simply because they contain documents rather than literary works (NEUMAN & MANGIAFICO tract electronic text projects). This confused usage reflects a rather loose handling of technical language that should be more precise. Nevertheless, small digital archives, actual and of the pseudo-archives variety, and more properly titled electronic editions of documentary collections (published archives) are appearing everywhere on the Internet. The Max-Planck Institute in Göttingen has a dozen projects currently to create a series of digital archives for German history from the fourteenth century onward. These are available in archives reading rooms on CD-ROM workstations and may be placed in CD towers for Internet access. THALLER (1996) chides historians who excuse themselves for lack of access to documentation, since such progress of retroconversion projects is increasing accesses worldwide. KERSEN asks if data archives on the Net are to be likened to the "Apocalypse or Apotheosis" because of apparent ease in access and use with attendant hidden pitfalls and subtle but pervasive problems in their systematic research. Sessions at AHC conferences are devoted regularly to such projects, ranging from medieval images (JARITZ, 1995, 1997) and Ancient Regime sources (THALLER, 1997) to twentieth-century registers for Holocaust studies (T. GROTUM) and photographic collections (NILSEN). Likewise, historians are increasingly concerned about accessibility issues, including interface design, retrievability, and discovery. S. ANDERSON *ET AL.* (1997) compare the search for historical material on the Internet/WWW with jumping "into the Great Wide Open." Historians are no longer foreigners in the land of high technology. Those who have taken to networking and electronic communications add a dimension to history computing that was totally absent from the Cliometric movement 20 years ago.

As a result of such progress as increased computer literacy, expanded memory capacity, high performance computing, and greater accessibility to computers and computing laboratories for support, History has now produced a sufficient supply of computer-using historians to change dramatically the milieu in which the great methodological debates occurred. The widespread acceptance of computing and the refinement of early quantification techniques make the concept of Historical Information Science less strange today than Cliometrics was 25 years ago. The old dichotomy between History *qua* Social Science or Humanity no longer seems valid as merging technologies and collaboration (GAFFIELD) alter the functional distinctiveness of institutions and fuse disciplines more than the integration of methodologies in interdisciplinary research or hybridization in multidisciplinary work (J. KLEIN). FINHOLT notices that time and geography, as well as hierarchies, seem to erode in electronic archives. Nor is the older juxtaposition of quantitative vs. qualitative as significant as it once was when textual and numerical data were so distinct (BOTZ; W. NEUMAN). Cross-disciplinary Historical Information Science may be an idea whose time has finally come.

The emergence of a holistic Historical Information Science from this milieu would cut across older specializations based on chronology and geography or nation states, and orientations like social, economic, political, military, intellectual, or cultural history (O. V. BURTON, 1991; DURANCE; EVANS, 1990). Indeed, the ideological persistence of a "discipline" with an identifiable core is a matter of considerable academic concern (MESSER-DAVIDOW, SHUMWAY, & SYLVAN), and cross-disciplinary studies are becoming increasingly common even when concealed under the guise of a traditional disciplinary specialization. Information Science as a syncretistic endeavor in the first place, has been subjected to similar pressures on self-identification (PRENTICE) as it relates to other fields, i.e., Communications (BORGMAN & RICE; BORGMAN & SCHEMENT; PAISLEY, 1990). History experiences similar pressures for reasons also related to its traditional syncretic nature and current influences on research as to market and consumption. As Michel de Certeau noted critically: "Historical production finds itself shared between the *literary* work which is 'authoritative' and the *scientific* esotericism which 'produces research" (CERTEAU, 1988, p. 65). Thus, it relates to most crosscurrents in academe precisely because all subject matter can be embraced in its scope. A fusion of History and Information Science is, therefore, a combination of two multi-disciplines for an even richer mix. The former extends the scope of the latter, while conversely the latter intensifies current inspection of the research processes and sources of History.

Significant influence from the information fields affecting historical scholarship may be identified as follows:

1. Information Science has already and will continue to examine the historical profession and institutions, the bibliography of historical literature, and the information behavior of historians; and conversely, historians are increasingly studying the history of information organizations and institutions, media, technology, processes, and profession. History and Information Science are not, upon second glance, an "odd couple" (STIEG, 1990) unless one accepts the dichotomy of two cultures, Science versus the Humanities, set up by C. P. Snow. They are diagramed as opposites when the Library of Congress classification system is conceived as a circular self-contained universe of knowledge. STIEG (p. 67) argues instead that although

they may be different, they can also be "mutually supporting and enriching." Opposites in a continuum, after all, usually balance each other.

2. Increased interest among historians in information communication as a mainstream rather than peripheral subject, coupled with an expanding interdisciplinarity (HORN & RITTER), is breaking down the intellectual barriers that are still maintained in academic departmentalization, providing an opportunity for greater dialogue between the academic fields and the professions, and offering a means of rapprochement. A number of joint-graduate degree programs, such as those pioneered in 1974 at the University of Maryland at College Park (UMCP), may be indicative of this willingness for at least cautionary collaboration. But more programs have failed than succeeded, and the UMCP experience has been fraught with perception and professional problems limiting genuine collaboration. It would be tragic if someday this were regarded as no more than a noble experiment, since the interdisciplinarity envisioned within professional degrees like the nascent Masters in Archival Science (MAS) degree programs is limited. Although historical studies about literacy (e.g., STOCK; MCKITTERICK; CLANCHY; SOMMERVILLE, etc.) are as much about recordkeeping and information systems as anything, their impact on cross-disciplinary studies, or those cutting across disciplines and into the professions, have been negligible. Increasingly inter-disciplinary subject interests by themselves do not guarantee increased communication across fields or lasting collaboration.

3. The burgeoning "new" socioeconomic and political history schools that previously used only numeric data, now under the pervasive influence of cultural anthropology as so long advocated by Eric R. Wolf and others who have sought the integration of Anthropology and History (SCHNEIDER & RAPP), are embracing themes and using sources once thought of as the purview of the Arts and Humanities rather than the Social Sciences (KERTZER *ET AL.*), so that numeric and descriptive analyses as well as quantified and narrative explanations are thriving together (the noted philosopher of History, Hayden White, never conceded the difference in the first place [H. WHITE, 1973]).

4. The related impact of cultural linguistics and "new" language studies *qua* communications, with the increased availability of digital textual sources which can be studied statistically with a scope never before realizable without computer assistance, is accelerating the breakdown of such older distinctions as quantitative versus narrative history, as it also blurs the divisions between various disciplines in academe (WINKLER; PRENTICE).

5. The changing nature of documents themselves and the notion of documentation (R. COX [1994c; 1996]; HINDING), the impact of electronic communications and recordkeeping (DOLLAR, 1992), and the proliferation of electronic archives and libraries, which is more pervasive than the older concentration of data archives in select research institutions, require major changes in historical research methods just as this phenomenon is creating tremendous change in libraries and librarianship (MARKEY DRABENSTOTT, 1994). The recent survey in 1994/95 of electronic records management in archives around the world by the INTERNATIONAL COUNCIL ON ARCHIVES lists 134 institutions. The retrospective conversion of sources into electronic form for convenience, compact storage, and preservation has already created an imperative for historians to engage information technology as never before.

6. Finally, growing comfort with and sophistication in the use of computers, and reliance on telecommunications in general, are slowly leading to reforms in graduate History training that emphasize computing as a prerequisite skill, like foreign languages or the so-called "auxiliary sciences" of History for both historical research and scholarly communications. The transition is less painful for the coming generation of historians than those caught in the throes of unexpected and fairly chaotic change when one had to rely on self-education to adopt to computing developed for accounting in business and industry rather than academic needs.

The following themes are woven throughout the subsequent discussion on:

1. The relationship between History and the Information Sciences devoted to the resources of archives, libraries, museums, and media centers

2. The possibility of the so-called "New Historicism" to accommodate new information technologies and scientific methodology for research that is increasingly a blend of quantitative and qualitative assessment

3. Technical concerns shared by the historical, archival, and library community related to source availability and the future of historical studies

4. The significance of these influences, concerns, and trends on education programs both in the teaching of history and in the training of the next generation of historians who may be reconceived as information professionals specializing in historical information and communications

Reflexive Inspection:

Information, Technology, and Culture

Having explored the potential relation of History and Information Science and laid out some of the background, potential ingredients, and combinations of studies that could be forged into a Historical Information Science, this chapter will explore the already existing study of History by Library, Archival, and Information Sciences, and the need in History for further study about the discipline's control over and use of its own literature and the problems resulting from mass and complexity as historians attempt inter-disciplinary studies. The idea presented here, however, is more than information scientist helping historians with their information retrieval problems, or historians reminding information professionals that they too have a history. These are important and shall be discussed, but the ideal sought is more than cross-disciplinary cooperation; it is genuine integration. Thus, this section first considers the volume of history literature, the nature of the History establishment, and the history of science and technology (Information Science and Information Technology in particular), which lend themselves to such integrated development. Might not these IS and IT strands of history be combined for mutual reinforcement? A corpus of use studies provides a potential beginning.

Another aspect to be considered is the minor, albeit potentially more influential, role History could play in Information Science: the history of information sources and consumption (history of books and reading), information processes in time and place (history of publishing, trade, communications), and information services and institutions (history of professionalization, associations, libraries, archives, and museums). These subjects already provide a rich historical literature and such study moves the information field away from its overconcentration on processes and techniques to sources and content. Recent efforts to revitalize the history of Information Science itself present new possibilities for collaboration and inter-disciplinary exchange.

Finally, a third component will be discussed as a possible addition to this amalgam, namely Organizational Culture studies from Administrative Science. Here one might look to a combination of Memory and Culture studies in History with Organizational Culture and Corporate Memory from Management, all of which focus on information and communication related to behavior and change, attitude and action. The resulting realignment of these quite disparate strands of research and entwinement with each other could produce a durable disciplinary thread of Historical Information Science.

HISTORY INFORMATION: BIBLIOGRAPHY AND USE

Literature Searching and Bibliographic Control

At the beginning of this decade 13,000 historical organizations were active in Canada and the United States alone (M. WHEELER). Unbelievable! So too is the fact that the United States, supposedly a young country without a profound sense of history, nevertheless has 50,000 sites that are declared to have historical significance (U.S. DEPARTMENT OF INTERIOR).

The absence of history in American life is a generalization that needs serious reconsideration. The real issue may be the lack of a large consumer audience for the works of professional historians and academic History outside the classroom, and what may be perceived as an overproduction of historical research as a literature in proportion to History's readership.

Even though historian Alan Brinkley in the aforementioned televised forum in 1996 thought that historians lacked a broad market for their opinions outside academic history, because of the public's perception of History as lacking "scientific legitimacy," they do constitute a major publishing industry in the West; although they may be concentrated in academia, history has a broader basis beyond academe than is often supposed. Just as there are a variety of histories, so there are several reading, listening, and viewing publics, and not all of these consume academic history. It is academic history, however, which has received most attention from Library and Information Science, as though this were all that matters.

History is a prolific field, both in terms of numbers of historians and their scholarly production, and as a staple of general studies from elementary through college education. Consider the situation in America. In 1993, rebounding from a low point in 1985, 27,774 students majored in History in United States colleges and universities and 2,952 received master's degrees. Five to seven hundred doctorates in History are awarded annually. Set into the Social Sciences where an empirical and quantitative ethos reigns, History would seem to be participating in an overall comeback that defies any lure of a strong job market. The United States Department of Education figures from 1995 indicate that 133,680 students earned their bachelor's degrees in History and the Social Sciences (an increase of 24 percent); 14,561 received master's degrees (up 32 percent); and 3,627 had Ph.D.s conferred upon them (a 26 percent increase), indicating growth rates higher than the national average of 15 percent for bachelor's degrees, 25 percent for master's, and 21 percent for doctorates (see the study of these data sponsored by the National Research Council and Conference Board of Associated Research Councils: GOLDBERGER, MAHER & FLATTAU, eds.).

Unfortunately, it is not possible to obtain cross-data between the Social Sciences/History and Computer/Information Sciences, which comprise a baccalaureate graduate class one-fifth the size of the former fields, but which at the master's level is nearly as large (10,416 compared with 14,561; fewer doctorates [810] were awarded in Computer Science than in History *per se*). Cross-over between these disciplines seems minimal, but this could increase if historical information science historians took advantage of such new curricula as the condensed "conversion" M.A. in Computer Science program at the University of Chicago. Those in Computer Science and Information Science likely to take an interest in History do so apart from their formal training, just as historians who enter these technical fields often do so only with rudimentary formal training, turning their amateur interests into professional expertise largely as a matter of continuing education. Peter Lyman has shown how in many cases computing simply reinforces existing work practices without introducing new problem solving, which he regards as a major failure in modern academe (LYMAN). William Graves argues that certain "ideologies of computerization" determine how new information technology is first employed rather than any technological determinism, and others argue that computers in student life fit into established patterns rather than revolutionize lives and learning (GRAVES, cited by SHIELDS). In short, teachers' beliefs about computing most often determines pedagogical change or lack thereof; the same may be said about research.

Regardless of its relation to the Social Sciences or Information Sciences, the complexion of History internally has changed. A 1989 survey showed the course array as 80 percent United States. and European History, whereas in 1995 the percentage had fallen to 66 percent (35 percent and 31 percent respectively) (TOWNSEND, 1996a, p. 9). History teaching, more than research, has undergone globalization in response to a variety of stimuli, but it has not necessarily reduced its Euro-American concentration. Instead, this concentration has been reduced in proportion to the whole curriculum by the expansion of other offerings. This reflects the new cross-disciplinary framework overtaking many fields as a world view exposes the limitations of existing theoretical approaches to a variety of subjects (KOFMAN & YOUNGS). The professorate has changed also: TOWNSEND's study (1996b, p. 11) depicts the "history cohort [as] larger, older, and more diverse" (even though 90 percent of all academic historians are white). All is not well with the discipline, however, since there is dissension in the ranks, widespread dissatisfaction with academe, severe employment problems, and modest earnings at best except in the upper echelon of full-professorships at leading universities even though more historians reach full professor rank (55 percent of the History faculties at doctoral granting institutions) than in other Social Science disciplines (the percentage is slightly higher, however, in traditional Humanities disciplines) (GOLDBERGER, MAHER, & FLATTAU). No History Department in the United States compares in size with the 300-member History faculty at Moscow State University which constitutes a school with its own dean. Historians in the United States are less concentrated in premier institutions. Some of the most prestigious are not the largest departments. Instead of large history factories, historians in the United States turn up in all institutions and their members are scattered in more than one department; they produce a steady stream of graduates at all levels of programs, and primarily earn their living by teaching rather than research. Ironically, however, it is their research rather than teaching that most often determines their promotion and rank. Among the implications of this distribution and scale characteristic of the historical profession in American higher education is that History departments are not large enough to command the resources to run historical computing and media laboratories of their own or even to have specialists in Historical Information Science, under this or any other rubric, work exclusively or even primarily for historical studies. Instead, they have to rely on shared generalists from user services in computer centers, or sometimes from academic computing, who may or may not have any familiarity with the problems of historical research and peculiarities of historical data. Historians in American universities are best served by history specialists in librarianship, by bibliographers and collection development officers, and by special collections and manuscript curators who often have graduate training in History. And they have been accustomed to thinking that archivists are "applied history" specialists serving them. They have no such illusions about computer specialists.

While the average 30-member History department in the United States has lost 3.2 faculty positions in the past decade, and doctorates per department have dropped from a high of 45.5 to 27.3, over 700 new Ph.D.s are entering, or are trying to enter the teaching field each year (increasing toward 800 in 1994 and then leveling off). Data are lacking about the technical training and skills levels achieved by this new cohort of historians. Doctorates awarded outnumber jobs advertised by more than 250 each year. This overproduction has continued since 1991, after a brief respite (1987-1991) when more jobs appeared than Ph.D.s were obtained, and when completion of doctoral programs dipped to a low in 1989. Although in 1993 a little over 10 percent of the History professorate were at retirement age (65-75 years old) in 1993, nearly 20 percent of History Ph.D.s in the United States were unemployed or only part-time employed (twice as many women than men are in this predicament, and overall gender differences persist with initial starting equity but men, in the course of 15 years from their doctorates, earn about 10 percent more than women). The greatest oversupply continues to be in American History, especially twentieth-century history, where three times as many recipients try to enter the field than there are academic jobs openings (TOWNSEND, 1996a, p. 8). In 1994, fewer than half of Ph.D.s in History had secured academic appointments upon completion of their dissertations.

Although historians earn more than most of their colleagues in the Humanities and averaged $48,200, they compared less favorably with peers in the Social Sciences. By 1996-1997 historians' average academic salaries had increased slightly to $49,765 in private and $49,893 in public institutions compared with all fields respectively at $48,850 and $51,512; the relative standing of historians *vis-à-vis* their colleagues in other fields had deteriorated, and set against the cost-of-living index, real compensation for History has actually declined (TOWNSEND,

1997, p. 17). Moreover, the better pay situation that once prevailed at private institutions has nearly disappeared. History competes well enough with Information Science *qua* Library Science, but traditionally comparison between the two hid some real differences. More library schools survived in public than private institutions, so when the difference between public and private pay scales was taken into account, the position of full-time library science faculty was slightly more competitive overall. Budgeting differs between these professional schools and History departments, of course, with totally different patterns in the use of adjunct faculty, graduate assistantships, and internships. Moreover, professional schools tended to run year-round programs, so their faculty had more summer school compensation as well as greater opportunities for consultancies. Calendar year salary comparisons from all sources of income, therefore, reveal a different picture than comparisons based on nine-month contractual data compiled by the College and University Personnel Association (CUPA). Finally, historian salaries do not compete as well with the more technical slant of Information Science, or with Computer Science and Management of Information Systems in Business. It is also interesting that historians as others in the Humanities earn considerably more when they leave academe, except in the nonprofit sector. From the average base inside academe and nonprofit organizations, average salaries in government are $6,000/year higher, and in the for-profit sector, where fewer venture, earnings increase by nearly $10,000/year (cf., INGRAM; TOWNSEND, 1996b; 1997). The disparity between Ph.D. production and job creation has increased recently, even though the number of history teaching jobs has increased slightly since the recession of the early 1990s (the ratio is still dismal, with an average 143 applicants for 23 jobs and over 100 applications per posting).

If these trends continue, more historians each year are seeking nonteaching positions; that is, "alternative" careers, as they are ridiculously called by academics when they indeed show greater flexibility than a single-track career, often lead to more lucrative options than teaching, and in business and government could result in greater influence for the promotion of History than is provided in higher education. The association between teaching and nonteaching historians should be encouraged, the dichotomy broken down, and a new model of historical scholarship encouraged (as discussed by E. BOYER on behalf of the CARNEGIE FOUNDATION, various AHA committees, and individual historians like E. RICE, BENDER, etc.; CORTADA [1997], a historian working as a technology consultant in IBM, offers sage advice for history departments to train historians purposefully for business and create effective placement programs for them). This characteristic of the modern job market is significant for the future of Historical Information Science, because young historians with computer and analytic skills who could form such a specialization within History are the very ones most capable of leaving academe for better paying jobs elsewhere.

The challenge to History in the United States is undeniable, if it continues to have one-quarter to one-third of its Ph.D. recipients enter occupations other than History teaching. Departments must consider their obligations to their own students and reconsider traditional curricula to make sure that a substantial component of its training includes skills that are transferable to other fields in ways other than the general application of historical knowledge. Already more and more contributions are being made in business and computing history, historical social studies, and professional studies of archives, libraries, and museums by scholars in nonteaching positions. Public History programs have tended to focus more on the consumption of history popularly, outside the classroom but also in continuing education, in its museums, parks, and thematic recreation. The focus discussed in this review, Historical Information Science, could provide a balance to this Public History *qua* history in the public sphere orientation, and an even more lucrative alternative to history teaching, in the research and organizational management sectors of business and government. It may be that the locus of such empirically oriented inter-disciplinary study will eventually fall outside History departments altogether. If so, this may accentuate the recent shift of History from the Social Sciences back to the Humanities and reorientation of History computing from quantification in socioe-conomic studies to newer forms of text and image analyses. As will be seen, parallel shifts in management may not mean that historians with interests and skills in the latter are necessarily restricted in their search for nonacademic employment.

In keeping with such trends and difficulty in characterizing the historical profession today, which is so much more diversified than ever, it is also difficult to profile historical literature, its consumers, or the whole profession based only on history teaching in higher education. Moreover, historical literature is not well studied from the vantage point of Information Science, and scholarly bibliography as a field within History is not firmly established. Although historical literature is increasingly serialized (STIEG, 1986), historians as humanists still value the printed book as their communication vehicle of choice, while those who are Social Science oriented are perhaps slightly more prone to serial publication. Either standards for publication increased with supply over demand in more recent years, or the increased sup-ply slipped in quality: the *American Historical Review's* rejection rate increased from 82 per-cent in 1941 to 90 percent in 1964 when submissions were nearly three times as many, but the number of articles published per year (i.e., twelve to sixteen) remained static (STIEG, 1995, p. 224). This increased pressure on core journals partially explains the rapid increase in the number and variety of history journals that began to appear after the 1960s (J. FYFE provides a useful analytical guide). However, while serial publication increased dramatically in History, historians held onto their preference with a value system favoring monographic publication. This dichotomy between reading preferences, communication formats and information behav-iors may reflect the age-old split over positivism, although no studies have tried to delineate practices and cognitive styles as they may align with philosophical leanings of historians.

The Humanities and Social Sciences are not in the same league with Science and Technology in mass production of scientific articles—some 6,000-7,000 per day worldwide. NAISBITT in 1982 (p. 24) noted an annual increase for the past decade of 13 percent and a doubling every five and a half years; actual proliferation has exceeded this. The increase is phenomenal if one includes electronic forms and Web-page postings. Nevertheless, the problems of bibliographic control and access are significant for the Humanities and Social Sciences. Apart from electronic forms, each year North American and European historians altogether generate nearly 10,000 monographic titles, increasing at a rate of 3 percent annually (HAAR). ABC-CLIO's databases (1992-1993 averages, covering 2,200-2,500 historical journals) are expanding annually with 22,600 entries (ca. 18,500 articles, 3,000 books, and 1,170 dissertations for *Historical Abstracts* non-American subjects after 1450 and for *America: History and Life* the counts for the past two years average 14,750 entries [ca. 7,000 articles, 6,000 book and media reviews, and 1,180 dissertations]). Actually this represents a decrease in monographic production from 1986-87 when 6,760 books in American history were published (and another 2,500 in Great Britain on various aspects of Anglo-American history). Historians were then producing over 20 percent of all books published in the Humanities and Social Sciences (41,000 titles) and 10 percent of total academic production in the United States (87,000 titles; 140,000 titles for all English language books, regardless of place of publication). Online or CD-ROM searching allows coverage as never before; at last glance in 1996, ABC-CLIO's *Historical Abstracts on Disc* (vols. 33-) contained 245,000 articles, 20,000 dissertations, 42,000 book citations, etc., or over 310,000 entries from more than 50 lan-guages (see the review of the CD-ROM version, 1982, by STILL, 1992).

The problem of mass, even within the field of History much less the entirety of inter-disciplinary scope historians often try to embrace, is bewildering. The goals of gaining a command over one's primary documentation in a field of research and of knowing the secondary literature to shape inter-pretation seem increasingly elusive. L. LEVINE notes that the ideal of a canon or core historical lit-erature is now *passé*. L. Hunt observes: "The explosion in publication has also pushed the prospect of better syntheses even further away. Some find this deeply disturbing, while for others it is simply the new condition of knowledge in the Information Age." She takes a position that I can appreciate but also doubt (HUNT, 1995, p. 1134):

> If historical knowledge is cumulative, as I believe it is, and if the purpose of historical knowledge is to promote greater understanding of how things came to be as they are, then the undeniable increase in knowledge should enable historians to write better syntheses as well as more telling analytical studies—better and more telling for the greater public as well as for fellow professionals.

Hunt relates this problem of bibliographic control even for increasingly narrow specializations to the French historiographic debates about "Forgetting and Remembering" in cultural history by noting how few students of history know much about the pioneer historians who broke ground for their own fields. She observes (p. 1119):

> For all their professional attention to the past, historians are a remarkably forgetful lot when it comes to the efforts of their predecessors. In the hundred or so years that have passed since the initial professionalization of the discipline of history, the span of historiography considered relevant in any given field has steadily contracted as the sheer amount of writing about the past has increased. This process of foreshortening is most apparent in those fields with a dense historiographical tradition, such as the French Revolution. Students of the revolution may have heard of Michelet, for example, but few read him; and, other than Tocqueville, few read any of the other nineteenth or even early twentieth-century historians of the event.
>
> The reasons for this neglect are obvious yet, nonetheless, paradoxical. We act like scientists, who fully expect their work to be superseded, and sooner rather than later, even though we are not sure that history is a science. To do something innovative in the scientific scheme of things is to do something different from, yet building on, the work of one's predecessors, usually defined as one's immediate predecessors. Thus the study of historians who published their findings in the preceding years or decades is essential; if one is not up-to-date, making a new move is by definition impossible....
>
> The imagined relevance of the historiography of any field now precipitously declines after twenty or thirty years reaching near zero forty or fifty years at the latest. Who among us can claim to have read the bulk of historical writing in our fields before the 1940s? This systematic forgetfulness characterizes everyone in the profession except those, of course, who professionally study the writing of history.

Lynn Hunt thus speculates that "systematic forgetfulness is a hallmark of historical study."

Unfortunately, Hunt's essay misconstrues an essential point: it mistakenly suggests that one can forget what one never knew, and her own observation is that historians have not read the pioneering work of their predecessors. Ignoring such work is different from forgetting it, but she could hardly say that systematic ignorance were a hallmark of historical study! Thus she treats the real issue of problematic coverage of a vast secondary literature charitably and apologetically. She provides no data to support her conclusions, nor does she cite any of the myriad studies about recall, relevance, or obsolescence, etc., that are so prolific in Information Science (e.g., MIZZARO's "whole history" of relevance is in fact confined to Informatics; but his rendition indicates how explicit the idea of relevance is in Information Science, compared with how loosely the term is used in History). Hunt's observation is unabashedly personal, a confessional musing almost, as she investigated the background of French Revolution studies that appeared in the *American Historical Review*. Unwittingly, Hunt, in voicing such concerns which are relatively untreated in historiographic literature, raises questions which come naturally to information scientists. Her questioning evolved from a perplexity about the modern predicament of historians confronting a massive litera- ture far too extensive to read, which is their ideal and burden at the same time, and from a wondering about how the obligations of currency and overwhelming immediacy affect con- tinuity in the field and long-term memory even for those whose expertise, by virtue of being historians, is expected to be historical, continuous, and synthetic.

While HUNT (1995) laments the forgetfulness of historians regarding their distant prede- cessors, she assumes that historians once knew the contributions of their immediate and more distant predecessors, and that they do know the work of their contemporaries within human limits given the volume of material to cover with modern production rates. She also raises an important question about self-reflection about one's ideological indebtedness, continuity and discontinuity in historical thought, and awareness of inheritance of scholarly paradigms from a previous generation's work, all of which forms the foundation for revision and reinterpreta- tion. She suggests that awareness, and perhaps acknowledgment, is important for more than immediate and direct borrowing. Her observations and contentions thus could relate to citation studies—especially those like CRONIN's exploration of the scholarly courtesy (1995) in cit- ing predecessors for indirect or pervasive influence as much as direct contributions. Some studies suggest, however, that historians ironically are not always aware of such indebtedness. A 1993-94 survey of American historians by the *Journal of American History* probed this issue of tracing influence of major historians and their works on the current generation of Americanists. A series of questions elicited short narrative responses from respondents, which BENDER (1994) attempted to generalize. He thought that the responses overall were captured by one respondent's characterization of the historical profession as "venturesome but cau- tious." Bender (p. 992), rather than analyzing the survey results scientifically (tallies are given in appended tables), reacted personally to the Americanist situation similarly to Hunt's assess- ment from a Europeanist perspective, but he reaches different conclusions:

> Although there is in the academy today much talk about secularism and post- Structuralism, among the American historians represented in this survey the Bible was named more frequently, by a wide margin, than any other book as a major intel- lectual influence. And the next most cited writings belonged not to Jacques Derrida, as teachers of Gertrude Himmelfarb, or even Peter Novick, might have suspected, but to Richard Hofstadter and Karl Marx. The name of Derrida did not appear at all, and Michel Foucault's books were cited for influence less often than J. R. R. Tolkien's *Lord of the Rings*.

If that is amusing, it is disturbing to find only four historians claiming to have been influ- enced by Max Weber, Sigmund Freud, or Hannah Arendt; only three by Marc Bloch; only one by Ruth Benedict, Pierre Bourdieu, or Robert Merton (though three by Thomas Merton); and none by Emile Durkheim, Karl Mannheim, Jurgen Habermas, or Hans-Georg Gadamar. It was heartening to discover the considerable influence of W. E. B. Du Bois, William Faulkner, Karl Marx, Mark Twain, and Alexis de Tocqueville (surprising now, in a way he would not have been in the 1950s). An impressive list, but not particularly contemporary. Historians need not and ought not chase current fads nor depend upon other disciplines for their ideas. Still, I regret that the responses of American historians did not reveal a fuller engagement with the most advanced transdisciplinary ideas of their own decade and their own century. The non-venture- some caution of the profession sometimes shades into conservatism and parochialism.

Ironically, given Bender's unflattering characterization, he also notes that "worry about the marginalization of history—in the university and in the larger public—pervades the responses to the survey. Respondents fear that historians are becoming self-enclosed.... Professional his- torians are becoming increasingly isolated form the general public and [their] writing [is] pri- marily for other historians." Bender concludes with "My plea to reconsider the ecology of intellectual life, to think more clearly about our relations to local public life and about the relationship of scholarship to public discourse...." It is a plea articulated before (BENDER, 1986; 1989; 1992; and especially in 1993). In any case, the kind of assumption made by HUNT (1995) about the currency of historian's acknowledged intellectual indebtedness, in contrast to possibly more far-reaching perspectives, is not supported by the *JAH* survey. In addition to a lack of synthesis in contemporary historical circles (at least of the kind GUTMAN, 1981, thought was missing), there seems to be a lack of system in the discipline's reading, carrying on tradition, or maintenance of the supposed continuity one might expect of History when it is characterized as conservative and cautious. Could it be that History is in trouble partially because it is poorly studied, and therefore poorly managed? Opinions vary, but no consensus seems forthcoming about intra- or inter-disciplinary information dissemination, transfer, or consumption. Nor can one identify systematic, empirical, objective, and scientific study about contemporary history information phenomena within the profession or the public at large except as historical studies of someone else's more distant past.

The implication of Lynn Hunt's realization is that contemporary historical literature is something to be searched more than to be read in the traditional sense, which in turn means that increasingly the task is one of strategy and technique. Thomas Bender's observations, however, do not indicate that historians employ systematic reading habits which might transfer to systematic and strategic information searching. One might expect that a goal of professional association would be to assist in this key activity. At its peak (1988-89), the bibliographic services of the American Historical Association surveyed 3,018 titles and was generating 3,500 entries for American History alone (MCCRANK, 1989). The American Historical Association Research Division nevertheless in 1990 rejected the recommendations of the American Association for the Bibliography of History (ABH) to automate and improve its services, and AHA subsequently disbanded its two major bibliographic surveys. This was justified largely on the supposition that ABC-CLIO and other sources provided adequate coverage, which also reflected opinions received by the *American Historical Review* about their listings. The ABH study (MCCRANK, 1989, p. 37), however, showed by overlap comparisons prepared by ABC-CLIO that 56.8 percent of the titles covered by AHA's *Recently Published Articles (RPA)* and *Writings on American History (WAH)* were *not* covered since 1964 by *Historical Abstracts* and *America: History and Life* (CD- ROM, 1982-). The latter now cover 2,100 serials (900 from North America) in forty languages; and from 1989 they included film and video reviews and citations for microforms as well. Consequently, online searching of the major bibliographic indexing and abstracting service in History generally can survey only 43.2 percent of the coverage once provided in the AHA manual tools, and the difference has to be found in a variety of special indexes that lack abstracts. Most are still manual tools, but some are converting to CD-ROM distribution. Part of the differences between AHA and ABC-CLIO coverage reflected scope policies, but several fields in History were poorly covered by either service, especially when contrasted to the often duplicated coverage of American History *per se*. Finally, the peculiar problems of indexing History literature might be noted, since the American Society of Indexers suggest that these are often more complicated than supposed, especially by historians who sometimes assume that anyone can produce a sound index (TOWERY, ed.). Professional indexers understand that these problems are complex, both because of the volume and variety of History literature, but also because of diversity of language usage among historians, differences between fields, and range from archaic to modern use with foreign phrases adopted liberally and a delight in uncommon expressions.

ABH also tried to assist AHA with a critical but positive study of the Association's *Recently Published Articles* and *Writings on American History* (MCCRANK, 1989b), but AHA councilors were surprised at the critique of the organs' problematic quality control, terminological consistency, name authority control, syndetic referencing, etc., and especially of the AHA's failure to adopt modern information technologies for their production and dissemination. As mentioned, the AHA Council rejected ABH's recommendations and discontinued these bibliographic operations. The *Guide* project funded by NEH would continue, but the AHA bibliographic series would endure only if taken over completely by Kraus International, the Association's collaborator for *WAH*. Both the traditional preferences of AHA's membership and financial considerations mitigated against AHA mounting a major automated bibliographic information service, but additionally the AHA Research Division considered that historians could easily turn to a series of indexes for consecutive coverage of historical publications: *L'Année Philologique* (1924-) for classical studies (CLAYMAN); *The International Medieval Bibliography* (1967-; on CD-ROM from the International Medieval Institute at Leeds University, 1995, which by 1999 will have incorporated all citations from 1967 onward) covering 3,000 periodicals and 200 collections each year. This can now be followed by *Iter, the Bibliography of Renaissance Europe (1300-1700)*, a Web-based project begun by the Renaissance Society of America which will eventually extend back into the Middle Ages (CASTELL); for post-1450 subjects, the aforementioned ABC-CLIO *Historical Abstracts* and *American: History and Life* (J. D. FALK) with their special coverage of twentieth-century happenings; and for contemporary coverage numerous indexes and abstracting services in the Social Sciences and current affairs. No empirical study other than that completed by the ABH was ever undertaken, so impression and opinion from personal experience largely from one particular subject domain ruled the day.

When ABC-CLIO undertook its *Historical Periodicals Directory* in 1981, the project to replace the pioneer 1961 survey by BOEHM & ADOLPHUS five years later, it controlled over 10,000 titles or almost three times more than the total number included in any indexing or abstracting services, including ABC-CLIO's. While Volume I covered the United States and Canada, each successive volume proved increasingly difficult to complete. Volume II (1982) contained 3,200 annotated title entries and 130,000 data elements in 15 languages for 22 countries in Western Europe, but editor Barbara Pope estimated that this monumental effort still covered only 30 percent of historical material produced in the continent that could fall into the scope of History. Volume III moved into Eastern Europe and the former Soviet Union; volume IV covered Africa and Latin America with less assurance of completeness; and Volume V surveyed international organizations.

In contrast, *History Source*, a CD-ROM service of EBSCO, covers only 50 titles, but these are supposedly the "leading historical journals." ALA's annual Periodical Price Index feature in *American Libraries* tracks 151 to 179 titles for its sample. The 1996 report (HAMMEL CARPENTER & ALEXANDER) indicates that History journals are still moderately priced; at an average of $50.76/title, they fall into the nineteenth rank among 25 subject categories, with the most expensive being Russian translations ($1099/title) and number 25, the least expensive, being children's periodicals ($21.65/title). These data remained relatively stable to 1997, with slight increased across the board. Since 1993 history journals have increased their prices slightly more than fields like Language and Literature, raising its rank to number 17, but tracking since 1987 shows that inflation has stabilized at ca. 6 percent/year after the 10-12 percent consecutive annual increases in pricing during 1990-1992. Three years of double digit inflation in history journal price increases raised the decade average to 7 percent, but this still reflects a slower pace than overall (9.8 percent) for American periodicals. In any one year, one can expect 32 percent of history journal titles to increase their prices. American history journals cost a third less than their non-American counterparts, partially because of higher inflation in European produced titles, but the average annual percentage of cost increase last year was higher for American history titles (8.7 percent versus 6.2 percent for non-American, which had already gone up a whopping 12.2 percent in 1994-95). Although such price trends may be alarming for historians, such increases in no way compare badly with the persistent and extraordinary rise in science journal prices which often crest 10 percent year. If a library subscribed to the core tracked by ALA, its annual investment in History periodicals would be $7,665 (1995 pricing).

The most recent price study (early 1998 data for a 1999 forecast) polls EBSCO's Publishing's *Academic Search* for 2,390 journals for smaller libraries as a sample from EBSCO's database of 256,000 serial titles, and uses ISI's *Social Science* and *Science Citation Index* for its 5,208 core list (see the tables in KETCHAM & BORN). Among its findings is the message of the study's title, "E-Journals Come of Age," since 24 percent (652 journals) in ISI's *Social Science Citation Index* now have an electronic version (midrange, compared with 10 percent or 150 titles in the *Arts and Humanities Citation Index* at the low end, and at the other end 30 percent or 900 titles in the *Science Citation Index*). Pricing for libraries is now being influenced by the phenomena of aggregation, that is the supply of group subscriptions to electronic journals through jobbers or middlemen (EBSCO, Blackwells, Faxon, University Microfilms, Swets, CARL, British Library, etc.) and a trend away from purchasing through subscriptions to licensing for access to materials not actually owned. The acquisition of research material is therefore far more complex than it was at the beginning of the decade since it involves a range of options from subscription ownership with separate pricing and terms for individual and institutional buyers; index, abstract, full-text, and full-text with graphics options; various copy restrictions and privileges; and a scale of pricing from separate articles to full access to entire runs of periodicals by title or class (subject sorts by Library of Congress Subject Headings rather than LC Classification).

History journals in this latest price study (201 titles in English constitute the modest sample) show a rise from an average of $76.83 in 1994 to $83.27 in 1995 (+8.38 percent) and $91.45 (+9.82 percent) by 1996 at three times the cost-of-living index for inflation, but then a slowdown in price increasing at 4.56 percent in 1997 and 3.81 percent for 1998 so that the average price now stands at $99.26/title/year (KETCHAM & BORN, Table 2, p. 41). This is higher than in Language and Literature but is still at the low end, especially when contrasted to the hard sciences (Chemistry, for example, at $1,577/title or Physics at $1,601/title). Journals (ISI titles) published in Europe often cost more than those in the United States, with those published in the Netherlands as the most expensive worldwide. Titles produced in England where the annual inflation increase has been 13-15 percent/year now cost nearly twice ($697) the composite figure ($334) for American productions (KETCHAM & BORN, Tables 3 and 4, pp. 41-42). In the Arts and Humanities, average per title costs are now $105.79 for United States productions and $224.28 for those from abroad (with a 1994-1998 percentage of change at 37.6 percent and 44.1 percent respective). For the Social Sciences the averages are more than double: $241.17 for United States productions (51.8 percent increase in four years) and $612.16 for foreign productions (+61 percent). Based on price history during this decade, European pricing is expected to increase by 13 percent plus another 3 percent for the impact of the currency conversion to a European Community standard. Currency fluctuation continues to make acquisitions from abroad problematic and encourages an imbalance of trade in ideas and publications by making American academic products comparatively cheaper and easier to acquire, and therefore to consume, in Europe (KETCHAM & BORN, Chart 1, p. 45). Continued price increases for American titles are projected at 8.4 percent for the Arts and Humanities, and 10.3 percent for the Social Sciences—still outstripping any likely increases in acquisitions budgets. The crisis continues to worsen; in History alone for medium-sized university libraries, the cost increase has been 30.18 percent over four years (KETCHAM & BORN, Table 10). These studies refer to "the cost of chaos" in academic publishing and libraries because those costs for institutions are far more than the price of periodicals, but labor, control and access systems, and an entirely different infrastructure that combines all media in information delivery internally and externally. Few constituencies, historians included, are satisfied with only electronic access, so in most cases hard copy and its electronic counterpart are both made available. The information technology costs are not offset by the modest discounts offered for electronic-only subscriptions.

Serials pricing, as distinct from periodicals, is also important since included in this category are indexes and abstracts to History literature. ALA tracks 1,280 serials titles with the help of major jobbers and suppliers and in 1996 used 800 as a core sample to show price trends over the past two decades (CHAFFIN). Historians tend to rely on three categories of serials: (1) General and the Humanities, where 116 titles now average $410.75/year registering a 7.6 percent increase last year against a run between 1978, when the increase was an all-time high of 25.2 percent in one year, through 1989 when these serials increased every year with double digit inflation; (2) Social Sciences, where 154 titles average $513.08/year and averaged a 5.3 percent price increase last year, against the 1979-1982 all-time highs of 10-15.8 percent; and (3) United States Documents, for which 170 titles average only $129.37/year with their government subsidies, and which have been more modest in price increases (e.g., 6.7 percent last year, but -0.6 percent in 1995). The overall average is $556.58/year for 1,280 titles and an expected increased of 6.6 percent *per annum.* Libraries which support historical studies may easily encumber $150,000 annually in just these categories. The problem, of course, is that budgets have not increased accordingly, and most libraries have faced a 3-4 percent gap between price and budget increases, so that each year acquisitions move money from book buying to serials and periodicals, which means fewer books purchased from booksellers and high prices per title. Moreover, this means that a field like History which has retained its orientation to monographic publishing is supported by an ever smaller percentage of total acquisition dollars (only 20-25 percent of most library acquisition budgets are devoted to monographs). For the past decade, libraries have trimmed subscriptions annually at a rate of circa 5 percent, which also drives up the per title costs for renewals. This has become a vicious cycle and a contentious political game on many campuses, in which History has not faired especially well (even though it takes for inflation alone nearly two cancellations of History titles to sustain a single Science subscription over a five-year period). The problem is similar in Europe where academic libraries have focused on national publications in their own languages, with generally poorer international collections than are built by American research libraries. This narrowing of scope by locale, region, and native language unwittingly supports local history over other genre and mitigates against comparative history and interdisciplinary, intercultural studies.

Such trends are influencing how historians research and disseminate their work. It has odd repercussions: Entering assistant professors are expected to have secured the interest of a publisher in their dissertation as a potential monograph, even if it were better released serially. Not only have we reached a preposterous situation in which today's entry-level assistant professor in the United States must meet criteria which sufficed for tenure ten years ago, but this means that much of the assessment for career entry and subsequent success has been shifted outside the university to academic presses. Competition for acceptance by a publisher of repute is keen, the time lag is considerable, and the cost per title is increasing at rates higher than in serial and periodical publishing. The impact on scholarly communications is considerable as well. This expectation restricts access by limiting the number of titles sold, and increases reliance on retrieval through reference mechanisms that historians resist using, which in turn lengthens the time required for works to enter into the field. This leads to adverse pricing trends resulting in decreased acquisitions, which further shift costs from collection development to operations whenever interlibrary loans are relied upon. History as a profession has no overall strategy for information dissemination, publications are diverse in format and content, standards vary tremendously, and bibliographic control is complicated. Access to all but the core literature can be problematic except at the largest research universities (whose development since World War II has been profiled by R. GEIGER; cf., GEIGER & WHISTON).

While historical research is prolific and widely distributed, local foci delimit the scope and usefulness of many articles, which in turn requires more extensive reading than ever to transcend the parochialism of regional studies and reading only in one's native language. Yet research collections tend to be highly centralized, sometimes collection strengths in secondary literatures do not correlate well with primary sources, and the location of special collections that are geographically focused can be far afield from the locales and regions they document (e.g., Western Americana in East Coast libraries, New England literature in Texas, etc.). Cornell University's A. KENNY holds that one of the most positive benefits of the digital library projects is in resource sharing and avoidance of duplication. If publications are posted but once and all copies are retrieved from the master electronically rather than from multiple locations, this will put tremendous strain on servers and require sophisticated indexing strategies and continuous investment in networks in order to navigate across multiple systems. Infrastructure expenditures and rising licensing costs have eroded any savings thought to be realized from electronic conversions. The National Federation of Abstracting and Information Services (NFAIS) is concerned about such trends and how publishing will be done in the next millennium (KASER). Libraries are especially concerned, both about the reality of the situation and the false premises held by administrators who seek relief from spiraling acquisitions budgets while believing that information technology saves money.

Such publishing trends in numbers and costs now create a climate in which alternatives are sought, such as in electronic publishing where often quality controls are lacking and in which accessibility through cataloging and indexing is woefully inadequate. Since 1995, the defunct bibliographic services of the AHA have been missed. Some H-Net people have wanted to resurrect *RPA* and *WAH* electronically and possibly to mount a current awareness service by carrying tables of contents for journals covered and by encouraging electronic reviewing that would be more timely than published reviews. At the same time, such listservs would compete with the *AHR* if H-Net, an AHA affiliate, were to establish an electronic review forum. The current H-Net review initiative (discussed later) is significant because it signals some dramatic changes in the profession, both in the use of electronic communications and in the expansion of historical discourse as an ongoing process rather than a series of packaged products, but it is too early to tell if such developments will lead to a scientific approach to criticism, analysis, and longitudinal study of historians themselves, their information bases and behaviors, assumptions and language, and general attitudes.

A few benchmarks exist by which to compare current developments, assess changes, and speculate about future developments. Historians serving as referees for the *American Historical Review* were asked by STIEG (1983) to describe and prioritize their values in reviewing, but answers were general and without enough clarity to be ranked. STIEG (1995, p. 222) in surveying referring practices subsequently summarized historian values for the *AHR* as "large scope and adequate research in sources, that were well-written, and in which the tone was appropriate," with the added criteria of significance, methodology, and presentation also being prominent.

Historians' generality in this regard, however, stands in sharp contrast, for example, to the twelve prioritized criteria operating in editorial boards of Psychology journals, which display an obvious penchant for scientific empiricism (LINDSEY & LINDSEY). STERN & KALOF review the methods, standards, and practice in evaluating Social Science research. NATOWITZ & CARLO (p. 332), in comparing the History reviews in the *AHR* and *JAH* with *Choice*, were able to arrive at a weighted comparative ranking of evaluative elements noted in 153 reviews, which in descending order from the most frequently mentioned were (1) analysis; (2) unity of thesis; (3) research; (4) objectivity; (5) readability; (6) historical content; and (7) editing. However, they could find no agreement among reviews of the same books in these three reviews, or for that matter between the two leading American History review journals, in the reviewers' selection of outstanding books or in their delivery of negative reviews. There is simply no consensus among historians and no pattern of consistency which can be identified in applying the promulgated criteria of the *AHR* or evaluative priorities reviewers say they employ. In the *JAH*, 74 percent of all reviews, 77 percent in the *AHR*, and 81 percent in *Choice* were favorable; of 459 reviews in the sample, only three books were uniformly rated as outstanding, and only three were condemned by being reviewed unfavorably. This proportion of favorable reviewing of about 80 percent of all History books reviewed has not changed much over the past 20 to 30 years (BIL-HARTZ; J. CASEY). *AHR* and *JAH* are seen to be more critical (only slightly more negative or unfavorable) and thorough in their reviewing (within their allotted 500-word limit per review, contrasted to *Choice*'s 200 words), but for this extended commentary one must wait eight to ten months respectively longer than the shorter reviews of *Choice* appear (which carries 6,000 reviews annually, in contrast to the *AHR* which reviews 1,000 of the 4,000 books it receives annually, and the 600 *JAH* reviews).

The descriptive and analytic bibliographic notes for all such reviewing are minimal. If free-form reviews were preferred by historians, which apparently is the case, a compromise would be to extend the bibliographic citation for analytics beyond customary bibliographic description to include graphic presentations, scope notes with a standard demarcation of geographic and chronological parameters, identification of methodologies and techniques, and perhaps a terminology for school of thought, persuasion, orientation, interpretation, and approach. These would enhance conceptual indexing and information retrieval by term matching in full-text searching. In the United States, historians have tended to approach their literature as Literature rather than a scientific information exchange, and they have refused to employ a grading system in reviewing or a selection from a specific set of recommendations that would affect selection and acquisitions. In other words, it may be a mistake to assume that historians who take to the Internet are automatically inclined toward the Social Sciences, quantification, or empiricism in their outlook, especially in self- and peer-evaluation or some formal attempt at quality control in the profession. Description may be preferred precisely because it allows for qualification in what is perceived to be a subjective task. So, moving to electronic reviewing may be another case of using the computer to do more of the same. Evaluation will not be speeded up necessarily, but publication will be faster. One might think that first-out electronic reviews might influence subsequent reviewing, but this has not been the case in print where *Choice* reviews appear so much earlier than those in History journals. In either case, manual or electronic, the means of dissemination may have no bearing on the quality of initial reviewing; the real change may come with interactive reviewing, where in an electronic forum, rejoinders can be fired off instantly rather than after a due interval for quiet reflection (SPINK, ROBINS & SCHAMBER explore implications of book reviewing in electronic publishing). H-Net, for example, provides a mechanism to review and rebut the reviewer more easily and quickly than is now afforded the person reviewed in letter replies to the editor. Given that studies have shown electronic discourse to be more aggressive and hostile than in print, one might see a change in the ratio of favorable to unfavorable reviews, and an upsurge in polemics and more personalized attacks than is the case in monitored reviewing. Many will not see such trends as promoting quality or being conducive to greater professionalism.

Will new information technology transform how History is done? Not automatically. SEGAL and others have seen all of this technology as a "mixed blessing." A new and more dynamic critique promises to democratize historical discourse, and this could transform the learning and teaching of History, but how such changes will affect historical research is not clear. The effect of one process upon the other, teaching and research, is not altogether clear. The potential of significant change for research lies in distance learning and interaction beyond one's own institution, collaboration during production, and prepublication review and criticism, which contributes to improved quality of mature work, rather than simply more criticism after the fact of publication when the work is prematurely published, requires revision, and should be enhanced. Indeed, current reviewing mechanisms mean that a negative or highly critical review never contributes to a better product, but it simply condemns the initial work to oblivion and damns its chances for re-edition in improved form. Unfortunately, such reviewing also has the same impact on career opportunities, and does not, therefore, invest in professional development except as a form of purging and excommunication. Prepublication electronic reviewing of drafts, formal publication in whatever format, and then ongoing discussion in an ever-enlarged circle not linked electronically to the original work would in essence serialize even monographic publication. This would be an improvement in the current publication reviewing practice for both research and teaching, and most of all, for historians' own continuing interactive education.

In any such projects, the older published forms or the new electronic versions envisioned by H-Net enthusiasts, scope definition is always a problem for History. If one were to expand the scope of such a purview to material culture, high and low, to accommodate public history, history of art, music and literature, and archeology and anthropology, the aforesaid problem of quantity and scale is magnified significantly. Already by the mid-1980s 30,000 museums in the world had published 642,000 books on every subject imaginable (CASTONGUAY, OIKAWA & VEZINA). Intellectual access to these artifacts via indexes to this vast and growing literature is becoming increasingly possible through *The Bibliography of the History of Art (BHA)* which cites 24,000 references annually. Literary and performance history traced through such sources as the *MLA Bibliography*, or classics and philology or language history in the *L'Année Philologique* (i.e., excluding titles not particularly historical), would add another 26,000 references annually. Relatively fewer publications in music and the performing arts are historical, since so much falls into the category of aesthetics and contemporary criticism, but nevertheless another 15,000 titles could be considered within the scope of Cultural History. In short, taking into consideration a 20-30 percent overlap in coverage of the main bibliographic sources, in any year nearly 110,000 published historical studies are indexed and abstracted! Publications often excluded from such bibliographic control include archival finding aids, local history studies, family genealogical materials, company and commemorative histories, newsletters expanding into quasi-journals, irregular series, private press work, and so-called "grey" literature. My consulting work for ABC-CLIO's *Historical Periodicals Directory* covering 600 titles from Spain and Portugal and decade-long bibliographic coverage of Iberian and Latin American titles for IFLA's *Annual History of Books and Printing* involved investigation of over 400 additional house publications and local and regional studies and comparison of their coverage in mainstream historical indexes, abstracts, and bibliographies. Over 60 percent of such local literature is not accessible through standard sources; 50 percent of such titles, many irregular, are not handled by subscription agencies; and 40 percent cannot be located in United States libraries, even in partial runs. The situation in reverse, namely ready access to local and regional American publications, is worse in European libraries. Access problems have increased with the serial budget problems of research libraries not only because of pricing, but also because of the splintering of research fields and specialization of readerships, higher production costs with smaller publications and print runs, and more titles which results in higher labor costs for acquisitions, bibliographic control, and collection maintenance; and access through indexing and abstracting are significantly higher than cataloging (access points are delineated by OCLC's *Cataloging* manual). The investment in collection development and bibliographic control by academic libraries is therefore significant. The sheer volume and level of in control and access are exponential problems. If all of the aforementioned areas are included, these might contribute another 15 percent to the total production of nearly 125,000 monographic publications annually.

In contrast to hardcopy publication, of the 8,261 commercially available databases holding 5.57 billion records, only 330 are in the Humanities (4 percent) including History's meager 29 titles (M. WILLIAMS, 1994a, p. xxvii) of which the largest are bibliographic (e.g., ABC-CLIO). Of course, most databases of socioeconomic historical data are usually classified under Social Science rather than History as such (e.g., Sociology-Historical data rather that Social History-Sources). Text bases of documents are seen as History's natural stuff.

More electronic Humanities products are coming each year (216 by 1990 or 4 percent of all databases: TIBBO, 1991, p. 299), but reported History production (34 of 3565 CD-ROMs, diskettes, tapes, etc., i.e., less than 1 percent) is minuscule (M. WILLIAMS, 1994b). History is underrepresented in these industrial surveys because local productions often have ineffective marketing mechanisms. Actually the current production of CD-ROMs in the former Soviet Union for Russian history alone, as demonstrated at the 1996 AHC conference in Moscow, has surpassed the dozen mark, but none of these are reported in the industry tallies. Even so, if counts were more thorough and listings were comprehensive, the percentage would still not rise higher than 3 percent, in stark contrast to the proportion of historical literature in traditional media. These data reflect the relative tardiness of historians entering the electronic information industry, and that their use of electronic information technology is predominantly to produce traditionally formatted and distributed publications, rather than to take advantage of electronic libraries or archives on their electronic desktops (WEISSMAN, 1990). Of course, this is also a reflection of economic options and the availability of financing in the disparity between Science and Technology and the Arts and Humanities.

As History catches up, it remains to be seen if current production rates level off and simply bifurcate between physical and electronic publication, or if the relative ease of electronic publication and the possible bypassing of peer review and the quality controls of academic presses result in even more publications. This potential increase is certainly predicted by H-Net activists. Electronic access by itself, however, does not guarantee more readers or intensified reading by current consumers, just more fluid dissemination. The latter is better justified for expanding readerships, not a stable one or even a constituency of declining numbers, which means that more is produced about less with greater specialization but is disseminated ever more widely without a realistic expectation of increased consumption. This does not make sense, except as a case of technology being used for its own sake. Such questioning places the issue of electronic publishing for historical studies squarely back into the realm of education and relative health of History in academe (see H. COLLIER for issues and trends in the electronic publishing industry). The prospects for History in electronic media are not at all clear. This massive and still growing volume is unbelievable and defies even the most rapacious of readers to do more than skim the surface. The results are largely dormant library collections awaiting use, as well as the widespread acquisition practice of "just in case" purchasing. The universities subsidize the process directly to university presses and indirectly through massive library acquisition budgets, and the cycle goes on without a strong correspondence between increased rates of acquisition and use. Conversion to electronic media makes "just in time" or "on demand" publishing available, if it is acknowledged that an unused file like a warehoused book does not reveal the real substance of publication. That is determined by actual use, reading, and presumably some understanding and impact. Measures of this are sorely wanting.

Is such prolific production warranted? Is such volume of history publication used effectively by historians for purposes other than regeneration of their secondary literature? What is its impact on teaching, synthesis, and learning outside professional history? Such questions are not readily answered from current studies because so little self-study and assessment is forthcoming from the profession which would assess the information process rather than the literature itself. History has in this regard operated like literary criticism rather than an information science. This is not a negative criticism of History, only an observation, but it suggests that there is much more to study than the literature of History. The history of History has yet to be told in terms of its dynamics, systems and processes, networking and infrastructure, etc., which might be studied through citation analyzes á la CRONIN (1984, 1995) for scientific communication, or with proper regard for its social impact and such issues as efficiency and effectiveness framed as larger questions than merely effective history teaching in the classroom. Bibliometric studies investigate communication patterns, identify research frontiers and the emergence of new fields, the histories of a subject domain, demarcate the boundaries between disciplines, and the evaluation of research activities by individuals, professionals, schools, and countries (L. SMITH, 1981; BORGMAN,

1990). VINKLER identified a decade ago some 39 different bibliometric measures. This methodology and its literature are reviewed by M. LIU and critiqued by the MACROBERTS team; see also the discussion of methodological issues such as the removal of duplicates in data set isolation and the recent literature review by INGWERSEN & CHRISTENSEN (1997; cf., CHRISTENSEN & INGWERSEN, 1995). Most recently VUKOVI'C relates classical distributions in bibliometrics (e.g., the "laws" of Pareto, 1895, Lotka, 1926, Bradford, 1934, and Zippf, 1949; cf., EGGHE's classification) to more general stochastic modeling used in modern informetrics (EGGHE & ROUSSEAU).

Classically, the interest of bibliometrics has been in the dispersion of articles by type and focus in scientific journals, i.e., how scientific journals are populated, or stated differently, observing the patterns or regularities of distributions in a literature (BOOKSTEIN, 1990a&b). History in particular, and the Humanities and Social Sciences in general, have come under bibliometric scrutiny only sporadically and sparingly. In fact, a bibliometric study of Bibliometrics would reveal a tremendous disciplinary bias, inbred citation patterns, and cocitation reinforcement that would suggest a redirection of research from saturated subject areas to less studied domains. A discipline like History might prove particularly challenging for in-depth study comparing fields by period, geography, type of history, and subject. It would be interesting to know, for example, how patterns change between fields; how open History is to other disciplines; how historians use literatures in other languages than their own; and what is the relationship between patterns of citations for original sources, published primary sources, and the secondary literature.

CRONIN's more recent study (1995) of the citation process, on the role of acknowledgment in "the primary communication process" (here using "primary" as in Information Science, i.e., History's secondary literature), incorporates some of the earlier work (1990) he did on History by inquiring into the *American Historical Review* in comparison with the *American Sociological Review, Mind*, and the *Psychological Review* over two decades (1971-1990). He employed a typology put forward in 1990 categorizing acknowledgments of "paymaster," moral supporter, "dogs body," technical expertise, "prime mover" or motivator, and the "trusted assessor" or reader. His third citation study analyzed 5,630 citations, in which 1,025 individuals were acknowledged by contributors to the *AHR*. Only 36 historians were mentioned three or more times, much fewer than those from other fields were mentioned by their peers, but in all of these disciplines a concentration of highly cited individuals appeared. The results for History, however, are perhaps influenced by the breadth of *AHR* coverage, and a greater cadre of multiple-cited historians would have emerged from a journal like *American History* or publications that devote more space to articles and less to reviews than does the *AHR*. Despite such variables, philosophers cite their peers the least, and psychologists and sociologists acknowledge intellectual indebtedness more than do historians. Again, since historians divide their citations between primary and secondary sources more than do practitioners in these other fields, there are possible explanations for these findings other than those provided by Cronin. Finally, Cronin's work used the *Social Sciences Citation Index* data pool, in which History is well-represented, but not nearly so well as Sociology and Psychology. These fields have therefore attracted more in-depth study than History. When Cronin supplemented his analysis of citations with a survey of faculty in major academic institutions, he discovered that most (68 percent) authors use citations to acknowledge properly major intellectual contributions which benefitted their work directly through some sort of collaboration short of co-authoring, or indirectly through their previous publications. Eighty-seven percent were aware of being cited by others, but less than 30 percent favored inclusion of acknowledgment data in promotion and tenure reviews. The most negative comments were in regard to perceived methodological problems (i.e., quantifiability), variance in significance of citations, and wrong use of such data. Only 8 percent admitted to failure in citing a significant contribution to their work, while 52 percent thought that they had made significant contributions which were used by others but which went uncited. Nevertheless, most thought that citations were a courtesy rather than a contractual obligation: hence, Cronin's title *The Scholar's Courtesy* (1995).

Such research is sadly underdeveloped in historical studies, where frequencies might reveal behaviors differing between specializations, relationships between primary source and secondary literature citations, and cultural differences related to sub-language, internal organization of a field's invisible college, information retrieval habits, and scholarly ethics. It is known, however, that 95 percent of all articles published in History which are tracked by Institute for Scientific Information (ISI) are *never* cited within five years of their appearance (SCHWARTZ, Table 2, p. 21). This is in keeping with the large-scale "uncitedness" in the Humanities in general (98 percent), which is far higher than in the Social Sciences (75 percent) and Physical Sciences (47 percent). Publications in narrower sub-disciplines or interdisciplinary fields have a higher citation index; 71 percent of articles in the history and philosophy of science, for example, are cited within five years of appearance. Likewise, when studies have disaggregated data for specializations within History, the uncitedness rate is slightly lower (91 percent), but not enough to argue away the problem in scholarly communications of a glut in publication compared with their cited use. In some fields citation rates rise significantly when one studies a specialty only; the problem of disaggregation and classification of disciplines and sub-disciplines is real in such statistical work. Of course, citation tracings do not indicate readership, only acknowledged indebtedness to someone else's research. T. BROOKS has explored the motivations in citing another's works: many, rather than genuinely tracing use and providing accountability for content, are perfunctory and even ritualistic or decorative. Cronin's typology of citation rationales admits this as well. If one consults the major professions' publication style manuals, one discovers more detail about how to cite something in a particular format than explanation of why or whom one should cite. Moreover, house rules of university publishers often intervene into personal preference for notes and citations, and these measures are often driven by economy (cost-containment) rather than intellectual accountability. Nor can rules be found in standard research methodology textbooks, but only sage advice of the sort one would expect from a conscientious mentor.

C. SCHWARTZ (p. 22) resurrects attention to a thesis about the incremental nature of advancement of disciplinary knowledge attributed to J. Ortega y Gasset's *The Revolt of the Masses* (1932), which maintains such progress is made "by a host of average scholars working on relatively unambitious projects." This seems like Peter Doorn's characterization of History as a "slow science." This means that uncited literature is not insignificant, as historians know when they go back in time to use literature that in other fields would be seen as outdated. On the other hand, during the 1970s, studies created another interpretation that only a few scholars in a discipline were responsible for its intellectual progress, in which case knowledge discovery is a product of the upper strata of publishing historians, for example, and the great mass of uncited studies can be dismissed (COLE & COLE). Reactions to citation data analyses are often mixed; some denounce the practice altogether, as is being done currently in the legal profession which just became aware of such tracking of law professors' publications and their citation to estimate their impact and the scholarly reputation of a faculty. Some law professors and deans scoffed at F. R. SHAPIRO's work, according to a *Wall Street Journal* report (January 22, 1997) about "Legal Citology" sweeping law schools, calling such study "an uncommonly silly fascination" and "fun to see" but a waste of time. Others heralded such analyses as a "milestone" legitimizing such scholarship about legal scholarship (like data about data, or metadata?). Some blame ISI's data gathering methodology; and some attribute large-scale uncitedness simply to normal statistical probability (high citedness correlates with Lotka's Law to measure research productivity). As in the case of Cronin's survey, many of the negative responses read like excuses to avoid further analysis and confrontation with some implications of the facts which are not especially flattering, such as narrower reading habits amid increased publication resulting in the dominance of just a few journals in each field (although all studies have shown a low correlation between a journal's impact and any article's citedness), or the increase ethnocentricity of reading, or at least of citation habits in America since the 1980s (which corresponds to the problem of declining foreign language utility) despite supposedly greater communication capabilities, globalization of curricula, and the tremendous investment by research libraries in serial literature collections (GAREAU).

In any case, citation analyses for a field like History reveal significant problems in scholarly communications, suggest some things about the sociology of the profession which are incongruent with some of its professional myths, and create difficulties for information scientists who might suggest structural and economic reform in scholarly History publishing. Citation analyses might also reveal significant finds for research and the use and referencing of primary sources, if citations to archival and published sources were traced to the same extent that citations to secondary literature are. It is perturbing to note how few citation studies are undertaken by archivists, manuscript curators, and special collection librarians to discover acknowledged indebtedness to their efforts and use of their sources. In any case, citation studies provide context unobtainable from reading a work alone, with no knowledge of its circulation, readings, and obligations created thereby, as revealed in referrals by other readers. What is unrevealed could be interesting as well, such as the point-to-point tracking or provenance tracing leading to retrieval through one citation to another. In History, since citations occur over a much longer time from publication than in other disciplines, and since there are more of them, such tracks could be long indeed. If it were possible to trace all such indebtedness as a kind of intellectual provenance, one would have a different kind of History of ideas than in the past.

From the publishing standpoint alone, History is big business. Yet we know relatively little about this History business, scholarly communications, and information behaviors of historians, their consumption and production habits, cognitive styles, documentation proficiency, the dynamics of idea exchanges in the literature, time lags in cross-disciplinary information exchange, characteristics of technological transfer in the field, shifts in vocabulary and style that reveal trends and influences, or the cost and efficiency of the whole enterprise. Little is known about the consumption of historical literature outside of academe and formal education, and even then, the available data are often limited to such book trade statistics as titles published and volumes sold. No studies exist from library circulation records or logs from online public access catalogs which would indicate user interests through actual document retrieval and perhaps something about reading and learning habits related to this vast literature. Even less is known about scholarly communications about history in an electronic environment (KAHIN). What impact does this cycle of production and acquisition have on teaching, on the synthesis, and refinement of the secondary literature, and on research producing new knowledge? Such questions are not really answerable from current use, citation, or bibliometric studies, nor is any kind of empirical assessment available from the historical profession. Again, History in this regard operates like literary criticism and a self-generating discourse rather than like an information science. Such critical self-study, totally separate from historiographic review, is sorely wanting. Standard titles in historiography, as histories of literature and criticism, say little about such issues.

Historians are increasingly aware of their markets, both enrollments in their classes and in the sale of History books. Despite large numbers, trends in both areas have been alarming. The French, in studying what began to be perceived after 1991 by NOIRIEL as a crisis in History today, both the infighting and its hypercritical tone are limiting the market of many history works to historians alone. The ensuing controversy has prompted a look at the consumption of history books and trends in History publishing for telltale signs of this supposed crisis. Thus, PROCHASSON has talked about the "crisis of the book" in this History crisis of History. From the viewpoint in France, he reflects (p. 11):

> In 1994 history books made up 2.3 percent of publications as a whole. And the trend is discouraging. Since 1988 this proportion has continually declined. Moreover, revenue from history books fell from 350 million francs to 320 million francs. The

number of new titles has declined from 671 in 1991 to 540 in 1994, although the average of sales per title increased. These days a history book is considered a success if it can sell five to six thousand copies. But again, one has to look at what kinds of works are being published.

Three old genres seem today to be surviving in the current history market: the dictionary, the biography, and the great thematic or national history. These publishing niches may not be the best or the most convenient for reflecting the vitality of contemporary history in France.

He maintains that France, unlike other markets, had long offered works of History and Social Sciences a "privileged position in publishing" that had entailed the possibility of "reaching a wider public than the closed circle of academic savants" that constitutes professional historians. This "exceptionism," he observes, is now called into question because of a variety of tendencies: the university system does not encourage historiographic innovation or intellectual adventurousness. Premature publishing has given rise to the "popular primers" which are no longer the master syntheses of master scholars, but resemble published survey courses. But more importantly, the popular genre of history "presents simple historical flavors to a finicky public" and "contradicts the current tendency to place doubt and complexity at the center of the historian's reflections" (pp. 10-11). The result is:

…important but more or less unreadable works, published by a small-circulation or minor university presses; on the other side…quickly published essays of dubious merit. Contributing to the crisis is the publication of numerous published monographs by a few specialized publishing houses. Often these are too quickly published dissertations, unimproved by the editorial assistance they would need to reach a public larger than a few dozen specialists.

This grim conclusion tends to lend credence to the controversial idea that there is a crisis of history in France.

Prochasson's short essay merited translation by the American Historical Association for its *Perspectives*, perhaps to do more than alert American historians of France to the situation there, but because his comments have some relevance for the scene in the United States as well.

Despite such contemporary critical observations and alarms, the history of History in terms of information production, dissemination, consumption, and impact, has yet to be told. PROCHASSON's charges, however stimulating they should be, hardly have support from evidence from the book trade, bibliometric study, or content or citation analysis on an international scale. Any number of his assertions cry out for serious research. Likewise, the profession's methods of scholarly communication through publications, conferencing, listservs and e-mail, correspondence, etc., has never been subjected to empirical investigation. MAY has studied humanist e-mail communications for the purpose of automatic classification of messages into question, response, announcement, and administrative types (using the HUMANIST listserv@brownvm.brown.edu). However, the efficiency, effectiveness, and extent and rate of intellectual and cultural change resulting from the historical enterprise are still unknowns. The History business in terms of investment and return (time, labor, personnel, etc., for teaching, research, and publication) from learning may be unmeasurable in some ways but not in every way. This is not as much a criticism of the historical profession so much as an observation about how much more there is to study than the literature of history. When reacting to this discussion, my colleague, Stephen Foster, saw these questions as falling into distinct categories: the behavioral, economic, intellectual, and technological models respectively. This alone illustrates the complexity of modern scholarly communications and points to possibilities of further study about historical discourse and communications from a vantage point outside History.

What is known seems not to be integrated by historians into course work about History. One might assume that Public History would be more concerned with such questions, but here too literature searching turns up very little other than casual observation and opinion pieces. One does not even find much to defend Public History from the criticism that it is sponsored by History departments largely to bolster enrollments rather than because of a genuine concern for the inclusion of history in public life and culture at large (MCCRANK, 1986). Placement of public historians in business and industry is still negligible. Moreover, a role for public history or any significant impact in the information industry and profession cannot even be identified. The most visible impact of historians in a practicing profession is in librarianship, in rare books and manuscripts, or historical and special collections, and secondly in reference and collection development, subject areas associated with History. Studies of starting salaries in historical societies, museums, etc., show no correlation between advanced studies and degrees with earnings. Salaries in these categories seem to be a function of size and financial stability of the cultural organizations, and a dramatic spread exists in the scale from curator to executive in historical organizations. The historical geography of most of these institutions in the United States and in Europe means that more jobs exist in local organizations at entry level and relatively low pay, and well-paying jobs are few in number. It is placement not in local historical societies and museums, but in government, public administration, business, and industry, where the opportunity for more rapid advancement exists, that raises junior historians' salaries in nonteaching jobs higher than average beginning professor levels. The problem of entrapment in particular career paths, whereby it is difficult to move back and forth between the private and public sector, in and out of academe, and between business and government, is stifling.

Until recently the American Historical Association paid little attention to self-study of graduate student and entry-level historians in the teaching field using placement data from History departments, but published analyses are still fairly rudimentary percentage comparisons of salaries by gender and tabulations of graduates versus known hires. Few socioeconomic analyses are available; few surveys canvas the field, so that profiles of the History profession are mostly descriptive, based on observation rather than empirical research. Fewer studies of historians in nonteaching roles have been taken, and professional surveys, e.g., in museum staffing, identify historians from those trained in other disciplines. Consequently, the transferability of skills learned in historical training and the application of subject knowledge itself are not well understood and many assumptions, often repeated, are not well grounded. For all of the arguments made for the applicability of History to archival appraisal, for example, no scientific studies prove the case or even demonstrate such a utility. This is one of the complaints voiced by HORSMAN about the difficulty in knowledge engineering and the development of decision support systems in archival appraisal. No studies have attempted to place historical reasoning or subject knowledge into the context of nonteaching jobs, their operations, functions, and responsibilities; or to relate history in such roles to other disciplines and professional training. The division between amateur and professional historians in such cases studies might be difficult to clarify. Historiography ignores whatever literature exists from nonteaching historians, and because the history of History has been largely a literary history focusing on production rather than consumption, important questions are often answered by no more than opinion. In such cases, History is a field in which, to paraphrase Peter Doorn talking about Social Science research, "data are golden" because we have precious little, but "opinions are free" because they are so abundant (DOORN, 1993). His scorn reflects the more subtle humor in a cartoon appearing in a spring 1996 issue of *The Chronicle of Higher Education* wherein a bartender in a pub across the street from a university posted a sign demanding that a little evidence be forthcoming with all of the opinion shared across his counter at this prestigious establishment. This subject of the practice of history, the profession at large rather than just in higher education, and a more sophisticated socioeconomic profile are still wide open and beg for serious study from Social Science perspectives. The kind of methodologies employed by Cliometricians to balance the dominance of largely uninformed narrative or quasi-case studies revealed in personal experiences and observations would reveal much about historians they do not know about themselves.

An admirable example of the kinds of inquiry that would be most informative is the collaboration between the Getty Trust Art History Information Program (AHIP, now folded into the Getty Research Institute) staff and the Brown University Institute for Research in Information and Scholarship (BAKEWELL *ET AL.*) in order to examine the practices of art historians. History has not been subjected to the same kind of rigorous studies of user requirements as in Art History, exemplified by LINDERMEIER & STEIN, for the design of automated information systems. No bibliometric or citation studies about historical scholarship compare with those by BUDD (1988) BUDD & SEAVEY or CULLARS (1985, 1989) for Literature (see WHITE & MCCAIN, 1989, for the kind of bibliometric scholarship which might be done). None employ the methodology recommended by MILSTEAD for analyzing subject bibliographic databases, or clustering algorithms often applied to other disciplines as illustrated by T. A. BROOKS, RASMUSSEN, etc., which involves the partitioning of literatures and inter- and co-citation mapping. These have not been done for History (see the methodology outlined by MCCAIN, 1991, and applied to Information Science in WHITE & MCCAIN); nor does one find empirical profiles of historical literature as a whole to study group identities in scientific change (e.g., GRIFFITH & MULLINS; and PLATT and C. MULLINS for Sociology in particular), or solid trend analysis (e.g., "domain analysis," as discussed by ARANGO & PRIETO-DIAZ [see fig. 1, p. 18] or BEGHTOL specifically for fiction) that can give credence to the casual observations one finds in History literature.

WHITE & MCCAIN (1998) among others characterize Anglo-American information scientists as either retrievalists or bibliometricians. They suggest that Information Science is comprised of these two subdisciplines, citation analysis and bibliometrics. Among others, P. WILSON has rejected such a characterization as too restrictive, but it is popular nevertheless. HARTER (1992) recognized this split as well and observes that the two "camps" are not well integrated.

Historical bibliometrics seems not to exist (i.e., comparative longitudinal sampling related to collection and institutional history) in Information Science, although WHITE & MCCAIN (1998, p. 327) provide such a comparative snapshot for the field of Information Science as narrowly defined by them (and their study is restricted to a core of English language journals that largely exclude historical treatments). This Drexel University team speaks of author co-citation analysis as producing a "history of the cliometric sort" when they trace co-citations between 1972 and 1995 among the most cited information scientists. By tracing connectedness between citers, mapping them into sectors, and grouping citation occurrences for 100 authors into time periods, of 1972-1979, 1980-1987, and 1988-1995 (rationale for the periodization is not clear), they "portray" the discipline with shifts of authors in and out of the most cited periods and shifts between sectors depending on the nature of their research. They posit the notion of capturing "the historical consensus" in author citation maps: "only what citers have recognized them for, not what they have actually done" (p. 329). They note interesting discrepancies between several authors' published work and how they are cited, often revealing a lag time in recognition of shifts in research emphases or a persistence in whatever initial citation patters where established. This phenomenon is different from the expected dwindling of citations as a literature ages (AVERSA). White and McCain are kind to the field in their observations rather than criticisms, and they fail to recognize the evidence produced by their own study of what may be taken as excessive inbreeding in the field among English speakers. The cultural limitations imposed on Information Science by such Anglo-American centricity with its inherent empiricism would tend to alienate such bibliometric Information

Science relying on citation analysis from the kind of history of ideas and intellectual diffusion current in New Cultural History. Bibliometricians have been interested in the phenomena of literature barriers revealed in citation maps, but not necessarily the barriers between Information Science and History. White and McCain conclude that "author co-citation analysis makes it difficult for information science, a rather evasive field, to evade such questions" and this is why certain authors as sets would fall into a thematic track or "history" of the field. Stated differently, one might wonder why there is no history in the field that would answer their question. Or conversely, why does History not have the kind of bibliometric study as exemplified by Howard and McCain that would inject into historiography some evidence from co-citation of preeminence of historians in their fields, their comings and goings as recognized by their citers, and the different shifts they make between types of research and how their work is received in the broader field across literature boundaries?

Within the field of Bibliometrics little has been done for History *per se* (as indicated by the lack of cited studies in surveys by BROADUS; BORGMAN, ed.; F. SHAPIRO; WHITE & MCCAIN (1989). This may be attributed to the difference between the ennumerative nature of Bibliography versus the quantification character of Bibliometrics; see DIODATO's recent *Dictionary of Bibliometrics* for an idea of the ahistorical nature of the latter. HERTZEL has explored the history of the idea and methodology of bibliometrics, and PIERCE pinpoints the origins of bibliometric indicators for measurement of information production and transfer in the Social Sciences. Most bibliometric research is in the Sciences, of course, secondly in the Social Sciences, and less in the Arts and Humanities, so part of the sparsity for empirical information about History as a discipline and the nature of its literature and communication is due to how few laborers in the Information Science field pay attention to History and the absence of bibliometric scholarly labor altogether in the discipline of History itself.

The relative lack of bibliometric research applied to History is unfortunate because such studies can be very telling for the design of effective information retrieval systems, acquisitions programs, and for communications. Consider, for example, BOULLE's analysis of the impact the celebration of the French Revolution and Rights of Man Bicentennial had on a surge of productivity by Canadian historians, but despite increased output, little apparent change was detected in research strategies or use of modern information technology to disseminate results. Heightened activity in History does not necessarily correlate with significant innovation in methodology; it simply increases coverage. Or, conversely, in order to apply historical inquiry to historical use patterns for longer range perspective, consider the interplay between History and Library Science while both evolved during the nineteenth century: the former influenced the latter profoundly in classification, but the latter may have equally but more subtly reversed this influence in how classification was applied. It would be interesting, for example, to study the dynamics between library classification systems, document management and retrieval, and how History has been conceived and taught. It might also be noted that History discussions about global periodization indicate no awareness of formal classification theory. Did the split between serialized and monographic literatures in library management in the late nineteenth century affect historians' deference to books rather than journals, in contrast to the placement of journals in laboratories and offices rather than libraries, which may have influenced the science and technical professions in their preference for the reverse? Or, did an objectified social institution of historical literature constitute at any time the same kind of "imaginary library" as A. KERNAN posits for Literature in American society, which consisted not only of a canon of authors, but notions of classification and appropriate use, the actual housing of kinds of documents and formats, and thereby the cultivation of certain practices and habits as History developed? Kernan's speculation for the interaction between formal libraries and conceptualization, canonization, and circulation of American and English literature suggests a variety of research topics relating History *per se* and Library History.

Bibliometric approaches have also been employed, including my own consultant work, in what some scholars may consider a more sinister analysis, i.e., to evaluate tenure potential for faculty—including historians. In this vein, the goal was to ascertain more than the fact that a scholar published, which is merely an issue of verification, but to show that his or her work had impact. Thus, citation tracing sought to reveal how fast after publication a scholar's work was cited by creating chronologs for citations of the contribution in question, noting how long the work stayed in vogue, and then through discipline mapping indicating how wide distribution was geographically, across disciplines and language barriers, and if those regarded as the esteemed elite in the field paid attention to the contribution. Clustering techniques identified peer groups based on mutual referral. Such research is usually unpublished, and the candidates seldom know the scrutiny their work received, not by content reading, but by the study of the academic circles which it attempted to enter, successfully penetrated and became a part, or failed to make its mark. Such bibliometric study of scholarly communications in History or any field would be revealing about how scholarship is disseminated, consumed, and propagated. If such information were available, beyond the practice of bibliography, it might have some impact on how research methodology is taught; it would assuredly influence advising about publication outlets, referees, reviewing, and strategies (which are largely matters of opinion now, without empirical foundations); and this might change how historians think about their own work, citation practices, and graduate training.

This bibliographic review provides some idea of the scope and size of the bibliography that must be surveyed by historians with cross-disciplinary interests and to keep up with more than one domain within History. Casual reading, browsing, and reliance on reviews and the citations of others will no longer suffice. A strategy must be designed and a regimen must be followed strenuously. Some bibliometric methods have been applied to this current bibliographic enterprise, but I must admit that the selection of citations herein is more akin to art than science. Moreover, the goal was not to write a thematic and bibliographic work, nor simply present a bibliography. For this present review online searches interrogated five bibliographic services covering 12,500 journal titles, plus OCLC was searched for holdings of its 37,000 libraries and for bibliographic verification in preparation of nearly 6,000 appended references. This is a sizeable bibliography by most standards, and yet it is relatively small when contrasted to what is available worldwide. These searches scanned more than 500,000 citations. This review surveyed firsthand more than 3,800 conference papers and articles, 1,600 monographs, and another 2,500 abstracts back to the 1970s and the early beginning and acceleration of History computing. Over 350 proceedings, bibliographies, and bibliographic reviews were studied for citation tracings, and recurrent citation did influence inclusion of many of the selections in this review. The total coverage is a small fraction of the available literature (only about 1 percent of references retrieved were selected for inclusion). This review concentrated on recent technical and methodological developments since the microcomputer revolution of the mid-1980s; literature identified as relating to the broad issues of Historical Information Science is a minor portion (2 percent) of the total available in History and must be augmented selectively from the Social Sciences and Information Science (for the latter, see the review by RULLER). Select references to past developments are those adding necessary background or complementing such previous reviews as in *The Annual Review of Information Science and Technology* that profile trends in Information Science (this survey, as already noted, is an extension of the short-form in *ARIST* (MCCRANK 1995; 30: 281-382). Inspection of the rapidly growing literature of Information Science and related research and project reports in computing (electronic records, data warehousing, enterprise networks, etc.) and engineering fields (pattern recognition, expert systems, visualization, software design, etc.) had to be highly selective, and could not be guided by citation tracing from the History literature because the latter is so spartan, out-of-date, and unreliable. Archival Science literature provides more avenues into technical literatures, but in contrast to what is available, such tracings are meager.

The current experience with online searching in a half-dozen databases revealed grave difficulties in identifying works relying on particular methodologies and techniques or specific technology, except for reports on these topics as such and the explicit treatment of methodology and technique required in dissertation proposals. By completion, however, specificity often gives way to generalization so that their abstracts often refer simply to the ubiquitous "analysis by computer" or "computer-generated analysis," etc., as if these were meaningful descriptors; in contrast, others identify the software down to the unrecognizable level of "SPSS\${x}\$," but never identify the specific methodologies employed. History reviews and indexes do not specifically note methodology except in broad terms like "quantification" or "computerized study." They lack review by set criteria, a failing shared with other fields (FURNHAM, p. 34). On the other hand, Information Science indexing and abstracting tools (*Information Science Abstracts* (1969-) and *Library and Information Science Abstracts* (1969-) treat History and related subjects like archives only tangentially, or they include only the history of information subjects.

No standards exist for such specification of method and technique, school of thought, or mode of interpretation. Nor is evaluation of the documentation base or use of evidence a universal ingredient in reviews. The American Historical Association, as the godfather of all historical associations in the United States, has never engaged in establishing "best practices" policies for the profession, so even if compliance were voluntary, there is little to guide one for emulation (see Appendix C). This is not simply the fault of reviewing. Such technical and methodological information is often implicit but is not explicit in actual publications, so that exploration of comparative methodology, borrowing and diffusion, and genuine innovation are difficult to search online or in History texts themselves. What is absent from reviews is also lacking in indexing. TIBBO's interviews do not even suggest that historians commonly search for specific methodological and technical information, or want such information supplied for cross-disciplinary research.

The searches for this survey encountered the same problems others (HANNEMYR & FLOOD) have confronted during the 1980s in citation studies of references to machine-readable documents that attempted to determine the rate of their use and changing habits of scholars in certain disciplines. At least most historians have adopted a style sheet for consistency in referencing, but at least four different styles are in vogue and in the transition to using more electronic information, all manner of citation syntax and form can be detected for electronic sources. LI & CRANE explore a variety of options in developing an "electronic style" based on APA's experience. Early projects to harness the chaotic information power of the Internet ran into the same problem of uniform citation practice, or lack thereof, and several projects have put forth their own preferences as would-be standards (e.g., EMORY UNIVERSITY's WWW project at http://www.cc.emory.edu/WHSCL/citation.formats.html). An Internet/WWW search turns up a variety of posted recommendations for citation styles: e.g., Janice Walker at the University of South Florida modifies the MLA style citations for electronic sources; Michael B. Quinion's "World Wide Words" includes citations for online sources; Haines Brown at Central Connecticut State University uses the *Chicago Manual of Style* as his basis for citation form; and Melvin Page of East Tennessee State University provides a guide specifically for History and the Humanities. In Europe, Mark Wainwright of Cambridge University tries to bring some control of citation style for Internet sources. Citation forms in practice followed several years behind changes in professional manuals (e.g., DODD, 1979, 1982; rev. 1990 for IASSIST). The Canadian History Association at the urging of José Igartua adopted a uniform but minimal citation style for electronic records, and for the Social Sciences the American Psychological Association has augmented its *APA Style Manual* for reference to electronic sources (and extensions have been added for Web sites, i.e., WEAPAS [Web Extension to American Psychological Association] by T. LAND). In 1994 an MLA-style citation format evolved in several literature related listservs, and although not yet an official standard of the Modern Language Association, a basic style sheet has been endorsed by the Alliance for

Computers & Writing (http://english.ttu.edu/acw.html. The basic format echoes the MLA arti-cle-in-compilation monographic rather than a serial format, where publisher name and address are replaced by protocol and addresses (e.g., http), followed by path, and in parentheses the file's retrieval or of visit to a particular WWW site.

More recently M. CROUSE has surveyed most of these ongoing projects for historians, with particular attention to their deference to the condensation of the *Chicago Manual* by Kate Turabian (sixth ed., 1996), which so many use for undergraduate teaching. Crouse relies on LI & CRANE, but makes some modifications, and he provides ample examples in a style sheet for historians. Of course, the problem is that a visitation date cannot be verified any more than one adds to a standard citation a checkout date from a library; and the state of the file when accessed cannot be reconstructed later. CROUSE (p. 22) cites HARNACK & KLEPPINGER for their caption "invisible revisability" to denote this problem. Thus, in the same way that the University of Colorado library homepage "Internet Connections" cautions users in citing elec-tronic information "Please note that only print resources can be considered authoritative" CROUSE concludes:

> Citations may, therefore, on occasion appear to be incorrect through no fault of the researcher. A reader may be hard pressed to distinguish between these innocent cases and cases in which the researcher is careless or even fraudulent in citing. For this reason, you should always give preference in citing to a printed version of the information. Cite electronic information only when a printed version does not exist or you cannot locate it or use it conveniently.

His advice is apparently for undergraduates writing history papers and the use of second-ary sources prevails, where concessions for convenience may override rules of evidence in any strict sense of the term; and the printed version so preferred, it would seem, should be some-thing more than a printout of the electronic source. Moreover, such well-meaning advice does not take into account the increasing change in scholarly communication where the print ver-sion is the analog of the primary electronic source (HURD & WELLER). This is why the Internet Archives project is so important, especially for historians using mutable electronic sources; it allows recall of an altered homepage (at least for the most visited sites) so one can check a source near to the date it was cited (approximate verification, but not the exact source). Or, consider the *Human Genome Project* that requires scientists to deposit their data in a data-bank precisely for its unaltered safekeeping and reverification. In such cases the electronic source should be considered the preferred source and any print version a copy at best but which very likely is altered in the process of printing and publication. Current efforts to create elec-tronic archives and electronic source repositories promise more reliable tracking and verifica-tion than calling up logbooks or in imitation of searching paper archives, having to request spe-cial services to search computer archives for backups at the home institution (a chancey proposition at best). In any case, since most sites are operating without an electronic archival program in place, this is not always possible—so we have citation style without bibliographic substance or verifiable content. This leaves the historian with information, but no evidence. In such dynamic media where access cannot be duplicated and content cannot be captured or replicated as presented before, the next best option to be able to retrieve still shots or time-set data views from electronic archives or third-party repositories such as the Internet Archives.

Regardless of this problematic issue of "revistability," a citation form can be no better than the data elements discernible in a source or bibliographic apparatus designed by a site's Webmaster or file provider. Most citation style sheets have not addressed the issue of file head-ers, self-dating update postings, title-page design, and homepage standards, etc., so even with a citation style agreed upon, the quality of metadata captured therein is still problematic. Some of the idiosyncrasy prevalent in electronic source creation, conveyance, and referencing may be normalized as Web pages and electronic sources are catalogued by librarians using such software as MARCIT (Nichols Technologies, Inc.), which allows one to view a site and cata- log it using a template which translates data elements into MARC formats for merging with online catalogs. It would be ideal if designers and creators filled out such catalog records for their own work at the time of release, like prepublication cataloging in books. Nevertheless, such cataloging provides metadata for retrieval more than authentification. These electronic forms fail in capturing the essence of older citation practices, namely reference for repeated retrievability of the same source, in the same form and format, unalterable, or when the file is not retrievable in the form originally cited, then reproducibility for verification and firsthand examination. Moreover, the citation style forms coming into place are for enumerative bibli- ography only. These should ideally dovetail into an advanced analytical bibliographic format or descriptive methodology (an electronic equivalent to Fredson Bower's scholarly bibliogra- phy, or extension of GASKELL's guide) so one could have for electronic media a counterpart for bibliographic authentification of print sources. Finally, it should be noted that most of these citation forms do not capture the kind of metadata specified in the new electronic Diplomatics (DURANTI; BLOUIN & DELMAS, eds.) advocated for the description of electronic archives.

Attention to citation style for electronic sources seems to assume that practices in citing print sources are so well established that they need little improvement. This is not the case, especially when sampling the variety of styles by discipline, language group, and national cul- tures, *vade mecum* tendencies among authors, and lack of strict editing for total quality con- trol by editors. Bibliography, like cataloging, is related to citation standards and practices and is an exacting art in its attention to detail, form, and style. Its discipline is too often unappre- ciated by historians and others who have likened it to mere list-making—and whose biblio- graphic habits very likely reflect this attitude. The practice of scholarly bibliography breeds respect and appreciation for the discipline involved. A standard requires more than consensus, but rather continued imitative practice. Key historical associations are in a position to set stan- dards, but as already noted, the American Historical Association, Organization of American Historians, etc., have not been active in this arena. Yet AHA's publications do establish quasi- standards through imitation and by virtue of their prestige and the stature of the organization.

Citation practices as exemplified by the *American Historical Review* could be enhanced sig- nificantly for retrieval purposes. *AHR* style is still quite traditional. Bibliographies are not pro- vided; citations are buried in footnotes. Review citation syntax includes: first and last name./quoted article title./italicized monograph title./locality of publication:/publisher name./year./pagination./ price. Citations in notes inconsistently supply state or country with localities, but omit publishers. One might contrast this format with APA style prevalent in the Social Sciences, with variations in engineering (IEEE) and information science (ASIS) for bib- liographies with complete citation data and parenthetic or hyperlinked reference by author name and date qualifier to full bibliographic entries listed only once. The syntax is as follows: last name, first name initials./(year).//article title./italicized monograph title./locality, state: pub- lisher; year.//pagination./price. ISBN; ISSN; CODEN; LC record numbers. Neither AHA, OAH, or ASIS list keywords for indexing and abstracting, but ASIS presents abstracts and bib- liographies. The AHA note form allows more explication, like a running hypertext, while APA style is largely for citations alone but can be expanded to include foot/endnotes with the same notation form in them as used in the text. *AHR* form could be improved by inclusion of certain features of the APA/ASIS variant, especially name standardization and inversion (surname first) and acquisition codes for document retrieval. More importantly, titles in Information Science are usually descriptive and straightforward, although authors are often addicted to their own sub-language and technical jargon. However, such entitling usually contains key words and a structured syntax that favors information retrieval from searching title entries only. The pen- chant in History is to use metaphor or catchy main titles for marketing, with the real descriptors after a colon in a subtitle. Content is often obscured rather than clarified by such practice. Likewise, Information Science abstracts tend to use whatever standardized vocabulary exists for the field in which the work falls, with tightly structured syntax and relatively simple sentence structure. Language use in abstracting by historians often reflects the character of the article like a précis or extract, so that the abstract does not always present an alternative pathway in information retrieval, so that retrieval of their work in electronic form is more dependent on term matching and searching is always more ambiguous.

European bibliographic citation habits are especially troublesome because of national preferences (or lack thereof) combined with those of the disciplines, but also because of a nonchalant attitude breeding inconsistency in data elements, incomplete data, and nonstandardization even in historical computing literature where one might expect greater precision. Both AHC and CNRS communications, for example, display erratic tracings and grave inconsistency in forms and style. Citations to electronic sources still lack standard formats and data elements, so online searches are greatly misconstrued. Authors, reviewers and abstractors do not use standardized vocabularies (e.g., *ASIS Thesaurus for Library and Information Science,* MILSTEAD, 1994; and many disciplines, such as Education, Psychology, Sociology, now have disciplinary thesauri) to describe these information science aspects of historical scholarship. Four distinct parallel vocabularies can be identified for historians, social scientists, computer scientists, and information scientists and their allies, librarians and archivists. These reflect quite different taxonomies, often more mental than explicit, about the same subjects. Therein topics are subordinated to different headings, variant terms are used synonymously, with little correspondence to standard headings used in libraries and archives. Classification and terminological tools are still lacking for collating diverse vocabularies, and mere term matching is an inadequate search procedure.

Consider the bibliography of computing in History since this relates so centrally to the idea of Historical Information Science. In searching for literature relating computing, research methods, and History, a pathway has been cleared with bibliographies by N. FITCH (1980), D. GARSON, C. L. CROSBY, S. R. GROSSBART, D. GREENSTEIN (1993a), and especially the ASSOCIATION OF HISTORY AND COMPUTING (AHC, 1993) *Historical Computing Bibliography* distributed electronically on diskette for the first time. This was being maintained by the Laboratoire d'Études et de Recherches sur l'Information et la Documentation (LERI-DOC) of the Université de Liège led by C. DESAMA (PASLEAU, 1987-1993). Unfortunately the initial AHC bibliographic database using Idealist software to manage a bibliography of more than 4,500 entries, is accessible only by word-matching, not genuine indexing; authority control is lacking; and many citations contain data entry errors, misattributions, and incomplete data. The 1995 update (covering 1994 contributions to 35 journals in socioeconomic history, linguistics within the humanities but not information science, and some social sciences but nothing from computer science) provides 629 citations, of which about a third contain bibliographic errors and deficiencies. A laudable project, it displays many of the classic problems in enumerative bibliography that are not rectifiable merely by computerization. Historians in Information Science must handle information precisely, for their own credibility if nothing else. Moreover, once such bibliographic databases are assembled and citation forms are standardized, these lend themselves to bibliometric analysis. This bibliographic foundation, therefore, not only underpins historical research and writing, but it is necessary for advances in the empirical or bibliometric study of historical literature, discourse between historians and scholarly communications, and the changing nature of the profession and discipline.

These aforementioned bibliographies, especially those that are classified, provide a framework for defining and delimiting Historical Information Science as related to the Social Sciences, but they largely ignore archival, library, museum, or other varieties of Information Science and therefore seem not to explore a wide range of potentially relevant research and applicable tools. This is partially because of the narrow identification of historical computing as simply the use of computers for historical research, rather than within the more holistic framework of Historical Information Science. They mistakenly limit their technical outreach to Computer Science but omit Computer and Electrical Engineering, largely to obtain what they need for project design and database management; but very little is accomplished inside History, even among the most devoted computing *aficionados*, that would qualify as Computer Science. That is a rare activity, and those with this technical capability easily migrate from History to the greater monetary rewards of the information profession and industry. In all, the bibliographic guides checked for computing applications to historical and art and literary history subjects include more than 6,000 citations, presumably a selective sample, but still no more than 2 percent of the available monographic literature. Moreover, such scholarly activity is growing exponentially and is becoming so integrated into scholarship overall, that computer methods and applications *per se* are not searchable qualifiers. These might be added to TIBBO's list (1994) of indexable elements for documents written by historians so retrieval can be performed as in archival indexing, around functional and operational aspects of documentation (as stressed by SAMUELS; BRUEMMER & HOCHHEISER; BEARMAN and other archivists, as distinct from the older structural analysis school represented by SCHELLEN-BERG, M. C. NORTON, etc.).

Of the various indexing and abstracting services, ABC-CLIO's *Historical Abstracts* and *America: History and Life* remain invaluable. It should be noted, however, that because of the nature of the field of History, the early distrust of abstracting by historians, and resistance to bibliographic and linguistic controls, ABC-CLIO chose not to develop History thesauri for either tool or to link archaic and modern language in their indexing. Term searching allows retrieval of author-used terms in titles, but notoriously most authors fail to take online information retrieval into account when entitling their studies. Otherwise term matches are with those selected by the abstractors, none of whom are guided by thesauri as a matter of policy. Other discipline-based tools than these comprehensive services must be used for specific subject domains, however, and in these subjects retrieval becomes even more problematic. In most cases these services provide access through term matching and limited use of standardized subject descriptors. In the general and specialized index and abstract services covering History, subjects are usually persons, places, and things, sometimes ideas, and rarely the methods, techniques, or technology used in the research. Computer-based methods are easily accessible only if the article is specifically on that topic. Even then, consistency in naming is lacking.

One might couple these discipline-based tools for History with *Library and Information Science Abstracts* (*LISA*), despite marginalization therein of our topics. New methods and technical applications can be found in *Computer Abstracts*, and in-depth investigations into the technologies themselves can be pursued through IEEE sources and *Computer and Electrical Engineering Abstracts*, but "history" in these indexes seldom appears and when it does, usage is commonly associated with computer memory and log mechanisms. Consequently, historical computing is not easily searched in modern information systems. *Revue historique* carries articles of interest that merge historical and archival interests, and the French journal that comes closest to the goal of inter-disciplinary study of the history of information, apart from the history of archives, libraries, and museums or the institutional aspect of such study for which there are many exemplars, is *L'Information historique*. These do not focus on primarily on research methodology, however, and therefore have no particular regard for the scientific aspects of historical studies or computer methods which tend to be found in those journals with Social Science orientations. For these concerns relevant articles are found predominantly in a handful of English-language journals (e.g., the OAH *American History* list [1988] is too limited and inbred): cf., *Historical Methods* (1978-) and *History and Theory* (1961-) generally, and more specifically *Social Science History* (1976-) and the *Journal of Interdisciplinary History* (1970-). These are the most fruitful for theoretical discussions in computing methods and interpretation.

The *Journal of Interdisciplinary History (JIH)*, having recently celebrated its twenty-fifth anniversary at the American Historical Association's 1995 conference, grew out of a 1966 discussion in the *Times Literary Supplement* on "New Ways in History." This set the tone "in the 'New History' style" for the next decades including special symposia on *Marriage and Fertility* and *Climate and History* (both 1980); *Hunger and History* (1983); *Art and History*, (1986); and *The Origin and Prevention of Wars* (1986). None has ever focused, however, specifically on historical information, its generation, structure, dissemination, etc.; and the articles indicate a traditional application of new methodology and computerization to fields defined as always within pre-established boundaries. Inter-disciplinarity has meant crossing these boundaries, more than the creation of new hybrids or genuinely new disciplines emerging from such border crossings. There is, however, a certain distinctiveness about scholarship at the edge of established disciplines in frontier zones. Nevertheless, contributions to *JIH* are predominantly from Americanists and American scholars who adhere to the traditional framework of historical studies and simply import methodology from the Social Sciences; there is little to indicate any engagement of modern Information Science or the hybrid of statistics and computational methodology called *Data and Knowledge Engineering* (cf., other IEEE publications; see KRUSKAL & TANUR for statistical terms and concepts). A quick comparison between terms now in use in information fields and in History reveals a linguistic gulf that no computer will bridge. This is a human and perception problem more than a technical issue, namely in giving proper credit to method and technique in historical research, and when these are borrowed from another discipline, to adopt the latter's terminology as well in order to talk across disciplinary boundaries and thereby to provide indexing as a means to follow such interdisciplinary discourse from one domain to the other.

Robert Fogel, in celebrating the journal's quarter-century of publishing cross-disciplinary work, turned naturally to counting and produced a short quasi-bibliometric rendition of its history. Its 20,000 pages have conveyed 734 articles "at the leading edge," claims FOGEL. They covered all fields, but the subject foci were predominantly North American and European (32 percent), while Asian and African inclusions constituted only 5 percent. The chronological focus is also predominantly modern and contemporary; ancient and medieval studies contributed only 4 percent. Subject orientations were political, economic, and demographic; and the quantification bent meant that 47 percent of its articles carried some kind of graphs and tables. But while these History journals focus on methodology, application, innovation, and new interpretation, they seldom get very technical. Notable exceptions include *JID*'s publication of D. LARSON's study which makes use of modern technical equipment for measuring climatic conditions in California to cross-check the accuracy of narrative reports from ship logs, miner's diaries, and missionary records for the past three centuries. Generally, however, for applicable technology one must turn to other sources.

More specific technical material appears in the conference proceedings and publications of the International Association for History and Computing's *History and Computing* (1989-) and the Cliometric *Social Science History* and *History Microcomputer Review*. The Humanities side is revealed in *Computers and Humanities* (*CHUM*, 1966-) coupled with *Literary and Linguistic Computing* and language reviews more nationally circumscribed like the *T.A.L. (Traitément Automatique des Langues)*. The largest dimension, the Social Sciences, is best covered by the *Social Science Computer Review* (*SSCORE*, 1982-) and its predecessors *Computing and the Social Sciences* and *Social Science Microcomputer Review*. *Historical Methods* (1978-) and *The Journal of Interdisciplinary History* should be read together to cover American historiography and methodological developments. A new journal, *Rethinking History*, may be relevant as it develops. *Technology and Culture*, the quarterly of the Society for the History of Technology, intermittently carries relevant studies, and its periodic "Current Bibliography in the History of Technology" special issues by H. LONGWOOD (1994, 1995) are especially useful for coverage in its sections number Two, 12, and 13, respectively, on Historiography and Documentation, Computing Technology, and Communication and Records (see also DAY & MCNEIL's biographic dictionary for the history of technology).

These titles can be compared with European publications, e.g., the Dutch *Gescheidenis en Informatica* journal of the Low Countries Association for History and Computing, the *Histoire et Mensure* of France's CENTRE NATIONAL DE LA RECHERCHE SCIENTIFIQUE (1990-), and the companion newsletter *Memoire Vive* of the ASSOCIATION FRANÇAISE POUR L'HISTOIRE ET L'INFORMATIQUE (1988-) which has hosted important international conferences at Bordeaux (1988), Montpellier (1989), and Rennes (1994). The bilingual *Historische Sozialforschung/Historical Social Research* (1979-) organ of QUANTUM is often explicitly concerned with empirical research methods and electronic data (cf., the related series, *Historish-Sozialwissenschaftliche Forschungen* from the Center by the same name), while the French *Annales* (New series, 1969-) often concerns methodology in a broader, philosophical sense and especially conceptualization and interpretation, but ironically often displays a certain inbreeding within French language circles and a lack of ready correspondence with German and English materials. To relate History to information and instructional technologies, turn to *EDUCOM Review, Cause/Effect, Education Technology*, and the *T.H.E. Journal*. Although not very accessible, *Archivi & Computer* (1991-) is devoted specifically to archival automation and data processing. *Archivaria* (ATHERTON), the Canadian professional organ, is considered by some to be the best journal in the archives field. The biannual *Archives & Manuscripts* provides an Australian perspective that is often at issue with European and American concepts (e.g., records continuum versus life cycle). Peruse *The American Archivist* (COX, 1994c), *Provenance* (SLY), *Archival Issues* (WURL), and *Primary Sources* (MCCRANK, 1994) for American electronic archives and archival automation (cf., COX's "Editor's Forum," 1994d, about these journals), plus the technical report series of national archives, international organizations like UNESCO's RAMP studies, and *Archives and Museum Informatics* (recently acquired by Kluwer Publishing).

Most countries have their own archives and professional organizations with their own respective journals, most of which seem to be trapped by language and culture within their own national traditions. This is limiting in some respects, but it is also natural for archives to reflect the cultures they document; however, a certain internationalism, like inter-disciplinarity, is a healthy antidote for nationalism and parochialism. Related developments in data archives can be monitored through the *IASSIST Quarterly*; this should be required reading for computing historians and social scientists, as well as electronic archivists (RULLER, p. 552). Otherwise, an alternative information strategy is to follow the publications of important historical research centers such as the Max-Planck-Institut für Geschichte in Göttingen; note particularly its important series *Halbgraue Reihe zur Historischen Fachinformatik* which, unfortunately, seems to be quite inaccessible in the United States. It might be noted also that the largest set of related publications is in teaching History with computers, or teaching computer use for History—without an obvious correspondence in results, i.e., computer-based historical research. Historians have taken to computers as a replacement for their typewriters, slides and overhead transparencies, etc., to enhance routine performance more than to change fundamentally their usual operations or to enhance their thinking, methodology, or qualitative aspects of research. Not only have qualitative and quantitative research methods merged, but both have become heavily dependent on computer technology. BICKMAN & ROG; J. CRESWELL; J. MASON; W. NEUMAN; and others, have linked quantitative and quantitative approaches in social research methodology. DENZIN & LINCOLN's handbook of qualitative research remains a popular introduction to an increasingly wide range of methodologies and techniques now available with modern computer capabilities. MILLER & FREDERICKS see the development of qualitative research methodology as "social epistemology and practical inquiry." GUBRIUM speaks of the "new language of qualitative method" which might be compared profitably with VOGT's dictionary of statistics and methodology for the Social Sciences; SCHWANDT supplies the vocabulary in his dictionary *Qualitative Inquiry*. GOLDEN-BIDDLE & LOCKE focus on the composition of qualitative research, as a counterpart to the more extensive literature about statistical analysis and interpretation and on graphic representation.

Granted that computing assists research greatly, historians need to aware of the fundamental changes and controlling factors inherent in word processing, many of which are highlighted by M. HEIM's *Electronic Word*.

Perhaps the main change in computational research is an enlargement of scope in data collection and analysis over what is possible to comprehend in a noncomputerized operation. Little experimentation to develop genuinely new methodologies or operations in History is ongoing, although a few historians are adopting developments from other fields which are new to History. This is a problem related to the traditional framing of domains by a subject area defined by periods and places, with the subordination of research methodology to these, rather than to develop a comparative methodologies specialization in its own right. This could serve as a proper umbrella for history computing. The recent exploration of data sets and analysis at the Historical Informatics Laboratory in Moscow, about which more will be said later, is illustrative of such cross-disciplinary adaptation (GARSKOVA & BORODKIN). But pure research in historical methods and computer operations is almost nonexistent, even in History Departments which claim to specialize in methodology; most of their output is more historiographic. What is needed, of course, is a laboratory to test new methodology, software applicability, and trial runs of test data to confirm computer-assisted analyses already published through re-runs, and to refine existing techniques. In short, we need research centers to do today what Franklin Jameson wanted History to accomplish a century ago, using modern information technology and historical data.

Lamentably, what has lapsed is the interdisciplinary forum in which information scientists in all Arts, Humanities, and Social Sciences once conversed with each other (and health sciences too, which related medicine especially to the Social Sciences through Demography): the series of international conferences on *Databases in the Humanities and Social Sciences (ICDBHSS*: cf., RABEN & MARKS, 1980; the intervening Spanish conference at the Facultad Politécnico de Madrid went unpublished; ALLEN, 1985; MOBERG, 1987; MCCRANK, 1989; BEST, MOCHMANN & THALLER, 1991) which was supposed to occur every other year in the United States and Europe. The brainchild of Joseph RABEN (1991), who continues to survey the broad landscape of humanities and social science computing, ICDBHSS proceedings were one of the best sources for reporting project development and encouraging cross-disciplinary information and technology transfer. The Cologne Computer Conference (BEST, MOCHMANN, THALLER), for example, brought together 500 participants worldwide into concurrent conferences: ICDBHSS (no. 6), AHC and INTERQUANT, and IFDO (International Federation of Data Organizations for the Social Sciences, no. 10). In 1994 a combined ACH and Association for Literary and Linguistic Computing (ALLC), founded in 1973 attracted 400 participants to the *Consensus ex Machina* conference in Paris to hear 140 speakers. The focus was still entirely on history and the humanities, largely on literary texts and statistical lexicology or leximetrics and stylistics without valuable intercourse with the Social Sciences or crossover into the Sciences through medical sciences. This need for the continuation of ICDBHSS or something on the same order, for cross-fertilization of ideas and technical applications to subject domains, both to foster technical transfer and to counteract current inbreeding, still exists. As is, historians at AHC, literature scholars at ACH, linguists at ALLC, social scientists at CSS, archivists at SAA, and librarians at ALA, ACRL, and Online conferences mostly talk with their own kind. ASIS often attracts an interesting mix, but where historians are underrepresented. Communicating across fields not only forces clarification of one's thought and discipline, and the use of incestuous jargon, but this sharing makes for a richer pool of ideas, approaches, and methods.

The History publication data also indicate how impossible it is to "cover" bibliographically any field within History without online retrieval and automated bibliographic control of historical literature. Although the claim is still made by some, it is preposterous. Even then, with systematic searching to identify priorities for one's reading list, the historian must either skim superficially and occasionally dive into the literature, or must be a voracious speed reader to gain depth and currency for a wider area. Historians may go through cycles of intense work with primary materials alternated with concentrated exploration of secondary literature, as needs change for course preparation and research projects. Reading habits tend to turn to the same core literature, however, and the disregard for formal access tools like indexes and abstracts would indicate that historians may be less prone to shift fields and explore new areas in any strategic manner or planned reading program. Few seem to set up their own Selective Dissemination of Information (SDI) services to canvas systematically broad fields or to operate inter-disciplinarily with simultaneous and equal coverage of both fields. This problem of mass is perhaps why most historians read narrowly in specific fields, and why they are consequently anxious about their obtaining adequate breadth even for generalized teaching.

The idealistic days described by Jesse H. Shera when historians could keep up with their field and leisurely explore others are long gone (SHERA). Yet historians still rely predominantly on reviews published in their own serials for their bibliographic surveys, even though in a typical year the AHA's *American Historical Review* (1895-) provides access to only about 800 books (e.g., 1993-94 academic year) or less than 7 percent of the total annual production. The Organization of American Historians' *Journal of American History* surveys 450 journal titles and reviews 600 books annually, so it assesses recent scholarship in American History on the basis of less than 10 percent of the available literature. This is presumably why, as mentioned before, H-Net participants are mounting an electronic review service with potentially 18,000 reviewers and readers. H-Net's goal would be to publish reviews electronically within six months of publication of the titles reviewed, and with any current awareness service, merge this with full-text retrieval of select files not protected by copyright which would be relevant to historians. It also seeks to create interactive reviewing, *à la* responses from authors, commentaries shared by reviewers, and even a readers' forum. Some see a "discussion thread" entwining such discussions, so that theoretically one review session could flow into another and expand indefinitely. They seek to change thereby the very nature of historical discourse until now. Four hundred reviews now form the core for such a beginning of a totally new reviewing strategy, but the scale of reviewing electronically is still inadequate given the scope of the subject and volume of production. In short, such reviewing at current rates will never come close to producing comprehensive online coverage. Discussions thus far have emphasized currency in electronic publishing but do not seem to realize the full potential of electronic reviewing for bibliometric analyses, other empirical approaches to content and discourse analyses, or objectified evaluation. Instead most historians tend to see the electronic forum simply as another but faster version of the reviewing business as usual. That, of course, would be a step forward. Now, however, even when historians supplement their coverage by reviews in specialized journals, they can perhaps survey but one quarter of historical literature through reviews. Most stay within their own fields, which demand enough of them.

A recent survey of faculty by BUDD & CONNAWAY attempted to discover current attitudes about the use of networked information and collaboration. Overall, faculty in all disciplines tended to remain conservative, but this was particularly evident outside the sciences in the submission of research to electronic journals for publication in nontraditional media. However, they found some evidence to indicate the beginnings of a geographic and disciplinary broadening in collaboration because of the impact of networked information. It still seems too early if these are the beginnings of the grand transformation NEGROPONTE and others see as almost inevitable. In any case, historians (16 percent of the population surveyed) were queried along with faculty from English, Psychology, Sociology, Physics and Chemistry in this study about faculty taking to the Internet for communication, information retrieval, and publication. BUDD & CONNAWAY (pp. 847-848) found that nearly 92 percent had access to the Internet and that 87 percent of the respondents now address some source via the Internet more than once weekly, but only a small percentage (13.7 percent) subscribe to electronic journals themselves. More of them, 23.4 percent, have read the content of electronic journals (17 percent do so from printouts). A majority of respondents (62.4 percent) report that their universities are not particularly willing to review electronic publishing equitably with print in their promotion and tenure evaluations. Yet 46.7 percent respond that their work patterns have changed since using networked information; of those who have changed work habits, 47 percent have now coauthored papers. Sixty percent believe that their disciplinary communities are undergoing change similarly, in reaching out beyond previous circles for collaboration and in becoming even more inter-disciplinary. Little change is detected in the pressure on faculty to publish, from 1987 when 87 percent of faculty in higher education reported to the American Council of Learned Societies that they felt strong or extremely strong pressure to publish (MORTON & PRICE). Physicists purport to see less change than other groups, but this is because their work changed earlier and they see current conditions as continuing established trends. This is not the case for historians, however, who are the most conservative of the faculties surveyed.

Historians, like their partners in English, Sociology and Psychology, are more aware of current change because change has come later to them than those in the hard sciences where online retrieval and networking in one form or the other has been predominant for more than a decade. Physicists, for example, rely most heavily on electronic journals (32 percent of them are subscribers, more than twice the number in other fields), in contrast to 5.8 percent in the aforementioned fields (of course, the number of electronic journals, 675 in 1995, is still relatively small: KING & KOVACS). Historians reported the least reliance on or regular use of electronic services to seek data and information sources of any of the fields studied (26.3 percent, compared with 31.8 percent in Psychology, 44.4 percent in English, 52.5 percent in Chemistry, 56.3 percent in Physics, and surprisingly, 64.3 percent in Sociology. Responses may be skewed because of proportions of older faculty in some disciplines; assistant professors report more Internet use (53.9 percent) than those in their senior ranks (44.9 percent for associate professors, and 37.9 percent for professors). Such increased use among younger historians can be placed in comparative perspective with trends in other disciplines in LAZINGER, BAR-ILAN & PERITZ's recent study of Internet activity. When asked about using networked information to seek funding for research, historians again admitted to the least use (18.8 percent), below English (25 percent) and Sociology (36.6 percent) faculties who were all well below responses in the sciences (50 percent+).

Regarding collaboration, 23.2 percent of historians queried thought that more collaboration was occurring, resulting in greater collegiality in their discipline. This again was low, in contrast to English (38.1 percent), Sociology (48.6 percent), Chemistry (50.5 percent), Psychology (55.2 percent), and Physics (69.6 percent). An interesting aside is an overall gender difference, in that women faculty search online library catalogs (OPACs) more than their male counterparts (69.4/56.7 percent), but this could reflect the greater number of women in text-oriented study fields rather than in the hard sciences. Women also perceive more change going on around them than do men. Historians, psychologists, and sociologists are positive in seeing change around them, but chose to aggregate responses, while those in Chemistry, English, and Physics report the most perceived changes for their disciplines. The greatest changes have been in intra-campus followed by inter-campus e-mail, more than the use of the Internet for access to sources. That may change as digital library and electronic archives initiatives provide more content in electronic form for Internet/WWW access. For now, however, historians are dependent on traditional means of information access and scholarly exchange. Change is slow in History. Habit prevails.

Electronic information sources for historians are a distant third in importance behind serials and especially books, their *sine qua non*. History books are already reviewed more than those in other fields: nearly a mean of five reviews per book in contrast to lows of 0.5 in the field of Mathematics to a range of means from 2.5-3.0 for other fields like Biology, Business, and

Education (THORNTON, p. 55). While some positive correlation has been found in research relating reviewing to purchasing by libraries, librarians are increasingly skeptical of reviews as a means of selection not only because of their lag time, but because Thornton's research finds little significant correlation between reviewing in all sources with circulation or use, and no correlation at all between reviews of history books in the scholarly review journals of the field with library circulation. Such studies have resulted in several recommendations for librarians engaged in collection development, which aims at use rather than comprehensive coverage to shift their time from using reviews in selection to promotion, and since comprehensive acquisitions can be geared toward publisher supply strategies rather than item selection, collection development librarians may well ignore reviews altogether for acquisitions work.

This means that History reviews have less utility than historians generally think and that their main purpose is to create a literature of criticism that is used primarily by historians themselves. This suggests a sociology of scholarly activity that is potentially damning for academe, if the divergence between prescription and practice is as widely spread as inferred from such library and archives use studies. Greater congruence between reviewing and use may result from electronically linking reviews to bibliography and prepublication cataloging, which could include encouraging publishers who solicit prepublication reviews for marketing purposes to publish the full reviews with the book publication, rather than simply extracts for advertising purposes. If linkage were also created between electronic reviews and MARC records in library catalogs, to augment spartan description in the assignment of subject headings, we would be moving toward the kind of holistic tool which would integrate reviews better into the bibliographic process. If citation tracings could also be linked to the main bibliographic records with reviews, and if these citations could pull with them the relevant text rather than merely identifying a citation in a footnote or endnote, one would have the running commentary within the core secondary literature combined with formal criticism. As is, reviewing functions more as a process of literary criticism and forms a remote tertiary source too unconnected by timing and placement to the main literature to be useful to a broader constituency. In short, historians must stop thinking so traditionally about reviewing as such, and think more in terms of designing and implementing a holistic History information system.

Historians not only study the past, but their reading is often historical in the sense of its being several years behind current production. Their current reviewing habits do not create a viable means of information retrieval for collection development, nor a current readers' advisory service. Moreover, reviews tend to duplicate each other and the lack of a coordinated strategy for reviewing other than distribution roughly by subject foci of books matched to those of journals means that all combined they do not produce anything close to a comprehensive review mechanism. Meanwhile, the problem of mass continues to perplex librarians and historians alike. Graduate students are simply intimidated, and, as LIMERICK expressed in the *Chronicle of Higher Education* not long ago, many historians like L. HUNT feel frustrated that they can never catch up. Indeed, they cannot even stay abreast. And librarians are left to ponder their expenditures of institutional and public funds to build comprehensive research collections of books that accumulate into ever larger collections, but for which some shocking studies have revealed half never circulate from their shelves within five years of purchase and cataloging (KENT *ET AL.*). They are bought because faculty expect reviewed books to be there (PARKER) in case of need, not that they necessarily are to be used. THORNTON's more recent work more reassuringly indicated at least five circulations for some 80 percent of the history books purchased by the Auraria academic library in Denver, even though those which were unreviewed circulated just as much as those which were not. Nevertheless, this means that up to 20 percent of history books bought are never read, and librarians have had to accept the famous truism of R. W. Trueswell's early bibliometric findings that 20-40 percent of a collection satisfies 80-100 percent of demand; this remains so with no significant impact on usage of reviewing in historical or any other journals.

Richard Cox has suggested to me that the same truism exists in archives, where perhaps only 20 percent of the pertinent literature is read. Far less would be applied. The recent study of *The American Archivist* by an SAA taskforce purports a much higher percentage of SAA's membership which reads this particular journal (TIBBO *ET AL.*, 1996). This may be because the scope of professional reading by American archivists is very narrow; they tend to read in only a few journals. They, like historians, rely on reviews which cover only a small fraction of pertinent literature, and citation studies of archival publications show little reference outside their native language. It is ironic, given this devote readership by archivists of a handful of archives journals, that the editors of these journals all complain about the dearth of publishable material. Historians whose field is other than the history of their own country and culture understandably read more broadly and in more languages, but archivists tend to be singularly parochial as specialists in their own nationalist histories and the subjects represented in their bailiwicks. They tend, therefore, to be more culture bound, less inclined to explore literatures in foreign languages, and narrow in their professional reading interests (to put the foreign language problem for English-speaking researchers in perspective, see GARFIELD & WELLJAMS-DOROF; etc.). No studies of which I am aware explore their leisure reading or outside interests; ironically, professional reading surveys framed from the vantage point of the profession, i.e., archives, would regard reading in history, other than what pertained to the content of the archives, as "outside" the professional scope. In this regard certainly archivists, and other professionals as well (e.g., librarianship), among whom many are trained as historians, do not regard themselves as historians.

The implications of such issues in bibliographic control, awareness, and use for historiography are enormous, potentially devastating, and at the very least disconcerting. Yet, few historians study the problem of History information, its production and dissemination, and standards of bibliographic control; strategies to balance surveying, speed reading interspersed with selective intensive reading or critical appraisals, reliance on extracts and abstracts; or new computer-assisted methods of scanning and downloading, building personalized textbases of secondary literature, using Boolean and other strategies for searching, and using hyperlinks to relate material of special interest to them. What is the relationship between the quasi-standards or values held by consensus rather than adherence to any comprehensive proscription, between evaluating historical writing, bibliographic control mechanisms, abstracting practice, etc., and these same procedures and practices in original research and examination of primary sources? We do not know. Continuity in historical research from the identification and retrieval of evidence through synthesis and interpretation, to scholarly communication and consumption, has not been studied scientifically. How are primary and secondary sources related in the research process? Can citation tracing, which has been studied more for other fields than History even though this is a common practice among historians, be automated more than through bibliographic linkages? Hypertext systems would seem to be an especially attractive enhancement of traditional reviewing in historical journals, since historians regularly link the works they review with other works and attempt to place them in larger trends, thematic contexts, and schools of thought (see the overview of hypertext by CONKLIN). Collaborative hypertext systems are available, e.g., *CHIRO* (MCKNIGHT, DILLON & RICHARDSON, 1990, 1991, and 1993, where they explore its psychological dimension). BELOVA & LAZAREV advocate hypertext as a means of electronic text archives management.

Systems analysis has influenced historical conceptualization of coherent units of study, and sometimes arguments for actual organic units, but the number of historians employing such methodology is relatively small (e.g., MCNEILL, 1976) and often display the influence of science and technology in their approaches (i.e., A. CROSBY, 1986). In the most recent discussions of historical periodization in 1995-96 (BENTLEY with reaction by P. MANNING), might have been placed into the intellectual arena of classification theory, but discussants seem unaware of the vast literature in classification theory (e.g., how classification and discrimination are entwined intellectual processes; cf., D. J. HAND, 1981, for discriminate analysis for classification and the construction of classification rules, HAND, 1997). MANNING (p. 778) cites P. CURTIN as among the most consistent of leading world historians in referring to "cultural areas," when he notes that some historians like Clark WISSLER, influenced by anthropology and attempts like MURDOCK's to classify cultural units by core characteristics (cf., the outline in the *Human Relations Area Files,* 1982, 1987, and ethnographic *Atlas,* 1981), have attempted to be systematic in their terminologies, but most make no such attempt. Taxonomies are not widely employed; terminologies are used less, and self-appointed authority for idiosyncratic definition rules the day. Hence concept indexing in historical literature has been problematic, and hyperlinks in electronic media reflect these problems of terminology—imprecision in usage, ambiguity and variable meanings at different times and in different places, and discontinuity (problems not dissimilar to those addressed by CHEN *ET AL.,*1998). Likewise, text processing assists historians in production, but the reverse is not true that historians use computers extensively to help them assimilate this greater quantity of literature. Nor do they seem to be teaching their students how to solve such overwhelming problems as information overload.

Searching is a different psychological and cognitive skill related directly to information storage and retrieval mechanisms and only indirectly to content; it is distinct from research or content analysis (KRIPPENDORF), but the two are often confused in history teaching and practice. Systematic browsing (BATES, 1981; MARCHIONINI, 1989), not random wandering, is a better approach to searching for ideas than for information; these two objectives are distinct. As Marcia Bates observed, "area scanning" in collections is similar to rapid perusals of full-text material to gain "a quick gestalt" or profile, much like librarians would use an encyclopedia article as a précis and prelude to a literature search (BATES, 1989, p. 417). Browsing and scanning skills are related to abstracting, and modern information systems are being designed to enable such rapid surveying of electronic information (BELKIN & CROFT), which can be assisted by historical constructs in classification such as chronological ordering, historical and modern term linkage in indexing, and association by genealogical connections or provenance. MARCHIONINI & SCHNEIDERMAN make the interesting distinction between "finding facts and browsing knowledge in hypertext systems." These are learnable and practical skills that are serious subjects of study (see the *ARIST* review by CHANG & RICE). They need to be incorporated explicitly and objectively in history teaching rather than being left at an unarticulated level of development or only a generalized capability implicit in historical reasoning. In a master's degree, certainly this basic skill of strategic information searching should be a required mastery because time, personal and that bought by others, must be expended wisely and efficiently partially to have time to browse and research, for serendipity and reflection, and for intellectual discourse at leisure. Historians, by not introducing students to standards of efficiency and economy as well as effectiveness in training them in searching and research, devalue their own talents, skills, and time. Resulting inefficiency may detract mightily from actual research and teaching, but few studies penetrate the information-seeking behavior of historians (habitual and otherwise), their values and attitudes, or their productivity measured against any objective standard. Consequently, reform is unlikely.

Library Science and Historian Use Studies

Although one may suspect that their values are such that the very thought of such critical self-appraisal is unappealing, in fact historians in the United States have been quite critical of themselves as users of modern information systems and services. Their own studies, however, have not been empirical, but have been largely a matter of conferencing to voice concerns and reach consensus and are occasionally bolstered by surveys. The few surveys on record are relatively limited, and few dovetail each other to make possible some sort of comparison over time. The AHA Committee on Graduate Education report by Dexter Perkins and John L. Snell in 1962 barely touched upon the issues raised in this work. The concerns voiced by historians did include the adequacy of research library resources, but their absence of concern about anything in the world of information technology suggests how unprepared the profession was for what was to transpire in the 1960s with mainframe computing and methodological advances in the Social Sciences. Little hint is provided of the controversies over Cliometrics which were to break out just a few years later. The introspection of American historians about information access other than library book budgets can be traced to the Belmont Conference of 1967 when the first survey research was conducted (of 300 historians contacted, only 50 responded; PERMAN, pp. 7-19).

The respondents then showed little interest in the bibliography of fields other than their own; most distrusted abstracts prepared by someone else and therefore refused to use index and abstracting services; ironically, they nevertheless liked lists of selected readings, and they cherished peer reviews. These preferences persisted despite visionaries like E. BOEHM who from his History incubus emerged as a pioneer in History information management, first as founder of the American Bibliographic Center and ABC-CLIO Press (R. BOEHM) that produces *America: History and Life* and *Historical Abstracts* (modeled initially after *Chemical Abstracts*; cf., FALK), and then as an educational leader in the information field (exemplified also by BOEHM & BUCKLAND) as founder of the accredited International School of Information Management (ISIM) that has been very creative in distance learning operations. However, at first librarians rather than historians were the major users and promoters of ABC-CLIO's indexes and abstracting tools. Conversion has been slow (TIBBO, 1991, pp. 298-300). Historians remained more interested in their own original research than current control of their subject literature; most develop their own customized if idiosyncratic means of keeping abreast of their fields. Such approaches, however, do not transfer well into systematic graduate training in bibliography, source criticism, and historical method.

RUNDELL's findings more than 25 years ago (1970) on the eve of the microcomputer revolution and the impact of the new Social Sciences on History, seemed to echo JAMESON's caveats which, although made a century before, still seem so relevant today. While great historians waged intellectual war on each other over issues in historical methodology and the philosophy of History, they did little to prepare their students for computer-assisted research, automated information retrieval, and new methodologies to accommodate new information technology. When I began working with Walt Rundell and his colleagues at the University of Maryland only five years after his study, he still had no clear idea about the relationship between studies of information storage and retrieval and the training of historians in information searching; online searching was just being introduced by the library science faculty but was unpracticed by historians there, and the History department had no computing facilities of its own. The potential for the alliance between History and Information Science was thought of almost entirely in terms of employment opportunities for historians in archives, rather than any strong intellectual reinforcement. Indeed, many of my colleagues wondered skeptically about the whole enterprise, and had little understanding of the early evolution of Information Science or its relationship between it and Library and Archival Science. Rundell, a historian open to new possibilities as his exploration of photographic archives to document his *Early Texas Oil* shows, admitted to me that historians were likely to appreciate training for better use of libraries and having historians as archivists, but the research undertaken by historians crossing over to the School of Library and Information Service, foreign territory across the mall, was not of interest to his colleagues in History. It was, after all, not History.

With hindsight, one might have expected more progressive attitudes and a somewhat different development and closer relationship earlier, but partnerships are often a long time in the making. Historians as library users remained material and source oriented, with less concern for and understanding of library organization, development, and technical services. Since at least one study (BOOSINGER) suggested a positive correlation between faculty who publish often with rising expectations of their peers and students in accomplished library use skills; the build-up of demand for historians to publish earlier and more, may have prompted more interest in user instruction in libraries and archives, but this self-serving attitude hardly promoted research perceived to be Information Science. Historians, of course, may not always see the connection between traditional library use and the modern and broader issue of information searching that today requires different conceptualization, basic algebra, linguistic skills, and use of computers everywhere. At the root, however, remains the critical skill and art of ennumerative bibliography which fell into disfavor as an historical endeavor.

The improvement of bibliography as a scholarly pursuit and bibliographic instruction in History (D'ANIELLO; cf., R. HARMON) was the aim of the Association for the Bibliography of History (ABH, 1976-), an affiliate of the American Historical Association (AHA). AHA (historians in America, studying all fields) and its ally, OAH (Organization of American Historians, (mostly historians of America, i.e., the United States), continue the reliance on reviews which their own membership produces). Historians' bibliographic enterprises to control intellectually their historical literature (e.g., *American History: A Bibliographic Review)* show a preference to synthesis and evaluation in such reviews, while distrusting evaluative abstracts and selective indexing. The reported contradictions are puzzling. Some misconstrue bibliography with mere listing or inventory control. In any case, AHA has never mounted a bibliographic effort comparable to the Modern Language Association (MLA) or undertaken documentation studies as thorough as the German inquiry into the intellectual and bibliographic accessibility of the literature of History (JUNGMANN-STADLER).

RUNDELL's gentlemanly critique was reinforced by subsequent Library Science studies of historians' poor knowledge of general reference tools, lack of search strategies, idiosyncratic use of libraries, and continued reliance on browsing. STIEG's survey of nearly a thousand historians (1981) provided one of the most severe; her findings indicated the likelihood that historians advising their undergraduate students about bibliographic searching for their term-paper projects, would misinform and misdirect their students because classroom faculty lacked basic reference skills themselves. Most recently, based on his observations working over a decade in reference at two academic libraries, D. BLEWETT addressed the AHA membership (1995, p. 25): "I have come to share the conclusion of others that history students, particularly graduate students, while perhaps skilled in evaluation and writing, are sadly lacking when it comes to information-gathering techniques."

Whereas in Rundell's day most historians distrusted computing as a means of information searching, now historians everywhere rely on automated techniques for bibliographic searching and increasingly for document retrieval also. The conservative bent of historians in resisting automated bibliographic control and surrogation in abstracts rather than reliance on reviews is displayed today in similar terms, arguments, and dispositions. Despite lipservice to the use of computers, for example, many historians still harbor strong reservations about the efficacy of computing and statements again and again betray a substantial discomfort with modern information technology. Once won over for information gathering, they are now fearful of computer-assisted weeding and information appraisal for selection into their analyses even though modern historians are swamped by the mass of records they confront. Most recently historian Paul Johnson articulated this distrust in the FORBES *ASAP* interviews:

> It is impossible to exaggerate the growing reliance on electronic storage systems for research historians. As more and more primary sources, printed and unprinted, are put into these systems, the research historian will gradually cease to be peripatetic. Rather, he will use his time, energy, and money traveling to and form libraries, public records offices, and other depositories of material. He soon will be able to carry out most of his research—eventually perhaps all of it—without leaving his study. Moreover, technology can also save precious time in classifying, analyzing, and presenting his material. It should make the results more accurate and dependable, for most errors in historical research arise form manual transcription

[i.e., "task performance error" in ROBBIN & FROST-KUMPF's typology]. The main result, however, will be an increase in the productivity of research historians and thus in the volume of specialist studies they publish.

...the synoptic historian is greatly dependent on modern technical aids "at second hand." But such technology has only limited, direct, firsthand value to general historians....The research historian filters and eliminates a vast amount of these activities and arranges what remains in some kind of order. New technology plays an enormously important part in this preliminary process.

But the synoptic historian, using all his analytical and literary skills, conducts the final process of selection that actually brings the period to meaningful and significant life. New technology does not help much here, except in a purely ancillary way. Ability to grasp the main themes while snatching at significant detail, to track the main themes while snatching at significant detail, to track the narrative camera over a huge area and time span at one moment, then move into close focus the next, to encapsulate character, to get to the root of institutional change, to identify key moments—the hinges on which history turns—to allow the historian actors to speak for themselves, all are techniques that conjure up vivid pictures in the reader's mind. These are feats of literary skill and historical judgment, which no machinery, however, sophisticated, can achieve.

The synoptic historian...sits on top of a vast pyramid of material compiled by researchers constantly using all the relevant new technologies. In the end, he has to reduce the pyramid to a few thousand cogent facts and figures by using his own unaided wits (FORBES *ASAP*, pp. 41, 69).

In other words, as noted previously, computers are used as a faster means to the same ends as before, with no substantial alteration in how historians think or work. P. Johnson, and so many other historians, see computing as an access tool, word processor, and assist to publishing in traditional formats. Computing may be used to gather information but not to eliminate it; and its organizational capabilities in database management systems are used only in perfunctory fashion. No indication of recent advances in Artificial Intelligence, Decision Support Systems, Expert Systems, use of decision trees, or techniques such as data mining, weighting, and filtering, etc., are present in Johnson's interview or any of the historians interviewed in 1996 by *FORBES*. The purpose of the interviews was to explore the prospects for digital technology in particular, but not a single historian interviewed seemed to know precisely what digital technology entailed. Moreover, all missed the point of computing, in that they chose to speak to the limitations of the machine more than to the enabling aspects of computers (as if "the computer" had a mind of its own or did anything by itself). The capacity of the computing talked about seems ever so limited, as though the computers historians had in mind were PC 386s or older. Acquaintance with software options seems equally limited. All juxtapose the historian versus the machine, or at best describe their computing experience as if it were an uneasy alliance.

John Keegan likewise stresses this common theme that computers cannot replace judgment, falsely assuming that this were ever suggested in the first place:

The excitement generated by Cliometrics, however, quickly passed, for the excellent reason that the one essential activity at which computers are notoriously bad is interpretation. The mere multiplication of facts, however securely stored, however diversely categorized, does not assist but may actually detract from the ultimate effort a historian must make, which is to see the woods among the trees....They may indeed come through long hours before a computer screen. They will not come, however, in any digitized way corresponding to the working of the human thought process, which remains as mysterious as ever (FORBES *ASAP*, pp. 37, 69).

Here again, the historian is quick to see computers as threatening, as replacements, rather than as assistants and extensions of human abilities, and *the* computer as thing is the focus of attention rather than the process, operation, and functionality. This tendency to impart to a computer a magical power and a menacing character smacks of fetishism that is hardly reconcilable with a view of objectivity in History. On the other hand, note that "judgment" is always described as a human quality only, as if Artificial Intelligence cannot replicate human judgment even for repeated, routine, and basic operations. Nor is the more telling issue of direct versus indirect intervention in data manipulation and interpretation raised, and there seems to be a prevalent confusion between computing and automation which is aimed more at routine operations. These interviews, and other sources, reveal a socially distributed bias among historians, indeed a collective mind set that presents a major obstacle to creating effective historical computing. Granted that software design and computing capabilities may still present problems to historians, but such attitudes mean that historians of such persuasion are not likely to resolve them, to advance technology specifically for History, or even to serve as critics who can communicate effectively with engineers, technologists, and software designers who might produce better products for historians to use. In such cases, note that as justification for not using computers adroitly, the attack is on their limitation without any sign that these respected historians know much about contemporary computing or the capabilities of other information technologies. Their lack of technical knowledge, however, does not stop historians from speaking out against technology. This defensive behavior is itself problematic.

The issues have changed slightly in the generation since Rundell's study, but it seems that the same kinds of prejudices are common. One of these is that the historian's work is so unique, existential, and rarified, that he or she cannot gain assistance from modern information technology except in preliminary ways, because in the end human judgment must prevail. I do not dispute the conclusion so much as its premises, when in fields facing life and death decisions as in medical diagnostics, civil and military defense, etc., and in the management of some of our most complex systems, computers are essential throughout the process and the entire organization. These historians beg the question that if the computer cannot assist them in historical work, then why not? Why have historians failed to develop computing for their own purposes as it has been developed for other fields, a development which requires equal amounts of imagination and judgment? Is the computer as machine at fault for the lack of judgment or imagination, or does the fault lie in the historical profession and its predisposition to tradition and reticence about technological change in History while studying it for everything else? Is the problem just the opposite of what these historians claim, namely the lack of imagination and judgment in the research and development of History as a field of inquiry because all of historians' attention is riveted on the history of other times and places than their own? Stephen Ambrose admitted; "For us [historians], even though we cannot always imagine *what* [his emphasis] technological changes will be made, we do expect their occurrence" (FORBES *ASAP*, p. 27). He quotes Henry Adams to make a point worthy noting here: "Great as were the material obstacles in the path of the United States, the greatest obstacle of all was in the human mind. Experience forced on men's minds the conviction that what had ever been must ever be."

Other concerns about information practices in History from an open-system perspective include (MCCRANK, 1985):

- Reliance on conferencing and the "invisible college" for personal recommendations about literature relevant to their needs is not typical only of historians; but it should be noted that information-for-fee via workshops and conferences is an extension of one's education that also continues forms of tuition, and may be considered distinct from free information services, self-reliant information access, and the disclosure of information in a truly public forum.

- The addiction to reviews, often tardy themselves and historians' perusal of them commonly later still, results in a considerable lag time between publication and consultation of up to five years or twice the so-called "shelf-life" of literature in more technical fields.

- This overreliance on someone else's reviewing seems to contradict historians' distrust of abstracts, but this can be remedied if time were taken to collate multiple reviews rather than rely on any single reviewing journal. As important, relying on reviews alone does not constitute a systematic survey of a field or cover a very great percentage of available literature; books reviewed are usually classified only by broad subject fields traditionally defined by period and geography, so there is little transference of information about methodology, technique, or source type across fields; and reviewing is a form of highlighting rather than a systematic, even, and thorough surveying.

- Historians' habitual tracing of others' citations rather than reliance on their own bibliographic survey work and analysis often comes under attack, somewhat unfairly and uncritically. Citation tracing by historians, however, occurs regularly as a form of document retrieval from articles, but such practice does not translate into regular use of citation indexes or into an appraisal of an article or other contribution measured by its circulation and use.

- The lag time in absorbing new contributions to History into the historiographic mainstream is more common to the Humanities than Social Sciences, and initially a monographic contribution's acceptance relies on approval by a relatively closed circle of authorities; no similar mechanism exists for valuative review of articles or research released serially and current practice often means duplication of publications in articles and monographs.

- The observation of waves or fads within History, as certain types of studies or subjects become "hot" topics while others fall out of popularity and are perceived as passé or as adoptions from other fields become the vogue of the day, is a characteristic shared with other disciplines. One might expect historians to be more concerned with thematic continuities in research, and with continuance or innovation in the applications of technology and methodologies which constitute tendencies and trends. The lure of the unique (which DOORN, 1997, regards as a myth or misunderstanding) works against such historical consciousness and continuity, and the discovery of new material seems to be valued higher than pioneering new methodology.

These paradigmatic shifts, ephemeral schools of thought, trends, etc., deserve study as historical phenomena themselves, but historiography seldom provides an empirical study of one's contemporary historical literature even though such assessments may be available for other literatures, professions, and long-gone movements. Historical discourse in the Renaissance because of its relation with Rhetoric, is studied more than contemporary History, but exceptions exist, of course, as in recent discussions about historical representation, the challenge of deconstructionism and relativism to history, and the debate about educational standards for history teaching (see J. POTTER for the connection between discourse, rhetoric and social constructions). History as current events is reported, however, more than analyzed. History may be self-critical, or receives criticism from the vantage point of the Philosophy of History, but the information and communication aspects of historical processes, functions, and thinking or the attributes of its literature and other forms of communications are not well known. Here is a case in point: the recent debates over the revision of history curricula, core courses and content, and basic textbooks associated with the Bill Clinton administration's Goal 2000 initiative, largely to incorporate minority viewpoints into a history criticized as that of "great white men," is based on a very shaky empirical foundation of self-study for either side, those for or opposed to a basic standard for elementary and secondary curricula. In this controversy emotions have run high, and political pressures are untempered by compelling evidence. It is another case emphasizing the divergence of academic history from a reading public, and the difference between memory and history about which so much is being written (the commingling of social and cultural history, e.g., P. STEARNS (1993), going back to Maurice Halbwachs in the late 1920s). Perhaps because of the interjection of historical metaphor into political debate by historians and Speaker of the House Newt Gingrich during 1995, American political candidates have been asked to react to proposed standards and historical revisionism; their reactions have been expressed almost always negatively, but the grounding is less historical and research-based than it is a politically adroit assessment of public mood. The current debate could be much better informed if a body of relevant research already existed. However, few benchmarks are in place by which to measure such controversial issues as under-representation, stereotyping, ratio management of content, classification based on relevance weighting, etc. How would one propose to measure the progress of any programs that may be implemented? There are research methods and strategies for unobtrusive study and both quantitative and qualitative research on these issues (J. MASON).

The assumption is that contemporary attitudes and behaviors are influenced indirectly or perhaps unconsciously by personal recollection of historical information and also directly through role modeling and imitation of historical precedents. This assumption remains largely untested. Where it has been debated, as in the case of degenerative media influence (e.g., pornography, easy sex, violence, class and racial stereotyping, confusion of work with socializing, etc.), the direct correlation between precedent and imitative behavior is difficult to make scientifically. REEVES & NASS claim that people encountering intelligent nonhuman entities more and more are likely to react the same as when interacting with humans, rather than suspending belief or not exercising personal judgment, but mediated information delivery does not bring about direct consequences like human interaction does. The same is characteristic of historical recall; it is remote, indirect, and therefore does not require the circumspection unless moved into the realm of interpersonal relations. Historical assumptions embedded into court proceedings, such as relating childhood experience to adult behaviors, are likewise problematic. Little research actually investigates the application of historical consciousness or more ambiguous and indirect influence of historical imagery on contemporary behavior, individual or group, and never within the realm of History itself. The crux of the problem is that historians have not studied History as practiced; have not engaged behaviorist research methodology regarding their own behaviors in information searching, research, and teaching; and have not studied their own literature bibliometrically or their scholarly discourse sociologically. Nor have they conducted similar research about the consumption of history by the public except as pastime, despite, ironically, the Public History movement. Such contemporary self-inspecting research, using many of the same methodologies employed to study past societies, might be used to great advantage for the advancement of History today. This may well come under the rubric of Historical Information Science.

While such concerns may not now have a solid base of empirical research, there is a growing literature about professional historians and their use of information resources and institutions within a broader literature about user needs and abilities (T. WILSON provides a half-century survey of this field within IS). Such research should be continued, but without any *a priori* assumptions that information gathering by historians would or must imitate behaviors in the natural sciences or medicine where timeliness rather than timelessness is a dominant value. Thinking of ideas is a different task than searching for information already known to exist; historians do not always differentiate between the two, but studies of historian information behaviors must do so. Concept indexing, for example, is a very different task than object indexing and conversely, a far more difficult task in information storage and retrieval. Indeed, one may use the expression "to look for ideas" only in a figurative sense, but "searching for information" is quite literal. Information scientists in studying historians seldom make such philosophical distinctions, however. Nor can historians be treated as a homogenous group as if History were a cohesive discipline. Coherence in historical scholarship and adherence in association and professional behavior may not always be related. BEVIR, speaking about the history of ideas, argues that historians should adopt a presumption of coherence and aim at constructing sets of beliefs as coherent wholes, but he does not bring his line of reasoning into the behavioral sphere. Nevertheless, historical information retrieval practice, admittedly conservative in a profession dedicated to the conservation and reuse of information, may be more congruent with its ethos and more consistent or systematic than is commonly recognized.

Just as similarities in cognitive styles exist between preferences for browsing (a legitimate approach to idea stimulation as distinct from information searching (cf., BATES; MARCHIONINI, etc.) and personal reference, conferencing, and reviewing, or historians' tracing of citations back through successive stages of their literatures (a referral approach using provenance as in archival information searching), nonstrategic information searching can be justified. Indeed, alternative, personal methods can provide an effective mechanism to establish continuity in search results, as recognized by E. GARFIELD and ISI citation indexing, and in the Soviet theory of bibliographical heuristics (GRECHIKHIN). In this tradition CLAUSEN used citations to measure the increasing influence after 1976 of the journal *Social Science History*. This procedure creates a lineage of use, a source genealogy back to origins, consistent with the principle of provenance in archival information retrieval. This is as powerful a strategy in information retrieval as content indexing, as R. LYTLE (1979, 1980) demonstrated and which software developers are rediscovering only now. Yale University programmers in 1996 applied these old principles as if they were new, apparently unaware of their archival connection, in designing *Lifestreams* software to store digital documents as a chronological stream that in essence tracks a document's digital life (e.g., a genuine electronic archives package). One graduate-student developer, Eric Freeman, who innocently proclaimed "People remember when something happened" as a principle for information retrieval, provided an alternative to traditional file structures (YOUNG, 1997, p. A20). The two, provenance and subject classification, are in fact complementary (BEARMAN & LYTLE; BEARMAN & SZARY). WIBERLEY & JONES (1989, p. 643), although seemingly unaware of this parallel research in archival information retrieval, note that historians commonly track material genealogically in keeping with their tendency to search literatures, manually or online, through proper names. KUHLTHAU advocates this timeline approach to study information seeking behavior; she is one of the few who uses history as a mechanism to study users, but does not necessarily see her approach as historical. In fact, a timeline mechanism is common in most series studies which use sequence as a basis for analysis, or any data sets as in MARKEY's use of computerized search logs to discover common errors, false searches, and misleads as a means to correct cataloging practices. The latter, however, does not use time as a factor in search analyses in the same way KUHLTHAU recommends, or in time studies related to group interaction as studied by MCGRATH (1984; 1994) and his associates. In the latter case, time and its attributed value are not studies so much as a historical sensibility or aid to making sense out of things, such as the use of chronology, as a matter of efficiency.

Efficiency in the sense of time-saving is not a value that seems to distinguish historians in their information retrieval habits (they may instead prefer thoroughness). Nor is timeliness in the same sense as in the business world, or in science and technology. Taking time allows for the combination of retrieval, thought, and strategy for the next instance of information retrieval into a more integral process than the paradigm of strategic planning, a direct search for a specific, targeted document, and analysis only after retrieval based on contents alone, rather than content analysis in the context of the search itself. Historians work in time, take time, and perceive time in ways not common in most settings, in a manner perhaps more akin to detective investigation than other kinds of information work. Information retrieval from clues is substantially different than by address or by existing search keys as studied by FIDEL. Consequently, values relating to time or the concept of place in history whether long-range or recent, seem very problematic in their transfer from one field to another. Some methods are more time-consuming than others, but a serial approach often does more than retrieve a single document, but going after a documentary string or what in archival methodology constitutes a record series. In short, two goals are working in such information retrieval: documents in a series and identification of the series (the proverbial trees and the forest) that provide a historical context above and beyond what each document would provide alone were it retrieved as though it were a self-contained, autonomous unit. The whole series, not a part, is of cardinal importance. A single record may be retrieved as a point of entry into a series, but what exists in proximity, before and after, is important. This is why some Key-Word in Context (KWIC) approaches to archival information retrieval are poorly designed or misapplied, since it makes a difference as to what level word linkage is made, i.e., to other terms within the document, to original vocabulary used throughout the series, or to a terminology ascribed to the series as metadata. In other words, document and information retrieval are often not the same, and historical searching should not be confused with simple document retrieval, as in so much of Information Science Information Storage and Retrieval (ISAR) research. Historians often neglect to make such distinctions in teaching methodology, and some comparisons and several user studies seem not to recognize these important differences.

This essentially historical, serial, and archival search methodology is used as well with registry systems (e.g., *The Federal Register*) to control and access federal and state government documents, whereby corporate entries replace personal names and a bureaucratic hierarchy substitutes for the natural family, although most librarians (a case in point is this confusion of archival and library approaches reflected in the CAUDLE & MARCHAND study) seem not to recognize the existence of Government Documents depositories as a published archives in their midst (COX, 1986). Unfortunately, this connotation is also lost in the draft assessment of formats and standards for the creation, dissemination, and accessibility of electronic "government information products" prepared for the United States National Commission on Libraries and Information Science (NCLIS) by the National Research Council.

Of course, historians and social scientists in general have been accused of neglecting government publications as primary sources (ZINK; HERNON), which some link to inadequate user instruction and development of information search skills (REELING; O'CONNOR). Much of this criticism comes from documents librarians who themselves sometimes seem to confuse the means of access to archives and documents with library methods as much as historians resist normalization in indexing and authority work in bibliographic control. Not surprisingly historians using computers for nominal linkage of their data records discovered problems that to them seemed new in the late 1970s, but which librarians had encountered decades earlier in cataloging and again as part of their efforts to link bibliographic records in online databases (WEINTRAUB). Few historians of the early era of historical computing related issues in bibliographic information retrieval, such as authority control or concept of main entry in classification, with historical database management. Archivists were likewise late, perhaps because of their affiliation and earlier training in History, to make such association between normalization and information retrieval (E. BLACK). Nor is it likely that historians are generally aware of how intellectual issues in nominal record linkage also pertain to their current information seeking behavior.

Studies have shown that historians, like literature scholars, rely on nominal data in information retrieval more heavily than anyone once suspected, and that the associative mental process used often reflects the procedural processing of nominal data in computerized research. This would suggest that historians should be explicitly aware of naming conventions, form of entry, syntax in nominal data elements for systematization, and normalization of orthography, etc., in referencing, citation stylistics, and in entitling their own work, but this does not seem to be the case. They need to minimize the orthographic impediments to information retrieval, namely the retrieval of their own production (such problems are reviewed by T. BROOKS, 1998). Style manuals and undergraduate term paper guides preferred by historians often assume that nominal entry is self-evident and does not require verification or normalization. Consequently their citations and references are often inconsistent in their own work, and are incongruent with the context in which they place their works (i.e., national bibliographic information systems, large research libraries, etc.; GRABOWSKI identifies the common elements in the regulation of written English). Because historians work with ambiguous data, especially in earlier periods when naming was not conventionalized or was conventional only by locales and no standards existed for the transfer of nominal data across borders, languages, and cultures with social mobility, they should be highly sensitive to the nuances of nominal data. Their sense of standards needs to be more developed than what might suffice for modern journalism. If that had been the case, an earlier transition by historians to online bibliographic searching would have triggered such associations in time to have assisted historians with the problems of nominal records linkage in nonbibliographic database design. This is not the case. Much needs to be learned from each other.

Recent studies more sympathetic to History (TIBBO, 1989/1990, 1993, 1994a-b), have recognized that historians use libraries more as humanists than as social scientists (see also CASE, 1986, 1991a-b), and thus place History in the Humanities when studying use behavior and information needs (cf., a series of such studies, not all complimentary, appeared as follows: BURCHARD, 1965; VICKERY, 1969; WEINTRAUB, 1980; STONE, 1980, 1982; STAM, 1984; STOAN, 1984; BROADBENT, 1986; FABIAN, 1986; BAKEWELL, BEEMAN & REESE, 1988; GOULD, 1988; WIBERLEY & JONES, 1989, 1994; GILMORE & CASE, 1992; FRANKLIN, 1993; SIEGFRIED, BATES & WILDE, 1993; etc.) and move away from unrealistic generalizations based on a homogeneity that does not exist (as indicated by the mixed profile by SIEGFRIED, BATES & WILDE, 1993, p. 277 and confirmed by WIBERLEY & JONES, 1994, p. 507) of end-user searching by humanities scholars. The one generality that holds, however, is that humanists and historians in particular make limited use of comprehensive online bibliographic sources, especially as endusers (WIBERLEY & JONES, 1994, p. 506 for the United States, citing somewhat incongruently S. STONE's dated study, which in 1980 drew similar conclusions about the United Kingdom; cf., EARLE & VICKERY for use of social science literature in the United Kingdom).

The stereotype or unitary profile of "the" historian, or "the" humanist, however, has been breaking down, partially because it is understood that (1) earlier studies were insensitive to cognitive styles associated with the various disciplines; (2) the very disciplinary nature of certain fields like History that relied on primary sources mitigated against use because access to such source material was then not well conveyed through online bibliographic information systems; and (3) information retrieval did not always need to be bibliographic. This is certainly true of art historians (BAKEWELL *ET AL.*; M. SCHMITT, 1988) whose recall may be initially more visual than verbal. Art historians when interviewed by Marilyn Schmitt understandably placed art objects before documents in their prioritization of source material, while historians are likely to invert these and rely more on primary textual documentation (SCHMITT, 1988). Donald Case stresses especially historians' tendency to use metaphor in recall and rely on personal memory for information retrieval rather than any sophisticated formal information system (CASE, 1991, pp. 662-64). He does not specifically relate this reliance on descriptive metaphors to forms of visualization, as in the use of word pictures, but others have explored the cognitive psychology involved in making sense through metaphors

(MACCORMAE; R. E. HASKELL). In his study of History's topologies, ANKERSMIT (1994), who has long studied historians' language (1983), traces "the rise and fall of metaphor" in historical usage. The flux he pictures is problematic for information retrieval because a historian's use may be personal creations as part of literary license, and acceptance into common usage among historians means that a metaphor becomes a cliche, falls into disuse therefore, and thus metaphors are unstable for consistent information retrieval over time. Case's initial findings might be explored further to discover how visuals assist in historical interpretation, i.e., visual thinking (FINKE; FINKE, WARD & SMITH; PETTERSON) and, in turn, how historical thinking lends itself to the burgeoning field of Knowledge Representation (BREWKA, ed.; CUMMINS, 1991 & 1996; GILLLET; NORWICH; PEARL & VERMA; cf., the international conferences devoted to the subject, i.e., CARLUCCI, DOYLE & SHAPRIRO, eds; DOYLE, SANDEWALL & TORASSO, eds.; and ANKERSMIT, 1989, who is not so much interested in visuals as language representation, especially when historians are prone to "getting the story crooked" rather than straight).

No use studies from an Information Science perspective have connected the use of primary source materials in library seminar rooms and archives with the kinds of metaphors Bonnie Smith does—gender preferential language and fantasies, masculine values and male exclusivity, progressive concepts of autonomy and male citizenship, and the language of love, obsession, and particularly, fetishism (B. SMITH, 1995). She argues, with ample quotes from nineteenth-century historians, that "the two practices of scientific history, the seminar and archival research, were as foundational to and influential in the profession as the ideals of truth and objectivity" (pp. 1150-51) and that "gender was constitutive of procedures in scientific history and that the complex uses of gender were pivotal to scientific advance" in explaining how history pursuits came to be, in J. H. Hexter's words, "pretty much stag affairs." She observes that "seminars and archives were spaces reserved mostly for professional men" (p. 1153) as workers and users, but does not investigate the counterpart in libraries where research has focused on them as women's places of work. (Smith instead refers to the female counterpart as the salon, which of course does have a connection with social reading, reading rooms, and the American public library movement.) Smith connects the nineteenth-century emphasis on scientific method by Leopold von Ranke, Herbert Baxter Adams, Ephraim Emerton, etc., with a social collectivity that was exclusionary, literally locked down inside seminar rooms and archives that were largely off limits to women. She further explores the language of work, documentary and archival research in particular, to reveal an imagery ranging from scenarios of pollution, danger, and mutilation, to sexual fantasies about exploring virgin territory in discovering unknown history. She quotes some of the most famous documentalists of the century as ravaging archives for their jewels, von Ranke's drive into archival research by "lust'" and "desire," and how Charles Seignobos and Langlois both found that "Each discovery [about finding an untouched document in a dusty archive] induces rapture" (p. 1172). One by one, colorful metaphors are extracted from historians' writings to indicate a mentality that seems to have been pervasive and certainly influenced more than one generation of researchers in library special collections and in the archives. If not sexual metaphor, then military bravado, chivalry, and machismo are revealed as in Lord Acton's description of history as "the heroic study of records." Smith concludes that "Expressions of objectivity were often made in highly sexed metaphors—metaphors that appeared 'natural' because modern ideology took sexual difference as natural."

Metaphors in language are still used in Organizational Culture studies to explore prevailing attitudes and pervasive mentalities; more will be said about this later. They may be used also like tropes and caricatures by survey researchers in marketing to build composite pictures of the public's perception of a product, or in the case of archives and libraries, of services and the professions (e.g., LEVY). Basic metaphors like clichés endure for long periods and exercise considerable influence on thought and behavior. As M. HESSE and

D. DAVIDSON have argued, and B. SMITH agrees, a metaphor is not simply decorative, but it is pertinent to cognition and knowledge formation, representation, and communication. CASE approaches the subject largely from the problem of language in information access, but the issue of metaphor use needs to be explored more widely in terms of cognitive psychology for user attitudes as well as behaviors. Moreover, the connection B. SMITH (1995) makes between objectivity as a value and the gendering of scientific inquiry should be explored as well for Information Science. Its metaphors, one suspects, may reveal similar traits to those who advocated scientific historicism and reliance on documentation as the preferred method of objective historical research.

Many studies of historians' information-seeking behavior and needs (profiled by TIBBO, 1989, 1994b) pertain mostly to libraries and secondary or tertiary materials. WIBERLEY & JONES more recently (1994) attribute the slowness of humanists in adopting information technology to the nature of their discipline and predict that as their sources are more and more products of information technology, they will adapt accordingly. They earlier stressed historians' use of large amounts of primary sources (as does FRANKLIN), information retrieval largely through proper names (WIBERLEY, 1988, p. 141; these findings were confirmed by SIEGFRIED & WILDE, 1990), and various heuristic approaches to information organization. These studies largely ignore archives use and research in unpublished primary sources as outlined by BROOKES some time ago or as advocated by DOWLER (1988), and more recently the socioeconomic historian's reliance on data archives (tentatively addressed by HEIM, 1980) or increased computer use (initially explored by MULLINGS), all of which circumvent traditional library use and bibliographic information retrieval. The aforementioned Getty Trust AHIP study with Brown University about the behavior of art historians (BAKEWELL *ET AL.*) is an important exception, since its interviews and case studies necessarily related art historians' work to works of art, and it explored the problems of museum-based research as well. Seldom is a holistic picture presented in such library-biased use studies that pertain only to one type of information service or institution; they treat only a portion of the information activity of most historians.

The fullest discussion of these issues is by TIBBO (1989, 1993) who notes the difference between American National Standards Institute (ANSI) and International Organization for Standardization (ISO) guidelines for abstracts, drawn up largely for the science fields, and the reality of natural language abstracting in History tools such as ABC-CLIO's services. Helen Tibbo's gleanings from interviews with historians at the University of Maryland shows how much they think of information retrieval in terms of objects, persons, events, and texts, rather than concepts, transactions and functions, and series or processes, much in the same way that MOLTO discovered that retrieval in family history by personal and kinship names is more prevalent than finding life-event terms. This supports WIBERLEY's findings about historians' preference for nominal rather than subject searching. TIBBO adopts her user-oriented findings to suggest design specifications for an optimal Information Storage and Retrieval (ISAR) system for History, and provides caveats about indexing for the Humanities (TIBBO, 1994a). She expands her study to online access to archives (TIBBO, 1994b) which she stresses as one of the most important developments of the past decade if only historians would systematically use techniques to create access tools, and then if they would use them.

The issue of Natural Language Processing (NLP), indexing and abstracting, and vocabulary control in information retrieval versus free text searching is a big question in searching historical secondary literature, and it has implications for historians' writing, teaching, and information retrieval (LANCASTER; again, see FIDEL about the use of search keys). Too often historians not trained in Information Science fail to appreciate the differences between free text and controlled vocabulary searching, or the implications of performance measures grounded in cognitive psychology like recall (the number of relevant concepts retrieved / the total relevant concepts) and precision (the number of relevant concepts retrieved/the total concepts retrieved) as reflected in HAAS (1995), H. CHEN & LYNCH's "cluster similarity function," and H. CHEN *ET AL*. (1998) in their approaches to information retrieval (cf., COMBER & STANFORD for records; KRISTENSON & JAERVELIN for newspapers). Few studies have been made specifically of full-text searching of historical writings, although MARCHIONINI's studies of full-text searching in hyperlinked encyclopedia may be applicable to the kind of work historians, or their students, do. MARCHIONINI (1995) found that people searching full-text electronic sources simply follow paths of least resistance, or in terms closer to their explanation, the path of least cognitive load. Scanning documents with headings, spaces, and highlighted keywords, for example, shifts the load from cognition and extraction of meaning to locate information to the perceptual system; this is easier for most people. Historical writing and presentation often requires a heavy cognitive load to retrieve information; histories are better read than browsed or used as databases for quick information retrieval. Histories are also laden with thick description, complex structures, varied vocabularies, and special terminologies, all of which impede easy information retrieval.

Using the text analysis package *Hum* developed by William Tuthill, S. HAAS (1995) studied History as one of eight disciplines to determine a methodology for identifying sublanguage domain terms and the patterns in which they occur. She extracted 5,696 domain terms from a set of 221 abstracts for History (an average of 44.2 domain specific words per abstract, more than for Biology and Economics, but less than for Electrical Engineering, Physics, Math, Sociology, and Psychology in that order); these domain terms were classified into 1,139 word types (the fewest of any of the disciplines, indicating its relative nontechnical nature and reliance on common language rather than domain specific discourse). She further broke her term base into five sets by subject matter and calculated averages to reveal again that History vocabulary tended to have the fewest domain specific terms (154) which constitutes 15.32 percent of all the words in the History abstracts studied. She then extracted "seed words" from the abstracts; that is, those words whose immediate contexts in the abstracts were searched for domain terms, e.g., "entry words." They were tagged as "marked" or those which appear in a standard dictionary, or "missing" when not included and for which one would have to turn to a specialized lexicon. History had the lowest percentage of seed terms adjoining domain terms (23.8 percent, as opposed to the highest, Physics, 53.4 percent); relatively low percentages of domain terms occurring in sequences of two words (20.5 percent), and almost no sequences of three or more terms (1.96 percent). Recall and precision measures based on VAN RIJSBERGEN's work resulted in an average score of 0.3752 above Sociology but well below the other disciplines, presumably because of the lack of sub-language terms that would give the field greater precision in communication and recall in information retrieval. The various measures all resulted in a consistency between the Social Sciences (Sociology) and Humanities (History) on the one hand, and the so-called hard Sciences on the other (Physics and Biology), which tend to have more domain terms that are predominantly used only in these disciplines or which have special meaning therein, and more terms used adjacently to designate concepts, specific technologies, and complex phenomena (BONZI). HAAS concludes that the extraction methods tested do not work well in History and Sociology, but do work well for the hard sciences.

Toni Petersen, who based on her experience with the *Art and Architecture Thesaurus* discovered similar divergence in sublanguage use between Art, which behaves like History because most text use is by art historians rather than practicing artists, and Architecture which uses more and more specific terms and is perhaps influenced by Engineering. PETERSEN advises that for these fields term classification and linkage are likely to be labor intensive because they require so much human intervention and editing. These findings have implications for automatic indexing and thesaurus construction which are not likely to be very automatic at all for History. Consider MOLTO's investigation of family histories as a genre within History. She found, among other conclusions, that word frequencies in a 20,000 word corpus indicate that family history literature differed significantly from general English writing, and usage indicates operation of a sub-language associated with genealogy. The characteristics of natural language usage in a sub-domain or specialty in History, therefore, do not necessarily apply to the discipline overall. Specific genre within History, such as the History of Technology, the History of Science, etc., are likely to produce different results than History would overall by displaying more specific language usage, more precise terms, and greater recall potential in information retrieval.

Historians seem unaware of the importance of such findings in their historical writing, which would become even more significant if such texts were converted to electronic form to become searchable tools as much as literary works. Their attitudes, often based on personal impression and experience rather than empirical research, influence projects in archives directed by historians or those whose judgment is content-based more than rooted in methodological side of the discipline. Note that if access to particular collections that are domain specific, for example, caters totally to those within particular disciplines, then the terminology taken from the corpus is likely to constitute a sub-language. Access by nonspeakers may depend on ample cross-referencing and term definitions rather than simply pulling key words out of context for rough indexes or full-text searching without assistance from a thesaurus. Moreover, such specialized access and sub-language terms need to be related to general access and common language to go from one collection and level of specialization to another (e.g., from a manuscripts collection or archives group to a LC-cataloged library). FRILING (1997), for example, has taken the position that term matching in full-text searching the Ben Gurion papers and Zionist collections on CD-ROM has been and is always totally satisfactory. This Ben Gurion project, however, is supported by a thesaurus. This creation of alternative means of access other than actual language in special collections is important, because so often one of the things that makes the collection "special" is its sub-language character.

TENOPIR (1985) specifies uses of sub-languages other than reading, such as identifying search keys in sub-disciplines which need to be related to general language and enhance subject searching in information retrieval systems. Sub-languages also provide linguistic data worthy of analysis in their own right. COLLANTES has shown that common naming behavior, even in technical fields where a greater language use conformity prevails than in the arts and humanities, produces such varied terms for the same concepts and document types, that information retrieval by any of these without coordinated indexing is very spotty. People reach consensus more easily about object naming, but texts or illustrations—even those with objects depicted—are especially problematic. Image retrieval based on captioning is indirectly based on object names, or semantic relationships based on naming, are likewise problematic (CHAMIS). Hence, information scientists are concerned with what is often simply referred to as the "vocabulary problem," i.e., the mismatch between human-system communications (FURNAS *ET AL.*). This is especially problematic for History and contributes to historians' skepticism about automatic information retrieval and such enhancements as weighting and filtering. Little evidence indicates that historians are addressing this "vocabulary problem"; however, either through its study generally or in any particular History domain: historical (i.e., abstracting something closer to technical writing than literary production); communication for cross-cultural teaching (which most history teaching is); or engineering solutions for decision support or expert systems development, to nurture expert historians who must master several foreign languages and in their speciality, sublanguages as well.

Indeed, historians seem to be among the worst offenders in creating mismatches between formalized descriptors in standard information retrieval systems and the vocabulary used in their scholarly communication. This is because historians tend to see their writing as a literary and creative activity, so they delight in varied expression, personal style, and often usage that reflects their being steeped in their historical sources such as when they retain classical terms when perfectly acceptable modern equivalents exist—a practice of "one-up-manship". Often archaic usage from primary sources creeps into their exposition, or more intentionally they adopt foreign terms and phrases more liberally than in other writing genre, often without providing parallel, searchable terms. Hopefully this is more than a case of feigned erudition; some foreign phrases capture meanings not easily rendered into a more empirical language like English; sometimes the adoption reflects common usage in a sub-language as in the case of Latin being retained in Law, Medicine, or Theology. At times the practice of quotation builds a sub-language vocabulary that specialist readers take for granted in the same way that English through Norman influence incorporated French phrases, if not native, as perfectly natural. This is why TIBBO warns about using abstracting and indexing methods and assumptions taken from research in the Sciences for work with secondary historical literature. Moreover, historians expect their works to be read like literature, not technical reports; and they expect them to be read *ad seriatim* rather than systematically searched and read piecemeal. Segmentation, partial reading, and limiting units of information to the page or paragraph, etc., are what often happens when reading electronic texts (BIRKERTS; cf., the fuller discussion of reading digital texts by BOLTER, 1987).

Eighteenth-century classical historians like Gibbon, and successors like Francis Parkman in American history, thought that one of the main purposes of history was to entertain, i.e., moral entertainment and exercising the mind though historical recall was a meditative and spiritual act. Their thinking might be invoked by modern proponents of "edutainment" (the combination of education and entertainment, but the notion of "fun" was lacking from the former and the idealism of the former is absent in the latter. Knowledge discovery in History, however, could be entertaining in reading and envisioning history, as it is in historical fiction converted to film. Perhaps the notion of "discovery" was a carryover from the medieval sense of "wonder" characterized by BYNUM (1997) in her recent AHA presidential address, just as the notion of the *exemplum* survives from the Middle Ages in the modern scenario that is meant to teach by example rather than definition and demonstration. But most *exempla* were known, expected, and their endings anticipated, and Carolyn Bynum is speaking about source-based views of the past which are not self-referential and like good modeling serve to reveal the unknown. There is a greater element of surprise in such research than that which simply verifies the known. Like good fiction which has its twists and turns as the plot unfolds, not all of history repeats the same old story.

Modern narrativists likewise stress the storytelling in History, which is also a resurrection of old emphases often placed in juxtaposition to scientific historicism as if one cannot have both, thorough analysis and a good story. On the contrary, one can have both. Cultural anthropologist Barbara Myerhoff relates the process of aging in all cultures with ritual and storytelling (MYERHOFF). This passing along tradition as a familial and cultural heritage is key to cultural continuity, and it is an ingrained act that is essential for so much of historical recall. Such reminiscences crystalize into stories, and when recorded, into documentation. SCHUMAN, BELLI & BISHCHOPING argue that this creates a generational basis for historical knowledge. Even if they are narrated long after the fact, family stories are still a form of witnessing and first-hand testimony. It is a revered tradition in itself, remembered in personal impression, repetition, and, as in a Normal Rockwell painting, in the visual arts as well.

In any case, History was edifying, more than merely being informative, and this feature still sets it off from so much of science and technology. Information scientists tend not to misunderstand this normative/descriptive tension in historical writing and historiography, stemming perhaps from History's formalization in the eighteenth century as a moral science. It has been suggested by LIVINGSTON that in such thinkers as Hume, moral philosophy and moral history are closely related, as they were in the *Federalist Papers* or in Jefferson and Hamilton's arguments based on history for the recommended Constitution of the United States. Information access was less a concern in such discourse than persuasion in the rhetorical tradition. Hence, style remains important in historical writing, and the genre requires more than journalism and mere reporting. While clarity is sought for readability, ambiguity may be used deliberately, metaphor is cherished, impression is valued as much as information. Term matching, or indexing by those unaware of the conventions of high style and rhetoric, or may fail to retrieve information that is subtle, embedded, or inferred, to say nothing of nuance. Hence, the common criticism about machine logic versus human judgment, and the mechanization of an art. So much of information retrieval falls short of the mark for human learning that is knowledge-based rather than merely databased. Computer Science as a data-oriented endeavor and Information Science, focused on information as communication at one time or in a relatively limited series or track, fail to provide the big picture, the whole story, or the moving picture and the storyline. In short, they often do not retrieve historical information so much as only information from history. The difference in these concepts, the ideal and the realty, is important and ought to point to the future direction of research in Information Science or, in particular, a new Historical Information Science.

Such traits pose significant challenges to information retrieval that perceives information as thing rather than process and that underestimates the interplay of power and communications. The emulation of historical writing of older styles rather than rigorous adherence to normalization may indeed hinder cross-cultural searching, and the absence of a core of key terms in free-text searching or availability of a commonly accepted thesaurus is problematic in history. The lack of such tools constructed according to established standards (NISO Z39.19-1993) pushes the burden of information retrieval entirely on the reader and user. In so doing, historians as authors face a paradox that in making history literary they may simultaneously limit the utility of their work, e.g., making it less accessible to readers for whom English is a second language (BLUME), for minorities who must accommodate formal academic English with its more complex structure and a vocabulary range exceeding their common usage, and readers in other times and places who must retrieve information from historical works remotely through mediated systems. They may inadvertently also limit the transferability of historical work across disciplines and to the more pragmatic professions. Thesauri act as intermediaries in such cases so novices can search for historical information in works produced by historians, and they relate specialized usage in one discipline or field to another (MANIEZ). Rather than something modern, thesauri are a time-tested redress to human communication difficulties (N. ROBERTS), but they are now being used differently in electronic environments (SVENONIUS). Vocabularies developed specifically for technical writing structurally geared at an eighth-grade level or a highly technical special-purpose language as used in the Sciences do not often work as well in the Humanities, Arts, and Social Sciences (experiments in automatic thesaurus generation (e.g., CHEN *ET AL.*, 1995) have not included mixing languages and within them both archaic and modern usages). Consequently, History as a field has a rich literature as indicated by the AHA *Guides,* but problematic information retrieval mechanisms except for bibliographic services such as those offered by ABC-CLIO Press which attempted term permutation to create search strings, rather than to operate with a thesaurus (FALK).

A case in point, as well as an illustration of sublanguage in History and historical conventions in classification and naming, may be the American Historical Association's most recent effort to guide novice historians through the maze of historical writing. The AHA's *Guide to Historical Literature*, first produced in 1955, only in 1995 after decades of outdated use (1961), was finally revised by an international team of historians funded by the National Endowment for the Humanities (NEH), Rockefeller Foundation, Andrew Mellon Foundation, and the Henry Luce Foundation. It was an exemplary collaborative effort, and the largest of its kind in North America, under the editorial leadership of Mary Beth Norton of Cornell University. ABH originally promoted this initiative (FALK, 1986a-b), but it was largely excluded from the project itself. Historians were encouraged to consider the scientific aspects of bibliographic control of their literature and new methods of dissemination, but the product was still traditional, resulting in a two-volume book format even though its compilation was electronic. Upon release, it was already two years out-of-date, and this was a single rather than sustained effort by the AHA in bibliographic control. Oxford University Press' promotional releases for the *Guide* claim that it is "the only reference [tool] to cover *every* field of history." It provides "easy access" in a two-column 7.5 x 10-inch page format (2,120 pages) to 27,000 "fully annotated citations," representing "the finest" and "the best historical literature available." It is heralded as a "keystone reference" work providing "unprecedented bibliographic guidance of extraordinary breadth, from prehistory to the 1990s." NORTON herself (*AHA Perspectives*, 1994; 32[8]: 1,6) hoped that the *Guide* will "serve the function of a colleague down the hall..." and would help to "break down some of the sub-disciplinary fields that have been built up over the last few years. It should show historians what is going on outside their fields."

The AHA *Guide* may be taken as an exemplary inter-disciplinary work presumably displaying historian prowess in bibliography and the application of library and information science principles, and also as an accurate depiction of how historians perceive their discipline. The guide is touted as "*the* place for anyone to start researching any topic in any field of history." Yet, it is designed more as a classified bibliography than a real guide that would, for example, incorporate "pathfinding" features, search strategies, and link levels of sources from tertiary to the primary. Therefore, this is not so much a research as a bibliographic search tool. Examination of the *Guide*'s taxonomy, citation formats and completeness, and indexing is therefore revealing of more than the book itself, but the mind set of the profession and the American Historical Association under whose aegis it was produced and how historians elected to handle some of the more vexing problems in bibliography and reference (e.g., problem handling against the background of reference research surveyed by J. RICHARDSON, 1995). Many could have been handled differently, of course, had an electronic reference tool been created.

The tool is laid out in 48 sections ostensibly "arranged by chronology and national and regional history." These act as classes, but the facets within it are not uniform or systematic from one section to another, and sequential numbering provides no clustering or readily discernable subordination. Subject orientations with fields of history that are usually described with adjectives, e.g., social, economic, political, ethnographic, etc., are subordinated as facets within classes, but not always as identifiable categories. Terminology in the annotations and indexes seems neither pre- or post-coordinated or controlled in the editing process, so the subject indexing does not overcome the problems of the taxonomy and classification. Subject terms do not seem related adequately internally, or to any external thesauri.

The ordering principle of the entire array is no more clear than some of the other design decisions. The classes begin with *Theory and Practice in Historical Study* by Richard T. Vann, the only general historiographic section *per se*, but each section has a short historiographic essay or overview. These are enlightening but do not by themselves or collectively provide guidance in any fashion similar to current trends in reference and bibliographic instruction movements, e.g., true taxonomies for organizational approaches to a subject, exemplary predesigned search strategies, preferences for key terms and relationships in searching the guide itself (other than the index's syndectic referencing) or online databases, record linking other than through general subject indexing, etc. After the introductory sections, then the guide moves to "Prehistory" (no. 2) in one instant, and to "World History" in another (no. 3). Then back again to "Ancient Near East" and an excursion through the Western Mediterranean (nos. 6-8) before turning East back to Byzantium (no. 8, while Medieval Europe is no 20) and venturing to "Central Asia" (no. 9) and China and Japan (two classes each, premodern and modern; nos. 10-13). Korea (no. 14) gets its own class, while the entire "Islamic World to 1500" is lumped together in another (no. 17) before moving to Africa. Islam is treated as a religio-cultural class. Ethnic classes are assigned to Jewish History, medieval and modern (no. 21), and to Native Americans, but no others.

"Native Peoples of the Americas" (section number 36) leads into a series on the New World, coming after the "Soviet Union" (no. 35) and before "Latin America to 1800" (no. 37) and "since 1800" (no. 38). Thereafter "Colonial North America" (no. 39) leads to sections on United States history from general (no. 40) to 1754- and since 1920 (nos. 41-44), and Canada (no. 45). Canada, however, is followed by "Australasia and Oceania" (no. 46) tucked between the North American series and sections "International Relations" from 1815 to, and then after 1920 (nos. 47-48).

While inclusions are patent for this work of "authoritative coverage of breathtaking scope," its subordination of entries, exclusions, and omissions are equally telling. Selections by policy are primarily in English, but key works in other languages are included especially for sections on non-Anglo-American cultures. The guide is dedicated to the published secondary literature in traditional outlets (i.e., journals and monographs), not original or primary sources—either edited materials or unpublished records. Coverage largely ignores interpretative literature in tertiary or reference tools like subject- and geographic-focused encyclopedia and encyclopedic dictionaries. Moreover, since the conceptualization of the project is so traditional, the *Guide* provides little guidance to electronic publishing, listservs and newer forms of scholarly communication, or access to the virtual libraries, archives, text and/or image databases that are widely available (e.g., more than two dozen digital library projects described by DRABEN-STOTT, MOHLENRICH, and others). Interpretive and synthetic works in tertiary tools are also omitted. The bias is toward single-authored monographs. Since so much of social science research is collaborative and communications in the information science fields are often through published proceedings, the selection criteria for the *Guide* like those for the *American Historical Review* discriminate against these fields, not because they are of inferior scholarship, but because of their mode of information dissemination. More than a quarter of the works cited in this survey are, for example, collections and collaborative thematic works likely to be ignored by the AHA *Guide* compilers. Contributors to these and newer forms of information services will doubtlessly feel slighted by such exclusion from the "finest" and "best" not because of the quality of their contributions, but on the basis of mode of communication. The major works cited in this survey's bibliography may serve as a partial corrective. The intent of supplying a sizeable bibliography to it is for it to serve as a bridge, sending historians into information science literature and information scientists into History, and both having entry points to the extensive and quickly changing information technology literature. The AHA *Guide* by virtue of its coverage allows this different focus and relieves me from covering each field of historical inquiry in depth. Instead, examples suffice, and selections included here serve as a complement to this earlier survey.

Other limitations are apparent even for more traditional coverage. Comparative history is reduced to "World History" (no. 3), although the *Guide* has ample cross-references between sections. "Science, Technology, and Medicine" has a class of its own (no. 4), but not Law, Religion or Theology, Philosophy or the History of Ideas/Intellectual History. Also excluded are splinter fields or those subjects identified as other disciplines, e.g., art history, music history, etc. Prehistory is included; archeology is not. The taxonomy is thereby skewed toward the political and technical at the expense of the cultural. Those fields that are methodologically focused or source-oriented are also excluded or are subordinated to geo-chronological classes: i.e., the so-called auxiliary sciences of history, e.g., codicology, paleography, diplomatics, and manuscripts studies; historical bibliography and typography; philately and numismatics; visual and documentary or deposition arts, and photography; oral history and sound recordings; historical geography and cartography; and the full range of documentation. Public History is likewise slighted, as are archives and museums. Entries in sections are arranged under headings, the syntactic construction and classification of which vary from section to section, and do not always relate to external subject headings in use such as *Library of Congress Subject Headings (LCSH)* generally and for History itself, *Medical Subject Headings (MESH)* for the History of

Medicine, or other specialty tools for theology and religion, social issues, and emerging fields, information formats, and new media (K. MARKEY & VIZINE-GOETZ for online information retrieval [using OCLC data]; see PETERSEN & MOLHOLT, eds. for subject access to nonbook formats). Terms like Historical Informatics, Historical Computer Science, or Historical Information Science are not found; citations about computing are mainly under Computers and Electronics as a subheading under the History of Technology (for this field's scope, cf., I. MCNEIL). Subjects like the history of information, artifacts, communications, and Information Science itself, are difficult to identify. Relevant coverage is slight. Finally, these volumes contain no empirical study of the literature surveyed or that cited, no bibliometric analysis or delineation of trends. Even a self-study of inclusions could have provided a weighted ranking of key journals, for example.

The citations themselves are arranged by author; some illustrate main entry and normalization problems. The style is hybrid, ordinarily running from citation number (section/item) used in indexing; uninverted author names without cognomen highlighting for easy scanning; short titles which are not always complete (series titles are often omitted); place (no country): publisher, and date; collation data is omitted for books, and article locations are cited by the common volume number (issue numbers omitted), year, and inclusive pagination. The inclusion of a mechanism of quick retrieval and reverification is commendable, i.e., the International Standard Serial (ISSN) or International Standard Book Numbers (ISBN). Short notations (subjects inferred) follow, with the initials of the selector/annotator. Admittedly detailed technical problems and some detailed errors always surface in a collaborative effort of this magnitude, but overall this is a clean, respectable bibliography which is clearly an improvement on the previous *Guide* in terms of scope, content, and presentation.

These observations are shared not to review the *Guide* negatively, since it is indeed a useful tool and worthwhile investment at a reasonable price; but instead to suggest that this work is less a model than it could have been had modern information science and technology been exploited more adroitly to produce a genuinely modern guide rather than a new guide in old form. Moreover, as presented, the *Guide* reflects attitudes, assumptions, and values typical of today's academic historian community, and as an "authoritative" tool demarcates the core territory of the History discipline, but becomes less reliable the more interdisciplinary the search. Perhaps the interplay between History with Literary Criticism for source and narrative explication is an exception to this generalization. The discipline has remained true to itself by producing a conservative, traditional retrospective compilation, without plans for continuation and currency. Bibliography for the AHA is an intermittent product more than a continuing process. This information access problem in research reflects a larger one in Education generally, and the disciplines in particular, which is essentially the same for American business in making the transition from total manufacturing to a combined production and information-based practice. It is easier to produce a single product one time than to sustain production of a continuous product. But education is a neverending process, not a single product. Academics individually and collectively, have had a difficult time facing the challenge from modern information technology that is changing the nature of scholarship in electronic media. And higher education has not reengineered on the same scale as in business and industry in order to adjust to a new reality.

Historical Information Science should include the scientific study of historian information-seeking behavior, attitudes, and literature. Additional research is required to understand: (1) the nature of historical literature and intellectual access to it, from perspectives other than content analysis; (2) patterns and timing of information exchange in the historical profession, measuring the accumulation of historical knowledge, extent of revisionism (e.g., what does this mean in terms of obsolescence?); and (3) changing and current practices and preferences of historians both as information seekers and providers, to monitor collective behavior and professional development. In the latter case, for example, the relation between information retrieval, assimilation, and integration into formal discourse and teaching would be of interest.

Such knowledge about historical information transfer needs to be assessed before attempting to modify such traditional and conservative information-seeking behavior, or conversely to customize tools for the dominant learning styles in the field. This is presumably what the AHA Research Division did in designing the new AHA *Guide* along traditional lines, but one suspects that the conceptualization of the project came from a generalized, intuited and discussed consensus of opinion rather than anything scientific. It would be interesting to know if citation reoccurrences before the *Guide*'s publication would indicate selection by the field at large coinciding with those by experts, or if citation patterns were at all altered after publication. Such citation studies might reveal if the *Guide* has any use beyond undergraduate reference. How would one justify to public funding agencies the cost of the *Guide* or any similar project, other than easily collectable data such as the number of volumes sold, number of reviews written, or other subjective criteria.

Enough is known, however, to call for a thorough reform of how historians teach information access and to change how graduate training prepares historians for the electronic intellectual world all around them. While traditional approaches may serve historians *qua* historians, the lessons learned in doing traditional historical research and attendant information searching may not be as transferable to other careers as much as they should be, if historians are to remain active in general education. Time management, precision, and recall in information retrieval, for example, are qualities left wanting in the typical historian's information searching fields other than his or her speciality. Thus the goal of transference, so often used to justify training in History as entry to other fields, may not be as great as commonly thought. This goal might be supported better if historians wielded more influence outside their classrooms, and if we could document how the production of historian literature directly influenced perception in and outside the field. How much more credibility History would have as a Social Science, if research could show that historical knowledge influenced decision making and behavior. We assume that it does as a matter of lore; we do not know how, in which specific instances, and to what effect.

Computer Literacy and History Computing Initiatives

The low priority given to bibliographic control of historical literature by United States historians and AHA's reliance on commercial ventures has meant that while bibliographic-minded historians have contributed to AHA's projects and are recruited by ABC-CLIO Inc. to serve as abstractors, the major historical associations in the United States have not developed within them a cadre of information professionals or developed a scientific approach to their own information needs. Other professional and scholarly associations have built such functions into their operations (MLA, APA, ALA, etc.) and prize them as basic services for their constituencies. In other fields, as in Education, think tanks have evolved into research laboratories exploring communications, media, information services, and teaching (e.g., the ten federally funded regional education laboratories in the United States). This is different from the situation in Europe where government-funded and corporate-assisted research centers such as France's Centre Nationale de Recherche Scientifique (CNRS) or the Max-Planck Institut für Geschichte at Göttingen have long engaged in bibliographic and source projects as integral to their research mission. This neglect of modern information technology and electronic resources is apparently reflected in History teaching and graduate training in the United States, and has retarded the growth of those purviews and operations identified here with Historical Information Science. A holistic unifying discipline that integrates bibliographic, numeric, textual, and image expertise cannot be built in the United States or elsewhere on weak and separated intellectual-technological foundations. Knowing and doing must be combined, it may be argued on grounds similar to those for the mutual reinforcement of faith and action.

Historians were and are still highly literate—textually; however, until recently requirements for other kinds of literacy—visual, computer, information literacy, etc.—were not recognized. Within the AHA it was assumed by committees promoting quantitative history that historians had to become more numerate (BOGUE, 1990), but the case for numeracy, even by Cliometricians, does not automatically transfer to the functional capabilities and ease of mind using modern technologies other than computerized calculation. American historians have been, therefore, largely ill-prepared to take advantage of the developing technology, which admittedly was not readily made available to them, and these factors partially explain the confusion and lag-time in their adoption of it for more than text processing. Their main avenue into the information field is intellectually through the overlap of Social Science History with the Social Sciences, and professionally through the Public History movement and relationship between History and archives. Although correction of this situation in the United States is much talked about, the solution is left largely to individuals. One cannot identify this as a major venue for the American Historical Association, for example, or its largest affiliates.

Many of the forward looking recommendations of the UNITED STATES. COMMISSION ON THE HUMANITIES for the 1980s, which used the *National Enquiry into Scholarly Communication* as its grounding, floundered so badly that a coherent national policy in the United States still cannot be identified. As a result in the 1990s the academic computing infrastructure is just being completed a decade behind previously envisioned schedules. The strict demarcation between the National Science Foundation (NSF) and National Endowments for the Humanities (NEH) and for the Arts (NEA) programs has not helped because interests in the technology to be applied are so split from the subject to which it is to be applied (projects using socioeconomic data in historical modeling would find more support in NSF, for example, but if image- or textbases were involved, NEH might be better, although until recently NEH never developed much acumen in computing). Joint funding for projects at the borderline between their purviews is rare. Moreover, the current federal administration's linkage of the National Information Infrastructure (NII) directly to economic development promises only incidental support for History as associated with the Social Sciences. The concept of NII as the National Research and Education Network (NREN) (CORBIN describes its development) originally held more promise for History and the Humanities in general, but NII and major projects like digital library initiatives are driven from the National Science Foundation (NSF). Since 1995 the current conservative regime in Washington, D.C. has targeted the National Endowment for the Arts (NEA) for elimination in an annual contest of wills. NEA survives, with unstable funding and a politicized future. Both agencies have had to weather the periodic storms in Washington, but the Arts and Humanities come under fire repeatedly, more regularly than scientific research. Science research funding recommendations are holding steady, however, including the Social Sciences, despite the budget cutting mood in the capital. While the decisive fate of the Arts and Humanities agencies are unclear in an era of budget constraints and politicized culture wars in the United States, both will continue to face perennial difficulty in obtaining government funding at all levels. Ironically, the United States Federal Government, particularly the White House, has continued the tradition of honoring American artists—a tradition begun by President J. F. Kennedy, but stable budgetary support lacks institutionalized commitment, varies from one administration to another, and seems always to be pitted against the goals to balance the budget and cut the national deficit even though the amounts in question are minuscule by any realistic comparison with these latter problems.

It must be recognized that NEH was itself tardy in promoting information technology and computing for the Humanities, and even when it began to do so, the amount of funding in contrast to the costs for such technology has always been disproportional. History has always found itself caught between NEH where anything too technical might dim chances for funding, and NSF where the technique and technology had to be emphasized and History recast totally as a Social Science to gain support. A coalition of learned societies (e.g., American

Council of Learned Societies or ACLS, including AHA) and some foundations like the Getty Trust, and the National Alliance, are fighting to save NEH as a separate funding agency, and increasingly professional associations, the information industry, and organizations allied with the National Science Foundation (NSF) have been brought into this alliance. Fortunately projects like the Digital Library Initiative which will assist the Arts and Humanities greatly, are sheltered under NSF's umbrella. It has been able to cooperate with NASA and the Defense Department's Advanced Research Project's Agency (DARPA) to pour $24.4 million in digital library development in the United States. These conversion projects (some of which are described later) are expensive, averaging $2-6/page, and require long-range, continual funding, rather than reliance on single benefactors and one-time grants. In the case of unilateral cooperation between project management and a patron, first-rate projects are tuned off and on intermittently depending on the will of the funding source or its financial health. Columbia University's digital Project Janus relied on a donated "Connection Machine 2" supercomputer with massive storage which had to be canceled when the hardware supplier, Thinking Machines, Inc., filed for bankruptcy. Recently the digital conversion projects at the Max-Planck Institute for History were threatened in 1995-1996 when the Foundation consolidated its operations and considered the fate of the Institute. It was spared in 1997—this time. Major programs initiated by the Kellog Foundation must work on short-term time frames because after three- or five-year cycles of grant support, their future is unknown. Initiatives are difficult to start up; projects are even more difficult to sustain as programs. The survival of such sponsored scholarship requires constant effort.

In any case, in the United States as in Europe the political stance of these allies for the NEH and its foreign philanthropic counterparts is necessarily defensive, even when the argument is essentially for the *status quo*. Perhaps the really important coalition that should form is even broader, cutting across the sciences, arts, and humanities for some kind of unified approach to funding a research infrastructure in the United States that is more coherent than what has evolved to date. Such a unidisciplinary vision does not and should not exclude culture. The federal funding of science research and technology without the arts and humanities, and without making science and technology available for cultural purposes, would seem tantamount to the government's intervention and stimulation of a single-dimension culture that is even more imbalanced than government funding policies have been in the past. The precarious interest of education and cultural endeavors in modern telecommunications, for example, is already under pressure from the rising use of the Internet for business and commercial transactions, with entertainment being second in use, and education a distant third.

POOLE describes the possibilities of global telecommunication, but problems exist everywhere (KOFMAN & YOUNGS). Many are technically rooted, but their resolution lies in policy and hence politics. The critical issue in modern telecommunications is to obtain broad band transmission sufficient for education's needs, rather than what modest band width and support the telecommunications industry wants to spare. The National Initiative for a Networked Cultural Heritage (NINCH) is being created to safeguard public interests in free access to the Internet (D. GREEN, 1997; cf., its articulated research agenda: NINCH, 1996; GETTY AHIP, 1996). It is symptomatic of the uneasy posture of government regarding information systems and services and also the divide between the technical communications side of the question and issues related to content. It is easier to support a technological advance for its own sake, than to relate the technology to content and support both. In short, behind funding problems and organizational approaches to information technology for the arts and humanities loom larger societal and political problems of perceptions, values, education, and rhetoric in public relations. Transcendence above these barriers and equitable global access are the goals of the Coalition for Networked Information (CNI) led by the late Paul Evan Peters, as also reflected in the ALA principles for the development of the National Information Infrastructure (NII) in the United States (Appendix A). Such coalitions like local collaborations are breaking down divisions between departments and disciplines, as well as the old and outdated distinction between "learned" and "professional" societies.

When the Vancouver Island History Project team BASKERVILLE & GAFFIELD (GAFFIELD *ET AL.*) in the late 1970s began investigation of building historical data archives, they were prompted to explore the work being done on MARC-AMC formats for archival description (OCLC *AMC Format*). They plunged anew into AACR-2, NSTF, MARC-AMC, field numbers, subject headings, descriptors, name authority control (LIBRARY OF CONGRESS, 1977/1997-; OCLC, *Name-authority*, third ed., 1984-), and thesauri, etc. (all related by GILCHRIST). GAFFIELD (p. 315) recalled later that "we found ourselves reading journals we had never even heard of, learning vocabularies of the 'foreign' language of other disciplines," referring to library and archival science. This, of course, is still largely the case, and is complicated by rapidly changing technology and usage variance, sometimes like local dialects, in the professional and technical journal literature.

Historians in the United States can avail themselves of academic computing centers and seem to be doing so in larger numbers, but computing staff are often as untrained in the Information Sciences as historians, and their library experience is likewise often no better developed than the amateur stage. As communications cross these disciplinary boundaries more and more, and sublanguages are learned by more people for cross-disciplinary discourse, such communication barriers will break down. Moreover, a broad common experience in library usage, more than in archives use, operates as a basis for understanding in the new information environment historians find themselves with such facilities as provided by H-Net. Libraries are interested in solving these problems and improving communications, access, and useability of information resources in all forms. Some (especially OCLC) are studying current traffic through FTP sites and are exploring enhancements of Internet capabilities such as file transfers (BISHOP). Nothing comparable to Hope N. Tilman and Sharyn Ladner's studies for special library use of telecommunications exists for historians' use, even for their own H-NET. In any case, History as a whole may not be professionally or intellectually ready to engage modern information technology full-scale, if such judgment is rendered from past library use and information-retrieval studies. A segment, however, is already so engaged, but the overall prognosis is mixed indeed. What is needed, however, is ongoing study of this development of electronic communication among historians as it unfolds, rather than waiting for an historical analysis of aged data sometime in the future.

European historians seem to have been better positioned intellectually with traditions of continuity between the human, social, and natural sciences, and respect for bibliographic scholarship, but not necessarily to engage information technology more easily than Americans. The European regard for History as part of both the Humaine and Social Sciences may have assisted financially, but complaints about inadequate funding for hardware and software are common on both sides of the Atlantic. Critics of the European situation portray an overall development of academic computing and information technology in higher education as no better than in the United States (GENET, 1995, 1996). Moreover, historians in the United Kingdom were initially no more receptive to information technology than Americans and historical computing there has been likewise a specialization of a minority of practitioners (SCHURER, 1990, pp. 172-173, citing the SOCIAL SCIENCE RESEARCH COUNCIL, 1970; cf. M. KATZEN). There, too, the earliest relationship with computer and information studies came through the Social Sciences rather than through librarianship or bibliographic endeavors. As in the United States, where J. HIGHAM observed that quantitative historians operated as an elite cadre unrelated to the rank and file of American historians, English computing historians like the American "Social Science Historians" were seen to operate at the fringe of the discipline. If they did not separate into their own organization voluntarily, it has often seen that they could be forced out of History with nowhere to reside. Yet, they were needed most firmly entrenched in the discipline, to operate as a fifth-column movement and bring about change from within rather than vilification from outside the profession.

Whether somewhat ostracized or not, computing historians in Great Britain in March, 1986, with help from the Nuffield and European Science Foundations, formed their own Association for History and Computing (AHC) at the second Westfield Conference at Queen Mary and Westfield College in the University of London. The first conference in Great Britain on "History and Computing" had been only the year before, but by 1986 the conference drew 300 people from 19 countries—"a galaxy of contact-starved historians," as DENLEY & HOPKIN recall the event (1995, p. 7). They "were able to discover colleagues working in other areas but with similar methodological and practical problems." AHC subsequently allied with French and German counterparts to establish national branches under the umbrella of an international AHC that now has about a thousand members in 25 countries. This organization has spread throughout Europe first from Austria (1986) immediately after the United Kingdom branch, and with an immediate alliance with the Verniging voor Geschiedenis en Informatica (VGI) or Low Countries Association for History and Computing that had evolved parallel to AHC. From these core foundations, the organization spread to France, Portugal, and Switzerland the next year, then the Commonwealth of Independent States (1988), Eastern Europe (1989), Canada (1990), to Spain (1990) and now to South America as well where incidentally the past two years have witnessed the greatest growth in sign-ons to the Internet. A chapter has been organized recently in the United States; its natural alliance would be with the Social Science History group. DENLEY & HOPKIN have attempted to stimulate interest in the United States through their introduction in 1995 of IAHC to the AHA; the contact person is Professor Janice Reiff of UCLA, the AHA's editor of its "Computing and History" forum (REIFF). IAHC's members seem to achieve a more fluid integration in both History and the Social Science organizations in Europe, although they are not well represented in the international archives arena, linguistics and terminology forums, or the information science community. Consequently their orientation remains closer to Social Science computing, but the traditional focus on numeric data has been expanded to textual and image computing in remarkable ways. This is a syncretist group that reflects the unidisciplinarity of historical computing as technique, methodology, and use of information technology regardless of field of application, which is so inherently interesting. It is therefore remarkable that it has had so little contact or relations with the Information Science communities of Europe and America (MCCRANK, 1994b). Historians seem unaware that there is even a much larger intra- and extra-academic information professional community sharing problems similar to those confronting computing historians.

Indicative of this larger context are developments in the United Kingdom concurrent with the development of AHC. To create a shortcut directly to information technology, the British History Association created an Advisory Body for Educational Technology (HABET), and the British Academy with the British Library Research and Development Department in 1990 (BRITISH LIBRARY, 1993, pp. 1-2, [37]) called together the Humanities Information Review Panel. Despite the British Library connection, it seems not to draw upon the United Kingdom's considerable Information Science community and its educational establishment (MACDOUGAL & BRITTAIN) as though there, as in the United States, the Humanities and Information Science are somewhat disjointed. Likewise, efforts of the British Library do not seem to be related to parallel efforts by the Public Records Office (PRO), such as its AD2001 program (Archives Direct by 2001 entailing Web access to PRO catalogs and guides, as well as a "virtual museum" of digitized images form the archives: see http://www.open.gov.uk/pro/prohome.htm). The archives/libraries dichotomy in Europe is as divisive as in America. Such fora were meant, however, to create interesting cross-disciplinary dialogues about information technology, but seem not to accomplish this task for History in particular, nor the Humanities generally, because the focus is on the information industry (BRITTAIN).

The 1990s seem like a remedial catch-up and acceleration simultaneously; these are exciting times for History, if it is serious about engaging information technology and relating to the Information Science community.

Historical computing in Europe has received tremendous invigoration but more modest financial support through several government and educational reform initiatives for this decade. The United Kingdom's development of the Joint Academic Network (JANET, soon to be SuperJANET), Computers and Teaching Initiative (orchestrated by the Information Systems Committee, ISC), and subsequent Technology Training Initiative (BRITISH LIBRARY, 1993), has had a stimulating effect on History and computing. The British Library Research and Development Department has also encouraged widespread debate about the impact of information technology on education, both generally and for information professionals, but its *Information UK 2000* report (MARTYN, VICKERS & FEENEY) does not relate very well a vision for a "proactive" information professional community with either the Social Science or Arts and Humanities except for language teaching. ELKIN criticized the report for being out of touch in other ways, especially pointing to the gulf between practitioners and library and information science educators. Continued efforts to spread computing capabilities throughout the United Kingdom educational system are noteworthy, such as the formation of a national data center for the Arts and Humanities under the direction of Daniel GREENSTEIN (1997).

France has concentrated its efforts in the Centre Nationale de Recherche Scientifique (CNRS) in Paris which actively promotes computerized history projects and, for its own operations and collections management, has developed a cadre of professionals in history and humanities computing that contribute regularly to international conferences. The CNRS venture into Artificial Intelligence (AI) applications and expert systems is particularly noteworthy, coupled with its extensive development of data dictionaries and textbases and its multidisciplinary scope. Examples of its wide-ranging activities are provided in a following discussion pertaining specifically to medieval studies (cf., BOURLET *ET AL.*). However, the situation in France seems not so progressive outside these few research centers. GENET (1995, 1996) has been especially critical of the *status quo* in France, especially the lack of development of a proper infrastructure for historical computing. Other historians are critical of the French school of History, which is highly divided. Some, like G. NOIRIEL, speak of a crisis in French History because of the rampant factionalization polarization of schools of thought (BOUTIER & JULIA discuss the various schools as "camps" waging intellectual warfare), which for all of their deconstruction and destruction (e.g., multi-directional attacks on the Annals school), have yet to come together for a new consensus, a common praxis, or set of methodologies. The problem is larger than the simpler question of use of computers by historians.

GENET does not address the work of French archivists with electronic records and computing, which is typical of commentaries by historians. Although Genet spoke about the situation in France in particular, but in continental Europe generally; and colleagues from the Low Countries participating in a panel discussion seem to agree with him about the inordinate lag time for technical information transfer across fields, the lack of state-of-the-art equipment, deficient training, and a general disaffection from empirical research. GUARNIERI (ACH, 1997) has painted a similarly dismal picture for Italy, where Humanities computing is dominated by a few institutes such as that for linguistics at Pisa. Historical computing projects have been undertaken in a few university research centers, but production of such scholarship has been sporadic. The integration of Information Science into the Humanities is not common, and Italian students have limited instructional tools for getting started. Guarnieri, whose dissertation work focuses on computing in the Humanities generally and History specifically, claims that fewer than 450 monographs in Italian deal with Informatics; most of these are manuals for specific software. Data processing in Italy as elsewhere offers only a "technology-conditioned" view, in his opinion. The deficiencies these historians lament point to the problem of an emerging field which requires fairly quick methodological solidification, coherent movement to form a lasting trend, and an enthusiasm general enough to create the transfer of funds and other resources needed to support historical computing. In short, computing in History requires a considerably larger investment, a longer gestation period, and a greater momentum to develop through adolescence into a mature science, but the support for such development has never been forthcoming from university administrations or national agencies.

In the United States as in Europe, History has lacked the resources to mount the necessary effort, and the initial foray into quantification studies met with such emotional resistance and unseemly contention that the discipline also lacked the accommodation if not the will and perseverance to adopt modern information technology. GENET's critique thus rings true for History in America as well as Europe. A movement toward descriptive anthropology, which has overtaken French social history (cf., ELEY & NIELD; KIRK; and P. JOYCE about the demise or transformation of Social History), is much easier to begin and to sustain precisely because it is not technologically dependent, is less costly, and can be accomplished individually. Like narrative history, it is the art of the possible. It requires neither the collaboration nor the laboratory support necessary for state-of-the-art computing, and less investment in methodological training and in database development before analysis. Few historians, however, have commented on recent trends in historiography as being a matter of convenience, limited investment, and within range of the possible, whereas alternatives were blocked because they were risky for immediate career advancement and even impossible given the relative poverty of History's research technical infrastructure in most countries. In the former Soviet Union momentum was achieved in a few select centers where History was allied closely with the Social Sciences, but there the lack of technology in academe generally was itself a constant drawback. Even today one must marvel at what Russian computing historians and their graduate students accomplish with so little (e.g., at Lomonsov State University with two classrooms converted to computing laboratories with a dozen and half PCs, in a school of 300 faculty). Thus what might have congealed earlier into an Historical Information Sciences seems to have had problems of theory and methodology and to have been out of synchronization with technology and technique in Science and Technology, in addition to the problem of congenial context and lack of a secure home base, compounded by the cost of technology, its rapid transformation, and inability of History to provide adequate training. All totaled, these are significant, formidable problems that would dampen the enthusiasm of even the most ardent devotee and stifle innovation in any discipline.

While the past decades have proven difficult and discouraging for some, certain developments need to be highlighted as encouraging signs. The European Economic Community (EEC, or sometimes just EC), which maintains its own computerized archives (PALAYRET), has supported conferences on the preservation and enhancement of historical records, for example the University of Bordeaux conference in 1989 on converting Inquisition records into data archives (DEDIEU & ROWLAND), and has long displayed an interest in electronic archives. It has also engaged the preservation field by sponsoring the VASARI project to monitor the effects of climate, especially light and humidity, on art objects in Europe's museums and has promoted data exchange between archives by funding the Remote Access to Museum Archives (RAMA) project (STARRE). EEC's computerized projects, especially work in machine translation (VOLLMER), have tremendous import for History, the Humanities, and other cultural endeavors even if they are undertaken for more practical international business concerns. One of the EEC's 24 directorates, the Commission of the European Communities (CEC), has two divisions that are especially involved in cultural and heritage matters: (1) DG X, the Cultural Action unit for information, communication and culture generally, is most important; but (2) DG XIII for technology is of obvious importance for such a topic as Historical Information Science. DG X and XIII have together supported the Network of Art Research Computer Image Systems in Europe (NARCISSE) and RAMA projects. Other directorates for marketing (DG III) and competition (DG IV) may affect cultural affairs because of involvement with the art trade, export of manuscripts and rare books considered to be cultural properties, etc. DG XI, because of its purview over environmental concerns, is relevant to preservation efforts. There is a tremendous potential for spin-off benefits from EEC activities to academic pursuits, such as the common market for higher education and tuition waivers allowing for the development of advanced studies programs and specialized centers more concentrated and larger than could be justified by smaller enrollments at multiple sites around Europe.

The inclusion of humanities and history computing in the EEC grants program reflects a continuing Western tradition of public and private patronage of the scholarly enterprise. Individual programs of interest to historians might be understood better when placed in the context of the overall strategy of the European Union (EU). Such a European perspective lacks the demarcation between the arts, humanities, and sciences that stultifies similar inter-disciplinarity in America and blocks the transfer of technology from business and industry or the professions such as medicine, to the whole of academe. This is unfortunate, because such fields as Medicine, well funded and endowed with so much intellectual talent, too often goes untapped by historians. Consider such diagnostic techniques and expert systems development from the Medical or Health Sciences that could be applied in History (see ROSSER MATTHEWS for quantification in the medical fields, which become extremely complex, as HECKERMAN's use of probability to study variables and similarities of complicated networks such as lymphatic systems). Given the tendency to model the whole of social experience upon individual behavior and to see parallels between human physiology and human organization (H. COLLINS), one might think that the historians and social scientists would turn to the medical sciences for methods and techniques, but this is not generally the case. Historians of Science and Medicine could serve History better as conduits between the fields. There are, however, well established alliances by which cross-disciplinarity works most often, and gulfs between other fields that impedes the exchange of ideas and transfer of ideas and technology.

The EEC in 1993 met in Brussels during December 1993 to consider a White Paper on "Growth, Competitiveness and Employment" which began a movement parallel to the United States' articulation in September of that same year of a "National Information Infrastructure" (NII, reframed in 1994 as Global Information Infrastructure, GII, to indicate cooperation in cross-border information exchange). Subsequently the EEC has launched an ambitious program under the direction of DG XIII (Telecommunications, Information Market, and Exploitation of Research) called *INFO2000*. Gunter Steven at the 1995 ASIS conference with the International Federation for Information and Documentation (FID) described its rationale on the basis of the changing business environment, maintaining that "Traditional foundations are being shaken" (G. STEVEN). He summarized these changes as follows: (1) data compression and broadband width now available means an abundance of information never before possible; (2) digitization and multimedia are producing a convergence of technologies that open up new possibilities as well; (3) deregulation and internationalization of information resources and flow means that the information market worldwide is increasingly open and competitive; and (4) the user now has more choices than at any other time because of the ability to be interactive and simultaneously to segment data and information. He points to changing values in the cost of information, indicating that between 1994 and the turn of the millennium equipment values will remain constant (14 percent), distribution costs will decrease significantly (from 38 percent a year ago), and content costs will rise dramatically (from the current 48 percent). Already the content industry (including publishing) in Europe is as large as the telecoms and computer hardware and software industry combined. It is indicative of the "scribe to screen" phenomena transforming international business, and which will have an equally thorough impact in academe. These trends are especially significant for historians because they have always been and are well positioned in the content business where the action will be, while the currently preponderant emphasis on the technology itself will decline. G. STEVEN (his slide 12) maintained "Content will be a key driver of demand" that will cater to full employment, competitiveness, cultural identities, linguistic diversity, and a new style, transnational democracy.

In light of these trends, the EEC in 1994 undertook several initiatives based on the so-called Bangemann report (June 24-25, 1994); the action plan "Europe's Way to the Information Society" outlined at the Brussels conference on July 19, 1994. This aims at creating a new regulatory and legal framework for information handling, a European-wide network, and programs for promoting the information society (which include social and cultural programming) and the EEC G-7 conference (February 25-26, 1995) on "The Global Information Society." In July 1995 an Information Society Forum of 124 experts in six working groups recommended a series of priority projects at the EU level, some of which are driven by comparisons between Europe and the United States. STEVEN reflects the EEC attitude that Europe in 1995 is three to five years behind the United States based of EU/US ratios such as 1/2.5 usage of electronic information services; 1/1.5-2 penetration of IT (Information Technology) equipment; 1/3 telephone use; and 1/.1 high capacity tariffs. One strategy of the EEC DG XIII is to take advantage of Europe's content industry by stimulating even more multimedia content by the year 2000—data, text, sound, images, mixed media, in analog or digital format, on a variety of carriers (paper, microfilm, magnetic or optical storage, etc.).

The EEC will therefore invest heavily in print as much as electronic publishing, including audiovisual, while the United States emphasis remains focused largely on technology. Actions include (1) stimulating demand and awareness in efforts to create new markets by demonstrating access capabilities: e.g., networks to all national organizations, clusters of pan-European users, etc., which is why the EU is so interested in transborder cooperation between cultural organizations; (2) exploiting public sector information, especially through common standards, interconnectivity, and integration of transaction systems; (3) creating catalysts for multimedia development in three pilot areas (cultural heritage, geographic information, and business opportunities including trade in intellectual property rights); and (4) supporting through public education and skills development under "Socrates" (Education policy) and "Leonardo" (Training Policy) programs. EU cultural policy falls under the name "Raphael." This EU nomenclature commemorating heroes in Western Civilization is another indication of the integration of cultural heritage in European thinking about the "information society" which is so often lacking in American ahistorical discussions where naming is more apt to invent another unintelligible acronym. In any case, the EEC understands the movement toward a knowledge intensive society and seeks to catalyze change as in moving into a reliable and global regulatory framework, focusing on information content as the key to future development, and trying to reach a consensus among member states about overarching goals. Its articulation of information policy seems more coherent than any American counterpart, and the discussion in Europe seems consciously less driven by technology for its own sake. G. STEVEN (OHT no. 8A) states the EEC position clearly: "The information society is about people—not about technology."

The former Soviet Union's "Campaign for Computerization, 1985," educational reform or *perestroika* called "informatization" has been less spectacular than originally conceived due to unforeseen political reorganization and attendant social turmoil, political unrest, and economic hard times. Y. LOGEL charts the history of the Soviet computing industry (cf., TIKHONOV *ET AL.*) with 1969 as a pivotal year leading to independent developments, and thence to increase cooperation within East Europe during the 1980s; however, WOLCOT points to numerous problems impeding the development of high performance computing before the more recent turn of political events, and GOODIN shows how the RAPIRA Project of the Group for School Informatics failed to inculcate in information technology revolution in Soviet secondary education. P. SPENCE RICHARDS covers the parallel development of Information Science in the former Soviet Union, which has had considerable influence on information theory in the United States. John Richardson is exploring further the growth of Information Science in the

Commonwealth of Independent States. RAKITOV has provided the chief overview of the Soviet vision of the "Information Society" just before the collapse of the USSR.

The reformation of the former Union into a Commonwealth of Independent States has changed the reality, but not the vision. The current catastrophic changes facing Russian archives are discussed with a sense of urgency by P. KENNEDY GRIMSTED (1989, 1990), including the questionable fate of the Russian Academy of Science's grand automation project, the *ArcheoBiblioBase*. In any case, computers in the Soviet Union were never readily available to arts and humanities scholars, and barely to social scientists, so progress has been as slow there as in the United States and elsewhere in bridging the gap between the rich and poor in access to information technology. What progress was made is now threatened by the financial crisis racking the Commonwealth's core states. Although unsuccessful at full-scale "informatization," the Soviet (now Russian) Academy of Science's inclusion of History in its support of research institutes was critical (BORODKIN, 1993). The survival of such research centers is very important in the continuous development of Historical Information Science, especially its empirical form, which Soviet prowess so well exemplified in socioeconomic studies (e.g., the methodology textbook of RAKITOV & GRIGORIIAN). Faculty exchanges assist in such continuity and sharing of methodologies and techniques, as in Borodkin's 1992-93 association with Harvard University. In 1994 the United States Information Agency (USIA) under the Freedom Support Act created a new exchange program for Russian Teaching Assistants (RTAP) hosted by American institutions. History is eligible, but Information Science is not mentioned in the program's scope statement. It would be ideal if such programs created continuing collaborative work across the Internet after such exchange occur, but the primary focus is to assist teaching English as a foreign language with classroom experience in the United States, and the conscious deployment of information technology to foster continued exchanges after personal visits, through Distant Learning technology and across the Internet, seems not to be a priority. That will hopefully change. Interestingly, post-Cold War international cooperation has produced an offering of assistance to Russian archives to resolve the intellectual access problem.

In 1992, the Hoover Institution and the Rosarkiv gently moved into some cooperative programs. Based on this detente, at the opening of 1995, the Research Libraries Group (RLG), announced an electronic link to the Russian State Archival Services to provide for shared cataloging, with Russian archival records being added to RLIN in return for access in Russia to the database's 67 million records. MircoMARC with a Cyrillic overlay is being employed in the State Archives of the Russian Federation (GARF) and the Russian Center for the Preservation and Study of Documents of Contemporary History (RtsKhIDNI), plus two Tver regional archival centers. The Russian archivist, Rudolf Pikhoia, thinks that this access alone will spur a re-evaluation of Soviet history, but such research requires full-text transmission of archival records. That is to be accomplished in a two-year pilot project, apparently not only for immediate access but as a preservation measure in case "something goes awry in Russia" (comment of Normal Naimark of Stanford, perhaps in awareness of the tragic loss in 1993 of the Sarajevo state library and archives in the Bosnian conflict). Consequently, Russian historians as well as American historians studying Russia, will have to become adroit Internet searchers and online RLIN users. They no doubt will do just that.

In short, despite problems the prospects of a major advance in the use of modern information technology by historians are really very good. The traditional lag time in adopting technology is shortening with each generation of historians in graduate studies. However, because History is commonly perceived as a nontechnical field, those attracted to historical studies are not often as prepared as one might expect to advance into the realm of Historical Information Science. In the United States, graduate studies must be supported by workshops and instruction in basic skills, and graduate courses in American institutions as in Europe still entail what might be regarded as remedial training. The acquisition of basic computer

skills and searching techniques, however, is not the same as evaluating information or understanding applications, sources, and research possibilities. It is a head start, nevertheless, over
the past generation of historians who for the most part were self-taught while technological
change outstripped their self-improvement, and who had to "learn on the fly" and through
continuing education to remedy their graduate training, without the myriad aids and educational opportunities that are available today.

HISTORY OF INFORMATION SCIENCE AND TECHNOLOGY

Most historical information is not preserved in its pristine original state, even for modern
history, unless it is a source that was seldom used. Unused sources are particularly troublesome
because they have no history themselves and, as in the case of unknown diaries, are difficult
to verify and authenticate. Unless the find is special or even spectacular, without prior use and
evidence of influence, it is not likely to be highly valued as a source. Unlike an *object d'art*
where, if the artifact is in a like-new condition, it is prized for its original state which is itself
evidence of the craftsmanship, art, or creation, most historical sources gain value for history
because of their initial use, continued reuse, and singular, dramatic, or repeated widespread
influence. Because historical information is subject to change in the course of its transmission
and use, the source documents history both in its origin and in every instance of use. In short,
sources tell history and have a history of their own, some of which must be told from other collaborating sources. This metahistory, or history of the source, is contextual; that is, its use in
time and place are interpreted so as to attribute value, importance, etc., to the source. Text and
context are interactive. This means that historians pay attention to the culture, organization,
and institution that created, preserved, and transmitted a source.

Archivists refer to this as provenance (extended as registration to preserve original order,
as in the German equivalent term *Registraturprinzip*), but source biography is often a larger
issue than chain of custody and ownership, especially when information derived from a
source is disembodied, so to speak, and relates to the source indirectly. This idea of tying
everything together for complete documentation, as opposed to disembodied information
transfer, is referred to by L. DURANTI (1997 a & b) as "the archival bond." She tersely
defines this as the "recursive identifying relationship of record" (1997b, glossary), but elab-
orates that this is "the original, necessary, and determined web of relationships that each
record has at the moment at which is it made or received with the records that belong in the
same aggregation. It is an incremental relationship...." The archival notion of provenance
has traditionally pertained to the source as a material witness, an object, or a thing.
Secondly, how a source is created and transmitted becomes equally important, and this is a
question of tracking that necessarily involves information technology. Formal criticism, document examination and authentification, forensics, and interpretation rely on a command of
technical information derived from and attributed to a source. Thirdly, historical information
is not conveyed through reversible processes. One cannot go from a final state back to the
initial state, and it is a given that only in totally reversible processes is all information recov-
erable. Historians, therefore, always confront the problems of imperfect and incomplete
data; because they cannot rely on a one-dimensional reverse (a tracking or chaining, or
duplication of an experiment) to observe a phenomenon or process again, they must rely on
a broad multisource information recovery mechanism, and even then, augment this with substitution, hypothesis, and sometimes speculation.

Every historian, therefore, must be a historian of information technology, and perhaps of
information science as well (i.e., whatever stood for the science of information and communication at the time). A multifaceted specialization in History must therefore include the
following: (1) knowledge of the core domain or the history of a subject in its time and place;

(2) the history of the sources that allow the historian to judge evidence and to reconstruct that history, i.e., a metahistory; (3) languages and linguistic competence to have access to internal content once appropriate sources are identified and retrieved; (4) the history of historical interpretation and writings about the subject, i.e., historiography; and (5) familiarity with a broad range of methodology. These should be developed in tandem, but too often the methodologies of source criticism and the technical knowledge of metahistory are not as well mastered as the subject area and its historiography, and search skills are often developed too narrowly in the area of primary research only. Certain fields, such as Medieval and Early Modern History where paleography, codicology, and diplomatics are often taught formally with expectations of linguistic skills and command of multiple languages, pay more attention to this aspect of historical study than others. American History is notoriously slack in teaching such skills and, most incredibly, it is not a strong component of most archivist education. Not only should this critical technical mastery be restored back to the core of historical education and training, but today an added crucial dimension in historical training must be accommodated: computing historians must understand thoroughly and critically modern information technology to comprehend the transformation of historical information from physical sources into electronic formats and transmission through telecommunications. Old specialties like paleography and typography must be extended to electronic codes and font conversions; diplomatics must be reinvented to study formatting, protocols, and software conventions; and programming languages have to be added to the historian's language repertoire (as advocated earlier by myself in the 1970s, and more recently by DURANTI and BLOUIN & DELMAS, 1997). Thus, the history of information and communication technology is an integral part of Historical Information Science.

The INTERNATIONAL TECHNOLOGY EDUCATION ASSOCIATION (ITEA) in 1996 attempted to provide a rationale and structure for the study of technology in its call for "technological literacy" for Americans (DYRENFURTH & KOZAK) parallel to and commensurate with the idea of "information literacy" (BRIEVIK & GEE). It defines technology (p. 16) as "human innovation in action. It involves the generation of knowledge and processes to develop systems that solve problems and extend human capabilities." As a foundation for its Technology for All Americans Project supported by the NSF and the National Aeronautics and Space Administration (NASA), ITEA's taskforce explains especially in regard to information technology (p. 1):

> Technological literacy is much more than just knowledge about computers and their application. It involves a vision where each citizen has a degree of knowledge about the nature, behavior, power, and consequences of technology from a broad perspective. Inherently, it involves educational programs where learners become engaged in critical thinking as they design and develop products, systems, and environments to solve practical problems.

Such a definition is in keeping with the increasing common approach to technology as an academic discipline and the integration of theory and experience in education. MITCHAM speaks of technology as a way of thinking; WIENS, leading a taskforce of the ITEA, argued for "technology as liberal education." The framework provided by the ITEA, as opposed to the older segregation of technology as material from anything ethereal which led to the misconception that technical matters were not intellectual, lends itself to the inter-disciplinary ideology underlying this essay. Indeed, the rationale and structure for the study of technology underscored by ITEA includes and promotes the history of technology as essential in its goal of technological literacy, especially to support its three components: use, management, and understanding of technology.

Technology is ever changing...

Part of the historical perspective of technology is an understanding of significant technological accomplishments throughout history. This can be an immense and significant undertaking. Moreover, what is considered significant may change according to the context in which it is placed. However, substantive technological milestones usually result in a combination of the following:

- An alteration of the way people create new products, systems, and environments

- An incorporation of new ways of doing work and recreation

- A widespread and dramatic impact on individuals, social systems, or the environment

- A significant impact on the progress in other subject fields

It is important that the nature and evolution of technology be included in the cognitive basis of the study of technology (p. 25).

The visualization of the knowledge structure of modern technology (p. 16) includes understanding "the nature and evolution of technology" and a cardinal skill is the ability to assess the impact and consequences of technological systems. The link between technological literacy and history computing with its use of computers, project management, and orientation toward modeling is clear when understood in terms of ITEA's description (p. 11) of "technologically literate people" as those who "use a strong systems-oriented approach to thinking about and solving technological problems." The systems approach is, of course, consistent with the argument for Historical Information Science based on technological convergence: "a system is a group of interrelated components that collectively achieve a goal" (p. 12). This explains the following look at the histories of information technology and information science as natural ingredients in Historical Information Science.

History of Information Institutions

The traditional framework for the study of information organizations, institutions, and related industries has been to devote attention to different kinds of institutions, i.e., libraries, archives, museums, etc., as though these were always unrelated even though their history is entwined, and in the modern era, their funding and governance are still related through parent authorities, corporate and often public, and their missions dovetail each other. A significant contextual history exists, but not a mature historiography or critical literature to draw upon in creating the history of Information Science, Communications, Computing, and Technology within such long-range and comparative vision. The basic contextual fields include (1) the history of ideas and intellectual history, especially those strains of Western thought that have imbued Information Science with its theoretical dimension; (2) the history of science and technology, which is increasingly written as part of the New Social or Political History (SUDDER) and includes information technology (MAHONEY); and (3) the rich inheritance of Information Science through Library Science and critical bibliography.

The International Federation of Library Associations (IFLA) sponsors the *Annual Bibliography of the History of the Printed Book and Libraries (ABHB*, ed. VERVLIET, 1969-) covering printed book and library history from ca. 1500; each year it provides access to more than 3,000 studies in 2,000 periodicals. Its counterpart for the manuscript period is the *Bulletin Codicologique* published in *Scriptorium* (1946/47-); and although there is no specialized extension for the bibliography for the history of modern electronic information and Information Science, this will come (e.g., *Journal of Electronic Publishing*). The twentieth-century *Historical Abstracts* is a mine for the history of modern information communication, media, organizations, technology, and science. Like ABC-CLIO's major indexes, *LISA* and *Library Abstracts* include such material. Bibliography for the Information Science counterpart to these culturally oriented humanities tools can be gleaned from basic references like the *Encyclopedia of Library and Information Science* and updated by *Information Science Abstracts*. One is led thereby to occasional, but not many, relevant articles in the *Bulletin of the American Society for Information Science* and the *Journal of the American Society for Information Science* (*JASIS*) (see the historical overview by A. W. ELIAS), and documentation publications in *Documentaliste* and the *Journal of Documentation* (reviewed historically by VICKERY, 1994).

If the idea of information is interpreted most broadly as formal human communication in keeping with the anthropological sense of culture, then other organizations might be associated with the traditional duo of archives and libraries, such as historical sites and parks, botanical gardens and zoos, and perhaps also the performing arts ranging from common to high culture. Zoos were revived in the West conterminously with the museum movement, but the former is not a subject associated with Information Science as much as the latter in recent years. BANN's study of the post-French Revolution museum which disembodied art and separated artifacts from any authentic context or sense of historical continuity, as part of a conscious reconstruction of the past, is as much a study of decontextualization of knowledge and fundamental objectification of visual information as it is a study of cultural institutions. His inquiry, ostensibly into museum history but really into larger information issues like the validity of representation *ex situ* and the nineteenth-century cultural reversion to recapture an authentic history that was to transform museums and archives with the professionalization of history (P. LEVINE), seems especially relevant to modern issues of computer visualization and context sensitivity. For another example, HOOPER-GREENHILL explores the impact of museums on both popular culture and knowledge organization (in keeping with trends in the sociology of knowledge, where as in the case of E. D. MCCARTHY knowledge is seen as culture). KATRIEL treats heritage museums in Israel as "cultural production centers" to study docents and their communications as a means to distinguish reflective history from modes of communication and methods of informing the public which are fundamentally opposed to History. The cultural critic Andreas Huyssen, who characterizes modernity as "a culture of amnesia," sees the phenomenal popularity of historical fiction in film and television while academic history plays to a decreased audience, and the growth of personal memoirs in the face of detachment and the passion for genealogy as family life fragments, as nostalgia in the place of formal History. Thus, he calls the increased popularity of museums in the last quarter of this century "Museummania" (HUYSSEN, p. 7).

The same distinction might be applied to the information milieu, where the thirst for information seems insatiable, but its utility and application once retrieved are not well understood; and the distance between such popular consumption and the formal, academic study of information resources, services, systems, etc., in Computer and Information Science seems to be increasing. Information Science, related to libraries and archives and thereby to the classical tradition, has traditionally emphasized formal knowledge and information systems rather than informal understanding and social systems that convey information, the focus on customer, service, clientele, etc., keeps the field's attention on consumption and the public. The tendency to treat information in the abstract or to pay more attention to the systems and operations behind the scenes and indirect services has been changing in the last decade with the subtle but pervasive influence of Anthropology. Both History and Information Science are paying more attention to informal communications, popular perceptions, and social circumstances that influence receptivity and interpretation of information. This is what Joyce Appleby recently called "public-minded history," as a subtle but perceptive distinction from Public History (APPLEBY, 1997b). In this regard, note likewise that popular culture and the performing arts cannot be easily segregated from radio, television, video, and other telecommunications.

Libraries have long engaged in public programs and see themselves as culture centers with exhibit and lecture programs stemming from the lyceum tradition, and performing arts as well are often featured in library programs. Library literature covers such events and programming, but seldom with formal program evaluation of the variety sanctioned in business and education, and this whole area is sadly neglected in Information Science literature. The bias is that such venues do not convey information, which is patently false, and public programming does not comprise information systems, which runs counter to the treatment of advertising in business and marketing, for example. Multimedia in public programming likewise gets little attention as distinct from its use in information systems. History, therefore, as a Social Science is more likely to receive attention then as one of the Humanities.

Historical Information Science should be more embracing in this regard than Information Science has been. Despite the pervasive influence of television in American life, one of the most elusive records in modern history is from television broadcasts (CATTERALL & MORRIS). Other communications technology would be included, with attention to their pre-electric antecedents. Current sensibilities appreciate oral or voice and visual or image communications, beyond the classically imposed restriction to textual information transfer and reliance on reading. The information contents of these purveyors of information and culture have usually been segregated from the organization, i.e., the history of books and printing or historical bibliography, and the history of literature or the arts has been taught separately as though content, medium, and dissemination are unrelated. Archival history, what little has been taught, is better integrated (e.g., R. COX, 1990), but it still reflects the division of such historical foci into categories defined by recent professionalization and academic departmentalization. Overall such history has been very fragmented not only because markets for historical information were splintered, separate, and mutually exclusive, but there was no unifying theme such as the modern concepts of communication and information provide. In short, Historical Information Science should follow the integrative and ecumenical domain-independent definitions of information and theoretically open and broad dimension of Information Science, and it should not be curtailed by the limitations of current practice.

Likewise, discipline-bound history must be re-conceptualized and integrated in the same way the *histoire du livre* movement (e.g., CHARTIER; N. Z. DAVIS; DARNTON; EISENSTEIN; FEBVRE & MARTIN; J. H. MARTIN, etc.) has transformed the history of the book into the study of reading (e.g., ISER; GRAFF; KASER; WEIGAND; etc.). Here "book" is a metaphor almost any conveyance of information and culture. Interestingly, the split between bibliography (BALSAMO) and documentation that occurred over the years has left a permanent schism in the information field; book history epitomized by the German *Lexikon des gesamten Buchwesens* (CORSTEN, PFLUG, & SCHMIDT-KUNSEMULLER) and documentation (à la DELMAS or MEYRIAT) often seem totally separated. Transposed into the culture of Information Science, however, the book becomes just one of many kinds of "interface media." The translation into French from more empirical English denotes a transformation in focus from the specific to the general, and an advance from the local even to the global with an ever more theoretical and abstract sense of ecology. The name change of the *Journal of the History of Libraries* to simply *Libraries and Culture* reflects such thinking. Ably edited by Donald Davis (1966-), it is in this larger reformed comparative and unidisciplinary framework that modern information science, technology, processes, and organizations must be studied today.

Apart from the History of the Book itself, beyond bibliography, Library history is the most prolific. The American scene is reviewed by D. DAVIS alone and by DAVIS & DAIN, which can be supplemented and updated by PASSET's bibliographies. MIKSA (1982) provides an older historiographic review, and M. HARRIS always challenges the complacency of conventional wisdom regarding library history. Expansion beyond the United States. is enabled by WIEGAND & DAVIS's encyclopedic and therefore global historical coverage, but few institutional histories can compete with the French penchant for synthesizing institutional and social history (e.g., POULAIN). Both SAA and ALA have their History round tables which stimulate lively exchanges in library and archives circles and beyond. Their conference papers are often featured in *Libraries and Culture*. Doctoral works in the library and information fields, many of which are historical or contain historical introductions and surveys of relevant literature leading into their case studies or technical treatments, were surveyed by YOUNG, whose compilation can be updated not only by *Dissertation Abstracts* but also reports on "Work in Progress" in the *Journal of Education for Library and Information Science*. Sometimes the thematic issues of *Library Trends* (see AULD) contain introductory chapters which are historical in nature. These examples reflect an ample bibliography for stimulating courses in the history of information thought, science, organizations, and technology, as illustrated not by the title but the content of "The History of Archives" taught by R. COX (1990) at the University of Pittsburgh, which brings history to the present and focuses on records, their function, and the institutionalization of documentation as information systems interwoven in fabric of the societies sustaining archives. It is this pervasive sense of continuity, contextualization, and the big picture that History can offer Information Science.

The "Bibliography of Writings on the History of Libraries, Librarianship, and Book Culture" is included annually in the *LHRT Newsletter* of the ALA Library History Round Table. Although it slights archives and manuscripts in favor of printed book and library history, its inclusions on literacy, communications, and technology in historical treatments often complement modern themes in Information Science. Although History within library and archives education was temporarily shunted from core to peripheral specialization, it is being revitalized for intrinsic interest and professional socialization purposes. Seventy-one studies appeared in 1996's listing for the United States library and book history; although coverage in foreign languages is much less thorough than for English publications, 48 works were listed that pertained to Europe; 14 to Asia, Africa and the Middle East; and 112 were thematic studies not specific to one area. Production of over 225 studies each year in this field indicates a certain vitality that is disproportionate to the status of historical inquiry in the library profession. Of course, the field is fed by historical studies of the book and of libraries from the English and Comparative Literature disciplines as well. Historical Bibliography *qua* History of Books and Printing, under impact of the New Social History has been transformed into *histoire du livre* and linked into the psycholinguistic history called, again in French precisely for its imprecision, that of *mentalité* (STRUEVER, 1979, p. 141).

Likewise, the appreciation of archives is now well coupled with semiology (TAYLOR, 1988; FOOTE, 1990; MCCRANK, 1994; O'TOOLE, 1994). In both fields, subspecialties exist that concentrate on the books and records themselves, i.e., analytical or critical bibliography and codicology, which can be broken down further into typography and paleography; or diplomatics with its extension into form criticism and forensic document examination. Some of the most innovative a trend-setting work in Diplomatics and linguistic computing is from the University of Strasbourg by B-M. TOCK (1997, cf., his report on the analysis of nearly 5,000 charters, 1998; and GUYOTJEANNIN, PYCKE & TOCK, eds.). While the latter focus on content, the contextual concern is what H. WHITE (1978) called *The Content of the Form*, which is so important in considering historical representation. This is demonstrated best in BEDOZ-REZAK's *Form and Order in Medieval France*, although the author is uninformed about contemporary form criticism within Information Science and Records Management. G. SPIEGEL, for another example from medieval France, stresses the importance of "social sites" where language is deployed, as in her attempt to search for "social logic" responsible for the production of discourse and textual representation. The continuity between the broad interpretation of history and the shifting of evidence and establishment of authenticity and decisions about use or admissibility at the microscopic level is too often implicit rather than explicit in scholarly exposition. A more conscious link between artworks and Art History seems to be more common than the parallel linkage between textual sources and Literature, or more common than manuscript, document, record, and artifact with History (as advocated by H. TAYLOR, 1979). PARINET and N. BARTLETT (1997) in this vein, make convincing cases for the application of Diplomatics to documentary art and photographs. Such approaches to codicology, for example, as an "archeology of text" are conscious means to make such linkage explicit (GRUJIS), reflecting Marshal McLuhan's more popularized connection between message and medium (MCLUHAN).

Now advanced technology is being applied in all of these areas, from the use of ultra-violet and infrared in order to discern illegible script and X-ray and phototransfer techniques to bring out latent patterns such as watermarks and to determine the structure and ingredients of information media, to digitization and script enhancement, computer-assisted collation and editing, and electronic publishing. As recently made evident at the first International Conference on the History, Function, and Study of Watermarks (MOSSER & SULLIVAN, 1997) at Virginia Tech's Center for Textual & Editorial Studies, even watermarks have come under electronic scrutiny. Of course analytical chemistry and applied physics are brought into play for the rare artifact, and artwork has long been subjected to scientific analysis more strenuously and frequently than in document examination, but modern technology and enhanced technique and refined methodologies are being applied at the microlevel to discrete entities (CARVALHO) and at the macrolevel for large-scale group analysis, and for the dissemination of results and continued scholarly communication. For example, a classic case of multi-disciplinary traditional and high-tech document authentification problems, and one of the most controversial, is delineated by P. MALONEY *ET AL.* ([199-]), i.e., the Shroud of Turin. The latter outlet is itself an example of changing technology's impact on publication and distribution and may be used to illustrate the relationship between information science and practice in information dissemination. Haworth Press moves these studies into publication from word-processed copy, edits and reformats it into an electronic on-demand publication, and disseminates the results in multiple formats under the trademark of Docuserial, e.g., separate text-based articles through telefax and photocopies, standing-order subscription in journal form of the whole collection, and traditionally as hardbound monographs (MCCRANK, 1994, 1995). As such, this organ bridges the gap between the traditional book, its serialized form, and electronic media. Such developments are historically noteworthy. Information technology has transformed how such scholarship is accomplished, and also how it is communicated. Who could predict the analysis of DNA as a tool of historical investigation as in tracing divergent genealogies from Thomas Jefferson?

Across great distance and time, the continuity of information communication is well treated historically in a variety of ways, but less capably when ideas are removed from their vehicles or disembodied from their receptacles. Recent, contemporary, and thereby short-term and too often discontinuous information and communication are the subjects of modern Information Science. Consideration of long-range communication and information dissemination, however, have not been commonly thought of as Historical Information Science. Yet historical information sources, processes, and institutions can be studied similarly in methodology to create a continuity to the present; and current concepts can be applied to historical phenomena to make contemporary sense of them. Examples of treatments under the guise of Humanities that approach such Information Science conceptualization, except that they predate modern information technology, may illustrate this point. Consider, for examples, the well studied issue of information transfer from the classical to medieval period and beyond, transformed into new media, as treated by REYNOLDS & WILSON's *Scribes and Scholars,* HAARMANN's *Early Civilization and Literacy in Europe,* or M. CLANCHY's *From Memory to Written Record*, so important for library and archival history. CLANCHY's works (the second edition contains such extensive rewriting and additions of new material, that both editions need to be read together to trace the evolution of his thinking), at least, are often cited by archivists (COX; DOLLAR, 1992, p. 36; MCCRANK, 1994) for historical insight into the transition from oral transaction to written act as a metaphor for the modern change from written to electronic records. Charles Dollar and others speculate about the social and cultural dimensions of transferring information between media, as something more than the technical issue of migrating data across systems (DOLLAR, 1993, 1995).

Perhaps the first introduction of American archivists to form criticism and Diplomatics occurred in 1976 at the University of Maryland in its MA+MLS program. In an advanced research methods seminar on Diplomatics, Codicology, and Analytical Bibliography, I introduced the topic and standard bibliography and presented a model form, formula, and protocol analysis of a twelfth-century diploma from a medieval cartulary. This was followed by an examination of letter writing for manuscript curators, based on secretarial handbooks and model letter collections in facsimile, which were also used to teach paleography. Then students had to date and localize a variety of manuscript hands from the twelfth century to twentieth-century personal papers, and then they had to select a twentieth-century product and do the same by examining both the technologies used to create the document and the form, protocols, format, medium, presentation, etc. complete diplomatic analysis of a modern record. In one book (1995), and one forthcoming, I speak of the need for a new diplomacy in modern electronic communications as well as the resurrection of the study of Diplomatics (which DURANTI, and others like DOLLAR, 1998, and COX, 1997b, have likewise contemplated) and association with cognate studies in other fields.

CHARTIER's recent collection of studies (1991/1997) of the evolution of forms of correspondence from the Middle Ages to the modern period is an excellent example of applying Diplomatics in New Cultural History (BOUREAU; DAUPHIN). Much of the evidence is derived from extant letter collections and model secretarial handbooks, parallel to Chartier's use of historical bibliography in his many contributions to the "new" history of the book. Diplomatics has been revived in relation to modern records by American archivists (BLOUIN & DELMAS, eds.), but without the kind of connection that ought to be made with current IS applications of Diplomatics under any other name to modern information systems and communication. An example of the latter, which takes a Diplomatics approach and may be seen as pertaining to Oral History, but which would never see itself in these terms, is ERICSSON's "protocol analysis" and treatment of verbal reports as data. Diplomatics as form criticism, for example, might be related also with the modern counterparts in Information Science (e.g., EVERETT & CARTER who advocate a topology of document retrieval systems and document types), which has little cognizance of the applicability or relationship to current endeavors such as automatic document classification (a field defined early by BORKO & BERNICK and explored as a form of pattern recognition by WINSTON). Text and document categorization are now associated more with natural language processing (NPL) than form criticism, but Diplomatics has always concerned itself with conventions, formula, and standardized phrases introducing readers to the type of business about to be conducted (the same approach, essentially, as taken by MAY to classify e-mail messages; P. JACOBS). The Japanese team, AOKI *ET AL.*, essentially used Diplomatics and form criticism in their approach to building an automatic index extraction system using layout structures. The same may be said about the need for an extension from typography, book design, and analytics as addressed in GASKELL's *New Bibliography*, which should be connected with graphic design and presentation, visualization, Graphic User Interface (GUI) research, and Computer-Assisted Drafting/Design (CAD) (EMMER). While we know that language and communication formats operate on the basis of continuity to be understood, it is surprising that so much discontinuity has developed between traditional fields of study and those now associated only with new technology, or how much cognitive distance has evolved between Information Science and the Humanities over the past decades.

An extensive literature also exists about literacy and communication, so germane to Information Science's inclusion of the humane component in information systems and people's behavior that is often culture bound. Linguists like J. C. NYIRI are therefore very interested in such historical treatments as B. STOCK's 1983 study of medieval literacy, even if they disagree, because prior experience delineated in such history and analysis has much to say to the contemporary reader. Cultural Linguistics have influenced History tremendously in the past decade, parallel to the anthropological infusion of Business with such historical inquiry and methodologies as used for organizational studies in Management in business and government circles, and which links Information with Social Science methodology (cf., H. BERNARD, 1988; KATZER, COOK, & CROUCH, 1991; and for archives administration, see DUFF; WALLACE). The old juxtaposition of historical and anthropological methodology (FABIAN; KERTZER *ET AL.*), and of relying on informants rather than using archives (BRETTELL) has given way as historical and anthropological methods blend not only in historical anthropology (SCHNEIDER & RAPP), but also in using documentation with survey and interview techniques in modern organizational culture and use studies that are no longer solely dependent on survey questionnaires. Both employ the same statistical procedures to analyze qualitative data (COFFEY & ATKINSON; K. W. TAYLOR & CHAPPELL; D. THOMAS). The historical record, informant transcript, and the oral interview may be treated similarly in computer-assisted analyses.

The empirical study of language as actually used in communications, records, etc., is common to Linguistics and Lexicology, Literature and History, Archival and Information Science, etc. MCARTHUR makes an excellent case for such inter-disciplinary linkage. Historians may be absorbing linguistic theory more generally than simply pursuing word studies, but the influence is permeating just as quantification has become less obtrusive but none the less influential. Even though some historians think that deconstructionism has permeated Text Criticism, but is less influential in History, the ubiquity of notions associated with Post-modernism (abetted by their ambiguity) in so much of modern scholarship is different from the conscious adoption of post-modern criticism or explicit citation of this or that theory (APPLEBY, 1997a). Postmodernism, especially its variants in relativism and textualism, has destablized most disciplines, or at least undermined their security in knowing anything for sure. So profuse is this identity crisis and insecurity that in the last decade more than three hundred books have been written in the subject-area of the sociology of knowledge. Only a tenth of that number have been devoted to epistemology as such, and fewer still have addressed the constructive development of methodology. The overwhelming trend has been to contest knowledge construction almost as a social or cultural exercise in make-believe. The most radical position is that virtually everything is a matter of language construction and that alone. Although this exclusivity and extremism can be rejected easily enough because it is so one-sided and almost fadish, the overstatement serves to spread the ferment from Linguistics and Literature to History and Sociology, and now all of the Social Sciences have all been penetrated (HOLLINGER). Even Information Science (WARNER, 1994) has been affected when considering full-text analyses for information searching and document retrieval, but nothing on the order of what has happened in History and other text-based fields of study. And no discipline is saturated like Literature and its specialty of text criticism.

Of course, this doubting of our ability to produce knowledge from text analysis that is not purely a reflection of our own culture comes at a time when texts from every culture are now more widely available than ever. Whereas relatively few full-text electronic sources were available in the early 1970s, mainly for law, these have proliferated during the 1980s to such an extent that now the selection numbers in the thousands (TENOPIR & RO). Search strategies designed for bibliographic files do not work as well in less standardized full-text sources, so apart from mark-up for term and section retrieval (an expanded version of keyword in context [KWIC], new forms of retrieval are being developed such as indexes with hyperlinks (e.g., LANCASTER; INGWERSEN; MARCHIONINI; SOERGEL) as though these forms of natural language retrieval with their explicit user orientation were not the epitome of presentism and what postmodernism criticizes most. But the business world does not care, its attention is short-range, and a practicality reigns in appreciation for what works at all, to say nothing about working perfectly in some philosophical sense. Moreover, postmodernism criticizes knowledge construction that mirrors the present, but that is the very essence of relevance in information science research and there it is a highly prized value. From this perspective, historical information is retrieved only because it can be made relevant to the modern user, and the retrieval itself depends on a frame of reference from the present. How else could an unknown from the past, distant or immediate, be retrieved? Even if possibly discoverable like some lost tomb waiting to be excavated because it is preserved, the past for the most part is lost when it is not continually referenced in the present. The past unknown is no history at all; it is simply what is forgotten.

As sources enlarge and become more complex, relevance in information retrieval remains a serious problem (MIZZARO claims it is a central issue, "if not *the* central issue"). SARACEVIC (1975) understood this in the earlier development of Information Science, and since then considerable research has explored this attribute of information (see the *ARIST* review by SCHAMBER, 1994; cf., A. SCHULTZ). FROELICH projects research agenda about relevance into the next millennium. It is an important concept to be made explicit in the research process. Relevance judgments are made throughout online searching and matching exercises (R. GREEN). Self-examination is required to discern what seems and actually is relevant to topical searching and research objectives (HARTER, 1992). JANES stresses how conscientious one must be during searching and research, especially of incremental judgments in reacting to documents as they present themselves. His recognition of the search process as being an informing act more than merely document retrieval is critical. BRUCE, C. BARRY, and others advocate a user-orientation and situational approach to determine what is relevant, but this largely ignores the intrinsic relevance already buried in documentation by records creators and initial users. Linkages internal to a record and links between records that form a series or what archivists perceive as an organic unity may be ignored if one assumes that collections are artificial, may operate somewhat differently in document retrieval archives or in historical research where the contextualization of data, information, and records is so important.

Recognizing the relevance of record creation to a creator's needs, to a continuum of use, and ultimately to a modern investigator in this continuum is a matter larger than ahistorical, situational, or user-centered relevance definitions. Historians are not unconcerned about these issues, practically or as intellectual questions to be studied, but their approach is to take a current issue to formulate a probe into the more distant past and expose the issue in historical context. While they often do not, unfortunately, use explicit operational definitions and the dynamic components inherent in situational definitions of relevance recommended by SCHAMBER, EISENBERG & NILAN or H. BRUCE, historians, like all information seekers, make relevance decisions all the time, both intuitively and objectively. They also operate within a disciplinary paradigm so that like other researchers, they would have more agreement about relevance for documents that are highly specific in content and fall clearly into one discipline (as SARACEVIC noted in 1975 and JANES confirmed in 1994). The sub-language of historians is different, their notions about relevance are complex because their perspective is farsighted, and their methodologies remain more descriptive than empirical by preference and because of the nature of their sources. These circumstances, however, are no excuses for operating with untested assumptions, relying purely on instinct or prior practice, or avoidance of explicit, objective thought about what is relevant when searching and selecting documentation or in the application of analytic approaches in research. Information scientists can help frame such intellectual questions, and in turn, historians can place these issues into larger contexts by probing extensions unseen by the former's nearsightedness.

Such research can connect History and Historical Information Science, as is well illustrated by M. OLSON (1989, 1991) and L.G. HARVEY (1991, 1992), individually and as a team (1988a-b). The have produced different kinds of studies using similar methodologies: one uses nineteenth-century library circulation records from Montreal converted into machine-readable form to analyze reading habits in Quebec and thereby illuminate French Canadian culture; another utilizes the *American and French Research on the Treasury of the French Language (ARTFL)* textbase of 1,500 works from the seventeenth through twentieth centuries (cf., *ARTFL* guides; SPOHER) in order to conduct word studies, checking frequencies of usage, clustering of preferences by periods, and shifts in vocabularies to indicate not only changes in French popular culture but in patterns of information communication such as political discourse. Few histories of information institutions and organizations, however, have employed cliometric analyses. Moreover, library history is most often interpreted as an institutional counterpart to literary history. Records management in the medical establishment or public government in court, county, and city clerks' offices, etc., seldom comes under the purview of such history which is aimed at elite art and acquired information rather than daily business of generating information. Therefore information technology inside library history is also limited to what happened in libraries. History that is professionally based or confined to certain types of institutions is usually self-limiting. Reading narrowly in one professional literature can lead to distortion about the importance of the institution, its history, and contributions at the exclusion of others, and the interpretation in such history can be very convoluted, as when studying information technology inside libraries rather than libraries inside the information establishment writ large. As the perspective changes, so too does interpretation. It is the proverbial "big fish in a small pond" syndrome. If one reads broadly and comparatively, one can grasp the larger picture and understand the history of information institutions, technology, and processes, but broad syntheses, now unavailable, would certainly help.

Is the historical metaphor reversible? Does this mean that those who studied such change and pioneered lasting innovation in documentation, communication, and record keeping such as the exchequers of old were proto-information scientists or for their times real information specialists under other titles? How can one understand the cultural basis for classification in Western thought without knowing the contributions of Scholasticism; is it so difficult to identify Hugh of St. Victor as a medieval information scientist (S. JACKSON, pp. 65-69) when for his *Didiscalicon* he struggled in the 1120s with one of the first taxonomies by which to access the whole corpus of Western knowledge?

It is interesting that VON RANKE in articulating his concept of scientific history was *ipso facto* drawn into the intellectual problems of historical classification in organizing his *Weltgeschichte* (1879-87). Or, consider a modern example, and ask why Arnold Toynbee, one of this century's greatest classifiers of historical knowledge who challenged the nationalist political assumptions in classifications used by Euro-American libraries today and sought to reconceptualize History as a field of comparative studies, has never been considered as an information scientist? Or for that matter, one might include H. G. WELLS whose *Outline of History* falls into the same era as SPENGLER's monumental work. TOYNBEE falls into an elite group of world systems conceptualizers (M. PERRY; SMURR; SANDERSON, ed.), with such company as William McNeill whose 1963 *Rise of the West* is argued by MANNING (MCNEILL, p. 775) to be "the beginning of systematic academic study of world history," through such recent spokesmen as Immanuel WALLERSTEIN (1994) (and such critics of "world systems theory" as P. KOHL). MCNIELL recently (1995) looked back to reconsider his supranational focus on Western Civilization and influence of his work over the past 20 years; he talks now about the concepts of global history and re-periodization (the historian's equivalent to reclassification). Such rethinking often comes back to the comprehensive work of Arnold Toynbee, the master reclassifier of this century whose comparative world perspective predated the move toward global history. TOYNBEE's *Reconsiderations* can be read, if not his whole multi-volume

History, as a treatise fundamentally important to Information Science. Toynbee's theory on cultural classification might be compared with RANGANATHAN's works, i.e., *A Librarian Looks Back,* but about as many in the IS community have read Toynbee as historians have read Ranganathan. One must transcend disciplinary boundaries to explore this potentially rich interplay between History and Information Science (MCCRANK, [199-]). Indeed, historians classify all the time as a matter of basic analysis, but they do not often use or develop classification systems as did Toynbee or classify systematically. He required a more explicit approach to confront the problem of mass information in world history.

The current uneasiness about rapidly changing technology and attendant anxiety about the increased volume of traffic and amounts of information have spawned a usual reflex in our society to check out the history of similar phenomena in other eras and areas as a way of understanding the current milieu. It is not surprising that under current awareness of the so-called "Information Age" (HAMMER) or "Information Revolution" (FORESTER) as if there were only one, historians have discovered others in the twelfth century (CLANCHY; MCCRANK, 1993), the late Renaissance (EISENSTEIN), the eighteenth century (CRAVEN; OBERLY), and nineteenth-century industrialization (STEIG, 1980). A. OSBORNE sees the current revolution caused by information technology as "running wild." Nonhistorical thinkers tend to view the modern predicament as unique; historians tend to see the Information Age as a paradigm that works and is meaningful because of similarities with past experience. The magnitude of the current information exchange, both in quantity of material and rate of transactions, seems to create different phenomena, however, or at least more complex ones, which require more robust sociocultural theory about diffusion of ideas, information transmission, and formation of understanding such as that attempted by those studying technological change (cf., ENGELSMAN & VAN RAAN; GRUBLER; MARCHETTI & NAKICENOVIC; KAUTZ & PRIES-HEJE, etc.). KAUFER & CARLEY's theory of constructuralism, however, has been subjected to the same salvos that have destroyed the work of other formalists and quantifiers; at least one reviewer, RESTIVO, congratulates them on the attempt and for their stimulation of further research and continued theorizing.

In short, the histories of ideas, books, printing, and cultural institutions (archives, libraries, museums, etc.) are plentiful, and no longer must literature be read *in vacuo.* Moreover, these histories are increasingly well informed from the Social Sciences, but relatively few fall into a genre where the dominant methodology is quantitative or where reliance on text also involves modern information technology. Nor are they well informed from Information Science, or *vice versa.* In distinguishing itself from Library Science, Information Science abandoned its roots in bibliography, just as scientific historicism in shunning antiquarianism abandoned genealogy—only to rediscover it a generation later in local and population history (PELLISSIER; BARTHELEMY & PINGAUD; GUYOT). Both fields shortchanged themselves in doing so. In this regard W. WIEGAND calls for a rapprochement to rediscover the relevance of reading in information studies and especially in library education.

History of Information Science

A professional or intellectual development without a history is not yet mature, or to use DE CERTEAU's metaphor (1973), its language is like being alone in the night. If consciousness of its own past seems lacking in modern Information Science (IS), so also are collective memory, culture, and confidence (e.g., as reflected by STEIG, 1992; 1993). The issue is not whether History is relevant for Information Science, since an answer obviously can be made in the affirmative, but it is a question of different perspectives and qualities of perception. Modern Information Science has been very nearsighted because it perceives itself as always current and therefore as new. IS therefore has a history, but no History. Historically minded people will be more aware of continuity than those who are not, as a matter of definition, scope of awareness, and self-actualization. All things are irrelevant to the forgetful and unconscious. IS research must be reminded of past ideas and even speculation about the future to achieve some circumspection and awareness that today was the future for someone in the past. Eugene Garfield, founder of the Institute for Scientific Information, told members of the American Society for Information Science (ASIS) at a recent conference (Baltimore, 1996), "if you would understand the future, study the past" (ASIS forum "Reflections on Our Future, moderated by C. DAVIS, Garfield quote, p. 22).

Not everyone in the information field would agree. ROUSE (1996), a proponent of collaborative planning on groupware, says people do not know how to plan change, and that often the assumption is "that the future would be pretty much like the past. The future might be a bit better or a bit worse than the past; nevertheless, it could be viewed as an extension of the past. Most people realize that this is not a good assumption when dealing with fundamental change (ROUSE, 1998, p. 832). This disavowal of continuity as a planning assumption is a problem in itself, since it justifies not planning for continuity. Equally contestable is his assumption (attributed to "most people") that fundamental change is inherently discontinuous. A problem he does not list in his evaluation of why people have difficulty in planning change and do not know what to do, is that they may not know the past very well (i.e., they know it superficially and only short-range, so they cannot use what they lack, historical knowledge, to project change). ROUSE's product planning process (1991) is devoid of historical knowledge, yet this is what is being packaged in decision support systems for change management (organizational change in business, strategic plans, and consensus building). Presentism rules the day rather than historicism. The results can be seen in discontinuity in technical development, discord between *vade mecum* solutions in information technology and social convention, alienation of traditional markets as new ones are targeted, disenchantment within organizations, fragmentation and insularity regarding specializations, and the isolation of disciplines.

J. LEE asks that computer scientists know about past developments, more a history of failure than success, and something more profound than merely a listing of "firsts," precisely for such knowledge's utility and future application. He argues for a proper contextualization, echoing Richard Hamming's 1978 presentation at the Los Alamos National Laboratory's early conference on the history of computing (METROPOLIS, HOWLETT & ROTA). He highlighted the need to know "what they thought when they did it" so that new information and different thinking might be gilded onto the old for new and different lines of development. In some cases such study is for incremental progress; in other cases, it is for inspiration to leapfrog across time by discovering older ideas that had been imagined more than thought, figuratively "before their time." The colloquialism about an idea "whose time has come" embodies the concepts not only of rethinking past options, but of refurbishing the old with new knowledge, insights, and means. It is an updating with modern technology. What had to be hypothetical only in one generation, because of limitations in technology or political barriers to acquire the means, might be realizable in the next. Context is the historian's framework to provide meaning for what others think is purely circumstantial. Lift an idea out of context to another with new possibilities, and history then may not simply repeat itself, but becomes inspirational and a form of renewal.

Illustrative cases are HIGGENBOTHAM's recall of nineteenth-century visions of technology which came into its own in our century; or for Library Science, MIKSA's reflections (1988) of Charles Cutter's speculation in 1883 of what access to collections in the Buffalo Public Library could be like a century later, i.e., in 1983. MUSMANN pulls together much of this early speculation for an "anecdotal history" from 1860 to 1960, thus contributing to a mythographic tradition in librarianship, but he does not cover science fiction or fanzine literature where futurism about technological innovation in the information field abounds, then and now; nor does his treatment provide the solid historical recall and modeling that lends itself to trends analysis and forecasting, thereby providing direction based on history for current thinking and speculation extending into the next millennium. His examples do, however, provide material for reflection on opportunities lost because past visionary thinking never found its way into actual development. RICE recalls early visions about where twentieth-century information technology was supposedly going, compared with actual developments and contrasted to where we went. General directions were fairly well forecasted; actual routes were not. Or history can remind us about major mistakes and accidental regression, as recalled by HORTON & LEWIS in their *Great Information Disasters*. History is not always a linear progression (indeed, Native American history is event-centered and does not operate strictly as linear history). Such disjunction suggests how sporadic progress is and offers a historical counterbalance to the basic but unproven assumptions in much of IS work about strategic planning, systematic development, and continually sustained progress. Forgetfulness like historical unconsciousness allows random regression and replay, duplication of effort and proverbial "reinvention of the wheel," and lacunae in the idealized continuum envisioned by most information scientists.

The crux of this continuity versus discontinuity problem in thinking is contextualization—the very thing threatened by major technological trends without human intervention and guidance to preserve memory because it has both immediate and enduring value as an internalized rather than vested interest. This point has been made in regard to History in the foregoing discussion, relating L. HUNT's recent observations about continuity in historiography; it must be raised now regarding Information Science and all information studies; and it will be raised again in relation to organizational culture and continuity in business activities.

This relevance of history to nonhistorical individual and organizational activities is an issue that might be placed into the historiographic debates over memory, history, and theory (LE GOFF, 1992; VIDAL-NAQUET; and others; cf., review by HUTTON). The issue has been called recently "the memory crisis" of the past century (GILDEA), and a problem of modernity in this century (TERDIMAN; cf., review of both by LEBOVICS). In a less alarmist fashion KAMMEN (1991) uses the metaphor "mystic chords of memory" to describe the transformation of tradition in America, to distinguish Americanist tradition and American history. LIPSITZ, writing at the same time as Kammen, does something along the same lines in his *Time Passages* with more attention to American popular culture, but equal concern for the tenuous relationship of history and collective memory.

A Europeanist perspective on American history is that its tradition back to the Old World is disjunctive at best. The trip across the Atlantic was often preceded by trauma and uprooting before relocation; the voyage took time and its own toll on memory, and thereafter isolation was common, and communications continued but with considerable time lag. The distortions of distance and time between settlements abroad and European roots on collective memory are also important for Australian history (e.g., DARIAN-SMITH, HAMILTON & CURTHOYS, eds.). While some certainly yearned for the world left behind, the westward and future orientation of New World settlers also meant a certain amount of disdain for the old and purposeful forgetfulness. Historical amnesia can be seen as an antidote to painful memory. And the dominant Protestant majority's accommodation for discontinuity in reform historicism predisposed acceptance of such breaches in cultural memory over the long term.

So much of this history writing is concerned with identity formation, and increasing the lack of a coherent and connecting identity in our time. KAMMEN (1987, 1992) wrestles with the peculiarities of this memory issue in the transformation of tradition by Americans, just as NORA struggles with the cultural memory in defining Frenchness. In this same vein BERCOVITCH explores *The Rites of Assent: Transformations in the Symbolic Construction of America*; J. BODNAR talks about *Remaking America* in terms of public memory, commemoration, and patriotism; and P. P. MILLER's *Landmarks of Women's History* adopts the public history metaphor as if events in the past could be viewed as historical sites, as indeed they can be in the form of memorials and commemorative acts (BROWNE).

More about such matters will be discussed later, specifically in a survey of developments in History and Organizational studies concerning collective memory and culture; the point here is simply to relate History and Information Science, to suggest a mutual relevance and potential symbiosis that seems lacking too often, and even to characterize certain strains in History as an Information Science. This point needs to be made conversely as well. In grappling with such mega-issues as collective culture, memory and identity, and behavioral and social structural modification, however, historians fail still to take into account the volume of research on organizational culture and corporate memory in nonhistorical literatures—organizational psychology, industrial sociology, human factors engineering, management in administrative science, and in information science, applications of cognitive psychology in groupware, decision support systems, and asynchronous interactive software design, or more generally the social ramifications of information products, systems, and services (historical and modern) for behavior modification and social restructuring. History excludes these fields as much as History is excluded by them, to the detriment of all. Consequently, this aspect of organizational culture in which information flourishes will be treated as an essential component of Historical Information Science.

The interrelationship of history and memory in current discussions has resulted in at least four, perhaps more, seminal notions: (1) memory as rectifier of misconstrued history (VIDAL-NAQUET) or conversely, History rectifying social misconstructions of reality (R. HAMILTON); (2) memory as a collective data pool from which historians select aspects to reconstruct a knowable past (LE GOFF, 1992); (3) history as the corrective to memory as unchecked myth (TERDIMAN); and (4) history as a counterbalance to unsubstantiated theorizing in the study of culture (GILDEA). Perhaps this carries the issue of historicism as an inherent component of any discipline too far into the theoretical and historiographic for many information scientists, but the point is that even for relatively immediate recall, some formal approach to memory assistance needs to be taken. As new cultural historians remind us, History, even that of the distant past, if recalled and made known, is always present. TERDIMAN (p. 9) states uncategorically: "No memory, no meaning." He argues that synchronic understanding of the type assumed by Information Scientists is simply not possible; there is no such thing as "timeless theory." KELLNER (1975) likens discontinuities in historical consciousness to be "time out" periods of unconsciousness. Inside Information Science this essential component of human cognition and identity is often explored only in an outward form, an intermediary transaction, or supportive technology, whether called "documentation" or some more technically sounding euphemism like retrospection, and perhaps contextualization, but seldom "History." HARRIS & HANNAH warn librarians against "the perils of ahistoricism" in the profession and WEST points to the need for historical perspective in framing questions in serialized research in Information Science. Similarly KRUMMEL chides researchers in Library and Information Science about the "Born Yesterday" fallacy. As in other instances, members in the Information Science community are now engaging in a more formal intra-disciplinary History because collective memory is failing after just a single shift between generations. At stake is the question of heritage, and therefore History has a vital role to play in Information Science. It always has, regardless of the neglect if not outright denial. The role is, moreover, interactive and reflexive. The past always lives in the present. That is precisely the key point of Terdiman's title, *Present Past,* or the paradox represented in the name of John Shideler's public history consulting firm, Future Past.

The common perception within the Information Science community of its own historical roots is extremely limited by language, culture, and disciplinarity. Although our intellectual heritage regarding information theory should have some depth to it, its classical components and medieval evolution are largely ignored because of the perception that science is an early modern phenomenon at best (MCCRANK, 1998). The historical parameters of information theory are often incorrectly curtailed by the history of information technology, and by the confusion of this with computing alone. Therefore both IS and IT are considered as modern phenomena, largely without histories. LOSEE (1997, p. 262) represents the commonplace in Information Science by reflecting back only to World War I and II for the origins of "Information Theory" with Harry Nyquist (1924) who investigated "the maximum speed of transmission of intelligence" for Bell Labs. His work and of other engineers like R. V. L. Hartley (1928), who switched emphasis in thought about information from psychology to physics, so Losee argues (that is, to natural entropies; cf., ACZAEL & DAROCZY), are the prototypes for the formalization of information theory by Claude Shannon in the 1940s (SHANNON & WEAVER). HARTLEY spoke of "the measurement of information" and addressed such concepts as precision, frequency, etc., now fundamental in information science research. He thought in terms of the number of symbols in sequences, which led to the channel model of information delivery which dominated telecommunications thinking to this day, and therefrom the larger dimension of Information Science.

Losee thus refers to Shannon's *Mathematical Theory of Communication* (1949) as "the founding document for much of the future work in information theory" (LOSEE, 1997, p. 263). He understands, however, that the channel-based process model that works in telecommunications does not work well elsewhere. He also separates communication from perception in the information process, which requires an occasion for observation (visual or audio). "Perceiving and observing by a sentient being (and in many nonsentient mechanisms) produce output having some relationship to the state of the world outside the observer" (p. 266) A "percept" in such thinking is a set of values in an output, i.e., information output about input. And he also discusses the difference between belief and knowledge (see ACKERMANN's much earlier, 1972, fuller discussion) in information theory: "Knowledge has been frequently described as 'justified true belief,' a belief held by an individual that is both true and for which they have some justification" (GETTIER)—an explanation that might recall Tertullian's second-century dictum about believing so that one might know, and *vice versa*. The subject is ageless (G. L. MILLER). Even though religion may be juxtaposed frequently to science, M. POLANYI (1964; 1974) suggested that faith and science go well together.

The idea that one must believe in order to know is not new theory, but it is often treated in Information Science as new and modern, and repeated in language better understood by information scientists than philosophical discourse or the intricacies of Christian apologetics. Even Shannon's channel-based model has its forerunners in Christian theory about wisdom as grace conveyed in streams of light, but theology and information science are not comfortable partners. Maybe they should get better acquainted. Modern consciousness of history's lingering presence even in areas like Information Science, which have been conspicuously presentist rather than genuinely circumspective, surfaces in odd ways. David Bennahum, a journalist rather than an historian, became aware of the loss of our most recent history in the current Information Revolution, so he opened a listserv discussion forum, to which over a thousand people have contributed, to create an account, not from the industry's perspective, but from user experiences, about the evolution of the Internet. It is, interestingly enough, called "Community Memory" (listserv@cpsr.org) for the networked community, to preserve its history. Bennahum likens his electronic forum to an "oral history" to recall how things began, where such terms as "hackers" really came from or were first used, and to let people reminisce for a future age about what it was like to use a computer for the first time or communicate across the Internet. How authoritative such a textbase can be, compiled as it is with unverifiable personal reflections and hearsay, makes the use of such a source problematic in the particular, but interesting in the aggregate.

Professional historians are not rushing to supply the information profession with a useable past. Indeed, modern information technology, much less information science, does not yet have a contingent of historians devoted to it. Instead, its history is being assembled by practitioners. The compilation by OLAISEN *ET AL.* is a start, presenting from the European perspective the rise of Information Science to discipline status and its relatively recent social interaction in institutions and professions other than those giving rise to it. It is one of the first to attempt a non- intradisciplinary exposition of the field. Even so, if BUCKLAND & LIU had stuck to "formal historical writing, the kind that professional historians produce" (p. 385) in surveying the history of Information Science, the bibliography would have been very short indeed. Few professional historians are among their citations because History has not paid any attention to IS. Moreover, such attention to the history of their own field by library, archives, and information educators and practitioners is relatively recent. Contributors to the Association for the History of Science and Technology (e.g., in *Technology and Culture*) have paid attention to Computer Science in connection with computer technology, but not Information Science. Nor does it figure into the History of Ideas, or as an extension to the *histoire du livre* movement. In short, Information Science has fallen through the cracks of traditional History and its subfields. This should be remedied.

Information Science is not without a history, so much as it has hitherto largely ignored continuity in information thought and processes and has just begun to search for its roots beyond the contemporary. This is somewhat ironic since the American Federation for Information Processing (AFIP) began promoting historical research and archival activity to document the information industry soon after its foundation in 1961, and by 1967 it funded research on the history of computers (CARLSON). Treatments in the 1974 *Encyclopedia of Library and Information Science* (updated by treatments through 1993) (KENT *ET AL.*) often included historical background, more than its abridged successor, the ALA *World Encyclopedia of Library and Information Services* (WEDGEWORTH, 1993), and this offers antidotes for a purely technological rendition. SHERA first, and H. CLEVELAND attempted to embed IS history into the discipline of Information Science, but not very successfully. Much more is available waiting to be discovered, most of its history has yet to be written, and what is available awaits a proper inter-disciplinary readership and inculcation into IS curricula.

A sign of Information Science's maturation is an awakening of its need for History, or at least its own history. Historical consciousness is, however, something more than the occasional commemoration, yet these historical events often trigger formal programs to recall the past and to provide the precondition for future theory. Finland's Tampere conference, celebrating in 1991 a twentieth anniversary of its library school, carried the theme *Conceptions of Library and Information Science*. Its proceedings placed historical reflection on equal footing with empirical research and theoretical discussion (VAKKARI & CRONIN), where MIKSA (1992) contrasted two paradigms in information studies, and thereby rehabilitated history as a legitimate descriptive approach to Information Science (as does STIELOW, 1994). One coeditor of these proceedings, VAKKARI (1994a & b), subsequently outlined the transition from Library to Information Science and based his generalizations on his own research on the German debates about the *Historia Literaria* in the transition from the traditional, classic, and humanistic basis of Library Science to the more empirical modern notions associated now with Information Science. VICKERY & VICKERY include historical background as obviously necessary for the theory and practice of Information Science, but more as adjunct to than part of the latter. While these studies are historical in orientation and methodology, they do not necessarily relate History and Information Science as co-disciplines.

In preparing for its centennial observations in 1995, the International Federation for Information and Documentation (FID) reviewed its 55 international conferences since the Brussels' Conference Bibliographique Internationale of 1895 (GOEDEGEBURE). Such commemorations coupled with a new millennium and present millenniarism have combined nostalgia with exuberance for the future in the information world. European information scientists, however, are consistently more aware of the history relating to their profession than are

Americans. FOSKETT, for example, employed history in typical fashion to compare "history, present status, and future prospects" of the Universal Decimal Classification (UDC) system. ASIS commemorated its own 50th anniversary in 1988 (CHARTRAND, HENDERSON & RESNICK), but sessions at ASIS conferences on the history of Information Science occurred only in 1992. In 1994 a preconference seminar on the History of Information Science was scheduled through the collaboration of two of ASIS' SIGs (Special Interest Groups), but with the impetus coming from Information Science educators. Moderated by Michael Buckland who promised then the welcomed contribution to the *Annual Review of Information Science and Technology* for 1995 on the history of Information Science (BUCKLAND & LIU), the Conference seminar explored such topics as scientific information in the Soviet Union under Stalin (SPENCE RICHARDS, 1994); the Termatrex Retrieval system (COVEY & WILLIAMS); information scientists in graduate library schools after 1960 (RICHARDSON); and the pioneers of the online systems (BOURNE & BELLARDO HAHN). ASIS is now funding a project to produce a directory of archival resources for the history of Information Science (R. WILLIAMS).

The editors BUCKLAND & BELLARDO HAHN of the first installment of the ASIS conference proceedings on the history of Information Science noted (1997, p. 285):

> Information Science has the curious property of perennially being widely regarded as a "new and emerging field," even a century after the beginning of the pioneering research and development program of what is now the International Federation for Information and Documentation (FID) by Paul Otlet and Henri La Fontaine. This is a dynamic and evolving field, but there has been widespread amnesia. Anything that has no known history will be regarded as new. If a field does not document its past, it will lack a history and also have a diminished sense of identity. If we ignore our own past, we should expect to remain continually regarded as "new and emerging."

> Ignoring our past has other disadvantages. As a practical matter, interesting ideas that lack immediately perceived utility are likely to be forgotten. Further, given the widespread desire for roots, heroes, and respectability, in the absence of carefully researched and documented history, we expect fanciful, mythic accounts, to take its place.

Otlet and La Fontaine's early endeavor to build a comprehensive ennumerative bibliography in 1895 and the development of the Universal Decimal Classification (UDC) to facilitate this (MCILWAINE) is another centennial this current investigation into the nexus between History and Information Science can celebrate.

Why now, in a professional association largely presentist in mind-set, is this interest in IS history and foundations surfacing as a legitimate concern of information scientists? It seems to be an issue of education, but a memorial sentiment is also at play. As a pioneer generation of information scientists passes, there is also a consciousness about the need for Oral History, lest personal testimony be limited to what has been published. Despite their tendency not to be concerned about history, a similar self- and group-awareness crept into the thinking of American physicists a generation ago that led to the establishment of the Center for the History of Physics. The late Larry Heilprin of the University of Maryland, one of the founders of the American Documentation Institute (HEILPRIN, 1985; cf., his appraisal of *ARIST,* 1988, through the 1980s), would have been pleased since he was among those like Gerard Salton and Charles Meadows who began to reflect that Information Science indeed had a history (SALTON; C. MEADOWS; and others). Secondly, there is awareness that, after the era of building information systems for "Big Science" throughout the 1960s, as described by De SOLA PRICE (cf., PAISLEY, 1990, p. 13; GALISON & HEVLY), with policy issues rising to the surface in the 1970s followed by recession that operated against forging ahead with some of the most innovative systems proposed by information scientists, there are watersheds that demarcate even recent development into recognizable periods. The current milieu has changed considerably since the widespread distribution of personal computing, growth of networking, and an internationalization of concerns, which are the same influences that have dramatically affected historical computing. Documentation and Information Science are not the reserves of the Anglo-American community, although increasing English is the *lingua franca* of the international community in this field, especially from Germany and Russia, but significant work is published still in Romance languages which does not make its way into the English-language self-citing circles. Although Americans tend to translate the Romance "Documentation" as "Information Science," this is a questionable practice because there is no need to translate a word which is the same in English, and the former term is a much more theoretical notion than the more empirical English entails; it includes, for example, the ideal and the practical, i.e., the embodiment of evidence (i.e., the form) which modern American Information Science has largely ignored. DELMAS (1992) focuses on the French idea of "Documentation" at the end of the past century, and BLANQUET widens this perspective

The Iberian arena is well represented by LOPEZ YEPES & MARTINEZ MONTALVO of Spain and DA COSTA of Portugal who provide both historical and international perspectives for a wider context than purely American developments. SAGREDO FERNANDEZ & GARCIA MORENO recently provided a select annotated bibliography for Spanish contributions since the establishment of Spain's first information center in 1952, but without the kind of synthesis that would have been more enlightening. CURRAS provides such a textbook explaining Spanish approaches to information from the perspective of the hard sciences and special libraries (including archives); this can be updated by LOPEZ YEPES; and historical overviews of development in the science and related training is provided by ABADAL (1993, 1994), which can be related to recent policy development since the Penna Report (1968) by ROS GARCIA & LOPEZ YEPES.

LILLEY & TRICE fail to provide a solid foundation with their uncritical biographic sketches and disjointed view of IS development, but FARKAS-CONN on Watson Davis and his involvement in the early American Documentation Institute provides a good start for a formal historiography for Information Science organization (e.g., the American Documentation Institute, the forerunner of ASIS). Such organization and institutional history does not necessarily encompass the whole of Information Science. These works do not provide any inkling of parallels between the Documentation and contemporary movements toward scientific historicism, for example; and oddly they trace the ideology of Documentation mainly to Library Science rather than into archives, records management, and other related developments which from within the field are not seen as mainstream. The historical perception within the IS community links Information Science to Library Science so much that this unilateral connection overshadows any other possible association (e.g., HAYES, 1985; MIKSA, 1985; RAYWARD, 1985; WRIGHT, 1985 [cf., WRIGHT, 1992]; whose positions are re-echoed by VAKKARI, 1994). This is predominantly because even when attempting an inter-disciplinary framework (e.g., MACHLUP & MANSFIELD), they frame their investigations within organizational histories and biographies which so far have formed the nucleus of such research. Moreover, these histories are from within the field by practitioners of Information Science first, and of History secondarily. Their viewpoints are, therefore, often intra-disciplinary and self-satisfying as when JAERVELEN & VAKKARI limit their content analysis of IS literature from 1965 to 1985 to a intradisciplinary core of journals.

These studies lack larger contextualization and the critical perspective that might be provided by an outsider looking in or an historian who from a more removed vantage point would examine Information Science in a broad, comparative framework. This is happening more and more, as evidenced by Michael Buckland's insights into the origins of modern Information Science in electronic technologies developed during and immediately after World War II (BUCKLAND, 1992), and in his broadening of the concept "document" to include any conveyor of information and meaning (BUCKLAND, 1991). However, there is little sign that Information Science is even discovered as a feasible subject for professional historians in their fora, even for intellectual history and the history of ideas, and only tangentially for the history of science and technology. This too must change.

The pioneer efforts (1976) of Joseph BECKER and Calvin MOOERS to capture the heritage of Information Science for ASIS members is more a rendition of the historical development of information technology than of the thinking behind it or in innovative applications, and their accounts are decidedly self-effacing since neither information scientist provides insight into his personal odyssey. Vannevar Bush receives continued attention (BUCKLAND, 1992; C. BURKE, 1992, 1994; NYCE & KAHN, 1989, 1991; SMITH, 1991), maybe more than is deserved by a purely historical assessment of MEMEX (which has never been linked to other forms of document collating, i.e., the Hillman collator) perhaps because of the presentism operating in IS thought that somehow considers BUSH and other visionaries as out of synchronization with their time and more in keeping with our own (C. BURKE, however, relates such hidden research in information retrieval to cryptanalysis and the war effort which originated some of this early theory and technology). Their thought is often disembodied and taken out of historical context in a wishful rethinking of historical development. The issue more historically framed is why such thought did not have greater impact than it did, more immediately, with greater continuity to subsequent developments without such need for rediscovery.

Project history, as in delineating the influence of *Chemical Abstracts* here and abroad (EGEREVA; WEISGERBER), has revealed the interaction of information technology and evolution of information services, and their societal impact. The late G. SALTON, himself a major innovator in information storage and retrieval (ISAR) research and technique developer, captured the history of his own field over the past three decades. His survey can be augmented by J. RICHARDSON's rendition over a wider time span, and by TENNER who relates the transition from manual ISAR techniques to automatic retrieval with the changing nature of mental work. BOURNE provides a historical treatment of the nexus between economics and technology in online systems. The development of AI research and applications is treated by HILKER and T. WALKER, and machine translation by HUTCHINS, but too often such surveys are limited to the library and information service arenas and serve merely as background to futuristic predictions about how such technology will revolutionize our lives. A case in point is N. SCUDDER's investigation of CAI/CAL in industrial education, which nevertheless is useful for the material pulled together and for a look outside the educational establishment. G. HARMON has related information science to the Sciences and Engineering. VINCENTI & ROSENBERG explored the early history of technical information dissemination, and VINCENTI returned to this theme using the field of Aeronautics as a case study specifically to examine how engineers think, how they learn, and what constitutes knowledge in Engineering. Their studies should be of interest to historians and project managers who must work with engineers in IT environments. An equally integral study fusing information science, specifically medical Informatics, with computer technology, is B. KAPLAN's examination of the complex relationship between medicine, information technology, and public policy in the health care field between 1950 and 1980; she concludes that the Flexnerian focus on basic research and the neglect of the clinical environment were major reasons why computerization lagged behind baselines established for implementation. The progress of medical computing seems to have been related more to particularities in medicine and public policy than to the technology itself.

The initial forays into Information Science history reveal the problems in documentation of the field, however young, when something is needed on the order of what has been done for other science fields like Physics such things as amassing correspondence files and publications in draft and final releases (WHEATON). The Information Science field, however, needs greater preservation of machine-readable records of its practitioners, and electronic archives in the future to enable such historical study; this study requires a contemporary awareness that is not pervasive and has not yet assisted in the creation of a viable archival record in a contemporary, ongoing, consistent manner. The Social Science dimension of Information Science has excluded it from the purview of agencies established to document science and technology, as at the University of California's Office for History of Science and Technology (Berkeley), so alternatives must be found. That presumably is one of the motivations for the ASIS *Directory* project. Moreover, in 1995-1996 three different publishing initiatives, coordinated by members of the ASIS division for the History and Theory of Information Science, are building a basic literature on the history of Information Science which undoubtedly will be a foundation for teaching, further studies, and hopefully a repositioning of history in the field. Then one might expect improved professional self-awareness minimally if not a genuine historicity in thinking about information issues from the technical and design aspect (history tools, historical reasoning, time and event analysis, etc.) to the human factor (trends analysis, organizational culture, corporate memory, etc.). A proper historical contextualization of information, uses, and users, for example, may change fundamental concepts within the Information Science field, such concepts as current notions of recall and precision in information retrieval which can be seen less as simply related attributes and more as contextually dependent variables themselves.

Rather than History for its own sake, historical awareness has been advocated by some in what has been called the "information industry" for very practical purposes. Altruistic and intellectual reasons be damned in environments where information is regarded as merely a product; here history is short-range recall from a week or month beforehand, perhaps a year, and the very term "archival" is reduced to a mere decade. Intergenerational communication is not the goal; rather history in this context is like a track record, score card, or crib sheet. It is merely a device to prompt recall, and does not constitute a record or provide real evidence. But any system where information is stored long enough so accumulation creates some continuity over any significant length of time and which relies on antecedent and precedent for retrieval and interpretation may be seen as historical. Therein lies a seed that could grow into genuine historical consciousness in information systems design and the integration of archives as an automatic component of current communications. In addition to some appreciation of History in terms of providing a perspective as in terms of commemorating developments in the information field (SALTON; MOOERS; MEADOWS; etc.) and computing (e.g., M. WILLIAMS, 1996), economic historical treatments have been applied to the information industry to assist management decision-making, e.g., in the library world as when the librarian considers an automation vendor's company stability and durability as a factor in awarding bids (RUSH). Or consider E. J. CHIKOFSKY's proposal that beyond immediate change management in software programming, programmers study the history of software to avoid continued reinvention and duplicated work (e.g., LEEBAERT includes the history of software in order to speculate about its future design). BOAR, like archivists, adopted the notion of "life cycle" to application prototyping. This is essentially the same reasoning used by J.A.N. LEE in calling for a history of computing supported by, among other things, software archives. S. SHAPIRO (1997) studied the "software crisis" of the late 1960s when computer manufacturers wanted "quick fixes" to make a case for "the historical necessity of synthesis in software engineering." C. PIDGEON has offered a scheme to analyze decision-making in the design process.

B. RAMESH (1992) likewise advocated a life-cycle approach to contemporary creation of an archival record during software design to capture project history in a systematic manner not for History *per se*, but as a decision-support mechanism (cf., FARRET). He presented a "formalism" called *REMAP (REpresentation and MAintenance of Process knowledge)* which uses *IBIS (Issue Based Information Systems)* methodology to record argumentation and thereby document deliberation and the detailed evolution of a design from concept to implementation. H. LEITNER likewise argued for the importance of "developmental history" when discussing

Brachman's Structured-Inheritance Network and consideration of "cultural posits" for use of the KNET representation formalism in "human-oriented" computer systems. This is the History of Ideas at the microlevel, combined with the use of electronic archives, cast in terms of modern Information Systems Management (ISM) in Business. The History in such presentations is so camouflaged that it is unrecognizable in any superficial reading, and such special-purpose language used inside a domain certainly impedes the transportability of the idea and methodology to another field, i.e., *REMAP*'s possible application in Intellectual History or Archival Science. Such practices, however, if embedded into the very processing of information through programming, could alleviate the kind of anxiety suffered now by archivists who do not see programmers as their allies. Bruce Dearstyne reflects the feelings of many archivists in lamenting, "The modern era is apparently not historical in the minds of many program managers, so recent materials—sometimes the entire twentieth century—are not collected" (DEARSTYNE 1993, p. 52). J. A. N. LEE (1996) laments the same tendency to dismiss the recent as nonhistorical. Automatic archives generation may be the key to countering this thinking.

Such collaboration across disciplines, however, is fraught with difficulty. Lingering bias in Information Science against the Humanities generally or History specifically may prohibit recognition of the merit of unidisciplinary thought and collaboration. Or conversely, the conservatism of History and its relatively slow accommodation of information technology remain barriers to cooperation in research and teaching. The recognition of common values are deterred by inadequate understanding of different sublanguages aligned to disciplines and technical specializations. Such terminological obstructions to cross-disciplinarity are legion: historians would understandably assume that a "Dynamic Belief Network" (BDN) had something to do with religion, perhaps social relations in sharing and spreading elements of religious faith, but it actually is used in inferential statistics and even more broadly in Information Science in ways that historians should pay attention to (HELM). Consider applications to robotics and sensing technology wherein "belief" is a probability distribution as in forecasting a missile trajectory (NICHOLSON) or a vehicle's forward motion on the basis of its previous path (ALMOND provides a guide to related software for probabilistic networks). The idea of "belief" is inferred because the real issue being treated is uncertainty (HELM). The range of issues associated with "belief" in this sense is addressed by ASSOCIATION FOR UNCERTAINTY IN ARTIFICIAL INTELLIGENCE (AUAI) at annual conferences, 1988-, and on its homepage: http://ww.auia.org); this field of study includes a complex methodology (HIRSHLEIFER & RILEY; KUIPERS) involving the parameters of structure, hidden variables, missing values, and incomplete data—such as historians often face in their research. Such graphical tracking is essentially a historical observation leading to path prediction based on past behavior, but the AI jargon even with an appreciation of metaphor hardly makes such theory or research available outside a specific inbred domain.

Historians for the most part have not availed themselves of this research and developed methodology. Yet, the decision science methodology and heuristics involved (e.g., KROZEL), and perhaps the model itself, could be applied in historical and archeological investigation in numerous ways, e.g., as in charting a course of a Spanish galleon lost at sea to assist in either a purely historical exercise or something more mundane like a treasure hunt, or plotting an itinerary from sporadic and incomplete data about a person's whereabouts (a methodology often employed in military maneuvers when intelligence is spotty). Modification of such a model, or software implementing it, and customization for a new application, would benefit from a thorough understanding of the decision process in development. Research, development, and operations are not mutually exclusive but are part of a continuum. Hence the rationale for such electronic documentation systems as *REMAP* is easily demonstrated; so too is the interplay between History, Computer Science, and Information Science in research projects of many kinds.

History of Information Technology

No information technology has been studied more thoroughly than printing, neither scribal production before the invention of printing and contemporary with it, or newer electronic means which coexist with print culture. Because coverage is so thorough and scholarly production so prolific in the history of books and printing, publishing, and libraries, the foregoing discussion has treated the subject broadly and has provided references to bibliographic sources for further exploration of specific works. This is more difficult to do in modern information technology, and therefore this discussion will delve into the secondary literature layer in a little more detail to provide an idea about what is available. Moreover, consider how such literature can be used as an extension of the more mature field of printing, book, and library history; that is, with their counterparts in electronic communications and production, image—text and databases, and network history. The history of technology, computing in particular, and Information Science generally, must be studied by electronic archivists and historians relying on electronic sources to equip themselves with the tools of modern electronic diplomatics and technical knowledge for electronic source criticism. One can argue that those engaged in modern information technology, media, and communications ought to have some historical background in their field of endeavor as a proper foundation for whatever they are doing. The same could be said for scientific inquiry. The history of Information Science, however, has been conceived as something decidedly different than its counterparts, either the history of information technology or of Computer Science, but these subjects are converging. They may be studied for their own sake, for a better understanding of specific technologies and industry, or for a historical consciousness about the relationship between information dissemination and technical innovation.

The close connection of information technology and science is reflected in current reflections on Alan Turing's early efforts in Artificial Intelligence and the rereading of other classic papers by Marvin Minsky and others (surveyed by FEIGENBAUM & FELDMAN), including John von Neumann's work on automata theory (ASPRAY & BURKS, eds.). W. ASPRAY, whose 1980 dissertation does so much more than provide a genealogy of computing machinery, delved into the multi-disciplinary formation of such new fields as communications theory, cybernetics, physiology and psychology, and a general speculative theory of information processing that was not purely mathematical. The popularity of VON NEUMANN's *The Computer and the Brain* (1959), for example, had influence far beyond the science and technology, but on the development of the Social Sciences that during the 1960s so much wanted to prove themselves genuinely scientific. MANNING (p. 775) links von Neumann to a host of subsequent developments; and BERTALANFFY's linkage of robots, minds, and men to the early systems analysis movement. The latter, of course, also influenced Anthropology and world history, i.e., World Systems theory. Other strains of influence from early computing to social thinking have been traced in an array of studies, a few of which are mentioned throughout this survey. PUGH & ASPRAY, for example, have more recently linked computer technology after its incubus in top-secret government think tanks during and after World War II with post-war industry in the United States, and thereafter with business and a worldwide market by focusing on the initial customer base by the mid-1960s. Slowly in such work socioeconomic history and the history of technology and business are being fused. Likewise, the cross-cultural study of P. CERUZZI on the "prehistory" of the digital computer from 1935 through the end of World War II and beyond to 1950 shows the transition from technology such as Konrad Zuse's relay machines in wartime Germany designed to meet specific military objectives (note the recent obituary by WEISS for Zuse, who died in 1995), to a more general approach to multiple applications and a theoretical perspective represented by John von Neuman (ASPRAY).

A totally different perspective, from the outside looking in with a sense of humor thinly veiling real social concerns about computer technology, is offered by GRUPPE who contributes to a genre in itself dating to the 1980s, mined the Cartoon Art Museums in San Francisco and Boca Raton to look at how computers and their applications faired in American comic strips and cartoons over the years. Among the continuing themes he identified are: "Pretender to the throne," or the machine that would be king; "Computer accuracy: If it computes, must it be true?"; and "Robots: Who's the boss?" He contrasts early themes (1940-1970) with those up to the present: i.e., "Competing for control: a brave new world,"; The computer humanized: Giving the tin man a heart"; "Trivial pursuits: Using a hammer to swat a fly"; "Think! (Before a machines does it for you)"; and "Neither depth nor diversity"; and more recently, "Intercomputer relations: Do you speak binary?"; "Us versus Them: Mutual hostility"; "Coexistence: 'Getting to know all about you'"; "Computer usage problems: A (dis)obedient servant"; "Realistic business applications: Hey, this thing really works!"; "A menagerie of users"; "Becoming a part of the landscape,"; and "Pardon me while I mutate" which frets about the loss of individuality. All of these themes are echoed as well in historiographical literature. GRUPE (p. 62) concludes: "Because of their often skewed perspective, they [cartoons] expose our fears and attitudes toward technology in a non-threatening way, not only mirroring our culture but also helping it to evolve... At their best, they amuse us, teach us, and force us to consider the implications of where our technology is headed."

Whereas "computoons" are an unorthodox source for the history of computing technology, such exploration of humor illustrates openness in the New Social History that combines with more orthodox reconstruction from technical and industrial sources. The nexus between information technology, computing and telecommunications and the history of Information Science can be explored with ample primary sources that pertain to the technology itself. These have been described preliminarily by the CHARLES BABBAGE INSTITUTE's *Resources for the History of Computing*; a historical and archival guide to study the rise of *The High-Tech Company* in America (BRUEMMER & HOCHHEISER) and creation of a *High-Tech Society* (FORESTER). Guides by IBM's J. W. CORTADA (1990) with E. JACKSON (1992) and M. S. MAHONEY (1983, 1993) to the pertinent bibliography and the conventional and data archives for computing technology history. The IEEE *ANNALS OF THE HISTORY OF COMPUTING* (1968-) is the mainstay for the history of the information industry and for histories of particular computer technologies, but often it has a narrow focus and limited integration of multi-disciplinary secondary literatures. The journal of the SOCIETY FOR THE HISTORY OF TECHNOLOGY, *Technology and Culture* (1959-), does a better job of placing information technologies in a broader historical context and treating the origins, dynamics, and consequences of technical change.

A good general background linking technological developments to their impact on socioeconomic history can be found in EAMES & EAMES (1973, updated in 1990) and GOLDSTINE's early work (1973). CORTADA's introduction to the history of data processing in his edited three-volume *Historical Dictionary of Data Processing* (1987) is the best place to begin, however, and one can augment this with a series of studies in the history of computing technology. More generally, note also from the early 1980s works by STERN & STERN, and a little later, FORESTER, which capture the enthusiasm of the so-called "computer revolution" on the eve of personal computing. RHEINGOLD in 1985, writing at the very onset of the microcomputer impact, sought to synthesize that background to his predicted "next computer revolution." A 1986 conference of the ACM was devoted totally to the history of the personal computing workstation (GOLDBERG, ed.). All such histories appear to be enamored with either "the Computer Age" or the "Information Age" and are entrapped by their contemporary and nationalist perspectives on technical revolution, so their scope is usually generation-bound with only flashbacks to post-World War II developments. Often several tensions can be discerned in such writing between technology and science (that is, practical versus theoretical concerns), things and ideas, and microhistory and macrohistory. Much of it is myopic and slow reading. The historiography is still adolescent at best, but it is rapidly maturing.

Some of this history of information technology is in the chronicler tradition, not always up to the standards of professional history today. The list compilation mentality that builds chronologies of "firsts" and "breakthroughs" (exhibited in Appendix F, a timetable of IT development included for convenience) is exemplified most recently by *BYTE* magazine's "20th anniversary report" (NEEDLEMAN). Eric Weirs, in his terse review for *Annals of the History of Computing* (1996: 18[2]); pp. 77-78), eschews this particular overview as a peculiar commemoration and a distortion of computing history: "Their [*BYTE* editors] heroes are not their teachers but the hackers, lone inventors, and successful entrepreneurs. The most important stuff is not that with the most intellectual content but whatever is the fastest, newest, has the most bells, whistles and the highest hype, works well, and sells massively." This is an extreme, meant to juxtapose popular culture from the academic, but both are important to the historian. IEEE's *Annals* hardly has the readership of *BYTE*. A vast quasi-academic literature exists standing midway between the popular and academic, which is sometimes all that there is to document socioeconomic and cultural movements affected by technical innovation. This is slighted here in favor of the academic, but even the latter sometimes exhibits only slight regard for contexts such as the history of the corporate developer, motive and precedent, market research and strategies, subsidiary technology integrated into the product, and usage. Note also that the chronicler stage of historiographic evolution is important, since it is the foundation for future conceptualization and revisionism.

A rudimentary chronological framework has evolved. Traditional accounts all harken back to Charles Babbage (1791-1871) and his "difference engine," and his assistant, Ada, Countess of Lovelace (1815-1852) and Lord Byron's daughter (HYMAN). Ada is sometimes touted as the world's first programmer, but as K. KATZ argues, this is largely lip service, as are the attempts to connect modern computing to Pascal's and Leibnitz's calculating machines. Many such attributions reflect anachronisms common in popular accounts of technology and lightweight historiography. She maintains that very little real historical continuity can be established between these early antecedents and twentieth-century accomplishments, but CERUZZI's *Computing before Computers* accomplishes this better. In reviewing historical background in basic computer science textbooks (scant at best), KATZ also notes that the standard rendition is not only deceiving and anachronistic by some of its inclusions and analogies, but it is woefully inadequate in other cases by serious omissions, such as in: not relating the evolution of the binary number system to computer design; skipping over the bridge of analog machines to earlier inventions and modern computers; slighting the connection of computer science and computer hardware development by downplaying Allen Turing (see HODGES) and other thinkers in favor of real computer people, but then also slighting the contributions of John Atanasoff, John W. Mauchly, J. Presper Eckert, etc.; ignoring external forces such as McCarthyism on the computer industry or the role of women which is only recently addressed (GURER); and an unwillingness to mention negative aspects of the computer revolution, e.g., worker displacement, the context of socioeconomic history (P. GRAHAM). She argues that it is important that computer science teachers impart to their students "the historical/societal context for the development of computer science to enable them to deal intelligently with the future. We must insist on the integrity of the historical material that is included in the texts we assign to our students to read" (K. KATZ, p. 19). To remedy such deficiencies, J. A. N. LEE (1996, p. 60) suggests a starting periodization by associating broad generations with decades:

1. 1940s with the emergence of the concept of computing

2. 1950s with a set of related but distinct disciplines and a central theme

3. 1960s brought in multi-disciplinary approaches

4. 1970s witnessed inter-disciplinary synthesis and

5. the 1980s saw the rise of specializations and the possible fragmentation of the general theme and relationships between disciplines

CERUZZI (1997) understands that chronological revision is difficult, partially because classification of computing into "generations" after 1960 (the generational metaphor predates this use, however), with the "first" generation being those with vacuum tubes, or everything dating from the UNIVAC in 1951, reinforces the common notion in computer science that whatever happened before more recent rapid advances in computer technology "was somehow mere prologue to the real history" (p. 5). Ceruzzi thinks that the usage of generations was solidified by IBM in 1964 when it introduced the System/360 numbered as the first of the "third-generation" machines. He shows that certain machines built in the 1930s and 1940s straddle such common chronological divisions as "ages" in computer evolution and have basic commonalities with computers employed after WWII.

LEE points to a similar sequence, although slightly longer lag time, for human/computer interaction developments. CORTADA (1996) amplifies this chronological scheme for development with a periodization for the spread of computing into the business marketplace: (1) pre-1945 is likewise just an idea stage when news about the ENIAC began to spread slowly with speculation about what computing might accomplish; (2) 1945-1952 is when "businesses meet the computer" when articles on digital computers doubled in a three-year period; (3) business adopts computers in 1952-1965 in accounting, banking, insurance, manufacturing, inventory control, and retail, in that order; (4) as evidenced by the spectacular growth of IBM, between 1965 and 1981 computers become ensconced in the corporate scene as a permanent fixture; and (5) from the mid-1980s onward personal computers reshape the industry. COR-TADA, LEE, NORBERG, and others imply a fundamental change in computers before and after WWII, which, Ceruzzi notes from the Computer Museum of Boston's attribution, is the "Newton-Maxwell Gap" meaning the difference in speeds based on mechanical devices governed by Newton's laws of motion to electronics governed by Maxwell's laws of electromagnetic radiation. He notes another significant change at this time in the architectural level of computing (i.e., a shift from serial to parallel data processing) associated with the von Neumann model. CERUZZI (1997, p. 6) sees this as a critical "architectural bridge across the chasm from computing's 'prehistoric' period to its modern era." Not only do such observations serve as reminders that it is not always historians who concoct chronologies, but that historical notions crystallize long before historians pay attention to them. In this case, academic historians were not the makers of computer history any more than what they did with computing made history at this time. Historians had not yet discovered the computer. Indeed, although CORTADA (1993a & b) details which businesses used computers in these periods, and for what purposes, it is obvious from his investigation that education was not a noticeable user in this larger scheme of big business. This lacuna in Cortada's chronology reflects LEE's observation (1996, p. 62) about old systems being handed down to the "less fortunate—to the biologists and educators"...and to latecomers like historians and archivists.

Although such chronological and conceptual work is far from stable and stages of development will undoubtedly be stretched out into more comprehensive periods as time goes on, some speculation about the historical processes of technical development and dissemination can be borrowed from process planning and control in product engineering and manufacturing. Based on his experience in product development, LEE (1996, p. 59) draws this time lag like a curve from a high point of perceived complexity when the original concept is still nebulous, to a radically descending timeline when understanding is increased and simplification occurs to make implementation possible. Then the development line begins to ascend again, but more slowly than it dropped originally, as enhancements are made, modifications are undertaken, and extensions are developed—all of which increase the complexity again. Although he does not continue his model indefinitely, one can understand that extensions like spin-offs start the process over again for related products. Products like all artifacts can be classified by components and substance, structure, function, operation and process, and manufacturing and sales. A resulting clustering and grouping of products as artifacts, creating a family from product lines based on an object genealogy, is one approach to studying technology. Computers have pedigrees, for example, related to trademarks and patents that may be likened to birth records and christenings; they are tracked like offspring with family names, product lines, model numbers, and modified extensions. Another, more closely related to intellectual history and akin to the archival notion of provenance, is to trace the concept from archetype to prototype and actual products, and to compare the parallelism between the multiplication of products and their modification with the growth of ideas and extent of revisionism, reconceptualization, and redesign (that is, the history of the idea entails its origin, extension in meaning, and diffusion; cf., SWEENEY). Documentation and artifacts, as in art history, must be combined to form all of the evidence needed for historical reconstruction and interpretation.

Such chronological and theoretical conceptualization is still very tentative, since much of this history is just passing out of its early documentation and collecting stage. The work of gathering documentation for computing history is relatively recent and still ongoing; J. LEE (1991) has attempted to provide some guidelines about what is needed, and these may serve to remind people in the industry who are not aware of their potential historical importance about what to preserve for posterity's sake. LEE (1996) and others know that preservation of sources is important, but that history goes beyond that to interpretation. The ability to interpret broadly and objectively based on multiple sources, however, is often hampered by how original documentation haphazardly survives, is artificially gathered, and is preserved as an afterthought and salvage operation. Even though computing is in the information business, and computer scientists see themselves as more than mechanical or electrical technicians, they have not individually or corporately always done well in systematically preserving their own records through effective archival information systems. This is partially a limitation of individual mind set, with an ethos that has been presentist and future oriented, and of cultural deprivation in the context of operating in government and industry first with overriding concerns for national security, secondly on business marketing and cost containment (PUGH & ASPRAY), and only recently with consciousness of a broader role in society and culture.

As in the case of information science, computer science circles are aware of thinning ranks among the pioneer computer builders (J. A. N. LEE, 1995; M .R. WILLIAMS), some of whom became conscious enough of their roles in science and technology to leave memoirs and autobiographies (e.g., K. ZUSE). Some have donated their papers to manuscript repositories, and some archives did preserve a continuous corporate record for successful companies. Business failures and unsuccessful experimentation are less well documented, as J. A. N. LEE (1996, pp. 57-59) laments. The IEEE Computer Society has attempted to create a documentary forum in its *Annals of the History of Computing* section for biographies edited by Eric Weirs (autobiographies, memoirs, and extensive obituaries including the demise of organizations and companies) "intended to celebrate a life." Another section is dedicated to Anecdotes, edited by James Tomayko, to provide "participants in the history of computing to contribute reminiscences of salient events." Both editors invite debate, varying opinion and recall, and evidence, but most are written from one perspective and are published as is, as anecdotes and reminiscences, as a sort of written oral history, without the scholarly editing that would insure their authority base as primary records (i.e., through the addition of a critical apparatus and supporting bibliography, annotation and verification of references, cross-checking facts and chronology, and peer review when possible). Lacking most regrettably is a link between such personal accounts and alternative sources for objectivity, such as reference to archival documentation. A great deal in the history of computing as with the history of other technology relies on citations of secondary material and published sources without recourse to the raw data, artifactual evidence, and actual records of the event or process they discuss. As in Information Science, published reports are considered "primary literature." Writing history from such sources alone results essentially in a literary history. Again, the archival discipline is often lacking in this worthwhile and praiseworthy enterprise, recall is sometimes all we have even for this contemporary history, and in time it will suffer form the same defects of other historical subject areas even though ironically this one embodies an information field. One might have expected something more from an information science, to be self-informing scientifically and to have had an information infrastructure that would not require salvage efforts on the scale now necessary to capture the history of a passing generation and of the very present. The flaw is endemic and lasting.

J. A. N. LEE (1996) and others (e.g., M.S. MAHONEY) have already called for a more sophisticated history of computing integrated into the history of technology and the larger scheme of things, but technicians turned historians cannot break with their own pasts. LEE, for example, cannot divorce computing history from his concept of a useable past, that is, to develop an historiography that is pertinent to the technical field, it must "begin to show usefulness and applicability to the modern world to begin to develop inroads into the field which it purports to investigate" (J. LEE, 1996, p. 62). His orientation is that of social scientist. History as technique and critique may be useful in such a persuasion, but history as intellectual inquiry for its own sake is still seen largely as irrelevant in the milieu of technology. Historical computing within Social Science History would seem to be the most respected in the history of technology, but ironically most work in this field is non-quantified, descriptive history based on documentary records. The history that Lee and others like him produce is narrative, despite its justification in Social Science terms. Perhaps this is because the underlying ethos in Technology, apart from the justifying rhetoric, is still as seen by STAUDENMAIER, dependent on storytelling within the organizational cultures of technical enterprises and within business corporations. The same is true of scientific communities where telling stories of historical development (as distinct from the study of History) was important for establishing associations and distinctions, as in Biology where biologist borrowed concepts from other domains and devised protocols that "included 'stories' of historical development of the current understanding about genes, proteins, processes, etc." (CHEN *ET AL*. [1997], p. 27). Information scientists use term association in such stories and protocols to study contexts and thereby to determine links in the design of information systems, referencing in conjoined thesauri, and indexing applications. In any case, one cannot automatically associate the history of technology with the technical practice of History, or the use of formal History with the historical elements in information systems design.

Computing history is still an insular field, isolated by its incorporation in the industry and departmentalization in academe, but also because it operates with an extensive and obtuse sublanguage of its own. It is, however, breaking out of its shell and emerging as a *bona fide* contributor to the larger world of historiography. Consider CORTADA's comparative study (1993a) of early computer companies (IBM, NCR, Burroughs, Remington Rand) and simultaneously published companion which places such business development in the broader context of the commercial marketplace in America (CORTADA, 1993b) and E. W. PUGH's recent insider's history of IBM (1995). FISHER, MCKIE & MANCKE's early work on IBM and the rise of the American data processing industry is notable; it is complemented by other IBM histories (R. SOBEL; E. PUGH [1995]). USSELMAN's award wining essay (1993) places IBM's leadership in the broader context of development of an international computer industry. Such work stands in contrast to much insider history that relies on personal experience and supplies anecdotal material, but which often lacks the big picture and context for broad, comparative interpretation. A recent example is H. OLDFIELD, director of General Electric's ERMA project, who recalls how this corporate giant vacillated when contemplating a move into the computer field in 1956 to accommodate one of GE's major customers, the Bank of America, with automated accounting; the new companies had been taunted by the press as being "the Seven Dwarfs" in comparison with IBM. He wrote his rendition partially in reaction to GROSCH's history of computer manufacturers of which he was highly critical. In any case, the GE fiasco has received attention here and elsewhere in the IEEE *Annals of the History of Computing* as a counterpoint to more common historical celebration of success stories.

The history of scientific computing received attention in a recent ACM conference (S. NASH, ed.) and CROARKEN provides a history of early scientific computing in Great Britain. The spread of computing into nonscientific areas is not well studied, however, even as an aspect of diffusion; and overall, computing in international business is not treated as well in history as for the American scene. Hardware history is also being compiled (RUNYAN; M. R. WILLIAMS), for applications in data conservation and a pragmatic concern in computer design largely for consumption inside the information industry (FLYNN, 1992). R. E. SMITH surveys the development of computer architecture, and FRIEDMAN & CORNFELD provide a history of computer systems development. It is understandable that with mainframe computing dominating the field, historians from the industry also write about dominant companies and the history of technology therefore is the history of large corporations. The historiography of computer technology must necessarily move from manufacturer to user studies, from traditional corporate history to business history broadly conceived, and from a history of applications and projects to a fusion of the history of ideas and New Social history. After all, communication, not things, is the essence of science and of Information Science in particular (GARVEY; GARVEY & GRIFFITH). HOLZMANN & PEHRSON have investigated the early history of signaling (fires, torches, beacons, to the telegraph) as a prehistory to data networks. C. MARVIN attempted to treat electrical engineering in the late nineteenth century sympathetically with how people then felt about new communication technology. The more recent impact of personal computing and networking, the Internet and World Wide Web, will assuredly cause considerable revision in such histories (e.g., COTTER's recounting of the origins of BITNET). HAUBEN & HAUBEN's forthcoming *Netizens* (an intentional play on Simon Schama's *Citizens*?) takes up the social impact of computer networking, and to do so, explores the history of the Internet. They ask in wonder: "The Past: Where has it all come from?"

The Smithsonian exhibition on the "Infoculture" in 1993 surveyed the major inventions associated with the so-called "Information Age" (LUBAR). Like AUGARTEN's older (1984) illustrated history of computing, this exhibition catalog is very useful for teaching. The history of hardware development has applications outside R&D operations in the case of preservation, not simply of museum pieces as visual artifacts on display at the Smithsonian (cf., TENNER review), but in selective retro-processing of electronic data. It is also often important to study operations and procedures in the appraisal of electronic records for archival retention (T. COOK, 1992), or for purely historical interpretation as in the history of science, technology, economics, etc., to understand fully historical data processing for analysis of its outcome. Although J. LEE (1996, p. 56) questions the value of preserving artifacts simply for deposit in museums, because he limits the functions of museums to general interpretation and education and to public relations rather than scholarship which he links more to archives and documentation. He does value the hands-on approach, however, of living museums, where one might experience history as in the case of using early software. Moreover, he recognizes that a danger exists in documentation in that they may "assume too much." Access to the artifact can therefore qualify interpretation of documentation. In essence, LEE argues for the preservation of software in archives as much as hardware and other artifacts in museums, on the "better safe than sorry" principle because one cannot foresee future value for something currently considered worthless such as old software. A better appraisal argument can be made by linking historic software, data processed, and content. One without the other is often inaccessible and unintelligible. The problem, of course, is that old bulky hardware lacking in aesthetics has not been seen as a collectible; and now some hardware is so minuscule that it cannot be seen as a collectible. It has no display and value and, in the case of firmware and software, lacks the normal attributes of what we associate with museum collections.

Much has been lost already, in the span of a single generation, and the acceleration of technical obsolescence compounds the problem. DOLLAR ([1998], p. 48), with an historian's perspective, observes "the history of digital technological innovation over the last four decades or so offers compelling evidence that technological change is inevitable and irreversible." Some of this is market driven and is artificially induced by the computer industry which has had little regard for the data losses incurred at their clients' and society's expense or since of archival goals other than to ensure "backward compatibility" between one or two versions of software upgrades. The software may be an upgrade, which too often causes a downgrade of archival objectives in information systems. Like lost artifacts from other generations, we may have to be content with metadata, secondary documentation, and surrogates such as photographic archives depicting machinery that is no more. Somehow such substitution for real things lost some time ago seems understandable as *fait accompli,* but like LEE, one should be uneasy about current loss and a lack of historical ecology in our throwaway society. When technological obsolescence threatens the survival of such important sources as the United States 1960 Census (on 7,300 UNIVAC II-A tape drives, which were left unsupported after 1975), one can no longer be complacent about this perennial problem. While archives in business and government bear the inordinate expense of salvaging electronic records from the perils of technological obsolescence, one must place much of the fault where it belongs, squarely with the profit-motivated leadership of a largely unaccountable computer industry.

The public history forum represented by the Smithsonian exhibition of information technology has its counterparts in the literature. While there is no need to duplicate the contents of the aforementioned bibliographies, a few citations may highlight trends and promote exemplary works. Not only does the history of telecommunications and related technology have decent foundations in the histories by OSLIN, POHL, ROGERS, and USSLEMAN (1995), but communications research has been surveyed by DELIA and *ARIST* has previously reviewed the development of telecommunications as well (CAWKELL, which now needs updating). COPELAND treats the history of sound recordings. Broadcasting, often left out of the IS picture but certainly important from the communications standpoint, is covered for America during a critical development over the turn of the last century by DOUGLAS and more fully by STERLING & KITTROSS. See also YOURDON's set of volumes on the broadcasting industry through the 1950s, which remains essential. J. DUNCAN provides a statistical background for the history of the radio in the United States, but for too short a time to draw lasting conclusions and without the kind of synthesis one would expect; radio, commercial and public, and HAM radio as well, deserves more historical research than it has received. The same neglect of these media in information science, as if information were only conveyed by text, is true of other forms of mass communication such as the news media and postal services (KIEL-BOWICZ, 1989, 1990). WASKO attempts to cover the contemporary history of motion picture and television, as well as home video production and distribution, by looking through somewhat Marxist spectacles primarily at Hollywood corporations and conglomerates that grew out of the film industry. Telephony is covered in a variety of ways, from C. S. FISCHER's prize-winning *American Calling,* a social history of the telephone to 1940 and treatments in labor and women's history exploring the period "When Women were Switches," to treatments of the technology itself (e.g., M. MUELLER). MALONE writes his history of the microprocessor from the viewpoint of the technology itself, as a "biography" of the microprocessor. He sees this as "a revolution in miniature."

Specific technologies have found their respective historians, from tracing writing instruments from pencils to ballpoint ink pens (DANIELS), typewriters (BLIVEN) to copying devices largely in nineteenth-century government bureaucracies (CRAIG), and more recently magnetic recordings (MORTON) and photocopying (CARLSON; MORT). Micro-formats seem to have been covered as well: microfilming (HIRTLE) and further miniaturization in the microdot inspired by espionage requirements during World War II through J. Edgar Hoover's

FBI (W. WHITE), micro-printing (LANDESMAN) such as on micro-cards (JAMISON), as well as newer technologies such as optical disks and CD-ROMs ("the new papyrus": LAMBERT & ROPIEQUET, eds.; cf., HARTIGAN 1993a & b; HOLTZ) and related standards (MORROW). Tele-facsimili developments are covered, albeit popularly, by HUNKIN. O'TOOLE (1994) relates this historiography of the copy tradition to archival theory. Whereas the history of such inventions and their early development are therefore well covered, H. SCHWARTZ takes such history of technology into the largest context possible by examining "the culture of the copy in the modern world." With similar scope and thorough integration of a technology and mechanical devices into the larger context of history, LANDES' *Revolution in Time* treats both the conceptualization of time and the history of clocks and time pieces. He writes the history of this technology from a social and cultural history perspective, but the same theme should be related to computing, especially timekeeping, serialization, synchronization, and temporal databases.

The relationship of modern visualization technologies to the older development of photography is possible by reading R. JENKINS's work on the American photographic industry over the turn of the last century (or consult J. SNYDER on the invention of photography) with KNEPPER's history of the Society for Information Display and updates such as provided by FRIEDHOFF & BENZON. While GOLDBERG points to the 1930s for serious work on visual information retrieval from photographic collections, RITCHIN connects photography and older research using images with computer visualization which he characterizes as an extension of photography rather than something totally new, i.e., *The Coming Revolution in Photography: How Computer Technology Is Changing Our View of the World*. Other areas are being addressed every day, since the history of technology has become a hot topic, it is now being merged with business history, and information technology is particularly of interest as the late twentieth century prepares for even more rapid acceleration in technological development during the next century. Some of this interest may be attributed to technology hype, but more so to an urge to take stock before leaping into the next millennium

Database evolution of interest to computing historians and historians of information science alike often starts with the invention of the Hollerith punched card (ADAMS; KISTERMANN), methods (ECKERT), and punched-card machinery (NORBERG). WIESELMAN & TOMASH have surveyed computerized printing; EISENBERG covers word processing in its early development (this topic needs updating); NEUFELD & CORNOC surveyed database design and development. SAMMET assembled an outline for the history of programming languages; and three important Association for Computing Machinery (ACM) conferences in 1978 about programming languages (WEXELBLAT, ed.), 1980 (METROPOLIS *ET AL.*), and 1993 (M. MAHONEY) prompted further exploration of the sources. The advent of personal computing is examined by PRESS. NORBERG (1996) relates early computing research and development to the Department of Defense (DOD) and related defense industry, especially Defense Advanced Research Projects Agency (DARPA); and USSELMAN (1996) relates such early government involvement with the continued support the industry receives as part of American public policy. CORTADA (1996, p. 27) recommends FLAMM's account of the relationship between government, industry, and "high technology" to be the best so far.

In the history of the library-based information industry PERRY discusses early computer-assisted searching and online information retrieval, and T. PETERS looks at the development of transaction log analysis as a means of studying search behaviors in automated environments. Document retrieval by call numbers is discussed by SATIJA. LEARN, in addressing library networking specifically includes a brief historical overview as background to his speculation about future development; his survey can be amplified by consulting the bibliography compiled by KRIETZ. FREEMAN offers reflections rather than a genuine history on the impact of older manual technologies (e.g., ink pens, keys, cards, etc.) on library operations before automation (surveyed by TEDD), and the evolution of cataloging techniques and classification systems have received considerable attention (GORMAN; OSBORN). One can reconstruct a continuum between such manual tools and the first large and complex databases kept in unwieldy card catalogs, to card retrieval systems, and then to online searching, and ultimately to search engines traversing the Internet looking for appropriate Web sites.

The history of Web search engines is provided by BELLARDO HAHN as a preview of a book in process by her and Charles Bourne on the early history of online systems (BOURNE & BELLARDO HAHN). They are trying to establish a basic timeline for developments in this past generation: "However, verifying dates, establishing priority of discovery and invention and giving proper credit to genuine trailblazers is a difficult and complex task" (p. 7). She traces such developments to Mike Kessler's use of Boolean operators and the development of TIP in 1964 and shortly thereafter, full-text searching of legal documents at Data Corporation and the early work of Richard Giering at Data Central (the precursor of LEXIS). From such modest beginnings came the development of word manipulation, browse capabilities, search refinement techniques, canned queries, and varied forms of display, as well as all enhanced retrieval and enlarged search engines as complex sets of operations. BELLARDO HAHN notes that many features in later online searching were conceptualized more than a decade before and were used first in serial searching in magnetic tape databases. The concepts themselves often have a much longer history. Such developments have taken even longer until their utility outside select research and development operations could be realized. Global access was demonstrated first in 1965, for example, even if it became a worldwide realty only in the 1990s.

The investigation of the evolution of a technology, i.e., object-oriented history, is more prevalent than the related Intellectual History or History of Ideas that would pertain more to the history of Information Science. Thus it is still easier to trace models, identify machinery, and delineate a technological trend from business and manufacturing reports, records, patents, etc., than it is to discern innovative thought, paradigm shifts, cultural mood swings, acceptance of assumptions and attitudinal change, and the altering of values, etc., that link human thought and behavior with their artifacts and technology. Many have recently called attention to the profound changes wrought by information technology, and have called upon history to make such changes understandable (e.g., SAXBY). The backgrounds, however, have sometimes proved unsettling since information systems management related to societal control through information management has not always supported popular assumptions about information and freedom. BENIGER links information systems to the economic origins and the control imperative. YATES (1989) likewise relates data processing and communications controls to the rise of the "system" in American business. LU (1990, 1991) explores more specifically the implications of Information Systems Management (ISM) in business models transferred from the Euro-American context to other cultures.

Considerable interest today focuses on this nexus between man and machine and the changing nature of work in the United States and its social implications. This connection is often subordinated under the rubric "Information Society," as in the work of SCHEMENT (1989, 1990) who tackles the problems of information technology in terms of the socioeconomic impact of computing in today's milieu by including historical briefings throughout his sociological treatment. More recently the collaboration of SCHEMENT & CURTIS has provided a contemporary political history of the Information Age, with its "tendencies and tensions." This work is not so absorbed in power politics in the question of media policy in the United States as is S. MILLER's recent *Civilizing Cyberspace* which has been questioned about its historical perspective and accuracy. Perhaps this treatment illustrates the problem of writing too close to the issues, in this case NII, reflecting a personal view from direct involvement, or indirectly that of the Computer Professionals for Social Responsibility (CPSR). The up-front, close, and personal variety of social and political commentary that enliven debate about contemporary issues may be put into broader, deeper perspective by other studies which are not histories as such but nevertheless provide valuable historical perspective. TENNER examines the impact of information storage and retrieval technology on how people do mental work. This theme is extended by ZUBOFF who relates the future of labor and power to "the smart machine." EDWARDS & SNYDER rely heavily on a combination of economic forecasting and the history of information technology for their futurism which describes ongoing changes in the home, workplace, and America at large (after H. SMITH's "rethinking America") to suggest what things may be like in 2010. This is the Social Science dimension of Information Science; it is also largely a matter of History.

Relevance interpreted only as geographic and chronological proximity, regardless of its objective measurement in Information Science, is a subjective value very difficult to realize. It is also often confused with cause. Proximity does not prove cause, and the pervasive influence of a historical event or larger development may be more relevant than any piece of information that is temporarily perceived as timely. The emphasis in current Information Science on the contemporary could therefore benefit from historical perspective. Conversely, History, reliant as it is on modern and historical information sources and a historical continuity in institutional survival for the preservation of sources and access to them, should pay more attention to developments in Information Science and information technology. Historians aware of contemporary information issues may well find insight into their own historical work and simultaneously provide much needed historical perspectives for those confronting modern information problems. Here is a case for classic symbiosis between Information Science as it has evolved thus far, and for Historical Information Science as it is could develop.

NEW CULTURAL STUDIES AND MANAGEMENT

In an anthropological sense, technology and culture go together. The former might exist without the other, but its use is another matter, i.e., a matter of culture. Dictionary definitions of "culture" often use the historic analogy of culture and cultivation to denote that the former requires care, attention, and even devotion in relation to the root term "cult" which is a belief system reinforced by ritual and ceremonies. KROEBER & KLUCKHOHN in 1952 counted more ways to define "culture" than anyone ever thought possible, more than the Nietzschean-Wittgenstein line of interpretation dominant in the Humanities. Anthropologists are still trying to narrow the "culture concept" down to a few working definitions (P. WATSON). GEUSS reminds us that German uses three different terms (*kultur* connected from Kant onward, 1790, with the shadow concept of Civilization; plus *bildung* and *geist,* i.e., diverse folkways of groups, development of individual talents and capacities, and aesthetic experience and judgment, respectively) for what is sometimes collapsed into the single English word. Stemming from the Latin *colo*, this past participle for placement together retains the idea of intention, action, and future expectation. Figuratively "to cultivate" means to improve and refine intellectually. Although closely related, a traditional distinction has always been made in letters and the sciences: one cultivates something that grows, and a culture is that in which it grows. Information may be an ingredient, so-called "food for thought," but it is not culture itself. The dominant focus in Information Science is often limited to the food itself, not nutrition, nor general health. This larger concern is a matter of culture, it is something history benefits, and this underscores the rationale of embedding history into information science and *vice versa*.

Historical information or formal knowledge of the past has its informal side in general memory and tradition, which are not ordinarily seen as information *per se*, but information also has a cultural dimension when one recalls the base meaning of the term: to inform is to give form, provide shape, and animate so as to communicate and instruct effectively, and thereby to make something known. If culture is the environment, and cultivation (i.e., teaching) refers to the technique, information is the means and history (that is, knowing by inquiry) is, as it was for the Greeks, the same as information. This approach to studying culture through its content (information), means (technology), and form (source criticism) is still more empirical than might be preferred by literary scholars who experience culture primarily through language and hence see everything as social discourse (e.g., GREENBLATT, 1990). Secondary teachers know that the narrative helps them convey history to students, in portraiture, contextualization, moralization, and interpretation, but the narrative is only one of many approaches to historical understanding and development of critical thinking (LEVSTIK). The narrative is the lead, not the analysis, and certainly not the conclusion in History.

Once culture is perceived as something which is developed, maintained, and indeed cultivated, then too the scientific impulse to control culture as a conditioned environment means one moves toward the idea of culture management. Then one can conceive of the business of culture and conversely culture in business as another aspect of disciplinary conversion. It is this extended conceptualization that is explored next, beyond Information Science and History, to relate Historical Information Science to such visual information resources and artifacts and to Business and especially to Management (SPOEHR & LEHMKUHLE). This nexus is useful in connecting types of institutions—libraries, archives, and museums—with something more than mere information dissemination or literary discourse, but in cultural regeneration. These institutions both serve and use history; they are historical information organizations subject to study from a variety of perspectives, both for the culture they support and reciprocally how culture supports them, and from the vantage point of management. In this broad sense Historical Information Science is the scientific study of the means by which civilization maintains itself. It is a refinement of History in general, focusing more narrowly on information sources and processes. The same holds true for smaller domains, i.e., cultures, societies, and groups. Thus Historical Information Science might be related properly to organizational culture at any level.

A significant distinction must be made between the history of something and history in it. In one case the referent is external, removed, and supposedly objective by its position as an observer rather than participant. This is largely the case in the history of technology and industry, although as has been argued there is a legitimate and necessary place for historical reasoning, perspective, and content within science and technology—especially in information science and technology. This case is reversed, however, when one talks about cultural history. There, history is an integral part of culture, an active ingredient, and consequently may operate more subjectively as both the subject of study and the referent. The latter kind of less objective history is therefore more difficult to conceptualize, analyze, and convey, and has often been seen as more introspective, descriptive, and anecdotal that it is totally humanistic and nonscientific. As science itself has become more circumspect and introspective as well, this dichotomy like so many others has failed to withstand trends toward convergence. Could one expect otherwise in an era when time itself has become less rigid, place is as much as state of mind as an actual location, and time travel of sorts through modern technology relies less and less on pure imagination. In such convergence might one not expect heightened awareness of the past in the present?

History, by touching both the Humanities and the Social Sciences at the same time, has occupied a unique position as a bridge for interdisciplinary studies, but so much of discipline-based scholarship has become interdisciplinary that its unique positioning is no longer the only or even primary conduit now available. It does retain special preeminence in retrospective studies, but even here, history is so diffuse and integrated into other disciplines that historical perspective and approach may not be identified with History as an organized field of study and formalized discipline. Information Science can also serve the same integrative role; so can Business if it had a mind to, and Education also offers mediation across traditional disciplinary boundaries. The diffused and pervasive influence of Anthropology in so many disciplines likewise functions as an inter-disciplinary mixer. This convergence of disciplines, a fusion resulting in considerable confusion, also entails a breakdown of the distinctiveness of hard and soft sciences, and sciences and nonsciences. No where is this more evident than in culture studies, where scientific approaches on framing questions, considering techniques, using technology, controlling observation, and methodologies in project management and analysis applied to social and ideological phenomena create newly expanded social sciences out of study areas traditionally seen as nonscientific and as situated squarely in the Arts and Humanities. Science is in every discipline, which means that is also more difficult to define what is scientific and what is not (CHALMERS). The same holds true for History; it too resides in every discipline. Its role in Business was largely that of background, but today Management and Cultural Studies offer new promise for increased awareness of History and contemporary uses in creating healthy organizational cultures.

Questions relating Culture, Cultural Memory, and History to information transmission and use can be posed to Information Science—where, however, they are seldom asked. Information scientists tend to assume that people act and make decisions based on information, and that the better informed they are, supposedly, the better decisions they make. It is a tacit assumption inherited from the progressive notion of education (J. BRUNER). Information Science, which remains largely behavioral in orientation, places people as users in the center of most investigation and utilizes Cognitive Psychology, from PIAGET onward, to a great extent (cf., these 1995 works: EYSENCK *ET AL.* for reference; J. BEST for introduction; and J. R. ANDERSEN for implications beyond the field itself); but information scientists have not adequately explored the cultural context in which information generators, providers, and systems operate. Such a notion seems totally foreign to Computer Science which tends to take almost a deist approach to a mechanized universe in which humans are adjuncts to the system. The notion of Culture, even in its anthropological sense, seems too abstract. Information scientists may understand social systems as contexts for their information studies, but the subtler and complex notion of a culture operating as a system, perpetuating itself, has not been explored to any extend comparable to trends in Cultural History or organizational studies in Management. Nor have the latter fields had much to do with each other. It is time for a rapprochement and fruitful interaction.

Collective Memory and Culture

The idea of "the collective" is implicit in all modeling, whenever the part is related to the whole. It is evident, for example, in such historical classics as *The Medieval Mind* by Henry Osborne Taylor, or any time historians talk about a civilization, culture, society, group, a mentality other than for a specific state of consciousness or character other than for an individual, and certainly when one talks about probability in terms of tendency, disposition, or propensity. The same may be said about ascribing personality to any organization, as when talking about *the* church, *the* university, and *the* company. Such a mental model of the collective is more pronounced in some historical studies than others, but the idea is pervasive whenever generalizations are made. JOHNSON-LAIRD (1988, 1993; cf., essays in his honor edited by OAKHILL & GARNHAM) stressed the importance of mental models in cognition. Although often associated with the Social Sciences that are group oriented, the idea is common to the Arts and Humanities as well whenever comparison is made between an entity and an archetype, or whenever classification occurs. In all cases the generality or schema are at odds with the exception or any unit examined individually. The universal tension is between the one and many, differences and commonalties, and concrete and the abstract as originally defined by Aristotle and Plato. We understand this philosophically, but the issue becomes more tense when removed from the abstract and applied to us individually if we do not share a sense of belonging. Tension is also heightened when one's sense of individuality is compromised. Such circumstances are discordant. This is what happens when master narratives become restrictive rather than inclusive. This flexible tension is sometimes, mistakenly, solidified into a false dichotomy in associating models only with the Sciences. Under this regimented thinking, History and Information Science have little to do with each other.

Nowhere in History has cognitive modeling become so pervasive and intense as in Cultural History, especially in the now common treatment of culture as memory, and societal memory as Collective Memory. CONFINO observes that "Memory" has become the leading guide word in Cultural History. For him and other cultural historians, the common denominator in such studies is "the way in which people construct a sense of the past" (CONFINO, p. 1386). P. HUTTON portrays History "as an Art of Memory." Although these cultural historians cite their indebtedness to Sociology and Cognitive Psychology, they continue to see themselves largely as Humanists because their subject matter is cultural. They often cannot or simply do not support their arguments through measurement, they prefer methodologies which do not tax them or their readers mathematically, and computing for them is largely text-processing rather than data analysis or computer-assisted problem solving. Few tacitly acknowledge the Social Science nature of their work because of the social context of the subject; how their assumptions and often speculative discourses are forged into models; or the relationship of contemporary work, which is largely descriptive, to relevant quantified studies or current applications as in Organizational Culture within Management. Some dislike the use of explicit models for fear that they appear too rigid and that interpretations based on modeling seem deterministic.

This apprehension is alleviated when one sees a model as a mode or method of explanation rather than as a static casting mold, when the form may be seen as more elastic and transformable than anything so rigid or prescriptive. POCOCK, for example, saw certain forms of political discourse as models that influenced thought and behavior, but he understood that the language used to capture the thought of the moment changed in time and that thought about the original event was ever changing. He reminded historians to move back and forth between the "context of language" and "content of experience" (POCOCK, p. 16; recently resurrected by J. M. SMITH [1997, p. 1417, n. 13]). Historical experience at the instant and all subsequent time influenced the political discourse. Ideas may achieve a form durable enough to be traced through History, but the cognition of them is another matter. Definition of an idea is not unlike a model, but its application and acceptance is interactive. The whole process is larger than any one input. CHARTIER (1989) warns that discourses, for example, as objects of analysis "cannot be reduced to the ideas they state or the themes they convey." He argues, of course, that people choose language strategically to project selected "representations," and act by "symbolic strategies" in naming, classifying, and disseminating. Representation and modeling are not that unlike, it seems, except in their presentation to different audiences from different perspectives, as if the sociocultural approaches were really so different from the Social Sciences.

Modern European and American cultural historians investigating culture as a distillation of Collective Memory, for example, seldom relate their work to older Marxist and communist history, but usually invoke pioneering works in Sociology. Collectivism understandably was an abiding interest of Soviet cultural and intellectual historicism in keeping with the orientation toward socialism and emphasis on socioeconomic History in a communist state (L. MILOV). History and Natural Science were fused in the endeavor to make sense out of the whole from individual history and case studies. The pronounced interest of Soviet scientists in brain size, for example, was motivated by the desire to explain human progress. When research failed to correlate any physical manifestations in the evolution of the human brain over the centuries which could explain either recent progress or mankind's overall social and political development, Soviet scientists moved from a physiological explanation of progress to a cultural one—namely, to emphasize the advancement of learning in common and the development of a collective intellect.

More recently such interests have been reemphasized in the West under a different guise, with the stronger interest by business and industry in teamwork and the orchestration of labor for common cause, rather than the older stress on individual accomplishment and entrepreneurialism. This movement, which advocates a certain conformity with a cultivated corporate culture, produces its own form of cultural collectivism. Moreover, historians in Europe and America have simultaneously with business theorists taken up the notion of accumulated social learning as an invisible but nevertheless real mainstay of culture. They have done so under the rubric of Cultural Memory when the topic is related to imagery, while the management counterpart has adopted the term Organizational Culture. In Social Psychology and Sociology the term "Collective Memory" is more in vogue. Not all collective memories need be historical; many are ahistorical in their lack of a clear time referent. S. CRANE (1992; 1997, p. 1375), following FUNKENSTEIN, identifies "historical memory" as one kind of Collective Memory. The latter she defines as "a conceptualization that expresses a sense of the continual presence of the past" (p. 1373). She acknowledges a basic "essential similarity," but sees a major difference between "lived experience (in Henri Bergson's sense) and the preservation of lived experience, its objectification..." (referring to BERGSON's *Matter and Memory* [1911]). Amos Funkenstein, prefers the "middle term" of "historical consciousness" in debates about the difference between History and Memory. Funkenstein sees "Western historical consciousness ... [as] a developed and organized form of it [i.e., collective memory]" (FUNKENSTEIN, p. 19).

This debate is reviewed by P. HAMILTON (1994), and GEDI & ELAM probe older positions to answer their question: "Collective Memory—What is It?" Some discussions may seem like hair-splitting, but the choice of term often reveals preferences for assumptions and in approaches. In Information Science SMITH & SAMUELSON examine similar phenomena in perception and remembering, but their approach entails such concepts as category stability, variability, and development, which do not appear in historians' discourse. Historians have discussed such issues more in the abstract, theoretically, without the same level of classification or precision in usage, and they have concentrated thus far on the large picture. Which came first? Does a prevailing culture condition a society to preselect what is preserved in its collective memory? Does the collected memory define the culture? Or, is it an interplay of both phenomena that forms collective consciousness and hence cultural memory? Such questions probe the innermost sanctuaries of the human mind and can be applied to almost anything: to archival appraisal, to issues of recall and relevance in Information Science, to ideological and technical diffusion, and to nonlinear pattern recognition in the study of some of the most complex phenomena known—those involving humans.

Just as the older forms of the History of Ideas and Intellectual History gave way, under the influence of Anthropology, to the history of meaning on the one hand (BOUWSMA, 1981), and on the other to a more contextualized Cultural History as in the history of *mentalité* during the 1980s (this historiographic shift is traced by P. HUTTON, 1981; CHARTIER, 1981; and while it was going on, by LE GOFF, 1974/1984). Some have linked this to the Annales paradigm, since Marc Bloch had used the concept in medieval history, but not all medievalists adopted this approach on the same scale as by early modern historians. LEGOFF & SCHMITT subsequently wondered why, when the idea of *mentalité* spread from France to Italy and Spain, and to Germany, that it never found a firm footing in England or in North America. At least no "school" can be identified with the *histoire d'mentalité*, but several strains in New Cultural History bear a resemblance to this European movement. Perhaps this genre was co-opted by a paradigm that struck a more strident cord in the Anglo-American world, where so much of history writing was being influenced by Cognitive Psychology more than just a cultural interpretation of intellectual history. The French concept of *mentalité* was interpreted elsewhere more concretely as a mind set of a society, and was thereafter transformed during the past decade into a question of History as Cultural Memory. In this case History is informal, and certainly not scientific historicism, but rather a far less intellectualized conglomerate which may not be organized extensively. ZERUBAVEL, for example, in rather fantastic imagery speaks of social perceptions as "social mindscapes" from the perspective of Cognitive Psychology. The concern has not been the formal apparati of social memory or factual verification, but collective opinion or consensus of the common man which operates like a social arsenal from which everyone can draw arms to defend a culture. This is construction in the its most ethereal sense.

VOVELLE makes important distinctions between *mentalities* and ideologies, even though the two are related conceptually and sometimes are thought of as the same. The latter are better articulated, take on a form through a formal literature, and therefore have authors and an authority base, while the former remain nebulous, are broader and resemble common property. This idea of a mentality transcends what needs to be documented because it is remembered, it is active in the social consciousness of people. It supersedes information, but not communication. Hence, news, reaction and commentary, and everyday discourse are important; the telltale signs of common thought are canonized; and the actuality of concern becomes the telling of the tale, the repetition, and the diffusion of a generalized notion, rather than anything than actually happened. It is the study of metaphysical *par excellence*, and metadata as data. Context is the subject. The history of archives, recordkeeping, libraries, documentation or anything like information systems and services germane to Information Science is thus conspicuously absent from this new field because the subject assumes a virtual world of ideas, perceptions, and feelings is dominant over anything more concrete and objective. The kind of documentation collected by manuscript repositories when appraisal ideology was imbued with a sense of the objective and appreciation for the unique, may therefore not appeal. Rare book collections assembled by notions of aesthetic quality may also miss the mark. Fine art in galleries may not be of as much interest for overall aesthetics, refined technique, or elevating subject matter, as for details of the unusual (or the usual, not or unusually depicted). Culturally oriented museums, however, because of their culture of things, and their artifact collections which create impressions and appeal to perception, their "show and tell" approach to public education through exhibits, and public history role in informing and experiential learning through audiovisual impression and group interaction, do find themselves under the scrutiny of modern cultural historians attracted to the notion of Cultural Memory. So does the film industry and other entertainments, i.e., past-times in the past. History as entertainment, visual representation, and even historical fiction is the subject more than anything historiographic, actual, or objective.

The irony in this transformation of a disciplinary field is profound. The emotional, irrational, impressionistic, fluid, pervasive, common, and ubiquitous have replaced the scientific, rational, formal, standardized, stable, rare, and exceptional, as the subject of study—even when that study is or pretends to be scientific. Such study may be of lasting impressions rather than well-formulated ideas or holistic ideologies. Hence, the notion does not necessarily entail the sense of order associated with positivism or the older quests of scientific inquiry. This modernist line of inquiry, moreover, may not be aligned with the notion of "collection" as used in Library Science where order is imposed from an external construct or system, for example, but may relate more closely with the sense of organic unity used by archivists to describe their collections. The material often seems to deal with more random and less structured pairings and looser relationships than anything resembling a controlled system. This is what makes the issue so complex, dynamic, and so ethereal. It is also what allows so much interplay of opinion, speculation, contention, and novelty in this increasingly popular but still largely undefined and undisciplined field. Its lack of cohesion may reflect its newness and immaturity, but also the late twentieth-century culture that gave rise to such non-disciplinary studies.

One might wonder if in the future historians of Cultural Memory might see the current frenzy of concerns over Memory as conditioned by subconscious millennialism as the year 2000 approaches. Others have criticized the field for similar reasons. CONFINO (p. 1387), a practitioner himself, recently charged that it "lacks critical reflection on method and theory, as well as systematic evaluation of the field's problems, approaches, and objects of study. It is largely defined now in terms of topics of inquiry.... One cannot avoid a sense that the choices of subjects is all too often governed by the fashion of the day." Echoing FURET's castigation of the earlier *histoire des mentalités* movement as "semantic prestidigitation," CONFINO (p. 1389) charges that "Like the history of *mentalités*, a great appeal of the history of memory appears to be its vagueness. And both histories have by themselves no additional explanatory value; their value depends on the problems posed and the methods used."

Whatever the exact rubric or approach, the underlying theme in Collective/Cultural Memory seems similar throughout the various disciplines which are turning to the central idea that collective attitudes and behaviors are created through shared experience, and that they are shared through common communications within a cohort of people who identify with a common history. PENNEBAKER explains that such a cohort can be identified for Americans, for example, whose youth was collectively influenced by the JFK assassination and the Vietnam War, but whose children are far less affected by these events. So the "collective" can be as small as a pledge class or grade in a school, an induction group in the military, or social clique; or as large as a generation, a whole society, and a nation. Examples extracted from the collection, whatever its dimension, are welded into a collective model. Sometimes this model is academic, as a study about a social entity which may or not have been conscious of group thinking, or the model is itself the entity's creation.

Contemporary studies edited by PENNEBAKER, PAEZ, & RIME and others all go back to S. FREUD's *Civilization and Its Discontents* for inspiration. Note W. MCDOUGALL's speculations in the 1920 about "The Group Mind" when articulating the principles of "collective psychology" to explain "national life and character," and C. G. JUNG's ideas about the collective unconscious. Although Jungian psychology popularized such notions, the French social psychologist Maurice Halbwachs, before WWII, was most responsible for giving these ideas form and definition when he wrote about social categories and collective memory in his *The Social Framework of Memory* (1925). There, and in his posthumously published works on *Collective Memory*, HALBWACHS maintained that all basic memory processes were social in that people remember mainly whatever they have discussed repeatedly and which is elaborated in their common discourse. All other events are forgotten in time. History, then, lives only through research, revision, and continued discourse. Nearly all historical studies about Cultural Memory go back to Halbwachs as their starting point, but few take up his notion that repetition and elaboration go together, that instances of both can be classified and counted, and hence that such phenomena are measurable. His approach stressed classification and analytic method. HALBWACHS, in an essay by the same name, did distinguish between "Historical Memory and Collective Memory" (1980, pp. 50-87); the latter, for him, is a deliberate separation from the memory of the group who lived and preserved memories, to form instead "a totality of past events...in a single record," defined less by the psychological life of the milieu in which they happened than by "the group's chronological and spatial outline of them." He laid the foundation for much more than highlighting case studies or describing exceptional examples, but to modeling based on empirical study, detailed content analysis, and close comparison. As S. CRANE (1997, p. 1377) astutely observed, Halbwachs' foundations allow for "multiple pasts" of personal recollection, group memory with lapses and operating by consensus, and a more mature anchoring of historical views in more objective frameworks at some later date, i.e., the difference between experience and memory of that experience, history, and History, all of which might be expressed better in the plural. The exception might be History, which Halbwachs argued should become total and unitary. In his view that historians ought to strive for an all-inclusive master narrative, he differs significantly from postmodern relativists who see such integration as ultimately excluding the individuals who made history from History in its most mature form. They would stay with description and multiple histories rather than advance toward a comprehensive model.

The transformation of Cultural History into a matter of memory is pervasive in recent scholarship. CARRUTHERS' *Book of Memory*, the title of which imitates medieval treatment, investigates classical notions of memory such as the *tabula memoriae* and the exercise of memory as recollection during the Middle Ages against a background of modern cognitive psychology (Carruthers cites, for example, BADDELEY; LURIA; MALCOLM; NORMAN) and with deference to early modern interpretations whose influence in modern historiography may require substantial revision. Mary Carruthers makes the important distinction between a book and a text, and challenges the notion that all texts were readings when the dominate culture was oral (a condition which she resolutely does not juxtapose against the idea of literate as did ONG, 1982). Her topic, however, is learned, formal memory more than collective memory. The two cannot be separated totally, but this is what has happened in two distinct streams of historiography and in the division between any historical concern as distinct from popular. YATES & ORLIKOWSKI provide useful distinctions for genres between these polarities in their structural approach to organizational communications. GILLIS (1994, 1996) treats the formation of individual personality, that is identity and memory as a historical relationship, to suggest how national identities are formed and maintained, but we do not have the same kind of structural approach as in organizational communication studies applied to regionalism or national cultures. M. CONWAY talks about recollection as an inventory of experience which reinforced memory and forms identity. MIDDLETON & EDWARDS and others explore some of these thorny issues of collective memory on a large scale, but somehow these studies do not relate well to intra-culture studies, inner organizational analysis, and social-networked communications. FENTRESS & WICKHAM connect individual memory with society's conventions and reinforcement, and hence "social memory" as a basis for group identity development and group behavior. CONNERTON likewise dissects the components and processes of social memory in his *How Societies Remember*.

Historical memory as a matter of Information Science, more than something about it, is important to other cognate fields as well, especially Psychology and Sociology. This issue has come into play in Organizational Culture studies with its focus on teamwork and in Information Science particularly with the advent of groupware and the dynamics of its use for distributed collaboration. In the latter case the issue is one of social bonding and culture generation without individual contact, but through communication over a distance. ZHANG (1998), for example, raises the question about defining group properties as a matter of research design when studying distributed computing and group problem solving. Such attributes as group identity and cohesion can grow from the experience of collaborative problem solving even when a group fails in solving a problem at hand. Something more is at stake than problem resolution alone, which may be of critical importance in preparation for the next task. Can the group be characterized entirely on the basis of the attributes of its individuals, or is something more added by the very act of collaboration? Is a group the same after having acted as a group? The reductionist approach is rejected by many who would ally themselves more with trends in Cultural Memory writing, namely that interaction produces emergent properties not identifiable for the group's members individually. The whole is greater than the sum of its parts, i.e., a society or a culture is something larger than the aggregation of membership. This interactionist view has been supported by recent work on distributed cognition (D.A. NORMAN suggests that interaction is one of the "things that makes us smart"). HUTCHINS; ZHANG (1996); and ZHANG & NORMAN have all studied phenomena described as "cognitive tasks that are distributed across the internal mind and the external environment, among a group of individuals, and across space and time" (ZHANG, 1998, p. 801). Examples of emergent group properties include the "group effect" (GEORGE, 1990); "collective efficacy" (BANDURA; GUZZO & SHEA); "transactive memory systems" (WEGNER); and "process gain" (STEINER). Several of these studies attribute the buildup of a dynamic and bonding for social organization through reiteration and the sharing common experience, which is very similar to the idea of a shared and retold history in Cultural Memory.

Memory studies have a clinical dimension that informs History and Information Science, but each tends to study memory in its own way. Recall, for example, is often treated in Information Science as though this process were disembodied. Individual forgetfulness has not been not so much the historian's concern as societal amnesia, or conversely, historians are concerned with individual remembering and witnesses as sources, and now with collective memory (e.g., FELMAN & LAUB's combination of literary criticism and psychoanalysis to examine "crises in witnessing" in their book, *Testimony*). Some problems of historical memory have been considered in source criticism, treatment of oral history methods and transcript *qua* documentary editing, and in reconciling variant testimony from multiple witnesses (BOTS). D. RITCHIE provides a current overview of oral history methods; and the implications of Memory research and Cultural Memory debates for Oral History are addressed especially in the essays published by T. BUTLER in 1989 and in FENTRESS & WICKAM's *Social Memory*. SOLOMON's collection of essays illustrating interdisciplinary approaches likewise uses the term "social memory." Related theorizing about distortion, deception, and reinforcement of idealized types in collective memory plays well with deconstructionism, relativism, and postmodernism on the one hand, and on the other allies with the conservative nature of human recollection, the social underpinning of "truth" in history, the effectiveness of History in distortion control, and the objective role of archives in society (HEALD).

Historians have become very aware of the implications of memory and cognitive studies in Psychology as allies in source criticism, deconstruction, and postmodern interpretation, but most often the arguments are to challenge accepted explanations, accounts, and generalizations, rather than to reinforce them. Less value is given to scholarship that affirms, it seems, than to revisionism, contention, and novel explanation. The stance is often that used in examining and discrediting evidence provided witnesses in court proceedings, as a prelude to introducing an equally speculative alternative that may or not be supported by first-hand witnessing as credible as that just discounted. Here lies the tricky business of discerning what is likely in terms of modern sensibilities as opposed to the testimony of historical witnesses, as value is added and detracted from original records in the process of interpretation. The authority of modern science, for example, is often juxtaposed against the authority of a historical text. J. WILKINSON chides historians of memory as treating interpretation based on evidence as just another choice between fictions.

The problem of values is compounded by what BEVIR (1992) castigates as "errors of linguistic contextualism," a form of presentism by attributing to an earlier period ideas that matured much later, as indicated by the words that eventually capture the idea. Not everyone handles this problem as well as S. KEMP in his explication of "Cognitive psychology" during the Middle Ages, when modern and archaic terms must be linked carefully to follow threads of thought, often through elaborate means, to make the case for continuity in the evolution of ideas that seems easily lost in changing vocabularies and translation through languages and across cultures. GOUWENS most recently tackled a similar problem in "perceiving the past," in this case Renaissance Humanism, "after the Cognitive Turn" where he stresses how much History has been affected by Cognitive Psychology in the last decade.

No field in History seems more affected than Social History turned into Cultural History that is largely language analysis of contemporary texts (note the exchange in *Past and Present* between L. STONE, P. JOYCE, C. KELLY, G. SPIEGEL, and others, about History and PostModernism (1991-1992); cf., ELEY & NIELD; KIRK; and P. JOYCE on the tribulations of Social History; and the review of J. SMITH about the impact of language study as the primary research method in New Cultural History). No topic has been so transformed in this warp between social and cultural history than the French Revolution, with subsequent fallout for all political discourse studies (cf., BAKER ET AL., eds., 1987-94, for a plentitude of examples demonstrating the linguistic emphases in historians' work on the French Revolution and subsequent political culture; and BAKER's *Inventing the French Revolution* which follows from L. HUNT, 1984). L. HUNT notes how the contemporary and current readings of political tracts and what passed for news in the eighteenth century has resulted then and today, not in a history, but multiple, often conflicting Histories.

History is not what is used to be. The extent of integration by historians of findings and insights from modern clinical and cognitive Psychology (e.g., WYER & SRULL) and other scientific disciplines like Medicine varies from mere lipservice in noting, for example, that the source of memory cannot be physically located in the brain (D. SCHACTER), to more extensive citation of modern secondary accounts and interpretative material (a parallel metahistory, but where mere reference for background does not always make clear the citations' relevance). No matter, citations of psychological, clinical, and medical findings are increasing, perhaps signaling that historians are finally beginning to use online searching for information outside their own discipline. Consider, for example, the attention given to the nature of autobiography in both Literature and Oral History; to the impact of traumatic experience on reconstructed memory (repression and exaggeration) in Psychology; to cult formation, religious conversion and indoctrination; to political campaigning, speech making and rhetoric in Political Science and Communications; and in Sociology to the emotional responses to memories that build into social movements. Thus History, Law, Psychology, and even Religion have had to address problems of historical memory in a larger inter-disciplinary context, which is a different matter than the history itself, or its formal description and analysis as History. In all of this debate, the cardinal element often lacking is the link between information technologies, information creation and dissemination, and its selective preservation and recall within social and political organizations. In turning so much to cognitive theory from a basis in intellectual history or the history of ideas, historians have been overly subjective and too involved in conjecture...thus slighting the objective by ignoring the history of information forms, technology, and organizations. Faulty memory as a lack of means and technology is a forgotten aspect in too much of this work.

Faulty memory is commonly seen as distinct from intentional fabrication, but invention may occur to fill voids; and such invention is precisely what constitutes fiction and "make-believe." In this regard, the problem can be related not only to Literature, but to statistics and modeling whenever a hypothetical model is placed into memory as a matter of substitution for what is unknown or not remembered. More than a matter of lack of data, this is an issue of imperfect data in original documentation that complicates interpretation in ways not resolvable by statistical operations. Common concerns related to imperfect data problems involve the improper substitution or misappropriation of data (manufactured and hypothetical data from models rather than real data, data out of context, etc.) which is difficult to detect and correct. Other phenomena need to be taken into account, however, such as the fabrication of data. In the sense of invention of history, faulty memory must be confronted as a contamination of the ongoing record and a source of misinterpretation. This possibility cannot be disregarded in the assessment of evidence, whether the fault is a break in the record or misinformation in the first place. The former involves examination of a chain of custody of the record, historiography revolving around the documentation, and an assessment of continuity and discontinuity in both the archival and meta-historical strains of information transfer. But faulty human recall when a record is created in the first instance is a different matter, for which historians are turning to Cognitive Psychology for assistance. Although they might handle this issue more like recall and precision in Information Science, they seldom do. Nor would information scientists be prone to treat recall as remembering, especially in such terms as expressed by LIRA for whom memory is a "passing back through the heart."

The problematic behaviors that may have influenced the quality of the historical record in the making, which today are considered abnormal and infrequent, are nevertheless diagnosed today as more and more prevalent. Is this just a matter of increased population and a proportional increase in instances recorded? Or, is this because of greater awareness resulting from improved communication and recordkeeping in public safety and health care, and because today we are willing to classify more microscopic deviance in behavior as different kinds of conditions and syndromes? Or are such phenomena actually more prevalent? Can it be assumed that historical records incorporate misinformation from faulty memory as often in history as today? This is an unknown, but historians can be aware that certain kinds of personal documentation close to trauma, or involving the later recall of traumatic events, are more likely to contain distortions from memory loss, imbalance, and embellishment, than other kinds of records such as those resulting from everyday business (cf., ANTZE & LAMBEK; CARUTH). Even without the influence of intense emotion, collective memory seems prone to distortion simply from inbreeding within groups where self-perspective lacks the objectivity of external vantage points and where, according to BAUMEISTER & HASTINGS, deception is abetted by flattery, among other things. Social psychologists deal with such problems in ghetto mentalities, cults, gangs, and other cadres, as in the military, where extremes of deflated or inflated self-images, bravado and single-mindedness, faith and hope, are spurred by emotional commitment with or without trauma, but which nevertheless forms and reforms collective memory. In the case of trauma, lawyers are taught to be aware of these phenomena for their cross-examination of witnesses, in either destroying or building a credible case, so it is argued that historians might do the same when confronting obviously traumatic experiences such as surviving personal assault or worse, mass atrocities (OSIEL), genocide (H. HIRSCH), war (cf., CHAUMONT; PIEHLER, who examines remembering war "the American way"), crime (GROSSER), or from natural calamity. The impact of emotion might erase memory, producing general amnesia or no memory at all, which is one problem; on the other hand, spotty blackouts which introduce discontinuity into a narrative record. In the case of children who have suffered abuse, one defense mechanism is a fabricated memory to overlay the truth entirely (GULLESTAD), or they develop multiple personalities with their own distinctive versions of memories (HACKING). Conversely, there may also be flashbacks of intensive and vivid recall which may not disturb a continuity, but these produce irregularity in emphasis, imbalance and unevenness. Does such intensity make the recalled memory more believable than others? It does for the remeberer. Does it for the listener, simply because of added emotional impact rather than information added or content value? Who is the examiner and examinee in such situations—the informer or the informed?

Such probing into the nature of collective memory is disturbing, because it seems that everything can be called into question and all things seem relative. Doubting or modern skepticism may seem excessive in some instances, perhaps symptomatic of postmodernism (in contrast to Modernism reconsidered by D. ROSS, 1994; cf., ROTH & ROSS, eds.). Relativism is abetted by the penchant for metaphor, which tries to elucidate past experience in terms of the modern or vice-versa. And History, examined so critically in its formation, seems bewilderingly complex. Consider how this modern fusion of cultural and social history, which is a shift from the older socioeconomic approach, coupled with heightened awareness for diversity, gender, and other touchy issues in our own age, has spawned new interest in personal testimonials in history which may be interpreted in light of modern clinical research. M. ROTH's *Ironist's Cage* (1995) covers an array of topics which relate memory, trauma, and the construction of history.

The more remote, historical case can be made more vivid and current by asking questions about contemporary traumatic events that must be traversed through personal memory to arrive at objective, useable evidence. Look at criminal cases and the growing literature about victimization, anger, guilt, and withdrawal, and the problems of self-image that affect memory. How does the trauma of rape create emotions that influence recollection, witnessing, and the narration of fact in trials? These are problematic, sensitive issues to be sure, which recently have been related increasingly, hypothetically and concretely, to the broader issue of historical reconstruction of the immediate and the more distant past. For example, the False Memory Syndrome Foundation in 1992 registered almost no accusations of sexual abuse against parents in the United States, but by the end of 1994, it had recorded nearly 12,000 cases. How does the sociologist or family historian make sense out of such phenomena, and what does the phenomenon of False Memory Syndrome mean for those concerned with memory, individual and collective? How does False Memory relate to the Repressed Memory Movements in societies longing to forget? Or, how does one diagnose through historical sources a witness whose testimony, unique and uncorroborated, may be suspected of so-called "flash-bulb" memories which even the witness cannot make sense of, and which therefore lack contextualization for sure interpretation (M. CONWAY). These are supposedly memories which are vividly impressed upon the mind by emotional intensity. Controversy surrounds the notion, whether such phenomena are real, to what extent, and how they impact other memories. WINOGRAD & NEISSER question the accuracy of recall in such flashbacks. When a momentary mental image is recalled repeatedly in an attempt to improve accuracy, does each repetition entail elaboration as HALBWACHS suggested for interactive group recollection?

Does this not occur when historians recall isolated testimony from sources, promote the incident's repeated discussion, and elaborate upon the original source throughout this process even to the point that the original source disappears into the background? Are all master narratives thereby delusional? Cannot all fragmentary sources in history be undermined by such suspicion and questions based on modern scientific research? Here the problems of source criticism confronted in the rise of scientific historicism are posed anew, in different light, and with a kind of scrutiny not possible a century ago. The assumption is that although documentation of such faulty memory phenomena exists today, it is likely that the phenomena themselves have a long undocumented history in Western and all societies. So, modern observations, clinical studies, and a growing specialization literature are now used to shed light or cast shadows on historical sources. Historians have confronted before such social phenomena as mass hysteria, pogroms, witch-hunts, Satanism, brainwashing, indoctrination, duping, etc., where they have had to weigh issues in determining actuality such as objectivity versus subjectivity; motivation and self-interest; make-believe; mistakes and faulty memory; deliberate falsification, forgery, fabrication and fraud, etc., where records do exist, in addition to the problem of non-extant records or imperfect and incomplete data.

This subject of ethnic and religious minority relations with the majority, often tied to regional and national identity development and the outbreak of internecine war, is usually a history of discord and friction which involves violence and trauma, individual and social. It is not surprising that such studies are now particularly influenced by modern Cognitive and Social Psychology as much as Sociology. Perhaps the most controversial application of false memory versus accurate recollection is in post-World War II history (e.g., the *Vichy Syndrome* by Henri ROUSSO; or more generally the reliability of war stories: MOELLER) and Holocaust studies (J. E. YOUNG on Holocaust memorials, another of which is now being erected in Berlin) where collective guilt and blame reign supreme in a continuing conflict. MAIER simply calls this quagmire "the unmasterable past." One the one hand is the motivation to keep memory of atrocities alive as a corrective and protective measure against their reoccurrence, which necessarily involves the regeneration of emotion so commitment is added to historical knowledge (L.LANGER regards Holocaust testimonies as "the ruins of memory"). On the other hand, deconstruction has been used for denial or at least the claim that those keeping Holocaust memories alive do so by exaggeration and overly concentrated foci that produces distortion in History. Or, in the case of reunified Germany, the quest to move on with life results in putting history behind and a recasting of priorities that to the victims and their families seems like denial (see the essays collected by GILLIS' *Commemorations* on German reaction to war movies, reminders such as concentration camps turned into historical sites, etc.). Jews, of course, have a history of tragedy to remember reaching much further back than the Holocaust, as VIDAL-NAQUET reminds us. D. NIREMBERG with this perspective from New Historicism, insights from social psychology, and interest very likely related to his own identity, investigated the treatment of minorities in late medieval northeast Spain or Catalunya and southern France where harmful incidents repeated, recounted, and elaborated upon, altered social discourse about human relations and in effect, wrought permanent change for the early-modern era in how Christian majorities regarded such minorities as the Jews in their midst. His highly regarded study is intriguing both for its subject matter and interpretation, and for why such history is being written currently. The subject ostensibly is set in the Middle Ages—but is it? The historian's spin seems very contemporary. There are two histories to be read here.

The peculiarities of Jewish culture that entwine History and Memory, where in modern post-Zionist times the former seems vanquished by the latter, are delineated by YERUSHALMI who in his disturbing 1982 commentary *Zakhor* (meaning "remember") saw "the invention of mythical pasts" and "deliberate distortion of the historical record" as "the aggressive rape of whatever memory remains" (pp. 197-198). He is embroiled in the challenge to Zionist historiography by "new historians" over the creation of Israel, creation of a new national identity (recounted by Y. ZERUBAVEL), and how Zionist ideology has handled relations with the Palestinians and other historical questions too close to contemporary events for comfort and objectivity (SHAPIRA and PAPPE in a 1995 historiographic collection in History and Memory; cf., WISTRICH & OHANA). SHAMIR recently investigated the importance of Israeli war memorials in the development of a national identity for Israel. CONFINO uses this particular controversy in Israel to illustrate the methodological and political problems with modern Collective Memory/Cultural History. The Spanish suffer similar agony over their discordant history for the past century and a half, especially the Civil War, which has influenced their own sense of identity and history profoundly (J. IGARTUA; PAEZ). AGUILAR FERNANDEZ contrasts remembering and forgetting the Civil War experience in the formation of modern Spain. The study of self and group identity is equally controversial, as when related to nationalism, racism, gender, and religion. Studies examining the collective memory of Jews in Israel engage all of these, with the history of anti-Semiticism and the Holocaust in the background. Classification is a dual process of inclusion and exclusion. What expertise from non-History disciplines do they bring to bear on these complicated issues? Considerable.

This recent concern of historians for cultural and collective memory, as distinct from formal History, has formed a distinctive genre within the discipline that illustrates the wide embrace of History (e.g., LE GOFF; GILDEA; TERDIMAN; NORA; etc.). NORA (1996) distinguishes between Collective Memory and History, but others do not. From a medievalist viewpoint, P. GEARY, for example, recently attacked Nora's distinction as a "false dichotomy." In Europe and America this persuasion of seeing history as somehow held in place within collective consciousness, as distinct from what really happened or views from different vantage points at other times, has been profoundly influenced by Cultural Anthropology and such thinking as GEERTZ's notion of "thick description" in cultural interpretation where layers upon layers must be pealed away and interpreted one at a time, like archeology and recording layers at a dig (an image exploited in the historical fiction by James Michener, where a "tell" tells a good story if not actual history, or, as employed by R. I. Burns [MCCRANK, 1996, p. 35] this is a metaphor for digging for evidence in an archives). In Michael Kammen's "transformation" of tradition in America, one can discern, for example, much more concern for historical fictions than history (KAMMEN, 1992). Fiction, when believed, becomes History in a relative sense. Unreality, given credibility, is imbued with a certain reality. Thus, as often expressed, historians are concerned with what is true, but also what is believed to be true. Sometimes the difference between recall and elaboration is like that between imitation and creation as in art history (e.g., where FARQUHAR attempts to evaluate innovation within traditional arts such as bookmaking and manuscript illumination). In both cases, the difference is difficult to discern. Does

a prototype have to be physically present to be copied approximately rather than exactly reproduced, or does an idealized archetype suffice?

Couple this notion of repetition and elaboration without recourse to the original source with
the commonplace understanding that people act not according to what is true, but by what they
think is true. Historians thus approach information, communication, and cultural transmission
issues far differently than in Information Science, where the assumption of document retrieval
as the main form of information dissemination and knowledge acquisition goes largely uncon-
tested. Likewise, historiography often assumes that formal history and historians control historical information and are the primary means of historical memory in cultural continuity.
KANSTEINER in reacting to MARWICK's contention that past human deeds are known only
through historian's accounts scoffs at the notion; he categorically denies this and maintains
instead that Western societies do not get information about the past through historical scholarship. As others do who criticize the state of academic history in North American and Europe
as elitist, he chides historians for their failure to reach larger audiences even when they resort
to narrative history. Do people need to know history to appreciate it and act according to historical generalization? Interpretation and conjecture are close cousins in this historiography.
What motivates people historically, apart from History, and to what extent do men and women
think historically or are influenced by their own sense of history in daily decisions? Is such
thought conscious, personal, concrete and rational, reflective, enlightening and stimulating, or
something resembling more an emotional attachment to the familiar that is less conscious,
somewhat irrational, compulsive, generalized and socially oriented as in bonding or identifying oneself with another? Is history supposed to be inspiring? Are both different dimensions
or faces of history? Or, is cultural memory something decidedly different?

Such questions have captured the attention of numerous historians, anthropologists, psychologists, and literary and art critics in recent years. CASEY reduces the field to phenomenological study, wherein the relationship between learning and remembering are explored in
modern terms, but which seems to resurrect old pedagogical debates about learning having to
be more than memorizing. YATES' *Art of Memory* (1966) is now almost classic, as is ONG's
The Word. Both relate memory and memorization to education, the former in a more secular
fashion and the latter in a philosophical and spiritual way. BRUNER reduces the whole problem of education to an issue of cultural transmission whereby education and culture play reciprocally. Debates about revisionism and views of History transmitted through education systems, therefore, can be related to issues of Cultural Memory and vice versa. Political
controversies about content in History curricula, seen thus, are debates over what is to be
remembered and if official systems will preserve this or that view of History. Unlike the False
Memory Syndrome, or the clinical treatment of amnesia for individuals, such issues about
what society will invest in to preserve its cultural memory relate to appraisal, selection, and
disposition in individual and group thought, in institutional memory such as in archives, or in
school curricula. Societal forgetfulness by accident or by purpose are two different things, as
are intentional omission and suppression or censorship. Thus archives, for example, are being
looked at in a Foucaultian light, because what archives they elect to save and how they preserve them, employ technology, and make them accessible is seen as a Cultural Memory issue
as much as one for History. Historians have come back to the notion of an archives as collected
if not collective memory (initially by FOUCAULD, then by mainstream historians like LE
GOFF, pp. 90-94, etc., and most venturesome, W. ERNST on electronic archives and the possibility of infinite selection of materials and, hence, histories).

An editorial for *The Economist* newspaper (1996) by nonhistorians looking at the phenomenon of history in society talks about the uses and abuses of History with regard to nationalism
and the case of Ireland which lives too much in its past, so some think, "when bygones aren't
bygones." They take up the question raised by Senator George Mitchel, ambassador to Ireland
who once lamented how little history school children in America knew, but who now wonders

if it is possible to have too much history. In reference also to the warring peoples of the Balkan states, the Israelis, Islamic fundamentalists, secessionists, and others, the editors ask:

> Is that evidence of too much history? Surely not. History is not like a medicine, which comes with a label on the bottle advising "Caution: dangerous to exceed the stated dose." History is what makes the nations what they are. It gives them their character, their institutions, their identity. You can misread it or misuse it, but you cannot have too much of it. On the contrary, it is countries that have too little that may fall prey to the temptation to invent it.

> ...confront your history, look it in the eye and then yourself likewise....

They take up the issues of revisionism and societal forgetfulness and controlled identity development as advocated in Organizational Culture circles, in the sense of overwriting history with artificial official history. They point to the nationalists and fundamentalists who take Oscar Wilde's wit seriously, when he said that "The one duty we owe to history is to rewrite it." They conclude:

> ...invented history is not peculiar to new nations, any more than misinterpreted history is peculiar to old ones.... Most others [Germany excepted for its coming to terms with its past] dwell on the laudable, suppress the inglorious, and embellish the rest. And those who do this to most disastrous effect are indeed those who are certainly addicted to the past. If it is not possible to have too much history, it is certainly possible to spend too much time looking into it. After all, the whole of the future remains to be rewritten.

In any case, the issue of how a society remembers and forgets often begs the question of whether whatever was supposed to be remembered was ever learned or experienced in the first place. Fantasy and memory could be juxtaposed more than they often are, and in today's hypercritical climate, their confusion is all too obvious for antihistory skeptics. Much of this humanistic exploration of memory and learning, or its related aspects in semiology, is so much better informed by Cognitive Psychology than ever before. This, however, has not really simplified the complex issues where History is embroiled in the contentions of modern society; indeed, inter-disciplinary perspectives have often complicated such issues.

If cultural memory is so affected by impression rather than formal information activities, then means of communication, stimulation of the senses, emotional reinforcement, and imagery emerge as important, if not more important, than texts, documents, and records. Things other than texts matter. The orientation of History is to place events in time and space; that is, to identify the occasion of recall and its stimuli, the reinforcement of memory through repetition, and the clarification and elaboration of what is remembered. The mode of operation is usually metaphoric, in giving to group memory the same attributes as individual memory. Thus the difference, for example, among individual memory, commemorization, and memorial is largely a matter of informal and official recognition, formalization, structure and scale, and restructuring and recreated permanence.

NORA's concept of "places" or "realms of memory" is reflected in several historian's interdisciplinary works that recently enlist environmental, psychology and sociology, as well as metaphorical and literal treatments from a romanticized countryside (BARNES & DUNCAN) to landscape architecture (SCHAMA, 1995), cityscapes (BOYER), and where authentic historical sites are unavailable, recreations for recreation as in theme parks but also anywhere that attributions are invented, tradition is accepted, and imagination is stimulated. In short, Nora's interpretation is very personal rather than official only, so that in the United States, for example, the 30,000 historical buildings, structures, and sites listed in the Historical American Buildings Survey and Historic American Engineering Record would only be a fraction of the endless possibilities (LIBRARY OF CONGRESS, 1995). BOURDIEU's concept of "habitus" similarly stresses the formative influence of special space and sense of place that is more local and personal than anything national and official. Bourdieu stresses how his concept can be used to frame empirical analysis (C. CALHOUN). In this regard, Simon Schama doubts the efficacy of computing and virtual reality, and he lauds the traditional "place of memory" for historians—the archives:

> [History] cannot work as it should (and cannot tell the vivid stories it must) unless it truly inhabits an archive[s] where we can touch the ink and the sealing wax; smell the must and the dust; and sense our dim kinship with the long lost. Only this direct, physical exposure to the fragile relics of vanished worlds has the power to summon the ghosts and make them substantial and eloquent. So while you can wire Clio till she's red hot and cybercool, if your make her virtual, the lady crashes (Schama interviewed in FORBES *ASAP*, p. 55).

This may sound like a historian's lament and seems highly subjective because Schama, while applauding the advances of modern information technology, also reveals a distrust and discomfort with it. Ironically, he also unveils an emotional attachment to the objects of history and displays awareness of immanence for all connections to the past, not simply the sacred, as important in stimulating historical imagination. One could argue, therefore, that this object-oriented (to borrow terminology from JAVA programming) mentality is "objective" in the sense that seeing is believing, and this means seeing real concrete objects rather than electronic out-of-place surrogates. Making the latter real requires imagery and imagination (cf., PYLSHYN; ROLLINS). On the other hand, museums retrieve objects from their natural habitats and display them in realistic but nonetheless reconstructed, replicated contexts. This is more acceptable than faking the central object of one's attention and devotion. Anthropologists, historians, art historians, and museologists who contribute to F. KAPLAN's collection of essays are all aware of this consciousness, connectedness, and awe that the past revealed in authentic objects and their presence brings to our present. She expresses this in the title of her book: *Museums and the Making of Ourselves*. Likewise, FINDLEN speaks of early modern specimen collecting as a means of "Possessing Nature." This idea of capturing history by encasing things and preserving them in a museum or one's personal keepsake shelf is a theme attracting considerable attention, largely because of the anthropological study of gifts, curios, mementos, etc., as a secular side of the sacred and notion of immanence. It is an object orientation common to all collecting, including rare book collecting, special collections in libraries, and the value placed on size of research library collections rather than on use.

Collecting might be extended to the use of information systems and the use of technology to do the same virtually, as in creating computerized photo albums and screen savers, or in the use of scanning to document personal property for insurance records while simultaneously creating a virtual treasury. The notion may be related as well to technology, including information technology and personal computing which has some unexplored parallels in modern visual programming and the use of icons to unveil hidden intellectual and technological treasures. Or, consider the value placed on processor speed, memory capacity, and potential analytic capability resulting from software collections in residence on a hard disk, not for actual use, but for possession's sake. Electronic collecting has yet to be studied from this perspective and is not normally considered from the vantage point of information science. It should be. Personal computing, after all, affords people with new ways of practicing history personally. PCs are used to create art, for example, that is not meant to last forever, any more than fleeting art forms such as liturgical reenactment, song and dance that are not formal performances, or ice sculpture or sand painting. Games such as cards, picture puzzles, etc., are valued for activity and entertainment, more than outcome. Likewise, activity and possession may be motivators unrecognized in Information Storage and Retrieval (ISAR). It plays into the ideology behind data acquisition, data warehousing, and the trend everyone to want more information, from more sources, and related in a greater variety of formats. The connoisseur more than the common user worries more about origin, chain of custody, authenticity, accountability, and all matters of discriminating taste and value-added when considering information in physical or electronic form.

Another aspect of object orientations, apart from modern software programming, related to such ideas in museology as when creating virtual heirlooms iconographically, is the idea of creating personalized virtual space and identifying this with places of the heart rather than simply an information storehouse. Continuities can be identified between past activities to collect and recollect the past with current use of IT to do the same virtually. ANDERSON & GALE speak about "inventing places" in cultural geography in the same sense of NORA's "realms of memory." The psychologist idea of cognitive mapping in learning theory has combined with cultural anthropology to inspire more literal metaphors between mental reconstruction, identification, and geography.

This thinking has found its way into Information Science for visual information retrieval and self-organization (CHEN; KOHONEN; LI; ORWIG, CHEN & NUNAMAKER). HARLEY, reminiscent of SCHAMA, speaks of the iconography of landscape in the same spirit as a tour guide recounts history on the spot, commemorating events and hallowing the place upon each telling, with tourists paying with time, attention, and money for the privilege of witnessing the recreation and somehow in their own minds and experience authenticating history with their credulity and acceptance of oral tradition. Visual reconstructive techniques used by observers, whether in a museum or outdoors on site, are discussed by CRARY; and these are applied to photographic interpretation whether for genealogical familiarization and family identity, forensics, historical visual documentation, or virtual reproduction (i.e., visualization) in "the post-photographic era" (W. MITCHELL). Photographs, capturing still life as they do, are often preferred to video for careful analysis by social psychologists who do everything from analyzing gesture and body language to proximity and groupings, to pinpoint telltale signs about the workings of their subjects. Investigators might apply LATANÉ's Sical Impact Theory, for example, in trying to ascertain the social influence one individual exerts over another by paying attention to immediacy (barrier-free physical proximity), group size which determines how much interaction is possible, strength of one or the other (perceived status), in addition to the extra information carried in face-to-face meetings above and beyond what is said. The methodology in photoanalysis of contemporary settings is little different from that used for historical ones, but the techniques are often more explicit and precisely taught in other disciplines than history, running from photojournalism to formal Photography as art, and from counseling to Psychology. The difference is often a refocus from artifact in photographs and the still life of staged historical photographs to the action in spontaneous photography and unobtrusive observation.

SHERMAN & ROGOFF edited a collection of modern essays about "museum culture" composed of histories, discourses, and spectacles. The treatment therein is reminiscent of the kind of socialcultural history before the heyday of ethnography or advent of the New Cultural History accomplished by Johann Huizinga in his classic, *Waning of the Middle Ages,* where pageant and commemoration are entwined with escapism and fantasy in a study of cultural memory. HUIZINGA's work predates the crystallization of the idea into a formal term or when this type of inquiry gelled into a genre of history, and well before the renewed interest in History as reenactment. KAPLAN *ET AL.* argue that museums, their collections and exhibitions, are both products and agents of social change. Likewise, remember that COLLING-WOOD thought sometimes as a metaphysical philosopher for whom reenactment and reimaging or imagination based on some evidence rather than flights of fantasy, were appropriate metaphors for understanding history. D. BATES notes that such ideas, including

Collingwood's spiritualism, has been marginalized in an age of modern secularism. Reenactment for Collingwood, according to Bates, connected his thought about ethical action, historical time, and a divine reality, so it had associations with religious liturgy.

The postmodern twist to such thinking about historical action and reenactment is an exploration of drama as historical fiction and recreated theatrical if not virtual reality. SAMUEL, for example, treats the "past and present in contemporary culture" in *Theatres of Memory* in a manner recalling parallels drawn in other works between historical imagery, tradition, cultural memory and self-identity. The theater itself, of course, regularly recreates history in its own way: reenactment. Its staging, script, directing, and interpretation produces ultimately a master narrative, which nevertheless changes from performance to performance with the interaction of actors and audience. The historical plays of Shakespeare, for example, bring history alive for more people than does academic, classroom history covering the same subjects. These are not commemorations, however, as is a Passion Play in Obergammerau, Bavaria; the Black Hills of South Dakota; the observation of Holy Week in any number of Christian churches; or as a Christmas story played by children whose instruction thus augments book-learning in Sunday school. It is doubtful if the hundreds of men and women who annually reenact famous battles from the Civil War or Euro-American and Native American conflict on the original battlefields upon their anniversaries, or their audiences, know or even care anything about postmodernism. They do, however, judging from the reenactment of a Seminole-American battle I attended two years ago on the Dade Historical Battlefield in central Florida, understand commemoration and the dedication of hallowed ground made sacred by those who died there. Nearly 20,000 volunteers are scheduled to act on the July 3-5 in the reenactment of the Battle of Gettysburg, the largest such event in the United States, on the nation's most commemorated battlefield, which is visited by more than two million people each year. Pilgrimages continue, shrines endure, and history lives in such places. Steven Spielberg's artistic film *Saving Private Ryan* (1998), graphic as it is in depicting the horrors of World War II, is built around the theme of actuality and recall. It opens and closes with acts of memory, and is itself a sober commemoration. It is a triumph in immersive filmography that takes people into History where they do not want or dare to go. History as personal reflection, continuing education, sentimentality, entertainment, and recreation are all combined in such phenomena in an order of magnitude incomparable with academic history.

All such studies related historical reenactment in actual "places of memory" (to use one translation of NORA's memorable phrase) pertain also to created ones, permanent memorials and exhibitions in archives and museums where, respectively, the themes of documentation, information retrieval, and recall are basic to historical reconstruction, and where selectivity, contextualization, representation, and interpretation are hotly debated now as they were in history. GABLE & HANDLER, noting how pluralistic history museums have become, point to the dependence of history portrayed in museums on the people responsible for interpretation. They argue, moreover, that skepticism about museum interpretation may be warranted because of the promotional aspects of museums that convert into a kind of advocacy for whatever is a museum's particular specialty. Likewise, although exhibits may draw on document collections for interpretation, these materials may be selected to support the viewpoint stressed by the institution. S. PEARCE (1993, 1994) argues for the intellectual rationale underlying museums as teaching institutions in keeping with modern notions of experiential learning outside the classroom, *in situ* in some cases, or in a fabrication, reconstruction, or simulation in others. She identifies archives and museums as two variations on the same theme, both of which have a reflexive relationship with society in being shaped by social forces and in turn providing social identity in ways other than purely intellectual reconstruction.

An appropriate metaphor may be in people's faith in paper currency because of historic guarantees; that is, warehouses of gold which do exist and which are important even if people have never used them or ever visited Fort Knox. But they still might be in awe of such a cache of bullion when standing before it. In this way people collectively may also "use" archives and museums, even those who have never visited one. In the same vein as many Renaissance historians have connected civic pride with archives and cultural institutions, the conversion of Holy Days into holidays, and other processes of secularization that ended the Middle Ages, O'TOOLE (1995) addressed the symbolic use of archives today, although more in terms of liturgy and ceremony (civic and religious) than those used by historians of cultural memory, but more like Renaissance historians who have investigated secular ceremony and pageantry in Italian city-states. O'Toole connects pervasive historical consciousness with documentation as related to the phenomenon of immanence illustrated in the pilgrimages of Americans to the National Archives to see the Declaration of Independence enshrined in its sanctuary on a secular altar in a state basilica. The religious and patriotic experience is similar. Moreover, a person who has religious sensibilities but does not belong to an organized religion, may still value the presence of churches in his or her surroundings. The actual and symbolic combine for multilayered meaning, and in such studies the empirical is seen as a limited outlook. In the terms of COOKE & WOLLEN concerning visual displays and representation, there is "culture beyond appearances."

Such interpretative work involves the idea of immanence appropriated from religion and sensibilities associated with shrine dedications, cult maintenance, and mystical interpretations blending surrealism with practical realism, which are usually, of course, properly secularized. This is not the case when dealing with Native American culture, which cannot be so easily secularized without grave distortion to the culture represented. Not only does the successful exhibition *Sacred Encounters* (J. PETERSON) illustrate this connection between museums as hallowed sanctuaries of culture and cultural memory, but it relates the idea of the sacred with nature, hallowed places, artifacts that promote recall, and experiential learning through simulation, visual and audio stimulation, and mood adjustment. In such museums there is controlled movement constricted by directions and pathways to follow, influenced by lighting and the lure of sound, and timed by programmed reactive and interactive presentations interspersed with quiet still life spots for reflection, where one walks through a reconstructed landscape filled with three-dimensional objects rather than viewing a two-dimensional static exhibit as in a picture gallery (an issue of design in PEARCE & PEARCE). The affected and attributed values to informative settings and objects are almost totally ignored in Information Science, although through visualization and sensory research in simulation, information conveyance by other than sight and literacy is being explored for new kinds of information technologies in the near future. Such explorations related to Public History (as by SCHLERETH) should be encouraged within the realm of Historical Information Science.

The field of cultural memory related to museums thus pertains to archives and special collections similarly, but to libraries as well, although rationalism and postmodern influence on their organizational culture have weakened their cultural traditions. Thus C. HEALD opens up the entire field of archival science to post-modern questioning, whether archives have a place in the post-modern world or if postmodernism fits at all into the archivist's paradigm of objectivity through official, authoritative documentation (BROTHMAN & BROWN in response ask if "postmodern archives" is indeed an oxymoron). K. WALSH, arguing for the relevance of museums in the world sees artifacts in museum exhibitions as representations through historic realities, whereas paintings in galleries, especially realism, would be representation more like photography and reproductive arts, or more similar to fiction than history. However, modern designers are now well aware of creating microclimates and spaces for viewing where the viewer as devotee can become part of the exhibit. Lighting, voice recordings, music and nature sounds, and slide shows and motion pictures all combine with the artifacts to create a mood that adds emotional dimension to transform passive viewing to active learning. The more creative book exhibits, for example, have moved away from displaying books as a treasury or static gallery in glass cases lined up along walls. Illustrative of this new immersion technique was a pioneering exhibition at the Walters Gallery in Baltimore in the 1980s which featured the miniature art of medieval *Books of Hours* and liturgical manuscripts. All were opened to the Office of the Dead, and were positioned on lecterns for the faithful to read, as architectural features of crypts, or, reminiscent of Eleanor of Aquitaine's funerary effigy, in the deceased's own hands. Each was showcased in context within a created monastic mausoleum and charnel house complete with graves, sepulchers, and monuments copied from the miniatures, with dried bones filling the space above the apses. Gregorian Chant wailed in the background. The viewers made their procession through this gallery with preconditioned silence and respect, and left with an engendered feeling of the intrusiveness of death, its ugliness and horrors, and its Christian conversion into something else, more than mere appreciation of a lost fine art. Likewise, in the aforementioned *Sacred Encounters* traveling exhibit is an illustrative case of the anthropologist at work, incorporating viewers as audience, pilgrims, and witnesses to history recreated. In both cases, such exhibits can be related to reenactment rather the just viewing, adding an emotional dimension to Cultural Memory more than through words and text alone. Meditation was encouraged with commemoration, in ways different from active learning in Living History museums which instruct by "show and tell" and by visitor participation in a controlled activity.

Museology has always entailed much more than public program and exhibition management, but active involvement in research, and often administration of archives, libraries, and artifact collections combined (HOOPER-GREENHILL). In recent years, museology has evolved more into a social and administrative science by venturing into visual and cognitive sciences for its own needs rather than continued total focus on the subject of the museum's material collections or the discipline it may serve, i.e., anthropology, archeology, history, or the arts. VERGO calls this regeneration and vigor "the new museology" reminiscent of the much earlier calls for "new" this and that with the impact of modern information technology. This may be new in the museum, but such developments rest of two decades of experience in artifact cataloging and archeology computing (STECKNER; HUGGETT & RYAN (eds.). RUGGLES & RAHTZ), which began large-scale database development in the early 1970s as indicated by BORILLO & GARDIN, eds.. Now the "wired museum" (JONES-GARMIL) is changing the paradigm of viewing things in a museum, from one perspective according to a display designer's decision, with one scene separate from others. Earlier work was primarily on data acquisition and organization; now the emphasis has shifted to information dissemination, representation, and interaction. This has meant a shift in computing activity from field work to the museum and out again to users' workstations everywhere, and a better balance between concerns for artifacts and cultures studied and those studying them today and modern museum goers.

The time lag is significant, since it relates not only to the will and means in museums to implement new technology, but also the advance of this technology to serve museum needs with recent progress in graphics and sound. Museums are catching up, with a vengeance—that is, they have bypassed the great expense and trauma of experimentation with intermediate technology, are taking advantage of their rich collections, and are providing quite a show. In riding a crest of interest and enthusiasm, they are also contributing significantly to visual learning theory, leisure studies, public history, and their role, according to the claim by HOOPER-GREENHILL, in "the shaping of knowledge." S. PEARCE (1990, 1993, 1994) has a set of interesting and provocative studies that deserve special mention, respectively one about archeology and another about the museum as a cultural institution; one falls into the area of organizational studies more than it realizes and the other focuses on object interpretation and collecting. Collecting itself is studied as a cultural phenomenon by ELSNER & CARDINAL's contributors. And audience receptivity is studied with marketing and educational assessment for political reasons. The peculiar confusion of politics and poetics in collected works by CLIFFORD & MARCUS and KARP & LAVINE is particularly interesting in developing the notion that there is power in the control of cultural perception. Museology, therefore, can be linked to this broad field of new cultural studies, visual culture specifically (JENKS), and to organizational studies in Business both for management of the museum business, but also management of people inside artifactually recreated historical worlds. In this sense, it is museology that has the longest experience with environmental psychology, collective culture management, and mass education outside the classroom.

The visual reconstruction and reinterpretation of culture have their counterpart in language arts, oral and written, in keeping with modern linguistic notions about the unbreakable connection between language and culture. HALBWACHS, for example, related information retrieval from collections with language and memory as "recollection." In this vein J. LE GOFF (1992) became extremely interested in the issue of social memory and culture as a field of historical inquiry partly because of his awareness of the modern impact of computerization, increased disk storage, and how much people now rely on referents outside themselves, that is artificial memory. It is almost as if Herbert Simon's classic on *The Sciences of the Artificial* were being connected with cultural-intellectual history (SIMON, 1996). The exploration of orality (as something more than message and communication of content, in the spirit of Walter Ong's theological enlargement of the subject of speech communication (ONG),) with literacy and the impact of writing technology has received new inspiration from awareness of the current conversion from written and printed formats to electronic communication. Thus, CLANCHY's work has achieved cult status in the archives world, EISENSTEIN's work inspires HEDSTROM, and medieval sensitivity to rites and symbols is recalled by American medievalists turned archivists, TAYLOR (1988) and MCCRANK (1995), and finds its way as well into American archives reinterpretations via Catholic sensibilities in O'TOOLE (1995).

If people cherish places and the memories they invoke, this lesson becomes important for education where the most effective places of learning are not classrooms and schools, but places where history resides. Hence, one has archives built as temples. In once sense, history lives there; in another, it comes to life elsewhere, i.e., where people live. The idea of memory is that something has been experienced and was learned before it could be remembered, and this raises the importance of *a priori* learning something of history before reenacting and reliving it. By extension to learning organizations in SENGE's terms, this aspect of public history also relates to places of work. This ideology, sometimes mystic and at others steeped in Psychology and Sociology, can simply celebrate history, or it can use history for cultural regeneration in very contrived and exploitative ways. This is not necessarily bad. Consider the impact of historical awareness and the stimulation of appreciation, mood, and motivation, and creation of comfort and a feeling of belonging, when historic sensibilities are incorporated into architecture and environmental design. Historic preservation and inclusion of historic continuity in design are all forms of simulation. Cultural simulation, like practice, breeds culture. Perspectives on the past are indeed informing and forming the present. History in this sense is especially vibrant beyond or outside the classroom in spaces not so confining or directly controlled by an authority figure. In such environments people explore history without historians. It is as HIMMELFARB, G. LERNER, and other historians have reminded their colleagues, that everyone is, after all, a historian. The issue is how authentic or fictitious the experience is, and recognition of real from make-believe or the surreal and hallucinatory.

This cultural theme's popularity is congruent with the deconstruction critique of the past decade and the relativism of this one, and it illustrates the convergence of contemporary interdisciplinary studies. It also has significance for History. The truth claim of History in this regard is largely irrelevant, except to what extent historians influence society at large. The metahistory is as important if not more so than the actual history. In short, it is the history of history's influence that falls into line with cultural memory studies, not historiography as usually conceived. Both the breadth and the depth of such influence of formal History on informal and intangible collective memory are very debatable. Historians write primarily for historians, and historical knowledge is not mostly transmitted textually, but rather orally in the classroom by lecture, and visually through images and media. Given this general situation, the overreliance of historians on monographic publication within narrow specializations seems somewhat reclusive, if not perverse, counterbalanced only by the grace of effective teaching and occasional recourse to audiovisual aids. History as a once gentlemanly profession has not been commented upon as gender discrimination, but as a lamenting that it is not a lucrative way to earn a living for either sex, unless another source of income affords the luxury of the historical enterprise. But History is elitist in other ways, cognitively and intellectually, and the historian's exercise of historical judgment and formation of historical views is truly remarkable and extraordinary. Equally remarkable but less studied and understood is how nonhistorians, everyday people, think historically every day, about themselves and their dreams, their social circle and circumstances, and their future lives and in retrospect. Amateur historians should enter the purview of library and archives use studies regarding History literature and historical information. This would offset the imbalance created by studying professional historians alone, and particularly teaching historians, as if they alone practiced History. This might also relate the influence, or lack thereof, of History in Cultural Memory formation, development, and survival.

Direct connections between historical research and publication and research and readership are difficult to make even in retrospect, and the relation between a historical work and an individual's thinking and behavior, collective thought and social action, or the development of consensus is often a matter of conjecture rather than substantiated fact. As already noted, few bibliometric or citation studies exist for History, and although the literature of History and historiography are well enough known, access to and dissemination of the literature of history are studied, but the integration, impact, or influence of historical information are not. Information Science, because of self-imposed limits on its purview within libraries and information systems, rather than expanding to cultural settings, has not invented a methodology to track recall and reference evoked by emotional responses to environmental stimuli, in natural situations or "places of memory," tourism and recreation at historical sites, or in experimental teaching where, for example, students read, see, hear, and smell history. Moreover, historical narrative's place in the history of reading has yet to be established. Instead, people seem to be influenced by history in general through a pervasive collective consciousness and social referral to historical phenomena almost as clichés, more than by any special knowledge of History. Most operate with little more than rudimentary outlines, complete with faulty chronology and misconstrued geography, without insight into history philosophically or scientifically beyond reaction to personal immediate experience. Do biographies still serve as exempla? J. F. Kennedy thought so when he wrote his *Profiles of Courage*. Popularized History? Yes, but that is the point.

Are personalized historiograms expanded and formalized more by the study of history, or by information communications, storytelling, and reminiscence? Are these forms of information processing worthy of study in Information Science? Or, as in the case of formal, scientific History, does inclusion of the popular, semiconscious, and routine make these studies somehow non-academic? Other than history electives for General Studies in higher education and required survey courses in Euro-American history in secondary schools, more people gain subsequent historical knowledge through entertainment in historical fiction, motion pictures, television, and museums or at historic sites while on vacation, rather than through the formal literature of History. KANSTEINER reminds us that academic History today is in search of an audience larger than its own practitioners. People whose recollection is reinforced and decisions are guided by documentation other than their own records or of their business, as in the case of relatively limited recourse to archives and formal information retrieval systems, are comparably few. Historians know this, and in keeping with social history's focus on the many rather than a few individuals, they are consequently interested not only in the formal process of history, but increasingly in the habitual, informal, sublime, and ubiquitous ways societies recall their own pasts, keep history alive for socialization purposes, and create a sense of continuity for their own children. Might historians be more successful in such an endeavor outside History departments and classrooms, through more firsthand experience with culture and society and contact more extensive than through teaching and writing?

Cultural Memory is not so much History, therefore, as a subject of her scrutiny. Socioeconomic and cultural historians are often like outside observers, looking in, studying a group in which they never participate—with empathy and sometimes envy. Historians may assume that they contribute to Cultural Memory, directly and indirectly, but how, to what extent, how pervasively and enduringly, are largely matters of conjecture.

Individuals may be influenced by a particular bit of history, a piece of literature, a lecture, or some awareness of a personal experience that is larger than oneself, and occasionally a historian's contribution reaches a wider public than the relatively narrow readerships of his or her specialization, a discipline, or the academic community as a whole, when an original contribution strikes a common cord and spawns imitators, a seminal idea or set of related ideas gain momentum, a movement is charged, and perhaps a school is born. Such developments create lasting impressions, regionally, nationally, and globally in an order of increasing rarity. However, as the philosopher Michael Polanyi argued, personal knowledge is most often based on "contrivances" (i.e., "classes of objects which embody a particular operational principle," M. POLANYI, p. 328) rather than scientific inquiry (see HILL & VON ENDE for an assessment of the Polanyi brothers contributions). If he is right, one cannot expect the average person to use historical paradigms other than those which suit his or her purpose at any given time, and the quest for a more objective, holistic history is a truly professional pursuit. Given also the bulk of historical research and writing and the few histories known to the reading public, to say nothing of the general population, one must count as truly exceptional the rise of any historian's contribution to acclaim outside his or her own field, let alone the public at large. Such cases are likely to be seen as part of the history of ideas or intellectual history as much as cultural history, and may not be construed as part of Cultural Memory studies. Indeed, other than heroes and saints, the pantheon of cultural memory is largely occupied by the anonymous. It is a field of historical activity once thought of as non-History or pseudo-History, where historians are reentering—but often only as observers and in a reactive and descriptive mode, and where information scientists are also treading—warily. Those who have moved from instructional technology to visualization and virtual reality, whether for entertainment or education (this distinction itself is no longer very credible), are leading the way. The union of Cultural Memory studies in History with parallel cultural studies in the Social Sciences and modern information technology may be cultivated profitably by those interested in Historical Information Science, especially in the reception and impact of historical information by the public at large.

How is culture recreated, refreshed, and passed along? Historians, like their colleagues in Anthropology, have come to regard these processes as something other than history, as if History *per se* or at least in its formal academic persona, fails in this mission. Similarly, technological diffusion in industrial studies and information dissemination in Information Science are studied as if these were something other than history. Nonsense! Equally nonsensical is denial of emotion and attitude in receptivity to and the assimilation of information. Academic history has had the same detachment or regard for emotionality as the antithesis of rationality as the business community, but ASHFORTH & HUMPHREY, among others, are seeking to change this pejorative view of emotion and instead see emotion in group dynamics as something useful for motivation and learning. When personal and social recollections take on a common identity in a society, and in turn provide identity for the individuals therein so they begin to conform and act in common self-interest, the phenomena altogether become Cultural Memory. Modern French sociocultural historians were among the first to see, as distinct from historical research and writing, the act of remembering, its personalization and collective counterpart, and the emotional response to memories as an issue of collective memory rather than history. Or, such socio-psychological phenomena are the subject of History. However, the reflexive relationship between the two, a common history and collective memory, makes such attempted clinical disassociation for the sake of objectivity somewhat contrived and difficult to maintain. This is essentially what deconstructionists argue, although usually in a different way, leading to relativism because of a confusion between that past as separate and objective and its incorporation as something personal and subjective at the same time. They rightly attack objective aspirations in History if historians do not also objectively study the subjective. Deconstructionism in the extreme is agnostic if not nihilistic, and needs to be tempered for sanity's sake. History needs to survive for the same reason.

This self-interest in history is often a matter of self-identity. No one in this generation of historians has contrasted History to heritage and memory more than Pierre Nora through his own historical essays and collection of more than a hundred contributions by colleagues about *Realms of Memory* (NORA, ed., 1988-1992). This "portmanteau" has been characterized as an incomparable "self-reflective enterprise" (LOWENTHAL, 1994, p. 8). This reviewer points to this "sparkling synthesis" as a convergence of perspectives "to mark France's passage from univocal patriotism to divers patrimonial pride" and describe's Nora's own contribution as seating "the current French historical mood in a shift from dazzling past toward global disengagement." Contributors thus explore "material and symbolic locales of national, local, ethnic and other identities" which students of organizational studies might find, if they were ever to read French or such volume of scholarship in seven tomes, totally relevant to their own academic pursuits. Lowenthal, who charges Nora and his Gallic historians with the practice of "exceptionalism" to the extreme, compares this French introspection with other national cultures, especially countries with less continuity than France, especially America "where nostalgia celebrates Nature and laments Native virtues." Although he contrasts the French self-awareness of its historical patrimony with German and Italian national discontinuity, and English insularity in building a self-proclaimed "national character," his comments about American sensibilities are worth quoting:

> American historians amputate their past into unlike, if not antipathetic, segments; native versus European, colonial versus national, antebellum versus Reconstruction. Continuity is slighted, overlap minimized; each stage disowns the last. The national past is a field of carnage littered with obsolete creeds.... New misgivings mark a yet more decisive breach.

> At whatever critical moment, the American past is seen sundered by some dividing line, boundary or watershed—a metaphorical barrier as awesome as the ocean that exiled newcomers from everything Familiar.

> Many Europeans felt the rupture of social change no less keenly, regretting or romancing times beyond recall, but European upheavals reinforce faith in continuity.... In contrast, Americans discount actual continuity while stressing the felt breach (LOWENTHAL, 1994, p. 8).

Lowenthal's commentary provides insights not only to Nora's work and his French school, his review and the entire recollection provided by Pierre Nora, which compelled his multinational comparison, reveals parallels in discussions about culture and memory in History with those in other fields which historians, as perusal of Nora's references and those of his collaborators attests, fail to consult. Of course, NORA's approach is personalized, as reflected in his own term *Essais d'ego-histoire* (1987), or fusion of autobiography and history for self-reflection in defiance of what he sees as feigned objectified history (POPKIN, 1996, p. 1140 paraphrases "Nora's contrast between completely self-effacing "objectivist" scholars and heroically self-reflexive ego-historians...").

One can lament but not chastise students fairly in these other fields for their failure to consult History or skepticism about historical perspective that is so unabashedly personalized and subjective. Instead, one might try to understand the cultures in which such introspective self-study occurs to discern their limitations and traditional strengths, prevailing tendencies, and fundamental assumptions. The French penchant for reveling in their heritage, if not actual History, and psychoanalytic and even confessional historiography stands in contrast to the colder and impersonal character of the Social Sciences, or to the ahistorical American cultural perceptivity as recently characterized by KAMMEN (1992) as *Mystical Chords of Memory* rather than genuine historical consciousness. The overriding character of American culture may, therefore, color organizational studies in America, by Americans, about American institutions and organizations, e.g., Americanist ahistorical approaches to corporate culture and organizational memory. The disassociation of history from contemporary American life or in such pursuits as business, or Information Science for that matter, is problematic from a historian's viewpoint, but so too should the disaffection by historians of History from the contemporary be equally problematic. Americans and French post-revolutionaries, Lowenthal remarks, share an inheritance from Musset's "enfants du siècle" in "revealing the past as gone, the present as new" (LOWENTHAL, p. 12). Not only are such observations pertinent for the study of American organizational culture and corporate memory in History, but also for Organizational studies in Management and in Information Science, Technology, and Services.

While historians have begun to study such cultural phenomena as collective memory and identity in large contexts, i.e., regions, countries, and subcontinents transposed into societies, nations, and entire civilizations, they also concentrate now on the local and in locales, but have been less active inside organizations. They do not see themselves as therapists, so others have assumed this role. Historians are sometimes accused of overstressing the unique, their penchant for "exceptionalism" in Lowenthal's words or, as one hyper critic chastised, revisionists for their "pursuit of attractive intellectual novelty." "In science it is the rule that counts; in history, often the exception" (LUKACS). However, trends in socioeconomic History toward local history have favored the unexceptional, commonplace, and generalized process, i.e., the rule, the norm, and the average. Like anthropologists who focus on communities, families, and groups, historians have become equally microscopic (see RUSSO, 1988, for the writing of local history in the United States, 1820s-1930s; cf., the work of the American Association for State and Local History [AASLH]). Local efforts to continue the New Urban History (a term first used in 1969), which THERNSTROM and DELZELL trace to Oscar Handlin's work in 1941, have been criticized in the late 1980s for not keeping up with the most sophisticated analyses when such rich data sources exist (CONZEN). MCDONALD provides a state-of-the-art overview of American urban history through this period. MOCH's combination of social and urban history in studying country to city migration was certainly an exception to Conzen's criticism. Since the late 1970s, urban history has exerted indirect influence on other foci, such as a juxtaposition to rural history, and a sense of space and proximity that goes beyond older uses of geography merely to locate actors and events (THERNSTROM).

Specialities like orality and alterity, and the construct of historical unconsciousness in primitive societies, are classically ethnographic notions (or, as DE CERTEAU, p. 209, stresses, *ethnography*). Emmanuel Le Roy Ladurie's trend-setting study of Languedocian peasants (LADURIE, 1966) took advantage of such awareness of territoriality and man's relation to earth, which he subsequently applied to historiography in general (LEROY LADURIE, 1973), in the tradition of Ferdnand Braudel whose panorama of northeastern Spain in the early modern era combined climatology, geography, demography, and traditional history (BRAUDEL). Such practice continues, as in the case of Jean Vilar's look at the same regional Catalan-Provencal culture for the modern period (VILAR). Moreover, such studies applied to rural populations the kinds of analyses first used only for urban history (HAUSER, ed.). Instead of census and employment records, such modern studies like their medieval and early modern counterparts turned to parish records (e.g., CHARBONNEAU & LAROSE for the computerization of parish registers in Canada; cf., FLEURY's *Manuel*; FLEURY & HENRY). Slowly, a merger between cultural anthropology and topography and family history or genealogy with the capabilities of computing gave rise by the 1990s to large anthroponomies or term banks with normalization and classification subroutines that allow nominal linkage as never before and the reconstruction of nuclear and extended families. Both urban and rural social history now exist largely as forms of local history, and they both focus on common people, i.e., primitive society, in anthropological terms, or in social terms, the working class. However, such geopolitical perspective on regional agrarian societies, now enabled by Geographic Information Systems (GIS) technology (GAFFNEY & STANCIC; MAGUIRE; MAGUIRE, GOODCHILD & RHIND) and a revolution in scientific cartography (HALL), has been refocused on the city as a microcosm of the larger culture (CHOAY), but without the classic notion of citified life necessarily being a high culture or civilization. Indeed, modern socioeconomic historiography has often used the metaphor of "jungle" for the urban scene, and its depiction in isometric proportion is one parallel to peaks and valleys with their skyscrapers and avenues. The city is seen as compaction, where proximity accelerates if not causes (stimulates is perhaps a better term) change more rapidly than in the countryside. While change has always attracted the historian's attention, so too has routine in the invention of "everyday" and "common man" history whether urban or rural. Rural local history has been largely demographic, however, because it is based on linkage between land and census records. Urban sources are more varied. Like all local studies, city data have called for quantification for traditional kinds of socioeconomic history, but more recent electronic sources are also more multifaceted.

Biography, except for the very notable, has become more of a literary pursuit, and less worthy individuals such as those laborers and commoners studied in WPA projects once deserved only "life stories" (RAPPORT). This has changed under the impact of anthropology and theorists like Clifford Geertz under whose influence the smallest is always joined to the largest in historical reconstruction, and thus everyday people must still be related to their overall culture. Thus, for example, COHEN & SCHEER construct a social history of American education through stories. NADEL argues that language and narrative always alter such study from fact-neutral undertakings to value-interpretative texts; he argues further:

> ...biography not only partakes in, but becomes a form of, cultural discourse through its recovery of the past which refigures the encoded values, traditions, and desires of an earlier culture. The biographer, in recreating the subject and contest of his subject, not only represents the past and its culture, and not only transmits it to his readers, but reorders it through its reconstruction. Biography reimagines the past while recovering it and creates a work that exists in history *as* history (NADEL, 1994, p. 74).

When individuals cannot have their personal histories retold, usually because lack of evidence, their tracings collectively are constructed into a social history that is often like a corporate biography. Analogies abound between individual and group behaviors. The group norm is inferred from individual actions, and when the individual cannot be known, he or she is given identity from the group. As in Europe, where "everyday history" enjoys increased popularity, in America the common is celebrated by Studs Terkel in his labor history and others who must rely on something other than written records to reconstruct their narratives and descriptions. Without a formal literature to document their lives or much in the way of archives, informants often rely on recall and narrate history orally, which then must be analyzed, sifted, integrated, and resynthesized into more formal history.

Oral History confronts this issue most directly, but all historians do because even written records are often recollections. Just as self-reflecting narrative often forms the basis of biography, memories form the social fabric of Cultural Memory. Is Social History just its formalization and academic rendering? But Cultural Memory tends to be what common people

share in common. It is their view of history; indeed, it is their history, in a personal possessive sense. Historians, therefore, often have to be concerned with three histories for all phenomena: (1) the informal, subjective and personal, perhaps designated with a lower case "h";
(2) actual and formally reconstructed History which may be capitalized to distinguish it from
the former, and (3) the history of this history which must be added to the usual concern for
the history of historical writing or historiography, interpretative traditions (informal and oral
discourse and visual transmission, and formal written History), and the archival counterpart,
the provenance of sources for such History (the latter is different from how H. WHITE (1973)
perceived metahistory, as imagined history parallel to and entwined with the actual).
Historians, of course, are not alone in studying such phenomena in everyday life; literary
scholars, art and music historians, etc., all study cultures of their day. i.e., popular culture, as
much as Culture in the capitalized, formal sense of the term. Their perspective is usually long-
range, their motive is purely academic, and they act more as onlookers, commentators and filters, shapers and conveyors, whose influence is subtle, gentle, indirect, and perhaps subversive, than as participants, instigators, doers and leaders. Most humanistic studies are
descriptive, however, and those in the social sciences are more empirical. Such a distinction
is blurring with recent trends in text analysis, but a lasting distinction may be made on the
basis of motivation and intent of such studies.

Among neglected subjects related to cultural memory of interest to information scientists
and deserving study by historians as well is the time lag in the movement of ideas, the means
of transmission, distortion in transit, and cognition and receptivity at the collective level
("unexplored terrain" as noted by SCHNEIDER & ANGELMAR). Judging from LINSTEAD
& GRAFTON-SMALL's interjection during the early 1990s of revisionist thinking by DER-
RIDA (1973, 1978, 1982) and DE CERTEAU (1984) into the milieu of organizational studies
in Management, the time lag to go from French to English and across disciplinary fields is
more than one decade. This holds as well for the transfer of such ideas as "life-cycle" from one
field to another in the 1960s, the impact of anthropology on organizational studies in the
1970s, and the converging ideas in the 1980s which reflect heavy borrowing from other fields.
Despite increased information technology, the growing mass of literature, and supposed acceleration of information dissemination in recent years, the time lag in the absorption of major
ideas into a discipline seems not to have shortened significantly. Moreover, it is difficult to discern reciprocal influence on a similar magnitude even in a decade's timespan that is ethnography taking as much from business administration as it has given, or a movement like deconstructionism being influenced by management literature. Exchange may take even longer than
unilateral borrowing. This is ironic in a field like organizational studies which supposedly has
a sense of timeliness in change management (HARVEY), unlike history which observes while
change unfolds. Certainly managers wishing for immediate organizational transformation who
look to organizational culture studies for speedy and direct assistance should be aware of the
relative slowness of genuine acculturation in their own field.

In the interplay between intellectual history and cultural memory a significant difference
exists between no memory and nothing to remember, slow recall and lack of recall, and
intentional substitution and forgetfulness versus cultural amnesia. Likewise, consciousness
of time lag calls attention to the difference between never having had the idea, borrowing
from another source, and the issue of recall as traditionally seen as internal to an information system. Can one remember what is unknown or not experienced? Ignorance, or the state
of not having learned yet, cannot not be disassociated from issues of cultural memory. Many
studies seem to assume common knowledge which is not in evidence, and that ideas are
widespread or are uniformly spread when they may be local, spotty, and trapped in a time
lag. Conceptualization of an idea and its local implant do not indicate reception beyond this
point or confines; broader dissemination and longevity need to be illustrated, and with the
repetition and spread, the changes made to the original should be mapped. A dynamic study

is required and dynamic means of representation and interpretation. Studying culture is hard enough; manipulating it for the right effect is difficult; being successful in cultural management is an art requiring every assistance from Social Science. That is the intent of Organizational Culture studies inside Business Management, both to provide stability and simultaneously to accelerate and direct change.

Business and industry cannot stay competitive or get the upper hand over competition by waiting for information exchange and technological diffusion to occur in the natural course of history; change in something requiring management and direction. Taking charge means making history, not merely studying it. But one might suppose that historical knowledge would help change agents shape history, but this is not that common an assumption in business and industry. The two remain isolated from each other. To remedy this and encourage greater interdisciplinarity these sections on collective Cultural Memory and History and on Corporate and Organizational Management are poised back to back.

Organizational Culture and Corporate Memory

Historians often explain their discipline as the study of change—as distinct from managing change (W. GREEN). In that pursuit, they are not alone; but historians in their descriptive mode tend not to operate like Social Scientists or administrators who explore the elements of change for management sake. Organizational culture studies are often undertaken by would-be change agents to apply what they have learned to accomplish immediate and covert goals: intervention and control, conversion or transformation (whatever the alteration is called), and lasting change. Their motive is for less esoteric purpose than pure History or as an Informative Science, but to change history. HARVEY in his practical guide to creating and managing "a positive change process" exemplifies the nonhistorical, nontheoretical approach, with discussion about overcoming resistance to change, "unfreezing" organizations, checklists for change management, strategies and things to avoid, and how to integrate or fuse change into an institution. He also exemplifies the "good advice" genre of this management literature, as distinct from theoretical foundations and basic research. Indeed, rather than operate as a social scientist, he reviews twelve pieces of "folk wisdom" about change, talks about "crafting" strategies, and speaks about how one becomes an "artisan of change." The ethos in such pragmatism separates this management literature from both History and the Social Sciences, and yet the subject matter in the context of organizations is universal. If History describes change as it has occurred, and Organizational Studies prescribe how to accomplish change at present, one would think there were common ground for mutual reinforcement and collaboration. Both, each from its own perspective, are inherent in how Cultural Memory affects change and how such change is remembered.

If not actual thought control, or direct manipulation of thinking, the intent is culture control and indirect manipulation of behavior. Students of organizational culture focus their attention on particular organizations, local contexts, shorter time spans and the contemporary; their methods are those of the Social Sciences, and they are future and results-oriented so that their interest in history is not for its own sake but as a necessary prelude to decisions, actions, and alterations. History, when employed, is used first to destroy the old and then to rebuild a new order (i.e., either unlearning precedes new learning and creates the need for it as argued by MEGILL & SLOCUM, or the process is more one of simultaneous substitution). As in conversion psychology, where a change of heart is often precipitated by crisis, studies in organizational culture transformation often entail internal and external forces that seem "to induce change or unfreeze the organization" (WILMS *ET AL.*, in their study of the New United Motor Manufacturing [NUMMI] joint venture between General Motors and Toyota). REGER *ET AL.* propose options between incremental change, which is too slow, and revolution, which is too extreme, for what they call a tectonic process and describe with the seismic metaphor of "creating earthquakes to change organizational mindsets." Enterprise consultants like W. B. ROUSE, as previously noted, often assume that fundamental change involves discontinuity, and little history is invoked in planning change because it is assumed that it is irrelevant or would be used to support the *status quo* (in which case its relevance is simply ignored). Theirs is an ahistorical mindset bent on changing history.

Change, however, is fundamentally a historical process. Change takes time, no matter how little or how much. Indeed, the rate of change is often the question. TYRE & ORLIKOWSKI in studying temporal patterns of adaptation in organizations have found that the rate of learning is high immediately after the introduction of novel elements, and slows as comfort levels increase. So, organizational studies of group learning curves suggest, as VON HIPPEL (1996) has observed for "learning by doing" in technological change, that as Marcie Tyre and Wanda Orlikowski's argue there are "windows of opportunity" of dramatic change that seem to be open only at the beginning of major changes. SCHEIN (1993a) maintains that to manage the anxieties of change, a new anxiety must be created such as a fear of not changing, remaining competitive, or being successful and profitable. He sees emotional conditioning and learned anxiety as a third stage of learning after (1) knowledge acquisition (e.g., relevant history) and (2) skill development combined with habit formation.

A common metaphor in organizational change management is that a cultural graft is like a new grape vine to a hearty stock. Change is a combination of gradual growth and attrition that is demarcated by certain junctures, or cultural transformation is likened to a branch, i.e., a change in course but within the same general direction. Cultural Memory similarly undergoes shifts in mood, emphasis, and reinterpretation, but with less consciousness about parallels with History. Practitioners, with their goal of intervention, have embedded the subject into the burgeoning field of Organizational Studies, and within the subspeciality of Organizational Culture, one studies Corporate Memory with the aim of forgetting and remembering as dual processes in organizational transformation. SMIRCICH and SCHEIN (1984) provide a good introduction to the overall layout of the field as it evolved in the 1980s. ST. CLAIR brings such surveys up to date and relates corporate memory to information management, and in particular, record-keeping technology. However, these treatments by management consultants do not always relate corporate memory with organizational culture, and although they attempt some comprehensiveness within organizations, they do not always place corporations into their broader social and cultural context as a historian would. Indeed, most management treatments of corporate memory ironically lack a strong sense of history except at the most stereotypical and official level. Historical consciousness is not what they are after so much as information retrieval and document delivery on the one hand, and on the other workforce commitment, unity of purpose, teamwork, and social cohesion within the organization. As such, these studies are introspective to a fault, and the culture and memory explored in the microcosm are very often wanting to fit into the larger scheme of things. Consequently, while organizational culture and information specialists using the framework of corporate memory use history sparingly or ignore History altogether, historians are likely to look upon the former's work as overly positivist if not actually deterministic, somewhat naive, and where history does come into play, as amateurish. From a consultant or change-agent viewpoint, most of what historians do and write about is largely irrelevant, not because this is so, but because historians fail to communicate with the corporate world in meaningful ways. Their primary audiences are different and different expectations keep the fields apart.

It is not so much that this field of Organizational Culture was taken away from History, as it grew outside History with little intercourse outside the core Social Sciences. From its perspective, History seems to belong more with the Humanities and is therefore less relevant to the pragmatic goals of Organizational Studies. This gap is closing...or is it? Perhaps, the gap is as wide as ever, and a bridge is needed, such as Historical Information Science that takes into account relevant aspects of Administrative Science such as organizational culture studies.

A leading consultant in Organizational Culture whose writings have played major roles in companies' change-of-thinking processes, according to BROKAW, is MIT's industrial psychologist Edgar Schein whose work in organizational psychology first appeared just when Cliometrics were taking off (SCHEIN, 1965; and Psychometrics too, e.g., COOMBS, DAWES, & TVERSKY, 1970). He now defines "culture" somewhat differently from anthropologists to bring the subject into the Social Sciences and in line with behavioralism: Culture is "a pattern of shared basic assumptions that the group learned as it solved problems of external adaptation and internal integration, that has worked well enough to be considered valuable and therefore to be taught to new members as the correct way to perceive, think, and feel in relation to those problems" (SCHEIN, 1992, p. 12). Of course, anthropologists like R. BENEDICT (whose interpretation of cultural order on the basis of dominant drives now seems like Taylorism and similar to Maslow's hierarchy of human needs as the key to motivation), tended to use "culture" inclusively, except in contrast to the Renaissance notion of high "Culture" (SINGER). MALINOWSKI was even more comprehensive. By 1952, KROEBER & KLUCKHOLN were able to count 160 anthropological definitions of culture. Clifford Geertz combined mood and aesthetics in his notion of ethos connected with culture: "A people's ethos is the tone, character, and quality of their life, its moral and aesthetic style and mood" (GEERTZ, 1973, p. 127). Culture is a positive concept, the opposite of pathos. All things have culture or are part of it (the debate on this distinction seems never ending), but the quality rating varies from good to bad and other polarities. However "culture" may be defined, the scale, so it is thought, can be influenced by interpreting "the sensory and aesthetic dimensions of corporate life" (i.e., the hermeneutics of organizational studies) and controlling "the relationship between artifacts and organizational action," i.e., pragmatics (GALIARDI, p. 13). European sociologists tend to retain this more theoretical and semiotic approach, while the American sensibility seems more pragmatic still. JESPERSEN says that the term "corporate culture" is often misused, but according to SCHEIN (1989), it should refer to "all of the assumptions about the goals of an organization and what has been learned through a company's successes and failures."

These ideas resemble ethnohistory in that learning is associated with the past as much as contemporary cross-fertilization and sources are often artifacts and symbols, but the literature, at least in Business and Management especially, seldom relates culture to history or the field of Organizational Culture with History. The frame of reference is usually ahistorical, but occasionally history is called upon to explain anecdotally evolution to a present position. Such anecdotes form raw material by which to construct history (FINEMAN), but in organizational studies anecdotes often are retold simply to convey a point and illustrate a situation rather than to reconstruct the organization's history. Such use falls into line with anecdotal history, and this use of interwoven stories to lay out a theme resembles the reaffirmation of the narrative in History (reaffirming because nineteenth-century history had been written mostly in narrative form as when Francis Parkman would tell a good story about the American West, before quantitative approaches were really possible on an equal scale). History and Management have more in common than Business History. However, ROWLINSON & HASSARD conclude that while the concept of culture in organizational studies promised to make corporate culture studies more historical, they did not. They attribute the failure to integrate business history and organizational studies to the social cognition and biases associated with the field. JONES & CANTELON attempt a rapprochement from Public History by arguing for the contemporary value of corporate history, but public historians have not successfully penetrated the Organizational Behavioral field in significant numbers. History, if studied at all, is studied scientifically to be applied; it is to be manipulated, if not actually made. Exceptions exist, of course, and not all corporate histories are abusive or sinister even when their explicit motive is identity development.

Consider the historiographic case study of Cadbury, an English confectionary family-owned company, where history and commemoration (especially a 1931 centenary) were used effectively to build a corporate culture by attributing the family's Quaker beliefs to corporate character. ROWLINSON & HASSARD, who cite the Cadbury example, use the historical concept of "invented traditions" to explore company histories. Thus, the histories generated by the company are seen as reconstructions to give meaning to the firm's labor-management institutions and as such, "inventions" themselves. Generally, however, the cognate field of "Public History" is unknown to those writing about culture in organizational studies. In covering a decade of publishing in twenty management journals, perusing 400 articles, and reviewing abstracts of another 500 for this essay, fewer than six references were found to the association or journal of *Public History*. Public historians appear a little more ecumenical since they include in their work more citations to these Management sources, but still, the crossover is not great. Most study corporate life as historians, from outside the corporate and management milieu. Again, notable exceptions exist; IBM's James CORTADA, whose studies of computer technology in American corporations share insider insight, comes to mind. Such contributors and their contributions are themselves cultural phenomena worthy of study in order to understand covert change agents, forms of academic expatriation, intellectual diaspora, and opportunities to use historical writing to make a difference.

Organization Culture studies developed independently from History, although contemporarily with New Social History during the 1970s, within the incubus of Business schools, and more specifically, Management departments, and particularly personnel management conterminously with the rise of Human Resource Development thinking. According to GUPTA & CHIN, such trends have antecedents dating to 1959 in such work as Haire's theorizing about the life-cycles of organizations. Archivists subsequently took over such thinking about the life cycle of records, documenting the seasons of their creator's life spans. Both predate History's concern for Cultural Memory by more than a decade. Organizational Culture in Management studies (e.g., TRICE & BEYER), or its counterpart to Cultural Memory, Corporate Memory, deserves attention in this discussion of Historical Information Science not only because of the parallels between it and New Social History methodology, but because the management of current documentation, i.e., future historical sources, also in Records Management and Archives Administration, is now being influenced as much, if not more so, by this field than by History. Moreover, as depicted by DEWIT, YATES, ZUBOFF and others, the interaction between information technology and organizational behavior is pervasive and mutually influential. One can hardly discuss the efficacy of archives or any information system without acknowledging their organizational context, the culture supporting or inhibiting their operational success, and how they contribute to the overall culture of the organization. The comparatively late engagement of electronic information systems and sources by historians, and their minority status and even scarcity in places where records are actually created, means that Organizational Culture, not History, is the likely determinant of the future of the historical record of corporate activity in the next millennium. In essence, for the sake of History, historians had better engage the field of Organizational Culture, co-opt it, and thereby insure that its perspectives become wider and longer range than they do now.

In addition to such avenues as business and organizational history and the history of technology, another entry might be made through the history of information for accountability, corroboration, and decision making. Likewise, the manuscript component of archives should benefit from Organizational Culture studies more than they do. If scholars in the latter field, many of whom identify with literary pursuits rather the Social Sciences, were more conscientious of the application of their materials to cultural profiling, their research could generate archival case studies and their exhibit programs would be tied to change management and marketing objectives rather than simply celebrating commemorative events. To date, this has not happened much in exhibit work and public programming. Most of the raw material for organizational cultural studies has simply disappeared after publication of findings, and as in Information Science, the publication itself is erroneously considered "primary publication." Primary sources, therefore, cannot be examined to verify such publication or for reuse in longitudinal study; nor do they contribute to the documentary basis for History. Consequently, historical input into Organizational Culture studies can enhance the former, and a closer relationship could be symbiotic and beneficial for both history and archives. The three fields, however, have developed along very different lines and symbiosis is now long overdue.

How did a folk literature in management practice move toward a Social Science? One can simply explain such divergence as historical, but this seems to beg the real question. Yet historical perspective does offer some explanation. The management literature has itself been subjected to discourse analysis by BARLEY & KUNDA to arrive at a historical outline and periodization for shifts or schools of thought that achieved dominance at one time or another. They show that new waves of thought in Management coincide with broad cycles of economic expansion and contraction, which is described almost like a Chinese *yin* and *yang* interpretation of history. They ascribe this vacillation back and forth from managerial theorizing to rational and normative rhetoric of control to "cultural antinomies fundamental to all Western industrial societies: that is, the oppositions between mechanistic and organic solidarity and between communalism and individualism." In this, they reflect the current fascination with paradoxes in human affairs.

In celebration of its fiftieth anniversary, the AMERICAN SOCIETY FOR TRAINING AND DEVELOPMENT in 1994 created a time line going back to 1700 to trace work-related learning. Such training in the workplace is closely entwined with shifts in management's thinking about management. Management theory, rooted in the Industrial Revolution, has been "field shaped" through "trial and error" practice rather than through science, and it still smacks of its nonacademic origin, pragmatic orientation, motivation for increased production, and traditional exploitation of labor. Its history has been outlined by AKTOUF; BARLEY & KUNDA; OWENS & SHAKESCHAFT; SANZGIRI & GOTTLIEB; M. WARNER, and others, although without the kind of in-depth analysis that would pass as solid historical research. In summary, a century ago the management movement in the United States began to coalesce experiential learning into a field of study, a science even, and began to combine business sense with a social conscience. As management science began to evolve conterminously with scientific historicism, it became introspective and studied human behavior out of enlightened self-interest. During the 1870s, for example, "industrial betterment" became a concern for improved management, and in sympathy with the kind of horrible conditions portrayed by Charles Dickens and so many others, business and charity combined in corporate philanthropy for social betterment as well. The two were seen increasingly as mutually advantageous, if for nothing else than to have a healthy industrious workforce. It was then during the so-called "Progressive era" that physiological elements were introduced to the psychological, such as notions of sanitation, public health, and physical fitness (DERICKSON). But the origin of scientific management usually dates later in the era from 1900 to 1923, when management seemed to divest itself of humanism and social welfare concerns in communities in favor of corporate growth, big business beyond localities, unheard of profits, and empire building by a new industrial aristocracy, and when nationalism combined with an instinctive international competitive posture. WARNER dates the beginnings of the human relations movement to the 1920-1930s. Others look to the years immediately thereafter for a throwing off older ideologies often related to class consciousness when military training crossed social class and gender boundaries to meet needs of the wartime effort.

This ended an unexplainable intellectual bondage to Taylorism and an odd separation of work from its intellectual conceptualization and initial learning phase (AMERICAN SOCIETY FOR TRAINING AND DEVELOPMENT). From then to 1955, emphases shifted again from human relations to welfare capitalism and concern for public relations. Industrialization imbued with nationalism was tempered by the aftermath of two world wars, the Great Depression provided a lasting, sobering lesson, and labor movements forced management to become more accountable. Patriotism fused with protectionism of markets and of American welfare during the Roosevelt era. After World War II through approximately 1955, older management ideas, including remarkably resilient Taylorism, were fused with the Social Sciences, especially behavioralism. Organizational behavior studies looked as though they were headed in a clear direction as a positivist Social Science. The field became addicted to self-determinism; that is basic to the very idea of management. SANZGIRI & GOTTLIEB attribute the following elements to organizational development theory of the 1950s and 1960s: (1) long-term orientation which eroded during the 1970s; (2) applied behavioral science emphasis; (3) change effort management from the top, which since has become multidirectional; (5) stress on action research, which has shifted toward content research; and (6) collaborative, facilitative changes which is still in vogue. After 1968, George Litwin and his associates worked on a causal model for inducing thorough, lasting, and pervasive change in organizations. Transformational change was thereafter seen as a response to the extended environment, i.e., context at large (P. BURKE; LITWIN). In summary, transactional variables, structure, and systems combine with transformational factors to affect motivation, which in turn influences performance and this accounts for change. Change is thereby brought about by manipulating variables in the internal operation of the organization and its relationship to its environment. The commingling of Management and Social Science (Sociology and Psychology, à la Social Psychology) in the 1970s, resulting in a Management Science as quasi-Social Science applied to Business, formed the background to developments in the 1980s (see HANCOCK ET AL. for the factors influencing research productivity in Management Science).

The evolution of this Management track in Business has been traced over the past 15 years by TRICE & BEYER. OWENS & SHAKESCHAFT argue that the "theory movement" forty years ago permanently separated the old management by trial and error from an era of empirical studies. Workplace experimentation was replaced with laboratory science and mathematical proofs. WARNER argues that only in the last 20 years has a "commonality of perspective" emerged, but HOFSTEDE offers balance to the parochialism that pervades the monolingual Anglo-American literature. He maintains that "Management" as used currently "is an American invention." United States management theory contains certain idiosyncracies such as foci on market processes, on the individual, and on managers rather than workers which make identification of the Americanist school fairly obvious, while what is considered normal and desirable in the United States may not be the norm elsewhere, and the application of American experience-bound theory to other national cultures therefore misses the mark. Hofstede's observation may explain why there is so little cross-influence between American management studies in English concerning organizational culture and memory and the French dominated historiographic school studying history and cultural memory.

When Social History came into vogue, the late 1970s witnessed social reform movements, labor consciousness, and public relations ideologies that fused with collective management strategies, the pervasive idea of teamwork, and emphasis on group dynamics. Psychology applied to individual motivation changed orientation from Taylorist gratification of basic needs to alignment of individual values with organizational practices or perceptions of corporate values. DOLENGA sees the information technology as having an impact on organization by allowing values to be shared with information, and on rising expectations of managers to be as sophisticated as the information technology they employ. Values are not always uniformly shared, however, or distributed evenly throughout the organization. Different levels of group interaction create aggregate values. SCHNEIDER & ANGELMAR argue that cognition at the collective level is also different from individual perception. Consequently HOFSTEDE ET AL. warn about the necessity to conduct analysis at the appropriate level. While organizations place individuals in workgroups for production (or by organized labor into unions), other social grouping occurs which is not controlled by management but is governed group dynamics. FIN-HOLT, SPROUL & KIESLER showed that Americans today belong to as many as 30 different workgroups, of the kind SUNDSTRÖM, DEMEUSE & FUTRELL (p. 120) describe as "teams" or "small groups of interdependent individuals who share the responsibility for outcomes for their organizations." Influence, if not actual control, can be exercised within or over these groups and individuals if the dynamics are understood and are manipulated. Such thinking dominates the interplay between Psychology for individual and Sociology for social control by management, but also to inform individuals and peer groups so they can manage themselves. The two fused into a hybrid, Social Psychology, which, when applied to industry, can fly under the banner of either Industrial Psychology or Sociology, or Organizational Studies. It can also inform Historical Information Science.

In America, first the Business academic community, followed soon afterward by corporate leadership seeking to change their organizations to become more competitive globally, picked up ideas from Cultural Anthropology which appealed as well to New Social History. Some date this beginning precisely to a specific issue of the *Administrative Science Quarterly* in 1979, but the movement cannot be delineated before the 1980s. BARLEY & KUNDA likewise separate the era of "systems rationalization" (1955-) from "organizational culture" dominance at the turn of the decade, i.e., 1980 (GRAVES early [1970]; OUCHI & JOHNSON, 1978; DEETZ, 1982; SMIRCICH, 1983; SCHEIN, 1985; etc.). OWENS & SHAKESHAFT see the change as an improvement "to newer, richer ways of understanding organizations and thinking about them" as opposed to the older emphases on "mathematical proof and ways of thinking borrowed from laboratory science." One can sense by this past decade's turn an erosion in organizing divisionally and into hierarchies, with an accompanying change in ethos where flexibility and adaptability became valued more than stability (cf., basic textbooks by BAIRD; POST & MAHON; HODGE & ANTHONY; DAVID; etc.). The most pervasive intervention technique to alter corporate cultures came with Total Quality Management (TQM), which swept through Management circles almost as fad, with all of the attributes of a cult movement (HARBER *ET AL.*). Currently dissatisfaction with older hierarchic forms of administration with their rigid reporting lines and governance by authority rather than persuasion has led to flatten organizations without former layers of middle management, increased decision making in work, and a transition to distributed systems and division by business function.

A shift in focus has occurred in planning as well, from long-range projections to short-term plans, contingencies, and opportunism comprising a new style of entrepreneurialism. Long-term plans of the five-year variety, made so intransigent and symbolic of unsuccessful planning by Soviet Marxist economic theorists, have been too often discredited by their own failures. They were replaced by short-range easier-to-achieve objectives and target-oriented strategies for incremental progress, replete with military terms like "strategy" and the kind of jargon about teamwork (e.g., "game plan") that infused competitive sports in America (KARLOF; BYARS; DAVID). This reorientation is less the product of scientific research than of reiteration and group persuasion, but one can sense a parallel movement in research trends. Because of the heightened interest in Psychology in regard to brainwashing and mind control, conformist behavior, gang formation, and techniques in religious cults, studies were done about teamwork, organizational force, and focus, while management became concerned with the symbols of corporate identity, dress codes, and membership. The jargon of the day often referred to the right "fit" between individuals recruited and the perceived culture of the organization as much as to matching individual abilities with organizational needs. This attitude seems to deny the probability of mutual adaptation and assumes an institutional and personality stability which may be tenuous at best (GIBBONS). As shown by LEWIN & STEPHENS and other students of social psychology, a reflexive relationship often exists between micro-properties in individual leaders which express themselves as choices in macro-level organization. An organization can reflect the personality of the executive, his or her character and also organizational preferences, while that person is simultaneously being molded by the organization he or she represents. Charisma may be an endowment of one's personality, but may also be a blessing of timing and context.

Another preoccupation occurred with mission and role statements (LEDFORD *ET AL.*), using terminology that sometimes seem more appropriate for arousing missionary zeal and religious proselytizing than corporate loyalty. The Nicene Creed is perhaps the epitome of an organizational mission statement. Although this did not hold Christians together organizationally or institutionally, it did give them a common identity contributing to an overall cultural cohesion in Christendom. While the efficacy of corporate mission statements is questioned, a crystallized philosophy is useful to guide behavior and decisions, to express cultural values, and to motivate employees, if one can make a philosophy statement compelling, keep good communications, and initiate a process for ongoing affirmation, renewal, or reinforcement of the values expressed. Here again the study of language usage, formal and official as well as the informal and off the record, is crucial; and semiotics should include the visual, iconic, and emblematic as well (CAMPBELL & ROLLINS, eds.).

Metaphors operating in the language of information systems, for example, are revealing; KENDALL & KENDALL identified six main metaphors: journey, war, game, organism, society, and machine. Information Science users also employ family, zoo, and jungle frequently. The "male" metaphors commonly used in motivational speech have been decidedly those of war and religion. Advertising and other presentations often play up the cold, metallic, and gleaming portrayal of computers and their peripherals as weaponry and present the clean room similar to war rooms. Apart from those sexually explicit images of male anatomy confused vulgarly with decision-making, which are the easiest to object to, such cultural environments have often made women uncomfortable in a "man's world" (F. WILSON). Just as gender distinctiveness may be seen as compromised in equity, so too is individualism in organizations where collectivism is overemphasized. Ironically, such trends in management may be seen to threaten entrepreneurialism and creativity by their focus on teamwork and social cohesion for increased productivity. This is a classic dilemma outlined 30 years ago by ARGYRIS, whose works are still being reprinted and read by many.

The rise of the Organization Culture, when set against this strategic, militarized and sexist background, with its divisional organization, ethos, and language, may be seen as a counter-movement, which entailed a reaction against the empiricism of the former (e.g., countering tendencies exemplified by FORGIONNE's *Quantitative Management*). N. DAVIS, KOTTE-MANN and REMUS, for example (cited by ATTWELL, p. A56) , have attacked the penchant for numerical modeling as "wrong-headed," in that managers have overestimated the superiority of computer models in search of "the illusion of control" suffering from "cognitive conceit." Such arguments, it seems, could have lifted directly from the debates in the late 1960s and early 1970s over Cliometrics. Business just experienced the same kind of backlash later. The "Productivity Paradox" has been determined as the cause for this disillusionment (NATIONAL RESEARCH COUNCIL). Business' deployment of information technologies with huge investments has not produced greater efficiency and a decrease in administrative work as promised by computer manufacturers, but rather it has displaced communication for really productive work and a requirement to upgrade technical competencies with attendant salary increases. Cost containment never occurred, and in reaction to this realization, skepticism has increased about automation and the kind of quantitative data and spreadsheet modeling that accompanied "management by numbers." Not only has such rethinking undermined the old assumption of administrators that computer-assisted modeling wrought better decisions, which has not proven true in all cases, but such skepticism in administrative circles is reinforced by similar reverberations in academe and qualification of quantitative methods in the Social Sciences. The balance between descriptive and quantitative approaches in History is more appealing now, and Organizational Culture studies in Business may be seen as one sign of such moderation.

At the same time, an extension of tendencies already in motion, such as toward greater flexibility and diversity, and individual semi-autonomy, worked against management of people as a numerical exercise or as attempts to mold them into a homogenous lot. J. GORDON maintains that enough research has been completed to conclude beyond doubt that well-managed heterogeneous groups are more productive than homogeneous ones. Managing well requires involvement, and diversity demands flexibility; both people-centered foci are distinct from process or the older concentration on product. Accordingly, some have seen an interjection of humanism, even "radical humanism" in such revised management theory (AKTOUF). The counter-culture moderating aspects of former tendencies can be seen in overtly different language, as when GALLAGAN searches for a "poetry of work." Affirmative action is part of the rationale in shifting approaches to human resource management and rethinking Organizational Culture as less homogenous than it once was. What were formerly thought of as subcultures on the basis of different cognitive styles (SACKMANN; TRICE), and even covert cultures which defy conformity but nevertheless have been found to energize research activities in some organizations (BEALE), must now be seen as somewhat mainstream as revision calls for thinking of the flow as many thematic currents rather than one, hopefully in the same general direction but with eddies and undercurrents, but not as a complete mix or unified movement where everything proceeds at the same pace.

SINCLAIR notes that some critics deny the very idea of organizational culture and maintain instead that organizations are little more than shifting coalitions of subcultures. FORTADO, who assumes that the superior-subordinate conflict is everywhere, argues that subcultures form when subordinates with similar problems join together for common resolution and develop effective interactions for a lasting infrastructure. This subculture may work and flourish despite perceived hierarchical power-oriented models which do not recognize them. Hence he calls for two-stage analyses, top-down and bottom-up, studying six cultural dimensions: (1) relationships; (2) truth-reality; (3) analytic determinations; (4) evidence; (5) time; and (6) the consequences of grieving. Put differently, the directed single cadence march has been replaced by something less orderly, and while percussion may still be heard, the drumbeat is less regular, rhythms vary, and sounds are more diverse. Integration and equity are no longer seen as sameness, and leadership in these circumstances is sometimes likened to orchestration and musical conducting. Noise, of course, is undesirable; dissonance and unresolved chords are also. The metaphor always evokes harmony. Management has had to respond accordingly and not only to accommodate subcultures, but also to view them positively as forms of enrichment. At the same time, like Janus being wary and two-faced while guarding the threshold, managers must also be aware of the dominant culture, beware of backlash against diversity, and know that many want a simpler time.

The new amalgam in management theory stresses social diversity, flexibility, values, and the dynamics of human relations in organizations. Complexity is acknowledged, and leadership rather than management is the commodity in demand (BEHN; R. LYNCH; NANUS; SCHEIN, 1993b). GIBBONS calls for a reorientation from management as control to an involvement paradigm, and he argues for a contingency theory of leadership to balance older die-hard beliefs that firms are masters of their own fates. Goals, objectives, and strategies are now complicated by several cultures or multiculturalism, and climates too (CHATTERJEE *ET AL.*). The contrived nomenclature seems artificial still, and mixed metaphors abound. The common agricultural metaphor of culture being produced by cultivation has led to talk about climates, as if so much watering and tilling can produce for certain desired crops. Social climates also change like the wind, but cultural management aims at governing prevailing tendencies. MORAN & VOLKWEIN argue that climate is more malleable and is therefore more properly targeted for short-term intervention through structural, perceptual, and interactive approaches, than the more pervasive and deeply rooted culture. SCHNEIDER *ET AL.* stress the priorities of quality service, innovation in research and marketing, and good citizenship in creating the proper climate for the culture of success. Such advice seems redundant throughout the literature. The typologies vary (cf., MARTIN; REDDING; SCHEIN; TRICE & BEYER) and like modeling, they may appear contrived and arbitrary. DOTY & GLICK nevertheless argue for the importance of topological theory building. In most cases, however, the basic thinking seems Pavlovian (which SCHEIN [1993] thinks is the most potent type of learning), and causal thinking is often two dimensional. Indeed, proximity of observables is sometimes mistaken for cause. Such proximity must have relationships to reveal cause, or what GLYMOUR (1987) calls "causal structure" (which underlies statistical modeling). In some cases as collaboration, proximity is an influential factor, but more as an increase in the probability of frequent communication and clarity because of reinforcement and lack of filters (mediation)—more than cause as such (KRAUT, EGIDO & GALEGHER). Repetition of phenomena may signal their importance, but their exact significance and repercussions are not so easily deduced.

Regardless of how long this current wave will last, goal shaping and total quality ideology have moved from production models to what Peter Senge made famous, the "learning organization" (SENGE), and onward to a new goal fit for today's globalization, i.e. "world-class" entities which combine the characteristics of total quality management and the learning organization (HODGETS *ET AL.*). NEVIS *ET AL.* advocate analyzing organizations as learning systems, in that the cycle of knowledge acquisition, dissemination, and utilization reveals a particular learning orientation and set of values. The World Class Executive Development study focuses on senior management and discusses the need to manage learning action and involvement cautiously (BAIRD *ET AL.*). In short, learning activities must occur at all levels of an organization to have world-class status. Workplace learning has taken six decades to come onto its own, according to the AMERICAN ASSOCIATION FOR TRAINING AND DEVELOPMENT, but training alone is not the same as organizational learning as described by ARGYRIS & SCHOEN. The hyperbole, as always, has been overblown in a search for new metaphors, e.g., the invention of the neologism "mentofacturing" by FORWARD *ET AL.* to stress the need for paradigms different from those associated with manufacturing. Others have referred to the "management of meaning" in organizations (MCCAULEY; SMIRCICH; SMIRCICH & MORGAN; contrast this usage with the philosophical inspection of "meaning" by POLANYI & PROSCH). Likewise, BLOOR & DAWSON talk about the dynamics of "professional belief systems" and "sense-making" as important in promoting professionalism in an organization's culture. BOYCE uses story analysis to examine the collective sense of structurally closed organizations. STAUDENMAIER alludes to this tradition of storytelling in technical fields, as distinct from formal history, as fundamental to "reweaving the human fabric." JEFFCUT identifies this shift from interpretation based on text to representation in organizational analysis as postmodernism. He argues that the "understanding of organization is inseparable from the organization of understanding" by showing the entanglement between organizing a textual study, which is based on a textual inscription of order in an organization. He is particularly critical of longstanding problems in methodology relating textual analysis and organizational symbolism.

What, then, constitutes Organizational Culture? SCHEIN (1985) identifies three "observables": (1) artifacts, including structures and processes so as to encompass everything from dress, manners, address, language usage, preferred vocabulary, etc., to products and technologies; (2) espoused values, best articulated when defended as justifications, which may signify idealized rather than actual behaviors; and (3) basic assumptions, usually internalized and untested, which are acted upon unconsciously like following a "mental map." A 1987 conference on "The Symbolics of Corporate Artifacts" attempted to delineate the main "observables" or "visible evidence" of corporate culture, to relate them to cultural codes of conduct, and to show how material culture is related to a model of cultural identity (GAGLIARDI). Its contributors reflected a heterogeneous lot of sociologists, psychologists, phenomenologists, and organizational studies specialists related through various associations. One, the European Group for Organizational Studies founded a Standing Conference on Organizational Symbolism (SCOS) in 1981. SCOS held its first conference in 1984.

Business Administration had discovered secular iconography, epitomized perhaps by ALVESSON & BERG's recent summation of work in organizational symbolism. Management studies have embraced semiotics; therefore, strange as it seems, Umberto Eco has a following in Business. Among foci are: the design of physical surroundings for organizations; a proper environment for socialization and work; the use of artifacts as cultural indicators for research; interpretation of these and other clues such as color coding and symbolism (SASSOON); communications and linguistic analysis (CZARNIAWSKA-JOERGES & JOERGES; ENGESTROM & MIDDLETON, eds.), with special attention to metaphors; the relationship between environmental control and organizational management; and the problem of dualism, paradoxes, and complexity in organizations. A sign of the times is an overwhelming sense of paradox in contemporary life, which appears in historiography with NORA *ET AL.* entertaining dialectical oppositional realms in everything they see (as noted by LOWENTHAL) as well as in management literature to such an extent that HANDY calls this decade "the age of paradox." BANTZ (p. 24) maintains that compliance with standards or "expectations" exerts tremendous peer pressure to conform, in that anyone seeks a comfort level with his or her surroundings and attempts to "fit" into context. He sees this as forming a kind of cultural logic, but not necessarily historical consciousness. DENISON and others declare this psychological tendency and its direction by management to be crucial for organizational effectiveness. However, organizations seeking a culture find the quest very illusive (THOMAS). Arguments pervade the literature about whether culture is something like an intellectual property that an organization has, or is like personality, describing what a company is (e.g., BRIGHT & COOPER). WALLACE (p. 12) sees a trend toward the former. The literature also displays a rift between those who argue that all cultures exhibit certain universals which enable comparative studies, and those who are more relativistic and see cultures as an interplay between the organization, its environment, and social contexts.

The concerns of modern Organization Culture studies seem to cluster into several themes. LINSTEAD & GRAFTON-SMALL summarize the trendy issues of the 1990s deriving momentum from the deconstructionism of the previous decade and an abiding relativism. In the field of organizational studies, they correctly discerned the impact first of ethnology and more recently sociopsychology and micro-studies of the kind called by Michael de Certeau for "tactics of everyday practice" (DE CERTEAU, 1984). However, corporate culture is distinguished as a pervasive space rather than merely a workplace, and in keeping with the times, Culture in both fields is also being described in terms of polarities, paradoxes, otherness, and discourse. Issues at play with each other include rationality versus irrational behavior, the constitution of common knowledge, cultural pluralities, power and ideology, individualism versus collectivism, and subjectivity which is somewhat ironically interpreted by objects and is supposedly to be studied objectively. In truth, many organizational studies are as subjective, notwithstanding a variety of critical apparati and feigned objectivity, as historical studies. Methodologies are similar as is the subject matter and the mix of analysis and description seems equally rich, but the scope and frames for organizational and historical studies differ; one can discern differences in theoretical proclivities and pragmatism, basic assumptions and philosophical orientations differ, and the audiences are really different. In short, the two fields share concerns, methods, and common ground and yet exhibit dramatic differences: they reflect two divergent academic and professional cultures.

Overall, considerable concern for typologies can be detected (GREENWOOD & HININGS), and for the taxonomy of the field itself (SCHEIN; TRICE & BEYER). The older monolithic concept of culture broke down very quickly, but the relationship of culture as a whole with components, subcultures, covert cultures, and the like is as debatable in this field as in History. GOFFEE & JONES accordingly argue that no one culture is best for all organizations, but that different corporate cultures range from networked, mercenary, fragmented, and communal organizations. Multiculturalism, for example, takes on the largest dimension, i.e., globalization and the cross-border management of international organizations (GALANT). Cross-cultural management is seen as especially problematic, since most research in the past has assumed one dominant culture or a constant bilateral mix. TAYEB points to common inadequacies in such research relating to conceptualization, project design and selection of methodologies, data collection, and interpretation. She is particularly sensitive to the employment of culture and social constructs. Management of multiculturalism within organizations is but a coinflip to multicultural organizations—or is it?

The issue is more complex than simply tracking increased multiple variables and identifying subcultures, or in creating a dynamic model. Both substance and presentation are involved in personality and identity, and stability is required of an entity for it to be recognized consistently in a changing context. This is difficult in multicultural organizations, for research design, or for practical management. Can a company maintain a dominant corporate culture across regional, national and continental boundaries, or does its internal and public character change according to cultural ingredients and contexts? CHATTERJEE *ET AL.* suggest that in view of the current trend toward tolerance of multiculturalism, any overemphasis on controlling newly acquired firms by imposing a new parent's goals outright or forcing conforming to the company image can now lead to dysfunctional management. Now, dominance of one corporate culture over another acquisition depends on comparable size in the merger, or weakness of one culture and strength of another. Equally strong cultural entities may result in the corporation looking more like a conglomerate with vibrant subcultures stronger than the overall parent's once dominant culture. In short, one can have a financial takeover triggering a covert cultural takeover in the reverse. When does such internal change and alteration of external cognitive features transform an entity into something else? Is the common and unspoken assumption that cultural transformations are mostly unilateral and lasting a valid foundation? FEDOR & WERTHER point to basic national cultural incompatibilities that fragment international organizations, including managers from subcultures in parent organizations, which are distinct from those which negotiated a cross-cultural alliance. This is a more subtle issue than something as obvious as how multilingualism, for example, can affect organizational culture that is very diffused. Or, consider the idea of cultural transplantation across different organizational cultures, which J. HARRISON likens to the accommodation problems faced by expatriates (an actual problem in multinational companies treated by GREGERSEN). These are new areas of research in modern management science. They concern information scientists as well and historians too.

Communication is always a concern in Organizational Culture studies, whether societal, across large organizations, or within groups. It receives attention from the top not only because it is a means by which organizations are managed, but because communication studies often reveal power structures in organizations other than what appear in organizational charts (MUMBY). A research area in Information Science has developed to support work in decision support systems development, especially interfaces to facilitate group dynamics in widespread modern organizations (JESSUP & VALACICH). Thus, as revealed by DAVENPORT & MCKIM's survey, groupware designers have become intensively interested in the dynamics of human interaction in groups through personal contact and via electronic communications, i.e., "connections" are central to networked organizations (SPROUL & KIESLER). HOFFER & VALACICH and MARSHALL *ET AL.* suggest that "group memory" be an overriding concept in groupware design. The thinking in such circles is the same as in corporate or collective memory, except that the group-focus is a microcosm at the opposite extreme from the macrocosm usually considered by historians of cultural memory. MENNECKE *ET AL.* provide some history of this socio-psychological movement in decision support systems research that parallels historical trends in memory research, but without reference to the work of historians who have shed light on precomputerized support group support systems in education, religion, and national organizations. Nor have H-Net historians and computing historians paid much attention to group-support research concerning project management and topics relevant to Internet conferencing. It would be interesting if information scientists interested in group memory and organizational culture were to join forces with social and cultural historians to study the foundations of consensus, values, cognition based on historical knowledge of all dimensions, and communications based on historical metaphors, which are brought to the table, or into the electronic conference as the case may be, for group decision-making. Moreover, group decision support technology and design of groupware has not tapped into the larger literature of organizational culture in Management any more than it has integrated work from History. Most of this research remains ahistorical and short-range, without proper regard for time and timing, and is the poorer for such shortsightedness. One suspects that group formation, socialization, and "sense making" do not happen as though the group existed in a vacuum without sense of time or space. If that were how modern groups are making decisions, they need all the help they can get, from computerized electronic support systems to group counseling and individual therapy! A prayer or two might be added for good measure! Indeed, the assumptions and belief systems underlying use of modern communication and information technology and one's reliance on unseen taskforces working independently (based on past performance and dependability, that is, the establishment of a trustworthy history) are worthy of serious consideration in future research.

SCHEIN (1993) stressed the need for dialogue across subcultural boundaries in organizations. Similarities exist between studying texts derived from organizations and studying the cultures more directly through observation. The one is more historical, the other anthropological. Indeed, LINSTEAD & GRAFTON-SMALL use the metaphor of "reading" an organizational culture as though it were a book. YATES & ORLIKOWSKI talk about "genre repertoires" as categories for study of thematic communication in organizations. In this regard, similar to trends in discourse analysis and modern literary studies, TOSEY, WILSON, and others study metaphors current in an organization's self-description. The love of metaphors for study show up in the studies themselves in new metaphorical language, such as TOSEY's "systemic metaphor" of "interfering with interferences." MARSHAK perceives "metaphorical systems" in organizations and highlights the need of administrators to manage "the metaphors of change." SCHEIN (1993) views dialogue as "central" in any model of organizational transformation and calls the need to dialogue across subcultural and hierarchical boundaries a pressing need. Thus he advocates the study of dialogue through mapping techniques.

As in History, narratology in the field of Organizational Culture is a dominant approach to understanding "how members make sense of social reality" (J. MEYER, p. 210). The link between socialization and literary motifs is made by HANSEN, INGERSOL & ADAMS, and BOYCE who like historians of children's literature try to discern what values are being conveyed in storytelling in Fortune 500 companies (HANSEN & KAHNWEILER). J. MEYER details a methodology to get members of organizations to tell stories and in so doing, to elicit from them descriptions of values. Clustering these into genre and types allows a study of reinforcement for harmony or of divergent strains to see if inconsistent values clash with one another to create conflict. SCHMIDT, who argues that stories from organizational experiences are among the best means to promote concrete and effective communication about values and ethics, juxtaposes such stories with argumentation and other forms of more rational, direct presentation of company lines to reveal an organization's most pervasive values. Sometimes it seems that sheer gossip is the subject, legitimized under the rubric of "narrative," and that several studies simply validate what is known from common sense (or "ordinary knowledge" as

MAFFESOLI calls it or "everyday understanding" in SEMIN & GERGEN's words). Often the formal treatment of common folk wisdom does illuminate. GAERTNER & RAMNARAYAN, for example, suggest that narratives back up arguments made more empirically; they maintain that organizational effectiveness is more dependent on stories about the organization's performance than any measures of production, sales, or profits.

Storytelling has always inculcated values systems in children and initiates to formal societies, and still does as exemplified by the Jasper Project at VANDERBILT UNIVERSITY which uses fabricated stories, i.e., the adventures of Jasper, as modern exempla. It seems only natural, therefore, that adult learning likewise be influenced by stories (which it is; see R. RICHEY on instructional design for adults). Humor, especially in jokes about organizations and its management, parodies, and manifestations of popular culture, are especially telling for ZINKHAN & JOHNSON. MITROFF & KILMANN emphasize that organization-specific stories may be keys to specific behaviors that contribute to the unique identity of the organizations in which they flourish. While the belief among academicians persists that practitioners are unconcerned about ethics in advertising, such research continues in the mainstream of Marketing, according to HYMAN *ET AL.* They search for better measures linking for such research and in so doing will contribute not only to advertising research but also to the history of popular culture. The history in such research, however, takes a back seat to story. BUSH & BUSH compare advertising with the internal story line in search of congruence, and see this issue as linked to, e.g., truth in advertising being less about a product's qualities, and more about representation of the organization to its public as posited by WILLIAMSON in the 1980s. Might one ask for similar congruence with an organization's history? The imagery in advertising may also be connected with visualization of an organization by its members. Image building and identification are related according to DUTTON *ET AL.* who relate two key images: what members believe is distinctive and enduring about their organization and the beliefs about what outsiders think about the organization. People assess the attractiveness of these images in terms of how they preserve their own self-image and enhance their self-esteem.

Much of this research is related through cognitive psychology to learning theory and visualization. In the way that researchers sometimes speak of "reading" a culture based on its documentary remains, SCHULTZ studies "pictures of culture" and sees graphic representation as more revealing than oral description or texts. The Johns Hopkins University symposium in 1991 on the "Relation of Mnemonic Functions to Pictorial Representation" connects remembering with representation as *Images of Memory* (KUECHLER & MELION, eds.). The literal dimension of this cultural study through imagery is reflected in photographic analysis, an increasingly common tool employed by organizational consultants (DOUGHERTY & KUNDA). Organizational management literature, however, contains few references to work on representation in social and cultural history (cf., COOKE & WOLLEN; FYFE & LAW). Still shots freeze emotions, gestures, expressions, etc., for detailed study of scenarios, portraits, and frames, differently than one might use video which replays a process. Slow motion allows one to see detail missed in full speed replay, but also motion pictures slowed down to consecutive frames can be studied similar to time-event and series analysis methodologies in other disciplines. The same technique, for example, can be employed by historians using historical photographs (TAGG). What is observed? Although it may be a matter of hearing, the sequence in which people in a group laugh at a joke, break into the conversation or bow out and distance themselves from colleagues or close ranks may also provide insight into social standing, power structure, and deference in social interaction. Body language, facial expressions, manners and protocols, and dress are the subject of study by RAFAELI & PRATT, since these are all taken as outward manifestations of the culture. The study of dress has become a trendy preoccupation of those fashion consultants writing "Dress for Success" books and those reading them in hope of success, but there is a more scholarly strain in cultural Anthropology as reflected by the recent works of EICHER (cf., BARNES & EICHER, eds.). Reflections in Management literature, however, are often unclear; and it is questionable whether they can be used as symptoms similar to diagnostics in medicine or as predictors of acceptance into a corporate culture. Dress, mannerism, and expression are all interactive variables.

The point is that these elements in human behavior are being studied as never before, and despite the obvious limitations of many of the contributions, they are having an effect on management practices. This is a common approach, for example, in conducting cultural audits of organizations, like physical checkups for healthy bodies (WILKINS). No such audits, however, move to the complexity of Verne Ray's 7,633 cultural element enumeration; instead they simplify like George Murdock's much earlier reduction to 30 key variables for cross-cultural mapping (cf., RAY; MURDOCK, 1981, 1982, 1987). From the viewpoint of serious cultural anthropology, much of this Management literature seems superficial. As studies progress, however, the field is changing and its scientific basis is developing rapidly.

All of these organizational traits are manifested in rituals, ceremonies, and programs (BROWN, 1993a & b). Ceremonies are performances, regularly scheduled, which are themselves symbolic (DEAL & KENNEDY); rites tend to be more elaborate, dramatic sets of activities. The borrowing from Anthropology is evident, as are parallels in this thinking with historians studying cultural memory. BROWN (1993a, 1994) discusses a dozen case studies to show how rites induce cognitive change in organizations by "transformational leaders," especially placing symbolic awards ceremonies into and designing a reward system as part of Manufacturing Resource Planning (MPR II) programs. These programs accentuate an organization's values, honor role models, award success, and allow management to preside in a very visual, public way (LANGE). Lange identified seven major rituals in business: rites of (1) passage (2) enhancement (3) degradation (4) conflict reduction (5) integration (6) renewal and (7) style.

DEHLER & WELSH stress the utility of rites to counterbalance the rationality in organizational behavior that has been emphasized traditionally in Management with an appeal to emotion. Indeed, it is this aspect that resembles religion and spirituality even in nonsectarian organizations (NILAKANT & RAO), and in which management may be seen more as an art than science. Just as Steven Covey has injected ethics back into business, not only as rules of conduct but as a deeper abiding concern, DEHLER & WELSH speak of "spirituality" as essential for management transformation, as distinct from organizational development. The current ethos is something more than a philosophy of management as perceived a decade ago, but rather an involvement with humanity. KOFMAN & SENGE talk today about "communities of commitment" as "the heart of learning organizations" in terms of transcendent human values (love, wonder, humility, compassion) that once were foreign to the vocabulary of business management. Ritual is an outward display of other values, such as trust between leadership and memberships in organizations, whether in religion or in marketing and sales (STRUTTON *ET AL.*; SCHNEIDER, B., *ET AL.*). The issue of ceremony, *qua* ritualistic programs, in modern management is not so much old-fashioned maternalism as mutual accountability in keeping with notions of teamwork, buddy systems, and camaraderie (SHAW, FISCHER & RANDOLPH).

Cultural cognition is reinforced by continuous recognition of proclaimed values. Thus HATCH (1990) stresses the architecture of business buildings, and environmental psychologists like SUNDSTROM also emphasize the importance of office design. BOISOT speaks of "information space" as a framework for learning in organizations. BERG & KREINER argue that architectural monuments for corporate headquarters are not simply vanity, but are assets; and DOXTATER points to the legitimate need for "ritual space" in such organizational arenas. Civic centers and corporate headquarters are the secular cathedrals in the language of semiology (GUIRARD). BUCKINGHAM examines historical stereotypes and the commemoration of historical events in this vein, his subject being "myths and anniversaries," but without acknowledged indebtedness to Organizational Culture studies. Managed national culture is often the subject of critique by historians because anti-nationalism has long been in vogue. If historians were to engage the field of Organizational Culture to study organizations and their cultures rather than Culture with its organizational supports, it is likely that their stance would be that of critics, and some would have difficulty with objectivity because of a basic suspicion and fear of manipulation through the management of organized culture. This is not a position automatically shared by all artists and humanists; musicians, for example, could not create grand music without acquiescence to a high degree of direction, indeed "orchestration," to play symphonic music. Once musicians learn a piece and play it together, however, then performance is as much evoked than directed by their leader. Such collaboration and harmony are achieved through practice, but historians may have little such experience. Cultural studies are nothing new to historians, but with the exception of practicing public historians, cultural management is. Conversely, cultural management may always have been part of an administrator's role, but outside academe, cultural studies are relatively new.

Management in such a milieu of contrived behaviors is more an issue of orchestration than direction, however, or in the field's language borrowed again from sports, coaching—the fashionable alternative term to guidance or counseling. The catch word of the day is "leadership" which is defined in as many ways as there are profiles of leaders (cf., A.BROWN; COVEY; DAVIS & GIBSON; HANDY; KOFMAN & SENGE; MOREAU & HUNT; NELSON, etc.). Chief executive officers today are expected to balance analysis and instinct (to avoid "extinction by instinct" and "paralysis by analysis" according to LANGLEY), and polarities like entrepreneurialism and collectivism (MORRIS *ET AL.*), or unity and cohesion with diversity, cooperation and competition, and other antitheses, all of which can lead to fragmentation. RICHARDSON warns how leaders must accommodate paradoxes and double-sided beliefs (e.g., managing people and production, democratically and autocratically, internally and externally, etc., and being innovative and visionary while also being supportive, adoptive and consensus building). EGGLESTON & BHAGAT distinguish between substantive and symbolic roles for leaders and show that in times or organizational reorientation the former are emphasized. Above all, executives must be experts in sensing and making sense out of an organization's culture, which includes understanding its "knowledge system" and its means of transmitting information (NESPOR). Rarely, however, are they expected by the theorists of today to know their organization's history. Instead, RASPA characterizes the modern CEO as the "corporate myth-maker."

This literature of Organizational Culture in the Management field is difficult to characterize but easy to criticize. One must read prolifically throughout the field to gain tidbits of knowledge which are not easily synthesized. Its language usage is not set, and often the field seems jargon ridden and prone to fads as authors compete for attention. Much of it appears to be good advice literature, without proper foundations in research of its own, or it displays too much uncritical borrowing from other fields. A lot is anecdotal, consisting of case studies that do not always support the generalizations drawn from them. And the bulk consists of small essays, serially produced, constituting an ongoing dialogue that generates consensus through repetition, rather than the weight of mature, self-contained, full-scale studies. One cannot but notice the consensus basis of such publications, where the study of group behavior seems to necessitate group study teams. Collaborative publications dominate the field, with the notable exceptions of a few authorities who rise to guru status. It is ironic that so many 10-page to 12-page essays require three to five authors to complete! The trend toward multiple authorship, so distinct from History, is not, however, as far gone as in Science where multiple authorship has crested over a hundred. Such extremes are not necessarily what is advocated here for a collaborative Historical Information Science. Many essays in this management literature explore modeling, typologies, and new terminology, as if to see if they catch on, without solid exercise of classification or terminological theory. This literature displays a penchant for neologisms, catchy phrases, memorable quotes, and even slogans. Finally, like most disciplines, it tends to be self-citing.

More substantively, the Organizational Culture movement in Management has been criticized severely as pseudo-science in the same vein as other Social Sciences have been regarded as "soft" from the vantage point of the so-called "hard" physical sciences and because the field is still so immature and derivative. Practitioners have been accused of narrow and partial perspectives, superficial analyses, simply conducting culture audits by plugging data into preconceived matrices that do not work well for particular situations (i.e., poor matches between instruments and methodologies selected and the subjects being studied, as cautioned by TAYEB), and merely doing empirical reporting without sufficient analysis. REDDING lists many of these problems as among those challenging the epistemology of organization studies. He also notes that despite its early inspiration from Anthropology, the field displays a bias against ethnographical fieldwork and favors instead survey questionnaire methods borrowed from Sociology. An added note would be that quite a few of these surveys could not stand the test of cross-examination in a court of law regarding their methodology and technique (DIAMOND). MARTIN & SIEHL have attempted to enhance quantitative methodologies in organizational culture studies with qualitative concerns, and SCHEIN (1987) has tried to improve the latter aspects of observation in organizational studies by giving it a "clinical perspective." The unsystematic and too often uncritical borrowing by Business from other disciplines, coupled with a weak theoretical development, undermines the field academically. Some see the view within Management as being too narrow and partial, and since it is usually one study per organization to respond to a crisis or set of undesirable circumstances, the methodology employed is static. Such criticism has been leveled caustically against "hit and run" diagnosticians who are seldom accountable for their ideas when converted to action in organizations. BOWER recalled the forces that launched management consulting on a large scale, and the "opprobrious term 'business doctors'" (e.g., quacks) such consultants had to live down.

A generation ago KUBLER (1962) had already stressed the idea of the cultural "array" of things as more important than any instance, and this is in keeping with the Social Science search for patterns in behaviors. BURKHARDT & BRASS wonder if phenomena studies are "changing patterns or patterns of change"—a question framed so aptly as to capture also the quandary of quantification studies in New Social History. Just as social history because of its Social Science orientation has been subjected to postmodern criticism, the same questions have been raised about organizational culture studies. From the perspective of historiography, the field of cultural studies applied to world history is both advanced and backward at the same time, especially in its handling of matters of interaction or its placement of diverse cultures into a single framework, may be culturally biased if not actually prejudiced (MANNING, p. 776), but the assumption is often that such an approach is safer when limited to a single organization than anything so broad or dynamic as society or culture at large. This assumption may be equally flawed, in assuming that any organization exists apart from its context, and such isolationist thinking has come increasingly under attack. It is similar to historical work concentrating on local history rather than risking the complexity involved in studying larger dimensions. As such, the localism of organizational culture reflects some of the greatest limitations of postmodernism (cf., the critiques of E. A. KAPLAN; D. HARVEY; F. JAMESON, etc.). SCHULTZ not only reminds management academics that the notion of corporate culture is neither new or unique to the business, but he questions the modernist assumption of corporate culture as patterns of meanings and values located supposedly at the depth of organizations, which nevertheless are revealed so superficially in symbols and artifacts. He levels a post-postmodern critique at the objective to regulate the behavior of members in an organization through meaningful events and internalized knowledge. On the other hand, HIGGINSON & WAXLER warn that if a split occurs between formal and informal "symbolic orders" mixed messages result in a neurotic organization.

Unlike New Social History and its attention to cultural memory, Organizational Culture has developed neither the desire or the apparatus to conduct in-depth, longitudinal research. These studies seldom consult archives or contribute to them for subsequent reexamination and proper historical bench marking. So, while timing is stressed as important in conducting change operations, in fact time is often overlooked as an important operational variable in research design (an exception being COFFEY, who studied time management as indicative of organizational values). One-time static views of dynamic continuing processes are simply inadequate, as realized by HATCH (1993) and others who, in reaction to Schein's 1985 model of organization culture as assumptions, values, and artifacts, focus more on symbols and processes or "symbolization," manifestations, and realization. However, current methods rely on one-time views and few studies include re-examination of other study's evidence to create a second look at the same case, phenomenon, or organization. Most of the syntheses in the literature are collages, with input from very different organizations which are assumed to share a commonality that is not always evident. So, the result is like using still-life paintings from art history as documentary evidence, where few alternative sources exist and the range of exploration is curtailed thereby, even though the subjects of modern organizational studies are alive and the possibilities for acquiring more data and capturing more active and longitudinal views are greater than in History. Indeed, if this were accomplished by contemporary Organizational Culture studies, history would be enriched with more comparative data than usually survive and future study could benefit by combining historical research and recurrent diagnostic checkups. Instead, excessive modeling, survey work, and overgeneralization make the field seem to others as rather superficial. It does not have to remain so, and perhaps this impression is because the field is still in adolescence.

Perhaps most ironic, however, is the criticism that too much of the work in Organizational Culture is so hypothetical when it claims to be an applied and practical field, and yet applications areas like human resource management are accused of lacking a coherent theoretical framework. WRIGHT & MCMAHAN point to six theoretical models at play: (1) behavioralism; (2) cybernetics; (3) agency-transaction cost models; (4) resource-based views; (5) power-resource dependence models; and (6) institutional theory, and they point to other theories as well, such as Marxism, population ecology, and interpretive theory. They agree, however, that despite such richness in modeling, the human resource field still lacks a strong theoretical foundation. On the other hand, an example of such ambivalent criticism, which is really a question of balance, is that so much of this organizational research seems more concerned with testing models or validating them with case studies than using models to explain organizational problems and assist in their resolution. Some critics esteem the pragmatism in the field that often seems lacking in academe. LEWIS challenged the basic notion in management literature that organizational culture has a direct and predicable effect on organizational performance. Her longitudinal study of an Australian college forced to transform itself into a university indicated that patterns of staff behavior could be changed without a corresponding positive change in values. The institution performed well according to stakeholders' criteria, despite widespread opposition to the changeover.

PRESTON's investigation of cultural symbols as a way to provide clear and persuasive pictures of corporate culture suggests that the link between management development and organizational culture is indirect at best. SCHULTE provides a postmodern critique of the field, charging like CRITCHLEY that its goals are an illusion, and that even the indirect control of human behavior through the manipulation of culture is simply absurd. CHATMAN & JEHN conclude also that the attempted use of organizational culture for a competitive advantage may be more constrained than researchers often assume. Historians might tend to agree, or at least share skepticism about the control impulse from management in such study of human affairs. The real fault lies in the field's radical reductionism, i.e., trying too hard to reduce complex phenomena into simple explanations so that management can act with only two or three generalizations in mind.

Cause is so easily confused with symptom in the diagnostic techniques employed. In the best light, enthusiasts expect too much; moderately, the field seems controlling and manipulative; at worst, it is simply naive.

Why, then, include this field into the spectrum envisioned as Historical Information Science? The altruistic answer is possible symbiosis and improvement of both fields, but the practical answer is that whatever the criticism, the field is well established in Management, has greater impact on thinking in corporate American than any historical work, and is a plausible bridge between Management Science and Information Science (i.e., the management of information versus the supportive computing and telecommunication technology). SCHOLZ shows that even in information technology, not everything that matters is simply information exchange: computers as artifacts play a role in organizational culture by displaying the technical prowess and modernity of the enterprise. CIBORA & LANZARA argue for such understanding in the design of computer software and representation, as in good advertising, on everything from user interfaces to HyperText Markup Language (HTML) homepages on the World Wide Web. Acknowledgment of these realities in modern culture warrants some discussion about the potential relationship of History and Organizational Culture studies through Historical Information Science.

Although organizational culture enthusiasts may invoke history for inspiration and as a tool for inducing change, SCHEIN and others in this school (BEHN, R. LYNCH, NANUS, etc.) seldom talk about formal History. The kind of quality business history as written by J. YATES is rarely cited in management literature, perhaps because her correlations between the rise of calculating and actuarial industries such as insurance companies with empiricism in America, both in research and as a preoccupation of management, are not seen as directly applicable even though her work reveals much about and provides significant insights into the cultures of post-World War II business organizations. Such studies often complicate rather than simplify. The consultant, change agent, or human resource manager is not likely to be immersed in history. Historians do not perceive of such work as being History, and members of the Institute of Management Consulting (1968-) hardly see themselves as historians. They have more in common than either group seems to realize, but the differences rather than commonalities are stressed most.

In a milieu where the pragmatic prevails, certain tendencies can be discerned which seem out of step with History today: (1) leaders and heroes are cherished, villains seem nonexistent, and judgments about good and bad often pertain to trends but not necessarily to people; (2) stories, myths, and legends compete with history for attention, credibility, and priority; and (3) cognitive orientations such as beliefs, values,and attitudes are transcendent over fact, objectivity, and the truth-claims of History. A. BROWN's "five sets of organizational phenomena" cluster such observables somewhat differently: (1) leaders and heroes; (2) stories, myths, and legends; (3) cognitive orientations such as beliefs, values, and attitudes; (4) behavioral orientations such as ceremonies, rites, and rituals; and (5) physical orientations such as architectural styles and office layouts. In such circumstances and in view of such criteria for the evaluation of corporate culture, academic History with its critical temperament, penchant for debate, rigorous individualism, and noticeable bent toward the liberal in politics is not always welcome as a ready ally for accomplishing the ulterior objectives of Management such as building consensus, harmony, camaraderie, social cohesion, and teamwork. Historians generally dislike the use of history for formation (in the sense used in Religion), reinforcement of preordained values and directed scenarios, or a possible role in unlearning as a prelude to learning something different in the reform process, even though these are precisely the same applications used to defend History in general education for character and civic development. Social Scientists often see this as "socialization," which is more acceptable to historians at a higher level of generalization than in specific instances and applications.

The pervasiveness of historical consciousness and its role in self-identity and socialization would seem to invite professional historians into the arena of organizational management as much as into education for general studies and civics. This nexus would seem to be even stronger today precisely because of historians' recent interests in history versus memory and self-interest in regenerating History's role in preserving and developing culture at all levels of our social structure. Few historians, even those of recent history or in the field of Public History, are active in the applied side of cultural organizational development except as contributors through lectures and suppliers of reading material. This despite greater rewards in the latter area where professional salaries in management surpass professorial compensation ranges by 20-50 percent. Moreover, some corporations have used reading programs effectively to change their cultures (BROKAW). Like bibliotherapy programs in health care, these have consisted of assigned readings and book-based discussions for focus on the same concerns by both managers and front-line workers. Most selections come from Management literature, Sociology for social action, the motivational genre from Psychology, and occasionally company histories, but seldom from History *per se*. The kind of writing rewarded in Business intentionally designed to reach a broad market and cut across educational levels inside non-academic organizations, might very well be disdained in History as mere popularization, even though they may be viewed more legitimately as an extension of classroom teaching activity to facilitate distance learning. In academe such activities are seen as service to be recognized as inferior to research and teaching in the traditional hierarchy of academic values, unless, of course, consulting through grants and contracts is lucrative for the institution as well. Archivists as information managers might move into this consultative role, if they were to discard traditional biases and overcome artificial limitations imposed upon them by training in History.

Where do organization culture recruits receive training? Most come from Psychology or Sociology, some from Anthropology if the focus of study were modern, and hybrid fields like Education, and they often work also with personnel or Human Resource management and training. More are now coming from Management programs in Business schools as Organizational studies become more ensconced, but it should be noted that few historians, even those in Business history, work in Business schools. Technical and production change is identified with "re-engineering" (HAMMER & CHAMPY; REVENAUGH) and the idea of an organizational "retrofit" (NEAL *ET AL.*), and therefore is associated in Technology with project management in Engineering. MARLOWE *ET AL.* identify, among other "re-ing" approaches to change, reinvention, reengineering, restructuring, etc., which all seem like variations of the same theme. Although these terms are often misapplied, in general usage they have come to mean any radical cross-functional rethinking and end-to-end restructuring of organizations as distinct from general reorganization or rearrangements. These make-overs are high-risk ventures; half of these total reorganizations fail, and with them, executives in their management positions. While salaries and compensation packages for CEO and top-level managers continue to climb, their job stability is deteriorating. This is a high-pressure environment for which few historians are well suited by training or perhaps by temperament. But if not the management of reengineering, one might expect more historical interest in the phenomena, past and present, and if such whole scale reorganization were studied historically, then greater transference of ideas and methodology than there seems to be now.

History is not an automatic ingredient in such training for Management any more than it is in Information Science. It should be, and the inclusion of Organizational Culture in this discussion of Historical Information Science calls for such innovation. Supposedly obvious relationships can be seen between cultural memory in History and (1) Anthropology (folklore and mythology, sometimes linked with Oral History and to Literature by language and linguistic studies, such as in popular culture), (2) Sociology (interpersonal communications and group activities), and (3) Communications as Speech and Language studies, but their connections with Organizational Culture in Management is less apparent. Segregation is often imposed the norm. Little attention in History is paid to what is happening in Business. The lack of cross-referencing in each other's literature indicates such a gulf, similar to that which exists between

History and Information Science. Sometimes actual disdain may be detected. Rapport between the traditional academic disciplines and the professions is often strained, and cross-fertilization is often wanting. This reflects the old division of the Liberal Arts from vocational, technical, and career oriented education. BARLEY, MEYER & GASH note that generally academicians part company with practitioners when it comes to the pragmatic implementation of normative control. It is one thing to study something; another to do it.

The linkage and cross-disciplinary features of Historical Information Science might strengthen such inter-disciplinary work by bringing formal history and archival information systems to the forefront of organizational management, while bringing from the latter into History and Archival Science deeper awareness of the manageability of culture within organizations and, to a lesser extent, society as well. The two have mutual concerns in civics in so much as historical awareness builds communities, and corporations, both private and public, have civic responsibilities to the communities they serve and in which they gain sustenance. Moreover, methodologies developed in management, such as cultural and communications audit procedures, like paradigm logic, are very applicable to historical projects. Conversely, one's self-awareness of one's context can be enhanced by the extension of time, i.e., history, to broaden the more limited awareness acquired by static environmental scanning. It is by comparison that change is measured, and the rate of change with its variables can only be mapped serially with multiple scans and corrective monitoring. In addition to the missing chronological component of organizational study, which is so noticeable when attempting historical comparison, many studies also lack adequate contextual referencing (more than just supplying dates but also in locating situations in historical context). Consciousness is too limited when based only on personal experience, and opinion prevails rather than considered synthesis from a rich mix of ideas. Even when social interaction is created in research design and a research team is truly representational of all aspects of a problem, the site is still trapped in time and context. Consequently, while historical investigations are too often untimely, seemingly unrelated to the present, and overly general, organizational culture studies are too often timeless, ahistorical, and unrelated to the past. The limitations of locality, presentism, inbreeding, and consensus that is self-informed and reinforced by repetition; the substitution of mythology for more objective history and project historiography; and the absence of an archival research record all undermine the current state-of-the-art organizational studies.

It is significant that the methods adopted by management in studying organizational culture are those of the anthropologist whose subjects often lack written records and whose methodology evolved to compensate for such lacunae. The transfer of anthropological method to modern organizations, which in most cases have more documentation than can be absorbed by the organization itself (let alone an external study team) incorporates certain assumptions that clash with formal Informational Science as much as History. The issue is the old dichotomy anthropologists employ to separate primitive from domestic societies. Primitive societies are often preliterate, lack formal histories but share a rich mythographic tradition, and communicate orally through sign language and a vocabulary of cultural symbols. The cynical assumption organization culture studies unconsciously make about modern organizations is that they are primitive—to such an extent that methods anthropologists developed to study uncivilized or nondomestic societies are best suited for understanding today's corporate life. The assumption made in not relying on formal information systems and communications is that the corporate culture being studied is illiterate, oral, and tribal. Indeed, REVENAUGH describes modern business precisely this way, on the basis of the "corporate tribes model."

This is a terrible indictment of Business education, and it perhaps goes hand in hand with the observation gleaned from MCCABE *ET AL*. that despite popular belief, business organizations composed largely of MBA graduates have less concern for ethics in the conduct of business than those with a cadre of lawyers. KURLAND notes how little research exists to explore the relationship between ethics and reward systems in business although preliminary findings show little connection. Given renewed management interest in business ethics (e.g., AGUILAR; HOFFMAN; J. O'TOOLE [1993], SINCLAIR), it would be interesting to know what impact on ethical considerations Liberal Arts graduates would have in business. Likewise, few organizational studies ever check the quality of information conveyed orally, visually, and symbolically with textual information and records, and information systems, or compare behaviors of literate and systematically informed organizations with the chaos of the primitive conditions they often explore. Many believe, for example, that computers and information systems are valuable in business just as information scientists often assume that information systems management benefit the organizations in which they operate. However, Paul Strassmann, Xerox Corporation's CIO, rightly drew attention away from the hardware and software *per se*, the capital investment that often cannot be justified by any direct connection to products, increased productivity, and profits, but may be justified by the synergism created, different operations and preparedness, and better management. He focuses on the critical issue, not of managing computers, but of management of the executive management of computers and information systems. STRASSMANN (1990, p. 519) provides the following caveats: "A computer is worth only what it can fetch at an auction. Its business value is its most economic alternative solution. Anything not worth doing is not worth doing well on a computer." His remarks are indicative of the movement in management circles to refocus on content rather than methodology and processing only and to integrate information into all projects and information systems into the very fabric of the organization. His comments seem equally cogent for historical and social science research project management.

Common untested assumptions about computerization and information systems also assume that corporate life as a whole is educated and therefore domesticated. WILENSKY posited that there is such a thing as "organizational intelligence," but this may not extend throughout the whole organization, e.g., to labor in all sectors. Those who share these perspectives but seldom look beyond their information systems to learn how their organizations operate seem culpable, but no less than organizational culture students who seem to exclude formal information exchange, information systems, and documentation from their purview. Their greatest concern in common is perhaps the study of resistance to change, but especially the fear of technology and of information technologies in particular. Both primitive and domestic cultures exist in many organizations, and often tension exists between them as they interact. In either case, a monolithic perspective is as problematic as a static view of a dynamic process. The same can be said for History and Information Science.

Common ground between Organizational Culture studies, History, and Information Science is easily found, although it is seldom occupied. A bridge to Information Science lies in cognitive psychology related to cooperation, collaboration, teamwork, and project management, and thereby to management and administration. From the foundations laid by PIAGET in the 1920s, developmental psychologists who followed in his footsteps and linguists interested in language acquisition (such as VYGOTSKY a little later, 1932,) believed that social interaction (parent and child, mentor and student, foreman and laborer) influenced cognitive development and this is related to language utility and communication (e.g., sublanguages). The field of social cognitive studies took off since the mid-1970s coterminous with Social Science history and Information Science (cf., JANIS & MANN; BUTTERWORTH & LIGHT; LOSEE & HAAS). LABVE (p. 1), who connects the process to empirical research through mathematics, defined social cognition as "the nexus of relations between the mind at work and the world in which it works" (cf., ROGOFF; ROGOFF & LABVE). Consider the study of social cognition, e.g., the proposition that cognition is socially distributed, (CICOUREL, 1974) as relevant to all information processing in organizations because "participants in collaborative work relationships are likely to vary in the knowledge they possess and must therefore engage each other in dialogues that allow them to pool resources and negotiate their differences to accomplish their tasks" (CICOUREL, 1990, p. 223). HUBER refers to this as "organizational learning" in the spirit of Peter Senge's notion of *The Fifth Discipline*. ROBBIN & FROST-KUMPF (p. 110) link communications, social knowledge, information acquisition, and error production and correction as critical to any information process in knowledge development. They assume "that knowledge is socially produced and derived from experiences with events, situations, activities, objects, people, and the use of data that describe these elements" (p. 113). This may be individual, but it is also, as they recognize, at the "social or collective level" of cognition and communications. What they do not recognize, is that what they are describing is history.

The link between this aspect of organizational culture and information studies with history can be seen in other commonalities. The kinds of evidence examined by organizational consultants is not that different from what historians look for today to supplement the written record. The one remains more documentary and fact oriented, and the other more survey prone and impression oriented, which means that the two may be more complementary than either knows. Both could appreciate the significance of signs and symbols, artifacts, ritual, formal and informal avenues of communication, social structures, common recall and consensus or stereotypes, and attitudes and morale generally (DEAL & KENNEDY). Subcultures are placed by both in context, countercultures are not disregarded (J. MARTIN & SIEHL), and the building of any model today takes into account variance and exceptions to any rule. Both must relate the specific with the general, and work back and forth. Interviewers and oral historians share common interests and techniques, and both operate at all levels of organizations from management to labor, with the understanding that both are managed in one way or another. Current trends toward cross-disciplinary studies would seem to beckon further cross-over between the disciplines and professions. The distance between History as a formal academic discipline and Organizational Culture as practiced in Business and Management is nevertheless inexplicably wide.

What could one expect of Organizational Studies applied to the History profession and organizations of historians? We lack Organizational Studies, for example, of history departments as either successful or dysfunctional organizations deserving emulation or in need of remediation respectively. How many academic administrators would inspect their departments this way, to determine their values, inner workings, cultural cohesion, camaraderie, objectives, and measured successes? How often are History faculties designed as organizations, other than by teaching specialities where appointments match the curriculum rather than where curricula take on the character of their organizational sponsors? Or consider the research possibilities for critical non-biographical examinations of historical research projects, which like autopsies lay open a corpus of material to see what worked or went wrong, to determine what should be avoided in future work and what might be transferred to other projects to enhance their chances for success. Evaluation reports for funded projects by NHPRC, NEH, NSF (Social Sciences), etc., fall short of this goal, but herein lies material waiting for such multiproject, cross-disciplinary study. In communication studies within organizations, such as informal colleges, reviewing networks, citation tracing, and now Internet communities as well, the possibilities are endless for the study of historians and of History in ways never considered in traditional historiography. Many historians seem defensive about such self-study, and certainly such study by management, and assuredly debates like those about Cliometrics over the selection of applications, appropriate methodologies, interpretation, and use, would be resurrected by such a prospect. Good! This may be just the ingredient needed in Organizational Studies to provide a needed external critique, to elevate the quality of research in this field, and broaden its scope to include more than modern business. Reciprocally, influence via Organizational Studies from Business and Management might provide historians with insights into their own organizational behavior and improve History project and organization management as well.

In addition to divergent preferences for the abstract and untried, and for the concrete and practical, the breakdown between historian and social scientist engaged in organizational culture studies often occurs over motive affecting interpretation and over specific occurrences, instances, and applications. Action linked to conclusion is where accountability really begins.

Because academics often need not act upon their findings, from the standpoint of management they often appear unaccountable. While historians gravitate toward "pure History" in their search for objectivity and impartiality, like a referee outside the game with no vested interest, the manager is a player and referee at the same time. The latter is seen by the former as more subjective, less academic and scholarly, having ulterior purposes, and operating in a way that a historian may disdain as manipulative and even clandestine. Image projection, public relations, culture and thought control, inference and information, bias and innuendo are associations historians may have about change agents and managers, whose historical imagery may be likened to "spin doctors" rather than history as such. Historians might approve of the use of History for affirmation and renewal, but would link anything leading to compulsive behavior as indoctrinative rather than purely informative. Indeed, change agents do study their organizations to induce change, make innovation comfortable, gain acceptance, and assist with morale during difficult times, encourage motivation and loyalty through means other than compensation, maintain civility in human relations, and to project positive corporate images not only for good marketing but also for *esprit d'corps*. Such manifold objectives require both Science and Art.

Nevertheless, despite such differences between academicians and practitioners, professionals all, the Organizational Culture field in or outside Administration Science and Management or in Information and Archival Science is a hybrid which must attract both the thinker and the doer, hopefully one and the same. Parallels between its thematic development and trends in historical research regarding Memory and Culture suggest ample opportunity for greater interplay across disciplinary boundaries than has occurred thus far. Historical Information Science is one arena in which convergence seems eminent, where new studies beckon crossing over disciplinary and professional lines, and where greater collaboration might occur.

Sources and Evidence:

Data and Electronic Archives

The foregoing discussions, having introduced the idea of Historical Information Science, have also addressed three overarching and integrated concerns in its purview:

1. Self-awareness is needed of the current milieu in which historical writing and analysis are undertaken, including more than the historiography to date, as well as an assessment of current attitudes, bibliographic tools available, and search strategy, in the planning of information searching and historical research as separate yet related processes. This initial assessment must address both gaining access to content in primary and secondary sources, and identification of appropriate methodologies and research techniques. This should include assessment of computing capabilities.

2. Interpretation depends on the study of historical information in context, with a continuity overview from creation to its reuse by the historian, which includes meta-knowledge about the means by which the information was created, preserved, and relayed through time and place to the historian. Source criticism depends on the history of the source, as a prerequisite for its use in reconstructing history. This should include awareness of metamorphoses in source transmission, such as translation between languages and transformation between media which play such an important role in global culture (BASSNET & LEFEVRE). The emphasis here has been on the information technology relating to historical records, especially the history of computing and telecommunications as an extension of previous attention to scribal and printing technologies.

3. Contextual interpretation of the present situation when history is reconstructed and the original setting when it transpired as well as the continuity of evidence between these two points in time, involves the interplay between the history and metahistory, i.e., source and source history, changing context of the source in the media conveying information and the technology of its making and transmission, and awareness of the changing environment of the source from creation, use, and current reuse in historical research. The emphasis here has been on the organizational context, separating cultural influences on and from the source itself, which influence the source's survival, preservation, transmission, and interpretation. This includes awareness of the current organizational culture at the time and place history is to be written.

Having explored this reflexive relationship between primary and secondary sources, access and document retrieval, information technology, and organizational culture, the following discussion turns to the issue of source preservation and the nature of evidence in its institutional, organizational context. This discussion focuses on archives, with awareness of parallel roles of galleries, museums, and other institutional forms, which can be in the same organization or operate separately. Each is identified primarily with a kind of media, but this discussion concentrates on numerate and textual sources, with some attention to visual and less to audio media. Given the focus on history and computing, attention here is primarily on recent developments in data and electronic archives that affect current and future historical research.

HISTORY-ARCHIVES RELATIONS

Providers and Users: Rising Mutual Expectations

The traditional triad or hierarchical levels from primary to tertiary and beyond are a conceptualization indigenous to History and Law that has spread also to librarianship, archival administration, and museology. Although some critics like G. WISE and S. GRIGG suggest that this approach should be discarded, it remains useful in reference work and for source appraisal (MCCRANK, 1994a). The primacy of a source lies first in its origins most proximate in time and place to the action recorded, even to the point of simultaneity, and second in its preservation in original form or surrogate that has a chain of custody and therefore an accountability that makes the allowance of substitution possible. Secondary sources are based on primary, and so forth, like an ancestry or chain of being documented in a critical apparatus that creates a genealogy for the information passed along and used. Reliable information has a pedigree.

This generational concept was never adopted by Information Science, however, where usage suggests that research literature, which would be considered secondary in History, is "primary" as if there were no first-hand evidence or original data to consider. This secondary literature is saved, but seldom are the original data preserved. Consequently few studies depend on new analysis of old data; nor are many really incremental, as if benchmarked over time using older data sets augmented by the new for trend analysis. Instead, most Information Science studies are snapshots, one at a time, in no special order. Historical preambles to Information Science research, apart from mere flashbacks, are literature reviews—not reviews of historical data. Although some large data sets exist for continuous research such as the pilot digital libraries, no Information Science data archives exists. Indeed, the data on which most Information Science research rests might not meet the tests of intrinsic or enduring value in archives appraisal, and most records managers would be prone to schedule such data for short-term retention only. The modern difference in usage about what constitutes a primary source or something worthy of archival deposition indicates the ahistorical thinking in Information Science. The cognitive rift between the two fields lies in the distinction between information and evidence. The commonplace reference to the first publication of research as primary in Information Science reveals a discontinuity in the intellectual development of the field and a rift with Library Science and Bibliography in particular, and a continuing problem in formulating historical perspective based on an accumulative record as distinct from a continuing and expanding literature. It also explains why Information Science is developing so few archives for multilevel, time-spanning longitudinal research, and instead misconstrues archives with the manuscript tradition of documenting a history of the profession.

Historians, on the other hand, pay verbal homage to reliance on primary sources and value original research in archives, which is commonly misconstrued to mean unpublished sources in the same casual way that historians seldom discern the real differences between literature searching and research per se. This focus on original sources is no defense of historians, however, since their citations to primary sources in proportion to secondary literature seems unrelated to purported scientific historicism based only on evidence. The secondary literature of History is also used authoritatively and similarly to primary literature in Information Science. Citations in the literature of History to primary sources in history are always fewer than to the field's secondary sources. Historians seldom cite tertiary sources as authoritative, even though these are the most synthesized and supposedly mature of these literature types, but tertiary sources synthesize the secondary literature and do not necessarily go back to primary or original sources. Like information scientists, historians tend to be self-citing or they cite references from a collegial pool, and seldom reexamine data and evidence thought to have been thoroughly exploited by the references they cite. Little actual verification occurs. Moreover, historians' use of archives and manuscript repositories in the United States now constitutes a minor fraction of total use (A. GORDON). Genealogists rank first.

Information scientists do not even constitute a recognizable constituency of archives—manuscript repositories, official archives, or electronic records. And the data sets generated in their research are seldom deposited in archives; therefore, no reverification work is possible even though a cardinal assumption in a science is repeatability of experimentation, simulation, and data analysis which makes results credible. Historical sources may be consulted repeatedly, and even if interpretation varies, a research tradition evolved that integrated primary and secondary sources in a constant revisiting of the past and continued mulching of old data considered with the new. The lack of "revisitability" in most Information Science research would be seen from a History perspective as a flaw, and the acceptance of previous research as authoritative without being able to verify it by consulting the same sources and reproducing the analysis would seem to be negligent. Such regard is the opposite of Information Science wondering about the relevance of historical data, except for the immediate past. This is where Information Science as practiced parts company with Historical Science. The conceptual chasm is one between information and evidence; the missing component in the former field is the archival. Historical Information Science should remedy this and integrate notions of evidence from Archival Science into Information Science.

The old regard of archivists for historians as the main users of archives has been one reason why archives have so poorly studied their constituencies or marketed their services to new ones. Repeatedly publications harken to an idyllic relationship between archivists and historians, sometimes in a paternalism that today seems antiquated, and at other times seemingly pure propaganda and mythology rather than good history. The disposition of RUNDELL, BRUBAKER, RUSSELL, BOLOTENKO, and others has been to celebrate common cause and encourage good relations. The repetition itself may indicate that the ideal is not actuality. Indeed, the two, archivists and historians, have had a shaky relationship for some time, and this has been exacerbated by the lure of modern Information Science and divisive influences resulting from trends in information technology. On the other hand, archives are often neglected by American information scientists because of the aforementioned difference in viewpoint and central concerns, and Information Science in the United States has produced little research in Archival Science. The kind of integration common in the European perspective, as represented by CURRAS (1988) in Spain, for example, is atypical of American Information Science approaches.

On the other hand, when historians study archives, they do so mainly as institutional histories or in reference to the relation of their holdings to their own research projects. Usually they think more in terms of the manuscripts' tradition than records management, and knowledge of archives operations is often lacking because it is not seen as immediately relevant to their information needs. They are not well represented in survey studies of archives user satisfaction unless they are a specifically targeted user group, but they often have disproportionate influence through appointments to advisory councils and through their teaching. Most historians who use archives acknowledge archivists who specifically helped them, but archival finding aids, descriptive material, etc., do not earn inclusion in most of their citation practices. Of course, citation studies have been concerned primarily with acknowledgment of people, not corporate authorship and citations of institutions or archives. Occasionally, sometimes vociferously, historians attack archives as unserviceable but most criticism is based on personal experience rather than empirical study. The "goodness" of an archives (in the same sense as BUCKLAND, 1991, considered library service) often rests on personal satisfaction, as in the case of customer satisfaction in consumerism rather than collegial professionalism, and seldom on overall objective assessment. An example is the recent diatribe by S. COMBE against French archivists who are accused of being agents of the state inhibiting research as much as promoting it. One would never know that she is talking about the same Archives Nationales described by FAVIER, the general director of the French archives, or the benign and service-oriented ASSOCIATION DES ARCHIVISTES FRANÇAIS. Her hypercritical review may have legitimate points, and presumably recounts some bitter experiences, but such vilification impedes its usefulness and defeats her own purpose, since only if tempered would her book be acceptable enough to French archivists that they might learn from it. This case is extreme, but others can be cited from conferences in American and in Europe.

At the 1996 IAHC conference in Moscow, as further examples, English archivists were condemned by socioeconomic quantitative historians as incompetent for their experimentation with sampling as a means of appraisal and for instituting sampling in records retention schedules; late twentieth-century German archivists were accused by German computing historians of being trapped in a nineteenth-century mentality; and digitization of historical documents was lauded by all, but partly justified as a technology to escape the mediation of archivists whose reference expertise, so it was generalized, was better suited for novices than experts. Overgeneralization often causes ill feelings, as when ostensibly to justify the full-text conversion of the Ben Gurion archives (100,000 pages of Ben Gurion's papers and Zionist records) FRILING castigated archives everywhere as woefully inadequate in their provision for information retrieval. According to him, archival information retrieval is largely a matter of perception and was usually highly subjective "depending on the mood of the archivist" and the organizational culture of the archives. He contrasted the value of direct access to every word in a textbase and its clarity, whereas in most archives researchers had not only to contend with archivists and their "obstruction to access," but also with description that was too general, misleading code words, and retrieval that was too vertical (linear or serial, as when working a records series) without adequate means to cut across record groups and series (horizontal collation). Hence, he predicted that digitization of archives would eventually make archival organization obsolete (it was unclear if he was speaking of archives as organizations, or organization meaning arrangement of archival records). His optimism for information retrieval based on term matching alone is misplaced and he is largely uninformed from Information Science, but worse, to make a positive case for the role of this new technology in archives he somehow felt obligated to go on the offensive.

In the United States national archivists stand accused of plotting against historical interests in their tardiness to declassify documents, and recently the AHA has confronted the NHPRC over the revision of its funding priorities in favoring electronic archives work over documentary editing projects. NHPRC funds have always been limited, but it has finally established proper archival priorities. The historians' arguments smack of "biting the hand the feeds you" because of the potential past tense: once having fed such projects, the "gravy train" (never really all that nourishing) might end. The problem is vexing, because continued progress of several award winning documentary editing projects is at stake. It is questionable whether subsidized documentary publishing should have been an NHPRC priority ever, given the poverty of government and institutional support of archives everywhere and NEH's involvement in resource publishing. In any case, the debate is reviving dissonance between archivists and historians. Professional divergence becomes periodically sensitized by such policy differences. At the same time, however, the AHA, OAH, and SAA have joined NARA in its legal action against the Internal Revenue Service (IRS), an adversary of stature enough to warrant common action. The IRS, the plaintives charge, is thwarting the mission and legal right of the United States National Archives to appraise agency records. Nevertheless, this alliance often seems fragile. In another instance, M. R. HILL in the Sage Qualitative Research Methods series maligned archivists by accusing them of an addiction to control, even to the point of lying about being unable to find certain documentation. He provides no proof for such defamation of a profession's character, not even verifiable anecdotal support. He advises young sociologists to "keep their cool" if they want to receive assistance from archivists "however incompetent and slow that help may be" (M. R. HILL, p. 51). Constructive criticism is usually welcome; the exposé is often distrusted; and destructive and impugnable forays always provoke reaction and opposition.

The reverse scenario can be provided, of course, when archivists are equally disparaging of historians and other researchers; they complain of their poor preparation before coming to an archives, their false expectations, their unrealistic demands for service, and even their *prima donna* behaviors. The more objective studies of and commentaries about user behavior indicate there is something to this (T. H. PETERSON, 1992), whereas the aforementioned railing against archivists seems to have little empirical foundation. Personal experience and personalized reaction must be seen for what they are. On the other hand, it is widely known that archivists trained by historians were provided with little practical experience in reference services. It would be interesting to have enough data to discern correlations between dissatisfied customers and negative user experiences with basic use skills levels of disgruntled patrons and with the kind of training received by the archivists of whom they are so critical. That shortfall in the training of archivists is changing (PUGH's SAA *Manual*, 1992; MALBIN reviews the literature on archival reference, which is not plentiful as noted by COX, 1992; TIBBO, 1995 carries the question into the electronic arena). One might hope that such mutual recrimination reflects poor experiences which are not the norm, but in these cases, it seems, improvement in relations is in order. As one of the most striking of recent examples, COMBE's treatise points out the longstanding love-hate relationship between archivists and historians. In the classroom, the historian is usually teacher and archivist student; in the archives, roles are reversed, to the discomfort of some historians who usually decry the possible negative results of intermediation, but cry as loudly when help is not provided. The confusion and reversals of roles requires a certain tact and diplomacy: who as provider is master or servant, and who as user and the recipient of service and documentation acts as either commander or supplicant? Whichever, each increasingly expects more of the other.

Far more objective studies than hearsay, offhand pejorative remarks, and individual experience, are needed regarding actual use, expectations, and plans for future developments. These are becoming more prevalent, partially because of calls to reform or to reinvent archives (BEARMAN & HEDSTROM; COX, 1995) as part of a general reinvention of government promoted by OSBORNE & GAEBLER. P. CONWAY (1986a & b), who first adopted library use study methodology to archives, identified multiple user groups for the National Archives, with appropriate discussions about how intellectual access to archival material may be improved (CONWAY, 1995). As a complement to the studies of NARA's use by A. GORDON and CONWAY, see MOLINE & OTTO who were the first to study remote users to determine current interest and future potential in electronic access to NARA's holdings, partially to justify the National Archives move toward offering more electronic services. Not only were Paul Conway's explorations welcomed since they showed that professional historians share the same problems of intellectual access with other users, but his work represents the kind of user study sadly lacking in archives. The exception seems to be academe where several user studies have been conducted (DOWLER; MAHER, 1986, 1992, etc.); YAKEL and BOST specifically addressed administrative use of academic archives. Like museums, archives track visitors by headcounts for the purpose of justifying budgets, monitoring staff needs, and planning for space utilization, but few institutions study their users systematically and continually either as a means to enhance services, diagnose information access problems, or contribute to the literature of use studies for overall assessment of the field. Finally, use studies that have been completed seem not to employ multivariate analysis techniques and discriminate adequately between types of users and uses; often historians as a group are simply folded into an overgeneralized population of academics to be distinguished not from each other, but from the general public.

Such a critical view by archivists of historians as users is reflected as well in their regard for historians as somewhat irrelevant teachers of archivists, especially when historians regard them as simply practitioners of applied history. This debate is actually centuries old, dating at least from the post-French Revolution when bureaucratic archivists sought to distance themselves and their principles from thematic and interpretative French history (POSNER, 1940; LOKKE). Their articulation of *provenance* and *respect du fonds* (BARTLETT, 1991) and their search for physical context in records rather than historical interpretation may be interpreted as an effort to free themselves from prevailing historical opinion, especially as vacillating as it was in the wake of political and ideological revolution and rampant revisionism. In many ways the position of archivists in the early nineteenth century paved the way for von Rankian reliance on historical records, archival research, revival of source criticism, and methodology associated with scientific historicism. This is why consideration of Historical Information Science must include Archival Science, not as a subset of History or mere auxiliary science, but as an ally and peer (as advocated by DELMAS, 1993).

A history of separatism but continued association, sometimes distant and polite and at others more amicable and collaborative, is usually traced to the French Revolution which was a disjuncture of the previous fusion between historian/archivist/curator and all-around public servant and savant. Sir Hilary Jenkinson came to express this polite anti-History sentiment among archivists by stating that the first duty of archivists is to the archives, not History, which he relegated to personal interest (JENKINSON). He was not so pronounced in his antihistorian persuasion as his countryman archivist, Felix Hull, who flatly stated later "The Archivist Should Not Be an Historian" (F. HULL). It was in this vein that Theodore Schellenberg, the dogmatist of American archivy, thought that archival and library science were more allied than history and archives from the practical viewpoint, largely because of parallels between library classification and arrangement and description which, although distinct approaches, were both nevertheless focused on the organization of knowledge rather than its interpretation (SCHELLENBERG, 1956, 1965). It was Margaret Cross Norton, however, who delivered the cruelest blow of all, when she argued for efficiency as any American administrator would, and placed archives into records management. NORTON juxtaposed archives and history by calling for the former to be scientific, at least as a form of Administration Science, whereas History was... well, history. She did not see History in league with the Social Sciences, since that strain was under vigorous attack and was retreating from its earlier position as the dominant form of New History. She would have understood, I suspect, the inclusion of both archives and organizational management as integral components of a new Historical Information Science.

The 1992 inquiry (GORDON) of the National Historical Publication and Records Commission (NHPRC) reflects this general disassociation of History and the archives professions that dates from the era of the great methodological debates of the late 1960s about Cliometrics and impact of computer technology, coterminous with the growing influence in the 1970s of Information Science. Coincidentally this professional separatism occurred when historians were hardly looking, so consumed were they with their great debates over quantification, appropriate methodology, and interpretation of American socioeconomic and political history; moreover, it occurred just after the first wave of information technology hit archives and they began to consider automation. Archives-History relations described incorrectly as always amicable by BRUBAKER have been strained periodically by conflict between historians' need to preserve and have access to historical records and archival custodial policies and administrative operations, but there has been a disaffection from History as the archival profession matured much like adolescence breeds independence from parents who are unfairly characterized as uncaring, indifferent, and unwise. Adulthood makes rapprochement easier. A benchmark exists since 1977 when the Society of American Archivists first dictated to History

Departments basic guidelines for graduate programs in archival administration other than for simple appreciation and use of archives. History still looks paternally down upon an archival career as a auxiliary occupation and Public History regards archives as its turf (HOWE, 41-51), but archivists see themselves increasingly as constituting a distinct information professional, although they retain an historicism in their work. The debate continues: the challenge of HULL provoked a counter thesis by BOLOTENKO who attempted to use history to defend History as the symbiotic ally if not the guardian of archivy, an attempt at moderation by M. RUSSELL, and an attack by COX (1984-85); a critical appraisal of historians' training of archivists by MCCRANK (1985), and continuing commentary by PEASE, GILLILAND-SWEETLAND, PETIT, etc. There is collaboration still, but also a distancing especially in professional separatism, education, and training (cf., BERNER, O'TOOLE).

After significant debate (cf., the background provided by H. G. JONES and SCHELLEN-BERG; continued by TAYLOR, 1977; WELCH; MCCRANK, 1979, 1985; T. COOK; COX, 1985-86, 1986; EASTWOOD, 1988, etc.) archivists' professional identity is now more aligned with the information profession rather than History (PEACE & FISCHER; GOGGIN), partially because of the latter's' fixation on college History teaching and neglect of historians going into the information profession, and also because of a polarizing influence from Information Science. A 1971 survey revealed that 51 percent of archivists in the United States had graduate degrees in History but only 12 percent in Library Science, but the 1989 SAA survey showed that over 36 percent now have MLS degrees and a greater mix of subject master's degrees; by 1992 18 percent of American archivists had doctorates. The practical nature of archives is indicated most recently, unfortunately, by the recent SAA salary survey (1996) showing that the most commonly sought academic background for employing archivists consists merely of three relevant courses; a Master's degree is required mainly for appointments in academe—often the MLS when the archivist is treated as a librarian. Short of a Ph.D., which sometimes opens doors to senior management, there is little correlation between academic degrees and salary. Experience is more important (LAWRENCE-LEITER INC.).

It was in 1977 that the Society of American Archivists (SAA) initiated its Committee on Automated Records and Technique (CART) that signaled the shift toward Information Science and technology in the 1980s (T. BROWN, 1993). While MCCRANK (1979, 1985) then saw Archival Science as a hybrid between History and Library/Information Science, such a view (still echoed here) has come under attack because of self-actualization pressures within the Society of American Archivists and a general movement toward greater professionalization by archivists everywhere. In any case, an opportunity was lost even when the University of Maryland's pioneer double Masters degree programs were initiated, because there was no strong link forged between Information Science and Social Science History as MCCRANK (1979) initially recommended and STIELOW later reiterated. This could have created a Historical Information Science much earlier in the United States. The HILS program at UMCP, for example, still has not accomplished this nexus (inexplicably each partner has continued to offer its own version of introductory graduate archives courses, and research generated seems this or that rather than a blend of History and one or more of the Information Sciences). Indeed, the historical and source criticism components of the Information side of this program have been weakened, and under the direction of the new HILS coordinator, Bruce DEARSTYNE, who sought advice for the program's reform from a variety of sources, the focus will be almost exclusively archival and records management connected with the nearby presence of the National Archives II complex, rather than the fuller array of Information Resource Management (IRM). While historical computing and diplomatics have been added to the History side by the addition of new faculty (BEDOS-REZAK), these are faculty interests rather than programmatic strengths, and their integration into the HILS program has been marginal. Both sides have major international strengths, but the archival focus has been almost exclusively American. The ideal envisioned has not been realized there—or elsewhere.

WALTERS suggests that the connection of Archival Science with History be made through Public History which, as a practical field, has often included archives and museums together in its purview. The technical component of Public History programs has been weak, however, and their dominant orientation is toward material culture studies, not documentary evidence. Moreover, these programs have not yet supported an information science component in their curricula, even though there are strong movements in quantification studies and modern information technology, especially image bases, in both cultural anthropology and archeology. The nexus between quantification in History, the initial engagement of electronic archives by archivists trained as social science historians, the innovative use of image bases in Anthropology and Archeology and their impact in other disciplines, and the current trend toward machine-readable records, which will dominate federal government output by the turn of the millennium, seems to be a proliferation of issues and a divergence of undertakings that simultaneously signal common interests and points for possible convergence. The current milieu appears somewhat chaotic, and this makes it difficult to see all of the possible connections and or to produce a convergence and synthesis from which to extract an application in educational reform. This cross-fertilization and richness problem exists in Europe as well where the tendency is to form yet another specialization rather than inter-disciplinary studies programs. It is difficult to pay attention to detail and see the whole picture at the same time.

Archivists have increasingly stressed for their own professionalism (GOGGIN; O'TOOLE) the need for a coherent Archival Science discipline (as argued by T. EASTWOOD and others), replete with separate identity. It is thought that this can be accomplished by improved education and credentialing, i.e., archivist certification (1987 plan; the Academy of Certified Archivists was begun in 1989). A movement, strongest in Canada, has established a Masters of Archival Science programs (initially at the University of British Columbia) distinct from Library Science or History degrees. In their quest for legitimate professional status and recognition, archivists do not want their field to continue as a "stepchild" of either History or Library Science. Current debate about archivist training and proposed curricular reform (O'TOOLE; BOLES, 1990; etc.) still fails to embrace a comprehensive approach to Historical Information Science as described by its advocates, and the most recent effort at rapprochement between History and Archives about educating archivists (BRIDGES *ET AL.*) and historians together by the Joint Committee On Historians and Archivists of AHA, OAH, and SAA (HAM, *ET AL.*) also misses the mark if for no other reason than its being too limited by the dominant "archival perspective" that is historical in ethos and aligned with the manuscripts tradition of archives development, and its input from History does not reflect the field's most technically advanced pursuits. The AHA/OAH/SAA Joint Committee rather casually dismisses the integration of "information science principles and techniques" as "beyond the scope of this study group" (HAM *ET AL.*, p. 728) as if Information Science had so little in common with History and Archives. American archivists are failing to make sense of the tremendous reform in Library and Information Science education in the last five years under the impact of new information technology, or to embrace a global vision to compare United States developments with those elsewhere (as described, for example, by MCGARY; A. MORRIS; WHITBECK; or cf., MAC-DOUGAL & BRITTAIN for the United Kingdom where so much Information Science education is at the undergraduate level). Moreover, there seems to be no unified vision in the United States about the potential of historical research using machine-readable sources except those accessioned into archives (e.g., artificially created and enhanced databases by and for historical research, retrospective conversions to electronic forms, linked data-text-image bases, etc.) as has evolved in Western and Eastern Europe.

Both SAA and the National Association of Government Archivists and Records Administrators (NAGARA) have reoriented themselves toward Information Science in their research agenda, although their annual conferences retain a broader scope. The practical orientation of previous discussion is being placed against a more theoretical background, and some but not enough crossover in treating archival concerns is evident in ASIS as well. The intensive dialogue begun at the University of Maryland a decade ago (MCCRANK, 1982; STIELOW, 1993) and continued at the University of Pittsburgh (COX *ET AL.*, 1994) is spreading and is being placed in a context larger than that traditionally exploited by archivists.

There is not, however, adequate integration of these concerns into mainstream History conferencing. During the 1980s a series of forums rehearsing intercourse between historians, archivists, and information scientists were placed into the programs of AHA, OAH, SAA, and ASIS, and panels played to full houses. Indicative of such collaboration was the coordination by ABH and AHC with AHA sponsorship, in order to penetrate the conservative historical bastion of the COMITE INTERNATIONAL DES SCIENCES HISTORIQUES (1990) with a Historical Information Science full-day "Informatique et Histoire" track in its 1990 Madrid congress (CISH, 1990, pp. 667-670). This attracted a standing-room only crowd of more than 200 Information Science-oriented historians and archivists and was actually adopted by CISH's International Committee for Bibliography as its official program. Previously CISH included only one panel on historical computing in its Stuttgart (1985) program, but at Montreal in 1995 the CISH conference could have featured an array of such sessions if only because AHC timed its international conference to coincide with the former's eighteenth congress. CISH 1995 was to have a decidedly Social Science History focus: "Family, Demography, and Social Reproduction," but apparently not any special focus on new methodology or information technology. Another attempt to integrate IS/IT issues into History; that is, into a Historical Information Science, is being made for CISH 2000 in Oslo, Norway. IAHC has petitioned CISH to become an affiliate society, which would presumably help insert such sessions in future international History conferences.

These are signs of changing times, growing awareness, genuine interest, but also conservatism, reaction, and resistance in traditional disciplines and at the core of their research, to information technology for its own sake. And IS/IT issues must compete by themselves, or under different rubrics, with so many other interests. The AHA, for example, turned down a proposal from AHC for joint sessions at the AHA 1994 conference (1993a, p. 258) on grounds that so many other proposals were judged more pertinent than the challenge to future History presented by the conversion to electronic recordkeeping. ZWEIG (1993a, p. 252) laments: "Our colleagues are usually unwilling even to acknowledge the transformation of the archival record" perhaps because the records "currently being generated by electronic systems will not become available until the leaders of the profession have retired." Signals, therefore, still seem mixed. However, such deliberate, formal outreach beyond one's specialized association and work place is important in producing a commonwealth of information about electronic information so crucial for the nexus between History, Archival Science, and Information Science, and to break down the isolationism of parallel but largely independent developments that somehow should coincide and reinforce each other.

Archives Access: Description, Automation, and Retro-Conversion

It is access to and use of electronic records where disagreements will arise between archivists and historians, but this is also where rapprochement could lie in common research agenda and technical applications (COX, 1990, 113-163). For the time being archivists still labor under the historical paradigm of archives, but this is costing them dearly in lack of technical integration into their organizations. One negative result of this delay in moving archives information technology along coterminously with developments in their parent organizations has been certain marginalization, and therefore, improper positioning to achieve their archival mission or records preservation and access. The problem is more serious than merely one of saving posterity and historical tradition, but at stake is continuous recall from past to present, organizational memory impairment and discontinuity, often accompanied by redundancy and inefficiency, and sometimes by catastrophic failure. Archivists have now been maneuvered into reactive positions as conservation movements, often after the damage is done, rather than being able to take active role in making the future as information is first produced, acquired, and used. Most of the work hitherto has been with electronic records as surrogates of physical documentation, or with the assumption that electronic records would remain close to known physical forms, i.e. continuity in developments of such as digital images being extensions of analogues or electronic pictures descending from photographs and paintings; or in text processing being merely text produced with electrical-mechanical assistance with the same essential continuity in the transition from manuscript or scribal to print and graphic culture.

Such assumptions appear less and less well founded, at least in terms of the rate of change which is so accelerated that a greater juncture may be occurring presently in a quarter century than in the industrial age, which took a full two centuries. Yet, the work on databases, textbases, and imagebases, which are really reconversions of old sources into new forms, is important for understanding the advent of genuinely new forms and sources for contemporary history. It is through such technological change that historians, and historically trained archivists, will be exposed to new information technologies, applications, and methodologies. With recent technological breakthroughs offer an invitation to soar or "bluesky" and experiment, historians and archivists should be running to lift off, but too many must go through the traditional stages from crawling to walking as they stumble along into the next millennium. Others who avoid looking forward resist the oncoming of this electrified Brave New World altogether, not realizing that for history makers it is already here. For the past half-century the paper based approach to information generation and record keeping has been giving way to electronic processing and formats, the rate of transfer is accelerating exponentially, and now most public information on paper is generated first electronically. The very nature of primacy in source criticism has been transformed, and most historians, regardless of the era they study, now rely on primary sources in secondary and tertiary formats rather than original sources. Archives hold the key to History's future and this future seems somewhat precarious right now.

Consider how and why today WHALEY speaks of "digitizing history" in reference to Virginia Commonwealth University's Multicultural Archives, which is comprised of digital renderings of documents borrowed (rather than securing their donation) from various African-American communities and are now being stored on optical discs. Over three dozen such archival projects are underway, and more are being announced monthly. The misattribution of the term "archives" begs many questions in such cases where nothing is official, and rather than originals, the records are all facsimiles, all converted into another more mutable media, and all rely on metadata and attestation for credibility and reliability in a new form of access which requires neither acquisition or accessioning as in traditional archives operations. The transformation of archives requires similar transformation in search strategies, in framing research questions and designing projects, and in research methodology. Searching for such records and working with such surrogates often from a distance, with or without traditional documentation, calls for a hypercritical eye, judgment based on criteria which are not yet totally clear, and a kind of trust and reliance on new forms of mediation not encountered before, at least to such an extent. "Virtual archives" require an unheard of virtuosity! The trend from direct examination of documents in original form to reliance on mutable electronic surrogates so that they can be manipulated in different ways for new kinds of analyses, constitutes not only a paradigm shift but also a transformation of research itself requiring the rethinking of criteria for evidence and proof, new forms of accountability in research, and new measures to deal with the dual ambiguities of language and interpretation and of documentation and reliability. Here the perplexing issue of electronic records shall be addressed first, and later the equally complicated and related issue of interpretation will be considered.

In such discussion, however, it is important to distinguish two kinds of electronic records relating to archives. Archival descriptive records in automated systems consist of tagged or coded descriptions which in North America are increasingly in Machine-readable Cataloging (MARC) Archives and Manuscripts Control (AMC) format for information exchange between autonomous archives and those in libraries about their holdings (over 100 archives in the United States have entered more than 250,000 AMC records into RLIN; see M. ROPER for a European perspective). Today the USMARC AMC is part of the Mixed Materials in the USMARC Integrated Format. These MARC-AMC records sometimes refer to text files of inventories, registers, and specialized indexes on local systems. Uncoded, nonexchangeable descriptions and a variety of inventories and registers exist, and they are far more numerous than MARC-formatted descriptions. Even when in electronic form, most of these appear much the same as when produced as typescripts. They are simply word-processed and may be placed on listservs for full-text retrieval, but they are not coded for retrieval of format or of conceptual elements, and they are not standardized. Although there is a general uniformity of practice that yields descriptions that appear somewhat alike, consistency, congruence, syntax, and levels of vocabulary sophistication vary according to region, institution, and the personal abilities of processing archivists. They display all of the challenges for automated information retrieval as any form of documentation generated by offices across America.

The variation in archival description is as varied as the characters of the 8,000 or more United States archives and manuscript libraries reporting to the NHPRC directory of archives and manuscript collections. The new *Directory of Archives and Manuscript Repositories in the US* (DAMRUS, compiled in 1988 and revised in 1995-96) lists 4,400 repositories. The *National Union Catalog of Manuscript Collections (NUCMC)* in the United States, begun in 1959 by the LIBRARY OF CONGRESS (1989/1997), now holds standardized collection-level descriptions of nearly 75,000 collections, which are now accessible electronically via *Archives USA,* which consists of the *NUCMC, National Inventory of Documentary Sources in the United States (NIDS)* or 52,000 finding aids for 42,000 collections in 300 repositories, via *DAMRUS* and its subject, corporate and personal name indexes (CHADWYCK-HEALEY, INC.). In 1997 the Library of Congress Manuscripts Division added its 10,000 records to *NUCMC.* Altogether these sources provide basic access to 100,000 manuscript collections in the United States.

This diversity is being challenged by movements for greater standardization, both of content and representation in archival description, and in communication formats for the exchange of descriptive data. HTML coding for display on Web site homepages has been a major motivator in bringing about conformity in syntax and structure in archival description, and other influences are working on content as well. Since it may never be possible to convert manual and text-processed finding aids into electronic forms that are normalized enough to search easily across systems, remote access to archival information remains at the collection level in most cases, and access at the item level is rare. Archival information retrieval remains more problematic than library searching of reasonably standardized item-level bibliographic information in most public access catalogs. Standardization for such archival description has progressed, but not to the same level as bibliographic description which in the case of serial records can be supplemented with electronic tables of contents, extensive indexing, and in some cases with scanned book indexes as well. Little evidence exists on the basis of demand, quality, or utility of electronic records over existing alternatives to justify the extraordinary costs associated with retrospective archives records conversion, especially if this were also to include editing and normalization to enhance information retrieval. Records conversion in most cases involves a data transfer from a dependent software to independent alternative or when a software is upgraded, but does alter the underlying bit stream.

The ideal is, however, to preserve structure and context in addition to the content. Most arguments for a monumental conversion effort are based on projected increased use because of convenience in remote searching via the Internet. In short, these projects are often motivated by the goal of greater immediate access, but not necessarily by a goal of long-term preservation for access through time. Moreover, electronic conversion does not automatically insure improved quality in information retrieval, just greater opportunity for more access. The archival problem is more akin to that confronting information users on the Internet where too often retrieval is dependent only on the most cursory of indexes and on term matching. Thus subject, corporate and personal name indexes to collection-level templates, remains the norm despite a generation of working on this problem of better access to records through greater specificity. This is why many researchers now want to bypass traditional archival description altogether and turn to automated retrieval by term matching in retroconverted full-text archives. However, the portion of electronically retrievable full-text records, distinct from digitized images of records which must still be retrieved through headings and indexing, to the total volume accessioned and acquired, is still relatively small.

A byproduct of the lack of precoordinated indexing and standardization in metadata records or access by record forms, is to shift the work from records creators to information searchers and the creation of a situation where even repeatable searches along strings of slightly altered search keys to create a drag-net, often results in incomplete searches even in the same files. Most archival information systems retrieve by searching nominal data item by item, sometimes creating sets but seldom do they have mechanisms for more than the most simplistic pattern matching. Some, with the aid of indexing and thesauri, do more than find like terms but progress toward subject and concept information retrieval. Given the nature of archives, where records by provenance come with their own vocabularies and where standardization across archives seems impossible and may not be desirable, different approaches to thesauri may be fruitful: RADECKI's older notion of a fuzzy thesaurus to relate sets of terms; automatic thesaurus generation from large corpora to produce what CROUCH called "global thesauri" cutting across domains; and CHAPLAN has explored mapping one thesaurus into another (i.e., vocabulary switching) as MCCRANK (1983) did a decade before with LSCH and Catholic and Jewish subject headings. All of these, even the most simple term-matching software that might assist the vocabulary problem in archives information retrieval systems, would be aided by standards in description, both record formats or structure, and content (i.e., preselected and coordinated vocabulary, and prescribed syntax in description, so that the originals are left as accessioned) for more precise recall and an improved satisfaction based on relevancy, when searching and browsing through large, poorly formed sets and disparate text corpora as commonly held in archives.

Secondly, the primary material to which these information systems refer may be in multiple forms ranging from artifacts to manuscripts and machine-readable records. The latter are both those created electronically in the first place and those maintained that way, but they can also be retrieved in paper printout. Conversely, paper records may be retrospectively converted into electronic form through word processing, scanning and optical character recognition, and voice input (NPL and voice processing technologies are reviewed by MILLER & WALKER, 1990). In both cases, one form of the record is a surrogate, a copy, rather than an original source, but both surrogate and original may be primary in the same sense that an edition is considered primary but not original (LEVITT & LABARRE). Just as documentary editions seem to replace recourse to the originals, electronic editions may supersede printed editions as in the case of the replacement of the *Washington Papers*, now a 28-volume set in the Presidents of the United States series, with a CD-ROM edition. Such migrations from original to primary source printed publication and then conversion to electronic text will undoubtedly be more direct from original and electronic primary source, but the problem of authentification and critical reliance on editions remains in either case.

The challenges of maintaining record structures across conversions, transporting context with data for interpretation, and the fragmentation of records and series all remain. The edited documentation of the Civil War, for example, included letters from famous generals in secretarial hands, considerably edited and cleaned up before they ever made it into print edition; without recourse to the autographed letters, many American historians have been fooled by the generals' secretaries and their unsuspecting editors that the documentary series actually reproduced what the correspondents wrote. Such problems in authentification and verification are not overcome simply because one has a text in electronic form. Indeed, the form is even more flexible than before, and capable of modification even when written on read-only media if they can be electronically copied, or even when only print copies can be made from them. The clean print copy can be scanned and easily transported to a read-write medium. Of course scholarly editing can be exacting, when in accord with analytical bibliographic standards (e.g., the British school embodied in the work of Fredson Bowers, and codified for literary scholars by TANSELLE), but historical documentary editing has not evolved to this level, and neither seems prepared to deal with such issues in a digital environment.

A. CUNNINGHAM and R. LANHAM's philosophical explorations of electronic text have shown that, even if one is more concerned with manuscripts than electronic records, the impact of modern information technology is still important.The trend toward electronic communication is constantly eroding the manuscript base of the overall historical record, as one moves from letter to telephone, and now to e-mail and to personal homepages. Personal papers are becoming increasing impersonal (HYRY & ONUF). The range of the communication circle is forever broadening so that locally produced "manuscripts" are less and less local in content and reference. They are increasingly amorphous in context and the media are increasingly impersonal. Conventions borrowed from the software rather than historical context tend to render electronic texts similar. The new media are savable if salvageable. However, such efforts require conscious intervention in creating an historical record at the onset rather than as a byproduct of everyday communications. Families, unlike organizations and institutions, do not naturally maintain information systems in the same way that they used to save momentos, scrapbooks, and letters. ONUF recently reminded archivists that little "legacy" data survive naturally.

Self-consciousness in this process of historical preservation and premeditated formation of archives changes the essential nature of the electronic equivalent of manuscripts. In formal communication such as literary production, constant overwriting proved to be a problem when only end-views survived, but saved drafts add significantly to the literary record. Saved changes are also collectable in manuscript, typescript, and printout forms if forethought exists. This implies a self-consciousness of history in the making, or making history, which is itself fodder for intellectual debate in the future. But this also means that manuscript curators and collectors must identify "collectable authors" early in the latter's careers, and this intervention, rather than the traditional postmortem collecting means a move toward fieldwork, donor relations with the creators rather than heirs, and an interactivity that changes forever the traditional roles of donor and patron in the way that a collector (individual or an institution) helps make a collectable author's reputation. Authors who achieve early recognition preempt those whose careers develop later in life, and business and social relationships between active collectors and living donors are often very complicated. Information technology, therefore, is forcing dramatic changes in collecting because the whole record, what is collectable, is no longer preserved as a natural byproduct of the creative process. Collecting by design is necessary, and this entails a certain engineering of history that has always existed to some degree, but never to the extent that this imperative exists today.

The aforementioned program priority setting by the NHPRC, in downplaying traditional documentary editing work or at least the subsidies for the publication of edited documents in traditional monographic formats, aggravates the current scene and highlights this issue of the fragility of current electronic documentation. The debate unfortunately seems to have split over this or that when a whole array of options exist: standards for the conversion of records to digital archives are evolving slowly; little thought is being given to techniques and standards for electronic text editing using modern visualization technology; and the creation of access tools other than simply coding old formats into HTML for Web retrieval begs for serious research (which is ongoing, as reported in LOGAN & POLLARD; HTML is a simple convention, criticized as "simplistic" because of its limitations in dividing text to appropriate levels [FLYNN, p. 617], but this is being addressed in current EAD projects). Thus far, as already mentioned, those working on document architecture standards have not taken text dissection down to the level of analytical bibliography or codicology to determine editions and states of document evolution. Such specialization will no doubt come in time, for these very specialized applications and relatively rare needs. I suspect that, with such new apparati, a scholarly criticism, which treats electronic text at various levels of detail will evolve, and it will be coupled with a forensic component of Information Technology for the evaluation of the integrity, authority, and reliability of electronic texts. Or will such concerns fall to the wayside as trivial, purely academic, and the worries only of a few experts whose critical work will never appeal to the masses? I hope not.

One can imagine a normal progression of technique and technology in analytical bibliography, from the first applications of optics to textual studies with the Hinman collator, the Vinton Collating machine, and Rothman's Houston Editing Desk and Editing Frame, to scanning and automated comparative work in Windows collating multiple texts simultaneously and using such methods as check-sum tests to verify exact duplication in electronic transmission of texts and images. Digital enlargement in many ways seems but an extension of the use of photographic blowups, and electronic fingerprinting for identification and security is not altogether different from the similar manual practices in rare book repositories (MCCRANK, 1979; R. HARMON, pp. 80-91). What is less understood, but which must be confronted squarely, is that sources artificially retroconverted into electronic form are no longer original sources in many cases, but are resources that are pliable copies. Transcript publication should be supplemented, therefore, with digitized reproduction of originals, and search techniques that locate information in parallel texts, original reproductions and annotated, edited documents. Even in the case of variants, hyperlinks can create new critical apparati that collate digitized excerpts of variant texts with the master edition. Or, as BELOVA & LAZAREV show, hypertext works well for controlling metadata and thereby managing electronic text collections. GOLOVANOV *ET AL.* likewise use hypertext for inventories of historical documents. In such applications a great attraction is the linkage of bibliographic controls with standards for critical bibliographic work, both cataloging and indexing—especially the design of syndetic systems.

The problems of the proverbial reinvention of the wheel, because of intra-disciplinary perspective and lack of continuity and congruence between manual and computer controlled systems, are endemic, because too many researchers have little training as database designers or in metadata operations. Technicians trained in the latter areas often have no experience in interdisciplinary information processing and control. Thus far, most CD-ROM documentary editing has simply entailed an electronic conversion of the former printed edition, so that modern information technology is used only for dissemination but not for the creation of a genuinely new scholarly tool. LIND discusses evolving standards for source editions, referring to what he believes are "text models," but too often the requirements discussed pertain to user friendliness of systems, graphic user interfaces, accessibility, etc., rather than appraisal, critical apparati, and practice of Diplomatics. COX reminds documentary editors that they are really publishing archives, to encourage them to rethink current practices in editing manuscripts. A reorientation from the system's to scholar's needs is what underlies "source-oriented" database design, versus conforming data in storage to the demands of models (positions which are mistakenly juxtaposed in DOORN's opinion [1997]). The real advantage of CD-ROM editions is when they have enough visual imagery and linkage to digital copies, or use sound and video clips to accompany texts, that they are multimedia and interactive. Without such enhancements, the mere transference of texts as textbases to CD-ROM and digital formats and display like electronic billboards seems not to take full advantage of the new media technology.

Likewise, in most cases, datasets deposited in data archives are not in original form. They have been edited and reformatted for easier use and for linkage with other datasets, and consequently data archives hold the electronic equivalent to edited manuscripts and fall into the manuscript library tradition rather than genuine archives. Data archives most often acquire rather than accession electronic data. All to often, as is the current case in the former Soviet Union, these are mounted as preservation efforts (BORODKIN, KOVAL'CHENKO & SOKOLOV; MOISEENKO). Methods of data handling, conversion, and description differ subtly but significantly between the two, and the change of custody often involves more than a changed context for the source, but also transformations of form, format, data structure, and completeness. These alterations and various kinds of "refreshing" should be documented as metadata for appraisal and interpretation. Various stages of data processing produce the equivalents to multiple states and editions of manuscript and printed sources. The common advocacy of reengineering data in business and industry needs to be tempered with the preservation principle of reversibility; that is, the reengineering should be done on a copy of the original data files, which when reengineered are stored as an enhancement or edition in a series. If the original file is overwritten by reengineered data, and the reengineering needs to be redone for whatever reason, one can not reverse the reengineering or scrap the faulty product and start over. If the metadata for the reengineering or reprocessing are not what they should be, without the original intact, the possibility of reconstruction or reconstitution of the enhancement at whatever stage is desirable, is remote. In the spirit of total quality management and ISO 9000 documentation standards, it is always better to be prepared for contingencies and nonconformity than to be sorry after the occurrence. File duplication and the creation of transferability and connectivity between legacy data and older systems and reengineering on new systems are prudent procedurally and cost effective as a sound principles in risk management.

Historians using such data in various stages of engineering, like those using published critical editions, should return more than they often do to original states to verify the integrity of their evidence in these altered forms. At the very least, a chain of custody and reverification of evidential values should be undertaken and documented in an historian's critical apparatus. However, data archives, as an artificial collection program and extension of the old manuscripts tradition described by BORDIN & WARNER, should not be confused with genuine electronic archives. Their procedures in data handling, refreshing, and conversion seem applicable, but as Charles Dollar rightly argues (NHPRC, 1991, p. 33), they cannot be used as a model for modern electronic records programs because the former development was driven by access rather than preservation concerns. They are created artificially after the fact rather than contemporary with records generation and as a natural byproduct of an entity's business. Such an approach is too little, too late, to achieve what the contemporary archivist must in documenting history as it is made. Historians often confuse the two parallel but distinct traditions; and in their overreliance on the former, have neglected development of the latter. Their ambivalence and late understanding of these issues is evident in the 1989 report of the National Coordinating Committee for the Promotion of History to NARA for the improvement of the United States National Archives from the perspective of "a community of users," i.e., historians.

Descriptive and provenance standards for such retrospectively converted source material have been lacking, however, and archival descriptive standards as they have evolved over the past half-decade are still lax in this regard. Moreover, description and appraisal as described by BOLES (1991) are not linked as solidly as commonly supposed with electronic archives management (BOOMS). HORSMAN is one of the few to attempt applications of knowledge engineering to archival appraisal. Indeed, old forms of appraisal and description seem incongruent with the new media being generated in electronic form originally, while they seem more appropriate for retrospectively converted data sets. HORSMAN and others working in the modern corporate world are vehement in their criticism of the gulf that has grown between academic archives with their history bent, and the so-called "real world," where history for its own sake is not a value readily identifiable. If it is, it is not a high priority. Altruistic motives often lie behind practical utility, direct application, the "need to know" basis, competitive advantage, and compliance and accountability issues. BROTHMAN (1991) proposed a hierarchy of scaled values for appraisal, which in essence quantifies or measures what is usually perceived as qualitative and is therefore mostly descriptive in archivist discussions.

Among a recent series of theoretical explorations of the relationship between appraisal, retention, and description pertaining to electronic archival records, one must start with challenges to basic notions related with appraisal which arose in the 1970s and 1980s contemporary with the mass explosion of government archives. RAPPORT, for example, delivered a fatal blow in 1981 to the notion that appraisal was a one-time verdict rather than a continuous process of re-assessment. Subsequently, one can trace the trend toward flexibility, and perhaps relativity also, in the reflective and persuasive writings of T. COOK (1984-85) when he proposed an "intellectual paradigm for archives" based on the early Knowledge-base movement (e.g., DAVIS & LENAT), and one can trace his publications in *Archivaria* over the decade to his 1992 "Mind Over Matter" classic essay on archival appraisal in the same vein, and follow innovations under his guidance at the National Archives of Canada (NAC) (see also HEDSTROM, 1989; and F. G. HAM's award winning introduction, 1992). R. BROWN similarly reexamines the practice of macro-appraisal (1995) which builds upon his earlier (1992) call for an "Archival Hermeneutics" in archival theory. HEDSTROM (1993) includes appraisal concerns throughout her discussions of description of electronic records, especially in integrating appraisal and description in archival processing. Most of this discussion in archives circles, which is prompted in part by a drive to control electronic records and which is admittedly self-citing and inbred, has yet to make much impact on communications in data archives circles among administrators in information systems management, or on History—even those sectors oriented toward the Social Sciences.

If the situation in archives appears somewhat messy (such characterization is actually charitable), it is worse in the Social Sciences, and therefore History as well, if one examines critical apparati of dissertations and publications based on artificially formed data archives and electronic archives manufactured as a natural byproduct of an organization's or institution's business. Just as problems abound in identifying precise methodologies used in research and analysis, it is often impossible to discern what sources were actually used, in what form, state or edition, or stage of data processing, and if the data pulled from a data set or electronic archives were substantially altered in the project's course. If delimited, streamlined, systematized, augmented, enhanced, and "refreshed" in any way, this is not regularly disclosed. Nor are such enhanced data sets commonly redeposited in the archives that provided the original set, so one cannot track use of originals or variant editions of files in its custody (and ordinarily archivists have not really been able to or wanted to). This is the same problem produced by carbon copies and printouts which may reflect different states than original manuscripts, and are kept in files as backups rather than primary evidence of the file's main business, except that in electronic form this problem is more difficult to detect. Research, therefore, can seldom be duplicated for verification; findings are usually modified from similar but not the same data or processing routines. Nor is meta-documentation commonly adequate for reuse of secondary data sets. Such issues need clarification, especially in strict identification of what is being described, retrieved and used, as part of archival descriptive and technical standards. Researchers themselves must confront this problem as a matter of objectivity and accountability and must fully disclose the state of the data that they use, just as those citing edited narrative materials should cite the edition and state of their sources. Simple location references are insufficient.

Computer historians are anxious to see what they still perceive would be "Historical Information Systems" in public archives and records offices, if for nothing more than to retrieve electronic information other than those already collected by data archives (e.g., BOONSTRA, 1990). Chad Gaffield called his information system a prototype of an "automated archivist" (GAFFIELD, 1988, p. 313). At the same time in the mid-1980s historians and data archivists were calling for "Intelligent Databases" that would have built into them search strategies and analytic capabilities. SUNDIN & WINCHESTER among others, wondered about the possibilities of natural language queries and expert systems so that access systems would not simply respond to precisely formulated searches but could "take hints" and react to suggestions, and offer interpretation which so long has been a taboo among many archivists in their construction of finding aids. It would reprogram itself to perform new analytic tasks requested by the research in his or her own language. Finally, an intelligent interface would actively aid in the coauthorship of papers! No such interactive archival agent exists, but a few archivists have begun to explore the use of expert and decision support systems for certain archival functions such as the appraisal of electronic records (GILLILAND-SWETLAND, 1995). Moreover, in applying such apparati to assist in electronics records management and in revised description when finding aids are converted to electronic form (e.g., SGML/ EAD projects), it seems prudent to recall the important distinction between the functions of archives and archival functions of documentation that Dutch archivists made earlier in this century

While computer-assisted appraisal may satisfy basic concerns and may help the interactive archivist, it does not always work for higher-order concerns. Appraisal based on current use does not always forecast future uses, as the past use of archival documentation has revealed time and again. Selection by tracking use, as in the case of the Internet Archives, mitigates against creating access to new materials; and conversely, newness itself often stimulates use, independently of any quality criteria or content analysis. Appraisal by use and use because of appraisal decisions are reflexive, and therefore impose self-limiting conditions. Moreover, current appraisal, whether machine-assisted or totally human, always impinges on interpretation since appraisal often determines if the historian will have anything to interpret. It would seem that all interpretation in history based on archival records must take into account appraisal criteria for retention, chain of custody, and criteria for selection as a tri-fold set in source criticism. Here archival metadata becomes crucial. Indeed, if one agrees that interpretation is a combination of source analysis with context, then appraisal and retention through time, transfer, and transmogrification or reengineering need to be taken into account. Thus O'TOOLE in 1989 challenged the notion than anything is really permanent in the original and really relevant; and more recently MCRANOR argued that even the notion of intrinsic value is actually attributed in the appraisal process. She places this value into the context or taxonomy of many values which change over time (ATTFIELD, J. O'NEILL), similarly to the thinking of SARACEVIC & KANTOR in evaluating information. The ideology of intrinsic value pertains to the notion of a source, a wellspring from which knowledge flows because of its contents as well as origins and history; whereas the spirituality and psychological aspect has to do with emanence—a feature that O'TOOLE (1993) extolled in his essay on the symbolic value of archives as artifacts. Such attributes have as much to do with organizational culture and continuing value systems than with original sources in the older objective sense or modern legal notions of evidence. Thus evaluation and appraisal may be linked to the interplay among museum culture, history and memory, historical sensibility, and organizational behavior discussed throughout this present essay.

Historians, however, are not of one mind on this issue of interpretative or subjective vs. factual and objective information retrieval or how to handle the fact that their evidence has been screened and preselected for them. Perhaps displaying historians' ambivalence between scientific historicism or Social Science History and History as part of the Humanities, or simply not being circumspective and introspective enough in primary research before interpretation, debates seem unclear about the real, core issues pertaining to functions of archives and the functions of archival records (WINCHESTER & WATELIET). Historians prefer their own reviews for secondary literature, which often delve into interpretation and historiographic debate as if to relish the subjective and interpretative, while traditionally disdaining abstracts on grounds that they may be subjective when abstracting attempts an objectivity more demanding than reviewing. Rarely are bibliographic and archival metadata ever critically reviewed by historians as forms of secondary or tertiary literature. In short, historiographic literature often reveals contradictory positions among historians, except for the general propensity to want it all—records, documentation, objective abstracts and notes, and interpretation—as well while retaining an often articulated but not well substantiated skepticism about any form of intermediation. Perhaps what is sought may be closer to the idea of information counseling inside retrieval systems, which provides more varied and complete reference service than in many archives' finding aids. Indeed, SUNDIN & WINCHESTER compare their envisioned intelligent system to an "historical archivist" like GAFFIELD's "automated archivist," except that they take the "user friendly" motif in automated systems development to the end degree; they want their "intelligent agents" not only to be archivist, programmer, and analyst, but also "co-historian and friend."

Archivists may be flattered by such compliments, or threatened if they see themselves co-opted by such integration or if they suspect as in the movement toward end-user computerized searching that historians want to rid themselves of archivists' intermediation between users and sources. This is one of the motivations mentioned most often in promoting digital archives and full-text searching. Increasingly, however, archivists like these historians see the interplay between electronic records and automated access and reference as mutually beneficial and that these processes with historical interpretation and teaching are part of the same continuum. Archival automation for access has come a long way since the University of Maryland ground-breaking conference nearly 20 years ago (MCCRANK, ed.,1981). Most of this progress occurred in an effort to dovetail MARC developments and to use or imitate library bibliographic networks: *MARCHON* (DURR, 1984) was among the earliest; *MicroMARC* came next from Michigan State University (recently adopted by the Hoover Institute and Russian Rosarkiv to exchange MARC data via RLIN for archival holdings; and *Cuadra Star*, etc., MARC-based pointers referred users from these short master records to older files of descriptions and to the archival records themselves, often in a hierarchical outline through a layered branching technique. Today more flexible multilevel, interactive, and dynamic systems are available. *GENCAT*, from Eloquent Systems, Inc., has adapted from Revelation Technologies, Inc. the idea of a toolkit separate from archival description files (the archives' archives) and the actual core of electronic archives or primary source material. It accommodates MARC ACM, RAD, and new international descriptive standards. Its latest release, version 4.0, uses hyperlinks to cross between local and network computing; hence it creates the ability for multilevel autonomy of electronic archives which recognizes the distinctiveness of an inherited source and yet allows linkage, use copies, and analysis across the larger system without compromising the integrity of the original records.

Again, it is modern information technology which is urging new combinations of processes such as information searching and research, archival appraisal and description, and online retrieval with data processing. This merging is creating an emergence of a new form of archives for the next millennium, consisting increasingly of digital records and electronic metadata (appraisal documentation, disposition tracking, use logs, and phased description, etc.; cf., LAW; NAVATHE & KERSCHBERG; VINDEN). MICHELSON & ROTHENBERG (pp. 245-246) argued for an integration of information retrieval and data processing and analysis or methods associated with historical computing, because "computing becomes an integral part of research.... Computation becomes part of the thought process itself...". The more dynamic information retrieval becomes, the more fluid the information system in moving data and merging documents into research sets, the more information searching (searching meta-data for document retrieval) and research itself (searching contents and analysis for interpre-tation) are integrated. Thus T. COOK (1993) proposed reconceptualization of the physical fonds or embodiment of information in records, as "conceptual" or "virtual fonds." Put another way, one may think of a trilogy in the knowledge production process: (1) physical information storage and retrieval through searching metadata; (2) enhancement of documentary content with contextual information and linkage to other records; and (3) the creation of artificial research sets of enhanced, restructured data which function as a knowledge base for interpre-tation, instruction, and become archives in themselves serving as the platform for the next stage of this continuing cycle (MCCRANK, 1987; H. TAYLOR, 1995).

From 1990 onward progress has been made in North American through collaboration of American and Canadian archivists in establishing standards for archival description (BUREAU OF CANADIAN ARCHIVISTS, 1985; CANADIAN ARCHIVAL ASSOCIA-TION, 1993; SOCIETY OF AMERICAN ARCHIVISTS, 1995). These standards are more amendable to electronic records than those previous descriptive practices that followed pro-cedures that were established for manuscripts a generation ago in the Library of Congress. Moreover, as these descriptions are now captured in electronic form, since most are prepared with modern word processing or may be scanned and converted to digital form, it is possible to interrelate and integrate metadata with content information in ways not previously possi-ble. HURLEY attempted to describe this new amalgam as "ambiance" which he defines as "the context of provenance." HEDSTROM (1993) explored what is essential in archival description, and following MICHELSON & ROTHENBERG, urged new conceptualization of "the possible" in blending old description with new standards and conjoining description with the records themselves through hypertext, as a means of going beyond operating with meta-data in one hand and content data in the other. HTML coding of description and metadata sources allows this retrieval of documentation and movement of data, text, image, and sound directly into contextual documents, or *vice versa*. H. MACNEIL speculated on the applica-bility of relational database management systems (RDBMS), which operate on the principle of a matrix, as a means of relating documents and provenance data (D. MAIER). She uses the metaphor of "weaving Provenancial and Documentary Relations" as if to anticipate such capabilities on the World Wide Web by using HTML. MAFTEI correctly warns against the archival use of RDBMS for the storage of archival data since the methodology is not source-oriented in that data are restructured into tables and because the matrix or tabularity itself makes such databases software dependent.

Several archives have produced Web pages allowing viewers to navigate through their find-ing aids and dive down into records in ways similar to data mining in data warehouses (a mixed metaphor common in this new IT jargon; see NEWING's glossary), or mechanisms used by data archives to pull data sets (e.g., census data) into support positions like underlying foot-notes or hypertext to support a narrative (more remains to be said about both). Indeed, when shareware DBMS applications are activated at the same time, the analysis can be performed at the moment as a kind of simulated replay to verify the procedure and support the narrative on the spot. The state archives of Oregon began experimenting with such relational retrieval of finding aids and direct access to textual documents using *MOSAIC* on the Internet (CANTRALLA), but Web technology with graphics capability increases the potential of such approaches extraordinarily. The National Archives of Canada has been exploring these added-value dimensions of Internet/Web access to both metadata and digital records, and creating hotlinks to other remote Web sites so relevant records can be imported into a researcher's workspace to produce artificial, holistic archives of the virtual kind envisioned by Terry Cook. Eventually one may add expert or a decision support system to assist with dynamic placement of hyperlinked URLs into metadata sources, which would work if archivists combined the-saurus controls and indexing strategies with HTML coding. Structured thesauri, for example, could relate general URLs for depositories and addresses to their major collections and records series through natural language pointers, and by using broader and narrower terms and precoordinated indexing and hierarchical subordination and synonymies simultaneously to create two- and three-dimensional paths for navigation. Three-dimensional navigation will be too complicated in a term-only interface, so this must be supplemented by a graphic user interface that supports good cognitive mapping for forward searching and recall for retracing, and each step must present opportunities for parallel side-stepping in the virtual space that will be the new search engine for archival information retrieval in the next millennium. The axiom in interface design these days is "Don't tell me; show me!"

The "automated archivist" foreseen by GAFFIELD need no longer be simply a vision; the prototypes for smart agents in a Web-linked Intranet environments are already tested and ready for imaginative applications. They are already in place in data warehouses across the United States and in Europe. The archives of the future are being invented in and outside the archives of today, largely outside of academe, and in organizations where historians rarely work. Historians of the future will have to use what the present provides, whatever that is (perhaps nothing more than storytelling, ritual, and vague social memory), unless they move out of academe into environments where history is lived and archives are made. This is where history belongs not to historians but to everyone as his or her own protagonist and historian; and to those who record it through time—archivists all, under this or another name.

ELECTRONIC RECORDS AND ARCHIVES

Historical Source Repositories: Confused Traditions

It is the data archives field, with its Social Science and Socioeconomic History background and continued historical mentality and application of historical method in documentation, and with increased exposure to Information Science and under pressure from the changing nature of modern records and impact of electronic communications and information technology, that should and indeed is spawning an increasingly strong information science component. Part of this is the growing recognition of a difference between data and electronic archives along older lines of historical manuscripts versus official records. This also is a recent phenomenon, dating no earlier than the late 1970s in the United States and a decade later in Europe.

American archivists have had the luxury (or handicap?) of thinking more about modern records unlike their European colleagues who must spread their attention to the whole historic spectrum of records back to the early Middle Ages (the European line can be traced also by national schools, but recently pan-Europeanism because of the EC is blending these into more universal statements of principles and practices, as reflected in LODOLINI). Managers like T. SCHELLENBERG inherited a European theoretical background, but performed little operations or pure research. Schellenberg's principles were inherited, but his New World context forced him and his colleagues to be highly critical of the confusion in European practice between manuscript curatorship and the administration of real archives. So his applications were born out of experience and practice in government archives more than they were strictly extensions of European archival thought. As such, both theory and practice in American archivy became less historical, and ultimately practice dominated theory.

Once codified as the bible of American archivists and sanctified by almost universal acceptance, Schellenberg's principles and practices were seldom tested, if even questioned. Euro-American archivists, even those with European doctorates like Ernst Posner who thought more theoretically and wrote about archives more broadly than his administrative experience would indicate, and those trained in the United States were above all pragmatic and rational in their approach to modern records management on a large scale. Their perspectives therefore were oriented more with what can today be identified with electronic records because it was modern, practical, and business-like, but it was not necessarily scientific, and the methodologies that were created to handle bulk data for social research, including socioeconomic history, were not applied readily to records management, appraisal, or archival administration. Unlike Europe where the tradition of gentleman historians in charge of archives as though they were given an honorific chair while so much of real archival work beneath them was performed at the technical and clerical level, or where they worked in manuscript collections and situations heavily imbued with a History ethos where the archives operation with official records was small scale, American archivists trained in History who entered government service had to push their historical interests to the background as they became above all managers of large-scale operations. Their archives served administrations and bureaucracies more than academia, or a clientele very diversified in which academics were a minority, so their organizations grew less and less like academe and more and more like bureaucracy. American archivy is a blended organizational culture, not to be confused with the intelligensia or the academic elite. And it has been treated by the latter, and is often still regarded as merely a service profession.

Most historians continue to call everything holding historical materials "archives" in a rather indiscriminate way, and sometimes the differences they perceive are less between genuine official archives and manuscript curatorship than they are distinctions between government archives and all others. But Schellenberg crystallized in the American mind-set and practice the distinction between manuscripts collections *qua* libraries and real, legitimate archives with their affinity to records management, and therefore between "manuscripts" and "documents" versus "records" and "archives." Many archivists today, inheriting a stronger European orientation or learning something about archives in a less empirical and defined way from History, do not always make this distinction. As reflected in the essays compiled by MCKEMMISH & UPWARD to share the Australian outlook, and others who have a less regimented or precise notion of what an archives is, find this Americanist distinction to be a "distracting division." Such a division is reinforced also in the separate establishment of archives and libraries, of course, and in them an often more manageable but less researchable segregation of records and documents by format, i.e., whether or not they are bound, rather than by function (i.e., adhering to older forms of structural organization, rather than more modern functional groupings (D. H. THOMAS, 1994).

Unlike librarians who focused on discrete, published bibliographic units rather than on collections except as these were compiled artificially by acquisitions (a transfer of property ownership), archivists were forced by sheer volume to concentrate attention on the aggregate in the first place and to confront the issue of presynthesis and unpublished information sources coming into archives through accessioning their parent organization's own material. But archivists too have been contemplating the need for description at the item level, just as librarians are undertaking analytics for microform and electronic resource collections. COX (1995) and others deplore this as misspent effort, displacing more urgent accomplishments in the archives agenda. Definitive description, transcription of records, and in-depth indexing of digital archives may be accomplished affordably for historical collections of finite size, but the same is not feasible for extensive series of official records. At the urging of the historical community which has its immediate self-interest at heart and thinks more in terms of manuscripts than archives, if such projects were undertaken at a massive scale, this would confuse methodologies and serve an immediate purpose at the expense of long-range fuller development of electronic archives. It is unfortunate to have to pit contemporary and future historical interests against each other, but with limited resources and a massive problem confronting archives today this is the case. We must balance preservation of the already past and of the passing.

The real distinctions that need to be kept in mind is the difference between primary research and all other derivative scholarly activities. Setting priorities must be concerned with the primacy of evidence, analysis and synthesis, and dissemination. Archivists work with "Clio in the raw" at the front-end of the information continuum (Hugh Taylor's phrase: TAYLOR, 1972). They adopted the European idea of preserving historic and organic unity as the basis for archival information management, expressed in French as the principles of *respect du fonds* and *provenance* (BARTLETT), but these conceptual frameworks are relatively meaningless for electronic records (T. H. PETERSON foretold the problems described by DOLLAR, 1990, pp. 6-11) unless reconceived as virtual fonds (as suggested by T. COOK, 1993). ZWEIG (1993a) argues that hybrid documents generated across agency lines, for example, force historians and archivists to broaden the concept of *provenance*, i.e., to combine the idea of the origin of records with tracking where they have been and, in the case of electronic multiplication, their parallel lives. Archivists for some time now have been keenly aware of the challenges in serialized information production (i.e., records series within or constituting records groups) and mass, as if anticipating librarianship's problems in dealing with increasingly serialized bulging library collections, but the complications of mixed genre, simultaneity of multiple versions, and variant strains, etc., are mind-boggling. They are also aware of the challenge created by the conversion to electronic media before the older backlogs of paper records could be handled so that now the problem of mass is compounded by the variety of media, accumulation and production, and spiraling costs for processing that requires a technically trained support staff and reeducated professional cadre.

Archivists' attention, therefore, is riveted on problems that are qualitatively and quantitatively different from historical collections and manuscripts libraries where some of the problems of retrospective conversion into digital form are, by comparison, easily scalable, solvable, and possible. This divergence of concern by scale, mass, and media is separating the continuum between manuscripts and archives which some archivists, especially those trained as historians, want to preserve. Such differences are being accentuated by currents of reform today, pulling modern archives further away from the historical manuscripts model toward information resource management and modern information systems. The situation is confusing, concepts are unclear, and the scholarly-professional dialogue is often muddled; the very definitions of archives and records and therefore their character are in question.

Current dialogue has not cultivated an understanding in North America between the two professions, history-oriented archivists clinging to the traditional spectrum and archivists aligned with information systems and records management. The capacity of Information Science to provide an umbrella for both went unrealized after 1980 with a breakthrough at the University of Maryland when more than a hundred archivists and information scientists met to discuss mutual problems and possible collaboration in solutions, but not many historians, even those teaching about archives, chose to participate. Its focus was on archival information storage and retrieval and information systems development: i.e., *Automating the Archives* (MCCRANK, ed., 1981). Its proceedings formed a *terminus post quem* for subsequent discussions (e.g., KESNER, 1984 and others), but its importance has not always been recognized in archival literature (e.g., the omissions in HICKERSON's *Manual* or in the chronology of SAA WGSAD, 1989, p. 447) because it occurred outside the routine pattern of activity within the Society of American Archivists. Nevertheless, thereafter key archivists in NARA and NHPRC began to think differently about archival information retrieval.

It was in this UMCP-CLIS conference's aftermath that the National Information Systems Task Force (NISTF) was formed. This development laid the foundation for different thinking about electronic records themselves and electronic records. More recently, however, archivists in the national archives have retreated from innovative approaches to information retrieval, partially because of costs and perhaps also because of risks to the *status quo*. The lack of such development may point to the recurrent leadership problem in the National Archives. A practical planning and program manual was provided shortly afterward by R. KESNER (1984), who earlier (1982) had also called historians to the task of putting the new technology to work and joining the Information Age. A decade latter, his call seems largely unheeded. Why?

After such stimulation in the early 1980s came some redirection of several developments and an abiding interest of archivists in Information Science, and a few—not many—information scientists seemed interested in the vexing problems of archives that reflected the larger world of information management in business and government more than in libraries. The relationship of intellectual and physical access and long-range preservation were intriguing research issues, yet few dissertations in the United States Library and Information Science schools have addressed problems particular to archives or special attention to Electronic Records Management (ERM).

Rethinking past experiences and future options stimulated a minority but cohesive movement within the archival profession, formalized by SAA into committees and taskforces, which concentrated first on information retrieval of paper records and then on the current preoccupation with electronic records management. SAA scheduled into its *Basic Manual* series volumes concentrating on archives automation (HICKERSON) and on machine-readable records (HEDSTROM, 1984); these are the bifurcated strains of Archival Science that overlap most with the interests of Historical Information Science. Disappointingly, involvement in archival automation for improved information access has not always promoted entry of archivists into electronic records management. The INTERNATIONAL COUNCIL ON ARCHIVES (ICA) *Guide* (1997) for the first time, after three years of negotiation, presents an international view on electronic archives consisting of four key roles for archivists: (1) involvement throughout life-cycle electronic records management; (2) an exerting of influence on records creators; (3) management of appraisal an an intellectual control over records; and (4) ensurance of preservation and continued access (MOHLENRICH). ICA, after releasing three reports on electronic records (an introduction of issues, a literature review, and a survey of programs) in 1996, is now addressing preferred techniques or "best practices" in its member organizations.

In 1983, the SAA National Information Systems Task Force's (NISTF, 1980-) work led not only to the MARC format (SAHLI) for Archives and Manuscripts Control (AMC) and the opening of automated bibliographic systems and networks such as RLIN and OCLC in 1984 to archivists, but also to a series of workshops, conference sessions, and working papers which stimulated a Renaissance in archival circles that can be characterized as an Information Science movement or, perhaps, the "new" archival science. In description, NISTF accomplishments were augmented by library cataloging accommodations for manuscripts and documentary art. In 1982 when AACR-2 interpretative manuals were being issued, Elisabeth Betz Parker's work in the Library of Congress on graphics materials were included for "original items" and "historical collections" (BETZ PARKER). It was not until 1988, however, that LC's *National Union Catalog of Manuscript Collections* (*NUCMC*) began using formal subject headings to merge archival topical access with library practice so one could retrieve in online systems both manuscript and print formats of the same materials. Today *NUCMC* searching in 75,000 collections is much easier as part of CHADWYCK-HEALEY's *Archives USA* on CD-ROM. MARC-AMC implementation was aided immeasurably by Steven Henson's cataloging manual for personal papers and manuscripts in libraries and historical societies (HENSON; revised in 1989 and endorsed by SAA as a standard, if not *the* standard, for manuscripts description; cf., the 1991 ICA standard; cf., ICA *ERM Guide* [1996]). Although this did not yet go into new media as extensions of old forms, the trend was clearly marked by the Library of Congress' revision of M. YEE's manual for "Moving Image" materials, namely films, but expanded for all types of instructional media as well. M. YEE recently completed her doctorate at UCLA with a dissertation that explores motion picture descriptive cataloging in detail.

While a vehicle to carry meta-information about archives was invented in the MARC-AMC format (really a tagged envelope that carries descriptive information), this accomplishment exposed grave problems in archival descriptive practices. At about the same time, national archivists considered MARC to be too limited to do all the record tracking they wanted in their information systems (NARA, 1986). The idea of a MARC record for archives and manuscripts and descriptive information exchange across bibliographic networks was ironically perceived as both too much and too little at the same time. But the inspection of MARC brought about an inspection of all standards, and with that, introspection about archival practices. Some had already placed greater emphasis on indexing and terminological control (e.g., use of thesauri) than was common among archivists. Exposure of the inadequate use of terminology in common archival descriptive practices, based in part on the foresighted work of Richard Berner, who thought more in terms of terminological and lexical access than traditional description (BERNER), called for an introduction of archivists to descriptive standards and vocabulary control, as was done very early by MCCRANK (1979, 1982) in American archival education at the University of Maryland in the mid-1970s and subsequently to the broader archival community through a series of workshops at UMCP and in 1981-82 for SAA at annual conferences. Unfortunately, the proposed manual in archival indexing was never commissioned by SAA; that could have accelerated progress by making available teaching tools customized to archival material and operations. Nevertheless, somewhat later and without direct continuity to the 1980-82 conferences and workshops at UMCP, in 1985 and 1987, the Canadian and American archival associations established committees and study groups to reexamine archival description, especially the structure of data elements and descriptive vocabularies. Such efforts led to the drafting of minimal standards for archival description, including enumeration of preferred data elements, which should have been translated into new citation formats as well, but were not for some time.

At least North American archivists coming into the 1990s had agreed to the proposition of operating by standards for archival description and access (SAA WGSAD report, 1989). By 1994 the committee, led by Victorian Irons Walch with Marion Matters, produced its handbook on standards for archival description (SAA WGSAD, 1994). The Canadians in 1990 established their *Rules for Archival Description (RAD)* (BUREAU OF CANADIAN ARCHIVISTS), which in 1992 was converted into a hypertext prototype, *HyperRAD*, for using the rules to produce machine-readable descriptions easily transported into online systems which can be tapped via Internet access (TOMS & DUFF, 1992, 1993; DUFF & TOMS). Archivists in the United Kingdom had already contributed greatly to the General International Standard for Archival Description, and in the same vein Australian archivists melded influences from both England and the United States to produce their own manual for "Australian Common Practice" (AUSTRALIAN SOCIETY OF ARCHIVISTS) and to address policy development on a large scale as a research issue and matter of politics (MOSCATO; O'SHEA) . Thus, perhaps indicative of a basic empiricism, the Anglo-American world seems to have moved with uncommon common direction toward sets of compatible standards for archival description and archival development through a proactive agenda and more vigorous organizational politics. Although that lengthy process took over a decade, it was necessary preparation for taking advantage of modern information technology that would not stand still to wait for archivists to catch up, so the work is still ongoing and needs to be elaborated for international, crosscultural, and multilingual archival information exchange.

This decade-long stress on standards evolution was very unsettling because revised practice was being initiated to take advantage of new computer and telecommunications technology before any theoretical revision really occurred. Theory seemed to be retrospective justification for changes in practice already adopted. MCCRANK in 1980 (pp. 323-329) predicted the outcome of adoption to new technology, with its requirements for systematization that had not been achieved by archivists through organizational consensus or required by manual finding aids, most of which were inconsistent internally, to say nothing about across a series. Debates on archival theory versus practice (F. BURKE; COX; GRÄNSTROM; MCCRANK; A. PEDERSON; STIELOW; TAYLOR, etc.; revitalized by a throwback from John ROBERTS) dramatically challenged complacent archival thinking and traditional practice. NISTF's former leader, David Bearman, continued the line of inquiry begun by the task force in a series of provocative articles (BEARMAN, 1989-1997), monographs (BEARMAN, 1987-1990), and technical reports such as the *Archives and Museum Informatics*, 1987- (reviewed by MCCRANK, 1990, and PEDERSON, 1990), the title of which reflects the link to the European notion of Informatics and archives (the term was adopted also by DOLLAR, 1990), and hence to Historical Information Science. Moreover, this development has been genuinely ecumenical, evangelic even, reaching out from the Social Science and History core of archives to the Arts and Humanities. However, electronic archivists are still concerned primarily with numbers and texts, and have yet to come to grips with the merging of digital sound archives (DUGGAN, beyond the treatment by STIELOW, 1986), or the transition in image archives from prints and photographs to digitized images (ARIS). In the digital world, sound, image, and text are all interchangeable.

Moreover, a whole generation of software has evolved in the past few years that makes traditional records management techniques nearly obsolete for modern records and project management: today archivists and records managers must be familiar with such "documentation management" systems and workflow software as *Documentum*, *In Concert*, *FileNet*, *Flowmark*, and *Watermark*, etc. (all of which are applicable as well to long-term collaborative historical research project control). These digital document management systems now work with imaging systems, distributed computing and networking, relational databases, and Internet/Intranet deployments to produce complex mega-systems which open new dimensions for Archival Science, require a wholly new archives paradigm, and mandate dramatically different training of archivists now and for the next generation of historians who hope to use sources generated in these multisite, multitasking, integrated and networked environments. Conversely, companies developing such systems, like PeopleSoft, IBM, and particularly Xerox Corporation, which has taken an interest in digital archives and libraries, need to incorporate archival standards and information requirements into their design and into the training their consultants and representatives provide.

This new impetus from digital technology, the fusion of multimedia, and the massive conversion in offices from paper to electronic communications is developing a reinvigorated Archival Science from what HEREDIA HERRERA (1992) called "archivology." This intellectual and technical transformation deserved review by ASIS in *ARIST* for its own merits, and at long last received the attention it deserved by MCCRANK (1995), but without the detail explored here. An international perspective has been offered by O. BUCCI (1992), but a brief enumeration here of important work by archivists serves mainly to tie together this trend and concerns for modern electronic records with the ongoing information needs of social scientists and computing historians for electronic data and separate development of economic, social, and political data archives, and both of these to the continuing manuscript and photograph collecting tradition converted into electronic text and image archives.

Major archives in the United States are developing staff expertise and research programs to assist their work: these include government institutions like the Smithsonian Institution, but most prominently the New York State Archives among the state institutions, the Bentley Library at the University of Michigan with its 15 years of Mellon Foundation support for summer institutes (unfortunately ending in 1997), and the University of Pittsburgh's education initiative in electronic archives. One must include NARA in this development, but not wholeheartedly or thoroughly throughout the ranks. The position of NARA archivists on the White House PROFS e-mail records indicate hesitancy to conceive of electronic records in all cases as archival, or at least deserving of archival appraisal for proper disposition. This may be because the National Archives, like so many state and institutional archives, lacks the means to address the issue, and so, it also lacks the will. Again, pragmatism prevails over intellectual argument in this case. On the other hand, historians have provided intellectual justification for a comprehensive approach to electronic records, but they have been ineffectual in providing any means.

The lead for development of electronic archives came not from historians, any historical society, or historical association, but from Social Science generally and the older alliance of Cliometric historians with Social Science History in the formation of data archives. The merging of data and electronic archives today is a consequence of computer applications in business and government more than in academe, and new information technology thereby is resurrecting the Cliometric movement in an expanded form using not just numerical data, but electronic text, sound, and image archives. As this area of interest expands and the volume of electronic records continues to surpass anything extant in the manuscript tradition of archives, historical repositories catering to traditional formats will become a small minority in the archives world, perhaps aligned as many manuscripts operations are today with rare book and special collections libraries. On the other hand, if more historical collections are digitized and converted into electronic form, they may be transmogrified into electronic archives. The organization of archives, the archival profession, and typology of institutions and their collections, will continue to change. Thus reformation in archives, caused by information technology and the merger of distinctive but inseparable archival traditions, will have a great impact on History. Indeed, it already has, and some historians seem to be taking notice. But the real test of archivist influence will not be in History, but rather in the world at large. Their success or failure will ultimately determine the history of the future and History in the future.

Data Archives

There is noticeable divergence still between comprehensive electronic and older data archives (cf., *GUIDE to Historical Datasets* series in *Historical Social Research*; and the older *RQ* "Selected List," 1982, of *Guides* to data archives and computerized reference service in History), and perhaps also libraries (COXON; RAYWARD), which in time will close. The former, representing the manuscripts tradition in archives transformed into machine readable files, was developed in the United States after 1963 with data collections going back to the 1930s (BOGUE, 1968, 1976, 1977; GEDA, 1979) as a Social Sciences infrastructure onto itself (formed by the Council of Social Science Data Archives), related to but independent from electronic archives (HEIM, 1980, 1982). Although the former development should be recognized as a repetition in the era of electronic records and databases of the prior anticipation of formal archives with records management by archives *qua* manuscript collections, common usage even by archivists is confusing. Usage in this essay reflects a respectful recognition of differences between "data archives" and "electronic archives" and a proper distinction between them. Historians as social scientists tend to use data archives, but have not exploited electronic archives as they might.

DOORN (1997) classifies modern electronic archives into four types, of which the first three are electronic extensions of the manuscript tradition in archives and are not official or

Repository type (age)	Content	Structure	Content	Treatment	Access
Social Science Data Archives (SSDA) (30 years)	Survey data	Tables Data sets	Coded interview returns; Code books & sheets	Segregated	Standard study Descriptions & SGML
Electronic Text Archives (ETA) (20 years)	Published literature	Markup texts	Literary works; Discreet Titles	SGML/TEI; Unified	SGML; Indexing; Catalogs
Historical Data Archives (HDA) (25 years)	Published & acquired sources	Mixed forms; Source dependent	Mixed genre	Discreet documents	Standard Study Descriptions
Public Records Offices (PRO) (25 years)	Produced & accessioned sources	Varied	Massive files	Combined & *in situ*	Inventories

true archives. His chart (see previous page) is useful in noting differences between types of archives, their status, and in how they approach records storage and description.

This table reflects a European view of archives from the historical manuscripts tradition, and does not recognize that official archives can be either public or private and that Historical Data Archives can contain formal archives by contract, and presumably they would also maintain their own archives in addition to acquired sources. So, such an attempted simplification always seems to have exceptions, and the forms and characteristics of operations are never quite as neat in reality as in such a model. It does, however, convey the idea that electronic archives of the public variety, mostly government, are neither the only kind of electronic records repository or the first. The first were artificially created data archives, salvage operations really, which were segregated from manuscripts repositories because of the latter's Humanities associations, and because of the technical demands of the media and sponsorship from Social Science foundations. For the purposes of greater clarification than in many discussions, the general terms "data archives" and "electronic archives" will be used here to distinguish between acquired collections and accessioned repositories of electronic information, and the qualifiers pertain to special media: "data" usually mean numerical information, while the assumption that only numerical data may be qualified is incorrect. So, "quantifiable" refers to operations rather than content and storage; "visual" encompasses image bases; "sound" includes oral and audio sources; and "text" refers, of course, to literate or alphabetic formats.

Certainly the most famous data archives in the United States, and perhaps worldwide, is the Inter-University Consortium for Political and Social Research (ICPSR, 1977). It was established at the University of Michigan in 1964 to collect and hold data sets for current and historical Social Science research (EULAU). It grew to over 200 institutional members by the 1980s (ROWE) and by its twenty-fifth anniversary (D. AUSTIN) it held data from 350 institutions documenting social and political phenomena in 130 countries, but of course, its strength is in United States sources. Early databases were scattered widely (SESSIONS) and had to be collected to be preserved (GEDA, AUSTIN & BLOUIN); it now has over 30,000 data sets, 1,000 of which are available over the Internet. There are now many more separate data archives (GEDA), represented by IASSIST and which collaborate internationally through the International Federation of Data Organizations (IFDO), such as at the University of North Carolina's Institute for Research in Social Science (IRSS, 1989-); but even more are developing as electronic archives components of institutional, government, and corporate archives or computer centers rather than as autonomous centers. The MicroCase social science data diskettes make a broad array of socioeconomic data available from such centers and the government. They are not produced specifically for historians, but they contain longitudinal data and, hence, are researched for historical interpretation by social scientists who in effect study history.

The early development of the machine-readable archives division of NARA imitated the ICPSR except that the National Archives did not have to acquire electronic records. It had what were then called machine-readable records in every format conceivable since the work of Hollerith in 1890. A separate division was established as an electronic counterpart to manuscripts, where electronic records were separated from other formats for the special handling and attention they required. Slowly, this office moved from a holdings operation to a research and development service for the National Archives and developed increasingly sophisticated ways to accession and appraise electronic government records. Today this national Center for Electronic Records has files for nearly 100 bureaus, departments, etc., especially of the executive branch, and a host of contracting agencies as well. Guides to the Center's holdings, such as that accessible on the Gopher (highlighted by DOORN, 1994, pp. 65-66 for access from Europe across the Internet), often emphasize for historical research potential the collections for:

1. Attitudinal data such as United States Information Agency (USIA) surveys from WW II onward;

2. Demographic data from both the Bureau of the Census and the Department of Commerce;

3. Education data collected by the federal government;

4. Health and social services data, especially related to specific programs;

5. International data gathered by the USIA and relating to trade;

6. Military data, post-WW II through the Vietnam War, including research sets from the 1960s; and

7. Scientific and technical data, including major surveys.

Partially in imitation of the Center for Electronic Records, and in part as a general movement to establish online archives, the European Economic Community (EEC) has made many of its holdings available on the Internet. The first to become accessible were the EEC's equivalents to OPACs: EURLIB (European Official Periodicals) is an EEC equivalent to international government documents online, complimented by EURISTOTE (Theses and Research on Europe), which provide reference access to full documentation, and research reports, such as EMIRE (European Employment and Industrial Research). DOORN (1994, p. 66) calls special attention to EURHISTAR (European Historical Data) which is an electronic archives begun in 1985 that makes available the most important EEC documents from the depository at the European University Institute, Florence, Italy. EURHISTAR is being augmented by work at the Institute to provide "grey" literature or unofficial publications by EEC agencies and subcontractors, and to mount digital image bases of its special collections of art and visual documentation (e.g., posters, pictures, photographs, maps, etc.). Such efforts are consistent with the EEC's patronage of the arts and humanities across Europe, and its progressive stance to promote a trans-European virtual library above and beyond efforts mounted by national governments.

These global, international, and national efforts should not obscure important developments at the local level where unique source material is plentiful but with attendant difficult access problems precisely because of its local nature. As noted previously, the very notion of culture and cultivation of civilization starts with seeding ideas, planting, and things taking root. In this sense all history is local, individual, and event based. Historical documentation, therefore, must encompass the spectrum from the highest levels to the lowest, from the general and aggregate to the specific and detailed. History associations have focused on communities in combination with museums, but mostly from the manuscripts tradition in archives rather than from documentation; local municipal and country records are for the most part a history disaster. Likewise, most historical societies and local associations have little influence over electronic records, either private or public sources. Yet, it is recognized in the archival professional today that electronic records management must begin at the grassroots level, at the moment of records creation. This ideal is not commonly realized. Data archives in the United States have sometimes grown inside regional and local studies centers such as the Center for Philadelphia Studies (HERSBERG, 1981) and the Baltimore Regional Institutional Studies Center (BRISC, now defunct; see DURR, 1981). Such hybrid and conglomerate archives, without secure institutional funding, endowments, or outside patronage, are difficult to develop and more difficult to sustain. Too often they are creations of single minds and energetic almost charismatic leadership, which lose their sense of direction and purpose and their chief catalyst for funding after their founders leave. Most of these local and regional research centers have been multimedia, but few have had genuine archives functions unless they are attached to university archives. Their acquisitiveness for material in all formats opens the possibility of their movement into electronic records, but many have lacked the funding, scale of operation, technology, technical background in personnel, or inclination to automate and to move into electronic records management. In other cases, electronic records have been created as the natural byproduct of local and regional historical and social research.

Local history, for example, was the focus of the Canadian Social History Project directed by Michael Katz. Early work in Canadian historical demography (IGARTUA *ET AL.*) led to the creation of an interuniversity cooperative (Institut de Recherche sur les Populations [IREP, formerly SOREP] CHARBONNEAU, 1988; ST.-HILLAIRE, 1993) and directed by Gerard Bouchard at the Université du Québec at Chicoutimi (BOUCHARD *ET AL.*, 1985, 1989; BOUCHARD, 1987). This followed a research and training program in historical demography directed by CHARBONNEAU & LEGARE at the Université de Montréal (L. HENRY's manuals, 1967, 1972, are still very useful, especially in relating such modern projects to early developments in the French historiographic school that pioneered in historical demography). IREP's origins are traced to 1971 when the Saguenay project was begun and the first research team was formed in 1977 (BOUCHARD, CASGRAIN & ROY, 1985). By 1979 this grew to an interuniversity endeavor between Laval, Québec, and McGill universities, and later these were joined also by the Universities of Montréal (1991), Concordia, and Sherbrooke (1994). Researchers collaborate in the building of a population database called *BALSAC* to support demographic, genetic, epidemiologic, and cultural studies, now totally over 5,000,000 public acts (birth, marriage, and death certificates, etc.). SOREP in Montréal developed a modified dBASE program, *SYGAP*, for handling prosopographic data, in cooperation with the Programme de Recherche Rendu-Osler de la Maison Rhone-Alpes des Sciences de l'Homme, the Centre Pierre Leon, and the Institut Européen des Genomutations in France (BIDEAU *ET AL.*). Population data were manipulated in *BALSAC*, an INGRES/INGRID system (BOUCHARD, *ET AL.*, 1989). Both BRISC and SOREP/IREP developed linguistic controls for intellectual access and records linking, masking for confidentiality, etc., and the latter developed software for family reconstitution along lines of relational database design that was truly innovative (BOUCHARD, 1985). Such pioneer research centers with their initial data archives have confronted early the challenge of local historical documentation and data archives management that continues to change fundamentally (D. MAYER). It is unfortunate not to benefit still from their sustained growth, but there are lessons to be learned in their floundering as well as their success.

It is often difficult to justify the expense of preserving local history data and making it accessible based on actual or potential use, without a clear notion of a user community and likelihood of use. Archives face the same problem as academic libraries of "just-in-case" collecting, which has become unaffordable because of the mass and high cost of serial information. This issue of economic scalability is not handled well in most archival operations, and it is largely ignored by the history profession. In most cases, the cost per use is extraordinary, and although historians may appreciate and acknowledge such support, expectations are often unrealistic. First use that produces a find is knowledge discovery, but its publication often discourages reuse as if the data can be mined for only lower grade ore.

Consider the not-so-hypothetical case of data sets acquired by a regional studies center; this became the foundation for a single doctoral dissertation which, once published, was often cited but the data were not revisited again for some time on the assumption that the first use was exhaustive. The repository had invested nearly one year's salary for a professional archivist to check the data, collate code books and other tools needed to access the data, provide an appraisal and introductory access guide which led the historian to his find: a half-year equivalent technician salary for data conversion from accompanying paper records and rewriting the total data to a stable medium for storage; and a quarter-year equivalent of a clerk-typist salary for data input. Add to this labor cost indirect costing for utilities and space, which runs minimally 10 to 20 percent but can rise to 50 percent and above, based on the base project cost. More labor costs could be added for the reference and personal assistance the use needed, especially technical support to assist in actual use, which could have been billed almost as a consultancy. An accountable reckoning of institutional support of that dissertation can be calculated at $48,000 for labor and $12,000 for indirect labor costs (benefits); $1,000 for data processing and storage; $500 for access and $1,000 prorated computer support, etc.; or ca. $62,500 base costs or total project cost of $81,250. Such an investment in a historian's work is hardly captured by the gratuity provided in most preface notes. Each page of the published product was, in this perspective, golden. In short, this archives investment can be justified only by continued use, so that this cost can be amortized over time and spread over several users; or such upfront costs must be defrayed by grants agencies, foundations, and perhaps transfers of funds from universities that collect graduate tuition for "directed studies" out of proportion to the direction given and without regard for the research assistance, access, and support from the repository.

The breadth and diversity of the sources and the variety of technologies used to record and convey them require staff flexibility and interdisciplinary training at increased levels of expertise from both data providers and users. Certainly models may be in the making now, e.g., the NEH-funded Newberry Library project for a history of Chicago and the historical components of the Information System for Los Angeles (ISLA) project in the United States, or a similar urban history project in the Max-Planck Institute, namely the digital city archives of Duderstadt, Germany, 1395-1650 (THALLER, 1997). In this latter project, the archival textbase is the result of digitizing 60,000 documents which are indexed and linked in accord with Geertz' notion of "thick description." Access can be through word matching, term retrieval, subject classification, or location. All household data are linked to addresses which are mapped, and an alternative form of visual access is created by touch-screen technology whereby one can zoom into a neighborhood from an overview map, touch the lot which retrieves the address, and in turn all hyperlinked documentation (displayed in either chronological or reverse chronological order) for families living at that location over the two centuries covered. These projects defy easy classification into one type of archives or another, and they are not conceived as archives; rather archives are their byproduct. In most cases, however, when the project is conceived as history first, the "archives" is really a historical source depository, and when the sources are electronic, they are usually surrogates rather than official records. What is amazing, however, is the continued lack of clarity brought to such projects in their design regarding institutionalization, organizational typology, legal status, content scope, description and access methods, and targeted audiences, identified clients, and studied user groups. Old confusions in the manuscript and paper realm have been transferred into the electronic.

Others research centers are imitating such early efforts in Baltimore and Philadelphia by beginning archives collections as part of regional and state history centers, and already established archives are adding manuscript collections to their operations. All seem to be exploring new technology to make their holdings graphically available across regional networks and the Internet. HEDSTROM, BEARMAN, and other archivists argue against collecting electronic records into such centers as electronic archives, but selected records may be copied into electronic hybrid sources in multimedia projects such as ISLA for Los Angeles, and history centers might still develop improved means of access to relevant records through the design of search engines and browsers for the Internet and WWW sites. Moreover, collaboration may come to pass between such centers and electronic archives holders in organizations that are not prepared for public service, whereby such service is outsourced to local and regional studies centers. In this way, an economy of scale could be achieved to warrant the staff development needed for technical, archival, and historical expertise to work with electronic records. But with today's networking capabilities, one no longer needs to operate on the older model of a centralized data archives.

Regional history centers with data and electronic text archives have been established in many European countries with the ICPSR as their model (MARKER, 1993, p. 190): among them might be noted:

- The Norwegian Social Science Data Services (NSD, 1991) in Bergen, founded in 1971 (HOLM; OLDERVOLL); the Stockholm Historical Database (SHD) for all Sweden (based on the Roteman Archives' 1.5 million entries), but which is part of the city archives, and a related research and training center, HISTLAB (FOGELVIK, 1989); and the Danish Data Archives (1,500+ datasets: DDA, 1986/1988) formed in 1973 at Odense (MARKER);

- In the United Kingdom, the Economic and Social Research Council Data Archives (ESRC, 1991) established at Essex in 1967 (S. ANDERSON, 1992; SCHURER & ANDERSON; LIEVESLEY), plus projects at Oxford (such as the Oxford Text Archives (BURNARD, 1988) and Cambridge universities (GREENSTEIN, 1989, 1990), and at the University of London's Center for Humanities Communications;

- The Netherlands Historical Data Archives (NHDA) in Leiden (DOORN) and Steinmetz Archives (2,100 datasets: STEINMETZ ARCHIVES, 1986);

- In France at the Archives Nationales and the Centre National de la Recherche Scientifique (CNRS) in Paris; in Belgium at the Université de Liège's Department of Social and Economic History (PASLEAU);

- The Zentralarchiv für Empirische Sozialforschung (1,700 post-WWII datasets: ZA, 1986) in Bonn and its counterpart at the University of Cologne, as well as the state Archives at Regensburg; the Historisches Institut in Bern, Switzerland, has its BERN-HIST project (PFISTER; PFISTER & SCHÜLE); in Austria in both Vienna, called WISDOM, founded in 1984 (NEMETH) and Graz (KROPAČ ET AL., eds., 1994);

- In Rome and Florence, Italy (GUARNIERI & TRAVASONI); and the Iberian peninsula in Barcelona, Madrid, Sevilla (VAZQUEZ DE LA PARGA; GONZALEZ), and Lisbon;

- Fifteen such centers are located in the Independent States of the former Soviet Union, but the most influential is still the Russian Historical Data Archives maintained by the Historical Informatics Laboratory at the Moscow State University (BORODKIN, 1993); and

- Others are being founded throughout Europe, at Israeli universities as well, and the phenomenon has also spread to Latin America (TYLER, 1977). Technically innovative, major archeological archives has been developed at Tokyo's National Museum of Ethnology (HONG ET AL.) and by the National Institute for Educational Research (OIKAWA).

From them is coming a steady stream of subject and methodological publications, databases and electronic texts, and software, which are not easily tracked and are not well covered by library and information science indexing and abstracting services. Technology transfer from the United States is still greater and easier than to the USA, perhaps reflecting the attitude of the American professorate that does not seek information outside the United States as much as do professors in other countries from outside their borders (CARNEGIE FOUNDATION; MONNEY, p. A38). In the case of Historical Information Science from the non-Americanist perspective, much of the most interesting work being accomplished is foreign precisely because of the modern historiographic trends toward local and regional studies. This attitudinal and disciplinary parochialism, however, also makes such information access and acquisition very problematic. Much of historical research, as in the case of Americans working in foreign territory, must be done locally for archival manual and electronic records, but also for locally published materials not accessible through bibliographic and interlibrary networks. Such historical "field work" and especially for data access and transfer usually requires personal contacts and increasing the mediation of reference archivists and specialized technicians. This dependency on nontransferable databases, local systems and expertise constitutes a barrier to international cross-border research, the Internet notwithstanding, as formidable as language differences and the unique character of local and regional documentation.

Data archivists have developed technical specialization in many of the processes and techniques that interest archivists as they now confront the task of accessioning, appraising, and preserving electronic records. The challenge is immediately translated into educational reform mandates which the North American archives profession is having some difficulty meeting (COX, 1994). SAA's CART (HEDSTROM; WALCH, 1994) has now embarked on a special Curriculum Development project to address this problem. Information Science programs could certainly do more than they have done, and closer working relations are also needed between archivists and Historical Information Science practitioners and the courses they are offering now in graduate History programs.

Although the archival focus of both data and electronic archivists has been on databases and electronic records series *per se* just as librarians work bibliographically with books and serials, all are necessarily interested in content use, information transfer, and interpretation, because of the reference function in archives and libraries. The technical components of accessing, opening, reading, and using archival data sets and records are so specialized, however, that direct user access and analysis will require competencies not widely developed outside these specialties. Most historians are not so trained technically, and as volume increases with the variety of technologies used to create these records, complete with problematic technical obsolescence and hardware incompatibility, all users will depend increasingly on archivists as intermediaries (MORRIS, 1993a, pp. 302-304). This will curtail freedom in research that historians cherish and will certainly be a source for increased frustration and conflict, but it will also be a motivation for increased collaboration between academic disciplines and the information professions. For now, however, historians are unable to tell archivists what they want for future history, short of the impossible "save everything." Archivists, on the other hand, are telling historians what they are going to have left, based not on information needs assessment, but on happenstance, practicality, and possibility within the limited means provided archives. Only a handful of archivists have promoted more systematic macro-appraisal approaches to the problem of mass and multimedia.

MICHELSON & ROTHENBERG have surveyed trends in scholarly research and the impact of New Social History in particular, to argue for changes in archival administration that are increasingly responsive to local and regional studies and the preservation of data which may once have been appraised as not having enduring value. HUSKAMP PETERSON unfortunately sees a decline in basic skills and certain negative trends in education, that will make user-centered service in archives increasingly difficult especially for nonscholars, for example, the problem of imprecision in knowing what a user wants, assuming that the potential user does know this. If they cannot retrieve needed information with face-to-face assistance, everyone wonders about the complications of computer interfaces and difficulties in unassisted remote access. NUNBERG (1996) and his collaborators go further in reviewing recent speculation about "the death of the book" including brick-and-mortar libraries, traditional publishers, linear narrative, authorship, and the identity of separate disciplines. D. GREENBERG (1993) questions the survival of library Special Collections (including Manuscripts departments) as research centers in the traditional sense where scholars come to examine sources not otherwise available, because researchers will want surrogates of these sources to travel to them electronically instead of costly trips to repositories. The clearinghouse model is often invoked, which has its reality test in automated reserve operations in libraries whereby texts, whole or parts, are licensed for reproduction and multiple use, are scanned, and are made accessible by computer for direct viewing in-house, downloading for individual use, and remote access via Web pages. The old reserve collection is thus replaced, and the traditionally centralized service is no more.

The massive conversion of primary sources into digital libraries and archives will operate the same way, whereby the electronic surrogate is the use copy and the original will supposedly reside undisturbed in a depository for safekeeping. The user in most cases is obliged to believe that what is delivered is an accurate and reliable rendering or an authentic document that continues to exist somewhere. The belief system involved is something like accepting currency with the assumption that gold bullion exists at Fort Knox in sufficient quantity to give otherwise worthless paper real value. If the system works, nobody checks the original. Instead the greatest concern is counterfeiting the surrogate currency. The fakes are detectable because of safeguards in reproduction of exact copies. Here the analogy breaks down because in electronic texts, images, and sound recordings where variety rather than uniformity is the norm, identification and reauthentification based on human pattern recognition and regulated electronic detection are not so likely to uncover fakes and forgeries, interpolations, graft and corruption. The analogy has another lesson, however, in that currency's acceptance is based on use and reuse; its reliability is related to what is commonplace. By implication, something unused does not remain current; unique things are not common. Use can be manipulated, as in marketing. Mass, saturation, and interaction are the cultural determinants. All surviving culture must be popular, or else protected, preferred, and elitist. Electronically available sources are likely to be used based on ease of access, not content or substance, highest degree of relevance, or authenticity.

In this sense, convenience, ready availability, and contemporary relevance may determine the basis of future scholarship, rather than what is pertinent long-term, basic or higher-order, or unique or rare. LANDOW & DELANY (p. 18) make the point that "Texts and even entire languages that do not transfer to a newly dominant information medium [i.e., digitization] become marginalized, unimportant, and virtually invisible." Speculation about the future of the texts, the book, and libraries has not commonly addressed evidence, records, or archives even though these information formats, organizational forms, and institutions are likely to merge into some new hybrid. The latter, however, are at a disadvantage; they already lack currency and for most, relevance, and hence value, to society at large. All of History is in jeopardy in such massive cultural and technical transformation—that is, history based on evidence and authentic records. History based on surrogates, common currency, remembrance and opinion will flourish. The former, highly artificial, is really quite fragile; the latter is durable precisely because of its pervasiveness, ubiquity, and mutability.

This critical issue of continuity through a major technological revolution and cultural shift relates to archives especially in valuation and appraisal, selective preservation, and activities such as retroconversion of old records that cannot survive in their original form, and particularly in copying and migration of electronic records. Because they are apprehensive about both choices made today and the reliability of technology over time, R. MORRIS (1993a) concludes, historians want everything. They want the mass and access together, i.e., bulk and convenience as well. He is rightly aware, however, that the issue is more complex than mere mass preservation, but also the guarantee of access to whatever is saved for posterity, in order to escape the dilemma of "Black Holes or Warehouses." He was perhaps advisedly leery about the new idiom of "data warehousing" in the information industry, but as will be seen, the choice is more than the void or the junkpile. The "warehouse" may be an unfortunate metaphor and indeed hide sloppy thinking in some cases, but the technological integration it invokes is encouraging. Such developments may provide useable data for future research, but it is this contemporary period, our time of rapid and rather haphazard transition that places late twentieth-century history in jeopardy. S. ROSS (1993, pp. 3-4) makes this same point by wondering what kind of socioeconomic contemporary history could be reconstructed from the records of VISA International which works with 18,000 banks and ten million merchants worldwide to generate six billion transactions annually (15 billion by the year 2000), if the records were not dumped every six months! S. MOSTOV was luckier to have the business archives of R. G. Dun and Company with their credit ratings preserved; these allowed him to analyze the socioeconomic condition of Cincinnati's Jewish community, 1840-1875. Such history, however, is based on data converted from manual records and falls into the tradition of electronic "manuscripts" research akin to what has been supported by data archives. But the survival of such data at the nonaggregate level is remarkable because it is uncommon, and so is the History produced from it.

The accomplishments of archivists in partially automating access to their holdings, improving description to take advantage of new information technologies, and arriving at basic standards for such description, all fall largely into the manuscripts tradition of archival development (L. GILLILAND-SWETLAND). They pertain less to genuine electronic archives, but rather to archivists fitting new media and electronic records into this older tradition. Data archives and this collecting tradition will persist, and pretwentieth century will rely on such retrospective conversion for paper records and the first generation of machine-readable records which used computerization like mechanization of discrete manual processes. Twentieth-century history too, will be largely a salvage operation and a matter of reconversion and dealing with incomplete records. The mess of late twentieth-century transitional information technologies makes this so. However, the pervasive changes of late-twentieth century information technology, in methodology integration, automation and hybridization of techniques, fusion of hardware and software, smart interactive systems, and scale and massive networking, really demarcate this century from what is rapidly approaching. Historical Information Science in delimiting itself to the historical may be the specialization of the next century to deal with the problems of records until now.

The future history of the twenty-first century lies in electronic archives. Here we face some very vexing problems. If Historical Information Science is to become both retrospective in its glance and forward thinking at the same time, using a Janus-like gaze to assist current developments, then every historian must also be an astute student of current events and expand historical hindsight incrementally, almost day by day. For self-interest and more altruistic concerns, historians must be active in a more integrative fashion, or to adopt somewhat redundant jargon of modern management circles for the sake of repeated emphases, they must be proactive. This is a central message of Helen SAMUEL's seminal case study, *Varsity Letters*, which also advocates a functions analysis approach to academic archives (a theme reinforced by A. GILLILAND-SWETLAND and KINNEY & WALLACH for documenting the academic community).

Crisis, Ferment, and Reform

If archivists are to confront the challenge of electronic archives, as many are now doing, many questions remain unanswered, educational reform is needed, and budgets fall short everywhere. Meanwhile, time is critical. How does one treat records so volatile and systems so nebulous with concrete plans and decisive action? Can historically based archival thinking relate to ahistorical thought and action in business, industry, and government? When so little has been done, much too late in view of the massive accumulation, where does one begin? How does archival action relate to history: is the issue to create a historical record, or other kinds of records that simply become historical as they age? Are historians credible players in this arena when they do not themselves create viable historical databases *qua* archives for a cumulative record of History (as distinct from a History literature and historiographic record)? Historians use archives more than they practice archival theory or operations, except when they become archivists. Can they expect nonhistorians in business, industry, government, etc., to work more responsibly and accountably for the sake of history? Historians should take note of the current milieu for vested interest sake, and Historical Information Science should relate to the research agenda of archives if archivists continue their role in creating and preserving the historical record, especially in electronic form.

Reacting to a series of state archives assessment projects in the 1980s that were hardly laudatory (reviewed by DEARSTYNE, 1997, pp. 25-59, who previously [1985] called the situation in the United States a "records wasteland"; see L. WEBER for summaries; cf., CONWAY for the 1985 census), coupled with the BURKEL & COOK's assessment of college and university archives (1983), the NHPRC began to redirect its priorities toward infrastructure development and fundamental issues related to the impact of modern technology on the archival record. The NHPRC consequently identified a short list of issues to create the agenda for funded research to assist archives in their entrance into the next century with improved capabilities to handle electronic records (1991). The basic questions were framed as follows:

1. What functions and data are required to manage electronic records in accord with archival requirements? Do data requirements and functions vary for different types of automated applications?

2. What are the technological, conceptual, and economic implications of capturing and retaining data, descriptive information, and contextual information in electronic form from a variety of applications?

3. How can software-dependent data objects be retained for future use?

4. How can data dictionaries, information resource directory systems, and other metadata systems be used to support electronic records management and archival requirements?

5. What archival requirements have been addressed in major systems development projects and why?

6. What policies best address archival concerns for the identification, retention, preservation, and research use of electronic records?

7. What functions and activities should be present in electronic records programs and how should they be evaluated?

8. What incentives can contribute to creator and user support for electronic records management concerns?

9. What barriers have prevented archivists from developing and implementing archival electronic programs?

10. What do archivists need to know about electronic records?

Accordingly, the NHPRC has begun to fund a number of electronic records grants: in 1995 awards were made to state historical societies and archives in Kansas, Indiana, and Ohio to develop and implement policies for electronic records generated by state government; to the DELAWARE PUBLIC ARCHIVES which is investigating the development of Records Life-Cycle tracking software (SALVIN; see the Delaware project at http://www.lib.de.us/ archives/); to the City of Philadelphia to do likewise at the municipal department of records level; to the South Carolina Department of Archives and History to develop a prototype information locator for the state; to the Bentley Historical Library and School of Information at the University of Michigan for an electronic records conference in 1996 (NHPRC, 1997); and to a collaborative project in New York between the state's Forum for Information Resource Management, Center for Technology in

Government, and Archives and Records Administration to develop a "system development model" for electronic record keeping embedded into statewide telecommunications systems and computing networks. Comparatively speaking, NHPRC grants are not large, they are often for start-up and feasibility projects, and outcome assessment has often been too weak to ensure transferability of lessons learned, but one can sense in these awards greater coherence, program direction, and potential than previously.

NHPRC is to be congratulated for this turnaround and its funding needs to be increased to sustain this momentum. If improved funding through NARA is not forthcoming, one might hope for closer collaboration with the National Science Foundation. NSF involvement could elevate the research components of these archival projects, engage computing historians and social scientists more in archival initiatives, and assist in wider information dissemination outside the archives and records management community. Attention to such archival issues by the National Commission on Libraries and Information Science (NCLIS) and other such bodies in the United States and other countries would not be out of the question. One might hope for cross-institutional studies and project comparisons and syntheses like benchmarking focusing on (1) quantitative analysis of costs, productivity with some objective definition, service with specific aims, quality assessment, and effectiveness; (2) inculcation of understanding "world-class" best practices to assist in filtering change by imitation and standards; and (3) how each project creates the next step or opportunity to learn more from the best practitioners (SPENDOLINI). All along NHPRC might have been building a database to enable benchmarking and to identify best practices, like some consulting companies (e.g., the Hackett Group), and if not entering into consulting directly, it might have created a consultant service not through SAA or other professional organizations, but by placing key archival consultants in consulting firms specializing in information technology, reengineering or change management, and work with the Fortune 500 league.

In each of the questions asked by the NHPRC one may substitute "computing historian" for "archivist" given that he or she essentially becomes a project archivist in the course of conducting research in an electronic environment with electronic records and data analysis. Moreover, the answers supplied to these questions by archivists will affect the very essence of future historical research. Perhaps one should substitute "historian" without qualification. Emphases in confronting such comprehensive issues are often bifurcated between intellectual access to electronic archival information, especially concerning description and standards, and the information itself, its format, preservation, and issues of transferability. The historian may be instinctively more interested in content, but the *a priori* concerns must be with meta-information, i.e., information about information, since that unlocks access and forms the parameters on both perceived utility and actual use.

Through its grants program, NHPRC is sponsoring interesting investigations into the base structure of descriptive records by a working group of archivists in technical services; special education for electronic archivists at the UNIVERSITY OF PITTSBURGH where at its new Center for Electronic Recordkeeping and Archival Research an outline of the "functional" requirements of archival information systems was developed between 1993 and 1996 (these really enumerate characteristics of records in the tradition of Diplomatics, but with new terms and an updated framework, more than they depict systems operations or functions; cf., the last version in COX, 1997, pp. 10-11; expanded by BARATA (1997), who incidentally maintains a bibliography for electronic records research in conjunction with the Pittsburgh Project, which is described succinctly by DUFF, 1996; see Appendix C for a synopsis of the "functional requirements" proposed); testing at the University of Indiana in a project directed by BANTIN (cf., www. Indiana.edu/~libarche/index.html); criteria for their evaluation are being developed at the University of Pittsburgh (COX & DUFF; COX & WILLIAMS). Interest has increased in model policies and standards that would articulate a "best practices" baseline for organizational accountability and performance in documenting its activities, e.g., "Acceptable Business

Communications" framework (BARATA, p. 16). Applications to municipal records may be followed in the model Philadelphia Electronic Records Project (GIGUERE) and for state records developments at New York's Archives and Records Administration (SARA) Center for Technology in Government working with such state agencies as the Adirondack Park Agency (KOWLOWITZ & KELLY). The World Bank's use of imaging technologies for record keeping (13,000 records in the test phase) independent of any particular technology (World Bank adopted Excalibur's Electronic Filing System [EFS] software because of its "fuzzy" search logic, operating with Oracle databases), in keeping with the "life cycle" concept, provides an international case since it operates offices in eighty-one countries. Australian archivists prefer their own concept of the "archival continuum" to the notion of a life cycle, which seems to suggest the arcane idea of dead records buried in musty archives after their active life (A. PETERSEN; F. UPWARD). The basic idea of a continuum is a continued resurrection in long-term reuse (cf., MCCRANK, 1985)

Likewise the NHPRC and the Canadian Social Science and Humanities Research Council have made generous grants to the archives program at the University of British Columbia to determine what a record is in an electronic information environment (i.e., "protecting electronic evidence"; see progress reports by DURANTI & EASTWOOD, 1995; DURANTI & MACNEIL, 1996). A team at UBC is now investigating the "Preservation of the *Integrity* of Electronic Records," which is obviously a more complex question than merely "archiving" in the computer center's sense of hanging a backup copy on magnetic tape in a vault. The issue of defining an electronic record seems simple enough at first glance, but in its simplicity lies such complexity that old cardinal concepts in archival theory and practice like accessioning, appraisal, and description are severely challenged. Led by DURANTI's European perspective (1997), Diplomatics plays a large role in bringing the documentary aspects of electronic archives to the foreground (DURANTI & MACNEIL). This is an approach which I find attractive because it is deeply rooted in historical practice and thought regarding evidentiary records, authentification, and the objectivity of historical events that requires recourse to a standard of proof other than personal recall and opinion.

Cardinal concepts exploited by Duranti and her coworkers are reliability and authenticity of records in all forms, including electronic. Duranti takes time-honored principles and practice and adopts them to modern times, revealing a flexibility even for electronic records which may be stored and conveyed as bytes and bits, but which must be rendered into intelligible form for human understanding and use. Thus, the UBC team provide templates for easy comparison of records in tradition form, subject to diplomatic analysis (templates 1-4), and records in electronic environments which can nevertheless be identified by their medium, content, form, persons (in the juridical sense), acts (evidence of action), archival bond or relationships, and mode of transmission (template 5). She advocates that complete electronic textual records need to conform to required diplomatic criteria: dates of creation, transmission, and receipt; attestation or statement of authorship; titling or address; inscriptions of senders, receivers, and intermediaries; and disposition or expression of will or judgment of the author. The record's reliability increases in proportion to its completeness and precision in such data, revealing control in its creation and transmission. Its authenticity is conferred by its mode, form, state of transmission or manner of preservation and custody. COX (1997) thinks that the problem is more than Diplomatics can resolve, but it is refreshing to see American archivists analytically discuss the components of documents, the essence of their "recordedness," in concrete terms in line with a rich intellectual heritage in historical Diplomatics and its kinship with Codicology and Analytical Bibliography—of which most knew nothing from their archival training and education in American History.

While some archivists, in awe of the challenges in electronic record keeping, have opted to throw out these concepts as obsolete or overthrown by current technology (KESNER, 1998), and have simultaneously opted to transmogrify the traditional role of the archivist, a perspective holding onto continuity would see principles as expandable rather than dogmatically defined once and for all time, so that appraisal needs to be accomplished in any case, and respect for "original order" in the old linear model may have to become a respect for disorder in nonlinear records creation. LIVELTON attempts to arrive at an archival theory based on epistemology, that is, the analysis of ideas rather than records or any particular form of document, and then to apply such analysis to the concept of records generally and more specifically, public records. JENKINSON's influence is apparent, especially in tying archives so closely to governance and the British notion of sovereignty rather in contrast to the American more secular notion of administration. This latest attempt to advance archival theory may crystallize one strain, but it falls short of contributing to the fundamental problem of an operational definition for electronic archives. After all, it is difficult to advocate record keeping when one lacks a useable definition of an electronic record; or, since it cannot be defined as a physical unity, it may be perceived to be an intellectual entity that is still fraught with problems when attempting to apply a purely theoretical notion to a real system. Knowledge of the relationship of an information system that acts as a model for subsequent retrieval (i.e., all information systems operate historically) to actual information exchange at the time of initial decisions, action, and recording of events is important. D. ROBERTS, specifically from an archival perspective, offers working definitions and distinctions between records, documents, and data. DURANTI's approach is to define a record by its characteristics, which constitute whatever is required for its acceptance by a juridical system: i.e., authorship or responsibility identification, the act itself, a stable medium, form, and context. The record is a natural byproduct of some action, which it records. ISO (ISA/DIS 15489) likewise uses the word being defined in the definition, which violates a cardinal rule of lexicology: i.e., a record is recorded information in any form, created, received, and maintained by an organization or person in the transaction of business and which is kept as evidence of that activity. Common usage in Computer Science is largely irrelevant, except that all of this must come together in some kind of representation.

The United Nations *Guidelines* (UN ACCIS, 1990, pp. 17-70) holds onto the amorphous definition (p. 19) from the 1968 United States legal definition adopted by the United Nations in 1984, that a record is "an item that documents the actions of an agency in the conduct of its business" and describes such as "documentary materials, regardless of physical type, received or originated by the United Nations, or by members of its staff...". NARA retention schedules (nos. 20, 23, 1988) hold onto the holistic definition option to cover entire classes of records described as things, materials, etc., but increasingly the notion is shifting toward definition by transaction, combining form and function to document activities. Apart from the old notion that a record is a thing, i.e., item with content, structure, and context, distinct from the more ethereal notion of information, such definitions attempt comprehensiveness and do not specify format, so electronic records are always presumed to be included. But as DEARSTYNE noted (1993, p. 225) from the NAPA study (p. 31): "An electronic document is not so much a 'thing' as it is a set of relationships." Archivists are thus having to return to fundamentals and basic conceptualizations to search for redefinition, similar to LOSEE's search for a domain independent definition of "information" more than a generation after the formation of Information Science. The archival notions of authenticity and integrity associated with a record by DURANTI & EASTWOOD, or reliability (DURANTI, 1995), are not so often included in discussions about information, but concepts of reception, relevance, and belief in Information Science can be related to the notion of trustworthiness in Archival Science and credibility in History. The philosophical hairsplitting between action and act, process and record, and reenactment versus replication are difficult to transfer to applications. The required move in thinking from object to process orientation in purely electronic environments "challenges traditional information science" and it certainly undermines the styles of critical apparatus and citation mechanisms that operate for printed materials. It challenges History, too, but each of these fields seems to be approaching the issue differently.

If archivists are now asking such basic questions as "What is an archival record?," the implications for historical research are tremendous. When answers are forthcoming, they could fundamentally alter the nature of archives, the mission of archival institutions, and the course of archives history. The issues translated into History are far more complex than sometimes understood; rather than merely finding an appropriate citation for a record used in historical research, the issue is what is the very "thing" being cited, which traditionally has always meant that "it" is retrievable for verification. Current archival thinking about appraisal, selection and retention, and document retrieval, whether in electronic or physical form, often skirts around the core issue of uncertainty and the truth-claim of history based on evidential research (see L. E. JOHNSON). Pierre Bayle raised such issues in the late seventeenth century, but Baylesian skepticism is seldom addressed by archivists directly. They often write as though their problems today are new, when their own historical backgrounds should alert them to the timelessness of their questions. But the new electronic environment is somewhat mind-boggling, either by intimidation or enormous attraction to modern information technology. Either seems to undermine an applied historicism.

Electronic archivists like HEDSTROM and MICHELSON, however, have grappled with comparisons of electronic records with predecessors in other form. Although continuity exists in content, discontinuity is obvious in process. The record as a coherent physical entity may not really exist, except as strings of 1/2s, +/-s, O/● s, etc. in strings, strewn throughout many systems and stored on a variety of media, that come together on command to create code that is translated for human recognition. Without the command function, a retrieval mechanism, the communications network, the synchronic operation of several host machines, and a power supply, the "record" does not exist, and the traditional citation referring to the non-existent record is largely meaningless. Nor is the late medieval concept of authorship which underpins bibliographic systems sacrosanct. Instead, the hybridization of documentation is returning to the early medieval milieu of composite documentation where an office, but not an individual, constitutes the authority for the creation of a document, its release, and dissemination.

Archivists now speak of the "competence" behind the information system, much like catalogers assign corporate entries to records for lack of an author, to move into more nebulous phraseology and thereby escape the empirical identification that authorship has come to mean. Future citations may be addresses and codes that trigger the interaction that recreates information on demand if all components necessary for such archival retrieval have been maintained. Or citations may have to appear like genealogies documenting the transference of information through successive stages in order to record a chain of custody as in the case of providing evidence for the admissibility of evidence in a court of law; i.e., documenting documentation, as BEARMAN & SOCHATS sum up the process of maintaining metadata or trace information. This obviously involves so much more than merely providing a URL address or standard citation form for referral, but a really critical apparatus will provide reference to documentation and assurance of the authenticity of the records being cited as evidence. If the electronic form cannot be retrieved as used originally, or in an authentic representation which has a documented record of transference, enhancement, or migration, the pretense of citing evidence authoritatively is delusional.

Increased rigor in research methods, and the teaching of these, needs to come about in historical reconstruction. Rather than the usual reliance on relatively weak instructional guides in our graduate History curricula on evidential theory and examination and presentation practices, historians, and archivists especially, require more thorough, legal training. MCCRANK (1997) has argued that if History is to prepare students for careers other than teaching, then the rigor of historical research methodology and published research itself must meet normative standards and those set outside academe for Social Science research. It has been recognized for some time that historians' conceptualization and use of evidence are different from those in actuarial and the legal professions, just as modes of argumentation and persuasion differ. By comparison, historical research methods often seem lax and historical reasoning is too often implicit rather than explicit. Whenever historical reconstruction is taken out of History circles (conference, classroom, or History publication) and is introduced to an actuarial or law environment such as an audit process, hearing, or courtroom, different expectations prevail. The point is underscored by J. SCHLEGEL who links empirical social science to American legal realism. Perhaps, therefore, the best textbook to adopt, with modification for historical research not based on the whims of historians but on the limitations of historical data and archival record, would be the FEDERAL JUDICIAL CENTER's *Reference Manual on Scientific Evidence.* Consider especially the *Manual*'s sections on the management of expert evidence, evidentiary frameworks, use of reference guides, survey research, statistics and particularly multiple regression, and the use of consultants and experts, as well as the caveats throughout about conflict of interest and ethics. Other court handbooks would be useful, such as those on rules of evidence (ROTHSTEIN), examination of witnesses (GONZALEZ), and those on intellectual property, e.g., patents, trademarks, and intellectual property litigation guides (United States CONGRESS. COMMITTEE ON THE JUDICIARY).

These legal guides do not address archival and historical research directly but may be applied to this area creatively and rather easily. Consider, for example, the techniques of a trial lawyer in examination of witnesses applied to historical accounts as the only witnesses the historian has, the benefits of cross-examination in mining limited documentation. Compare such guides with either textbooks on historical methodology or books about archival appraisal, and one will immediately understand the relative lack of rigor, discipline and standards in much of historical research and archival work. If such rules have not been applied to documentary evidence in traditional formats, tried and tested, revised and retried, then the field is ill-prepared to tackle the even more complex electronic forms entering the archival arena. Most archival concern today is on technical procedure simply to acquire and save electronic files, to say nothing of appraisal for value and potential use, the evolution of a critical apparatus for use, and the evaluation and assessment techniques for appropriate use and interpretation of such evidence. In short, the critical apparatus upon which modern scholarship has come to rely is being severely tested by new technologies which require remediation and progress at the same time. Old standards and forms are being dismantled without anything immediately to take its place, while most academics proceed as if their enterprise were immune from such substantial and pervasive change. At least archivists have come to recognize the problem and include electronic records management in such textbooks as by DEARSTYNE (1993, pp. 222-241) and WILSTED & NOLTE. Inclusion is important, as is asking questions as the first step in problem resolution.

Electronic archives research agenda have been framed generally by HEDSTROM (1991) in one of the most insightful essays available. It can be used nicely as a platform on which to base any discussion of these disturbing and complex issues. She postulated the following (NHPRC, 1991, p. 30) for research on electronic issues:

1. The goal of archival research...is to develop generalized policies, practices, methods, and applications for the management, preservation, and dissemination of electronic records.

2. Research...should anticipate rather than react to technological trends.

3. Research...must account for the social, economic, and political aspects of organizational life that influence how information technologies are adopted and used by organizations.

4. Research...can build on what records managers and archivists already know about organizational information handling practices because [these] are evolutionary in nature.

5. Research must be interdisciplinary and draw on conclusions reached by other fields.

6. Research agenda must recognize that resources—expertise, funding, power to influence, and response time—are limited and [must] maximize the effective use of those resources.

Using the metaphor of "Understanding Electronic Incunabula" inspired by EISENSTEIN's work (whose inquiry incidentally was spurred onward by Bridenbaugh's attack on Cliometrics [p. ix]) which compared the printing press to the computer as "an agent of change," HEDSTROM (1991) maintains that because current technology trends are creating sharper distinctions between conventional and electronic files (echoing GAVREL, 1990 and observations of DOL-LAR best articulated in 1992), new approaches and techniques must be found, archivists must intervene into the implementation of information systems to guarantee the archival mandate's viability, and archival concerns must be embedded into descriptive and exchange standards for electronic records. She does not provide the answers to her thoughtful questions, but her essay abounds with hints of a direction for development. Charles Dollar (NHPRC, 1991, pp. 33-34) took exception to the metaphor "incunabula" and the paradigm of transitions in book publishing because they were more gradual and less massive than what is being experienced in electronic records (e.g., two centuries in contrast to a single generation). He suggested alternatives like the adoption of carbon copying within 20 years at the turn of the century which revolutionized office recordkeeping. He also disagreed that archivists (or historians for that matter) can have any impact whatsoever on the marketplace. He does not believe the thrust by archivists on standards will be enough to insure the archival preservation of modern electronic records.

The promise of digital preservation through comparatively inexpensive reliance on CD-ROMs seems premature, as CONWAY (1995) cautions. Whereas Conway's admonition is based largely on manufacturing processes which do not insure an archival product for long-term preservation, ROTHENBERG (1995) warns that whenever digital bit streams are translated to other media, as is done in some preservation programs for electronic records, something is lost each time. Eventually the original system is not maintainable. M. MILLER recently warned archivists not to mistake imaging technology as an easy answer to records management, appraisal for archival retention, or conservation, but stresses the need to know thoroughly the physical characteristics and uses of documents before transferring them to digital format. ZIMMERMAN concludes, regarding her investigation of Global Information Systems (GIS) preservation, that a critical technological and methodological gap exists here, which in essence means that all digital resources not transferred to another medium entirely are at risk. Digital library and archival projects, therefore, must be seen for the time being as access programs, not preservation programs.

This preservation issue seems to beg the question whether data are being captured at all in genuine archival programs for long-term retention. There are mechanisms to embed archival functional processes into the overall operations of a corporate entity or an individual's creativity on his or her workstation. These fall into a range of possibilities with decision support and design tools, but BEARMAN does not think archivists have used them to any real advantage. Nevertheless, the National Archives of Canada since 1988, reflecting the approach taken by Canada's Treasury Board, has taken the stand that it is the records creators who bear the initial responsibility to identify records properly at the so-called "item level" which retains a packaging connotation, but also attempts to embrace a content-oriented definition (J. MCDONALD). In 1996, the National Archives of Canada issued its *Guideline on the Management of Electronic Records in the Electronic Work Environment* (EWE) to provide strategies in offices to incorporate record keeping requirements in automated business practices (J. MCDONALD, 1996). The focus is on the "live environment" and process of records creation in a functional framework, not simply an appraisal of content in records or series, since related information in networked environments is now spread out over so many offices, agencies, and systems that a comprehensive approach is required and work habits must be influenced from the start (J. MCDONALD, 1997). Content is not always predicable and a total content approach has been criticized for a failure to supply evidence of activities, but only results (NOLTE; FAGERLUND). Moreover, full-text storage and term-matching retrieval returns one to the item-level approach. So there seems to be no escape from some kind of combination of content orientation with package retrieval.

Archivists in Ottawa as elsewhere now call for software designers to create dialogue screens which assign records to appropriate organizational components automatically upon creation, with built-in expert system components that operate on organizational models. The stress is on life-cycle landmarks which archivists maintain are unaltered in the conversion from manual to electronic communications. However, the item-level description and disposition tactic does not seem feasible, and at the same time stress on files as reflecting layers in management are less meaningful given the trend to flatten organizations, reform old hierarchies, and distribute work across interactive systems. Consequently, archivists call for a *coup de grace* (UN ACCIS, p. 24) in DBMS operations and file management so that components of files, when manipulated in parts and by function in various areas of an organization, are automatically documented and linked. Perhaps the solution is the application of control points for system-defined transactions in data processing, as at "save" commands or final use when deleted from RAM (BENDER). In any case, archivists have been warned (BIKSON *ET AL.*, 1985; MANKIN *ET AL.*, 1988) against any attempt to limit user options or system functions to preserve records since that would create political backlash and assuredly undermine an organizational approach to archives.

Uniformly archivists have gravitated by default and conscious adaptation toward the industry's use of metadata systems, i.e., Information Resource Directory Systems (IRDS; ANSI approved in 1988; FIPS 156 approved in 1989 [Federal Information Processing Standards]) or Data Dictionary/Data-Directory Systems as their key strategy (WERTZ; OSBORNE, ROSEN & GALLAGHER). The 1995 Metadata Invitational Workshop hosted by OCLC (hence, sometimes referred to as the "Dublin Standard" accessible at http://purl.oclc.org/metadata/ dublin.core) produced the Dublin Metadata Element List (DMEL) for describing electronic documents, with a controlled vocabulary, including a semantic header (an application of SGML in 1990) as conceived as part of HTML for Web documents (DESAI, 1994, 1995, 1997, p. 194). The Dublin conference was followed by another in the United Kingdom, resulting in the so-called "Warick Framework" (http://www.ub2.lu.se/tk/warick.html) aiming at a comprehensive and hence international infrastructure of "Network Resource Description." The approach is to conceive electronic records in networked environments as fixed information objects, hence documents, which seem to indicate compatibility between such description and extensions built upon this model, with Business Acceptable Communications as derived from the University of Pittsburgh project (BEARMAN, 1997). These evolving standards for descriptions of electronic documents at least provide foundations for systems audits and unobtrusive means of policy enforcement. They also indicate trends toward consensus and international cooperation, and a merger of archival and library interests in access to electronic information over the duration.

New data management tools have as many implications for archivists, and therefore historians, too, as for engineering, since they track the technical execution of design in manufacturing. i.e., "Design Evolution Management" (e.g., RAMESH). One prototype, IADEMS, has been experimented with at the University of Illinois (THOMPSON). It integrates input from multiple designers, tracks workflow, records decisions, schedules, traces revisions and alternatives explored but not acted upon, generates an explanatory record useful later in the technical writing of manuals, and in essence creates a "design process history" of the kind archivists dream about in contemporary and integrated documentation strategies. It is similar in purpose to Ramesh's aforementioned integration of design and simultaneous documentation in software design. These are directed specifically at group engineering processes to support decision making by documenting not only decisions themselves but what led to them.

Similar processes are being applied to all kinds of collaboration for distributed enterprise management. In some cases group actions are charted in what has been compared to mapping techniques (SAMBURTHY & POOLE), especially in cause analysis in corporate environments (EDEN, ACKERMANN & CROPPER). In other cases, meetings audits are circulated before subsequent meetings so that contributors all start from the same basis. This cyclical post-meeting reporting became the basis of *Group Systems V* from Ventana Corporation, originally from collaboration between IBM and the Electronic Meeting Systems (EMS) laboratory at the University of Arizona (NUNAMAKER *ET AL.*, 1987, 1989), which displays documents to participants in meetings while they are ongoing and records minutes, documents retrieval, tracks editions and additions, etc., in the course of the meeting for synthesis thereafter and recall of the dynamics of the discussion and decision-making. Such practices are now studied sociologically and psychologically by information scientists to enable shareware to act as groupware, in keeping with modern trends toward teamwork in large-scale organizations. MCGRATH & KELLY point to the influence of time on such dynamics in electronic discourse; their attempt to delve into the social psychology of time is as important for the understanding of historical events and processes as it is for such practical applications as managing meetings. Indeed, it is time management that is driving some of this reliance on electronic conferencing and related research.

The larger the enterprise and group, the greater the need to formalize such traditions and procedures as enabling mechanism for information sharing and supporting healthy group dynamics. In so doing, such groupware designers are unwittingly creating the kind of tools archivists need to document modern organizations (the history of such developments is recounted by MENNECKE, HOFFER & WYNNE). Indeed, MARSHALL, SHIPMAN & COOMBS describe one such hypertext system, *Aquanet*, as a "tool to hold your knowledge in place." Their thinking falls short of anything genuinely archival, but that description is not a bad definition of an archives. The problem with such development is that these solutions all seem software dependent. The move toward systematic use of metadata and external referents is to free records from such hardware or software dependence, to guarantee "least-loss" migration across systems over time (BRODIE & STONEBRAKER).

The COMMISSION ON PRESERVATION AND ACCESS in 1996 sought to clarify previously confused techniques and methods lumped under the ambiguous term "refreshing" data, to define "migration" as the periodic transfer of digital materials from one hardware platform or software configuration to another, usually across generations of technical development. Specifically the purpose of migration is to preserve "the integrity of digital objects" for future retrieval and display despite constantly changing technology. BRODIE & STONEBRAKER clear up some confusion in saving data from old systems by making it accessible through new systems, through a host of processes too often subordinated under the umbrella term "migration"—copying, reformatting, converting, and migrating records. The latter alone involves the following: analysis of legacy data, systems functions, and structure; decomposition of the original structure; designing target interfaces, applications, and new database structure; installation of the target system with necessary gateways; and the actual migration of legacy data, applications, and interfaces with an aftermath of checking and verification of a successful migration. This is not push-button technology. The implications of BRODIE & STONEBRAKER's enumeration of steps in this complicated process are important. One connotation is that the so-called "legacy" computing requires handling systems which resist modification and change and are therefore difficult to manage in new computing environments. This means that inclusion of archival objectives in electronic records management complicates computing significantly.

Archival information systems, which pay attention to records integrity and authenticity to avoid substantive change in transferring data between computing environments, invoke a higher standard (choices and operations are outlined by DOLLAR, 1999, incorporating recent reports by U. ANDERSSON and C. GRÄNSTROM).

Such mutual concerns for data, records, and project management have merged with the widespread adoption of groupware for collaborative research and distributed projects (MANSELL). Such convergence has refocused attention on the seminal importance of archives, not so much for long-term preservation, but for immediate needs in that all collaborators should operate from the same knowledge base. DAVENPORT & MCKIM in their benchmark review of groupware for ASIS in 1995 discuss this issue of convergence and rightly focus on the centrality of archives, although they treat this incorrectly under "the emergence of new issues."

This new issue is actually old and seems to be a constant in human affairs. The problem is twofold: (1) the development and maintenance of the archival base for collaborative research, and (2) project history and organizational memory, which CONKIN, DAVENPORT, HOFFER & VALACICH, MENNECKE *ET AL.*, and others discuss as an important issue in Information Science under any neologism possible rather than call it a matter of history. DERVIN & NILAN, entrapped in typical Information Science thinking and jargon, argue for historical reconstruction when analyzing why people turn to formal information resources or create formal information structures and products, but the process is never recognized as historical as such. In another case DERVIN (1977, 1988) argues for a "user-driven narrative" as a means of recall in decision making, described by DAVENPORT & MCKIM (p. 122) as "a revisiting of the sequence of events and perceptions that have brought individuals together on a given quest." Ah, historical recollection by any other name is now palatable within Information Science and has been rediscovered as a new issue! And the utility of historical narrative in information retrieval, long understood in archives, seems to be just dawning in Information Science, when in History the role of a dominant narrative is under attack. All of this seems very ironic.

Those who study group dynamics and collaborative work in "sense-making" (as opposed by WEICK [1985] to electronic nonsense) have become aware as well of the socialization dimension of group interaction as part of the design of decision support systems and groupware (DERVIN, 1992). WEICK (1969) is a strong advocate of history in sense-making, although he seems not to realize this, since he refers to the historical dimension in human interaction as "the reflective glance" and treats historical recall and reasoning as "retrospective sense-making." This reflects the milieu of Organizational Culture in Management, as discussed earlier. If such interest in recall, replay, and information management for group interaction and collective decision making were understood as a matter of history and historical relevance in a hermeneutic framework linking History and Information Science, one would have not only a basis for Historical Information Science in contemporary settings, but also the opportunity to embed in groupware design sound archival information systems.

The use of *Lotus Notes* is a case in point. Its features as a client-server network and asynchronous replication are especially inviting for archivist intervention, and because there is no structured group interaction mandated but provides a development framework for shared document-based data, an archivist can retrieve and organize "official" views and record use based on security clearances, message-passing, and workflow in collaborative settings. *Lotus Notes* was also upgraded in 1992 when the Zeta software company took over this groupware technology. Zeta's Customer Services Department developed a new real-time Incident Tracking Support System (ITSS) to log customer calls and thereby retain a history of service programming or, in essence, an archives. The introduction of ITSS spun off other changes that augmented the log and created a trouble-shooting database of solutions provided for customers, which was in turn upgraded by the introduction of quality-control systems, conventions such as rating levels of documentation supporting a logged-in solution (e.g., fully documented, documented by certain individuals, and customer verification). Ultimately as the case study provided by ORLIKOWSKI & HOFMAN indicates, managers began to rely on this "electronic archives" for performance evaluation in which documentation skills came to be considered as critical. Although not recognized as such, *Lotus Notes* as used by Zeta employees, produced a living archives; it grew naturally out of the operations of the corporation, became increasingly formalized and integrated into functions across the organization, and grew as a continually augmentable information resource.

While archivists struggle to leave the print paradigm behind and recognize that rather than primarily text the records of the future will be multimedia, the very notion of capturing a record means that the dominant thinking is still about a static view, e.g., a screen or a data array as it is in current Web "pages." Interactivity is a feature which still defies the archival imagination. The fluidity of information formats streaming past in 3-D virtual space, guided by intelligent agents, which the Internet 2 can support, will make even today's Web look like a traditional library with its addressed containers, serial retrieval, and page captures on a screen (GAUCH). Internet 2 is an academic initiative now sheltered by EDUCOM, which began in 1996 with 33 universities and is now supported by over 100 institutions. It aims to develop networked "gigapop" centers (high-speed transmission relays, OC12; high capacity, reliability with predictable performance, data streaming and security or authentification means) to support collaborative, inter-institutional research without the problems of today's Internet (40 percent loss of packets at some intersections, traffic congestion and overcrowding of education and research by entertainment and commercial concerns). Internet 2 will be dedicated to distributed multimedia learning, remote collaboration and teleimmersion, remote instrumentation and telescience, cooperative processing, telemedicine, and digital libraries (S. LYNN). Internet 2 is a vehicle meant to carry information and facilitate work that must be captured somehow as archival records despite the speed and volume it portends. More than anything else, for archivists and all archivally concerned researchers Internet 2 should flag the need to develop radically new methods for electronic records management in short order.

The new networked media of the next millennium, already well in sight during this decade, will merge the instructional and entertainment forms we are accustomed to distinguishing as independent media. KELLY & WOLF, editors of *Wired Magazine* (p. 17), predict a "radical future of media beyond the Web" in which networked media "are not archival, but immersive" (an odd juxtaposition, reflecting rather loose thinking and the popular rather than professional notion of what is "archival"). They advise:

> The image to hold in mind is an amusement park, full of experiences and information coming at you in many forms, some scripted, some serendipitous. It may be intense, it may be ambient, but it always assumes you are available. Push media arrive automatically—on your desktop, in your e-mail, via your pager. You won't choose whether to turn them on, only whether to turn them off. And there will be many incentives not to.

> Foremost is relief from boredom. Push media will penetrate environments that have, in the past, been media free—work, school, church, the solitude of a country walk. Through cheap wireless technologies, push media are already colonizing the world's last quiet nooks and crannies.

What is the source for this bombardment of information, images, and allures? What is driving this search for a new paradigm which archivists must consider? Again KELLY & WOLF provide an answer and advise a new way of thinking about multimedia in the near future:

> ...the 150 million Web pages now in existence won't disappear. They'll only proliferate, and at an increasing rate worldwide. We can expect a billion Web

pages by 2000. Some of them will even be worth reading. But superseding those billion pages will be a zillion nonpage items of information and entertainment. Think video. Think text flickering over your walls. Think games at work. Think anything where a staid, link-based browser is useless.

...The browser becomes invisible by becoming ubiquitous.

It is difficult to think of archives this way. The paradigm shift required is similar to museums becoming experiential and living museums, or moving into simulations, theatrical presentations (remember the combination of the Folger Shakespeare Library and Theater), theme parks, and scenarios such as the Renaissance Pleasure Faire and Living History Center in California ("history immersion" according to PAHL [1994] is an effective teaching method). Archivists have not made such a transition, and have not really caught up with the Web or how to figure out how to capture something this transient, unstable and volatile, which is simultaneously growing at exponential rates unthinkable for any other media. Archivists since 1992 have used sites to allow users to browse through documents, both finding aids and select records, but largely in imitation of online retrieval. Now we are told that browsers which retrieve two-dimensional information and which might have been the instruments for capturing archival samples will be phased out and replaced by "many-to-many" media: "anything flows from anyone to anyone—from anywhere to anywhere—anytime" in environments where information no longer "flows" but "cascades" and in a world where information is not broadcast or retrieved, but works its way across vast networks, always operative, ever present, through "ambient publishing."

Archival Science today has neither the impression or the paradigm by which to plot a future reaction to such developments; archivists do not even share the same vocabulary with the Silicon Valley 20-year-olds who are forging this multimedia world. History as a profession is not helping them. This is not a world by design nor accident but, more simply, a happening out of a complex milieu of latter twentieth-century technological developments. It is and will be a struggle to relate old concepts to this new information technology and interactivity. History often seems unrelated to such futuristic development, but all of this is history in the making. The more modern media becomes interactive and instantaneous, history is simultaneously made and destroyed. As in primitive, oral societies, the word, gesture, and image are communicated briefly and then pass into fading memory or oblivion unless intervention is also at the instant, immediate, and interactive. Like archivists, or perhaps as archivists, historians must insert themselves into living history at present, or History will continue to become fading memory and distant reconstruction. One must begin by taking stock of what exists now, and setting priorities that cannot include all things for all people and that cannot hope to save everything in pristine state, original order, or even in the same media. Tolerances for ambiguity and incompleteness, guided information transfer, tracking indirect provenance, and layered archives with degrees of completeness, reliability, accessibility, etc., may be in order for a new era of networked ubiquitous archives. Meanwhile, one must assess the current state of archival thinking to consolidate a foundation for such bold thinking, radical revisionism, and new initiatives. Archives cannot be recording after the fact; they must become, paraphrasing Hugh TAYLOR's capture of the medieval principle, "the very act and deed."

Evidence and Risk Management

What is the prospect for archivists to interject themselves in project collaboration and insure that groupware incorporate an archival program? Good, if archivists distinguish themselves from manuscripts curatorship and history, and they, instead, focus on modern records and information management. They must redirect their interest from a remote past to the immediately passing.

Part of this reorientation is good public relations, since without this modern face the power brokers in information technology and systems management are unlikely to admit archivists into their closed circle. But this refocus is not merely a pretense or a face-lift; it is a doubling of the knowledge base of Archival Science, a matching of modern technique and methodology to traditional theory and practice, and a commitment to continuing education to keep pace with the rapid development of information technology and to increased political activity to garner the financial resources needed to get the job done. Of course the personal and professional dilemma is how does one accomplish this without neglecting other responsibilities, including those to the historical record already accumulated? The divide between manuscripts curatorship and modern records management seems to be intensifying, calling for two or more sets of credentials (languages, methodological specializations, etc.) and areas of expertise (multiple degrees, double majors rather than a major with a minor field, etc.), similar to the specialization that has occurred in rare book curatorship within librarianship. It is no longer sufficient to be a generic archivist.

Although archivists in all fields are turning to modern information technology for various activities, including digitization of historical records for preservation and access, an elite cadre of North American archivists has developed expertise in electronic records. Many have been trained on the job as in national archives, some have retooled through continuing education, and a new generation of technically better-equipped graduates of Archival Science graduate programs has emerged. These archivists are interested in modern records almost exclusively and are obviously now searching for alternative approaches to electronic archives than those they inherited from a few fledgling operations for electronic records and the nonarchival approaches of most computer centers (DOLLAR, 1990, 1992, 1993, [1998]; BEARMAN, 1989, 1993; COX *ET AL.*, 1994). They are doing so with increasingly less input from historians, but their immediate concern is how to avoid creating a historical record after the fact. Increasingly they see the record as the *de facto* creation of action to be captured as a natural byproduct of the business at hand. Archivists are instead turning to trends in business and government and are relying on adherence to "best practices" to create archives conterminously with original documentation, not for the altruistic use of history, but for quality control and standards like ISO 9000 (HOYLE; W. PERRY), organizational effectiveness, and risk management.

The UNIVERSITY OF PITTSBURGH Center for Electronic Recordkeeping and Archives has developed a "Framework for Business Acceptable Communications" (BARATA. p. 16; see www://www.lis.pitt/edu~nhprc/. File name: Example.txt [e.g., version dated 4/21/97]) based on the legal concept of a "warrant," which in ordinary language is an assurance or guarantee against harm, loss, or injury (DUFF, 1997; in contrast to BEGHTOL's use for literary warrant). Coming from medieval customary law, it is like a bodyguard pledge, except here *corpus* means a body of information that serves as evidence.

In more specialized legal usage a warrant also conveys authority, which is usually in the form of proof, to justify a decision or action as in a sanction or when providing a representative with the warrant of attorney. It is in this vein that R. WILLIAMS cites state laws regarding the legality of optical storage and microfilm used in modern litigation. The warrant itself is an instrument which invests power, an act of authorization, as in a warrant for arrest in the case of wrongdoing. The warrant is itself a record, which requires further record keeping to document decision and actions taken to comply with custom, tradition, law, or in modern business, best practices as determined by an external party as an objective standard. Requirement 6 of the Functional Requirements of Recordkeeping rests on "literary warrant" explained as a "requirement [which] derives from the law, customs, standards and professional best practices accepted by society and codified in the literature of different professions concerned with records and record keeping," i.e., the American Institute of Certified Accountants (Auditing Standard 55); EDI security control standards; United States Department of Commerce Technology Administration and NISO standards for Open Document Architecture (ODA) interchange (which has lacked a broad commercial base) and Raster Document Application Profile (DAP); and, of course, endorsements of these by professional associations (ASIS,

ARMA, SAA, etc.) and adoptions by influential organizations such as NARA, of course, but more so the Department of Defense contracting where the difference between compliance and non-compliance means loss of major business income (DUFF).

Historians might consider what this would mean if such a requirement were embedded into grants that support their research, if the NHPRC imposed this on documentary editing projects as good business practices, and if university tenure and promotion reviews considered such requirements as a means to ensure quality research and publication as an extension of the warrant required of graduate students by graduate schools mandating a prescribed standard for the proper presentation of a thesis or dissertation (but more than form control would be warranted in filing electronic research, theses and dissertations, or publications for faculty review files). If historians were to apply their craft in historical teaching, research, and publication "up to standard," according to the federal and state rules of evidence and warrants in state records laws, a radical transformation of professional practice would be in order. The point is that to submit historical and social science research based on records, paper or electronic, to the test of legal evidence is precisely what is required, not by academe apparently or our professional associations, but by our laws and courts. If historians train themselves for work outside the classroom, or train archivists who assuredly will work beyond the classroom, such standards must be taken into account in graduate education, research practice, and information resource management. While integrity may remain a personal attribute, compliance may be self-imposed but also mandated externally. Standards, always existing as "the other" to adopt a postmodern popular way of phrasing it, are objective in the sense that they lie beyond the pale of personal consideration, whim, influence, or limited expertise.

The specification of quality controls may be dated back to 1951 with the work of J. M. Juran and developed mainly in military specifications in RFPs (Request For Proposals) and bid processes. The Quality movement gained momentum in the 1980s, but took on an especially strong record keeping and even archival form (although the term "archives" is seldom used in the basic manuals) in industry and manufacturing, both as a safeguard against liability and for enhancement of corporate and product reputations for competition in a free market. The shortest working definition may be that by HOYLE (p. 5): "fitness for use" which encompasses notions of excellence, conformance with requirements, freedom from defects, and customer satisfaction. However, products cannot meet ISO 9000 standards; organizations can, since these are process oriented. ISO standards came about in 1987 and have evolved in the development of an organizational quality management system as they were adopted in more than 100 countries. Hence "quality standards (e.g., SAE ARD 9000 for Quality System Regulation itself, and layers of industry specific standards, e.g., 9000 for production, 9000-1 quality management assurance, 9002-3 for Quality Systems models, and 9004-1 to 7 for system elements, etc.) are now being adopted by educational programs as well (e.g., York County Area Technical Vocational School using ISO 9002-1996). Briefly Level 1 includes Quality policies and assignment of responsibilities; Level 2 contains Quality procedures; Level 3 consists of job instructions; and Level 4 is a records management system demonstrating and documenting compliance. They are applicable to any research project and to archives operations themselves. If interpreted and applied properly, they entail the establishment of an archival information management system within an ISO compliant organization even though the standards do not see themselves as promoting archives *per se*. Here again, as in the case of "history" under any other name in the information fields, "archives" assume a new identity under Total Quality Management, perhaps because of their association with distant history, rather than historical information in its original form and first-generation use.

The elements of ISO 9000-1 are (HOYLE, pp. 38-39):

4.1. Management responsibility entails a "buy-in" and guarantee of support from top-level management.

4.2. Quality System is the overall design for policies, procedures, documentation, and audits or evaluations.

4.3. Contract review schedules are formal and routine expert reviews by disinterested third parties to maintain ISO registration through external audits, inspection, and assessment.

4.4. Design Control establishes the Quality system, its functions, operations, and maintenance.

4.5. Document control is often expressed in terms of records management, but increasingly in terms of automated systems (Information, sometimes Integrated Systems Technology (IST) known collectively as Document/Data Processing Management/Electronic Document Management (DPM/EDM).

4.6. Purchasing procedures, vendor selection, etc. favor using ISO registered suppliers. Of course this element can be interpreted for information work like data "acquisition" and archives accessioning.

4.7. Customer-supplied product procedures for verification, storage, and maintenance of the product can be reinterpreted for archival purposes as appraisal, but more if "verification" is taken to mean assessment of quality, e.g., reliability and conformance to requirements. This element is to protect the organization from faulty "input" whether raw materials, component parts, or poor records, bad data, and unreliable information.

4.8. Product Identification and traceability, which librarians would see as cataloging and tracking to a publisher, are what archivists would call description and the application of the principles of provenance and respect du fonds (origin, original order, integrity, consistency, context, chain of custody, and record linkage for inference and reference).

4.9. Process Control includes identifying and planning production under controlled circumstances to insure quality in processing, manufacturing, and production of any product, including information sources.

4.10. Inspection and Testing must be done before a product is used or processed until it has been inspected (e.g., in data sets, loading data to insure readability and basic DBMS functionality).

4.11. Inspection, Measuring and Test Equipment standards for control, calibration, inspection, and guarantee of accuracy of tools are used to perform inspection and testing (e.g., something so simple as checking calendar and clock settings on the computer to ensure accurate dating in record processing).

4.12. Inspection and Test status reports create a historical or time/series metadata self- documenting file.

4.13. Control of Nonconforming Product(s) entails problem solving and contingency planning and constitutes a risk management subprogram.

4.14. Corrective Action includes procedures for remediation.

4.15. Handling, Storage, Packaging & Delivery processes, e.g., information storage and retrieval.

4.16. Quality Records or metahistory of production and processes allow evaluation of products and judgment about their quality.

4.17. Internal Quality Audits set up a mechanism for self-examination and control, which may be reviewed also in audits by external inspectors.

4.18. Training, which is also programmatic and is distinct from generalized education, pertains to work defined above as specific tasks (policy, procedure, process, etc.). Addresses specific training needs for all personnel performing activities that affect quality.

4.19. Servicing involves verification that service (performance and results) meets specified standards.

4.20. Statistical Techniques entail a match between data and proper measurement techniques and interpretative methodology.

Altogether these elements attempt to comprise a comprehensive quality assurance program. In business and industry, but increasingly in social services as well, and now education too, organizations that implement quality management programs and are approved through the external audit procedures are registered as ISO compliant companies. The registration, like a seal of "Good Housekeeping," can be used in marketing and supposedly adds prestige that can be converted through reputation into profitability. Archives have difficulty with the latter application, of course, but as an integral component of an overall ISO 9000 program they can justify their existence and cost on grounds more persuasive than for the sake of history. Yet, if such standards are met, one result may be quality data, records, and information on which to base better documented history. In fact, if history research projects adopted similar standards in conjunction with archives, better history all around may be the result. Moreover, graduate experiential training in laboratories, that is, History projects in which project management was taught as such and by example and quality control systems were used, would allow historians to develop skills and expertise marketable outside the classroom. This would seem especially relevant for those intending to practice History rather than teach it, in Public History, and particularly in Archives and the information professions.

This Quality approach to document and data control parallels established records management practices, but often falls short of producing a quality archives. Performance characteristics in quality systems (e.g., robustness, complexity, maintainability, reliability, flexibility, vulnerability, consistency, compliance, usability, traceability, as listed by HOYLE, p. 22) are similar to the functional requirements specified in the Pittsburgh project. In the archives field the overall goal has been labeled as one of "accountability." Archivists have not turned to the computer and information industry as such, except to ask for improved data management software adoptable to an organization's structure, perhaps because customarily a computer technician's concept of an archives or "archiving" is a backup or the act of copying data to magnetic tape and hanging it on a rack in a secured vault for safekeeping (indeed, downloading to a server is now called "vaulting" synonymously with "archiving"). Equally limited is the perception of archival preservation as meaning duration of a little more than a decade and archives internal to systems have been developed only as logs and diagnostic tools for repair and data recovery in case of damaged equipment. The computer industry and systems operators in organizations overall have been particularly obtuse in understanding long range, societal, and ethical dimensions of their technology, to a point that one wonders how they ever appropriated the name "information" for their offices and functions. That posture is changing, however, as the industry itself undergoes change in understanding public accountability and service as part of good business. Increasingly there is concern for archival preservation in big business, as exemplified by Xerox Corporation's collaborative venture with research libraries to explore using digitized media as appropriate preservation strategies (KENNEY & PERSONIUS).

For the time, however, digitization must be considered an access strategy rather than a preservation technology. This may be understood in the retro-conversion of sources in other formats to digital media, but it spells disaster for digital data which exist in no other form. Funding exists for retrospective conversion and development of digital libraries from already existing media, but not for the conversion of digital data to more stable media with life expectancies beyond a single generation. The National Media Lab reports that digital media can have a life expectancy of 20 years if properly stored in a controlled environment of 25 percent relative humidity at 40 degrees Fahrenheit (VAN BOGART, 1996), which entails considerable cost for a relatively short duration. For archival criteria, namely longevity and attendant readability, when modern electronic communication and information technologies are compared with other media and with information technologies now regarded as primitive (parchment, paper, codification, microforms, print, etc.), recent progress appears as massive regression. The information explosion may be just that, an explosion, with rapid combustion and massive destruction of the information mass produced. Man's technologies to destroy have always been greater than those to create and preserve.

CONWAY (1996), in a recent report for ACCIS relating to the Commission's tracking source conversion in its *Digital Collections Inventory,* warns especially against stamped CD copies, and prefers laser produced master recordings. Copying data between optical media is also more time consuming than transfers between magnetic tapes (DOLLAR [1998] compares costs for data transfer between magnetic tapes and CD-ROMs for large files, e.g., a terabyte of data, showing that optic media costs for the storage devices and the labor are fifteen to twenty times higher than for magnetic media). Electronic archives, therefore, still prefer magnetic media for long-term storage. More and more one sees better understanding of the connectivity between the technical creation of information and its immediate use, with reuse and long-term preservation, and with cost-factors that determine how long an institution can maintain electronic records. It has been estimated that the annual cost of managing one megabyte of electronic data is $7 in an active mode; the cost of use versus storage is considerably more, given that 80 percent of data on a typical network is accessed less than once a month, and 50 percent remains unused for more than a half-year (BALOUGH). Balough estimates as well that it costs (1997 prices) $2,400 to scan one linear foot of archival documents, not including preparation and indexing. So, retrospective conversion to electronic form is not always cost effective and it may increase access but also preservation risk; and conversion of electronic data to paper can be cost effective and better for preservation, but with a loss of convenience in access. The latter saves time but is costly. This is often justified by a claim to efficiency and greater productivity, but study after study has failed to substantiate this claim.

This theme of preservation related to access over time was the subject, for example, of a special seminar offered in spring 1997 by the Northeast Center for Preservation. Likewise the Rochester Institute of Technology Image Permanence Institute (RIT-IPI) in 1997 offered an intensive workshop on "Preserving Photographs in a Digital World" with the subtitle "Balancing Traditional Preservation with Digital Access." Such forums where business and industry meets with the preservation and user communities are relatively recent, given that digital conversion of archives has been undertaken for more than a decade. Media obsolescence, as S. ROSS observes, means that preservation of electronic records through periodic intervention is a neverending task. Software independence does not negate the increased dependency of all electronic media on human caretaking that is far more labor intensive, technically demanding, and expensive than physical record keeping.

This educational process of awareness for historical information related to present access in business and industry, even in the information industry, has been slow and difficult. Likewise, awareness backed by adequate technical information has grown slowly among historians and other user groups with a long-term vested interest in the survival of digital media. This tardiness is again the Achilles heel of History; it is always after the fact. This cross-divisional communication process has not been made easier by the close association of archives with History and by isolation from Business and the information industry, or by the common low regard among Business school faculty and manufacturers for archives and records management as a lower-level function than administration when in fact the two should be highly integrated. BEARMAN's association of archives and records management with risk management is an interesting ploy to reposition the archival enterprise in both Business education and corporations everywhere.

A cardinal issue is long-term information access rather than immediacy, which is a distinction that may not be appreciated by the business enterprise unless accountability over time is enforced by public policy and government. Similarly, C. LYNCH (1986) advocates the idea of differential investment in information by a corporation balanced against assessment of the potential cost of misjudgment or failure to retain the necessary levels of accountability and objectivity. These points are brought home for Australians by RENEHAN whose case study of the Victorian Audit Office (1988-1992) showed how poor record keeping can have dire consequences. All such appeals are to gambling strategies to hedge one's bet and play the odds, but no archivist or records manager has argued this case using probability methods. Instead, this is an emotional appeal under the guise of modern business prudence and accepted image of conservative management, to an important instinct or risk aversion. Archives, in this sense, are the ultimate form of "just in case" preservation of information in evidential form, so one can respond "just in time" during a liability crisis. P. L. BERNSTEIN, who sees "risk" in terms of the history of ideas, would place archives into Western development as a means to achieve control over one's future, to beat chance: "risk has always been a matter of measurement and gut" (p. 7). This is an era when "the very structure of the world as we have known it seems to be trembling at its foundations, intensifying the search for novel risk management techniques at all levels of human activity." This holds true as well in the preservation of information and evidence, hence, archives.

Electronic archivists, on the other hand, are also approaching data as their institution's intellectual property, or that which is held in the public trust, which may be licensed for use or may be freely used (but access may not be free), much like the medieval notion of *usufruct* which provided for widespread use but safeguarded ecclesiastical rights by guarding against the alienation of property. The Japanese futurist Yoneji MASUDA (p. 55) stated the issue in modern terms noting the multiplicative nature of information: "goods are consumed in being used, but information remains however much it is used." The real qualifications here are "use" which insures access in time, or disuse which reduces future access to chance; and the verb "remains" which suggests that information has a locus and original state which should not be destroyed in use. Information transfer, then, does not move information in the same way one transports goods; it is really a process of extension. Historical discussions seem to imply not only that electronic archives are alienable physically, when they do not exist physically, and may be hardware dependent in more ways than simply a technical compatibility issue. The data, software, and hardware may be so closely interrelated, as in the design of many expert systems, that the stored database, without the organizing retrieval system and interpretive display software, is useless. Even if read, context is lost, so original use is never recreated; the transfer involved in essence creates another intellectual entity from old data. In that case, it is a grave distortion of evidence to assume that a source remains inviolate through such restructuring or transmigration between systems. Here the deconstructionist critique of text, and of history as nothing more than reconstruction might be reconsidered. If taken, to an extreme, deconstructionism with its disbelief in truth would undermine not only history but the basic assumptions that sustain our society and culture. Total denial of the truth-claim of history is like abandoning good faith in business and the notion of accountability in human affairs. Not only would the need for archives disappear, but also the justification for accountants, actuarial managers, etc., and in most cases, lawyers and courts, since the possibility of reconstruction from evidence and critical judgment based thereon are so fundamentally questioned.

History working through archives, therefore, is a not a singular occupation of historians, and the concern of professional historians for the integrity of archival evidence may be less than that of other professions. Their concern, given the nature of modern electronic information systems, should be heightened when they understand that few information systems preserve evidence—they simply convey information. Just as a truth-in-lending ethic is involved in business transactions, so too must a similar truthfulness prevail in the transfer of data and information that preserve what archivists call the "recordedness" of evidence (COOK). In integrated multimedia systems where aural, visual, textual, and numeric data are interdependent, often a whole system must be transferred as a holistic record. Data preservation, as summarily treated in computer center operations, falls far short of this goal. Or, the reverse may be better because of the complexity and risk in transferring whole systems to other keepers. Do not transfer such databases or attempt duplication of such systems; instead, maintain them by mandate and organizational compliance, and provide access through some kind of reference service, and then arrange some form of research mediation. Document the documentation as used, so there is a record for the critical apparatus of the research, i.e., project archives, not just footnotes, so that one has living archives rather than unused records. Insure that the record of use in a continual enhancement of the archives (MCCRANK, 1985). Users, therefore, should contribute to the archives they use; and archivists should exploit their users by insisting on a reciprocal relationship and value-added payback. KROPAČ ([1997]) agrees indirectly when he describes sources as "living documents" whereby the original and commentary tradition interact continually. This may be extended to electronic media and to the kind of hyper linkage envisioned by H-Net participants who want to link reviews to books. A logical extension, not yet articulated by H-Net promoters, would be to link all secondary literature with primary sources, commentary with evidence, and hence text and data, and original data with enhanced data sets.

This model involves a reconceptualization of traditional archives as repositories, a creation of ancient temples or more relevant except for the facades of archival buildings perpetuating classical mythography, the castle keeps of medieval Europe. The modern model would be less conspicuous and more ubiquitous, like electronic records and modern communications. If surrogate records can be accessed for multi-institutional access and need not be exchanged to be used, and one can search electronic records hosted by any agency, increasingly the idea of a centralized archives whereto all archival records are sent in an accessioning process, is, as BEARMAN (1991) eloquently portrayed, an "indefensible bastion." This is because of the cost in transfer from an archives back into a research office, with attendant redundancy, technical problems in retrospective conversion of electronic data, and contextual distortion, is as great as in accessioning such from the offices in which they were created, or more accurately, from the systems where they developed. Moreover, most large archives are already coping with such backlogs in appraisal, accessioning, and description that they are not even dealing well with the records they have or their retro-conversion into electronic form for flexible use and preservation. Archival arrangement patterned after paper records is nonsensical, so traditional description for access records seems equally suspect. It is an argument that attacks the establishment and has some takers in America, a small following in Australia, and fewer still who can be identified in Europe. This is not so much to protect the establishment of formal archives; this is to promote the lesson of history showing time and again how perishable archives are and how much more vulnerable archives are in that critical stage when they pass from first to secondary use. Much more appealing to archivists generally is to police this transition with authority obtained by law or the highest level of administration in organizations, to reposition themselves in organizational structures so they can influence records creation, and to argue on the basis of risk management the needs for evidence and in cultural terms to keep long-term memory in tact. The archives, true to its ancient metaphoric tradition, is the proper locus for such memory.

Already major changes seem imminent as indicated by the Standard Data Description format used by historical data archives which are moving toward incorporation of Standard Generalized Markup Language (SGML) coding invented by Charles Goldfarb and colleagues at IBM's Cambridge Scientific Center from the precursor, GML, which was adopted as an ISO standard in 1986: ISO 8879 (GOLDFARB, 1985), or embedded metadata rather than traditional separate descriptions (GOLDFARB's *Handbook,* 1990/1991; see GOLDFARB [1990, 1997] and MOSHER & PETERSON for recollections relating to SGML's history). SGML has now overtaken its rival, Open Document Archival (ODA), formerly Office Document Architecture (ISO 8613 standard), which for the sake of "blind exchange" of documents restricts the character sets and notations used (see CAMPBELL-GRANT for ODA; MARCOUX & SEVIGNY, pp. 588-589, compare the two standards; the TRAVIS & WALDT *SGML Implementation Guide* treats SGML migration; see VAN HERWIJEN; SENGUPTA & DILLON, etc. for applications).

The SGML-based Encoded Archival Description (EAD) project in the United States promises to provide guidelines for the use of text coding in archival description (sample HTML and SGML encoded finding aids can be viewed at http://sunsite.berkeley.edu/Finding Aids/index.html). EAD Document Type Definition (DTD) was developed at the University of California, Berkeley, as related by D. PITTI (1995, 1997), one of the principals in the UC project (using DynaText software, 1995-); but it achieved momentum in the archival world after a group fellowship award enabled several archivists interested in description to convene in 1995 at the Bentley Library at the University of Michigan, and at an invitational conference on finding aids at Berkeley that same year (DOOLEY). Both Harvard and Yale Universities are using EAD and Softquad's Panorama Pro viewers and search tools and OpenText/LiveLinks server and software to create unified (but not uniform) finding aids to their massive legacy files of metadata (324 paper finding aids have been converted at Yale for the Sterling, Beinecke, and Divinity library collections), working across multiple depositories in their institutions that have their own autonomy, subject collections, persuasions, and traditions. (Harvard, for example, has 98 separate libraries and 49 archival repositories with 14,000 finding aids of which only 21 percent are electronic (N. BOUCHE and L. MORRIS respectively for Yale and Harvard), in contrast to a small repository implementation at the University of Vermont (E. DOW). The NEH-funded American Heritage Project among the Universities of Virginia to where Pitti has moved, California-Berkeley, Duke and Stanford are likewise using EAD to create electronic access to their guides (500 have been converted to date) and digitized collections (e.g., Jefferson letters at U.VA: SEAMAN). Their integration of EAD projects with their OPACs is influencing how they use MARC cataloging. An SAA CAIE Working Group on Encoded Archival Description is attempting to formalize EAD into an archival standard (KIESLING), and in 1998 the Society hopes to offer a series EAD workshops around the country. S. HENSEN laid out there a rationale for a seamless web of online descriptions for access to archives via the Internet/WWW. The Library of Congress also lent impetus to this development by adopting EAD in its Prints and Photographs Division (A. MITCHELL; J. RUTH), and Harvard and Yale Universities have adopted SGML tools to develop a finding aids system that cut across their many different repositories (L. MORRIS; N. BOUCHE). Many of these projects were reported to SAA members at the 1996 and 1997 conferences as a prelude to the 1998 education effort.

The SGML/EAD DTD can provide archivists and their users with fuller description (text now, but also image) than MARC ACM description, which can be used in a complementary fashion as a boilerplate for the more extensive metadata captured in a DTD. Or, the SGML/EAD DTD can function independently of MARC-based systems in the Internet/Web environment. Keyword searching, however, needs to be complimented with predefined and designed cataloging and finding aids. Context information and navigation guides must be provided as well as free-term association and subject-heading matches. While the coding and format of

SGML/EAD DTD are being enhanced (e.g., links to authority records), and this can serve as the preferred record syntax for archival information exchange between computers, MAFTEI (1997) reminds us that coding itself, especially elaborate coding, produces technology dependence. Only code-free data can be stored independently, so when possible data should be separated from coding (in the same way that in machine-translation systems since the turn of the decade have always separated text from layout for storage and manipulation; the two are reassembled only for display). He notes that for the time the only completely hardware and software independent data exchange format is the *Abstract Syntax Notation* (ASN.1) for the description of structured data. Maftei suggests that EAD DTD be harmonized with the General International Standard Archival Description (ISAD) and International Standard Archival Authority Record for Corporate Bodies, Persons, and Families (ISAAR/CPF) descriptive standards (see his Archival Data Model, fig. 2, p. 13); and that EAD tags explicitly support multiple levels of description. These would be in keeping with MCCRANK's recommendations over a decade ago (1988) for linking bibliographic and archival descriptive cataloging and fuller diplomatic and codicological descriptions through stratified vocabularies and authority records, and for phased or multitiered cataloging and formatted descriptions so metadata grow incrementally and inferential systems become dynamic. MAFTEI (p. 7) also recommends that archivists redesign their finding aids, but now to take advantage of hypertext/hyperlink capabilities of Web browsers. Most discerningly, he warns against promotion of SGML/EAD DTD as an archival descriptive standard in the same way MARC became a descriptive cataloging standard, rather than EAD's more promising role as a communication format.

These applications are abetted by solid foundations in standards development beforehand. NISO provided a toolkit for developing customized SGML applications (NISO/ANSI/ISO 12083, replacing Z39.59-1988; VAN HERWIJEN provides an annotated version, a history of the standard, and examples; see also ALSCHULER for case studies). Finally software has been developed to insert SGML coding based on standard word processing commands (NISO's SGML *TagPerfect*). Such ready-made tools would allow archivists, for example, to customize formats and combine these with such coding devices for an online toolkit available to archivists and historians everywhere. SEAMAN, based on his experience with the NEH-funded cooperative American Heritage Project hopes to add content guidelines to encourage best practices in all coding projects. J. D. MASON reviews the ongoing work of ISO's Document Processing and Related Communications working group of the Joint Technical Committee 1, Information Technology (also sponsored by the International Electro-technical Commission [IEC]) for the development of (1) Document Style Semantics and Specification Language (DSSL): ISO/IEC 10779; see ADLER for its functions in providing a transformation language, specifications for formatting characteristics, query language Standard Document Query Language (SDQL), and an expression language; (2) hypermedia languages like *HyTime* (developed initially in 1992; ISO/IEC 10744; DEROSE & DURAND to provide a users' guide to *HyTime*; see KIMBER & WOODS for its hyperlink applicability to historical writing); and (3) SGML itself related to the UNICODE application (developed by Xerox and Apple as a 16-bit scheme) of ISO/IEC 10646 character encoding standard for multilingual computing.

Consequently, archivists focusing their attention on electronic records are looking to records creators for assistance, by indirect control through policy rather than through direct custody of electronic records, new mechanisms for intellectual access, and use of networking for access across distributed depositories and offices throughout an organization. An appropriate model may be the aforementioned ISO 9000 approach to insuring proper documentation in manufacturing through standards, voluntary compliance, and certification based on information audits and inspections. The idea is that if an agency creates records it has the obligation to do so according to standards so they can be kept, and the agency assumes responsibility for maintenance and supplying electronic access according to established procedures and policies; transfer and disposition to a central archives is a process of last resort such as when the agency is shut down and the records are in danger. This applies to history project management as well. Moreover, the agency has presumably already created some kind of access system which requires some form of description, tagging, coding, and cataloging. Archival description is usually a second-time processing, much like a re-editing and standardization for user convenience. It is time consuming and costly; efforts might be better spent at the front end of the records creation process rather than at the back end when records become less active. Improvements in up-front description and adherence to standards might increase and prolong use. In such cases the old distinction between active and inactive records to demarcate the difference between recorded information systems and records management from archives, becomes blurred. So too does the distinction between original use and historical uses, resulting in what North American archivists have come to think of as "continuing" rather than "permanent" value. The former term recognizes multiple phases for different kinds of usage of recorded information, rather than a simple dichotomy. It also co-opts office managers into the archival process and shifts the age-old stress on historical uses for archives to contemporary use.

Such a paradigm shift in the archives community is tantamount to revolution of the archives: it is more than a redirection of emphases, but a realignment of professional values. The new management model is one of distributed archives and networking, sharing of records management responsibility through organization policy formulation and adherence to best practices, and electronic access and reference. Such a reformulation of the modern archives will distance these organizations from data archives and the historical manuscript variety of archival depositories, and from History too, as archival management completes this process of integration into management and identification with the information profession. On the other hand, the long-term results should benefit history, so it has been argued, by providing a more comprehensive, balanced documentation, by saving more and better records that have an increased chance of survival, and by improving access from remote sites across our expanding networks.

Such revisionist thinking is apparent in several case studies and reports from the UNITED NATIONS, the United States NATIONAL ARCHIVES AND RECORDS ADMINISTRATION (NARA), and reports from Australia during this past decade. These provide a historical perspective on archival thinking about large-scale organizational electronic archives, which despite their recent vintage, seem now like a prologue to the fast breaking developments of Internet/WWW in the last half of this decade. The acceleration of such developments in information technology and networking in particular have hardly allowed archivists' thinking to gel into any kind of consensus before new problems are thrust upon them. GAVREL's RAMP study for UNESCO and the international archival community in 1990 on "conceptual problems" posed by electronic records framed the important questions, as in HEDSTROM's subsequent essay that acknowledges indebtedness to this report. Both show that coming into this decade archivists had yet to reach any consensus about electronic records, except perhaps agreement with Charles Dollar's arguments, which were articulated in his 1992 survey of electronic media and technical trends, that old approaches will not work (DOLLAR, 1994).

The UNITED NATIONS Advisory Committee for the Coordination of Information Systems (ACCIS) report (1990) had concluded the same. The ACCIS Technical Panel survey begun in 1988 (1990, p. 11) found that in the United Nations alone eighteen different agencies were using 22 different e-mail systems, not necessarily interoperable (only a third had networking operations in place), but overall use was increasing at a rate of 3 to 5 percent every year. Not only were current communications not working systemwide, but only a fourth of the agencies had long-term retention policies. Most offices were following vendor-driven policies without prioritization of the organization's holistic needs. United Nations surveyors also found that despite prophecies of the "paperless office," most agencies relied on paper controls (e.g., print indexes, traditional files, etc.) for managing their electronic records. In their implementation of automation, office managers lacked the know-how and even when knowing better, they still lacked the time to develop new methodologies consistent with the technology they were employing. Many were simply waiting for vendors to supply software that supported such record keeping procedures. Meanwhile, for nearly a decade communications were scrambled, records were lost, and even for those saved, finding aids were incongruent with the format of the records themselves. Anyone studying United Nation functions, policy making, etc. for the past decade whether as self-study for assessment and improvement, legal background work, or subsequent historical inquiry faces serious obstacles in this case, and presumably in many others as well. One might regard the United Nations, like other large governmental organizations, to have been simply a stereotypical mess, but state and local situations are as sad if not worse, and universities and library systems, which supposedly are more adroit in their approach to information and business, may be no better; hence, they are no more accountable. If archivists cannot continue to do what they have been taught based on experience with paper records, what then are they to do?

In 1989 a task force organized by the NATIONAL ACADEMY OF PUBLIC ADMINIS-TRATION (NAPA) had voiced concern about the preservation of federal records in electronic form in response to a Committee on the Records of Government which had earlier (1985) concluded (NAPA, 1991, p. iii) that "the proliferation of electronic technology with the federal establishment posed a danger to the historical record." The 1985 report (p. iii) said "NARA must seize the initiative" and reassess its own capability to master "knowledge of emerging technologies...". The Committee's recommendations were for:

1. Development of a systematic, long-term plan with Office of Management and Budget (OMB), General Services Administration (GSA), National Institute of Standards and Technology (NIST), etc.

2. Sponsorship of document prototype record keeping projects

3. Review with OMB of federal requirements for records management

4. Initiation of outreach programs to provide guidance in offices generating electronic records.

5. Provision of detailed, practical guidelines for agency use such as summaries of laws and regulations, checklists for audits and self-inspection, definitions and procedures, and preliminary retention schedules.

6. Development of software models for built-in record keeping rules

7. Involvement in federal standards formulation

8. Technology assessment projects, at least every three years, to stay current

9. Research programs in NARA and outside through contracts

10. Cooperation with OMB to obtain legislation for better records management

11. Encouragement of the transfer to NARA of electronic records from agencies and review of older schedules and "rules of thumb"

12. Creation of indexing schemes for information storage and retrieval

13. Initiation of job audits to create a chain of command for records responsibility

14. With the help of the appropriate professional organizations, sponsorship of a reexamination of the relationships between archivists, historians, librarians, records managers, systems personnel, and other technology specialists. The goal of this

re-examination would be to promote understanding between these professions and to develop methods and avenues of cooperation" (p. 14)

15. development of collaborative mission statements between NARA, GSA, and the Academy and electronic user groups, action recommendations, etc., for incoming administrations

16. Creation of "single point contacts in agencies" and use of "account executives" and "desk officers" to monitor information flow

17. Continued assessment of NARA's staff capabilities, administrative leadership, management functions, efficiencies, and allocation of resources.

The 1989 NAPA panel of 14 archivists, historians, and information scientists was in effect a result of the 1985 recommendations. This group concluded "… the wholesale loss of historically important documents has not yet occurred. But the panel believes that unless steps are taken soon valuable documents will be lost." Somewhat inconsistently the report declared, "This is a time of urgency and NARA must take meaningful, realistic action." It recommended that NARA "seize the initiative, seek new rules and regulations, issue guidelines, and begin educational programs—both self-education and the education of others." Panelists recommended as well the extension of NARA's research efforts to gain a better understanding of electronic technology. NAPA President Ray Cline noted (NAPA, 1989, p. iii) the lack of "historical awareness" in government agencies as the underlying problem. After interviewing 142 government officials, 90 program administrators, nine information managers, 20 records managers, and 18 historians, and formulating some consensus with the information at hand, NARA was encouraged to work with the OMB, the GSA, and NIST to embrace a vision, to define objectives for electronic record keeping, and to sponsor prototype projects in federal agencies. The recommendations formed a two-pronged attack on the problem: (1) outreach, cooperation, etc., for influence leading to compliance to guidelines promulgated by archivists and (2) enforcement through federal requirements, program regulation, and if need be, law.

Most significantly for research, NARA was advised to use the National Historical Publications and Records Commission (NHPRC) to encourage external research. In all seventeen recommendations came forth, half of which were statements advising NARA to undertake various forms of assessment, including circumspection of its own capabilities to manage a federal electronic records program. The report did not address the more fundamental problem raised by some archivists, namely that due to its historical mentality NARA is confused about its mission and character: it sees itself as a cultural rather than a service agency, with larger obligations to the American people to preserve an intellectual and documentary heritage, than as the archives of the federal government that first and foremost serves the information and records needs of the government. The results of some of this thinking can be seen in more recent planning announcements by the archivist of the United States, John W. Carlin, a new NARA Vision statement, and a ten-year strategic plan (cf., CARLIN; NARA, etc., and Web site postings at http://www.nara.gov/nara). It is apparent as well in the differences between NARA and the AHA regarding such access issues as records appraisal and documentary editing.

In 1991, another inter-disciplinary NAPA panel of 25 subject experts reported to NARA about a consensus or NEH-style panel review appraisal strategy for 900 federal databases, or rather what information could be had from inventories and descriptions from creating agencies (many of which resisted the very notion of having their databases evaluated); the panel recommended permanent retention of half of these. Ironically for a study managed by public administrators, those selected for retention were not valued because of the administrative functions of the offices that generated them, but because of the programs they documented. The disposition of subject experts was predictably biased toward subject or content analysis, not the authority-based appraisal often used by archivists or even the functional analysis that is more in vogue (as is recommended for art objects as well by STAM, 1989; 1991, p. 129). Such approaches take their cue from the communications model in information science that evolved in the 1980s. Unlike any appraisal of use, which may be misconstrued as the cardinal criterion in the notion of "continuing value" if one relies heavily from library literature about collection management, this panel focused on subject and content analysis relating to a preconceived set of activities: (1) diplomatic and foreign affairs; (2) fiscal and economic policies; (3) military operations and defense; (4) the use and conservation of natural resources and science; and (5) social and judicial concerns. This is a functions approach resting on assumptions, not well defined and left unmeasured, regarding priorities drawn from notions about historical categories and their inferred importance. History as such was not a categorized concern, nor were the arts and humanities, but in fact concern for the historical record pervades the study and downplays administrative issues.

Historical-thinking archivists and historians in their approach to appraisal hold in the background some notion of use, but it is seldom explicit and it is therefore not measurable. It is based largely on personal experience, and therefore on the collective experience of the panel of experts queried. The foundation, therefore, is on the authority, by office, of the person's standing in a profession, and formal education and personal reputation, rather than use a study or extensive study of user communities. This polling of a historical-oriented representation is not based in Social Science methodology; nor is it really humanistic. Archivists have tended not to relate their thinking about appraisal to the larger philosophical field of axiology or the theory of value (ATTFIELD; BROTHMAN; DEBREU; WITTGESTEIN, 1980; R. PERRY; cf., FEENEY & GRIEVES for values of information from the library perspective; and REPO for information evaluation in economics, accounting, and management science). Information Science continues to be concerned with this nagging problem of defining "value" for information and of information services so necessary for program evaluation, assessment, and cost justification. SARACEVIC & KANTOR (cf., KANTOR) have recently worked on a use-oriented value of information schematic, but without recourse to archival literature on appraisal or the notion of evidence as information with added value (as suggested by R. TAYLOR in 1986 but not carried far enough into the ideology of records, proof, evidence, belief and trust). The result is ahistorical. These information scientists do, however, pay attention to the idea of relevance and distinguish between intrinsic, extrinsic or instrumental, inherent, and contributory values. They designed a *Derived Taxonomy of Value in Using Library and Information Services*. The approach, method, and suppositions brought to bear on this project stand in sharp contrast to the NARA/NAPA approach to understanding value and producing working definitions for evaluation and appraisal purposes.

In reviewing the NAPA report MINNICK (1994) also questioned the representational character of the panel, but more constructively pointed to the report's strength in delineating a process rather than just a general approach to electronic records appraisal. He concluded that this investigation of using panel review mechanisms was not really successful; NAPA failed to produce anything that can be seen as a model. He saw NAPA "turning the information pyramid on its head," referring (p.151) to a model of administrative decisions forming the apex and program data composing a broad base. Of course, the pyramid is so flat in today's management theory that it may not have a recognizable head or apex. One might also question that reliance on panel review by subject experts whose credibility generally is not substantiated by user studies or by their knowledge or use of archives, or the reliance on rating systems based predominantly on technical requirements. Panel review and rating systems should determine, as the report incorrectly purports to describe, "the archives of the future."

NARA itself had to reconsider other possibilities, including the ICPSR "Documentation Rating System." Here, however, lies the aforementioned confusion of the manuscript tradition in archives being transferred into the electronic arena. ICPSR can be selective and acquire databases meeting criteria external to the context of their creation; an electronic archives cannot. If a database is faulty and cannot be assimilated into the working operations of a data archives, it can be rejected, discarded, or altered significantly; if the same approach were used by NARA contextual evidence of the faulty operations of an office would be destroyed along with the data themselves. Likewise, the NAPA panel showed little concern for the historical evaluation of government operations themselves. It is precarious, it would seem, to study American foreign policy as if it operated in a vacuum or purely in a theoretical mode, without knowing about policy makers and the routines and operations of their offices. Can one have diplomacy without diplomats and diplomas? One could not have, then, such telling reconstructions as by Herbert Feis, for example, about the communications problems in Washington, D.C., that contributed to the Japanese successful surprise at Pearl Harbor in 1941. As *Foreign Relations of the United States (FRUS)* points out, this is presumably why Public Law 102-138 (the Foreign Relations Authorization Act) in 1991 created the series with a historical Advisory Committee to insure the completeness and "timeliness" of the record (which is in fact published 30 years after the fact; cf., Committee report, *AHA Perspectives*, 1994 Nov.; 32(8): 16-18).

The harbinger for change in archives is the rate of conversion to electronic communications and documentation in everyday business and government practice. The problem and opportunity are increased amounts of information, moving faster through a greater variety of media and in more formats, and an attendant intensification in information use in decision-making even at ranks previously excluded from such participatory management based on information exchange. W. Edwards Deming's extension of Taylorism to all aspects of an organization and work means that previous hierarchical forms of information production, dissemination, tracking, and retrieval for documentation will not suffice. Many studies of records management inside today's organizations have been triggered by Total Quality Management (TQM) efforts (e.g., at MIT: FELKER). Observers of the contemporary scene in the United States (EDWARDS & SNYDER, 1984 & 1992) point to information intensive work and the phenomena collectively known as the rise of knowledge workers, as distinct from those employed in traditional industry. This, again, is in keeping with SENGE's idea of a "learning organization." Archivists since the mid-1980s have become acutely aware of these developments; these are not some future trends but changes already engulfing them, and they are attempting to alter how archives are conceived and organized to cope with such changes. Critics argue that old methods and practices have really never worked in the United States given the sheer mass of documentation created and size of its governmental organizations and counterparts in the private sector. Moreover, the assumption is that ongoing approaches to paper records cannot be applied to electronic archives, mainly because of limited resources given to archives, although in truth little study has tested current methods and practices on electronic records.

The issue of archival methodological transferability from paper to electronic archives is not empirically known. Some like T. H. PETERSON have argued a continuity thesis; more have opted for discontinuity and revolution in the archives because they are dismayed that evolution has been so painfully slow and that the problem has gotten out of hand. Archives are not known for their innovation but for their natural conservatism. Historical and analytical studies of archives operations, such as that by HOUSE on the origins of records scheduling in American government archives (NARA especially), show that the evolution of systematic procedures across archives and agencies took a long time, well over a generation to form, take hold, and be realized. Such slow-paced innovation when reform is called for could be disastrous, as it was for federal records which were destroyed randomly by calamity and neglect for most of the United States' history while procedures and conformance came about painfully and sporadically. Electronic records of the twentieth century seem equally at peril, not for lack of deliberation, but for lack of timely action. Thinking historically about records as historical documents does not compel timely action, but it allows modern records to age, whereby their very survival becomes the criterion for their preservation. Hindsight is easier than foresight in historical thought, and sustained deliberation unfortunately can delay action. As in academic collegial governance, in team-based records management, one can have situations in which death by expertise occurs.

Perhaps no other challenger to the *status quo* in American archives has had as much influence as David BEARMAN in the post-NISTF decade, through his consulting, conducting workshops, presenting at major conferences, editing the *Archives and Museum Informatics* series, and a consecutive series of "thought papers" or essays based less on empirical research than on circumspection. Articles written between 1989 and 1993 have been gathered into a single book: *Electronic Evidence. Strategies for Managing Records in Contemporary Organizations.* In effect, although this book ostensibly eschews History, it is also about the management of History's future in so much as historical research continues to be based on contemporary evidence, documentation, and an information system permitting source retrieval volume for greater impact. Bearman's preaching has taken hold at least among a group of disciples engaged in electronic archives, perhaps because the field lacks the knowledge workers needed to keep up with trends already well established, and has so few thinkers, much less a plentitude of prophets. As BEARMAN indicates (p. 4) his ideas began to crystallize while consulting for the United Nations Administrative Coordinating Committee on Information Systems Technical Panel for Electronic Records Management (ACCIS TP/REM) in 1988-1989. His contribution to the U.N. policy (1990) on electronic archives was thus included as chapter 3 in his *Electronic Evidence.* Since then he has advocated the delineation of basic functional requirements of electronic records management systems (Appendix C) through the use of policy, project design, systematic implementation and adherence to technical standards. His gospel took up a cardinal lesson from indexing theory in paying attention to functions and operations, that is action, rather than things or records themselves or software as the basis for documentation systems and the future evolution of "non-custodial" archives (BEARMAN, 1991). He called for a new mind-set or mentality that would have to be far more flexible in dealing with virtual documents than hitherto required by paper archives.

The absence of such thinking and the neglect in developing systems capable of meeting the test for electronic archives were for BEARMAN (1993) revealed in the decisions of the United States District Court of Appeals regarding e-mail logs generated by the White House IBM PROFS system. The need for archives to preserve official electronic communications was not so much recognized by archivists, and was in many ways disavowed by the National Archives, as by the court in its evidentiary requirements that were not met by a records system that anticipated such needs. Thus, BEARMAN and others, especially HEDSTROM (1993a & b), called for a "reinventing of archives." Some of their suggestions, which seem radical in view of the conservative nature of archives history, seem mandated by the ubiquitous and fluid nature of electronic records. While BEARMAN (1994) castigates the United States National Archives for adherence to a passive approach to archives, and the confusion of archives with what information is in a central repository, other national archives such as the National Archives of Australia, and also those of Canada and the Netherlands, are already moving away from attempting to accession electronic archives into a central archives except as last resort and are moving toward inspecting and influencing information management at the level of its originator and time of its creation through a strategy of "documenting documentation" which in essence creates an archives for archives.

At the 1994 SAA conference in Indianapolis, BEARMAN (1995) outlined his "Archival Strategies" and engaged in lively forum with reactors Eric Ketelaar from the Netherlands, Ian Wilson from Canada, and Ann Pederson from Australia (cf., I. WILSON, 1990-91, 1995; A. PEDERSON, 1995). The discussion flowed from Bearman's *Archival Methods* (1989) written five years before and from Bearman's assessment of the influence of his message over the past five years. Despite a surge in citations and a lot of discussion which Pederson teasingly refers to "Bearmania" (PEDERSON, 1995, p. 433, n. 6), Bearman himself was less sure of actual results or substantive change in the archival profession at large, rather than pockets of innovation or leadership of only a few change agents in North American archives. In essence, he buttressed his arguments against documentation strategies in selection and appraisal as inherently flawed, based on premises drawn from deconstructionism (BROTHMAN, 1993) and fundamental misconstructions characterized by T. COOK (1994) as a problem of "Electronic Records, Paper Minds." COOK (1997a) later assessed Bearman's work as revolutionary and praised him as one of the century's leading archival thinkers—a high accolade indeed, from an archivist known himself as a critical archival thinker. COOK (1997b) is unwilling to concentrate on the evidential value of records at the expense of cultural values, which is a total shift from the archival guardianship of culture to information management that appears to be selfish, i.e., short-term service to a particular master, rather than long-term service to society. He recently urged archivists not to forsake such professional values and warned against too narrow an approach to appraisal when "Our past is truncated by our self-imposed operational definitions."

These caveats are not specifically anti-Bearman and Terry Cook has not disaffected from this camp, but his reconsideration reflects a view that relishes traditions in the archives that are reflected in records management and which are nonextant in information systems management. Cook is deferring in his comments but notices that the kind of operation Bearman envisions is still a ways off; no system software in broad application now meets the requirements, and a projection of a decade is not unrealistic in seeing archival operations encoded into widely used software. Cook, unlike Hedstrom and Bearman, is unwilling to write off a decade of this century's history. Thus not everyone is so enamored with Bearman's guru-like status in the field of modern records and electronic archives, and some archivists fear an unreflective, immoderate revolution in the archives. Some critics have been less accommodating than Terry Cook. Recently Linda Henry of the National Archives, under the guise of good humor, was particularly outspoken. She likened the circle of writers who echo Bearman's themes to a "cohort" because it is a self-selective, relatively small, highly vocal or published, self-citing group that operates in strategic fashion, often through invitation-only working conferences—hence, the military term—and her own application of Ann Pederson's coined phenomenological term to David's devotees as "Bearmaniacs" (HENRY, 1997) for those who would dispense with history and tradition. She was especially critical of the cohort's use of "scare tactics" to coerce radical change. Henry sees herself not as reactionary, but in the moderate middle-ground staked out perhaps best by Trudy Peterson of the National Archives (T. H. PETERSON).

Bearman revisited his earlier treatise and asked of archivists the same probing questions as before (BEARMAN, 1995, p. 383):

1. Assuming our best methods succeeded in every respect, to what extent would we meet the challenges we [archivists] have identified?

2. If our current methods will not achieve our aims, how can either our goals or our methods be redefined in order to be achievable?

His position is (p. 383): "… it is necessary to accept that we are shaping the documentary record and [we need to] be explicit about the rules by which conscious shaping of the record is operating."

Bearman attempts again to persuade archivists to adopt "strategic thinking" using "societal mechanisms or levers" (external: costs, bad press, law suits, models; proof of concept; internal: standards and protocols, demonstrated savings, articulated problem or solution). One of his fundamental points is the archival goal of creating evidence "in the first place" rather than record keeping after the fact. So, he challenges archivists (1) to identify evidence (as distinct from appraisal or selection of records, which he declares is a "bankrupt" method; (2) to document activity; (3) to maintain evidence, which he interprets more broadly than material preservation only; (4) to enable use; and (5) to measure success. For each of these he suggests tactics that together form strategies. This all would add up to "reinventing archives" (p. 396) while archivists "ride the communications revolution" (p. 413). I. WILSON comments largely from his perspective from within the Ontario provincial archives, where the keywords in Bearman's regimen strike a chord; and PEDERSON analyzes the Bearman change manifesto in terms of "innovation diffusion" by noting the time lag between problem admission, identification of solutions ("Re-purposing the archival enterprise; Re-Defining Locus, Function, and Activities; Re-Aligning and Sharing Responsibilities," pp. 440-444), the preaching of a message for reform, risk taking and moving to action, and finally, seeing results. She hopes that the "ailing" archival profession is ready for recovery.

Recourse to metadata or surrogate documentation for access to actual records is a strategy on which not everyone agrees, especially in view of the transience of information, the volatility of documentation, and the ineffective appraisal methods that would trigger the documentation process when records are created. Moreover, such a process of documentation is insufficient as a single act but must be a continuous process to insure immediate access, subsequent access for ulterior purposes, the saving of editions in a series as the document record or contracts, and the creation of expanded or alternate access for reuse over time. Finally, documenting functions and creating evidence rather than appraising and describing records as in the old regime, are different propositions for many archivists than their historical preparation entailed. Advocates of such proactive archives ultimately move toward a position of archives as enforcement agencies, when traditionally in government as in most other organizations they have been powerless to enforce policies and statutes already on the books. The Canadian approach, close to the American position, backs away from strong-arm tactics and endorses more of a goal-oriented approach to "best practices" and an accountability ethic that goes hand in hand with movements toward Total Quality Management (TQM) and other quality control measures. With a sense that perhaps the line prevails too often in such decision making, the American experience thinks management needs some external incentive. Trends in benchmarking provide this; so does corporate commitment to ISO 9000 compliance. Just as DURANTI (1995) has at a recent SAA conference, one can discern key differences between the United States, Canadian, and Australian national positions, and these may be contrasted with the older European tradition regarding adherence to archival policies, compliance with mandates, and voluntary cooperation.

In any case, draft statements of functional requirements for recordkeeping have been forthcoming from the University of Pittsburgh project (1993, 1994) and have been promulgated by BEARMAN (1994, pp. 60-61) in a variety of public fora with diverse audiences: at SAA for professional archivists, at IACH in Montreal for computing historians, and at the workshop series on electronic recordkeeping for business and industry information officers and consultants, and internationally in Australia. These are included in an appendix to this work because if they suffice for organizational records management, they apply as well to research and development projects and as well to historical research projects. For the latter they add a dimension seldom discussed by historians who embark on data based projects (MCCRANK, 1996). As paraphrased from the summary by COX & WILLIAMS (Appendix A), these requirements are that:

1.   A compliant organization or project adheres to the legal and administrative requirements for record keeping defined by the jurisdictions in which they operate.

2.   *Accountable* systems are

2.1. Responsible by having policies, assigned responsibilities, and formal methodologies for their management

2.2. Implemented systems that are employed consistently in the normal course of business, are procedural, and conform to accepted practice in the sector in which they function

2.3. Reliable in that they have quality control over the information used and processes, so that records are credible

3. *Functional records* are

3.1. Comprehensive, being created for all transactions

3.2. Complete, meaning that they capture all information generated, including meta-information about their context, creation, and conveyance as structures information for human cognition and understanding

3.3. Identifiable, in that records are unique and have boundaries

3.4. Authentic, or can be proved to have originated with the records creator or authority

3.5. Sound, as in having integrity, and they are protected over time from corruption, damage, and unauthorized modification

3.6. Auditable, having a traceable history both for their creation and transfer, and also use

3.7. Exportable, or transferable using appropriate data representation standards and communications protocols

3.8. Removable, meaning they can be deleted with appropriate permission and authority, but such deletion would leave audit trails to document prior existence

3.9. Available, retrievable, and accessible

3.10. Usable, because they are logically reconstructible from documented and preserved structure and context relationships

3.11. Understandable, both in the representation or views they would have had for their creators when created

3.12. Redactable or capable of being masked to safeguard confidentiality, security, privacy, or other limitations on access, without deterioration of content

As the UNIVERSITY OF PITTSBURGH (1993, fig. 2) project group stated: "The functional requirements were specifically developed in order to provide guidance for the management of electronic record keeping systems, although they are equally applicable to manual systems. Information system professionals should note that business functions, business processes, business transactions and business records rather than systems functions, systems processes, systems transactions, or systems records, are the consistent focus of record keeping." DOLLAR ([1998]) focuses more on electronic records than information systems, for archival preservation. He consolidates the essential characteristics into a short list: archival records need to be readable, intelligible, identifiable, encapsulated (e.g., SGML), retrievable, capable of reconstruction, understandable, and authentic. Once having system functional requirements in mind, or more accurately a substantive notion about what an archival record is, the next step is to identify a strategy for implementation and maintenance.

Ultimately, therefore, an organization (project team or lone researcher) has to buy into the concept of archival systems that combine information systems with evidential record keeping systems, and enforcement or self-discipline must be matters of organizational commitment, policy, and character. Rather than rely on external or internal top-down enforcement for compliance,

successful implementation and continuation may rely instead on creating an organizational culture that understands and appreciates archives for the evidential information they supply and the
organizational memory they keep intact. This is why the aforesaid functional requirements project draws upon the organizational memory and culture research (DUFF & WALLACE).
Organizational culture is itself treated as a major variable in creating a reflexive records program.
One can argue for either enlightened self-interest or more altruistically for societal good, but in
a client-server, distributed, and personal computing environment, record keeping will always be
a matter of personal compunction as much as systems requirements, organizational policy, or
archival *desiderata*. R. Floud's idea of "every man his own historian" would therefore rest on the
assumption that first every person must be his or own personal archivist. Organizational culture
as a whole depends on its parts; people ultimately make the difference. Historically minded people are likely to make a more positive difference than those who think within a contemporary
frame of mind. Ultimately goals like having compliant, accountable, and functional records and
evidence upon which to base personal recall and historical reconstruction tie into the effectiveness of History in education for society at large and especially for leaders, administrators, and
managers. Given the relative absence of history from American business education, this is an
unlikely development. This is why in government and business circles history and altruism are
played down by archival advocates, who instead turn to such motivation as business efficiency
tied to profit, risk management, and corporate effectiveness.

Having delineated the problem in more detail than can sometimes be digested, especially
given the magnitude of quantity of the electronic information already generated but which is
not readily retrievable over the long haul, BEARMAN proposed a generalized strategy using
policy formulation, design principles, systematic implementation, and national and international standards. The problem of tying archival record keeping to comprehensive information
policy questions whether an organization's ability to formulate policy in its own best interest
or society's. If the slowness of the United States government in developing an Internet policy
is any indication (reviewed by BRAMAN), the placement of archival concerns in the context
of overall information policy is fraught with intrigue and paranoia, politics and vested interest,
and layers of traditional procedures and bureaucratic labyrinths. R. MARKS criticizes current
legal and legislative apparati in the United Kingdom, for example, as being an "eighteenth century process" attempting to deal with high technology. Likewise M. MACNEIL points to the
clash of "old and new worlds" in Britain's attempts to resolve information policy issues and
understand high technology in a collection of essays contrasting "enterprise and heritage" in
the "crosscurrents of national culture" (CORNER & HARVEY, eds.). The incongruence is
amazing, myriad agenda are bewildering, and the wide variance in people's level of technical
understanding is daunting in both government and in large corporations.

The reorientation in archival thought is partially a capitulation to the overwhelming odds
archivists face in controlling the vast amounts of records created today, and it strives to take
advantage of trends in technology rather than to assume the impossible task of controlling information technology in an organization for the ulterior idealism of archives, but it also is in keeping with management trends in flattening organizations, distributing decision-making authority,
and in collegial or participatory management. But it not only calls for organizational change of
considerable magnitude, but an even greater transformation of archivists from records managers
to change agents and policy designers (see HUBER & GLICK, eds. to relate the redesign of
information services to organizational structures). Thus, the University of Pittsburgh project
(1994) exhibits concern for organization culture as a key variable in the ability of an organization to manage change and to change how it generates and records its own information. Thus,
the connection is made in this essay between Corporate Memory and Organizational Culture
with archives, history, and information work, or Historical Information Science. COX (1995)
understandably shows equal concern for the organizational culture of archivists themselves.

Such revisionist archives thinking displaces historians from their former status as preferred users but does not eliminate them from use or the safekeeping of electronic records as a viable historical record *en toto*. If they are to engage modern archives, historians like archivists have to leave their safe havens, classrooms, and archives to infiltrate the very highest echelons of government or public and private administration. This is "going public" and advocacy more like a missionary than is role commonly assigned to Public History, or in AHA President Joyce Appleby's musing about all History being public (APPLEBY, 1997b). This is a more daring and risky venture. Moreover, such an ethic demands that historians teach by example, as in managing their own records, course management, service functions, and of course research. Each historian must be his or her own archivist for historical projects. How historians manage their own practice, teaching, and research therefore matters. Formal project management is an important issue in historians' work, both as a training ground for students, but also for integration of such projects into the research programs of their parent organizations as distinct from totally individualized and private research. This has implications as well for how universities manage research, and how they ensure its coordination with teaching, support scholarly communications, and build a knowledge base for future generations.

These agenda set a goal far more demanding than merely citation tracing through a properly formatted critical apparatus in a book but require metadata for the whole research process and a reconfiguration of our research institutions. It implies the kind of reform in research methods that some historians have already conformed to with the use of personal computers, and the transfer of field data and research notes into files which ultimately become the critical apparatus of a finished product. Rather than destroy the infrastructure of a study after publication, however, the extension of the logic in the functional requirements approach to historian's work means that the metadata remains accessible to support the official record, i.e., the book, article, or final edition of a database. Research notes, data sets, etc., could be made available via a researcher's homepage on the Web, for example, so that after publication of a historical monograph one could examine the evidence directly, not indirectly through citation tracings, for review and criticism, and most importantly, for a foundation to subsequent work.

BEARMAN (1993) argues persuasively that the cardinal value in appraisal reform, records maintenance, policy formulation, and new approaches to description for electronic access to archives, which would achieve this paradigm shift, rests on the notion of evidence (as distinct from information alone). COX (1994b, p. 9) hails this "rediscovery of records as evidence." Historians should be able to relate to this value too, but BEARMAN advocates a rapprochment with neither historians or the information profession, but rather with the actuarial and legal areas of upper and middle management: lawyers, accountants, auditors, and risk managers who require evidence and are establishing legal standards for its electronic form (SKUPSKY, 1995, 1996). BEARMAN seems to think that the historical value of archives is almost incidental, or that it is a natural byproduct of their evidential value but that organizations will not invest in archives for purely altruistic motives—or invest enough to fulfill the accountability imperative. Administrators will, however, invest to the point where it will cost them more if they risk not having preserved information for which they are accountable and which makes their organizations accountable. Memorialization as history is nice, but "accountability" as embraced by MCKEMMISH & UPWARD (1993) is a different matter. Perhaps Bearman occasionally overstates his case in an effort to drive home his points and partially in reaction to the singular history-oriented mind-set of so many archivists. He is even more brazen, pointing to judiciary censures, penalties, and other forms of retribution resulting in the loss of assets and revenues resulting from information malpractice and lack of documentary accountability as immediate, relevant, and understood in a totally different dimension in America—in terms of cold, hard cash!

The ferment over electronic evidence is not to be found in History; indeed, one barely finds general awareness of the key issues in historical literature. MCCRANK (1996) has addressed such concerns in History forums, but too often historians react to the problems contemplated as someone else's, too remote for immediate concern, and unrelated to their current research without understanding their importance in relevant teaching. Faculty are generally fearful about accountability, not in the abstract, but in application; however, the invisibility of performance accountability and assumption of equivalence between competence and credentials in academe for students means that the opportunity to teach by example is often lost. This can be corrected by the conscious insertion of information citation and referral in teaching. Good metadata practice and referral habits are too important to be exercised in research and publication alone. This should include the constant appraisal of information sources for retention and use, citation and critique of provenance and format for current presentation, whereby teaching in the classroom, like teaching peers through presentation at professional and scholarly conferences or in oral demonstrations in business meetings, is viewed as part of the formal information process. Accountability should apply to all such situations.

If one finds such concerns taken for granted in academe, then one will see a different heightened concern for accountability in board rooms of corporate America, Europe, and Japan; in lawyers and accountants' offices, in law enforcement agencies, and in our courts. The closest daily parallel is patent examination to guarantee protection over intellectual property, reexamination of patents compared with later products developed to study possible infringement by second parties, and litigation to establish fault and the value of claims. In such processes, the filing of patents establishes by strict standards a meta-information source, a technical archives, where each document has an official capacity, a legality, as a potential witness to a historic development—an invention, a product or commodity, and a value. The patent itself becomes a surrogate for the actual thing because it translates physical evidence from the artifact into language and it describes more than the thing, but the idea and intellectual effort that went into the object's conception, design and development, production and marketing. Nothing is so damaging to a defendant as for a claimant to prove that the rival corporation knowingly copied a patented product and neglected to buy rights to do so. In determining potential liability in the Research & Development (R&D) stage, the defendant should have searched patents of similar make, determined degrees of sameness and difference to ascertain potential liability, and then if significantly altered to be patentable separately proceed to file a patent and if not, to proceed into negotiation with the patent holder to buy rights for reproduction, integration, reuse, or whatever.

Little training in document examination and evidence analysis in History is ever so thorough, standardized, or exacting; nor is most historical research subject to such vigorous reexamination; the stakes simply are not there to warrant such effort apart from the integrity of the historian and the solid, lasting nature of his or her work. Nor do most archivists engage in such analytic rigor in appraisal, partially because appraisal standards are so often geared toward cultural values, which are difficult to define and which have equal difficulty in accepting. When personal accountability such as job security and personal liability enter the picture, usually such standards change instantly, as when a manuscript curator appraises a potentially valuable document and invests an annual salary or more in its purchase, when the piece always has the potential of being bogus and a forgery; or when a museum curator mortgages five years of acquisitions funds to purchase a work of art which had better be authentic. In both scenarios, the record examiner, document appraiser, or curator risks reputation, livelihood, and more if a conflict of interest enters into the proceedings. Similarly, if a corporate archivist, lawyer, or other official enters false documentation into court proceedings without being able to substantiate the record's official nature, its chain of custody, and its inherent integrity, not only does the party risk having the information dismissed but could face penalties if any collusion can be determined in falsifying evidence and polluting the record overall. Intent to do harm, willful neglect, and incompetence in that order are ranked by degree of duplicity and fault, and resulting damages are set accordingly.

This is why the past decade has witnessed continuing education efforts for corporate administrators and information systems management, such as the Australian Electronic Records Management Conference in 1994 (YORKE). In the United States, COHASSET ASSOCIATES, INC., has offered its *Managing Electronic Records* (MER) conferences since 1992. The subtitle for this annual conference in 1996 is telling: "Diffusing the Corporate Time Bomb!" (taken from the title of JESSEN's new book about e-mail management). Likewise several research centers, such as the Cyberspace Law Institute, have sprung up because of the problem in relating issues created by new information technology and operations with established doctrine. PERRITT has provided one of the best legal guides in the United States, to steer one through the maze of copyright, trademark, patent, secrets law, privacy, fort and criminal liability, information crimes, dispute resolution, and cross-border information transfer in electronic commerce. No guide can keep up with precedents being set daily or the expanding technology, but Perritt's work is integrative and he provides an analytical framework for applying basic legal principles to the new situations arising from the deployment of new information technology before its socioeconomic impact is known.

The implications from recent litigation for electronic archivists were made most clear, by the celebrated Exxon case in 1990-1991 over liabilities of the corporation for the natural disaster that occurred with the 1989 oil spills from the tanker *Valdez* whose crude oil lapped onto the Alaskan shoreline, killing countless waterfowl and mammals and costing millions of dollars for cleanup and environment repair. Exxon was liable, of course, but the amount was to be determined not necessarily in accord with cleanup costs alone since, if this had been purely accidental, such costs would have been shared. Since the spill did occur, the damage was done, the issue was not if reparations were owed, but how much, and this determination would rest on the resetting of the historical stage and playing the "what if" scenario. Was the incident simply the occurrence of an accident waiting to happen? Was this particular accident preventable? The burden of proof therefore shifted from the state to the company which had to show that its procedures and policies were in place, were being adhered to, and that they were adequate in most cases, barring an "Act of God," to protect against such as a disaster. The state attacked on the basis of known risks with cartage of crude oil on tankers, and the corporation had to counter with evidence of risk management, including selection and training of its personnel. Critical to the case, as it happened, was the record of the captain in charge, his health and judgment, and whether Exxon knew that his personal problems in such emergency situations created higher risk of calamity. If the company knew about problems contributing to such a potential scenario then it was at fault to a greater degree by virtue of negligence.

In this case as now in so many, attorneys increasingly targeted electronic records in discovery actions. The result was a $5 billion verdict against Exxon, resulting largely from persuasion by the plaintiffs that Exxon officials knew about potential liabilities from personnel problems but took no preventive action. The telling evidence came from corporate e-mail records, which John H. JESSEN of Electronic Evidence Discovery, Inc., has called "the largest unfunded liability" in America. Lawyer B. O'NEILL of the firm Faegre & Bensen attributes his success entirely to electronic evidence, and the ability to manage over 2.5 million electronic documents that became part of this litigation. Key processes in these proceedings brought to light the importance of metadata including the operations of an archives and records management system which can establish the admissibility of electronic evidence by virtue of the objectivity and completeness of the system regardless of any particular case. In other words, the efficacy of the documentation depends only in part on internal evidence, but also objectivity based on its context, semiautonomous operation, and inviolate protection from vested interest in data acquisition, appraisal and retention, disposition and accessibility. O'NEILL refers to these management issues as "upstream" because they are determined at the startup of an information system, at the water's pure source, long before the information flow grows, and certainly before any issue of contamination is raised. Through

COHASSET ASSOCIATES, HULBERT, a noted trial attorney, has provided a tutorial on how in such litigation a trail lawyer could and would attack an agency or company on how it manages its electronic records. "We try to find holes in your system, in your process for keeping records. It's how we're going to try to win our case (p. 1)."

Particularly interesting in such discovery, apart from so-called official documents, were records which attested their use and impact. Hence e-mail records were among the most revealing. This is why JESSEN labeled e-mail logs as a "liability" of untold proportion especially in America which has led the way in electronic communications and commerce. It was important to have official records such as policies, contracts, etc., but also to show how they were used, and therefore to document information flow—retrieval, circulation, points of contact, interpretation, decisions, and actions related to their contents. It is important to document functions not simply in outline form as in organizational charts, but to demonstrate functionality and operations by recreation of information flows, genealogies of decision-making, or decisive events where individuals assume accountability lest liability be attributable to the entire organization. Therefore, lawyers are now advising corporations and their archivists and records managers about evolving guidelines for the legal acceptance of electronic records that depends on situational circumstances. R. FISHER and R. F. WILLIAMS of COHASSET ASSOCIATES, Inc., advise that "electronic records management systems must include the functional capabilities to meet all legal provisos," including certain "foundational requirements" included in federal and state laws and regulations that govern the life-cycle of electronic records.

Such legislation is growing as states such as California and Texas, which are modifying their discovery rules, are confronting the issues involved in electronic evidence. Arizona is mandating that information systems be subject to sweeps as due process and a matter of course and as an essential component automatic discovery action in major litigation. Revised Rule 26 of the *Federal Rules of Civil Procedures* is seen to have widespread impact and the United States Department of Justice is now setting guidelines on computer evidence. The issues are complex, such as mandated discovery possibly violating privacy rights or requiring search warrants. The cost of such discovery must be defrayed by someone, meaning that the issue of responsibility and cost liability is linked to decisions about when full searching and disclosure are warranted by proper or reasonable suspicion and cause. Some courts, protecting their own interests, are trying to place 100 percent of the discovery costs on business. Finally, even when limited, certain kinds of data discovery can be camouflaged in requests for documentation, and the act of discovery itself can be damaging as in revealing trade secrets, patented formulas, and design principles, or in the case of covert action, industrial or governmental, of espionage strategies, and personnel identifications.

The very linkage that documents information flow and functionality can also disclose what might be properly protected. JESSEN therefore has attempted to create a "risk-reduction plan" based on his experience with 400 cases involving pretrial discovery action and what he labels as "discovery blackmail" as in coercing default because of an executive's fears about what a corporate information system might actually reveal. He advocates a "proactive" plan involving understanding high risk problems, i.e., "smoking guns," records appraisal on the basis of risk, knowledge of court orders and their implications (including those that are too broad, need definition and refinement, etc.) to create strategies for compliance and resistance when necessary. John Phillips of Martin Marietta Energy Systems, Inc., suggests that comprehensive strategies to insure that electronic document-based information systems are assets rather than liabilities to an enterprise must include: (1) evaluation of new technologies for their impact on system management; (2) policies that include insight into future environments; (3) procedures that adapt today's "custodial operating procedures" to include the new world of "virtual distributed information"; (4) consideration of available standards and selection of which ones to follow; (5) integration of document management systems and assurance for effectiveness of the overall system;

and (6) ongoing training for personnel. The organization and its information system are coterminous and inseparable in such holistic views.

The legal implications of such recent litigation and evolving rules of evidence for electronic records are not easily divorced from the rapidly evolving technology. Because the idea of an original source in unalterable form in the paper evidence world is so compromised in the electronic environment, it is difficult to prove that any one electronic record is pure and inviolate, that is, it has not been subjected to illegitimate tampering and interpolation in the processes of its creation, edition, expansion, and transfer across systems and into different kinds of formats and media. A case in point is the admissibility of electronic signatures as binding, which raises issues from procurement and initial authentification and verification, to retention and transfer from one source to another and to accounts payable. MCBRIDE, BAKER & COLES, INC., reports that more than 21 states in the United States now have legislation on the use of digital signatures, and as noted by HAMMOND-BAKER (pp. 240-241), a uniform law is in the draft stage. Just as complex is the parallel issue of electronic signatures of documents or mechanisms in electronic form that clandestinely accompany electronic records as meta-records of a document's origins and evolution, life-cycle or history, and interaction with other records. In the case of digital records, the integrity of bit streams is the question. Can both context and structure of digital documents be kept over time? What is "bootstrapping" in passing bit streams from one system to another? How dependent is a digital record's acceptability and veracity on coding schemes, cross-referencing methodologies, and invisible but parallel "ghost" records that must accompany an official record like body and soul, forever attached, to make digital information whole and reliable? How idiosyncratic are such meta-systems, and if unique, how does one verify their efficacy apart from design and operations which are part of the very system being evaluated? If one is able to "read" an electronic document in the future, will the reader have the same assurances then as when the record was active? When bits are migrated across system, the process is hardly the same as making a copy in a transfer process that defies intervention (DOLLAR, [1998] makes clear the distinction between copying and migrating electronic records).

So, the two archival strategies that have evolved thus far, i.e., documenting documentation and of preserving bit streams in records transfer, are hardly foolproof. They are indeed less reliable than processes associated with paper records that are entirely dependent on human intervention. In the latter case, it is the human act that requires explicit intervention—directions and specifications, choice of materials, selection of processes, and specific times for the event. Change in electronic records, especially digital media, can be ubiquitous, clandestine, instantaneous, and as easy for editorial change as for eradication (something more than simple erasure from visible work spaces).

Awareness of the transmutability of the modern archival record is causing reconsideration of assumptions about the uniqueness of older records. Thus O'TOOLE (1994) takes up the issue of the "elusive" original record articulated first by Hugh Taylor in humanistic terms and rephrased technically at the same time (H. TAYLOR, 1988a & b), and in confronting the dilemma of today's uses of history may lead modern archivists into a better understanding of the illusion of uniqueness and the rarity of originality in archives. In all copying, with whatever technology, from scribal days through printing but especially with photography and photocopying and most importantly word processing, not only has authority been compromised but the ideal of authorship as well. Rather than reliance on the original, the critical question is one of authenticity through processing over time. As in the Middle Ages, texts were associated with authors, but perhaps more so with the traditions that passed on information and an authority for its acceptability than individual authors as sole creators. The modern technology ironically may involve a return to to more nebulous times even though we think of information technology as being more exacting, precise, and empirical—and having an authority of its own. Both M. HEIM (1987) and BOLTER (1987) have explored the desultory effects of modern multiform technology on stability in human communications. Archival Science holds onto the ideal of stable and hence reliable information. This was not always the case in the past; it may not always be possible in the future.

These concerns over malleability, mutability, and intangibility then ultimately translate not only into the systematization of operations in systems, where timing is of the essence, but point to the issue of control of such systems and raise important issues of security. R. F. WILLIAMS lists seven major concerns in electronic records management:

1. Legality of systems versus the legality of media or the distinction of information and its meta-information and how the two go hand in hand;

2. Original document disposition, pertaining to when the original can be destroyed and a surrogate kept (i.e., computer output in print format or microform for original electronic records that are erased, or destruction of paper record originals when transferred to copies in other formats, including scanning and transfer via electronic media);

3. Unique legal issues pertaining to electronic records, such as logical documents versus physical documents, compound documents, transient compound documents, etc., to which may be added the problem of disparate documents whose parts are on different systems in diverse places only to be assembled on demand;

4. Policies and procedures to respond to discovery actions, which seemingly would also pertain to discovery in historical research rather than simply legal discovery in court action;

5. Security issues, such as in discerning the difference between system and media security (illicit access to a system versus intervention into a document within a system, i.e. system malfunctions versus record tampering); distinctions in record annotation (add-ons), enhancement (editions, erasures and substitutions, interpolations, etc.), and manipulation (dating, addressing, placement, replacement, duplication, etc.); and maintaining distinctions between software and hardware and their influence on both the records, (the media) and the system;

6. Users operational responsibilities, as distinct from record keeping requirements and operations; and

7. Legal responsibilities, including current laws and important considerations about what is missing in today's laws.

In addressing American archivists, R. F. WILLIAMS (1997) adopted the language and approach coming from the working conferences on electronic records management in which he participated (e.g., the concept of the archival bond), and elaborated from his editing work regarding the legality of microfilm (1979 with 28 subsequent updates) and optical storage (1987 with ten subsequent updates) and collaboration with AIIM (1993) on the disposition of optically stored records. He noted a change in United States courts' focus regarding optical storage trends, from the admissibility of optical media to the question of credibility of the information retained on any electronic storage systems. He also noted a change in the evolution of the law, from concentration on a record to a conceptual framework entailing acceptance of electronic records, adherence to standards of proof, and consideration in decisions of content, form or structure, type, and both the totality of the record and the nature of the recordkeeping operation. In a move away from individual testimony and personal knowledge which are subject to faulty recall and partial picture given the volume and mass of information to be considered as well as the increased transience in the workplace, there is greater reliance on corporate memory, which is seen as more stable and comprehensive, in the form of data and records. If an organization relied on its data and records to conduct its business, this can create circumstantial probability for acceptance of such documentation providing that its creation and maintenance is regular, its use is continuous in that it supported actual experience, and that there was a dutiful recording of its creation and use. Thus, as Robert Williams advocates, in industry one must strive for an effective partnering of business and records management. Examples he points to include the case of tampering with Tylenol containers where Neal, Inc., was exonerated because it could show consistency in safeguard packaging, or after the bizarre sabotage of Halloween treats, when an alleged razor in a Snickers bar was shown to be bogus because Mars company subjects all of its candy bars to metal detection before shipment.

Thus, R. F. WILLIAMS argues, records management is the management of evidence, which calls for the switch from reactive to proactive activities such as (1) monitoring the tremendous increase in state statutes over the past decade and laws like the *Uniform Business Records as Evidence Act (UBREA)*, the *Uniform Photographic Copies of Business and Public Records as Evidence Act (UPA)*, and *Uniform Preservation of Private Business Records Act (UPPBRA)*; (2) supplementing content with management evidence; and (3) investing in records programs that deal with regulatory compliance and can respond to discovery. This means preparedness, systematic implementations, and the maintenance of operations in accord with approved standards under direction of a systems administrator; quality control through regular internal and external audits; the documentation of the chain of custody; and fulfilment of all compliance obligations (backups, safe off-site storage, audit trails, system documentation [policies and procedures, user and security manuals, access records and a history of changes, training materials, service and repair records, indexing, migration paths, etc.]). R. F. WILLIAMS adds a fourth leg to the image of a three-legged chair to make it stable, i.e., accountability added to the usual objectives of speed, low cost, and pleasing presentation in the production of computer-generated documents.

COHASSET ASSOCIATES, INC. (p. 2) claims that "most records are documents that are created for legal reasons: to anticipate disputes and possible litigation or to achieve regulatory compliance." This assertion assumes an honesty and forthright intention in documentation, which may be absent as is apparently the case in contemporary litigation over access to corporate archives in the American tobacco industry where disclosure may also prove culpability based on foreknowledge. This lawyer's approach also supports the administrative viewpoint and displays understanding of the archival nature of information systems more than is common inside Information Science or Computer Science, but does not adequately concern itself with knowledge for its own sake or in informing an organization about itself. Again, the larger concern is building the "learning organization" as advocated by SENGE and societal good as stressed by COOK (1997).

This legal perspective may also miss the point driven home so well by public policy analyst Francis Fukuyama that "trust still counts in a virtual environment" (FORBES *ASAP*, p. 33). Elsewhere FUKUYAMA also speculates about "The End of History," but in an interview about the future of digital technology he challenges the rosy depictions of an electronic global marketplace based entirely on technology without proper regard for the people element. After hearing one network executive extoll the virtues of electronic conferencing and business transactions, Fukuyama's reaction was to compare this scenario with his own fear of his credit card being lost and discovered again by a bunch of high schoolers: "The virtual corporation that the executive described falls on its face for much the same reason: an absence of trust.... Trust becomes all the more important in a high tech environment." This, as he rightly observes, is a different issue from security alone, but it does pertain to the concern for credibility of digital information raised throughout this current essay. Not all human transactions can be achieved by data processing, and the attributed value to information lies outside the information technology itself. It does reside in the information system if it is to be truly functional, and is an attribute of corporate culture. He argues that "trust often arises from moral reciprocity" and from experience (e.g., the idea of an established track record, which in effect is a combination personal and corporate history). He wants a system of "branding" to assist with discrimination about such issues as competence, reliability and judgment. "Smart machines by themselves can't substitute for the human judgment and human contact that is ultimately the basis of trust." The same arguments were voiced, of course, when substituting paper currency for coinage in the late Middle Ages, or in the thirteenth-century paper for vellum in documentation, or for quality book production during the late Renaissance.

Historically, people have conveyed trust through surrogates for personal mediation and direct communication, and historians too accept such documentation technology as trustworthy. The argument today would include trust in information systems to relay authentic reliable documentation beyond what programmers consider their critical issue of data integrity. This archival concern and higher value based on morality needs to be interjected into any discussion of accountability and risk management. Even in business, good name, character, and reputation are assets worth protecting. Throughout history and in History today, these are among the most relied upon criteria in source appraisal.

Most assuredly, this corporate legalistic approach to archives and risk management through records or an accountability ethic in administration has little concern for History as long-range perspective. This means that information is not rehearsed and documentation is not prepared ostensibly to influence history as such, but it could be. And such a motive is more apparent in the destruction of incriminating documents. This always makes the burden of proof more difficult for the prosecution and for the historian. Retention goals are usually more immediate, but they can be influenced by external authority as compliance standards, as in the case of data retention standards for pharmaceutical firms doing drug testing, where the requirement is more than one generation so as to trace genetic effects. Ironically, the lack of concern for historical commemorization contributes to the objectivity of historical reconstruction, and greater awareness of historical perception in an organizational culture could lead to contamination of records. History is best served by an awareness of historicity in the sense of actuality in documentation and archival operations. This reorientation toward the world that produces information and evidence rather than those who study it long after the fact does not mean that archivists think that history is irrelevant for their cause or that archivist-historians are an "endangered species" as decried by PETTIT, but that History is being relegated to a different position in the user community that reflects actual use. It does mean, however, that archivists require in their professional education more vigorous training in document examination, procedural methodology, and criteria for evidence than is commonly provided in educating historians. Perhaps this should not be, but the issue of accountability in the so-called "real world" is very different from that in academic argument in historical circles. And the realization that records creators, not historians, are the primary users of their own records cannot but change archivist attitudes toward historians. Historical use is secondary, and by extension, historians therefore are not the preferred users they think themselves to be.

History's significance is more indirect and reflexive than immediately pertinent or direct. It is contextual, and therefore does relate to the issue of organizational culture more than historians are aware and more pervasively that is realized by corporate management. Just as some historians (e.g., TEMIN; CAMPBELL-KELLY) have been investigating the use of information in government and business, HEDSTROM (1991, pp. 338-343) relies on the sociopolitical history of technology in general, and of information technology particularly and extending back to the invention of printing, for contextualization of such archival issues. To drive home her point that information handling is more evolutionary than revolutionary, she quotes (p. 344) Xerox Corporation's D. LEVY (p. 4) who recognizes that "our literate culture retains and reinvests in its technological heritage, since the cost of discontinuous change is so high." He is among many sharing such a sentiment, expressed variously that history is of "paramount importance" in a world of "such complex developmental interactions" (LEWINTON, ROSE & KAMIN cited by HAWORTH, pp. 101-102); or that "Continuous change is comfortable change, the past is then the guide to the future" (HANDY, p. 3) which reflects NELSON & WINTER's evolutionary theory of change.

Such are testimonials for the relevance of historical perspective in business management, science and technology transfer, and to Information Science as well. These are the lingerings of historicism in archival thought, but not the pandering of archivists to historians that once placed them in the category of a service occupation or merely an adjunct field less respectable than History itself because archivists had to apply their learning in daily practice other than teaching. If historicism is to remain as an underpinning of archival theory, and the cause of History is to be retained as an appraisal consideration in keeping records, the relationship between these two professions must improve. That was indeed the seminal message of the joint committee on Archives and History (BRIDGES *ET AL.*). More important than collegial rhetoric, however, is the need for historians to insure that the records they want retained are appraised by archivists as having continuing value because they are continually used. The historians only real case for continued long-term service is as consumer. Otherwise, as in the past, archival survival for history's sake is largely a matter of chance, not strategy for the public's best interest, and certainly not risk management for private vested interest.

Data Warehouses: Re-engineering Electronic Archives

The old paradigm to which History has grown accustomed is, rapidly changing: nowadays two parallel traditions, manuscripts and archives, operate together under one roof, and the same person may need to wear two hats: one of curator and one of record keeper. People in this position must reconcile two mind-sets or must struggle to coordinate two disparate operations, there is an uneasy tension between archives as an institutionalized centralization of operations and collections of final, official records and the decentralized or distributed mode in which most original-state documentation is actually created in stages, on the job, on-site, and in an evolutionary process often not documented by the ultimate record. Such change does not necessarily mean the disassociation of Archival Science and History because archives and history remain entwined, but developments in the former will affect the latter profoundly. The crisis facing archivists is not the benign neglect of historians or trends in modern historiography that seem to lessen the importance of archives in History, but all alliances need to be reinforced today because the archival problem, although seen largely as technical, is very historical. The problem is to develop electronic archives that integrate history into the information profession and provide for the continuity of information flow from past to present and into the future. The argument that all of this must be done for history's sake will very likely fail no matter how eloquently presented. That argument should be made but adopted to the audience, with acknowledgment that other fields use terms like "legacy data" for their historical information. The dimensions of time and place in information creation, dissemination, retrieval, and integration are relevant still, but they are understood as timeliness and proximity more than something distant. The "now" of history must be emphasized.

Is it now possible to record processes and documentation, to track and map communications and interaction in temporal databases which create historical views at the moment and add to them in serial form as events unfold, to relate all of these despite the obvious complexity of modern organizations and the happenstance that makes systems interesting rather than simply robotic, and to incorporate in history the interaction of humans with their information technology, i.e., man-machine communications?

These are the challenges of modern archives. The shared responsibility of History would be to integrate the research and analysis processes into archival administration and services to create more than archival information systems, but rather archives coupled with decision support systems capable of sustaining interactive research outside the archives with archival data and records, access, and analytic tools. By comparison with these agenda, the more common small-project foci of historical retrospective conversion and electronic publication, to say nothing of traditional document editing projects so dear to historian's immediate vested interest, pale in significance. Digitized manuscript collections and historical data files are relatively small compared with current records production and the capacity needed for future mega-archives. Just as technological advances are making it possible to bypass older limitations on digital historical publication projects, recent advances in intranet design and both legacy and enterprise computing make possible the holding of massive electronic archives in distributive client-server architectures, which was at the turn of this decade impossible.

Consider the dramatic changes that have occurred in the period covered by this survey alone. Whereas the PC mini-revolution underway by 1984 would proliferate small-scale computing, fragment electronic archives down to the personal and project levels, and make information organization and synthesis more difficult than ever while access was accelerated geometrically and mass compounded annually, it took a decade until 1993 and after, to engineer software capable of dealing with the resulting mass, complexity, and fragmentation at the current state. Nevertheless, these problems are evolving unabated. From all this personalization of computing, accommodation of personal idiosyncracies by flexible software, and adoption to local systems and organizations that are neither really systematic or organized well, we have had to reconceptualize the very notion of "system" and to reinvent information systems as networks. These function increasingly parallel to human networks, from person to person, people to people, group to group, and interorganization communications. We now distinguish between Intranets and the Internet to deal with the complexity of computerized information systems within modern organizations, which are themselves widely distributed and somewhat amorphous as they cross borders, grow and contract, absorb and split, and continually reshape themselves. The distinction but five years ago, between Local Area Networks (LANs) and Wide Area Networks (WANs), has already been rendered obsolete by this new interconnectivity, which Microsoft Inc. calls "NT" for "New Technology." Ah, the lure of all things new—New History, New Science, etc., all must have new methods, techniques, and technology! The quest for newness is troublesome for History—and a never-ending issue in Information Science as well.

The new era of internetworking since the turn of this decade brings with it ease and difficulty, connectivity and isolation, and information and confusion, all at the same time. Continuity and contextualization remain problems and this purports things to come. If, in History as in global business and other disciplines that are expanding their scope, the goal is a more holistic approach to the study of human affairs, then the challenge is to confront mass and complexity at the same time. It has been estimated that the amount of information in the world now doubles every twenty months and the size and number of databases are increasing even faster (DILLY, pt. 1.1). The result is what BRACKETT has called "Data Chaos." Once this is acknowledged, it is a relatively simple step to move onto the conclusion that data access and management, research, and analysis must be done differently than in the past. Modern business, seeking to be intelligent, now perceives knowledge as an asset and is redesigning business processes accordingly. Academe, which supposedly has always recognized this, has not, however, perceived education as a business or see knowledge as something with an architecture and management dimension (M. JONES). Attitudes must change, the business of education must be reengineered, and the processes of scholarship likewise need to be reconsidered.

Developments in the past decade conducive for archives, and therefore for history, include legacy and enterprise computing which in the first case attempt continuity between old and new systems and in the second aim for holistic and highly integrative solutions to modern information problems (MARTIN & LEBEN). Electronic archivists must inject these with archival goals, principles, strategies, and use approaches associated with knowledge engineering and data warehousing (MIMNO, 1995a-c). Briefly, the idea of legacy computing is to provide continuity in the use of older mainframe and mid-frame hardware and their software to glide to new distributed models, networks, and client-server architectures utilizing PCs. By aiming at blending old and new systems, it provides opportunities to recover old data and transfer it to the new hybrid architecture. The business goal is to avoid redundancy of work caused by loss of data. While this may not be expressed in archival terms, the idea is essentially continuity based and is therefore compatible with archival goals. Whereas operations once performed on mainframes and in computer centers are now performed on PCs of Pentium Plus grade with peripherals for scanning and enhanced storage, the problems of synchronization, coordination, and systematic informing through timely reporting and alerts remain as major challenges in enterprise computing.

While businesses are often not developing actual archives, in the conversion to client-server architectures and the use of Web-based Intranets they are turning to new Electronic Document Management Systems (EDMS) for current records management which can be expanded for archival document management as well. Good EDMS packages today combine document storage, work flow control, and indexing capabilities for fast retrieval, e.g., *Metaphase* DPM/EDM software (see W. B. GREEN's introduction to EDMS). In short, EDMS is a combination of complementary technologies that can expand into a combined records management and electronic archives system. In EDMS design a repository stores, controls, and manages documents; work copies are checked in and out and most now offer version control which includes a history of all instances a document changes over time (J. BOYLE). Increasingly repository management software offers control as well over relationships between documents and their components (whole and parts, add-ons, etc.), so that the concept of an electronic document in such systems is one of containment (i.e., a document is a container for multiple forms, various content, organized and linked in some way). Vendors design EDMS as two-tier or three-tier systems: in the former the client does more of the work; in the latter the server does. The Document Management Alliance is working toward a set of interfaces that will allow multivendor configurations in one system. A database separate from the document repository itself houses metadata files using pointers that can retrieve in demand, often down to paragraph levels. Most desktop applications today are OLE (Open Document) compliant. Open Document Management (ODM) API standards allow for an interface now between desktop applications and document management clients without recourse to a separate application. These refer to inter-operability, while SGML/HTML refer to content formatting for independence from platforms and applications. Document linkage and pointing for information storage and retrieval can be as simple or detailed as one wants, and some integrated publishing-oriented systems (BOYLE likes *Interleaf;* see also *Documentum* software) capture automatically with document creation the metadata appropriate for retrieval. Workflow is enhanced by viewing documents in parallel rather than serially; alerts can notify users whenever a new version is available; audit trails can be created recording use and running commentary as well as editing histories; and some workflow engines come mounted with repositories (e.g., *OpenText* or *NovaSoft*; *Saros* and *PC Docs*, etc., use third parties). Standards to increase workflow efficiency are being worked on by the Workflow Management Coalition. Searching is also made more efficient by confining searches to documents with specific attributes, rather than by ransacking entire files *ad seriatim*. Newer search engines combine RDBMS techniques with word searches and now are integrating such refinements with Web site interfaces as well (*Fulcrum, Verity*, etc.).

Archivist's interests are also better served by more sophisticated Web publishing of documents that generates full repositories of native and viewable documents. R. BOYLE (pp. 76-78) compares three architectures or models in Web site management: (1) in the manual model, whereby a Webmaster simply posts documents and changed them by downloading a version, editing it, and replacing it on the homepage (this is easy to implement, but is error-prone, time-consuming, and involves no document control); (2) in the publishing model a repository is built to store and manage documents, and publication is done by extracting a document for mounting on the Web site (e.g., a batch process using a workflow engine which updates in real time), but retrieval of online information requires duplicated indexing and such systems do not capture attributes from the repository (nor do they automatically provide context pointers); and ideally (3) in an "access model" all documents in a repository are viewable through a browser that allows drilling down into a file to appropriate levels (multilevel data inheritance, in MAFTEI's terms, 1997, p. 13) for relevant information by using attributes, hierarchical relationships, and pathways shaped by recurrent use (navigation queries). In other words, as the software becomes more sophisticated to retrieve documents in real time, the greater is the propensity to build an archival repository from which to draw documents for online viewing and for creating data views. These are what MAFTEI (1997, p. 7) calls "network relational database management systems," as distinct from tabular RDBMS designs (he describes, p. 23, *GENCAT* as "one of the best implementations of the network relational model" because of its "dynamic array" offered by the *Advanced Revelation* Database Management System of Revelation Technologies, Inc., which Eloquent Systems Inc. used to build this archives automation software).

Network relational database management systems are recommended for electronic archives and history computing because by relating networks that provide indirect access to database or identifiable, autonomous electronic archives:

1.   Data structures can be left undisturbed for permanent storage and, hence, can preserve the archival integrity of the source without the compromise chanced in data transfer and restructuring.

2.   Components of electronic archives that happen to be technology dependent can be isolated from those that are independent (hence dependency and interdependencies are not increased) and the appropriate software for dependent data can be stored and preserved as a separate component.

3.   Both hierarchical and contextual information can be provided to users independently of the data archived or any particular data set, and the distinction between original metadata and subsequent enhancements are made clear (in short, multisource inherited and generated metadata can be kept in multilevel databases to avoid contamination with original data or an archives' archives or records of its own data management).

The repository is left intact in such processes or is added to by subsequent versions; but it is less vulnerable than before to overwriting, purging, and accidental deletion. All of these newer technologies, without any overt archival consciousness by their developers, are nevertheless conforming to an archives model of long-term information storage and retrieval based on the idea of a primary or base source, a respected *fonds*, preservation of original order, and records linkage or contextual information retrieval. Increasingly EDMS environments hold actual archives, but under any name other than "archives." Some danger lies in this nonrecognition, namely in potential discontinuity in systems management for long-term retention. Foreknowledge of archival intent and purpose in information systems design is important, since once compromised, the archival integrity of electronic records may not be able to be recovered. Mere data recovery as a technique and process, and the sanctity of electronic archives (accountability, chain of custody, original character and autonomy, contextual relations and linkage, assurance and trustworthiness, etc.), are related, but they certainly are not the same.

This trend toward convergence between modern electronic records and network database management systems, leading to fully developed electronic archives and creation of mega-archives, is furthered by the enlargement of intranets to enterprise proportions and beyond (as in the case of the Internet Archives). One approach to synthesize text, image, and data electronic resources is to create an intranet that allows front-end search engines for data acquisition within a corporate system and to design a strategy of discovery in large-sale, complex systems that may be used as in the aforementioned example of the Exxon *Valdez* affair, or from the corporate vantage point more positively to exploit information resources for ever more effective research and development operations, marketing, and informed executive decision making congruent with decisions taken at all other levels of complex organizations. The conglomerates absorb archives into larger entities, like records groups into an archives. We really do not have a good term for archives of archives or concept of databases and electronic archives that are larger than their parent organizations because of ongoing data acquisition from external sources. Enterprise computing attempts to network the entire system of the entity. Data warehousing is a collateral attempt to build a mega-information resource that may be fragmented and distributed, but that appears seamless to users because of intelligent intermediary search engines, expert systems, and other AI applications (HAYLES & MICHIE; HAYES-ROTH; WATERMAN & LENAT). The idea is to use trends in "open systems" to create hybrid systems which are expansive networks of networks, in which the old serial processes of information searching and research are genuinely integrated. The convergence of all of these developments into systematic large-scale, distributed operations is sometimes called "data warehousing," which in many ways seems like what archivists are talking about in the reinvention of electronic archives (MCCRANK [forthcoming]; KESNER [1998]).

Data warehouse architects still argue about what data warehousing is and is not. Sometimes the term is used comprehensively to include all aspects of data storage and data mining, and at other times it refers primarily to data storage and processing only. The two terms, to adopt a cliché, represent two sides of the same coin: i.e., information storage and retrieval. Data mining refers more properly to the latter; as defined by RAGHAVAN, DEOGUN & SEVER (1998, p. 402), it is "the process of deriving useful knowledge from real-world databases through the application of pattern extraction techniques." It is sometimes used in conjunction with "knowledge discovery" which connotes the ability to discern patterns and to derive meaning from sources too large and complex to do so manually or without computer assistance. Data warehousing, however, only makes sense if placed in a large context, one of integration, and where information access and analysis are combined. Conversely, new approaches to integrative and large-scale analyses depend on easy access to large amounts of data. W. H. Inmon, President of Pine Cone Systems, is often credited with being the "father" of data warehousing, or at least as the man who in 1993 pulled the myriad components together in a unified concept which has propelled so much of the development of large networked systems in business and industry during this decade (IMMON).

In his classic-status textbook in business circles, *Building the Data Warehouse*, IMMON stresses four characteristics of a data warehouse: (1) subject-oriented data (instead of an application orientation); (2) integration through consistent coding conventions; (3) time-variant research possibilities created by long-term data acquisitions and storage; and (4) non-volatile data, in that databases are loaded, increased incrementally, and accessed, but they are not deleted, updated, or changed (i.e, they are essentially electronic archives, although Inmon does not use this term). He is fond of using the metaphor of farmers or explorers to describe people's approach to data storage and retrieval; either one grows and harvests data internally, or one seeks it externally and brings it back to one's own storehouse. Commonly, both approaches are used now simultaneously. DILLY (pt. 1.4.6) expands upon Inmon's characteristics to include:

1.   Load performance that controls incremental loading with no degradation of system response times;

2. Seamless load processing—the jobs of data conversions, filtering, reformatting, integrity checks, physical storage, automatic indexing, and metadata updating;

3. Data quality management to ensure local and global consistency and referential integrity;

4. High-speed query performance;

5. Terabyte scalability to accommodate the exponential growth in data (e.g., through optical disk storage, hierarchical storage management devices, etc.);

6. Mass user scalability for thousands of concurrent users;

7. Networked data warehousing or cooperatives within the overall system architecture which are nevertheless managed from single control stations;

8. Warehouse administrations with controls for resource limits, charge backs, query prioritization, workload tracking and tuning, etc. for uninhibited user access;

9. Integrated dimensional analysis (i.e., ROLAP use); and

10. Advanced query functionality to accommodate analytic calculations, sequential and comparative analyses, and consistent access to segregated or detailed and integrated or summary data.

MATTISON provides a current methodological overview of what is euphemistically referred to as "the Big Database in the Sky," but which requires a "feet-firmly-on-the-ground" approach to up development. The complex and risky management aspect of data warehouses is treated by IMMON & IMHOFF (see the Tech Topic series by PRISM SOLUTIONS which Bill Inmon initiated, especially for management roles and responsibilities). See the *CIO Magazine's* Data Warehousing Resource Center (http://www.cio.com) for over 20 relevant URLs and lists of major vendors, including 50 "white papers" on the latest technology including OLAP and data mining, and electronic books on building data warehouses by Bill Inmon and others. Unfortunately some of these are rather superficial and one tends to find inconsistencies in usage, some jargon still but less hype, and lead-ins to consulting services rather than the kind of treatments one would consider genuinely academic (they often lack, for example, appropriate critical apparati or even standard bibliographic style when references are provided; cf. NEWING's data warehouse glossary; KENAN SYSTEMS' OLAP Council's terminology). Sometimes this is because the pitch is to the executive decision maker, the CEO or funder rather than a Chief Information Officer (CIO) or architect and implementor, or another information professional at the operational level. As such, they provide useful overviews even if occasionally somewhat evangelistic lures into large-scale information technology initiatives where databases crest more than a terabyte. The GARTNER GROUP in its series of consultative reports recently provided one on data warehouses for executives to cut through the hype and discuss in cold, clear terms the objectives of modern business intelligence—at the cost of $2,000 per report!

The series of course books adopted for the annual DATA WAREHOUSING INSTITUTE Training Conferences are useful in gaining an overview of new technologies and trends toward their integration ((LIVINGSTON & RADEN; MIMNO, 1995a-b; WATSON and the INSTITUTE's *Evaluation Reports*, especially the 1995 *Guide*). Moreover, the major vendors of data warehouse management software have all produced series of "White Papers" which are available directly from AT&T, Computer Associates, Hewlett Packhard, IBM, Software AG, Sybase, Tandem, Brio Technology, Cognos, EMC, Information Advantage, MicroStrategy, Prism Solutions, and Vality. PRIME MARKETING makes available a convenient *Data Warehouse Glossary* in its *Conspectus*. K. ORR provides a synopsis of the technology involved, as does KIMBALL's *Toolkit*. R. MATTISON, who provides one of the best introductions to data warehousing from the perspective of a practitioner, predicts that leading-edge information architectures will be the key to the survival of many twenty-first century businesses. One must read broadly and critically, but it is intriguing to put the researcher into the position of the CIO to speculate about what history would be like if electronic archives worked like large data warehouses with data mining capabilities, knowledge acquisition (expert systems), and Decision Support Systems (DSS) which are available to many corporate executives today (see FAYYAD for the advances to date in knowledge discovery and data mining AI techniques; M. PALMER provides a comprehensive reference and bibliography for expert system development coming into this decade). Indeed, the whole idea is to make all researchers, regardless of title and office held, his and her own executive in charge of their data and research projects.

The main ideas in enterprise computing and data warehouses include (1) studying corporate information generation and how this has been accomplished, e.g., a legacy issue; (2) creating a data warehouse and operational data store (two separate co-dependent entities), and appropriate data marts (subsets of data downloaded to more localized operations to reduce traffic across the system overall); and (3) tracking and producing documentation, when the metadata derived from the whole enterprise but safeguarded are also integrated so one can make sense of the data pulled in from the various parts of the corporation. The goal, according to K. ORR (1994, pt. 2.2) "is to free the information that is locked up in the operational databases and to mix it with information from other, often external, sources of data."

The architecture of a data warehouse represents the overall structure of data, communication, processing, and presentation for the entire enterprise. Its interconnected parts or layers include:

1. An operational database (external database layer)

2. The information access layer for end users which connects the various data components in the data warehouse through a common data language to those tools normally used (e.g., spreadsheets like Excel, Lotus 1-2-3, Focus, etc.; Access; SAS, SPSS; etc.)

3. Data access, usually SQL, now coupled with a variety of filters such as EDA/SQL (ANSI standard)

4. A data directory (metadata)

5. Process management for job control (a scheduler for processes and procedures)

6. "Middleware" for application messaging or information transport around the enterprise

7. The core data or warehouse itself consisting of the physical (electronic) data and virtual or logical views, stored either on mainframes or on client/server platforms

8. A data staging area for replication or copy management which may or not involve data quality analysis or filters preliminarily identifying patterns and structures within operational data.

Definitions and rules are often seen as forming a procedural repository, which when stored by keyword and their definitions, are seen as prescriptive dictionaries. Data dictionaries are sometimes likened to the Rosetta Stone because the logical linkage created between terms, rules, operations, and data allow translation between human queries and computer responses. The iterative nature of data warehouses is always emphasized, in that the conversion of a theoretical architecture to a real structure and information system takes time and repetitious processing. For example, data harvesting, like records scheduling and retention in archives, is an ongoing, repetitive operation. It is the massive data accumulation that makes large-scale computing necessary but also desirable to make new findings possible (and in business, profitable). Data acquisition and processing are constants; analyses may be periodic. Finally, although the "warehouse" idea stresses storage and retrieval, it is always linked to analysis. Now, with OnLine Analytical Processing (OLAP) in particular (see ARBOR SOFTWARE's "keys" to the rapid deployment of enterprise information systems), this makes analysis more regular as well, as part of everyday business.

So, what does data warehousing entail? One answer is everything required of an enterprise-wide electronic archives. In distributed computing, three models are prevalent. The first is the application/server, which makes available a single DBMS on a server which is transferred to a user for data operations but does not reside on the user's PC, and the user must also navigate through the system also to retrieve required data which increases network traffic, but the processing is run locally. The second model is the file/server setup, which uses local applications but posts changes to files stored on the server client/server environments, which process queries on the server with the back-end and front-end computers working together in a two-tiered architecture (sometimes an intermediate level is added for business processes), sharing the work by distributing different tasks to each other, such as the following: SQL, report writers, spreadsheets, graphics subsystems, statistical packages, and CASE tools on the client; DML, data storage, security, backup and recovery utilities are on the server.

In actuality, however, these models, themselves hybrids, are often mixed in large systems. *ACCESS*, for example, provides a continuum to support a single user continuously but scales up from the first to second model, for modest computing projects. Other software families are needed for large-scale enterprise computing projects and information systems. Scale and capacity, information mass and proliferation of database structures, multitype networking and interdependencies of institutions and technologies, and rapid innovation make the current milieu very complex. UMAR provides a good overview of the new distributed computing environment and its many management challenges.

IBM's Open Blueprint™ is an example of the elaborate interoperable, open systems architecture which is coming into place (IBM, 1995a-d, 1996) and which makes these conglomerate super systems possible. IBM's idea is to provide a planning guide for the migration from mainframe to decentralized client/server computing, both to protect investments already made and to insure wise investments based on continuity in their glide to new technology. The Open Blueprint relies on network services (SNA APPN, TCP/IP. OSI, NET BIOS IPX) built on a physical network of multiple systems, all of which support common transport semantics or protocol-independent communications through distributed systems, and a sub-network to facilitate the choice of transmission facilities and connections to services for communications (conversational communication, Remote Procedure Call, and Queuing); object management including transparent access to local and remote objects (Life-Cycle and Externalization services); and distribution services that provide common functions for directory, security, time, and transaction management. These layers of network and distributed systems services support, in IBM's schema, data access to hierarchical, relational or object databases; applications (software, transaction monitoring, event services, document support, etc.) and presentations (user interfaces, viewing, printing, multimedia, etc.), and application enabling services such as workgroup and workflow management through electronic mail, conferencing, distance learning, telephony, and digital library support. Although computer companies like IBM may want to make such processes as migration of data from system to system as transparent as possible, or the creation of software that integrates legacy data with that in new systems, this subterfuge could hinder the archivists in making metadata documentation more difficult and in discerning real alterations of the data being restructured and transformed in the process of systems migration. Such interventions may transfer data but not the complete archival record, such as context and structure in original development and use, and hence any radical treatment of legacy data becomes a disjuncture in the supposed continuity of this record. Archivists are just now distinguishing between the different processes of refreshing, transference, and migration in records maintenance, and how to combine legacy computing with migration strategies

(COMMISSION ON PRESERVATION AND ACCESS (CPA), 1996; cf., DOLLAR, 1997; HEDSTROM, 1997; MAKARENKO; BINNS, BOWEN & MURDOCK; for review migration technology for legacy systems, see BRODIE & STONEBRAKER; DOLLAR [1998] addresses this issue specifically from an electronic archives perspective).

In an interactive corporate computing environment the enterprise is not really circum-scribed by organizational boundaries since one can reach out through the Internet. Partnerships are often reinforced by direct communications and even shared databases. Data acquisition is therefore both internal and external at the same time, and its use creates hybrid records and new forms of information which must be kept as they grow. The goal of a dynamic data warehouse is to create a gigantic pool of networked, interactive, integrative information resources of gigantic dimension, wherein data is augmented continuously. John Bernardi of EMC Corporation claims that Data Warehouse (DW) storage requires up to four times more space than operational data from conventional business process systems (DATA WAREHOUSING INSTITUTE, 1995, p. 16). Original data and additional data are kept, not necessarily together, but so they can be combined on demand and acted upon with whatever combinations of software are desirable, from a repeat of original processing or alternative choices, so that originals and alterations are all retrievable. It is this integrative, additive (serial), and open systems approach which essentially makes modern DW into archives. It is simply that computing engineers often miss this essential transformation of databases into electronic archives because of their limited and misconceived notions about what archives are, i.e., off-line, static data instead of a long-term, in-depth, dynamic information system. The key difference in the design of an information system and an electronic archives is not the technology itself, but the regard for evidence.

Data cleansing is largely a matter of eliminating unnecessary duplication in operational data such as low-level transaction information that slows down query processing, which can be com-pared to the easiest selection and retention decisions in archival appraisal based on originals versus copies and discard of multiple copies of directional materials. It is the data transforma-tion stage that might worry archivists, since project design can attempt to store data in original form and transform it for certain uses when called into action (in which case transformation occurs only in research subsets, not in the raw storage). Alternatively, and with grave archival implications, data could be massaged, transformed, and reengineered for storage so sets could be recalled ready for interaction with other data. If the latter procedures are introduced, then metadata and documentation of the original data sets becomes critical, as is a mechanism for retroformation whenever a particular data set needed to be examined in its original state. As with any preservation concern, data transformation should be reversible. An alternative is to store data sets in original and transformed states. This is likely to bring opposition in business applications because of increased cost and data redundancy not justified by use, unless the aforementioned concern for evidence and the appeal of risk management are raised.

If transformed data in subsets are the basis for research and decisions, then documentation and preservation efforts must be aimed at retaining the ability to recreate the subset and duplicate data processing to replicate results as required, or the results themselves must be saved with proper documentation about how they were derived. Each has its trade-off: the former requires more processing and operations capabilities over time, and the latter involves more data duplication; both require the same kinds of documentation. Otherwise, data warehouse managers are likely to dismiss historical data as simply "old style" and to regard any preserved original as the archives, and unfortunately as an independent operation from the warehouse. The two must be merged, since use of transformed data based on an archival set is an added dimension of the data and must be tracked as archival in itself. This can be done technically, but often is not; this is largely a mat-ter of awareness, education, and enlightened policy. Increasingly researchers want equal access to structured transaction-oriented data in legacy and relational databases and nonstructured data (e.g., text files), and new approaches are being worked out to take the best of data and text retrieval systems to handle a broad range of data types (J. DAVIS).

Data integrity consists of two "flavors" in programmer's jargon, physical and logical. In the first case the issue is the safety of data, placed under the protection of a DBMS file manager, which in turn relies on the database primary, relationship or referential, domain (sets of values), and user or business (rules) integrity. Archivists have something more in mind. So do the courts, so should serious researchers, and ultimately, so should users in the business community who rely on data without knowing as much as they should about its integrity other than this common reliance on data management programs. Total quality management (TQM) should pertain to the quality of the data itself, not simply the security of database management: data worth warehousing should have immediate value that is enhanced by breadth and depth at the same time.

Data Warehouses (DW) are expensive to implement and maintain because they are so complex and encompassing, and this means in turn that few archivists and almost no historians are ever trained in environments to provide experience with this kind of magnitude and complexity. This limitation calls for new kinds of post-degree training opportunities, post-appointment advance-level internships, and in-depth technical training in one or more areas of legacy and enterprise computing and data warehousing. Archivists need to become part of the information team to gain such experience on the job, and historians to use such information sources need to follow suit and get out of the classroom and academe and into environments where historical data are first being generated, used, and warehoused. Their after-the-fact research has to find some linkage with source creation and preservation, and their research itself has to have greater continuity between past and present. Granted that their research topic might be historical and set in the past, but the research itself is, or should be, a current event.

Data warehouses are becoming increasingly common in government, corporations, and now in public sector enterprises as well. Because they often involve one to two years implementation and a redesign of enterprise computing, and cost up to $3 million depending on size, scale, and distribution, the large investment in data warehousing is sometimes difficult to justify even in the for-profit sector. Arguments include bonding with the customer through information services, enabling workers to perform better and smarter, identifying hidden business opportunities, being precise in marketing, and rapidly responding to events within and outside the organization; there should also be an improved ability to respond to market and technology trends. All of these could justify such development as well in academe and in archives, and could be translated into terms making sense for historical research as well. Less convincing is needed now in the business world than five years ago when the first moves toward DW were often high risk ventures and, therefore, did not seem to be attractive models for electronic archives. At DW conferences, Hal Daniels, who directs The Associate Group's DW project, passes along the common caveat that half of DW projects fail within eighteen months of implementation (DATA WAREHOUSING INSTITUTE, 1995, p. 19). He attributes such failures to common problems, such as the following:"paralysis by analysis"; politics (or "all-out war") inside organizations; unclear or inconsistent short-term goals (deliverables) and inhibition created by slavish adherence to long-term strategies; overconfidence in "bleeding edge" hardware technology not tested enough in the field; mistaken beliefs in benchmarking and competitive price/performance evaluations; confusing "off-the-shelf" and open-systems components with "do-it-yourself" on-the-job education for staff development and for gaining needed expertise; lack of user analysis and query methodology; and using summary and sample data as the basis for DW design, instead of relying on transactional data. He plays on the term "warehouse" and common variations of this theme (enterprise data warehouses, two-tiered data warehouses, distributed data warehouses, etc.) to construct a unique vocabulary for classifying such failures in a continuum from jazzy misnomers like information factory and data mart, to data outhouses, basements, mausoleums, tenements, shacks, cottages, condominia, and jailhouses guarded by the local IT department, and "DW street people" whose numbers are declining but who are characterized as "conference groupies" and prolific authors and speakers who are ignored by their bosses because of their failure to understand the actual business benefits of data warehouses.

Allan Paller of the CIO Institute, in a popular workshop warned against the "Ten Mistakes to Avoid for Data Warehouse Managers" (PALLER; see also SHAH & MILSTEIN):

1. Wrong sponsorship by management lacking the resources to sustain the project

2. Working with wrong expectations, that are unobtainable rather than realistic

3. Political naive behavior

4. Overloading the warehouse (unnecessary data storage and lack of records management)

5. Confusing database design for warehousing with transactional design

6. Incorrect choice of managers

7. Old-style data requiring transformation (which is where archival concerns should appear)

8. Overlapping and confusing data definitions

9. Believing vendor performance promises

10. Short-term views of data warehouse development

11. Missing alert opportunities (rather than reporting) for management

He teasingly adds more than ten caveats to his list to illustrate that still another mistake is to believe that one could encounter only a certain number of problems.

Data mining in some ways is the buzzword for AI applications and statistical research in business. Some have said, mistakingly, that Information Systems Management (or ISM) is data mining (DARLING). Others relate it to Decision Support Systems which developed so rapidly in the 1980s (ALTER; BENNET; KEEN & SCOTT-MORTON; SPRAGUE & CARLSON; updated for Decision Support Analysis or DSA by MEADOR, GUYOTE & ROSENFELD). It is the research operations working on a data warehouse, in league with policies, procedures, strategies, etc., business operations, and ongoing transactions. What makes this development different is employment of AI techniques and Social Science research methodology in massive databases, use of high-performance computing that includes Machine Learning (ML) for improved efficiencies, and broad integration. The metaphor is based on the analogy of shifting through large amounts of data to find valuable patterns and regularities in sets of data, in the same way that a miner digs through rock or a panner shifts through large amounts of gravel to find a vein or precious nuggets of gold. The ingredients have been evolving for two decades now, but the current innovation is in combination, integration, and application. TRYBULA recently surveyed the literature on data mining and knowledge discovery. It is truly amazing how fast this technology and related methodologies have developed.

Traditional methods are sometimes classified by functions:

1. Classification using predicted attributes denoting the class of a tuple and inferring rules that govern classes (exact, strong, and probabilistic rules)

2. Associations or operations against sets of records which identify existing affinities or patterns, as in IBM's Market Basket Analysis using transaction logs to create correspondences in purchasing products together, usually expressed in percentages

3. Sequential or temporal pattern recognition to identify trends

4. Clustering or segmentation by creating a partition so all members in each set are similar according to some metric or because of their similarity or proximity, which can include rules to calculate degrees of membership in a group (ARABIE, HUBERT & SOETE, eds)

HAHN & CHATER notice the paradox in using similarity to explain concepts and *vice versa*, concepts to explain similarity. This may prove unsettling for those who understand how similarity underpins the operationalization of fuzziness relating to relevance in information retrieval. It is this thorny issue of identification of information on the basis of similarity, even when the comparison is fuzzy, that also pertains to the use of historical metaphor to explain the present. Since history does not repeat itself exactly, what is perceived to be relevant, and especially what may be seen as generally repetitious, relies on degrees of similarity. Retrieval of historical information, therefore, rests to some extent on conceptualizing similarity as a working methodology in large-scale longitudinal databases.

Information retrieval based on similarity and metaphor is far more complex than term matching and automatic comparison of numeric data, and the complexity of modern information retrieval is increased by the volume of data, multiple entwined methodologies, and the goal to accomplish more than information retrieval, namely that of acquiring new knowledge. Knowledge acquisition relies on information retrieval but is often seen as a separate, higher-level enterprise. Various methodologies employed are too often subsumed under the far too general term "data mining." The following components make data mining technology work today. The first are neural networks, which are mathematical structures of links between input, hidden, and output layers that have the ability to learn from past history, have evolved greatly since their infancy in the 1960s. The second is use of induction and deduction in decision trees—mostly Classification and Regression Trees (CART) that structure two-way decisions and label nodes, edges, and leaves. The last are Chi Square Automatic Interaction Detection (CHAID) for multi-way decisions, rule induction ("if-then" rules), genetic algorithms or optimization techniques based on concepts of genetic combination, mutation, and natural selection; and classification techniques sometimes called "nearest neighbor" approaches, which match new records with characteristics of historical datasets on the basis of greatest similarity.

Online Transaction Processing (OLTP) is the conventional data acquisition and reporting scheme with relatively simple security requirements, problems with concurrency, and noticeable degradation in performance as use increases; juxtapose this to OLAP (or, ROLAP [MICROSTRATEGY]) which is often confused with the overly general but popular term "data warehousing." ROLAP might be identified better with Decision Support Systems (DSS) or Executive Information Systems (EIS, coined by American Management Consultants John Rockart and Michael Tracy in 1982; cf., ROCKART; ROCKART & DELONG) which propelled this development. BIRD provides a useful update covering the first decade of EIS progress (see also BUCHANAN; ROLPH & BARTRAN; GRAY). Basically, EIS consists of eight components (CITY UNIVERSITY OF LONDON):

1. Intuitive and natural interfaces (e.g., touch screens, mouse/click mechanism, infrared keypads, etc.) for easy navigation by busy executives who often dislike computers and cannot invest the time to learn anything too complicated

2. Executive database for predetermined data views quickly retrieved

3. Data collection from different sources and consolidation in integrated views

4. Variety of presentation options (graphs, charts, maps, etc.)

5. Investigation techniques (drill-down capabilities)

6. Planning using modeling for different scenarios

7. Communications (e-mail with pre-formatted messages and easy attachment links)

8. Development tools for new applications and screen formats

Behind the scene, however, more complicated data processing and information management are taking place.

OLAP/ROLAP may be juxtaposed to older OLTP purposes to run a business with the former's design to analyze business. OLTP's purpose is running day-to-day operations, it usually relies on relational database structures and normalized data and uses IBM's SQL or variant for access, and in the process of daily business the data are incomplete and forever changing. Whereas OLTP design represents data in tables and columns which support relational linkage (data, descriptor, and characteristics tables), OLAP is designed for human inquiry and stores data by dimensions (views) and measures (numeric variables). Data warehouse operations differ from OLTP in that the purpose is informational rather than operational; that is, the aim is not processing but analysis; an RDBMS is also used, but the data model is multi-dimensional; SQL is used in combination with data analysis extensions; and the condition of the data is descriptive, historical, and indeed, archival (DILLY, pt. 1.4.3). OLAP may be applied to a data warehouse, but is separate from data warehouse operations; it pertains to methods of data analysis performed online after a data warehouse provides appropriate data in electronic work spaces as research sets, and in business settings result sharing through a decision support or executive information system (where data representation is all important).

OLAP technology is now in its second generational wave, having been born in the convergence of three technologies: Symmetric MultiProcessing (SMP), data transformation with metadata tool development, and multi-dimensional end-user packages. The term was coined by E. F. Codd in 1993 and defined as "the dynamic synthesis, analysis and consolidation of large volumes of multi-dimensional data" (CODD). He mixes technology prescriptions with application requirements (first enumerated as 12 rules or features, then eighteen, and the list keeps expanding) as criteria for OLAP systems, which should include a multidimensional conceptual view, transparency, accessibility, consistency in reporting performance, client/server architecture, generic dimensionality, dynamic sparse matrix handling, multiuser support, unrestricted cross-dimensional operations, intuitive browsing and searching using agents with exception reporting and periodic agents reporting predefined conditions when found or by set schedule as in monthly reporting, data manipulation (based usually on mining hierarchies), flexible scheduling and reporting, and unlimited dimensions and aggregation levels.

What was once a wish list has now become, in Codd's terms, an "IT Mandate" (CODD, CODD, & SALLEY). Based largely on CODD's criteria, OLAP functionality has been charactered by the OLAP COUNCIL's *Guide to OLAP Terminology* provided by Kenan Systems (p. 1) as a dynamic multi-dimensional analysis of consolidated enterprise data supporting end user analytical and navigational activities including:

- Calculations and modeling applied across dimensions [structural attribute of cubes], through hierarchies and/or across members

- Trend analysis over sequential time periods

- Slicing subsets [a slice is a subset of a multidimensional array corresponding to a single value for one or more members of the dimensions not in the subset] for on-screen viewing

- Drill-down to deeper [most detailed] levels of consolidation [or drill up to sum-marized data]

- Reach-through [extension of accessible data] to underlying detail data

- Rotation [changing the dimensional orientation of a report or page display, e.g., X and Y axes] to new dimensional comparisons in the viewing area

> OLAP is implemented in a multiuser client/server mode and offers consistently rapid response to queries, regardless of database size and complexity. OLAP helps the user synthesize enterprise information through comparative, personalized viewing, as well as through analysis of historical and projected data in various "what-if" scenarios. This is achieved through the use of an OLAP Server.

As this technology keeps developing, the concept of OLAP keeps enlarging. Recently MATTISON & CREETH proposed a new acronym for OLAP and a redefinition: FASMI or Fast Analysis of Shared Multidimensional Information. They add to the basic OLAP family and client/server architecture such techniques as time-series analysis, object orientation, parallel processing, optimized proprietary data storage, and multi-threading.

One of the big issues in such approaches is the issue of multidimensionality, or how associations between dissimilar components of information are built using predefined business rules about the information. Data can be stored relationally and still be viewed multi-dimensionally. Multi-dimensional architectures are often described as cubes (each defined by three dimensions) forming ever larger building blocks which can be "sliced and diced" interactively by calling for multiple page displays through specification of slices via rotations and drilling down or up in research operations. With multi-dimensional databases, one wants the management tools needed to ensure integrity through backup and restoration capabilities, tuning for optimal performance, security at multiple levels, and access defined by user classes of user privileges. Other requirements include: flexible retrieval from aggregate to atomic levels of detail; incremental database refreshment capabilities that do not rewrite or reload data already resident; support for multiple arrays (e.g., relational architectures typically permit definition up to 256 tables in a single database); database joins to overcome limitations in query flexibility; subset selection; local data support; and SQL interface. When all such features are provided one has something different than older database management systems. OLTP structures surmise that users know what they want when they query their data; OLAP does not assume this, but attempts to offer fast responses to complex queries across huge data stores. Whereas OLTP operational data need to be cleaned and transformed (denormalized and aggregated) when transported into OLAP environments, OLAP accommodates all kinds of actual data transfers from multiple databases, tabular and descriptive varieties, images and video, and sound because it stores data in different systems. OLAP, and particularly relational OLAP (ROLAP) which has already overtaken OLAP in percentage of new installations, is therefore a preferred archival approach to multi-database management in a diverse warehouse.

Multi-Dimensional Databases (MDD) are broken into header and data storage blocks, with pointers from headers to appropriate blocks and various indexing mechanisms to retrieve quickly from these blocks. Metadata pointer structures create the illusion that a query acts directly on data, but in fact the query is processed through an intermediary redefinition of relational tables and columns and sets of dimensions, members, and measures, to "map" a direction for the query to appropriate data. Programmers, unaware of similar conventions in bibliography, libraries and archives, often adopt the so-called "Hungarian Naming convention" of Charles Simonyi which attaches a prefix tag to the front of an object or variable to classify it. Since 1993 a somewhat more complex convention has gained acceptance in the *Visual Basic* and *Access* (Microsoft) arena, the Leszynski/Reddick nomenclature method in English which uses four-part naming with two levels of names (general and specific) to form a lower-case string (no spaces) with the syntax of prefix, tag, base name, and qualifier (POOLET & REILLY, ch. 5 tables). All elements in these strings use a conventional abbreviation by consonants surrounding a single vowel or three consonants omitting interspersed vowels for mnemonic assistance, i.e., break =brk, document = doc, field = fld, table = tbl, or yes/no = ysn.

Data mining techniques developed in business for understanding customer behavior and improving market effectiveness are essentially forms of data modeling of the same vintage as used in historical computing, and indeed, data mining relies heavily on historical data to create and validate models. DILLY provides a good introduction for the business context and a European perspective. MCGUFF offers an overview of how data modeling fits into data warehousing. R. G. ROSS speaks of "entity modeling," which is very conducive to historical computing, although with his focus on business he does not realize this. His entity-relationship approach, however, is based on careful consideration of intersection data derived from modeling time and events. He speaks of "entity life histories" with their time dimension, and the need to handle "complex event histories" and to coordinate them with state information. He advocates an "organizing history" approach to documenting data models, which is basically an archival approach that has been used throughout this half-century, but he does not see these techniques as necessarily archival. Instead, "archiving" to him is capturing data views or snapshots. Among his concerns in modeling are points-in-time versus series analysis, event streams and aging.

The reliance on the so-called "Entity-Relationship" in data modeling has come under attack, however, because of its denial of the domain concept and disregard for intra-database relationships (CODD, CODD & SALLEY, pt. 3). The Codd husband and wife team regard this as a "fundamental flaw." They argue for an even more flexible information synthesis and dynamic analysis and call for an increasingly robust OLAP development for analysis, as opposed to still more variants on relational database management systems. It is the speculative dimension of inquiry they seek to exploit for knowledge discovery.

The basic uses of data mining in business for marketing (market segmentation, customer turnover prediction, fraud detection, direct and interactive marketing, "basket" analysis [determining what products are commonly bought together], and trend analysis for forecasting, etc.) exploit customer data and rely on techniques well known in social research. In some cases business is simply catching up to Social Science research methodology, but has the advantage of custombuilt databases. In others, such practical applications are combining with more theoretical approaches to develop future possibilities in Artificial Intelligence (AI) (R&D applications are reviewed by KENDALL & WALKER). Data mining is this combination of research using statistics, databases, machine learning, and advanced AI techniques (induction; FURUKAWA, MICHIE & MUGGLETON, eds.; MICHIE, SPIEGELHALTER & TAYLOR, eds.). As already mentioned, all together the approaches are now being called "Knowledge Discovery" (i.e., mining databases to identify knowledge not known before, such as latent pattern recognition), as related to Knowledge Engineering (i.e., building databases that offer such potential; see the aforementioned literature review by TRYBULA). FAYYAD *ET AL.* and ARABIE, HUBERT & SOETE, eds., provide case studies and discussions of the latest developments in classification and clustering (cf., BIJNEN; EVERITT; LORR; MIRKIN), trend and deviation analysis, dependency modeling, integrated discovery systems, and the potential of "next generation" databases. P. COHEN surveys the empirical methods now being employed in AI research, including classical parametric methods, computer-intensive resampling methods, statistical hypothesis testing, performance analyses, and predictive programs including causal models. Statistical models and information discovery are methods to go beyond *ad hoc* inquiries of databases. They produce "virtual data," that are derived from queries to produce certain data views, which in turn grow the archives in accord with use.

Lessons in the use of data warehouses represent similar approaches as in historical computing: often historical precedents are identified, sampling is used, derived variables are examined to identify the best indicators, and data views are studied often in a series. But modern data mining techniques rely increasingly on new technologies, rather than regression analyses, such as mentioned above: neural nets, tree-based methods, example prototyping, rule-based searches, and a combination for optimal results. A big push in the industry is to integrate decision support into production, which means integrating modeling in data warehousing. This in turn has meant a dramatic turn toward OLAP technology in the past few years (the *OLAP Report* [MATTISON & CREETH] surveys the current market, covering thirty potential contenders and reviewing 23 in detail).

A recent survey of businesses in the United States indicates that of those embarking on data warehousing, 43 percent use ROLAP and 40 percent of those planning installations will use it; 46 percent of current installations use query tools, and 55 percent of planned projects will; 37 percent now model data, but 44 percent plan to; 30 percent do scheduling and 33 percent of those installing systems will do the same, and 14 percent of current operations have multi-dimensional databases, but 31 percent of new installations will go in this direction. Data mining, or combinations of search and analysis tools, have been used to date by only 17 percent of companies having data warehouses in place; but 31 percent of those planning such development expect to go into data mining (MCCARTHY, 1997). The latter is especially attractive to pharmaceutical companies where social and medical data are combined for genuine leaps in the knowledge companies have about their potential markets, and for banks where transaction logs provide customer profiles of long-term individual and aggregate behavior. Bank of America, for example, has conducted research on the Hispanic surname population in California that has caused the corporation to debunk all previous notions about this growing market segment.

Executives are therefore interested in tying research results directly to modifications in policies and program design. Scoring techniques are often advocated, distributed models are used increasingly, and self-tuning systems are being developed. Much of this is subordinated under the rubric "Decision Science, which today focuses on multi-dimensional models in finance, sales, marketing, retail, subscription and inventory studies" (theory of choice: see HEAP, *ET AL.*; RESNIK; see also game theory). The interrelationships are sometimes envisioned in the "multicube" (using *Essbase*, *Express*, etc.), i.e., a cube composed of smaller cubes, so that each of the six sides is a matrix of cells than can be related to each other and to the whole at the same time. The issues are similar to other models drawn from econometrics: defining relationships, adjusting to changing dimensions, handling sparsity, predicting size and performance, and flexibility amid research. Whereas older research methods stressed data aggregation, newer techniques distinguish this from data consolidation. In data warehousing this means leaving data in separate databases and copying it into operational databases for research. Star schematics are often viewed as the best design for relational databases, augmented by indexing, tuning query performance, and the use of summary tables. All of this is in anticipation of the next generation of information technology that will include data visualization inconceivable only a decade ago, generic algorithms, and reliance on simulation as distinct from traditional data analyses.

True data warehouses are read only and in this sense of security are archival; data updates come from the operational database and are appended to the original data blocks, but they do not merge, integrate, or overwrite the original. In the cubic model, data would not be overwritten to add new data, but additives are appended by joining cells to enlarge the original cube, i.e., a multicube cube. Thus, data corpora are grown by combination rather than interpolation or expansion by integration. While the whole complex thus ingests new data and grows, its components retain their original state. The growth process is less one of cellular division than a form of cloning and augmentation, and joining through neural nets. Memory is thus always an aggregate of discrete cells, and data retrieved results from multiple searches and many integrations to build customized data sets. If the new amalgamation in a workspace is stored, it can be stored entirely as a new cell, or to avoid data redundancy new data only would be stored with the instructions for repeated performance in data processing, i.e., pulling the same data from another cell and repeating the same operations to replicate the results. It is in the customization of data sets to specific inquiries that knowledge discovery usually occurs. New data sets or new documents are thus composed on demand. If useful, these are stored anew, so that the archives grows with the thinking that is applied to its data. The new paradigm is closer to how human memory works with the grown of brain cells stimulated by intellectual activity and with intelligence increasing through the growth of neural connections. In this sense, data warehouses are living archives. They seek to build a corporate intelligence.

Because data processing for analysis occurs in work spaces and localized marts (mini-warehouses), the problem in data warehouse management is often one of traffic control and data replication. This also means that the new data warehouse architecture is essentially historical, and is very conducive for presenting data trends, just as data mining is often explained in genealogical and family terms (parents, children, generations, etc.), and multi-dimensional architectures invariably use time and place as two of their dimensions (i.e., historical relationships). This development was not consciously to create an archival type of storage, but because no reliable software was available at the turn of the decade to synchronize end-user updating. Piped-in denormalized data can mean extensive data duplication, and synchronizing even commonly duplicated data like names and addresses can be a difficult task. If processing and mass storage capabilities continue to expand exponentially, these may simply overcome the need for synchronization or reduction of data redundancy. Data warehouse management, therefore, may not be constrained by storage space considerations parallel to conventional paper archives. Performance is the critical issue. This because with all that data, more questions are being asked of increased complexity, requiring more metadata and indexing to be scanned, and this often overloads a network. All experts warn that successful data warehouse projects breed increased demand so that spiraling expectations place great pressure on the system for continued expansion and development. In large organizations traffic or an exponential query load, not storage, is the critical management problem.

An array of products exist today to support large-scale, integrated and open-systems computing architecture. Indeed, it is the prepackaged software that has enabled industry to break into this kind of computing on a large-scale as opposed to previous reliance on AI laboratory results for limited applications and periodic runs. As exclaimed by one enthusiast with a certain anti-intellectualism and typical disdain for actually understanding the methodology one employs: "Thankfully, we're past the bleeding edge stage. You no longer have to hire Ph.D.s in statistics and artificial intelligence away from academia, set them up in a lab somewhere, sprinkle liberally with money, and hope for the best. There's packaged technology out there—a bewildering variety of packaged technology, in fact. The trick is to find a product that you can turn into a business solution" (DARLING, p. 54).

The growing selection may be reviewed briefly to illustrate the rapid development of this field and why data warehouses and data mining are more feasible today than just five years ago (cf., MATTISON & CREETH).

1.   Data storage, moving, and staging

1.1. Data origination, acquisition, transformation and storage

Data origins are traditionally thought of as internal, but now data are commonly imported. Imported and internally generated data are often combined with a variety of information forms: commercial databases, syndicated data, news feed, contracted market research, e-mail, Internet communications, text files, video, and voice. Although it is no longer assumed that information storage will be primarily data files, most information storage is assembled into some kind of database. In the United States, traditional databases are likely to be created on software from *ADABAS*, AllBase, AS/400. AT&T *Teradata*, Computer Associate's CA-*DATA-COM*, CA-*IDMS*, *DB2*, Focus, IMS, Informix, Model 204, Oracle, PCS, SAP *R/3*, SAS, Sybase, TOTAL, and Rdb. Any such list reminds one of alphabet soup, and the metaphor is apt since vegetable soup has an infinite variety of recipes and *ad hoc* combinations. The idea is to take data created on any of these platforms and be able to mix and match it with other databases for whatever combination is wanted.

1.2.   Data extraction, transformation, and cleaning

Data are either held in their original form and are transformed when retrieved for certain applications that requires another format, or they are transformed when stored as generic data ready-made for reuse. Common data extraction and transformation tools include AT&T *Teradata's FastLoad/MultiLoad*; CA-Ingres *Replicator*; Carleton *Passport*; COBOL; Comshare *Commander OLAP*; Digital *Access Works*; ETI: Evolutionary Technology's *Extract*; Focus; IBM's *Data Replication Solution* and *Visual Warehouse*; NATURAL; Oracle *7 Symmetric Replication*; Praxis *Omni Replicator*; Prism *Warehouse Manager*; SAS; Software AG *SourcePoin*t; Sybase *System 10 Replication* Server; Trinzic *InfoPump*; and VSAM *Transparency*. Data reengineering and authentication tools include *Apertus* and Vality Technology products.

1.2.1.   Source linkage

Certain software are ideal for linking data stored in different sources in a warehouse. Sometimes called "middleware," the following are common in business: CA-IngresNET and *Gateways*; Cupta *DB2 Gateway*; IBI EDA/SQL; IBM *Datajoiner*, *DRDA*, and *Visual Warehouse*; Informix *Enterprise Gateway*; Intersolv *Q&E*; Microsoft ODBC; Oracle *Open Connect*; Praxis *Omni replicator*; SAS *Connect*; Software AG *Entire Middleware* and *SourcePoint*; Standard Technology *Metacube*; Sybase *Enterprise Connect* (MDI); TechGnosis *PCSequeLink*; and Trinzic (a division of Platinum Inc.) *InfoHub*.

1.3.   Data storage

Data may be stored on conventional disks, in disk array with RAID (EMC), or systems such as IBM's AdStar *Distributed Storage Manager*. Multidimensional database engines are made by Arbor's *Essbase*; Comshare *Commander OLAP*; IRI (a division of Oracle, Inc.) *Express*; Pilot (a division of Dun and Bradstreet) *Lightship* server; Planning Sciences *Gentium*; and SAS systems. Servers are usually scaled by the size of databases to be handled. Medium-range servers include ADABAS; AT&T *Teradata* (UNIX edition); Computer Associate's *CA-Ingres*; Focus; IBM DB2 family; Informix; Lotus *Notes*; Microsoft *Access* and *SQL/server*; Oracle; Red Brick; SAS; Sybase; and Tandem. Large-scale warehouse servers include ADABAS; AT&T *Teradata*; CA *Datacom* and *IDMS*; IBM *DB2* for MVS and for OS/400, and *DB2 Parallel* edition for AIX/6000; Informix; MasPar; Model 204; Red Brick; Tandem; and White Cross.

2.   Information access

2.1.   Speed

Information retrieval engines are often selected for the fastest retrieval given a particular environment. Optimization is achieved by a variety of means: enlarged physical access space (Digital *Alpha*; *DB2* for MVS etc.); Bitwise indices (Sybase, Model 204, etc.); DBMS parallel computing; global heterogeneous access optimization (e.g., IBM *Datajoiner*); intelligent data partitioning (Informix; *DB2* family); intelligent storage systems (EMC); multi-pass SQL execution plans (MicroStrategy); pre-processing (e.g., complex time-series indices, multidimensional engines); static SQL (IBM *DB2* family); and statistical query optimizers (DB2, CA-*Ingres*, Tandem *MDAM*). Combinations of techniques are used to speed retrieval in large projects by: AT&T *Teradata*'s Advanced Parallel Optimizer; Borland International's *Delphi*; *Dynasty; Forte* from Forte software; HP *Intelligent Warehouse*; and Star Index and Pattern Index (Red Brick).

2.2. Search engines

Apart from printed guides and metadata dictionaries, among search engines in large-scale projects are: Brio/*Query*; Digital *Info-Harvester*; IBM *DataGuide*; Prism *Directory Manager*; SAS/*ACCESS*; Software AG *Esperant*; and Trinzic *Forest & Trees*.

2.3. Development tools

Over fifty development tools exist to create applications for information delivery, EIS and DSS, but the following is a representative list: Brio *Data Edit*; CA OpenROAD; Comshare *Command Center*; Grupta *SQL/Windows*; IBM *Data Interpretation System*, Visual Age, Visualizer, and *VisualGen*; Information Advantage *Decision Suite*; Informix *NewEra*; Microsoft *Visual Basic*; MicroStrategy *DSS Architect* and DSS Executive; NATURAL; Oracle *CDE*; Pilot *Lightship*; *Powerbuilder*; and SAS/*AF* and SAS/EIS.

2.4. ROLAP servers and linking middleware

Relational OLAP servers and software linking RDBMS and tools include HP *Intelligent Warehouse* (middleware); Information Advantage *Axsys* (ROLAP server); MicroStrategy *DSS Server* (ROLAP); and Stanford Technology Group's *Metacube* (ROLAP server).

2.5. Information delivery

Of more than one hundred tools from which to select, the Data Warehousing Institute lists these: Andyne *GQL* and *Pablo*; Brio *Business Objects*; Cognos *Impromptu* and *PowerPlay;* Comshare *Commander OLAP*; Focus *EIS*; Holos; IBM *Data Interpretation System* and *Visualizer*; Information Advantage *Decision Suite*; IRI *Express EIS* and *Express View*; Lotus 123 and *Notes*; Microsoft *Access, Excel, Word, PowerPoint*, etc.; MicroStrategy *DSS Architect* and *DSS Executive*; Pilot *Lightship*; SAS EIS, *ASSIST*, and *AF Software*; Software AG *Esperant*; and Trinzic *Forest & Trees*.

2.6. Alert systems

Timely information alerts rather than staggered more lengthy reports are advised for business executives. Several vendors have produced alert systems which are triggered by significant changes in specified databases as they are augmented or when routine processing checks results in unexpected changes. Among these "value added" alert systems are: Comshare *Alerts*; Information Advantage *InfoAgent*; MicroStrategy *Intelligent Agents* and *Alerts*; IBM DB2 *Event Alerters*; Information Advantage *InfoAlert*; and Trinzic *Forest & Trees*.

3. DBMS and Warehouse management

Process managers include AT&T *Data Base Query Manager* and *TOP END*; Digital *Information Catalogue*; HP *Intelligent Warehouse*; IBM *FlowMark* and *Visual Warehouse*; Prism *Directory Manager*; Sequent *Decision Point*; and Software AG *SourcePoint*. Systems managers include AT&T *OneVision*; CA *Unicenter*; HP *OpenView*; IBM *DataHub* and *NetView*; and Tivoli.

Of course such a classification is never very stable, because increasingly products are being packaged in such a way as to encompass myriad operations. IBM's Intelligent Data Miner and Silicon Graphics' MineSet, for example, combine data preparation and data mining tools.

Some vendors dominate particular industry applications, but many hybrid systems are coming into place. A few exemplary case studies are offered by the DATA WAREHOUSING INSTITUTE (1995-; 1997) and DATA WAREHOUSING INFORMATION CENTER to show that these complex structures are now not only feasible, but are operational, productive, and spreading:

1. The *Société Nationale des Chemins de Fer Français* (SNCF) or French National Railroad Thales System which in 1991 began using AT&T's *Global Information System* with a *Teradata* database for decision support and what it calls an "Enterprise Information Factory" for real-time high-performance management applications to control bookings and routings of 400 TGVs (*Train à Grande Vitesse*), which have traveled up to 515 kph; and 1,200 classical trains throughout France.

2. Ingram Book Company's Visual Warehouse using an IBM 320 Pentium, a Novell *NetWare* LAN, Token Ring connection to an IBM MVS/ESA mainframe and server using OS/2, incorporating distributed *DB2*, Oracle, and Sybase data based operations and all kinds of files, to serve 48,000 retail outlets and libraries internationally and meet their demand for 147M books and media each year.

3. 3M Corporation's Intelligent Warehouse backbone relying on HP's *Open Warehouse* solutions on a HP 9000 model T500 class system (70 gigabytes, or GB, of disk; 1 GB of memory initially) to assist with the company's $15 billion annual sales by creating configurable data independent of underlying physical structures, optimization of data summaries, security management for business views and yet an open system for its knowledge workers throughout the corporation, and a stable environment for end users.

4. Woolworth's move in 1994 from its E-POS (Electronic Point-of-Sale) system in 779 retail stores to an enlarged system to exploit accumulated data for analysis of purchasing patterns and market predictions throughout the United Kingdom, using the Tandem K20000 system running the NonStop SQL/MP Relational DBMS as its platform (250GB database) and operating over 20 interfaces.

5. Energy Services, the fifth largest electric utility in the United States ($6 billion in revenues) serving 2.5 million customers, after 1992 confronted deregulation of the industry by using data warehousing to enhance its competitive ability, using four Sybase SQL servers (i.e., four warehouses or relational databases for financial data, revenue, customer market, and human resource operations) on a SunSPARC 2000 machine, to run a warehouse expected to create 100GB of data by 1996, made accessible by Microsoft *Access* and by using applications from Powersoft *PowerBuilder*.

6. Ertl Company, a $220 million Iowa toy manufacturer, claimed that it paid for 18,000 hours of labor annually to generate reports before it sought a 50 percent improvement in productivity by implementing data warehousing strategies using Software AG's *ADABAS* fourth-generation language-constructed data management system.

7. Harris Semiconductor Manufacturing Company won an award in 1995 for its presentation as Best Data Warehousing Project which it undertook in 1992 to link five worldwide manufacturing sites with its Melbourne, Florida, headquarters by using Computer Associate's *CA-Ingres* DBMS and a suite of products to

standardize data services for its engineers, including extensive automated data mining capabilities.

8. J. M. Huber Inc., a Fortune 500 manufacturing company which moved its operations onto IBM RS6000s and Sun Microsystem UNIX servers while trying to reengineer legacy data for accurate consolidated views of its clients and business operations, provided a case study about Return-On-Investment (ROI) analysis to justify data warehousing costs by business value (removal of limitations on performance, capacity, scalability, reliability, manageability) and the benefits of its *Integrity Data Reengineering Tools* from Vality Technology, Inc., which address the same problems archivists and historians have in nominal records linkage by using parsing, pattern matching, lexical analysis, and statistical matching to clean its messy and inaccurate databases.

9. The Associated [Insurance] Group works with 6 million people in the United States through its health care, insurance, and financial services has confronted the problem of integrating a variety of data warehouses distributed across many platforms so they work together through the Prism *Warehouse Manager.*

10. Home Box Office (HBO) implemented Oracle solutions on an IBM AIX RISC 6000 host using Brio Technology's *BrioQuery* tool to assist 200 distributors of HBO programming.

11. Sara Lee, a $15.5 billion company, with ten subsidiaries, adopted Information Advantage (IA) *Decision Suite* on a UNIX server to perform OLAP processing directly on a variety of data warehouses.

12. Transamerica Commercial Finance Corporation unified its information services into a DW architecture with approximately 50GB using Hewlett-Packard's *Informix* system.

13. United States West Communications in Denver uses Oracle 7 for scalable, parallel data warehousing on an IBM SP2 connected to a 30-node network of data marts, to study data on its 25 million customers in 14 western states to determine customer needs, trends based on household characteristics.

14. Bank of America headquartered in San Francisco uses powerful NeXT clients with SQL tools and OLAP from Angoss, Business Objects, Microsoft, and SAS, and Quantrix multi-dimensional spreadsheets with Lighthouse Design's modeling package in order to track checking activities and to customize offers to its clientele.

15. Merck-Medco Managed Care, a pharmaceutical insurance and prescription mail-order component of the drug giant Merck, based in Montvale, New Jersey, installed an NCR *Teradata 5100* data warehouse using off-the-shelf OLAP and query tools to study its customer base and health trends as a means to identify less expensive alternatives to brand prescriptions and thereby help patients deal with deep cuts in federal assistance programs.

16. The California State University system of 22 campuses adopted Brio*Query* and Brio *Enterprise* to capture and to disseminate real-time financial information, or what Brio Technology's Katherine Glassey calls "business intelligence," across this far-flung network, by using standard Web browsers to connect through a CSU intranet a variety of indigenous systems, many different databases, and software operations.

17. Rich Products selected a prefabricated warehouse architecture (which the Data Warehouse Institute refers to as "shrink wrapped" solutions) created with a combination of Data General and QAD for its manufacturing enterprise, aiming primarily at accurate inventory control as a critical improvement for its customer services.

18. Fidelity Investments chose Information Advantage's *Decision Suite* and WebOLAP of its 20,000 employees engaged in financial data analysis, timely reporting, and rapid trading; its 400GB warehouse is expected to expand by 3-4GB/month.

19. PHH Corporation uses ETI's *Extract* to assist 2,600 clients manage huge vehicle fleets by converting operational data to strategic information to predict need, response times, availability, and to plot solutions.

20. Hallmark Cards employs an NCR Data Warehouse on a WorldMark 5100M parallel processor to manage 300GB of data for the distribution of 40,000 products to 45,600 outlets nationwide, and in keeping with its personal touch mission, to "get in-touch" with its customers.

21. United Parcel Service (UPS) since 1986 invested $1.5 billion into its information infrastructure, which was seen as mission critical for its handling of a billion packages each year, routed through 1,500 facilities worldwide, for speedy delivery. Its quality insurance program, adopted in 1994, required accurate tracking and reporting for 1,600 monitors. The data utilize 300GB in a warehouse residing on a Sequent Symmetry 5000 SMP computer running UNIX with Oracle as the database manager, which by 1997 will disseminate information to 3,000 users across the UPS intranet.

22. Police in Delaware now tune into a Software AG *ADABAS* data warehouse for Criminal Intelligence in 1.5 million records created over a three-year period. Officers use *esperant* and SourcePoint for data retrieval, scheduling, and mapping. Information management is critical, not just for tracking 200 arrests each day, but in major crimes like homicide where investigations longer than three days face a condition of deteriorating evidence that makes crime solution increasingly problematic as time marches on; research therefore is under a tight deadline.

Briefly, then, this is the business and government milieu in which modern information is being created, used, and analyzed. Data analysis occurs often in manners similar to operations undertaken by socioeconomic historians who have traditionally used socioeconomic and family historical data, but who have not sought or have been denied access to contemporary mass data held by modern corporations. Moreover, few historical investigations are conducted under such stress, deadlines, risk, or accountability. In business, the implications and impact of data warehousing and data mining or knowledge discovery operations have often necessitated reorganization of the enterprise itself, or at least Business Process Reengineering. History does not prepare historians for such milieu because History is not operated as a business; or put differently, the business of History is not so much mismanaged as unmanaged. As such, historical content and analysis are appropriate for information managers of historical or longitudinal data, but History is a poor training ground. As a laboratory, it lacks the proper environment, access, tools, and ethos for large-scale electronic records and databased research. If electronic archives were to implement similar strategies or if electronic archivists are to interject themselves into business processes as information resource managers as KESNER (199-, forthcoming) advocates, one could expect the same rigor, standards, and scalability in training as the business of managing archival information. It is a milieu in which the historical and contemporary are contingent, and where, therefore, archivists must be competent to work for both modern records sake and the future of history. However, not a single history computing project in the past decade can be identified to qualify for inclusion in such large-scale, complex operations as model data warehouses or electronic archives. Indeed, no current archives, state or national, so qualifies; and even corporate archives in organizations building such enterprises, since most of these are being shunted into the background for one reason or another. This includes use of products like *DataMind* and Angoss' *Knowledge Seeker* which are desktop and client/server programs. Only a handful of historical computing projects even have access to the software packages and technical support needed for the larger applications requiring parallel processing.

It is unlikely that traditional historians who are not using such information technology to advantage are qualified to train archivists today—even those limited to the manuscripts tradition who must embrace modern digital technologies for access and preservation. Most assuredly historians in average history departments with a few PCs and a minority of faculty colleagues equipped to do more than word processing are ill-equipped to deal with modern electronic archives. Most lack the technical competence and management experience to direct such critical programs. They should retire from the archivist training business, except perhaps for introductory archives appreciation courses and introductory user training. If computing historians move into these areas, use these tools, and can train with them, and have access to such first-class commercial, industrial, and government operations as described above, for internships and on-the-job training, they may be able to train the next generation of electronic archivists. If not, then computing historians will need training by such electronic archivists. But from where will they come? From leading History Department graduate programs? Unlikely. From graduate schools of Information Science? Some, perhaps. But only a dozen have archival educators aboard full-time, and only two schools have on their full-time faculties archivists with electronic archives expertise. From MIS programs in Business schools (Information Systems Management)? Not unless business and management schools rehabilitate records management and overcome their stereotyping of this concern as a mere extension of old secretarial schooling. Computer Science programs? Not likely, unless research into the data warehouse phenomenon takes off. In all of these cases, the overall answer is: Possibly by personal preference and interest, but not because of program orientations. Then what about newly minted M.A. programs in Archival Science? One would think so, but not if these adhere to the minimal professional guidelines now in vogue or reach an economy of scale to expand their small faculties and achieve genuine specialization. Thus, this educational problem looms large, so that more must be said about it later when considering educational programming.

Might not the health and vigor of history computing itself be judged in light of such recent developments in complex, integrated and open systems technology? Compare the magnitude of data handled and the scale of operations in legacy and enterprise computing today with normal history computing projects. The comparison becomes laughable except when also considering the magnitude of history, the scope of historical questions, and the myriad data and information sources that exist but which are beyond the control of the single historian no matter how much he or she labors under the illusion of mastery. Then such comparison is depressing. The disorganization of History, the fragmentation of history, the lack of coordinated historical enterprise, and the price paid for individuality and personal creativity instead of collaboration across disciplines and institutions are all quite sad. Can historians, working individually and under the guidance of lone mentors, advance to the level of mastery over modern information technology and methodology needed to mount research projects beyond those associated with traditional manuscript sources converted into electronic data? Can they go beyond traditional cliometric analysis of limited datasets to more sophisticated research in multiple databases, integrate visual and oral sources, and work with intelligent systems? Is the concept of a historical data warehouse *qua* electronic archives feasible as a multilevel, distributed internetwork of client-servers using Internet/WWW communications?

Data warehousing, then, has obvious implications for electronic archives, history computing, and indeed, all History.

What is needed in the United States and in Europe are a select few advanced studies centers with well equipped and technically supported laboratories for simulation and other research capabilities to teach in genuinely modern archival science and to blend this with historical/legacy data to develop an advanced Historical Information Science. Then, perhaps, virtual visions of a really new "New History" can become real.

New Historicism and Unidisciplinary History

DIFFUSION AND CONFUSION

Since change and history are interchangeable, change in History is happening—even if at a rate insufficient for historians (or anyone else) to catch up with modern information technology or to work more effectively with electronic archives in the near future. The rate of change through the dissemination of ideas alone, without the requirement of adopting new technologies or modifying methods, can be sudden and seem revolutionary, but there is always a time lag for such ideological dissemination to take hold in some practical way. Ideas by themselves can flow through publication and conferencing much easier than when they acquire baggage such as hardware, software, and training requirements. E. M. Rogers, for example, studied not new technologies for their own sake, but how they reveal the process of change or "diffusion of innovation." He defines diffusion as "the process by which an innovation is communicated through certain channels over time among the members of a social system. It is a special type of communication, in that the messages are concerned with new ideas (ROGERS, 1986, p. 5).

This theme of new technical information transfer and adoption and adaptation of new technologies themselves is the focus of PACEY's *Technology in World Civilization*. Diffusion can also be studied with a speculative eye on the future. Consider, for example, the two- to five-year lag time between the first encounter with new research, absorption into one's own research, and application in teaching. If one were to add to this ideological transference the technological dimension whereby proof of understanding through application in some physical production were demanded, one would expect of an astute student of cultural and technical diffusion that the temporal patterns of the diffusion of technological and methodological innovation within a discipline, across disciplines, and from disciplines to professions and practice would take significantly longer in each case respectively. As such, the study of diffusion is especially amendable to time-space mapping techniques (e.g., ENGELSMAN & VAN RAAN). Another example of the connection between the spread of ideas and growth of ideology, or the forging of a social mentality so central to New Cultural History and inherent in modern Organizational Culture studies, with parallel lines of inquiry in the History of Technology and Information Science is the aforementioned application of time-pattern analysis in citation studies and the mapping of the influence of trend-setting works in various literatures and prototypes such as major inventions.

Research productivity, information transfer, and technical adaptation are all phenomena related to the overall process of cultural and intellectual diffusion. Herbert Simon in 1957 first proposed a model, which came to be known as the Simon-Yule process (CHEN), that has been elaborated upon over the years. This "Cumulative Advantage" model is known popularly as "Success breeds Success" has been applied to Informetrics (e.g., J. TAGUE, 1981; EGGHE & ROUSSEAU, 1995), and most recently by J. HUBER (1998) whose major concern is with invention. As in the case of cohort analysis relying on social data, historical data sets have not often included time-pattern data, so the limitations of extant database restricts such study. Nor are they random samples, so as M. PAO (1985) suspected, data selection bias taints most databases in any case. Finally, the model which infers increased rates of production with experience, Huber claims, is not confirmed for inventors (whose individual productivity follows a Poisson distribution, and rate of production across a wider population fits the Gamma distribution). He and others note the similarity of such investigations to LOTKA in 1926, who for scientific publishing claimed that the number of authors falls as the square of the number of papers produced. The late M. PAO (1986) rationalized this as an inverse power function with an exponent range from 1.8 to 3.8. As noted before, Lotka's work has inspired many studies for different literatures which attempt to delineate production over time, with the assumption that the earlier entry into a field and accumulation of experience could be tracked like an exponential curve. That would look like cumulative advantage in action, but such "laws" as Lotka's hardly seem universally applicable. Increased attention has been paid therefore to explaining variances in distributions and production histories using time pattern analysis. Moreover, when tied to Social Science today, rather than geared to older ideas about a more deterministic model, such studies reveal a diversity that has been connected with inequality and disproportional opportunities for research and production (e.g., P. ALLSION, 1980). STEPHAN & LEVIN stress this importance of being at the right age, place, and time to strike the mother lode in science. Of course, historians have commented similarly in cases of political opportunity.

This issue of opportunity, of course, can be related to technical support and information access among the many variables that have been studied regarding academic productivity. Information transfer may be seen as both intellectual and technical diffusion combined (the idea and its conveyance), but the two processes do not seem to be related in Information Science research. Consider studies of research productivity in academe. Survey research coming out of the 1970s identified most of the important variables in an individual's scholarly productivity (WARNER, LEWIS & GREGORIO): biological age of authors and their professional age (usually determined by the date a Ph.D. was awarded); the "load" balance between research and teaching or other competing activities and the prestige or orientation of the institution from which one graduated which in time is overtaken in importance by that in which one works, e.g., the Carnegie classification for higher education in the United States, CAUSE, 1996). These studies and their criteria are reviewed by REBNE.

Some interesting correlations have been uncovered, but many appear to be merely verifications of common sense assumptions: for example, institutional stature when correlated with improved resources to support research and decreased teaching loads does make for greater scholarly productivity (measured purely by publication, as in GARLAND & RIKE for Library and Information Science). Although a positive relation was thought to exist between teaching and research, this is largely a value attested in questionnaire responses (a study of perceptions more than actuality, as indicated by BONZI), and more empirical data shows that prolific publishers spend up to a third less time teaching than those who teach full time but publish much less than their research-oriented colleagues (HANCOCK *ET AL.*). Few of these studies actually establish a correlation between information resources readily available onsite (e.g., library collections, acquisition expenditures, etc.) with alternatives such as interlibrary loan, proximity to other resources in urban centers, more distant travel to sources, or conferencing and the delivery of papers. A recent exception is KAMINER & BRAUNSTEIN's effort to correlate Internet use with research productivity in the natural sciences at the University of California, Berkeley (cf., J. COHEN). But for the most part these are snapshot studies without a balance between the data sample and biographic case or longitudinal studies of scholarship embodied in scholars, continuities and traditions, or good historical syntheses. Most of these studies pertain to the sciences and engineering, and, unfortunately, the aforementioned use studies of historians have not tied their findings into research on scholarly productivity. None relate information production with information consumption, tie such inquiries together with citation analyses that better provide an input/output correlation that might portray a continuum in information dissemination and accumulation, tap the histories of higher education or the disciplines, or place their study in the context of cultural, intellectual, or technical diffusion. They provide information that might be used in sociocultural and intellectual history, but by comparison they seem procedural and sterile. Most Information Science articles provide a history of the research literature about scholarly productivity, but they do not provide a history of the phenomena studied. Here again lie opportunities for the mutual enrichment of Information Science and Cultural-Intellectual History in Historical Information Science.

Scholarly productivity without the diffusion of ideas and innovation resulting from research hardly seems worthwhile. The overall process of diffusion does not mean the simple and direct transfer of information, but its modification in the process of adoption and referral. Arnulf Grubler and his colleagues at the International Institute for Applied Systems Analysis in Austria generalize that "No innovation spreads instantaneously" but instead a typical "S" temporal pattern is most common when one visualizes such change (GRUBLER, 1996, p. 29-30). The pattern itself appears invariant, but its regularity and timing vary greatly. Diffusion is understood as a spatial and temporal phenomenon, and spread is usually seen as a linear dynamic from an innovation center to subcenters and outward to a periphery. While adoption is later on the periphery, there are gains available from previous learning and experience so adoption and adaptation speed up considerably. Diffusion clusters and lumps with overlaps, back drafts, diversions, and setbacks; it is not smooth even though it is "a process of imitation and homogenization." In GRUBLER's words (p. 30):

> The densities of application remain discontinuous in time and heterogeneous in space among the population of potential adopters and across different social strata. In fact, overall development trajectories appear necessarily punctuated by crises that emerge in transitional periods. As such, diffusion and its discontinuities may be among the inherent features of the evolutionary process that governs social behavior.

> Nevertheless, appropriate incentives and policies may nurture the development of more benign technologies and their diffusion, and many changes can be implemented over a time frame of two to three decades.

He notes differences between incremental change and attempts at more radical departures: "The interdependence between individual artifacts and long-lived infrastructures creates our dilemma" of selecting avenues for innovation and change. His historical insights lead him to comment further: "There are times of change and times for change, and unless our individual and collective behavior is modified, these times will remain to frustrate and excite us." He is talking about technological, methodological, and productive change mostly in regard to industry, but his observations are applicable as well to intellectual disciplines such as History or professions such as Archives adapting and adopting to technology.

One would expect to find more about diffusion in Information Science as well, but when information is studied in the abstract or *in vacuo*, this is not the case. Moreover, diffusion studies in technology tend to treat information as a thing, again to adopt Michael Buckland's phrase, which is parallel to study of the book trade, but not necessarily information dissemination. Grubler's comments are germane as well when contemplating changing times in history, and time for change in History, when thinking about old and new science—in this case, Historical Information Science. Revisionism in History, new methodologies and research trends, etc., all reflect the phenomena of cultural diffusion and information transfer between disciplines and from one generation to the next. The new, when contrasted to the old, usually defines a period of change. This is essential in historical thought about historical developments, and it pertains as well to the development of History.

When reflecting about progress in developing new methodologies and revising old ones, or applying new technologies, N. ZEMON DAVIS (attribution in CISH, 1990, II p. 667) commented about how rapidly History has changed in only a decade, so that in the 1990s she too had to discern differences between the *old* and *new* "New Social History"! In the reaction to L. STONE's "New Old History" (1979), E. JOHNSON (1989) likewise refers to recent quantitative Social Science History as "old 'new history'" that was described during the 1980s by RABB (1983a), HIMMELFARB and others as still burgeoning.

FOGEL (1995), the Nobel Laureate, traces the origins of New History (that is, Socio-Economic History) back to pre-World War I, however, to those who broke tradition with the scientific historicism that largely focused on document examination and textual criticism espoused by Leopold Von Ranke and Herbert Baxter Adams, to the "manifesto" of James Harvey Robinson, and to the socioeconomic historical debates from the 1920s in the United States. He notes that the Scandinavians, for example, pioneered in the accumulation of social data in the 1920s. As do many, he also sees the Social Science History Research Council's *Theory and Practice in History*, often referred to simply as that famous "Bulletin 54" in 1946, as pivotal. However, Fogel in his reflective years has longer range perspective and appreciation for continuity than did contemporaries of the self-proclaimed methodological and intellectual "revolution" after the mid-century. He now sees the "New Histories" as being an upsurge with post-World War II family reconstition histories (as pioneered in 1956 by Louis HENRY in Genoese studies) rather than totally new phenomena in the 1950s and 1960s, which is easily linked to the Annales school in France, the Fabian economic historians of England, United States social historians, and Soviet socioeconomic quantifiers. He would point to breakthroughs as Edward P. Thompson's *History of the Working Class* (1966) as trend setters, but not as first exemplars (E. THOMPSON). The "newness" according to Fogel, were the new statistical techniques developed during the late 1960s and applied in the early 1970s, and the combination of these with computing, especially as the arcane language of early computer programming was surpassed, to greatly expand the range of Cliometrics. He reflected in 1995 about the situation 20 years earlier, and the fierce debates that ensued, remarking that "stunning surprises were bound to be controversial," and that "new information must justify itself through baptism by fire."

The terminology is convoluted and confusing, and from an Information Science perspective, the wordplay may appear somewhat contrived and silly. The "old" refers to the first-generation Cliometricians who thought they were doing something new, from the 1970s when the AHA Committee on Quantitative Data was at work and the Social Science History Association was founded (AYDELOTTE, 1971; BERKHOFER, 1969; BOGUE, 1983 which goes back to the 1960s; FOGEL, 1975; LORWIN & PRICE; etc.; cf., CROUZET for the 1970s and before, ROTHSTEIN), until the microcomputer revolution of the 1980s (RABB; ROTHBERG). The same aging of the once "new" ideology as novelty wears off can be said for the old New Political History, Econometrics, etc. (BOGUE, 1973, 1980), and more recently, New Literary History (MINK, 1969-1970), and when this linguistic bent combined with cognitive psychology is turned on History itself, "New Historical Literacy" (COX & REYNOLDS).

The array of new specialties and inter-disciplinary studies combining the Arts, Archeology, Anthropology (especially Ethnology), cognitive Psychology, Linguistics, Biography and Demography combined, and Geographic Information Systems (GIS), with History is what *en toto* some herald as the "New Historicism" (VEESER). The term "New Historicism" is often attributed to GREENBLATT (1982), but J. MARTIN (1997, p. 1313, n. 13) is correct that the idea was more prevalent and the term was deployed so rapidly that it is better to think in terms of a school of literary historians than one guru and his disciples. Some hail FOUCAULT a decade earlier, for example, as the progenitor of New Historicism. MONTROSE speaks of "New Historicisms" in the plural. Moreover, Steven Greenblatt himself somewhat disavowed the term in favor of something more literary, namely the "cultural poetics" (VEENSTRA) which sounds like a move away from what is commonly perceived as scientific in any empirical sense.

New Historicism, despite its textual base, or rather because of its foundations in textual crit-icism and study of language and communications to discern content and intent, meanings and processes, can be very scientific and closely identified with the Social Sciences. The more emphasis on method, perhaps (especially empirical approaches to word study and discourse analysis), the more closely identified New Historicism might be with the Social Sciences; and the more it is identified with the close reading of texts and the discovery of creative insights, the more it seems allied with the Humanities. Some, like myself, see it as bridging both, and therefore a theme needed to be explored in relation to the idea of Historical Information Science as a unidiscipline. What about its newness? Every continuity has something new added, or it is not continuous. OLABARRI also takes a continuity approach to all of this new-ness and shows common philosophical ideas in the schools of history that arose from the 1920s to the 1970s with nineteenth- and twentieth-century historiography; he argues for a basic con-tinuity back to the German notion of *historismus*. He sees this basic continuity extending through the newer schools coming after the 1970s, despite their innovative ideas and enlarge-ment of scope. But the overuse of the adjective "new" seems somewhat anti-historical and is certainly a terminological problem since newness does not really describe anything uniquely. E. GOODHEART pokes fun at such convoluted nomenclature by referring to the "New" as another "old-fashioned topic."

In addition to these hybrid disciplines, schools of thought, and catchy phases surveyed by IGGERS (1983), Konrad Jarausch discerns national "styles" of quantitative History that "com-plicate the transnational dialogue" and a blending of these into an international interdiscipli-narity (JARAUSCH, 1985; 1991, pp. 199-203). ANKERSMIT attempts to reconcile German and Anglo-Saxon historicism as complementary. GALTUNG likewise discerns such proclivi-ties of national style in approaches to biography. RUSEN maintains that historians must acknowledge cultural differences in historiography when approaching intercultural or com-parative historiography. Illustrative of this cultural preference is the more mathematical and theoretical approach applied by the Soviet school to very pragmatic subjects like agricultural reform, under the lasting influence of KOVAL'CHENKO (1972), the History counterpart to A. I. MIKHAILOV in Science Informatics. Contrast this to the French *nouvelle histoire* serializa-tion of History (CHAUNU, 1964) across all usual chronological and geographical limits to search out grand themes, or the pervasive *mentalité* influence (SAMARAN, pp. 937-66) in new cultural history in Europe (COUTEAU-BEGARIE; L. HUNT, 1989). JARAUSH (1991, p. 201) also contrasts German *Wissenschaft* as "systematic scholarship" with the American notion of hard science and hence its more behavioralist approach to social history. He thinks of British quantitative history "as a technically advanced variant of a common Anglo-American pattern."

History today is as varied as ever and no less syncretist and eclectic than Information Science (GREENSTEIN, 1993b, p. 149); both present formidable difficulty for the indexer and classi-fier since historians themselves lack proper taxonomies and terminologies or control thereof in their discourse. If Historical Information Science were to be added to the list of specialties, for-bearance would dictate avoidance of the adjective "new." What would the "old" version have been when Information Science in its library derivative or genesis from computer technology has been so ahistorical? Yet the amalgam suggested here is indeed "new" when compared with the New History of previous decades or the status of historical Informatics as perceived in Europe as simply history computing as an extension of the old Cliometric movement. The foun-dations for the Historical Information Science components of these movements rest in the ori-gins of computer applications to History and the aforementioned great debate coming into the 1970s, as well as the institutionalization of quantification studies as an accepted component of History practice. JARAUSCH (1990) is even cautiously optimistic about a "reawakening" of the role of quantitative methodology in this decade's History. Cliometricians captured widespread attention in their respective arenas by focusing on: serfdom and agricultural reform in the

USSR; politics and vacillation from democratic movements to Nazi totalitarianism in Germany; social classes and personal relationships in France; demography and trade in Great Britain; and first slavery, then transportation and markets, and finally labor and politics in the United States. Statistical work on census and poll data continued unabated despite the rounds of criticism first during then 1970s about the methodology employed, then during the late 1970s and into the 1980s confrontations with Marxist schools in socioeconomic historiography, and finally challenges by deconstruction theorists. From the late 1960s into the 1970s, social mobility and population studies, founded upon work after World War II (reviewed by P-A. ROSENTHAL), supposedly revealed the power of computing and quantification in analysis of complex phenomena, but they also exposed the limitations of quantification based on sociological methods.

The new socioeconomic and demographic history focusing of labor, class formation, and mobility were subjected to severe criticism in History unlike anything experienced by Sociology itself: (1) classification of social categories (e.g., social classes themselves) proved difficult and seemingly arbitrary, or idiosyncratic in being customized to a particular case and not generalized to any system for which there was widespread consensus (JENNY provides an essay on social classification from the French perspective; BIJNEN and LORR evaluate clustering techniques specifically for Sociology); (2) quantification historians, like their Social Science colleagues, tended to ignore traditional, nonempirical sources such as contemporary descriptive accounts which offered conflicting evidence detracting from the generalizations reached by counters; and (3) studies tended to become repetitive, applying the same methodology without substantial improvement to a new geographic area and to increasingly smaller time frames, without accounting for known regional differences or encountering the rise of ethno-historiography that played up cultural regionalism. A brief enlargement of foci occurred with microcomputing when historians could control more information to enlarge the scope of their studies, but this phase never returned to the grand comparative framework of earlier years, and indeed, seems to have receded back into microhistory which is subject to the same criticism now as 20 years ago. Moreover, quantification historians still use computing largely to link and calculate data rather than to synthesize sources and create information systems. Elaborate quantification studies have been undertaken with increased adroitness in statistical manipulation, reliability checking, and attention to variance, but the basic methodology itself has not evolved to take full advantage of modern information technology beyond data processing and analysis. Historical Information Science should entail much more than assumed under the older rubric of quantified history transmogrified into Social Science History or the mere combination of History and computing as used initially by those involved in the formation of the AHC. The development process tends to move on—inexorably and perpetually.

By the 1990s the aforementioned shift in History had occurred toward cultural studies, ethno-historiography and the history of popular thought fusing with social historians' focus on the family: first during the 1980s with the rise of the history of *mentalités* (P. HUTTON, 1981; LE GOFF, 1984; SAMARAN) rather than through a philosophy of ideas (P. BURKE), or a cultural rather than an intellectual history. All has been democratized. This trend had gained momentum since the 1960s with Philippe Aries' work on childhood and family life in the Ancien Régime (ARIES; cf., MUCHEMBLED) and continued with the plebeian interest in everyday living to produce a history of that post-Enlightenment abstraction—life. Despite the promises of the Annales school (and "beyond" according to FURET, 1983) and the French intention to integrate everything (BOURDELAIS), historians like PROST have mirrored L. STONE's earlier disenchantment with quantification; one wonders whatever happened to the grand synthesis of the French social historiographic movement that pledged to place empirical socioeconomic and political history into the mainstream. According to the mapping of the "French trajectories" in Intellectual History or Sociocultural History in France by R. CHARTIER (1982), the Annales line seems to have become mighty thin by this century's end. Current French historiography was become decidedly textual, narrative, and discursive, but there are wholesome reactions to the Derridan view of everything as only linguistic reconstruction. American historians have been struggling with the same problem of a balanced interaction between specialization and generalization that has plagued so much of higher education, according to BOK. The larger issue is reflected within History as fragmented studies and overarching synthesis, as revealed by T. BENDER and enough detractors to form an OAH Round Table response (1987).

Lawrence Levine in his presidential address before the Organization of American Historians characterized the "canon" on modern historiography to be one of process, large plots, incorporation, and continuing reinterpretation, etc., reflecting the new relativism that has pervaded recent historiographic thought (L. LEVINE, 1993; see also LEVINE's important work [1988] on the cultural hierarchy in America). But historians wisely have not totally embraced either deconstructionism or postmodernist theory except to qualify their interpretation and to question evidence ever more critically. When historians like D. W. COHEN have advanced a postmodern critique of traditional History and substituted instead a more personalized reading of history as an appropriate approach, they provoke immediate detractors (HENIGE). Most historians seem to retain a healthy skepticism as they hold onto a sense of realism in their introspective and interconnecting role between past and present. Recently John Higham congratulated them for that (AHA, 1995), and historians like LEBOVICS (p. 1,276) in reviewing the work of TERDIMAN on history and memory, regarded "radical historical relativism" as a sign of "theoretical innocence."

On the other hand, although the former debates about the inclusion of Social Science research methods and quantification of everything now seem somewhat passé possibly because such methods are now so widely accepted, historians have not moved to a solidly empirical or neo-positivist position. They often operate as moderates in an intermediate range between these extremes, but without coalescing into any consensus or middle ground. They are aware of the problems of distortion resulting from any number of limitations on historical reconstruction, since they are often reminded of these by philosophers of history (e.g., RICOUR, 1984). Historians are also aware of the larger problem resulting from no historical sense whatsoever. One always assumes the risk of being wrong when venturing an opinion and explanation, but one misses the mark always for every opportunity not taken. Older concerns about quantification and continued debates about data relevance, objectivity, interpretation seem irrelevant to some whose attention has been captured by feminist critiques, literary theory, deconstructionism, and the nebulous and amorphous mix called postmodernism. Some like B. PALMER have risen to the occasion to challenge to defend history and attack the relativism of Derridan linguistic interpretation, or what Elizabeth Fox-Genovese in reviewing his book, called "the fashionable tendency to substitute language for history"—a criticism that sounds much like those railing a generation ago against the substitution of numbers for history!

It is against such recent free-flowing and relativistic dialogue that three protagonists react in their *Telling the Truth About History* (APPLEBY, HUNT & JACOB, 1994). Their attack on postmodernism and relativism marks a swing back to a moderate center in the debates about language, reality, and objectivity. They posit a middle ground, so to speak, between words and things, which they characterize as "practical realism." It seems that the mentalité of New Social History will survive this most recent intellectual buffeting (cf., BUNZEL; HIGHAM [1995]; B. G. SMITH; and the rejoinder by APPLEBY, HUNT & JACOB, 1995). HIGHAM (1995) sees their construction of relativism as problematic and their methodology as monist, and overall their collaborative effort as another attempt at a "collective program" that lies somewhere between party platforms and exploratory arguments. Higham and the trio of women historians, according to their reply, seem optimistic that History as a field is expanding and is rising to a new gender-free, multicultural, democratic level.

More recently Thomas Haskell took up this question of difference between "thing" and "knower" as a constant tension which he traces to ancient Greece, but he sees the pretensions of postmodernism and fictional delusion as far more dangerous than conventional approaches to history (T. HASKELL). Like the former trio of women apologists, he argues for a moderate historicism as he uses historiographic case studies to evoke from historians more thought about their methodology, theory, and mode of explanation. Yet, while confronting knotty issues like moral obligation, interest and self-interest, representation, and formalism, he does not speak precisely about specific methods as much as he does about theory and broad interpretation. Although he chides historians who merely "report from the archives," he keeps the time-honored demarcation between fact and fiction and expands such discrimination to make also a distinction between history and propaganda. But as the title of his treatise maintains, T. HASKELL makes clear that *Objectivity Is Not Neutrality*. The possibility, therefore, of an amalgam like Historical Information Science is still very plausible because an underlying empiricism is being retained in the historical discipline which might be coupled with its ecumenism. Indeed, the pursuit of objectivity may be reinforced by an overt reaction to deconstructionism and postmodernism, and this may make possible a fresh start in the new millennium which optimizes new information technology and experimental methodologies without reactionary hyper-criticism and unbearable negativity.

While such discussions in History may seem factional and tedious to some, it would be refreshing to see such introspective critical debate carried into the Information Science arena. There positivism survives intact, without the tempering effect from the same critical challenge which confronted positivist tendencies in History. Not only is the history of Information Science not well known because history plays such a little role in it (an exception being the aforementioned recent survey by BUCKLAND & LIU), but few information scientists realize their indebtedness to positivism. Indeed, the ideology of Information Science as ecumenical and applicable to all fields reminds one of the 1930s movement of positivists like Otto Neurath and his circle (HEMPEL, 1952) to undergird all disciplines with a scientific basis, if not actually to unify them into one holistic science. The idea of a unifying technical and methodological core running through inter-disciplinary history is therefore not new or revolutionary. It reflects the synthesis advocated by Herbert Baxter Adams and the thinking at Johns Hopkins University that promoted the seminar as an inter-disciplinary thinktank, except that they lacked the means now made available by modern information technology. Now, in retrospect, the unity of technique and method, technology and history, and ever enlarged synthesis of disciplinary perspectives and scope of study seems like the next logical stage of cognition in historiographic development. It is a continuation since the 1890s of history's enlargement beyond political studies, the New Histories movement since the 1960s, and the increased interdisciplinarity of the past two decades, but now this syncretism can be coupled with the accelerated advances in computerization, digital source conversion technology, and networking through modern telecommunications.

While working with archivists on his Vancouver Island Project (VIP), Chad Gaffield, began to understand the difference between conventional historical research as "unhurried harrowing" and "romantic research" *vis-à-vis* systematic history, i.e., strategic searches for relevant sources (GAFFIELD, 1988, p. 313). The former was not rejected, but it was considered incomplete. The same can be said of how most history is constructed by the lone historian, then critiqued by peer review, is revised and published, critiqued again and thereafter integrated into historiographic corpora but often in oblique, indirect ways which are difficult to trace. Instead, historical research could have been constructed collaboratively in the first place with the critique built into the initial research process as it is in dissertation mentoring, then reviewed in electronic draft, and finally disseminated as revised in a mature form and with links to reviews, criticism, rebuttal, and references illustrating its integration into the field. In short, both the nature and timing of historical critique and the process of historical information dissemination must change. Moreover, the collaborative, unifying component might be interjected more profitably into the initial research than at its end, after publication. This aspect of Historical

Information Science is why organizational studies generally, and project management particularly, seem so relevant to multiyear, multi-institutional, and multi-disciplinary collaborative projects (cf., SHAPRIO on *Collaborative Computing* today).

GAFFIELD & BASKERVILLE and their colleagues came to realize in the mid-1980s:

> …we sought the admittedly unattainable goal of systematic identification of all the relevant sources, just as we strove for the ever elusive achievement of clearly articulated concepts and rigorous methodologies in our own research.
>
> In this way, we created somewhat unconsciously a small but complex world of archivists, computer system analysts and programmers, librarians, historians, and an array of other specialists. Slowly, we came to see the possibilities with the creation of records and extending to their ultimate use when they become redefined as historical sources. In this research paradigm, archival information is the "lifeblood" of a system which links the producers, managers, and uses of that information. Since the system depends upon circulation (access) of that information, computerization becomes more than heuristic; it begins to take on a life of its own. (GAFFIELD [1988] p. 313)

This experience reflects my own sentiment, in that as technology is itself merging, so too are information sources themselves, and the old divisions between curatorial, archival, critical and interpretative, and teaching roles are breaking down to a common information science (GAVEN). GAFFIELD (1988, pp. 316-317) points to the softening of the so-called "hard sciences" and the "soft sciences" like History are being reconsidered as epistemologically closer to such sciences as biology, but Physics as well (WINCHESTER, 1984), so that "Disciplinary boundaries are no longer simply assumed." History, as an underpinning of and component in all disciplines, offers a comprehensive synchretic capability of achieving a unidisciplinary character. The inter-disciplinary research trend with its "collaboration of machines and minds" of which Gaffield speaks (p. 317), which he, as a typical computer enthusiast, exclaims is a "truly revolutionary paradigm shift," is one that I characterize as Historical Information Science.

People may never be able to study themselves or their affairs in the same objective way they study other phenomena, objects or "the other" in TODOROV's terms (cf., MCGRANE). This has translated into an emphasis on alterity, rather than heritage or common ground, and in stressing the different, strange, and alien, old commonalities and continuities are rapidly disappearing. So while one can point to a convergence in methodological developments and a breaking down of disciplinary identities, the other side of this development is increased atomism, fragmentation, and a certain isolation and unconnectedness in contemporary scholarship. In that sense, history no longer provides the foundations it once did for disciplinary learning, and therefore modern scholarly constructions often seem to lack a firm grounding in anything. Priorities are not clear, nor an order of importance because the referents are no longer the background to something current, and the bizarre, short-term, and grotesque rival the importance of the representative, long-term, and recognizable in history. Deconstructionism and postmodernism have not been mere aberrations, therefore, but will have a lasting impact on how the world is viewed. They seem not to be passing away so much as they are being assimilated into common skepticism, antiscientific thinking, and inter-disciplinary debate that degenerates so much into the subjective that common ground for understanding is lost. Deconstructionism and modern relativism will survive as critical subcurrents of intellectual ferment in our culture, and I predict they will rise up again in a new guise, not as an attack on history by comparative literature and co-option of history as historical fiction, but in multimedia and in the use of imaging technology and digitization to create a virtual reality that is ahistorical. Then, as can be seen in some current events during the 1990s, history as impression becomes less a matter of knowledge and more a question of taste, personal recall and persuasion, and ultimately of politics. Amidst all the globalization are diametrically opposite trends toward the microcosm, the particular, and the unimportant in the larger view. Like our information technology, scholarship has become digital.

Technological convergence promotes such grinding down of old edifices, and it is presumed that such intellectual mulching is good because it is technical, and therefore new. Not all historians are so sure that everything coming out of these technically driven changes is good, such as the breakdown of method into technique and processing at such a minute level that overriding concerns are difficult to track and keep in mind. In 1991 quantification buffs like BEST and JARAUSCH prudently made technology subservient to methodology, and both were subordinated under historical interpretation, in the accepted hierarchy of historian values that resist any subservience of mind to machine. That the Cliometric movement never totally monopolized History has meant that the discipline remained open to the possibility for non-quantified descriptive disciplines like Anthropology, which now routinely quantify qualitative data, to have major influences on the History profession.

KEESING, who defines Anthropology as "the science of custom," traces what MANNING (p. 777) calls "a remarkable set of conceptual shifts. Paradigms labeled as evolutionism, historicalism [e.g., WISSLER], diffusionism, functionalism, and configurationalism succeeded each other from the 1870s through the 1950s." Movements like Structuralism (DOSSE) and such variations as structuration (GIDDENS, 1976, 1979) have supposedly run their course into PostStructuralism (POSTER, 1989, 1990) with accommodations for quantification (but are still applied in Business, e.g., ORLIKOWSKI, 1995), and even Deconstructionism uses such methodology while questioning interpretation in all aspects and attacking data models as much as those built from descriptive sources. Deconstructionism, relativism, and postmodernism will all leave their mark on historiography because the latter is quintessentially syncretist. Rather than destroy History, one might hope that such movements are continually absorbed by her (KUKLICK). In other cases, critical cross-disciplinary examination of anthropological concepts, especially by social historians, has encouraged their abandonment (e.g., A. KUPER). With an increase in Social Science research that has been estimated without exaggeration to be a million-fold since 1950 (STEWART & KAMINS), all of the Social Sciences, not only Anthropology, will continue to exert tremendous and pervasive influence in History even on those areas given to relativism and subjectivism in the extreme. This will serve as a counter-current within History to the cultural historiogaphy that continues to revel in novel interpretation of every text subjected to another reading without the benefit of an empirical analysis, a rigorous scientific methodology, and a weighing of evidence for proper contextualization.

When the founders of *The Journal of Interdisciplinary History* approached the MIT press, they wanted to publish historians "who were transforming the field," by drawing upon every technique available. Its inter-disciplinary ethos has been characterized by its founding editors Robert I. Rotberg and Theodore K. Rabb "to employ the methods and insights of other disciplines in the study of past times and to bring a historical perspective to those other disciplines." The MIT press release for its twenty-fifth (1995) characterizes the *JIH* forum as "Always subject to contention and modification—the methods, techniques, and sources used in historical study change as other disciplines augment and revise them, continually and cumulatively." As in the case of the Braudel Center's focus on unidisciplinary history, the journal's use of "inter-disciplinary" studies approaches the same meaning and likewise downplays the impact of information technology on the transformation of the discipline(s). Historians tend not to recognize such cross-fertilization as a discipline itself because our curricula organize scholarship into cells, rather than nodes or connections, external links, and processes; and History is departmentalized like any other discipline when indeed its inter-disciplinary or unidisciplinary nature makes it quite unique, without boundaries of time, place, subject, or language. Historians are drawn to large questions, which they often try to answer from small domains.

Historians seek to master only relatively small intellectual specialties, which they constantly enrich through the importation of ideas and methodologies from other fields. They export historical views, but seldom reciprocate with genuinely innovative research methodologies or techniques.

While examples can be provided to illustrate the more pervasive movements in contemporary historical thought and practice that lend themselves to the development of Historical Information Science that transcends traditional foci defined by time and place, the following focuses more on methodology and use of information technology as a means to balance the more common intellectualization of inter-disciplinary History.

QUANTIFIED SOCIAL SCIENCE HISTORY

As expected, the Social Science fields, except for Anthropology, have remained preoccupied with numerical data, quantification techniques, and statistical analysis. It is not coincidental that it is Anthropology, the least quantitative of the Social Sciences, which has most influenced History and Literature in recent years. In any case, historians especially retain a healthy skepticism about pure quantification without qualification that keeps the use of statistics in check (e.g., N. FITCH's challenging question, "Statistical Fantasies and Historical Facts?"). Ever since HUFF's now classic treatise on how to lie with statistics (1954), such skepticism generally prevails when confronted with arguments by numbers which are not made clear and understandable. Perhaps in imitation of Mark Twain's acid humor about the numbers game, a genre of sayings and books has developed about the "dos and don'ts" in statistics (e.g., S. CAMPBELL; KIMBLE; REICHARD). Important caveats have been articulated about the transfer of statistical methods developed in experimental science, precisely to analyze data from experimentation, to non-experimental fields like History where at best one deals in statistical inference (ALKER [1984]; OAKES; cf., EARMAN, ed. and HESSE [1974] for inference and induction in science) rather than empirical proof and what have been described as "quasi-experiments" (COOK & CAMPBELL; ACHEN; cf., review by G. W. COX).

Because of previous criticism of cliometricians wanting to quantify everything, historians are now wary of when they select a quantified approach to their sources (HARTEL, 1974) and often perform test runs as emphasized by M. THALLER (1982) to ascertain the viability of a computerized project beforehand so they are not continually accused of making much ado about nothing, i.e., lacking sensitivity to congruence between the problem being explored and overkill technology brought to bear on it. When these pilot studies are published, they often contain the most interesting discussions of source criticism and methodology germane to information science interests, which seem to get suppressed or condemned to footnotes in final studies. In other cases the test serves as a dissertation itself, as did W. BROOKMAN's exploration a decade ago of the *Scientific Information Retrieval (SIR)* program as a viable tool for analyzing 293 4,000-year-old cuneiform tablets from Ur III—an example purposely selected here to illustrate not only the interesting combination of the old and the new, but the admirable reaching into other fields for software solutions to historical computing. The task is to find a congruence between the problem, source, analytic method, and technology, assuming that the decision to compute is warranted in the first place (FIELDING & LEE; ROHRS & DARCY).

Charles Tilly recognized this sizing or "fit" problem early on (TILLY, 1972), and since then a "rule of thumb" has evolved (JARAUSCH, 1991, p. 27) that a data set should have ten times as many observations as variables before lending itself to computerization (DAVEN-PORT provides a history of the quantitative study of variation). At the opposite extreme is the problem of mass warned against by A. PHILIPS, with so much data that the results of cross-tabulation, categorization, and independent variable sorts are overwhelming. Historians were at first reluctant to resort to sampling to solve the latter dilemma (BODE and GINTER), but especially when working with large data sets like census reports (SCHMITZ & SCHOFIELD; SCHAEFER; R. C. JOHNSON), random and systematic samples are now often used, producing what D. S. SMITH called "a mean and random past." W. B. HILL recently relied on a 10 percent sample of the black households in Charleston listed in decennial population schedules from 1880 through 1910 to study post-Reconstruction changes in this town's Black community. For obvious reasons, historians do not usually interview or do survey samples as do modern social and information scientists, except when studying recent and current phenomena to compare with their histories (e.g., M. KELLY's study of rural craft education in Ireland on regional economies; L. LINDSEY's use of immigration questionnaires; CHILDS' assessment of Black Studies programs in History, both using SPSS-X to analyze survey returns); but they do interrogate sources and can sample what they have from past surveys, inventories, and registers. Despite such procedures as outlined by R. C. JOHNSON, History is limited by the past and historians always have to ask the probing question posed by W. H. WILLIAMS, "How bad can *good* data really be?"

In addition to judging the efficacy of data, they must also ask "What constitutes "good" research?" This is a question that goes beyond the bibliometric study of scholarly productivity, citation tracking, or any other singular approach to such a complicated issue. In addition to the evaluation of published results, this question probes myriad issues associated with the Information Sciences, such as access, selection, analysis, technique, project management, and then, ultimately, results. These are judged in the broader context of a discipline, research trends, and notions about relevance of research questions to current intellectual curiosity and information needs. These are the contributions History can make for itself and for all disciplines and lines of inquiry.

Ultimately, however, the core issue is something more than information as this is commonly understood, or simply technique. The argument must be based on evidence—or better yet, scientific evidence—and ultimately the weighing of this evidence to reach a conclusion. What does this mean? Measurement in one form or another.

Historical and Scientific Evidence

Answers to such questions as those posed above lie in legal guidebooks regarding the admissibility of evidence in courts of law. DIAMOND, a psychologist and lawyer who has explored methods for the empirical study of law, provides excellent guidelines for survey research and cites research on questionnaire design, sampling techniques, and the cognitive bases for answers to surveys (TANUR). Generally researchers might heed the court's ruling about "scientific evidence" expressed in Daubert versus Merrel Dow Pharmaceuticals, Inc. (113 S. Ct. 2786, 2795, 1993) which has been expressed at length outside the archival and historical fields (e.g., BLACK; FRIEDMAN; POULTER). The aforementioned "fit" problem raised by TILLY 20 years ago was a central issue in this legal debate. Note also the court's admonitions about reliability as "the reproducibility of results" (KAYE & FREEDMAN, p. 341), which would require the archival preservation of project data and its accessibility, documentation of research procedures and methods, availability of software for reuse, and the ability to replicate analysis. All of these requirements should be met in archival based historical research. It is disheartening to note that in all of the reviewing done by historians of historical and archival research, how seldom these criteria are mentioned. If one were to apply these criteria in dissertation examinations and to many of the monographs reviewed positively in the *American Historical Review* and other review journals, how many could pass the test? Would Information Science bear such scrutiny any better?

The courts have also hammered out rulings on problem areas in statistical research which are useful to review as a checklist of where attention must be placed in conducting scientific historical research using Statistics, that is the field's three major components of (1) theory, or the study of mathematical properties of statistical procedures; (2) probability, where the most difficulty resides (cf., basic textbooks, e.g., LOEVE; FALK & FALK; FELLER, etc.); and (3) applications, where issues of congruence, consistency and "fit" become problematic (see KRUSKAL & TANUR for terms and usage in Statistics). Because so many historical studies seems to either ignore or not make explicit how these issues are addressed, a brief review may helpful. A summary list follows, extracted from the FEDERAL JUDICIAL CENTER's *Reference Manual on Scientific Evidence* (1994, pp. 221-388, esp. BERGER; DIAMOND; KAYE & FREEDMAN; RUBINFELD):

1. Statistical testimony needs to be objective, which requires that the researcher maintain a professional autonomy.

2. Expertise can be established by formal credentials, but most importantly by experience.

3. Testimony can be enhanced by collaboration, that is, "two-expert" cases of inter-locking testimony.

4. Full disclosure of all analyses, fruitful and false runs should be represented as a history of the development of the statistical approach finally used (i.e., a metahistory of a historical work).

5. As in disclosure prior to a trial, alternative modes of analyses should be explored before presentation of a case and interpretation of results.

6. Although the *Federal Rules of Evidence* do not prescribe the exact order of presentation, a traditional ordering is what is commonly expected, namely that witnesses (any witness which credibility and ability to testify, i.e., a person in court, or documentary evidence used by an historian) are presented first and then are cross-examined by specific questions rather than by extended narration. Analysis is reserved for after all testimony is heard, or read.

What do these general procedures mean for statistical research and presentation when arguing a case?

1. The measurement process must be demonstrated as reliable, that is, reproducible.

2. Validity must be established to ensure accuracy by proving that an instrument (test instrument, but also a survey, an historical record) does or did what it is supposed to do or have done in the past.

3. Is data collection adequate? This question refers to how data are coded, logged, recorded, and preserved.

Only when these tests have been answered in the affirmative can inferences begin to be made.

Surveys and census returns, the most common form of data used in historical research, or any analyses of large populations of people or objects require thorough description and analysis to answer the foregoing questions.

1. A census by definition surveys every unit in a population. Does it? If not, then it is a survey, and surveys are more difficult because they involve sampling. A sampling framework must provide explicitly the listing used and lottery method used for selection (i.e., random selection, convenience samples where bias must be confronted at the onset, and probability sampling, which is a random sampling from a preselected sample to ensure a representative final sample).

2. Use of a survey, rather than a census, requires that the researcher convince the reader that an appropriate population has been studied, selection is unbiased, data gathering has been validated, and the units studied are representative.

3. Census and survey research may provide descriptive results without answering the question of causation. Here historians contend that they have problems not pertaining to Social Science research on contemporary subjects, because the latter can attempt to establish cause through experimentation. If modern experimentation to establish cause in certain present circumstances is used in historical research, the issue of "fit" in applicability arises immediately, just as it would if a modern researcher took a historical experiment and applied it to a contemporary case. Indeed, "off-the-shelf" (that is, by definition, historical) cases are used all the time. If controlled experiments are not possible, then the next best is a well-designed one, and demonstration of how variables in one case might change if applied in another so that one can compensate for the time discrepancy in interpretation.

4. Variables, dependent and independent, must be analyzed thoroughly when attempting to show a cause-and-effect relationship. It is useful to list variables to identify clearly which factors are under control and which are not and could mask causal relations or give false appearances of causes.

5. Confounding variables must be handled separately by correlating them with independent and dependent variables because confounding changes are often two-way or reciprocal. Historians, of course, cannot always check their control groups or control themselves the variables at play in a data set. They may be able to provide more convincing cases, however, by presenting more than one well designed study. Comparisons are essential.

6. Can the results of one experiment or research based on one sample be generalized? This raises the issue of "external validity." The rule of thumb is that confidence, in the appropriateness of extrapolation, cannot come from the experiment itself, but it can come from context and it is here that historical expertise is all important.

7. In court most statistical studies are observational, rather than experimental; so too in history, if one thinks about observing situations through the eyes of documented witnessing. In both cases, current and historical observation, the observer has little control if any over the population being observed. The same is true for evidence produced from field work. A compelling case based on observation can be made when associations can be made between different groups, several studies, etc., so one does not suspect a defect in one study or a peculiarity in a group of subjects. Appropriate statistical techniques to account for the effects of confounding variables add credibility. Subjects can often be treated as a control group. Plausible explanations are to be provided for the effects of independent variables, and causal links should not depend on the observed association alone. However, in observed cases, statistics by themselves do not prove cause in any association.

Apart from the research itself, the related issues of interpretation and presentation remain.

1. The data display should be sufficiently complete, so that selective presentation is not like quoting someone out of context.

2. Rates and percentages must be properly interpreted.

3. Graphs, the most common of which for distributions is the histogram, must fairly portray data. Trend displays are particularly susceptible to misinterpretation when their scales or axes alter appearances of the same data.

4. An appropriate measure must be used for the center (mean, median, mode) of a distribution.

5. An appropriate measure of variability (range, interquartile range, mean absolute deviation, and standard deviation which describe variables in isolation) must be used.

6. An appropriate measure of association (percentages, proportions, ratios, correlations, and slopes of regression lines) must be used. Multiple regression techniques are essential for historical research which invariably must understand the relationships between two or more variables. Multiple regression is useful in determining whether a particular effect is present, the magnitude of such an effect, and in forecasting what a particular effect would be if it were not for an intervening event (the "what ifs" of history).

7. Protection against random error must be provided by applying the laws of probability in one or more acceptable methods: standard errors, confidence intervals, significance probabilities, hypothesis tests, and posterior probability distributions.

These diverse aspects of statistical research need not be explored in detail here, because one can resort to numerous aids from encyclopedic treatments (KRUSKAL & TANUR) to layman introductions (RUNYON, 1996; ZEISEL) and a wide selection of standard general textbooks (e.g., FREEDMAN; FREEDMAN, PISANI & PURVES; D. MOORE; MOORE & MCCABE) and those specifically addressing Social Science research (e.g., KATZER, COOK & CROUCH; OAKES). Moreover, historians wishing to examine research design and archival documentation issues for their own work might take advantage of litigated use of statistical analyses in areas of their concern: antitrust litigation where econometics abound; employment discrimination cases which hold ample material for labor historians; in racial and sex discrimination so germane for a variety of social history projects; and voting rights cases which employ demographic data and a variety of statistical methodologies. Not only do historians not incorporate such methodological resources explicitly into their work, but quantitative historical research has not been adequately studied to determine the sufficiency of graduate education in statistics, the effectiveness of such research, or bias in the research community.

Historians tend to distrust published data, including that supplied by ICPSR and census samples, almost as much as they refused once to rely on abstracts and indexes. This is ironic because RUNDELL found that in the 1970s historians totally trusted documentary editions so much that they ceased checking sources in their original formats once they had been published. The distrust of both numerical data and abstracted information may be related to cognitive style, but also to professional cohesion in accepting the work of other historians with more trust than historical work from outside the field. In any case, this critical or even skeptical attitude would assuredly produce some appraisal methodology for data sets such as developed by H. JACOB and others to evaluate prepared data sources and correct some of their deficiencies. Moreover, initial exploration for training can be done in prepared samples such as those disseminated from North Carolina State University's National Collegiate Software Clearinghouse (GARSON, 1989). SCHURER & ANDERSON have attempted to guide historians to the most readily available data files in machine-readable form, which tend to be those collected in data archives but not the many more machine-readable files in electronic archives waiting to be appraised, inventoried, and cataloged.

Analytic Tools

Whereas programs like *SPSS* and *SAS* are commonly thought of as the quantification historian's basic toolkit, the increased sophistication of spreadsheet (e.g., *LOTUS 1-2-3,* now *1-4; EXCEL, PARADOX,* etc.) and relational database software (e.g., *R-BASE 1-4*), attendant graphing capabilities offer alternatives for the analysis of fiscal data and menu-based toolkits (e.g., *FoxPro*) offer alternatives to having to use programming languages. Inexpensive packages employed widely in other fields, like *KwikStat* (DOS) and *Winks* (Windows) from TexaSoft, Inc., (http://www.texasoft.com/homepage) and its Windows version (WINKS 4.1), Microsoft's *Statistica,* and others, seem not to be used as much by historians, despite their adaptation like SPSS 7.0 for Windows to personal computing and their packing of so much into comprehensive programs. *Statview* v4.5 from Abacus Concepts, Inc., (http://www. abacus.com) became especially popular after its first release in 1985 for Macintosh computers because of its spreadsheet-like data management whereby changes in data sets automatically result in reconfigured outputs so "what-if" scenarios can come into play easily, customizable graphs and tables in a complete drawing environment for explanation and very effective presentation (but only two-dimensional at present), and an archival operations feature which means that results as "action objects" retain in memory all steps used to create results (useful for regenerating analyses, creating related analyses, and as a methodological critical apparatus for teaching, footnoting, etc.). It is available for Mac users also with SuperANOVA, and the new release for Windows is totally re-engineered to bring over 90 data analysis and graphing templates to the screen on a moment's command. Neither of these software packages contain programming or macro language, but they operate from menus which invoke standardized procedures and operations. They are affordable for individual researchers. Both are more than a decade old, so their relative nonuse in quantitative History is puzzling. Perhaps it is because their utility so exceeds expectations. Such PC-loadable comprehensive packages now contain an arsenal of tools far more elaborate and of greater variety than would have been available in mainframe environments where many historians received their training, and their capability enables the best talent in statistical research and strains the novice. They simply go beyond what is commonly taught in statistics strictly for historical research and outdate standard texts from only five years ago. In fact, none of the methods textbooks used most commonly today in History graduate courses cover more than half of the procedures, methods, and tests included in such packages.

Now standard features in comprehensive statistical analysis software suites include:

- Descriptive statistics—a variety of mean calculations (harmonic, geometric, trimmed, etc.), standard deviation, variance and coefficient of variance, median, minimum and maximum measures and range, missing values, kurtosis, skewness, percentiles, etc., with histogram, plotting, and graphics capabilities.

- Database management such as dBASE files, with import capabilities from American Standard Code for Information Interchange (ASCII) and other files

- Frequency distribution, with specifications of number and widths of intervals

- Independent single and multiple group T-tests, paired and unpaired

- Analysis of variance including Chi-square for one samples, F-test for unpaired samples, and both one-tail or two-tail tests

- Pearson correlation, whole and partial covariance, with selections from listwise or pairwise deletion

- Regression analysis from simple and linear to multiple (any number of predictors), and polynomial or stepwise (e.g., forward and backward) procedures; Correlation matrix, R-square, and adjusted R-square, Pearson's and Spearman's coefficient tests for significance; and ANOVA tables and a variety of outputs (e.g., coefficients or regression, standardized coefficients, confidence intervals for coefficients, and serial auto-correlation)

- Graphics, including scatter plots that include bands for the slope of a regression line and the mean of the dependent variable, and other plotting forms (regression, residuals versus fitted values; dependent versus fitted values, etc.)

Advanced Analysis of Variance (ANOVA) and other enhancements include these features:

- Choices from factorial or repeated measure models, with more than a dozen factors at play

- Cell models for balanced and unbalanced data

- A variety of tests, such as the Fischer PLSD exact test, Tukey HSD, Scheffe's F, Dunnett, Bonferroni/ Dunn, etc.

- Graphic output as interaction plots, with bar and line charts for easy comparison

- Frequency and cross-tabulation tables, including two-way contingency tables and summary statistics (with Yate's Chi-square, G statistic, contingency coefficient tests; e.g., Goodness of fit testing, McNemar's test, Fischer exact test, Phi and Cramer's V, Relative Risk, Odds Ratio, etc.)

- Cross-tab output including counts, and row, column, and overall percentages, post hoc cell contributions and cellular Chi-squares

- Nonparametric tests of a growing variety, now numbering a dozen in some packages (Mann-Whitney, Kruskal-Willis analyzes, Friedman's test for paired or repeated measures, Chochran's Q test for dichotomous data analysis, etc.)

- Time-series procedures for plotting and auto-correlations, estimating parameters, forecasting, differencing, Box-Jenkins type models, etc.

- Exploratory factor analysis using Harris and Kaiser image approaches, integrated principal axis analysis with orthogonal and oblique transformations; varimax, equamax and quartimax rotations; correlation matrix, etc. The generation of unrotated, orthogonal and oblique factor plots, screen plots, etc.

Survival analytics include three major groupings of methodologies:

- Nonparametric methods including actuarial estimates, linear rank tests for cross-group comparisons including log rank, stratification

- A variety of tables illustrating survival function and related quantities, quantiles, and summary data, such as Kaplan-Meier life tables and comparison of survival curves

- Plotting of cumulative survival and hazard, density, and censor/response patterns

- Regression models including proportional hazards, exponential, log normal, logistic Stepwise options, stratification, etc. with likelihood ration joint significance tests, residuals, deviance, and score options, etc., again demonstrable in a variety of tables and plots (baseline cumulative survival and hazard, residual plots, etc.)

Quality control measures are increasingly included:

- Subgroup measurements, user specifiable tests for special causes, extending to graphs and tables whose reconfiguration and comparisons between forms act as checks (e.g., X-Bar, R-, S-, I-, and P-charts)

- Automatic calculation of three-sigma limits

- Individual measurements, including control over parameters

- P/NP, C/U controls, and Pareto analysis (charts and tables) to determine priorities for improvements.

Little evidence indicates use of still more sophisticated and comprehensive database management systems (Oracle, Sybase, Informix, Ingres, etc.) for multiple database integration or use of software such as Visigenic's ODBC driver set for working across multiple platforms. Perhaps such ODBC-compliant applications will become more prevalent as genuine collaboration increases, which requires linkage between researchers and multiple historical centers. The increased prevalence of client-server architectures and distributed computing will make such collaboration and multisite project work ever more convenient and desirable. For the time being, most historical computing is dedicated to single projects which operate from unified databases even when multiple data sets are correlated, and such work is usually directed by individual researchers with their graduate students and perhaps intermittent help from a computing center programmer. Most of the statistical packages used on PCs are not considered "industrial strength" today, but they are more powerful than mainframe capabilities were in the past decade. The problem is that the possibilities for large-scale computing have increased to such an extent, and digital corpora are growing so fast, that the scale of commercial, industrial, and government computing today still leaves historical computing with its finite data sets in incomparable standing. Most history projects, by comparison, are minuscule. However, if ever integrated, they could constitute sizeable multimedia corpora requiring a data warehouse approach. Even with their small-scale databases, however, desktop tools today offer historians high-powered analysis.

Technical developments which counteract the promotion of collaborative computing because of new client-server architectures, mega-networks, and multiplatform integration include not only the increased capacity of personal computers, but the expansion of toolboxes which provide compatible sets of software (e.g., Borland's *Officemate* package; Corel's *WordPerfect* Suite, Microsoft's *Windows* NT, etc.) that increase the self-sufficiency of the lone computer user (J. SHAPIRO). Moreover, some software packages are increasing in sophistication and subroutines, that the full range of their applications for historical research has yet to be explored. KURTZMAN, for example, recently studied spreadsheets for the representation of historical accounting data. He presents a spreadsheet history scheme as a model consisting of sequences of computation tuples. When continuous data are not possible to produce a series, but cross-sections are periodically available, audits of accounting records can be very revealing. As an illustrative case I offer my audit of the *Rationes Decimarum Hispania* (1279-80), a medieval crusade tax collected by the Church in northeastern Spain, which could be compared with a later royal crusade tax in the following century which also used dioceses as tax collection districts (MCCRANK, 1990). A spreadsheet approach allowed each diocese to be compared with all others at both times, and the interval allowed these two distinct cross-sections to be compared with each other as in a three-dimensional matrix (fiscal data, geographic unit, time differential between two similar taxations). The comparisons revealed shifts in financial capabilities and corporate wealth geographically over a half-century, suggesting the impact of ecclesiastical reorganization during the Reconquest on the future fiscal capabilities of the dioceses, and substantial differences in church finance between old and new

Catalunya. Such cross-sectional data did not lend themselves to the same statistical analysis as longitudinal data or the application of *SPSS*, but fit nicely into spreadsheet analytic methods.

Variables and variation are key concerns in such research because once a norm is described, the exceptions become especially interesting and allow refinement of the generalization, further minute analysis, modeling, and spinoff studies. The Cambridge Group for the History of Population and Social Structure, following the leads of Peter Laslett and Richard Wall, pioneered computerization of what have been called prosaic records, especially to study individual households (i.e., their life cycles) in sufficient number or cross-section in one period to generalize about a given society. Thus, models have been developed for the early modern household, the pre-industrialist city, the changing countryside, etc., which once built seemed to encourage a second round of investigation using similar methodologies but perhaps a different sample or perhaps from another locale, for further confirmation, slight revision, and occasionally a major assault upon the model often with a critique of previously employed analytic methods (e.g., L. Berkner attacking P. Laslett). This cyclical historiography is apparent, for example, in S. COOPER's critique of early modern social history, before she contributes to the same genre with similar minute revision and refinement of earlier work by J. Patten and G. Sjøberg, based on her investigation of the English seaport, King's Lynn, 1689-1702.

Not all variant analysis works in the microcosm of local history; some applications are global in scale. TABER, for example, applied the expert system *Policy Arguer (POLI)* to model international situational data from the 1950s and relate these to belief systems operating in United States foreign policy during that decade; *POLI*'s "predictions" were 86 percent accurate when compared with actual history. The logical "debate" simulated by *POLI* could be analyzed for explication of hypothetical causes and connections not easily made by normal procedures, and these pointed direction to future study of narrative sources for collaboration or rebuttal of hypotheses generated by such modeling. D. THOMAS (1974) talks about "predicting the past" in this sense, when speaking about anthropological archeology; that is, the anthropologist, archeologist, and the historian all predict certain findings in given situations based on what they know about similar cases. In this sense historians predict relevant finds in archives just like archeologists do in the field. These thought processes are often subtle and left unarticulated, and are perhaps ascribed to hunches or the like. Computerization of such processes requires explicit, precise operations. All of the common variable analytic techniques are used in machine prediction and learning; frequency distribution along time lines is a natural historical inquiry, as suggested by the term "histogram" for bar-charted results for continuous variables. The automatic generation of tabular, linear, and mapped data in image form is more problematic than often assumed and requires sophisticated training and awareness, both for presentation and interpretation.

Edward Tufte has shown how important it is to visualize data accurately and effectively (1983; 1990; 1997); based on his own consulting experiences, he has related the significance of graphics design and effective presentation especially to political science history and policy analysis (1974). His illustrated lectures demonstrate how people, even when presented with accurate data and capable analyses, have missed the point because of poor presentation. In some cases, he makes his point by showing the disastrous consequences of misinterpretation of visualized data. He thus makes the case for graphics standards (as in description, cf., LOHSE & WALKER), and for training in visual presentation and graphics interpretation. His work is significant for its combination of visualization and statistical inference in the presentation of scientific evidence, but the rapid innovation in computer graphics has caused his work to be quickly superseded in technical aspects (but not principles). So, TUFTE converted his duo into a trilogy by adding *Visual Explanations* in 1997, which explores the depiction of data relating cause and effect in new computer interfaces design and use of graphics, narratives, and animation entwined. He represents his works as "pictures of numbers...of nouns,...of verbs" because they proceed from statistics (charts, graphs, tables), to data maps, design of high-dimensional data, and the idea of information depth, and finally interactive graphics for decision-making. Thus, they are marketed as "Images and Quantities, Evidence, and Narrative" with the same concerns as taken up bibliographically in this essay. Such benchmark work as Tufte's must nevertheless be updated by studies in cognitive mapping or utility of displays for information retrieval (H. FISHER; KOHONEN [1995]; X. LIN; MARCHIONINI, SOERGEL & LIN; ORWIG, CHEN & NUNAMAKER), electronic data presentation (FREI & JAUSLIN; FOLWER, FOLWER & WILSON), and visualization technology (FU & KUNII; KUNII; VEITH), including reliance on depth perception and motion in 3-D animated imagery (ROBERTSON, CARD & MACKLINAY). Graphic organizers created specifically to guide historical research have been explored by CLARKE, MARTEL & WILLEY. They provide a scheme for sequencing research steps, fact tours, time lines, diagrams, etc. for students to learn how to propose defensible answers to difficult questions, rather than simply to retrieve or recite facts. Like all tools, they can be used well but also abused.

Since TUFTE's early works appeared in 1983, numerous guides have presented the "dos and don'ts" in graphic presentations from viewpoints both of aesthetics and clarity, in both two and three dimensional visualization, and with variety to explore much more than traditional quantification graphs, but combinations of video, art and models, animation, and combinations of visuals (BROWN *ET AL.*). Software like *StatView* for Windows now comes with both statistical tools like spreadsheets and DBMS capabilities combined with powerful graphics and presentation tools that even allow for transparent overlays, choices of presentations from different windows, 3-D interactive graphics, etc., which may be used with new plotting software like *Tecplot* that replaces older CAD drawings with new capabilities in visualization technology. Although promoted as scientific tools, because many of these developments are aimed at persuasion through visual stimulation, they increase the probability of subjective presentation and misrepresentation over the kinds of traditional graphics discussed initially by TUFTE (1990; cf., TUFTE, 1997). Such technical developments call for the parallel development of a new speciality, visual criticism, i.e., a form of source criticism for new visualization training people for critical interpretation and presenting guidelines for the close analytic and philosophic examination required in complex visuals based on sophisticated statistical computation. Such guidance would be a counterweight to art design for attention only, or overemphasis on showy presentations, and would act as a complement to the cognitive concerns in Graphic User Interface (GUI) design.

In the past five years, a field of visual science has evolved rapidly, sometimes called "Visualization," which relates to data display or what has been called more traditionally "representation" (EMMER; FAUGERAS; GALLAGHER; NIELSON *ET AL.*) Usage varies, although a tendency exists among visual technologists in research laboratories and in Information Science to think of scientific visualization as dealing with Science, and everything else as nonscientific. In their recent review of visualization literature, J. WILLIAMS *ET AL.* (p. 163, 165) make this distinction by identifying empirical research with precision and Science and deal with more abstraction and textual data as "nonscientific visualization." That dichotomy is unfortunate but understandable given the divisions between the disciplines, and the lag time for techniques and technology in science and technology developed for industry to travel into other areas, i.e., from industrial design to architecture and to the arts.

The more general or abstract the definition of visualization, the more ecumenical the term seems to be, but visualizing, like graphing, now generally connotes some form of mediation and use of computing, rather than envisioning, depicting, drawing, illustrating, or other generic terms. WILLIAMS *ET AL.* paraphrase ROSSIGNAC & NOVAK, speaking from an engineering perspective, to define visualization as "the mapping of discrete values computed over an n-dimensional domain onto pixel colors via a dimension-reducing process justified by its dependence on human perceptual capacities for extracting information from visual stimuli."

They are speaking of processes more complex than merely using traditional graphs and charts to display comparative data. This approach and an array of new visual technology open myriad possibilities to do so much more than merely graph information in traditional ways. The trend is illustrated by the conversion of two-dimensional or flat bar graphs shown straight on, to three-dimensional shown from an angle from above that multiple bars may be compared in clusters or a stack. Each three-dimensional bar can be a multiplex unit like a cable made of many strands. Such methods attempt to preserve more complexity in their representation while simultaneously illustrating an overall simplicity. Pattern graphs are still more abstract and complex, for example, and take on the characteristics of abstract art. Their interpretation demands more than merely comparing the relative sizes of different slices of a pie or which bars are longer. Add color, density, and texture to these forms of data representation to illustrate the variables and the commonalities at the same time, and one has something more appropriate for complex modeling that indeed resembles art. Many specific techniques and methodologies can be incorporated into such complex graphics. In turn, the character of an image, representative or illustrative, can be used for image retrieval just like letters, words, and phrases supply the means of text retrieval.

Certainly some of the most sophisticated attempts to track variables apply to artwork itself, but their application can be anything from graphs to engineering and architectural drawings to full renderings, real-life paintings, and abstract forms. Color spectra, for example, are difficult variables to track visually but can be used precisely with computer technology where measurement is exact: see O'GORMAN & KASTURI for pixel-level processing and feature analysis. CORRIDONI *ET AL.* base their work on the color classification theories and feature analysis of Johannes Itten who applied these to picture and painting analysis in the 1960s (ITTEN). Image segmentation (HARALICK & SHAPIRO; RISEMAN & ARBIB) and facet analysis (CHANG & LIU) of pictorial data are typical approaches, but recently it is the relationship between facets, proximity of images within partitions of an overall image, and linkage between images organized by genre, artist, region and period, which produces a basis for semantic retrieval that has attracted the attention of cultural information scientists (cf., LIU & PICARD for texture; HIRATA & KATO; MEHROTA & MCGAHEY, L.; DEL BIMBO & PALA for shape similarities; JAIN & VAILAYA and NIBLACK for combining shape, texture, and color features). Thus, an image semantics language (i.e., based on semantic relationships between imaged objects) is developing to support complex iconic indexing and cognitive mapping (CHANG, SHI & YAN; CHANG & LIU; SWAIN). SWAIN & BALLARDO approach indexing and information retrieval on the basis of primary colors and on the relationships between them. Recent information retrieval by color, in addition to classification (e.g., Itten-Runge chromatic sphere, Phillip Otto Runge's use of a reference set of 180 colors), uses semantics and fuzzy logic for rough sets (BINAGHI, GAGLIARDI & SCHETTINI). This combination of approaches mitigates against the need for exact matching when searching by color and takes into account hues, tones, luminance, and saturation (amount of color).

Image retrieval has become very sophisticated, therefore, combining color matching that includes approximation with pattern recognition or shape recognition that accommodates some ambiguity for general feature analysis, plus subject descriptors and object classification. Such systems as the Query by Image Content (NIBLACK; CODY; FLICKER *ET AL.*) also combine image partition, segmentation techniques (RISEMAN & ARBIB; HARALICK & SHAPIRO), spatial arrangements, content analysis, and color properties to retrieve images. These hybrid approaches go far beyond the idea of image-object classification (SWAIN & BALLARD use this in combination with color descriptors as a kind of search string). CHANG, JUNGERT & TORTORA address image information retrieval and spatial reasoning using their system of Symbolic Projection in a way that dovetails historian's work on the symbolic and memory and organization culturalists in their study of symbols, arrangements, and space. More generally, if it is a transfer of the symbolic into the geometric to observe simulations and computations that are not ordinarily seen, scientists especially praise this approach as an enrichment of the process of discovery and fostering insights. As such, it can be used by historians as well.

Such innovative approaches to image information retrieval assist in traditional forms such as paintings and sketches, but they are even more necessary because of the variety of techniques used in electronic imaging. Although Visualization may include artistic representation through computer-assisted rendering, coloring, and texturizing, which scientists use as well as art historians, computer artists and designers, etc., Science visualization is closer to how quantification historians would be likely to use visual technology as Social Scientists—that is, to enhance data representation. Current surveys of methods and techniques are available at the introductory levels by RUSS (1995) and at the more advanced technical level for science and medicine, industry and manufacturing from the Visualization Society of Japan (NAKAYAMA & TANIDA).

WILLIAMS *ET AL.* (p. 164) provide a useful model for visualization components (e.g., data, model, system, interface, and users), and list basic graphic rendering techniques in use (pp. 174-77): (1) light source positioning and shading; (2) removal and addition of hidden lines and surfaces; (3) depth and size cuing; (4) projection and clipping of lines and surfaces; (5) shadowing; (6) motion production; (7) anti-aliasing and stereopsis; and (8) volume reconstruction. Supposedly accurate data interpretation and presentation override aesthetics, but object displays may be realistic or designed as visual metaphors. Multivariate analysis can be displayed through a variety of options, and various displays can be checked to discover patterns in data which are not ordinarily detectable (BRAY & MAXWELL). P. ROBERTSON discusses a methodology for the selection of appropriate data representations. Data preparation is all important, as in any quantification research. Since the issue is one of mapping domain data onto a geometry where it is rendered and displayed, data management, structure, and selection of visualization technique and structure are critical issues. In some cases, for example, one wants to visualize something already known theoretically, and in other cases, the visualization is itself theoretical and exploratory. Data handling by registration, classification, segmentation, etc., common in quantification research are all related to problems in volume analysis in visualization as in non-visualized projects. Toolkits, such as *DataFlow* (DYER), allow the mapping of data to geometrical contracts to enable visualization. As more visualization is undertaken, the literature is expanding with advice on selection of techniques, tools, and data processing for visualized research (NIELSON *ET AL.*; updated, e.g., by the series from CRC Press, http://www.crcpress.com), but ROBERTSON *ET AL.* nevertheless point to the need for benchmarks and standardized means to evaluate visualization systems. The same is true for criteria in formal criticism, especially the nexus between data sources, representation, and interpretation. A new visual acuity is required of historians, as by scientists, in the use of visualization technology. Such techniques are described in basic textbooks for visualization (e.g., J. D. FOLEY *ET AL.*). KELLER & KELLER address the selection of different techniques on the basis of "visual cues." The technology has advanced so fast that equally sophisticated review and criticism have lagged far behind (see NIELSON *ET AL.*).

Complex motion analysis as in space exploration and interactive systems still rely on large mainframe environments for data processing, but increasingly a variety of sophisticated visual toolkits are available for Pentium-grade PCs (e.g., PV-WAVE and C-SIMPLEPLOT at the lower end to more sophisticated toolkits: *Minimum Reality*; *Spyglass Transform*; *DADisp*; VIS-AGE system; *Data Explorer*; *SuperGlue*; *SemNet*; *Visualizer*; etc.). R. ROSS provides a useful handbook of software for engineers and scientists which is equally useful for historians as a foundation from which to explore visualization software. This can be updated by magazines, such as *Computer Graphics, Visualization,* or *3-D Design* (cf., www.3d-design.com) which capture the imagination of every would-be virtual reality designer. Visualization software characteristics and functionality include support for 2-D or 3-D and volumetric environments;

viewpoint setting capabilities; navigation mechanisms for changing views; graphic transformation for modifying scalar properties; data transformation applications for statistical analysis, filtering, smoothing, etc.; grouping capability; rendering to work with color, texture, illumination, shading, etc.; mapping data to standard scales (Cartesian, logarithmic, polar, spherical mechanisms); animation for time-oriented data and whole dynamic data sets; import and export means for data exchange; and some kind of database management system (DBMS) that has a flexible interface, seamless sub-processes, and allows for user control. Advanced projects such as the Research on Interactive Visual Environments (RIVERS) at the University of Illinois National Center for Supercomputing Applications (NCSA) are producing new techniques that require, in HABER & MCNAB's words, "visualization idioms."

Applications of *LightWave* 5.5 with such plug-ins as Immersion's *VertiSketch* or its *Microscribe 3D*, and *3D Studio MAX*, and *After Effects* combine 3-D graphics with motion through digital video make productions once reserved for the most sophisticated studios now a possibility for household industries. They certainly make the use of transparencies or old slide shows dated and comparatively uninteresting, although these still have their place because of their simplicity and technical independence. These new software products are increasingly available in campus media production centers so that historical simulations can be produced for course support; or, in some cases, with expertise provided in media laboratories, projects can be added to courses whereby students engage in 3-D modeling and interactive video projects to explore history visually. This pertains to object rendering, real-life visualization, dynamic mapping, and statistical modeling—all of which may be used together today (to be discussed further in relation to art and image bases).

A common concern is if History so constructed is thereby converted into a media technology course which simply uses some historical content, where does the technology instruction begins to dominate and therefore replace subject matter? This is why it may be necessary to sequence and pair courses, which requires better coordination of curricular offerings and course selection through controls and advising rather than a smorgasboard approach to course selection. To be sure, the applications of such visual technology are hardly limited to formal education, so exposure to them has often come from outside schooling. This technology is instead being driven by the digital entertainment industry (as described by T. E. KINNEY): animation, filmmaking, interactive television, multimedia CDs, video games, virtual reality theme parks, etc., and secondarily by designers, artists, and media specialists. Formal education is adopting such technology only after it has been developed in the industry, tried and proven, and after it has found a popular market that defrays the development cost and thereby makes it affordable for educational institutions. Moreover, they are becoming increasing common so their lack of integration in History will be come more and more noticeable (more than the lack of serious history integrated into visual media production outside History). Active 3-D graphic representation today is an extension of yesterday's 2-D static graphs, diagrams, and maps, but the lag time in adopting new visual technology for teaching often makes education seem outdated. Good presentation, data representation, and visualization keep history from becoming passé. But such pedagogic concerns (discussed more in relation to teaching history; cf., L. LLOYD; CARLSON & FALK, etc. for technology and education) may miss the point here if they are believed to belong only to secondary and undergraduate teaching. These technologies should be combined with History as historical method. Research and teaching in this case do go hand in hand.

Historians have been slow to use advanced visualization techniques, but such applications are nearby judging from some of the quantification work that is being done and the need for improved representation of statistical models and serialized rather than static views. Such developments will eventually lead to more historical modeling and simulation. What are the research trends that might lend themselves to modern visualization? Stated differently, how can modern vizualization technology be applied to History as practiced now to make it relevant in tomorrow's increasingly visual and less textual world?

Consider how quantification and qualitative historical research may be related to newer forms of data representation and the visualization of narrative history. One connection is by understanding how history, through complex serial processes, must be studied as frozen frames like a unit in a motion picture or as snapshots in a broken series because the historical record is incomplete. Both time and place must be manipulated for full comprehension. The ideal is to add forward motion, i.e., to animate a dead or static past, and at other times to be able to freeze-frame life to study it in detail one step at a time. Another is to remember that in historical narrative, like storytelling, imagination is stimulated and mental imaging occurs as a necessary ingredient for learning, and that modeling and graphic visualization are means of making the implicit explicit. Finally, metaphor in language has its counterpart as substitution in data representation and visualization where objects can be representative or figurative (dots and lines for real things, numbers and dimensional objects for spatial coverage, or animated models standing in for historical persons).

The archival notion of life-cycle of records in appraisal is similar to "life course" research composed of "event history analysis" as proposed in P. D. ALLISON's useful text (1984; cf., BLOSSFELD *ET AL.*), described in essays edited by MAYER & TUMA, or in C.TILLY's (1993) time series analysis in the study of European revolutions which combined quantification with regional time-series narratives (episodes). Many statistical approaches in applications not thought of as historical are nevertheless history-based as convincingly argued by RAFFALOVICH & KNOKE; indeed, all regression analysis is historical because no organic data exist for "progression" analysis. We can, of course, supply data projections, but these too are based on historical precedent. Such clustering and directional path techniques have been statistically and descriptively applied to family history (CORNELL) to specific families and family types under the rubric "cohort analysis" (see GLENN for introduction and H. GOLDSTEIN for problem areas), to show change over time (in Social Science jargon, "longitudinal event data"), such as in childbearing and rearing patterns and ratios of family size to income that infer standards of living. When such data are mapped and visualized in digital form, the techniques used in their analysis are not substantially different than those used in any image analysis, whether an abstract painting or an abstract data model. For example, if data in either were recognizable by color because of original application or by color coding, whether they represent flecks of pigment on a canvas or people migrating across a terrain, combinations of color classification, pattern recognition and shape matching, density and flow or directional mapping, relationships between them based on spatial analysis or semantics based on object or color, etc., all apply. From one perspective, depiction and modeling, whether in art or data composition, are both matters of representation. The major difference between the first and second examples is that the first is static and the second active. It is still far easier to study the former, and then to move as in motion picture technology to a comparison of frames one after the other, and finally to continual motion (the combination of time and space) that characterizes history.

Social historians have developed statistical techniques to study groups over time, but few projects have applied the latest technologies in image and time-series analysis. Visualization technology for new data representation is being applied to social and cultural history, however, and will change older methods considerably. COLLENTEUR (1997) explores well developed cohort analysis techniques for a "large-scale project on small-scale communities." Such a methodology evolved in structural social history after heavy borrowing from modern Sociology. Such work provides the basis on which modern visualization, data representation, and image analysis techniques will be overlaid. Cohort analysis measures as many observations as possible for particular subsets of data, from which data for cohorts are extrapolated and are linked by cross-sectional analysis. The technique is like cross-sectional analysis except that the methodology is tailored to longitudinal analysis and relies on measures of repeatable data over some time. Thus, a control set displaying the same observable phenomena is required. Subsets of data, representing cohorts or subjects moving through time together, are studied to reveal patterns and generalities as well as deviation from the norm. Cross-sectional data reveal little about instances of change. Another problem is that most social cohorts suffer from atrophy through time, resulting in a loss of data and therefore asymmetrical data (e.g., higher male death rates produce gender asymmetry, as does the tendency for more males to migrate than females), which must be adjusted to study life activities. The isolation of data on age, period, and group interaction is problematic since one influences the other. Consequently, this kind of research requires measures that are repeatable over time for time-series analysis, rather sophisticated statistical procedures, and continuous data sources that display the same observations over time.

Multiple variables evoke an immediate suspicions about possible relationships and hence measures of association. Because historians think constantly by relating time to place, two-dimensional matrix plotting, as in scatter diagrams, are likewise naturally preferred for the envisioning of data. Outliers may be discarded for generalization, but they often invite separate investigation because historians are so often intrigued with the novel and exceptional while social scientists are more comfortable studying norms in the aggregate. Aberrant behaviors often require such individual and customized study that they do not lend themselves to continued quantification. More complex multivariable and multiregression analysis and covariance analysis are increasingly common (see introduction by IVERSEN & NORPOTH) because of *SPSS ANOVA* (Analysis of Variance) commands and routines (well explained by ANDREWS *ET AL.*; cf., HAND & TAYLOR). R. JENSEN (1991) adopted such variable analysis techniques to what historians, like information scientists, often think of as classification issues or a literature broken into genres, as when studying social classes and wanting to break them down into smaller groups (as R. SIMMONS did on a county basis to study class structure along the Ohio River from 1840 to 1850). C. H. ACHEN in 1986 explained regression analysis for historians in nonmathematical terms that still make sense (as do SCHROEDER *ET AL.*). JARAUSCH (1991, pp. 140-142) summarizes the four basic questions historians ask of their analysis: (1) what is the predictability of three or more variables from those already known; (2) how is accuracy reflected in variable analysis; (3) what causal relationships can be identified for causal models; and (4) what interaction between variables can be described. Today researchers can turn to expert systems (SOWIZRAL) to assist them in designing their research program, choice of appropriate methodology, selection of variables likely to be so related as to produce the inference of cause, and testing the features of any linear model (SCHEINES). Part of methods selection and project design must entail risk analysis, i.e., as in determining risk in policy analyses (MORGAN & HENRION). Such concerns have been relatively weak in methodological training and historical quantitative research; instead more emphasis has been placed customarily on the nature of the data.

Historians generally have not carried their work theoretically as far into Bayesian statistics (BERNARDO *ET AL.*) and networks, or fully into Artificial Intelligence (FRANKLIN), as current statistical theory (HAND; HAND, ed.) and expert systems applications allow (surveyed by MICHIE) to explore causal information and heuristics (HECKERMAN & SHACHTER; KAHNEMAN *ET AL.*; SPIRTES *ET AL.*), inference (CASELLA & BERGER; TANNER), knowledge discovery through "data mining" (BUNTINE, 1991; FAYYAD *ET AL.*; HECKERMAN; and others, in their work for Microsoft, Inc.), and graphic modeling (R. EDWARDS). Nor has their regression analysis generally incorporated the most advanced features of classification and regression trees (FRIEDMAN *ET AL.*). Indeed, historians seem uncomfortable with what was once viewed as the "quantification of judgment" at the beginning of the Cliometric movement (R. WINKLER), but which is now more commonly called probabilistic reasoning to deal with uncertainty (HIRSHLEIFER & RILEY; KAHNEMAN *ET AL.*; NEAPOLITAN); such notions as "inferred causality" (PEARL & VERMA); or in seeing historical reconstruction from partial data to be similar in method and thought processes to forecasting in reverse (for causal reasoning in AI applications, cf., G.

SHAFER; FREUDER & MACKWORTH). While historians remind everyone of the need to study the past, TOFFLER urged that there be a similar role in education for the study of the future. For him, forecasting the future or constructing it is similar to reconstructing the past. Likewise, the past-present-future linear progression always needs to be broadened. The connection between historical reasoning and contextual analysis is often the interplay between linear temporal projection and geographic expansion of the moment. This involves variable analyses and what statisticians think of as temporal reasoning or temporal influences in modeling. Only the former Soviet school of Cliometricians, for example, has employed Markov Chains to any extent in property analysis and graphic representation of historical data (see D. FREEDMAN, 1983, on Markov processes).

Part of the problem is taking general historical discourse which takes method and reasoning too much for granted, down to a proper level of explicit, detailed, logical argumentation where the reasoning process is not assumed, but is made absolutely clear. Historians tend to pay more attention in citations to referencing sources than to explication of method and explicit deduction and induction dissected into a step-by-step procedure or technique that can retraced, replicated, and therefore programmed. Research into historical reasoning in this empirical manner, distinct from argumentation presented in the philosophy of history, is almost nonexistent; therefore, we have little software development for historical research and coverage of historical reasoning in teaching historical methods is woefully inadequate. Proper course materials do not even exist. Examples of what needs to be done would be explicit explorations of spatial and temporal reasoning precise enough to be used in developing an historical component of AI research. Consider D. CASE's observation about historians' penchant for using metaphors to express themselves, in distinction from the use of analogy in research. When addressing similarity, analogy is the comparative reasoning process or perception, while the metaphor is the figure of speech that reflects the determination of the degree of sameness in things recognized as separate and distinct. Sameness, as in the case of gender issues, is not the same as equity.

When historians use metaphors based on analogies, they are engaging in modeling. Moreover, when they teach, historians often reinforce their lectures with diagraming, time-lines, other forms of graphic representation, and many appeal to mental imagery for historical reconstruction on the part of their listeners through the invocation to "picture this." HOLYOAK & THAGARD treat analogy as recalling familiar past situations to deal with novel ones. Their approach from the perspective of cognitive science is highly applicable to historical reasoning in problem solving, explanation, and general communication. What they see as "mental leaps" that are creative but also risky are of interest to any researcher using models, since analogy making is the recognition of sameness or degree to which things, processes, people, and events appear to be the same. R. SCHOLZ recommends several "cognitive strategies for stochastic thinking." FRENCH, for another example, attempts to use analogy as a basis for computer model development and representation. He sees data linkage through analogy as important for stochastic processing, distributed computing, and simulated parallelism and parallel processing. In essence, he attempts to offer a computational model of mechanisms underlying these subtle processes in perceiving sameness. To do so, he and others working with analogy in human thinking for applications in Artificial Intelligence have had to study the phenomenon and explain it more explicitly than historians do even when they are discussing historical reasoning.

When one understands this problem of imprecision in historical discourse as a carryover from and camouflage of precision problems in historical research, then it becomes clear why historians have not engaged AI research for their own purposes, why so little software exists for historical work, why too much of historical method is left vague and is never reduced to technique and systematic process, and why so many historians regard their work as insightful, creative, inspirational, and relying on personal judgment in close identification with the Humanities rather than subjecting their information processing to closer scrutiny. The issue is more than empowerment and access to technology, but a shift in the discipline's culture. The solution rests on the early initiation of historians as undergraduates in technically enhanced coursework, formal training in graduate education and retraining of those who lacked a strong technical component, and securing the nexus between technique, engineering, and technology with insight, inspiration, and motivation.

The kind of integration of History and Information Science called for in this essay may be more difficult, therefore, than it would first seem. Mastering a historical field with its attendant methodologies and languages, etc., and achieving competence in information technology at the same time, are difficult. At the same time, the possibilities for major contributions to History and the interjection of historical interests into Information, Computer, and Cognitive Sciences are indeed luring (see B.L. ALLEN's recent *ARIST* survey of cognitive research in Information Science). Are such intellectual and inspirational motives enough? Hardly. Exemplary programs must evolve, the award system must change, job opportunities must materialize, and then talent, now available, can be attracted to this kind of History and Information Science, i.e., Historical Information Science.

Problematic Data: Use and Interpretation

It is doubtful that historical analytic work to date has contributed greatly to statistical theory (reviews of knowledge engineering literature by statisticians, e.g., BLUNTINE, 1996, acknowledge no contributions whatsoever), but History certainly can provide opportunity for widening the range of applications, bringing more and different kinds of data under systematic and normalized scrutiny (e.g., tabular data for reference: FIENBERG), and enriching interpretation in History (cf., P. LASLETT; BLALOCK). Some historians, like R. ZEMSKY very early (1969) and M. THALLER more recently, have advocated development of methodology and theory that are specifically historical. As already mentioned, at the most recent IAHC meeting in Moscow, KROPAČ (1996) and DOORN (1996) contemplated the basic elements and synthesis of a underpinning theory for historical computing. Like psychologists in approaching IQ measurement as a composite latent variable, historians are usually skeptical of single-answer explanations because their data defy such precise measurement or unilateral relationships. Factor analysis has been deployed to eliminate some variables and to focus on others to provide an ideal linear trajectory. Sometimes such diagnostics through the weighting of indicators approach Artificial Intelligence (AI) techniques in building fuzzy expert systems, whereby possibilities are not excluded but are ranked in an order of likelihood based on number of occurrences and interrelationships between them (KANDEL).

The historian to confront these knotty problems of records linkage before anyone else was D. HERLIHY (1980) in the early 1970s while examining fourteenth-century Tuscan fiscal records. Such work fused with socio-cultural historiography of the family reconstruction ilk represented by G. DUBY and K. F. WERNER. Medievalists have had some of the most difficult problems to overcome simply because of the nature of their discipline and historical sources and difficulty in generating data from the archives. Data streams can be found in rich veins within these archives, but they are not readily identifiable from the surface of things; the veins meander through mighty tough rock at times (colloquial Latin, illegible and highly abbreviated script, incomplete records or redundant copies, etc.), and data must be mined under difficult conditions (no simultaneity in multi-site research; everything is asynchonous at first). ORNATO (p. 27), speaks of the problem of "information flow" referring to continuity between diverse fonds in many different archives and continuous extraction of linked data to create cultural term and personal name banks (i.e., anthroponomies). Coordination of work in different mines is difficult, mining at any one site produces sporadic results, and once retrieved the nuggets are usually imperfect. Data extraction and refining can be helped by modern information analytic techniques, and the whole field has developed an impressive array of methods and systems commensurate with the increase of personal computing power during the last decade.

Inspired also by methods worked out for modern labor history, and especially demographic studies in French Canada (i.e., SOREP; e.g., BOUCHARD, CASGRAIN & ROY's methodological essay, 1985, on family reconstitution studies in Saguenayenne Quebec is often quoted in French circles), a panhellenic or international school of French-speaking historians have shared their trade secrets with each other and all other computing historians. New techniques are being applied recently to fuzzy data in prosopography and family history. Once can point to the early project pioneered by Gian Piero Zarri after 1975 and still ongoing, *RESADA*, which has developed some sophisticated combinatorics and equivalency tables for sorting self-references and signatory qualifiers in official records (e.g., an APL program designed by Lucia Zarri-Baldi) (*RESEDA* reports by the CNRS and ZARRI; cf., the recent update by ORNATO); PELISSIER's programming in 1983; and at the end of the decade the first of four successive versions of the *LEGIA I-IV* database and information retrieval system designed by Claude Desama and his colleagues at Liège (PASLEAU, 1989); BOURLET *ET AL.* (1991) for the developing CNRS- IRHT expert system; N. HURON and his collaborators at Tours under the direction of Monique Bourin in developing *NOMEN* software to interrogate cartularies; and finally note Jean-Philippe Genet's project at the University of Paris (cf., GENET & LOTTES, eds.). BECK (1994) provides a methodological overview of recent studies and evolving methodology. M. SELZ and SELZ & LAMAISON, and contributers to BARTHELEMY & PINGUAD discuss this recent alliance between "informatique" and geneaology in demographic, family, and socio-cultural history.

A number of innovative doctoral dissertations and subsequent studies have been completed using prosopography and anthroponomy (BOURIN, ed., 1990-[1998]; MARTIN & MENANT) used in genealogy and family reconstruction (any indication of parentage, i.e., marriage and business records in church and family archives, inheritance and property records, tax records, orthography and syntax in early naming developments, allowing the reconstruction of family trees and extended lineages for wider applications in social and cultural history and regional studies). As one moves about Europe regionally from south of the Pyrenees to the western Mediterranean then to central France and eastward, cf., J. M. MARTIN and BOLOS I MASCI & MORAN I OCERINJAUREGUI for their anthoponomies from Catalunya and MARTINEZ SOPENA, ed., for Castile-León; BOURIN, MARTIN & MENANT, eds., for the Mediterranean world and MARTIN & MENANT ed., for Italy DUHAMEL-AMADO's impressive dissertation on the Viscounts of Beziers and Agde for medieval Languedoc; BARTHELEMY for Vendôme; and LE JAN for central medieval Frankland and BOZZOLO, LOYAU & ORNATO for the same area in early modern France; MORSEL for Franconia (all reviewed by BOURIN & CHAREILLE). Imprecise dating as in author and artist attributions is treated by SIGNORE & BARTOLI. For nominal record linkage in census files beyond the 80 percent of links that ordinarily can be made by simple matching (M. THALLER's generalization, 1987, p. 151; echoed by JARAUSCH, 1991, p. 60) or by common methods of collating orthographic variants, probabilities are employed for intelligent guesswork. At issue is the precise identification of individual people and artifacts, their social belonging in a specific historical milieu, and therefore their use as primary witnesses and evidence in historical argumentation (the important of context, as argued early by WRIGLEY, 1969, 1972, 1973; and by WINCHESTER, 1970, 1985).

In older historical quantification, traditional sets were compiled by deciding if an entity belonged or did not; classification was a simple either/or decision. Fuzzy sets, however, call for degrees of membership in a set, and can accommodate partial membership in more than one set (KANDEL; MIYAMOTO; DUBOIS & PRADE); therefore, such a methodology accommodates historical social data much better than the more rigid traditional set compilation based on strict "in" and "out" decisions. More work with incomplete data and imperfect information, which are the majority of cases in historical research, may proceed to new levels of inquiry and use of inference as exemplified by analysis of fuzzy data sets at the Historical Informatics Laboratory in Moscow (GARSKOVA & BORODKIN). The Laboratory's package *Fuzzyclass* is now available on Windows (ZAVALISHIN & BORODKIN). Its availability will assuredly encourage historians to explore more historical data which until now have not seemed viable for analysis because of their problematic lacunae. Imperfect data overlooked because of complications for traditional analyses should be reinvestigated as these new methodologies evolve to compensate for certain types of error.

Economists and decision theory scholars speak of "perfect information" as error free (AHI-TUV & WAND; BACHARACH; HOFFMAN & MESHKOV; NERMUTH; J. PHILIPS; J. SENGUPTA), but data gathering does not always result in this ideal (e.g., consider the heroic attempts at accurate counting over the past fifty years in economic measurement, celebrated recently at the Conference on Research in Income and Wealth: BERNDT & TRIPLETT). LOSEE (1990; 1997, p. 266) explains: "Perfect information about a source domain X exists when there is a one-to-one mapping in a noiseless environment for the source X onto the destination set Y. Information may be said to be incomplete when the mapping from X is into Y, not onto Y." This is hardly the language historians would use to discuss incomplete and imperfect data, but their concerns are the same. DRETSKE, among others, makes the important distinction between information and its antithesis, false information, and between misinformation and disinformation (as does HERNON [1995] for Internet findings). These, he stresses, are not varieties of information. LOSEE (1997, p. 267) attempts to reconcile these factors with his all-encompassing operational definition of information, to note differences between problems such as "when what is transmitted is not received as sent," as in the case of information loss; or when the loss is in producing a particular output characteristic in a noisy environment wherein "the value taken on by the characteristic is determined by a random or error component." Misinformation may be seen as tainted, or as partially or wholly false (C. FOX, 1983). Finally, Losee notes that another form of misinformation is unjustified information: "If one believes something for the wrong reasons, one may be said to be misinformed." GETTIER asks "Is justified true belief knowledge?" As in the aforementioned work on error analysis in search of means not to correct error so much as to deal with it, thinking about information in Information Science tends to take on a language of its own, a form of methodological inspection aimed toward operations, and a technical bent not common in historians' discourse about similar if not the very same problems. The difference is that the Information Science approach often lends itself to modeling and computer operations in ways historical discourse does not.

The latest discussions in History about imperfect transmission of information tend toward the philosophical in an attempt to deal with the limitations on historical knowledge. By focusing almost exclusively on the recipient, rather than the transmitter and process of transmission, this human-oriented approach to imperfect and incomplete information provides little resolution other than to admit the obvious, that historical knowledge is derived through nonreversible processes and is therefore imperfect. But this does not mean that it is unreliable and useless. Moreover, with preservation of adequate sources and the linguistic, statistical, and analytic skills to penetrate them, one can reconstruct historical knowledge in a process of simulation that approximates reversibility. Reinterpretation and revisionism require this. While perfection is the ideal, one can rationalize that the goals in historical reconstruction are approximation and an objective handling of factors that contribute to distortion. Precision is a matter of degree, and genuine knowledge by definition is generalized more than concrete data and tends to be more synthesized than structured information. Objectivity neither requires denial of imperfection and incompleteness or submission to their inhibiting influences, but rather acknowledgment of their presence and rising to the challenge of their neutralization or proper accommodation. How do historians tackle this problem? LORENZ, for example, bases his concept of "internal realism" in History on acceptance of such limitations. His position in some respects reflects thinking in APPLEBY, HUNT & JACOB's argument for pragmatic realism and its reiteration by APPLEBY (1997a). Recognition of the problem, however, does not necessarily deal with it, and passive acceptance of limitations initially imposed by imperfect data as some kind of resignation does nothing to improve historical research methodology. Here is the really critical problem that must be addressed.

A considerable amount of research has been done in database management (DBMS) and the Artificial Intelligence communities, both of which have developed a variety of methodologies for dealing with problematic data of the variety frequently encountered by historians—uncertain, incomplete, or imprecise (as classified by BONNISSONE & TONG). BOSC, DUBOIS & PRADE add vagueness and inconsistency to this classification of imperfections; DUBOIS, PRADE & ROSSAZZA treat vagueness, typicality and uncertainty in class hierarchies. CLOGG (and CLOGG & DAJANI) discuss the problems of uncertainty particularly for social studies (i.e., see also D. DUNCAN, 1975, 1984, for modeling in Sociology; cf., J. B.THOMPSON and DANZIGER for Psychology). It is, however, difficult to find historians, even in Historiography, and with the exception of the Philosophy of History, discussing their information and source problems the same way these are discussed in the Social Sciences that compute, or in Computer Science and Engineering, or in Information Science. Historians, while employing subsystems and building databases to handle imperfect and uncertain data, are unlikely to associate their work with "knowledge and data engineering" (to say nothing about publishing their work in such sources as the Institute of Electrical and Electronics Engineering [IEEE] journal by this very name). Conversely, those readily identifying themselves as Knowledge Engineers seem to know little about historical knowledge except as expressed in terms of time series, temporal reasoning, and time-dependent or temporal databases. These are unfortunately never considered in the computing and information science literatures as historical databases. More cross-disciplinary dialogue is needed.

Uncertainty, which may be inherently subjective, is a lack of enough information about the state of the world or whatever dimension is being studied, so that without knowing if something is true of false, all that can be done is to measure numerically the degree of surety or speculation about the proposition. It is uncertainty which underlies the labeling of deductive procedures and inference programs as "belief" networks, etc., rather than knowledge-based systems—a term which suggests that the bases are known facts. Uncertainty often arises from an agent constructing a subjective opinion about something which he or she did not know for certain as true. SENGUPTA (1985) correctly sees the goal of reasoning under conditions of uncertainty not as arriving at a correct answer or truth in any absolute sense, but the goal is to make "optimal decisions" based on reason rather than "judgment calls" based on one's psychology (MCGRATH, 1982). BELL, RAIFFA, & TVERSKY as editors of a collection of essays about decision-making classified them into descriptive, normative, and prescriptive interactions based on information but also influences during the decision making process. Even with certain and complete data, the process may introduce uncertainty. H. SIMON (1982) perceived models that worked in such ambiguous environments as "models of bounded rationality." Such observations, from a different perspective, reflect the arguments over objectivity in History and need for pragmatic realism even in empirical research. RICOUR (1974) in his lectures in the United States on hermeneutics confronted the same issue on a larger scale than uncertain data, in how to resolve conflict between differing interpretations.

The next two problems can be described objectively to one degree or another. Incompleteness, the absence of information, can exist when the value of an attribute is unknown or is universal as when all instances of particular attributes are unknown. Imprecision can be valued in intervals (e.g., somewhere between this or that parameter); fuzzy valued, which happens frequently in historical descriptive information where qualifiers are imprecise (e.g., "quite young" or "somewhat educated"); or discrete as when a source guesses someone's age and gives the reader two or three choices ("eighteen, nineteen, or perhaps even twenty") as though the historian's guess would be as good as any, including the original estimate. Some describe imprecision as a linguistic problem, i.e., the granularity of language both of the provider and of the inquirer (i.e., information retrieval, as discussed by BELKIN & CROFT). Imprecision and uncertainty often appear together (BORDOGNA & PASI). Vagueness can be thought of, as do BOSC & PRADE, as fuzzy-valued imprecision related to some undefinable or immeasurable predictions. Repeated usage of the same qualifiers, especially when consistent, often allows one to construct values to clarify data. Inconsistency, however, is itself problematic, as when two or more conflicting values are applied in a source to the same variable. PARSONS (p. 35) notes that the literature he surveyed sometimes refers to ignorance as a sixth form of imperfection; he defines this as a lack of knowledge, particularly about the relative certainty of a number of statements. Note that reliability is an attributed value to be ascertained, which is not necessarily inherent in the data but may reside in one's research methodology.

PARSONS (1996) recently surveyed these problems in the design of databases and in the application of Artificial Intelligence (expert, diagnostic, and decision support systems) to these problems of imperfect information. He pays particular attention to medical research (which is of interest for its investigation of case histories and genetic research which relates to demography and biography) and the hard sciences, but includes no regard for the particular features of historical information such as context sensitivity, cultural entrapment, translation and paraphrase differentiation, technical dependency, or the relevance of time as a factor in the origins of the aforementioned imperfections (an exception being WILLIAMS & KONG [1991] who link the issues of time and incompleteness). PARSONS, like those he cites from within the Engineering field, seems unaware of the interests in handling imperfect information by BORODKIN, PASLEAU, THALLER, and others; or interest in Artificial Intelligence as explored by ENNALS and other quantification historians. On the other hand, several developments in Parsons' surveys are worth mentioning here because they are important breakthroughs apparently little known in the History community. No historical methods textbook, for example, examines data problems as precisely and objectively as is required in database design and analytic methodology. Nor would the vocabulary of historians automatically translate into Information Science and *vice versa*. Indeed, although similar problems are discussed in both fields, dialogue between them is spartan if it exists at all, and the sub-language of each speciality is so different that it is possible to read in both fields without connecting the similarity of the problems faced or approaches to their solutions. Historians, for example, while confronting the aforementioned problems in their research have no taxonomy by which to analyze these problems. They are often run together and confused, while customized solutions demand precision in framing questions about data.

PARSONS notes that the boundary in the IS literature between sorting imperfect data in databases and work on reasoning with imperfect data in Artificial Intelligence is not clear-cut, but he sees the approaches as distinct enough to separate them into two camps. Historians have worked predominantly in the former mode (i.e., DBMS), but are increasingly entertaining AI approaches to their data analysis. MOATRO argues tersely, as if constructing a theorem, that "Uncertainty permeates our understanding of the real world. The purpose of information systems is to model the real world. Hence, information systems must be able to deal with uncertainty." Rather than make certain, which many historians think they are doing in the sense of proof, the reverse is a logical approach, i.e., to reduce uncertainty. If one were to construct historical knowledge only from perfect data, our history would be small indeed. RIGNEY's essay about the varieties of historical ignorance recalls Thomas Carlyle's musings about this human predicament, "ignorance in the face of the past," to suggest that the very limitedness of historical representation creates a distinctive aesthetic effect for History, which she calls "the historical sublime." She thinks this is particular to historical writing which may be simulated for rhetorical purposes (and theoretical modeling as well?), but which is rooted in its cognitive function.

SMITHSON points out, as noted by PARSONS (p. 353), that much intellectualization in Western Civilization involves building attractive models based upon realizations never approached in reality. These often operate as general paradigms, but the problem is more acute in quantification and in modeling which achieve elegance by ignoring uncertainty and clarity by ignoring what in reality is messy. Again, such work underscores why such deductive procedures and inference systems are called "belief" networks and ties into the previous discussion of cultural memory versus history. Belief networks balance speculation and supposition with proposition and plausibility, and hence distinguish between different aspects of knowledge. Applications of such knowledge-based work relying on imperfect information to history also give new meaning to the distinction in History between what is true and what people think is true. The difference, of course, is the basis upon which belief rests, how it is supported, and when and how it is applied. The approach is at odds with deconstructionism, postmodernism, and agnosticism. It accepts the imperfection of data and of our knowledge, deals with it, and nevertheless proceeds to extend our knowledge based on what we have. This is the essence of knowledge bases. Thus, while seeming highly theoretical, knowledge and data engineering are eminently practical given the epistemological problems of historical sources, reconstruction, and ultimately an imperfect knowledge of the past which requires continual refinement.

Modeling imperfection in databases, following PARSONS' attack on the problem of organizing a literature which is difficult to summarize, involves storing incomplete information, which he links to: (1) nonmonotonic reasoning (BREWKA; GINSBERG); (2) imprecise information increasingly handled as fuzzy sets through approximate reasoning (the principles for which have been worked out since the 1980s, e.g., ZADEH, 1965, 1978, 1983; and applied in AI and expert systems; ZADEH & SANCHEZ; MANDAMI & GAINES; cf., ZADEH & YAGER, eds., for views on fuzzy logic related to knowledge representation); and (3) uncertainty (also handled by fuzzy logic: ZADEH & KACPRZYK), which involves probability, possibility, and a theory of evidence more formal than is usually articulated in archives or historical work look for such articulation in standard methodological textbooks, e.g., G. SCHAFER, to understand the relative neglect of historical methodology in lieu of historiography). PARSONS (p. 360) summarizes the four basic ways to handle imperfect information, each of which has several variations (with either a number or symbol to indicate): (1) the degree to which an attribute is known to satisfy a relation; (2) the strength of the relation between the attributes; and (3) the strength of the inheritance; or (4) to derive the appropriate number or symbol resulting from a query.

In the case of incompleteness, most schemes since CODD's work in 1979 focus on the null value simply to occupy the place of absent data, but this often leaves unresolved the value of the "place-holder" since an unknown value could also be nonexistent. ETHERINGTON surveys the reasoning behind current approaches. A number of algorithms have been developed to establish boundaries for assigning inferred values in cases of missing attribute values, or answers are provided as rough sets. NEAPOLITAN reviews the algorithms commonly used in expert systems. Deductive databases sometimes create a self-checking set of sets composed of substitutions of all legal values for the unknown (WILLIAMS & KONG, 1988). In other cases, such as in *Prolog* systems, null values are replaced with inferred negation or yes/no queries, to implement what has been called by REITER "the closed world assumption" which produces consistency in data-based answers even when incompleteness exists. Otherwise, if relevant information were missing, no answer at all may be forthcoming. LASKEY & LEHNER explain the distinctions between assumptions, beliefs, and probabilities in such approaches.

In the case of impression, convention calls for fuzzy logic and fuzzy sets as employed by *Fuzzyclass* where an object's degree of membership in a class is calculated or when classes are combined logically, the degree of membership is determined for the enlarged set (MORRISEY). In databases, the fuzzy degree of membership is associated with each tuple of a relation. The degree of the relation may be used as a measure of certainty about the information stored or an estimate of how typical a tuple is for a relationship. In handling vagueness in natural language some systems adopt predictions logic by assigning varying values to fuzzy terms and thereby creating fuzzy sets which operate on all relations and essentially turn textbases into relational databases. The elements of fuzzy logic employed in such treatments include specification of fuzzy relationships where membership is by degree, the mapping of object names to fuzzy objects, assignment of variables to fuzzy sets, and formulae which weight classes, connections, etc. (see DUBOIS *ET AL*.; ZEMANKOVA & KANDEL; about weighting and extension of fuzzy to possibility logic; cf., NILSSON).

Sometimes a measure of similarities or proximities between fuzzy relationships is used to calculate how interchangeable (ensuring that relations are reflexive, symmetric, and transitive) one might be for the other (cf., PETRY & BOSC, 1996; SHENOI & MELTON). This approach has been extended to pattern matching. Uncertainty is different from incomplete data and requires different methods for resolution. PRADE & TESTAMALE advocated attaching a possibility degree to every value of every attribute to create a possibility distribution and a model that can also take incompleteness into account. The exhaustion of all possibilities in analysis does not yield probability, which is further quantification of a database's uncertainty. Methods of modeling and simulating with incomplete data have been evolving for fifteen years, with considerable success for physical systems and continuous mechanisms, but KUIPERS explores such techniques for qualitative reasoning. The idea is to create a qualitative model and then find all possible behaviors consistent with the knowledge embodied in the model. The more consistency found in type and quantity tends to validate the model.

AI approaches to imperfect information split into two groups according to PARSONS: those who deal symbolically with the incomplete information problem and those who deal numerically with imprecise and uncertain information. As in History, the split occurred in the 1970s between those in the mainstream who disliked purely quantitative approaches and those who champion numerical methodology. Most incomplete data problems are handled by non-monotonic logics such as REITER's default logic (cf., BESNARD), which are extensions of classical logic that augment inference mechanisms to include assumptions about what is missing. Specific defaults refer to sets of rules which control what assumptions may be made (POOLE). Circumspection is another nonmonotonic reasoning approach whereby the failure to derive particular facts allows their negation to be assumed (E. D. MCCARTHY). Usually a set of rules pertaining to plausible conjecture are applied. Work on imprecision, following ZADEH's lead in creating fuzzy sets to allow inferences from what is known to what is known only imprecisely. Meanwhile, possibility theory has been applied to the uncertainty problem (DUBOIS & PRADE; BOSC & KACPRZYK; WOLKENHAUER) to good advantage over probabilistic logic, the foundations of which were laid by NILSSON. Both rely on deductive reasoning. PEARL (1988) best related probability theory to causal relations which are so interesting to historians (see CAVALLO & PITARELLI for a concise review of theory relating to probabilistic databases). Numerical approaches are less reliant on deduction, but instead employ inference derived from classical statistics. PARSONS (p. 364) notes that the relatively recent development of Bayesian belief networks has won wider acceptance of quantification methods by the IA community. PEARL's work remains the benchmark reference for belief networks, which may be updated by LAURITZEN & SPIEGELHALTER. Networks tend to be correct for a given point in time and ordinarily do not accommodate changes very well, so that recently attention has been turned toward dynamic models which require interactive and dynamic construction and maintenance.

All of these approaches pertain to historical modeling and reconstruction using imperfect information. Historians have dealt with some of these issues, but in terms different from the data engineering community and with their attention riveted on specific problems rather than the aforementioned broad issues which encompass them. Moreover, it is difficult to find database construction and AI theory expressly linked to practice in History, or when historical reasoning is applied in expert and decision support systems, to have it recognized as such.

Whereas knowledge engineering once was directed solely toward building large databases that would be searched mainly for information already somewhat known when the data were assembled (at least some relevant information retrieval was anticipated and latent patterns were expected) more recent work focuses on retrieval methodology for large heterogeneous networks or warehouses of different databases. This switches the focus on the data and on the structure of a particular database, to the strategy, method, and flexibility of inquiry which uses fuzzy logic. A possibility is the development of a metabase from data retrieved from original databases; this artificial database, built by selective processes, can yield results not as easily obtained from the originals. Moreover, it can be manipulated without damage to the original data or database structures. Once removed from the original, it may be more abstract, but thereby more pliable. This is the idea behind OLAP applied to data warehouses. For example, missing data can be supplied from inference, probability theory can be applied to clear up ambiguity, and data can be transformed into a variety of structures, without contamination of an original set. Add to these possibilities an interrogation that can be designed like a series of queries, with varying degrees of vagueness or precision, inclusiveness or exclusion, or a synonymy to increase the richness of the vocabulary in these searches to match the wealth of terms found is some textbases. A variety of kinds of queries are now recognized: classification, characterization, association, and clustering (for the latter see ANDERBERG; RASMUSSEN [1992]; VAN RIJSBERGEN and others). Sometimes these approaches are all lumped together under the general rubric "data mining," or "harvesting," or into a contrived "discipline" called by some "Knowledge Discovery in Databases," or KDD (see the circle of FAYYAD, PIATET-SKY-SHAPIRO, SMYTH & UTHURUSAMY; FRAWLEY, PIATETSKY-SHAPIRO & MATHEUS; MATHEUS, CHAN & PIATETSKY-SHAPIRO).

The movement toward such flexible information retrieval dates to 1982 with PAWLAK's "rough set theory" (cf., PAWLAK, 1982; 1992). Whereas fuzziness refers to uncertainties in natural language, rough sets are related to categorical structures of knowledge used in information retrieval. The two are often used together. Rough set theory now enjoys considerable vogue among data miners and is used in combination with decision support systems (e.g., SLOWINSKI) to classify relations and identify dependencies (recently [1998] explored by special issues of *JASIS*, ed. by RAGHAVAN, DEOGUN & SEVER: therein BELL & GUAN use decision tables; LINGRAS & YAO rely on equivalence relations; CHOUBEY *ET AL.* use feature selection to amplify PAWLAK's approach to query classification; and WU uses a heuristic, attribute-based program called HCV [version 2] with its induction algorithm rather than decision trees to discriminate sets and subsets of variable values). Another *JASIS* special issue in 1998, edited by BORDOGNA & PASI, explores the management of uncertainty and imprecision through clustering, rough sets, and fuzziness in information retrieval.

No problem of imperfect information has occupied the attention of quantification historians like naming and classification, that is, nominal linkage. Historians, however, have tackled this issue largely without recourse to IS literature and independently without assistance from either the DBMS or the AI communities where similar problems have long been discussed as "term association" in information retrieval (DOYLE; LESK, 1969; STILES) using associative logic (COURTIAL & POMIAN). Naming has received considerable in-depth attention in Information Science as a matter of linkage and reference (i.e., Onomasiology, often related to Psycholinguistics; cf., J. CARROLL; MOROT; J. MACNAMARA), in ways that would benefit historians in tackling their particular problems (cf., KRIPKE; A. W. MOORE; J. F. ROSEN-BERG). G. W. FITCH relates naming with believing, since it captures an identity and is the embodiment of personality, character, and ideas. The assumption is that if someone or something is properly named and he, she, or it is retrieved, one gets what is expected. The retrieval itself is initiated because of belief vested in a name, naming conventions, and that names are permanent, religious and legal attributes. This is what underpins the stability in nomenclatures over time. Otherwise chaos reigns, socially, intellectually, and in all information retrieval by names.

Term ambiguity in textbases and indexing are problems for which solutions have been addressed, but the primary focus of historians has been on people identification that they have not associated naming with the broader issues of terminology any more than they put addresses together with classification theory. They have therefore ignored relevant research in Information Science, just as information scientists have ignored records linkage work in historical computing because the problem is not recognized as one of relational indexing and term disambiguation. The historical vocabulary problem is not substantially different from the modern one discussed so much in Information Science as this relates to information storage and retrieval. Moreover, the historical and modern problems are related in that the retrieval of historical information often depends on modern usage for search keys linked to terms used in the past differently, with different meaning, connotation, and context, and different orthography.

The problems highlighted by Terrence Brooks for online information retrieval—"word conundrums" as he calls them—are truly seditious in foiling the best intentioned information retrieval from texts, historical or modern (T. BROOKS [1998]). These include differentiation between words and tokens in indexing or retrieval schema; simple normalization such as upper and lower cases; single word and multi-word phrases (or in relation to naming, particularly first, middle, last name, baptismal and confirmation names, official versus used names, etc.); and what most think of as basic punctuation (cf., G. NUNBERG; and C. MEYER for American English practices and idiosyncracies), e.g., a consistent working definition of what constitutes a sentence, and if a period really is a stop function (i.e., stop-lists for "reading" electronic text: BRUTHIAUX; C. FOX). T. BROOKS points to other problems and pertinent literature for solutions: the understanding of acronyms, hyphenated words, and inverted phrases using commas or varied punctuation; the troublesome apostrophe (G. LITTLE; SKLAR) and hyphen (MCINTOSH) in any case; normalization between "white space" and lexemes, which are varied and irregular spacing between words and phrases—really a problem for medievalists working with unspaced running text or punctuation before standards were widely achieved; correcting or ameliorating unwanted consequences of normalization; linking normalized texts where the norms vary (a flagrant example, use of colons, semi-colons, etc., in titles; cf., DILLON for the colon and its overuse); the especially difficult problem of translating spoken language into normalized text or retrieval using norms for retrieval of verbatim language like transcripts which is not normalized; the difference between the interpretation of spaces by humans reading a text and a computer parsing it (HINDLE); and filing order and consistency in pre-computer ordering. The orthographic challenges to information retrieval from unconstrained text are becoming really apparent for information scientists in the development of Internet archives. Archivists have been aware of the problems for some time, but have not developed any scientific means to confront the challenge of free text. Computing historians have focused on normalization and nominal linkage in historical data sources, as in lists, inventories, registers, etc., where some normalization was already imposed on entry, but they have not until recently widened their focus to historical full-text work.

Although historians may use gazetteers for place-names, there is little to indicate that historians resort to official toponomies such as the thesauri developed by the United States Board on Geographic Names partially to assist in mapping and the kind of total disambiguation of place names required which of defense systems (e.g., United States Defense Mapping System). Personal and place names can be problematic enough, but they are part of a larger issue. The intellectual problem of ambiguous keywords is that defined by FURNAS *ET AL.* in 1987; they fail in discriminating semantic content. Consequently document retrieval through indexing riddled with the problems of polysomy (when a number of concepts can be indexed by a single term) and synonymy (when a number of terms can index a single concept) is plagued with performance problems, similar to faulty information retrieval from historical data sets were nominal linkage is similarly flawed, i.e., where one name can indicate several people (i.e., polysomy), and where the same people have used multiple names as they move about, marry, divorce, etc. (synonymy). Information scientists have tended to resolve these problems by several approaches that avoid simple reliance on term matching (according to the classification and examples used by BARTRELL *ET AL.*):

1. The building of thesauri automatically or manually and modifying these with semantically similar terms (SALTON & LESK in the early 1970s; cf., WANG, VANDEN-DORPE & EVENS in the mid-1980s; and P. NELSON reporting for the 1990s), just like a historian might build a directory to check confirmed identifications and expand upon relations as family memberships are discovered.

2. Automatic term disambiguation into term senses (MCDONALD *ET AL.*; VORHEES), which is a technique also employed by computing historians as when applying occupational coding. The method common in Information Science of positing vectors of multi-dimensional semantic space and classifying documents (treated simply as term banks) into them, so that semantic relatedness is determined by location and hence similarities within vectors (SALTON, 1983), seems unexplored by computing historians.

3. Augmentation of terms with explicit associations (BELEW; KWOK), which historians do with people when documents such as marriage certificates record such associations, so that birth, medical, marriage, and tax records may all be linked to expand searches and create a dynamic architecture in a database.

4. Newer approaches using relevance feedback information, such as ranking and weighting, in attempts to identify the interests of the inquirer (HARMAN; SALTON & BUCKLEY), which have been used only in a few institutional historical computing projects such as by PASLEAU and her colleagues at Liège, but which seem not to be employed in individual research projects.

One problem with the methods commonly adopted from SALTON's pioneering research is that only documents which share terms are considered semantically related, but in these cases co-occurrence constrains how a retrieval system is able to estimate relatedness between texts. So, an array of more advanced methods have evolved to cope with this problem (e.g., automatic document classification; concept mapping, latent semantic indexing, and metric similarity modeling). They attempt to represent documents in a multi-dimensional space so that two vectors may be similar even if they do not share terms. Hence they predict semantic associations more than those implied by simple term co-occurrence. It is this area of document representation, term expansion to semantic similarities, and advanced modeling, which historians need to explore as means of information retrieval from their imperfect databases.

History databases are, thus, often weaker in design and multifunctionality for research because they are customized for the project for which the data were culled and normalized, they are constrained by traditional sets, and the reflexive relationships between the concrete and general are not always as reciprocal in data processing as they should be for multipurpose analysis. Often data are normalized in the building of a database to enable information retrieval through preordained methods (as in library cataloging producing a clean master record whereby original data may be edited based on external conventions, or in precoordinated indexing), whereas source-oriented databases attempt to leave data in original form, even if dirty and "obviously" inconsistent at first glance, so that the variations themselves can be used (for example, evolution of variant to normalized orthographies in standardizing naming conventions). Like postcoordinate indexing, data extraction methods in such source-oriented databases would rely on normalized metadata that leave the original in tact. Just as the significance of the individual is amplified by the many in an array of social data, and the macroscopic and microscopic must be understood together (GAGAN), there is a social history of things that grows out of nominal linkage with each other and to makers, conveyers, and owners.

Naming is an intellectual function (J. M. CARROLL; G. W. FITCH; MACNAMARA) that becomes all too obvious when one engages nominal linkage in vast amounts of data, and when this linkage combines personal names to places, objects, and texts, and especially when links are forged to concepts. MOROT related naming, indicating, and perceiving with reference which can be problematic when naming is done poorly. FURNAS (1982) in probing the methodology of historical semantics for automatic thesaurus construction asked, "How can a computer use what people name things to guess what things people mean when they name things?" PRUDOVSKY questions the propriety of ascribing ideas, developments, etc., which are named later to those who preceded the mature development when those who may be antecedents are not progenitors because they lacked the linguistic means to express themselves as later convention would. This is always a problem in classification and linkage in terminologies that link archaic terms with modern ones for the sake of information retrieval or for data analysis. It is the old philosophical conundrum in studying the origin of things and ideas of whether someone could have a thought without the accompanying linguistic means to express it, or is something what we call it before it is so named. Or, when naming something dynamic like a process or something constantly changing, the name seems to make it static. Thus life is divided into stages, so one must distinguish recognize that "boy" and "man" are both male, but they are yet not the same. Nevertheless, the boy may envision himself as a man before coming of age, which is set by puberty and social convention; his designation as boy, man, or simply male locks him into history. How does naming and reference in an information system retrieve the whole dynamic being, its past, present, and future?

Historians, however, have been largely preoccupied with simpler questions than concept linkage, and term association rather than with identification of people in history and disambiguation of nominal data. Among the identification methods used to link personal names are algorithms designed in European data archives by G. GUTH, J. OLDERVOLL, and U. PORTMANN (see a comparison of methods by BRON & OLSEN), but other approaches include hypertext linkage (L. HUGHES), masking variants to collate by roots, searching on sequential consonants in names or using truncation for full-name collation similar to OCLC searching. THALLER (1987, p. 151) observes that this problem of nominal record linkage gets the most attention in Social Science History methodological literature (BASKERVILLE *ET AL.*) and quantification textbooks (WINCHESTER), but it deserves it least because so many solutions exist. RUUSALEPP more recently resurrected this issue because he wants more interactive linking of records than older tagging practices. He is working on a method to link data clusters as well as discrete data, to record confidence levels for links, and to maintain decision logs for long-term projects. The idea is to objectify linkage, minimize bias, and resort to automatic reconstitution which also minimizes inconsistencies.

Such current work on automatic tagging and linkage seems to be similar but unfortunately unrelated to ongoing automatic indexing research and approaches to vocabulary control (CHAMIS). Historians have seen their work as unique, but the uniqueness lies in code rule generation and codebook design to control tagging, not in the routine execution of tagging and coding. They have not turned to external assistance in their database development work, partially because of this misconception, and partially for lack of funding. So they devalue their own labor by moving from design into production. This underscores again the need for project management in historian training. If not automatic, manual operations more efficient than in small graduate student sweatshops are now readily available. Commercial firms like Access Innovations, Inc., which has been in the database production business since 1978, offer a full range of records conversion, tagging, coding and indexing services. In 1996, this firm alone tagged more than a million pages of technical documents for intranet access (with the guarantee of "99.95 percent accuracy"!). In 1997, it started seeking Encoded Archival Description (EAD) contracts to expand its SGML/HTML markup work. Several monastic communities have also sought out-sourced contracts in database development, Web homepage design, retrospective conversion, documenting encoding, and translation services. The Cistercians and Trappists have thus completed such work arranged through an external agent, producing a new kind of Scriptorium, Inc., during this decade. In essence, all legacy data capture and conversion efforts are historical enterprises and have more in common than is commonly recognized with Dom David Knowles' *Great Historical Enterprises* of the Maurists and Bollandists (KNOWLES). Or, conversely, the great *Acta Sanctorum* in this sense was in response to a data imperfection problem and was a process of historical data clean-up and normalization of history.

In some cases, normalization occurs in data entry, similar to data cleaning practices in data warehousing, although this is often directed simply at reduced data duplication; both result in storage of data which are altered for the sake of retrieval. Some historians, for example, have resorted to *SOUNDEX* for data entry, whereby a normalization occurs automatically in translating sound to characters by prescribed procedures or algorithms rather than a phonetic code (which means that its implementation must be adjusted for the phonetic character of each language used and especially for culturally distinctive patronymics). In some cases, such as at the University of Tromso in Norway, a speech generator has been used to read transcriptions while they are being proofread. Such approaches approximate library solutions which suppress variant data by subjecting entries to authority control; this produces results not always well suited to historical research or archival information control (M. EVANS) if main entry access is the only means provided. Historians need the collocation benefit of authority control in searching and merging files, but they must be able to desegregate such files at will to reclassify subsets and analyze the very variables that such editorial alteration would destroy. Moreover, historians speak about "record linkage" because nominal data are the primary means of such collocation just as personal names are used in cataloging to collate publications by author, but historians are actually referring to linking content data of records rather than the records themselves and their usage is closer to that in indexing than cataloging. The problems are related, methodologies are similar, but the fields learn little from each other.

The whole field of History could use the kind of program developed by the Getty Trust Art History Information Program (AHIP) for improvement of communication among art historians who talk about the same artists under a variety of names: *Synoname* is a term-matching software using twelve routines from the simple to the complex (i.e., character omission and substitution to word approximation) that links variable usage with name authority control. Voice input could benefit from the same kind of computer-assisted correctional programs as spell-checkers for text processing, and both mechanisms can be customized to save and collate variants rather than destroy them. Historians need to couple voice input with text correctional software applied to their problem of conversion of historical records to machine-readable form. Interesting possibilities exist in machine-translation programs and CAI systems for instructional assistance as in the case of Y. LEE's *Ill-Formed Input Handling System (IFIHS)* developed in 1990 for understanding ill-formed natural language input from first-year medical students whose mistakes required a XEROX 1108 AI machine using *Interlisp-D* language with a spell-checker, parser, and an "understander" to edit a final product.

All of this can be related to data acquisition in Information Science and to the controversial issues surrounding data transformation in transfers from one format to another. A case in point for the problematic input of historical data into numeric and textual files is the considerable attention paid to coding occupations in labor history databases (SCHURER & DIEDERICKS) for socioeconomic and political research (M. B. KATZ). Here terminological and classification problems in thesaurus construction abound because activities known now by one name were not called that when they began, nomenclatures change over time and differ by language and regional dialect, natural colloquialisms and more artificial technical vocabularies require correspondence that may have been more implicit than explicit in sources, and the aforementioned nominal data problems in orthography and syntax pertain to all census rolls, poll books, registers, and job lists (BLUMIN; MORRIS, 1990, 1993; NAULT & DESJARDINS; SCHURER, 1990). Indexing strategies are being adopted in complex databases, as in the case of NERI & TRAVASONI's use of *Calliope* software, but WEUSTEN warns against disadvantages of using overly extensive thesauri for linkage. Early classification schedules by historians were quite elaborate (SCHURER & DIEDERIKS point to DAUMAND & FURET's relationship structure for eighteenth-century Parisian professions, as an example of such schema), but were usually *vade mecums* for specific book projects and were never generalizable enough to be used as tools in the information field even though they have been widely imitated in other works. Consider, for example, the evolution of the so-called BOOTH-ARMSTRONG system (MORRIS, 1990, p. 18), or the elaboration of simple schemes into more mature classification schedules for professions and occupations used in socioeconomic, labor, and demographic history (BOUCHARD, 1985a). These act as historical thesauri but usually are not called such by historians nor have their inventors formally studied indexing and thesaurus construction and indexing.

Such skills were learned on the project, seldom beforehand, and the consequently each taxonomy, classification format, and terminology tends to be idiosyncratic. This made integration and revision difficult, and often one project's work has been simply adopted for another, so terminological work has not always seemed really to mature as its use spreads. Problems of consistency and congruence abound, and normalization often creates unilateral rather than multidimensional links. Moreover, most code sheets lack the taxonomies for flexible classification and easy revision, the kind of subordination of terms and clustering reflected in the *Art & Architecture Thesaurus* for professions, or effective connections to related subject thesauri. Moreover, they are seldom collated with modern rubrics or *vice versa*, so there is little congruence between general terminology in historians' works or their book indexes, even when focused on special topics, and formal search terms from special purpose vocabularies employed in modern information retrieval. This limits transferability to other projects without necessarily dictating similar research methodologies. None of these nominal linkage systems are automatic or approach the expert systems design in, for example, the aforementioned prototype of AHIP's *Synoname* for artists, terminological matching used in machine translation or lexicology, or in medical information systems. The work of AHIP in this area of terminological control should be looked upon as a model, adopted and expanded. Increasingly, database developers are aware of terminological editing problems from past experience and on selections of solutions before embarking on data entry. BREURE (1995), for example, has investigated *Altis* as a model-based approach to flexible historical data entry; ERLACH & REISEN-LEITNER advocate a relational approach to linking genealogical, family, or other forms of social bonding without relying on standardization of nomenclature. MARKER has likewise found ways to enter data from sources with attention to the integrity of original forms and still be able to provide linkage between variants in his database design.

Nevertheless, the potential contribution of the extensive Library and Information Science literature about classification, indexing and thesaurus construction is an important perspective absent, for example, from MANDEMAKERS' discussion of classification and scaling, but he does relate (pp. 42-44) historical schedules with modern tools such as the *International Standard Classification of Occupations (ISCO)* related by H. Fenijn (unpublished reports) between the Historical Sample of the Population of the Netherlands with the 1984 Beroepen classification. The *EUROCIT* (European City histories) project may have enough collaboration to produce more formal European instruments (e.g., the Leicester University Centre for Urban History's *English Small Town Project* described by P. CLARK), and indeed, S. ANDERSON (1993) of the Cambridge Group for the History of Population and Social Structure has suggested thesaurus construction to assist with the terminological problems in coding occupational data. A prototype exists in the work of T. DURR and P. ROSENBERG from 1977 at BRISC, which given such current discussions seems to have been way ahead of its time. The Italian National Research Council's Instituto per la Documentazione Giuridica is already implementing a thesaurus of law terms that will affect legal history (CAMMELLI & PARENTI) and because of such terminological standardization, this field is rapidly implementing expert systems to aid research (HARDY) beyond its advanced bibliographic services. The precoordinated structure advocated by P. DOORN (1993, pp. 84-85) for the Social, Demographic, and Economic Groups (SODEC) concept may provide the needed bridge between the historical and modern. The proceedings of the Cambridge discussion fora, however, show little awareness of applicable terminological work already accomplished (e.g., BUDIN; DURR & ROSENBERG; NEDOBITY; RIGGS; GETTY TRUST AHIP, 1992; etc.) or the considerable Information Science literature on this topic.

New tools are sure to be built (hopefully not in a vacuum by historians, who claim heightened sensitivity to contextualization), but with what connection to existing tools it is difficult to say. On the other hand, most modern thesauri are designed with so little historical consciousness that it is perhaps unfair to chide historians for not being mindful of modern information thesauri. Most thesauri link synonyms in contemporary usage, whereas historians need linkage with archaic terms, translated equivalents, and contextually sensitive cultural terms as well. DIEDERIKS & TJALSMA (p. 30) remind us that coding data as a fundamental activity of research, "has been in existence much longer than making data machine-readable and allocating them a code." They miss the point, however, that mere coding is not necessarily classification, and that the latter is an intellectual task now easily automated, and has become a very sophisticated aspect of information storage and retrieval. Classified terminologies combine indexing and classification for information storage and retrieval. An example of classified tagging which could be used by historians in business and socioeconomic history are the United States Department of Commerce's Standard Industrial Code (SIC) tags that could be used to link products with occupations. Moreover, one has ready-made databases and decision support tools in such software packages as *Marketplace* to be used with Dunn and Bradstreet's business database of businesses in the United States (cf., *American Business Directory*, *Hoover Directory*, etc. all on CD-ROMs). One can use this standard reference tool for marketing to introduce students to occupational coding and product classification, and such operations as query design, creation of data sets, and basic analysis, which includes random sampling techniques. One could expand the SIC tags for historical antecedents, parallels and synonyms, to build a classified historical thesaurus and expanded tags to relate historical and modern terminology rather than to build occupational codes from scratch or which are so customized to individual projects that they cannot be used to integrate diverse projects and relate them to modern circumstances. Moreover, few devices contrived by historians for their individual projects measure up to international standards, have the flexibility of faceted classification in such systems as *PRECIS,* or contain the relationships built into thesauri hierarchies as exemplified by the *Art & Architecture Thesaurus.*

Socioeconomic history database development as in labor history (e.g., KOVAL'CHENKO, BOVYKIN & LAGRANZH's statistical work on strikes and lockouts in Russia) and social mobility studies (e.g., R. SIMMONS; combined with gender studies, e.g., T. SNYDER; LINDSEY, etc.), which combine data from census returns with that gleaned from immigration questionnaires, industry personnel files, land records and wills are replete with ambiguity and quality control problems which multiply and become more complex as one goes back in time. Modern records are more numerous, but the same kinds of problems appear throughout a series; the problem may have more instances of occurrence without necessarily changing its fundamental nature or complexity. Many of these problems are treated by IGARTUA (1987) in his studies about aluminum workers in Quebec. The increased size of a database does justify turning to computerization for resolution of identification and classification problems. Detail, seemingly down to the level of trivia, can add up for significant findings. Social data are often imperfect in some way, and historical data are also usually incomplete.

Two areas of current endeavor supporting a Historical Information Science are theoretical approaches to such fuzzy data (BORODKIN *ET AL.*; CANDLIN & MORGAN), linking non-quantitative approaches to modeling (TIKHONOV), and ambiguous or vague sources (requiring "thinking ambiguously" when making information retrieval work to provide unambiguous answers: BUSCH, 1994). A new twist on the old problem of relativity is what C. GORDON (1991) has called "variable truth," and the congruence between a historical entity and modern equivalency by which to make sense of it. Indeed, modeling involves speculation, hopefully sound, and such exploration of virgin data and unchartered theoretical territory requires the adoption or creation of software that is particularly appropriate for handling large amounts of such data through associative logic and clustering, pattern recognition, path prediction, and temporal reasoning. An extremely interesting example by GRIBAUDI (1987) of spatial reasoning employed in the study of social systems and stratification research, which incorporates both quantification methods such as clustering and association (from data provided in marriage registers) and structural linguistics centers on the formation of the Italian working class (see also the methodological discussion by GRIBAUDI, 1993). This social history emphasis on everyday living and the common man is also exemplified in the work of LASZLOVSZKY (1991) who has tied such social stratification to material culture studies in medieval Hungary. Josef Laszlovsky's work provides an interesting model in computerized research linking archeology, anthropology, and socioeconomic history.

This inter-disciplinary approach is typical of the "Everyday Life" motif in medieval and early modern studies, which concerns itself with much the same foci as in modern social, labor, and urban history reflected in five sessions on the history of social mobility at the 1994 AHC conference *Structures and Contingencies in Computerized Historical Research* in Nijmegen (BOONSTRA *ET AL.*). There the speakers, the majority from the former Soviet Union, were all concerned with structures, strata, patterns, classifications, dimensions of space and time, and models for historical interpretation of elites and gentries, the peasants and the disenfranchised, women workers and other laborers. All sought to discern the "dynamics" of people's movement in certain locales and periods of history as explanation for larger questions. Such work, judging from the 1996 Moscow AHC conference, continues unabated (cf. BOKAREV; GREBENICHENKO; SOKOLOV *ET AL.*, etc.) and they are spreading such work to the United States through immigration and appointments in American graduate schools (e.g., Vladimir TREML; SZYRMER) and through cross-border collaboration (e.g., HOCH *ET AL.*; and efforts by myself and Leonid Borodkin to publish a set of essays from the former Soviet Union displaying the current prowess of this school of quantification historians in historical computing such as BORODKIN *ET AL.*).

While social studies can be vertically oriented along lines of class structure and mobility trends in one place over time, others look for patterns at the same time over a wider geographic domain. Trend and pattern analyses are similar in methodology but use chronology and geography interchangeably. A fascination with latent or unrecognizable patterns is understandable because bringing them into view is a certain kind of discovery with its own inherent satisfaction. At the 1994 Nijmegen AHC conference (BOONSTRA *ET AL.*, 1995) one theme addressed new methods for "Uncovering Structures" (e.g., BELOVA). At ACH IX, José Igartua spoke of "uncovering patterns of sociability" in studying residences in a Canadian company town, Arvida (IGARTUA, 1993, 1995). T. MOISEENKO turned to multi-dimensional data analysis to discern "hidden structures" while BORODKIN & SVISCHOV used Marchov chains in simulations of social mobility in the early Soviet Union of the 1920s. Cluster analysis (CRAVEN; EVERITT; JAMBU) is another approach used to visualize similarities and differences (e.g., DARU), to find groups in data (ROMESBURG; KAUFMAN & ROUSSEEUW), to compare and contrast in multi-dimensional scaling. R. TRYON used cluster analysis very early (1955) to study social grouping in the San Francisco Bay area. Variations of such methodologies continue to be applied today. Correspondence analysis was used by H. BEST (1994) to discern not so much geographic migration as upward social mobility, i.e., climbing the political ladder, to see if German politicians kept their friends from student days as later political allies. If a cluster or group were already known, then reverse approaches are used such as discriminate function analysis, which requires highly stable and normal variables, and logistic regression, which uses the group or classification as a dependent variable. I. BRODER and A. J. LICHTMAN did an excellent job in making sense out of regression analysis for historical reconstruction. But the rigorous statistical analyses of series with regression techniques that are particularly historical (as explained by BEVERDIGE & SWEETING) is not all that common even though its application has been demonstrated successfully by several historians such as F. GOUDA & P. H. SMITH's combination of demographic data with multi-variables—in their case, gender, crime fluctuation, and periods of famine in nineteenth-century France.

Of course, the idea of cause and structure is a highly controversial issue in data analysis (PEARL; SPIRTES, GLYMOUR & SCHEINES) often related to probabilistic reasoning (PEARL, 1988). BUNTINE offers a recent guide through the voluminous statistical and computing literature. FREUDER & MACKWORTH explore automated reasoning in AI research as "constraint-based reasoning," including: design, planning and scheduling; temporal and spatial reasoning (J. BERRY; S. CHENG); defeasible and causal reasoning; machine vision and language understanding; qualitative and diagnostic reasoning; and expert systems. SHAFER particularly elucidates "causal conjecture" as a field of probability statistics and notes that the various disciplines that use causal reasoning vary in their relative weighting of the security and precision of knowledge as opposed to timeliness of action. The Social Sciences, which he sees as different from practical science such as engineering, business and medicine, which deal with limited knowledge, seek a high level of certainty for causes and expect high levels of precision in the measurement of their effects. He articulates a careful language for causal explanation. However, much of the debate among historians is more philosophically than methodologically oriented, and its language is anything but controlled. The two disciplinary environments in which causality is considered (excluding the "hard" sciences) cannot be disassociated, but historians often discuss the nature of history less in terms of abstract method than through case studies, and their vocabulary tends to conform to the subject discourse encapsulating a theoretical discussion. Their reasoning about cause and effect, therefore, is often less than explicit and without clarification of meaning and precision in language usage; they are ill-prepared to apply causal reasoning in computing.

Considerable historiographic debate has been engendered about causation, for example, in terms of historical agency, meaning who or what causes something and with what power, from what source, and to what effect. RIGBY notes that historians sometimes argue about the establishment of a hierarchy of causes to isolate the primary cause of historical events. He rejects this because of the interdependence of events, and uses Marxist "historical materialism" as a case study to illustrate his point that complex phenomena cannot be explained so simply. He reflects the linear thinking of many historians about cause and effect, and thinks of classification merely as ranking into single scales. He is right because such thinking is too simplistic to deal with more complicated historical phenomena. W. H. DRAY (1995) explored historians' concepts of causation, and A. GIDDENS offered a theory of structuration to cast in the role of agent a line of development greater than a single person. British social anthropology in a complementary way had also stressed functionalism (STOCKING, ed.). C. LLOYD says that historians in practice tacitly seem to accept the structuration theory in some form, but this does not produce consensus among historians about an individual's agency power or lack thereof (cf, ORLIKOWSKI's application in organizational studies).

POMPER investigates such discussions around two powerful agents who are seen to have changed the course of history significantly, Hitler and Stalin. He notes the interest, perhaps influenced by Soviet historiography and its inclination to find a physical basis for historical explanation in genetics or the strand of historiography that concentrates on the collective to explain everything, including individuals who stand out from the general background of human history. The debate over agency and causation tends to see such powerful figures either as agents acting on their own will to change history, or as acting out a role charted by larger forces in history. Pomper points to works by A. J. P. Taylor and Isaac Deutscher, and an interesting inclusion, the Getty's exhibit designers, to show how some historians reduce or nullify agential power. It is in rare cases, however, that such discussion is brought down to methodological issues as dissected and clear as in computer literature in the AI field. Many of the issues are similar, but approaches, assumptions, frameworks, and vocabularies are very different. It is easily understood that correlations, like circumstances, do not necessarily translate into cause and effect relationships. The relationship of cause and effect itself is not that clear.

Although most applications are in forecasting (data history pattern recognition, e.g., AL-JABRI) rather than in studies of historical trends, time-series or event history analysis by multiple regression techniques would seem to have special appeal to historians who appreciate long-term social change (MAYER & AMEY; ALLISON; ANDRESS) and use chronology and timespans as basic concepts (i.e., BOSWELL for colonization patterns; KLEMM for agrarian history with the interplay of weather and crop failure or plenty). Historians tend to be hyper-critical of hypothetical means to fill in gaps in a series or other kinds of structured historical data where lacunae from missing documentation (i.e., occasional rather than serial lists, e.g., registers, probate records, tax roles, price lists, inventories, manifests, etc.) are filled in by expert systems drawing conclusions deductively and inductively by inference from the series that is intact or the data accumulated from actual evidence. Two methods of "machine learning" exist: explanation-based and similarity-based learning, which can be used in an integrated fashion for building databases and converting discontinuous files into continuous series (DANYLUK). Inferred data, as distinct from actualized data, can be identified in graphing, etc., as well as a time series is graphed linearly and the years for which no data are available can be filled in according to pre-gap and post-gap patterns.

While advanced technology has been used to analyze series, little evidence exists to indicate that historians have used such techniques in building or enhancing their files. Older practices in such quantification methods are just beginning to change as new tools are adopted (BURTON & FINNEGAN, 1989; STIER). In her study of property ownership and land survey records, however, L. FOX recently explored the criteria and design of information systems which would produce time lines, noting the utility of such databases for genealogical and demographic, sociological and anthropological, folklore and even local religious research and special research and instruction, but she also stressed the use of such tools by abstract companies, attorneys, realtors, and mineral and petroleum companies. KNOERL advocates "mapping history" using GIS technology. BERTINO discusses data mapping and simulation techniques for analyzing and illustrating dynamic relief population shifts and movements, i.e., large and small demographic changes. DRAKE's use of a parcel-based Geographic Information System, as an example of such practical utility, applies land use history in environmental science. GIS applications are also now common in archeology in combination with geography (LOCK & STANCIC, eds.; MASCHNER, ed.) and CAD rendering (e.g., GIL). See MOELLERING (1987) for references to digital cartographic data standards and the work of the Numerical Cartography Laboratory at Ohio State University.

Russian demographic history is flourishing (ARSENTIEV; ROWNEY, etc.), and a special project on Russian population history (1700-1917) has been mounted at Tambov (HOCH *ET AL.*; KANUISHTECHEV & PROTASOV). This cross-sectional approach to regional studies might be compared with a longitudinal study of one site as in the case of J. RAINEY's study of the English entrenchment at Calais in the fifteenth century, or a centralized corporation encompassing multiple sites in a locale as by J. NEWMAN who studied the Wadsworth estate in New York's Genesee Valley during a latter era. In other cases, historians want to overlay a static geographic map with dynamic mapping of social migration (WATTEL & VAN REENEN). This mapping of social relationships and overlay on cartographic maps to illustrate spatial relationships is explored by FYFE & LAW, although this technique must be used wisely. As noted before, proximity does not always show cause and relationships, such as a familial tie that is in name only, a one-time business deal rather than continued but intermittent transactions that are difficult to detect, or attenuated transactions that are often not used as parallel series do not depict effective social conduits of emotion or power. Sometimes a connection maps possibilities and potential alliances rather than actual ones. The historian cannot transfer to mapping the intangible and nonphysical the same stability implied by the Western concept of land mapping. Such mapping techniques are not, therefore, so straight forward as might be assumed initially. When applied to tribal and nomadic societies favoring communal properties, associations via tangibles needed for linkage of interstices on a matrix resulting in socioeconomic mapping are clusters rather than individuals and the dynamics may be quite different than for individuals and small familial groups. In such cases, even geographic boundaries are fuzzy; borders become borderlands and frontiers, rather than surveyed lines and fenced properties.

In such cases it is useful to be able to relate such fuzzy geographic data to contour maps so that one can infer more precise boundaries in historical geography from natural geography. It is possible thereby for historians to reconstruct old flood plains and dried lakes, travel routes and river crossings, navigable sections of rivers whose character has been changed by engineering, and ports that are now inland or are under water today; and even to use simulation to indicate seasonal and periodic changes. However, mapping the activities of larger social units often allows large-scale comparison with natural geographies which cannot be done satisfactorily when action is limited to one locale unless one reduces scale to the minute, as when linking households and neighborhoods in urban social history because one has street maps and addresses. Longitudes and latitudes are often being incorporated into directory databases today precisely so they can be linked to GIS (e.g., Dunn and Bradstreet's *Marketplace* or the *American Business Directory* linked to city maps for directions). Location coordinates can be inserted to historical databases for similar linkage and visual collation of an underlying historical landscape or cityscape with the modern scene. PICKLES and his group therefore examine the social implications of GIS today and in the study of the past as well, qualifying the assumption that maps actually convey always what is purported to be "Ground truth." Maps, the possession of them, their interpretation, and the assumption that one knows where one is in time and space, are tools of control as noted by HARLEY (1988) and others. This is the same notion as the power of information. Thus, like legal instruments and written documents, maps act as codifiers of information. Their spatial visualizations and representations have been subjected to the same deconstructive criticism as texts (HARLEY, 1992).

LIND explores historical concepts of space when working with computer-based maps which may be reconstructed not to show modern depiction and projections but rather historical and regional projections which represent world views much different from our own. Indeed, recent argument over Euro-centric projections in mapping (i.e., Mercator projection) reflect the continued interplay between subjective and objective mapping which can contrast conceptions of space and geography based on human perspective with those mathematically modeled which are in fact never actually perceived except in models. BOZZI & SAPUPPO link visualization in "word-images" to mapping by linking geographic description in historical lexicons with place-names, locations, and later mathematical models to illustrate the difference between perspectives from specific points of observation and world views particular to certain regions and times with standardized maps, dominant projections, and scientific geographic mapping. For example, the assumption that early explorers and travelers labored under the same viewpoints and mental models as we do when consulting modern maps can bring great distortion into historical interpretation. So, at times, it is preferable to project locations, place-names, and scales onto historic maps to reproduce historic perceptions that for the time constituted spatial reality for a people. Such reconstructive approaches both use historic maps and surveys and land records similarly, but they start from different premises with orientations in the first case that is prosopographic; in the second, geographic; and the latter two, combinations. François Furet and Pierre Chaunu advocated that historians construct such chronologs or time series as the basis for linear analysis, as outlined by LUNDGREEN, and for a continuous story line in narrative (FURET; CHAUNU, 1964). The series, of course, is an intellectual tool also basic to archives methodology, but it has not therein come under similar scrutiny. In the latter case, where transactions and functions rather than records themselves are the key to effective indexing, actions in series become processes which are governed by policies; so, action or event analysis is crucial to archival information systems design. Acts and events in series or some data structure constitutes what has been called "indexical" as distinct from "objective knowledge" (LESPER-ANCE, or the degree of "indexicality" is important: BUCKLAND, 1997).

In other cases, spatial relationships need to be studied for themselves, since they reveal patterns of space in time that are too often ignored in historical, archeological, and anthropological research. Cultural and physical boundaries are not always the same, and reference points and relations between sites often vary by direction depending upon or independent from natural geography (e.g., in facing churches East toward the rising sun, placing monasteries on mountain tops, or other layouts and situations where belief factors override natural terrain dictates). In this aspect of unpredictability and unrecognizable inherent patterns, historical geographic and intellectual, cognitive, and information mapping require techniques more flexible than reliance on sight, simple unilateral relations, or two-dimensional thinking (MAGUIRE, GOODCHILD & RHIND). Spatial relations in maps and pictures share similar properties and in both cases direction and topology can be used to draw inference about what would appear to be very different subject matter (SHARMA & FLEWELLING). See, for example, COBB & PETRY who use a fuzzy framework based on J. F. ALLEN's temporal intervals (1983) and direction sets to model spatial relationships such as disjointed proximity, tangent closeness, overlaps, and containment (cf., GUESGEN). Such approaches can be used to map relationships between records in an archives, given the archival notion of context in place and time, for new approaches to document retrieval or for analysis. The properties of spatial relationships in a variety of settings are themselves revealing of information hidden from view except by such modeling.

Such empirical approaches have not been used to test archival information systems, even though the concept of a records series is used generally and the criterion of continuity in action, i.e., process, is applied almost intuitively in archival appraisal. But for socioeconomic history it seems that such series analysis coupled with GIS technology is a powerful combination. Yet, new tools like *Spyglass Slicer* for the IBM PC and compatibles with Windows, a volumetric analysis tool that renders data in volumes, slices, isometric surfaces, etc., can mask variables or make designated values transparent, translucent, or opaque and can produce animation from data frames, etc. It is now being used by scientists and engineers to visualize different scenarios by playing "what-if" games with their data by changing the role of values and variables in analyses (see M. OSBORNE & RUBINSTEIN and HEAP & VAROUFAKIS for game theory, that is set into the wider context of Artificial Intelligence research by FAGIN *ET AL.*). Although it is not apparent that historians have yet turned to such data-analysis tools that support dynamic visualization and multiple hypothetical renditions, in short time this technology will transfer from the scientific and technical fields to the Social Sciences and to History.

Because of historians' contextual orientation and instinct for geographically placing events in history in more than a chronological series, regional variance is important in telling history that is complex, comparative, and is really an interrelated set of histories. Demarcated areas and periods have been likened to ecologies, in which the Social Science orientation is to discern ecosystems at work. Since W. P. SHIVELY in 1969 suggested that a statistically reconstituted ecology determined, or so it could be inferred, group behavior, the deployment of such regression analysis has been controversial. Does this discrimination and alignment smack of a serious intellectual issue popularly thought of as "guilt by association"? Even in courts of law, such proximity proves only opportunity, but not cause or actuality. The evidential problem is even more complex when talking about groups and whole societies. Ecological regression analysis has been applied especially to the behavior of different electorates in political history (E. JONES; R. ROTH). Early applications in the 1970s also opened a continuing debate not only about statistical methods (SHADE and KOUSSER & LICHTMAN) which have since been greatly refined, but over the applicability of methodology meant for analysis of group behavior to studying individuals and ascribing to them characteristics of the group with which they could be associated (cf., KOUSSER, 1973; BRODER & LICHTMAN; and KOUSSER & LICHTMAN). How much can one infer individual behavior from group behavior or relate a subgroup to a whole and explain the dynamics between the two? The issue is the use or misuse of association to derive an associated behavior (FLANAGAN & ZINGALE, critiques by KOUSSER, 1986) by explicit relationships as memberships in organizations, or implicitly inferred from religious affiliations or preferences exhibited in other practices.

This methodology is related to prosopography and the cardinal issue of nominal record linkage of individuals to each other to reconstitute family life and other social organizations; add social mobility and then the element of exercising power as in voting, and one moves quickly from local prosopography to regional demography and from Sociology to Political Science (FARR & SEIDELMAN). The classic study that pioneered much of this methodology was Stephan THERNSTROM's *Poverty and Progress* (1964), when all such nominal linkage had to be done first hand. Now, several programs exist for genealogy that generate family tree structures and link individuals through kinship (FINDLER & MCKINZIE; SELZ-LAURIERE & FLAVIGNY; RYAN; WINCHESTER; WILLIGAN & LYNCH). Genealogists have their choice of several programs; one of the most used is *Personal Ancestral File* software written in 1986 (Release 2.2, 1989) by the Mormon Church's Family History Department. It links individuals to families and connects families, charts pedigrees and family trees, sorts and indexes, and controls individual biographical records in relation to larger structures. But programs written for practicing genealogists often lack the kind of nominal records linkage used in demographic and social science research, and are usually meant for smaller databases than dumps of vast amounts of census data to be matched with parish, employment, and health records. Moreover, genealogical work on one's family line often ignores context; the techniques for family reconstruction are similar, but the enlargement of family to social history requires linkage to more contextual data and statistical analyses which are seldom applied in everyday genealogy. Still, one cannot approach the latter without a methodological background in the former, whether the interest is personal in one's own family or for genetics research or social history. In all of these endeavors nominal records linkage is a technical problem related to statistical series analysis, but it is also an issue of linking disciplines.

The intellectual and procedural issues are the same for social history, bibliographic control in archives and libraries, and family genealogy. Because of such hypersensitivity to context in historical interpretation, historians have been especially influenced by Edward Tufte's demonstrations of graphic displays of statistical data (TUFTE, 1983, 1990), but they did not delve too deeply in the field of knowledge representation as it is evolving in Information Science (cf., PYLYSHYN; ROLLINS). Instead, historiographic debate has been concerned largely with the attack of relativistic textualists and the attributed relationship between historical reconstruction and fiction. In this vein, they are closer in thinking about visualization as in cognition related to art and art appreciation than to cognitive psychology as used in Information Science (for the art viewpoint, see FINKE; PETERSEN). Although statisticians have studied graphic representation historically (e.g., BENIGER & ROBYN; ANDREWS *ET AL.*, 1980), historians still seem as interested in the "how to" (e.g., H. CLEVELAND's influential textbook) and aesthetics, as in the logical correlation between their data and graphs. As mentioned, little in Historical Methods literature indicates application of cognitive psychology to such visualization, and historians' use of graphs tends to be traditional and two-dimensional (e.g., bar graphs, pie charts, organizational structure outlines, chronologs, etc.) rather than advances into more complicated relational and overlap (Venn) diagraming, GANTT charts, and 3-D graphic models, etc., and only computing historians use scatter diagrams, etc. Historians' reviews, moreover, seldom critique such displays, on the basis of Tufte's criteria or another other, as though these are mere supplements to the text rather than substantive components of the case.

If statistics "lie," the proverbial "damn lie" is in their graphing and visualization; or, conversely, graphs provide a formalization of ideas not otherwise discernible, as argued back and forth in the *Zeitsgeschichte* debate between Karl Stuhlpfarrer and Siegfried Mattl (ARDELT). Historians certainly have not abandoned graphics for presenting their findings, but given the caveats of M. THALLER (1987, p. 148) and others, more are on guard against misrepresentation and are now evolving what has been called by M. DARU, an "historical graphicacy" so that complex graphs and diagrams based on equally complex mathematics are not regarded as unconnected to "real" History. The same argument has been used against literary method in text analysis. Indeed, a relationship exists between modeling and paradigm development in history, pattern recognition, mapping and graphic representation in that they all form a theoretical hypertext or layer to historical interpretation that can sometimes seem removed from the story line in historical narrative. All forms of theoretical reconstruction, whether the theoretical model or graph, the dissection or layering in Structuralism, or the use of rich metaphor to relate the past to the present, need to relate to the story line, and all need to be supported by a critical under-layer of references to original sources.

TUFTE's caveats about misrepresentation of quantifiable data in graphics can be applied as well to word study and image analysis. Coloration, proportion and depth perception in illustration, for example, are measurable; so are word selection categorized for intensity and ranges of comparative description (i.e., smallest, smaller, small, average, big, bigger, biggest) in word imagery. While historians have been alerted to issues of representation in the presentation of their findings and in interpreting historical presentations (AUERBACH's classic, *Mimesis; The Representation of Reality in Western Culture*; cf., S. GREENBLATT's inter-disciplinary journal *Representations*), they have yet to engage the field of Knowledge Representation in Information Science in a significant way (e.g., IEEE *Knowledge Engineering, Visualization,* etc.). BAIN (1996) is one of the few archivists to employ visualization techniques and solicit reactions to graphic representations in "visualizing archival work" to Archival Science. Is this late exploration of the cognitive and technical aspects of visual communications due to an addiction to text and recent preference for narrative? Is such tardiness simply lack of interest and identification of such applications with History, or does it also relate to lack of know-how? History has content that deserves new and interesting presentation beyond traditional graphics and warrants exploration of new imagery capabilities, and modeling in History lends itself to visualization and new forms of knowledge representation perhaps more than in most disciplines.

Finally, ever since L. BENSON's very early work (1961) explaining New York State voting behaviors in Jacksonian democracy on the basis of economic motivation, model building to synthesize hypotheses and test them is an important part of Social Science historical research (e.g., MCCLELLAND's early work (1975) in model building for New Economic History), but historians were and still are generally put off by statistical models that are so theoretical they cannot also be described and illustrated by historical example (BOGUE, ed., 1973). They are skeptical of data they cannot trace by themselves from source to model and are distrustful of conclusions too automatically generated. And they often see causal explanation as being too singular if a model cannot accommodate multiple variables and offer multiple plausible explanations. Simply put, model building often omits the story line. MARCOULIDES & HERSBERGER provide a more successful approach than most, by making the math understandable, contrasting univariate and multivariate techniques, providing many examples, and exploiting software such as *SAS*. Just as the examples with real data in this 1997 textbook make statistical methodology understandable and acceptable, ABBOT (1994) claims that the mutually reinforcing interplay between quantification and narrative description is the most convincing case to be made for adopting statistical approaches and retaining narrative. RAGIN has argued this when criticizing the overuse of multivariate techniques to resolve issues better handled by simpler Boolean logic to explain deviance and varied developments in history. The character of the methodological approach, whether old or new, is often a question of which dominates— quantitative analysis supporting the narrative, or narrative description explicating a model built or conclusions reached quantitatively. IGARTUA (1991) stresses the fundamental importance of the initial decision about why and when to quantify and turn to computing for the historian's work. The Humanity component of History that wrestles with its Social Science side remains suspicious of process for its own sake, methodological overkill, and jargon, as reflected in the work of D. N. MCCLOSKEY (1985) and essays he subsequently edited (1990) attacking positivism in the Social Sciences and particularly in Econometrics (*à la* MADDALA)—collective flaws labeled simply as "modernism."

Such debates, as already noted, often miss the mark or overstress polarization at extremes rather than the continuum. The arguments over models, reconstructions, paradigms and graphic presentations are often over the fine points of interpretation, methodological application, and reliability. They are valid in their own right and such discussion needs to go on, but the overriding issue and larger picture that seems to escape the data-minded and those riveted to minutia are that such work has been static. It aims both at capturing a slice of history for close inspection, as though time stood still, and the presentation has therefore also been static. Moreover, the traditional paradigm is always linear, and most of the statistical techniques applied to historical data have been based on linear algebra. The most sophisticated historical research today is still largely confined to relational database schema and is conceived as a terminal project rather than an ongoing enterprise. Consequently, most historians and archivists as well do not seem to be prepared for the mental shift required to take advantage of OLAP/ROLAP technology and data extraction tools now available to them. They do discover and generate knowledge, but seldom with Knowledge Discovery tools and methodology. Often their data do not allow it, but there are other limitations as well.

To take advantage of these technologies, rather than to consider data modeling entirely from a philosophical viewpoint that too often assumes that current limitations are to be with us always, approaches to data modeling must be more progressive. Consider, for example, how to transform thinking about relational models into star architecture for data warehousing and integrated analysis. Traditional modeling techniques relying on entity relationships, for example, must be translated into the world of dimensional data analysis and physical models based on different guidelines than most historical computing was based on within the past decade. MCGUFF recommends the works by architect Christopher Alexander for such reconceptualization and the design of complex "things" (objects) with seemingly conflicting requirements (C. ALEXANDER, 1975, 1977; 1979). His concept of repetitive (not duplicated) objects seems to have predicted the move toward object-oriented programming, so more than decade after his writing, Alexander has become very popular in computing circles. One can understand this from his dictate (1975): "The principle of organic order: Planning and construction will be guided by a process which allows the whole to emerge gradually from local acts." This seems applicable as well in socioeconomic, bottom-up history that relies on the particular for the general, or in non-Western historiography which is highly localized, event-centered, and which is not so systematized as History has become in the West during the first generation of cliometrician activity. This is the goal of contemporary modeling and simulation in social history as advocated by Robert Axtell, i.e., "a new, generative kind of social science" (EPSTEIN & AXTELL).

To move from a static to a dynamic model the focus must switch from things to processes or the connections between things, their relatedness, interaction, and influence. This caveat needed in the business world is already well understood by historians, but their modeling techniques have not always implemented such thinking. The difference is that between OLTP and OLAP/ROLAP processing, and the use of data in greater amounts and with more versatility than has been common in historical computing projects. First, the kind of model developed can be customized to the phenomena being studied. This does not entail asking oneself or end users what they want to see, since they are likely to answer whatever they have seen in the past. This blocks knowledge discovery from the onset. Moreover, once having seen what they ask for, they will immediately ask for something else. So, it is a fallacy to build a model for knowledge discovery around user demand in the same way one might study user expectations for design and information storage and retrieval system that provides access to prepackaged information in set formats. To avoid such obsolescence in modeling and large-scale multiple-user information systems such as data warehouses, rather than beginning with questions asked by users based on prior experience, one would consider the array of questions which could be asked. MCGUFF, for example, makes a distinction between questions one can ask, those we want to ask, and finally, what should be asked. Information needs and desires are not the same. A need is far more limiting an idea than the latter, but both are experiential. A totally source-centered approach would be to ask what the data can answer, but this too is limited to data structures as they exist rather than as enhanced in operations and analyses. This would simply mean asking the same questions as those who gathered the data in the first place. One might instead focus on functional requirements today and data optimization. Moreover, multi-dimensional modeling overcomes most of the aforementioned limitations of traditional modeling. Such multi-dimensional dynamic modeling can resolve some of the constraints, for example, attributed by J. SMITH (1997, p. 1438) to the linguistic approach to political culture, "a two-dimensional model of human agency, a model that is unable to account adequately for linguistic innovation or cultural change."

In dimensional modeling, one first develops structural dimensions as is normally done in relational databases. This often involved denormalization and reliance on the generational concept in dimensional table definitions (parents and children, considered as genealogy in provenance relationships when applying archival principles). A simple vertical model uses the traditional time dimension broken into all components of the largest whole which provides for drilling up and down along a continuum of time units from the smallest to the largest in any data set (e.g., seconds to millennial) by using a parent ID self-join with time units. Any time dimension aggregation is thereby possible. A simple horizontal model uses the leaf members in a genealogy or decision tree to identify associations and ancestries, which can also be aggregated to produce any social unit desired above the individual level. Again, the idea is to provide for drilling operations with a single join along one of many possible dimensions. Finally, one can combine these for multilevel drilling. Such an approach is within normal relational modeling and is a recursive structure which can be represented in a normal table form or tree structure (but depending on data available, the structure may be balanced or imbalanced and may have to be addressed by creative aggregation strategies). Types and subtypes can also be used in any entity-relationship model when entities are nonheterogeneous; this model may be used in data warehousing as a one of several possible categorical dimensions which are used typically to support analytical processing. Informational dimensions must also be accommodated in star architectures, which are inhibited in standard relational models. Many tools are available to assist in modeling structural dimensions so necessary for relational databases, but the concepts of changed relations, changing attributes, and complexity over time are not well accommodated in relational databases. This is why process modeling must be combined with data modeling, and thus the rationale for turning to OLAP/ROLAP technologies for queries of data, formation of data sets for analysis, and their exploitation by multiple operations and methodologies rather than a single predetermined approach.

In all such data and processing modeling a plaguing set of entwined problems consists of handling imperfect data and of proper conceptualization. Both are significant. Yet, in many of the Social Sciences and in Information Science too, especially Informetrics, a number of regularities occur frequently in the form of mathematical approximations that may be aspects of a single mathematical form. As BOOKSTEIN remarks (1997, p. 2), this regularity displays some remarkable properties that make it possible to work even with the most ambiguous of data (for an information scientist's perspective on ambiguity, congruent with thinking throughout the Social Sciences, see BOOKSTEIN's treatments in 1990a-b). Although the method is deterministic, it is tempered with awareness of imperfections in data acquisition and hence in measurement regardless of technique. Random error always influences measurement perfection, and a whole array of impediments are included. Each has an accepted resolution in statistical procedures. Other errors producing imperfect data are social and project-bound; communication failures are especially prevalent, social cognition problems create others, often relevant data are ignored, data are misclassified, and a project may be flawed by poor decision-making (NORMAN, 1988; ROBBIN & FROST-KUMPF, pp. 97-98).

Statistics has been developed essentially to cope with most of these, including incomplete and imperfect data, and corrections or checks on communications and interpretations, but others such as poor decision-making and miscommunication may be detected statistically but are not usually corrected by statistical adjustments alone (see H. LEWIS for a simplified approach to probability, game theory, reasoning with incomplete data, etc., in everyday decision-making). The laws of probability, however, deal with randomness where the equation is often expressed as an actual measure equal to the true measure times a random-error variable, which assumes that variation is in fact governed by the law of probability (FELLER). Or, expressed differently, error in computer-human interaction is inevitable and some variation caused by error must be taken into account in all statistical operations (NORMAN, 1983, 1986, 1988). Imperfection in data, not to be confused with probabilistic uncertainty, has prompted the development of fuzzy logic. A major premise in such thinking is that fuzzy concepts by definition are imprecise, but they are certain. From 1965 on, since the critical observations of ZADEH's in information studies, many concepts cannot be expressed in tradition sets, and therefore the theory of fuzzy sets evolved. In other words, in fuzzy thinking an item can belong to a set by degree; in traditional thinking an item is in or is outside a set which forces a definitive classification when such cannot really be justified on the basis of the information at hand. So, this idea of partial membership in one or more sets really pertains to ambiguity rather than probability.

Ambiguity can derive from imperfect data, but can as easily result from weaknesses in the conceptual basis for measurement (following BOOKSTEIN's concise coverage of these problems, 1997, pp. 3-4, summarizing his earlier treatments, 1990a-b). Bookstein examines the laws of Informetrics (i.e., the "counting laws" of BRADFORD, 1934; LOTKA, 1926; and ZIPF, 1935), and speculates that we may have evolved modes of analysis which are insensitive to conceptual weakness or poorly defined ideas. He argues that all of these laws reveal a single regularity that is sturdy and resistant to data ambiguity (most fully explored in BOOKSTEIN, 1990a) "given proper conceptualization" of the problem studied (the caveat is stress by BOOKSTEIN, 1997, p. 4). He created a hypothetical well-behaved target group of subjects that produced like a Lotka population and then introduced irregularities or distortion into the control group to show that the basic form of regularity remained, leading him to conclude that even when not detected, some distortion was always present. He then examined the stochastic properties of Informetric Laws and resilient distributions to conclude that all mathematical relationships are approximate, and that we have simply developed adaptations to uncertainly which is ubiquitous in all of the Social Sciences. He argues for the creation of functional forms which are not affected too severely by imperfect conceptualization, so we can survive in an ambiguous world. Bookstein concentrates on Informetrics inside Information Science as a Social Science, so the theoretical problems he addresses are pervasive and pertain as well to measurement and conceptualization problems in Historical Information Science. The difference, it may be argued, is that the historian is even less in control of data collection than the social or information scientist who studies contemporary phenomena. Historians, therefore, need to be even more critical of their data and sources. However, if Bookstein's observations can be applied to the historian's work, perhaps more critical than analysis of data are self-analysis and critical appraisal of problem conceptualizations.

New History and New Science

What might bring historians, especially those capable of computerized reconstruction of generalization from minutiae to conceive of history differently? And can a "new science" develop without the discord that contested past innovations? Are the social factors in the origins of New Science described by BEN-DAVID & COLLINS conducive for change in synchronization with the revolution in information technology that surrounds us? Current unrest, discomfort, and perplexity suggest that change is still difficult in History where change management is improvisational rather than planned (going back to ORLIKOWSKI & HOFMAN's model). It is also more difficult to achieve change in a field like History when historians are themselves students of change. Innovation in such environments might suffer the fate of what a decanal colleague of mine called "death by expertise." This is as fatal as what another dean termed "learned helplessness."

One sign of adaptability would be the exploration of nonlinear models of history. Non-linearity does not mean the same as unsystematic history, but the referent for systematization may be other than chronological time, or the entrapment by a series, or a grid. Mythography can, for example, achieve a history of its own that is increasingly systematic and consistent, but which is not necessarily chronological. Its ordering principle may be spatial and geographic. This is the case of much Native American historiography, which when tested by Western geo-chronological systematization is often considered primitive. One reason is that Indian myths so often collapse real-time history when irrelevant time-spans occur, or because events may not be seen as causal, so they need not be proximate or sequential. Much of tribal history is event-centered, as in the case of ancient mythology and much of Greek and Roman history, and certainly early medieval history, all of which which required synthesis and synchronization. Local history is often event-centered, and its framework is not universal, comparative, or long-range linear history, but in a regional context, short-ranged, and somewhat in a time-warp with more formal, larger, encompassing stabilized or set history. Moreover, while certain events may be seen as causal and this causality requires them to be seen one after another as time marches on, to be understood, others involve a retrogression of sorts, where a modern event triggers reinterpretation of an older one. Thought is not so time-bound as other phenomena in human affairs.

Ironically, new technology is aiding a breakdown of systematic and linear history, often seen in the fragmentation of master narratives. Local historians, of course, work at the opposite end of this spectrum, before a master narrative is even constructed. They are often the ones doing the construction. If new forms of information retrieval operate by subject without context (place, date, original circumstances, structures, or presentations, etc.), they are essentially ahistorical if the criteria for "historical" are traditionally Western. Put another way in archival terms, they lack the criteria of evidence as identified in the notion of the archival bond (original content, context, and structure altogether in a chain of custody) which may be multi-directional rather than strictly linear. Such "history" has often been relegated to non-historical or quasi-historical status, especially when related to oral tradition rather than written records. However, many kinds of modern information retrieval operate without this kind of archival integrity or sense of historicity, but the information retrieved is considered authoritative and reliable nonetheless. Forward and backward chaining in information retrieval systems or computing using a simple chronometer may assume a linear direction in all processes and causality thereby that are not necessarily there. Neither would, for example, automatically detect horizontal influences or simultaneity unless another more contextual system were used for ordering than linear time. However, within the Western tradition, order that is not chronological (i.e., linear) is not seen as historical; yet linear time traces only one track at a time. Parallel developments are thought to occur at the same time, but such phenomena hardly include all similar developments. We make sense out of concurrent developments, for example, based on previous events and perceive similitude either within one tradition or another. Comparative history usually refers to parallel developments, concurrency, that is multiple tracks (places, areas, and regions) in the same periods, but it also entails comparing different periods in the same tradition. Classification is one attempt at creating vertical and horizontal order at the same time. Even in the West, sense-making does not always operate on linear time alone.

Scenarios like anecdotal information can be retrieved and used as in field of Organizational Culture, to represent archetypes, stereotypes, generalizations, and metaphors or exempla rather than chronological history. Consider, for example, the effectiveness of inculcating collective culture in Native American storytelling where in the midst of narration some allusion sparks a digression or an addition from a hearer to expand the story but also to incorporate the contributor into the narrative and hence the corporate memory. Or, think of when a referent to an important ancestor triggers an honor song so that collective memory and liturgy are interwoven spontaneously. This form of nonlinear linkage, thought of as digression by those thinking only in linear time, may be synchronized later or not, depending on the information needs of the moment, the strength of the tradition to bring things back on track or at least to make them relevant, and the culture surrounding the linkage which operates like a pathway through the forest of data that might be possibly be called into play. Native Americans were fascinated by Roman Catholic liturgy not only because of its drama, but its conscious reenactment of historical event in the consecration during the Mass, its invoking collective memory in the Collect, its lessons through Biblical readings (operating by subject retrieval, not chronological rendition but cyclical genre in the Church Year, etc.; cf., MCCRANK, [1999], on interactive media and cross-cultural religious conversion). In short, nonlinearity characterizes many uses of the past, chaotic and nonlinear histories abound, and the professional historians' work of synthesis, systematization, reinterpretation may be seen from the vantage point of the source, the story giver, as unwarranted editing, control, and objectivity in the extreme on the one hand, and on the other a peculiar form of subjectivity.

Consider what happens to a master narrative encoded with SGML or HTML for hypertext additions or links that short-circuit, retro-flash, leap forward, side-step and divert, repeat cycles, and isolate segments in a linear progression or whole continuum. An example of modeling this nonlinear thinking and alternative form of history is the Tribal History project at the D'Arcy McNickle Center for American Indian History at the Newberry Library (C. HOWE). Its director, Craig Howe, a Lakota Sioux with experience at the University of Michigan using hypercard to document Native American narratives, is attempting to capture the oral traditions of four Plains tribes (two Sioux, the Crow, and Cheyenne, all of which may be juxtaposed to Euro-American renditions) as well as the tribal perspective of "doing history," which is certainly different from European perspectives. Because tribal histories are collective and continuing, a definitive master narrative is not possible. Referents in tribal histories are spatial, social, and experiential; although they may operate chronologically by remembering an "epitomizing event" each year, to produce an annual cumulation so to speak, they are not necessarily linear within these general time references. They are not frozen in space in the European surveyor mentality, but are nomadic and operate like travelogues with key geological landmarks as referents characterized differently by each people. Nor are these tribal histories universal, comparative, or systematized outside their own realm of collective experience; and they are authoritative only as a collective narrative. Each has multiple voices.

When systematized into master narratives or codified into linear history in the European method of writing history, Native American histories from the perspectives of those who inherited this history undergo grave distortion in their migration across cultures and different media. One master narrative is told with one authoritative voice. Hypertext/video allows multiple, even conflicting stories to exist simultaneously without preordering, selection, and systematization. The reader/viewer/hearer can experience tribal history through such media more closely to the original tradition than through book form, and enter into the experiential realm by adding to it, becoming his or her own historian in working out syntheses for themselves, and if done socially and interactively with media and other people, authoritative history may be worked out by consensus. This smacks of the ultimate in relativism, of course, and is a little like contemporary chronologs being constructed on Web sites without any research into historical documentation whatsoever, but by putting requests out on the Internet for personal recall and taking as the right answer the response most frequently given. The result may not portray reality, but in the absence of any other source such a reconstruction will be accepted as authoritative. There is method here, in both cases, and even a certain objectivity which ironically appears to be highly subjective. Is a new form of History being born from such information technology, which is chaotic in appearance at the onset, but which is self-ordering in time and space? What are professional historians to make of such phenomena, which seem contemporary and postmodern because of new technology, but which also seem as old as the ancients themselves? As in the case of literature, historians will assuredly differ (cf., LANDOW, M. JOYCE, etc., for discussions about hypertext and literary pedagogy).

Having deliberately introduced the idea of nonlinear history from an anthropological perspective rather than borrowing from the hard sciences, let us now consider how such premodern and postmodern historiography and information technology relate to Social Science History perspectives being influenced by modern science. In the realm of physical science, nonlinearity is often associated with Chaos Theory (GLEICK provided a forecast in 1978 of intellectual developments to come, as did BRIGGS & PEAT in 1981 in the heyday of history computing; cf., R. LEWIN; WALDROP). Most thinking about chaos and its formalization into theory harkens back to the prodigious work of Herbert Simon, but only more recently has it caught the imagination of those outside the physical sciences. It has been hailed as "the New Science" (PRIGOGINE & HOLTE, eds.). Thinking about chaos takes a certain paradigm shift from traditional linear thinking, and FINKE & BETTLE even suggest that it takes a certain cognitive style to deal with the change (i.e., how some people process information as distinct from others). In 1986, scientists at a London conference about chaos devised a seemingly paradoxical definition of it (I. STEWART, p. 17): chaos is "Stochastic behaviour occurring in a deterministic system." Stewart and others reasoned that since "stochastic behaviour is" ... lawless and irregular" and "deterministic behaviour is rule by exact and unbreakable law," then "chaos is 'lawless behaviour governed entirely by law.'" This, SHERMER (1995) points out, is an obvious contradiction, except that scientists use the word chaos to mean not something lawless, but chaos as apparent lawlessness. KELLERT more recently defines Chaos Theory as "the qualitative [i.e., geometric] study of nonstable aperiodic behavior in deterministic nonlinear dynamical systems" wherein the key words are "dynamic system" which suggests different processes operating locally and interacting at a higher level. B. BELL (p. 18) simplifies an overview of the characteristics of chaotic systems as:

1. Behavior of individual components (autonomous agents) follow a few simple rules—in effect, a widely distributed but mundane intelligence.

2. The systems (sometimes called "natural systems") are inherently synergistic, generally unpredictable, and quite different from the actions of components. Small variations in initial conditions or inputs can eventually cause huge differences in system behavior

3. Such systems do show some order if properly analyzed. State space paths of system variables will occupy regions know as attractors.

For those seeing no structure, repetition, pattern, or consistency in human affairs, at first glance chaos theory seemed to offer justification for staying with the local, event, and situational in history, except that chaos theory does not mean, as popularly misconstrued, sheer randomness. Chaos Theory aims to bring some rationale to what appears purely as chance. (RUELLE makes the important distinction between chance and chaos.) HOLLAND stresses the continuity between chaos and order. Moreover, even randomness operates by certain principles and can be reduced to mathematical statements; natural calamities, for example, may not be predictable at exact time and location, but can be predicted in terms of likely frequency and general region. Thus, farmers in certain parts of the country plan on a bad harvest at least once every seven years and prorate their income accordingly and insurance companies set their rates by estimating their future liability. In this sense, examples in Catastrophe Theory are often drawn from weather forecasting (ARNOLD; DEFACIO; POSTON & STEWART; WOODCOCK & POSTON). The problem is that accuracy in such predictive calculation breaks down over longer periods of time and when applied to larger geographic areas. The same is true for post-diction or historical explanation (the reverse of prediction). So, rather than perceiving highly complex milieu that seem to defy description and explanation as chaotic generally, the attempt has been to see such phenomena objectively, hence Chaos Theory. This has required the development of new methodologies and means of data analysis (OTT, SAUER & YORKE, eds.).

Recent refinement in this field of theoretical mathematics has contributed to an otherwise philosophically based Complexity Theory as an extension of Chaos Theory that limits the range and field of investigation to increase post- or predictability (a key point made by REISCH, 1991, and responded to by SHERMER, 1995). Sometimes the terms Chaos and Complexity are used synonymously, but the latter may be seen as a later refinement of the former, especially in scaling down an inquiry to what may be perceived as a system or an identifiable complex where interdependence and influences are most apparent (NICOLIS and PRIGOGINE provide a useful introduction to Complexity Theory; see also the studies honoring Juris Hartmanis edited by SELMAN). An entire complex therefore becomes a systems of systems where the study of transference of influence is similar to studying communications in internetworks (BAR-YAM; KUSHILEVITZ & NISAN). This segregation and improved scalability makes chaos more manageable for study.

How is complexity theory defined as a science? What is its scope? The electronic journal *Complexity International* is devoted to complex systems research, the scope of which embraces artificial life, cellular automata, chaos theory, control theory, evolutionary programming, fractals, genetic algorithms, information systems, neural networks, nonlinear dynamics, and parallel computation studied as such or applied to any field. The journal *Complex Systems* (1987-) focuses predominantly on parallel processing, sequential machine theory, and cellular automata. John Wiley's new physical bimonthly journal *Complexity* devotes itself to "the rapidly expanding science of complex adaptive systems" and raises complexity from a theory within Science to a science itself (http://journals/wiley.com/1076-2787/aims.html). The "Science of Complexity" focuses on methodological themes such as chaos and the same topics as its electronic counterpart. The journal welcomes papers "integrating conceptual themes and applications that cross traditional disciplinary boundaries" but the editors, revealing some antagonism between popular culture and science and perhaps with the humanities (e.g., NATOLI's attempt to see fractals in the complexities of literature), explicitly maintain that *Complexity* is not "a forum for speculation and vague analogies between works like 'chaos,' 'self-organization,' and 'emergence,' that are often used in completely different ways in science and in daily life." As shall be seen, that would exclude much of the discussion about complexity in History at this point. Others are more tolerant of the speculative and see in "the patterns of chaos: [*sic*] a new aesthetic of art, science, and nature" (J. BRIGGS).

Chaos Theory evolved out of the hard sciences, Physics in particular, which made its direct applicability to the Social Sciences difficult and to History uncomfortable and, so it has been argued, inappropriate. The kind of mathematical complexity involved in Physics, for example, made the concept in practice seem irreducible to the Social Sciences. One can understand this better by consulting CLAUSEN & SHOKROLLAHI who focus on "algebraic complexity theory" for advanced work; STOYAN & STOYAN and BANDT, GRAF & ZAHLE provide courses in stochastic methodology of geometrical statistics for random shapes and order-disorder models; and N. JONES treats computability in terms of complexity from the vantage point of programming. Software for exploring fractals on the Macintosh is touted by WAHL; BARNSLEY (1992) and others. One can find a bridge for Complexity Theory between the physical and biological sciences in Genetics research, which when linked through geography to demography may be related to History and thereby to the kind of New Social History associated with quantification and study of minutia through modeling (as already discussed; see also BURGISSER).

Chaos and, hence, Complexity Theory is now largely dependent upon the idea of fractals or geometrical objects in nature that are self-similar under changing scales. Such thought has developed parallel with information and visualization technology during this generation. See MANDELBROT (1982) especially for breakthrough thinking; then see CROWNOVER (1995) to understand the development of this field over the last decade (the phenomenon, of course, has required its own journal, *Fractals*, 1993-). It is the difference in vantage points not unlike what has been made possible in 3-D virtual modeling, which may take on different meaning in new light. Or, different scalability allows one to discern form for and order in what otherwise, in a different scale with different dimensions, seems entirely disorderly or without form. Hence, disorder-order modeling. BARNSLEY (1988) maintains that *Fractals* [are] *Everywhere*.

The idea becomes more understandable for historians when removed from Physics and explored in Geography (e.g., HIRST & MANDELBROT's title, *Fractal Landscapes*). A confluence of rivers at the water's edge seems chaotic and turbulent, but the rivers from a nearby hill top appear more calm and regular, and still more orderly from an aerial photograph, and finally as viewed from space entire drainage systems appear (LAM & DECOLA, eds.; cf., BARTON & LAPOINTE for Geology). The same imagery and scalability is being applied by Medicine to the human circulation and lymphatic system. Another popular explanation is to uses a segment of rugged coastline viewed from different levels. One cannot get down to a micro-level beyond grains of sand, but the upper limit of macro-levels is determined more by definition than natural particles (B. WEST; WEST & DEERING). In the natural sciences, as illustrated by this example, natural objects are random versions of mathematical fractals; that is, in a statistical sense, given a sufficiently large sample, some magnification of a part of the sample can be matched closely with some other part of the sample, or some examples with some other members of the ensemble (BARNSLEY; CROWNOVER; G. EDGAR; PEITGEN, JÜRGENS, & SAUPE; PICKOVER, ed.).

New possibilities exist for historians as well, in more open access to space imaging technology such as remote sensing of monuments in context, pathways, settlement patterns, whole terrains, and regions. NASA's Landsat and France's SPOT satellites have resolution limits of 16 to 32 feet in size, but the IKONOS satellite, for example, from its 400-mile orbit can resolve objects that are as small as three feet in diameter. No longer the monopoly of the military and espionage community, such high-resolution remote sensing products are now available commercially from Space Imaging, Inc., in Colorado (explore such possibilities on the Web site, "Unofficial Space at www.discovery.com/stories/unofficialspace.html"). The costs are still high, and government scrutiny enforces "shutter control" regarding politically and militarily sensitive areas (archeological sites close up, for example, but not whole sectors of Israel; castle fortifications, but no military or airforce bases) or the invasion of personal privacy (candid shots of nudist beaches, private celebrity weddings, etc.). But consider how different the effect is in teaching a unit on Native American and French voyageur canoe trade on the river systems and great lakes of North America with a two-dimensional map and chalkboard, or with a layered fractal approach controlled in computer graphics like a zoom lense on the Great Lakes from 400 miles above the earth that reveals everything from artifacts the size of a totem or canoe to the rapids on every stream or shallow in each bay?

A critical issue, of course, is scaling, or how big must the overview be? Or, as asked in Intellimation video from a 1986-88 Annenberg COMAP Project, "How big is too big?" (CONSORTIUM FOR MATHEMATICS AND ITS APPLICATIONS). Fractal geometry is a mathematical means to explore the dynamics of turbulent flow, chaotic motion, and nonlinear systems (e.g., percolation clusters, especially in physiology, climatology, etc.). Rather than Newtonian determinism, such thinking seems to follow J. C. Maxwell's dictum that "The true logic of this world is the calculus of probabilities." P. KOCH (p. 1) observes that in the realm of space physics, "unpredictable randomness is overwhelmingly the most common behavior." Is this also the case in history? Are perceptions of order and disorder in history largely problems of scalability and resemblance that rely on the level of overview achieved or particular perspective assumed? In History's parlance, such technology and approaches are really throwing new light on old things. Physical attributes like size, color, and shape change, and so does the traditional concept of time as an even, linear progression. This adds a new twist to postmodern relativism!

My own thinking about historical phenomena I studied previously has been influenced by Mandelbrot's notion of fractals and scalability applied to historical geography. I had, for example, studied Christian expansionism in the frontier of New Catalonia along Spain's Mediterranean coast (MCCRANK, 1996). Working at ground level with rather mundane documentation from the archives, mainly kept in Barcelona but also those in Madrid holding the rich *fondos* of the Cistercian monasteries of Santes Creus and Poblet, I had detailed zones of reconquest activity down to the level of natural boundary lines traceable today from twelfth-century descriptions in the charters of surviving landmarks—rivers, outcroppings, mountain ranges, and castle ruins. I had thought of the Reconquest as piecemeal, which it was, without being able to discern any overall strategy except what might be explained by the rugged terrain of the region. Moreover, I had been led to believe by military historians that strategy was a modern invention, so I did not expect to find evidence for strategy in the Reconquista. Then I began to take an overview as though I were in aerial reconnaissance over the area where Muslims had offered the stiffest resistance to military takeover and continuing cultural resistance to cultural integration over the next several centuries. I began to see patterns not discerned before, of four distinct zones of Christian encroachment against Islam, each with its own character, customs, social clique, and power base.

As I subsequently argued when giving the Lowe lecture at Western Michigan University (MCCRANK, 1990), four bands of reconquest activity could be discerned from the coast to the hinterland: allied city-states, Catalan marcher lords, reformed monastic orders, and then the military orders. Mapping post-conquest landholdings demarcated these zones well enough, and natural geography filled in the missing borderlands. The charters read by themselves seemed to provide no overall strategy, but reread together with this paradigm in mind, they revealed ample evidence that the zoning was intentional and that the Christians operated their alliance system to provide concerted actions rather than a simple mass movement along lines dictated by regional geography. I hope to demonstrate the inner dynamics of this interaction through dynamic modeling of social-military alliance structures by tracing the names of signatories in these medieval charters to show how extended families operated in their own domains and together to hold onto the frontier they had wrestled from its Muslim conquerors. It would be ideal in a Braudelian way to present graphically and interactively a two-century-long process of expansion and solidification as both a time-motion simulation and a dynamic map of land holdings. The Christian fortified, surveyed, and bounded lands versus Muslim communal occupation of more open territory (not unlike Euro-American landholding super-imposed over the Native American, a counterpart to the Muslim familial and tribal way) could each be superimposed graphically over a three-dimensional scaled rendering of the region's geography. Chaotic pinpoints and fractal settlements would appear to self-organize as a new regime replaced the old Muslim march, thus History would come alive. Modern information technology, knowledge discovery techniques, and historical research are integral in such research. Such is my current project for the medieval frontier of New Catalunya using military maps and three-dimension reconstitution using CAD software, and perhaps one day, when affordable, remote satellite images of the same region.

Recent elaboration of Complexity Theory beyond the physical sciences are significant for studying historical processes, therefore, especially in modeling order-disorder systems (BUNDE & HAVLIN). For example, diffusion: in uniform space diffusion is proportional to lapsed time, but it is easily recognized that the rate of change will vary as the terrain differs or if barriers are present (as in the study of technological diffusion: B. H. KAYE). Think in terms of geographic and cultural variables that would affect diffusion as being a lattice of conducting links, or deflecting and obstructing links, perhaps like a pinball machine on which the game hardly depends only on the speed and direction of the ball. Moreover, several balls can be in play at the same time: in this example, both the agents and their environment are interactive. Hence, the topic is one of chaotic dynamics as well as fractals (BARNSLEY & DEMKO). The time factor can change randomly according to contact with these differing links, momentum, size of cluster, etc., in ways not normally tracked in linear systems or addressed by linear thinking. Much of complexity systems research aims at exposing and clarifying time-dependent effects in disordered materials (the title of a NATO Advanced Study Institute conference in 1987: PYNN & RISTE, eds).

Historians have thought in terms which are not totally alien to fractal geometry when they aggregate people into groups and generalize about them, and they understand side effects that accompany linear developments. Generally, however, when historical phenomena are studied geographically and chronologically, both dimensions are treated linearly as though the two interact with each other on a controlled matrix. Intersections are the most complex conjunctions of time and space that such thought can track. It seems impossible to track side effects in all directions at once along a trajectory of any development. This two-dimensional linear perspective assumes an environmental control by a third element that is never explicitly addressed. Moreover, historians are not often mathematically precise in their controls on scale, levels of descriptive generalization, or specific vantage point for every observation. Such multi-dimensional interactive viewing of history is simply too complex for older methodologies. As SIMPSON notes, technologies have evolved to handle more complex notions of time than simply a single, constant linear progression as perceived in Western culture. When we talk about "changing times," there is a double meaning in these words.

Complexity Theory seems compatible with New Historicism, but not quantification as conceived in the early 1980s, because understanding complexity requires a paradigm shift from linear equations and programming in quantification studies hitherto dominant in historical linear computing to something even more radical than accommodating fuzzy data in data modeling or developments in source-oriented programming. The very essence of historical computing may be reoriented with a reconceptualization of History, or rather, a full realization of what historians have always known and those with Social Science orientations have always assumed: human affairs are indeed very complex; they are at once localized and global; change is constant but not steady or even; and to understand the particular and the general one must constantly relate detail to the big picture. Moreover, while it is easier to describe isolated events than complex processes, meaning is derived from both. Often one is more secure working from a source or informant, an artifact, or a coherent body of evidence, than one is trying to make sense out of complex phenomena.

Statistical inference, modeling, and graphic projection, etc., are means of extending knowledge even into areas of history where surety will never exist, but where feasibility, plausibility, and understanding can be enhanced by cross-checking approaches more reassuring than pure or untested speculation. Probabilistic networks based on Bayesian thinking offer an avenue to new explorations of old data (BERNARDO & SMITH). HECKERMAN's tutorial (1995) points the way. Finally, while our senses search for a thing and take comfort in something concrete, our rationality recognizes processes, influences, and synergistic entities that are not real in the same concrete sense. A similar challenge confronts the hard sciences (EFRON & TIBSHIRANI), given recent findings in Physics which now predict discovery of particles without substance—a seemingly antithetical notion, but which is projected from current knowledge and is an extension of relativity theory. The same applies to modern Medicine, since people do not exist in isolation from each other, disease and ailments do not exist in vacuums, and what happens in controlled environments and test tubes often works differently in real life (hence the older notion of knowledge-coupling in medical information systems). Consequently, some geneticists, for example, think Medicine as practiced today, with its simplistic unilateral association of symptom and treatment, requires total rethinking.

Such rethinking has been affecting History as well, especially because we now have the tools to assist us in complex thinking and problem solving. Reconsideration of older quantification applications in the Social Sciences have already begun in Economics, even in applied areas like investments where some banks, for example, have fired linear algebraic programmers to replace them with those who can work with dynamic systems and open-ended modeling. Forecasting like diagnosis is understood to be too complex to operate simply on linear projections like target practice with one-time aim and single shots, regardless of the skill and precision, if one is confronted with multiple, moving targets. Instead, to follow the same metaphor, a shotgun approach is being adopted of directional blasting a wider area to achieve surer results. Still, for all of the discussion about chaos and complexity theory in History, historians have not been very productive in actual applications and they have not been active inside such think tanks as the Santa Fe Institute West. (Dick Morely, founder of Flavors Technology, in 1995 announced plans for a Santa Fe Institute East in Boston.) John Casti, one of SFI's founders, informed Michael Shermer in 1994 that no historian had ever worked at the Institute, perhaps because, as SHERMER (1995, p. 7) indicates, "No historian has produced a major work on chaos and history." Although founded by physicists, SFI has now included Social Sciences (especially Economics) and socioeconomic behaviors studies from massive data such as produced by the modern banking industry with electronic charge card transactions. Studying behavior of contemporary Americans through VISA transaction logs makes OPAC log-analysis in Library Science seem like child's play.

Those drawn to speculative and experimental forums like the Santa Fe Institute are not, however, disinterested in History. Hayward Alker of the University of Southern California's School of International Relations recently began investigating the modeling techniques employed at the Institute to understand the complex phenomena of "historicity" in the history of international affairs, i.e. defined by Frederich Olafson as "the sense of time-ordered self-understanding shared among members of a continuous human society" (SFI electronic *Bulletin*, fall 1996). ALKER's inspiration came from H. WHITE's *Metahistory* (1973) and W. FIKENTSCHER's *Modes of Thought*. Working with SFI postdoctoral fellow Simon Fraser for programming and

George Lakoff for parallel processing, Alker is exploring how memories and histories can be incorporated into artificial life simulations (based on the Mac *Tierra* model developed by Tom Ray, and ECHO simulation developed by John Holland). In the words of the SFI *Bulletin* (http://www.santafe.edu/sfi/publications/Bulletin/bulletin- fall96/history.html):

> … Alker argues that agent-based models [e.g.., *Swarm* software in beta testing] may encourage a new kind of sustainability-sensitive social science modeling appropriate in an age of increasingly constraining ecological limits. Falling within a tradition of modeling that goes back to Gottfried Leibnitz, the "godfather of cybernetics," this approach achieved exceptional mathematical clarity in the von Neumann-Burks Theory of Self-reproducing Automata. The parallel processing computer architectures used by Lakoff and his students to model meaningful historical constructions reflect the common origins of a modeling tradition oriented toward multicellular dynamics, the reconstruction of evolutionary history and a greater appreciation of the way human cognition reflectively understands and transforms both itself and the natural world of which it is a part.

Part of the collaborative effort between the Sante Fe Institute and the Brookings Institution with the World Resources Institute in the so-called *2050 Project* (EPSTEIN & AXTELL) is a modeling capability to use agent-based simulation like field study, to examine "what-if" scenarios. A current application is to artificially create a small society of Anasazi people whose culture flourished in the the American southwest, 400-1400 A.D. Each agent or person interacts with each other according to whatever social relationships are typical and particularities are known (growth, marriage, offspring and extension of family life, death, etc.), with normal activities in the base simulation interrupted by external forces such as shifts in climatic conditions and migrations. In such simulations history is repeatable; virtual history can be replayed, slowed down and speeded up, and each replay can be altered to study single or combined stimuli, responses, and effects. Of course, the simulation can only mimic actuality, but large processes can be observed in ways not possible through documentary historical reconstruction, analysis, and narrative. History is thus reduced to a laboratory to discern patterns, typicality, frequency and probability which can be used in new historical explanations. Moreover, rather than merely explain something, it can be shown. "Show and tell" are thus combined dynamically.

One can point also to significant work by BORODKIN (1997) and his school (BORODKIN & LEONARD; ANDREEV *ET AL.*; LEVANDOVSKY; etc.) experimenting with chaos theory to explore the nonlinear dynamics of Russian labor history. IZMESTIEV applies such methodology from Russian Cliometricians to American economic history by modeling data about United States flour exports in the nineteenth century. The crux of such thinking is often stated simply—small events can have large effects—sometimes to counter the traditional thinking that large events must have large inputs. No one seems very interested in large events that have small effects. Immediate and long-range context, therefore, give significance to an otherwise insignificant datum. If it were not for the aftermath, the original event would seem less important, and the initial conditions surrounding that event would not attract interest. From the perspective of both the Physical and Social Sciences one reason for historical applications is to increase awareness about what to look for in present settings that may have significance later. Space and time have properties which contradict our common sense and contravene our abilities to observe history around us.

The problem is greater than simply imperfect data resulting from lack of preservation or even accumulation of initial observances. Multi-dimensional phenomena are particularly likely to deceive us. Inspired by Karl Popper and even Leibnitz before him, these ideas are not new but the technology by which to explore them is. The goal is not to postulate universal laws so exacting or precise as Hempel would have liked, but the ability to deal with nonlinear dynamics, hence, unexpected events and results with two perspectives. These quests are related: in one, the historical, the goal is explanation both for what happened and also greater understanding through "what-if" scenarios or alternative histories which allow one to put actuality into perspective; in the other, the present, the goal is a combination of explanation for understanding and prediction for preparedness. In the sciences, prediction is often the dominant goal because the study is often driven (funded) by the motive for control, although altruistic understanding, one would hope, is an ever present goal. If we cannot alter our history, can we influence our destiny? This is an ageless question posed by the ancients who felt more awe and perceived themselves as more helpless than we do when regarding the forces of nature.

Medieval thinkers explored the same theme, with various explanations including one metaphor which we can associate with gaming theory and beating the odds, that is, the wheel of fortune. They did not have the mathematical means to address statistical probability, the calculators to assist in handling differential equations, or computing power to manipulate the data stores we have, but their curiosity, speculative thought, and intellect set the foundations for thinking about chaos, the complex, and the difficulties of simplicity which lie at the core of such research today. The medieval mind was persuaded by St. Augustine and other Fathers about the linearity of time, but the spectrum of medieval thought was never entirely wedded to the determinism in linearity that dominated post-Reformation developments or Newtonian science. Moreover, older concepts of linearity were more general, directional like bands rather than narrow lines and single trajectories, where interplay was taken for granted.

Is the world purely accidental? Or, does the problem lie in our inability to perceive order from our vantage point as agents living in History? In chaos theory, tenets may be prevalent, but not necessarily laws. The basic thrust of historical questioning in this mode, according to ANDREEV, switches from "why" to "how" and uncertainty is treated as a kind of postmodernism in science. Instead of straining for the absolute, one learns to live with ambiguity, and with an ambiguous history and quasi-predictable future. Directions may be forecast, perhaps even selections of paths, but not certain steps. Surety is proportional to size of generalization, pattern, and phenomena; uncertainty increases as one moves closer to a particular instance. LEVANDOVSKY thus looked at strike movements in Russian history between 1895 to 1908 in terms of nonlinear dynamic models. He noticed that when graphing events in a time series or spectrum analysis, peaks of activity deviated enormously from most data fluctuations. Using Stochastic procedures borrowed from biological research in epidemiology and a mathematical system of differential equations, he graphed real data under a superimposed model of system data to show how the system indicated build-ups to these radical fluctuations that could not be seen in data modeled by traditional methods. The peaks in the real data spectrum thus appeared more predictable, except that this is the case only with hindsight and theoretical modeling.

The methods used in applying complexity theory to social history seem similar to some used to study the dissemination of information. Whereas older approaches would have relied on person-to-person contacts for linkage, the search for information system data did not rely on personal contact but on the spread of ideas, rumor, tension, and fear. The case in point was the 1905 shooting of a worker that in retrospect proved to be a turning point in the strike movements, even though treated in isolation this was a relatively small, isolated event. Its news created a large effect, disproportional to the incident itself. News did not spread chaotically, but through very complex systems influenced by external impulses. Levandovsky specifically likens the problem to the study of information dissemination, and thus makes a key link between such historical inquiry and Information Science. While the phenomena studied appear to operate in a system and exhibit intrinsic or inherent properties, the influence of externals on the system and on specific happenings is unclear. Of course, this methodology generates numerous questions. How well understood are the differential equations used in such complex modeling? To what degree is such extreme abstraction acceptable? How many cases are required to validate a model? What does such a paradigm shift do to causal thinking about historical processes in

History? Is chaos theory too relativistic? And can more linear models representing cause and effect be reconciled or used together with nonlinear chaos or complexity modeling?

Events occurring in a system, even though it is too complex to be seen as such, or for that matter to see connections between various phenomena, may not be simply chaotic in the sense of random occurrences. As in the case of imperfect data where fuzzy logic assists not so much in filling lacuna, but instead in leaping across them, making sense out of certain complicated, intricate, and interwoven events as part of an identifiable phenomenon, is often hindered by our inability to focus on detail and the big picture at the same time. Usually we have to move back and forth from detail to generality, when they in fact coexist simultaneously. It is our observation capabilities, thought, and sense making that are time-bound and sequential, rather than the events themselves. Moreover, by necessity we must study events in a series to mirror actual processes that are more involved and convoluted than we can discern by our unaided powers of observation. Such limitations are ours, not the historical situation studied; and this does not necessarily make happenings random. Thus, many theorists are turning from chaos, theory to such variations as complexity theory to investigate highly complex milieu and seemingly chaotic phenomena that occur in proximity in time and space (perceived as clusters or systems?). Complexity theory, reduced here ironically to simple terms and simplified in my explanation paradoxically to the point of naive simplicity, rests on three critical reconsideration of the universe, physical and biological, and therefore social as well:

1. Reclassification of "things" (originally perceived in Physics as particles, but because the concept applies to energy as well, when the idea is transferred to the Social Sciences one need not think necessarily in terms of people or objects, but objectified events, processes, happenings, and lives) based on the concept of granularity or coarseness, which in turn affects categorization of phenomena, better describes the universe than the antiquated notion of anything being strictly solid or constantly in any particular state. In such thinking, scaling from small to large with infinity in either dimension is not limited to a linear model or singular direction; changing mass is multi-directional and may not be constant or consistent, but tends to be congruent with its environment. Moreover, every whole has its components; systems are networks of systems, pervasive and discreet, larger and smaller, encompassing and subordinate, active and dormant, actively and reactively engaged with each other.

2. Behaviors are not static progressions, but they change in accord with differing sizes, mass, energy, and degree of interactivity. Past performance, i.e., history, is not the best explanation or foundation for prediction unless it accounts for the state of the subject at the time of each observation from every possible angle and measurement. Most views are intermittent, like still photographs from one camera angle, taken in sequence to produce something like a motion picture that our poor sight takes for constant motion and an accurate depiction of change. Instead our vision is limited by our own perspective, too much remains unseen, and perception is based only on appearance rather than substance.

3. Change, therefore, is always context sensitive. The whole and the part must be related all of the time, from all angles, with the understanding that both act upon and react to each other. Relationships are reflexive. Moreover, the whole is indeed more than the sum of its parts (water is not simply a combination of hydrogen and oxygen. And its liquid properties differ significantly from its gaseous state), but borders, limitations, confinements, and definition seen as "definements," are neither static or absolute. The ideas of individuality, corporation, wholeness, and completion, or the opposite end of a spectrum, i.e., of particles, parts and particulars,

are abstractions, constructs, and models which simply enable humans to think alone and collectively. Complex entity modeling, therefore, must be conceived not so much as chaos, but as systems of systems, interacting at different speeds, depending on the amount of interaction and directions of forces or actions upon each other.

One avenue deserving more explicit exploration than has been given to it in history literature, perhaps because the methodology is so mathematical, is this subtle move from Chaos to Complexity theory in the physical and biological sciences (GLEICK; HAND). The difference has implications for History and Information Science as well for the concept of Historical Information Science explored here. Herbert Simon in laying the foundations for Artificial Intelligence in 1979 justified modeling alternative models of thought to deal with the complex (SIMON, 1979), and, as already noted, what he more recently called "bounded rationality" (SIMON, 1991), has contributed to the evolution of various notions that have gelled into an increasingly formal Complexity Theory. BROCK and BAUMOL & BENHABIB used the theory to explain economic change in history. This thinking has made Chaos Theory applicable, for example, or organizations, and hence to management theory. So, key articles in the business sections of leading journals in the United States have recently run headlines about "Complexity meets the Business World" which convert Chaos Theory into "a new business science" (BROWNLEE; OVERMAN). Hence, Coopers & Lybrand consultants, Thinking Tools, Inc., of California, worked with complexity theorists at the Santa Fe Institute to produce software, *TeleSim*, for introducing executives to competition in a deregulated marketplace (cf., *Exploring Chaos* by MECC with its components: Mosaic Madness, Game of Life, Random Walk 1-2, and Chaos Game). Approaches related to Complexity Theory are extolled at Ernst & Young's Center for Business Innovation, so more and more corporations are now mining their company's customer records and data warehouses using nonlinear programs. Mathematicians are applying such approaches to everything from the stock market to flexible designs for assembly plants. S. KAUFFMAN, in his book *Management for the Millennium*, encourages businesses to embrace the principles of complexity theory to manage more creatively; thus the glossary of terms and phrases he coined is recommended in "Creativity at the Edge of Chaos" to *Working Women's* readers (1997 Feb.; 22[2]:46-52) as a working vocabulary for tomorrow's managers. HAYLES (1991) warns against such popularization and the "deprofessionalization" of the term's usage, but to little avail.

The Chaos metaphor is now widely used in business, far more than in History or Information Science (BEHN; KIEL); its spread has been fanned by a series of financial management and administrative science books since 1992 (PRIESTMEYER; WHEATLEY; OVERMAN & LORAINE; DANEKE; etc), which have advocated "postmodern...administration" (FOX & MILLER). OVERMAN (1996, p. 4) claims that within three years certain shifts in thinking inside the corporate world are noticeable: he maintains that Chaos Theory has added significantly to the understanding of administrative behaviors, for example:

> ...appreciation, not distrust of chaos and of uncertain stressful times in organizations and management...real change and new structures are found in the very chaos they [managers] try to prevent...certain faith in self-organization; this is not complacency but the knowledge that small actions can redouble many times over to create large results in what chaos theorists call the butterfly effect...the context of control and prediction changes from short-term outcomes to a much larger sense of scale and order. Administrative issues like diversity and accountability are viewed in the larger social and political context.

"The world of quantum administration is even stranger than that of administrative chaos" he exclaims; and in a pronouncement that sounds almost religious, he explains this phenomenon in relation to the aforementioned discussion about organizational culture:

> Quantum administration is a world with different foci: on energy, not matter; on becoming, not being; on coincidence, not causes; on constructivism, not determinism; and on new states of awareness and consciousness. In many aspects, quantum administration shifts focus from structural and functional aspects of organization to the spiritual characteristics and qualities of organizational life. As bizarre and weird as all this sounds, it is already part of our scientific practice and everyday personal and administrative lives.

Examples abound for contemporary interest in such nonlinear dynamic modeling: in stock market prediction, distribution and production, and product marketing in business (K. BALL; cf., the proceedings of the Annual Chaos Conferences in Manufacturing); communication loads on telecommunication systems and networks in Information Technology; social mobility for long-term demographic trends in Sociology and short-term tourism in Hospitality Management; political trends and voting behaviors (T. BECKER); the interplay between Psychology, Sociology, and Biology (S. BARTON; HALASZ) and epidemiology and genetic research in Medicine (STITES) and the organization of health care (CHOPRA; OVERMAN & CAHILL). MORIN (1996) relates "the art of complexity" to "a new way of thinking" in information theory and cybernetics, as an antidote to determinism which he incorrectly assumes to mean a denial of random factors by a purely mechanistic logic (when many see chaos theory as quite deterministic, e.g., outcomes as factors of combinatorics). In any case, all such developments have implications for teaching and curricula, as described by R. IANNONE.

M. S. FOX, influenced by Simon's ideas, approached distributed computing from the point of view that simultaneous and parallel data processing were needed to manipulate complex data sets. Complexity in this computational approach was defined as "excessive demands on rationality. That is, the task requirements exceed current bounds on computational capacity" (M. FOX, 1981, p. 75). The same might be said for the perception of complexity as too taxing on the human brain and its computational capacity, which in turn requires computing and thereafter computers of increased power to contend with increasingly complex and massive data. The information complexity approach has become popular among engineers and computer scientists who learn coding and information theory, and who have been taught to pay attention to such minimum complexity measures as code and message length (RISSANEN). Information scientists have borrowed the idea of complexity from them, but equally from the Social Sciences where data have always been perceived as among the most complex. ROBBIN & FROST-KUMPF (p. 96), relying on M. DAVID (cf., DAVID & ROBBIN), use census data to illustrate what they mean by data complexity:

> millions of observations, thousands of data elements with numerous interdependent relationships, and intricate logical conditions on the measurement process. Data complexity connotes an interdependence of organizational, social, cognitive, and technical requirements for understanding, retrieving, and use data. These very requirements have, however, resulted in underutilization, misuse, and nonuse of complex data by data users (secondary analysts).

Stochastic and Bayesian methods are related, as in search bounds, extension of likelihood approaches, and learning networks based on resampling schemes (BUNTINE, 1996, p. 205). Such a transition in thinking would break away from the historian's tendency to model human behavior in the aggregate on individual behavior as if the two were automatically the same, and it could accommodate the complexity known by historians to exist by virtue of the numerous variables in human affairs they have attempted to account for when arriving at generalization.

Complexity theory and cross validation through resampling are logical progressions from the past decade's multivariate statistics. Likewise, the notion of concurrency has developed from simple serial to parallel processing and now to multiple linear processing whereby each event, moment, progression, and entire series must be related to all counterparts in other linear developments. Finally, consider these elements as interactive and interdependent. The increased complexity boggles the mind, both rationality and imagination, and in becoming aware of the bounds on one's individual intellect to track, and more, to comprehend such complex interaction, reliance on artificially created assistance seems to be the only recourse that is rational. Relying simply on a single historian's prowess, no matter how diligent and learned, or on his or her own unaided judgment becomes a preposterous proposition.

One could venture into the difference between chaos and complexity in either philosophical or religious terms, but this would not simplify matters for considering how such thinking might translate into historical computing. A visual model of something more concrete may assist here, especially since so much of this thought comes from the physical sciences. Consider gravity as a linear force and the calculation of a free fall; then enter variants into the equation to make this model more complex. The wind is blowing, but not from one direction; wind currents are changing and the impact on the falling object is neither constant or from one direction only. As the object falls, it descends through layers of varying resistance from thin to heavier atmosphere and into something even denser, perhaps water, before reaching its destination. Finally, the object is not falling by itself, but is one of many like a hail shower, with one ball bumping into the other. The calculation of destination, even more complex in space travel, is far removed from the original linear equations and projections. Likewise, the description of where something has been or how it developed is equally complex. However, historians in most computing are still operating at the level of thought required by the former relatively simple situation of single entities in free fall without obstruction or influence, rather than the complex world they are really studying. Such thinking should have appeal to quantification historians and encourage them to engage the next generation of computing for complex analyses, interactive modeling, and dynamic visualization associated with multi-dimensional virtual reality.

Consider, for example, what complexity theory says about variance, and how reconceptualization of variants in nonlinear terms should alter currently limited approaches to data modeling, pattern recognition, and the static concepts of structure. Variants must be treated by size, mass, interaction, and motion as dynamic clusters. Reclassification of variants is required, in a subtle but pervasive shift from thinking of things to functions, actions, processes, and relationships. Types of interaction may be discerned and categorized. Sequencing stressed in linear programming need not be replaced with randomness, but rather with greater variation to account for exchanging places rather than rigid line-ups. Location becomes a matter of distance, proximity, interactivity, and in the study of intelligent life, awareness.

Causality in linear thinking is therefore changed as dramatically in historical work as in holistic medicine where a diagnosis is no longer simply a set of symptoms reduced to a single generic problem as if all people were average (when relatively few are, since distributions in life do not appear as perfected Bell curves), linked unilaterally to a prescription for a projected cure. Differing prognoses are entertained, timing is important, and choices are made based on multiple variables—actual age, weight, intake (other medicines, foods, etc), and case histories of an individual's health rather than a statistical average, matched against an array of responses, some natural, others pharmaceutical, in combinations with natural remedies. As is being realized slowly in Medicine, changing contexts and interactions of systems produce new circumstances which continue to alter dynamics of interactive systems. Such alterations can be noticed in both the properties of the things studies and in the phenomena surrounding them, i.e., changed behaviors. Projections reached by linear programming toward single solutions and predicted results often miss the mark. Or, when they seem to work, they obscure the possibilities of other alternatives working similarly well or better.

A new paradigm more compatible with the complexity of human affairs would see input as a range of actions (as in activity theory, which is now being applied to human computer interaction) from inaction, continued action, reaction, to intensified and altered actions that feed into an array of filters or scenarios that change combinations with each other and inputs, resulting in possibilities, projections, contingencies, and alternatives sorted out by artificial intelligence operators and "if that, then this" logic (Contingency theory) and priorities as likelihoods based on the inputs, intensity, timing, and interactivity recorded. The result is a far more dynamic model than can be achieved in linear programming, a better analysis because more possibilities are covered, and projections that can be related to other potentially viable alternatives. Such an approach is decidedly different from working with fuzzy data to produce reliable averages and hypothetical explanatory models for which no particular or actual case exists in known history. It is also different from the current emphasis on structures, static as they often are, or on pattern recognition, as if the pattern were a template controlling human affairs as distinct from a descriptive model or more general explanation. For historians complexity theory means multiple explanations for phenomena, the composite of which produces the fullest range of explanation possible. Weighted multiple explanations may be seen as inherently better than description only or single cause explanations which so often seem overly simplistic with the benefit of hindsight. Finally, the emphasis on context sensitivity *en toto* means moving beyond the relatively simple two-dimensional interplay between linear time and single place of an agent whose history is largely constructed from its own vantage point to a multi-dimensional universe in which circumspective agents are active and reactive, i.e., in space and dynamic situations that are forever changing. Explanations of historical phenomena, like any observed contemporaneously or foreseen through some kind of predictive modeling and projection, are not so easily rehearsed as in linear programming or so simply explained as by linear thinking.

The physical sciences have likewise encountered phenomena which are also unexplained by linear logic and programming, but they have been more creative in seeking alternative ways of looking at things and developing innovative methodologies; these have been adapted increasingly to socioeconomic studies. From chaos and complexity theories have sprung such revisions and refinements as antichaos and self-organized criticality where "many composite systems naturally evolve to a critical state in which a minor event starts a chain reaction that can affect any number of elements in the system" (BAK & CHEN), which should interest historians in that real and perceived chaos seems not to be tolerated for long before order is either reintroduced to stabilize situations or underlying order rises to the surface where is it more evident than at first glance. Creation and destruction are interactive. PRIGOGINE introduced the idea of self-organization from disorder, as distinct from John von Neuman's idea of self-regeneration, Heinz Von Foerster's "order from noise," or Henri Atlan's "random organization." COHEN & STEWART in their *Collapse of Chaos* argue the paradox that from the interaction of chaos and complexity comes simplicity. S. KAUFFMAN suggests that complex living systems (e.g., human societies) arise by virtue of their own laws of assembly, interaction, and self-correction.

Moreover, interest in feedback mechanisms in physical and economic phenomena are surprisingly parallel with research in Information Science on similar phenomena; for example, imbalanced equilibria and seemingly chaotic situations seem almost self-correcting and restabilizing or what the economist W. B. ARTHUR refers to as "adaptive systems" (ARTHUR, DURLAUF & LANE). Chaos theoreticians have likened these intra-movements or fluctuations like ebbs and flows or rises and falls in systems to be similar to subcultures making their influence felt inside cultures (PRIGOGINE stressed the importance of these "fluctuating" subsystems). CASTI's *Complexification* explores such timed events and processes as catastrophes, chaos, paradoxes, irreducibility, emergence, and interaction, etc., by suggesting correspondences between physical and social-historical phenomena. SFI researchers have tossed out numerous challenges for historians and information scientists to take up; many of the problems raised are more like unanswered questions which require a combination of History and

Information Science to be addressed. Nonlinear dynamics were first explored for historical research in the United States during the late 1980s, but only in this decade when such methods and their underlying principles gained popularity in the Social Sciences have historians investigated such modeling more thoroughly (SHERMER). The result has been a resurrection of old methodological debates, including some of the very same bugaboos from the earlier Cliometric controversy. It has been criticized for merging science and history, too often seen as opposites. In other cases, historians have objected because, in Shermer's words (p. 60), "The integration of chaos and history uses a theory of present change to explain past change."

The assumption, of course, is that change as a historical process does possess certain characteristics which can be applied to all time, e.g., the measurement of change by time itself. As when modeling events for which not every instance is known or when confronting the problems of imperfect or incomplete data, inference is used, which in effect substitutes something known from one time period and similar situation for another less known period, or in cases of short duration, unknown developments, nonlinear dynamic modeling often relies of data exchange to fill missing pieces of the puzzle. This is the objection of historians whose credulity is limited to complete data, but then what can be known of history is often very little. If one grants the objection, this is tantamount to not trying to find out something simply because data seem insufficient to document every instance. Very little knowledge is so completely documented. As we live with a certain amount of ambiguity in our everyday lives, so too must we accommodate an ambiguous history in many of its phases. Generalized notions about what happened, however, are usually taken as better than no notion at all. Like scientists appreciating a solidly constructed hypothesis, historians understand the importance of rational speculation. A good guess is a credit, more than simply admitting ignorance. Without guess work, after all, in many cases historians are left with nothing. The same can be argued for modeling.

As already mentioned, the dominant notion prevailing in such instances, however, is that time marches on in a linear direction, or at least we can trace events usually only along a trajectory, path, or something wider and less delimited, such as a movement or something vague as an orientation. Linearity is common to all of these notions about history, and implicit therein is a cause and effect relation between what transpired before and after. History becomes more complicated when several paths are explored, and when movement on them is uneven, or worse, two-directional. Intersections are intriguing because of the mix that can occur, but too many, as in lattice work, become disturbing and confusing like a maze. Too much movement, too many directions, variable timing, and disorder prohibiting a story line and a progression of historical narrative as explanation (i.e., causal stories) are all disturbing (MCCLOSKEY, 1990, p. 19). Nonlinear thinking upsets the pervasive Augustinian paradigm. Historians have long been aware of alternative approaches to historical explanation and have ascribed certain phenomena to chaos in the same way that medieval historians explained certain events as mysteries. But they have not, generally investigated chaotic history as just that; instead, the chaotic period is seen as an interregnum, an abnormality, and a fluctuation from the usual course of human events. KELLERT explains this tardiness of historians in terms of similar reactions in the hard sciences where physicists, for example, "had not learned to look for chaos. What they did not look for, they did not find."

Even though the idea of chaos had surfaced in late nineteenth-century physics, it was argued away as so much "noise" in the classically defined orderly universe. Historians reacted no differently. Kellert argues that it was not until the 1960s that nonlinearity was deemed worthy of scientific experimentation, when science began to give up the "metaphysical comforts of determinism." He adopts a feminist interpretation of science (noted in SHERMER's critique, p. 3), that is, when women began entering science increasingly notions of a mechanistic universe were being discarded as a means of dominating nature rather than living with her. The same tardiness to adopt less deterministic models for historical research may be observed in Information Science, even though women were well represented in this profession and the field always claimed to be a science (at least a Social Science). Kellert argues that in the late 1970s and early 1980s, science, technology, and culture were ready for chaos. In Shermer's paraphrase, "...meaningless noise became meaningful data." At the same time, of course, quantitative historians were exploiting local data and even trivia as never before. Early Cliometricians, however, operated almost exclusively along linear lines—not curves, waves, or circles, and certainly not intricate multi-directional laces. When they did conceive of patterns and worked to discover latent patterns where they could not be seen without the help of a computer such patterns like good fabrics such good patterns were still expected to have a grain in their weave. Their objectives were largely deterministic. The same might be said still for Information Science. Why would chaos theory be more acceptable now than then? KELLERT explains that the influence came from "extra scientific parts of society," as if women entering the sciences brought in a fresh look and a host of things not previously considered legitimate science, disorder being one of these curious phenomena. Shermer quotes Kellert, accepting his explanation, that chaos theory became attractive because it "yields qualitative predictions for systems where detailed quantitative predictions are impossible." K. HAYLES (1984, 1990) likewise views the rise of chaos theory as a parallel movement with Postmodernism in tune with the aftermath of literary deconstructionism which indeed seems to have made History chaotic.

Even though it is difficult to point to many works that have employed chaos/complexity theory to advantage in actual case studies, the idea of such applications has generated a metahistory literature worth exploring. Oddly enough, it reveals that Hempelian notions are alive and well, although their expression is transmuted from exacting and all-covering laws to a more generalized notion of order in the universe, if for no other reason than to provide a counterthesis to chaos as popularly treated, namely as sheer lack of order. Instead, the academic version of chaos theory maintains the suspicion that latent patterns underlie what is immediately and directly observable and that some order is operable despite the apparent lack thereof to contemporary informers about historical phenomena and participants in the system being explored. Those oriented toward Social Sciences still explore to enhance predictability, or if not forecasting, more modestly post-dictability as a means of explanation and an alternative to pure description and narrative. T. JACKSON, on the other hand, sees the two as compatible in that the introduction of chaos theory into the writing of history (in this case, historical fiction), helps to "unravel" the importance of history in narrative.

Recently numerous articles have propelled chaos theory into historical circles which have a Social Science orientation and where historical computing flourishes. SHERMER points to Ilyra Prigogine and Isabelle Stenger's widely read *Order Out of Chaos* as a stimulus and bridge between the "extra scientific" and scientific (PRIGOGINE & STENGER). He notes as well that in the same year, 1984, Alvin Saperstein suggested that "war be viewed as a breakdown in predictability, a situation in which small perturbations of initial conditions, such as malfunctions of early warning radar systems or irrational acts of individuals disobeying orders, lead to large unforeseen changes in the solutions to the dynamical equations and mode" (SAPERSTEIN, pp. 303-305). BEAUMONT takes a similar view that the history of war is a study of chaos. EPSTEIN (1985) spoke of "the calculus of conventional war" when advocating methods for dynamic analysis or scenario-driven war games in anticipation of modern video games and simulation capability. Although Saperstein does not make this connection, here is chaos theory applied to what TOYNBEE much earlier in his *Change and Habit* attributed to uncontrolled acceleration of human events, in contrast to habit which was predictable. Toynbee never espoused chaos theory as such but came close to the same conclusions based on his multilineal conceptualization of history (cf., for example, OTT). The same idea is reflected in HANN's title for a collection of case studies: *When History Accelerates: Essays on Rapid Social Change, Complexity, and Creativity.*

To continue with Shermer's chronolog, LOYE & EISLER in 1987 published their paper on "Chaos and Transformation" using history to support their futuristic generalizations. SHERMER (1988) published his application of such thinking to formal history (first given as a paper at the "Interface Conference" in Atlanta—how apropos!), viewing historical happenings as events resulting from movement on a matrix rather than moments in movement along straight lines, to form "A Theory of Historical Contingency." SHERMER (1995, p. 8) later frames the issues in terms of the interrelationship between "contingent-necessity"—taken to mean a conjuncture of events compelling a certain course of action by constraining prior conditions—and the polarization of randomness and predictability. Contingency is a trigger for change, and the "trigger" point is a bifurcation in an historical sequence where previous well-established necessities, according to SHERMER, have been challenged by others to produce (cause?) a change in course (or when thinking linearly, direction). Another related characteristic of chaos is "sensitive dependency" which is captured in another metaphor of nonlinear dynamics, namely, the proverbial "straw that breaks the camel's back."

By the opening of this decade, there was increased awareness of chaos theory in History, as a theoretical reversal of the standard "great man" and "large event, great impact" explanations of historical change. In 1990, BEYERCHEN heralded this as "a new intellectual vision," and HAYLES spoke about the "paradigm shift of remarkable scope and significance" at the beginning of this decade. Unfortunately, proponents of nonlinear dynamic modeling fell into the same trap as all enthusiasts by proclaiming chaos studies to be the "new science." In true form for historians, critics rose to the challenge and to reject the hype, reminding everyone of passing fads in the previous decades about catastrophe theory (ARNOLD; POSTON & STEWART), collision theory (M. GOLDBERGER & WATSON), and the like, which caught on only for short times (M. W. HIRSCH; and more recently, ROTH & RYCKMAN, n. 3). Shermer retrospectively assures us that a conservative reaction could have been expected: "... such cross disciplinary integration usually received in the scholarly community" such a reception. That, in History, was predicable (and may be predicted as well for this present attempt to argue the cross-disciplinary case for Historical Information Science).

In 1990, DYKE, whom Shermer claims was the first (perhaps first in English) to take a serious look at the historical applications of chaos theory, published his "Strange Attraction, Curious Liaison: Clio Meets Chaos." While being skeptical and even sarcastic in the spirit of the older Cliometric debates, Dyke nevertheless provided chaos theory with some credibility in blending the idea of "great men" of history with the idea of happenstance or, as he called it, "special circumstance" that provoked their action and thus evoked their greatness. All of this attention to what was still new and novel for many historians naturally led to a forum at the American Historical Association on January 9, 1994, on "Chaos Theory and History" which despite poor placement on the schedule, panelists SHERMER (chair), ROTH & RYCKMAN, and REISCH played to a standing-room only audience (it was, as the chairman recalled, a small room—indicative of AHA's incorrect prediction of low interest among today's historians). The panel was convened precisely to encourage debate about nonlinear historical computing under the guise of the applicability of chaos/complexity theory to the modern study of History. Debate they did—and still do.

In its February 1991 special issue, *History and Theory* published a must-read forum on *Chaos Theory and History* featuring Professors George Reisch and Donald McCloskey whose views have provoked comment ever since. The debate often focuses on two theses: (1) Causal theory whereby one sees cause and effect in a proportional linear harmony (as the saying goes, "one [your choice of explicative] thing leads to another"); and (2) Convergence theory, whose proponents like MCCLOSKEY, BEYERCHEN, ROTH, WALLERSTEIN, etc., hold out the promise of a reconciliation between a law-governed universe and unpredictable history ("conflicting intuitions," as ROTH & RYCKMAN call them, p. 2). REISCH (1995) attacked both Hempelian notions of covering-laws (thus indicating that the old issue is not really dead, but periodically is pushed underground and surfaces anew) and explanations based only on initial conditions (e.g., the so-called "butterfly effect"), and he favors the use of narration in History. More importantly, "covering-law explanations must be resolved into narrative temporal structures." SCHERMER (1995, p. 8) likewise reminds us that scientists have also turned to constructing the equivalents to scientific narratives of systems rather than chasing the elusive universal form.

REISCH (1991) argues that historical processes do exhibit dependence on initial conditions and that history is chaotic, but accurate prediction is not possible beyond very short temporal spans because of the problems of incomplete and imperfect data, which is my paraphrase to tie his arguments to aforementioned themes in Historical Information Science (cf., the rendition and rebuttal by ROTH & RYCKMAN, a rejoinder by REISCH and moderation by SCHERMER, 1995). The assumption is that accuracy depends on accurate local data, but requisite detail is seldom available (as if the limitation of modern history were always a matter of inadequate archives). Approximation and generalization, then, are the characteristics of most valid and reliable historical explanation, rather than either absolute continuous recall or predictability. REISCH therefore argues in somewhat of a circuitous route from hypothetical covering-laws that are inherently faulty as predictors, but may suffice for explanation as "global contours" or "narrative temporal structures."

MCCLOSKEY (1991) on the other hand attempts an understanding of historians steeped in linear thinking, educated in what he calls "a rhetoric of linear differential equations" that teaches them to think that "large results must have large causes." Of course he would like to reform such thinking. He shares George Reisch's doubts about the possibilities to acquire sufficient data for accuracy in predictive historical modeling or forecasting, and even with an abundance of data he foresees problems in determining which events are explainable, which causes might be invoked, and whether systems (parts of the world in certain periods) are linear or nonlinear (as if they must be one or the other). But departing from Reisch, Donald McCloskey rejects the idea that narrative is appropriate for nonlinear history. The problem is twofold and paradoxical: unbounded sets can incorporate anything and in chaotic systems stories are untellable (precisely because story lines are linear, but also because one is overwhelmed by detail). He adds another challenge, the "paradox of foreknowledge" common in science fiction wherein time travelers play with history and alter its course, and thereby destroy the very predictability that enabled them supposedly to control their lives. In *Star Trek*, remember, the prime directive of noninterference was justified by this same reason. McCloskey does not invoke the Federation of Planets as an authority, but he does wonder if actors in a system could themselves predict and act on their knowledge, how would it affect the system. Ultimately, McCloskey advocated the use of "formal models as metaphors" rather than narratives for historical explanation, and thereby he finds a cardinal commonality between the Humanities and Science.

In reviewing the Reisch-McCloskey forum, ROTH & RYCKMAN conclude that the former simply establishes that "scientific" history moves in small steps (that is, covering short periods, that his arguments do not stand up to scrutiny, and that as the debate continues, simulations of complex phenomena (e.g., stocks and commodities markets) are being developed as imitative models which do not resolve the issues he stresses into narrative explanations. They likewise conclude that the latter succeeded only in "the replacement of one dogma (linear proportionality) by another (nonlinear dynamics). They conclude, therefore, from this initial round of debate, that it is still unclear if Chaos Theory has really anything genuinely new or insightful to offer History; and "as goes the Causal thesis so goes Convergence." They conclude (p. 41-2), therefore:

> Deep conceptual difficulties are inherent in the apparently suggestive analogy between nonlinear systems and historical events. The promised benefits of chaos theory vis-à-vis history are at best an extremely loose heuristic which easily

seduces the unwary into taking at face value terms and concepts that have a especially precise meaning only within the confines of mathematical theory. Outside of this context the use of these terms and concepts furthers tendencies to promote pseudoscientific "accounts" of the character of history, accounts which some of the more circumspect exponents of the "chaotic paradigm" in historical studies take some pains to eschew.

Beyond this threatening obfuscation, the primary intellectual issue joined by the promotion of the chaotic paradigm in historical studies seems to be spurred by desires to resist the tired hegemonies of "global" meta-narrative histories, whether by driving yet another nail in the coffin of the Hempelian covering-law model of historical explanation (an enterprise we thought was long ago passé), or by opposing the viability of structuralist or "social force" theories of historical determinism. While we sympathize with these latter aspirations, we remain decidedly skeptical that any truly beneficial assistance to metahistorical studies will be rendered by overblown comparisons with the dynamics of nonlinear systems.

Here one has a conclusion drawn from philosophical debate in Platonic style about premises and methods so generalized that one wonders about the real understanding of them, with no reference to actual pilot studies, no testing, and no contribution to the development of method which might overcome objections to the general approach. Classical skepticism, conclusions largely based on opinion, positions of authority in the teaching establishment, and the personal reading of historical theory literature dominate this initial round of debate which thwarts the development of methodology, however experimental, before it even has a chance to transform itself in the process of transference or to emerge from within History itself. One can immediately sense a *dejà vu* from earlier Cliometric debates, however bridled the reactionary impulse is. The negativism may be veiled by academic civility more than before. There is again a core conservatism of the historical enterprise, a propensity toward criticism, and a timidity of historians at large to engage quantification, modeling, and experimental methodologies or to interject themselves into non-History environs where historical perspective might be valuable but where such discussion would have to occur on a different level.

It is as the University of Chicago's William McNeill observed, somewhat saddened that History is so much a craft learned in the apprenticeship mode where mastery comes only with practice: "...in general we [historians] are an untheoretical profession; [we] learn by apprenticeship and reflect little on the larger epistemological contest of our inherited terms" (personal correspondence cited by SHERMER, 1995, n. 5). He commends Schermer for trying to illuminate the profession, "but [I] suspect most of my colleagues will not even try to understand!" This may seem somewhat harsh, unless it is taken as a statement about the human condition generally, since similar remarks have been heard in Information Science circles about practitioners in the field. It may be hard to fly with one's nose to the grindstone, but an open mind is required for the reception of ideas from other fields. The synthetic nature of History requires this, but one might also hope for more indigenous methodological experimentation and interdisciplinary development where historians were not so content with taking new thought from other fields, subjecting it to such hypercriticism that its death rather than modification is the result, or conversely, simply applying a contemporary mode of thought to the past and serving it up always as New History.

While ROTH & RYCKMAN recently referred to historical explanation based on chaos theory as "scientistic illusions of understanding," REISCH (1995) has responded by advocating "Scientism without tears" (of fears?). The former react badly to what they see as a false analogy between history and chaos theory, when advocates argue that the adoption of chaos theory lessens History's deviations from Science. Their argument confuses several things, most obviously chaos theory with chaos observed in history and the notion that History is or has a unified theory. As mentioned, they divide advocates of chaos theory applications to the study of historical phenomena into two camps: those constructing models which adopt a causal thesis, and those who feel compelled to adopt such approaches on the basis of convergence theory. (I would, supposedly, fall into this latter camp in advocating a unifying Historical Information Science which might use at least for purposes of exploration and methodological development both linear and nonlinear approaches associated with chaos theory.)

REISCH, after analyzing the problems ROTH & RYCKMAN propose, concludes that they, as others, have "hurled baseless accusations" against the use of dynamic nonlinear modeling. He goes further in his counterattack to argue that there is no basis for the contention that scientific concepts cannot be used in explaining historical events. All parties in this debate, of course, miss an essential point: regardless of what historians think about the applicability of chaos and complexity theory to History, grappling with these theories is a necessity for historians because all other disciplines are engaging them. If Physics and Astronomy, Biology and Genetics, Political science, Sociology, Organizational Management, Manufacturing and distributed production, and Information Science, and in some circles Literature as well, all absorb elements of chaos theory into their thinking, operations, applications, and production, what choice has History but to engage such studies if for nothing else than to be able to continue an understanding of modern culture? To ignore something so pervasive, or worse, to maintain that it has nothing to do with History, is perverse. The test of historical inquisitiveness and adaptation will be if historians in America explore such concepts only to study their subjects, or if they experiment with new techniques and applications of information technology similar to young scholars in Russia, in order to produce pilot studies that enable us to refine such methods and enhance the technology needed for theoretical modeling and a mutually reinforcing interplay between quantitative and qualitative interpretations (as explored by KING, KEOHANE & VERBA in Political Science and History).

SCHERMER (1993, 1995) admirably attempts to move thinking about chaos and complexity in History beyond apologetics and polemics by producing a model that addresses some of the queries raised by REISCH (p. 18) and others. His model of "contingency-necessity" to connect early pervasive contingencies with later local necessities, which vary over time, proposes six corollaries (1995, p. 9):

1. The earlier in the development of any historical sequence the more chaotic are the actions of the individual elements of that sequence and the less predictable are future actions and necessities.

2. The later in the development of any historical sequence the more ordered are the actions of the individual elements of that sequence and the more predictable are future actions and necessities.

3. The actions of the individual elements of any historical sequence are generally postdictable but not specifically predictable, as regulated by Corollaries one and two.

4. Change in historical sequences from chaotic to ordered is common, gradual, followed by relative stasis, and tends to occur at points where poorly established necessities give way to dominant ones so that a contingency will have little effect in altering the direction of the sequence.

5. Change in historical sequences from ordered to chaotic is rare, sudden, followed by relative nonstasis, and tends to occur at points where previously well-established necessities have been challenged by others so that a contingency may push the sequence in one direction or the other.

6. At the beginning of any historical sequence, actions of the individual elements are chaotic, unpredictable, and have a powerful influence on the future development of that sequence. As the sequence gradually develops and the pathways slowly become more worn, out of chaos comes order. The individual elements sort themselves into their allotted positions, as dictated solely by what came before—the unique and characteristic sum and substance of history, driven forward on the entropic arrow of time by the interplay of contingency and necessity.

Once a historian chooses to delimit his or her study, or adopt a rational boundary (an area and time, a culture, etc.), SHERMER proposes the model of contingent-necessity and the above quote corollaries can be used "as a heuristic framework for representing what happened between these limits. A historical sequence is a time frame determined by the focal point and the boundaries of the subject under investigation." He is here echoing PRIGOGINE & STENGER (p. 169) who observe that in chaos "the mixture of necessity and chance constitutes the history of the system."

One might rephrase this in making a case for Historical Information Science, namely that by necessity History must study such systems to continue to study history as it unfolds lest it encourage chaos in the worst sense of the word in bringing about the demise of history. If information today is imbued with the notions of chaos and complexity, and this is the stuff of history tomorrow, historians had best engage such developments sooner than later. Even if its chief role is as detractor and critic, New History cannot ignore this "New Science."

MULTI-DIMENSIONAL VIEWS

In addition to new information technology, analytic methods, and modeling based on an alternative thinking as a means to create a new historicism, there remains the conjunctive problems of presentation of nonlinear events in serial media which are inherently linear, the reconciliation of opposing views, or at least the accommodation of differing views in the notion of historical truth. Data mining and knowledge discovery, modeling, and knowledge representation are closely entwined in learning. Those who attack mathematical modeling must remember that modeling is also done linguistically and through imagery, and combinations thereof as in word pictures, parables, and storytelling. Modern computer graphics now make modeling neither textual or verbal, but actively audiovisual, totally multidimensional, and interactive (FALCIDIENO & KUNNI, eds.)

The pervasive book mentality, shaped by a Judeo-Christian communications technology designed to capture and preserve for all time the Christ-event and to guard against tampering with the oral/aural-visual evidence converted to text has so captured the mentality of Western historiography that historians cannot break away from this model even for their own presentation of their interpretations. Thus, a numerate representation is still commonly inserted into text-blocks as a static, unchanging picture of the event or series of events studied. The codex, with its binding of signatures, controlled layout, checks for completeness such as tables of contents, chapter divisions, titling, and serial pagination, not only preserves content but it controls readers for sequential consumption of information. The sequencing is always linear, and history is usually Augustinian in its layout and progression, even though we know that when people read books they defy the control built into binding by paging backwards, browsing and skimming, viewing pictures first before reading the text, and surveying tables and contents and indexes to read in the book rather than from cover to cover. Just as objects are meant to be viewed as a whole, books were made to be read sequentially, and serials and archival series were meant to be consulted serially. But libraries were and are different, since they are multi-source, diverse, and contextual, so that reading in a library is a substantially different experience than reading a book, consulting archival records, or examining museum exhibition. The three have their own unique characteristics, presentation strengths and weaknesses, controls, histories, and cultures; yet they are all related. And they are being integrated more and more by modern information technology.

The pervasive mind-set of historians is solidly locked into this book tradition with preference for text, even when their methodologies are quantified rather than purely descriptive. This holds as well for work with images, which are often serialized as in film, one after the other, when actuality may appear more kaleidoscopic from their perspective of the agent. In this vein, BATY has argued, based on her work with historical photographs for the critical examination of all still-images and their placement, whenever possible, into a series so one interprets their historical data from the equivalent to a motion picture. Such sequencing represents historical thinking that is codified; it simplifies by bringing order to things perhaps less orderly than historical analysis would allow them to remain. The result is a particular view that is two-dimensional at best. However, today's technology allows for multi-dimensional thinking, analysis, and representation. Again, this change is challenging the dominant linear notion of history.

Note, for example, that not all human data acquisition is serial, and even it were, time is often unnoticed and views may be taken in and recognized in an order other than how we make sense of our observations. Even when one glances about, circumspection allows the mind to comprehend several scenarios at once, each frame by the direction in which one looks. One scene is retained mentally while another is viewed, and the mind reconstructs a sort of cinerama or circumferential view greater than what can actually be seen at once. Each direction may be viewed sequentially, but recall is from an integrated mental panorama. In short, we know that human information processing and acquisition are different, and that neither is always sequential, linear, or chronological as commonly thought. Why, then, is history always viewed traditionally in these terms? Is it a matter of simplicity and avoiding mental overload? History recognized as complex requires a higher order of complex thinking, including more complex information retrieval. This is difficult, as when contemplating comparative history, which is really a form of parallel processing. One-track mindedness is easier; so is a serial one, and hence two-dimensional history. Multivariant, multi-dimensional history is difficult to perceive, synthesize, and make sense of, when relying only on our natural powers of observation or older technologies.

When quantified studies have been undertaken in history, the goal is usually a conversion back into narrative, textual codification, and the subjugation of graphics to text. This is a pickling process, and it preserves history but does not bring it alive. The Christian notion of revelation, i.e., retaking something intangible from the physical vellum in the process of reading, was something more than the secular idea of reading denotes: it entailed breathing spirit into the past and resurrecting it anew in one's own time. This is why the Bible was read aloud, priests "said" Mass, and the Gospel was proclaimed. Preaching has thus been largely oral, with a textual basis, and teaching has usually been mediated by a variety of means (hence, multimedia). The text alone is thus packaged or codified, and is static or dead; but it has the potential to become dynamic. Late-antique Latin scribes used to experiment with story lines and scripted images, glosses or running commentaries, and other metadata. Medieval scribes invented the prototypes for hypertextuality in their compartmentalization, marginalia, and footnote apparati; or, as in the last of the antique manuscript era that produced the famous *Codex Amelianus* where illustration plays such an important role, when scribes broke with their classical tradition to experiment with the relation between text and image and mingled serialized illustrations resembling comic strips with their texts to create continuity between the spoken word and its written communication. They attempt to interject such dynamism into a preservation medium, and recapture the spirit of the times about which they wrote, but their technology was too limited. The movement from plain song to polyphony illustrates the same point. Presentations continued to integrate media throughout the Middle Ages, moving texts into parallel columns, collating the Gospels by tables, inserting prayer and music into texts for reflection and acclamation and, in scholarly works, inventing a variety of notation systems and ultimately indexing totally separate works. Alterity is as much a goal as eternity; or expressed in the modern equivalent, preservation and access are mutual goals. The two must be balanced properly. Today's electronic interaction of media, formats, and changing forms, is what was once only dreamed of, but it may be at the expense of what late-antique and medieval scribes accomplished for long-term preservation.

The idea of accessing multiple works and the practice of reading and rendering parallel texts simultaneously with audio-visual enhancement are hardly new. The technology is. It is for the conversion of static serial text into dynamic or interactive multi-dimensional parallel texts that more resemble group conversations with their reversions, asides, spontaneity, and simultaneity, that hypertext was reinvented electronically. Its extension to hypermedia merges texts and images, but the real breakthrough is interactivity (RAMAIAH provides a useful overview of interactive media, although not much historical perspective). Hypertext editing allows one similarly to link text with image and to invoke responses; both track a mainline with running commentary while saving the original produce something new, integrative, and creative. There are drawbacks, however, since its use requires parallel thinking abilities, somewhat like parallel computing, in tracking more than one linear stream of information at a time (MCKNIGHT, DILLON & RICHARDSON, 1993). Hypertext layered on hypertext, as when links are used in notes, becomes problematic and disorienting. Sidetracking is one negative effect counteracting the benefits of hypertext in complex documents. In narrative or discourse which relies on consecutive explanation, as in history when chronologically organized, the same problem appears as digression one upon the other, which can obfuscate the storyline altogether. LANDOW applies a modified textual criticism to hypertexts and has reservations about hypertext systems similar to those who comment on the negative cognitive and psychological effects of textprocessing. M. JOYCE sees hypertext as allowing two parallel minds to coexist in literary interpretation without ever needing reconciliation.

The notion of a master narrative in debates about authority in interpretation does not mean that the dominant exposition is straightforward, but it is usually linear; nor that the story line is necessarily simple, since there are always variations on the theme. Scribes and printers have long used chronological tables to collate historical events, but such synchronism does not automatically provide explanation. Coordinated periodization proves difficult as one moves toward globalization. This is more perplexing problem than simply information management. Complexity seems to thwart easy classification at higher levels of abstraction. Linking the microcosm with the macrocosm is a never ending problem. Historians today struggle with such problems as did their medieval scribal predecessors. Old techniques using linear thinking often unilaterally connected one object, event, or thought with another as in codification, sequencing and chaining, or string indexing. Now electronic technologies are presenting other possibilities, both for research and its presentation. H. S. HUGHES advocates the use of hypertext "to remove the structures of historical data" or to create alternative structures from the same data when the data structure seems to come from data collection strategies and techniques rather than from the phenomena being recorded.

Consider what such visualization technology means even for history that is considered static because of the nature of the sources, especially if an audio dimension were added as well. Oral history likewise can be reduced to a textual track for abstracting into narrative and book format. Or *vice versa*, a repeated narrative such as a scripted presentation can be studied to ascertain the relationship between this "master narrative" and localized "object stories." Some materials such as liturgy and social occasions governed by a high degree of protocol lend themselves to such study. KATRIEL, for example, uses such techniques to study museum interpretation and its use of "a rhetoric of factuality" and "the narrative appropriation of objects" to establish the indexical relationship between a collection view and discreet objects. Or, an archival series can be visualized in ways previously inconceivable by archivists a decade ago. Oral assessments of a record series utility by certain users may reveal uses not perceived by a reference archivist; exit interviews can be translated into graphic organizers and map displays to enhance subsequent retrieval.

Consider the work of M. OLSEN *ET AL.* which illustrates the methodology of determining word frequencies in a document collection, computes a distance measure between occurrences and their documents, and uses rectangular icons to display relational features in a multi-dimensional space mapped either to a 2-D or 3-D space. ROMAN & COX provide another example of non-Science visualization pointed out by WILLIAMS, SOCHATS & MORSE (pp. 163-64), whereby computer programs are placed into a visual array for retrieval based on their classified features: scope, abstractions, specification methods, interfaces, and presentations. Content-based image data modeling as described by Rajiv Mehrota's Museum data model merges image and text retrieval, and because of its comparison of shapes for retrieval (framed pictures, diagrams and abstractions, text blocks and page layouts that combine image and text), it is very flexible. It uses what he calls a "multilevel abstraction hierarchy," which functions like a thesaurus. Complex or simple images can be retrieved from one source and mapped to another, to produce hybrid sources; or conversely, to break apart complex sources into more manageable dissected sources. The MARS project exploits feature extraction techniques to use color, texture, shape, and layout which can be applied to any image, pictures, calligraphic manuscript, or type fonts. Reports on these interesting projects appear in the work of editors HEIDORN & SANDORE. Such integrated approaches offer new possibilities for archivists and historians working with electronic records and large-scale computerized projects where previously text and images were handled separately.

The critical issue to be understood, requiring a paradigm shift of tremendous dimension, is to reinvent dynamic history with the new technologies available. What is required is the same shift as when one goes from images or pictures, real or mental, to moving pictures and visual communications, where text may remain the basis but is not the sole form of communication. Thus, demographic historians should not use a plotter simply to produce a printed, static picture of a single point in time, but myriad sequential portraits of change that allows space and time to interact as a reflection of these dimensions in the actual events as they unfolded. A program and saved file can do this; a single view cannot, and a series of views can but poorly illustrate history in motion like an off-speed film or jerky video. VAN STEENDEREN makes an important distinction between "open and closed hypermedia systems" where a closed text or view, to preserve an original in its historical state, can be conserved but also altered at the same time. The operation is performed on a work copy without affecting the master, and each work draft can be saved as an overlay, thus creating a series of views, but always keeping open the possibility of activating change in another work copy. The dual goals of preservation and access are thus achieved. To return to the metaphor of moving pictures, this may be like using transparencies and overlays to reveal stages, progressions, and transitions not discernible to the historian today anymore than they could be seen by the people caught in the history these presentations depict. The difference is between studying anatomy from Gray's classic tome or from the dynamic digitized *Human Body* project.

To go further, data captured graphically can be activated digitally and imposed on backgrounds that also recreate staging areas, such as when settlement patterns are controlled by place and time indicators which recreate a process in actual time by aligning a settlement with a dot, a geographic site with an intersection of a grid map, and time of settlement with a timing sequence in a running program. The result is a dynamic history, more impressionable and substantially different than plot diagrams and maps printed in a book. The quantified methods employed now as means to a printed end should be reconsidered as sets of methodologies to be incorporated into ever larger projects and systems, and as subsets to knowledge-based and expert systems that potentially can go beyond any individually conceived and orchestrated project. In this light, a quantified model based on regression analysis must be turned into a regression of data that unfolds in real time and allows for observation of and participation in the process of discovery. This is decidedly different from preparing data for a program run, analysis of results, and presentation of interpretation. The historian, so keenly interested in time, must begin subjecting historical reconstruction to the rigors and recreation aspects of time-event analysis, replay, and simulation runs with altered variables in dynamic visualizations. In this trend, such tools as currently relied upon, SPSS and SAS for example, are inadequate. Or at best, they are tools to be used with a greater array of even more sophisticated technologies at our disposal.

New visual technology allows historians to look in multiple directions at the same time, closer to actual human interaction with surroundings. Likewise, multi-dimensional data processing requires multidirectional viewing and a new way of thinking about historical simultaneity and envisioning history. Images, including photography, have come under inspection in a variety of ways, resulting in a new genre of visual source criticism (cf., W. J. MITCHELL [1994]; TAGG; etc.). Likewise, quantifiable data in series may be graphed as three-dimensional moving data pictures in a new kind of dynamic knowledge representation. Movement from two-dimensional to three-dimensional thinking is difficult enough, but going to multidimensional representation that is not static but interactive requires whole new tools. Rather than display 3-D objects without phenomena or change as in moving from a simple matrix sheet to a holographic box, one needs to add interaction which would display the box as wave action with its sides writhing to and fro. Such technology is now available for engineering and design in dynamic 3-D CAD systems, but it seems not yet to be used much by historians. That will come shortly. The technology is now affordable and mountable on PCs Pentium 75 grade and above, using Windows 3.1, Win 95 or NT, for under $750.

The point is that neither historical Informatics or quantified Social Science History when interpreted as computing what was previously configured manually, or adherence to presenting findings as business-as-usual in oral narrative or textual rendition, are employing modern information technology to its fullest. They often focus on the data acquisition, analytic software, and procedures at the expense of presentation software, technique, and artistry. Moreover, the common dichotomy between research and teaching as made by many as a real demarcation is a false differentiation because even the presentation of research at conferences is a form of teaching one's peers. Searching, research and analysis, synthesis, presentation, criticism, confirmation, and reinterpretation are stages in a continuum. Research design and project development today must include foresight for the following: (1) archival processing for data preservation, to provide for accountability and enable verification, and to ensure re-usability for continuing and nonduplicate studies; (2) for both traditional oral and print presentation, but also dynamic modeling and the electronic incorporation of one's research into larger projected interactive virtual environments; and (3) for the integration of text, image, numeric data into holistic designs, where one's work may be used as a building block in different research projects or enveloping ones in the future.

In this sense Historical Information Science is meant to change profoundly the very nature of History as commonly practiced today, to move practice into the areas already envisioned by current conceptual and technical trends and to transform even those elements like the quantification social science historians that consider themselves to be leaders in such innovation. The old "New History" is not getting younger or older; it is simply trapped in its own time. It is the stepping stone for the always new and yet to be realized. Historians should not fool themselves again by believing that this new "New" History is the last of what is new. The next stage, it seems, is Virtual History, and the debate will continue as it must, with progenitors and critics who wonder if this is genuinely and authentically historical at all. Our technology and methodology will not answer those questions. But given the persistence of oral communications, and tendency to rely increasingly on visual communications in preference to the dominance of textual sources, Virtual History may be the only history that is assimilated and which therefore endures.

Thus, examination of what has transpired in quantified social science history seems but a prelude to what is transpiring in the interplay between textuality, visualization, and interactive media.

NARRATION AND VISUALIZATION: TEXT AND IMAGE ANALYSIS

At the opening of the 1980s when the American Historical Association sponsored a state-of-the-art review of History in the United States (KAMMEN, 1980), psycho-history, quantitative social-scientific history, and comparative history had made enough impression on historians to deserve their own niches in the survey, but literary history and the history of the arts were still excluded from cultural and intellectual history. The full impact of deconstructionism leading toward the literary critique and linguistic assault on objective historicism had yet to be felt. Computing in history was limited to the old socioeconomic and political and labor history schools where computational text analysis, to say nothing of graphics, was not extant. Image research, even when there were a few pioneering photo-essays such as Walter Rundell's aforementioned exploration of early Texan oil fields, was still largely a matter of picture research to support teaching serialized history in a "show and tell" mode. At one time the average historian thought of media as no more than supplemental to the lecture. Slides and transparencies were merely supports to oral discourse. H. TAYLOR in his 1977 presidential address before the Society of American Archivists envisioned something more in his fluid interpretation of documentary art. O'TOOLE in 1995 reminded American archivists again about the symbolic significance of archives in the modern world, and at the same time I provided a case history which demonstrated that this was how it was meant to be by the medieval inventors of modern archives—artifact and content, art and text, object and impression, are inextricably bound together (MCCRANK, 1995). Actual representation and effective presentation are equally important.

Times have surely changed in the last decade. This cliché hardly captures the magnitude of the change, however, since media technology finally does for us what has been wanted but unrealized for aeons. New media provide interactivity—replay on demand, remodeling, immersion into a virtual environment, and a level of artificial intelligence that fools us into behaving with machines as we would with humans. In the same way that quantified and narrative historical styles are undergoing a rapprochement, historians will use graphics to make their cases convincing, as well as using images for research with their textual records in ways both less subjective and more empirical, and *vice versa*. DAVIES, BATHURST & BATHURST argue that a major current trend is a redress of the previous imbalance between picture and text in the post-Victorian era of education with its neo-classical emphasis on text over image. The adage of a "picture worth a thousand words" has new meaning in digital environments, so that some call documentary art "the telling image" to suggest the information role of visual documentation beyond or in addition to the aesthetic. The increased interest in visual thinking and hence in visual interface design in information retrieval (GILLESPIE) means increasing integration of text and image and heightened awareness of their interplay and interpretation. This trend is affecting everything in information searching, research, and teaching (FRIEDHOFF & BENZON).

Inter-disciplinary history means a greater mix of sources, source criticism, and methodologies. For example, a chronological arrangement of photographs of a historical site taken over time might be studied as if it were a statistical time series, counting changes depicted therein as if these were variables in the life of a town, for example. This time-series and chronologically based technique is not substantially different from those employed in comparative "before" and "after" shots in architectural remodeling or in crime scene analysis, or in unobtrusive video- and photo-observation in therapy or organizational studies. Misuse of image sources can occur, of course, even in the best reproductions as in Ken Burns' popular documentary film *The Civil War*, which was criticized by BATY, 1994 for misplaced scenes (cf., his newer productions, *The West* and *Baseball*). The same is true of sequential texts which can be studied logically as a series, such as when they are periodical, are organically similar (e.g., works of a given author; an archival series of records from an agency, etc.), or can be related by association explicitly by a source like an independent variable or inferred statistically as though linking a dependent variable to its controller. In the first case, historians borrow heavily from cognitive psychology; in the second, from philology and now applied linguistics and historical lexicology. Such approaches produce an affinity, for example, between Social and Art History with Psychology and components of Information Science like Knowledge Representation or Visualization in Information Technology. In the second example, such scholarship exploits the relationships between the History of Ideas and Intellectual History with historical bibliography, the history of texts and literary history, and in communications and discourse analysis (e.g., R. BARTHES; cf., M. STUBBS). All have mutual concerns in such information technology as scanning and Optical Character Recognition (OCR) for input, data/text/image-base management for analysis, and high resolution graphics for output (WALKER & MILLER).

These interdisciplinary developments are also contributing to a Historical Information Science; or the same might be argued for subsets of Information Science like Art or Literary History, whenever "science" is interpreted generally as systematic, disciplined scholarship, which is largely concerned with information source analysis, informing processes and communication, assimilation and learning using modern information technology.

Historians who decried the limitations of quantitative history more than a decade ago invited the return of the narrative to History to balance what they saw as disjointed Social Science approaches resulting in a fragmented history. They have had their way in the post-structuralist era (KELLNER, 1987; POSTER, 1989)—perhaps. They might be equally put off, however, by the idea of "narratology," or learning how History's stories are being treated critically and scientifically as a literary genre (ONEGA JAEN & GARCIA LANDA, eds.; PRINCE). History today may be less structural and empirical than in its New Social Science days only a decade ago, and modeling is still prevalent except that descriptive rather than quantitative models are more in vogue. Some devotees of quantification see the era of the great debates as a Golden Age rather than what it was, merely a beginning and, thus, regard recent trends as a decline toward narration and description, and now to depictions rather than explanations. It does not have to be viewed so; instead the interplay between data, text, and image improvises an increasingly enriched History today.

The historical profession while intellectually robust is fraught with a crisis mentality and fragmentation. Despite a public that is consuming history in its arts and entertainment, academic History has severe pragmatic, financial, organizational, and identity problems. Historical literature has become ethnohistorical and more descriptive; the shift is from society to culture (BRETTELL). These trends favor the merging of text and image in a holistic analysis, and offer the possibility of descriptive and quantified methodologies to complement each other. History thus continues to serve as a bridge between the Social Sciences and Humanities, but the two-directional traffic flow, at various speeds, is often uneven. Nevertheless, History serves as a major conduit of influence from the former to the latter. Whereas in the 1970s the Social Sciences prevailed and History was imbued with a quantitative quality, the 1980s witnessed a new mix and by the 1990s it seems this earlier flow has been reversed and the major influence is coming from literary theory. Applied linguistics may provide a new balance by the end of the decade. History in the next millennium will be a far richer mix than anything experienced this past century. Interactive media will enable revising and a re-envisioning of history which is bound to be simulating and stimulating, innovative and creative, simultaneously precise in depiction and detail but ambiguous in meaning, pervasive and ubiquitous, and therefore upsetting and controversial.

Historical narrative is very literary and colorful, sometimes bordering on the surrealistic and subject to the same criticism of "fantasy" that N. FITCH attributed to quantitative New Social History. It can be highly theoretical and abstract, if not obtuse, due to the impact of post-structuralists and deconstructionists operating from the vantage point of comparative literature and for whom history and fiction are part of the same humanistic continuum. RIGNEY understands that history is more difficult, because it is necessarily selective and incomplete in respect to the real world because not everything is known or can be included in a discourse, so a history is never whole or complete. On the other hand, fictional representations are by definition complete in themselves. The work is bounded by its own scope, without regard to the boundless realm of history. Can fiction be used like modeling and projections to fill in gaps in historical knowledge, without total confusion between the two? Perhaps. Older distinctiveness between intellectual history and the history of ideas seem to have blurred as they were merged with local and regional social history, literary history and criticism. GEERTZ (1983) pointed out this tendency to create "blurred genres" at the local level of knowledge where more is known about less. But rather than a generic mix or blend of diverse cultures where commonalities override differences, diversity itself is in vogue, resulting in emphasis on local and personal identities, particularism, and parochialism, and microscopic studies are everywhere. Thus, historians are increasingly aware that although they once were critical of themselves for contributing to such overarching identification as nationalism, deconstructionist History has torn down identities without replacing them with any alternative structure. History is thus subject to severe criticism as being hypercritical and destructive rather than synthetic and creative precisely because of fragmentation and concentration on the local. It is this problem which HIGHAM (1994) attempted to resolve by suggesting that one could, for example, transcend nationalism by focusing less on the state and more on the importance of American national culture, so as to preserve the national framework without over-politicization on the one hand or reactionary descent to the regional and local on the other. One is forever confronted in the modern landscape with distinguishing between the forest and the trees, while wanting to see and comprehend both. The technologist can understand this tension by seeing an analogy in digital technology for imagery and the relationship of pixels and pictures. This is an issue of modeling, of course, but with images and description rather than with numbers alone. Intra-disciplinary studies contribute to inter-disciplinary enrichment, which in turn provides new frameworks and stimulates new questions that cause the disciplines to grow. Convergence does not have to eradicate individual identities in the disciplines any more than the commingling of peoples has to erase individualism or equity must mean sameness.

An example of recent introspection about the ascendancy of the particular and different over the whole and the common related to the issue of social and cultural modeling is the NEH-funded symposia sponsored by UCLA's Center for Medieval and Renaissance Studies, "Creating Ethnicity: the Use and Abuse of History." Michael Moss began the series by examining ethnicity in late antiquity and how categorization by Gallo-Roman historians or early "ethnographers" formed a basis for modern classification. Such debate has moved from the older framework of social class within a culture to one culture over the other in a global context, and interestingly approaches fundamental current social issues which impinge also on classification criticism in Information Science by placing potentially sensitive questions into a more remote historical laboratory for analysis and discussion. STOLKE postulates "a propensity in human nature to reject strangers" as one explanation for "the rhetoric of exclusion" in Europe. C. LEVI-STRAUSS (1996) was recently compelled to comment on history in relation to the contemporary link between racism and cultural diversity to pronounce that no people can claim that they alone developed world civilization, since this was and still is a convergence of different cultures, each with its own distinctness. The remoteness of one historical case, therefore, seems always bound with its contemporary viewing. The large picture frames the detail, and both interact with the persuasions of the viewer, personally based on his or her own experience or educationally if framed by one discipline or several. This classification problem of part and whole can be examined in so many different ways. It is questionable, however, if the discovery and exposition of the unique is worthwhile when one has to strain in demonstrating its significance. Is this the residue of scientific historicism and computerization decried by those wanting balance with narrative history? The problem seems no different than that facing quantification history that exploits minutia without building to generalization, or archival appraisal without linking selection for retention with potential use. It is an ageless intellectual question of moderation and balance between the particular and general, between data and information, between technology and science, and one discipline with another or all others.

In any case, an irony underlies these current trends toward new uses of and reliance on texts and images to balance mere numbers in that texts are being converted to machine-readable form as never before and textbases are used like new editions (sometimes uncritically, literary texts and historical records alike), and these are being analyzed by computerized methods engineered in applied linguistics that are heavily statistical and use many of the same quantitative approaches of the Social Sciences (BOOKSTEIN, 1995; SPOHER). Morphemes, words, phrases, and whole texts have become what numeric data were to Social Science historians, and number crunching has a new version in word crunching for text analysis. Variation in both speech and writing has been studied to identify domain usage characteristics to assist information retrieval, but also to reveal the character of particular literary genre, cultures, disciplines, and organizations (BIBER). The techniques and methodologies used by Statistical Linguistics, text analysis in Literature, and Natural Language Processing (NLP) in Information Science, are similar, but cross-referencing between these domains is not as common as one might suppose (P. JACOBS; LEVINE & RHEINGOLD).

The grounding of communication theory in Linguistics dates back to the 1950s and the movement in Language and Literature to study language empirically in the 1960s was parallel to the Cliometric movement in History. New History and New Literary History have assumed the old objectives of scientific historicism and methodology of quantitative research in the Social Sciences, but with consequences for the old way of conceptualizing sources as primarily numerical. Now the sources can be sound, image, text, or numerical, and mixed, all of which can be converted to quantifiable metadata. Where does one work begin and another end, if they are merged and analyzed not as independent, separate texts, but altogether as a sampler, a documentary series, or a chronolog? What happens to authorship and the distinctiveness of texts, or other questions asked by NUNBERG *ET AL.*, when individual sources are submerged into a collection or split among several electronic corpora where the whole is of greater importance than any of its components? Of course, such integration has always camouflaged authorship and readership when such generalizations were employed as "the medieval mind" or "the American author," etc., without an empirical basis for the hypothetical archetype. Yet, such considerations today have forced some (DEROSE, DURAND & MYLONAS) to ask again, "What is Text, Really?" The question rings familiar: remember that the archivist (e.g., COX, 1994) is asking at the same time, "What is a record, really?" and BUCKLAND (1997), reflecting similar questioning by information scientists, has had to re-ask "What is a document?" Each technological advance seems to force us back to basics, redefinition, a host of operational definitions, and in attempts at integration and consensus generic definitions that seem so general that they can be applied to everything and anything.

The idea of a "text" is not immune to this problem of definition and conceptualization. Likewise "image" becomes difficult to define. Consider the complexity of discourse, text, and imagery in terms of discussing a text to create an image of what happened, and then going on to explain the event's significance then and the relevance of this history today. Digitization of texts means that manuscripts *qua* images can be used as analogues themselves, integrated as textual supports linked-like hypermedia to form a new kind of critical apparatus (DELANEY & LANDOW). Mark Olsen's expansion of and research in the ARTFL textbase of French literature is illustrative of this trend (OSLEN), even though such terminological methodologies have been hotly contested (i.e., RODGERS' *Contested Truths,* the reaction by OLSEN & HARVEY, and rejoinder by RODGERS [1998]). Does it matter that patterns discernible today could not be discerned when the texts were written and read originally? What is the significance of sound when no one heard it? Or, for that matter, the significance of a surviving text if nobody read it previously? Should an assessment of a text or discourse be altered significantly by what we now know about them statistically, when readers and listeners had no such influential knowledge?

Such automated research methods in text analysis are the same as those used in Information Science for content analysis and the study of natural language textbases, sub-language usage, and indexing and abstracting effectiveness (e.g., mutual or shared information techniques used by DAMERAU; syntactic information used by DAGAN & CHURCH for technical vocabularies; and a combination or collocation information). As more digitized texts become searchable, they become important sources for such word studies in Information Science as well as Discourse Analysis in Applied Linguistics (i.e., sociolinguistics applied to natural language: M. STUBBS). As many exist now, users need to know how the thesauri are constructed or indexing has been done to understand the nature of their information retrieval using the access tools supplied. Word retrieval can provide one kind of metadata about a source, distinct from content, which can be mapped to produce a picture of a source or a sort of road map. Word pictures can be diagrammed, relationships among terminology, descriptors, and metaphors can be mapped, frequencies can be graphed, and spectrograms can provide information not visible when reading a text. And whole literatures can be visualized (WHITE & MCCAIN). Is such information gleaned from computerized word study not so much retrieved or discovered as it is manufactured? Like a picture supposedly worth a thousand words but never equal to a text, data representation in a model is like a picture, that is, different from what it represents.

More basically, text, image, and numbers in such modeling become interchangeable. When incorporated by Semiotics as signs in language (KRISTEVA), images become integral to texts rather than mere supports as in the case of comic strips or storyboards where script and illustration are conjoined. LEE & URBAN argue for their centrality rather than ornamentation, and in certain disciplines like Journalism symbols operate with recognizable structure and precision in meaning that makes them part of language rather than decoration (J. LINK). Image and text readings therefore go hand in hand, as when one describes the visual orally and in turn uses metaphors and allusions that can be pictured mentally. The translation back and forth from image to text, however, may operate precisely only within one culture and its language; or more generally, across certain cultures. The International Association for Semiotic Studies has produced six conference proceedings; the Fifth Congress held in 1994 at the University of California stressed the need to unify approaches and definitions for a more systematic study of Semiotics around the world rather than within only one culture (RAUCH & CARR, eds.).

Current historiography since the 1970s (GREIMAS) is reflecting these shifting paradigms, changes in the use of sources, and the dynamism of variable, interchangeable, and interpolated presentation. Both text bases and image bases are now as important as databases in historical computing. Visual, textual, and numeric information from the past all can fall under the purview of Historical Information Science, but the approach, methodology, and resulting interpretations will most likely differ significantly from Postmodernism in literary studies and its impact via descriptive anthropology on narrative history as practiced by those riding the crest of the current wave of enthusiasm for the subjective. In any case, encoded texts and digitized imagery go hand in hand and are therefore considered together in this essay against a backdrop not only of what is happening in the Arts and Humanities, but in applied linguistics and semiotics in

Organizational Culture within Management, in Visualization in Information Technology, and Information Storage and Retrieval in Information Science.

Encoded Texts for Discourse and Literary Analysis

The interplay between history and literary studies in text-based, computer-assisted analytic work may be discussed, therefore, in a different framework than Literature for its own sake, or from within the Humanities. The application of technique, especially measurement and quantified content analysis, makes such study different from a reading. A broader perspective might be offered by bringing into the discussion the parallel movements in the Social Sciences, Information Science, Education, and Management. Under the influence of Anthropology (especially Ethnography), Applied Linguistics as in Lexicology, and Rhetoric (SPILLNER) transformed into Communications, a new field called Discourse Analysis (BEAUGRANDE; BROWN & YULE; LINK, HORISCH & POTT; VAN DIJK; etc.) has impacted both Social-Intellectual History (R. BARTHES) and Language (SEBEOK) and historically oriented Literature studies (L. HALASZ). In the modern era, Emile BENVENISTE is perhaps most responsible for its cohesion as a research methodology, although elements of today's approaches can be traced to Descartes' *Discourse de la méthode*. Such developments rest on formalist language studies and Linguistics theorizing based on the groundwork of L. BLOOMFIELD, F. DE SAUSSURE, and N. CHOMSKY (1972) and the evolution of the idea of a species-specific language and emphasis on performance or processing which impacted History and Literature as much as Information Science.

Discourse Analysis evolved out of literary criticism and a fusion with communications theory exactly at the time of quantification debates in History and the intrusion of Information Science on librarianship during the 1970s. It is contemporary with early linguistic computing and the European influence not dissimilar from that of the Annales school on American New Social History or the *histoire du livre* movement on historical bibliography. A decade ago, GARNHAM recognized that discourse analysis entailed a kind of modeling, mental if not actually quantified, for representation of elements in text as a kind of hybrid virtual text. This modern notion resembles the old German construct of the *uhrtext* in philology and early textual criticism, that is a text no longer extant from which all surveying variants sprung. Over a century ago, such thinking was based on genealogy; it used decision trees to diagram how a text changed in time to result in a regional variant. The method was a form of deconstructionism, used to identify clearly the pieces before reconstructing an edited text. Such editions were, and are, models. They are artificial reconstructions in words, which can also be reconstructed mathematically by classifying, counting, and measuring those words. Thus the world of quantitative and qualitative models model often converge. It may seem inappropriate to think of the two methodologies, but beyond its numbers, Mathematics is often thought of as a language, as in the reading of visuals, tables, and graphs is perceived as a form of literacy (N. CLARK). Yet DOLBY, CLARK & ROGERS speak of "the language of data." Nor should contemporary methods be considered so unique to the modern world; most methodology has a long incubation period and a historical evolution, so that the history of method, technique, and practice always has a bearing on modern research if only our memories and recall were more historical (LAVE). Presentism is a shortsightedness that seldom enhances science. It detracts from modern Information Science, and it has also limited some studies in discourse analysis and modern textual studies when the text or discourse studies are mere samples, but the conclusions drawn therefrom are applied universally. In short, what can be known from the present is assumed to pertain to all time; because it has been said and repeated, it must have been so; and current knowledge is always better than in the past (thus confusing the issues of quality or integrity of information with relevance and currency).

R. DE BEAUGRANDE in 1980 presented Discourse Analysis as "a multidisciplinary science of texts," and by 1988 when at UNESCO's INFOTERM conference (CZAP & GALINSKI) he, as a keynote speaker, also reached back to de Saussure, N. Chomsky, and J. Piaget as well, before pulling ideas from thermodynamics, quantum theory, and molecular biology to reorient linguistic theory toward a systems approach and incorporate terminology and special purposes languages under the umbrella of Linguistics. He took the position that process rather than product (i.e., communication rather than a thesaurus, lexicon, or vocabulary) was most important. His purpose was to situate the idea of "control" at the center of language theory for understanding complex systems operations not dissimilar from Library and Information Science's previous placement of authority control over language variation at the heart of information systems design. The emphasis in linguistics theory, however, is less practical and more concerned with the "understanding of understanding" (p. 21). Similarly, the idea of "interpreting interpretation" (W. ROGERS) and treatment of language as system which is so common in all Linguistics now pervades the current approach to texts, historical and modern. The new spin is to see texts not as products, as in the older History of the Book, but as communication vehicles and their reading as information processes throughout history.

An elaborate methodology has thus evolved in linguistic computing from what early practitioners like KUCERA (1967) called "computational analysis" of English or use of any other language. Leximetric studies are increasingly common. Most rely enough on a body of common techniques to warrant the production of special software like *LEXICO1* for the Macintosh; it was originally designed by the LABORATOIRE DE LEXICOMETRIE POLITIQUE specifically to diagnose political discourse. Thus, words in texts may be counted and checked for frequency in usage and changes in meaning when used at different times to reveal paradigm shifts and dynamic rather than static thought. Such methodologies are outlined in early guides in the 1980s (FRANCIS & KUCERA), K. JENSEN & JANKOWSKI's handbook (1991), or a number of basic textbooks (e.g., OAKMAN; RENKEMA; SALEM & LEBART). These deconstruction methods are somewhat the reverse of those used to create sources and access them, but the latter are not known explicitly until a text is fully examined, as a whole and all of its parts. Concordances collate terms for access to words by extracting terms one by one and collating their uses, just the opposite of placing them into a text. Classification control on a concordance produces an index that accesses concepts more than words. Variants are commonly collated with computer assistance and a variety of programs (HOCKEY, 1980, pp. 144-167; LANCASHIRE, 1988, pp. 108-10); special software, *Collate*, has been designed to accommodate simultaneous multi-text variant analysis (ROBINSON, 1994; 1995). Concordancing like the quantitative historian's records linkage is a common methodology; such word study is pursued as well in Information Science to study domain literatures (ARANGO & PRIETO-DIAZ; DAMERAU) to aid indexing and classification.

A text viewed as a term bank can be desegregated, terms can be segregated into sets, and quantified analysis can proceed to glean information only indirectly related to the purpose of the text, e.g., the learning of an individual author or a defined group, more than the subject analysis of the texts themselves. TOMITA & HATTORI used such techniques early (1975) in treating indexes as term banks and checking frequency of keywords usage and their relationships with conceptual terms for what they called a "quasi-quantitative" historical study of technical and scientific information transfer in Japan after 1965. Texts *qua* collections move such analysis from terminologies as such to individual biography and thence to social-cultural and intellectual history if they are literary, and if more documentary, the analysis might be socioeconomic and political in orientation; or a blending of sources could produce a composite, ultra-disciplinary overview. When moved into the contemporary applied sphere, as when analyzing current formal documents such as mission statements and current electronic records such as e-mail, in discerning the culture of an organization to assist management in selecting strategies that will work in their businesses or bureaucracies, or when studying search behaviors of individuals and groups by analyzing OPAC logs (e.g.,

MARKEY, DRABENSTOTT), this approach leaves History *per se*, but the methodology, interpretation, and implications of such work are the same as when a historian employs similar discourse or text analysis techniques to historic documents and reaches conclusions about failures and successes of past generations. One might think of all such research as historical—"short history" as distinct from the *long durée*.

Such a comprehensive view approaches History largely as a history of texts, which blends well with certain fields such as Renaissance studies where Rhetoric and public discourse were always key interests (STRUEVER, 1970). Historical writing has itself been subjected to such analysis quite early by R. BARTHES (1967, 1981) to place History in the Social Sciences or by STRUEVER (1985) as a study of contemporary academic discourse, just as BAZERMAN & PARADIS have used such techniques to trace technical and professional communications between the professions. Recent history textbooks have been similarly inspected by educators like M. WILLS (1992). She used *WordScan* to create a textbase of 1,400 pages from ten sample textbooks on American colonial history and word frequency to check on the use of 338 terms denoting religious values, groups, and people to study changes between the 1960s and 1990s especially in the treatment of the Great Awakening. She concluded that although the magnitude of treatment had stayed the same, unfavorable bias against the Great Awakening had increased as determined by the values of tone, feeling, and attitude.

This burgeoning field, as already indicated, has also entered the business world in such areas as organizational management, industrial psychology, and marketing under the guise of "organizational culture" studies. It has its counterpart in Information Science in content analysis and the study of domain literatures. Its empirical techniques and methodologies for natural-language processing find their way into courts: when studying answers to questionnaires provided to prospective jurors as seen in the O. J. Simpson trial publicity; when evidential problems arise from contested e-mail testimony (REED); or when forensic document examination laboratories discern forgeries and frauds from the authentic according by measuring internal evidence (A. MORTON), such as the correspondence between word frequencies and syntax usage between contested documents and those proven previously to be authentic. Connections between Discourse Analysis and Information Science abound in indexing, abstracting, classification, and terminological work like thesaurus construction, and information retrieval generally. Quantified textual analysis exemplifies many of the cross-disciplinary trends that are so evident in breaking down the dichotomy between the Humanities and Social Sciences that also undercut previous assumptions that History could be only a background support for Information Science. As such assumptions erode, the fusion implied in a Historical Information Science becomes more understandable, and hopefully more attractive.

DE CERTEAU in his *L'Écriture de l'histoire* underscored the "power-structure" of historiography almost in Machiavellian terms, not too dissimilar in ethos from M. FOUCAULT's likening possession of things and power to madness in his *Histoire de la folie a l'âge classique*. Historians of printing and publication have long praised the "power" of the printed word to the point of making it a cliché, but not with the adulation of modern journalists or information scientists who have commandeered this ideological rhetoric for themselves by referring to "information power" and to certain access methods as "powerful." This is a normal expression in the field, and has been employed as well in this essay. Similar interest is accordingly manifested in "computing power" and the exercise of authority through technology. Indeed, "empowerment" is a legitimate research concern in information management (cf., ASIS workshop by MENOU; INTERNATIONAL DEVELOPMENT RESEARCH CENTRE). Such usage invites discourse analysis and a psychological probe into the police or militaristic *mentalité* of these users, and perhaps also of such neologisms as bibliographic "control" to describe means of intellectual facilitation, functions and operations in terms of strategies, or tools, mechanisms, and weapons. Linguists, cultural anthropologists, psychologists, and historians of language are more interested in such nuance than ever and have become increasing sensitive to dominance in language as one result of the feminist critique of history. They would have a field day with T. E. TURNER's recent (1991) characterization of integrated imaging technology as "a strategic information systems weapon"! More seriously, RICHARDS (1988, 1989, 1994) has carved out a thematic stream of research linking wartime efforts, espionage and "intelligence" operations with the development of Information Science during World War II and immediately afterward to capture scientific and technological information for American industrial and government purposes. This controlling aspect of the IS mentality has been seen in business as well, sometimes as revealed in the connection between wartime economies, post-WW II industrialization, and the use of information systems in the development of large corporations (YATES, 1989). Historical realities loom large behind the rhetoric of the information profession.

While CORTADA some time ago (1979) showed how computers had affected the conduct of foreign policy and transformed diplomacy and diplomatics, discourse analysis has been used interestingly by P. EDWARDS to examine the "cognitive revolution" after World War II, the ideology of Artificial Intelligence, the creation of a "cultural politics" impacted by the redistribution of power resulting from computer accessibility and lack thereof, and the influence of systems analysis on political thought (his global findings seem to be reflected in campus politics as well!). Similar thinking and content analysis approaches to texts appear in GRAY's dissertation (1991) on *Computers as Weapons and Metaphors* to delineate the interdependence of science/technology and the military as central to postmodern warfare. In the same vein, NOBLE explored the military approach to problem solving in the late 1950s and the evolution of computer-based education programs in the United States, resulting, he concludes, in the subordinations of educational to advanced technological research, educational practice to human engineering, and people to the cognitive requirements of information technologies. Such use of computers for content analysis of texts and interviews are extensions of older quantified techniques used since the late 1970s in Social Science history, as exemplified in the case of diplomatic history by the work of SMALL & LAUREN, or the methods handbook by KRIPPENDORF (1980). More recently this literature on content analysis of databases has been reviewed by P. JACSÓ.

Likewise, the convertibility of texts and oral discourse has been understood for some time, but the diagnostic technology and methodology are more recent. Some time ago, for example, Richard Jensen, long before supporting historical discourse on a listserv, called attention to the possibilities of innovative research by linking Oral History to quantification (JENSEN, 1981). He criticized the elitist mode of Oral History interviewing with the movements in social history that might benefit from sampling in more broadly conceived interview programs. Moreover, JENSEN has advocated automated techniques for text management (1991) by historians, regardless of the source, textual or oral. Here he is joined by archivists and others in the information profession who have been critical of Oral History for its lack of concern about intellectual access in its documentation techniques. BRUEMMER (*American Archivist* Forum, 1993 fall; 56[4]: 564), for example, asks the question, "Why belabor the complex (i.e., "a more complex view of access of oral history" suggested by F. STIELOW in an earlier *American Archivist* Forum, 1992) when faced with the simple fact that for most oral historians access is an afterthought?" He suggests that at least a simple MARC record be prepared to locate oral interviews, perhaps with improvements being developed by NHPRC funding, to form the national network of oral history sources envisioned by STIELOW (1986, p. 73). JENSEN, however, is recommending much more: namely, that oral history transcripts be treated like textual archives, digitized and encoded for full-text searching, discourse analysis, and such applied linguistic research as for dialectology and lexicology.

The transition from language to communication studies has been pervasive and this pertains both to the academic disciplines and to information professions. The fusion with Anthropology for specification of cultural contexts or communities (MACFARLANE) and even Philosophy in the quest for meaning in language use meant that the influence on History was, in N. STRUEVER's words (1979, p. 127), "not altogether simple and straightforward." While targeting C. LEVI-STRAUSS with criticism of causal modeling likened to "naive determinism," she weaves together influences of J. HABERMAS (1967; 1968), E. VERNON, E. BENVENISTE, L. WITTGEN-STEIN, etc., to suggest the theoretical implications of the ferment in Linguistics for History. J. M. SMITH (1997, p. 1,417) argues for "the circumvention of the frustrating and ultimately false choice between 'social' and 'linguistic' determinism." Nevertheless, he notes that most debates about history and language are phrased in these terms, although most historians would never admit to a strict determinist philosophy. B. SMITH (1995, p. 1,419) notes that CHARTIER (1988, 1989), like BIA-GIOLI in his provocative representation of Galileo as a courtier rather than the pure scientist later ages made him out to be, rejects "the cognitive autonomy of the individual" while staying clear of social and linguistic determinism. Smith, following the acknowledgments of Roger Chartier and Mario Biagioli to Norbert Elias's earlier work on court society which paid so much attention to the jockeying at court through language, i.e., strategies, tactics and social posturing, which ultimately were seen as operations and maneuvers, like logistics, in a social system (N. ELIAS, 1983). N.ELIAS (1994) likewise studied etiquette, manners, and protocols as forms of control and social organization, producing networks of "interdependencies" which, as J. SMITH summarized, altered individual behavior, increased self-consciousness, and transformed power structures.

It is interesting that Norbert Elias, and his pervasive influence through Roger Chartier and his school, has had no influence whatsoever in Organizational Culture studies in Management and Information Sciences; few references to these influential cultural historians can be found in this parallel professional literature. On the other hand, examination of citations in the works of these historians or in those contributing to the recent *American Historical Review*'s forum on New Cultural History (*AHR*, 1997; 105 [2]), reveals an equal lack of integration of the prodigious work of organizational-behavior sociologists and psychologists addressing modern equivalents of older elites, courts, coteries, corps, and other social groups whose language, behavioral norms, dress, gesture, etc., likewise provide the data to characterize moments and movements in sociocultural history.

The influential probe of language and meaning into all aspects of History, in the form of deconstructionism (DERRIDA, stemming from his early criticism in 1971 of J. L. AUSTIN's speech-act theory, 1961), was felt in exposing the common juxtaposition of the "I" and "you," or "Self" and "Other" that TODOROV made so famous, and the feigned objectivity attempted in historical writing through the use of the third person and preterit tense. Particularly subjective but inviting is the inextricable connection between signifiers in language and their explicit, implicit, inferred, and contextual meanings. The refractional effects of linguistics scholarship, in sharp contrast to debates over the Saussurean idea of "collective memory" and variations on this universal theme that could have been unifying, went hand in hand with localism and regionalism in historical studies (GILDEA). THIBAULT stressed in Saussure's work the idea that signs in social life are dynamic. They are not used passively but creatively, and although their use reflects continuity with the past signs operate in living traditions. Likewise, Linguistic interest in metaphors like a literary scholar's focus on tropes played well in intellectual historiography and the minds of textual historians. Linguistic theory was for them an external rationale *qua* science; it could play the same role as statistics and mathematical modeling did for socioeconomic and political historians who wanted their work to appear scientific.

The subsequent fusion of linguistic and historical textual scholarship (surveyed by RABEN) is no less real than the educated public's general reception to the ideas of Marshall McLuhan and Umberto Eco (cf., MCLUHAN; ECO). Nancy Struever points to the "New" book historians (E. EISENSTEIN, N. ZEMON DAVIS, R. DARNTON, R. CHARTIER, etc.) who combine social history with their attention to readings, publics, text and bibliographic scholarship, and linguistic theory in their provocative studies of information dissemination in the earlier age of print media (STRUEVER). By contrast, the reading of texts as signs as by Tzvetan Todorov, whom some historians think should have stuck with his studies of the

Fantastic (cf., TODOROV's theories, 1967; 1975; 1978/1990; 1995, applied in 1984 in his highly controversial *The Conquest of America*) has led to some very misleading and superficial history and abuse of sources as though they were never read at all (or worse, charges of deliberate distortion: L. LYNCH, 1994). Such is the case in the most recent debates over the Quincentennial interpretations of Discovery versus Encounter, imperial conquest as holocaust, etc. in the works of S. GREENBLATT reflecting the extremes of new "New Historicism," and K. SALE and D. E. STANNARD where poetic license borrowed from Literature can be contested as very detestable history. As J. LEE notes, the anecdote occupies a central position in the New Historicism because it is used so much to illuminate historical ideas. Selection of which anecdotes are told and how they are used, however, are highly subjective, and Lee comments that in the case of Stephen Greenblatt and others the flexible meaning of anecdotes protects the narrator from rigorous criticism. In so much of this kind of history writing it is often difficult to distinguish surmise and speculation from reconstruction based on the kind of evidence that would stand the tests discussed previously. And even when several incidents are cited, unless their number, frequency, pattern, and caliber are put into some kind of comparative framework, one is uninformed about the representative or unique character of the phenomena considered. In short, examples may abound, but without quantitative analysis the argument is as unfulfilling as quantity without quality or numbers without explanation and description. Narration and description need not be devoid of an empirical foundation.

DE CERTEAU (1988; paraphrased by his translator, Tom Conley, p. xi) argued that the aims of historiography and literature have been converging since the Enlightenment. Indeed some historians (e.g., TREPANIER) in arguing for refined style in historical writing as a literature, have argued that History is an art of narration and description as if History were Literature. De Certeau claimed that History (that is, the discipline, not history *per se*) is a style of discourse, and he suggested that historians are like courtiers courting favor, persuading, and convincing. Such gnostic tendencies, skepticism, and deliberate historical and literary (con)fusion hardly seem to make the case for a Historical Information Science very compelling. In their extreme, they mitigate against the very notion of humane sciences and the notion of the objective, as they reduce everything to a matter of language. Language and literature are not the same, however, since depending on perspective, one may be perceived as broader than the other. It is somewhat like confusing History with its secondary literature, or confusing literature, which even if contemporary is still created and artificial, as primary on the same order as sources produced as natural byproducts of human affairs. Just as Anthropology has changed History pervasively, it (with Linguistics) adds a scientific dimension to both oral and written communication to the study of Literature. The objective has entered into the subjective and *vice versa*. One can be objective about subjectivity, and study it scientifically, or layer the already subjective with more subjectivity. Obviously, the orientation of a Historical Information Science would be the former, but this does not mean an orientation toward numeric data alone. It does betray a tendency to measure and thereby to apply quantification techniques to qualitative subjects, including narrative and discourse.

Such historical *qua* literary work characterized by Greenblatt and others, reflects the controversial impact of Linguistics on textual historiography, although not necessarily the empirical methodologies adopted by less impressionable discourse analysts. In such discourse, History has often become the handmaiden of mythography and servant of propaganda in the building of contemporary consciousness along politicized, ethnic, and psychological lines. In such cases the truth claim or integrity of history is at stake; such debates have been characterized, regardless of their content, as scholarship versus political activism. It is such agenda in Afrocentrism to which LEFKOWITZ reacted so strongly, on the assumption that truth mattered still today in such debates about the interaction of cultures in history. One noted commentator, George F. Will, argued, "Afrocentrism rests on something even worse than the idea that the truth of a proposition matters less than the utility of the proposition in serving a political agenda. Afrocentrism is another weed fertilized by the idea that there is no such thing as truth, only competing 'narratives'; that power decides which narratives prevail; ...and that such concoctions begin with and depend on, disdain for historical methodology" (WILL, p. 78). On the other hand, K. L. KLEIN notes that the terms "master narrative" and "metanarrative" have been employed pejoratively in recent Western scholarship, like past disclaimers for older ideas about Universal History, to distinguish between Western-style historicity from non-Western or nonhistorical discourse.

In Anthropology, as reflected in the work of Claude Levi-Strauss who critiqued "capital-H History" and celebrated everything local and primitive and created lasting antimonies (e.g., science versus savagism as distinct from savagery), in the work of Jean-François Lyotard who defined Postmodernism as "incredulity toward metanarratives" (including science with its own mode of discourse distinct from narrative), and in the work of James Clifford (Klein adds Francis Fukuyama to this list), the idea of a master narrative pertains less to formal principles that differentiate one culture from another than to dominance in a pragmatic sense (cf., CLIFFORD, 1988; LYOTARD, 1979/1984). BENDER (1995), based on the aforementioned *JAH* survey, thinks that American historians seek a "synthetic sensibility in a variety of histories, not a single synthesis." Local narratives can achieve the same dominance in their own sphere, of course, but by definition they attract less attention and are therefore easier to propagate, refine, and perpetuate. J. CLIFFORD in 1986, adopted the metaphor also popularized by Stephen Greenblatt that narratives, paradigms, and cultural antimonies "oscillate" between distinctive forms more than the synthesis that occurs in historical dialogue (J. CLIFFORD, 1988, thus juxtaposes History and Anthropology). Clifford parts company with LEVI-STRAUSS who lamented the obliteration of cultural difference as History's tragedy, by postulating that difference remains and simply rises and ebbs in time like subcultures within any dominant culture.

This most controversial component of such theorizing and in ethnohistorical research and writing is the sociopolitical and intellectual problem investigated by a UCLA forum on ethnicity and History. The use of history, similar to the old schools which used it for moral rectitude and political persuasion, is seen as subversive by those who hold onto a sense of historicism that is more objectively rooted in the sources and less subjectively given to contemporary currents in interpretation. Objectivity and neutrality are often confused in this regard. History as narrative, or more currently as discourse itself, is unlikely ever to return unscathed to the premises of the turn-of-the-century scientific historicism (as argued by H. WHITE), but advocates of scientific text studies might argue otherwise. Those who simply read texts for their impression and style of personal interaction to share equally personal insights are more likely to see history, especially its narrative form, as a genre of literature. They are not prone to use modern computer-assisted text analysis to check their impressions and they usually ask different kinds of questions about their material than those imbued with a scientific, empirical bent toward proof other than the expertise of the witness. Moreover, such controversy has shifted many a historian's perspective from introspection of a Euro-American framework to a global one that requires comparative perspective and admittedly different sensibilities when moving beyond one's own culture. Thus, Caroline Walker Bynum as AHA president characterized the professorate today as America's "last Eurocentric generation" in remarks assured to draw rebuttal, and perhaps even furor (BYNUM). Her remarks seem more in the spirit of Eric WOLF who, in John Gillis words, intended "to restore to non-Western peoples some rightful measure of historical agency, to remove them from the category of the 'other' to which they had been previously assigned" (GILLIS, p. 5). The globalization of European history calls for new integration, to be sure, but not the radical revisionism that casts out historical methodology, its science, and replaces the very notion of history with just another story.

Has such postmodernism affected the practice of history? Most assuredly. Has New Criticism resulted in changes in History? It has, if Simon Schama's *Dead Certainties: Unwarranted Speculations* is any indication of the willingness of historians to investigate their own historiography and challenge even the most stable of historical perceptions through the years (SCHAMA, 1991). But some of this revisionism is extended postmodernism and skepticism unbridled rather than New Historicism based on scientific methodology. Or, the schizophrenia of academic history is caught between an historicism close to Von Ranke's theory of historical knowledge based on epistemological idealism where meanings are based directly on evidence in a real, concrete form; or something closer to the existentialism of the post-Heidigger school as in the thought of Otto Gerhard Oexle (IGGERS, 1995). In both cases History provides a critical literature, but in the latter variety it is more akin to Literary Criticism where the criticism becomes a literature in and of itself, paralleling and haunting the primary literature it criticizes. This is a different phenomena than the reexamination of texts through numeric computation or relying on the prestige of quantification rather than personal insight, that is, the "pursuit of objectivity in science and public life" studied by T. PORTER (1986).

MAZA (1996) recently treated this continuing tension between historical and literary studies, noting (p. 1,512) that it is the study of genre where the two fields overlap most comfortably. She describes (p. 1,494) some of this work in a specific genre as "combining traditional narrative with postmodern experiment." The deconstructionist/constructionist debates of the late 1980s into the 1990s about history as literature therefore have more of a connection than is often realized with the debates of the 1970s over quantification. MAZA notes that a new generation of literary critics are turning from foci purely on literary texts and "transhistorical studies" to include noncanonical literatures of interest to social historians as well (sentimental and "dime" novels, captivity narratives, etc.), so she speculates about the advent of renewed convergence of the humanistic disciplines that emphasizes "stories in history." Such recent historiography seems trapped in the Humanities without awareness of similar movements in the Social Sciences, or even in such mundane fields like Business, away from cause and effect analysis, linear explanations, and one-dimensional explanation. The movement toward nonlinear programming in applied fields and the embrace of chaos and complexity theory by the most recent generation of Cliometricians, may be seen as parallel to, yet not really integrated with movements in text analysis and narrative history toward more complex multilayered readings of sources. Moreover, historians oriented toward the Social Sciences like DOORN (1996, p, 69), who refers to VRIES to argue that they are not as monothetic in theory as they sometimes claim to be, often seem to bear less antagonism with narrative history than narrativists do with quantification. DOORN, in the aforementioned forum, sees the arguments too skewed and differences too sharply drawn when description or narration and quantification are compatible. Nevertheless, old "misunderstandings" seem to persist, divisions in the past generation of historians have been inherited by the present as indicated by MAZA, and one must wonder if such polarized perspectives are rooted in individual psychologies to create, not misunderstandings in Doorn's words, but continual misunderstanding which displays a pervasive cognitive dissonance in the study of human affairs (a position staked out elsewhere: MCCRANK, 1996).

Some of this tension may result from classification problems and territoriality, but when explained in terms of psychology it seems like an identity crisis. If History is so impacted by literature via a circuitous route through cultural anthropology, resulting in the tension Maza describes, such discomfort may be exacerbated when Literature influenced by Linguistics, especially statistical linguistics of the variety pioneered by French lexicographers and thesaurus constructionists in studying the classics (GUIARD; P. MULLER; DELATTE and his school at Liège; DENOOZ; LAFON; MICHEL; TOMBEUR, etc.), displays a technical bent. To ameliorate this situation, GREENBERG & SCHACTERLE put together a collection of essays at the beginning of this decade in an effort to break down the antithesis of *Literature and Technology*. The juxtaposition criticized is Literature as imaginative and subjective versus rigorous but mechanistic Technology. The contributors seem to assume that postmodern approaches to literature are more analytic and objective, and describe them as "technological" and focused on the "techniques of literary expression."

One reviewer reacted to these attempts at rapproachment between technology and literature, often a literary treatment of a technology, as difficult to understand as subatomic physics! The complexity of argument, often convoluted and inferred from unexplained paradigms or what S. TURNER sees as "superindividual entities" like "practice" or "culture" which are inherently unobjective, often does make purported objective treatments difficult to follow. Narrativist and descriptive history mixed with critical analysis can read like a novel with main characters, dominant themes, befuddled with diversions, cameo appearances, and interwoven subplots. It may be that complexity theory needs to be applied to current post-modern confusion between history, literature, linguistics, statistics, and technology.

Whereas in humanistic circles the debate between History and everything else, which is itself symptomatic of the identity problems in the discipline, often centers around reinterpretation of old texts and the past in general according to new paradigms. As in science the issue is often revisionism, wherein the tension is increased by the rate of change, i.e., how radical the revision seems to be, as distinct from incremental reinterpretation. Consider the following: Lynn Hunt's use of Freud's "family romance" to detect mythology operating in the French Revolution (HUNT); Judith Walkowitz' combination of feminism and Foucauldian discourse analysis to understand male narratives for female audiences in *fin-de-siécle* London (WALKOWITZ); the process of going from Early Modern to Medieval; Caroline Walker Bynum's exploration of religious and secular imagery from texts to arrive at new interpretations of gender-differentiated spiritualism (BYNUM); or Gabrielle Spiegel's recent use of genre to explore the rise of narrative history in France (SPIEGEL). Much of this research is based solidly on archival documents, as exemplified by Natalie Zemon Davis's trendsetting exegesis of pardoner's tales from court records (N. ZEMON DAVIS, 1987). In the latter case, official records were themselves fictional, but not fictitious.

None of these well-received studies have employed techniques evolving from computer applications in text analysis, to say nothing of the full array of methods now available with modern information technology: series analysis, word or phrase study, frequency correlations, concept analysis based on thesauri or other linkages, disambiguation, discourse mapping, formula and pattern detection, or form analysis. Much of this revisionism is a "rereading" of known texts, highly informed from other disciplines, but it is also highly subjective. These are histories written like literary works, as one-person creations that borrow from other disciplines but that are not genuinely multi-disciplinary where one viewpoint would operate as a check on the other or where methods are always explicit. They are insightful and innovative, but are they scientific? In some ways, yes, such as in their experimental mode and willingness to take a new look at old assumptions, applied linguistics, and fertilization from cognitive psychology and cultural anthropology, but these are largely mind experiments representing the traditional way of doing "arm-chair" history because of the limitations of the sources they encounter. They are largely text-based and easily fall into the trap of postmodernism, namely that all knowledge is conditioned by its textuality. Are they thus limiting by source survival, method, and technique? Might such studies be tested by more empirical means, with computer-assisted analysis of texts and their cross-check with others, linguistic and lexical modeling, and further refined or revised? The two approaches could ultimately produce a balanced synthesis, even for those subjects which seem to be totally dependent upon texts.

None of these historical treatments, although they treat of information and communications issues, are well informed from Information Science (of course, neither is Information Science well informed from such studies). They may connect through mutual interests in reading, bibliography and literature, or the history of the book in Library Science, but the time lag for citations to appear across this great divide is nearly a decade. Some, like Mary Carruthers' work on historical memory, delve into related disciplines like cognitive psychology, but since her focus is medieval it will not be seen as relevant to a field that is so present minded (CARRUTHERS). It is unknown if concepts from contemporary Western psychology, which explain much older transcultural mentalities for our understanding, would have provided any understanding whatsoever for the subjects being studied. The subject of cognitive psychology has been modern man, so the application across cultures is always fraught with danger. This may explain a reluctance to use modern Information Science for historical studies, except that no one would expect a simple overlay of conclusions drawn from modern information behavior to another era without accommodation. Such reluctance may explain the lack of inter-disciplinary reciprocity in one direction, but it does not explain why more borrowing has not occurred in the opposite direction, from those areas in Information Science which are textually oriented into History that is also text-based and chooses to operate in narrative mode. Is this because the latter is so focused on the vehicle, the text, rather than the process of information dissemination and the function of being informed? This is especially curious in those studies that purport to take interest in more than the text and context, but also the agent and activity. Perhaps the real reason is simply lack of familiarity with cross-disciplinary information transfer and adaptation methodology, in the same way that so much of contemporary information work is simply uninformed by the more remote past. Or, are such works doomed to a specialized audience, and are thus marginalized, because of the current cultural environment of national commitment to innovation and a pervasive sense that relevance pertains only to whatever is immediate?

These comments are not meant as criticism in any negative sense, but several musings that may be shared. Among other observations, note that the majority of recent contributions in these narrative-centered histories constitute a feminine critique departing from male dominated historiography; the descriptive mode is today dominated by female scholars, in contrast to the male domination of previous quantification studies in History and Social Science historiography. Some of this is a conscious and deliberate "engendering" of history and thus reveals gender preferences in modern History writing. Is text-based revisionism only a matter of source survival, or is it also resulting from the current gender mix and diversification as distinct from the older dominance by Euro-American males? Are subject preferences (e.g., social and cultural history versus older political, military, and economic varieties) and reliance on literate means rather than numeric analyses also skewed along gender lines today? Is the difference something like the bifurcation noticeable in male-dominated Electrical Engineering and Computer Science versus Information Science where at least in its library-orientation women scholars are more numerous? However, one detects less consciousness about the gender correlations or engendering of a discipline in Information Science. The exception would be the self-consciousness of Library Science as pertaining to libraries, and hence association with librarianship which historically has been a predominantly women's profession. It is this strain, for example, that inserts into Information Science the study of children using information sources and systems. A similar gender differentiation may be discerned in the distinction between Information Management and Information Services, or directing versus nurturing, and recent trends in acceptable management styles. It is controversial, nevertheless, to suggest that these disciplinary, subject interests, or methodological orientations are totally or even partially a male/female polarization, and that gender plays an important role in method selection and orientation toward either qualitative or quantitative approaches.

More than one feminist historian has dared to penetrate this minefield where men are afraid to tread. B. SMITH in arguing that Scientific History was driven not by the quest for objectivity alone, but also by fantastical ingredients, points to the contradictions apparent in the use of sex-laden and power-oriented metaphors by the early exponents of scientific historicism—all men. She suggests "In the spaces left open by these contradictions and by the inescapable reliance on metaphor, the innovative or those who were merely different might try to find new direction" (B. SMITH, 1995, p. 1176). The rise of the narrative and subjective retelling of history by the aforementioned women historians may reflect this new direction. In this vein, the new criticism seems to envelope a personalized and even hypersensitivity based on the close scrutiny of texts, always against a methodological paradigm borrowed from another field. The result is a literary excursus which falls within the framework of the

Humanities rather than the Social Sciences. Rather than being grounded upon statistical linguistics and quantification methodologies, the dominant method is to describe and illustrate rather than count and demonstrate.

Debates about method often reveal a division between cognitive preferences toward segregation or integration which has been described in deliberately nonscientific terms by Lynn Hunt as "a contrast between splitters and lumpers" (HUNT, 1995). Are they, then, counters? Not usually. In effect, text-based historians contributing to this recent wave of literary historicism have not engaged in computerized text analysis as fully as their literary and linguistic colleagues; their chief sources are literary rather than documentary texts, and they largely ignore nontextual archival records. Their works form a genre of their own, representing a different mentality than that reflected in quantified studies, and their treatment of text is therefore decidedly different from how an information scientist would treat similar subject matter. It is doubtful if disciplinary preference in scientific historicism or in a leaning toward Social Sciences as evident in Information Science or tendencies toward objective and empirical history versus subjective and narrative history can ever be equated to something so dichotomous as the infamous battle of the sexes, but a certain dialectic is discernible even if one shuns labeling one persuasion as feminine and another as masculine. The alignment of studies characterized by method and style with gender, however, would seem to be a perfectly legitimate subject for empirical study and a matter for Information Science, and Historical Information Science especially, to investigate. The results, no doubt, will be controversial.

Such a division of the historian's house into this or that camp is often a juxtaposition of the Humanities versus the Social Sciences, describers versus counters, or Platonism versus Aristotelianism, as much as the methodological positions described humorously by Lynn Hunt. Another characterization of such polarization is provided by Simon Schama who specifically relates preferences to information technology and computing:

> Traditionally, historians have come in two basic models: the hang glider and the truffle hunter, and both can be helped out by electronic technology. Truffle hunters are excavators, resolute at extracting some small savory gobbet of truth from an improbably hidden source, but so committed to going from hole to hole that they miss the broader landscape in between. Hang gliders, by contrast, bob about on breezy thermals of generalization, taking in the lay of the land, but never actually descending to inspect its gritty details. But with the computer's help, the truffle hunter's horizons can be broadened and the hang glider's focus sharpened (SCHAMA quoted in FORBES *ASAP*, p. 55).

The same might be applied to the data miners, i.e., "truffle hunters," versus the theorists or "hang gliders" in Information work. Both Hunt and Schama capture something of the dualism and tension in historical studies reflected in the misunderstandings cited by DOORN (1996) and cognitive dissonance described by MCCRANK (1996). Like the proverbial battle of the sexes, this difference in how one views the world and its history from another, seems eternal. Information technology enables people to see things differently, but perhaps only if a need is felt for a change in perspective. Either the view must change, or the viewer must move. It would be interesting to know how historians hold onto their preferences or change positions at different times of their lives, cross-over the divide and come back again, and how those on mid-ground combine persuasions that are so often seen as opposites into a personal dialectic. Short of Hegelian metaphysics, one unifying force has been the intervention of Anthropology into both the Social Sciences and the Humanities to stress a topic in common, namely culture.

It is ironic that History, so impacted by quantification methodology from the Social Sciences at one turn, should be so influenced at another by literary studies which are decidedly nonquantified, while movements in Literature, not previously enamored with empirical methodology, should be taking to computerized text analysis with a vengeance. Both, it seems, have been invaded by cultural Anthropology; the chief *guru* judging by citation analysis, is Clifford Geertz who was enchanted with something other than power in human activities, but instead, their "poetics" (GEERTZ, 1973). It is ironic also that this emphasis on narration in text-based History should be influenced so extensively by Anthropology, which is ostensibly a Social Science aiming at objectivity via Literary Studies which are so subjective.

While some see convergence in these cross-disciplinary studies, a divergence in language, both vocabulary and usage, can be detected in History to argue that the recent literary impact on History, following the invasion of cultural Anthropology, has further polarized narrative and quantified history and further distanced literary or textual historians from their databased and quantification-prone counterparts. It remains to be seen if some of the subjective readings of texts and interesting interpretations, which are interspersed with semiotics, ethnology, and cognitive psychology, and based largely on selective quotation, extensive description, and anecdotal paraphrase interwoven into a new criticism, can be and will ever be reexamined with more empirical methods which might meet the scientific requirements of evidence, i.e., measurement, model building and testing, and reproducibility of results. Otherwise, this swing in historiography toward the narrative, personalized interpretation, and subjectivity, may simply be a phase, a counterpoint to unjustified belief in numbers, seen from non-Western eyes as a *yin* and *yang* movement. The ideal, speaking as a moderate, is balance and harmony between the two extremes. Multitype text-based, image-based, and data-based probes mutually reinforcing and checking each other are in order.

Has textuality simply replaced numeracy as the current focal point in many of these methodological discussions among text-based historians? Given the current awareness of word imagery more than when AUSTIN and others first explored such phenomena in the 1960s, then an unheard counterpoint against the rise of quantification, trends now indicate even greater potential interplay between textual exegesis, image analysis, and data modeling in the future. Contemporary foci on genre, myth, and mystic, with image, imagination, and cognition are not as exclusive from quantified models as one might think from the French school (or American specialists in French History) now dominating European History intellectual and sociocultural historiography. Both image and narrative, however, are subject to scientific analysis and can be quantified in one way or another if historians skilled in textual analysis were also expert in mathematical techniques. An imbalance exists today, with a skewing toward the descriptive and narrative as much as when the pendulum previously swung in favor of quantification, when Lawrence Stone, nearly 20 years ago, prophesied the "revival of the narrative."

MAZA (1996, p. 1493) rightly proclaims, "Storytelling, or in academic parlance 'narrative,' has returned to the historical discipline with a vengeance." She does not notice the similar revival in Management, as noted earlier, or storytelling as an organizational therapy. However, a resurgence of quantification mingled with textual studies could be in order, if historians were adequately trained in mathematics and statistics as much as in language and literature. That does not seem to be the case. If, as MONTROSE discerned in the New Historicism (VEESER), the dual foci on "the historicity of texts and the textuality of history," so too one might notice trends in applied linguistics that may well resurrect quantified methodology applied more and more surreptitiously to both literary and nonliterary historical texts in such things as pattern recognition and mapping ideas as though a narrative were a landscape, and to treat word and graphic images similarly. The point is that those who envelope themselves solely in text and are confident that literary and nonliterary or documentary historical text analysis involved word study only are mistaken. The interplay between text, image, mapping and quantified modeling is much larger than is often represented in current debates framed traditionally as a matter solely of text studies with traditional humanistic tools and methodologies. All of these issues in Information Science are sometimes treated as matters of representation, and in Computer Science as interfaces.

Even when using linguistic methods to analyze texts, historians have a regard for documentary sources as something other than (perhaps, more than) fictional texts. All texts, from all places and periods, can be subjected to computer-assisted systematic linguistic analysis to extract patterns, themes, mentalities, etc., not plainly seen by a reader or knowingly implanted by an author; they are cultural attributes naturally absorbed, conveyed, and understood differently when recontextualized (BOURQUE & DUCHASTEL; SALEM & LEBART). The historian would prefer the modern reader keep a historical piece in the context of its origin while evaluating it, before proceeding to further consideration in the contemporary context. But in Literature as Religion the contemporary context is deemed more important, so a text may be lifted from historical context if it "speaks" to the reader. Such texts are seen to transcend history from one perspective; from another, the contemporary is always an historical referent. History too, to be relevant, attempts to relate past and present. In so doing, reconstructed "actual" history and "virtual" reality may often be confused, especially with modern technological recreations such as holography or in cinematography where actual and virtual will share an exchangeable reality in the near future. Already historical fiction, like modeling, provide a range of interpretation extending beyond the actual, resulting also in criticism that history is fiction in the sense that it is artificially contrived, reconstructed, and reinterpreted in light of contemporary sensibilities. It is this relativism to which many historians react critically (e.g., APPLEBY, HUNT & JACOB), if not vociferously (B. PALMER).

This subjectivity and relativism also creates problems in public history, i.e., how one relates to the audience. Consumers of history in public presentation as much as in academic pursuits, are less convinced than ever that historians' selection is objective, to say nothing about their interpretation, especially when it challenges core history, the old canon, or hallowed tradition. In the United States, such trends became evident in the public reaction against the 1991 National Museum of American Art's exhibition "The West As America" which challenged romantic mythography about the American West. The 1992 controversy over the Quincentennial of Columbus, his discovery, exploration, encounter, exploitation or whatever, was a real debacle to behold with opinion substituting for information at every turn of event in the public debate, distortion entering school curricula by design, and celebrated secondary works masquerading as historical research without recourse to the original record, archival or published (L. LYNCH; MCCRANK, 1994). This was but a prelude to what has been called the "pyrotechnics" over the Smithsonian Institution's Enola Gay exhibition and its ignominious cancellation (T. A. WOODS).

All of this commotion would seem to prove that history does matter, and it is a personal as much as a public matter. LINENTHAL & ENGELHARDT allude to the Enola Gay and similar controversies between those who experienced an episode of history and those who represent it later as modern "History Wars." Thus the debate at the 1996 AHA conference about "Who Owns History?" is a question posed by *The New York Times* in 1995 (HANLEY). The issue in historical information science, given its reliance on new technologies and mediation more than selection of actual artifacts and presentation of a revisionist interpretation, is more complex because the possibility of preordained selection controlled not by the documentation itself but the search strategy, of countless interpretations and seemingly endless reinterpretation, and scenarios that can be rehearsed faster than any exhibit could be mounted (or an exhibit that is digitized and re-arranged, edited, and interpolated into others). It is also an issue of document authentification and selection more complex than in the realm of using a few authenticated real manuscripts and printed records, which can be altered after authentification in transit through a variety of media, and which can take on new meaning in accord with recontextualization. The debatable aspects of history reconstructed technologically may not be as apparent to most consumers in the same way a history lesson is in the classroom or an exhibit in a Smithsonian Institution museum may be, but it is this subtle, ubiquitous aspect that should be most alarming.

New information and instructional technology assists in recall, precision, and document retrieval, or conversely it can assist one in forgetting. When it comes to national history according to KOVEN, the needs to remember and to forget are equally strong. He likens amnesty in past situations to sanctioned amnesia, i.e. forgive and forget. The problem, of course, is not confined to the United States. KOVEN points to the French who have "a special aptitude for forgetting embarrassing episodes in their history, or having short memories," which is perhaps why it is French historians who are the forefront of Memory and History studies and why historians like NORA (1989), who is especially antagonistic with the objectivist paradigm, are especially sensitive to this issue in more than formal academic history. He adds to his list of "places of memory" not only monuments and shrines, but passages in textbooks, proverbs, folktales, and the French national anthem. The French, of course, point to the Americans who seem to have adjusted to the trauma of Vietnam more easily than to a critical history of how the West was won. They jokingly make their point by reminding Americans that it should be easier to deal with their history when it is so short! On the other hand, the French, Germans, Canadians, and Americans perhaps share similar problems in historical memory due to recurring crises of unity and identity, such as those highlighted for the French by Henry Rousso's *The Vichy Syndrome*. In information science the question is raised about the efficacy of the right amount of information, lest one be deluged on the one hand or only skim the surface on the other; in history circles a similar debate is occurring about how much memory is good for a people, whether purging is better than pardoning, or social catharsis is preferred to consensus—in sum, according to KOVEN (p. 59), "remembering versus forgetting."

The choices KOVEN provides are not so clearcut as this or that, but some of this and that. Moreover, these treatments do not, however, interject the technical dimension to the crises of historical memory they address (except, perhaps, for filmography and the visual arts). In Information technology, as pointed out in the case of electronic records, archives, and data warehousing, the issue may be one of overwriting more than deletion. Let us amplify the discussion by precisely such inclusion. Consider the tutorial system Story Making Interactive LanguagE (SMILE), which is used in the Moscow State University to provide documentary and narrative snapshots of "seventeen moments of Russian history" (IZMESTIEV). The authors present SMILE as a tool for "programming tutorial systems in History." History and storytelling are still entwined in new information technology, and the issue of discernment between the two, verification, and evidential historicity remain critically important. Couple story generating software with virtual reality in visualization and the prospect for history's alteration increases significantly, more than at any other time except when history was simply forgotten because the technology did not exist to record it; it never passed into corporate memory through folklore and the arts, and individual memory died with the witnesses. In NORA's treatment, the interplay between history and memory is, by comparison with what is possible with new technology (i.e., local and global recall, alteration, and obliteration) relatively conventional and mundane.

Document verification is difficult in any case, but new technology makes old problems even more complicated. The benefits of visual computing research has provided forensics with advances that would prove useful for historians if they were initially trained in document examination better than most are. J. M. FOURNIER demonstrated the utility of such techniques years ago (1977) in relation to the Dreyfus Affair. As in the case of trying to authenticate a recently found funerary oration now attributed to Shakespeare, while others think of the Shakespearean corpora as a collective enterprise, the analytic techniques are similar.

Historians suspecting forgeries and interpolations will want to avail themselves of such technology to reveal more than can be seen under a magnifying glass, racking light, or ultraviolet inspection. Applications include computer recognition of fingerprints for the FBI (MEGDAL), which is a concept that was applied much earlier to rare book and manuscript identification (MCCRANK, 1978; R. HARMON, pp. 80-91) and now to data files as well (W.

VAUGHAN; ZWEIG, 1993b); signature verification in check writing for banks (BROCKLE-HURST; PAQUET & LECOURTIER) and other security purposes or sorting mail for the post office by scanning zip codes and addresses also have transfer potential for manuscripts research and information retrieval beyond human abilities. Several history projects are already appropriating such technology as fast as it is developed, but lone historians without proper laboratory and research support, which are not provided as often by research libraries and archives as they should, cannot get the training or tap the collaborative expertise they need to verify their primary sources. Historians have assisted the relatively few laboratories working on historical documentation by providing source material and they lend their expertise in paleography, calligraphy, and diplomatics. But the critical scale needed to develop proper software for document verification, including electronic file integrity, has not been attained in History or the whole of academic research. One must reach into other fields where forensics are important, as in banking and criminology in order to discover technology and methodologies that can be adapted to a wide array of historical documentation.

Even when verification and authentification are attempted, new technology makes forgery detection ever more technical and difficult. New forensic and analytic methodologies are not being invented as rapidly as the technology for records creation (invention?) is developing. Moreover, forensic approaches to electronic documentation must work across databases, textbases, and imagebases since digital technology merges all three into hybrid documents, and no presentation is immune from radical alteration, either in editing (which needs to be documented with metadata) or intentional interpolation and forgery (which, of course, will not be documented but should be detected nonetheless). Everyone is now aware of the easy changes made with text processing and the need to distinguish between electronic editions and states just as in print, and most understand that data presentations likewise have editions and states that should be identified. Moreover, reading processes include rechecking text where comprehension fails, repetition, and critical thinking skills that are taught with reading. Likewise, the statistical interpretation of data requires one to slow down, take a critical look, and recheck the array if comprehension fails. People understand that data are easily manipulated and nongraphic data presentations are usually looked at more closely to be understood, but this is often not the case in graphic representations as TUFTE has made so clear. Originals, copies, editions, states, etc., for visual presentations are seldom identified, whether in more traditional media like prints and photographs, or Web sites. And because people see all the time, it is assumed, incorrectly, that they comprehend what they see. Sometimes a second look is possible, but often not, and a stare is socially discouraged so that people usually do not "read" an image but glance at it and full comprehension is dependent on visual recall from memory—faulty as that may be. Visual accuracy and memory can be trained as a form of literacy, but this is often a neglected area of our education. Most people have training in reading text and data but operate with whatever skills they manage on their own for visual acuity, comprehension, and interpretation. Visual information transfer often sacrifices one for the other, the whole picture or detail, when with training both need to be seen and understood. Ironically, therefore, it is the graphic representation and the image that are most easily accepted uncritically and are the least checked for forgery. Because images and texts are merged more easily that data arrays, narration and visualization or text and image analysis are thus treated together in this essay. Historians and other analysts using visual information must learn to read images critically and technically.

Although more will be said later about the possibilities and problems in using image resources, the point here is to stress the mutual reinforcement of image and text information, their merged and volatile character in a digital environment, and the need for the critical and technical examination of both. Consider software such as *"Picture It!"* on CD-ROM from Microsoft which enables users to do advanced image editing in Windows environments, and "fix" everything from tinting to "red eye" including erasure of unwanted details. Historical images scanned into Web pages are thereby equally subject to interpolation as text. Using digital photography, Western Pro

Imaging Labs of Vancouver, B.C., has developed a unique service, Divorce X as it is called, to expunge undesirable sources (or mother-in-laws, ex-lovers, or anyone else's face one wants forgotten) from photos. Its president, Keith Guelpa, explained in an interview carried by *The Wall Street Journal* and other newspapers for the 1995 New Year, that if a couple got together again— no problem: the offending party could be reinserted by the same process. MCDONALD & COLE offer instruction on *"How to Make Old-Time Photos."* So much for the family photo album as authentic evidence for family history! The movie *Rising Sun* in 1993 introduced the general public to the problems of forensics and document authentification in the case of digital video, when the character played by Sean Connery had to turn to high-tech professionals to find out how evidence in video tapes had been altered by making a killer disappear from the images recorded by surveillance cameras. The technical task was to recover masked visual data from doctored video disks removed from a security system, and thereby identify the murderer. The general exposure of the public to such technology, the spectrum from use to abuse, is interesting because of people's acceptance of the idea, its deployment, and apparent willingness to adapt. The general moviegoing public acknowledged that this is modern reality, not fiction, and that modern technology, virtual reality, and the real world are likely to become even more mixed up (M. HEIM, 1993). Distortion may be discerned, but deliberate forgery is less obvious.

Multimedia recreation, simulation exercises, and modeling are variations on the same theme and can rely on similar methodologies and technologies. The implications of such confusion are enormous. The epistemological dimensions of such interactive media when refined as they are becoming appear to be so complex that discernment seems increasingly dependent on the subtle rather than obvious because normal common sense-tested assumptions are no longer reliable. People's reality check is dependent on their objective sense of history, but the more subjective this sensibility is, the more problematic is discernment between real and make-believe. Deconstructionist thought like this, coupled with modern multimedia and information technology, highlights the enormity of the contemporary crisis facing History which historians seem barely to acknowledge. Historians still rely too heavily on their historical common sense, and too often have not been trained well enough in diplomatics and formal criticism, analytical science, and forensics to have a basis for developing new epistemology for new kinds of technically-dependent documentation and their mediation. Consequently, little work is being done in History to develop the critical technical skills needed to authenticate electronic communications, digitized documentation, interactive sources, and machine-dependent media.

New methodologies are required, and a new historical epistemology must be invented. The distinction between depositional or documentary image and art, which has often allowed historians to avoid dealing with interpretative elements in paintings for example, and which blurred in turning to photographs as supposedly more stable historical evidence even though scenes could be staged, cannot be so easily circumvented for modern history or for any other period when the primary source is conveyed secondarily through digital technology. Personal, corporate, and government historical sources captured in image and text can be altered so easily in a digital, virtual world that old assumptions, standard research methodologies, and examination of primary sources before use will no longer suffice to create a documentary, evidential base for history. Perhaps it is a nagging paranoia or having dealt with too many forgeries in my own work that caused me to misread an advertisement (AHA *Perspectives*, 1995: 33(2); 5) by the George Washington University Center for the History of Media and the National Gallery of Art summer seminar on "Learn to Make Historical Documentaries" as "Learn to Make Historical Documents"! In the slang of the day, CONNEL talks about "Doing Texts," which conjures up the colloquialism "doing someone in," but which was meant more in the vein of HEXTER's "Doing History." The evidentiary issues at hand, however, need to be taken seriously.

Document examination and formal source criticism, not well taught in most graduate History curricula, must become part of the historian's natural repertoire rehearsed in research even before one gets to the knotty questions of subjectivity and objectivity in interpretation. The choice is not possible, of course, if objectivity is not attempted at the start, in the creation and maintenance of archives, without the appraisal and security of the object (i.e., record). One then has only the subjective option left. The issue then becomes being objective about the subjective, and *vice versa*. Authentification and verification, two related but not synonymous processes, must be practiced with more diligence than ever in electronic environments if the concept of evidence is to be preserved in the modern sense of proof or provability will become merely a matter of probability. Reliability of a credible witness in the particular for a specific instance is necessary even in an array of data where the testimony of a single act, record, and rendering is tempered by context and the sometimes confused notion of likelihood that lies somewhere between possibility and probability. Historians, like courts of law, must now consider the admissibility of evidence by appraising not only internal criticism of content and externals of form, but provenance and meta-information that affords one some guarantee of authenticity. The watchword is for non-doctoring when the technology favors interpolation. The methodology that has evolved for data transfer and preservation is for convenience in use but provides no guarantee against doctoring. Security systems are being developed to guard against viruses and hackers to safeguard electronic data from mutilation and destruction, but less for internal tampering, discontinuity in tracking and chain of custody, and preservation of authenticity and the authority of a record or data set (see the primers on Internet security by FLOOD; SCHNEIER; RUSSELL & GANGEMI). DENNING & DENNING recently brought together a 34-chapter book to educated network administrators about security breaches, including new security checking software such as *Tripwire, Secure Analysis Tool for Auditing Networks (SATAN),* and *Pretty Good Privacy (PGP)* (GARFINKEL; STALLINGS; P. R. ZIMMERMANN). But hacker infiltration cases are different from the purely spurious invention one finds on the Internet: i.e., the *Internet hoaxes* to which one is alerted by the COMPUTER INTERNET ADVISORY CAPABILITY (CIACH) or the scams tracked by the FEDERAL TRADE COMMISSION.

The conveyance of digital information today relies on relatively few techniques to safeguard the authenticity of the information seen remotely. First, electronic records can be rendered "read-only" for transit through a client-server system, but that limits utility. Second, a checksum mechanism can be employed as in telecommunications to ensure accurate transmission, where a one-byte representation of the decimal value of each character in a specified segment of a record is added to the record. When checked by a computer, a viewer is alerted if this sum has changed even by one byte. Third, one-way (i.e., irreversible) hashing similarly checks two sums and compares them to detect alterations. This involves compressing a digital object (e.g., using MD5 or SAH has digest algorithms) when sent and when received, to ensure that the uncompressed record to be used is authentic. Finally, digital time-stamping is a one-way hash digest of a record that is registered with a third-party agency for certification of authenticity (e.g., Surety Technologies' *Digital Notary Record Authentication System*). The third party is used for objectivity, since then even the repository can use the service to recheck authenticity of its own records and guard against internal security breaches. Digital libraries have not always provided these means for authentication of their sources. However, if documents in digital libraries are relied upon for research as primary sources (e.g., critical electronic editions), as in the case of archival electronic records conveyed digitally researchers need to authenticate their images and texts before relying upon them. Such methods should be added to the researcher's repertoire just as one would examine paper documents to authenticate recorded information before considering such sources as evidential.

As digital technology develops and more sources are made available digitally, new techniques for authentication need to be established. Fraud is best prevented by stable media, but this is not likely in media so pliable that interpolation is invited as an attribute of the technology. So, protection must be added after the fact, so to speak, but its effectiveness also relies on awareness and precautions of the user. Electronic forgery, interpolation of electronic documents, scams and hoaxes will continue to plague users and take in the innocent who believe that anything relayed by computer must be so; this problem of will bedevil historians ever more, and they need to develop habits of multisource verification and the means to authenticate information delivered electronically. Electronic archives should be developing surety services in this regard. Security and authentication operations may be seen as improved when turned over to surety agencies, independent of any vested interest in the records themselves, purveyor or user. For this reason alone electronic archives must be provided with a degree of independence for objective value-neutral operations which are subject to regular audit.

Indeed, the person controlling the technology can control reality, and thus has great power to alter history by performing what was colloquially called "salting" the archives in the era of paper records. The metaphor is from ancient times when fields of the conquered enemy were salted to make them barren, thereby crippling their enemy's recovery for years to come. The veracity of an archives, once its security is breached and the records are salted, is likewise ruined. Charles Polzer of Arizona's Museum of Anthropology has recounted cases of contested southwest land claims where legitimacy could be contrived not by destroying records, but by adding forgeries and interpolations to a series in the Mexican archives (POLZER). When called upon by an American court, the archives would be microfilmed and notarized and thus accepted as an authentic historical record in settling disputes. Civil War historians who rely on old but standard documentary editions of correspondences from Union and Confederate generals and other important witnesses may unknowingly rely on secretarial copies. Without verifying originals, they may base their work on interpolated material. If these interpolations in old records series often go undetected, how many electronic interpolations may be undetected in modern records or in the electronic renderings of historical records? The lack of critical document examination in historical research and the lack of methodology to do so with modern information technology seem to be far more serious affronts to the objectivity of historical writing than the interpretative issues raised by deconstructionists and postmodernists.

How serious is this problem in modern research? In 1996, several major projects in pharmaceutical research, NIH-funded genetic research to control inherited disease, and cancer research were set back by the scandalous falsification of data resulting in skewed and unreliable interpretations. Francis Collins, director of the National Center for Human Genome Research, withdrew five papers on leukemia research after his research teams uncovered problems of concocted data by an graduate student employed by the Center. Numerous other cases of fraud in scientific research, as examined by GRAYSON, caused Congress to appoint a Commission on Research Integrity which expanded the list of malfeasance from the traditional trilogy of fabrication, falsification, and plagiarism to include theft of, or damage to, research facilities, equipment, and projects, as well as misconduct and self-interest in proposal reviewing. Thus, federal rules of misconduct are evolving, to the chagrin of the university community and other researchers who continue to minimize the problem without much study of the alleged issue overall. GUNSALUS, in a recent symposium on "Science in Crisis at the Millennium," warns against continuing problems and future scandals, but points to the inadequacy of current definitions and inoperability of current quality-control and oversight programs.

ZAGORIN, reflecting on several hundred studies about lying and deception from the vantage point of social psychology, recently subjected fraud and misrepresentation to a systematic literature overview. This was in response to the perceived increase in deception and attendant distrust of government, medicine, business, and other professions by Americans, which reflects also in their skepticism about history and the historical profession. ZAGORIN's identification of dissimulation as one of the "ways of lying" in early modern Europe reflects his interest in the phenomena of social disassembly due to various kinds of persecution in another era, but his investigation was inspired by events in our time.

History, of course, is not above charges of deception and misrepresentation as many current debates indicate; nor is it immune from corruption in research practices and similar sabotage in data preparation and handling which are much less scrutinized than peer reviewing of results or conclusions. In my own experience in doctoral examinations I have been alerted to possible inclusion of interpolated records from a bound, otherwise legitimate series, into a documentary edition because the methodologies associated with diplomatics, codicology and analytical bibliography were not practiced—indeed, they had not been taught. Cases of blatant lying or fabrication of citations to nonextant sources (materials that never existed, as distinct from deception through forgeries) seem rare compared with plagiarism which periodically scandalizes the historian community. Although professional historical interpretation has been challenged in a variety of ways, historical research *per se* has not been subjected to the same scrutiny in the sciences or medicine in regard to research methods, reverification, and double or blind-referencing to check sources; critical apparati in historical writing, editing, and reviewing are not designed to check routinely for such problems as falsification of sources and extrapolated evidence. History does not have the same kind of monitoring, checking, and quality-control agency at work as the National Institute of Health, and data sets are seldom submitted with written results.

It seems doubtful that studies relying on electronic surrogates check their corresponding original sources, and it is questionable whether historians are being trained with the technical skills or project management techniques to conduct authentification, verification, and reliability checks for their data and other sources. This is easier to do in electronic scholarship than citations to unpublished archival material and may be a future requirement. These possible shortcomings go to the heart of the issue, i.e., competence in source examination and handling of evidence, rather than the ability to move on to artfully crafted criticism based on a reading of a text or judgments based on surface, style, and presentation, or highly subjective personalized interpretation.

One can point to few innovations where historians are using technology adroitly to safeguard the integrity of their documentation, rather than to interpolate it at will and with impunity. One of the few models would be the Holocaust digital archives project at the Max Planck Institut which invested the time and funds to design a security check-sum measure with their digital editions of Nazi detention camp records (THALLER, 1997; REHBEIN). Here is a case where historians have understood the potential for falsification, interpolation and other forms of fraud by those into Holocaust denial; and where modern information technology, information science, history, and political savvy all came together. This is an issue of quality control. Readers as consumers deserve such quality assurance in historical research and writing. If the production of History were in compliance with a ISO-9000 standard, such assurances would be mandated.

The mainstream of critical debate in contemporary historiography, however, seems less concerned about the primacy, authenticity, and purity of evidence than in the motives and critical temperament involved in its contemporary interpretation. The two are connected, however, since the very notion of evidence presupposes some objective standards of truth. Historians have always been concerned in internal and external criticism of their documentation with the issue of motive in the creation of documentation to determine reliability of evidence. However, radical deconstructionists have attacked not the primacy of evidence in original documentation, or practices in document examination, but more the subjectivity in interpretation by historians during historical reconstruction. Motives are tied to ideology, including both the creation of evidence and also why the historian wants to investigate the phenomena in the first place. It is like a defense lawyer suspecting all testimony about evidence elicited by the prosecution because the examiner tested evidence with the motive to convict, but may have ignored exculpating evidence, and *vice versa*.

This relativism in reading history as literature and historical description as fabricated mental imagery like any art work seems especially relevant to linguistic computing applied to texts, which so easily interpolates and can thereby just as easily misconstrue historical and contemporary contexts, so that the same skepticism applied to quantification and data modeling is now applied to reconstructed or highly edited texts. It may pertain to the historian's use of metaphor and anecdote, word pictures, and narratives told as exempla. If one were to buy into the relativism of De Certeau and deconstructive criticism of J. Derrida, quantified models would be no different than historical narrative in being suspect as reconstructions. Such criticism certainly can be applied with potentially destructive results to artistic historical reconstruction in the visual arts, whether an artist's rendition for *National Geographic* or a courtroom artist's rendition for a newspaper, and especially for computer synthesized recreations of monuments from archeological traces, holographs and visual models, and document enhancement whether textual or image. Such criticism has been leveled not only against models built on word studies (SHILLINGSBURG), but against the kind of historical narration advocated by L. STONE when he proposed in 1979 that an alternative to quantification of many data from a broad spectrum of events would be to describe in detail a representative event and then let it reflect on the larger development. From the viewpoint of scientific historicism, the critical issue here would be the key word "representative" and how that were determined. Such extrapolations and historical constructions imitate literary modeling, and both can be decried as fictional in the same way that mathematical models in quantified socioeconomic history were assailed. Both may be attacked on the grounds of too great a reliance on a hunch or too much artistic license on one hand, or on the other, too heavy a reliance on computer simulation, reconstruction, and modeling.

Never before have the issues of authenticity, verification, and source identification been so entwined with questions of appraisal, selection and rejection, use and interpretation, where the subjective and objective are indivisible. Note that such study can act as a philosophical critique as well of most modern Information Science, if detractors were to muster the destructive power of deconstructionism and combine it with unbridled skepticism. Information Science is not immune, only somewhat nonreflective, and deflective as well. Historical Information Science, with its affinity to History and contentions therein, will certainly be drawn into such debate as it was with the advent of quantification. It is perhaps because of such circumspection that historians do reach out to auxiliary fields and other disciplines to augment historical argumentation. Technique, technology, and methodology all combine in lending credence to historical interpretation.

In other cases, initial overextensions of such methodologies have served to undermine the credibility of historical scholarship. FOMENKO & RACHEV applied discourse analysis to electronic versions of texts from ninth-century to seventeenth-century Russian chronicles to measure divisions and time periods, check word frequencies and shifts in usage between them, and analyze degrees of correspondence between them to determine how narratives for the same period were related, and those for different periods borrowed from one another. They, thus, attempted to delineate an historiographic tradition similarly to a time series analysis. They concluded that time was disjointed in the chronicler tradition, that parallel developments were sometimes placed into serial order while at other times serial processes were collapsed into parallel developments. Events had been dislocated as well. In short, history had been really messed up by early historians who attempted to make sense of the transition from late antiquity through the Byzantine period and to late medieval Russian times. Radical revision was called for, which could be justified as well by turning to natural science.

FOMENKO's historical works and the ensuing controversy in the former Soviet Union are an interesting case of modern revisionism that combined postmodern critique in the extreme on the one hand, with overconfidence in mathematical modeling and projection on the other. The historical works of this mathematician, now numbering seven volumes since the 1980s, constitute an interesting experiment in the fusion of textual exegesis with empirical methodology. Fomenko's works have achieved an unprecedented popularity, especially surprising given their burden of mathematical proofs and methodological excursions, while in the Russian Academy of Sciences he is held in utter disdain. His goal was to reformulate history by reconceptualizing traditional chronology by synchronizing it with the few hard facts that would allow the restructuring of time, namely astronomical observations. Time as expressed in traditional chronologies is for Fomenko an entrapment of local observations rationalized into time lines as though chronicled events unfolded in a chronological series. He suspected that local time and events have overlapped with each other more than is commonly perceived. Parallel history was, in this view, recorded erroneously as serial. Thus he has sought to collapse tradition chronology by nearly a millennium, by a close reading of the chronicles and examination of texts which reminds one of the promises made in New Criticism for a rewriting and re-envisioning of traditional History. For his resynchronization of chronologies, with attendant arguments that different historical personages of note were really the same people perceived differently, he has been scoffed at as a sheer dilettante, despite the elaborate critical apparatus and mathematical reconstructions. Most of the attackers, established historians, however, failed to penetrate the method or counter the argument, but simply railed against madness.

Recently PONOMAREV, a graduate student, met Fomenko on his own ground in the hard sciences to deliver the most decisive rebuttal. One of Fomenko's foundations was the reworking of chronology from the second century on, by redating the accounts of Claudius Ptolemeaus in the *Almagest* (http://sunsite.unc.edu/expo/vatican.exhibit) to the seventh through the eleventh centuries based on the Greek chronicler's recording of astronomical observances which supposedly anchor his accounts in true time. Once late antique events were thus redated, most of medieval history had to be compressed to reconcile this revision with modern times. Andrey Ponomarev read Fomenko as closely as the latter claimed to read Ptolemy and targeted nine major miscalculations in the mathematician's work. One argument in particular demonstrates creativity in the use of modern information technology in History polemics.

The debate centered around a sighting of Venus dated by Fomenko in 887. A NASA astronomical program projecting constellation configurations (*Home Planet 2* at http://www.rahul. net) was found to be capable of recalculating backward as much as predicting stellar alignments, and reconstructing sky maps from vantage points on Earth. The eclipse of the star Virgo by Venus was confirmed for 887 as Fomenko had argued, but this phenomenon could not be observed from Earth, then or now, because of the position of the sun. Likewise, in checking 18 lunar eclipses, eight could never have been observed in Egypt because of the angle over the horizon. One by one such reexamination of the evidence and argument left Fomenko's reconstruction of multilevel history lacking the solid foundation he claimed to have discovered in astronomical correlation. But Fomenko's books are still widely read and many Russians on his authority have accepted a radical re-arrangement of their historical consciousness. Why? At a time when the Commonwealth of Independent States is altering its path in history, many Russians are also concerned intensely with their history and altering it as well. The popular discourse and the science in History seem to be the real multilevel incongruence at hand. Fomenko's influence and the resulting debate, therefore, would seem to be good material for discourse analysis and the study of history in the popular psychology of the Russian people during this time of trouble. Parallel time and geographic relativism leading to multilevel history, like time warps in science fiction, are poised for a shakeup of the corporate world view; all of these phenomena seem worthy of serious study amid all of the intercourse between History and Literature, and in this case, between History and Science which find themselves at various times, closer and more distant, as each is in flux (paraphrasing J. MARGOLIS). This departure of virtual history from reality or actuality has occurred at other times and has attracted historians' attention as an intriguing field of study. AUERBACH as early as 1968 laid the groundwork for such an inquiry from historical perspective into the representation of reality in Literature, long before deconstructionists from literacy schools began their attack on historical reconstruction as predominantly relative representation. F. R. Ankersmit undertook a semantic analysis of historians' language use and subsequently examined the role of metaphor in historical description and language constructions in historiographic representation (ANKERSMIT, 1983; 1989; 1994). The French coined the term "the social imaginary" as a concept to study a widely held virtual reality that does not correspond to reality except as a commonplace in popular imagination. The perception is real, but not the thing perceived. The research is directed, therefore, toward proof of the social discourse, sometimes without recourse to underlying, documented reality. Sometimes only the hyperlevel can be documented because it exists independently of actuality. There are always two parallel texts to examine, the one speaking from the historical past, and the historian's interpretation of that past for the present audience.

Examples of such discourse analysis for the study of fiction in the history of popular culture include K. KELLEY's examination of best-sellers from 1850 to 1920 to identify American "success models" and their gender differentiation. J. D. ORTEN's more recent dissertation (1989) provides another example of such crossover between communications, historical, and literary research; he studied the rhetorical ideal of "plain language" in Elizabethan Puritanism by contrasting what was said about language with actual use based on statistical analysis of a 90,000-word corpus that allow some differentiation between Anglican and Puritan tastes such as the former's richer vocabulary and the latter's reliance on more Anglo-Saxon terms. R. COOK applied a similar methodology to study American "Puritans and Pragmatists" in nineteenth-century Iowa by computer-assisted examination of roll calls and partisan rhetoric in that state's legislature. BOURQUE & DUCHASTEL approached the political rhetoric of the Duplessis regime in Québec in much the same way in order to identify and juxtapose the traditional and progressive positions of the day. BERLANSTEIN pulled together contributions that merged discourse analysis and social class studies to "rethink labor history."

VAN DIJK analyzed newspapers to treat "news as discourse," just as SPURR treated journalism and travelogues similarly to produce a social study of "the rhetoric of empire" in the heyday of European colonialism. So too with historians today, critical of the sensationalist view of history projected by news media, have to sort news and history into their appropriate categories while teaching. The same discrimination will no doubt be a key activity of future historians looking back upon this era. As media coverage grows, sensationalism continues, and we continue to witness the waning of historical perspective in modern journalism and television; historians will have to confront the mediation of history as a common problem. Lessons may be learned from history of other ages, when the mythical element in history was perpetuated by other than electronic means, especially ritual performance repeated so often that human recall is the rehearsed surrogate rather than based on the actual event or documentation thereof.

Myths and rituals, oral evidence turned into texts, were studied in these ways by anthropologist G. URBAN to gain insight into the culture of South American Indians who could not rely on written documentation. But the availability of writing technology does not preclude similar activities in literate cultures. LINK & WULFING collected studies of nineteenth-century German myths and symbols to trace the origins of race identity and connect this with rising nationalism. More recently as part of the return to narrative studies in French Social History, CHEVALIER borrowed ideas from Victor Hugo's *Les Miserables* to relate labor classes with perceptions of dangerous behavior, and REID followed in a similar vein to reveal what Parisians conjured up from their city's sewers. WALKOWITZ's *City of Dreadful Delight* examines sensationalism in Victorian journalism that created myths that assumed a quasi-reality in how they affected people's behaviors. In all such work, the relationships between text and context, agent and action, real and invented are all important. Such multilevel history renderings can explore actuality and contemporary perception as well as continued historical perception created by continuous reading and rereading of a genre long after the events they purport to describe.

Much of this layered history that relies on texts and their reading, a continually reinforced narrative, depends on the study of reading itself, more as an issue of cognition and belief than literacy *per se*. Semiotics and linguistics are merged in treating words in descriptions as pictures and images described as texts (GUIRAUD), including such abstract notions as "reading" space and time as advocated by PINTO, which should interest historians. And reading itself, now understood as a creative interaction between reader and author mediated by text and controlled by particular technologies, has been totally revamped into what is sometimes called the New Literary History (THOMPSON). Such trends are likely to fuse with treatment of texts as landscapes, somewhat in the tradition of good graphics design. Such history would seem to be liable to the same critique of statistical representation and modeling *à la* E. TUFTE (1990), but with the added element in multilevel history of layered and stratified texts that operate like GIS overlays. Rather than collate text like an electronic version of a Hinman collator working with two editions laid side by side, digitized texts can be superimposed in layers, compared automatically by pattern recognition software that retrieves maps as images (BRACK; B. MORRIS) and linked by interwoven terminological interfaces that operate as indexes (MCCRANK, 1987) not unlike methods developed to collate layers of archeological evidence from strata in a dig (e.g., GALINE). Spatial relationships in information retrieval are now being applied to bibliographic information retrieval, and this has prompted renewed interest in geographic terminology and criticism of extant indexing tools that retrieve information largely through spatial indicators (HILL & RASMUSSEN). Here again, linguistics, terminology, and subject-domain knowledge become fused in improving database design for effective information retrieval and representation.

Behavioralists are not immune from such trends, either in their own behaviors or those of their subjects. Psychologists want to go "beyond attitudes and behavior" (POTTER & M. WETHERELL) to get into the mind through discourse analysis of written and spoken communications in the same way they have wanted to use images to provoke responses that as verbalized texts can be studied as an indirect discourse with art or their own flashback recollections. Sociologists use similar "ethno-methodology" to study such mundane "talk" as transcribed telephone conversations or directions to discern "structure-in-action" in organizations (BODEN & ZIMMERMAN) or the American home (VARENNE, HILL & BYERS), just as Xerox Corporation employees discovered that their e-mail was being analyzed for studies of morale in the ranks and to clarify virtual information communities in the company and networking across the country ostensibly for benign organizational management, but suspicions were otherwise. The point can be brought closer to home for academics, as mentioned before, when considering citation tracing and similar analyses of their scholarship used to gauge more than whether a professor had published, which in a research university is assumed, but if such publications had enough influence to warrant tenure and promotion.

Government documents and technical literatures are being studied similarly, for security reasons and to check the efficacy of scholarly communications or as in patent texts or pharmaceutical labels and prescription directions, as quality control in information dissemination. Now, with electronic surveillance in text, checking for plagiarism can be equally automatic. In 1995-1996 in the United States, several cases have already come to light, and the techniques of discourse analysis and computerized word study have been employed in ways that are intriguing and disturbing. Thus far, historians have not employed such technology as much as one might have wished in the field of analytical bibliography (as distinct from ennumerative bibliography), for source verification and provenance checking. While literary scholars have developed the methodology into a highly sophisticated art for typographical works of literature, with findings that have warranted reediting several works, such applications to documentary collections are rare. This is perhaps because the historical profession has relegated bibliography and editing to second-class citizenship in an ironic twist for a profession that claims to be based on records, documents, and testimony from the past. Little research can be identified in History on developing critical methodologies for handling electronic sources.

Other fields than History have voiced legitimate concerns in effective and legal technical information transfer and its authentification. In this regard during the 1970s the general public in America was exposed to the potential of optical scanning and term collation or concordancing technology applied to whole texts, perhaps most widely with political implications by the movie *Three Days of the Condor* staring Robert Redford where the application was in espionage. In this thriller, techniques were adopted such as surveillance operations to spot formula and secret code hidden innocuously in imported and exported books. The plot seemed not too far fetched during the last days of the Cold War, or when the CIA was indeed caught influencing the texts disseminated by previously reputable American publishers. There are indeed Orwellian overtones in such techniques being applied to one's writing like a profiler to determine psychological outlook, or to study religious conviction, political persuasion, or correctness. The predicament of our own times is treated with dark humor in J. F. GARNER's *Politically Correct Bedtime Stories: Modern Tales for Our Life and Times*. But it is harder to laugh when the analyses seem intrusive or when the aftereffect is personally experienced, as when word study, discourse analysis, and phrase matching with psychological profiles are applied to materials submitted for the clandestine review of job applications or for tenure and promotion. Such inspection of standard textbooks has occurred precisely to make them standardized. This is a controversial practice, which can be closely associated with recent political debates over language and culture: in Canada, and Québec in particular, about 'language police" enforcing laws to preserve the Frenchness of Québecois culture; in France, the issue is likewise the debasement of a pure language; in Spain, where regional dialect and languages (Basque, Catalan, Gallego, Andalusian, etc.) have resurfaced since Franco's days; and in the United States, most recently California, public debates have occurred over bilingual education. Such technology has also been employed to support political arguments, and in the courts about censorship of music groups, arts programs, and television, based on analyses of their lyrics, descriptions of content, and scripts; and the appropriateness of certain authors in public library children's and young adult collections. Note the technology's employment in the debates over a standardized history curriculum for elementary and secondary schools or for general studies curricula at the college level. In teaching and editing, such empirical findings or rather the use of such data, is complicated by issues related to academic freedom. Empirical evidence is difficult to dispute except on methodological grounds; but the interpretation and use of such evidence is always open to question.

Coupled with access over the Internet to electronic archives, raw records, and more formally published documents, in addition to these text corpora, the prospect for increased text analysis is no longer a distant vision. Some archivists are still balking, arguing again that their material is unique as they did when opposing uniform descriptive standards and MARC cataloging, or that the investment therefore is too great given the quantity of their holdings. Others are paying attention to the pilot digital archives projects already undertaken and to the increased cost-effectiveness of the technology and capacity of electronic storage, and consequently to the recognized increased feasibility every year for records conversion. The potential for new forms of information discovery using intelligent browsers and collators is largely untested, however, for historical research. Such technology is being exploited in business administration, risk management, and in litigation of law suits in combination, however, with techniques developed in discourse analysis. This may range from sampling corporate correspondence or internal e-mail communications to spot check morale or the state of organization culture in an organization, or adversely, to show how a corporate culture is habitually racist, sexist, or whatever, based on word frequencies and patterns in usage within large-scale corpora.

Such methodology and technology are common to all disciplines. Some applications may be controversial; the purpose and motivation are entwined with such judgment. The subjective and objective in such decisions are inextricably fused. Such analyses seem less encroaching on individual privacy and less threatening if the sources are historical in the sense of well-aged and removed from the contemporary scene. Remember, that recently historians very much wanted the National Archives to save the Nixon tapes and currently want government archivists to accession e-mail files as important historical resources. Their reactions are predictably different, however, at the prospect of university archivists treating faculty files similarly, or in having their lectures, writings, and official correspondence analyzed similarly with techniques that have also been applied in intelligence operations. Unobtrusive observation and espionage can employ similar techniques in data collection; motivation, goals and objectives, and planned application make a difference. So does historical distance from the contemporary and geographic distance from an individual.

HAMMIT (p. 138) indicates that in United States courts in terms of the privacy/access issue, "the balance has been tilted in favor of privacy over time." HAMMON BAKER (p. 239) in her discussion of access to government information points to a case of interest to historians and archivists alike. In a 1989 decision *(Department of Justice vs. Reported Committee for Freedom of the Press)*, the Supreme Court denied access to a computer file (a rap sheet which contained all kinds of personal information), arguing that even if this information is publically available in disparate locations and the diligent researcher might put it together, "the task can be impossible as a practical matter." The Court reasoned that

> ...the issue here is whether the compilation of otherwise hard-to-obtain information alters the privacy interest implicated by disclosure of that information. Plainly there is a vast difference between the public records that might be found after a diligent search of courthouse files, country [*sic*, i.e. county] archives, and local police stations throughout the country and a computerized summary located in as ingle clearinghouse of information.

In other words, the court made a distinction between fragmented and collated information, and between paper and electronic records on the basis of ease of use and greater accessibility, so that the kind of records conversion into digital form, and improved metadata or finding aids, and the kind of synthesis undertaken in historical research where myriad sources are pulled together for a telling exposé heighten the court's concern for increased possibilities of infringement on personal privacy. Such thinking has great potential for impact on the future of social research and Social History based on the automated compilation of personal data. Privacy rulings and legislation might insure that all such research is truly historical, that is, one or more generations old.

Personal privacy issues relating to contemporary history researched through modern information systems and online search capabilities are treated by B. FLOOD (1997) and her contributors to a special issue of the *ASIS Bulletin*, including "Creeping Peoplebases" which compares database development with privacy loss. This might be read, by way of contrast, as comparable to what is possible, e.g., as outlined by C. LANE's *Naked in Cyberspace* about personal records research and market competitive intelligence. These reflect the popular mood and professional concerns in the information field, but not the same attention to legality and formal policy development that one finds in archival literature or law reviews. Government archivists are treading a fine line these days as the privacy/access issue becomes more and more complicated, since moves toward "open government" can open the governments information resources about the citizenry—in detail. Moreover, it is easy to find reference and guide literature that are diametrically opposed: the one advising about how to find out anything about anyone, and the other telling you how to protect your privacy. SCHNEIER, for example, outlines methods for creating security for e-mail systems and safeguards for personal message privacy. Several insure privacy, but in shutting out third-party monitoring they also inhibit automatic archival appraisal and retention of e-mail communications as official records. Remove the buffer of time and personal research or biography seems more intrusive than in History practice; but trends in New Social History and concurrent documentation strategies (record generation contemporary with the living experience) make current controversies over privacy a potentially significant issue for the future of History. One need only recall Bill Gates' apprehension of "documented lives."

The access versus privacy issue affects history, therefore, now and in the future. Historical source generation, access, and use are always concerns, but these may be heightened now with the trend in archives toward accountability and the onus of record keeping on the records creator. So, too, are the issues of records generation and record keeping with disclosure, future use, and possible interpretation. Historians have had to contend with loss and imperfect data because of the non-creation of permanent information and records, the loss of documentation because of faulty record keeping, and occasionally the fabrication of records and forgery. But the number of people who have left a historical record because of self-awareness of their potential historical importance is relatively few. Theirs is the elite history of the greats. But recent historiography has shown a permanent shift from such history to that of the common man, all men and women, in all walks and stages of life. Their records, often byproducts of daily existence, constitute the historical record for such history, but most are not created as public records or with a historian's use in mind. A certain objectivity survives that increases their value for History, and their use by historians bestows on them an added value beyond their official purpose; but their use may also entail an invasion of privacy, and the making of a historical record of something never intended for such. These ethical and philosophical issues cannot be suborned in the prevalent concern for the information technology and the preservation of all information. The technical and economic ability to save everything may be ours sooner than anyone thought, but that still begs the question that not every item of information was meant to survive, become a record, or be noteworthy in any way as history.

Despite the issue possibility of saving everything for historical study, this is unlikely. It seems more probable that accidental preservation will remain a chief characteristic of History's resources. However, the historical record may be consciously created by those to be studied, to impact History purposefully, as never before, by saving and possibly altering records, or deleting them; and saving them in encrypted files, in formats, or on media which guarantees that they cannot be read now or over time. Nixon in post-Watergate interviews admitted that he would not have saved White House tapes had he thought anything in them would point to illegal activity—so much for the reliability of archival record keeping by records creators themselves. Yet, in most cases, dependency of the historical record on the creator is a given. This contradicts a basic tenet of objectivity, namely reliance on a physical manifestation other than one's own intelligence and on someone not party to the case. This third-party issue always connotes the thought of a watchful "big-brother" problem in data collection and the mastering of evidence. Historians want to be able to examine the communications of others more than they generally would want to be examined themselves. While scholars revel in the possibilities of new techniques for computer-assisted analyses of text as discourse, the idea of self-study with the same proficiency seems abhorrent. The same is likely for all disciplines. Such is human nature. Thus the fields of information policy and law are bound to grow, and security and access will remain dialectically opposed to each other. It is one thing for material placed into the public domain to be digitized and converted to searchable text, but another in the case of personal papers, records, and electronic communications not meant for public consumption, or business and administrative files that are not public records in the first place. Because of the emphasis on digitization for access, electronic conversion often entails a conversion in the status of records, from private to public, and in their decontextualization with indiscriminate use, a reduction of their stature from evidence to mere information.

Such trends in historical and applied linguistic studies have tremendous import for archives, including data archives. Electronic archivists and historians who use modern documentation must reconsider their previous concentration on numerical data sets in support of Social Science research. Only two decades ago one could hardly envision how text processing, electronic publishing, and e-mail would automatically produce a machine-readable text archives for contemporary studies, or how Social Science History would engage the retrospective conversion of printed material to electronic sources for such linguistic computing applications as employed in Discourse Analysis. Such developments were anticipated in the establishment of text archives at Oxford (BURNARD, 1988) and Rutgers Universities, and later at the University of Virginia. They have now attracted the interest of the Research Libraries Group. With the advances in the past decade of voice recognition technology beyond *SOUNDEX*, documents, oral history, radio and television news, etc. are increasingly transferable sources because the media are interchangeable, or as multimedia they can be used together. Thus converging technologies are merging organizations dedicated to specific kinds of media, such as sound, visual, text and data archives, as much as they are fostering an ever more thorough mix of the disciplines.

Many projects can be cited to illustrate the trend to convert traditional sources into digital formats and others for coding and conversion into changeable text. Digital libraries (information in the public domain) are the easiest in terms of the provision of access because the issues are largely technical and economic; digital archives will remain more complicated because of the public versus private issue, and because their limited potential use will not as easily justify the investment. The Computerized Information Retrieval System was illustrative of specialized projects that artificially create an electronic corpus around specific themes. TIRADO assembled sources on Columbus and the Age of Discovery, which combined enumerative bibliography with textbases of reviews, editions of literary and documentary texts to provide a lasting scholar's resource from the Quincentenary activities of 1992. Other projects are more organic, in that they convert collections already assembled physically, as in library Special Collections. An example is Sheffield University's Hartlib Papers project in conjunction with the British Library's multimedia initiatives, whereby 25,000 manuscript sheets are translated and text processed into optical disc storage for free-text and thesaurus controlled searching (PATERSON). It includes subsidiary projects in multimedia presentations. At the other end of the scale are comprehensive endeavors at integration and access. The H-Net project aims at both creating source banks and WWW linkage to those held elsewhere. One of the largest and most ambitious multibase programs is T. HART's *Project Gutenberg* which aims to provide the seemingly fantastic objective of *one trillion* texts, including a million books identified as "classic," freely distributed as the next century's "Every Man's Library" accessible from every home (now via the University of Minnesota Gopher/Libraries/Electronic Books/[title]/ Historical Documents; cf., HART, 1990; HAMILTON, 1997).

The feasibility of conversion of literary corpora to ever larger textbases has been demonstrated by numerous projects (e.g., DRABENSTOTT's review of twenty-six such digital projects in libraries), from special corpora to grander schemes (see CUADRA's *Directory*, especially for what MARTYN identifies as "source databases"). KIBIRGE most recently places the phenomenal conversion to full-text electronic access to massive source material into the context of national public policy, networking, and problems in the information and telecommunications industry. The Council on Library Resources (CLR) and ACCIS tracked smaller digital library projects and resulting collections through a major inventory project. Not only are there numerous commercially available projects such as *The Library of the Future Series* with 950 unabridged works, including literary and religious classics, but also works by famous historians (KOLTAY). Quanta Press has produced CD-ROM series on the *United States War* (1990-1991) and *European Monarchs* (1992). Full-text journals (e.g., Information Access Company's *ASAP*, Wilson's indexes and full-text service, UMI's or EBSCO's services, etc.) and newspapers (including America Online) are readily available.

The massive conversion undertaken as combined access and conservation project by scanning brittle books in major research libraries (KENNY & PERSONIUS) is making an electronic corpus available for "just-in-time" reprint publishing by Xerox Corporation and as test bases for computerized content and form content analyses. XEROX has developed a new digital scanner for books that can hold them semi-opened in a cradle and insert a photo-wedge with its own light source into a textblock without damaging bindings. Such combinations of conservation design, applications, mass duplication, and dissemination make digital technology increasingly feasible for historical collections. Thus, the Yale University project directed by Don Waters has already digitized 4,500 or the 10,000 titles it plans to make available electronically. Cornell University is doing the same. Case Western, Harvard, Stanford Universities, and the University of California at Davis are already scanning 20,000 pages of publications into document servers hosted on networked PCs that make their libraries "reserve" materials available across campuses, into dormitories (via a WEB server at IUPUI, for example) and to homes as well.

A partnership between the Library of Congress and Ameritech Corporation has resulted in ten awards in 1996-1997 of up to $600,000 each to convert major holdings in African American sheet music (1,500 images, 1870-1920 at Brown University and other nineteenth-century sheet music from Duke (3,000 images) into digital collections. Other conversions are: the addition of 7,500 images to the 48,000 previously digitized photographs from the Denver Public Library featuring the history of mining and Rocky Mountain and Plains Indians; the Robert Runyon photographic collection from the University of Texas documenting the Rio Grande Texan-Mexican borderland, 1900-1920; 900 records from North Dakota State University documenting the settlement of the Great Plains; 100 first-person narratives from the South during the 1800s at the University of North Carolina; stereoscopic views of small-town America (1850-1910) from the New York Public Library's Dennis Collection (11,552 images), coupled with materials from the LC *American Memory* project; Ohio Historical Society's 22,000 pages of text and images of African American experience in that state; Harvard University's collections on American Landscape and Architectural Design (2,500 images, 1850-1920); and 5,800 environmental photographs (1897-1931) from the University of Chicago. These visual libraries of 112,000 images documenting late nineteenth and early twentieth-century American history are open, thereby, 24 hours every day. If such digitized texts were searchable internally, as when converted to characters or by image indexes to sectors and objects, one might expect that word and object by automated collation would become as common as spell-checking today. That day will come.

Read-write jukeboxes with expandable storage, which handle CD-ROM and optical disks to mix media seem to have unlimited potential even though some predicted that compact discs would be a transitory technology. In effect, CD-ROM backup on personal computers creates personal archives possibilities that beckon exploration of archival sound software design for a new generation of users. One practice already tried and tested is that of compiling correspondence archives which could be subjected to word study and discourse analysis to observe linguistic phenomena such as expressions of loyalty, emulation, motivation, and descriptors revealing mood, or tendencies in negotiation which like nervous quirks in a poker game disclose one's hand, etc., for use in gaining the upper hand in business deals, rehearsing witnesses for testifying, dealing with the news media, and in diplomatic negotiations. Even transcribed telephone conversations are studied to observe tendencies toward entrenchment, flexibility, empathy and resentment to calculate the continuing discourse. Psychologists can and do analyze taped sessions in this way. One could, for example, analyze one's own discourse as a form of self-study and increased awareness, not only for improved recall but self-improvement in ways not contemplated by information scientists, e.g., forms of introspection associated with self-meditation, since one could talk with oneself, so to speak, over time. The result is an interactive psycho-history and biographic therapy, following Greek notions of self-healing. The flexibility in record keeping with personal text archives is far greater than simple old-fashioned diary writing. Self-actualization through every one being his or her own electronic archivist in turn has implications for electronic archivists at large and for future historians studying turn-of-the-millennium history when everyone could be his or own historian, auto[matic]biographer, and self-analyst. Psycho-historians could have a field day with such sources! One can only guess where these developments could lead us.

Current enthusiasm for digital libraries and personal electronic archives reminds one of the early work of FID pioneers Robert Goldschmidt and Paul Otlet who, having first proposed standards for microfiche in 1905, in 1925 advocated the first use of portable libraries in micro-formats equal to 468 meters of conventionally shelved books. OTLET in his 1934 principal work *Traité de Documentation* anticipated hypertext linkage in his "vision of Xanadu" as RAYWARD (1994) calls his futuristic speculation about bibliographic possibilities, but Otlet could not foretell how miniaturization in microfiche could be seen as an antecedent to electronic libraries and archives (Otlet's pioneering work, brought to light mainly by RAYWARD's translation of his works [1990] and subsequent series of studies [1994, 1997]; cf., RIEUSSET-LEMARIE; R. DAY). He did, however, understand the complex social origins of the book, multimedia variations on the basic conceptual design of the codex, and the consequences of reading different ways and in different environments ("social spaces" as R. DAY argues).

Then, as now, there were problems to work out more than for the technology itself, but in the intellectual operations accompanying source conversion. The processes of standardization, authentification, and verification seem as messy now as before, and without having benefitted from the study of the history of information science and technology, contemporary digital enthusiasts seem unaware of the parallels and of history repeating itself. (T. D. WALKER illustrates the essential continuity by tracing some of this development in information storage technology leading to the American Library Association's *Journal of Documentary Reproduction*, 1938-1942, the forerunner of *American Documentation*, 1950-1969, and *JASIS*, 1969-). His data about the occupations of *JDR* contributors (WALKER, p. 365) reminds us of the once close collaboration between librarians, museum curators, archivists, and historians in early documentation studies; archivists and historians (including art historians and historical society personnel) combined constituted the second largest occupation group contributing (second only to academic librarians, at 30 percent of all contributions) who were responsible for nearly 21 percent of the journal's content. This jumps to 30 percent if one were to add the contributing administrators, librarians, and editors trained as historians. JDR's editor, Vernon D. Tate, for example, had his Ph.D. in History. Today's unawareness of this close association, made more tragic by the connection between awareness as the initial step in learning, is why it seems sad that History and Information Science do not inform each other better than they have over the past two decades or do now.

While digital technology is being used to make such exemplary sources, its application in mass retro-conversion of endangered and high-use documentation as both a means of preservation and mass dissemination will most dramatically alter the future of historical research. Such integrated technologies applied to historical materials are featured in aforementioned retrospective full-text conversion of brittle books in major American libraries, as well as the publishing of archives and backfiles such as in University Microfilm International (UMI) Digital Library Project or Chadwyck-Healey's source-conversion projects. The latter has recently partnered with the University of Virginia to disseminated 560 digital works from UVA's special collections as the *Electronic Archives of Early American Fiction*. Other collaborative electronic publishing ventures coupling electronic publishers and library special collections include Primary Source Media (PSM) and Cornell University who have produced the *Witchcraft in Europe and America* collection as first in a series of Rare Books Online series. The greatest activity, however, is in access to electronic journals. The Institute of Scientific Information (ISI) recently announced development by IBM at its Almaden Research Center in San Jose of an electronic client/server full-image service for 1,350 journals in ISI's Life

Sciences program. As libraries become more accustomed to serving digital resources and in converting their own holdings into digital media, they may also be in a position to create research archives from ongoing projects. They can earn royalties up to 20 percent for sales of their collections in electronic form. Moreover, conversion project costs are coming down as more projects are undertaken. Research project directors have less and less excuse not to create data archives on CD-ROMs, since the disk-mastering technology costs have come down to around $3,000 and more and more research libraries have access to such conversion technology. Libraries and archives, however, tend to think in terms of what they have, in retrospective conversion of their holdings, or in acquisitions from other sources, rather than creating collections anew directly from ongoing research on their own campuses and in their communities. Moreover, funding often most be justified by the importance of what already exists, rather than the potential of what might be. Finally, digital access is a preliminary step only; digitization does not mean that the electronic data, images, and texts can be manipulated for analysis. This requires character recognition and translation, coding, and cleaning, after retro-conversion.

Currently the main thrust in the United States is the Digital Library Initiative (DLI) funded at a million dollars per year (NSF IR194-11330 cooperative agreement), originally for six projects of seventy-three proposed, through cooperation of the National Science Foundation (NSF), Advanced Research Projects Agency (ARPA), and National Aeronautics and Space Administration (NASA), and six university sites: Carnegie Mellon University, University of California at Berkeley and at Santa Barbara, University of Illinois at Champagne-Urbana, University of Michigan, and Stanford University (SCHATZ & CHEN). The idea, articulated by a NSF "white paper" by William Wulf on national collaboratories, i.e., university testbeds, IT companies, publishers, and user groups are to cooperate in forming the next millennium's "knowledge repositories" (W. ARMS reporting through the electronic *Digital Library Magazine* at http:www.dlib.org). These digital libraries are not service organizations, but are massive text and image bases used for experimentation and research. A research agenda was formed in May 1995 by the INFORMATION INFRASTRUCTURE TECHNOLOGY AND APPLICATIONS (IITA) work group, NII's highest technical committee (reported through http:/www-giglib.stanford.edu/diglib/pub/reports/iita-dlw/main.html). The goal was to form a network of distributed repositories where objects of any type could be searched within and across indexed collections, achieving "deep semantic interoperability" requiring breakthroughs in descriptive techniques, retrieval operations, object interchange and retrieval protocols, uniform metadata, and federation of heterogeneous repositories (e.g., SHETH & LARSON). Funded research tends to meet the so-called DARPA test, i.e., what would the industry do? If it would happen anyhow, driven by trends in the industry, it does not need funding. But if funding is needed to spur a catalyst for change that might not otherwise happen, then a project is a primary candidate for the Digital Library's initiative support. Project details are available through the DLI National Synchronization Effort homepage (http://www.grainer.uiuc.edu/dli/national.htm).

The ultimate goal is to create national, international, and global collaboration, and to consider the Internet and World Wide Web both as a vehicle and a vast yet single virtual collection. Different sites are approaching the project in complementary fashion: for example, the Berkeley team is focusing on information retrieval from automatically recognized image documents, including photographs (R. WILENSKY), while at Illinois the focus is on manually structured text documents for scientific literature (SCHATZ & CHEN). Carnegie-Mellon's team is investigating the digital integration of video, audio, and text resources (WACTLAR *ET AL.*), including formal testing of visual retrieval demonstrated in CHEN's *Emperor I* project a decade ago, like face detection in rapid image displays, text skimming as a form of information retrieval, image registration, code applications, and speech recognition. The Santa Barbara team's Alexandria Digital Library Project concentrates on retrieval of geographic information by terms using USMARC and FGDC standards for library retrieval and geospatial metadata respectively, with effective graphic display (T. SMITH; C. FISCHER). Stanford University's group is exploring object technology and software (e.g., JAVA) for an interoperable digital library using Object Management Group's CORBA™ to provide interface uniformity while giving implementers a wide latitude in performance and service profiles. Additionally the Stanford project has prototyped Glossary of Servers Server (GLOSS) to assist in identifying appropriate library sites, and SCAM (Copy Detection by digital overlays to compare documents and determine unfair use and plagiarism) and Copyright Protection System (COPS) to support evolving economic schemes which would support digital libraries and make it viable for producers to share sources across the network. These protection programs are linked to online payment and other transaction schemes. The University of Michigan focuses on library services through interactive software agents (interfaces for users, mediators and facilitators, and collections, e.g., WIERERHOLD), focusing initially on secondary school science curricula, space-science laboratories, and user services in the University of Michigan libraries (ATKINS *ET AL.*). Other projects in the United States more specifically address historical books and manuscripts, tying access to preservation, such as the *Digital Scriptorium* project, a collaboration between Consuelo Dutschke and Charles Faulhaber respectively from Columbia University and the University of California's Bancroft Library funded by the Mellon Foundation to digitize 10,000 images from 700 codices and 2,000 documents stretching back seven centuries. A second grant to the Hill Monastic Manuscript Library at St. John's University will allow its *Electronic Access to Medieval Manuscripts* project directed by Hope Mayo to join with the Vatican Film Library at St. Louis University and the Columbia-Berkeley collaboration. Funds from the Mellon Foundation are also driving the *Making of America Project* (*MOA*) between the University of Michigan and Cornell University. This has already made 5,000 volumes published in the United States between 1850 and 1877 available on the Web and major serials from the same period (cf., http://www.umdl.umich.edu/moa/and http://www.moa.cit.cornell.edu). Cross-collection searching became available in late 1997 when the page count of this digital project is expected to crest 650,000.

Whereas initially the digital library and text archives were largely concerned with the literary canon, just as galleries would select choice art and image bases that have been predominantly built to access unique and exemplary artworks (W. VAUGHAN, 1987). Digital texts can be supplemented with digital images increasingly made available by such digital "image library" projects as the Art Museum Image Consortium (AMICO) which has a testbed of 20,000 high-resolution images to go online in 1999-2000. Founded by the Association of Art Museum Directors Educational Foundation, Inc., AMICO's founding members are the Art Institute of Chicago, the Center for Creative Photography in Tucson; the George Eastman House in Rochester; the J. Paul Getty Museum; the Metropolitan Museum of Art in New York; Montreal's Museum of Fine Arts; and Canada's National Gallery of Art. AMICO will license Web access to institutions for $2,500-5,000 based on size of potential user population. The digital library initiatives in the United States are now becoming more archival in content, with their conversion of maps, aerial photographs, reports, and documents into electronic form (the main access to which is still the OCLC *Maps* format, 1980-). Moreover, because the retro-conversion is also a conservation as much as an access initiative, and so much of nineteenth-century material is at risk from embrittlement and acidic deterioration, the bulk of the digital library in the United States has become historical in nature. The issues related to documentary art and a wider sample of voice records, images, and everyday texts are decidedly different from retrospective conversion of a literary canon or electronic portfolio of choice artworks.

If MICHELSON & ROTHENBERG's advice about local documentation strategies to accommodate trends in socioeconomic history for national, regional, and local studies is extended to family history, biography, and micro-levels for organizational culture studies or even to the individual subconscious for psycho-history, then textual archives must be assembled and made accessible at the ultimate micro-levels as well. Paper archives cannot go to such levels; electronic archives can. Such capability is not only a matter of data compression and storage capacity, but automatic means of data collection such as the video surveillance of business meetings, conferences, or any meeting, or more specific operations such as surgery or court room transactions instead of mere transcriptions, and for security and enforcement. Remote Video Inspection (RVI) systems are already in widespread use in the technical service industry, and such packages as Videoimagescope™ systems are sure to find their way into historical sites work, conservation, and archeology. The hardware is very portable, cameras are worn just like viziers on construction caps; they access ports as small as .236 inches and inspect as deep as 52 feet. They relay to home base in real time, and a variety of image management software is available. The issue accompanying this versatility and ease in video-recording for data acquisition is the same as in surveillance, namely the balance between individual privacy and public information, whether contemporary or historical.

In most archives, with closure only to protect the rights of the current generation, privacy for the dead is not a concern of the living. If it were, History would be a different matter altogether. Historians in the past relied on records surviving as much by chance as by intention, often almost as random sampling, but with the archivist moving into records creation for retention, armed with new technologies, documentation strategies today take on the aura of predetermining History. Archival appraisal leading to disposal rather than retention decisions and societal lobotomies are not exclusive concepts. Nor is archival appraisal leading to the retention of everything unrelated to societal forgetfulness because of overload and the richness syndrome. Before, technological limits on information transfer, storage, and retrieval produced a natural economy of historical information. Now, without such an economy of means, the quandary facing the future of History is as much an intellectual task of policy-making and control to produce an artificially contrived economy and efficiency, which means striking some compromise that will automatically limit the level to which micro-history can descend and the scope it can embrace. If accessioning and storage are not the limitations, then the dependency of future access on the maintenance of information retrieval systems will be the great economizer. Saving more in a greater number of transferable formats means that more historical data may become even more hidden like the proverbial needle in the haystack to an extent in electronic cyberspace unbelievable in paper archives. Such probing thought certainly poses significant research problems blending Archival and Historical Information Science.

Such trends have also meant that the preoccupation of quantitative historians with coding data for computer manipulation has likewise become the concern called "mark-up" by linguists, literary scholars, and text-oriented historians. In both cases the issue is about metadata. Tagging was the dominant technique developed during the 1960s, but text coding has been used as an indexing device since the 1970s (FOSSIER & ZARRI) to retrieve information from historical documents. Techniques have become more varied and sophisticated in recent years (R. JENSEN, 1990), but no less cumbersome and tedious in the preparation phase.

The most significant development in this area is the international Text Encoding Initiative (TEI, 1987-) of the Association for Computing in the Humanities (ACH), the Association of Computational Linguistics (ACL), and Association of Literary and Linguistic Computing, which the Association of History and Computing (AHC) has also supported. This initiative has been funded by both the European Community, the United States National Endowment for the Humanities, the Canadian Social Sciences and Humanities Research Council, and private contributors such as the Mellon Foundation (IDE & SPERBERG-MCQUEEN; cf., GOLDFARB). Coordinated by C. M. SPERBERG-MCQUEEN and L. BURNARD, the TEI working groups in which historians are active, adopted the Standard Generalized Markup Language (SGML = ISO 8879; cf., *The SGML Primer* at http://www.sq.com/sgmlinfo/ primbody.html)) as the syntax platform underlying textbase editing and means to the higher ends, namely questions of "*what* should be encoded in an electronic text, and *how* that encoding should be represented for interchange" (BURNARD, p. 106). TEI's 1990 draft *Guidelines for Text Encoding for*

Interchange has been circulated widely, discussed in countless conferences, and is finally ready as a basic reference manual available by anonymous File Transfer Protocol (FTP) (cf.., BARNARD & IDE; IDE & SPERBERG-MCQUEEN; IDE & VERONIS, etc., for the background of TEI). The TEI guidelines, first envisioned in 1987, are now influencing work in modeling historical data (BEARMAN, 1990; GREENSTEIN, 1991) and descriptive standards for the exchange of historical data sets (MARKER; VAN HALL), as well as the whole arena of editing and publishing where full-text search capabilities is the objective (MARIN-NAVARRO & ALEVANTIS). Such coding, hypertext linkage, front-end search engines, and expert systems will enhance full-text information retrieval (DETEMPLE). Historical textbases must take advantage of such advances. KIMBER & WOODS, in arguing for the adoption of *HyTime* for the source representation of hyperdocuments, address History specifically to show how hypertext can link text and context, historical narration with historical analysis, and current historical literature with its historiograhic underpinning. For them "Historical writing and analysis is problematic hypertext" (p. 604):

> The study of history is, ultimately, the study of relationships. Why things happened the way they did, why people behaved the way they did, and what forces combined to influence events in a particular way. Any work of historical analysis is an application of historians' world view and the web of relationships that they think are important, interesting, and relevant, to the objects they think apply to a particular relationship.

> Historical analysis is, thus, a natural candidate for expression as hypertext. Historical analysis also has the property that, in general, the analysis is as important as the primary sources to which it refers, meaning that the focus of a person studying history is not only on the historical objects, but also on what other historians have thought about them. This means that the study of history is also the study of the thought of historians. One of the difficulties in this study is that the relationships, the web of hyperlinks, that represent a given historian's thought on a particular topic are often obscured by the form of the presentation, namely the printed prose. Compounding this problem is the difficulty of comparing one historian's web to another's.

> ...history is inherently time-based, which leads to some simple but effective practical applications of HyTime's time-based functionality.

Before an American audience, M. THALLER (1988) astutely raised the issue for scholars everywhere working with texts, historical or literary of whether they should be producing critical paper editions with the text-processed version inaccessible or only through an electronic archives in a form that still required conversion for use elsewhere, or databases in which case a published book is the byproduct rather than the chief or sole objective of the textual work. This issue is especially important for documentary editors working with history sources, and agencies like NARA's National Historical Publications and Records Commission (NHPRC), since the co-production of books and textbases can save costly retrospective conversion and assist immediately the kind of research illustrated by recent trends in Discourse Analysis. It also impacts future bibliographic scholarship in which electronic versions like manuscript drafts must be considered in critical edition work.

Libraries are beginning to understand the potential affects of such changes because it affects their collection development and future mission. Librarians as consumers, however, have not been effective in influencing product design any more than archivists have influenced records creation. Libraries, as service organizations, are conservative and rather than take a risk or be leaders in technology transformation, they often follow and wait for demand to come from their customer base. Indeed, a 1996 survey funded by the Kellogg Foundation indicated that Americans did not expect their public libraries to test new technology or want them to (BENTON FOUNDATION). Nevertheless, libraries are taking a lead in digitizing collections and providing electronic access. Special libraries, which also moved faster into online services than other libraries, are responding to more coherent professional constituencies which seem to adapt to technological innovation faster than the general public or even universities as whole entities. Not all problems presented by digital alternatives are solved for user services, collection management, or preservation. The digital library project's importance to archives is yet to become clear, although large-scale digital conversion of records such as at the Archivo de las Indias in Sevilla point the way. GILLILAND-SWETLAND (1995, p. 43) notes that while this technology is being adopted to such large projects, under premises that are questionable: she understands that while perceptions are frequently cited, we still actually know quite little about electronic communities, the contemporary impact of networks on ongoing activities like scholarly research, or future preservation and care for the "recordedness" of digital sources. The basis on which future History must depend is being transformed today, without much input from this community except perhaps with assistance in content selection for such projects.

The difference today from when information technology was developed mainly as an academic enterprise may lie outside academe altogether in the mass market and popular consumption, as reflected in the entertainment industry, especially music and video as KINNEY noted. This necessarily means that for historians to get involved in the larger societal, technical, and industrial issues affecting the future of their discipline, they must get out of academe more and more and not regard such activity as an "alternative" career. Such outreach and purposeful interjection of the historian's concerns into industry and the marketplace might well be considered the career of choice rather than applying History only by teaching. Such provocative revisionism challenges the academic culture that pervades History, and required rethinking and redirecting of young historians much like a church turns much of its young talent to the mission field rather than returning all to the seminary. Likewise, a more expansive view of the field's research possibilities beckons new studies that are not entirely placed in the past. Political, economic, market, and professional problems abound in this area of electronic publishing in the academic enterprise, teaching with technologies accepted in the home before the classroom, and the accommodation of individual preference and consumption. Information policy issues loom larger than ever. A component of Historical Information Science may well be the politics of historical information dissemination, policy issues protecting sources and enabling the future of historical scholarship, and the interplay between academic and public history. These are, however, among the weakest venues of the historical profession's performance today.

Finally, the sheer mass of available resources, the variety of media in which they are stored, and the choices of access are mind-boggling. The possibilities far exceed the individual's capacity to explore all that pertains to large-framed topics, so that practical management considerations and the desire to complete a project contribute to the increasingly common microview in History. A reversal of this trend in view of the expanding universe of knowledge to be explored will depend on collaboration, groupware, and assistance from Artificial Intelligence research in creating intelligent agents for distributed information systems (GAUCH; HAVERKAMP & GAUCH; O'HARE & JENNINGS); this is nothing short of reengineering History. Yet, fields within historical studies such as text-based research, which has focused on the narrative both the historical and the contemporary [hi]story telling—show little movement toward technically based innovation. They are, in fact, more introspective and individually based than ever. The problem historical scholarship faces is no longer one of technical feasibility; it is conceptual. How within a discipline prone to award individual creativity associated with the Humanities with an award system that supports such independence and even eccentricity are such habits changed? In a field that looks backward for its subject matter, how can one encourage forward thinking to assist the next generation of historians who must confront issues of intellectual access and multimedia in their research on a scale far greater and with complexity unknown by the current generation of teaching historians?

The complication of online retrieval in a standardless but rapidly expanding universe of data, text, and images bases, is sometimes described as the "richness syndrome." TOYNBEE (pp. 103-135) grappled with the same "problem of quantity in the study of human affairs" as early as the 1930s. In typical historian fashion and as a classicist, he invoked the lament of Hippocrates about the inadequacy of the human mind to comprehend the totality of human experience (p. 103) despite archives and information technologies: "The quantity of the phenomena is out of all proportion to the capacity of any single mind to deal with them in a single working lifetime. *Ars longs, vita brevis*."

How frustrating!...and sad. This is precisely why the next generation of historians must employ information technology in the service of History better than their teachers. They could be assisted in this endeavor if a coherent Historical Information Science were informed by History and Information Science. Some of the greatest potential for this lies in the current surge of creativity in textual or narrative History influenced by Anthropology, if it were to move beyond its literary phase and focus on texts to absorb from New Literary Criticism and Discourse Analysis some of the more empirical means at its disposal and to exploit more technical linguistic modes of analyses and computer applications in natural language processing, information retrieval, and textbase design.

Images, Artifacts, and Art Information

Multimedia developments have been influencing education generally because of visualization's reinforcement of literacy and text-based learning, but it has also profoundly influenced the arts, arts organizations, and public consumption of visuals (BEARMAN, ed., 1995). As expected, it is having an impact on History as well. The most viable link between multimedia and History, outside of teaching in formal education, is undoubtedly through Public History and museums. But today media also affect research relying on new techniques of visualization and forms of visual modeling, i.e., knowledge representation, as well as the presentation of that research or electronic publishing. Although this connection between History and media is not well made, the history of multimedia over the past 30 years is recounted by HARTIGAN (1993b). REISMAN brings this overview up to date and projects developments into the twenty-first century. Inspiration may harken back to H. G. Wells, but concrete developments are linked more with names like Ted Nelson.

All of this imaging technology has been brought into the practical realm of educational applications by the process of windowing which began in the 1970s, at least the rough idea stage, at Xerox's Palo Alto Research Center (PARC) with Alan Kays work on man-machine interfaces, Douglas Engelbart's use of a "mouse" rather than keyboard, and Rand Corporation's use of graphic tablets. Steven Jobs put such disparate technology together into one package called Apple Computers. Computer graphics have since then changed the playing field for the arts, Art History, History generally, and New History particularly, but academicians by and large have joined the game very late. As in the case of early computing, when they did not have easy access to computers until after the PC outbreak, one decade later historians find themselves without access to multimedia computers and adequate software libraries, and their entry into visualization technology is again lagging behind the more affluent and technologically adroit Sciences. If one harkens back to speculations made by Engelbart, whose contributions over this half-century were recently recognized by a special ASIS award, all of this started more than a generation ago.

The lag time has been almost a decade after some of these initial developments made their way from information technology into applications in fields like the Arts and Humanities. Even five years would have been far-out thinking, given this enormous lag time in contrast to the expanding vision for "augmentation" technology that is now finally affecting the arts (e.g., at the Human Augmentation Institute: ENGELBART & ENGLISH, 1988; 1994). As N. Hays has commented, art and science are converging in modern information technology. Thus EMMER pulls together artists and mathematicians to discuss "the visual mind" and its production from drawings to computer graphics. Finally, computer vision, neuroscience, and cognitive psychology have all jumped into debates about imagery, namely the relation between mental imagery and visual perception in how the human brain interprets the world (e.g., A. WATSON relating human vision to digital image compression; cf., the essays in M. BRADY and the standard textbook by BRUCE, GREEN & GEORGESON). Progress in computer visualization is largely responsible for this debate. It pertains as well to historian's discussions about memory and commemoration, teachers' questions about illustration and demonstration, museum concerns about visual learning from exhibits, and the artist's interests in rendering and depiction which are flipsides to the computer graphic designer's concern for representation.

Historians of art and artifacts of all kinds have not made adequate use of Computer Assisted Drafting/Design (CAD) and early drafting technologies, despite major advances in standard software packages like *AutoCAD* in moving from two- to three-dimensional drawing ("stereo computer vision," according to O. FAUGERAS), and the wider availability of software once thought of as rather exotic and too expensive for the arts and humanities. Basic CAD training, stripped of special applications like drafting standards, can be accomplished in a matter of weeks, and it does not take much nowadays to have a CAD workstation in place and plotters for drawings, and systems for placement of renderings into context as architects do while still in the design phase. Earlier application of CAD would have prepared historians in general, as it did for some historians of art and architecture, to advance more easily into modern visualization technologies. Historians who have remained text bound are further behind. What they have missed is the exploration of "visual thinking with computers" in the words of Richard Mark Friedhoff (FRIEDHOFF & BENZON, p. 12).

What is the art of illusion in computer graphics and modern visualization is also a powerful learning tool (GOMBRICH), requiring less "make-believe" than was once necessary, and instead of substitution for imagination (i.e., imag[en]gin[er]ation, hence "imagineering"), modern tools are releasing creativity never before utilized. This is a proverbial problem and blessing at the same time for historians. Control mechanisms for the formation of world views, already dismantled by television and modern communications, are degenerating, including reliance on the traditional classroom, lecture, textbook, and library-based search exercise. Rampant individualism brings with it accelerated relativism, which furthers the dissolution of history down to the microlevel and condenses long range sensibilities to immediacy and brief experiences. Specificity without simultaneous generality is trivialization; the general without the concrete is equally meaningless. We have always found it difficult to have both at the same time; we usually toggle between the two. People need assistance with this intellectual feat, and multimedia technology is evolving to meet this test.

Computer graphics offer education a new visual vocabulary that challenges the primacy of text in every field. Among the many offerings are run-length encoding for recurring values, Lempel-Ziv-Welch compression for Tagged Image File Format (TIFF) and Graphics Interchange Format (GIF) image files, CCITT Group 4 compression, Joint Bi-tonal Image Group (JBIG), Joint Photographic Experts Group (JPEG), Motion Picture Experts Group (MPEG), TIFF, and GIF. The challenge to primary text is true for images, sound, and video-on-demand and construction of large digital imagebases (KHOSHAFIAN & BAKER). In the Internet world, this can be seen in the transition to a "post-HTML environment," still dominated by pages of information, to something more three-dimensional, interactive, and continuous than we even have the words to describe properly.

KELLY & WOLF inform us about the impact of greater communication capabilities that will make media displays larger and more dynamic; expanding networks that will form a new information ecology; and that will allow convenience and reliability on ready-made sources rather than do-it-yourself technology. They contrast "pull media (the current Web, and all sorts of information retrieval) to "push media" (TV, radio, movies, and especially video) as the promise of the future already indicated in *BackWeb* and *Pointcast*, and in 1996 by Netscape's *Constellation* interface for desktop computers, which does not need to launch a browser, and Microsoft's *Active Desktop* scheduled for late 1997. The latter does not frame a static page in a window but captures ongoing streams in 3-D space. Around the corner in the next millennium, visionaries see a media-scape of push-pull, active objects, virtual space, and ambient broadcasting where one can be active and retrieve information in all forms, or more passively have information (i.e., "move from invoked to evoked content" [KELLY & WOLF, p.15]) flow from previous encounter, having been guided by intelligent agents, through interfaces which "'play' human attention" (cf., ETZIONI & WELD's predictions; HAVERKAMP & GAUCH review the development of information agents). Stories (no interaction) or interaction (no stories) is not a polarization that must be so in the new media world being created. New technologies allow for interactive, growing narrative much like mythmaking in Native American oral tradition, with the addition of an electronic archives to backup faulty human memory and correct contamination through new means of historical research.

Multimedia enrich interpretation and complicate it at the same time, when impression is so immediate and impacting in a matter of seconds, while analysis and reflection are so time consuming. Media technologists like instant impact, impression, stimulation, and assume that seeing is believing, while anyone using digitized images for research must be more wary. Image bases require the same kind of archival integrity that is more commonly associated with textual records, and a new skill of visual literacy, more expansive that previously conceived graphic literacy, must be added to the repertoire required of modern researchers. Seeing in virtual environments should not be misconstrued with believing as a matter of course (or fact). Such notions contain the same problems inherent in the use (or abuse?) of natural language by the computer community when employing print metaphors for new technologies. When thinking about image bases and object-oriented modeling and analysis, remember the earlier connection made between data representation and envisioning surrogates (KHOSHAFIAN; KHOSHAFIAN & ABNOUS). The same caveats may be extended to the use of imagery in belief systems. Virtual representations may be included in this discussion of art and artifacts, because they are the artifacts of the computer age and the artistic products of new technology, but the discussion needs to go beyond merely issues of electronic reproduction of images just as the implications of digital text raise serious issues of authenticity, actuality, integrity, and evidence.

The visual arts have been impacted considerably, from simpler paint systems (pixel-based graphics) and "cut and paste" procedures which are photocopy-based approaches to object-based systems which rely on computer storage of the geometry of objects (that is, the computer stores measurements, not images) to recreate images on command. Object-based geometry is three dimensional; a z-axis is added to x and y axes, and all geometric forms are stored by formula and take on specific dimensions (see BOWYER & AHUJA for the latest advances in imaging technology and the need to develop a new "image understanding" in human-machine intelligence for image segmentation and feature extraction, conversion from two- to three-dimensional images and object recognition). *PhotoModeler* 2.1 by Eos Systems, for example, is a three-dimensional modeling software that can create realistic virtual models by applying textures from actual photos of objects. In one demonstration of this software six shots of a house, from different angles or overlapping views, were used to create a VRML model which can be depicted either as a three-dimensional image or as a architectural frame house if one exported the model (.DXF file) to a CAD or a rendering program. Standard 33mm photos are scanned into digital form with something like a Kodak PhotoCD, a camera simulator that indicates where pictures were taken, and for which form and perspective data are calculated automatically. Once rendered into digital form, the image is pliable. Any historical structure or artifact (codices, for example) can be reproduced for detailed study in such ways, including changing the color spectra, trajectories, and intensities of light sources, and hence shading, to reflect indoor and outside environments, cloudy or sunny skies, time of day, and season.

Objects must be described in every detail precisely for computer visualization whereby a projection is calculated using old techniques developed since the Renaissance. The user specifies a point of view, and the computer calculates projectors passing through the image plane and thereby determines values for each pixel forming the resultant image. Cartesian coordinates allow renderings that are seemingly three-dimensional because pixel values are determined from the vantage point to create the illusion of distance and depth perception. This technology reproduced objects, shapes, and surreal images, which are then enhanced by another illusion that light is falling on the object's surface, i.e., shading techniques, like Lambert shading from Johann Heinrich Lambert's eighteenth-century optics principles, whereby surfaces are provided by interlocking polygons that are brightened or darkened according to their placement relating to the vector of illumination. Gouraud shading is more subtle by adjusting vortex instead of surface illumination. Highlighting is added by Phong shading which takes into account the source of illumination and the position of the observer. In addition to these techniques, texture mapping incorporates real world textures, grains, and patterns and computer geometric memory to "wrap" an object with whatever surface is required. Finally, reality is simulated further by ray-tracing, whereby the optical properties of different materials are figured into the equation for surface rendering which is computationally expensive since the computer must calculate all reflection and refraction of every combination of pixels. Imagine, if you will, fractal mountains recreated first as two-dimensional objects, transformed into three-dimensions by a randomly added inner form, then broken into geometric patterns to provide a skeletal structure on which a textured, shaded surface is added. Any historic place can be so recreated by such fractal techniques, and restored like new or properly aged. Indeed, a three-dimensional scene can be transformed from old to new as the viewer wants.

The next step is conversion to full simulation and animation by recalculating frames to supply altered views for "motion pictures." The fashion industry has now created libraries of different textiles flowing as when worn on a fashion show runway, so that virtual models can show off new fashions with full motion imitating the performance of a garment before it is ever actually made. Clouds have now been video-recorded, classified, and mixed virtually for speeded-up storms in movies and for TV weather programs. The critical test now, so it is thought among visual technologists, is to recreate smoke virtually wafting as it were, through a virtual breeze. This is more subtle than adding fire or explosions to a scene (e.g., from Artbeat's *ReelExplosions* or *Reelfire* CDs) in digital video. Each enhancement is a step beyond the previous technique. This gives new meaning to the historian's older notions, from only two decades ago, about "making history."

Whereas psychologists once treated this idea skeptically, they have passed through this hypercritical phase, and now it is widely recognized that mental imagery works in a variety of ways, differing from one individual to the other and that it is important in scientific speculation as well as artistic creativity. There seems to be an intimate relation between "object recognition" and perception of three-dimensionality and, although depth perception from flat surfaced images, as in making sense of a photograph from monocular cues (e.g., linear perspective, interposition of oculation, contrast and shadow hints, detail and aerial perspectives, etc.), is not well understood, it is an important gift for the artist and art historian alike. Students applying to technical schools offering CAD training are often given perception tests to see if they can think visually. The gist is to see an object and to be able to rotate it in the mind, to view it from all angles mentally, and then apply reasoning to the mental model so that basic questions can be asked: e.g., whether two objects pictured differently were in fact identical. The goal is to substitute perception and visual thinking for real world action, i.e., to use illusion theoretically and rationally to save labor and wasted effort. The thrust of most applications is futuristic, so it is commonly thought, except that sequential perceptions are always retrospective and are therefore historical.

Historians also require such capabilities, not only for their use of photographs and documentary art but also in aerial photography and interpretation of newer technical visual reproduction or recreations, as in Side-Imaging Radar (SIR) techniques for high resolution depth perception of terrains which cannot be seen from ground level, or digital reproduction and enhancements. Ensemble processing now enables the historical geographer to view terrain from great distances, and following techniques used in mechanical text collation for critical editing, computerized images made at different times can be superimposed for detailed comparison and isolation of states to determine the differences time can make. Multi-spectral scanning (superimposition of images recorded with different wave lengths) has created color maps that are truly amazing for their depiction of land formations and seas that, for example, enable historians of trade and commerce in ways unheard of only a decade ago, to interpret information about ports, harbors, travel routes, etc.—even those long buried under water. Now with satellite images of the earth the historian can arrange for synthetic flyovers that combine the latest in image processing and computer graphics.

Image processing today combines digitization, enhancement, restoration, and compression techniques (BLACKLEDGE; GOMEZ & VELHO; SONKA, HLAVAC & BOYLE; D. PEARSON). The SOCIETY OF PHOTO-OPTICAL INSTRUMENTATION ENGINEERS (SPIE) cover advances in image storage and retrieval. BOYLE & THOMAS provide a "first course" on computer vision (cf., M. BRADY). Basically, in digitization, reflected light from a controlled scanned area is recorded by a photodetector and the signal is digitized to eight bits, for example, for a possible 256 gray levels. The smaller the spot, the finer the scan. Numbers represent the brightness value for each spot (pixel); a typical digital image may have 512 x 512 or 250,000 pixels. Output is determined by point to point rendering, a cluster of pixels may be used to localize operations, or globally all pixels determine the output image. Other than making an image more visually appealing by eradicating "noise" by reconfiguring a set of pixel values to arrive at an artificial mean used in filtering rather than the actual recording, enhancement is making visual data more evident by contrast manipulation, adding color to black-and-white images, and assigning color to gray levels (as in thermography where hot spots by convention appear red and cold as blue). Restoration, as the term implies, uses information about an original image's creation and ideal or uncorrupted image by eradicating any imperfections that were part of the original manufacture. Point-spread functions can reduce blurring, or eradicate it through inverse filtering or selectively filtering specific types of noise (e.g., using Fourier transforms). Compression represents an image with fewer numbers and thereby minimizes degradation of the image's information. The number of bits per pixel is reduced, often with a result of one-fifth the total number. This can be done selectively, reducing noncontent areas around the wall or jacket of an image most, and leaving the face alone (resulting in a "broken image"). Compressed digital images that require less storage can be returned to original states for viewing by reverse processing.

Related digital technology like edge detection has become critical not only in the authentification of art works but also through pixel analysis the same approach has been applied to forgery in digital images. Fourier-domain operations treat each pixel in relation to patterns and whole images to determine electronic composition in visualizations. To allow flexible manipulation at the granular level for image enhancement, out-of-focus pictures can be sharpened by increasing high spatial frequencies, along edges, for example, and in deblurring or correcting blurs. Such techniques have been applied to stellar skyscapes, and conversely to reading illegible manuscripts and Dead Sea Scroll fragments. Computed tomography uses Fourier analysis in many fields for 3-D viewing, especially in medicine connected with X-ray; the same technology has also been applied to three-dimensional art objects to create 3-D renderings on screen which are like look-ing at hollow wire sculpture or tubes that resemble coils. In the same way that surface tracings are used to create patterns and reconstruct or replicate them in a three-dimensional image, the use of light waves to reflect such recreated surface images is the basis for holography.

Recent advances in laser technology bring life to the visions of Dennis Gabor, who in 1948 thought of reconstructed light waves as a means to form images. All of these present means to manipulate visual reality are being used in reprographics, advertising, and modern art, but not very much in historical reconstruction (consider the analysis by MESSARIS of the role of images in advertising for "visual persuasion," which is a different concern than good GUI design). While scientific and aesthetic possibilities are opened up by such technology, so too are possibilities for fraud and deception. FRIEDHOFF (p. 77) recalled one of the earliest con-troversies when in 1982 *National Geographic* "moved" two Egyptian pyramids closer together, so they fit better on the magazine's cover, by altering the image rather than just reshooting the photograph from a different angle (at considerably additional expense and delay). Budget considerations, not actuality, prevailed. The end justified the means. In most cases photographic alteration is done to make the image clearer or more striking, but in others the motive is sheer propaganda and deployment of the power of the picture (DEBRAY), proverbially worth more than a thousand words, to distort history. Photographic historians and philosophers of image sources have warned the public about being misled by image manipu-lation (cf., JAUBERT; LE MAREC; PARINET; QUEAU).

Whereas it is now relatively mundane to scan an image or to photograph an object digitally and transfer the image to a screen, with control of trajectories and light sources beyond camera location, this manipulation of flat or two-dimensional images has been converted by three-dimensional graphics technology to transfer objects back and forth from the real and virtual worlds. Real objects are now easily digitized by using such digitizers as Immersion Corporation's *Microscribe-3D,* which is essentially a robotic arm with counterweights and stylus or light pen with which one traces around an object while sensors capture the actual dimensions and recon-struct a three-dimensional orthographic projection on screen (a mesh image) that can be saved as files in standard formats such as IDES and DXF. Immersion Inc. claims that *Microscribe* renders relatively large objects (i.e., countertop variety) over a good-sized workspace with spatial accu-racy to .009" (.23 mm). Objects transferred to orthographic projections using this software can be manipulated further, reshaped and redesigned using polygons and lines, splines, or NURBs, etc.. Such three-dimensional images, faithfully replicated or enhanced, can superimposed on any two-dimensional background or transferred into moving images or digital video for animation, gaming, and simulation. *Microscribe* (priced at ca. $3,000) works with its own MAX plug-in or that from 3D Studio, and with *3D Studio, Lightwave*, *Alias*, *SoftImage*, *Strata* and other packages and on PC, Mac or SGI platforms. For smaller objects that cannot be traced easily because of dexterity limitations or the convoluted shape of complex objects, one can select such alternatives as Roland Corporation's PICZA 3D, a piezoelectric device for limited area scanning (24 inches or 6 x 4 inches), which sells for under $1,500.

More than visual reproduction is involved in this modern image technology, but replication is as well. Laser cutters have been used for some time now to produce models of buildings from three-dimensional CAD renderings. Modern technology for computer-assisted manufac-turing is also relevant for the arts. Consider, for example, that modern stereolythogram tech-nology allows not only the relay of text and visual information, but also three-dimensional objects. Either robotic scanners for large objects or six-dimension scanners are used for smaller objects placed in scanning boxes. They measure surfaces of the object in relation to distance from surrounding enclosures or the platforms for moving scanners, they calculate pro-jectiles for laser beams to go the same distance, point by point, and they transmit these meas-urements and coordinates to a stereolithographic compositor where the artifact is to be repli-cated in actual size and exact dimensions. Stereolithography reproduces the object in a manner that is the opposite of injection mold technology. Instead, a base of liquid plastic or resin is slowly pushed up from a flat surface; a laser beam encircles the resin, moving in and out in accord with measurements sent to its controller, and this seals the resin or plastic layer by layer until the object is built *en toto* from head to foot. Color can be added to the surface by a variety of finishing processes to replicate the original. The sealed, hardened, and formed plastic object is removed from its incubus, so that the object, like any mold or model, can be studied, used, altered, and reproduced at will.

A similar process is used at the supercomputing laboratory at the University of California, San Diego, where paper laminate is used instead of plastic in order to create three-dimensional models of everything from protein to relief maps of Death Valley (D. WILSON). In this case, the reverse of the aforementioned plastic technique is used; instead of building the model layer by layer from unformed resin, the model is sculpted from a stack of paper with a laser beam that burns a controlled path around the stack, one sheet at a time, until the remaining stack is shaped exactly by the prescribed dimensions. The Laminated Object Manufacturing (LOM) system built by Helisys, Inc., was first used as a "prototyper" to envision things that were not yet here, but it was quickly learned that such technology could also be used to envision things which have passed away. Moreover, such technology once reserved for industrial manufacturing has become affordable and almost a toy in small laboratories. Roland Corporation's MODELA 3D plotter, for example, which works with the company's PICZA 3D scanner, converts scanned objects to prototypes using styrofoam, balsa wood, or other modeling material. Because it imports .DFX files, one can create objects virtually and then real models, or *vice versa*.

Although these object-rendering and object-fax technologies have been developed to assist manufacturing at distant sites, it also can be used by museums to send replicas instead of images only. Just as one plant can be connected to separate design operations in distributed manufacturing, the on-location field trip, design studio, laboratory, the museum, archives, and library special collections, and classroom can all be interconnected. The high costs involved are not the technology itself, but this infrastructure development and textbase, imagebase, object base, and database development that conveys information aesthetically and multidimensionally (FLORANCE & DUCKWALL). The payoff in learning is considerable. The opportunities for the blind are obvious, but we are all somewhat visually impaired. Scientists are awed by how much more they notice when turning a model in their hands and interacting with it, rather than just viewing it statically from afar or on screen even with the use of three-dimensional glasses. In this case, the sense of feeling is added to sight, and visualization thereby rises to a new plane of interactive sense perception. Of course, they are discovering what artists have long understood in modeling, sculpting, and in turning ethereal entities into three-dimensional artifacts to give them objectivity. Such artifices, like models of the atom or of the solar system, are not unlike the visualization of history in Western Christian and classic traditions of resurrecting the holy and revered dead to be manifest to the living as life-size statutes. The difference is that now these recreations can be animated, contextualized, and rehearsed as never before. History can come alive in virtual reality. Replication and simulation, not exact repetition, is a possibility today. History can be fabricated thereby in the worst sense of the term, rather than the best, but this has always been the case even in simple recollection, interpretation of text, and any historical reconstruction.

Replication then, not just visualization and simulation, may be where historical modeling is headed and where education is going as well. Libraries, archives, and museums one day may have replicators as imagined in Star Trek's Enterprise suites, to provide for their patrons on site or to telefax as easily as we now send documents which, after all, are indeed three-dimensional artifacts. This is not quite the counterpart to digital music where reproduction is so exact, and tactility is yet limited to shape rather than more subtle sensory capabilities in touch. But it has its uses. Think of how a small clay model is often used to produce a large sculpture, and consider this process in the reverse. If this is where computer graphics and the industry have come, where does education fit it? Is education merely a market, following such developments, or has it spawned such changes, participated in the development, and played a significant leadership role? Where in this framework do the historical arts fit? Historical Science?

Such questions beckon a survey of current developments in History and especially Art History, historical institutions, and historical research using visual arts and new media. Museums, galleries, and other cultural institutions are subjected to the tremendous pressure to catch up to this surge in digital technology, which they are now doing with great speed, exhilaration, and cost. One pressure is the inter-disciplinary exchange between Art History and Archeology (GREENHALGH; GUIMIER-SORBETS), the visual and cognitive sciences, as well as History (the symbiosis here is reflected in the combination forming in the United Kingdom CTICH's Center for History, Art and Archeology Computing). Anthropology is as much a bridge as History in these inter-disciplinary connections.

Computing in these disciplines tends to be interdisciplinary, so that the trends in information technology applied to a discipline influence automation in cultural institutions and *vice versa*. See DORAN & HODSON; GINOUVES & GUIMIER-SORBETS, eds.; and ROSS, MOFFETT & HENDERSON, eds., for modern quantitative methods and computer applications in archeology. Today, these methods may not be so statistical but are nevertheless empirical because of whole image and feature matching, information based on color and other forms of measurement not expressed overtly as mathematically as they actually are in computer-assisted recognition, and pattern recognition whether in a GIS overview of a site or the scanning of a museum artifact as though its surface were a terrain. Rather than a matter of aesthetics or personal taste, the approach is often critical and analytic, comparative and relying on formal classification and topologies. WATSON provides a good explanation of the scientific method in archeology; and HOOPES considers the future of Archeology and Anthropology on the Web.

While greater strides in individual computerized projects have been made than in institutional information systems development, networking, and automation on a large scale, that trend is about to be reversed. E. S. ORE and others are envisioning a worldwide supra-institutional structure for image processing and retrieval for the arts and humanities. Advanced projects like the medieval image bank at Krems have demonstrated such feasibility, not only for full images but partials which may be separated to form segmented visual archives, i.e., to search for things like tools, dishes, furniture; caricatures and personal features like faces, headdress, costume, and even gesture (JARITZ, 1997). It is now relatively easy to use such an image base, to select objects classified by time and place, and to recreate a virtual environment such as setting a medieval table, or more instructive, a series of tables depending of the rank and station of those about to eat or dine. Stereotyped persons can be costumed for any age and occasion for which an historical image exists. One can similarly outfit a horse or different horses depending on use, from the wild to any domestic situation, from first use in pulling a plow to full battle gear to display the evolution of medieval cavalry and warfare. The old show and tell can now be done interactively, forward and backward, and simultaneously for instantaneous comparison and contrast. Such applications are placing demands on image retrieval as never before, from all sources, in ways beyond older picture research.

As already mentioned in the case of CHEN's demonstrations, classified images may be retrieved visually by humans and with computers through pattern and shape comparison. The aforementioned Symbolic Projection approach to image information retrieval uses spatial reasoning (CHANG & JUNGERT), so that descriptions of image content are related to spatial relationships between objects in pictorial presentations. The application may be more immediate in medical image archives, CAD and GIS, or robotics even, but the potential for object retrieval combined with pattern recognition in the arts is significant. If one can do this for objects in one picture, one can do it as well for objects in organized collections, mapped landscapes, graphic user interfaces, and virtual galleries. The collection components and technology for such a structure seem already extant and the trend toward multi-institutional cooperation seems to have reversed the once highly individualized and competitive posture of most art institutions (SAUNDERS & HAMBER); the political and fiscal means are still wanting, but developments toward such a possibility seem to be accelerating.

Textual elements in image retrieval remain important, especially in naming and classifying objects depicted, standardizing a nomenclature for technical methods employed, and conceptual indexing representations of ideas by things. Standardized classification and descriptive methods for art, often based on the foundations laid by Robert Chenhall (CHENHALL, updated by AMERICAN ASSOCIATION FOR STATE AND LOCAL HISTORY), are enhanced when using the *Art and Architecture Thesaurus*, but their utility to users outside a museum or research center is not well understood. Their application need not be restricted to massive institutional computerization, but with the possibilities provided by client-server designs and networking they should be utilized in projects mounted on personal computers. Several museum DBMS packages like *Stipple* (CANON-BROOKES) and *Questor* have indeed evolved into full-scale cultural information management systems (R. PALMER) for the institutions that implement them, but regional, national, and international networking on the scale of the library world is what it will takes to create a scholarly milieu where museums, archives, and libraries are equally accessible to historians. Some of this is accomplished by archives and museums using library networks and utilities to exchange bibliographic information formatted into special versions of Machine-Readable Catalog (MARC) records (e.g., Archives and Manuscripts Control [AMC-MARC]). However, even in their transformation to Universal MARC (UNIMARC), this standard for carrying textual information is still too limited for conveying full-text documents, images, and combinations. Thus the attention to File Transfer Protocol (FTP), coding and mark-up standards, and description guidelines are coupled with terminological control. It is likely that MARC records may serve merely as pointers and act as a directory system so one can retrieve the actual documentation needed on the Internet from MARC-supplied addresses. While such developments are ongoing, museums have lagged far behind libraries, and a little behind archives in global networking and descriptive standards. The latter made significant advances in the United States by adopting AMC-MARC to use bibliographic networks, but museums in the past five years now seem to be moving ahead of archives, especially in Europe, in standards development, networking, and computerized cataloging (cf., KAMISHER; A. ROBERTS; ABELL-SEDDON; SZRAJBERT, 1992; etc.).

By and large, however, both archives and museums are in the same predicament of not having developed the technical and personnel infrastructure to take advantage of the most recent advances in information and telecommunications technology that make PC image bases affordable for educators and researchers. Hewlett-Packard has begun placement of photo-scanners in its desktop computers as a standard option, so it is now relatively easy to build personal photo-archives and to transmit visual information alone or embedded into electronic text. Whereas in 1988 when with few exceptions the scale of projects was relatively small compared with today, scanning speed was not considered a major issue in contrast to cost and resolution. Scanning 100 pages per day was acceptable then, but no longer. Digital cameras at resolutions of 300 dpi or higher can still be costly and are by today's expectations, slow scanners. The next generation promises half-second per page scanning, but costs are still high (above $15,000). If the same cost reductions are seen for scanners as for computers, by the end of this decade one can expect these costs to be cut in half. Such high-speed scanners will no doubt become as ubiquitous as photocopiers in libraries, archives, and media centers. Such developments raise expectations and seem to pressure institutions to deliver their intellectual wares in electronic form complete with visualization. Contextualization often means visualization, and *vice versa*.

Major efforts are now underway to develop the technical standards, conventions, and guidelines needed for international sharing of art, object, and documentary information textually and visually (A. ROBERTS). Most of these in North America, and Europe as well, are tracked by the Clearinghouse on Art Documentation and Computerization directed by Patricia Barnett at the T. J. Watson Library of the Metropolitan Museum of Art. It supplies directories and bibliographies on broad topics cutting across many institutions. Some of the arts agencies in the United States in the late 1970s envisioned a national arts information system (COK *ET AL.*) based on a national standard for Arts Information Exchange (pp. 105-167) which is still unrealized as a separate system. Its goals are being met, however, through integration and collaboration with other networks (BEARMAN, 1990). Significant players in North America include the Getty Trust AHIP (now the Getty Research Institute) through the Art Information Task Force (AITF) working with the Museum Computer Network (MCN), the Visual Resources Association (VRA); the Art Libraries Society of North America (ARLIS/NA); and the Canadian and American archivists professional associations, especially the SAA standards board and affiliates, the Committee on Automated Records and Technique (CART), the *ad hoc* Working Group on Standards for Archival Description (WGSAD), and the Committee on Archival Information Exchange (CAIE) which works primarily with MARC AMC refinements; and the American Association for State and Local History (AASLH) Common Agenda for History Museums. As in the case of archival information exchange *per se,* major historical associations are conspicuous by their lack of involvement in museum information exchange developments (see Appendix D).

Some of the most progressive initiatives in the museum world have been forthcoming from Canada. Government involvement in cultural resource management and the preservation of historical records is exemplified there by an enlightened and progressive cultural properties act that has had such meritorious effects as the creation of the Hudson Bay Company archives at the Manitoba Provincial Archives (MOOSEBERGER *ET AL.*). Canadian networking and cooperation across provincial and linguistic boundaries are also exemplary. The Museum Computer Network (MCN) since 1990 has promoted a standards project, Computer Interchange of Museum Information (CIMI), that would allow multiple institutions to build databases in common and develop integrated museum information retrieval systems (BLACKABY & SANDORE). Attempts in the 1980s toward coordination of already decade-old systems in individual institutions to build a national model seem to be paying huge information dividends (CASTONGUAY, OIKAWA, & VEZINA; BESSER). This is a collaborative effort of the National Library of Canada; the Canadian Heritage Information Network (CHIN, which is part of the Arts and Heritage Sector of Communications Canada) of 150 museums; the National Museums Corporation; the Canadian Institute for Scientific and Technical Information (CISTI); a commercial partner, QL Systems, Ltd.; and the University of Toronto Automated System (UTAS) to use already existing library networks and standards for shared cataloging and bibliographic information, but also for inventories, registrations, and image relay, as well as informal discourse among curators. CHIN collaborates with Conservation Information Network (CIN), CIDOC and its parent, ICOM, in a variety of programs. Museums, at least the larger and better funded among them, seem to be moving ahead of archives in their quest for visual access especially with the employment of video and development of interactive media applications for their publics (BEARMAN, 1992).

The impact of multimedia technology on cultural institutions is discussed in BARRET & REDMOND, some of which expands upon a theme W. BARRETT develops elsewhere, the "social construction of knowledge." They are particularly interested in innovative multimedia systems rather than single terminal displays, to develop "interactive transformational environments." Some of the most innovative are in businesses where corporate sponsorship supplies the necessary cash to be truly innovative and experimental. Companies interested in developing corporate culture often use their monumental headquarters like museums, for display and tours, and have invested a great deal of money in visual programs and interactive media. If the R&D effort is too costly for cultural institutions to finance from scratch, they might well turn to corporate sponsors (which many have) to ask for time and talent as much as cash. Imitation is often cheaper than creation.

In any case, museums are moving into multimedia as rapidly as possible. *ITEM*, a news service from INTERNATIONAL VISUAL ARTS INFORMATION NETWORK (IVAIN), since 1990 has reported on more than 127 interactive multimedia projects in museums and galleries worldwide, but predominantly in Europe. The survey covers supposedly the best and brightest, but with the increased affordability of multimedia production and the continuing connection between creativity and individual effort, it maybe that some of the most innovative projects are in smaller institutions.

Museums' overriding concern for a general viewing public rather than the individual researcher promotes such investment, as does the arts' competition for leisure time with and involvement in the entertainment business. However, the Art and Photography Division of the National Archives of Canada is moving ahead with its ArchiVISTA program using AT&T graphic processors with IBM PC/DOS integration into the archives' office automation, in order to build image bases from its rich collections of cartoon drawings, beginning with a pilot project of 20,000 scanned images from its array of 13.5 million photographs and documentary images (G. STONE; STONE & SYLVAIN). The National Archives through this project is demonstrating the possible fusion of archives and museums with the creative use of technology to enlarge their public. In 1986 the division established the Canadian Museum of Caricature to present its original cartoons in both exhibits and interactive visual displays; within two years of opening, it hosted 25,000 visitors annually. Moreover, this use of digital imagery for the public is having spin-off impact on search procedures available to researchers, including shortcuts through an otherwise impregnable processing backlog when normal procedures broke down after the archives accessioned more than a million more images in a single month. This created such a need to reconfigure its access systems and services, including consideration of the image itself as a substitution for archival group description and item cataloging, that the ArchiVISTA project pointed to ways of bypassing traditional archival methods to combine terminological control (not unlike that advocated years ago by Richard BERNER) in indexing with image retrieval. CHEN's *Emperor I* project has demonstrated how powerful interactive media, first video and now CD-ROM image bases, could be for classified image retrieval. RORVIG (1987, 1990, 1993) and others (RODDY; SMALL, etc.) have indeed argued for the feasible substitution of visual for textual retrieval; the ArchiVISTA project seems to provide a demonstration for such substitution or at least enhancement of literate processes with visual information retrieval.

One can predict where image technology is taking us in education from what has already happened in the entertainment industry and is transpiring in libraries and museums the world over with the creation of virtual tours, first with transparencies and slides, then automation of such images with software like *PowerPoint*, the addition of simulation, and now virtual exhibits and tours. The next step, already evident is theme parks, is beyond sound to add motion, climate control, and other sensory perceptions such as smell. The trend, if one can project this from current developments, is to bring people into totally recreated environments, into an "immersive telepresence" in IEEE *Multimedia* language (also abbreviated as IT, which is easily confused therefore with Information or Instructional Technology; cf., KANADE, RANDER & NARAYANAN; MOEZZI; JAIN, 1997). MOEZZI's teams at Visual Computing Laboratory at the University of California, San Diego, have produced virtual views from scratch, while others model three-dimensional views from two-dimensional camera input. HIROSE *ET AL*. review the techniques used in such "Virtual World Generation." His team in Tokyo has been experimenting with generating synthetic sensations.

Some projects are still in the laboratories, but other developments are moving out into the classroom, library, and museum. D. CAMPBELL at the Human Interface Technology (HIT) Laboratory at the University of Washington has created a virtual gallery with architecture design software (Autodesk's *AutoCAD* 12+, *3D Studio,* and Greenspace software displayed with the Silicon Graphics Onyx Reality Engine 2 system). While students in MIT's Media Lab work at their *MetaDesk* with two-dimensional rear-projected maps illuminating their screens under their clear desk tops, with the added tangibility of plexiglass models rising from the map below, and "information lens" which glide across the surface to lift images onto a monitor that displays a converted three-dimensional image of the scene, object, or alteration on demand (DAVENPORT & BRADLEY). Students in Des Moine, Iowa, experience Niagara Falls in their own virtual dome, and in other places the museum is brought into schools similarly via three-dimensional video projection and surrounding sound (HIROSE *ET AL.*). In such environments experiential learning and imagination are combined. The vision from children's literature is increasingly real, where a young reader enters into a book and becomes part of the story. This too has been envisioned in *Star Trek* scenarios where for recreation and learning through simulation twenty-fourth century characters experience realities from previous times, recreated to the finest detail in the starship's holideck. Good science fiction is always rooted in history, and in this case such scenarios are believable in part because we already have rudimentary technology that allows history replay. The most unbelievable part of this science fiction aboard the *Enterprise* is not about the technology, but pertains to History. One doubts that historical preservation in our time or during the next millennium will be much better than in previous ages; the history is not going to be detailed enough for such technology to replicate any such scenarios except as recreations and historical fiction. All such future replays will have to be three-dimensional models with hypothetical simulations. The fault will not be in technological know-how, it will be the lack of knowledge and our imperfect data from the past because of inadequate contemporary documentation in history.

This observation brings the other end of the spectrum into perspective, i.e., to switch from presentation in the future to data acquisition at present. Another trend to note is equipping the viewer to be his or her own documentation expert, image collector, and editor. Remote Visual Inspection (RVI) technology can be used to document archeological digs, geographic surveys, forensic inspections such as autopsies and proceedings like trials, or to capture historical events as they unfold. The technology is simply a step beyond the tourist camcorder and the reporter's TV coverage. Consider such technology in all field work, but do not limit its applications to work only in the field: include archives and their documentation as the field, or if one prefers the metaphor from data mining combined with "archeology of the book," the dig. Historical sites, archives, and museums could equip historians with such technology to be used to advantage as much as it can be used by technicians to inspect machinery in the field. Olympus Industrial RVI systems can be carried like briefcases on shoulder straps, and viewers either take in what the wearer sees through a visor, or through handheld cameras that can squeeze into ports as small as .236 inches, or can inspect objects at a distance of 52 feet with blowups that show amazing detail. Such image gathering technology allows visual data acquisition in volume far surpassing photography. Video clips can be inserted easily into homepages for visual reinforcement of textual information, and multidirection video capture during a walk-through can supply simultaneous video screens for virtual reality laboratories. Such developments are extensions of everyday occurrences such as creating one's own screen savers with personalized photo albums scanned into an image base.

More applied to History, the archival researcher may simply put on a video pack and their camera fitted helmet, so that while they inspect their manuscripts firsthand, they capture them folio by folio for subsequent scanning and analysis. Whole archival series could be transferred to individual workstations with such RVI technology. Moreover, as espionage forms of this video-capture technology become available to the wider public, the camera will fit into eyeglass frames, and shoulder bags or back packs required today will snap on one's belt. The technology is here, and its price is dropping rapidly. Several companies are now using digital video to relay information back and forth between engineers in the field and their home offices. Their field inspectors are equipped with video cameras and voice communications to record what is seen, heard, and described on site, to build an instant record for later analysis (an example of the distinction between information searching and research). In keeping with current distributed computing, client-server architectures, and miniaturization, engineers in the field and military scouts will soon be wearing an eyepiece display monitor with their cameras in their headgear, with an information feed from small, compact but powerful minicomputers on their belts or in their pockets. Xybernaut Corporation has already announced that such a Sony product is in development. Wearable computers are no longer science fiction or of a privileged few at MIT's Media Lab.

If an archives, gallery, or library were to make such equipment available to researchers the benefit for both would be enormous. This development requires rethinking of reference and user services, the way work is performed in networked environments, and a holistic integration not envisioned by most organizations now (SPROUL & KIESLER). Consider, however, how such reader enhancement could also improve institution operations. Video camera relay to digital databases could be tracked for added electronic surveillance and improved security, and more positively to create logs of researchers' foci and attention given to certain records, documents, and images. Such metadata could be used to select automatically what original material should be retrospectively converted to digital form. One can imagine automation of the process where instead of user studies after the fact, user interest measured in real time would capture images for the institution's electronic archives simultaneous with a viewer's decision to upload a record into a personal image base. Dual video-monitoring is already employed in hospital operating rooms, where a video-log of a surgical procedure is kept archivally for risk management (a safeguard against malpractice), and still frames from living specimen are selected for image enhancement and subsequent teaching purposes. Current developments in high-cost industries such as medicine and space technology will result in subsequent wider utilization and lower cost applications. Such applications illustrate the impact of new technology on merging methods, integrating collections of artifacts and documents, and creating a real continuum between types of information institutions. This same blending is also evident in the merging of disciplines and the boundary crossing of unidisciplinary think tanks such as the MIT Media Lab. Sound, image, text, and movement from dance to gesture and body language, are all to be integrated into a new, rich information base for future access, learning, and action.

Consider recent developments leading to the next millennium's integration of sound- and image-based research into the textually dominated practices of today. While specific technologies are coming down in cost, the investment for developing comprehensive studios or visual production laboratories is still too much for most educational and cultural institutions to bear. The Media Center for Art History at Columbia University was recently featured by the *Chronicle of Higher Education*'s regular focus on information technology (GUERNSEY). She reports on an exemplary model project by three Columbia students and two faculty advisors to create a thirteen-minute computer-animated video tour of Amiens' medieval Gothic cathedral for a required Arts Humanities course. One segment reconstructs in five minutes some 50 years of actual construction. Another "computerized cinematography" project aims to let the viewer "fly into" the two-dimensional landscapes of Rafael, which are known for their three-dimensional perspective. Another speculated about letting viewers "fly around" inside the Vatican. Teachers and students proclaim that this video technology "transforms the teaching of Art History," but administrators note the costs. The Media Center was developed with an estimated investment of $2.3 million, of which $575,000 came from an NEH challenge grant; and the Amiens project itself was supported by NEH and university grants of $138,000, mostly to buy time and talent. When such tools are combined with data banks, books and libraries, enthusiastic faculty, and project teams, the experience is understandably heralded as a "transformation."

The means to create visual access to art and artifacts transformed into new media are placing tremendous pressure on image information providers to create dynamic access to their historical sites and collections for distance learning, enhanced viewing, and new techniques of analysis. This has refocused attention on cataloging and description, terminology, and the parallel development of information systems to provide text analyzes with visual communications. Because collections are distributed and information resource sharing is the name of the game today, new forms of collaboration are occurring beyond regional and national borders. Image information is being globalized. The International Council of Museums (ICOM) hosted by UNESCO, with its affiliate, International Confederation of Architectural Museums (ICAM), provides links across borders for a genuine ecumenical approach to cultural heritage information and preservation. CIDOC, ICOM's 500-member organization has spread throughout fifty countries. It has been working, for example, on standards for site documentation with archeological groups, national monuments organizations, and government agencies such as parks services. Its Data Model working group proposes to develop an international standard structure for data exchange among museums. And a related terminology working group has already created a draft standard for art and archeology that has been tested by the Network Art Research Computer Image Systems in Europe (NARCISSE), a project of the European Economic Community (EEC) aimed at high resolution image banks and multilingual information retrieval. Likewise, CIDOC working groups exist for iconographic classification (all of which is based on the original conceptions of Erwin PANOFSKY formulated in 1939), cooperatively but independent from the ICONOCLASS Research and Development group that since 1990 has been responsible for the constant revision and updating of the ICONOCLASS database (developed in the Netherlands by H. van de Waal, ICONOCLASS is a hierarchical scheme that includes headings for art works, descriptive notes, and index terms).

How might all this fit together internationally? One indication is the Remote Access to Museum Archives (RAMA) project begun in 1992 with EEC (DG XIII) backing for an even larger umbrella initiative, RACE (Research and development in Advanced Communication technologies in Europe). One of RACE II's projects that began in 1990 is named the Mona Lisa for Modeling Natural Images for Syntheses and Animation; this project brings together nine European industrial, broadcasting, and academic institutions (United Kingdom's BBC and Queen Mary and Westfield College; Siemens and Daimler-Benz, Video Art Production and Digitale Videosysteme with the University of Hanover from Germany; Thomson Broadcast Systems from France; and the University of the Balearic Islands, Spain). Mona Lisa is to become a three-dimensional virtual studio where an entire set is generated electronically with the illusion of camera motion in a real setting, but where in fact images from multiple sites are electronically merged: archives of three-dimensional models and textures; automatic three-dimensional modelers and dynamic modeling; interactive software; scene generation tools, etc., combined with real-time cameras shooting action against blue backgrounds for transposition, camera tracking for positing, perspective controls, and mixing modules, resulting in what has been called "synthetic TV" (BLONDE *ET AL.*). The result is a coherent broadcast which actually never exists or happens. It is the historian's dream and nightmare at the same time. Broadcasting of such electronic virtual realities will be made possible by new telecommunications configurations. RAMA, for example, is a telecommunications cooperative cutting across six countries that supports an open systems interface and international standards, while attempting also to serve individual museums with their traditional inventories, descriptors, data structures, etc. Participating museums in the pilot project include the Musée d'Orsay in Paris, the Prado and Museo Arqueológico Nacional in Madrid, the Pergamon Museum in Berlin, the Museon in The Hague, and the Beszley Archive in Oxford. ICOM's international character means that it serves similar purposes as and cooperates with its counterparts in the archives and library worlds, i.e., the International Council on Archives (ICA) and International Federation of Library Associations and Institutions (IFLA) respectively.

Currently, the plethora of organizations, task forces, working groups, and committees, all with their own projects and acronyms which seem to comprise yet another language, form a maze that is truly amazing. One may very well feel like navigating through a labyrinth, but a general hierarchical schematic can be discerned with each committee or task force somehow being sponsored by or reporting to a parent archival, library, or museum organization at the national level, and each of these has an international counterpart. While the connection between national and international levels is not always strong, modern communications technology is forging stronger connections. The weakest links have not been along vertical lines, but been horizontal divisions between types of institutions and the failure of professionals to override these for concerted action and influence on national agenda especially in policy formulation and resource allocation. The acceleration of interest in standards, terminology, and data exchange can be attributed in part to the Internet/WWW and its explosive international growth which has caught museums, and most of the art and architecture, art history, and archeology fields, unprepared to reap the benefits of new communications technology as archives were a decade ago. Libraries have been in front of the latter two for nearly two or more decades, but they need allies too and a common cause in cultural and information resource management is widely recognized. Standards for cooperation on a global scale had simply not developed conterminously with the technological advances experienced over the past decade. While the catch-up may appear confusing, and it often is indeed, the variety of organizations involved from grassroots movements to larger umbrella associations is necessary for the broad education that must be achieved.

How does such a flurry of international institutional activity relate to individual researchers and subject-domain projects? Is there a connection between the macrocosm and microcosms? In the conversion of Art History to the history of arts in an anthropological sense, a greater consciousness of inter-disciplinarity among all of the Arts is linking audio and the visual as never before. The *Art and History* (1986) volume of the *Journal of Interdisciplinary History* may be used as a point of departure to study recent developments. A contemporary movement in History toward greater appreciation of material culture and the anthropological strain in Art History have much in common. F. HASKELL delineates at least three great shifts in historiography that have affected how art is employed in History. The final one is cultural history in a pervasive sense rather than portraiture for heroic biographic history. Special interests include the social functions of art, the history of cognition, the idea of visual narrative, and iconology as allegory and representation (as explored by S. GREENBLATT, 1981).

The neat classifications of the turn-of-the-century simply have not sufficed in this transition one century later. Have they ever really sufficed? Have not the divisions erected by such classification and the departmentalization of disciplines in our schools always had their detractors and interdisciplinary minds that transcended such boundaries? Remember that Aby Wartburg (1866-1929) who placed the arts into the context of culture in an anthropological sense (cf., K. FORSTER; R. GOMBRICH) like an historical anthropologist (P. BURKE, 1990), thus always related artworks to liturgy and religion, whether in everyday folk life or the most elite expressions of Western Culture (K. FORSTER). Thus F. GILBERT thought that Wartburg had taken "Art History to the History of Civilization" like CASSIRER and PANOFSKY (FERRETTI). WARTBURG also thought like a New Culture historian (DIERS) who would have liked the construct of Historical Information Science, as indicated by the projection of his *Mnemosgne* picture atlas of social memory (*soziales Gedächtnis*) (BAUERLE), which never materialized, and for which adequate information and image technology exists only now. He was a proverbial man before his time. It is no wonder that the Getty Research Institute is now republishing Wartburg's works when his supra-disciplinary perspective resonates so well with trends dominant one century later. CONFINO (p. 1390-91), for example, like GINZBURG (p. 21), uses Warburg's methodology to interpret art (rejecting formalism or the "autonomy of aesthetic values") as indicative of how modern cultural historians might improve the field of Cultural Memory.

Part of the so-called "Information Explosion" is really an implosion involving a greater variety of researchers wanting access to what hitherto was the domain of a select specialization. Consider, for example, that formerly retrieval of an art object was by its name or that of its maker, which would provide a brief standardized description. Now the same objects are described in much greater detail and one can retrieve information about like objects based on so much more than artists and titles: manufacturing dates, materials, structures, processes and techniques, symbolism, design, color and even texture. Color classification as a means of identification and information retrieval is hardly new; David Ramsay Hay, for example, advocated a color code in the early 1800s (D. R. HAY, second ed., 1846), although nothing so sophisticated to encompass the color array possible today (ITTEN), with hues, shading, and degrees of brightness that can be measured precisely. Paintings can be computerized easily into paint-by-number representations. Three-dimensional artworks present even more complex problems. Sculpture databases now use over 300 tags for description (SCOTT, 1988); fiber art may require more (LUNIN, 1994, p. 67). If is not so much more new knowledge or simply a matter of more information, but information in a greater variety of detail, forms, languages, and modes of transferability, used by more and different kinds of people, that is changing older more unitary communications that were once unilateral into something so multifaceted that the variety and intensity of usage are being magnified. Art History, for example, assisted by the pervasive influence of the notion of "culture" in the anthropological sense of B. MALINOWSKI or as popularized by R. BENEDICT, has led allied fields like History in viewing information in image-based sources as essential rather than merely supportive of their textual research and communication of their work (BERG ET AL.). While in Psychology and Education, studies of perception and cognition, and art and imagery merge as an issue of representational meaning; in History, art appreciation has given way to image analysis and semiotics, i.e., documentary art (CAMPBELL & ROLLINS, eds.; FREEDBERG [1989]).

Language and the oral, the visual and the artifact, sound and oral sources, are all being interwoven on a scale once possible only within a rather confined geographic and chronological specialization. When the documentation aspect of depositional art is communicated verbally, such discourse based on visual cognition has its own referents, structure, and character which have been analyzed for the development of expert systems applied to art information retrieval (M. WILSON). The ethnohistorical bent in modern historiography and focus on locale have moved attention away from great art of the masters, which will remain but as an elitist preoccupation rather than social concern, just as grand themes and great men in History seem to be disappearing into the common man—"people's history" as FLOUD (1984) calls it. Art works in series, collections, and the aggregate, treated as artifactual reflections of the societies producing them and semiotic signage, and the contextualization of art in history and literature (i.e., the visual described textually) are trends affecting cultural institutions, their programs and constituencies, and the dynamics of art information systems and services. Moreover, the Arts like other disciplines are losing their distinctiveness when transformed by or created in new multimedia.

The leadership of such organizations as the J. PAUL GETTY TRUST's Art History Information Program (AHIP, 1983-) is having a significant impact on the automation of comprehensive (registration, curatorial management, conservation, photographs and image documentation, education and public programs) collection management systems (R. PALMER). The complexity of the current situation linking research, artworks, and cultural resource management is reflected in the Getty Trust's organization in seven entities extending from the original museum, to include conservation, arts management, art education, philanthropy, the humanistic study of art, and most important for our purposes, the Art History Information Program. AHIP is itself divided into specialties for issues study and policy formulation, standards and the development of information resources such as promoting inventories of art objects (e.g., CORTI; CORTI & SCHMITT), creation of research databases, and research and development of information technologies to support art information. The organizational structure of the Trust and of its programs reflects the purviews combined into an Art History Information Science.

Perhaps best known is its *Art and Architecture Thesaurus* (see review by WEINBERG), a project as important as a stimulus for worldwide collaboration and concentration of thought about the information needs of art historians (BAKEWELL *ET AL.*) as for its results and intended applications in archival description and indexing (PETERSEN & BARNETT). This decade-long (1979-) award-winning project guided by Pat Moholt and its current director, Toni PETERSEN, was funded by NEH, the Council on Library Resources (CLR), the Andrew Mellon Foundations, and the J. Paul Getty Trust: it was a monumental financial, intellectual, and political task. Modeled after the National Library of Medicine's *Medical Subject Headings (MeSH)*, it was published in 1990 as a three-volume print edition. Its CD-ROM companion authority file was released in 1992. It is being updated continuously (BUSCH, 1992b). The second edition in 1994 expanded the original 23 hierarchies or conceptual categories to 33, organized in seven facets, which together classify 90,000 terms from art, architecture, museology, archives, and conservation, with British and American equivalents in English usage, into rankings from broad and narrow. Its facets include: associated concepts; styles and periods; agents (people and organizations); activities; materials; objects; built environment (landscapes, complexes, districts, etc.); furnishings and equipment; and visual and verbal communication. Certain vocabularies have potential for widespread application in historical documentation beyond art and architecture, perhaps with some expansion: e.g., professions in the people hierarchy; the entire activities facet for disciplines, functions, events, and techniques; the weapons and ammunition hierarchy for military historians; or that of exchange media for economic historians. As are most thesauri, the *ATT* is also expandable and thus adaptable for a variety of purposes. However, its use by historians is, unfortunately, still negligible.

When it was developing its programs a decade ago, AHIP's studies confirmed D. STAM's dissertation findings (1984) about the inter-disciplinarity of the field that is so representative of all History. Consequently, the Humanities are included in the GETTY TRUST's purview to provide a proper context for Art History (e.g., as denoted in the 1997 reorganization as separate entities moved into its new campus, the Getty Research Institute for the History of Art and Humanities was constituted). This new Research Institute now works with its counterpart, the Getty Information Institute, to bridge the gap once existing between humanities scholarship and information technology. Ongoing collaborative efforts between art institutions, art libraries, and archives and museums holding extensive image collections (especially photographs) are consequently moving toward joint efforts in Canada and the United States to provide better intellectual access to their sources through information sharing, conferencing, and authority work (cf., BEARMAN & SZARY on cataloging for online systems; see STAM, 1984, 1991, also for the history of cataloging art objects and a recommended typology; cf., SUNDERLAND; BUSCH, 1994, p. 32).

The Art Information Task Force (AITF), a coalition formed in 1990 between the Getty Trust AHIP and the College Art Association (CAA), including also the Visual Resources Association (VRA), the Art Libraries Society of North America (ARLIS/NA), and the Museum Computer Network (MCN), promises a full-range, far-reaching report on what scholars and the general public will expect from tomorrow's "virtual museum." It is hoped that this will establish an international standard for the categories of description for works of art. Its surveys were largely of art historians and concerned mainly art works rather than artifacts or documentary and disposition art, but its attempt to create an information framework from academic, museum, and art information communities, holds promise as well to historians who under the influence from anthropology are increasingly concerned with material culture. One of the problems, however, has been that the taxonomies and terminologies used in Anthropology lack correspondence with library classifications and subject headings, so that nonobject descriptors for classes, subclasses, and genre for behavior and practices, and synonymies linking these across diverse cultures were not well developed coming into the first era of library and archival automation (RAO). While Art History's strides in classification, description, language control, and information retrieval will help History, their mutual alliance with Anthropology still points to weaknesses in most information systems. People and things, for example, are still more easily retrieved in most art information systems than are groups, collective and individual actions, aesthetics, values, ideas, or beliefs.

Among AHIP programs are Art Information Task Force (AITF) goals and priorities, which works with the College Art Association (CAA). The Image and Information Standards Initiative will work to formulate recommendations for a standard description of an image file to compensate for differences in image capturing hardware, color fidelity, and resolution quality (BESSER & TRANT). Howard Besser is now the principal investigator in a Andrew W. Mellon funded collaborative project between seven museums and seven universities to explore art information sharing over digital networks; it is called the Museum Educational Site Licensing Project, 1995-1997 (TRANT, 1997). These were recently reviewed in the University of Illinois 1996 Clinic on Library Applications of Data Processing in which Besser, Jennifer Trant, Lois F. Lunin participated with key papers that capture the state of the art, its problems and progress (others concentrated on specific projects and technical issues more than overview of ongoing collaborations: HEIDORN & SANDORE, eds.). Besser himself admitted that just a decade ago the realization of large image bases seemed terribly remote; in his words, "farfetched."

Such digital-image projects go hand in hand with efforts toward uniform standards for description of cultural objects and architectural drawings (PORTER & THORNES), for the protection of cultural property and conservation practices. In the same vein, the Provenance Documentation Collaborative provides over 350,000 ownership tracings for 11,000 paintings in the United States and 32,000 primarily in American and British museum collections (L. JONES; SZRAJBERT, 1990), but the related files on private collectors is not automated (which would support biographies of collectors as in R. PURCEL, ed.). Spin-offs from its Provenance Index, directed by Burton Fredericksen, are forming a series entitled *Documents for the History of Collecting*. In addition to the *Art & Architecture Thesaurus* (1990; 2nd ed., 1994) and its companion *ATT: Authority Reference Tool* (1992), the Getty Trust supports a host of Authority Reference Tools: the bilingual *Bibliography of the History of Art (BHA*, 1991-; successor to *RILA* and *RAA*, available as file 191 on DIALOG) which is done with the French CNRS Institut de Information Scientifique et Technique (INIST), and also makes available its *Subject Headings* (1992); and the *Witt Computer Index* to the American school component of 67,000 photographic mounts (57,000 art works by 3,800 artists, late 1600s-, controlled by 160,000 associated authority records and 6,500 vocabulary terms: C. GORDON, 1991) of the Courtauld Institute's collection (founded in the 1890s), containing over 1.7 million black and white reproductions of Western art to the twelfth century, is a computer-index project directed by her; a *Union List of Artist Names* ([*ULAN*] 1994) with 200,000 artists and architects, 70,000 sources and bibliography, which grew out of nine AHIP project authority files; a related *Thesaurus of Geographic Names* (*TGN*, for 1995 CD-ROM release) which provides a geographic hierarchy (relating locations with regions) for 300,000 modern and 15,000 historical place-names (1987-) and will grow with planned massive data entries from Times Books and Rand McNally files (cf., the United States Board on Geographic Names and Defense Mapping Agency thesauri); and the CD-ROM *Avery Index (to Architectural Periodicals) on Disc* (COLUMBIA UNIVERSITY, 1977-; from G. K. Hall or online via RLIN or DIALOG) provides 155,000 records covering 700 journals. The Getty's ongoing *Census of Antique Art and Architecture Known to the Renaissance* project (1982-), a collaboration with the Warburg Institute of the University of London and Rome's Bibliotheca Hertziana directed by Arnold Nesselrath, now contains 45,000 records and 25,000 associated images on videodisc. The AHIP search tools have been adopted for several external projects of note, such as Academic Press' *Image Directory* and online *Visual Image Bank* (http:/www.imagedir.com) which now contains 60,000 records as it is still under development. It was anticipated to hold 100,000 by 1998 when officially launched with the directory in both electronic form and a print version.

Finally, AHIP has entered into another collaboration with The American Council of Learned Societies (ACLS is a federation of 52 scholarly organizations in the United States) and the Coalition for Networked Information (CNI: Association of Research Libraries [ARL], CAUSE and EDUCOM with a task force of 170 institutions and organizations) in *The Humanities and Arts on the Information Highways* initiative to influence the development of the National Information Infrastructure (NII) (AHIP, ACLS & CNI) so electronic resources will be nationally available in the United States both because of government support and the adherence to technical standards for data exchange.

Computing in art history projects has grown phenomenally, as illustrated by VAUGHAN, HAMBER, MYLES & VAUGHAN especially for cataloging artworks, but increasingly also in their analysis. The GETTY TRUST AHIP with the Scuola Normale Superiore of Pisa (CORTI *ET AL.*, 1984) from 1984 onward has tried to provide a directory to data processing projects in the history of art and related disciplines. Its extensively indexed final report in 1988 (CORTI *ET AL.*, 1988) describes more than 240 such projects. Each entry provides identification of the researchers, information managers, and systems developers, software and hardware used, data recording methods, and language of the database; also provided are narrative descriptions, scope (chronological and geographical coverage), and means of access. Since publication the number of such projects has perhaps increased half again as many, and a broader coverage of related work in History and Archeology would have doubled the directory's size. Its focus is on Art with a capital "A" rather than attempting a sweep of all such projects in material culture which would have also had to include Anthropology. Nevertheless, this was a model survey project it and set a high standard for similar reporting.

Art and text composition programs largely as ways of mastering facts by sets of rules in Artificial Intelligence applications have been compared when developing both information systems and support systems for creative design and composition (FARRET). This is a very nebulous task environment for rules and facts to work well together. Progress thus far has obvious implications for engineering management or technical execution of design, but more experimental and potentially significant is its support of computer-assisted artistic creativity in and out of academe. The IADEMS prototype (J. THOMPSON), for example, in creating a "design process history" can be applied to create a contemporary history of art if artists were self-aware enough to document their own creativity. Perhaps that is too much to expect, since this would seems to contradict the very notion of spontaneity in artistic creation, but it would have more applicability in documentary art, and most interestingly in architecture or museology. In the former, such design management tools could document a building from inception to completion, with all variable stages in between, and acknowledgment that the finished product is much more than the singular creation of an architect or architectural firm, but is often negotiated with patron, developer, owner, etc., and is a sociological phenomenon. In the latter case, for example, curators could create art historical sources with such tools by documenting provenance, tracking exhibits, recording viewer reactions in exhibitions, placing a work in variable contexts, etc., simultaneously with the maintenance of security and insurance records, itineraries and schedules, and other operations. Such tracking systems are not dissimilar in purpose to RAMESH's aforementioned integration of design and simultaneous documentation in software design. Both reflect capabilities to generate archives as a contemporary byproduct of action. The result is useful for evaluation, but some react adversely to having an equivalent of Big Brother watching viewers at the museum.

The point deserves repeating, that very few processes, even those of human creativity in the arts, have escaped such study, and the processes of forming something and informing some communication, and extracting or assimilating information, are reversible processes. History has been largely an endeavor to inform, moving from a concrete reality to an artificial or recreated image of it; conversely, History can also be informed from artificial models, imagined scenarios or simulations, and virtual reality. A visual image described may be treated like a special documentary or technical literature in abstracting and indexing (THIEL; DUGGAN; P. SMALL), a discourse in oral communications, and a cognitive bitmap at the convergence of psychology and reprographic technology; the reverse is not uncommon, as in going from descriptive language to artwork when a police artist reconstructs a portrait from a the recall of a witness, an artistic rendition of a lost historical site is created by a documentary artist for *National Geographic*, or holographic pyramids and monumental artworks are virtually reconstructed by computers from thousands of photographed artifacts or descriptions in historical travelogues. Thus the same methods are used to retrieve actual images, information about images, and imagined visuals, all of which are an aid to and product of art history in its largest dimension.

All of these methods and theories may be assumed under the rubric "Historical Information Science," when the subject is historical; specific techniques and methodologies are employed, and information technology is used. In short, most images would be included under such an umbrella. An example of the kind of quantified historical research using SPSS, fusing text analysis with material culture studies, which has practical import for museology, is L. TAYLOR's study of fashion magazines (1860-1880) to determine the prevalence of certain fabrics, periodization, and dominance of certain styles and designs, and references for documentation of museum holdings. The result is useful for museum conservation, and collection strategies, and such documentation is especially useful in connecting artifacts with illustrations that provide historical social context. Art History, it seems, should relate to this theme in a manner similar to History. Perhaps the additional qualifier "Art" can be used when the historical research is object centered (e.g., Art Historical Information Science). The same may be true of the histories of all of the arts, as in the case of merging music, oral discourse such as storytelling or liturgical recitation, voice recognition technology and sound visualization, and analytical methodologies.

Art historians, indeed all historians, relying on desktop textbases and databases want images at their immediate disposal as well, not just information about them, for both their teaching and research (BERG *ET AL.*). The integration of digitized images into the evolving historical workstation project of the Max-Planck Institute illustrates this line of development (FIKFAK & JARITZ). Using a model of networking for multi-institutional cooperation (JARITZ, 1991), much of this work is centered in the Institut für Mittelalterliche Realienkunde in Krems, Austria, under the direction of Gerhard Jaritz. The center's focus on medieval art provides a testing ground for some of the most difficult problems in art history and image technology, and perspectives drawn from both art specialists and medieval and early-modern historians using art as documentation. His project sponsored by the Austrian Academy has now digitized over 40,000 manuscript pages with artwork from the medieval and early modern periods. Jaritz is greatly influenced by semiotics because of the importance of symbolism in medieval works of art. He approaches his material from the vantage point of social history and prosopography, as indicated in the title of his 1988 presentation before the International Medieval Studies conference at Western Michigan University, "Finding the Signs: Pictures of Medieval Life"—meaning daily living documented in realism of Gothic miniatures and artwork for history, as distinct from art for its own sake (JARITZ, 1988). For retrieval purposes, this means the analysis of images as artifacts, depictions for thematic and conceptual meaning, and symbolic significance: indexing using vocabulary control such as the *Art and Architecture Thesaurus* and motif and iconographic reference sources (i.e., *ICONOCLASS*); cataloging for access through library networks as well as archival inventories (THALLER, 1993), as well as retrieval of available electronic texts digitized from hard-copy publications; and perhaps fingerprinting or use of unique identifiers (VAUGHAN).

Art, archeology, anthropology, sociology, and history are all combined in material culture studies, wherein the artifact is "read" as evidence with the texts that provide context, to create a history that attempts to recreate contemporary environments for interpretation (JANSEN; PIPPONIER). Such intellectual techniques, where the historian envisions a scenario in his or her mind's eye, are the forerunners of more technologically enhanced Virtual Reality approaches whereby the imagery is not purely mental or so individualized (WALKER & MILLER). ZUBOFF has effectively argued that all computerization is a generic kind of alternative if not virtual reality; so are theatrical plays, movies, video games, and TV, claims Michael SPRING who tries to use history to create more ease with the new multiple realities (virtual, artificial, alternate, cyber-, etc.) from which we can now choose. He cites (pp. 238-40) these technologies as antecedents, and also shows how science fiction since William Gibson's introduction in 1984 of the term "cyberspace" in his *Neromancer* (an intentional play on "necromancer") has also prepared society for what is coming. For him, and many more, history and fiction play the roles. They have not, however, really used the same level of technologies. Historians, are as much constrained by their sense of reality in such developments as by their lack of technical expertise and funding. For the time being, the primary focus of historians is getting an electronic hold on their material, more than using it in innovative applications or creating new forms of understanding history. Old paradigms understandably grip historians in their own historical vices.

The movement toward virtual reality in history can be seen, however, in the pervasive trend to incorporate electronically visual documentation into a previously text-dominated discipline. Using *KLIEU* software (anglicized as *CLIO* for the muse of History) and its object- oriented programmed Image Analysis System (IAS) (cf., THALLER and JARITZ, 1993), the Institute's REAL databases are constructed as sign finders (p. 21) meaning retrieval is for series, single artworks, and pictographic details from within these sources. The kinds of problems addressed, for example, are access to inferred meaning as in fashion statements whereby the torturers of a saint are dressed to display negative values derived from late medieval sumptuary laws, such as prescription of pointed shoes that may suggest blame on non-European minorities, namely medieval Jews, for the acts being portrayed. The access may be to retrieve what is no longer visible, as in the case of censorship through erasure, etc. (JARITZ, 1993, pp. 12-14 provides examples from REAL's digitized images). REAL's bilingual (German with English translations in preparation) indexing, then, is based both on actuality and intentionality for full explanations (COOK; BAXANDALL) so that unrealistic art can still be accessible by purpose and use in addition to traditional assignments of artist (often attributed at best), place (origin, itinerary, and present location), date (usually expressed as a fuzzy attribute), and physical description. Moreover, coding is being applied to image details like icons for retrieval (i.e., the *ICONOCLASS* model: cf., GARNIER and COUPRIE) or the use of tags quantitatively by SPSS or other statistical software for cluster analysis as suggested by THALLER (1982). Moreover, the center's extensive photo-archives of 20,000 slides and illustrations from published sources are being scanned using the Kurzweil Data Entry Machine (KDEM), the use of which M. THALLER had advocated since 1983, to produce electronic corpora which may be distributed through a variety of mechanisms. JARITZ pleads for an "open system" free from copyright restrictions on the distribution of digitized images and a host of other problems arising from the notion of information as intellectual property (which WALDEN discusses from the British legal point of view).

Several European libraries like the Bodleian at Oxford are contemplating similar programs of digitizing their manuscripts and creating access systems that combine textual and visual sources (BUZZETTI). The Vatican Library, for example, is also producing a videodisc of 150,000 of its manuscripts, and will create other CD-ROM products from its 2,000,000 books and 100,000 prints and in addition to access through its Web site (http://www.software.ibm.com/is/dig-lib/vatical.html). Three videodiscs are already available, each with 25,000 images for consulting more than 6,000 manuscripts described by a research team from the École des Hautes Études en Sciences Sociales at Paris. The image data banks will be connected to its online catalog and other supporting collections such as that of the papal Catholic University of Rio de Janeiro in Brazil. Another project is underway at the Vatican Microfilm

Library at St. Louis University contributing to the *Electronic Access to Medieval Manuscripts* project funded by the Andrew W. Mellon Foundation. This will also make MARC AACR2-compatible catalog descriptions available through RLIN.

A variety of database designs and technical methods have evolved to retrieval image and text together (reviewed by THALLER, 1992), including digitized images of manuscript and transcribed texts. Judging from recent AHC and ALLC conference abstracts, there is considerable interest in such OCR technology and potentially numerous projects, but electronic transcriptions present problems of their own, both from the variable content of prepublication "fluid" texts, legibility especially for the capture of archival records, capturing the structures of documents, and high resolution requirements. Presentation can be chaotic in accessing specific manuscripts electronically, keeping track of verso and recto images and out-of-sequence material, and creating tree structures (EISNER) to connect variant manuscripts (which sometimes is resolved by resorting to the ISO Office Document Architecture standard (ISO no. 8813) drafted in 1986 (ANDRE, FURUTA & QUINT) as a blueprint for DBMS design. Several imagebase software packages are available (LUNIN, 1987), most having their own peculiar limitations: MIDAS is commonly used in Germany, but ORBIS has been adopted recently for several projects because of its PC adaptability (HRASKO & SAJO). Some photogrammetric software like Rollei-metric, are especially useful in architecture, archeology, and the decorative arts because of their three-dimensional reconstructive capabilities. Virtual models can be viewed from all angles, just like isometric landscapes recreated as webbed-net models from detailed satellite data. Image-based systems are therefore also being deployed in archeological, anthropological, and history museums for retrieval of textual and visual information about artifacts from the smallest amulet to architecture on the grand scale (TRANT).

Archaeologists are equally interested as historians and curators in standards (RICHARDS & RYAN) for artifact information retrieval and correspondence with bibliographic systems (MARTLEW) and in-house textbases which are growing as archaeologists record field notes electronically, often on portables in the field and then in an editing and enhancement by indexing as files are transferred to main systems (LOCK & WILCOCK). Historians in an archives now do the same (CLARK), and accordingly notes are often blended automatically into publications, but research files are often larger than what is published so these project logs should be deposited like manuscript collections into appropriate repositories. Archeological survey data (BOISMIER & REILLY) are often handled like census records, but their context sensitivity is as much spatial (for the idea of "archeological space" see J. ARNOLD) as time related. Elaborate coding schema and classification systems have been devised for pottery from archeological digs (LEENHARDT) for given areas and periods, but these have not yet been normalized for broad comparative study across computer networks even though their images can be transferred (NEES). J. KNOERL's aforementioned idea of using GIS technology for "mapping history" is not just for Geography, but extends to placing information spatially, i.e., where documentation in all media, texts and artifacts, may be used to locate human events and put them in exact geographic situation complete with their surroundings or total context. Modeling spatial data has become a keen interest of social-economic historians who display their data in graphs but also on maps.

Computer mapping is used to show migrations and invasions resulting in changed boundaries, settlement and landholding patterns, changing population density, and overlaying historical maps to create dynamic virtual mapping programs corresponding to time series. PFISTER's tracing of people's migration on the grand scale from 1500 to 1800, for example, would come to life if animated. The AHC conference in Moscow featured seven projects in Russian history (PIOTUKH; PETROV & TROIANOVSKY; ROWNEY; VLADIMIROV, etc.), Canadian population studies (ROBICHAUD & WAYWELL), and the relationship of objects to indigenous locales (NICCOLUCCI & BENVENUTI). There is great appeal in using Geographic Information Systems (GIS) as a computerized counterpart to the cognitive idea of mental mapping, where mental constructs are aided by three-dimensional visualization (QUESADA). Thus *Klieu* is being used by S. GORDON to model museum documentation, relating it to images and to geographic reference systems to reconstitute an artifact's current location for inventory and security purposes, and origins *in situ* for its history and placement. Such reference systems need to be more than symbolic, however, if they relate to actual geography; to be objective referencing must relate to neutral, external fixtures (cf., D. MAGUIRE's overview; GOODCHILD & GOPAL's critique of the accuracy of spatial databases). Most recently fuzzy relationships have been worked into geo-spatial modeling (COBB & PETRY). The issue is more than scientific precision, since information retrieval problems persist because of unmitigated individualism, entrapment by regionalism, and overspecialization. In any use of GIS technology one might advocate adoption of new standards for geo-spatial metadata as promulgated by the United States GEOGRAPHIC SERVICES, which are part of a larger international collaboration (MOELLERING).

Because of chronological and spatial calculations, archeology has always been as much a numerate as visual study (FLETCHER & LOCK; ANDRESEN, ET. AL.). The trend is toward graphics analysis combined with clustering methods to determine spatial proximity that reveals horizontal layers of homogeneous development and vertical overlayers that add the dimension of time and chronological development (cf., ANDRESEN *ET AL.*; COOPER & RICHARDS; RICHARDS & RYAN). The goal of such perspective has been longstanding, but static representation prohibited its accomplishment. Still, as José Igartua reminds me, one can point to exceptional attempts such as the eighteenth-century three-dimensional rendering of Montreal's cityscape in the Canadian Centre for Architecture, which is carefully based on land titles and building contracts converted to individual pictures and then to a full-blown composition. Now such reconstruction can be accomplished routinely with sophisticated Computer-assisted Design (CAD) software such as *AutoCAD* 14 and such peripherals as symbol and components libraries. These allow three- dimensional representation from blueprints, drawings, and other schematics, and provide for approximate visualization with realistic perspective and conventional shapes and models. These symbols and standard shapes can be customized to approach any scenario, real or imagined, without starting a drawing from scratch. Scale and perspective are automatically calculated into the automated rendering.

CAD systems, based on vector graphics, seem especially powerful tools for historical reconstruction when used in combination with Geographic Information Systems (GIS). Archaeologists (e.g., OZAWA) also have long been very much interested in developing multi-layered (i.e., surface but also various strata to control data from excavations by depth which translates into time) GIS applications and systems designed for flood control and transportation planning for obvious conservation reasons. Such multi-dimensional GIS systems can coordinate: (1) underground utilities with archeological digs; (2) surface construction, habitation layouts, and transportation; and (3) sky control such as airport approach paths whereby air traffic can be steered away from wildlife areas, historic sites, or densely populated areas to save waterfowl and guard against accidents between airplanes and flying flocks, or save monuments from stress due to vibration and to save people from noise pollution. Apart from such applications, some cultural and others more pragmatic, these systems can also recreate simulations according to known patterns of flooding, storm paths, etc., correlated with human settlement and migration patterns, to assist the historian. Generally, however, historians have been less creative in the use of such technology than archeologists because the latter were more comfortable borrowing three-dimensional image technology from drafting and architecture. Archaeologists now seek to do more effectively with GIS systems what was done by plotters a decade ago (EFFLAND) by using CAD applications especially for modern urban architectural archeology (STENVERT). When they also employ holography to retain interactive three-dimensional information and present scenarios dynamically, sometimes from the vantage point of a tourist, the results are spectacular. Like architects and urban planners, they are also interested in topography or surface features as keys to whatever lies underneath new structures. Consequently, they are also taking advantage of satellite survey data, the production of isometric maps, and now digitized landscaping as well.

While these developments in industry and technology for surveying and other engineering and construction applications are not specifically designed for Anthropology and Archeology, these two fields are finding ready use for such technology. The time-lag, however, for such technical transfer has been about one decade. That is beginning to shorten, not because of industry's concern for these fields, but because of the technical training now being embedded into these disciplines. Particularly promising for history modeling and teaching is the evolution of integrated spatial information systems (LAURINI & THOMPSON) with visualization (BLONDE *ET AL.*). These involve the merger of geography and mapping by satellite positioning, archeology and site photography and video, sound, and animation all in one (KRAAK). The current development of "electro-techture" three-dimensional active maps used for military simulation will one day be available to relate historical scenarios with intervening and today's contours, events, and monuments.

No artifact or site seems impervious to new geo-historical visual analyses and representation. Not only are local history and archeological materials of interest to professional historians, but also to genealogists especially when museums and history centers record gravestone inscriptions (DUNK & RAHTZ) with interests more than to document brass rubbing templates, but also to see cemetery sculpture as commemorative art (J. WILSON) and to relate such images to prosopographical databases. G. STONE collated 40 variables in data elements coded from 4,500 photographs of tombstones to create a motif index by which to compare ten religious and polythematic areas for signs of socioeconomic status of the deceased and iconographic preferences linked to lineage. Low-tech less expensive projects in material culture and conservation have proven useful for historic preservation programs, as at the University of Manitoba, where images from the university's photographic archives were scanned into a campus information program for its physical plant operations (MOOSEBERGER & THOMPSON). When repair work or campus planning took place, the life-history of the campus and its buildings and grounds (original design, construction, and maintenance record over the years, complete with images, location grids, maps, and aerial views) is readily available to administrators and engineers alike. Such historical preservation databases attached to GIS systems are already evolving as intricate integrated urban information systems in Europe combining engineering with historical preservation (ARLAUD, HAMMARCHE & LUROL). In Lyon, France, such systems track ground-level mapping with underground archeological surveys and even traffic patterns in the sky overhead so that historic landmarks are protected from vibration deterioration from overhead, traffic can be rerouted to stop pollution on ground, and potential digs remain inviolate from street repairs and excavation for construction until their possibilities are examined.

More elaborate projects are likewise being developed at the larger research museums, and their applications are being adopted or imitated in state and local museums and history centers in America and throughout Europe. It is no more uncommon to find computer-assisted guides and reference supports in museums than to see kiosks with public-access terminals pulling data for customers from the *All Music Guide* in music stores. Or, consider the GIS system for the metropolitan area of St. Louis, which has been customized as a locator reference tool in the St. Louis Public Library for direct access by patrons.

The general public is beginning to expect more elaborate, interactive information access in libraries and museums (HOLSINGER); educated people will expect it of historical information as well, in all kinds of settings including their homes. While most instructional technology and design studies pertain to classroom use, S. PURCEL in exploring public instruction built a model system for the Virginia Museum of Natural History at VPI. His analyses were both to produce a digital motion-video product and to document the design process, so he was also able to provide a useful set of media-development guidelines for public historians and museum personnel. SCRAMNet-LX offers a multi-computer and video camera system capability to project a background environment with floor and ceiling, and to place three-dimensional moving objects in the foreground so that action filmed in one location can be superimposed into a setting filmed entirely separate, to create situations which seem real enough, but which never actually happened. Sense8, a California manufacturer of Virtual Reality software for microcomputers, has already demonstrated its three-dimensional tour capabilities for art galleries, with a three-dimensional sensibility that you are there seeing what the camera does and hearing soundtracks both of background noise and foreground commentary. Disney World has been using such technology to create simulated rides, by placing the viewer on moving platforms that rock and roll in accord with three-dimensional views and Dolbystereo sound tracks. Such amusements are hits with the American public who then expect simulation in education to be equally sophisticated—and equally entertaining. Public historians have been forewarned by the California Cultural Heritage Data Management Advisory Committee (1986) to keep abreast with information technology such as GIS development because it is impacting archeology, anthropology, and historic preservation (C. WETHERELL). Educators have also been warned that "virtual education" may be equally unreal and short-lived.

The University of Illinois' development of the CAVE prototype ("Cave," named after Plato's concept of cultural formation circumscribed by the space in which one is reared) for multi-dimensional Virtual Reality projection on four walls and the ceiling allows the viewer to get inside the creation. This is the breakthrough for the immersive media touted for the next millennium. It, like the Habitat project of Lukas Films, Inc., or the work going on at MIT's Media Lab (BRAND), represents the movement beyond Cinerama and widescreen film projection and Dolby stereo sound toward insertion of the viewer/listener into the middle of the environment, where he or she is transformed into an "experiencer" in history (or historical fiction) by participating with the surrounding interactive media. As already hinted, one can imagine the track of such developmental research leading to something like the holideck envisioned by *Star Trek* writers (FARMER; HENDERSEN). Its uses were always altruistic; viewers were not introduced to the downside of human uses for such technology as experienced with the trafficking of pornography over the Internet and its widespread marketing via the Web. Unfortunately, Virtual Reality applications in the games and entertainment industry, under criticism for their propensity to display graphic violence so actively and realistically, or to display explicit sex indiscriminately for a nondiscriminating audience, seem to be proliferating far faster than cultural and educational applications. So, the trajectory for such technical development does not seem that clear, despite good intentions.

Deviations and turns can come with remarkably short notice. When more data visualization systems become affordable and advance to the stage of the IBM prototype (REILLY & WALTER) of the Roman baths at Bath, England, wherein a viewer can virtually "walk" through the model (depicted as the actual ruins or idealized restorations, where virtual reality enhancements in the electronically reconstructed models present problems for those wanting a reality check, such as R. D. SPICER), they will contribute to computer-assisted research, education, and public programs—as IBM-UK demonstrated in 1988 so well at the Cologne Computer Conference with what has been called the "Sid and Dora's Bath Show." The demonstration has been retired before it could even generate enough interest and capital investment for implementation in History and Archeology education. The high prototype costs came down dramatically, but within a half-decade this technology, which dazzled historians then, was superseded within three years. It is a far cry from other immersive archeological virtual-reality projects such as that recreating Pompeii before its destruction in 79 B.C. "Virtual Pompeii" can be toured at Carnegie Mellon University's SimLab headed by Carl Loeffler.

Since the decade-old experimentation with virtual recreations such as the baths of Bath, IBM has expanded its vista by backing Scott Ross' new company, Digital Domain, for enterprises more profitable than History and Archeology. Prototyping such technology may be accomplished in the laboratory within academe but it cannot be sustained without fruitful application. One neglected ally is the entertainment industry where scale affords experimentation greater than what can be done inside the university, similar to the absorption of initial high costs in CD-ROM technology by a few companies and the dramatic reduction in cost when a huge market was found by the music industry. The education establishment cannot accomplish such development alone, and must co-opt the entertainment industry. Such applications of visualization and immersive technology to history simply pale in contrast to the innovations associated with George Lucas, "the magician" whose Industrial Light and Magic Corporation is "erasing the line between fantasy and reality" (LANE, p. 122).

Hollywood deception has become so good that viewers cannot tell anymore if something is filmed on site, in a studio, or in computer simulation. Consider a recent time line of make-belief events which could be applied to depictions of historical events or inserted into any visual record: *Star Wars* (1977) saw motion control of cameras for action-packed and breathtaking simulated battle scenes; *Star Trek II: the Wrath of Kahn*'s Genesis sequence (1982) was the first completely computer-generated scene; the 1985 version of *Young Sherlock Holmes* had the intrepid hero meeting the first computer-generated character, the stained glass man; *Willow* (1988) and the *Abyss* (1989) introduced the American public to "Morfing" to produce three-dimensional characters; *Terminator 2: Judgment Day* (1991) had morfed amorphous characters dissolving into their surroundings; *The Young Indiana Jones Chronicles (1992),* unlike *Gone with the Wind* which used wax dummies for extras, "simply" replicated digitally the extras and placed them on digitally created backgrounds; in 1993 *Death Becomes Her* characters sport digitally created skin and twirling heads; and *Jurassic Park* (1993) brought all of these accomplishments together in one blockbuster and its sequel in 1997 provided a second look at the same physical models and virtual creatures produced by a combination of modeling, puppeteering, and virtual duplication, that magically through modern history and prehistory together as only dreamed by H. G. Wells. In 1995, *Casper* accomplished what hitherto had stymied human digital replication, namely hair, replicated strand by strand, and "standing on end."

Forest Gump (1994) was the first time that history was purposefully distorted by digital recreation, however, when the hero was made to meet President John F. Kennedy. In this presentation digital editing made a double-amputation look real on a moving character, crowds at football games were replicated, for once and always Ping-Pong balls moved as they were supposed to, and helicopters flew without the expense of flying any into the set (LANE). It is in the encounter with the unknown, the alien, that such imagery has been used most spectacularly, with the understated charm of *ET* to overstated catastrophe in *Independence Day*. The year 1997 brought an array of fast action yarns with the greatest mix of real and surreal ever. When the virtual is also outlandish and surreal as in the recreation of the comic book *Men in Black*, it is indeed comical and is easily dismissed as unreal; when it is carefully disguised as real, the distinction between real and virtual in many viewers' eyes becomes blurred, the mind's eye becomes confused, and the possibilities for historical reconstruction, deconstruction, distortion, and substitution, become threatening and sinister. Now such virtual inserts into film are considered normal; they are expected to be there; and they are expected to be as undetectable as ubiquitous. Spielberg's collaboration with Dreamworks to recreate history on film as in *Saving Private Ryan* is the most recent illustration of how far such visualization technology has come, where the test of virtual reality is the emotional response so strong that the recreation is accepted as real…for the moment, and in lingering flashbacks. In *Star Wars, Episode I: The Phantom Menace* (1999) the entire film by George Lucas mixes virtual reality with animation and motion-picture recording all in the name of future history: "We, the members of the Jedi Council, have created this record of those terrible events. This recording device has captured the images and sounds of the struggle, so that future generations will remember (script by J. Whiman & M. Oppenheimer, in film prologue).

Seeing is no longer believing. Or, seeing the unreal, recreated, imitative, or virtual may induce belief and emotion as strong as actual experience. Some hold that "Show me" is better than any other method of explanation; this is the proverbial Doubting Thomas position. But "Show and tell" seem to go together best. Even so, knowing and believing may not always go together. That does distinguish modern sensibilities from turn-of-the-century notions about objective history and actuality. Indeed, belief itself is not a constant, but needs to be suspended regularly. The difference, however, between "make-believe" and "made to believe" is that in the former situation the viewer has control; in the latter, the viewer is controlled. Studies have explored how children differentiate the virtual from real, as in television, more than they have for adults. In the latter cases, concern has been on destructive role images, as in drug use, or on violence and the virtual predisposition of viewers for violent action. Fewer studies have explored the media's impact on historical understanding except for historical fiction and films, but not at greater depth in exploring the impact of virtual reality and immersive technology.

The impact of virtuality and fiction on history and representation of evidence is everywhere. Virtual reality is influencing how documentation is represented visually in information systems design. The graphical display of bibliographic data is often of current interest to library information science, for example, and increasingly the visual mapping of concepts with the display of real objects and texts is creating a new interplay between traditional media. Information storage and retrieval systems thereby are converted into dynamic, interactive decision-support and learning multimedia systems (for a unified conceptualization, cf., F. HALASZ; SOERGEL, etc.) that enable a flexibility described by CARLSON & RAM as "hyperintelligence." Thus ISAR and CAI/CAL are becoming two aspects of the same integrated process (H. BURTON). The subject matter is often historical so that when archival documentation, images, and texts are digitized to form "Virtual Libraries" with increasingly sophisticated search capabilities and multi-window and multi-screen displays, a remarkable informative, educational, and entertaining product is delivered. Windowing, for example, now allows simultaneous searching of online databases and OPACs while retaining reference screens from other searches or one's work space in full view. Larger screens make feasible multiple windows and the addition of dynamic images such as video along side still frames for visual searching. People are capable of pattern match scans at remarkable speeds when visual frames in classified order as demonstrated by CHEN in locating museum objects and art from classified frames matched against frozen frames from video. The same techniques work in automated tours of buildings, exhibits, and terrains when combined with GIS technology.

The Smithsonian Institution began using video to document oral history sessions and interviews in the early 1980s, so that it now has amassed a considerable image resource by which to compose "videohistory" (SCHORZMAN). The most interesting applications are well beyond this stage, however, in flight and driving simulations, services for the physically handicapped, for medical and sports diagnostics, and new forms of three-dimensional virtual reality rides in Disney World. Unfortunately for education and the world of archives, libraries, and museums, much of the relevant literature is still in the "how-to" stage, with a focus on the technology itself, pervasive worry about start-up costs, and a tendency to "wow" prospective audiences and funding agencies. Hopefully, research on utility, effectiveness, and interplay with other media and traditional library and archives materials will follow. For now, such developments are proceeding largely as self-motivated technical experiments on the basis of assumptions rather than on hard evidence or well constructed theory, but certainly there are a plethora of untested futuristic promises.

One of the most promising projects, because of the collaboration in its development if for nothing more, is the University of Southern California's new *Information System for Los Angeles (ISLA)* which envisions a multimedia databased collection for the history of Los Angeles. *ISLA* will become, so its originators proclaim, a comprehensive and integrated electronic source for texts, photographs, maps, datasets, etc., which is supposed to allow users "to analyze the history and social dynamics of Los Angeles in new ways" (unpublished *ISLA* prospectus, fall 1994). "This new type of library research collection will be based upon networked state-of-the-art computer hardware and software including database, search-and-retrieval, and analytical systems; it will require the development of new kinds of data structures allowing readers to understand the relationship of multimedia archival documents with a subject/space/time indexing system." It is an undertaking of USC's Center for Scholarly Technology (CST) within the University Library, which expects input from fourteen disciplines and collaboration between the library and the university's computer services. It is the kind of people's history envisioned by FLOUD and others but in a different, expanded sense of collaborative scholarship, and it is a "doing history" production on the grand scale, larger than could have been forecast by HEXTER. Moreover, it also represents both the syncretism and fragmentation of History today, in that historical documentation is thus retrievable, and such systems may provide assistance in analysis as well as collation of records, but it does not produce a history as such or guarantee any synthesis, problem resolution, or specific outcome. Its purpose is mainly to inform and enlighten, but not necessarily to interpret for the viewer or reader, and thus it could be subject to the same limitations of chronicles in supplying fact with implicit appraisal for data selection, but not explicit analysis, as distinct from histories. Or, in its richness, the experience may produce what Andre VIEL called "nonoriented time and ambivalence." Instead of a history, its supports multiple histories, and thus champions the notion of every man being his or her own historian.

Similarly, such projects as the Packard Humanities Institute's *American Founding Fathers Project* makes every user his or her own editor, since its CD-ROMs provide the unedited papers of Franklin, Adams, Washington, Madison, and Jefferson. The traditional intermediary, the professional historian or documentary editor, could be removed to a consultancy or deistic role for such systems, rather than remaining integral to the ongoing information and teaching, unless placed into the process by some institutional authority. Users at home or in libraries will seek recourse to historians at their discretion, and if historians are in their offices or classrooms, the convenience factor will mitigate against this interaction. The historian's role may be confined to the canned interview as part of the program, unless forms of interactivity are designed other than adherence to classroom lecturing and mere copying of this environment into a scripted and taped video that runs sequentially. Proverbial "talking heads" are easily captured on video, edited, and spliced into such media presentations; real personalities and engaging teachers are well preserved in this pickling process. While such media present some dangers, they also are opportunities. Such virtual libraries and archives may be used as teaching and epistemological laboratories, but they are dependent on a certain heuristics which come from previous experience or are transferred by creative methods into the new media. For all of the discussion about active learning and the arsenal already at our disposal (surveyed in a later discussion on history teaching), relatively little is known about the learning of history through multimedia, the formation of culture and acculturation from the point of view in the Humanities and Arts, or history's utility from the Social Science vantage point, other than certain shopworn clichés about using the past for present decisions to influence the future. Think tanks such as the MIT Media Lab need to direct serious research toward such history and learning issues and investigate the interplay between textuality, orality, and visualization specifically in regard to History.

The significance of pilot projects, therefore, goes way beyond the technology itself; they forecast a newer "New History," of History forever renewed, for which we have not even invented a proper vocabulary. Nor have we reformed teaching habits and expansion to new modes of service as in Distance Learning to prepare for such change. From one perspective, is not all History distance learning? Is the substantive difference in how this metaphor is used today only a matter of electronic technology? Or, is it a question of multiple technologies which have their own histories from which to learn? Converging technologies may be forcing a convergence of disciplines and professional roles, especially with the current trend away from any form of personal intermediation and increased reliance on multimedia and therefore, mediation by software. Little research is being conducted on current mediation in the study of history, but historians are studying such issues in other areas, at other times. The future will have histories, but perhaps no unifying history. The degree of interaction with historians remains to be seen, and in the resolution of this question lies the fate of the professional historian. The result may be even greater fragmentation, increased relativism, and heightened individual isolationism or lack of identity, while nevertheless being very well informed, visually stimulated, and technically hopped up—and technologically dependent.

Although such current projects as mentioned in this survey point to the future, it is difficult to track a small number of them and more difficult still to make sense of the current milieu. The line of development and the cast for the future scenario can be seen in the history of some productions. An early model program for visual information retrieval was developed to handle over 10,000 archeological surveys from Japan at the National Research Institute in Tokyo (OIKAWA) which holds scanned analog images and drawings for all artifacts which are stored in microfilm, relates them to schematic drawings and photographs of digs, and to full-test information retrieval including electronic transcriptions of notebooks. Yet, this pioneer project saw little duplication despite efforts by its creators to highlight its features at numerous conferences. Few historians were equipped to understand the technology, and even if they wanted to, access to developmental laboratories for such enhanced historical research were limited. The limitations were more than technical; they were also financial, assuredly; but more, they have been conceptual. Some of these earlier analog-based projects are converting to digitized programs to make use of greater flexibility in recently developed technologies. Such collections as surveys with line-drawing and schematic sketches such as architectural drawings and certain kinds of maps, are liable to retrieval by pattern recognition compared with user's input drawings with light pens or outlines using "graph browsers" (BAGG & RYAN) rather than keyboarding terms and text *(BYTE)*. Standards for descriptions of architectural drawings (PORTER & THORNES) have been devised mainly by two working groups in the United States: the Architectural Drawings Group (ADAG) and the Foundation for Documents of Architecture (FDA) at the Center for Advanced Study in the Visual Arts at the National Gallery of Art in Washington, D.C. The human communications and cultural political problem is how to relate the one project in the United States to another, in Japan for example, to create a globally accessible multimedia resource. Standardized description for textual retrieval combined with pattern and outline searching, with full image retrieval, would create a dynamic tool for architectural history. Moreover, the AI components of such systems development will have broad applications to engineering as well, so the architectural, artistic, and technological components of material culture may soon come together in interactive systems. What has History to contribute to such developments? Potentially much; probably nothing unless within History a Historical Information Science evolves that is inter-disciplinary, collaborative, and technically advanced.

AI applications are also being employed to use pattern matching algorithms to retrieve by shapes (GRACA *ET AL.*), often in conjunction with cataloging data identifying images and electronic version of older microcards that stored miniature digital photo-inserts on them, so users see a Boolean-searched set of images (e.g., known portraits of certain individuals, sorted to satisfy a query specifying when someone was young or old) displayed and ranked from highest to least probability of matches based on image descriptive elements, patterns, and textual information. Such developments are parallel but somewhat anachronistic with others. Medical diagnostic systems were among the first expert systems to connect image bases with text retrieval and natural-language enquiry, as when a surgeon needs an immediate comparison of an exposed tissue or damaged organ with one that is normal and an array of abnormalities. Slide projection hardly sufficed in such situations; analog image retrieval did better, and digitized manipulatable imagery does even better now. Such image-based systems operate with matching programs by sorting variants (size, coloration, etc.) with scanned images from the actual operation, they arrange images in schema measured by degrees of similarity and statistical probability, and they collate image-based information with parallel interactive databases such as case histories, symptoms, and current condition. In most cases these are decision-support systems rather than automatic diagnostic tools. The incorporation of pixels to hold a digitized image in a textual record and the inclusion of a combination of texts and images in relational databases (sometimes called a BLOB, for "Binary Large Object Database") provides depiction and description together, and requires a combination of key word, subject, and image retrieval systems working together (R. CATTELL).

Such systems, pioneered in medicine and space research, are being applied to other fields such as art, archaeology, forensics, and conservation (LUNIN, 1992; 1994, p. 66). What works on a lunar landscape is applicable to Earth geography as well; surgical procedural documentation and feedback mechanisms work also for forensics other than pathology such as in book and art conservation; and autopsy techniques or oral and visual documentation can be transferred to archaeological sites. Such information technology transfer is ongoing at a rate and scale hitherto impossible especially as the technology moves from high-cost innovative projects to duplicated application areas. History by itself may not be able to pioneer such high-tech solutions to its problems, but it can be more adoptive than it is. In such sophisticated hybrid multi-based systems, art, artifact, geographic location and landscape for context, and comparable images are retrieved similar to multi-media projects that are also archaeological and anthropologically oriented (i.e., CHEN). Object-oriented programming is promoting such transference surrogates (KHOSHAFIAN; KHOSHAFIAN & ABNOUS). Analog and digital technology are used together, and hypertext interfaces are proving popular for linking text and image in information retrieval systems (MOLINE, 1989). Special attention in IBM's Tokyo Research Laboratory is being paid to high resolution color windows suitable for ethnographic material and museum artifacts (HONG & SUGITA). The same approach is being contemplated for digital libraries of manuscripts and archives such as *ISLA*, which will destabilize texts but will also reconstruct them with images transported from other contexts. Possibly confusing, mostly enhancing, and always with intriguing interaction. Rather than text removed from the medium which originally carried it, digitized facsimile reproduction can convey text and artifactual context not possible in paper edition and which will conserve detailed variance usually suppressed and lost in critical edition work as this has evolved since the Middle Ages. It is likely, based on prototypes already tested, that future expert systems will be integrated into complex technologies that scan manuscripts, date and analyze scripts, use pattern recognition and feature diagnostics for smart retrieval of exemplars for further refinement and integration of data, text, and image, and will learn from saved searches. Already past the experimental stage in space exploration, medical research, and engineering, which are absorbing the development costs, such technology is now finding its way into social science, humanities, and art applications.

Perhaps no development in electronic image sources and photo-archives has stirred speculation more than Bill Gates' purchase in 1995 of the famous Otto Bettman Archives, which hold an estimated 16 million images, including major runs of image documentation for social history dating from 1935, and of significance for the arts as well. Many of its treasures such as Matthew Brady's Civil War pictures and shots of Rosa Parks' historic bus ride in Montgomery, Alabama, have been featured in many documentary films. In 1989, Gates quietly formed a privately held company separate from Microsoft, Inc., called Corbis Corporation, under CEO Doug Rowan, who explains that the venture into photo-archives will lead to the pursuit of film, video, and audio sources as well, all to be digitized and distributed, for a price, over the Internet. Rowan is quoted by *Fortune* (1995 Dec. 11; 132[12], p. 38) as saying: "We want to capture the entire human experience throughout history." The core of the Corbis Mission statement is "one company serving as collector, distributor and storyteller...to provide digital access to the images of yesterday, today and tomorrow" (http://www.corbis.com). It was the Bettman acquisition that called major attention to Corbis, but in fact the company had already amassed holdings of more than 500,000 images before the deal, including nonexclusive rights to images from St. Petersburg Hermitage Museum to MIT School of Architecture and Planning's drawings. Other deals are being struck weekly with museums for nonexclusive electronic distribution of their holdings in exchange for royalties. Award winning CD-ROM products are already available from Corbis (e.g., *Passion for Art: Renoir, Cezanne, Matisse* paintings from the Barnes collection; *Critical Mass: America's Race to Build the Atomic Bomb*; *Volcanoes: Life on the Edge*; *FDR*; and *Leonardo da Vinci*). *Times* (1995 Oct.; 146[17], p. 107) called the merger of Gate's bankroll, image archives, and Microsoft technology "a marriage made in cyberheaven" and *Fortune* magazine has called attention to Gate's strategy in creating convenience for "one-stop shopping" in the world's audiovisual and art marketplace. Today, the visual archives already hold more than 17 million images!

It remains to be seen what kinds of intellectual access are created to retrieve images from such a massive mega-collection, but one suspects that the pioneer efforts of individual museums to date to create image archives will pale by comparison. Moreover, the sheer mass of such a resource makes possible an integration of visuals never before possible, so that combined with new technology and movement into virtual systems, one is hard pressed to imagine what history in the future will look like. One certainty is clear, however, is that such developments spell a major re-alignment between text and image if not actual merger in the future reconstruction of history. It also is indicative of a new development in public/private history turned entrepreneurial, where access to historical material will be a fee-paid service. Such developments may further divide the two traditions in archives, where the manuscripts strain becomes more businesslike and records management, already in business, may become even more private except in government.

Such developments challenge historians in ways not previously thought possible, to reconceptualize how history is done and presented. The movement to interactive user-controlled virtual systems offers viewers unbridled access to a rich storehouse of historical data, documents, and texts, images and sounds, but not always structure, schematics, or even sequence. These resources reflect both the syncretism and fragmentation of History today, in that historical documentation is thus retrievable, and such systems may provide assistance as well as collation of records, but do not produce a history as such, or guarantee any synthesis, problem resolution, or specific outcome. Their purpose is mainly to inform and enrich but not necessarily to interpret for the viewer or reader, so it may not enlighten or enhance understanding unless some sense of context, continuity, and perspective is brought to bear on data acquisition. Otherwise such information even when delivered in new formats and a variety of media can still be subject to the limitations of chronicles of old in supplying fact with implicit appraisal behind the data selection, but no rationale, explicit analysis, or reinterpretation as one should get in histories. Historian commentaries are often interspersed in history-telling so one receives the story line and explication at the same time; the image in word or illustration is usually not left to speak for itself.

Readers have always had the option of going after the story line with less attention to the running commentary, but in new media the historian's history, as distinct from the raw materials of the past, can be bypassed altogether and ignored. Optional History is likely to produce fragmented histories and a free reign of impressionism, rich in imagery but poor in sense making. In such richness is the common experience what VIEL calls "nonoriented time and ambivalence?" Instead of a history, these tools form recollections, they support multiple histories, and thus this trend seems to champion the notion of everyone being his or her own historian by shifting the burden of historical reconstruction to the receiver, viewer, and hearer. The assumption from past generations, of course, was that this pertained to educated men and women already equipped with a critical sense, practiced judgment, perspective, and context from a broad, liberal arts education. Such assumptions no longer seem justified. What this means sociologically at a greater depth than its immediate entertainment possibilities, a romanticized democratic appeal, or superficial satisfaction of human curiosity, is not well understood.

The integration of data, text, and image in historical research requires a breadth that is difficult to achieve. Today's technological advances, however, have made low-end applications more simple, so beginning is easier; they have expanded the high-end options, so there is more to accomplish when moving beyond neophyte status toward expertise. Mastery must be reached in a technological field, an array of techniques and methodology, and a discipline-based domain as well. If graduate training in History continues to be intra-disciplinary with attempts to achieve a mastery over content rather than methodology, such technical expertise may be impossible to acquire within the confines of traditionally conceived programs. It may make more sense to focus on methodological and technical training in degree programs and to acknowledge that content must be self-mastered during life-long learning. Moreover, to bridge the traditional gap between disciplines and cut through the departmentalization that characterizes academe, History needs to develop a field of studies capable of building the methodological and technological expertise to relate to this larger world of information organizations, standards, systems, networks, and exchange. The transfer of technology information and technology itself to History are processes worthy of specialization in their own right. Otherwise, such important work is left to professional historians who are amateurs outside their fields, or conversely, when technologists with no historical training engage in the practice of History, the result may be equally problematic. It is easier, however, to train a computer literate and interested historian in Computer Science, than it is to foster the opposite transition. Such specialization in source-oriented computing is what THALLER calls for, which he calls Historical Computer Science.

The development of Historical Information Science might be conceived even more broadly. It would bridge the gap between computing and history by applying the former to the latter, but would also assist in nurturing computer science development of software appropriate for historical research and archives, would embed a historical dimension in program design and an archival component in information systems, and would expand historical research capabilities to control more data in multi-formats especially with more involvement in the protection of and creation of access to its own sources. It would do the following: include self-study of historians and the historical profession, practice, and communication; develop new methodologies and explore knowledge representation for improved communication of results; and it would create career options other than teaching history and professional flexibility that enhance History and those areas into which historians would venture because of their technical training and broad education. It would ideally promote technological transference between fields and provide computing with an intellectual dimension it now lacks. History, thus, could fulfill better its traditional role of syncretism and synthesis among the various disciplines and between the Social Sciences and the Arts and Humanities. That is a cardinal role of a unidiscipline.

MEDIEVAL STUDIES AND ELECTRONIC SOURCES: EXEMPLARY SYNCRETISM

Medieval studies are often seen as esoteric and marginal by those imbued with the modernist notions of presentism, relevance of the contemporary, and stereotyping of such interests as antiquarian (meaning that they lack potential for innovation). One might be surprised that a field rooted in dead languages and a distant past, indeed "dark ages" made more remote by such notions, widespread ignorance and lack of historical knowledge, could be quite "with it" in terms of new thinking, methods, and information technology. Perhaps no historical field of study brings together traditionally disparate disciplines in the fusion process characterizing modern scholarship, or illustrates some of the most difficult intellectual and technical problems in database development and computer-assisted analysis, as does Medieval Studies. This is perhaps because of an intellectual preparation by the Annalistes interjecting geography, cultural anthropology, and quantification into studies of the Middle Ages, but also because medieval history in particular, and related studies in art, religion, and literature, tend to be comparative and hence interdisciplinary at the onset, reliant on a facility in foreign languages and philology, difficult comparative methodologies, and seemingly impenetrable sources that require refined criticism. Other fields may be selected to illustrate similar points, but a field so complex as medieval studies seems to make the case for the integration of information technology and the fusion of Social Science methodologies into what is commonly seen as part of the Humanities even more compelling. If medievalists with their language and source problems, and seemingly esoteric studies, can adopt to modern information technology and analytical methods, could not those in less demanding fields? Moreover, medieval history is a field which I know well enough to illustrate my case for an integral Historical Information Science.

Formed in the United States at the turn of the century (or in CANTOR's words, "invented") as one of the first fields of comparative history and inter-disciplinarity, while the Middle Ages were treated in Europe predominantly within the chronological periodization of national histories (i.e., medieval parallel to colonial history), Medieval History often explores the origins of things even before their development allows a vocabulary to mature that defines and describes them: when personal naming and authorship were coming out of conceptual stages but were hardly standardized in practice either by convention or orthography and place-names were far from official but were largely a matter of custom; when even initial punctuation was an enhancement of text transmission, if texts could be found; when the raw data shelved for centuries in archives are encrypted in highly abbreviated and barely legible scripts as well as a variety of languages with evolving grammars and vocabularies; and when the sources appear as worn and sometimes fragmentary documents, and as often in loose piles and tied bundles as in bound codices. It has a rich, diverse, multicultural and multilingual historiography (as exemplified *par excellence* by the 1989 international congress on medieval historiography at the University of Paris [GENET, ed., 1991]), but where modern information technology was largely ignored.

In addition to the problems of source criticism in reconstructing medieval history is the perennial debate about when the Middle Ages began and ended—if they ever did or, if the conceptualization is valid at all, other than as a reaction against the concept of the Renaissance. C. HOLLISTER most recently argued for reconsideration of the Middle Ages as a really distinctive phase in European history. PIRENNE took up this issue of periodization and classification as perhaps no other medievalist, but although his famous thesis about the beginning of the Middle Ages found widespread acceptance in Medieval History, his broader conceptualization of world history as thematic processes, classifying history into "currents"(1948) more fluidly and dynamically conceived than organic units, entities, or periods, never received the attention it deserved even when his theme was resurrected for the 1990 world Congress of Historical Sciences (CISH). The metaphor of "seasons" applied to human life cycles is sometimes applied to societies, cultures, and civilizations, in which everyone and everything has a "Middle Age" that is more expandable and contractible, depending on health and longevity, than a simply biologically conditioned or preordained period.

The point is again to illustrate how historical conceptualization and periodization are fundamental to classification, even though this historiographic debate made no impact on the neoclassicists who had a few years earlier embedded nineteenth-century notions into both the Dewey and Library of Congress classification schemes. Continued debate about classification and periodization in History remains so theoretical and uninformed from Information Science that it has had little impact on operating systems or on the terminologies that govern our information retrieval systems. Whether it is politically correct to substitute "encounter" for "discovery" in historical jargon has had little impact on information systems outside of projects inside given specialties. Historians have normally followed social and political trends, as when using designated official languages or reverting to sub-languages and regional languages, without the kind of input they could contribute to formal systems. Medievalists, of course, have always had the option, a luxury and as such an elitist opportunity, to revert to Latin for standardization. But even then, problems of regionalism and states of language development and standardization in the Middle Ages make this issue more complex than it would first appear, especially if R. WRIGHT is correct in seeing standard Latin as an overlay on indigenous Romance. Such linguistic issues are not only a question of formal literature, as too commonly presumed, but should be inspected from the vantage point of Information Science for information handling, systems formation and maintenance, communications, and administrative history in the conduct of human affairs.

In the United States, Medieval History evolved contemporary with scientific historicism, and thus reacted with aversion to nineteenth-century Romanticism even though the latter remained important for its growth in America. Some of the attraction of the Middle Ages lay in their difference from modernity, and medieval studies often acted as a form of social criticism around the turn of the century. Its antimodernism has remained a cultural contrapuntal trait. The early phase of medieval studies focused on law and institutional forms of government, including the formation of Western values such as primitive democracy in German tribalism. The field was heavily reliant on philology and source criticism in the German tradition since Henry Adams and Herbert Baxter Adams studied there. This orientation of American medievalists switched to France after World War II, but it adhered to the established interpretative program of continuity whereby medieval Europe was viewed as the incubus for American values (COURTENAY surveys the growth of medieval studies, 1870-1930). Thus, the Middle Ages were not a pre-history for American history, they were its not-so-far-off progenitor.

Continuity between the New and Old Worlds was a fundamental assumption after Charles H. Haskins so demonstrably attacked in his *Renaissance of the Twelfth Century* the Burkhardian discontinuity thesis that the early-modern Renaissance, had been a significant break between medieval and modern times. Haskins and his protoégés thought of American history as an extension of the West since its late antique/early medieval foundation (cf., his biography by VAUGHAN). The textbook of his outstanding student, Joseph Strayer, formed a canonical core for medieval history, and a generation of medievalists trained by him dominated the field through the 1970s (CANTOR, pp. 245-286). K. MORRISON, in a study that actually classified and counted dissertations and Haskins' medals from the Medieval Academy is one of the earliest and closest approximations to a bibliometric analysis taken by an historian to historiography, portrayed this academic oligarchy during the 1960s and 1970s and its research agenda which supplied Americans with a recognizable past in early-modern and medieval England. This monolithic interpretation of the Middle Ages began to break down, however, after the 1970s, when the variety of medieval cultures was reemphasized (CONSTABLE). Moreover, the rest of Europe including its frontiers and borderlands with other cultures came under study with a dramatic shift of attention, methodology, and interpetation from the old geographic concentration on England and northern France, and that one exception to the secular state, the medieval papacy. A notable rediscovery of the Mediterranean world by German historians at the Frei Universitat in Berlin brought back the Crusades, now in the larger context of the continuing encounter between Islam and the Christian regimes of the East and West. Southern French historians from Toulouse crossed over the Pyrenees with ease turning their backs toward Paris to reorient themselves to how Catalan and Provencal cultures had been more united culturally and politically for most of the Middle Ages than between the north and south of modern France. And in Anglo-American medieval historiography, Luso-Hispanic studies experienced a Renaissance with renewed interest in socioeconomic and cultural history rolled into one and consideration of Christian, Muslim, and Jewish interaction. Since 1970, some 45 Iberian-focused dissertations were written in English at the universities of Cambridge, Toronto, Fordham, Princeton, Virginia, and California (Berkeley and Los Angeles), with the most notable impact on the profession coming from UCLA where R. I. Burns produced a stream of trend-setting ethnohistorical works and coached 25 doctoral recipients through their research (MCCRANK, 1995). Since then medieval studies have tended to delve into specific areas and times, and with this specialization has come not only a breakdown of older general-izations stretching across too large a territory and time, but an appreciation for local and regional culture. Moreover, the comfortable homogeneity of the older synthesis has given way to as much attention to differences as commonalities, and discontinuities and even strangeness (the "grotesque" in P. FREEDMAN's characterization) which make the history of the Middle Ages more like opening up the X-Files than an excursion through a familiar past.

The latest characterization of medieval studies in America by FREEDMAN & SPEIGEL takes up several themes woven into this bibliographic essay. They stress the renewal of the older notion of medieval "alterity" from modern times, but with several interpretative twists and as part of a larger movement in scholarship in recent time:

> Unlike the attention devoted to the state of individuality, the distinction between a tolerant and an intolerant Middle Ages has survived and even flourished. Indeed, it has proven central to the deployment of a new notion of medieval "alterity," whose beginnings can be traced to the late 1970s and which has created a new landscape of concerns that could have been anticipated. What has not survived is the optimistic belief in a progressive Middle Ages embodying pluralism, rational-ity, and self-knowledge. In its place is a renewed emphasis on a reiterated strange-ness....The changes it experienced were part of a much broader movement, which, from the perspective of the 1990s, can be seen as the importation and adaptation of postmodernism into the heart of American scholarship in all fields (p. 693)....

> ...the most powerful sense of the Middle Ages current in the academy is what goes under the name of its alterity, for that alterity offers the best means of escaping from the model of total identification that was the chief mode of studying the Middle Ages in the past. What has changed in the postmodern understanding of medieval alterity, and serves sharply to distinguish it from the earlier construction of it, is the simultaneity of our desire for history and the recognition of its irrepara-ble loss, a loss we longer can, or care to, mask beneath the modernist guise of con-tinuity and progress (p. 703).

They note (pp. 694-97) that medieval historians "were slow to take up the challenge of post-modernism." But they do attribute the dramatic changes of the last few years to the following: (1) the emergence of feminist historiography and gender studies; (2) "the rejection of possitivist certainties and foundationalism of the 'old' historicism—together with its implicit, universaliz-ing humanism—in favor of a 'new' historicism that took its lead from the creation of 'discourse' studies" in cultural history; and (3) the so-called "linguistic turn" which they term as "a trans-formation in the understanding of documents as texts rather than sources." In all three respects, their insight mirrors what has been said in this essay, but in this case from the specific vantage point of contemporary medieval studies. The wording may change, as when causality translates into "foundationalism" or "search for origins" as a sign of the presence of positivism no matter how well it is disguised (history used in the quest for cultural foundations is described by FRANTZEN; or, put in another way, "the construction of social identity" as in the case of Anglo-Saxonism revived in the nineteenth century to define Englishness, as described by those contributing to a collection of essays assembled by FRANTZEN & NILES, eds.). In any case, these respected medievalists also appreciate the reflexive nature of historical discourse, as noted so clearly in the relationship between current political awareness and the framing of questions by historians.

This reflexivity also pertains to presentation of the more distant past and its relevance to the contemporary reader, listener, or viewer, and adoption of the term "representation" with a slightly different slant than as used in information fields like graphic-user interface design, modeling, and mediation.

> As a result of this development, the idea of history has been transformed from narration to representation, based on the conviction that the investigation of the past occurs only through the mediatory and mediating texts it bequeaths, and, therefore, what is "recovered" is not so much the truth of the past as the images of itself that the past produces (FREEDMAN & SPIEGEL, p. 697).

They quote E. VANCE (p. 227) in reference to this "new medievalism" that is "a science not of things and deeds but of discourses; an art not of facts but of encoding of facts." In this sense, historians seem to have discovered what has been known in Information Science for some time, namely the difference between data and metadata, the pervasive need to model for comparison and contrast in order to construct knowledge, and the importance of representation in communication with a user community. These phenomena are not new; their recognition in History is. And historians approach such issues differently, less technically and more philosophically, than in Information Science. The main difference, however, is enlarged perspective enabled by time and distance, leading to generality not always appreciated by those more focused on immediate applications such as data representation in modern graphics.

FREEDMAN & SPEIGEL note that these changes in outlook and inquiry have characterized American historiography in general from the mid-1970s onward. They thus point, through their analysis of recent medieval historiography from the 1980s up to circa 1996 coterminous with this essay, to the current milieu which would be introspective, subjective, and more comfortable with description than causal explanation or anything smacking of old-style positivism. Their characterization of American medieval-studies scholarship can be contrasted to that in Europe, especially to the aforementioned flurry of computational work in medieval family and social history at research centers in the Sorbonne and CNRS, and the major French universities as well as those in Spain, where the establishment of fact, however local, is still a primary endeavor. The subjective and introspective movement in America depicted by Freedman and Spiegel is obviously a potential problem in advocating something like Historical Information Science in an era when dominant trends seem very nostalgic, nonscientific, and in some ways perhaps even antiscience. Such a conclusion would miss the broadening of information searching and its systematization to create such a cross-fertilization and integration of such a range of sources and secondary literature, which only a generation ago would have been nearly impossible. It would also slight the underlying research in medieval studies and History in general, with their combing of sources and consideration of evidence more readily available and varied than ever before (i.e., the richness syndrome), in deference to the end product, namely a secondary literature temporarily caught in a postmodern morass. Of course, a review of the secondary literature was their intent, but one can recognize modern revisionism without celebrating postmodernism with such positivism. This is not to dispute their commentary, so much as to note that this overview does not present the whole picture. What is questionable is their portrayal of a strain, vocal and articulate, as mainstream and as a permanent orientation.

Few historiographic essays penetrate the presentation layer to explore the actual research, overall methodology, or specific techniques used unconsciously or explicitly. Indeed, one could surmise from the lacuna in such an essay as by Paul Freedman and Gabriele Spiegel (theirs is representative of the genre) and lack of anything in the United States as coherent as a movement or school comparable to that represented in *Le Médiéviste et l'Ordinateur* that American medievalists might be unequipped methodologically and technically to conduct studies that would take advantage of modern information technology, empirical approaches, and computer-assisted analyses. What about any influence by computing and information technology on the whole of medieval studies in the last half of this century and the period on which they concentrate? Such activity is not misrepresented; it is not mentioned. Typical of such historiographic essays, these authors offer no bibliometric evidence of the shift they observe based on their reading in the field (an impressionistic approach, in vivid contrast to the aforementioned approach to domain analysis by MCCAIN, WHITE & MCCAIN, etc.); and their reading as reflected in their post-1980 citations is skewed toward New Cultural History. The literature cited is really a thematic literature, a strain, however enlarged that may be. It ignores the stream of intercultural socioeconomic and cultural-political histories such as the aforementioned Burns' production from UCLA, or for that matter, the solid archival-based research on the peasantry of medieval Catalunya produced by Freeman himself—none of which really fall into the characterization ascribed to recent postmodern medieval historiography. Thus, their essay reflects an obvious bias and rather personalized selection by orientation rather than a real sample in any empirical sense (the review illustrates the antipositivism it ascribes to others, and the authors place themselves in the mainstream they depict rather than assume a position of objective observers). Their analysis therefore seems unbalanced in that all works cited are cultural and textually based, none is socioeconomic or empirical, and few rely on charter evidence or official records from archives (as distinct from manuscripts texts) except for those representing the old school. From this, one might suspect that empirical, archival-based research has gone out of style. Not so. Finally, the essay totally ignores whatever quantification has occurred and is continuing, or those studies that retain a Social Science orientation. Or, is it that these might not be considered historical any longer, in view of the themes Freedman and Spiegel portray as dominating this field of historical inquiry? Is this an unconscious remnant of subjective review or a more conscious but unspoken practice of exclusionary social politics in the discipline? The non-postmodern would seem not to be in the favor any longer, or at least in the agenda of these medievalists in their description of "old and new medievalisms" (cf., ROSENTHAL & SZARMACH for the American variety and WORKMAN; WORKMAN & VERDUIN, eds., for European medievalism).

In any case, FREEDMAN & SPIEGEL's essay reflects the rarified milieu in which they work, in that their primary focus is modern historians' concerns as they explore the past, not necessarily the past itself and certainly not in Rankian terms, and not historians' research methods, techniques, or critical handling of evidence associated with scientific historicism. Instead, theirs is a philosophical bent, and their overriding concern is the "theoretical context out of which to work" (p. 703). In essence they are talking about the same thing as modeling, and are rejecting one model in favor of another, more complex and nebulous variety, but they do not think in these terms. Their vocabulary reflects thought of a different ilk than can be found in information science. They surmise that postmodernism seems viable for this generation of medievalists because it invites people to contemplate the "fantasy" of previous historical construction, so that "the alterity of the Middle Ages, it would appear, is our own estrangement from that fantasy writ large." So, current historiographic movements are reduced to a matter of social psychology (psychosis?) and disillusionment with contemporary society, which forces reinterpretation of other societies and a distancing from the past. Unfortunately, as an *a priori* assumption, negation is valued more than anything affirming.

Is history with a difference a profound revelation? Not really. It confirms how so much revisionism is inspired and reiterates of the historians' quest for continual relevance, or more cynically the need to establish oneself as revisionist and one's work as new. What is interesting but unsaid is whether all this distancing of medieval from modern is the result of or is generating anything methodologically innovative? References to methodology are mostly oblique and general (again going back to FREEDMAN & SPIEGEL's essay, but merely as a case to illustrate the point), e.g., to linguistics, semiotics, etc.. They are occasionally more specific, e.g., "symbolic anthropology of the Geerzian sort," "Derridean deconstruction," or Foucauldian perspective of "normalization," and they seldom delve into epistemology. Perhaps among the most important of their references for the philosophical basis of research methodology and interpretation would be the important work of B. STOCK (1983), notably his most recent contribution to the perennial debates about "the uses of the past." Entitled *Listening for the Text* (1997), Brian Stock calls into question common prejudgments or assumptions in the selection and execution of methodologies in textual research. Despite the relevance of the orality/literacy debate to historical modeling based on text, and of such questions to information retrieval in all ages, there is little hint of any informing of medieval studies by Information Science (nor of such considerations entering Information Science). Even so, many of the concerns voiced in these studies are informational questions; the strengths of philosophical reflection and source criticism lies in History, and of linguistics and technical methodology in Information Science—hence the potential alliance. But no mention is made by FREEDMAN & SPIEGEL (nor in the historiographic essays they cite) of any impact of modern information studies or technology on this field. Even if historians are not rushing to use the latest technology and automated technique for computer-assisted analysis, greater information access (larger research libraries and interlibrary service, more open archives and easier travel, reprographics and electronic access to catalogs and finding aids), the influence of information technology on History is a phenomenon too important to ignore.

In fact, digital technologies and modern communications are impacting medieval studies in ways not totally clear. If medievalists were genuinely interested in studying the effects of mediation and information transmission on their sources, their retrieval, and on interpretation beyond the fields they traditionally engage, they would study information preservation, retrieval, and dissemination, and explore modern Information Science for its relevance to their complicated task. Medievalists and classicists share many common concerns, sources, and research methods, but apart from ancient languages, the quantity and order of magnitude of problems tackled by medievalists have made Classics seem relatively simple and self-contained by comparison. Classical studies, like medieval studies, have become increasingly computerized (J. SOLOMON). Perhaps it is precisely because of this scope, quantity of sources, and magnitude of technical and intellectual problems that medievalists, already multilingual and usually trained in paleography, diplomatics, and archival skills, took readily to computers. Their training is far more methodological, comparative, and linguistically oriented than, say, for American historians of United States History, and this methodological and linguistic background lends itself easily to computing.

At the onset of the 1970s, more than 24 large-scale quantified and computerized projects in medieval and early-modern socioeconomic history were underway in Europe alone (IRSIGLER). Thus, it was for a concordance of St. Thomas Aquinas that the first great modern computer-sorted (six million punched cards replacing handwritten slips) reference project was undertaken by Roberto BUSA, S.J., just after World War II in 1949. According to his own story, Fr. Busa obtained IBM's support from its chief executive Thomas Watson, Sr., originator of Big Blue's THINK signs, by using another of the corporation's mottos as his final argument: "The difficult we do right away; the impossible takes a little longer." His initial run in 1951 of classifying by ritual and collating hymnal texts cited by the scholastic master is a landmark in Humanities computing history. When his complete concordance was printed out, 80,000 pages unfurled as if a monumental recreation of the ancient scroll. Today all this fits comfortably into one CD-ROM product.

Two decades later it was another medievalist, Robert Benton, at Cal-Poly State University in San Luis Obispo, CA, where early NASA space imagery work was ongoing, who was invited to see if any exploration technology could have spin-off value for the Humanities (BENTON). He was allowed to experiment in 1974 with a new kind of photographic technology before the term "digitization" was in use, to read a previously erased text by Arnau de

Vilanova on an illegible twelfth-century palimpsest by blocking out the surface text as though it were unwanted electrostatic interference in a shot of the moon. The resulting reconstruction allowed the then visible undertext to be enhanced by contrast adjustments, and Arnau's words were revealed from that manuscript for the first time in seven centuries. I recall personally Benton's enthusiasm and my incredulity at seeing the first results in 1973 when we visited together at Mt. Angel Abbey, Oregon.

At the same time another pioneer, the late David Herlihy, before his tours of duty at Harvard and Brown Universities, came from the University of Texas to the University of Wisconsin where he met the Americanist Cliometrician, A. Bogue (HERLIHY, 1976, 1978, 1981). Herlihy used techniques drawn from the first quantitative socioeconomic historians in America and theory borrowed from the French Annalistes, both of which were applied to Florentine and Pistoian household tax records, the *catasto*, for a fresh look at the social structure of late medieval towns in Italy (HERLIHY, 1967 on Pistoia, and 1985 for medieval households generally). Herlihy in a personal conversation with me discussed the steep learning curve required of historians entering historical computing in its early days, and he lamented the labor intensity of such projects as his investigation of late medieval tax records. The archival research required in late medieval and early modern Latin and vernacular records was difficult enough, but the tedious and exacting work of data transcription and normalization took its toll. Herlihy claimed that these processes took more time than his data analysis or the writing of his books. His investment was freely shared with his students and all others who asked for help. His work on late medieval tax records has found successors among graduate students at the University of Chicago, and his methodological influence can be detected in one of the last dissertations he advised at Harvard University—namely B. VENARDE's quantitative survey of women's monastic foundations in medieval western Europe.

As these three vignettes indicate, Medievalists had taken to the computer. Their history illustrates the problem of technical information transfer and self-imposed limitations against comparative inter-disciplinary learning since many were begun almost accidentally and hence idiosyncratically, they were often imbued with the personal preferences of initial project managers without recourse to any broadly based scientific study, and many reflected cultural norms of their own intellectual and social environments.

The French Centre National de la Recherche Scientifique (CNRS) Institut de Recherche et d'Histoire des Textes (IRHT) has been collecting microfilms of medieval manuscripts since its foundation in 1937 partially as a preservation movement through the two world wars. Today this collection has grown to 42,000 microfilmed manuscripts (50,000 reels), of which 25,000 texts from 10,500 manuscripts have been analyzed. These are searchable online, once a password has been secured, through a system called MEDIUM (GUILLAUMONT & MINEL) which provides access by it 2,738 authors, titles, and subject cataloging; by manuscript identification and descriptive elements; provenance tracings; microfilm and archival data; and special features including citation tracings through secondary literature to the original source. Standardization work has been ongoing since the first colloquies were organized in 1953 to normalize main entries for 1,195 holding libraries and archival repositories in 614 cities, references to their local catalogs, authorship and toponymies, and title format, as well as to encourage the use of international taxonomies and terminologies for script identification in paleography. With its *Bulletin de recherche et d'histoire des textes* (1953-) the Institut produces an international *Repertoire* of directory of medievalists, and publishes series of manuscript studies, critical editions of document collections and narrative sources, inventories and catalogs, methodological handbooks (e.g., documentary forensics, onomastics, diplomatics, paleography, codicology, etc.), and combinations of focused studies with appended texts for institutional, legal, economic, social, and cultural history. The practical experience gained in such work has been shared through a special *Serie Informatique et Documentation Textuelle*, which begins with the early work on automatic indexing by FOSSIER & ZARRI and its guide for cataloging and descriptors (1977), and within its series are treatments of automated schematic indexing including such complicated subjects as Arabic nomenclature, transliteration, and programming techniques for biographic work related to bibliographic control. The RESEDA System, for example, operates on a biographic database for France, 1350-1450 A.D., using inference procedures that reportedly "mirror the intellectual processes of an historian" in personal identification (LEE).

IRHT in 1965 also began tracking experimental computerized work in medieval studies in its *Le Médiéviste et L'Ordinateur* (33 issues to date) with its logo showing a medieval monk in his scriptorium with a keyboard beside his easel, a terminal instead of a window, and a mainframe tucked inside his armarium (a popular metaphor used also, for example, by HAHN and interestingly by the editors of *JASIS* who, while improving the journal's high-gloss cover, became enamored with combining medieval manuscripts with modern computer graphics to suggest continuity in information dissemination, despite the relative lack of historical content in the journal itself). This newsletter was joined in 1973 by Montreal's *Informatique et études médiévales*. A spin-off bibliography in 1982 generated 1,250 entries (BOURLET *ET AL.*). Subsequent interest in computing for medieval studies produced in that same year the first of two special collections of essays edited by A. GILMOUR-BRYSON, which were devoted to this topic. Subsequently, computer-assisted medieval studies have proliferated to such an extent that they are innocuous in conference proceedings and bibliographies, but reports on special projects appear periodically in conference proceedings like that edited by FOLKERTS & KUHNE for computerized access to medieval and Renaissance manuscripts, and such fora as *Primary Sources and Original Works* where W. STEVENS (1992) and J. HAMESSE ([199?]) provide further case studies and discussions of problems in computerizing access to and the texts and images of manuscript sources. KIERNAN (1994) surveys progress in the digitization of medieval manuscripts. I have surveyed Informatics' progress in such work before, and attempted to link codicology and analytical bibliography with bibliographic networks and utilities, international cataloging and descriptive standards, and special collections with archives (MCCRANK, 1988, 1990, 1991). Representative of such effort is MAYO's tests (1991, 1992; cf., SHATFORD LAYNE) of the MARC format's capability to record sufficient data to catalog medieval codices. Such cataloging efforts may be contrasted to access by incipits and their automation.

Other reports illustrate database and digitization work ongoing at centers in Princeton, Rutgers, and St. John's (MN) Universities, and the Universities of California (Berkeley, CA) in the United States and Toronto in Canada; and in Europe at Oxford, Louvain, Nïjmegen, Wöffenbuttel, Munich, Krems, Paris, Liège, Pisa, Florence, Rome, Sevilla, and Lisbon. In most of these cases, however, although the numbers of documents are large, they are still finite. The applicability of such approaches to the geometric increase in data accumulation by the United States federal government, or such agencies as NASA, is not a matter of simple transferability. The greatest success has been with historical archives or in the manuscripts tradition, rather than the larger expanse of archives *per se*, and no real telling experience whatsoever with electronic archives.

In the mid-1980s, CNRS began a "Discography" to track CD-ROM products supporting medieval studies (PELLEN; see also the listings by PANIJEL; cf., the reviews and interviews by Elisabeth Lalou periodically in *Le Médiéviste et l'Ordinateur*). The basic cache by 1993 for a medievalist's composite workstation for an investment of ca. $30,000 in hardware (which has decreased by 40 percent in the past five years), $50,000 in software and ongoing subscription costs of $5,000/year (which is increasing at 5 percent per year), would hold about 50 titles on 75 disks for bibliographic access to 25,000 journals and five million book catalog entries, 175,000 theses and dissertations, with additional abstracts from 10,000 titles and another 10,000 articles just for socioeconomic and social history methodology and interpretation; 7.5 million dictionary terms in a dozen languages including medieval Latin, with the *OED* and for current usage, Webster's 9th *Collegiate Dictionary*; seven centuries of music history with scores; 350,000 Anglo-Saxon and English poems from 600 A.D. onward; incipits to the works of 400,000 authors. There is also access to 99 percent of all extant classical Greek authors in full-text and onsite all of the works by the Greek and Latin Fathers of the Church and their medieval successors including Thomas Aquinas' 108 opera and another 60 contemporary commentaries on his work to go with BUSA's concordance, the *Index Thomisticus*, available from the Editorio Elettronica Editel; the Bible in full-text with concordancing, with the Packard Humanities Institute's multiple versions PHI version 5.3 (Vulgate, Septuagint, Greek New Testament, Hebrew and the English King James and Standard versions, and the New Testament in Coptic with referencing to 362 Latin authors working with Biblical exegesis (and Milton's works are thrown in to boot!); about 10,000 images for display, 1,500 manuscript miniatures from the late Middle Ages and early Renaissance, and another 5,000 analytics for medieval images.

Included among the most important CD-ROM textbases (reviewed by BEGUIN; POIREL) would be the complete *Patrologia Latina* of J. P. Migne's 221 volumes from Chadwyck-Healey, Inc., once a perfected release is available; and BRÉPOLS Corporation's CETEDOC (Centre de Traitément Electronique des Documents directed by Paul Tombeur at the Université Catholique de Louvain-la-Neuve, which is part of the Laboratoire d'Informatique en Sciences Humaines de l'Université Catholique de Louvain [Louvain-la-Neuve]) *Corpus Christianorum: Series Latina & Continuatio Medievalis* or *Library of Christian Latin Texts* (*CLCLT*, 2nd. ed., 1994: 28 million words with five million more added every two years; CLCCLT-3 for Windows [December 1996] added 600 new texts from 120 authors not in previous releases, for a total of 1,900 titles). This growing electronic library can be augmented by the company's publications of the Royal Irish Academy's *Archives of Celtic-Latin Literature* (1300 texts from 400-1200 A.D.), the CNRS-IHRT's *Index to Latin Forms* (a thesaurus of 50 million words including Neo-Latin from 1500 to the present), and its *Incipit Index of Latin Texts* (400,000 incipits) has been expanded to *In Principio* (again edited by Brépols) to 360,000 incipits from medieval manuscripts. This tool is growing by nearly 100,000 new incipits each year from the Hill Monastic Manuscript Library which had amassed a card file of 400,000 incipits. The *Thesaurus Fontium Cisterciensium,* released in 1998 on IX centenary of the founding of Cîteaux, provides all the major Cistercian edited texts in machine-readable form (some of which are from the *CLCLT*). Since 1996 medievalists have also had access through Brépols to the *Monumenta Germaniae Historica* in electronic form: e*MGH*-1 is the electronic analog to the paper edition but can be searched full-text using Boolean operators, or through the elaborate index.

BRÉPOLS has more recently announced release of its CETEDOC *Index of Latin Forms / Thesaurus formarum totius latinitatis a Plauto usque ad saeculum XXum* for $2,000 (CD-ROM of 70 million Latin forms and a printed word list divided into Ancient, Patristic, Medieval, and Neo-Latin), which uses retrieval software by Dataware Technologies and the Orda-B System database and functional design by the Cetedoc team itself. It is, as the publishers predicted, "indispensable" for the history of words, languages, thought, and institutional development. An array of cognate tools are being developed by Brépols Electronic Publishing such as the *Thesaurus Diplomaticus* (September 1997), a digital collection of 6,000 medieval charters with parallel transcriptions, the study of which is supported by document analyses for 13,000 documents comprising a database of 1.7 million words, plus iconographic presentations from 2,400 seventh through twelfth-century charters. The first release costs $1,400. The Diplomatic File contains descriptive analyses of each document in the database (authors, recipients, parties of the act, dates in the document itself and those attributed to it, and lists of key persons, measurements, places, and institutions, plus references to published texts. The Text File supplies transcribed texts from the medieval Latin dictionary project in Belgium, all of which are searchable full-text and may be linked to the metadata in the Diplomatic File and to an Image File or a numbered series of photographs of the originals. The *Thesaurus Diplomaticus* is an electronic extension of work begun as an editing project in 1866 by A. Wauters for the Belgian Commission Royale d'histoire and continued after 1983 by the Belgian Comité national of the *Dictionaire du Latin médiéval* and CETEDOC. As such, the core of this corpus is from the Low Countries, but the scope has already spread through Luxembourg and northern France, and the consortium hopes to bring into its expanding scope all corpora (edited and unedited charters) for the rest of medieval Europe.

Products now seem to be appearing faster than budgets are growing to buy and mount them. The *Dictionnaire du latin belge* is an international enterprise being coordinated with the French *Nouveau Du Cange* project, expanding upon the *Index scriptorium operumque latino- belgicorum medii aevi...* (Brussels, 1973-79) directed by L. Genicot and Paul Tombeur and their collaborators Collections of Latin documents are forthcoming, as heralded by the *Progetto Archidata* for canonists (the Lombardic councils from 1100 to 1800, from Teledata Srl. Group), but initial production of CD-ROMs has been oriented toward language, philosophy, and literary studies. A database of medieval epigraphy from the eighth through thirteenth centuries has been built from 1969 to 1974 by the Centre d'Études Superieures de Civilisation Médiévale at Poitiers; this has been reworked since 1991 and is scheduled for 1996 release as the *Corpus des Inscriptions de la France Médiévale*. The Adriano Capelli and Auguste Pelzer dictionaries of Latin abbreviations, now superseded, would be replaced electronically by O. PLUTA's *Abbreviations* (edited by Brépols) Apple-based text and script-image retrieval system. The medieval foci can be expanded to the classics by the *Opera Latina* CD-ROM (Editions Hachette) from Laboratoire d'Analyse Statistique des Langues Anciennes (LASLA) at the University of Liège, which publishes the periodical *Organisation internationale pour l'Étude des Langues anciennes par Ordinateur (RELO)*, which contains 77 classical works. CAUQUIL's essential Latin vocabulary will be available shortly on CD-ROM, along with MARTIN's *Les Mots Latins*. This classical and medieval Latin research library can be augmented with Greek through the aforementioned *Perseus* CD-ROM and the 700 works provided by the *Thesaurus Linguae Graecae (TLG)*.

All of these CD-ROM products should be augmented by Internet access to Web sites that are serving up thousands of documents in digital form, translations, and access to analytic tools such as the *Dictionnaire Automatique du Latin (DAL)* which contains the cumulative language base of Latin from Plautus to Vatican Council II based on the work of CETEDOC at Louvain-la-Neuve over the past three decades. The term base contains 161,230 forms now and 27,082 lemmitizations. Work on the *opera* of St. Jerome and St. Bernard of Clairvaux, and the charters of the diocese of Arras, is ongoing now. The *CLCLT* holds 28 million variant forms, and the *Thesaurus formarum* being produced is expected to crest at 60-70 million terms. The ARTEM project at Nancy is expanding these text bases to include more and more medieval charters. Much of this work is described by CHARPIN, especially for the research group Linguistique et Traitement Automatique des Langues Anciennes (LITALA). French Latinists and linguists have been especially adaptive at concordancing software and methodology from wherever they can find it, and when borrowing is not the answer, in creating it for their own purposes (e.g., the lexicometric packages *PISTES* [P. MULLER]; *LOGITEXTE* by the CNDP and INRP, etc.). They have also been at the forefront of statistical lexicography (cf., DELATTE *ET AL.*; DENOOZ; GUIRAUD; LAFON; J-H. MICHEL; P. TOMBEUR, etc.; cf., C. MULLER's pioneer work in statistical linguistics).

Examples of the URLs (periodically reported by PANIJEL) which a connected medievalist would have in his or her preference address lists or bookmarks are, for classical background, are M.C. Panelia's *Electronic Resources for Classicists* maintained at the University of New Hampshire (http://www. circe.uns.edu/classics/resources.html), and the classics homepage at the University of Michigan (http://rome. classics.lsa.umich.edu/welcome.html), etc. One can search for *Latin Sources on the Internet,* an index at http://www.prodworks.com/community/ pla/plalatin.html), or *WWW Medieval Resources* (http://ebbs.english.vt.edu/medieval/medieval. ebbs.html). The University of Georgetown *Labyrinth Library: Latin Texts* (http://www.George

town.edu/ labyrinth/library/latin/latin-lib.html) now makes available about fifty medieval texts in addition to proceedings such as the 1995 Cultural Frictions conference, James O'Donnell at the University of Pennsylvania displays hypertext late medieval documents in a collection called *Later Latin Texts and Contexts* (http://ccat.sas.upenn.edu//jod/recentiores.html), and Haines Brown is collecting documents for his *Feudalism in World History* (http://neal.ctstateus.edu/ history/world-history/feudalism.html). Lynn Nelson's medieval workshop at the University of Kansas is putting up texts such as the *Rule of Hospitalers* at the Royal Monastery of Sigena in Aragón (http://kufacts.cc.ukans.edu/ftp/pub/history/Europe/Medieval/latintexts), which may be augmented with documentary texts for medieval Hispanists going up on the Web page of the American Academy of Research Historians of Medieval Spain (AARHMS) and Northwestern University's literary-oriented *Medieval Iberia Resources* (http://ftp.acns.nwu. ed/oub/ NUacademics/hispanic.studies/index.html). Every study group in time will have a homepage, it seems, and will provide source material for its members and everyone else. Thus one can search with hits for fabliaux, the Holy Grail, exempla, Reinhard, and Piers Plowman, etc. The *Electronic Beowulf* is exemplary (KIERNAN, 1995). ARTFL is not to be overlooked by medievalists (SPO-HER) since it contains such aids as the Nicot *Dictionnaire français-latin* (1606) (http://humani-ties. uchicago.edu/ARTFL/ARTFL.html). And, of course, one would keep track of the home-pages and access through the major research libraries for medievalists: Vatican's aforementioned page; research centers like the CNRS itself (http://dodge. grenet.fr.8001) or the *Monumenta Germaniae Historica* in Munich via Columbia University (http:/www.columbia. edu/cu/libraries/ indiv/manc/mgh.html); the Hill Monastic Manuscript Library at St. John's Abbey and University (http://www.csbju.edu.hmml/); the Bibliothèque Nationale de France for its 1,000 illuminations online (http://www.bnf/fr/enluminiures/acccueil. html); and the Bodleian Library at Oxford (http://www.rsl.ox.ac.uk/imacat. html).

Everyday more sites appear on the Internet/WWW. Unfortunately, search engines like *Yahoo!* with its classified catalog often do not catch such academic sites, and full-indexes searched by *Altavista*, for example, still leave the problem of multiple languages in term matching. Moreover, many of these sites come and go, and they are unstable. Most are relatively new, so their contents are still meager. Many available electronic texts lack reliable critical apparati, are not critical editions, and display idiosyncracies in selection and presentation. For all such deficiencies, they promise better things to come.

Teaching and research in electronic sources are often inseparable. *Medieval Model* might be mounted for simulation and course preparation; *Medieval Realms* would be a nice complement for visuals along with the Vatican Library's videodisc of its manuscripts. Fototeca Sotrica Nazionale (1991) has produced a CD-ROM of 250 select miniatures from the eleventh through the sixteenth centuries, the *Storia delle Miniatura Mediovale dei Codici Membranacei*, which is very useful to teaching. In addition to a selection of word processors, including *Nota Bene* for foreign languages and Microsoft *Word* for the integration of graphics and text, and a bibliographic formatting package like *Procite*, the workstation would use HISTCAL for control of chronologies and calendars (DONCHE; cf., BRUNING), and perhaps something like OXFORD UNIVERSITY's *Micro-Concordance Program* (*MCP*) for text analysis (HOCKEY & MARTIN) and ROBINSON's *COLLATE* to track and collate variables. Moreover, with INTERNET connectivity, the modern workstation need not hold all of its sources in residence but would provide avenues to RLG and the *Medieval and Early Modern Data Bank* (*MEMDB*), and to medievalists communicating on the University of Kansas listserv for medieval studies, or to tap any of the hundred-plus electronic discussion groups that would be relevant to some aspect of medieval history. Global people-networking for collegial intercourse and online reference assistance and for importing data worldwide is increasingly commonplace in historical research.

These tools present interesting reference and intermediation problems; free text, keyword, and controlled vocabulary searching with Boolean operators in medieval Latin can boggle the mind enough for these edited texts, but other sources are much less standardized, and directions are not always in English. Trilingualism is not enough. For example, more is to come, such as major recon-projects providing regional and national corpora, e.g., Spain's *ADMYTE* program (*Archivo Digital de Manuscritos y Textos Españoles*) has its first CD-ROMs available for incunabula and early printed books from the major peninsular libraries, especially the Biblioteca Nacional in Madrid (FAULHABER & MARCOS-MARIN). This project is often overshadowed by the massive undertaking of the ARCHIVO GENERAL DE INDIAS (IGA) in Sevilla to convert its *ficheros* and selected records from its fondos of eight million documents and volumes (82 million pages and 7,000 maps and drawings) to machine-readable form for online searching (GONZALEZ). The IGA project, funded by the Ramón Arces Foundation, the Ministry of Culture, and the IBM Spain Scientific Center in Madrid, has been duplicated for the important municipal archives of Puebla, Mexico, using the same IBM technology and approach (Programa ARHIMP is Archivo Histórico del Municipio de Puebla, 1531-). The Puebla team of over 20 archivists, paleographers, technicians, and clerical assistants has divided its project into three stages: the Actas de Cabildo from 1533 to 1821, 1822 to 1910, and the modern records from 1911 to 1996. Such retrospective conversion unfortunately has not entailed thorough editing and standardization, nor translation between old and modern vernaculars. Digitization is a proven conservation aid and improvement in user services, but these projects have not necessarily modernized methods for information retrieval with new storage techniques except for searching *à la* word matching. They use late-twentieth technology to retrieve only by fifteenth to seventeenth century access points and traditional indexing. These projects continue to be revised and expanded, however, and initial digitization makes possible subsequent improvements in intellectual access and document retrieval as adept as modern narrative text coding and retrieval (ASHFORD & WILLETT).

Archival information retrieval is more complex than text searching, however, since individual records must be tracked in relation to their series, identified by record format, and linked by more than dating. This is a different matter from treating manuscript sources bibliographically. Archival records linkage involves more complex data preparation than cataloging. Official records, for example, supersede one another without the same kind of substitution that satisfies most text searchers, with the important exception of literary editors. Record retrieval within series is at a greater level of specificity than bibliographic retrieval. Therefore, the contextual issues in archival information storage and retrieval require a different kind of analysis and description to build archival databases that serve effective information systems. Retrospective conversion to digital formats alone is insufficient. This is only half of the task.

Apart from access to standard literary texts, medieval historians are especially interested in cartularies and other forms of medieval records, both for their own analysis and to build large corpora of archival documentation in machine-readable form so that large comparative studies can be undertaken. Among the many long-range projects initiated might be mentioned the English *DEEDS* project studying English records of the military orders (GERVERS, LONG & MCCULLOCH). Jacques André at Rennes has demonstrated the utility of the GRIF program and hypertext approaches to the digitized cartulary of Geoffrey de Saint-Laurent. An exemplary project was directed by I. KROPAČ (1990): the lemmatized text (ca. 3,000 pages) of the medieval cartulary of the Duchy of Styria, now available in electronic edition from the Austrian Institut fur Historische Hilfswissenschaft. In the course of this work, KROPAČ issued a series of studies on computer-assisted instruction (1987), database architecture (1990), medieval historical modeling (1991), and information system development for historical research (1992). Linguists at the international institute in Pisa since 1981 had begun the Latin Lexical Database (RELAL) project to automate methods to analyze Latin morphology and syntax based on a 60,000 word core or dictionary (BOZZI & CAPPELLI). The Max-Planck Institut für Geschichte's early use of standardized text encoding to make available machine-readable collections of medieval High German sermons (WISBEY) plus a prosopographical database of over 450,000 medieval people based on nine electronic editions of records from the following: the monasteries of St. Gallen, Reichenau, Fabaria, Remiremont, St. Peter (Salzburg), Corvey, and Fulda (some of which are in the *Monumenta Germaniae Historica* computer-edited series described by REUTER; cf. e*MGH*-1); Cluniac necrologies and those from Munich, Merseburg, Magdeburg, Luneburg, Regensberg, Moissac and Piacenza; and the cartularies of Fulda, St. Gallen, Lauresham, and Cluny.

A photographic archives of 20,000 images from the Krems Institut für Mittelälterliche Realienkunde (JARITZ, 1988) provides a portrait of "Daily Life in the Middle Ages"through a catalog of 5,000 of them and a forthcoming WORM distribution of what currently is available in slide sets (THALLER, 1987). IBM's research laboratory at Winchester, England, has provided the Austrian Academy of Science's Institut für Mittelalterliche Realienkunde with prototype software and use of its *IMPART* image processing capability to develop image enhancement, close-ups, and pattern recognition functionality (i.e., more than analogs or simply window pictures). The GETTY CENTER AHIP project since 1983 has assiduously collected manuscript art in a color photographic collection now exceeding 90,000 images, mostly French, Italian and Flemish from the thirteenth to fifteenth centuries, all individually catalogued and related to a classified manuscript file (STEELE). The Departement des Manuscrits of the Bibliothèque Nationale since 1989 has been developing its own database, *MANDRAGORE*, to access its vast manuscript collection through 10,000 descriptors (6,000 proper names) beyond the former capability of the manual catalogs (1980, 1983, 1984, 1987) produced by the library's Centre de Recherche sur les Manuscrits Enlumines (CRME). The *Index of Medieval Medical Images (IMMI)* is an outstanding project relating image access, indexing techniques, terminological research, and controlled vocabularies or thesauri (INFUSINO, SHATFORD LAYNE & O'NEILL)—in this case, *MeSH* (National Library of Medicine's *Medical Subject Headings*, 1990) and *LCSH* (Library of Congress *Subject Headings*, 1988-).

While digital technology is being used to make such exemplary sources as Catholic University of America's collections of Gregorian Chant (the *CANTUS* project) more accessible, its application in mass retroconversion of endangered and high-use documentation as both a means of preservation and mass dissemination will most dramatically alter the future of historical research. Consider the APIS project (Advanced Papyrological Information System, 1997-) partially supported by NEH ($300,000 toward a $3 million project) to digitize 30,000 fourth to eighth-century papyri (10 percent of all known fragments) at Columbia (from where Roger Bagnall coordinates the project), Duke, Princeton, Yale, and the Universities of Michigan and California. Oxford University has embarked on an ambitious project funded by the British Library to provide full access to medieval manuscripts, not just artwork, through exhaustive (30,000 ms. pages) digitization of whole codices, beginning with eighty manuscript and incunable versions and editions of the *Canterbury Tales* (BLAKE & ROBINSON; DEEGAN & ROBINSON) to be made available on CD-ROMs in Cambridge University's Electronic Edition series (1994-). Specifications for such large digitization projects were compiled by ROBINSON (1993) from a study of the Office for Humanities Communication of Oxford University's Centre for Humanities Computing. Other electronic edition projects include the *Herbarium*, a popular medieval medical treatise ascribed to pseudo-Apuleius, and a hypermedia teaching edition of Old English poem, *The Dream of the Rood* (DEEGAN, TIMBRELL & WARREN).

Images thereby become a real component of multimedia visual and textual research wherein image is used almost interchangeably with text. Certainly that is the trend in gliding some projects such as the *Index to British Art* (A. M. LOGAN) from mainframe-hosted indexes to PC workstations and CD-ROM with indexes that operate as bridges or translators, often called image interfaces, between the textual and visual. Text can be treated as image as in the case of manuscript reproduction, and image almost as text when images are retrieved to support a narrative as a kind of hyperlinked storyboard or consecutively framed cartoon strip.

Medieval studies never looked so good, and they are looking even better with three-dimensional reconstructions of ruins like the aforementioned holographs of Bath or the famous abbey of Cluny. Classical and medieval archaeologists, especially in France (BECK) and Italy (GOTTARELLI), are now reconstructing the late antique and medieval milieu in virtual reality using storyboard animation and tools like *TDImage*, *E-D Catia*, *TERR*, etc., on Apple, AT, IBM, and Sun workstations. Photogrammetric opportunities were perhaps first envisioned because of the surviving plans for such monastic layouts as St. Gall, but were early realized in applications at Cluny (K. J. Conant's plans were digitized in 1991 and enhanced by CAD applications; e.g., for Cluny IV, see SAPIN), and more recently at sites in the Loire Valley (JUFFARD; ZADORA-RIO), and the MATOS system which uses *Paradox* software at St.-Germain at Auxerre (PETIDENT). Such tools as *Arkeoplan* (ARROYO-BISHOP & LANTADA) combine photography with scanning, taga boards, and high-resolution color imagery to project, for example, complete towers from their extant bases, full walls from partial remains, and multistoried buildings from first-floor foundations, even with textures from medieval masonry added from what remains through vertical "textual mapping" (GRUEL & BUCHSENSCHUTZ) or a combination of Computer-Assisted Design (CAD) and mapping techniques similar to methods used to develop GIS programs developed for horizontal plains and contoured landscapes to keep track of spatial relations between finds in rectangular digs and larger surveys if there are multiple explorations.

In my own research of the twelfth-century Iberian frontier of the Reconquest, I am exploring the use of such tools to reconstruct the rugged landscape and numerous castles and fortifications which exist in ruins and sometimes only traces today (MCCRANK, 1996). Using techniques originally pioneered to reconstruct piecemeal the monumental architecture and facades of ancient Egypt from crumbled remains strewn on the ground, stones are typed, measured, and numbered; weights are calculated; and repeatable patterns with projected proportions are thereby depicted. The 1988 CNRS virtual reconstruction of the temple of Karnak demonstrated how far such technology has come from the movie studios into academe. It is what the French call "infography" (SAPIN, p. 53). Major headway in the applications of survey and engineering technology and AutoCAD applied to medieval archeology, with refinement of techniques, is exemplified by the digitized video used for stratification mapping by Antonio GOTTARELLI (1992, 1994) to reconstruct the medieval commune of Sienna. Imagery and history are thus fused in illusion and reality. FORTE characterizes all such developments simply as "virtual archeology."

Such combinations of technology are expanding historical knowledge, but have practical applications as well in historic preservation. A major impetus for such development, for example, came in 1984-1988 with the expansion of the underground transportation system or metro in Lyon, France, when the city later wanted to build parking garages underground with parks on their surface. While the Lyonese were immediately worried about the city's underground utilities and drainage system, they wanted to foster tourism by not scarring their historic cityscape, and were also concerned about destroying the evidence of their city's history that lay beneath in layers of centuries-old construction. Such urban renewal thus created impetus for a continuously developing historico-archaeological information system, the aforementioned *Lyonais Projet d'Archéologie* (ARLAUD; ARLAUD, HAMMARCHE, & LUROL). France very early in 1975 envisioned a national image and database to safeguard its national patrimony (GUILLOT, 1992); begun in 1978, it is being maintained by the Ministry of Culture at the national computer center, Fontainebleau. A UNIX Risc-6000 hosted textbase using Oracle, *DRACAR* (1991-), relates research (MAGNAN) to sites controlled with a GIS (PC Arc/Info.) contour mapping and statistical package (GUILLOT, 1994). In other areas, e.g. Hungary (BLENDA, LASZLOVSKY & ROMHANYI; LASZLOVSKY & ROMHANYI) *Klieu* is being customized to accommodate such projects, to create the a database of the "material civilization" of bygone ages. *Klieu* has been used for over 30 major historical computing projects in Germany since

1986 when the AHC first took interest in it. Peter Denley's commendable initiative to translate manuals, etc., and provide workshops in English at Queen Mary and Westfield College in London will help spread the use of this software.

Such richness is already overwhelming and the conversion to machine-readable form is only in its first decade. The Research Libraries Group (RLG) has now taken an interest in all of this activity, with sponsorship of easy access to *The Medieval and Early Modern Data Bank (MEMDB*, 1985-; the project scopes is 800-1800 A.D. and contains such data sets as 13,000 currency exchange rates collected by P. Spufford, and MARC records for cataloged electronic files of medieval tabular data) at Rutgers University (CARLIN; BELL & VAN CAUWEN-BERGE). This last example might be used to relate high-tech medieval studies with the general goal of improved information systems for future multidisciplinary scholarship. Numismatics, always a matter of accounting, is essentially a combined statistical research and museological endeavor (LEESE), so the next logical step in development of the MEMDB currency database is to combine such data with images to produce a virtual catalog of coinage which can be activated by an expert system to locate exemplars, calculate exchanges on spreadsheets, and present coins and bills as icons that can be manipulated with a mouse individually and as sums (e.g., show a quarter with any mathematical combinations of smaller coins, nickels, dimes and pennies, which can add up to the 25 cents). Such a system might be expanded for exchanges in kind to show commodities and their monetary values for any period and location that such historical data exists. This is technically possible now and digital catalogs of major numismatic collections in Vienna, Oslo, and New York will form the basis for such interactive systems. Such development is close enough to be beyond the speculation stage in the *Coins and Computers Newsletter*. Such development is in keeping with the direction of current research and development trends; and such a project illustrates the utility of history, archaeology, and museology in multimedia information systems development.

The point may also be made that more is being provided now than can be assimilated readily into teaching and the retraining of faculty whose graduate education preceded all this. Everything mentioned can be tapped generally for medieval studies or, because of their interdisciplinarity, for a variety of other applications in other fields. Method, technique, and selection of specific technologies are often transferable. One problem for historians interested in doing this is that project reporting is very fragmented, often in newsletters and other in-house publications which are difficult to obtain. Project information clearinghouses have not been well developed in History, and even journals like *Computers and the Humanities* have not featured work in History other than for occasional thematic issues of conference papers (IGAR-TUA, 1996), and they are not systematically reviewed. This communications problem in the profession may be remedied by tapping into listservs and discussion groups through H-Net and this network's initiatives in electronic reviewing may include project reporting more than has been common in review journals. Even so, History specifically and the Humanities generally have not developed standards for project description, including citing technologies selected or in identifying techniques employed. Project demonstrations and workshops are not featured in History association conferencing, except for the Association of History and Computing. The Medieval Conference at Western Michigan University and its European counterpart at the University of Leeds would be ideal places to feature projects in medieval studies, and some showings have occurred there. However, History has nothing comparable to trade shows associated with conferences in the information industry: CAUSE and EDUCOM separately or in their current amalgam, Computers and Libraries, Online, etc. AHA exhibits are still publisher dominated, with little exposure of historians to the information world outside of traditional formats, other than occasional material for secondary teaching. Once can only envision and hope for the day when this situation might change.

Adroit use of current technology can assist in information retrieval, collation, assessment, and analysis, rather than simply supplying electronically what was accessible previously, albeit in more limited fashion, without computer assistance. New masteries are required in addition to rather than as replacements of old methodologies and specialty skills. Such development should leapfrog intervening stages if possible, which it is by replacing actual incremental stages of development with models and simulations (WHICKER & SIGELMAN) and using these to achieve really major advances. That, as argued more than a decade ago (MCCRANK, 1986c), is the difference between simple computerization and automation. Again, it is the difference in what ZUBOFF more recently called "informating"—meaning that the information relayed also informs the system to enable a process of continued self-improvement through AI applications. In adopting such approaches, the academy, which assumes that it is already an adept learning organization, can assure itself of fulfilling such a role. I come back again to what SENGE envisions as a "learning organization" as distinct from a learned individual working alone in the traditional artisan style of humanistic scholarship. The prospect is simultaneously daunting and exciting.

The challenges of digital conversion of sources and electronic access, computerization and new forms of analyses where images, texts, and data are interchangeable, and enhanced prospects for inter-disciplinary and intra-disciplinary collaboration may not be met if, as recent characterizations of the field of medieval studies indicate, the mainstream of historical scholarship is simply not ready. Its unreadiness may be a lack of technical education and means but most assuredly also rests of its current *mentalité*. Scholars must develop standards and greater accountability outside their own opinion no matter how expert, a more explicit methodology for the scientific rather than personalized study of sources and the predominantly literary interpretation of history as either narration or representation, and a middle ground between old positivism in scientific historicism and its overly strident ambition in the first wave of cliometrics, and its total rejection and enmity to all empiricism for the sake of unbridled impressionism under the guise of ingenuity and personal insight. In short, while recognizing the tenuous nature of representation and that modeling is a continuous process, historical scholarship must escape the traps of postmodernism which undermine the fundamental nature of knowledge discovery and learning.

Historical Information Science Issues

TECHNOLOGY

The crux of historical computing is collocation and comparison of whatever is being studied to produce generalization, coupled with the isolation and description of variables to note exceptions to the rule, and when variations fall into clusters and patterns to group like variance into geographic and chronological entities that may be subjected to further analysis. IGARTUA (1991) outlines the process and reduces complex procedures and intricate methodologies simply to "the historian's work." The intellectual process is one of classification and description, while the technical process is largely organizational, i.e., aggregation versus segregation of data of either numeric figures like costs and commodities, or people and their related data, and these are connected by time and place. If such information can be related as well to thought and culture through texts, images, and artifacts, so much the better. The more and varied the data, the larger the database and more complex the management and analytic operations will be, but so too the richer the History. In such operations, the critical ability lies in data and records linkage, but one must get the data into machine-readable form in the first place and have the necessary hardware and software by which to perform these complex operations, and a methodology by which to analyze and interpret the data. Such computer-assisted historical research reveals several major, cross-disciplinary concerns that are the domain of a nonsubject specific but methodologically oriented and technical Historical Information Science.

Data conversion is a significant problem because mass converts to high costs. Digitization as a replacement for analog conversion (e.g., microfilming, photo-analogs, etc.) has advantages such as image enhancement, but in the large digital projects which are largely conservation oriented, the contents of the documents themselves are unaltered. Low-level technicians can be employed and once trained, the operation is largely routine. There is no editorial cleanup, which may be required in the preparation of large data runs and data sets for research. In the latter case, the problem becomes one of high-level technical operations, increased labor cost, slower production, and the assembly of a critical apparatus to indicate appropriately all data transformations, editing, and normalization. Data are seldom what they appear or claim to be. Precision is usually wanting and must be remedied by extensive and intensive editorial work unless in an computerized environment these tasks can be automated. Even then one must distinguish between work and enabling tasks, as advised by WHITEFIELD, ESGATE & DENLEY (cf., DENLEY & WHITEFIELD).

There are definitely problems. They may be with input and recording processes as when a clerk can not spell or keyboard operator mistypes, or with the very nature of the data. An example might be when personal names in oral and preliterate societies may be pronounced but have never been spelled before resulting in varied orthography for the same name and indeed the very same person. Ambiguities like this abound in historical database construction even more so than in bibliographic databases where one is assured of working with literate authors by definition and the ambiguities are more easily recognized by different language and transliteration than misidentification because the original recorded identification was the very first ever for the people so documented. Recent Social Science datasets at least have some control built into them at the time of their production; taxpayers and collectors at least got names approximately right. However, similar problems exist for linking nicknames, baptismal and legal names, name changes resulting from marriage, and those taken from variant sources such as church, birth, census, tax, and employment records.

By comparison, archival and historical databases are far more difficult than library and bibliographic files to impose some control over, manage, and analyze. Usually a coded, tagged, and edited electronic archival *Uhrtext* or original database is prepared, from which a surrogate is produced that normalization can be imposed upon; its data are enhanced by linkage to other databases, resulting in a data complex that is then analyzed. So there are at least three stages of database building before one is ready for analysis. As THALLER (1993b) correctly observed, this work is so source, data, and labor intensive that often computational historians work with fewer sources than those relying on published texts.

The easiest aggregation is simply adding similar data for subtotals by period or subject to yield totals, and performing basic statistical analysis like percentages, ratios, or slightly more interesting, to work with spreadsheet formats. But the most basic variable, as in counting money with different currencies, requires an auxiliary database of conversion ratios for normalization of all monetary data. Such operations become very complex when identifying people, let alone categorizing them, because of faulty data and ambiguity. Early historical computing developed first when analyzing census and tax records that were originally meant to be counted for accounting; they could be readily cleaned up in parallel runs for editorial checking, much like copy cataloging in automated libraries or checking authority records, or audit procedures. But in most historical computing, the source by which subsequent authority control might be based, must be done from scratch. Moreover, most historical data based work is highly individualized rather than collaborative, so currently there is no economy of scale reached as in shared library cataloging. There is, however, an economy to be achieved in multisite use that helps to justify production costs.

This situation could change with increased value given to collaborative projects, as indeed the National Endowment for the Humanities has done by earmarking some funds for such work, and more effective use of the Internet for project management (MCCRANK, 1994). The Social Sciences have been more adept at large-scale collaborative project management than History, but no such collaboration in either field compares with the monumental effort and success of library networking and shared cataloging or the tremendous multi-institutional investment put into retrospective conversion, editing, and reformatting of catalog data. Such efforts are being rewarded now with interlibrary searching of OPACs across the Internet. OPACs are the most systematic and standardized databases searchable from anywhere. Such effort might be emulated. Despite the complexity of historical research and distinctiveness of every project, certain common themes and problems have emerged that when addressed produce a meta-discipline independent of the geopolitical and chronologically defined field being studied. More emphasis on commonalities and less adulation of project uniqueness is a mental hurdle historians, like archivists most recently, must overcome.

Technological Obsolescence and Preservation

Preservation has become a field unto itself in the last decade. Although it has been a concern in museum and archives longer than it has in the library, the latter has made great strides since the 1976 inception of preservation courses in professional library education with Paul Banks at Columbia University (whose program moved to the University of Texas). The University of Maryland with myself and Christopher Clarkson (UMCP-CLIS has retained preservation management as an integral component of its History/Library Science advanced studies program, but failed to realize the projected full-scale program in Preservation conceived in 1978 with the UMCP Art History Department and program in Museology with the Smithsonian Institution). Whereas these early initiatives lacked appropriate literatures altogether even for basic training in archives and library preservation, this literature has expanded during the past decade, and the infusion of management and technology into the preservation arena during the 1980s brought about an unprecedented sophistication and full-blown multidisciplinarity requiring specialization of its own. My own work with the Library of Congress Office of Preservation (Peter Waters and Don Etherington) for summer workshops (1978-80) was perhaps the earliest attempt to adapt Social Science research methods from Demography to mass preservation program development through condition surveys and statistical analysis for project design and budgeting (MCCRANK, 1981, 1984), and thereby to convert a craft focused on the conservation of artifacts into a management science tending to collections.

The history of technology and manufacturing is especially important in training conservators, and as in the case of archives, subject-area history and History overall are often perceived as the key to appraisal and contextual interpretation. Conservation, however, required a history focusing on technology, manufacturing, and physical collections, rather than on content; hence, such applied history focused on subject matter being incorporated into codicology for manuscript studies and analytical bibliography for printed media, e.g., writing techniques (paleography) and materials (instruments, inks, parchment, paper, etc.), packaging and binding (structure and materials), mass production and publication (typography), and transport and storage pertaining to the artifacts at the time of their creation and all intermediate steps when physical condition was altered. This formed a foundation as anatomy and biology do for the medical sciences. This historical technical knowledge had to be coupled with current science and engineering studies for scientific study (forensics), intervention, and treatment. Traditional history as taught in most History departments was not what was needed, so much as a customized blending of the history of technology, science, business, and art. Such a blend was called for then, and now also, to study the medium more than the message. In other words, the emphases need to be reversed for most History, or a better balance between content and mode or means of communication needs to be achieved as in Art or Music History. Or, in the case of the modern *histoire du livre*, older more formalized styles of the history of the book, closer to analytical bibliography, are what is required. A chronicle-style classified form of historical knowledge distilled into a reference tool for easy access and application is more useful than histories as written today. Yet, this is precisely the kind of historical research and presentation that is undervalued in History today. This hybridization and integration of historical and scientific information was not available as part of the growing field of Information Science any more than it came from traditional History. This is still the case. Information Science, like History, underestimates the value of such critical and often empirical research. Both ignore the lasting value of such contributions.

The required inter-disciplinary mix and combination of analytic and descriptive methodologies necessary for metadata tools could be assumed under the umbrella of Historical Information Science. In this regard, it may be argued, History becomes synonymous with metadata. But the range of media and the technology considered in Preservation must be extended to electronic media and formats. New technology associated with nonprint media requires new research, learning, and specialization. This field is still in its infancy, unfortunately, because it is a demanding specialization requiring more expertise than can be provided from Archival Science and Museum programs, especially those under the purview of History and Art History unless supplemented extensively by forensic science. Nor can the preservation of sound recordings be a minor concern inside traditional Music archives (D. THOMAS). The needed inter-disciplinarity must reach out to Electrical Engineering and Industrial Technology. A product's manufacturing technology must be understood for proper intervention, since so much of conservation is a reversal of undesirable processes. This is why the history of information technology has been included in this work, which stresses the conservation of information. The extent to which this has been done and higher education has responded to this need for training and expertise, is sorry indeed.

It is not my purpose to review the entire field of Preservation here, but to relate it with the aforementioned concerns of Historical Information Science. The late Suzan Swartzburg managed to capture the state of the art for library preservation (SWARTZBURG), and RITZENTHALLER's SAA manual attempted to do the same for archives. BUCKNER HIGGENBOTHAM has provided a solid overview of preservation and conservation topics articulated by experts in this burgeoning field, although the history of the field itself is not well covered. Although it includes a chapter on how science and technology are assisting preservation today, and another on the use of technology for managing preservation programs, the traditional association of preservation with Art and History does not always favor the interjection of preservation sensibilities, ethics, and product quality concern into manufacturing and industry at large. This could be accomplished, of course, as part of ISO 9000 compliance. This connection between quality and permanence is often made best by a focus on material science, often through chemistry related to product engineering, design, and production, most weakly in relation to the production of information sources except in book design and paper quality where the contemporary problem of brittle books resulting from acidic paper and improper environmental conditions has threatened our library collections with natural disaster. Ironically this has spawned library interest in digitization as both an access and preservation technology.

Thus, in early 1997, the Northeast Conservation Center joined with other organizations to explore the impact of digitization for information preservation and access. The transfer from a physical information technology based on paper to an electronic one actually exacerbates the scope content, and educational problems in Preservation. Concern for electronic data, records, and converted documents remain neglected, as reflected in the lacunae in the otherwise laudable collection of essays edited by BUCKNER HIGGENBOTHAM. Moreover, like ecology and environmental science relating to everyday life, or in the matter of injecting an archival concern even into routine activity, it is important to create a broad awareness of preservation and conservation issues to inculcate an ethic in the public at large, which is a task closely related to History education. People unconscious of history seldom think about preservation and conservation, and when such consciousness raising is asynchronous, preservation becomes an afterthought and conservative reaction indeed. So in this sense the state of History is important for preservation, and *vice versa*. What are still needed, of course, are interventions into manufacturing to ensure product quality, prevention and care in use, and environmental quality control for long-range preservation.

The redux of the historical preservation problem for electronic sources is the presentist mind set of contemporary computing industry and computer science community, illustrated in abuse of historical terminology, and hence thought, such as turning the noun "archives" into a verb as a catchall for a host of specific archival functions and operations, and thinking of "archival" as a timespan of no more than a few years. As P. JERMANN remarks (p. 11) about digital image products:

> The source for digital image's strength is also the source of its weakness. The machine readability and digital nature of the electronic record represent potential preservation nightmares. Whereas microfilm can be accessed with as little technology as a magnifying glass, reading data from an optical disk requires an international industrial effort. The industry driving this technology is highly competitive and driven by market forces that continually demand greater storage and processing capabilities. In this market, the needs of libraries and archives [and historians, too] are largely irrelevant. The technology that reads today's optical disk will certainly be replaced by new technologies. Today's improved access could easily be tomorrow's unreadable disk.

> The nature of digital data compounds the problems posed by machine readability. At its most basic level, digital data is [*sic*] simply an unrelenting, undifferentiated, essentially meaningless string of zeroes and ones. Digital data must be translated to be meaningful and this translation is anything but straightforward....Unless we know the language of translation, our digital data is [*sic*] meaningless and useless.

> The currently undefined life span of the optical disk on which the digital data resides [*sic*] is another cause for concern. Estimates for the life span of an optical disk vary from a doomsayer's two to three years to an optimist's 100 years. Neither paper nor microfilm, with potential lives of 300 to 500 years, would be considered remotely archival with this life expectancy.

Thus, the archival nature of optical disks for long-range preservation is still controversial, despite widespread applications in records management and technical improvements in the medium as described by SAFFADY(1996a & b). Saffady reviews the options and evaluation processes required to select appropriate storage media for electronic record keeping today, including outsourcing work to imaging vendors. One must choose from the following: magnetic disks (floppy disks, hard drives, disk cartridge drives); magnetic tapes (nine-track; .5 inch data cartridges, digital linear tape, QIC formats, .8mm data cartridge, digital audio tape); and optical disks (3.5, 5.25, 12- and 14-inch optical disks; CD-ROM, CR-R., DVD disks, and MD data disks). No one contests the advantage of storage density, however. Whereas one magnetic tape holds 6,250 bits/inch or 112,500,000 characters (i.e., bpi readings), one 12" optical disk stores the equivalent of 5,000 magnetic tapes or one terabyte of data. The new CD-size Digital Video Disk (DVD) can provide menu access to anthologies, multiple sound tracks (multilanguages and subtitles) and can hold four feature-length films (133 minutes) with its 30-fold increase in the number of pits on two sides of a dual-layer disk (each read by a changed angle and focus of the light source and receiver). This increased capacity of dual-layer 18 GB disks makes possible ample storage for document and image frames with item-level retrieval. Storage capacity, therefore, seems to be progressing nicely. The critical questions are: storage for how long, under which conditions, and with what transferability after a decade, century, or more?

This is why some (WILLIS for the Commission on Preservation and Access) argue for combinations of programs for access in electronic form while simultaneously adhering to more permanent formats like paper and microfilm for preservation and conversion to digital form purely for dissemination and access (CONWAY & WEAVER). Moreover, the continuous reformatting required of electronic media (DOLLAR, 1999; LESK; SAFFADY, 1997) for long-range retention depends on the stability of our institutions, continuity of programs, and such machinery dependence, that one could find little in history to predict success over bygone generations. CONWAY (1996) in a recent report for ACCIS relating to the Commission's tracking source conversion projects in its *Digital Collections Inventory*, warns especially against stamped CD copies, and prefers laser produced master recordings. More and more one sees better understanding of the connectivity between the technical creation of information and its immediate use, with reuse and long-term preservation. Historical preservation, however, is not a driving force in any technological development and has little impact on the immediate marketplace. So, preservation must be built into products as a mark of quality, and perhaps its higher cost should be absorbed into pricing with good advertising that markets total product quality as worth the investment.

As T. E. KINNEY has indicated, the future of information services is not being driven so much by business information needs as one may suspect but by the entertainment industry. This could actually assist in preservation since entertainment involves the arts, even if the popular culture variety which today could still exploit everyone's self-interest in long-term enjoyment, both everyday consumers and true *aficionados*, so that a preservation ingredient cost could be buried discreetly in overall pricing rather than handled as a surcharge or cultural preservation program added long after the initial purchase. Entertainment has a different "line" mentality, and increasingly the once stark difference between entertainment and information service is blurring. Learning and fun are not as exclusive as once thought. Not only would History be well served by incorporating an archival quality control in production of entertainment and information products, but in addition to information and education, history in its most democratized distribution as entertainment, if properly packaged and marketed, could help itself more than it does through support of historical preservation in all of its electronic formatting and media distribution.

Indeed, given the difficulty in information transfer from one generation of hardware to another within transitions of less than three years in some cases, the problem is one of belated historical consciousness as an ideal but failure to apply this while designing, implementing, maintaining and changing computer technology. It is a management problem of pervasive insensitivity to time and the evolutionary nature of effective change, including technological glide. Hewlett-Packard, Inc., which today makes 25,000 products, says that half of these are derived from products delivered in the previous two years. When a HP computer is manufactured and marketed, only so many are released in accord with sales projections, and the model's life-span is calculated at no more than six months when its sequel goes into production. Consider this problem in terms of the multiplicity of vendors and products, their slow adoption of standards for compatibility, and the added complexity of software upgrades for personal computers, i.e., whether this is a strategic glide or happenstance changeover. Microsoft introduced the Windows operating system in 1985 but it did not take off until Windows 3.0 in 1990; by 1993, Windows supplanted DOS. DOS files are convertible to Windows, and presumably most formatting and tags, etc., in use are transferable, so little must be done to recapture operations capability with older files. This was important for user satisfaction and still is since Windows for certain operations such as indexing and search/replace routines in large textbases is slow and inefficient compared with DOS operations. What about original DOS files from the vantage point of records management and archives? What has happened to them? What will happen to them, even if retained, if and when DOS disappears? What metadata are lost in this translation? The decreased cost of personal computers and software, increasing reliance on electronic communications even for household accounting and ordinary communications, the selection of software and choices between upgrades and changeovers and a move to client-server architectures in local networks mean that the problem of continuity in electronic resource management at the individual micro-level has become seemingly hopeless as much as it appears overly complex at the organizational or macro-level.

Consider the current malaise resulting from the oversight (dare one say stupidity? as many have when venting their frustration in this case) of software programmers who shortened to two digits input for dating by years (omitting the millennium and century designators), to make their codes more efficient so it was thought, without foresight to the glide to the next millennium. Consequently, without correction by the year 2000 annual dates between the twentieth and twenty-first centuries cannot be differentiated (ULLRICH & HAYES call this snafu "the challenge of the century"). Of course, the greatest fear was that the timing devices in computers in flipping to a triple zero may trigger shutdowns because some programming used double zeros in a two-character field to do just that. It is estimated that in the United States $400 *billion* had to be spent on programmers time to fix code and avoid disaster! Correcting faulty chronology in computer systems has become a major industry! The intended frugality of saving two characters in keyboarding and coding dates now seems like the greatest false economy measure of all time. Popular speculation talked about traffic signals not working, banking transactions being interrupted, and other kinds of doomsday prognoses. Little thought has been turned to the number of electronic files that may be dumped, erased, and overwritten simply because they are judged to be historical rather than relevant to contemporary business. Given the time pressure of an approaching millennium, any kind of systematic appraisal seemed improbable except to protect immediate financial interest. The randomness of data preservation in such an unstable environment bodes ill for the future of archives and history. Already new products are available for the re-development of dating in code and automated computer run-books, testing, and audits. Either data elements for the year designations had to be converted to four-character representation and leaving the software logic intact, which requires programming changes to systems so that the new year designations are recognized, or software logic had to be modified to handle the two-character representations correctly. Workshops and seminars appeared on the circuit as computer center staffs everywhere were pulled off other projects to accomplish the big fix of the millennium. One sponsored by Barnett Data Systems carried the ironic title that sounds preposterous on its own, "Planning and Implementing the Year 2000"! They were not talking about a Times Square celebration.

It is ironic that IBM has called its architecture of systems to link mainframe computers with newer client-server networked systems as a "Legacy" environment. While this may suggest that data transfer and preservation are key concerns, IBM seminars reveal that the main motive is prolonging the life of old hardware, namely mainframe computers, in distributed computing environments during an era of budgetary constraints. The archival transfer of electronic data is seen as an application issue, disassociated from the problem of hardware obsolescence. The IBM strategy is to get a few more years use out of mainframes by incorporating them into networks and reminding everyone that a mainframe computer is also a client server. Such an approach could assist the electronic archivist if indeed the application side of the problem were addressed, but often the implication is that the mainframe would be kept in use only for the active life of current data. Stretching the life-span of older equipment and phasing it out when the utility of the data expires absolves systems administrators from the difficult and potentially costly problem of long-range data preservation and transfer across hosts and systems. Hardware upkeep is therefore contingent upon data utility as originally intended, with little regard to secondary use or historical value. In such scenarios, data banks may be destroyed when their hosts are terminated. Data appraisal, thereby, becomes inextricably linked to maintenance costs, technical feasibility, and business efficiency.

Historic preservation of electronic archives in such scenarios is not "business critical," as systems people say, unless made so by concerns other than those arising from the information systems technology itself. In the free marketplace and in business where capitalist values dominate, these fail miserably in regard to archival concerns when altruistic sociocultural values are called for in addition to economic motivation. Rhetoric aside, the proverbial almighty dollar reigns and short-range implementation for expediency and efficiency prevail over long-term preservation. This is the danger in seeing electronic or any archives as only serving an immediate constituency, or in confusing information and historic values with the cost of technology. One can take little consolation that the prospects for preservation of the modern record for history's sake is thus no better or worse than it was when most communication was oral and equally fleeting. Information technology over the past 30 years has not been used well for archival purposes, and the design of systems architecture only for immediate needs, often with a vision of merely a few years, poorly serves its owner and heirs. The legacy of continued imprudent planning for technological glide will be one of chaos and forgetfulness.

Charles Dollar and others, however, concede that archivists (and historians) constitute such a small market, and most decisions in the production of electronic information is market driven, and the best tactic archivists can take is not to talk about the altruistic virtues of history for posterity, but to make a case for the more immediate good of the organization and adherence to "best practices" standards established through professional associations and standards organizations (DOLLAR, 1992). The difference in arguments for best practices and for history's sake is not altogether apparent, except in taking a short versus long view of what is best and for whom. Now or posterity; and for us or our children? The more idealistic argument takes on notions from religion, namely the Biblical notion of good stewardship (DEARSTYNE, 1993, p. 230). The conundrum is similar to those who argue for environment conservation as self-interested preservation or for discussions over passing the national debt onto our children. But these comparisons trivialize the problem, since both are familiar and in one way or the other classic problems confronting society. One suspects in the latter case that the inheritance of debt may be more predictable than the future of History based on contemporary electronic documentation and reconverted sources. The production of so much electronic information in the last of this century without regard to its preservation is a massive problem for the future of history and societal memory, which cannot be remedied only by the aforementioned catch-up efforts of electronic archives and education. Archival organizations are setting priorities as advocated by RITZENTHALER; some are making practical decisions to ignore what they cannot accomplish as a logical component of appraisal. DOLLAR's outlook, for example, suggests what archivists may have to do with information recently generated or which is still being produced without provision for future preservation; he moves beyond the problem of electronic records trapped in the transition period just experienced, to focus on improvements in the next century. The late twentieth century, therefore, may become a black hole for future historians.

The dilemma confronting historians in particular, who are not facing the challenge in any meaningful way, pertains to us all, and the danger of choices now cannot be underestimated. It is, I think, impossible to be too alarmist in this case. The problem is unprecedented in that the very technology we have invented to generate so much information is the very source of its interpolation and unreliability. The very technology that has allowed us to create so much information is ironically the very instrument for its destruction. Today's information in raw form is data, which are now so minute, parochial, and customized that in the smallest dimension they are genuinely trivial, but in the larger picture it is such detail that provides a potential clarity which no other generation has ever had. This is profoundly ironic. In other eras the technologies adopted for communication aimed at permanence, not mutability; even so, the sources produced were still perishable, but this was not the intent. Wax tablets were reusable for practice, but they were not the medium of choice for information that was potentially reusable. In the electronic era the media of choice are precisely those designed initially for constant, different reuse rather than repetition or continuity between one use and the next. Their very instability made them highly useable, and simultaneously very perishable. Given what has happened even to records deemed permanent by their creators, one cannot expect better from deliberately transient media. Why would one expect longevity of an information source intended by its medium to be short-lived? Literature about the sociology of knowledge seems to sanction selection and suppression of knowledge as a matter of necessity, but as in library selection such decisions are conscious, rationale, and within parameters of organizational missions and goals. This is not the case in the loss of electronic data due to the lack of appraisal and retention in organizations, inherent perishability and dependence on obsolete technology, and requirements for constant care and attention for preservation. The point of jeopardy is the transition from primary to secondary use. At issue more than the preservation of records or of their information, but the very historical consciousness of Western culture (KELLNER, 1975). Thus, this essay deliberately incorporates Organization Culture in Management into the purview of Historical Information Science.

In the case of classical culture surviving into the Middle Ages only in pockets and then mere traces and fragments, when intellectuals lamented the loss of the past they blamed such destruction on the barbarian invasions. The real culprit, however, may not have been the overt destruction of archives, libraries, literatures and documents, art and monuments, but the destruction of the infrastructure that sustained classical culture. The real destroyer was not so much intentional as it was a neglect of those institutions and organizations that would have regenerated and restored such losses. The effects of incidental destruction therefore became cumulative. The failure of classical civilization may be attributed to its veneer rather than penetrating character, and thus its erosion when scratched and dented by the invasions. Gibbon first, like Arnold Toynbee much later, attributed the causes to internal breakdowns more than external assaults. The transition and rebuilding of civilization in the West took half a millennium; the Carolingians tried, but it was only by the twelfth century, in what Charles Homer Haskins declared to be a real "Renaissance," that the intelligentsia began a massive recovery effort to save what was left of classical culture. In so doing, they resuscitated their own, including the redevelopment of archives, the institution of written law, the spread of literacy, and record keeping as a matter of course. As demonstrated in the case of northeastern Spain, such developments were largely indigenous, with little real continuity to the classical world (MCCRANK, 1995). Thereafter, a scribal ethic was thereafter inculcated in school children everywhere to record their transactions and thoughts, conduct themselves in business objectively, and settle disputes through historical reconstruction based on evidence. There was a distinction between writing for mere communication and creating a record. The real lament of those wishing a greater inheritance from the classical world was not the neglect of culture by the ancients, but the failure of the immediate inheritors to preserve what they received and took over during their infiltrations and conquests. The losses in great battles, fires, and destruction of cities were commemorated because they were known, seen, and understood; but equally destructive, invisible, and less understood was the sheer neglect of cultural preservation by the populace at large. Therein lies the real tragedy that should ring warnings for today's society. No invasion, no catastrophic atomic war, or series of fires in the archives is required now to destroy continuity in the historical record; simple deletion in mass, lack of policies for preservation and technological glide, and in the transition, the unthinking discarding of electronic files one after the other. Convenience, neglect, and shortsightedness are the culprits, abetted now by computer technology.

The preservation issue of mass is therefore complicated by machine-dependence and the rapidity of technological obsolescence. This is attracting the attention of historians whose sources are in electronic form created on first-generation hardware but, among historians at large, these constitute a minority. The problems of working with census data, when for example the 1960 electronic census is in jeopardy, are being recreated not only by formal research archives captured only in electronic formats, but to an even larger extent by modern e-mail (HIGGS). Examples abound, such as the inability of the National Aeronautics and Space Administration (NASA) to read over a thousand of its magnetic tapes holding data from early space exploration. As RAYWARD points out, society has placed the burden not on records creators, but on archives, libraries, and museums which must cooperate given the magnitude of the scale and the discrepancy between obligation and means facing these organizations. This was the approach of the American Federation for Information Processing Societies (AFIPS) which funded historical research into computing at the Charles Babbage Institute, Boston's Computer Museum (which has a West Coast branch, the Computer Museum History Center which opened in 1996), and the Smithsonian (which is interested in such research, but not necessarily in amassing a large collection of computer artifacts), but was less influential in the industry itself. The trade journalist Frederic Davis is developing another player in this arena, the San Francisco Computer Museum (PICARILLE). J. BOWEN tracts developments in computing history and museology in his *Virtual Museum of Computing* (http://www.icom.org/vlmp/computing.html).

The assumption is that preservation lies in an aftermath of collecting activity rather in information production, and few think of it as an integral corporate responsibility that should be part of today's thinking about Total Quality Management (TQM) and adherence to "best practices." Moreover, a mental division has always separated historical computing and the use of electronic records from the machinery which created and supported them. That ignores the issue of historical context, namely the common interdependency of software and hardware, and the constraints of original use which should affect historical interpretation. The shift in today's archival thinking about archival retention and preservation is redistributing the burden and placing a lion's share on the records creator. This would apply as well to historians creating databases which have been called "recyclable" (MCCRANK, 1988). They have not assumed such responsibilities very well, given how few projects make use of reusable databases from historical research projects. Data archivists at recent workshops like the 1996 *Archives in Cyberspace* meeting in Moscow (DOORN, 1997) still wonder how to get deposits of databases into the archives for continual reuse. Part of the problem has been machine-dependency and non-transferability of databases, but these limitations are less severe than they were only a decade ago. On the other hand, attitude and awareness problems seem unabated.

As MORELLI argues, this previous notion of electronic records existing somehow as separate from computer systems, is no longer viable. WEISSMAN (1990) calls attention to firmware developments where the two cannot be so distinguished. Examples abound of magnetic tape still in storage that cannot be read, not because of the media, but because no working hardware exists. Thus LESK (1997) and his colleagues at Bell Laboratories (now Lucent Technologies) reported to the Commission on Preservation and Access that archives must preserve more than records, but also the technology that supports them. That is, archives must enter the living museums business, or collaborating museums must not just collect dead machinery as shells for display, but must be living museums with functional obsolete equipment and trained staff for maintenance and operation. The fault for such awkward technical glide and rapid obsolescence, such as in the haphazard and opportunistic development of operating systems (especially DOS), lies with the computer industry where the lack of concern for the ecology of information may be likened to the failure in social responsibilities of companies which exploited the present without investing in environmental conservation for future generations. The computing industry has not been called to task for the technological mess that so threatens late twentieth-century history; its corporate philanthropy has not identified archives and the preservation of electronic records as a worthwhile programmatic objective of redeeming virtue. Little evidence points to acknowledgment of the industry's contribution to the problem or comprehension of possible contributions to its correction. Like historians, but only in reverse, manufacturers of hardware divorce their products from software and the electronic information they hold and convey.

Because of the historical development of computing, therefore, the preservation imperative calls for more than electronic record keeping. SWADE (1993, pp. 94-95) argues that the case for collecting software in science museums can be made on the basis of the broad mandate to "maintain a material record of technological change" even though there are those who question the materiality of software in light of the object-oriented culture of a museum. He likens the problem to the justification of saving samples of drugs to document pharmaceutical science, where also "function is not manifest in physical form." This initiative in Great Britain has its counterparts in the United States where BEARMAN calls for the same measure to assure the future ability of archivists to access to their electronic files. J. A. N. LEE (p. 56) reports similar discussions at the same time over the History of Computing Listserv *SHOT*. In a 1993 posting, pioneer computer builder Willis Ware proclaimed "Software is unquestionably among the most important contributions of recent generations to the history of mankind. Yet little thought or effort has been devoted to how it should be preserved...if there is value in doing so." He asks what might be learned from the software itself versus its documentation, manuals, and books reporting about it, but he realizes that "the answer is not at all obvious." The arguments differ in particulars but all have the same thrust. More than a purest impulse, as in the case of historical re-enactment or building a log cabin with pioneer tools as a demonstration project, the goal is to assure that the enabling tools are preserved with raw material because their modern descendants are no longer compatible with the original formats and the greater the distance between one generation and another, the more software and hardware incompatibility becomes a barrier to historical research.

One approach for creating continuity is through reprocessing. However, reformatting continually to read old data with modern machines and tools runs the risk of altering the very form and substance of the original source. In some cases form and content cannot be divorced without damage to the original entity, so that the observation of BUCKLAND (1991) who critiqued the notion of "information as thing" as a misconception seems not to apply to all cases. Economists like Malcolm Getz, formerly university librarian at Vanderbilt, have argued the opposite, that information must be valued as things, namely economic things. The value may be attributed, not intrinsic as archivists once asserted, but instead associated with concrete form as in the case of copyright, patents, and other forms of intellectual property. Moreover, the entity or what archivists call the record, in electronic media is often a combination of things which must work in tandem: electronic files, software agents and data readers, auxiliary files like codes and tables, and skilled interpreters. The plurality or rather multiplicity of the electronic source (the equivalent of inventory, content, container, packaging and labeling, and log of use) makes sense when one remembers the archivists' observation that all records are byproducts of the actions they document. Actions are very often complex phenomena. Such records by themselves, without the controlling software, documentation of origin and purpose (provenance), context (fonds), etc. are incomplete. The case in electronic records, especially those generated by object-oriented programming, calls for software acquisition with machine-readable records.

Once the argument is made and wisely accepted for software collections, hardware collecting follows by definition in the same manner that sound archives must have working phonographs if they are to hear music from phono-records, and listeners if we are to have interpretation. Or, hardware documentation as a surrogate of the real machinery is necessary, to enable a rewrite and transfer to a different host which may emulate original processing. Commensurately with the Smithsonian, the Computer Museum in Boston, and the Charles Babbage Institute, all of which have saved computers and all sorts of media to document information, computer, and communications sciences, the British Science Museum collaborated with the British Computer Society to found the Computer Conservation Society. Together they have restored, for example, a Ferranti Pegasus machine from 1958 which is now in working order and is reading data not capable of being read since the 1960s. This is expensive, however, so research teams continue to study means of simulation on modern machines to replicate old processes, thereby creating new ways to access old data, and perhaps even to improve upon old methods and enhance the utility of the data through such technological glide.

The spectrum of choice from physical storage of data in original form or media having continuity with the original, executable programs in original but superseded program languages or converted into new programs, and original conserved and restored hosts or those capable of simulated processing and reprocessing, means adopting a very flexible mental approach to historical records that do not really become inactive like some playwright's notion of mythical sleep, waiting to be reawakened in unchanged form but in a new state and altered circumstance; the more apt metaphor, not well accommodated in Western historical and philosophical thought, is more like reincarnation, where old life is placed in a new body and one has to observe the effects of this on personality. Or, restated the old notion of a life-cycle of records as really circular, with beginning and end at the connection, needs to be re-envisioned as a continuing spiral that features continuity in the strand and has an overall direction distinct from the twists and turns therein, but whose coils also display distinct stages with their own diameter, spring, and elasticity. Simulation is a replay, a new stage, and cannot be confused with sameness; nor can the preservation of electronic records be misconstrued with the paper paradigm (EATON, 1994). ROSS & HIGGS indicate the entwinement between technical, theoretical, and legal issues in preserving "the past's future." Such concerns have an interplay and convergence so that like trends toward unidisciplinary research, the distinctiveness between archives, museums, and libraries is quickly eroding (RAYWARD, 1993). So, too, is the notion common to archives, art, criticism, and critical editing work, that content and format are forever connected when in electronic form, sound, visual art, textual material, and numeric files are often stored as desperate pieces only to come together as a "virtual document" upon command. The "thing of it all" is not thing at all, but process. To capture that, a multifaceted approach must be taken which includes the conscious destruction of records, the conservation of some in original form with attendant hardware and software, and the transformation of others.

Large commercial ventures in corporations are proving the utility of digitization for massive retro-conversion projects coupled with the creation of online retrieval systems on a scale never before feasible. Caterpillar Corporation's reengineering of its documentation systems now supports online maintenance in the field, complete with retrieval of diagrams and schematics from its electronic archives. Such technology has resulted in substantive changes in how work is accomplished. XEROX Corporation in the United States and internationally, with ongoing research at its laboratories in Palo Alto, California, and Europark in Cambridge, England, has been redefining itself from a photocopy company to a documentation firm using digital technologies integrated with other companies' products to create virtual libraries and archives (CANTRELL). The redirection, or perhaps an acceleration in the same direction from old Xerox processes, is exemplified in a new logo, a digitized X emerging from its particle base as if existing in cyberspace. XEROX is competing with several players like KODAK, Inc., in an increasingly competitive high-tech business where costs seem astronomical. Baseline costs will decrease, however, as projects come out of their pilot stages. Moreover, the trend is toward integrated technologies, i.e., building customized distributed systems from components supplied by several specialist companies, which archives and libraries will be able to afford. Xyonnics software, for example, is commonly used by larger companies for image compression. The former limitations imposed by storage and transmission requirements of image transfer are being overcome very rapidly. As imagery and telecommunications technologies combine for lower cost and higher speed transmission (WALKER & MILLER), libraries and archives will reengineer themselves also. These changes will require researchers, historians included, to change their traditional research habits. For preservation purposes, for example, readers may be obliged to conduct all preliminary research in electronic surrogates, even when they are at the archives. They can just as well do such initial consultation from their local library, offices, or home.

Just as documents are being created on Document Assemblers, they are as easily modified with "cut and paste" routines in Windows Clipboards and similar programs designed for continual editing, interpolation, and redesign. New Document Manager systems for the creation of records automatically generate retrieval points as well for a variety of searching options, including use of "wildcards" through truncation. The very flexibility and creativity with such technology is both a blessing and curse for historical research. As with all technologies, use and abuse are more ethical than technical. Today collaborative behaviors have become central to Information Science because of such technology (MCNEESE; see particularly DENLEY & WHITEFIELD on multimedia document production). The forensic techniques for source authentification have been developed, but their availability in academe is limited to the hard sciences. One may expect the same lag time as experienced during the last decades in the slow growth of access to mainframe computers by humanists, to occur in the spread of this technology to documentalists.

"Dry-cleaning" techniques with such software as *Scan Fix* by Sequoia, Inc., have been developed to eliminate speckles, static traces, etc. in the conversion of documents to digital images. In one XEROX test case for document reproduction, to create electronically a facsimile of a manuscript dated in 1320 which is now in the Gregorian University Library at the Vatican, engineers failed to understand both the aesthetics and evidential values of their work and mistakenly cleaned the images in the process of scanning and thereby enhanced the electronic version. The image was then printed on pure white paper just as pristine as when the image was reconstituted at 600+ dpi. The conservation component of the project, which was to produce a physical surrogate for the reduction of stress on the original from unnecessary use, had to be redone. The engineers had to replace the blemishes as they appeared on the original, and they reprinted it both on new but pseudo-parchment paper and on actually aged paper to recreate surrogates that preserved both text and image plus context. The very same processes used to create such marvelous facsimiles of the *Doomsday Book* and other historical treasures, of course, are those which can also be used to forge entirely new "historical" documents in facsimile, and more transparently, as virtual documents which cannot be easily differentiated from originals in online retrieval. Such technology carries with it an implicit trust, and lacking this at face value, an increasingly elaborate metadata system for documentation and surety of provenance much like a seal was used to verify medieval writing and trademarks authenticated name brand manufacture. The implications of computer hacking and electronic forgery and piracy of intellectual property are not matters only of security, profit, and trade as in the 1995 agreements between the United States and China, but they also pertain to the very nature of proof and evidence, verification and authenticity, documentation, appraisal and selection, admissibility, and citation or referencing. Yet most documentary scholarship relying on facsimile and surrogation has not relied upon very precise rules of evidence for admissibility and use, similar to those in Law regarding microfilm and electronic records (R. WILLIAMS). At stake is the very survival of documentary historicism and the discernment between historical fact and fiction.

Consequently preservation and security issues seem to go hand in hand. They pertain to the process of conversion, more than the concern for data integrity as meant by systems managers and programmers whose perspective is limited to the post-conversion transfer of data. Most of recent research on data security and maintenance of the integrity of digital data has been accomplished in criminology concerning computer fraud and in the financial sector rather than in electronic archives. One project, however, deserves special mention in this regard. The aforementioned Holocaust Documentation project in Germany guarantees data integrity with invisible embedded protection against data tampering and an elaboration of the check-sum method for reauthentication (REHBEIN, [1997]). The dual approach there was to create both an electronic "watermark" and a seal as a form of user registration. The watermark component relies on a technique of using the surface display of a digitized document, which can be divided into columns and rows to make cells. The granularity of dots per inch (dpi) determining resolution in printing, of course, becomes a matter of pixels in electronic displays. Therefore, this technique compares the resolution of these cells to provide pixel values as the means of data proofing. A random check on at least four cells per frame creates a bit sum which is embedded into the image. When an image is tampered with and this sum is altered, the ratio of black to white pixels is altered and the grayscale changes; although undetectable to the naked eye, a computer can easily detect the attempted alteration of a text. Such attempted unauthorized alteration results in the image dissolving and the data are rendered irretrievable. The seal, on the other hand, is like a license predicated on authorization of use by IP addresses. A user's logon identification is compared with the embedded seal (a list of authorizations) in the database. The watermark is used primarily for distributed digital texts on CD-ROMs, and the seals work well for Internet access just as check-sum methods have worked in telecommunications previously.

Xerox and other companies, from the 1988 federal government's interest in document engineering and the Department of Defense (DOD) Computer-aided Acquisitions and Logistical Support (CALS) Initiative, have had to consider how to handle formal texts by type and component in large textbases in order to retrieve and manipulate digital documents. XEROX information scientists refer to the problem as "Formalizing the Figural" which requires taking an abstract like "form" which is visually apparent but seldom defined, and reducing it to standard forms. The information industry has not widely adopted SGML or TEI approaches to markup text as in academic circles. Instead, it has retained the United States DOD technical standards based on Raster Document-Object codes that segment electronic text files into their physical counterparts of monographs or for series, issues, down to chapters or articles, and then pages, and allow segregation of images and forms from their related texts (i.e., stripping them of context). These texts, as whole documents and their parts, dispersed as they may be, must be linked and tracked across networks as they are assembled, transmitted and received, reassembled, and resent, etc. The problem becomes nightmarish as documents become more and more complex, evolving into multimedia presentations.

In response to this trend, highly specified Document Type Definitions (DTD) have evolved for engineering schematics and industrial drawings that are combined with renderings and computer generated models that approach virtual reality. Such multimedia documents are not read, they are shown, heard, demonstrated, and interrogated. The business world, therefore, is moving far beyond the academic reliance on traditional texts for information dissemination. These are the sources for future historians must use. Although the Text Encoding Initiative (TEI) expanding upon SGML is gaining acceptance, publishers have generally adhered to a less complex set of codes developed by the American Association of Publishers. Meanwhile WordPerfect 6.1+ for Windows 3.1+ with SGML allows authors to create standardized markup texts and peer-to-peer file transfer of such texts across the Internet, bypassing the older formality of traditional publication. Windows 95 onward make HTML coding and information posting to Web pages even easier. The problem of coding texts and images similarly, simply, and efficiently remains one of consensus and voluntary compliance. Increasingly, however, if one wants to escape machine and software dependency for information transfer with the greatest flexibility and maximum reach, conformity to mark-up schema that work across systems is required. This means simplicity in basic coding for formatting, based on what programmers adopted from typesetting and word processing. Such markup methods control format and presentation, and some style as well, but not necessarily a typology of documentation for the kind of form control, convention, protocol, and classification associated with Diplomatics (a weighting of credibility by the presence of diverse elements, identified in basic manuals by GIRY, BOUARD, TESSIER, etc., updated by GUYOTJEANNIN, PYCKE & TOCK). Nor does it remotely approach what is required by analytical bibliography. Conveyance is the goal, more than analysis. This has been the case for most new communication forms, which in time have had to be formalized and which congealed into a system as usage spread and the communication field broadened. These are not new problems, but they are more complex than before, in precomputing or in the early days of computing. Initiatives aimed solely at text transference are missing the mark, of course, for the purposes of analyses. In the 1970s, when experiments (e.g., MCCRANK, 1982) with large text files and different manipulation for a variety of faceted indexing schemes preceded such elaboration of standards, best practices, and subsequent normalization, there was no choice but to invent *vade mecum* codes and proceed as one could. That is not the situation today.

Other byproducts than markup codes are being developed to handle massive electronic text files and related digital images. Built-in toolkit archival information systems, under the guidance of Operation Management Systems, are being designed to handle copyright permissions, for example, in massive digital projects. Both IBM and Xerox corporations have designed what amounts to an internal archives management system for security control and risk management into their document delivery systems. In an open system, permissions to copy proprietary information are usually controlled by encryption (Data Inscription Standard). In short, new systems can be designed to document documentation automatically, and these can be adopted for other functions required by archival standards. The output of these meta-information components of documentation systems will thus be critical for future historical research, and almost as important as the documents themselves since they attest distribution, use, and are the keys to their access. Encryption is a two-edged sword; it is the secrecy (privacy, confidentiality, intellectual property protection, etc.) versus access (freedom of information, public interest, research agenda, etc.) dilemma. It can serve the archivist only from within the system producing coded information, when archivists share the code. This highlights the current concern of archivists about their integration into the information production business rather than being on the receiving end only. Historians had better assist them in this effort, since historians are usually on the outside looking in, after the fact, and if their data sources are encrypted without the means to break codes and translate into normal numerical and linguistic data, historians will be worse off than archeologists deciphering dead languages and archaic symbols (SCALERA).

The current controversy is heated because computer security overall is such a hot topic. According to the American Society for Industrial Security (ASIS), since 1992 computer break-ins have increased 323 percent and insiders are involved 46 percent of the time, the industrial spy business is booming, losses are estimated at over $5 billion annually in theft of the following targets in priority order: strategic plans, R&D reports, manufacturing processes, marketing plans, intellectual property, financial data, customer lists, and personnel documentation (J. YOUNG). Management Analytics, a consulting firm specializing in computer system security, estimates the loss at much higher, ca. $10 billion a year! The tele-spy business has its own "newspeak" wherein "social engineering" means impersonating an authorized user and lying so skillfully over the telephone as to secure passwords and other security information. In self-defense, companies are hiring "tiger teams" to test their security before hostile "telecommandos" do. A host of counterintelligence measures are being taken beyond the usual controlled access by distributed passwords, such as new methods of authenticating another party, using biometric devices for fingerprinting or retinal scans, challenge-response sequences, entrapment programs embedded into files, and the use of "sniffers" to monitor network traffic. Encryption is just one of many options, often used in combination with other methods to ensure security; in this process mathematical manipulation by complex algorithms transforms original text (called in the jargon of the day, "plaintext') into unintelligible "ciphertext." Its all part of risk management—and electronic archives management, too.

The so-called "crypto factor" may entail legally binding electronic signatures, decipherment codes, electronic "fingerprints" in documents, triggers acting like invisible hotlinks in coded text, etc., which could assist preserving electronic records or damn them to obscurity after their immediate life span. Archivist and historian concerns seem unnoticed compared with the heightened sensibility of law enforcement, surveillance, and national security, and other sectors of government as well, so when SCHEIER's manual on cryptography was released, a common spin, as in *Wired Magazine* (see its home page: http://hotwired.com/clipper/) was that this book was something the National Security Agency (NSA) never wanted published. Encryption has been growing since the 1970s, but recent concern has been heightened by the spread of public-key encryption and the supposedly "uncrackable" RSA algorithms. The United States Federal Government has responded with the Clipper Chip proposal which in essence would license encryption codes and create an archives of these which could be accessed by proper authorities through appeal to the courts similar to applying for wire taps.

The debate has raised an Orwellian specter often covering up real issues of importance to archivists and historians, but these communities have not raised their voice in this fray. Watchdog groups like the Electronic Frontier Foundation (http://www.eff.org) monitor related developments daily, but historians seem unaware of its implications, and archivists are only beginning to understand them. When so many bureaus and companies pass into oblivion or are taken over by other entities, their archives disappear as well or are often rescued as a salvage attempt rather than smooth transition through a donation arrangement, deposit, or another kind of custody transfer. Even if saved, if the electronic archives were well secured through encryption other means, they may never be accessible for future research. Such access versus security concerns, therefore, relate directly to preservation efforts, archives, and the future of so much socioeconomic history that current inattention by historians and archivists seems very shortsighted indeed.

The means to transmit and protect electronic information inside the corporate world and government also pertains to how information is handled in public utilities and on the Internet. Remember that forms of textual fingerprinting and entrapment codes used as security measures are interpolations that border on forgery; if they do not limit access, they can nevertheless distort what is retrieved. This is an increasingly common approach to deter video piracy. The most sinister forms of deception used in the digital environment are like old tricks in "salting" paper archives, employing substitution mechanisms like hypertext whereby challenged access, improperly met, does not result in lock-out, but in retrieval of hyper-misinformation which as a counterstrike attempts to sabotage illicit users. Anti-scam procedures designed to protect copyrighted material on the Internet can both block access or, failing this, falsify retrieved information or present contaminated or marked data; this is an electronic equivalent to marking currency to trace in robbery cases or implanting viruses that explode similar to paint canisters can when a bank's money bag is opened without authorization. The intended culprit could be an unsuspecting future historian researching the present, which after all, is something like spying from a distance but with unharmful intentions. The same may be applied to electronic archivists who want to embed their equivalent to a "logic bomb" into users' files (a resident computer program that is usually dormant but, when activated, triggers a save to a remote archival retriever (a gatherer; or a server acting as a client for an archival guardian serving an ulterior purpose), who want to use their own version of a "sniffer" program, or who invent their own "Trojan Horse" program to repetitiously exploit security programs precisely for archival retention.

The idea in most of these electronic document distribution systems is to digitize hard copies of both books and manuscripts, from originals and from microfilm, as well as images which are often separate because of different resolution requirements, and to publish on demand using the "Just-in-Time" concept from modern business which abhors large inventories such as maintained by libraries in expectancy of user needs. Digital masters are ideal for such on-demand service. Output can be telecommunicated for electronic reproduction on screen, laser printouts, and regeneration of hardcopy facsimiles through high-speed printers, automatic collators and binders, and mail distribution. But if security management systems are not transferred to archives with digital documents and coded data, the latter will not be available for future use. To use a metaphor to exemplify the potential frustration for historians, it would be like knowing from transit manifests and other meta-documentation that important original documents have been put in a safe for safekeeping, learning where the safe is, but lacking the keys or finding out that the combination has been lost. Then the equivalent to a safecracker must be brought in—ironically, the computer hacker then becomes the historian's ally! Computer fraud today may be tomorrow's research strategy in electronic records research.

Encrypted transmissions are meant to be used as composed, but other forms of documentation in open systems exchange are more complex and fluid. Harvard University's Law School is already transmitting case studies to the University of Pennsylvania's Wharton School, and they are sending "floptical" read-write CD-ROMs back and forth where the case file grows and contracts as commentaries are added and obsolescent material is deleted. The CD-ROM records are therefore dynamic, being interchangeable with host systems after transmission, and like round-robin letters for lack of a better metaphor, become intellectual entities devoid of authorship in the old sense of the word. They are individually written conglomerates which at best would be catalogued by today's AACR-II standards under corporate entry. The CD-ROM cannot be catalogued as a physical record or a stable intellectual entity even as a series unless an archival agent intervenes and captures electronic "snapshots" of the dialogue in the reusable media. A background competence or sponsorship may be identified, but contributors may not always be linked to each contribution, and the information itself is so mutable that it seems impossible to track each mutation as a variant edition or to log intermittent use after periods of dormancy. Archival concepts like "record group," may be applied simply to avoid responsibility for any kind of analytics. Archival concepts like provenance, original order, and *respect du fonds* or preservation of original context are often seem meaningless for such dynamic documents. Almost no operations research has been conducted to find out for sure. Simulated tests of various procedures and methods might be conducted to evaluate the effectiveness of older concepts and approaches to electronic records, but no systematic research program has been articulated. Traditional methods of bibliographic control are fraught with equally perplexing problems.

What, in this milieu, is an archival record? COX (1994b, p. 592) adds, "and why should we care?" What is the unit, measurement, category, or class for appropriate intellectual control of electronic archives? Archivist decisions about these questions will affect historians and all other scholars using such records. To what does the researcher refer? How does one cite such a source, and why, if when retrieved it is different from when sent and when cited? How does one capture a state of an editorial process that is basically never static but is just periodically dormant, or an issue in a series of such minute issues that the changes are only meaningful when aggregated beyond the microscopic level? How does one describe something always in the status of flux? Does whatever descriptive method derived necessarily involve issues of relativity since time and motion are so intrinsic to the new media? COX (1994a) believes that the archival record, as concept and thing, is still evolving. Into what? We are uncertain. The new descriptive methodologies are likely to become mathematical and symbolic more than descriptive and immediately understandable to the researcher, and contents may become so encrypted that machine translation is required for all archival research. Control of bit streams in data flow is beyond the comprehension of most users and custodians of archives, and of electronic and data archives as well, but such are the approaches are being considered currently. Records generated by high-technology today will most likely remain technologically dependent in the future.

Methods similar to time-lapse photography have been discussed; these would require clocking devices for differentiation of stages in the transposition of data, but such technical solutions do not resolve the intellectual judgment about when a fluid and dynamic text or image has changed substantially and substantively to become an essentially different document. The issue is somewhat like the automobile collector who starts out with an original, and in the process of restoration exchanges so may parts that the refurbished car, like an enhanced document, resembles the original but in fact no longer has the same physical components as before. The object is objectively altered, but subjectively preserved. Carried to an even more perplexing level, if cloning is developed and transplants are increasingly common, when would a body become a different person? Or, in human and historical terms, body cells grow, replicate, and die in personal growth, and an intellect matures with age and may decline with age; we think of such life transitions as natural and that the person remains constant even while life is dynamic. We distinguish between thoughts of the immature and mature person and can treat thought as evolutionary and isolate stages in a series with chronology, yet we commonly treat data derived from dynamic life-cycles as if they were static. There are parallels by which to think about dynamic information systems and records, and the very technology making such flexible systems and fluid documents available can also be redesigned and reapplied to meta-documentation systems by which to make sense of them historically. This is meta-history unlike whatever has been conceived before.

While historians will probably welcome the retro-conversion of microfilmed documents to digital form for convenience if nothing else, they must consider the evidential aspects of transmutable documents, the chain of custody, the strength of information systems and organizations for endurance of the records they hold, and citation and reference issues in how scholarship is sustained, critically evaluated, verified, and transmitted. The intellectual aspects of documentation in electronic media seem not to be progressing in tandem with technological advancement. New protocols and an entirely revised Diplomatics must be invented for human as well as man-machine communications (DURANTI, 1988-91; MCCRANK, 1994). These perhaps need to entail the electronic equivalent of notarization and registration, so if data and metadata do not check out, one is alerted to data tampering. Such methods can be employed with licensing or authorization of use, and archives dispersing their holdings in digital form can create online test beds by which users can reverify their data before accepting it for their research. A reverified source could be given a dated seal of "Good Housekeeping" which is updated whenever the data sources are collated for verification. Whenever a seal or notarization was compromised, or when data integrity came into question, a new download from the quality-controlled source could be arranged as a matter of course. Digital technology is now altering and will continue to change the nature of archives, libraries, and documentation; it must necessarily change how historical information searching is undertaken, how research is conducted, and how historians teach and prepare students for a new era of history.

While it is easy to be enthusiastic about new technology (or intimidated, as the case may be), some wariness is justified both because of the problems facing scholars in the intellectual control of their sources and of their own intellectual property, and in the selection and application of technologies for their own projects. Just as businesses must be realistic in bringing viable products to the marketplace, scholars must be realistic in assessing technology and in project design to relate research to productivity and to their intellectual marketplace. Pilot projects are expensive and risky, and they require advanced research to guard against duplication. Technological innovation requires greater investment than transfer and adaptation, so most technical progress is incremental. Studies about technical information transfer show that this difficult task of technology assessment, selection, and integration is often ill performed in business and industry and is equally problematic in academe. Sometimes projects, especially academic endeavors where being first to secure patent rights and market shares is less important than in manufacturing and industry, are better served by adoption of "tried-and-true" rather than cutting edge technology. The ability to glide from one technological base to another is just as critical, however. Such concerns require historians and other academicians mounting research projects using modern information technology to develop technical abilities beyond what they usually possess individually, and therefore to rely on research support centers, technical support staffs, and project assistants. In this milieu, collaborative project management is an art needing to be explored, studied, and developed. It is a competency required of computing historians and electronic archivists as well.

Retrospective Source Conversion

Although the term "retrospective conversion" has been used in the library world since the transition from card to online catalogs and the editing of bibliographic data to conform to AACR II, it did not connote the transformation of physical into virtual libraries because librarians concentrated first on their meta-information structures rather than source content; nor was it used until recently, as by ROSS (1993, pp. 6-8), to describe Document Image Processing (DIP) or the task of converting hard-copy print and manuscript records into machine-readable form. The historical task is threefold: (1) to create a surrogate record from the original for retrieval as metadata and format these into library cataloging and archival inventory controls; (2) to transform the physical record into machine-readable form; and (3) to normalize the information therein so it can be transferred, collated, and analyzed, which usually means tagging and coding already published materials, but can also entail transcription, transliteration, and translation of archival sources. It is usually assumed that such coordination, transformation, and visualization were pre-storage operations, but technology today affords customized storage with both pre-processing and post-processing. In keeping with archival principles original data may be stored with minimal alteration, and search interfaces can work between one format and another, the content and a query. Reformatting and assembly now go hand in hand more with retrieval than with storage. Moreover, storage condensation now allows one to store originals as analog digital images linked to converted parallels such as OCR-processed and coded documents without the kind of distortion originals sources were once subjected to in retrospective conversion or transformation to electronic form.

Many technologists who use the term "conversion" to describe digital processes fail to understand the implications of the term culturally; as in religious conversion it means embracing the new means and turning one's back on the old. They may assume that they can do likewise, rather than seeing the converted documentation as an extension of the older forms in a continuous record. Historians and archivists rightly think more in terms of continuity. It is significant that most historical institutions making records available in digital form are therefore keeping originals and often microfilm copies as well. Digital conversion is an expansionist rather than a replacement technology in history-related endeavors: continuity is a cardinal ethic, which may embrace the archival principles of *respect du fonds* and *provenance* to preserve original order, document integrity, and genealogy. Hence, "conversion" is not really the correct cultural term to apply to such transferral of historical documentation into electronic forms. Conversion, a turnaround, entails a rejection of the old in favor of the new (from *convertere*). Especially in religion, it is a starting over, new beginning, and whole-scale, thorough alteration, and it emphasizes discontinuity. It does not refer to the outer form, but the inner substance, intellectual matter, and character.

Adherence would be a more correct term meaning, that although one moves onward, the old form is respected, retained, augmented and enhanced. Adherence is incremental, transitional, and stresses continuity. One thereby supports tradition, i.e., a living carrying forth, rather than destruction of the past, the old, and everything former, for the sake of the new. The misuse of the term "retrospective conversion" in librarianship is a case in point; it often is taken to mean the changeover of bibliographic records from manual to electronic form, but it actually includes conversion from nonstandard bibliographic description to *Anglo-American Cataloging Rules* II. If old records are merely transferred to new media, where is the conversion? It is a technical transformation, perhaps, with increased access, but not a substantive change in information quality. Of course it was argued by many that much local information in manual bibliographic records was lost, especially when fuller description was replaced with scant Library of Congress cataloging. Conversion usually implies change for the better, but in rejecting the old, the historical past is always endangered. If in Electronic Archival Description (EAD) old description is merely made available electronically through HTML coding, without substantial editing, improvement of the record, and enhancement of the metadata, likewise the transfer to new media is not a genuine conversion. If archivists practiced their own principles in their archives' archives (i.e., their metadata or information systems), they would edit their records serially and keep the series intact. Old descriptions would be retained, either manually, or for continuity in access, in coded form as a linked record to revised, upgraded, and new EAD records.

Hence, more than simply being new, digitization properly managed is a means of renewal. As BASSNETT & LEFEVRE's colleagues indicate, such transfer work like translation is not purely mechanical; even machine-translation with human intervention and editing requires more than simply knowing languages, but also understanding cultures. Creating information systems that transcend the cultures of records creators and transmitters and that aim beyond the immediate culture of the contemporary user is complex. So, when records are converted to other forms, one must also understand that a transformation is undertaken, of documentation and the cultures to which it relates. Technology provides tools for change, and as such technology is itself a force to be reckoned with in cultural evolution. Converting records between media, formats, and language will, as G. NUNBERG (1996) and his associates maintain, cause some wrenching social and cultural dislocations.

Early historical computing entail laborious transfer of data onto code-sheets and then on to punched cards (the "precursors of Electronic Records" according to ADAMS). The latter have disappeared, but not keyboarding and the laborious task of data transfer. Now, however, historians are keenly interested in Optical Character Recognition and scanning in expectation that original scripted, drawn, and printed sources even if microfilmed (which is being investigated at the University of Birmingham, as reported by LAFLIN, 1993, 1995a, 1995b) can be "read" into machine-readable form and output in print characters, and they want to be able to code and tag such converted data as easily as correcting student term papers. Once thought impossible, this is now probable on a scale unbelievable just a decade ago but as technical capabilities (reviewed by GOODALL) increase, so do aspirations and the issue of mass conversion is still daunting. These problems remain: high resolution is still costly as is all image storage; long-term preservation is more labor intensive and organization dependent than print media; and distribution systems are still in their infancy, as concluded by a recent report (1993) of NARA's COMMISSION ON PRESERVATION AND ACCESS (p. 14; cf. earlier report to the Commission by LESK).

Despite the common misconception that scanners "read" documents and such processes are automatic (corrected by GIUNTA & HACKER), retrospective conversion from manuscript or printed historical records to machine-readable data files is a multistep and labor intensive process as described by M. OLSEN (1993, pp. 94-97) from experience building the ARTFL database. In some cases, as OLSEN (1991) demonstrates with formally published French literature, an economy of scale is never reached to decrease costs by volume, and at times manual keyboarding is still more cost-effective than high-tech solutions especially if such work can be subcontracted to foreign workshops for savings on input labor. Manuscript work cannot be outsourced in most cases because of the special skills required even to read historical materials, so the closest alternative is to exploit student labor where in major universities' higher costs can also be justified as advanced training and continuing education (STEPHENSON). In other cases such as the Bakunin manuscript project at the International Institute of Social History in Leyden (BOS), it made sense to pay for transcription and normalization work to be done manually and to farm out the work by language to native-speakers of the four principle languages used by Tat'jan Alexandrev Bakunin (1814-1876), founder of the anarchist movement. BOS & VAN DER MOER claims that manual transcription in Russia proved to be a lot cheaper than OCR, but computers have been employed for 11,000 pages of printed text of which 3,500 have already been converted and normalized. The *Arkiv Bakunin* of 100,200 letters, to be edited with French translations, cost five million gilders (overrunning its $3.5 million gilder budget for an intended five-year project) and consisted of seven volumes by 1981, and was falling further and further behind production schedules. After a hiatus in 1992, the project was resurrected but converted to CD-ROM production, which also made conveyance of pictures, portraits, and sketches by some 430 artists much easier and more economical. Savings in reproduction and processing were transferred into better indexing. Nevertheless, because of volume and desire to transfer costs from labor intensive input and processing to error detection and postprocessing editing for quality control, computing historians are intensely interested in computer visual science and the practical Optical Character Recognition (OCR) applications. Digitized sources, of course, are not searchable until translated by OCR applications or what has sometimes been called Intelligent Character Recognition (ICR) to distinguish simpler preservation technology that reproduces text digitally but which operates like an analog, from readable or manipulated text.

While progress in recognizing type or print in standard fonts is considerable, recent work on manuscript is also significant. Prospects appeared promising by the mid-1980s for fairly conforming stylized pre-twentieth-century secretarial handwriting in United States National Archives, as reported by M. ALLEN. Since then, considerable progress has been made on scripts presenting even greater calligraphic variety and levels of difficulty such as mixtures of Cyrillic and Latin alphabets for Russian and Polish sources (BORODKIN *ET AL.*, 1993; BOS *ET AL.*) and medieval Gothic Latin book hands such as textura script (FRIEDMAN, 1993) or Renaissance incunabula and modern German Gothics (VAN HORIK, 1992), but still harder challenges lay in the archives with early-modern highly abbreviated scribbles that frustrate the most capable paleographer, the nonstandardized scripts of the Middle Ages, or epigraphical evidence in archeological museums. ROBINSON doubts if scanning technology, especially pattern recognition, will ever suffice for medieval hands. However, the same skepticism was applied to Arabic script and Chinese characters; in the latter case, progress has been significant (HSIEH). Moreover, NATO's Scientific Laboratories have pursued OCR for all kinds of handwriting, especially for identification purposes (e.g., NATO SCIENTIFIC AFFAIRS DIVISION Institute on the Fundamentals of Handwriting Recognition conference at the Château de Bonas, France, in 1993). Longhand and secretarial or notarial hands present difficulty levels far more complex than fine medieval book hands. Once intractable problems are giving way to significant progress. In all instances, the costly and laborious tasks of transcription and input are bottlenecks in the current state of technology that keep the art from achieving the potential envisioned.

The history of OCR development through the early 1990s is outlined by MORI *ET AL.*, which may be supplemented by the review of current OCR research by GOVINDAN & SHIV-APRASAD and H. C. OGG's useful reference guide to the OCR field (1992). Another useful overview is provided by R. PLAMONDON specifically for handwritten documentation, for which A. SENIOR (1992) makes available electronically an evaluative report on several applicable OCR systems. Two recent conferences provide reports and case studies from a variety of projects in or related to History: the first *International Conference on Document Analysis and Recognition* at Saint Malo, France, in 1991 (INTERNATIONAL CONFERENCE), and the 1993 international AHC-sponsored workshop hosted by Leyden University through the joint efforts of the Nijmegen Institute for Cognition and Information (NICI, founded in 1986) and the Netherlands Historical Data Archives (NHDA), which produced the proceedings *Optical Character Recognition in the Historical Discipline* (DOORN *ET AL.*, eds.).

The evolution of OCR technology occurred along two competing lines: (1) feature extraction programs that dentify characters by recognizing components in a font design and are, therefore, font dependent; versus (2) pattern recognition which requires training before conversion, but which is not font dependent. Hence, the term "omnifont" came into use in the United States for the pattern approach, even though the name is misleading. Four generations of OCR can be identified to date. The earliest trial-and-error period focused on analog solutions whereby light passed through masks and was captured on photosensitive film. During the 1970s dedicated systems were common, each for specific fonts, using very clear shapes; but a limited amount of training was attempted to expand from specific fonts to families of type design. Limited success encouraged the pattern recognition approach, but too many calculations were required for easy glide to PC machines in the 1980s. PCs for OCR had to be equipped with extra memory, dedicated scanners, etc., but experimentation continued to improve performance. Consequently, in the 1990s when more powerful PCs came onto the mass market, OCR technology could be mounted in self-contained workstations for the first time. Some cost surveys indicate that between 1986 and 1992 OCR costs dropped by a factor of ten every two years, from $4,000 to $400 for software, so that since 1993 the market has seen a variety of software and hardware configurations that make widespread use of OCR for source conversion more feasible than ever. Indeed, some software like *Cuneiform* 2 can be downloaded for free trial use (http://www.ocr.com).

Most OCR operations contain the following program elements: (1) image files are fed into a recognition engine which de-skews and cleans the image (box and line removal, etc.); (2) base structure or formatting is analyzed to determine page layout (e.g., double columns require a different reading order than single column documents); (3) zones or windows and templates are created, so work can be chunked into controllable sizes; (4) a variety of operations can be performed for training (adjustments are made when "guesses" are verified, so repeated sightings are recognized with more confidence), lexical information can be applied from external sources (e.g., from dictionaries which feed spell-checker operations), and ranges can be established for all or special features (alpha, numeric, or alpha-numeric, and symbolic) for efficiency and accuracy (e.g., range setting eliminated common errors, such as "5" and "S" or "0" and "O," which can be confused easily); (5) confidence evaluations can be calculated; and (6) editing assistants can be had, which double-check wherever the system hesitated.

A variety of hardware and software can be identified in historical records projects: different models of the Kurzweil Document Editing Machine (KDEM) through the K5200 series were most common and were employed relatively early by the Max-Planck Institut, for example (THALLER, 1989); Gigaread 1.52, a matrix matching package has been upstaged largely by Pro-Lector 1.2; and scanners in use include ReadStar, Omnipage, Apple's Macintosh One Scanner, Fujitsu's Image Scanner, Caere Typist and Typist Plus graphics, and Hewlett Packard IIp and IIc machines, etc. (VAN HORIK, 1992a). Many case studies report evaluations of such technology for their specific applications such as VAN HORIK's reviews for the NHDA (1992b, 1996), usually more as justification for decision making in projects than systematic review and assessment of needs not being met by vendors. The Association for Information and Image Management (AIIM), however, provides neutral and objective assessments of the current technology (i.e., buying guides and state of the industry reports, having moved well beyond micrographics as reviewed by VILHAUER), and help literature such as what is recommended practice (p. 1,198) for quality control of image scanners and the proper role for facsimile [1989] (see its *Journal of Information and Image Management* [*JIIM*] and note the AIIM *Glossary of Imaging Technology,* 1992).

History and archives have always posed significant problems for OCR and optical disk developers because the storage medium is not archival or human readable in any sense, so its machine-dependency is a counterweight to its pliability in electronic form. Also, many of the original sources to be converted are contextually sensitive. For example, multilingual texts in culture-formed and individualized connected cursive scripts are far more difficult than handwritten blocked or printed character recognition from standardized fonts of discrete designed letters. Consequently, historical sources are still classified as among the most difficult to read by OCR, and sometimes examples are pulled from old material as test samples for new technology. The Information Science Research Institute in Las Vegas evaluates such technology for the United States Departments of Defense and Energy by drawing samples from a five million character database (test results can be found at http://www.isri.unlv.edu/isri). In all, 50-75 percent of all mistakes occur in 20 percent of the most difficult documents to read because of broken characters, interlining, smudges, erasures, etc., which are common in historical documents. Most of these problems will not be resolved specifically for History, but by adaptations of applications to forensics and document examination concerns in other fields.

Problems being resolved currently are those presented by tables, curved lines, speckling, small print, reverse video, and creative type fonts that do not fall into well-classified design families. Solutions are in place for the most common problems: non-Latin and "creative" fonts are studied with training algorithms so the recognition learning only has to occur once; shady backgrounds or yellow pages are treated with a variable grey scale and by dropping out color in scanning; grey scale OCR also compensates for many broken characters; range testing deals with numerical tables; separation functions have been built into OCR software to divide adjoining characters such as ligatures; digital filtering takes care of many stains in so-called "enhancement" processing; and bleeding is increasingly controlled by adaptive contrast settings. Work on signatures is still in progress. Mistakes are classified as insertions, substitutions, and rejections. Nearly 100 percent may never be reached, but accuracy is improving and several programs (*Textbridge*, *Omnipage*, OCRON, *Recognita*, etc.) have now tested at above 90 percent. *Recognita* 3 has proven good for Eastern European languages, and *Cuneiform* 2 has performed well on Cyrillic and seems well suited for degraded material. Moreover, for fine work and small-point text (e.g., below 6 pt.) requiring upgrades from the standard range of 300-400 dpi resolution to 600, not only do equipment prices increase, but the storage space required jumps astronomically (800 times the space for a standard page of keyboarded text

[5000 bytes] without compression; 200 times with compression). But new 5.25-inch optical disks can store 500 million bytes, or ca. twenty-five 5,300-page books.

Experience with converting printed materials is extensive enough to have produced tables of acceptable error and speed rates for the most common formats (OGG, 1993, pp. 85-86). Errors are corrected in a variety of proofing mechanisms from matches with personal reading by an editor, oral readings with a second corrections editor, and double-entry routines such as over-typing, to more technical means like spell-checkers operating with customized dictionaries, global search and replace commands for common misreadings (the ARTFL project does this for several hundred transformations for its software: OLSEN, 1993, p. 107), replacement of second readers altogether by duplicate scanning and voice replay for the editor, and multiple scannings and automatic collations or synchronization which can reduce errors by as much as 70 percent, beyond which expert editors intervene into a semi-automatic reprocessing to produce the final version as in most machine-translation editing (HANDLEY & HICKEY; BRADFORD & NARTKER; CONCEPCION & D'AMATO). Editing converted text files usually requires some personal guidance because global search and replace routines to normalize orthography and standardize terminologies, designed for document production wherein variables are assumed to be merely keyboarding errors, are not what historians always want. They must discriminate between mechanical misreadings in the conversion process and indigenous variables that are not errors but constitute evidence. Likewise, automatic correction routines in firmware like Hewlett Packard's scanners can prove problematic. In most cases they want the machine-readable form to remain truthful to the original, with variables in spelling and vocabularies intact for special study. The normalization *qua* modernization is largely a contrivance for information retrieval, which may be done in a surrogate overlay or indexing additive, without misconstruing original data. Such modifications like the current trend toward typeface and resolution enhancement for bit-mapped characters, are better left to post-processing as improvements of output rather than use where they constitute a corruption of the database.

Early aims may have been too high with the immediate expectation of total automation of a manual process. The ideal is technology that informs itself during its own applications, rather than automates repetitiously; i.e., something more than performing faster and more consistently than manual processing, the technology generates new information about what accomplishes the work and thereby increases efficiency and refines technique. OCR relying on pattern recognition may be described as automation because the process is basically static and repetitive, while relying on vector analysis may be a case of informed and dynamic processing, requiring "smart" technology. The midway between these technologies is computer-assisted processing, where the "smarts" are supplied through human intervention into an otherwise automated process. Some of the most satisfying applications seem to be in such human-machine interactive technologies. Developments in machine-translation projects as at Siemens Corporation and its TEAM Terminology Data Bank (BRINKMANN), which grew out of technical information transfer efforts that once appeared as industrial espionage in order to translate technical specifications for major industrial designs like airplane schematics, have successfully scanned and separated format from text and replaced the translated version back in the same formats in electronically reconstructed documents. This same technology is replicated whereby layout features such as column dividers are screened out to allow OCR information retrieval from tax forms, census polls, and voting registrations that contain readily convertible numeric and prosopographic data so important for socioeconomic and political history. Historians often need to retain a document's format for editing and evidential purposes, but D. KELLER points to other technical reasons, as when an index is already available and need not be redone if the electronic text is reconstituted in the same page format. Finally, such technology has become sophisticated enough to convert medieval scribal to modern music notation (MCGEE & MERKLEY, 1991, 1993), which is much more difficult than earlier conversions from engraved music (PRERAU), as a spin-off from applications to text. It is this versatility, increased accuracy, and speed that are revolutionizing historical source conversion.

While progress in OCR conversion of standard Latin fonts has progressed, and this may be employed where it is a viable tool for source conversion to electronic form, the outstanding problem for most historians and archivists is script conversion by means other than manual transcription and keyboarding. Based on such foundations as Fourier transforms and Bezier curvatures, handwriting has been studied from several perspectives (SRIHARI & BOZINOVIC), as a repetitive and oscillating process, separate from the words or products of such processing. Slowly a "grammar of action," as it has been called by E. Helsper and L. Schomaker, has been developed (DOORN *ET AL.*, 1993). This can be applied to pen strokes, which can be isolated optically (PETIER & CAMILLERAPP), to create a Virtual Handwriting System envisioned for the near future. Instead of graphic images bit-mapped or recognized by a static pattern (dependent on considerable standardization in penmanship not to be expected from most sources in dynamic interactive systems developed from early studies of human kinematics for artwork [FREYD; LACQUANTI *ET AL.*] that use vector-oriented algorithms) pen movements are traced, once with an electronic stylus but now with scanners. These movements, like other trajectories (e.g., an airplane's flight pattern), are broken into directional leads, angles, and scaled from light to heavy strokes, which like simulations (SENIOR, 1992) or animations (REEVES) are matched against previously computerized models of similar behavior and character formation (SCHOMAKER, 1991 & 1993; SCHOMAKER & TEULINGS) or the application of neural nets. The problems of segmentation and connectivity remain, making script more difficult than hand printing because of irregular spacing and horizontal glide in letter and word formation. Size variables like height are handled by adhering to baselines (EDELMAN, FLASH & ULLMAN) and creating histograms (SENIOR, 1992 & 1993) to study ranges and displacements created in certain scripts. In most cases such techniques are employed to "teach" a system to recognize scripts not seen before so that transliteration is made accurate, but for massive conversion projects teachable programs have been replaced by newer omnifont pattern recognition software with such capabilities as feature extraction and fragment analysis subroutines (OGG, 1993, p. 87).

Newness in technical development does not always mean the best match for particular applications. For example, the older user-trainable procedures for OCR have been employed in identification of scripts and individual handwriting for their own sake (FRIEDMAN, 1993), as in the critical edition of a medieval manuscript and with computer assistance discerning a sequence of different scribes in its production by the patterns of variables that appear in their handwriting or when using scanners like old Hinman collators to compare typographic variants. The buildup of seemingly trivial data from variants and their patterns makes a case for the origin (location and time of manufacture) of manuscripts on the basis of scribal characteristics that add precision to examination procedures already practiced by diplomaticists and paleographers. Indeed, knowledge of conventions controlling format and structure as taught in Diplomatics, and of title page design with borders, rules, and other forms of compartmentalization as studied in Descriptive and Analytical Bibliography (the F. BOWERS and P. HASKELL tradition), are useful when manipulating scanned text independently from its original state, context, and historical format. Pure SGML coded text or ASCII files, for example, are more readily searchable than blocked and compartmentalized text. If OCR prepared text were to be reconstituted electronically for a historic visual representation, it is possible to develop coding for typographic design and use tags to retrieve printer's devices or scribal embellishments from an imagebase as when importing visuals from electronic libraries of drawings and schematics for CAD constructions, to recreate an electronic facsimile on demand. Theoretically, the borders, rules, and compartments could be studied independently of text for investigations of composition and production, and attributions to printers and other workshops. However, when not needed, text could likewise be searched independently by machine or read by a human in whatever script or font one wanted, in larger type, and with enhancements for legibility and clarity.

Associative memory for organizing auxiliary databases of patterns, as described by T. KOHONEN, and generative clustering techniques applied to the such variables in handwriting as height and elongation, ductus or directional curvature of an individual stroke within a character, weight of pen to parchment or paper, etc., produce "uncertain reasoning" algorithms (KAHNEMAN, SLOVIC & TVERSKY; SHAFER & TVERSKY), which allow approximations for ambiguous characters and fuzzy transliteration or problematic illegibility as when organic inks fade into their supports or bleed-throughs hinder making sense out of a verso. Possible readings can be analyzed morphologically (CONCEPTION *ET AL.*), matched against stored whole-word dictionaries that may use words either as character sets or symbols (O'HAIR & KABRISKY) or phrases and whole sentences (PAQUET & LECOURTIER) for things like addresses and quotations respectively, so systems like a Viterbi decoder can "guess" the most likely choices to produce a meaningful word or phrase and can mark variables and present candidates for subsequent selection in manual editing. Differences in transliteration and orthography can be confused easily, however, so errors will always occur.

VAN HORIK (1993, p. 164) and others predict a rapid improvement in OCR technology that will produce even more flexibility in records conversion to electronic form, from automatic adjustment of contrast settings in scanning operations and better "noise" filters to combinations of linear approaches of reading character by character by classification and static pattern matching that will always be necessary backups for diacriticals and such embellishments as flourishes and gross capitals, with dynamic readers that will be trainable through text runs to adjust to a document's regular scripts and typefaces, spacing, layouts, and repeated orthographic variables. Such advances will assuredly accelerate the already rapid deployment of OCR technology to historical records and will ultimately enable historians to concentrate more on source criticism and editorial processes than on the technology itself. A few centers monitor recent advances in OCR technology. The NHDA, for example, takes on text conversion projects by contract, may be mentioned here. Work at the NHDA has included: digitization of over 20,000 historical photographs and the creation of a retrieval system for these; enhancing digitized census records with character recognition for data manipulation; recording text data from birth, death and marriage certificates; conversion of a massive Dutch bibliography into CD-ROM for redistribution; and undertaking a pilot project to convert 60,000 pages of parliamentary records from 1996 into electronic form.

In 1996, VAN HORIK provided a state-of-the-art assessment for the NHDA and shared his findings for computing historians who contemplate using OCR to build large test bases. He notes several new developments that make OCR feasible even in small archives and for moderate-sized projects. First, three-dimensional OCR is being developed, where grey scale and image input are mixable, so that a range of choices can be made for other than black or white pixels. This will increase accuracy and may have applications in type-overs, erasures, and palimpsests if OCR is perfected for scripts. Second, the kinds of external knowledge brought to bear on a scanned text make ICR, despite the marketing hype, approach what appears to be intelligent renderings of difficult texts. New software programs include multilingual dictionaries, specialty lexicons for sub-languages, classifiers, segmentation programs, and those which aim at ambiguity resolution. Third, fuzzy matching after the fact allows an OCR operation to leave a string in memory which deviates from matches, so retrieval of the string need not be exactly as read in the viewable text. For example, trigrams, three-character segments in search strings that can be retrieved without absolute accuracy, are used. Fourth, voting systems are being employed where multiple engines scan a text and the reading which is taken as the majority becomes the preferred rendering. Other readings are not necessarily obliterated but are arranged by confidence levels calculated by filters, spell-checkers, and algorithms. Sometimes, these are combined with manual selection as in Machine-Translation

(MT) systems for human intervention in editing. Manual labor is therefore decreased and is expended only at critical points where human expertise is required. OCR combined with MT means that in preparing electronic versions, one can create electronic translations by expending human labor to enhance the total product. If full translation is not required, keyword hypertext or indexing can be multilingual to enhance information retrieval.

Such technology may be deployed in the reverse, for other uses which are "cool" but potentially dangerous for historical research. It can be used to imitate scribes, medieval and modern, including your handwriting, and create computerized manuscript facsimiles. Thus scanning and character recognition to produce imitations can be used to prepare instructional materials for courses in paleography, calligraphy, and typography. A calligrapher or anyone willing to pay an average price for personalized software to Signature Software, Inc. (Hood River, OR), can submit a rendition of someone's handwriting as a specimen sheet to be scanned for the design of a font resembling the original. Or, anyone can submit his or her signature and 26 specified sample words and seven ligatures handwritten on blueline matrices. The selection is designed to encompass the alphabet in capitals and lowercase letters, most ligatures occurring in English, punctuation, and special signs ordinarily displayed on a keyboard. The company supplies *Personal Font* version 1.1, which matches standard ASCII characters with electronic imitations from the supplied samples. The result is a "personal font" that one names for him or herself; it duplicates not letter formation as with script fonts for typewriters, but word formations that appear handwritten complete with the idiosyncracies of one's personal hand with or without optional spell-checking. Or if you do not like your handwriting, select an elegant recreated hand from the company's *SUPERScript* cursive Font package. Once installed, the font can be selected for laser printers like any other option. Ostensibly, such a personalized manuscript has some popular appeal, as in making believe that annual holiday letters are original and handwritten, but it could also be used by secretaries inserting "signatures" to text-processed letters for their bosses. In this regard, security would seem a little worrisome, as still another test of signature identification technology is provided. It is no wonder that security and endorsement systems are converting to fingerprinting, voice recognition, or as introduced in spy dramas, retinal scanning for identification. Such technology also means that for the moderate price of a software package, and MAC or PC workstation, and a high-resolution laser printer, anyone can manufacture an altered facsimile of the Gettysburg Address or any other historical document for which facsimiles exist by which to make a cut-out specimen sheet. Of course, if for fraud, the work would have to be done a little better than in 1996 when three Columbia University students used the school's high-resolution color photocopiers to manufacturer their own currency. The United States Treasury Department was quick to intervene, but not before several counterfeit bills had been passed to an unsuspecting public. Now, of course, currency engraving has gone high-tech with additions to visible design and decoration of an arsenal of invisible watermarks, fingerprints, rules of various length and thickness, and double-checking serial numbers to be scanned electronically, with deliberately skewed overprinting to produce fuzziness and blurs, and selection of certain colors over backgrounds into which the foreground fades, and carefully placed micro-flaws into otherwise flawless design, just to defy the latest in OCR and related technologies. In short, traditional authentification means are usually lost in OCR processing and visualization. In the case of guarding against facsimiles that serve as counterfeit, other means should be invented so that historical documentation in surrogate has some identification other than face value.

This prospect of fraud, together with substandard work and incompetence when this technology is so available to the amateur, adds new meaning to document examination for archivists and historians in the future of appraisal and evidence consideration in a world of electronic records. But consider also the positive uses for teaching, the convenience of electronic surrogates for readers who commonly disdain microfilm, and the transportability. Or, consider, with the ethics involved and proper disclosure, the justifiable reproduction on artificially aged paper of facsimiles to be displayed in an exhibit, which would save the original from over-exposure and the prolonged access to precious documents conserved better because of their decreased actual use. Consider promotional uses. An archives or manuscripts library with extensive holdings of the papers of certain individuals, for example, can create specimen sheets by scanning or high-resolution xerography, have a personal font composed for the original hand, and then reproduce manuscripts from electronic transcriptions. Then the visitor could ask the Manuscripts Division of the Library of Congress, for example, for a OCR-reproduced presidential manuscript, or a facsimile autograph, as a keepsake. A character recognized can be matched against customized fonts built from OCR input into image bases of this or that person's handwriting or type from any historic printshop. The library or museum shop could as easily provide a fake personal note wishing Season's Greetings to patrons from long-dead historical figures, prerequisite documents for the most prestigious genealogy, or a land grant from authorities long ago. A thin line divides facsimiles from fakes and electronic reproduction from fraud.

Less innocently, abuse of such technology may threaten the continuation of handwritten checks, or at least their cashing, because of this slender difference between facsimile reproduction and forgery that is increasingly nonexistent except in intention of use to enhance or to defraud. The problems created by such rapidly developing facsimile technology make those surveyed by RAPPORT, who 20 years ago pointed to the difficulties in discerning between forgeries, fakes, and facsimiles, pale by comparison. Every archivist and curator will have to be a forensics expert as well as a technical wizard. O'TOOLE (1994) examined the archival ideal of uniqueness in paper, and punctured this myth so that it will never survive as before, but his analysis is only a prelude to understanding that uniqueness in the electronic world is a theoretical notion so far removed from paper archives that metaphors linking physical and electronic formats fail archivists miserably. Ideas about data integrity as perceived in computer science are equally limited. Technology is slowly grappling with the problems created by the flexibility of modern digital forms because these problems are just becoming clear. Contemporary historians have not been thinking about them as much as accountants, bankers, document examiners, lawyers, and the courts, but the next generation of historians most assuredly must confront the problem of evidence in electronic documentation.

Such are the prospects of new optical character and vector analysis graphic technology in the near future of historical and modern documentation. These speculations illustrate the proverbial wisdom in associating both a curse and blessing with technology. Not only should the contemporary archivist, curator, and historian be equipped with forensic skills in technical document examination, reading rooms will have to be equipped like laboratories with workstations for document verification and authentification before records are entered into evidence in courtrooms or history books. After all, "salting" an archives is an ageless game played by land swindlers and unethical researchers alike. Now one does not even need to be a calligraphically skilled artisan to attempt a little counterfeit on the unsuspecting. Technology assists even amateurs in faking mastery. This phenomenon, too, adds to the case for the revival of Diplomatics as advocated by L. DURANTI (1989-1990) at the turn of this decade, but also extended into electronic documentation studies and a new forging of science into an Historical Information Science on a different magnitude than encompassed by current Social Science computing. Retrospective conversion projects will add to this future questioning, unless project documentation is kept meticulously, and this becomes part of the whole record as metadata assuring chain of custody, quality control, high standards, and personal integrity so that documents read electronically may also be trusted.

Description, Terminology, and Data Exchange

Although the master recordkeeper Sir Hilary Jenkinson very early reminded historians that "archives were not drawn up in their interest or for the information of Posterity" (JENKINSON,

p. 11), historians have always thought otherwise. Their difficulty in using data compiled in the past is often blamed on poor documentation and design on the part of the creators who, however, never had such future use in mind. Such criticism is somewhat antihistorical, but the problems encountered because of such lack of foresight are considerable and some historians and data archivists today call for intervention and education so contemporary database developers will not repeat the mistakes of the past and will describe and document their data for future use (HEDSTROM, 1992; ROSS, 1993; ANDERSON, 1994). The same caveat, however, must be applied to data archivists and information science historians whose use of a data set may entail enhancements which like subsequent revised editions of monographs, should also be saved and catalogued. The fruits of recurring historical efforts must be cumulative for added value (LIEVESLEY) in a repetitive process (more than secondary use, but tertiary, etc.); thus the idea of "recycling databases" (MCCRANK, 1987; supported by HOLM, p. 317). Note similar attempts in historical lexicology to recover corpora for machine-translation purposes (VOLLMER); each work is a building block for something greater. Secondary use of data should result in a value-added dimension to the primary data because of a continuing provenance and record of reuse that can be portrayed as an oscillating series (MCCRANK, 1987). Description of contents and formats for sustained access must be a continual process, e.g., description of reformatting, upgrades, and enhanced separate editions. Data archives must not fall into the habit of thinking that their historical files are best or most valuable only if immediately reusable by inappropriately borrowing criteria of use from librarianship, complete with its presentist fallacy (MARKER, 1993, p. 190).

The current emphasis in the American archival community on "continuing value" is susceptible to this present-mindedness, largely as a matter of expediency. In most cases records created for one intent, even when well described for their original purpose, must be described again for alternative uses. Otherwise, appraisal based on continuing use or nonuse may reflect the adequacy or inadequacy of description and intellectual access, which has everything to do with the efficiency and fulfillment of mission of an archival program and little intrinsically with the records themselves. Indeed, continued use may require continued promotion, not just passive intellectual access. Such effort, however, is more than just public relations and marketing. It involves terminological links within and between series (BUDIN), and a further linkage between past and potential use by relating published research with records series. Such a programmatic access apparatus is imperative for electronic records which can not be seen, understood, or used without some sort of mediation. This requires different sets of subject descriptors as well as standards for description of the source itself, i.e., meta-information or surrogate documentation, whether for manuscript, print, or electronic files. MORELLI calls attention to this need of a special-purpose language in defining electronic records as a whole, including the computer system as basic rather than external to such definition, as when old databases are glided onto new hosts. BEARMAN (1995) suggests in essence adopting the expediency that a record is one when the creator/sender says so in a mandatory protocol at the beginning of an official transmission. This is essentially what MCCRANK (1994) called for in the invention of a new electronic diplomacy. Agreements about such boilerplating, however, still leave unsettled such matters as internal consistency, readability, and compatibility; and continuity in meaning and interpretation even if data can be transferred from place to place and from one time to another. Here again the specter of language standardization is raised, or one must consider alternatives such as hyperlinkage to extensive meta-documentation.

The transportability of records across systems and adherence to standards have been major concerns of the electronic archives community (NARA, 1990; UNITED NATIONS, 1990) throughout this decade and before, but these issues took time to move toward center stage in discussions in the history computing community. They are essential as rules for a common playing ground of technical and intellectual interaction. This approach involves intervention and regulation. Whereas historians are still at the stage of understanding the very idea of specified standards rather than a generalized ethical code of conduct (i.e., the creation of "an electronic records culture," (UNITED NATIONS ACCIS, pp. 26-27), archivists working with other components of the information profession recognize a variety of standards issues that may be classified into four main categories (GETTY TRUST AHIP & ICOM CIDOC, 1993):

1.   Information system standards for the functions and operations of an information system

2.   Data standards, which pertain to the information itself, its record structure, content which is determined by rules of data entry into fields and elements, and values of the vocabulary used in fields

3.   Procedural standards for management and policy enforcement

4.   Information exchange standards (such as X12, etc., discussed subsequently) that allow institutions and systems to share information, e.g., ISO-8879 or SGML; ISO-2709 for cataloging data, and Electronic Data Interchange for Administration, Commerce, and Transport (EDIFACT) that merged X12 with the United Nations Trade Data Interchange (UN/TDI) standard.

Discussions on standards in general often confuse these because they are indeed interrelated, just as discussions about electric records sometimes seem to confuse the content or records of an archives, or the actual information and the surrogate records that document that information, i.e., the meta-information. Whereas the latter dominated discussions during the past decade for the establishment of the AMC-MARC format by which archives could use bibliographic networks to share information about their holdings, increasingly the electronic archives community has refocused attention on the former. Discussions in circles of computer historians tend to bypass descriptive standards and meta-information to aim immediately at the exchange of data sets, still adhering as most do to the concept of databases being similar to an electronic version of a manuscript or text file, and that somehow the researcher possesses his or her data. An exception to this generalization was the cross-disciplinary history-archives dialogue ensuing from the Vancouver Island Project (IGARTUA *ET AL.*), and the willingness a decade ago of GAFFIELD *ET AL.* to approach database management from an archival perspective rather than simply according to the dictates of available DBMS software.

Past efforts toward historical database description and subject control in data archives have been disjointed and often unconnected with the experience in archives and libraries with cataloging standards, subject control, indexing, and thesaurus construction. Vocabulary variety rather than control for specificity has been prized in the Humanities (WIBERLEY), but the problem is much more than personal taste and predilection. It is an issue of cultural and contextual sensitivity. Tests using rotational and permutation string indexing for standardized descriptors of historical material, relating current access to Library of Congress Subject Headings (LCSH) and other standardized subject headings, revealed significant problems (MCCRANK, 1984, vol. 2), more complex than orthographic variance, but reflecting issues in historical lexicology (BOGURAEV & BRISCO) such as linking archaic usage to contemporary terms either by direct correspondence (VASILEVA) or indirectly coupling parallel but time-differentiated vocabularies which could now be treated as hypertexts (MCCRANK, 1988). BOZZI & SAPUPPO have exploited old dictionaries to create links between historical terms and images, in order to create visual lexicons. Historical indexes and historical literary concordances have the same problems of object or image and subject term coordination as in nominal record linkage issues that confront quantified historical research.

Since 1974, the Social Sciences have undertaken subject terminological work, which is related to UNESCO's INFOTERM initiatives, especially to establish standardized descriptors for concepts, methods, and sources as proposed by F. RIGGS. The aim was to clarify ambiguity between overlapping concepts and terms in general usage for more precise communication, especially in Political Science (SARTORI; RIGGS & TEUNE). Those contributing to the anthology of essays about History as an "indexing Specialty" point out the extent of the language problem for History (TOWERY). The late W. KUEHL, a respected bibliographer of History dissertations in 1965, 1970, and 1980, proposed to NEH that under the auspices of ABH with the collaboration of ABC-CLIO, Inc., a universal History Thesaurus be compiled. He envisioned a PC-based "Linking System for Historical Literature" like an electronic notebook facilitating historians' research and ties into bibliographic systems and databases. The technical viability of such an approach using UNIX, even with portable PCs used in fieldwork for later transfer to main files, and integration of library (MARC format) and historical methods (free-text notes) with standardized descriptors (LSCH), was subsequently demonstrated by D. CLARK (1991a-b) in a pilot *History Database* project at the California Historical Society. Despite enthusiastic support from OAH (HOFF-WILSON, who thought Nixon administrators would not regard this as a "sexy proposal" since Washington bureaucrats hold that "computerized records management, data archives, bibliographic files, and library systems are deadly dull subjects"!) and endorsement from AHA, the planning grant was unfunded, and ABH did not regroup to try again after the untimely death of its visionary project leader. The project would have provided a broad contextual tool to facilitate standardized description of electronic historical sources. Perhaps the AHC will take up such an effort, as S. ANDERSON has recently proposed, but the task is daunting. It would be achieved best, perhaps, as a networked project of electively integrating existing thesauri for specific domains and editing them for compatibility. These could be customized for historical research by adding historical terms and then creating syndectic references from archaic terms to modern equivalents and *vice versa*. These could be enhanced by integrating synonymies, and either creating hyperlinks to an embedded historical level or multilevels as the case may be, or creating links between parallel vocabularies that could be built from historic lexicons (e.g., for English and most European languages since the Renaissance, the Cordell Collection of dictionaries at Indiana State University, which Warren Cordell built as an archives of language). This is why the inclusion of contemporary French dictionaries with the ARTFL textbases makes such sense.

Despite such foundations and false starts, little connection can be made between these early terminological standardization efforts and current experiments in individual data archives (ANDERSON, 1993/94) for source terms and similar efforts in the rare book and manuscript sector of the Anglo-American library world (e.g., ACRL-RBMS, 1983 & 1991 for Genre Terms and Provenance evidence respectively; e.g., LIBRARY OF CONGRESS, 1996, *TGM* [*Thesaurus of Graphic Materials*], I-II, which provides 600 genre and physical characteristic terms with 400 cross-references, and 5,500 subject descriptors with 4,300 cross-references) related to cataloguing standards for historical material (text and graphic) and the application of controlled descriptors (MCCRANK, 1985, 1988, 1992). Nor is there coordination of terms from other source banks such as the GETTY TRUST AHIP's *Art and Architectural Thesaurus* and related *Authority Reference Tool*, which would allow congruence for more than text archives but for image and artifact retrieval as well. Finally, source types that classify documentation and records should have continuity with original usage and the typologies and taxonomies that have developed over the centuries in Law and Administration (e.g., Diplomatics; cf., SKEMER; DURANTI, 1989-1992; BLOUIN & DELMAS), and Lexicography (e.g., basic for *The Order of Things*). KROPAČ's handling of cartulary data displays such awareness of classification and terminology. Continuity with previous descriptive standards is advisable, and congruence and consistency between descriptors used in library OPACs for published historical sources and applied in the MARC-AMC format for historical manuscripts and archival documentation (SAHLI; EVANS & WEBER) with those used for electronic records and data archives would be very valuable. Unfortunately, the focus on the exchange of historical databases has been mostly on hardware compatibility and transfers between historical research centers and data archives, without adequate attention to cross-system, i.e. library-archives-museum exchange.

Historians are now concerned with description for information exchange rather than only technical transferability (GENET); the connection between these facets is now generally recognized. Although some European data archives like the ESRC catalog their files using the MARC format and IFLA's ISBD standard, and employ AACR II, this is an accommodation to share information through bibliographic networks and does not, according to B. WINSTAN-LEY, signify any satisfaction by historians with such descriptive practice. The dated cataloging standard for Machine-Readable Data Files (MRDF) (DODD, 1982; cf., OCLC *MRDF* format, 1986-; OCLC *Computer Files* format, 1989) may serve as a basis for such international collaboration through IASSIST (e.g., the 1993 IASSIST Conference workshop on "Creating Documentation Guidelines for Data Procedures"), since its editor, S. DODD (1990-), has repeatedly called for its revision and expansion, and current discussions are bridging the communication barriers between the Anglo-American and continental worlds and between libraries and manuscript depositories, archives, and data archives. Some, like VAN HALL (1989, 1991), point out that unlike most data sets for the Social Sciences, which are two-dimensional, most historical data sets are largely relational. Such a difference needs to be accommodated in a descriptive standard.

Ongoing deliberations promoted by the Association of History and Computing among Dutch, British, Russian, and Danish data archives to collaborate in a Standard Study Description project aim at international standards for documenting historical data files (REINKE, 1981; SCHURER, MARKER; HAUSMANN *ET AL.*; VAN HALL, 1989, 1991). The original proposal for such a Standard Study Description is now over 20 years old, having been made by Per Nielsen in 1974—which might set some kind of record in standards development history. The work has slowed because of the shift in historiography during the 1980s away from quantification to cultural studies, the lack of prior experience in setting technical standards and the inherent problem in gaining international consensus when there has not been an international organization with sufficient influence to shepherd a proposal through the international bureaucratic maze. KAHIN & ABBATE explore the social and political processes of standards development (for the Harvard Information Infrastructure project, bringing together social scientists, technologists, and policy makers; see also related case studies in KAHIN & WILSON). CISH is useless for such practical outcomes; the collaboration of AHC, ALLC, ACH, and IASSIST following the TEI model performance should be pursued. A basic *Guidelines for Documenting Historical Data Files* (ANDERSON, 1993/1994, p. 4-5) has been circulated for use after an initial pilot project headed by P. DOORN and N. VAN HALL (cf., VAN HORIK; DOORN *ET AL.*) which developed a Historical Data Set Description Scheme (HDDS) for use on a "Do-It-Yourself" program at the Netherlands Historical Data Archives (NHDA). The European initiative seems to have no North American involvement or that of the archives community, so its internationalism seems very Eurocentric. Unfortunately, the scheme is woefully inadequate, does not relate to international standards in other fields, and fails to achieve anything as sophisticated as that completed in the last ten years (BUREAU OF CANADIAN ARCHIVISTS, 1985) by the Canadian and American archivists with their recently promulgated CAA *Rules for Archival Description* (*RAD*) and *HyperRAD*, and the SAA *Handbook* for archival descriptive standards. It ignores descriptive terminologies in use for a decade in many archival information systems or common data elements used in automated archival information retrieval, e.g., ISAD (G) and ISAAR (CPF).

Such repetition occurs in History circles despite BUDIN's attempt to enlist historians' interests in INFOTERM's activities, because they may want descriptive information to satisfy their own needs, but historians have resisted language (syntax and vocabulary) standardization to describe history, and this predilection carries into their difficulty with standardized description of their sources. However, the automated systems component of a data archives operation needs congruence between paper and electronic source controls. Homegrown systems often preserve the idiosyncracies of local practice, complicated by the uniqueness of the vocabularies of the sources themselves (archaisms with corresponding equivalents or historical synonyms), native and original languages with orthographic variants, and personal preferences. It is easier to agree upon the basic data elements required to describe technically a machine-readable file for inter-institutional transfer of data (P. BECKER; M. COOK). Moreover, any such History initiative should be practical in that standards being adopted in business and the information industry should apply, albeit with modification, since sheer numbers of potential users will determine adoption. In this regard, note the current discussions on electronic commerce across the Internet and how electronic data interchange will be accomplished as reviewed by V. MCCARTHY and in the electronic RFC by HOUSER, GRIFFIN & HAGE (ftp://ds.internic.net/rfc/rfc1865.txt.). Such multi-institutional collaborative efforts are the only way to reach consensus and to work toward standardized subject descriptors, source terms, and descriptive data elements for electronic archives for them to have a chance at widespread implementation. They are also the means by which endorsement may come about for historical data interchange as part of a larger commercial practice.

In the Commonwealth of Independent States (CIS) or Federated States (FSU) a similar national collaboration is occurring: the Russian (formerly Soviet) Historical Data Archive (GARSKOVA, 1993/1994) formed in 1992 to replace the 1989 aborted Consortium on Data Bases in History. Initial collaboration will be an extensive inventory of machine-readable data files by the History faculty at the Moscow State University, the Academy of Sciences Institute for History, and the Moscow State Institute for Historical Archives. The coordination of such efforts with those of the Rosarchiv and the Hoover Institute for the use of *MicroMARC* for input into RLIN (cf. TARASOV for a brief report of Rosarchiv international activities), or with the INTAS-funded (INTernational ASsociation in Brussels) History and Computing project (1994-) is unclear. The survey instrument circulated in 1995 follows the 1989 questionnaire on Historical Data Sets in Europe (GARSKOVA, p. 4). Once historical databases are identified, the issue of actual exchange requires coding or tagging for exchange. Most European historical data archivists assume that such editorial work for textual files would adhere to the Text Encoding Initiative (TEI) using SGML and a model being developed currently (GREENSTEIN, 1991). MOISEENKO, a liaison between the CIS and Europe through her position in the Inter Documentation Company in Leyden, where she works closely with the NHDA, reports on the INTAS project's progress to standardize documentation for computer files in the CIS. Studies are being undertaken on the following: the preservation of context of MRDFs; the appraisal of electronic records; storage problems, particularly dependency, and others regarding hardware; cataloging and descriptive practices; and reference services for electronic archives. The study committee notes particularly the lack of coherent policy following the breakup of the USSR (cf., SOKOLOV), so that leaders in History are calling for the creation of "a common information space of Russia" (MOISEENKO, p. 40) beginning with updating state standards (so-called GOST, seven of which already prescribe the use of thesauri; eight refer to bibliographic description of documents). In 1991, a directory of major MRDF producers and current electronic and data archives was produced by the Russian Information and State Statistical Committee (ROSKOMINFORM & GOSKOMSTAT) and it covered an estimated 30 percent of extant MRDFs of potential historical value. About 85 percent of the inventoried files are Social Science databases created and maintained on mainframes (15 percent of which were IBM). Russian archivists want to preserve original draft descriptions by records creators, to prepare technical descriptions on files organization and data recording, and finally to provide content descriptions of the data as information. In all of these cases, the meta-information of History is of vital concern in the evolution of global historical information systems.

While descriptive standards can always be refined and customized for specific kinds of information and purposes, and markup codes and tagging principles can evolve to various levels of precision for retrospective application, the critical developments now are in standardization for data exchange independent of hardware and the insurance of software and hardware interoperability now and in the future. This issue goes to the heart of other problems such as long-range retention of files, retro-conversion, international project collaboration, full use of the INTERNET for data communications, verification procedures, and technological glide that supports cumulative progress. Moreover, the economic and political problems in standards formulation for data exchange are complex and the collaboration needed to achieve them seems tantamount to yet another overlay in worldwide governance. However, standards compliance in this area is largely a matter of volunteerism except where antitrust issues are involved. Standards formulation therefore has had to involve consumers and producers, the public and private sectors, and the most altruistic among entrepreneurs who foresee long-range advantages in standardization over immediate profit from small, temporary markets. Historians are latecomers to this arena because their awareness is really only emerging as the possibilities of networking are seen more clearly, and they have not and probably never will comprise a significant component of the hardware market. Yet, as discussions at recent ACH conferences attest, computing historians have joined their voices to those of other and larger constituencies to support national and international standards for data exchange. The political pressure applied, however, seems insignificant compared with the larger market forces of a transition toward open systems (i.e., Open Systems Interface or OSI), distributed computing and decline of mainframe dependency, global networking, and client-server architecture in information systems.

Certainly, the prospects for the Z39.50 protocol standard approved by the American National Standards Institute (ANSI) in July 1992 and upgraded in 1995 (NISO Z39.50-1995), are encouraging for historians and others who want expanded access to electronic information. Z39.50-compliant systems are *ipso facto* oriented toward interoperability and vendor-independence (E. TURNER; WARD). Originally a protocol or set of "attributes" by which information is searched, retrieved, and relayed, was promoted for interlibrary exchange of bibliographic data; work has already begun to use the same approach to convey full text and images through Z39.50 searching. Some have described Z39.50 as a transparent translator which allows searches to be initiated locally in a manner accustomed by the user. Searches are reformatted into a flexible hierarchy of attributes, to enable a system to seek information stored in other ways, but which can be retrieved and reformatted into the neutral form. The information is finally reformatted again from the neutral carrier format, into the format expected by the software and hardware of the sender's workstation. NISO has provided guides for implementation (MOEN) and case studies of such experience (NISO Pub. 500-229). Z39.50 already applies to MARC formats, and when registered, may soon apply as well with SGML/EAD Document-Type Descriptions (DTDs) for archives.

Genuine standards are not those achieved *de facto* through vendor dominance, but through consensus building and general compliance in any organization or project. Historians have often operated by vendor standards without realizing the difference, until they want to exchange data with other projects that do not use the same vendor for software and hardware. The goal, of course, is to use what hardware and software one wants in an open system where one can mix and match according to one's taste and means. Standards are usually not forced on a project by the hardware but are adopted as a matter of best practice. Those standards ready for general compliance are usually approved by accrediting standards organizations at the national and international levels (hence, the interplay between ANSI or American National Standards Institute and ISO, the International Standards Organization). Government can force suppliers into standards by virtue of its purchasing power, as has been done by the United States Department of Defense but equally important is FIPS (Federal Information Processing Standards of the UNITED STATES NATIONAL BUREAU OF STANDARDS) and the ISO adaptation by the federal government, i.e., Government Open Systems Interconnection Profile (GOSIP). The implementor of FIPS and other standards such as OSI is the United States

Department of Commerce National Institute of Standards and Technology (NIST). The OSI standard has evolved from the 1970s to a standard in 1979 (ISO 7498) and now into what is described as an "environment" or seven-layered outline or "architecture" for collating similar functions which act according to other standards, each level building on the previous layers its cumulative foundation. The OSI reference model aims at standardizing the relationships between the following layers: physical, data links, networking, transporting, session, presentation, and applications. Each layer has its own rules and conventions that if followed, allow any vendor to design systems that at any level can relate to another vendor's system. Even the terminology (e.g., a protocol consisting of rules and conventions) is derived from Diplomatics, so historians should be comfortable with the idea. To sell hybrid systems, the computer industry is generally forging ahead with standards that will improve the situation for widespread data exchange. For developments in the United States which now affect worldwide production, one must follow the activities of Electronics Industries Association (EIA) and for telecommunications, the Consultative Committee on International Telephone and Telegraph (CCITT).

Sometimes this whole array of existing standards and quasi-standards from consensus, definition, and tradition seems confusing. They are constantly evolving with new technology. Moreover, the somewhat disjointed work on continuing standardization by myriad organizations, even within one industry, seems difficult to coordinate with those of other fields. Standards setting is easier than gaining acceptance or compliance. One area of collaboration important for historians and archivists is the alliance between libraries and the book trade. COMPTON describes this arena as an "alphabet soup of organizations, Electronic Data Interchange for Libraries and Booksellers in Europe (EDLIBE), Pan-American Book Sector EDI Group (EDItEUR), International Committee on EDI for Serials (ICEDIS), Book Industry Systems Advisory Committee (BISAC), CSISAC, and Serials Industry Systems Advisory Committee (SISAC),"—which is actually a short list—and this "soup" is treated under the general rubric of Electronic Data Interchange (EDI). This formal acronym sounds more ambitious than the common goal of data exchange, but Friedemann Weigel, the information systems director of Harrassowitz, summed up the issue best: "EDI is paperless trade" (WEIGEL, p. 142). He predicts that by the end of this decade 50-80 percent of communication between librarians and agents will be handled as EDI transactions. If a book is ordered this way, as a complete product or as electronic text to be assembled by the recipient and redistributed, such developments contributing to the library's function as an electronic clearinghouse are well underway.

Such developments will serve historians and all scholars relying on electronic sources if direct electronic document delivery is the result, rather than simply electronic book ordering, and if the source is standardized for data exchange. Historians essentially want to trade data, texts, images, and ideas, similar to the objectives of archivists, curators, librarians, booksellers, and others engaged in intellectual and academic business. It seems doubtful that historians need to organize yet another standard setting organization since they lack the clout to have such standards widely adopted, but they should be participating in the conversation about standards and should pay special attention to the book trade library world (BLUH). An example would be Book Industry Communication (BIC) in the United Kingdom that evolved from the 1986 "Avoiding the Electronic Babel" seminar (B. GREEN). The Biblical "Babel" problem is with us still and will not be solved simply by telecommunications and electronic communication standards. The issue of quality control is still a people problem. FITTS likens the grappling of large-scale EDI operations to "dancing with a gorilla" and points to a 1995 study by MAYOR for the LTD Group which showed that in a survey to test the ability of clients to do electronic ordering, 59 percent of 1,560 responses contained human errors. The goal of SISAC is to streamline processing and eliminate the paper shuffle that requires such a large investment in the human infrastructure. Direct ordering in an EDI environment may prove more efficient for the clearinghouse, and more problematic for the inquirer who must become his or her own ordering agent, user of standards, and negotiator of multiple systems, and who then must assume responsibility for such typical error ratios.

Such progress in standardization for data interchange is laudable but very late in the development of computing. The dominant trade groups are concerned with publishing and already existent trade rather than potential trade in commodities which are never really published or acquired but are accessioned and often exist in the public domain. Moreover, the standards setting process as described by CRAWFORD and others has been an obstacle to archivists who like historians have largely been excluded from the controlling interests in technical standardization. The process has been quite exclusionary, if not by intent, then indirectly the very nature of the discussion, and standards governing future technology are influenced by what is in research and development now. Since archivists are outside the R&D loop, they are not well positioned to participate actively in standards formation except in reaction to proposals already progressing toward adoption. Historians ought to be in the R&D loop also, but as single researchers they lack a unified voice and any trade association to operate for their interest. In essence they turn over their goods to publishers who govern the trade. Their best interests are served from within the publishing industry, by historians who work as acquisition agents, as editors, and in marketing, and thereby gain a more technical and practical training than in History. Archivists have similar problems when they publish their holdings or allow them to be published electronically, on microfilm, or traditionally in books of edition documents. Direct electronic access to archival sources bypasses the usual publishing cycle, including profit making, so investment is still waiting for a scale that will make networked electronic archives a realty soon. When the value of an archives is based on in-house users, direct external access may indeed operate against the immediate interests of archives administration. Resource sharing is often an altruistic objective, rather than a practical strategy.

Finally, archivists often lack training in publishing generally, so their ability to work with technical standards for data exchange is also limited by their backgrounds. This can be changed, of course, by improving professional education for those working in History but whose career whose focus is on activities other than teaching. The issue, therefore, has never been purely technical. Problems lie in the academic infrastructure of our universities, the fragmentary organization of research organizations, and the training of researchers without practical skills in project management, and the overemphasis on individualism unbalanced by the sustained growth of collaboratories.

Nevertheless, between professional associations, government, standards accrediting agencies, and industrial cooperatives, a host of standards other than Z39.50 have evolved. A foundation exists for such collaborative, networked, historical work. The United Nations ACCIS Technical Panel on Electronic Records Management (1990) identified 13 standards of greatest significance for electronic archives and hence for historical computing. These affect current data exchange and thus the future of collaborative historical research across the INTERNET (MCCRANK, 1995). MOLINE's NIST Report (1988-3851) enumerated nineteen essential standards for document and graphics interchange, and M. LAW, for her 1989 "Framework for the Exchange and Preservation of Electronic Records," (Attachment B, 30 pages) reviewed ten of these for the United States National Archives to consider (cf., EATON, 1993). Already mentioned are SGML (ISO 8879) and AMC- MARC (ANSI Z39.2 parallel to ISO 2709) for standardized markup of content text, coupled with the database interrogator Structured Query Language (SQL, developed from earlier Boolean keyword retrieval software such as SEQUEL) (ANSI X3.135-135-1986 /ISO 9075/ FIPS PUB 127). Consider also the CTITT recommendations of X-400-X.430, ODA/ODIF, etc., for reference description and bibliographic information exchange, plus MHS (Data Communications Networks Message Handling System) for e-mail. The Database Language standard (NDL: ANSI X3.133-1986/ ISO 8907/ FIPS PUB 126) guards against the common *vade mecum* programming that revels in the unique and idiosyncratic that insures non-transferability of files. The Data Descriptive

Format (DDF), i.e., ANSI/ISO 8211; FIPS PUB 123 approved in 1982) is important for splitting computer generated records into components using file headers and tag sets, but it has lacked a broad commercial base for widespread implementation. But this development did open the way for Open Systems architectures in 1986 (i.e., Open Systems Interconnection [OSI]). For transfer of data files, common standards include File Transfer, Access and Management [FTAM], i.e., ISO 8571) and the ISO cluster Information Processing System Open Systems Interconnection Series of Virtual Terminal (VT) Standards (ISO/DIS 9040-41) governing graphics interfaces. In the business world, ISO 1030 has become increasingly important. Developed mainly in Germany and Sweden for Industrial Automation Systems and Integration/Industrial Design in aircraft and automobile manufacturing (and incidentally, pharmaceuticals), its common name is the Standard for the Exchange of Product Model Data (STEP). This development's extension to a new computer language, *EXPRESS*, holds promise for records authentication and electronic archives because of developers' emphases on long-term access for liability protection for the life of a product and beyond, i.e., life of product users or at least one generation or more.

Those data project managers who take seriously their responsibility to insure the creation of a meta-information database for their projects (as recommended by OSBORNE, ROSEN & GALLAGHER) should observe the Information Resource Directory System or IRDS (ANSI X3.138-1988/ FIPS PUB 156; cf. GOLDFINE & KONIG) to insure compliance across local and regional boundaries. The list of standards, created, evolving, and yet to come, is as expandable as the technologies that require them. The acronyms (SPDL, SGML, ODA/ODIF, CGM, etc.) which form a shorthand to denote sometimes equally meaningless names, seem perplexing and daunting for all but the fully initiated. Such initiation is now made easier by V. Irons Walch and her collaborators for SAA WGSAD; its *Handbook* (1994) reviews 86 standards in detail and provides short descriptions for another 157 covering automated systems and network specifications, stressing open systems interconnectivity and summarizing the General International Standard for Archival Description. MOEN places IT standards in the Federal government into the framework of an evolving federal information policy in the United States.

As we move from twentieth-century static documentation to the next century's dynamic documents (or animated, as they have been called, because of the interchange between text, still image, and digitized video clips), the standards will proliferate but will also undergo a classification and packaging similar to the trend set by the OSI movement. Historians may want to get involved in standards formation, but it is more important that they become engrossed in standards implementation. First, a rudimentary education must take place, so that their discussions are more informed than they have been and they do not try to reinvent the wheel when the vehicles they use are already so equipped. Those engaged in archival education have no choice but to educate themselves and their students, or fail in their educational mission to produce competent archivists. The few electronic archivists we do have are educating themselves in the business of standards and self-interest or enlightened compliance for electronic records transfer; so too should historians, partially for review and support, mostly for implementation. At least make sure an electronic archivist is on the project team, and if none are available, grow your own. Necessity may indeed be the mother of invention in this case.

Software Solutions

The medieval historian Emmanuel Le Roy Ladurie who became the director of the Bibliothèque Nationale, 20 years ago erroneously predicted that all historians would have to become their own programmers, because then quantitative historians lacked software which properly enabled them to achieve their objectives (LADURIE, 1973, pp. 13-14). In technical circles, his misprognostication may be remembered more than his imaginative and trendsetting approaches to medieval social history. When he entered historical computing, it was still common for first-generation projects to have customized programs written as a one-shot effort. Historians still face an unusually difficult problem in identifying software to match their sources and solve their problems.

VOORBIJ (p. 37) blames the instability of software development and habitual new releases which do no always work well in mid-project upgrades, as a factor inhibiting computer-assisted research in the Humanities. W. PERRY (1986) provided a step-by-step guide to test software packages to be assured that "they do what *you* want." Locating software through bibliographic systems is not especially helpful because functional terms are too general, naming software is an advertising gimmick rather than information retrieval mechanism, and jargon and colloquialism pervade the computing world; but one can turn via BITNET to the Online Academic Software Information Service (OASIS) database for educational software, numerous software reviews and catalogs by vendors, and such guides as produced by SPAETH (1991) specially for historians. Now the richness syndrome is exacerbating this issue: there is so much from which to choose, but shopping is a really frustrating trial and error process after an initial evaluation effort based on reviews and profiles. Intellectual access to shareware, such as PC-SIG (Software Interest Group) which provides ca. 6,000 shareware packages, for example, is only through broad terms, and then loading the software to scan instructions and help screens. Test runs take an up-front speculative investment for purchased software that may not be useable, plus tremendous amounts of time, and even then, one cannot be sure that the best software solution to a set of problems is properly identified. Personal referral is still the most common selection strategy, increasing through electronic bulletin boards and listservs, and as in archival provenance or citation tracing a copy tradition is well established: successful use in one project often means subsequent adoption by another, sometimes despite substantial differences in needs. Convenience and comfort levels are equally influential factors. The description and analytics of software is a major weakness of current technical information systems that if improved, would greatly benefit historians—and other consumers as well.

LEEBAERT and his collaborating observers of trends in the software industry attempt to forecast the most important developments. This is difficult, because nobody really foresaw the breakthroughs of the past five years such as the swing toward object-oriented programming under the influence of JAVA or the increased capacity of microprocessors. It has been difficult to shift common paradigms from the mechanical age to understand that today smaller is bigger, and more powerful. Nor could anyone foresee the complications necessitating standards, the complexity of groupware, security issues, simultaneous market expansion and contraction, the impact of giants such as Microsoft having as much influence on computing as the hardware industry did a decade ago, or the archival and legal implications of the developments during a mere half-decade.

One of the perplexing current dilemmas is the divergence between relational database management systems and object-oriented technology which offer a semantically richer data modeling capability (KHOSHAFIAN & BAKER). In moving from data analysis to visualization one is confronted with an awkward glide between the two. Relational database management systems have features worth retaining: they preserve data independence, are amendable to algebraic operations, allow for query optimization, and are conducive to standardization. On the other hand, as TEUHOLA (p. 446) points out, developments in CAD/CAM/CIM and CASE tools point to deficiencies in relational database work. In the DBMS environment: the number of cells is high and processing loads are heavy, whereas connections between relations are logical, direct pointers are faster; reassembly of a composite object (which is necessarily fragmented across many relations in a relational database) requires many expensive joins; concurrence and recovery strategies are heavy and unsuited for long transactions; and answers to queries consist of copies of tuples in the database. These are defects in most DBMS operations which are being addressed, with the result that a new class of systems is emerging called "object-relational" which attempt to have the best of both worlds. Some knowledge engineers point to clustering of composite objects as the natural reason for the superiority of object-based systems over relational databases, but both approaches can achieve this. In short, in today's world historians will want to preserve relational theory and the features of relational databases, while obtaining the new flexibility of object-oriented technology and its visualization capabilities. Archivists must do the same. Until now, however, computing historians have been more concerned with traditional DBMS packages and statistical operations because of their Cliometric backgrounds. Very little software engineering is paying attention to specific needs of historians, and little evidence indicates that they know what they need and want or make any sort of consolidated effort to get it.

Software engineering is a speciality in itself, going well beyond the historian's concept of programming to obtain certain operations for their data sets; today, it is customized for specific projects. More than a growing IT specialization, some think that it is a discipline in itself (SHAW & GARLAN). Ladurie was not wrong, as so often claimed by those who revel in the arrival of DBMS/RDBMS packages in the 1980s, in stressing the need for programming capabilities in History; he was wrong is suggesting that every historian should be his or her own programmer. That would be a call for dilettante, when an expert programmer is needed. Computers should not turn good historians into lousy programmers, but should invite collaboration between good historians and good programmers. Ladurie did not mean this in a trifling way, however, but in the sense of loving what computer software could accomplish in specific instances without understanding its real complications and potential beyond an immediate, highly specialized application. Nor did most computing historians understand the extent of the need in fields like History and Archival Science, which deal with some of the most complex data anywhere, in myriad formats, and now they confront unheralded mass as well. It was wasteful then, and is more so today, to think in terms of customized programming for every conceivable historical research project; the redundancy is unbelievable, and although the projects may contribute advances to their field of inquiry, the infrastructure does not exist whereby the supporting apparatus (specifications, programs and software, testing data, codebooks, etc.) could be shared efficiently to maximize the return on the investment. It is furthermore naive to think that a relatively unsupported field like History could command the funds for sophisticated software design given the limited scale of most historical research, so constrained as it is by the individuality of its undertaking.

History does not need to have all historians become programmers, but it does need, to quote the Marines, "a few good men [and women]" to apply their programming expertise to History and engage in historical software engineering. This is a development which needs to be managed for the sake of archival information management and historical computing, and not left to helter-skelter trial-and-error experiments all over the place (see PUTNAM & MYERS' "executive briefing" about controlling software development). This might be accomplished best in a few research centers where software engineers and computing historians can collaborate over time to produce whole toolboxes or a sustained series of software releases to historians everywhere to use. Again, supercomputing laboratories at major United States universities would be places where scale might afford some attention to History. A few schools of information studies like Syracuse, Drexel, and Michigan where there is interest in software engineering for information storage and retrieval could support the research required for new developments, especially if their faculties collaborated with History departments and young computer-capable historians were directed into such research. History would benefit also by alliances with the Social Sciences, Arts, and Humanities to exploit academic computing centers on their campuses or developments like the new Media Union at Ann Arbor. Most of these are application driven and are working laboratories for teaching and small research projects rather than advanced research, but they pool together the talent needed for collaborative work which can outshine their original intent. Moreover, these are training grounds for the future generation of computing historians. The kind of development advocated here, however, requires preliminary study which has not been accomplished, to classify historical data and research problems in such a way that a generic typology could evolve. This would provide the needed framework to evaluate existing software for types of historical projects, and direct research and development in software engineering for archival studies and historical research which would not duplicate needlessly the capabilities already provided by existing software. In addition to creating new software packages, many of the needs in historical computing would be in refreshing and there is a need to update older software attached to hardware-dependent data files and to decide which one wants to reuse, migrate across systems, and employ to recapture lost or unusable historical data (i.e., reengineering: R. ARNOLD). Repackaging is often needed to bring together separate software applications into comprehensive solutions and whole suites of software.

To understand what needs to be done, one might explore the literature of software engineering but do not expect to find there any concern for historical computing and renovation of old programs. For that one might turn to the IAHC workshop proceedings from Tromso, Norway (OLDERVOLL, ed., 1992). Otherwise, the mind-set is entirely futuristic. A good start for such investigation is the IEEE Software and Engineering Management series. DORFMAN & THRAYER (1996) provide a good overview of the software life-cycle: requirements specification, design, coding, validation, verification, testing, and maintenance. It not only introduces the formal methods used in software engineering, but includes object-oriented development and structured development (see SIGFRIED for object-oriented techniques), and covers management issues like quality assurance, configuration management, standards (especially ISO 9000 and 9001 [see SCHMAUCH and JENNER respectively]; the 26 most common standards are collected in one edition by IEEE, 1994), metrics (OMAN & PFLEEGER on the what, how, when and why of appropriate measurements in this process), and the accommodation of emerging technologies. THAYER & DORFMAN's discussion of the education needed for software engineers might be amplified by the need to train a few such engineers specifically for historical data and research. Alternatives include REIFER's popular *Software Management* book, now in its fourth edition, and one may always turn to MARCINIAK's *Encyclopedia of Software Engineering* for specifics and for recent structured techniques to YOURDON (1986; YOURDON, 1979, earlier pulled together the "classics" in software engineering). The THAYER & DORFMAN team has produced a companion volume specifically about software requirements engineering, which is the science and discipline of establishing and documenting what new software is to do, before approaching the issue of how to accomplish these tasks (see also the case studies assembled by THAYER).

The current trend is toward user-oriented development, where research would consist of the study of historians and history computing projects to determine what has been done in the past and what expectations exit for the future. This might be difficult in the case of historical studies, for the many reasons surveyed in this essay, and it is something that historians should perhaps do for themselves through self-study. The crux of the problem would be to transform the disjunctive discussion historians have engaged in for years into something definable in order to write software requirements in such a way that solutions could be engineered. Each requirement would need to be clarified and documented precisely. Then the process of writing programs could begin by selecting appropriate methods and tools, using software system engineering models, applying standards, and taking the necessary steps to ensure quality throughout the whole process. PERRY, POSTON & LYU treat software testing, now accomplished with an array of software reliability tools; see also M. S. DEUTSCH, who stresses a life-cycle approach to software quality engineering. The Software Engineering Institute (SEI) at Carnegie-Mellon University produces a series of colloquia and monographs about such work, and one can point to such programs as at Drexel's School of Information Studies for specialized graduate programs, beyond programming, in software design.

One compilation by A. W. BROWN advocates an approach which seems appealing for history and archives, namely component-based software engineering. This seems to be compatible with Deutsch's focus on evolutionary (historical?) models for software project management. The idea is the evaluation of software components already existing for assembly into appropriate software architecture, and the subsequent development of whole systems. This latter step would move into configuration management, namely the selection of software, firmware, and hardware for a system (BUCKLEY). GARG & JAZAYERI advocate "process-centered software engineering" that combines project management with software and process engineering in specific work environments. This is especially appropriate for history research centers which in sustaining long-term projects could develop useful software as a byproduct to be applied elsewhere. In short, this endeavor is much more complicated than simply having a few lines of code written to solve a few problems in specific data sets. The expertise needed to write good software is considerable, and for complex fields like history which require complex sets of interactive software, the high cost of labor alone means that few centers can create such software, and then only if the project were subsidized or if a market existed to guarantee a return on the investment. This situation explains why so little software has been created for historical research.

The computing field is open to influence from applications fields, if historians, archivists, and documentalists were better enabled to define their needs. The *Computing the Future* report by HARTMANNIS & LIN recommended balancing the core in computing research with a broadening the field by exploring more possibilities in demand-driven applications areas, although some object to any dilution of long-term research for short-term applied objectives. Twenty-two working groups met at the MIT Laboratory for Computer Science in 1996 to chart strategic directions of computing research, but representation from electronic archives or computing historians through any of their organizations was not to be seen (WEGNER & DOYLE report on resulting computing survey research). The fiftieth anniversary of the Association of Computing Machinery (ACM) seems like another opportunity lost to interject History's needs into the consciousness of computer engineers.

If one were to undertake software engineering for History, how would the state of the art be assessed? Then how would one articulate need for future development? Certainly, the widespread availability of the *Statistical Package for the Social Sciences* (*SPSS*) was of major importance for quantitative history, and its distribution as *SPSS/PC* for personal computers and use with Windows will insure its use over competitors. Since 1985, SAS has gained in use because of easier input of files, database management, and for generating reports; historians have turned to a host of specialized programs for quantification. Database management systems with nonfixed length fields are preferred (SPAETH, 1991, lists forty-two DBMS programs and twenty-six text handlers in his guide for historians); *dBase* III-IV are commonly used, but *R-BASE* is liked because of its matrix design and relational abilities for linkage (GREENSTEIN, 1989; GUTMANN; REIFF, 1991, pp. 130-136). However, not all historical computing is following the relational model. Other packages are in use, like *ASK SAM*, etc., but increasingly historians are turning to academic and humanities computing centers to supply them with an array of software and consulting as well to adopt and adapt and to employ combinations of packages in their multi-task projects. Unfortunately all databases that operate on a tabular basis, designed to handle simple hierarchies, break down when expected to manipulate complex data and open hierarchical data structures. Excessive coding and deposit of data in cells defined by matrices create significant problems for long-term data storage. These are not archival, so data should be stored separately for preservation and reuse over time.

Relatively few uses of major mainframe software suites like *ORACLE* or *SYBASE* can be identified; the *Deeds Project* and Southampton Media Lab's *Microcosm* project and *HiDes* application would be noteworthy exceptions (Multicosm Ltd.'s homepage is at http://www.multicosm.com). Historians often complain that a computer center staff usually underestimates the complexity of historical research (SCHURER). Computer support staff often assume that *SPSS* is the answer to everything on the assumption that historians will need no more than a little matrix algebra and basic statistics and that their files are indeed going to be numeric and therefore exact. Moreover, computer centers are accustomed to short-range projects, sometimes only for the current academic term, rather than those lasting for years and decades. When I first began large mainframe computing in the 1970s, a constant problem was the regular and timely but premature "archiving" of my project data while the database was still being built. An exception had to be made for my work, as for so many other historical projects that seem to go on and on, and the routines required were indeed not routine at all. Systems people regularly took down projects at quarter breaks so special arrangements had to be made to glide from term to term. Customization of software and procedures had to accommodate my multi-year projects.

At the opening of this decade, SPAETH (1991) surveyed some 314 packages classified broadly into computer-assisted instruction, numerical analysis, and database management categories. He subsequently expanded this to include textbase management systems (SPAETH, 1992). Inclusions were deemed especially relevant to historical work, but many more could have been included and his project will have to be updated periodically. Most importantly, such a perspective on software appropriate for historical computing is too self-limiting (OLDERVOLL, ed., 1992). KUNNE (1992) is convinced that the gap between ideally flexible software and historical computing needs is lessening. Historians still ignore, as do archivists, the software packages now available for data warehousing and data mining, many of which are applicable to historical projects because they rely so heavily on Artificial Intelligence breakthroughs, decision support systems especially, and methodologies that have evolved to handle socioeconomic data in business. These are often expensive, but are really quite useful for historians because the types of data and queries they are designed to handle resemble the needs of computing historians. Historical data structures are often not as unique as historians make them out to be; the data are unique, but not necessarily their structure or the problems presented in their analyses. Some of this limitation results from the isolation of academic computing from larger administrative computing, and the relatively small database development in History and other disciplines in contrast to the mega-databases accumulated by big business.

Legacy computing is a modern metaphor for everything leftover from mainframe operations. It does not refer to anything systematic, but just the opposite, a combination of different systems to allow the old and new to work together without a complete retro-conversion of databases in an enterprise. This eloquent euphemism hides the lack of continuity in bridging the gap between one generation and the next of computing systems. Indeed, even the term "system" lacks operational definition, as is being discovered by testers tackling the Year 2000 problem. Sometimes, the reference is to everything mounted in one CPU; at other times, the framework is the local network. It may refer to the hardware configuration only, or to the combination of certain hardware and software; in the most generic sense, "system" is used as a catchall to include everything in computing. Many of these so-called systems are not systematic, but constitute add-ons at one end, and at the other entail embedded systems which are quite hidden and serve as adjuncts for certain operations. These are like modern plug-ins, but without their built-in compatibility. In any case, legacy computing seems to have little to do with historical computing over the duration or with History computing. Too bad.

The computer industry has not helped historical computing, because rather than bring historians into large-scale computing in nonacademic contexts, academe has been viewed as a potential market place of its own, albeit rather small in comparison with business, industry, and government. Even when philanthropy has been involved, computer laboratories for academic computing have not entailed the kind of software and hardware capable of data warehouses and data mining. As a result, historical computing has remained, unfortunately, nonintegrated, vendor-dependent, and a relatively small affair. IBM in Europe, which is more actively involved in national centers and AHC branches than in the United States, has been particularly influential in hardware installations and therefore software selection. Even in graphics and interactive media where Apple excelled, CD-ROM software used in History splits 70 percent IBM or IBM-compatible, and only 30 percent Macintosh (PELLEN, p. 13), but there is little indication that this reliance on IBM computers has any correlation with the use of IBM advanced systems or software like IBM's *Data Miner*. DOS, Windows, and UNIX operating systems are all in use. The Getty Trust's AHIP laboratories are migrating all database projects to a Sun/Sybase common platform. The Getty Trust is one of the few collaboratories that is developing an IT infrastructure capable of advanced electronic research in historical data. Others which have potential, so far not achieved, are departments of History in universities with NSF Supercomputing Laboratories such as the University of Illinois, or those like the University of Michigan that can tap similar computing resources. Unfortunately, little software development or project design for advanced historical computing on the scale of data warehousing and data mining has been forthcoming from these institutions. The problem is not the technology itself but the access to it; and not the need, but awareness of it. Even in our best institutions of higher education, the problem is technical education outside Information Technology itself.

Historical research centers require an economy of scale to have the engineers and programmers to design their own sophisticated software. Oddly, these have not developed in the United States, except in conjunction with the Social Sciences (this alignment may reflect federal funding through NSF). Most historical research centers buy prepackaged software on the open international market and users accommodate their projects to what is at hand. J. T. LINDBLAD notes the many shortcomings of software not designed specifically for historical research. AHA and other professional historical organizations have not, as has MLA in the case of *NOTA BENE*, established a technical R&D operation or backed software development. Only a few archives (NARA, ICPSR, BRISC, Michigan State University, the Smithsonian Institution in the United States; the NHDA in Leyden, CNRS in Paris, etc.) have developed their own archival information storage and retrieval systems. These are not included in SPAETH's guide (1991), but his coverage can be augmented by: BEARMAN, 1987/88; LIGHT *ET AL.*; the COX & BEARMAN directory of archival software; and CIBBARELLI (who annually reviews more than 300 packages ostensibly for library software, but this includes full-text retrieval, citation and records management programs). Rarely does such technology development inside an archives spawn a separate software company, as in the entrepreneurial cases of Ted Durr's *MARCON* system (AIRS, Inc., 1984) with thesaurus capability (DURR). Michigan State University's *MicroMARC* has now found its way via RLG into Russian archives. Both offer AMC-MARC format compatibility. Consider also David Clark's UNIX-based *History Project* that lets historians take electronic notes, organize and link them to MARC-compatible tables for easy construction of a critical apparatus, and move their sorted texts directly into draft publications and note taking through an editing process directly into a full manuscript (CLARK, 1994).

In the United States the Getty Trust AHIP has developed its own project software, especially for terminologies and authority control, and for creating census records across a distributed system of participants in Europe and America. The Center for Electronic Texts in the Humanities (CETH), a cooperative between Rutgers and Princeton Universities, does both software evaluation and training. The Getty Trust, ACLS, CNI National Initiative (p. 24) recommends CETH as a model. The ISPCR at the University of Michigan remains the model for data archives. The United States National Archives and Records Administration released a Request For Proposal (RFP) for up to $10 million to develop an archives information system, presumably for public access, but in the fall of 1994 NARA withdrew its RFP because of the cost, administrative problems perhaps related to the Clinton administration's failure to appoint an archivist of the United States for nearly two years, and the stated purpose that NARA's priorities had changed to upgrade its administrative systems.

Think tanks like the Santa Fe Institute may develop software for the historian's use. In May 1996, SFI released its *SWARM* software which consists of a free set of software libraries for building multi-agent simulations (it can be downloaded from http://www.santafe.edu/projects/swarm; over 200 copies were downloaded in the first week of its availability). It is domain-independent and has been tested for modeling in ecology, anthropology, economics, political science, and evolutionary systems in addition to the hard sciences. A team consisting of Chris Langton, Nelson Minar, Manor Askensai and Roger Burkhart took over two years to develop *SWARM*, and it was beta-tested internationally at UCLA, the University of Michigan, Yale, Washington State, and Monash University in Australia and at the University of Venice. *SWARM* is intended for dynamic modeling generally, but subsequent development will tailor versions for specific kinds of simulations.

The European historical research centers that are exceptions to this picture and have engaged in software review and development are: the Historical Informatics Laboratory in Moscow (BORODKIN *ET AL.*); the Graz Institut für Geschichte workshop and Krems laboratory for medieval art history (HARTEL; KROPAČ; JARITZ); the Centre National de Recherche Scientifique (CNRS-IHRT) in Paris; and the Max-Planck Institute für Geschichte in Göttingen (THALLER *ET AL.*); and in the British Isles there is specifically the Development of Software for History (DISH) project at the Historical Computing Laboratory at the University of Glasgow (TRAINOR, 1988; MORGAN); plus the Cambridge and Oxford University groups, especially the latter with its text archives initiative and the specialized division of the Oxford University Press in electronic publishing. The Pisan Instituto Linguistica Computazionale is noteworthy because its linguistic work has fed so ably into European historical computing (BOZZI & CAPPELLI). The French centers for computational linguistics funded by the CNRS and following the pioneer example of Charles MÜLLER have likewise forged links between literary and historical computing. At the University of Groningen a Department of Alpha-Informatics has been formed in the Faculty of Arts where computer scientists, linguists, text experts, art historians and historians all work together. There Historical Computing has been interpreted as an independent discipline focusing on software development rather than on the production of historical knowledge. In addition to testing such software as *Klieu* and *Histcal*, researchers there are developing Graphic User Interfaces (GUIs) to make software use easier for historians. The ideas is to allow historians to develop their own interfaces without programming, but using modern toolboxes.

The Max-Planck Institute's Center for Historical Research, which unfortunately since 1996 has been threatened with closure because of the Foundation's financial difficulties, has become the most prolific and influential developer since 1978 under the leadership of Manfred Thaller, its former research fellow for Historical Information Science (his own self-description) and past president of AHC. The Institut is a branch of the Max-Planck Gesellschaft founded for "fundamental research" (THALLER, 1990, p. 1), a mission which it fulfilled by "infrastructure services" like bibliographic publication and model studies that are inherently interdisciplinary, more recently post-graduate training, and now software development as well. THALLER (1994) conceives of an "historical computer science" in his own image, or modeled after his own career, which is a distinct, technical approach to historical computing through the development of appropriate software. His approach rests of four explicit assumptions (1994, p. 31):

1.   The application of computers in history shall *either* make the results of historical research more easily verifiable inter-subjectively or allow the integration of a larger corpus of historical sources into one statement of the researcher than would be possible in studies which do not use a computer.

2. To do so, a formalization of historical reasoning, as well as a formalized understanding of the content of historical sources is required.

3. For such formalizations historians draw upon the experience of computer science (and statistics, where applicable) as far as possible.

4. If a historical research problem or a historical source cannot be properly formalized by known concepts of computer science, new concepts of computer science are needed; neither new historical problems, nor new historical sources.

5. Most fundamental and most general, with excuse of exception: *Software has to be adapted to the needs of History; not History to popular trends in the software industry* [Thaller's emphasis].

After 1978, when the Institut had undertaken four related projects employing "microanalytical" methods which THALLER (p. 1) defines as "attempts to explain long-term changes in an historical community by a detailed analysis of individuals and their fates," common agenda were identified from the pool of scholars drawn there for collaborative research. The methodological issues and technical problems identified were so great that a new concept, the "historical workstation," project was born. The idea was to develop a machine-independent database management system that provided an organizational framework for complex, long-term historical computing projects that would themselves develop growth of the core programs. Programming in C+ began in 1986, the first release was in 1987 under the name of the Greek muse *Klieu* (i.e., Clio), the patroness of History. Funding from Volkswagen, Inc., enabled a project that began in 1988 to rewrite previously developed software into C and create more as a three-year project: "Software Development for the Historical Disciplines." C+ (now C++), a programming language closer to natural language and more readable than older business programming, lends itself both to a strict addressing of the machines in commands but also to handling abstract data types, and it is thus often preferred for data abstraction and problem solving (CARRANO). Included are the following: prototypes for handling character strings containing alphabetic characters beyond the modern 26-character set plus icons; CMATCH, a pattern matching system; a parsing system for irregular input; FuzzNet, a generalized tool for handling abstract data of fuzzy sets; and Q-NET, a C-additive managing large dictionaries needed for morphological analysis. Another stand-alone "pre-processor" system written in C, Standard Format Exchange Program (StanFEP), was unveiled at the Montpelier AHC Conference as part of *Klieu* version 4; it allows the processing of precoded data such as texts prepared for electronic typesetting or using SGML or TEI codes by neutralizing the marking so that alternative DBMS packages not ready to handle a particular formatting can still handle the file (WERNER).

In 1992, *Klieu* Version 5.1.1 was released in English, with StanFEP, on 3.5-inch disks for PCs of 386 or above specifications, and an Image Analysis System (UNIX based), through a joint effort of the Max-Planck Institut, the British Academy and Royal Historical Society, and faculty from the Universities of Southampton and London's Queen Mary and Westfield College. THALLER (1992) has produced a reference manual for it, and WOOLARD and DENLEY have written a tutorial; the image manual is by G. JARITZ (1992). Although in the public domain, *Klieu* in English is not free, but the cost is an unbelievably affordable 30 pounds.

Attention to the environment in which such software would be used expanded the project from just software to the idea of an all-comprehensive desktop workstation. THALLER (1992, p. 4) wanted a DBMS that would accommodate large databases close to original form with the following: as little coding as possible; interactive access to read-only databases for contextual information and reference; interactive databases for data transfer; Artificial Intelligence applications to make subsystem interplay transparent to users; and highly integrated interfaces with a desktop publishing system and statistical software. THALLER presents several scenarios illustrating the difference in source-oriented software from most DBMS packages that would not respect the considerable differences of historical from modern databases such as their size, variable length, many attributes, multiple equivalencies for data commonly entered in a single field, plus the great variation in content. He defines the goal as follows (1994, p. 33):

> Source oriented data processing [cf., GREENSTEIN, 1994] attempts to model the complete amount of information contained in a historical source on a computer; it tries to administer such sources for the widest variety of purposes feasible. While providing tools for different types of analysis, it does not force the historian at the time he or she creates a database to decide already which methods shall be applied later.

Klieu, of course, is his prime example. It is based on a data model close to semantic networks, which uses names in a meaningful way, allows subgroups of data within a database that are discreet entities with their own characteristics, facilitates even arbitrary connection between databases and data groups, and provides special tools for hierarchical and relational data structures. He also shows how different their operations must be for variable context sensitivity, when most DBMS programs assume they will operate in a singular modern context, including dealing with variable calendars for time sequencing, algorithms for orthographic variation, multiple languages and dialects, calculation of currency exchanges, and sequential processing to refine data according to what would appear to most programmers as very idiosyncratic sets of rules.

THALLER (1994, p. 39) outlines *Klieu*'s operation as working a historian's query through database software to a knowledge environment (local orthography, calendar, social terminology applicable currencies and lemmatization of source languages, etc.), resulting in uninterpreted strings as database which can then be analyzed and interpreted. The enhanced architecture of this working database will reconnect to primary sources as bound images or "bit-mapped manuscripts" (p. 43) to allow for easy checking of sources while working with extracted data. He, thereby, defines *Klieu* (p. 38) as follows:

> In *Klieu* a historical source is administered by transcribing various parts of a source, assigned to individual elements of a database, as literally as possible. All knowledge about the meaning of the transcribed items is administered separately in a layer of the system which is specifically dedicated to the administration of knowledge. Any query the user makes, any command that has to access the data which are stored in the transcribed source, is interpreted to the knowledge stored about the source.

For the enhanced version in progress, he adds (p. 42):

> The visual reproduction of the transcribed source resides within the database; parts of it can be reproduced on a suitable output medium as a result of any such way of accessing the transcription as implied above. Once the reproduction of part of the source has been selected and displayed, it can be modified by subsystems incorporating the full power of image processing.

The entire *Klieu* workstation and integrated source databases, therefore, include:

1. Archives consisting of primary sources that resemble lists connected through a central catalog

2. Archives that are unregistered sources like running texts, which also have similar links through a central catalog

3. Museum inventories related to image processing

4. Libraries or connections to bibliographic databases through keyword linkage, cataloging and subject headings or thesauri, relating books and articles to the archival sources and museum objects in other databases incorporated into the system

Pilot studies have been conducted since 1991 to test the entwined operations of *Klieu* with some of the most difficult modern sources imaginable, namely the so-called Gypsy Camp deportation records (two vols.) from Auschwitz-Birkenau and the related *Sterbebücher* death certificate registers (46 vols., 40,000 photographs, etc., connected with the prisoner roll-calls or *Staerkebücher* records) which in 1992 were returned from the former Soviet Union to the concentration camp memorial. The archival microfilm of the records contains 430,000 frames, and may be augmented by similar records from three other concentration camps. One of the early efforts was to reach consensus on naming conventions so a seamless set of databases could be built that would enable easy data transfer between several archives. REHBEIN (1997) explains that the project has attempted to produce a homogenous database and source edition in machine-readable form not only for better access, but also to preserve originals. The idea of an electronic source includes the raw data or text files from converted sources, as well as a fairly detailed description for enhanced information retrieval. Work has concentrated on the equivalent to a catalog with linkage between data and metadata, but rather than item description, the team has opted for a quasi-series approach by artificially grouping documents into clusters and providing summaries for these record groups. In addition to these summaries, "thumb-nail" miniatures of documents are included with descriptions, so one can visualized the original sources with their descriptions. This has required emphasis on high resolution. Finally, their approach has been to utilize Self-Documenting Image Files (SDIF, based on TIF files).

Thaller, who now works out of Bergen, Norway, understood that no single comprehensive project like the Historical Workstation could find sufficient funding in one place, so the strategy has been to network and coordinate such development with a variety of centers from Austria to England and most recently Russia. Intern-institutional cooperation championed by the IAHC has produced in Europe a prototype of the "collaboratory" before the United States NATIONAL RESEARCH COUNCIL began promoting this concept. While attention has been riveted on the use of historical data converted to machine-readable form, not enough consideration has yet been paid to the process of retrospective conversion creating databases that are subject to preservation problems and need to be adhere to the archival standards evolving for electronic records. Research institutions engaged in such retrospective conversion of historical records must do so with progressive vision and understanding that they are creating electronic archives anew. These need to be administered as such. This is especially important as international resource sharing and collaboration become more common across the Internet. Cross-Atlantic collaboration, however, is still limited at present. The only pan-America-Europe coordinated venture has been the Text Encoding Initiative. The historical computing community is fragmented and transfer in technique, method, and technological application is too easily blocked by the limitations of American historians in reading foreign languages and outside their own traditionally defined fields. The American information science community has unfortunately also remained uninvolved in this international development. In some ways it may be perceived as a model collaborative program; in others, it is still individually driven and has rested primarily on the extraordinary energy and persistence of Manfred Thaller. It is a development too important to ignore, and it illustrates the maturation of a semi-autonomous Historical Informatics in the European sense, as Historical Computer Science, but also a larger Historical Information Science bridging History, Computer Science, and Information Science.

EDUCATION AND TRAINING

So many of the problems in this transition stage of electronic records and historical research are blamed on a lack of proper training in graduate History programs, including insufficient integration of computing and instructional technology in History undergraduate and secondary teaching, i.e., Computer-Assisted Instruction or Learning (CAI/CAL). Education is often blamed generally, but the fault is both programmatic and personal, and can be assigned to faculty and students alike. This is a problem more complex than the often simplistic blame on technophobia that supposedly haunts the Arts and Humanities more than other faculties. Even graduate students are prone to blame shortcomings on others, especially their teachers, like children whose problems are forever attributable to bad parenting. Accountability, however, always rests with the individual. Students and faculty exert influence on each other, one by teaching and mentoring, and the other through the selection of schools, programs, and mentors, and by a willingness to be taught. Moreover, much of graduate work is self-teaching. So shortfalls like not acquiring an array of methodological skills for research, acquaintance with a variety of techniques, or familiarity with modern information technology, take a certain unspoken collusion. Correction will also take cooperation. If not required, a computer background can be voluntarily acquired. However, if this is done by accident rather than design, training may be haphazard. Still, in retrospect, this would be better than nothing.

These concerns may be related to the CARNEGIE FOUNDATION (1994) four-fold definition of scholarship that includes innovative teaching with research applied to teaching (may archivists and librarians expand this also to informing) as co-equals with theoretical research. One way to accomplish a better balance between teaching and research is to reconsider the latter as peer teaching. Historians and colleagues interested in using Information technology to bridge this gap are exploring this theme at the 1997 H-Net Conference at Michigan State University. H-Net listservs and discussion groups already move freely between teaching concerns and research issues, and are now incorporating information and instructional technology as well with more theoretical material from allied disciplines.

Finally, the nexus between teaching and information sharing is reflected in a parallel alignment between Information Science and Education in several graduate schools (e.g., UCLA, SUNY Buffalo, etc.), which may be expressed in the double meaning of IT, i.e., both Information Technology and Instructional Technology. Other schools relate both Education and Information Science to the Social Sciences (e.g., UC-Berkeley, SUNY-Albany with Public Policy, etc.). Information Science usually studies information use and behavior in the aggregate, more than the individual, which aligns it more with Sociology than Psychology, or with a blend like Organizational Psychology or Cognitive Psychology. Its ethos, as already stated, is present-minded, not historical, so a connection between History and Information Science is often indirect, through a Social Science, and often through Education because of the nexus between informing and teaching.

D. NEUMAN's recent Delphi study to clarify the main issues in the use of information resources in education, in this case searching online and CD-ROM databases by secondary students, makes the point well that database designers have considered "a host of issues ranging from knowledge organization to human-computer interaction, [but] they typically frame their considerations in terms of access to and retrieval of information rather than effective use of that information" (p. 297). She advocates a conscious link, because of natural convergence is occurring anyway, between information systems design and Instructional Systems Design (ISD). She adopts M. FLEMING's five categories of effective instructional presentations: referential (iconic, digital, visual, auditory symbolic systems to represent content); informational (the quality of content organization and presentation); relational (especially synonymy, but all relationships expressed); demand (expectations of users, from low to higher level cognitive processing); and image-of-the-other (the designer's concept of the user based on the foregoing four categories of information). These presentations summarize a number of findings about human behavior and learning. Each one needs to be addressed in instructional and information systems design, and by every information professional and teacher conveying information to students. As such, the problems investigated and solutions provide criteria by which to review instructional media. This integration of an information and instructional approach to media and dual evaluation of information sources as instructional tools is perhaps represented best in the award-winning studies of Neuman's colleague then at the University of Maryland, Gary Marchionini, not only on the *Perseus Project*, but in examining Web technology, digital presentations of whole collections as interactive exhibits (e.g., Library of Congress), and hypertext applications and full-text searching in electronic encyclopedia (MARCHIONINI, 1989). Although his work has not focused specifically on History, his subjects have ranged through the Arts and Humanities and his findings seem pertinent for appropriate for historical work in electronic media and History teaching with instructional media (e.g., MARCHIONINI, 1994).

Teaching historians will find in his discussions a common chord, more than in most IS literature, to relate Information Science concerns and approaches with issues discussed, for example, in H-Net AHA fora on teaching History. D. NEUMAN provides (pp. 284, 298) a bibliography or core literature that bridges the continuum between information, communication, and instruction, from the classics in ISD from the late 1970s and early 1980s when computing was dramatically affecting instructional technology (selected references include ANGLIN; L. BRIGGS; DICK & CAREY; FLEMING & LEVIE; GAGNE; REIGELUTH; RICHEY; SALOMON, etc.), to listing the graduate schools in the United States with flourishing research programs in instructional technology. She notes that one now has over 100 design models from which to choose when producing or using instructional media (GUSTAFSON), and expert assistance can be gleaned from a variety of associations: e.g., the Association for Educational Communications and Technology, the National Society for Performance and Instruction, and the Society for Applied Learning Technology.

Neuman's Delphi study identified the most important student problems in learning today and the most significant policy and curricular issues of which administrators and teachers are most concerned. Each major concern is linked to potential solutions. Among the top in these problem/concern categories are: planning effective search strategies; screen design issues relating segments of information and searching; overcoming mismatches between personal ideas and how information is actually organized; generating proper search terms and mastering new terminologies; and accommodation for the many variables of individual motivation, abilities, and goals. In some cases, the student problem is simply understanding how to begin. Instructional concerns that unified all parties queried were mastery of higher-order thinking skills, in designing, conducting, and interpreting research; familiarization with the variety of databases and their possibilities; and the formalization of instruction for information searching as part of the overall curricular, course, or unit goal. In short, information sources have always been instructional resources requiring good design from layout, typography, to directions and packaging. Today's interactive electronic media are more powerful, but they are also more complicated, and simultaneously liberating and frustrating, fulfilling and inundating. They are easy to use initially, superficially, and by themselves, but difficult to use together and collaboratively, with sophistication and expertise.

Teaching History

It makes eminent sense to turn to Computer-Assisted Instruction (CAI), Computer-Assisted Teaching (CAT), and Computer-Assisted Learning (CAL) methods and technology for teaching computer use and initiating students to the world of electronic information (the "knowing how" of History according to YEAGER & MORRIS). Indeed, today there is little rationale choice but to do so. The electronic classroom once envisioned as something for tomorrow is here with a full range of emerging technologies (BOSCHMANN). Packages, their design and content, may focus on information access more than delivery, massive or highly selective content, straight-forward presentation or more advanced forms of visualization, and may operate as closed, syn-dectic systems or be open-ended. Some are more vendor and hardware dependent than others, the technologies have changed too rapidly to produce any lull long enough to achieve integra-tion, and while still in the infancy stage of instructional multimedia with its rampant experi-mentation and complicated market, the whole venture of instructional support in any form is still expensive. Information and instructional technologies are often difficult to differentiate. Being informed, after all, is a precondition for informed learning.

While the requirement to use computerized information technology is in many ways being dictated to historians and other academicians by those controlling information systems, libraries and archives, and museums, this is less the case with instructional technology in the classroom where academic freedom and professorial prerogatives prevail. The availability of information and instructional technology and the access to information, however, do not answer questions about what to use or access, how, when, to what advantage, or how to eval-uate the whole process. Indeed, sheer availability and accessibility bring with them a subtle imperative for use, if for nothing more than to justify the investment. More positively, justifi-cation is often provided by those arguing for "active" learning in laboratory settings or studios rather than "passive" old-style learning in lecture halls and control-designed classrooms (this literature, like some propaganda campaign from Education and Educational Psychology, is vast and can be accessed via *ERIC* and other indexes in Education; entry can also be made through BONWELL & EISON; MEYERS & JONES; etc.). Of course, faculty privilege can be used to dismiss the possibilities of instructional technology to enhance traditional courseware, the lecture, which takes a beating from the action crowd. Recently in the AHA "Teaching Innovations Forum," TRIFAN was both highly critical of the "active learning" message and several of its suppositions, and in retaliation defended lecture methods as "active" against those assailants who assumed that the activities of listening, viewing, and reading were some-how dormant (rejoinders and extensions were offered by J. Oberly and R. Marchand). More recently another historian and dean of Humanities and Social Sciences, K. STUNKEL, has taken the rebuttal of interactive-learning theory advocates to a larger audience, namely the readership of the *Chronicle of Higher Education*, with his defense of "The Lecture: a Powerful Tool for Intellectual Liberation."

These debates surrounding teaching content and methods are more than mere turf protec-tion, however, or defense of the *status quo*; they focus on some of the most difficult and core issues of education at all levels and on History's role in cultural formation and regeneration. They are, unfortunately, largely philosophical debates exchanging personal opinion formed mainly by personal experience as quasi-individual case studies. Emotional conviction may be evident in such discussions, but a firm basis on research is often lacking. Indeed, very little empirical comparative research or formal assessment of innovative methods exists for history teaching beyond secondary Social Studies curricula. This lacuna is gaping in comparison with that for information resource and systems usage by historians, and most of the aforementioned use studies do not differentiate between usage for research or teaching.

What empirical research does exists seems woefully inadequate to convince either camp of the other's position It is unfortunate that such polarization has reduced this complex issue into this or that, or extremes of totally mediated courses and teacherless instruction or "guide on the side" coaching peer groups versus the controlling mode ridiculed as "sage on the stage" authoritarian presentation that lacks any mediation save the instructor's talking head. The arguments seem the same, whether over instructional television in the late 1960s or computer-assisted instruction now. Given that student groups are so varied, it would seem common sense to use varied styles of pres-entation, media, and exercises from the purely mental to the individually active and interactive, and to modulate the serialization of course delivery by engineering complementary and supplemental alternatives and additives to traditional classes (like homework, assigned reading outside of class, library use any time individually or in groups, or CAI modules and electronic fora). There is a high cost in such redundancy, however, which is an overarching problem in an era of fiscal constraint.

One experimental case study by J. SCHUTTE at CSU-Northridge in 1996 is illustrative of the problem. He randomly split a class in his Social Statistics course into two control groups: one a "virtual" class relying on e-mail, hypernews, WWW form-controlled submissions, and a moderated Internet Relay Chat (IRC) forum; and the other a traditional face-to-face lecture/discussion class, both scheduled over a 14-week semester. To his surprise, test results seemed to indicate that the "virtual interaction produced better results" by a degree of 20 percent. His small study was posted online, picked up by the *Chronicle of Higher Education* and the popular press in early 1997, and became a centerpiece for electronic discussion groups nationwide. It was praised as conclusive evidence and attacked as "artless...comparative research" because it actually reiterated what is well known, namely the positive correlation between more time on a task yielding improved performance (E. NEAL). The attention it gained was blown totally out of proportion to the actual research project or significance of his findings in one instance.

E. NEAL (a historian by training, and now director of faculty development at the University of North Carolina-Chapel Hill) has likewise attacked T. Russell's survey of research on this subject which is often used for claiming that no significant difference can be found between mediated and nonmediated instruction. Neal notes that control groups in academe are really not controlled in such comparative research, and he warns that the variable of quality in delivery influences outcome (not all faculty are equally talented in, nor are students equally receptive to, all things). The methodological weakness of too many studies is why KIES investigated empirical methods for evaluating mediated collaborative work; these may also be applied to interactive, mediated learning. Learning is not guaranteed by the mere presence of critical activities, such as those highlighted by the American Association for Higher Education (AAHE) *Flashlight Project*: (1) interaction between student and expert/teacher; (2) student-student interaction; (3) active learning; (4) time on task; (5) rich, rapid feedback; (6) high expectations of the student's ability to learn; and (7) respect for different talents and ways of learning (cognitive styles). One can administer diagnostic pretests, then measure these variables as inputs, and use post-tests to evaluate desired outputs. Positive correlations can thereby be made, but not necessarily the comparisons that have been made, or to obtain the kind of controlled and re-verifiable results that would sustain many of the conclusions that have been drawn from case studies or those generalized from their aggregation. This is not an easy field of inquiry when it comes to research design.

Subtle but important differences exist between mere interaction and genuine collaboration (as reflected in the essays edited by MCNEESE), and it is the latter that I advocate throughout this essay. The means to this higher goal are: the Internet and its local variation; Intranets composed of WANS and LANS; supporting groupware; both real-time and asynchronous communications; and the World Wide Web for access to electronic information backup. Educators have been called to seek an accommodation with the "new realities" in the business world described by P. DRUCKER (e.g., the emergence of the "knowledge worker" in the "information society") and the emergence of self-managed teams (MANKIN, COHEN & BIKSON; NAVARRO). MORRISSEY has studied the impact of Internet and collaborative technology on management education in the United States which relies heavily on case studies (i.e., very localized and discreet histories, from a historian's perspective). He concludes on the basis of three studies of individuals and four of groups that the most consistent finding overall "was the improved performance of the electronic meeting students over the traditional face-to-face students in decision quality tasks. The outcome is consistent with the meta-analyses of similar studies on other populations." He is referring to the link between group process and productivity made long ago by STEINER (1972). In effect, the kind of improved results through collaboration achieved in the role-playing games of survival scenarios in the wilderness (comparing the decisions of a single person in jeopardy with a group-consensus in the same situation, judged against the opinion of experts) can be had in the conduct of most business (the metaphor of wilderness survival for the business "jungle" is used here intentionally).

Most business research has been on synchronous interaction in meetings, not the "any time, any place" virtual environment of international business, but networking technology has changed this emphasis. The major qualitative difference was in the attitude of participants who liked the self-pacing, the clarity brought to bear on task assignments in order to make the system work (too often assumed in synchronous discourse), and the support of document management tools, all of which produce an efficiency and save time for more qualitative and social aspects of business and learning in face-to-face meetings. In certain collaborative learning situations such as brainstorming, groups that interact electronically have outperformed those meeting face-to-face (HOFFER & VALACICH; JESSUP & VALACICH; GALLUPE *ET AL.*; NUNAMAKER, APPLEGATE & KONSYNSKI). Concurrency seems to work better in some situations than others. In other studies computer-mediated communication seems to have resulted in decisions of equal quality (HILTZ *ET AL.*; SIEGEL *ET AL.*), and in one study higher quality (GALLUPE *ET AL.*), but the underlying reasons are not known (cited also by CITERA). These aspects of asynchronous collaborative work should widen the dimension of older studies about audiovisuals, mediated instruction, and computer-assisted learning such as CBT (Computer-Based Training) modules, but for whatever reason, experiential learning in mediated teamwork environments has not been related well to research about active learning or CAI/CAL.

The use of instructional technology is often drawn into and is framed by these larger methodological debates, as if the use of a computer were tantamount in itself to an "active learning" persuasion or, equally fallacious, that the computer learns for people. Moreover, most of the debate is about one-way/one-time delivery and synchronous interaction, without the added benefits of asynchonous collaboration. Detractors are quick to point out deficiencies in multimedia more than they propose solutions, and often criticisms are so overgeneralized that it is problematic to decipher what is needed and wanted (two different questions, and for which audiences and user groups?), so that research and development, and marketing too, can be directed for the mutual advantage of producer and consumer. Mark Helprin of the Hudson Institute recently railed against the paradigm of computer-assisted and multimedia instructional support, in sharp contrast to a scenario of traveling to London to experience the sights, sounds, and smells of England complete with Shakespearean theater in person. He makes an eloquent case for experiential learning (HELPRIN):

> A life lived with these understood, even if vaguely [a specific environment and a harmony in elements that relate to us and of which we are often unaware], will have the grace that a life lived unaware of them will not. When expanding one's powers, as we are in the midst of now doing by many orders of magnitude in the mastery of information, we must always be aware of our natural limitations, mortal requirements, and humane preferences (FORBES, *ASAP*, p. 20).

Like a mediaeval *sic et non* exposition, he goes back and forth between extremes to illustrate choices. But he assumes that one paradigm is exclusive of the other, when to achieve the full awareness he advocates, one may want both the actual experience and the mediated surrogate. The latter, for example, could prepare the viewer for what is to be seen and afterward remind him or her of what was seen, without either the visit or the virtual tour necessarily being the only choice. The case for multimedia can be made precisely because of our awareness of "our natural limitations, mortal requirements, and humane preferences [i.e., choice]." Moreover, gaming and simulation technology aims at precisely this objective, that is, experiential learning (SCHLENE). HELPRIN derides CAI technology, however, by stating the obvious for all learning, as if this requirement pertained only to machine-assisted learning: "Most multimedia is appalling. It endeavors to do the integrative work that used to be the province of the intellect, and that, if it is not in fact accomplished by the intellect, is of absolutely no value."

It is doubtful that instructional media will solve the basic problems in teaching and learning which are endemic to human nature; some of the criticism leveled against multimedia pertain to all mediated instruction regardless of the level of technology employed, from chalk to white board, from slide and overhead transparency projectors to LCDs and PowerPoint presentations, and from static or interactive personal lectures to video presentations, and onward toward Learning Caves and Holidecks. Rather than make the challenging task of good, creative teaching easier, much of the thrust has been enrichment rather than convenience, and with the greater array of media available, the more complicated teaching becomes because well integrated multimedia instruction requires up-front investment, collaboration with support services, and superior personal management on the part of teachers who must understand their own abilities, their students, and the organization culture in which both are teaching and learning. Consequently one must consider the broader issue of history in education, rather than just instructional method and technology in history. Unfortunately, a shift in focus from method to content does not make life easier for the History teacher. If content knowledge and research methodology are two requirements for a well-trained historian, a third would be presentation skills through writing, speaking, illustration, and multimedia. Direct, indirect, and mediated instruction and dissemination of research require different competencies, sensibilities, and sets of technical skills.

The application of computer information and instructional technology in History teaching was slighted in *The National Standards for History* project (NSH), but perhaps this omission was a blessing. Certainly the English writing for *The Economist* in 1996 who characterized "Americans, eternally at ease with their history, are also good at re-examining it," have not paid attention to the United States milieu since 1994. Indeed, the furor over quantification studies in History during the late 1960s and early 1970s has been superseded in intensity, ferocity, vindictiveness, and sheer nastiness over the teaching of History in American elementary and secondary schools. FERRO's treatise in 1981 on how the past is taught, especially to children, as either an open inquiry or closed preferred history (i.e, the use and abuse of History), addressed bias in textbooks related to prejudices in children. His commentary a decade before the great debate over history teaching in the United States seems very relevant even though his focus was mainly on European education. Granted that historical interpretation of historical episodes such as the Enola Gay exhibit at the Smithsonian have generated some heated controversy, such reactions seemed like small preludes to the general outcry precipitated by an attempt to find a standard for teaching History as an antidote for the perceived lack of historical knowledge among young Americans.

History as a matter of social construction is extremely important and, hence, controversial, especially when translated into school curricula where the teaching of history has so much to do with the transmission of culture and formation of social perception (GOODSON). Little has seemed more controversial in History than the issuance in November 1994 and revision in 1996 of base standards for K-12 history teaching in American schools (NATIONAL CENTER FOR HISTORY). The National Standards Project was conceived in the George Bush administration, but was instituted in President Bill Clinton's *Goals 2000: Educate America Act* backed by an initial $1.6 initial and total $2.2 million in funding through grants from the Department of Education and the National Endowment for the Humanities. Its principal spokesman and project guide, Gary B. Nash of UCLA, more than codirector Charlotte Crabtree and assistant Lynda Symcox, has been on the defensive ever since the three-volume work was released in October 1994, but more so after Lynn Cheney, formerly of NEH, led the conservative charge against the standards (CHENEY; NASH & DUNN). The national tempest had already been stirred by local whirlwinds since 1990 in California and in New York (NEW YORK STATE.

SOCIAL STUDIES REVIEW AND DEVELOPMENT COMMITTEE). BICOUVARIS (1994) traces the growth of these skirmishes into the larger conflagration and the stage by stage revision to the initial draft under fire from several fronts. NASH (1996) and his colleagues have recounted their embroilment in the decade's "culture war" with more dispassion than many combatants. The intensity of the debate caught many off-guard, especially given the diminished role of History in general studies, lasting employment problems in academic history, and a malaise in the profession that laments how little History is taught at all. When many claim that History in general is in crisis, the sudden tempest over emphases and the particular seems ironic and dumbfounding. It is an episode that deserves further inspection within a broader context of American cultural and intellectual history, and from the vantage points of organizational culture and information science as well.

The politicalization of this affair grew when Senator Bob Dole essentially labeled revisionists as traitors for their tampering with America's history (H. KAYE). The debate intensified after more ammunition for conservative reactionaries was supplied by John Fonte's Committee to Review National Standards, as critics took exception to the proposed curriculum's globalization at the expense of former dominant Euro-American core in history teaching (FONTE & LERNER). They accuse it both of imbalance and an ultraliberal bias (JOST). Revisions after the initial uproar were mostly cosmetic, as Nash himself admitted. LONDON and others called for further reform, rather than merely removing the Standards' "propagandistic" overtones. The critical factors, apart from point by point debates about assertions, assumptions, and proof or absence thereof, seem to have centered on such issues as balance, revision rather than radical alteration, and the pervasive charge of presentism. Many detractors were upset by the NSH's debunking or worse, ignoring traditional heroes in American national history, and resurrecting from obscurity new unsung heroes from countercultures and subcultures in the name of diversity. Some accuse the standards simply of misrepresenting American history. The very citations of works seen as innovative and refreshing by some are viewed by others as poor interpretations or worse, radical and ultraliberal. Here the aforementioned problems of data selection from the mass and dealing with imperfect data on the other hand, which challenge all historians in doing history, confront History's consumer's as well. LUSTICK takes a typical Social Science approach to this problem of "selection bias" by suggesting that strategies are needed to select from partially inconsistent historical monographs a hybrid account or "background narrative" which either transcends the works of individual historians or underpins them. The idea almost sounds like a consumer's guide with ratings by explicit criteria, except that rather than simply rate books as a means to sort alternatives, the goal would be to provide a hybrid model with the best of all exemplars. Such solutions, however, have not worked in manufacturing, for example in using selection and criteria to produce the ideal automobile; or in education when teachers teach students to pass a known standardized test.

In any case, the standards have been scrutinized like no other work in History within the United States, including discourse analysis, term frequency, classification study, and other computer-assisted methods mentioned in this survey. Apart from the standards themselves, these debates have set a tone for public discourse and a hypercritical milieu in which all media representing history are judged. DIGGINS, one of the most eloquent, castigates history for defrocking the Social Sciences in one instant, and being usurped by them in another under the guise of New Social history. He attacks the "roots" mystique as well (a new form of Romanticism), and a host of other causes of the ill fortune to befall the Standards project which lie in the recent history of History. H. KAYE reminds everyone "to make sense of the furor we must think historically and politically," which he sees as not just an intense discussion of pedagogical guidelines, but a class war in America over "the very purpose and promise of historical education and, even beyond that, the vision we hope to pass on to our children of America's past, present, and possible futures." His rendition, of course, added fuel to the fire which has burned on, and whenever dying out, it lies smoldering still just under the surface of things. Throughout this episode, scientific historicism died a hundred deaths. Information Science, it seems, never knew about the controversy; the field displayed no sense of its potential relation to anything other than History and education...certainly not to information.

SMYTH, surveying the British situation, maintains that history has always been influenced by political agenda, either in revisionism or the removal of recreations of the past (for example, the Victorian reworking of Alfred the Great to support modern British imperialism). But in the United Kingdom debates since 1994 seem to run a parallel course to those in the United States. Although equally virulent and contentious, more discussion seems to be going on about a "history-teaching crisis" in England particularly, which is more about teaching method than content (FITZGERALD & FLINT). A recent survey of United Kingdom History departments gathered information about assessment, modularization, use of information technology, and career prospects for history majors (FITZGERALD & HINGLEY). Its approach is reminiscent of RUNDELL's study for the American Historical Association 20 years ago, but such data gathering is being used to suggest curricular remodeling and educational reform at all levels. The School Curriculum and Assessment Authority has created a new history curriculum for British education that seems to generate as much controversy as the National Standards in the United States. C. WHITE points out that concerns are expressed by teachers especially about increased flexibility about what to cover in stage 1 and reductions in coverage at stage 2, with greater emphasis on improving critical thinking skills and use of historical knowledge than merely its accumulation. The reduction in content is said to result partially for a reduction of what was seen as overload, but also to appease differences between rightists and leftists about certain subjects and their emphases. Stage 3 still gives such importance to British history that the issue of balance is questioned given trends toward globalization and the particular problem this creates for British imperial history, colonization, and interaction with the Third World (*TIMES*). Matters once instilling pride may now turn to greater circumspection and creation of self-doubt and recrimination in the same way that reexamination of the American westward expansion and encounter with Native Americans has created similar problems for revision in American history education.

Such revisionism and debate about applications in the schools have been less contentious than the British High Education Funding Council's Quality Assessment initiatives, first to rate research productivity, and then teaching quality in the process of "modularisation" of curricula (FITZGERALD & HINGLEY). The TQA process, entailing a rather crude ranking system, has been described with a range of adjectives from "inadequate" to "bloody awful." Computerized research and computer-assisted teaching issues have been involved in these assessments. FITZGERALD & HINGLEY (p. 6) explain: "There is a certain amount of schizophrenia in history departments over the role of new technology in teaching. While some universities are leading the way with computing courses and research departments [e.g., Glasgow, where the Teaching and Learning Technology Programme (TLTP) History Coursework Consortium is based], others are at best agnostic about the benefits technology can offer the average history student." While some historians have embraced CD-ROM projects, the Open University's critic, Arthur Marwick, spurns "most of the CD-ROM teaching stuff..." as "pretty trivial." Nevertheless, instructional technology is being adopted widely if not always enthusiastically in Great Britain.

In the former Soviet Union, of course, the problem of national politicalization of history and its influence on general education is even more hotly contended than in the Anglo-world. There, former Soviet republics are trying to reclaim their own histories, reconcile them with the official histories of the post-Stalinist era, and figure out how revision should be placed into school systems to create historical views that assist in building a new commonwealth. PETRE observes that socialist control of nationalist history destroyed the citizens' critical view of history: "Reviving historical awareness in the post-communist era promises to be a monumental task." Historians and educators there also debate the orientation of their history, once so nationalist and self-indemnifying, to Europe, or to a more broadly and multicultural global history given their neighbors and the rival cultures and separatism within CIS borders. Historians in the Commonwealth of Independent States, therefore, face larger challenges than the tension between conservative and liberal polarizations in the United States. Searching for a way to reconstruct an entire multinational history within an intellectual context of globalization is heart-wrenching and mind-boggling. The Council of Europe recently convoked a conference with representatives from 47 countries to explore "The Mutual Understanding and Teaching of European History"; the Council generally agreed that students must be able to interpret history from divergent sources and from all sides of conflicts. Some of the most perplexing concerns related to children and the level at which conflict resolution should be introduced, for example, in forming value judgments about Hitler, etc. (RAFFERTY).

Content rather than method has dominated the standards debate in the United States, whether delivery is traditionally oral and textual or computerized. W. MCDOUGALL, however, raises points germane to this discussion of historical information science regarding the skills History seeks to develop. The opening chapters of the standards establish a duality of purpose, and a tension between them, in understanding why history matters: (1) "Knowledge of history is the precondition of political intelligence," which Walter McDougall interprets as helping one to make "intelligent political choices"; and (2) "History is the only laboratory we have in which to test the consequences of thought," which McDougall sees as the corrective to possible presentism in the first. More generally "Historical memory" is labeled as the key to our "connectedness with all *hu*mankind." Teaching is to be rooted in chronology, so pupils apprehend patterns and cause-and-effect relationships, strike a balance between broad themes and specific events, and imbue such scholarly values as evaluating evidence, logical argument, interpretive balance, comparative analysis, comprehension, and "issues-analysis and decision-making" which are "historical thinking skills" (p. 854) to be applied to everyday life in detecting bias, weighing evidence, evaluating arguments, and "to sniff out spurious appeals to history by partisan pleaders, and to distinguish between anecdote and analysis." These goals, with their decidedly Social Science orientation and sense of purpose (McDougall also notes a deemphasis on the history of ideas), are to be accomplished with assignments requiring students to:

1. Identify the source of a historical document and assess its credibility

2. Contrast the differing values, behaviors, and institutions involved

3. Differentiate between historical facts and interpretations

4. Consider multiple perspectives of various people

5. Analyze cause-and-effect relationships and multiple cause

6. Challenge arguments of historical inevitability

7. Compare competing historical narratives

8. Hold interpretations of history as tentative

9. Evaluate major debates among historians

10. Hypothesize the influence of the past

W. MCDOUGALL astutely remarks: "This splendid instructional guide for a Ph.D. thesis defense is what the Standards aim to require of all 5th to 12th graders...In practice, this curriculum would overtax the capabilities of most teachers, not to mention pupils...."

One could indeed use these goals as much for training historians than teaching history in primary and secondary education, and could expect to see some congruence between the two and consistency in standards at three levels, with the higher standard for graduate training and subsequent practice to stress the critical apparati, techniques, and methods for source appraisal, selection of appropriate methodologies and the techniques for their implementation, congruence between such analyses, information input and output, and a plan for effective information dissemination (choice of communications, appropriate channels, well-designed media, which altogether form a strategy). In short, apart from content and balance arguments, these standards do seem formidable, but they in no way encompass all that needs to be accomplished for doctoral work. Multilevel, tiered, and graded work, reinforcement and the addition of new material for greater depth and increased scope are implicit in the notion of graduate work, as is the idea that this all begins at elementary levels, secondary, and other intervening levels. If there is anything limiting about the idea of graduate education, it is the false notion that one ever completes it.

The standards controversy could be even more complicated than it has become, if issues of information and instructional technology were added to the debate, as they well might be. In addition to what should be taught and why, are issues of how, and if these questions point to information skills development combined with conceptualization and the interpretation of history, the focus of the current debate is enlarged considerably. It is not the purpose here to review this debate *per se* but only to provide another dimension stemming from the notion of Historical Information Science which may be applied at all levels of instruction. For example, the aforementioned inadequacies of history graduate students in information retrieval are hardly limited to their graduate experience. The criticism by archivists and librarians is that graduate studies often do not remedy deficiencies from earlier education. The charge is that information technical skills are not developed conterminously with subject knowledge so students can replenish and expand this knowledge base at will, independently of formalized schooling or an education institutional incubus. At issue is congruent maturation and creation of an intellectual self-informing individuality that is not only independent in thinking, but continually informed thinking. Here one wishes for more empirical research that would clarify rather than complicate questions about the efficacy of computer-assisted instruction in tandem with the considerably more enlightening research in information science about user behaviors and automated information retrieval processes.

Note that this public discourse about history in education is occurring when the shift in academic History and current historiography generally has been away from empiricism and Social Science history, to the closer link of History with the Humanities. Consequently, even though in secondary education the tendency is to see History as part of Social Studies education, the discussion is oriented toward historical reasoning predominantly as a textual and language methodology and a philosophical persuasion. Logic is understood as important, both deduction and induction, but the dominant focus is microscopic and on local and regional studies, and the viewpoint is serial more than parallel despite lip service to globalization which should favor the latter thinking (BENITEZ outlines six approaches to globalization). Finally, numerate reasoning and statistics for inference, modeling, and probability are lacking balanced attention in these debates. It is as if mathematics were part of another dimension totally and the worlds of numbers and letters do not overlap. One of the few to bridge this gap is B. C. HOLLISTER who argues that mathematical data can be combined effectively with social issues in the classroom to facilitate a better understanding of historical events. He argues especially for the integration of "social math" into history teaching at all levels, elementary through college level teaching. PERMAN & PERMAN use historical scenarios to teach math (projections, linear algebra, etc.), as in applying game theory to the voyage of Ferdinand Magellan and other narratives, where the goal is to use math to identify feasible options and to explain thereby the strategies selected in history. While the focus of historians has been on the lack of history literacy, more attention might be paid to the pervasive problem of historical numeracy.

A variety of teaching strategies exist to accommodate the styles of both teachers and students in engaging information and instructional technology, as they are both learners in this experience (ROHRS). Moreover, as this survey demonstrates, the array of electronic resources now available is so vast that appraisal, selection, and application are difficult problems in addition to technique and appropriate technology—all questions related to solid pedagogy. The aforementioned library use studies suggest serious problems in teaching students to access historical literature, and more difficulty in identifying primary sources. Source appraisal in any form is difficult to do and to teach, and electronic media make these tasks no easier. Just the opposite: in creating easier access and mass, and by adding yet another layer of mediation and technique plus a choice in formats, they complicate research significantly. Reliance on general studies education for foundations, i.e., bibliographic skills, which seem to be so unevenly developed, has been criticized severely. Historians are accused by themselves (e.g., G. BAIN, 1995) of having ignored and missed out on the genuine revolution that occurred in the bibliographic instruction movement in academic libraries (BREVIK & GEE), and for their confusion when discussing methodology of such basic distinctions as between searching and research (MCCRANK, 1992a). BAIN claims that from his experience in a university archives and library that many of the problems identified by W. RUNDELL 20 years ago have yet to be remedied. Access to historical sources and literature does not play into some of the recent debates about history teaching in America (KRAMER, REID & BARNEY). BLEWETT concludes similarly that the structuring of information, and hence its searching, are not well-developed skills among history graduate students even though the library is "the historian's laboratory" (p. 27). One may suspect that if such foundations are not mastered in libraries with walls, the problem is exacerbated by the Internet/WWW or universal library without walls, governance, or organization.

Efforts in the classroom dovetail initiatives in the library Bibliographic Instruction movement toward Information Literacy (BREIVIK & GEE; MCCRANK, 1992a) more than simply computer use. The Association for the Bibliography of History (ABH) attempted some remedy (D'ANIELLO *ET AL.*), and ample opportunities are provided by ABC-CLIO such as discounted access to its databases for instruction, sample publications, and free examination copies (c.f., the Getty Trust AHIP's free *Art and Architecture Thesaurus* demonstration diskettes). Most companies now offer some form of instructional aid with their products. SWIERENGA and others like TUCKER recommended a decade ago the combination of bibliographic instruction with history in general studies. They attested good experiences in incorporating the then nascent bibliographic instruction movement into their undergraduate history teaching, but modules aimed a remedying deficiencies in library use skills do not go far enough to create computer literacy or even the same ease and comfort level as when a student grew up with computer games. The laboratory or practice component is critical, and such practice must not be simply remedial or repetitious. The best experience seems to be sequential exposure to ever more challenging software and richer sources through one's formal education. The choices available today are far richer than a decade ago.

Online searching and techniques for full-text versus controlled vocabulary searching are seen by most historians as the purview of librarians so these skills are often taught tutorially when tools are first used, or in short demonstration modules as part of libraries' Bibliographic Instruction programs. Some are evolving into holistic Information Literacy programs (MCCRANK, 1993) in which historians should be active players. Librarians are often addicted to bibliographic searching and sometimes do not engage specialized full-text bases any more readily than historians. The former often understand classification and terminological control better, and the latter know the domain literature more thoroughly, so there is plenty of opportunity for fruitful collaboration here. Full-text searching often results in higher recall but lower precision (HOOD; PAGELL), but other studies (WAGERS; TENOPIR, 1985, 1988) indicate that free-text and controlled-term search performances are complementary and must be used together for ultimate results. Such findings suggest the need to teach multiple search techniques in an overall strategy when one investigates historical literature. Moreover, a search strategy may have to be adapted to the characteristics of historical sources; MOLTO's research in family histories, for example, concluded that there are significant differences in searching males and females because search term frequencies differ according to gender. Synonyms, homographs, form variations, and co-occurrence patterns are all issues to be confronted in searching historical literature. It is not a straightforward, simple task as too often assumed by historians. History as a knowledge domain is not restricted enough to hold great promise for natural language analyzers and database query engines to facilitate effective automatic searching. Users therefore have to become acquainted with menu, Boolean-formed set, keyword and controlled terminology as well as free-text information retrieval, and to learn to distinguish quickly between relevant hits and noise in winnowing results.

Most importantly, given studies about negative attitudes, technophobia, cognitive dissonance, and other psychological and emotional issues preventing comfort and ease in online or CD-ROM searching, timing and presentation are important in course design (E. JACOBS based on full-text searching in Law). What is known about overcoming resistance to technological change in the workplace (FINE) should be applied in the classroom as well, and certainly in the design of instructional technology (BAKER). Technostress has been recognized as something legitimate to be confronted in the workplace; it must be recognized as an issue in education as well (SETHI). Parallels exist between using self-paced learning and interactive CAI/CAL systems with decision support systems in management which have been well-developed since the 1970s (M. MORTON; KEEN & MORTON; ROCKART & DELONG trace their deployment in business as CBT [Computer-Based Training], but academic applications are rare), but which still encounter resistance to use (PINNICK). The problem lies in both human-computer communication and peculiarities of the knowledge domain (G. FISCHER). Granted a fear of misinformation may be legitimate, as ACKOFF warned in early developments, but this is precisely why critical judgment skills must be developed. Awareness of such possibilities is simply savvy. Such apprehension might be positive; it would certainly promote critical usage and temper any overreliance on a support system which by definition is not meant to make definitive decisions by themselves.

Some of these systems are simply memory assists, systematic prompts, and directional guides, as distinct from the later development of expert systems that interact with knowledge bases. Some follow the basic rules of "direct teaching" which like good rhetorical tactics, explains first what will be said, says it, and then repeats what was said by way of summary and reinforcement. This can be enhanced visually on screen as much as writing outlines on wallboards. Nevertheless, technological phobia are common. Irrationality and anxiety are often camouflaged by seemingly critical objections. Prominent factors include a common personal-history reflex in human behavior: a poor prior experience is often recalled and negative emotional reactions to the first instance are transposed to the second. An explicit outline of objectives and schedules predicting change, a personal touch, and creation of a supportive social context is equally important. And environmental psychologists would also point to a hospitable learning environment, which is often lacking in computer laboratories set up more for the efficiency of cabling and security of equipment than the comfort of the learner.

Few studies exist that examine syllabi, interactive *practica*, lecture delivery, or testing and evaluation in history teaching at the college level. Thus the supposedly easy conversion of manual courseware to electronic media is not a given. What may be assumed to be a redesign may indeed be the design from scratch or the first formalization of ongoing instruction that has operated largely as free flowing conversational discourse. Librarians, for example, commonly complain that course syllabi are too often vague in their instruction and lack standard citation elements in their references. When reserve lists have been automated, as in Xerox Corporation's deployment of electronic textbases instead of photocopy files, the task of editing syllabi, authority work, and correcting citations and linking them to MARC records can be formidable when setting up a campuswide system. The same is true when scanning course descriptions and syllabi into a fully electronic catalog. The editing, standardization, and data acquisition in such projects are far more complicated than mastering the technology. It is difficult to assess the prowess of historians in developing courseware, since most activity is hidden within academic computing, media laboratories, and do-it-yourself personal computing. Subsequent studies need to address actual use, impact on teaching and research, and the greater access or also new possibilities for innovative techniques and research methodologies that the new media provide. This is the question posed by historians like S. ANDERSON *ET AL.*1997; KERSEN; MARKER, 1997; OLDERVOLL, 1997; and SEAMAN, etc., who devoted a session at the recent IAHC conference to "History on the Internet." Others are taking note of the Internet as a history teaching tool as well as communications vehicle. VLADIMIROV praises the Internet for allowing "East and West [to meet] in Cyberspace."

It is possible to identify popular packages, relate use to certain computer-active historians, and correlate some courseware with survey courses more than with more specialized offerings, but it is very difficult to discern holistic instructional delivery systems in higher education similar to those being implemented in large corporations. The conservative nature of university faculty and skepticism about self-paced training in academic disciplines and the relative slow advance of computer-assisted instruction in colleges and universities are not the only reasons. The nature of university teaching where instructional labor costs in the Liberal Arts and General Studies are still relatively cheap compared with technical fields, and delivery on a single campus can be personal and coordinated reasonably well. The move of universities to multi-campus and off-campus instruction, and greater deployment of distance learning programs, will alter this situation and compel university administrators to seek more efficient ways to deliver courses through mediated instruction, distance learning technology, and comprehensive delivery systems beyond classroom scheduling. Within the Computer-Based Training (CBT) industry, however, such educational endeavors do not yet constitute a very large market in relation to technology being applied to productivity in the workplace, occupational training, and consulting. Large corporations with thousands of employees in multiple sites confronting steady turnover and escalating demands on workers' knowledge bases and skills levels are turning to large distributed instructional systems. Continuing education is being merged with staff development in Human Resource Department (HRD) operations. Some universities are following suit already; others will assuredly follow.

The most recent *Computer-Based Training Report* (CB COMMUNICATIONS, 1996) does indicate some interesting trends, however, such as the mixing of authoring tools. First, about 70 percent of those who develop courseware use two products, and 44 percent use three in their toolkits. Second, divergence is widening between preferences for authoring tools based on the experience of the users; more experienced authors prefer *IconAuthor*, *Phoenix*, *Quest*, and *TenCORE*, while less experienced users rate *Authorware*, *Director*, *Toolbook*, and *Visual Basic* more highly. Third, the report claims that "person hours needed to develop an hour of courseware are directly and positively related to years of experience in developing it." In other words, organizations with more experience actually require *more* time developing courseware, which is the opposite of what one might expect. This is because courseware designed and programmed by experts is becoming ever more complex and sophisticated, user expectations have risen significantly with greater exposure to CAI support, and courseware has become increasingly interactive and multimedia-based.

Historians, experts in their fields, are still mostly amateurs in mediated instruction; they can develop courseware on their own, but increasingly the best products are team-based, pilot-tested, revised, and distributed, and then require support systems to assist users, train trainers, and update the product. Multimedia are especially gaining acceptance in history survey courses (EVANS & BROWN). In corporate style, HRD operations have spawned whole media and computer-based training staffs just as universities have had to develop teaching support and academic computing centers. These add significantly to the overall cost of course delivery; coupled with library support, the factor may be as high as one-third. Administrators influenced by the for-profit business model mistakenly regard these as "cost centers" rather than product quality control and enhancement operations.

This leads to the fourth trend affecting CAI, namely the increased reliance on local-area networks for courseware delivery and use of the Internet/WWW for tutorial distance learning. In 1995 43 percent of courseware developers expected delivery over LANs, but in turning to Internet delivery, CD-ROM use is falling off from 59 percent to 41 percent at the beginning of 1995 and now only 37 percent. Widespread use of the Internet/WWW technology and delivery into the home seems to be the wave of the future. On the other hand, CD-ROMs on file servers in a client/server architecture, available on Intranets, offer a means to provide local access without competing for time over long-range networks. The two means of distribution, therefore, may be seen as complementary rather than distinct one-or-the-other alternatives. Historians, however, are not using this technology so much for collaborative research as for inexpensive and convenient asynchronous communications to build support groups; their main use of the Internet is for listservs and electronic conferencing among themselves, rather than for enabling their students or teaching them through the new media. Relatively few faculty, for example, conduct counseling, receive student reports and term papers, provide correction and accept rewrites electronically. Yet, such technology is well tested, often in place, and is used successfully in universities offering off-campus programs, in contrast to accomplishing the same tasks electronically on campus. It was gratifying, therefore, to see at the recent IACH a growing awareness of the Internet's utility for mediated instruction and the activities of H-Net devotees at AHA and OAH conferences.

One might check to see what is available before creating customized media, but even this can be problematic. More traditional media are being converted into digital format for computer relay, and with permission photographs can be scanned into computer programs and with proper licensing video can be captured for CAI programs and delivery from Web sites. Only a small fraction of slide sets, film, and video are retro-converted into digital form. The NATIONAL INFORMATION CENTER FOR EDUCATIONAL MEDIA (NICEM) attempts to track educational media from 20,000 producers and distributors in the United States alone; its database of 420,000 entries is edited annually at a rate of about 5 percent or more than 20,000 additions and corrections. NICEM (http://www.nicem.com) also produces an *International Directory of Educational Audiovisuals* (*IDEA*) on CD-ROM for media produced since 1985 which may still be available. To provide some idea of how prolific recent production has been, *IDEA* 's multimedia coverage has tripled since 1993; over 60 languages are represented in this database, which is now updated quarterly. Most of this is targeted for K-12 education, but more is slanted toward general adult education at a beginning college level. Subject indexes do not reveal what may be relevant for history teaching, and indexing by discipline is also problematic because History as a heading and the field itself is so inter-disciplinary.

Beyond bibliographic instruction and information literacy for proper foundations, what exists for teaching skills associated closely with History or History itself? CAI developments are so prolific that a thorough review is not possible here (one might use the Carnegie Commission's 1975 report on computers and learning in American higher education as an early benchmark [ROCKART, ed.]; see BLOW & DICKENSON, updated by the NATIONAL COUNCIL FOR EDUCATIONAL TECHNOLOGY directory, 1991; cf., SCHENE's ERIC sample, 1992), but a sampling may illustrate trends and increased interest in History games and simulation to teach more than historical facts like mere renditions of names, dates, and events, but instead to inculcate historical awareness and develop the ability for historical reasoning (SEMOCHE). On the other hand. detractors warn against market pressures to pander to commercial success rather than uphold standards of accuracy (MALI). GAVRISH has devised a seven-step "detective" approach to history thinking skills, which may have utility like older crime detection games like *Clue*. Frances BLOW (1990) stresses the use of computerized sources in teaching pattern recognition as a cardinal concept in historical thought, while others (RAMOS & WHEELER) emphasize the enhancement of learning historical content in a comparative mode. KLIER begins such a process by requiring history students to use online searching and prepare senior-level seminar papers with Writer's Workbench. W. COPELAND also stresses the utility of computerized pedagogy to teach the "inquiry method" so important for historical thinking. MCEACHERN uses simple branching techniques to accomplish similar goals; a more complex scheme using graphic organizers is proposed by CLARKE *ET AL.*, which is a methodology fusing instructional technology with information storage and retrieval using map displays (LIN). CENSER at George Mason University, using the French Revolution as the subject matter, contrasts a traditional approach of literature investigation of issues and a short paper in his course on Historiography and Methodology with a module using e-mail to have students engage in debate and simultaneously practice logic and writing skills about things historical. C. NELSON adopts literacy skills for history teaching. Finally, many teachers use narrative history and historical fiction to introduce their topics (KORNFELD), and this practice provides an easy transition to the use of historical film, video, and digital programs. Kits are available which provide textbooks, learning modules, handouts, video-discs and CD-ROMs for a selection among storage and delivery media, and Learning Resource Centers often build whole collections of such media to mix and match for customized lessons (PARHAM).

Papers on CAI/CAL appear in countless forums across the United States and Europe, so much that specialization in certain fields is now common. They are not, however, particularly well informed by Information Science. In History such development is exemplified by the United Kingdom's Computers in Teaching Initiative (CTI) Center for History with Archaeology and Art History (CTICH), which publishes a biennial newsletter, *Craft* (1989-) and through a consortium arrangement specializes in courseware design and production. The multifaceted *HiDES Project* within the expanding array of applications offered by Microcosm entails both a research enterprise using primary documentation, heuristic tools, and teaching opportunities (COLSON). It admirably embraces the whole spectrum of historical work and exemplifies the benefits of cooperation between government through grant support, creative instructional programs, a university Media Lab, and private industry. It is another model experimentation with the concept of the "collaboratory" so touted by the NATIONAL RESEARCH COUNCIL.

Interest in such developments seems to be growing, partially in response to a recognized crisis in history teaching in the United States and reinvigoration of the American Historical Association's Teaching Division (see Appendix C). Still, such activity in the United States does not seem to compare with what is happening in Europe. Three international conferences have been held in Europe just on "Computers in the History Classroom," one hosting over 500 participants from 20 countries in Lisbon during April 1993, sponsored by the Fundação Gulbenkian and the Associação Portuguesa de Historia e Informatica (CANAVILHAS) with 170 speakers (but only one American project report) in tracks devoted to Information Technologies and the Curriculum, the Practice of Teaching and Learning, Teacher Training, Software and Hardware developments, and a subject focus on The Age of Discovery—Fifteenth and Sixteenth Centuries featuring demonstrations of five CAI packages in maritime and discovery History sparked by the Quincentennial in 1992. Such conferences illustrate the widespread interest computer-assisted History teaching and prolific activity in project development in Europe. The American scene is more difficult to assess because such interests are scattered through so many different areas. Conferences such as that sponsored in 1997 by H-Net and periodically monitoring its electronic conferencing provide some clues. Such conferences, however, concentrate such interests and heighten activities, often in the short run, so these are not always indicative of overall trends and the state-of-the-art in common practice.

Computer-assisted History teaching is in the same state as other disciplines, having developed numerous packages and completed some testing, but not yet a systematic theory or uniform set of applications. Computer-Assisted Language Learning (CALL) or Instruction seems to be at the same stage, although it has been helped by computer applications in Linguistics more directly than early quantification has helped History in this regard (cf., HIGGENS & JOHNS; LINE & WALMANSBERGER; STEPPI; and WYATT for CALL). Moreover, European education with its need to develop multilingual capabilities early has been especially active in CALL development, whereas in the United States this concern is left to a smaller cadre of foreign language teachers. In any case, most language instruction today also teaches the culture of that language, and hence, historical content is usually prevalent. One might expect non-Americanist historians interested in CAI to be allied closely with those working in CALL, but this does not seem to be the case since the teaching of foreign history is still done in English without prerequisites for parallel language studies of the cultures studied. Many workshops have been conducted and ample good advice literature exists about how to teach History with computing (see, RAHTZ and SCHICK for comprehensive approaches, although the latter has been severely criticized for lack of focus [YEAGER & MORRIS citing PAHL's review]; cf., surveys by GUTMANN; TRAINOR, 1990; MIDDLETON & WARDLEY; and FLYNN for socioeconomic and political history teaching). O. V. BURTON, who started over a decade ago to use census returns to teach history studies how to translate manuscript to electronic sources (1980-81), but now he uses "canned" or databased exercises to teach a wide range of historical research methods (BURTON *ET AL*, 1987). Like T. ARMSTRONG, Burton has used SPSS analysis of census data to build exercises for American history students.

CROZIER was among the first to introduce undergraduates to quantified research and computing with census data for comparison of upper Mississippi River towns (e.g., Winona, MN and Dubuque, IA). His coursework followed directions set by Chad Gaffield and Ian Winchester's Canadian Social History Project and Theodore Hersberg's Philadelphia Social History Project. The "Interactive" Census Database Project is used in introductory history courses at Williams College to teach the fundamentals of historical investigation to correct deficiencies among today's students who are, ABEL maintains, poorly equipped to evaluate large events and their historiography because they have so little idea about how historical narratives are developed. She revised her incorporation of database construction documenting a small agrarian community in the nineteenth century, and replaced it into a course on culture and technology in Victorian America focusing on Dalton, Massachusetts. In the course of contributing to the database, each class is exposed to variety of primary documentation to support the census data used, and simple DBMS operations in *Filemaker Pro* and data representation using *Cricket Graph*. It is important to notice how long-term quantified research projects have benefitted teaching both for undergraduates and as training ground for research assistants. In one case, J. REIFF (1988) makes the reverse case for teaching microcomputing through History. W. BARNES took a similar stand a decade ago when using CAI/CAL approaches to teach the history of the computer revolution by letting middle school students experience, for example, the differences between batch processing and time sharing.

History is concerned with more than data, of course, so considerable interest is directed at other kinds of sources. The electronic relay of archival documentation, manuscripts, and photographs, as in the Library of Congress *American Memory* project (1990-) (FLEISCHAUER) falls into a longstanding effort by archivists to get historians to teach with primary sources in hand (TAYLOR, 1972; ARMOUR POLLY & LYON; ROE), and may be seen as an instructional technology response to the soul-searching of American educators (HIRSCH; RAVITCH & FINN) and historians especially about what Americans ought to remember, but seem not to, as a matter of basic "civil literacy" (THELEN). Some historians blame themselves or rather their colleagues for the current situation. Echoing David McCullough's earlier link (1993) between History's elitism and the decline of comprehension by United States citizens of their history, W. C. RICE asserts that "historical illiteracy" has been aided by the insider nature of academic history, i.e., historians in "the small world of academic history" writing for their peers rather than wider audiences. Similar criticism is leveled in Great Britain against historians who are themselves blamed for the decline of historian knowledge in the populace at large (although FITZGERALD & FLINT's criticism was leveled more at how than what was taught).

One of the few structured studies available about how multiple documentary sources influence the teaching of historical reasoning skills is by ROUET *ET AL.* Two groups of college students read control sets of readings, one consisting of contemporary participant accounts and historians' essays about them, and other only the historians' analytic essays which cited the primary sources. Students were asked to examine their readings, rate their trustworthiness and usefulness, and to write their own essay about the controversy described in their readings. The results revealed significant differences between the two control groups, in that the presence of the actual documentation with the historian's analyses made a difference in how students read the latter and rated the whole experience. The study group concluded that history learning is indeed enhanced by the use of primary documentation, but this study did not explore further the difference between reading transcribed and published sources with secondary accounts, *vis-à-vis* recourse to document facsimiles. Use of computerized analog forms and digitized reproductions may be seen as an extension of earlier efforts to distribute facsimiles by the National Archives (E. FREEMAN), and such progressive state archives as in New York which actively encourages teachers to use documents and records in their courses at all levels (ROE). Most recently SARA produced a manual, *Consider the Source: Historical Records in the Classroom*, to assist teachers along with annual "teaching-with-historical-records" workshops (NEW YORK STATE ARCHIVES AND RECORDS ADMINISTRATION). Perhaps its incubus in the New York Department of Education has encouraged such uncommon initiative. Moreover, sustaining such a program is an entirely different matter from producing a one-time product.

The identification of historical documents as the most important form of primary source in History can be balanced with artifacts in museums, as is often done through field trips. But History in Evidence, Inc., also assists teachers by supplying replicas of historical objects for use in the classroom, to get "a real feel for history" (*TIMES*, 1994). Students can examine close up personally replicated artifacts from Egypt, Rome, Greece, etc., or the American colonies without traveling to Jamestown or Williamsburg. Of course, the production and sale of historical replicas are being promoted by the museum business and a healthy mail-order catalog industry, so the costs of replicated historical artifacts is coming down. Historical dress-up is not limited to children playing cowboys and Indians in poorly imitative customs. Middle-class Americans proudly wear museum replicated jewelry and clothing, and home decorator shops are replete with historical replicates to create historical moods in interior design. As the market for such has expanded, costs have dropped, and it is now feasible for school media centers to stock galleries of their own. As computer reproduction and CIM techniques become more common in education and cultural institutions, the issue will not be the transport of measurements to photo-replicators and laser-cutting mold machines, but policy and intellectual property rights pertaining to historian artifacts. *Realia* are on the comeback, as is historical costuming and role playing. Just as volunteers in historian societies can raise log cabins with original instruments and their hard labor, for entertainment through experiential learning, facsimile documents, for example, can be reproduced in historical handpresses or by hand with quill pens and aged, watermarked, laid paper, by candlelight if mood is required, to revitalize reenactment as a teaching experience or socialcultural ritual. Museum, theater, archives, library, and classroom are all different stages of and for similar experiences. Alternatives exist for those who do not want to do everything virtually on computer.

Such series as the commercial *JACKDAW* thematic kits consist of time lines, documents, maps, engravings, and photographs from the archives, together with study guides, lesson plans, thought and discussion questions. These "portfolios of Historical Documents" are to support "thematic hands-on multicultural inter-disciplinary cooperative learning" in the fields of United States History (32 modules were available for 1995), World History (22 packets); Ancient, Cultural & Religious History (11 portfolios); Government, Law and Civil Rights (17 titles); Labor and Industry (seven completed to date); and Rebellion and War in all ages (21 modules, one of which, namely "Martin Luther", seems arbitrarily placed). Such facsimile reprints in Jackdaw kits, with their accompanying notes and lessons, seem especially amenable to transfer to digital form and hypertext applications. This is essentially what has been done on a grander scale by the Library of Congress digital library project, when one uses its online exhibits, for example, in combination with access to the thousands of digital documents being made available, or by museums which are providing three-dimensional renderings of their precious artifacts.

The electronic media now available is far more dynamic than the "show and tell" display of facsimiles, however, and customization of such sources into lesson plans and presentations requires effort far beyond the traditional lecture. The well-crafted lecture survives as the unifying narrative, but it can now be presented in living color, motion, parallel windows for comparison, close-ups, blow-ups, overlays, and with text, image, and sound track interspersed. WISSENBURG & SPAETH therefore use the metaphor of "the enriched lecture" for hypermedia use. Such metaphors display a reluctance to leave the traditional classroom where conventional media are smaller, controllable, and identifiable from other stimulants such as the teacher speaking. Virtual reality simulations as big as life, however, convert the entire classroom into a six-dimension studio in which student and teacher are participants together.

Such studios are already being prefabricated, and systems such as SCRAMNet-LX Network connect computer controlled projectors for synchronization of projections all around the viewer. Microsoft is using its *SOFTIMAGE* to create virtual theater, or the classroom of the future. In such situations one does not want a lecture, but interactive commentary, dialogue, and discussion that enrich what is seen. Moreover, advances in modeling virtual humans, as with the European Union's funded program MARILYN (a three-dimensional computer graphics program which articulates a model of Marilyn Monroe), may soon place a simulated human into the picture. Jeff Kleiser and Diana Walczak's "synthespian" concept from the late 1980s has been developed to such an extent that Synthespian Studios now creates computer-generated characters for Hollywood. Their three-dimensional full-body scan of Sylvester Stallone to create Judge Dredd won worldwide acclaim. They are now working on introducing synthespians into real-time virtual environments. Avatar worlds are already on the Internet, and students are familiar with such technology before their college days. Teaching in such multi-mediated environments calls for every historian to become a production artist, director, actor, and critic all at the same time. In all of this, time management seems crucial. Moreover, such teaching relies on teamwork rather than the lone teacher; the support cast now must consist of librarians, archivists, computer and instructional technicians, and directors, etc.—and many more dollars than traditional methods ever required, new learning environments that date most facilities, and total institutional commitment to quality teaching.

Older efforts to disseminate documents from our archives or photographs of museum collections now seem meager given the Library of Congress decision to convert its premier collections into digital form; the pilot project, *American Memory*, even seems diminutive in contrast to the fiscal resources being devoted to this initiative: five million of the Library's 110 million items are scheduled to go online by the year 2000. The cost: $60 million., of which $15 million has been pledged by Congress, and the Library of Congress must raise $45 million from private sources, so that, in James Billington's words "...everybody gets a look at the American past" at LC (http://www/loc.gov). The original project provided electronic access to digitized Americana from the Mathew Brady Civil War photographs, the motion picture footage of the 1906 San Francisco earthquake, documents from the Constitutional Convention of 1789, post-Civil War African-American political pamphlets, and Works Progress Administration (WPA) interviews with Americans during the Great Depression. These are supported by the results of the 1991-1993 user evaluation from 44 sites nationwide; the "White papers" which are reports about digital technology, standards (1994), reproduction-quality issues (1992), finding aids (1994), and proceedings of a 1992 workshop on the conversion of textual historical materials to electronic form.

Librarian of Congress James Billington in the fall of 1994 announced major private funding for the project: $5 million from the David and Lucille Packard Foundation, $5 million from the chairman of Multimedia Inc., John W. Kluge; and $3 million from the W. K. Kellogg Foundation. Kodak, Inc., added another million dollars in late 1995. The pilot project has been expanded to the National Digital Library project, described as making available multimedia historical collections from the Library of Congress. Of the Library's 110 million items, 75 million are described as primary source materials in nonbook formats (photographs, manuscripts, rare books, maps, sound recordings, motion pictures, etc.); of these special items, 220,000 are digitized. Six major collections have been made available since 1994 on the LC World Wide Web (http://www.loc.gov). The LIBRARY OF CONGRESS (1995) has also used five demonstration projects to explore distribution on CD-ROMs, commercial online services which now provide access to six online exhibits such as *African-American Culture and History* and *In the Beginning was the Word: The Russian Church and Native Alaskan Cultures*, cable television and regional telephone companies, including the CD-ROM titles *Selected Civil War Photographs* (Stokes Imaging Services) and a series of personal narratives (1849-1900) in *California as I Saw It*. Other collections are in production: (1) *Shaping the Twentieth Century*; (2) *America from the First through the Second World War*; (3) *Nineteenth-century America*; and (4) *Eighteenth-Century America*. In 1997 the project was expanded through a grant program offering on a competitive basis up to $75,000 for individual institutions and $150,000 for consortia to digitize collections that would expand the *American Memory* resources beyond the Library of Congress.

Moreover, the Library of Congress is developing its version of "the electronic library of the future" in its *Global Electronic Library* project that links WWW meta-indexes and search tools with federal and state government information, and LC Access/LOCIS or online catalog of 40 million records. Its graphic interface ACCESS connects to LOCIS, the Library of Congress Information System, and the LC OPAC. Users can already access LC *MARVEL* (*MAchine-Assisted Realization of the Virtual Electronic Library*, i.e., LC's Gopher) on the Internet for image and text files. *THOMAS*, a WWW site (http://thomas.loc.gov.) named "in the spirit of Thomas Jefferson," is a service of the United States Congress (initiated by the 104th Congress) in conjunction with the Library, making available across the Internet the full-text base of all legislation and the *Congressional Record*. In addition to an online tutorial on "How our Laws Are Made," it uses the University of Massachusetts' relevancy ranking search system to order retrieved items, combines full-text and indexing strategies for searches, and provides "links" to "Hot Legislation" by bill numbers, short titles, and calendars for weekly agenda in both the House and Senate.

Behind the scenes the Library of Congress is pioneering several technology projects in test phase, such as the Electronic Copyright Management System (ECMS) and Electronic Cataloging in Publication (CIP) which would allow manuscripts to be transmitted to the Library for pre-publication cataloging while a press prepared them for publication. In case of the latter service, historians and other authors interested in how their titles and subject access would allow retrieval in large information systems, prepublication cataloging data could be searched in test runs to determine retrievability and issues of misidentification arising from the too common habit of cute and artfully contrived but nondescriptive titles. One result of such testing would assuredly be many last minute title changes to avoid the problematic loss of one's work like a proverbial needle in a haystack because a title looked sharp as a gimmick in initial advertizing. This is simply an example of the detailed and practical use of such programs, in juxtaposition to the great and theoretical use of L.C. electronic offerings for teaching. The Library of Congress projects hold great portent for the future information access that is longer range, contextual, and voluminous which will only increase in complexity, richness, size and scope as other national libraries follow suit. The opening of its Digital Library Visitor's Center on October 13, 1994, heralded an new era when the general public was introduced to digital libraries. Assessment of LC's digital document access programs thus far has been along the lines of feasibility and public acceptance. While access to digital versions broadens access and assists preservation by limiting wear on the original, nevertheless enthusiasts for digital libraries often overstate their case by thinking of digital surrogates as total replacements rather than substitutions and only one of multiple forms of which others may be preferred. Thus, critics caution against the mythology of the virtual library as something other than a real library's complement. The issues are different, however, when the original is digital and no conversion takes place for access, but only in use when readers produce their own print versions and electronic copies. In most use, questions about originality, authenticity, primacy, and evidential values will be ignored—if they are ever raised at all.

With the general public so educated through library, archives, and museum Visitor's Centers, one might expect academe at least to keep abreast with such developments in its educational programs. Interactive learning is often construed to mean activity between students or student and teacher, but today's information technology requires us to broaden that meaning to interaction with computerized systems, digital sources, and smart teaching agents, and virtual environments. Advocacy of experiential learning in such contexts is not revolutionary. Henry Baxter Adams urged this for his graduate students in the 1880s. A century later, however, this exposure to History's potential public and the practice of history other than its writing, through exhibits, interpretation, media production, etc., or through archives and the creation of historical content and nuance in information systems, are generally not the case. Graduate programs in history which continue to see such applied history as undesirable, second-rate, or as an "alternative" for their less than brilliant Ph.D. candidates in an overcrowded job market for history teachers are missing the point. Even if under the guise of enriching the teaching arsenal of historians beyond lectures, discussion groups, term papers or the means to share research through more than written articles and conventional books, graduate studies in History should include in the methodological repertoire such standard tools of SGML/HTML coding, visualization techniques, and groupware use. In short, historians must be provided with the means to interact with their audiences indirectly, asynchronously at the user's convenience, and through a variety of media. Mediated learning in virtual environments must be seen as an extension of experiential learning possibilities in real environs, but these environments make classrooms of yesterday and today seem like sterile, sequestering prisons. Without widespread attitudinal change among historians, experiential learning will be relegated to on-the-job training; except for first appointments in historical societies, special collections, and archives, this may translate to self-help. Moreover, nonteaching historians, archivists, and others who take their historical training beyond the classroom into the field, whether the information field or another, will continue to be marginalized by this attitude or, by definition, ostracized as nonhistorians. Meanwhile, advances in information technology, and multimedia technology especially in the entertainment industry have left education far behind.

Still, several projects like the LC Digital Library initiative beg for acceptance, adoption, use, feedback, and continuous improvement. Yet historians are beginning to realize that they can do serious historical research (C. SMITH) and interesting History teaching (P. SEED) with a selective array of Web sites (cf., MCMICHAEL). Most digital projects are not specifically history oriented, nor do they have a single use in mind. The collaborative *Making of America* project, for example, between Cornell University and the University of Michigan libraries involves the conversion of 5,000 volumes from between 1850 and 1870, including difficult to find journals such as *Scribner's Monthly* which are so useful for their engravings of nine-teenth-century American life. The range of applications and creative uses seems infinite, if only the adoption of instructional technology were to transcend radically the plateau of the overhead transparency and slide projector. The Library of Congress effort reflects trends to use information technology for access and preservation combined, and while its scale may be awe-some, other significant projects are being developed in all major research libraries and archives so electronic surrogates exist in addition to the original primary source collection. Examples include the Canadian optical-disk Jean Talon project for twentieth-century Canadian history, or by way of contrast, the aforementioned Vatican Library projects. Or consider the British Broadcasting Company's support of the *Domesday* Project (1986-) which will provide access to 54,000 photographs, 24,000 maps, and 10,000 data sets and moving images with sound. The British Library similarly makes its priceless *Beowulf* manuscript available for electronic view-ing (http://portico.bl.uk/access/beowulf/electronic-beowulf.html). Their use and substitution of wear on originals has a positive effect on artifact preservation, other than the possibility of long-term preservation only in surrogate form. But the real revolution is access not only for research by the privileged academic elite, but their potential for teaching and as part of a cul-tural heritage made available to all. Their very availability will affect the popular notion of his-tory, with or without the mediation of professional historians. FLOUD (1984) had no idea of the potential significance of his concept of "people's history" realizable through modern information technology.

The flagship leadership of the Library of Congress in the United States has had an effect on academic libraries both in preservation and access, and presumably an influence on user behavior, teaching, and research will be noticeable within a couple of years. United States aca-demic libraries and corporations, individually and cooperatively, have inaugurated nearly two dozen major digital library projects that signal tremendous change for how instruction and research will be undertaken in the near future. These are symptoms of what DRABENSTOTT characterized as "the Access Paradigm Shift," as distinct from past unsuccessful efforts by research libraries to build their own comprehensive collections.

Less ambitious projects nevertheless indicate what can be done with such retroconverted sources. Commercial products are proliferating rapidly. Manual reference tools converted to electronic form include Microsoft's *Bookshelf '94* which supplies dictionaries of language and quotations, thesauri, almanacs, atlases, concise encyclopedia, and *The People's Chronology*. The host of newly created, more specialized tools relevant to History may be illustrated by the initial releases by IVERSON SOFTWARE INC., of its "HyperTextBooks" for Apple Newton computers. These electronic tertiary tools are described as "interactive reference books" because one can search by index terms or along pathways created by automatic hyperlinks. Its Anthropology volume covers 250 topics; the Archaeology release adds 80 more; and an indica-tion of series' development includes a volume devoted to Afghanistan for international studies (in this case 100 topics). Or, consider Voyager Company's *"For All Mankind"* electronic docu-mentary history of the Apollo moon mission (1968-1972) with its interviews, film footage, pho-tographs from the NASA Archives, etc., supported by glossaries of technical terms, diagrams of spacecraft, maps of launching and laboratory sites and biographical sketches on astronauts. Creative Multimedia (1994) has made available on CD-ROM 4,000 photographs from *Life* mag-azine plus 2,000 letters to the editor and some video footage, thus creating a collage for teach-ing in the period 1936 to 1972. Some titles are devoted to specific literary works, like *The Essential Frankenstein* that supplies Mary Shelley's novel in full text and notes; it contains reproduced graphic renderings from the past, and updates these with film clips and interviews and in the true spirit of southern California adds a video game. Carnegie Mellon's *Informedia Digital Video Library* is one of the most dynamic interactive library access systems that conveys an increasing amount of full-text material linked to catalogs and references to information still in traditional formats. These are both reference and teaching and self-educating tools.

Although slow to start, History CD-ROMs are now being produced in a steady stream. These are reviewed regularly in standard selection tools (cf., ALA's *Choice*; *Library Journal*; *PC Magazine*. For example, LAGUARDIA & TALLENT recommend the following: American Heritage's *Civil War*; Compton Encyclopedia's *American History*; *History Alive: The Northwest Passage; a House Divided: The Lincoln-Douglas Debates*; and the simulation *Oregon Trail* I-II). ROZENZWEIG evaluates 16 CD-ROMs, especially Electronic Book products (e.g., *African American Experience*; *Black American History*; *Roosevelt: History Maker*; Sony Imagesoft's *The Haldeman Diaries* [one of the best rated], etc.), clip art from the archives (e.g., *Archives of History*), and entertainment or hobby software which has value in history teaching such as cuttings from old films (e.g., *Ephemeral Films, 1931-1960*), collections from news coverage and films made during the Wars (*USA Wars*), and products in music history aimed at listener edification (e.g., *History of the Blues*). RABINOVITZ in tracking the "Top 100 CD-ROMs" includes those in History, noting also Medio Multimedia's *JFK Assassination* as superior in its user interface, content, multimedia implementation, use of system resources, and user friendliness (examples of the kinds of criteria used for rating such products from the perspective of information technology). Compact Publishing's *Time Almanac of the 20th Century* received good marks and is an interesting example of the fusion of reference resource and learning tool. Although most products are for modern history for which electronic resources are plentiful, one might mention CD-ROMs for other periods such as Cambrix Publishing's *Anglo-Saxons* and Microsoft's *Ancient Lands*. More and more such multipurpose tools are being created, but their review and evaluation are difficult, and most are not as valuable as stand-alone products as they could be when part of software libraries, coherent collections, and well-designed interactive instructional laboratories.

Part of the learning process may be in customization of electronic projects that combine texts, audios and visuals as a new form of research paper. Electronic texts of historical sources, for example, can be augmented by historical visual references from distributed electronic archives, manuscripts, and rare books. For example, USA Software Publishing, Inc., which says it is dedicated to the preservation of historical graphics has converted William Cullen Bryant's 1873 picture book, *Picturesque America* (1994), with its 1,000 woodcuts and steel engravings, into a CD-ROM with "copy and paste" graphics and text for a flexible teaching and reference tool. Digitized forms, thus, create even more transmutable possibilities, but from the historian, archival, and preservation perspectives that very mutability which makes the medium so interesting also threatens the notions of documentation, objectivity, and durability or permanence which underpin historical thought. Students can locate scenes in *Picturesque America* through its new indexing, CD-ROM allows enhancement of illustrations and removal from their originally bound context, etc., but they cannot experience the book as originally presented or perhaps understand as well its privileged use to escape upperclass living rooms by the few who owned its 700 copies. On the other hand, more than a privileged few can get access to these historical illustrations on CD-ROM and through networks than could use them in today's rare book libraries. And CDs as collections can have a cumulative affect, as when the Bryant portraits of America are used with Research Publication's *American Journey: Westward Expansion* (1994) which goes back to Columbus and comes forward to the twentieth century as its depictions also move from east to west. The dramatic differences are: (1) the numbers of users potentially using hitherto inaccessible materials, which in itself illustrates the democratization of such technology in moving historical sources out of the repository and provides access to them directly and more freely for the individual than through a classroom, a course, or even a field trip; and (2) direct interactivity between the learner and source bank in an electronic environment where a different kind of mediation is required of teachers—if teachers are needed at all. If so, teachers as facilitators may serve as enhancements to the media rather than *vice versa*. Personalization and human interaction will remain important, but perhaps not so dominant in years to come as in the classrooms of this or the past century.

The reluctance of historians to study as objectively as possible their own discourse for more than the ideas exchanged, but the method and effectiveness of communication and presentation, means that the communication of historical awareness and knowledge may not be well taught. Historiography in the Anglo-American tradition has customarily studied historical writing as Literature, not Communication, and as an art more than as a technique, method, or information system. It is ironic that this seems not be changing when the New Social History movements of the *histoire d'livre* variety have become concerned with communications and address the dissemination of ideas as much as the ideas themselves. Historians engaging such studies understand the proverbial question about the significance of sound if there are no hearers, or equally to the point, of writing if there are no readers. The kind of library use studies to which historians have been subjected seem not to exist for teaching effectiveness. The AHA Teaching Division has been aware of this problem for a long time, and has initiated programs, written articles in the AHA newsletter, etc., about innovative teaching. However, such coverage itself indicates the conservatism of History teaching and problematic integration of electronic tools into traditional methods, or the conversion of traditional methods to more dynamic fora and transferable media. Nor are media and modern diagnostic techniques applied to the teaching and communication of history for its improvement. Education research literature is embarrassingly sparse regarding History teaching beyond K-12, and seemingly non-extant for adult learning outside the classroom. Likewise within Information studies the effectiveness, efficiency, and impact of History information dissemination and programming are non-issues. Museum programs generate some evaluations, but nothing that is gelling into a body of literature that would support systematic study of the efficacy of History. One might think that something like the value of History, taken so much for granted, would be more demonstrable than it is.

History as a literature, as a form of composition and written discourse, seems to be more prevalent an art form than History in its grand rhetorical tradition or as a basis for debate and declamation. Little use of discourse generation software seems to be made in History despite progress in knowledge-based tutoring systems that can be adapted to a specific domain (Y. ZHANG). Such adaptation, however, would require more terminological work in History and discourse analysis, not of historical records, but of historiographic literature, lectures, and discussion. The sub-languages of historical specializations need to be analyzed, as do the interplay between cognitive styles and their related expressions in discussing textual and visual sources; the transference of historical thought to present understanding needs to be more explicit, as in linking archaic with modern usage in one language and in translation across languages and cultures. In addition, the historical profession must itself be subjected to rigorous study as a source for oral history and discourse analysis, to discern influences, fads, trends, adaptability, inter-disciplinary exchange, mood and temperament rather than merely continuing to classify historical writing in one ideological camp or the other, all to benefit the teaching of history and the transition to computerized smart intermediaries, tutors, and expert systems that are modeled on History by historians.

Efforts to create mediated instructional tools and large-scale accessibility to historical sources electronically achieved notoriety with W. REINHOLT's seven-disk *Culture 1.0: The Hypermedia Guide to Western Civilization* whose accompanying workbook humorously juxtaposes this modern technology to Victorian educational objectives with the title *Interdisciplinary Lessons Covering Various and Sundry Things Every Secondary School Student Should Learn and Every College Student Should Know*. Behind this humor and delightful software, however, lurks alarming motivation such as the Gallup Poll's findings that 25 percent of American college seniors could not date Columbus' voyages to the New World before 1500 A.D. and more (50 percent) failed to place chronologically the American Civil War in the period 1850-1900

(LEWIS). FINNEGAN stresses computerized map work because students taking American History surveys lack the basic geographic knowledge to link even the best known events. These startling surveys and a series of books in 1987 (BLOOM; HIRSCH; RAVITCH & FINN; CHENEY; etc., reviewed by MULCAHY and ZILVERSMIT) bashing American education for its failure to produce a "civic literacy" in the United States, prompt such investment into teaching and instructional technology. REINHOLD advertised his courseware as "Goods of the Mind" or "structured information for contextual cultural literacy" aimed at the "canon" or "core" of a liberal arts education.

At real risk is the very reality of cultural heritage, which may be conveyed from one generation to another through a variety of means, but by definition must be kept alive, have a continuity insured, and be safeguarded from becoming so elite and rarified that it is therefore fragile and extinguishable precisely because it is not made and kept relevant for an entire people. Mediated instruction, as through the entertainment media, is a means of such conveyance and cultural transfer, and because it can be interactive, such learning can also be fun. It may not be for everyone, since cognitive psychology has taught us that different people have different cognitive styles as well as learning speeds, and at different times are more receptive to different kinds of stimulation. Strict adherence to the traditional lecture method, without variety, excludes the possibility of people whose cognitive abilities are not attune to oral, serial delivery or to text only, from reaching their potentials. Variety is called for if historians or any educators are to reach a varied audience.

Early exploration of hypertext for history teaching dates no further back than the late 1980s, such as the *Project Jefferson* (BYRNE, KINNELL, & CHIGNELL; CHIGNELL & LACY; W. COPELAND), which demonstrated that even basic indexing proved somewhat problematic because of the language problems presented by History. The most difficult, perhaps, is the relationship of usage between historical time and place with the present. Hypertext is one means of relating past and present usage in parallel descriptions to relate contemporary renderings with original sources (L. HUGHES) or images (BITTER-RIJPKEMA). SKRAEMM praises hypertext not only as a means of structuring historical data for research, but also as an assist to students in searching original sources with modern language descriptors. A laudable example of recent work is AYER's hyperlinked resource package *Valley of the Shadow: Living the Civil War in Virginia and Pennsylvania*, with local records from two contiguous counties which faced each other across the Potomac River, to provide a microcosm of the North and South where the two came into daily contact. At last report, this project continues to grow.

Several notable projects, some reviewed by WARD, can exemplify these points. Some have been greatly elaborated by integrating text and image, and now sound as well, by such "electronic books" turning into full course packages like *Perseus* for classical studies at Yale University (CRANE); *Sources in History: The Medieval Realms* CD-ROM support for a national curriculum in History in the United Kingdom (PROCHASKA, p. 171); or the student-developed *Civil War Hypermedia Project* in American history which became a centerpiece for the New York Dalton School's New Laboratory for Teaching and Learning (LIEPOLT). Certainly the *Perseus Project* is among the most thoroughly evaluated for human-computer interaction and graphic-user interface (GUI) design (MARCHIONINI & CRANE). *Perseus-2* on CD-ROM (1996) contains more than 25,000 full-screen images; the complete works of 31 Greek authors in Greek with English translation supported by a 35,000-word lexicon; an atlas featuring schematic, satellite, and topographic maps of ancient and modern Greece; and a catalog of 1,420 vases and 366 sculptures; an encyclopedia for reference; and a bibliography of 3,000 citations—all for $350 (http://www.perseus.tufts.edu).

William Andrews, using his *Triad-Project* which integrated computer applications and audio-video programs for independent learning and colloquia or discussion classes for American history survey courses taught since 1985, formerly studied the impact of CAI/CAL initiatives on outcomes by assessing student evaluations, test scores, and professional observations of his classes (W. ANDREWS). He focused mainly on interactive video because it was considered most innovative, and certainly was the most labor intensive component of course preparation. Students responded positively but seemed to have gained only a marginal advantage over control groups not experiencing such multifaceted instruction. He had to question the return, less than expected, compared with the high cost of such modest-tech media and the time invested to do original development. The cost issue is frequently raised (e.g., MIDDLETON, 1989), and there's the rub! CAI/CAL instruction must be packaged and commercialized for widespread distribution and use to achieve an educational return for the dollar. The infrastructure in academe has not been so entrepreneurial and supportive.

Nevertheless, the instructional possibilities of such technology are undeniable, even if proven results are much contested. CAI innovation is one response to teaching the *Nintendo* generation. The first applications of gaming and simulation were in political history, using voting and poll data to recreate actual events and manipulation of that data to alter the real outcome of an election, as in the early case of *The Election of 1912* or much more elaborate *Great American History Machine* (D. MILLER; MILLER & MODELL; SCHLATTERER) that, among other sources, uses ICPSR data sets 0001-0003 for census returns between 1840 and 1970. The interplay of demographics and public health can be experienced in *1665: The Great Plague of London* (COATES). Examples of the best productions are those winning awards from EDUCOM's NCRIPTAL such as CTICH's *Salem Dataset* which allows students to experience a witchcraft trial, and a counterpart for European history is C. LOUGEE's award-winning *The Would-Be Gentleman* for life in the court of Louis XIV. Although the title comes from an accusation of pretense, the software's educational utility comes from its ability to allow the user to pretend, make believe, and if not to alter history, to imagine an alternative to it, and thereby achieve comparison not otherwise likely except for the most imaginative. Others dislike such open-ended programs. When students work through the hypercard tutorial *Fort Sumter* by R. LATNER, they play Abraham Lincoln before the Civil War; but after getting advice from all the Cabinet members about five key problems and selecting a course of action, they are then shown Lincoln's own decision. Students cannot "change history" by their decisions. Not all packages are equally lauded; some are very controversial. *Palestine 1947* by Longmans, Inc., allows users to play with 1,800 policy issues but ultimately only four outcomes are possible (critiqued by F. BLOW, 1987, pp. 286-288; cf., RITTER; MORRIS, 1991). Of these, World War III could explode, but the mental constraints of the creators would not allow the possibility of the peaceful creation of a separate Muslim state as actually occurred just a few years later. This illustrates the risk in computer-managed learning systems where the fault rests with the author, not the user, because control of the variables is never released and indeed exploration of all possible variables is not allowed. Apparently hindsight does not always create foresight. Computerization does not alter this human condition.

Multiuse commercialized packages like Xiphias' *Timetable of Science and Innovation* can serve as library reference tools, tutorial workstations, or for teaching. Gale Research's *Discovering World History* CD-ROM is another electronic reference tool that can be used as instructional media. As an historical encyclopedia it contains colored images, chronologies, and primary documents to support its secondary coverage of world events. The older use of computers to display documents more in the information retrieval mode of OPACs has given way fully to windowing, hypermedia, and interactive media using text, image, and sound altogether (e.g., IRIS intermedia). Thus a project like *Perseus* is nicely complemented by *Daedalus*, a video-imagebase of ancient Greek sculpture created by the Ashmole Archives in London. Combine these with the *Thesaurus Linguae Graecae (TGL)* for the electronic texts of 3,157 authors (Homer to 600 A.D.) and their 57 million surviving words (99 percent of the extant literature), and the *Database of Classical Bibliography* (CLAYMAN) assembled by the American Philological Association and the publishers of *L'Année Philologique* (Société Internationale de Bibliographie Classique), one has an information-rich environment never before achievable even in the greatest of classics libraries. Text collation in Windows provides instant comparison as never before, as in the case of searching the CD-ROM *Oxford English Dictionary* (2nd ed.) for some of its 60 million words. Another example of combination for a geometric enhancement effect would be *OED*'s use with the Oxford University Press *Electronic Text Library* from modern back to Chaucer, or Chadwyk Healey's electronic full-text *Poetry Database* for 1,350 Anglo-Saxon poets, one has a radically different learning and teaching environment than with the traditional humanities library. As in a library where using a collection is a decidedly different experience than reading a book, learning in a well-designed, integrated multimedia environment (rather than segregated as when electronic media are separate from nonelectronic sources) is substantially different than using a single tool in the sterile environments commonly created for the technology rather than the user. Disney, Inc., understands the difference; it is about time the educational establishment learns this as well.

Some projects are already combining and absorbing sources in two decades of growth. Perhaps the most inspiring of the early interactive media ventures that has expanded continually from the early 1980s is C. CHEN's impressive *Emperor I* project which combines reference tools such as a virtual encyclopedia and dictionaries, bilingual narration, textbases, detailed indexing with thesaurus control down to levels below screen recall for sector and item retrieval, windowing for motion and still-frame video for comparison, and assimilation of interviews, news events, and oral histories, with ample ability for customization for formal class presentations or for individual exploration. It is an excellent example of the breakdown of old disciplinarity, cutting across the fields of geography, archeology, anthropology, history, and art history and integrating museums and their artifacts with field work and the context of their origins. A second equally exemplary project is L. MADOX's NSF-funded *Global Jukebox* that is a worldwide survey of dancing and dance music from the vantage point of comparative cultural anthropology and history. Beginning modestly as an exploration of the origins of American jazz in African cultures, this project expanded from sound archives to active image bases to capture dance sequences in full motion, color, and sound. It, too, has an elaborate information structure behind the screen, classifying dance, cultures, and sites into a complicated taxonomy, but with a variety of means for searching and recall. It bears the same name as the University of Alaska's noteworthy *Project Jukebox* (KNOKE, SCHNEIDER & MUDD, 1991; CHEN, 1992) that is a multimedia presentation of 6,000 audio and video recordings, maps and photographs, texts, and interviews about Alaskan history. *Global Jukebox* is inspiring other applications, as at Indiana University's Music Library which plans to make available digitized scores put into full-motion synchronized with digital audio in a media spectacular called *Variations*. When linked to bibliographic databases, one can retrieve citations to be linked to reference textbases, and perhaps image bases of portraits, the score and parts, and perhaps a choice of recordings and soundtracks which can be heard altogether or split apart by voice and instrumentation, and by sections and parts.

These projects are truly remarkable, but commonly they are used in electronic environments like media-intensive classrooms or auditoriums, too isolated from other media like the archives, libraries, museums, and stages that could connect the surrogate with the real source, and present in person interactively with electronic display. But plans call for *Variations* to be put across the networks, and home users accustomed to playing games on their personal computers already have their soundboards installed. The technical among them are hooking them up to their stereo speakers in anticipation of the kind of educational entertainment to be provided by projects like *Variations*. Teaching, performing, and engineering are thereby merged, as are traditionally separate places. The endangered species is not the source-rich people-centered, active library, archives, theater, or museum, but the comparatively sterile classroom and the assembly-line model of education from the industrial age.

While such projects allow virtual exploration of other peoples, cultures, places, and events, they are essentially interactive retrieval designs which impress by the array of visual and oral stimuli added to textual information delivered by multimedia in intensive learning environments (GUTMANN, 1988a). They are entertaining as well as educational, and work both for group presentations and individual use (PURCEL). They differ in purpose and design from software intended more for individual use and the development historical logic hosted entirely on PCs. Here is where gaming and simulation interplay with History (HANNEMAN & HOLLINGSWORTH) in the sense of reenactment to gain experience in historical inference as advocated 20 years ago by R. MARTIN, in keeping with R. COLLINGWOOD's *Idea of History* (1945), namely "imagining history."

An impressive example of such simulation technology and computational modeling exists in Political Science history. The aforementioned program *Policy Arguer (POLI)* is an expert system conceived as a research tool to forecast policy orientation, but it has great teaching potential. Going beyond standard modeling techniques and incorporating discourse and textual analytic methods, contextual information is used to create environments in which scenarios run, decision makers are characterized by *a priori* beliefs or sets of assumptions they are thought to have brought to the tables where decisions were made, and sets of possible options are thereby analyzed to predict both specific actions and a strategy or course of action (TABER). The testing of hypothetical replays and computer generated predictions against known history, as in the case of United States involvement in Asia after the 1950s, is especially intriguing. In such cases historical knowledge is used to build a system and confirm conclusions drawn by expert systems. The "game" of running such simulation models lies in the ability to alter historical scenarios by introducing fictional variables elements, which may be a means of scouting for latent variables which may not be fictional at all but simply unobservable using traditional means (OSBORNE & RUBENSTEIN). The learning aspect comes with both make-believe and non-confirmation of history, the thrill of discovery and revisionist interpretation of history, and speculation about possible futures. This is an example of how technology now allows historians to re-image history as well as stimulate imaginations in ways even more interactive than lecturing no matter how graphic and dynamic. The teaching strategy is to add to the dimension of what was in History by postulating "what if" scenarios and then simulating courses of events different from those tracked by conventional History. Here, as in certain uses of literature as historical documentation, fiction and history blend as historical fiction to teach possibilities, probabilities, and eventualities as added dimensions to History as it is known.

These tools reflect the same problems raised in the study of "realty" in fiction (RIFFATERRE) and raise questions about excessive relativity and subjectivity that are topics for debate both in education and social analysis (ROSALDO). If fiction can be written interactively in *Storyspace*, so too can history. The philosophical issue seems the same as outlined by Karl Popper 60 years ago in his "critical rationalism" which held that all knowledge claims are subject to falsification (POPPER). Extending Popper's reasoning, some have attacked historical writing as a form of falsification promoted by good intentions. No doubt such debate will continue. The deconstructionist and relativist argument that attempts to reduce history to literature and raise reconstructed fiction to truth is attractive for those not wanting to muster evidence for their premises and (mis)constructions, but is not really compelling because everything thereby becomes so subjective. Its rejection does not necessarily mean nonappreciation of "recreational" history, however. Historians adhering to an older, timeless construct of historicity as attempted truthfulness in representation of fact and intellectual honesty in interpretation, whether the recently promoted pragmatic realism or a more explicit historicism based on a sense of immanence and high value on documentation more akin to turn-of-the-century scientific historicism, will always have reservations about "historical scenarios" not solidly linked to evidence of actual happenings and supported by meta-documentation.

Does the cultural antithesis of Real versus Virtual reflect the Western polarization of science and literary fiction? The rhetoric of science would always posit the real with the scientific, and see a clear divide between these and the artistic, imaginative, and fictional. This polarity and segregation exist in historical narrative, but some think that the demarcation between fiction and history is not very clear-cut. The confusion or grey area in a narrative continuum from pure fantasy to historical reconstruction may be illustrated by the substitution of mythography and story telling for history as History, e.g., Salmon Rushdie's work, as a means of making sense out of the past. Thus R. T. KELLEY sees as a technical extension of "magical realism" in novels. This confusion of magic and visualization technology in a Disneysque motif seems to echo Gibson's *Necromancer* and, likewise, plays to human inquisitiveness and arouses suspicions and fear at the same time. Like the radio interviewer from Vienna who in 1993 at the IAHC Conference, in Graz, wanted to know what I thought as a historian about the prospect for time travel, I replied that in the United States we already had time travel—we had Steven Spielberg! It was a timely quip, since *Jurassic Park* had just opened that very week in Vienna! I am not alone in recognizing the possibilities of modern media for history, or for that matter in voicing skepticism about future applications. SAPIN (p. 53) and others saw in *Jurassic Park* the new wave of history.

We are well beyond the fictive musings of Jack Finney whose novel *Time and Again* suggests how, through immersion in contrived material cultural environments coupled with training of the mind to exclude from the cognitive process all artifacts and effects of a certain age, one can, in effect, travel in time. Professor Ron Davis uses this fascinating novel in his courses at Western Michigan University to stimulate history students' thinking about history. Commonplaces like time, place, and individual perception become complicated by issues like parallel contexts, simultaneity, uniqueness and reoccurrence, repetition and redundancy in human experience. I have likewise used Miller's novel *A Canticle for Liebowitz* for archives students, to explore the significance of loss of organization and cultural memory in human affairs and to challenge the notion of continual progress. In this case, futuristic priests chant a canticle which has retained only symbolic meaning (*ápropos* to the argument of O'TOOLE (1993) about the symbolic significance versus the literal meaning of archives), since in fact it is a grocery list of a Polish worker which is the only extant writing (hence, Scripture) from before a nuclear holocaust. What human sensibility attributes to artifacts and sees in them is often imaginative and yet historical, but modern technology now goes beyond fiction and exercise of the imagination. Holography and virtual reality will soon take historical reconstruction and deconstructionism to a new dimension where reality and fiction, belief and make-believe, and personal subjective experience and objective human discernment are difficult to distinguish. Although visuals and visualization have long been part of the historians repertoire for both research and teaching, the historian's cognitive praxis is about to require a major overhaul.

The technology is taking one beyond recreation through re-creation, toward expanded experiential learning that forces us to evolve both ontological and epistemological thinking (M. HEIM). Some think that the prospects ahead hold the antithesis of history rather than its vindication. Certainly, cyberspace challenges historical thinking because it is non-Euclidian (MCFADDEN), or as SPRINGER says, "recursive, almost fractal" rather than merely repetitive; "neither a natural direction or flow of time nor entopic flow exists" (p. 250). Such observations do confront historians with perplexing issue of time and relativity, carrying to a new dimension the debates about fact and fiction begun by the linguistic deconstructionists. This literature/virtual versus history/literal reality dichotomy exists now in dynamic instructional media to an extent never dreamed possible, since computer-generated multisensory Virtual Reality freed from physical reality mixes substantive and imaginative elements at will (see the literature review by NEWBY). Vernor Vinges' epistemological probe in 1987, *True Names and Other Dangers*, delved into the implications of theoretical constructs then perceived more traditionally and textually than as visually today with computer-reconstructed surrealities, and it asked some basic questions that are becoming more disturbing as these technologies develop. No less a mind than Hayden White has been attracted to the conundrum presented by representational technology (FRIEDLANDER), and the Annenberg Scholars

Program at the University of Pennsylvania chose "The Future of Fact" for its theme in 1996 because of the realization that there is no representation without interpretation. One resultant study by N. DAVIES explored "media literacy" in children ages six through 11 to determine how they discerned the real from unreal especially in televised narratives, which is different from year to year as they are exposed to real life, history, literature, and the arts. But the issues go further than, for example, the potential ill effects of violence on television. Fact makes fantasy believable; the one elucidates the other, but does fantasy makes fact acceptable and *vice versa*? The issues of "make-believe" affect journalism, especially documentary reporting; law, and both the theory and forensics of evidence; and the sciences. History often lies at the very crux of the debate over actuality and representation, although historians are hardly the only stakeholders. Information Science should be involved but has still distanced itself from such unsettling introspection.

From the viewpoint of historical realism, Virtual Reality, depending on editorial control of the author or the user, is a form of visual misinformation if known reality is deliberately distorted (as feared an editorial in *The LANCET*; cf., GRAY & DRISCOLL). Philippe QUEAU has warned against "dangerous illusions" as a substitute for actual history. ZWEIG (1992) asked similar questions about the substitution of fake sources for authentic ones in the new VR media and the dire consequences for subsequent interpretation as history is fabricated at the source rather than in the interpretative stage where criticism can set the record straight. As already discerned in previous comments about evidence in electronic form and the perils of digitized text, the issue is far more ominous than academic questions about proper interpretation, presentation, and visualization. NORA's "places" or "sites of memory" can be transferred now from real places to imaginary settings, may be replaced at will and whim with altered states, and history is recreated literally in the eye of the beholder. Fantasy, fiction, and history blur in such multi-dimensional VR worlds. Few historians address the implications of the new media and its pliability in the hands of the receptor and learner, with the exception of BIDDICK who fears "the haunting of Virtual Worlds" as a nearby prospect.

How close are we to such a specter? The virtual replay of history envisioned by Charles Dickens in *The Christmas Carol* relied on ghosts rather than VR technology to teach a powerful lesson through "what if" scenarios so Scrooge could choose a future brighter than any portrayed based on his past. The most recent television film versions of Dickens' work, of course, employ visual trickery with the latest technology for effects never dreamed of a few years ago. Consider how behavior modification through attitude adjustment, stimulated by envisioning alternative histories, was achieved in this classic. The reader and viewers of the film versions suspend belief in the actual and substitute acceptance of the virtual in such cases. When the interlude has lasting effect, the experience is akin to religious conversion. The methods employed are age-old, common in cult formation and brainwashing, but the technology is now so sophisticated and subtle that visualization, as intended, stimulate visions. The good is obvious when one sees education as personal reformation; the danger seems to reside not in such fantasy recognized as such, or in resorting to virtual reality to teach important lessons dynamically by playing with history, but in the consciousness of the act, the ability to discern the difference between the actual and the virtual, and the objective versus the subjective use of the hypothetical. Formation, reformation, and deformation have their parallels in information, reformatting, and misinformation or more sinister, disinformation. Plenty of instances of the latter two are readily available on the Internet (HERNON, 1995). Likewise, it is not the fantasy that seems threatening, but flights into fantasy or escapism and an unwillingness or inability to return to reality that might be feared. Virtual Reality, it seems, offers the best and the worst for our consideration. The possibilities add a new, as yet unexplored dimension to the tension between History and Literature as explored by MAZA (1996).

Apart from the high-tech entertainment world and the opposite extreme of low-tech media for instruction, consider mid-range alternatives that place manipulative abilities into the hands of the viewer and learner who experience virtual reality. Like so much of technology, which is amoral in itself, the good and the bad lies in human intention and the use. The *Alternate Reality Kit (ARK)* designed by XEROX Corporation's Palo Alto Research Center (PARC), was created specifically to allow students to dispense with the laws of nature and engage in visual experiments (M. SMITH) of a different sort than simulation in science and engineering (DEFANTI *ET AL.*) where as in laboratories the goal is repetitive viewing for repeated observations to enable learning. *ARK's* aim is creativity, not reality in any traditional, scientific, or historical sense. While some find this seemingly boundless mind experience intriguing, it poses problems for historians and their idea of history as essentially learning from past experience. So, in reaction to such highly individualized and free-form visualization, many instructors want to embed control into their design, for a form that is sometimes called "Computer *Managed* Learning" rather than "assisted." Conversely, they may distrust software for collaborative writing, that in replacing individual word processors may make it difficult to distinguish a student's own term paper from corporately or "ghost" written submissions unless, perhaps, instructors also resort to automated text analysis for authentification before producing a grade. They are adhering to the medieval invention of singular authorship with the discovery of the individual, to such an extent that the validity of the collective creation is devalued.

Older issues like plagiarism, so ensnaring for the historical profession in the past couple of years and as complex as ever because such debates involve academe in ethics, are not totally unrelated to issues of credit, accountability, and identification of authorship and authority in representation issues. Nor are they removed from such teaching methods as impersonation, whether in reenactments as in the case of annual Lincoln-Douglas debates celebrated in Illinois, countless skits performed on National History Day, or in the Professor W. Gregory Monahan's masquerading in the classroom as a reincarnated Christopher Columbus (MONA-HAN). His costumed rendition of historical persona in the role of "historian as performer" can be seen as an active and recreative version of what Ken Wolf calls " the Old-Fashioned Way—Through Biography" (WOLF). Both are examples of "Redrawing Professional Boundaries to Revitalize History Education" (FINK & KRAMER) that can be related to what is transpiring in visual technology, except that in the latter the learner is the actor, the teacher is removed not as some Deistic manipulator as in conventional computer-assisted instruction, but as the behind-the-curtain orchestrator of a multimedia learning environment.

The Annenberg program calls attention likewise to the "boundary-blurring genres of docu-drama, talk shows, media events, imagined biography, virtual reality, home-and-garden supplements, and the other forms of infotainment" (program announcement for 1995-1995). To use the famous medieval metaphor of the garden alluded to, whether for earthly delights as in courtly love or transcendent contemplation in a cloister, the historian is removed from the action like a caretaker who may tend the garden but whose presence and persistent mediation for its exploration and enjoyment are not necessary. Teaching, a matter of both presentation and representation, relates the conceptual issues of deconstructionist debates with historical interpretation in real practice. The same issues persist, evermore complex, in virtual time.

Elihu Katz, director of the Annenberg Scholars Program at the University of Pennsylvania, asks a series of intriguing questions (E. KATZ):

> Is the distinction between fact and fiction still tenable? Are the genres of fact and fiction interchangeable? What do we know about how "readers" decode them? How can the truth-claims of factual genres be validated? What is the role of methodology in the production (representation) of facts? Can the information needs of citizens be reconciled with the blurring of generic boundaries?

Manfred Thaller in his plenary address before the IX AHC conferees grappled with such issues in the historian's approach not only to image technology but also such methodology as data modeling and simulation: "Virtual Reality? The mind of the historian and the conflict between 'data' and 'reality'" (THALLER, 1995). Potential use and abuse of the technology evokes new ethical concerns, educational issues, and different approaches to role definition among professionals, teachers, and students. Intention and use, apart from the technology itself, separate Virtual Reality tools from modeling and simulation, and the conviction of being able to inform really, that is a faithful sense of reality, is what distinguishes education and information from entertainment and "infotainment," mediated instruction from games, and lamentably too often, learning from fun. The issue is complex. The technology will make it more so, and the problem seems ever more innocuous than watching movies or television where historical fiction reigns in popular culture and the documentary struggles to maintain its select audience.

Perhaps this is why 75 historians met with filmmakers, screenwriters, playwrights, and visual technologists at the California Institute of Technology workshop on "Narrating Histories," (ROSENSTONE *ET AL.*, 1994; 1995) where panels discussed "The Temptation of Fiction," and "Revisioning History." M. FERRO (1984, 1988) provides a European perspective on the same subject. The CalTech workshop investigated "self-reflexive history, fragmented or postmodern history, history as theater or screenplay, history of a sort we cannot name" while groping with issues known in more familiar literary contexts and in terms of textuality rather than visual representation. The book *Past Imperfect* reviews 60 films, each by a different historian, to critique how well Hollywood did in historical reconstruction and representation (CARNES & FARAGHER). Mistakes galore were uncovered; stereotyping was commonplace, and historical accuracy usually suffered for expediency and story line or the overall goal of entertainment over edification. The problem is, of course, the two cannot be easily divorced.

One discussion between father and daughter illustrates my point here (retold by CARNES & FARAGHER):

Daughter: "Did that really happen?"

Father: "I don't know. If it's a good story, does it have to be true?"

Daughter: No answer.

Father: "I mean, does it really matter to you whether the story was true?"

Daughter: "Dad, is this some sort of psychology question?"

The authors summarize: "Only a professor could ask a question of such ponderous silliness. Of course, we want stories to be true"—the affirmation of an historian. Or, they offer a compromise in James Axtell's critique of *Black Robe* when he noted that the movie "convincingly depicted not an event but a cultural process" of Jesuit missionary and Huron interaction in 1634 Canada. This is the same argument used to justify modeling.

This forum, as most, largely exchanged opinion—expert no doubt, but these colloquia often fall into the genre of literary criticism more than anything scientific. Indeed, the reaction in the industry to historians' criticism was that the academics were nitpicking; indeed, historians in their film reviews, which began only in 1986 in such organs as the *Journal of American History* because film reviewing was considered journalistic rather than a scholarly endeavor, have tended to see themselves as critics for accuracy's sake (WINKLER, 1995). J. O'CONNOR (1990) attempted to lay out a basis for the historical analysis of film and television in his *Image as Artifact* for the American Historical Association (cf., J. O'CONNOR, 1983; O'CONNOR & JACKSON). ROSENSTONE's approach is somewhat different, in tempering the viewpoint of historian as hypercritic. Instead, as the titles of the compilations he has edited indicate (e.g., *Revisioning History* and *Visions of the Past*), he has attempted in the spirit of Public History to see filmmakers as historians and, in particular, to understand how they can do certain things through film that historians operating in conventional ways cannot. Natalie Zemon Davis, who began teaching a course on Film and History at Princeton University after *The Return of Martin Guerre* was filmed, uses Rosellini's *The Rise of Louis XIV* in her teaching. Likewise, ATTREED & POWERS, recalling the 1991 AHA annual meeting session chaired by Zemon Davis on "The Medieval Film: Its Uses and Abuses" in which Charlton Heston participated before a standing-room-only crowd, use film to teach medieval history and have for a decade organized annually a Medieval Film series at the College of Holy Cross. While they applaud film as a "powerful tool," they are circumspect still about the use of fiction in motion pictures, "reel life," to study real life (p. 11). If Hollywood productions do not assist in, at least, the use of film by historians, this means that History teaches students something about "better cinemagraphic taste for our maturing students."

The focus of such discussions, while exploratory and a sign of the times themselves, have yet, therefore, to engage fully the state of the art of modern information/instructional technology or the science of visualization. If expanded and placed into an even more contemporary media setting, discriminating taste in film should be developed into critical skills and the exercise of judgment in all things visual, and the historians' critique of filmmaking should be extended to the whole field of visualization and imagery. This requires a combination of historical, cognitive psychological, and technical knowledge beyond the level yet discussed in historiography and discussions of representation. Moreover, very little empirical evidence is brought to bear upon anything objective (i.e., measurable results, positive outcomes, etc.) in these discussions; they are largely discourses themselves, and rehearsals of personal opinion, experience, and imagination, unsubstantiated by evidence about emotional impact, impression, conveyance of meaning, attitudinal change, and altered states of historical consciousness. The idea of envisioning history as a form of recall, once a framework is assembled and historical pictures are rendered is interesting, since we know that mental visualization reinforces memory.

The lessons of cognitive psychology seem relevant to the current history/memory dichotomy we hear so much of today, but they seem to be used more to support deconstructionist theory than bolster history or add to the historian's teaching repertoire. Indeed, although such studies use methodologies common to the social sciences and information science, historians have not employed them for their own professional concerns. Nor have they developed critical means to evaluate the conveyance of historical lessons in the new technologies such as Virtual Reality. The lofty goals of the National Standards that students be taught to discern historical documentation and assess the credibility of sources will in the next millennium require highly computerized media laboratories with diagnostic software and techniques not yet invented. Those embroiled in the current debate about history teaching and politicians who wage the culture war for the ascendancy of this or that interpretation and mix for the "right" balance in content, are missing the point entirely. Their concerns are those of the century past, not the beginning of the new millennium.

The prelude for future concern is being played now, however, and it seems to be a question of relating academic to popular culture, or perhaps integration is the theme to follow. Academic historians are often aware of the widespread consumption of nonacademic history through media, outside the classroom, while academic history remains in crisis. In cyberspace and the electronic marketplace, consumerism will have an even greater impact on history than in academe where authority and controls dictate selection or at least guided learning—more so, when the control is pushbutton or a joystick handheld by the consumer. Librarians accustomed to working in an open-systems environment rather than the sterile confines of most classrooms have understood such implications of developing information and instructional technology, but they too are troubled by the fusion of information and entertainment, infomercials that combine reporting and advertising, and the circumvention of the library like the classroom as the main conveyances of these related functions of information and instruction.

In just a few years, libraries are going to be wide open, day in and out, with or without librarians as they have been in the past years, and all fields, not just history, will be a free-for-all.

The Getty AHIP team on December 23, 1994, announced a collaborative project with MUSE Educational Media to study the use of, educational impact, and widespread implications of access to museum images over networks to discern "common solutions to problems no inhibiting the development of computer-based learning tools for the study of art and culture." It is endorsed by the Association of Art Museum Directors, the American Association of Museums, and Coalition for Networked Information. The pilot project, the Museum Educational Site Licensing Project (1995-1997), plans to test the distribution of 3,000 art images from six museums (Fowler Museum in Los Angeles, CA; George Eastman House photography museum in Rochester, NY; Harvard University's art museums; Houston Museum of Fine Arts; National Gallery of Art; and National Museum of American Art in Washington, D.C., each of which are providing 500 images from its collections) to seven universities (American, Columbia, and Cornell Universities, and Universities of Illinois, Maryland, Michigan, and Virginia) where faculty have committed themselves to using the test images in their classes, to study such issues as intellectual property rights, network security, information standards, conditions for educational use, etc. (SORKOW). The goal, of course, is to continue to clear a way for the "Virtual Museum" envision by MUSE's Karl Katz. The target is a viable model site licensing agreement that can be adopted widely and make possible the online-classroom of the near future.

Tom Hickerson, in commenting about this project, correctly understands that the issues are larger than legal and technical, but that "We are not going to see the resources devoted to developing large databases of material [in digital form] until we can demonstrate their value." The tests may prove more positive if only in Art History Departments where visionary experience and image documents are paramount than if image work is incorporated into History Departments and Literature where the image has traditionally been subservient to text. Resistance factors may be more varied and complex than when working with faculty and students already preconditioned to visual information relay and analysis. Moreover, the test sites are at major universities where teaching loads are less, time for research and development is made more readily available to faculty, and where student bodies are highly selective. So one may hope that after this pilot study, others are conducted to aim less on the legal issue concerning the art museum community, and more on the use effectiveness and cost-benefit concerns of teachers and learners. Given the recent ventures of historians into visual documentation and CAI/CAL applications, coupled with their traditional skepticism and conservatism, History Departments would be an ideal, tough test environment to learn more about interactive media, image bases, and mediated instruction with and without direction from instructors.

In such developmental technology and applications for both information dissemination and instruction lie much more than mere information access and transfer, therefore, but the testing of perception and reality of both creators and users, the growing need for mental imaging or imagination in the process of information retrieval, and a dynamic personalized hermeneutics for self-directed learning. The challenge is not only the student's, since the old dichotomy between student and teacher is becoming more confused as well. Role reversals are potentially possible at almost any time because of the facile utility of information technology and knowledge or expertise defined by a subject domain. Equal access is a great democratizer. Faculty, supposedly more perceptive with experience, should be the most challenged. Teachers at all levels must learn how to integrate such CAI/CAL technology into a course, curriculum, and program, and to understand that thereby the teacher is no longer the main information provider. As learners expect more experiential learning to be incorporated into their formal education, they will see the traditional classroom as inherently restricting, and traditional course structures as controlling and indoctrinating. Both teacher and student must understand that no field of knowledge is knowable in the old sense of mastery, and no discipline stands alone. Yet, given the plentitude of information and multiple means of access, never was there greater need for guidance, mentoring, and strategizing in the learning process. It is understandable why the CARNEGIE FOUNDATION so emphasizes today the need for research and innovation in teaching, and why a conservative profession like History, with its book and lecture orientation, is so challenged by this wave of CAI/CAL choices. AHA's Teaching Division is more active than ever, and it has made an overt effort to involve secondary History and Social Studies teachers and accord them the professional status they deserve. The Division has not, however, been aggressive in the CAI/CAL field. Moreover, AHA and allied professional associations have a far more difficult time influencing the quality of History teaching in higher education.

Although blamed on the research emphasis in History as though this were inimical to effective teaching, this misperception is a false dichotomy. The real problem is time management. Content, method, and communication are related. Research and publication may be perceived more wholesomely as the means by which historians teach their peers. The media through which that is accomplished should be more diversified than book production, and History must acknowledge the variety of scholarship advocated by the CARNEGIE FOUNDATION. Historical Information Science must engage CAI/CAL, especially as Virtual Reality systems replace our now comparatively meager attempts at simulation, in case historians sense of research limit them to discovery and interpretation, but not communication, and thus neglect the most deliberate and formal information dissemination, i.e., teaching.

Training Historians

It would seem that a call to reform graduate training of historians has been almost continual in one forum or another (VAN TASSEL). The need for improved information skills among new historians was argued by RUNDELL, but not as vigorously and without the same effect that those arguing a century ago for documentation and critical analytic skills had on scientific historicism. Among the most vocal and critical of the profession at large are those who engage in history-computing or who have entered the information profession (e.g., MCCRANK, 1985; STIELOW, 1985; REIFF, 1993; GREENSTEIN, 1994; GENET, 1995; VOORBIJ). They join those who have had reason to be defensive given the reverse discrimination they confront when the majority of their peers, steeped in traditional methodologies and practice, judge innovative and controversial or early and experimental work against the standards of well-established History. SHIELDS in a collaborative "social construction of academic computing" in higher education argues, like so many, for a change in the reward structure of academe to encourage educational innovation.

This value-system problem is so great that it has attracted the attention of the American Association for Higher Education (AAHE), but the arguments are mostly over the balance between teaching and research rather than the difference among investments, activities, and products which require technical expertise beyond what is commonly required by traditional intra-disciplinary training (DIAMOND & BRONWYN). Historian Eugene Rice, in reacting to BOYER's reconsideration of scholarship in 1990, called for academics to move beyond the simplistic debate over research versus teaching to concentrate instead on the scholarly work of faculty on several points: their advancement of knowledge; its integration, transformation, and application; and, it might be added, its transference. Recognition of the value-added dimension of achieving competence in information technology in addition to content expertise is often neglected in these discussions.

Many careers have been sacrificed because of experimentation with computing (HOPKINS, 1989), and the retraining required after doctorates which did not introduce young historians to computing or the full range of methodologies and techniques here subordinated under the rubric of Information Science History. It was once impossible even to build a database, let alone produce meaningful or mature research results within the time constraints of merely six years allowed assistant professors for promotion and tenure review. VOORBIJ among others laments the lack of understanding among academics about the up-front investment required for computing in the Humanities, the time needed to develop robust computer training modules, and the equitable value that should be placed on electronic editions with other forms misjudged to be more scholarly. The selection of research topics suitable for quantification, for example, has to consider the required investment of time, effort, and funds for source conversion against the time without stable income one could afford for dissertation research and thereafter against the timetable for professorial advancement, so that already converted numerical data (census records, surveys, economic statistics, prepared data sets, etc.) were more reasonable subjects than sources which had to be mined from the archives, translated, coded and tagged, and structured into a database before analysis could even begin.

VOORBIJ (p. 41) warns that "We are still far, far away from plug and play humanities." He takes aim at three miscomprehensions common in considering academic computing: (1) "mismastering the computer," in following technical specialists who act as factotums in promising more than can be delivered; (2) "misappreciation of humanities computing," generally by oversimplification and by not understanding the complexity of the issues involved and therefore equal complexity of the computing employed; and (3) "misunderstanding of computer aided instruction" which should be value-added instruction in the long run to offset the enormous upfront investment. In this regard computing historians share complains with information professionals on twelve month contracts, like academic librarians, who are often disadvantaged by regimens and reward systems geared toward research productivity.

In the United States, considerable faculty ferment across the disciplines is promoting reexamination of faculty evaluation and reward systems (promotion, tenure, sabbaticals and other leaves, equity in competition for research support, etc.), as indicated by Carnegie Foundation for the Advancement of Teaching initiatives (BOYER), perspectives aired through the American Association of Higher Education (DIAMOND & BRONWYN, 1993 and 1995), and the Institutional Priorities and Faculty Rewards Project coordinated by Syracuse University's Center for Instructional Development which has garnered statements from 15 professional associations about the range of activities appropriate for their disciplines. The Scholarly Publishing and Academic Resources Coalition (SPARC) has likewise challenged the traditional relationship between tenure and promotion with scholarly communication, and SPARC initiatives have received endorsement from the Association of University Presses, the American Council of Learned Societies, and the Association of Research Libraries in part to relieve the pressure on faculty for premature publication, to credit publication in more than a few professional, elite, and high-cost outlets, and to open possibilities for electronic communications for short-life publications and thereby halt the spiraling cost of serials. Such efforts may bring about the distinction between publication of work in progress and mature, synthetic, and long-life publication, create a recognized continuum of publication from service to pure research and different formats for various levels of scholarly communication, and credit the role of certain kinds of publication as peer teaching.

Effective teaching, of course, is the chief rival to the alleged overemphasis on research and publications, and this concern is related to computer-assisted instruction and other technologies, but not enough attention is being paid to the up-front investment required for certain kinds of risky business in research itself: exploring alternative technologies, developing methodologies, building databases and information resources, crossing disciplinary boundaries, and innovation in technique and adaptation of technology that are creative and potentially significant even though the first test cases or pilot studies were less than desired. The practice of judging pioneer studies that try new methodology and apply technology in new ways against achievements and practices in established fields is contradictory when creativity, innovation, and entrepreneurship should be encouraged. Indeed, such practices are deadly.

Practitioners in historical computing have been as nearsighted as their more traditional peers, however, by not realizing that in such quantification efforts not one, but two intellectual products were being developed for publication. One is the database itself, which if properly designed and deposited into a data archives, and made public, should be recognized as a publication in itself, not unlike documentary editing. It is an objective intellectual product capable of standing by itself, of being modified, reused like any primary source, and the results of endeavors can be assimilated similarly into the mainstream of historical scholarship. If historians genuinely prize the primacy of original sources and their accessibility, this should be the foremost goal of a computerized history project. The second product is more properly the secondary source: i.e., the study normally associated with historical research, a dissertation, series of articles, or monograph, which is the subjective and interpretative product. The common discarding of the first product, or failure to bring it to publication standards, undermines the second by destroying any ability for verification and genuinely critical review not based simply on peer review or expert opinion. It is also simply wasteful.

It is this verification problem that Lawrence Stone played up when he attacked historical computing (STONE, 1979, p. 11; 1995); it has been dismissed as "absurd" by Manfred Thaller because historians even in reviewing do so little verification work and never return to archives to check on citations to primary sources (THALLER, 1994, p. 31). That may be, lamentably so, but the training of historians must include this ethic of verifiability and evidence as an intellectual and moral underpinning of their discipline, and History must also develop and maintain as sense of "best practices" and accountability as in government, business, and archives. Now through electronic means, such verification may be easier than it ever was in narrative history with traditional sources and library retrieval or with archives and their previous inability to be of service in this regard. Finally, THALLER's more positive and compelling argument for historical computing is to be noted (p. 31), namely that "the objectivity and verifiability of computer-based calculations [have been] for decades...an argument why such methods are less open for [sic] subjective influences."

However, quantified history has not commonly develop the normal practice of dual publication of data sets and all meta-information documentation through either deposition in or donation to a public repository. It is exemplary that one can retrieve from the ICPSR the original data sets of a 576 cases drawn from a thousand days of activity and a random tenth of others used by Charles Tilly in his earliest studies during 1966 of social violence in nineteenth-century France (ICPSR Data file 0051 and codebook; C. TILLY, 1965). One could check his conclusions by reworking his data from his intensive and general samples, or one could add to the sets to clarify such study for a longer period or wider territory, or use these data as a sample compared with a similar set of data drawn from a different area or era. Minimally one could examine the data and operations performed on them (even replication if the software were available) as part of dissertation defenses and the publication review process. The mere offering of data for such examination is, I think, a mark of integrity.

Given these possibilities, it would be interesting to have access to the use records of these data sets to see how and how often historians and social scientists have indeed reused data from previous research. Instead, each researcher normally goes back to the original source for the data—the census or whatever—and recreates a customized data set for his or her particular study. Little data set enhancement is thus accomplished, methodological treatments tend to be imitative by transposition to a different set of data for another area or another time, but such studies do not build upon each other except by summarizing the conclusions of prior investigations. In short, most revisionism is a revision of conclusions, not based on revised or expanded data. Opinions are refined, clarified, or altered, usually without recourse to the data they are based upon in the same way that a narrative source may be reread again and again to amplify its meaning. The benefit of data-based research is not really as cumulative as it might be. Such practice is very shortsighted, and this needs to change. It is somewhat like a corporate

Research and Development reinventing something, often at considerable expense, and encroaching upon another's intellectual property, often in the case of patent infringement with severe financial penalties. This happens all too often in business and industry because engineers are not taught to search patents beforehand, but leave this task until the last and to the legal department when preparing to file for their own patent. Their research and development does not rest on a continuum larger than their own experience, and the developmental process is flawed because the literature and data search was inappropriately timed.

The problem is similar in historical and social science research, but the consequences are not so dire. Indeed, Research and Development (R&D) project administration and electronic records management must become part of the historian's basic professional training. This requires a rehabilitation of archives and records management training at the proper professional level in universities, which in turn requires a change in attitude by many academics about the tedious nature and presumed low-level work of records management (KNOPPERS, 1983; DURANTI, 1989; PEMBERTON, 1989, 1991). Such change would also alter perception about how data-based research is undertaken, within what time periods, and what credit or value can be placed on projects that are innovative in both content and methodology and result in two intellectual products instead of the traditional one. It is not accidental that the subject foci of early quantified socioeconomic or political studies were geared toward datasets readily convertible to a specific use; they were providential selections, resulting in a certain redundancy. Thus political practicalities of career advancement have not favored the growth of what may be called the "new" scientific history within academic History, and this in turn has exacerbated the problem of reform and readiness to adapt to changing times and technologies. Nor have they favored constant enhancement of our data resources.

The early Cliometricians wanted reform within core requirements of graduate History programs that would make computing a required skill, often by substituting computer programming languages for foreign language requirements (LANDES & TILLY). Such arguments were not successful, even though the foreign language proficiency of graduate students declined in any case. Now such arguments are largely irrelevant since programming is not what is really required, but instead a far more complex array of information management and archival skills to handle electronic records. GAVREL (1990, p. 8) seems to understate such requirements: "A certain level of technical knowledge is required by the researcher in order to use machine-readable records in secondary analysis." For modern and contemporary history, for example, it is necessary to know how records haven been handled over the past 20 years. Current or state-of-the-art computer science technical expertise is good for only five years without constant rejuvenation, since the "shelf-life" of technical knowledge is increasingly shorter. Some say that even a half-decade is optimistic. The historian, however, cannot substitute one period's technical information for another; instead, the process is incremental and continually augmentable and cumulative as past data is transmogrified into current systems. Statistical reasoning is still required, moreover, and must be developed as an aptitude one way or another. Although basic Statistics was introduced in Historical Methods courses (E. SHORTER's then novel but now passé textbook was widely adopted in the United States; R. FLOUD's introduction in 1971 with its revision [1979] for the 1980s remained in use longer), the application was often accomplished tutorially and adopted for specific projects, thesis, and dissertation work.

As already noted, more advanced techniques were taught in workshops outside History curricula in the United States at the Newberry Library and Northwestern University in Chicago, the ICPSR in Ann Arbor, Michigan, and other centers allied with the Social Sciences. The organizational phenomenon of historical quantification in the United States was curiously a Midwestern growth, with roots in West Lafayette, Indiana, Ann Arbor, Michigan, and Madison, Wisconsin, often in confrontation with the East Coast History establishment. This perhaps reflects the pioneer methodological work by social scientists at the University of

Chicago in the 1920s and 1930s (BULMER), but that would mean that the time lag for such methodology to penetrate History was over 30 years. This may be true as well of technology transfer, that it took the turnover of a generation of historians before computing could come into wider use, and as experimentation increased and pioneer studies threatened accepted wisdom, so did a counter-movement gain impetus. Attacks like Lawrence Stone's turning-point critique of 1979, in Sara Maza's recent acknowledgment, "accurately predicted the end of the hegemony of structural, material-determinist, and quantified approaches to history" (MAZA, 1996, p. 1493). Cliometricians would never have guessed that they held any such hegemony in the field, but more to the point here, historians in attacking methodology then and later, often disguised their discomfort with the technology that made such methodology possible. The subsequent enabling of more historians to increase their comfort level with computing with the personal computer revolution of the mid-1980s, tempered the hypercriticism at the beginning of the decade. Nevertheless, computers remained in short supply, and PCs were just what their name implied, for personal computing. Their use in teaching, a social activity, was neglected in History. Computing as an essential research methodology, other than word processing where computers were simply a replacement for the typewriter, has taken nearly a generation to recover what Cliometricians thought should be its proper role in training historians and furthering research beyond the capabilities of the lone historian. The widespread application to computing to history teaching is taking even longer.

The same delayed reaction was true in Europe where research institutes sometimes affiliated with universities, but largely semiautonomous centers in Paris, London, Cologne, Bonn, Tubingen, Göttingen, Florence, Pisa, etc., were the main providers of advanced techniques in historical and social science computing to university curricula (cf., SPAETH, ed., 1992; V. DAVIS, 1993). Historians in the European-based Association for History and Computing complain about the same problems of resistance to computing and information technology there as in American academe (GREENSTEIN, 1994, p. 6 speaks about "Computing for the Terrified"!). Certainly the workshop of M. THALLER at the MAX-PLANCK INSTITUT für Geschichte is the most important of these autonomous workshops; with support from IBM Deutschland, it offers a special "Quellenstudium per computer" program which has been the post-doctoral training camp for many computer historians in summer schools (1989-) at Göttingen, Cologne, and Salzburg (BOTZ *ET AL.*). Five tutorials have been developed there by P. BECKER *ET AL.* (1989) based on the Institut's medieval databases. Its influence is far more widespread because of THALLER's participation in so many of the other centers, its prolific publication program, and the distribution of software. The availability of *Klieu* in English has contributed to the growth of a similar program at the University of London (DENLEY).

This pattern also held for archivists engaging electronic records for the first time. They operated with the same handicap in training as historians with a time-lag of nearly a decade in adjusting to the changes in records production, and only a few historians whose social historical bent had led them into computing early were available to lead any educational or programmatic effort (T. BROWN, 1984, 1993). GREENSTEIN (1994, p. 12) complains still about the dearth of History professors in Europe capable of teaching basic historical computing and consequently, trapped in self-perpetuating cycle, few graduate students are being trained adequately for next generation. This reflects the situation in the United States described by COX (1994), where archivists have had to disassociate themselves from History to seek better technical nurturing elsewhere. Thus the National Archives was the first to confront the massive transition to electronic records production that occurred with Robert MacNamara's influence and the Vietnam War (HARRISON). SAA committees since 1969 were addressing the issues raised by the prospect of increased data archives, but it was only in response to C. DOLLAR's first proposal in 1979 for a seminar at SAA conferences on "Appraisal of Machine-Readable Records" that a real educational program was formed (endorsed by SAA in 1981: BROWN, 1993, p. 412) through cooperation with ICPSR's C. GEDA and other CART activists.

At the same time the first requirements of graduate students majoring in Archival Science to include in their programs Information Science courses such as Information Storage and Retrieval were introduced at the University of Maryland between 1978 and 1980, and the curriculum there began to address electronic records issues (MCCRANK, 1979, 1980, 1985; STIELOW, 1993). The 1981 SAA endorsement envisioned four levels of instruction from general knowledge of automated systems to a specialization in machine-readable records; this became articulated later as a spectrum from introductory conceptual information to "High-Tech Applications." Learning objectives were delineated for each level both for electronic records management and their appraisal (BROWN, 1984; updated in 1993, pp. 414-421). Workshops were designed by the SAA Committee on Automated Records and Techniques (CART) for the following: (1) Description and Documentation of electronic records; (2) Access; and (3) Preservation (WALCH, 1993). A series of workshops were presented at SAA annual conferences, regional archivist conferences, and at IASSIST. From these workshops, components found their way into courses offered in Archival Science at a variety of schools of Library and Information Science. Eight of these schools now have full-time Archival Science faculty aboard. Elsewhere, archivists themselves may do the instruction. HEDSTROM (1993) observes that many of them are not familiar with teaching methods (nor teaching methodology); REID (1995, p. 329) agrees, and recommends retooling especially for teaching adult learners. The Australian archivists have developed similar curricula and teaching initiatives (AUSTRALIAN ARCHIVES).

Charles Dollar, in reflecting on such trends in the archives and his own personal experience in historical computing, called upon historians and archivists to collaborate in the creation of new data-based documentation. This experience of electronic archivists in creating a core curriculum for themselves during the 1980s (T. COOK), that eventually led to the ability to specialize within graduate degree programs for archivists in the 1990s, is being repeated a decade later by computing historians seeking similar specialization in the preparation of a new generation of research historians. DOLLAR (1988) advocated throughout the 1980s that historians respond to changes in the historical record by preparing their students to use new information technologies. Most programs, outgrowths of single advanced courses in quantification methodology that follow a more general Historical Methods offering, cannot be identified before then, the mid-1980s in most curricula, and such specialization is still only possible in the largest universities where academic computing laboratories made such teaching possible on a scale larger than one to one.

A 1992 survey of the 143 History Ph.D. granting institutions in the United States (75 percent response rate) undertaken by the Joint Committee on Historians and Archivists revealed that research methodology is taught twice as much in seminars as in other class formats; although it may be generalizable, instruction usually relates specifically to the topic at hand. Offerings in general methodological courses are rarer (DICHTL, summarized by BRIDGES *ET AL.*, pp. 734-738; which incidentally displays serious problems in survey research methodology and analysis of results, and shows no awareness of the aforementioned body of use studies about historian attitudes about information and information seeking behaviors in the United States). Under the guise of research, bibliographic sources and use of archival materials dominated course content by more than three times the attention to the other three possible ingredients queried about: use of cataloging systems (classification systems, natural language information retrieval, or online, automated, or manual systems?); use of computerized databases and finding aids (without adequate distinction in the questions or responses to ascertain what was wanted or what the replies really meant); and quantitative techniques (as synonymous with methodology, but not with enough segregation to isolate textual from numeric quantification, the wider range of technologies available than older statistical computing, or the range in methodology from mere data tabulation to the more abstract and advanced statistics and analytical methods employed in the Social Sciences). The use of computers, automated systems, and quantitative techniques were a decided third choice for most respondents and could not garner more than three percent of first choice options.

The AHA-SAA committee examined over 24 syllabi to clarify their survey results, concluding (E. BRIDGES *ET AL.*, p. 734) that "one conspicuous similarity in the courses was a relative inattention to the complexities of how records are created and organized and the nuances of archival finding aids. The disparity between what history departments say and what they do is an indication of the lack of agreement about how to train students in the necessary competencies and the lack of attention given to this issue." Although most historians (53 percent) thought that graduate students should receive broad research training, their responses to how their departments actually handled such training shows great inconsistency between the ideal of breadth and its actual accomplishment. Of the historians profiling their departments, 37 percent claimed to use archivists and librarians "systematically" (i.e., consistently?) in graduate training, while 39 percent did so only occasionally, and 24 percent never did. No inquiry was ever contemplated about the role of Information Science in historical training or vice versa. If this survey, intentionally simple, had gone after more detailed information using terminology from Information Science, it is doubtful if historians could have responded meaningfully. The committee concluded "The real problem is that the historical profession [in the United States] no longer has a core understanding of research principles and practices that are essential for graduate students." It is in this same vein that BLEWETT recommends that in their graduate training historians should take courses in Library Science, not only to remedy search skills, but to study the structure and organization of information, theories of learning, and modern information technology to bolster historical research capabilities. He also points to the "increasing interdisciplinary nature of research in academics" as underpinning such a recommendation.

Archivists proposed that historians introduce their graduate students to the following principles and practices to remedy this haphazard approach to graduate training regarding the use of archives: (1) uniqueness of archives; (2) provenance; (3) functions of records; (4) original order; (5) collections or the aggregation of records; (6) context for appraisal and interpretation; and (7) connectedness between records, collections, and institutions (E. BRIDGES *ET AL.*, pp. 738-739, relying on reference instruction modules developed at the University of Michigan's Bentley Library by M. J. Pugh and N. Bartlett). Although these "broad archival concepts, not universal truths" resemble concerns in Historical Information Science, they are framed very traditionally within an archival perspective and some of these principles as expressed do not apply well to electronic records. Of course, this survey was intended to solicit information only about history and archives in a traditional framework; it did not explore the nexus between quantified research and data archives or the possible connection with electronic records. It exhibits some of the same binocular focus problems apparent in library use studies, this time from the perspective of archivists. However flawed, such a study does suggest concern for and growing current awareness about the problems confronting graduate education in History in the United States. Discussions in Europe about training historians raise similar concerns.

One cannot discern in the United States any developments in History Departments or archives education embedded in them that might compare with the ferment in Library Science graduate education transformed into Information studies (MARCUM). To create a new type of information professional for the next millennium, the Kellogg Foundation in 1994 created its Human Resources for Information Systems Management (HRISM) with four large grants to the schools of information studies at the Universities of Michigan and Illinois, Drexel University, and Florida State University to test innovative approaches in curricular transformation. The University of Michigan, like the University of Maryland a generation ago, has redesigned its faculty for greater inter-disciplinarity like older "think tanks" to concentrate on the potential and problems of digital information. Historians have been invited into the circle to focus on electronic archives, but to a lesser extent on the history of information technology and policy. Its new curriculum, implemented in 1997, retains an integrated core, and will allow students studying information storage and retrieval and information systems management to apply their learning to specific settings to gain specialization as archivists, librarians, systems managers, etc. The refocus of emphases from these specific settings to the main processes is reflected in its name change to the School of Information. Drexel University's College of Information Science and Technology uses consumerism and market analysis to reshape its curriculum and is creating a distinctive continuity between undergraduate and graduate programs in Information Science. Although its former dean, Richard Lytle, was trained as an historian of technology and was formerly an archivist and leader in the aforementioned NISTF movement, the College displays no real attention to History, but like its parent concentrates on business and industry. Lytle remarks that the emphasis is on the inquiring and designing professional as distinct from the technical person. Florida State University like Drexel has begun building an undergraduate degree program to meet the needs in the state. The University of Illinois LEEP3 curriculum stresses the social, systems, organizational and access issues in information work. An added Fund for the Improvement of Post-Secondary Education (FIPSE) has created a program for information consulting. In an era of contracting enrollments in traditional fields and problematic placement, these schools are expanding. All insist they have not abandoned Library Science, but they have expanded its boundaries and placed it in an enlarged context. Such change is characterized as an infusion, of more than external funding, but rather of instruction, methodology, and technology from all other areas.

Such a picture of invigorated information studies should be alluring to History. Yet the aforementioned survey results about traditional research methods and knowledge about primary and secondary sources indicate that advanced historical computing training in American universities is still very diffuse, largely centering around key professors engaged in computing (hence the dominant seminar approach) rather than formal curricula. The apprenticeship model continues. Little evidence exists for anything coalescing into an Historical Information Science as coherent academic programs in History. One can achieve a formal education in history computing at such places as the University of Illinois (Urbana and Chicago campuses), but almost tutorially through directed study and research. Specialized training in textbases is now available at the Center for Electronic Texts in the Humanities (CETH) at Rutgers and Princeton Universities, but such offerings fall into the workshop variety rather than a systematic curricular program. Online searching of *Dissertation Abstracts* reveals a steady stream of doctoral dissertations using a variety of computing methods and packages, but no real concentration of activity. Only 3-5 percent of the dissertations, at least those abstracted in *Dissertation Abstracts International* which were assigned to History categories in the five years between 1988 and 1993, seem to be computer based and heavily reliant on computational methodologies for data, texts, or images. Moreover, of these, nearly one-third are historically oriented dissertations not produced in History Departments.

Given the aforementioned problems in searching these bibliographic databases for methodology, one might suspect that a higher percentage of dissertations use computers for other than word processing, but the component is not significant enough to warrant emphasis in their abstracts. This seems to be the case as indicated by the lists of dissertations in progress surveyed by the AMERICAN HISTORICAL ASSOCIATION, but the old AHA forms do not gather the kind of technical and methodological information that would assist in such an evaluation. Nevertheless, one would expect a more pronounced production of scholarship in historical computing at highly technical universities like Carnegie-Mellon and Drexel Universities, the Virginia and California Polytechnics, and the Georgia, Illinois, and Massachusetts Institutes of Technology, or the British polytechnics, but History is not emphasized in such environments. One might expect a series of such dissertations from major American and British universities where there are well-established social and behavioral research centers such as at Stanford, Minnesota, Washington, D.C., and the research triangles in Michigan and North Carolina in the United States. Despite concentrations on both

Mathematics and History in the Institute of Advanced Studies at Princeton, the Institute has never been a catalyst for some sort of symbiosis between the two. The same is true for the most prestigious universities in Great Britain. No significant production of doctorally trained historians can be identified either for those institutions like St. Andrews, Oxford, London, and Essex universities that now have computing laboratories and programs in historical computing. Such dissertations can be linked with a small cadre of mentors at the largest institutions, many of whom are named in this present survey. However, other than a intermittent string of doctorates under the guidance of these computing historians, one is hard pressed to find evidence of any real concentration identifying a continually productive program.

Nor can a strong correlation be found between scholarship in areas related to Historical Information Science (except for Archival Science) with any of the institutions granting doctorates in Library and Information Science in either the North America or Great Britain. The University of Maryland may be somewhat the exception with dissertations by LYTLE, TIBBO, and others, but UMCP has not become the center of advanced archival studies one might have wished for, even with the adjacent NARA II facility and its reserve of trained professionals. It, nor any comparable school, is no power-house producing a series of scholars who have had a systematic, dynamic impact on the profession in this regard. No school of information studies really compares well with those graduate schools where one or two key scholars have produced a line of historians at one time or another, in different fields, whose work as researchers and teachers has altered the discipline (e.g., in the aforementioned case of medieval studies, think of Brian Tierney's production from Cornell, Richard Sullivan's line out of Michigan State, or the more than 24 Ph.D. recipients mentored at UCLA by Fr. R. I. Burns). The University of Michigan has more recently entered the electronic archives field in connection with its digital library initiative (e.g., GILLILAND-SWETLAND, who is now adding this dimension to the UCLA program). A series of masters theses from the University of British Columbia often find themselves in *Archivaria* and an occasional short monograph; some of these pertain to electronic records but do not seem to use advanced information technology or computational methodologies for their completion. A few theses are identifiable from Western Washington University's program, mostly reflecting the ex-NARA character of its faculty. Most studies coming from these programs are still reflective and synthetic pieces based on traditional archival documentary research. However useful these may be, they are not the kind of operations research and re-engineering that are so badly needed. Richard Cox as past editor of *The American Archivist* continues to bemoan the plight of the leading professional journal in securing genuine research articles for publication (COX, 1994d). *History and Computing,* like *Computers and the Humanities,* also displays a penchant for case studies, thematic essays, and mere commentaries rather than operations research, substantive lasting contributions, or broad, comparative syntheses.

Past SAA president Eddie HEDLIN in her 1994 presidential address boldly challenged the Society of American Archivists to approach American businesses for sustained support of several archives and records management research institutes where teaching was ongoing, such as at College Park in conjunction with the NARA II installation, for government information, or the University of Michigan with its Bentley fellowship program supported by the Mellon Foundation for 15 years (now defunct). However, that this was a call to action rather than praise of actual accomplishment is itself telling. Since then the University of Pittsburgh, led by Richard Cox and abetted by a research team formed to complete NHPRC grant projects, including David Bearman as a principal investigator, has founded such a center. It appears to be independent of any History entity. It remains to be seen how it thrives, perhaps depending on outside sources for income. This is a start, but the field has had many false starts before, and sustaining and developing such a venture is perhaps more difficult than a tiny beginning. Only a few are needed; quality rather than quantity should be the goal.

Coupled with the uneven diffusion in curricular development and relatively immature approaches to advanced training, such a review does not lend support to any contention of a syncretistic movement, however slight, in the United States and Canada parallel to that in Western Europe or the East (i.e., the former Soviet Union and its block) that links electronic archives, computational methodologies, and historical computing; or which makes the latter, by whatever name, Informatics or Information Science, into a distinct discipline. On the other hand, academic concern in America over adequate skills in quantitative reasoning for entering graduate students is so great that the Educational Testing Service is creating a separate module for the Social Sciences, separate from one addressing aptitude in hard mathematics, to augment its three other core testing foci in the Graduate Record Examinations. The goal is to inculcate greater proficiency in mathematical reasoning which would lend itself to easier use of computational methodology and historical computing by graduate students. One wonders if such an examination approach will have the desired effect if the professorate in fields like History are prone to ignore such applications in their own coursework and graduate student mentoring. Does the resident faculty have the prerequisite numerate skills now demanded of incoming graduate students? Would a sample survey and basic skills test in mathematics and computational methodology to academic historians, similar to the study by M. STEIG about basic bibliographic skills for undergraduate teaching and advising, reveal another embarrassing lacuna of the same dimension that she found a decade ago?

Janet Reiff, representing an American viewpoint from Social Science History computing and quantification, stressed a four-fold clarification between "computer literate" and "computer trained" historians, quantitative historians, and computer historians depending on specific combinations of methodological and technical expertise (REIFF, 1993, pp. 21-26). Reiff's recommendations may be taken as a continued lobby for increased numeracy among historians, from the earlier entreaty of L. BENSON and A. BOGUE (repeated in 1990), to N. FITCH (1988) who offers as a model a course using quantitative methods and technology in the history curriculum. Robert Fogel put it simply in his commentary commemorating the anniversary of *The Journal of Interdisciplinary History* at the 1995 AHA conference: "One is in real trouble if you cannot count" (FOGEL, 1995). Alternative sets of distinguishing characteristics for various levels of training were levels advocated by those more text oriented for documentary history, images and art history, geography and mapping and oral history. GREENSTEIN (1994) humorously split levels of computing in History into the categories of introductions "for the terrified" as a sometimes necessary antecedent to Historical Computing *per se* as methodological and technical training, or when computing is integrated into traditionally framed courses, i.e., "Computers in the History of Blah" as he calls them somewhat disparagingly. He distinguishes between Historical Computing and Humanities Computing (p. 14); his criteria are not clear but seem to be positioned along the old divide between quantification of socioeconomic data as the proper historical orientation allied with the Social Sciences, and the computerized inspection of text and images as somehow pertaining only to the Humanities. That framework is highly subjective and should be reexamined. Accordingly, however, courses and curricula take on different content foci depending on their teachers and program directors, but a general consensus may be evolving about a basic set of competencies in quantitative reasoning cutting across the disciplinary and subject parameters. This is a basic requirement, however, rather than consensus about advanced training.

One suspects that historians need breadth and depth equal to or greater than offered in many American Information Science programs, plus the content knowledge of a historical field. How this is accomplished in an individual's program, however, is left largely to individual aspiration, advising and mentoring, and chance. Thus as noted by GREENSTEIN (1995), there are major differences between European and American approaches to curricular development and the concept of what properly constitutes an academic program. Perhaps one agreement exists across national circles, and that is the distinction made by VOORBIJ (p. 36): "Research involves data processing, not using computers." He, like others, would like to see methodology at the core of discussions in historical computing, rather than this or that technology, and he is especially critical of turning over training to computer technicians who know little about research. "More attention should be paid to methodology, from the very moment that scholars start to work with computers" (VOORBIJ, p. 37).

Universities in the United Kingdom as in the Netherlands (BREURE) and Scandinavian countries are witnessing a revival of computing in the classroom and in research, thanks to government intervention in the former, and a traditionally progressive attitude toward computing in the latter two countries coupled with economies that afford computing technology in education. GREENSTEIN (1994, p. 4) surmises that "Historical computing is probably [better] developed in Britain than anywhere else in Europe as a result of government policies. Still, coverage is patchy." This is because, as SPAETH (1992, p. 9-12) has noted also, it is only in connection with centers that some universities can acquire proper staff support and faculty expertise to mount actual programs.

This focus on select centers (Besançon, Montpelier, Rennes, Paris, etc.) is also the approach in France, where early educational developments were described by GENET (1978) whose more recent assessment of historical computing (1995) is very discouraging. The interplay between research centers and university life flows freely in France, i.e., it is difficult to separate formal education in History curricula with laboratory and practical training "on the job" in project work at centers that attracts a pool of talent through a variety of mechanisms from assistantships to subcontracting and outsourcing. The pervasive influence of the Annalistes remains, and government supported humanistic database and online projects certainly create an atmosphere of acceptance of historical computing in France, but the recent shift in French historiography back to textual source criticism seems to have diluted any real resurgence of traditional quantification in History or movement toward more formalized academic programs that resemble something more structured than apprenticeship to a mentor who is computer-literate.

GENET (1995) in his most recent assessment of the situation in France, based on a survey of 32 educational centers, is quite pessimistic. He acknowledges that the formation of historical informatics is not easy, and he vacillates between hope and despair when contemplating developments over the last decade. While contemplating activities elsewhere, most notably relating to the Association for History and Computing, he concludes (1995, p. 33 [my translation]) "In totality, the situation for historians seems altogether unfavorable in France concerning the field of Informatics: reading journals and acts of specialized colloquia is in this regard revealing, and the situation of the French historians is conspicuous by their absence." He criticizes the situation in three ways: (1) continuation of the tension between descriptive and documentary sciences and the social sciences, and the lack of integration of history into the hard sciences where computing was well supported, while French historiography reveled in historiographic review and revisionism, the history of mentalities, and microscopic studies of dubious merit; (2) poor training in computerization, despite national projects after 1986/87 to distribute personal computers widely (the plan "Informatique pour tous" or IPF); and (3) an unserving institutional infrastructure and bureaucratic maze between such research centers as the CNRS and France's universities. He chides his French compatriots and historians for their lack of participation in the international information highway, while they isolate themselves within their own language and protection of the French national cultural patrimony.

In contrast to the American scene, several full-blown graduate curricula have evolved on the continent. A "Historical and Cultural Informatics" program has arisen at the University of Groningen in its Alpha-Informatica Department, i.e., Computing in Humanities (WELLING, 1993a). A specialization in an already detailed and segmented curriculum is developing there in Computational Linguistics and Artificial Intelligence for History as any field in the Humanities. The language orientation of such programs prefers uses of *LISP, Scheme, Prolog*, etc., concentration of telecommunications, and linguistics fields like syntax and semantics as well as logic (for logic programming, cf., HARVEY & WRIGHT, and FRIEDMAN & FELLEISEN [1996a & b] for *Scheme*; R. GABRIEL; JONES, MAYNARD & STEWART; and STEELE for the modern dialect of *LISP;* and STERLING & SHAPIRO for *Prolog*). The University of Leyden in 1991 built a "transnational" graduate program upon an undergraduate base of six-year-long courses for 150 students in a track (LIND). At Liège, full-year courses by S. PASLEAU (1993) in statistics and computer science applied to History focus on modern and contemporary history only. Embedded into a larger program on "Communication Art and Science," there is allowance for specialization by combining historical computing with "Book" and "Documentary Sciences." The options are essentially divided along the lines of bibliographic and archival studies. Since 1980 at the Karl-Franzen-Josef University in Graz, and 1984 in Vienna, workshops were organized, the *Quantkurs* which expanded purely quantitative to computational history which included source criticism, descriptive statistics, personal computing and use of standard packages like SAS and SPSS, introduction to *Klieu* software, analysis and interpretation of results (KROPAČ, 1987). Since 1991, students at the University of Vienna can pursue a university-wide inter-disciplinary program overseen by a Research Commission (FUCHS, 1993) with a core in quantitative methods, databases and systems, information retrieval, text and image content analysis, historical cartography, and image processing. The literature searching courses focus on several documentation systems, and include CD-ROM bibliographical tools like *BIP*, ABC- CLIO's indexes and abstracts, etc.; they also use DIALOG for online searching; and these burgeoning info-historians travel across the Internet to learn American OPACs, to create self-sufficiency in an electronic information world. Much of the training looks like Library and Information Science coursework in the United States (WHITBECK, 1991). Such curricular progress in German universities is very spotty, however, and BUSCHE characterizes the overall situation as "poor" in his assessment of German historians' responsiveness to information technology and the methodologies of historical computing. GUARNIERI says that no courses in Historical Informatics are taught in Italy.

Progress in the former Soviet Union, described nationally and region by region by BORODKIN & LEVERMANN (cf., BORODKIN & GARSKOVA, 1992, specifically in the experience at Moscow's Lomonosov University), was delayed by tardiness of the microcomputer revolution that perpetuated historians' lack of access to computers. BORODKIN (1993, p. 2) laments this technical handicap on Russian historical Informatics and project work, but the theoretical and mathematical prowess of the Russian Cliometricians is internationally respected as recognized by ROWNEY. They move into chaos theory applications and fuzzy set analysis in ways just being contemplated in the West (GARSKOVA & BORODKIN). From 1979 to the hundredth meeting in 1992 the All-Union Seminar on Quantitative History, organized by Moscow State University's history faculty and the Academy of Sciences' Commission on the Application of Mathematical Methods and Computers in Historical Research, has had a major impact especially in training a young generation of computer-literate historians. BORODKIN (1993, p. 9) claims that throughout this time an integral part of "Quantitative History" was the study of problems generated by the "meeting point of the historical source and computer, which formed the core of historical information science." The Moscow State University Historical Informatics Laboratory continues to train about 120 undergraduates, 40 graduate students, and 20 post-graduate faculty from around the Commonwealth in Historical Information Science. A general course surveys the following: usage and applications; microcomputer "architectonics" and text processing for content analysis of documents; database management using *dBase III+* and *ClioMetr* for bibliography, as well as prosopographical files; spreadsheets using *Lotus* 1-4; and AI applications such as expert systems, e.g., *Hydronimicon* and *Fuzzyclass*; OCR and image processing, and source-oriented software, namely *Klieu*. An advanced course focuses specially on quantification and statistical methodology: data analysis such as crosstabulation; descriptive statistics (e.g., variance); sampling; correlation and regression analysis;

multidimensional statistical analysis like factoring, cluster analysis, and scaling; and time series analysis. Other advanced study centers in the former Soviet block have evolved in the University of Warsaw (KOPCZINSKI) and Lorand Eotvos University in Budapest (BENDA *ET AL.*). The latter, which developed from the work of G. GRANASZTOI, now has 41 ongoing databased projects in which students gain experience.

In Europe as in the American archival education movement, a multilevel approach is being taken to evolve a more uniform transborder or international curriculum (V. DAVIS *ET AL.*) such as discussed at an AHC conference in Glasgow (1992). THALLER (1993, pp. 7-9) also makes a distinction between basic and advanced curricula. The first focuses on operating systems and numerical data handling, text files, statistical inference and graphic representation, use of hypermedia or nonstandard equipment like OCR and scanning devices, and some demonstration of application ability in one area of basic competence. For advanced outcomes, the working group's consensus wanted the following: awareness of the diversity of software and solutions to historical computing problems; the ability to take a data set through the whole process of formalization of a problem, design of a data structure and entry, analysis, and presentation of results; and a "computer literacy" thought of as self-help in learning new software by oneself. These outcomes could be reached through courses and modules embedded into larger curricula, "explicit curricula" like a track or special dedicated seminars, or interdisciplinary curricula that would provide a high-level programming language, familiarity with two areas of computer applications such as image processing and databasing, and dissertation work with explicit integration of computer science into the subject. The commonalities based on general consensus are considerable; yet the differences in formalization are significant.

Any number of curricular programs could be designed to train historians in Historical Information Science that would accomplish a balanced combination of technical competence with research methodologies and subject-domain expertise. A "program" is decidedly different from the common apprenticeship approach ensconced inside the total degree program as common in American graduate studies in History. By program, I mean a course of action that is announced beforehand, rather than made up as one goes along. And the course, traditionally consisting of courses that have some unity to make an organic and intellectual whole, should be coherent, congruent, systematic, and outcome-oriented. In the case of Historical Information Science, since the conceptualization is new and terminology unsettled, the desired specific outcomes may not yet be entirely clear but the array of knowledge bases and skills has been identified and the scope of a History subject-domain as traditionally defined seems acceptable. The combination of these, however produces a formidable want-list of accomplishments for graduates. The desired specialization (actually correlated and coordinated specializations) can hardly be done in one year within the confines of a single Masters of Arts program as commonly contrived in the United States (e.g., 36 semester credit-hours, of which six can be external like a minor field, six for a research or thesis component, leaving 24 for both methodology and content coursework). The double master's (MA + MLS) program earlier advocated by MCCRANK (1979) and recently endorsed by BLEWETT (1994) has its merits, but a mix of coursework does not always guarantee a proper blend since not all professional studies curricula have the desired archival component that is as well-developed as at the University of Maryland and at only handful of other schools. So, these programs are not necessary easily available. Nor does a mere inter-disciplinary course mixture, especially if they are all introductory, insure the kind of advanced research application seen as essential by computing historians.

What is accomplished inside a graduate program may depend on prerequisites, or as in the case of foreign language proficiency requirements, these may be done for nongraduate credit parallel to the graduate program. Remedial coursework might be arranged through audits. In dual-master's two-year programs it is common to omit the external field requirement since the entire program by definition is inter-disciplinary, so the total credit count usually hovers in the range of 54-60 credit hours. Likewise, doctoral programs building on a separate and substantial master's degree previously earned, can accommodate flexibly the same kind of course sequencing set-up for a dual master's program. Tracks cutting vertically across layered courses (surveys, colloquia, practica, seminars, etc.) produce a matrix that can provide for an orderly progression through a program and still accommodate diversity and choice in subject specialization. This program architecture allows greater opportunity for course sequencing into tracks and thereby insuring an advance toward genuine specialization. An economy of scale is required both for the clustering of incoming graduate students into cohorts who move along somewhat together and provide mutual support for each other, but also for cost-efficiency in the use of faculty talent and justification of considerable investment in computer laboratories, software libraries, and technical support services.

It does not seem desirable to dictate any particular design to a school, since programs always have to be tailored to local circumstances, overall requirements, and available talent. Moreover, standardization need not produce such uniformity that personal choice and institutional character are unaccommodated. But it is advisable to do what professional organizations have done, or what the IAHC has contemplated (V. DAVIS *ET AL.*; SPAETH *ET AL.*), in producing a programmatic "framework" for graduate studies so graduates will satisfy common expectations regarding broad coverage, special expertise and mastery, and practical experience.

Library Information Science once identified three areas as a core, although they resulted in various course clusters: (1) bibliography and reference; (2) cataloging and classification; and (3) management or administration. This foundation was then built upon for specialization by type of library or organization, a function, or a subject area. The only technological specialization that was commonplace was instructional technology and media for school librarianship. Under the impact of information technology, this has changed drastically, not only with the focus on Information Technology becoming a specialty itself, but indeed a whole array of specializations, of which some area is now considered an essential addition to the core. The field is undergoing redefinition, but a consensus about the core has yet to develop and it may be subsumed under Information Science, i.e. as applied in libraries (CRONIN, 1995). As mentioned, schools have increasingly allied themselves with other units to avoid elimination during recent budget crises: with Computer Science (Pittsburgh), Communications (Rutgers), Education (e.g., South Florida, UCLA), etc., while others are amalgamations with Social Sciences and policy studies (e.g., University of California, Berkeley; SUNY, Albany). The University of Maryland continues its alliance between History and Information Science for its dual master's program for archivist training, but no mergers have linked History and Information Science in any structural reorganization. The University of Michigan recently restyled itself simply as the School of Information. Association of Library and Information Science Education (ALISE) continues to debate the core curriculum concept and the context for future information studies.

In the United Kingdom, a Transbinary Group working in 1985 with universities and polytechnic schools advised on curricular reform in Information Science to accommodate the rapidly changing world of information technology. It outlined a process of curricular reform entailing four stages of transition:

1. Information storage and retrieval (ISAR) absorbs classification, terminology, description, cataloging, indexing, abstracting, etc., which were reconceived as specialized functions and types of approaches within a larger focus, and which were all taken to be automated operations.

2. Development of a broad background in information technologies of all types should include a basic competency in computing in particular.

3.   Integration of information technology should be contained in all courses, as sort of a "writing across the curriculum" requirement to teach composition and insure practice and development of language skills. Thus students would be exposed to applications in special fields and would gain a comparative perspective.

4.   The design of new courses would have to be particularly oriented to new information systems and services and management of these. The management aspect is being conceived as especially oriented toward communication and interpersonal skills.

Under the influence of Information Systems Management (ISM) as articulated in Business schools, the following clusters are evolving (T. WILSON):

1.   Subject domains as fields defined less by traditional discipline and more by functions and services, which are seen as specialized fields of application (banking and finance, health, education, etc.)

2.   The economics of information and finance, information law and policy development, and evaluation and assessment more than of technology itself (e.g., needs, performance, outcomes, etc.), but also of the corporate and larger social environment for its implementation and use

3.   Information users, uses, and communities, communications

4.   Information, media, and telecommunications technologies themselves

5.   Information systems, systems theory, and research methodologies

In the United States, however, graduate library schools have come under attack from administrations seeking to balance over-stressed budgets and struggling to understand the proliferation of seemingly compatible but separate degree programs from various providers in their universities: Information Systems Management often in Business Schools; Computer Science which can be alone or allied with Mathematics or Business; and Library and Information Science that usually stood alone at small professional schools but which has been forced to partner with Education, Communications, Political Science and Policy Studies, and Computer Science. Moreover, relatively few institutions of higher education in the United States offer doctoral programs (16 to 20 schools), and only a few are in institutions also supporting premier History departments. The latter nonalignment, however, may make little difference, since the premier departments have often showed the least inclination toward developing any technical prowess until most recently. Options for genuine doctoral work fusing historical studies and information science, therefore, are largely individual rather than programmatic. There is no consensus or set of guidelines for program prerequisites, content, design, and outcomes of desired competencies.

In 1977, American archivists provided initial guidelines for graduate programs claiming to educate archivists. The guidelines were then so weak as to undermine the more advanced programs in the United States, but they at least provided a minimum for Departments of History that in response to the academic employment crisis after the 1974 recession tried to place history graduates in archives with no particular specialization. While not discounting the value of general courses on archives use and appreciation, archivists did not regard these one-course efforts, even when combined with some kind of field study or apprenticeship, as sufficient training. The baseline was set at some introductory course, a practicum for supervised and guided laboratory experience, and then some form of experiential training doing archival work.

The guidelines were imminently practical, embodied no research component, and made no move toward electronic records management in the recommendations.

The professionalization movement among archivists in the 1980s that led to the certification plan of 1987 and implementation by 1989 through an Academy of Certified Archivists, bypassed the previous attempt to move toward program certification that was to have been tested by the SAA Committee on Education at the Universities of Maryland and Wisconsin and at Wayne State University where self-studies for program evaluation had been undertaken by L. J. McCrank, J. Ham, and P. Mason, respectively, but which were never used. Without adequate support from SAA standards, weak as they were, the certification mechanism by default sanctioned as a certified archivist anyone who could pass a comprehensive examination on basic archival literature, theory, and practice, regardless of formal specialized education. While it was still assumed that professional archivists would have a master's degree, undergraduate programs in records management and a few in library science could adequately prepare a graduate to pass such an examination (but not for the profession, if one accepts the arguments of PEMBERTON, 1981, 1983; 1991; cf., similar arguments about the fusion of archives and records management with the information science component of librarianship, resulting in a long discussion that failed to produce maximum results, e.g., PEACE & FISHER; BUCKLAND, 1982; F. EVANS, 1984; BERNER, 1986; MCCRANK, 1979, 1986). As in librarianship, the MA was seen to be terminal degree, suggesting mastery while in fact taking a minimalist approach to methodological development, refinement of technique and improvement of practice, and exploration of new information technology. No attention was paid to research and advanced studies beyond the practitioner degree. Archival Science, therefore, did not develop so much as an Archival Administration (or perhaps more accurately, management), and the research orientation of those with doctorates in the profession remained that of History which was traditionally content rather than methodologically focused. Because History Departments were so poorly prepared to employ or engage the issues created by modern information technology, the best educated among American archivists were still ill-prepared to confront the challenges of electronic records as COX's study (1994) indicates. Moreover, the widespread mutual enrichment of the Social Science history and archives that I envisioned in the 1970s never occurred. If it had, a larger cadre of computer-literate archivists would have taken up the electronic records challenge.

The SAA *Directory* (1995-96) identifies 38 multi-course graduate programs in archival studies in the United States and Canada, plus SAA for continuing education and two providers of post-appointment training. Not all offer coherent programs in archival administration, and most continue to embed this specialization in either History of Library/Information Science. Such hybridization has come under attack because many of these programs were taught by adjunct professors, schools and departments failed to support genuine specialization and research by appointing archival specialists to their faculties, and the field itself has expanded greatly over the past two decades. Consequently, SAA (1995-1996) adopted a new set of guidelines for development specifically of M.A.S. (Masters of Archival Studies) degrees. Note: the substitution of "studies" for "science" is significant, not that the research component is largely a *laissez-faire* matter, but it is subordinated to an overall goal of blending the theoretical with the practical. Notably for the first time scholarly research is an issue of professionalism, and research methodology is considered as an important complementary knowledge base. Scholarly research is advocated as "an essential component of the archival studies curriculum because it established in the student the habit of thinking critically and rigorously about archival issues." The guidelines thus recommend a thesis requirement in the master's program. The research methods recommended are those of the Social Sciences (p. 13, p. 15 n. 12).

The guidelines (pp. 9-15) pertain to the following: the nature of materials for which the archivist is responsible; the nature of the activities that generate these materials and the contexts in which they are generated; and the nature of archival work. The proposed curriculum would consist of five components: (1) contextual knowledge (United States History focusing on organizations, legal and financial systems; (2) archival knowledge, which is subdivided into the history of archives, their organization, legislation, and character of the profession, combined with records management and archival science; and (3) complementary knowledge, which is enumerated as conservation, library and information science, management, research methods, and History; (4) Practicum; and (5) Scholarly research.

One can take issue with the cardinal assumption drawn from the writings of Richard COX, put succinctly by the SAA Education Committee (1995, p. 12) as a rationale for the core focus on "Archival Knowledge."

> The identity of a profession is founded on a body of knowledge belonging exclusively to it, and on a professional culture that arises from a common history, a united purpose, a shared language, and collective values, norms, and standards.

Particularly controversial should be the idea that knowledge is owned and possessed, and that the ingredients of archival history, records management, and archival science are exclusive to the profession. The critical problem is the employment of would-be archivists who have inadequate training in archives, who lack a thorough understanding of archival principles so they can apply them to specific cases, and who while trained in history know nothing about the history of their field in particular or of information studies generally. However, for the purpose of discussing ingredients in Historical Information Science, attention must be focused on how Archival Science is defined. The crux of this component lies in "fundamental ideas about the nature of archives, archival documents, and archival functions (archival theory); the analysis of ideas for performing archival functions (archival methodology); and the study of practical implications and implementations of theory and method in actual circumstances (archival practice)" (SAA EDUCATION COMMITTEE). What is most important is that "proper attention should be given to the development of new records formats, due to changing information technologies for the creation, maintenance, and use of records, and to emerging automated systems for archives. The challenge posed by these two phenomena to archival thinking and practice must be explored." For the latter educators are referred to the model curriculum recommended by the Committee on Automated Records and Techniques (CART). In all professional education there is a pronounced emphasis on experiential learning or "learning by doing" in laboratory settings and on-the-job training that runs so contrary to the prevalent mode in History departments across the United States.

With these trends in mind within Library, Archives, and Information Sciences, historians might reconceptualize their own approaches to the training and education of historians in Historical Information Science. What might the range of curricular options be for History departments that want to support the aforementioned specializations in the information profession? What might be accomplished more than through conventional curricula? Can the historical profession carve out an academic niche for historians in the information marketplace? Such objectives can be addressed more effectively than through the current tendency toward an unsystematic and nonprogrammatic integration of historical computing into traditionally framed courses. The choices listed in the appended curricular guide (Appendix C) are aligned with American graduate and professional education rather than the European model, they deliberately embrace the larger concept of Historical Information Science rather than the narrower European interpretation of Historical Informatics as simply Computer Science, and they attempt to indicate the array of choices available rather than to dictate a specific program architecture or selection of courses. Nor does this guide eschew the options of specialization in accord with guidelines specifically for careers in librarianship, archives and museum administration, or conversely the kind of technical specialization advocated by THALLER (1994) for Historical Computer Science. The idea here is to represent the possibilities for a hybrid unidisciplinary specialization here called Historical Information Science, stressing the preparation needed for historical research project funding and management, technical execution, and proper augmentation of historical data in electronic archives, coupled with the content knowledge of a traditionally framed historical field of study and the methodological and theoretical knowledge of both social science and humanistic research (i.e., the *humane sciences*). Course names are suggestive of content and organization of knowledge and teaching areas, but they reflect courses now offered in American graduate schools and therefore, a current nomenclature.

The ultimate goal in training historians or other information professionals in Historical Information Science is to create a coherent, congruent educational experience in a systematic program. That will always rely on the efficacy of academic mentoring, but there should be a balance between pure apprenticeship to a master scholar and operating within programmatic guidelines that insure that work with a key faculty member still takes advantage of an entire faculty. Finally, an academic program in Historical Information Science requires a certain symbiosis between a talented faculty and their institutional context. This includes not only recruitment of faculty expertise and nurturing of a dynamic, collaborative culture, but the integration of technical and methodological expertise across a faculty and departmental lines to create a genuine inter-disciplinarity. Success requires a proper institutional setting and financial support, i.e., laboratory facilities in addition to a variety of classroom settings, technical resources and assistance from organized support services (academic computing, media production and distribution, teaching and faculty development centers), mature and exemplary libraries and archives for information access and services but also as instructional laboratories themselves, flexible scheduling for course development and laboratory and fieldwork supervision. Finally, once the faculty is ready, the setting is prepared, opportunities are created, etc., one must have talented, creative, intellectually curious, and technically oriented students who are able and willing to learn.

A new generation of historians can be trained who are far more capable of engaging modern information technology in their research and teaching, and who can migrate with greater ease in and outside academe as opportunities present themselves.

The Future of the Past

CONCLUSION

In this bibliographic review and essay, I have surveyed those developments in the past decade especially, and a few years beyond, which seem to purport things to come in the new millennium. One of these is a merging of technologies which is causing a blending of traditional disciplines by a unifying metadiscipline or what I have called a unidiscipline following the lead of modern Annalistes—empirical, methodological, technical, and historically oriented information studies cutting across established boundaries. It is therefore more than multidisciplinary as such combinations are usually perceived; that is, borrowing from one discipline to assist work in another, like minor fields subordinated to a major field of study. Instead, the goal is a holistic view of information and communication in history to the very present, or from the present back in time, which is longitudinal and long range in perspective, context sensitive, multicultural, and highly synthetic and syncretist. This hybrid, I suggest, may be called Historical Information Science, as an extension of older notions of scientific historicism combined with modern Information Science, with the application of modern Social Science research methodology and state-of-the-art information technology.

This would require a blending of the following:

1. Subject knowledge from a domain in History

2. Archival Science, especially for converted sources and electronic archives

3. Library Science for bibliographic reference, adroit information searching through any medium, and special acumen in terminology, classification, and bibliographic control

4. Social Science quantitative research methodology

5. Information Science (IS) especially for information storage and retrieval, visualization, data and knowledge engineering, combined with a basic competence in database design and management or basic management of information systems (MIS)

6. Administrative Science for large-scale project management and organizational development

Historical Information Science as conceived here is broader and more integrative than simply historical computing as a practical art or in European usage of Historical Informatics as quantifiable historical research conducted with computer assistance. In most cases, the research focus of historical computing has been traditionally very centered in a particular domain, into which methodologies developed elsewhere are imported. Originality lies in the application and in exploiting data not studied before or studied completely with the capability afforded by new technology. Historical Information Science focuses more on:

1. Operations such as project management, exploration of methodologies, testing potential applications, developing technique, and defining procedures for strategic research

2. Source criticism and structural analysis, including appropriate metadata, for data-bases, textbases, and imagebases

3. Experimentation to develop processes and products for historical research which may be broadly applicable or customized for problems in specific domains and certain kinds of sources

4. Publication of research results in traditional formats such as monographs and journals, but also to contribute to the technical literature in the form of reports, reviews, and test results

5. Resource development through retrospective conversion of source material into electronic form; enhancement of data sets, text base, image files, and sound recordings; standardization and normalization; and improved access by terminological work, thesaurus construction, indexing and abstracting

6. The deposit of data, files, programming, shareware, etc., in appropriate archives and research centers so that one contributes to the cumulative resource base available to historians everywhere

7. The administration of research, project management, and organizational development using history in non-History enterprises and in historical agencies, archives, and museums, for the advancement of History and dissemination of historical information for the sustenance of culture

When conceived as a methodological orientation rather than traditional specialization in a particular domain, the historical foci are necessarily comparative. Moreover, the scope is on information in all forms, contexts, and times, with its information technologies and systems at the time related to current capabilities, with attention to medium, context, communication, dissemination, impact, and influence. Information, communications, and media are the real subjects. To accomplish this one must have attendant development of theory and applications including experimental approaches such as simulation and modeling, new statistical and analytical methodologies and enabling techniques, and testing and evaluation of information structures, formats, technology, software, and operations management strategies which can enhance research and publication, history teaching and learning, and the preservation, dissemination, and retrieval of historical information.

The encompassing embrace of Historical Information Science, as I envision it, is suggested by my inclusion in this discussion and coverage of:

1.1. Historiography that is less literature oriented, pays more attention to the methods, techniques, technology, and information components of History, and provides a background for contemporary capabilities, such as the origins of quantified methodologies in the Cliometric movement, parallel developments in Information Science, or the advent and spread of academic computing

1.2. Methodology, especially developments of new technologies, techniques, and innovative applications, which has contributed to History in the past and which are at the cutting edge now, and which potentially respond to the increased scope of modern History and the critical problem of data mass

2.1. Bibliographic control and improved access to historical literature and information retrieval

2.2. Information use, with continued studies of historians and related academic and professional communities (e.g., in the information profession), and user groups not identified with professional history in the public (e.g., genealogists, museum patrons) and private sectors (e.g. in business, government)

2.3. Computer literacy, training, and the state of academic computing including software development and access, and capability of assessment for applications in historical research

3.1. Professional relations between allied academic and professional communities (e.g., historical agencies, archives, libraries, museums, foundations, and research organizations)

3.2. Archival Science, the resource base for historical research, record keeping and documentation, and records management

3.3. Electronic records, retrospective conversion projects, and data and electronic archives

4.1. History of information formats, media, and systems

4.2. History of information producers, distributors, and information dissemination

4.3. History information sciences and technologies

4.4. Underlying philosophy, assumptions, and missions

5.1. Cultural and organizational management studies in Administrative Science

5.2. History and memory studies entwining cognitive psychology, sociology, and History

5.3. Project management, research and development operations, etc.

6.1. Historical data processing and quantification in Social Science History

6.2. Text and image analyses for History in the Arts and Humanities

6.3. Integration and new uses of historical sources in electronic form

7.1. Problem resolution in information handling an technological dependencies

7.2. Source problems, preservation and conversion projects

7.3. Description, access, and data transfer

7.4. Software design and use

8.1. History teaching using computer technology and multimedia

8.2. Training historians and archivists with new technologies and methodologies

8.3. Research evaluation, standards, publication, and information dissemination

These issues are categorized in accord with current classification and professional divisions that govern information searching in established disciplines and subject domains, but the discussion of them has been deliberately excursive, inter-disciplinary, and critical with attempted linkage of publications, projects, technologies, and methodologies across a wide purview, but with a chronological limitation primarily to the last decade and to Europe and America. The extent of relevant activity is remarkable in itself, but so is the increased sophistication and technical prowess of historical studies using information technology and computer-assisted analysis. Indeed, it is no wonder why so few have attempted overviews and syntheses such as the one attempted here; the task is daunting, even for such a modest time frame as that since the spread of personal computing. While this survey was exhaustive, using all relevant databases and online systems available, the resulting coverage has been necessarily selective. The citations provided tie into the discussion and do not, therefore, constitute a comprehensive guide to all relevant sources in the disparate literatures of History and the Social Sciences, Arts and Humanities, Business and Administration, Computer Sciences and Engineering, and Information Science, pertaining to historical agencies and organizations, archives, libraries, and museums. Moreover, it has been impossible also to cover by detail or even mention the prodigious cumulative publication output of historians over the past decade; only a few relatively references could be included to illustrate key points. The problems of scope, mass, and detail addressed in this essay are self-evident in this work itself.

In the spirit of unitary studies as proposed here, with concentrated foci on source criticism, analytic methodology, techniques and operations, experimentation, and uses of information sources and technology, the aforementioned chapters could be reformulated into larger, more philosophical categories as follows:

1. The examination of historical sources which includes source criticism from Diplomatics and Codicology for manuscript, and Descriptive and Analytical bibliography for print materials, external or form and internal or content criticism for audio and visual materials as well, and forensic science and technology, all of which must be extended and applied also to electronic media in metadata as a combination of description and analytics. All of these should relate to verification, authentification, confirmation, and interpretation as matters of evidence, epistemology, and heuristics.

2. The study of information searching and retrieval, those of who seek and use historical information, their motivations and behaviors, actual usage and trends, etc., to study History in the past and at present beyond historiography as historical literature, to sustain historical inquiry, and to advance its capabilities and influence. These concerns constitute the heuristic dimension of such studies.

3. The tracking of information through history, production, and formation or production in physical form, its provenance and dissemination, preservation and organization, and its transference, translation, and transmutation across distance and through time, across cultures and in different languages, through technical transformations, and diverse organizations and institutions. This should compose a genealogical meta-database for research, tracking recordings, chain of custody, and tradition, which relates to evidential theory and law, social norms and organizational cultures, credibility and the truth claim of History or an objective view of the past subject to challenge and criticism and hence revision, and the very foundations of knowledge based on historical sources. Such concerns pertain to accountability, documentation, and epistemology.

4. The history of methodologies and techniques for communication, record keeping, preservation, edition, publication, and the transmission of primary sources, secondary literature based on them, syntheses into tertiary reference materials, and how such documentation and evidence relates to a variety of constituencies and cultures (academic, professional, popular, etc.).

5. Exploration of analytic and research methodologies, data processing, operations and techniques of any period, as these relate to he above topics, but especially of our own time as a means to advance and improve our knowledge of the past and thereby comprehension of the present. Forecasting, prediction, and speculation are legitimate concerns in this vein, both past occurrences and current attempts. This extends beyond the content information in History, but builds an arsenal of tools, methods, and techniques that advance historical inquiry and historical mindedness.

6. *Quo vadis?* Speculation about the past and present always relates to the future, since an underlying tenet of all historical thought is one of continuity through time. The progressive assumption in such thought is that we can improve the future through choices made now based on knowledge of the past. More than knowledge for its own sake, therefore, the idea in Historical Information Science contains an optimism and perhaps even a certain determinism to direct change, and hence to apply what is learned, and to re-engineer the present for continual betterment. It anticipates Knowledge Management (KM), one of the latest buzzwords in business and, in terms of project management and coordinated research and scholarly communications, does address the business of History as much as history in business or organizational management.

Those drawn to the idea of Historical Information Science, which admittedly has an underlying ideology inherent in the relationship between science and technology (i.e., science in action), would presumably have an idealistic ethos. In using information technology to accomplish what cannot be done otherwise, they would be committed to extending the human capacity to understand the past as an enhancement of the present and betterment of the future. At the same time practitioners would have to be practical and enjoy problem solving through technology, engineering, and science beyond description or narration, but also explanation. The orientation is ecumenical, comparative, engaging, and multidisciplinary precisely to accomplish unidisciplinary collaboration and synthesis. It entails reciprocity, that is, applying archives, library, museum, information, and administration sciences to History and *vice versa*, providing them with a useable history and embedding into these fields a pervasive historical consciousness. Finally, reflecting the difficulty in defining Historical Information Science within traditional disciplinary frameworks, it embodies a *mentalité*, character and cognitive style, which above all must be comfortable with the unknown, untried, and experimental, and understanding of the paradox that in a unidiscipline generality is in fact *the* specialization.

Epilogue

More and more history is done with a combination of the following: (1) evaluation of raw historical sources and data which are converted into machine-readable form; (2) some method of quantification or statistical analytics and collation or aggregation, and (3) the use of computers for processing, analysis, and communicating historical information. All forms of historical sources are being exploited—numeric, textual, visual, and oral. No period, subject, or area is left untouched. Every technology and methodology seems susceptible to adoption by historians, adaptation for historical research, and for use in communicating historical scholarship. No limits but the self-imposed are in sight. One of the most perplexing problems facing historians is that of "richness"—too much, too quickly, and too complex—because History is accumulative. Perhaps most lacking in their training is the organization of historical information itself, project management, and adroit use of modern information services to access historical literature and primary sources, for their own welfare, their teaching, and their research.

Historians will always be more interested in content analysis, interpretation, and the essence of History than in technology for its own sake or process for novelty. As they go on, historians will always look back; that is their fascination. It is not only what historians do, that is who they are. Reflection, research, analysis, synthesis, and new order from old; how they do this, or with what technology, is often coincidental. They will use whatever means and sources are at their disposal. The articulation of a Historical Information Science would entail a more deliberate, coherent, and strategic expansion of methodologies, creation of electronic sources, and application of information technology than is often the case now. The result may be ever more complicated history delving into its intricacies with more detail than could be managed by man alone, an enlargement of scope beyond the perception of the single seer, and recall greater than any previous generation could imagine.

This will take several of the collaboratories of the kind envisioned by the NATIONAL RESEARCH COUNCIL, a different model than what historians are accustomed to, rather than the kind of segregated and segmented teaching and research undertaken in most history departments, the individualized fellowship and grants programs of research libraries, the pension support of senior scholars by the Institute of Advanced Historical Studies at Princeton and its clones, or random mix of pursuits supported by fellowships at the National Center for the Humanities. Some historians, stimulated by the *Human Genome Project* for which the federal government in the United States spent $152 million in 1995 alone (COURTEAU; WILKIE), or the *Global Climate Change* and *Biological Diversity Documentation* initiatives that are commanding as much as $231 million, are now envisioning an electronically navigable *History of the Human Race* on an even larger scale than the current biogenetic or weather networks, which will require similar innovation and progress as in biological science, perhaps through a piggybacking of projects and combination of genetic and prosopographic research interests. Moreover, the *Human Genome Project* is exemplary in its self-documentation by its requirement to deposit data for research published (WELLER). Thus both a data and an electronic archives are produced as co-products of this research initiative. The historians who point to the *Human Genome Project* as a model are dreaming of a historical enterprise comparable to the growth of "big science" after the 1960s (GALISON & HEVLY)—which has never come to pass.

"Little Science," to adopt DE SOLA PRICE's contrasting terms, has had to suffice, even when the aspiration was global. Smaller projects, like the world immigration and migration project directed by Aristide Zolberg and Charles Tilly and funded by the MacArthur Foundation, if they were properly designed for later integration, may build eventually into such mega-sources through a bottom-up architecture. It is more likely, however, that because of scale, scope, and mass, the future will be one of Intranet communications for collaborative research in relatively small think tanks (perhaps more like pods really) and specialization centers, using Internet navigation between ever enlarged and complex multi-networks in an archival cyberspace resembling one interactive constellation after another. The management of such research, assuming that it should be managed collaboratively, will be difficult in any case; it will be almost impossible if such an art is not practiced by historians from their early careers, preferably from graduate school onward. Currently, historical research overall is unmanaged, and one must wonder also about project management in particular cases. I do not advocate micro-management, external direct control, or intervention that may be regarded as interference, so much as the management of the means, opportunity, and cooperation so important to large-scale collaborative History. Above all, I advocate explicit and objective self-management by historians and researchers themselves.

History might be served best not by overly managed research, therefore, so much as the development of guiding framework and the collaborative use of templates to build networked registries of historical databases, factual geo-chronological tools that could operate like historical thesauri, standards in methods and techniques for the construction of software toolkits and intelligent agents, and criteria for evidence, that would serve like metadata for reference, benchmarking, and specific kinds of historical analyses and methodologies. The new information technology affords opportunities now which historians have not had before. What is possible in contemplating the future of a "Networked Cultural Heritage"? Consider, for example, a metadata standard for biographic description in an HTML template that would capture not the essence of a person or attributes, but his or her defining characteristics similar to how one catalogs a book, i.e., cataloging a person as an information source but with event histories attached. This could be applied retrospectively to create a networked biographic dictionary on a scale never realizable before, with links, for example, from historical personages who were authors to bibliographic records of their works, updated by self-registration or data migration from census records. Or consider an historical place-name registry that similarly cataloged communities with chronologs, supporting a larger GIS that linked underground, surface, and aerial information with geo-biological and climatic information systems. Consider how research could be conducted if such a person, place, and time set of databases worked like data warehouses, in which data mining or new kinds of information retrieval and extraction techniques could be applied. Go further to conceive how such historical information systems might be linked to archives, libraries, and museums for document retrieval in any media. Understand the implications for new forms of critical apparati in the publication of historical research that do more than reference sources, but retrieves them, and thereby bring about historical research that is ever more auditable, accountable, verifiable, reliable, and re-countable because its use of evidence, methods of analysis, and logic in argumentation are traceable. Think about such possibilities on a global scale. Think systems, networks, mass, and speed in historical information retrieval to enable historians' work to enhance the archival-historical record, add the qualitative dimension, synthesize and interpret, debate and refine, in a continuous sense-making enterprise that is reflective, circumspect, and speculative. To achieve such a vision, the business of History must be transformed.

Meanwhile, as a realistic counterweight to such blue-sky envisioning, the *Humanities and Arts on the Information Highways Initiative* taskforce is skeptical about prospects for adequate funding even to have easy access to "information highway," to say nothing about what it would provide access to. The report concludes (p. 34):

> The humanities and arts require investment in the technologies that will permit consistent, reliable and widespread digital representation of our cultural heritage and enable that resource to be exploited with ease. This in turn requires understanding of the special characteristics of humanities and arts information (which demands precision of reference, preservation of context, and multiplicity of viewpoints) and appreciation of the barriers to its access (including connectivity of institutions holding such information, methods for protecting intellectual property, and open systems).

Although one might laugh at the naivete in thinking that the American federal government would ever spend the money needed to mount such an effort, one can dream and work toward making dreams reality. In this case, not even Virtual Reality will become real without such vision and united action. One can readily imagine, as done some time ago by Gene Roddenberry in his *Quaestor Tapes* or more recently in *Star Trek: The New Generation*, the future "historical workstation" as something well beyond any Virtual Reality envisioned now. A decade ago information scientists were beginning to react to coordinate indexing as passé, and were envisioning "the Global Brain" (GULL), while others remained skeptics about the historic and human limitations inherent in information retrieval. SWANSON characterized the fantasy in such speculation as "the Future of an Illusion." The illusion still exists, alluring as it is, but historical hindsight over just the last decade assists in pushing new visions further into the future and making older visions realities in our own time.

Historians should appreciate the popular bumper-sticker wisdom: "The future is not what it used to be." Envisioning possibilities, however, does not make them happen. The pragmatic realism that guides change constructively and with a sense of purpose and direction rests on historical sensibility. We know about future development, if we know our past; and we know that today's information technology is relatively primitive compared with what is to come shortly. It is critical that we take our past with us into the future, for sanity's sake, for self-identity and self-actualization, individually and collectively, and for retention of a critical circumspection. This requires engagement of past and current information technology, preservation of information on a massive scale never before possible in human affairs, and a monumental effort in retrieval, synthesis, and interpretation of which we are not yet capable but will be in the next millennium. Not only does the infrastructure have to be built, but educational reform must proceed, and an ease with and accommodation of technical change must find an accord between our own human nature, adaptability to change wrought by our own technology, continued imagination and creativity—and science too, even in History, and especially for historical information.

If History is indeed to participate in the development of the next millennium's heralded "Information Age," as it must, now is not too soon to reexamine its traditional posture, to reform itself, and to transcend current self-imposed limitations. It needs to strengthen its bridges between the Arts and Humanities and the Social Sciences, and the Sciences too, and while remaining syncretist and multi-disciplinary, find a unifying core of methods and achieve a graceful ease in applying information technology to its own needs. Such progress could be assisted by an identifiable or formalized unifying discipline, already called Historical Information Science, which places emphasis on methodology and technology equal to and proportional with traditional subject-area foci. Information Science and History would be mutually enhanced by such development. So, too, would modern society be enriched with better assurance that in the future with technique and technology we would also have culture and memory.

We could thereby guarantee continuous knowledge of the past and have a history upon which to reflect at present, so we might envision always brighter futures.

Appendices

APPENDIX A

Principles for NII Development in the United States

The following set of recommendations is distributed by the American Library Association and the Society of American Archivists as a public policy document relating to the establishment in the United States of the National Information Infrastructure (NII).

Principles for the Development of the National Information Infrastructure (NII)

First Amendment and Intellectual Freedom	Privacy	Intellectual Property	Ubiquity	Equitable Access	Interoperability
1. Access to the NII should be available and affordable to all regardless of age, religion, disability, sexual orientation, social and political views, national origin, economic status, location, information literacy, etc. **2.** The NII service providers must guarantee the free flow of information protected by the First Amendment. **3.** Individuals should have the right to choose what information to receive through the NII.	**1.** Privacy should be carefully protected and extended. **2.** Comprehensive policies should be developed to ensure that the privacy of all people is protected. **3.** Personal data collected to provide specific services should be limited to the minimum necessary. **4.** Sharing data collected from individuals should only be permitted with their information consent. **5.** Individuals should have the right to inspect and correct data files about themselves. **6.** Transaction data should remain confidential.	**1.** Intellectual property rights and protections are independent of the form of publication or distribution. **2.** The intellectual property system should ensure a fair and equitable balance between rights of creators and other copyright owners and the needs of users. **3.** Fair use and other exceptions to owners' rights in the copyright law should continue in the electronic environment. **4.** Compensation systems must provide a fair and reasonable return to copyright owners.	**1.** Libraries should preserve and enhance their traditional roles in providing access to information regardless of format. **2.** Network access costs for libraries, educational organization, government entities, and nonprofit groups should be stable, predictable, and location insensitive. **3.** Resources must be allocated to provide basic public access in fostering the development of the information infrastructure.	**1.** The NII should support and encourage a diversity of information providers in order to guarantee an open, fair, and competitive marketplace, with a full range of viewpoints. **2.** Diversity of access should be protected through use of nonproprietary protocols. **3.** Access to basic network services should be affordable to all. **4.** Basic network access should be made available independent of geographic location. **5.** The NII should ensure private, government, and nonprofit participation in governance of the network. **6.** Electronic information should be appropriately documented, organized, and archived through cooperative endeavors of information service providers and libraries.	**1.** The design of NII should facilitate two-way audio, video and data communication from anyone, easily and effectively. **2.** Interoperability standards should be encouraged and tied to incentives for the use of those standards in awards for federal funding. **3.** A transition phase should provide compatibility between leading-edge technology and trailing-edge technology to allow users reasonable protection from precipitate change. **4.** The federal government should encourage interoperability standards and should tie incentives to the use of those standards. **5.** Federal government information dissemination programs should adhere to interoperability standards. **6.** Principles of interoperability should require directory locator services and nonproprietary search protocols, as well as a minimal set of data elements for the description of databases.
Reprinted with permission from the American Library Association					

APPENDIX B

Internet/WWW Information Sources: A Select List of URLs

Key reference sites are noted by an asterisk for their guidance to other sites.

GENERAL INTERNET/WWW INFORMATION

SAVETZ, KEVIN, comp. 1993-. *Unofficial Internet Book List.* Redwoods, CA; 1993-. Accessible at http//redwood.northcoast.com/savetz/booklist/. Ongoing bibliography of 500+ reference tools about the Internet and World Wide Web, including reviews.

History of the Internet. 1995-. Tucson, AZ: University of Arizona, 1995-. Accessible at http://ccit.arizona.edu/Internet/inhist.html.

ARCHIVES SITES (see L. MILLER)

* INTERNATIONAL COUNCIL ON ARCHIVES (IAC). COMMITTEE ON ELEC-TRONIC RECORDS. 199-. *Electronic Records Management.* Paris, FR: ICA; 199-. Accessible at http://www.archives.ca/ica/english.html. See the literature review about electronic records management, coverage through 1996, by Alf Erlandson; and 1994-95 survey of electronic records programs in archives.

* NATIONAL ARCHIVES AND RECORDS ADMINISTRATION (NARA). 1996-. *NARA.* Washington, DC: NARA; 1996-. Accessible at http://www.nara.gov. See for NARA's holdings. Extensions go directly to specific formats, e.g.,.../nara/nail.html for the Audiovisual Information Locator Database (NAIL);.../gils.html for Government Information Locator (GILS); and for electronic records title lists use http://gopher.nara.gov:70/1/inform/dc/electr.

* NATIONAL ARCHIVES AND RECORDS ADMINISTRATION (NARA). NATIONAL HISTORICAL PUBLICATIONS AND RECORDS COMMISSION (NHPRC). 1996-. *NHPRC Homepage.* Maintained at the University of Pittsburgh. Accessible at http://www.lis.pitt. edu/~nhprc/.

* NATIONAL ARCHIVES OF CANADA. 199-. *Managing Electronic Records.* Ottawa, CAN: NAC, 199-. Accessible at http://www.archives.ca.

* NATIONAL ARCHIVES OF CANADA. 1996-. *Open Government.* Ottawa, CAN: NAC, 1996-. Accessible at http://www.opengov.ca.

* *NET GO.* 1995-. Miller, Leon C., ed. New Orleans, LA: Tulane University Archives; 1995-. Accessible at http://www.tulane.edu/~lmiller/ReadyNetGo.html. Miller claims this site is for "one-stop shopping" for archival Internet sources, with hyperlinks to all relevant sources for Archives, but also to History sites. Supersedes older archives gopher sites such as gopher://una.hh.lib.umich.edu:70/00/inetdirsstacks/archives% Akaynthony, an early standby which ceased updating in 1994.

* SITE D'INFORMATION SUR LA GESTION DES DOCUMENTS ADMINISTRAT-IFS ET DES DOCUMENTS D'ARCHIVES. 1995-. Roberge, Michel, ed. [Paris] FR; CNRT; [1995]-. Accessible at http://www.medium.qc.ca/~ robergem/sigda.html. SIGDA claims to be a premier international cybersite for administrative documentation and archival documents.

* SOCIETY OF AMERICAN ARCHIVISTS. 1994-. *US-SAA*. Austin, TX: University of Texas SAA Student Chapter for SAA; 1994-. Accessible at http://volvo.gslis. ute.edu/~us-saa/. Contains SAA membership, and annual conference information.

* SOCIETY OF AUSTRALIAN ARCHIVISTS. 1995-. *Australian Archives*. Sydney: SAA; 1995-. Accessible at http://www.aa.au-//WWW/aa-home-page.html. Cf., http://www.aa. gov.au.

* SOCIETY OF SOUTHWEST ARCHIVISTS. [1995]-. *Daybook*. Miller, Lee, ed. New Orleans, LA: Tulane University Archives for SSA; [1995}-. Accessible at http:// www.tulane.edu/-lmiller/Daybook.html. Derived from "Archivist's Daybook" feature of the *Southwestern Archivist*.

* UNITED STATES DEPARTMENT OF DEFENSE. 1997-. *Records Management*. Washington, D.C.: DOD. 1997-. Accessible at http://www.dtic.dla.mil/c3i/recmgmt. html.

* UNIVERSITY OF TEXAS. GRADUATE SCHOOL OF LIBRARY & INFORMA-TION SCIENCE. [1995]-. *Archives and Special Collections*. Nacke, Laura, ed. Austin, TX: University of Texas GSLIS; [1995]-. Accessible at http://volvo.gslis.utex.edu/ ~epcss/list.html. Sublist of University of Texas SAA Student Chapter homepage *US-SAA*, with instructions for using listservs.

* UTAH STATE ARCHIVES. 199-. *Archives Reference*. Salt Lake City, UT: Utah State Archives, 199-. Accessible at http://utstdpwww.state.us/~archives/referenc/!archive. htm. Numerous pointers to other archives sites.

ARTS SITES (see also museums)

* *Artsource*. 199-. Lexington, KY: University of Kentucky, 1999-. http://www.uky. edu/Artsource/general.html.

* GETTY ART HISTORY INFORMATION PROJECT (AHIP). 1993-. Los Angeles, CA; The Getty Trust; 1993-. Accessible at http://www.ahip.getty.edu/ahip.

* NEW YORK FOUNDATION FOR THE ARTS. 1994-. *Arts Wire*. New York, NY: NY Foundation for the Arts; 1994-. Available as subscription at http://www.tmn. com/Artswire/ www/awfront.html.

* SMITHSONIAN INSTITUTION. ARCHIVES OF AMERICAN ART. 1995-. *Art Archives*. Washington, DC: Smithsonian Institution; 1995-. Accessible via telnet:// sirs.si.edu, and select "archives" from menu.

* SMITHSONIAN INSTITUTION. NATIONAL MUSEUM OF AMERICAN ART. 1994-. *Inventory of American Painting and Sculpture*. Washington, DC: Smithsonian Institution Museum of American Art; 1994-. Accessible at http://www.nmaa.si.edu. Database of 300,000 American artist paintings and sculpture.

* *WORLD WIDE ARTS RESOURCES*. [1994]-. World Wide Arts Resources, Inc.; 1994-. Accessible at http://www.concourse.com/wwar/defaultnew.html. Provides 9,000 classified arts resources.

HISTORY SITES

* *Historical Text Archives.* [1994]-. Mawbry, Dan, ed. State University, MS: Mississippi State University College of Arts and Sciences and Computing Center; 1994-. Accessible at http://www.msstate. edu/Archives/History.index.html. ASCII historical document textfiles, American historical papers, diaries, bibliographies, etc., with hyperlinks to other sites.

* *History Computerization Project.* 1995. Accessible at http://www.directnet.com/ history. Index for history resources, History department homepages, and teaching materials.

* *History Resources.* 1993-. Lawrence KS: University of Kansas; 1993-. Accessible at http://history.cc.ukans.edu/history/WWW-history-main.html. WWW consortium approved history resource page, with links to listservs, discussion lists, conferences, and sites around the world selected for history content.

* *Journal of Artificial Societies and Social Simulation (JASSS).* 1998-. Surrey, UK; January 1998-. Accessible at http://www.soc.surrey.ac.uk/JASSS/

LIBRARY SITES

INTERNATIONAL FEDERATION OF LIBRARY ASSOCIATIONS AND INSTITUTIONS (IFLA). 1993-. IFLA Web Site. IFLA, 1993. Accessible at http://www.nlc-bnc.ca/ ifla/home.htm. LIBRARY OF CONGRESS. 1993. *American Special Collections.* Washington, DC: LC; 1993-. Accessible at http://lcweb.loc.gov/spcollhome.html. Linked to main LC site.

* LIBRARY OF CONGRESS. 1993. *American Memory Project.* Washington, DC: LC; 1993-. Accessible at http://rs6.loc.gov/amhome.html. Linked to main LC site.

* LIBRARY OF CONGRESS. 1993. *Library of Congress Homepage.* Washington, DC: LC; 1993-. Accessible at http://lcweb.loc.gov/homepage/lchp.html. Main LC site, linked to *American Special Collections* and *American Memory Project.*

* UNIVERSITY OF WASHINGTON. 1995-. *Library an Archives Exhibits.* Prietto, Carole, ed. Seattle,WA; University of Washington; 1995-. Accessible at http:// library.wustl.edu/~prietto/exhibits. Exhibits listed alphabetically by title in libraries, archives and museums that are viewable on a Web site.

MUSEUM SITES (see reference: KALFATOVIC)

* MUSEUM COMPUTER NETWORK. 1995-. Accessible via http://world.std.com/ %7Emcn/MCN.html.

* SMITHSONIAN INSTITUTION. 1993-. *Smithsonian Institution Homepage.* Washington, DC: Smithsonian Institution; 1993-. Accessible at http://www.si.edu. Links are provided to extensive system of Web pages for each museum in the system.

* UNIVERSITY OF NORTH CAROLINA. 1994-. *Web Museum Network.* Accessible at http://sunsite.unc.edu//wm/.

* OXFORD UNIVERSITY. 1994-. *Museums Page.* Oxford, UK: Oxford University; 1994-. Accessible at http://www.comlab.ox.ac.uk/archive/other/museums.html.

WWW Virtual Library Museums Page traces online exhibitions; indexes museum homepages.

PROJECT SITES

TEXT ENCODING INITIATIVE. 1995-. *Text Encoding Initiative Homepage* (Electronic file). Available at: http://www.uic.edu:80/orgs/tei/.

* N-Net, c. 1996-. *H-Net Homepage*. East Lansing, MI: Michigan State University; c. 1996-. Available at http://h-net2.edu.

H-Net Lists January 1, 1996

For these lists, send subscribe message to LISTSERV@UICVM.UIC.EDU

1.	H-Antis	Antisemitism
2.	H-Italy	Italian history and culture
3.	H-Urban	Urban history
4.	HOLOCAUS	Holocaust studies
5,	H-Ideas	Intellectual history
6.	IEAHCnet	Colonial; 17-18th century Americas

For these lists, send subscribe message to LISTSERV@MSU.EDU

7.	H-Africa	African history
8.	H-Albion	British and Irish history
9.	H-AmReI	American religious history
10.	H-AmStdy	American studies
11.	H-Asia	Asian studies & history
12.	H-Canada	Canadian history & studies
13.	H-C lvWar	US Civil War
14.	H-C LC	Comparative literature & computing
15.	H-Demog	Demographic history
16.	H-DlpIo	Diplomatic history, International affairs
17.	H-Ethnic	Ethnic, immigration & emigration studies
18.	H-Film	Scholarly studies & uses of media
19.	H-German	German history
20.	H-Grad	For graduate students only
21.	H-High-S	Teaching high school history/social studies
22.	H-Judaic	Judaica, Jewish History
23.	H-Labor	Labor history
24.	H-LatAm	Latin American history
25.	H-Law	Legal and constitutional history
26.	H-Local	State and local history & museums
27.	H-Mac	Macintosh users
28.	H-M Media	High-tech. teaching; multimedia; CD-ROM
29.	H-NZ-OZ	New Zealand & Australian history

30. H-PCAACA	Popular Culture Assoc. & American Culture Assn.	
31. H-RevIew	H-Net book reviews (reviews only, no discussions)	
32. H-Rhetor	History of rhetoric & communications	
33. H-Rural	Rural and agricultural history	
34. H-Russia	Russian history	
35. H-SAE	European anthropology	
36. H-SHGAPE	US Gilded Age & Progressive Era	
37. H-South	US South	
38. H-Survey	Teaching US Survey	
39. H-State	Welfare state; "putting the state back in"	
40. H-Teach	Teaching college history	
41. H-W-Civ	Teaching Western Civilization	
42. H-West	US West frontiers	
43. H-Women	Women's history	
44. H-World	World history	

For these lists, send subscribe to LISTSERV@KSUVM.KSU.EDU

45. H-Pol	American politics	
46. H-War	Military history	

For these lists, send subscribe to LISTSERV@VM.CC.PURDUE.EDU

47. H-France	French history	
48. Habsburg	Austro-Hungarian Empire	

For this affiliated list (reviews only, no discussion),
write LISTSERV@LISTSERV.ACNS.NWU.EDU

49. LPBR-L	Law & Politics Book Review	

For this affiliated list write to H-MEXICO@5ERVIDOR.UNAM.MX

50. H-MEXICO	Mexican history and studies	

For these affiliated Cliometric Society lists, send subscribe message to
LISTSOCS.MUOHIO.EDU

51. H-Business	Business history (cosponsored by H-Net)	
52. Databases	Design & management of historical databases	
53. EH.RES	Economic history short research notes & queries	
54. EH.DISC	Economic history extended discussion	
55. EH.NEWS	Economic history bulletin board	
56.		
57.		
58. EconHist.Student	Students & faculty in economic history	
59. EconHlst.Teach	Teaching economic history	
60. GIobaI.change	Economic history dimensions of global change	

61. Quanhist.recurrent   Comparative recurrent phenomena

PLANNING STAGE: (FOR 1996) (INQUIRIES TO H-NETOUICVM.UIC.EDU)

62. H-Af-Am   African American studies
63. H-Amlnt   American Intellectual history
64. APPALNET   Appalachian studies
65. H-Ed   History of Education
66. H-Japan   Japanese studies
67. H-MusText   Lyrical texts; opera
68. H-SHEAR   Early American Republic
69. H-Skand   Scandinavian history & culture
70. H-UC LEA   Labor Studies
71. H-Ukraln   Ukrainian studies
72. H-Major   For Undergraduate history majors
73. H-USA   For Teaching American History
                    and Studies Abroad

H-Net Gophers: try the H-Net gopher at H-Net.msu.edu
H-Net's WWW home page: hffp://h-net.msu.edu

APPENDIX C

Functional Requirements of Recordkeeping Systems

The following guidelines encapsulate the work of D. BEARMAN (1994, Appendix, pp. 294-304) related to the NHPRC-funded University of Pittsburgh *Recordkeeping Functional Requirements Project* (vol. 1, 1994; vol. 2, 1995). It is reproduced in this appendix as a recommendation for all databased historical research projects for the effective transfer of databases to electronic archives. The version below is a synopsis of the draft on November 10, 1994 for "Pure Form tactics" (vol. 2 [1995], pp. 85-104).

Organization

1.   Compliant

Accountable Record Keeping System

2.   Responsible
3.   Implemented
4.   Reliable

Captured Records

5.   Comprehensive
6.   Identifiable
7.   Complete
   7a.   Accurate
   7b.   Understandable
   7c.   Meaningful
8.   Authentic

Maintained Records

9.   Preserved
   9a.   Inviolate
   9b.   Coherent
   9c.   Auditable
10.   Removable

Usable Records

11.   Exportable
12.   Accessible
   12a.   Available
   12b.   Renderable
   12c.   Evidential
13.   Redactable

David Bearman
University of Pittsburgh Electronic Records Project
1994 DRAFT SPECIFICATIONS

Functional Requirements for Recordkeeping
1994 DRAFT SPECIFICATIONS

Functional Requirements for Recordkeeping

Organization—Compliance

1.   Compliant: Organizations must comply with the legal and administrative requirements for recordkeeping within the jurisdictions in which they operate, and demonstrate awareness of best practices for the industry or business sector to which they belong and the business functions in which they are engaged.

   1a)   External recordkeeping requirements are known.

      1a1)   Laws of jurisdictions with authority over the record creating organizations are known.

1a2) Regulatory issuances of entities with administrative authority over the record creating organizations are known.

1a3) Best practices of recordkeeping established by professional and business organizations within the industry and business functions of the organization are known.

1b) Records created by organizational business transactions which are governed by an external recordkeeping requirements are linked to an internal retention rule referencing the documented law, regulation, or statement of best practice.

1c) Laws, regulations, and statements of best practice with requirements for recordkeeping are tracked so that changes to them are reflected in updated internal recordkeeping instructions.

Record Keeping Systems—Accountability

2. Responsible: Recordkeeping systems must have accurately documented policies, assigned responsibilities, and formal methodologies for their management.

2a) System policies and procedures are written and changes to them are maintained and current.

2b) A person or office is designated in writing as responsible for satisfying recordkeeping requirements in each system.

2c) System management methods are defined for all routine tasks.

2d) System management methods are defined for events m which the primary system fails.

3. Implemented: Recordkeeping systems must be exclusively employed in the normal course of business.

3a) Business transactions are conducted only through the documented recordkeeping system and its documented exception procedures.

3b) No records can be created in the recordkeeping systems except through execution of a business transaction.

3c) Recordkeeping systems and/or documented exception procedures can be demonstrated to have been operating at all times.

4. Reliable: Recordkeeping systems must process information in a fashion that assures that the records they create are credible.

4a) Identical data processes permitted by the system must produce identical outcomes regardless of the conditions under which they are executed.

4b) Results of executing Systems logic are demonstrable outside the system.

4c) All operational failures to execute instructions are reported by the system.

4d) In the event of system failures, processes under way are recovered and re-executed.

Records—Captured

5. Comprehensive: Records must be created for all business transactions.

5a)   Communications in the conduct of business between two people, between a person and a store of information available to others, and between a source of information and a person, generate a record.

5b)   Data interchanged within and between computers under the control of software employed in the conduct of business creates a record when the consequence of the data processing function is to modify records subsequently employed by people in the conduct of business.

6.   Identifiable: Records must be bounded by linkage to a transaction which used all the data in the record and only that data.

6a)   There exists a discrete record, representing the sum of all communications associated with a business transaction.

6b)   All data in the record belongs to the same transaction.

6c)   Each record is uniquely identified.

7.   Complete: Records must contain the content, structure and context generated by the transaction they document.

7a)   Accurate: The content of records must be quality controlled at input to ensure that information in the system correctly reflects what was communicated in the transaction.

7al)   Data capture practices and system indictions ensure that source data is exactly replicated by system or corrected to reflect values established in system authority files.

7b)   Understandable: The relationship between elements of information content must be represented in a way that supports their intended meaning.

7bl)   Meaning conveyed by placement or appearance of data are retained or represented

7b2)   System defined views or permissions are retained and the effects are reflected in the record are represented.

7b3)   Logical relations defined across physical records are retained or represented.

7b4)   Software functionality invoked by data values in the content of the record are supported or represented.

7c)   Meaningful: The contextual linkages of records must carry information necessary to correctly understand the transactions that created and used them.

7cl)   The business niles for transactions, which minially locate the transaction within a business function, are maintained.

7c2)   A representation of the source and time of the transaction which generated a record is maintained.

7c3)   Links between records which comprised a business activity are retained.

8.   Authentic: An authorized records creator must have originated all records.

8a)   All records have creators which are documented.

8b)   Records creators must have been authorized to engage in the business transaction that generated the record.

8c) A knowledge-base of persons authorized to engage in business transactions is maintained and either operates as a control over system functions such that transactions could not occur without being authorized and/or documents the authorization of the creator as part of the record.

Records—Maintained

9. Preserved: Records must continue to reflect content structure and context within any systems by which the record are retained over time.

9a) Inviolate: Records are protected from accidental or intended damage or destruction and from any modification.

9a1) No data within a record may be deleted, altered or lost once the transaction which generated it has occurred.

9b) Coherent: The information content and structure of records must be retained in reconstructable relations.

9b1) If records are migrated to new software environments, content, structure and context information must be lied to software functionality that preserves their executable connections or representations of their relations must enable humans to reconstruct the relations that pertained in the original software environment.

9b2) Logical record boundaries must be preserved regardless of physical representations.

9c) Auditable: Record context represents all processes in which records participated.

9c1) All uses of records are transactions.

9c2) Transactions which index, classify, schedule, file, view, copy, distribute, or move a record without altering it are documented by audit trails attached to the original record.

9.c3) Transactions which execute a records disposition instruction whether for retention or destruction are documented by audit trails attached to the original record.

10. Removable: Records content and structure supporting the meaning of content must be deletable.

10a) Authority for deletion of record content and structure exists.

10b) Deletion transactions are documented as audit trails.

10c) Deletion transactions remove the content and structural information of records without removing audit trails reflecting context.

Records—Usable

11. Exportable: It must be possible to transmit records to other systems without loss of information.

11a) Exporting protocols should be reversible or the lost functionality should be represented in a fashion that produces the same result in the target system as in the originating environment.

12. Accessible: It must be possible to output record content, structure and context.

12a) Available: Records must be retrievable.

12al) The system must be able to retrieve the record of any transaction at any later date.

12b) Renderable: Records must display, print or be abstractly represented as they originally appeared at the time of creation and initial receipt.

12bl) The structure of data in a record must appear to subsequent users as it appeared to the recipient of the record in the original transaction or a human meaningful representation of that original rendering should accompany the presentation of the original content.

12c) Evidential: Records must reflect the context of their creation and use.

12c1) A human meaningful representation of the contextual audit trail of a record must accompany all displays or printed output.

13. Redactable: Records must be masked when it is necessary to deliver censored copies and the version as released must be documented in a linked transaction.

13a) The release of redacted versions of a record is a discrete business transaction.

13b) The fact of the release of a redacted version of a record is an auditable use of the original record and therefore results in creation of an audit trail with a link to the transaction which released the redaction.

APPENDIX D

Action Recommendations for Historical Associations

MEMBERSHIP

- Personally improve computing skills beyond word processing, actively use the INTERNET, and engage in an H-Net listserv of interest.

- Encourage faculty development through offerings to improve information skills from local computer centers, libraries, archives, and media centers.

- Actively participate in library, archives, historical society boards, advisory committees, and Friends groups.

- Integrate bibliographic instruction in course work and ally with the Information Literacy movement.

- Form alliances with resource allocators for development of information services, computing assistance, and access to information technology for faculty and students alike. Develop local and online support groups.

- Attend conferences and contribute to association activities in the information professions, to insert historical concerns in their agenda and foster History awareness among their memberships.

- Specify in published work the exact methodologies used with justification, and standardize referencing to datasets and electronic records for retrieval, verification, and reuse.

ASSOCIATIONS

- Form standing committees, task forces, and division-level policy making groups for Historical Information concerns, to monitor technological development, policies, funding, etc., and make news systematically available to the membership. Draw upon overlapping memberships from associations such as the Association for the Bibliography of History (ABH), International Association for History and Computing (IAHC), Association for Computing and the Humanities (ACH), and the Social Science History Association.

- Develop in-house expertise and a cadre of information professionals devoted to historical information issues, services, and project consultation.

- Participate with formal delegations to EDUCOM and CAUSE (now combined as EDUCAUSE) and the National Coalition for Networked Information.

- Participate organizationally in national and international standards formulation and development.

- Develop standards other than stylistic preferences for citation and reference, especially to electronic records; create guidelines and criteria for reviews; and promote use of standard thesauri for improved communications and information retrieval from historiographic literature.

- Use a listserv and the H-Net to post briefings on information technology, science, and policy issues affecting the History community. Prepare White Papers and position statements on key issues.

- Monitor legislation and lobby for funding for technology and research.

- Improve professional association-sponsored bibliographic control of History literature.

- Strengthen bonds between AHA/OAH, ALA, SAA, and ASIS for cooperative interdisciplinary programs and a coalition to support progressive information policies, technology support, and information and cultural institutions (archives, libraries, museums).

- Support the visibility of information technology, methods, and issues in international fora such as Comité International de Sciences Historiques (CISH), and insert historical issues into international information professional fora such as International Federation of Library Associations (IFLA), International Congress of Archives (ICA), etc.

- Adopt "best practice" standards for information management in historical associations themselves, to lead by example.

- Mount affordable continuing education programs relating information technology to historical research interests, scheduled with national conferences; some of these could be cooperative ventures with information profession associations.

- Identify universities with commitments to advanced education, research, and continuing education in fields relating to Historical Information Science to promote selected national centers of excellence. Seek NSF support for these technical support centers and INTERNET nodes, to create a network to assist historians in and out of academe with educational programs, workshops, online tutorials and reference assistance, and promotion of Historical Computer Science with attendant software development and impact on the information industry. Perhaps use the Medieval Academy of America's approach to networking Centers of Medieval Studies as a prototype.

- Promote the appointment of computer-literate and computing historians to faculties of Library and Information Science, Archival studies, ISM faculty in Business schools, Computer Science, and in academic libraries, academic computing centers, and archives.

- Participate in cross-disciplinary political action and lobby groups such as the Coalition for Networked Information, CAUSE, NINCH, and other alliances to further the best interests of libraries, archives, museums, and related academic computing to build a proper infrastructure for source preservation, global networking, and linked collaboratories; and to keep open telecommunications and networks to insure access to sources and the free flow of information.

APPENDIX E

Historical Information Science Graduate Program Curricular Guide

Knowledge Area   Course Array   Competencies and Skills   Experiences,   Examples

Prerequisites   Undergraduate degree (BA or BS) with acceptable major, including:

History Survey Knowledge of Western Civilization
Foreign Language(s) (reading proficiency)
Algebra and Basic Statistics (college level)
English Composition (mastery)
Introduction to Computing (minimum: clerical utility)

History Fields

Historical fields of study chronologically and geographically defined, which may aim for comprehensive coverage therein or may specialize further by matching a field with a subject area. Field definitions are usually constructed from a Western Civilization core branching out to non-Western areas as follows:

Ancient/Classical History (Near East to Mediterranean)
Medieval History (Latin and Byzantine), subdivided by region and rough periodization of early, high, and late eras.
Early Modern Europe and Expansion History
Modern Europe (national histories by century) with scope extended to Slavic areas.
American History (United States and Canada, Latin America): periodization roughly by centuries (colonial, early independence, national, etc.) broken down further by country and region.
Non-Western History: African and Asian History subdivided by region and culture.

Subject Areas Matched with History Fields:

Social, Political, Economic, Cultural, Intellectual, etc. (and combinations thereof, i.e., socioeconomic). These orientations often suggest coursework outside History Departments *per se*, in the aligned discipline (e.g., Sociology, Political Science and Government, Economics, etc.). This inter-disciplinarity can be extended to a degree that History *per se* is simply *primus inter pares* in the program, as it often is in Medieval or American Studies programs. Cultural History traditionally allies with Language and Literature, rather than Art or Music History although this is changing. History of ... (discipline of profession) courses (Art, Music, Law, Business, Commerce, etc. are especially useful.

Courses: *Historiography* (History of History); *Bibliography of History* (distinct from Historical Bibliography); Colloquia (discussion fora); Seminars (group research); Directed Research (tutorial); Practica (laboratory), Field Work, Assistantships (project setting) and Internships (work setting).

History Specializations

Courses designed around a special form, process, subject (distinct from topic), etc. for concentrated focus and detailed exposure to exemplars and examination and appraisal criteria and techniques.

> <u>Courses:</u>
>
> *Historical Bibliography* (History of formal/academic communications, manuscripts, books, scribal production, printing, publishing, author biography, etc.)
>
> *History of Science, Technology and Production* (history of artifacts, products, design and development, applications of technique and method, manufacturing, production and distribution, use, and business, etc.)
>
> *Legal History* (Laws, Codes, interpretation, courts, biography, etc.)
>
> *Archives History* (history of archives literature, recordkeeping, records management, use, archival institutions, profiles and biography, professions, etc.)
>
> *Library History* (history of library literature, librarianship, collections, libraries, librarians, professions, etc.)
>
> *Museum/Gallery History* (history of art and artifact collections, collectors, institutions, profession, including anthropological or historical, and art museums)
>
> *History of [Process* or form specialization] (e.g., Photography, Computing, Writing, Printing, Telecommunications)
>
> > <u>Competencies and skills:</u> Field content and survey knowledge; Literature and ennumerative bibliography survey knowledge; source identification, reading, and interpretation; historical conceptualization and hypothesis framing; argumentation and logic; basic data collection and analysis; historiographic writing and presentation.
> >
> > <u>Experiences:</u> Library use; Archives use; online use; Reading, interpreting, discussing primary and secondary literature; bibliographic surveys; analytic and expository writing (critical reviews, essays, term papers, research projects; thesis and dissertation or capstone projects.

Source Criticism and Research Methods

Methodological courses designed for specific information formats where a general competence is acquired in a methodological discipline, and research is attempted and practiced in a History field and subject-area.

> *Statistics* (advanced, i.e., to regression, multivariate and time/series analyses, validation tests, stochastic models, probability, etc.)
>
> *Graphics and Image Analysis* (knowledge representation, graphics interpretation, cognition, etc.)
>
> *Art Interpretation and Iconography*
>
> *Codicology and Analytical Bibliography* (Codification, physical bibliography [manuscript and printed])
>
> *Diplomatics and Paleography* (format criticism; script interpretation and classification)
>
> *Numismatics* (currency history, valuation, exchange)
>
> *Cartography* (maps, charts, GIS tools)
>
> *Chronology* (Calendaring; periodization and Time/Series Analysis)
>
> *Legal and Forensic Evidence* (Appraisal, admissibility, use)
>
> *Literary and textual criticism* (in appropriate languages)
>
> *Discourse Analysis and Applied Linguistics*
>
> *Semiotics*

Lexicology, Lexicography (word studies, especially for historical vocabularies, terminologies, orthography, etc.)

Competencies and skills: Statistical modeling; regression, frequency, probability, and variant analysis; Text processing, coding, mark-up, and source dissection; Translation and transliteration; Content analysis, concordancing, collocation; Standardization, records linkage, data conversion, etc. Contextual historical knowledge (actors and actions; original purposes and intentions, functions and operations, techniques and technology; institutional settings, provenance, etc.). Aesthetics and diplomacy in publication, formal presentation, and information delivery.

Experiences: Use of basic statistical packages like *SAS*, *SPSS*, *Histcal*, spreadsheets, etc.; e-mail communications and listserv participation; use of basic media technology (video, film, etc.) to test a research proposal with a trial run, sample experiment, etc., then to complete a study using appropriate methodologies, techniques, technology, etc., and finally to present it both in scholarly form for publication and personally as either a course module or conference presentation.

Information Science

Coursework aimed at objectives such as: (1) the management of information resources for access, dissemination, and use including research projects and teaching; (2) the study of human communications and information behaviors as well as the systems and technologies that enhance communication, information storage and retrieval, access, use, and learning; and (3) the design, implementation, and evaluation of instructional technology, information systems, and large-scale, long-range institutionalized research projects.

Courses:
Reference and Instructional Services
Classification and Cataloging AACR, (taxonomies, descriptive standards)
Information Storage and Retrieval (including Indexing, Abstracting, Thesauri)
Information Theory and Design
Knowledge Representation (Graphics, interfaces, etc.)
Archives and Records Management (electronic records emphasis)
Administration of Information Systems and Services (all settings, stress on automation)
Information Behaviors and Use
Research and Development (R&D) (Project design and management)
Information Policy and Law
Scholarly Communications
Cognitive Psychology and Learning Theory
Information/Instructional Media and Interactive Technology

Competencies and skills: use of taxonomies, controlled vocabularies, syntax, and association/relational logic; application of knowledge of behavioral aspects of information processing; unobtrusive and qualitative research methods; survey analysis; application of learning theory to information transfer and education; etc.

Experiences: online searching; use studies; interviewing; teaching and reference practica; performance appraisal (direct observation, video, time-motion studies, traffic flow analyses, etc.), briefing simulations; proposal drafts; diagnostic exercises (measurement and evaluation); etc.

Computer Science and Technology

Courses aimed at the provision of technical competence in computing and telecommunications.

> Courses:
>
> *Programming* (languages plus toolkit use)
> *DBMS* (DataBase Management Systems)
> *CAD* (Computer-Assisted Design/Drafting; Visualization)
> *Data Structures* and Computer Organization
> *Software Engineering* (Design and Appraisal)
> *Computer Graphics and Interfaces*
> *Artificial Intelligence* (Expert and Decision Support Systems)
> *Knowledge Engineering* (DataBase design)
> *Telecommunications and Networking*
> *Hardware and system diagnostics* (troubleshooting)
> *Computational Mathematics & Operations*
> *Computational Linguistics* (semantic and syntactic structures)
> *Modeling and Simulation (Knowledge Management)*
>
>> Competencies and skills: utility of *Access, BASIC* or *C+*, plus toolkits like *FoxPro*; files management; data conversion and transfer, normalization of data; query language utility; interface modification and design; history tree structures; OCR, *LISP/Scheme, Prolog;* and Natural Language Processing (NLP); digitization, scanning, and CD-ROM mastering; specification development, installation and testing of software, etc.
>>
>> Experiences: laboratory exercises and exposure to a variety of software first through demonstration and leading to self-teaching, software evaluation, and appraisal of packages for specific applications; games and simulations, etc.

Capstone Project / Thesis / Dissertation

These options at the culmination of formal study entail directed research in a chosen historical field and subject area, leading to a useable demonstration project or publishable study that demonstrates mastery and application of research methods and techniques, the application of information technology and the use of computing operations. The difference between a thesis and dissertation may be a matter of scope and size, the former being smaller, exploratory, and perhaps a prelude to the latter, but not a substantive difference in quality. The examining committee should be inter-disciplinary, including extra-departmental faculty, reflecting the distribution of course work outlined above. A Capstone project for a non-thesis master's with a practice rather than theoretical research reorientation nevertheless entails directed research. The project, like a thesis, should involve design, data collection and analysis, implementation, and evaluation, parallel to the processes of research design, data collection and analysis, synthesis and writing, presentation and defense in a thesis program. The dissertation, culminating doctoral work, should demonstrate not only mastery at the level of a master's degree, but also self-direction and initiative resulting in a mature production accepted by peer review, plus demonstration of capacity and potential for continued research and productivity.

APPENDIX F

Information Technology (IT) Development Timeline

Time	General	Corporate	Hardware	Software	Networking
1500	DaVinci's sketches	Wheel-based calculator			
1600s	Music notation systems	Programmed music boxes			
					Earliest step-by-step programming
1642	B. Pascal's math	Mechanical calculator			
1672	G. W. Leibnitz' Calculus	Business calculators			
1700s	Industrialization				
1725	Bouchon's programs	Programmable weaving machine			
1785	Cartwright's	Programmed power loom			
1800s	Business applications				
1804	J-M. Jacquard's applications	Programmable loom			
1820	T. de Colmar's work	Arithometer machine			
1822	C. Babbage	Analytical or Difference Engine-1833			
1840s				Ada Byron's speculations about programming	
1847-	G. Boole's Algebra (-1851)				
1987	D. E. Felt's Computations	Comptometer patented			
1890	H. Hollerith's inventions	Tabulating machine & Hollerith punched cards			
1890s		Computing-Tabulating-Recording Company formed (forerunner of IBM)			
1892		W. Burroughs adding machines			
1911		CTR (Computer-Tabulating Machines) forerunner of IBM			
1924		CTR renamed IBM			
1930	V. Bush		Differential analyzer		
1937	H. Aiken's mechanical computer project-1944				
			Harvard Mark I		
1938	Bell Lab's work		Relay-based computers		
	J. Atansopff & C. Berry's collaboration		Electronic digital calculator		
	K. Zuse's work		Z1 machine		
1939			Zuse's Vacuum tube computer		
1941			Z3 Program-controlled calculator		
1942	J. Atanasopf & C. Berry's work		ABC digital computer		
1943	T. H. Flower's British		Colossus cipher machine	Electronic clocked logic	
	J. Mauchly & S. P. Eckert's work at Penn's Moore School				
1944	H. Aiken at IBM		Mark I (ASCC) successful testing		
1945	V. Bush's Memex idea (MIT)				
1946			Electronic Numerical Integrator & Computer (ENIAC,-1955) co-invented by J. Maulchy & J. Presper Eckert		
				Decimal-based computing	
		Bell Lab's Model V			
	Bell Lab team:		Transistors		
	J. Barden, W. Schockley & W. Brattain				
1947		ACM (Assn. for Computing Machinery)-			
1948	H. Aitken's redesigns at IBM	Harvard Mark II relay machine			
	A. M. Turing Machine			AI beginnings	
1950s			Several types of relay machines		
	J. Forrester's real-time work at MIT		Whirlwind system		

Time	General	Corporate	Hardware	Software	Networking
1950s	W. B. Shockley's work		Transistors and semiconductors		
			Magnetic core memory		
1951			EDVAC (Electronic Discrete Variable Automatic Computer)		
			Binary-base computer		
			UNIVAC (Universal Automatic Computer)		
1953		IBM begins making computers			
1955		Remington Rand and Sperry merger=Sperry Rand Corporation			
				E. Dijkstra's programmer's terminology	
1957	USSR launches Sputnik			G. Hopper's compiler programming	
	US sci-tech initiatives			J. Backus develops FORTRAN at IBM	
		ARPA (Advanced Research Projects Agency) in US DOD			
		SAGE (Semi-Automatic Ground Environment) defense system—1983			
		Digital Equipment Corp (DEC) founded by K. Olsen			
1958				J. McCarthy's creation of LISP	
1959	C. Strachey's Time-sharing concept			Basis for interactive computing	
	F. Corbato's work at MIT				resource sharing
1960s				COBOL programming language	
1961		AFIPS (American Fed. of Information Processing)-1990			
1962	D. C. Englebart's pre-PC publications				Packet-switching evolves
1963	I. Sutherland's Sketchpad			Graphic users interface (GUI) initiatives	
		SRI System		Zoning screen displays	
1964		IBM designs	IBM System/360		
		G. Amdahl	Integrated circuits in computers		
				J. Kemeny & T. Kurtz write BASIC language	
				M. Kessler's development of TIP	
	Boolean operators in online searching			Earliest automatic citation searching in Law	
		TEXTIR system		Relevance feedback in online searching	
1965			Time-sharing computers		
				"Wildcards" to correct erroneous term searches	
				Synonyms added for bifurcated term searching	
				Stop words eliminated in searching	
				Record grouping in screen displays	
		MICRO systems		Automatic retrieval of microfilm	
		NASA document retrieval systems		Online ordering of microfilm-print documents	
1966		Lockheed's DIALOG system		Numbered sets in online retrieval	
				BOLD system's online thesaurus	
	N. Prywes' MultiList system			Document display by hierarchical relationships	
1967		UK National Physical Laboratory			NPL Data Network
1969	Lawrence Robert's network design				ARPANET commissioned - 1900; four network hosts
					MERIT founded
					X.25 base in MI

Time	General	Corporate	Hardware	Software	Networking
1969		Data Corporation, OH		R. Giering's proximity operators in term searching	
				Numeric tag searching: early encoding of text	
				Highlighting introduced in screen displays	
1970s					ALOHANet in HA
		Xerox PARC (Palo Alto Research Ctr.)			Ethernet
			Intel's 4004 microprocessor		Workgroup computing
	E. Roberts USAF work			PROLOG programming language	
			Micro Instrumentation Telemetry Systems (MITS Inc., -1977)		
		Digital Equipment Corp. (DEC)			
		Intel Corp. founded by R. Noyce & G. Moore			
			Intel 4004 microprocessor chip		
1972	Computer games - Atari Inc. founded by B. Nolan				
	Minicomputer development				TELNET specification
			S. Cray Research Inc.'s Cray 1		
		IBM's STAIRS system		Case sensitivity for precision in text searching	
1973					ARPANET goes international
	G. Kildall			CP/M operating systems	
1974		Digital Research Corp.			
			8080 & Z80 microprocessors		
			64K storage reached		
	Microcomputing-		MITS' Altair 8800 kit		TELNET operational
	V. Cerf & R. Kahn's protocol work			Trans. Control Protocol (TCP)	
1975		Robert's Altair 8080 (pre-Intel)			
		AT&T Bell Laboratories work			
			Multi-board Bus structures UUCP (UNIX to UNIX)		
			IBM introduced laser printer		
		B. Gates & P. Allen team		BASIC programming for Altair 8800	
		Microsoft Inc. founded			
			I. Yermish's work at U. PA		
				Introduction of "likeness" in online searching	
1976		S. Jobs & S. Wozniak experimentation			
1977		Apple Computer founded			THEORYNET at U. WI.
		Tandy's Radio Shack		G. Kildahl's CP/M operating system	
			Apple II microcomputers -1993		
			Motorola's MOS 6502 microprocessor		
			Megahertz speed reached		
			Concurrent DOS multitasking		
			DEC VAX series introduced		
		Tymeshare			Tymnet
		Commodore Computers -1994			
			Pet PCs -1981		
		Tandy/Radio Shack -1993			
			TRS-80 PCs		
1978	Spreadsheets			D. Bricklin's VisiCalc	
1980s		Apple re-engineering		B. Stroustrup's C programming language	

Time	General	Corporate	Hardware	Software	Networking
1980s				Applications of fuzzy logic and sets	
			Motorola's MC68000 microprocessor		
	Internet Configuration Control Bd. (ICCB)				MUD 1 from U. Essex, UK
1981		IBM licenses MS-DOS from Microsoft; Underprices DOS to replace CP/M			
			IBM-PC introduced		Computer Sc. Network (CSNET)
			File transfers		Because Its There Net (BITNET)
1982					European UNIX net (EUNet)
					France's Minitel network
				Transmission Control Protocol (TCP)	
				Internet Protocol (IP)	
	Laser applications		Compact discs		
1983					Europe Acad. Research (EARN)
1984	W. Gibson's *Neuromancer*		Apple's PCs MacIntosh introduced		
			IBM uses Intel 8080 microprocessors		
	Personal computing		IBM-PCjr. introduced		Domain Name Server (DNS)
					JUNET in Japan
					JANET in UK
1985-	Desktop publishing coined by P. Brainerd			Aldus PageMaker	
	IBM-compatible field broadens				
		Compaq Computers		BIOS published	
	High performance computing		Cray 2 supercomputer		
1986		5 NSF Supercomputing centers			NSFNET created (56kps)
					first Freenet (Cleveland, OH)
1987	Home computing		IBM PS/1-2 generations of PCs		
			NSFNET + MERIT Network Inc. and MCI found ANS		
					1000+ BITNET hosts
1988		DOD adopts OSI			TCP/IP interim status
		Computer Emergency Response Team (CERT)			
				T1 upgrade for NSFNET	
				Virtual Reality prototypes	
				CAD development-	
1990			Electronic Frontier Foundation founded by M. Kapor		
				Archie from McGill U., CN	
				Hytelnet by P. Scott	
			DOD migration to OSI		
				ISODE (ISO Development Environment)	
1991			Thinking Machines Inc.	WAIS(Wide-area Info. Servs.)	
				Gopher from U. MN.	
			CERN, SW	WWW (World Wide Web)	
				T3 upgrade for NSFNET	
1992			Digital Research acquired by Novell		
	Internet Society (ISOC) chartered			Veronica from U. NV	
	J. Amour Polly's Surfing the Internet		SQML adoption		

Time	General	Corporate	Hardware	Software	Networking
1993		Commodore Computers liquidated			InterNIC founded by NSF
		AST Research acquires Tandy computers			
			Worms, Spiders, Wanderers, Crawlers, Snakes		
			Mosaic from U. IL.		
	WWW explodes				Electronic communities:
			Intel Pentium 64-bit microprocessors		E.g. Lexington, VA
1994	WWW surpasses TELNET use	Altavista, Excite, InfoSeek, Lycos, etc.			
		Trans-European Research and Education Network Assn. (TERENA)			
			3-D CAD development		
1995	Interconnected	Network providers proliferate		NSFNET reform: research focus	
				BNS (Backbone Netwk Ser.)	
	Listservs and news groups proliferate			"Supermarket" indexes expand	
		HOTBOT etc.			
		Netscape		Browsers and search engines proliferate	
		Compuserve, America Online, Prodigy, etc.			
		Microsoft, Inc. expansion		Windows '95	
	Government homepages			HyperText Markup Language (HTML)	
	Text Encoding initiatives & Digitization projects proliferate				
		Library of Congress American Memory			
	Virtual Libraries			JAVA & Object-oriented software	
				Groupware	
1996	Communications Decency Act (CDA) controversy				
	Security issues proliferate with increased hacker activity				
	Privacy issues			Encryption	
		Netscape & Microsoft browser competition			
			Pentium Pro		
	Internet Phone services				
		Internet businesses and marketing expand			
				Internet II	
1997		Antitrust suit against Microsoft			
	PUSH technologies				American Registry for Internet Numbers (ARIN) 134,365 networks 828,000 domains 16,146,000 Internet hosts 171 countries Internet connected 1,117,259 WWW sites
	International Internet/WWW communications				
1998	Cost reductions for hardware & software			Windows 98	
1999	Virtual libraries, museums, and universities				
2000	Microsoft loses case			Y2K Crisis	
2000-	Continued progress				

Glossary

DEFINITIONS
(in an ascending order)

Data are what is given in the smallest units, from digits to arrays and points to lines, and bits of information which are encountered, collected, or inferred and manufactured, that are neither facts nor constitute evidence by themselves. These are the raw material for building information.

Information pertains less to things themselves or content, i.e., the "what," but more to the "how" and the processes of packaging, storage, access, and retrieval, presentation, animation and even inspiration for communication and reception to produce knowledge. It is constituted by structured data for interpretation, but may be seen as separate from interpretation itself. It is also the act or process of informing and relaying intelligence, or to make the distinction in another way, the message and format rather than disembodied content or thought. Its importance is increased by accuracy, precision, and relevance. Information is a positive attribute and value which is assumed to be truthful; its negative counterparts are often expressed as misinformation or mistaken or inaccurate information; and disinformation or the deliberate supplanting of false information for nefarious ends.

Facts are things done, that is deeds or acts made into something known (from *facere*, to make, so something made), which have had or do have actual existence, and are true and pertain to objective reality. Facts are conveyed by information, although not all information is factual. Whereas facts are supposedly stable, actual, and real and can therefore be made evident (they are not represented but must be presented), **factors** are the agents, makers, or doers, different from variables, which act on data to make fact.

Evidence is whatever furnishes proof, separate from the information itself or in addition to it, and is constituted by outward sign(s) (*evidentia*). When something (fact) is "in evidence," it is, as the root (*vide*) implies, seen or viewed; it is manifest, conspicuous, or prominent, and therefore public in some way. Something is made evident through testimony, more than merely delivering information (i.e., testifying, verifying, accounting for, placing in context, reconstructing its history, supplying its metadata and provenance). Evidence is the foundation for proof.

Proof (from *probare*) is the cogency of evidence or demonstration of relationships of something tested that compels acceptance as fact or truth; it establishes validity and induces certainty.

Knowledge is the higher-order condition or cognizance of facts and something as a whole, awareness of and acquaintance with relevant evidence, understanding of proof, and even familiarity for comprehension and comfort with what is known both hypothetically and for certain. It is complex and operates on data using metadata and integrates information from multiple sources to achieve objectivity. But more than a command of the facts, knowledge is an overall perspective and a synthesis, or at least an accommodation, for interpretation and application.

Belief, a term that is often trivialized by misuse, is the mental act of acceptance as true and acting or living accordingly. Such action tacitly assents to facts as tenets, or holding something as true, with cognizance and commitment. It can be distinguished from faith, a systematized set of beliefs or a religious creed.

Wisdom should be considered as a higher dimension still, beyond knowledge or belief alone but in some combination, which is demonstrated in wise judgments or decisions based on knowledge as its Anglo-Saxon root and suffix indicate (*wit* applied as *wis-dom* or use of knowledge domain). It is a concept imbued with religious meaning, related to character and morality.

CRITERIA FOR SCIENTIFIC EVIDENCE

Summary extracted from the Federal Judicial Center's *Reference Manual on Scientific Evidence* (1994, pp. 221-388). These apply to all forms of data and information: numerative, textual, audio or visual; quantitative and qualitative; and historical and contemporary.

Basic criteria

1. Statistical testimony needs to be **objective**, which requires that the researcher maintain a **professional autonomy**.

2. **Expertise** can be established by formal **credentials**, but most importantly by **experience**.

3. **Testimony** can be enhanced by **corroboration**, i.e., "two-expert" cases of interlocking testimony.

4. **Full disclosure** of all **analyses**, fruitful and false runs, should be represented as a **history** of the development of the statistical approach used (i.e., a meta-history of a historical work).

5. As in disclosure prior to a trial, **alternative modes of analyses** should be explored before presentation of a case and interpretation of results.

6. Although such established rules of evidence do not prescribe the exact order of **presentation**, a traditional ordering is what is commonly expected, namely that witnesses (any witness with credibility and ability to testify, i.e., a person in court, or documentary evidence used by an historian) are presented first and then are cross-examined by specific questions rather than extended narration. Analysis is reserved for after all testimony is collected, entered, heard, or read.

Procedural criteria

1. The measurement process must be demonstrated as **reliable**, that is reproducible.

2. Validity must be established to ensure **accuracy** by providing that an instrument (test instrument, but also a survey, an historical record) does or did what it is supposed to do or have done in the past.

3. Data **collection** must be deemed **adequate**. This question refers to how data are coded, logged, recorded, and preserved.

Description and analyses

1. A **census** surveys every unit in a population; it accounts for all data. If it does not, it is a survey, which is more difficult because surveying involves sampling. A **sampling** framework must provide explicitly the listing used and lottery method for selection (i.e., random selection, convenience samples where bias must be confronted at the onset, and probability sampling which is a random sampling from a preselected sample to ensure a representative final sample).

2. Use of a survey rather than a census requires that the researcher convince the reader, judge, or recipient that an **appropriate** population has been studied, selection is **unbiased**, data gathering has been **validated**, and that the units are **representative**.

3. Census/consensus and survey research may provide descriptive results without answering the question of causation. Here historians contend that they have problems not present in Social Science research on contemporary subjects, because the latter can attempt to establish cause through **experimentation**. **Simulation** may substitute for experimentation. In either case the issue of "**fit**" in **applicability** arises immediately, just as if a modern researcher took a historical experiment and applied it to a contemporary case. Indeed, "off-the-shelf" (that is by definition, historical) cases (or software) are used all the time. If controlled experiments and simulation are not possible, then the next best is a well designed one, even if a thought-out rather than actual experiment, and demonstration of how variables in one case might change if applied to another, so that one can compensate for the time discrepancy in interpretation.

4. **Variables**, dependent and independent, must be analyzed thoroughly when there is an attempt to show a **cause-and-effect relationship**. It is useful to list variables to identify clearly which factors are under control and which are not and could mask causal relations or give false appearances of causes.

5. **Confounding variables** must be handled separately by correlating them with independent and dependent variables because confounding changes are often two-way or reciprocal. Historians, of course, may not be able to check their control groups except in simulations, but they can control the variables at play in a data set and analyses. They may be able to provide more convincing cases by presenting more than one well-designed study or case. Comparisons are essential.

6. The issue of **external validity** is the question if the results or conclusions from one case, experiment, or research project based on one sample or subject can or should be generalized. The rule of thumb is that confidence in the appropriateness of extrapolation cannot come from the experiment or study itself, but it can come from context and it is here that historical expertise is all important.

7. In formal court proceedings or the court of public opinion statistical studies are **observational** rather than **experimental**; so too in history, if one thinks about observing situations through the eyes of documented witnessing. In both cases, current and historical observation, the observer has little control if any over the population being observed. The same is true for evidence produced from field work. A compelling case based on observation can be made when associations can be shown between different groups, several studies, etc., so one does not suspect a defect in one study or a peculiarity in a group of subjects. Appropriate statistical techniques to account for the effects of confounding variables add credibility. Subjects can often be treated as a control group. Plausible explanations are to be provided for the effects of independent variables, and causal links should not depend on the observed associations alone. However, in observed cases, statistics by themselves do not prove cause in any association. These principles can be adapted for narration and description as explanation.

Data and Records Management concerns

1. Legality of systems versus legality of the media or the distinction of information and its meta-information, data and meta-data, facts and interpretation, and how these go hand-in-hand as pairs.

2. **Original documentation** and **disposition**, pertaining to extant records, when the original can be destroyed and a surrogate accepted. Surrogation methods and transfer processes must be documented. This involves computer output in any form (printout, mircroform, download); erasure, alteration, and destruction of records, and the destruction of a prior form to favor a subsequent copy, surrogate, or imitation, including photocopying, reentry, scanning, and transfer via electronic media.

3. Unique legal issues pertaining to the **composition of records** as logical documents versus physical documentation, compound documents, transient compound documents, etc., to which may be added the problem of disparate documents whose parts are on different systems in diverse places only to be assembled on demand.

4. **Policies** and **procedures** to respond to **discovery action** which seemingly would also pertain to discovery in historical research (e.g., privacy issues) rather than simply legal discovery in court actions.

5. **Security** issues, such as in discerning the differences between system and media security (illicit access to a system versus intervention into a document within a system, i.e., system malfunctions versus record tampering); distinctions in record annotation (add-ons), enhancement (editions, erasures, and substitutions, interpolations, etc.), and manipulation (dating, addressing, placement, replacement, duplication, etc.); and maintaining distinctions between software and hardware and their influence on both the records or media and the system.

6. **User responsibilities**, as distinct from recordkeeping requirements and operations, which includes awareness of research trends and methods, and service which aids and abets research and information disclosure.

7. **Legal responsibilities**, which includes current laws and considerations about what is missing from today's laws, or which may be **moral responsibilities** beyond explicit legal obligations.

References

This bibliography is selective, reflecting what is mentioned in the essay rather than being a comprehensive guide; hence its title, "References." Because it includes some citations operating as reference rather than referral or bibliographic recommendation, as in the case of popularization and report literature, anomalies will be apparent in this bibliography by the inclusion of references from special mention and occasionally negative review rather than purely a critical selection of the literature's best. However, the indexing of both the text and the citations attempts to create a tool that can still serve as a guide. Citations are listed alphabetically by author/editor entry (sometimes corporate author) rather than being classified, for easier access from either the index or the essay. Editors are treated as authors when an entire compilation is cited. Only when authors or editors are not identifiable or the work is obviously issued under institutional authority are corporate authors used. Corporate author entries in the bibliography are not automatically duplicated as subject entries in the index. The foci of the chapters and references therein act as a classification of sorts. The result is a reading guide and reference tool covering almost 6,000 citations. While not purporting to be exhaustive or claiming controlled balance in selection, the following efforts have been made:

1. to integrate works from Computing and Information Systems Management, Library, Archives, Museum, and Information Sciences, the Social Sciences, Literary Criticism, Art History and History (Music History is admittedly slighted) to illustrate the value of crossover between disciplines and professional literatures;

2. to provide a European perspective with the North American, and therefore to cite relevant literatures other than those in English. Selection of works to be cited often gravitated toward those which, like literature reviews, act as conduits into other areas that while being potentially useful to Historical Information Science, could not be explored in detail within the scope of this essay. Despite a multiple language facility, my personal limits in reading languages requiring transliteration still impose limitations on this review's coverage; and

3. to bring up-to-date coverage while ensuring preparation of final copy in 1998 for publication in 1999 as a benchmark survey leading into the new millennium. Theoretically coverage could be continuous, but then the work would never be completed and would not achieve its purpose of a synthetic snapshot of what has transpired since the arrival in 1983-1984 of the personal computers in academe and the impact of information technology and new methodology during the decade thereafter. The original cut-off date was envisioned as 1995. However, no cut-off date was strictly imposed and additions were made during the typescript's revision, but coverage tapers off in 1997 and only advance copy and early 1998 releases could be included selectively. Since many academic journals

are behind in their publication schedules set by their frequency, some by more than a full calendar year, coverage past 1997 is necessarily spotty. Already a file of another hundred publications relevant to this survey has been compiled, perhaps for a sequel covering the crossing of the threshold and the forthcoming first decade of the new millennium.

A modified American Psychological Association (APA) style is employed here, resembling closely the American Society for Information Science (ASIS) style sheet used for *ARIST*. This seemed expedient given the nexus between History *qua* science and the Social Sciences, and usage in Information Science. Alphabetized citations have been numbered alpha-numerically for referencing that is distinguishable from page references so they can be differentiated in the index from page references to the text. Thus the index correlates both commentary and citations. APA and ASIS conventions call for full bibliographic citations to appear in the references with International Standard Book Number (ISBN) and International Standard Serial Number (ISSN) numbers and order information to assist retrieval of these materials. In most cases these are provided; sometimes Library of Congress Card Number (LCCN) (sometimes the call number for older citations) record numbers are provided instead, or CODEN and Government Document numbers. Note that references to print-version pagination may be inexact when the electronic text was used. Most providers of electronic serials still do not provide exact pagination, but only the beginning page of the original, and electronic versions often lack tables, illustrations, enlarged headings, etc., so page lengths differ in any case. Moreover, there is no correspondence between original pagination and screen displays or print-outs. Citations attempt to provide access to physical print whenever possible since this medium still tends to be more complete and reliable than electronic surrogates.

Geographic designations of places of publication use the standard two-digit abbreviations for U.S. states and international codes for countries, some of which may be expanded to three digits to avoid confusion with state abbreviations: Australia (AU); Austria (AT); Belgium (BE); Canada (CN); Czech Republic (CZ); Denmark (DK); Finland (FI); France (FR); Germany (DEU); Hungary (HU); Italy (IT); Mexico (MX); Netherlands (NL); New Zealand (NZ); Norway (NO); Portugal (PT); Russian Federation (RU [USSR is used for older material; CIS for Commonwealth of Independent States may also be used]); Spain (ES); Sweden (SE); Switzerland (CH); United Kingdom (UK); United States (US), etc.

Document retrieval via citation tracing is still hampered by faulty and inexact references in too much of the literature, and in Europe by personal styles or a *vade mecum* in citation formats rather than strict adherence to a professional, national, or international bibliographic standard (e.g., IFLA). In all, more than 30 different citation formats—not counting purely idiosyncratic syntax and styles—were encountered while doing this literature survey. Some seem to engage in creative rather than technical writing in their critical apparati. Consistency in syntax and form, fullness of information and provision of all standard data elements for complete citation, and accuracy as well, are universal problems. Editing acumen seems to vary tremendously by country, discipline, and publisher. The problem is exacerbated by electronic publishing in which too much is prematurely shared without self-discipline for quality control or without the scrutiny of some external editorial authority.

As much as authors who are unaccustomed to academic critical apparati, formal standards, and bibliographic rigor, many historians can be faulted here even though they document their work more profusely than those in other disciplines. One might expect rigorously enforced bibliographic requirements that comply with formal bibliographic standards in Information Science, but even in *JASIS* there appear citations with compulsory data missing. Engineers, computing gurus, consultants, and those popularizing their views on the public speaking circuit seem to be among the most unreliable in referencing or citation accuracy. Strict editing and verification sampling in the more reputable journals provide some quality control, but collections of essays and compilations seem less trustworthy. The problem is significant: nearly 30 percent of citations traced from references by historians in their writings proved to be faulty, either as incomplete or erroneous. This observation points to a problem of precision requiring remedy if citation tracing remains a principle method for historians to track down their material. Hopefully, this bibliographic compilation is an improvement over this contemporary situation, but I cannot claim this to be a perfect bibliography—if such ever existed. I am well aware of the practical impossibility of producing an error-free bibliography of this size or maintaining absolute consistency when the compilation extended over several years of reading. Indeed, anyone who has attempted such a bibliographic undertaking understands the possibilities for the occasional blind reference, misattribution, incorrect orthography and variance in transliteration, and the insurmountable problem of citing electronic sources which lack proper style and even the most basic of bibliographic elements. Most monographic citations herein have been checked against MARC records, but even some of these carried mistakes into the world of copy cataloging. Article references are more difficult to verify, but a sample check against major bibliographies was undertaken. In both serial and monographic treatment, international standard book and serial numbers have been supplied, and when unavailable the citation often refer to catalog copy. I apologize if anything egregious misleads anyone using this as a guide.

I am indebted to colleagues at Ferris State University's A. S. Timme Library for their assistance: Mary Gallagher in Interlibrary Loan for literally hundreds of loans, with thanks also to the libraries which made their collections so available; and Librarians Richard Perrin for online searching and bibliographic verification of articles, and Scott Atwell for OCLC searching to check citations against MARC records and to supply ISBN/ISSN data for the easy retrieval of the materials included in this bibliography. ASIS was supplied by Knight's DIALOGUE with a generous account for online searching, ample enough for an *ARIST* article (MCCRANK, 1995) and for this larger survey. University Microfilms, Inc. (UMI) (Ann Arbor, MI) also provided, by way of a demonstration and trial period, two months of free searching in *Proquest* for its electronic periodical files before OCLC's *FirstSearch* was readily available to me through Access Michigan.

My appreciation is also extended to *PSOW* Board members and referees who read this essay before publication, and to colleagues who read parts or the whole of this essay while in draft. I have benefitted from their comments since the breadth of its coverage defies one person's range of competence. Responsibility for error or misrepresentation, of course, always remains with the author. I hope that the critical temperament of readers who discern problems beyond the unavoidable human mistakes inherent in such a review, or who disagree with my observations as my overview seems to glide along the surface as it intentionally does, will be balanced with credit for what is accomplished here. That is, as stated at the onset, this bibliographic essay is meant as a review of a wide, potentially integrative purview, and in doing so it is a preview to the future. If one reader, at my suggestion, incorporates an idea from another field and applies it to historical research, or conversely takes an historical approach to problems posed in Information Science, then this essay will have begun to serve its very important purpose.

-A-

A1
ABADAL FALGUERAS, ERNEST. 1993. La Formación en Biblioteconomía y Documentación en España [The Formation of Library Science and Documentation in Spain]. *Documentación de las Ciencias de la Información* (ES). 1993; 16: 9-46. (In Spanish).

A2
ABADAL FALGUERAS, ERNEST. 1994. *La Documentación en España* [Documentation in Spain]. Madrid, ES: CIN-DOC; 1994. 200p. (In Spanish). ISBN: 3400074319. Based on his dissertation: *Orígines i evolucío de la informacío i documentacío a l'estat espanyol* [Origins and Evolution of Information Science and Documentation in Spain]. Barcelona, ES; Universitat Autonoma de Barcelona; 1991. (In Catalan).

A3
ABBATE, JANET. 1999. [*Inventing of the Internet* ISBN: 026W11727; LCCN: 98047647]. Cambridge, MA: MIT Press; [1999. 264p.].

A4
ABBOT, ANDREW D. 1988. *The System of Professions: An Essay on the Division of Expert Labor.* Chicago, IL; University of Chicago Press; 1988. 435p. ISBN: 0226000680 (hbk.); 022600699 (pbk.); LCCN: 87030206.

A5
ABBOT, ANDREW D. 1990. Conception of Time and Events in Social Science Methods: Causal and Narrative Approaches. *Historical Methods.* 1990; 23: 140-150. ISSN: 0161-5440.

A6
ABEL, TRUDI J. 1997. Students as Historians: Lessons from an "Interactive" Census Database Project. *AHA Perspectives.* 1997 March; 35(3): 1, 10-13. ISSN: 0743-7021.

A7
ABELL-SEDDON, B. 1989. Reforming Collection Documentation: A New Approach. *The International Journal of Museum Management and Curatorship.* 1989; 8(1): 63-67. ISSN: 0260-4779.

A8
ABOBA, BERNARD. 1993. *The Online Users' Encyclopedia: Bulletin Boards and Beyond.* Reading, MA: Addison-Wesley Publishers; 1993. 806p. ISBN: 0201622149.

A9
ABRAHAM, RALPH H.; GARDINI, LAURA; MIRA, CHRISTIAN. 1997. *Chaos in Discrete Dynamical Systems. A Visual Introduction in 2 Dimensions.* Santa Clara, CA: TELOS / New York, NY: Springer Verlag; 1997. 246p. and CD-ROM. ISBN: 0-387-94300-5 (hbk.).

A10
ABRAMS, PHILIPS. 1982. *Historical Sociology.* Somerset, NJ: Open Books; 1982. 353p. ISBN: 0-72910-11-8; 0-729101-06-1 (pbk.).

A11
ABU-MOSTAFA, YASER S. [1988]. *Complexity in Information Theory.* New York, NY: Springer-Verlag; [c1988]. 131p. LCCN: 86003746.

A12
ABUKHANFUSA, KERSTIN; SYDBECK, JAN, eds. 1994. *The Principle of Provenance: Report from the first Stockholm conference on Archival Theory and the Principle of Provenance* (2-3 September 1993). Skrifter utgivna av Svenskka Riksarkivet, 10. Stockholm, SE: Swedish National Archives; 1994. ISBN: 91-88366-11-1; ISSN: 0346-8488.

A13
ACADEMIC PRESS. 1997/[1998]. *Image Directory.* San Diego, CA: Academic Press; 1997. Print directory, [1998 forthcoming]. Electronic file and directory accessible at http://www.imagedir.com.

A14
ACHEN, CHRISTOPHER H. 1986. *The Statistical Analysis of Quasi-Experiments.* Berkeley, CA: University of California Press; 1986. 172p. ISBN: 0-52004-723-0; 0-52004-724-9 (pbk.); LCCN: 85-14150.

A15
ACHINSTEIN, PETER; SNYDER, LAURA J., eds. 1994. *Scientific Methods: Conceptual and Historical Problems.* Melbourne, FL: Krieger Publishing Co.; 1994. 168p. ISBN: 0-89464-822-5.

A16
ACHLEITER, H. K., ed. 1987. *Intellectual Foundation for Information Professionals.* New York, NY: Columbia University Press; 1987. 213p. ISBN: 0880339578; LC: f7060631

A17
ACKERMANN, ROBERT J. 1972. *Belief and Knowledge*. Garden City, NY: Anchor Books; 1972. 149p. LCCN: 79-175407.

A18
ACKLAND, GLENDA. 1992. Managing the Record rather than the Relic. *Archives and Manuscripts*. 1992; 20 (1): 57-63. ISSN: 0157-6895.

A19
ACKOFF, RUSSEL L. 1967. Management Misinformation. *Systems Management Science*. 1967; 14 (4): B147-B156.

A20
ACZAEL, J.; DAROCZY, Z. 1975. *On Measures of Information and Their Characterization*. New York, NY: Academic Press; 1975. 234p. ISBN: 0120437600.

A21
ADAM, NABEL R.; BHARGAVA, BHARAT. K. 1993. *Advanced Database Systems*. Berlin, DEU; New York, NY: Springer-Verlag; 1993. 451p. ISBN: 038757073 (USA).

A22
ADAM, NABEL R.; BHARGAVA, BHARAT K.; HALEM, H.; YESHA, Y., eds. 1995. *Advances in Digital Libraries*. New York, NY: Springer-Verlag; 1995. ISBN: 3548614109.

A23
ADAMO, GIOVANNI. 1994. *Bibliografia di Informatica umanistica* [Bibliography of Humanistic Informatics]. In: *Informatica e disciplina umanistiche*, 5. [Rome]:Bulzoni Editore; 1994. 420p. (In Italian).

A24
ADAMS, ROBERT M. 1996. *Paths of Fire. An Anthropologist's Inquiry into Western Technology*. Princeton, NJ: Princeton University Press; 1996. ISBN: 0-691-02634-3.

A25
ADLER, SHARON C. 1997. The "ABCs" of DSSSL. See reference: LOGAN, E.; POLLARD, M., eds. 1997b: 597-602.

A26
AGUILAR, FRANCIS J. 1991/1994. *Supercharging Corporate Performance: Business Ethics in Action*. New York, NY; 1991. Rev. ed. *Managing Corporate Ethics: Learning from America's Ethical Companies how to Supercharge Business Performance*. New York, NY: Oxford University Press; 1994. 177p. ISBN: 019598345.

A27
AGUILAR FERNANDEZ, PALOMA. 1996. *Memoría y olvido de la guerra civil espsañola* (Memory and Forgetting about the Spanish Civil War). Madrid, ES: Alianza; 1996. 435p. (In Spanish). ISBN: 8420694681. Based on Ph.D. dissertation at the Universidad Nacional de Educación a Distancía; 1995.

A28
AHITUV, N.; WAND, Y. 1981. Information Evaluation and Decision Makers Objectives. *Interfaces*. 1981; 11 (3): 24-33. ISSN: 0092-2102.

A29
AIRS (Automated Information Reference Systems), INC. 1984. *MARCON* (Micro Archives and Records Collections Online). Users Manual and 2 floppy disks. Baltimore, MD: AIRS, Inc.; 1984. (Software includes thesaurus construction module). Available from AIRS, Inc. P.O. Box 16322, Baltimore MD 21210.

A30
AITKIN, ANGUS J., ed. 1972. *The Computer and Literary Studies*. 2nd Symposium on the Uses of Computers in Literary Research, University of Edinburgh Institute for Advanced Studies in the Humanities. Edinburgh, Scotland: University of Edinburgh; 1972. ISBN: 08522422328; LCCN: 72-79287; OCLC: 668098.

A31
AKTOUF, OMAR. 1992. Management and Theories of Organization in the 1990s: Toward a Critical Radical Humanism? *Academy of Management Review*. 1992 July; 17 (3): 407-431. ISSN: 036307425.

A32
AL-JABRI, IBRAHIM M. 1991. *An Expert System for Forecasting*. Chicago, IL: Illinois Institute of Technology; 1991. 190p. (Ph.D. dissertation; DAI, vol. 53/03-A: 875). Available from: University Microfilms, Ann Arbor, MI; Order no. AAD92-22168.

A33
ALBRECH, P. 1984. Opportunity and Impediment in Graduate Program Innovation. In: *New Directions for Higher Education* [v. 11]. San Francisco, CA: Jossey-Bass; 1984. ISSN: 0271-0560.

A34
ALEXANDER, CHRISTOPHER W. 1964. *Notes on the Synthesis of Form*. Cambridge, MA: Harvard University Press; 1964. Reprint, 1970. ISBN: 0674627512.

A35
ALEXANDER, CHRISTOPHER W. 1977. *A Pattern Language*. New York, NY: Oxford University Press; 1977. 117p. ISBN: 0195019199; LCCN: 74022874.

A36
ALEXANDER, CHRISTOPHER W. 1979. *The Timeless Way of Building*. New York, NY: Oxford University Press; 1979. 552p. (On symbolic semiotics). ISBN: 0195024028; LCCN: 7604265.

A37
ALEXANDER, JEFFREY C.; BOUDON, RAYMOND; CHERKAQUI, MOHAMMED. 1997. *The Classical Tradition in Sociology*. Pt. 1: *The American Tradition*. J. C. Alexander., ed. 4 vols., 1664p. Pt. 2: *The European Tradition*. R. Boudon, ed. 4 vols., 1664p. Thousand Oaks, CA: Sage Publications; 1997. 8 vol. set, each vol. 416p. See URL = http://www.sagepub.com.

A38
ALKER, HAYWARD R., Jr. [1965]. *Mathematics and Politics*. New York, NY: Macmillan; [1965]. 152p. LC call no. JA73.A39.

A39
ALKER, HAYWARD R., Jr. 1984. Historical Argumentation and Statistical Inference: Towards More [Ap]propriate Logic for Historical Research. *Historical Methods*. 1984; 17(4): 164- 173. ISSN: 0161-5440.

A40
ALKER, HAYWARD R., Jr.; DEUTSCH, KARL W.; STOETZEL, ANTOINE H. 1974. *Mathematical Approaches to Politics*. San Franciso, CA: Jossey-Bass; 1973. 475p. ISBN: 0875891764.

A41
ALLEN, B. L. 1991. Cognitive Research in Information Science: Implications for Design. In: Willliams, M., ed. *Annual Review of Information Science and Technology* (26: 3-37). Medford, NJ: Information Today for ASIS; 1991. ISSN: 0066-4200.

A42
ALLEN, BARRY. 1993. *Truth in Philosophy*. Cambridge, MA: Harvard University Press; 1993. ISBN: 0674910907.

A43
ALLEN, J. F. 1983. Maintaining Knowledge about Temporal Intervals. *Communications of the ACM (Assn. of Computing Machinery)*. 1983; 26: 832-843. ISSN: 0001-0782.

A44
ALLEN, JAMES. 1987. *Natural Language Understanding*. Menlo Park, CA: Benjamin/Cummings Publishing Co., Inc.; 1987. 574p. ISBN: 0-8053-0330-8.

A45
ALLEN, M. 1993. Critical and Tradition Science: Implications for Communication Research. *Western Journal of Communication*. 1993; 57: 200-208. ISSN: 1057-0314.

A46
ALLEN, MARIE. 1987. Optical Character Recognition: Technology with New Relevance for Archival Automation Projects. *The American Archivist*. 1987; 50(1): 88-99. ISSN: 0360-9081.

A47
ALLEN, MARIE; BAUMAN, ROLAND M. 1991. Evolving Appraisal and Accessioning Policies of Society Archives. *The American Archivist*. 1991 winter; 54(10): 96-111. ISSN: 0360-9081.

A48
ALLEN, ROBERT F. 1988. The Stylo-Statistical Method of Literary Analysis. *Computers and Humanities* (Netherlands). 1988; 22(1): 1-10. ISSN: 0010-4817.

A49
ALLEN, ROBERT F., ed. 1985. *The International Conference on Data Bases in the Humanities and Social Sciences, 1983 at Rutgers, the State University* [NJ]. ICDBHSS,'83, [2]. Osprey, FL: Paradigm Press; 1985. 434p. ISSN: 0-931351-00-6. Now available from Learned Information, Inc., Medford, NJ.

A50
ALLEN, RODNEY F. FLETON, RANDALL G. 1991. Photographs as Historical Documents. *OAH Magazine of History*. 1991 winter; 5(3): 7-12. ISSN: 0882-228X.

A51
ALLEN, THOMAS J. 1977. *Managing the Flow of Technology: Technology Transfer and the Dissemination of Technological Information within the R&D Organization.* Cambridge, MA: MIT Press; 1977. 320p. ISBN: 0262010488.

A52
ALLEN, THOMAS J.; SCOTT, MICHAEL S., eds. 1994. *Information Technology and the Corporation in the 1990s.* Oxford, UK: Oxford University Press; 1994. 532p. ISBN: 0195068068; LCCN: 94-46832.

A53
ALLISON, PAUL D. 1980. Inequality and Scientific Productivity. *Social Studies of Science.* 1980; 10: 163-179. ISSN: 0306-3127.

A54
ALLISON, PAUL D. 1984. *Event History Analysis: Regression for Longitudinal Event Data. Quantitative Applications in the Social Sciences.* Sage University Papers, vol. 07-046. Beverley Hills, CA: Sage Publications; 1984. 87p. ISBN: 0803920555 (pbk). LCCN: 84-51704/r89.

A55
ALLISON, PAUL D.; LONG, J. S.; KRAUZE, T. K. 1982. Cumulative Advantage and Inequality in Science. *American Sociological Review.* 1982; 47: 615-625. ISSN: 0004-1224.

A56
ALMOND, GABRIEL A. 1990. *A Discipline Divided: Schools and Sects in Political Science.* Newbury Park, CA: Sage Publ.; 1990. 348p. ISBN: 0803933010.

A57
ALMOND, R. 1995-. *Software for Belief Networks.* Accessible at: http://bayes.stat.washington.edu/almond/belief. html.

A58
ALSCHULER, LIORA. [1995]. *ABCD. SGML.* Oxon Hall, MD: NISO Press, [1995]. 414p. ISBN: 1-850-32197-3.

A59
ALTER, STEVEN L. 1980. *Decision Support Systems: Current Practice and Continuing Challenge.* Reading, MA: Addison-Wesley, Inc.; 1980. 316p. (Addison Wesley Series on Decision Support). ISBN: 0201001934; LCCN: 78-067690.

A60
ALTER, STEVEN L. 1999. *Information Systems: A Management Perspective.* 3rd ed. Reading, MA: Addison Wesley; c1999. 523p. ISBN: 0201351099; LCCN: 98-036555. See also for companion text, reference: KNAB, R. W. 1992.

A61
ALVESSON, MATS; BERG, PER OLAF. 1992. *Corporate Culture and Organizational Symbolism.* New York, NY: Walter de Gruyter; 1992. 258p. LCCN: 91-27140.

A62
AMBOS-SPIES, KLAUS; HOMER, STEVEN; SCHOENING, UWE, eds. 1993. *Complexity Theory: Current Research.* Cambridge, UK and New York, NY: Cambridge University Press; 1993. 313p. ISBN: 0521442205; LCCN: 94167857.

A63
AMERICAN AND FRENCH RESEARCH ON THE TREASURY OF THE FRENCH LANGUAGE (ARTFL). 1993a. *Bibliography of the ARTFL Database.* Chicago, IL: University of Chicago and the CNRS Institut National de la Langue Francaise; 1993. 62p. Available from: ARTFL, University of Chicago Dept. of Romance Languages and Literature, 1050 E. 59th St., Chicago IL 60637.

A64
AMERICAN AND FRENCH RESEARCH ON THE TREASURY OF THE FRENCH LANGUAGE (ARTFL). 1993b. *User's Guide to Philologic 2.0.* Chicago, IL: University of Chicago and the CNRS Institut National de la Langue Francaise; 1993. 62p. No ISBN. Available from ARTFL, University of Chicago Dept. of Romance Languages and Literature, 1050 E. 59th St., Chicago IL 60637.

A65
AMERICAN ASSOCIATION FOR STATE AND LOCAL HISTORY (AASLH). 1988. *The Revised Nomenclature for Museum Cataloguing: A Revised and Expanded Version of Robert G. Chenhall's System for Classifying Man-made Objects.* Blackaby, James R.; Greeno, Patricia, eds. Nashville, TN: American Association for State and Local History; 1988. ISBN: 90910050937; LCCN: 88-14625; OCLC: 17953996. Available from: AASLH, 172 2nd Ave. N. Suite 102, Nashville, TN 37201.

A66
AMERICAN ASSOCIATION FOR STATE AND LOCAL HISTORY (AASLH). 1991. *Documentation Practices in Historical Collections.* Report from the Common Agenda. AASLH Technical Leaflet, v. 176. Nashville, TN:

AASLH; 1991 January/February. (Contains sample Common Agenda Documentation Survey.) Also inserted in *History News*. 1991; 46(1). ISSN: 0363-7492; LCCN: 51-4632/r852; OCLC: 246430665.

A67
AMERICAN ASSOCIATION FOR HIGHER EDUCATION (AAHE). 1996. *The Disciplines Speak: Rewarding the Scholarly Professional and Creative Work of Faculty*. Diamond, Robert M.; Adam, Bronwyn, eds. Washington, D.C.: AAHE; 1996. Available in ERIC microfiche, ED406957.

A68
AMERICAN ASSOCIATION OF MUSEUMS (AAM). 1924-. *Museum News*. Washington, D.C.: AAM; 1924-. Semi-monthly (1924-1976); 6x/yr (1976-). ISSN: 0027-4089; LCCN: 26-18042; OCLC: 1758869. Available from: AAM, 1225 Eye St. NW, Suite 200, Washington, DC 20005.

A69
AMERICAN ASSOCIATION OF MUSEUMS (AAM). 1998. *American Strategy*. Washington, D.C.: AAM & The Getty Information Institute; 1998. Accessible at: http://artsedge.kennedy-center.org/american.

A70
AMERICAN BIBLIOGRAPHIC CENTER / CLIO PRESS (ABC-CLIO). 1964-; 1982-. *American: History and Life*. Santa Barbara, CA: ABC-Clio Press; 1964-. Available as DIALOG File 38 and Knowledge Index (FileHIST 1), 1964. (Updated 4x/year). ISSN: 0002-7065; DLC: 84-640891. Now *America: History and Life on Disc* (CD-ROM); 1982-. (Updated 3x/year).

A71
AMERICAN BIBLIOGRAPHIC CENTER / CLIO PRESS (ABC-CLIO). 1964-; 1982-. *Historical Abstracts*. Santa Barbara, CA: ABC-Clio Press; 1964-. Available as DIALOG File 39 and Knowledge Index (File HIST 2). (Updated 6x/year). Now available as *Historical Abstracts on Disc* (CD-ROM); 1982-. (Updated 3x/year).

A72
AMERICAN BIBLIOGRAPHIC CENTER / CLIO PRESS (ABC-CLIO). 1981-1985. *Historical Periodicals Directory*. Boehm, Eric H.; Pope, Barbara H.; Ensign, Marie S., eds. Santa Barbara, CA: ABC-Clio Press; 1981-1985. 5 vols. ISBN: 0-87436-018-8 (v. 1); 0-87436-019-6 (v. 2), etc.; LCCN: 81-12892.

A73
AMERICAN COUNCIL OF LEARNED SOCIETIES (ACLS); J. PAUL GETTY TRUST. 1992. *Technology, Scholarship, and the Humanities: The Implications of Electronic Information*. Summary of Proceedings. University of California at Irvine, Sept. 30-Oct. 2, 1992. Falls Church, VA: Keens Co. for ACLS and the Getty Trust; 1992. 43p. IBSN: 0-9632792-1-1.

A74
AMERICAN FEDERATION OF INFORMATION PROCESSING SOCIETIES (AFIPS). 1979-. *Annals of the History of Computing*. New York, NY: Springer-Verlag for AFIPS; 1979-. Quarterly. ISSN: 0164-1239; LCCN: 80-643390; OCLC: 4583089.

A75
AMERICAN HISTORICAL ASSOCIATION (AHA). 1985-. *The American Historical Review*. Washington, D.C.: AHA; 1985-. Qtly. ISSN: 0002-8762.

A76
AMERICAN HISTORICAL ASSOCIATION (AHA). 1961, 1962. *Guide to Historical Literature*. Howe, F., *ET AL.*, eds. New York: Macmillan, Co.; 1961/1962. 962p. (First AHA Guide dates to 1931). LCCN: 61-7602; OCLC: 556092.

A77
AMERICAN HISTORICAL ASSOCIATION (AHA). 1974-[1990]. *Writings on American History: A Subject Bibliography of Articles*. Dadian, C.; Dougherty, J., Price, A., eds. Milwood and White Plains, NY: Kraus International Publications; 1962-1973/1974-.

A78
AMERICAN HISTORICAL ASSOCIATION (AHA). 1975-1990. *Recently Published Articles*. Dadian, C. D., ed. Washington, D.C.: William Byrd Press for the AHA; 1975-1990. 3x/yr., 15 vols. ISSN: 0145-5311; LCCN: 76-648505; OCLC: 2280829.

A79
AMERICAN HISTORICAL ASSOCIATION (AHA). 1994a. *Directory of History Departments and Organizations in the United States and Canada*. 20th ed. Washington, D.C.: AHA; 1994. 19th ed.; 1993/1994. 733p. OCLC: 30023045. Annual. ISSN: 1077-8500; DLC: 77-151141; OCLC: 3243851.

A80
AMERICAN HISTORICAL ASSOCIATION (AHA). 1994b. *Doctoral Dissertations in History.* Washington, D.C.: AHA; 1976-. 18th ed., vols. 18-19. Annual. ISSN: 0145-9929; LCCN: 77-640363; OCLC: 2429011. Available from: AHA Institutional Services Program, 400 A. St. SE, Washington, DC 20003.

A81
AMERICAN HISTORICAL ASSOCIATION (AHA). 1995. *Guide to Historical Literature.* Norton, Mary Beth, *et al.*, eds. 3rd ed. New York, NY: Oxford University Press; 1995. 2 vols. (References chiefly from 1961-1992). ISBN: 01959057279 (set); LCCN: 94-3670; OCLC: 31133049.

A82
AMERICAN HISTORICAL ASSOCIATION (AHA). 1996. Guidelines for Affiliation with the AHA. *AHA Perspectives.* 1996 March; 34 (3): 23. ISSN: 0743-7021.

A83
AMERICAN HISTORICAL ASSOCIATION (AHA). 1997. *Directory of History Departments and Organizations in the United States and Canada.* Washington, D.C.: AHA; 1997. (Note: 15,000 names, 780 institutions; includes *Doctoral Dissertations in History*, formerly separate. Compare with 1994 ed.). OCLC: 30023045.

A84
AMERICAN HISTORICAL ASSOCIATION (AHA). 1998. New Technologies and the Practice of History. In: Townsend, Robert, ed. *AHA Perspectives.* 1998 February; 36 (2): 2-39. (Entire issue on title topic). ISSN: 0743-7021.

A85
AMERICAN HISTORICAL ASSOCIATION (AHA). COMMITTEE ON REDEFINING SCHOLARLY WORK. 1994. Redefining Historical Scholarship. *AHA Perspectives.* 1994 March; 32:19-23. ISSN: 0743-7021.

A86
AMERICAN NATIONAL STANDARDS INSTITUTE (ANSI). 1986a. *Information Technology—Database Languages—Structured Query Language (SQL).* New York, NY: ANSI; 1986. Available from ANSI.

A87
AMERICAN NATIONAL STANDARDS INSTITUTE (ANSI). 1986b. *Specification for a Data Descriptive File for Information Interchange.* New York, NY: ANSI; February 1986. ANSI/ISO 8211-1985; FIP PUB 123.

A88
AMERICAN NATIONAL STANDARDS INSTITUTE (ANSI). 1988. *Information Resource Directory System (IRDS).* New York, NY: ANSI; 1988. ANSI; X3.138-1988.

A89
AMERICAN SOCIETY FOR INFORMATION SCIENCE. 1950-/1970-. *American Documentation.* Washington, DC: American Documentation Institute; 1950-1969. Quarterly. ISSN: 0096-946X; OCLC: 1479779. Continued by: *Journal of the American Society for Information Science (JASIS).* Silver Spring, MD: ASIS; 1970-. 10x/yr. ISSN: 0002-8231.

A90
AMERICAN SOCIETY FOR TRAINING AND DEVELOPMENT. 1994. The Coming of Age of Workplace Learning: A Time Line. *Training & Development.* 1994 May; 48 (5): S4-S12. ISSN: 1055-9760; OCLC: 2343625; LCCN: 91-641384.

A91
ANDERBERG, MICHAEL A. 1973. *Cluster Analysis for Applications.* New York, NY: Academic Press; 1973. 359p. (Publication of Ph.D. Dissertation, University of Texas; 1971). ISBN: 0120576503.

A92
ANDERSEN, PERRY. 1992. The Ends of History. In: *A Zone of Engagement* (pp. 279-375). London, UK: Verso Books; 1992. ISBN: 086091956.

A93
ANDERSEN, PETER B.; HOLMQUIST, BERIT; JENSEN, JENS. F., eds. 1993. *The Computer as Medium.* Cambridge, UK: Cambridge University Press; 1993. 495p. ISBN: 0521419956; LCCN: 93025989.

A94
ANDERSON, CHARLES W. 1993. *Prescribing the Life of the Mind: An Essay on the Purpose of the University, the Aims of Liberal Education, the Competence of Citizens, and the Cultivation of Practical Reason.* Madison, WI: University of Wisconsin Press; 1993. 173p. ISBN:02999138305 (hbk.); 0299138348 (pbk.)

A95
ANDERSON, J. A., ed. 1977-. *Communication Yearbook.* Newbury Park, CA: Sage; 1977-. Annual. ISBN: 0147-4642.

A96
ANDERSON, JAMES. D. 1985. Indexing Systems: Extensions of the Mind's Organizing Power. *Information and Behavior.* 1985; 1: 287-323. ISSN: 0740-5502.

A97
ANDERSON, JAMES D. 1997. *Guidelines for Indexes and Related Information Retrieval Devices.* Oxon Hill, MD: NISO Press; 1997. (NISO Technical Report [TR-02]). ISBN: 1-8801124-36-X. Available from NISO Press at 1-800-282-NISO; Fax 301-567-9553.

A98
ANDERSON, JOHN R. 1973. *Human Associative Memory.* Washington, D.C.: V. H. Winson, distributed by Halsted Press; 1973. 424p. (Experimental Psychology series). ISBN: 0470028920.

A99
ANDERSON, JOHN R. 1976. *Language, Memory, and Thought.* Hillsdale, NJ: L. Erlbaum Associates, distributed by Halsted Press; 1976. 546p. (Experimental Psychology series). ISBN: 0470151870.

A100
ANDERSON, JOHN R. 1983. *The Architecture of Cognition.* Cambridge, MA: Harvard University Press; 1983. 345p. (Cognitive Science series, 5). ISBN: 0674044258.

A101
ANDERSON, JOHN R. 1985/1995. *Cognitive Psychology and Its Implications.* 2nd ed. New York, NY: W. H. Freeman; 1985. 472p. ISBN: 0716716860. 3rd ed. Hillsdale, NJ: L. Erlbaum Associates; 1990. 276p. ISBN: 0805804196. 4th ed. New York, NY: Freeman; 1995. (Note: editions vary tremendously).

A102
ANDERSON, JOHN R. 1995. *Learning and Memory: An Integrated Approach.* New York, NY: J. Wiley; 1995. 488p. ISBN: 0471586854.

A103
ANDERSON, KAY; GALE, FAY, eds. 1992. *Inventing Places. Studies in Cultural Geography.* Melbourne, AU: Longman Cheshire; Halsted Press; 1992. 285p. ISBN: 0582868750 / 0470218711.

A104
ANDERSON, M. 1978. Occupational Classification in the United States Census, 1870-1940. *Journal of Interdisciplinary History.* 1978; 8: 111-130. ISSN: 0022-1953.

A105
ANDERSON, MICHAEL Q. 1982. *Quantitative Management Decision Making, with Models and Applications.* Monterey, CA: Brooks/Cole Pub. Co.; 1982. 623p. ISBN: 0818504358.

A106
ANDERSON, MICHAEL Q. 1986. *Quantitative Management: An Introduction.* 2nd ed. Boston, MA: Kent Pub. Co.; 1986. 662p. ISBN: 0534059589.

A107
ANDERSON, PHILIP W.; ARROW, KENNETH J.; PINES, DAVID, eds. 1988. *The Economy as an Evolving Complex System* [I]. Santa Fe, NM: Santa Fe Institute (SFI); 1988. (Santa Fe Institute Studies in the Science of Complexity). ISBN: 0-201-15685-7 (pbk.). For sequel, see reference: ARTHUR, W. B.; DURLAUF, S. N.; LANE, D. A., eds. 1997.

A108
ANDERSON, SHEILA J. 1992. The Future of the Present—The ERSC Data Archive as a Resource Centre for the Future. *History and Computing.* 1992; 4: 191-196. ISSN: 0957-0144.

A109
ANDERSON, SHEILA J. 1994. Documenting Data for Secondary Analysis: The Primary Producer's Role and Responsibility. *IASSIST Quarterly.* 1994; ISSN: 0739-1137.

A110
ANDERSON, SHEILA J.; TOWNSEND, SEAN; STRUIJVE, OSCAR. 1996. Into the Great Wide Open—Exploring History on the Web. See reference: BORODKIN, L., ed. 1996. Session A3.

A111
ANDERSON, SHEILA J.; WINSTANLEY, BRIDGET. 1993. Problems and Possibilities of a Historical Thesaurus. See reference: MARKER, ed. 1993/1994: [1-21]. Discussion continued below.

A112
ANDERSON, SHIELA J.; WINSTANLEY, BRIDGET. 1995. Problems and Possibilities of a Historical Thesaurus. See reference: JARITZ, G. *ET AL.,* eds. 1995: 411-430.

A113
ANDERSSON, SUNE. 1987. The Swedish Land Data Bank. In: *International Journal of Geographical Information Systems*. 1987 July-September; 1(3). (Entire issue on title topic). ISSN: 02698-3798.

A114
ANDERSSON, ULF. 1996. *SESAM: Philosophy and Rules Concerning Electronic Archives and Authenticity*. Stockholm, SE: ASTRA Inc.; 1996. (Based on the University of Pittsburgh project and D. Bearman's work).

A115
ANDERSSON, ULF, ed. 1997. *Workshop on Electronic Archiving: An Evaluation of the SESAM*. Stockholm, SE: ASTRA Inc.; 1997.

A116
ANDRE, JACQUES. R.; FURUTA, RICHARD; QUINT, VINCENT. , eds. 1989. *Structured Documents*. Series in Electronic Publishing. Cambridge, UK; New York, NY: Cambridge University Press; 1989. 220p. ISBN: 0521365546.

A117
ANDREANO, RALPH L., ed. [1970]. *The New Economic History: Recent Papers in Methodology*. New York, NY: J. Wiley; [1970]. 178p. (American Economic History series). Essays first appeared in *Explorations in Entrepreneurial History*, 2nd series. LC: HB75.A557.

A118
ANDREEV, ANDREY; BORODKIN, LEONID; LEVANDOSKY, MIKHAIL. 1996 [199-]. Modelling Unstable Historical Processes using Methods of Nonlinear Dynamics (Application fo Chaos Theory in the Analysis of the Worker's Movement in Pre-revolutionary Russia). See reference: BORODKIN, L., ed. 1996: Abstract of presentation, 82-83; paper [199- forthcoming].

A119
ANDRESEN, JENS; MADSEN, TORSTEN.; SCOLLAR, IRWIN, eds. 1992. *Computing the Past: Computer Applications and Quantitative Methods in Archaeology: CAA'92*. Selected Papers from the 20th Computer Applications in Archeology Conference, held March 27-29, 1992, at Aarhus Universitet, Aarhus, Denmark. Aarhus, DK: University Press; 1992. 469p. IBSN: 8772881127; OCLC: 28233374.

A120
ANDRESS, JANS-JÜRGEN. 1992. *Einführung in die Verlaufsdatananalyse: Statistische Grundlagen und Anwendungsbeispiele zur langsschnittanalyse kategorialer Daten* [Introduction to Historical Data Analysis: Statistical Foundations and Applications illustrated by Longitudinal Analysis of Categorized Data] . In: *Historische Sozialforschung/ Historical Social Research*. Koln, DEU: Zentrum für Historische Sozialforschung; 1992. 328p. (HRS Supplement 5). (In German). ISSN: 0172-6404; OCLC: 28912064.

A121
ANDREWS, D.; GREENHALGH, M. 1987. *Computing for Non-scientific Applications*. Leicester, UK: University of Leicester; 1987. 346p. ISBN: 0-7185-1252-9.

A122
ANDREWS, F. M.; MORGAN, J. N.; SOUQUIST, J. A.; KLEM, L. 1973. *Multiple Classification Analysis: A Report on a Computer Program for Multiple Regression using Categorical Predictors*. 2nd ed. Ann Arbor, MI: Institute for Social Research; 1973. 102p.(On OSIRIS and SPSS analysis of variance capabilities). ISBN: 0879441488; pbk. 0879440554; LCCN: 73-620206; OCLC: 19740415.

A123
ANDREWS, WILLIAM X. 1991. *The His-Triad Project: The Experiment and the Experience*. Mufreesboro, TN: Middle Tennessee State University; 1991. 431p. (D.A. dissertation; DAI, vol. 53/12-A: 4287). Available from: University Microfilms, Ann Arbor, MI (order no. AAD92-12842).

A124
ANDRIESSEN, J. H. ERIK; KOOMAN, PAUL L., eds. 1997. *The Introduction of Information and Communication Technology (ICT) in Organizations*. In: *Work and Organizational Psychology*. Mahwah, NJ: Lawrence Erlbaum Associates, Inc.; 1997. 144p. (Entire issue on title topic). ISBN: 0-86377-949-2.

A125
ANGLIN, GARY. J., ed. 1991. *Instructional Technology: Past, Present, and Future*. Englewood, CO: Libraries Unlimited; 1991. 399p. ISBN: 0872878201.

A126
ANIEL, JEAN-PIERRE. [199-]. *Mandragore*: An Iconographic Database for the Manuscripts in the Bibliotheque Nationale, Paris. See reference: HAMESSE, J., ed., [199-] forthcoming.

A127
ANKERSMIT, FRANK R. 1983. *Narrative Logic: A Semantic Analysis of the Historian's Language*. The Hague, NL; Boston, MA: M. Nijhoff; 1983. 265p. ISBN: 9024727316.

A128
ANKERSMIT, FRANK R. 1989. *The Reality of Effect in the Writing of History: The Dynamics of Historiographical Topology*. Amsterdam, NL: Koninklijke Nederlandse Akademie van Wetenschape; 1989. (Medeldelingen van de Afdeling Letterkunde; nieuse reeks, d. 52, no. 1). ISBN: 0444857044.

A129
ANKERSMIT, FRANK R. 1994. *History and Topology: The Rise and Fall of Metaphor*. Berkeley, CA: University of California Press; c1994. ISBN: 0520082044.

A130
ANKERSMIT, FRANK R. 1995. Historicism: An Attempt at Synthesis. *History and Theory*. 1995 October; 34(3): 143-161. (Commentaries follow; critique by IGGERS. GEORG, and reply and Ankersmit about the reconciliation of German and Anglo-Saxon historicism). ISSN: 0018-2656.

A131
ANKERSMIT, FRANK R.; KELLNER, HANS. 1995. *A New Philosophy of History*. London, UK: Reaktion Books; 1995. 289p. ISBN: 0948462787.

A132
ANSCOMBE, GERTRUDE E. M. 1957/1963. *Intention*. Oxford, UK: Blackwell; 1957. 2nd ed., 1963. 94p.

A133
ANSCOMBE, GERTRUDE E. M. 1971. *Causality and Determination: An Inaugural Lecture* [at Cambridge University, 6 May 1971]. Cambridge, UK: Cambridge University Press; 1971. 30p.

A134
ANTENUCCI, JOHN C; BROWN, KAY; CROSWELL, PETER L.; KEVANY, MICHAEL J.; ARCHER, HUGH. *Geographic Information Systems: A Guide to the Technology*. New York, NY: Van Nostrand Reinhold; 1991. 301p. ISBN: 0442997566.

A135
ANTZE, PAUL; LAMBEK, MICHAEL, eds. 1996. *Tense Past: Cultural Essays in Trauma and Memory*. New York, NY: n.p.; 1996. 266p. ISBN: 10415915627 (hbk.); 10415915635 (pbk.); LCCN: 95026249.

A136
AOKI, T.; TANAKA, T.; NISHI, T.; TSUKADA, M.; NAKAMURA, O.; MIKNAMI, T. 1988. Automatic Text Extraction System using Layout Structure. *Research Report of Kogakuin University*. 1988; 64: 297-302.

A137
APPADURAI, ARJUN. 1986. *The Social Life of Things: Commodities in Cultural Perspective*. Cambridge, UK / New York, NY: Cambridge University Press; 1986. 329p. ISBN: 0521323517; LCCN: 85019529.

A138
APPLEBY, JOYCE O. 1997. Public-Minded History. *AHA Perspectives*. Washington, D.C.: AHA. 1997; 1: 2-3. ISSN: 0743-7021.

A139
APPLEBY, JOYCE O. 1998. The Power of History. *American Historical Review*. 1998 Feb; 103 (1): 1-14. ISSN: 0002-8762.

A140
APPLEBY, JOYCE O., ed. 1996. *Knowledge and Postmodernism: In Historical Perspective*. New York, NY: Routledge; 1996. 559p. ISBN: 0415913829 (hbk.); 0415913837 (pbk.).

A141
APPLEBY, JOYCE O.; HUNT, LYNN; JACOB, MARGARET. 1994. *Telling the Truth About History*. New York, NY: W. W. Norton & Co.; 1994. 322p. ISBN: 0393036154.

A142
APPLEBY, JOYCE; HUNT, LYNN; JACOB, MARGARET. 1995. Response [to reviews by BUNZL, SMITH, and HIGHAM]. *Journal of the History of Ideas*. 1995 October; 56 (4): 675-681. ISSN: 0022-5037.

A143
APPLIED COMPUTER RESEARCH, INC. 1970-. *Computer Literature Index. A Subject/Author Index to Computer and Data Processing Literature* . [NY]: ACR, Inc.; 1970-. Annual Cumulation, 1996. 1997; 26: 326p. (Covers books and articles). ISSN: 0270-4846.

A144
ARABIE, PHIPPS; HUBERT, LAWRENCE J.; SOETE, GEERT DE. 1996. *Clustering and Classification*. River Edge, NJ: World Scientific; 1996. 490p. ISBN: 9810212879 (hbk.); 9810213549 (pbk.).

A145
ARANGO, G.; PRIETO-DIAZ, R. 1991. Introduction and Overview: Domain Analysis Concepts and Research Directions. In: Prieto-Diaz, R.; Arango, G., eds. *Domain Analysis and Software Systems Modeling* (pp. 9-26). Los Alamitos, CA: IEEE Computer Society Press; 1991. 299p. ISBN: 081868996x.

A146
ARBIB, MICHAEL A.; HESSE, MARY B. 1986. *The Construction of Reality*. Cambridge, UK: Cambridge University Press; 1986. 286p. ISBN: 0521326893.

A147
ARBOR SOFTWARE INC. [1996]. *The Role of the Multidimensional Database in a Data Warehousing Solution* (Electronic file). Sunnyvale, CA: Arbor Software, Inc.; [1996]. (Arbor Software White Paper). Available from Arbor Software Corporation at http://www .arborsoft.com/wht_ppr/ wareTOC.html (viewed June 1997).

A148
ARBOR SOFTWARE, INC. [1997a]. *Data Warehousing and OLAP: The Keys to Rapid Deployment of Enterprise-Scale Information Delivery Systems*. Sunnyvale, CA: Arbor Software, Inc.; [1997]. Accessible at http://olapasap.arbor soft.com.

A149
ARBOR SOFTWARE, INC. [1997b]. *Increasing Corporate Intelligence with the World Wide Web*. Sunnyvale, CA: Arbor Software, Inc.; [1997]. 8p.(An Arbor Software White Paper). Accessible at http://olapasap.arborsoft.com.

A150
ARCHIVES DES FRANCE. 1970. *Manuel d'archivistique: Théorie et practique des archives en France* [Archival Science Manual: Theory and Practice in the Archives of France]. Sponsored by the Association des archivistes français. Paris, FR: S.E.V.P.E.N.; 1970. 805p. (In French). LC no.: CD1191.A85.

A151
ARDELT, RUDOLF G. 1987. Die Grafische Darstellung-ein Hilfmittle des Unterristches ein Methodisches Instrumenter Geschichts-wissenschaft? [Graphic Representation: A Teaching Aid and Methodological Tool for the Science of History?]. *Zeitgeschichte* [Vienna, AT: Geyer-Edition]. 1987; 14(5): 198-210. (In German). ISSN: 0256-5250; LCCN: 74-640279/r90.

A152
ARGYRIS, CHRIS. 1957/1976. *Personality and Organization: The Conflict between the System and the Individual*. New York, NY: Harper and Row; 1957. Reprint: New York, NY: Harper-Collins; 1976. ISBN: 0060302100.

A153
ARGYRIS, CHRIS. 1964/1990. *Integrating the Individual and the Organization*. New York, NY: John Wiley & Sons; 1964. 327p. LCCN: 64-13209. New edition. New York, NY: Transactional Publications; 1990. ISBN: 0887388035.

A154
ARGYRIS, CHRIS. 1974. *The Applicability of Organizational Sociology*. New York, NY: Cambridge University Press; 1974. ISBN: 0521084482.

A155
ARGYRIS, CHRIS. 1983. Action Science and Intervention. *Journal of Applied Behavioral Sciences*. 1983; 19(2): 115-140. ISSN: 0021-8863.

A156
ARGYRIS, CHRIS. 1994. *On Organizational Learning*. Reprint. London, UK: Blackwell; 1994. ISBN: 1557866635 (pbk.).

A157
ARGYRIS, CHRIS; PUTNAM, ROBERT; SMITH, DIANA MCLAIN. 1985. *Action Science*. Jossey-Bass Social and Behavioral Science series. San Francisco, CA: Jossey-Bass; 1985. ISBN: 0875896650.

A158
ARGYRIS, CHRIS; SCHOEN, D. A. 1978/1994. *Organizational Learning: A Theory of Action Perspective*. Reading, MA: Addison-Wesley; 1978. Reprint. New York and London, UK: Blackwells; 1994. ISBN: 1557866675. Based on their *Organizational Learning: Theory, Method and Practice*. Reading, MA: Addison-Wesley Publishers; 1966. ISBN: 02016729836.

A159
ARIES, PHILIPPE. [1960]. *L'Enfant et la Vie Familiale sous l'Ancien Régime* [The Child and Family Life in the Ancient Régime]. Paris, FR: Plon; [1960]. 503p. LCCN: 62-25542/L; OCLC: 265129.

A160
ARIS, JOHN. 1990. Animating the Archives. *ASLIB Proceedings*. 1990 January; 42(1): 1-15. ISSN: 0001-253x.

A161
ARLAUD, C. 1993. Les Fouilles de la Presui'ile a Lyon [The Archeological Digs of the Island of Lyon]. *Archéologi*. 1993 October; 294: 58-66. (In French). ISSN: 0570-6270; LCCN: 64-9499; OCLC: 19760326.

A162
ARLAUD, C.; HAMMARCHE, M.; LUROL, J.-M. 1994. *L.P. Arch'*: Un Système de Gestion Informatisée des Données Archéologiques en milieu urbain, à Lyon (1991-1994) [Arch(aeology): An Information Management System for Archaeological Data in an Urban Milieu: Lyon]. (In French). See reference: BECK, P., ed. 1994: 28-31.

A163
ARMON-JONES, CLAIRE. 1986. The Thesis of Constructionism. In: Harre, Rom, ed. *The Social Construction of Emotions* New York, NY: Oxford University Press; 1986. 2-40. ISBN: 0631165851.

A164
ARMOUR POLLY, JEAN; LYON, ELAINE. 1992. Out of the Archives and into the Streets. American memory in American Libraries. *Online*. 1992 September; 16(5): 51-57. ISSN: 0146-5422.

A165
ARMSTRONG, C. J.; FENTON, R. R., eds. [1996]. *World Databases in Social Sciences*. London, UK: Bowker-Saur; c. 1996. 793p. ISBN: 1857391160; LCCN: 96148588.

A166
ARMSTRONG, DAVID M. 1989. *A Combinatorial Theory of Possibility*. Cambridge, UK/New York, NY: Cambridge University Press; 1989. 156p. ISBN: 052111374278 (hbk.); 0521377803 (pbk.); LCCN: 89000708.

A167
ARMSTRONG, THOMAS F. 1983. They Tell Me It's Fun: History Students and Information Technology in and Classroom Computer Use. In: *Proceedings and Papers of the Georgia Association of Historians* Atlanta, GA: Assn. of Georgia Historians; 1983. 88-91. ISBN: 0275-3863; LCCN: 81-643246; OCLC: 7142549.

A168
ARMSTRONG, W. A. 1972. The Use of Information about Occupation: Occupational Classifications. In: Wrigley, Edward A., ed. *Nineteenth-century Society: Essays in the Use of Quantitative Methods for the Study of Social Data* Cambridge, UK: Cambridge University Press for the Cambridge Group for the History of Population and Social Structure; 1972. 191-310. (See for the so-called Booth-Armstrong classification of occupations). ISBN: 0521084121; LCCN: 72-24552; OCLC: 16211907.

A169
ARNHEIM, RUDOLF. 1954. *Art and Visual Perception: A Psychology of the Creative Eye*. Berkeley, CA: University of California; 1954. 408p. LC no.: N70.A7.

A170
ARNHEIM, RUDOLF. 1970. *Visual Thinking*. London, UK: Faber; 1970. 345p. ISBN: 057100993655; LCCN: 78588335.

A171
ARNHEIM, RUDOLF. 1986. A Plea for Visual Thinking. In his: *New Essays on the Psychology of Art* Berkeley, CA: University of California Press; 1986. 135-152. ISBN: 052005535 (hbk.); 052005543 (pbk.).

A172
ARNHEIM, RUDOLF. 1988. Visual Dynamics. *American Scientist*. 1988; 76 (6): 585-591. ISSN: 0003-0996.

A173
ARNOLD, J. B. III. 1979. Archeological Applications of Computer-Drawn Contour and Three Dimensional Perspective Plots. In: Upham, Stedman, ed. *Computer Graphics in Archeology: Statistical Cartographic Applications to Spatial Analysis in Archeological Contexts* Tempe, AZ: Arizona State University; 1979. 1-15. (ASU Anthropological Research Papers, 15). ISSN: 0271-0641.

A174
ARNOLD, ROBERT S., ed. 1993. *Software Re-engineering*. Los Alamitos, CA: IEEE; 1993. 688p. ISBN: 0-8186-3272-0.

A175
ARNOLD, V. I. 1992. *Catastrophe Theory*. Wasserman, G. S., trans. 3rd ed. Berlin, DEU; New York, NY: Springer Verlag; 1992. 150p. ISBN:0387548114.

A176
ARROYO-BISHOP, DANIEL; LANTADA-ZARZOSA, M. T. 1994. *Quelque pas dans l'enregistrement et l'analyse architecturale, apports du projet ArcheoDATA* [About the Registration and Analysis of Archeological Data shared

from the *ArcheoDATA* Project]. In: *Les Nouvelles de l'Archéologie*. 1995; 54. (In French). ISSN: 0242-7702; LCCN: 85-60428; OCLC: 9362344. Available from: Maison des sciences de l'homme, 54, Blvd. Raspail, F-75270 Paris Cedex 06, France.

A177
ARSENT'EV, NIKOLAY M. 1994. *Zamoskovnyi gorni okrung: zavodovladeltsy i rabochie* [Workers Northeast of Moscow: Professions and Miners]. Saransk, RU: Izdatelstvo Mordovskogo universiteta; 1994. 233p. (in Russian) ISBN: 5710301876.

A178
ARSENT'EV, NIKOLAY M. 1996 [199-]. Processing Russian Demographical Sources: Family Structure in the Volga Region, 180-19 centuries. See reference: BORODKIN, L., ed. 1996: Abstract of presentation, 16; paper [199- forthcoming].

A179
ARTANDI, SUSAN. 1973. Information Concepts and Their Utility. *Journal of the American Society for Information Science*. 1993; 24: 242-245. ISSN: 0002-8231.

A180
ARTHUR, W. BRIAN; DURLAUF, STEVEN N.; LANE, DAVID A., eds. 1997. *The Economy as an Evolving Complex System* II. Santa Fe Institute Studies in the Science of Complexity. Santa Fe, NM: Santa Fe Institute (SFI); 1997. ISBN: 0-201-15685-7 (pbk.). For vol. I, see reference: ANDERSON, P. W.; ARROW, K. J.; PINES, D., eds., 1988.

A181
ASHFORD, J.; WILLETT, P. 1988. *Text Retrieval and Document Databases*. London, UK: Chartwell-Bratt; 1988. ISBN: 0-86238-204-1.

A182
ASHFORTH, BLAKE R.; HUMPHREY, RONALD H. 1995. Emotion in the Workplace: A Reappraisal. *Human Relations*. 1995 February; 48 (2): 97-125. ISSN: 0018-7267.

A183
ASPRAY, WILLIAM F., Jr. 1980. *From Mathematical Constructivity to Computer Science: Alan Turing, John von Neumann, and the Origins of Computer Science in Mathematical Logic*. Madison, WI: University of Wisconsin; 1980. (Ph.D. dissertation; DAI, vol. 41/10-A: 4478). Available from: University Microfilms, Ann Arbor, MI: Order no. AAD81-05257.

A184
ASPRAY, WILLIAM F. 1991. *John von Neumann and the Origins of Modern Computing*. Cambridge, MA: MIT Press; 1991. 376p. ISBN: 0262011212.

A185
ASPRAY, WILLLIAM F., ed. 1990. *Computing before Computers*. Ames IA: Iowa State University Press; 1990. 266p. ISBN: 0-8138-0047-1.

A186
ASPRAY, WILLIAM F.; BURKS, ARTHUR, eds. 1987. *Papers of John von Neumann and Computer Theory*. Cambridge, MA: MIT Press; 1987. 624p. (Charles Babbage Institute Reprint Series for the History of Computing, 12). ISBN: 026222030X; LCCN: 86- 8588/r87; OCLC: 13582096.

A187
ASPRAY, WILLIAM F.; CAMPBELL-KELLY, MARTIN. 1996/1997. *Computers: A History of the Information Machine*. New York, NY: Basic Books; 1996. 2nd ed. New York, NY: Harper-Collins; 1997. ISBN: 0465029906.

A188
ASSOCIATION FOR COMPUTING AND THE HUMANITIES (ACH). 1966-. *Computers and the Humanities* [*CHum*]. New York, NY: Pergamon; Dordrecht, NL: Kluwer Academic Publishers; 1966-. Qtly. ISSN: 0010-4817.

A189
ASSOCIATION FOR DOCUMENTARY EDITING. 1984-. *Documentary Editing*. Lexington, VA: Association for Documentary Editing; 1984-. Qtly. ISSN: 0196-7134; LCCN: 85-11011; OCLC: 10685677.

A190
ASSOCIATION FOR HISTORY AND COMPUTING (AHC). 1988 (1989-). *History and Computing*. Morris, Robert J., ed. Eynsham, Oxford, UK: University of London; 1989-. Semi-annual. ISSN: 0957-0144; LCCN: 92-659037; OCLC: 22659624. See also references to proceedings and volumes of collected essays by editors DENLEY, P.; HOPKIN, D.1987; DENLEY, FOGELVIK, HARVEY. 1989; etc.

A191

ASSOCIATION FOR HISTORY AND COMPUTING (AHC). 1993. *A Historical Computing Bibliography* (Electronic file). Denley, P., ed. London, UK: AHC and the University of London QMW Humanities Computing Center; 1993. (Diskette; Version 1.0). Available from: IAHC, History Department, College of Queen Mary, London UK.

A192

ASSOCIATION FOR INFORMATION AND IMAGE MANAGEMENT (AIIM). 1967-. *Journal of Information and Image Management* (JIIM). Silver Springs, MD: AIIM; 1967-. (Formerly *Journal of Micrographics*). ISSN: 082-3876.

A193

ASSOCIATION FOR INFORMATION AND IMAGE MANAGEMENT (AIIM). [1988]. *Recommended Practice for Quality Control of Image Scanners*. Silver Spring, MD: AIIM; [1988]. 19p. ANSI/AIIM Standard MS44-1988.

A194

ASSOCIATION FOR INFORMATION AND IMAGE MANAGEMENT (AIIM). 1989a. Facsimile and its Role in Electronic Imaging. Silver Springs, MD: AIIM; 1989. 36p. AIIM Technical Report TR170-1989.

A195

ASSOCIATION FOR INFORMATION AND IMAGE MANAGEMENT (AIIM). 1989b. *Information and Image Management: the State of the Industry*. Silver Spring, MD: AIIM; 1989. 88p. AIIM Cat. DO30.

A196

ASSOCIATION FOR INFORMATION AND IMAGE MANAGEMENT (AIIM). 1992. *Glossary of Imaging Technology*. Silver Spring, MD: AIIM; 1992. 79p. ISBN: 089258243X; AIIM Cat.7TR2.

A197

ASSOCIATION FOR INFORMATION AND IMAGE MANAGEMENT (AIIM). 1994a. *Performance Guidelines for the Legal Acceptance of Records Produced by Information Technology Systems*. Pt. III: *Implementation [ANSI/AIIM TR31-1994]*. Silver Spring, MD: AIIM; 1994.

A198

ASSOCIATION FOR INFORMATION AND IMAGE MANAGEMENT (AIIM). 1994b. *AIIM Buying Guide and Membership Directory*. Silver Spring, MD: AIIM; 1994. (Annual). ISSN: 0897-3177

A199

ASSOCIATION FOR LITERARY AND LINGUISTIC COMPUTING (ALLC). 1985. *Computers in Literary and Linguistic Computing/Ordinateur et les Recherches Literaires et Linguistiques*. Proceedings, 11th International Conference, Universite Catholique de Louvain (Louvain-la-Nueve), 2-6 April, 1984. Paris, FR: Champion/Geneva, CH: Slatkine; 1985. 404p. (French and English). ISBN: 2051007039; LCCN: 88136699.

A200

ASSOCIATION FOR LITERARY AND LINGUISTIC COMPUTING (ALLC). 1986-. *Literary and Linguistic Computing*. Oxford, UK: Oxford University Press; 1986-. Qtly. ISSN: 0268-1145; LCCN: 87-647341; OCLC: 14082151.

A201

ASSOCIATION FOR LITERARY AND LINGUISTIC COMPUTING (ALLC). 1988. *Computers in Literary and Linguistic Computing / Ordinateur et les Recherches Literaires et Linguistiques*. Roper, John, ed. Proceedings, 13th International Conference, University pf East Anglia, 1-4 April, 1986. Paris, FR: Champion/Geneva, CH: Slatkine; 1988. 181p. (Travaux de Linguistique Quantitative, 39). (French and English). ISBN: 2051009945; LCCN: 88194841.

A202

ASSOCIATION FOR UNCERTAINTY IN ARTIFICIAL INTELLIGENCE (AUAI). [1990-]. *Conferences on Uncertainty in Artificial Intelligence*. San Mateo, CA: Morgan Kaufmann Pub.; 1990-. Cf., *AUAI Home Page*. Berkeley, CA: Thinkbank; 1995-. Accessible at http://www.auai.org/.

A203

ASSOCIATION FRANÇAIS POUR L'HISTOIRE ET L'INFORMATIQUE. 1990-. *Mémoire Vive [Living Memory]* (FR). Bourlet, Caroline, ed. Paris, FR: CNRS Institut de Recherche et d'histoire des textes; 1990-. (Bulletin de l'Association). Available from: CNRS, Paris, FR.

A204

ASSOCIATION OF CANADIAN ARCHIVISTS. 1975/76-. *Archivaria*. Ottawa, CN: ACA; 1975/76-. (Semi-annual). ISSN: 0318-6954; LCCN: 84-643294; OCLC: 3247908. Available from: ACA Secretary, Public Archives of Canada, 395 Wellington St., Ottawa, Ontario, Canada K1G 0E7.

A205
ASSOCIATION OF COLLEGE AND RESEARCH LIBRARIES (ACRL). RARE BOOKS AND MANUSCRIPTS
SECTION (RBMS). 1991. *Genre Terms: A Thesaurus for Use in Rare Book and Special Collections Cataloguing.*
2nd ed. Prepared by the ACRL Bibliographic Standards Committee of the Rare Books and Manuscripts Section.
Chicago, IL: ALA/ACRL; 1991. 78p. ISBN: 083897516X; LCCN: 91-193471; OCLC: 19910909. See also:
College and Research Libraries News. 1983; 9: 322-325. ISSN: 0099-0086.

A206
ASSOCIATION OF COLLEGE AND RESEARCH LIBRARIES (ACRL). RARE BOOKS AND MANUSCRIPT
SECTION (RBMS). 1988. *Provenance Evidence: A Thesaurus for Use in Rare Book and Special Collections
Cataloguing.* Prepared by the Standards Committee of the Rare Books and Manuscripts Section. Chicago, IL:
ALA-ACRL; 1988. 19p. ISBN: 083897239X; LCCN: 89-162538; OCLC: 19489177.

A207
ASSOCIATION OF RESEARCH LIBRARIES (ARL). 1993. *Directory of Electronic Journals, Newsletters and
Academic Discussion Lists.* M. Strangelove; D. Kovacs, comps.; A. Okerson, ed. 3rd ed. Washington, D.C.: ARL,
1993. 355p. OCLC: 19930630.

A208
ASSOCIATION OF RESEARCH LIBRARIES (ARL). 1997. *Monograph and Serial Costs in ARL Libraries, 1986-
1997.* Accessible at: http://www.arl.org/stats/arlstat/1997_t2.html.

A209
ATHERTON, JAY. 1994. The Contribution of *Archivaria* to the Development of the Canadian Archival Profession. See
reference: COX, ed., 1994d. 270-277.

A210
ATKINS, DANIEL E.; BIRMINGHAM, WILLIAM P.; DURFEE, EDMUND H.; GLOVER, ERIC J.; MULLEN,
TRACY; RUNDENSTEINER, ELKE A.; SOLOWAY, ELLIOT; VIDAL, JOSE M.; WALLACE, RAVEN; WELL-
MAN, MICHAEL P. 1996. Toward Inquiry-based Education through Interacting Software Agents. See reference:
SCHATZ, B.; CHEN, H., eds. 1996: 69-76.

A211
ATKINSON, A. C. 1985. *Plots, Transformations, and Regression: An Introduction to Graphical Methods of Diagnostic
Regression Analysis.* New York, NY: Oxford University Press; 1985. 282p. ISBN: 0-198533-59-4; LCCN: 85-5140;
OCLC: 11867011.

A212
ATTFIELD, ROBIN. 1987. *A Theory of Value and Obligation.* London, UK: Routledge, Kegan & Paul; 1987. ISBN:
0709905726.

A213
ATTREED, LORRAINE; POWERS, JAMES F. 1997. Lessons in the Dark: Teaching the Middle Ages with Film. *AHA
Perspectives.* 1997 January; 35 (1): 11-16. ISSN: 0743- 7021.

A214
ATTWELL, PAUL A. 1996. "The Productivity Paradox." *The Chronicle for Higher Education.* 1995, March 15; 42
(27): A56. ISSN: 0009-5982.

A215
AUDET, MICHEL; BOUCHIKHI, HAMID, eds. 1993. *Structuration du Social et Modernité Avancée: Autour des
Travaux d'Anthony Giddens* [Structuration of Social Advancement and Modernity: Based on the Work of Anthony
Giddens]. Sainte-Foy, Québec, CN: Presses de l'Université Laval; 1993. 537p. ISBN: 2763773192.

A216
AUERBACH, ERICH. 1953. *Mimesis: The Representation of Reality in Western Literature.* Trask, W. R., trans.
Princeton, NJ: Princeton University Press; 1953. 563p. LCCN: 52013152.

A217
AUGARTEN, STAN. 1984. *Bit by Bit; An Illustrated History of Computers.* New York, NY: Ticknor & Fields; 1984.
324p. ISBN: 0-899192-68-8; 0-8999193-02-1 (pbk.); LCCN: 84- 2508; OCLC: 10695774.

A218
AUGER, PIERRE; ROUSSEAU, LOUIS. 1978. *Méthodologie de la recherche terminologique* [Methodology for
Terminological Research]. Québec, CN: Office de la Langue Français, Editeur officiel du Québec; 1978. 80p.
(Etudes recherches et documentation). (In French). ISBN: 0775427977.

A219
AULD, LAWRENCE W. S. 1988. Library Trends Past and Present: A Descriptive Study. *Library Trends.* 1988 Spring;
36(4): 853-868. ISSN: 0024-2594.

A220
AURELL, MARTIN. 1995. *Les noces du comte: marriage et pouvoir en Catalogne (785-1213)* [Comital Nuptials: Marriage and Power in Catalunya]. In: *Histoire ancienne et medievale*, 32. Paris, FR: Publications de la Sorbonne; 1995. (In French).

A221
AUSTIN, ERICK W. 1992. The ICPSR Historical Data Archive: What can be learned from its 25 years. *Cahier VGI* [*Vereniging voor Geschiedenis en Informatica* (Low Countries Association for History and Computing)]. Hilversum, NE: Uitgeverij Verloren; 1992.

A222
AUSTIN, JOHN L. 1961/1979. *Philsophical Papers*. Urmson, J. O.; Warnock, G. J., eds. Oxford, UK; Clarendon Press; 1961. 3rd ed. 1979. 306p. ISBN: 019283021X (pbk.); 0198246277 (hbk.).

A223
AUSTIN, JOHN L. 1962a. *How to Do Things with Words*. Cambridge, MA: Harvard University Press; 1962. 166p. (William James Lectures [1955]). 2nd ed. Oxford, UK: Clarendon Press; 1975. 168p. ISBN: 019824553X.

A224
AUSTIN, JOHN L. 1962b. *Sense and Sensibilia*. Warnock, G. J., ed. Oxford, UK: Clarendon Press; 1962. 144p.

A225
AUSTRALIAN SOCIETY OF ARCHIVISTS. 1993. *Australian Common Practice Manual*. Sydney, AT: ASA; 1993.

A226
AVERSA, ELIZABETH. 1985. Citation Patterns of Highly Cited Papers and Their Relationship to Literature Aging. A Study of the Working Literature. *Scientometrics*. 1985; 7: 383-389. ISSN: 0378-5939.

A227
AXELROD, ROBERT. 1985. *The Evolution of Cooperation*. New York, NY: Basic Books; 1985. ISBN: 045021212.

A228
AYDELOTTE, WILLIAM O. 1971. *Quantification in History*. Reading, MA: Addison Welsey; 1971. 181p.LCCN: 76-150517; OCLC: 147530.

A229
AYDELOTTE, WILLIAM O., BOGUE, ALLEN G.; FOGEL, ROBERT W., eds. 1972. *The Dimensions of Quantitative Research in History*. Princeton, NJ: Princeton University Press; 1972. 435p. (Quantitative Studies in History, s.n.). ISBN: 0691075441; LCCN: 75-166370; OCLC: 579815.

A230
AYER, ALFRED J. [1959]. *Logical Positivism*. Glencoe, IL: Free Press; {c1959]. 455p. LCCN: 58006479. Reprint in Library of Philosophical Movements. Westport, CT: Greenwood Press; 1978. ISBN: 0313204624; LCCN: 78006321.

A231
AYTON, ANDREW. 1989. Computing for History Undergraduates: A Strategy for Database Integration. *Historische Sozialforschung / Historical Social Research*. 1989; 14: 46-51. ISSN: 0172-6404.

-B-

B1
BAACHUS, FAHEIM. 1990. *Representing and Reasoning with Probabilistic Knowledge: A Logical Approach to Probabilities*. Cambridge, MA: MIT Press; c1990. 233p. (Artificial Intelligence series). ISBN: 0262023172; LCCN: 900103555.

B2
BAAYEN, HAROLD. 1992. Statistical Models for Word Frequency Distribution: A Linguistic Evaluation. *Computers and Humanities*. 1992; 26 (5-6): 347-364. ISSN: 0010-4817.

B3
BABBIE, EARL R. 1998. *The Basics of Social Research*. 8th ed. Belmont, CA: Wadsworth Publishing; 1999. 473p. Rev. of *The Practice of Social Research*. 1998. ISBN: 0534559530; LCCN: 98-024155.

B4
BABBIE, EARL R.; HALLEY, FRED. 1998. *Adventures in Social Research: Data Analysis using SPSS for Windows 95*. Thousand Oaks, CA: Pine Forge Press; c1998. 326p., disk (includes data set from the 1996 GSS). ISBN: 0761985247; LCCN: 98-140153.

B5

BABBIE, EARL R.; WAGENAAR, T. H. 1983. *Practicing Social Science Research.* 3rd ed. Belmont, CA: Wadsworth; 1983.

B6

BACHARACH, MICHAEL; HURLEY, SUSAN, eds. 1991/1993. *Foundations of Decision Theory: Issues and Advances.* Oxford, UK: Basil Blackwell; 1991. Reprint, 1993. ISBN: 0631190635.

B7

BADDELEY, ALAN D. 1976. *The Psychology of Memory.* New York, NY: Basic Books; 1976. 430p. ISBN: 0465067360.

B8

BADDELEY, ALAN D. 1990/1997. *Human Memory: Theory and Practice.* Boston, MA: Allyn and Bacon; 1990. 515p. ISBN: 0205123120(pbk). Hove, UK: Psychology Press; 1997. ISBN: 0863774318 (pbk.).

B9

BAGG, JANET; RYAN, NICK. 1991. Interacting with Diagrams: Using a Graph Browser with a Research Database. See reference: BEST, H., *ET AL.*, eds., 1991. 280-285.

B10

BAILEY, CHARLES W. Jr. 1996-1997. *Scholarly Electronic Publishing Bibliography.* [Electronic file, version 6:3/1/97]. Accessible at http://info.lib.uh.edu/sepb.html.

B11

BAILEY, KENNETH. D. 1994. *Typologies and Taxonomies. An Introduction to Classification Techniques.* Thousand Oaks, CA: Sage Publications; 1994. ISBN: 0803952597.

B12

BAILEY, LARRY P. 1995. Auditing in a Microcomputer Environment. In: *Miller GAAS Guide: A Comprehensive Restatement of Generally Accepted Auditing Standards* (8.05). Altamonte Springs, FL: Institute of Internal Auditors; 1995. (Revision of the IIA Comprehensive GAAS Guidelines). ISBN: 0156024306

B13

BAILYN, B. 1982. The Challenge of Modern Historiography. *American Historical Review.* 1982; 87: 1-24. ISSN: 0002-8762.

B14

BAIN, GEORGE. 1996. Visualizing the Archival Work Process: A Survey and Interpretation. *Archival Issues.* 1996; 21 (1) : 47-60. ISSN: 1067-4993.

B15

BAIRD, LLOYD; BRISCOE, JON: TUDEN, LYDIA: ROSANSKY, L. M. H. 1994. World Class Executive Development. *Human Resource Planning.* 1994; 17 (1): 1-15. ISSN: 0199- 8986.

B16

BAIRD, LLOYD S.; POST, JAMES E.; MAHON, JOHN F. 1990. *Management: Functions and Responsibilities.* New York, NY: Harper & Row; 1990. ISBN: 0060404388

B17

BAK, PER; CHEN, KAN. 1991. Self-organized Criticality. *Scientific American.* 1991 Jan.; 264 (1): 46-. ISSN: 0036-8733.

B18

BAKER, JULIA. 1991. *Processes of Change: An Anthropological Inquiry into Resistance to Technological Changes in an Organization.* Boulder, CO: University of Colorado; 1991. 280p. (Ph.D. dissertation; *DAI,* vol. 52/09-A: 3328). 267p. Available from: University Microfilms, Ann Arbor, MI (Order no. AAD92-06596).

B19

BAKER, KEITH M. Memory and Practice. *Representations.* 1985 summer; 11: 134-159. ISSN: 0734-6018.

B20

BAKER, KEITH M. 1990. *Inventing the French Revolution: Essays on French Political Culture in the Eighteenth Century.* Cambridge, UK: Cambridge University Press; 1990. 372p. ISBN: 0521346185 (hbk.); 0521385784 (pbk.).

B21

BAKER, KEITH M.; LUCAS, COLIN; FURET, FRANCOIS; OZOUF, MONA, eds. 1987-1994. *The French Revolution and the Creation of Modern Political Culture.* Colloquium on the Political Culture of the Old Regime, Chicago, Sept. 11-15, 1986. Oxford, UK; Oxford University Press / New York, NY: Pergamon Press; 1987-1994. 4 vols. ISBN: 0080342582.; LCCN: 87-016080.

B22
BAKER, R. S. 1997. History and periodization [review article]. *Clio.* 1997; 26: 135-141. ISSN: 0884-2043.

B23
BAKEWELL, ELIZABETH; BEEMAN, WILLIAM O.; REESE MCMICHAEL, CAROL; SCHMITT, MARILYN, eds. 1988. *Object, Image, Inquiry: The Art Historian at Work.* Report on a collaborative study by the Getty Art History Information Program (AHIP) and the Institute for Research in Information and Scholarship (IRIS), Brown University. Santa Monica, CA: Getty Trust, AHIP; 1988. 199p. ISBN: 0-89236-135-2; LCCN: 88-1101; OCLC: 17412977. Available from: Getty Trust Publications Distribution Center, P.O. Box 2112, Santa Monica, CA 90407-2112.

B24
BALLAND, GERARD; BELLIS, GIL; BRAEKELEER, MARC; DEPOID, FRANÇOISE; LEFEBVRE, MONIQUE; SEQUY, ISABELLE. 1996. *Généalogies et reconstitutions des familles. Analyses des besoins* [Genealogies and Family Reconstructions. Analyzes of Necessities]. Paris, FR: INED; 1996. (Dossiers et Recherches, 54). (In French).

B25
BALOUGH, ANN. 1997. Cost of Information Management. *Records & Information Management Report.* 1997 December; 13 (10): 1. ISSN: 8756-0089.

B26
BALSAMO, LUIGI. 1990. *Bibliography: History of a Tradition.* Trans. from Italian by W. A. Pettas. Berkeley, CA: Bernard M. Rosenthal; 1990. 209p. ISBN: 0-9600094-2-6.

B27
BAMBACH, CHARLES R. 1995. *Heidegger, Dilthey, and the Crisis of Historicism.* Ithaca, NY: Cornell University Press; 1995. 297p. ISBN: 0801430798.

B28
BANDT, C.; GRAF, S,; ZAHLE, M., eds. 1995. *Fractal Geometry and Stochastics.* Conference proceedings, Finsterbergen, Germany, June 12-18, 1994. Basel, CH / Boston, MA; Birkauser Verlag; 1995. 245p. ISBN: 0817652639.

B29
BANN, STEPHEN. 1984. *The Clothing of Clio: A Study of the Representation of History in Nineteenth-Cenury Britain and France.* Cambridge, UK: Cambridge University Press; 1984. ISBN: 052125616x (pbk.).

B30
BANNISTER, ROBERT C. 1987. *Sociology and Scientism.* Chapel Hill, NC: University of North Carolina Press; 1987. ISBN: 0807817333.

B31
BANTZ, CHARLES R.; PEPPER, GERALD. 1993. *Understanding Organizations: Interpreting Organizational Communication Cultures.* Columbia, SC: University of South Carolina Press; 1993. (Studies in Communication Processes). ISBN: 0872498794.

B32
BAR-HILLEL, Y. 1955. An Examination of Information Theory. *Philosophy of Science.* 1955; 22: 86-105. ISSN: 0031-8248.

B33
BAR-HILLEL, YEHOSHUA., ed. 1964. *Language and Information: Selected Essays on their Theory and Application.* Reading, MA: Addison-Wesley Co.; 1964. 388p. (Addison-Wesley series in Logic). LCCN: 64-55085.

B34
BAR-YAM, YANEER. 1997. *Dynamics of Complex Systems. Studies in Nonlinearity.* Studies in Nonlinearity series. Reading, MA: Addison, Wesley, Longman; 1997. ISBN: 0-201-55748 (hbk.).

B35
BARATA, KIMBERLY, comp. 1997a. Bibliography of Electronic Records Research to May of 1997. See reference: BEARMAN, D.; TRANT, J., eds. 1997: 323-346.

B36
BARATA, KIMBERLY, comp. 1997b. *Working Electronic Records Research Resources, 1997* [Electronic file]. Pittsburgh, PA: Archives and Museum Informatics; 1997. (CD-ROM).

B37
BARBONI, E. J. 1992. *Information Technologies in Independent, Liberal Arts Colleges. A Summary Analysis of Comparative Data.* Washington, D.C.: Council of Independent Colleges; 1992. Available from: CIC, Washington, D.C.

B38
BARBUT, MARC. 1994. Sur la formalisation dans les sciences sociales [Formalization in the Social Sciences]. *Histoire et Mesure.* 1994; 9 (1): 5-12. (In French). ISSN: 0982-1782.

B39
BARDET, JEAN-PIERRE; HAINSWORTH, MICHAEL. 1981. *Logiciel CASOAR. Calculs et Analyses sur Ordinateur Appliqués aux Reconstitutions* [CASOAR Software: Calculations and Analyzes in Computer Applications to Reconstitutions [models]). In: *Cahier des annales de démographie historique*, 1. Paris, FR: Société de démographique historique; 1981. (In French).

B40
BARKER, JOHN. 1982. *The Superhistorians: Makers of our Past.* New York, NY: Charles Scribners and Sons; 1982. 365p. ISBN:068416664X; LCCN: 82-5461; OCLC: 8345175.

B41
BARLEY, STEPHEN R.: KUNDA, GIDEON. 1992. Design and Devotion: Surges of Rational and Normative Ideologies of Control in Managerial Discourse. *Administrative Science Quarterly.* 1992 September; 37 (3): 363-399. ISSN: 0001-8392.

B42
BARLEY, STEPHEN R.; MEYER, GORDON W.; GASH, DEBRA C. 1988. Cultures of Culture: Academics, Practitioners and the Pragmatics of Normative Control. *Administrative Science Quarterly.* 1988 March; 33: 24-60. ISSN: 0001-8392.

B43
BARNARD, DAVID T.; IDE, NANCY M. 1997. The Text Encoding Initiative: Flexible and Extensible Document Encoding. See reference: LOGAN, E.; POLLARD, M. 1997b: 622-628.

B44
BARNES, J. A. 1994/1995. *A Pack of Lies: Towards a Sociology of Lying.* Cambridge, UK: Cambridge University Press; 1994. 200p. 1995 ed. (Themes in the Social Sciences series). ISBN: 0521459788 (pbk.).

B45
BARNES, RUTH; EICHER, JOANNE B., eds. 1993. *Dress and Gender: Making and Meaning.* London, UK: Berg; 1993. 204p. ISBN: 0-85496-720-6 (hbk.); 0-85496-865-2 (pbk.).

B46
BARNES, SUSAN B. 1995. *The Development of Graphical User Interfaces from 1970 to 1993, and Some of its Social Consequences in Offices, Schools, and the Graphic Arts.* New York, NY: New York University; 1995 (Ph.D. dissertation). 383p. Available from University Microfilms, Ann Arbor, MI.

B47
BARNES, TREVOR J.; DUNCAN, JAMES S., eds. 1992. *Writing Worlds. Discourse, Text and Metaphor in the Representation of Landscape.* London, UK: Routledge; 1992. ISBN: 0415069831.

B48
BARNES, WILLIAM H. 1982. *The Computer and Society: The Implications for Humankind. A Supplemental Curriculum for Students in Eighth-grade Junior-high/Middle-school American History Courses.* Pittsburgh, PA: Carnegie-Mellon University; 1982. 389p. (D.A. dissertation; DAI, vol. 43/10-A; 3396). Available from: University Microfilms, Ann Arbor, MI (Order no. AAD83-22673).

B49
BARNOUW, ERIC. 1966. *A Tower in Babel: A History of Broadcasting in the United States to 1933.* New York, NY: Oxford University Press; 1966. In: *A History of Broadcasting in the United States*: Vol. 1. New York, NY: Oxford University Press; 1966-1970. LC call no.: HE8689.8.B36.

B50
BARNOUW, ERIC. 1968/1970. *The Golden Web: A History of Broadcasting in the United States, 1933-1953.* New York, NY: 1968. 391p. *The Image Empire, from 1953-.* In: *A History of Broadcasting in the United States.* Vols. 2-3. New York, NY: Oxford University Press; 1966-1970. LC call no.: HE8689.8.B36.

B51
BARNOUW, ERIC. 1974/1983. *Documentary: A History of the Non-Fiction Film.* Rev. ed. Oxford, UK: Oxford University Press; 1974. 332p. Reprinted, 1983. 360p. ISBN: 0195033019 (pbk.).

B52
BARNSLEY, MICHAEL F. 1988. *Fractals Everywhere.* Boston, MA: Academic Press; 1988. 394p. ISBN: 0120790629.

B53
BARNSLEY, MICHAEL F. 1992. *The Desktop Fractal Design System* (electronic file). Boston, MA: Academic Press; 1992. 44p. (Handbook and 3.5 disk). ISBN: 0120790653.

B54
BARNSLEY, MICHAEL F.; DEMKO, STEPHEN G., eds. 1986. *Chaotic Dynamics and Fractals*. Proceedings of a conference at Georgia Institute of Technology, March 25-29, 1985. Orlando, FL: Academic Press; 1986. 292p. ISBN: 0120790602.

B55
BARON, STANLEY N.; KRIVOCHEEV, MARK I. 1996. *Digital Image and Audio Communications: Toward a Global Information Infrastructure*. New York, NY: Van Nostrand Reinhold; 1996. 288p. ISBN: 0-442-021206-2.

B56
BARROS, CARLOS. 1995. La historia que viene [The History to Come]. See BARROS, C., ed. 1995: 95-117.

B57
BARROS, CARLOS, ed. 1995. *Historia a Debate* [History under Debate]. I: Pasado y Futuro. Actes del Congreso Internacional "A Historia d Debate" 1-11 de Julio de 1993, Santiago de Compostela. La Coruna, ES: Graficas Sementeira, S. A.; 1995. 353p. ISBN: 920572-2-X.

B58
BARQUIN, RAMON; EDELSTEIN, HERB. 1997. *Planning and Designing the Data Warehouse*. Saddle River, NJ: Prentice Hall; 1997. 311p. ISBN: 0132557460.

B59
BARRETT, ANTHONY N. 1991. *Computer Vision and Image Processing*. London, UK and New York, NY: Chapman and Hall; 1991. 304p. ISBN: 0412377306.

B60
BARRET, EDWARD; REDMOND, MARIE. 1995. *Contextual Media. Multimedia and Interpretation*. Cambridge, MA: MIT Press; 1995. 300p. ISBN: 0-262-02383-0.

B61
BARRETT, WILLIAM. 1978. The Illusion of Technique. *A Search for Meaning in a Technological Civilization*. Garden City, NY: Anchor Press/Doubleday; 1978. 355p. ISBN: 0-385-11201-7; LCCN: 77-27765.

B62
BARRON, D. 1989. Why use SGML? *Electronic Publishing*. 1989; 2(1): 3-24. ISSN: 0260- 6658.

B63
BARRY, C. L. 1994. User-defined Relevance Criteria: An Exploratory Study. *Journal of the American Society for Information Science*. 1994; 45: 149-159. ISSN: 0002-8231.

B64
BARRY, JOHN A. 1991. *Technobabble*. Cambridge, MA: MIT Press; 1991. 268p. ISBN: 022023334; LCCN: 91-12488; OCLC: 23383826.

B65
BARRY, RICHARD E. 1993. Getting It Right: Managing Organizations in a Runaway Electronic Age. See reference: MENNE-HARITZ, A., ed. 1993: 27-55.

B66
BARRY, RICHARD E., dir. [1995]. *Electronic Records Management in the New Millennium: Managing Documents for Business and Government* [Video]. Thurston, Anne, contributor. London, UK: University of London for the British Library Board; [1995]. Booklet, 27p. ISBN: 0-902090-03-8.

B67
BARRY, RICHARD E. 1996. Making the Distinctions between Information Management and Records Management [draft ARMA conference paper, electronic file]. *Barry Associates Homepage*. Arlington, VA: Barry Associates; 1996. 5p. Accessible at http://www. mlrsi.com/rickbarry/IMT-ARM1/MT-ARM1.html.

B68
BARTHELEMY, DOMINIQUE. 1993. *La Société dans le Comte de Vendôme: de l'an mil au XIV siècle* [Society in the County of Vendôme from 1000 to 1300]. Paris, FR: Fayard; 1995. (In French).

B69
BARTHELEMY, DOMINIQUE; PINGAUD, MARIE-CLAUDE, eds. 1997. *La Généalogie entre Science and Passion* [Genealogy between Science and Passion (i.e., emotional motivation)]. Paris, FR: Editions du Comite des travaux historiques et scientifiques; 1997. (In French).

B70
BARTHES, ROLAND. 1967. Le Discours de l'histoire [The Discourse of History]. *Information sur les sciences sociales/Social Science Information*. 1967; 6(4): 65-75. (In French). ISSN: 0539-0184; LCCN: 86-649437; OCLC: 2450595. Reprinted with other related essays in *Le Bruissement de la Langue [*The Noise of Language*]*. Paris: Seuil; 1984.LCCN: 84-241299/r89; OCLC: 2855557. Cf., *The Discourse of History*. Bann, Stephen, trans.

In: Schaffer, Elinor, ed. *Rhetoric and History: Comparative Criticism Yearbook* (pp. 3-20). Cambridge, UK: Cambridge University Press; 1981.

B71
BARTHES, ROLAND. 1970/1983. *L'Empire des Signes*. Paris, 1970. Trans. as: *The Empire of Signs*. New York, NY: Farrer, Strauss & Geroux; 1983. ISBN: 0374522073 (pbk.).

B72
BARTHES, ROLAND. 1981. The Theory of the Text. *Untying the Text*. Young, Robert, ed. London: RAP; 1981. 31-47. ISBN: 7071000804x; 0710008058.

B73
BARTHES, ROLAND. 1988/1994. *The Semiotic Challenge*. Ploward, Richard, trans. Berkeley, CA: University of California Press; 1994. 293p. ISBN: 0520087844.

B74
BARTLE, RACHEL. 1983. *Computer Applications in Archives: A Survey*. Liverpool, UK: University of Liverpool; 1983. 58p. (British Library Research & Development Report, no. 5749). ISBN: 0907156010.

B75
BARTLETT, NANCY. 1991. *Respect des Fonds*: The Origin of the Modern Archival Principal of Provenance. See reference: MCCRANK, L., ed. 1991:107-115. Also published as *Primary Sources and Original Works*. 1991: 1 (1/2): 107-115. ISSN: 1042-8216.

B76
BARTLETT, NANCY. 1996. Diplomatics for Photographic Images: Academic Exoticism? See reference: BLOUIN, F.; DELMAS, B. 1996: 486-494.

B77
BARTON, CHRISTOPHER; LAPOINTE, P. R., eds. 1995. *Fractals in the Earth Sciences*. New York, NY: Plenum Press; 1995. 265p. ISBN: 0306448653.

B78
BARTON, SCOTT. 1994. Chaos, Self-Organization, and Psychology. *The American Psychologist*. 1994 January; 49(1): 5-15. ISSN: 0003-3066.

B79
BARTRELL, BRIAN T.; COTTRELL, GARRISON W.; BELEW, RICHARD K. 1995. Representing Documents Using an Explicit Model of Their Similarities. *Journal of the American Society for Information Science*. 1995; 46 (4): 254-271. ISSN: 0002-8231.

B80
BARZUN, JACQUES. 1972/1974. History: The Muse and Her Doctors. *American Historical Review,* 1972 February; 77: 36-64. ISSN: 0002-8762. Expanded into: *Clio and the Doctors: Psycho-History, Quanto-History, and History*. Chicago, IL: University of Chicago; 1974. 173p. LCCN: 74-5723; OCLC: 1069140.

B81
BARZUN, JACQUES; PELIKAN, JAROSLAV; FRANKLIN, JOHN HOPE. *Scholarship Today: The Humanities and Social Sciences*. Washington, D.C.: Library of Congress; 1987. 48p. (Occasional Papers of the Council of Scholars, 5). ISBN: 0844405639; LCCN: 87600153.

B82
BASALLA, GEORGE. 1988/1989. *The Evolution of Technology*. Cambridge, UK: Cambridge University Press; 1988. Pbk. ed., 1989. 248p. ISBN: 052129681.

B83
BASCH, EVA. 1991. Books Online: Visions, Plans and Perspectives for Electronic Text. *Online*. 1991 July; 15 (4): 13-24. ISSN: 0146-5422.

B84
BASKERVILLE, PETER; GAFFIELD, CHAD. 1983-84. The Vancouver Island Project: Historical Research and Archival Practice. *Archivaria*. 1983-84; 17: 173-87. ISSN: 0318-6954.

B85
BASKERVILLE, PETER; GAFFIELD, CHAD. 1985. Shifting Paradigms and Emergent Technologies. Introduction to Baskerville, P.; Gaffield, C., eds. *Archives, Automation, and Access*. Victoria, CAN: University of Victoria, BC; 1985.

B86
BASKERVILLE, S. W.; HUDSON, PAT; MORRIS, ROBERT J., eds. 1992. Record Linkage. In: *History and Computing*. 1992: 4 (1): 2-51. (Entire issue on title topic). ISSN: 0957-0144.

B87
BASSNETT, SUSAN; LEFEVRE, ANDRE, eds. 1995. *Translation, History and Culture*. London, UK: Cassell; 1995. 224p. ISBN: 0-304-33622-X.

B88
BASTIEN, HERVE, ed. 1996. *Droit des Archives* [Archival Law]. Paris, FR: Directions des Archives de France; 1996. 192p. ISBN: 291160105-X.

B89
BATEMAN, ROGER M..; GOTTMAN, JOHN M. 1986/1997. *Observing Interaction: An Introduction to Sequential Analysis*. Cambridge, UK: Cambridge University Press; 1986. LCCN: 85-22362. 1997 reprint. 207p. ISBN: 052145008X; LCCN: 96-26084.

B90
BATES, DAVID. 1996. Rediscovering Collingwood's Spiritual History. *History and Theory*. 1996 February; 35 (1): 29-56. ISSN: 0018-2656.

B91
BATES, MARCIA J. 1981. Search Techniques. In: Williams, Martha E., ed. *Annual Review of Information Science and Technology* (16: 139-170). White Plains, NY: Knowledge Industry Publications, Inc., for the American Society for Information Science; 1981. ISSN: 0066-4200.

B92
BATES, MARCIA J. 1989. The Design of Browsing and Berrypicking Techniques for the Online Search Interface. *Online Review*. 1989; 13(5): 407-24. ISSN: 0309-314.

B93
BATES, MARCIA J. 1999. The Invisible Substrate of Information Science. See reference: BATES, M., ed. 1999. Pt. 2: 1043-1050.

B94
BATES, MARCIA J., ed. 1999. *The 50ʰ Anniversary of the Journal of the American Society for Information Science*. Pt. 1: *The Journal, Its Society and the Future of Print*. Pt. 2: *Paradigms, Models, and Methods of Information Science*. Special issues of *The Journal of the American Society for Information Science*. 1999; 50(11-12): 960-1162. ISSN: 0002- 8231.

B95
BATESON, GREGORY. 1972/1987/1990. *Steps to an Ecology of Mind: Collected Essays in Anthropology, Psychology, Evolution, and Epistemology*. New York, NY: Jason Aronson; 1987. ISBN: 0876689500. Re-edition. New York, NY: Ballantine Books; 1990. ISBN: 0345332911.

B96
BATT, FRED; MARTELL, CHARLES, eds. 1991. *Libraries and the Humanities in the 1990s. Library Hi Tech* (Consecutive issue 33). 1991; 9(1): 112p. (Entire issue on title topic). ISSN: 0737-8831; LCCN: 83-645580; OCLC: 25736572.

B97
BATY, LAURA A. [199-]. Photographs are NOT Wallpaper. Paper presented in the session "Use and Misuse of Primary Sources," Society of American Archivists Conference, Indianapolis, IN, September 10, 1994. Publication forthcoming [199-].

B98
BAUER, MARTIN, ed. 1995. *Resistance to New Technology: Nuclear Power, Information Technology, and Biotechnology*. Cambridge, UK / New York, NY: Cambridge University Press; 1995. 422p. ISBN: 0521455189 (pbk); LCCN: 94026745.

B99
BAUERSFELD, PENNY. 1994. *Software by Design. Creating People Friendly Software for the MacIntosh*. New York, NY: M&T Books; 1994. ISBN: 1558282963.

B100
BAUMEISTER, ROY F.; HASTINGS, STEPHEN. 1997. Distortions of Collective Memory; How Groups Flatter and Deceive Themselves. See reference: PENNEBAKER, J. W., *ET AL.*, eds. 1997.

B101
BAUMOL, WILLLIAM; BENHABIB, JESS. 1989. Chaos: Significance, Mechanism, and Economic Applications. *Journal of Economic Perspectives*. 1989; 3(1): 77-105. ISSN: 0895-5309.

B102
BAWDEN, DAVID. 1990. Computer Output Devices. See reference: KENT, A., ed. 1990; 45: 64-82.

B103
BAXANDALL, MICHAEL. 1991. [Art History Reviews]. *English Historical Review*. 1991 July; 106(420):763. ISSN: 0085-3042.

B104
BAZERMAN, CHARLES; PARADIS, JAMES, ed. 1991. *Textual Dynamics of the Professions: Historical and Contemporary Studies of Writing in Processional Communities* Madison, WI: University of Wisconsin Press; 1991. 390p.(. Rhetoric of the Human Science series). ISBN: 0299125904; 0299125947 (pbk.); LCCN: 90-50079; OCLC: 22310639.

B105
BEACH, W. W. 1980. A Second Look: The Agenda for Social Science History. *Social Science History*. 1980; 4: 357-364. ISSN: 0145-5532; LCCN: 77-640161; OCLC: 2761258.

B106
BEAGRIE, NEIL; GREENSTEIN, DANIEL. 1998. *Digital Collections: A Strategic Policy Framework for Creating and Preserving Digital Resources* (Electronic file). Accessible at http://www/ahds.ac.uk/manage/framework/html.

B107
BEALE, WILLIAM M. 1990. *Overt and Covert Organizational Culture: A Case Study of the Office of Technology Assessment.* Blacksburg, VA: Virginia Polytechnic Institute and State University; 1990. 254 pp. (Ph.D. dissertation; *DAI*, vol. 51, no. 06-A, p. 2152). Available form University Microfilms, Ann Arbor, MI.

B108
BEARD, CHARLES. 1934. Written History as an Act of Faith. *American Historical Review.* 1934 January; 39:219-231. (Beard's 1933 AHA Presidential Address). ISSN: 0002-8762.

B109
BEARMAN, DAVID. 1987a. *Collecting Software: A New Challenges for Archives & Museums.* Pittsburgh, PA: Archives & Museum Informatics; 1987. 80p. *(*Archival Informatics Technical Report [August 1985]. 1987; 1, no. 2). ISSN: 1042-1459.

B110
BEARMAN, DAVID. 1987b. *Towards a National Information System for Archives and Manuscripts Repositories: The National Information Systems Task Force (NISTF) Papers, 1981-84.* Chicago, IL: Society of American Archivists; 1987. 119p. ISBN: 0-931828-39- 2.

B111
BEARMAN, DAVID. 1987c. *Optical Media: Their Implications for Archives and Museums.* Pittsburgh, PA: Archives and Museums Informatics; 1987, c1989. 74p. (Archives and Museum Informatics Technical Report, 1 [originally Vol. 1, no. 1]). ISSN: 1042-1459.

B112
BEARMAN, DAVID. 1987/1988. *Automated Systems for Archives and Museums: Acquisitions and Implementation Issues.* Pittsburgh, PA: Archives & Museum Informatics; 1987/1988, c1989. 88p.(Archives and Museum Informatics Technical Report, 4 [originally vol. 1, no. 4]). ISSN: 1042-1459.

B113
BEARMAN, DAVID. 1989a. *Archival Methods.* Pittsburgh, PA: Archives & Museum Informatics; 1989. 67p. (Archives & Museum Informatics Technical Report 3, no. 1). ISSN: 1042-1459.

B114
BEARMAN, DAVID. 1989b. Archives and Manuscripts Control with Bibliographic Utilities: Challenges and Opportunities. *The American Archivist.* 1989; 52 (1): 26-39. ISSN: 0360- 9081.

B115
BEARMAN, DAVID. 1990a. *Archives & Museum Data Models and Dictionaries.* Pittsburgh, PA: Archives & Museum Informatics; 1990. 100p. (Archives & Museum Informatics Technical Report, 10). ISSN: 1042-1459.

B116
BEARMAN, DAVID. 1990b. Management of Electronic Records: Issues and Guidelines. See reference: UNITED NATIONS. 1990: 17-70, 89-107, 135-189.

B117
BEARMAN, DAVID. 1991. An Indefensible Bastion: Archives as Repositories in the Electronic Age. In: *Archives and Museum Informatics*. Pittsburgh, PA: Archives & Museum Informatics; 1991. 14-24. Technical report 13. ISSN: 1042-1459

B118
BEARMAN, DAVID. 1993a. Archival Data Management to Achieve Organizational Accountability for Electronic Records. *Archives and Manuscripts.* 1993; 21 (1): 14-28. ISSN: 0157-6895. See reprint in reference: BEARMAN, 1994. 12-33.

B119
BEARMAN, DAVID. 1993b. Archival Principles and the Electronic Office. See reference: MENNE-HARITZ, A., ed. 1993: 177-193.

B120
BEARMAN, DAVID. 1994. *Electronic Evidence. Strategies for Managing Records in Contemporary Organizations.* Walch, Victoria Irons, ed. Pittsburgh, PA: Archives and Museum Informatics; 1994. 314p. ISBN: 1-885626-08-8.

B121
BEARMAN, DAVID. 1995a. Archival Strategies. *The American Archivist.* 1995; 58 (4): 380- 413. ISSN: 0360-9081. See commentaries by WILSON, I.; PEDERSON A.; and KETELAAR, E. (pp. 454-456).

B122
BEARMAN, DAVID. 1995b. Thesaurally Mediated Retrieval. *Visual resources.* 1995; 10: 295-307. ISSN: 0197-3762.

B123
BEARMAN, DAVID. 1996a. Archiving and Authenticity. See reference: BEARMAN, D., ed. 1996: 63-67.

B124
BEARMAN, DAVID. 1996b. Item Level Control and Electronic Recordkeeping. *Archives and Museum Informatics.* 1996; 10: 195-245. ISSN: 1042-1459.

B125
BEARMAN, DAVID. 1997a. Capturing Records' Metadata: Unresolved Questions and Proposals for Research. See reference: BEARMAN, D.; TRANT, J., eds. 1997: 271-285.

B126
BEARMAN, DAVID. 1997b. Electronic Records Research Issues. See reference: BEARMAN, D.; TRANT, J., eds. 1997: 201-204.

B127
BEARMAN, DAVID. 1997c. New Economic Models for Administering Cultural Intellectual Property. See reference: JONES-GARMIL, K., ed. 1997: 231-266.

B128
BEARMAN, DAVID. [199-]. Towards a Reference Model for Business Acceptable Communications. *The American Archivist.* [199-; forthcoming]. ISSN: 0360-9081.

B129
BEARMAN, DAVID, ed. 1987-. *Archives and Museum Informatics.* Newsletter and Technical Reports. Pittsburgh, PA: Archives and Museum Informatics; 1987-; 1-. Irregular series. ISSN: 1042-1459. See reviews by MCCRANK, 1990; PEDERSON, 1990.

B130
BEARMAN, DAVID, ed. 1991. *Archival Management of Electronic Records.*Pittsburgh, PA: Archives & Museum Informatics; 1991. 56p. (Archives and Museum Informatics Technical Report, 13). ISSN: 1042-1459.

B131
BEARMAN, DAVID, ed. 1995. *Multimedia Computing and Museums.* Selected Papers from the Third International Conference on Hypermedia and Interactivity in Museums (ICHIM'95-MCN'95), San Diego, CA, October 9-13, 1995. Pittsburgh, PA: Archives & Museum Informatics; 1995. 388p. (Archives & Museum Informatics series). ISBN: 1885626118.

B132
BEARMAN, DAVID; DUFF, WENDY. 1996. Grounding Archival Description in the Functional Requirements for Evidence. *Archivaria.* 1996 spring; 41: 275-303. ISSN: 0318-6954.

B133
BEARMAN, DAVID; HEDSTROM, MARGARET. 1993. Reinventing Archives for Electronic Records: Alternative Service Delivery Options. See reference: HEDSTROM, M., ed. 1993: 82-98.

B134
BEARMAN, DAVID; LYTLE, RICHARD. 1985. The Power of the Principle of Provenance. *Archivaria.* 1985; 21: 14-27. ISSN: 0318-6954.

B135
BEARMAN, DAVID; SOCHATS, KEN. [1996]. *Metadata Specifications derived from Functional Requirements: A Referene Model for Business Acceptable Communications* (electronic file). Accessible at http//www.lis.pitt.edu/ ~nhprc.papers/model.html.

B136
BEARMAN, DAVID; SZARY, RICHARD. 1987. Beyond Authorized Headings: Authorities as Reference Files in a Multi-Disciplinary Setting. In: Muller, Karen, ed. *Authority Control Symposium.* (pp. 69-78). Symposium of the

ARLIS Cataloging and Indexing Systems Special Interest Group and Cataloging Advisory Committee. Tucson, AZ: Art Libraries of North America; 1987. 138p. (ARLIS Occasional Papers, 6). ISBN: ISBN: 094274005X (pbk.).

B137
BEARMAN, DAVID; TRANT, JENNIFER. 1998. Electronic Records Research Working Meeting, May 28-30, 1997: A Report from the Archives Community. *Bulletin of the American Society for Information Science*. 1998 Feb./Mar.; 24 (3): 13-17. ISSN: 0095- 4403.

B138
BEARMAN, DAVID; TRANT, JENNIFER, eds. 1997. Proceedings from the Working Meeting on Electronic Records Research, Pittsburgh, PA, May 1997. In: *Archives and Museum Informatics: Cultural Heritage Informatics Quarterly*. 1997: 11 (3-4): 201-362. (Entire issue on title topic). ISSN: 1042-1467; CODEN: AMUIEA.

B139
BEAUGRANDE, ROBERT-ALAIN de. 1980. *Text, Discourse, and Process: Toward a Multidisciplinary Science of Texts*. Freedle, R. O., ed. Norwood, NJ: Ablex Publishers; 1980. 351p. (Advances in Discourse Processes, 4). ISSN: 0164-0224; ISBN:0893910333; LCCN: 80-154170; OCLC: 6558322.

B140
BEAUGRANDE, ROBERT-ALAIN de. 1981. Linguistic Theory and Meta-theory for a Science of Texts. *Text* (NL). 1981; 1/2: 113-161. ISSN:0165-4888; LCCN: 82-644597; OCLC: 7365246.

B141
BEAUGRANDE, ROBERT-ALAIN; DRESSLER, WOLFGANG ULRICH. 1981. *Introduction to Text Linguistics*. New York, NY and London, UK: Longman; 1981. (Longman Linguistics Library, 26). (Translation from the 1972 German edition; Dressler's contribution is translated from *Einfuhrung in die Textlinguistik*). ISBN: 0582554861; pbk. 0582554853.

B142
BEAUMONT, ROGER A. 1994. *War, Chaos, and History*. Westport, CT: Praeger; 1994. 214p. ISBN: 0275949494.

B143
BECHER, T. 1989. *Academic Tribes and Territories: Intellectual Enquiry and the Cultures of Disciplines*. Bristol, PA: Society for Research into Higher Education and Open University Press; 1989.

B144
BECK, PATRICE, ed. 1994. L'Informatique et l'Archéologie. In: *Le Médiéviste et l'Ordinateur.* 1994 spring; 29: 1-60. (Entire issue on title topic). ISSN: 0223-3843.

B145
BECKER, CARL. 1932/1972. Everyman His Own Historian. *American Historical Review.* 1931 January; 37: 221-236. (Becker's 1931 AHA Presidential Address). ISSN: 0002-8762. Also in his: *Detachment and the Writing of History: Essays and Letters of Carl L. Becker.* Snyder, Phil L., ed. Ithaca, NY: Cornell University Press; [1958]. Reprinted. Westport, CT: Greenwood; 1972. 240p. (See also: What are Historical Facts?).

B146
BECKER, JOSEPH. 1976. The Rich Heritage of Information Science. *Information Science in America. Bulletin of the American Society for Information Science.* 1976 March; 2(8): 9- 13. (Entire issue on title topic). ISSN: 0095-4403.

B147
BECKER, JOSEPH. 1984. An Information Scientist's View on Evolving Information Technology. *Journal of the American Society for Information Science.* 1984. 35 (3): 164-169. ISSN: 0002-8231.

B148
BECKER, PETER. 1987. Formen und Mögligkeiten der Standardisierung bei Metaquellen [Forms and Possibilities in the Standardization of Metadata]. See reference: HAUSMANN *ET AL.*, eds. 1987: 18-27.

B149
BECKER, PETER; WERNER, THOMAS; GROTUM, THOMAS; NEMITZ, JÜRGEN; SCHUH, BARBARA. 1989. Tutorials. (Electronic files, in irregular series). Göttingen: Max-Planck-Institut für Geschichte; 1989-. Available from: Max-Planck-Institut für Geschichte, Hermann-Foge Weg 11, D200 Gottingen, DEU.

B150
BECKER, THEODORE L., ed. 1991. *Quantum Politics: Applying Quantum Theory to Political Phenomena*. New York, NY: Praeger; 1991. ISBN: 0275933105.

B151
BECKETT, J. V. 1990. The Computer and the Local Historian. *Archives*. 1990; 19: 192-198.

B152
BEDERIDA, FRANÇOIS, ed. 1995. *L'histoire et le métier d'historien en France, 1945-1995* [History and Method of Historians in France, 1945-1995]. Paris, FR: Editions de la maison des sciences de l'homme; 1995.

B153
BEDOS-REZAK, BRIGITTE. 1993. *Form and Order in Medieval France: Studies in Social and Quantitative Sigillography*. Aldershot, UK: Variorum; c1993. (Collected Studies, 424). ISBN: 0860783553; LCCN: 93-005706.

B154
BEGHTOL, C. 1995. Domain Analysis, Literary Warrant, and Consensus: The Case of Fiction Studies. *Journal of the American Society for Information Science*. 1995; 46: 30-44. ISSN: 0002-8231.

B155
BEGUIN, DANIEL. 1994. Le *CLCLT* de Brépols. La Litterature latine patristique et médiévale sur CD-ROM [The Brépols *CLCLT*. Patristic and Medieval Latin Literature on CD-ROM]. *Revue d'Histoire des Textes*. 1994; 24: 485-493. ISSN: 0373-6075.

B156
BEHN, ROBERT. 1994 . *Leadership Counts: Lessons for Public Managers from the Massachusetts Welfare Training and Employment Program*. Cambridge, MA: Harvard University Press; 1994. ISBN: 0674518535.

B157
BELEW, RICHARD K. 1989. Adaptive Information Retrieval: Using a Connnectionist Representation to Retrieve and Learn about Documents. In: *Proceedings of ACM* SIGIR Cambridge, MA: ACM (Association of Computing Machinery) Press; 1989. 11-20.

B158
BELEW, RICHARD K.; MITCHELL, eds. 1996. *Adaptive Individuals in Evolving Populations. Models and Algorithms*. Reprints of class essays and presentations at the Santa Fe summer institute, 1993. Santa Fe, NM: Santa Fe Institute (SFI); 1996. (Santa Fe Institute Studies in the Science of Complexity). ISBN: 0-201-15685-7 (pbk.).

B159
BELKIN, N. J. 1990. The Cognitive Viewpoint in Information Science. *Journal of Information Science* (UK). 1990; 16: 11-15. ISSN: 1352-7460.

B160
BELKIN, N. J. BROOKS, H.; DANIELS, P. 1987. Knowledge Elicitation Using Discourse Analysis. *International Journal of Man-Machine Studies*. 1987; 27: 127-144. ISSN: 0020-7373.

B161
BELKIN, N. J.; CROFT, W. B. 1987. Retrieval Techniques. In: Williams, Martha, ed. *Annual Review of Information Science and Technology* Amsterdam, NL: Elsevier; 1987. 22: 109-145. ISSN: 0066-4200.

B162
BELKIN, N. J.; ROBERTSON, S. E. 1976. Information Science and the Phenomenon of Information. *Journal of the American Society for Information Science*. 1976; 27: 197-204. ISSN: 0002-8231.

B163
BELL, D. A.; GUAN, J. W. 1998. Computational Methods for Rough Classification and Discovery. See reference: RAGHAVEN, V.; DEOGUN, J.; SEVER, H., eds. 1998: 403-414.

B164
BELL, DANIEL. 1973/1976. *The Coming of Post-Industrial Society. A Venture in Social Forecasting*. New York, NY: Basic Books; 1973. Pbk. Ed., 1976. 507p. ISBN: 0465097138.

B165
BELL, DANIEL. 1982. *The Social Sciences since the Second World War*. New Brunswick, NJ: Transaction Books; 1982. ISBN: 878554262.

B166
BELL, DANIEL J. 1980. *Teletext: The New Networks of Information & Knowledge in a Computer Society*. New York, NY: Basic Books; 1980. ISBN: 0465084028.

B167
BELL, DANIEL J. 1991. *Mathematics of Linear and Non-Linear Systems: For Engineering and Applied Scientists*. Oxford, UK: Oxford University Press; 1991. ISBN: 0198563639.

B168
BELL, DAVID E.; RAIFFA, HOWARD; TVERSKY, AMOS. 1988. *Decision Making: Descriptive, Normative, and Prescriptive Interactions*. Cambridge, UK; New York, NY: Cambridge University Press; 1988. 623p. ISBN: 0521351499.

B169
BELL, RUDOLPH; VAN CAUWENBERGHE, EDDY H. G. 1990. *The Medieval and Early Modern Data Bank* (*MEMDB*). *Tijdschrift voor Geschiedenis* (Groningen, NL: P.Noordhoff). 1990; 103: 260-278. ISSN: 0040-7518; LCCN: 09-2870/r43.

B170
BELL, RUDOLPH; VAN CAUWENBERGHE, EDDY H. G. 1991. The *Medieval and Early Modern Data Bank* in Europe and North America. See reference: BEST, H., *ET AL.*, eds., 1991: 92-95.

B171
BELLARDO, LEWIS J.; BELLARDO, LYNN LADY, eds. 1992. *A Glossary for Archivists, Manuscript Curators, and Records Managers.* Chicago, IL: Society of American Archivists; 1992. 45p. ISBN: 0931828791.

B172
BELLARDO HAHN, TRUDI. 1998. Text Retrieval Online: Historical Perspective on Web Search Engines. *Bulletin of the American Society for Information Science.* 1998 April/May; 24 (4): 7-10. ISSN: 0095-4403.

B173
BELLARDO HAHN, TRUDI. 1998. Pioneers of the Online Age. See reference: BELLARDO-HAHN, T.; BUCKLAND, M., eds. 1998. 116-131.

B174
BELLARDO HAHN, TRUDI; BUCKLAND, MICHAEL, eds. 1998. *Historical Studies in Information Science.* Medford, NJ: Information Today, Inc. for the American Society for Information Science; 1998. 326p. ASIS Monograph Series. ISBN: 1-57387-062-5.

B175
BELOVA, EUGENIA. 1995. Qualitative Data Analysis with *QualiDatE.* See reference: BOONSTRA, O.; COLLENTEUR, G.; VAN ELDEREN, B., eds. 1995. 43-54.

B176
BELOVA, EUGENIA B.; LAZAREV, VALERY V. 1995. Software for Historical Research. Specifics of Behaviour and Interface. See reference: JARITZ, G. *ET AL.*, eds. 1995. 300-306.

B177
BELOVA, EUGENIA B.; LAZAREV, VALERY V. 1996 [199-]. From Hypertext to Hyperarchives: A Software System for Electronic Text Archives Management. See reference: BORODKIN, L., ed. 1996. English abstract of presentation, 54-55; paper in Russian [199- forthcoming].

B178
BEN-DAVID, JOSPEH; COLLINS, RANDALL. 1966. Social Factors in the Origins of a New Science. *American Sociological Review.* 1966; 31: 451-465. ISSN: 0004-1224.

B179
BENDER, THOMAS. 1984. The New History-Then and Now. *Reviews in American History.* 1984 December; 12: 612-622. ISSN:0048-7511.

B180
BENDER, THOMAS. 1986. Wholes and Parts: The Need for Synthesis in American History. *Journal of American History.* 1986 June. 73: 120-136. ISSN: 0021-8723.

B181
BENDER, THOMAS. 1993. *Intellect and Public Life: Essays on the Social History of Academic Intellectuals in the United States.* Baltimore, MD: The Johns Hopkins Press; 1993. 179p. ISBN: 0801844339 (pbk.).

B182
BENDER, THOMAS. 1994. "Venturesome and Cautious:" American History in the 1990s. *The Journal of American History.* 1994 December; 81(3): 992-1003. ISSN: 0021-8723.

B183
BENEDICT, RUTH. 1934/1960. *Patterns of Culture.* Boston, MA: Houghton Mifflin; 1934. Repr. New York: Penguin Books. 272p. OCLC: 25686649. Repr. New York: New American Library; 1960. 254p. OCLC: 1909519.

B184
BENEDICKT, M., ed. 1990. *Cyberspace: First Steps.* Cambridge, MA: MIT Press; 1990. ISBN: 0262521776.

B185
BENEDON, WILLIAM. 1978. Management in Information: An Interdisciplinary Approach. *Records Management Quarterly.* 1978 October; 12(4): 5-10. ISSN: 1050-2343.

B186
BENIGER, JAMES R. 1986. *The Control Revolution: Technological and Economic Origins of the Information Society.* Cambridge, MA: Harvard University Press; 1986. 492p. ISBN: 0-674-16985-9.

B187
BENIGER, JAMES R.; ROBYN, D. L. 1978. Quantitative Graphics in Statistics: A Brief History. *The American Statistician.* 1978; 32(1): 1-11. ISSN: 0003-1305.

B188
BENITEZ, HELENA. Globalization of United States History: Six Strategies. *Social Education*. 1994 March; 58 (3): 142-145. ISSN: 0037-7724.

B189
BENJAMIN, WALTER. 1972-89. *Thesen zur Geschichte* [Theses in History]. In his: *Gesammelte Schriften*. Tiedmann, Rolf; Schweppenhauser, Hans, eds. Frankfurt am Main, DEU; Suhrkamp; 1972-1989.

B190
BENNER, MARTHA L. 1996/1997. *The Lincoln Legal Papers* and the New Age of Documentary Editing. See reference: IGARTUA, J. E., ed. 1996/1997. 365-372.

B191
BENNET, WILLIAM J.; FAIR, WILLARD; FINN, CHESTER; FLAKE, FLOYD H.; HIRSCH, E. D.; MARSHALL, WILL; RAVITCH, DIANE. 1998. A National Still At Risk. *Policy Review*. 1998, July-Aug.; 90: 23-29.

B192
BENNETT, GEORGE. E. 1988. *Librarians in Search of Science and Identity: The Elusive Profession*. Metuchen, NJ: Scarecrow Pres; 1988. 221p. ISBN: 0810820757.

B193
BENNETT, JOHN L. 1983. *Building Decision Support Systems*. Reading, MA: Addison- Wesley, Inc.; 1983. 277p. ISBN: 0201005638.

B194
BENNETT, SIMON. 1996. The History of Psychiatry: An Opportunity for Self-reflection and Interdisciplinary Dialogue (Review essay). *Psychiatry*. 1996 Winter; 59(4); 336-357. ISSN: 0033-2747.

B195
BENSON, LEE. 1972. *Toward the Scientific Study of History*. Philadelphia, PA: J.P. Lippincott; 1972. 352p. ISBN: 039747265-X; 0397472234 (pbk.); LCCN: 73-1611415; OCLC: 267303.

B196
BENSON, T. LLOYD. 1997. Information Technology and the Liberal Arts College (Electronic file). In Vision section of *Microsoft in Higher Education*. 1997 August; 6 pp. Accessible at http://www.mircrosoft.com/education/hed/vision.htm.

B197
BENTLEY, JERRY. 1996. Cross-Cultural Interaction and Periodization in World History. AHR Forum. *American Historical Review*. 1996 June; 101(3): 749-770. ISSN: 0002-8762.

B198
BENTON, JOHN F. 1979. Digital Image Processing Applied to the Photography of Manuscripts, with Examples drawn from the Pincus Manuscript of Arnold of Vilanova. *Scriptorium*. 1979; 33: 40-55. ISSN: 0036-9772.

B199
BENVENISTE, EMILE. 1966/1971. *Problèmes de linguistique générale*. Paris, FR: Gallimard; 1966. Meek, M. E., trans. *Problems in General Linguistics*. Miami, FL: University of Miami Press; 1971. 317p. ISBN: 087024132X; LCCN: 77-102692/r842; OCLC: 19711001.

B200
BERCOVITCH, SACVAN. 1993. *The Rites of Assent: Transformations in the Symbolic Construction of America*. New York, NY: Routledge; 1993. 424p. ISBN: 041590014 (hbk); 0415900158 (pbk); LCCN: 92019999.

B201
BERG, J. VAN DEN; BRANDHORST, H; HUISSTEDE, P. VAN. 1992. Image Processing and the (Art) Historical Discipline. See reference: THALLER, M., ed., 1992a. 5-40.

B202
BERG, R. DREYER. 1994. Our Computational Culture: from Descartes to the Computer. *Review of General Semantics*. 1994 Summer; 51(2); 123-145.

B203
BERGER, MARGARET A. 1994. Evidentiary Framework. See reference: FEDERAL JUDICIAL CENTER, 1994. 37-119.

B204
BERGER, PETER L.; LUCKMANN, THOMAS. 1966/1967. *The Social Construction of Reality: A Treatise in the Sociology of Knowledge*. Garden City, NY: Doubleday; 1966. Pbk. Ed., 1967. 219p. ISBN: 0385158985.

B205
BERGERON, LOUIS; REVEL, JACQUES, eds. *L'Espace Français* [The French Space]. Histoire de France series. Paris, FR: Seuil; 1989. 669p. ISBN: 2020102366.

B206
BEREITER, CARL; SCARDAMALIA, MARLENE. 1987. *The Psychology of Written Composition*. Hillsdale, NJ: Laurence Erlbaum; 1987. 389p. ISBN: 0898596475.

B207
BERINGER, RICHARD E. 1987. *Historical Analysis: Contemporary Approaches to Clio's Craft*. New York, NY: John Wiley; 1978. 317p. ISBN: 0471069957 (hbk.); 0471069965 (pbk.).

B208
BERINSTEIN, PAULA. 1996. *Finding Images Online*. Medford, NJ: Information Today, Inc.; 1996. 357 p. ISBN: 0-910965-21-8.

B209
BERINSTEIN, PAULA. [1998]. *Finding Statistics Online: How to Locate the Elusive Numbers You Need*. Medford, NJ: Information Today, Inc.; [1998]. 320 p. ISBN: 0-91096-25-0.

B210
BERKELEY MUSEUM INFORMATICS PROJECT. 1996-. Standards for Museum & Cultural Heritage Information [electronic file]. Berkeley, CA: University of California; 1996-. http://www.mip.berkeley.edu/ mip/standard.html.

B211
BERKENKOTTER, CAROL; HUCKIN, THOMAS N. 1995. *Genre Knowledge in Disciplinary Communication: Cognition / Culture / Power*. Hillsdale, NJ; Lawrence Erlbaum Associates, 1995. 190p. ISBN: 0805816119 (pbk.); 0805816127 (hbk.); LCCN: 94016549.

B212
BERKHOFER, ROBERT F. 1969. *A Behavioral Approach to Historical Analysis*. New York, NY: Free Press; 339p. ISBN: 0029029708; LCCN: 69-11485; OCLC: 4143.

B213
BERKHOFER, ROBERT F. 1983. The Two New Histories: Competing Paradigms for interpreting the American Past. *OAH Newsletter*. 1983 May: 9-12. ISSN: 1059-1125.

B214
BERKHOFER, ROBERT F. 1990. *Beyond the Great Story: History as Text and Discourse*. Cambridge, MA: Harvard University Belknap Press; 1990. 366p. ISBN: 0674069072; LCCN: 95-002005.

B215
BERLANSTEIN, LENARD R., ed. 1993. *Rethinking Labor History: Essays on Discourse and Class Analysis*. Urbana, IL: University of Illinois Press; 1993. 235p. ISBN: 025201975- X; pbk. 0252062795; LCCN: 92-24297; OCLC: 26160785.

B216
BERLIN, ISAIAH. 1960-61. History and Theory: The concept of Scientific Historicism. *History and Theory*. 1960-61; 1(1): 1-31. ISSN: 0018-2656.

B217
BERLIOZ, JACQUES; AVRIL, JOSEPH. 1994. *Identifier sources et citations* [Identifying Sources and their Citations]. In: *Ateliér du médiéviste*, 1. [Turnhout], BE: Brépols; 1994. 336p. (Entire issuè on title topic; In French). ISBN: 250350311X.

B218
BERNARD, H. RUSSELL. 1988. *Research Methods in Cultural Anthropology*. Newbury Park, CA: Sage Publications; 1988. 520p. ISBN: 0803929773; pbk. 0803929781; LCCN: 87-23735; OCLC: 16684930.

B219
BERNARD, P.; HANKS, S., eds. 1995. *Proceedings of the Eleventh Conference on Uncertainty in Artificial Intelligence*. San Francisco, CA: Morgan Kaufmann; 1995.

B220
BERNARDO, JOSÉ. M.; BERGER, J. O.; DAVID, A. P.; SMITH, A. F. M., eds. 1980-1994-. *Bayesian Statistics*, 1-4. Valencian International Meetings on Bayesian Statistics. Irregular; publishers vary. No. 1 (1979): 647p. Valencia, ES; 1980. ISBN: 843700722. No. 2 (1983): 778p. New York, NY: North Holland; 1983. ISBN: 044877460. No. 3 (1987): 778p. . ISBN: 0198522207. No. 4 (1991): 859p. Oxford, UK: Oxford University Press; 1992. ISBN: 0198522665.

B221
BERNARDO, JOSÉ. M.; SMITH, ADRIAN. F. M. 1994. *Bayesian Theory*. Chichester, UK: John Wiley; 1994. ISBN: 0471924164.

B222
BERNDT, ERNST R.; TRIPLETT, JACK E., eds. 1992. *Fifty Years of Economic Measurement: The Jubilee of the Conference on Research in Income and Wealth.* Chicago, IL: University of Chicago Press; 1992. ISBN: 0226043851.

B223
BERNER, RICHARD C. 1983. *Archival Theory and Practice in the United States: A Historical Analysis.* Seattle, WA: University of Washington; 1983. 219p. ISBN: 0-295-95992-4.

B224
BERNSTEIN, PETER L. 1995. Risk as a History of Ideas. *Financial Analysts Journal.* 1995 Jan./Feb.; 51(1): 7-13. ISSN: 0015-198X.

B225
BERRY, JOSEPH K. 1995. *Spatial Reasoning for Effective GIS.* With a collection of mathematical formulae by Nigel Waters. Fort Collins, CO: GIS World Books; 1995. 208p. ISBN: 1882610148.

B226
BERTALANFFY, L. 1968. *General Systems Theory: Foundations, Development, Applications.* New York, NY: George Braziller; 1968.

B227
BESNARD, P.; HANKS, S., eds. *Uncertainty in Artificial Intelligence: Proceedings*, Eleventh Conference. Montreal, CA: AI Press; 1995.

B228
BESSER, HOWARD. 1991. Imaging: Fine Arts. *Journal of the American Society for Information Science.* 1991 September; 42 (8): 589-596. ISSN: 0002-8231.

B229
BESSER, HOWARD. 1997a. The Changing Role of Photographic Collections with the Advent of Digitization. See reference: JONES-GARMIL, K., ed. 1997. 115-128.

B230
BESSER, HOWARD. 1997b. The Transformation of the Museum and the Way its Perceived. See reference: JONES-GARMIL, K., ed. 1997. 153-170.

B231
BESSER, HOWARD. [199- forthcoming]. *Image Databases.* ASIS Monograph series. Medford, NJ: Learned Information, Inc. for the American Society for Information Science; [199-, forthcoming].

B232
BESSER, HOWARD; TRANT, JENNIFER. 1995. *Introduction to Imaging: Issues in Constructing an Image Database.* Santa Monica, CA: Getty Art History Information Program; 1995. 48p. ISBN: 0892363614.

B233
BEST, HEINRICH. 1991. Technology or Methodology? Quantitative Historical Social Research in Germany. *Computers and the Humanities.* 1991; 25(2-3): 163-71. ISSN: 0010-4817. Published also under slightly altered title: Technique or Method? Quantitative Historical Social Research in Germany. See reference: KRAUSE, J. ed. 1991. 163-172.

B234
BEST, HEINRICH. 1995. From the "Kulturnation" to the "Staatsnation": Universities and National Integration in Mid-nineteenth century Germany. See reference: JARITZ, G., *ET AL.*, eds. 1995. 109-118. See abstract in JARITZ, G., *ET AL.*, 1993: 54.

B235
BEST, HEINRICH; MANN, REINHARD, eds. 1977. *Quantitativ Methoden in der Historisch- Sozialwissenschaften Forschungen* [Quantitative Methods in Historical Social Science]. Stuttgart, DEU: Klett-Cotta; 1977. 254p. LCCN: 81-459369/r882; OCLC: 4783368.

B236
BEST, HEINRICH; MOCHMANN, EKKEHARD; THALLER, MANFRED, eds. 1988. *Cologne Computer Conference, September 7th-10th, 1988. Abstracts.* Cologne, DEU: Druck u. Verarbeitung/Hundt Druck GmbH for the University of Cologne; 1988. Irregular pagination, sections A-F [ca. 500p.]. (Ltd. distribution to conference participants only). OCLC: 25292040.

B237
BEST, HEINRICH; MOCHMANN, EKKEHARD; THALLER, MANFRED, eds. 1989. Computer Applications in the Historical Sciences: Selected Contributions to the Cologne Computer Conference, 1988. In: *Historisches Sozialforschung / Historical Social Research (DEU).* 1989; 14(3): 5-104. (Entire issue on title topic). ISSN: 0172-6404.

B238
BEST, HEINRICH; MOCHMANN, EKKEHARD; THALLER, MANFRED, eds. 1991. *Computers in the Humanities and the Social Sciences. Achievements of the 1980s, Prospects for the 1990s.* Proceedings of the Cologne Computer Conference 1988, Uses of the Computer in the Humanities and Social Sciences held at the University of Cologne, September 1988. Munich, London, New York, Paris: K. G. Saur; 1991. 520p. ISBN: 3-598-11041-3. Other conference contributions were published by same editors [above reference] for the Zentrum für Historische Sozialforschung [Cologne] in its *Historische Sozialforschung/ Historical Social Research,* 14 [1989] and 15 [1990] (DEU). ISSN: 0172-6404; OCLC: 24937324. See also revised versions in references: BEST,H.; THOME,H., eds., 1991.

B239
BEST, HEINRICH; SCHRADER, W. H. 1987. Quantitative Historical Social Research: The German Experience. See reference: JARAUSCH, K; SCHRADER, W. H., eds. 1987. 30-48.

B240
BEST, HEINRICH; THOME, HELMUT, eds. 1991. *Historische Sozialforschung* [Historical Social Research]. St. Katharinen [Göttingen]: Max-Planck-Institut für Geschichte in Kommission bei Scripta Mercaturae Verlag; 1991. 379p. (Halbgraue Reihe zur historischen Fackinformatik. Serie A: Historische Quellenkunden, Band 231). ISBN: 392266184-X; LCCN: 92-145356; OCLC: 25746527.

B241
BEST, JOHN B. 1986/1995. *Cognitive Psychology.* 3rd ed. St. Paul, MN: West Pub. Co.; 1992. 4th ed. Minneapolis, MN: University of Minnesota Press; 1995. ISBN: 0314908943; LCCN: 91022955.

B242
BESTOUGEFF, HELENE; LIGOZAT, GERARD. 1992. *Outils Logiques pour le Traitément du Temps.* Trans.: *Logical Tools for Temporal Knowledge Representation.* New York, NY: Ellis Horwood; 1992. ISBN: 013541699X; LCCN: 92033968.

B243
BEVIR, MARK. 1992. The Errors of Linguistic Contextualism. *History and Theory.* 1992; 31: 276-298. ISSN: 0018-2656.

B244
BEVIR, MARK. 1994. Objectivity in History. *History and Theory.* 1994 October; 33 (3): 328- 335. ISSN: 0018-2656.

B245
BEVIR, MARK. 1997. Mind and Method in the History of Ideas. *History and Theory.* 1997 May; 36(2): 167-190. (About the presumption of coherence). ISSN: 0018-2656.

B246
BEVERDIGE, ANDREW A.; SWEETING, GEORGE V. 1985. Running Records and the Automated Reconstruction of Historical Narrative. *Historische Sozialforschung/ Historical Social Research.* 1985 July; 35: 31-44. ISSN: 0172-6404.

B247
BEYERCHEN, ALAN D. 1990. Nonlinear Science and the Unfolding of a New Intellectual Vision. *Papers in Comparative Studies.* 1990; 6: 25-49.

B248
BEZDEK, JAMES C. 1981. *Pattern Recognition with Fuzzy Objective Function Algorithms.* New York, NY: Plenum Press; 1981. 256p. ISBN: 0306406713.

B249
BEZDEK, JAMES C., ed. 1987. *Analysis of Fuzzy Information.* International Fuzzy Systems Assn. (IFSA) Conference, Kauai, 1984. FIP-84. Boca Raton, FL: CRC Press; 1987. 3 vols. ISBN: 0849362962.

B250
BIAGIOLI, MARIO. 1993. *Galileo, Courtier: The Practice of Science in the Culture of Absolutism.* Chicago, IL: University of Chicago Press; 1993. 402p. ISBN: 0226045595.

B251
BIBER, DOUGLAS. 1988/1992. *Variation across Speech and Writing.* Cambridge, MA: Cambridge University Press; 1988. Pbk. ed., 1992. ISBN: 0521425565 (pbk.).

B252
BICKMAN, LEONARD; ROG, DEBRA J. 1997. *Handbook of Applied Social Research Methods.* Thousand Oaks, CA: Sage Publications; 1997. 604p. ISBN: 0-7619-0672-X (pbk.).

B253
BICOUVARIS, MARY V. 1994. *Building a Consensus for the Development of National Standards in History.* Ann Arbor, MI: University Microfilms; 1994.

B254
BICOUVARIS, MARY V. 1996. National Standards for History: The Struggles behind the Scenes. *The Clearing House.* 1996 Jan.-Feb.; 69(3): 136-140. ISSN: 0009-8655.

B255
BIDDICK, KATHLEEN. 1993. Humanist History and the Haunting of Virtual Worlds: Problems of Memory and Rememoration. *Genders.* 1993; 18: 47-66. ISSN: 0894-9832.

B256
BIDEAU, ALAIN; BRUNET, GUY; GUILLEMETTE, ANDRE; HEYER, EVELYNE; LEGARE, JACQUES; POULARD, SERGE. 1991. *SYGAP. Système de Gestion et d'Analyse de Population* [SYGAP: Database System and Population Analyses].[Lyons, FR]: Programme Rhone-Alpes; 1991. *(*Recherches en Sciences Humaines, 6). (In French).

B257
BIERSACK, ALETTA. 1989. Local Knowledge, Local History: Geertz and Beyond. See reference, HUNT, L., ed., 1989. 72-96.

B258
BIJKER, WIEBE E.; HUGHES, THOMAS; PINCH, TREVOR, eds. 1987. *The Social Construction of Technical Systems: New Directions in the Sociology and History of Technology.* Cambridge, MA: MIT Press; 1987. 372p. ISBN: 0262022621; LCCN: 86- 27600; OCLC: 14819149.

B259
BIJNEN, E. J. 1973. *Cluster Analysis.* Tilburg, DEU: Tilburg University Press; 1973. 112p. ISBN: 9023729129. Note: For Sociology.

B260
BIKSON, TORA K.; EVELAND, J. D.; GUTEK, BARBARA A. 1988. Flexible Interactive Technologies for Multi-Person Tasks: Current Problems and Future Prospects. Olson, Margrethe H., ed. *Technological Support for Work Group Collaboration.* Hillsdale, NJ: Lawrence Erlbaum; 1988. 377-394. ISBN: 0-8058-0304-1.

B261
BIKSON, TORA K.; EVELAND, J. D. 1990. Interplay of Work Group Structures and Computer Support. See reference: GALEGHER, J.; KRAUT, R. E.; EGIDO, C., eds. 1990. 245-290.

B262
BIKSON, TORA K.; FRINKING, E. J. 1993. *Preserving the Present: Toward Viable Electronic Records.* The Hague, NL: Edu Uitgeverij Publishers; 1993. 169p. ISBN: 903990487.

B263
BILDARCHIV FOTO MARBURG. [1998]. *Digital Information System for Art and Social History (DISKUS)* [CD-ROM]. Jubilee ed. Marburg, DEU: Philipps-Universität Marburg, Deutsches Dokumentationzentrum für Kungstgeschichte; [1998]. 5 discs. ISBN: 3-598-40320-8

B264
BILHARTZ, TERRY. 1984. In 500 Words of Less: Academic Book Reviewing in American History. *History Teacher.* 1984 August; 17(4): 526-536. ISSN: 0018-2745.

B265
BILL, R. 1994. Multimedia GIS—Definition, Requirements, and Applications. In: *1994 European GIS Yearbook* London, UK: Taylor & Francis; 1994. 151-154. LC call no.: G70.2 E9.

B266
BINAGHI, E.; GAGLIARDI, I.; SCHETTINI, R. 1992. Indexing and Fuzzy-logic based Retrieval of Color Images. *Visual Database Systems II.* Amsterdam, NL: Elsevier; 1992. 70-92. (IFIP Transactions, A-7)

B267
BINFORD, LEWIS R. 1972. *An Archeological Perspective.* New York, NY: Academic Press; 1972. ISBN: 0127850422.

B268
BINFORD, LEWIS R. 1983/1984. *In Present of the Past: Decoding the Archeological Record.* London, UK: 1983. Pbk. ed. New York, NY: W. W. Norton; 1984. ISBN: 0500274940 (pbk.).

B269
BINFORD, LEWIS R. 1989. *Debating Archeology.* New York, NY: Academic Press; 1989. ISBN: 0121000451.

B270
BINNS, S. E.; BOWEN, D. V.; MURDOCK, A. 1997. Migration Strategies within an Electronic Archive: Practical Experience and Future Research. See reference: BEARMAN, D.; TRANT, J., eds. 1997: 301-306.

B271
BIRCH, D.; DENLEY, PETER, compilers. 1993. *A Historical Computing Bibliography* (Electronic file). London, UK: Association for History and Computing; 1993. (Disk: Version 1.0).

B272
BIRD, JILL. 1991. *Executive Information Systems Management Handbook*. London, UK: Blackwell Publishers; 1991. ISBN: 0850127890.

B273
BIRDSALL, WILLIAM F. 1975. The Two Sides of the Desk: The Archivist and the Historian, 1909-1935. *American Archivist*. 1975 April; 38: 159-173. ISSN: 0360-9081.

B274
BIRKERTS, SVEN. 1994/1995. *The Gutenberg Elegies: The Fate of Reading in an Electronic Age*. New York, NY: Fawcett Columbine Books; 1994. 231p. Pbk. ed., 1995. ISBN: 0449910091.

B275
BIROU, ALAIN. [1966]. *Vocabulaire pratique des sciences sociales* [Practical Vocabulary of the Social Sciences]. Paris, FR: Editions Economie et Humanisme; [1966]. 314p. LCCN: 66050690.

B276
BISHOP, ANN P.; STAR, L. S. 1996. Social Informatics for Digital Libraries. Williams, Martha, ed. *Annual Review of Information Science and Technology* (*ARIST*). Medford, NJ: Information Today for ASIS; 1996. 31: 301-403. ISBN: 1-57387-019-6; ISSN: 0066-4200; CODEN: ARISBC; LC no. 66-25096.

B277
BISHOP, ANN P., ed. 1994. *Emerging Communities: Integrating Networked Information into Library Services*. 30th Annual Clinic on Library Applications of Data Processing. Urbana-Champagne, IL: University of Illinois Graduate School of Library and Information Science; 1994. 304p. ISBN: 0-87845-094-7.

B278
BISKUP, PETER, ed. 1995. *Debates and Discourses: Selected Australian Writings on Archival Theory, 1951-1990*. Sidney, AU: Australian Society of Archivists; 1995. 230p.

B279
BITTER-RIJPKEMA, MARIE-ELISE. 1995. Art History Study: Design and Development of Flexible Multimedia Learning material—a Strategy. See reference: BOONSTRA, O.; COLLENTEUR, G.; VAN ELDEREN, B., eds., 1995. 299-305.

B280
BLACK, BERT; AYALA, FRANCISCO; SAFFRAN, R.; BRINKS, CAROL. 1994. Science and the Law in the Wake of Daubert: A New Search for Scientific Knowledge. *Texas Law Review*. 1994; 72(4): 715-802. ISSN: 0040-4411.

B281
BLACK, ELIZABETH. 1991. *Authority Control: A Manual for Archivists / Le Controle d'autorité: Un manual destiné aux archivistes*. [Ottawa, CN]: Bureau of Canadian Archivists, Planning Committee on Descriptive Standards; 1991. 73p. (English and French parallel texts). ISBN: 0969079753; LCCN: 91-90310; OCLC: 23974675.

B282
BLACK, J. B.; BERN, H. 1981. Causal Coherence and Memory for Events in Narratives. *Journal of Verbal Learning and Verbal Behavior*. 1981; 20: 267-275. ISSN: 0022-5371.

B283
BLACKABY, JIM; SANDORE, BETH. 1997. Building Integrated Museum Information Retrieval Systems: Practical Approaches to Data Organization and Access. See reference: TRANT, J., ed. 1997: 117-146.

B284
BLACKLEDGE, JONATHAN M., ed. 1997. *Image Processing: Mathematical Methods and Applications*. IMA Conference on Image Processing, Mathematical Methods and Applications, Cranfield University, September 1994. Oxford, UK: Clarendon Press; 1997. 516p. (Institute of Mathematics and Its Applications conference series, 61). ISBN: 0198511973.

B285
BLACKER, F. 1995. Knowledge, Knowledge Work and Organization: An Overview and Interpretation. *Organizational Studies*. 1995; 16(6): 1021-1046. ISSN: 0170-8406. Note: On Activity Theory.

B286
BLACKWELL, DAVID; GIRSHICK, MEYER A. 1954/1979. *Theory of Games and Statistical Decisions*. New York, NY: John Wiley; 1954. Reprint, 1979. 355p. (Wiley Publications in Statistics). ISBN: 048663816; LCCN: 79087808.

B287
BLAIR, DAVID C. 1990. *Language and Representation in Information Retrieval*. New York, NY: Elsevier Science; 1990. 335p. ISBN: 0444884378.

B288
BLAKE, C.; KEOGH, E.; MERZ, C. J. 1998-. UCI Repository of Machine Learning Databases [Electronic file]. Irvine, CA: University of California, Dept. of Information and Computer Science; 1998-. Accessible at: http://www.ics.edu/~mlearn/MLRepository. html.

B289
BLAKE, NORMAN; ROBINSON, PETER. 1993. *The Canterbury Tales*. Oxford, UK: Oxford University Centre for Humanities Computing; 1993. (Project Occasional Papers, 1). Available from Oxford University Humanities Centre.

B290
BLALOCK, HUBERT M., Jr. 1982. *Conceptualization and Measurement in the Social Sciences*. Beverley Hills, CA: Sage Publications; 1982. 279p. ISBN: 0803918046; LCCN: 81-23269; OCLC: 8114676.

B291
BLANNING, ROBERT W.; KING, DAVID R., ed. 1996. *Organizational Intelligence. AI in Organizational Design, Modeling, and Control*. Los Alamitos, CA: IEEE, 1996. 320p. ISBN: 0-8186-7069-X.

B292
BLANQUET, M. F. 1993. La Fonction Documentaire. Étude dans un perspective historique [The Information Science Function. Study from an Historical Perective]. *Documentaliste*. 1993; 30 (4-5): 199-204. (In French). ISSN: 0012-4508.

B293
BLEDSTEIN, BURTON J. 1976. *The Culture of Professionalism: The Middle Class and the Development of Higher Education in America*. New York, NY: Norton; 1976. 354p. ISBN: 0393055744.

B294
BLENDA, GYULA; LASZLOVSZKY, JOZSEF; ROMHANYI, BEATRIX. 1993. History and Computing in Hungary. See reference: BORODKIN, L.; LEVERMANN, eds., 1993. 39-60.

B295
BLEWETT, DANIEL K. 1995. Why History Students Should Take Library Science Classes. *AHA Perspectives*. 1995 February; 33(2): 25-27. ISSN: 0743-7021.

B296
BLIVEN, BRUCE, Jr. 1954. *The Wonderful Writing Machine*. New York, NY: Random House; 1954. (History of the typewriter).

B297
BLOCH, HOWARD R. 1985. Naturalism, Nationalism, and Medievalism. *Romanic Review*. 1985; 76: 341-360. ISSN: 0035-8118.

B298
BLOCH, HOWARD R.; NICHOLS, STEPHEN G., eds. 1996. *Medievalism and the Modernist Temper*. Baltimore, MD: The Johns Hopkins University Press; 1996. 496p. ISBN: 080185086X (hbk.); 0801850878 (pbk.).

B299
BLOCH, MARC L. 1962. *The Historian's Craft*. P. Putnam, P., trans. New York, NY: Knopf; 1962. 197p. (Translation of *Apologie pour l'histoire*). OCLC 3742366.

B300
BLONDE, LAURENT; BUCK, MATTHIAS; GALLI, RICARDO; NIEM, WOLFGANG; PAKER, YAKUP; HEAN-SHAWAND, H. M.; UNWIN, D. J., eds. 1994. *Visualization in Geographical Information Systems*. London, UK: John Wiley; 1994.

B301
BLONSKY, MARSHALL. 1985. *On Signs*. Baltimore, MD: Johns Hopkins University Press; 1985. 536p. ISBN: 0801830060 (hbk.); 0801830079 (pbk.).

B302
BLOOMBERG, J. 1995. Ethnography: Aligning Field Studies of Work and Systems Design. In: Monk, A.; Gilbert, G. N., eds. *Perspectives on HCI: Diverse Approaches*. New York, NY: Academic Press; 1995.

B303
BLOOMFIELD, MORTON W. [1953]. *Form and Idea*. New York, NY: Macmillan; [1953]. 288p. LCCN: 53001030. Reprint, [1961]. 390p. LCCN: 61005388.

B304
BLOOR, GEOFFREY; DAWSON, PATRICK. 1994. Understanding Professional Culture in Organizational Context. *Organizational Studies*. 1994; 15 (2): 275-295. ISSN: 0170-8406.

B305
BLOSSFELD, HANS-PETER; HAMERLE, ALFRED; MAYER, KARL U. 1988/1989. *Event History Analysis: Statistical Theory and Applications in the Social Sciences*. Hillsdale, NJ: Erlbaum Associates; 1988 (c.1989). 297p. ISBN: 080580126-X; LCCN: 88-7073; OCLC: 17650674.

B306
BLOUIN, FRANCIS X. 1996. A Framework for a Consideration of Diplomatics in the Electronic Environment. See reference: BLOUIN, F.; DELMAS, B. 1996. 466-479.

B307
BLOUIN, FRANCIS X.; DELMAS, BRUNO, eds. 1996[1997]. *Diplomatics and Modern Records*. In: *The American Archivist*. 1996 fall [1997]; 59 (4): 412-494. (Entire issue on title topic). ISSN: 0360-9081.

B308
BLOW, FRANCES. 1987. A Fertile Error is More Productive than a Barren Truth: A Strategy for Database Integration. See reference: DENLEY, P.; HOPKIN, D., eds., 1987. 285-288.

B309
BLOW, FRANCES. 1990. Seeking Patterns, Making Meanings: Using Computerized Sources in Teaching History in Secondary Schools. See reference: MAWDSLEY, E. *ET AL.*, eds., 1990. 92-98.

B310
BLOW, FRANCES; DICKENSEN, ALARIC, eds. 1986. *New History and New Technology*. London, UK: Historical Association; 1986. 76p. ISBN: 0-85278-282-9.

B311
BLUH, PAMELA, ed. 1996. *EDI*. Special section in: *Library Administration & Management* (pp. 138-174). 1996 Summer; 10(3). ISSN: 0888-4463.

B312
BLUM, BRUCE I.; DUNCAN, KAREN A., eds. 1987. *A History of Medical Informatics*. Proceedings of the AMC (Association of Computing Machinery) Conference on the History of Medical Informatics, National Library of Medicine, 1987. New York, NY: AMC Press; 1987. 455p. ISBN: 021501287; LCCN: 89-17960; OCLC: 20392347.

B313
BLUME, PETER. 1986. Sogning i udenlandske daabaser [Searching in Foreign Language Databases]. *DF-REVY* (Aarhus, DK: Denmarks Forskningsbiblioteksforening). 1986 October; 9(8): 158-59. ISSN: 0106-0503.

B314
BLUMER, MARTIN. 1981. Quantification and Chicago Social Science in the 1920s: A Neglected Tradition. *Journal of the History of the Behavioral Sciences*. 1981; 17(3): 312- 31. ISSN: 0022-5061; LCCN: 65-9867; OCLC: 1783134.

B315
BLUMER, MARTIN. 1984. *The Chicago School of Sociology*. Chicago, IL: University of Chicago Press; 1984.

B316
BLUMFIELD, M. W. 1976. Stylistics and the Theory of Literature. *New Literary History*. 1976; 7: 271-311. ISSN: 0028-6087.

B317
BLUMIN, STEVEN. 1976. *The Urban Threshold: Growth and Change in a Nineteenth-century American Community*. Chicago, IL: University of Chicago Press; 1976. 298p. ISBN: 0226061698.

B318
BLUMIN, STEVEN. 1989. *The Emergence of the Middle Class: Social Experience in the American City, 1760-1900*. Cambridge, UK: Cambridge University Press; 1989. 434p. (Interdisciplinary Perspectives on Modern History series). ISBN: 0521250757 (hbk.); 0521376122 (pbk.).

B319
BLUMIN, STEVEN. 1990. The Classification of Occupations in Past Time: Problems of Fission and Fusion. See reference: MAWDSLEY, E., *ET AL.*, eds., 1990. 83-89.

B320
BOAR, B. 1986. Application prototyping: A Life Cycle Perspective. *Journal of Systems Management*. 1986 February; 37: 25-31. ISSN: 0022-4839.

B321
BOAST, R. B.; LUCY, S. 1996. Teaching with Objects. See reference: KAMERMANS, H.; FENNEMA, K., eds. 1996: 479-486.

B322
BOBINSKI, GEORGE. 1985. An Analysis of the 105 Major U.S. Journals in Library and Information Science. *Library Science Annual*. 1985; 1: 29-41.

B323
BOCCHI, FRANCESCA.; DENLEY, PETER, eds. 1994. *Storia e Multimedia* [History and Multimedia]. Atti del Settimo Congresso Internazionale del Association for History and Computing, Bologna, 29 agosto-2 setembre 1992. Bologna, IT: Italian AHC chapter; 1994. 860p. (Papers in Italian, French, and English). ISBN: 8880810006.

B324
BOCCIGNONE, G.; CHIANESE, A.; CORDELLA, L. P.; MARCELLI, A. 1993. Recovering Dynamic Information from Static Handwriting. *Pattern Recognition*. 1993; 26(3): 409- 418. ISSN: 0031-3203.

B325
BODEN, DEIRDRE; ZIMMERMAN, DON, eds. 1991. *Talk and Social Structure: Studies in Ethno-methodology and Conversation Analysis*. Berkeley, CA: University of California Press; 1991. 305p. ISBN: 0-52007-506-4; LCCN: 91-50423; OCLC: 24930251.

B326
BODENHAUSEN, G. V.; WYER, R. S. 1987. Social Cognition and Social Reality: Information Acquisition and Use in the Laboratory and the Real World. See reference: HIPPLER, H.-J.; SCWARTZ, N.; SUDMAN, E., eds. 1987. 8-41.

B327
BODMER, WALTER F.; MCKIE, ROBIN. 1995. *The Book of Man: The Human Genome Project and the Quest to Discover our Genetic Heritage*. New York, NY: C. Scribner; 1995. 259p. ISBN: 0684801027.

B328
BOEHM, ERIC H. 1965. *Blueprint for Bibliography: A System for the Social Sciences and Humanities*. Santa Barbara,CA: Clio Press; 1965. 22p. (Bibliography and Reference Series, 1). LC call no.: Z1009.B587 no. 1.

B329
BOEHM, ERIC H. 1967. *The Cue System for Bibliography and Indexing*. Santa Barbara, CA: Clio Press; 1967. 45p. (Bibliography and Reference Series, 7). LC call no.: Z1009.B587 no. 7.

B330
BOEHM, ERIC H. 1978. Twenty-five years of History Indexing: A Practitioner's Report. *The Indexer*. 1978; 11 (1): 33-39. ISSN: 0019-4131.

B331
BOEHM, ERIC H.; ADOLPHUS, LALIT. 1961. *Historical Periodicals: An Annotated World List of Historical and Related Serial Publications*. Santa Barbara, CA: ABC-Clio Press; 1961. 618p. LC call no.: Z6205.B67.

B332
BOEHM, ERIC H.; BUCKLAND, MICHAEL K., eds. 1983. *Education for Information Management. Directions for the Future*. Record of a conference cosponsored by the Information Institute, International Academy at Santa Barbara, and the Association of American Library Schools. Santa Barbara, CA: Information Institute; 1983. 125p. ISBN: 0961059001 (pbk.); LCCN: 88-80146; OCLC: 9479992.

B333
BOEHM, RONALD. 1981. *ABC-CLIO: A 25 Year History*. Santa Barbara CA: ABC-CLIO; 1981. 95p. IBSN: 0-87436-325-X.

B334
BOGUE, ALLAN G. 1968. United States: the "New" Political History. *Journal of Contemporary History*. 1968; 3(1): 5-27. ISSN: 0022-0094.

B335
BOGUE, ALLAN G., ed. 1973. Emerging Theoretical Models in Social and Political History. In: *American Behavioral Scientist*. 1973; 16(5). (Entire issue on title topic). ISSN: 0002- 7642. Republished as a monograph: Beverley Hills, CA: Sage Publications. 152p. ISBN: 0803903219; LCCN: 73-87857; OCLC: 969509.

B336
BOGUE, ALLAN G. 1976, 1977. The Historian and Social Science Data Archives in the United States. *American Behavioral Scientists*. 1976; 19(4): 419-42. ISSN: 0002-7642. Revision published in *Library Trends*. April 1977; 25(4): 847-88. ISSN: 0024-2594.

B337
BOGUE, ALLAN G. 1980. The New Political history in the 1970s. See reference: KAMMEN, M., ed. 1980. 231-251.

B338
BOGUE, ALLAN G. 1983. *Clio and the Bitch Goddess: Quantification in American Political History.* Beverly Hills, CA: Sage Publications in cooperation with the Social Science History Association; 1983. 279p. (New Approaches to Social Science History, vol. 3). ISBN: 08-0392-089-X; 08-0392-0903 (pbk.); LCCN: 83-13757; OCLC: 9758881. Title in reaction to the C. BRIDENBAUGH attack of Cliometrics.

B339
BOGUE, ALLAN G. 1987. Great Expectations and Secular Depression: The First 10 Years of the Social Science History Association. *Social Science History.* 1987; 11: ISSN: 0145-5532; LCCN: 77-640161.

B340
BOGUE, ALLAN G. 1990. The Quest for Numeracy: Data and Methods in American Political History. *Journal of Interdisciplinary History.* 1990; 21(1): 89-116. ISSN: 0022-1953.

B341
BOGURAEV, BRAN; BRISCOE, TED, eds. 1989. *Computational Lexicography for Natural Language Processing.* London, UK and New York, NY: Longman and John Wiley & Sons, Inc.; 1989. 310p. ISBN: 0-582-02248-7.

B342
BOISMIER, W. A.; REILLY, P. 1988. Expanding the Role of Computer Graphics in the Analysis of Survey Data (pp. 221-225). In: Ruggles, C. N. L.; Rahtz, S. P. Q., eds. *Computing and Quantitative Methods in Archeology.* 1987 Computer Applications in Archeology (CAA) Conference at the University of Leicester. Oxford, UK: BAR; 1988. 393p. ISBN: 086054075.

B343
BOISOT, MAX. 1995. *Information Space: A Framework for Learning in Organizations, Institutions, and Culture.* London, UK / New York, NY: Routledge; 1995. 550p. ISBN: 041511490X.

B344
BOK, SISSELA. 1978/1995. *Lying. Moral Choice in Private and Public Life.* New York, NY: Pantheon Books; 1978. 326p. ISBN: 0394413700.

B345
BOK, SISSELA. 1987. *Secrets: On the Ethics of Concealment and Revelation.* New York, NY: Pantheon Books; 1987. 332p. ISBN: 0394515811.

B346
BOKAREV, YURY. 1996 [199-]. The Models of Russian History Turnpoints. See reference: BORODKIN, L., ed. 1996: Abstract of presentation, 79-81; paper [199- forthcoming].

B347
BOLES, FRANK. 1990. Archival Education: Basic Characteristics and Core Curriculum. *AHA Perspectives.* 1990 October; 28: 1-11. ISSN: 0743-7021.

B348
BOLES, FRANK. 1991. *Archival Appraisal.* In association with Julia Marks Young. New York, NY: Neal-Schuman Publishers, Inc.; 1991. 118p. ISBN: 1-55570-064-0.

B349
BOLES, FRANK. 1996. Making Hard Choices: Continuing Education and the Archival Profession. *Archival Issues.* 1996; 21 (1) : 7-24. ISSN: 1067-4993. Cf., rejoinder by HORN, D., pp. 25-31.

B350
BOLOS I MASCI, JORDI; MORAN I OCERINJAUREGUI, JOSEP. 1994. *Repertori d'antroponims catalans* [Repertory of Catalan Anthroponomies]. Barcelona, ES: Institut d'Estudis Catalans; 1994. (In Catalan)

B351
BOLOTENKO, GEORGE. 1983. Archivists and Historians: Keepers of the Well. *Archivaria.* 1983 Summer; 16: 5-25. ISSN: 0318-6954.

B352
BOLTER, JAY DAVID. 1984. *Turing's Man: Western Civilization in the Computer Age.* London, UK: Duckworth; 1984. 266p. ISBN: 071569179.

B353
BOLTER, JAY DAVID. 1987. Text and Technology: Reading and Writing in the Electronic Age. *Library Resources and Technical Services.* 1987 January/March; 31: 12-23. ISSN: 0024-2527.

B354
BOLTER, JAY DAVID. 1991. *Writing Space: The Computer, Hypertext, and the History of Writing.* Hillside, NJ: Lawrence Erlbaum Associates; 1991. 258p. ISBN: 0805804277 (hbk.); 0805804285 (pbk.).

B355
BOMMELJÉ, BASTIAAN. 1987. *De sfinx op de rots: over geschiedensis en het menselijkk tekort* [historiography]. Amsterdam, NL: Contact; 1987. 190p. (In Dutch). ISBN: 9025465692; LCCN: 87-177400.

B356
BONWELL, CHARLES C.; EISON, JAMES A. 1991. *Active Learning: Creating Excitement in the Classroom.* Washington, DC: ASHE; 1991. (ASHE-ERIC Higher Education Report, 1). ISBN: 187830087 (pbk.).

B357
BONWELL, CHARLES C.; SUTHERLAND; TRACEY E., ed. 1996. *Using Active Learning in the Classroom: A Range of Options for Faculty.* San Francisco, CA: Jossey-Bass; 1996. 101p.

B358
BONZI, S. 1992. Senior Faculty Perception of Research Productivity. *Proceedings of the ASIS Annual Meeting* (vol.29) . Washington, D.C.; Knowledge Industry Publications, Inc.; 1992. 206-211.

B359
BOOK, RONALD V., ed. 1986. *Studies in Complexity Theory.* London, UK / New York, NY: John Wiley; 1986. 226p. ISBN: 0470202939 (pbk); LCCN: 85031478.

B360
BOOKSTEIN, ABRAHAM. 1976. The Bibliometric Distributions. *Library Quarterly.* 1976; 46: 4126-423. ISSN: 0024-2519.

B361
BOOKSTEIN, ABRAHAM. 1990a-b. Informetric Distributions.   Pt. 1: Unified Overview (pp. 368-75). Pt. 2: Resilience to Ambiguity (pp. 376-88). *Journal of the American Society for Information Science.* 1990; 41: 368-388. ISSN: 0002-8231.

B362
BOOKSTEIN, ABRAHAM. 1995. Ambiguity in Measurement of Social Science Phenomena. In: M. Koenig & A. Bookstein, eds. *Proceeedings of the Fiftieth Biennial Conference of the International Society for Scientometrics and Informetrics.* Rosary College, River Forest, IL, June 7-10, 1995. Medford, NJ: Learned Information; 1995. 73-82.

B363
BOOKSTEIN, ABRAHAM. 1996. Bibliocryptography. *Journal of the American Society for Information Science.* 1996 Dec.; 47 (12): 886-895. ISSN: 0002-8231.

B364
BOOKSTEIN, ABRAHAM. 1997. Informetric Distributions, III. Ambiguity and Randomness. *Journal of the American Society for Information Science.* 1997 Jan.; 48 (1): 2-10. ISSN: 0002-8231.

B365
BOOKSTEIN, ABRAHAM, ed. [1991]. *Research and Development in Information Retrieval.* SIGIR '91 Proceedings, 14th International ACM/SIGIR Conference, Chicago, IL, October 13-16, 1991. New York, NY: ACM Press; [c.1991]. 359p. ISBN: 0897914481; LCCN: 93108083. Available from ACM Order no. 606910.

B366
BOOMS, HANS. 1977. *Aus de Arbeit der Archiv. Beitrage zur Archivwessen, zur Quellenkunde, und zur Geschichte* [About the Work of Archives: Contribution to Archival Science, its Development and History]. Boppard am Rhein, DEU: Bolt; 1977. (Schriften des Bundesarchiv, 25). (In German). ISBN: 3764616903.

B367
BOOMS, HANS. 1987. Society and the Formation of a Documentary Heritage: Issues in the Appraisal of Archival Sources. *Archivaria.* 1987 Summer; 24: 105-25. ISSN:0318-6954.

B368
BOOMS, HANS; BUBERACH, HEINZ. 1968. *Das Bundesarchiv und seine Bestände: Ubersicht* [The German National Archives and Its Holdings: An Overview]. Boppard am Rhein, DEU: Bolt; 1968. 376p. (Bundesarchiv Schriften, 10).

B369
BOON, KEVIN A. 1997. *Chaos Theory and the Interpretation of Literary Texts: The Case of Kurt Vonnegut.* Studies in American Literature, 27. Lewiston, NY: Edwin Mellen Press; c1996. 191p. ISBN: 0773485538; LCCN: 970377565.

B370
BOONE, MARY E. 1993. *Leadership and the Computer.* Rocklin, CA: Prima Publishing; 1993. 397p. ISBN: 155958081.

B371
BOONSTRA, ONNO W. A. 1990. Supply-side Historical Information Systems: The Use of Historical Databases in a Public Record Office. *Historisch Sozialforschung/ Historical Social Research.* 1990; 15: 20-30. ISSN: 0172-6404.

B372
BOONSTRA, ONNO W. A.; COLLENTEUR, GEURT; VAN ELDEREN, BART, eds. 1995. *Structures and Contingencies in Computerized Historical Research.* Proceedings of the IX International Conference of the Association for History & Computing, Nijmegen 1994. *Cahier VGI [Vereniging voor Geschiedenis en Informatica* (Low Countries Association for History and Computing)], 9. Hilversum, NL: Uitgeverij Verloren; 1995. 315p. (Entire issue on title topic). ISBN: 90-6550-142-8.

B373
BOONSTRA, ONNO W. A.; COLLUNTEUR, GEURT; JANSSENS, ANGELIQUE; VAN ELDEREN, BART; MAN-DEMAKERS, KEES; STEVES, GEERT, eds. 1995. *Structures and Contingencies in Computerized Historical Research.* Proceedings of the IX International Conference of the Association for History and Computing, August 30-September 2, 1994, University of Nijmegen. Hilversum, NL: Uitgeverij Verloren; 1995. 320p. (Vereniging voor Geschiedenis en Informatica series). ISBN: 9065501428.

B374
BOOSINGER, MARCIA L. 1990. Associations Between Faculty Publishing Output and Opinions Regarding Student Library Skills. *College and Research Libraries.* 1990 September; 51(5): 471-481. ISSN: 0010-0870.

B375
BOOTH, A. 1967. A "Law" of Occurrence for Words of Low Frequency. *Information and Control.* 1967; 10: 368-393.

B376
BOOTH, ALAN; HYLAND, PAUL, eds. 1996. *History in Higher Education: New Directions in Teaching and Learning.* Oxford, UK/Cambirdge, MA: Blackwell Publishers; 1996. 327p. ISBN: 0631191356 (hbk.); 0631191364 (pbk.); LCCN: 95017968.

B377
BOOTH, SHIRLEY. 1997. *Learning and Awareness.* Educational Psychology series. Mahwah, NJ: Lawrence Erlbaum Associates, Inc.; 1997. 240p. ISBN: 0-8058-2455-3 (pbk.).

B378
BORDOGNA, GLORIA; GALIARDI, I.; MERELLI, D.; MUSSIO, P.; NALDI, F; PADULA, M. 1990. Pictorial Indexing for an Integrated Pictorial and Textual IT Environment. *Journal of Information Science* (UK). 1990; 16 (3): 165-174. ISSN: 1352-7460.

B379
BORDOGNA, GLORIA; PASI, GABRIELLA. 1993. A Fuzzy Linguistic Approach Generalizing Boolean Information Retrieval: A Model and its Evaluation. *Journal of the American Society for Information Science.* 1993 Mar.; 44 (20): 70-83. ISSN: 0002-8231.

B380
BORGMAN, CHRISTINE L. 1984. Psychological Research in Human-Computer Interaction. In: Williams, Martha E., ed. *Annual Review of Information Science and Technology.* White Plains, NY: Knowledge Industry Publications for ASIS; 1984; 19: 33-64. ISBN: 0-86729-093-5; ISSN: 0066-4200.

B381
BORGMAN, CHRISTINE. 1989. Cognitive Science and Psychology. *Bulletin of the American Society for Information Science.* 1989 Oct./Nov.; 16 (1): 16-. ISSN: 0095-4403.

B382
BORGMAN, CHRISTINE; SIEGFRIED, SUSAN L. 1992. Getty's Synoname and Its Cousins: A Survey of Applications of Personal Name-Matching Algorithms. *Journal of the American Society for Information Science.* 1992 Aug.; 43 (7): 459-77. ISSN: 0002-8231.

B383
BORGMAN, CHRISTINE L., ed. 1990. *Scholarly Communication and Bibliometrics.* Newbury Park, CA: Sage; 1990. 363p. ISBN: 0803938799. Revision of special issue of *Communication Research.* 1989: 16 (5). ISSN: 0093-6502.

B384
BORGMAN, CHRISTINE L.; MOGHDAM, DINEH; CORBETT, PATTI K. 1984. *Effective Online Searching.* New York, NY: M. Dekker; 1984. 201p. ISBN: 0824771427.

B385
BORGMAN, CHRISTINE L.; RICE, RONALD E. 1992. The Convergence of Information Science and Communication: A Bibliographic Analysis. *Journal of the American Society for Information Science.* 1992 July; 43: 397-411. ISSN: 0002-8231.

B386
BORILLO, MARIO; GARDIN, JEAN CLAUDE. 1984. *Banques de données archéologiques* [Archeological Databases]. Colloques nationaux 932 de Centre national de la recherche scientifique: Marseille, 12-14 juin 1972. Paris, FR: CNRS; 1974. 331p. (In French, with English summaries). ISBN: 2222016614.

B387
BORKO, HAROLD. 1968. Information Science: What is It? *American Documentation.* 1968 January; 19: 5. ISSN: 0022-8231.

B388
BORKO, HAROLD. 1977. Toward a Theory of Indexing. *Journal of the American Society for Information Science.* 1977; 13 (6): 355-365. ISSN: 0002-8231.

B389
BORKO, HAROLD; BERNICK, M. 1963. Automatic Document Classification. *Journal of the* ACM (Assn. of Computing Machinery). 1963; 10: 151-162. ISSN: 0001-0782.

B390
BORLUND, PIA; INGWERSEN, PETER. 1997. The Development of a Method for the Evaluation of Interactive Information Retrieval Systems. *Journal of Documentation* (UK). 1997 June; 53: 225-250. ISSN: 0022-0418.

B391
BORODKIN, LEONID I. 1992. Istorik i komp'iuter: noye rubezhi 90-kh godov [The historian and the computer: new horizons of the 90s]. In: *Informatsionnyi Biulletin' Komissii po primeneniiu matematischeskikh metodov i EVM v istoriseskikh issledovaniiakh pri otdelenii istorii RAN* [Information Bulletin of the Russian AHC-Branch and the Russian Academy of Sciences' Commission on the Application of Mathematical Methods and Computers in Historical Research], no. 4. Moscow, RU: Russian Academy of Sciences; 1992.

B392
BORODKIN, LEONID I. 1993. History and Computing in the USSR and Russia: Retrospect, State of the Art, Perspectives. See reference: BORODKIN, L.; LEVERMANN, eds., 1993. 7-20.

B393
BORODKIN, LEONID I. 1993. Istoriceskaja informatika v SSSE/Rossii: Reropektiva, sostojanie, perspektivy [Historical Informatics in the USSR/Russia: Retrospective overview and perspectives]. In: Borodkin, L; Levermann, V., eds. *Istorija I komjuter: Novye Informacionnye technologii v istoriceskick issledovanijach I obrazovanii* [History and Computers: New Information Technology and Historical Development and Work] [Gottingen, DEU] St. Katharinen: Scripta Mercaturae Verlag; 1993. 251-275.

B394
BORODKIN, LEONID I. 1996a. XI Mezdunarodnaya Konferencija "History and Computing": Novyi Etap v Razvitii Istoicheskoi Informatiki [The 11th International Conference on "History and Computing": A New Era in the Development of Historical Informatics]. See reference: BORODKIN, L. I., ed. 1996. 3-4.

B395
BORODKIN, LEONID I. 1996b. Istoricheskkaja Informatika v Metodologischeskih Izmereniajah [Historical Informatics in Methodological Surveys]. See reference: BORODKIN, L. I., ed. 1996. 101-111. (In Russian).

B396
BORODKIN, LEONID I., ed. 1996/ [199-]. *Data Modelling/Modelling History.* XI International Conference of the Association for History and Computing, August 20-24, 1996, Moscow State University. *Abstracts.*146p. *Proceedings* Moscow, RU: Moscow State University; [199-, forthcoming?]. Selections edited in *Informatsionnyi biulletin assoctsiastsii "Istoria i komputer"* [Information Science Bulletin of the History and Computing Association]. Spetsialny vypusk Biulletenia, posviaschehennyi XI Mezhdunarodnoi konferentsii "History and Computing" Moscow, MGU im. M. W. Lononosova 20-24 Aug. 1996y. Moscow, RU: Associtotsia "Istoria i komuter"; 1996 Nov. 19. 239p. ISBN: 57228006729. (In Russian).

B397
BORODKIN, LEONID I., ed. 2000. *Historical Computing in the Former Soviet Union.* In: *Primary Sources and Original Works.* Binghamton, NY: Haworth Press, [199-, forthcoming]. Ca. 275pp. (Entire issue on title topic). ISSN: 1042-8216.

B398
BORODKIN, LEONID I; KOVAL'CHENKO, IVAN; SOKOLOV, A. 1983. Mass Historical Sources and the Problems of Historical Data Archives. In: Kovalchenko, I., ed. *Aktualnye problemy istochniovedieniia* [Actual Problems in Historical Data Collections]. Moscow, RU: [Moscow State University]; 1983. *Tezisy dokladov IV Vsesoiuznoi konferentsii* (series). (In Russian).

B399
BORODKIN, LEONID I.; LAZAREV, VALERY; ZLOBIN, EVGENY. 1993. Applications of OCR in Russian Historical Sources: A Comparison of Various Programs. See reference: DOORN, P., *ET AL.*, eds. 1993. 139-146.

B400
BORODKIN, LEONID I.; LEVERMANN, WOLFGANG, eds. 1993. *History and Computing in Eastern Europe.* St. Katharinen [Göttingen, DEU]: Max-Planck-Institut für Geschichte in Kommission bei Scripta Mercaturae Verlag; 1993. 150p. (Halbgraue Reihe zur historischen Fackinformatik. Serie A: Historische Quellenkunden, Band 21). ISBN:3- 928134-94-9.

B401
BORODKIN, LEONID I.; MILOV, L. V. 1984. Some Aspects of the Application of Quantitative Methods and Computers in the Analysis of Narrative Texts. See reference: ROWNEY, D. K., ed. 1984. 186-207.

B402
BORODKIN, LEONID I.; SVISCHOV, M. [199-]. Computer-Assisted Simulation of Social Mobility in the NEP Period (1920s); using Markov Chains. See reference: BOONSTRA *ET AL.*, eds. [199-, forthcoming].

B403
BORODKIN, LEONID I.; TIAZHEL, NIKOVA, V. S., eds. 1995. *Krug idei: razvitie istoricheskoi informatiki:* trudy II konferenstii Assoctsiastsii "Istoriia i kimputer" [Circle of Ideas: Models and Technologies of Historical Informatics: proceedings of the 2nd Conference of the Association of History and Computing]. Moscow, RU: Izdatellstvo Moskovskogo gorodskogo arkhivov; 1995. 485p. ISBN: 5-7228-0030-9; LCCN: 96101810.

B404
BOS, BERNADINE; VAN DER MOER, ANKE. 1996 [199-]. OCR or Manual Data Entry: Experiences of the Bakunin-Project. See reference: BORODKIN, L., ed. 1996: Abstract of presentation, 55-56; paper [199- forthcoming].

B405
BOSC, PATRICK; DUBOIS, DIDIER; PRADE, HENRI. 1998. Fuzzy Functional Dependencies and Redundancy Elimination. *Journal of the American Society for Information Science.* 1998; 49 (3); 217-235. ISSN: 0002-8231.

B406
BOSC, PATRICK; KACPRZYK, JANUSZ. 1995. *Fuzzy Sets and Possibility Theory in Database Management Systems.* Heidelberg, DEU: Physica-Verlag; 1995. See also: Fuziness in Database Management Systems. Hedelberg, DEU: Physica-Verlag; c1995. 433p. ISBN: 379080858X; LCCN: 952066009.

B407
BOSC, PATRICK; PIVERT, O. 1992. Some Approaches for [*sic*] Relational Databases Flexible Quering. *Journal of Intelligent Information Systems.* 1992; 1: 323-354. ISSN: 0925-9902.

B408
BOSC, PATRICK; PIVERT, O. 1995. SQLf: A Relational Database Language for Fuzzy Querying. *IEEE Transactions on Fuzzy Systems.* 1995; 3:1-7.

B409
BOSCHMANN, ERWIN, ed. 1995. *The Electronic Classroom. A Handbook for Education in the Electronic Environment.* Medford, NJ: Information Today, Inc.; 1995. 240p. ISBN: 0-938734-89-x.

B410
BOSWELL, TERRY. 1989. Colonial Empires and the Capitalist World-Economy: A Time Series Analysis of Colonization, 1640-1960. *American Sociological Review.* 1989; 54: 180-196. ISSN: 0003-1224.

B411
BOTS, HANS. 1993. Editions de correspondence aux XIXe et XX siècles. Méthodes et strategies [Editing 19-20th century Correspondence: Methods and Strategies]. *XVIII Siècle.* 1993 January-March; 178: 119-129.

B412
BOTZ, GERHARD, ed. 1988. *"Qualität und Quantität": Zur Praxis der Methoden der Historischen Sozialwissenschaft* [Quality and Quantity: Toward Methodological Development in Historical Social Science] Frankfurt, DEU / New York, NY: University Press; 1988. 366p. (Bund. 10). ISBN: 3-59333-880-7; LCCN: 89-1811295; OCLC: 21340753.

B413
BOTZ, GERHARD; SCHMID, GEORG; SCHROEDER, WILHELM; THALLER, MANFRED. 1989. Göttingen Summer School '90 [pamphlet]. Göttingen, DEU: Max-Planck-Institut für Geschichte; 1989. 39p. Available from: Max-Planck-Institut für Geschichte, Hermann-Foge Weg 11, D200 Göttingen, DEU.

B414
BOTZEM, SUSANNE; KURSCHEL, HENRIETTE. 1995. The ICE-Project. See reference: JARITZ, G. *ET AL.*, eds. 1995. 397-410.

B415
BOUARD, ALAIN DE. *Manuel de Diplomatique Français et Pontificale* [Manual of French and Pontifical Diplomatics]. Paris, FR: A. Picard; 1929. 2 v. (In French).

B416
BOUCHARD, GERARD. 1985. *La reconstitution automatique des familles: Le système SOREP* [The Automatic Reconstruction of Families: The SOREP System]. Chicoutimi, CN: Universite du Québec a Chicoutimi; 1985. 2 vols. 745p. (In French).

B417
BOUCHARD, GERARD. 1987. Le development de SOREP comme centre de recherche multidisciplinaire et interinstitutionel [The Development of SOREP as a Multidisciplinary Interinstitutional Research Center]. *Les Centres de recherche universitaires en sciences humaines*. Ottawa, Ontario CN; Les Presses de l'Universite de Ottawa; 1987. 33-47. (In French).

B418
BOUCHARD, GERARD. 1988. Les fichiers-reseaux de population: Un retour à individualité [Data from Population registers: The return of individualism]. *Histoire sociale / Social History* (CN). 1988 November; 21 (42): 287-294. (In French). ISSN: 0018-2557.

B419
BOUCHARD, GERARD. 1996. *Tous les métiers du monde: le traitement des données professionnelles en histoire sociale* [All the Measures of the World: The Treatment of Professional Data in Social History]. [Sainte Foy, Québec], CN: Presses de l'Université Laval; 1996. 323p. ISBN: 2763774695. (In French).

B420
BOUCHARD, GERARD; GASGRAIN, BERNARD; HUBERT, MICHAEL; ROY, RAYMOND. 1989. Fichier de population et structures de gestion de base de données: le fichier-reseau *BALSAC* et le Systéme INGRES/INGRID [Population Files and Database Structures: the File system of INGRES/INGRID]. *Histoire et Mesure*. 1989; 4(2): 39-57. (In French). ISSN: 0982-1782.

B421
BOUCHARD, GERARD; GASGRAIN, BERNARD; ROY, RAYMOND. 1985a. *Reconstitution automatique des familles: données saguenayennes* [Automated Reconstitution of Families: Data from the Saguenay]. Montréal, CN: SOREP, Université du Québec a Chicoutimi and Universite de Laval; 1985. (In French).

B422
BOUCHARD, GERARD; GASGRAIN, BERNARD; ROY, RAYMOND. 1985b. *Reconstitution automatique des familles: Le systéme SOREP* [Automated Reconstitution of Families: the SOREP System]. Chicoutimi, CN: Université du Québec a Chicoutimi; 1985. 2 vols. Dossier, 2. (In French).

B423
BOUCHARD, GERARD; CONVILLE, SERGE, eds. 1993. *La Construction d'une culture: Le Québec et Amerique Français* [Construction of a Culture: Québec and French America]. Congres: Identité collective. St. Foy, Québec, CN: Université de Laval; 1993. 645p. (In French). ISBN: 2763773060.

B424
BOUCHE, NICOLE. 1997 [1998]. When Parallel Lines Meet: Implementing the EAD in the Yale University Library. See reference: DOOLEY, J., ed. 1997 [1998].

B425
BOULDING, L. 1956. *The Image: Knowledge in Life and Society*. Ann Arbor, MI: University of Michigan Press; 1956.

B426
BOULLE, PIERRE H. 1992. Canada Looks at the French Revolution: Analysis of Canadian Imprints, 1889-1989. See reference: MCCRANK, L., ed. 1992: 15-32. Also published as *Primary Sources & Original Works*, 1 (2/3): 15-32. ISBN: 1-56024-150-0.

B427
BOURDELAIS, PATRICE. 1984. French Quantitative History: Problems and Promises. *Social Science History*. 1984; 8: 179-192. ISSN: 0145-5532.

B428
BOURDIEU, PIERRE. 1972/1977. *Esquisse d'une théorie de la practique*. 2nd ed. Paris, FR: Droz; 1972. 269p. (Travaux de droit économie, de sociologie, et des sciences politiques). Trans. as. *Outline of a Theory of Practice*. New York, NY: Cambridge University Press; 1977. 248p. ISBN: 0521211786 (hbk.); 052129166x (pbk.).

B429
BOURDIEU, PIERRE. 1979/1984. *La Distinction: Critique Social du Jugement*. Paris, FR: Minuit Eds.;1979. (Le Sens Comun series). ISBN: 2707302759. Trans as: *A Social Critique of the Judgement of Taste*. Cambridge, MA: Harvard University Press; 1984. 613p. ISBN: 0674212800 (pbk.).

B430
BOURDIEU, PIERRE. 1984. *Homo academicus*. Paris, FR: Minuit Eds.; 1984. 302p. (Le Sens Comun series). (In French). ISBN: 2707306967.

B431
BOURDIEU, PIERRE. 1990. *In Other Words: Essays Towards a Reflexive Sociology*. Palo Alto, CA: Stanford University Press; 1990. 223p. (Translation of *Chosé dites*). ISBN: 0806715572 (hbk.); 0806717257 (pbk.).

B432
BOURDIEU, PIERRE. 1994. *Academic Discourse, Linguistic Understanding, and Professional Power*. Passeron, J.-P.; St. Martin, Monique des, trans. Cambridge, UK: Polity Press; 1994. 136p. (Translation from *Homo Academicus*). ISBN: 0745608205.

B433
BOURDIEU, PIERRE; CHARTIER, ROGER; DARNTON, ROBERT. 1985. Dialogue à propos de l'histoire culturelle [Dialog about Cultural History]. *Actes de la recherche en sciences sociales*. 1985; 59: 86-93. ISSN: 0335-5322.

B434
BOUREAU, ALAIN. 1991/1997. The Letter-writing Norm: A Medieval Invention. See reference: CHARTIER, R., ed. 1991/1997.

B435
BOURIN, MONIQUE, ed. 1989-[1998]. *Genèse médiévale del'anthroponymie moderne* [The Medieval Beginnings of Modern Anthroponomy]. Vol. 1 of series by the same title, in *Études d'anthroponomie médiévalle*, 1-4. Vol. 1, rev. ed., 1990. Vol. 2, pt. 1: *Presistances du nom unique: le cas de la Bretagne, L'anthroponymie des clercs* [Persistence of unique names: the case of Britain, the Anthroponymy of Clerics]. 1992. Vol. 2.., pt. 2: *Designation et anthroponymie des femmes: Méthodes statistques pour l'anthroponymie* [Designation of Feminine names: Statistical Methods for the Anthroponomy]. 1992. Vol. 3: *Enquêtes généalogiues et données prosopographiques* [Genaological Investigations and Prosocopographic Data]. 1995. Vol. 4: *Anthroponymie dependance et stigmatisation sociale* [Anthroponomic dependence and Social Stigma] [forthcoming, 1998]. Azay-le- Ferron/Tours, FR: [Presse de la Universite]; 1989-[1998]. (In French).

B436
BOURIN, MONIQUE; CHAREILLE, PASCAL. 1997. Les systèmes de gestion de base de données anthroponomiques [Systems to create Anthroponomical Databases]. (In French). See reference: BOURIN, M.; CHAREILLE, P., eds. 1997. 19-27.

B437
BOURIN, MONIQUE; CHAREILLE, PASCAL, eds. 1997. *Généalogie et Informatique* [Genealogy and Computing]. In: *Le Médiéviste et l'Ordinateur* [The Medievalist and the Computer]. 1997 winter; 36: 39 pp. (Entire issue on title topic; In French). ISSN: 0223-3843.

B438
BOURIN, MONIQUE; MARTIN, JEAN-MARIE; MENANT, FRANCOIS, eds. 1996. L'Anthroponymie: Document de l'histoire sociale des mondes mediterranéens medievaux [Anthroponomy: Documentation of the Social History of the medieval Mediterranean World]. Acts du colloque international, Palais Farnese, École française de Rome, 6-8 octubre, 1994 (GDR 955 du CNRS). In: *Collection de l'École française de Rome, 226*. Rome, IT: École française de Rome; 1996. 502p. (Entire issue on title topic). (In French). ISSN: 0223-5099; ISBN: 2728303614.

B439
BOURLET, CAROLINE; DOUTREPONT, CHARLES; LUSIGNAN, SERGE, comps. 1982. *Ordinateur et études médiévales: Bibliographie* [Computing and Medieval Studies: A Bibliography]. Montréal, CN: Université de Montréal, Institut d'études médiévales. 178p. ISBN 2-920409-00-X. (Collates 1250 entries from *Computers and Medieval Data Processing/Informatique et etudes medievales* [CADAP/INFEM], 1973-). ISSN: 0223- 5099; ISBN: 2728303614. See also reference: UNIVERSITÉ DE MONTRÉAL, 1973-.

B440
BOURLET, CAROLINE; GUILLAUMONT, AGNES; FAUGERES, ARLETTE; MAGDELAINE, MICHELLE; SELZ-LAURIERE, MARION. 1991. Construction of an Individual Identifications Help System. See reference: BEST, H., *ET AL.*, eds., 1991. 343-350.

B441
BOURLET, CAROLINE; MINEL, JEAN-LUC. 1990. From an Historian's Know-How to a Knowledge Base: Using a Shell. See reference: MAWDSLEY *ET AL.* eds. 1990. 55-59.

B442
BOURNE, CHARLES P. 1980. On-line Systems: History, Technology, and Economics. *Journal of the American Society for Information Science*. 1980 May; 31(3): 155-160. ISSN: 0002-8231.

B443
BOURNE, CHARLES P.; BELLARDO HAHN, TRUDI. [199-]. Pioneers of the Online Age. In: Pre-conference seminar on *The History of Information Science*, at the Conference of the American Society for Information Science, October 17-20, 1994, Alexandria, VA. Forthcoming in: *The History of the Development of Online Systems and Services in the U.S.* New York, NY: Academic Press; [199-, forthcoming].

B444
BOURNE, EDWARD G. [1967]. [Leopold von] Ranke and the Beginning of the Seminary Method in Teaching History. In.: *Essays in Historical Criticism*. Freeport, NY: Books for Libraries Press; [1967], 304p. LCCN: 67023183.

B445
BOURQUE, GILLES; DUCHASTEL, JULES. 1994. *La Société liberale Duplessité, 1944- 1960*. Montréal, Québec, CN: Presses de l'Université de Montréal; 1994. 435p. ISBN: 276061644.

B446
BOURQUE, GILLES; DUCHASTEL, JULES; PLANTE, PIERRE. 1988. *Restons traditionnels et progressifs. Pour un novelle analyze du discours politique: Le cas du régime Duplessis au Québec* [Traditional and Progressive Remains. Toward a New Analysis of Political Discourse: The Case of the Duplessis Regime in Quebec]. Montreal, Quebec, CN: Boreal; 1988. 399p. ISBN: 289052227X; LCCN: 89-147697.

B447
BOUTIER, JEAN; JULIA, DOMINIQUE, eds. 1995. *Passé recomposes: Champs et chantiers de l'histoire* [The Reconstituted Past: Fields and Interpretative areas of History]. Paris, FR: Autrement; 1995.

B448
BOUWSMA, WILLIAM J. 1981. From History of Ideas to History of Meaning. *Journal of Interdisciplinary History*. 1981; 12: 20-30. ISSN: 0022-1953.

B449
BOVE, PAUL A. 1990. Discourse. See reference: LENTRICCHIA, F.; MCLAUGHLIN, T., eds. 1990. 50-65.

B450
BOWEN, J. P., ed. 199-. *The Virtual Museum of Computing* [electronic file]. Reading, UK; 1997. Accessible at http://www.icom.org/vlmp/computing.html.

B451
BOWERS, RICHARD A. 1995. A History of Media & Media Technology. *CD-ROM Professional*. 1995 July; 8: 109-116. ISSN: 1049-0833.

B452
BOWKER, GEOFFREY C.; STAR, S. L.; TURNER, W.; GASSER, L., eds. 1997. *Social Science, Technical Systems, and Cooperative Work: Beyond the Great Divide*. Mahwah, NJ: Lawrence Earlbaum Associates; 1997. 470p. (Computers, Cognition, Work series). ISBN: 0805824022 (hbk.); 0805824030 (pbk.).

B453
BOWSER, EILEEN; KUIPER, JOHN, eds. 1991. *A Handbook for Film Archives*. New York, NY: Garland; 1991. 1201p. ISBN: 082403533X; LCCN: 91-13493.

B454
BOWYER, KEVIN; AHUJA, NARENDRA, eds. 1996. *Advances in Image Understanding. A Festschrift for Aziel Rosenfeld*. Los Alamitos, CA: IEEE; 1996. 352p. ISBN: 0-8186- 7644-2.

B455
BOYARIN, JONATHAN. 1993. Placing Reading: Ancient Israel and Medieval Europe. In: Boyarin, J., ed. *The Ethnography of Reading*. Berkeley, CA: University of California Press; 1993. 285p. ISBN: 0520079588 (hbk.); 05200813331 (pbk.).

B456
BOYARIN, JONATHAN. 1994. *Remapping Memory: The Politics of Timespace*. Minneapolis, MN: University of Minnesota Press; 1994. 250p. (Commentary by Charles Tilly). ISBN: 0816624526 (hbk.); 0816624534 (pbk.).

B457
BOYCE, BERT R.; MEADOW, CHARLES T.; KRAFT, DONALD H. 1994. *Measurement in Information Sciences*. San Diego, CA: Academic Press; 1994. 283p. (Library and Information Sciences series). ISBN: 0-12-121450-8; LCCN: 94017976..

B458
BOYCE, MARY E. 1995. Collective Centering and Collective Sense-making in the Stories and Storytelling of One Organization. *Organization Studies*. 1995; 16 (1): 107-137. ISSN: 0170-8406.

B459
BOYER, M. CHRISTINE. 1994. *The City of Collective Memory. Its Historical Imagery and Architectural Entertainments*. Cambridge, MA: MIT Press; 1994. 560p. ISBN: 0262023717.

B460
BOYER, ERNEST L. 1990. *Scholarship Reconsidered: Priorities of the Professorate*. Princeton, NJ: Carnegie Foundation for the Advancement of Teaching; 1990. See also: CARNEGIE FOUNDATION.

B461
BOYLE, JAMES. 1996. *Shamans, Software, and Spleens. Law and the Construction of the Information Society.* Cambridge, MA: Harvard University Press; 1996. 270p. ISBN: 0676805224 (hbk.).

B462
BOYLE, JAMES. 1997. A Blueprint for Managing Documents. *BYTE.* 1997 May; 22(5): 75-80. ISSN: 0360-5280.

B463
BOYLE, ROGER; THOMAS RICHARD C. 1988. *Computer Vision: A First Course.* Boston, MA / Oxford, UK: Blackwell Scientific Publications; 1988. 210p. ISBN: 06320017554 (hbk.); 0632015772 (pbk.).

B464
BOZINOVIC, R. M.; SRIHARI, S. N. 1989. Off-line Cursive Word Recognition. *IEEE PAMI.* 1989; 11(1): 68-83. ISSN: 0018-9219.

B465
BOZZI, ANDREA; GAPPELLI, GIUSEPPE. 1988a. A Latin Morphological Analyzer. See reference:THALLER, M., ed. 1988. 47-54.

B466
BOZZI, ANDREA; CAPPELLI, GIUSEPPI. 1988b. Machine-readable Textual Archives and Exchange of Data: Some Experiences at the ILC-Pisa. See reference: GENET, J.-P., ed., 1988. 195-190.

B467
BOZZI, ANDREA; CAPPELLI, GUISEPPE. 1991. Automatic Lemmatization of Latin Texts. See Reference: BEST, H. *ET AL.*, eds. 1991. 373-378.

B468
BOZZI, ANDREA: SAPUPPO, ANTONIO. 1995. Word-Image Linkage in the Computerized Analysis of Old Printed Dictionaries. See reference: BOONSTRA, O.; COLENTEUR, G.; VAN ELDEREN, B., eds., 1995. 223-230.

B469
BOZZOLO, CARLA; LOYAU, HELENE.; ORNATO, MONIQUE. 1995. Hommes de culture et hommes de pouvoir parisiens à la Cour amoureuse. I. Une approche prosopographique (CBMO). II: Un approches monographique: Bureau de Dammartin [Parisian Men of Culture and Men of Power in the Court of Love: A Prosopographic Approach and Monographic Approaches]. In: *Pratiques de la culture écrite en France au XV siècle.* Louvain-la-Nueve, BE: FIDEM; 1995. *Textes et etudes du Moyen Âge.* 1995; 2: 245-278. (In French). (Entire issue on title topic).

B470
BRACK, E. V., ed. 1987. *Mapfinder: The Use of Computer Graphics in an Automated Map Retrieval System: Final Report.* Shefield, UK: University of Shefield Department of Information Studies; February 1987. 57p. (British Library Research & Development Department, Project SI/G/700). OCLC: 17828817.

B471
BRACKETT, MICHAEL H. 1987. *Developing Data Structured Databases.* Englewood Cliffs, NJ: Prentice-Hall; 1987. 226p. ISBN: 0132043971.

B472
BRACKETT, MICHAEL H. 1996. *The Data Warehouse Challenge: Taming Data Chaos.* New York, NY: John Wiley & Sons; 1996. 579p. ISBN: 0471127442 (pbk.).

B473
BRADFORD, R.; NARTKER, T. [1991]. Error Correlation in Contemporary OCR Systems. In: *First International Conference on Document Analysis and Recognition, September 30- October 2, 1991 [IDCAR I at Saint Malo, France].* Organized by AFCET (Association francaise pour la cybernetique, economique et technique); IRISA-INRIA, Rennes; and Telecom, Paris. [Paris], FR: Ecoles nationale Superieure des Telecommunications; [1991]. 2 vols. (French abstracts). OCLC: 30688707.

B474
BRADFORD, S. C. 1934. Sources of Information on Specific Subjects. *Engineering.* 1934; 137: 85-86. ISSN: 0013-7782.

B475
BRADSHER, JAMES G., ed. 1988/1989. *Managing Archives and Archival Institutions.* London, UK: Mansell; 1988. Chicago, IL: University of Chicago Press; 1989. 304p. ISBN: 0720119650 (hbk.); 0720119871 (pbk.).

B476
BRADY, MICHAEL, ed. 1981. *Computer Vision.* Amsterdam, NL: North-Holland; 1981. 508p. Reprinted from : *Artificial Intelligence.* 1981 Aug.; v. 17. (Entire issue on title topic).

B477
BRAND, MYLES; HARNISH, ROBERT M., eds. 1986. *The Representation of Knowledge and Belief.* Tucson, AZ: University of Arizona Press; c1986. 368p. ISBN: 081665099979; LCCN: 86024961.

B478
BRAND, STEWART. 1987. *The Media Lab: Inventing the Future at MIT.* New York, NY: Viking Penguin; 1987. 285p. ISBN: 0670814423; LCCN: 87-40017.

B479
BRANDS, H. W. 1995. *The Reckless Decade: America in the 1890s.* New York, NY: St. Martin's Press; 1995. 375p. ISBN: 0312135947.

B480
BRANSCOMB, LEWIS M.; KELLER, JAMES, eds. 1996. *Converging Infrastructures. Intelligent Transportation and the National Information Infrastructure.* Cambridge, MA: MIT Press for the Harvard Information Infrastructure Project; 1996. 320p. ISBN: 0-262-52215-2.

B481
BRATLEY, P.; HAMESSE, JACQUELINE. 1990. The Computerisation of Manuscript Incipits. In: Chaueka, Yaacov., ed. *Computers in Literary and Linguistic Research.* Acts de la XVe Conference Internationale, Jerusalem, 5-9 Juin, 1988. Paris, FR / Geneva, CH: Champion-Slatkine; 1990. 138-145. (Travaux de linguistique quantitative, 44 : 383p). ISBN: 205101079x.

B482
BRAUDEL, FERNAND. 1958/1980. Histoire et Sciences Sociales: La Longue Durée [History and the social sciences: the *longue durée*]. *Annales: Sociétés, Économies, Civilisations.* 1958; 26: 725-753. ISSN:0395-2649. Included in his *Écrits sur l'histoire* [1969]. Matthews, Sarah, trans. *On History* Chicago, IL: University of Chicago Press; 1980. 6- 22. ISBN: 0226071502; LCCN: 80-11201/r83; OCLC: 6092168. Released also in London, UK: Weidenfeld & Nicolson; 1980.

B483
BRAUDEL, FERNAND. 1969. L'Histoire des civilisations: le Passé explique le present [The History of Civilizations: The Past explains the Present]. In his: *Écrits sur l'histoire.* Paris, FR: Flammarion; 1969. 25-314. Translated in *On History* (1980); See reference: BRAUDEL, 1958/1980.

B484
BRAUDEL, FERNAND. 1976. *La Mediterranée et le monde a l'époque de Philippe II.* 3rd. ed. in 2 vols. Paris, FR: A. Colin; 1976. 578p. LCCN: 78-342712/r92; OCLC: 3060794.

B485
BRAY, JAMES H.; MAXWELL, SCOTT E. 1985. *Multivariate Analysis of Variance.* Beverly Hills, CA: Sage; 1985. 80p. (Quantitative Applications for the Social Sciences, 54). ISBN: 0803923104.

B486
BREITENSTEIN, MIKEL. 1999. From Revolution to Orthodoxy: An Evolutionary History of the *International Encyclopedia of Unified Sciences.* See reference: WOODS, LARRY, ed. 1999. 783-797.

B487
BREIVIK, PATRICIA SENN. 1994. *Information Literacy: Educating Children for the 21st Century.* New York, NY: Scholastic; 1994. 198p. ISBN: 0590492764

B488
BREIVIK, PATRICIA SENN; GEE, E. GORDON. 1989. *Information Literacy. Revolution in the Library.* London, UK / New York, NY: Collier Macmillan Publishers, for the American Council on Education. 250p. ISBN: 0-02-911440-3.

B489
BRENT, EDWARD E., Jr.; ANDERSON, RONALD E. 1990. *Computer Applications in the Social Sciences.* Philadelphia, PA: Temple University Press; 1990. 471p. ISBN: 0-87722- 666-0; LCCN: 89-38772; OCLC: 20262071.

B490
BRÉPOLS ELECTRONIC PUBLISHING COMPANY. 1990-. *CETEDOC Library of Christian Latin Texts.* (Electronic files on optical disk). Turnhout, BE: Brépols, Inc. for the New Catholic University of Louvain; 1990. Contains volumes from *Corpus Christianorum Series Latina* and *Continuatio Mediaevalis.* P. Tombeur, *User's Guide.* Tournhout: Brépols; 1991. 93p. Available from: Brépols, Inc., Steenweg op Tielen 68, 2300 Turnhout, BE; fax. no. 014-42 89 19.

B491
BRÉPOLS ELECTRONIC PUBLISHING COMPANY. 1993-. *Royal Irish Academy Archive of Celtic-Latin Literature.* (Electronic files on optical disk). Turnhout, BE: Brépols, Inc.; 1993-. 23 files, from 1787-. OCLC: 26670948.

B492
BRÉPOLS ELECTRONIC PUBLISHING COMPANY. 1993/1994. *In Principio: Incipit Index of Latin Texts,* (electronic files on optical disk or CD-ROMs). Turnhout, BE: Brépols, Inc.; 1993-. (A-L made available in 1993; A-Z in 1994). 400,000 incipits from card files of the IRHT, Paris. (Users manual in French and English). OCLC: 30418211.

B493
BRÉPOLS ELECTRONIC PUBLISHING COMPANY. [1994]. *CETEDOC Index of Latin Forms* (electronic file). Turnhout, BE: Brépols, Inc.; [1994]. See reference: BREPOLS. 1993/1994.

B494
BRETTELL, C. B. 1992. Archives and Informants. Reflections on Juxtaposing the Methods of Anthropology and History. *Historical Methods.* 1992; 25 (1): 28-36. ISSN: 0161-5440.

B495
BREURE, LEEN. 1992. Tools for the Tower of Babel: Some Reflections on Historical Software Engineering. See reference: OLDERVOLL, J., ed. 1992: 23-36.

B496
BREURE, LEEN. 1995. Altis. A Model-based Approach to Historical Data Entry. See reference: BOONSTRA, O.; COLENTEUR, G.; VAN ELDEREN, B., eds. 1995. 178-188.

B497
BREWKE, GERHARD, ed. 1996. *Principles of Knowledge Representation.* Palo Alto, CA: Stanford University Press; 1996. 318p. ISBN: 1575860570 (hbk.); 157860562 (pbk.).

B498
BRIDENBAUGH, CARL. 1963. The Great Mutation. *American Historical Review.* 1963; 68: 1-10. ISSN: 0002-8762.

B499
BRIDGES, EDWIN; HUNTER, GREGORY S.; MILLER, PAGE PUTNAM; THELEN, DAVID; WEINBERG, GERHARD. 1993. Toward Better Documenting and Interpreting of the Past: What History Graduate Programs in the Twenty-First Century Should Teach about Archival Practices. *The American Archivist.* 1993 Fall; 56(4): 730-749. ISSN: 2832-4808.

B500
BRIDGES, WILLIAM. 1991. *Managing Transitions: Making the Most of Change.* Reading, MA: Addison-Wesley; 1991. 130p. ISBN: 0201550733.

B501
BRIDGES, WILLIAM. 1994. *Job Shift: How to Prosper in a Workplace without Jobs.* Reading, MA: Addison-Wesley; 1994. 257p. ISBN: 0201626675.

B502
BRIET, SUZANNE. 1951. Qu'est-ce que la documentation? [What is Documentation?]. Paris, FR: EDIT; 1951.

B503
BRIGGS, JOHN. 1992. *Fractals; The Patterns of Chaos: A New Science of Art, Science, and Nature.* New York, NY: Simon Y Schuster; 1991. 192p. ISBN: 06671742183 (hbk.); 0671742175 (pbk.).

B504
BRIGGS, JOHN; PEAT, F. DAVID. 1989. *Turbulent Mirror: An Illustrated Guide to Chaos Theory and the Science of Wholeness.* New York, NY: Harper & Row; c1989. 222p. ISBN: 0060160616.

B505
BRIGGS, JOHN; PEAT, F. DAVID. [1999]. *Seven Life Lessons of Chaos: Timeless Wisdom from the Science of Change.* New York, NY: Harper Collins Publishers; c1999. 207p. ISBN: 0060182466; LCCN: 97052983.

B506
BRIGGS, LESLIE J. 1967. *Handbook of Procedures for the Design of Instruction.* Pittsburgh, PA: American Institutes for Research; 1967. 176p. (Research in the Behavioral Sciences, Monograph 2). LCCN: 79019583.

B507
BRIGGS, LESLIE J.; GUSTAFSON, KENT L.; TILLMAN, MURRAY, eds. 1977/1981/1991. *Instructional Design: Principles and Applications.* Englewood Cliffs, NJ: Educational technology Publications; 1977. 2nd ed., 1981. 261p. ISBN:0877781774. Rev. ed., 1991. 487p. ISBN: 087778230X; LCCN: 90023255.

B508
BRIGHT, KEVIN; COOPER, CARY L. 1993. Organizational Culture and the Management of Quality. *Journal of Managerial Psychology*. 1993; 8 (6): 21-27. ISSN: 0268-3946.

B509
BRILLOUIN, LEON. 1956. *Science and information Theory*. New York, NY: Academic Press; 1956. 320p. LC call no.: TK5101.B86.

B510
BRINKMANN, KARL-HEINZ. 1981. Use of the TEAM Terminology Data Bank for the Terminology work of DIN [Deutsches Institut für Normung (Standards)]. *International Forum on Information and Documentation*. 1981 April; 6(2): 28-29. ISSN: 0304-9701.

B511
BRITISH LIBRARY & BRITISH ACADEMY. 1993. *Information Technology in Humanities Scholarship. British Achievements, Prospects, and Barriers*. London, UK: The British Library, Research and Development Department; 1993. 50p.(Library and Information Research Report 6097). ISBN: 1-897791-03-08.

B512
BRITT, DAVID W. 1997. *A Conceptual Introduction to Modeling. Qualitative and Quantitative Perspectives*. Mahwah, NJ: Lawrence Earlbaum Associates, Inc.; 1997. 224p. ISBN: 0-8058-1937-1 (hbk.); 0-8058-1938-x (pbk.).

B513
BRITTAIN, J. MICHAEL, ed. 1989. *Curriculum Development in Information Science to Meet the Needs of the Information Industries in the 1990s*. London, UK: British Library Board; 1989. 220p. ISSN: 0263-1709; ISBN: 0-7123-3170-0; LCCN: 89-214030; OCLC: 28798881.

B514
BROADBENT, ELAINE. 1986. A Study of Humanities Faculty Library Information Seeking Behavior. *Cataloging and Classification Quarterly*. 1986 Spring, 6(3): 23-37. ISSN: 0163-9374.

B515
BROADUS, ROBERT N. 1987a. Information Needs of Humanities Scholars: A Study of Requests Made at the National Humanities Center. *Library and Information Science Research*. 1987 April-June; 9(2): 113-129. ISSN: 0740-8188.

B516
BROADUS, ROBERT N. 1987b. Early Approaches to Bibliometrics. *Journal of the American Society for Information Science*. 1987 March. 38(2): 127-129. ISSN: 0002-8231.

B517
BROCKLEHURST, E. 1985. Computer Methods of Signature Verification. *Journal of Forensic Sciences*. 1985; 30: 445-457. LCCN: 58-27459/r872; OCLC: 1754597.

B518
BRODER, I.; LICHTMAN, A. J. 1983. Modeling the Past: The Specification of Functional Form. *Journal of Interdisciplinary History*. 1983; 13: 489-502. ISSN: 0022-1953.

B519
BRODIE, MICHAEL; STONEBRAKER, MICHAEL. 1995. *Migrating Legacy Systems: Gateways, Interfaces, & the Incremental Approach*. San Francisco, CA: Morgan Kaufmann Publ.; 1995. 210p. ISBN: 1558603301.

B520
BROKAW, LESLIE. 1991. Books that Transform Companies. *Inc*. 1991 July; 13 (7): 30-40. ISSN: 0162-8968.

B521
BRON, D. DE; OLSEN, M. 1986. The Guth Algorithm and the Nominal Record Linkage of Historical Records. *Historical Methods*. 1986; 19: 20-24. ISSN: 0161-5440.

B522
BROOKES, BERTRAM C. 1972. Information Science (Excluding IR). In: Whatley, Herbert A., ed. *British Librarianship and Information Science, 1966-1970* (pp. 137-149). London: British Library Association; 1972. 712p. OCLC: 498526.

B523
BROOKES, BERTRAM C. 1980-81. The Foundations of Information Science. *Journal of Information Science*. 1980-81; 2: 125-133, 209-221, 269-275; 3: 3-12. ISSN: 1352-7460.

B524
BROOKES, BERTRAM C. 1984. Lenin: The Founder of Informatics. *Journal of Information Science* (NL). 1984 June; 8: 221-223. ISSN: 0165-5515.

B525
BROOKES, BERTRAM C. 1990. Biblio-, Sciento-, Infor-metrics? What are We Talking About? In: Egghe, Leo; Rousseau, Ronald, eds. *Informetrics 89/90*: Selection of Papers submitted for the 2nd International Conference on Bibliometrics, Scientometrics and Informetrics; 1989 July 5-7; London, Ontario; New York, NY: Elsevier; 1990. 31-44. ISBN: 0-444-88460-2.

B526
BROOKMAN, WILLIAM R. 1984. *The Umma Industry: Studies in Neo-Summerian Texts*. Minneapolis, MN: University of Minnesota; 1984. 528 pp. (Ph.D. dissertation; *DAI*, vol. 45/05-A: 1489). Available from: University Microfilms, Ann Arbor, MI; Order no. AAD84-18451.

B527
BROOKS, PHILIP C. 1969. *Research in Archives: The Use of Unpublished Primary Sources*. Chicago, IL: University of Chicago Press; 1969. 127p. LC call no.: D16.B88.

B528
BROOKS, TERRENCE A. 1990. Clustering in Comprehensive Bibliographies and Related Literatures. *Journal of the American Society for Information Science*. 1990; 41 (3): 183-192. ISSN: 0002-8231.

B529
BROOKS, TERRENCE A. 1998. Orthography as a Fundamental Impediment to Online Information Retrieval. *Journal of the American Society for Information Science*. 1998 June; 49 (8): 731- 741. ISSN: 0002-8231; CODEN: AISJB6.

B530
BROTHMAN, BRIEN. 1991. Orders of Value: Probing the Theoretical Terms of Archival Practice. *Archivaria*. 1991 Summer; 32: 80-85. ISSN: 0318-6954.

B531
BROTHMAN, BRIEN. 1993. The Limits of Limits: Derridean Deconstruction and the Archival Institution. *Archivaria* (CAN). 36 Autumn; 35: 205-220. ISSN: 0318-6954.

B532
BROTHMAN, BRIEN; BROWN, RICHARD. 1996. Archives and Postmodernism. *The American Archivist*. 1996 fall; 59: 388-390. (Commentary on C. HEALD's article). ISSN: 0360-9081.

B533
BROWN, ALAN W., ed. 1996. *Component-based Software Engineering.* Los Alamitos, CA: IEEE; 1996. 152p. ISBN: 0-8186-7718-4.

B534
BROWN, ANDREW D. 1993a. Leading Technological Change. *Leadership & Organization Development Journal*. 1993; 14 (4): 21-26. ISSN: 0143-7739.

B535
BROWN, ANDREW D. 1993b. Managing Culture through Training Programs: The Digital Experience. *Training & Management Development Methods*. 1993; 7 (1): 2.11-2.19. ISSN: 0951-3507.

B536
BROWN, ANDREW D. 1994. Implementing MRPII: Leadership, Rites, and Cognitive Change. *Logistics Information Management*. 1994; 7 (2): 6-11. ISSN: 0957-6053.

B537
BROWN, GILLIAN; YULE, GEORGE, eds. 1983. *Discourse Analysis*. Cambridge, UK: Cambridge University Press; 1983. 288p. ISBN: 0521241448; 0521284759 (pbk.); LCCN: 82-23571; OCLC: 9131532.

B538
BROWN, JUDITH. 1990. *The I in Science: Training to Utilize Subjectivity in Research*. Oslo: NO: Scandinavia Universities Press; 1990. 199p. ISBN: 8200276611.

B539
BROWN, JUDITH R.; EARNSHAW, RAE; JERN, MICHAEL; VINCE, JOHN. 1995. *Visualization. Using Computer Graphics to Explore Data and Present Information*. Sommerset, NJ: J. Wiley & Sons, Inc.; 1995. 287p. and CD-ROM. ISBN: 0471129917 (pbk.).

B540
BROWN, M. H. 1990. Defining Stories in Organizations: Characteristics and Functions. In: See reference, ANDERSON, J. A., ed. 1990. 13: 162-190.

B541
BROWN, RICHARD. 1991-1992. Records Acquisitions Strategy and Its Theoretical Foundation: The Case for a Concept of Archival Hermeneutics. *Archivaria*. 1991-1192 Winter; 33: 34- 56. ISSN: 0318-6954.

B542
BROWN, RICHARD. 1995. Macro-Appraisal Theory and the Context of the Public Records Creator. *Archivaria* (CAN). 1995 Fall; 40: 132-145. ISSN: 0318-6954.

B543
BROWN, RICHARD D. 1989. *Knowledge is Power: The Diffusion of Information in Early America, 1700-1865*. New York, NY: Oxford University Press; 1989. 327p. ISBN: 0- 19-504417-1.

B544
BROWN, ROGER. 1958. How Shall a Thing be Called? *Psychological Review*. 1958. 65: 14-21. ISSN: 0033-295X.

B545
BROWN, THOMAS E. 1984. The Society of American Archivists confronts the Computer. *The American Archivist*. 1984; 47 (4): 366-383. ISSN: 0360-9081.

B546
BROWN, THOMAS E. 1993. A Decade of Development: Educational Programs for Automated Records and Techniques within the Society of American Archivists. *The American Archivist*. 1993; 56(3): 410-423. ISSN: 0360-9081.

B547
BROWNE, STEPHEN H. 1995. Reading, Rhetoric, and the Texture of Public Memory. *The Quarterly Journal of Speech*. 1995 May; 81 (2): 237-251. ISSN: 0033-5630.

B548
BROWNLEE, SHANNON. 1996. Complexity Meets the Business World: A New Business Science is Shedding Light on Commerce. *U.S. News and World Report*. 1996 Sept. 30; 121(13): 57. ISSN: 0041-5537.

B549
BRUBAKER, ROBERT L. 1976. Historians and the Information Profession. See reference: CLARK, R.,ed., 1976. 174-180.

B550
BRUCE, H. W. 1994. A Cognitive View of the Situational Dynamism of User-centered Relevance Estimation. *Journal of the American Society for Information Science*. 1994; 45: 142-148. ISSN: 0002-8231.

B551
BRUCE, VICKI; GREEN, PATRICK R.; GEORGESON, MARK. 1997. *Visual Perception. Physiology, Psychology, and Ecology*. 3rd ed. Mahwah, NJ: Lawrence Erlbaum Associates, Inc.; 1997. 448p. ISBN: 0-86377-450-4 (hbk.); 0-86377-451-2 (pbk.).

B552
BRUEMMER, BRUCE H.; HOCHHEISER, SHELDON. 1989. *The High-Technology Company: A Historical Research and Archival Guide*. Minneapolis, MN: Charles Babbage Institute; 1989. 131p. (NHPRC Grant project 87-47). OCLC: 20324985. Available from: SAA, Chicago, IL.

B553
BRUNER, JEROME S. 1960. *The Process of Education*. New York, NY: Vintage Books; 1960. 97p. Reprinted, Cambridge, MA: Harvard University Press; 1960. LC call no.: LB855.B75.

B554
BRUNER, JEROME S. 1996. *The Culture of Education*. Cambridge, MA: Harvard University Press; 1996. 224p. ISBN: 0674179528.

B555
BRUNET, E. 1991. What do Statistics Tell Us? See reference: HOCKEY, S., ed. 1991. 70-92.

B556
BRUNING, GERT. 1985. Moderne Instrumente der Historischen Chronologie-Tashencomputer ersetzen umfangreiche Tabellenwerk [Modern Tools of Historical Chronology: Computing extenisve substitution Tables]. *Historische Sozialforschung/Historical Social Research*. 1985; 35: 67-81. (In German; English abstracts). ISSN:0172-6404.

B557
BRUNTON, PAUL; ROBINSON, TIM. 1993. Arrangement and Description. See reference: ELLIS, J., ed. 1993: [210-230].

B558
BRUTHIAUX, P. 1993. Knowing when to Stop: Investigating the nature of Punctuation. *Language & Communication*. 1993: 13: 27-43. ISSN: 0271-5309. Available at http:// peak.umd/umich.edu/cgi-bin/peak/listjournal/ 02715309

B559
BRYMAN, ALAN; CRAMER, DUNCAN. 1990. Quantitative Data Analysis for Social Scientists. London, UK / New York, NY: Routledge; 1990. 290p. ISBN: 0415026644; 0415926652 (pbk.); LCCN: 89-27683; OCLC: 20453663.

B560
BUCCI, ODILO, ed. 1992. *Archival Science on the Threshold of the Year 2000.* Proceedings of the International Conference, Macerata, 3-8 September 1990. Macerata, IT: University of Macerata; 1992.

B561
BUCHANAN, WILLIAM. 1974. *Understanding Political Variables.* 2nd ed. New York, NY: C. Scribner; 1974. 305p. ISBN: 0684136546.

B562
BUCKINGHAM, WILLIAM. 1996. Myths and Anniversaries. *History Today* (UK). 1996 May; 46(3): 11-13. ISSN: 0018-2753.

B563
BUCKLAND, MICHAEL K. 1983. *Library Services in Theory and Context.* Elmsford, NY: Pergamon Press, Inc., Maxwell House. 202 p.(Pergamon International Library of Science, Technology, Engineering and Social Studies). ISBN: 0-08-030134-7; 0-08- 030133-9 (pbk.).

B564
BUCKLAND, MICHAEL K. 1991a. Information as Thing. *Journal of the Society for Information Science.* 1991; 42: 351-60. ISSN: 0002-8231.

B565
BUCKLAND, MICHAEL K. 1991b. *Information and Information Systems.* New York: Greenwood Press; 1991. 225p. ISBN: 0-313274-63-0.

B566
BUCKLAND, MICHAEL K. 1991c. Information retrieval of more than text. *Journal of the Society for Information Science.* 1991 September; 42:8, 586-588. ISSN: 0002-8231.

B567
BUCKLAND, MICHAEL K. 1992. Emmanuel Goldberg, Electronic Document Retrieval, and Vannevar Bush's Memex. *Journal of the American Society for Information Science.* 1992 May; 43(4): 284-94. ISSN: 0002-8231.

B568
BUCKLAND, MICHAEL K. 1995. Documentation, Information Science, and Library Science in the U.S,A. *Information Processing & Management.* 1995: 32 (1): 63-76. ISSN: 0306- 4573. See also in reference: BELLARDO HAHN, T.; BUCKLAND, M., ed. 1998. 159-172.

B569
BUCKLAND, MICHAEL K. 1997/1998. What is a "Document"? See reference: BUCKLAND, M.; BELLARDO HAHN, eds., pt. 2. 1997. 804-809. See also reference: BELLARDO HAHN, T.; BUCKLAND, M., ed. 1998. 215-220.

B570
BUCKLAND, MICHAEL K. 1999. The Landscape of Information Science: The American Society for Information Science. See reference: BATES, M., ed. 1999. Pt. 1: 965-969.

B571
BUCKLAND, MICHAEL K.; BELLARDO HAHN, TRUDI, eds. 1997. *History of Documentation and Information Science,* pts. 1-2. *Journal of the Association for Information Science.* 1997. 48 (4): 285-379. (Entire issue on title topic). ISSN: 0002-8231.

B572
BUCKLAND, MICHAEL K.; LIU, ZIMING. 1995. History of Information Science. In: Williams, Martha E., ed. *Annual Review of Information Science and Technology.* Medford, NJ: Information Today, Inc. for ASIS; 1995; 30: 385-416. ISBN: 1-57387-019-6; ISSN: 0066- 4200; CODEN: ARISBC; LCCN: 66-25096.

B573
BUCKLEY, FLETCHER J. 1996. *Implementing Configuration Management. Hardware, Software, and Firmware.* 2nd ed. Los Alamitos, CA: IEEE; 1996. 408p. ISBN: 0- 8186-7186-6.

B574
BUCKNER HIGGINBOTHAM, BARBRA, ed. 1995. *Advances in Preservation and Access, II.* Medford, NJ: Information Today, Inc.; 1995. 427p. ISBN: 0-038734-88.

B575
BUDD, JOHN M. 1986. Characteristics of Written Scholarship in American Literature: A Citation Study. *Library and Information Science Research.* 1986; 8: 189-211. ISSN: 0740-8188.

B576
BUDD, JOHN M. 1988. Publication in Library and Information Science: The State of the Literature. *Library Journal.*
1988 September; 113(14): 125-131. ISSN: 0363-0277.

B577
BUDD, JOHN M.; SEAVY, C. A. 1996. Productivity of U.S. Library and Information Science Faculty: The Hays
Study Revisited. *Library Quarterly.* 1996; 66: 1-20. ISSN: 0024-2519.

B578
BUDD, JOHN M.; SILIPIGNI CONNAWAY, LYNN. 1997. University Faculty and Networked Information: Results
of a Survey. *Journal of the American Society for Information Science.* 1997; 48(9): 843-852. ISSN: 0002-8231.

B579
BUDIN, GERHARD. 1991. The Application of Terminology-Based Knowledge Data Bases in the Humanities and
Social Sciences and its Impact on Research Methods. See reference: BEST, H., *ET AL.*, eds., 1991. 337-342.

B580
BULMER, MARTIN. 1981. Quantification and Chicago Social Science in the 1920s: A Neglected Tradition. *Journal
of the History of the Behavioral Sciences.* 1981; 17: 312-331. ISSN: 0022-5061.

B581
BUNDE, ARMIN; HAVLIN, SHLOMO. 1996. *Fractals and Disordered Systems.* 2nd ed. Berlin, DEU / New York,
NY: Springer Verlag; c1996. 408p. ISBN: 3540562192; LCCN: 95041926.

B582
BUNTINE, RAY L. 1995. Graphical Models for Discovering Knowledge. See reference: FAYYAD, U. M., *ET AL.*,
eds. 1995.

B583
BUNZL, MARTIN. 1995. Pragmatism to the Rescue? *Journal of the History of Ideas.* 1995 October; 56 (4): 651-660.
(Review of APPLEBY, HUNT & JACOB). ISSN: 0022- 5037.

B584
BURCHARD, J. E. 1965. How Humanists Use a Library (pp. 219-223). In: Overhage, Carl; Harmon, R. Joyce, eds.
Intrex: Planning Conference on Information Transfer Experiments (Sept. 3, 1965). Boston, MA: MIT Press;
[1965]. 276p. IBSN: 1-450087-9; LCCN: 65-28409; OCLC: 317756.

B585
BURDEA, GRIGORE; COIFFET, PHILIPPE. 1994. *Virtual Reality Technology.* New York, NY: John Wiley.; c1994.
ISBN: 0471086320 (pbk.); LCCN: 94018004.

B586
BUREAU OF CANADIAN ARCHIVISTS. COMMITTEE ON DESCRIPTIVE STANDARDS. 1985. *Toward
Descriptive Standards: Report and Recommendations of the Canadian Working Group on Archival Descriptive
Standards.* Ottawa, CAN: Bureau of Canadian Archivists; 1985. 192p. (Extensive bibliography, pp. 103-192). ISBN:
0889256802. See also references: BLACK, E., 1991; EASTWOOD, T., 1992.

B587
BUREAU OF CANADIAN ARCHIVISTS. COMMITTEE ON DESCRIPTIVE STANDARDS. 1990-. *Rules for
Archival Description.* Ottawa, CAN: Bureau of Canadian Archivists; 1990-. 1 vol. (Looseleaf; irregularly updat-
ed). ISBN: 0969079737.

B588
BUREAU OF CANADIAN ARCHIVISTS. COMMITTEE ON DESCRIPTIVE STANDARDS. 1992. *Subject
Indexing for Archives: The Report of the Subject Indexing Working Group.* Bureau Publication no. 4. Ottawa,
CAN: Bureau of Canadian Archivists; 1992. 144p. ISBN: 0-0690797-7-X.

B589
BUREAU OF ELECTRONIC PUBLISHING. 1990. *History of the World on CD-ROM* [electronic file]. CD-ROM.
New York, NY: BEP; 1990.

B590
BURGELMAN, ROBERT A. 1988. *Strategic Management of Technology and Innovation.* Homewood, IL: Irwin;
1988. 604p. ISBN: 0256034818.

B591
BURGISSER, PETER. 1997. *Algebraic Complexity Theory.* Berlin, DEU / New York, NY: Springer-Verlag; 1997.
618p. ISBN: 3540605827.

B592

BURKE, COLIN. 1992. The Other MEMEX: The Tangled Career of Vannevar Bush's Information Machine, The Rapid Selector. *Journal of the American Society for Information Science*. 1992 December; 43(10): 648-657. ISSN: 0002-8231.

B593

BURKE, COLIN. 1994. *Information and Secrecy: Vanevar Bush, ULTRA and the other Memex*. Metuchen, NJ: Scarecrow Press; 1994. 446p. ISBN: 0810827832.

B594

BURKE, FRANK G. 1981. The Future Course of Archival Theory in the United States. *The American Archivist*. 1981; 44: 40-46. ISSN: 0360-9081.

B595

BURKE, FRANK G. 1997. *Research and the Manuscript Tradition*. Lanham, MD: Scarecrow Press for SAA; 1997. 320p. ISBN: 0-8108-3348-4.

B596

BURKE, PETER. 1980. *Sociology and History*. London, UK/Boston, MA: G. Allen & Unwin; 1980. 116p. ISBN: 0034011144 (hbk.); 0043011152 (pbk.); LCCN: 80040105.

B597

BURKE, PETER. 1990. *The French Historical Revolution: The Annales School, 1929-89*. Cambridge, UK: Polity Press; 1990. 152p. ISBN: 0804718369 (hbk.); 0804718377 (pbk.). Reprint. Stanford, CA: Stanford University Press; 1990. 152p. ISBN: 0804718369; LCCN: 90070699.

B598

BURKE, PETER. 1993. *History and Social Theory*. Ithaca, NY: Cornel University Press; 1993. 198p. ISBN: 0801428610 (hbk.); 0801481007 (pbk.); LCCN: 92054434.

B599

BURKE, PETER, ed. 1991/1992. *New Perspectives on Historical Writing*. Cambridge, UK: Polity Press; 1991. 254p. ISBN: 074560501X. University Park, PA: Pennsylvania State University Press; 1992. ISBN: 027100827X (hbk.); 0271008342 (pbk.); LCCN: 91029380.

B600

BURKHARDT, MARLENE E.; BRASS, DANIEL J. 1990. Changing Patters of Patterns of Change: The Effects of a Change in Technology on Social Network Structure and Power. *Administrative Science Quarterly*. 1990 March; 35: 104-127. ISSN: 0001-8392.

B601

BURNARD, LOU D. 1988. The Oxford Text Archive: Principles and Prospects. See reference: GENET, J.-P., ed. 1988. 191-203.

B602

BURNARD, LOU D. 1991. What is SGML and How Does It Help? See reference: GREENSTEIN, D., ed. 1991a. 65-80.

B603

BURNARD, LOU D. 1992. Tools and Techniques for Computer-Assisted Text Processing. Butler, C. S., ed. *Computers and Written Texts*. Oxford, UK: Oxford University Press; 1991. 1-28.

B604

BURNARD, LOU D. 1993. The Text Encoding Initiative: Towards an Extensible Standard for the Encoding of Texts. See reference: ROSS, S.; HIGGS, E., eds. 1993. 105-118.

B605

BURNARD, LOU D.; SPERBERG-McQUEEN, MICHAEL C., eds. 1990. *Guidelines for the Encoding and Interchange of Machine-readable Texts*. Sponsored by ACH (Association for Computers and Humanities); ACL (Association for Computational Linguistics); and ALLC (Association for Literary and Linguistic Computing). [Chicago, IL and Oxford, UK]: Text Encoding Initiative; July 15, 1990 (corrected Aug. 6, 1990). 280p. OCLC: 25559340. Revised: SPERBEG-MCQUEEN, C. MICHAEL; BURNARD, LOU. 1994. *Guidelines for Electronic Text Encoding and Interchange (TEI P3)*. Chicago, IL/Oxford, UK: ACH-ACL-ALLC Text Encoding Initiative; 1994.

B606

BURTON, HILIARY D. 1988. Virtual Information Systems: Unlimited Resources for Information Retrieval. In: Kinder, Robin; Katz, Bill, eds. *Information Brokers and Reference Services*. Binghamton, NY: Haworth Press; 1988. 125-131. ISBN: 0-86656-739-5.

B607
BURTON, O. VERNON. 1980-81. Using the Computer and Manuscript Census returns to teach American Social History. *Indiana Social Studies Quarterly*. 1980-81; 33(3): 21-37. ISSN: 0019-6746.

B608
BURTON, O. VERNON. 1987. Historical Research Techniques: Teaching with Database Exercises on the Microcomputer. *Social Science History*. 1987; 11(4): 433-448. ISSN: 0145-5532.

B609
BURTON, O. VERNON. 1991. Computers, History, and Historians: Converging Cultures? *History Microcomputer Review*. 1991; 7(2): 11-23. ISSN: 0887-1078.

B610
BURTON, O. VERNON. 1992. Quantitative Methods for Historians: A Review Essay. *Historical Methods*. 1992; 25(4): 181-188. ISSN: 0161-5440.

B611
BURTON, O. VERNON; BLOMEAGER, R.; FUHADO, A; WHITE, S. J. 1987. Historical Research Techniques: Teaching with Database Exercises on a Microcomputer. *Social Science History*. 1987; 11: 433-438. ISSN: 0145-5532.

B612
BURTON, O. VERNON; FINNEGAN, TERENCE. 1989. New Tools for "New" History: Computers and the Teaching of Quantitative Historical Methods. *History Microcomputer Review*. 1989; 5(1): 13-18. ISSN: 0887-1078.

B613
BURTON, O. VERNON; FINNEGAN, TERENCE. 1991. Supercomputing and the U.S. Manuscript Census. *Social Science Computer Review*. 1991 Spring; 9: 1-12. ISSN:0894- 4393.

B614
BURY, J. B. 1902. *The Science of History*. Inaugural lecture, Divinity School, Cambridge University. Cambridge University Press; 1903. 42p. LCCN: 03-31259; OCLC: 1169484. See reference: STERN, S., ed., 1970.

B615
BUSA, ROBERTO. 1949. *La Terminologia Tomistica dell'interiorita. Saggi di methodo per una interpretazione della metafisica della presenza* [The Terminology of St. Thomas in the Interior. Essay about Methodology for an Interpretation of the Metaphysics of the Presence]. Milan: Bocca; 1949.

B616
BUSA, ROBERTO. 1951. *S. Thomae Aq. hymnorum ritualium varia specimina concordantiarum.* [Various Specimen of Concordances for the Hymns and Rites of St. Thomas Aquinas]. *A first example of word index automatically compiled and printed by IBM punched card machines.* Milan, IT: Fratelli Bocca, Editori; 1951. 175p. (Archivium Philosophicum Aloisianum). OCLC: 19831006.

B617
BUSA, ROBERTO, ed. 1982. *Global Linguistic Statistical Methods to Locate Style Identities*. Proceedings of an International Seminar. Rome: Edizioni dell'Ateneo; 1982. 111p. (Lesseco intellectuale europea, 29).

B618
BUSA, ROBERTO. 1990. Informatics and New Philology. In: Humanities Computing in Italy (pp. 339-344). *Computers and Humanities*. 1990; 24 (5-6). (Entire issue on title topic). ISSN: 0010-4817.

B619
BUSCH, JOSEPH A., ed. 1992a. Art Information and Information Systems in Cultural Institutions. *Bulletin of the American Society for Information Science*. 1992 December/January; 18 (2): 22-30. ISSN: 0095-4403.

B620
BUSCH, JOSEPH A. 1992b. Updating the Art and Architecture Thesaurus for Use in Object and Image Documentation. See reference: STONE, S.; BUCKLAND, M., eds. 1992. 1-8.

B621
BUSCH, JOSPEH A. 1992c. Use of a Relational Database System to Model the Variability of Historical Source Information. Paper for the 2nd Biennial Meeting of the International Society for Knowledge Organization, Madras, India. August 26-28, 1992. 34p.

B622
BUSCH, JOSEPH A. 1994. Thinking Ambiguously: Organizing Source Materials for Historical Research. See reference: FIDEL *ET AL*, eds., 1994. 23-56.

B623
BUSCHE, K.-P. 1992. Teaching History and Computing at German Universities: A Brief Description of a Poor Situation. See reference: SPAETH, DENLE; DAVIS, TRAINOR, eds., 1991. 15-16.

B624
BUSH, ALAN J.; BUSH, VICTORIA DAVIES. 1994. The Narrative Paradigm as a Perspective for Improving Ethical Evaluations of Advertisements. *Journal of Advertising*. 1994 September; 23 (3): 31-41. ISSN: 0091-3367.

B625
BUSH, VANNEVAR. 1945. As We May Think. *Atlanta Monthly*. 1945 July; 176: 101-108. ISSN: 0004-6795.

B626
BUTLER, CHRISTOPHER S., ed. 1985. *Computers in Linguistics*. Cambridge, MA / Oxford, UK: Blackwell; 1985. 266p. ISBN: 0-6311-4266-5; LCCN: 85-7540; OCLC: 12021956.

B627
BUTLER, CHRISTOPHER S., ed. 1992. *Computers and Written Texts*. Cambridge, MA / Oxford, UK: Blackwell; 1992. 305p. IBSN: 0631163816; LCCN: 91-23292; OCLC: 24066698.

B628
BUTLER, THOMAS, ed. 1989. *Memory: History, Culture and the Mind*. Oxford, UK: B. Blackwells; 1989. 189p. (Wolfson College Lectures). ISBN: 063464421; LCCN: 88028786.

B629
BUTTERWORTH, GEORGE. 1992. *Context and Cognition: Ways of Knowing and Learning*. Hillsdale, NJ: Lawrence Erlbaum Associates; 1992. 186p. ISBN: 0805813926 (hbk.); 0805813934 (pbk.).

B630
BUTTERWORTH, GEORGE.; LIGHT, PAUL., eds. 1982. *Social Cognition: Studies of the Development of Understanding*. Chicago, IL: University of Chicago Press; 1982. 261p. ISBN: 0226086097.

B631
BUZZETTI, DINO. 1993. Image Processing and the Study of Manuscript Textual Traditions. See reference: FIKFAK, J.; JARITZ, G., eds. 1993. 45-63.

B632
BYARS, LLOYD L. 1987. *Strategic Management: Planning and Implementation, Concepts and Cases*. 2nd ed. New York, NY: Harper & Row Publishers; 1987. 320p. ISBN: 000410957 (pbk.).

B633
BYNUM, CAROLINE WALKER. 1996. Presidential Editorial. AHA *Perspectives*. 1996, February; 34 (2):2-3. ISSN: 0743-7021.

B634
BYRNE, PAMELA R.; KINNEL, SUSAN K; CHIGNEL, MARK. 1989. An Expert System for Online Retrieval in the Humanities: the first year of Project Jefferson. See reference: MCCRANK, L. J., ed., 1989. 99-108.

B635
BYTE. 1990. *Computing without Keyboards*. In: *BYTE* (Magazine [Special Issue]). 1990 July; 15(7): 202-52. (Entire issue on title topic). ISSN: 0007-7135.

-C-

C1
CAGNON, PAUL, ed. 1989. *Historical Literacy: The Case for History in American Education*. Bradley Commission on History in Schools. New York, NY: Macmillan; 1989. 338p. ISBN: 002542115.

C2
CALHOUN, CRAIG. 1996. A Different Poststructuralism. *Contemporary Sociology*. 1996 May; 25(3): 302-6. (Review of P. BOURDIEU's *Outline of a Theory of Practice*). ISSN: 0094- 3061.

C3
CALLINICOS, ALEX. 1988. *Making History: Agency, Structure, and Change in Social History*. Ithaca, NY: Cornell University Press; 1988. 275p. ISBN: 0801421217; LCCN: 87047766.

C4
CALLINICOS, ALEX. 1989. *Against Postmodernism: A Marxist Critique*. Cambridge, UK: Polity Press; 1989. 207p. ISBN: 074560613X (hbk.); 0745606148 (pbk.); LCCN: 90129273.

C5
CALLINICOS, ALEX. 1995. *Theories and Narratives: Reflections on the Philosophy of History*. Durham NC: Duke University Press; 1995. 252p. ISBN: 0822316315 (hbk.); 0822316455 (pbk.); LCCN: 94024970.

C6
CAMBRIDGE SCIENTIFIC ABSTRACTS & ENGINEERING INFORMATION, INC. 1992-. *Computer and Information Systems Abstracts*. Bethesda, MA: Cambridge Scientific Abstracts; 1992 - ; 40- (Qtly.). ISSN: 0191-9776.

C7
CAMIC, CHARLES. 1989. Reshaping the History of American Sociology. *Social Epistemology*. 1994; 8: 9-18. ISSN: 0269-1728.

C8
CAMIC, CHARLES. 1995. Three Departments in Search of a Discipline: Localism and Interdisciplinary Interaction in American Sociology, 1890-1940. *Social Research*. 1995 Winter; 62(4): 1003-124. ISSN: 0037-783X

C9
CAMIC, CHARLES; XIE, YU. 1994. The Statistical Turn in American Social Science: Columbia University, 1890 to 1915. *American Sociological Review*. 1994 October; 59(5): 773-801. ISSN: 0003-1224.

C10
CAMMELLI, ANTONIO; PARENTI, LUIGI. 1991. *Thes[aurus] Giur[uidica]*: An Experimental Thesaurus of Legal Terms. See reference: BEST, H., *ET AL.*, eds., 1991. 351-355.

C11
CAMPBELL, DACE A. 1997. Explorations into Virtual Architecture: A HIT Lab Gallery. See reference: MOEZZI, S., ed. 1997. 74-76.

C12
CAMPBELL, DONALD T. 1969. Ethnocentrism of Disciplines and the Fish-Scale Model of Omniscience. See reference: SHERIF & SHERIF, eds. 1969. 328-348.

C13
CAMPBELL, DONALD T. 1988. *Methodology and Epistemology for Social Sciences: Selected Papers*. Oberman, E. Samuel., ed. Chicago, IL: University of Illinois Press; 1988. 609p. ISBN: 0226092488; LCCN: 88001127.

C14
CAMPBELL, MARY B.; ROLLINS, MARK, eds. 1989. *Begetting Images: Studies in the Art and Science of Symbol Production*. New York, NY: Peter Lang; 1989. 249p. ISBN: 0- 820410-454.

C15
CAMPBELL, RUTH; CONWAY, MARTIN A., eds. 1995. *Broken Memories; Case Studies in Memory Impairment*. Oxford, UK / Cambridge, MA: Blackwell; 1995. 444p. ISBN: 0631187227 (hbk.); 0631187235 (pbk.).

C16
CAMPBELL, STEPHEN K. 1974. *Flaws and Fallacies in Statistical Thinking*. Englewood Cliffs, NJ: Prentice-Hall; 1974. 200p. ISBN: 013327214.

C17
CAMPBELL-GRANT, I. R. 1991. Introducing ODA. *Computer Standards and Interfaces*. 1991; 11: 149-157. ISSN: 0920-5489.

C18
CAMPBELL-KELLY, MARTIN. 1990. Punched Card Machinery. See reference: ASPRAY, W., ed. 1990. Ch. 4.

C19
CAMPBELL-KELLY, MARTIN. 1993. Information in the Business Enterprise. See reference: ROSS, S; HIGGS, E., eds. 1993. 261-268.

C20
CAMPBELL-KELLY, MARTIN; ASPRAY, WILLIAM. 1996. *Computer. A History of the Information Machine*. New York, NY: Basic Books; 1996. 342p. (Alfred P. Sloan Foundation Technology series). ISBN: 0465029892.

C21
CANADA. PUBLIC ARCHIVES. RECORDS MANAGEMENT BRANCH. 1976. *Records Organization and Operations*. Ottawa, CN: Minister of Supply and Services; 1976. 154p. See also reference: CANADA. TREASURY BOARD; MCDONALD, JOHN.

C22
CANADA. TREASURY BOARD. 1987. *Strategic Direction in Information Technology Management in the Government of Canada.* Ottawa, CN: Treasury Board of Canada; 1987.

C23
CANADA. TREASURY BOARD. 1989. *Management of Government Information Holdings*. Ottawa, CN: Treasury Board of Canada; 1989. See also reference: BUREAU OF CANADIAN ARCHIVISTS.

C24
CANARY, ROBERT H.; KOZICKI, HENRY, eds. 1978. Introduction. In: *Writing of History: Literary Form and Historical Understanding* (pp. 3-30). Madison, WI: University of Wisconsin Press; 1978. ISBN: 0299075702; LCCN: 78-4590; OCLC: 3748290.

C25
CANAVILHAS, CONCEIÇÃO, ed. [199-]. *Computers in the History Classroom.* Proceedings of the 3rd International Conference, Lisbon, Portugal, April 14-16, 1993. Lisbon, PT: Associação Portuguesa de Historia e Informatica and the Fundação para a Divulgação das Tecnologias da Informação; [199- forthcoming].

C26
CANDLIN, FRANCIS; MORGAN, NICHOLAS. 1990. Messy Data—Clean Software—Brilliant Results. *Historisch Sozialforschung/ Historical Social Research* (DEU). 1990; 15: 72-78. ISSN: 0172-6404.

C27
CANNON, JOHN A.., ed. 1980. *The Historian at Work.* London, UK / Boston, MA: Allen & Unwin; 1980. 210p. ISBN: 0049010255 (hbk.); 0049010263 (pbk.); LCCN: 81217031.

C28
CANO, VIRGINIA. 1989. Citation Behavior: Classification, Utility and Location. *Journal of the American Society for Information Science.* 1989; 40: 284-290. ISSN: 0002-8231.

C29
CANO, VIRGINIA. 1990/1993. *Citation Life Cycle: Use of Citations through Time.* London, Ontario, CAN: University of Western Ontario School of Library and Information Science; 1990. 133p. (Ph.D. Dissertation). Available from: University Microfilms, Ann Arbor, MI.

C30
CANON-BROOKES, PETER. 1991. Museum-Databases Constructed Using *STIPPLE.* See reference: BEST, H., *ET AL.*, eds., 1991. 48-52.

C31
CANTOR, NORMAN. 1991. *Inventing the Middle Ages: The Lives, Works, and Ideas of Great Medievalists of the Twentieth Century.* New York, NY: William Morrow & Co.; 1991. 477p. ISBN: 0688094066; LCCN: 91-22748; OCLC: 23975292.

C32
CAPERS, JONES. 1998. *The Year 2000 Software Problem; Quantifying the Costs and Assessing the Consequences.* New York, NY: ACM Press; Reading, MA: Addison-Wesley; 1998. 335p. ISBN: 0201309645.

C33
CARANDE, ROBERT J. 1993. *Information Sources for Virtual Reality: A Research Guide.* Westport, CT: Greenwood Press; 1993. 157p. ISBN: 0313288046 (pbk.); LCCN: 92045083.

C34
CARGILL, CARL F. 1989. *Information Technology Standardization: Theory, Process, and Organization.* Bedford, MA: Digital Press; 1989. 252p. ISBN: 15558022X.

C35
CARLIN, M. 1989. The Medieval and Early Modern Data Bank. *AHA Perspectives.* 1989; 12: 12. ISSN: 0743-7021.

C36
CARLSON, CHESTER F. 1965. History of the Electrostatic Recording. Dessauer, John H.; Clark, Harold E., eds. *Xerography and Related Processes.* London, UK: Focal Press; 1965. 15-49. LC call no.: TR1045.D475.

C37
CARLSON, DAVID A.; RAM, SUDITA. 1990. Hyper-intelligence: The next Frontier. *Communications of the Association for Computing Machinery.* 1990 March; 33(3): 311-321. ISSN: 0001-0782.

C38
CARLSON, HELEN; FALK, DENNIS R. 1995. *Multimedia in Higher Education.* Medford, MI: Information Today, Inc.; 1995. 176 p. ISBN: 1-57387002-1.

C39
CARLSON, WALTER M. 1986. Why AFIPS Invested in History. *Annals of the History of Computing.* 1986; 8(3): 270-74. ISSN: 0164-1239.

C40
CARLUCCI AIELLO, LUIGIA; DOYLE, JON; SHAPIRO, STUART C. 1996. *Principles of Knowledge Representation and Reasoning.* Proceedings of the Fifth International Conference on Knowledge Representation and Reasoning, Cambridge, MA, 1995. San Francisco, CA: Morgan Kaufmann Pub.; 1996. 671p. ISBN: 1558604219.

C41
CARLYLE, R. E. 1985. Bringing History to Life. *Datamation*. 1985 March 1; 31(5): 145-146. (Review). ISSN: 0011-6963.

C42
CARNAP, RUDOLPH. 1934/1995. *The Unity of Science*. Black, M., trans. London, UK: Thoemmes; 1995. 101p. ISBN: 1-85506-391-3.

C43
CARNAP, RUDOLPH. 1934. *The Unity of Science*. London, UK: K. Paul Trench, Trubner & Co., Ltd.; 1934. 101p. LCCN: 35008996.

C44
CARNAP, RUDOLPH. [1972a]. Empiricism, Semantics, and Ontology. See reference: MORICK, H., ed. 1972; ch. 1.

C45
CARNAP, RUDOLPH. [1972b]. Logical Foundations of the Unity of Science. See reference: MARRAS, A., ed. 1972.

C46
CARNAP, RUDOLPH. 1995. *Philosophical Foundations of Physics: An Introduction to the Philosophy of Science*. Gardner, Martin, ed. New York, NY: Dover; 1995. 300p. ISBN: 0486283186 (pbk); LCCN: 94039458

C47
CARNAP, RUDOLPH; MORRIS, CHARLES, eds. [1941]. *Foundations of the Unity of Science*. Vols. 1-II: *International Encyclopedia of Unified Science*. Chicago, IL: University of Chicago Press; [1941]. LCCN: 74132777.

C48
CARNEGIE FOUNDATION FOR THE ADVANCEMENT OF TEACHING. 1990. *Scholarship Reconsidered: Priorities of the Professorate*. Princeton, NJ: The Carnegie Foundation; 1990. 147p. ISBN: 093105043x.

C49
CARNEGIE FOUNDATION FOR THE ADVANCEMENT OF TEACHING. 1994. *The Academic Profession: An International Perspective*. E. L. Boyer, P. G. Altbach, M. J. Whitelaw, eds. Princeton, NJ: The Carnegie Foundation; 1994. (Report of 1992 survey). ISBN: 0931050472; LCCN: 94-40363; OCLC: 31375878.

C50
CARNES, MARK C., ed. 1995. *Past Imperfect: History according to the Movies*. New York, NY: H. Holt; 1995. 304p. ISBN: 0805037594.

C51
CARNES, MARK C.; FARAGHER, JOHN MACK. 1995. Hollywood History. *American Heritage*. 1995 September; 46(5): 74-85. ISSN: 0002-8738. Available in: IAC, *General Periodicals*, 17170109.

C52
CARO BAROJA, JULIO. 1992. *Las falsificaciones de la historia* [Falsifications of History]. Barcelona, ES: Seiz-Barral; 1992. 2 vols. (In Spanish).

C53
CARPENTER, RONALD H. 1995. *History as Rhetoric: Style, Narrative, and Persuasion*. Columbus, SC: University of South Carolina Press; 1995. 350p. (Studies in Rhetoric and Communication). ISBN: 1570030324.

C54
CARR, DAVID. 1986. *Time, Narrative, and History*. Bloomington, IN: Indiana University Press; c1986. 189p. ISBN: 0253360242; LCCN: 85045742.

C55
CARR, EDWARD H. 1964. *What Is History?* Hamondsworth, UK: Penguin Books; 1964. 159p. (George Macaulay Trevelyan Lecture). OCLC: 19790430.

C56
CARRANO, FRANK M. 1995. *Data Abstraction and Problem Solving with C++: Walls and Mirrors*. New York, NY: John Wiley; 1995. 768p. ISBN: 0-8053-1226-9.

C57
CARRARD, PHILIPPE. 1992. *Poetics of the New History: French Historical Discourse from Braudel to Chartier*. Baltimore, MD: Parallax University Press; 1992. 256p. ISBN: 0801842549; LCCN: 91020585.

C58
CARROLL, JOHN. M. 1985. *What's in a name: An Essay in the Psychology of Reference*. New York, NY: W. H. Freeman; 1985. 209p. ISBN:0716716879.

C59
CARROLL, N. 1997. Periodizing postmodernism? *Clio.* 1997 winter; 26: 143-165. ISSN: 0884- 2043.

C60
CARRUTHERS, MARY. 1990/1996. *The Book of Memory. A Study of Memory in Medieval Culture.* Cambridge, UK: Cambridge University Press; 1990; pbk., 1992; repr. 1996. (Cambridge Studies in Medieval Literature, 10). ISBN: 0521-38282-3 (hbk.); 0-521- 42973-0 (pbk.).

C61
CARTWRIGHT, NANCY; CAT, JORDI; FLECK, LOLA; UEBEL, THOMAS E. 1996. *Otto Neurath. Philosophy between Science and Politics.* Cambridge, UK / New York, NY: Cambridge University Press; 1996. 288p. (Ideas in Context series, 38). ISBN: 0521451744.; LCCN: 95008505.

C62
CARUTH, CATHY. 1991. *Empirical Truths and Critical Fictions: Locke, Wordsworth, Kant, and Freud.* Baltimore, MD: The Johns Hopkins University Press; 1991. 167p. ISBN: 0801840805.

C63
CARUTH, CATHY. 1996. *Unclaimed Experience: Trauma, Narrative and History.* Baltimore, MD: The Johns Hopkins University Press; 1996. 154p. ISBN: 0801852463 (hbk.); 0801852471 (pbk.).

C64
CARUTH, CATHY, ed. 1995. *Trauma: Explorations in Memory.* Baltimore, MD: The Johns Hopkins University Press; 1995. 277p. ISBN: 0801850096 (hbk.); 080185007X (pbk.).

C65
CARVALHO, JOAQUIM. 1989. Expert Systems and Community Reconstruction Studies. See reference: HARVEY, C. *ET AL.,* eds. 1989. 97-102.

C66
CARVALHO, JOAQUIM. 1991. Soluzioni informatiche per micro-storici [Computer Science Solutions for Micro-History]. *Quaderni Storici* (Ancona, IT). 1991; 26: 761-791. (In Italian with English summaries). ISSN: 0301-6307.

C67
CASDEGLI, MARTIN; EUBANK, STEPHEN, eds. 1992. *Nonlinear Modeling and Forecasting.* Santa Fe, NM: Santa Fe Institute (SFI); 1992. ISBN: 0-201-52764-4 (hbk.); 0-201-58788-2 (pbk.).

C68
CASE, DONALD O. 1986. Collection and Organization of Written Information by Social Scientists and Humanists: A Review and Exploratory Study. *Journal of Information Science.* 1986; 12(3): 97-104. ISSN: 0165-5515.

C69
CASE, DONALD O. 1988. How Do Experts Do It? The Use of Ethnographic Methods as an Aid to Understanding the Cognitive Processing and Retrieval of Large Bodies of Text. In: Chiaramella, Yves, ed. *SIGIR'88: Proceedings of the Association for Computing Machinery.* 11th International Conference on Research and Development in Information Retrieval; 1988 June 13-15 in Grenoble, France. New York, NY: ACM; 1988; 127-133. ISBN: 2- 7061-0309-4.

C70
CASE, DONALD O. 1991a. The Collection and Use of Information Sources by Some American Historians: A Study of Motives and Methods. *Library Quarterly.* 1991 January; 61(1): 61- 82. ISSN: 0024-2519.

C71
CASE, DONALD O. 1991b. Conceptual Organization and Retrieval of Text by Historians: The Role of Memory and Metaphor. *Journal of the American Society for Information Science.* 1991 October; 42(9): 657-668. ISSN: 0002-8231.

C72
CASELLA, GEORGE; BERGER, ROGER L. 1990. *Statistical Inference.* Belmont, CA: Wadsworth & Brooks / Cole Co.; 1990. ISBN: 0534119581.

C73
CASEY, EDWARD S. 1976. *Imagining: A Phenomenological Study.* Bloomington, IN: Indiana University Press; 1976. 260p. ISBN: 025332914.

C74
CASEY, EDWARD S. 1987. *Remembering: A Phenomenological Study.* Bloomington, IN: Indiana University Press; 1987. 362p. ISBN: 0253349627 (hbk.); 0253204097 (pbk.).

C75
CASEY, EDWARD S. 1997. *The Fate of Place: A Philosophical History.* Berkeley, CA: University of California Press; 1997. 488p. ISBN: 05202002961.

C76
CASEY, JAMES B. 1985. *Assessment of Quality in Book Selection: An Evaluation of the Effectiveness of Opinions Rendered by Peer Review in American History Journals.* Cleveland, OH: Case Western Reserve University School of Library Science; 1985. (Ph.D. Dissertation). Available from: University Microfilms, Ann Arbor, MI.

C77
CASSELL, JUSTINE. 1991. *The Development of the Expression of Time and Event in Narrative.* Ph.D. Thesis. Chicago, IL: University of Chicago; 1991. 233p. LCCN: 9295501. Microfilm available from Regenstein Library, Photo-duplication, University of Chicago, IL.

C78
CASSIRER, ERNST. 1944. *An Essay on Man: An Introduction to the Philosophy of Human Culture.* New Haven, CT: Yale University Press / London, UK: Oxford University Press; 1944. 237p. LCCN: 44005386.

C79
CASSIRER, ERNST. 1950. *Das Erkenntnisproblem in der Philosophie und Wissenschaft der neueren Zeit.* Woglom, W. H.; Hendel, Chares W., trans. *The Problem of Knowledge; Philosophy, Science, and History since Hegel.* New Haven, CT: Yale University Press; 1950. 334p. LCCN: 50007218.

C80
CASSIRER, ERNST. 1953/1996. *Philosophie der Symbolischen Formen.* Manheim, Ralph, trans. *The Philosophy of Symbolic Forms.* New Haven, CT: Yale University Press; 1953. 3 vols. *The Metaphysics of Symbolic Forms.* Verene, Donald P., trans. Yale University Press; [c.1996], vol. 4. ISBN: 0300062788 (vol. 4); LCCN: 52013969.

C81
CASSIRER, ERNST. 1961. *Logik der Kulturwissenschaften.* Smith Howe, Clarence, trans. *The Logic of the Humanities.* New Haven, CT: Yale University Press; 1961. 217p. LCCN: 61006311.

C82
CASSON, HERBERT N. [1971]. *The History of the Telephone.* Freeport, NY: Books for Libraries Press; [1971]. 315p. ISBN: 0836966082; LCCN: 76175693.

C83
CASTELL, TRACY. [1997]. Maintaining Web-based Bibliographies: A Case Study of *Iter, the Bibliography of Renaissance Europe.* In: *Digital Collections: Implications for Users, Funders, Developers and Maintainers.* Proceedings of the 60th ASIS Annual Meeting. Washington, D.C., November 1-6, 1997. Schwartz, C; Rorvig, M., eds. Medford, NJ: Information Today, Inc.; 1997. 34: 174-182

C84
CASTI, JOHN L 1994. *Complexification: Explaining a Paradoxical World through the Science of Surprise.* New York, NY: Harper-Collins; 1994. 320p. ISBN: 6060168889.

C85
CASTONGUAY, DENIS; OIKAWA, AKIFUMI; VEZINA, RAYMOND. 1983. Information and Communications Technology Serving the Needs of Canada's Museum Curators and Researchers. *Information Services & Use.* 1983 Spring; 3(1/2): 29-47. ISSN: 0167-5265.

C86
CASTRIGIANO, DOMENICO P.L. 1993. *Catastrophe Theory.* Preface by R. Thom and A. Hayes. Reading, MA: Addison Wesley Longman; 1993. ISBN: 0-201-55590-5 (hbk.).

C87
CATTEL, RODERIC G. G. 1991/1994. *Object Data Management: Object-oriented Relational Database Systems.* Reading, MA: Addison-Wesley; 1991. 318p. ISBN: 0201530929. Rev. ed., 1994. 389p. ISBN: 0201547481.

C88
CATTELL, RODERIC G. G.; ATWOOD, TOM 1994. *The Object Database Standard ODMG-93.* San Mateo, CA: Morgan Kaufmann Publishers; 1994. 169p. ISBN: 1558603026.

C89
CATTERALL, PETER; MORRIS, KATE. 1996. Flickering Images? *History Today* (UK). 1996 October; 10 (4): 4-7. (Concerns TV broadcast records). ISSN: 0018-2753.

C90
CAUDLE, SHARON L.; MARCHAND, DONALD. 1989. *Managing Information Resources: New Directions in State Government— A National Study of State Government Information Resources Management.* Syracuse, NY: Syracuse University School of Information Studies; 1989. 307p. ISBN: 0962380709.

C91
CAUQUIL, GUILLAUM. 1992. *Vocabulaire essentiel du latin* [Essential Latin Vocabulary]. Paris, FR: Hachette; 1992.

C92
CAUSE (Association for Managing and Using Information Resources in Higher Education). 1996. *Institutions by Carnegie Classification*. Denver, CO: CAUSE; 1996. Accessible at http://cause-www.colorado.edu/member-dir/carnegie/doc.2_institutions.html.

C93
CAUSE / EDUCOM. [1994]. *Evaluation Guidelines for Institutional Information Technology Resources*. Available from CAUSE at http://www.cause.org/information-resources/ir-library. See reference: FLEIT, LINDA. [1994]: appendix.

C94
CAVANAUGH, TOM. 1995. *Fading Away: The Preservation and Enhanced Use of Canada's Audiovisual Heritage*. Ottawa, CAN: National Archives of Canada; 1995.

C95
CAWKELL, ANTHONY. 1980. Information Technology and Communications. In: Williams, Martha E., ed. *Annual Review of Information Science and Technology*. White Plains, NY: Knowledge Industry Publications, Inc., for the American Society for Information Science; 1980; 15: 37-65. ISBN: 1-57387-019-6; ISSN: 0066-4200; CODEN: ARISBC; LCCN: 66-25096.

C96
CENSER, JACK R. 1997. Teaching Historiography and Methodology: The Electronic French Revolution. *AHA Perspectives*. 1997 January; 35 (1): 1, 6-8. 16. ISSN: 0743-7021.

C97
CENTRE D'ÉTUDES DES MANUSCRITS. 1946/47-. *Scriptorium: Revue internationale des études aux manuscrits* [International review of manuscript studies] (BE). F. Lyna, dir. Bruxelles, BE: Centre d'études des manuscrits; 1946/47-. 2x/year. (In English, French, German or Italian). ISSN: 0036-9772; LCCN: 49-17121; OCLC: 1714630.

C98
CENTRE NATIONAL DE LA RECHERCHE SCIENTIFIQUE (CNRS). 1979-. *Histoire moderne et contemporaine informatique*[Modern History and Contemporary Informatics] (FR). Paris, FR: Laboratoire d'Informatique pour les sciences de l'homme; 1979-. 3x/yr. ISSN: 86-20021; OCLC: 12994901.

C99
CENTRE NATIONAL DE LA RECHERCHE SCIENTIFIQUE (CNRS). 1985-86. *Méthodes Quantitatives et Informatiques dans l'étude des Textes. En Hommage Charles Müller* [Quantitative Methods and Informatics in the Study of Texts: Studies dedicated to Charles Müller]. Colloqui internationale CNRS de Universite de Nice, 5-8 Juine 1985 [Computers in Literary and Linguistic Research]. Geneva, CH: Slatkine; Paris, FR: Champion; 1985. Paris, FR: CNRS; 1986. 2 vols. (Travaux de Linquistique Quantatives, 35). (In French and English). ISBN: 2051007306 (set).

C100
CENTRE NATIONAL DE LA RECHERCHE SCIENTIFIQUE (CNRS). 1986-. *Histoire et Mesure* [History and Measurement](FR). Paris, FR: CNRS; 1986-. Qtly. (In French; summaries in English and French). ISSN: 0982-1782.

C101
CENTRE NATIONAL DE LA RECHERCHE SCIENTIFIQUE (CNRS). INSTITUT DE RECHERCHE ET HIS-TOIRE DES TEXTES (IRHT). 1965-. *Le Médiéviste et l'Ordinateur* [The Medievalist and the Computer] (FR). Chareille, Pascal, ed. Orleans, FR: CNRS-IHRT; 1965-. Qtrly. (In French). ISSN: 0223-3842. Electronic version available at http://irht.cnrs-orleans.fr.

C102
CENTRE NATIONAL DE LA RECHERCHE SCIENTIFIQUE (CNRS). INSTITUT DE RECHERCHE ET HIS-TOIRE DES TEXTES (IRHT). 1977. *Guide pour d'élaboration d'une notice de manuscrit* [Guide for the Elaboration of Manuscript Citation]. Paris, FR: CNRS-IHRT; 1977. 52p. ISBN: 2-222-02228-2. Available free from IHRT, Paris, FR.

C103
CENTRE NATIONAL DE LA RECHERCHE SCIENTIFIQUE (CNRS). INSTITUT DE RECHERCHE ET HIS-TOIRE DES TEXTES (IRHT). [1985-]. *MEDIUM. Base de données sur le manuscrit médiéval* [*MEDIUM* Database for Medieval Manuscripts] (electronic file hosted on CIRCE, Orsay, France). Paris, FR: CNRS, IHRT. Available via INTERNET with passwords from IHRT, Section Informatique, 40 Avenue d'Iena, 75116 Paris-FRANCE (telephone no. [1] 47.23/61.04)

C104
CENTRE NATIONAL DE LA RECHERCHE SCIENTIFIQUE (CNRS). INSTITUT DE RECHERCHE ET HIS-TOIRE DES TEXTES (IRHT). 1971-. *Revue d'histoire des textes* [Review of the History of Texts] (FR). New series, 1971-. Vol. 1-. Supersedes: *Bulletin d'information de l'Institut de recherche et d'histoire des textes*, 1952-1966; vols. 1-14 and *Bulletin de Institut de recherche et d'histoire des textes*, 1967-1968; vol. 15. Annual [Irregular]. ISSN: 0373-6075; separate ISBNs for each volume in series begin in 1971 with 2-222-01395-X.

C105
CERCONE, NICK. 1983. *Computational Linguistics*. Oxford, UK / New York, NY: Pergamon Press; 1983. 245p. (International series in Modern Applied Mathematics and Computer Science, v. 5). ISBN: 0080302253X.

C106
CERCONE, NICK; MACALLA, GORDON. 1987. *The Knowledge Frontier: Essays in the Representation of Knowledge*. New York, NY: Springer-Verlag; 1987. 512p. (Symbolic Computation series). ISBN: 0387965572.

C107
CERTEAU, MICHEL DE. 1970. Making History. Problems of Method and Problems of Meaning. *Recherches de science religieuse*. 1970; 58: 481-520. Also in: CERTEAU. 1975/1988. ISBN: 0-231-05574-9.

C108
CERTEAU, MICHEL DE. 1973. Le Noir soleil du language: Michel Foucault. In: *L'Absent de l'histoire* [Absence of History] (pp. 115-132). Paris, FR: Mame; 1973.

C109
CERTEAU, MICHEL DE. 1974. The Historical Operation. See reference: LE GOFF, J.; NORA, P., eds., 1974. 1: 3-41. Revised translated version as "Historiographical Operation", see reference: CERTEAU. 1975/1988. 56-113.

C110
CERTEAU, MICHEL DE. 1975. *Une politique de la langue: La Revolution française et les patois, l'enquête de Gregoire* [The Politics of Language: The French Revolution and the French Language: An Inquiry into [Henri] Gregoire]. Julia, Dominique; Revel, Jacques, eds. Paris, FR: Gallimard; 1975. 317p. LC call no.: PC2711.C4.

C111
CERTEAU, MICHEL DE. 1975/1988. L'operation historigraphique (The Historiographic Operation]. *L'écriture de l'histoire* (pp. 63-120). Paris, FR: Editions Gallimard; 1975. Conley, Tom, trans. *The Writing of History*. New York, NY: Columbia University Press; 1988. 368p. ISBN. 0-231-05574-9.

C112
CERTEAU, MICHEL DE. 1984. *Arts de faire*. Rendall. Steven, trans. *The Practice of Everyday Life*. Berkeley, CA: University of California Press; 1984. 229p. ISBN: 0520047508.

C113
CERTEAU, MICHEL DE. 1986. *Heterologies: Discourse on the Other*. Massumi, Brian, trans. Minneapolis, MN: University of Minnesota Press; 1986. 276p. ISBN: 0816614040; LCCN: 85-16457; OCLC: 12344807.

C114
CERUZZI, PAUL E. 1981. *The Prehistory of the Digital Computer, 1935-1945: A Cross- cultural Study*. Lawrence, KS: University of Kansas; 1981. 393p. (Ph.D. dissertation; abstracted in *DAI*, 42/08-A: 3726). Available from: University Microfilms, Ann Arbor, MI (Order no. AAD82-02578).

C115
CERUZZI, PAUL E. 1983. *Reckoners: The Prehistory of the Digital Computer, from Relays to the Stored Program Concept, 1935-1945*. Westport, CT: Greenwood Press; 1983. 181p. (Contributions to Computer Science series). ISBN: 0313233829; LCCN: 82020980.

C116
CERUZZI, PAUL E. 1997. Crossing the Divide: Architectural Issues and the Emergence of the Stored Program Computer, 1935-1955. *Annals of the History of Computing*. 1997; 19(1): 5-12. ISSN: 1058-6180.

C117
CHADWYCK-HEALEY, INC. 1996. *Archives USA*.(Electronic file). Alexandria, VA: Chadwyck-Healey, Inc.; 1996. ISBN: 0-89887-156-5. Contents: *DAMRUS (Directory of Archives and Manuscript Repositories in the U.S.)* (updated from 1988); *NUCMC (National Union Catalog of Manuscript Collections)* (1959-1995); and *NIDS (National Inventory of Documentary Sources in the United States)*. Annual updates from NIDS microfiche collection which is updated 5x/year. Web edition available by subscription.

C118
CHAFFIN, NANCY J. 1996. U.S. Serial Services Price Index for 1996. *American Libraries*. 1996 May; 27 (5):106-107. ISSN: 0002-9769.

C119
CHAIKLIN, SETH.; LAVE, JEAN, eds. 1993. *Understanding Practice: Perspectives on Activity and Context*. Cambridge, UK: Cambridge University Press; 1993. 414p. (Learning in Doing series). ISBN: 0521392632; LCCN: 92010606.

C120

CHALMERS, ALAN F. 1982/1991. *What is This Thing Called Science? An Assessment of the Nature and Status of Science and its Methods* 2nd ed. Auckland, NZ: University of Queensland Press; 1991. (First published in 1976). ISBN: 070221834.

C121

CHALMERS, ALAN F. 1990. *Science and Its Fabrication.* Bristol, PA: M. Keynes for the Open University; 1990. 192p. ISBN: 0335093183 (hbk.); 0335093175 (pbk.).

C122

CHAMIS, ALICE YANOSKO. 1991. *Vocabulary Control and Search Strategies in Online Searching.* In*: New Directions in information Management,* 27. Westport, CT: Greenwood Press; 1991. 121p. (Entire issue of title topic). ISBN: 0313254907; LCCN: 90-25224; OCLC: 22813304.

C123

CHANG, SHAN-JU; RICE, RONALD E. 1993. Browsing: A Multidimensional Framework. In: Williams, Martha E., ed. *Annual Review of Information Science and Technology* (vol. 28:.231-276) Medford, NJ: Learned Information, Inc. for the American Society for Information Science; 1993. ISBN: 0-939734-75-X; ISSN: 0066-4200.

C124

CHANG, SHI KUO; LIU, S. H. 1984. Picture Indexing and Abstracting Techniques for Pictorial Databases. *IEEE Transactions on Pattern Analysis and Machine Intelligence.* 1984; 6(4): 250-60. ISSN: 00162-8828.

C125

CHANG, SHI KUO; SHI, Q. Y.; YAN, C. W. 1987. Iconic Indexing by 2-D Strings. *IEEE Transactions on Pattern Analysis and Machine Intelligence.* 1987; 9(3): 413-428. ISSN: 00162-8828.

C126

CHANG, SHI KUO; JUNGERT, ERLAND; TORTORA, GENOVESSA. 1996. *Intelligent Image Database Systems.* Singapore and River Edge, NJ: World Scientific; 1996. 302p. (Software Engineering and Knowledge Engineering series, vol. 5). ISBN: 9810223900.

C127

CHAPLAN, M. A. 1995. Mapping Laborline Thesaurus terms to Library of Congress Subject Headings: Implications for Vocabulary Switching. *Library Quarterly.* 1995; 65 (1): 39061. ISSN: 0024-2519.

C128

CHARBONNEAU, HUBERT. 1988. Le registre de population de Québec ancien. Bilan de vingt annees de recherches [The Population Registers of Old Quebec. A Summary Account of 20 Years of Research]. *Histoire sociale / Social History* (CN). 1988 November; 21(42): 295-299. (In French). ISSN: 0018-2557.

C129

CHARBONNEAU, HUBERT. 1993. *The First French Canadians: Pioneers in the St. Lawrence Valley.* Newark, NJ: University of Delaware; 1993. 236p. ISBN: 0874134544 (pbk.).

C130

CHARBONNEAU, HUBERT; LAROSE, ANDRE. 1980. *Du manuscrit a l'ordinateur: depouillement des registres paroissiaux aux fins de l'exploitation automatique. Programme de recherche en démographie historique* [From Manuscript to Computer: Document Analysis of the Parish Registers after their Automatic Exploitation. Research Program in Historical Demography] In: *Études et recherches archivistiques,* 3. Quebec, CN: Archives nationales du Québec; 1980. 229p. (In French). (Entire issue on title topic).

C131

CHARBONNEAU, HUBERT; LEGARE, JACQUES. 1980-1987. *Repertoire des actes de baptême, marriage, sepulture et des recensements du Québec ancien. Programme de recherche en démographique historique* [Repertory of the Acts of Baptism, Marriage, Burial, and relating to Sickness in Old Québec. Research Program in Historical Demography]. Montréal, Québec, CN: Les Presses de l'Université de Montréal; 1980-87. 45 vols. (Covering 1700-1800). Rev. ed., 1991. 15 vols. ISBN: 276061570,-5353, -5876,-4714 etc.

C132

CHARBONNEAU, HUBERT; MARCILLIO, MARIA L. 1979. *Démographie historique* [Historical Demography]. 2nd ed. Rouen, FR: Presses Universitaires de France; 1979. 213p. (In French). ISBN: 2130360769.

C133

CHARLES BABBAGE INSTITUTE. 1987. *Resources for the History of Computing: A Guide to U.S. and Canadian Records.* Bruemmer, Bruce H., comp. with T. Traub and C. Brosenne. Minneapolis, MN: University of Minnesota Charles Babbage Institute; 1987. 187p. (Includes: Selected Readings in the History of Computing). LCCN: 88-102769; OCLC: 16962545.

C134
CHARNIAK, EUGENE. 1994. *Statistical Language Learning*. Cambridge, MA: Bradford Book; 1994. 192p. ISBN: 0-262-53141-0. Distributed by MIT Press.

C135
CHARPIN, FRANÇOIS. 1994. La pratique de l'informatique dans l'enseignement des langues anciennes [Computing Applications in the Teaching of Ancient Languages]. In: *Recherches en Linguistique et Traitement automatique des langues anciennes (LITALA)*. Paris, FR: LITALA; 1994. 39-53. (In French).

C136
CHARTIER, ROGER. 1982. Intellectual History or Socio-cultural History? The French Trajectories. See reference: LACAPRA, D.; KAPLAN, S. L., eds. 1982. 25-45.

C137
CHARTIER, ROGER. 1983. Histoire intellectuelle et histoire des mentalite. Trajectoires et questions [Intellectual History and the History of Mentalities: Trajectories and Questions]. *Revue de Syntheses*. 1983; 111-112, 277-208. (In French).

C138
CHARTIER, ROGER. 1985. Texts, Symbols, and Frenchness. *Journal of Modern History*. 1985; 57:685-695. ISSN: 0022-2801.

C139
CHARTIER, ROGER. 1988. *Cultural History: Between Practice and Representations*. Cochrane, Lydia G., trans. Cambridge, UK: Polity Press; 1988. 209p. ISBN: 0745604226.

C140
CHARTIER, ROGER. 1989. Le monde comme representation [The World as Representation}. *Annales E. S. C.* 1989 Nov.-Dec.; 6: 1505-1520. (In French). ISSN: 0395-2649.

C141
CHARTIER, ROGER. 1991/1997. Secretaries for the People? See reference: CHARTIER, R., ed. 1991/1997.

C142
CHARTIER, ROGER. 1994. *Culture, écrite et société: l'ordre des livres XIVe-XVIIIe siècles.* Cochrane, L. G., trans. *The Order of Books: Readers, Authors, and Libraries in Europe between the Fourteen and Eighteenth Centuries.* Stanford, CA: Stanford University Press; 1994. 126p. ISBN: 0745610986.

C143
CHARTIER, ROGER, ed. 1991/1997. *La Correspondance: Les Usages de la lettre au XIXe siècle.* Paris, FR; 1991. Trans. of 3 chapters as: *Correspondence: Models of Letter-writing form the Middle Ages to the Nineteenth Century.* Cambridge, UK: Polity Press; 1997. 162p. ISBN: 0745612253.

C144
CHARTIER, ROGER. 1995a. *Forms and Meanings: Texts, Performances, and Audiences from Codex to Computer.* Philadelphia, PA: University of Pennsylvania; 1995. 128p. ISBN: 0812233026 (hbk.); 08121546x (pbk.).

C145
CHARTIER, ROGER. 1995b. L'histoire aujourd'hui: doutes, defis, propositions [History Today: Doubts, Definitions, and Propositions]. (In French). See reference: BARROS, C., ed. 1995: 119-130.

C146
CHARTIER, ROGER. 1997. *On the Edge of the Cliff: History, Languages, and Practices.* Baltimore, MD: The Johns Hopkins University; 1997. 191p. ISBN: 0801854350 (hbk.); 0801854369 (pbk.).

C147
CHARTRAND, ROBERT LEE; HENDERSON, MADELINE M; RESNIK, LINDA, eds. 1988. ASIS 50th Anniversary Issue. *Bulletin of the American Society for Information* Science. 1988 June-July; 14(5): 1-68. ISSN: 0095-4403.

C148
CHATFIELD, C. 1989. *The Analysis of Time Series: An Introduction.* 4th ed. New York, NY: Chapman and Hall; 1989. 241p. ISBN: 0824044878; 0412318202 (pbk.); LCCN: 89-7142; OCLC: 19518654.

C149
CHATMAN, E. A. 1986. Diffusion Theory: A Review and Test of a Conceptual Model in Information Diffusion. *Journal of the American Society for Information Science*. 1986; 37: 377-386. ISSN: 0002-8231.

C150
CHATMAN, JENNIFER A.; JEHN, KAREN A. 1994. Assessing the Relationship between Industry Characteristics and Organizational Culture. How Different Can You Be? *Academy of Management Journal*. 1994 June; 37 (3): 522-553. ISSN: 0001-4273.

C151
CHATTERJEE, SAYAN; LUBATKIN, MICHAEL H.; SCHWEIGER, DAVID M.; WEBER, YAAKOV. 1992. Cultural Differences and Shareholder Value in Related Mergers: Linking Equity and Human Capital. *Strategic Management Journal* (UK). 1992 June; 13 (5): 319- 334. ISSN: 0143-2095.

C152
CHAUMONT, JEAN-MICHEL. 1997. *La Concurrence des Victimes: Genocide, Identité, Reconnaissance* [The Concurrence of Victims: Genocide, Identity, and Remembering]. Paris, FR: Ed. La Decouverté; 1997. 380p. ISBN: 270712690X. (In French).

C153
CHAUNU, PIERRE. 1964. Histoire quantitative et histoire serielle [Quantitative and Serial History]. *Cahiers Vilfredo Pareto. Revue Européen d'histoire des sciences sociales.* 1964; 3: 165-175. ISSN: 0008-0497.

C154
CHAUNU, PIERRE. 1974. *Histoire, science sociale: la durée, l'espace et l'homme a l'époque moderne* [History, Social Science: The Period, Space, and Man in the Modern Age]. Paris, FR: Société d'edition d'enseignement superieur; 1974. 437p. ISBN: 27-1811-527-66; LCCN: 75-502155; OCLC: 1491675.

C155
CHEN, C. 1992. Computer Technology to Preserve and Access Endangered Oral History in Alaska. *Microcomputers for Information Management.* 1992; 9(3): 191-95. ISSN: 0742- 2342.

C156
CHEN, CHING-CHIH, ex. prod. 1985;[1991]. *The First Emperor of China* [Qin Shi Huang Di](Videodisc). B. Davis; M. Mackay, production. N.p.: Voyager Company; c1991. Laser disc, 30 minutes, plus video picture library. Composite version of 2-disc release in 1985.ISBN: 1-55940-219-9; LCCN: 96520690; Voyager cat. no. V1051L.

C157
CHEN, CHING-CHIH. 1990. Effective Management of Image Databases: Incorporating Visual Images into Information Systems and Services. In: Gorman, Michael, ed. *Videotechnology and Libraries.* 2nd National Conference of LITA, October 2-6, 1988, Boston, MA. Chicago, IL: American Library Assn.; 1990. LCCN: 90172449.

C158
CHEN, HSINCHUN. 1994. Collaborative Systems: Solving the Vocabulary Problem. *IEEE Computer.* 1994; 27 (4): 58-66. ISSN: 0180-9162.

C159
CHEN, HSINCHUN. 1994. Collaborative Systems: Solving the Vocabulary Problem. In: *Computer Supported Cooperative Work (CSWC).* Special issue of *IEEE Computer.* 1994; 27 (5): 58- 66. (Entire issue on title topic). ISSN: 0180-9162.

C160
CHEN, HSINCHUN; HOUSTON, ANDREA; NUNAMAKER, JAY, Jr.; YEN, JEROME. Toward Intelligent Meeting Agents. *Computer.* 1996 August; 29 (8): 62-71. ISSN: 0018-9162.

C161
CHEN, HSINCHUN; LYNCH, K. J. 1992. Automatic Construction of Networks of Concepts Characterizing Document Databases. *IEEE Transactions on Systems, Man and Cybernetics.* 1992; 22(50: 885-902. ISSN: 0018-9472.

C162
CHEN, HSINCHUN; MARTINEZ, JOANNE; KIRCHHOFF, AMY; NG, TOBUN D.; SCHATZ, BRUCE R. 1998. Alleviating Search Uncertainty through Concept Associations: Automatic Indexing, Co-occurrence analysis, and Parallel Computing. *Journal of the American Society for Information Science.* 1998; 49 (3); 206-216. ISSN: 0002-8231.

C163
CHEN, HSINCHUN; NUNAMAKER, JAY, Jr.; ORWIG, RICHARD; TUKOVA, OLGA. 1998. Information Visualization for Collaborative Computing. *Computer.* 1998 August; 31 (8), 75-83. ISSN: 0018-9162.

C164
CHEN, HSINCHUN; SCHATZ, BRUCE R.; YIM, T.; FRYE, D. 1995. Automatic Thesaurus Generation for an Electronic Community. *Journal of the American Society for Information Science.* 1995; 46; 175-193. ISSN: 0002-8231.

C165
CHEN, Y. S. 1989. Analysis of Lotka's Law. *Information Processing & Management.* 1989; 25: 527-544. ISSN: 0306-4573.

C166
CHENEY, LYNNE. 1987. American Memory: A Report on the Humanities in the Nation's Public Schools. Washington, D.C.: NEH; 1987. 29p. SUDOC: NF3.2:AM312.

C167
CHENEY, LYNNE. 1995. *Telling the Truth: Why Our Culture and Our Country Have Stopped Making Sense, and What We can do about It.* New York, NY: Simon & Schuster; 1995. 255p. ISBN: 0684811014.

C168
CHENG, SU-SHING, ed. 1990. *Advances in Spatial Reasoning.* Norwood, NJ: Ablex Publ. Corp.; 1990. 2 vols. ISBN: 0893915726 and 0893915734.

C169
CHENHALL. ROBERT G. 1978. *Nomenclature for Museum Cataloging: A System for Classifying Man-made Objects.* Nashville, TN: American Association for State and Local History; 1978. 512p. ISBN: 0910050309; LCCN: 77-20097; OCLC: 3380221. Updated ed. Blackaby, James R.; Greeno, Patricia, eds. *The Revised Nomenclature for Museum Cataloging: A Revised and Expanded Version of Robert G. Chenhall's System for Classifying Man-made Objects.* Nashville, KY: AASLH; 1988. ISBN: 0910050937; LCCN: 88-14625; OCLC: 17953996.

C170
CHENHALL, ROBERT G. 1981. Computerized Data Bank Management. In: Sylvia, W., ed. *Data Bank Applications in Archeology.* Tucson, AZ: University of Arizona Press; 1981. 1-8. ISBN: 0-8165-0686-8.

C171
CHENHALL, ROBERT G.; VANCE, DAVID. 1988. *Museum Collections and Today's Computers.* Westport, CT: Greenwood Press; 1988. 169p. ISBN: 0313253390; LCCN: 88-3091; OCLC: 17546303.

C172
CHERNAIK, W.; DAVIS, C; DEEGAN, M., eds. 1993. *The Politics of the Electronic Text.* London, UK: University of London Office for Humanities Publications and Center for English Studies; 1933. (Office for Humanities Communication Publications, no. 3). ISBN: 1-897791-04-6.

C173
CHESEBRO, JAMES W.; BONSALL, DONALD G. 1989. *Computer-Mediated Communication. Human Relationships in Computerized World.* Tuscaloosa, AL: University of Alabama; 1989. 275p. (Studies in Rhetoric and Communication). ISBN: 0-8173-0460-6; LCCN: 89- 32991.

C174
CHESTER, MICHAEL. [1975]. *Deeper than Speech: Frontiers of Language and Communication.* New York, NY: Macmillan; [1975]. 90p. ISBN: 0027183106.

C175
CHEUMSKY, ELEANOR; SHADISH, WILLIAM R. 1997. *Evaluation for the 21st Century.* Thousand Oaks, CA: Sage Publications; 1997. 540p. ISBN: 0-7619-0611-8 (pbk.).

C176
CHIGNELL, MARK H.; LACY, RICHARD M. 1988. Project Jefferson: Integration Research and Instruction. *Academic Computing.* 1988 October 2; 3: 12-17, 40-45. ISSN: 0892- 4694.

C177
CHIKOFSKY, ELLIOT J. 1992. Software History Should be Required Reading. *IEEE Software.* May 1992; 9(3): 96-98. ISSN: 0740-7459.

C178
CHILD, MARGARET S., comp. 1993. *Directory of Information Sources on Scientific Research Related to the Preservation of Sound Recordings, Still and Moving Images, and Magnetic Tape.* Washington, DC: Commission on Preservation and Access; c1993. 14p. LCCN: 94113951.

C179
CHILDS, SANDRA L. 1992. *A Descriptive Study of Black Studies Units in the Southeastern Region of the United States.* Atlanta, GA: Georgia State University; 1992. 154p. (Ph.D. dissertation). *DAI,* 53/05-A: 1333. Available from: University Microfilms, Ann Arbor, MI; (Order no. AAD92-28132).

C180
CHING-CHUN, HSIEH. 1985. Full-text Searching of Chinese Language: An Experimental System for Studying Chinese History Literatures. *Journal of Library and Information Science.* 1985 October; 11(2): 125-42. ISSN: 0363-3640.

C181
CHISHOLM, R. M. [1972]. Notes on the Logic of Believing. See reference: MARRAS, A., ed. [1972]: ch. 4.

C182
CHOAY, FRANÇOISE. 1970. L'Histoire et la méthode en urbanisme [History and Methodology in Urbanism]. In: *Histoire et Civilisation. Annales: Sociétés, Économies, Civilisations.* 1970; 25: 1143-54. (Entire issue on title topic). ISSN: 0395-2649.

C183
CHODOROW, STANLEY. 1996. The Medieval Future of Intellectual Culture: Scholars and Librarians in the Age of the Electron. *ARL Newlsetter*. 1996 December; 189: 1-3. ISSN: 1050-6098.

C184
CHOMSKY, NOAM. 1972. *Language and Mind*. New York, NY: Harcourt Brace Jovanovich; 1972. 194p. ISBN:0151478104; 0155492578 (pbk.); LCCN: 70-187121; OCLC: 303573.

C185
CHOMSKY, NOAM. 1975. *Reflections on Language*. New York, NY: Pantheon Books; 1975. 269p. ISBN: 0394499565; 0394731239 (pbk.); LCCN: 75-10268; OCLC: 1582533.

C186
CHRIST, CARL F. 1985. Early Progress in Estimating Quantitative Economic Relationships in America. *American Economic Review*. 1985; 75: 39-52. ISSN: 0002-8282.

C187
CHRISTENSEN, RONALD. 1984. *Order and Time: A General Theory of Prediction*. Lincoln, MA: Entropy; c1984. (Entropy Minimax Sourcebook, 10). ISBN: 0938876198; LCCN: 85150679.

C188
CHRISTENSEN-SZAALANSKI, JAY J.; WILLHAM, CYNTHIA FOBIAN. 1991. The Hindsight Bias: A Meta-Analysis. *Organizational Behavior and Human Decision Processes*. 1991 Feb.; 48 (1): 147-169. ISSN: 07495978.

C189
CHRONICLE OF HIGHER EDUCATION (CHE). 1981-. Washington, D.C.: CHE; 1981-. 48x/yr. ISSN: 0009-5982; OCLC: 1554535. (Note regular feature column, "Information Technology").

C190
CHUA, TAT-SENG; PUNG, HUNG KENG; KUNII, TOSHIYASU. *Multimedia Modeling: Towards Information Superhighway*. Internet Congress, Singapore, 14-17 November, 1995. Singapore; River Edge, NJ: World Scientific; 1995. 428p. ISBN: 9810225024.

C191
CHUBIN, DARYL. E., ed. 1983. *Sociology of the Disciplines: An Annotated Bibliography, 1972-1981*. New York, NY: Garland; 1983. 202p. ISBN: 0824092236 (pbk.).

C192
CIBBARELLI, PAMELA. 1994. *Directory of Library Automation Software, Systems, and Services*. Medford, NJ: Learned Information, Inc.; 1994. 374p. (Published biannually since 1983). ISBN: 0-938734-82-2.

C193
CIBORA, CLAUDIO U.; LANZARA, GIOVAN FRANCESCO. 1990. Designing Dynamic Artifacts: Computer Systems as Formative Contexts. See reference: GAGLIARDI, P., ed., 1990. 147-163.

C194
CICOUREL, AARON V. 1973/1974. *Cognitive Sociology: Language and Meaning in Social Interaction*. [Hammonsworth] UK: Penguin Editions; 1973. 191p. New York, NY: Free Press; 1974. ISBN: 0140809929.

C195
CICOUREL, AARON V. 1981. *Advances in Social Theory and Methodology. Toward an Integration of Micro- and Macro-Sociologies*. Boston, MA: Routledge; 1981. 325p. ISBN: 0710009461 (hbk.); 071000947x (pbk.).

C196
CICOUREL, AARON V. 1990. The Integration of Distributed Knowledge in Collaborative Medical Diagnosis. In: GALEGHER, J.; KRAUT, R. E.,; EGIDO, C., eds. 1990. 222-242.

C197
CIO [Chief Information Officer] *MAGAZINE*. 1996-. *Data Warehouse Executive Resource Center* (Electronic file). Santosus, Megan, comp. CIO Communications, Inc.; 1996-. Accessible at http://www.cio.com/CIO/rc-dw.html.

C198
CITERA, MARYALICE. 1998. Distributed Teamwork: The Impact of Communication Media on Influence and Decision Quality. See reference: MCNEESE, M. D., ed. 1998. 792-800.

C199
CITY UNIVERSITY OF LONDON. SCHOOL OF INFORMATICS. [1996]. *Executive Informaton Systems* (Electronic file). Group G. London, UK: City University, [1996]. (Information Management Module, section 4). Accessible at http://www.soi.city.ac.uk.homes/ ec586/EIS.html.

C200
CLANCEY, WILLIAM J. 1997. *Situated Cognition: On Human Knowledge and Computer Representations.* Cambridge, UK / New Yoirk, NY: Cambridge University Press; 1997. 406p. (Learning in Doing series). ISBN: 0521444004 (hbk.); 0521448719 (pbk.); LCCN: 96035839.

C201
CLANCHY, MICHAEL T. 1979/1993. *From Memory to Written Record: England, 1066-1307.* Cambridge, MA; Harvard University Press / London UK: Edward Arnold; 1979. 330p. ISBN: 0674325109. Rev. ed. Cambridge, UK: Blackwell; 1993. 407p. ISBN: 0631178236 (hbk.); 0631178575 (pbk.); LCCN: 92-20180.

C202
CLARK, DAVID L. 1991a. Computer Database Management for Historical Research and Writing. *AHA Perspectives.* 1991 April; 29: 10-12. ISSN: 0743-7021.

C203
CLARK, DAVID L. 1991b. *Database Design: Applications of Library Cataloging Techniques.* New York, NY: McGraw-Hill; 1991. 330p. ISBN: 0830634436; LCCN: 91-19894; OCLC: 23901651.

C204
CLARK, DAVID L. 1994. *History Computerization Project.* CA: Reed Reference Publishing; 1994. (Manual for Los Angeles Historical Society retrospective conversion).

C205
CLARK, FRANKLIN; DILIBERTO, KEN. 1996. *Investigating Computer Crime.* Geberth, V. J., ed. Boca Raton, FL: CRC Press; 1996. 256p. (Practical Aspects of Criminal and Forensic Investigation series). ISBN: 0-8493-8158-4.

C206
CLARK, M. A. 1978. Occupational Classification in the United States Census: 1870-1940. *Journal of Interdisciplinary History.* 1978; 9: 111-130. ISSN: 0022-1953.

C207
CLARK, N. 1986. Tables and Graphs as Language. In: *Proceedings of the 18th Symposium on Interfaces.* Ft. Collins, CO: American Statistical Association; 1986. 83-89.

C208
CLARK, PETER. 1993. Occupations and the English Small Towns Project at Leicester University. See reference: SCHURER, K.; DIEDERIKS, H., eds., 1993. 23-28.

C209
CLARK, ROBERT, ed. 1976. *Archive-History Relations.* New York, NY: Bowker; 1976. 218p. ISBN: 083520776; LCCN: 76-18806; OCLC: 253998.

C210
CLARK, WILLIAM. 1989. On the Dialectological Origins of the Research Seminar. *History of Science.* 1989; 27: 111-154. ISSN: 0073-2753.

C211
CLARKE, JOHN; MARTELL, KEVIN; WILLEY, CAROL. 1994. Sequencing Graphic Organizers to Guide Historical Research. *The Social Studies.* 1994 March-April; 85 (2): 70-76. ISSN: 0037-7996.

C212
CLAUSEN, A. R. 1988. Social Science History: Citation Record, 1976-1985. *Social Science History.* 1988; 12: 97-215. ISSN: 0145-5532.

C213
CLAYMAN, DEE L. [199-]. Automated Bibliography for Ancient and Medieval Studies. See reference: HAMESSE, J., ed. [199-] (Forthcoming).

C214
CLESTIN, TINA; GODBOUT, GILLES; VACHON-L'HEUREUX, PIERRETTE. 1984. *Méthodologie de la recherche terminologique pontuelle. Essai de definition* [Methodology for Terminological Construction Research]. Auger, Pierre, project dir. Québec, CN: Office de la Langue Française, Editeur officiel du Québec; 1984.

C215
CLEVELAND, DONALD B.; CLEVELAND, ANA D. 1990. *Introduction to Indexing and Abstracting.* Engelwood, CO: Libraries Unlimited; 1990. 209p. ISBN: 0872873463.

C216
CLEVELAND, HARLAND. 1985. *The Knowledge Executive: Leadership in an Information Society.* New York, NY: Truman Talley Books; 1985. 261p. LCCN: 85-4442.

C217
CLIFFORD, JAMES. 1988. *The Predicament of Culture: Twentieth-century Ethnography, Literature, and Art.* Cambridge MA: Harvard University Press; 1988. 311p. ISBN: 0674698428 (hbk.); 0674698436 (pbk.).

C218
CLIFFORD, JAMES; MARCUS, GEORGE E., eds. 1986. *Writing Culture: The Poetics and Politics of Ethnography.* Berkeley, CA: University of California Press; 1986. 305p. ISBN: 0520056525 (pbk.).

C219
CLOCKSIN, WILLIAM F. 1997. *Clause and Effect: Prolog Programming for the Working Programmer.* New York, NY: Springer-Verlag; 1997. ISBN: 3540629718 (pbk.); LCCN: 97035795.

C220
CLOGG, CLIFFORD C. 1992. The Impact of Sociological Methodology on Statistical Methodology. *Statistical Science.* 1992; 7: 183-196. ISSN: 0883-4237.

C221
CLOGG, CLIFFORD C.; DAJANI, AREF N. 1991. Sources of Uncertainty in Modeling Social Statistics. *Journal of Official Statistics.* 1991; 7: 7-24. ISSN: 0282-4234.

C222
CLUBB, JEROME M. 1974. Quantification and the "New History": A Review Essay. *The American Archivist.* 1974; 37(1): 15-25. ISSN: 0360-9081.

C223
CLUBB, JEROME M. 1986. Computer Technology and the Source Materials of Social Science History. *Social Science History.* 1986; 10: 97-114. ISSN: 0145-5532.

C224
CLUBB, JEROME M.; BOGUE, ALLAN G. 1977. History, Quantification, and the Social Sciences. *American Behavioral Scientist.* 1977; 21(2): 167-85. ISSN: 0002-7642; OCLC: 2204054.

C225
CLUBB, JEROME M.; SCHEUCH, E. K., eds. 1980. *Historical Sociological Research: The Use of Historical Process Produced Data.* Stuttgart, DEU: Klett-Cotta; 1980. 536p. (Historisch-sozialwissenschaftliche Forschungen, Bd. 6). ISBN: 31-2911-060-7 (pbk.); LCCN: 80-508716; OCLC: 19801113.

C226
COALITION OF HISTORY EDITORS FOR PUBLISHING IN THE FUTURE. 1998. Statement on Intellectual Diversity. *AHA Perspectives.* 1998 Feb.; 36(2): 36. ISSN: 0743-7021.

C227
COATES, LES. 1990. "1665: The Great Plague of London": Classroom Observations from the Program's Authors and an Evaluation by a Student Teacher. *Teaching History* (UK). 1990; 21: 33-35. ISSN: 0040-0610.

C228
COBB, MARIA A.; PETRY, FREDERICK E. 1998. Modeling Spatial Relationships within a Fuzzy Framework. *Journal of the American Society for Information Science.* 1998; 49 (3); 253- 266. ISSN: 0002-8231.

C229
COCKS, GEOFREY; JARAUSCH, KONRAD H., eds. 1990. *German professions, 1800-1950.* New York, NY: Oxford Universitiy Press; 1990. 360p. ISBN: 0195055969.

C230
CODD, EDGAR F. [1996]. Extending the Database Relational Model to Capture More Meaning (Electronic file). Accessible at Data Warehousing Institute homepage; [1996] (viewed June 1997).

C231
CODD, EDGAR F.; CODD, S. B.; SALLEY, C. T. [1993]. *Providing OLAP (On-Line Analytical Processing) to User-Analysis: An IT Mandate* (Electronic file). 6 pts. E. F. Codd & Associates; 1993. Available from Arbor Software Corporation at http://www. arborsoft.c.e/wht_ppr/coddTOC.html.

C232
COFFEY, AMANDA J. 1994. "Timing is Everything." Graduate Accountants, Time, and Organizational Commitment. *Journal of the British Sociological Association.* 1994 November; 28 (4): 943-956. ISSN: 0038-0385.

C233
COFFEY, AMANDA J.; ATKINSON, PAUL. 1996. *Making Sense of Qualitative Data: Complementary Research Strategies.* Thousand Oaks, CA: Sage Publications; 1996. 206p. ISBN: 0803970528 (hbk.); 0803970536 (pbk.).

C234
COHASSET ASSOCIATES, INC.; IMAGINGWORLD. 1995. *Managing Electronic Records: Diffusing the Corporate Time Bomb (MER'95)* (Brochure). Third National Conference, Chicago, IL, November 6-8, 1995. 15p. Available from: Cohasset Associates, 3806 Lake Point Tower, 505 N. Lake Shore Drive, Chicago, IL 60611; Fax 312-527-1552.

C235
COHEN, IRA J. 1989. *Structuration Theory: Anthony Giddens and the Constitution of Social Life*. Houndmills, Hampshire UK: Macmillan; 1989. 307p. ISBN: 033371208 (hbk.); 0333371216 (pbk.).

C236
COHEN, J. 1996. Computer mediated Communication and Publication Productivity among Faculty. *Internet Research: Electronic Networking Application and Policy*. 1996; 6 (2/3): 41-63.

C237
COHEN, JACK; STEWART, IAN. 1994a. *The Collapse of Chaos: Discovering Simplicity in a Complex World*. New York, NY: Viking Books; 1994. 495p. ISBN: 0670844839; LCCN: 93-33511.

C238
COHEN, JACK; STEWART, IAN. 1994b. Why are there Simple Rules in a Complicated Universe? *Futures*. 1994 Jul/Aug.; 26 (6): 648-65. (About modeling, chaos theory, and consciousness). ISSN: 0212-1346.

C239
COHEN, JACOB. 1988. *Statistical Power Analysis for the Behavioral Sciences*. 2nd ed. Hillsdale, NJ: Lawrence Erlbaum Associates; 1988. 567p. ISBN: 0805202835; LCCN: 88-12110.

C240
COHEN, MICHAEL; SPROUL, LEE. 1996. *Organizational Learning*. Thousand Oaks, CA: Sage Pub.; 1996. 611p. ISBN: 0803970889 (hbk.); 0803970897 (pbk.).

C241
COHEN, PAUL R. 1995. *Empirical Methods for Artificial Intelligence*. Cambridge, MA: Bradford Book; 1995. 560p. ISBN: 0-262-03225-2. Distributed by MIT Press.

C242
COHEN, RALPH; ROTH, MICHAEL S. 1995. *History and.. ; Histories within the Human Sciences*. Charlottesville, VA: University of Virginia Press; 1995. 413p. ISBN: 0813914981 (hbk.); 081391499X (pbk.).

C243
COHEN, ROSETTA M.; SCHEER, SAMUEL, eds. 1997. *The Work of Teachers in America. A Social History through Stories*. Mahwah, NJ: Lawrence Erlbaum Associates, Inc.; 1997. 352p. ISBN: 0-8058-2690-4 (hbk.); 0-8058-2250-X (pbk.).

C244
COK, MARY VAN SOMEREN; BROMELKAMP, HENRY A.; THURTON, ELLEN; WOLF, THOMAS. 1981. *All in Order: Information Systems for the Arts*. Washington, D.C: National Assembly of State Arts Agencies (NASAA); 1981. 167p. ISBN: 0-89062-132-2.

C245
COLE, JONATHAN R.; COLE, STEPHEN. 1972. The Ortega Hypothesis: Citation Analysis Suggests that only a Few Scientists Contribute to Scientific Progress. *Science*. 1972 October 27; 178: 368-375. ISSN: 0036-8075.

C246
COLES, ROBERT. 1995. *Doing Documentary Work*. New York, NY / Oxford, UK: Oxford University Press; 1995. 278p. ISBN: 0195116291.

C247
COLLANTES, LOURDES Y. 1995. Degree of Agreement in Naming Objects and Concepts for Information Retrieval. *Journal of the American Society for Information Science*. 1995 March; 46(2); 116-132. ISSN: 0002-8231.

C248
COLLIER, HARRY. 1991; 1993;[1998]. *The Electronic Publishing Maze. Strategies in the Electronic Publishing Industry*. 3rd ed. Tetbury, UK: Infonortics Ltd.; [1998]. 200p. ISBN: 1-873699-43-3.

C249
COLLINGWOOD, R. G. 1924. *Speculum mentis: The Map of Knowledge*. Oxford, UK: Clarendon Press; 1924.

C250
COLLINGWOOD, R. G. 1933/1995. *An Essay on Philosophical Method*. London, UK: Thoemmes; 1995 reprint. ISBN: 1-85506-392-1.

C251
COLLINGWOOD, R. G. 1945. Human Nature and Human History. In: *The Idea of History*. London and Oxford: Clarendon Press; 1945. 1-16. OCLC: 1030684.

C252
COLLINS, HARRY M. 1990. *Artificial Experts: Social Knowledge and Intelligent Machines*. Cambridge, MA: MIT Press; 1990. 266p. ISBN: 026203168X.

C253
COLLINS, JAMES C.; PORRAS, JERRY. 1994. *Built to Last: Successful Habits of Visionary Companies*. New York, NY: Harper Business; 1994. 322p. ISBN: 08873067713; LCCN: 94-70571.

C254
COLSON, JEAN; COLSON, R. FRANK. 1996. Perspectives on Processing the "Digital Image" as a Problem at the Intersection of "Meaning" and "Technology". See references: BORODKIN, L., ed., 1996; BORODKIN, L., ed.[199- forthcoming]. Note: Projects from the Digital Library Research Centre, University of Southampton, UK.

C255
COLSON, R. FRANK; COLSON, JEAN; WEAL, MARK. 1994. Underpinning Interpretation: the Emergence of Microcosm. See reference: OLDERVOLL, J., ed. 1994. 52-58.

C256
COLSON, R. FRANK; HALL, WENDY. 1992. Pictorial Information Systems and the Teaching Imperative. See reference: THALLER, M., ed. 1992. 73-86.

C257
COLUMBIA UNIVERSITY. AVERY ARCHITECTURAL AND FINE ARTS LIBRARY. 1977-. *Avery Index to Architectural Periodicals*. Goodman, T., ed. Riverside, NJ: G. K. Hall & Co.; 1983-. ca. 2,500-3,000p. in 4 vols./year. 1983-84 ISBN: 0-8161-0456-5. *Avery Index on Disc* (CD-ROM); 1993-. ISSN: 0-7838-2122-0; 5.25" diskette: 07838-2126-3. Available from: G. K. Hall & Co., Attn. D. Rose, Macmillan Publishing Co., 866 3rd Ave, fl. 17, New York, NY 10022. Available also online as: DIALOG file 178.

C258
COMBE, SONIA. 1994. *Archives Interdites: Les Peurs Francaises face à l'Histoire Contemporaine* [Archives Prohibited: The French Fears visible to Contemporary History]. Paris, FR: Albin Michel; 1994. 327p. ISBN: 2226075380.

C259
COMBER, DENIS; STANFORD, JOY. 1989. A Comparison between Free Text and a Thesaurus Controlled Vocabulary in Searching an Online Records Management Database. *Records Management Quarterly*. 1989 Autumn; 1(3): 113-20. ISSN:0034-172X.

C260
COMITÉ INTERNATIONAL DES SCIENCES HISTORIQUES (CISH). 1926-. *International Bibliographie des Sciences Historiques / Internationale Bibliographie der Geschichts-wissenschaften / International Bibliography of Historical Sciences*. Paris, FR: Libraire Armand Colin. Annual (suspended, 1940-1946). ISSN: 0074-2015. 1931-. *International Bibliography of Historical Sciences*. London, UK: K. G. Saur; 1931-. (59 volumes to date with coverage through 1990; volumes are also treated separately rather than as a serial. E.g., 1994; 59. 281p.). ISBN: 3-598-22651-9.

C261
COMITÉ INTERNATIONAL DES SCIENCES HISTORIQUES. 1990. *Rapports et abrégés: 17e Congrès International des Sciences Historiques* [Reports and Abstracts of the Seventeenth International Congress of the Historical Sciences]. 4 vols. in 2. Madrid, ES: Comité International des Sciences Historiques; 1990. (Section Chronologique, I-II, 1203p.; Grands Themes, I-II, 700p.). ISBN 84-600-7529-X.

C262
COMITÉ INTERNATIONAL DES SCIENCES HISTORIQUES. 1990, 1992. *17o Congreso Internacional de Ciencias Historicas / 17e Congrès International des Sciences Historiques / 17th International Congress of Historical Sciences*. E. Benito Ruano & M. Espadas Burgos, eds. Pt. 1: Sections Chronologiques. Madrid, ES; CISH; 1992. Vols. 1-2, 1203p. ISBN: 84-600-8153-2. Pt. 2: Sections Chronologiques 2, Organismes Affilies, Commisiones Internes, Tables Rondes. Rapports et abrégés. Vols. 1-2. 700p. ISBN: 84-600-7529-X (same number as abstracts).

C263
COMMISSION ON THE HUMANITIES. 1980. *The Humanities in American Life*. Berkeley, CA: University of California Press; 1980. 192p. ISBN: 0-520-04183-6; pbk. 0-520-04208- 5.

C264
COMMISSION ON PRESERVATION AND ACCESS. 1988-. *Newsletter*. Washington, DC: Commission; 1988-. (Mthly.). ISSN: 1045-1919. Available free from the Commission, 1785 Massachusetts Ave., NW, suite 313. Washington, DC 20036.

C265
COMMISSION ON PRESERVATION AND ACCESS. 1993. *Preserving the Intellectual Heritage*. A Report of the
Ballagio Conference, June 7-10, 1993, held at the Rockefeller Foundation Study and Conference Center.
Washington, DC: Commission; October 1993. 36p. LCCN: 94-187647; OCLC: 2930537.

C266
COMMISSION ON PRESERVATION AND ACCESS. 1995. *Archiving Digital Information*. Report of the Task Force
on Digital Information. Washington, D.C.: Commission and the Research Libraries Group. Draft report release,
August 23, 1995.

C267
COMPTON, BRUCE. 1996. The ILS Vendor and EDI: A Perspective. See reference: BLUH, P., ed. 1996. 164-168.

C268
COMPUTER INCIDENT ADVISORY COMMITTEE (CIAC). 1997-. *Internet Hoaxes* [Online]. Accessible at
http://ciac.llnl.gov/ciac/CIACHoaxes.html.

C269
COMPUTERS AND THE HUMANITIES. 1966-. New York, NY: Pergamon; 1974-. Dordrecht, NL: Kluwer Academic
Publishers; 1990-. (Qtly.). ISSN: 0010-4817.

C270
COMPUTERS AND TEACHING INITIATIVE (CTISS). 1992. *Computers in University Teaching: Core Tools for
Core Activities*. Oxford, UK: CTISS; 1992.

C271
CONCEPCION, VINCENTE P.; D'AMATO, DONALD P. 1993. Symbol Correspondence for Integrating Multiple
OCR Outputs. See reference: DOORN, P. *ET AL.*, eds. 1993. 113- 130.

C272
CONCEPCION, VINCENTE P.; GRZECH, M. P.; D'AMATO, DONALD P. 1991. Using Morphology in Document
Image Processing. In: Kou-Hu Tzou; Toschio Koga, eds. *Proceedings of Visual Communications and Image
Processing '91: Image Processing, November 11-13, 1991*. Sponsored by SPIE (International Society for Optical
Engineering) with IEEE and EURASIP (European Association for Signal Processing). Bellingham WA: SPIE;
1991. 2 vols, 1094p. (SPIE Proceedings series). ISBN: 0819407437 (pbk.); LCCN: 91-641811; OCLC: 25138997.

C273
CONFINO, ALON. 1997. Collective Memory and Cultural History: Problems of Method. *American Historical
Review*. 1997 Dec.; 102 (5): 1386-1412. ISSN: 0002-8762.

C274
CONKLIN, J. 1987. Hypertext: An Introduction and Survey. *Computer*. 1987; 20: 17-41. ISSN: 0018-9162.

C275
CONNER, DARYL R. 1992. *Managing at the Speed of Change: How Resilient Managers Succeed and Prosper where
others Fail*. New York, NY: Villard Books; 1992. 282p. ISBN: 0679406540; LCCN: 92-20753.

C276
CONNERTON, PAUL. 1989/1991. *How Societies Remember*. Cambridge, MA: Cambridge University Press; 1989.
2nd ed., 1991. 121p. ISBN: 0521249480 (hbk.); 0521270936 (pbk.); LCCN: 89007070.

C277
CONSORTIUM FOR MATHEMATICS AND ITS APPLICATIONS, INC. (COMAP). 1988. *Overview; How Big is
Too Big?* [Video]. S. Garfunkel, host. Annenberg/CPB Collection. Santa Barbara, CA: Intellimation; 1988.
Videocassette (60 min.).

C278
CONSORTIUM FOR THE INTERCHANGE OF MUSEUM INFORMATION (CIMI). 1993-. Cultural Heritage
Information Online (CHIO) project. Accessible at http://www.cimi.org.

C279
CONSTABLE, GILES. 1995. The Many Middle Ages: Medieval Studies in Europe as Seen from America. See reference: HAMESSE, J. ed. 1995. 1-22.

C280
CONVERSE, JEAN M. 1987. *Survey Research in the United States: Roots and Emergence, 1890-1960*. Berkeley, CA:
University of California Press; 1987. 564p. ISBN: 0520053990; LCCN: 85-24500.

C281
CONWAY, MARTIN A. 1990. *Autobiographical Memory: An Introduction*. Philadelphia, PA: Open University Press;
1990. 200p. ISBN: 0335098495 (hbk.); 03350998487 (pbk.).

C282
CONWAY, MARTIN A. 1995. *Flashbulb Memories*. Hillsdale, NJ: Lawrence Earlbaum; 1995. 140p. ISBN: 0863773532.

C283
CONWAY, MARTIN A. 1997a. The Inventory of Experience: Memory and Identity. See reference: PENNEBAKER, J. W., *ET AL.*, eds. 1997.

C284
CONWAY, MARTIN A. 1997b. *Recovered Memories and False Memories*. Oxford, UK; New York, NY: Oxford University Press; 1997. ISBN: 0198523874.

C285
CONWAY, MARTIN A., ed. 1992. *Theoretical Perspectives on Autobiographical Memory*. Proceedings of the NATO Advanced Research Workshops on Autobiographical Memory, held at Grange-over-Sands, UK, 4-12 July, 1991. Dordrecht, NL: Kluwer Academic Publishers; 1992. 502p. ISBN: 0792316460.

C286
CONWAY, MARTIN A., ed. 1997. *Cognitive Models of Memory*. Hove, UK: Psychology Press; 1997. 369p. ISBN: 0863774873 (hbk.); 0262032457 (pbk.).

C287
CONWAY, PAUL. 1986a. Facts and Frameworks: An Approach to Studying the Users of Archives. *American Archivist*. 1986 Fall; 49: 393-408. ISSN: 0360-9081.

C288
CONWAY, PAUL. 1986b. Research in Presidential Libraries: A User Survey. *Midwestern Archivist*. 1986; 11: 35-56. ISSN: 1067-4993.

C289
CONWAY, PAUL. 1987. Perspectives on Archival Resources: The 1985 Census of Archival Institutions. *American Archivist*. 1987 spring; 50: 174-191. ISSN: 0360-9081.

C290
CONWAY, PAUL. 1991. *Archival Preservation in the United States and the Role of Information Sources*. Ann Arbor, MI.: University of Michigan; 1991. (Ph.D. Dissertation). Available from: University Microfilms, Ann Arbor, MI (Order no. 9208522).

C291
CONWAY, PAUL. 1994. *Partners in Research: Improving Access to the Nation's Archives. User Studies of the National Archives and Records Administration*. Pittsburgh, PA: Archives & Museum Informatics; 1994. 156p. ISBN: 1885626096; OCLC: 31183348. Available from: SAA Publications, Chicago, IL.

C292
CONWAY, PAUL. 1995. *Preservation in the Digital World*. Washington, DC: ACCIS; 1996. 24p. ISBN: 1887334691.

C293
CONWAY, PAUL. 1996. *Conversion of Microfilm to Digital Imagery: A Demonstration Project. Performance Report on the Production Conversion Phase of Project Open Book*. New Haven, CT: Yale University Press; 1996. 22p., facsims.

C294
CONWAY, PAUL; WEAVER, SHARI. 1994. *The Setup Phase of Project Open Book. A Report to the Commission on Preservation and Access on the Status of an Effort to Convert Microfilm to Digital Imagery*. Washington, DC: Commission on Preservation an Access; 1994. 24p. (Report on Yale University Library pilot conversion project). OCLC: 30789775.

C295
COOK, MICHAEL. 1988a. *Archives and the Computer*. 2nd ed. London, UK: Butterworths-Heinemann, Ltd.; 1988. 170p. ISBN: 0-408-10882-7.

C296
COOK, MICHAEL. 1988b. *The Management of Information from Archives*. Brookfield, VT: Gower Publishing; 1988. 234p. ISBN: 0566035069.

C297
COOK, MICHAEL. 1989. *A Manual of Archival Description*. 2nd ed. Aldershot, UK: Gower; 1989. 291p. ISBN: 0566036347.

C298
COOK, MICHAEL. 1991. Towards International Archival Data Exchange: Descriptive Standards. *Archivi & Computer*. 1991; 1(1): 18-25. ISSN: 1121-2462.

C299
COOK, MICHAEL. 1992. Towards International Data Exchange: Description Standards. See reference: ENMARK, R., ed. 1992. 167-178.

C300
COOK, MICHAEL. 1993. *Information Management and Archival Data.* London, UK: Library Association Publ.; 1993. 210p. ISBN: 1856040534.

C301
COOK, MICHAEL, ed. 1987. *Computer Generated Records.* London, UK: Society of Archivists; 1987. (Approaches to Problems in Records Management, no. 2).

C302
COOK, ROBERT J. 1986. *Puritans, Pragmatists, and Progress: The Republican Coalition in Iowa, 1854-1878.* Oxford, UK: Oxford University. 351p. (D. Phil. dissertation). *DAI*, vol. 49/08-A, p. 2364. Available from: University Microfilms, Ann Arbor, MI (Order no. AADD-83177).

C303
COOK, TERRY. 1990-1991. The Rites of Passage: The Archivist and the Information Age. *Archivaria* (CAN). 1990; 31. ISSN: 0318-6954.

C304
COOK, TERRY. 1991a. Appraisal in the Information Age: A Canadian Commentary. *Archives & Museum Informatics.* 1991; 13: 50-56. (Technical Report, 13). ISSN: 1042-1467.

C305
COOK, TERRY 1991b. *The Archival Appraisal of Records Containing Personal Information.* Paris: UNESCO; 1991. 94p. (RAMP Study PG1-91/WS/3 for the General Information Programme and UNISIST). OCLC: 25120279. Available from: UNESCO Federal Information Programme, 7 Place de Fontenoy, 75700 Paris, FR.

C306
COOK, TERRY. 1991c. Viewing the World Upside Down: Reflections on the Theoretical Underpinnings of Archival Public Programming. *Archivaria* (CAN). 1990-91 Winter; 31: 123-135. ISSN: 0318-6954.

C307
COOK, TERRY. 1991-92. Easy to Byte, Harder to Chew: the Second Generation of Electronic Records Archives. *Archivaria* (CAN). 1991-92 Winter; 33: 202-216. ISSN: 0318-6954.

C308
COOK, TERRY. 1992/1993. The Concept of the Archival Fonds: Theory, Description, and Provenance in the Post-Custodial Era. See reference: EASTWOOD, T., ed. 1992: [1-38]. See also: The Concept of the Archival Fonds in the Post-Custodial Era: Theory, Problems, and Solutions. *Archivaria* (CAN). 1993 Spring; 35: 24-37. ISSN: 0318-6954.

C309
COOK, TERRY. 1994. Electronic Records, Paper Minds: The Revolution in Information Management and Archives in the Post-Custodial and Post-Modernist Era. *Archives and Manuscripts* (AUS). 1994 November; 22: 300-328. ISSN: 0157-6895.

C310
COOK, TERRY. 1997. The Impact of David Bearman on Modern Archival Thinking: An Essay of Personal Reflection and Change. *Archives and Museum Informatics.* 1997; 11 (1): 15-37. ISSN: 1042-1467.

C311
COOK, THOMAS D.; CAMPBELL, DONALD T. 1979. *Quasi-Experimentation: Design and Analysis Issues for Field Settings.* New York, NY: John Wiley; 1979. 405p. ISBN: 0528620533.

C312
COOK, THOMAS D.; REICHARDT, CHARLES S. 1979. *Qualitative and Quantitative Methods in Evaluation Research.* Beverly Hills, CA: Sage Pub.; 1979. 160p. ISBN: 0803913001 (hbk.); 080391391X (pbk.).

C313
COOK, SAMUEL. 1996. Technological Revolution and the Gutenberg Myth. See reference: STEFIK, M., ed. 1996.

C314
COOKE, LYNNE; WOLLEN, PETER. 1995. *Visual Display. Culture Beyond Appearances.* Seattle, WA: Bay Press; 1995. 351p. ISBN: 0941920321.

C315
COOMBS, CLYDE H.; DAWES, ROBYN M.; TVERSKY, AMOS. [1970]. *Mathematical Psychology: An Elementary Introduction.* Englewood Cliffs, NJ: Prentice-Hall; [1970]. 419p. Cf., *Frontiers of Mathematical Psychology: Essays in Honor of Clyde Coombs.* Brown, D. R.; Smith, J. E. K., eds. New York, NY: Springer-Verlag; 1991. 202p. ISBN: 0387974512.

C316
COONAN, GERT DE; DE RUAN, ETIENNE E.K., eds. 1995. *Foundations and Applications of Possibility Theory.* Proceedings of FAPT'95, Ghent, Belgium, Dec. 1995. River Edge, NJ: World Scientific; c1995. 328p. ISBN: 9810222890; LCCN: 95038390.

C317
COONTZ, S. 1992. *The Way We Never Were: American Families and the Nostalgia Trap.* New York, NY: Basic Books; 1992.

C318
COOPER, ALAN. 1995. *About Face. The Essentials of User Interface Design.* Foster City, CA: Programmers Press; 1995. 580p. ISBN: 1-56884-322-4.

C319
COOPER, MALCOLM; RICHARDS, JULIAN, eds. 1985. *Current Issues in Archeological Computing.* [Proceedings of] the 3rd Annual Conference on Techniques of Archeological Excavation, 1984 December 8, Birmingham, England. (BAR International Series, 271). Oxford, UK: BAR (British Archeological Reports, Ltd.); 1985. ISBN: 0-86054-344-7.

C320
COOPER, NECIA GRANT, ed. 1994. *The Human Genome Project: Deciphering the Blueprint of Heredity.* Mill Valley, CA: University Science Books; 1994. 360p. ISBN: 0935702296.

C321
COOPER, SHIELA M. 1985. *Family, Household, and Occupation in Pre-industrial England: Social Structure in King's Lynn, 1689-1702.* Bloomington, IN: Indiana University; 1985. 300p. (Ph.D. dissertation; *DAI,* vol. 46/12-A: 338). Available from: University Microfilms, Ann Arbor, MI (Order no. AAD86-02434).

C322
COOPER, WILLIAM S. 1971. A Definition of Relevance for Information Retrieval. *Information Storage & Retrieval.* 1971; 7: 19-37.

C323
COPELAND, PETER. 1993. *Sound Recordings.* London, UK: British Library; 1993. 80p. ISBN: 0712302255 (pbk.).

C324
COPELAND, WILLIS D. 1985. Teaching Students to "Do" History: The Teacher and the Computer in Partnership. *History Teacher.* 1985; 18(2): 189-98. ISSN: 0018-2745.

C325
CORBIN, ROBERTA A. 1991. The Development of the National Research and Education Network. *Information Technology and Libraries.* 1991 September; 10 (3): 212-220. ISSN: 0730-9295.

C326
CORCORAN, ELIZABETH. 1991. Ordering Chaos. *Scientific American.* 1991 August; 96-98. ISSN: 0036-8733.

C327
CORKHILL, C.; MANN, M. 1978. *Information Needs in the Humanities: Two Postal Surveys.* Sheffield, UK: University of Sheffield Center for Research on User Studies; 1978. 174p. (British Library Research and Development Report, no. 5455. CRUS Occasional Paper). ISBN: 09-060880-11; LCCN: 79-315563; OCLC: 568774.

C328
CORLETT, J. ANGELO. 1996. *Analyzing Social Knowledge.* Lanham, MD: Rowman & Littlefield; 1996. 167p. ISBN: 087682935 (hbk.); 0847682943 (pbk.).

C329
CORNELL, L. L. 1990. Analyzing the Consequences of Family Structure with Event-History Methods. *Historical Methods.* 1990; 23: 53-62. ISSN: ISSN: 0161-5440.

C330
CORNELL WAY, EILEEN. 1991. *Knowledge Representation and Metaphor.* Dordrecht, NE / Boston, MA: Kluwer Academic Publishers; c1991. 271p. ISBN: 0792310055 (pbk.); LCCN: 90048010.

C331
CORRIDONI, JACOPO M.; DEL BIMBO, ALBERTO; VICARIO, ENRICO. 1998. Image Retrieval by Color Semantics with Incomplete Knowledge. *Journal of the American Society for Information Science.* 1998; 49 (3); 267-282. ISSN: 0002-8231.

C332
CORRIVEAU, JEAN-PIERRE. 1995. *Time-constrained Memory: A Reader-based Approach to Text Comprehension* [Discourse Analysis]. Hillsdale, NJ: Lawrence Erlbaum Associates; 1995. 408p. ISBN: 08058817115 (hbk.); 0805817123 (pbk.); LCCN: 95019949.

C333
CORSTEN, SEVERIN; PFLUG, GUNTHER; SCHMIDT-KUNSEMULLER, FRIEDERICH ADOLF. 1985-. *Lexikon des gesamten Buchwesens: LGB2* [Dictionary of Collected Book Knowledge]. Rev. ed. Stuttgart, DEU: A. Hiersemann; 1985-. Irregular. (In German). ISBN: 3-7772-8527-7.

C334
CORTADA, JAMES W. 1979. The Impact of Computer Technology on the Research of Diplomatic History. *Society for the History of American Foreign Relations Newsletter.* 1979; 10(1): 1-11. ISSN: 0740-6169.

C335
CORTADA, JAMES W. 1983. *An Annotated Bibliography on the History of Data Processing.* Westport, CT: Greenwood Press; 1983. 215p. ISBN: 0313240019. For expanded version, see reference: CORTADA, J. 1990b.

C336
CORTADA, JAMES W. 1987. An Introduction to the History of the Data Processing Industry. In: *Historical Dictionary of Data Processing* (pp. 1-44). Westport, CT: Greenwood, CT; 1987. 309p. ISBN: 0313233039.

C337
CORTADA, JAMES W. 1990a. *Archives of Data-Processing History: A Guide to Major U.S. Collections.* Westport, CT: Greenwood Press; 1990. 181p. ISBN: 0-313-25923-2.

C338
CORTADA, JAMES W. 1990b. *Bibliographic Guide to the History of Computing, Computers, and the Information Processing Industry.* New York, NY: Greenwood Press; 1990. 644p. ISBN: 031326810X. Expanded version of earlier compilation: see reference CORTADA, J. 1983.

C339
CORTADA, JAMES W. 1993a. *Before the Computer: IBM, NCR, Burroughs, and Remington Rand and the Industry They Created, 1965-1956.* Princeton, NJ: Princeton University Press; 1993. 644p. ISBN: 0-691-04807-X.

C340
CORTADA, JAMES W. 1993b. *The Computer in the United States: From Laboratory to Market, 1930 to 1960.* Armonk, NJ: M. E. Sharp; 1993. 183p. ISBN: 1563242346 (hbk.); 1563242354 (pbk.).

C341
CORTADA, JAMES W. 1996a. *A Bibliographic Guide to the History of Computer Applications, 1950-1990.* Westport, CT: Greenwood Press; 1996. 278p. (Bibliographies and Indexes in Science and Technology, 10). ISBN: 0-313-29226-4.

C342
CORTADA, JAMES W. 1996b. Commercial Applications of the Digital Computer in American Corporations, 1945-1995. See reference: WILLIAMS, MICHAEL R., ed. 1996. 18-29.

C343
CORTADA, JAMES W.; JACKSON, EUGENE B. 1990. *A Bibliographic Guide to the History of Computing, Computers, and the Information Processing Industry.* Westport, CT: Greenwood; 1990. 644p. (Bibliographies and Indexes in Science and Technology, 6). ISBN: 031326810X (pbk.); LCCN: 90-3093; OCLC: 21334516.

C344
CORTADA, JAMES W.; MAHONEY, MICHAEL S. 1983. *An Annotated Bibliography on the History of Data Processing.* Westport, CT: Greenwood; 1983. 215p. ISBN: 0313240019; LCCN: 83-8539; OCLC: 9557821.

C345
CORTES ALONSO, VICENTA. 1980. *Documentacion & Documentos* (Documentation and Documents). Madrid, ES: Ministerio de Cultura, Direccion General de Bellas Artes, Archivos y Bibliotecas; 1980. 80p. (In Spanish). ISBN: 84-7.483-151-2.

C346
CORTEZ, EDWIN M. 1999. Planning and Implementing a High Performance Knowledge Base. See reference: WOODS, LARRY, ed. 1999. 161-171.

C347
CORTI, LAURA, ed. 1984. *Census Computerization in the History of Art.* Pisa, IT / Santa Monica, CA: Scuola Normale Superiore de Pisa and the Getty Trust AHIP; 1984. 427p. OCLC: 13628530.

C348
CORTI, LAURA; SCHMITT, MARILYN, eds. 1984. *International Conference in Automatic Processing of Art History Data and Documents. Proceedings.* Pisa, IT / Santa Monica, CA: Scuola Normale Superiore de Pisa and the Getty Trust AHIP; 1984. 2 vols.

C349
CORTI, LAURA; WILDE, DEBORAH; PARRINI, UMBERTO; SCHMITT, MARILYN, comps. *1988. SN/G Report on Data Processing Projects in Art.* Pisa, IT/ Santa Monica, CA: Scuola Normale Superiore de Pisa and the Getty

Trust AHIP; 1988. 645p. in 2 vols. Available from: Officio Publicazioni, Scuola Normale Superiore, Piazza dei Cavalieri, 7, 56100 Pisa, IT.

C350
COSSON, S. 1994. A Real Feel for History. *Times Educational Supplement* (UK). 1994 March 11; 4054: B20-21. ISSN: 0040-7887.

C351
COSTELLO, PAUL. 1993. *World historians and their Goals.* Dekalb, IL: Northern Illinois University Press; 1993. 295p. ISBN: 75801730; LCCN: 92-015134.

C352
COTTER, H. 1988. Birth of a Network: A History of BITNET. *CUNY Computer Center Communications.* 1988; 14: 1-10.

C353
COTTRELL, GARRISON W. 1989. *A Connectionist Approach to Word Sense Disambiguation.* London, UK: Pitman / San Mateo, CA: Morgan Kauffmann Publishers; c1989. 220p. ISBN: 0934613613; LCCN: 87031084.

C354
COUNCIL OF STATE HISTORICAL RECORDS COORDINATORS (COSHRC). 1996. *Maintaining State Records in an Era of Change: A National Challenge* (Electronic file). Accessible on the NHPRC Website at http://www.nara.gov/nara/nhprc/shrabs.html.

C355
COUPRIE, LEENDERT D. 1978. Constructing and Editing an Alphabetical Index to the Iconographic Classification with the Aid of Electronic Data Processing. In: *First International Conference in Automatic Processing of Art History Data and Documents:* vol. 2. Pisa and Los Angeles, CA: Getty Trust, AHIP; 1978. 151-181. Available from: the Getty Trust, AHIP, Santa Monica, CA.

C356
COURTEAU, J. 1991. Genome Databases. *Science.* 1991; 24: 201-207. ISSN: 0036-8075.

C357
COURTENAY, WILLIAM J. 1982. The Virgin and the Dynamo: The Growth of Medieval Studies in North America, 1870-1930. In: Gentry, Francis G.; Kleinhenz, Christopher, eds. *Medieval Studies in North America: Past, Present, and Future* (pp. 1-15). Kalamazoo, MI: Western Michigan University; 1982. 252p ISBN: 0918720175 (pbk.).

C358
COURTIAL, J. P.; POMIAN, J. 1987. A System based on Association Logic for the Interrogation of Databases. *Journal of Information Science* (NE). 1987; 26 (5): 629-640. ISSN: 0165-5515.

C359
COUTEAU-BEGARIE, HERVI. 1983. *Le Phénomène "Nouvelle Histoire": Stratégie et Idéologie des nouveaux historiens* [The Phenomenon of "New History": Strategy and Ideology of the New Historians]. Paris, FR: Economica; 1983. 354p. (Based on thesis at the University of Bordeaux; 1980). ISBN: 2717806504; LCCN: 83-219773; OCLC: 10181051.

C360
COVEY, STEPHEN. 1990. *The Seven Habits of Highly Effective People: Restoring the Character Ethic.* 1st. Fireside ed. New York, NY: Simon and Schuster; c. 1989, 1990. 358p. ISBN: 0671708635 (pbk.).

C361
COVEY, STEPHEN. 1991. *Principle-centered Leadership.* New York, NY: Summit Books; 1991. 334p. ISBN: 0671749102.

C362
COVEY, HELEN CLAIRE; WILLIAMS, ROBERT V. 1994. *The Termatrex Retrieval System: History and Demonstration.* New York, NY. n.p.; 1994.

C363
COWAN, GEORGE A.; PINES, DAVID: MELTZER, DAVID, eds. 1994. *Complexity: Metaphors, Models, and Reality.* Santa Fe, NM: Santa Fe Institute (SFI); 1994. ISBN: 0-201-6626-5 (hbk.); 0-201-62606-3 (pbk.).

C364
COX, GARY W. 1988. Recent Developments in Statistical Inference: Quasi-experiments and Perquimans County. *Historical Methods.* 1988; 21(3): 140-42. ISSN: 0161-5440.

C365
COX, JEFFREY N.; REYNOLDS, LARRY J., eds. *New Historical Literary Study: Essays on Reproducing Texts, Representing History.* Princeton, NJ: Princeton University Press; 1993. 337p. ISBN: 0691069912; 0691015465 (pbk.); LCCN: 92-42580; OCLC: 27034965.

C366
COX, LYNN; BEARMAN, DAVID, comps., eds. 1990. *1990 Directory of Software for Archives and Museums.*. Pittsburgh, PA: Archives & Informatics; 1990. 196p. (Technical Report, 12 [originally published as vol. 4, no. 4]). ISSN: 1042-1459.

C367
COX, RICHARD J. 1983. American Archival History: Its Development, Needs, and Opportunities. *The American Archivist.* 1983; 46(1): 31-41. ISSN: 0360-9081.

C368
COX, RICHARD J. 1984-85. Archivists and Historians: A View from the United States. *Archivaria* (CAN). 1984-85 winter; 19: 185-90. ISSN: 0318-6954.

C369
COX, RICHARD J. 1986a. Government Publications as Archives: A Case for Cooperation between Archivists and Librarians. See reference: MCCRANK, L., ed. 1986. 111-128.

C370
COX, RICHARD J. 1986b. Archivists and Public Historians in the United States. *The Public Historian.* 1986 Summer; 8: 43-56. ISSN: 0272-3433.

C371
COX, RICHARD J. 1990a. A History of Primary Sources in Graduate Education: An Archival Perspective. Special *Collections/Primary Sources & Original Works.* 1990; 4(2): 39-78. (Includes syllabus for course on the History of Record Keeping and Archival Administration). ISSN: 1042-8216.

C372
COX, RICHARD J. 1990b. *American Archival Analysis: The Recent Development of the Archival Profession in the United States.* Metuchen, NJ: Scarecrow Press; 1991. 347p. ISBN: 0810823381 (pbk.); LCCN: 90-36213; OCLC: 21600983.

C373
COX, RICHARD J. 1992a. The Archival Profession and Information Technology Standards. *Journal of the Society for Information Science.* 1992 September; 43: 571-575. ISSN: 0002-8231.

C374
COX, RICHARD J. 1992b. *Managing Institutional Archives: Foundational Principles and Practices.* Westport, CT: Greenwood Press; 1992. 306 p. (Library management Collection). ISSN: 0894-2986; ISBN: 0-313-27251.

C375
COX, RICHARD J. 1992c. Researching Archival Reference as an Information Function: Observations on Needs and Opportunities. *RQ.* 1992 spring; 31: 388-96. ISSN:0033- 7072

C376
COX, RICHARD J. 1993. The Master of Archival Studies and American Education Standards: An Argument for the Continued Development of Graduate Archival Education in the United States. *Archivaria* (CAN). 1993 Autumn; 36: 221-231. ISSN: 0318-6954.

C377
COX, RICHARD J. 1994a. An Analysis of Archival Research, 1970-92, and the Role and Function of *the American Archivist.* See reference: COX, ed., 1994d. 278-289.

C378
COX, RICHARD J. 1994b. *Electronic Archives. The Challenges to Archival Education and Research.* Binghamton, NY: Haworth Press; 1994. 232p. ISBN: 1-56024-644-8. Also in: *Primary Sources & Original Works.* 1994; 3 (3-4). (Entire issue on title topic). ISSN: 1042-8216.

C379
COX, RICHARD J. 1994c. The Record: Is It Evolving? *The Records & Retrieval Report. The Newsletter for Professional Information Managers.* 1994 March; 10(3): 1-16. ISSN: 8756- 0089.

C380
COX, RICHARD J. 1994d. What Is an Archival Record, and Why Should We Care? *American Archivist.* 1994; 57 (4):592-594. ISSN: 0360-9081.

C381
COX, RICHARD J. 1995. Archives and Archivists in the Twenty-First Century: What Will We Become? *Archival Issues.* 1995 [1996]; 20(2): 97-114. ISSN: 1067-4993.

C382
COX, RICHARD J. 1996. *Documenting Localities.* Lanham, MD: Scarecrow Press for SAA; 1996. 224p. (Society of American Archivists series). ISBN: 0-8108-3043-4.

C383
COX, RICHARD J. 1996. The Record in the Information Age: A Progress Report on Research. *The Records & Retrieval Report. The Newsletter for Professional Information Managers*. 1996 Jan.; 12 (1): 1-16. ISSN: 8756-0089.

C384
COX, RICHARD J. 1997a. Electronic Systems and Records Management in the Information Age: An Introduction. See reference: TRAVIS, I., ed. 1997. 7-11.

C385
COX, RICHARD J. 1997b. More than Diplomatic: Functional Requirements for Evidence in Recordkeeping. *Records Management Journal*. 1997 April; 7: 31-57.

C386
COX, RICHARD J., ed. 1994d. Editor's Forum on Needs in Archival Research and Publications. *The American Archivist*. 1994 Spring; 57(2): 268-308.(Essays by editors profiling the five main North American journals in archival studies). ISSN: 0360-9081.

C387
COX, RICHARD J.; DUFF, WENDY. 1997. Warrant and the Definition of Electronic Records: Questions Arising from the Pittsburgh Project. See reference: BEARMAN, D.; TRANT, J., eds. 1997. 223-231.

C388
COX, RICHARD J.; RASMUSSEN, EDIE. 1997. Reinventing the Information Profession and the Argument for Specialization in LIS Education: Case Studies in Archives and Information Technology. *Journal of Education for Library and Information Science*. 1997; 37: 255-267. ISSN: 0748-5786.

R389
COX, RICHARD J; WILLIAMS, JAMES, project directors. 1994. *University of Pittsburgh Recordkeeping Functional Requirements Project: Reports and Working Papers*. Pittsburgh, PA: University of Pittsburgh School of Library and Information Science; Sept. 1994. Irregular pagination. ISSN: 0896-6117.

C390
COXON, HOWARD. 1983. Information Services from Numeric Data Bases: The U.S. Experience. *Australian Library Journal* (AU). 1983 November; 32(4): 5-12. ISSN: 0004-9670

C391
COYNE, RICHARD. 1995. *Designing Information Technology in the Postmodern Age*. Cambridge, MA: MIT Press; 1995. 408p. ISBN: 0-262-03228-7.

C392
COZZENS, SUSAN F. 1989. What do Citations Count? The Rhetoric-first Model. *Scientometrics*. 1989; 15: 437-447. ISSN: 0138-9130.

C393
COZZENS, SUSAN F., ed. 1990. *The Research System in Transition*. NATO Advanced Study Institute on managing Science in the Steady State. Conference in Il Ciocco, IT, 1989. Dordrecht, NL: Kluwer Academic Publishers; 1990. 407p. (NATO ASI Series, Behavioral and Social Sciences, no. 57). ISBN: 0792308581.

C394
COZZENS, SUSAN F.; GIERYN, THOMAS F., eds. 1990. *Theories of Science in Society*. Bloomington, IN: Indiana University Press; 1990. 264p. ISBN: 0253314712.

C395
CRAIG, BARBARA L. 1992. The Introduction of Copying Devices into the British Civil Service, 1877-1889. In: Craig, Barbara, ed. *The Archival Imagination. Essays in Honour of Hugh Taylor* (pp. 105-133). Ottawa, CA: Association of Canadian Archivists; 1992. 263p. ISBN: 1-895382-06-8.

C396
CRANACH, MARION VON; DOISE, WILLEM; MUGNY, GABRIEL, eds. 1992. *Social Representations and the Social Basis of Knowledge*. Lewiston, NY: Hogrefe & Huber; 1992. 220p. (Swiss Monographs in Psychology, v. 1). ISBN: 0889370702 (hbk.); 3456821050 (pbk.).

C397
CRANE, GREGORY. 1990a. Challenging the Individual: the Tradition of Hypermedia Databases. *Academic Computing*. 1990 January; 4: 22-23, 31-32, 34-38. ISSN: 0892- 4694.

C398
CRANE, GREGORY. 1990b. "Hypermedia" and "Scholarly Publishing." *Scholarly Publishing* (CAN). 1990 April; 21: 131-155. ISSN: 0036-634X.

C399
CRANE, GREGORY; MYLONAS, ELLI. 1988. The Perseus Project: An Interactive curriculum on classical Greek civilization. *Educational Technology*. 1988 November; 28(11): 25-32. ISSN: 0013-1962.

C400
CRANE, SUSAN A. 1992. *Collecting and Historical Consciousness: New Forms for Collective Memory in Early Nineteenth-century Germany.* Chicago, IL: University of Chicago; 1992. (Ph.D. dissertation). Available from: University Microfilms, Ann Arbor, MI.

C401
CRANE, SUSAN A. 1996. (Not) Writing History: Rethinking the Intersections of Personal History and Collective Memory with Hans von Auffsess. *History and Memory*. 1996 Spring/Summer; 8: 5-92. (Concerning autobiography as history). ISSN: 0935-560X.

C402
CRANE, SUSAN A. 1997a. Memory, Distortion, and History in the Museum. *History and Theory*. [1997 Dec.]. (forthcoming). ISSN: 0018-2656.

C403
CRANE, SUSAN A. 1997b. Writing the Individual Back into Collective Memory. *American Historical Review.* 1997 Dec.; 102 (5): 1372-1385. ISSN: 0002-8762. C290

C404
CRARY, JONATHAN. 1992. *Techniques of the Observer. On Vision and Modernity in the Nineteenth Century.* Cambridge, MA: MIT Press; 1992. 171p. ISBN: 0262031695; LCCN: 90-6164.

C405
CRAVEN, KENNETH. 1992. *Jonathan Swift and the Millennium of Madness: the Information Age in Swift's Tale of a Tub.* Leiden, NL: E. J. Brill; 1992. 238p. (Brill's Studies in Intellectual History, 30). ISBN: 9004095241; LCCN: 91-43722; OCLC: 24907856.

C406
CRAVEN, PAUL. 1995. A General Purpose Conceptual Clustering Engine. See reference: BOONSTRA, O.; COLLENTEUR, G.; VAN ELDEREN, B., eds. 1995. 33-42.

C407
CRAWFORD, SUSAN Y.; HURD, JULIE M.; WELLER, ANN C. 1996. *From Print to Electronic: The Transformation of Scientific Communication.* Medford, NJ: Information Today, Inc.; 1996. 117p. ISBN: 1-57387-030-7.

C408
CRAWFORD, WALT. 1989. Standards, Innovation and Optical Media. *The Laserdisk Professional.* 1989, January; 2 (1): 31-38. ISSN: 10490833.

C409
CRESWELL, JOHN W. 1997. *Qualitative Inquiry and Research Design. Choosing Among Five Traditions.* Thousand Oaks, CA: Sage Publications; 1997. 416p. ISBN: 0-7619-0144-2 (pbk.).

C410
CRITCHLEY, BILL. 1993. Managing Organizational Culture—Is It just an Illusion? *Leadership & Organization Development Journal.* 1993; 14 (1): i-iii. ISSN: 0143-7739.

C411
CROARKEN, MARY. 1990. *Early Scientific Computing in Britain.* 1990. Oxford, UK: Clarendon Press; 1990. 160p. ISBN: 019853484.

C412
CROCKETT, MARGARET. 1993. The Theory of electronic records in the information age. *Journal of the Society of Archivists* (UK). 1993 Autumn; 14 (2): [130-140]. ISSN: 0037- 9816.

C413
CRONIN, BLAISE. 1984. *The Citation Process: The Role and Significance of Citations in Scientific Communication.* London, UK: Taylor Graham; 1984. 103p. ISBN: 0947568018.

C414
CRONIN, BLAISE. 1985/1992. *Information Management: From Strategies to Action, 1-2.* London, UK: ASLIB; 1985 [vol. 1]. ISBN: 0851421938. 1992; 2: 221p. ISBN: 0851422810.

C415
CRONIN, BLAISE. 1991. *Elements of Information Management.* Metuchen, NJ: Scarecrow Press; 1991. 207p. ISBN: 081082406X.

C416
CRONIN, BLAISE. 1995a. *The Scholar's Courtesy: The Role of Acknowledgment in the Primary Communication Process*. London, UK: Taylor Graham; 1995. 124p. ISSN: 0-94756-66-2.

C417
CRONIN, BLAISE. 1995b. Shibboleth and Substance in North American Library and Information Science Education. *Libri*. 1995; 45: 45-63. See attack by CROWLEY, W. 1999.

C418
CRONIN, BLAISE; DAVENPORT, L. 1989. Profiling the Professors. *Journal of Information Science* (UK). 1989; 15: 13-20. ISSN: 1352-7460.

C419
CROSBY, ALFRED W. 1997. *The Measure of Reality: Quantification and Western Society, 1250-1600*. Cambridge, UK: Cambridge University Press; 1997. 272p. ISBN: 0-521- 55427-6.

C420
CROSBY, CONNIE L. 1989. *A Guide to Computer Applications for Humanities Students*. Waterloo, Ontario, CAN: University of Guelph; 1989. 230p. (M.A. Thesis; *DAI* file 35, Masters Abstracts, vol. 30/03: 469). ISBN: 0-315-62238-5. Available from: University Microfilms, Ann Arbor, MI (Order no. AADMM-62238).

C421
CROUCH, C, J. 1990. An Approach to the Automatic Construction of Global Thesauri. *Information Processing and Management*. 1990; 26 (5): 629-640. ISSN: 0306-4573.

C422
CROUSE, MAURICE. 1995-98. *Citing Electronic Information in History Papers*. Memphis, TN: University of Memphis, TN. Updated March 26, 1998. 24p. Accessible at http://www.people.memphis.edu/~mcrouse/ elcite.html (viewed April 1998).

C423
CROUZET, FRANÇOIS. 1983. Cliometrie et Revolution Industrielle [Cliometry and the Industrial Revolution]. *Histoire, Économie et Société* (FR). 1983: 2(4): 607-24. (In French). LCCN: 83-641547; OCLC: 8924328.

C424
CROWLEY, WILLIAM. 1999. The Control and Direction of Professional Education. See reference: BATES, M., ed. 1999. 1127-1135. Note: the Library Science vs. Information Science controversy.

C425
CROWNOVER, RICHARD M. 1995. *Introduction to Fractals and Chaos*. Boston, MA: Jones & Barlett; 1995. 306p. ISBN: 0867204648

C426
CROZIER, WILLIAM L. 1996 [199-]. Minnesota River Towns to Manhattan: Historical Data Modeling for Research and Teaching. See reference: BORODKIN, L., ed. 1996: Abstract of presentation, 83-84; paper [199- forthcoming].

C427
CROZIER, WILLIAM L.; GAFFIELD, CHAD. 1990. The Lower Manhattan Project: A New Approach to Computer-Assisted Learning in History Classrooms. *Historical Methods*. 1990 Spring; 23: 72-77. ISSN: 0161-5440.

C428
CRUM, LAURIE BROOKE. 1995. Digital Revolution: Changing Roles and Challenges for Archivists in the Age of Global Networking. See reference: GILLILAND-SWETLAND, ANNE, ed. 1995. 51-64.

C429
CSIKSZENTMIHALYI, MIHALY. 1990. *Flow: The Psychology of Optimal Experience*. New York, NY: Harper & Row; c1990. 303p. ISBN: 0060162538; LCCN: 89045645.

C430
CSIKSZENTMIHALYI, MIHALY. 1993. *The Evolving Self: A Psychology for the Third Millennium*. New York, NY: Harper Collins; c1993. 358p. ISBN: 0060166770; LCCN: 92056220.

C431
CUADRA ASSOCIATES. [196-]; [1989]. *Directory of Online Databases*. Landau, Ruth, comp. [Santa Monica, CA]; Cuadra Associates; [n.d.].LCCN: 79054776. Cf., *Online Database Selection: A User's Guide to the Directory of Online Databases*. New York, NY: Cuadra/Elsevier; [c1989]. ISBN: 0444015035; LCCN: 89012044.

C432
CULLARS, JOHN. 1985. Characteristics of the Monographic Literature of British and American Literary Studies. *College and Research Libraries*. 1985 November; 46(6): 511-522. ISSN: 0010-0870.

C433
CULLARS, JOHN. 1989. Citation Characteristics of French and German Literary Monographs. *Library Quarterly.* 1989; 59: 305-325. ISSN: 0024-2519.

C434
CUMMINGS, L. L.; FROST, PETER J., eds. 1985. *Publishing in the Organizational Sciences.* Homewood, IL: Richard D. Irwin; 1985. 794p. ISBN: 0-256-03308-0.

C435
CUMMINS, ROBERT. 1983. *The Nature of Psychological Explanation.* Cambridge, MA: MIT Press; 1983. 219p. ISBN: 0262030942.

C436
CUMMINS, ROBERT. 1991. *Meaning and Mental Representation.* Cambridge, MA: MIT Press; 1991. 180p. ISBN: 0262031396.

C437
CUMMINS, ROBERT. 1996. *Representations, Targets, and Attitudes.* Cambridge, MA: MIT Press; 1996. 153p. ISBN: 026203225X.

C438
CURRAS, EMILIA. 1982. *Las Ciencias de la Documentación: Bibliotecología, Archivología, Documentación e Información* [The Documentation Sciences: Library, Archival, Documentation, and Information Sciences]. Barcelona, ES: Ed. Mitre; 1982. 249p. (In Spanish).LCCN: 84-17034.

C439
CURRAS, EMILIA. 1988. *La Información en sus Nuevos Aspectos* [Information in its New Aspects]. Madrid, ES: Paraninfo; 1988. 307p. (In Spanish). ISBN: 84-283-1600-7.

C440
CURRAS, EMILIA. 1996. *Tratado sobre Ciencia de la Información* [Treatise on Information Science]. Rosario, Argentina: National University; 1996. 400p. (In Spanish).

C441
CURRENT, RICHARD N. 1954/1988. *The Typewriter and the Men Who Made It.* Urbana, IL: University of Illinois; 1954. 2nd ed. Arcadia, CA: Post-Era Books; 1988. 149p. ISBN: 0911160884.

C442
CUSHING, STEVEN. 1991. "Minds and Machines" for Humanities Majors: A Liberal Arts Course in Computers and Cognition. *Computers and Humanities.* 1991; 25 (5): 275-281. ISSN: 0010-4817.

C443
CUTRAIN, P. 1984. Depth, Span, and Relevance. *American Historical Review.* 1984; 89: 1-9. ISSN: 0002-8762.

C444
CZAP, HANS; GALINSKI, CHRISTIAN, eds. 1988. *Terminology and Knowledge Engineering.* Proceedings: International Congress on Terminology and Knowledge Engineering, 29 Sept.-1 Oct. 1987, University of Trier. Frankfurt am Main: INDEKS Verlag for UNESCO INFOTERM and Association for Terminology and Knowledge Transfer. 435p; Suppl. 255p. (Irregular series from first INFOTERM symposium in 1975).LCCN: 88- 160321; OCLC: 1887265.

C445
CZARNIAWSKA-JOERGES, BARBARA; JOERGES, BERNWARD. 1990. Linguistic Artifacts at [the] Service of Organizational Control. See reference: GAGLIARDI, P., ed. 1990. 339-363.

-D-

D1
D'AMICO, HELEN; ZAVADIL, JOSEPH B., eds. *Medieval Scholarship: Biographical Studies on the Formation of a Discipline.* Vol. 1: *History.* New York, NY: Garland; 1995. (Garland Reference Library of the Humanities, 1350). ISBN: 0824068947.

D2
D'ANIELLO, CHARLES A., ed. 1993. *Teaching Bibliographic Skills in History: A Sourcebook for Historians and Librarians.* Westport, CT: Greenwood Press; 1993. 385p. (Project of the Association for the Bibliography of History). ISBN: 0313252661; LCCN: 92-8833; OCLC: 25508227.

D3
DA COSTA, A. F. C. 1990. Ciencia da Infomação: o Passado e a Atualidade [Information Science: From the Past to Actuality]. *Ciencia da Informação* (Brazil). 1990 July-December; 19(2):137-144. (In Portuguese, English abstracts). ISSN: 0100-1965.

D4
DAGAN, I.; CHURCH, K. 1995. *Termight*: Identifying and Translating Technical Terminology. In: *Proceedings of the Fourth Conference on Applied Natural Language Processing*. N.p.: Association for Computational Linguistics; 1995. 34-40. LC call no.: P98.A57.

D5
DAHLBERG, INGETRAUT. [199-]. The Historical Paradigm in the Philosophy of Classification. Paper in session on: *Toward a Modern Philosophy of Classification*, at the American Society for Information Conference, October 17-20, 1994, at Alexandria, VA; [199-]. (forthcoming).

D6
DALE, ANDREW I. 1991. *A History of Inverse Probability: from Thomas Bayes to Karl Pearson*. New York, NY: Springer-Verlag; c1991. 495p. ISBN: 0387976205; LCCN: 91017794.

D7
DAMERAU, F. 1990. Evaluation Computer-generated Domain-oriented Vocabularies. *Information Processing and Management*. 1990; 26 (6): 791-801. ISSN: 0306-4573.

D8
DAMERAU, F. 1993. Generating and Evaluating Domain-oriented Multi-word Terms from Texts. *Information Processing & Management*. 1993; 29 (4): 433-447. ISSN: 0306-4573.

D9
DANDRIDGE, T. C. 1983. Symbol's Function and Use. In: Pondy, L. R.; Frost, P. J.; Morgan, G.; Dandridge, T. C., eds. *Organizational Symbolism* (pp. 69-79). Greenwich, CT: JAI Press; 1983. 307p. ISBN: 0892323663.

D10
DANEKE, GREGORY A. 1994/[1999]. *The Agathon Agenda: Non-Linear Dynamics and Practical Policy*. London, UK: Oxford University Press; 1994. Rev. as: *Systematic Choices: Nonlinear Dynamics and Practical Management*. Ann Arbor, MI: University of Michigan Press; [1999]. ISBN: 0472110497; LCCN: 99-033759.

D11
DANISH DATA ARCHIVES (DDA). 1986/1988. *Danish Data Guide*. Odense, DK: DDA; 1986. *Danish Data Guide Update*. Odense, DK: DDA; 1988. (See also the DDA newsletter, *DDA-Nyt*, available from: DDA, Odense, DK).

D12
DANT, TIM. 1991. *Knowledge Ideology and Discourse: A Sociological Perspective*. London and New York: Routledge; 1991. 253p. ISBN: 0415947861; 0415064589 (pbk.); LCCN: 90-24337; OCLC: 222810610.

D13
DANYLUK, ANDREA P. 1992. *Extraction and Use of Contextual Attributes for Theory Completion: An Integration of Explanation-based and Similarity-based Learning*. New York, NY: Columbia University; 1992. 282p. (Ph.D. dissertation; *DAI*, vol. 53/06-B: 2979). Available from: University Microfilms, Ann Arbor, MI (Order no. AAD92-31991).

D14
DANZIGER, KURT. 1987. Statistical Method and the Historical Development of Research Practice in American Psychology. In: Kruger, L.; Gigerenzer, G.; Morgan, M. S., eds. *The Probabilistic Revolution*. Vol. 1: *Ideas in History*. Vol. 2: *The Ideas of Science*). Cambridge, MA: MIT Press; 1987. 35-47. ISBN: 0262111187; LCCN: 86-17972.

D15
DANZIGER, KURT. 1990. *Constructing the Subject: Historical Origins of Psychological Research*. Cambridge, UK: Cambridge University Press; 1990. 354p. (Cambridge Studies in Historical Psychology). ISBN: 0521363586; LCCN: 89-22160.

D16
DARIAN-SMITH, KATE; HAMILTON, PAULA; CURTHOYS, ANN, eds. 1994. *Memory and History in Twentieth-Century Australia*. New York, NY / Melbourne, AS: Oxford University Press; 1994. 255p. ISBN: 0195535693.

D17
DARLING, CHARLES B. 1997. Datamining for the Masses. *Datamation*. 1997 February; 43 (2): 52-56. ISSN: 0011-6963.

D18
DARNTON, ROBERT. 1980. Intellectual and Cultural History. See reference: KAMMEN, M., ed., 1980. 334-346.

D19
DARNTON, ROBERT. 1982. *The Literary Underground of the Old Regime*. Cambridge, MA: Harvard University Press; 1982. 258p. ISBN: 0674536568.

D20
DARNTON, ROBERT. 1986. The Symbolic Element in History. *Journal of Modern History*. 1986; 58: 218-234. ISSN: 0022-2801.

D21
DARNTON, ROBERT. 1995. *The Forbidden Bestsellers of Pre-revolutionary France*. New York, NY: W. W. Norton; [1995]. 440p. ISBN: 0393037207.

D22
DARROCH, GORDON. 1988. A Study of Census Manuscript Data for Central Ontario, 1861-1871. Reflections on a Project and on Historical Archives. *Histoire sociale / Social History* (CAN). 1988 November; 21(42): 304-311. ISSN: 0018-2557.

D23
DARROCH, A. GORDON; ORNSTEIN, MICHAEL D. 1979. Error in Historical Data Files: A Research Note on the Automatic Detection of Error and on the Nature and Sources of Errors in Coding. *Historical Methods*. 1979; 12: 157-167. ISSN: 0161-5440.

D24
DARU, MYRIAM. 1995a. Historical Graphicacy. About the Art of Translating Historical Facts into Revealing, Attractive and Correct Graphics and the Ability to Interpret Them. See reference: JARITZ, G., *ET AL.*, eds. 1995. 271-287. See also abstract in reference: JARITZ *ET AL*. 1993. 72-74.

D25
DARU, MYRIAM. 1995b. Graphic Explorative Modeling of Historical Data. See reference: BOONSTRA, O.; COLLENTEUR, G.; VAN ELDEREN, B., eds. 1995. 55-66.

D26
DATA WAREHOUSING INFORMATION CENTER. 1995-. *White Papers on Data Warehousing* (Electronic file). Greenfield, Larry, comp. 11p. Courtesy of LGI Systems Inc. Accessible at http://www.starnetinc.com.larryg/whitepap.html.

D27
DATA WAREHOUSING INSTITUTE. 1996a. *1995 Annual Conference Proceedings*. Bethesda, MD: Data Warehousing Institute; 1996. 590p.

D28
DATA WAREHOUSING INSTITUTE. 1996b. *Data Warehousing*. Crofts, Steven, president. Gaithersburg, MD: Data Warehousing Institute; 1996-. Available with membership from DWI, 9158 Rothbury Drive 200, Gaithersburg, MD 20879. Accessible at http://www.dw-institute.com.

D29
DATA WAREHOUSING INSTITUTE. 1996c. *A Guide to Data Warehouse Development and Information Directory Products*. Bethesda, MD: Data Warehousing Institute; 1996. (Product Evaluation Reports, 4). Available from: Data Warehousing Institute 9158 Rothbury Drive 200, Gaithersburg, MD 20879. Accessible at http://www.dw-institute.com.

D30
DATA WAREHOUSING INSTITUTE. 1997. What Works? An Unprecedented Collection of Case Studies and Persepctives from Leading Companies Worldwide. In: *Data Warehousing*, vol. 3: 65p. (Entire issue on title topic).

D31
DAUMAND, A.; FURET, FRANCOIS. 1961. *S*tructures et relations sociales a Paris au XVIIIe siecle [Social Structures and Relations in Paris in the Eighteenth Century]. In: *Cahiers des Annales* (FR). 1961; 18: 97p..(Entire issue on title topic). OCLC: 29112068.

D32
DAUPHIN, CECILE. 1991/1997. Letter-writing Manuals in the Nineteenth Century. See reference: CHARTIER, R., ed. 1991/1997.

D33
DAVENPORT, ELISABETH. 1992a. Extending Corporate Memory. Cronin, Blaise, ed. *Information Management: From Strategies to Action II*. London, UK: ASLIB; 1992. 33- 52. ISBN: 0-85142-281-0.

D34
DAVENPORT, ELISABETH. 1992b. What Do We Look at When We Do Information Science? See reference: VAKKARI, PERTTI; CRONIN, BLAISE, eds. 1992. 286-298.

D35

DAVENPORT, ELISABETH; MCKIM, GEOFFREY. 1995. Groupware. In: Williams, Martha E., ed. *Annual Review of Information Science and Technology*: volume 30. Medford, NJ: Information Today, Inc. for ASIS; 1995. 115-159. ISBN: 1-57387-019-6; ISSN: 0066-4200; CODEN: ARISBC; LCCN: 66-25096.

D36

DAVENPORT, THOMAS H. 1993. *Process Innovation: Re-engineering Work through Information Technology.* Boston, MA: Harvard Business School Press; 1993. 337p. ISBN: 087843662.

D37

DAVENPORT, THOMAS H.; PRUSAK, LAURENCE. 1997. *Information Ecology: Mastering Information and the Knowledge Environment.* Oxford, UK: Oxford University Press; 1997. 255p. ISBN: 0195111680; LCCN: 96-45169.

D38

DAVENPORT, THOMAS H.; PRUSAK, LAURENCE. 1998. *Working Knowledge: How Organizations Manage What They Know.* Boston, MA: Harvard University Press; 1998. 199p. ISBN: 0875846556; LCCN: 97010781.

D39

DAVID, FRED R. 1993. *Strategic Management.* 6th ed. New York, NY: Macmillan Publishing Company; 1993. 352p. ISBN: 013486011X; LCCN: 96-36834.

D40

DAVID, M. H. 1980. Access to Data: The Frustration and Utopia of the Researcher. *Review of Public Data Use.* 1980; 8: 327-337. ISSN: 0092-2846.

D41

DAVID, M. H. 1991. The Science of Data Sharing: Documentation. See reference: SIEBER, J. E., ed. 1991. 91-115.

D42

DAVID, M. H.; ROBBIN, A. 1990. Database Design for Large-scale Complex Data. *Proceedings of the 21st Symposium on the Interface between Statistics and the Computer.* April 1989, Orlando, FL. Alexandria, VA: American Statistical Association; 1990.

D43

DAVID, PAUL. 1990. *Computer and Dynamo: The Modern Productivity Paradox in a Not-Too- Distant Mirror.* Palo Alto, CA: Stanford University Center for Economic Policy Research; 1990. (Publication 172).

D44

DAVIDSON, DONALD. 1984. What Metaphors Mean. In his: *Inquiries into Truth and Interpretation.* Oxford, UK: Clarendon; 1984. 292p. ISBN: 01924617X (hbk.); 0198750463 (pbk.); LCCN: 83-15136.

D45

DAVIES, DUNCAN; BATHURST, DIANA; BATHURST, ROBIN. 1990. *The Telling Image: The Changing Balance between Pictures and Words.* Oxford, UK: Clarendon Press; 1990. 166p. ISBN: 0198583397; LCCN: 90-7598.

D46

DAVIES, MARIE MESSENGER. 1997. *Fake, Fact, and Fantasy. Children's Interpretations of Television Reality.* Mahwah, NJ: Lawrence Erlbaum Associates, Inc.; 1997. 256p.(LEA Communication Series: Media Education). ISBN: 0-8058-2047-7 (pbk.).

D47

DAVIS, BOB; WESSEL, DAVID. *Prosperity: The Coming 20-year Boom and What It Means to You.* Random House/Times Business; 1998. ISBN: 0812928199.

D48

DAVIS, CHARLES, moderator. 1996/1997. Reflections on Our Future. *Bulletin of the American Society for Information Science.* 1997 December/January; 23 (2): 16-23. ISBN: 0095-4403; CODEN: BASICR

D49

DAVIS, DONALD G. 1991. Seventy-Five Years of Education for the Profession: Reflections on the Early Years. *Journal of Education for Library and Information Science.* 1991 Fall/Winter; 32(3/4): 157-177. ISSN: 0748-5786.

D50

DAVIS, DONALD G., ed. 1966-. *Libraries and Culture.* Austin, TX: University of Texas Press; 1966-. Qtly. (Formerly, *Journal of Library History*). ISSN: 0022-2259.

D51

DAVIS, DONALD G.; DAIN, PHYLLIS, eds. 1986. History of Library and Information Science. In: *Library Trends.* 1986 Winter; 34(3): 357-531. (Entire issue on special topic). ISSN: 0024-2594.

D52
DAVIS, DONALD G.; TUCKER, JOHN M., eds. 1989. *American Library History: a Comprehensive Guide to the Literature.* Santa Barbara, CA: ABC-CLIO, Inc.; 1989. 471p. ISBN: 0-87436-142-7. (7150 entries, revising the 1978 bibliography; updated by W. WIEGAND's annual bibliographical essays and J. PASSET's bibliographies in *Libraries and Culture*).

D53
DAVIS, FRED. 1979. *Yearning for Yesterday: A Sociology of Nostalgia.* New York, NY: Free Press; 1979. 146p. ISBN: 0029069505; LCCN: 78-19038.

D54
DAVIS, JUDITH. 1996. *Textbases* (Electronic file). Report accessible at http.www.psgroup.com. Includes *Open Information Systems* feature report summary.

D55
DAVIS, LANCE E.; ENGERMANN, STANLEY. 1987. Cliometrics: The State of the Science (or Is IT Art or, perhaps, Witchcraft?). *Historical Methods.* 1987 Summer; 20(3): 97- 106. ISSN: 0161-5440.

D56
DAVIS, NATALIE ZEMON. 1981. Anthropology and History in the 1980s: The Possibilities of the Past. *Journal of Interdisciplinary History.* 1981; 11: 267-275. ISSN: 0022-1953.

D57
DAVIS, NATALIE ZEMON. 1987. *Fiction in the Archives: Pardon Tales and Their Tellers in Sixteenth-Century France.* Stanford, CA: Stanford University Press; 1987. 217p. ISBN: 0804714126 (pbk.).

D58
DAVIS, NATALIE ZEMON; STARN, RANDOLPH, eds. 1989. Memory and Counter-Memory. In: *Representations.* 1989 Spring; 26. (Entire issue of title topic). ISSN: 0734-6018.

D59
DAVIS, RANDALL; LENAT, DOUGLAS B. 1982. *Knowledge-based Systems in Artificial Intelligence* [Case studies]. New York, NY: McGraw-Hill; 1982. 490p. ISBN: 0070155577.

D60
DAVIS, VIRGINIA; DENLEY, PETER; SPAETH, DONALD; TRAINOR, RICHARD, eds. 1992. *Towards an International Curriculum for History and Computing* St. Katharinen [Göttingen, DEU]: Max-Planck-Institut für Geschichte in Kommission bei Scripta Mercaturae Verlag; 1992. 150p. (Halbgraue Reihe zur historischen Fackinformatik. Serie A: Historische Quellenkunden). See related reference: DAVIS, V. 1993.

D61
DAVIS, VIRGINIA; DENLEY, PETER; SPAETH, DONALD; TRAINOR, RICHARD, eds. 1993. *The Teaching of Historical Computing: An International Framework.* St. Katharinen [Göttingen, DEU]: Max-Planck-Institut für Geschichte in Kommission bei Scripta Mercaturae Verlag; 1993. 137p. (Halbgraue Reihe zur historischen Fackinformatik. Serie A: Historische Quellenkunden, Band 17). ISBN: 3-928134-98-1. See related reference: DAVIS, V. 1992.

D62
DAY, J. M.; WALTON, G.; EDWARDS, C. 1997. The Culture of Convergence. *International Journal of Electronic Library Research.* 1997; 1(1); 43-62.

D63
DAY, LANCE; MCNEIL, IAN. 1996. *Biographical Dictionary of the History of Technology.* London, UK: Longmans; 1996. 844p. ISBN: 0415060427.

D64
DAY, RON. 1997. Paul Otlet's Book and the Writing of Social Space. See reference: BUCKLAND, M.; BELLARDO HAHN, eds. 1997. 310-317.

D65
DE CORTE, ERIK, ed. 1992. *Computer-based Learning Environments and Problem Solving.* Berlin, DEU / New York, NY: Springer-Verlag; 1992. 484p. (NATO ASI (Scientific Affairs Division) series F, Computer and System Sciences, 84). ISBN: 3540550488; LCCN: 92019166.

D66
DE VRIES, JAN. 1984. *European Urbanization, 1500-1800.* Cambridge, MA: Harvard University Press; 1984. 398p. ISBN: 0674270150; LCCN: 84010774.

D67
DEAL, TERRENCE E.; KENNEDY, ALAN A. 1982. *Corporate Cultures: The Rites and Rituals of Corporate Life.* Reading, MA: Addison-Wesley Publishing Co.; 1982. 232 p. ISBN: 0201102773.

D68
DEAN, THOMAS; ALLEN, JAMES; ALOIMONOS, YIANNIS. 1995. *Artificial Intelligence Theory and Practice.* Redwood City, CA: The Benjamin Cummings Publishing Co., Inc.; 1995. 563p. ISBN: 0805325476.

D69
DEARSTYNE, BRUCE. 1993. *The Archival Enterprise. Modern Archival Principles, Practices, and Management Techniques.* Chicago, IL: American Library Association; 1993. 295p. ISBN: 0-8389-0602-8; LCCN: 92-24279. (Note especially, "Electronic Records: A Challenge for Archivists," pp. 222-241).

D70
DEARSTYNE, BRUCE W., ed. 1997 [1998]. State Archival Programs. In: *The American Archivist.* 1997 Spring [1998]; 60 (2): 130-252. (Entire issue on title topic). ISSN: 0360- 9081.

D71
DEAVEN, LARRY L. 1994. Computation and the Genome Project—a Shotgun Wedding. See reference: COOPER, N. G., ed. 1994.

D72
DEBOLLA, PETER. 1986. Disfiguring History. *Diacritics.* 1986; 16(4): 49-58. ISSN: 0300- 7162.

D73
DEBONS, ANTHONY. 1990. Advances in Information Science. In: *Advances in Computers.* 1990; 3: 307-360.

D74
DEBONS, ANTHONY; HORNE, ESTHER E.; CRONENWETH, SCOTT. 1988. *Information Science: An Integrated View.* Boston, MA: G. K. Hall; 1988. 172p. ISBN: 0816118574 (hbk.); 0816118779 (pbk.).

D75
DEBONS, ANTHONY; HORNE, ESTHER E. 1997. NATO Advanced Study Institute of Information Science and Foundations of Information Science. See reference: BUCKLAND, M.; BELLARDO, HAHN, eds. Pt. 2, 1997. 794-803.

D76
DEBONS, ANTHONY., ed. 1974. *Information Science: Search for Identity.* Proceedings of the 1972 NATO Advanced Study Institute in Information Science, Seven Springs, Champion, PA, August 12-20, 1972. New York, NY: M. Dekker; 1974. 491p. ISBN: 0824760964; LCCN: 73085383..

D77
DEBRAY, REGIS. 1987. *Le Pouvir de l'image* [The Power of the Image]. Paris, FR: Gallimard; 1993.

D78
DEBRAY, REGIS. 1996. *Manifestos médiologiques.* Trans. Rauth, Eric. *Media Manifestos: On the Technological Transmission of Cultural Forms.* London, UK / New York, NY: Verso; 1996. 179p. ISBN: 1859849725 (hbk.); 1859840876 (pbk.); LCCN: 95-51442.

D79
DEDIEU, JEAN PIERRE; ROWLAND, ROBERT, eds. 1990. *L'Ordinateur et le Métier d'Historien* [The Computer and the Practice of the Historian]. IVe Congres "History and Computing," 14-16 Septembre 1989. Bordeaux, FR: CNRS and the Maison des Pays Iberiques; 1990.

D80
DEEGAN, MARILYN; TIMBRELL, NICOLA; WARREN, LORRAINE. 1992. *Hypermedia in the Humanities.* Oxford, UK: Oxford Computing Services; and Hull; University of Hull, CALL Unit; 1992. 82p. ISBN: 1858890004 (pbk.); OCLC: 29018549.

D81
DEEGAN, MARILYN; ROBINSON, PETER. [199-]. Computerized Image Projects at Oxford University. See reference: HAMMESE, J., ed. [199-] forthcoming.

D82
DEEMTER, KEES VAN; PETERS, STANLEY, eds. 1996. *Semantic Ambiguity and Underspecification.* Stanford CA: CSLI Publications; c1996. 272p. (CSLI Lecture Notes, 55). ISBN: 1575860295 (hbk.); 1575860287 (pbk.); LCCN: 95049881.

D83
DEETZ, S. 1988. Cultural Studies: Studying Meaning and Action in Organizations. See reference: ANDERSON, J. A., ed. 1988. 11: 335-345.

D84
DEFACIO, BRIAN. 1994. Catastrophe Theory. In: *Encyclopedia of Science and Technology* [electronic file]. New York, NY: McGraw-Hill; 1994. CD-ROM, 3p.

D85
DEFANTI, T.; BROWN, M.; MCCORMICK, B. 1989. Visualization: Expanding Scientific and Engineering Research Opportunities. *Computer.* 1989 August; 22(6): 12-26. ISSN: 0018- 9162.

D86
DEHLER, GORDON E.; WELSH, M. ANN. 1994. Spirituality and Organizational Transformation: Implications for the New Management Paradigm. *Journal of Managerial Psychology.* 1994; 9 (6): 17-26. ISSN: 0268-3946.

D87
DEJONG, GERALD, ed. 1993. *Investigating Explanation-based Learning.* Boston, MA: Kluwer Academic Publishers; c1993. 438p. ISBN: 079239125X (pbk.); LCCN: 90048514.

D88
DEL BIMBO, A.; PALA, P. 1987. Visual Image Retrieval by Elasting [*sic,* Elastic] Matching of User Sketches. *IEEE Transactions on Pattern Analysis and Machine Intelligence.* 1987; 19(2): 121-132. ISSN: 00162-8828.

D89
DELAISSE, L. M. J.; MARROW, JAMES; DEWIT, JOHN. 1977. *Illuminated Manuscripts: The James A de Rothschild Collection at Waddeston Manor.* Fribourg, DEU: National Trust; 1977. (Exemplifies codicological layout and format for manuscript description).

D90
DELANY, PAUL; LANDOW, GEORGE P., eds. 1991. *Hypermedia and Literary Studies.* Cambridge, MA: MIT Press; 1991. 352p. ISBN: 0262041197.

D91
DELATTE, LOUIS. 1961. Un Laboratoire d'analyse statistique des langues anciennes a l'Université de Liège [A Laboratory for the Statistical Analysis of Classical Languages at the University of Liège]. *Antiquite classique.* 1961; 30: 429-444. ISSN: 0770-2817.

D92
DELATTE, LOUIS.; GOVAERTS, S.; DENOOZ, J. 1985. Étude statistique de la proposition subordonée chez quinze auteurs latins [Statistical Study of the subordination proposition in fifty Latin authors]. *Syntaxe et Latin. Actes du IIe Congrès International de Linguistique Latine,* Aix-en-Provence, 28-31 Mars 1983. Aix-en-Provence, FR: CNRS; 1985. 125-278.

D93
DELCOURT, CHRISTIAN. 1992. About Statistical Analysis of Co-occurrence. *Computers and the Humanities.* 1992; 26(1): 21-30. ISSN: 0010-4819.

D94
DELGADO, ROBERTO; LYNCH, BEVERLY P. 1999. Future Historians: Their Quest for Information. *College & Research Libraries.* 1999; 60 (3): 245-259. ISSN: 0010-0870.

D95
DELIA, JESSE G. 1987. Communication Research: A History. In: Berger, Chares R.; Chaffee, Steven H., eds. *Handbook of Communication Science.* Beverly Hills, CA: Sage Publications; 1987. 20-98. ISBN: 0-8039-2199-3.

D96
DELMAS, BRUNO. 1987. Les nouvelles archives. Problèmes de definitions [The New Archives. Problems and Definitions]. In: *Les Nouvelles archives, formation et collecte.* Actes du XXVIIIe Congrès national des Archives francais. Paris, FR: Archives nationales; 1987. (In French).

D97
DELMAS, BRUNO, dir. 1991. *Dictionnaire des archives, de l'archivage aux systèmes d'information, français-anglais-allemand* [Dictionary of Archives, from archival practice to information systems, in French, English, and German]. Paris, FR: Anfor for the Ecole de Chartes; 1991. (Trilingual).

D98
DELMAS, BRUNO. 1992a. Bilan et perspectives de l'archivistique française au seuil du troisième millénaire [Inquiry and Perspectives on French Archival Science at the beginning of the third millennium]. See reference: BUCCI, O., ed. 1992. 81-109.

D99
DELMAS, BRUNO. 1992b. Une fonction nouvelle: Genèse et developement des centres de documentation [A New Function: The Genesis and Development of Documentation Centers]. In: Poulain, Martine, ed. *Histoire des bib-liothèques françaises,* vol. 4: *Les bibliothèques au XXe siècle, 1914-1990.* Paris: Promodis Editions du Cercle de la Librarire; 1992; 178-193. ISBN: 2-7654-0510-7.

D100
DELMAS, BRUNO. 1993. Archival Science and Information Technologies. See reference: MENNE-HARITZ, A., ed. 1993. 168-176.

D101
DELMAS, BRUNO. 1996. Manifesto for a Contemporary Diplomatics: From Institutional Documents to Organized Information. See reference: BLOUIN, F.; DELMAS, B. 1996. 438-452.

D102
DELOUGHRY, THOMAS J. 1994. History, Post-Print. *The Chronicle of Higher Education.* 1994 January 12; 40 (19): A12-21. ISSN: 0009-5982; OCLC: 1554535; GST no.: R-129-572-830.

D103
DEMM, EBERHARD. 1971. Neue Wege in der Amerikanischen Gesichtswissenschaft [New Trends in the American Historical Discipline]. *Saeculum: Jahrbuch für Universalgeschichte* (Freiburg, DEU). 1971; 22(4): 342-76. ISSN: 0080-5319.

D104
DENISON, DANIEL R. 1990. *Corporate Culture and Organizational Effectiveness.* New York, NY: John Wiley & Sons; 1990. 267p. ISBN: 047180021X.

D105
DENLEY, IAN; WHITEFIELD, ANDY. 1998. A Case History in Applying Task Analysis in the Design of a Multimedia Cooperative Document Production System. See reference: MCNEESE, M. D., ed. 1998. 817-831.

D106
DENLEY, PETER 1989. Computing as a Discipline. *Communications of the ACM.*1989; 32 (1): 9-23. ISSN: 0001-0782.

D107
DENLEY, PETER. 1990. The Computer Revolution and "Redefining the Humanities." See reference: MAILL, D. S., ed., 1990.

D108
DENLEY, PETER. 1995. Historical Computing as a New Language for History? See reference: JARTIZ, G. *ET AL.,* eds. 1995. 18-28.

D109
DENLEY, PETER; FOGELVIK, STEFAN; HARVEY, CHARLES, eds. 1989. *History and Computing,* II. Manchester, UK: University of Manchester Press; 1989. 290p. ISBN: 0-7190-2877-9; (pbk) 0-7190-2971-6. (Distributed exclusively in the U.S. by St. Martin's Press).

D110
DENLEY, PETER; HOPKIN, DEIAN. 1995. History and Computing: A Learned Society and a European Perspective. In column "Computers and Software," ed. Janice Reiff. *AHA Perspectives.* 1995 January; 33(1): 1, 7-9. ISSN: 0743-7021.

D111
DENLEY, PETER; HOPKIN, DEIAN, eds. 1987. *History and Computing* [I]. Manchester, UK: University of Manchester Press; 1987. 224p. ISBN: 0-7190-2484-6. (Distributed exclusively in the U.S. by St. Martin's Press).

D112
DENNING, DOROTHY E.; BRANSTAD, DENNIS K. 1996. A Taxonomy for Key Escrow Encryption Systems. *Communications of the ACM* (Association for Computing Machinery). 1996; 39 (4): 34-. ISSN: 0001-0782.

D113
DENNING, DOROTHY E.; DENNING, PETER J., eds. 1998. *Internet Besieged: Countering Cyberspace Scofflaws* [Computer crime]. New York, NY: ACM Press [Association for Computing Machinery] / Reading, MA: Addison Wesley; c1998. 547p. ISBN: 0201308207 (pbk.); LCCN: 07027279.

D114
DENOOZ, J. 1988. Application des méthodes d'analyse factorielle a la frequence des categores grammaticales en latin [The Application of factoral analysis methods to the frequency of grammatical categories in Latin]. *Les Cahiers de l'Analyse des Données.* 1988; 13 (1): 19-40.

D115
DENZIN, NORMAN K.; LINCOLN, YVONNA S., eds. 1994. *Handbook of Qualitative Research.* 5th printing. Thousand Oaks, CA: Sage Publications; 1994. 656p. ISBN: 0-8039-4679-1 (hbk.).

D116
DEOGUN, J. S.; RAGHAVAN, J. S.; SARKAR, A.; SEVER, H. 1997. Data Mining: Research Trends, Challenges, and Applications. See reference: LIN, T.; CERCONE, N., eds. 1997. 9-45.

D117
DERICKSON, ALAN. 1994. Physiological Science and Scientific Management in the Progressive Era: Frederic S. Lee and the Committee on Industrial Fatigue. *Business Historical Review*. 1994 Winter; 69 (4): 483-514. ISSN: 0007-6805.

D118
DEROSE, STEVEN J.; DURAND, DAVID G. 1994. *Making Hypermedia Work: A User's Guide to HyTime*. Boston, MA: Kluwer Academic Publishers; 1994. 384p. ISBN: 0792394321.

D119
DEROSE, STEVEN J.; DURAND, DAVID G.; MYLONAS, E; RENEAR, A. H. 1990. What is Text, Really? *Journal of Computing in Higher Education*. 1990; 1(2): 3-26. ISSN: 1042-1726.

D120
DEROSE, WILLIAM. [1996]. *Structured Information: Navigation, Access, and Control* [electronic file]. Berkeley, CA: University of California; [1996]. Accessible at http://sunsite/berkeley.edu/ FindingAids/EAD/derose. html.

D121
DERRIDA, JACQUES. 1967/1976. *De la Grammatologie*. Paris, FR: Editions de Minuit; 1967. 118p. Spivak, Gayatri, trans. *Of Grammatology*. Baltimore, MD: The Johns Hopkins Press; 1976. ISBN: 0801818419.

D122
DERRIDA, JACQUES. 1967/1978. *L'Écriture et la différence*. Paris: Seuil; 1967. Bass, A., trans. *Writing and Difference*. Chicago, IL: University of Chicago Press; 1978. 342p. ISBN:0710000804; OCLC: 4913312.

D123
DERRIDA, JACQUES. 1977. Signature Event Context. *Glyph*. 1977; 1: 172-197. (Critique of speech-act theory).

D124
DERRIDA, JACQUES. 1981. *La Dissemination*. Trans. as: *Dissemination*. Chicago, IL: University of Chicago Press; 1981. 366p. ISBN: 0226143279.

D125
DERRIDA, JACQUES. 1996. *Mal d'archive*. Trans. as: *Archive Fever: A Freudian Expression*. Lecture at the international colloquium: Memory: The Question of Archives, London, June 5, 1995. Chicago, IL: University of Chicago Press; 1996. 113p. ISBN: 0226143368.

D126
DERVIN, BRENDA. 1977. Use Theory for Librarianship: Communication, not Information. *Drexel Library Quarterly*. 1977; 13: 16-32. ISSN: 0012-6160.

D127
DERVIN, BRENDA. 1983. Information as a User Construct: The Relevance of Perceived Information Needs to Synthesis and Interpretation. In: Ward, S.A.; Reed, L. J., eds. *Knowledge Structure and the Implication for Synthesis and Interpretation*. Philadelphia, PA: Temple University Press; 1983. 155-188. ISBN: 0877223319.

D128
DERVIN, BRENDA. 1989. *Rethinking Communication*. Newbury Park, CA: Sage Publ. With the International Communication Assn.; 1989. 2 vols. ISBN: 0803930321 (vol. 1); 0803930313 (vol. 2).

D129
DERVIN, BRENDA. 1992. From the Mind's Eye of the User: The Sense-Making Qualitative-Quantitative Methodology. In: Glazier, Jack D.; Powell, Ronald R., eds. *Qualitative Research in Information Management*. Englewood, CO: Libraries Unlimited; 1992. 61-84. ISBN: 0-87287-806-6.

D130
DERVIN, BRENDA. 1994. Information — Democracy: An Examination of Underlying Assumptions. *Journal of the American Society for Information Science*. 1994; 45: 369-385. ISSN: 0002-8231.

D131
DESAI, BIPIN C. 1995. *Report of the Metadata Workshop*. Electronic file. Dublin, OH: OCLC; 1995 March. Accessible at http//ww.es.concordia.ca/~faculty/bdesai/test-of-index-systems.html.

D132
DESAI, BIPIN C. 1997. Supporting Discovery in Virtual Libraries. *Journal of the American Society for Information Science*. 1997 March; 48 (3): 189-199. ISSN: 0002-8231.

D133
DESJARDINS, BERTAND. 1979. Introduction des micro-ordinateurs dans l'elaboration des données au Programme de recherche en démographie historique [Introduction to microcomputers for the elaboration of databases for a Research Program in Historical Demography] . *Cahiers québecois de démogaphique*. 1979 December; 8(3): 39-57.

D134
DETEMPLE, WENDELIN. 1989. Future Enhancements for Full-text Databases. *Online Review*. 1989 April; 13(2): 155-60. ISSN: 0309-314x.

D135
DEUTSCH, MICHAEL S. 1982. *Software Verification and Validation: Realistic Project Approaches*. Englewood Cliffs, NJ: Prentice Hall Publ.; 1982. 327p. ISBN: 0138220727.

D136
DEUTSCH, MICHAEL S.; WILLIS, RONALD R. 1980. *Software Quality Engineering: A Total Technical and Management Approach*. Englewood Cliffs, NJ: Prentice Hall Publ.; 1980. 317p. ISBN: 0138232040.

D137
DEVANEY, ROBERT L. 1989. *An Introduction to Chaotic Dynamic Systems*. 2nd ed. Reading, MA: Addison, Wesley, Longman; 1989. (Studies in Nonlinearity series). ISBN: 0-201-13046-7 (hbk.).

D138
DEVANEY, ROBERT L. 1989. *An Introduction to Chaotic Dynamical Systems*. Redwood City, CA: Addison-Wesley; c1989. 336p. ISBN: 0201130467; LCCN: 89-14928.

D139
DEVANEY, ROBERT L. 1992. *A First Course in Chaotic Dynamical Systems. Theory and Experiment*. Reading, MA: Addison, Wesley, Longman; 1992. (Studies in Nonlinearity series). ISBN: 0-201-55406-2 (hbk.).

D140
DEVIJVER, PIERRE A.; KITTLER, JOSEF. 1982. *Pattern Recognition: A Statistical Approach*. London, UK: Prentice Hall; 1982. 448p. ISBN: 0136542360.

D141
DEVLIN, BARRY. 1997. *Data Warehouse: From Architecture to Implementation*. Reading, MA: Addison-Wesley; 1997. 432p. ISBN: 0201964252.

D142
DEVLIN, K. 1991. *Logic and Information*. Cambridge, UK: Cambridge University Press; 1991. 307p. ISBN: 0521410304.

D143
DEWE, MICHAEL. 1987. Local Studies and the New Technology: The British Experience. *Information Development*. 1987 January; 3(1): 23-29. ISSN: 0266-6669.

D144
DEWIRE, DAWNA T. 1994. *Text Management*. New York, NY: McGraw-Hill; 1994. 301p. ISBN: 0070167311.

D145
DEWIT, DIRK. 1994. *The Shaping of Automation: A Historical Analysis of the Interaction between Technology and Organization, 1950-1985*. Roterdam, NL: Uitgeverij/ Hilversum: Verloren; 1994. 409p. ISBN: 9065504141; LCCN: 94-287465.

D146
DEY, IAN. 1993. *Qualitative Data Analysis: A User-friendly Guide for Social Scientists*. London, UK / New York, NY: Routledge; 1993. 285p. ISBN: 0415058511 (hbk.); 041505852X (pbk.); LCCN: 920226082.

D147
DIAMON, ROBERT M. 1989. *Designing and Improving Courses and Curricula in Higher Education: A Systematic Approach*. San Francisco, CA: Jossey-Bass; 1989. 279p. ISBN: 1555421296.

D148
DIAMOND, ROBERT M.; BRONWYN, E. ADAM. 1993. *Recognizing Faculty Work: Reward Systems for the Year 2000*. San Francisco, CA: Jossey-Bass: 1993. 125p. ISBN: 1555426813.

D149
DIAMOND, SHARI SEIDMAN. 1986. Methods for the Empirical Study of Law. In: Lipson, Leon; Wheeler, Stanton, eds. *Law and the Social Sciences*. New York, NY: Russel Sage Foundation; 1986. 740p. ISBN: 0871545284; LCCN: 85-62807.

D150
DIAMOND, SHARI SEIDMAN. 1994. Reference Guide on Survey Research. See reference: FEDERAL JUDICIAL CENTER. 1994. 221-272.

D151
DICK, WALTER; CAREY, LOU. 1978/1991. *The Systematic Design of Instruction*. 3rd ed. Glenview, IL: Scott-Foresman; 1991. ISBN: 0673151220.

D152
DIEDERIKS, HERMAN A.; TJALSMA, H. D. 1993. The Classification and Coding of Occupations of the Past: Some Experiences and Thoughts. See reference: SCHURER, K.; DIEDERIKS, H., eds. 1993. 29-40.

D153
DIEHL, CARL. 1978. *Americans and German Scholarship, 1770-1870.* New Haven, CT: Yale University Press; 1978. 194p. (Yale Historical Publications, 115). ISBN: 0300020791.

D154
DIESING, PAUL. 1971. *Patterns of Discovery in the Social Sciences.* Chicago, IL: Aldine Atherton; 1971. 350p. ISBN: 020230101X.

D155
DIESING, PAUL. 1991. *How does Social Science Work? Reflections on Practice.* Pittsburgh, PA: University of Pittsburgh Press; 1991. 414p. ISBN: 0822936615.

D156
DIGGINS, JOHN PATRICK. 1996. The National History Standards. *American Scholar.* 1996 Autumn; 65 (40: 495-523. ISSN: 0299-3466.

D157
DIGGINS, JOHN PATRICK. 1997. Can the Social Historian Get It Right? *Society.* 1997 Jan.- Feb.; 34(2): 9-20. ISSN: 0147-2011.

D158
DIJK, TEUN A. VAN. 1980. *Textwissenschaft: eine interdisziplinare Einfuhrung* [Text Science: An Interdisciplinary Undertaking]. Munchen, DEU: Deutscher Taschenbuch Verlag; 1980. 284p. (In German).

D159
DIJK, TEUN A. VAN. 1988a. *New Analysis: Case Studies of International and National News in the Press.* Hillsdale, NJ: L. Erlbaum; 1988. 325p. ISBN: 080580046.

D160
DIJK, TEUN A. VAN. 1988b. *News as Discourse.* Hillsdale, NJ: L. Erlbaum Associates; 1988. 200p. ISBN: 0805800654.

D161
DIJK, TEUN A. VAN, ed. 1985a. *Discourse and Communication: New Approaches to the Analysis of Mass Media Discourse and Communication.* Berlin, DEU: W. De Gruyter; 1985. 367p. ISBN: 0899251056.

D162a
DIJK, TEUN A. VAN, ed. 1985b. Discourse and Literature. In: *Critical Theory,* vol. 3. Amsterdam, NL: J. Benjamins Pub. Co.; 1985. 245p. ISBN: 0915027542 (hbk.); 0915027559 (pbk.).

D162b
DIJK, TEUN A. VAN, ed. 1985c. *Handbook for Discourse Analysis.* London, UK: Academic Press; 1985. 4 vols. ISBN: 0127120017; LCCN: 84-6482; OCLC: 10727035.

D163
DILLON, ANDREW. 1994. *Designing Useable Electronic Text: Ergonomic Aspects of Human Information Usage.* London and Bristol, UK: Taylor & Francis; 1994. 195p. ISBN: 0- 7484-0113-X.

D164
DILLON, J. T. 1982. In Pursuit of the Colon: A Century of Scholarly Progress: 1880-1980. *Journal of Higher Education.* 1982: 53: 93-99.

D165
DILLON, LISA Y. 1996/1997. Integrating Nineteenth-Century Canadian and American Census Data Sets. See reference: IGARTUA, J. E., ed. 1996/1997. 381-392.

D166
DILLON, MARTIN. 1993. *Assessing Information on the Internet: Toward Providing Library Services for Computer-mediated Communication.* Dublin, OH: OCLC Office of Research; 1993. 1 vol. OCLC Report no. OR/RR-93/1.

D167
DILLY, RUTH. 1995. *Data Mining. An Introduction* (Electronic file, version 2). Belfast, UK: Parallel Computer Centre, Queens University; 1995. 5 pts. Accessible at http://www.pcc.qub.ac.uk/tec/courses/datamining/ohp/dm-OH

D168
DIODATO, VERGIL P. 1984. Impact and Scholarliness in Arts and Humanities Book Reviews: A Citation Analysis. *Proceedings of the Annual Meeting of the American Society for Information Science.* 1984; 21: 217-221. ISSN: 0147-2011.

D169
DIODATO, VERGIL P., ed. 1996. *Dictionary of Bibliometrics*. Binghamton, NY: Haworth Press; 1996. 185p. ISBN: 1560248521 (hbk.); 156024853X (pbk.).

D170
DOCK, JULIE BATES, ed. 1996. *The Press of Ideas: Readings for Writers on Print Culture and the Information Age*. Bedford, MA: St. Martin's Press; 1996. 679p. ISBN: 0312133197 (pbk.); LCCN: 95-080792.

D171
DODD, SUE A. 1979. Bibliographic References for Numeric Social Science Data Files: Suggested Guidelines. *Journal of the American Society for Information Science*. 1979; 30: 77-82. ISSN: 0002-8231.

D172
DODD, SUE A. 1982. *Cataloguing Machine-Readable Files: An Interpretive Manual*. Chicago, IL: ALA; 1982. 247p. ISBN: 0838903657 (pbk.). See reference: DODD, S.; DANDBERG-FOX, A. 1985. (To be revised and updated further).

D173
DODD, SUE A. 1990. Bibliographic References for Computer Files in the Social Sciences: A Discussion paper. Chapel Hill, NC: Institute for Research in Social Science; 1990 May. 5p. Available from the author: usdodd@uncvm1.bitnet. (Draft discussion paper for IASSIST 1990 meeting based on ICPSR Representatives E-Mail discussion group).

D174
DODD, SUE A.; SANDBERG-FOX, ANN M. 1985. *Cataloging Microcomputer Files: A Manual of Interpretation for AACR2*. Chicago, IL: ALA; 1985. 272p. ISBN: 0838904017; OCLC: 11728340.

D175
DOEBLER, ROLAND WAGNER. 1997. Science-Technology Coupling: The Case of Mathematical Logic and Computer Science. *Journal of the American Society for Information Science*. 1997 February; 48 (2): 171-183. ISSN: 0002-8231.

D176
DOISE, WILLEM. 1993. *The Quantitative Analysis of Social Representations*. Hemel Hemstead, Hertfordshire, UK: Harvester Wheatsheaf; 1993. 170p. (European Monographs in Social Psychology series). ISBN: 0745013473.

D177
DOLBY, J. L.: CLARK, N.; ROGERS, W. H. 1986. The Language of Data: A General Theory of Data. In: *Proceedings of the 18th Symposium on Interfaces*. Ft. Collins, CO: American Statistical Association; 1986. 83-89.

D178
DOLENGA, HAROLD E. 1992. Management Paradigms and Practices in the Information Age. *SAM Advanced Management Journal*. 1992 Winter; 57 (1): 25-29. ISSN: 0036-0805.

D179
DOLLAR, CHARLES M. 1968/1971. Innovation in Historical Research: A Computer Approach. *Computers and the Humanities*. 1968; 3: 139-151. ISSN: 0010-4817. Incorporated into his: *Historian's Guide to Statistics; Quantitative Analysis and Historical Research*. New York, NY: Holt, Rinehart, and Winston; 1971. 332p. Reprinted. Huntington, NY: R. E. Kreiger Pub. Co.; 1974.

D180
DOLLAR, CHARLES M. 1986. *Electronic Records Management and Archives in International Organizations. A RAMP Study with Guidelines*. Paris, FR: UNESCO General Information Programme and UNISIST; 1986. 160p. Available from: UNESCO Federal Information Programme, 7 Place de Fontenoy, 75700 Paris, FR.

D181
DOLLAR, CHARLES M. 1988. The Impact of New Technologies on the National Archives and Federal Government Documentation. *American History: A Bibliographic Review*. 1988; 4: 14-22. ISSN: 0748-6731.

D182
DOLLAR, CHARLES M. 1992. *Archival Theory and Information Technologies: The Impact of Information Technologies on Archival Principles and Methods*. Bucci, Odilo, ed. Ancona, IT: University of Macerata; 1992. 117p. Available from: the Society of American Archivists, T. Brinati, Managing Editor, 600 S. Federal, Suite 504, Chicago, IL 60605).

D183
DOLLAR, CHARLES M. 1993a. Archivists and Records Managers in the Information Age. *Archivaria* (CAN). 1993 Winter; 36: 36-54. ISSN: 0318-6954.

D184
DOLLAR, CHARLES M. 1993b. New Developments and the Implication of Information handling. See reference: MENNE-HARITZ, A., ed. 1993. 56-66.

D185
DOLLAR, CHARLES M. 1994. Electronic Memory and the Redefinition of Preservation. Morelli, Gregoria, ed. *L'Eclisse Della Memoria.* Gius, IT: Laterza and Figli; 1994.

D186
DOLLAR, CHARLES M. 1999. *Authentic Electronic Records: Strategies for Long-term Access.* Chicago, IL: Cohasset Associates; 1999. 248p. (Draft copy provided by author, Dec. 1997). LCCN: 99-75846.

D187
DOLLAR, CHARLES M.; JENSEN, RICHARD. 1971. *Historian's Guide to Statistics: Quantitative Analysis in Historical Research.* 332p. New York: Holt, Rinehart, and Winston; [1971]. ISBN: 0030780209; OCLC: 139225.

D188
DOLLAR, CHARLES M.; SKAGGS, DEBORAH S. 1996. *Using Information Technologies to Build Strategic Collaborations: The State of Alabama as a Test Case.* Chicago, IL: SAA; 1996. 48p.; teaching notes, 9p. (A Case Study in Archives Management).

D189
DOLLAR, CHARLES M.; WILLIAMS, ROBERT. 1995. A New Strategy for Migrating Long-term Electronic Records: Meeting Operational Needs with Less Risk at Lower Costs. In: *Proceedings of the 1995 Managing Electronic Records Conference.* Chicago, IL: Cohasset Associates; 1995.

D190
DONCHE, P. 1990. *HISTCAL,* A Program for Historical Chronology. *History and Computing.* 1990; 2: 97-106. ISSN: 0957-0144.

D191
DONDIS, DONIS A. 1973. *A Primer of Visual Literacy.* Cambridge, MA: MIT Press; 1973. 194p. ISBN: 0262040409; LCCN: 72011579.

D192
DOOLEY, JACKIE, ed. 1997[1998]. Encoded Archival Description (EAD). Papers from the 1995 UC-Berkeley EAD Conference and sessions at the 1996 and 1997 SAA Conferences. In: *The American Archivist.* 1997 [1998]: 60 (3-4). (Entire issue on title topic). ISSN: 0360-9081.

D193
DOORN, PETER. 1992. Data are Sacred, Opinion is Free: The Netherlands Historical Data Archive. *Cahier verniging voor Geschiedenis en Informatica* (NL). 1992; 5: 20-42.

D194
DOORN, PETER. 1993a. History and Computing at the University of Leiden. See reference: DAVIS, DENLEY, SPAETH & TRAINOR, eds., 1993. 91-96.

D195
DOORN, PETER. 1993b. Social Structure and the Labour Market: Occupational Ladders, Pyramids and Onions. See reference: SCHURER, K.; DIEDERIKS, H., eds. 1993. 75-100.

D196
DOORN, PETER. 1994. Opportunities and Pitfalls of the Internet for Historians. See reference: OLDERVOLL, J., ed., 1994. 59-69.

D197
DOORN, PETER. 1996a. Jeschche Raz o Metodologii: Staoje i Prekrasnoje: "Mylnaja Opera" o Neponimanii Mezhdu Istotikami i Modelami [Once More about Methdology—The Bold and Beautiful: A "Soap Opera" about the Misunderstandings among Historians about Models]. See reference: BORODKIN, L.I., ed. 1996. 61-85. Followed by commentaries from 21 reactors, pp. 86-195. (In Russian).

D198
DOORN, PETER. 1996b [199-]. The Bold and the Beautiful: A Soap Opera About Misunderstandings between Historians and Models. See reference: BORODKIN, L., ed. 1996: Abstract of presentation, 114-115; paper [199-forthcoming].

D199
DOORN, PETER, ed. 1990. *NHDA II.* Chronos Historical Data Archive System: A Handbook to a Prototype. In; *Cahier vereniging voor Geschiedenis en Informatica* (NL). Amsterdam, NL: SWIDOC/ Steinmetzarchief; 1990. (Entire issue on title topic).

D200
DOORN, PETER; HELSPER, ERIC; VAN HORIK, RENE; LEENARTS, ELLEN; VERUGDE, CARLO; RIEKERK, ERIK, eds. 1993. *Optical Character Recognition in the Historical Discipline.* Proceedings of an International Workshop organized by: Netherlands Historical Data Archive and Nijmegen Institute for Cognition and

Information. St. Katharinen [Göttingen, DEU]: Max-Planck-Institut für Geschichte in Kommission bei Scripta Mercaturae Verlag; 1993. 165p. (Halbgraue Reihe zur historischen Fackinformatik. Serie A: Historische Quellenkunden, Band 18). ISBN: 3-928134-97-3.

D201
DOORN, PETER; KLUTS, CELESTE; LEENARTS, ELLEN, eds. 1992. Data, Computers, and the Past. *Cahier Vereniging voor Geschiedenis en Informatica* (NL). Hilversum, NL: Uitgeverij Verloren; 1992.

D202
DOORN, PETER K.; LINDBLAD, J. T. 1990. Computertoepassingen in de economische geschiedenis. in het bizonder bij tijdreeksanalyse [Computer Processing in Economic History: Toward a Theory of Analysis]. *Tijdscrift voor Geschiedenis* (NL). 1990; 103: 326-341. (In Dutch). ISSN: 0040-7518.

D203
DORAN, J. E.; HODSON, F. R. [1975]. *Mathematics and Computers in Archeology.* Edinburgh, UK: Edinburgh University Press; [1975]. 381p. ISBN: 0852242506.

D204
DORFMAN, MERLIN; THAYER, RICHARD H., eds. 1996. *Software Engineering.* Los Alamitos, CA: IEEE; 1996. 552p. ISBN: 0-8186-7609-4.

D205
DORN, GEORG W. [1997]. *Deductive, Probabilistic, and Inductive Dependence: An Axiomatic Study in Probability Semantics.* Frankfurt am Main, DEU/New York, NY: P. Lang; c1997. 361p. ISBN: 0820432059; LCCN: 97003777.

D206
DOSSÉ, FRANÇOIS. 1987/1994. *L'histoire en Miettes: Des "Annales" a la "Nouvelle Histoire.* Paris, FR: Editions la Decouverté; 1987. 268p. ISBN: 2707116750. Conroy, Peter V., trans. *New History in France: The Triumph of the "Annales".* Urbana, IL: University of Illinois Press; 1994. 232p. ISBN: 0252019075 (hbk.); 0252063732 (pbk.); LCCN: 93035586.

D207
DOSSÉ, FRANÇOIS. 1991/1997. *Histoire du Structuralisme.* Paris, FR: La Decouverte; 1991. ISBN: 2707120626. Glassman, D., trans. *History of Structuralism.* Minneapolis, MN: University of Minnesota Press; 1997. 2 vols. ISBN: 081662240X (set); LCCN: 96051477.

D208
DOSZKOCS, THOMAS E. 1986. Natural Language Processing in Information Retrieval. *Journal of the American Society for Information Science.* 1986; 37: 161-186. ISSN: 0002-8231.

D209
DOTY, D. HAROLD; GLICK, WILLIAM H. 1994. Typologies as a Unique Form of Theory Building: Toward Improved Understanding and Modeling. *Academy of Management Review.* 1994 April; 19 (2): 230-251. ISSN: 036307425.

D210
DOUGHERTY, DEBORAH; KUNDA, GIDEON. 1990. Photographic Analysis: A Method to Capture Organizational Belief Systems. See reference: GAGLIARDI, P., ed. 1990. 185-205

D211
DOUGLAS, MARY. 1986. *How Institutions Think.* Syracuse, NY: Syracuse University Press; 1986. 146p. ISBN: 0815623690 (hbk.); 08156020665 (pbk.).

D212
DOUGLAS, MARY; HULL, DAVID L. 1992. *How Classification Works: Nelson Goodman among the Social Sciences.* Edinburgh, UK: Edinburgh University Press; 1992. ISBN: 0748603514.

D213
DOUGLAS, SUSAN J. 1987. *Inventing American Broadcasting, 1899-1922.* Baltimore, MD: The Johns Hopkins Press; 1987. 363p. ISBN: 0-8018-3387-6.

D214
DOWLER, LAWRENCE. 1988. The Role of Use in Defining Archival Practice and Principles: A Research Agenda. *American Archivist.* 1988 Winter; 51(1-2): 74-86. (Cf., Commentaries by Jacqueline Goggin, pp. 87-90; and by Anne R. Kenney, pp. 91-95). ISSN: 0360-9081.

D215
DOWLER, LAWRENCE. 1996. Our Edifice at the Precipice. *Library Journal.* 1996 February 15; 121 (3): 118-120. ISSN: 0363-0277.

D216
DOWLER, LAWRENCE, ed. 1996. *Gateways to Knowledge. The Role of Academic Libraries in Teaching, Learning, and Research*. Cambridge, MA: MIT Press; 1996. 250p. ISBN: 0-262-04159-6.

D217
DOWNES, NICK. 1992. *Big Science*. Washington, D.C.: AAAS Press; 1992. 120p. ISBN: 0871685027.

D218
DOXTATER, DENNIS. 1990. Meaning of the Workplace: Using Ideas of Ritual Space in Design. See reference: GAGLIARDI, P., ed. 1990. 107-128.

D219
DOYLE, JON; SANDEWALL, ERIK; TORASSO, PIETRO. 1994. *Principles of Knowledge Representation and Reasoning*. Proceedings of the Fourth International Conference on Knowledge Representation and Reasoning, Bonn, Germany, May 24-27, 1994. San Francisco, CA: Morgan Kaufmann Publ.;1994. 655p. ISBN: 155860328X.

D220
DOYLE, L. B. 1962. Indexing and Abstracting by Association. *American Documentation*. 1962; 13 (4): 378-390. ISSN: 0096-946X; OCLC: 1479779.

D221
DRAKE, BARBARA JOHNSON. 1992. *Use and Data Quality Analysis of a Parcel-based Land Information System for Identification of Potential Remediation Sites*. NY: SUNY College of Environmental Science and Forestry; 1992. 246p. (M.S. thesis; Masters Abstracts, 31/03: 1184). Available from: University Microfilms, Ann Arbor, MI; Order no. AAD13-51700.

D222
DRAY, WILLIAM H. 1957. *Laws and Explanation in History*. London, UK: Oxford University Press; 1957. 174p. See review by POMPER, PHILLIP. 1996.

D223
DRAY, WILLIAM H. 1974. The Historical Explanation of Actions Reconsidered. See reference: GARDINER, P., ed. 1974. 66-89.

D224
DRAY, WILLIAM H. 1989. *On History and Philosophers of History*. Leiden, NL: Brill; 1989. 237p. ISBN: 9004090002.

D225
DRAY. WILLIAM H. 1995. *History as Re-enactment: R. G. Collingwood's Idea of History*. Oxford, UK: Clarendon Press; 1995. 347p. ISBN: 019824293X.

D226
DRAY, WILLIAM H., ed. 1966. *Philosophical Analysis and History*. New York, NY: Harper & Row; 1966. 390p. (Sources in Contemporary Philosophy). LC call no.: D16.8.D76.

D227
DRETSKE, F. I. 1981. *Knowledge and the Flow of Information*. Cambridge, MA: MIT Press; 1981. 273p. ISBN: 0262040638; LCCN: 80-21633. Precis published in *Behavioral and Brain Sciences*. 1983; 6: 55-90. ISSN: 0140-525X.

D228
DREYFUS, HUBERT L. 1992. *What Computers Still Can't Do*. Cambridge, MA: MIT Press; 1992. 409p. ISBN: 0-262-54067-3.

D229
DROYSEN, J. G. 1858/1977. *Grundriss der Historick*. Jena: Fromann. Rev. ed. Leipzig: Veit & Comp.; 1882. Trans., Andrews, Elisha B. *Outline of the principles of history*. Boston, MA: Ginn & Co.; 1897. 122p. 2nd and 3rd eds. as *Historik; Vorlesungen uber enzykopädie und methdologie der geschichte*. Munich, DEU: R. Oldenbourg; 1943 and 1958. Reprinted, Stuttgart, DEU: Fromann-Holzboog; 1977. 7th rev. ed., Hubner, Rudolf, ed. *Historik: Vorlesungen über Enzyklopädie und Methodologie der Geschichte*. Darmstadt, DEU: Wissenschaftliche Buchgesellschaft; 1977. 444p. ISBN: 3486408585.

D230
DRUCKER, PETER F. 1959. *Landmarks of Tomorrow*. New York, NY: Harper; [1959]. 270p. LCCN: 58012444. Reprint with subtitle: *A Report on the New "Post-Modern" World*. New Brunswick, NJ: Transaction Publishers; c1996. ISBN: 1560006226.

D231
DRUCKER, PETER F. 1969. *The Age of Discontinuity: Guidelines to our Changing Society*. New York, NY: Harper & Row; [1969]. 402p. LCCN: 71-007708.

D232
DRUCKER, PETER F. 1980. *Managing in Turbulent Times*. New York, NY: Harper & Row; 1980. 239p. ISBN: 0060110945.

D233
DRUCKER, PETER F. 1985. *Innovation an Entrepreneurship: Practice and Principles*. New York, NY: Harper & Row; 1985. 277p. ISBN: 0060154284.

D234
DRUCKER, PETER F. 1986. *The Frontiers of Management: Where Tomorrow's Decisions are being Shaped Today*. New York, NY: Truman Talley Books; 1986. 368p. ISBN: 0525244638.

D235
DRUCKER, PETER F. 1989. *The New Realities. In Government and Politics, in Economics and Society, in Business, Technology and World View*. New York, NY: Harper and Row; 1989. 226p. ISBN: 0060161299.

D236
DRUCKER, PETER F. 1993. *Post-Capitalist Society*. New York, NY: Harper Business; 1993. 232p. ISBN: 0887306209.

D237
DUBLIN, ROBERT. 1969/1978. *Theory Building*. New York, NY: Free Press; 1969. Rev. ed., 1978. 304p. ISBN: 0-02-907620-X (hbk.); LCCN: 77-90010.

D238
DUBOIS, DIDIER; PRADE, HENRI. 1988. *Théorie des possibilités*. Collaboration with Farreny, Henri; Martin-Clouaire, Roger; Testemale, Claudette. Trans. Harding, E. F. *Possibility Theory: An Approach to Computerized Processing of Uncertainty*. New York, NY: Plenum Press; c1988. 263p. ISBN: 0306425203; LCCN: 87032179.

D239
DUBOIS, DIDIER.; PRADE, HENRI. 1990. Rough Fuzzy Sets and Fuzzy Rough Sets. *International Journal of General Systems*. 1990; 17: 191-209. ISSN: 0308-1079.

D240
DUBOIS, DIDIER; PRADE, HENRI. 1992. Gradual Inference Rules in Approximate Reasoning. *Information Sciences*. 1992; 61 (1-2): 103-122. ISSN: 1069-0115.

D241
DUBOIS, DIDIER; PRADE, HENRI.; ROSSAZZA, J.-P. 1991. Vagueness, Typicality, and Uncertainty in Class Hierarchies. *International Journal of Intelligence Systems*. 1991; 6: 167-183.

D242
DUBY, GEORGES. 1982. Geschichte und Geschichteswissenschaft [History and Historical Science]. In: *Suhrkamp Taschenbuch Wissenschaft*, 409. Frankfurt am Main, DEU: Suhrkamp; 1982. (In German; translation of *L'histoire et des méthodes*). ISBN: 3518280090.

D243
DUBY, GEORGES. 1994. *Histoire Continue*. Trans as: *History Continues*. Chicago, IL: University of Chicago Press; 1994. 149p. ISBN: 0226167775; LCCN: 94-3893.

D244
DUBY, GEORGES, ed. 1961. *L'histoire et ses méthodes* [History and its Methods]. Paris, FR: Gallimard-Pleiade; 1961. (In French).

D245
DUCHEIN, MICHEL. 1983. Theoretical Principles and Practical Problems of *Respect des Fonds* in Archival Science. *Archivaria* (CAN). 1983 Summer; 16: 64-81. ISSN: 0318-6954.

D246
DUCROT, OSWALD; TODOROV, TZVETAN. 1972. *Dictionnaire Encyclopédique des Sciences du Language* [Encyclopedic Dictionary of the Sciences of Language]. Paris, FR: Editions du Seuil; 1972. 469p. (In French).

D247
DUFF, WENDY M. 1996a. *The Influence of Literary Warrant on the Acceptance and Credibility of the Functional Requirements for Recordkeeping*. School of Library and Information Science. Pittsburgh, PA: University of Pittsburgh; 1996. (Ph.D. Dissertation). Available from: University Microfilms, Ann Arbor, MI.

D248
DUFF, WENDY M. 1996b. Reliable Evidence: A Research Project funded by the NHPRC. *Archivaria*. 1996 Fall; 42: 28-45. ISSN: 0318-6954.

D249

DUFF, WENDY M. 1997. Compiling Warrant in Support of the Functional Requirements for Recordkeeping. See reference: TRAVIS, I., ed. 1997. 12-16.

D250

DUFF, WENDY M.; TOMS, ELAINE G. 1992. *HyperRad*: An Hypertext Application for the Effective and Efficient Use of the Rules for Archival Description. *Archivaria* (CAN). 1992; 34: 252-265. ISSN: 0318-6954.

D251

DUFF, WENDY M.; TOMS, ELAINE G. 1993. *HyperRad: An Automated Text Retrieval Hypertext Prototype for the Rules of Archival Description.* Ottawa, CAN: Canadian Council of Archives, August 1994. (Project report).

D252

DUFF, WENDY M.; TOMS, ELAINE G. 1995. *HyperRAD*: A Case Study in Developing Electronic Manuals for Archives. *American Archivist.* 1995 Summer; 58 (2):242-256. ISSN: 0350-9081.

D253

DUGGAN MARY KAY. 1992. Access to Sound and Image Databases. See reference: STONE, S.; BUCKLAND, M., eds. 1992. 83-97.

D254

DUHAMMEL-AMADO, CLAUDIE. 1995 [1998-1999]. *La famille aristocratique languedociénne. Parenté et patrimonie dans les viscomtes de Béziers et d'Agde (900-1170)* [An Aristocratic Family of Languedoc: Parentage and Patrimony of the Viscounts of Béziers and Adge]. Université de Paris IV-Sorbonne, February 1995. These d'État (Doctoral dissertation) completed under the name C. AMADO. Toulouse, FR: Framespa; [forthcoming, 1998-1999]. 2 vols. (In French).

D255

DUHAMMEL-AMADO, CLAUDIE. 1997. Construire une généalogia: faire flèche de tout bois [To Constuct a Geneaology: Making a Straight Arrow from all the Wood (e.g., which wood to use to make a straight arrow shaft? —an untranslatable turn of phrase playing on the French expression "Tout bois n'est pas bon à faire" which means that one must know how to distinguish between people)]. See reference: BOURIN, M.; CHAREILLE, P., eds. 1997. 4-11. (In French).

D256

DUNCAN, JAMES H. 1982. *Radio in the United States, 1976-1982; a Statistical History.* Kalamazoo, MI: Duncan Media Productions; 1982. 192p. LC call no.: HE8698.D92.

D257

DUNCAN, JAMES S.; LEY, DAVID, eds. 1993. *Place / Culture / Representation.* London, UK: Routledge; 1993. 341p. ISBN: 041509450 (hbk.); 0415094518 (pbk.).

D258

DUNCAN, OTIS D. 1975. *Introduction to Structural Equation Models.* New York, NY: Academic Press; 1975. 180p. ISBN: 0122241509.

D259

DUNCAN, OTIS D. 1984. *Notes of Social Measurement: Historical and Critical.* New York, NY: Sage Publications; 1984. ISBN: 0871542196.

D260

DUNK, JULIE; RAHTZ, SEBASTIAN. 1989. Strategies for Gravestone Recording. See reference: DENLEY, P., *ET AL.*, eds., 1989. 72-80.

D261

DUNN, ROBERT G. 1998. *Identity Crises: A Social Critique of Postmodernity.* Minneapolis, MN: University of Minnesota Press; 1998. 291p. ISBN: 0816630720 (hbk); 0816630739 (pbk.).

D262

DUNN, ROSS E. 1985. Periodization and Chronological Coverage in a World History Course. In: Konvitz, Josef W., ed. *What Americans Should Know: Western Civilization or World History?* Proceedings of a Conference at Michigan State University, April 21-23, 1985 (pp. 129-140). Lansing, MI: Michigan State University; 1985. 270p. LCCN: 86-62260.

D263

DUNNETTE, M. D.; HOUGH, L., eds. 1990/1992. *Handbook of Industrial and Organizational Psychology.* Palo Alto, CA: Consulting Psychologists Press; 1990. 2 vols. 2nd ed., 1992. 3 vols. ISBN: 0891060417 (hbk.); 0891060421 (pbk.).

D264
DURANCE, CYNTHIA J., ed. 1990. *Management of Recorded Information: Converging Disciplines.* Proceedings of the 1989 International Council on Archives, Symposium on Current Records, held at the National Archives of Canada, Ottawa 15-17 May, 1998. New York, NY: K. G. Saur; 1990. 218p. ISBN: 3598108974; LCCN: 90-175457; OCLC: 22116028.

D265
DURANTI, LUCIANA. 1989-1990. Diplomatics: New Uses for an Old Science. In: *Archivaria.* 1989; 28: 7-27; 29: 4-17; 30: 4-20; 31: 10-35; 32: 6-24; 33: 6-24. ISSN: 0318-6954.

D266
DURANTI, LUCIANA. 1989a. Is There a Records Management Theory? In: *Proceedings of the 35th Conference of ARMA International* (November 5-8, 1989). Washington, D.C: ARMA; 1989. 814-822. ISBN: 0933887434.

D267
DURANTI, LUCIANA. 1989b. The Odyssey of Records Management. *Records Management Quarterly.* Pt. I: 1989 July; 23(3): 3-6, 8-11. Pt. II: 1989 October; 23(4): 3-6, 8-11. ISSN: 0034-172X.

D268
DURANTI, LUCIANA. 1993. The Archival Body of Knowledge: Archival Theory, Method, and Practice, and Graduate and Continuing Education. *Journal of Education for Library and information Science.* 1993 Winter; 34(1): 8-24. ISSN: 0748-5786.

D269
DURANTI, LUCIANA. 1995. Reliability and Authenticity: Their Concepts and Implications. *Archivaria* (CAN). 1995 Spring; 39: [1-12]. ISSN: 0318-6954.

D270
DURANTI, LUCIANA. 1997a. The Archival Bond. See reference: BEARMAN, D.; TRANT, J., eds. 1997. 213-218.

D271
DURANTI, LUCIANA. 1997b. Archival Science. *Encyclopedia of Library and Information Science.* New York, NY: Dekker; 1997; 59: 1-19. ISBN: 0-8247-2045-8.

D272
DURANTI, LUCIANA; EASTWOOD, TERRY. 1995. Protecting Electronic Evidence: A Progress Report on a Research Study and its Methodology. *Archivi & Computer* (IT). 1995: 3: [200- 214]. ISSN: 1121-2462.

D273
DURANTI, LUCIANA; MACNIEL, HEATHER. 1996. The Protection of the Integrity of Electronic Records: An Overview of the UBC-MAS Research Project. *Archivaria* (CAN). 1996 Fall; 42: 46-67. ISSN: 0318-6954.

D274
DURANTI, LUCIANA; MACNIEL, HEATHER; UNDERWOOD, WILLIAM. 1996. Protecting Electronic Evidence: A Second Progress Report on a Research Study and its Methodology. *Archivi & Computer* (IT). 1996; 6(10): 37-67. ISSN: 1121-2462.

D275
DURKHEIM, ÉMILE. 1982. *Regles de la méthode sociologique.* Trans., Lukes, Steven. *The Rules of Sociological Method; and selected texts on Sociology and its Method.* London, UK: Macmillan Press; 1982. 264p. ISBN: 0333280717 (hbk.); 0333280725 (pbk.).

D276
DURR, WILLIAM T. 1981. Baltimore Regional Institutional Studies Center. See reference: MCCRANK, L., ed. 1981. 73-84.

D277
DURR, WILLIAM T. 1984. Some Thoughts and Designs about Archives and Automation. *The American Archivist.* 1984; 47(3): 271-289. ISSN: 0360-9081.

D278
DURR, WILLIAM T.; ROSENBERG, PAUL M. 1977. *The Urban Information Thesaurus. A Vocabulary for Social Documentation.* Westport, CT: Greenwood Press for the Baltimore Regional Institutional Studies Center, University of Baltimore; 1977. 375p. ISBN: 0-8371-9483-0.

D279
DUTTON, JANE E.; DUKERICH, JANET M.: HARQUAIL, CELIA V. 1994. Organizational Images and Member Identification. *Administrative Science Quarterly.* 1994 June; 39 (2): 239-263. ISSN: 0001-8392.

D280
DUSZAK, ANNA, ed. 1997. *Culture and Style in Academic Discourse.* New York, NY: Mouton de Gruyter; 1997. ISBN: 3110152495; LCCN: 97-16350.

D281
DYKE, CHARLES. 1988. *The Evolutionary Dynamics of Complex Systems.* Oxford, UK: Oxford University Press; 1988. 161p. ISBN: 0195951769; LCCN: 87-20394. About Socio-biology.

D282
DYKE, CHARLES. 1990. Strange Attraction, Curious Liaison: Clio meets Chaos. *Philosophical Forum.* 1990; 21: 369-392. ISSN:0031-806X.

-E-

E1
EAMES, CHARLES; EAMES, RAY. 1990. *A Computer Perspective: Background to the Computer Age.* New edition. Cambridge, MA: Harvard University Press; 1990. 174p. ISBN: 0-674-15626-9.

E2
EARMAN, JOHN. 1986. *A Primer on Determinism.* Amsterdam, NL: Kluwer Academic Press; 1986. 273p. (University of Western Ontario Series on Philosophy of Science). ISBN: 9027722404.

E3
EARMAN, JOHN. 1992. *Inference, Explanation, and other Philosophical Frustrations: Essays in the Philosophy of Science.* Berkeley, CA: University of California Press; 1992. 301p. (Pittsburgh Series in Philosophy and History of Science, 14). ISBN: 052007757773.

E4
EARMAN, JOHN; GLYMOUR, CLARK N; STACHEL, JOHN J., eds. 1977. *Foundations of Space-Time Theories.* Conferences on Space-Time Theories sponsored by the Minnesota Center for Philosophy of Science in Minneapolis, MN, May 9-11, 1974 and Boston University, June 3-5, 1974. Minneapolis, MN: University of Minnesota Press; 1974. 459p. ISBN: 0816608075.

E5
EARNSHAW, RAE A.; WISEMAN, NORMAN 1992. *An Introductory Guide to Scientific Visualization.* Berlin, DEU/ New York, NY: Springer-Verlag; 1992. 156p. ISBN: 0-387- 54664-2.

E6
EASTERBY, RONALD; ZWAGA, HARM, eds. 1984. *Information Design: The Design and Evaluation of Signs and Printed Material.* NATO Conference on Visual Perception of Information, The Netherlands, 1978. Chichester, UK: John Wiley & Sons, Ltd.; 1984. 588p. ISBN: 0471104310; LCCN: 82-17408.

E7
EASTHOPE, GARY. 1974. *A History of Social Research Methods.* London, UK: Longman; 1974. 169p. ISBN: 0582484804 (hbk.); 0582484812 (pbk.).

E8
EASTON PRESS. 1994. *Treasures of the Library of Congress.* Norwalk, CT: The Easton Press; 1994. Pamphlet, 13p. Available form Easton Press, 47 Richards Ave., Norwalk, CT 06857.

E9
EASTWOOD, TERRY. 1988. Nurturing Archival Education in the University. *The American Archivist.* 1988; 51 (3): 228-252. ISSN: 0360-9081.

E10
EASTWOOD, TERRY, ed. 1992. *The Archival Fonds; from Theory to Practice.* Ottawa, CA: Bureau of Canadian Archivists Planning Committee on Descriptive Standards; 1992. (In French and English). ISBN: 0-9690797-6-1.

E11
EATON, FYNNETTE. 1993. The National Archives and Electronic Records for Preservation. See reference: MOHLENRICH, J., ed. 1993. 41-62.

E12
EATON, FYNNETTE. 1994. Preserving Electronic Records: Not the Easiest Task. In: Kobler, Benjamin; Hariharan, P. C., eds. *Third NASA Goddard Conference on Mass Storage Systems and Technologies.* Atkinson, WI: Highsmith Press; 1993. 99-102. (NASA conference publication: N94-31964).

E13
ECKERT, WALTAR J. 1984. *Punched Card Methods in Scientific Computation.* Cambridge, MA: MIT Press; 1984. 136p. (First published: New York, NY: Columbia University Press; 1940).

E14
ECO, UMBERTO. 1976. *A Theory of Semiotics*. Bloomington, IN: University of Indiana Press; 1976. 354p. ISBN: 0253359554; LCCN: 74-22833; OCLC: 1195082.

E15
ECONOMIC AND SOCIAL RESEARCH COUNCIL DATA ARCHIVE (ESRC). 1992. *User Guide and Catalogue*. Essex, UK: University of Essex, ESRC; 1992-. Catalogue updated periodically; see references: SCHURER,K., 1992; ANDERSON, S., 1992.

E16
ECONOMIST NEWSPAPER LTD. 1996. Nations and Theory Past: The Uses and Abuses of History. *The Economist* (UK). 1996 Dec. 21; 341 (7997): 71-75. ISSN: 0013-0613.

E17
EDELMAN, S.; FLASH, T. 1987. A Model of Handwriting. *Biological Cybernetics*. 1987; 57: 25-36. ISSN: 0340-1200.

E18
EDELMAN, S.; FLASH, T.; ULLMAN, S. 1990. Reading Cursive Handwriting by Alignment of Letter Prototypes. *International Journal of Computer Vision*. 1990; 5(3): 303-331. ISSN: 0920-5691.

E19
EDEN, COLIN; ACKERMANN, FRAN; CROPPER, STEVE. 1992. The Analysis of Cause Maps. *Journal of Management Studies*. 1992 May; 29(3): 310-325. ISSN: 0022-2380.

E20
EDGAR, GERALD A., ed. 1993. *Classics on Fractals*. Studies in Nonlinearity. Reading, MA: Addison-Wesley; 1993. 366p. ISBN: 0201587017.

E21
EDGAR, WILLIAM J. 1980. *Evidence*. Lanham, MD: University Press of America; 1980. 459p. ISBN: 0819112925 (hbk.); 0819112933 (pbk.).

E22
EDWARDS, DAVID. 1995. *Introduction to Graphical Modeling*. New York, NY: Springer- Verlag; 1995. 274p. ISBN: 0387944839.

E23
EDWARDS, DEREK. 1992. *Discursive Psychology*. Newbury Park, CA/London, UK: Sage Publications; 1992. 200p. ISBN: 08039984421 (hbk.); 0803998443X (pbk.).

E24
EDWARDS, GREGG; SNYDER, DAVID P. 1984. *Future Forces: An Association Executive's Guide to a Decade of Change and Choice*. Washington, D.C.: Foundation of the American Society of Association Executives; 1984. 109p. LCCN: 88-180106; OCLC: 11560699.

E25
EDWARDS, GREGG: SNYDER, DAVID PEARCE. 1992. *America in the 1990's. An Economy in Transition, a Society Under Stress*. Washington, D.C.: Es-Press for the American Society for Association Executives; 1992. 26p. (Updates *Future Forces*, 1984). Available from authors: D. Snyder Family Enterprise, 8628 Garfield St., Bethesda, MD 20818-6704; G. Edwards, dir., Academy for Advanced Strategic Studies, 1647 Lamont St. NW, Washington, DC 20010-2796.

E26
EDWARDS, GREGG; SNYDER, DAVID PEARCE. 1997 [199-]. *Roller Coaster 2000. Forces Re-shaping Daily Life and Work in America, 1990 to 2010*. Bethesda, MD: Snyder Family Enterprise; 1997 [forthcoming 199-8].

E27
EDWARDS, PAUL N. 1988. *The Closed World: Computers and the Politics of Discourse*. Santa Cruz, CA: University of California, Santa Cruz; 1988. 301p. (Ph.D. dissertation; *DAI*, vol. 49/12-A: 3849). Available from: University Microfilms, Ann Arbor, MI (Order no. AAD89-05620).

E28
EELLS, ELLERY. 1991. *Probabilistic Causality*. Cambridge Studies in Probability, Induction, and Decision Theory. Cambridge, UK: Cambridge University Press; 1991. 413p. ISBN: 0521392446; LCCN: 90039238.

E29
EEROLA, MERVI. 1994. *Probabilistic Causality in Longitudinal Studies*. New York, NY: Springer-Verlag; c1994. 131p. (Lecture Notes in Statistics series, 92). ISBN: 0387943676; LCCN: 94031763.

E30
EFRON, B.; TIBSHIRANI, R. 1991. Statistical Data Analysis in the Computer Age. *Science*. 1991; 253: 390-395. ISSN:0036-8075.

E31
EGEREVA, T. A. 1976. Otraslevaya informatsionnaya sluzba i ee vliyanie na organizatsiyu spravochno-informat-sionnogo obsluzhivaniya spetsialistov (na primere Chemical Abstracts Service) [A Specialized Information Service and Its Influence on the Organization of Reference and information Work with Specialists (based on Chemical Abstracts Service)]. *Nauchnyo Teknicheskie Biblioteki SSSR*. 1976; 1: 23-32.

E32
EGGHE, LEO; RONALD ROUSSEAU. 1990. *Introduction to Informetrics: Quantification methods in Library, Documentation, and Information Science*. Amsterdam, NL / New York, NY: Elsevier, Science Publishers; 1990. 450p. ISBN: 0444884939; LCCN: 90-3250; OCLC: 21376663.

E33
EGGHE, LEO; RONALD ROUSSEAU. 1995. Generalized Success-Breeds-Success Principle Leading to Time-dependent Distributions. *Journal of the American Society for Information Science*. 1995; 46: 426-435. ISSN: 0002-8231; CODEN: AISJB6.

E34
EGGLESTON, KATHRYN K; BHAGAT, RABI S. 1993. Organizational Contexts and Contingent Leadership Roles: A Theoretical Exploration. *Human Relations*. 1993 October; 46 (10): 1177-1192. ISSN: 0018-7267.

E35
EHRLICH, HEYWARD. 1991. An Interdisciplinary Bibliography for Computers and the Humanities Courses. *Computers and the Humanities*. 1991; 25 (5): 315-327. ISSN: 0010- 4817.

E36
EICHER, JOANNE B., ed. 1995. *Dress and Ethnicity. Change across Space of Time*. London, UK: Berg; 1995. 256p. ISBN: 0-85496-87902 (hdk.); 1-85973-003-5 (pbk.).

E37
EISENBERG, DANIEL. 1992. History of Word Processing. See reference: KENT, A., ed., 1992. 42: 268-278.

E38
EISENBERG, M. B. 1988. Measuring Relevance Judgements. *Information Processing & Management*. 1988; 24(4): 272-289. ISSN: 0306-4573.

E39
EISENSTEIN, ELIZABETH. 1979/1980. *The Printing Press as an Agent of Change: Communication and Cultural Transformation in Early Modern Europe*. Cambridge, UK: Cambridge University Press; 1979. 2 vols. Combined as one paperback volume, 1980. ISBN: 0-521-21967-1; 0-521-21967-8 (separate vols.); 0-521-22044-0 (set); 0-521-29955-1 (pbk.).

E40
EISNER, MICHAEL. 1991. The ARBOR Information System for Classical Archeology and History of Art (or Tree Structures as Documents). See reference: BEST, H., *ET AL.*, eds., 1991. 36-41.

E41
ELECTRONIC ARCHIVES DESCRIPTION (EAD). [1996-]. *EAD Homepage* [electronic file]. Washington, D.C.: Library of Congress; [1996-]. Accessible at http://lcweb.loc.gov/ loc/standards/ead.

E42
ELEY, GEOFF; NIELD, KETIH. 1995. Starting Over: The Present, the Post-Modern and the Moment of Social History. *Social History*. 1995; 20: 355-364. ISSN: 0022-4529.

E43
ELIAS, A. W. 1987. Fifty Years of ASIS—Thirty-Eight Years of *JASIS*. *Journal of the American Society for Information Science*. 1987 September; 38(5): 385-386. ISSN: 0002- 8231.

E44
ELIAS, NORBERT. 1978. *Was ist Soziologie?* Trans.: *What is Sociology?* London, UK: Hutchinson; 1978. 187p. ISBN: 0091331102 (hbk.); 0091331110 (pbk.).

E45
ELIAS, NORBERT. 1978/1994. *Über den Prozess der Zivilisation*. Trans as: *The Civilizing Process*. New York, NY: Urizen Books; 1978. (American ed. was initially entitled: *The History of Manners*). Jephcott, Edmund, trans. Oxford, UK: Oxford University Press; 1994. 2 vols. in 1.

E46
ELIAS, NORBERT. 1983. *Die höfische Gesellschaft*. Trans as: *The Court Society*. Jephcott, Edmund, trans. New York, NY & Oxford, UK: Blackwell; 1983. 301p. ISBN: 0631196706.

E47

ELIAS, NORBERT. 1986. *The Quest for Excitement: Sport and Leisure in the Civilizing Process*. Oxford, UK: Blackwell; 1986. 313p. ISBN: 0631146547.

E48

ELIAS, NORBERT. 1991. *The Symbol Theory*. London, UK/Newbury Park, CA: Sage Publications; 1991. 147p. ISBN: 0803984189 (hbk.); 08039984197 (pbk.).

E49

ELIAS, NORBERT. 1991. *La société des individus* [The Society of Individuals]. Paris FR: Fayard; 1991.

E50

ELIAS, NORBERT. 1992. *Time: An Essay*. Oxford, UK: Blackwell; 1992. 216p. ISBN: 0631157980.

E51

ELIAS, NORBERT. 1996. *Studien über die Deutschen*. Trans as: *The Germans: Power Struggles and the Development of Habitus in the nineteenth and Twentieth Centuries*. Cambridge, UK: Polity Press; 1996. 494p. ISBN: 0745609953.

E52

ELIAS, NORBERT. 1998. *On Civilization, Power, and Knowledge: Selected Writings*. Mennell, Stephen; Goudsblom, Johan, eds. Chicago, IL: University of Chicago Press; 1998. 302p. (Heritage of Sociology series). ISBN: 0226204316.

E53

ELIAS, NORBERT; MARTINS, HERMINO; WHITELY, RICHARD, eds 1982. *Scientific Establishments and Hierarchies*. Dortrecht, NL; D. Reidel Pub. Co.; 1982. 368p. (Sociology of the Sciences, 6). ISBN: 9027713227 (hbk.); 90277132335 (pbk.).

E54

ELKIN, JUDITH. 1992. Information UK 2000: Response on Behalf of the Education Committee of the Library Association. *Personal Training and Education* (UK). 1992; 9(1): 18-24. ISSN: 0264-8466.

E55

ELL, PAUL; BARTLEY, KEN; LEE, JANETTE. 1996 [199-]. The Future of Large Historical Databases. See reference: BORODKIN, L., ed. 1996: English abstract of presentation, 122-123; paper in Russian [199- forthcoming].

E56

ELLIS, DAVID. 1989. A Behavioural Approach to Information Retrieval System Design. *Journal of Documentation* (UK). 1989; 45: 171-212. ISSN: 0022-0418.

E57

ELLIS, DAVID. 1991. Hypertext: Origins and Use. *International Journal of Information Management*. 1991 March; 11(1): 5-13. ISSN: 0268-4012.

E58

ELLIS, DAVID; ALLEN, DAVID; WILSON, TOM. 1999. Information Science and Information Systems: Conjunct Subjects Disjunct Disciplines. See reference: BATES, M., ed. 1999. Pt. 2: 1095-1107.

E59

ELLIS, JUDITH, ed. 1993. *Keeping Archives*. Victoria, AU: D. W. Thorpe and Australian Assn. of Archivists, Inc.; 1993. ISBN: 1-875589-15-5.

E60

ELOQUENT SYSTEMS, INC. [1996-]. *GENCAT* [software]. See http://gencat.eloquent- systems.com.

E61

ELSNER, JOHN; CARDINAL, ROGER, eds. 1994. *The Cultures of Collecting*. Cambridge, MA: Harvard University Press / London, UK: Realktion Books; 1994. 312p. ISBN: 098462507.

E62

ELTON, GEOFFREY R. 1969. *The Practice of History*. New York, NY: Fontana; [c. 1967], 1969. 223p. ISBN: 0006319238; OCLC: 25444691.

E63

EMMER, MICHELE, ed. 1993. *The Visual Mind. Art and Mathematics*. Cambridge, MA: Leonardo Book; 1993. 294p. ISBN: 0-262-05048-X. Distributed by MIT Press.

E64

EMORY UNIVERSITY. WORLD WIDE WEB PROJECT. [1993-]. Citation Formats. In: *Field Guide to Sources On, About, and On the Internet*. Accessible at: http://www.cc.emory.edu //WHSCL/citation.html (1996).

E65
ENDRES-NIGGEMEYER, BRIGITTE; NEUGEBAUER, ELISABETH. 1998. Professional Summarizing: No Cognitive Simulation without Observation. *Journal of the American Society for Information Science.* 1998; 49 (6):486-506. ISSN: 0002-8231.

E66
ENGELBART, DOUGLAS C. ; ENGLISH, WILLIAM K. 1988. A Research Center for Augmenting Human Intellect. Reprint from: Gried, Irene, ed. *Computer-Supported Cooperative Work: A Book of Readings.* San Mateo, CA: Morgan Kaufmann; 1988. ISBN: 0-934613-57-5. Cf., *A Research Center for Augmenting Human Intellect.* Video, 1994. Available from: Bootstrap Institute, 6505 Kaiser Dr., Fremont, CA 94555.

E67
ENGELSMAN, E. C.; VAN RAAN, A. F. J. 1991. *Mapping Technology. A First Exploration of Knowledge Diffusion amongst Fields of Technology.* The Hague, NL: Netherlands Ministry of Economic Affairs; 1991. 71p. (Beleidsstudies technologie economie, 15). ISSN: 0923-3164.

E68
ENGERMANN, STANLEY. 1977. Recent Developments in American Economic History. *Social Science History.* 1977; 1: 72-89. ISSN: 0145-5532.

E69
ENGESTROM, YRJO; MIDDLETON, DAVID. 1996. *Cognition and Communication at Work.* Cambridge, UK: Cambridge University Press; 1996. 346p. ISBN: 0521441048.

E70
ENGESTROM, YRJO; MIETTINEN, REIJO; PUNAMAKI, RAIJA-LEENA, eds. 1999. *Perspectives on Activity Theory.* International Congress for Research on Activity Theory (2nd), Lahti, Finland. Cambridge, UK / New York, NY: Cambridge University Press; c1999. 462p. (Learning in Doing series). ISBN: 0521431271 (hbk.); 052143730X (pbk.); LCCN: 97040981.

E71
ENMARK, ROMULO, ed. 1992. *Humanities Information—Cultural Heritage and Humanities Research: Problems and Possibilities in Light of New Technology.* London, UK: British Library; 1992. 197p. (British Library Research Report, 6075). OCLC: 27906551. Cf., same title with subtitle: Proceedings of the Fourth Anglo-Nordic Seminar, held in Copenhagen, DK, 7-9 June 1991. Esbo, FI: NORDINFORs Secretariat; 1992. ISBN: 9514759451; LCCN: 92-227229; OCLC: 27384857.

E72
ENNALS, RICHARD. 1985. *Artificial Intelligence: Applications to Logical Reasoning and Historical Research.* Computers and Their Applications series. Chichester, UK: Ellis Horwood Research. 172p. ISBN: 0-470-20181-9.

E73
ENNALS, RICHARD; GARDIN, JEAN-CLAUDE, eds. 1990. *Interpretation in the Humanities: Perspectives from Artificial Intelligence.* London: The British Library; 1990. 367p. (Library and Information Research Report, 71). ISBN: 0712331867; LCCN: 90- 115622; OCLC: 23770982.

E74
ENSER, P. G. B. 1995. Progress in Documentation: Pictorial Information Retrieval. *Journal of Documentation.* 1995: 51(2): 126-170. ISSN: 0022-0418.

E75
ENTWISTLE, NOEL J. 1981. *Styles of Learning and Teaching.* London, UK: J. Wiley; 1981.

E76
ENTWISTLE, NOEL J., ed. 1990. *Handbook of Educational Ideas and Practices.* London, UK / New York, NY: Routledge; 1990. 1140p. ISBN: 0414030611; LCCN: 89010482.

E77
EPSTEIN, JOSHUA M. 1985. *The Calculus of Conventional War: Dynamic Analysis without Lanchester Theory.* Washington, D.C.: Brookings Institution; c1985. 31p. ISBN: 0815724519 (pbk.); LCCN: 85-072707.

E78
EPSTEIN, JOSHUA M. 1997. *Nonlinear Dynamics, Mathematical Biology, and Social Science.* Santa Fe, NM: Santa Fe Institute (SFI); 1988. (Santa Fe Institute Studies in the Science of Complexity). ISBN: O-201-95989-5 (hbk.); 0-201-41988-2 (15685-7 (pbk.).

E79
EPSTEIN, JOSHUA M.; AXTELL, ROBERT. 1996. *Growing Artificial Societies: Social Science from the Bottom Up.* Washington, D.C.: Brookings Institution Press; 1996. 208p. ISBN: 0262050526 (hbk.); 0262550253 (pbk.); 0262550261 (CD).

E80
ERICSSON, KARL ANDERS. 1993. *Protocol Analysis: Verbal Reports as Data*. Rev. ed. Cambridge, MA: MIT Press; 1993. ISBN: 0262050471 (hbk.); 0262550237 (pbk.).

E81
ERLACH, DANIELA; REISENLEITNER, MARKUS. 1995. A Relational Approach to Computer-based Studies of Geneaology, Family Patterns, and Social Bonding. See reference: BOONSTRA, O.; COLLENTEUR, G.; VAN ELDEREN, B., eds. 1995. 199-207.

E82
ETZIONI, O.; WELD, D. 1995. Intelligent Agents on the Internet: Fact, Fiction, and Forecast. *IEEE Expert: Intelligent Systems and Applications*. 1995; 10 (4): 44-49. ISSN: 0885-9000.

E83
EULAU, HEINZ, ed. 1989. *Crossroads of Social Science: The ICPSR 25th Anniversary Volume*. New York, NY: Agathon Press. 1989. 177p. ISBN: 0875860907; 0875860915 (pbk.); LCCN: 88-7421; OCLC: 18497429.

E84
EVANS, CHARLES T.; BROWN, ROBERT. 1998. Teaching the History Survey Course using Multimedia Techniques. See reference: AHA. 1998. 17-20.

E85
EVANS, FRANK B. 1990. Records and administrative processes: Retrospect and prospects. See reference: DURANCE, C., ed. 1990. 27-36.

E86
EVANS, FRANK; WARNER, ROBERT. 1971. American Archivists and Their Society. *The American Archivist*. 1971; 34: 169. ISSN: 0360-9081.

E87
EVANS, MAX. 1986. Authority Control: An Alternative to the Record Group Concept. *The American Archivist*. 1986; 49(3): 249-261. ISSN: 0360-9081.

E88
EVANS, MAX J.; WEBER, LISA B. 1985. *MARC for Archives and Manuscripts: A Compendium of Practice*. Madison, WI: State Historical Society of Wisconsin.; 1985. 262p. ISBN: 0-87020-232-4. (Distributed by SAA, 600 S. Federal St. 505, Chicago, IL 60605).

E89
EVANS-PRITCHARD, EDWARD E. 1961/1962. *Anthropology and History*. Manchester, UK: University of Manchester; 1961. 22p. OCLC: 611153. Reprinted in his *Essays in Social Anthropology*. London: Faber and Faber; 1962. 233p. ISBN: 0571089933; LCCN: 63-669; OCLC: 19721108.

E90
EVERDELL, WILLIAM R. 1997. *The First Moderns: Profiles in the Origins of Twentieth- century Thought*. Chicago, IL: University of Chicago Press; c1997. 501p. ISBN: 0226224805; LCCN: 96044334.

E91
EVERETT, DANIEL M.; CARTER, STEVEN C. 1992. Topology of Document Retrieval Systems. *Journal of the American Society for Information Science*. 1992 Dec.; 43 (10): 658-74. ISSN: 00065-0876.

E92
EVERETT, JIM. 1996. *Handlist of Electronic Teaching Resources for Teachers of History, Archeology, and Art History*. Glasgow, UK: CTICH Centre for History, Archaeology and Art History; 1996. Available from: CTICH, 1 University Gardens, University of Glasgow, G12 8QQ UK; Email = ctich@gla.ac.uk.

E93
EVERITT, BRIAN. 1980/1993. *Cluster Analysis*. 2nd ed. London, UK: Heinemann Educational Books; 1980. 3rd ed. London, UK: E. Arnold/Halstead Books; 1993. 170p. ISBN: 0340584793 (hbk.); 0470220430 (pbk.); LCCN: 93-168652.

E94
EVERITT, BRIAN. 1991. *Applied Multivariate Data Analysis*. London, UK: Edward Arnold; 1991. 304p. ISBN: 0340545291; LCCN: 95-221711.

E95
EVERITT, BRIAN. 1992. *Talking about Statistics: A Psychologist's Guide to Data Analysis*. London, UK: E. Arnold; 1992. 130p. LCCN: 92-231800.

E96

EVERTSZ, CARL J. G.; PEITGEN, HEINZ-OTTO; VOSS, RICHARD F., eds. 1996. *Fractal Geometry and Analysis: The Mandelbrot Festschrift, Curação, 1995.* River Ridge, NJ: World Scientific; c1996. 512p. ISBN: 9810224346; LCCN: 96210568.

E97

EYSENCK, MICHAEL W.; ELLIS, ANDREW W.; HUNT, EARL B.; JOHNSON-LAIRD, P. N., eds. 1995. *The Blackwell Dictionary of Cognitive Psychology.* Oxford, UK: Blackwell; 1995. 390p. ISBN: 0631156828.

-F-

F1

FABIAN, BERNHARD. 1986. Libraries and Humanistic Scholarship. *Journal of Librarianship* (UK). 1986 April; 18: 79-92. ISSN: 0022-2232.

F2

FABIAN, JOHANNES. 1983. *Time and the Other: How Anthropology Makes its Object.* New York, NY: Columbia University Press; 1983. 205p. ISBN: 0231055900 (hbk.); 0231055919 (pbk.).

F3

FAGIN, RONALD; HALPERN, JOSEPH Y.; MOSES, TORAM; VARDI, MOSHE Y. 1995. *Reasoning about Knowledge.* Cambridge, MA: MIT Press; 1995. 500p. ISBN: 0-262- 06162-7.

F4

FAIRTHORNE, ROBERT A. 1961. *Towards Information Retrieval.* London: Butterworths; 1961. 211p. LCCN: 62-53666; OCLC: 1401062.

F5

FAIRTHORNE, ROBERT A. 1969. Content Analysis, Specification, and Control. In: WILLIAMS, M., ed. *Annual Review of Information Science and Technology:* vol. 4. Medford, NJ: Information Today; 1969. ISBN: 1-57387-019-6; ISSN: 0066-4200; CODEN: ARISBC; LCCN: 66-25096.

F6

FALCIDIENO, BIANCA; KUNNI, TOSHIYASU. 1993. *Modeling in Computer Graphics: Methods and Applications.* Conference proceedings: Modeling in Computer Graphics, Genoa, June 28 - July 1, 1993. Berlin, DEU / New York, NY: Springer-Verlag; 1993. 475p. ISBN: 3540565299 (GM); 0387565299 (USA).

F7

FALK, JOYCE DUNCAN. 1981a. Computer-assisted Production of Bibliographic Databases in History. *Indexer* (UK). 1981 April; 12(3): 131-39. ISSN: 0019-4131.

F8

FALK, JOYCE DUNCAN. 1981b. In Search of History: Bibliographic Databases. *History Teacher.* 1981; 5(1): 523-44. ISSN: 0018-2745.

F9

FALK, JOYCE DUNCAN. 1982a. Computer Usage in Advanced History Courses. *RQ.* 1982 Summer; 21: 342-364. ISSN: 0033-6807.

F10

FALK, JOYCE DUNCAN. 1982b. The Historian Enters the Electronic Age: Bibliographical and Database Publishing. *The Public Historian.* 1982 Spring; 4: 35-42. ISSN: 0272-3433.

F11

FALK, JOYCE DUNCAN. 1986a. *A Guide to Historical Literature and other Issues in History Bibliography.* Report of the Association for the Bibliography of History to the American Historical Association Research Division. April 12, 1986. Available from: ERIC, no. ED 305-303.

F12

FALK, JOYCE DUNCAN. 1986b. Librarians and Historians at the American Historical Association. *College and Research Libraries News.* 1986 September; 47: 501-503. ISSN: 0010-0870. (Summarizes discussion between ABH and AHA members related to the Guide project).

F13

FALK, JOYCE DUNCAN. 1988. Data Bases for History: An Overview and Implications. *American History: A Bibliographic Review.* 1988; 4: 1-13. ISSN: 0748-6731.

F14
FALK, RUMA; FALK, RAPHAEL. 1993. *Understanding Probability and Statistics. A Book of Problems*. New York, NY: A. K. Peters; 1993. 239p. ISBN: 1568810180.

F15
FANDERL, H. K. FISCHER; KAMPER, J. 1992. The Open Document Architecture: From Standardization to the Market. *IBM Systems Journal*. 1992; 31(4): 728-753. ISSN: 0018- 8670.

F16
FARRADANE, JASON E. L. 1953. Information Service in Industry. *Research* (UK). 1953; 6: 327-330. Note: coined "Information Science."

F17
FARRADANE, JASON E. L. 1955. Professional Education for Information Scientists. In: *Congrès des bibliothéques et des centres de documentation*. The Hague, NL: Martinus Nijhoff; 1955; 2B: 76-81

F18
FARADANE, J. 1980. Knowledge, Information, and Information Science. *Journal of Information Science* (UK). 1980: 2: 75-80. ISSN: 1352-7460.

F19
FARKAS-CONN, IRENE S. 1990. *From Documentation to Information Science: the Beginnings and early development of the American Society for Information Science.* New York, NY: Greenwood Press; 1990. 229p. (Contributions in Librarianship and Information Science series). ISBN: 0313255059; LCCN: 89-25666; OCLC: 2061864.

F20
FARQUHAR, JAMES D. 1976 . *Creation and Imitation: The Work of a Fifteenth-century Illuminator.* Ft. Lauderdale, FL: Nova University Press; 1976. 198p. (Nova University Studies in the Humanities, 1).

F21
FARR, JAMES; SEIDELMAN, RAYMOND. 1993. *Discipline and History: Political Science in the United States.* Ann Arbor, MI: University of Michigan Press; 1993. 427p. ISBN: 04732095129 (hbk.); 0472065122 (pbk.).

F22
FARRET, PETER W. 1990. *Intentional Composer: A System for Acquiring Creative Design Knowledge*. Kingston, Ontario, CAN: Queens University; 1990. 141p. (Ph.D. dissertation; DAI, vol. 52/11-B: 5926). Available from: University Microfilms, Ann Arbor, MI (order no. AADNN-61575). ISBN: 0-315-61575-3.

F23
FARROW, J. 1991. A Cognitive Process Model of Document Indexing. *Journal of Documentation*. 1991; 47: 149-166. ISSN: 0022-0418.

F24
FAUGERAS, A.; MAGDELAINE, M. 1992. Application d'un systéme expert à la resolution d'une problème d'identification des individus dans un corpus historique [Application of an Expert System to resolve the Problem of Identification of Individuals in an Historical Source]. See reference: SMETS, J., ed. 1992. 455-461.

F25
FAUGERAS, OLIVIER. 1993. *Three-Dimensional Computer Vision*. Cambridge, MA: MIT Press; 1993. 695p.(Artificial Intelligence series). ISBN: 0-262-06158-9.

F26
FAULHABER, CHARLES. 1996. Distance Learning and Digital Libraries: Two Sides of ta Single Coin. *Journal of the American Society for Information Science*. 1996 Nov.; 47: 854-856. ISSN: 0002-8231.

F27
FAUSEY, JON; SHAFER, KEITH. All My Data is in SGML. Now What? See reference: LOGAN, E.; POLLARD, M. 1997b. 638-643.

F28
FAVIER, JEAN, ed. 1993. *La pratique archivistique Française* [French Archival Practice]. Paris, FR: Archives Nationales; 1993. 630p. ISBN: 2-86000-205-1.

F29
FAYYAD, USAMA M. 1996. Data Mining and Knowledge Discovery: Making Sense out of Data. *IEEE Expert*. 1996; 10: 20-25. ISSN: 0665-9000.

F30
FAYYAD, USAMA M.; PIATETSKY-SHAPIRO, GREGORY; SMYTH, PAHRAIC; UTHURUSAMY, RAMASAMY. 1996. *Advances in Knowledge Discovery and Data Mining*. Cambridge, MA: AAAI Press; 1996. 560p. ISBN: 0-262-56097-6. Distributed by MIT Press.

F31
FAYYAD, USAMA M.; UTHURUSAMY, R., eds. *1995. Knowledge Discovery and Data Mining.* First International Conference on Knowledge Discovery and Data Mining, at Montreal, Quebec, CAN / Menlo Park, CA: AAAI Press; 1995.

F32
FEATHER, JOHN; STURGES, RODNEY P., eds. 1997. *International Encyclopedia of Information and Library Science.* London, UK / New York, NY: Routledge; 1997. 492p. ISBN: 0415098602; LCCN: 95053290.

F33
FEDERAL GEOGRAPHIC DATA COMMITTEE (FGDC). 1994. *Content Standards for Spatial Metadata.* Reston, VA: FGDC Secretariat; 1994. Available from the FGDC, telephone no. 703-648-5725.

F34
FEDERAL JUDICIAL CENTER. 1994. *Reference Manual on Scientific Evidence.* Deerfield, IL: Clark Boardman Callaghan; 1994 . 637p. ISBN: 0-87632-269-0.

F35
FEDERAL JUDICIAL CENTER. 1995. *Manual for Complex Litigation.* Deerfield, Il.: Clark Boardman Collaghan; 1995.

F36
FEDERAL TRADE COMMISSION. 1996a-. *Cybershopping: Protecting yourself when buying online*[Online]. Accessible at http://www.ftc.gov/bcp/conline/pubs/buying/cycbersho.htm.

F37
FEDERAL TRADE COMMISSION. 1996b-. *Online scams: Potholes on the Information highway* [Online]. Accessible at http://www.ftc.gov/bcp/conline/pubs/services/online.htm.

F38
FEENEY, MARY; GRIEVES, MAUREEN, eds. 1994. *The Value and Impact of Information.* London, UK: Bowker Saur; 1994. 303p. ISBN: 1857390849.

F39
FEENEY, MARY; MERRY, KAREN, eds. 1990. *Information Technology and the Research Process.* London: K. G. Saur; 1990. 340p. (British Library Research series). ISBN: 0- 86291-474-0.

F40
FEENEY, MARY; ROSS, SEAMUS. 1993. *Information Technology in Humanities Scholarship: British Achievements, Prospects, and Barriers.* London, UK: The British Library Research and Development Department and the British Academy; 1993. (Report, 3).

F41
FEFFER, ANDREW. 1993. *The Chicago Pragmatists and American Progressivism.* Ithaca, NY: Cornell University Press; 1993. 279p. ISBN: 0801425026; LCCN: 92-54974.

F42
FEIGENBAUM, EDWARD A.; FELDMAN, JULIAN, eds. 1995. *Computers and Thought.* Cambridge, MA: AAAI Press; 1995. 550p. ISBN: 0-262-56092-5. Distributed by MIT Press.

F43
FELDMAN, DAVID H.; CSIKSZENTMIHALYI, MIHALY; GARDNER, HOWARD. 1994. *Changing the World: A Framework for the Study of Creativity.* Westport, CT: Praeger; 1994. 180p. ISBN: 0275947696 (hbk.); 0275947750 (pbk.); LCCN: 93011868.

F44
FELDMAN, MARTHA S.; MARCH, JAMES G. 1981. Information in Organizations as Signal and Symbol. *Administrative Science Quarterly.* 1981: 26 (2): 171-186. ISSN: 0001- 8392.

F45
FELDMAN, S. P. 1986. Management in Context: An Essay on the Relevance of Culture to the Understanding of Organizational Change. *Journal of Management Studie*s (UK). 1986; 23: 587-607. ISSN: 0022-2380.

F46
FELKER, CHRISTOPHER D. 1993. *Report on Archival Policy and Records Management in Development Research Offices* (Electronic file). Cambridge, MA: MIT Resource Development Office; 1993. (Records Management Report).

F47
FELLER, W. 1968. *Introduction to Probability and Its Application.* 3rd ed. New York, NY: Wiley; 1968. (Wiley Series in Probability and Mathematical Statistics).

F48
FELMAN, SHOSHANA; LAUB, LORI. 1992. *Testimony: Crises of Witnessing in Literature: Psychoanalysis and History.* New York, NY; 1992. 294p. ISBN: 0415903912 (hbk).; 0415903920 (pbk.).

F49
FENTRESS, JAMES; WICKHAM, CHRIS. 1992/1994. *Social Memory.* 2nd ed. Oxford, UK: Blackwell; 1994. 229p. ISBN: 0631166181 (hbk.); 063116619X (pbk.); LCCN: 91-27041.

F50
FERGUSON, EUGENE S., ed. [1968]. *Bibliography of the History of Technology.* Cambridge, MA: Society for the History of Technology; [1968]. 347p. LCCN: 68-21559.

F51
FERNAND BRAUDEL CENTER for the Study of Economies, Historical Systems, and Civilizations. 1976-. *Newsletter.* Binghamton, NY: State University of New York at Binghamton; 1976- . Nos. 16-17 cited. Available, as is its *Review*, from the F. Braudel Center, Binghamton University, P.O. Box 6000, Binghamton, NY 13902-6000.

F52
FERRO, MARC. 1981/1984. *Comment on Raconté l'Histoire aux Enfants* [Comment on Retelling History to Children]. Trans. *The Use and Abuse of History: or, How the Past is Taught.* London, UK; Boston, MA: Routledge & Kegan Paul; 1984. 257p. ISBN: 0710096585.

F53
FERRO, MARC. 1984/1988. *Film et histoire.* Series: Histoire et ses representations. Paris, FR: Editions de l'École des Hautes Études en Sciences Sociales; 1984. Rev. ed., trans. as *Cinema and History.* Detroit, MI: Wayne State University Press; 1988. 175p. ISBN: 081431904 (hbk.); 081431905X (pbk.).

F54
FERRO, MARC. 1985. *L'Histoire sour Surveillance: Science et Conscience de l'Histoire* [History under Surveillance: The Science and Conscience of History]. Paris, FR: Calmann-Levy; 1985. 216p. ISBN: 2702013931.

F55
FEYERABEND, PAUL K. [1972]. Science without Experience: How to be a Good Empiricist—A Plea for Tolerance in Matters Epistemological. See reference: MORICK, H., ed. [1972]. ch. 5.

F56
FEYERABEND, PAUL K. 1975/1993. *Against Method: Outline of An Anarchistic Theory of Knowledge.* Atlantic Highlands, NJ: Humanities Press; c1974. 339p. ISBN: 039100381X. London, UK: Verso; 1975, reprint 1978. 3rd ed., 1993. 279p. ISBN: 0860916464; LCCN: 93033557.

F57
FIDEL, RAYA. 1991. Searchers' Selection of Search Keys: 2. Controlled Vocabulary or Free- Text Searching. *Journal of the American Society for Information Science.* 1991; 42(7): 501-514. ISSN: 0002-8231.

F58
FIDEL, RAYA. 1993. Qualitative Methods in Information Retrieval Research. *Library and Information Science Research.* 1993; 15(3): 219-247. ISSN: 0740-8188.

F59
FIDEL, RAYA; BELLARDO HAHN, TRUDI; RASMUSSEN, EDIE M.; SMITH, PHILIP J., eds. 1994. *Challenges in Indexing Electronic Text and Images.* Medford, NJ: Learned Information, Inc. for the American Society for Information Science; 1994. 306p. (ASIS Monograph series). ISBN: 0-938734-76-8.

F60
FIELDING, NIGEL G.; LEE, RAYMOND M., eds. 1991. *Using Computers in Qualitative Research.* Newbury Park, CA: Sage Publications; 1991. 216p. ISBN: 0803984243; 0803984251 (pbk.); LCCN: 90-53679; OCLC: 24054742.

F61
FIENBERG, S. E. 1971. A Statistical Technique for Historians: Standardizing Tables of Counts. *Journal of Interdisciplinary History.* 1971; 1: 305-316. ISSN: 0022-1953.

F62
FIKENTSCHER, WOLFGANG. [1988]. *Modes of Thought in law and Justice: A Preliminary Report on a Study in Legal Anthropology.* 56th Colloquy, 16 April 1987, University of California and the Graduate Theological Union. Wuellner, Wilhelm, ed. Berkeley, CA: Center for Hermeneutical Studies in Hellenistic and Modern Culture; c1988. 84p. (Colloquy series). ISBN: 089242057X; LCCN: 88-035306.

F63
FIKFAK, JURIJ. 1996. Multimedia Presentations of Historical Demography Issues. See reference: BORODKIN, L., ed. 1996. Abstract, p. 1126-127. 2000.

F64

FIKFAK, JURIJ; JARITZ, GERHARD, eds. 1993. *Image Processing in History: Towards Open Systems*. St. Katharinen [Göttingen]: Max-Planck-Institut für Geschichte in Kommission bei Scripta Mercaturae Verlag; 1993. 80p. (Halbgraue Reihe zur historischen Fackinformatik. Serie A: Historische Quellenkunden, Band 16). ISBN: 3-928134-99-X.

F65

FINDLEN, PAULA. 1989. The Museum: Its Classical Etymology and Renaissance Genealogy. *Journal of the History of Collections*. 1989; 1: 59-78. ISSN: 0954-6650.

F66

FINDLEN, PAULA. 1994. *Possessing Nature: Museums, Collecting, and Scientific Culture in Early Modern Italy*. Berkeley, CA: University of California Press; 1994. 449p. (Studies on the History of Society and Culture, 20). ISBN: 05200733347.

F67

FINDLEN, PAULA. 1998. Possessing the Past: The Material World of the Italian Renaissance. *American Historical Review*. 1998 Feb,; 103 (1): 83-114. ISSN: 0002-8762.

F68

FINDLER, NICHOLAS V.; MCKINSIE, WILEY R. 1969. On a computer program that generates and queries kinship structures. *Behavioral Science*. 1969; 14: 334-340. ISSN: 0005-7940.

F69

FINE, SARAH. 1986. Technological Innovation, Diffusion and Resistance: An Historical Perspective. *Journal of Library Administration*. 1986 Spring; 7: 83-108. ISSN: 0193-0826.

F70

FINEMAN, JOEL. 1989. The History of the Anecdote. In: Vesser, H. Aram, ed. *The New Historicism* (49-76). New York, NY / London, UK: Routledge; 1989. 317p. ISBN: 0415900697 (hbk.); 0415900700 (pbk.).

F71

FINHOLT, TOM. 1993. The Erosion of Time, Geography and Hierarchy: Sharing Information through an Electronic Archive. See reference: MENNE-HARITZ, A., ed. 1993. 67-90.

F72

FINHOLT, TOM; SPROULL, L.; KIESLER, S. 1990. Communication and Performance in *ad hoc* Groups. See reference: GALEGHER, J.; KRAUT, R. E.; EGIDO, C., eds. 1990. 291-325.

F73

FINK, LEON; KRAMER, LLOYD. 1994. Redrawing Professional Boundaries to Revitalize Education. *AHA Perspectives*. 1994 May/June; 32(5): 13-15. ISSN: 0743-7021.

F74

FINKE, RONALD A. 1990. *Creative Imagery: Discoveries and Inventions in Visualization*. Hillsdale, NJ: Lawrence Erlbaum Associates; 1990. 188p. ISBN: 08805807721.

F75

FINKE, RONALD A.; BETTLE, JONATHAN. 1996. *Chaotic Cognition: Principles and Applications*. Mahwah, NJ: Lawrence Erlbaum Associates; 1996. 224p. ISBN: 080581739 (hbk.); 0805817409 (pbk.).

F76

FINKE, RONALD A.; WARD, THOMAS B.; SMITH, STEVEN M. 1992. *Creative Cognition: Theory, Research, and Applications*. Cambridge, MA: MIT Press; 1992. 239p. (Bradford Book). ISBN: 0262061503

F77

FINLEY, MOSES I. [1952]. *Studies in Land and Credit in Ancient Athens, 500-200 B.C.* New Brunswick, NJ: Rutgers University Press; [1952]. 332p. LCCN: 52008908.

F78

FINN, CHESTER E; RAVITCH, DIANE. *What do our 17-year-olds Know? A Report on the First National Assessment of History and Literature*. New York, NY: Harper & Row; c1987. 293p. ISBN: 006015892; LCCN: 87045432.

F79

FINN, CHESTER E; RAVITCH, DIANE; HOLLEY ROBERT, P. 1985. *Challenges to the Humanities*. New York, NY: Holmes and Meier; 1985. 223p. ISBN: 0841910179 (hbk.); 0841910198 (pbk.); LCCN: 84029065.

F80

FINNEGAN, TERENCE. 1990. Developing Computer-assisted Instructional Materials in the American History Surveys. *History Teacher*. 1990; 24(1): 67-78. ISSN: 0018-2745.

F81
FISCHER, C. 1995. Alexandria Digital Library: Rapid Prototype and Metadata Schema. *Proceedings of the Forum on Research and Technology Advances in Digital Libraries (ADL)*. Secaucus, NJ: Springer-Verlag; 1995.

F82
FISCHER, CLAUDE S. 1992/1995. *America Calling. A Social History of the Telephone to 1940*. Los Alamitos, CA: IEEE Computer Society; 1992. Berkeley, CA: University of California Press; 1995. 424p. ISBN: 050079337 (pbk.); LCCN: 91038355.

F83
FISCHER, G. 1984. Human-Computer Communication and Knowledge-based Systems. In: H. J. Otway and M. Peltu, eds. *The Managerial Challenge of New Office Technology* (pp. 54- 79). London, UK: Butterworths; 1984. 246p. ISBN: 0408015330; LCCN: 84-9596; OCLC: 10780828.

F84
FISCHHOFF, B. 1982. For Those Condemned to Study the Past; Heuristics and Biases in Hindsight. See reference: KAHNEMAN, SLOVIC & TVERSKY. 1982.

F85
FISHBEIN, MARTIN; AJZEN, ICEK. [1975]. *Belief, Attitude, Intention, and Behavior: An Introduction to Theory and Research*. Reading, MA: Addison-Wesley; [1975]. 578p. ISBN: 0201020890.

F86
FISHBEIN, MYRON H. 1985. *A Model Curriculum for the Education and Training of Archivists in Automation: A RAMP Study*. Paris, FR: UNESCO General Information Programme and UNISIST; November 1985. 33p. PGI-85/WS/27. Available from: UNESCO Federal Information Programme, 7 Place de Fontenoy, 75700 Paris, FR.

F87
FISHER, DAVID E.; FISHER, MARSHALL JON. 1995/1996. *Tube. The Invention of Television*. New York, NY: Basic Books; 1995 / Washington, D.C.: Counterpoint; 1996. 427p.(Alfred P. Sloan Foundation Technology series). ISBN: 1887178191.

F88
FISHER, FRANKLIN M.; MCKIE, JAMES W.; MANCKE, RICHARD B. 1983. *IBM and the U.S. Data Processing Industry: An Economic History*. New York, NY: Praeger; 1983. 532p. ISBN: 0030630592.

F89
FISHER, H. T. 1982. *Mapping Information: The Graphic Display of Quantitative Information*. Cambridge, MA: Abt Associates; 1982. 384p. ISBN: 0890115710; LCCN: 82-6858.

F90
FITCH, G. W. 1987. *Naming and Believing*. Philosophical Series, vol. 36. Dordrecht, NL / Boston, MA: R. Reidel; 1987. 215p. ISBN: 9027723494. Distributed by Kluwer Academic Publishers..

F91
FITCH, NANCY E. 1980. Statistical and Mathematical Methods for Historians: An Annotated Bibliography of Selected Books and Articles. *Historical Methods*. 1980; 13: 222-231. ISSN: 0161-5440.

F92
FITCH, NANCY E. 1984. Statistical Fantasies and Historical Facts: History in Crisis and its Methodological Implications. *Historical Methods*. 1984; 17(4): 239-254. ISSN: 0161- 5440.

F93
FITCH, NANCY E. 1988. The Crisis in History: Its Pedagogical Implications. *Historical Methods*. 1988 Summer; 21(3): 104-11. ISSN: 0161-5440.

F94
FITTS, JOHN. 1996. Dancing with a Gorilla: EDI in the Retail Sector. See reference: BLUH, P., ed. 1996. 171-174.

F95
FITZGERALD, IAN. 1997. Virtual History. [Report on the 2nd Annual Virtual Heritage Conference, London, UK]. *History Today*. 1997 March; 47 (1): 31-33. ISSN: 0018-2753.

F96
FITZGERALD, IAN; FLINT, ADAM. 1995. British University History Now. *History Today* (UK). 1995 August; 45 (8): 53-75. ISSN: 0018-2753.

F97
FITZGERALD, IAN; HINGLEY, VICKI. 1996. [British] University History 1996. *History Today* (UK). 1996 August; 46 (8): 50-55. ISSN: 0018-2753.

F98
FITZPATRICK, PAUL J. 1955. The Early Teaching of Statistics in American Colleges and Universities. *American Statistician*. 1955; 5(2): 12-18. ISSN: 0162-1459.

F99
FLAMM, KENNETH. 1988. *Creating the Computer: Government, Industry, and High Technology*. Washington, D.C.: Brookings Institution; 1988. 282p. ISBN: 085728506 (hbk.); 0815728492 (pbk.).

F100
FLANAGAN, W. H. 1984. The Conduct of Inquiry in Social Science History. *Social Science History*. 1984; 8: 323-339. ISSN: 0145-5532.

F101
FLANAGAN, W. H.; ZINGALE, N. H. 1985. Alchemist's Gold: Inferring Individual Relationships from Aggregate Data. *Social Science History*. 1985; 9: 71-91. ISSN: 0145- 5532. (See critique by J. M. KOUSSER, 1986).

F102
FLAVELL, JULIE M.; SPAETH, DONALD A. 1996/1997. *New York, New Immigrants* 1900: *A Teaching Framework for Historical Datasets*. See reference: IGARTUA, J. E., ed. 1996/1997. 393-399. *New York, New Immigrants* is available from CTICH, 1 University Gardens, University of Glasgow, G12 8QQ UK; Email = ctich@gla.ac.uk.

F103
FLEISCHAURER, CARL. 1992. *American Memory* (electronic file). Washington, D.C.: Library of Congress; 1992. Accessible through Library of Congress homepage.

F104
FLEISCHAUER, CARL; BRANNAN, BEVERLY W.; LEVINE, LAWRENCE; TRACHTENBERG, ALAN. 1988. *Documenting America, 1935-1943*. Berkeley, CA: University of California Press; 1988. 361p. ISBN: 052002205.

F105
FLEIT, LINDA H. [1994]. *Self-Assessment for Campus Information Technology Services*. Denver, CO: CAUSE; [1994]. 26p. (CAUSE Professional Paper Series, no. 12 [PUB3012]. Study sponsored by Datatel, Inc.). Includes CAUSE/EDUCOM *Evaluation Guidelines for Institutional Information Technology Resources*. Available from CAUSE at http://www.cause.org/information-resources/ir-library.

F106
FLEMING, MALCOLM L. 1981. Characteristics of Effective Instructional Presentation: What We Know and What We Need to Know. *Educational Technology*. 1981; 21: 33-38. ISSN: 0013-1962.

F107
FLEMING, MALCOLM L.; LEVIE, W. HOWARD, eds. 1993. *Instructional Message Design: Principles from the Behavioral and Cognitive Sciences*. 2nd ed. Englewood Cliffs, NJ: Educational Technology Publications; 1993. 331p. ISBN: 0877781044; LCCN: 77-26089.

F108
FLEMING, ROBIN. 1995. Picturesque History and the Medieval in Nineteenth-century America. *American Historical Review*. 1990 October; 100: 1061-1094. ISSN: 0002-8762.

F109
FLEMMING, CANDACE C.; VON HALLE, BARBARA. 1989. *Handbook of Relational Database Design*. New York, NY: Addison-Wesley; 1989. 605p. ISBN: 0201114384.

F110
FLETCHER, MICHAEL; LOCK, GARY R. 1991. *Digging Numbers: Elementary Statistics for Archaeologists*. Oxford, UK: Oxford University Committee for Archeology; 1991. 187p. ISBN: 094781633X.

F111
FLEURY, MICHEL; HENRY, LOUIS. 1956. *Des registres paroissaux a l'histoire de la population: Manuel de depouillement et d'exploration de l'etat civil ancien* [Parish Registers and the History of Population: Manual of Data Extraction and Exploration of Data from the Old Civil State]. Paris, FR: Institut National d'Etudes Demographiques; 1956.

F112
FLEURY, MICHEL; HENRY, LOUIS. 1956/1976/1985. *Manuel de Dépouillement et d'Exploitation de l'État Civil Ancien* [Manual on Extraction and Exploitation of Data from the Old Civil State]. 1st ed. Paris, FR: INED; 1956. *Nouveau Manuel de dépouillement et d'exploitation de l'état civil ancien*. Rev.ed., 1976. 3rd ed. Paris, FR: Institut National d'Études Démographiques (INED); 1985. 202p. ISBN: 2733220071.

F113
FLOOD, BARBARA, ed. 1997. Personal Privacy, Integrity and Data Security. In: *Bulletin of the American Society for Information Science*. 1997 Feb./March; 23(3): 3-27. (Entire issue on title topic). ISSN: 0095-4403; CODEN: BASICR.

F114
FLORANCE, VALERIE; DUCKWALL, ROB. 1992. Conversion of Artwork to Electronic Form: A Case Study of Costs and Aesthetic Factors. See reference: STONE, S.; BUCKLAND, M., eds. 1992. 171-183.

F115
FLOUD, RODERICK. 1971/1979. *An Introduction to Quantitative Methods for Historians*. Princeton, NJ: Princeton University Press. 220p. 2nd ed. London: Methuen; 1979. 237p. ISBN: 0416716601; 0416716709 (pbk.): LCCN: 80-494261; OCLC: 6077265.

F116
FLOUD, RODERICK. 1984. Quantitative History and People's History. *Social Science History*. 1984; 8: 151-168. ISSN: 0145-5532.

F117
FLYNN, MARY K. 1992. History Lessons: New Books on Microcomputer History (Review). *PC Magazine*. 1992 May 26; 11 (10): 32. ISSN: 0745-2500.

F118
FLYNN, PETER. 1995. *The World-Wide Web Handbook: A Guide for Users, Authors, and Publishers*. London, UK: International Thompson Computer Press; 1995. 351p. ISBN: 1850322058.

F119
FLYNN, PETER. 1997. W[h]ither the Web? The Extension or Replacement of HRML.   See reference: LOGAN, E.; POLLARD, M., eds. 1997b. 614-621.

F120
FODOR, JERRY A. 1975. *The Language of Thought*. Cambridge, MA: Harvard University Press; 1975.

F121
FOGEL, ROBERT W. 1960. *The Union Pacific Railroad: A Case in Premature Enterprise*. Baltimore, MD: The Johns Hopkins University Press; 1960. 129p. LCCN: 60-14850; OCLC: 238063.

F122
FOGEL, ROBERT W. 1966. The New Economic History: its Findings and Methods. *Economic History Review*. 1966; 2nd series, 19: 642-56. ISSN: 0013-0117. Reprinted in reference: FOGEL, R. W.; ENGERMAN, S. L., eds., 1971. 1-12. See the review by Edward Kirkland, *American Historical Review*. 1967 July; 72 : 1494-6. ISSN: 0002-8762.

F123
FOGEL, ROBERT W. 1970. History and Retrospective Econometrics. *History and Theory*. 1970; 3: 245-264. ISSN: 0018-2656; LCCN: 63-47837.

F124
FOGEL, ROBERT W. 1975. The Limits of Quantitative History. *American Historical Review*. 1975; 80: 329-350. ISSN: 0002-8762.

F125
FOGEL, ROBERT W.; ELTON, GEOFFREY R. 1983. *Which Road to the Past? Two Views of History*. New Haven, CT: Yale University Press; 1983. 136p. ISBN: 0300030118; LCCN: 1983-3573; OCLC: 9324412.

F126
FOGEL, ROBERT W.; ENGERMANN, STANLEY. 1974. *Time on the Cross: The Economics of American Negro Slavery*. Boston, MA: Little, Brown, Co.; [1974]. 286p. ISBN: 0316287008; LCCN: 83-18347; OCLC: 741011.

F127
FOGEL, ROBERT W.; ENGERMANN, STANLEY, eds. 1971. *The Reinterpretation of American Economic History*. New York, NY: Harper & Row; 1971. ISBN: 0060421096; LCCN: 75-141166; OCLC: 154724.

F128
FOGELVIK, STEFAN. 1988. The Archive at your Desk. See reference: GENET, J.-P., ed. 1988.

F129
FOGELVIK, STEFAN. 1989a. The Stockholm Historical Database at Work. *History and Computing*. 1989; 2: 256-265. ISSN: 0957-0144.

F130
FOGELVIK, STEFAN. 1989b. Studier och handlingar roerande [Data Handling Studies]. *Stockholms Historia* (SE). 1989; 6: 13-28.

F131
FOGERTY, JAMES, ed. 1997[1998]. Archives and Business Records. In: *The American Archivist*. 1997 Winter [1998]; 60 (1):1-110. (Entire issue on title topic). ISSN: 0360- 9081. Essays expanding beyond the Records of American Business Project, directed by James Fogerty of the Minnesota Historical Society and Michael Nash of the Hagley Museum and Library, with an international scope.

F132
FOLKERTS, M.; KUHNE, A., eds. 1990. The Use of Computers in Cataloging Medieval and Renaissance Manuscripts. Papers from the International Workshop in Munich, 10-12 August 1989. In: *Algorismus, Studien zur Geschichte der Mathematik under der Naturwissenschaften*. Munich, DEU: Institut für Geschichte der Naturwissenschaften; 1990. 179p. (Entire issue on title topic). ISBN: 3892410038; LCCN: 92-239269; OCLC: 24096514.

F133
FOLWER, R. H.; FOLWER, W. A.; WILSON, B. A. 1991. Integrating Query, Thesaurus, and Documents through a Common Visual Representation. In: *Proceedings of the Fourteenth Annual International ACM/SIGIR Conference on Research and Development in Information Retrieval*. New York, NY: ACM; 1991. 142-151.

F134
FOMENKO, ANATOLI T. [1994]. *Empirico-statistical Analysis of Narrative Material and its Applications to Historical Dating*. Efimov, O., trans. Dordrecht, NL / Boston, MA: Kluwer Academic; c1994. 2 v. : *Development of the Statistical Tools* and *The Analysis of Ancient and Medieval Records*. ISBN: 0792326067 (set); LCCN: 93043470.

F135
FOMENKO, ANATOLI T.; RACHEV, SVETLOZAR. 1990. Volume functions of historical texts and the Amplitude Correlation Principle. *Computers and the Humanities* (NL). 1990; 24: 187-206. ISSN: 0010-4817.

F136
FONER, ERIC. 1990/1997. *The New American History*. Philadelphia, PA: Temple University Press; 1990. ISBN: 0877226989 (hbk.); 0877226997 (pbk.); LCCN: 89-20563. Rev. ed., 1997. 292p. LCCN: 96-52059.

F137
FONTE, JOHN D.; LERNER, ROBERT. 1997. History Standards are not Fixed. *Society*. 1997 Jan.-Feb.; 34(2): 20-26. ISSN: 0147-2011.

F138
FOOTE, KENNETH E. 1990. To Remember and Forget: Archives, Memory, and Culture. *The American Archivist*. 1990; 53(3): 378-392. ISSN: 0360-9081.

F139
FOOTE, KENNETH E. 1992. Mapping the Past: A Survey of Microcomputer Cartography. *Historical Methods*. 1992; 25(3): 121-131. ISSN: 0161-5440.

F140
FORBES. 1996. The Digital Revolution: Where do we go from here? *The Big Issue: Forbes Supplement on the Information Age*. Karlgaard, Rich, ed. *FORBES ASAP*. 1996, December 2; sn: 13-296. ISSN: 0015-6914 . Interviews with "53 Seers & sages on the Techno-Future"; pt. 1, History & politics.

F141
FORESTER, TOM. 1987. *High-Tech Society: The Story of the Information Technology Revolution*. Cambridge, MA: MIT Press; 1987. 311p. ISBN: 0262560445 (pbk.); OCLC: 20900994.

F142
FORGIONNE, GUISSEPPI A. 1990. *Quantitative Management*. Chicago, IL: Dryden Press; c1990. 912p. ISBN: 0030266491; LCCN: 89-1635.

F143
FORSYTH, D.; MALIK, J.; WILENSKY, R. 1997. Searching for Digital Pictures. *Scientific American*. 1997; 276 (6): 88-93. ISSN: 0036-8733.

F144
FORSYTH, WILLIAM. 1874. *The Rules of Evidence as Applicable to the Credibility of History*. London, UK: R. Hardwicke; 1874. 36p. (Victorian Institute Transactions).

F145
FORTADO, BRUCE. 1992. Subordinate Views in Supervisory Conflict Situations: Peering into the Subcultural Chasm. *Human Relations*. 1992 November; 45 (11): 1141-1167. ISSN: 0018- 7267.

F146
FORTE, MAURIZIO; SILIOTTI, ALBERTO, eds. 1997. *Virtual Archeology. Re-creating Ancient Worlds*. New York, NY: J. Wiley; 1997. 288p. New York, NY: H. N. Abrams; 1997. 294p (Translation of: *Archeologia: percorsi virtuali nelle civilita scomparse*). ISBN: 0810939436.

F147
FORWARD, GORDON E.; BEACH, DENNIS E.; GRAY, DAVID A.; QUICK, JAMES CAMPBELL. 1991. Mentofacturing: A Vision for American Industrial Excellence. *Academy of Management Executive*. 1991 August; 5 (3): 32-44. ISSN: 0896-3789.

F148
FOSKETT, ANTHONY C. 1973. *The Universal Decimal Classification: The history, present status, and general classification scheme.* London, UK: Clive Bingley; 1973.

F149
FOSKETT, ANTHONY C. 1977/1982; 1996. *Subject Approach to Information.* 3rd ed. London, UK: Clive Bingley; 1977. 476p. 4th ed., 1982. 574p. 5th ed. London, UK: Library Assn. Publishing; 1996. ISBN: 0208019340 (hbk.); 0208019207 (pbk.).

F150
FOSKETT, D. J., ed. 1990. *The Information Environment: A World View: Studies in honour of Professor A. I. Mikhailov, director of VINITI* [Academy of Sciences State Committee on Science and Technology] , *1956-1988, vice-president of FID, 1969-1976, 1981-1988.* FID series, 685. Amsterdam, NL / New York, NY: Elsevier; 1990. 198p. ISBN: 0444883045; LCCN: 90048904.

F151
FOSSIER, LUCIEN; ZARRI, GIAN PIERO. 1975. *L'indexation automatique des sources documentaires anciennes* [Automatic Indexing of Ancient Documentary Sources]. Paris, FR: Editions du Centre national de la recherche scientifique (CNRS-IHRT); 1975. 87p. (Serie Informatique et Documentation Textuelle, Cb1). (In French). ISBN: 2-222-01881-1.

F152
FOUCAULT, MICHEL. 1961/1972. *Folie et déraison: Histoire de la folie a l'âge classique.* Paris: Plon; 1961. 2nd French ed., Paris: Gallimard; 1972. R. Howard, trans. *Madness and Civilization.* New York, NY: Pantheon Books; 1965. 299p. LCCN: 65-10199; OCLC: 8899259.

F153
FOUCAULT, MICHEL. 1966/1970. *Les Mots et les choses.* Bibliotheque des sciences humaines. Paris: Gallimard; 1966. 400p. LCCN: 66-86458; OCLC: 575851. Translated as: *The Order of Things.* New York, NY: Vintage Books; 1970. 387p. OCLC: 18820153.

F154
FOUCAULT, MICHEL. 1969/1972. *L'Archéologie du savoir.* Paris: Gallimard; 1969. 285p. LCCN: 77-409589; OCLC: 751834. A. M. Sheridan Smith, trans. *The Archeology of Knowledge.* New York, NY: Pantheon; 1972. 245p. ISBN: 0394471180; LCCN: 72- 1135; OCLC: 511209.

F155
FOUCAULT, MICHEL. 1977a. The Fantasia of the Library. In: Bouchard, D. F.; Simon, Sherry, trans. *Language, Counter-Memory, Practice: Selected Essays and Interviews by Michel Foucault.* Donald F. Bouchard, ed. Ithaca, NY: Cornell University Press; 1977.

F156
FOUCAULT, MICHEL. 1977b. *What is an Author?* In: *Language, Counter-memory, Practice: Selected Essays and Interviews.* Bouchard, Donald F; Simon, Sherry, trans. Ithaca, NY: Cornell University Press; 1977. 240p. ISBN: 0801409799.

F157
FOUCAULT, MICHEL. 1980. Truth and Power. In: Gordon, C., ed. *Power/Knowledge: Selected Interviews and Other Writings 1972-1977* [by Michel Foucault]. Brighton, UK: Harvester Press; 1980; 109-133.

F158
FOURNIER, JEAN-MARC. 1977. New Progress in Optical Writing Appraisal applied to the "Dreyfus Affair". In: Marom, E., ed. *Applications of Holography and Optical Data Processing.* Oxford, UK: Pergamon Press; 1977. 549-554. ISBN: 0080216250; LCCN: 77-1864; OCLC: 2818397; 109-133.

F159
FOX, C. 1992. Lexical Analysis and Stoplists. In: Frakes, William B.; Baeza-Yates, Ricardo, eds. *Information Retrieval: Data Structure & Algorithms* (pp. 102-130). Englewood-Cliffs, NJ: Prentice Hall; 1992. 504p. ISBN: 0134638379.

F160
FOX, CHARLES J.; MILLER, HUGH T. 1995. *Post-Modern Public Administration: Toward Discourse.* Beverly Hills, CA: Sage Publications; 1995. 175p. ISBN: 0803958013 (hbk.); 0803958021 (pbk.).

F161
FOX, CHRISTOPHER J. 1983. *Information and Misinformation: An Investigation of the Notions of Information, Misinformaiton, Informing, and Misinforming.* Westport, CT: Greenwood; 1983. 223p. ISBN: 0313239282.

F162
FOX, J., ed. 1990. *Educational Technology in Modern Language Learning.* Sheffield, UK: Sheffield University Press; 1990.

F163
FOX, LOUISE WATSON. 1993. *Development of a System for Producing Property-owner Time Lines with Educational Applications.* Ed.D. dissertation. East Texas State University. 290p. *DAI*, 54/09-A: 2865 (order no. AAD94-00451).

F164
FOX, M. S. 1981. An Organizational View of Distributed Systems. *IEEE Transactions on Systems, Man, and Cybernetics.* 1981; 11 (1): 70-80. ISSN: 0018-9472.

F165
FRAENKEL, ABRAHAM A.; BAR-HILLEL, YEHOSHUA; LEVEY, AZRIEL. 1973. *Foundations of Set Theory.* 2nd ed. Amsterdam, NL: Noord-Hollandsche U. M.; 1973. 404p. ISBN: 0720422701; LCCN: 68054505.

F166
FRAKES, WILLIAM B.; BAEZA-YATES, RICARDO, eds. 1992. *Information Retrieval: Data Structures and Algorithms.* Englewood Cliffs, NJ: Prentice-Hall; 1992. 504p. ISBN: 0134638379.

F167
FRANCIS, LEE: 1996. *Native Time: A Historical Time Line of Native America.* New York, NY: St. Martin's Press; 1996. 356p. ISBN: 0312131291; LCCN: 950080027.

F168
FRANCIS, WILLIAM N.; KUCERA, HENRY. 1982. *Frequency Analysis of English Usage: Lexicon and English Grammar.* Boston, MA: Houghton Mifflin; 1982. Rev. of *Computational Analysis of Present-Day American English.* Providence, RI: Brown University Press; 1967. 424p.

F169
FRANK, A. G.; GILLS, B. K. 1990. The Cumulation of Accumulation: Theses and research agenda for 5000 years of World System History. *Dialectical Anthropology.* 1990; 15: 19-42.

F170
FRANK, PETER R., ed. 1978. *Von der Systematischen Bibliographie zur Dokumentation* [From Systematic Bibliography to Documentation]. Darmstadt, DEU: Wissenschaftliche Buchgesellschaft; 1978. 556p. (Weg der Forschung, 144). (In German). ISBN: 3-534-05579-9.

F171
FRANKLIN, PHYLLIS. 1993. Scholars, Librarians, and the Future Use of Primary Records. *College & Research Libraries.* 1993 September; 54: 397-406. ISSN: 0010-0870.

F172
FRANKLIN, STAN. 1995. *Artificial Minds.* Cambridge, MA: Bradford Book; 1995. 464p. ISBN: 0-262-56109-3. Distributed by MIT Press.

F173
FRANTZEN, ALLEN J. 1990. *Desire for Origins: New Language, Old English, and Teaching the Tradition.* New Brunswick, NJ: Rutgers University Press; 1990. 260p. ISBN: 0813515904 (hbk.); 0813515912 (pbk.)

F174
FRANTZEN, ALLEN J.; NILES, JOHN D., eds. 1997. *Anglo-Saxonism and the Construction of Social Identity.* Gainesville, FL: Univeristy of Florida Press; 1997. 242p. ISBN: 0813015324 (hbk.).

F175
FRAWLEY, WILLIAM J. 1992. *Linguistic Semantics.* Hillsdale, NJ: Lawrence Erlbaum Associates, Inc.; 1992. 533p. ISBN: 0805810749 (hbk.); 0805810757 (pbk.).

F176
FRAWLEY, WILLIAM J.; PIATETSKY-SHAPIRO, GREGORY; MATHEUS, C. J. 1991. Knowledge Discovery in Databases: An Overview. See reference: PIATETSKY-SHPAIRO, G.; FRAWLEY, W. J., eds. 1991. 1-27.

F177
FREEDBERG, DAVID. 1989. *The Power of Images. Studies in the History and Theory of Response.* Chicago, IL / London, UK: University of Chicago Press; 1989. 534p. ISBN: 0226261441; LCCN: 88-27638; OCLC: 18441236.

F178
FREEDMAN, DAVID. 1983. *Markov Chains.* New York, NY: Springer-Verlag; 1983. 382p. ISBN: 0387908080.

F179
FREEDMAN, DAVID. 1991. *Statistics.* New York, NY: Norton; 1978. 506p. ISBN: 0393090760. 2nd ed.; 1991. ISBN: 0393960439.

F180
FREEDMAN, PAUL. 1995. The Return of the Grotesque in Medieval Historiography. In: Barros, Carlos, ed. *Historia à Debate* [History under debate], I-IV. Vol. 4: *Medieval* (pp. 9-19). Proceedings of an international conference, July 7-11, 1993. Santiago de Compostela, ES: Universidad de Santiago de Compostela; 1995. ISBN: 849205738.

F181
FREEDMAN, PAUL; SPIEGEL, GABRIELLE M. 1998. Medievalisms Old and New: The Rediscovery of Alterity in North American Medieval Studies. *American Historical Review*. 1998 June; 103 (3): 677-704. ISSN: 0002-8762.

F182
FREEMAN [FINCH], ELSIE T. 1991a. Soap and Education: Archival Training, Public Service, and the Profession—An Essay. *The Midwestern Archivist*. 1991; 12(2): 87-94. ISSN: 0363-888X.

F183
FREEMAN [FINCH], ELSIE T. 1991b. Teaching with Documents. Due Process and Students Rights: Syllabus of the Goss vs. Lopez Decision. *Social Education*. 1991 March; 55(3): 161-163. ISSN: 0037-7724.

F184
FREEMAN [FINCH], ELSIE. 1994. *Advocating Archives: An Introduction to Public Relations for Archivists*. Lanham, MD: Scarecrow Press for SAA; 1994. 208p. ISBN: 0-8108-2935-4: LCCN: 94003797.

F185
FREEMAN, MICHAEL S. 1991. Pen, Ink, Keys, and Cards: Some Reflections on Library Technology. *College & Research Libraries*. 1991 July; 52(4): 328-335. ISSN: 0010- 0870.

F186
FREI, HANS P.; JAUSLIN, J. F. 1983. Graphical Representation of Information Services: A User-oriented Interface. *Information Technology*. 1983; 2 (1): 23-42.

F187
FRENCH, ROBERT M. 1995. *The Subtlety of Sameness. A Theory and Computer Model of Analogy-making*. Cambridge, MA: Bradford Book; 1995. 320p. ISBN: 0-262-06180-5. Distributed by MIT Press.

F188
FRENKEL, K. A. 1991. The Human Genome Project and Informatics. *Communications of the ACM* (Assn. of Computing Machinery). 1991; 34 (11): 41-51. ISSN: 0001-0782.

F189
FRETWELL-DOWNING DATA SYSTEMS, INC. 1997. *Z39.50 for Archival Applications*. London, UK: Fretwell-Downing, Inc.; 1997.

F190
FREUD, SIGMUND. [1989]. *Das Unbehagen in der Kultur*. Trans. as: *Civilization and its Discontents*. Strachey, James; Gay, Peter, trans. New York, NY: W. W. Norton; [1989]. 127p. ISBN: 0393301583 (pbk.).

F191
FREUDER, EUGENE C.; MACWORTH, ALAN K., eds. 1994. *Constraint-based Reasoning*. Cambridge, MA: MIT Press; 1994. 409p. ISBN: 0-262-56075-5.

F192
FREYD, J. J. 1983. Representing the Dynamics of a Static Form. *Memory and Cognition*. 1983; 11(4): 342-436. ISSN: 0090-502X.

F193
FRICKE, MARTIN. 1997. Information Using Likeness Measures. *Journal of the American Society for Information Science*. 1997 October; 48(10): 882-892. ISSN: 0002-8231.

F194
FRIEDEN, ROB. 1996. *International Telecommunications Handbook*. Boston, MA: Artech House; 1996. 419p. (Artech Telecommunications Library). ISBN: 0890065683; LCCN: 95041686.

F195
FRIEDHOFF, RICHARD; BENZON, WILLIAM. 1989/1991. *Visualization: The Second Computer Revolution*. New York: NY: Abrams; 1989. 215p. ISBN: 0-8109-1709-2. New York, NY: W. H. Freeman; 1991. ISBN: 0716722312; LCCN: 90049785.

F196
FRIEDLANDER, SAUL. 1997. *Nazi Germany and the Jews*. Vol 1: *The Years of Persecution*. New York, NY: Harper Collins; 1997. 436p. ISBN: 0-06-019042-6.

F197
FRIEDLANDER, SAUL, ed. 1992. *Probing the Limits of Representation: Nazism and the "Final Solution."* Papers from Conference on topic, UCLA, April 26-29, 1990. 407p. ISBN: 0674707664 (pbk.); LCCN: 91029609.

F198
FRIEDMAN, ANDREW L.; CORNFELD, DOMINIC S. 1989. *Computer Systems Development: History, Organization, and Implementation.* New York, NY: John Wiley & Sons; 1989. 420p. ISBN: 0471923990.

F199
FRIEDMAN, DANIEL; FELLEISEN, MATTHIAS. 1996a. *The Little Schemer.* 4th ed. Cambridge, MA: MIT Press; 1994. 224p. ISBN: 0-262-56099-2.

F200
FRIEDMAN, DANIEL; FELLEISEN, MATTHIAS. 1996b. *The Seasoned Schemer.* Cambridge, MA: MIT Press; 1996. 224p. ISBN: 0-262-56100-X.

F201
FRIEDMAN, JEROME M.; OLSHEN, R. A.; STONE, C. J. 1984. *Classification and Regression Trees.* Belmont, CA: Wadsworth; 1984. 358p. ISBN: 0534980546 (hbk.); 0534980538 (pbk.).

F202
FRIEDMAN, JOHN B. 1991. Electronic Sleuthing in Medieval Scriptoria. *Scriptsit: The triannual Journal of the Washington Calligraphers Guild.* 1991; 15 (2): 15-18.

F203
FRIEDMAN, JOHN B. 1992. Cluster Analysis and Manuscript Chronology of William du Stiphel, a Fourteenth-century Scribe at Durham. *History and Computing.* 1992; 4: 75-97. ISSN: 0957-0144.

F204
FRIEDMAN, JOHN B. 1993. Computerized Script Analysis and Classification: Some Directions for Research. See reference: DOORN, P., *ET AL.*, eds. 1993. 67-81.

F205
FRIJHOFF, WILLEM. 1995. Structures and Contingencies in Historical Research. See reference: BOONSTRA, O.; COLLENEUR, G.; VAN ELDEREN, B., eds. 1995. 10-22.

F206
FRILING, TUVIA. 1996 [199-]. History and Computing: Steps toward a less relative Discipline. See reference: BORODKIN, L., ed. 1996: Abstract of presentation, 128-129; paper [199- forthcoming].

F207
FRODEMAN, R. 1995. Geological reasoning: Geology as an interpretative and historical science. *Geological Society of America Bulletin.* 1995; 107 (8): 960-968.

F208
FROELICH, T. J. 1994. Relevance Reconsidered—Towards an Agenda for the 21st century: Introduction to Special Topic Issue on Relevance Research. *Journal of the American Society for Information Science.* 1994; 45: 124-134. (Entire issue on title topic). ISSN: 0002-8231.

F209
FUCHS, EDUARD. 1993. Teaching History & Computing at the Viennese Departments of History. See reference: DAVIS, DENLEY, SPAETH & TRAINOR, eds. 1993. 103-106.

F210
FUCHS, STEPHAN. 1992. *The Professional Quest for Truth: A Social Theory of Science and Knowledge.* Albany, NY: SUNY Press; 1992. 254p. ISBN: 0791409236 (hbk.); 0791409244 (pbk.).

F211
FUKUYAMA, FRANCIS. 1992. *The End of History and the Last Man.* New York, NY: Free Press; 1992. 418p. ISBN: 002909752.

F212
FUKUYAMA, FRANCIS. 1995. *Trust: Social Virtues and the Creation of Prosperity.* New York, NY: Free Press; 1995. 457p. ISBN: 0029109760.

F213
FULD, LEONARD. 1995. *The New Competitor Intelligence: The Complete Resource of Finding, Analyzing and Using Information about your Competitors.* New York, NY: John Wiley & Sons; 1995. 428p. ISBN: 0471585084 (hbk.); 0471585092 (pbk.); LCCN: 94-18292.

F214
FUNKENSTEIN, AMOS. 1989. Collective Memory and Historical Consciousness. *History and Memory*. 1989 Spring/Summer; 1: 5-26. ISSN: 0935-560X.

F215
FURET, FRANÇOIS. 1971. Quantitative History. *Daedalus*. 1971; 100: 151-167. ISSN: 0011- 5266.

F216
FURET, FRANÇOIS. 1974. L'Histoire quantitative et la construction du fait historique [Quantitative History and the Construction of Historical Fact]. See reference: LE GOFF, J.; NORA, P., eds., 1974: 35-49.

F217
FURET, FRANÇOIS. 1983. Beyond the *Annales*. *Journal of Modern History*. 1983; 55: 389- 410. ISSN: 0022-2801.

F218
FURET, FRANÇOIS. 1984. *Atelier de l'Histoire*. Mandelbaum, Jonathon, trans. *In the Workshop of History*. Chicago, IL: University of Chicago Press; 1984. 259p. ISBN: 02262733369; LCCN: 84-2638; OCLC: 10725318..

F219
FURET, FRANÇOIS; OZOOUF, JACQUES. 1977. *Lire et écrire: L'Alphabetisation français* [Reading and Writing: The French Alphabetization]. Paris, FR: Editions de Minuit; 1977. 2 vols., 372p. ISBN: 2707301892; LCCN: 78-349723; OCLC: 3913118.

F220
FURNAS, G. W.; LANDAUER, T. K.; GOMEZ, L. M.; DUMAIS, S. T. 1987. The Vocabulary Problem in Human-system Communications. *Communications of the* ACM (Assn. of Computing Machinery). 1987; 30: 964-971. ISSN: 0001-0782.

F221
FURNHAM, A. 1986. Book Reviews as a Selection Tool for Librarians: Comments from a Psychologist. *Collection Management*. 1986; 8(1): 33-43. ISSN: 0146-2679.

F222
FURSTENBERG, G. M. VON, ed. 1989. *Acting under Uncertainty: Multidisciplinary Conceptions*. Boston, MA: Kluwer Academic Publ.; 1989. 485p. ISBN: 079239036.

F223
FURUKAWA, KOICHI; MICHIE, DONALD; MUGGLEON, STEPHEN, eds. 1994. *Machine Intelligence 13: Machine Intelligence and Inductive Learning*. 13th Machine Intelligence workshop, Loch Lomond, Scotland, 1992. Oxford, UK: Clarendon Press; 1994. 478p. ISBN: 0198538502.

F224
FYFE, GORDON; LAW, JOHN. 1988. Picturing Power: Visual Depiction and Social Relations. In: *Sociological Review*. New York, NY and London, UK: Routledge; 1988. 281p. (Monograph no.35). (Entire issue on title topic). ISBN: 0415031443 (pbk.).

F225
FYFE, JANET. 1986. *History Journals and Serials: An Analytical Guide*. New York, NY: Greenwood Press; 1986. (Annotated Bibliographies of serials, 8). 351p. ISBN: 0313239991.

-G-

G1
GABLE, ERIC; HANDLER, RICHARD. 1994. The Authority of Documents at some American History Museums. *Journal of American History*. 1994 June; 81(1): 118-128. ISSN: 0021- 8723.

G2
GABOWITSCH, MISCHA. 1997. Mathematics contra Chronology. *Moscow News*. 1997 July 31; p. 6. (About Anatoly Fomenko's theories).

G3
GABRIEL, RICHARD P. 1985. *Performance and Evaluation of LISP Systems*. Cambridge, MA: MIT Press; 1985. 285p. ISBN: 0262070936 (pbk.).

G4
GABRIEL, RICHARD P. 1996. *Patterns of Software: Tales from the Software Community*. New York, NY: Oxford University Press; 1996. 235p. ISBN: 019510269X; LCCN: 95-41883.

G5
GADAMAR, HANS-GEORG. 1975/1989. *Wahrheit und Methode.* Weinsheimer, J.; Marshall, D., trans. *Truth and Method.* Barden, G.; Cumming, J., eds. London, UK: Sheed & Ward; 1975. Reprint: New York, NY: Crossroad; 1989. ISBN: 07227076002; LCCN: 7636169.

G6
GADAMAR, HANS-GEORG, ed. 1972. *Verité et historicité.* Trans. *Truth and Historicity.* The Hague, NL: Martinus Nijhoff; 1972. 79p. ISBN: 9024712025; LCCN: 73321924. (English, French and German).

G7
GAFFIELD, CHAD. 1982. Theory and Method in Canadian Historical Demography. *Archivaria.* 1982; 14: 123-136. ISSN: 0318-6954.

G8
GAFFIELD, CHAD. 1988. Machines and Minds: Historians and the Merging Collaboration. *Histoire sociale / Social History* (CAN). 1988 November; 21 (42): 312-317. ISSN: 0018- 2557.

G9
GAFFIELD, CHAD. 1993. *Aux Origines de l'identité Franco-Ontarienne: Education, Culture et Économie* [The Origins of the French-Ontarian Identity: Education, Culture and Economy]. Ottawa, CN: Presses de l'Université d'Ottawa; 1993. 284p. (In French). ISBN: 2760302555.

G10
GAFFIELD, CHAD; BASKERVILLE, PETER A. 1985. The Automated Archivist: Interdisciplinarity and the Process of Historical Research. *Social Science History.* 1985 spring; 9: 167-184. ISSN: 0145-5532.

G11
GAFFIELD, CHAD; BASKERVILLE, PETER A.; PANTER, CATHERINE; SHEPHERD, PAULINE. 1985. *Field Definitions and Data Entry for Archival Material.* Victoria, BC: VIP (Vancouver Island Project); 1985. Related to: *Vancouver Island Project System: Project Design Manual* and *VIPS: User Guide.* Victoria, BC, CN: University of Victoria Computing and Systems Services; 1987.

G12
GAFFNEY, VINCENT; STANCIC, ZORAN. 1991. *GIS Approaches to Regional Analysis: A Case Study of the Island of Hvar* [Croatia]. Ljubljana: University of Ljubljana Research Institute of the Faculty of Arts; 1991. 100p. OCLC: 27562640.

G13
GAGAN, DAVID. 1988. Some Comments on the Canadian Experience with Historical Databases. *Histoire sociale / Social History* (CAN). 1988 November; 21(42): 300-303. ISSN: 0018-2557.

G14
GAGLIARDI, PASQUALE. 1990a. Artifacts as Pathways and Remains of Organizational Life. See reference: GAGLIARDI, P., ed. 1990b. 3-40.

G15
GAGLIARDI, PASQUALE, ed. 1990b. *Symbols and Artifacts: Views of the Corporate Landscape.* Third International Conference on Organizational Symbolism and Corporate Culture, University of Milan, June 24-26, 1987. New York, NY: Aldine de Gruter; 1990. 428p. ISBN: 0-202-30428-0; LCCN: 91-44078.

G16
GAGNE, ROBERT. M., ed. *Instructional Technology: Foundations.* Hillsdale, NJ: Erlbaum; 1987. 473p. ISBN: 0898596262 (hbk.); 0898598788 (pbk.).

G17
GAGNON, PAUL A. 1987. *Democracy's Untold Story: What World History Textbooks Neglect.* Washington, D.C.: American Federation of Teachers; 1987. 142p. (Publication of the Education for Democracy Project). LC call no.: JC423.G171.

G18
GAGNON, PAUL A., ed. 1989. *Historical Literacy: The Case for History in American Education.* New York, NY: Columbia University Press; 1989. 338p. (Report of the Bradley Commission on History in Schools). ISSN: 0025-4215.

G19
GALE, S. 1990. Human Aspects of Interactive Multimedia Communication. *Interacting with Computers.* 1990; 2(2): 175-189. ISSN: 0953-5438. Available also online at http://peak.umdl.umich.edu/cgi-bin/peak/list journal/09535438.

G20
GALE GROUP, INC. [2000-]. *Historical Resource Center* (electronic file). Detroit, MI: Gale Group, Inc.; [2000-forthcoming]. Publisher's website and CD-ROM, produced with subsidiary, Primary Source Multimedia, Inc., initially for U.S. History; contains secondary literature, reference tools, documents, and bibliographic links.

G21

GALEGHER, JOLENE; KRAUT, ROBERT E.,; EGIDO, CARMEN, eds. 1990. *Intellectual Teamwork: Social and Technological Foundations of Cooperative Work*. Hillsdale, NJ: Lawrence Erbaum Associates; 1990. 542p. ISBN: 0805805338 (hbk.); 0805805346 (pbk.).

G22

GALINE, HENRI. 1980. De la Stratigraphie a la Chronologie [Concerning Stratigraphy and Chronology]. In: Schnapp, A., ed. *L'Archeologie aujourd d'hui* [Archeology Today]. Paris, FR: Editions Errance; 1980. ISBN: 2877720616; OCLC: 26198331; 63-86.

G23

GALISON, PETER L.; HEVLY, BRUCE W., eds. 1992. *Big Science: The Growth of Large- Scale Research*. Stanford, CA: Stanford University Press; 1992. 392p. ISBN: 0804718792.

G24

GALLAGAN, PATRICIA A. 1993. The Search for the Poetry of Work. *Training & Development*. 1993; 47 (10): 33-37. ISSN: 1055-9760. Note: a response to the 1982 report on U.S. education, *A Nation at Risk*, by the Institute for Research on Learning (IRL).

G25

GALLAGHER, PATRICK J.; D'AMICO, HELEN, eds. *Hermeneutics and Medieval Culture*. Albany, NY: State University of New York Press; 1989. 287p. ISBN: 0887067433 (hbk.); 088706745X (pbk.).

G26

GALLAGHER, RICHARD S., ed. 1995. *Computer Visualization. Graphic Techniques for Engineering and Scientific Analysis*. Los Alamitos, CA: IEEE; 1995. 352p. ISBN: 0-8493-9050-8.

G27

GALLOWAY, EDWARD A.; MICHALEK, GABRIELLE V. 1995. The Heinz Electronic Library Interactive Online System (HELIOS): Building a Digital Archive Using OCR and Natural Language Processing Technologies. *The Public-Access Computer Systems Review* (electronic journal). 1995; 6 (4): unpaginated. Accessible athttp://info.lib.ub.edu/ pr/v6/n4/gall6n4.html.

G28

GALLUPE, R. B.; DENNIS, A. R.; COOPER, W. H.; VALACICH, J. S.; BASTIANUTTI, L. M.; NUNAMAKER, J. F., Jr. 1992. Electronic Brainstorming and Group Size. *Academy of Management Journal*. 1992; 35: 350-369. ISSN: 0001-4273.

G29

GALTUNG, JOHAN. 1981. Structure, Culture, and Intellectual Style: An Essay Comparing Saxonic, Teutonic, Gallic, and Nipponic Approaches. *Social Sciences Information*. 1981; 26 (6): 817-856.

G30

GALTUNG, JOHAN. 1990. Macro-History as Metaphor for Biography: An Essay on Macro- and Micro-History. *Biography*. 1990 Fall; 13 (4): 283-299.

G31

GALVIN, THOMAS J.; KAHN, RUSSELL L. 1996. *Electronic Records Management as Strategic Opportunity: A Case Study of the State University of New York Office of Archives and Records Management*. Chicgao, IL: SAA; 1996. Case study, 22p; Teaching notes, 14 p. Available from: SAA Publications, Chicago, Il.

G32

GARDINER, PATRICK. 1961. *The Nature of Historical Explanation*. London: Oxford University Press; 1961. 142p. OCLC: 269800.

G33

GARDINER, PATRICK, ed. 1974. *The Philosophy of History*. New York, NY: Oxford University Press; 1974. 224p. ISBN 0-19-875031-5.

G34

GAREAU, WILLIAM: 1983. The Increasing Ethnocentrism of American Social Science. *International Journal of Comparative Sociology*. 1983 September; 24: 248-260. ISSN: 0020-7152.

G35

GARFIELD, EUGENE. 1979. *Citation Indexing—Its Theory and Application in Science, Technology, and Humanities*. New York, NY: Wiley; 1979. 274p. ISBN: 0471025593.

G36

GARFIELD, EUGENE. 1980. Is Information Retrieval in the Arts and Humanities Inherently Different from that in Science? The Effect that ISI's *Citation Index for the Arts and Humanities* is Expected to Have on Future Scholarship. *Library Quarterly*. 1980 January; 50(1): 40-57. ISSN: 0024-2519.

G37
GARFIELD, EUGENE. 1991. To Be an Uncited Scientist is No Cause for Shame. In: Garfield, E., ed. *Essays of an Information Scientist*. Philadelphia, PA: ISI Press; 1991; 14: 390-391. 15 vols. ISBN: 0894950002 (set).

G38
GARFIELD, EUGENE; WELLJAMS-DOROF, A. 1990. Language Use in International Research: A citation analysis. *AAPSS Annual*. 1990; 51: 10-24.

G39
GARFINKEL, SIMSON. 1995. *PGP: Pretty Good Privacy.* Sebastopol, CA: O'Reilly & Associates; 1995. 393 p. ISBN: 1565970988.

G40
GARG, PANKAJ; JAZAYERI, MEHDI, eds. 1995. *Process-centered Software Engineering Environments*. Los Alamitos, CA: IEEE; 1995. 424p. ISBN: 0-8186-7103-3.

G41
GARLAND, K.; RIKE, G. E. 1987. Scholarly Productivity of Faculty at ALA-accredited Programs of Library and Information Science. *Journal of Education for Library and Information Science*. 1987; 28 (2): 87-98. ISSN: 0748-5786.

G42
GARNER, J. F. 1994. *Politically correct bedtime stories*. New York, NY: Macmillan Publishing Co.; 1994. 79 pp. ISBN: 0-02-542730-X.

G43
GARNHAM, ALAN. 1987. *Mental Models as Representations of Discourse and Text*. New York, NY: John Wiley and Sons; 1987. 205p. (Ellis Horwood series in cognitive science). ISBN: 0745802095.

G44
GARNIER, FRANCOIS. 1984. *Thésaurus Iconographique, systéme descriptif des representation* [Iconographic Thesaurus: Descriptive System of Representations]. Paris, FR: Leopard d'Or; 1984. 239p. ISSN: 2863770322; LCCN: 84-239484; OCLC: 11217800.

G45
GARSIDE, ROGER; LEECH, GEOFFREY; SAMPSON, GEOFFREY, eds. 1987. *The Computational Analysis of English: A Corpus-based Approach*. London, UK: Longman Group UK, Ltd.; 1987. 196p. ISBN: 0-582-29149-6.

G46
GARSKOVA, IRINA. 1993/1994. Problems and Perspectives of Machine-Readable Data Archiving in Russia. See reference: MARKER, ed. 1993/1194. [1-10].

G47
GARSKOVA, IRINA M., ed. 1994. *Bazy I banki dannych v istoriceskich isledovanijach* [Data banks and Historical Research Developments]. Moscow, RU: M. V. Lomononsova Universitet; 1994. 214p.

G48
GARSKOVA, IRINA M.; BELOVA, EVGENIA B.; BORODKIN, LEONID I., eds. 1996. *Istoricheskaia informatika* [Historical Informatics].Moscow, RU: Mosgorarkkkhiv; 1996. 395p. (Desiat novykh uchebnikov po istoricheskim distsiplinam [The New Disciples of the Historical Scientific Discipline]). ISBN: 5-7228-0031-7.

G49
GARSKOVA, IRINA; BORODKIN, LEONID. 1993. *FUZZYCLASS*: A New Tool for Typological Analysis in Historical Research. See reference: BORODKIN, L.; LEVERMAN, W., eds. 1993. 71-86.

G50
GARSON, G. DAVID. 1986. *Academic Microcomputing: A Resource Guide*. Newbury Park, CA: Sage Publications, Inc; 1986. 175p. ISBN: 0803929277; 0803929285 (pbk.); LCCN: 86-13087; OCLC: 17225088.

G51
GARSON, G. DAVID. 1989. Data Archives, Transfer, and Analysis in the Social Sciences: The NCSC Dataset Program for Research Instruction. See reference: MCCRANK, L., ed. 1989. 247-252.

G52
GARSON, G. DAVID. 1997. *Computer Technology and Social Issues*. Hershey, PA: Idea Group Publishing; 1997. 456p. ISBN: 1-878289-28-4.

G53
GARSON, G. DAVID; OBERMAN, E. SAMUEL. 1983. *Public Management Research in the United States*. New York, NY: F. Praeger; 1983. 194p. ISBN: 0030621593; LCCN: 83002400.

G54

GARTNER, R. 1993. Moves Toward the Electronic Bodleian: Introducing Digital Imaging into the Bodleian Library. ACH-ALLC'93 Joint International Conference, Georgetown University, Washington, D.C. 16-19 June, 1993. (Conference handout).

G55

GARTNER GROUP, INC. 1996. *Data Warehouse, Data Mining, and Business Intelligence: The Hype Stops Here* (Electronic file). N.p.: Gartner Group; October 1996. (Gartner report in Business Applications). Accessible at http://www.gartner.com/hotc/ alphasars.html.

G56

GARVEY, WILLIAM D. 1979. *Communication: The Essence of Science. Facilitating Information Exchange between Librarians, Scientists, Engineers, and Students.* New York, NY: Pergamon Presss; 1979. 332p. ISBN: 0080225441 (hbk.); 0080233449 (pbk.).

G57

GARVEY, WILLIAM D.; GRIFFITH, BELVER C. 1972. Communication and Information Processing within Scientific Disciplines: Empirical Findings for Psychology. *Information Storage & Retrieval.* 1972; 8: 123-126. ISSN: 0020-0271.

G58

GATES, BILL; MYHRVOLD, NATHAN; RINEARSON, PETER. 1995. *The Road Ahead.* New York, NY: Penguin Books; 1995. 332 pp. and CD-ROM. ISBN: 0-670-77289-5 (hbk.); 0-14-2-6040 (pbk.) .

G59

GAUCH, SUSAN. 1992. Intelligent Information Retrieval: An Introduction. *Journal of the American Society for Information Science.* 1992; 43: 1775-182. ISSN: 0002-8231.

G60

GAVREL, KATHERINE. 1990. *Conceptual Problems Posed by Electronic Records. A RAMP Study.* Paris, FR: UNESCO General Information Programme and UNISIST; April 1990. 46p.+ 3p. PGI-90/WS/12. LCCN: 90-220432; OCLC: 22617085. Available from: UNESCO Federal Information Programme, 7 Place de Fontenoy, 75700 Paris, FR.

G61

GAVRISH, MICHAEL J. ARRATO. 1995. The Historian as Detective: An Introduction to Historical Methodology. *Social Education.* 1995 March; 59 (3): 151-154. ISSN: 0037-7724.

G62

GEARHART, SUZANNE. 1987. History as Criticism: The Dialogue of History and Literature. *Diacritics.* 1987; 17(3): 56-65. ISSN: 0300-7162.

G63

GEARY, PATRICK J. 1994. *Phantoms of Remembrance: Memory and Oblivion at the End of the First Millennium.* Princeton, NJ: Princeton University Press; 1994. 248p. ISBN: 0691034222.

G64

GEDA, CAROLYN. 1979. Social Science Data Archives. *The American Archivist.* April 1979; 42 (2): 158-66. ISSN: 0360-9081.

G65

GEDA, CAROLYN; AUSTIN, ERICK W.; BLOUIN, FRANCIS X. 1980. *Archives and Machine Readable Records.* Proceedings of the Conference on Archival management of Machine-Readable Records, February 7-10, 1979. Chicago, IL: SAA; 1980. 248p. ISBN: 0931828198; OCLC: 7095423.

G66

GEDI, NOA; ELAM, YIGAL. 1996. Collective Memory—What is It? *History and Memory.* 1996 Spring/Summer; 8: 30-50. ISSN: 0935-560X.

G67

GEERTZ, CLIFFORD. 1973/1979. *The Interpretation of Cultures.* New York, NY: Basic Books; 1973. Reprint, 1979. 470p. ISBN: 046503425X.

G68

GEERTZ, CLIFFORD. 1983. *Local Knowledge.* New York, NY: Basic Books; 1983. 244p. ISBN: 0465041582.

G69

GEIGER, ROGER L. 1986. *To Advance Knowledge: The Growth of American Research Universities, 1900-1940.* Oxford, UK: Oxford University Press; 1986. 321p. ISBN: 0195938037.

G70
GEIGER, ROGER L. 1993. *Research and Relevant Knowledge: American Research Universities since World War II.* New York, NY: Oxford University Press; 1993. 411p. ISBN: 019505346X.

G71
GELL, ALFRED. 1992. *The Anthropology of Time. Cultural Construction of Temporal Maps and Images.* London, UK: Berg; 1992. 341p. ISBN: 0-85496-890-3.

G72
GENET, JEAN-PHILIPPE. 1978. L'Historien et l'ordinateur [The Historian and the Computer]. *Historiens et Géographies* (FR). 1978; 270: 125-142. (In French).

G73
GENET, JEAN-PHILIPPE. 1992. Sources, Metasources, Textes, et Histoire [Sources, Meta-sources, Texts, and History]. (In French). See reference: BOCCHI, F.; DENLEY, P., eds. 1992. 3-12.

G74
GENET, JEAN-PHILIPPE. 1995. La Formation des Historiens a l'Informatique en France: Espoir ou Désespoir? [Training of Historians in Informatics in France: Hope or Despair?]. *Le Médiéviste et l'Ordinateur* (FR). 1995 Printemps-Automne; 31-32: 32- 36. (In French). ISSN: 0223-3843.

G75
GENET, JEAN-PHILIPPE, ed. 1988. *Standardisation et Échange des Bases de Donées Historiques: Actes de la Troisiéme Table Ronde International Tenue au L.I.S.H.* [Standardization and Change in Historical Databases: Acts of the Third International Round Table head at L.I.S.H.]. Paris, FR: Centre National de la Recherche Scientifique; 1988. (In French). ISBN: 2-222-04222-4.

G76
GENET, JEAN-PHILIPPE, ed. 1991. *L'Historiographie médiévale en Europe* [Medieval Historiography in Europe]. Actes du colloque organisé par la Fondation Européenne de la Science, au Centre de recherches historiques et juridiques de l'Université Paris I, du 29 mars au 1er avril 1989. Paris, FR: Editions du CNRS; 1991. 342 p. (In French, English, German and Italian). ISBN: 2222046092.

G77
GENET, JEAN-PHILIPPE; LOTTES, G., eds. 1996. L'État moderne et les elites XIIe- XVIIIe siècles: apports et limite de la méthode prosopographique [The Modern State and Elites in the 12-18th centuries: Depositions and the Limits of Prosopographic methodology]. In: *Actes du colloque international CNRS*, Paris, 16-19 octobre 1991. Paris, FR: Publications de la Sorbonne; 1996. 79-94. (In French).

G78
GENET, JEAN-PHILIPPE; ZAMPOLLI, ANTONIO, eds. 1992. *Computers and the Humanities* (NL). Aldershot and Dartmouth for the European Science Foundation; 1992. 139p. ISBN: 1855212897; LCCN: 93-122882; 31045716. Distributed in the U.S. by Ashgate Publishing Co.

G79
GEORGES, JAMES; JOHNSON, DEL. 1992. *Dynamical Systems Software. A First Course in Chaotic Dynamical Systems Software Labs: 1-6.* Reading, MA: Addison, Wesley, Longman; 1992. (Guide with Macintosh disc). (Studies in Nonlinearity series). ISBN: 0-201-52767-7 (hbk.).

G80
GEORGES, R.; JONES, M. 1995. *Folkloristics: An Introduction.* Bloomington, IN: Indiana University Press; 1995.

G81
GEROVITCH, SLAVA. 1996. Perestroika of the History of Technology and Science in the USSR: Changes in the Discourse. *History and Culture.* 1996 January; 37(1): 102-134. ISSN: 0040-165X.

G82
GERVERS, MICHAEL; LONG, GILLIAN; MCCULLOCH, MICHAEL. 1990. The *DEEDS* Database of Medieval Charters. History and Computing: Design and Coding of the RDBMS Oracle 5. 1990; 2: 1-11. See reference: DENLEY, P. *ET AL.*, eds. 1990. 1- 11.

G83
GETTIER, E. L. 1963. Is Justified True Belief Knowledge? *Analysis.* 1963; 23: 121-123. ISSN: 0003-2638.

G84
GETTY TRUST, J. PAUL. ART HISTORY INFORMATION PROGRAM (AHIP). 1990-1997. *Art & Architecture Thesaurus.* New York, NY and Oxford, UK: Oxford University Press; 1990. 1782p. in 3 vols. plus supplement; 1992. ISBN: 0-19-506403-8. 2nd expanded and revised ed.; 1994. ISBN: 0-19-508884-0. *ATT:ART 2.0* (Electronic edition); 1994. ISBN: 0-19-508885-9 for singles users; 0-19-508998-7 for networks. *ATT:USMARC 2.0* (US MARC Authority Format; diskette); 1994. ISBN: 0- 89236-306-1 (-X for 5.25" diskette). *ATT:REC 2.0* (Authority

Record Format Version; diskette); 1994. ISBN: 089236-309-6 (-X for 5.25" diskette). All are available from: ATT User Services Dept., Oxford University Press Electronic Publishing, 200 Madison Ave., New York, NY 10016.

G85
GETTY TRUST, J. PAUL. ART HISTORY INFORMATION PROGRAM (AHIP). 1991-. *Bibliography of the History of Art/Bibliographie d'Histoire del'Art* (*BHA*). Paris: Centre National de la Recherche Scientifique, (CNRS), Institut de l'Information Scientific et Technique (INIST); 1991-. 4 vols. annually. ISSN: 1150-1588. (Continues *RILA: Repertoire International de Literature d'Art*). Available from: INIST Diffusion, 2 Allee du Parc de Brabois, F-54514 Vandoeuvre-les-Nancy Cedex, France.

G86
GETTY TRUST, J. PAUL. ART HISTORY INFORMATION PROGRAM (AHIP). 1992a. *Art & Architecture Thesaurus: Authority Reference Tool edition* (software). New York, NY: Oxford University Press for AHIP; 1992. ISBN: 0-19-508144-7. (Includes *ULAN: Union List of Artists Names*). Available from: Oxford University Press Electronic Publishing, 200 Madison Ave., New York, NY 10016.

G87
GETTY TRUST, J. PAUL. ART HISTORY INFORMATION PROGRAM (AHIP). 1992b. *The Getty Art History Information Program* (brochure). Santa Monica, CA: Getty Trust AHIP; 1992. 12p. Available from: the Getty Trust, 401 Wilshire Blvd., Suite 1100, Santa Monica CA 90401-1455.

G88
GETTY TRUST, J. PAUL. ART HISTORY INFORMATION PROGRAM (AHIP). 1992c. *Bibliography of the History of Art/Bibliographie d'Histoire del'Art: BHA Subject Headings English/BHA Mots cles materière Français.* Santa Monica, CA: AHIP; 1992-. ISSN: 1150-1588. Available from: K. Buckwalter, BHA Managing Editor, Clark Art Institute, Williamstown, MA 01267.

G89
GETTY TRUST, J. PAUL. ART HISTORY INFORMATION PROGRAM (AHIP). 1996. *Research Agenda for Networked Cultural Heritage.* Santa Monica, CA: Getty AHIP; 1996. Available from: the Getty Trust, 401 Wilshire Blvd., Suite 1100, Santa Monica CA 90401-1455.

G90
GETTY TRUST, J. PAUL. ART HISTORY INFORMATION PROGRAM (AHIP); COLLEGE ART ASSOCIATION. ART INFORMATION TASK FORCE. 1996a. *Categories for the Description of Works of Art* (electronic file). Baca, M.; Harping, P., eds. Santa Monica, CA: AHIP & CAA; 1996. 2 3.5 disks for Windows 3.1; reference card. ISBN: 0892364068. Available also as package with *Visual Resources.* 1996; 11 (3-4). Cf. "Standards" at http://www.getty/edu/gri/research/icres. htm.

G91
GETTY TRUST, J. PAUL. ART HISTORY INFORMATION PROGRAM (AHIP). 1996b. *Research Agenda for Networked Cultural Heritage.* Bearman, David, ed. Santa Monica, CA: Getty AHIP; 1996. 80p. ISBN: 0892303149.

G92
GETTY TRUST, J. PAUL. ART HISTORY INFORMATION PROGRAM (AHIP); THE AMERICAN COUNCIL OF LEARNED SOCIETIES (ACLS); THE COALITION FOR NETWORKED INFORMATION (CNI). 1994. *Humanities and Arts on the Information Highways. A Profile.* Santa Monica, CA: J. Paul Getty Trust AHIP; 1994. 48p. Available from: J. Paul Getty Trust AHIP, 401 Wilshire Blvd., Suite 1100, Santa Monica CA 90401-1455.

G93
GETTY TRUST, J. PAUL. ART HISTORY INFORMATION PROGRAM (AHIP); INTERNATIONAL COUNCIL OF MUSEUMS (ICOM). INTERNATIONAL DOCUMENTATION COMMITTEE (CIDOC). 1993. *Developments in International Museum and Cultural Heritage Information Standards* (brochure). Santa Monica, CA: Getty Trust AHIP; 1993. 32p. Available from: Getty Trust AHIP, 401 Wilshire Blvd. 1100, Santa Monica CA 90401-1455.

G94
GETTY TRUST, J. PAUL. ART INFORMATION TASK FORCE (AITF). [199-]. *Categories for the Description of Works of Art.* Santa Monica, CA: Getty Trust AHIP; (Forthcoming). Information available from the project manager, Deborah Wilde, Getty Trust via E-Mail at dwilde@getty.edu.

G95
GEU, THOMAS E. 1998. Chaos, Complexity, and Coevolution: The Web of Law, Management Theory, and Law Related Services at the Millennium. *Tennessee Law Review.* 1998; 66 (1): 137-. ISSN: 0040-3288.

G96
GEUENICH, DIETER. 1991. A Data Base for Research on Persons and Groups of Persons in the Middle Ages. See reference: H. BEST *ET AL.*, eds., 1991. 103-108.

G97
GEUSS, RAYMOND. 1996. Kultur, Bildung, Geist [Culture, Formation, and Taste]. *History and Theory*. 1996 May; 35(2): 151-167. ISSN: 0018-2656.

G98
GEYER, MICHAEL; BRIGHT, CHARLES. 1995. World History in a Global Age. *American Historical Review*. 1995 October; 100 (4):1034-1058. ISSN: 0018-2656.

G99
GIBBONS, PATRICK T. 1992. Impacts of Organization Evolution on Leadership Roles and Behaviors. *Human Relations*. 1992 January; 45 (1); 1-18. ISSN: 0018-7267.

G100
GIBBS, BRIAN H.; SINGER, J. DAVID. 1993. *Empirical Knowledge on World Politics: A Summary of Quantitative Research, 1970-1991*. Westport, CT: Greenwood Press; 1993. 453p. ISBN: 0313272271; LCCN: 93-25478; OCLC: 28416400.

G101
GIDDENS, ANTHONY. 1976. *New Rules of Sociological Method: A Positive Critique of Interpretative Sociologies*. New York, NY: Basic Books; 1976. 192p. ISBN: 0465050832.

G102
GIDDENS, ANTHONY. 1979. *Central Problems in Social Theory: Action, Structure, and Contradiction in Social Analysis*. Berkeley, CA: University of California Press; 1979. 294p. ISBN: 0520039726 (hbk.); 0520039750 (hbk.).

G103
GIDDENS, ANTHONY. 1990. *The Consequences of Modernity*. Stanford CA: Stanford University Press; 1990. 186p. ISBN: 0804717621.

G104
GIDDENS, ANTHONY. 1995. *A Contemporary Critique of Historical Materialism*. 2nd ed. Basingstroke, UK: Macmillan; 1995. 294p. ISBN: 0333625536 (pbk.); 0333625544 (hbk.).

G105
GIDDENS, ANTHONY; TURNER, JONATHAN H., eds. 1987. *Social Theory Today*. Stanford, CA: Stanford University Press; 1987. 428p. ISBN: 0804713979.

G106
GIGERENZER, GERD. 1989. *The Empire of Chance: How Probability Changed Science and Everyday Life*. Cambridge, UK: Cambridge University Press; 1989. 360p. LCCN: 88- 16928.

G107
GIGERENZER, GERD; MURRAY, D. J. 1987. *Cognition as Intuitive Statistics*. Hillsdale, NJ: Lawrence Erlbaum; 1987. 214p. ISBN: 0898595703; LCCN: 86-23927.

G108
GIGUERE, MARK D. 1997. Automating Electronic Records Management in a Transactional Environment: The Philadelphia Story. See reference: TRAVIS, I., ed. 1997. 17-19.

G109
GILBERT, E. N. 1966. Information Theory after 18 Years. *Science*. 1966; 152: 320-326. ISSN: 0036-8075.

G110
GILBERT, FELIX. 1977. *History: Choice and Commitment*. Cambridge, MA: Harvard University Belknap Press; 1977. 549p. ISBN: 0674396561; LCCN: 67027352.

G111
GILCHRIST, ALAN D. 1994. Classifications and Thesauri. See reference: VICKERY, B. C., ed. 1994. 85-118.

G112
GILDEA, ROBERT. 1994. *The Past in French History*. New Haven, CT: Yale University Press; 1994. 418p. ISBN: 0300057997.

G113
GILHOOLEY, IAN A. 1991. *Information Systems Management, Control and Audit*. Altamonte Springs, FL: Institute of Internal Auditors; 1991. 507p. ISBN: 6894132369.

G114
GILL, PHILIP J. 1998. Archeology Finds Riches in AutoCAD. *Education by Design*. San Rafael, CA: Autodesk, Inc. 1998 Spring; s.n.: 6-7, 11. Refering to archeology sites at URLs for the Texas Historical Commission (THC) underwater exploration of Matagorda Bay and LaSalle Shipwreck project at www.thc.state.tx.us/belle; the Pompeii

Forum project at http://pompeii.virginia.edu;www.brynmawr.edu/csa; and Bir el Fouta church project outside Carthage at www.rmwc.edu.

G115
GILLESPIE, THOMAS K. 1991. *Mapping Thoughts: Visual Interfaces for Information Retrieval*. Berkeley, CA: University of California; 254p. (Ph.D. dissertation. *DAI*, 53/05-A: 1305). Available from University Microfilms, Ann Arbor, MI (order no. AAD92-28661).

G116
GILLETT, GRANT. 1992. *Representation, Meaning and Thought*. Oxford, UK: Clarendon Press; 1992. 213p. ISBN: 0198239939.

G117
GILLEY, SHERIDAN. 1996. History without Morality, History without Truth. *History Today* (UK). 1996 May; 46(5): 11-14. ISSN: 0018-2753.

G118
GILLILAND-SWETLAND, ANNE J. 1992. Archivy and the Computer: A Citation Analysis of North American Archival Periodical Literature. *Archival Issues*. 1992; 17: 95-112. ISSN: 1067-4993.

G119
GILLILAND-SWETLAND, ANNE J. 1995a. *Development of an Expert Assistant for Archival Appraisal of Electronic Communications: an Exploratory Study.* Ann Arbor, MI: University of Michigan Information and Library Studies; 1995. (Ph.D. Dissertation). Available from University Microfilms, Ann Arbor, MI; or from the University of Michigan Library, DISS 25889 (FILM 31157).

G120
GILLILAND-SWETLAND, ANNE. 1995b. Digital Communications: Documentary Opportunities Not to be Missed. See reference: GILLILAND-SWETLAND, ANNE, ed. 1995. 39-50.

G121
GILLILAND-SWETLAND, ANNE J. 1996. *Policy and Politics: The Archival Implications of Digital Communications and Culture at the University of Michigan*. Chicago, IL: Society of American Archivists; 1996. 36p.

G122
GILLILAND[-SWETLAND], ANNE J., ed. 1988. Automating Intellectual Access to Archives. In: *Library Trends*. 1988 Winter. (Entire issue on title topic). ISSN: 0024- 2594.

G123
GILLILAND-SWETLAND, ANNE J., ed. 1995. *Archival Issues*. 1995; 20(1): 1-78. (Entire issue on title topic; Papers on digital archives and libraries from the University of Michigan School of Information doctoral program). ISSN: 1067-4993.

G124
GILLILAND-SWETLAND, ANNE; KINNEY, GREGORY T.; WALLACH, WILLIAM K. 1992. *Uses of Electronic Communication to Document an Academic Community*. Final Report to the National Historical Publications and Records Commission, grant no. 91-113; University of Michigan Division of Research and Development DRDA grant no. 91-539. Ann Arbor, MI: University of Michigan Bentley Historical Library; 1992. 2 vols.

G125
GILLILAND-SWETLAND, LUKE J. 1991. The Provenance of a Profession: The Permanence of the Public Archives and Historical Manuscript Traditions in American Archival History. *The American Archivist*. 1991; 54(2): 160-175. ISSN: 0360-9081.

G126
GILLIS, JOHN R. 1996. The Future of European History. *AHA Perspectives*. 1996 April; 34 (4): 1, 4-6. ISSN: 0743-7021.

G127
GILLIS, JOHN R., ed. 1994. *Commemorations. The Politics of National Identity*. Princeton, NJ: Princeton University Press; 1994. 290p. ISBN: 0691032009 (pbk.).

G128
GILMORE, MATTHEW. 1988. Increasing Access to Archival Records in Library Online Public Access Catalogs. *Library Trends*. 1988; 36: 609-623. ISSN: 0024-2594.

G129
GILMORE, MATTHEW B.; CASE, DONALD O. 1992. Historians, Books, Computers, and the Library. See reference: STOVER, M. 1992. 667-686.

G130
GILMOUR-BRYSON, ANNE, ed. 1978. *Medieval Studies and the Computer. Computers and the Humanities*. 1978. 12. (Entire issue on title topic). ISSN: 0010-4817.

G131
GILMOUR-BRYSON, ANNE, ed. 1984. *Computer Applications to Medieval Studies. Studies in Medieval Culture*, 17. Kalamazoo, MI: Western Michigan University, Medieval Institute; 1984. 194p. ISBN: 0-918720-25-7; (pbk.) 0-918720-18-4.

G132
GINOUVES, RENE; GUIMIER-SORBETS, ANNE MARIE. 1978. *La Constitution des données en Archéologie Classique* [The Structure of Data in Classical Archeology]. Paris, FR: Editions du CNRS; 1978. 161p. ISBN: 2222023211.

G133
GINZBURG, CARLO. 1989. *Miti, emblemi, spie*. Trans. as*: Clues, Myths, and the Historical Method*. John and Anne C. Tedeschi, trans. Baltimore, MD: The Johns Hopkins University Press; 1989. 231p. ISBN: 0-8018-3458-9 (hbk.); 0-8018-4388-X (pbk.).

G134
GINZBERG, CARLO. 1991. Representation: Le mot, l'idée, la chose [Representation: The word, idea, and thing]. *Annales E. S. C.* 1991 Nov.-Dec.; 6: 1219-1234. ISSN: 0395- 2649. (In French).

G135
GIORDANO, FRANK R.; WEIR, MAURICE D.; FOX, WILLIAM P. 1997. *A First Course in Mathematical Modeling*. 2nd ed. Pacific Grove, CA: Brooks/Cole Publishing Co.; 1997. 525p. ISBN: 0-534-22248-X (hbk.).

G136
GIRY, ARTHUR. 1925. *Manuel de Diplomatique diplomes et chartres, chronologie technique, elements critiques et parties constitutives de la teneur des chartes, les chancelleries, les actes privés* [Manual of Diplomatic: Diplomas, charters, technology of chronology, criticial elements and constitutive parts of the basis of charters, chancelleries, and private acts]. Paris, FR: F. Alan; 1925. 1 v. in 2. 944p. (In French; Latin documents).

G137
GIUNTA, MARY A; HACKER, BEVERLEY S. 1991. Using Computer Technology to "Read" Documents: The Optiram Example. *Documentary Editing*. 1991 September; 12(3): 65-67. ISSN: 0196-7134.

G138
GLADNEY, H. 1998. Digital Access to Antiquities. *Communications of the ACM*. 1998; 41: 49-57. ISSN: 0001-0782.

G139
GLASER, BARNEY G.; STRAUSS, ANSELM L. 1967/1980. *The Discovery of Grounded Theory: Strategies for Qualitative Research*. 11th ed. New York, NY: Aldine Atherton; 1980. 271p. LC call no.: HM48.G54.

G140
GLASER, BARNEY G.; STRAUSS, ANSELM L. 1992. *Emergence vs. Forging: Basics of Grounded Theory Analysis*. Mill Valley, CA: Sociology Press; 1992. 129p. LC call no.: HM48.G44.

G141
GLASSIC, CHARLES. 1993. *The Four Kinds of Scholarship*. Presentation for the Carnegie Commission for Higher Education before the annual conference of the Association of Business Schools, Washington, D.C.; 1993.

G142
GLEICK, JAMES. 1978/1987. *Chaos: Making a New Science*. New York, NY: Viking Press; 1978. Rev. ed. *Chaos: Making a New Source*. New York, NY: Penguin; 1987. 352p. ISBN: 0670811785. See related software: *Chaos* (Electronic file). [Sausalito, CA]: Autodesk; c. 1990, 1991. Version 1.01, 4 5.25" diskettes and guide.

G143
GLENISSON, JEAN. 1965. L'Historiographie française contemporaine en France de 1940 a 1965 [Contemporary French Historiography, 1940-1965]. In: Comité français des sciences historiques. *La recherche historique en France de 1940 a 1965* (pp. ix-lxiv). Paris, FR: Centre National de la Recherche Scientifique (CNRS); 1965. 477p. OCLC: 1172034.

G144
GLENISSON, JEAN. 1979. *France*. Day, John, trans. See reference: IGGERS, G; PARKER, eds. 1979. 175-192.

G145
GLENN, N. D. 1977. *Cohort Analysis*. Sage University Papers, ser. 07-005. Beverly Hills, CA: Sage Publications; 1977. 72p. ISBN: 080390794X. OCLC: 3154556.

G146
GLYMOUR, CLARK N. 1980. *Theory and Evidence*. Princeton, NJ: Princeton University Press; 1980. 383p. ISBN: 069107240X (hbk.); 0691100772 (hbk.).

G147
GLYMOUR, CLARK N., ed. *Discovering Causal Structure: Artificial Intelligence, Philosophy of Science, and Statistical Modeling*. Orlando, FL: Academic Press; 1987. 394p. ISBN: 0122869621.

G148
GLYMOUR, CLARK N.; SCHEINES, RICHARD; SPIRTES, PETER.; KELLY, K. 1987/1993. *Discovering Causal Structure: Artificial Intelligence, Philosophy of Science, and Statistical Modeling*. San Diego, CA: Morgan Academic Press; 1987. 391p. Rev. ed. New York, NY: Springer-Verlag; 1993. 526p. with disk. (Lecture Notes in Statistics, vol. 81). ISBN: 0122869621.

G149
GOEDEGEBEURE, BEN G. 1994. FID approaching its 100th Anniversary. *FID News Bulletin*. 1994; 44: 10, 217-220. ISSN: 0014-5874.

G150
GOFFEE, ROB; JONES, GARETH. 1996. What holds the Modern Company Together? [corporate culture]. *Harvard Business Review*. 1996 November-December; 74(6): 133- 139. ISSN: 0017-8012.

G151
GOGGIN, JACQUELINE. 1984. That We Shall Truly Deserve the Title of the "Profession": The Training and Education of Archivists. *American Archivist*. 1984 Summer; 47(3): 243-254. ISSN: 0360-0810.

G152
GOLDBERG, ADELE, ed. 1988. *A History of Personal Workstations*. New York, NY: ACM Press/ Reading, MA: Addison-Wesley Pub. Co.; 1988. 537p. ISBN: 0201112590.

G153
GOLDBERGER, ARTHUR S. 1964. *Econometric Theory*. New York, NY: Wiley; 1964. 399p. LC call no.: HB74.M3G6.

G154
GOLDBERGER, ARTHUR S. 1991. *A Course in Econometrics*. Cambridge, MA: Harvard University Press; 1991. 405p. ISBN: 0674175441.

G155
GOLDBERGER, MARVIN L.; MAHER, BRENDAN A.; FLATTAU, PAMELA E., eds. 1995. *Research Doctorate Programs in the United States: Continuity and Change*. Committee for the Study of Research Doctorate Programs in the United States sponsored by the Conference Board of Associated Research Councils. Conducted by the National Research Council. Washington, D.C.: National Academic Press; 1995. 740p. ISBN: 0309050944.

G156
GOLDBERGER, MARVIN L.; WATSON, KENNETH M. 1964. *Collision Theory*. New York, NY: Wiley; 1964. 919p. LC call no.: QC794.G63.

G157
GOLDEN-BRIDDLE, KAREN; LOCKE, KAREN. 1997. *Composing Qualitative Research*. Thousand Oaks, CA: Sage Publications; 1997. 145p. ISBN: 08003974302 (hbk.); 0803974310 (pbk.).

G158
GOLDFARB, CHARLES F. 1985. *The Standard Generalized Markup Language: ISO 8879*. Geneva, CH: ISO; 1985. Available from: ISO, Geneva, CH.

G159
GOLDFARB, CHARLES F. 1990. *The SGML Handbook*. Rubinsky, Yuri, ed. Oxford, UK: Clarendon Press; 1990. 663p. ISBN: 01998537379.

G160
GOLDFARB, CHARLES F. 1997. SGML: The Reason Why and the First Published Hint. See reference: LOGAN, E.; POLLARD, M. 1997b. 656-661.

G161
GOLDFARB, CHARLES F., ed. 1995. The Text Encoding Initiative. In: *Computers and the Humanities* (NL). 1995; vol. 29. (Entire issue on title topic). ISSN: 0010-4817.

G162
GOLDFARB, CHARLES F.; RUBINSKY, YURI. 1990/1991. *The SGML Handbook*. New York, NY: Oxford University Press; 1990. Reprint, 1991. 663p. ISBN: 0198537379.

G163
GOLDFINE, A.; KONIG, P. 1988. *A Technical Overview of the Information Resource Dictionary System*. 2nd ed. Washington, D.C.: U.S. Dept. of Commerce NTIS; January 1988. NBSIR: 88-3700.

G164
GOLDSTEIN, H. 1979. Age, Period, and Cohort Effects: A Confounded Confusion. *BIAS: Bulletin in Applied Statistics* (UK). 1979; 6: 19-24. LCCN: 86-15909; OCLC: 27165329.

G165
GOLDSTINE, HERMAN H. 1972. *The Computer from Pascal to Von Neuman*. Princeton, NJ: Princeton University Press; 1972. ISBN: 0691081042.

G166
GOLDSTINE, HERMAN H. 1977. *A History of Numerical Analysis from the 16th through the 19th century*. New York, NY: Springer-Verlag; c1977. 348p. LC call no.: QA297.G641.

G167
GOMBRICH, ERNST H. 1966a. *Aby Wartburg*. Hamburg, DEU: Hamburg Universitat; 1966. (Hamburger Universitatsreden, 34). LCCN: 715808.

G168
GOMBRICH, ERNST H. 1966b. *Norm and Form*. London, UK: Phaidon Press; 1966. 4th ed. Chicago, IL: University of Chicago Press; 1985. 164p. (Studies in the Art of the Renaissance, 1). ISBN: 0226302164 (pbk.); LCCN: 84028113.

G169
GOMBRICH, ERNST H. 1982. *The Image and the Eye. Further Studies in the Psychology of Pictorial Representation*. Oxford, UK: Phaidon Press; 1982. 320p. ISBN: 0714822459; LCCN: 82152563.

G170
GOMEZ, JONAS; VELHO, LUIZ. 1997. *Image Processing for Computer Graphics*. New York, NY: Springer-Verlag; 1997. 352p. ISBN: 038794546.

G171
GOMEZ, L. M.; LOCHMAN, C. C.; LANDAUER, T. K. 1990. All the Right Words: Finding what you want as a Function of the Richness of Indexing Vocabulary. *Journal of the American Society for Information Science*. 1990; 41: 547-559. ISSN: 0002-8231.

G172
GONZALEZ, PEDRO A. 1992. The Digital Processing of Images and Archives and Libraries. See reference: THALLER, M., ed. 1992a. 97-121.

G173
GONZALES, RICHARD A. 1989. *Examination of Witnesses*. Gallaghan's Trial Practice series. Deerfield, IL: Clark Boardman Callaghan; 1989. Loose-leaf vol. LCCN: 89-23998.

G174
GOODALL, I. 1993. Applying Recognition Technology for Automatic Data Entry. *Information Management and Technology* (UK). 1993 March; 26(2): 83-87. ISSN: 0959-2350.

G175
GOODCHILD, MICHAEL F. [1992]. *Spatial Analysis using GIS: Seminar Workbook*. Santa Barbara, CA: National Center for Geographic Information & Analysis; [1992]April. 1 v. (pagination varies). (NSF grant funded project).

G176
GOODCHILD, MICHAEL F.; GOPAL, SUCHARITA, eds. 1989. *The Accuracy of Spatial Databases*. National Center for Geographic Information and Analysis Conference proceedings, Montecito, CA, Dec., 1988. London, UK: Taylor and Francis; 1989. 290p. ISBN: 0850668476.

G177
GOODCHILD, MICHAEL F.; PARKS, BRADLEY O.; STEVAERT, LOUIS T. 1993. *Environmental Modeling with GIS*. New York, NY: Oxford University Press; 1993. 488p. ISBN: 0195080076.

G178
GOODHEART, EUGENE. 1992. New Historicism: And Other Old-Fashioned Topics. *CLIO*. 1992 Spring; 21(3): 305-309. ISSN: 0884-2043.

G179
GOODIN, LAURA E. 1991. *Teaching a Nation to Compute: The Rapira Project and Soviet Information-Technology Education*. Washington, D.C.: American University; 1991. 104p. (M.A. Thesis; *DAI* file 35, Master Abstracts, vol. 29/04: 544). Available from: University Microfilms, Ann Arbor, MI (order no. AAD13-43945).

G180
GOODMAN, N. 1976. *Languages of Art. An Approach to a Theory of Symbols.* 2nd ed. Indianapolis, IN: Hacken; 1976.

G181
GOODSON, IVOR. 1997. *The Changing Curriculum: Studies in Social Construction.* New York, NY: P. Lang; 1997. 210p. (Counterpoints, v. 18). ISBN: 0820426091.

G182
GORDON, ANN D. 1992. *Using the Nation's Documentary Heritage: The Report of the Historical Documents Study.* Washington, D.C.: National Historical Publications and Records Commission; 1992. 112p. OCLC: 25679206.

G183
GORDON, CATHERINE. 1991. Dealing with Variable Truth: The Witt Computer Index. *Computers and the History of Art.* 1991; 2(1): 21-27. ISSN: 1048-6798

G184
GORDON, JACK. 1992. Rethinking Diversity. *Training.* 1992 January; 29 (1): 23-30. ISSN: 0095-5892.

G185
GORDON, MICHAEL D.; DUMAIS, SUSAN. 1998. Using Latent Semantic Indexing for Literature Based Discovery. *Journal of the American Society for Information Science.* 1998 June; 49 (8): 674-685. ISSN: 0002-8231; CODEN: AISJB6.

G186
GORI, FRANCO; GALEOTTI, MARCELLO; GERONAZZO, LUCIO, eds. 1993. *Nonlinear Dynamics in Economics and Social Sciences.* Berlin, DEU: Springer- Verlag; 1993. 367p. ISBN: 0387567046.

G187
GORMAN, MICHAEL. 1989. Yesterday's Heresy—Today's Orthodoxy: An Essay on the Changing Face of Descriptive Cataloging. *College & Research Libraries.* 1989 November; 50(6): 626-634. ISSN: 0010-0870.

G188
GOSE, EARL; JOHNSONBAUGH, RICHARD; JOST, STEVE. 1996. *Pattern Recognition and Image Analysis.* Upper Saddle River, NJ: Prentice-Hall PTR; 1996. 484p. and disk. ISBN: 011132364158.

G189
GOSSMAN, LIONEL. 1978. History and Literature: Reproduction or Signification. See reference: CANARY, R. H.; KOZICKI, H., eds. 1978. 3-30.

G190
GOTTARELLI, ANTONIO. 1992. La Video-documentazione Elettronica dello Scavo Archeologico [Electronic Video-Documentation of an Archeological Dig]. Studi ed Esperienze per il Progetto di una Periferica Dedicata. *Archeologia e Calcolatori.* 1992; 3: 77-99. LCCN: 91-648685; OCLC: 22885582.

G191
GOTTARELLI, ANTONIO. 1994. La Video Documentazione Elettronica dello Scavo Archeologico Modelli Interpretativi e Processamento Digitale [Electronic Video Documentaton of an Archeological Dig. The Digital Process and Interpretation of Models in Archeology]. See reference: BECK, P., ed. 1994. 19-25.

G192
GOTTSCHALK, LOUIS R. 1961. *Understanding History: A Primer of Historical Method.* New York, NY: Alfred Knopf; 1961. reprinted, 1963. 298p. OCLC: 15186462; 9238818.

G193
GOUDA, F.; SMITH, P. H. 1983. Famine, Crime and Gender in Nineteenth-century France: Explorations in Time-series Analysis. *Historical Methods.* 1983; 16: 59-73. ISSN: 0161-5440.

G194
GOULD, CONSTANCE. C. 1988. *Information Needs in the Humanities: An Assessment.* Stanford, CA: The Research Libraries Group, Inc.; 1988. 62p. LCCN: 89-109468; OCLC: 21043946.

G195
GOULD, STEPHEN J. 1996. *Full House: The Spread of Excellence from Plato to Darwin.* New York, NY: Harmony Books; 1996. 244p. ISBN: 0517703947.

G196
GOUWENS, KENNETH. 1998. Perceiving the Past: Renaissance Humanism after the "Cognitive Turn." *American Historical Review.* 1998 Feb.; 103 (1): 55-82. ISSN: 0002-8762.

G197
GRABOWSKI, J. 1996. Writing and Speaking: Common Grounds and Differences toward a Regulation Theory of Written Language Production. In: Levy, C. Michael; Ransdell, Sarah., eds. *The Science of Writing: Theories,*

Methods, Individual Differences, and Applications. Mahwah, NJ: Lawrence Erlbaum; 1996. 432p. ISBN: 0805821042 (hbk.); 0805821090 (pbk.).

G198
GRACA, L.; LAUDAN, K.-H.; ZAMPERONI, P.; KAMPFFMEYER, U.; TEEGEN, W.-R. 1991. On the Computer-Aided Classification of Pottery Shapes. See reference: BEST, H., *ET AL.* 1991. 21-27.

G199
GRAENSTROM, CLAES. 1993. Will Archival Theory Be Sufficient in the Future? See reference: MENNE-HARITZ, A., ed. 1993. 159-167.

G200
GRAENSTROM, CLAES. 1994. The Janus Syndrome. See reference: ABUKHANFUSA, K.; SYDBECK, J., eds. 1994. 1-15.

G201
GRAENSTROM, CLAES. 1997. *Reformatting: Preservation of New Media and Migration.* Conference program abstracts (pp. 12-13). European Conference on Archives, Barcelona, May 1997.

G202
GRAFF, HARVEY; MONACO, PAUL. 1980. *Quantification and Psychology: Toward a "New" History.* Washington, D.C.: University Press of America; 1980. 516p. ISBN: 0819109428; LCCN: 79-3854; OCLC: 5846349.

G203
GRAFTON, ANTHONY. 1990. *Forgers and Critics: Creativity and Duplicity in Western Scholarship.* Princeton, NJ: Princeton University Press; 1990. 157p. ISBN: 0691055440.

G204
GRAFTON, ANTHONY. 1991. *Defenders of the Text: The Traditions of Scholarship in an Age of Science, 1450-1800.* Cambridge, MA: Harvard University Press; 1991. 330p. ISBN: 0674195442.

G205
GRAFTON, ANTHONY. 1992. *New Worlds, Ancient Texts: The Power of Tradition and the Shock of Discovery.* Cambridge, MA: Harvard University Press; 1992. 282p. ISBN: 0674618750.

G206
GRAFTON, ANTHONY. 1997. *The Footnote; a Curious History.* Rev. ed. Cambridge, MA: Harvard University Press; 1997. 241p. ISBN: 0674902157.

G207
GRAHAM, PETER S. 1994. *Intellectual Preservation: Electronic Preservation of the Third Kind.* Washington, D.C.: Commission on Preservation and Access; 1994 March. 7p. Available from the Commission.

G208
GRAHAM, RONALD L.; GROETSCHEL, MARTIN; LOVASZ, LASZLO. 1996. *Handbook of Combinatorics.* Leiden, NL: Elsevier Science B.V.; 1996. 2 vols., 2,350p. ISBN: 0-262-07169-X. Distributed in U.S. by MIT Press.

G209
GRANASZTOI, GYORGY. 1972. Computers in the Historical Sciences. *Tortenelmi Szemle* (Budapest, HU). 1972; 14: 29-47. (Summaries in Russian and French). ISSN: 0040-9634.

G210
GRATTAN-GUINESS, I., ed. 1994. *Companion Encyclopedia of the History and Philosophy of Mathematical Sciences.* London, UK / New York, NY: Routledge; 1994. 2 vols., 1806p. ISBN: 0415037859 (set); LCCN: 92-13707.

G211
GRAY, CHRIS H. 1991. *Computers as Weapons and Metaphors: The United States Military, 1940-1990, and Post-Modern War.* Santa Cruz, CA: University of California at Santa Cruz; 1991. 539p. (Ph.D. dissertation; DAI, vol. 52/06-A: 2255). Available from: University Microfilms, Ann Arbor, MI (order no. AAD91-32415).

G212
GRAY, CHRIS H., ed. 1996. *Technohistory: Using the History of American Technology in Interdisciplinary Research.* Melbourne, FL: Krieger Publishing Co.; 1996. 280p. ISBN: 0-89464-853-5 (pbk.).

G213
GRAY, CHRIS H.; DRISCOLL, MARK. 1992. What's Real about Virtual Reality" Anthropology of, and in, Cyperspace. *Visual Anthropology Review.* 1992 Fall; 8(2): 39-49. ISSN: 1053-7147.

G214
GRAY, PAUL, ed. 1994. *Decision Support and Executive Information Systems.* Conference proceedings. Englewood Cliffs, NJ: Prentice-Hall; 1994. 469p. ISBN: 0132387895; LCCN: 93-1929.

G215
GRAYSON, LESLEY. 1996. *Scientific Deception. An Overview and Guide to the Literature of Misconduct and Fraud in Scientific Research.* Mahwah, NJ: Lawrence Erlbaum Associates, Inc.; 1996. 120p. ISBN: 0-7123-0831-8 (pbk.).

G216
GRAZIELLA; ENZO, LOMBARDO. 1990. Graphiques et analyze démographique: Quelques elements d'histoire et d'actualité [Graphics and Demographic Analysis. Some Elements of History and Actuality]. *Population.* 1990; 45: 399-414. ISSN: 0032-4663.

G217
GREBENICHENKO, SERGEY. 1996 [199-]. A New Method of Revealing Alternatives and Bifurcation Points in the Management of Macroeconomic Processes: Dynamic Modeling of Soviet Economic Regulation in the 1920s. See reference: BORODKIN, L., ed. 1996: English abstract of presentation, 103-104; paper in Russian [199- forthcoming].

G218
GRECHIKHIN, A. 1982. Bibliografischeskaya evristika: istoriya, sistema, vozmozhnosti [Bibliographical Heuristic: History, Systems, and Potential]. *Bibliotekar* (RU). 1982; 7: 35-37. ISSN: 0006-1808.

G219
GREEN, BRIAN. 1996. News from across the Pond: The U.K. Experience. See reference: BLUH, P., ed. 1996. 151-154.

G220
GREEN, DAVID. 1997. Technology, Scholarship, and Politics: The National Initiative for a Networked Cultural Heritage. *AHA Perspectives.* 1997 April; 35(4): 40, 42-43. ISSN: 0743-7021.

G221
GREEN, KENNETH C. 1990-. *Campus Computing Survey.* 1996 Survey available from principles: K. Green c/o Campus Computing, P.O. Box 261241. Encinco, CA 91426-1242. See precis: Supporting Instruction and Assisting Users: The Major Technology Challenge Confronting US Colleges and Universities (Electronic file). In Vision section of *Microsoft in Higher Education.* 1997 March; 7p. Accessible at http://www.microsoft.com/education/hed/news/march/support.htm.

G222
GREEN, REBECCA. 1995. Topical Relevance Relationships. I: Why Topic Matching Fails. *Journal of the American Society for Information Science.* 1995; 46: 646-653. ISSN: 0002-8231.

G223
GREEN, WILLIAM A. 1995a. History, Historians, and the Dynamics of Change. *History and Theory.* 1995 October; 34(3): 271-. ISSN: 0018-2656.

G224
GREEN, WILLIAM A. 1995b. Periodizing world history. *History and Theory.* 1995 May; 34 (2): 99-112. ISSN: 0018-2656.

G225
GREEN, WILLIAM B. 1993. *Introduction to Electronic Document Management Systems.* San Diego, CA: Academic Press; 1993. 250p. ISBN: 0-12-298180-4.

G226
GREENBERG, DOUGLAS. 1993. Get Out of the Way if You Can't Lend a Hand: The Changing Nature of Scholarship and the Significance of Special Collections. *Journal of Library Administration.* 1993; 19(1): 83-98. Also in LEE, S., ed. 1994.

G227
GREENBERG, MARK; SCHACHTERLE, LANCE. 1992. *Literature and Technology.* Bethlehem, PA / Canbury, CT: Lehigh University Press and Associated University Presses; 1992. 322p. ISBN: 0934223203; LCCN: 91-60584.

G228
GREENBLATT, STEPHEN J. 1981. *Allegory and Representation.* Baltimore, MD: The Johns Hopkins University Press; 1981. 193p. ISBN: 080182642X.

G229
GREENBLATT, STEPHEN J. 1990a. Culture. See reference: LENTRICCHIA, F.; MCLAUGHLIN, T., eds. 1990. 225-232.

G230
GREENBLATT, STEPHEN J. 1990b. *Learning to Curse: Essays in Early Modern Culture.* New York, NY: 1990. 188p. ISBN: 0415901731.

G231
GREENBLATT, STEPHEN J., ed. 1993. *New World Encounters.* Berkeley, CA: University fo California Press; 1993. 344p. ISBN: 0520080203 (hbk.); 0520080211 (pbk.).

G232
GREENBLATT, STEPHEN; GUNN, GILES, eds. 1992. *Redrawing the Boundaries: The Transformation of English and American Literary Studies*. New York, NY: Modern Language Association; 1992. 595p.(bibliography, pp. 525-580). ISBN: 0873523954 (hbk.); 0873523962 (pbk.).

G233
GREENE, WILLIAM A. 1992. Periodization in European and World History. *Journal of World History*. 1992; 3: 99-111. ISSN: 1045-6007.

G234
GREENHALGH, MICHAEL. 1982. New Technologies for Data and Image Storage and their Application to the History of Art. *Art Libraries Journal*. 1982 Summer; 7(2): 67-81. ISSN: 0307-4722.

G235
GREENSTEIN, DANIEL I. 1989. A Source-Oriented Approach to History and Computing: The Relational Database. *Historische Sozialforschung / Historical Social Research* (DEU). 1989; 14(3): 9-16. ISSN: 0172-6404.

G236
GREENSTEIN, DANIEL I., ed. 1991a. *Modeling Historical Data: Towards a Standard for Encoding and Exchanging Machine-Readable Texts*. St. Katharinen [Gottingen, DEU]: Max-Planck-Institut fur Geschichte in Kommission bei Scripta Mercaturae Verlag; 1991. (Halbgraue Reihe zur historischen Fackinformatik. Serie A: Historische Quellenkunden, Band 11). ISBN: 3-928134-45-0.

G237
GREENSTEIN, DANIEL I. 1991b. Standard, Meta-Standard: A Framework for Coding Occupational Data. *Historische Sozialforschung / Historical Social Research* (DEU). 1991; 16: 3-22. ISSN: 0172-6404.

G238
GREENSTEIN, DANIEL I. 1993a. A Guide to Historical Computing Resources. See reference: DAVIS, DENLEY, SPAETH, D.; TRAINOR, eds. 1993. 135-137.

G239
GREENSTEIN, DANIEL I. 1993b. Electronic Information Resources and Historians: A Consumers View. See reference: ROSS, S.; HIGGS, E., eds. 1993. 149-160.

G240
GREENSTEIN, DANIEL I. 1994a. *A Historian's Guide to Computers* Oxford, UK: Oxford University Press; 1994. 268p. (Bibliography, pp. 239-263). (Oxford Guides to Computing in the Humanities). ISBN: 0198242352 (hbk.); 10982355216.

G241
GREENSTEIN, DANIEL I. 1994b. Four Courses in Search of a Discipline: European Approaches to Teaching History and Computing. See reference: OLDERVOLL, J., ed., 1994. 3-18.

G242
GREENSTEIN, DANIEL I. 1996 [199-]. The Arts and Humanities Data Service: A Collaborative Interdisciplinary Scholarly Venture. See reference: BORODKIN, L., ed. 1996: Abstract of presentation, 23-24; paper [199- forthcoming].

G243
GREENSTEIN, DANIEL I. 1996/1997 [1998]. Bringing Bacon Home: The Divergent Progress of Computer-Aided Historical Research in Europe and the United States. See reference: IGARTUA, J. E., ed. 1996/1997. 351-364.

G244
GREENWOOD, ROYSTON: HININGS C. R. 1993. Understanding Strategic Change: The Contribution of Archetypes. *Academy of Management Journal*. 1993 October; 36 (5): 1052-1081. ISSN: 0001-4273.

G245
GREETHAM, D. C. 1996. Textual Forensics. *Publications of the Modern Language Association of America* (PMLA). 1996 January; 111(1): 32-42. ISSN: 0030-8129.

G246
GREGERSEN, HAL B. 1992. Commitments to a Parent Company and a Local Work Unit during Repatriation. *Personnel Psychology*. 1992 Spring; 45 (1): 29-54. ISSN: 0031-5826.

G247
GREGORY, RICHARD L.; GOMBRICH, ERNST H., eds. [1973]. *Illusion in Nature and Art*. London, UK: Duckworth; [1973]. 288p. ISBN: 0715607558 (hbk.); 0715607556 (pbk.); LCCN: 74159251.

G248
GREIMAS, ALGIRDAS J. 1970. Histoire et structure. In his: *Du Sens: Essais sémiotiques* [Of the Senses: Semiotic Essays]. Paris, FR: Editions du Seuil; 1970. 2: 103-116. 2 vols. ISBN: 20206559 (set); 2020065495 (vol. 2 only); LCCN: 75-495601; OCLC: 366688.

G249

GREIMAS, ALGIRDAS J. 1979. *Introduction à l'analyse du Discours en Sciences Sociales* [Introduction to Discourse Analysis in the Social Sciences]. Paris, FR: Classiques Hachette; 1979. 254p. LC call no.: H62.I63.

G250

GREIMAS, ALGIRDAS J. 1986. *On Meaning: Selected Writings in Semiotic Theory.* Perron, P. J.; Collins, F. H., translators. Minneapolis, MN: University of Minnesota Press; 1986. 237p. (Theory and History of Literature, 38). ISBN: 0861879201.

G251

GREW, R. 1995. *World Historians and their Goals* [review article]. *History and Theory.* 1995; *34*: 1- 19. ISSN: 0018-2656.

G252

GRIBAUDI, MAURIZIO. 1987. Itineraires ouviers: éspaces et groupes sociaux a Turin au debut du XXe siècle [Itineraries of workers: Space and social Groups in Turin at the beginning of the 20th century]. M-C. Rykebusch, trans. Paris: Editions de l'École des haute études en sciences sociales; 1987. 264p. ISBN: 2713208920; OCLC: 18818882.

G253

GRIBAUDI, MAURIZIO. 1993. Social Stratification and Complex Systems: A Model for the Analysis of Relational Data. See reference: SCHURER, K.; DIEDERIKS, H., eds. 1993. 53-74.

G254

GRIFFIN, JANE. 1997. MetaData: Capturing the Heart of the Data Warehouse. *Application Development Trends.* 1997 January; (3): 70-74. ISSN: 1073-9564.

G255

GRIFFIN, LARRY J. 1995. How is Sociology informed by History? *Social Forces.* 1995 June; 73 (4): 1245-1255. ISSN: 0037-7732

G256

GRIFFITH, BELVER C.; MULLINS, N. C. 1972. Coherent Social Groups in Scientific Change. *Science.* 1972; 177: 959-964. ISSN: 0036-8075.

G257

GRIGG, SUSAN. 1991. Archival Practice and the Foundations of Historical Method. *Journal of American History.* 1991 June; 78: 228-239. ISSN: 0021-8723.

G258

GROSCH, HERBERT R. J. 1990. *Computer: Bit Slice from a Life.* Novato, CA: Third Millennium Book; 1990. ISBN: 0887330851; LCCN: 89020523.

G259

GROSSBART, S. R. 1992. Quantification and Social Science Methods for Historians: An Annotated Bibliography of Selected Books and Articles. *Historical Methods.* 1992; 25: 100-120. ISSN: 0161-5440. Continues the bibliographic survey by N. FITCH, 1980.

G260

GROSSER, ALFRED. 1990. *Le Crime et la Memoire* (Crime and Memory). Translated to German as: *Ermordung der Menschheit: der Genozid im Gedächtnis der Volker* (Reminiscence of the People: Genocide in Folk Memory). Munich, DEU: C. Hanser; 1990. 308p. (In German). ISBN: 3446153047.

G261

GROSSMAN, DAVID; FRIEDER, OPHIR; HOLMES, DAVID; ROBERTS, DAVID C. 1997. Integrating Structured Data and Text: A Relational Approach. *Journal of the American Society for Information Science.* 1997; 48 (2): 122-132. ISSN: 0002-8231.

G262

GROTUM, THOMAS. 1993. The Memorial Data Base of the Archives of the Concentration Camp Auschwitz. See reference: JARITZ, GERHARD; KROPAČ, INGO H.; TEIBENBACHER, PETER, eds. 1993. Abstract, pp.123-124.

G263

GROVES, ROBERT M. 1989. *Survey Errors and Survey Costs.* New York, NY: John Wiley and Sons; 1989. 560p. ISBN: 0471611719.

G264

GRUBER, WILLIAM H.; MARQUIS, DONALD G., eds. *Factors in the Transfer of Technology.* Cambridge, MA: MIT Press; 1969. 289p. LC call no.: T174.M12.

G265
GRUBLER, ARNULF. 1990. *The Rise and Fall of Infrastructures, Dynamics of Evolution, and Technological Change in Transport.* Heidelberg, DEU: Physica Verlag; 1990. 305p. ISSN: 3790804797. New York, NY: Springer-Verlag; 1990. 305p. ISBN: 0387913762.

G266
GRUBLER, ARNULF. 1991. Diffusion: Long-Term Patterns and Discontinuities. T*echnological Forecasting and Social Change.* 1991; 39: 159-180. ISSN: 0040-1625.

G267
GRUBLER, ARNULF. 1995/1996. Time for a Change: On the Patterns of Diffusion of Innovation. *Daedalus.* 1996 Summer; 125(3): 19-31. ISBN: 0011-5266. Extended version (WP-95-82) available from the International Institute for Applied Systems Analysis, Lexenburg, AT.

G268
GRUEL, KATHERINE; BUCHSENSCHUTZ, OLIVIER. 1994. De l'Usage d'ARKEOPLAN pour l'enregistrement d'elements en Elevation: Étude d'un Mur du Convent du Mont Beauvray (Bourgogne) [Use of ARKEPLAN for the registration of Elevation Data: Study of the Walls of the Convent of Mont Beauvray, Burgundy]. See reference: BECK, P., ed. 1994. 12-18.

G269
GRUPPE, FRITZ H. 1996. Computoons. The Evolving Image of Computers in Cartoons. *IEEE Computer.* 1996 April; 29 (4): 55-62. ISSN: 0180-9162.

G270
GRUPP, HARIOLF, ed. 1992. *Dynamics of Science-based Innovation.* Berlin and Heidelberg, DEU: Springer-Verlag; 1992. 321p. ISBN: 0387550623; LCCN: 91-45677.

G271
GUAN, J. W.; BELL, D. A. 1992. *Evidence Theory and Its Application.* Leiden, NL: North-Holland; 1992. (Studies in Computer Sciences and Artificial Intelligence, vol. 8). ISBN: 0444896414.

G272
GUBRIUM, JABER E.; HOLSTEIN, JAMES A. 1997. *The New Language of Qualitative Method.* New York, NY: Oxford University Press; 1997. 244p. ISBN: 0195999931 (hbk.); 019509994X (pbk.).

G273
GUELKE, LEONARD. 1997. The Relations between Geography and History Reconsidered. *History and Theory.* 1997 May; 36(2): 216-235. ISSN: 0018-2656.

G274
GUERCIO, MARIA. 1994. Archival Theory and the Principle of Provenance for current records. See reference: ABUKHANFUSA, K.; SYDBECK, J., eds. 1994. [70-80].

G275
GUERNSEY, LISA. 1997. Video Technology Transforms the Teaching of Art History. *Chronicle of Higher Education.* 1997 February 14; 43 (23): A20-22. ISSN: 0009- 5982.

G276
GUESGEN, HANS W. 1989. *Spatial Reasoning Based on Allen's Temporal Logic.* Berkeley, CA: International Computer Science Institute; 1989. (Technical Report no. TR 89-1049).

G277
GUESGEN, HANS W. 1992. *A Perspective on Constraint-based Reasoning: An Introductory Tutorial.* Hertzberg, Joachim, contributer. Berlin, DEU / New York, NY: Springer-Verlag; 1992. 123p. (Lecture Notes in Computer Science/Artificial Intelligence, 597). ISBN: 3540555102 (pbk.).

G278
GUILLAUMONT, AGNES; MINEL, JEAN-LUC. 1996. *MEDIUM* (Medieval Mss. Database). *Le Médiéviste et l'Ordinateur* (FR). 1996 Printemps-Automne; 33. (In French). ISSN: 0223-3843.

G279
GUILLOT, DOMINIQUE. 1994. La Carte Archéologique de la France: Une Base de Données au Service da la Gestion du Patronomie Archéologique [The Archeological Papers of France: A Data Base for the Generation of an Archeological Patrimony]. See reference: BECK, P., ed. 1994. 43-47.

G280
GUIMIER-SORBETS, ANNE MARIE. 1990. *Les Bases de Données en Archéologie. Conception et Mise en Oeuvre* [Data Bases in Archeology. Conception and Work in Progress]. Paris, FR: Centre Nationale de Recherches Scientifique (CNRS); 1990. 272p. ISBN: 2222044812; LCCN: 91-131037; OCLC: 23975800.

G281
GUIRAUD, PIERRE. 1954/1960. *Les caracteres statistiques du vocabulaire* [The Statistical Character of Vocabulary]. Paris, FR: Presses universitatires de France. 116p. Reprinted, Paris, FR: CNRS; 1960. Companion to his *Bibliographie critique de la statistique linguistique*. Utrecht, NL: Editions Spectrum; 1954. 121p. LC call no.: Z7001.G96.

G282
GUIRAUD, PIERRE. 1975. *La Sémiologie*. Trans. *Semiology*. London, UK: Routledge & K. Paul; 1975. 106p. ISBN: 0710080050 (hbk.); 0710080115 (pbk.).

G283
GULL, CLOYD D. 1987. Information Science and Technology: From Coordinate Indexing to the Global Brain. *Journal of the American Society for Information Science*. 1987 September; 38(5): 340-366. ISSN: 0002-8231.

G284
GULLESTAD, MARIANNE, ed. 1996. *Imagined Childhoods: Self and Society in Autobiographical Accounts*. Proceedings from a workshop on "Constructions of Childhood in Autobiographical Accounts," Norsk senter for barneforskning (Norwegian Ctr. For Childhood Research), Voss, Norway, May 10-12, 1992. Boston, MA; Oslo, NO: Scandinavian University Press; 1996. 244p. ISBN: 8200226301.

G285
GUMERMAN, GEORGE J.; GELL-MANN, MURRAY, eds. 1994. *Understanding Complexity in the Prehistoric Southwest*. Santa Fe, NM: Santa Fe Institute (SFI); 1994. (Santa Fe Institute Studies in the Science of Complexity). ISBN: 0-201-87039-8 (hbk.); 0-201-87040-1 (pbk.). See also reference: TAINTER, J. A.; BAGLEY, B. TAINTER, eds. 1996.

G286
GUNDLACH, ROLF; LUEKERATH, CARL A. 1976. *Historische Wissenschaften und Elektronische Datanverarbeitung* [Historical Science and Electronic Data Processing]. Frankfurt am Main, DEU / Vienna, AT: Ullstein-Buch; 1976. 406p. ISBN: 3548033199; LCCN: 78-380-367; OCLC: 3797347.

G287
GUNSALUS, C. K. 1997. Rethinking Unscientific Attitudes about Scientific Misconduct. *Chronicle of Higher Education*. 1997; 43(29): 4-5. ISSN: 0009-5982.

G288
GUPTA, A.; JAIN, R. 1997. Visual Information Retrieval. *Communications of the ACM* (Assn. for Computing Machinery). 1997; 40(5): 70-79. ISSN: 0001-0782.

G289
GUPTA, YASH P.; CHIN, DAVID C. W. 1994. Organizational Life Cycle: A Review and Proposed Directions for Research. *Mid-Atlantic Journal of Business*. 1994 December; 30 (30): 269-294. ISSN: 0732-9334.

G290
GURER, DENISE W. 1995. Pioneering Women in Computer Science. *Communications of the ACM* (Assn. for Computing Machinery). 1995 January; 38 (1): 45-. ISSN: 0001- 0782.

G291
GUREVICH, AARON. 1992. Historical Anthropology and the Science of History. *Historical Anthropology of the Middle Ages* (pp. 3-49). Cambridge, UK: Cambridge University Press; 1992. (Translated from Russian). 247p. ISBN: 002263100833; LCCN: 92007664.

G292
GUSKEY, THOMAS; HUBERMAN, A. M., eds. 1995. *Professional Development in Education: New Paradigm and Practices*. New York, NY: Teachers College Press; 1995. 290p. ISBN: 0807734268 (hbk.); 080773425X (pbk.).

G293
GUTH, GLORIA. 1976/1977. Surname Spellings and Computerized Record Linkage. *Historical Methods Newsletter*. 1976/77; 10: 10-16. ISSN: 0161-5440.

G294
GUTMAN, HERBERT G. 1981. The Missing Synthesis: Whatever Happened to History? *Nation*. 1981 November 21; 521, 555-556. ISSN: 0027-8378.

G295
GUTMANN, MYRON P. 1988a. Teaching Historical Research Skills to Undergraduates: Thoughts on Microcomputers and the Classroom. *American Quarterly*. 1988 September; 41: 502-521. ISSN: 0003-0678.

G296
GUTMANN, MYRON P. 1988b. Teaching Historical Research Skills of Undergraduates. *Historical Methods*. 1988; 21: 112-180. ISSN: 0161-5440.

G297
GUTMANN, MYRON P. 1990. Computer-based History Teaching in Higher Education: The United States. *History and Computing.* 1990; 2(1): 24-30. ISSN: 0957-0144.

G298
GUTMANN, MYRON P.; FLIESS, KENNETH H.; HOLMES, AMY E.; FAIRCHILD, AMY L.; TEAS, WENDY A. 1989. Keeping Track of Our Treasures: Managing Historical Data with Relational Database Software. *Historical Methods.* 1989 Fall; 22(4): 128-143. ISSN: 0161-5440.

G299
GUYOT, XAVIER. 1996. Généalogie et informatique [Genealogy and Computing]. *Revue Français de Généalogie* (FR). 1996 Oct.-Nov.; 106 supplement; 1-16. (In French).

G300
GUYOTJEANNIN, OLIVIER. 1996a. La Diplomatique Médiévale: et l'Elargissement de son Champ [Medieval Diplomatics: The Enlargement of Its Field]. In: *La Gazette des Archives* (FR). 1996; 172.

G301
GUYOTJEANNIN, OLIVIER. 1996b. The Expansion of Diplomatics as a Discipline. See reference: BLOUIN, F.; DELMAS, B. 1996. 414-421.

G302
GUYOTJEANNIN, OLIVIER; PYCKE, JACQUES; TOCK, BENOIT-MICHEL. 1993. Diplomatique médiévale [Medieval Diplomatics]. In: *L'Atelier du Médiéviste*, 1. Turhout, BE: Brepols; 1993. 442p. 2nd printing; 1995. (In French). (Entire issue on title topic). ISBN: 2503503128.

G303
GUZZO, R. A.; SHEA, G. P. 1992. Group Performance and Intergroup Relations in Organizations. See reference: DUNNETTE, M. D.; HOUGH, L. M., eds. 1992. 3: 269-313.

-H-

H1
H-NET [HUMANITIES ONLINE; formerly *HISTORY NETWORK].* 1995/96-. *H-NET WHATIS* [electronic file]. R. Jensen, Exec. Dir. Chicago, IL: University of Illinois at Chicago Circle; 1995/96-. Listserv@uicvm.uic.edu. (See *H-NET* flyers distributed at the American Historical Assn. Conference, Atlanta, Jan. 6-9, 1996). Subscription E-Mail address: H-Net@msu.edu. See also: H-NET Homepage at http:www//h-net.msu.edu.

H2
HAAR, JOHN. 1993. Prices of U.S. and Foreign Published Materials. Book Trade Research and Statistics. In: Barr, Catherine, ed., *Bowker Annual: Library and Book Trade Almanac.* New Providence, NJ: R. R. Bowker; 1993. 477-498. ISBN: 0-8352-3345-6.

H3
HAARMANN, HARALD. 1979. *Sprachenstatistik in Geschichte und Gegenwart* [Language Statistics in History and the Present]. Hamburg, DEU: Buske; c1979. 402p. (About Discourse analysis; in German). ISBN: 3871183687; LCCN: 80141075.

H4
HAARMANN, HARALD. 1990. *Language in its Cultural Embedding: Explorations in the Relativity of Signs and Sign Systems.* Berlin, DEU / New York, NY: Mouton de Gruyter; 1990. 276p. (Studies in Anthropological Linguistics, 4). ISBN: 3110120860; LCCN: 90013442.

H5
HAARMANN, HARALD. 1996. *Early Civilization and Literacy in Europe: An Inquiry into Cultural Continuity in the Mediterranean World.* Berlin, DEU / New York, NY: Mouton de Gruyter; 1996. 207 [184]p. (Approaches to Semiotics, 124). ISBN: 3110146517; LCCN: 95042928.

H6
HAAS, STEPHANIE W. 1995. Domain Terminology Patterns in different Disciplines: Evidence from Abstracts. *Journal of the American Society for Information Science.* 1995; 44(1): 67-79. ISSN: 0002-8231.

H7
HAAS, STEPHANIE W. 1997. Disciplinary Variation in Automatic Sublanguage Term Identification. *Journal of the American Society for Information Science.* 1997; 48(1): 67-79. ISSN: 0002-8231.

H8
HABERMAS, JURGEN. 1967. *Zur Logik der Sozialwissenschaft* [*Logic of the Social Sciences*]. Tubingen, DEU: Mohr; 1967. 195p. (Philosophische Rundschau, Beiheft 5). OCLC: 12490193.

H9
HABERMAS, JURGEN. 1968. *Technik und Wissenschaft als "Ideologie"* [*Technique and Science of Ideology*]. Frankfurt-am-Main, DEU: Suhrkamp; 1968. 169p. LCCN: 73-371159; OCLC: 940074.

H10
HACKING, IAN. 1995. *Rewriting the Soul: Multiple Personality and the Sciences of Memory.* Princeton, NJ: Princeton University Press; 1995. 336p. ISBN: 069103642X.

H11
HAERD, MIKEL. 1994. Technology as Practice. *Social Studies of Science.* 1994; 24: 549- 585. ISSN: 0306-3127.

H12
HAFER, GLENN. 1996. *The Art of Causal Conjecture.* Cambridge MA: MIT Press; 1996. 552p. ISBN: 0-262-19368-X.

H13
HAGLER, RONALD. 1991. *The Bibliographic Record and Information Technology.* 2nd ed. Adamantine Studies in Information Technology and Library Science. Twickenham, UK: Adamantine; 1991. 331p. ISBN: 0744900379; OCLC: 27071522.

H14
HAHN, NAN L. 1981. From Medieval Scribe to Microcomputer. *Perspectives in Computing.* 1981; 1(3): 20-29. ISSN: 0273-4621.

H15
HAHN, ULRIKE; CHATER, NICK. 1997. Concepts and Similarity. See reference: LAMBERT, K.; SHANKS, D., eds. 1997.

H16
HAINS, DAVID, ed. 1990. *Information Sources in Information Technology.* New York, NY/ London, UK: Bowker-Saur; 1990. 350p. ISBN: 0408032855.

H17
HAJEK, PETR.; HAVRANEK, TOMAS.; JIROUSEK, RADIM. 1992. *Uncertain Information Processing in Expert Systems.* Boca Raton, FL: CRC Press; 1992. 285p. ISBN: 0849363683.

H18
HAJO, CATHY MORGAN. 1991. Computerizing Control over Authority Names at the Margaret Sanger Papers. *Documentary Editing.* 1991 June; 31(2): 35-39. ISSN: 0196- 7134.

H19
HAKALA, JUHA; HUSBY, OLE; KOCK, TRAUGOTT. 1996. Warwick Framework and Dublin Core Set Provide a Comprehensive Infrastructure for Network Resource Description. *Report from the Metadata Workshop, II.* Warwick, UK, April 1-3, 1996 (electronic file). Accessible at http://www.ub2.lu.se/tk.warwick.html.

H20
HALASZ, FRANK G. 1988. Reflections on Notecards: Seven Issues for the Next Generation of Hypermedia Systems. *Communications of the AMC.* 1988; 31(7): 836-852. ISSN: 0001- 0782.

H21
HALASZ, LAZLO, ed. 1987. *Literary Discourse: Aspects of Cognitive and Social Psychological Approaches.* Berlin, DEU / New York, NY: W. de Gruyter; 1987. 242p. (Research in Text Theory / Unteruschungen zur Texttheorie, 11). ISSN: 0179-4167; ISBN: 0899253253; OCLC: 15015286

H22
HALASZ, MICHAEL F. 1995. Nonlinear Dynamics in Behavioral Systems. *The American Psychologist.* 1995; 50(2): 107-109. ISSN: 0003-066X.

H23
HALBWACHS, MAURICE. 1925/1935. *Les Cadres Sociaux de la Mémoire* [The Social Framework of Memory]. . Paris, FR: F. Alcan; 1925. Nouvelle ed.; 1935. 404p. LC call no.: BF371.H157

H24
HALBWACHS, MAURICE. 1962/1992. Historical Memory and Collective Memory. In: Coser, Llewis A., ed. & trans. *On Collective Memory* (pp. 50-87). Chicago, IL: University of Chicago Press; 1992. 244p. ISBN: 0226155941 (hbk.); 0226115958 (pbk.).

H25
HALBWACHS, MAURICE. 1968/1992. *Le Mémoire collective.* 2nd ed. Paris, FR: Presses Universitaires de France; 1968. 204p. Coser, Llewis A., ed. & trans. *On Collective Memory.* Chicago, IL: University of Chicago Press; 1992. 244p. ISBN: 0226115941 (hbk.); 0226115968 (pbk.). Selections from *Les Cadres Sociaux de la Mémoire* and *La Topographie Legendaire des Evangiles en Terre Sainte.*

H26
HALBWACHS, MAURICE. 1980. *Memoire collective*. Ditter, F. J.; Ditter, V.Y., trans. *The Collective Memory*. New York, NY: Harper & Row; c1980. 186p. ISBN: 0060908009 (pbk.); LCCN: 74018576.

H27
HALL, B. J. 1992. Theories of Culture and Communication. *Communication Theory*. 1992; 2: 50- 70. ISSN: 1050-3293.

H28
HALL, PETER G.; PRESTON, PASCHAL. 1988. *The Carrier Wave: New Information Technology and the Geography of Innovation, 1846-2003*. London, UK / Boston, MA: Unwin Hyman; 1988. 305p. ISBN: 0-04-445081-8.

H29
HALL, STEPHEN S. 1992. How Technique is Changing Science. *Science*. 1992 July 17; 27: 344-349. ISSN: 0036-8075.

H30
HALL, STEPHEN S. 1993. *Mapping the Next Millennium: How Computer-Driven Cartography is Revolutionizing the Face of Science*. New York, NY: Vintage Books; 1993. 477p. ISBN: 06797421755 (pbk.); LCCN: 92-50610; OCLC: 27012791.

H31
HAM, F. GERALD. 1975. The Archival Edge. *The American Archivist*. 1975 January; 38: 5-13. ISSN: 0360-9081.

H32
HAM, F. GERALD. 1993. *Selecting and Appraising Archives and Manuscripts*. Archives Fundamentals series. Chicago, IL: Society of American Archivists; 1993. 106p. ISBN: 0931828848.

H33
HAMBER, ANTHONY; MYLES, JEAN; VAUGHAN, WILLIAM., eds. 1989. *Computers and the History of Art*. London, UK / New York, NY: Mansell; 1989. 213p. ISBN: 0-7201-1980-4; LCCN: 89-35093; OCLC: 19922120.

H34
HAMESSE, JACQUELINE, ed. 1995 *Bilan et perspectives des études médiévales en Europe* (Inquiry and Perspectives of Medieval Studies in Europe] . Louvain-la-Nueve, BE: Universitaire de Louvain; 1995.

H35
HAMESSE, JACQUELINE, ed. [199-, forthcoming]. *Texts and Images. Computer-assisted Manuscript Studies*. Binghamton, NY: Haworth Press; [199- forthcoming]. To be co-published in: *Primary Sources and Original Works*. [199-],: ca. 180p. ISSN: 1042-8216.

H36
HAMILTON, DAVID P. 1991. Research Papers: Who's United Now. *Science*. 1991, January 4; 251: 25-30. ISSN: 0036-8075.

H37
HAMILTON, PAULA. 1994. The Knife Edge: Debates about Memory and History. See reference: DARIAN-SMITH, K.; HAMILTON, P.; CURTHOYS, A., eds. 1994.

H38
HAMILTON, PAULA; DARIAN-SMITH, KATE, eds. 1994. *Memory and History in Twentieth- Century Australia*. Melbourne, AU / Oxford, UK: Oxford University Press; 1994. 255p. ISBN: 0195535693.

H39
HAMILTON, RICHARD E. 1996. *The Social Misconstruction of Reality: Validity and Verification in the Scholarly Community*. New Haven, CT: Yale University Press; 1996. 289p. ISBN: 0300063458.

H40
HAMMEL CARPENTER, KATHRYN; ALEXANDER, ADRIAN W. 1996. U.S. Periodical Price Index for 1996. *American Libraries*. 1996 May; 27 (5):197-105. ISSN: 0002-9769.

H41
HAMMER, DONALD P., ed. 1976. *The Information Age, its Development, its Impact*. Metuchen, NJ: Scarecrow Press; 1976. 275p. ISBN: 0810809451; LCCN: 76-10603; OCLC: 2137100.

H42
HAMMER, ERIC M. 1995. *Logic and Visual Information*. Stanford, CA: CSLI Publications; c1995. 124p. (Studies in Logic, Language and Information series). ISBN: 1881526879 (pbk.); LCCN: 95024761.

H43
HAMMER, MICHAEL; CHAMPY, JAMES. 1993/1994. *Re-engineering the Corporation: A Manifesto for Business Revolution*. New York, NY: Harper Business; 1993. LCCN: 92-54748. 2nd rev. ed. New York, NY: Harper Business; 1994. 223p. ISBN: 0887306403.

H44
HAMMER, MICHAEL; STANTON, STEVEN A. 1995. *The Re-engineering Revolution*. New York, NY: Harper Business; 1995. 223p. ISBN: 0887306403.

H45
HAMMIT, HARRY A. 1996. Integrating the Disciplines: Analysis of the Proceedings. In: *Report of the National Privacy and Public Policy Symposium*. Hartford, CT: The Connecticut Foundation for Open Government, Inc; 1996.

H46
HAMMOND BAKER, KATHRYN. 1997. The Business of Government and the Future of Government Archives. See reference: DEARSTYNE, BRUCE, ed. 1997 [1998]. 234-252.

H47
HAND, D. J. 1981. *Discrimination and Classification*. Chichester, UK: J. Wiley; 1981. 218p. ISBN: 0471280488.

H48
HAND, D. J. 1985. *Artificial Intelligence and Psychiatry*. Cambridge, UK: Cambridge University Press; 1985. 266p. ISBN: 0521258715.

H49
HAND, D. J. 1987. *Multivariate Analysis of Variance and Repeated Measures*. London, UK: Chapman & Hall; 1987. 262p. ISBN: 0412258102 (hbk.); 0412258005 (pbk.).

H50
HAND, D. J. 1997. *Construction and Assessment of Classification Rules*. Chichester, UK: J. Wiley; 1997. 214p. ISBN: 0471965839.

H51
HAND, D. J., ed. 1991. *Artificial Intelligence Frontiers in Statistics*. London, UK: Chapman & Hall; 1991. 410p. (Artificial Intelligence and Statistics, 3). ISBN: 04122407108.

H52
HAND, D. J., ed. 1994. *AI and Computer Power*. London Conference, Mar. 13-14, 1991. London, UK: Chapman & Hall; 1994. 212p. ISBN: 0412455501.

H53
HANDLEY, J. C.; HICKEY, T. B. 1991. Merging Optical Character Recognition Outputs for Improved Accuracy. In: A. Lichnerowicz. ed. *Proceedings, Intelligent Text and Image Handling "RIAO '91 Conference, Barcelona, Spain, April 2-5, 1991*. Sponsored by the EEC (Commission of the European Communities); CID (Centre de hautes etudes internationales d'Informatique documentaire); and CASIS (Center for the Advanced Study of Information Systems). Amsterdam, NE / New York, NY: Elsevier; 1991. 999p. ISBN: 044489361X; LCCN: 92-101636; OCLC: 27938169.

H54
HANDLIN, OSCAR. 1971. History: A Discipline in Crisis? *American Scholar*. 1971; 40(3): 447-65. ISSN: 0003-0937.

H55
HANDLIN, OSCAR. 1975. The Capacity of Quantitative History. *Perspectives in American History*. 1975; 9: 7-26. ISSN: 0079-0990.

H56
HANDY, CHARLES. 1990. *The Age of Unreason*. Boston: Harvard Business School Press; 1990. 278p. ISBN: 0875843018; OCLC: 25961120.

H57
HANLEY, SARAH. 1996. Who Owns History? History in the Museum and the Classroom. *AHA Perspectives*. 1996 October; 34 (7): 1, 6. ISSN: 0743-7021.

H58
HANN, C. M., ed. 1994. *When History Accelerates: Essays on Rapid Social Change, Complexity, and Creativity*. London, UK: Athlone Press; 1994. 325p. ISBN: 048511464X.

H59
HANNEMAN, R.; HOLINGSWORTH, J. R. 1984. Modeling and Simulation in Historical Inquiry. *Historical Methods*. 1984; 17 (3): 150-163. ISSN: 0161-5440.

H60
HANNESTAD, STEPHEN E. 1993. The Evolution of Archival Practice. See reference: KENT, A., ed. 1993. 124-154.

H61
HANSEN, CAROL D.; KAHNWEILER, WILLIAM M. 1993. Storytelling: An Instrument for Understanding the Dynamics of Corporate Relationships. *Human Relations*. 1993 December; 46 (12): 1391-1409. ISSN: 0018-7267.

H62
HANTAIS, LINDA; MANGEN, STEPHEN, eds. 1996. *Cross-National Research Methods in the Social Sciences.* London, UK: Cassell; 1996. 288p. ISBN: 1-85567-354-2.

H63
HARALICK, R. M.; SHAPIRO, L. 1980. Image Segmentation Techniques. *Computer Vision, Graphics, Image Processing.* 1980; 12: 100-132. ISSN: 0734-189x.

H64
HARBER, DOUG; BURGESS, KEVIN; BARCLAY, DAPHNE. 1993. Total Quality Management as a Cultural Intervention: An Integrative View. *Asia Pacific Journal of Quality Management.* 1993; 2 (1): 17-27. ISSN: 0965-3570.

H65
HARDEE, A. MAYNOR; HENRY, FREEMAN G., eds. 1990. Narratology and Narrative. In: *French Literature:* vol. 17. Columbia, SC: University of South Carolina; 1990. 152p. (Entire issue on title topic; in French and English). ISSN: 0271-6607.

H66
HARDESTY, D.; WINDEATT, S. 1989. *CALL* [Computer-Assisted Language Learning]. Oxford, UK: Oxford University Press; 1989.

H67
HARDY, I. T. 1993. Creating an Expert System for Legislative History Research: Project CLEAR's "Lexpert". *Law Library Journal.* 1993 Spring; 85(2): 239-73. ISSN: 0023- 9283.

H68
HAREVAN, TAMARA. 1991. The History of the Family and the Complexity of Social Change. *The American Historical Review.* 1991; 96: 95-124. ISSN: 0002-8762.

H69
HARLAN, DAVID. 1988. Intellectual History and the Return of Literature. *American Historical Review.* 1989 June; 94: 879-907. ISSN: 0002-8762.

H70
HARLEY, J. B. 1988. Maps, Knowledge, and Power. In: Cosgrove, Denis; Daniels, Stephen, eds. *The Iconography of Landscape: Essays on the Symbolic Representation, Design, and Use of Past Environments* (pp. 277-312). Cambridge, UK: Cambridge University Press; 1988. 318p. ISBN: 0521324378.

H71
HARLEY, J. B. 1992. De-constructing the Map. See reference: TREVOR, J. BARNES; DUNCAN, JAMES S., eds. 1992. 231-247. Rev. ed. from *Cartographica.* 1989; 26: 1-20.

H72
HARM0N, D. 1992. Relevance Feedback revisited. In: *Proceedings of ACM SIGIR*). Copenhagen, NY: ACM Press; 1992. 1-10.

H73
HARMON, D. 1995. Overview of the Second Text Retrieval Conference (TREC-2). *Information Processing & Management.* 1995; 31: 271-289. ISSN: 0306-4573.

H74
HARMON, GLYNN. 1971. On the Evolution of Information Science. *Journal of the American Society for Information Science.* 1971 July-August; 22(4): 235-241. ISSN: 0002-8231.

H75
HARMON, GLYNN. 1984. The Measurement of Information. *Information Processing and Management.* 1984; 20 (1-2): 193-198. ISSN: 0306-4573.

H76
HARMON, GLYNN. 1986. The Interdisciplinary Study of Information: A Review Essay. *Journal of Library History.* 1986 Spring; 22: 206-277. ISSN: 0022-2259. (Extensive review of MACHLUP & MANSFIELD, eds. 1983).

H77
HARMON, ROBERT B. 1989. *Elements of Bibliography: A Simplified Approach.* Rev. ed. Metuchen, NJ / London, UK: Scarecrow Press, Inc.; 1989. 288p. ISBN: 0-8108-2218-0.

H78
HARNACK, ANDREW; KLEPPINGER, EUGENE. 1996. *Beyond the MLA Handbook: Documenting Electronic Sources on the Internet.* 1996, Nov. 25. Accessible at http://falcon.eku.edu /honors/beyond-mla.

H79
HARPING, PATRICIA. 1999. Resistance is Futile: Inescapable Networked Information Made Accessible Using the Getty Vocabularies. See WOODS, LARRY, ed. 1999. 833-847.

H80
HARRINGTON, H. JAMES; MATHERS, DWAYNE D. 1997. *ISO 9000 and Beyond: From Compliance to Performance Improvement.* New York, NY: McGraw-Hill; 1997. 359p. ISBN: 0070267774; LCCN: 97-136226.

H81
HARRIS, JESSICA. 1982. Information Science. *Academic American Encyclopedia.* Danbury, CT: Grolier, Inc.; 1982. 172-173. ISBN: 0717220001; LCCN: 79-27430; OCLC: 8984158.

H82
HARRIS, MICHAEL H. 1986. State, Class, and Cultural Reproduction: Toward a Theory of Library Service in the United States. In: Simonton, Wesley, ed. *Advances in Librarianship.* 1986; 14: 211-252. ISSN: 0065-2830; ISBN: 0-12-024614-7.

H83
HARRIS, MICHAEL H.; HANNAH, STAN A. 1992. Why Do We Study the History of Libraries? A Meditation on the Perils of Ahistoricism in the Information Era. *Library & Information Science Research.* 1992 April-June; 14(2): 123-130. ISSN: 0740-8188.

H84
HARRIS, MICHAEL H.; HANNAH, STAN A. 1993. *Into the Future: The Foundations of Library and Information Services in the Post-Industrial Era.* Information Management, Policy and Services [series]. Norwood, NJ: Ablex Corporation; 1993. 182p. ISBN: 0893919705; LCCN: 93-170220; OCLC: 28386645.

H85
HARRIS, ROY. 1986. *The Origin of Writing.* London, UK: Duckworth; 1986. Reprint. LaSalle, IL: Open Court; 1986. 166p. ISBN: 0812690354; LCCN: 86-002439..

H86
HARRISON, DONALD F. 1989. Machine-Readable Sources for the Study of the War in Vietnam. See reference: MCCRANK, L., ed. 1989. 279-292.

H87
HARRISON, J. KLINE. 1994. Developing Successful Expatriate Managers: A Framework for the Structural Design and Strategic Alignment of Cross-cultural Training Programs. *Human Resource Planning.* 1994; 17 (3): 17-35. ISSN: 0199-8986.

H88
HART, MICHAEL, dir. 1971-. *Project Gutenberg.* [Urbana, IL; 1971-]. See e-text archives of 2,500+ online titles accessible at: www.gutenberg.net.

H89
HART, MICHAEL. 1990. Project Gutenberg: Access to Electronic Texts. *Database.* 1990 Dec.; 13: 6-9. ISSN: 0162-4105.

H90
HART, THOMAS, ed. 1989-. *Project Gutenberg* [Newsletter]. N.p.; 1989-. Irregular. Available from: D. Turner, OSB, Illinois Benedictine College, 5700 College Rd., Lisle IL 60532-0900.

H91
HARTEL, REINHARD. 1989. To Treat or not to Treat: The Historical Source before the Input. *Historische Sozialforschung/Historical Social Research* (DEU). 1989; 14(2): 35-38. ISSN: 0172-6404.

H92
HARTEL, REINHARD. 1991. The Demands of the Historical Disciplines on Machine Readable Sources and the Consequence for Their Standardization. See reference: BEST, H., *ET AL.*, eds. 1991. 491-495.

H93
HARTER, STEPHEN P. 1992. Psychological Relevance and Information Science. *Journal of the American Society for Information Science.* 1992; 43: 602-653. ISSN: 0002-8231.

H94
HARTIGAN, JOHN M. 1993a. Compact Disc Recording: A Technical Overview. *CD-ROM Professional.* 1993 September; 6(5): 102-106. ISSN: 1049-0833.

H95
HARTIGAN, JOHN M. 1993b. Multimedia: The Marriage Broker for Television and Computers. *CD-ROM Professional.* 1993 May; 6(3): 69-71. ISSN: 1049-0833.

H96
HARTLAND, P.; HARVEY, C. 1989. Information Engineering and Historical Databases. *History and Computing*. 1989; 2: 44-62. ISSN: 0957-0144.

H97
HARTLEY, R. V. L. 1928. Transmission of Information. *Bell System Technical Journal*. 1928; 7: 535-563.

H98
HARTMANN, HEIDI; KRAUT, ROBERT E.; TILLY, LOUISE, eds. 1986. *Computer Chips and Paper Clips; Technology and Women's Employment* Washington, DC: National Academy Press; 1986. 2 v. (National Research Council Committee on Women's Employment and Related Social Issues). ISBN: 0309036887.

H99
HARTMANNIS, JURIS, ed. 1989. *Computational Complexity Theory*. Lectures for the American Mathematical Society, Jan. 5-6, 1988. Providence, RI: American Mathematical Society; [c1989]. 128p. ISBN: 0821801317; LCCN: 89006857.

H100
HARTMANNIS, JURIS; LIN, HERBERT., eds. 1992. *Computing the Future: A Broader Agenda for Computer Science and Engineering*. Washington, D.C.: National Academic Press for the National Research Council; 1992. 272p. ISBN: 030904740X. See also reference: SELMAN, A., 1990.

H101
HARVEY, BRIAN; WRIGHT, MATTHEW. 1994. *Simply Scheme. Introducing Computer Science*. Cambridge, MA: MIT Press; 1994. 615p. ISBN: 0-262-08226-8.

H102
HARVEY, C. 1990. The Nature and Future of Historical Computing. See reference: MAWDSLEY, E. *ET AL*., eds, 1990.

H103
HARVEY, C.; PRESS, J. 1992. Relational Data Analysis: Value, Concepts and Methods. *History and Computing*. 1992; 4: 98-109. ISSN: 0957-0144.

H104
HARVEY, DAVID. 1989. *The Condition of Postmodernity: An Inquiry into the Origins of Cultural Change*. Oxford, UK: Oxford University Press; 1989. 378p. ISBN: 0631162925 (hbk.); 0631162941 (pbk.).

H105
HARVEY, JOHN H. 1996. *Embracing their Memory: Loss and the Social Psychology of Storytelling*. Boston, MA: Allyn & Bacon; c1996. 232p. ISBN: 0205174787; LCCN: 95024025.

H106
HARVEY, LOUIS-GEORGES. 1991, 1992. Books and Culture in French Canada: The Library of the Institut-Canadien de Montreal, 1852-1880. See reference: MCCRANK, L., ed.1992: 153-174. Also published in *Primary Sources & Original Works*. 1991; 1(2/3): 153-174. ISBN: 1-56024-150-0.

H107
HARVEY, LOUIS-GEORGES; OLSON, MARK. 1988. Computers and Intellectual History: Lexical Statistics and the Analysis of Political Discourse. *Journal of Interdisciplinary History*. 1988; 18: 449-464. ISSN: 0022-1953.

H108
HARVEY, THOMAS R. 1995. *Checklist for Change: A Pragmatic Approach to Creating and Controlling Change*. 2nd ed. New York: Technomic Publishing Co., Inc.; 1995. 188p. ISBN: 1-56676-281-2.

H109
HASAN, H. 1998. Activity Theory: A Basis for Contextual Study of Information Systems in Organizations. See reference: HASAN, H.; GOULD, E.; HYLAND, P., eds. 1998. 19-38.

H110
HASAN, H.; GOULD, E.; HYLAND, P., eds. 1998. *Information Systems and Activity Theory: Tools in Context*. Wollongong, AU: University of Wollongong Press; 1998.

H111
HASKELL, FRANCIS. 1993. *History and Its Images: Art and the Interpretation of the Past*. New Haven, CT: Yale University Press; 1993. 558p. ISBN: 0300055404; LCCN: 92- 41145; OCLC: 27171634.

H112
HASKELL, ROBERT E., ed. 1987. *Cognition and Symbolic Structures: The Pyschology of Metaphoric Transformation*. Norwood, NJ: Ablex Publishing Co.; 1987. 304p. ISBN: 0893913685; LCCN: 87-011486.

H113
HASKELL, THOMAS L. 1997. *Objectivity is not Neutrality. Explanatory Schemes in History.* Baltimore, MD: The Johns Hopkins University Press; 1997. 440p. ISBN: 0-8018-5681-7.

H114
HASKINS, CHARLES H. 1923. European History and American Scholarship. *American Historical Review.* 1923 January; 28: 205-220. ISSN: 0002-8762.

H115
HASTORF, ALBERT. H.; ISEN, ALICE. M., eds. 1982. *Cognitive Social Psychology.* New York, NY: Elsevier North Holland; 1982. 462p. ISBN: 0444006176.

H116
HATCH, MARY JO. 1990. The Symbolics of Office Design: An Empirical Exploration. See reference: GAGLIARDI, P., ed. 1990. 129-146.

H117
HATCH, MARY JO. 1993. The Dynamics of Organizational Culture. *Academy of Management Review.* 1993 October; 18 (4): 657-693. ISSN: 0363-7425.

H118
HAUBEN, MICHAEL; HAUBEN, RONDA. 1997. *Netizens. On the History and Impact of Usenet and Internet.* Los Alamitos, CA: IEEE Computer Society; 1997. 384p. ISBN: 0-8186-7706-6.

H119
HAUGER, JAMES S. 1995. *Reading Machines for the Blind: A Study of Federally Supported Technology Development and Innovation.* (Ph.D. dissertation). Blacksburg, VA: Virginia Polytechnic Institute and State University; 1995. 398p. Available form UMI, Ann Arbor, MI.

H120
HAUSER, JACK. 1996. Text Retrieval Dreams. *CD-ROM Professional.* 1996 June; 9(6): 52-62. ISSN: 1049-0833.

H121
HAUSER, PHILIP M.; DUNCAN, OTIS D., eds. 1959. *The Study of Population: An Inventory and Appraisal.* Chicago, IL: University of Chicago Press; 1959. 864p. LCCN: 58011949.

H122
HAUSMANN, FREDERICK; HARTEL, REINHARD; KROPAČ , INGO H.; BECKER, PETER. eds. 1986. *Datennetze für die historischen Wissenschaften? Probleme und Möglichkeiten bei Standardisierung und Transfer maschinenlesbarer Daten / Data Networks for the Historical Disciplines? Problems and Feasibilities in the Standardization and Exchange of Machine Readable Data.* Conference proceedings, Karl-Franzens- Universität, Graz, 30 May-1 June, 1986. Graz, AT: Leykam-Verlag for the Karl-Franz University; 1986. 271p. (Papers in German and English). ISBN: 3701100012; LCCN: 87-203875; OCLC: 21048425.

H123
HAVERKAMP, DONNA S.; GAUCH, SUSAN. 1998. Intelligent Information Agents: Review and Challenges for Distributed Information Sources. *Journal of the American Society for Information Science.* 1998; 49 (4): 304-311. ISSN: 0002-8231.

H124
HAWGOOD, DAVID. 1992. *Computers for Family History: An Introduction.* London, UK: D. Hawgood; 1992. 60p. ISBNL 0948151080; LCCN: 95-217835.

H125
HAWKES, DOUGLAS K. 1994. Information Literacy in Business Schools. *Journal of Education for Business.* 1994 September; 70(1): 54-62. ISSN: 0883-2323.

H126
HAWKINS, JOHN A.; GELL-MANN, MURRAY, eds. 1992. *Evolution of Human Languages.* Santa Fe Institute Studies in the Science of Complexity. Santa Fe, NM: Santa Fe Institute (SFI); 1992. ISBN: 0-201-52572-0 (hbk.); 0-201-52573-9 (pbk.).

H127
HAWORTH, KENT. M. 1992. The Principles Speak for Themselves: Articulating a Language of Purpose in Archives. See reference: CRAIG, B., ed., 1992. 90-104.

H128
HAY, DAVID C. 1996. *Data Model Patterns: Conventions of Thought.* London, UK: Dorset House Publishing; 1996. 268p. ISBN: 0932633293; LCCN: 95-24983.

H129
HAY, DAVID R. 1846. *A Nomenclature of Colours Applicable to the Arts and Natural Sciences, to Manufacturers, and other Purposes of general Utility.* 2nd ed. Edingburgh, UK: W. Blackwood & Sons; 1846. 72p. LCCN: 11032931.

H130
HAYES, J. R.; FLOWER, L. S. 1980. Identifying the Organization of Writing Processes. In: Gregg, Lee W.; Steinberg, Erwin R., eds. *Cognitive Processes in Writing.* Hillsdale, NJ: Erlbaum; 1980. 3-29. ISBN: 0898590329; LCCN: 80-018624.

H131
HAYES, ROBERT M. 1985. The History of Library and Information Science: A Commentary. *Journal of Library History.* 1985 Spring; 20(2): 173-178. ISSN: 0275-3650.

H132
HAYES, ROBERT M. 1994. Information Science and Librarianship. See reference: WIEGAND, W.; DAVIS, D., eds. 1994. 275-280.

H133
HAYES-ROTH, FREDERICH.; WATERMAN, D.A.; LENAT, DOUGLAS B. 1983. *Building Expert Systems.* Reading, MA: Addison-Wesley; 1983. 444p. (Teknowledge Series in Knowledge Engineering, 1). ISBN: 0201106868.

H134
HAYKIN, SIMON. 1994. *Neural Networks. A Comprehensive Foundation.* Los Alamitos, CA: IEEE; 1994. 720p. ISBN: 0-02-352761-7

H135
HAYLES, JEAN E.; MICHIE, DONALD; SPERRY LTD. 1983. *Intelligent Systems: The Unprecedented Opportunity.* Chichester, UK: E. Horwood / West Sussex, NY: Halsted Press; 1983. 206p. ISBN 0853126461 (UK); 0470275014 (USA).

H136
HAYLES, N. KATHERINE. 1984. *The Cosmic Web: Scientific Field Models and Literary Strategies in the Twentieth Century.* Ithaca, NY: Cornell University Press; 1984. 209p. ISBN: 0801417422.

H137
HAYLES, N. KATHERINE. 1990. *Chaos Bound: Orderly Disorder in Contemporary Literature and Science.* Ithaca, NY: Cornell University Press; 1990. 309p. ISBN: 0801422620 (hbk.); 0901497019 (pbk.).

H138
HAYLES, N. KATHERINE. 1991. Complex Dynamics in Literature and Science. In: Hayles, K., ed. *Chaos and Order: Complex Dynamics in Literature and Science.* Chicago, IL: University of Chicago Press; 1991. 308p. ISBN: 0226321 (hbk.); 0631183221 (pbk.).

H139
HAYTHORNWAITE, CAROLINE; BOWKER, GEOFFREY; JENKINS, CHRISTINE; RAYWARD, W. BOYD. 1999. Mapping the Dimensions of a Dynamic Field. See reference: BATES, M., ed. 1999. Pt. 2: 1092-1094.

H140
HEALD, CAROLYN. 1996. Is There Room for Archives in the Postmodern World? *The American Archivist.* 1996 Winter; 59: 88-101. ISSN: 0360-9081. See response by BROTHMAN & BROWN. 1997.

H141
HEALY, CHRIS. 1994. Histories and Collecting: Museums, Objects, and Memories. See reference: HAMILTON, P.; DARIAN-SMITH, K., eds. 1994.

H142
HEALY, CHRIS. 1997. *From the Ruins of Colonialism: History as Social Memory.* Cambridge, UK / New York, NY: Cambridge University Press; 1997. 249p. ISBN: 0521562783; LCCN: 96020475.

H143
HEAP, SHAUN H.; HOLLIS, M.; LYONS, B.; SUGDEN, R.; WEALE, A. 1992. *The Theory of Choice: A Critical Guide.* Oxford, UK: Basil Blackwell; 1992. 398p. ISBN: 0631171746 (hbk.); 0631183221 (pbk.).

H144
HEAP, SHAUN H.; VAROUFAKIS, YANIS. 1995. *Game Theory: A Critical Introduction.* London, UK: Routledge; 1995. 282p. ISBN: 041509402X (hbk.); 0415094038 (pbk.).

H145
HEARNSHAW, HILARY M; UNWIN, DAVID J., eds. 1994. *Visualization in Geographical Information Systems.* Workshop of the UK Assn. for Geographical Information, Burleigh Court, University of Loughborough, 1992. Chichester, UK / New York, NY: Wiley and Sons; c1994. 243p. ISBN: 0471944351; LCCN: 94-04624

H146
HECKERMAN, DAVID E. 1995a. Bayesian Networks for Knowledge Representation and Learning. See reference: FAYYAD, U. M., *ET AL.*, eds. Extended version: Microsoft Research Advanced Technology Division, MSR-TR.

H147
HECKERMAN, DAVID E. 1995b. A Tutorial on Learning Bayesian Networks. In: *Microsoft Research*. Microsoft, Inc., Advanced Technology Division; 1995 March. Available as: Microsoft Technical Report MSR-TR-95-06.

H148
HECKERMAN, DAVID E.; SHACHTER, R. 1995. A Definition and Graphical Representation for Causality. In : Besnard, P.; Hanks, S., eds. *Uncertainty in Artificial Intelligence: Proceedings, Eleventh Conference.* Montreal, CAN: 1995.

H149
HEDLIN, EDDIE. 1994 [1995]. Presidential Address. The Society of American Archivists annual conference, Indianapolis, September 8, 1994. *The American Archivist.* [1995]; 58(1): 10-15. ISSN: 0360-9081.

H150
HEDSTROM, MARGARET. 1984. *Archives & Manuscripts: Machine-Readable Records.* SAA Basic Manual series. Chicago, IL: SAA; 1984. 75p. ISBN: 0931828600.

B151
HEDSTROM, MARGARET. 1991. Understanding Electronic Incunabula: A Framework for Research on Electronic Records. *The American Archivist.* 1991 Summer; 54(3): 334-354. ISSN: 0360-9081.

H152
HEDSTROM, MARGARET. 1993a. The Electronic Records Challenge. *History News.* 1993 July/August; 48 (4): 5-8.

H153
HEDSTROM, MARGARET. 1993b. Descriptive Practices for Electronic Records: Deciding What is Essential and Imagining What is Possible. *Archivaria.* 36 Autumn; 36: 53-63. ISSN: 0318-6954.

H154
HEDSTROM, MARGARET. 1993c. Reinventing Archives for Electronic Records: Alternative Service Delivery Options. See reference: HEDSTROM, M., ed. 1993. 82-98

H155
HEDSTROM, MARGARET. 1994. *Management and Preservation of Nevada's Electronic Public Records: A Report to the Nevada Historical Records Advisory Board.* Carson City, NV: NHRVB; 1994. 28p. LCCN: 95-621257.

H156
HEDSTROM, MARGARET. 1996/1997. *Migration Strategies and Electronic Records* (electronics file). Paper presented at the 1996 Fermo conference, and at the Pittsburgh Electronic Records Conference, May 22-24, 1997. Accessible at http://www.lis.pitt.edu/~cerar/ statement.html.

H157
HEDSTROM, MARGARET. 1997. Research Issues in Migration and Long-Term Preservation. See reference: BEARMAN, D.; TRANT, J., eds. 1997. 287-291.

H158
HEDSTROM, MARGARET, ed. 1993. *Electronic Records Management Program Strategies.* Pittsburgh, PA: Archives & Museum Informatics; 1993. 156p. (Archives and Museum Informatics Technical Report, 18). ISSN: 1042-1459.

H159
HEDSTROM, MARGARET, ed. 1994. *2020 Vision. The American Archivist.* 1994 Winter; 57(1): 1-164. (Entire issue on title topic). ISSN: 0360-9081.

H160
HEDSTROM, MARGARET; WALCH, VICTORIA I., eds. 1993. Automated Records and Techniques Curriculum Project. In: *The American Archivist.* 1993; 56(3): 397-559. (Entire issue on title topic). ISSN: 0360-9081.

H161
HEEHS, PETER. 1994. Myth, History, and Theory. *History and Theory.* 1994 February; 33 (1): 1-19. ISSN: 0018-2656.

H162
HEIDORN, P. BRYAN; SANDORE, BETH, eds. 1997. *Digital Image Access & Retrieval*. Urbana-Champagne, IL: Graduate School of Library and Information Science; 1997. 191p. (Clinic on Library Applications of Data Processing, March 24-25, 1996). ISBN: 0-87845-100-5.

H163
HEILPRIN, LAURENCE B., ed. 1985. *Toward Foundations of Information Science*. White Plains, NY: Knowledge Industry Publications, Inc. for ASIS; 1985. 232p. ISBN:0867291494; LCCN: 85-12612/r89; OCLC: 12160960.

H164
HEILPRIN, LAURENCE B. 1988. Early Historical Perspectives: *Annual Review of Information Science and Technology (ARIST)*. *Journal of the American Society for Information Science*. 1988 July; 39(4): 273-280. ISSN: 0002-8231.

H165
HEIM, KATHLEEN M. 1980. *Social Science Data Archives: A User Study*. Ph.D. dissertation. Madison, WI: University of Wisconsin; 304p. *DAI*, 42/01-A: 5. Available from University Microfilms, Ann Arbor, MI: Order no. AAD81-10079.

H166
HEIM, KATHLEEN M., ed. 1982. Data Libraries for Social Sciences. In: *Library Trends*, 30(3). Urbana-Champagne, IL: University of Illinois Graduate School of Library and Information Science; 1982. 509p. (Entire issue on title topic). ISSN: 0024-2594; OCLC: 8380219.

H167
HEIM, KATHLEEN M. 1987. Social Scientific Information Needs for Numeric Data: The Evolution of the International Data Archive Infrastructure. *Collection Management*. Spring 1987; 9: 1-53. ISSN: 0146-2679.

H168
HEIM, MICHAEL. 1987. *Electric Language: A Philosophical Study of Word Processing*. New Haven, CT: Yale University Press; 1987. 305p. ISBN: 0300038356.

H169
HEIM, MICHAEL. 1990. The Erotic Ontology of Cyberspace. See reference: UNIVERSITY OF TEXAS, 1990. 38-39.

H170
HEIM, MICHAEL. 1993/1994. *The Metaphysics of Virtual Reality*. New York, NY: Oxford University Press; 1993. Reprint, 1994. 175p. ISBN: 0195081781.

H171
HEISE, DAVID R. 1988. Computer Analysis of Cultural Structures. *Social Science Computer Review*. 1988 Spring; 6: 18-96. ISSN: 0894-4393.

H172
HELM, PAUL. 1994. *Belief Policies*. Cambridge, UK: Cambridge University Press; 1994. 226p. ISBN: 052146028X.

H173
HELPRIN, MARK. 1996. The Acceleration of Tranquility (Technological Advances and the Pace of Life). *Forbes ASAP*. 1996 Dec. 2; 158(13): S14-21. ISSN: 0015-6914.

H174
HELPSER, ERIC; SCHOMAKER, LAMBERT. 1993. Off-line and On-line Handwritten [*sic*] Recognition. See reference: DOORN, P. *ET AL*. 1993. 39-52.

H175
HEMPEL, CARL G. 1942. The Function of General Laws in History. *Journal of Philosophy, Psychology, and Scientific Methods*. 1942; 39: 35-48. ISSN: 0160-9335.

H176
HEMPEL, CARL G. 1952. *Fundamentals of Concept Formation in Empirical Science*. International Encyclopedia of Unified Science. Chicago, IL: University of Chicago Press; 1952. 93p. (Foundations of the unity of science, 2[7]). LCCN: 52-13426; OCLC: 170573.

H177
HEMPEL, CARL G. 1965. *Aspects of Scientific Explanation and other Essays in the Philosophy of Science*. New York, NY: Free Press: 1965. 504p. LCCN: 65-015441. Reprint, 1970.

H178
HEMPEL, CARL. [1972]. On the Logic of Explanation. In: MacKinnon, Edward, ed. *The Problem of Scientific Realism*. New York, NY: Appleton-Century-Crofts; [1972]. 301p. ISBN: 0390585416; LCCN: 72089135.

H179
HEMPEL, CARL G. 1974. Reasons and Covering Laws in Historical Explanation. See reference: GARDNER, P., ed. 1974. 90-105. This extrapolates main ideas from his earlier works: *Aspects of Scientific Explanation,* 1965; and his *Fundamentals of Concept Formation in Empirical Science*, 1952.

H180
HENIGE, DAVID. 1995. Omphaloskepsis and the Infantalizing of History. *The Journal of African History* (UK). 1995 May; 36 (2): 311-319. ISSN: 0021-8537.

H181
HENRY, LOUIS. 1956. *Anciennes familles genevoises. Étude démographique: XVI-XX siècles* [Ancient Genovese Families: Demographic Study from the Sixteenth to Twentieth Centuries]. Paris, FR: Presses Universitaires de France; 1956.(Cahier 26 de I.N.E.D.). (In French). ISSN: 0021-8537.

H182
HENRY, LOUIS. 1967. *Manuel de démographie historique* [Manual of Historical Demography]. Paris, FR: Droz for the Centre de Recherches d'Histoire et de Philosophie; 1967. 148p. (Hautes etudes medievales et modernes, 3). (In French).

H183
HENRY, LOUIS. 1972. *Démographie: Analyse et Modeles* [Demography: Analysis and Models]. Paris, FR: Larousse; 1972. 240p. (In French). Trans. Van de Walle, Etienne; Jones, Elise F. *Population: Analysis and Models*. New York, NY: Academic Press; c1976. 291p. ISBN: 0123412501; LCCN: 76-043172.

H184
HENSEN, STEVEN L. 1989. *Archives, Personal papers, and Manuscripts: A Cataloging Manual for Archival Repositories, Historical Societies, and Manuscript Libraries*. 2nd ed. Chicago, IL: Society of American Archivists; 1989. 196p. ISBN: 0931828732; LCCN: 89-63416; OCLC: 20899791.

H185
HENSEN, STEVEN L. 1997 [1998]. EAD and Web-access to Archival Materials. See reference: DOOLEY, J., ed. 1997 [1998].

H186
HERBST, JUERGEN. 1965. *The German Historical School in American Scholarship: A Study in the Transfer of Culture*. Ithaca, NY: Cornell University Press; 1965. 262p. ISBN: 0804616663; LCCN: 79-159072,

H187
HERLIHY, DAVID. 1976. *Medieval and Renaissance Pistoia: The Social History of an Italian Town, 1200-1430*. New Haven, CT: Yale University Press; 1967. 297p.

H188
HERLIHY, DAVID. 1976/1992. Computer-Assisted Analysis of Statistical Documents of Medieval Society. In: Powell, J. M., ed. *Medieval Studies: An Introduction*. Syracuse, NY: Syracuse University Press; 1976. Rev. ed., 1992; 185-212. ISBN: 0815621752; 0815621760 (pbk.); LCCN: 76-8870; OCLC: 2272959.

H189
HERLIHY, DAVID. 1978a. Computation in History: Styles and Methods. *Computers and Humanities*. 1978; 11: 8-18. ISSN: 0010-4817.

H190
HERLIHY, DAVID. 1980. Problems of Record Linkages in Tuscan Fiscal Records of the Fifteenth Century. In his collected essays: *Cities and Society in Medieval Italy*. Ashgate / London, UK: Variorum Press; 1980. (Variorum reprint series, 10).

H191
HERLIHY, DAVID. 1981. Quantification in the 1980s: Numerical and Formal Analysis in European History. *Journal of Interdisciplinary History*. 1981; 12: 115-136. ISSN: 0022-1953.

H192
HERLIHY, DAVID. 1985. *Medieval Households*. Cambridge, MA: Harvard University Press; 1985. 227p. ISBN: 0674563751 (hbk.); 067456376X (pbk.).

H193
HERLIHY, DAVID; KLAPISCH-ZUBER, CHRISTIANE. 1978b. *Les toscans et leurs familles. Une étude du catasto florentin de 1427* [Tuscans and their Families: A Study of Florentine Household Tax of 1427]. Paris, FR: Foundation Nationale des Sciences Politiques, École de Hautes Études en Science Sociales, École des hautes études en sciences sociales; 1978. 702p. ISBN: 2724604008; 2713206847; LCCN: 79-374836; OCLC: 5618011.

H194
HERNER, SAUL. 1984. Brief History of Information Science. *Journal of the American Society for Information Science.* 1984; 35(3): 157-163. ISSN: 0002-8231.

H195
HERNON, PETER. 1984. Information Needs and Gathering Patterns of Academic Social Scientists, with Special Emphasis Given to Historians and Their Use of U.S. Government Publications. *Government Information Quarterly.* 1984; 1: 401-429. ISSN: 0740-624X.

H196
HERNON, PETER; MCCLURE, CHARLES R. 1993. Electronic U.S. Government Information: Policy Issues and Directions. In: Williams, Martha, ed. *Annual Review of Information Science and Technology (ARIST)* (28: 45-101). Medford, NJ: Information Today for ASIS; 1993. ISBN: 1-57387-019-6; ISSN: 0066-4200; CODEN: ARISBC; LC no. 66-25096

H197
HERSBERG, THEODORE. 1981. Archival Automation and the Researcher. See reference: MCCRANK, L., ed., 1981. 35-66.

H198
HERSBERG, THEODORE, ed. 1981. *Philadelphia: Work, Space, Family, and Group Experience in the Nineteenth Century: Essays Toward an Interdisciplinary History of the City.* New York, NY: Oxford University Press; 1981. 525p. ISBN: 0195027523; 0195927531 (pbk.); LCCN: 90-10843; OCLC: 6042821.

H199
HERTZEL, DOROTHY H. 1985. *Bibliographical Approach to the History of Idea Development in Bibliometrics.* Cleveland, OH: Case Western Reserve University; 1985. 222p. (Ph.D. Dissertation). Available from: University Microfilms International, Ann Arbor, MI (UMI order no. 85-10095).

H200
HERUBEL, J-P. V. M.; GOEDEKEN, E. A. 1993. Trends in historical scholarship as evidenced in the *American Historical Review*, 1896-1990. *Serials Review.* 1993; 18 (2): 79-84.

H201
HERWIJEN, ERIC VAN. 1990/1994. *Practical SGML.* Dordrecht and Boston: Kluwer; 1990. 397p. ISBN: 079230635X. 2nd ed. Norwell, MA: Kluwer Academic Publishers; 1994. 288p. ISBN: 0792394348; LCCN: 93-047579.

H202
HERWIJEN, ERIC VAN. 1995. *The Annotated ISO 12083: The Gateway to SGML Publishing* (Electronic diskettes). Geneva, CH: International Standards Organization (ISO); 1995. 2 disks. ISBN: 92-67-10215-X

H203
HESKE, TED; NEPORENT HESKE, JILL. 1996. *Fuzzy Logic for Real-World Design.* New York, NY: Annabooks; 1996. 428p.; 1 disk. ISBN: 0929392248; LCCN: 06148482. Available from: http://annabooks.com. [Embedded systems].

H204
HESSE, MARY. 1974. *The Structure of Scientific Inference.* Berkeley, CA: University of California Press; 1974. 309p. ISBN: 0520025822.

H205
HESSE, MARY. 1980. *Revolutions and Reconstructions in the Philosophy of Science.* Bloomington, IN: University of Indiana; 1980. Brighton, UK: Harvester Press; 1980. 271p. ISBN: 085272686.

H206
HETERICK, ROBERT C., Jr., ed. 1993. *Re-engineering Teaching and Learning in Higher Ed: Sheltered Groves, Windmills, and Malls.* Denver, CO: CAUSE; 1993. 46p. (CAUSE Professional Paper Series, no. 1 [PUB3001]. Study sponsored by Digital Equipment Corporation). Accessible at http://www.cause.org/information-resources/ir-library.

H207
HEWER, S. 1989. *Making the Most out of IT Skills* [Information Technology]. London, UK: n.p.;1989.

H208
HEXTER, JACK H. 1971a. *The History Primer.* New York: Basic Books; 1971. 297p. ISBN: 0465030270; LCCN: 74-13551; OCLC: 135553.

H209
HEXTER, JACK H. 1971b. *Doing History.* Bloomington, IN: University of Indiana Press; 1971. 182p. ISBN: 0253318203; LCCN: 70-1665049; OCLC: 216632.

H210
HEXTER, JACK H. 1979. *Reappraisals in History: New Views on History and Society in Early Modern Europe.* 2nd ed. Chicago, IL: University of Chicago Press; 1979. 278p. ISBN: 0- 226-33232-2.

H211
HICKERSON, THOMAS H. 1981. *Archives & Manuscripts: An Introduction to Automated Access.* Chicago, IL: SAA; 1981. 60p. (SAA Basic Manual series). ISBN: 0931828295 (pbk.); LCCN: 81-52113; OCLC: 7761468.

H212
HIGGENBOTHAM, BARBRA B. 1989. "You Have Only to Touch the Keys...": Nineteenth- century Visions of Twentieth-century Technology. *Urban Academic Librarian.* 1989 Winter; 7(2); 40-45. ISSN: 0276-9298.

H213
HIGGENS, J.; JOHNS, T. 1984. *Computers in Language Learning.* London, UK: Collins ELT / [Reading, MA]: Addison-Wesley World Language Division; 1984. 192p. ISBN: 02101046482.

H214
HIGGINSON, THOMAS J.; WAXLER, ROBERT P. 1993. Corporate Cultures for the 1990s: What is Needed? *Industrial Management.* 1993 January-February; 35 (1): 11-13. ISSN: 0019-8471.

H215
HIGGS, EDWARD. 1992. Machine Readable Records, Archives, and Historical Memory. *History and Computing.* 1992; 4(3): 183-190. ISSN: 0957-0144.

H216
HIGGS, EDWARD, ed. 1998. *History and Electronic Artifacts.* Oxford, UK: Oxford University Press; 1998. 345p. ISBN: 0198236336 (hbk.); 0198236344 (pbk.); LCCN: 97-1470.

H217
HIGHAM, JOHN. 1965/1986. *History: Professional Scholarship in America.* New York, NY: Prentice Hall; 1965. Reprinted from 1965 first Torchback ed. New York: Harper & Row; 1973. Reprinted: Baltimore, MD: The Johns Hopkins University Press; 1986. 272p. ISBN: 0-8018-3462-7.

H218
HIGHAM, JOHN. 1994. The Future of American History. *Journal of American History.* 1994 March; 80(4): 1289-1310. ISSN: 0021-8723.

H219
HIGHAM, JOHN. 1995. The Limits of Relativism: Restatement and Remembrance. *Journal of the History of Ideas.* 1995 October; 56 (4): 669-675. ISSN: 0022-5037. Review of APPLEBY, HUNT & JACOB, 1994.

H220
HILKER, EMERSON. 1986. Artificial Intelligence: A Review of Current Information Sources. *Collection Building.* 1986; 7(3): 14-30. ISSN: 0160-4953.

H221
HILL, LEWIS E.; VON ENDE, ELEANOR T. 1994. Towards a Personal Knowledge of Economic History: Reflections on our Intellectual Heritage from the Polanyi Brothers. *The American Journal of Economics and Sociology.* 1994 January; 53 (1): 17-27. ISSN: 0002-9246.

H222
HILL, LINDA L. 1990. *Access to Geographic Concepts in Online Bibliographic Files: Effectiveness of Current Practices and the Potential of a Graphic Interface.* Pittsburgh, PA: University of Pittsburgh; 1990. 200f. (Ph.D. Dissertation. *DAI:* 91-20481). OCLC: 27762875. Available in microfiche from: University Microfilms International, Ann Arbor, MI.

H223
HILL, LINDA L.; RASMUSSEN, EDIE M. 1992. Geographic Indexing Terms as Spatial Indicators. See reference: STONE, S; BUCKLAND, M., eds. 1992. 9-20.

H224
HILL, MICHAEL R. 1993. *Archival Strategies and Techniques.* Newbury Park, CA: Sage Publications; 1993. 88p. (Qualitative Research Methods Series, 31). ISBN: 080-3948- 255.

H225
HILL, W. 1994. History-enriched Digital Objects: Prototype and Policy Issues. *The Information Society.* 1994; 10: 139-145.

H226
HILL, WALTER B. 1989. *Family, Life, and Work Culture: Black Charleston, South Carolina, 1880 to 1910.* College Park, MD: University of Maryland; 1989. 452p. (Ph.D. dissertation; *DAI*, vol. 50/07-A: 2184). Available from: University Microfilms, Ann Arbor, MI (Order no. AAD89-24164).

H227
HILTZ, S. R.; JOHNSON, K.; TUROFF, M. 1986. Experiments in Group Decision Making: Communication Process and Outcome in Face-to-face Versus Computerized Conferences. *Human Communication Research*. 1986; 13: 225-252.

H228
HIMMELFARB, GERTRUDE. 1987. *The New History and the Old*. Cambridge, MA: Harvard University Belknap Press; 1987. 209p. ISBN: 0674615808 (pbk.); LCCN: 87-327; OCLC: 15107685.

H229
HINCHMAN, L. P.; HINCHMAN, S. K., eds. 1997. *Memory, Identity, Community: The Idea of the Narrative in the Human Sciences*. Albany, NY: State University of New York Press; 1997.

H230
HINDING, ANDREA. 1993. Inventing the Concept of Documentation. *Journal of American History*. 1993; 80(1): 168-179. ISSN: 0021-8723.

H231
HINDLE, D. 1994. A Parser for Text Corpora. In: Atkins, B. T. S.; Zampolli, A., eds. *Computational Approaches to the Lexicon*. Oxford, UK: Oxford University Press; 1994. 103-151. ISBN: 0198238793 (hbk.); LCCN: 94-001852.

H232
HIPPLER, HANA-J.; SCHWARZ, NORBERT; SUDMAN, SEYMOUR, eds. 1987. *Social Information Processing and Survey Methodology*. New York, NY: Springer-Verlag; 1987. 223p. ISBN: 038796570X.

H233
HIROSE, MICHITAKA. 1997. Image-Based Virtual World Generation. See reference: MOEZZI, S., ed. 1997. 27-33.

H234
HIRSCH, HERBERT. 1995. *Genocide and the Politics of Memory: Studying Death to Preserve Life*. Chapel Hill, NC: University of North Carolina Press; 1995. 240p. ISBN: 0807821985(hbk.); 0807845051(pbk.); LCCN: 94029750..

H235
HIRSCH, MORRIS W. 1989. Chaos, Rigor, and Hype. *The Mathematical Intelligencer*. 1989; 11: 6-8. ISSN: 0343-6993.

H236
HIRSCHHEIM, RUDY A.; KLEIN, HEINZ-KARL; LYYTINEN, KALLE. 1995. *Information Systems Development and Data Modeling*. Cambridge, UK / New York, NY: Cambridge University Press; 1995. 289p. ISBN: 0521373697; LCCN: 94033321.

H237
HIRSCHHEIM, RUDY A.; SMITHSON, STEVE; WHITEHOUSE, DIANE. 1990. *Microcomputers and the Humanities: Survey and Recommendations*. New York, NY: E. Horwood; 1990. 165p. (Horwood series in Computers and their Applications). ISBN: 0135825377; LCCN: 90030884.

H238
HIRSHLEIFER, JACK; RILEY, J. G. 1992. *The Analytics of Uncertainty and Information*. Cambridge, UK: Cambridge University Press; 1992. 465p. (Cambridge Surveys of Economic Literature). ISBN: 0521239567 (hbk.); 0521239567 (pbk.); LCCN: 96-23754.

H239
HIRST, WILLIAM; MANDELBROT, BENOIT B. 1994. *Fractal Landscapes from the Real World*. Touring Exhibition, 1994-1996: Catalog. Manchester, UK: Cornerhouse; 1994. 1 vol., ills. ISBN: 00948797231.

H240
HIRTLE, PETER B. 1989. Atherton Seidell and the Photoduplication of Library material. *Journal of the American Society for Information Science*. 1989 November; 40(6): 424-431. ISSN: 0002-8231.

H241
HISTORICAL COMPUTER SOCIETY. 1995-. *Historically Brewed*. Jacksonsville, FL: HCS; 1995-. Available from: HCS, 3649 Herschel St., Jacksonville, FL 32205.

H242
HISTORICAL METHODS. 1978-. Washington, DC: Heldref Publications; 1978-. Qtly. ISSN: 0161-5440; LCCN: 78-645392.

H243
HISTORICAL METHODS NEWSLETTER. 1967-1977. Pittsburgh, PA: University of Pittsburgh Center for International Studies and Department of History; 1967-1977. ISSN: 0018-2494.

H244

HISTORISCHE SOZIALFORSCHUNG / HISTORICAL SOCIAL RESEARCH. 1979-. Co- sponsored by the Zentrum für Historische Sozialforschung (Cologne) and Informationszentrum Sozialwissenschaften (Bonn). Stuttgart, DEU: Klett-Cotta; 1979-. Annual. (In German and English). ISSN: 0173-2145; LCCN: 82-644125; OCLC: 8593669.

H245

HISTORY AND MEMORY. Studies in Representation of the Past. 1989-. Bloomington, IN: University of Indiana Press; Frankfurt am Main, DEU: Athenaeum. 1989-: 1-. ISSN: 0935-560X.

H246

HISTORY ASSOCIATION. 1988. *Update of Computer Software for History.* London: Microelectronics Education Support Unit; 1988. Updated by references: NATIONAL COUNCIL FOR EDUCATIONAL TECHNOLOGY, 1991; and SPAETH, D. 1991.

H247

HISTORY COURSEWARE CONSORTIUM. 1992-. *Core Resources for Historians* (electronic files). Glasgow, UK: University of Glasgow; 1992-. (Funded by the UK Higher Education Council Teaching and Learning with Technology Programme [TLTP]). 12 CD-ROMs with primary documents, tutorials, secondary literature, select bibliographies, and data sets viewable also in HTML, produced on Women's History; Mass Politics; Industrialization, Urbanization, and Migration; and the Pre-modern period (Papacy, Reformation, and Early Modern English Towns). ISBNs include 095175-1441, -1468, -1476, -1484, -1492, etc. Available at www.gla.ac.uk/~histtltp/.

H248

HISTORY COURSEWARE CONSORTIUM. [1998-]. *Newsletter.* Glasgow, UK: University of Glasgow; [1998-]. Membership distribution for users of *Core Resources for Historians.* Accessible at www.gla.ac.uk/~histtltp/.

H249

HITCHCOCK, TIM. 1993. "She's Gotta Have I.T.": Teaching Information Technology to Undergraduate History Students. *History and Computing* (UK). 1993; 5: 193-198. ISSN: 0957-0144.

H250

HJÖRLAND, B.; ALBRECHTSEN, H. 1995. Toward a New Horizon in Information Science: Domain Analysis. *Journal of the American Society for Information Science.* 1995; 46: 400- 435. ISSN: 0002-8231.

H251

HOBSBAWN, E. J. 1971. From Social History to the History of Society. *Daedalus.* 1971; 100: 20-45. ISSN: 0199-9818.

H252

HOCH, STEVEN L.; KASHCHENKO, SERGEY; MIZIS, YURY. 1996 [1999-]. Project in Russian Population History, 1700-1917: Preliminary Results. See reference: BORODKIN, L., ed. 1996: English abstract of presentation, 89-90; paper in Russian [199- forthcoming].

H253

HOCKEY, SUSAN, ed. 1980. *A Guide to Computer Applications in the Humanities.* London, UK: Duckworth; 1980. 248p. ISBN: 0715613154; 07156131903 (pbk.); LCCN: 80-473910; OCLC: 6204014. Rev.ed. Baltimore, MD: The Johns Hopkins Press; 1980. 248p. ISBN: 0801823463; 0801828910 (pbk.); LCCN: 79-3378; OCLC: 6182716. Updated and rev. ed., 1983. ISBN: 0801828910 (pbk.); OCLC: 9907611.

H254

HOCKEY, SUSAN; IDE, NANCY; LANCASHIRE, IAN, eds. 1991, 1994. *Research in Humanities Computing,* 1-4. New York and Oxford: Oxford University Press; 1991-1994. ISBN: 0-1982-425-14; OCLC: 24923149.

H255

HOCKEY, SUSAN; MARRIOTT, IAN. 1988. *Oxford Concordance Program. OCP User's Manual.* Versions 1. Version 2 with MARTIN, JEREMEY. Oxford, UK: Oxford University Computing Services; 1988. 367p. OCLC: 2369707.

H256

HODGE, BILLY J.; ANTHONY, WILLIAM P.; GALES, LAWRENCE M. 1991/1995. *Organization Theory: A Strategic Approach.* 4th ed. Boston, MA: Alyyn and Bacon; c1991. 5th ed. Upper Saddle River, NJ: Prentice-Hall, Ltd.; 1995. 482p. ISBN: 0205152740; LCCN: 95-51122.

H257

HODGES, PARKER. 1988 The New Maturity of Computer Science. *Datamation.* 1988 Sept. 15; 34 (18): 37-41. ISSN: 0011-6963.

H258

HODGETS, RICHARD M.; LUTHANS, FRED; LEE, SANG M. 1994. New Paradigm Organizations: From Total Quality to Learning to World-class. *Organizational Dynamics.* 1994 Winter; 22 (3): 5-19. ISSN: 0090-2616.

H259
HOFF-WILSON, JOAN. 1985. The Plight of a Mom and Pop Operation. *OAH Newsletter*. 1985 May; 4. ISSN: 1059-1125.

H260
HOFFER, JEFFREY; VALACICH, JOSEPH S. 1993. Group Memory in Group Support Systems: A Foundation for Design. In: Jessup, Leonard; M. Valacich, Joseph S., eds. *Group Support Systems: New Perspectives*. New York, NY: Macmillan; 1993. 214-229. ISBN: 0-02- 360625-8.

H261
HOFFMAN, K. H.; MESHKOV, N. 1987. Problem[s] from Empirical Economics: II. Determining Uncertainties arising from Incomplete Data using Information Theory. *Resources and Energy* (NE). 1987; 9 (4): 379-395.

H262
HOFSTADTER, RICHARD. 1972. History and the Social Sciences. See reference: STERN, F. 1972. 360-372.

H263
HOFSTEDE, GEERT. 1993. Cultural Constraints in Management Theories. *Academy of Management Executives*. 1993 February; 7 (1): 81-94. ISSN: 0896-3789; OCLC: 15500779; LCCN: 93-91573.

H264
HOFSTEDE, GEERT; BOND, MICHAEL HARRIS; LUK, CHUNG-LEUNG. 1993. Individual Perceptions of Organizational Cultures: A Methodological Treatise of Levels of Analysis. *Organization Studies*. 1993; 14 (4): 483-503. ISSN: 0170-8405.

H265
HOLLAND, JOHN H. 1998. *Emergence: from Chaos to Order*. New York, NY: John Wiley & Sons; 1998. 224p ISBN: 0201149435; LCCN: 97-021350.

H266
HOLLANDS, ROBIN. 1996. *The Virtual Reality Homebrewer's Handbook*. New York, NY: John Wiley & Sons; 1996. 362p. plus CD-ROM. ISBN: 0-471-95871-9.

H267
HOLLINGER, ROBERT. 1994. *Postmodernism and the Social Sciences: A Thematic Approach*. Thousand Oaks, CA: Sage; 1994. 192p. (Contemporary Social Theory, 4). ISBN: 0803946376 (hbk.); 0803946384 (pbk.).

H268
HOLLISTER, BERNARD C. 1995. Social Math in the History Classroom. *Social Education*. 1995 January; 59(1): 14-17. ISSN: 0037-7727.

H269
HOLLISTER, C. WARREN. 1992. The Phases of European History and the Nonexistence of the Middle Ages. *Pacific Historical Review*. 1992; 61: 1-22. ISSN: 0030-8684.

H270
HOLM, LARS W. 1989. The Norwegian Census Data Bank and the Norwegian Social Science Data Service. See reference: MCCRANK, L. J., ed. 1989. 317-325.

H271
HOLM, LIV A. 1996. *Models for Open System Protocol Development*. UDT Series on Data Communication Technologies and Standards for Libraries. The Hague, NTD: IFLA; 1996. 109p. ISBN: 1-9694214-7-8.

H272
HOLMES, OLIVER W. 1964. Archival Arrangement—Five different operations at five different levels. *American Archivist*. 1964; 27: 1-25. ISSN: 0360-9081.

G273
HOLSCHER, L. 1997. The new annalistic: A sketch of a theory of history. *History and Theory*. 1997 Oct.; 36 (2): 317-335. ISSN: 0018-2656.

H274
HOLSINGER, ERIC. 1992. Virtual Travel Takes Kiosks to New Dimension. *MacWeek*. 1992 June; 6(25): 36-38. ISSN: 0892-8118.

H275
HOLSTI, OLE R. 1969. *Content Analysis for the Social Sciences and Humanities*. Reading, MA: Addison-Wesley; 1969. 235p. LCCN: 69-018008.

H276
HOLT, WILLIAM STULL. 1938. *Historical Scholarship in the United States, 1876-1901: As Revealed in the Correspondence of Herbert B. Adams*. Baltimore, MD: Johns Hopkins University Press; 1938. 314p. (Historical

and Political Science Series, 56). LCCN: 39-0011218. Rev. ed. *Historical Scholarship in the United States, and other essays.* Seattle, WA: University of Washington; [1967]. 184p. LCCN: 67-01314.

H277
HOLT, WILLIAM STULL. 1940. The Idea of Scientific History in America. *Journal of the History of Ideas.* 1940; 1: 352-362. ISSN: 0022-5037.

H278
HOLTZ, FREDERICK. 1988. Optical Disc Technology: The Past, Present, and Future. In: Holtz, F., ed. *CD-ROM: Breakthrough in Information Storage.* Blue Ridge Summit, PA: Tab Books, Inc.; 1988. 93-142. ISBN: 0-8306-1426-5.

H279
HOLYOAK, KEITH J.; THAGARD, PAUL. 1994. *Mental Leaps. Analogy in Creative Thought.* Cambridge, MA: Bradford Book; 1994. 336p. ISBN: 0-262-58144-2. Distributed by MIT Press.

H280
HOLZMANN, GERARD; PEHRSON, BJOERN. 1994. *The Early History of Data Networks.* Los Alamitos, CA: IEEE; 1994. 304p. ISBN: 0-8186-6782-6.

H281
HONG, JUNGOKOOK K.; HASHIHARA, H.; IOKA, M.; KUROKAWA, M.; SATO, M; SUGITA, S.; KUBO, M; TAMAOTO, Y. 1988. A Color Image Database for an Ethnology Museum. See reference: BEST, MOCHMANN, THALLER, eds. 1988. Abstracts B5. 1-2.

H282
HONG, JUNGOKOOK K.; SUGITA, SIGEHARU. 1991. A Colour Image Database for an Ethnology Museum— A Multi-Window System for Electronic Cataloguing and Browsing of Ethnographic Samples on the PC. See reference: BEST, H., *ET AL.*, eds. 1991. 53-60.

H283
HOOD, WILLIAM. 1987. Full-text Searching in Bibliographic Databases. *LASIE (Library Automated System Information Exchange).* 1987 October; 18(2): 42-48. ISSN: 0047- 3774.

H284
HOOPER-GREENHILL, EILEAN. 1991. *Museum and Gallery Education.* Leicester, UK: Leicester University Press; 1991.

H285
HOOPER-GREENHILL, EILEAN. 1992. *Museums and the Shaping of Knowledge.* London, UK /New York: NY;:Routledge; 1992. 232p. ISBN: 0-415-06145-8; 0-415-07031-7 (pbk.).

H286
HOOPES, JOHN W. The Future of the Past: Archeology and Anthropology on the World Wide Web. See reference: TRANT, J., ed. 1997. 87-105.

H287
HOPKINS, DEIAN. 1989. The Politics of Historical Computing. *History and Computing.* 1989; 1: 42-49. ISSN: 0957-0144.

H288
HOPKINS, DEIAN. 1992. The Future of the Past. See reference: BOCCHI, F.; DENLEY, P., eds. 1992. 759-764.

H289
HOPKINS, TERENCE K.; WALLERSTEIN, IMMANUEL; BACH, ROBERT L. 1982. *World-systems Analysis: Theory and Methodology.* Beverley Hills, CA: Sage Publications; c1982. 200p. ISBN: 0802918100 (hbk.); 0803918119 (pbk.); LCCN: 82000670.

H290
HORAN, P. M. 1987. Theoretical Models in Social History Research. *Social Science History.* 1987; 11: 379-398. ISSN: 0145-5532.

H291
HORN, DAVID. 1996. Education for Archivists: Hard Choices and Hard Work. *Archival Issues.* 1996; 21(1): 25-31 ISSN: 1067-4993.

H292
HORN, L. 1989. *A Natural History of Negation.* Chicago, IL: University of Chicago; 1989.

H293
HORN, T. C. R.; RITTER, HARRY. 1986. Interdisciplinary History: A Historiographical Review. *History Teacher.* 1986; 19: 427-448. ISSN: 0018-2745.

H294
HORSMAN, PETER. 1994. Taming the Elephant: An Orthodox Approach to the Principle of Provenance. In: Abukhansfa, K.; Sydbeck, J., eds. *The Principle of Provenance*. Boras, SE: Swedish National Archives; 1994; 45-55. ISBN: 91-88366-11-1; ISSN: 0346-8488.

H295
HORSMAN, PETER. 1997a. *The Application of Knowledge Engineering in Archival Appraisal*. Gravenhage, NE: n.p.; 1997.

H296
HORSMAN, PETER. 1997b. Digital Longevity: Policies on Electronic Records in the Netherlands. See reference: BEARMAN, D.; TRANT, J., eds. 1997. 235-240.

H297
HORTON, FOREST W.; LEWIS, DENNIS, 3eds. 1991. *Great Information Disasters*. London, UK: Aslib; 1991. 218p. ISBN: 0-85142-255-1.

H298
HORTON, WILLIAM K. 1991. *Illustrating Computer Documentation: The Art of Presenting Information Graphically on Paper and Online*. New York, NY: John Wiley & Sons, Inc.; 1991. 313p. ISBN: 0471538469 (hbk.); 0471538450 (pbk.); LCCN: 91015425.

H299
HORVITZ, E.; JENSEN, F. V., eds. 1996. *Proceedings of the Twelfth Conference on Uncertainty in Artificial Intelligence*. San Francisco, CA; Morgan Kaufmann; 1996.

H300
HOUSE, KENNETH J. 1990. *The Development of Records Disposition Procedures and Legislation at the United States Archives, 1934-1945*. Bellingham. WA: Western Washington University; 1990. 335p. (M.S. Thesis). Rev. ed. forthcoming in *Primary Sources and Original Works* [199-].

H301
HOUSER, LLOYD J.; SCRADER, ALVIN M. 1978. *The Search for a Scientific Profession: Library Science Education in the U.S. and Canada*. Metuchen, NJ: Scarecrow Press; 1978. 180p. ISBN: 081081062X; LCCN: 77-17563.

H302
HOUSER, W.; GRIFFIN, J.; HAGE, CARL. 1996. *EDI Meets the Internet: Frequently Asked Questions about Electronic Data Interchange on the Internet* (Electronic file). January 1996. 41 p. Accessible as ftp://ds.internic.net/rfc/rfc1865.txt.

H303
HOWE, BARBARA. 1989. *Careers for Students of History*. Washington, D.C.: American Historical Association; 1989. 94p. ISBN: 0872290441; LCCN: 89-81697; OCLC: 21299988.

H304
HOYLE, DAVID. 1994. *ISO 9000 Quality Systems Handbook*. 2nd ed. Oxford, UK: Butterworth-Heinemann Ltd.; 1994. 498p. ISBN: 0-7506-2130-3.

H305
HRASKO, GABOR; SAJO, TAMAS. 1993. The ORBIS Database Project. For a Computer Catalogue of Hungarian Artistic and Historical Collections. See reference: FIKFAK, J.; JARITZ, G., eds., 1993: 68-76.

H306
HUBER, GEORGE P. 1991. Organizational Learning: The Contributing Processes and the Literatures. *Organization Science*. 1991; 2 (1): 88-115. ISSN: 1047-7039.

H307
HUBER, GEORGE P. 1993. Understanding and Predicting Organizational Change. In: Huber, George P.; Glick, William H., eds. *Organizational Change and Redesign: Ideas and Insights for Improving Performance*. New York, NY: Oxford University Press; 1993. 450p. ISBN: 0195072855.

H308
HUBER, GEORGE P.; VAN DE VEN, ANDREW H. 1995. *Longitudinal Field Research Methods: Studying Processes of Organizational Change*. Thousand Oaks, CA: Sage Publications; 1995. 373p. ISBN: 0803970900 (hbk.); 0803970919 (pbk.).

H309
HUBER, JOHN C. 1998. Cumulative Advantage and Success-Breeds-Success: The Value of Time Pattern Analysis. *Journal of the American Society for Information Science*. 1998; 49 (5): 471-476. ISSN: 0002-8231; CODEN: AISJB6.

H310
HUCHINS, W. J. 1978. Progress in Documentation: Machine-translation and Machine-assisted Translation. *Journal of Documentation* (UK). 1978 June; 34(2): 119-59. ISSN: 0022- 0418.

H311
HUFF, CHUCK.; FINOLT, THOMAS., eds. 1994. *Social Issues in Computing: Putting Computing in Its Place.* New York, NY: McGraw-Hill; 1994. 726p. (Computers and Civilization). ISBN: 0070308632; LCCN: 93049600.

H312
HUFF, DARRELL. 1954. *How to Lie with Statistics.* New York, NY: Norton; 1954. 192p. ISBN: 039309426X.

H313
HUGGETT, JEREMY; RYAN, NICK S., eds. 1995. *Computer Applications and Quantitative Analysis in Archeology.* Conference proceedings, CAA 94, University of Glasgow, March 23-26, 1994. Oxford, UK: Tempus Reparatum; 1995. 257p. (British Archaeological Reports International Series, 600). ISBN: 0860547779.

H314
HUGHES, H[ENRY]. STUART. 1958. *Consciousness and Society: The Reorientation of European Social Thought, 1890-1930.* New York, NY: Knopf; 1958. 433p. LCCN: 58- 010976.

H315
HUGHES, H. STUART. 1963. The Historian and the Social Scientist. See reference: RIASANOVSKY, A; RIZNIK, B., eds. 1963.

H316
HUGHES, H. STUART. 1964. *History as Art and as Science: Twin Vistas on the Past.* World Perspectives, v. 32. New York, NY: Harper and Row; 1964. 107p. LCCN: 63- 20291; OCLC: 392872.

H317
HUGHES, LORNA M. 1995. Using Hypertext to Remove the Structures of Historical Data. See reference: BOON- STRA, O.; COLLENTEUR, G.; VAN ELDEREN, B., eds. 1995. 273-279.

H318
HUGHES, THOMAS P. 1989. *American Genius: A Century of Invention and Technological Enthusiasm, 1870-1970.* New York, NY: Viking; 1989. 529p. ISBN: 0670814784.

H319
HUIZINGA, JOHAN. 1924/1952/1954/1996. *Hertsttij der Middeleeuwen.* Trans. as: *The Waning of the Middle Ages: A study of Form of Life, Thought, and Art in France and the Netherlands in the 14th and 15th centuries.* London, UK: Edward Arnold & Co.; 1952. 328p. Reprint. Garden City, NY: Doubleday; 1954. 362p. Trans. as: *The Autumn of the Middle Ages.* Chicago, IL: University of Chicago Press; 1996. 467p. ISBN: 0226359921.

H320
HULBERT, BRADLEY J. [1997]. *As a Trial Attorney, How Would I Attack the Way You Manage Your Electronic Records?* [Electronic file]. Chicago, IL: McDonnell Boehnen Hulbert & Berghoff, Inc.; [1997]. 36p. Accessible through Cohasset Homepage at http://www.cohasset/com.hulbert/hulbert.html.

H321
HULL, DANIEL M. 1995. *Who are You Calling Stupid?* Waco, TX: Center for Occupational Research and Development (CORD); 1995.

H322
HULL, FELIX. 1980. The Archivist Should Not be an Historian. *Journal of the Society of Archivists* (UK). 1980 April; 8: 250-262. ISSN: 0037-9816.

H323
HUMPHREYS, S. C. 1969. History, Economics, and Anthropology: The Work of Karl Polanyi. *History and Theory.* 1969; 8: 166-212. ISSN: 0018-2656.

H324
HUNT, LYNN. 1986. French History in the Last Twenty Years: The Rise and Fall of the *Annales* Paradigm. *Journal of Contemporary History.* 1986; 21: 209-224. ISSN: 0022- 0094.

H325
HUNT, LYNN. 1995. Forgetting and Remembering: The French Revolution Then and Now. *American Historical Review.* 1995; 100(4): 1119-1135. ISSN: 0002-8762.

H326
HUNT, LYNN. 1997. Democratization and Decline? The Consequences of Demographic Change in the Humanities. See reference: KERNAN, A., ed. 1997.

H327
HUNT, LYNN, ed. 1989. *The New Cultural History.* Berkeley and Los Angeles, CA: University of California Press; 1989. 244p. ISBN: 0-520-06428-3; pbk. 0-520-06429. See especially her introduction: History, Culture, and Text (pp. 1-22).

H328
HUNTER, GREG S. 1996/1997. *Developing and Maintaining Practical Archives: A How-to-do- it Manual.* New York, NY: Neal-Schuman Publ.; 1997. 283p. ISBN: 1855702120.

H329
HUNTER, TIM. 1993. Just Give Me the Fax. *New Scientist.* 1993 February 13; 137(1860): 33-37. ISSN: 0262-4079.

H330
HURON, NICOLAS. *NOMEN* (computer file). Memoire de DEA. Tours, FR: Universite de Tours; 1991. (In French)

H331
HUTCHINS, E. 1991. The Social Organization of Distributed Cognition. In: Resnick, L. B.; Levine, J. M.; Teasley, S.D., eds. *Perspectives on Socially Shared Cognition.* APA Conference Proceedings, University of Pittsburgh; 1989 (pp. 283-307). Washington, D.C.: American Psychological Association; 1991. 429p. ISBN: 1557981213.

H332
HUTTON, PATRICK H. 1993. *History as an Art of Memory.* Hanover, VT: University Press of New England; 1993. 229p. ISBN: 0874516315 (hbk.); 0874516374 (pbk.); LCCN: 93017246.

H333
HUTTON, PATRICK H. 1994. [Review]. *History and Theory.* 1994; 33: 95-107. ISSN: 0018- 2656. Review of LE GOFF, 1992 and VIDAL-NAQUET, 1992.

H334
HUYSSEN, ANDREAS. 1986. *After the Great Divide: Modernism, Mass Culture, Postmodernism.* Bloomington, IN: Indiana University Press; 1986. 244p. ISBN: 0253100577 (hbk.); 0253203996 (pbk.).

H335
HUYSSEN, ANDREAS. 1995. *Twilight Memories: Marking Time in a Culture of Amnesia.* New York, NY: Routledge; 1995. ISBN: 0415909341 (pbk.); 041590935X (hbk.).

H336
HUYSSEN, ANDREAS; BATHRICK, DAVID. 1989. *Modernity and the Text: Revisions of German Modernism.* New York, NY: Columbia University Press; 1989. 244p. ISBN: 0231066449.

H337
HYMAN, ANTHONY. 1982. *Charles Babbage, Pioneer of the Computer.* Princeton, NJ: Princeton University Press; 1982. 287p. ISBN: 0691083037; LCCN: 81-048078.

H338
HYMAN, MICHAEL R.; TANSEY, RICHARD; CLARK, JAMES W. 1994. Research on Advertising: Past, Present, and Future. *Journal of Advertising.* 1994 September; 23(3): 5- 15. ISSN: 0091-3367.

H339
HYRY, TOM; ONUF, RACHEL. 1997. The Personality of Electronic Records: The Impact of New Information Technology on Personal Records. *Archival Issues.* 1997; 22(1): 37-44. ISSN: 106677-4993.

-I-

I1
IACONO, S; KLING, ROB. 1996. Computerization Movements and Tales of Technological Utopianism. See reference: KLING, R.; DUNLOP, C., eds. 1996. 85-105.

I2
IACOVINA, LIVIA. 1993. Appraisal of Public Archives. See reference: KENT, A., ed., 1993. 52: 1-12.

I3
IANNONE, RON. 1995. Chaos Theory and its Implications for Curriculum and Teaching. *Education.* 1995 Summer; 115(4): 541-548. ISSN: 0013-1172.

I4
ICONCLASS. 1966. *ICONCLASS* [Icon Classification system]. Utrecht & Leiden, NL: ICONCLASS Research & Development Group; 1996. Accessible at http://iconclass.let.uu.nl.

I5
IDE, NANCY M.; SPERBERG-MCQUEEN, MICHAEL C. 1991. Development of a Standard for Encoding Literary and Linguistic Materials. See reference: BEST, H., *ET AL.*, eds. 1991. 511-512.

I6
IDE, NANCY M.; SPERBERG-MCQUEEN, MICHAEL C. 1995. The Text Encoding Initiative: Its History, Goals, and Future Development. See reference: IDE, NANCY; VERONIS, JEAN, eds. 1995. 5-15.

I7
IDE, NANCY M.; VERONIS, JEAN., eds. 1995. The Text Encoding Initiative: Background and Context. In: *Computers and the Humanities*. 1995; 29 (1-3). (Entire issue on title topic). ISSN: 0010-4817. Published separately. Dordrecht, NL: Kluwer Academic Publishers; 1995. 242p. ISBN: 0792336895 (hbk.); LCCN: 95-031289.

I8
IEEE ANNALS OF THE HISTORY OF COMPUTING. 1992-. Los Alamitos, CA: IEEE Computer Society; 1992-. ISSN: 1058-6180. (Continues the *Annals of the History of Computing*).

I9
IEEE COMPUTER SOCIETY. 1996. *Fuzzy Logic CD-ROM Library* (Electronic file). Los Alamitos, CA: IEEE; 1996. CD-ROM. ISBN: 0-12-059755-1. Contains machine-readable popular textbooks by Cox, McNeill & Thro, Zadeh, and Dubois & Prade.

I10
IGARTUA, JOSÉ E. 1988. Table ronde-Round Table. Les Bases de donnees historiques: L'experience canadienne depuis quinze ans / Historical Databases: The Canadian Experience Since Fifteen Years. Igartua, Jose ed. *Histoire sociale / Social History* (CAN). 1988 November; 21 (42): 283-317. (Entire issue of title topic). ISSN: 0018-2557.

I11
IGARTUA, JOSÉ E. 1995. Uncovering Patterns of Sociability: Residential Structures in a Company Town, Arvida, Canada; 1925-1940. See reference: BOONSTRA, O., *ET AL.*, eds. 1995. 116-126.

I12
IGARTUA, JOSÉ E., ed. 1996/1997 [1998]. Computers and Historians. In: *Computers and the Humanities* (NL). 1996/1997 [1998]; 30 (5): 347-399. (Entire issue on title topic). ISSN: 0010-4817; CODEN: COHAUD.

I13
IGARTUA, JUANJO; PAÉZ, DARIO. 1997. Art and Remembering Traumatic Collective Events: The Case of the Spanish Civil War. See reference: PENNEBAKER, J. W., *ET AL.*, eds. 1997.

I14
IGGERS, GEORG G. 1975/1978/1984. *New Directions in European Historiography.* Middletown, CT: Wesleyan University Press; 1975. German ed.: *Neue Geschichtswissenschaft. vom Historismus zur historischen Sozialwissenschaft: Ein Internationaler Vergleich,* [New History: From Historismus to Historical Social Science. An International Overview]. Munich, DEU: Deutscher Taschenbuch Verlag; 1978. 275p. ISBN: 3423043083; OCLC: 10565512. Rev. expanded English ed.: *New Directions in European Historiography.* Middletown, CT: Welsyean University Press; 1984. 267p. ISBN: 0819560715.

I15
IGGERS, GEORG G. 1983. *The German Conception of History: The National Tradition of Historical Thought from Herder to the Present.* Middleton, CT: Wesleyan University Press; 1983. 388p. ISBN: 0819560804.

I16
IGGERS, GEORG G. 1990. The Crisis of the Ranke Paradigm in the Nineteenth-century. In: Iggers, Georg G.; Powell, James M., eds. *Leopold von Ranke and the Shaping of the Historical Discipline.* Syracuse, NY: Syracuse University Press; 1990. 223p. ISBN: 0815624697.

I17
IGGERS, GEORG G. 1993/1997. *Gechichtswissenschaft im 20. Jahrhundert.* Rev., expanded English version: *Historiogaphy in the Twentieth Century: from Scientific Objectivity to the Postmodern Challenge.* Hanover, NH: Wesleyan University Press; 1997. 182p. ISBN: 0819553026 (hbk.); 0819563064 (hbk.).

I18
IGGERS, GEORG G. 1995. Historicism: the History and Meaning of the Term. *Journal of the History of Ideas.* 1995 January; 56(1): 129-153. ISSN: 0022-5037.

I19
IGGERS, GEORG G.; PARKER, HAROLD. T., eds. 1979. *International Handbook of Historical Studies. Contemporary Research and Theory.* Westport, CT: Greenwood Press; 1979. 452p. ISBN: 0-313-21367-4.

I20

IMMON, WILLIAM H. 1992. *Building the Data Warehouse*. Boston, MA: QED Publishing Group; 1992. 272p. ISBN: 0894354043.

I21

IMMON, WILLIAM H.; IMHOFF, CLAUDIA. 1996. *Building the Operational Data Store*. New York, NY: Wiley; 1996. 276p. ISBN: 0471128228.

I22

IMMON, WILLIAM H.; WELCH, WILLIAM H.; GLASSEY, KATHERINE L. 1997. *Managing the Data Warehouse*. New York, NY: John Wiley; 1997. 386p. ISBN: 0471163104.

I23

IMPEDOVO, SEBASTIANO, ed. 1994. *Fundamentals in Handwriting Recognition*. Proceedings of NATO Advanced Study Institute on Handwriting Recognition, Chateau de Bonas, Fr., June 21-July 3, 1993. Berlin, DEU / New York, NY: Springer-Verlag for the NATO Scientific Affairs Division; 1994. (NATO Series F, Computer and Systems Sciences, no. 124). ISBN: 0387574506 (US); 3540574506 (DGR).

I24

IMPEY, OLIVER; MACGREGOR, ARTHUR, eds. 1985. *The Origins of Museums: The Cabinet of Curiosities in Sixteenth-and Seventeenth-Century Europe*. New York, NY: Oxford University Press; 1985. 335p. ISBN: 0199521085; LCCN: 85-230059.

I25

INFORMATION INFRASTRUCTURE TECHNOLOGY AND APPLICATIONS (IITA). 1995. *Interoperability, Scaling, and the Digital Library Research Agenda* (electronic file). NII- IITA Report, 1995. Accessible at http:/www-diglib.stanford.edu/diglib/pub/reports/ iitapdlw/main. html.

I26

INFORMATION SCIENCE ABSTRACTS. 1969-. Philadelphia, PA: Documentation Abstracts; 1969-; 1-. Monthly. (Continues *Documentation and Information Science Abstracts*). ISSN: 0020-0239.

I27

INFORMATION SCIENCES, APPLICATIONS. 1994-. New York, NY: Elsevier Science; 1995- . 6x/yr. ISSN: 0020-0255; OCLC: 1753138. Electronic version (ISSN: 1069-0115) Accessible at http://peak.umdl.umich.edu.cgi-bin/peak/listjournal/10690115.

I28

INFORMATION TECHNOLOGY ASSOCIATION. 1997. Help Wanted: The IT Workforce Gap at the Dawn of a New Century (electronic file). Washington, D.C.: ITAA; 1997. Accessible at http://www.itaa.org; and in hard copy from ITAA, 1616 N. Ft. Myer Drive, suite 1300, Arlington, VA 22209.

I29

INGERSOLL, VIRGINIA HILL; ADAMS, GUY B. 1992. The Child is "Father" to the Manager: Images of Organizations in U.S. Children's Literature. *Organization Studies*. 1992; 13 (4): 497-519. ISSN: 0170-8406.

I30

INGRAHAM, PATRICIA W.; ROMZEK, BARBARA. S. 1994. *New Paradigms for Government*. San Francisco, CA: Jossey-Bass Publishers; 1994. 352p. ISBN: 01555426565.

I31

INGRAM, LINDA, ed. 1995. *Humanities Doctorates in the United States: 1993 Profile*. Washington, DC: National Academy Press; 1995.

I32

INGWERSEN, PETER. 1992a. Information and Information Science in Context. *Libri* (DK). 1992 April-June; 42(2): 99-135. ISSN: 0024-2667.

I33

INGWERSEN, PETER. 1992b. *Information Retrieval Interaction*. London, UK: Taylor Graham; 1992. 246p. ISBN: 0947568549 (pbk.).

I34

INGWERSEN, PETER. 1997. Europe and Information Science. *Journal of the American Society for Information Science*. 1997 Dec.; 48: 1139-1141. ISSN: 0002-8231.

I35

INGWERSEN, PETER. 1998. The Calculation of Web Impact Factors. *Journal of Documentation* (UK). 1998 March; 54 (2): 236-243. ISSN: 0022-0418.

I36
INSTITUT D'ÉTUDES MÉDIÉVALES, UNIVERSITÉ DE MONTRÉAL. 1973-. *Computers and Medieval Data Processing/Informatique et études médiévales (CAMPAP/INFEM)*. Montréal, CN: Institut d'études médiévales, Université de Montréal; 1973-; 1-. Biennial. ISSN: 0384-5060.

I37
INSTITUTE OF INTERNAL AUDITORS RESEARCH FOUNDATION. 1990. *Audit, Control, and Security of Paperless Systems: Trends, Guidelines, Practices, and Techniques*. Based on the Proceedings of the 1990 Advanced Technology Forum, Orlando, FL, September 17-19, 1990. Altamonte Springs, FL: IAA Foundation; 1990. 140p. LCCN: 91182349.

I38
INSTITUTE OF INTERNAL AUDITORS RESEARCH FOUNDATION. 1991. *Managing Computer Resources*. Altamonte Springs, FL: Institute of Internal Auditors; 1991.

I39
INTERNATIONAL ASSOCIATION FOR SOCIAL SCIENCE INFORMATION SERVICE AND TECHNOLOGY (IASSIST). 1976-. *IASSIST Quarterly*. Santa Monica, CA: Rand Corporation for IASSIST; 1976-. Qtly. ISSN: 0739-1137; LCCN: 83-4258; OCLC: 9693936. See also *IASSIST Newsletter*. ISSN: 0024-2179.

I40
INTERNATIONAL COUNCIL ON ARCHIVES (ICA). 1988. *Dictionary of Archival Terminology*. Munich, DEU: Saur; 1988.

I41
INTERNATIONAL COUNCIL ON ARCHIVES (ICA). 1991. Statement of Principals Regarding Archival Description. *Archivi & Computer*. 1991; 1(fasc.1): 8-12. ISSN: 1121-2462.

I42
INTERNATIONAL COUNCIL OF ARCHIVES (ICA). 1993. *Les archives et les archivistes au service de la protection du patrimonie culturel et naturel: actes de la vingt-septiemme conferences internationale de la table ronde des archivies*. [Archives and Archivists serving the Protection of the Cultural and Natural Heritages: Proceedings of the 25th International Conference of the Round Table on Archives]. Dresden conference, 1990. Rome, IT: ICA; 1993. 186p.

I43
INTERNATIONAL COUNCIL ON ARCHIVES (ICA). 1996. *Guide for Managing Electronic Records from an Archival Perspective*. Paris, FR: ICA; 1996. Accessible at http://www.archives.ca.

I44
INTERNATIONAL COUNCIL OF ARCHIVES (ICA). 1997. *Planning for Information Technology in Archives*. Ottawa, CAN: National Archives of Canada for the ICA; 1997.

I45
INTERNATIONAL COUNCIL ON ARCHIVES (ICA). COMMISSION ON DESCRIPTIVE STANDARDS. 1995. *ISAAR (CPF): International Standard Archival Authority Record for Corporate Bodies, Persons, and Families*. Ottawa, CAN: National Archives of Canada for the ICA; 1995.

I46
INTERNATIONAL DEVELOPMENT RESEARCH CENTRE (CAN). *1993. Measuring the Impact of Information on Development*. Ottawa, CAN: IDRC Books. Inc.; 1993 ISBN: 0-88936-708-6. Available from: IDRC Books, ox 8500 Ottawa KIG 3H9 or UNIPUB, 4611-F Assembly Drive, Lanham, MD 20706-4391.

I47
INTERNATIONAL FEDERATION FOR DOCUMENTATION (FID). 1975. *Problems of Information Science* [Information Science, its Scope, Objects of Research, and Problems]. Proceedings, FID Congress. Moscow, USSR: FID; 1975. 363p. (In Russian and English). Available from: FID, Pub. 530.

I48
INTERNATIONAL FEDERATION OF LIBRARY ASSOCIATIONS AND INSTITUTIONS (IFLA). 1977. *Names of Persons: National Usages for Entry into Catalogues*. Rev. ed. London, UK: IFLA International Office for UBC; 1977. 193p. ISBN: 0903043106. Based on earlier work of Arthur H. Chaplin (1963); rev. ed. by D. Anderson, *Names of Persons* (1967).

I49
INTERNATIONAL FEDERATION OF LIBRARY ASSOCIATIONS AND INSTITUTIONS (IFLA). 1987. *ISBD (CF): International Standard for Bibliographic Description of Computer Files*. London, UK: IFLA International Office for UBC; 1987.

I50
INTERNATIONAL MEDIEVAL BIBLIOGRAPHY. 1967-. Leeds, UK: University of Leeds School of History; 1967-; 1. Annual. (Available cardsets, hardcover monographic series, or CD-ROM). ISSN: 0020-7950; LCCN: 70-462591; OCLC: 1783429.

I51
INTERNATIONAL SOCIAL SCIENCE COUNCIL. 1967-. *Social Science Information*. Paris, FR: the Council; 1967. Qtly. ISSN: 0539-0184; LCCN: 86-649437; OCLC: 2450595.

I52
INTERNATIONAL STANDARDS ORGANIZATION (ISO). 1985. *ISO Standard 5963-1985 (E). Documentation— Methods for Examining Documents, Determining their Subjects, and Selecting Index Terms*. Geneva, CH: ISO; 1985. Available from ISO, Rue de Varembe, num. 56, CH-1121 Geneva 20, CH. Accessible at http://www.iso.ch.

I53
INTERNATIONAL STANDARDS ORGANIZATION (ISO). 1986. *Information Processing—Text and Office Systems—Standard Generalized Markup Language (SGML)*. 1st ed. Geneva, CH: ISO; 1986. Ref. No.: ISO 8879: 1986. Available from: ISO, Rue de Varembe, num. 56, CH-1121 Geneva 20, CH. Accessible at http://www.iso.ch.

I54
INTERNATIONAL STANDARDS ORGANIZATION (ISO). 1987. *Information Processing Systems—Open Systems Interconnection*. Geneva, CH: ISO; May 19, 1987. ISO: 2024 and 2025. Available from ISO, Rue de Varembe, num. 56, CH-1121 Geneva 20, CH. Accessible at http://www.iso.ch.

I55
INTERNATIONAL STANDARDS ORGANIZATION (ISO). 1989. *Information Processing—Text and Office Systems—Open Documents Architecture (ODA) and Interchange Format*. Geneva, CH: ISO; 1989. Ref. no.: ISO 8613: 1989.

I56
INTERNATIONAL STANDARDS ORGANIZATION (ISO). 1996. *Draft International Standard (ISA/DIS) 15489: Records Management*, pt. 1. Geneva, CH: ISO; 1996. Available from ISO, Rue de Varembe, num. 56, CH-1121 Geneva 20, CH. Accessible at http://www.iso.ch.

I57
INTERNATIONAL STANDARDS ORGANIZATION (ISO). 1996. *Unicode/ISO 10646* (electronic file). Washington, CD: ISO; 1996 October 17. Accessible at http://www.gy/ com.www/w1/ww2/unne.html.

I58
INTERNATIONAL STANDARDS ORGANIZATION (ISO); INTERNATIONAL ELECTROTECHNICAL COM-MISSION (IEC). 1992. *Information Technology—Hypermedia/time-based structuring language (HyTime)*. Geneva, CH: ISO; 1992. Available from ISO, Rue de Varembe, num. 56, CH-1121 Geneva 20, CH. Accessible at http://www.iso.ch. Ref. : ISO/IEC 10744: 1992.

I59
INTERNATIONAL STANDARDS ORGANIZATION (ISO); INTERNATIONAL ELECTROTECHNICAL COM-MISSION (IEC). 1996a. *Information Technology—Document Style and Semantic Specification Language (DSSL)*. Geneva, CH: ISO; 1996. Available form ISO, Rue de Varembe, num. 56, CH-1121 Geneva 20, CH. Accessible at http://www.iso.ch. Ref. : ISO/IEC 10779: 1996.

I60
INTERNATIONAL STANDARDS ORGANIZATION (ISO). JOINT BI-LEVEL IMAGE GROUP. 1997. *The JBIG Compression Standard: The Future for Document Imaging* (White paper, electronic file). Washington, D.C.: ISO; 1997. Accessible at http://www.pdsimage/com/html/news/jbig/wtpaper.html.

I61
INTERNATIONAL VISUAL ARTS INFORMATION NETWORK (IVAIN). 1994. *Image Technology in Museums and Art Galleries (ITEM)*. Rees, Jeremy, director. Newsletter published in conjunction with CIDOC. Ipswich, Suffolk, UK: IVAIN. 1994; 1-. Biennial. Reports on 127 multi-media projects since 1990. Available in hardcopy or floppy disc from IVAIN, The Library, Rope Walk, Ipswich, Suffolk, IP4 1LT (E-Mail: ivainjr@gn.apc.org).

I62
INTER-UNIVERSITY CONSORTIUM FOR POLITICAL AND SOCIAL RESEARCH (ICPSR). 1977-. *Guide to Resources and Services, 1976-1977*. Ann Arbor, MI: ICPSR; 386p. Updated 1991-1992. ISSN: 0362-8736. (See also reference: EULAU, H., 1989; Online catalog is searchable via Internet Gopher at ICPSR.ICPSR.UMICH.EDU).

I63
INTER-UNIVERSITY CONSORTIUM FOR POLITICAL AND SOCIAL RESEARCH (ICPSR). 1986. *CDNet Search: Using SPIRES to Search the ICPSR Databases*. Ann Arbor, MI: ICPSR; 1986. 36p. OCLC: 15984549.

I64
IRSIGLER, FRANZ. 1976. *Elektronische Datenverarbeitung in der Wirtschafts- und Sozialgeschichte des Mittelalters und in der Frühen Neuzeit*. Bericht uber eine Arbeitstagung im Buekefekder Zentrum für Interdisciplinare Forschung am 23. und 24 Oktober 1976. [Electronic data processing in Medieval and Early Modern Economic and Social History: Report on a Conference in the Bielefeld Center for Interdisciplinary Research]. *Blätter für Deutsche Landesgeschichte* 1979; 115: 121-62. ISSN: 0006-4408; OCLC: 2568986.

I65
IRWIN-ZARECKA, IWONA. 1994. *Frames of Remembrance: The Dynamics of Collective Memory*. New Brunswick, NJ: Transaction Publishers; 1994. 214p. ISBN: 1560001380; LCCN: 93008802.

I66
ISENSON, R. S. 1969. Project Hindsight. See reference: GRUBER, W. H.; MARQUIS, D. G., eds. 1969. 155-176.

I67
ISER, WOLFGANG. 1978. *The Act of Reading: A Theory of Aesthetic Response*. Baltimore, MD: The Johns Hopkins University Press; 1978. 239p. ISBN: 0801821010.

I68
ITTEN, JOHANNES. 196/19731. *Kunst der Farbe*. Ravensburg, DEU: Otto Maier Verlag; 1961. Van Haagen, Ernest, trans. *The Art of Color: The Subjective Experience and Objective Rationale of Color*. New York, NY: Van Nostrand Reinhold; 1973. ISBN: 0442240376.

I69
ITTEN, JOHANNES. 1972/1978. *Werke und Schriften*. Itten, Annaliese, comp.; Rotzler, Willie, ed. Zurich, CH: O. Fuessli; 1972. 2nd ed., 1978. 447p. ISBN: 3280010004.

I70
IVERSON, GUDMUND. R.; NORPOTH, HELMUT. 1987. *Analysis of Variance*. 2nd ed. Newbury Park, CA: Sage Publications; 1987. 94p. (Sage University papers. Quantitative Applications in the Social Sciences, no. 07-001). ISBN: 0803930011 (pbk.); LCCN: 87- 61276; OCLC: 16237356.

I71
IVERSON SOFTWARE, INC. 1994. *Anthropology HyperTextBook*. *Archeology HyperTextBook* (Apple Newton software packages). Rice Lake, WI: Iverson Software; 1994. Available from publisher, P.O. 3, Rice Lake, WI 54868-0003 (E-MAIL: J5RSON@eworld.com).

I72
IZMESTIEV, DMITRY. 1995. Programming Tutorial Systems in History with SMILE (Story Making Interactive LanguagE). See reference: JARITZ, G. *ET AL.*, eds. 1995. 267-270. Abstracted in JARITZ, KROPAČ, TEIBEN-BACHER, eds. 1993.

I73
IZQUIERDO ARROYO, J. M. 1995. *La Organización Documental del Conocimiento*. [The Documental Organization of Knowledge], Madrid, ES: Tecnidoc; 1995.

-J-

J1
JACKSON, M. C. 1997. Critical Systems Thinking and IS Research. See reference: MINGERS, J.; STOWELL, F., eds. 1997. 201-238.

J2
JACKSON, SYDNEY. 1974. *Libraries and Librarianship in the West. A Brief History*. New York, NY: McGraw-Hill Book Company; 1974. 489p. (McGraw-Hill Series in Library Education). ISBN: 0-07-032118-3.

J3
JACOB, ELIN K.; SHAW, DEBORAH. 1998. Socio-cognitive Perspectives on Representation. In: Williams, Martha E., ed. *Annual Review of Information Science and Technology* (*ARIST*; vol. 33). Medford, NJ: Information Today, Inc.; 1998. ISBN: 1-57387-065-X.

J4
JACOBS, EDWARD. 1988. Teaching Students to Use Full-text Online Databases. *Law Librarian* (UK). 1988 August; 19(2): 49-58. ISSN: 0023-9275.

J5
JACOBS, P. 1992. Joining Statistics with NLP [Natural Language Processing] for Text Categorization. In: *Proceedings of the Third Conference on Applied Natural Language Processing*. Association for Computational Linguistics; 1992. 178-185. LC call no.: P98.A57.

J6
JAERVELIN, KALERVO; VAKKARI, PERTTI. 1992. The Evolution of Library and Information Science, 1965-1985: A Content Analysis of Journal Articles. See reference: VAKKARI, P.; CRONIN, B., eds. 1992. 109-125.

J7
JAIN, A. K.; VAILAYA, A. 1996. Image Retrieval using Color and Shape. *Pattern Recognition*. 1996; 29 (8): 1233-1244. ISSN: 0031-3203.

J8
JAMBU, MICHEL. 1983. *Cluster Analysis*. New York, NY / Amsterdam, NL: North-Holland Pub. Co.; 1983. 898p. ISBN: 044866345.

J9
JAMES, MIKE. 1985. *Classification Algorithms*. New York, NY: J. Wiley; 1985. 209p. (Wiley Interscience series). ISBN: 0471847992 (hbk.). London, UK: Collins; 1985. ISBN: 00038300543 (pbk.).

J10
JAMES, MIKE. 1988. *Pattern Recognition*. New York, NY: Wiley; 1988. 144p. (Wiley Interscience series). ISBN: 0471611204.

J11
JAMESON, FREDRIC. 1981. *The Political Unconscious: Narrative as a Socially Symbolic Act*. Ithaca, NY: Cornell University Press; 1981. 305p. ISBN: 0801412331.

J12
JAMESON, JOHN FRANKLIN. 1891. *The History of Historical Writing in America*. Boston, MA: Houghton, Mifflin and Co.; 1891. 160p. LCCN: 03-18645; OCLC: 2922474.

J13
JAMISON, MARTIN. 1988. The Microcard: Fremont Rider's Pre-computer Revolution. *Libraries & Culture*. 1988 Winter; 23(1): 1-17. ISSN: 0894-8631.

J14
JANES, JOSPEH W. 1991. Relevance Judgements and the Incremental Presentation of Document Representations. *Information Processing & Management*. 1991; 27: 629-646. ISSN: 0306-4573.

J15
JANIS, IRVING L.; MANN, LEON. 1977. *Decision Making: A Psychological Analysis of Conflict, Choice, and Commitment*. New York, NY: Free Press; 1977. 488p. ISBN: 0029161606.

J16
JANSEN, HANS-LOUIS. 1990. Medieval Culture and the Problem of the Historical Interpretation of Archaeological Evidence. In: Jartiz, Gerhard, ed. *Mensch und Objekt im Mittelalter und in der frühen Neuzeit: Leben-Altag-Kulture*. Internationaler Kongress Krems an der Donau 27. bis 30. September 1988 (pp. 397-409). Vienna, AT: Institut fur Mittelalterliche Realienkunde Osterreichs; 1990. 454p. (Ver öffentlichen des Instituts für Mittelalterliche Realienkunde Osterreichs, 13). (In German). ISBN: 3- 700117-99-X; OCLC: 22997724.

J17
JARAUSCH, KONRAD H. 1984. The International Dimension of Quantitative History: Some Introductory Reflections (pp. 123-132). In: Jarausch, K., ed., *Quantitative History in International Perspective*. In: *Social Science History*. 1984; 8: 123-215. (Entire issue on Title topic). ISSN: 0145-5532.

J18
JARAUSCH, KONRAD H. 1985a. The Great Change: Quantitative Approaches to the Transformation of European Society. *Historische Sozialforschung/ Historical Social Research* (DEU). 1985; 33: 4-10. ISSN: 0172-6404.

J19
JARAUSCH, KONRAD H. 1985b. (Inter)national Styles of Quantitative History. *Historical Methods*. 1985; 18: 13-19. ISSN: 0161-5440.

J20
JARAUSCH, KONRAD H. 1986. Some Reflections on Coding. See reference: THALLER, M., ed. 1986. 175-178.

J21
JARAUSCH, KONRAD H. 1990. The Role of Quantitative Methods in History: Decline or Reawakening? *Storia della Storiographia* (IT). 1990; 18: 43-60. ISSN: 0392-8926.

J22
JARAUSCH, KONRAD H., ed. 1976. *Quantifizierung in der Geschichtswissenschaft: Probleme und Mögligkeiten* [Quantification in Historical Science: Problems and Possibilities]. Dusseldorf, DEU: Droste; 1976. 365p. (In German). ISBN: 3-770003-57-8; OCLC: 2625784.

J23
JARAUSCH, KONRAD H.; ARMINGER, GERHARD; THALLER, MANFRED. 1985. *Quantitative Methoden in der Geschichtswissenschaft: eine Einführung in die Forschung, Datenverarbeitung und Statistik* [Quantitative Methods in the Historical Science: An Introduction to the Research Field, Datenbased Work, and Statistics]. Die

Geschichtswissenschaft, s.n. Darmstadt, DEU: Wissenschaftliche Buchgesellschaft; 1985. 211p. ISBN: 3534091639; OCLC: 1309054.

J24
JARAUSCH, KONRAD H.; HARDY, KENNETH A. 1991. *Quantitative Methods for Historians: A Guide to Research, Data, and Statistics.* Chapel Hill, NC: University of North Carolina Press; 1991. 247p. ISBN: 0807819476; 0807843091 (pbk,); LCCN: 90-40746; OCLC: 21951098.

J25
JARAUSCH, KONRAD H.; SCHRADER, W. H., eds. 1987. *Quantitative History of Society and Economy: Some International Studies.* St. Katharinen [Göttingen, DE]; Scripta Mercaturae Verlag [Max Planck Institut für Geschichte; 1987. *(Historisch- Sozialwissenschaften Forschungen*, Bd. 21). ISBN: 3-922661-40-8.

J26
JARITZ, GERHARD. 1988. Finding the Signs: Pictures of Medieval Life. Published twice: see reference: THALLER, M., ed., 1988. 15-28 (with photos). See also reference: BEST, H., *ET AL.*, eds. 1991. 61-67 (without photos).

J27
JARITZ, GERHARD. 1991. Medieval Image Databases. Aspects of Cooperation and Exchange. *Literary and Linguistic Computing.* 1991; 6(1): 15-19. ISSN: 0268-1145.

J28
JARITZ, GERHARD. 1993a. *Images. A Primer of Computer-Supported Analysis with KLIEU IAS.* (Electronic diskette; part of the *KLIEU* 5.1.1 package). St. Katharinen [Göttingen, DEU]: Max-Planck-Institut für Geschichte in Kommission bei Scripta Mercaturae Verlag; 1993. (Halbgraue Reihe zur historischen Fackinformatik. Serie A: Historische Quellenkunden, Band 22).

J29
JARITZ, GERHARD. 1993b. Scratched Images or: Instead of an Introduction. See reference: FIKFAK, L. J.; JARITZ, G., eds. 1993. 9-20.

J30
JARITZ, GERHARD; KROPAČ, INGO H.; TEIBENBACHER, PETER, eds. 1993. *The Art of Communication.* Abstracts of the VIII International AHC-Conference, Graz, Austria, August 24-27, 1993. Graz, AT: History and Computing Austria; 1993. 205p. Limited distribution to conference attendees.

J31
JARITZ, GERHARD; KROPAČ, INGO H.; TEIBENBACHER, PETER, eds. 1995. *The Art of Communication.* Proceedings of the VIII International Conference of the Association for History and Computing, Graz, Austria, August 24-27, 1993. Graz, AT:Akademische Druck-u. Verlagsanstalt; 1995. 537p. ISBN: 3-201-01646-2.

J32
JAUBERT, ALAIN. 1986/1989. *Le Commissariat aux archives.* Paris, FR: Barrault; 1986. (In French). Trans. as: *The Commissary for the Archives. Making People Disappear: An Amazing Chronicle of Photographic Deception.* Washington, D.C.: Pergamon-Brassey's International Defense Publishers; c1989. 190p. ISBN: 0080374301; LCCN: 89-008458.

J33
JEFFCUTT, PAUL. 1994. From Interpretation to Representation in Organizational Analysis: Postmodernism, Ethnography and Organizational Symbolism. *Organizational Studies.* 1994; 15 (2): 241-274. ISSN: 0170-8406.

J34
JENG, LING HWEY. 1996. A Converging Vision of Cataloging in the Electronic World. *Information Technology and Libraries.* 1996 December; 15(4): 222-231. ISSN: 0730- 9295.

J35
JENKS, CHRIS, ed. 1995. *Visual Culture.* New York, NY and London, UK: Routledge; 1995. 269p. ISBN: 0415106222 (hbk.); 0415106230 (pbk.).

J36
JENKINS, GEORGE, ed. 1997. *Information Systems, Policies, and Procedures Manual.* 2nd ed. Englewood Cliffs, NJ: Prentice-Hall; 1997. Irregular pagination. ISBN: 0132558459.

J37
JENKINS, KEITH. 1991. *Re-thinking History.* London, UK: Routledge; 1991. 77p. ISBN: 0415067782; LCCN: 91-10051; OCLC: 23355830.

J38
JENKINS, REESE V. 1975. *Images and Enterprise: Technology and the American Photographic Industry, 1839-1925.* Baltimore, MD: Johns Hopkins University Press; 1975. 371p. ISBN: 0-8018-1588-6.

J39
JENKINSON, HILARY. 1922/1966. *A Manual of Archive Administration*. Shotwell, James T., ed. Publication of the Carnegie Endowment for International Peace, Division of Economics and History (British series). Oxford, UK: Clarendon Press; 1922. 243p. LCCN: 22-16884; OCLC: 932628. Rev. ed. London: P. Lund, Humphries, & Co.; 1937. 256p. Reprint. London, UK: Humphries & Co.; 1966. OCLC: 1406396.

J40
JENNER, MICHAEL G. 1995. *Software Quality Management and ISO 9001*. Los Alamitos, CA: IEEE; 1995. 256p. ISBN: 0-471-11888-5

J41
JENNY, JACQUES. 1997. Méthodes et pratiques formalisées d'analyse de contenu et de discours dans la recherche sociologique française contemporaine. Etat des lieux et essai de classification [Methodology and Formal Techniques of Analyzes of the Contents and Discourse in Contemporary French Sociological Research] . *Bulletin de Méthodologie Sociologique* (FR). 1997; 54: 64-122. (In French).

J42
JENSEN, KLAUS B.; JANKOWSKI, NICHOLAS W., eds. 1991. *A Handbook of Qualitative Methodologies for Mass Communication*. London, UK / New York, NY: Routledge; 1991. 272p. ISBN: 0415054044; 0415054052 (pbk.); LCCN: 91-3686; OCLC: 23650408.

J43
JENSEN, RICHARD. 1978. New Presses for Old Grapes: Multiple Classification Analysis. *Historical Methods*. 1978; 11: 174-176. ISSN: 0161-5440.

J44
JENSEN, RICHARD. 1981. Oral History, Quantification, and the New Social History. *Oral History Review*. 1981; 9: 13-25. ISSN: 0094-0798.

J45
JENSEN, RICHARD. 1983a. The Historian and the Microcomputer. *Journal of American History*. 1983; 14. ISSN: 0021-8723.

J46
JENSEN, RICHARD. 1983b. The Microcomputer Revolution for Historians. *Journal of Interdisciplinary History*. 1983; 14(1): 91-112. ISSN: 0022-1953.

J47
JENSEN, RICHARD. 1991. Text Management. *Journal of Interdisciplinary History*. 1991; 22: 711-722. ISSN: 0022-1953.

J48
JERMANN, PETER. 1994. Digital Imaging Basics. NDCC *Technical Leaflet*. Andover, MA: Northeast Document Conservation Center; 1994. Reprinted in: *Archival Outlook*. 1994 January; s.n.: 10-11. ISSN: 0091-5971.

J49
JESPERSEN, FRED F. 1989. Corporate Culture is the Real Key to Creativity. *Business Month*. 1989 May; 133 (5): 73-75. ISSN: 0892-4090.

J50
JESSEN, JOHN H. [199- forthcoming]. *Defusing the Time Bomb: A Practical Guide to Electronic Mail Issues*. N.p.; [199-, forthcoming].

J51
JESSUP, LEONARD M.; VALACICH, JOSEPH D., eds. 1993. *Group Support Systems: New Perspectives*. New York, NY: Macmillan; 1993. 365p. ISBN: 0-02-360625-8.

J52
JICK, T. D. 1979. Mixing Qualitative and Quantitative Methods. Triangulation in Action. *Administrative Science Quarterly*. 1979; 24: 601-611. ISSN: 0001-8392.

J53
JIMERSON, RANDALL C. 1989. Redefining Archival Identity: Meeting User Needs in the Information Society. *American Archivist*. 1989 Summer; 52: 332-340. ISSN: 0360- 9081.

J54
JING, JUN. 1996. *The Temple of Memories: History, Power, and Morality in a Chinese Village*. Palo Alto, CA: Stanford University Press; 1996. 217p. ISBN: 0804727562.

J55

JOHN, R. R. 1994. American Historians and the Concept of the Communications Revolution. In: Bud-Frierman, Lisa., ed. *Information Acumen: The Understanding and Use of Knowledge in Modern Business* (pp. 98-112). London, UK: Routledge; 1994. 254p. ISBN: 0415077885; LCCN: 93010558.

J56

JOHNSON, ERIC A. 1988a. Counting 'how it really was": Quantitative History in West Germany. *Historical Methods.* 1988; 21: 61-79. ISSN: 0161-5440.

J57

JOHNSON, ERIC A. 1988b. Quantitative German History in the United States and the United Kingdom. *Central European History*. 1988; 21: 396-420. ISSN: 0008-9389.

J58

JOHNSON, ERIC A. 1989. Reflections on an old "new history": Quantitative Social Science History in postmodern Middle Ages. In: *German Histories: Challenges in Theory, Practice, Technique* (pp. 408-427). *Central European History*. 1989; 22(3-4). (Entire issue on title topic). ISSN: 0008-9389.

J59

JOHNSON, LAWRENCE E. 1992. *Focusing on Truth*. London, UK: Routledge; 1992. 279p. ISBN: 0415072522 (hbk.); 0415072539 (pbk.).

J60

JOHNSON, PAUL. 1991 . *The Birth of the Modern World Society. 1815-1830*. New York, NY: Harper Collins Publ.; 1991. 1095p. ISBN: 006016574X.

J61

JOHNSON, PAUL. 19 . *Modern Times: The World from the Twenties to the Eighties*. New York, NY: Harper & Row; 1993. 817p. ISBN: 6060151595.

J62

JOHNSON, R. C. 1978. A Procedure for Sampling the Manuscript Census Schedules. *Journal of Interdisciplinary History*. 1978; 8: 515-530. ISSN: 0022-1953.

J63

JOHNSON-LAIRD, PHILIP N. 1983. *Mental Models: Towards a Cognitive Science of Language, Inference and Consciousness*. Cambridge, MA: Harvard University Press; 1983. 513p. ISBN: 054241235; LCCN: 83-672488, See also reference: OAKHILL, J.; GARNHAM, A., eds. 1996.

J64

JOHNSON-LAIRD, PHILIP N. 1988. *The Computer and the Mind: An Introduction to Cognitive Science*. Cambridge, MA: Harvard University Press; 1988. 444p. ISBN: 0674156153.

J65

JOHNSON-LAIRD, PHILIP N. 1993. *Human and Machine Thinking*. Hillsdale, NJ: L. Erlbaum Associates; 1993. 189p. ISBN: 080580921X.

J66

JONES, ARNITA A.; CANTELON, PHILIP L., eds. 1993. *Corporate Archives and History: Making the Past Work*. Malabar, FL: Krieger Publishing Co.; 1993. 211p. ISBN: 0894643533.

J67

JONES, E. T. 1972. Ecological Inference and Electoral Analysis. *Journal of Interdisciplinary History*. 1972; 2: 249-262. ISSN: 0022-1953.

J68

JONES, HOUSTON G. 1968. Archival Training in American Universities, 1938-1968. *The American Archivist*. 1968; 31: 135-154. ISSN: 0360-9081.

J69

JONES, HOUSTON G., ed. 1995. *Historical Consciousness in the Early Republic: The Origins of State Historical Societies, Museums, and Collections, 1791-1861*. Chapel Hill, NC: University of North Carolina Press for the North Caroliniana Society and North Carolina Collection; 1995. 262p. (North Caroliniana Society Imprints, 25). LCCN: 96-128630.

J70

JONES, L. D. 1989. Computerizing the British Museum. *Computers and the History of Art*. 1989; 10: 13-20. ISSN: 7081-239.

J71
JONES, MARTYN. [199-]. Information: Its Architecture and Management. In: Jones, Martyn. *Knowledge Asset Management and Corporate Memory*. [Forthcoming, 199-]. Excerpt as electronic file, Accessible at http://hispacom.es:80/MARTYN/.

J72
JONES, NIEL D. 1997. *Computability and Complexity: From a Programming Perspective*. Cambridge, MA: MIT Press; 1997. 466p. ISBN: 0262100649.

J73
JONES, ROBIN; MAYNARD, CLIVE; STEWART, IAN. 1990. *The Art of LISP Programming*. London, UK / New York, NT; Springer-Verlag; 1990. 169p. ISBN: 0387195688.

J74
JONES, STEVEN G., ed. 1995. *Cybersociety: Computer-mediated Communication and Community*. Thousand Oaks, CA: Sage Publications; 1993. 241p. ISBN: 080399556762 (hbk.); 0803956770 (pbk.).

J75
JONES-GARMIL, KATHERINE. 1997. Laying the Foundation: Three Decades of Computer Technology in the Museum. See reference: JONES-GARMIL, K., ed. 1997. 11-34.

J76
JONES-GARMIL, KATHERINE, ed. 1997. *The Wired Museum: Emerging Technology and Changing Paradigms*. London, UK: 1997. Washington, D.C.: American Association of Museums; 1997. 278p. ISBN: 00931201111365.

J77
JORAVSKY, DAVID. 1994. Knowing Ourselves: Literary Art vs. Social Science. See reference: ROSS, DOROTHY, ed. 1994.

J78
JOST, KENNETH. 1995. Teaching History. *CQ [Congressional Quarterly] Researcher*. 1995 September 29; 5(36): 851-868. Available in: IAC, *General periodicals*, 17416584.

J79
JOURNAL OF INTERDISCIPLINARY HISTORY. 1970-. Cambridge, MA: MIT Press for the School of Humanities and Social Sciences; 1970-. Qtly. ISSN: 0022-1953; LCCN: 77-120540; OCLC: 1799976.

J80
JOURNAL OF THE HISTORY OF COLLECTIONS. 1989-. Oxford, UK: Oxford University Press; 1989-. 2x/yr. ISSN: 0954-6650.

J81
JOYCE, MICHAEL. 1995. *Of Two Minds: Hypertext, Pedagogy and Poetics*. Ann Arbor, MI: University of Michigan Press; 1995. 277p. ISBN: 0472095781.

J82
JOYCE, PATRICK. 1991. History and Post-Modernism I. *Past and Present*. 1991; 133: 204- 209. ISSN: 0031-2746. Response to STONE, L. (1991); see also references: KELLY, C.; SPIEGEL, G. 1992.

J83
JOYCE, PATRICK. 1995. The End of Social History? *Social History*. 1995; 20: 73-91. ISSN: 0022-4529.

J84
JUDT, TONY. 1979. A Clown in Regal Purple: Social History and the Historians. *History Workshop Journal* (UK). 1979; 7: 66-94. No OCLC record.

J85
JUFFARD, OLIVIER. 1994. L'Enregistrement par l'Image relevée Architecturaux assistés par Ordinateur [Computer Assisted Registration of Relief Images in Architecture]. See reference: BECK, P., ed. 1994. 2-6.

J86
JUNG, CARL G. 1953-[1966]. *Collected Works* (Vols. 12-20). New York, NY: Pantheon Books; 1953-[1965]. Princeton, NJ: Princeton University Press; 1966-. (Bollingen series, 20 vols.).

J87
JUNG, CARL G. [1959]. *Basic Writings*. New York, NY: Modern Library; [1959-1965]. Vols. 1-12: 552p.

J88
JUNGMANN-STADLER, F. 1980. *Documentation of Literature in the Historical Sciences. Analysis of the Current Services and Concept Utilization of an Information and Documentation System* [trans.]. Munich, DEU: Arbeitsgemeinschaft Ausseruniv. Historischer Forschungseinrichtungen; 1980. 116p. NTIS report, N82-10954.

-K-

K1

KACPRYZYK, JANUSZ; FEDRIZZI, MARIO, eds. 1988. *Combining Fuzzy Imprecision with Probabilistic Uncertainty in Decision Making.* Berlin, DEU / New York, NY: Springer- Verlag; c1988. 399p. ISBN: 0387500057; LCCN: 88020092.

K2

KAHIN, BRIAN. 1992. Scholarly Communication in a Networked Environment: Issues of Principal, Policy, and Practice. *Electronic Library.* 1992 October; 10: 275-286. ISSN: 0264-0473.

K3

KAHLENBERG, FRIEDERICH, ed. 1989. Festschrift für Hans Booms. *Aus de Arbeit der Archiv. Beitrage zur Archivwessen, zur Quellenkunde, und zur Geschichte* [About the Work of Archives: Contribution to Archival Science, its Development and History]. Boppard am Rhein, DEU: Bolt; 1989. 988p. (Schriften des Bundesarchiv, 36). (In English, French and German). ISBN: 3764618922.

K4

KAHNEMAN, DAVID.; SLOVIC, P.; TVERSKY, AMOS. 1982. *Judgement under Uncertainty: Heuristics and Biases.* Cambridge, UK: Cambridge University Press; 1982. 535p. ISBN: 0521240646 (HBK.); 0521284147 (pbk.)

K5

KALAYINIKOV, W. W.; NOSOVSKII, G. V.; FOMENKO, A. T. 1995. *Datirowka svesdnogo cataloga "Almagesta" Statistiecki i geometricveckii analis* [Statistical and geometric analysis of the Periodization in the Almagest catalog]. Moscow, RU: Izd-vo "Faktorial"; 1995. 286p. ISBN: 5-88688-005-4. (In Russian).

K6

KALFATOVIC, MARTIN R. 1996. Internet Resources in the Visual Arts. *College and Research Libraries News.* 1996; 57 (5): 289-293. ISSN: 0099-0086. Guide to museums, galleries, and arts information sites.

K7

KAMERMANS, H.; FENNEMA, K., eds. 1996. *Computer Applications and Quantitative Methods in Archaeology.* CAA `95. Leiden, NL: University of Leiden; 1996. In special issue of: *Analecta Praehistoria Leidensia,* 28.

K8

KAMINER, NOAM; BRAUNSTEIN, YALE M. 1998. Bibliometric Analysis of the Impact of Internet Use on Scholarly Productivity. *Journal of the American Society for Information Science.* 1998 June; 49 (8): 720-730. ISSN: 0002-8231; CODEN: AISJB6. Based in part on Kaminer's dissertation, *Network Use and Scholar's Productivity.* Berkeley, CA: University of California; 1997.

K9

KAMISHER, L. M. 1989. A Model for the Computerization of Museum Collections. *The International Journal of Museum Management and Curatorship.* 1989; 8(1): 45-56. ISSN: 0260-4779.

K10

KAMMEN, MICHAEL G., ed. 1980. *The Past Before Us: Contemporary Historical Writing in the U.S.* Prepared for the 15th CISH conference in Bucharest, Romania, August 1980. Ithaca, NY: Cornell University Press for the American Historical Association; 1980. 524p. ISBN: 0801412242; LCCN: 79-25785; OCLC: 5800037.

K11

KAMMEN, MICHAEL G. 1987. *Selvages & Biases: The Fabric of History in American Culture.* Ithaca, NY: Cornell University Press; 1987. 336p. ISBN: 0801419247.

K12

KAMMEN, MICHAEL G. 1988. *Sovereignty and Liberty: Constitutional Discourse in American Culture.* Madison, WI: University of Wisconsin Press; 1988. 231p. ISBN: 0299117308.

K13

KAMMEN, MICHAEL G. 1991. *Mystic Chords of Memory. The Transformation of Tradition in American Culture.* New York, NY: Alfred A. Knopf; 1991. 864p. ISBN: 0394577698.

K14

KAMMEN, MICHAEL G. 1992. *Meadows of Memory: Images of Time and Tradition in American Art and Culture.* Austin, TX: University of Texas Press; 1992. 192p. (Anne Burnett Tandy Lectures in American Civilization, no. 11). ISBN: 0292751397.

K15

KAMMEN, MICHAEL G. 1997. *In the Past Lane: Historical Perspectives on American Culture.* New York, NY: Oxford University Press; 1997. ISBN: 0195111117; LCCN: 97021613.

K16
KANADE, TAKEO; RANDER, PETER; NARAYANAN, P. J. 1997. Virtualized Reality: Constructing Virtual Worlds from Real Scenes. See reference: MOEZZI, S., ed. 1997: 34-47.

K17
KANDEL, ABRAHAM. 1986. *Fuzzy Mathematical Techniques with Applications*. Reading, MA: Addison-Wesley Publ.; 1986. ISBN: 0201117525.

K18
KANDEL, ABRAHAM, ed. 1992. *Fuzzy Expert Systems*. Boca Raton, FL: CRC Press; 1992. 316p. ISBN: 084934297X.

K19
KANDEL, ABRAHAM; LANGHOLZ, GIDEON, eds. 1992. *Hybrid Architectures for Intelligent Systems*. Boca Raton, FL: CRC Press; 1992. 420p. ISBN: 0849342295.

K20
KANISHTCHEV, VALERY; PROTASOV, STANISLAV. 1996 [199-]. A Project of Integral History on [the] Local Level: Preliminary Results of Data Collection and Computer Analysis. See reference: BORODKIN, L., ed. 1996: English Abstract of presentation, 91-92; paper [199- forthcoming in Russian].

K21
KANN-RASMUSSEN, LARS; LARSEN, CARSTEN. 1991. Photography and Image Database Documentation Project at the National Museum of Denmark. *Archeological Computing Newsletter* (DK). 1991 March; 26: 1-7. ISSN: 0952-3332.

K22
KANSTEINER, WULF. 1996. Searching for an Audience: the Historical Profession in the Media Age— a Comment on Arthur Marwick and Hayden White. *Journal of Contemporary History*. 1996 January; 31 (1): 215-220. ISSN:

K23
KANTOR, PAUL B. 1994. Information Retrieval Techniques. In: Williams, Martha ed. *Annual Review of Information Science and Technology*: vol. 29. Medford, NJ: Learned Information, Inc. for ASIS; 1994. 53-90. ISBN: 1-57387-019-6; ISSN: 0066-4200; LCCN: 66-25096; CODEN: ARISBC.

K24
KAPLAN, ABRAHAM. 1964. *The Conduct of Inquiry: Methodology for Behavioral Science*. San Francisco, CA: Chandler; 1964.

K25
KAPLAN, BONNIE MAE. 1983. *Computers in Medicine, 1950-1980: The Relationship between History and Policy*. Chicago, IL: University of Chicago; 1983. (Ph.D. dissertation; *DAI*, vol. 44/11-A: 3472). Not available from UMI; contact the University of Chicago Regenstein Library ILL services.

K26
KAPLAN, E. ANN, ed. 1988. *Postmodernism and Its Discontents: Theories, Practices*. London, UK: n.p.; 1988. 188p. (Haymarket series). ISBN: 0860912116 (hbk.); 0860919250 (pbk.).

K27
KAPLAN, ELISABETH; MIFFLIN, JEFFREY. 1996. "Mind and Sight": Visual Literacy and the Archivist. *Archival Issues*. 1996; 21(2): 105-127. ISSN: 1067-4993.

K28
KAPLAN, FLORA S. 1996. *Museums and the Making of Ourselves: The Role of Objects in National Identity*. London, UK: Cassell; 1996. 448p. ISBN: 0-7185-0039-3.

K29
KARAMUFTUOGLU, MURAT. 1998. Collaborative Information Retrieval: Toward a Social Informatics View of IR Interaction. *Journal of the American Society for Information Science*. 1998 Oct.; 49(12): 1070-1080. ISSN: 0002-8231.

K30
KARL, FREDERICK R.,ed. 1994. *Biography and Source Studies*. New York, NY: AMS Press; 1994. ISBN: 0-404-63411-7; ISSN: 1075-3451.

K31
KARP, IVAN; LAVINE, STEVEN D., eds. 1991. *Exhibiting Cultures. The Poetics and Politics of Museum Display*. Conference on Poetics and Politics of Representation, Smithsonian Institution, September 26-28, 1988. Washington, DC: Smithsonian Institution; 1991. 468p. ISBN: 1560980206 (hbk.); 1560980214 (pbk.).

K32
KASABOV, NIKOLA K. 1996. *Foundations of Neural Networks, Fuzzy Systems, and Knowledge Engineering*. Cambridge, MA: Bradford Book; 1996. 544p. ISBN: 0- 262-1121204. Distributed by MIT Press.

K33

KASER, RICHARD, ed. 1996. *Publishing in the New Millenium.* Philadelphia, PA: NFAIS (National Federation of Abstracting and Information Services); 1996. Report available directly from NFAIS, 1518 Walnut St. no. 307, Philadelphia, PA 19102.

K34

KASTURI, RANGACHAR; JAIN, RAMESH, eds. 1991. *Computer Vision.* Los Alamitos, CA: IEEE Computer Society; 1991. 2 vols. (IEEE Computer Society Press Tutorial series). ISBN: 0818691034.

K35

KATRIEL, TAMAR. 1994. Sites of Memory: Discourses of the Past in Israeli Pioneering Settlement Museums. *Quarterly Journal of Speech.* 1994 February; 80 (1): 1-20. ISSN: 0033-5630.

K36

KATZ, ELIHU. 1987. Communications Research since [Paul] Lazarsfeld. *Public Opinion Quarterly.* 1987 Winter; 51 (4): S25. ISSN: 00033362X.

K37

KATZ, ELIHU. 1997. *Annenberg Scholars Program* [flyer]. Philadelphia, PA: University of Pennsylvannia; 1997. [4p.].

K38

KATZ, KAILA. 1997. Historical Content in Computer Science Texts: A Concern. *Annals of the History of Computing.* 1997; 19 (1): 16-19. ISSN: 1058-6180.

K39

KATZ, M. B. 1972/1973. Occupational Classification in History. *Journal of Interdisciplinary History.* 1972/73; 3: 63-88. ISSN: 0022-1953.

K40

KATZ, R.; TUSHMAN, M. 1979. Communication Patterns, Project Performance, and Task Characteristics: An Empirical Evaluation and Integration in an R&D Setting. *Organizational Behavior and Human Performance.* 1979; 23: 139-162. ISSN: 0030- 5073.

K41

KATZ, STANLEY N. 1995. Do Disciplines Matter? History and the Social Sciences. *Social Sciences Quarterly.* 1995 December; 76 (4): 863-878. ISSN:

K42

KATZEN, MARY. 1985. *Technology and Communication in the Humanities: Training and Services in Universities and Polytechnics in the UK.* London, UK: The British Library; 1985. 121p. (Library and Information Research Report, 32). ISSN: 0263- 1709; ISBN: 0712330461 (pbk.); OCLC: 12946172.

K43

KATZEN, MARY. 1986. The Application of Computers in the Humanities: A View from Britain. *Information Processing and Management* (UK). 1986; 22(2): 259-267. ISSN: 0306-4573.

K44

KATZEN, MARY, ed. 1991. *Scholarship and Technology in the Humanities.* London, UK: K. G. Saur; 1991. 196p.(British Library Research series). ISBN: 0-8291-625-9.

K45

KATZER, JEFFREY; COOK, KENNETH H.; CROUCH, WAYNE W. 1978/1982/1991. *Evaluating Information: A Guide for Users of Social Science Research.* Reading, MA: Addison-Wesley Publ.; 1978. ISBN: 02100948X. 2nd ed. 1982. 3rd ed. New York, NY: McGraw-Hill, Inc.; 1991. 272p. ISBN: 0070335885; LCCN: 90-31519; OCLC: 21118885.

K46

KAUFER, DAVID. S.; CARLEY, KATHLEEN, M. 1993. *The Influence of Print on Socio-cultural Organization and Change.* Hillsdale, NJ: Lawrence Erlbaum; 1993. 474p. ISBN: 0-8058-1273-3; 0-8058-1238-5 (pbk.).

K47

KAUFMAN, LEONARD; ROUSSEEUW, PETER J. 1990. *Finding Groups in Data: An Introduction to Cluster Analysis.* New York, NY: John Wiley and Sons; 1990. 342p. ISBN: 0471878766.

K48

KAUFFMAN, STUART. 1991. Antichaos and Adaptation. *Scientific American.* 1991 August; 265: 64-70. ISSN: 0036-8733.

K49

KAUFFMAN, STUART A. 1993. *The Origins of Order: Self-Organization and Selection in Evolution.* New York, NY: Oxford University Press; 1993. ISBN: 019505819 (hbk.); 0195079515 (pbk.); LCCN: 91011148.

K50
KAUFFMAN, STUART. 1995. *At Home in the Universe: The Search for the Laws of Self-Organization and Complexity*. New York, NY: Oxford University Press; 1995. 321p. ISBN: 0195095995; LCCN: 94-025268.

K51
KAUTZ, KARLHEINZ; PRIES-HEJE, JAN, eds. 1996. *Diffusion and Adoption of Information Technology*. Proceedings of the first IFIP WG8.6 Working Conference on the Diffusion and Adoption of Information Technology. Oslo, Norway, October 1995. New York, NY & London, UK: Chapman & Hall; 1996. 219p. ISBN: 0412756005.

K52
KAYE, BRIAN H. 1993. *Chaos & Complexity: Discovering the Surprising Patterns of Science and Technology*. New York, NY: VCH; 1993. 593p. ISBN: 15608117992.

K53
KAYE, DAVID H.; FREEDMAN, DAVID A. 1994. Reference Guide on Statistics. See reference: FEDERAL JUDICIAL CENTER. 1994. 331-414.

K54
KAYE, HARVEY J. 1996. Whose History is It? *Monthly Review*. 1996 Nov.; 48(60): 16-31. ISSN: 0027-0520.

K55
KEANEY, M. 1996. The Poverty of Rhetoricism: Popper, Mises, and the Riches of Historicism. Glasgow, UK: Glasgow Caledonian University Dept. of Social Sciences; 1996. 27p. ISBN: 0948255978.

K56
KEARL, MICHAEL. [1998-]. *An Investigation into Collective Historical Knowledge and Implications of its Ignorance* [electronic file]. [Sant Antonio, TX: Trinity University Dept. of Sociology and Anthropology; [1998-]. Accessible at http://www.trinity.edu /~mkearl/histgnr.html.

K57
KEEN, PETER G. W.; SCOTT-MORTON, MICHAEL S. 1978. *Decision Support Systems: An Organizational Perspective*. Reading, MA: Addison-Wesley Publ.; 1978. 264p. ISBN: 0201036673.

K58
KELLER, DONALD. 1993. High Speed OCR Systems Have Flexibility and Accuracy. *Document Image Automation*. 1993 Spring; 13(2). ISSN: 1054-9692.

K59
KELLER, PETER R.; KELLER, MARY M. 1993. *Visual Cues. Practical Data Vizualization*. Los Alamitos, CA: IEEE; 1993. 350p. ISBN: 0-8186-3102-3.

K60
KELLERT, STEPHEN H. 1993. *In the Wake of Chaos: Unpredictable Order in Dynamic Systems*. Chicago, IL: University of Illinois Press; 1993. 176p. ISBN: 0226429741 (hbk.); 0226429768 (pbk.).

K61
KELLEY, KAROL L. 1981. *Self-made Man? True Woman? Historical Approaches to the Creation of American Success Models*. Bowling Green State University; 1981. 483p. (Ph.D. dissertation; *DAI*, 42/01-A: 346). Available from: University Microfilms, Ann Arbor, MI (Order no. AAD81-14532).

K62
KELLEY, ROBERT THOMAS. 1992. *Virtual Realism: Virtual Reality, Magical Realism, and Late Twentieth-century Technologies of Representation*. Bloomington, IN: University of Indiana; 1992. 292p. (Ph.D. dissertation; *DAI*, 53/09: 3209). Available from: University Microfilms, Ann Arbor, MI (Order no. AAD93-01454).

K63
KELLNER, HANS. 1975. Time Out: the Discontinuity of Historical Consciousness. *History and Theory*. 1975; 14: 275-296. ISBN: 0018-2656.

K64
KELLNER, HANS. 1987. Narrativity in History: Post-Structuralism and Since. *History and Theory*. 1987; 26: 1-29. ISSN: 0018-2656.

K65
KELLNER, HANS. 1989. *Language and Historical Representation: Getting the Story Crooked*. Madison, WI: University of Wisconsin Press; 1989. 339p. ISBN: 0299120503.

K66
KELLNER, DOUGLAS. 1995. *Media Culture: Cultural Studies, Identity, and Politics between the Modern and Postmodern*. London, UK / New York, NY: Routledge; 1995. 357p. ISBN: 04151005692 (hbk.); 0415105706 (pbk.).

K67
KELLY, CATRIONA. 1991. History and Post-Modernism III. *Past and Present.* 1991; 133: 209-213. ISSN: 0031-2746.

K68
KELLY, KEVIN; WOLF, GARY. 1997. Push! *Wired.* 1997 March; s.n.: [12-23]. ISSN: 1059-1028.

K69
KELLY, MARY ANN. 1992. *Effects of Continuing Education in a Rural Development Project in Northwest Connemaria, Ireland.* Ithaca, NY: Cornell University; 1992. 178p. (Ph.D. dissertation; *DAI,* 53/10-A: 344). Available from: University Microfilms, Ann Arbor, MI (order no. AAD93-00849).

K70
KELLY, SEAN. 1996. *Data Warehousing in Action: The Route to Mass Customization.* Chichester, UK: John Wiley; 1996. 186p. ISBN: 0471950823.

K71
KEMENY, ANNE MARIE. 1993. *S(t)imulating Subjects: The Mechanization of the Body in Postmodern Discourse.* Stony Brook, NY: State University of New York at Stony Brook; 1993. 285p. (Ph.D. dissertation; *DAI,* 54/05-A: 1805). Available from: University Microfilms, Ann Arbor, MI (order no. AAD93-28165).

K72
KEMP, SIMON. 1996. *Cognitive Psychology in the Middle Ages.* Westport, CT: Greenwood; 1996. 139p. ISBN: 0313300518.

K73
KEMPSTER, MARK. [1996]. Storage Trends into the 21st Century (electronic file). Accessible at http://www2.ari.net/thicz/.

K74
KEMPSTER, MARK; KEMPSTER, LINDA. 1997. *Advanced Storage Requirements and Capabilities: A White Paper prepared for the Association for Information and Image Management.* Silver Springs, MD: AIIM; 1997. Available from AIIM, Silver Spring, MD.

K75
KENDALL, JULIE E.; KENDALL, KENNETH E. 1993. Metaphors and Methodologies: Living beyond the Systems Machine. *MIS Quarterly.* 1993 June; 17 (2): 149-171. ISSN: 0276-7783.

K76
KENNEDY GRIMSTED, PATRICIA. 1989. *A Handbook for Archival Research in the USSR.* [New York, NY]; International Research and Exchange Board; [Washington, DC]: Kennan Institute for Advanced Russian Studies; c1989. 430p. LCCN: 89181729.

K77
KENNEY, ANNE R.; CHAPMAN, STEPHEN. 1996. *Digital Imaging for Libraries and Archives.* Ithaca, NY: Cornel University Library, Dept. of Preservation and Conservation; 1996. Loose-leaf, 207p.-. Workshop notebook, 1995-1996. Available from: SAA, Chicago, IL. Publication no. 326.

K78
KENNEY, ANNE R.; FRIEDMAN, MICHAEL A.; POUCHER, SUE A. 1993. *Preserving Archival Material through Digital Technology: Final Report.* [Ithaca, NY]: Cornell University Library, Dept. of Preservation and Conservation, for the New York State Program for the Conservation and Presentation of Library Research materials; 1993. 1 vol., loose-leaf.

K79
KENNEY, ANNE R.; PERSONIUS, LYNNE K. 1992. *The Cornel/Xerox/Commission on Preservation and Access Joint Study in Digital Preservation*. Report: Phase 1 (January 1990-December 1991). *Digital Capture, Paper Facsimiles, and Network Access.* Washington, D.C.: Commission on Preservation and Access; 1992. 47p. No ISBN; OCLC 26816888. Available from: CPA at 1400 16th St. NW 740, Washington D.C. 20026-2117 or through Olin Library 215, Cornel University, Ithaca, NY 14853.

K80
KENNY, ANTHONY J. P. 1982. *The Computation of Style: An Introduction to Statistics for Students of Literature and Humanities.* Oxford, UK: Pergamon Press; 176p. (Pergamon International Library of Science, Technology, Engineering, and Social Sciences). ISBN: 0-08-024282-0; ISBN: 0-08-024281-2 (pbk).

K81
KENNY, ANTHONY J. P. 1992. *Computers and the Humanities.* IX British Library Research Lecture. London, UK: The British Library; 1992. 12p. ISBN: 0712332677; LCCN: 92-45443; OCLC: 25997498.

K82
KENT, ALLEN; COHEN, J.; MONTGOMERY, K. L.; WILLIAMS, J. G.; BULICK, S.; FLYNN, R. R.; SABOR, W. N.; MANSFIELD, U. 1979. *Use of Library Materials*. New York, NY: Marcel Dekker, Inc.; 1979. Sometimes referred to in Library Science literature simply as "the Pittsburgh Study."

K83
KENT, ALLEN; LANCOUR, HAROLD; DAILY, J. E., eds. 1968-93. *The Encyclopedia of Library and Information Science*. New York, NY: Marcel Dekker; 1968-92. 53 vols. ISBN: 0-8247-2045-8.

K84
KENT, GEORGE O., ed. 1991. *Historians and Archivists: Essays in Modern German History and Archival Policy*. Fairfax, VA: George Mason University Press; 1991. 349p. ISBN: 091396932X; LCCN: 91-11032; OCLC: 23463230.

K85
KENTUCKY INFORMATION SYSTEMS COMMISSION. 1990. *Managing Information Resources for Kentucky. Strategies for the Future, 1990-1992*. Dooley, Stephen N., chair. Developed in partnership with the Agencies of State Government. Frankfort, KY: Kentucky Information Systems Commission; April 1990. 91p.; append. A: Information Policy, 4p.; append. B: Information Resources Architecture, 42p. Kentucky state doc. no. 351.00722; OCLC: 22204366. Available from: KY Information Systems Commission, 101 Cold Harbor Drive, Frankfort, KY 40601-3050.

K86
KEOGH, JAMES E. 1997. *Solving the Year 2000 Problem*. Boston, MA: AP Professional; 1997. 264 p. ISBN: 0125755600.

K87
KEPPEL, G. 1991/1992. *Design and Analysis: A Researchers's Handbook*. 3rd ed. Englewood Cliffs, NJ: Prentice Hall; 1991. Rep. 1992. 594p. ISBN: 0132007754; LCCN: 90022248.

K88
KERN, STEPHEN. 1983. *The Culture of Time and Space, 1880-1918*. Cambridge, MA: Harvard University Press; 1983. 372p. ISBN: 0674179722; LCCN: 83000303.

K89
KERNAN, A. B. 1982. *The Imaginary Library: An Essay on Literature and Society*. Princeton, NJ: Princeton University Press; 1982. 186p. ISBN: 0691065047; LCCN: 81-47928.

K90
KERNAN, ALVIN. 1996. *What's Happened to the Humanities?* Princeton, NJ: Princeton University Press; 1996. 267p. ISBN: 0691011559; LCCN: 96-28325.

K91
KERTZER, D. I.; SILVERMAN, S.; RUTMAN, D. B.; PLAKANS, A. 1986. History and Anthropology: A Dialogue. *Historical Methods*. 1986; 19(3): 119-128. ISSN: 0161- 5440.

K92
KESNER, RICHARD M. 1982. Historians in the Information Age: Putting the New Technology to Work. *The Public Historian*. 1982; 4(3): 31-48. ISSN: 0272-3433.

K93
KESNER, RICHARD M. 1984. *Automation for Archivists and Records Managers: Planning and Implementation Strategies*. Chicago, IL: American Library Association; 1984. 222p. ISBN: 0-0389-0406-8.

K94
KESNER, RICHARD M. 1984/1985. Automated Information Management: Is there a Role for the Archivist in the Office of the Future. *Archivaria* (CN). 1984/85 Winter: 19: 162-172. ISSN: 0318-6954.

K95
KESNER, RICHARD M. 1993. The Changing Face of Office Documentation: Electronic/Optical Information Technologies. See reference: MENNE-HARITZ, A., ed. 1993. 112-127.

K96
KESNER, RICHARD M. 1993 [1995]. Teaching Archivists about Information Technology Concepts: A Needs Assessment. *The American Archivist*. 1993 Summer [1995]: 46((3): 434-443. ISSN: 0360-9081.

K97
KESNER, RICHARD M. 1995. Group Work, Groupware, and the Transformation of Information Resource Management. *The American Archivist*. 1995 Spring; 58(2): 154-169. ISSN: 0360-9081.

K98

KESNER, RICHARD M. 199-. Information Resource Management in the Electronic Workplace: A personal Perspective on "Archives in the Information Society." *American Archivist*. [199-: 16 pp., forthcoming]. ISSN: 0360-9081.

K99

KETCHAM-VAN ORDEL, LEE; BORN, KATHLEEN. 1998. E-Journals Come of Age. Periodical Price Survey, 1998. *Library Journal*. 1998, April 15; 123: 40-45. ISSN: 0363-0277.

K100

KETELAAR, ERIC. 1985. *Archival and Records Management Legislation and Regulations: A RAMP Study with Guidelines*. Paris, FR: UNESCO General Information Programme and UNISIST; 1985. 117p. (Report PGI-85/WS/9). Available from: UNESCO Federal Information Programme, 7 Place de Fontenoy, 75700 Paris, FR.

K101

KETELAAR, ERIC. 1997. *The Archival Image: Collected Essays*. Bos,-Rops, Yvonne, ed. Amsterdam, NL: Hilversum Verloren; 1997. 124p. ISBN: 9065505652.

K102

KETTL, DONALD F. 1994. Managing on the Frontiers of Knowledge: The Learning Organization. See reference: INGRAHAM, P. W.; ROMZEK, B. S. 1994. 1-26.

K103

KEVLES, DANIEL J.; HOOD, LEROY E., eds. 1992. *The Code of Codes: Scientific and Social Issues in the Human Genome Project*. Cambridge, MA: Harvard University Press; 1992. 397p. ISBN: 0674136454.

K104

KEYLOR, WILLIAM R. 1975. *Academy and Community: The Foundation of the French Historical Profession*. Cambridge, MA; 1975. 286p. ISBN: 0674002555.

K105

KHOSHAFIAN, SETRAG. 1993. *Object-Oriented Databases*. New York, NY: J. Wiley; 1993. 362p. ISBN: 041570567 (hbk.); 0471570583 (pbk.).

K106

KHOSHAFIAN, SETRAG; ABNOUS, RAZMIK. 1995. *Object Orientation: Concepts, Analysis & Design, Languages, Databases, Graphical User Interfaces, Standards*. New York, NY: J. Wiley; 1995. 504p. ISBN: 0471078344.

K107

KHOSHAFIAN, SETRAG; BAKER, A. BRAD. 1996. *Multimedia and Imaging Databases*. San Francisco, CA: Morgan Kaufmann Publ.; 1996. 586p. ISBN: 1558603123.

K108

KHOSHAFIAN, SETRAG; BUCKIEWICZ, MAREK. 1995. *Introduction to Groupware, Workflow, and Workgroup Computing*. New York, NY: Wiley; 1995. 376p. ISBN: 0471029467.

K109

KIBIRIGE, HARRY M. 1996. *Foundations of Full-Text Electronic Information Delivery Systems: Implications for Information Professionals*. New York, NY: Neal-Schuman Publishers, Inc.; 1996. 221p. ISBN: 1555702082; LCCN: 96028444.

K110

KIDWELL, PEGGY ALDRICH; CERUZZI, PAUL. E., eds. 1994. *Landmarks in Digital Computing: A Smithsonian Pictorial History*. Washington, D.C: Smithsonian Institution Press; 1994. 148p. ISBN: 1560983116; LCCN: 93-025428.

K111

KIEL, L. DOUGLAS. 1994. *Managing Chaos and Complexity in Government: A New Paradigm for Managing Change, Innovation, and Organizational Renewal*. San Francisco, CA: Jossey-Bass Publishers; 1994. 246p. ISBN: 0787900230; LCCN: 94-21303.

K112

KIEL, L. DOUGLAS. 1996. *Chaos Theory in the Social Sciences: Foundations and Applications*. Ann Arbor, MI: University of Michigan; 1996. 349p. ISBN: 0472106384; LCCN: 95-35470.

K113

KIEL, L. DOUGLAS; SELDON, BARRY J. 1998. Measuring Temporal Complexity in the External Environment: Nonlinearity and the Bounds of Rational Action. *American Review of Public Administration*. 1998 Sept.; 28 (3): 246-266.

K114
KIES, JONATHAN K. 1997. *Empirical Methods for Evaluating Video-mediated Collaborative Work.* Blacksburg, VA: Virginia Tech University; 1997. (Ph.D. dissertation). Available from University Microfilms, Ann Arbor, MI.

K115
KIES, JONATHAN K.; WILLIGES, ROBERT C.; ROSSON, MARY BETH. 1998. Coordinating Computer-Supported Cooperative Work: A Review of Research Issues and Strategies. See reference: MCNEESE, M. D., ed. 1998. 773-775.

K116
KIESLER, SARA., ed. 1997. *Culture of the Internet.* Mahwah, NJ: Lawrence Earlbaum Associates; 1997. 463p. ISBN: 0805816356; LCCN: 96031388.

K117
KIESLING, KRIS. 1997 [1998]. SAA's CAIE Working Group on EAD Documentation. See reference: DOOLEY, J., ed. 1997 [1998].

K118
KILMANN, RALPH H.; PONDY, LOUIS R.; SLEVIN, DENIS P., eds. 1976. *The Management of Organizational Design.* Conference on Organizational Design, University of Pittsburgh, October 1974. New York, NY: North Holland; 1976. 2 vols. ISBN: 0444001883.

K119
KILMANN, RALPH H.; SAXTON, MARY J.; SHERPA, ROY; & ASSOCIATES (eds.). 1985. *Gaining Control of the Corporate Culture.* Conference proceedings, University of Pittsburgh Graduate School of Business, October 24-27. San Francisco, CA: Jossey-Bass; 1985. 451p. ISBN: 0875896669.

K120
KIMBALL, BRUCE A. 1992. *The "True Professional Ideal" in America: A History.* Oxford, UK: Blackwell; 1992. 429p. ISBN: 1-55786-182-X; LCCN: 91-25259.

K121
KIMBALL, RALPH H. 1996. *The Data Warehouse Toolkit.* New York, NY: John Wiley & Sons; 1996. 388p. and disk. ISBN: 0471153370; LCCN: 95-50557.

K122
KIMBER, W. ELIOT. 1995. *SGML. Comp.text.sgml* [Electronic file]. Accessible at http://www.uss.ie/info/net/markup.html.

K123
KIMBER, W. ELIOT. 1996. *Practical Hypermedia: An Introduction to HyTime.* Englewood Cliffs, NJ: Prentice-Hall; 1996. LCCN: 94-26771.

K124
KIMBER, W. ELIOT; WOODS, JULIA A. 1997. Application of HyTime Hyperlinks and Finite Coordinate Spaces to Historical Writing, Analysis, and Presentation. See reference: LOGAN, E.; POLLARD, M., eds. 1997b. 603-613.

K125
KIMBLE, GREGORY A. 1978. *How to Use (and Misuse) Statistics.* Englewood Cliffs, NJ: Prentice-Hall Pub.; 1978. 290p. ISBN: 0134362047 (hbk.); 0134361962 (pbk.).

K126
KING, GARY; KEOHANE, ROBERT O.; VERBA, SIDNEY. 1994. *Designing Social Inquiry: Scientific Inference in Qualitative Research.* Princeton, NJ: Princeton University Press; 1994. 265p. ISBN: 0691034702 (hbk.); 0691034710 (pbk.).

K127
KINNEL, SUSAN K.; FRANKLIN, CARL. 1992. Hypercard and Hypertext: A New Technology for the 1990s. See reference: KENT, A., ed. 1992. 278-295.

K128
KINNEY, THOMAS E. 1995. *Entertainment Technology and Tomorrow's Information Services.* Medford, NJ: Information Today, Inc.; 1995. 128p. (ASIS Monograph series). ISBN: 1-57387-006-4.

K129
KINTSCH, WALTER. 1970/1977. *Learning, Memory, and Conceptual Processes.* New York, NY: John Wiley; 1970. 498p. ISBN: 047480703. Rev. ed. as: *Memory and Cognition.* New York, NY: John Wiley; 1977. 490p. ISBN: 047148072x.

K130
KINTSCH, WALTER. 1997. *Comprehension: A Paradigm for Cognition.* Boulder, CO: Cambridge Univeristy Press; 1997. ISBN: 0521583608 (hbk.); 05216299861 (pbk.).

K131
KINTSCH, WALTER; VAN DIJK, TEUN A. 1983. *Strategies of Discourse Comprehension*. Orlando, FL: Academic Press; 1983. 418p. ISBN: 0127120505.

K132
KIPFER, BARBARA A. 1997. *The Order of Things: How Everything in the World is Organized—into Hierarchies, Structures, and Pecking Orders*. New York, NY: Random House; 1997. 389p. ISBN: 0679444785.

K133
KIRK, NEVILLE. 1994. History, Language, Ideas and Post-Modernism. *Social History*. 1993; 18: 219-213. ISSN: 0022-4529.

K134
KIRKWOOD, W. G. 1992. Narrative and the Rhetoric of Possibility. *Communication Monographs*. 1992; 59: 30-47. ISSN: 0363-7751.

K135
KISTERMANN, F. W. 1991. The Invention and Development of the Hollerith Punched Card. *Annals of the History of Computing*. 1991; 13(3). ISSN: 1058-6180.

K136
KLAHR, DAVID; KOTOVSKY, KENNETH, eds. 1989. *Complex Information Processing: The Impact of Herbert A. Simon*. Hillsdale, NJ: L. Erlbaum Associates; 1989. 459p. (21st Carnegie Mellon Symposium on Cognition). ISBN: 0805801782 (hbk.); 0805801790 (pbk.); LCCN: 88031004.

K137
KLAMER, ARIO; MCCLOSKEY, DONALD N.; SOLOW, ROBERT M., eds. 1988. *The Consequences of Economic Rhetoric*. Cambridge, UK: Cambridge University Press; 1988. 305p. ISBN: 0521342864.

K138
KLEIN, JULIE T. 1990. *Interdisciplinarity: History, Theory and Practice*. Detroit, MI: Wayne State University Press; 1990. 331p. ISBN: 0814320872; LCCN: 89-35166; OCLC: 19975811.

K139
KLEIN, KERWIN LEE. 1995. In Search of Narrative Mastery: Postmodernism and the People without History. *History and Theory*. 1995 December; 34 (4): 275-299. ISSN: 0018-2656.

K140
KLEIN, NORMAN M. 1997. *The History of Forgetting: Los Angeles and the Erasure of Memory*. New York, NY: Verso; 1997. 330p. (Haymarket series). ISBN: 1859841759 (pbk.).

K141
KLEIN, WALDO C.; BLOOM, MARTIN. 1994. Social Work as Applied Social Science: A Historical Analysis. *Social Work*. 1994 July; 39(4): 421-432. ISSN: 0037-8046.

K142
KLIER, JOHN D. 1989. Computer Usage in Advanced History Courses. *History Microcomputer Review*. 1989 Fall; 5(2): 49-53. ISSN: 0887-1078.

K143
KLINE, MARY-JO. 1987. *A Guide to Documentary Editing*. Baltimore, MD: The Johns Hopkins Press; 1987. 228p. ISBN: 0801833418.

K144
KLING, ROB. 1994. Reading "All About" Computerization: How Genre Conventions Shape Nonfiction Social Analysis. *The Information Society*. 1994; 10(3): 147-172.

K145
KLING, ROB; CRAWFORD, HOLLY. 1999. From Retrieval to Communication: The Development, Use, and Consequences of Digital Documentary Systems. See reference: BATES, M., ed. 1999. 1121-1122.

K146
KLING, ROB; MCKIM, GEOFFREY. 1999. Scholarly Communication and the Continuum of Electronic Publishing. *Journal of the American Society for Information Science*. 1999; 10(10): 890-906. ISSN: 0002-8231.

K147
KLING, ROB; ROSENBAUM, H.; HART, C. 1998. Social Informatics in Information Science: An Introduction. *Journal of the American Society for Information Science*. 1998; 49: 1047-1052. ISSN: 0002-8231.

K148

KLING, ROB; CRAWFORD, H.; ROSENBAUM, H.; SAWYER, S; WEISBAND, S. 1999. *Information Technologies in Human Context: Learning from Organizational and Social Informatics*. Bloomington, IN: Indiana University Center for Social Informatics. Accessible at: http://www.slis.indiana.edu/CSI.

K149

KLING, ROB; DUNLOP C., eds. 1996. *Computerization and Controversy. Value, Conflicts, and Social Choices*. 2nd ed. San Diego, CA: Academic Press; 1996. 961p. ISBN: 0-12- 415040-3.

K150

KLIR, GEORGE J.; FOLGER, TINA A. 1988. *Fuzzy Sets, Uncertainty, and Information*. London, UK: Prentice-Hall International Editions; 1988. 355p. ISBN: 01334598435.

K151

KLIR, GEORGE J.; ST. CLAIR, UTE H.; YUAN, BO. 1997. *Fuzzy Set Theory: Foundations and Applications*. Upper Saddle River, NJ: Prentice Hall; 1997. 245p. ISBN: 0133410587.

K152

KLIR, GEORGE J.; YUAN, BO. 1995. *Fuzzy Sets and Fuzzy Logic: Theory and Applications*. Upper Saddle River, NJ: Prentice Hall; 1995. 547p. ISBN: 0131011715.

K153

KLOPPENBERG, JAMES T. 1987. Deconstructive and Hermeneutic Strategies for Intellectual History: The Recent Work on Dominick LaCapra and David Hollinger. *Intellectual History Newsletter*. 1987; 9: 56-65. OCLC: 9752362; DLC: 830117491.

K154

KNAB, RAYMOND W. 1992. *Spreadsheet and Database Cases for Information Systems*. Reading, MA: Addison-Wesley Pub. Co.; c1992. 150p., disk. ISBN: 0201581779; LCCN: 92-009907.

K155

KNEPPER, ROBERT C. 1987. History of the Society for Information Display. *Information Display*. 1987 April; 3(4): 12-16. ISSN: 0362-0972.

K156

KNIGHT, K. 1990. Connectionist Ideas and Algorithms. *Communications of the ACM* (Assn. of Computing Machinery). 1990; 33 (11): 59-74. ISSN: 0001-0782.

K157

KNIGHTS, DAVID. 1997. Organization Theory in the Age of Deconstruction: Dualism, Gender, and Postmodernism Revisited. *Organizational Studies*. 1997; 18(1): 1-19. ISSN: 0170-8406.

K158

KNOERL, JOHN J. 1991. Mapping History using Geographic Information Systems. *The Public Historian*. 1991 Summer; 13(3): 97-108. ISSN: 0272-3433.

K159

KNOKE, PETER J.; SCHNEIDER, W.; MUDD, ISABELLE. 1991. PROJECT JUKEBOX: Technology for Oral History Preservation and Access. *Audiovisual Librarian*. 1992 May; 17(2): 108-13. ISSN: 0302-3451.

K160

KNOPPERS, JAKE. 1983. Integrating Technologies = Integrating Disciplines? *ARMA Records Management Quarterly*. 1983 April; 17(1): 5-7, 26. ISSN: 1050-2343.

K161

KNOWLES, DAVID. 1963. *Great Historical Enterprises: Problems in Monastic History*. London, UK: T. Nelson; 1963. 231p.

K162

KOCH, PETER M. 1994. Chaos. In: *Encyclopedia of Science and Technology* [electronic file]. New York, NY: McGraw Hill; 1994. CD-ROM; 10pp.

K163

KOCH, WALTER A., comp. 1972. *Strukurelle Textanalyse: Analyse du écrit; Discourse Analysis* [Structural Text Analysis: Analysis of Writing; Discourse Analysis]. *Studia Semiotica*. Hildesheim, DEU: G. OLMS; 1972. 486p. (Collecta semiotica, 1). (Entire work on title topics; in English, French, and German; one study each in Czech and Russian). ISBN: 3487042916.

K164

KOCKA, JURGEN. 1980. Quantitative Social Scientific History. See reference: KAMMEN, M., ed. 1980. 169-178.

K165

KOCKA, JURGEN. 1984a. The Revivalism of Narrative: A Response to Recent Criticism of Quantitative History. *Social Science History.* 1984; 8: 133-149. ISSN: 0145-5532.

K166

KOCKA, JURGEN. 1984b. Theories and Quantification in History. *Social Science History.* 1984; 8(2): 169-178. ISSN: 0145-5532.

K167

KOCKA, JURGEN. 1989. The State of Social Science History in the Late 1980s. *Historical Methods.* 1989; 22: 13-19. ISSN: 0161-5440.

K168

KOFMAN, ELEONORE; YOUNGS, GILLIAN, eds. 1996. *Globalization: Theory and Practice.* London, UK: Cassell; 1996. 339p. ISBN: 1855673460 (hbk.); 1855673479 (pbk.).

K169

KOFMAN, FRED; SENGE, PETER M. 1993. Communities of Commitment: The Heart of Learning Organizations. *Organizational Dynamics.* 1993 Autumn; 22 (2): 5-23. ISSN: 0090-2616

K170

KOHONEN, TEUVO. 1989. *Self Organization and Associative Memory.* 3rd ed. New York, NY: Springer-Verlag; 1989. 312p. (Springer series in Information Sciences, 8). ISBN: 0387513876; LCCN: 89-19681; OCLC: 20015322.

K171

KOHONEN, TEUVO. 1995/1997. *Self-Organization Maps.* Berlin & Heidelberg, DEU: Springer-Verlag; 1995. 2nd ed., 1997. 426p. ISBN: 3540620176 (pbk.); LCCN: 96-53987.

K172

KOLTAY, Z. 1992. Library of the Future Series, Second Edition. *CD-ROM Librarian.* September 1992; 7(8): 47-49. ISSN: 0893-9934.

K173

KOMOROWSKI, JAN; SYTKOW, JAN M., eds. 1997. *Principles of Data Mining and Knowledge Discovery.* First European Conference, RKDD'97, Trondheim, Norway, June 24-27, 1997. Berlin, DEU / New York, NY: Springer-Verlag; 1997. 396p. (Lecture Notes in Computer Science series). ISBN: 35406322399 (pbk.).

K174

KOPCZINSKI, MICHAL. 1993. History and Computing at the Department of History, University of Warsaw. See reference: DAVIS *ET AL.,* eds. 1993. 107-112.

K175

KOPOSSOV, NIKOLAI. 1995. Vers l'Anthropologie de la Raison Historique [Toward an Anthropology of Historical Reasoning]. (In French). See reference: BARROS, C., ed. 1995. 263-268.

K176

KORFAGE, ROBERT F. 1997. *Information Storage and Retrieval.* New York, NY: John Wiley & Sons, Inc.; 1997. 349p. ISBN: 04711433838.

K177

KORNFELD, EVE. 1995. History and the Humanities: The Politics of Objectivity and the Promise of Subjectivity. *New England Journal of History.* 1995; 51 (3): 44-55.

K178

KORNFELD, JOHN. 1994. Using Fiction to Teach History: Multi-cultural and Global Perspectives of World War II. *Social Education.* 1994 September; 58 (5): 281-287. ISSN: 0037-7724.

K179

KOSELLECK, REINHARD. 1985. *Vergangene Zukunft.* Tribe, Keith, trans. *Futures Past: On the Semantics of Historical Time.* Cambridge, MA: MIT Press; c1985. 330p. ISBN: 0262111004; LCCN: 85005195.

K180

KOSSLYN, S. M. 1980. *Image and Mind.* Cambridge, UK: Cambridge University Press; 1980. 500p. ISBN: 0674443659; LCCN: 80010329.

K181

KOSSLYN, S. M. 1985. Graphics and Human Information Processing. *Journal of the American Statistical Association.* 1985; 80: 499-512. ISSN: 0162-1459.

K182
KOSSLYN, S. M. 1989. Understanding Charts and Graphs. *Applied Cognitive Psychology*. 1989; 3: 183-226. ISSN: 0888-4080.

K183
KOUSSER, J. MORGAN. 1973. Ecological Regression and the Analysis of Past Politics. *Journal of Interdisciplinary History*. 1973; 4: 237-262. ISSN: 0022-1953.

K184
KOUSSER, J. MORGAN. 1977. The Agenda for Social Science History. *Social Science History*. 1977; 1: 383-391. ISSN: 0145-5532.

K185
KOUSSER, J. MORGAN. 1984. The Revivalism of the Narrative: A Response to Recent Criticisms of Quantitative History. *Social Science History*. 1984; 8: 113-149. ISSN: 0145-5532.

K186
KOUSSER, J. MORGAN. 1986. Comment and Debate on Flanigan's and Zingales's "Alchemists Gold." *Social Science History*. 1986; 10: 71-84. ISSN: 0145-5543.

K187
KOUSSER, J. MORGAN. 1989. The State of Social Science History in the Late 1980s. *Historical Methods*. 1989; 22: 13-20. ISSN: 0161-5440.

K188
KOUSSER, J. MORGAN; LICHTMAN, J. A. 1983. "New Political History": Some Statistical Questions Answered. *Social Science History*. 1983; 7: 321-344. (Reply to W. G. SHADE, 1981). ISSN: 0145-5532.

K189
KOVAL'CHENKO, IVAN D. 1972/ 1987. *Matematicheskie metody v istorischeskikh issledovani i akh: sbornik statethi* [Mathmatical Methods of Historical Data Processing: Statistical Modeling]. Moscow, USSR: Akademiia nauk SSSR. Komissi i a po primeneni i u matematicheskikhmetodov i elektronnovychislitel nykh mashin v istorischeskikh issledovani i akh; 1972. 234p. Rev. eds., 1984. 382p. Reprint, 1987.LCCN: 84-206155; OCLC: 14081405. (In Russian). Koval'chenko collaborated with L. Borodkin and I. Rafi-Zade to produce a similar text-book in Azerbaijanian to support the Historical Informatics Center in Baku: *Sovremennyre methody izucheniia istoricheskih istochnikov pri pomoshchi EVM* [Baku, 1991].

K190
KOVAL'CHENKO, IVAN D. 1977. *Matematischeskie metody v istoriko-ekonomicheskikh I istoriko-kulturnykh isslde-dovaniiiakh* [Sbornik statethi] [Mathematical Methodology and Data Processing for Economic and Cultural History: Statistical Modeling]. Moscow, USSR; Akademiii nauk SSSR. Komissi i a po primeneni i u matematich-eskikhmetodov i elektronnovychislitel nykh mashin v istorischeskikh issledovani i akh; 1977. 384p. (In Russian).

K191
KOVAL'CHENKO, IVAN D. 1982. *Istorischeskii istochnikov svete ucheniia ob informatsi* [Historical Reasoning for Information]. In: *Istoriia SSSR*, 3. Moscow, USSR: Lomonsov University; 1982. (Entire issue of title topic; in Russian).

K192
KOVAL'CHENKO, IVAN D. 1985. *Matematischeskie metody I 8EVM v istoricheskikh issledovaniiiakh: sbornik statethi* [Mathematical Methodology for the 8EVM and Historical Data Processing: Statistical Modeling]. Moscow, USSR: Akaemiiia nauk SSSR; 1985. 341p. (In Russian).

K193
KOVAL'CHENKO, IVAN D. 1987. *Metody istoricheskogo issledovaniiia* [Historical Methodology and Historiography]. Moscow, USSR: Akademiiia nauk SSSR. Otdelenie istorii; 1987. 438p. (In Russian).

K194
KOVAL'CHENKO, IVAN D. 1991. The Role of Quantitative Methods in Historical Research. *Historical Social Research/ Historische Sozialforschung* (DEU). 1991; 16: 5-16. ISSN: 0172-6404.

K195
KOVAL'CHENKO, IVAN D.; BOVYKIN, VALERITHI I.; LAGRANZH I. 1986. *Statistika stachek v Rossii I v indus-trialnykh stranakh Evropy I v SshA* [Statistical Servicies for the Study of Russian Industrial Strikes]. Moscow, USSR: Akademiia nauk SSSR, Institut istorii; 1986. 148p. (In Russian).

K196
KOVAL'CHENKO, IVAN D.; MILOV, LEONID; BORODKIN, LEONID; GARSKOVA, IRENA. 1983. [Quantitative methods of historical research]. Moscow, USSR: Moscow State University; 1983. (In Russian).

K197

KOVAL'CHENKO, IVAN D.; SHIKLO, ALLA E. 1985/1990. *Sbornik materialov po istorii istoricheskothi mauki v SSSR:konetis XIX-nachalo XX v.* [Source Material and Historiography in the Soviet Union for the 19th-20th Centuries]. Moscow, RU: Vysshaiia Shkola; 1990. 303p . *Sbornik materialov po istorii istoricheskothi mauki v SSSR: konetis XVIII-pervaiia tret XIX v* [Source Material and Historiography in the Soviet Union for the 18-19th Centuries]. Moscow, USSR: Vysshaiia Shkola; 1990. 285p. (About approved standard textbooks). (In Russian). ISBN: 5060016080.

K198

KOVAL'CHENKO, IVAN D.; TISHKOV, VALERI A. 1983. *Kolichestvennye metody v sovestskoi i amerikanskoi isto-riografi* [Quantitative Methods in Soviet and American Historiography]. Moscow, USSR: Akademi i a nauk SSSR; 1983. 424p.LCCN: 84-171033; OCLC: 11725818.

K199

KOVEN, RONALD. 1995. National Memory: the Duty to Remember, the Need to Forget. *Society.* 1995, Sept.-Oct.: 32(6): 52-59. Available in: IAC, *Magazine Collection,* no. 17370521.

K200

KOWALSKI, GERALD. 1997. *Information Retrieval Systems: Theory and Implementation.* Boston, MA: Kluwer Academic Publishers; 1997. 282p. ISBN: 0-7923-9926-9.

K201

KOWLOWITZ, ALAN. 1988. *Archival Appraisal of Online Information Systems.* Commentary by John McDonald. Pittsburgh, PA: Archives and Museum Informatics; 1988. 74p. (Archives and Informatics Technical Report, 2[no.3]). OCLC: 20369464.

K202

KOWLOWITZ, ALAN; KELLY, KRISTINE. 1997. *Models for Action*: Developing Practical Approaches to Electronic Records Management and Preservation. See reference: TRAVIS, I., ed. 1997. 20-24.

K203

KRAAK, MENNO-JAN. 1996. Integrating Multimedia in Geographical Information Systems. *IEEE Multmedia.* 1996 Summer; 3 (2): 59-65. ISSN: 1070-986X.

K204

KRAJICEK, JAN. 1995. *Bounded Arithmetic, Propositional Logic, and Complexity Theory.* Cambridge, UK / New York, NY: Cambridge University Press; 1995. 343p. ISBN: 0521452058; LCCN: 94047054.

K205

KRAMER, LLOYD S. 1989. Literature, Criticism, and Historical Imagination: The Literary Challenge of Hayden White and Dominick LaCapra. See reference: HUNT, L., ed. 1989. 97-128.

K206

KRAMER, LLOYD S.; REID, DONALD; BARNEY, WILLIAM L., eds. 1994. *Learning History in America: Schools, Cultures, and Politics.* Minneapolis, MN: University of Minnesota Press; 1994. 225p. ISBN: 0816623635 (hbk.); 0816623643 (pbk.).

K207

KRAUS, R. M.; FUSSELL, S. R. 1990. Mutual Knowledge and Communicative Effectiveness. In: GALEGHER, R. J.; KRAUT, R.E.; EGIDO, C., eds. 1990. 111-145.

K208

KRAUSE, J., ed. 1991. *Computers and the Humanities in Germany.* In: *Computing and the Humanities.* 1991; 25(1/2). (Entire issue on title topic). ISSN: 0010-4817.

K209

KRAUT, R. E.; EGIDO, C.; GALEGHER, J. 1990. Patterns of Contact and Communication in Scientific Research Collaborations. In: GALEGHER, R. J.; KRAUT, R.E.; EGIDO, C., eds. 1990. 149-172.

K210

KREITZ, PATRICIA A. 1992. An Annotated Bibliography on Networking: Past, Present, and Future. *Resource Sharing and Information Networks.* 1992; 8(1): 159-1887. ISSN: 0737-7797.

K211

KREPS, G. 1990. Stories as Repositories of Organizational Intelligence: Implications for Organizational Development. See reference: ANDERSON, J., ed. 1990. 13: 191-202.

K212

KRIPKE, S. A. 1980. *Naming and Necessity.* Cambridge, MA: Harvard University Press; 1980. 172p. ISBN: 0674598458.

K213
KRIPPENDORFF, KLAUS. 1980. *Content Analysis: An Introduction to its Methodology.* Beverley Hills, CA: 1980. 191p. ISBN: 0803914970; 0803914989 (pbk.); LCCN: 80-19166; OCLC: 6581330.

K214
KRISTENSEN, JOANA; JAERVELIN, KALERVO. 1990. The Effectiveness of a Searching Thesaurus in Free-text Searching in a Full-text Database. *International Classification.* 1990; 17(2): 77-84. ISSN: 0340-0050.

K215
KRISTEVA, JULIA. 1980. *Desire in Language: A Semiotics Approach to Literature and Art.* trans. New York, NY: Columbia University Press; 1980. 305p. ISBN: 0231048068; LCCN: 80-10689; OCLC: 6016349.

K216
KROEBER, ALFRED; KLUCKHOHN, CLYDE. 1952. Culture: A Critical Review of Concepts and Definitions. In: *Papers of the Peabody Museum of American Archeology and Ethnology,* vol. 47. Cambridge, MA: Harvard University Peabody Museum; 1952.

K217
KRONFELD, MICHAEL. 1990. *Reference and Computation. An Essay in Applied Philosophy of Language.* Studies in Natural Language Processing. New York, NY: Cambridge University Press; 1990. 185p. ISBN: 0-521-36636-4 (hdk); 0-521-39982-3 (pbk); LCCN: 89-78246.

K218
KROPAČ, INGO H. 1987a. Computers in the Lecture Room: Basic Considerations on the Concept of Teaching Computational History. In: *Computerized Information Systems in University Education.* Proceedings of a Symposium held in Zagreb, October 22-23, 1987 (pp. 43-47). Zagreb, YU: ALPS-ADRIA Rectorial Conference; 1987. 271p. LCCN: 88-156394; OCLC: 26398244.

K219
KROPAČ, INGO H. 1987b. Vorschlage für Standortbestimmung einer Historischen Fachinformatik [Proposal for the Position of Historical Informatics]. In: Erwinka, G,; Hoflechner, W.; Pickl, O.; Wiesflecker, H.; Hartel, R., eds. *Geschichte und ihre Quellen. Festschrift für Friedrich Hausmann zum 70. Geburtstag.* Graz, AT: Akademische Druck-u. Verlagsanstalt; 1987. 601-610. (In German). ISBN: 3201014141; OCLC: 22167406.

K220
KROPAČ, INGO H. 1990. Die Datenbank UHRTEXT: Das Urkundenbuch des Herzogstums Steiermark [The Account Books of the Steier March Commandery]. In: Kropač , I. H., ed. *Das Urkundenbuch des Herzogstums Steiermark. Eine Textdatenbank.* St. Katharinen [Göttingen, DEU]: Max-Planck-Institut für Geschichte in Kommission bei Scripta Mercaturae Verlag; 1990. 1-15. (Halbgraue Reihe zur historischen Fackinformatik. Serie C: Historische Quellenkunden, Band 18). (In German).

K221
KROPAČ, INGO H. 1991a. Homo ex Machina: Prosopography and Chartularies. See reference: BEST, H., *ET AL.,* eds. 1991. 97-102.

K222
KROPAČ, INGO H. 1991b. Medieval Documents. See reference: GREENSTEIN, D., 1991. 117-127.

K223
KROPAČ, INGO H. 1992. Zur Konzeption von Informationsystemen in der Geschichtswissenschaft [The Concept of Information Systems in the Historical Discipline]. In: Kaser, Karl; Stocker, Karl, eds. *Clios Rache. Neue Aspekte strukurgeschichtlicher und theoriegeleiteler Geschichtsforschung in Osterreich* (pp. 87- 129) Vienna, AT / Cologne, DEU: Bohlaus Verlag Gesellschaft m.b.H. und Co.; 1992. 244p. (Bolhaus zeitgeschichtliche Bibliothek, Band 22). (In German). ISBN: 3205054865; OCLC: 28935913.

K224
KROPAČ, INGO H. 1996 [199-]. Cognition, Imagination or Illusion? History from a Formal Point of View. See reference: BORODKIN, L., ed. 1996: Abstract of presentation, 115-16; paper [199- forthcoming].

K225
KROPAČ, INGO; JARITZ, GERHARD; TEIBENBACHER, PETER, eds. 1995. *The Art of Communication.* Proceedings of the VIII International Conference of the Association for History and Computing, Graz, AT, August 24-27, 1993. Graz, AT: Akademische Druck-u. Verlagsanstalt; 1995. 537p. (Grazer Grundwissenschaftliche Forschungen). ISBN: 3-201-01646-2.

K226
KROZEL, JAMES A. 1992. *Intelligent Path Prediction for Vehicular Travel.* Lafayette, IN: Purdue University; 1992. 102p. (Ph.D. dissertation; *DAI,* vol. 53/05-B: 2419). Available from: University Microfilm, Ann Arbor, MI (Order no. AAD92-29147).

K227

KRUEGER, MYRON W. 1991. *Artificial Reality II*. Reading, MA: Addison-Wesley Publishing Co.; 1991. 286p. ISBN: 0-201-52260-8.

K228

KRUGER, LORENZ; DARTON, LORRAINE; GIGERENZER, GERD; HEIDELBERGER, MICHAEL; MORGAN, MARY S., eds. 1987. *The Probabilistic Revolution*. Vol. 1: *Ideas in History*. Vol. 2: *The Ideas of Science*. Cambridge, MA: MIT Press; 1987. 2 vols. ISBN: 0262111187 (hbk.); 0262111195 (pbk.); LCCN: 86-17972.

K229

KRUMMEL, DONALD W. 1993. Born Yesterday and Other Forms of Original Sin: Two Perspectives on Library Research. *Journal of Education for Library and Information Science*. 1993 Fall; 34(4): 279-286. ISSN: 0748-5786.

K230

KRUPAT, ARNOLD. 1992. *Ethnocriticism: Ethnography, History, and Literature*. Berkeley, CA: University of California Press; 1992. 273p. ISBN: 0520074475 (hbk.); 0520076664 (pbk.).

K231

KRUSE, SUSAN E. 1991. Computing and History Courses for Undergraduates: Issues of Course Design. *History and Computing*. 1991; 3: 104-112. ISSN: 0957-0144.

K232

KRUSKAL, WILIAM; TANUR, JUDITH M. 1978. *International Encyclopedia of Statistics*. New York, NY: Free Press; 1978. 2 vols., 1350p. ISBN: 0029179602.

K233

KRYZAK, ADAM; KASYAND, T.; SUEN, CHING Y., eds. 1989. *Computer Vision and Shape Recognition*. Selected papers from the Vision Interface `88 conference, Edmonton, Alberta, CA, June 6-10, 1988. 451p. (Computer Science series, 14). ISBN: 9971508621.

K234

KUBLER, GEORGE. 1962. *The Shape of Time: Remarks on the History of Things*. New Haven, CT: Yale University Press; 1962. 136p. LCCN: 62-008250.

K235

KUCERA, HENRY. 1967. *Computational Analysis of Present-day American English*. Providence, RI: Brown University Press; 1967. 424p. LCCN: 67010213.

K236

KUECHLER, SUSANNE; MELION, WALTER S., eds. 1991. *Images of Memory: On Remembering and Representation*. Symposium on "Relation of Mnemonic Functions to Pictorial Representation" organized by the Johns Hopkins University Program in Art History and Anthropology. Washington, D.C.: Smithsonian Institution Press; 1991. 265p. ISBN: 1560980273; LCCN: 90022943.

K237

KUEHL, WARREN L. 1985. *Access to Historical Literature: A Planning Study for a History Thesaurus*. Proposal submitted to the Division of Research Programs, National Endowment for the Humanities, June 25, 1985. Akron, OH: Dept. Of History, University of Akron; 1985. Typescript, [32p.].

K238

KUHLTHAU, CAROL C. 1987. *Information Skills for an Information Society: A Review of the Research*. Syracuse, NY: Syracuse University School of Education and School of Information Studies; 1987. (Report no. IR-74).

K239

KUHLTHAU, CAROL C. 1990. The Information Search Process: From Theory to Practice. *Journal of Education for Library and Information Science*. 1990; 31: 72-75. ISSN: 0748-5786.

K240

KUHLTHAU, CAROL C. 1993. *Seeking Meaning: A Process Approach to Library and Information Services*. Norwood, NJ: Ablex Publishing Corp.; 1993. 199p. ISBN: 0893919683 (hbk.); 1567500196 (pbk.).

K241

KUHN, THOMAS S. 1962. The Structure of Scientific Revolutions. In: *International Encyclopedia of Unified Science*, vol. 2. Chicago, IL: University of Chicago Press; 1962. 172p. 3rd ed.; 212p. ISBN: 0226458075 (hbk.); 0226458083 (pbk.).

K242

KUHN, THOMAS S. [1972]. Incommensurability and Paradigms. See reference: MORICK, H., ed. [1972]; ch. 6.

K243

KUHN, THOMAS S. 1977. *The Essential Tension: Selected Studies in Scientific Tradition and Change*. Chicago, IL: University of Chicago Press; 1977. 366p. ISBN: 0226458059.

K244
KUIPERS, BENJAMIN. 1994. *Qualitative Reasoning. Modeling and Simulation with Incomplete Knowledge.* Cambridge, MA: MIT Press; 1994. 450p. ISBN: 0-262- 11190-X.

K245
KUNII, TOSHIYASU I. 1989. *Visual Database Systems.* FIP Proceedings, Working Conference, Tokyo, 3-7 April 1989. New York, NY: North-Holland Publ.; 1989. 546p. ISBN: 04448733341; LCCN: 89-2951.

K246
KUNII, TOSHIYASU I. 1992. *Visual Computing: Integrating Computer Graphics with Computer Vision.* Tokyo, JA: New York, NY: Springer-Verlag; 1992. 963p. ISBN: 0387701036.

K247
KURAN, TIMUR. 1995. *Private Truths; Public Lies. The Social Consequences of Preference Falsification.* Cambridge, MA: Harvard University Press; 1995. 423p. ISBN: 0674707575.

K248
KURLAND, NANCY B. 1995. The Unexplored Territory linking Rewards and Ethical Behavior: A Review and a Diagnostic Model. *Business & Society.* 1995 April; 34 (10): 34-50. ISSN: 0007-6503.

K249
KURTZMAN, STEPHEN J. II. 1991. *Properties of Spreadsheet Histories.* Los Angeles, CA: University of Southern California. (Ph.D. dissertation; *DAI,* vol. 52/08-B: 4314). Available from: USC Doheny Library Micrographics Dept., Los Angeles, CA 90089-0182.

K250
KUSHILEVITZ, EYAL; NISAN, NOAM. 1997. *Communication Complexity.* New York, NY: Cambridge University Press; 1997. 189p. ISBN: 0521560675.

K251
KWOK, K. L. 1991. Query Modification and Expansion in a Network with Adaptive Architecture. In: *Proceedings of ACM SIGIR.* Chicago, IL: ACM; 1991. 192-201.

-L-

L1
LABORATOIRE D'ÉTUDES ET DE RECHERCHES SUR L'INFORMATION ET LA DOCUMENTATION (LERI-DOCS). 1995. *History and Computing. An International Bibliography.* St. Katharinen (Göttingen), DEU: Max Planck Institut für Geschichte; 1995. (Halbgraue Reihe zur Historischen Fachinformatik, A28).

L2
LACAPRA, DOMINICK. 1983. *Rethinking Intellectual History: Texts, Contexts, and Language.* Ithaca, NY: Cornell University Press; 1983. 350p. ISBN: 080141587X; 0801498864 (pbk.): LCCN: 83-7218; OCLC: 9442497.

L3
LACAPRA, DOMINICK. 1985. Is Everyone a Mentalite Case? Transference and Cultural Concept. In his: *History and Criticism* (pp. 71-94). Ithaca, NY: Cornell University Press; 1985. 145p. ISBN: 18070230; 0801417880 (pbk.); LCCN: 84-16990; OCLC: 11030789.

L4
LACQUANIATI, F.; TERZUOLO, C.; VIVIANI, P. 1993. The Law relating the Kinematic and Figural Aspects of Drawing Movements. *Acta Psychologica: An International Journal of Psychonomics* (NL). 1993; 54: 51-67. ISSN: 0001-6918.

L5
LAFLIN, SUSAN. 1993b. An Interactive System for Recognition of Manuscripts. See reference: DOORN, P., *ET AL.,* eds. 1993. 53-58.

L6
LAFLIN, SUSAN. 1995a. An Interactive System for Off-Line Text Recognition. See reference: JARITZ, G., *ET AL.,* eds., 1995: 257-263. Abstract in JARTIZ, G. *ET AL.* 1993. 40-41.

L7
LAFLIN, SUSAN. 1995b. The Generation of Gothic Text. See reference: BOONSTRA, O., *ET AL.,* eds. 1995. 231-237.

L8
LAFOLETTE, MARCEL C. 1992. *Stealing into Print. Fraud, Plagarism, and Misconduct in Scientific Publishing.* Berkeley, CA: University of California; 1992. 293p. ISBN: 052008314.

L9

LAFON, PIERRE. 1984. *Dépouillements et statistiques en lexicometrie* [Document Analysis and Statistics in Lexicometry]. Geneva, CH; Paris, FR: Slatkine; 1984. (Travaux de Linguistique Quantative). (In French). ISBN: 2-05-1000613-X.

L10

LAGUARDIA, CHERYL; TALLENT, ED. 1996. CD-ROM Review [History on CD-ROMS]. *Library Journal*. 1996 October 1; 121 (6): 134-136. ISSN: 0363-0277.

L11

LAIRD, PHILIP D. 1988. *Learning from Good and Bad Data*. International Series in Engineering and Computer Science, 47. Boston, MA: Kluwer Academic Publishers; c1988. 211p. ISBN: 0898382637; LCCN: 87035103.

L12

LAKOFF, GEORGE. 1987. *Women, Fire, and Dangerous Things: What Categories Reveal about the Mind*. Chicago, IL: University of Chicago Press; 1987. 614p. ISBN: 0226468038; LCCN: 86019136.

L13

LAKOFF, GEORGE; JOHNSON, MARK. 1980. *Metaphors We Live By*. Chicago, IL: University of Chicago Press; 1980. 242p. ISBN: 0226468011.

L14

LAKOFF, GEORGE; JOHNSON, MARK. 1999. *Philosophy in the Flesh: The Embodied Mind and its Challenge to Western Thought*. New York, NY: Basic Books; c1999. 624p. ISBN: 0465056733.

L15

LAM, NINA S.N.; DECOLA, LEE, eds. 1993. *Fractals in Geography*. Engelwood Cliffs, NJ: PTR Prentice Hall; 1993. 308p. ISBN: 01310588673.

L16

LAMBERT, STEVE; ROPIEQUET, SUZANNE, eds. 1986-1987. *CR-ROM*. Forward by Bill Gates. Redmond, WA: Microsoft Press; 1986-87. Vol.1: *The New Papyrus: the Current and Future State of the Art*; vol. 2: *Optical Publishing: A Practical Approach to Developing CD-ROM Applications*. ISBN: 0914845748 (pbk., v. 1); 1556150008 (pbk., v. 2).

L17

LAMBERTS, KOEN; SHANKS, DAVID, eds. 1997. *Knowledge, Concepts, and Categories*. Cambridge, MA: the MIT Press; 1976. 464p. ISBN: 0-262-62118-5.

L18

LAMPSON, BUTLER. 1992. Authentification in Distributed Systems: Theory and Practice. *ACM Transactions on Computer Systems*. 1992 November; 10 (4): 265-310. ISSN: 0734-2071.

L19

LANCASHIRE, IAN; MCCARTY, WILLARD, eds. 1988-. *The Humanities Computing Yearbook. A Comprehensive Guide to Software and other Resources*. 1st ed., 1988; 2nd ed., 1990; 3rd ed., 1991. New York, NY: Oxford University Press; 1988-1991. 396p. ISBN: 0-19-824442-8.

L20

LANCASTER, F. WILFRID. 1977/1978. Toward Paperless Information Systems. In: *Occasional Papers*, 127. Urbana, IL: Graduate School of library and Information Science; 1977. 27p. Rev. expanded ed. New York, NY: Academic Press; 1978. 179p. ISBN: 0124360505.

L21

LANCASTER, F. WILFRID. 1968/1979. *Information Retrieval Systems: Characteristics, Testing, and Evaluation*. New York, NY: Wiley; 1968. ISBN: 0471512400. 2nd ed. New York, NY: Wiley; 1979. ISBN: 0471046736.

L22

LANCASTER, F. WILFRID. 1981. *Investigative Methods in Library and Information Science*. Arlington, VA: Information Resources Press; 1981. 260p. ISBN: 0878150358.

L23

LANCASTER, F. WILFRID. 1986. *Vocabulary Control for Information Retrieval*. Arlington, VA: Information Resources Press; 1986. 270p. ISBN: 0878150536.

L24

LANCASTER, F. WILFRID. 1991. *Indexing and Abstracting in Theory and Practice*. London, UK: Library Association; 1991. 328p. ISBN: 1856040046.

L25
LANCASTER, F. WILFRID; WARNER, AMY J. 1993. *Information Retrieval Systems: Characteristics , Testing and Evaluation*. Rev. ed. *Information Retrieval Today*. Arlington, VA: Information Resources Press; 1993. 341p. ISBN: 0878150641.

L26
LANCET, THE. 1991. Being and Believing: Ethics of Virtual Reality. *The Lancet*. 1991 August 3; 338: 283-84. (Editorial). ISSN: 0023-7507.

L27
LANDAUER, THOMAS K. 1998. The trouble with Computers: Usefulness, Usability, and Productivity. *Isis*. 1998; 89(1): 93-. ISSN: 0021-1753.

L28
LANDES, DAVID S. 1983. *Revolution in Time: Clocks and the Making of the Modern World*. Cambridge, MA: Harvard University Belknap Press; 1983. 482p. ISBN: 06777476800 (pbk.); LCCN: 83008489.

L29
LANDES, DAVID S.; TILLY, CHARLES, eds. [1971]. *History as Social Science*. Behavioral and Social Sciences Survey: History Panel. Englewood Cliffs, NJ: Prentice-Hall, Inc.; [1971]. 152p. ISBN: 0133891224; LCCN: 76-140267; OCLC: 127955.

L30
LANDESMAN, KAYLA. 1988. Readex Microprint: An Historic Perspective. *Government Publications Review*. 1988 September-October; 15(5): 463-469. ISSN: 0277-9390.

L31
LANDIS, WILLIAM E.; ROYCE, ROBERT. 1995. Recommendations for an Electronic Records Management System: A Case Study of a Small Business. See reference: GILLILAND-SWETLAND, ANNE, ed. 1995. 7-22.

L32
LANDOW, GEORGE P. *Hypertext 2.0: The Convergence of Critical Theory and Technology*. Baltimore, MD: The Johns Hopkins University Press; 1997.

L33
LANDOW, GEORGE P., ed. 1994. *Hyper/Text/Theory*. Baltimore, MD: The Johns Hopkins University Press; 1994. 377p. ISBN: 0801848377 (hbk.); 0801848385 (pbk.).

L34
LANDOW, GEORGE P.; DELANY, PAUL. 1993. Managing the Digital Word: The Text in an Age of Electronic Reproduction. Introduction to *The Digital Word*. See LANDOW, GEORGE P.; DELANY, PAUL. 1993. 1-20.

L35
LANDOW, GEORGE P.; DELANY, PAUL. 1993. *The Digital Word: Text-based Computing in the Humanities*. Cambridge, MA: MIT Press; 1993. 362p. ISBN: 0262125176X. See also DELANY & LANDOW.

L36
LANE, CAROLE A. 1997. *Naked in Cyberspace. How to Find Personal Information Online*. Wilton, CT: Pemberton Press; 1997. 544p. ISBN: 0-910965-17-X.

L37
LANE, MICHAEL, ed. [1970]. *An Introduction to Structuralism*. New York, NY: Basic Books; [1970]. 456p. ISBN: 0465035760; LCCN: 71135624.

L38
LANE, RANDALL. 1996. The Magician. *Forbes Magazine*. 1966 March 11; 157 no. 5: 122-128. ISSN: 0015-6914.

L39
LANG, EWALD; CARSTENSEN, KAI-UWE; SIMMONS, GEOFFREY. 1991. *Modeling Spatial Knowledge on a Linguistic Basis: Theory, Prototype, Integration*. Computer Science series, 481. Berlin, DEU / New York, NY: Springer-Verlag; c1991. 137p. ISBN: 038753718X (pbk.); LCCN: 91006725.

L40
LANGE, CHRISTIAN. 1991. Ritual in Business: Building a Corporate Culture through Symbolic Management. *Industrial Management*. 1991 July-August; 33(4): 21-23. ISSN: 0019-8471.

L41
LANGER, LAWRENCE L. 1991. *Holocaust Testimonies: The Ruins of Memory*. New Haven, CT: Yale University Press; 1991. 216p. ISBN: 0300049668.

L42
LANGLEY, ANN. 1995. Between "Paralysis by Analysis" and "Extinction by Instinct." *Sloan Management Review*. 1995 Spring; 36(3): 63-76. ISSN: 0019-848X.

L43

LANGRIDGE, DEREK W. 1989. *Subject-analysis: Principles and Procedures*. London, UK: Bowker-Saur; 1989. Revision of *Classification and indexing in the Humanities*. London, UK: Butterworths; 1976. 143p. LCCN:76-375295.

L44

LANHAM, RICHARD A. 1993. The Extraordinary Convergence: Democracy, Technology, Theory, and the University Curriculum. In his *The Electronic Word: Democracy, Technology, and the Arts*. Chicago, IL: University of Chicago Press; 1993. 285p.; floppy disk. ISBN: 0226468836 (hbk.); 0226468844 (pbk.).

L45

LANZI, E. 1998. *Introduction to Vocabularies: Enhancing Access to Cultural Heritage Information*. Los Angeles, CA: Getty Information Institute; 1998. 46ff. Available from the Institute.

L46

LARSEN, POUL STEEN. 1999. Bosok and Bytes; Preserving Documents for Posterity. See reference: BATES, M., ed. 1999. Pts. 1: 1020-1027.

L47

LARSON, DANIEL O. 1995. California Climatic Reconstruction. *Journal of Interdisciplinary History*. 1995; 25(2). ISSN: 0022-1953.

L48

LASOTA, ANDRZEJ; MACKAY, MICHAEL C. 1994. *Chaos, Fractals, and Noise: Stochastic Aspects of Dynamics*. New York, NY: Springer-Verlag; c1994. ISBN: 0387940499 (pbk); LCCN: 93010432. Revision of *Probabilistic Properties of Deterministic Systems*, 1985

L49

LASZLOVSKY, JOZSEF. 1991. Social Stratification and Material Culture in 10th-14th century Hungary. In: Kubinyi, Andreas; Laszlovsky, Jozsef, eds. *Altag und materielle Kultur im Mittelalterlichen Ungarn*. In: *Medium Aevum Quotidianum* (Krems, AT). 1991; 22. (Entire issue on title topic). OCLC: 30949256.

L50

LASZLOVSKY, JOZSEF; ROMHANYI, BEATRIX. 1994. La Civilisation matérielle de la Hongrie Médiévale sur Ordinateur (Questions Theoriques, Méthodologiques et Pratiques). See reference: BECK, P., ed. 1994. 47-52.

L51

LATNER, RICHARD. 1988. Witches, History and Microcomputers: A Computer-Assisted Course on the Salem Witchcraft Trials. *The History Teacher*. 1988 February; 21: 173-193. ISSN: 0018-2745.

L52

LATOUR, BRUNO. 1979. *Laboratory Life: The Social Construction of Scientific Facts*. Beverly Hills, CA: Sage Publications; 1979. (Sage Library of Social Research, 80). ISBN: 08003909934 (hbk.); 008039009942 (pbk.).

L53

LATOUR, BRUNO. 1993. *Nous n'avons jamais été modernes*. Trans as: *We Have Never Been Modern*. New York, NY: Harvester Wheatsheaf; 1993. 157p. ISBN: 074501322lX.

L54

LAURINI, ROBERT; THOMPSON, DEREK. 1991. *Fundamentals of Spatial Information Systems*. London, UK: Academic Press; 1991. 680p. (APIC Series, 37). ISBN: 0124383807.

L55

LAURITZEN, ASTRID B.; GLUE, BIRTHE E., eds. 1980. *Danish Data Guide: Excerpts from the DDA Holdings of Machine Readable Standard Study Descriptions of Danish Social Science Data*. Odense, DK: Odense Universitet, Danish Data Archives; 1980. 224p. LCCN: 82204744.

L56

LAVE, CHARLES A.; MARCH, JAMES G. 1975. *An Introduction to Models in the Social Sciences*. Lanham, MD: University Presses of America; 1975. 421p. ISBN: 0819103814; LCCN: 91-40855.

L57

LAW, AVERILL M.; KELTON, W. DAVID. 1982. *Simulation Modeling and Analysis*. New York, NY: McGraw-Hill; 1982. 400p. ISBN: 0070366969.

L58

LAW, JOHN; LODGE, P. 1984. *Science for Social Scientists*. London, UK: Macmillan; 1984. ISBN: 0333351002.

L59

LAW, MARGARET H. 1988. *Guide to Information Resource Dictionary Applications: General Concepts and Strategic Planning*. Washington, D.C.: National Bureau of Standards; 1988 April; NBS Special Publication 500-152.

L60
LAW, MARGARET H. 1989. *Database, Data Dictionary, Interchange, and Use Interface Standards: Description and Status.* Assisted by L. Gallagher and T. Boland. Prepared for NARA by the NIST Information Systems Engineering Division. Gaithersburg, MD: NIST [National Institute of Standards and Technology]; 1989. 30p. See reference: LAW, M.; ROSEN, B. 1989: Attachment B.

L61
LAW, MARGARET H.; ROSEN, BRUCE K. 1989. *Framework and Policy Recommendations for the Exchange and Preservation of Electronic Records.* Prepared by the NIST National Computer Systems Laboratory for NARA. [Gaithersburg, MD]: The Laboratory / Washington, D.C.: National Institute of Standards and Technology; March 1989. 48p.; attachments A-D (ca. 180p). LC call no.: CD973.D3L38; OCLC: 22902656.

L62
LAZINGER, SUSAN; BAR-ILAN, JUDIT; PETIZ, BLUMA C. 1997. Internet Use by Faculty Members in Various Disciplines: A Comparative Case Study. *Journal of the American Society for Information Science.* 1997 January; 48(6): 508-518. ISSN: 0002-8231; CODEN: AISJB6.

L63
LE COADIC, YVES F. 1993/1994. Histoire des sciences et histoire de la science de l'information [History of Science and the History of Information Science]. *Documentaliste* (FR). 1993 July/Oct.; 30 (3-4): 205-209. ISSN: 0012-4508. Incorporated into: *La Science de l'Information* [Information Science]. Paris, FR: Presses Universitaires de France; 1994. 127p. (Que sais-je? series; in French). ISBN: 2-13-046381-9.

L64
LE GOFF, JACQUES. 1973. L'Historien et l'homme quotidien [The Historian and Everyday Man]. In his: *L'Historien entre l'ethnologie et le futurologie* [The Historian between Ethnology and Futurology]. The Hague, NL: Mouton; 1973.

L65
LE GOFF, JACQUES. 1992. *Storia e memoria.* Rendall, Steven; Claman, Elizabeth, trans. *History and Memory.* New York. NY: Columbia University Press; 1992. 265p. (European Perspectives). ISBN: 0231075901; LCCN: 92019887.

L66
LE GOFF, JACQUES; NORA, PIERRE, eds. 1974. *Faire de l'histoire* [The Making of History]. Paris, FR: Gallimard; 1974. 3 vols. ISBN: 2070323757l; LCCN: 74-170552; OCLC: 980781.

L67
LE JAN, REGINE. 1995. *Famille et pouvoir dans le monde Franc (VII-Xe siècle). Essai d'anthropologie sociale* [Family and Power in Frankland, 7-10th centuries. An essay in social anthropology]. Paris, FR: Publications de la Sorbonne; 1995. (Histoire ancienne et médiévale, 33). (In French). ISBN: 02859442685.

L68
LE MAREC, GERARD. 1985. *Les Photos Truquées. Un siècle de propaganda par l'image* [Touched-up Photos: A Century of Propaganda through the Image]. Paris, FR: Editions Atlas; 1985. (In French).

L69
LE ROY LADURIE, EMMANUEL. 1966. *Les Paysans de Languedoc.* Paris, FR: Sevpen; 1966. 2 vols., 1037p. No ISBN; LCCN: 67-107998; OCLC: 244593. Rev. ed., J. Day, trans. *The Peasants of Languedoc.* Urbana, IL: University of Illinois Press; [1974]. 370p. ISBN: 0252004116; LCCN: 74-4286; OCLC: 858725.

L70
LE ROY LADURIE, EMMANUEL. 1973/ 1974/ 1979. *Le Territoire de l'historien.* Paris, FR: Gallimard; 1973. 2 vols. LCCN: 73-173195; OCLC: 9677998. Reynolds, Ben and Sian, trans. *The Territory of the Historian.* Chicago, IL: University of Chicago Press; 1979. 345 p. ISBN: 0226467899; 0226473252 (pbk.); LCCN: 78-31362; 81-449; OCLC: 4549419; 17937367. Selection of 9 from 15 essays republished as *The Mind and the Method of the Historian.* Reynolds, Sian, trans. Chicago, IL: University of Chicago; 1979. Rev. ed., Harvester; 1981. 310p. LCCN: 81-4419.

L71
LEARN, LARRY L. 1990. The Role of Telecommunications in Library Automation: Past, Present, and Future Perspectives. *Library Technology Reports.* 1990 July; 26(4): 503- 516. ISSN: 0024-2586.

L72
LEARY, DAVID. E. 1995. Naming and knowing: Giving forms to things unknown. *Social Research.* 1995 Summer; 62 (2): 267-298. ISSN: 0037-783X.

L73
LEBOVICS, HERMAN. 1994. [Untitled featured review of TERDIMAN (1993) and GILDEA (1994)]. *American Historical Review.* 1994 October; 99(4): 1276-1278. ISSN: 0002-8762.

L74

LEDFORD, GERALD E., Jr.; WENDENHOF, JON R.; STRAHLEY, JAMES T. 1995. Realizing a Corporate Philosophy. *Organizational Dynamics*. 1995 Winter; 23(3): 4-19. ISSN: 0090-2616.

L75

LEE, ALISON. 1992. *Investigations into History Tools for User Support*. Toronto, ONT: University of Toronto; 1992. 242p. (Ph.D. dissertation; *DAI*, 53/12-B: 6395). Available from: University of Toronto Library. ISBN: 0-315-73815-4.

L76

LEE, BENJAMIN; URBAN, GREG, eds. 1989. *Semiotics, Self, and Society*. Berlin, GW; New York, NY: Mouton de Gruyter; 1989. 311p. ISBN: 0899255604.

L77

LEE, BRAD. 1993. *Virtual Communities: Computer-Mediated Communication and Communities*. Bloomington, IN: Indiana University; 1993. (Ph.D. dissertation; *DAI*, 54/04-A: 1134). Available from: University Microfilms, Ann Arbor, MI (Order no. AAD93-23232).

L78

LEE, CARL D.; SMAGORINSKY, PETER, eds. [1999]. *Vygotskian Perspectives on Literacy Research: Constructing Meaning through Collaborative Inquiry*. Cambridge, UK / New York, NY: Cambridge University Press; [1999]. ISBN: 0521630959 (hbk.); 052163878X (pbk.); LCCN: 99012568.

L79

LEE, GEORGES. 1982. Artificial Intelligence, History, and Knowledge Representation. *Computers and the Humanities*. 1982; 16(1): 25-34. ISSN: 0010-4817.

L80

LEE, JAY. 1993. Geographic Information Systems: An Introduction. *Art References Services Quarterly*. 1993: 1(3): 69-79. ISSN: 1050-3548.

L81

LEE, JOHN. 1995. The Man Who Mistook his Hat: Stephen Greenblatt and Anecdote. *Essays in Criticism*. 1995 October; 45 (4): 285-301. ISSN: 0014-0856.

L82

LEE, JOHN A.N. 1995. *Computer Pioneers*. Los Alamitos, CA: IEEE Computer Society; 1995. 782p. ISBN: 0-8186-6357-X.

L83

LEE, JOHN A. N. 1996. "Those Who Forget the Lessons of History are Doomed to Repeat It" or Why I Study the History of Computing. *IEEE Annals of the History of Computing*. 1996 Summer; 18 (2): 54-62. ISSN: 1058-6180. See reference: WILLIAMS, MICHAEL, ed. 1996: 54-62.

L84

LEE, SUL H., ed. 1993. *The Role and Future of Special Collections in Research Libraries: British and American Perspectives*. Binghamton, NY: Haworth Press; 1993. 98p. ISBN: 1560244798; LCCN: 93-30716.

L85

LEE, YOON-HEE. 1990. *Handling Ill-formed Natural Language Input for an Intelligent Tutoring System*. Illinois Institute of Technology. 110p. (Ph.D. dissertation; *DAI*, vol. 51/09-B: 4449). Available from: University Microfilms, Ann Arbor, MI (Order no. AAD91-05328).

L86

LEEBAERT, DEREK, ed. 1995. *The Future of Software*. Cambridge, MA: MIT Press; 1995. 320p. ISBN: 0-262-62109-6.

L87

LEENHARDT, MARIE. 1969. *Code pour le classement et l'étude des poteries médiévales: nord et nord-ouest de l'Europe* [Classification Code for the Study of Medieval Pottery from the North and Northwest of Europe]. Caen, FR: Centre de Recherches Archeologiques Médiévales; 1969. 94p. OCLC: 4324411.

L88

LEESE, MORVEN N. 1983. Statistical Methodology in Numismatic Studies. *Journal of Archeological Science*. 1983; 10: 29-33. ISSN: 0305-4403.

L89

LEFF, GORDON. [1969]. *History and Social Theory*. University, AL: University of Alabama Press; 1969. 240p. ISBN: 0817366059; LCCN: 78076586.

L90
LEFKOWITZ, MARY R.. 1992a/1997. *Not Out of Africa: How Afrocentrism became an Excuse to Teach Myth as History.* New York, NY: Basic Books; 1992. 222p. New ed., 1997. (New Republic Book). 297p. ISBN: 046509838X (pbk.); LCCN: 97183099.

L91
LEFKOWITZ, MARY R. 1992b. Afrocentrism Poses a Threat to the Rationalist Tradition. *Chronicle of Higher Education.*1992 May 6; 38 (35): A52. ISSN: 00095982.

L92
LEGARE, JACQUES. 1981. Le programme de recherche en démographique historique de l'Université de Montréal: fondements, méthodes, moyens et resultats [The Research Program in Demographic History at the University of Montréal: Foundations, Methods, Works, and Results]. *Études Canadiennes / Canadian Studies* (CAN). 1981 June; 10; 149-182. ISSN: 0225-3054.

L93
LEITNER, HENRY H. 1982. *A Knowledge Representation Formalism for Human-oriented Computer Systems.* Cambridge, MA: Harvard University; 1982. 358 p. (Ph.D. dissertation. *DAI*, vol. 43/02-B, p. 471). Available form University Microfilms, Ann Arbor, MI (Order no. AAD82-16195).

L94
LEMANN, NICHOLAS. 1995. History Solo: Non-Academic Historians. *American Historical Review.* 1995 June; 100 (3): 788-799. ISSN: 0002-8762.

L95
LENAT, DOUGLAS. B.; CUHA, R. V. 1990. *Building Large Knowledge-Based Systems: Representation and Inference in the CYC Project.* Reading, MA: Addison-Wesley; 1990. 372p. ISBN: 0201517523.

L96
LENTRICCHIA, FRANK; MCLAUGHLIN, THOMAS, eds. 1990. *Critical Terms for Literary Study.* Chicago, IL: University of Chicago Press; 1990. 2nd ed., 1995. 486p. ISBN: 0226472043; LCCN: 94-43640.

L97
LEONARD-BARTON, DOROTHY. 1988. Implementation as Mutual Adaption of Technology and Organization. *Research Policy* (NL). 1988;17: 251-65. ISSN: 0048- 7333.

L98
LEROUX, M.; SALOME, J.; BADARD, J. 1991. Recognition of Cursive Script Words in a Small Lexicon. In: *First International Conference on Document Analysis and Recognition.* Actes de la conference, September 30-October 2, 1991, Sant-Malo, France. Sponsored by AFCET, IRISA-INRIA, and Telecom. Paris, FR: Ecole Nationale Superieure des Telecommunications; [1991]; 2: 774-782. 2 vols. ISBN: 29036771002; OCLC: 30688707.

L99
LESK, MICHAEL E. 1969. Word-word Association in Document Retrieval Systems. *American Documentation.* 1969; 20 (1): 27-38. ISSN: 0096-946X; OCLC: 1479779.

L100
LESK, MICHAEL E. 1992. *Preservation of New Technology: A Report of the Technology Assessment Advisory Committee to the Commission on Preservation and Access.* Washington, DC: National Archives and Records Administration (NARA), Commission on Preservation and Access; October 1992. 19p. OCLC: 27001231. Available from NARA, Washington, D.C.

L101
LESK, MICHAEL E. 1994. Which Way to the Future? The Control of Scholarly Publication. In: Nabil, R. A.; Bharat, K. B.; Yelana, Y., eds. *Lecture Notes in Computer Science.* New York, NY: Springer; 1994. 33-49.

L102
LESK, MICHAEL E. 1997. *Practical Digital Libraries: Books, Bytes, and Bucks.* San Francisco, CA: Morgan Kaufmann, Pub.; 1997. ISBN: 1558604596 (pbk.).

L103
LESPERANCE, YVES. 1991. *A Formal Theory of Indexical Knowledge and Action.* Toronto, Ontario CAN: University of Toronto; 1991. 189p. (Ph.D. dissertation; *DAI*, vol. 53/02-B: 936). Available from: University Microfilms, Ann Arbor, MI (Order no. AADNN-65931).

L104
LEUNG, CLEMENT H. C.; SO, W. W. W. 1997. Characteristics and Architectural Components of Visual Information Systems. See reference: LEUNG, CLEMENT H. C., ed. 1997.

L105
LEUNG, CLEMENT H. C., ed. 1997. *Visual Information Systems*. First International Conference on Visual Information Systems, February 1996. Berlin, DEU / New York, NY: Springer Verlag; 1997. 274p. (Lecture notes in Computer Science, 1306). ISSN: 0302-9743. ISBN: 3540636366.

L106
LEVANDOVSKY, MIKHAIL. 1996 [199-]. Visualisation of Nonlinear Dynamic Models: The Applications of Chaos Theory in Historical Research. See reference: BORODKIN, L., ed. 1996: English abstract of presentation, 19; paper in Russian [199- forthcoming].

L107
LEVERMANN, WOLFGANG; GROTUM, THOMAS; PARCER, JAN. 1995. Preservation and Improved Accessibility of the Archives in the Memorial Oswiecim/Brzezinka (Auschwitz/Birkenau). See reference: JARTIZ, G. *ET AL.*, eds. 1995. 141-149.

L108
LEVI-STRAUSS, CLAUDE. 1958/1963. *Anthropologie structurale*. Rev. ed.[from 1953 ed.]. Paris, FR: Plon; 1958. 435p. Laton, M. trans. *Structural Anthropology*. New York, NY: Anchor Books; 1963; reprint 1967. 413p. Revised ed., New York, NY: Doubleday; 1969. 2 vols. ISBN: 0465082300 (set)

L109
LEVI-STRAUSS, CLAUDE. 1966. *La Pensée Savauge*. Trans. as: *The Savage Mind*. Chicago, IL: Univeristy of Chicago Press; 1966. 290p. LCCN: 66-066893.

L110
LEVI-STRAUSS, CLAUDE. 1996. Race, History, and Culture. *UNESCO Courier*. 1996 March; sn; 30-34. ISSN: 0041-5278.

L111
LEVINE, HOWARD; RHEINGOLD, HOWARD. 1987. *The Cognitive Connection: Thought and Language in Man and Machine*. New York, NY: Prentice Hall Press; 1987. 276p. ISBN: 0131396196.

L112
LEVINE, LAWRENCE W. 1988. *Highbrow/Lowbrow: The Emergence of Cultural Hierarchy in America*. Cambridge, MA: Harvard University Press; 1988. 293p. ISBN: 0674390760 (pbk.).

L113
LEVINE, LAWRENCE W. 1993. Clio, Canons, and Culture. *Journal of American History*. 1993; 80: 849-867. ISSN: 0021-8723.

L114
LEVINE, M. M. 1977. The Informative Act and its Aftermath: Toward a Predictive Science of Information. *Journal of the American Society for Information Science*. 1977: 28: 101-106. ISSN: 0002-8231.

L115
LEVINE, PHILLIPA. 1986. *The Amateur and the Professional: Antiquarians, Historians and Archaeologists in Victorian England, 1838-1886*. Cambridge, UK: Cambridge University Press; 1986.

L116
LEVITT, J. H.; LABARRE, C. E. 1975. Building a Data File from Historical Archives. *Computers and the Humanities*. 1975; 9: 77-82. ISSN: 0010-4817.

L117
LEVSTIK, LINDA S. 1995. Narrative Constructions: Cultural Frames for History. *The Social Studies*. 1995 May-June; 86(3): 113-117. ISSN: 0037-7996.

L118
LEVY, DAVID M. 1988. *Topics in Document Research*. Palo Alto, CA: Xerox Corp., System Sciences Laboratory; 1988. (Report 8.31.1039).

L119
LEVY, DAVID M. 1994. Fixed or Fluid? Document Stability and New Media. In: *Proceedings of the European Conference on Hypertext Technology, 1994*. New York, NY: Assn. for Computing Machinery [ACM]; 1994. 24-31.

L120
LEWIN, ARIE Y.; STEPHENS, CARROLL U. 1994. CEO Attitudes as Determinants of Organizational Design: An Integrated Model. *Organizational Studies*. 1994; 15 (2): 183- 212. ISSN: 0170-8406.

L121
LEWIN, ROGER. 1992. *Complexity: Life at the Edge of Chaos*. New York, NY: Macmillan Pub. Co.; c1992. 208p. ISBN: 0025704850; ICCN: 92030314.

L122
LEWIS, DIANNE S. 1994. Organizational Change: Relationship between Reactions, Behavior, and Organizational Performance. *Journal of Organizational Change Management.* 1994; 7 (5): 41-55. ISSN: 0953-4814.

L123
LEWIS, HAROLD W. 1997. *Why Flip a Coin? The Art and Science of Good Decisions.* New York, NY: J. Wiley & Sons; 1997. 224p. ISBN: 0471165972; LCCN: 96029444.

L124
LEWIS, PETER H. 1989. Wrinkles in Time. A Hard Look and Software. Educational Life column. *New York Times.* 1989 November 5. ISSN: 0362-4331.

L125
LEYDEN, PETER. [1996]. On the Second Renaissance. In: *On the Edge of the Digital Age* (electronic file). Accessible at http://www.startribune.com/stonline/html/digage.main4.htm. (Interviews and bibliorgaphy).

L126
LI, XIA; CRANE, NANCY B. 1993. *Electronic Style: A Guide to Citing Electronic Information.* Westport, CT: Meckler; 1993. 65p. ISBN: 08836909X.

L127
LI, XIA; CRANE, NANCY B. 1996/1997. *Electronic Style: A Handbook to Citing Electronic Information.* Medford, NJ: Information Today, Inc.; 1996. 250p. ISBN: 1-57387-027-7. Cf., their *Electronic Sources: APA Style of Citation* (1996, July 27) and *MLA Style of Citation* (1997, Oct. 21). Available respectively http://www.uvm.edu/~sli/reference/apa.html for the APA style; and the MLA equivalent at the same address with extension mla.html.

L128
LIBERMAN, MICHAEL; SCHABES, Y., eds. 1993. *Statistical Methods in Natural Language Processing.* Sixth Conference of the European Chapter of the Association for Computational Linguistics, EACL '93 Tutorial. Utrecht, NL: EACL; 1993.

L129
LIBRARY AND INFORMATION SCIENCE ABSTRACTS (LISA). 1969-. Moore, N. L., ed. London, UK: Library Association and ASLIB. LISA Plus (CD-ROM). Available from K. G. Saur, no. DL1110. (Includes backfiles to 1989 plus abstracts from *Current Research in Library and Information Science,* 1981-). ISSN: 0024-2179.

L130
LIBRARY OF CONGRESS. 1977-1996/1997-. *Name Authorities* [electronic file]. Washington, D.C.: LC; 1977-1996. 1997-. 3,900,000 retrospective records; updated by ca. 350,000 records annually.

L131
LIBRARY OF CONGRESS. 1987-1990. *Classification Schedules. D: History.* Washington, D.C.: LC; 1987-1990. ISBN: 0-8444-06383-X; 0-8444-0579-5; 08444-0685-6; 0-8444-0574-4; 0-8444-0649-X.

L132
LIBRARY OF CONGRESS. 1989/1997-. *National Union Catalog of Manuscript Collections (NUCMC) and LC Manuscripts* [electronic file]. Washington, D.C.: LC; 1989/1997-. 18,000 records, 1989-1996; 12,000 records plus 10,000 LC Mss. Records.

L133
LIBRARY OF CONGRESS. 1991. *Descriptive Cataloging of Rare Books.* 2nd ed. Washington, D.C.: LC; 1991. ISBN: 0-8444-0690-2.

L134
LIBRARY OF CONGRESS. 1991-. *American Memory.* Fleischhauer, Carl, coordinator. Washington, D.C.: Library of Congress American Memory Program; 1991-. Available on the Library of Congress homepage.

L135
LIBRARY OF CONGRESS. 1994-. *National Digital Library.* Washington, D.C.: National Digital Library; 1994-. For further information, contact L.C. National Digital Library, Washington, D.C. 20540 (Phone 202-707-3300).

L136
LIBRARY OF CONGRESS. 1995a. 1994 in Review. In: *Library of Congress Information Bulletin.* 1995 January 9; 54(1): 23p. (Entire issue on title topic.) ISSN: 0041-7904.

L137
LIBRARY OF CONGRESS. 1995b. *America Preserved: A Checklist of Historic Buildings, Structures, and Sites.* Washington, D.C.: LC; 1995. 1184p. 30,000 entries through 1994 from the Historic American Buildings Survey and Historical American Engineering Record.

L138
LIBRARY OF CONGRESS. 1995c. *Classification Schedules. E-F: History, America*. Washington, D.C.: LC; 1995.
ISBN: 0-8444-0896-4.

L139
LIBRARY OF CONGRESS. 1996a. *Classification Schedules. C: Auxiliary Sciences of History*. Washington, D.C.:
LC; 1996. ISBN: 0-8444-0914-6.

L140
LIBRARY OF CONGRESS. 1996b. *Thesaurus for Graphic Materials*. TGM I: *Subject Terms*. TGM II: *Genre and
Physical Characteristic Terms*. Washington, D.C.: Library of Congress Cataloging Distribution Service; 1996.
556p. ISBN: 0-8444-08889-1.

L141
LICHTMAN, ALLAN J.; FRENCH, VALERIE. 1978. *Historians and the Living Past: The Theory and Practice of
Historical Study*. Arlington Heights, IL: AHM Pub. Corp.; c19978. 267p. ISBN: 0882957732; LCCN: 77086035.
Reprint, 1986. ISBN: 088295772 (pbk.); LCCN: 86019796.

L142
LIEBSCHER, P.; MARCHIONINI, G. 1988. Browse and Analytical Search Strategies in a Full-text CD-ROM
Encyclopedia. *School Library Media Quarterly*. 1988; 16: 223-233. ISSN: 0278-4823.

L143
LIENTZ, BENNET P.; REA, KATHRYN P. 1995. *Project Management for the 21st Century*. San Diego, CA:
Academic Press; 1995 reprint. 308p. ISBN: 0-12-449965-1.

L144
LIEPOLT, W. 1993. A Civil War CD at the Dalton School. *CD-ROM*. October 1993; 8(9): 60-64. ISSN: 0893-9934.

L145
LIEVESLEY, DENISE. 1993. Increasing the Value of Data. See reference: ROSS, S.; HIGGS, E., eds. 1993. 205-217.

L146
LIGHT, RICHARD B.; ROBERTS, D. ANDREW; STEWART, JENNIFER D. 1986. *Museum Documentation Systems:
Developments and Applications*. London, UK: Butterworths & Co., LTD.; 1986. 332p. ISBN: 0-408-10815-0.

L147
LILLEY, DOROTHY B.; TRICE, RONALD. 1989. *A History of Information Science, 1945-1985*. Library and Information
Science [series]. San Diego, CA: Academic Press; 1989. 181p. ISBN: 0-12-450060-9.

L148
LIMERICK, PATRICIA. 1992. Information Overload is a Prime Factor in our Culture Wars. *The Chronicle of Higher
Education*. 1992 July 29; 38 (47): A32. ISSN: 00095982.

L149
LIN, HERBERT. 1997. Emerging Legal and Public Policy Issues in Developing the National Information Infrastructure.
Plenary session paper at ASIS, Mid-Year Conference, Scottsdale, AZ, 1997.

L150
LIN, T. Y.; CERCONE, NICK, eds. 1997. *Rough Sets and Data Mining: Analysis for Imprecise Data*. Boston, MA:
Kluwer Academic; 1997. 436p. ISBN: 0792398076.

L151
LIN, XIA. 1993. *Self-organizing Semantic Maps as Graphical Interfaces for Information Retrieval*. College Park, MD:
University of Maryland CLIS; 1993. (Doctoral dissertation). Available form University Microfilms, Ann Arbor, MI.

L152
LIN, XIA. 1997. Map Displays for Information Retrieval. *Journal of the American Society for Information Science*.
1997; 48 (1): 40-54. ISSN: 0002-8231.

L153
LIN, XIA; MARCHIONINI, GARY; SOERGEL, DAGOBERT. 1993. Category-based and Association-based Map
Displays by Human Subjects. In: *Proceedings of the 4th SIG/CR Classification Research Workshop*. Silver Springs,
MD: ASIS; 1993. 147-164.

L154
LINCOLN, YVONNA S.; GUBA, EGON G. 1985. *Naturalistic Inquiry*. Beverly Hills, CA: Sage Pub.; 1985. 416p. ISBN:
0803924313.

L155
LIND, GUNNER. 1995. Historical Concepts of Space and Computer-based Maps. See reference: BOONSTRA, O., ed.
1995. 238-244.

L156
LIND, GUNNER. 1996 [199-]. Text Models for Source Edition: Requirements and Availability. See reference: BOROD-KIN, L., ed. 1996: English abstract of presentation, 30-31; paper in Russian [199- forthcoming].

L157
LINDBLAD, J. THOMAS. 1990. Computer Applications in Expansion History. *International Journal of Maritime History.* 1990; 2(1): 207-214. ISSN: 0843-8714.

L158
LINDBLOM, CHARLES E. 1997. Political Science in the 1940s and 1950s. *Daedalus.* 1997 Winter; 126(1): 225-242. ISSN: 0011-5266.

L159
LINDERMEIER, R.; STEIN, C. 1991. User Requirement Analysis in the Museum and Art History Field for Advanced Computer System Design. *Computers and the History of Art.* 1991; 1. pt. 2: 39-53. ISBN: 3-7186-5185-8.

L160
LINDSEY, DUNCAN; LINDSEY, THOMAS. 1978. The Outlook of Journal Editors and Referees on the Normative Criteria of Scientific Craftsmanship. *Quality and Quantity.* 1978; 12: 45-62. ISSN: 0033-5177.

L161
LINDSEY, LYDIA. 1992. *The Role of Immigration Policy, Race, Class, and Gender in Shaping the Status of Jamaican Immigrant Women in Birmingham, England.* Chapel Hill, NC: University of North Carolina; 1992. 718p. (Ph.D. dissertation; *DAI,* 53/09- A: 3339). Available from: University Microfilms, Ann Arbor, MI (Order no. AAD92-34988).

L162
LINGRAS, P. J. 1996. Belief and Probability Based Database Mining. *Proceedings of the Ninth Florida Artificial Intelligence Symposium (FLAIRS'96).* Key West, FL, May 20-22. St. Petersburg, FL: Eckerd College Press; 1996. 316-320.

L163
LINHART, H.; ZUCCHINI, W. 1986. *Model Selection.* Chichester, UK: John Wiley; 1986. 301p. ISBN: 471837229.

L164
LINK, JURGEN. 1978. *Die Struktur des Symbols in der Sprache des Journalismus: zum Verhaltnis literartur und pragmatic Symbole* [The Structure of Symbols in the Language of Journalism: toward a Relation between Literature and Pragmatic Symbolism]. Munich, DEU: Fink; 1978. 268p.(In German). ISBN: 3770515013.

L165
LINK, JURGEN; HORISCH, JOCHEN; POTT, HANS-GEORG. 1983. *Elementaire Literatur und Generative Diskursanalyse* [Elementary Literary and Generative Discourse Analysis]. Munich, DEU: F. Wink; 1983. 187p. (In German). ISBN: 3770521420.

L166
LINK, JURGEN; WULFING, WULF, eds. 1991. *Nationale Mythen und Symbole in der zweiten Halfte des Jahrhunderts: Sturkurten und Funktionen von Konzepten nationaler Identität* [National Myths and Symbols in the second half of the Century: Endurance and Function in the Concept of National Identity]. Stuttgart, DEU: Klett-Cotta; 1991. 311p. (Sprache und Geschichte, Band 16).

L167
LINSTEAD, STEPHEN A.; GRAFTON-SMALL, ROBERT. 1990. Theory as Artifact; Artifact as Theory. See reference: GAGLIARDI, P., ed. 1990b. 387-412.

L168
LINSTEAD, STEPHEN A.; GRAFTON-SMALL, ROBERT. 1992. On Reading Organizational Culture. *Organizational Studies.* 1992; 13 (3): 331-355. ISSN: 1070-8406.

L169
LINSTROM, R. W.; WOODLEY, M. S. 1999. Irrestible Metadata: Guidelines for Usage of the Dublin Core Metadata in Online Exhibitions. *Spectra: Journal of the Museum Computer Network.* 1999 Spring; 26: 19-31.

L170
LIPSITZ, GEORGE. 1990. *Time Passages: Collective Memory and American Popular Culture.* Minneapolis, MN: University of Minnesota Press; 1990. 306p. (American Culture series). ISBN: 0816618054 (hbk.); 0816618062 (pbk.); LCCN: 890055209.

L171
LIPSTADT, DEBORAH E. 1993/1994. *Denying the Holocaust: The Growing Assault on Truth and Memory.* New York, NY: Free Press; 1993. New ed., New York, NY: Plime; c1993. 278p. ISBN: 0452272742; LCCN: 93045586.

L172
LIRA, ELIZABETH. 1997. Remembering: Passing back through the Heart. See reference: PENNEBAKER, J. W., *ET AL.*, eds. 1997.

L173
LITTLE, G. D. 1986. The Ambivalent Apostrophe. *English Today*. 1986; 8: 15-17. ISSN: 0266-0784.

L174
LIU, M. 1993. The Complexities of Citation Practice: A Review of Citation Studies. *Journal of Documentation* (UK). 1993; 49: 370-408. ISSN: 0022-0418.

L175
LIVELTON, TREVOR. 1996. *Archival Theory, Records, and the Public*. Society of American Archivists series. Lanham, MD: Scarecrow Press; 1996. 192p. ISBN: 0-8108-3051-5.

L176
LIVINGSTON, GLEN; RADEN, NEIL. 1995. *Database Design for Data Warehousing*. Bethesda, MD: Data Warehousing Institute; 1995. 80p.

L177
LLOYD, CHISTOPHER. 1986. *Explanation in Social History*. New York, NY: B. Blackwell; 1986. ISBN: 0631131132; LCCN: 85-13359; OCLC: 12189279.

L178
LLOYD, LES, ed. 1997. *Technology and Teaching*. Medford, NJ: Information Today, Inc.; 1997. 366 p. ISBN: 1-57387-014-5.

L179
LLOYD, LES, ed. [199- forthcoming]. *Teaching with Technology: Rethinking Tradition*. Medford, NJ: Information Today, Inc.; [199- forthcoming]. ISBN: 57387-068-4.

L180
LOCK, GARY R.; STANCIC, ZORAN. 1995. *Archeology and Geographic Information Systems: A European Perspective*. London, UK: Taylor & Francis; 1995. 392p. ISBN: 074840208X.

L181
LOCK, GARY R.; WILCOCK, JOHN. 1987. *Computer Archeology*. Shire Archeology series. Alesbury, UK: Shire Publications, Ltd.; 1987. 64p. ISBN: 0-85263-877-9.

L182
LOCKYEAR, K.; RAHTZ, S. P. Q., eds. 1991. *Computer Applications and Quantitative Methods in Archaeology*. Oxford, UK: Oxford University; 1991. (British Archaeological Reports. International series, 565).

L183
LODOLINI, ELIO. 1995. *Archivistica, Principi, e Problemi* [Archival Science, Principles and Problems]. 7th ed. Milano, IT: Franco Angeli; 1995. 438 p. (Series: Manuali professionali Franco Angeli, 59). ISBN: 8820433788.

L184
LOEFFEN, ARJAM. 1994. Text Databases: A Survey of Text Models and Systems. *SIGMOD Record*. 1994 March; 23(1): 97-106.

L185
LOEVE, MICHAEL. 1963. *Probability Theory*. 2nd ed., 1960. 3rd ed. Princeton, NJ: Van Nostrand; 1963. 685p.

L186
LOGAN, A.-M. 1991. Building a Computerized Index of British Art. From Mainframe to PC/AT to PS/2 to CD-ROM, CD-I, and Image Interface in the Near Future. In: Turk, C., ed. *Humanities Research Using Computers*. London, UK / New York, NY: Chapman & Hall; 1991; 95-114. ISBN: 0-412-37830-2; 0-442-31350-0.

L187
LOGAN, ELISABETH; POLLARD, MARVIN. 1997a. Evolving Concept of the Document. See reference: LOGAN, E.; POLLARD, M., eds. 1997b. 581-582.

L188
LOGAN, ELISABETH; POLLARD, MARVIN, eds. 1997b. Structured Information/Standards for Document Architectures. In: *Journal of the American Society for Information Science*. 1997 July; 48(7): 581-661. (Entire issue of title topic). ISSN: 0002-8231; CODEN: AISJB6.

L189
LOGEL, YVES. 1987. Les Ordinateurs Sovietiques: Histoire obligée de trois décennies [Soviet Computers: History over Three Decades]. *Revue d'Études Comparatives Est-Ouest*. 1987; 18(4): 53-75. ISSN: 0338-0599.

L190
LOHSE, GERALD; WALKER, NEFF. 1993. Classifying Graphical Knowledge. See reference: KENT, A., ed., 1993. 53. 38-82.

L191
LOKKE, CARL. 1968. Archives and the French Revolution. *American Archivist.* 1968 January; 31: 23-31. ISSN: 0360-9081.

L192
LONDON, HERBERT. 1997. National Standards are Judged Again. *Society.* 1997 Jan.-Feb.; 34(2): 27-30. ISSN: 0325-6472.

L193
LONDON, HERBERT; ROGERS, FREDERICK A. 1989. *Social Science Theory: Structure and Application.* New Brunswick, NJ: Transaction Publishers; 1989. 361p. ISBN: 0887383348; LCCN: 88-29179.

L194
LONG, S. J.; ALLISON, P. D.; MCGINNIS, R. 1979. Entrance into the Academic Career. *American Sociological Review.* 1979; 44: 816-830. ISSN: 0004-1224.

L195
LONGLEY, DENNIS. 1982/1989. *Dictionary of Information Technology.* New York, NY: John Wiley; 1982. 379p. ISBN: 0471895741. 2nd ed., 1985. 3rd ed. *Macmillan Dictionary of Information technology.* London, UK: Macmillan; 1989. 566p. ISBN: 0333449711 (hbk.); 0333460502 (pbk.).

L196
LOOMES, G.; SUGDEN, R. 1982. Regret Theory: An Alternative Theory of Rationale Choice under Uncertainty. *Economic Journal* [UK]. 1982; 92: 805-824. ISSN: 0013-1033.

L197
LOPEZ YEPES, JOSÉ. 1995. *La Documentación como Disciplina. Teoría e Historia* [Documentation as a Discipline: Theory and History]. Pamplona, ES: EUNSA (Ediciones de la Universidad de Navarra); 1995. (In Spanish). 337p. ISBN: 8431313285; LCCN: 95-158762.

L198
LOPEZ YEPES, JOSÉ; MARTINEZ MONTALVO, ESPERANZA. 1994. Prorgama y Metodologia Docente para la Disciplina: Teoria e Historia de la Documentacion [Programmatic and Instruction Methodology for the Discipline: Theory and History of Documentation]. *Revista General de Informacion y Documentacion.* 1994; 4(1): 9-42. (In Spanish).

L199
LOPEZ YEPES, JOSÉ; ROS GARCIA, JUAN. 1993. *Que es Documentación? Teoría e Historia del Concepto en España* [What is Documentation? The Theory and History of the Concept in Spain]. Madrid, ES: Sintesis; 1993. (In Spanish). Expansion from: *Teoria de la documentacion* [Theory of Documentation]. Pamplona, ES: Universdiad de Navarra; 1978. ISBN: 843130541X.

L200
LOPEZ YEPES, JOSÉ; ROS GARCIA, J. [1994]. *Politicas de Información y Documentación* [The Politics of Information and Documentation]. Madrid, ES: Sintesis; [1994]. 191p. (In Spanish). ISBN: 8477382239; LCCN: 95-228442.

L201
LORENZ, CHRIS. 1994. Historical Knowledge and Historical Reality: A Plea for "Internal Realism." *History and Theory.* 1994 October; 33(3): 297-328. ISSN: 0018-2656.

L202
LORR, MAURICE. 1983. *Cluster Analysis for Social Scientists.* San Francisco, CA: Jossey-Bass; 1983. 233p. ISBN: 0875895662.

L203
LORWIN, VAL R.; PRICE, JACOB M., eds. 1972. *The Dimensions of the Past: Materials, Problems, and Opportunities for Quantitative Work in History.* Essays presented to the American Historical Association's Committee on Quantitative Data. New Haven, CT: Yale University Press; 1972. 568p. ISBN: 6855653; LCCN: 78-151587; OCLC: 533397.

L204
LOSEE, ROBERT M. 1990. *The Science of Information: Measurement and Applications.* New York, NY: Academic Press; 1990. 293p. ISBN: 0124557716; LCCN: 90-227.

L205
LOSEE, ROBERT M. 1995. The Development and Migration of Concepts from Donor to Borrower Disciplines: Sublanguage Term Use in Hard & Soft Sciences. In: KOENIG, M. E. D.; BOOKSTEIN, A., eds. *Proceedings of the Fifth International Conference on Scientometrics and Informetrics.* 1995: 265-274.

L206
LOSEE, ROBERT M. 1997. A Discipline Independent Definition of Information. *Journal of the American Society for Information Science.* 1997 March; 48(3): 254-269. ISSN: 0002-8231.

L207
LOSEE, ROBERT M.; HAAS, S. W. 1995. Sublanguage Terms: Dictionaries, Usage, and Automatic Classification. *Journal of the American Society for Information Science*. 1995; 46: 519-529. ISSN: 0002-8231.

L208
LOTKA, A. J. 1926. The Frequency Distribution of Scientific Productivity. *Journal of the Washington Academy of Sciences*. 1926; 16: 317-323.

L209
LOUCH, A. R. [1967]. *Explanation and Human Action*. Oxford, UK: Blackwell; [1967]. 243p. LCCN: 67077360.

L210
LOUCH, A. R. 1969. History as Narrative. *History and Theory*. 1969: 8(1): 54-70. ISSN: 0018-2656.

L211
LOUGUEE, CAROLYN C. 1988. "The Would-Be Gentleman": A Historical Simulation of the France of Louis XIV. *History Microcomputer Review*. 1988 Spring; 4: 7-14. ISSN: 0887-1078.

L212
LOWENTHAL, DAVID. 1994a. Distorted Mirrors. *History Today* (UK). 1994 February; 44(2): 8-12. ISSN: 0018-2753. Available also in: IAC *General Periodicals ASAP*, no. 72F0267.

L213
LOWENTHAL, DAVID. 1994b. *The Past is a Foreign Country*. Cambridge, UK: Cambridge University Press; 1994. 489p. ISBN: 0521224152 (hb.); 052129480 (pbk.).

L214
LOYE, DAVID; EISLER, RIANE. 1987. Chaos and Transformation: Implications of Non-equilibrium Theory for Social Science and Society. *Behavioral Science*. 1987; 32: 53-65. ISSN: 0005-7940.

L215
LU, TAIHONG. 1990. Four Milestones in the Development of Information Science. *Journal of the China Society for Scientific and Technical Information* (CH). 1990 October; 9(5); 394-400. (In Chinese; English abstract). ISSN: 1000-0135.

L216
LU, TAIHONG. 1991. The Evolution and Trends of MIS. *Information Science* (CH). 1991; 12(4): 53-60. (In Chinese). ISSN: 1000-8489.

L217
LUBAR, STEVEN. 1993. *Infoculture: The Smithsonian Book of Information Age Inventions*. Boston, MA: Houghton Mifflin; 1993. 408p. ISBN: 0-395-57072-5.

L218
LUCAS, R. 1998. Digital Imaging: How Libraries, Museums, and Other Image Banks are Managing a Digital World. *Syllabus*. 1998; 11: 39-46.

L219
LUHN, H. P. 1957. A Statistical Approach to Mechanized Encoding and Searching of Literary Information. *IBM Journal of Research and Development*. 1957; 1: 309-317. ISSN: 0018-8646.

L220
LUKACS, JOHN. 1994. Revising the Twentieth Century. *American Heritage*. 1994 September; 45(5): 83-89. ISSN: 0002-8738. Available in: IAC, *General Periodicals* ASAP, no. 75B1738.

L221
LUNDGREEN, PETER. 1976. Quantifizierung in der Sozialgeschichte der Bildung [Quantification in the Social History of Education]. *Vierteljahrschrift für Sozial- und Wirtschafts Geschichte*. 1976; 63(4): 433-53. ISSN: 0042-5699.

L222
LUNIN, LOIS F. 1987. Electronic Image Information. In: Williams, M., ed. *Annual Review of Information Science and Technology*. Amsterdam, NL: Elsevier; 1987; 24: 179-224. ISBN: 1-57387-019-6; ISSN: 0066-4200; CODEN: ARISBC; LC no. 66-25096

L223
LUNIN, LOIS F. 1992. Image Overview '92. In: *Proceedings of the Thirteenth National Online Meeting*. New York, NY, May 5-7, 1992 (pp. 195-202). Medford, NJ: Learned Information, Inc.; 1992. ISBN: 0938734636; OCLC: 19920616.

L224
LUNIN, LOIS F. 1994. Analyzing Art Objects for an Image Database. See reference: FIDEL, R., *ET AL*., eds., 1994. 57-72.

L225
LUPPRIAN, KARL-ERNST. 1995. Developing Computer-based Finding Aids for Modern Archival Records: A Project of the Bavarian State Archives Administration. See reference: JARITZ, G. *ET AL.*, eds. 1995. 367-375.

L226
LUSTICK, IAN S. 1996. History, Historiography, and Political Science: Multiple Historical Records and the Problem of Selection Bias. *American Political Science Review*. 1996 September; 90(3): 605-619. ISSN: 000-0018.

L227
LYDECKER, KENT. 1994. Impact and Implications of Multimedia. In: Lees, Diane, ed. *Museums and Interactive Multimedia*. Proceedings of an International Conference held in Cambridge, 20-24 September 1993 (6th International Conference of the MDA and 2nd International Conference on Hypermedia and Interactivity in Museums [ICHIM'93]). Cambridge, UK: University of Cambridge Press / Pittsburgh, PA: Archives & Museum Informatics; 1994. 290-294. ISBN: 090596389X.

L228
LYDESDORFF, LOET. 1989. Words and Co-Words as Indicators of Intellectual Organization. *Research Policy* (NE). 1989; 18: 209-223. ISSN: 0048-7333.

L229
LYDESDORFF, LOET. 1992. Knowledge Representation, Bayesian Inferences, and Empirical Science Studies. *Social Science Information*. 1992; 31: 213-237. ISSN: 0539-0184.

L230
LYDESDORFF, LOET. 1995. *The Challenges of Scientometrics: The Development, Measurement, and Self-Organization of Scientific Communications*. Leiden, NL: Leiden University DSWO Press; 1995. 231p. ISBN: 9066951125.

L231
LYNCH, CLIFFORD A. 1995. The TULIP Project: Context, History, and Perspective. *Library Hi-Tech*. 1995; 13(4): 8-24. ISSN: 0737-8831.

L232
LYNCH, CLIFFORD A. 1997. The Uncertain Future for Digital Visual Collections in the University. *Archives and Museum Informatics*. 1997; 11(1): 5-13. ISSN: 1042-1467.

L233
LYNCH, DANIEL C.; LUNDQUEST, LESIE. 1996. *Digital Money. The New Era of Internet Commerce*. Los Alamitos, CA: IEEE Computer Society; 1996. 285p. ISBN: 0-471-14178-X.

L234
LYNCH, KATHERINE A. 1994. The Family and the History of Public Life. *The Journal of Interdisciplinary History*. 1994 Spring; 24 (40): 665-685. ISSN: 0022-1953.

L235
LYNCH, LAWRENCE D. 1993. Columbus in Myth and History. In: McCrank, L., ed. *Discovery in the Archives of Spain and Portugal: Quincentenary Essays, 1492-1992*. Binghamton, NY: Haworth Press; 1993; 227-287. ISBN: 1-56024-643-X. Co-published as *Primary Sources & Original Works*. 1993; 2(1-2): 227-287. ISSN: 1042- 8216.

L236
LYNCH, RICHARD. 1993. *LEAD! How Public and Nonprofit Managers Can Bring Out the Best in Themselves and Their Organizations*. San Francisco, CA: Jossey-Bass Publishers; 1993. 213p. ISBN: 1555424945.

L237
LYNN, STUART. 1990. The Relationship between Digital and Other Media Conversion Processes: A Structured Glossary of Technical Terms. *Information Technology and Libraries*. 1990 Dec.; 9: 315, 321. ISSN: 0730-9295.

L238
LYON, G. REID; KRASNEGOR, NORMAN A. 1996. Attention, Memory, and Executive Function. Baltimore, MD: P. H. Brookes Pub. Co.; 1996. 424p. ISBN: 1557661987.

L239
LYOTARD, JEAN-FRANÇOIS. 1979/1984. *La Condition postmoderne: Rapport sur le savoir*. Paris, FR: Editions de Minuit; 1979. 109p. Bennington, Geoff; Massumi, Brian, trans. *The Postmodern Condition: A Report on Knowledge*. Theory and the History of Literature, 10. Minneapolis, MN: University of Minnesota Press; 1984. ISBN: 0816611661 (hbk.); 0816611734 (pbk.).

L240
LYOTARD, JEAN-FRANÇOIS. 1985. Histoire universelle et Differences Culturelles [Universal History and Cultural Differences]. *Critique* (FR). 1985 May; 41: 559-568. ISSN: 0011-1619.

L241

LYOTARD, JEAN-FRANÇOIS. 1991a. *L'Inhuman: Causeries sur le Temps*. Trans. as: *The Inhuman: Reflection on Time*. Palo Alto, CA: Stanford University Press; 1991. 216p. ISBN: 0804720088.

L242

LYOTARD, JEAN-FRANÇOIS. 1991b. *La Phenomenologie*. Trans. as: *Phénoménology*. Albany, NY: State University of New York Press; 1991. 147p. ISBN: 0791408051 (hbk.); 079140806X (pbk.).

L243

LYSAKOWSKI, RICHARD; SCHMIDT, STEVEN. 1996. *Automating 21st Century Science- The Legal, Regulatory, Technical and Social Aspects of Electronic Laboratory Notebooks and Collaborative Computing in R&D*. N.P.: Team Science Publishing; 1996.

L244

LYTLE, RICHARD H. 1979. *Subject Retrieval in Archives: A Comparison of the Provenance and Content Indexing Methods*. College Park, MD: College of Library and Information Services; 1979. 189p. (Ph.D. Dissertation). Available from University Microfilms, Ann Arbor, MI.

L245

LYTLE, RICHARD H. 1980. Intellectual Access to Archives, pt. 1: Provenance and Content Indexing Methods of Subject Retrieval. *American Archivist*. 1980; 43(1): 64-75. Pt. 2: Report of an Experiment Comparing Provenance and Content Indexing Methods of Subject Retrieval. *American Archivist*. 1980; 43(2): 191-207. ISSN: 0360-9081.

L246

LYU, MICHAEL R. 1996. *Handbook of Software Reliability Engineering*. Los Alamitos, CA: IEEE; 1996. 875p. and CD-ROM. ISBN: 0-07-039400-8.

-M-

M1

MACCORMAC, EARL R. 1985. *A Cognitive Theory of Metaphor*. Cambridge, MA: MIT Press; 1985. 254p. ISBN: 0262132125; LCCN: 85-7984.

M2

MACDONALD, GEORGE F. 1991. The Museum as an Information Utility. *Museum Management and Curatorship*. 1991; 10: 305-311.

M3

MACDONALD, GEORGE F. 1992. Change and Challenge: Museums in the Information Society. In: *Museums and Communities*. Washington, D.C.: Smithsonian Institution Press; 1992; 158-181.

M4

MACDONALD, GEORGE F.; ALSFORD, STEPHEN. 1997. Toward the Meta-Museum. See reference: JONES-GARMIL, K., ed. 1997. 267-278.

M5

MACDOUGAL, JENNIFER; BRITTAIN, J. MICHAEL. 1993. Library and Information Science Education in the United Kingdom. In: WILLIAMS, M. E., ed. *Annual Review of Information Science and Technology*. Medford, NJ: Learned Information, Inc. for the American Society for Information Science; 1993; 27: 361-390. ISBN: 0-938734-75-X; ISSN: 0066-4200.

M6

MACFARLANE, ALAN. 1977. History, Anthropology and the Study of Communities. *Social History* (UK). 1977; 5: 631—652. ISSN: 0307-1022.

M7

MACHLUP, FRITZ. 1962. *The Production and Distribution of Knowledge in the United States*. Princeton, NJ: Princeton University Press; 1962. 416p. LCCN: 63007072.

M8

MACHLUP, FRITZ. 1980. *Knowledge and Knowledge Production*. Princeton, NJ: Princeton University Press; c1980. 272p. ISBN: 0691042268; LCCN: 82122044.

M9

MACHLUP, FRITZ. 1980-1984. *Knowledge, Its Creation, Distribution, and Economic Significance*. Princeton, NJ: Princeton University Press; c1980-1984. 3 v. ISBN: 0691042268; LCCN: 80007544.

M10
MACHLUP, FRITZ. 1982. *The Branches of Learning.* Princeton, NJ: Princeton University Press; c.1982. 205p. ISBN: 0691042306; LCCN: 82003695. Also v. 2 in reference: MACHLUP, FRITZ. 1980-1984.

M11
MACHLUP, FRITZ. 1984. *The Economics of Information and Human Capital.* Princeton, NJ: Princeton University Press; c1984. 644p. ISBN: 0691042330; LCCN: 83042588. Also v. 3 in reference: MACHLUP, FRITZ. 1980-1984.

M12
MACHLUP, FRITZ; LEESON, KENNETH. 1978-1980. *Information through the Printed Word: The Dissemination of Scholarly, Scientific, and Intellectual Knowledge.* New York, NY: Praeger Publishers; 1978-1980. 4v. ISBN: 0030474019; LCCN: 78019460.

M13
MACHLUP, FRITZ; MANSFIELD, UNA, eds. 1983. *The Study of Information: Interdisciplinary Messages.* New York, NY: Wiley; 1983. 743p. (Wiley Interscience Publication). ISBN: 047188717X; LCCN: 83012147.

M14
MACKENZIE, DONALD. 1996. *Knowing Machines: Essays on Technical Change.* Cambridge, MI: MIT Press; 1996. 338p. ISBN: 0-262-13315-6.

M15
MACKINTOSH, IAN. 1986. *Sunrise Europe. The Dynamics of Information Technology.* Oxford, UK: Basil Blackwell; 1986. 288p. ISBN: 0-631-14406-4; LCCN: 86-6077.

M16
MACLEOD, DUNCAN J. 1975. Measuring Slavery. *History Journal.* 1975; 18(1): 202- 05.

M17
MACNAMARA, JOHN T. 1981. *Names for Things: A Study of Human Learning.* Cambridge, MA: MIT Press; 1981. 275p. ISBN: 026131692 (hbk.); 0262630923 (pbk.).

M18
MACNEIL, HEATHER. 1992. Weaving Provenancial and Documentary Relations. *Archivaria.* 1992 Summer; 34: 197. ISSN: 0318-6954.

M19
MACNEIL, HEATHER. 1992. *Without Consent. The Ethics of Disclosing Personal Information in Public Archives.* Lanham, MD: Scarecrow Press for SAA; 1992. 230 p. ISBN: 0-8108-2581-3.

M20
MACNEIL, HEATHER. 1996. Implications of the UBC Research Results for Archival Description in General and the Canadian Rules for Archival Description in Particular. *Archivi & Computer* (IT). 1996: 6 (3-4): 240-250. ISSN: 1121-2462.

M21
MACROBERTS, MICHAEL H.; MACROBERTS, BARBARA. 1987. Another Test of Normative Theory of Citing. *Journal of the American Society for Information Science.* 1987 July; 38: 305-306. ISSN: 0002-8231.

M22
MACROBERTS, MICHAEL H.; MACROBERTS, BARBARA. 1989. Problems of Citation Analysis: A Critical Review. *Journal of the American Society for Information Science.* 1989 Sept.; 40: 342-349. ISSN: 0002-8231.

M23
MADDALA, G. S. 1992. *Econometrics.* 2nd ed. New York, NY: Macmillan; 1992. 631p. ISBN: 0023745452; LCCN: 91-23860; OCLC: 24009460.

M24
MADUREIRA, NUNO L. 1995. Knowledge Representation and History. See reference: JARTIZ, G. *ET AL.*, eds. 1995. 237-256.

M25
MAFFESOLI, MICHEL. *La Connaissance Ordinaire.* Trans. as: *Ordinary Knowledge: An Introduction to Interpretative Sociology.* Cambridge, UK: Blackwell Publishers/Cambridge, MA; Polity Press; 1996. 196p. ISBN: 0745611184.

M26
MAFTEI, NICOLAS. 1994. Software Requirements for Multi-level Descriptions and Context Presentation. *Archivi & Computer* (IT). 1994; 4: 324-338. ISSN: 1121-2462.

M27
MAFTEI, NICOLAS. 1997. *Technology and Standards for Archives Automation. A Status Report.* Nicolas Maftei Consulting, Inc. 1997 November. 32 pp. (Paper supplied by C. Dollar).

M28
MAGUIRE, CARMEL; KAZLAUSKAS, EDWARD J.; WEIR, ANTHONY D. 1994. *Information Services for Innovative Organizations.* New York, NY: Academic Press; 1994. 319p. ISBN: 0724650309; LCCN: 93-38540.

M29
MAGUIRE, DAVID J. 1989. *Computers in Geography.* Harlow, UK: Longman Scientific & Technical; J. Wiley; 1989. 248p. ISBN: 0470211946.

M30
MAGUIRE, DAVID J. 1991. An Overview and Definition of GIS. See reference: MAGUIRE, D.; GOODCHILD, M.; RHIND, D., eds. 1991. 9-20.

M31
MAGUIRE, DAVID J.; GOODCHILD, MICHAEL F.; RHIND, DAVID, eds. 1991. *Geographic Information Systems: Principles and Applications.* Essex, UK: Longman; New York, NY: Wiley; 1991. 2 vols. ISBN: 0582056616 (set).

M32
MAHER, WILLIAM J. 1986. The Use of Use Studies. *Midwestern Archivist.* 1986; 11: 17 ISSN:1067-4993.

M33
MAHER, WILLIAM J. 1992. *The Management of College and University Archives.* Metuchen, NJ: Scarecrow Press for SAA; 1992. 448p. ISBN: 0-8108-2568-6.

M34
MAHN, HOLBROOK; JOHN-STEINER, VERA. 1996. Psychological Uses of Complexity Theory. *The American Journal of Psychology.* 1996 Fall; 109(3): 465-. ISSN: 0002-9556.

M35
MAHONEY, MICHAEL S. 1988. The History of Computing in the History of Technology. *Annals of the History of Computing.* 1988; 10(2): 113-25. ISSN: 0164-1239.

M36
MAHONEY, MICHAEL S. 1993. "What Makes History?" In: *The Second History of Programming Languages Conference (HOP-II). ACM SIGPLAN Notices.* 1993 March; 28 (3): x-xii.

M37
MAI, JENS-ERIK. 1999. A Postmodern Theory of Knowledge Organization. See reference: WOODS, LARRY, ed. 1999. 547-556.

M38
MAIER, DAVID. 1983. *The Theory of Relational Databases.* Rockville, MD: Computer Science Press; 1983. 637p. ISBN: 0914894420.

M39
MAILL, DAVID S., ed. 1990. *Humanities and the Computer: New Directions.* Oxford, UK: Clarendon Press; 1990. 222p. ISBN: 0198242441; LCCN: 89-71302.

M40
MAINES, D.; SURGUE, N.; KATOVICH, M. 1983. The Sociological Impact of G. H. Mead's Theory of the Past. *American Sociological Review.* 1983; 48: 161-173. ISSN: 0003-1224.

M41
MAINZER, KLAUS. 1996. *Thinking in Complexity: The Complex Dynamics of Matter, Mind, and Mankind.* 2nd rev. ed. Berlin, DEU; New York, NY: Springer-Verlag; 1996. 349p. ISBN: 3540606378.

M42
MALBIN, SUSAN L. 1997. The Reference Interview in Archival Literature. *College & Research Libraries.* 1997 January; 59(1): 69-80. ISSN: 0010-0970.

M43
MALI, ANYA. 1995. Aspen Forum: History's Future in [the] Electronic Age. *Publishers Weekly.* 1995 April 10; 242 (15): 13. ISSN: 000-0019. Report from the Jerusalem International Book Fair, 1995.

M44
MALINOWSKI, BRONISLAV. 1926. *Myth in Primitive Psychology.* London, UK: Kegan Paul, Trench, Trubner & Co., Ltd.; 1926. 128p.

M45
MALINOWSKI, BRONISLAV. 1944. *A Scientific Theory of Culture and other Essays*. Chapel Hill, NC: University of North Carolina; 1944. 228p. LCCN: 44-8385; OCLC: 279667.

M46
MALLINSON, JOHN C. 1989. Preserving Machine-Readable Archival Records for the Millenia. *Archivaria* (CAN). 1989; 22: 147-152. ISSN: 0318-6954.

M47
MALONE, MICHAEL S. 1996. *The Microprocessor. A Biography*. Los Alamitos, CA: IEEE; 1996. 333p. ISBN: 0-387-94342-0.

M48
MALONEY, PAUL, ed. [199- forthcoming]. *The Shroud of Turin: A Case Study in Document Authentification.* McCrank, L. J., series ed. Binghamton, NY, PA: Haworth Press; [199-]. [300p.].

M49
MANDELBAUM, MAURICE. 1965. The History of Ideas, Intellectual History, and the History of Philosophy. *History and Theory*. 1965; 5: 33-66. ISSN: 0018-2656.

M50
MANDELBAUM, MAURICE. 1974. The Problem of "Covering Laws." See reference: GARDNER, P., ed. 1974. 51-65.

M51
MANDELBAUM, MAURICE. 1977. *The Anatomy of Historical Knowledge*. Baltimore, MD: The Johns Hopkins University Press; 1977. 230p. ISBN: 080189296; LCCN: 76-46945; OCLC: 2525245.

M52
MANDELBROT, BENOIT B. 1953. An Informational Theory of the Statistical Structure of Language. In: Jackson, W., ed. *Proceedings of the Symposium on Applications in Communication Theory*. London, UK: Butterworths; 1953; 486-502. ISBN: 10503293.

M53
MANDELBROT, BENOIT B. 1977/1982. *Fractals*. 1977. Rev. ed. *The Fractal Geometry of Nature*. San Francisco, CA: W. H. Freeman; 1982. 460p. ISBN: 0716711869.

M54
MANDEMAKERS, KEES. 1993. Basic Elements of a Scheme for a Successful Classification of Occupational Titles in an Interdisciplinary, Historical and International Perspective. See reference: SCHURER, K.; DIEDERIKS, H., eds. 1993. 41-48.

M55
MANGUEL, ALBERTO. 1996. *A History of Reading*. London, UK: Harper-Collins; 1996. 372p. ISBN: 0-00-255006-7.

M56
MANIEZ, J. 1993. L'Evolution des Langages Documentaries [The Evolution of Documentation Languages]. *Documentaliste* (FR). 1993 July-October; 30(4-5): 254- 259. (In French). ISSN: 0012-4508.

M57
MANKIN, DON.; COHEN, SWAN G.; BIKSON, TORA K. 1996. *Teams and Technology*. Boston, MA: Harvard Business School Press; 1996. 284p. ISBN: 0875843999.

M58
MANN, W. C.; THOMPSON, S. A. 1987. Rhetorical Structure Theory. A Theory of Text Organization. In: Polany, L., ed. *The Structure of Discourse*. Norwood, NJ: Ablex; 1987.

M59
MANNHEIM, KARL. 1928/1952. The Problem of Generations. In his: *Essays on the Sociology of Knowledge*. London, UK: Routledge & Kegan Paul; 1952; 276-322.

M60
MANNING, PATRICK. 1996. The Problem of Interactions in World History. *AHR* Forum. *American Historical Review*. 1996 June; 101(3): 771-782. ISSN: 0002-8762.

M61
MANSAND, B.; LINOFF, G.; WALTZ, D. 1992. Classifying News Stories Using Memory-based Reasoning. In: Belkin, N.; Ingwersen, P.; Pejtersen, A. M., eds. *Proceedings of the Fifteenth Annual International ACM SIGIUR Conference on Research and Development in Information Retrieval*. New York, NY: ACM; 1991. 51-58.

M62
MANSELL, ROBIN, ed. 1994. *Management of Information and Communication Technologies: Emerging Patterns of Control*. London, UK: Aslib; 1994. 362p. ISBN: 0-85142-312-4.

M63
MANSFIELD, EDWIN. 1961. Technological Change and the Rate of Imitation. *Econometrica*. 1961; 29(4): 741-766. ISSN: 0012-9682.

M64
MANSFIELD, EDWIN. 1968/1993. *The Economics of Technological Change*. New York, NY: W. W. Norton & Co.; 1968. Rev. ed. Aldershot, UK: Elgar Pub.; 1993. 489p. ISBN: 185278283X; LCCN: 93-22664.

M65
MARARNEKO, ANN MARIE. 1997. Research Issues in Systems Implementation: Risks and Tradeoffs. See reference: BEARMAN, D.; TRANT, J., eds. 1997. 293-300.

M66
MARCELLA, ALBERT, Jr.; CHAN, SALLY. 1993. *EDI Security Control and Audit*. Boston, MA: Artech House; 1993. 212p. ISBN: 0890066108.

M67
MARCH, JAMES G.; SIMON, HERBERT A. [1958]. *Organizations*. Guetzkow, Harold, contributer. New York, NY: John Wiley; [1958]. 262p. March's essays are republished in : *Decisions and Organizations*. New York, NY: Blackwell; 1988. 458p. ISBN: 063115812X; 0631168567 (pbk.).

M68
MARCHAND, ROLAND. [2000]. *Creating the Corporate Soul*. Berkeley, CA: University of California Press; 2000.

M69
MARCHAND, SUZANNE L. 1996. *Down from Olympus: Archeology and Philhellenism in Germany, 1750-1970*. Princeton, NJ: Princeton University Press; 1996. 400p. ISBN: 0691043930.

M70
MARCHETTI, CESARE. 1980. Society as a Learning System: Discovery, Invention, and Innovation Cycles Revisited. *Technological Forecasting and Social Change*. 1980; 18: 267-282. ISSN: 0040-1625.

M71
MARCHIONINI, GARY. 1987. An Invitation to Browse: Designing Full-text Systems for Novice Users. *The Canadian Journal of Information Science*. 1987; 12(3/4): 69-79. ISSN: 0380-9218.

M72
MARCHIONINI, GARY. 1989. Information-seeking Strategies on Novices using a Full-text Electronic Encyclopedia. *Journal of the American Society for Information Science*. 1989; 40 (1): 54-66. ISSN: 0002-8231.

M73
MARCHIONINI, GARY. 1994. Designing Hypertexts: Start with an Index. See reference: FIDEL, R. *ET AL.*, eds. 1994. 77-90.

M74
MARCHIONINI, GARY. 1995. *Information Seeking in Electronic Environments*. Cambridge, UK: Cambridge University Press; 1995. 224p. (Cambridge series on human-computer interaction, 9). ISBN: 0521443725; LCCN: 94044629.

M75
MARCHIONINI, GARY. 1997. Bringing Treasures to the Surface: Library of Congress National Digital Library Program. Paper at the 14th *Symposium on the Advanced in Human-Computer Interface Design*, University of Maryland, College Park, MD; May 30, 1997. Accessible at http://www.cs.umd.edu/projects/hcil/.

M76
MARCHIONINI, GARY; CRANE, GREGORY. 1994. Evaluation of the Perseus Project. *Library Science & Technology*. 1994.

M77
MARCHIONINI, GARY; DWIGGINS, S.; KATZ, A.; LIN, X. 1993. Information Seeking in Full-text End-user Search Systems: The Roles of Domain and Search Expertise. *Library and Information Science Research*. 1993; 15: 35-69. ISSN: 0740-8188.

M78
MARCHIONINI, GARY; KOMLODI, ANITA. 1998. Design of Interfaces for Information Seeking. In: Williams, Martha E., ed. *Annual Review of Information Science and Technology* (*ARIST*; vol. 33). Medford, NJ: Information Today, Inc.; 1998. ISBN: 1-57387-065-X.

M79
MARCHIONINI, GARY; PLAISANT, CATHERINE; KOMLODI, ANITA. 1998. Interfaces and Tools for the Library of Congress National Digital Library Program. *Information Processing & Management*. 1998 Sept.; 34 (5): 535-555. ISBN: 0306-4573.

M80
MARCHIONINI, GARY; SCHNEIDERMAN, BEN. 1988. Finding Facts vs. Browsing in Hypertext Systems. *IEEE Computer.* 1988 January; 21: 7-80. ISSN: 0018-9162. Also in: B. Schneiderman, ed. *Sparks of Innovation in Human-Computer Interaction.* Norwood, NJ: Ablex Publishing; 1993. 102-122. ISBN: 156750078 (pbk.); 156750079X.

M81
MARCINIAK, JOHN J., ed. 1995. *Encyclopedia of Software Engineering.* Los Alamitos, CA: IEEE; 1988. 2 vols., 1500p. ISBN: 0-471-54004-8.

M82
MARCOS MARIN, FRANCISCO A. 1994. *Informatica y Humanidades* [Information Science and the Humanities]. Madrid, ES: Gredos; c1994. 816p. ISBN: 8424916654; LCCN: 95126916. (In Spanish).

M83
MARCOULIDES, GEORGE A.; HERSBERGER, SCOTT L. 1997. *Multivariate Statistical Methods: A First Course.* Mahwah, NJ: Lawrence Earlbaum Associates, Inc.; 1997. 336p. ISBN: 0-8058-2571-1 (hbk.); 0-8058-2752-X (pbk.).

M84
MARCOUX, YVES; SEVIGNY, MARTIN. 1997. Why SGML? Why Now? See reference: LOGAN, E.; POLLARD, M., eds. 1997b. 584-592.

M85
MARCUM, DEANNA B. 1997. Transforming the Curriculum; Transforming the Profession. *American Libraries.* 1997 January; 27(1): 35-38. ISSN: 0002-9769.

M86
MARCUS, GEORGE E.; FISCHER, MICHAEL M. J. 1986. *Anthropology as Cultural Critique: An Experimental Moment in the Human Sciences.* Chicago, IL: University of Chicago Press; 1986. 205p. ISBN: 0725504484 (hbk.); 0226504492 (pbk.).

M87
MARECHAL, DENIS. 1986. *La Photographie: quelle source pour l'histoire* [Photography: A source for history]. Paris, FR: IEP (Institute d'Etudes politiques de Paris); 1986. (These de 3o cycle). (In French).

M88
MARGOLIS, JOSEPH. 1993. *The Flux of History and the Flux of Science.* Berkeley, CA: University of California Press; 1993. 238p. ISBN: 0520083199.

M89
MARGOLIS, JOSEPH. 1995. *Historied Thought, Constructed World: A Conceptual Primer for the Turn of the Millennium.* Berkeley, CA: University of California Press; 1995. 377p. ISBN: 0520201132.

M90
MARIENSTRAS, ELISE; ROSSIGNOL, MARIE-JEANNE, eds. 1994. *Mémoire privee, Mémoire collective, dans l'Amerique pre-industrielle* (Private Memory/Collective Memory: In Pre-Industrial America). Paris, FR: Berg International with the University of Paris and the CNRS; 1994. 303p. (Collection "Frontieres"). (In French). ISBN: 2900269946.

M91
MARIN, MARCOS. 1995. *Informatica y humanidades* [Computers and Humanities]. Madrid, ES: np; 1995.

M92
MARIN-NAVARRO, JOSE; ALEVANTIS, P. E. 1991. Alice in the Wonderland of SGML: Streamlining Text Entry in the CELEX Databases. *Electronic Library: The International Journal for Minicomputer, Microcomputer, and Software Applications in Libraries.* June 1991; 9(3): 155-60. ISSN: 0264-0473.

M93
MARK, D. M.; FRANK, A. U. 1990. Concepts of space and spatial language. In: *Auto-carto[graphy] 9 Conference Proceedings,* Baltimore, MD, 1989 (pp. 538-556). Falls Church, VA: ASPRS/ACSM; 1990.

M94
MARKER, HANS-JORGEN. 1991a. Study Description Adjustments for Historical Research. See reference: BEST, H., *ET AL.*, eds., 1991. 502-506.

M95
MARKER, HANS-JORGEN. 1991b. Encoding Standards for the "Generalist" and the "Specialist": Complex Compound Documents as a Test Case. See reference: GREENSTEIN, D., ed., 1991. 147-162.

M96
MARKER, HANS-JORGEN. 1993. Data Conservation at a Traditional Data Archive. See reference: ROSS, S.; HIGGS, E.,eds., 1993. 187-193.

M97
MARKER, HANS-JORGEN, ed. [1993-]. Historical Data Archives on Common Ground. Copenhagen, DK: Danish Data Archives; 199- (Forthcoming). [52p.] (Pre-publication proofs distributed at the IACH Conference at Graz, 1993).

M98
MARKER, HANS-JORGEN. 1995. The Source Entry Project. See reference: BOONSTRA, O., *ET AL.*, eds. 1995. 189-198.

M99
MARKER, HANS-JORGEN; REINKE, HERBERT; SCHURER, KEVIN. 1987. Making Sense out of Historical Information: Towards Standards for the Description and Documentation of Machine-Readable Historical Sources and Data. In: Hausmann, F.; Hartel, R.; Kropač, I.; Becker, P., eds. *Datennetze für die Historischen Wissenschaften?*. *Probleme und Möglichkeiten bei Standardisierung und Transfer Maschinenlesbarer Daten* [Data Networks for Historical Science? Problems and Possibilities for the Standardization and Transfer of Machine-readable Data]. Graz, AT: Keykam-Verlag; 1987. 152-158. ISBN: 3-0711-0001-2.

M100
MARKER, HANS-JORGEN; REINKE, HERBERT; SCHURER, KEVIN. 1988. Sources and Data: Description and Documentation Requirements in Historical Social Research. See reference: GENET, J.-P., ed. 1988. 71-86.

M101
MARKEY DRABENSTOTT, KAREN. 1994. *Analytical Review of the Library of the Future*. Washington, D.C.: Council on Library Resources; 1994. 200p. Available also on anonymous FTP: sils.umich.edu

M102
MARKEY DRABENSTOTT, KAREN; VIZINE-GOETZ, DIANE. 1994. *Using Subject Headings for Online Retrieval: Theory, Practice, and Potential*. San Diego, CA: Academic Press under OCLC auspices; 1994. 365p. ISBN: 0122215702.

M103
MARKS, RICHARD D. 1994. High Technology Legislation as an Eighteenth-century Process. *Stanford Law & Policy Review*. 1994; 6(1): 17-23. ISSN: 1044-4386.

M104
MARLOWE, HERBERT, Jr.; NYHAN, RONALD C.; ARRINGTON, LAWRENCE; PAMMER, WILLIAM J. 1994. The Re-ing of Local Government: Understanding and Shaping Governmental Change. *Public Productivity & Management Review*. 1994 Spring; 17(3): 299-1311. ISSN: 1044-8039.

M105
MARRAS, AUSONIO, ed. [1972]. *Intentionality, Mind, and Language*. Urbana, IL: University of Illinois Press; [1972]. 527p. ISBN: 0252002113; LCCN: 79165043.

M106
MARROU, HENRI-IRENEE. 1961. Qu'est-ce qu'un fait historique? [What is in the Making of History?] See reference: DUBY, GEORGES, ed. 1961. 1494-1500.

M107
MARROU, HENRI-IRENEE. 1965. Théorie et practique de l'histoire [The Theory and Practice of History]. *Revue historique* (FR). 1965; 89: 139-170. ISSN: 0035-3264. (In French).

M108
MARSHAK, ROBERT J. 1993. Managing the Metaphors of Change. *Organizational Dynamics*. 1993 Summer; 22 (1): 44-56. ISSN: 0090-2616.

M109
MARSHALL, CATHERINE; SHIPMAN, FRANK M., III; COOMBS, JAMES H. 1994. *VIKI*: Spatial Hypertext Supporting Emergent Structure. In: Chamber, Teresa; Moreno, Carmen, eds. *Proceedings of the European Conference on Hypermedia Technology*; 1994 September 18-023, Edinburgh, Scotland; New York, NY: Association for Computing Machinery; 1994. 13-23. ISBN: 0-89791-640-9.

M110
MARSHALL, JOSEPH. 1997. Creativity at the Edge of Chaos. *Working Woman*. 1997 Feb.; 22(2): 46-52. ISSN: 0145-5761.

M111
MARTIN, F. 1937/1995. *Les mots latins [Latin Words]*. First ed. Paris, FR: Hachette; 1932. Converted to Electronic file for MacIntosh, 1995.

M112
MARTIN, HENRI-JEAN. 1988/1994. *Histoire et pouvoirs de l'écrit*. Paris, FR: Perrin; 1988. Cochrane, Lydia G., trans. *The History and Power of Writing*. Chicago, IL: University of Chicago Press; 1994. 592p. ISBN: 0276508358.

M113
MARTIN, JAMES. 1993. *Principles of Object-Oriented Analysis and Design*. Englewood Cliffs, NJ: Prentice-Hall; 1993. 412p. ISBN: 0132088715.

M114
MARTIN, JAMES; LEBEN, JOE. 1995. *Client/Server Databases: Enterprise Computing*. Englewood Cliffs, NJ: Prentice-Hall; 1995. 352p. ISBN: 0-13-305160-9.

M115
MARTIN, JAY. 1994. Historical Truth and Narrative Reliability: Three Biographical Stories. See reference: KARL, F., ed. 1994. 25-72.

M116
MARTIN, JEAN-MARIE; MENANT, FRANÇOIS, ed. 1994-95. Génese médiévale de l'Anthroponymie moderne: L'éspace italién [Medieval Beginnings of Modern Anthroponomy: The Italian Space]. In: *Melanges de l'École frnçise de Rome—Moyen Âge* [MEFRM] Rome, IT: École française de Rome; 1994-95. 2 vols. (In French).

M117
MARTIN, JOANNE. 1993. *Cultures in Organizations: Three Perspectives*. New York, NY: Oxford University Press; 1993. 228p. ISBN: 0195071638 (hbk.); 0195071646 (pbk.); LCCN: 92-6604.

M118
MARTIN, JOANNE.; SIEHL, C. 1983. Organizational Culture and Counterculture: An Uneasy Symbiosis. *Organizational Dynamics*. 1983; 12 (2): 52-64. ISSN: 0090-2616.

M119
MARTIN, JOHN. 1997. Inventing Sincerity, Refashioning Prudence: The Discovery of the Individual in Renaissance Europe. *American Historical Review*.1997; 102(5): 1309-1342. ISSN: 0002-8762.

M120
MARTIN, REX. 1977. *Historical Explanation: Re-enactment and Practical Inference*. Ithaca, NY: Cornell University Press; 1977. 267p. ISBN: 0801410843; LCCN: 77-3121; OCLC: 2984518.

M121
MARTINEZ SOPENA, PASCUAL, ed. 1995. *Antroponimía y sociedad. Sistemas de indentificación hispano-cristianos en los siglos IX a XIII* [Anthroponomy and Society. Systems of Identification of Hispano-Christians in the 11-13th centuries]. Valladolid, ES: Universidades de Santiago de Compostella and Valladolid; 1995. (In Spanish).

M122
MARTINO, JOSEPH A. [1995]. A Technology Audit: Key to Technology Planning. In: *National Aereospace and Electronics, 1994 Conference* (NAECON). Washington, DC: NAECON; [1995]. 1241-1247.

M123
MARTLEW, ROGER, ed. 1984. *Information Systems in Archeology*. Gloucester, UK: Alan Sutton Publishing Ltd.; 1984. 159p.(New Standard Archeology series). ISBN: 0- 86299-116-1; LCCN: 84-131183; OCLC: 11376666.

M124
MARTON, FERENCE; BOOTH, SHIRLEY. 1997. *Learning and Awareness*. Mahwah, NJ: Lawrence Earlbaum Associates, Inc.; 1997. 240p. (Educational Psychology Series). ISBN: 0-8058-2454-5 (hbk.); 0-8058-2455-3 (pbk.).

M125
MARTY, PAUL F. 1999. Museum Informatics and Collaborative Technologies: The Emerging Socio-Technological Dimension of Information Science in Museum Environments. See reference: BATES, M., ed. 1999. Pt. 2: 1083-1091.

M126
MARTYN, JOHN. 1985. Factual Databases. *ASLIB* [Association of Special Libraries and Information Bureaux] *Proceedings* (UK). 1985 May; 37(5): 231-38. ISSN: 0001-253X.

M127
MARTYN, JOHN; VICKERS, PETER; FEENEY, MARY, eds. 1990. *Information UK 2000*. London, UK; K. G. Saur; 1990. 293p.(British Library Research series). ISBN: 0-86291-620-8.

M128
MARVIN, CAROLYN. 1988. *When Old Technologies Were New: Thinking about Electronic Communication in the Late Nineteenth Century*. New York, NY: Oxford University Press; 1988. 269. ISBN: 0195044681.

M129
MARWICK, ARTHUR. 1971/1984/1989. *The Nature of History*. New York, NY: Alfred Knopf; c1970. Reprints. London, UK: Macmillan; 1984. 316p. ISBN: 0333323726 (pbk.); LCCN: 86673467. Chicago, IL: Lyceum Books; 1989. 442p. ISBN: 0925065005; LCCN: 89002786.

M130
MARWICK, ARTHUR. 1995. Two Approaches to Historical Study: The Metaphysical and the Historical. *Journal of Contemporary History*. 1995 January; 30 (1): 5-36. ISSN: 0022-0094.

M131
MASCHNER, HERBERT D. G., ed. 1996. *New Methods, Old Problems: Geographic Information Systems in Modern Archeological Research*. Tenth Annual Visiting Scholar Conference, March 12-13, 1993. Carbondale, IL: Southern Illinois University Center for Archaeological Investigations; 1996. 315p. (Occasional Papers, no. 23). ISBN: 0881040797.

M132
MASCIA-LEES, FRANCES; SHARPE, PATRICIA. 1992. Culture, Power, and Text: Anthropology and Literature Confront Each "Other". *American Literary History*. 1992 Winter; 4: 678-696. ISSN: 0896-7148.

M133
MASON, JAMES D. 1997. SGML and Related Standards: New Directions as the Second Decade Begins. See reference: LOGAN, E.; POLLARD, M., eds. 1997b: 593-596.

M134
MASON, JENNIFER. 1996. *Qualitative Researching*. Thousand Oaks, CA: Sage; 1996. 180p. ISBN: 0803989865 (pbk.).

M135
MASON, K. O. 1973. Some Methodological Issues in Cohort Analysis of Archival Data. *American Sociological Review*. 1973; 38: 242-258. ISSN: 0003-1224.

M136
MASTERPASQUA, FANK; PERMA, PHYLLIS A., eds. 1997. *The Psychological Meaning of Chaos: Translating Theory into Practice*. Washington, D.C.; American Psychological Association; 1997. 353p. ISBN: 15579984298.

M137
MASUCH, MICHAEL; POLOS, LASZLO, eds. 1994. *Knowledge Representation and Reasoing under Uncertainty: Logic at Work*. Berlin, DEU / New York, NY: Springer- Verlag; c1994. 237p. ISBN: 0387580956 (pbk.); LCCN: 94020068.

M138
MATHEUS, C. J.; CHAN, P. K.; PIATETSKY-SHAPIRO, GREGORY. 1993. Systems for Knowledge Discovery in Databases. *IEEE Transactions on Knowledge and Data Engineering*. 1993; 5 (6): 903-912. ISSN: 1041-4347.

M139
MATSUDA, MATT K. 1996. *The Memory of the Modern*. New York, NY: Oxford University Press; 1996. 255p. ISBN: 019509364X (hbk.); 0195093658 (pbk.); LCCN: 95030287.

M140
MATTERS, MARION, ed. 1990. *Automated Records and Techniques in Archives: A Resource Directory*. Brown, Thomas E., contributer. Chicago, IL: SAA; 1990. 75p. LC call no.: Z699.5.A7A911.

M141
MATTERS, MARION. 1995. *Oral History Cataloging Manual*. Chicago, IL: Society of American Archivists; 1995. 109p. ISBN: 093182897X; LCCN: 95-8072.

M142
MATTISON, ROB. 1996. *Data Warehousing Strategies, Technologies, and Techniques*. Los Alamitos, CA: IEEE Computer Society; 1996. 510p. ISBN: 0-07-041034-8.

M143
MATTISON, ROB; CREETH, RICHARD. 1996. *The OLAP Report*. Synopsis [electronic file]. Accessible at http://www.busintel.com/busintel/syn4.htm.

M144
MAURO, FREDERIC. 1971. Conceptualisation et Quantification en Histoire Economique [Conceptualization and Quantification in Economic History]. *Revista de la Universidad Complutense de Madrid* (ES). 1971; 20(79): 65-78. (In French).

M145
MAWDSLEY, EVAN; MORGAN, NICOLAS; RICHMOND, LESLEY; TRAINOR, RICHARD, eds. 1990. *History and Computing, III: Historians, Computers and Data. Applications in Research and Training*. Manchester, UK and New York, NY: Manchester University Press; 1990. 213p. ISBN: 0-7190-3051-X; 0-7190-3211-3 (pbk.).

M146
MAWDSLEY, EVAN; MUNCK, THOMAS. 1993. *Computing for Historians: An Introductory Guide.* Manchester, UK: University of Manchester Press / New York, NY: St. Martin's Press; 1993. 227p. (Bibliography, pp. 222-227). ISBN: 0719035473; 0719035473 (pbk.); LCCN: 92-38789; OCLC: 26975528.

M147
MAX-PLANCK-INSTITUT FÜR GESCHICHTE. [1989]. *Quellenstudium per Computer* [Course of Study in Computing](flyer). Gottingen, DEU: IBM Deutschland GmbH; [1989]. 7p. Available from the Institute.

M148
MAX-PLANCK-INSTITUT FÜR GESCHICHTE. [199-]. *Halbgraue Reihe zur historischen Fackinformatik* [Series of Undertakings in Historical Informatics]. Serie A-B: Historische Quellenkunden, Band 1-[25]. Serie C: Datenbasen als Editionem (Machine-Readable Texts), Band 1-[20]. St. Katharinen [Göttingen, DEU]: Max-Planck-Institut für Geschichte in Kommission bei Scripta Mercaturae Verlag; [199-]. Irregular series. (See author main entries for contents of series). (In German and English). ISBN: 3-928134-xx-x.

M149
MAYER, DALE. 1985. The New Social History: Implications for Archivists. *The American Archivist.* 1985; 48(4): 388-399. ISSN: 0360-9081.

M150
MAYER, KARL U.; TUMA, NANCY B., eds. 1989. *Event History Analysis in Life Course Research.* Selected papers from Human Development and Education conference at the Max-Planck Institute, Berlin, June 5-7, 1986. Madison, WI: University of Wisconsin Press; 1989. 297p. ISBN: 029912200X; 0299122042 (pbk.); LCCN: 89-40261; OCLC: 20294662.

M151
MAYER, T. F.; AMEY, W. R. 1974. Spectral Analysis and the Study of Social Change. In: Costner, H. L., ed. *Sociological Methodology, 1973-1974.* San Francisco, CA: Jossey-Bass; 1974. 410p. ISBN: 0875891977; LCCN: 73-9071; OCLC: 930177.

M152
MAYO, HOPE. 1991/1992. MARC Cataloguing for Medieval Manuscripts: An Evaluation. See reference: STEVENS, W.,ed. 1991/1992. 93-152.

M153
MAYO, HOPE. 1991. Medieval Manuscript Cataloging and the MARC Format. *Rare Books & Manuscript Librarianship.* 1991; 6(1): 11-22. ISSN: 0884-450X.

M154
MAYOR, TRACY. 1995. The Economics of EDI. *CIO Magazine.* 1995 May 1; 8 (13): 62- 72. Accessible at http://www.cio.com.

M155
MAZA, SARAH. 1996. Stories in History: Cultural Narratives in Recent Works in European History. *American Historical Review.* 1996 December; 101(5): 1493- 1515. ISSN: 0002-8762.

M156
MAZLISH, BRUCE. [1963]. *Psychoanalysis and History.* Englewood Cliffs, NJ: Prentice- Hall; [1963]. 183p. LCCN: 63009223.

M157
MAZLISH, BRUCE. 1989/1993. *A New Science: The Breakdown of Connections and the Birth of Sociology.* New York, NY: Oxford University Press; 1989. 319p. Republished. University Park, PA: Pennsylvania State University Press; 1993. 333p. ISBN: 0271010924; LCCN: 93003773.

M158
MAZLISH, BRUCE. 1998. Comparing global history to world history. *The Journal of Interdisciplinary History.* 1998 Winter; 28(3): 385-396.ISSN: 0022-1953.

M159
MAZLISH, BRUCE; BULLTJENS, R. eds. 1993. *Conceptualizing Global History.* Boulder, CO: Westview Press; 1993. 253p. (Global History series). ISBN: 0813316839 (hbk.); 0813316847 (pbk.).

M160
MCADAMS, STEPHEN; BIGAND, EMMANUEL, eds. 1993. *Thinking in Sound: The Cognitive Psychology of Human Audition.* Oxford, UK: Oxford University Press; 1993. 354p. ISBN: 0198522584 (hbk.); 0198522576 (pbk.).

M161
MCARTHUR, TOM. 1986. *Worlds of Reference: Lexicology, Learning, and Language from the Clay Tablet to the Computer.* Cambridge & New York: Cambridge University Press; 1986. 230p. ISBN: 0-521-30637-X.

M162
MCAULEY, JOHN. 1994. Exploring Issues in Culture and Competence. *Human Relations*. 1994 April: 47(4): 417-430. ISSN: 0018-7267.

M163
MCBRIDE, BAKER & COLES, INC. 1997. State-by-state Summary of Digital Signature Legislation. *Government Technology*. 1997 April; 10: [40-60]. Cf. National Conference of Commissioners on Uniform State Laws accessible at http://www.law.upenn.edu/ library/ulc/uecicta/ect897.htm.

M164
MCCABE, DONALD L.; DUKERICH, JANET; DUTTON, JANE E. 1994. The Effects of Professional Education on Values and the Resolution of Ethical Dilemmas: Business School vs. Law School Students. *Journal of Business Ethics*. 1994 September; 13(9): 693-700. ISSN: 0167-4544.

M165
MCCAIN, KATHERINE W. 1990. Mapping Authors in Intellectual Space: A Technical Review. *Journal of the American Society for Information Science*. 1990; 41: 433-443. ISSN: 0002-8231.

M166
MCCAIN, KATHERINE W. 1995. Biotechnology in Context: A Database-Filtering Approach to Identifying Core and Productive Non-Core Journals Supporting Multidisciplinary R & D. *Journal of the American Society for Information Science*. 1995; 46(4): 306-317. ISSN: 0002-8231.

M167
MCCARN, DAVID. [1997]. *Toward a Universion Data Format [UDF] for Preservation* (electronic file). Boston, MA: WGBH Educational Foundation; [1997]. Accessible at http://info.wgbh.org/PDF. (NHPRC grant-funded Video preservation project).

M168
MCCARTHY, E. DOYLE. *Knowledge as Culture: The New Sociology of Knowledge*. London, UK / New York, NY: Routledge; 1996. 130p. ISBN: 0415064961 (hbk.); 041506497X (pbk.).

M169
MCCARTHY, VANCE. 1995. The Web: Open for Business. *Datamation*. 1995 December 1; 41(22): 30-36. ISSN: 0011-6963.

M170
MCCARTHY, VANCE. 1997. Strike it Rich. *Datamation*. 1997 February; 43(2): 44-50. ISSN: 0011-6963.

M171
MCCAULEY, JOHN. 1994. Exploring Issues in Culture and Competence. *Human Relations*. 1994 April; 47(4): 417-430. ISSN: 0018-7267.

M172
MCCLELLAND, CHARLES E. 1991. *The German Experience of Professionalization: Modern Learned Professions and Their Organizations from the Early Nineteenth Century to the Hitler Era*. Cambridge, UK: Cambridge University Press; 1991. 253p. ISBN: 052194570.

M173
MCCLELLAND, PETER D. 1975. *Causal Explanation and Model Building in History, Economics, and the New Economic History*. Ithaca, NY: Cornell University Press; 1975. 290p. ISBN: 0801409292.

M174
MCCLOSKEY, DONALD N. 1985. *The Rhetoric of Economics*. Madison, WI: University of Wisconsin Press; 1985. 209p. ISBN: 0299103803; LCCN: 85-40373; OCLC: 12724735.

M175
MCCLOSKEY, DONALD N. 1990a. Ancients and Moderns. *Social Science History*. 1990; 14: 289-303. ISSN: 0145-5532.

M176
MCCLOSKEY, DONALD N. 1990b. *A Bibliography of Historical Economics to 1980*. Cambridge, UK: Cambridge University Press; 1990. 505p. ISBN: 0521403278.

M177
MCCLOSKEY, DONALD N. 1990c. *If You're So Smart: The Narrative of Economic Expertise*. Chicago, IL: University of Chicago; 1990. 180p. ISBN: 0226556700; LCCN: 90-33041; OCLC: 21226865.

M178
MCCLOSKEY, DONALD N. 1991. History, Differential Equations, and the Problem of Narration. The "New Science" and the Historical Social Sciences. In: *History and Theory*. 1991; 30: 21-36. (Entire issue on title topic). ISSN: 0018-2656.

M179
MCCLOSKEY, DONALD N. 1994. *Knowledge and Persuasion in Economics*. Cambridge, UK: Cambridge University Press; 1994. 445p. ISBN: 0521434750 (hbk.); 0521436036 (pbk.).

M180
MCCLURE, CHARLES R.; LOPATA, CYNTHIA L. 1996. *Assessing the Academic Networked Environment: Strategies and Options*. Washington, DC: Coalition for Networked Information; 1996. 133p. ISBN: 0918006287.

M181
MCCRAE, HAMISH. 1994. *The World of 2020: Power, Culture, and Prosperity*. Boston, MA: Harvard Business School Press; 1994.

M182
MCCRANK, LAWRENCE J. 1979a. Analytical and Historical Bibliography: A State of the Art Review. In: Carbonneau, Denis, ed. *Annual Report of the American Rare, Antiquarian and Out-of-Print Book Trade, 1978/79* (pp. 175-185). New York, NY: BCAR Publications; 1979. 233p. ISBN: 0-930986-02-4;(pbk.) 0-930986-03-2.

M183
MCCRANK, LAWRENCE J. 1979b. The Prospects for Integrating Historical and Information Studies in Archival Education. *The American Archivist*. 1979; 42(2): 443- 455. ISSN: 0360-9081.

M184
MCCRANK, LAWRENCE J. 1980a. *Education for Rare Book Librarianship: A Re-examination of Trends and Problems*. R. Stevens, ed. Champaign-Urbana, IL: University of Illinois; 1980. 92p. (Occasional Papers of the University of Illinois Graduate School of Library Science, 144). ISSN: 0073 5310.

M185
MCCRANK, LAWRENCE J. 1980b. The Future Care of the Past: Present Developments in Archival Education. In: Fyfe, J., ed. *Proceedings: A Symposium on Archival Education (July 28, 1979)* (pp. 11-41). London, Ontario CAN: University of Western Ontario, School of Library and Information Science; 1980. 67p. ISBN: 0-7714-0169-8.

M186
MCCRANK, LAWRENCE J., ed. 1981. *Automating the Archives. Issues and Problems in Computer Applications*. White Plains, NY: Knowledge Industry Publications, Inc. for ASIS; 1981. 363p. ISBN: 0-914236-95-4; 0-914236-86-5 (pbk.).

M187
MCCRANK, LAWRENCE J. 1979- 1982. *Archival Indexing and Terminology in Archives Description*. College Park, MD: College of Library and Information Services; 1979-1982. Revised; 1982. 140p. (Course syllabi and workshop manuals; limited distribution to enrollees).

M188
MCCRANK, LAWRENCE J. 1983. *The Rare Book and Manuscript Collection of the Mt. Angel Abbey Library: A Catalogue and Index*. 5 fiche program, 421p. Appended to: *Mt. Angel Abbey: A Centennial History of the Benedictine Community and its Library*. Wilmington, DE: Scholarly Resources, Inc.; 1983. 176p. ISBN: 0-8429-2212-0.

M189
MCCRANK, LAWRENCE J. 1984a. Integrating Conservation and Collection Management: An Experimental Workshop Report. *Archives and Library Security*. 1984; 6(1): 23-48.

M190
MCCRANK, LAWRENCE J. 1984b. Rare Book Cataloging: Improved Standards and Rising Costs. *Cataloging and Classification Quarterly*. 1984; 5(1): 27-51.

M191
MCCRANK, LAWRENCE J. 1985a. Strategic Planning for Networking of Rare Book and Historical Manuscript Data Resources. See reference: ALLEN, R. F., ed. 1985. 193-208.

M192
MCCRANK, LAWRENCE J. 1985b. Historians as Information Professionals: Problems in Education and Credentials. *The Public Historian*. 1985; 7: 7-22. ISSN: 0272-3433. Note "Public Historians and Information Science," in reference HOWE, B. 1989. 13- 15.

M193
MCCRANK, LAWRENCE J. 1986. La anatomía fiscal de periodo de post-restauración de la Iglesia de Tarragona. Una revision de las *Rationes Decimarum Hispaniae* (1279-80) [The Fiscal Anatomy of the Church of Tarragona in the Post-Restoration Period]. *Hispania: Revista Española de Historia*. 1986; 45: 245-97. (In Spanish) ISSN: 0018-2141. English version in *The Medieval Frontier in New Catalonia*. London, England: Variorum Press; 1997. 245-303. ISBN: 0-86078-582-3; LCCN: 96-1437.

M194

MCCRANK, LAWRENCE J. 1986. The Impact of Automation: Integrating Archival and Bibliographic Systems. See reference: MCCRANK, L., ed. 1986. 61-98.

M195

MCCRANK, LAWRENCE J. 1987. Turning Archives into Databases. See reference: MOBERG, T., ed. 1987. 268-75.

M196

MCCRANK, LAWRENCE J. 1988. Linking bibliographic and archival information systems: Indexing terms and stratified vocabularies. See reference: CZAP, H.; GALINSKI, C., eds. 1988. 2: 128-132.

M197

MCCRANK, LAWRENCE J. 1989. *The Bibliographic Services of the American Historical Association: Recently Published Articles (RPA) and Writings on American History (WAH)*. Association for the Bibliography of History task force report to the Research Division of the American Historical Association. Washington, DC: ABH; 1989. 51p. ERIC no. ED312-200.

M198

MCCRANK, LAWRENCE J. 1990. *Archival and Museum Informatics*. Review Essay. *Special Collections/Primary Sources & Original Works*. 1990; 4(2): 117-132. ISSN: 0270-3157.

M199

MCCRANK, LAWRENCE J., ed. 1991. *Bibliographical Foundations of French Historical Studies. Bicentennial of the French Revolution*. Annual Conference of the Association for the Bibliography of History, 1989. Binghamton, NY: Haworth Press; 1991. ISBN: 1-56024-150-0. Co-published in *Primary Sources & Original Works*. 1991; 1(2/3). ISSN: 1042-8216.

M200

MCCRANK, LAWRENCE J. 1991/1992. Manuscripts and Informatics: Progress and Prospects. See reference: STEVENS,W., ed., 1991/1992. 159-180.

M201

MCCRANK, LAWRENCE J. 1992a. Academic Programs for Information Literacy: Theory and Structure. In: Reichel, M., ed. Library Literacy Forum. *RQ [Reference Quarterly]*. 1992; 31(4): 485-497. ISSN: 0033-7072.

M202

MCCRANK, LAWRENCE J. 1992b. Knowledge Engineering: The Interplay of Historical and Information Science in the Study of Change. In: Shaw, D. *et al.*, eds. *ASIS '92*. Proceedings of the American Society for Information Science, Pittsburgh, PA, October 26-29, 1992 (pp. 277-287). Medford, NJ: Learned Information, Inc.; 1992. 357p. ISSN: 0044-7870; ISBN: 0938734695; OCLC: 26905960.

M203

MCCRANK, LAWRENCE J. 1993. Documenting Reconquest and Reform: The Growth of the Archives of the Crown of Aragón. *The American Archivist*. 1993; 56(2): 256-318. ISSN: 0360-9081. Rev. ed., The Medieval Information Revolution: European Expansion and Documentation in the Crown of Aragón. See reference: MCCRANK, L. J., ed., 1993. 256-318.

M204

MCCRANK, LAWRENCE J. 1994a. Historical Information Science and Communications—A Report and Review Essay. *The International Information & Library Review*. 1994; 26: 1-14. ISSN: 0020-7837.

M205

MCCRANK, LAWRENCE J. 1994b. Primary Sources and Original Works: A Docuserial concerning Archives, Documentation, and Scholarship. See reference: COX, ed., 1994d. 290-299.

M206

MCCRANK, LAWRENCE J. 1995a. Parallel Processing: Collaborative Research across the Internet. (1993 IAHC plenary address). See reference: JARITZ, G. *ET AL.*, eds. 1995. 319-351.

M207

MCCRANK, LAWRENCE J. 1995b. History, Archives, and Information Science. In: Williams, Martha, ed. *Annual Review of Information Science and Technology (ARIST)*: vol. 30. Medford, NJ: Information Today, Inc. for ASIS; 1995 [1996]. 281-382. ISBN: 1-57387-019-6; ISSN: 0066-4200; CODEN: ARISBC; LC no. 66-25096..

M208

MCCRANK, LAWRENCE J. 1996. "Nepravilnoje Ponimanije" v Istorii Raznoglasija v Posnanii [Cognitive Dissonance and Misunderstandings in History]. See reference: BORODKIN, L.I., ed. 1996. 134-39. (In Russian).

M209
MCCRANK, LAWRENCE J. 1996 [1999-]. The Future of Fact: Archives, Electronic Evidence, and Historical Research. See reference: BORODKIN, L., ed. 1996 [199-]. English abstract of presentation, 132-133; paper in Russian [199-, forthcoming].

M210
MCCRANK, LAWRENCE J. [1999]. Historical Information Science: Information Science in History and History in Information Science. *AHA Perspectives.* [1999 forthcoming]: 37(9): 14 pp. ISSN: 0743-7021.

M211
MCCRANK, LAWRENCE J. [2000- forthcoming]. *Abandoned Heritage, Lost Theory: Thinking about Information in Ages Past.* [In progress, 2000-].

M212
MCCRANK, LAWRENCE J. [2000-]. *Conversions: Information, Education, and Transformation of Culture in the Catholic Mission to Oregon, 1835-1885.* [199-, forthcoming].

M213
MCCRANK, LAWRENCE J. [2000-]. *Data Warehousing and Electronic Archives: the Case for Symbiosis.* [199-, forthcoming].

M214
MCCRANK, LAWRENCE J. [2000-]. *Diplomatics, Old and New: Form Criticism and Structural Analysis in Documentation.* [n.p.: forthcoming].

M215
MCCRANK, LAWRENCE J. [2000-]. *The Historian as Information Scientist and Historical Topology as Classification: The Case of Arnold Toynbee.* [2000-forthcoming].

M216
MCCRANK, LAWRENCE J., ed. 1986. Archives and Library Administration: Divergent Traditions and Common Concerns. *Journal of Library Administration.* 1986; 7(2/3). 184p. (Entire issue on title topic). ISSN: 0193-0826.

M217
MCCRANK, LAWRENCE J., ed. 1989. *Databases in the Humanities and Social Sciences.* Proceedings of the International Conference on Databases in the Humanities and Social Sciences held at Auburn University at Montgomery [AL], July 1987. ICDBHSS, 4. Medford, NJ: Learned Information, Inc.; 1989. 718p. ISBN 0-938734-37-7.

M218
MCCRANK, LAWRENCE J., ed. 1991. *Bibliographic Foundations of French Historical Studies.* Conference Proceedings of the Association for the Bibliography of History at the American Historical Association, San Francisco, CA, December 27-28, 1989. Binghamton, NY: Haworth Press; 1991. 255p. ISBN: 0-7890-6042-6 (pbk.). Co-published in *Primary Sources and Original Works.* 1991; 1(1/2): 255p. ISSN: 1042- 8216.

M219
MCCRANK, LAWRENCE. J., ed. 1993. *Discovery in the Archives of Spain and Portugal: Quincentenary Essays, 1492-1992.* Binghamton, NY: Haworth Press; 1993. 590p. ISBN: 1-56024-643-X. Co-published in *Primary Sources & Original Works.* 1993; 3(1-4): 19-102. ISSN: 1042-8216.

M220
MCCRANK, LAWRENCE J., ed. 1999-. History, Information Science, & Technology (column opener). *AHA Perspectives.* 1999 May-. [Column opener] 1999; 37(5): 39- 40. ISSN: 0743-7021.

M221
MCCARTHY, J. PATRICK. [1999]. Commercial Publishers Websites for Teaching U.S. History Surveys. *AHA Perspectives.* [1999 forthcoming]; 37(9): 12 pp. ISSN: 0743- 7021.

M222
MCCULLAGH, C. BEHAN. 1978. Colligation and Classification in History. *History and Theory.* 1978: 17 (3): 267-284. ISSN: 0018-2656.

M223
MCCULLAGH, C. BEHAN. 1987. The Truth of Historical Narratives. *History and Theory.* 1987; 26:30-46. ISSN: 0018-2656.

M224
MCDONALD, JOHN. 1991. *Operational Plan Framework for the National Archives of Canada.* Ottawa, CAN: National Archives of Canada; 1991. Available from the National Archives of Canada.

M225
MCDONALD, JOHN. 1993. Managing Information in an Office Systems Environment. See reference: MENNE-HARITZ, A., ed. 1993. 138-151.

M226
MCDONALD, JOHN. 1995. Managing Information in an office systems environment: The IMOSA Project. *American Archivist.* 1995 Spring; 58(2): 142-153. ISSN: 0360-9081.

M227
MCDONALD, JOHN. 1996a. *Guideline on the Management of Electronic Records in the Electronic Work Environment.* Ottawa, CAN: National Archives of Canada; 1996.

M228
MCDONALD, JOHN. 1996b. *Vision of Record Keeping in the Electronic Work Environment.* Ottawa, CAN: National Archives of Canada; 1996.

M229
MCDONALD, JOHN. 1997. Towards Automated Record Keeping, Interfaces for the Capture of Records of Business Processes. See reference: BEARMAN, D.; TRANT, J., eds. 1997. 277-285.

M230
MCDONALD, JOHN J.; COLE, MELBA SMITH 1981. *How to Make Old-Time Photos.* Blue Ridge Summit, PA: McGraw-Hill TAB Books; 1981. 264p. ISBN: 0830697926 (hbk.); 0830610391 (pbk.).

M231
MCDONALD, TERRENCE J. [1988a]. *The Burdens of Urban History: The Theory of the State in Recent American Social History.* Ann Arbor, MI: University of Michigan; [1988]. 42p. (Transformations CSST [Comparative Study of Social Transformations] Workinig paper, no. 5; CRSO Working Paper, no. 355).

M232
MCDONALD, TERRENCE J. [1988b]. *What we talk about when we talk about History: the Conversations of History and Sociology.* Ann Arbor, MI: University of Michigan; [1988]. 29p. (Transformations CSST [Comparative Study of Social Transformations] Working paper, no. 52; CRSO Working Paper, no. 422).

M233
MCDONALD, TERRENCE J. 1996. *The Historic Turn in the Human Sciences.* Conference of the University of Michigan Program for the Comparative Study of Social Transformations. Ann Arbor, MI: University of Michigan Press; 1996. 417p. ISBN: 047209632X (hbk.); 0472066323 (pbk.).

M234
MCDONOUGH, JEROME P. 1999. Designer Selves: Construction of Technologically Mediated Identity within Graphical, Ultiuser Virtual Environments. *Journal of the American Society for Information Science.* 1999; 50(10): 855-869. ISSN: 0002-8231.

M235
MCDOUGALL, WALTER A. 1995. Whose History? Whose Standards? *Commentary.* 1995 May; 99(5): 36-44. ISSN: 0010-2601. Available in IAC, *General Periodicals*, 79A0575.

M236
MCDOUGALL, WALTER A. 1996. What Johnny Still Won't Know about History. *Commentary.* 1996 July; 102(1): 32-37. ISSN: 0010-2601.

M237
MCDOUGALL, WILLIAM. 1920/1973. *The Group Mind, A Sketch of the Principles of Collective Psychology, with some attempt to apply them to the Interpretation of National Life and Character.* 1st and 2nd rev. eds. New York, NY / London, UK: G. P. Putnam's Sons; 1920. 418p. Reprint ed. New York, NY: Arno Press; 1973. ISBN: 0405051484.

M238
MCEACHERN, CAMERON. 1996 [1999-]. Students Authoring Projects to Nurture History Skills: Opinion-Making, Reflective Thinking, Brainstorming, and others—Classroom experience. See reference: BORODKIN, L., ed. 1996: English abstract of presentation, 111-112; paper in Russian [199- forthcoming].

M239
MCFADDEN, T. 1990. The Structure of Cyberspace and the Ballistic Actors Model—An Extended Abstract. See reference: UNIVERSITY OF TEXAS. 1990. 60-62.

M240
MCGARY, KEVIN J. 1987. Curriculum Theory and Library and Information Science. *Education for Information.* 1987; 5(1): 139-156. ISSN: 0167-8329. See also his related editorial: 1987; 5[2]: 87-90.

M241
MCGEE, WILLIAM; MERKLEY, PAUL. 1993. Optical Recognition of Music. See reference: DOORN, P., *ET AL.*, eds. 1993. 147-154.

M242
MCGOVERN, NANCY; RULLER, TOM. [1996]. *Electronic Records Bibliography* [Electronic file]. Ann Arbor, MI: School of Information; [1996]. 5p. Accessible at http:// http2.sils.umich.edu/HCH/ERECS-Bib/bib.html.

M243
MCGRANE, BERNARD. 1989. *Beyond Anthropology: Society and the Other.* New York: Columbia University Press; 1989. 150p. ISBN: 0231066848.

M244
MCGRATH, JOSEPH E. 1982. *Judgement Calls in Research.* Studying Organizations, vol. 2. Beverly Hills, CA: Sage Publ.; 1982. 127p. ISBN: 0803918739 (hbk.); 0803918747 (pbk.).

M245
MCGRATH, JOSEPH E. 1984. *Groups: Interaction and Performance.* Englewood Cliffs, NJ: Prentice-Hall; 1984. 287p. ISBN: 0-13-365700-0.

M246
MCGRATH, JOSEPH E. 1990. Time Matters in Groups. In: Gallagher, Jolene R.; Kraut, Robert E.; Egido, Carmen, eds. *Intellectual Teamwork: Social and Technological Foundations of Cooperative Work.* Hillsdale, NJ: Lawrence Erlbaum; 1990. 23-78. ISBN: 0-8085-0533-8.

M247
MCGRATH, JOSEPH E.; KELLY, JANICE R. 1986. *Time and Human Interaction: Toward a Social Psychology of Time.* New York, NY: Guiford Press; 1986. 183p. ISBN: 0- 89862-111-9.

M248
MCGUFF, FRANK. 1996. *Data Modeling for Data Warehouses* (Electronic file). 10pts. Accessible at http://members.aol.com/fmcguff/dwmodel.htm.

M249
MCGUIRE, MICHAEL. 1990. *Chaos, Fractals, and Dynamics. Computer Experiments in Mathematics.* Reading, MA: Addison, Wesley, Longman; 1990.(Studies in Nonlinearity series). ISBN: 0-201-232288-X (pbk.).

M250
MCILWAIN, CHARLES H. 1937. The Historian's Part in a Changing World. *American Historical Review.* 1937 January; 42: 207-224. (McIlwain's 1936 AHA presidential address). ISSN: 0002-8762.

M251
MCILWAIN, CHARLES H. 1941. Medieval Institutions in the Modern World. *Speculum.* 1941; 16: 275-283. ISSN: 0038-7134.

M252
MCILWAINE, I. C. 1997. The Universal Decimal Classification: Some Factors Concerning its Origins, Development, and Influence. See reference: BUCKLAND, M.; BELLARDO HAHN, eds. 1997. 331-339.

M253
MCINTIRE, C. T.; PERRY, MARVIN. 1989. *Toynbee: Reappraisals.* Toronto, CA: University of Toronto Press; 1989. 254p. ISBN: 0802057853.

M254
MCINTOSH, R. 1990. *Hyphenation.* Bradford, UK: Computer Hyphenation Ltd.; 1990.

M255
MCKEMMISH, SUE; UPWARD, FRANK, eds. 1993. *Archival Documents: Providing Accountability Through Recordkeeping.* Melbourne, AU: Ancora Press; 1993. 247p. (Monash Occasional Papers in Librarianship, Recordkeeping and Bibliography, 3). ISSN: 1036-2037; ISBN:0-86862-016-5: OCLC: 29623524.

M256
MCKENZIE, D. F. 1986. *Bibliography and the Sociology of Texts.* London, UK: British Library; 1986. 70p. (The Panizzi lectures). ISBN: 0712300856.

M257
MCKIM, VAUGHN R.; TURNER, STEPHEN P. 1996. *Causality in Crisis?: Statistical Methods and the Search for Causal Knowledge in the Social Sciences.* Notre Dame, IN: University of Notre Dame Press for the Reilly Center for Science, Technology, and Values; 1996. (Studies in Science and the Humanities, 4). ISBN: 0268008132; LCCN: 95043072.

M258
MCKNIGHT, CLIFF; DILLON, ANDREW; RICHARDSON, JOHN. [1990]. *CHIRO: Collaborative Hypertext in Research Organizations: Progress Report*. Loughborough, UK: Loughborough University HSUAT Research Institute; [1990]. 23f. (British Library Research & Development Report, no. 6007).

M259
MCKNIGHT, CLIFF; DILLON, ANDREW; RICHARDSON, JOHN. 1991. *Hypertext in Context*. Cambridge Series on Electronic Publishing. Cambridge, UK: Cambridge University Press; 1991. 166p. ISBN: 052137488X.

M260
MCKNIGHT, CLIFF; DILLON, ANDREW; RICHARDSON, JOHN. 1993. *Hypertext: A Psychological Perspective*. New York, NY: E. Horwood; 1993. 202p. ISBN: 01334416503 (hbk.); 0134416430 (pbk.).

M261
MCLELLAN, HILARY. 1992. *Virtual Reality: A Selected Bibliography*. Englewood Cliffs, NJ: Educational Technology Publications; 1992. 60p. (ET Bibliography series, 6). ISBN: 00877782466; LCCN: 92008488.

M262
MCLUHAN, MARSHALL. 1962. *The Gutenberg Galaxy*. Toronto, CA: University of Toronto Press; 1962. 293p. LCCN: 62-4860; OCLC: 428949.

M263
MCLUHAN, MARSHALL. 1964/1994. *Understanding Media. The Extensions of Man*. Introduction by Lewis H. Lapham. Cambridge, MA: MIT Press; 1994. 392p. ISBN: 0-262-63159-8.

M264
MCMICHAEL, ANDREW. 1998. The Historian, the Internet, and the Web: a Reassessment. See reference: AHA. 1998. 29-32.

M265
MCNEESE, MICHAEL D., ed. 1998. *User-centered Cooperative Systems*. In: *Journal of the American Society for Information Science*. 1998 June; 49(9): 796-864. (Entire issue on title topic). ISSN: 0002-8231; CODEN: AISJB6.

M266
MCNEIL, IAN, ed. 1990. *An Encyclopedia of the History of Technology*. London, UK: Routledge; 1990. 1062p. ISBN: 041501362.

M267
MCNEIL, MAUREEN. 1991. The Old and New Worlds of Information Technology in Britain. In: Corner, John; Harvey, Sylvia, eds. *Enterprise and Heritage: Crosscurrents of National Culture*. London, UK: Routledge; 1991; 116-136. ISBN: 0-415-04702-1.

M268
MCNEILL, WILLIAM H. 1989. *Arnold Toynbee—A Life*. New York, NY: Oxford University Press; 1989. 346p. ISBN: 095058631; LCCN: 88023188.

M269
MCNEILL, WILLIAM H. 1990. The Rise of the West after Twenty-Five Years. *Journal of World History*. 1990; 1: 1-21. ISSN: 0022-5436.

M270
MCNEILL, WILLIAM H. 1995. The changing shape of world history. *History and Theory*. 1995 May; 34(2): 9-27. ISSN: 0018-2656.

M271
MCNEILL, WILLIAM H. 1995. Periodizing World History. *History and Theory*. 1995; 34: 99-111. ISSN: 0018-2656.

M272
MEAD, RICHARD. 1990. *Cross Cultural Management Communication*. New York, NY: John Wiley & Sons; 1990. 273p. ISBN: 0471926604.

M273
MEAD, RICHARD. 1994. *International Business Management: Cross-Cultural Dimensions*. Cambridge, MA: Blackwells; 1994. 525p. ISBN: 063118368X (hbk.); 0631183698 (pbk.); LCCN: 93-44208.

M274
MEADOR, C. LAWRENCE; GUYOTE, MARTIN J.; ROSENFELD, WILLIAM T. 1996. *Decision Support Planning & Analysis: The Problem of Getting Large-Scale DSS Started* (Electronic file). Management Support Technology Corp.; 1996 June 14. 6 pts. Accessible at htt://www.mstnet.com/MST/wp_ds.htm

M275
MEADOW, CHARLES T. 1988. Back to the Future: Marking and Interpreting the Database Industry Timeline. *Database*. 1988; 11(5): 14-16, 19-31. ISSN: 0162-4105.

M276
MEADOW, CHARLES T. 1992. *Text Information Retrieval Systems*. San Diego, CA: Academic Press; 1992. 302p. ISBN: 012487410X; LCCN: 91024494.

M277
MEADOW, CHARLES, T. 1987. *The Origins of Information Science*. London, UK: Taylor Graham; 1987.

M278
MEADOWS, ARTHUR JACK, ed. 1987. *The Origins of Information Science*. London, UK: Taylor Graham for the Institute of Information Scientists; 1987. 261p. (Foundations of Information Science, 1). ISBN: 0947568131; OCLC: 16639007.

M279
MEDHI, JYOTIPRASAD. 1994/1995. *Stochastic Processes*. 2nd ed. New York, NY: J. Wiley; [1994]. 598p. ISBN: 0470220538; LCCN: 92036071.

M280
MEDUSHEVSKII, A. N. 1990. *Administravnye rformy v Rossii xviii-xix vv. U sravnitel'no- istorischeskai perspektiv: nauchno-analecticheskii ob zu Mosco* [Administrative Reform in Russia during the 18-19th centuries from the Perspective of New History: a Scientific Data Analysis from Moscow]. Moiseenko, Tatayana, ed. Moskau, RU: Akademiia nauk SSSR, In-trauch. Informatsii po shchestvennyn naukam; 1990. 46p. ISBN: 0.40 RUS; LCCN: 91-215596.

M281
MEGDAL, BARRY B. 1983. *VLSI Computational Structures Applied to Fingerprint Image Analysis*. Pasadena, CA: California Institute of Technology; 1983. 289p. (Ph.D. dissertation; *DAI*, vol. 44/06-B: 1892). Available from: University Microfilms, Ann Arbor, MI (Order no. AAD83-22673).

M282
MEGILL, ALLAN. 1985. *Prophets of Extremity: Nietzche, Heidegger, Foucault, Derrida*. Berkeley, CA: University of California Press; 1985. 399p. ISBN: 0520052390.

M283
MEGILL, KENNETH A. 1997. *The Corporate Memory: Information Management in the Electronic Age*. New Providence, NJ: Bowker-Saur; 1997. ISBN: 1-85739-158-6.

M284
MEHAN, H. 1984. Institutional Decision-making. See reference: ROGOFF, B.; LABVE, J., eds. 1984. 41-66.

M285
MELTZER, B. N. 1949. The Productivity of Social Scientists. *American Journal of Sociology*. 1949; 55: 25-29. ISSN: 0002-9602.

M286
MENEZES, ALFRED J.; VAN OORSCHOT, PAUL C.; VANSTONE, SCOTT A. 1996. *Handbook of Applied Cryptography*. Boca Raton, FL: CRC Press; 1996. 632p. ISBN: 0-8493-8523-7.

M287
MENGES, ROBERT J.; WEIMER, MARVELLEN. 1996. *Teaching on Solid Ground: Using Scholarship to Improve Practice*. Higher and Adult Education series. San Francisco, CA: Jossey-Bass; 1996. 406p. ISBN: 07887901334.

M288
MENNE-HARITZ, ANGELIKA, ed. 1993. *Information Handling in Offices and Archives*. Munich, London, Paris, and New York: Saur; 1993. 197p. ISBN: 3-598-11146-0.

M289
MENNECKE, BRIAN E.; HOFFER, JEFFREY A.; WYNNE, BAYARD E. 1992. The Implications of Group Development and History for Group Support System Theory and Practice. *Small Group Research*. 1992 November; 23(4): 524-572. ISSN: 1046-4964.

M290
MENNINGER, W. WALTER. 1996. Memory and History: What can You Believe? *Archival Issues*. 1996; 21(2): 97-106. ISSN: 1067-4993.

M291
MERIT. 1995. *NSFNET History of Usage by Service*. Ann Arbor, MI: MERIT network at the University of Michigan; 1995. Accessible at http://nic.merit.edu/nsfnet/statistics/ history.ports.

M292
MERTES, K. 1998. Saints, Kings, and Peasants: Indexing Medieval and Renaissance History. See reference: TOW-ERY, MARGE, ed. 1998: 1-10.

M293
MERTON, ROBERT K. 1973. *The Sociology of Science: Theoretical and Empirical Investigation.* Chicago, IL: University of Chicago Press; 1973.

M294
MESSARIS, PAUL. 1994. *Visual `Literacy': Image, Mind, Reality.* Boulder, CO: Westview Press; 1994. 208p. ISBN: 08133166771 (hbk.); 0813319374 (pbk.); LCCN: 93026069.

M295
MESSARIS, PAUL. 1997. *Visual Persuasion: The Role of Images in Advertising.* Thousand oaks, CA: Sage Publ.; 1997. 297p. ISBN: 0803972458 (hbk.); 0803972466 (pbk.).

M296
MESSENGER DAVIES, MAIRE. 1997. *Fake, Fact, and Fantasy. Children's Interpretations of Television Reality.* Mahwah, NJ: Lawrence Erlbaum Associates, Inc.; 1997. 256p. ISBN: 0-8058-2047-7 (pbk.).

M297
MESSER-DAVIDOW, ELLEN; SHUMWAY, DAVID R.; SYLVAN, DAVID J., eds. 1993. *Knowledge: Historical and Critical Studies in Disciplinarity. Knowledge: Disciplinarity and Beyond.* Charlottesville, VA: University of Virginia Press; 1993. 466p. ISBN: 0813914280 (hbk.); 0813914299 (pbk.); LCCN: 92-466606; OCLC: 27226392.

M298
METROPOLIS, NICHOLAS; HOWLETT, JACK; ROTA, GIAN-CARLO, eds. 1980. *A History of Computing in the Twentieth Century: A Collection of Essays.* International Research Conference on the History of Computing, Los Alamitos, CA.; 1976. New York, NY: Academic Press; 1980. 659p. ISBN: 0124916503. Bibliography, pp. 629-659.

M299
METROPOLITAN MUSEUM OF ART. 1968. *Computers and Their Potential Applications in Museums.* New York, NY: Arno Press; 1968.

M300
METZ, RAINIER; VAN CAUWENBERGE, EDDY; VAN DER VOORT, ROEL, eds. 1990. *Historical Information Systems.* Sessions B-12B. Proceedings of the Tenth International Economic History Congress, Leuven, August 1990. Leuven, NL: Leuven University Press; 1990. 118p. ISBN: 9061863880; OCLC: 30885116.

M301
MEYER, CHARLES. F. 1987. *A Linguistic Study of American Punctuation.* New York, NY: Peter Lang; 1987. 159p. ISBN: 0820405221.

M302
MEYER, JOHN C. 1995. Tell Me a Story: Eliciting Organizational Values from Narratives. *Communication Quarterly.* 1995 Spring; 43(2): 210-225. ISSN: 0146-3373.

M303
MEYER, N. DEAN; BOONE, MARY E. 1987. *The Information Edge.* New York., NY: McGraw-Hill Pub.; 1987. 333p. ISBN: 0070417822; LCCN: 86-222546.

M304
MEYER, T.; SPENCER, J. 1996. A Citation Analysis Study of Library Science: Who Cites Librarians? *College & Research Libraries.* 1996; 57: 23-32. ISSN: 0010-0870.

M305
MEYERS, CHET; JONES, THOMAS B. 1993. *Promoting Active Learning: Strategies for the College Classroom.* San Francisco, CA: Jossey-Bass; 1993. 192p. ISBN: 1555425240.

M306
MEYRIAT, JEAN. 1993a. Les Formations à la Documentation en France. Aperçu Historique [Foundations for Documentation in France: A Brief History]. *Documentaliste* (FR). 1993 July-October; 30(4): 213-217. (In French). ISSN: 0012- 4508.

M307
MEYRIAT, JEAN. 1993b. Un Siècle de Documentation: la Chose et le Mot [A Century of Documentation: the Thing and the Word]. *Documentaliste* (FR). 1993 July-October; 30(4-5): 192-198. (In French). ISSN: 0012-4508.

M308
MIALL, DAVID S., ed. 1990. *Humanities and the Computer: New Directions.* Oxford, UK: Clarendon Press; 1990. 222p. ISBN: 0-19-824344-1; LCCN: 90-45127; OCLC: 22278590.

M309
MICHAEL, JAMES J.; HINNESBUSCH,, MARK. 1996. *From A to Z39.50: A Networking Primer.* Oxon Hill, MD: NISO Press; 1996. 166p. ISBN: 0-88736-766-6.

M310
MICHAILOV, O. 1992. *Vlijane informacsonnoj technologii na teoriju I praktiku archivnogo dela: analiticeskij obzor.* [Application of information technology to the theory and practice of archivology: An analytical Work]. Moscow, RU: Gosarchiv, Rosijaskij naucno-issledovatel'kij centr kosmiceskoj dokumentacii; 1992. 26p.

M311
MICHEL, JACQUES-HENRI. 1984-85. *Premiers elements d'une Introduction a l'informatique appliquée aux textes* [Primary Elements of an Introduction to Informatics Applied to Texts]. In: *Philosophie classique* (BE). Brussels, BE: Presses Universitaires de Bruxelles; 1984-85. (Entire issue on topic).

M312
MICHELSON, AVRA. 1987. Description and Reference in the Age of Automation. *The American Archivist.* 1987 Spring; 50(2): 192-203. ISSN: 0360-9081.

M313
MICHELSON, AVRA, ed. 1988. *Archives and Authority Control: Issues and Problems in Computer Applications.* Pittsburgh, PA: Archives and Museum Informatics; 1988, c1989. 63p. (Archives and Museum Informatics Technical Report, 6). ISSN: 1042-1459.

M314
MICHELSON, AVRA; ROTHENBERG, JEFF. 1992. Scholarly Communication and Information Technology: Exploring the Impact of Changes in the Research Process on Archives. *The American Archivist.* 1992; 55(2): 236-315. ISSN: 0360-9081.

M315
MICHENER, JAMES A. 1965/1967. *The Source.* Greenwich, CT: Fawcett; 1965. New York, NY: Fawcett Crest; 1967.

M316
MICHIE, DONALD. 1987. Current Developments in Expert Systems. In: Quinlan, John R., ed. *Applications of Expert Systems.* 2nd Australian Conference on Applications of Expert Systems. London, UK: Addison-Wesley Turing Institute Press; 1987. 237p. ISBN: 0201174499.

M317
MICHIE, DONALD; SPIEGELHALTER, D. J.; TAYLOR, C. C. 1994. *Machine Learning, Neural and Statistical Classification.* Englewood Cliffs, NJ: Prentice Hall; 1994. 289p. (Horwood series in Artificial Intelligence). ISBN: 013106360X; LCCN: 94007096..

M318
MICROSTRATEGY, INC. 1995. *Relational OLAP: An Enterprise-Wide Data Delivery Architecture* [Electronic file]. MicroStrategy White Paper, III. Vienna, VA: MicroStrategy, Inc.; 1995. 8 pts. Accessible at http://www.strategy.com/wp_a_il.htm.

M319
MIDDLETON, DAVID; EDWARDS, DEREK, eds. 1990. *Collective Remembering.* London, UK: Sage Publications; 1990. 230p. ISBN: 0803982348 (hbk.); 080392356 (pbk.); LCCN: 90154419.

M320
MIDDLETON, ROGER. 1989. Computer Techniques and Economic Theory in Historical Analysis. *History and Computing.* 1989; 1(1): 19-37. ISSN: 0957-0144.

M321
MIDDLETON, ROGER; WARDLEY, PETER. 1990. Information Technology in Economic and Social History: The Computer as Philosopher's Stone or Pandora's Box? *Economic History Review.* 2nd series. 1990; 43(4): 667-696. ISSN: 0013-0117.

M322
MIDDLETON, ROGER; WARDLEY, PETER, eds. 1991-. Information Technology Reviews. In: *Economic History Review.* Spreadsheets. 1991-; 44: 343-393. Databases. 1992; 45: 378-412. Computer-assisted Learning. 1993; 46: 379-409. *Econometrics.* 1994; 47: 374-407. ISSN: 0012-9682.

M323
MIE, FREDERICH. 1985. Zur Terminologie und Typographie von Facteninformationssystemen [Toward a Terminology and Typography *(sic,* i.e. Topology) for Data Information Systems]. *Nachrichten für Dokumentation* (DEU). 1985; 36 (2): 66-72. ISSN: 0027-7436.

M324

MIKHAILOV, ALEXANDR I.; CHERNYI, ARKADII I.; GILJAREVSKII, RUDZHERO S. 1969. Informatics: Its Scope and Methods. In: *On Theoretical Problems of Informatics* (pp. 7-24). Moscow: All-Union Institute for Scientific and Technical Information; 1969. 190p. FID 435. LCCN: 72-184275; OCLC: 38075.

M325

MIKHAILOV, ALEXANDR I; CHERNYI, ARKADII I; GILJAREVSKII, RUDZHERO S. 1976, 1982. *Nauchnye kommunikatsii i informatika.* Moscow, USSR: Vseso i uzny i institut Nauchno i teknichesko i informatsii; 1976. Burger, Robert H., trans. *Scientific Communications and Informatics.* Arlington, VA: Information Resources Press; 1984. 402p. ISBN: 0878150463; LCCN: 83-81012; OCLC: 10530973.

M326

MIKHAILOV, ALEXANDR I.; GILJAREVSKIJ, RUDZHERO S. 1971. *An Introductory Course on Informatics/ Documentation.* The Hague, NL: International Federation for Documentation; 1971. 204p. LCCN: 72197718.

M327

MIKHAILOV, ALEXANDR I.; LOSKUTOV, ALEXANDER YU 1990. *Foundations of Synergetics* [System theory]. Berlin, DEU / New York, NY: Springer-Verlag; 1990-. 2 vols.: Active Systems; Complex Patterns. ISBN: 0387527753. LCCN: 90010102.

M328

MIKHAILOV, ALEXANDR I., ed. 1969. *On Theoretical Problems of Informatics.* Moscow, USSR: All-Union Institute for Scientific and Technical Information; 1969. 190p. (International Federation for Documentation series, 435). LCCN: 72184275.

M329

MIKHAILOV, ALEXANDR I., ed. 1975. *Problems of Information User Needs / Problems of Information Science.* Moscow, USSR: All-Union Institute for Scientific and Technical Information; 1975. 165p. (International Federation for Documentation series, 501). LCCN: 81162752.

M330

MIKSA, FRANCIS L. 1982. The Interpretations of American Library History. In: Robins Carter, Jane, ed. *Public Librarianship: A Reader.* Littleton, CO: Libraries Unlimited; 1982. 73-90. ISBN: 0-87287-246-7.

M331

MIKSA, FRANCIS L. 1985. Machlup's Categories of Knowledge as a Framework for Viewing Library and Information Science History. *Journal of Library History.* 1985 Spring; 20(2): 157-172. ISSN: 0275-3650.

M332

MIKSA, FRANCIS L. 1988. Information Access Requirements: An Historical and Future Perspective. In: Hewitt, Joe, ed. *Advances in Library Automation and Networking:* volume 2. Greenwich, CT: JAI Press Inc.; 1988. 45-68. ISBN: 0-89232-673-5.

M333

MIKSA, FRANCIS L. 1992a. The Concept of the Universe of Knowledge and the Purpose of LIS Classification. In: *5th International study conference on classification research*, Toronto, CAN/Amsterdam, NL: Elsevier Publishing Co.; 1992.

M334

MIKSA, FRANCIS L. 1992b. Library and Information Science: Two Paradigms. See reference: VAKKARI, P.; CRONIN, B., eds. 1992. 229-252.

M335

MIKSA, FRANCIS L. 1994. Classification. See reference: WIEGAND, W.; DAVIS, D., eds. 1994. 144-153.

M336

MILES, MATTHEW B.; HUBERMAN, A. M. 1984. *Qualitative Data Analysis: A Sourcebook of New Methods.* Beverly Hills, CA: Sage; 1984. 263p. ISBN: 0803922744.

M337

MILES, MATTHEW B.; HUBERMAN, A. MICHAEL. 1994. *Qualitative Data Analysis: An Expanded Sourcebook.* Thousand Oaks, CA: Sage Publications; c1994. 338p. ISBN: 0803946538 (hbk.); 0803955405 (pbk.); LCCN: 93041204.

M338

MILIC, L. T. 1991. Progress in Stylistics, Statistics, Computers. *Computers and the Humanities.* 1991; 25: 393-400. ISSN: 0010-4817.

M339

MILLER, DAVID W.; MODELL, JOHN. 1988. Teaching United States History with the Great American History Machine. *Historical Methods.* 1988 Summer; 21(3): 121-34. ISSN: 0161-5440.

M340
MILLER, FREDERICK M. 1981. Social History: Implications for Archivists. *American Archivist.* 1981 Spring; 44: 113-124. ISSN: 0360-9081.

M341
MILLER, GEORGE A. 1963. Information and Memory. *Scientific American.* 1963 August; 42-46. ISSN:0036-8733.

M342
MILLER, G. L. 1987. *Resonance, Information, and the Primacy of Process: Ancient Light on Modern Information and Communication Theory and Technology.* Rutgers, NY: Rutgers University; 1987. (Doctoral dissertation). Available from University Microfilms, Ann Arbor, MI.

M343
MILLER, JERRY, ed. 2000. *Millennium Intelligence: Understanding & Conducting Competitive Intelligence in the Digital Age.* Medford, NJ: Information Today, Inc.; 2000. ISBN: 0-910965-28-5.

M344
MILLER, LEON C. 1996. Cyberspace for Archivists. *Archival Outlook.* 1996 May; s.n.: 12-13. ISSN: 0091-5971. Annotated list of 14 Internet/WWW sites for archival interests.

M345
MILLER, MICHAEL L. 1991. Is the Past Prologue? Appraisal and the New Technologies. See reference: BEARMAN, D., ed., 1991. 38-49.

M346
MILLER, MICHAEL L. 1995. Disc Players, the Records Manager/Archivist, and the Development of Optical Imaging Applications. *American Archivist.* 1995 Spring: 58(2): 170-180. ISSN: 0360-9081.

M347
MILLER, PAGE PUTNAM, ed. 1992. *Reclaiming the Past: Landmarks of Women's History.* Bloomington, IN: Indiana University Press; c1992. 232p. ISBN: 0253338425; LCCN: 91046604.

M348
MILLER, RICHARD K.; WALKER, TERRI C. 1988. *Artificial Intelligence Applications in Research and Development.* Madison, GA: SEAI Technical Publications; 1988. Reprint. Lilburn, GA: Fairmont Press; 1988. 213p.

M349
MILLER, RICHARD K.; WALKER, TERRI C. 1987/1990. *Natural Language and Voice Processing; An Assessment of Technology and Applications.* Madison, WI: SEAI Tecnical Publications; 1987. Rev. ed. Lilburn, CA: Fairmont Press; 1990. ISBN: 0881731021. Distributed by Prentice-Hall.

M350
MILLER, STEVEN E. 1996. *Civilizing Cyberspace: Policy, Power, and the Information Superhighway.* New York, NY: ACM Press; 1996. 413p. ISBN: 0-201-84760-4.

M351
MILLER, STEVEN I.; FREDERICKS, MARCEL A. 1994. *Qualitative Research Methods: Social Epistemology and Practical Inquiry.* New York, NY: P. Lang; 1994. 159p. ISBN: 0820423262 (hbk.).

M352
MILLET, HELENE, ed. 1985. *Informatique et Prosopographie: Actes de la Table ronde du CNRS, Paris, 25-26 Octobre 1984* [Informatics and Prosopography: Acts of the CNRS Roundtable]. Paris, FR: Editions du CNRS; 1985. 360p. ISBN: 222203759X; LCCN: 86-210505; OCLC: 15161970.

M353
MILOV, LEONID. 1996 [199-]. Quantitative History: Past and Present. See reference: BORODKIN, L., ed. 1996: English abstract of presentation, 18; paper in Russian [199- forthcoming].

M354
MILOV, LEONID V.; BULGAKOV, M. B.; GARSKOVA, IRINA M. 1986. *Tendentisii agrarnogo razviutiiia Rossii pervothi poloviny XVIII stoletiia: istoriografiiia, kompu'iuter i metody issedovaniia* [Tendencies in the Agrarian Reforms in the Russian Federation throughout the 18th century; Historiography, Computer Applications, and Methods in Data Modeling (Cadastres data)]. Moskau, USSR; Izd-vo Moskovskogo universiteta; 1986. 303p.

M355
MILSTEAD, J. L. 1992. Methodologies for Subject Analysis in Bibliographic Databases. *Information Processing & Management.* 1992; 28(3): 407-431. ISSN: 0306-4573. Distributed earlier in draft from the Department of Energy Office of Scientific and Technical Information, Oak Ridge, TN. Publication no. ETDE/OA-58.

M356
MILSTEAD, J. L., comp. 1994. *ASIS Thesaurus of Information Science and Librarianship.* Medford, NJ: Learned Information, Inc., for ASIS; 1994. ISBN: OCLC: 30264864.

M357
MIMNO, PIETER R. 1995a. *How to Build Enterprise Applications with Client/Server Technology.* Bethesda, MD: Data Warehousing Institute; 1995. 119p. Available from the Institute.

M358
MIMNO, PIETER R. 1995b. *Rapid Application Development.*   Bethesda, MD: Data Warehousing Institute; 1995. 95p. Available from the Institute.

M359
MIMNO, PIETER R. 1995c. *Twelve Technologies You Should Know.* Bethesda, MD: Data Warehousing Institute; 1995. 95p. Available from the Institute.

M360
MINGERS, JOHN; GILL ANTHONY, eds. 1997. *Multi-methodology: The Theory and Practice of Combining Management Science Methodologies.* Chichester, NY: Wiley; c1997. 442p. ISBN: 0471974900; LCCN: 97009288.

M361
MINGERS, JOHN; STOWELL, F., eds. 1997. *Information Systems: An Emerging Discipline.* Berkshire, UK: McGraw-Hill; 1997.

M362
MINICK, N. 1997. The Early History of the Vygotskian School: The Relationahsip between Mind and Activity. In: Cole, Michael; Engestroem, Yrjo; Vazquez, Olga, eds. *Mind, Culture, and Activity: Seminal Papers from the Laboratory of Comparative Human Cognition* (pp. 117-127). Cambridge, UK / New York, NY: Cambridge University Press; 1997. 501p. IBSN: 0521552389 (hbk.); 0521558239 (pbk.); LCCN: 96038956.

M363
MINK, LOUIS O. 1969-1970. History and Fiction as Modes of Comprehension. *New Literary History.* 1969-1970; 1: 541-558. ISSN: 0028-6087.

M364
MINK, LOUIS O. 1977. Philosophy and Theory of History. See reference: IGGERS, G. S.; PARKER, H. T. eds. 1979. 17-27.

M365
MINNICK, AL. 1994. Review of: NAPA, *The Archives of the Future;* 1991. *American Archivist.* 1994 Winter; 57(1): 150-151. ISSN: 0360-9081.

M366
MIRA, CHRISTIAN. 1987. *Chaotic Dynamics: From the One-dimensional Endomorphism to the Two-dimensional Diffeomorphism.* Teaneck, NJ: World-Scientific; 1987.

M367
MIRA, CHRISTIAN; GARDINI, LAURA; BARUGOLA, A.; CATHALA, J.C. 1996. *Chaotic Dynamics: Two-dimensional Noninvertible Maps.* Teaneck, NJ: World Scientific; 1996.

M368
MIRKIN, BORIS G. 1996. *Mathematical Classificaton and Clustering.* Nonconvex Optimizations and its Applications, vol. 11. Dortrecht, NL: Kluwer Academic Publishers; 1996. 428. ISBN: 0792341597.

M369
MITCHELL, ANN. 1997 [1998]. EAD in LC's Prints and Photographs Division. See reference: DOOLEY, J., ed. 1997 [1998].

M370
MITCHELL, B. R., ed. 1998. *International Historical Statistics, 1750-1993.* New York, NY: Groves Dictionaries, Inc.; 1998. 3 vols., 3,150 p. ISBN: 1-56159-233-1 (set). Vol. 1: *Africa, Asia & Oceania.* 1050 p. ISBN: 1-56159-234-X. Vol. 2: *The Americas.* 1,050 p. ISBN: 1-56159-235-8. Vol. 3: *Europe.* 1,050 p. ISBN: 1-156159-236-6.

M371
MITCHELL, WILLIAM J. 1992. *The Reconfigured Eye. Visual Truth in the Post- Photographic Era.* Cambridge, MA: MIT Press; 1992. 273p. ISBN: 0262132869.

M372
MITCHELL, WILLIAM J. 1994. When is Seeing Believing? *Scientific American.* 1994 February; 270: 68-73. ISSN: 0036-8733.

M373
MITCHELL, WILLIAM J. 1995. *City of Bits: Space, Place, and the Infobahn.* Cambridge, MA: MIT Press; 1995. 225p. ISBN: 0262133091.

M374
MITRANI, ISI. *Probabilistic Modeling*. New York, NY: Cambridge University Press; 1997. ISBN: 0521585112; LCCN: 97026099.

M375
MITROFF, IAN I.; KILMANN, RALPH H. 1975. Stories Managers Tell: A New Tool for Organizational Problem Solving. *Management Review*. 1975 July; 64; 18-28. ISBN: 0025-1895.

M376
MIYAMOTO, SADAAKI. 1990. *Fuzzy Sets in Information Retrieval and Cluster Analysis*. Dordrecht, NL: Kluwer; 1990. 259p. (Theory and Decision Library series D, vol. 4). ISBN: 0792307216.

M377
MIYAMOTO, SADAAKI. 1998. Application of Rough Sets to Information Retrieval. *Journal of the American Society for Information Science*. 1998; 49(3); 195-205. ISSN: 0002- 8231.

M378
MIZZARO, STEFANO. 1996/1997. *Relevance: The Whole (Hi)story*. Udine, IT: Udine University Dept. Of Mathematics and Computer Science, 1996. (Research report UDMI/12/96/RR). See also reference: BUCKLAND, M.; BELLAR-DO HAHN, T.,eds., pt. 2. 1997. 810-832.

M379
MOBERG, THOMAS F., ed. 1987. *The International Conference on Data Bases in the Humanities and Social Sciences, 1985* [held at Grinnel College, IA]. Osprey, FL: Paradigm Press; 1987. 533p. (ICBHSS, 3). ISBN: 0-93111351-02-2 (pbk.). Available from: Learned Information, Inc., Medford, NJ.

M380
MOCH, LESLIE PAGE. 1983. Paths to the City: Regional Migration in Nineteenth-century France. In: *New Approaches to Social Science History, 2*. Beverly Hills, CA: Sage Publications; 1983. 261p. ISBN: 0803919859; LCCN: 83-2959; OCLC: 9219352.

M381
MODIS, THEODORE. 1992. *Predictions: Society's Telltale Signature Reveals the Past and Forecasts the Future*. New York, NY: Simon & Schuster; 1992. 300p. ISBN: 0671759175; LCCN: 92-18321.

M382
MOELLERING, HAROLD. [1987]. *A Final Bibliography for Digital Cartographic Data Standards*. Columbus, OH: Ohio State University Numerical Cartography Laboratory for the National Committee for Digital Cartographic Standards; [1987]. 71p. (U.S. Geological Survey, 9). LC call no.: Z6004.D36.

M383
MOELLERING, HAROLD, ed. 1991. *Spatial Data Transfer Standards: Current International Status*. New York, NY: Elsevier for the International Cartographic Association; 1991. 247p. ISBN: 185166677X.

M384
MOEN, WILLIAM E. [1995]. *A Guide to the ANSI/NISO Z39.50 Protocol: Information Retrieval in the Information Infrastructure*. Oxon Hall, MD: NISO Press; 1995. 12p. LC call no.: Z674.8.M64. Available from NISO, Gaithersburg, MD.

M385
MOEN, WILLIAM E. 1998. Accessing Distributed Cultural Heritage Information. *Communications of the ACM*. 1998; 41: 45-48. ISSN: 0001-0782.

M386
MOEN, WILLIAM E., ed. 1993. *Information Technology Standards in the Federal Government: Components of Federal Information Policy*. Proceedings of the American Society for Information Science Annual Conference. Silver Springs, MD: ASIS; 1993.

M387
MOEN, WILLIAM E.; TUCKER, MORGAN S. 1997. *A Guide to Global Z39.50*. Oxon Hill, MD: NISO Press; 1997. ISBN: 1-880124-35-1.

M388
MOEZZI, SAIED, ed. 1997. Immersive Telepresence. In: *IEEE Multimedia*. 1997 January-March: 4(1): 88p. (Entire issue on title topic). ISSN: 1070-98X.

M389
MOHLENRICH, JANICE, ed. 1993. *Preservation of Electronic Formats and Electronic Records*. Fort Atkinson, WI: Highsmith Press; 1993. 144p. ISBN: 0917846176; LCCN: 92-38498.

M390

MOISEENKO, TATYANA. 1996. *Russian Archives and Electronic Records.* A Report for the INTAS Project on "History and Computing." Nederlands Historisch Data Archief (NHDA) Rapporten III. Leiden, NL; NHDA; 1996. Draft (no. ISBN) distributed at the International Workshop, Archives in Cyberspace, Moscow, 4-6 January 1996. Available from the NHDA, Soelensteeg 16, 2311 VL Leiden or Postbus 9515, 2300 RA Leiden, The Netherlands.

M391

MOISEENKO, TATYANA. [199-]. Hidden Structures of the Russian Peasantry (an application of multidimensional statistical analysis). See reference: BOONSTRA, O., ed. [199-, forthcoming].

M392

MOISEYEV, NIKITA. 1996. Modeling Historical Social Processes in the Context of [the] Information Society. Plenary session paper at AHC XI. See reference: BORODKIN, L., ed. 1996. Paper forthcoming, 199-. (In Russian).

M393

MOISSIS, ALEX: READ, CRISPIN. 1997. *Business Intelligence and the Web. The Convergence of Two Technologies that will Change the way we make Decisions.* Technical White Paper. N.p., USA: Business Objects; 1997. 20p. See http://www.businessobjects.com.

M394

MOLINE, JUDI. 1988. *Document Interchange Standards: Description and Status of Major Document and Graphics Standards.* Gaithersburg, MD: U.S. Dept. of Commerce, National Institute of Standards and Technology (NIST) National Computer and Telecommunications Laboratory; September 1988. 44p. NISTIR 88-3851. See also reference: LAW, M. H.; ROSEN, B. K. 1989; Attachment A.

M395

MOLINE, JUDI. 1989. Recommendations for Document Transfer Standards and Their Integration into National Archives Policy. 30 pp. See reference: LAW; ROSEN. 1989. Attachment C.

M396

MOLINE, JUDI. 1991. The User Interface: A Hypertext Model Linking Art Objects and Related Information. In: Dillon, Martin, ed. *Interfaces for Information Retrieval and Online Systems: The State of the Art.* New York and Westport, CT: Greenwood Publishing Co. for ASIS; 1991. 337p. ISBN: 0313274940; LCCN: 91-8240; OCLC: 23220681.

M397

MOLINE, JUDI; OTTO, STEVE. 1994. *A User Study: Informational Needs of Remote National Archives and Records Administration Customers.* Gaithersburg, MD: National Institute of Standards and Technology Systems and Software Technology Division, Computer Systems Laboratory; 1994 November. 125p. (NIST Publication 500-221). Available from GPO: no. 003-003-03305-7.

M398

MOLTO, MAVIS B. 1989. *Textual Regularities Applicable to Full-text Searching: The Case of Family History Literature.* Los Angeles, CA: University of California at Los Angeles. 354p. (Ph.D. dissertation. *DAI,* 50/12-A: 3778). Available from University Microfilms, Ann Arbor, MI (Order no. AAD90-14211).

M399

MONAHAN, W. GREGORY. 1994. The Historian as Performer: Bringing Historical Characters to Life in the Classroom. *AHA Perspectives.* 1994 December; 32(9): 11-15. ISSN: 0743-7021.

M400

MONKKONEN, ERIC H.,ed. 1994. *Engaging the Past: The Uses of History Across the Social Sciences.* Durham, NC: Duke University Press; 1994. 196p. ISBN: 0822314401 (hbk.); 0822314312 (pbk.).

M401

MONMONIER, MARK S. 1991/1996. *How to Lie with Maps.* Chicago, IL/London, UK: 1991. 1776p. LCCN: 90-40687. 2nd ed., 1996. 207p. ISBN: 0226534200 (hbk.); 0226534219 (pbk); LCCN: 95-32199.

M402

MONTROLL, ELLIOT W. 1978. Social Dynamics and the Quantifying of Social Forces. *Proceedings of the National Academy of Sciences of the United States of America.* 1978; 75: 4633-4637. ISSN: 0027-8424.

M403

MONTROSE, LOUIS ADRIAN. 1992. New Historicisms. See reference: GREENBLATT, S.; GUNN, G., eds. 1992. 392-418.

M404

MONTUORI, ALFONSO. 1993. The Psychotherapeutic Model of Time, Space, and Knowledge. In: *Mastery of Mind: Perspectives on Time, Space and Knowledge.* Berekeley, CA: Dharma Pub.; c1993. (Perspective on TSK series). ISBN: 089002567 (hbk.); 08898002451 (pbk.); LCCN: 93010597.

M405
MOOERS, CALVIN. 1976. Technology of Information Handling: A Pioneer's View. Information Science in America. In: *Bulletin of the American Society for Information Science*. 1976 March; 2(8): 18-19. (Entire issue on title topic). ISSN: 0095-4403.

M406
MOONEY, CAROLYN J. 1994. The Shared Consensus of Scholars. International column. *Chronicle of Higher Education*. 1994 June 22; 40: A34-A38. See reference: CARNEGIE FOUNDATION. 1994.

M407
MOORE, A. W. 1993. *Meaning and Reference*. Oxford, UK: Oxford University Press; 1993. 302p. ISBN: 0198751249 (hbk.); 0198751257 (pbk.).

M408
MOORE, DAVID S. 1985/1991. *Statistics: Concepts and Controversies*. New York, NY: W. H. Freeman; 1985. 2nd ed., 1991. 313p. ISBN: 0716721996 (hbk.); 0716721988 (pbk.).

M409
MOORE, DAVID S.; MCCABE, GEORGE P. 1993. *Introduction to the Practice of Statistics*. 2nd ed. New York, NY: W. H. Freeman; 1993. 854p. ISBN: 071672250X.

M410
MOORES, SHAUN. 1993. *Interpreting Audiences: The Ethnography of Media Consumption*. London, UK: Sage; 1993. ISBN: 0803984464 (hbk.); 0803984472 (pbk.).

M411
MOOSEBERGER, MICHAEL, ed. [199-]. Cultural Properties Law and Policy in Canada: The Case of the Donation of the Hudson Bay Company Archives. In: *Primary Sources and Original Works*. Binghamton, NY: Haworth Press; [199- forthcoming]. (Entire issue on title topic). ISSN: 1042-8216.

M412
MOOSEBERGER, MICHAEL; THOMPSON, WILLIAM. 1990. The University of Manitoba Historical Buildings Database: A Case Study of Cross-Institutional Cooperation. *Special Collections*. 1990; 4(2): 99-106. ISSN: 0270-3157.

M413
MORAN, E. THOMAS; VOLKWEIN, J. FREDERICKS. 1992. The Cultural Approach to the Formation of Organizational Climate. *Human Relations*. 1992 January; 45 (1): 19-47. ISSN: 0018-7267.

M414
MORAZE, CHARLES. 1968. L'Histoire et l'unite des sciences de l'homme [History and the Unity of Human Sciences]. *Annales: Economies, Societes, Civilisations*. 1968; 23(2): 233-240. ISSN: 0395-2649.

M415
MOREAU, RENE. 1984. *The Computer Comes of Age: The People, the Hardware, and the Software*. Cambridge, MA: MIT Press; 1984. 227p. ISBN: 0262131943.

M416
MORELLI, J. D. 1993. Defining Electronic Records: A Terminology Problem .. or Something More." See reference: ROSS, S.; HIGGS, E., eds. 1993. 83-93.

M417
MORGAN, MILLET G.; HENRION, MAX; SMALL, MITCHELL. 1990. *Uncertainty: A Guide to Dealing with Uncertainty in Quantitative Risk and Policy Analysis*. Cambridge, UK: Cambridge University Press; 1990. 332p. ISBN: 0521365422.

M418
MORGAN, N. J. 1987. Sources and Resources: the DISH Project at Glasgow. See reference: DENLEY,P.; HOPKINS, D., eds. 1987. 302-308.

M419
MORI, SHUNJI; SUEN, C. Y.; YAMAMOTO, K. 1992. Historical Overview of OCR Research and Development. *Proceedings of the IEEE* [Institute of Electrical and Electronics Engineers]. 1992; 7: 1029-1058. ISSN: 0018-9219.

M420
MORICK, HAROLD, ed. [1972]. *Challenges to Empiricism*. Bellmont, CA: Wadsworth Publishing Co.; [1972]. 329p. ISBN: 0534001874; LCCN: 72080652.

M421
MORIN, EDGAR. 1984. *Sociologie* [Sociology]. Paris, FR: Fayand; 1984. 465p. (In French). ISBN: 223014620; LCCN: 85-150072.

M422
MORIN, EDGAR. 1986. La Connaissance de la Connaissance [Knowledge about Knowledge]. In: *La Methode*, vol. 3. Paris, FR: Editions du Seuil; 1986. (In French). ISBN: 2020092573; LCCN: 88-103302.

M423
MORIN, EDGAR. 1990. *Introduction a la Pensée Complexe* [Introduction to Complex Thought]. Paris, FR: ESF; 1990. (In French).

M424
MORIN, EDGAR. 1991. *Les idées: leur Habitat, leur Vie, leus Moeurs, leur Organisation* [Ideas: Their Habitat, Life, Death, and Organization]. In *La Méthode*, vol. 4. Paris, FR: Editions du Seuil; 1991. 261p. ISBN: 2020136694 (hbk.); 2020056380 (pbk.); LCCN: 92-145881.

M425
MORIN, EDGAR. 1994. *La Complexité Humaine* [Human Complexity]. Paris, FR: Flammarion; 1994.

M426
MORIN, EDGAR. 1996. A New Way of Thinking [Complexity]. *UNESCO Courier*. 1996 February; s.n.: 10-15. ISSN: 0041-5278.

M427
MOROT, EDOUARD. 1995. *The Imagination of Reference: Perceiving, Indicating, Naming*. Gainsville, FL: University of Florida Press; 1995. 218p. ISBN: 081301014069.

M428
MORRIS, ANNE. 1993. The Teaching of IT in Departments of Information and Library Studies in the UK. *Journal of Information Science* (UK). 1993; 19: 211-224. ISSN: 0165-5515.

M429
MORRIS, BARBARA. 1988. CARTO-NET: Graphic Retrieval and Management in an Automated Map Library. *Bulletin of the Geography and Map Division of the Special Library Association*. 1988; 152: 19-35. ISSN: 0038-6758.

M430
MORRIS, CHARLES. 1966. *Otto Neurath and the Unity of Science Movement*. A Collection Commemorating Otto Neurath's Place in the Unity of Science Movement. Jerusalem, IS: n.p.; 1966. (Association for Unification and Automation in Science, 5). LCCN: 68004052.

M431
MORRIS, LESLIE. 1997 [1998]. Developing a Cooperative Intra-institutional Approach to EAD Implementation [Harvard University project]. See reference: DOOLEY, J., ed. 1997 [1998].

M432
MORRIS, MICHAEL H.; DAVIS, DUANE L.; ALLEN, JEFFREY W. 1994. Fostering Corporate Entrepreneurship: Cross-cultural Comparisons of the Importance of Individualism versus Collectivism. *Journal of International Business Studies*. 1994; 25 (1): 65-89. ISSN: 0047-2506.

M433
MORRIS, PETER E.; CONWAY, MARTIN A., eds. 1993. *The Psychology of Memory*. New York, NY: New York University Press; 1993. 3 vols. ISBN: 0814754961 (set).

M434
MORRIS, ROBERT J. 1985. Does Nineteenth-century Nominal Record Linkage have Lessons for the Machine-readable Century? *Journal of the Society of Archivists* (UK). 1985; 7: 503-512. ISSN: 0037-9816.

M435
MORRIS, ROBERT J. 1990. Occupational Coding: Principles and Examples. *Historische Sozialforschung/ Historical Social Research* (DEU). 1990; 15: 3-29. ISSN: 0173-2145.

M436
MORRIS, ROBERT J. 1991. History and Computing Expansion and Achievements. *Social Science History*. 1991; 9(2): 215-230. ISSN: 0145-5532.

M437
MORRIS, ROBERT J. 1992. The Historian at Belshazzar's Feast: A Data-archive for the Year 2001. *Cahiers van de Vereniging voor Geschiedenis en Informatica* (NL). 1992; 5: 42-52.

M438
MORRIS, ROBERT J. 1993a. Electronic Records and the History of the Late 20th Century. Black holes or warehouses—What do historians really want? See reference: S. ROSS & E. HIGGS. 1993. 302-316.

M439
MORRIS, ROBERT J. 1993b. Fuller Values, Questions and Contexts: Occupations Coding and the Historian. See reference: SCHURER, K.; H. DIEDERIKS, H., eds. 1993. 5-22.

M440
MORRISON, KARL F. 1980. Fragmentation and Unity in American Medievalism. See reference: KAMMEN, MICHAEL, ed. 1980. 2-60.

M441
MORRISSEY, CHARLES A. 1998. The Impact of the Internet on Management Education: What the Research Shows. *Microsoft in Higher Education* [electronic journal]. 1998 June: 6 pp. Accessible at http://www.microsoft. com/education/hed/action.htm

M442
MORROW, BLAINE V. 1993. Standards for CD-ROM Retrieval. See reference: KENT, A., ed. 1993. 51: 380-389.

M443
MORSEL, JOSEPH. 1993. *Une société politique en Franconie a la fin du Moyen Âge: Les Thungen, leurs princes, leurs pairs et leurs hommes (1275-1525)* [Political Society in Franconia at the end of the Middle Ages: The Thungen, their princes, matchmaking, and people). Paris, FR: Sorbonne; 1993. (Doctoral dissertation, Universite de Paris IV-Sorbonne). (In French).

M444
MORT, J. 1989. *The Anatomy of Xerography: Its Invention and Evolution.* Jefferson, NC: McFarland Press; 1989. 226p. ISBN: 0899504426.

M445
MORTIMER, ANDREW J. 1993. *Information Structure Design for Databases: A Practical Guide to Data Modeling.* Oxford, UK: Butterworth-Heinemann, Ltd.; 1993. 221p. ISBN: 0750606835.

M446
MORTON, ANDREW Q. 1978. *Literary Detection: How to Prove Authorship and Fraud in Literature and Documents.* New York, NY: Charles Scribner's Sons; 1978. 223p. ISBN: 0-684-15516-8.

M447
MORTON, DAVID LINDSEY, Jr. 1995. *The History of Magnetic Recording in the United States, 1888-1978.* Athens, GA: University of Georgia; 1995. 552p. (Ph.D. Dissertation). Available from University Microfilms, Ann Arbor, MI.

M448
MORTON, HERBERT C.; PRICE, ANNE J. 1989. *The ACLS Survey of Scholars: Final Report of Views on Publications, Computers, and Libraries.* Washington, DC: American Council of Learned Societies; 1989. 137p. ISBN: 0-8191-7260-X; 0-8191-7261-8 (pbk.).

M449
MORTON, MICHAEL S. 1971. *Management Decision Systems: Computer Based Support for Decision Making.* Cambridge, MA: Harvard University Press; 1971.

M450
MOSCATO, LUISA. 1997. Australian Approaches to Policy Development and Resulting Research Issues. See reference: BEARMAN, D.; TRANT, J., eds. 1997. 241-250.

M451
MOSSER, DABIEL W.; SULLIVAN, ERNEST W. [199-]. *Proceedings of the First International Conference on the History, Function, and Study of Watermarks.* [Blacksburg, VA: Center for Textual & Editorial Studies, Virginia Polytechnic Institute and State University; 199-, forthcoming].

M452
MOSTELLER, FREDERICK; TUKEY, JOHN W. 1977. *Data Analysis and Regression: A Second Course in Statistics.* Reading, MA: Addison-Wesley Pub. Co.; 1977. 588p. ISBN: 020104854X.

M453
MOSTOV, STEPHEN G. 1981. *A "Jerusalem" on the Ohio: The Social and Economic History of Cincinnati's Jewish Community, 1840-1875.* Waltham, MA: Brandeis University; 1981. 309p. (Ph.D. dissertation; DAI, 42/06-A: 2821. Available from: University Microfilms, Ann Arbor, MI (Order no. AAD81-26888).

M454
MOWERY, DAVID C., ed. 1996. *The International Computer Software Industry: A Comparative Study of Industry Evolution and Structure.* Oxford, UK and New York, NY: Oxford University Press; 1996. 324p. ISBN: 0-19-509410-7.

M455
MUCHEMBLED, ROBERT. 1974. Famille et Histoire des Mentalités (XVIe-XVIIIe siècles): État Present des Recherches [Family History and the History of Mentalities (16-18th centuries): The Present State of Research]. *Revue des Études Sud-Est Européennes* (RM). 1974; 12(3): 349-70. ISSN: 0035-2063.

M456
MULCAHY, KEVIN V. 1989. Civic Literacy and the American Cultural Heritage. *Journal of Politics*. 1989; 51(1): 177-87. ISSN: 0022-3816.

M457
MÜLLER, CHARLES. 1968/1973. *Initiation à la statistique linguistique* [Introduction to Statistical Linguistics]. Paris, FR: Larousse; 1968. 249p. Rev. expanded ed. *Initiation aux méthodes de la statistique linguistique*. Paris, FR: Larouse; 1973. See also reference: CNRS. 1985.

M458
MULLER, HARRO; CROMPTON, JOE. 1996. Walter Benjamen's Critique of Historicism: A Rereading. *The Germanic Review*. 1996 Fall; 71(4): 243-252. ISSN: 0016-8890.

M459
MULLER, PIERRE. 1989. *PISTES*, pur une investigation systematique des textes [*PISTES* for a systematic invesitgation of texts]. In: *Logitexte*. Paris, FR: CNDP and INRP; 1989.

M460
MULLER, SAMUEL; FEITH, JOHANN A.; FRUIN, ROBERT. 1968. *Handleidung voor het ordinen en beschrijven van archiven*. 2nd ed. Groningen, NL: Netherlands Association of Archivists; 1898. A. K. Leavitt, trans. *Manual for the Arrangement and Description of Archives*. New York, NY: H. W. Wilson Co.; 1968. 225p.

M461
MULLINGS. CHRISTINE. 1992. *Computers and Communications in the Humanities: A Survey of Use*. [Oxford, UK]: Oxford University Computing Services, Office for Humanities Communications; 1992. 86p. (Humanities Communications publications, no. 1). ISBN: 1897791003 (pbk.); LCCN: 93-1001; OCLC: 28224317.

M462
MULLINS, NICHOLAS C. 1972/1973. *Theory and Theory Groups in Contemporary American Sociology*. New York, NY: Harper & Row; 1972.

M463
MULLINS, NICHOLAS C. [1973]. *Science: Some Sociological Perspectives*. Indianapolis, IN: Bobbs-Merril; [1973]. 40p. ISBN: 0672612054 (pbk.).

M464
MUMBY, DENNIS K. 1988. *Communication and Power in Organizations: Discourse, Ideology, and Domination*. Norwood, NJ: Ablex Pub. Corp.; 1988. 194p. ISBN: 08993914800.

M465
MUMBY, DENNIS K. 1993. *Narrative and Social Control: Critical Perspectives*. Newbury Park, CA: Sage; 1993. 244p. ISBN:0803949316(hbk.); 0803949324 (hbk.).

M466
MUNEVAR, GONZALO, ed. 1991. *Beyond Reason: Essays on the Philosophy of Paul Feyerabend*. Doordrecht, NL: Kluwer Academic Publishers; c1991. 535p. (Boston Studies in the Philosophy of Science, c. 132). ISBN: 0792312724. Translated selections from Duerr, Hans Peter, ed. *Versuchungen Aufsatze zur Philosophie Paul Feyerabends*. Frankfurt am Main, DEU: Shurkamp Verlag; 1980.

M467
MUNSTERBERG, HUGO. 1994. *Psychology and History*. In: *Psychological Review*. 1994 April; 101(2): 230-237. (Entire Centennial issue of special topic). ISSN: 0033-295X.

M468
MURDOCK, GEORGE P. 1949. *Social Structure*. New York, NY: Macmillan; 1949. 387p. LCCN: 49-009317.

M469
MURDOCK, GEORGE P. 1967/1981. *Ethnographic Atlas*. Rev. ed. *Atlas of World Cultures*. Pittsburgh, PA: University of Pittsburgh Press; 1981. 151p. ISBN: 0822934329.

M470
MURDOCK, GEORGE P., ed. 1987. *Outline of Cultural Materials*. 5th rev. ed. New Haven, CT: Human Relations Area Files; 1987. 247p. ISBN: 0875366546.

M471
MURPHY, G. G. S. [1970]. The New History. See reference: ANDREANO, R. L., ed. [1970]. 1-20.

M472
MURPHEY, MURRAY G. 1973. *Our Knowledge of the Historical Past.* Indianapolis, IN: Bobbs-Merrill; 1973. 209p. ISBN: 0672612690; LCCN: 72080408.

M473
MURPHEY, MURRAY G. 1986. Explanation, Causes and Covering Laws. *History and Theory.* 1986; 25: 43-57. ISSN: 0018-2656.

M474
MURPHEY, MURRAY G. 1994. *Philosophical Foundations of Historical Knowledge.* Albany, NY: State University of New York; c1994. 344p. ISBN: 0791419193 (hbk.); 0791419207 (pbk.); LCCN: 93005321.

M475
MUSEUM COMPUTER NETWORK (MCN). 1993. *Standards Framework for the Computer Interchange of Museum Information.* Washington, D.C.: MCN [Museum Computing Network]; 1993 May.

M476
MUSMANN, KLAUS. 1993. *Technological Innovations in Libraries, 1860-1960; An Anecdotal History.* New York, NY: Neal-Schuman Publishers, Inc.; 1993. 240p. ISBN: 0-313-28015-0.

M477
MYBURGH, SUSAN. Metadata and Its Meaning for Records Managers. *Records and Information Management.* 1998 May. (Report 14).

M478
MYERHOFF, BARBARA. 1992. *Remembered Lives: The Work of Ritual, Storytelling, and Growing Older.* Ann Arbor, MI: University of Michigan Press; 1992. 387p. ISBN: 0472103172 (hbk.); 0472081772 (pbk.).

M479
MYERHOFF, BARBARA; SIMIE, ANDREI, eds. 1978. *Life's Career— Aging: Cultural Variations on Growing Old.* Beverly Hills, CA: Sage Publications; 1978. 252p. ISBN: 0803908679.

M480
MYLONAS, ELLI. 1989. The *Perseus Project*: Developing Version 2.0. *Proceedings of Hypertext '93.* Pittsburgh, PA, November 5-8, 1989. Baltimore, MD: Association for Computing Machinery [ACM] Press; 1989. 249-257. (Technical Briefing).

M481
MYLONAS, ELLI. 1992. An Interface to Classical Greek Civilization. *Journal of the American Society for Information Science.* 1992; 43: 192-201. ISSN: 0002-8231.

M482
MYLONAS, ELLI; CRANE, GREGORY; MORRELL, KENNY; SMITH, D. NEEL. 1991. *The Perseus Project: Data in the Electronic Age* (brochure). [Cambridge MA: Harvard University]; 1991. 19p. Available from: Perseus Project, Dept. of Classics, 319 Boylston Hall, Harvard University, Cambridge MA 02138. See *Perseus.2.*

M483
MYRDAL, GUNNAR. 1958. *Value in Social Theory: A Selection of Essays and Methodology.* London, UK: Routledge & F. Paul; 1958. 269p. LCC: 58-002336.

-N-

N1
NACHMIAS, DAVID; NACHMIAS, CHAVA 1976/1981/1987. *Research Methods in the Social Sciences.* 3rd ed. New York, NY: St. Martins Press; 1987. 355p. ISBN: 0312676212.

N2
NADEL, IRA B. 1984. *Biography, Fiction, Fact & Form.* New York, NY: St. Martin's Press; 1984. 248p. ISBN: 0312078684.

N3
NADEL, IRA B. 1994. Biography as Cultural Discourse. See reference: KARL, FREDRICK R., ed. 1994. 73-84.

N4
NAISBITT, JOHN. 1994. *Global Paradox: The bigger the World Economy, the More Powerful its Smallest Players.* New York, NY: W. Morrow; 1994. 304p. ISBN: 0688127916 (hbk.); 068807220 (hbk.).

N5

NAKAYAMA, YASUKI; TANIDA, YOSHIMICHI, eds. 1996. *Atlas of Visualization, II*. Boca Raton, FL: CRC Press for the Visualization Society of Japan; 1996. 240p. ISBN: 0-8493-2656.

N6

NAKICENOVIC, NEBOJSA; GRÜBLER, ARNULF, eds. 1991. *Diffusion of Technologies and Social Behavior*. Papers from a conference at the International Institute for Applied Systems Analysis, Lexenburg, Austria, June 1989. Berlin, DEU / New York, NY: Springer-Verlag; 1991. 603p. ISBN: 3540538461(Berlin); 0387538461 (US).

N7

NANUS, BURT. 1992. *Visionary Leadership: Creating a Compelling Sense of Direction for Your Organization*. San Francisco, CA: Jossey-Bass; 1992. 237p. ISBN: 1555424600.

N8

NARDI, BONNIE A.; O'DAY, VICKI L. 1999. *Information Ecologies: Using Technology with Heart*. Cambridge, MA: MIT Press; c1999. 232p. ISBN: 0262140667; LCCN: 98029318.

N9

NARDI, BONNIE A., ed. 1996. *Context and Consciousness: Activity Theory and Human- computer Interaction*. Cambridge, MA: MIT Press; 1996. 400p. ISBN: 02621400586; LCCN: 95010974.

N10

NARIN, F.; NOMA, E. 1985. Is Technology becoming Science? *Scientometrics* (NL). 1985; 7: 369-381. ISSN: 0138-9130.

N11

NASH, C. J. 1992. Interactive Media in Museums: Looking Backwards, Forwards, and Sideways. *Museum Management and Curatorship*. 1992; 11: 171-184.

N12

NASH, GARY B.; CRABTREE, CHARLOTTE; DUNN, ROSS E. 1997. *History on Trial: National Identity, Culture War, and the Teaching of the Past*. New York, NY: Alfred Knopf, distributed by Random House; 1997. LCCN: 97-2819.

N13

NASH, GARY B.; DUNN, ROSS E. 1995. History Standards and Culture Wars. *Social Education*. 1995 January; 59 (1): 5-8. ISSN: 0037-7724.

N14

NASH, RONALD H., ed. 1969. *Ideas of History*. New York, NY: Dutton; 1969. 2 v. LCCN: 69017929.

N15

NASH, STEPHEN, ed. 1990. *A History of Scientific Computing*. ACM Conference on the History of Scientific and Numeric Computation, Princeton, NJ; 1987. Reading, MA: Addison-Wesley Pub. Co.; 1990. 359p. ISBN: 0201508141.

N16

NATHAN, N. M. L. 1980. *Evidence and Assurance*. Cambridge, UK: Cambridge University Press; 1980. 194p. ISBN: 0521225175.

N17

NATIONAL ACADEMY OF PUBLIC ADMINISTRATION (NAPA). 1989. *The Effects of Electronic Recordkeeping on the Historic Record of the United States*. [Washington, DC]: NAPA for NARA; January 1989. 69p., appendices. (Report for the National Archives and Records Administration [NARA]: Contract no. NAXXOP8800009). OCLC: 19372104.

N18

NATIONAL ACADEMY OF PUBLIC ADMINISTRATION (NAPA). 1991. *The Archives of the Future: Archival Strategies for the Treatment of Electronic Databases*. Washington, DC: NAPA for NARA; 1991. 156p. (Report for the National Archives and Records Administration. NTIS: PB92-178631LEU.

N19

NATIONAL ACADEMY OF PUBLIC ADMINISTRATION (NAPA). 1996. *Information Management Performance Measures: Developing Performance Measures and Management Controls for Migration Systems, Data Standards, and Process Improvement*. Washington, D.C.: NAPA; 1996. Available from NAPA.

N20

NATIONAL ARCHIVES AND RECORDS ADMINISTRATION (NARA). 1986. *[The] MARC Format and Life Cycle Tracking at the National Archives: A Study*. Washington, D.C.: NARA; 1986 spring. 11 pp. (A Report of the Archival Research and Evaluation Staff to the Archivist of the United States).

N21

NATIONAL ARCHIVES AND RECORDS ADMINISTRATION (NARA). 1990. *A National Archives Strategy for the Development of Standards for the Creation, Transfer, Access, and Long-Term Storage of Electronic Records of the*

Federal Government. Washington, D.C.: NARA; 1990. 22f. (Archival Research and Evaluation Staff, Technical Information Paper, no. 8). OCLC: 22204421.

N22
NATIONAL ARCHIVES AND RECORDS ADMINISTRATION (NARA). 1991. *Strategy for Electronic Records.* Washington, DC: NARA; 1991. 47p. Available from NARA.

N23
NATIONAL ARCHIVES AND RECORDS ADMINISTRATION (NARA). 1996. *Ready Access to Essential Evidence: The Strategic Plan of the National Archives and Records Administration, 1997-2000* (Electronic file). View at NARA Web site: http://www. nara.gov/nara/vision/naraplan.html.

N24
NATIONAL ARCHIVES AND RECORDS ADMINISTRATION (NARA). NATIONAL HISTORICAL PUBLICA-TIONS AND RECORDS COMMISSION (NHPRC). 1990. *Electronic Records Issues. A Report to the Commission.* Weber, Lisa, ed. Washington, DC: NHRPC; March 1990. 11p. (NHRPC Reports and Papers, 4).

N25
NATIONAL ARCHIVES AND RECORDS ADMINISTRATION (NARA). NATIONAL HISTORICAL PUBLICA-TIONS AND RECORDS COMMISSION (NHPRC). 1991. *Research Issues in Electronic Records.* Conference report: Working Meeting on Research Issues in Electronic Records, January 24-25, 1991. St. Paul, MN: Historical Society for NHPRC; 1991. vi, 37p. OCLC: 27794177.

N26
NATIONAL ARCHIVES AND RECORDS ADMINISTRATION (NARA). NATIONAL HISTORICAL PUBLICA-TIONS AND RECORDS COMMISSION (NHPRC). 1997. *Electronic Records Research and Development: Final Report of the 1996 Ann Arbor Conference.* Ann Arbor, MI: University of Michigan; 1997. 42p.

N27
NATIONAL ARCHIVES AND RECORDS ADMINISTRATION (NARA). OFFICE OF RECORDS ADMINISTRA-TION. 1990. *Managing Electronic Records.* 32p., appendices A-G. (NARA Instructional Guide Series). Available from: GPO, doc. 1992 0-329-445.

N28
NATIONAL ARCHIVES AND RECORDS ADMINISTRATION (NARA). OFFICE OF RECORDS ADMINISTRA-TION. [1990]. *The Management of Electronic Records in the 1990s.* A Report of a Conference held June 21-23, 1989, Easton, MD. Washington, DC: NARA Office of Records Administration; [1990]. 34p. LCCN: 90602997.

N29
NATIONAL ARCHIVES AND RECORDS ADMINISTRATION (NARA). OFFICE OF RECORDS ADMINISTRA-TION. 1992. *Archival Information System (AIS) Prototype.* Report by Standard Technology Inc., and SYSCON Corporation. Washington, DC: SYSCON; 20 July 1992. 2 vols. OCLC: 28539935.

N30
NATIONAL ASSOCIATION OF GOVERNMENT ARCHIVES AND RECORDS ADMINISTRATORS (NAGARA). 1989. *Archival Administration in the Electronic Age: An Advanced Institute for Government Archivists.* (Pamphlet). Co-sponsored by the School of Library and Information Science, University of Pittsburgh. Pittsburgh, PA: NAGARA; 1989. (Grant funded by Council on Library Resources).

N31
NATIONAL ASSOCIATION OF GOVERNMENT ARCHIVES AND RECORDS ADMINISTRATORS (NAGARA). 1990. *A New Age: Electronic Information Systems, State Government, and the Preservation of the Archival Record* (Pamphlet). Lexington, KY: Council of State Governments; 1990. 11p.

N32
NATIONAL ASSOCIATION OF GOVERNMENT ARCHIVES AND RECORDS ADMINISTRATORS (NAGARA). 1991. *Digital Imaging and Optical Media Storage Systems: Guidelines for State and Local Government Agencies.* Albany, NY: NAGARA; 1991. Available from NAGARA.

N33
NATIONAL CENTER FOR HISTORY IN THE SCHOOLS (U.S.). 1994. *United States History: Exploring the American Experience.* Gary B. Nash, director. Los Angeles, CA: The Center at the University of California, Los Angeles; 1994. 3 vols. (National Standards for History). See references: NATIONAL COUNCIL FOR HISTORY STANDARDS. 1991-1992.

N34
NATIONAL COORDINATING COMMITTEE FOR THE PROMOTION OF HISTORY. 1989. *Developing a Premier National Institution: A Report from the User Community to the National Archives.* Putnam Miller, Page, ed. Washington, D.C.: NCCPH; 1989. 39p. (About NARA). LCCN: 89060457. Available from the NCCPH, Washington, D.C.

N35

NATIONAL COUNCIL FOR EDUCATIONAL TECHNOLOGY (NCET). 1991. *Educational Software: A Directory of Currently Available Software for Primary and Secondary Education.* London, UK: J. Whitaker & Sons; 1991. 384p. ISBN: 0850212138 (pbk.):LCCN: 91-65917; OCLC: 24954228.

N36

NATIONAL COUNCIL FOR HISTORY STANDARDS. 1992. *Criteria for Standards (Amended).* Los Angeles, CA: National Center for History in the Schools, 1992 May. Cf., *Progress Report and Sample Standards*, 1993 July & Oct. Available from the Center, 10880 Wilshire Blvd., suite 761, Los Angeles, CA 90024-4108.

N37

NATIONAL COUNCIL FOR HISTORY STANDARDS. 1994. *National Standards for World History.* Los Angeles, CA: National Center for History in the Schools; 1994 October. Available from the Center, 10880 Wilshire Blvd., suite 761, Los Angeles, CA 90024-4108.

N38

NATIONAL COUNCIL FOR PUBLIC HISTORY. 1978-. *The Public Historian.* Santa Barbara, CA: University of California at Santa Barbara for the Council; 1978-. Qtly. ISSN: 0272-3433; LCCN: 81-640706; OCLC: 4617561.

N39

NATIONAL INFORMATION CENTER FOR EDUCATIONAL MEDIA (NICEM). 1996. *International Directory of Educational Audiovisuals (IDEA).* CD-ROM. Albuquerque, NM: NICEM; 1996. Available from NICEM, O.O. Box 8640, Albuquerque, NM 87198-8640. Online access: http://www.nlightn.com; and as *AV-Online* via Knight Rider, File 46, or CompuServe's Knowledge Index, File KI046; and as a CD-ROM it is distributed by Silver Platter, BiblioFile, etc.

N40

NATIONAL INFORMATION STANDARDS ORGANIZATION (NISO). 1988-. *Information Standards Quarterly.* Oxon Hall, MD: NISO Press; 1988-. Qtly. ISSN: 1041-0031.

N41

NATIONAL INFORMATION STANDARDS ORGANIZATION (NISO). 1993. *Z39.19-1993. Guidelines for the Construction, Format, and Management of Monolingual Thesauri.* Oxon Hill, MD: NISO Press; 1993. 84p. ISBN: 1-8801124-04-1. Available from NISO Press at 1-800-282-NISO; Fax 301-567-9553.

N42

NATIONAL INFORMATION STANDARDS ORGANIZATION (NISO). 1994. *Z39.53-1994. Codes for the Representation of Languages for Information Interchange.* Oxon Hill, MD: NISO Press; 1994. 12p. ISBN: 1-8801124-10-6. (Covers codes for 28 languages). Available from NISO Press at 1-800-282-NISO; Fax 301-567-9553.

N43

NATIONAL INFORMATION STANDARDS ORGANIZATION (NISO). 1995a. *SISAC X12 Implementation Guidelines for Electronic Data Interchange (EDI).* Oxon Hill, MD: NISO Press; 1995. ISBN: 0-940016-49-4. 1996 ed., ISBN: 0-940016-62-1. Used with EDI Transaction Subsets (ANSI X12 EDI): *SISAC X12 Implementation Guidelines for EDI.* ISBN: 0-94—16-57-5.

N44

NATIONAL INFORMATION STANDARDS ORGANIZATION (NISO). [1995]b. *NISO/ANSI/ISO 12083 Electronic Manuscript Preparation and Markup.* Oxon Hall, MD: NISO Press; 1995. 200p. ISBN: 1-880124-20-3.

N45

NATIONAL INFORMATION STANDARDS ORGANIZATION (NISO). [1995]c. *SGML TagPerfect.* Oxon Hall, MD: NISO Press; [1995]. Diskette and manual. Available from NISO Press at 1-800-282-NISO; Fax 301-567-9553.

N46

NATIONAL INFORMATION STANDARDS ORGANIZATION (NISO). 1995d. *Z39.50- 1995. Information Retrieval (Z39.50): Application Service Definitiona nd Protocol Specification.* Oxon Hill, MD: NISO Press; 1995. 180p. ISBN: 1-880124-22-X. The same as ANSI/NISO/ISO 23950 adopted in 1997 in the U.S. See guides by MOEN & TUCKER and MICHAEL & HINNEBUSCH.

N47

NATIONAL INFORMATION STANDARDS ORGANIZATION (NISO). 1996a. *ANSI/NISO/ISO 3166 Codes for the Representation of Names of Countries.* Oxon Hill, MD: NISO Press; 1996. 32p. ISBN: 1-880124-19-X. Available from NISO Press at 1-800-282-NISO; Fax 301-567-9553.

N48

NATIONAL INFORMATION STANDARDS ORGANIZATION (NISO). 1996b. *SGML Europe '96 Conference Proceedings: Electronic and Paper.* Oxon Hall, MD: NISO Press; 1996. 264p. And 4 diskettes (Dynatext browser). Available from NISO Press at 1-800-282-NISO; Fax 301-567-9553.

N49
NATIONAL INFORMATION STANDARDS ORGANIZATION (NISO). 1997a. *ANSI/NISO/ISO 12083. Electronic Manuscript Preparation and Markup.* Oxon Hill, MD: NISO Press; 1997. 200p. ISBN: 1-880124-20-3. Available from NISO Press at 1-800-282-NISO; Fax 301-567-9553.

N50
NATIONAL INFORMATION STANDARDS ORGANIZATION (NISO). 1997b. *Catalog.* Oxon Hill, MD: NISO Press; 1997. 36p. Available from NISO Press at 1-800-282-NISO; Fax 301-567-9553.

N51
NATIONAL INFORMATION STANDARDS ORGANIZATION (NISO). 1997c. *The Unicode Standard (version 2.0).* Oxon Hill, MD: NISO Press; 1997. 960p. plus CD-ROM. ISBN: 0-201-48345-9. Software development standard.

N52
NATIONAL INFORMATION STANDARDS ORGANIZATION (NISO). 1997d. *Guidelines for Abstracts.* Oxon Hill, MD: NISO Press; 1997. 24p. ISBN: 1-880124-31-9.

N53
NATIONAL INFORMATION STANDARDS ORGANIZATION (NISO). [1997e]. *Z39.29- 199X. Bibliographic References* (revision of ANSI X39.29-1979). Oxon Hill, MD: NISO Press; 1997 [forthcoming]. Available from NISO Press at 1-800-282-NISO; Fax: 301-567-9553.

N54
NATIONAL INFRASTRUCTURE TASK FORCE. 1993. *The National Information Infrastructure: Agenda for Action* (pamphlet). [Washington, D.C.: NITF]; 1993 Sept. 15.

N55
NATIONAL INSTITUTE OF STANDARDS AND TECHNOLOGY (NIST). 1989. *Framework and Policy Recommendations for the Exchange and Preservation of Electronic Records.* Prepared for NARA. Bethesda, MD: NIST; 1989.

N56
NATIONAL INSTITUTE OF STANDARDS AND TECHNOLOGY (NIST). 1991a. *Proposed American National Standard Guidelines for the Construction, Format, and Management of Monolingual Thesauri. ANSI/NISO Z39.19-199X.* Bethesda, MD: NIST; 1991. 126p. OCLC: 26187127. See NISO Z39.19 (1993).

N57
NATIONAL INSTITUTE OF STANDARDS AND TECHNOLOGY (NIST). 1991b. *Application Portability Profile (APP): The U.S. Government's Open System Environment Profile. OSE/1, version 1.0.* Gaithersburg, MD: NIST Computer Systems Laboratory; April 1991. 67p. (NIST Special Publication, no. 500-187). ISBN: 003- 003-03083-0; LCCN: 91-601082; OCLC: 2531925.

N58
NATIONAL INSTITUTE OF STANDARDS AND TECHNOLOGY (NIST). [1996]. Arts, Humanities, and Culture on the NII. In: *The Information Infrastructure: Reaching Society's Goals.* Report of the Information Infrastructure Task Force Committee on Applications and Technology. Gaithersburg, MD: NIST; [1996]. 117-142. SP857 doc. No. PB941-63-383; SN 003-003-03267-1. Available via Gopher at iitf.doc.gov.

N59
NATIONAL LIBRARY OF EDUCATION. 1996. *World Wide Web Server Standards and Guidelines* [Bibliography]. Washington, D.C.; Dept. of Education, Office of Educational Research and Improvement; 1996.

N60
NATIONAL RESEARCH COUNCIL. 1995. *Preserving Scientific Data in Our Physical Universe: A New Strategy for Archiving the Nation's Scientific Information Resources.* Report of the Steering Committee for the Study of Long-term Retention of Selected Government and Technical Records of the Federal Government. Washington, D.C.: National Academy Press; 1995. 67p. ISBN: 030905186X.

N61
NATIONAL RESEARCH COUNCIL. COMMISSION ON PHYSICAL SCIENCES, MATHEMATICS, AND APPLICATIONS. 1995. *Preserving Scientific Data on our Physical Universe.* Washington, D.C.: National Academy Press; 1995. 67p. ISBN: 030905186X.

N62
NATIONAL RESEARCH COUNCIL. COMMITTEE ON HUMAN FACTORS. 1994. *Organizational Linkages: Understanding the Productivity Paradox.* Harris, Doug, ed. New York: National Academy Press; 1994. 310p. ISBN: 0309049342.

N63

NATIONAL RESEARCH COUNCIL. COMMITTEE ON A NATIONAL COLLABORATORY. 1993. *National Collaboratories: Applying Information Technology for Scientific Research.* Washington, D.C.: National Academy Press; 1993. 105p. ISBN: 0309048486. Note: See Appendix A: Elements of a Functional Collaboratory

N64

NATIONAL RESEARCH COUNCIL. COMPUTER SCIENCE AND TELECOMMUNICATIONS BOARD (CSTB). 1996. *Cryptography's Role in Security in the Information Society (CRISIS).* Washington, DC: NRC; 1996. See http://www2.nas.edu/cstweb. Report available from CSTB: call 1-800-624-6242.

N65

NATIONAL TECHNOLOGY AND SCIENCE COUNCIL (NTSC). 1994. *A Window to the Future.* Papers for a Conference on Managing Electronic Information, 20-24 June 1994. E. Shepherd, ed. London, UK: University College; 1995. 66p.

N66

NATOLI, JOSEPH P. 1992. *Mots d'ordre; Disorder in Literary Worlds.* SUNY series: The Margins of Literature. Albany, NY: SUNY; 1992. 290p. ISBN: 0791411117 (hbk.); 079111411125 (pbk.).

N67

NATOWITZ, ALLEN; WHEELER CARLO, PAULA. 1997. Evaluating Review Content for Book Selection: An Analysis of American History Reviews in *Choice,* the *American Historical Review,* and the *Journal of American History. College & Research Libraries.* 1997 July; 58(4): 323-337. ISSN: 0010-0870.

N68

NATTER, WOLGANG; SCHATZKI, THEODORE; JONES III, JOHN PAUL. 1996. *Objectivity and Its Other.* New York, NY: Guilford Press; c1995. 214p. ISBN: 089625424 (hbk.); 0898625459 (pbk.).

N69

NAUGLER, HAROLD. 1984. *The Archival Appraisal of Machine-Readable Records: A RAMP Study with Guidelines.* Paris, FR: UNESCO General Information Programme and UNISIST; November 1984. 161p. UNESCO no: PGI-84/WS/27.LCCN: 85-243954; OCLC: 13497372. Available from: UNESCO Federal Information Programme, 7 Place de Fontenoy, 75700 Paris, FR.

N70

NAULT, FRANÇOIS; DESJARDINS, BERTRAND. 1988. Recent Advances in Computerized Population Registers. *Historical Methods.* 1988 Winter; 21(3): 29-33. ISSN: 0161-5440.

N71

NAULT, FRANÇOIS; DESJARDINS, BERTRAND. 1989. Computers and Historical Demography: The Reconstitution of the Early Québec Population. *History and Computing.* 1989; 2: 143-148. ISSN: 0957-0144.

N72

NAVARRO, J. J. 1994. Computer Supported Self-Managing Teams. *Journal of Organizational Computing.* 1994; 4 (3): 317-342.

N73

NEAL, ARTHUR G. [1998]. *National Trauma and Collective Memory: Major Events in the American Century.* Armonk, NY: M. E. Sharpe; 1998. ISBN: 0765602865 (hbk.); 0765602873 (pbk.); LCCN: 97046625.

N74

NEAL, ED. 1998. Does Using Technology in Instruction Enhance Learning? Or, The Artless State of Comparative Research. *Microsoft in Higher Education* [electronic journal]. 1998 June; 6 pp. Accessible at http://www.microsoft.com/education/hed/comment.htm

N75

NEAL, JUDITH; TROMLEY, CHERYL L.; LOPEZ, ERNIE; RUSSELL, JEANNE. 1995. From Incremental Change to Retrofit: Creating High-performance Work Systems. Executive Commentary. *Academy of Management Executive.* 1995 February; 9(1): 42- 54. ISSN: 0896-3789.

N76

NEAPOLITAN, RICHARD. 1990. *Probabilistic Reasoning in Expert Systems.* New York, NY: J. Wiley; 1990. 433p. (Wiley Interscience series). ISBN: 0471618403.

N77

NEDERLANDER RIJKARCHIEFDIENST. 1997. *European Expert's Meeting on Electronic Records, Proceedings.* The Hague, NL: Rijkarhiefdienst; 1997.

N78

NEDOBITY, WOLFGANG. 1989. Terminological Data Banks as Knowledge Bases: Terminology and Information/Knowledge Management. See reference: MCCRANK, L., ed. 1989. 493-499.

N79
NEEDLEMAN, RAPHAEL. 1995. *BYTE*, 20th Anniversary Report. *BYTE*. 1995 September; 20(9): 53-165. ISSN: 0360-5280.

N80
NEES, RICHARD J. 1994. *Electronic Image Communications: A Guide to Networking Image Files*. Medford, NJ: Information Today, Inc.; 1994. 95p. ISBN: 0-938734-87- 3.

N81
NEILSON, ROBERT E. 1997. *Collaborative Technologies and Organizational Learning*. Hershey, PA: Idea Group Publishing; 1997. 200p. ISBN: 1-878289-39-X

N82
NEISSER, ULRIC; WINOGRAD, EUGENE, eds. 1988. *Remembering reconsidered; Ecological and Traditional Approaches to the Study of Memory*. New York, NY / Cambridge, UK: Cambridge University Press; 1988. 390p. ISBN: 0521330319.

N83
NELSON, CYNTHIA STEARNS. 1994. Historical Literacy: A Journey of Discovery. *The Reading Teacher*. 1994 April; 47 (7): 552-557. ISSN:0886-0246.

N84
NELSON, JOHN S.; MEGILL, ALLAN; MCCLOSKY, DONALD N., eds. *The Rhetoric of the Human Sciences: Language and Argument in Scholarship and Public Affairs*. Madison, WI: University of Wisconsin Press; 1987. 445p. ISBN: 0299110206.

N85
NELSON, P. E. 1993. Text Retrieval Conference Site Report. In: Harman, D. K., ed. *The First Text Retrieval Conference (TREC-1)*. Washington, D.C.: NIST; 1993. (NIST Special Publication 500-207).

N86
NELSON, REED E. 1993. Authority, Organization, and Societal Context in Multinational Churches. *Administrative Science Quarterly*. 1993 December; 38(4); 653-682. ISSN: 0001-8392.

N87
NELSON, THEODORE H. 1980. Replacing the Printed Word: A Complete Literary System. In: Lavington, S., ed. *Information Processing 80: Proceedings of the IFIP Congress; 1980 October 6-9, Melbourne, Australia*. New York, NY: North Holland; 1980; 1013-1025. ISBN: 0-444-86034-7.

N88
NELSON, THEODORE H. 1983. *Literary Machines*. Swathmore, PA: Ted Nelson; 1983.

N89
NEMETH, GUNTHER. 1993. The Austrian Archives and its Data. (About the Wiener Institut fur Sozialwissenschaftliche Dokumentation und Methodik [WISDOM]). See reference: ROSS, S.; HIGGS, E., eds. 1993. 195-203.

N90
NERI, SILVIA; TRAVASONI, STEFANO. 1995. *Calliope*: An Informatics Tool for Complex Indexes. See reference: BOONSTRA, O., *ET AL*., eds. 1995. 208-214.

N91
NERMUTH, MANFRED. 1981. *Information Structures in Economics: Studies in the Theory of Markets with Imperfect Information*. Berlin, DEU: Springer-Verlag; 1981. 236p. ISBN: 0387111867 (pbk.); LCCN: 81-23247.

N92
NESMITH, THOMAS. 1982. Archives from the Bottom Up: Social History and Archival Scholarship. *Archivaria (CN)*. 1982 Summer; 14/15: 5-26. ISSN: 0318-6954.

N93
NESMITH, THOMAS, ed. 1993. *Canadian Archival Studies and the Rediscovery of Provenance*. Lanham, MD: Scarecrow Press for SAA; 1993. 526 p. ISBN: 0-8108- 2660-7.

N94
NESPOR, JAN KENT. 1985. *The Construction of Knowledge in School Settings*. Austin, TX: University of Texas; 1985. 327 p. (Ph.D. Dissertation. *DAI*, vol. 46 no. 10-A, p. 3074). Available form University Microfilms, Ann Arbor, MI.

N95
NEUFELD, M. LYNNE; CORNOC, MARTHA. 1986. Database History: From Dinosaurs to Compact Discs. *Journal of the American Society for Information Science*. 1986 July; 37(4): 183-190. ISSN: 0002-8231.

N96
NEUMAN, DELIA. 1995. High School Students' Use of Databases: Results of a National Delphi Study. *Journal of the American Society for Information Science*. 1995; 46 (4): 284-298. ISSN: 0002-8231

N97
NEUMAN, WILLIAM L. 1997. *Social Research Methods: Qualitative and Quantitative Approaches*. 3rd ed. Boston, MA: Allyn and Bacon; 1997. 560p. ISBN: 0205193560.

N98
NEURATH, OTTO; CARNAP, RUDOLPH; MORRIS, CHARLES, eds. 1955. *The International Encyclopedia of Unified Science*. Vol. 1, nos. 1-10. Chicago, IL: University of Chicago Press; 1955.

N99
NEURATH, OTTO; CARNAP, RUDOLPH; MORRIS, CHARLES, eds. 1969-1970. *Foundations of the Unity of Science: Toward an International Encyclopedia of Unified Science*. Chicago, IL: University of Chicago Press; 1969-70. 2 vols.

N100
NEVIS, EDWIN C.; DIBELLA, ANTHONY J.; GOULD, JANET M. 1995. Understanding Organizations as Learning Systems. *Sloan Management Review*. 1995 Winter; 36 (2): 73-85. ISSN: 0019-848X; OCLC: 3527106; LCCN: 91-28424.

N101
NEW SOUTH WALES. ARCHIVES AUTHORITY. 1995. *Documenting the Future—Policy and Strategies for Electronic Recordkeeping in the New South Wales Public Sector*. Roberts, David, ed. Sydney, AU: Archives Authority of New South Wales; 1995.

N102
NEW YORK STATE. ARCHIVES AND RECORDS ADMINISTRATION (SARP). 1995. *Managing Records in E-Mail Systems* (Electronic file, WordPerfect 5.1). Albany, NY: SARA; 1995. Accessible at ftp.sara.nysed.gov in the public directory, filename: email.wp5. 1 Research Council; 1996. *Summary Report, 1994*, available from NRC, 2101 Constitutional Ave., NW, Washington, D.C. 20418.

N103
NEW YORK STATE. ARCHIVES AND RECORDS ADMINISTRATION (SARA). 1996. *Consider the Source: Historical Records in the Classroom*. Albany, NY: SARA; 1996. Available from SARA, Albany, NY 12203.

N104
NEW YORK STATE. CENTER FOR TECHNOLOGY IN GOVERNMENT. 1996. *Making Smart IT Choices*. Albany, NY: State University of New York at Albany; 1996. Available from the Center, SUNY-Albany, NY 12203.

N105
NEW YORK STATE. FORUM FOR INFORMATION RESOURCE MANAGEMENT. 1992. *The New York State Sourcebook Pilot Project: A Metadata Approach to Information Management*. [Albany, NY: NYS Forum for Information Resource Management; March 1992. 20p., app. (example of 148 source descriptions completed). State doc., s.n. (NHPRC Grant funded project). Report summarized larger evaluation and feasibility studies. All are available from: New York State Forum, Rockefeller Institute, 411 State St., Albany, NY 12203.

N106
NEWBY, GREGORY B. 1993. Virtual Reality. In: Williams, Martha E., ed. *Annual Review of Information Science and Technology*. Medford, NJ: Learned Information, Inc. for the American Society for Information Science; 1993; 28: 187-230. ISBN: 0-938734-75-X; ISSN: 0066-4200.

N107
NEWELL, ALLEN E.; SIMON, HERBERT A. 1961. *Computer Simulation of Human Thinking*. Santa Monica, CA: Rand Corporation; 1961. 23p. LCCN: 64047172.

N108
NEWELL, ALLEN E.; SIMON, HERBERT A. 1972. *Human Problem Solving*. Englewood Cliffs, NJ: Prenctice- Hall; 1972. 920p. ISBN: 0134454030.

N109
NEWING, ROD. 1996. *Conspectus Data Warehouse Glossary* [electronic file]. [London], UK: Internet Global Services, Ltd.; c1996. 3p. Short version of 15 terms, accessible at http://www.pmp.co.uk/feb48.htm. Full conspectus of 200 definitions available from Prime Marketing Publications (no. 01923-285323).

N110
NEWMAN, D. R.; JOHNSON, CHRIS; WEBB, BRIAN; COCHRANE, CLIVE. 1997. Evaluating the Quality of Learning in Computer Support Co-operative Learning. *Jounral of the American Society for Information Science*. 1997 January; 48(6): 484-495. ISSN: 0002-8231

N111
NEWMAN, JAMES J. 1988. *"To Plow the Same Five Times": Estate Management and Agricultural Change in the Genesee Valley of New York State, 1810-1865.* Rochester, NY: University of Rochester; 1988. 266p. (Ph.D. dissertation; *DAI*, vol. 49/07-A: 1940). Available from: University Microfilms, Ann Arbor, MI (Order no. AAD88-17510).

N112
NIBLACK, W. 1993-95. The QBIC Project: Querying Images by Content using Color, Texture and Shape. In: *Storage and Retrieval for Image and Video Databases.* Proceedings of SPIE conference, February 1993. Bellingham, WA: SPIE; 1993-95; 173-187. ISSN: 1084-2926.

N113
NICOLIS, G. 1989. *Exploring Complexity: An Introduction.* New York. NY: W. H. Freeman; 1989. 313p. ISBN: 0716718596 (hbk.); 071671860X (pbk.).

N114
NIELSON, GREGORY M.; HAGEN, HANS; MÜLLER, HEINRICH, eds. 1997. *Scientific Visualization. Overviews, Methodologies, and Techniques.* Los Alamitos, CA: IEEE; 1997. 700p. ISBN: 0-8186-7777-5.

N115
NIESSEN, JAMES P.; ROBERTS, SUZANNE F. 1999. Challenges and Constraints for History Selectors. Accessible at http://wwwcri.uchicago.edu/info/awcconf/Atlanta%20Papers/ texyales5.htm.

N116
NIESSEN, JAMES P.; VAN ORDEN, RICHARD 1997. *Use of Historical Information Study.* Dublin, OH: OCLC; 1997 Spring. (Unpublished survey report).

N117
NILES, JOHN D. 1997. Appropriations: A Concept of Culture. See reference: FRANTZEN, A.; NILES, J. D., eds. 1997.

N118
NILSON, L. B. [199-]. *Teaching at its Best: A Research-based Resource for College Instructors.* Bolton, MA: Anker; [199- forthcoming].

N119
NISBETT, R. E.; ROSS, L. 1980. *Human Inference: Strategies and Shortcomings of Social Judgement.* Englewood Cliffs, NJ: Prentice-Hall; 1980. 334p. ISBN: 0134451309.

N120
NOBLE, DAVID F. 1977. *America by Design: Science, Technology, and the Rise of Corporate Capitalism.* New York, NY: Alfred Knopf; 1977. 384p. ISBN: 0394499832; LCCN: 76-47928.

N121
NOBLE, DAVID F. 1984/1986. *Forces of Production: A Social History of Industrial Automation.* New York, NY: A. Knopf; 1984. 409p. ISBN: 0394512626 (hbk.); 019504046 (pbk.). 2nd ed. New York, NY: Oxford University Press; 1986. LCCN: 85-29759.

N122
NOBLE, DAVID F. 1997. *The Religion of Technology: The Mythical Foundations of a Modern Obsession.* New York, NY: Alfred Knopf; 1997. ISBN: 0679425640; LCCN: 96-48019.

N123
NOBLE, DOUGLAS D. 1990. *Military Research and the Development of Computer-based Education.* Rochester, NY: University of Rochester; 1990. 421p. (Ph.D. dissertation; *DAI*, vol. 51/06-A: 1930). Available from: University Microfilms, Ann Arbor, MI (Order no. AAD90-32774).

N124
NOIRIEL, GERARD. 1994. Foucault and History: the Lessons of a Disillusion. *The Journal of Modern History.* 1994 September; 66 (3): 547-569. ISSN: 0022-2801.

N125
NOLTE, WILLIAM. 1987. High-Speed Search Systems and their Archival Implications. *The American Archivist.* 1987 Fall; 50(4): 580-584. ISSN: 0360-9081.

N126
NORA, PIERRE. 1989. Between History and Memory: *Les Lieux de Mémorie. Representations.* 1989 Spring; 26: 7-25. ISSN: 0734-6018.

N127
NORA, PIERRE, ed. 1984-92. *Les Lieux de Mémoire.* Paris, FR: Gallimard; 1984-1992. 7 vols. Kritzman, Lawrence, ed., trans. *Realms of Memory: Rethinking the French Past.* New York, NY: Columbia University Press; 1993. ISBN: 0231084048. (Commonly referred to as *Places of Memory*).

N128

NORA, PIERRE; AGULHOR, MAURICE, eds. 1987. *Essais d'ego-histoire* [Essays on Historiographic/Autobiographic History]. Paris, FR: Gallimard; 1987. 375p. (In French). ISBN: 2070711722.

N129

NORBERG, ARTHUR L. 1990. High-Technology Calculation in the Early 20th Century: Punched Card Machinery in Business and Government. *Technology and Culture.* 1990 October; 31(4): 753-779. ISSN: 0040-165X.

N130

NORBERG, ARTHUR L. 1996. Changing Community: The Computing Community and DARPA. See reference: WILLIAMS, MICHAEL, ed. 1996. 40-53.

N131

NORBERG, ARTHUR L.; O'NEILL, JUDY E.; FREEDMAN, KERRY J. 1996. *Transforming Computer Technology: Information Processing for the Pentagon, 1962-1986.* Baltimore, MD: The Johns Hopkins University Press; 1996. 384p. ISBN: 0- 8018-5152-1.

N132

NORDIC COUNCIL FOR SCIENTIFIC INFORMATION. 1996. *To Preserve and Provide Access to Electronic Records.* [Oslo, NO]: Nordic Council; 1996. (In Scandinavian languages with 14-page English summary). Available from the Nordic Council (paper supplied by Charles Dollar).

N133

NORIEL, GERARD. 1996. *Sur la "crise" de l'histoire* [Concerning the Crisis in History]. Paris, FR: Belin; 1996. 343p. ISBN: 2701117992.

N134

NORMAN, DONALD A. 1983. Design Rules based on Analysis of Human Error. *Communications of the ACM* (Assn. of Computing Machinery). 1983; 4: 254-258. ISSN: 0001-0782.

N135

NORMAN, DONALD A. 1986. Cognitive Engineering. In: Norman, D. A.; Draper, S. W., eds. *User Centered System Design: New Perspectives on Human-computer Interaction* (pp. 31-62). Hillsdale, NJ: Lawrence Erlbaum Associates; 1986. 526p. ISBN: 0898597811 (pbk.); LCCN: 85-25207.

N136

NORMAN, DONALD A. 1988/1990. *The Design of Everyday Things.* New York, NY: Basic Books; 1988. 257p. ISBN: 0465067093. Reprint. *The Psychology of Everyday Things* New York, NY: Doubleday; 1990. 257p. ISBN: 0385267746; LCCN: 91-38762.

N137

NORMAN, DONALD A. 1993. *Things that Make us Smart: Defending Human Attributes in the Age of the Machine.* Reading, MA: Addison-Wesley; 1993. 290p. ISBN: 0-201-89859-781-1.

N138

NORTHROP, FILMORE S. C. 1947; 1969/1979. *The Logic of the Sciences and the Humanities.* Cleveland, OH: World Publishing Co.; 1969. Reprint: Westport, CT: Greenwood Press; 1979. 402p. ISBN: 0313211612; LCCN: 78-21524; OCLC: 4494637.

N139

NORTON, MARGARET CROSS. 1975. *Norton on Archives: The Writings of Margaret Cross Norton on Archival Records and Records Management.* Thornton W. Mitchell, ed. Carbondale, IL: University of Southern Illinois Press; 1975. 288p. ISBN: 0809307383.

N140

NORTON, MARY BETH. 1994. AHA *Guide to Historical Literature. AHA Perspectives.* 1994; 32(8): 1, 6. ISSN: 0743-7021. See AMERICAN HISTORICAL ASSOCIATION for the *Guide.*

N141

NORUSIS, MARIJA J. 1991. *The SPSS Guide to Data Analysis for SPSS/PC+.* 2nd ed. Chicago, IL: SPSS, Inc.; 1991. 499p. ISBN: 0923967346; LCCN: 91-66147; OCLC: 25006399.

N142

NORWEGIAN SOCIAL SCIENCE DATA SERVICES (NSD). 1991. *Catalogue.* Bergen: NSD; 1991. Updated by its newsletter, *NSD Brukermelding* (NW). (In Norwegian). Available from the NSD, Bergen, NW.

N143

NORWICH, KENNETH H. 1993. *Information, Sensation, and Perception.* San Diego, CA: Academic Press; 1993. 326p. ISBN: 0125218907.

N144
NOSOVSKII, GLEB V.; FOMENKO, ANATOLI T. 1996. *Imperiia: Rus', Turtsiia, Kitai, Evropa, Egipet: Novaia matematischeskaia khronologiia drevosti* [Imperia: Russia, Turtstan, Kitai, Egypt: New Mathematically derived Chronologies]. Moscow, RU: Izd-vo "Faktorial"; 1996. 751p.(In Russian). ISBN: 5886880100; OCLC: 36751751; LCCN: 97180975.

N145
NOVELLI, VITTORIO. 1983. Informatica e documentazione, 1974-1983 [Information and Documentation]. *Informatica e documentazione* (IT). 1983; 10(4): 270-291. (In Italian). ISSN: 0390-2439.

N146
NOVICK, PETER. 1988. *That Noble Dream: The "Objectivity Question" and the American Historical Profession.* Cambridge, UK: Cambridge University Press; 1988. 648p. ISBN: 0521343283; 0521357454 (pbk.); LCCN: 88-2606; OCLC: 17441827.

N147
NUNAMAKER, JAY F. Jr.; APPLEGATE, LYNDA M.; KONSYNSKI, BENN R. 1987. Facilitating Group Creativity: Experience with a Group Decision Support System. *Journal of Management Information Systems.* 1987 December; 3(4): 5-29. ISSN: 0742-1222.

N148
NUNAMAKER, JAY F. Jr.; VOGEL, DOUGLAS R.; KONSYNSKI, BENN R. 1989. Interaction of Task and Technology to.Support Large Groups. *Decision Support Systems.* 1989; 5(2): 183-196. ISSN: 0167-9236.

N149
NUNBERG, GEOFFREY. 1990. *The Linguistics of Punctuation.* Menlo Park, CA: Center for the Study of Language and Information; 1990. 141p. ISBN: 0937073474 (hbk.); 0937073466 (pbk.).

N150
NUNBERG, GEOFFREY, ed. 1996. *The Future of the Book.* Berkeley, CA: University of California Press; 1996. 306p. ISBN: 05202045061 (hbk.); 0520204514 (pbk.); LCCN: 95-45461.

N151
NUNEZ, M. 1991. The Use of Background Knowledge in Decision Tree Induction. *Machine Learning.* 1991; 5: 231-250. ISSN: 0885-6125.

N152
NUTT, PAUL C. 1992. *Strategic Management of Public and Third Sector Organizations: A Handbook for Leaders.* San Francisco, CA: Jossey-Bass Publishers; 1992. 486p. ISBN: 1555423868.

N153
NYCE, JAMES M.: KAHN, PAUL, eds. 1991. *From Memex to Hypertext: Vannevar Bush and the Mind's Machine.* San Diego, CA: Academic Press, Inc.; 1991. 367p. ISBN: 0-12-523270-5.

N154
NYGAARD, L. 1992. Name Standardization in Record Linking: An Improved Algorithmic Strategy. *History and Computing.* 1992; 4: 63-74. ISSN: 0957-0144.

N155
NYIRI, JANOS C. 1995. Tradition and Social Communications. (Keynote address, Graz IAHC Conference, 1992). See reference: JARTIZ, G. *ET AL.*, eds. 1995. 3-17.

-O-

O1
O'CONNOR, JOHN E. 1976/1987/1996. *Teaching History with Film and Television.* Washington D.C.: American Historical Assn.; 1976. 74p. JACKSON, MARTIN A., ed. Rev. eds., 1987; 1996. 86p. ISBN: 0872290409.

O2
O'CONNOR, JOHN E. 1990. *Image as Artifact: the Historical Analysis of Film and Television.* Malabar, FL: R. E. Krieger Pub. Co.; 1990. 344p. ISBN: 089463126 (hbk.); 0894643134 (pbk.).

O3
O'CONNOR, JOHN E., ed. 1983. *American History, American Television: Interpreting the Video Past.* New York, NY: Ungar; 1983. 420p. ISBN: 0804426686 (hbk.); 0804466211 (pbk.).

O4
O'CONNOR, JOHN E.; JACKSON,MARTIN A. 1988. *American History/American Film: Interpreting the Hollywood Image.* New Expanded ed. New York, NY: Ungar; 306p. ISBN: 0804426724 (pbk.).

O5

O'CONNOR, MARY A. 1992. Markup, SGML, and Hypertext for Full-text Databases. Pts. 1-3. *Professional CD-ROM*. 1992 May; 5(3): 112-13. ISSN: 1049-0833.

O6

O'HAIR, J.; KABRISKY, M. 1991. Recognizing Whole Words as Single Symbols. In: *First International Conference on Document Analysis and Recognition* (Vol. 2:774-782). Actes de la conference, September 30-October 2, 1991, Sant-Malo, France. Sponsored by AFCET, IRISA-INRIA, and Telecom. Paris, FR: Ecole Nationale Superieure des Telecommunications; [1991]. 2 vols. ISBN: 29036771002; OCLC: 30688707.

O7

O'HARA-DEVEREAUX, MARY; JOHANSEN, ROBERT. 1994. *Global Work: Bridging Distance, Culture and Time.* San Francisco, CA: Jossey-Bass Publ.; 1994. 439p. ISBN: 1555426-26.

O8

O'HARE, GREG M. P.; JENNINGS, NICK R., eds. 1996. *Foundations of Distributed Artificial Intelligence.* New York, NY: John Wiley & Sons, Inc.; 1996. 576p. (Wiley Interscience series). ISBN: 0471006750 (pbk.).

O9

O'SHEA, GREG. 1997. Research Issues in Australian Approaches to Policy Development. See reference: BEARMAN, D.; TRANT, J., eds. 1997. 251-257.

O10

O'SHEA, GREG; ROBERTS, DAVID. 1996. Living in the Digital World. *Archives and Manuscripts*. 1996 Nov.; 24: [300-310]. ISSN: 0157-6895.

O11

O'TOOLE, JAMES. 1993. *The Executive's Compass: Business and the Good Society.* New York, NY: Oxford University Press; 1993. 163p. ISBN: 0195081196.

O12

O'TOOLE, JAMES M. 1990. *Understanding Archives and Manuscripts.* Chicago, IL: Society of American Archivists; 1990. 79p. (SAA Basic Manual series). ISBN: 0- 931828-77-5.

O13

O'TOOLE, JAMES M. 1993. The Symbolic Significance of Archives. *The American Archivist*. 1993; 56(2): 234-255. ISSN: 0360-9081.

O14

O'TOOLE, JAMES M. 1994. On the Idea of Uniqueness. *The American Archivist*. 1994; 57(4): 632-658. ISSN: 0360-408.

O15

OAKES, MICHAEL W. 1986/1990. *Statistical Inference: A Commentary for the Social and Behavioral Sciences.* New York, NY: John Wiley; 1986. Chestnut Hill, MA: Epidemiology Resources, Inc.; 1990 reprint. 185p. ISBN: 0917227042.

O16

OAKHILL, JANE; GARNHAM, ALAN, eds. 1992. *Discourse Representation and Text Processing.* Hove, UK: Lawrence Erlbaum; 1992. 395p. ISBN: 086377900X.

O17

OAKHILL, JANE; GARNHAM, ALAN, eds. 1996. *Mental Models in Cognitive Science: Essays in Honor of Phil Johnson-Laird.* Hove, UK: Psychology Press; 1996. 336p. ISBN: 0863774482.

O18

OAKMAN, ROBERT L. 1984. *Computer Methods for Literary Research.* Rev. pbk. ed. Athens, GA: University of Georgia Press; 1984. 235p. ISBN: 0-8203-0686-X (pbk.).

O19

OARD, DOUGLAS W.; DIEKEMA, ANNE R. Cross-Language Information Retrieval. In: Williams, Martha E., ed. *Annual Review of Information Science and Technology (ARIST*; vol. 33). Medford, NJ: Information Today, Inc.; 1998. ISBN: 1-57387-065-X.

O20

OBERLY, JAMES W. 1982. The Information Revolution in Historical Perspective. *[ARMA] Records Management Quarterly*. 1982; 16(4): 5-7. ISSN: 0297-1503.

O21

ODDIE, GRAHAM J. 1986. *Likeness to Truth.* Boston, MA: D. Reidel; 1986. About verisimilitude controversy.

O22
OGG, HAROLD C. 1992. *Optical Character Recognition: A Librarian's Guide*. Westport, CT: Greenwood; 1992. 171p. ISBN: 088736778X; LCCN: 91-36276; OCLC: 24544674.

O23
OGG, HAROLD C. 1993. Pre- and Post-Processing in the Conversion Process for Optical Character Recognition. See reference: DOORN, P., *ET AL.*, eds. 1993. 83-112.

O24
OHLY, H. P. 1993. Knowledge-Based Systems: Another Data Approach for Social Scientists. *Social Science Computer Review*. 1993; 11(1): 84-94. ISSN: 0894-4393.

O25
OIKAWA, AKIFUMI. 1989. [An] Archeological Image Database System. See reference: MCCRANK, L., ed. 1989. 501-507.

O26
OLABARRI, IGNACIO. "New" New History: A "longue durée" structure. *History and Theory*. 1995 February; 34(1): 1-29. ISSN: 0018-2656.

O27
OLAISEN, JOHAN; MUNCH-PETERSEN, ERLAND; WILSON, PATRICK , eds. 1995. *Information Science: From the Development of the Discipline to Social Interaction*. Oslo, NO: Scandinavian University Press; 1995. 281 p. ISBN: 82-00-03939-0 (pbk.).

O28
OLAP COUNCIL [On-Line Analytical Processing]. 1995. *Guide to OLAP Terminology* (Electronic file). Kenan Systems, 12 pp. Accessible at URL: http://www.kenan.com/ acumate/olaptrms.htm. OLAP Council homepage is accessible at http://www. olapcouncil.org/index.html; telephone no.: 1-800-474-6257.

O29
OLDERVOLL, JAN. 1985. Automatic Record Linkage of 18th Century Nominal Records. See reference: ALLEN, R., ed. 1985. 335-340.

O30
OLDERVOLL, JAN, ed. 1992a. Eden or Babylon? On Future Software for Highly Structured Historical Databases. In: *Halbgraue Reihe zur historischen Fackinformatik*.St. Katharinen [Göttingen]: Max-Planck-Institut füΔ876r Geschichte in Kommission bei Scripta Mercaturae Verlag; 1992. (Serie A: Historische Quellenkunden, Band 13). Available from the Institute.

O31
OLDERVOLL, JAN. 1992b. *CenSys. Eine Softwarenwelt für die Analyze historischer Daten* [CenSys. A Software package for the analysis of Historical Data]. St. Katharinen [Göttingen]: Max-Planck-Institut für Geschichte in Kommission bei Scripta Mercaturae Verlag; 1992. (Halbgraue Reihe zur historischen Fackinformatik. Serie B: Historische Quellenkunden, Band 9). (In German). Available from the Institute.

O32
OLDERVOLL, JAN, ed. [1994]. *Historical Informatics: an Essential Tool for Historians?* A Panel Convened by the Association for History and Computing at the nineteenth Annual Meeting of the Social Science History Association, Atlanta, GA (October 14th, 1994). [Bergen, NO: University of Bergen Department of History for the AHC, 1994]. 69p. No ISBN. Available from IACH or editor at the University of Bergen, Sydnesplass 9, N-5007, Bergen, NO (E-Mail: oldervoll@hi.uib.no; telephone: +47.55212322 / fax: +47.55901445).

O33
OLDFIELD, HOMER R. 1996. *King of the Seven Dwarfs: General Electric's Ambiguous Challenge to the Computer Industry*. Los Alamitos, CA: IEEE Computer Society Press; 1996. 252p. ISBN: 0-8186-7383-4.

O34
OLIVEIRA, J. N. 1992. *HITEX*: Um Sistema em Desenvolvimento para Historiadores e Arquivistas [HITX: A Retrieval System for Historians and Archivists.] *Ler Historia* (PG). 1992; 23: 127-138. (In Portuguese).

O35
OLIVIA, LAWRENCE. 1992. *Partners Not Competitors: The Age of Teamwork and Technology*. Hershey, PA: Idea Group Publishing; 1992. 256p. ISBN: 1-878289-09-8.

O36
OLSON, DAVID R.; TORRANCE, NANCY. 1996. *Modes of Thought: Explorations in Culture and Cognition*. Cambridge, UK: Cambridge University Press; 1996. 305p. ISBN: 052149601 (hbk.); 0521566444 (pbk.).

O37

OLSEN, MARK V. 1988-1989. The History of Meaning: Computational and Quantitative Methods in Intellectual History. *Journal of History and Politics*. 1988-1989; 6: 121- 154. Reprinted in: Woolf, D. R., ed., *Intellectual History: New Perspectives*. Lampeter, Wales UK: Edwin Mellen Press; 1989. 121-154. ISBN: 23143558; LC: 91-112877; OCLC: 20771421.

O38

OLSEN, MARK V. 1991. The French Revolution of the Library: The *Trésor de la Langue Francaise*. See reference: MCCRANK, L., ed. 1991c. 33-55.

O39

OLSEN, MARK V. 1993. Scanning, Keyboarding, and Data Verification: Factors in Selecting Data Collection Technologies. See reference: DOORN, P., *ET AL.*, eds. 1993. 93-112.

O40

OLSEN, MARK V.; HARVEY, LOUIS-GEORGES. 1988a. Computers in Intellectual History: Lexical Statistics and the Analysis of Political Discourse. *Journal of Interdisciplinary History*. 1988; 18: 449-464. ISSN: 0022-1952.

O41

OLSEN, MARK V.; HARVEY, LOUIS-GEORGES. 1988b. Contested Methods: A discussion of Daniel T. Rodgers' *Contested Truths*, Keywords in American Politics Since Independence. *Journal of History of Ideas*. 1988 October/December; 44: 653-668. ISSN: 0022-5037. See rejoinder by RODGERS, D..

O42

OLSEN, MARK V.; LEBLANC, PHYLLIS. 1988. La Collecte et la verification semi-automatisée des données quantitatives [The Collection and Semi-Automatic Verification of Quantified Data]. *Histoire Sociale/Social History*(CN). 1988; 41: 137-143. (In French). ISSN: 0018-2257.

O43

OLSEN, MARK V.; McLEAN, ALICE M.; THOMAS, JEAN-JACQUES. 1993. Optical Character Scanning: A Discussion of Efficiency and Politics. *Computers and Humanities*. 1993; 27 (2): 121-128. ISSN: 0010-4817. Alternate version: Scanning, Keyboarding, and Data Verification: Factors in Selecting Data Collection Technologies. See reference: NETHERLANDS HDA & NICI. 1993: 93-112.

O44

OLSON, GARY M; OLSON, JUDY S.; CARTER, MARK R. 1992. Small Group Design Meetings: An Analysis of Collaboration. *Human-Computer Interaction*. 1992 Winter; 7(4); 347-374. ISSN: 0737-0024.

O45

OLSSON, LARS O. 1995. *Undergraduate Teaching of the History of Technology: A Survey of the Teaching at Some Universities in the USA in 1993*. Gothenberg, SE: Chalmers University of Technology Dept. of History of Technology and Industry; 1995. 69p. (Updates similar survey in 1978).

O46

ONEGA JAEN, SUSANA; GARCIA LANDA, JOSÉ A. 1996. *Narratology: An Introduction*. London, UK: Longman; 1996. 324p. ISBN: 05822555422.

O47

ONG, WALTER. 1967. *The Presence of the Word: Some Prolegomena for Cultural and Religious History*. Terry Lectures. New Haven, CT: Yale University; 1967. 360p. Reprinted. Minneapolis, MN: University of Minnesota Press; 1981. 360p. ISBN: 0816610436 (pbk.); LCCN: 81-003017.

O48

ONG, WALTER. 1977. *Interfaces of the Word: Studies in the Evolution of Consciousness and Culture*. Ithaca, NY: Cornell University Press; 1977. 352p. ISBN: 080141105X.

O49

ONG, WALTER J. 1982. *Orality and Literacy: Technologizing the Word*. London, UK: Methuen; 1982. 201p. ISBN: 041671370X (hbk.); 0416713807 (pbk.).

O50

ONLINE COMPUTER LIBRARY CENTER (OCLC) INC. 1979-. *Cataloging: User Manual*. Dublin, OH: OCLC; 1979-. Loose-leaf vol. ISBN: 0933418019.

O51

ONLINE COMPUTER LIBRARY CENTER (OCLC) INC. 1980-. *Maps Format*. Columbus, OH: OCLC; 1980-. Loose-leaf vol. ISBN: 093418167.

O52

ONLINE COMPUTER LIBRARY CENTER (OCLC) INC. 1984-. *Name-Authority: User Manual*. Columbus, OH: OCLC; 1980-. Loose-leaf vol. ISBN: 0933418000 (set); 0933418078.

O53
ONLINE COMPUTER LIBRARY CENTER (OCLC) INC. 1986-a. *Archives and Manuscript Control Format.* Dublin, OH: OCLC; 1986-. Loose-leaf vol. ISBN: 0933418000 (set); 0933418884.

O54
ONLINE COMPUTER LIBRARY CENTER (OCLC) INC. 1986-b. *Machine-readable Data Files Format.* 2nd ed. Dublin, OH: OCLC; 1986-. Loose-leaf vol. ISBN: 0933418000 (Set); 0933418892.

O55
ONLINE COMPUTER LIBRARY CENTER (OCLC) INC. 1989. *A Guide to Special Collections in the OCLC Database.* Schieber, P.; Voedisch, V. G.; Wright, B. A., comps. Dublin, OH: OCLC; 1989. 120p. ISBN: 1556530250 (pbk.).

056
ONLINE COMPUTER LIBRARY CENTER (OCLC) INC. 1989. *Computer Files Format.* Dublin, OH: OCLC; 1989. Loose-leaf vol. ISBN: 0933418000 (Set).

O57
ONLINE COMPUTER LIBRARY CENTER (OCLC) INC. 1993. *Building a Catalog of Internet-accessible Materials.* A Proposal to the U.S. Dept. Of Education Research and Improvement, Library Programs. Dublin, OH: OCLC; 1993. 28p.

O58
ONLINE COMPUTER LIBRARY CENTER (OCLC) INC. 1995. *The New Electronic Scholarship.* Dublin, OH: OCLC; 1995.

O59
ONLINE COMPUTER LIBRARY CENTER (OCLC) INC. 1999. *The Dublin Core Metadata Initiative.* Dublin, OH: OCLC Office of Research and Special Projects; 1999. Accessible at http://purl.org.DC.

O60
ORAVEC, JO ANN. 1996. *Virtual Individuals, Virtual Groups: Human Dimensions of Groupware and Computer Networking.* Cambridge, UK: Cambridge University Press; 1996. 389p. ISBN: 0-521-4593-X.

O61
ORBACH, BARBARA C. 1991. The View from the Researcher's Desk: Historians' Perceptions of Research and Repositories. *The American Archivist.* 1991 Winter; 54: 28-43. ISSN: 0360-9081.

O62
ORBANZ, EVA, ed. 1988. *Archiving the Audio-Visual Heritage; A Joint Technical Symposium: FIAF* [Federation internationale des archives du film]; *FIAT* [Federation internationale des archives de television]; *IASA* [International Association of Sound Archives], May 20-22, 1987 in Berlin. Organized by the Stiftung Deutsche Kinemathek. M. Hagen, trans. Berlin, DEU: Stiftung Deutsche Kinemathek; c1988. 169p. LCCN: 92196017.

O63
ORE, E. S. 1992. A Supra-institutional Infrastructure for Image Processing in the Humanities? See reference: THALLER, M., ed., 1992a. 135-142.

O64
ORGANIZATION FOR ECONOMIC CO-OPERATION AND DEVELOPMENT (OECD). 1995. *The Global Human Genome Programme.* Megascience: the OECD Forum. Paris, FR: OECD; 1995. 75p. ISBN: 9264145753.

O65
ORGANIZATION OF AMERICAN HISTORIANS (OAH). 1981-. *OAH Newsletter.* Bloomington, IN: OAH; 1981-. Qtly. ISSN: 1059-1125; LCCN: 93-648046; OCLC: 7981472. Available from: OAH, 112 N. Bryan St., Bloomington, IN 47401.

O66
ORGANIZATION OF AMERICAN HISTORIANS (OAH). 1993. Computing Journals for the Historian. *American History: A Bibliographic Review.* 1993; 4: 37-45. ISSN: 0748-6731.

O67
ORLIKOWSKI, WANDA J. 1992. The Duality of Technology: Rethinking the Concept of Technology in Organizations. *Organization Science.* 1992; 3: 398-427. ISSN: 1047- 7039.

O68
ORLIKOWSKI, WANDA J. 1993. Learning from Notes: Organizational Issues in Groupware Implementation. *The Information Society.* 1993; 9(3): 237-250.

O69
ORLIKOWSKI, WANDA J. 1995. Structuration Theory in Practice: Exploring Organizations with a Structural Lens (Video recording). ICOS Seminar series, Nov. 17, 1995. Ann Arbor, MI: University of Michigan Interdisciplinary Committee on Organizational Studies; 1995. 1 Video cassette (106 minutes). Based on ORLIKOWSKI, 1992; and ORLIKOWSKI, W.; YATES, J. 1992.

O70
ORLIKOWSKI, WANDA J.; BAROUDI, J. J. 1991. Studying IT In Organizations: Research Approaches and Assumptions. *Information Systems Research*. 1991; 2: 1-28. ISSN: 1047-7074.

O71
ORLIKOWSKI, WANDA J.; HOFMAN, J. DEBRA. 1997. An Improvisational Model for Change Management: The Case of Groupware Technologies. *Sloan Management Review*. 1997 Winter; 38(2): 11-26. ISSN: 0019848X.

O72
ORLIKOWSKI, WANDA J.; YATES, JOANNE. 1992. Genres of Organizational Communication: A Structuration Approach to Studying Communication and Media. *Academy of Management Review*. 1992; 17: 299-326. ISNN: 0363-7425.

O73
ORLIKOWSKI, WANDA J.; YATES, JOANNE. 1994. Genre Repertoire: The Structuring of Communicative Practices in Organizations. *Administrative Science Quarterly*. 1994 December; 39(4): 541-574. ISSN: 0001-8392; OCLC: 1461102; LCCN: 57-59224.

O74
ORNA, ELIZABETH; PETTIT, CHARLES. 1980. *Information Handling in Museums*. New York, NY: C. Bingley; 1980. 190p. ISBN: 0851573002. New York, NY: KG Saur; 1980. ISBN: 0896644405. LCCN: 81-140240; OCLC: 9041997.

O75
ORNSTEIN, ROBERT. 1983/1986/1991. *The Evolution of Consciousness: Darwin, Freud, and Cranial Lere on the Origins of the Way We Think*. New York, NY: Prentice-Hall Press; 1991. 305p. ISBN: 0135875692; LCCN: 91-11306.

O76
ORR, KEN. 1977. *Structured Systems Development*. New York, NY: Yourdon Press; 1977. 170p. ISBN: 091707265.

O77
ORR, KEN. [1996]. *Data Warehousing Techology: A White Paper* (Electronic file, text and Powerpoint images). Ken Orr Institute, [1996]. 7 pts. Accessible at http://www.kenorrinst.com/wp/dwt/dwt1-1.html.

O78
ORTEN, JON D. 1989. *Elizabethan Puritanism and the Plain Style*. Minneapolis, MN: University of Minnesota; 1989. 255p. (Ph.D. dissertation; *DAI*, vol. 50/11-A: 3605). Available from: University Microfilms, Ann Arbor, MI (Order no. AAD90-08291).

O79
ORTONY, ANDREV, ed. 1979/1993. *Metaphor and Thought*. New York, NY: Cambridge University Press; 1979. 2nd ed., 1993. 678p. ISBN: 05214054775 (hbk.); 0521405610 (pbk.); LCCN: 92037625.

O80
ORWIG, RICHARD; CHEN, HSINCHUN; NUNAMAKER, JAY F. 1997. A Graphical Self-Organizing Approach to Classifying Electronic Meeting Output. *Journal of the American Society for Information Science*. 1997 February; 48 (2): 157-170. ISSN: 0002-8231.

O81
OSBORNE, ADAM. 1979. *Running Wild: The Next Industrial Revolution*. Berkeley, CA: McGraw-Hill Inc.; 1979. 181p. ISBN: 0-931988-28-4.

O82
OSBORNE, ANDREW D. 1991. From Cutter and Dewey to Mortimer Traube and Beyond: A Complete Century of Change in Cataloging and Classification. *Cataloging and Classification Quarterly*. 1991; 12(3-4): 35-50. ISSN: 0163-9374.

O83
OSBORNE, DAVID; GAEBLER, T. 1992. *Reinventing Government: How the Entrepreneurial Spirit is Transforming the Public Sector*. New York, NY: Plume Books; 1992. Reading, MA: Addison-Wesley Pub. Co; 1992. 405p. ISBN: 0201523819.

O84
OSBORNE, MARTIN J.; RUBINSTEIN, ARIEL. 1994. *A Course in Game Theory*. Cambridge, MA: MIT Press; 1994. 368p. ISBN: 0-262-65040-1.

O85
OSBORNE, WILMA; ROSEN, BRUCE; GALLAGHER, LEONARD. [1989]. Recommendations for Database and Data Dictionary Standards and Their Integration into National Archives Policy. See reference: LAW & ROSEN, 1989: Attachment D. (18p).

O86
OSIEL, MARK. 1997. *Mass Atrocity, Collective Memory, and the Law*. New Brunswick, NJ: Transaction Publishers; 1997. 317p. ISBN: 1560003227; LCCN: 96050097.

O87
OSLIN, GEORGE P. 1992. *The Story of Telecommunications*. Macon, GA: Mercer University Press; 1992. 507p. ISBN: 0-8654-418-2.

O88
OTLET, PAUL. 1934; repr. 1989. *Traité de documentation: La Livre sur le livre, théories, et pratique*. Bruxelles, BE: Editions Mundaneum; 1934. Repr., Liège, BE: Centre de Lecture Publique de la Communauté Française; 1989. 431lp. (In French)

O89
OTLET, PAUL. 1990. *International Organization and Dissemination of Knowledge: Selected Essays*. W. Boyd Rayward, trans. and ed. Amsterdam, NL: Elsevier; 1990. 256p. FID pub. 684. ISBN:0-444-88678-8.

O90
OTT, EDWARD. 1993. *Chaos in Dynamical Systems*. Cambridge, UK: Cambridge University Press; 1993. 385p. ISBN: 0521432154 (hbk.); 0521437997 (hbk.).

O91
OTT, EDWARD; SAUER, TIM; YORKE, JAMES A. 1994. *Coping with Chaos; Analysis of Chaotic Data and the Exploitation of Chaotic Systems*. New York, NY: J. Wiley; 1994. ISBN: 0471025569.

O92
OUKSEL, A.; NAIMAN, C. F. 1994. Coordinating Context building in Heterogeneous Information Systems. *Journal of Intelligent Information Systems*. 1994; 3: 151-183. ISSN: 0925-9902.

O93
OUY, GILBERT. 1978. Comment render les manuscrits médiévaux accessibles aux chercheurs [How to make medieval manuscripts accessible to researchers]. In. Guys, Albert.; Gumbert, J. P., ed. *Codicologica 4: Essais méthodologiques:* vol. 9. Leiden, NL: E. J. Brill; 1978. 9-58.

O94
OVERMAN, E. SAM. 1996. The New Science of Administration: Chaos and Quantum Theory. *Public Administration Review*. 1996 September; 56(5): 487-492. ISSN: 0033-3352.

O95
OWENS, ROBERT; SHAKESHAFT, CAROL. 1992. The New "Revolution" in Administrative Theory. *Journal of Educational Administration*.1992; 30(2): 4-17. ISSN: 0957-8234.

O96
OXFORD UNIVERSITY PRESS. 1990. *Micro-OCP (Oxford Concordance Program)*. (Electronic software). New York, NY: Oxford University Press; 1990. 175p. and disk. ISBN: 0198249993; LCCN: 87-47374; OCLC: 16923730. Available from: Oxford University Press, 200 Madison Ave., New York, NY.

O97
OZAWA, KAZUMASA. 1991. An Archeological Research Support System with Databases of Japanese Ancient Tombs and Geography. See reference: BEST, H. *ET AL.*, eds., 1991. 13-20.

-P-

P1
PACEY, ARNOLD. 1975/1992. *The Maze of Ingenuity: Ideas and Idealism in the Development of Technology*. New York, NY: Holmes & Meier; 1975. 350p. ISBN: 0841901813. 2nd ed. Cambridge, MA: MIT Press; 1992. 306p. ISBN: 0262161281 (hbk.); 026266075X (pbk.).

P2
PACEY, ARNOLD. 1983. *The Culture of Technology*. Cambridge, MA: MIT Press; 1983. 210p. ISBN: 0262160935; LCCN: 83-11393; OCLC: 9576234.

P3
PACEY, ARNOLD. 1990. *Technology in World Civilization: A Thousand Year History*. Cambridge, MA: MIT Press; 1990. 238 p. ISBN: 0262161176; LCCN: 89012801.

P4
PADAGAS, BARBARA. 1992. *Sequel Server* and *Visual Basic* (electronic software). Seattle, WA: Microsoft, Inc.; 1992.

P5

PAEPCKE, ANDREAS; COUSINS, STEVE B.; GARCIA-MOLINA, HECTOR; HASSAN, SCOTT W.; KETCH-PEL, SCHATZ, BRUCE; MISCHO, WILLIAM H.; COLE, TIMOTHY W.; HARDIN, JOSEPH B.; BISHOP, ANN P.; CHEN, HSINCHUN. 1996. Federating Diverse Collections of Scientific Literature. See reference: SCHATZ, B.; CHEN, H., eds. 1996. 28-36.

P6

PAEZ, DARIO; BASABE, NEKAME; GONZALEZ, JOSÉ LUIZ. 1997. Social Processes and Collective Memory: A Cross-Cultural Approach to Remembering Political Events. See reference: PENNEBAKER, J. W., *ET AL.*, eds. 1997.

P7

PAGE, CARL. 1995. *Philosophical Historicism and the Betrayal of First Philosophy*. University Park, PA: University of Pennsylvania Press; 1995. 235p. ISBN: 0271013303 (pbk.); 0271011300 (pbk.).

P8

PAGELL, R. A. 1988. Primary Full-text Information: Databases for the End-user. In: *Online Information 88. Proceedings of the 12th International Online Information meeting, London, 6-9 December 1988* (pp. 255-62). Oxford, UK: Learned Information (Europe); 1988. 2 vols., 412p. ISBN: 0904933687; OCLC: 19787338.

P9

PAHL, RONALD H. 1994. Forsooth! An Exploration into Living History. *The Social Studies*. 1994 Jan.-Feb.; 85(1); 21-25. ISSN: 0037-7996.

P10

PAISLEY, WILLIAM J. 1965. *The Flow of [Behavioral] Science Information: A Review of the Research Literature*. Stanford, CA: Stanford University Press for the Institute for Communication Research; 1965.

P11

PAISLEY, WILLIAM J. 1986. The Convergence of Communication and Information Science. In: Edelman, Hendrik, ed. *Libraries and Information Science in the Electronic Age* (pp. 122-152). Philadelphia, PA: ISI Press; 1986. 177p. ISBN: 0894950584.

P12

PAISLEY, WILLIAM J. 1990a. Information Science as a Multi-discipline. See reference: PEMBERTON, J. M.; PRENTICE. 1990. 3-24.

P13

PAISLEY, WILLIAM J. 1990b. An Oasis where Many Trails Cross: The Improbable Co-citation Networks of a Multi-discipline. *Journal of the American Society for Information Science*. 1990; 42: 459-468. ISSN: 0002-8231.

P14

PAISLEY, WILLIAM J.; BUTLER, MATILDA. *Knowledge Utilization Systems in Education: Dissemination, Technical Assistance, Networking*. Beverly Hill, CA: Sage Pub.; 1983. 312p. ISBN: 0803919441.

P15

PALAYRET, J. M. 1991. The European Community Historical Archives: An Experience with Computerization. *Archivi & Computer* (IT). 1991; 1(2): 115-123. ISSN: 1121- 2462.

P16

PALLER, B. T. 1989. Visual Perception, Observation Systems, and Empiricism. *Philosophical Studies* (NL). 1989; 55: 65-80. ISSN: 0031-8116.

P17

PALMER, BRYAN D. 1990. *Descent into Discourse: The Reification of Language and the Writing of Social History*. Philadelphia, PA: Temple University Press; 1990. 289p. ISBN: 0877226784.

P18

PALMER, R. G. 1992. Automation in the Arts: Coordinating the Experts. *Art Documentation*. 1992; 11(3): 121-23. ISSN: 0730-7187.

P19

PAMONDON, REJEAN., ed. 1993. Handwriting, Processing, and Recognition. In: *Pattern Recognition*. 1993; 26. (Entire issue on title topic). ISSN: 0031-3203.

P20

PANIJEL, CLAIRE. 1996. Documents Electroniques pour Latinistes [Electronic Documents for Latinists]. *Le Medieviste et Ordinateur* (FR). 1996; 33: 49-51. (In French). ISSN: 0223-3843.

P21

PANOFSKY, ERWIN. 1970. *Meaning and the Visual Arts*. London, UK: Penguin; 1970. 407p. ISBN: 014050879 (pbk.); LCCN: 84-11864; OCLC: 7325588.

P22
PAO, MIRANDA L. 1985. Lotka's Law: A Testing Procedure. *Information Processing & Management*. 1985; 21: 305-320. ISSN: 0306-4573.

P23
PAO, MIRANDA L. 1986. An Empirical Examination of Lotka's Law. *Journal of the American Society for Information Science*. 1986; 37: 26-33. ISSN: 0002-8231; CODEN: AISJB6.

P24
PAQUET, T.; LECOURTIER, Y. 1991. Handwriting Recognition: Application on Bank Checques. In: *First International Conference on Document Analysis and Recognition*. Actes de la conference, September 30-October 2, 1991, Sant-Malo, France. Sponsored by AFCET, IRISA-INRIA, and Telecom. Paris, FR: École Nationale Superieure des Telecommunications; [1991]; 2: 749-757. 2 vols. ISBN: 29036771002; OCLC: 30688707.

P25
PARCER, JAN; LEERMANN, WOLFGANG; GROTUM, THOMAS. 1994. Remembering the Holocaust: Preservation and Improved Accessibility of the Archives in the Memorial Oswiecim/Brzezinka (Auschwitz/Birkenau). See reference: OLDERVOLL, J., ed. 1994. 44-51.

P26
PARER, DAGMAR; TERRY, RON, eds. 1993. *Managing Electronic Records: Papers from a Workshop on Managing Electronic Records of Archival Value*. Sydney, AT: Australian Council of Archives Inc. and Australian Society of Archivists Inc.; 1993.

P27
PARHAM, CHARLES. 1994. Ten Views of the Past: Software that Brings History to Life (Review). *Technology and Learning*. 1994 March; 14(6): 36-42. ISSN: 1053-6728.

P28
PARINET, ELISABETH. 1996 [1997]. Diplomatique et Photos Institutionelles. La Gazette des Archives. 1996; 172. Rev. trans. as: Diplomatics and Institutional Photos. See reference: BLOUIN, F.; DELMAS, B., eds. 1996. 480-485.

P29
PARIS, S. G.; LIPSON, M. Y.; WIXSON, K. K. 1983. Becoming a Strategic Reader. *Contemporary Educational Psychology*. 1983; 8: 293-316. ISSN: 0361-476x.

P30
PARK, T. K. 1994. Toward a Theory of User-based Relevance: A Call for a New Paradigm of Inquiry. *Journal of the American Society for Information Science*. 1994; 45: 135-141. ISSN: 0002-8231.

P31
PARKER, J. M. 1989. Scholarly Book Reviews in Literature Journals as Collection Development Sources for Librarians. *Collection Management*. 1989; 11(1/2): 41-57. ISSN: 0146-2679.

P32
PARROT, KEITH. 1993. The Networked Access Model [of Archives]. See reference: PARER, D.; TERRY, R., eds. 1993. 111-114.

P33
PASLEAU, SUZY. 1987. *LEGIA II. La gestion automatique des données en histoire. Collection du CIPL* [*Legia II*: The Automatic Management of Data in History.] Serie du Laboratoire d'informatique documentaire et d'histoire quantitative, 1. Liège, BE: University of Liège CIPL; 1987. 110p. LCCN: 87-190399; OCLC: 25026457. (In French). LEGIA III-IV packages are available from the Laboratory.

P34
PASLEAU, SUZY. 1988. *Les Bases et Données en Sciences Humaines* [Data Bases in the Humanities]. Liege, BE: University of Liège; 1988. (In French)

P35
PASLEAU, SUZY. 1989a. Demographic Research Methodology, Data Manipulation, and Interpretation. See reference: MCCRANK, L., ed. 1989. 521-526.

P36
PASLEAU, SUZY. 1989b. Historical Data Bases as a Field for Structured Query Language. *Historische Sozialforschung / Historical Social Research* (DEU). 1989; 14: 23-29. ISSN: 0172-6404.

P37
PASLEAU, SUZY. 1989c. Le Traitement informatique des registres de population du XIXe siècle: Premieres étapes et perspectives d'avenir [Data Processing of 19th century Population Registers: First stages and future outlook]. *Histoire et Mesure*. 1989; 4(1- 2): 21-38. (In French). ISSN: 0982-1782.

P38

PASLEAU, SUZY. 1993. Informatics and the Humanities at the University of Liege. See reference: DAVIS, DENLEY, SPAETH, & TRAINOR, eds. 1993. 97-100.

P39

PASSET, JOANNE E. 1992, 1994. The Literature of American Library History. Pt. 1: 1989-1990. *Libraries & Culture.* 1992 Fall; 27(4): 405-429. Pt. 2: 1991-92. *Libraries & Culture.* 1994 Fall; 29(4): 415-439. ISSN: 0894-8631.

P40

PASSMORE, JOHN. 1978. *Science and Its Critics.* Mason Welch Gross Lectureship Series. New Brunswick, NJ: Rutgers University Press; 1978. 100p. ISBN: 0-8135-0852-5; LCCN: 77-12049.

P41

PASSMORE, JOHN. 1979. The Objectivity of History. See reference: IGGERS, G.; PARKER, eds. 1979. 145-160.

P42

PASSMORE, JOHN. 1987. Narratives and Events. *History and Theory.* 1987; 26: 68-74. ISSN: 0018-2656.

P43

PATERSON, A. 1992. Windowing the Past: A Seventeenth-century Technological Archive and its Electronic Exploitation. In: Lucker, J. K., ed. *IATUL Proceedings: 14th Biennial Conference, Cambridge, MA, 8-12 July, 1991.* New Series. 1992; 1: 164-68. ISSN: 0018-8476.

P44

PATTERSON, LEE. 1987. *Negotiating the Past: The Historical Understanding of Medieval Literature.* Madison, WI: University of Wisconsin Press; 1987. 239p. ISBN: 029940400 (hbk.); 029110443 (pbk.).

P45

PATTERSON, LEE. 1990. Critical Historicism and Medieval Studies. In: Patterson, Lee, ed. *Literary Practice and Social Change in Britain, 1380-1530* (pp. 1-15). Berkeley, CA: University of California Press; 1990. 345p. ISBN: 0520064860.

P46

PATTON, PETER C.; HOLLIEN, RENEE A., eds. 1981. *Computing in the Humanities.* Lexington, MA: Lexington Books; 1981. 404p. ISBN: 0669033979.

P47

PAVLIK, JOHN V.; DENNIS, EVERETT E. 1992. *Demystifying Media Technology: Readings from the Freedom Forum Center.* Mountain View, CA: Mayfield Publishing; 1992. 194p. ISBN: 1559341459; LCCN: 92-25132.

P48

PAWLAK, ZACHEUSEZ. 1982. Rough Sets. *International Journal of Computer and Information Sciences.* 1982; 11: 341-356.

P49

PAWLAK, ZACHEUSEZ. 1992. Rough Sets: A New Approach to Vagueness. See reference: ZADEH, L.A.; KACPRYZK, J., eds. 1992. 105-118.

P50

PAWLAK, ZDZISLAW 1991. *Rough Sets: Theoretical Aspects of Reasoning about Data.* Dordrecht, NL: Kluwer; 1991. 229p. (Theory and Decision Library, Series D: System Theory, Knowledge Engineering, and Problem Solving, 9). ISBN: 0792314727; LCCN: 91034107.

P51

PEACE, NANCY E.; FISHER CHUDACOFF, NANCY. 1979. Archivists and Librarians: A Common Mission, a Common Education. *The American Archivist.* 1979; 42(4): 456- 462. ISSN: 0360-9081.

P52

PEACH, ROBERT W. 1992/1996/1997. *The ISO 9000 Handbook.* Fairfax, VA: CEEM Information Services; 1992. 496p. 2nd ed. New York, NY: McGraw-Hill, Inc.; 1996. 674p. 3rd. ed. Chicago, IL; Irwin; 1997. 1008p. ISBN: 0786307862; LCCN: 96-23785.

P53

PEARCE, PETER; PEARCE SUSAN M. 1980. *Experiments in Form: A Foundation Course in Three-Dimensional Design.* New York, NY: Van Nostrand Reinhold Co.; 1980. 146p. ISBN: 0442264976.

P54

PEARCE, SUSAN M. 1990. *Archeological Curatorship.* Leicester Museum Studies series. Leicester, UK: Leicester University press; 1990. 223p. ISBN: 0718512987.

P55
PEARCE, SUSAN M. 1992/1993. *Museums, Objects and Collections: A Cultural Study*. Leicester, UK: Leicester University Press; 1992. Reprinted ed. Washington, D: Smithsonian Institution Press; 1993. 296p. ISBN: 1560983302; LCCN: 93-119114.

P56
PEARCE, SUSAN M. 1994. *Art in Museums*. New Research in Museum Studies, 5. London, UK: Althone Pub.; 1994. 292p. ISBN: 048590005X; LCCN: 94-48-59.

P57
PEARCE, SUSAN M. 1995a. *Exploring Science in Museums*. London, UK: Athlone Pub.; 1995. 207p. ISBN: 0485900068; LCCN: 95-30352.

P58
PEARCE, SUSAN M. 1995b. *On Collecting: An Investigation on Collecting in the European Tradition*. London, UK: Routledge; 1995. 440p. ISBN: 0415075602; LCCN: 96- 35151.

P59
PEARCE, SUSAN M. 1997. *Experiencing Material Culture in the Western World*. New York, NY: Leicester University Press; 1997. ISBN: 07185002101 (hbk.); 0718500299 (pbk.); LCCN: 96-26727.

P60
PEARCE, SUSAN M., ed. 1989. *Museum Studies in Material Culture*. London, UK: Leicester University Press; 1989. 174p. ISBN: 071851288X.

P61
PEARCE, SUSAN M., ed. 1990. *Objects of Knowledge*. London, UK: Athlone Press; 1990. 235p. (New Research in Museum Studies, 1). ISBN: 0485900017; LCCN: 90-001021.

P62
PEARCE, SUSAN M., ed. 1992. *Museums and Europe 1992*. London, UK: Athlone Press; 1992. 232p. ISBN: 0485900033.

P63
PEARCE, SUSAN M., ed. 1993. *Museums and the Appropriation of Culture*. London, UK: Athlone Pub.; 1993. 265p. (New Research in Museum Studies, 4). ISBN: 0485900041; LCCN: 93-39430.

P64
PEARCE, SUSAN M., ed. 1994. *Interpreting Objects and Collections*. London, UK: Routledge; 1994. 343p. LCCN: 94-11658.

P65
PEARL, JUDEA. 1984a. *Search and Heuristics*. New York, NY: North Holland Pub./Elsevier; 1983. 269p. ISBN: 04448666205; LCCN: 83-6217.

P66
PEARL, JUDEA. 1984b. *Heuristics: Intelligent Search Strategies for Computer Problem Solving*. Reading, MA: Addison-Wesley; 1984. 383p. ISBN: 6201055945; LCCN: 83-12217.

P67
PEARL, JUDEA. 1988. *Probabilistic Reasoning in Intelligent Systems: Networks of Plausible Interference*. San Mateo, CA: Morgan Kaufmann; 1988. 552p. ISBN: 0934613777; LCCN: 88-13069.

P68
PEARL, JUDEA. 1993. Graphical Models, Causality, and Intervention. *Statistical Science*. 1993; 8(3): 266-273. ISSN: 0883-4237.

P69
PEARL, JUDEA; SHAFER, GLENN, eds. 1990. *Readings in Uncertain Reasoning*. San Mateo, CA: Morgan Kaufmann; 1990. 768p. ISBN: 1558601252; LCCN: 90-33564.

P70
PEARL, JUDEA.; VERMA, T. S. 1991. A Theory of Inferred Causation. In: Allen, J. A.; Fikes, R.; Sandewall, E., eds. *Principles of Knowledge Representation and Reasoning: Proceedings*, Second International Conference. San Mateo, CA: Morgan Kaufmann; 1991. ISBN: 1559601651; LCCN: 91-013453.

P71
PEARSON, DONALD E. 1991. *Image Processing*. London, UK; New York, NY: McGraw-Hill; 1991. 314p. (Essex Series in Telecommunications and Information Systems). ISBN: 0077073231.

P72
PEDERSON, ANN. 1990. Do *Real* Archivists Need *Archives and Museum Informatics?* [review]. *The American Archivist.* 1990 Fall; 53: 666-675. ISSN: 0360-9081.

P73
PEDERSON, ANN. 1995. Empowering Archival Effectiveness: *Archival Strategies* as Innovation. *The American Archivist.* 1995; 58(4): 430-453. (Commentary on BEARMAN, D., 1995). ISSN: 0360-9081.

P74
PEEK, ROBIN P.; NEWBY, GREGORY B., eds. 1997. *Scholarly Publishing: The Electronic Frontier.* Cambridge, MA: MIT Press for ASIS; 1997. 365p. ISBN: 0-262-16157-5.

P75
PEITGEN, HEINZ-OTTO; JÜRGENS, HARTMUT; SAUPE, DIETMAR. 1992. *Chaos and Fractals: New Frontiers of Science.* New York, NY: Springer-Verlag; c1992. 984p. ISBN: 0387979034; LCCN: 920223277.

P76
PEITGEN, HEINZ-OTTO; RICHTER, PETER H., eds. 1986. *The Beauty of Fractals: Images of Complex Dynamical Systems.* Berlin, DEU / New York, NY: Springer-Verlag; c1986. 199p. ISBN: 0387158510; LCCN: 86003917.

P77
PELIKAN, JAROSLAV J. 1983. *Scholarship and its Survival: Questions on the Idea of Graduate Education.* Princeton, NJ: Carnegie Foundation for the Advancement of Teaching; c1983. 100p. (Carnegie Foundation essay). ISBN: 0931050243; LCCN: 83015211.

P78
PELIKAN, JAROSLAV J. 1992. *The Idea of the University: A Reexamination.* New Haven, CT: Yale University Press; 1992. 238p. (Commentary on John Henry Cardinal Newman's *The Idea of a University*). ISBN: 0300057253; LCCN: 92002928.

P79
PELISSIER, JEAN-PIERRE. 1983. *Démographie. Généalogie. Micro-Informatique* [Demography. Geneaology. Micro-computing]. Paris, FR: Société de démographie historique; 1983. (Cahier des annales de démographie historique, 2). (In French).

P80
PELLEN, RENE. 1993. Les CD-ROM pour Médiévistes: Premiers elements d'une Discographie [CD-ROMS for Medievalists: Bases for a Discographie]. *Le Médiéviste et l'Ordinateur* (FR). 1993 Fall; 28: 13-18. (In French). ISSN: 0223-3843.

P81
PEMBERTON, J. MICHAEL. 1989. Records Management: Planet in an Information Solar System. In: *Proceedings of the 35th Conference of ARMA International* (November 5-8, 1989). Washington, D.C.: ARMA; 1989. 823-839.

P82
PEMBERTON, J. MICHAEL. 1991. Education for Records Management: Rigor Mortis or New Direction? *ARMA Records Management Quarterly.* 1991 July; 25(3):50-57. ISSN: 1050-2343.

P83
PEMBERTON, J. MICHAEL. 1997. Chief Knowledge Officer: The Climax to your Career? *ARMA Records Management Quarterly.* 1997 April; 31(2): 66-72. ISSN: 1050-2343.

P84
PEMBERTON, J. MICHAEL; PRENTICE, ANN E., eds. 1990. *Information Science: The Interdisciplinary Context.* New York, NY: Neal Schuman; 1990. 189p.(Some papers are from the 1987 ALISE Conference). ISBN: 1-55570-048-9; LCCN: 89-13291; OCLC: 20422185.

B85
PENA, ALONSO; TALLABS, FELIPE A. 1996 [199-]. Historians as Complex Adaptive Systems. See reference: BORODKIN, L., ed. 1996: English abstract of presentation, 130-131; paper in Russian [199- forthcoming].

P86
PENN, IRA A.; PENNIX, GAIL; COULSON, JIM. 1994. *Records Management Handbook.* 2nd ed. London, UK: Ashgate Publishing Co.; Aldershot, Hants, UK / Brookfield, VT: Gower; c1994. 303p. ISBN: 0566075105; LCCN: 93048279.

P87
PENN, LISHA B. 1991. *Descriptive Practices at the National Archives: Past, Present, and Future.* Washington, DC: NARA; 1991. 57p. Available from NARA.

P88
PENNEBAKER, JAMES W.; BANASIK, B. L. 1997. On the Creation and Maintenance of Collective Memories: History as Social Psychology. In: PENNEBACKER, J. W.; PAEZ, D.; RIME, B., eds. 1997. 1-20.

P89
PENNEBAKER, JAMES W.; PAEZ, DARIO; RIME, BERNARD, eds. 1997. *Collective Memory of Political Events. Social Psychological Perspectives.* Mahwah, NJ: Lawrence Erlbaum Associates, Inc.; 1997. 312p. ISBN: 0-8058-2182-1; LCCN: 96029389..

P90
PENROD, JAMES I.; DOLENCE, MICHAEL G. 1991. *Re-engineering: A Process for Transforming Higher Education.* Study sponsored by Coopers & Lybrand, Inc. Denver, CO: CAUSE; 1991. 36p. CAUSE Professional Paper Series, no. 9 (PUB3009) Accessible at http://www.cause.org/information-resources/ir-library.

P91
PEREIRA, FERNANDO; GROSZ, BARBARA, eds. 1994. *Natural Language Processing.* Cambridge, MA: Bradford Book; 1994. 537p. ISBN: 0-262-66092-X. Distributed by MIT Press.

P92
PERHAM, ARNOLD E.; PERHAM, BERNADETTE H. 1995. Discrete Mathematics and Historical Analysis: A Study of Magellan. *Mathematics Teacher.* 1995 February; 88(2): 106-113. ISSN: 0025-5769.

P93
PERITZ, BLUMA; EGGHE, LEO, eds. 1997. *Proceedings of the Sixth Conference of the International Society for Scientometrics and Informetrics, Jerusalem, June 16-19, 1997.* Jerusalem, IS: Hebrew University of Jerusalem, School of Library, Archive, and Information Studies; 1997. 540p. ISBN: 965-222-793-5. Abstracts are accessible at http:// shum.huji.ac.il/~bluer/ISSI/.

P94
PERKIN, HAROLD. 1989. *The Rise of the Professional Society in England since 1880.* London, UK: Routledge; 1989. 604p. ISBN: 0415008905.

P95
PERKINS, D.; SPAETH, D. A.; TRAINER, R. H. 1992. Computers and the Teaching of History and Archaeology in Higher Education. *Computers & Education.* 1992 July- August; 19: 153-162.

P96
PERKINS, PHIL. 1995. The Development of Computer Assisted Learning Materials for Archaeology and Art History. *Computers and the History of Art.* 1995; 5(2): 79-91.

P97
PERKINS, PHIL. 1997. University Archaeological Education, CD-ROMs, and Digital Media. *Antiquity* (UK). 1997 Dec.; 71: 1066-1070. Special issue on *Electronic Archaeology.*

P98
PERMAN, DAGMAR H., ed. 1968. *Bibliography and the Historian: The Conference at Belmont of the Joint Committee on Bibliographical Services to History, May 1967.* Santa Barbara, CA: ABC-CLIO Press; 1968. 1776p. LCCN: 68-12982; OCLC: 409168.

P99
PERRITT, HENRY H. 1996. *Law and the Information Superhighway: Privacy, Access, Intellectual Property, Commerce, and Liability.* Somerset, NJ: J. Wiley & Sons, Inc.; 1996. 848 p. (Annual supplements forthcoming). LCCN: 95-38871.

P100
PERRY, MARVIN. 1996. *Arnold Toynbee and the Western Tradition.* New York, NY: P. Lang; 1996. 145p. (American University studies, series V: Philosophy, 169). ISBN: 0820426717; LCCN: 95001698.

P101
PERRY, RALPH B. [1926]. *General Theory of Value: Its Meaning and Basic Principles Construed in Terms of Interest.* New York, NY: Longmans, Green & Co.; [1926]. 702p. ISBN: N/A.

P102
PERRY, RALPH B. 1954. *Realms of Value: A Critique of Human Civilization.* Cambridge, MA: Harvard University Press; 1954. 497p. ISBN: N/A.

P103
PERRY, WILLIAM E. 1983a. *Effective Methods of EDP Quality Assurance.* Englewood Cliffs, NJ: Prentice-Hall; 1983. 378p. (QED Series). ISBN: 0132443368.

P104

PERRY, WILLIAM E. 1983b. *Ensuring Data Base Integrity.* New York, NY: J. Wiley; 1983. 378p. ISBN: 0471865265.

P105

PERRY, WILLIAM E. 1986. *How to Test Software Packages: A Step-by-step Guide to Assuring They Do What you Want.* New York, NY: J. Wiley; 1986. 231p. ISBN: 0471817848.

P106

PERRY, WILLIAM E. 1991. *Quality Assurance for Information Systems: Methods, Tools, and Techniques.* Boston, MA: QED Technical Pub. Group; 1991. 814p. ISBN: 0894353470.

P107

PERRY, WILLIAM E. 1995. *Effective Methods for Software Testing.* Los Alamitos, CA: IEEE; 1995. 556p. ISBN: 0-471-06097-6.

P108

PERSEUS PROJECT. [1997]. *Perseus 2.0* (CD-ROM). New Haven, CT: Yale University Press; [1997]. Accessible at www.yale.edu/yup/.

P109

PETERS, JOHN D. 1988. Information: Notes toward a Critical History. *Journal of Communication Inquiry.* 1988 Summer; 12(2): 9-23. ISSN: 1096-5759.

P110

PETERS, THOMAS A. 1993. The History and Development of Transaction Log Analysis. *Library Hi-Tech.* 1993; 11(2): 41-66. ISSN: 0737-8831.

P111

PETERSEN, TONI. 1990. Developing a New Thesaurus for Art and Architecture. *Library Trends.* 1990; 38(4): 644-658. ISSN: 0024-2594.

P112

PETERSEN, TONI, dir. 1994. *Art and Architecture Thesaurus with the Authority Reference Tool* [electronic files]. New York, NY: Oxford University Press; 1994. Manual and 6 diskettes. ISBN: 619508832; AAT alone: 0195091558. Also available as a 5-volume set. ISBN: 019587569. See also reference: GETTY TRUST. AHIP.

P113

PETERSEN, TONI; BARNETT, PATRICIA J. 1994. *Guide to Indexing and Cataloging with the Art and Architecture Thesaurus.* New York, NY: Oxford University Press; 1994. 397p. ISBN: 0-19-508880-8; LCCN: 93-30635; OCLC: 28633722.

P114

PETERSEN, TONI; MOLHOLT, PAT, eds. 1990. *Beyond the Book: Extending MARC for Subject Access.* Boston, MA: G. K. Hall; 1990. 275p. ISBN: 0816119244 (hbk.); 0816119252 (pbk.).

P115

PETERSON, JACQUELINE; PEERS, LAURA L. 1993. *Sacred Encounters: Father DeSmet and the Indians of the Rocky Mountains West.* Norman, OK: University of Oklahoma Press; 1993. 192p. ISBN: 08061257561 (hbk.); 0806125764 (pbk.).

P116

PETERSON, TRUDY HUSKAMP. 1984. Archival Principals and Records of the New Technology. *American Archivist.* 1984 Fall; 47(4): [380-390]. ISSN: 0346-8488.

P117

PETERSON, TRUDY HUSKAMP. 1992. Reading, Riting, and 'Rithmetic: Speculations on Change in Research Processes. *American Archivist.* 1992 Summer; 55: 414-419. ISSN: 0360-9081.

P118

PETIDENT, YVES. 1994. Le Systéme de Gestion des Données de Fouilles a Auxerre [A Data Base Management System for the Excavations at Auxerre]. See reference: BECK, P., ed. 1994. 36-42.

P119

PETIER, J.; CAMILLERAPP, J. 1991. An Optimal Detector to Localize Handwriting Strokes. In*: First International Conference on Document Analysis and Recognition.* Actes de la conference, September 30-October 2, 1991, Sant-Malo, France. Sponsored by AFCET, IRISA-INRIA, and Telecom. Paris, FR: École Nationale Superieure des Telecommunications; [1991]; 2: 710-718. 2 vols.(In English and French). ISBN: 29036771002; OCLC: 30688707.

P120
PETRE, ZOE. 1994. Past Imperfect. *UNESCO Courier*. 1994 May; sn: 16-20. (Note: About historical reconstruction in former Soviet Union). ISSN: 0041-5278.

P121
PETROV, MIKHAIL. 1996a. The New Image of Archives or Ili Vpechchatlenija a Sektsii A2 "Digital Archives" [Impressions from Section A2 about Digital Archives]. (In Russian). See reference: BORODKIN, L. I., ed. 1996. 16-18.

P122
PETROV, MIKHAIL; TROIANOVSKY, SERGEY. [1996b/199-]. Surface Modelling of Pre- Occupied Territory of the Novgorod Kremlin. See reference: BORODKIN, L., ed. 1996: English abstract of presentation, 96-97; paper in Russian [199-, forthcoming?].

P123
PETRY, FREDERICK E; BOSC, PATRICK. 1996. *Fuzzy Databases; Principles and Applications*. Boston, MA: Kluwer Academic Publishers; 1996. 226p. ISBN: 0792396677; LCCN: 95045774..

P124
PETTERSSON, RUNE. 1993. *Visual Information*. 2nd ed. Englewood Cliffs, NJ: Educational Technology Publications; 1993. 374p. ISBN: 0877782628; LCCN: 93-19822.

P125
PETTIT, MARILYN H. 1991. Archivist-Historians: An Endangered Species? *OAH Newsletter*. 1991 November; 19(4): 8-9, 18. ISSN: 1059-1125.

P126
PFISTER, CHRISTIAN. 1993. *BERNHIST*. Geographisch-Historisches Informationssystem für den Kanton Bern/ Système d'information geographique et historique pour le canton Berne [BERNHIST. Geographical-Historical Information System for Canon Bern]. Bern, CH: Historisches Institut; 1993. 16p. (Distributed paper from the author). See also reference: DENLEY, FOLGEVIK & HARVEY. 1989.

P127
PFISTER, CHRISTIAN. 1994. *Bevolkerungsgeschichte und Historische Demographie, 1500-1800* [People's Migrations and Historical Demography, 1500-1800]. In: *Enzyklopädie desutcher Geschichte*, bd. 28. Munich, DEU: Oldenbourg; 1994. 151p. ISBN: 3486550144.

P128
PFLEEGER, CHARLES P. 1997. *Security in Computing*. Upper Saddle River, NJ: Prentice Hall; c1997. 574p.(1st ed., 1989). ISBN: 0-13-337486-6; LCCN: 96032910.

P129
PFLEEGER, SHARI LAWRENCE; JEFFERY, ROSS; CURTIS, BILL; KITCHENHAM, BARBARA. 1997. Status Report on Software Measurement. *IEEE Software*. 1997 March-April; 14(2): 33-44. (2nd Software Metrics Symposium).

P130
PHELAN, PEATER; REYNOLDS, PETER J. 1996. *Argument and Evidence: Critical Analysis for the Social Sciences*. London, UK: Routledge; 1996. 247p. ISBN: 0415113725 (hbk.); 0415113733 (pbk.).

P131
PHILIPS, J. A. 1979. Achieving a Critical Mass while Avoiding and Explosion: Letter-cluster Sampling and Nominal Record Linkage. *Journal of Interdisciplinary History*. 1979; 9: 493-508. ISSN: 0022-1953.

P132
PHILIPS, LOUIS. 1988. *The Economics of Imperfect Information*. Cambridge, UK: Cambridge University Press; 1988. 281p. ISBN: 05213092047 (hbk.); 0521312003 (pbk.).

P133
PHILLIPS, JOHN T. 1995. Metadata—Information about electronic records. *Records Management Quarterly*. 1995 October: 29(4): [45-55]. ISSN: 1050-2343.

P134
PHILLIPS, JOHN T. 1997. What's in that Data Warehouse? *Records Management Quarterly*. 1997 April: 31(2): [45-55]. ISSN: 1050-2343.

P135
PHILLIPSON, NICOLAS T.; SKINNER, QUENTIN. 1993. *Political Discourse in Early Modern Britain*. Cambridge, UK: Cambridge University Press; 1993. 444p. (Ideas in context series). ISBN: 052139242X.

P136

PIAGET, JEAN. 1926/1955. *Langage et la pensée chez l'enfant.* Cabrain, M., trans. *The Language and Thought of a Child.* New York, NY: Harcourt Brace; 1926. 246p. LCCN: 26014531. Reprint: New York, NY: Meridian; 1955. LCCN: 55- 007703. See also reference: SINGER, D., ed. 1997.

P137

PIATETSKY-SHAPIRO, GREGORY; FRAWLEY, WILLIAM J., eds. 1991. *Knowledge Discovery in Databases.* Cambridge, MA: IAAA Press; 1991. 525p. (See esp. introduction: Knowledge Discovery in Databases: An Overview). ISBN: 0262660709.

P138

PIATTELLI-PALMARINI, MASSIMO. 1994. *Inevitable Illusions. How Mistakes of Reason Rule our Minds.* Piatelli-Palmarini and Botsford, K., trans. New York, NY: John Wiley & Sons, Inc.; 1994. 242p. ISBN: 0-471-58126-7; LCCN: 94-12759.

P139

PICARILLE, LISA. 1997. Archival Rivals. *Computerworld.* 1997 January 20; 31(3): 83-85. (About the Ars Electronica Center [computer museum] in Austria). ISSN: 0010-4841.

P140

PICKLES, JOHN, ed. 1995. *Ground Truth: The Social Implications of Geographic Information Systems.* New York, NY / London, UK: The Guilford Press; 1995. 248p. ISBN: 0898622948 (hbk.); 0898622956 (pbk.).

P141

PICKOVER, CLIFFORD A., ed. 1996. *Fractal Horizons: The Future of Use of Fractals.* New York, NY: St. Martin's Press; 1996. 355p. ISBN: 0312125992.

P142

PIEHLER, G. KURT. 1995. *Remembering War the American Way.* Washington, D.C.: Smithsonian Institution Press; 1995. 233p. ISBN: 1560984619; LCCN: 94010755..

P143

PIERCE, SYNDEY J. 1992. On the Origin and Meaning of Bibliometric Indicators: Journals in the Social Sciences, 1886-1985. *Journal of the American Society for Information Science.* 1992 August; 43(7): 477-487. ISSN: 0002-8231.

P144

PIGEON, CHRISTOPHER W. 1990. *Analyzing Decision-Making in Software Design.* Irvine, CA: University of California at Irvine; 1990. 132p. (Ph.D. dissertation; DAI, vol. 51/03-B: 1363). Available from: University Microfilms, Ann Arbor, MI; Order no. AAD90-22317.

P145

PINNICK, DONALD R. 1992. *Assessment of Perceived Barriers to the Adoption of a Computer-based Decision Support System.* Bloomington, IN: Indiana University; 1992. 137p. (Ed.D. dissertation; *DAI,* vol. 53/05-A: 1351). Available from: University Microfilms, Ann Arbor, MI; Order no. AAD92-28009.

P146

PINTO MOLINA, M. 1995. Document Abstracting: Toward a Methodological Model.   *Journal of the American Society for Information Science.* 1995; 46: 225-234. ISSN: 0002-8231.

P147

PIPPONIER, FRANÇOISE. 1984. Les Sources de l'histoire de la Culture Matérielle a la luminiere des Recherches Recentes [Sources for the History of Material Culture illuminated by Recent Research]. In: *Die Erforschung von Altag und Sachkultur des Mittelalters.* Vienna, AT: Institut für mittelalterliche Realienkunde Osterreichs; 1976. 23-33. (Ver öffentlichungen des Instituts für mittelalterliche Realienkunde Osterreichs, 6). (Entire issue on title topic). LCCN: 76-646494; OCLC: 7115254.

P148

PIRENNE, HENRI. 1948/1962-1965. *Les grands courants de l'histoire universelle.* Brussels, BE; 1948. 5 vols. Parsons, T.; Smelser, N. J., trans. *The Tides of History.* New York, NY: Allen & Unwin; 1962-65. Excerpts in 2 vols. LCCN: 62-007800.

P149

PISANO, J.-B. 1994. The *TABELLION* System: Database and the Automated Database Management for Legal, Economic and Social Elements in Notarized Information. See reference: BOCCHI, F.; DENLEY, P., eds. 1994.

P150

PITKIN, GARY M., ed. 1996. *The National Electronic Library: A Guide to the Future for Library Managers.* Westport, CT: Greenwood Presss; 1996. ISBN: 0313296138; LCCN: 95-40028.

P151
PITKIN, HANNA FENICHEL. 1967/1969. *The Concept of Representation.* Berkeley, CA: University of California Press; 1967. 323p. New York, NY: Atherton Press; 1969. 202p.

P152
PITTI, DANIEL. [1995]. *Overview of SGML* (electronic file). Berkeley, CA: University of California; [1995]. Available in 3 formats as file *sgmlintr* at ftp://library.berkley.edu/ pub/sgml/rlgfast.

P153
PITTI, DANIEL. 1997 [1998]. The Origins of EAD [Electronic Archival Description]. See reference: DOOLEY, J., ed. 1997[1998].

P154
PLAMONDON, REJEAN; LEEDHAM, C. GRAHAM., eds. 1990. *Computer Processing of Handwriting.* Papers from the Fourth International Graphonomics Society Conference at Tronheim, Norway, July 24-26, 1989. Teaneck, NJ: World Scientific; c1990. 412p. ISBN: 9810204086; LC: 90047340.

P155
PLAMONDON, REJEAN; PRIVITERA, CLAUDIO. 1999. The Segmentation of Cursive Handwriting: An Approach based on offline Recovery of the Motor-temporal Information. *IEEE Transactions on Image Processing.* 1999 Jan.; 8: 80-.

P156
PLATT, JENNIFER. 1976. *Realities of Social Research: An Empirical Study of British Sociologists.* [London], UK: Sussex University Press; 1976. Reprint. New York, NY: Riley; 1976. 223p. ISBN: 0470691190.

P157
PLATT, JENNIFER. 1992. "Case Study" in American Methodological Thought. *Current Sociology.* 1992; 40: 17-48. ISSN: 0011-3921.

P158
PLATT, JENNIFER. 1996. *A History of Sociological Research in America, 1920-1960.* Cambridge, UK: Cambridge University Press; 1996. 333p. ISBN: 0521441730.

P159
PLUTA, OLAF. [199-]. *Abbreviations*: The First Electronic Dictionary of Medieval Latin Abbreviations. See reference: HAMMESSE, J., ed. [199-, forthcoming].

P160
POCOCK, JOHN G. A. 1971/1973. *Politics, Language, and Time: Essays on Political Thought and History.* New York, NY: Atheneum; 1971. Reprint, 1973. 290p. ISBN: 0416666809.

P161
POHJOLA, RAIMO. 1994. The Principle of Provenance and the Arrangement of Records / Archives. See reference: ABUKHANFUSA, K.; SYDBECK, J., eds. 1994: [80-91].

P162
POHL, HANS, ed. 1989. *Die Bedeutung der Kommunication für Wirtschaft und Gesellschaft* [The Significance of Communication for Management and Society]. Stuttgart, DE: Franz Steiner Verlag; 1989. 485p. (In German). ISBN: 3-515-05320-4.

P163
POINCARE, HENRI. 1996. *Science and Method.* London, UK: Thoemmes.; 1996. 288p.(Key Texts series). ISBN: 1-85506-431-6.

P164
POIREl, DOMINIQUE. 1996. Le *CLCLT* et la *PLD*: Libres reflecions d'un utilisateur [The *Corpus Christianorum* and Migne's *Patrologia Latina* on CD-ROM: Free Thoughts from a User]. *Le Médiéviste et Ordinateur.* 1996; 33: 54-56. (In French). ISSN: 0223-3843.

P165
POLANYI, KARL. 1944. *The Great Transformation.* New York, NY: Farrar & Rinehart; 1944. 305p. Reprint. Boston, MA: Beacon Press; [1985]. 315p. ISBN: 080705690 (pbk.); LCCN: 84-028381.

P166
POLANYI, MICHAEL. 1958/1962. *Personal Knowledge: Towards a Post-Critical Philosophy.* Chicago, IL: University of Chicago Press; 1958. 2nd corrected ed. London, UK: Routledge and Kegan Paul; 1962. 428p.

P167
POLANYI, MICHAEL. 1964. *Science, Faith, and Society.* Chicago, IL: University of Chicago Press; 1964. 96p. LCCN: 64-022254.

P168
POLANYI, MICHAEL. 1974. *Scientific Thought and Social Reality: Essays*. In: *Psychological Issues*, vol. 8. New York, NY: International Universities Press; 1974. 157p. (Entire issue on title topic). ISBN: 0823660052.

P169
POLANYI, MICHAEL; PROSCH, HARRY. 1975. *Meaning*. Chicago, IL: University of Chicago Press; 1975. 246p. ISBN: 0226672948.

P170
POLLOCK, J. K. 1986. *Contemporary Theories of Knowledge*. London, UK: Hutchinson; 1986. ISBN: 0091729319. Totowa, NY: Rowman & Littlefield; 1986. 208p. ISBN: 084767425 (hbk.); 0847674533 (pbk.); LCCN: 88-10221.

P171
POLZER, CHARLES W.; BARNES, THOMAS C.; NAYLOR, THOMAS H. 1977. *The Documentary Relations of the Southwest: Project Manual*. Tucson, AZ: Universiyt of Arizona Press; 1977. 160p. LCCN: 77622113.

P172
POMPER, PHILIP. 1985. *The Structure of Mind in History: Five Major Figures in Psychohistory*. New York, NY: Columbia University press; 1985. 192p. ISBN: 0231060645.

P173
POMPER, PHILIP, ed. 1995. World Historians and their Critics. Selected paper from the World History Conference at Wesleyan University, March 25-26, 1994. In: *History and Theory*. 1995; 34. (Entire issue on title subject). ISSN: 0018-2656.

P174
POMPER, PHILIP. 1996. Historians and Individual Agency. *History and Theory*. 1996 October; 35(3): 282-309. ISSN: 0018-2656.

P175
PONOMAREV, ANDREY. 1996 [199-]. Internet Against Historical Sensation Generated by Mathematicians: On Re-examining Ptolemaeus' *Almagest*. See reference: BORODKIN, L., ed. 1996: Abstract of presentation, 41-42; paper in Russian [199- forthcoming].

P176
POOL, R. 1994. Turning an Info-Glut into a Library. *Science*. 1994 October 7; 20-22. ISSN: 0036-8075.

P177
POOLET, MICHELLE A.; REILLY, MICHAEL. 1996. *Access 95 Client/Server Development*. Indianapolis, IN: QUE Corp; 1996. 640p. ISBN: 0-7897-0366-1. Note Tables 5.1-7 for the Leszynski/Reddick naming convention.

P178
POPKIN, JERMEY D. 1996. Égo-Histoire and Beyond: Contemporary French Historian- Autobiographers. *French Historical Studies*. 1996 Fall; 19(4): 1139-1158. ISSN: 0016- 1071.

P179
POPPER, KARL R. 1934. *Logik der Forschung*. Vienna, AT: Springer; 1934. 248p. LCCN: 35-38115; OCLC: 4180218. Translated in expanded version as: *The Logic of Scientific Discovery*. London, UK: Hutchinson; 1959. 479p. Reprint. New York, NY: Basic Books; [1959]. 479p. OCLC: 5089675.

P180
POPPER, KARL R. 1957/1960. *The Poverty of Historicism*. Boston, MA: Beacon Press; 1957. 2nd ed. London, UK: Routledge & K. Paul; 1960. 169p. Harper Torchbook ed. New York, NY: Harper & Row; 1961. 166p. Reprinted, 1969. Rev. ed., 1972; reprinted, 1976. German trans. *Das Elend des Historizismus*. Tubingen, DEU: J. C. B. Mohr.; 1965. 132p. (Die Einheit der Gesellschaftswissenschaften, Bd. 3).

P181
POPPER, KARL R. 1963. *Conjectures and Refutations*. London, UK: Routledge and Kegan Paul; 1963.

P182
POPPER, KARL R. 1972. *Objective Knowledge; An Evolutionary Approach*. Oxford, UK: Clarendon Press; 1972. 380p. ISBN: 0198243707.

P183
PORRAS, JERRY I. 1987. *Stream Analysis: A Powerful Way to Diagnose and Manage Organizational Change*. Reading, MA: Addison-Wesley; 1987. 163p. ISBN: 0201056933; LCCN: 86-271183.

P184
PORTER, ELSA A., chair [1991]. *The Archives of the Future: Archival Strategies for the Treatment of Electronic Databases. A Study of Major Automated Databases maintained by agencies of the U.S. Government*. Washington, DC: National Academy of Public Administration; [1991]. (Irregular pagination) (Report for the National Archives and Records Administration; contract NAXXOP90000159).

P185
PORTER, THEODORE M. 1986. *The Rise of Statistical Thinking, 1820-1900*. Princeton, NJ: Princeton University Press; 1986. 333p. ISBN: 0691084165.

P186
PORTER, THEODORE M. 1995. Information Cultures: A Review Essay. *Accounting, Organizations and Society*. 1995 January; 20(1): 83-93. ISSN: 0361-3682.

P187
PORTER, THEODORE M. 1995/1996. *Trust in Numbers. The Pursuit of Objectivity in Science and Public Life*. Princeton, NJ: Princeton University Press; 1995. ISBN: 0691037760. Reprint, 1996. 310p. ISBN: 0-691-02908-3.

P188
PORTER, VICKI; THORNES, ROBIN. 1993. *A Guide to the Description of Architectural Drawings*. Santa Monica, CA: Getty Trust AHIP; 1993. 324p. ISBN: 0816106231; LCCN: 94-7769; OCLC: 30078904.

P189
PORTMANN, URS. 1981. The Identification of Persons in the Middle Ages: Results from the First "Freiburger Burgerbuch" (1341-1416). *Historische Socialforschung / Historical Social Research* (DEU). 1981 April; 18: 11-26. ISSN: 0172-6404.

P190
POSNER, ERNST. 1940. Some Aspects of Archival Development since the French Revolution. *The American Archivist*. 1940 July; 3: 161-170. ISSN: 0360-9081.

P191
POSTAN, MICHAEL M. 1970. *Fact and Relevance: Essays on Historical Method*. Cambridge, UK: Cambridge University Press; 1970. 187p. ISBN: 0521078415; LCCN: 75-145603; OCLC: 117334.

P192
POSTER, MARK. 1984. *Foucault, Marxism, and History: Mode of Production versus Mode of Information*. Cambridge, UK: Polity Press; 1984. 173p. ISBN: 0745600174 (hbk.); 0745600182 (pbk.).

P193
POSTER, MARK. 1989. *Critical Theory and Post Structuralism: In Search of a Context*. Ithaca, NY: Cornell University Press; 1989. 172p. ISBN: 0801423368 (hbk.); 0801495881 (pbk.).

P194
POSTER, MARK. 1990. *The Mode of Information: Poststructuralism and Social Context*. Chicago, IL: University of Chicago Press; 1900. 179p. ISBN: 0226675955 (hbk); 02266755963 (pbk.).

P195
POSTER, MARK. 1995. *The Second Media Age*. Cambridge, MA: Polity Press; 1995. 186p. ISBN: 0745613950 (hbk.); 0745613969 (pbk.).

P196
POSTER, MARK. 1997. *Cultural History and Postmodernity: Disciplinary Readings and Challenges*. New York, NY: Columbia University Press; 1997. 173p. ISBN: 0231108826 (pbk.).

P197
POSTMAN, NEIL. 1993. *The Surrender of Culture to Technology*. New York, NY: Alfred A. Knopf; 1993. 222p. ISBN: 0-394-58272-1.

P198
POSTON, ROBERT M. 1996. *Automating Specification Based Software Testing*. Los Alamitos, CA: IEEE; 1996. 240p. ISBN: 0-8186-7531-4.

P199
POSTON, T.; STEWART, IAN. 1978. *Catastrophe Theory and Its Applications*. London, UK; San Francisco, CA: Pitman; 1978. 491p. ISBN: 0273010298.

P200
POTTER, JONATHAN. 1996. *Representing Reality: Discourse, Rhetoric, and Social Construction*. London, UK; Thousand Oaks, CA: Sage; 1996. 253p. ISBN: 08039841003 (hbk.); 0803984111 (pbk.).

P201
POTTER, JONATHAN; WETHERELL, MARGARET. 1987. *Discourse and Social Psychology: Beyond Attitudes and Behaviour*. London and Newbury Park, CA: Sage Publications; 1987. 216p. ISBN: 0803980558; 0803980566 (pbk.). LCCN: 87-60198; OCLC: 16462607.

P202
POTTER, ROSANNE G., ed. 1989. *Literary Computing and Literary Criticism: Theoretical and Practical Essays on Theme and Rhetoric*. Philadelphia, PA: University of Pennsylvania Press; 1989. 276p. ISBN: 081228156X.

P203
POULAIN, MARTIN, ed. 1992. *Histoire des bibliothèques françaises* [History of French Libraries]. Paris, FR: Promodis Editions du Circle de la Libraire; 1992.(In French). ISBN: 2-7654-0510-7.

P204
POUYEZ, CHRISTIAN; LAVOIE, YOLANDE; BOUCHARD, GERARD. 1983. *Les Saguenayens: Introduction à l'histoire des populations du Saguenay, XVIe-XXe siècles* [The Saguenayen People: Introduction to the history of population of the Saguenay, 16- 20th centuries]. Sillery, Quebec, CN: Presses de l'Université du Québec; 1983. 368p. + 4 microfiche appendices, pp. 391-1025. Bibliography, pp. [xxiv]-xxxiii. (In French). ISBN: 2760503291.

P205
POWICKE, FREDERICK M. 1955/1976. *Modern Historians and the Study of History: Essays and Papers*. London, UK: Odhams Press; 1955. Reprinted. Westport, CT: Greenwood Press; 1976. 256p. ISBN: 0837184282; LCCN: 75025496.

P206
PRATT, ALLAN D. 1982. *The Information of the Image*. Norwood, NY: Ablex; 1982. 117p. ISBN: 00893910554.

P207
PRENTICE, ANN E. 1990. Introduction [to: *Information Science. The Interdisciplinary Context*]. See reference: PEMBERTON, J. M.; PRENTICE, A. E., eds. 1990. vii- xxvi.

P208
PRERAU, D. 1975. "*DO-RE-MI*": A Program that Recognizes Music Notation. *Computers and the Humanities*. 1975; 9(1): 25-29. ISSN: 0010-4817. Based on 1970 dissertation at MIT.

P209
PRESS, LARRY. 1993. Before the Altar: The History of Personal Computing. *Communications of the ACM* [Association for Computing Machinery]. 1993 September; 36(9): 27-33. ISSN: 0001-0782.

P210
PRESTON, DIANE. 1993. Management Development Structures as Symbols of Organizational Culture. *Personnel Review*. 1993; 22(1): 18-30. ISSN: 0048-3486.

P211
PRICE, DEREK JOHN DE SOLA. 1963. *Little Science, Big Science*. Gerge B. Pegram Lectures, 1962. New York, NY: Columbia University Press; 1963. 119p. LCCN: 63-1-524; OCLC: 522357.

P212
PRICE, DEREK JOHN DE SOLA. 1976. A General Theory of Bibliometric and Other Cumulative Advantage Processes. *Journal of the American Society for Information Science*. 1976; 27: 292-306. ISSN: 0002-8231; CODEN: AISJB6.

P213
PRIGOGINE, ILYA; HOLTE, JOHN, eds. *Chaos: The New Science*. Nobel Conference, Gustavus Adolphus College, St. Peter, MN, 1990. Lanham, MD: University Press of America; 1993. 127p. ISBN: 0819189340 (pbk.).

P214
PRIGOGINE, ILYA; STENGER, ISABELLE. 1984. *Order Out of Chaos: Man's New Dialogue with Nature*. New York, NY: Bantam Books; 1984. 349p. ISBN: 0553340824. Published also with alternative subtitle: *The Evolution Paradigm and the Physical Sciences*. ISBN: 0553340824.

P215
PRIME MARKETING PUBLICATIONS. [1995]. Conspectus Glossary. Newing, Rod, comp. In: *The Conspectus [of] Data Warehousing & Decision Support Environment*. 200 definitions; core list, 3 pp. Accessible at http://www.pmp.co.uk/feb48.htm

P216
PRINCE, GERALD. 1982. *Narratology: The Forum and Functioning of Narrative*. Berlin, DEU; New York, NY: Mouton; 1982. 184p. ISBN: 9027930902.

P217
PRINCE, GERALD, ed. 1987. *A Dictionary of Narratology*. Lincoln, NL: University of Nebraska Press; 1987. 118p. ISBN: 0803236786; LCCN: 87-4998; OCLC: 15109449.

P218
PRISM SOLUTIONS, INC. [1997]. Data Warehouse Roles and Responsibilities. *Prism Tech Topics*. Sunnyvale, CA: Prism Solutions, Inc.; [1996-]. 1997: Vol. 1, no. 30. Series originated by Bill Inmon. Available for $20 ea. or all

on one CD-ROM for $195 from Prism Solutions, 1000 Hamlin Ct., Sunnyvale, CA 94089; telephone: 800-995-2938; fax.: 408-752-1875.

P219
PRITCHETT, PRICE. [1995]. *The Employee Handbook of New Work Habits for a Radically Changing World*. Dallas, TX: Pritchett & Associates, Inc.; [1995]. 52p. Series available from: Pritchett & Associates, Inc., 13155 Noel Rd. Suite 1600, Dallas, TX 75240.

P220
PROCHASKA, ALICE. 1993. The British Library and the Challenge of Electronic Media: A View from the Perspective of Special Collections. See reference: ROSS, S.; HIGGS, E., eds. 1993. 167-173.

P221
PROCHASSON, CHRISTOPHE. 1997/1998. Is there a "Crisis" of History in France? Gilman, Nils, trans. *AHA Perspectives*. 1998 May; 36(5): 9-12. ISSN: 0743-7021.

P222
PROJECT GUTENBERG. [1988-]. Gopher address: University of Minnesota Gopher/Libraries/Electronic Books/By Title/Historical Documents.

P223
PROST, ANTOINE. 1992. What has Happened to French Social History? *Historical Journal* (UK). 1992; 35: 671-679. ISSN: 0018-246X / 0440-9302.

P224
PRUDOVSKY, GAD. 1997. Can We Ascribe to Past Thinkers Concepts they had no Linguistic Means to Express? *History and Theory*. 1997 February; 36(1): 15-32. ISSN: 0018-2656.

P225
PRZELECKI, MARIAN; SZANIAWSKI, KLEMENS; WOJICKI, RYSZARD, eds. 1976. *Formal Methods in the Methodology of Empirical Sciences*. Proceedings of the Conference for Formal Methods, Warsaw, Poland, June 17-21, 1974. Dordrecht, NL: D. Reidel; 1976. 457p. (Synthese Library, v. 103). ISBN: 9027706980; LCCN: 76004586.

P226
PTASYNSKI, JAMES G. 1997. Critical Strategic and Tactical Elements for Successfully Integrating Technology into Teaching and Learning. Commentary (Electronic file). *Microsoft in Higher Education*. 1997 August; 5p. Accessible at http://www. microsoft.com/education/hed.

P227
PTASYNSKI, JAMES G., ed. 1997. *Technology Tools for Today's Campuses* (CD-ROM). Redmond, WA: Microsoft Inc.; 1997. 70 articles on CAI, also featured in Microsoft's *Online Technology Colloquium*, 1997-. Accessible at http://www.microsoft.com/ education/hed.

P228
PUGH, ALEXANDER K. 1978. *Silent Reading: An Introduction to its Study and Teaching*. London, UK: Heinemann; 1978. 122p. ISBN: 0435107194; LCCN: 69-306587.

P229
PUGH, EMERSON W. 1995. *Building IBM: Shaping an Industry and Its Technology*. Cambridge, MA: MIT Press; 1995. 405p. ISBN: 026216478.

P230
PUGH, EMERSON W.; ASPRAY, WILLIAM. 1996. Creating the Computer Industry. See reference: WILLIAMS, MICHAEL, ed. 1996. 7-17.

P231
PUGH, EMERSON W.; WINSLOW, GEORGE H. [1966]. *The Analysis of Physical Measurements*. Reading, MA: Addison-Wesley; [1966]. 246p.

P232
PURCEL, ROSAMOND WOLFF. 1992. *Finders, Keepers: Eight Collectors*. New York, NY: W. W. Norton; 1992. 155p. ISSN: 0303030547.

P233
PURCEL, STEVEN L. 1993. *Integrating Digital Images into Computer-based Instruction: Adapting an Instructional Design Model to Reflect New Media Development Guidelines and Strategies*. Blacksburg, VA: Virginia Polytechnical Institute and State University; 1993. 125p. (Ph.D. dissertation; *DAI*, 54/06-A: 2124). Available from: University Microfilms, Ann Arbor, MI (Order no. AAD93-31473).

P234
PUTERMAN, ZALMA M. 1977. *The Concept of Causal Connection.* Doctoral dissertation. Uppsala, SE: University of Lodz; 1977. 2 v. LCCN: 7812162.

P235
PUTNAM, HILARY. 1981. *Reason, Truth and History.* Cambridge, UK: Cambridge University Press; 1981. 222p. ISBN: 0521230351 (hbk.); 0521297761 (pbk.).

P236
PUTNAM, LAWRENCE H.; MYERS, WARE. 1996. *Controlling Software Development. An Executive Briefing.* Los Alamitos, CA: IEEE; 1996. 90p. ISBN: 0-8186-7452-0.

P237
PYLYSHYN, ZENON W. 1984. *Computation and Cognition: Toward a Foundation for Cognitive Science.* Cambridge, MA: MIT Press; 1984. 292p. ISBN: 0262160986.

P238
PYNN, R.; RISTE, T., eds. 1987. *Time-dependent Effects in Disordered Materials.* NATO Advanced Study Institute at Geilo, NO. New York, NY: Plenium Press; 12987. 504p. (NATO ASI Series, B Physics, v. 167). ISBN: 030006427826.

-Q-

Q1
QUANTUM (ASSOCIATION FOR QUANTIFICATION AND METHODS IN HISTORICAL AND SOCIAL RESEARCH). 1973-. *Historische Sozialforschung /Hisorical Social Research* (DEU). Bick, W.; Muller, P. J.; Reinke, H., *et al.*, eds. Stuttgart, DEU: Klett-Cotta; 1973-. Alt. Title: *Quantum Dokumentation,* 1973-. Attached irregular series, e.g., *Historisch-Sozialwissenschaft Forschungen,* Bd. 1-.1984-. ISBN: 312911050X.

Q2
QUANTUM 1979-. *Historische Sozialforschung/ Historical Social Research.* Cologne, DEU: Universität zu Koln, QUANTUM , and the Zentrum für Historische Sozialforschung; 1979-. Irregular Supplements. (In German and English). ISSN: 0172-6404; LCCN: 83-644046; OCLC: 19811110. Available from the Center for Historical Social Research, 40, D-5000 Koln, DEU.

Q3
QUANTUM. 1989-1992. A Guide to Historical Datasets in U.S. and European Science Data Archives. In*: Historische Sozialforschung/ Historical Social Research* (DEU). Cologne, DEU: 1989-1992. ISSN: 0172-6404. Contents: Pt. 1: Inter-University Consortium for Political and Social Research, Ann Arbor, MI (ICPSR). 1989; 14(2): 168-81. Pt. 2: Economic and Social Science Research Council (ESRC) Data Archive, University of Essex. 1989; 14(4): 143-55. Pt. 3: Electronic Records in the National Archives. Pt. 1: Center for Electronic Records, National Archives and Records Administration, Washington, D.C. 1991; 16(3): 159-164. Pt. 4: Norsk Samfunnsvitenskapelig Datajeneste [Norwegian Social Science Data Service]. 1990; 15(2): 83-88. Pt. 5: Svensk Samhallsvetenskaplig Datajanst [Swedish Social Science Data Service]. 1990; 15(3): 199-202. Pt.6: The Netherlands Historical Data Archive. 1990; 15(4): 197-200. Pt. 9: The Roper Center for Public Opinion Research, Storrs. CT. 1992; 17(2): 95-120, (3): 106-13. (In German, English, Norwegian, Swedish).

Q4
QUEAU, PHILIPPE. 1993a. Les Illusions Dangereuses [Dangerous Illusions]. *Telerama* [FR]. 1993; 20: 10-16. (In French). ISSN:0040-2699.

Q5
QUEAU, PHILLIPPE. 1993b. *Le Virtuel, Vertus, et Vertiges* [The Virtual, the Truthful, and the Dazzling]. Seyssel, FR: Champ Vallon; 1993. (In French)

Q6
QUESADA, ARLI. 1998. Learning to see in 3D: How Mental Images become Photorealistic. *Education by Design.* San Rafael, CA: Autodesk, Inc.*;* 1998 Spring; s.n.: 2-5. Cf., Autodesk's website at www.autodesk.com.

Q7
QUESTOR SYSTEMS, Inc. 1994. *QUESTOR* (Software). Available from: Questor Systems, Inc., 899 El Centro St. Suite 101, South Pasadena, CA 91030.

Q8
QUINN, JAMES B. 1980. *Strategies for Change: Logical Incrementalism.* Boston, MA: Richard D. Irwin; 1980. 222p. ISBN: 0870942204 (hbk.); 0256025436 (pbk.); LCCN: 80-82098.

Q9

QUITNER, JOSHUA. 1993. Far Out: Welcome to Their World Built of MUD. *Newsday*. 1993 November 7. Gopher address: University of Koln/About MUDS, MOOS, and MUSES in Education/Selected Papers/Newsday (1995).

-R-

R1

RABB, THEODORE K. 1983a. The Development of Quantification in Historical Research. *Journal of Interdisciplinary History*. 1983; 13: 591-601. ISSN: 0022-1953.

R2

RABB, THEODORE K., ed. 1983b. The Measure of American History. In: *Journal of Interdisciplinary History*. 1983; 14(4). (Entire issue on title topic). ISSN: 0022-1953.

R3

RABB, THEODORE K.; ROTBERG, ROBERT I. 1982. *The New History, the 1980s and Beyond: Studies in Interdisciplinary History*. Princeton, NJ: Princeton University Press; 1982. 332p. ISBN: 0691053707; 0691007942 (pbk.); LCCN: 82-47634; OCLC: 9139110.

R4

RABEN, JOSEPH. 1991. Humanities Computing 25 Years Later. Silver Anniversary issue of *Computers and Humanities*. 1991; 25(6): 341-351. ISSN: 0010-4817.

R5

RABEN, JOSEPH; BURTON, SARAH. 1981. Information Systems and Services in the Arts and Humanities. Williams, Martha E., ed. *Annual Review of Information Science and Technology*. White Plains, NY: Knowledge Industry Publications, Inc., for the American Society for Information Science; 1981; 16: 247-266. ISBN: 1-57387-019-6; ISSN: 0066-4200; CODEN: ARISBC; LC no. 66-25096

R6

RABEN, JOSEPH; MARKS, GREGORY., eds. 1980. *IFIP Working Conference on Data Bases in the Humanities and Social Sciences*. Dartmouth College, NH 23-24 August, 1979. ICBHSS, 1. New York, NY/Amsterdam, NL: Elsevier-North Holland. 329p. LCCN: 80-16205; OCLC: 6331627.

R7

RABINOVITZ, RUBIN. 1994. History. In Buyer's Guide section: The Top 100 CD-ROMS. *PC Magazine*. 1994 September 13; 13(15): 148-150. ISSN: 0888-8507.

R8

RADECKI, T. 1976. Mathematical Model of Information Retrieval System Based on the Concept of [a] Fuzzy Thesaurus. *Information Processing and Management*. 1976; 12: 313-318. ISSN: 0306-4573.

R9

RAFAELI, ANAT; PRATT, MICHAEL G. 1993. Tailored Meanings: On the Meaning and Impact of Organizational Dress. *Academy of Management Review*. 1993 January; 18(1): 32-55. ISSN: 0363-7425.

R10

RAFFALOVICH, L. E.; KNOKE, D. 1983. Quantitative Methods for the Analysis of Historical Change. *Historical Methods*. 1983; 16: 149-154. ISSN: 0161-5440.

R11

RAFFERTY, FRANCES. 1995. "Hopes of our Shared History." *Times Educational Supplement* (UK). 1995 November 10; 4141; 18. ISSN: 0040-7887.

R12

RAGHAVAN, VIJAY V.; DEOGUN, JITENDER S.; SEVER, HAYRI, eds. 1998. Knowledge Discovery and Data Mining. In: *Journal of the American Society for Information Science*. 1998; 49(5): 397-470. (Entire issue of title topic). ISSN: 0002-8231; CODEN: AISJB6.

R13

RAGIN, CHARLES C. 1987. *The Comparative Method: Moving Beyond Qualitative and Quantitative History*. Berkeley, CA: University of California Press; 1987. 185p. ISBN: 0520058348; LCCN: 86-30800; OCLC: 15017459.

R14

RAHTZ, SEBASTIAN, ed. 1987. *Information Technology in the Humanities: Tools, Techniques and Applications*. Computers and their Applications series. Chichester, UK: Ellis Horwood; 1987. 188p. ISBN: 0-7458-0148-X.

R15
RAINEY, JOHN R., Jr. 1987. *The Defense of Calais, 1436-1477.* Newark, NJ: Rutgers University; 1987. 284p. (Ph.D. dissertation; *DAI*, vol. 48/07-A: 1862). Available from: University Microfilm, Ann Arbor, MI (Order no. AAD87-23298).

R16
RAISH, MARTIN, ed. 1996. *Key Guide to Electronic Resources: Art and Art History.* Ensor, P., ed. Medford, NJ: Information Today, Inc.; 1996. 120 p. (Key Guide series). ISBN: 1-57387-022-6.

R17
RAKITOV, ANATOLITHI I. 1987. Metodologiia Istoriko-Nauchnykh Issledovaii v Epokhu Komp'iuternoi Revoliutsii [The Methodology of Historical-scientific Research in the Era of the Computer Revolution]. *Voprosy Istorii Estestvoznaniia i Tekhniki.* 1987; 3: 32-41. (In Russian). ISSN: 0042-8779.

R18
RAMAIAH, C. K. 1992. An Overview of Hypertext and Hypermedia. *International Information, Communication & Education.* 1992 March; 11(1): 26-42. ISSN: 0970- 1850.

R19
RAMESH, BALASUBRAMANIAM. 1992. *Process Knowledge-based Support for Systems Development.* New York, NY: New York University; 1992. 155p. (Ph.D. dissertation; DAI, 53/11-A). Available from: University Microfilms, Ann Arbor, MI.

R20
RAMM, AGATHA. 1980. Leopold Von Ranke. See reference: CANNON, JOHN, ed. 1980.

R21
RAMOS, DONALD; WHEELER, ROBERT A. 1989. Integrating Microcomputers into the History Curriculum. *History Teacher.* 1989; 22(2): 177-88. ISSN: 0018-2745.

R22
RANCIERE, JACQUES. 1992. *Les mots de l'histoire. Essai poetique du savoir.* Paris, FR: Editions du Seuil; 1992. Mellehy, Hassan, trans. *The Names of History: On the Poetics of Knowledge.* Minneapolis, MN: University of Minnesota Press; c1994. 114p. ISBN: 0816624011 (hbk.); 0816624038 (pbk.); LCCN: 94007212.

R23
RANGANATHAN, S. R. 1992. *A Librarian Looks Back: An Autobiography of Dr. S. R. Ranganathan.* New Delhi, India: ABC Publishing House; 1992. 485p. ISBN: 81- 7123-048-2.

R24
RAO, C. R. 1971. Taxonomy in Anthropology. In: Hodson, F. R.; Kendall, D. G.; Tautu, P., eds. *Mathematics in the Archeological and Historical Sciences.* Proceedings of the Anglo-Romanian Conference, Mamaia, 1970 (pp. 19-29). Edinburgh, UK: Edinburgh University Press; 1971. ISBN: 085224-213-1.

R25
RAO, I. K. R. 1980. The Distribution of Scientific Productivity and Social Change. *Journal of the American Society for Information Science.* 1980; 31: 111-122. ISSN: 0002-8231; CODEN: AISJB6.

R26
RAPHAEL, LUTZ. 1996. *Die Erben von Bloch und Febre: "Annales" Geschichtsschreibung und "Nouvelle Histoire" in Frankreich, 1945-1980* [The Heritage of Bloch and Febre: Annales Historical Writing and New History in France, 1945-1980]. Munich, DEU: 1996. (In German). 635p. ISBN: 3608913041.

R27
RAPPORT, LEONARD. [199-]. *Rapport with Archives: Documenting an Archivist's Intellectual Odyssey — The "Life Story" of Leonard Rapport.* L. J. McCrank, ed. Binghamton, NY: Haworth Press; [199-, forthcoming]. 213 pp. Co-published in: *Primary Sources and Original Works.* 199- . ISSN: 1042-8216.

R28
RAS, ZBIGNIEW; ZEMANKOVA, MARIA. 1990. *Intelligent Systems: State of the Art and Future Directions.* New York, NY: E. Horwood; 1990. 529p. (Ellis Horwood series in Artificial Intelligence). ISBN: 013659317; LCCN: 90-044158.

R29
RAS, ZBIGNIEW; ZEMANKOVA, MARIA, eds. 1994. *Methodologies for Intelligent Systems.* 8th International Symposium, ISMIS'94, Charlotte, NC, October 16-19, 1994. New York, NY: Springer-Verlag; 1994. 613p. ISBN: 0387584951.

R30
RASMUSSEN, EDDIE. 1992. Clustering algorithms. See reference: FRAKES, W.; BAEZA-YATES, R., eds. 1992.

R31
RASPA, RICHARD. 1990. The C.E.O. as Corporate Myth-Maker: Negotiating the Boundaries of Work and Play at Domino's Pizza Company. See reference: GAGLIARDI, P., ed. 1990: 273-280.

R32
RATIKOV, ANATOLITHI I. 1989-1990. *Perspektivy informatizatisii obshchestva: referativnythi sbornik* [Perspectives on the Information Society: Abstracted References]. Series: Informatisiiia, nauka, obshchestvo. Moscow, USSR: Akadameiia nauk SSSR, In-t nauch. Informatisii po obshchestvennymnaukam; 1989-1990. 2 vols.

R33
RATIKOV, ANATOLITHI I; GRIGORIIAN, E. R. 1982. *Statisticheskie metody v obshchestvennykh naukakh: sbornik obzorov* [Statistical methods for the Social Sciences]. Series: Informatisiiia, nauka, obshchestvo. Moscow, USSR: Akademiia nauk SSSR, In-t nauch informatisii po obshchestvennym naukam; 1982. 159p. (In Russian).

R34
RAUCH, IRMENGARD; CARR, GERALD F., eds. 1997. *Semiotics around the World: Synthesis in Diversity.* Proceedings of the Fifth Congress of the International Association for Semiotic Studies, University of California, Berkeley, CA, 1994. Berlin, DEU; New York, NY: Mouton de Gruyter; 1997. 2 vols. ISBN: 31101122235.

R35
RAUZIER, JEAN-MICHEL, ed. 1993. Contributions à l'histoire de la Documentation en France [Contributions to the History of Documentation in France]. *Documentaliste* (FR). 1993 July-October; 30(4-5): 191-262. (In French). ISSN: 0012-4508.

R36
RAVICHANDRA RAO, INNA K. 1983. *Quantitative Methods for Library and Information Science.* New York, NY: John Riley; 1983. 271p. ISBN: 0852767495; LCCN: 83- 906299.

R37
RAVVIN, NORMAN. 1997. *A House of Words: Jewish Writing, Identity and Memory.* Montreal, CAN: McGill-Queen's University Press; 1997. 191p. ISBN: 0773516654 (pbk.); 0773516646 (hbk.).

R38
RAY, RABINDRA. 1988. *Memory and the Intelligibility of Historical Time.* Allahabad, India: Govind Ballabh Pant Social Science Institute; 1988. 21 p. LCCN: 89910817.

R39
RAY, VERNE F. 1942. Culture Element Distributions. *Anthropological Records.* 1942; 8: 99- 258.

R40
RAYWARD, W. BOYD. 1975. *The Universe of Information: The Work of Paul Otlet for Documentation and International Organization.* Moscow, USSR: VINIT [All Union Institute for Scientific and Technical Information]; 1975. 389p. (FID pub. 520). LCCN:77-363924.

R41
RAYWARD, W. BOYD. 1983. The Development of Library and Information Science: Disciplinary Differentiation, Competition and Convergence. See reference: MACHLUP, F.; MANSFIELD, U., eds. 1983.

R42
RAYWARD, W. BOYD. 1993. Electronic Information and the Functional Integration of Libraries, Museums, and Archives. See reference: ROSS, S.; HIGGS, E., eds., 1993: 227-243.

R43
RAYWARD, W. BOYD. 1994a. Visions of Xanadu: Paul Otlet (1868-1944) and Hypertext. *Journal of the American Society for Information Science.* 1994; 45(4): 235-250. ISSN: 0002-8231.

R44
RAYWARD, W. BOYD. 1994b. Some Schemes for Reconstructing and Mobilising Information in Documents: A Historical Perspective. *Information Processing & Management.* 1994; 30(2): 163-175. ISSN: 0306-4573.

R45
RAYWARD, W. BOYD. 1996. The History and Historiography of Information Science: Some Reflections. Special issue of *Information Processing & Management* (pp. 1-88). 1996; 32 (1): 3-18. ISSN: 0306-4573. See also reference: BELLARDO HAHN, T.; BUCKLAND, M., eds. 1998. 7-21.

R46
RAYWARD, W. BOYD. 1997. The Origins of Information Science and the International Institute of Bibliography/ International Federation for Information and Documentation (FID). See reference: BUCKLAND, M.; BELLARDO HAHN, eds., 1997. 289-300.

R47
RAYWARD, W. BOYD. 1998. Electronic Information and the Functional Integration of Libraries, Museums, and Archives. See reference: HIGGS, E., ed. 1998. 207-224.

R48
RAYWARD, W. BOYD. [1999]. The Noble Brow of History: The History and Heritage of Science Information Systems. Report on History of Information Science pre-conference, Pittsburgh, 1998. *Bulletin of the American Society for Information Science*. 1999 Dec.; 25(2): 19-22. ISSN: 0095-4403.

R49
REBNE, DOUGLAS. 1990. *Determinants of Individual Productivity: A Study of Academic Researchers*. Los Angeles, CA: Institute of Industrial Relations, University of California at Los Angeles; 1990. 155p. (Monograph & Research series, 53). (Revision of Ph.D. dissertation at UCLA, 1988). ISBN: 0892151625.

R50
REDDING, S. GORDON. 1994. Comparative Management Theory: Jungle, Zoo or Fossil Bed? *Organization Studies*. 1994; 15 (3): 323-359. ISSN: 0170-840; OCLC: 6172557; LCCN: 82-20032.

R51
REDER, LYNNE M., ed. 1996. *Implicit Memory and Meta cognition*. Papers of the 27th Carnegie Symposium on Cognition, Carnegie-Mellon University, 1995. Mahwah, NJ: Lawrence Erlbaum; 1996. 362p. ISBN: 080518596 (hbk.); 080581860x (pbk.).

R52
REDMOND, A. D. 1985. American Society for Information Science—History. See reference: KENT, A. *ET AL.*, eds. 1985. 38: 11-31.

R53
REED, BARBARA. Metadata: Core Record or Core Business? *Archives and Manuscripts* (AU). 1997; 25: 218-241. ISSN: 0157-6895.

R54
REED, BARBARA; ROBERTS, DAVID, eds. 1991. *Keeping Data: Papers from a Workshop on Appraising Computer-based Records*. Dickston, AU: Australian Council of Archives and the Australian Society of Archivists; 1991. 122p. ISBN: 094721903X.

R55
REED, C. 1989. Authenticating Electronic Mail Messages—Some Evidential Problems. *Modern Law Review*. 1989 September; 52: 649-660. ISSN: 0026-7961.

R56
REELING, PATRICIA; O'CONNOR, DANIEL. 1991. Use of Government Publications in an Academic Setting. *Government Publications Review*. 1991; 18(5): 489-515. ISSN: 0277-9390.

R57
REEVES, BYRON; NASS, CLIFFORD. 1996. *The Media Equation: How People Treat Computers, Television, and New Media Like Real People and Places*. New York, NY: Cambridge University Press; 1996. 305p. ISBN: 1-57586-052-X.

R58
REEVES, WAYNE W. 1996. *Cognition and Complexity: The Cognitive Science of Managing Complexity*. Lanham, MD: Scarecrow Press; 1996. ISBN: 0-08108-3101-5.

R59
REFERENCE QUARTERLY (RQ). 1982. Selected List of Guides to Databases and Data Archives, [and] Computer-assisted Reference Service in History. *RQ*. 1982; 21(4): 342-64. ISSN: 0033-7072.

R60
REHBEIN, MALTE. 1996 [1999-]. The Modern Document: Digital Archives for Mass Sources from the Holocaust. Paper at the XI International AHC Conference Programme, Moscow, August 20-24, 1996. See reference: BOROD-KIN, L., ed. [1998] 1996: English presentation, 13; paper in Russian [199- forthcoming].

R61
REICHARD, ROBERT S. 1974. *The Figure Finaglers*. New York, NY: McGraw-Hill; 1974. 274p. ISBN: 0070517770.

R62
REICHENBACH, MARIA. *The Direction of Time*. Berkeley, CA: University of California Press; 1991. 280p. ISBN: 0520018397; LCCN: 91009335.

R63
REID, LYDIA J. E. 1995. Electronic Records Training: Suggestions for the Implementation of the CART Curriculum. *American Archivist*. 1995; 58(3): 326-340. ISSN: 0360- 9081.

R64
REIF, FREDERICK. 1980. Theoretical and Education Concerns with Problem Solving: Bridging the Gaps between Human Cognitive Engineering. In: Tuma, D. T.; Reif, F., eds. *Problem Solving and Education: Issues in Teaching and Research* (pp. 39-52). Carnegie Mellon University Conference proceedings. Hillsdale, NJ: Lawrence Erlbaum Associates; 1980. 212p. ISBN: 089590086 (hbk.); 0470269189 (pbk.); LCCN: 79-22461.

R65
REIFER, DONALD J. 1993. *Software Management.* 4th ed. Los Alamitos, CA: IEEE; 1993. 664p. ISBN: 0-8186-3342-5.

R66
REIFF, JANICE, ed. 1988a. History, Microcomputers, and Teaching. In: *Historical Methods.* 1988 Summer; 21: 140p. (Entire issue on title topic). ISSN: 0161-5440.

R67
REIFF, JANICE L. 1988b. Using History to Teach Microcomputers. *Historical Methods.* 1988; 21: 135-139. ISSN: 0161-5440.

R68
REIFF, JANICE L. 1991. *Structuring the Past: The Use of Computers in History.* Washington, D.C.: American Historical Association; 1991. 149p. ISBN: 0-87229-050-6.

R69
REIFF, JANICE L. 1993. Numbers in the Historical Computing Curriculum. See reference: DAVIS, V. *ET AL.,* eds. 1993. 19-27.

R70
REIFF, JANICE L. 1998. Riding the "Wave of the Present." See reference: AHA. 1998. 3-4.

R71
REIFF, JANICE L. 1999. *Digitizing the Past: The Use of Computers and Communication Technologies in History.* Washington, D.C.: American Historical Association; 1999. ISBN: 0-87229-104-9-8.

R72
REIGELUTH, CHARLES M., ed. 1983. *Instructional-Design Theories and Models: An Overview of their Current Status.* Hillsdale, NJ: Lawrence Erlbaum; 1983. 487p. ISBN: 089592755; LCCN: 83-14185.

R73
REIGELUTH, CHARLES M.; BANALBY, BELA H.; OLSON, JEANETTE R., eds. 1993. *Comprehensive Systems Design: A New Educational Technology.* Berlin, DEU / New York, NY: Springer-Verlag; 1993. 436p. Workshop proceedings, NATO Scientific Affairs Division. ISBN: 3540566775 (GW); 0387566775 (US); LCCN: 93-11329.

R74
REILLY, PAUL. 1988. *Data Visualization: Recent Advances in the Application of Graphic Systems to Archeological Data.* IBM UK Scientific Centre Report, 185. Winchester, UK: IBM; 1988.

R75
REILLY, PAUL; WALTER, ANDREW. 1987. Three-Dimensional Recording in the Field: Preliminary Results. *Archeological Computing Newsletter.* 1987; 10: 7-12. ISSN: 0952-3332.

R76
REILLY, PAUL; WALTER, ANDREW. 1991. Data Visualization in Archeology. See reference: BEST, H., *ET AL.,* eds. 1991. 7-12.

R77
REILLY, PAUL; PALTZ, SEBASTIAN P. Q., eds. 1992. *Archeology and the Information Age: A Global Perspective.* Derived from the 2nd World Archeological Congress, Barquisimeto, Venezuela, Sept. 1990. London UK: Routledge; 1992. 395p. (One World Archeology, 21). ISBN: 041507858X; LCCN: 91-41648; OCLC: 24701744.

R78
REINGRUBER, MICHAEL C.; GREGORY, WILLIAM W. 1994. *The Data Modeling Handbook: A Best Procedure Approach to Building Quality Data Models.* New York, NY: John Wiley & Sons; 1994. 362p. ISBN: 0471052906; LCCN: 94-12669.

R79
REINHOLT, WALTER W. 1988. *Culture 1.0: The Hypermedia Guide to Western Civilization.* 7 diskettes plus users manual (26p.). Scotch Plains, NY: Cultural Resources, Inc.; 1988. OCLC: 20335295.

R80
REINITZ, RICHARD. 1972. A Note on the Impact of Quantification on the Methodology of Non-Quantitative History. *Pennsylvania History.* 1972; 39(3): 363-66. ISSN: 0031-4528.

R81
REINKE, HERBERT. 1981. Towards Standards for the Description of Machine-readable Historical Data. *Historisches Sozialforschungen /Historical Social Research* (DEU). 1981; 18: 3-10. ISSN: 0172-6404.

R82
REINKE, HERBERT. 1986. Datenbeschreibung und Datendokumentation in der historischen Sozialforschung, Problembeschreibung und Empfelungen für die Forschung [Data Bases and Documentation in the Historical Social Sciences. Problems and Recommendations for Research]. See reference: THALLER, M., ed. 1986.

R83
REINKE, HERBERT; SCHURER, KEVIN; MARKER, HANS-JÖRGEN. 1986. Making Sense out of Historical Documentation. See reference: HAUSMANN *ET AL.*, eds. 1986.

R84
REISCH, GEORGE. 1991. Chaos, History, and Narrative. The "New Science" and the Historical Social Sciences. In: *History and Theory.* 1991; 30: 1-20. (Entire issue on title topic). ISSN: 0018-2656. See rejoinders by ROTH, PAUL A.; RYCKMAN, THOMAS A.

R85
REISCH, GEORGE. 1995. Scientism without Tears: A Reply to Roth and Ryckman. *History and Theory.* 1995 February; 34 (1): 45-59. ISSN: 0018-2656.

R86
REISER, MORTON F. 1984. *Mind, Brain, Body: Toward a Convergence of Psychoanalysis and Neurobiology.* New York, NY: Basic Books; 1984. 228p. ISBN: 0465046037.

R87
REISER, MORTON F. 1994. *Memory in Mind and Brain: What Dream Imagery Reveals.* New Haven, CT: Yale University Press; 1994. 218p. ISBN: 0300060327.

R88
REISER, R. A. 1987. Instructional Technology: A History. See reference: GAGNE, R. M., ed., 1987. 11-48.

R89
REISMAN, SOREL. 1996. *Multimedia Computing: Preparing for the 21st Century.* Hershey, PA: Idea Group Publishing; 1996. 600p. ISBN: 1-878289-5.

R90
RENAISSANCE SOCIETY OF AMERICA. 1995-. *Iter, the Bibliography of Renaissance Europe* (electronic file). Toronto, CAN: University of Toronto Center for Reformation and Renaissance Studies (CRRS); 1995-. 60,000 records. Accessible at http://www. library.utoronto.ca/iter/. Collaborative project between CRRS, Arizona State University's Ctr. For Medieval and Renaissance Studies (ACMRS), and the University of Toronto Library and Faculty of Information Studies (FIS), which plans to extend coverage to the Middle Ages.

R91
RENKEMA, JAN. 1993. *Discourse Studies: An Introductory Textbook.* Amsterdam, NL/Philadelphia, PA: J. Benjamins; 1993. 224p. ISBN: 1556194927 (hbk.); 1556194935 (pbk.); LCCN: 93001453.

R92
REPO, A. J. 1989. The Value of Information: Approaches in Economics, Accounting, and Management Science. *Journal of the American Society for Information Science.* 1989; 40: 68-85. ISSN: 0002-8231.

R93
RESCHER, NICHOLAS. 1975. *A Theory of Possibility: A Constructivistic and Conceptualistic Account of Possible Individuals and Possible Worlds.* [Pittsburgh, PA]: University of Pittsburgh Press; 1975. 255p. ISBN: 0822911221; LCCN: 75010540.

R94
RESCHER, NICHOLAS; JOYNT, CAREY B. 1959. Evidence in History and Law. *The Journal of Philosophy.* 1959 June; 56: 561-578. ISSN: 0160-9335.

R95
RESEARCH LIBRARIES GROUP (RLG). 1987. The Medieval and Early Modern Data Bank. *The Research Libraries Group News.* 1987 January; 12: 8-10. ISSN: 0196- 173X. Available from RLG.

R96
RESEARCH LIBRARIES GROUP (RLG). 1993. *Using RLIN for Archival Reference.* Mountain View, CA: RLG; 1993. Loose-leaf binder and 4 disks. LCCN: 93-107156; OCLC: 24765373.

R97
RESNIK, MICHAEL D. 1987. *Choices: An Introduction to Decision Science.* Minneapolis, MN: University of Minnesota Press; 1987. 221p. ISBN: 0816614393 (hbk.); 0816614407 (pbk.).

R98
RESNIKOFF, H. L. 1989. *The Illusion of Reality*. New York, NY: Springer-Verlag; 1989. 339p. ISBN: 0383963987; LCCN: 87-9681.

R99
RETTIG, SALOMON. 1990. *The Discursive Social Psychology of Evidence: Symbolic Construction of Reality*. Cognition and Language series. New York, NY: Plenum Press; 1990. 231p. ISBN: 0306437015.

R100
REULAND, ERIC J.; ABRAHAM, WERNER; ANKERSMIT, FRANK R., eds. 1993. *Knowledge and Language*. Proceedings, Conference on Knowledge and Language at the University of Groningen, May 21-25, 1989. Dordrecht, NL: Kluwer Academic; 1993. 3 vols. ISBN: 0792318889 (set).

R101
REUTER, TIMOTHY. 1987. Computer-Assisted Editions of Medieval Historical Texts. See reference: DENLEY, P.; HOPKIN, D., eds., 1989. 251-261. Concerning the *MGH* project.

R102
REVEL, JACQUES. 1986. Mentalites. *Dictionnaire des sciences historiques*. Burguiere, A., ed. Paris, FR: Presses Universitaires de France; 1986; 450-456. (In French).

R103
REVEL, JACQUES; CHARTIER, ROGER. 1986. Annales. *Dictionnaire des sciences historiques*. Burguiere, A., ed. Paris, FR; 1986; 30-31. (In French).

R104
REVEL, JACQUES; HUNT, LYNN A., eds. 1995. *Histories: French Constructions of the Past*. New York, NY; 1995. 654p. (New Press postwar French Thought series, v. 1). ISBN: 156841956; LCCN: 95071802.

R105
REVEL, JACQUES; WACHTEL, NATHAN; AUGE, MARC, eds. 1996. *Une école pour les sciences sociales: de la vie section a l'École des hautes études en Sciences Sociales* [A School for the Social Sciences: the 4th section of Advanced Studies in the Social Sciences]. Paris, FR: Les Editions du Cerf; 1996. 554p.(Sciences humaines et religions series). ISBN: 220405268X.

R106
REVENAUGH, D. LANCE. 1994. Implementing Major Organizational Change—Can We Really Do It? *TQM Magazine*. 1994; 6(6): 38-48. ISSN: 0954-478X.

R107
REYNOLDS, L. D.; WILSON, N. G. 1975. *Scribes and Scholars. A Guide to the Transmission of Greek and Latin Literature*. London, UK: Oxford University Press; 1968. 2nd rev. ed. 1974, repr. 1975. 275p. ISBN: 0-19-814372-9.

R108
RHEINGOLD, HOWARD. 1985. *Tools for Thought: The People and Ideas behind the Next Computer Revolution*. New York, NY: Simon & Schuster Computer Book Division; 1985. 335p. ISBN: 0671492926.

R109
RHEINGOLD, HOWARD. 1991. *Virtual Reality*. New York, NY: Summit Books; 1991. 415p. ISBN: 0671693638; LCCN: 91-10955.

R110
RHEINGOLD, HOWARD. 1993/1994. *The Virtual Community: Homesteading on the Electronic Frontier*. Reading, PA: Addison-Wesley; 1993. 325p. ISBN: 0201608707. Rev. ed. New York, NY: Harper Perennial; 1994. 335p. ISBN: 0201608707; LCCN: 94-25495.

R111
RIASANOVSKY, ALEXANDER V.; RIZNIK, BARNES, eds. [1963]. *Generalizations in Historical Writing*. Philadelphia, PA: University of Pennsylvania Press; [1963]. 239p.

R112
RICE, EUGENE R. 1996. *Making a Place for the New American Scholar*. Washington, D.C.: American Association for Higher Education; 1996. (AAHE Working Paper, 1).

R113
RICE, JAMES. 1991. The Evolution of Early Visions: An Historical Perspective on Today's Information Technology. *Reference Librarian*. 1991; 33: 111-124. ISSN: 0276-3877.

R114
RICE, JOHN A. 1995. *Mathematical Statistics and Data Analysis*. Belmont, CA: Duxbury Press; 1995. 594p. (Wadsworth & Brooks/Cole Statistics/Probability series). ISBN: 0534082475.

R115
RICE, WILLIAM CRAIG. 1995. Who Killed History? An Academic Autopsy. *The Virginia Quarterly Review*. 1995 Autumn; 71(4): 601-616. ISSN: 0042-675X See affirmative response: The Small World of Academic History. *The Wilson Quarterly*. 1996 Winter; 20(1): 123-125. ISSN: 0363-3276.

R116
RICHARDS, JULIAN D.; RYAN, NICK S. 1985. *Data Processing in Archaeology*. New York, NY: Cambridge University Press; 1985. 232p. ISBN: 0521257697; LCCN: 84-9523; OCLC: 10723804.

R117
RICHARDS, PAMELA S. 1989. ASLIB at War: The Brief But Intrepid Career of a Library Organization as a Hub of Allied Scientific Intelligence, 1942-1945. *Journal of Education for Library and Information Science*. 1989 Spring; 29(4): 279-296. ISSN: 0784-5786.

R118
RICHARDS, PAMELA S. 1994. *Scientific Information in Wartime: The Allied-German Rivalry, 1939-1945*. Westport, CT: Greenwood Press; 1994. 192p. (Contributions in Military Studies, 151). ISSN: 0083-6884; ISBN: 0-313-29062-8.

R119
RICHARDSON, BILL. 1995. Paradox Management for Crisis Avoidance. *Management Decision*. 1995; 33(1): 3-18. ISSN: 0025-1747.

R120
RICHARDSON, GEORGE P. 1991. *Feedback Thought in Social Science and Systems Theory*. Philadelphia, PA: University of Pennsylvania Press; 1991. 374p. ISBN: 0812230531 (hbk.); 0812213327 (pbk.).

R121
RICHARDSON, JOHN V., Jr. 1995. *Knowledge-Based Systems for General Reference Work: Applications, Problems, and Progress*. San Diego, CA: Academic Press; 1995. 355p. ISBN: 0-12-588460-5.

R122
RICHARDSON, JOHN V., Jr. [199- forthcoming]. The Information Scientists in North American Graduate Schools of Librarianship, 1960-1990. Paper in: pre-conference seminar on the History of Information Science, at the Conference of the American Society for Information Science, October 17-20, 1994, Alexandria, VA.

R123
RICHEY, RITA C. 1986. *The Theoretical and Conceptual Bases of Instructional Design*. London, UK: Kogan Page; 1986. 227p. ISBN: 0893972487.

R124
RICHEY, RITA C. 1992. *Designing Instruction for the Adult Learner: Systematic Training, Theory, and Practice*. London, UK: Kegan Paul; 1992. 246p. ISBN: 0749404779.

R125
RICOEUR, PAUL. 1965/1966. *Histoire et verité*. Paris, FR: Editions du Seuil [1965/66]. Trans. as. *History and Truth* [Essays]. Evanston, IL: Northwestern University Press; 1965. (Northwestern University Studies in Phenomenology and Existential Philosophy). ISBN: 0810104423; LCCN: 68-139199.

R126
RICOEUR, PAUL. 1974. *Le Conflit des Interpretations*. Trans. as: *The Conflict of Interpretations: Essays in Hermeneutics*. Ihde, Don, ed. Evanston, IL: Northwestern University Press; 1974. 512p. (Northwestern University Studies in Phenomenology and Existential Philosophy). ISBN: 0810104423.

R127
RICOEUR, PAUL. 1976. *Interpretation Theory: Discourse and the Surplus of Meaning*. Fort Worth, TX: Texas Christian University Press; 1976. 107p. (Expanded 1973 Centennial Lectures). LC call no.: BD241.R52.

R128
RICOEUR, PAUL. 1977. *La Métaphora Vive*. Czerny, Robert, trans. *The Rule of Metaphor: Multidisciplinary Studies of the Creation of Meaning in Language*. Toronto, CN: University of Toronto Press; 1977. 384p. ISBN: 0802053262.

R129
RICOEUR, PAUL. 1978. The Metaphorical Process as Cognition, Imagination, and Feeling. *Critical Inquiry*. 1978; 5 (1): 141-157. ISSN: 0093-1896.

R130
RICOEUR, PAUL. 1984. *The Reality of the Historical Past*. Milwaukee, WI: Marquette University Press; 1984. 51p. (Aquinas Lecture).

R131
RICOEUR, PAUL. 1984-1988. *Temps et écrit.* McLaughlin, Kathleen; Pellauer, David, trans. *Time and Narrative.* Chicago, IL: University of Illinois; 1984-1988. ISBN: 0226713318; LCCN: 83017995.

R132
RICOEUR, PAUL. 1991. *Du Texte a l'Action.* Trans. as: *From Text to Action.* Evanston, IL: Northwestern University Press; 1991. 346p. ISBN: 0810109786 (hbk.); 0810109921 (pbk.).

R133
RIDGEWAY, WHITMAN H. 1974. Numerophilia: A Review of Recent Books on Quantitative History. *Maryland Historian.* 1974: 5(1): 53-62. ISSN: 0025-424X.

R134
RIEUSSET-LEMARIE, ISABELLE. 1997. P. Otlet's *Mundaneuum* and the International Perspective in the History of Documentation and Information Science. See reference: BUCKLAND, M.; BELLARDO, HAHN, eds. 1997. 301-309.

R135
RIFFATERRE, MICHAEL. 1990. *Fictional Truth.* Baltimore, MD: Johns Hopkins University Press; 1990. 137p. (Parallax series). ISBN: 0801839335; 0801839343 (pbk.); LCCN: 89-36929; OCLC: 20057588.

R136
RIFKIN, JEREMY. 1995. *The End of Work: The Decline of the Global Labor Force and the Dawn of the Post-Market Era.* New York, NY: Putnam's Sons; 1995. 250p. ISBN: 08777798.

R137
RIGBY, S. H. 1995. Historical Causation: Is One Thing More Important than Another? *History: The Journal of the Historical Association* (UK). 1995 June; 80(259): 227-243. ISSN: 0018-2648.

R138
RIGGS, FRED W. 1988. Terminology for Social Scientists: The Problem and a Solution. See reference: CZAP, H.; GALINSKI, C., eds. Suppl.: 133-142.

R139
RIGGS, FRED W., ed. 1982. *The CONTA Conference: Proceedings of the Conference on Conceptual and Terminological Analysis in the Social Sciences at Bielefeld, FRG, May 24-27, 1981.* Frankfurt am Main, DEU: INDEKS Verlag; 1982. 368p. (Vol. 1 of the proposed *INTERCOCTA Encyclopedia*). ISBN: 3886722007; OCLC: 10422946.

R140
RIGGS, FRED W.; SARTORI, GIOVANNI; TEUNE, HENRY. 1975. *The Tower of Babel: On the Definition and Analysis of Concepts in Social Sciences.* Pittsburgh, PA: International Studies Association; 1975. 107p. (International Studies Association Occasional Paper, no. 6). OCLC: 2050157.

R141
RIGNEY, ANN. The Untenanted Places of the Past: Thomas Carlyle and the Varieties of Historical Ignorance. *History and Theory.* 1996 October; 35(3): 338-358. ISSN: 0018-2656.

R142
RIPLEY, BRIAN D. 1981. *Spatial Statistics.* New York, NY: Wiley; 1981. 252p. ISBN: 0471083674.

R143
RIPS, LANCE A. 1989. Similarity, Typicality, and Categorization. In: Vosniadov, Stella; Ortony, Andrev, eds. *Similarity and Analogical Reasoning.* Cambridge, UK: Cambridge University Press; 1989. 592p. ISBN: 0521362954 (hbk.); 0521389756 (pbk.); LCCN: 88-11813.

R144
RIPS, LANCE A. 1994. *The Psychology of Proof: Deduction, Reason, and Human Thinking.* Cambridge, MA: MIT; 1994. 449p. ISBN: 0267181533; LCCN: 93-5811.

R145
RISEMAN, E.; ARBIB, M. 1977. Segmentation of Static Scenes. *Computer Vision, Graphics, Image Processing.* 1977; 6: 221-276. ISSN: 0734-189x.

R146
RISSANEN, J. 1987. Stochastic Complexity. *Journal of the Royal Statistical Society.* 1987; 49(3): 223-239.

R147
RITCHIE, DAVID. 1986a. *The Computer Pioneers: The Making of the Modern Corporation.* New York, NY: Simon and Schuster; 1986. 238p. ISBN: 067152397X; LCCN: 85-22239.

R148
RITCHIE, DAVID. 1986b. Shannon and Weaver: Unraveling the Paradox of Information. *Communication Research.* 1986; 13(2): 278-298. ISSN: 0093-6502.

R149
RITCHIE, DAVID. 1991. *Information*. Newbury Park, CA: Sage Publ; 1991.

R150
RITCHIE, DAVID A. 1995. *Doing Oral History*. New York, NY: Twayne Publ.; 1995. 265p. (Twayne's Oral History series, 15). ISBN: 0805791248 (hbk.); 0805791280 (pbk.); LCCN: 94020304..

R151
RITCHIN, FRED. 1990. *In Our Own Image: The Coming Revolution in Photography. How Computer Technology is Changing Our View of the World*. New York, NY: Aperture; 1990. 158p. ISSN: 089381982 (hbk.); 08938113990 (pbk.).

R152
RITTER, HARRY. 1986. *Dictionary of Concepts in History*. Westport, CT: Greenwood Press; 1986. 490p. (Reference Sources for the Social Sciences and Humanities, 3). ISBN: 0313227004; LCCN: 85027305.

R153
RITTER, LEONORA. 1988. Simulation as a Teaching Aid. *Computing and History Today*. 1988; 4: 31-34.

R154
RITZENTHALLER, MARY L. 1983. *Archives & Manuscripts: Conservation. A Manual on Physical Care and Management*. Chicago, IL: Society of American Archivists; 1983. 144p. (Archives & Manuscripts series). ISBN: 0931828589 (pbk.); LCCN: 83050878.

R155
RITZENTHALLER, MARY L. 1984. *Archives & Manuscripts: Administration of Photographic Collections*. Chicago, IL: Society of American Archivists; 1984. 173p. (Archives & Manuscripts series). ISBN: 0931828619 (pbk.); LCCN: 84051384.

R156
RITZENTHALLER, MARY L. 1990. *Preservation of Archival Records: Holdings Maintenance at the National Archives*. Washington, DC: National Archives and Records Administration; 1990. 29p. (NARA Technical Information Paper, 6). NTIS: PB90-168733. OCLC: 22441880.

R157
RITZENTHALLER, MARY L. 1993. *Preserving Archives and Manuscripts*. Chicago, IL: Society of American Archivists; 1993. 225p. (Archival Fundamentals series) ISBN: 0931828954; LCCN: 94151026.

R158
ROBBIN, ALICE. 1992. Social Scientists at Work on Electronic Research Networks. *Electronic Networking Research: Applications and Policy*. 1992; 2(2): 6-30. ISSN: 1051-4805.

R159
ROBBIN, ALICE; FROST-KUMPF, LEE. 1997. Extending Theory for User-Centered Information Services: Diagnosing and Learning from Error in Complex Statistical Data. *Journal of the American Society for Information Science*. 1997 February; 48(2): 96-212. ISSN: 0002-8231.

R160
ROBERTS, DAVID.; LIGHT, R. B. 1980. Museum Documentation. *Journal of Documentation* (UK). 1980; 36(1): 42-84. ISSN: 0022-0418.

R161
ROBERTS, DAVID. 1992. International and National Developments in Museum Information Standards. *Computers and the History of Art*. 1992; 3(2): 3-6. ISBN: 3-7186-5363-X; ISSN: 1048-6798.

R162
ROBERTS, DAVID. 1993. Managing records in special formats. See reference: ELLIS, J., ed. 1993: [380-390].

R163
ROBERTS, DAVID. 1994. Defining Electronic Records, Documents, and Data. *Archives and Manuscripts* (AU). 1994 May; 22(1): 14-26. ISSN: 0157-6895.

R164
ROBERTS, GEOFFREY. 1996. Narrative History as a Way of Life. *Journal of Contemporary History*. 1996 January; 31(1): 221-229. (Comment on the Marwick- White debate). ISSN: 0022-0094.

R165
ROBERTS, J. 1964. The Self-Management of Cultures. In: Goodenough, W., ed. *Explorations in Cultural Anthropology: Essays in Honor of George Peter Murdock*. New York, NY: McGraw-Hill; 1964. 433-454. LC call no.: GN8.G65.

R166
ROBERTS, JOHN W. 1987. Archival Theory: Much Ado About Shelving. *The American Archivist*. 1987 Winter; 50: 66-74. ISSN: 0360-9081.

R167
ROBERTS, N. 1984. Historical Studies in Documentation: The Pre-history of the Information Retrieval Thesaurus. *Journal of Documentation* (UK). 1984; 40: 271-285. ISSN: 0022-0418.

R168
ROBERTSON, G. G.; CARD, S. K.; MACKLINAY, J. D. 1993. Information Visualization using 3D Interactive Animation. *Communications of the* ACM (Assn. of Computing Machinery). 1993; 36 (4): 57-71. ISSN: 0001-0782.

R169
ROBERTSON, ROLAND. 1992. *Globalization: Social Theory and Global Culture*. London, UK: Sage; 1992. 211p. ISBN: 0803981864 (hbk.); 0803981872 (pbk.); LCCN: 02050327.

R170
ROBEY, DAVID, ed. 1973. *Structuralism: An Introduction*. Oxford, UK: Clarendon Press; 1973. 154p. ISBN: 0198740123; LCCN: 73173608.

R171
ROBIN, R. 1973. *Histoire et linguistique* [History and Linquistics]. Paris, FR: A. Colin; 1973. 306p. LCCN: 74-150292; OCLC: 811154.

R172
ROBINSON, PETER. 1993. *The Digitization of Primary Textual Sources*. Oxford, UK: Oxford University Office for Humanities Communications; 1993. 104p. (Humanities Communications, 4). ISBN: 1897791054 (pbk.); LCCN: 94-3292; OCLC: 29704458.

R173
ROBINSON, PETER M. W. 1994. *Collate*: A Program for Interactive Collation of Large Textual Traditions. In: S. Hockey and N. Ide, eds. *Research in Humanities Computing*, 4. Oxford, UK: Clarendon Press; 1994. LCCN: 92-643990; OCLC: 24868195.

R174
ROBINSON, PETER M. W. [199-]. Collation, Textual Scholarship, and the Electronic Edition. See reference: HAMESSE, J., ed. [199-, forthcoming].

R175
ROBINSON, V. 1988. Implications of Fuzzy Set Theory Applied to Geographic Databases. *Computers, Environment, and Urban Systems*. 1988; 12: 89-98. ISSN: 0198-9715.

R176
ROCCA, A. M. 1994. Integrating History and Geography. *Social Education*. 1994 February; 58 (2); 114-117. ISSN: 0037-7724.

R177
ROCKART, JOHN F. [1975]. *Computers and the Learning Process in Higher Education: A Report to the Carnegie Commission on Higher Education*. New York, NY: McGraw- Hill; [1975]. 356p. ISBN: 0070101221.

R178
ROCKART, JOHN F. 1979. Chief Executives Define their Own Data Needs. *Harvard Business Review.* 1979 March-April; 57(2): 81-93. ISSN: 0017-8012.

R179
ROCKART, JOHN F.; DELONG, DAVID. 1988. *Executive Support Systems: The Emergence of Top Management Computer Use*. Homewood, IL: Dow-Jones Irwin; 1988. 280p. ISBN: 0870949551; LCCN: 87-77026..

R180
RODDY, KEVIN. 1991. Subject Access to Visual Resources. What the `90s Might Portend. *Library Hi-Tech*. 1991; 9(1): 45-49. ISSN: 0737-8831.

R181
RODGERS, DANIEL T. 1987. *Contested Truths: Keywords in American Politics since Independence*. New York, NY: Basic Books; c1987. 270p. ISBN: 0465014151; LCCN: 87047522.

R182
RODGERS, DANIEL T. 1988. Keywords: A Reply. *Journal of the History of Ideas*. 1988 October/September; 49: 200-202. ISSN: 0022-5037. Rejoinder to OLSEN & HARVEY, 1988.

R183
ROE, KATHLEEN. 1981. *Teaching with Historical Records*. Albany, NY: NY State Education Dept.; 1981.

R184

ROGERS, EVERETT M. 1986. *Communication Technology: The New Media in Society.* New York, NY: The Free Press; 1986. 273p. ISBN: 0-02-927110-X.

R185

ROGERS, EVERETT M. 1994. *A History of Communication Study: A Biographical Approach.* New York, NY: Free Press; 1994. 576p. ISBN: 0029267358; LCCN: 93- 43281.

R186

ROGERS, EVERETT M.; RICE, RONALD E. 1988. *Research Methods and New Media.* New York, NY: Free Press; 1988. 21p. ISBN: 0029353377 (hbk.); 0029353319 (pbk); LCCN: 88-11260.

R187

ROGERS, EVERETT M.; SHOEMAKER, FLOYD. 1961/1994. *Diffusion of Innovations: A Cross-Cultural Approach.* New York, NY: Glencoe; 1961. Reprint, 1962. *Communication of Innovations.* 2nd ed.; 1971. 3rd ed.; 1983. 4th ed. New York, NY: The Free Press; 1994. 476p. ISBN: 0028740762 (hbk.); 0029266718 (pbk.).

R188

ROGERS, WILLIAM ELFORD. 1994. *Interpreting Interpretation: Textual Hermeneutics as an Ascetic Discipline.* University Park, PA: Pennsylvania State University Press; 1994. 240p. ISBN: 0271010592; 0271010614 (pbk.); LCCN: 92-41210; OCLC: 27150236.

R189

ROGOFF, BARBARA. 1990. *Apprenticeship in Thinking: Cognitive Development in Social Context.* New York, NY: Oxford University Press; 1990. 242p. ISBN: 0195059735.

R190

ROGOFF, BARBARA; LABVE, J. 1984. *Everyday Cognition: Its Development in Social Context.* Cambridge, MA: Harvard University Press; 1984. 314p. ISBN: 0674270304.

R191

ROHRS, RICHARD. C. 1987. Sources and Strategies for Computer-Aided Instruction. *Historical Methods.* 1987; 20: 79-83. ISSN: 0161-5440.

R192

ROHRS, RICHARD C.; DARCY, ROBERT. 1990/1995. *Guide to Quantitative History.* Santa Barbara, CA: ABC-CLIO Press; 1990. Rev. ed. Westport, CT: Praeger; 1995. ISBN: 275948978; 0275952371 (pbk.); LCCN: 93-50069; OCLC: 29636656.

R193

ROLLINS, MARK. 1989. *Mental Imagery: On the Limits of Cognitive Science.* New Haven, CT: Yale University Press; 1989. 170p. ISBN: 0300044917.

R194

ROLPH, PAUL; BARTRAM, PETER. 1992. *How to Choose and Use an Executive Information System.* London, UK: Mercury; 1992. 154p. ISBN: 1852511761; LCCN: 93-153184.

R195

ROMESBURG, H. CHARLES. 1984. *Cluster Analysis for Researchers.* London, UK: Lifetime Learning Publications; 1984. 334p. ISBN: 05340324886.

R196

ROPER, JOHN P. G.; ZAMPOLLI, ANTONIO; HAMESSE, JACQUELINE, eds. 1988. *Computers in Literary and Linguistic Research.* Proceedings, 13th International Conference L'Ordinateur et les recherches litteraires et linguistiques, at the University of East Anglia, Norwich (UK), April 1-4, 1986. Paris, FR; Champion; and Geneva, CH: Slatkine; 1988. 181p. ISBN: 2051009945.

R197

ROPER, MICHAEL. 1993. Automation and Archives: Progress and Policy. *Archivi & Computer.* 1993; 3(1): 2-14. ISSN: 1121-2462.

R198

RORTY, RICHARD. 1991. *Objectivity, Relativism, and Truth.* Cambridge, UK: Cambridge University Press; 1991. 226p. ISBN: 0521353696 (hbk.); 0521358779)pbk.); LCCN: 90-41632. About New Pragmatism.

R199

RORTY, RICHARD; SCHNEEWIND, JEROME B.; SKINNER, QUENTIN. 1984. *Philosophy in History: Essays on the Historiography of Philosophy.* Lectures at The Johns Hopkins University, 1982-1984. Cambridge, UK: Cambridge University Press; 1984. 403p. ISBN: 0521253527 (hbk.); 0521273307 (hbk.).

R200
RORVIG, MARK E. 1987. The Substitutibility of Images for Textual Descriptions of Archival Materials in an MS-DOS Environment. In: Lehman, L.; Strohl-Goebel, H., eds. *The Application of Microcomputers in Information, Documentation and Libraries* (pp. 407-415). Amsterdam, NL: North Holland Press; 1987. 813p. ISBN: 044470134; LCCN: 87-33876; OCLC: 16472285.

R201
RORVIG, MARK E. 1990. Intellectual Access to Graphic Information. Introduction. *Library Trends.* 1990; 38: 639-643. ISSN: 0024-2594.

R202
RORVIG, MARK E. 1993. A Method for Automatically Abstracting Visual Documents. *Journal of the American Society for Information Science.* 1993; 22: 139-141. ISSN: 002-8231.

R203
ROSALDO, RENATO. 1989. *Culture and Truth: The Remaking of Social Analysis.* Boston, MA: Beacon Press; 1989. 253p. ISBN: 0807046086; LCCN: 88-47659; OCLC: 18835508.

R204
ROSEN, BRUCE K.; FONG, ELISABETH. 1988. *Guide to Distributed Database Management.* Gaithersburg, MD: NISO Press; 1988. 27p. (NISO Pub.: 500-154). CODEN: XNBSAV.

R205
ROSEN, BRUCE K.; FONTAINIS, ISABELLA DE 1989. *Guide to Data Administration.* Gaithersburg, MD: NISO Press; 1989. 73p. (NISO Pub.: 500-197). LCCN: 89-600766.

R206
ROSEN, BRUCE K.; LAW, MARGARET. 1991. *Guide to Schema and Schema Extensibility.* Gaithersburg, MD: NISO Press; 1991. 25p. (NISO Pub.: 500-173). LCCN: 92-600008.

R207
ROSENBERG, JAY F. 1994. *Beyond Formalism: Naming and Necessity for Human Beings.* Philadelphia, PA: Temple University Press; 1994. 241p. ISBN: 1566391180.

R208
ROSENBERG, NATHAN. 1979. Technological Interdependence in the American Economy. *Technology and Culture.* 1979; 20: 25-50. ISSN: 0040-165X).

R209
ROSENBERG, NATHAN; VINCENI, WALTER G. 1978. *The Britannica Bridge: The Generation and Diffusion of Technological Knowledge.* Cambridge, MA: MIT Press; 1978. 107p. ISBN: 0262181871.

R210
ROSENBERG, RICHARD. 1997. *The Social Impact of Computers.* 2nd ed. San Diego, CA: Academic Press; 1997. 448p. ISBN: 0-12-597131-1.

R211
ROSENOER, JONATHAN. 1996. *CyberLaw. The Law of the Internet.* Los Alamitos, CA: IEEE; 1996. 365p. ISBN: 0-387-94832-5.

R212
ROSENSTONE, ROBERT A. 1988. History in Images/History in Words. *American Historical Review.* 1988 December; 93: ISSN: 0002-8762.

R213
ROSENSTONE, ROBERT A. 1995. The Historical Film as Real History. *Film and History.* 1995; 5: 5-23. ISSN: 0360-3695.

R214
ROSENSTONE, ROBERT A., ed. 1994a. Experiments in Narrating Histories: A workshop. *AHA Perspectives.* 1994 Sept.; 7-10. (Report on the California Institute of Technology workshop, April 1994). ISSN: 0743-7021.

R215
ROSENSTONE, ROBERT A., ed. 1994b. *Revisioning History: Film and the Construction of a New Past.* Princeton, NJ: Princeton University Press; 1994. 255p. ISBN: 069108629X (hbk.); 0691025347 (pbk.).

R216
ROSENSTONE, ROBERT A., ed. 1995. *Visions of the Past: The Challenge of Film to Our Idea of History.* Cambridge, MA: Harvard University Press; 1995. 271p. ISBN: 0674940970 (hbk.); 067490989 (pbk.).

R217

ROSENSTONE, ROBERT A.; SIMON, BRYANT; SLUHOVSKY, MOSHE. 1994. Experiments in Narrating Histories: A Workshop. *AHA Perspectives*. 1994 September; 32(6): 7-10. ISSN: 0743-7021. Further information is available from: R. Rosenstone, Division of the Humanities and Social Sciences, CalTech, Pasadena, CA 91125.

R218

ROSENTHAL, BERNARD; SZARMACH, PAUL E., eds. 1989. *Medievalism in American Culture*. Papers from the 18th Annual Conference of the Center for Medieval and Early Renaissance Studies, SUNY Binghamton, NY. Binghamton, NY: SUNY at Binghamton; 1989. 301p. (Medieval & Renaissance Texts & Studies, v. 55). ISBN: 08669980393.

R219

ROSENTHAL, PAUL-ANDRE. 1996. Treize ans de reflexion: de l'histoire des populations a la démographie historique française (1945-1958) [Thirty Years of Reflection on French Population and Demographic History]. *Population*. 1996; 6: 1211-1238. (In French). ISSN: 0032-4663.

R220

ROSING, INA; PRICE, DEREK JOHN DE SOLLA. 1977. *Science, Technology, and Society; A Cross-disciplinary Perspective*. London, UK / Beverly Hills, CA: Sage Publications; c1977. 607p. (International Council for Society Policy Studies). ISBN: 0803998589; LCCN: 76055928.

R221

ROSKOMMEN INFORM. 1991. *Directory of Soviet Databases*. [Moscow, RU]: All-Union Institute for Inter-Industrial Information; 1991.

R222

ROSS, DOROTHY. 1984. Historical Consciousness in Nineteenth-century America. *American Historical Review*. 1984 October; 89: 909-928. ISSN: 0002-8762.

R223

ROSS, DOROTHY. 1988. On the Misunderstanding of Ranke and the Origins of the Historical Profession in America. *Syracuse Scholar*. 1988; 9: 31-41. ISSN: 0276- 6345.

R224

ROSS, DOROTHY. 1991. *The Origins of American Social Science*. Cambridge, UK: Cambridge University Press; 1991. 508p. ISBN: 0521350921.

R225

ROSS, DOROTHY. 1994a. Modernism Reconsidered. See reference: ROSS, DOROTHY, ed. 1994.

R226

ROSS, DOROTHY. 1994b. Modernist Social Science in the Land of the New/Old. See reference: ROSS, DOROTHY, ed. 1994.

R227

ROSS, DOROTHY, ed. 1994. *Modernist Impulses in the Human Sciences, 1870-1930*. Baltimore, MD: The Johns Hopkins University Press; 1994. ISBN: 0801847443 (hbk.); 0801847451 (pbk.).

R228

ROSS, RONALD G. 1987. *Entity Modeling: Techniques and Applications*. Boston, MA: Database Research Group; 1987. 218p. ISBN: 0941049000; LCCN: 87-402022.

R229

ROSS, SEAMUS. 1993. Historians, Machine-Readable Information, and the Past's Future. See reference: ROSS, S.; HIGGS, E., eds. 1993. 1-20.

R230

ROSS, SEAMUS. 1995a. Intelligent Graphical user Interfaces: Opportunities for the Interface between the Historian and the Machine. See reference: JARTIZ, G. *ET AL.*, eds. 1995. 207-222.

R231

ROSS, SEAMUS. 1995b. Preserving and Maintaining Electronic Resources in the Visual Arts for the Next Century. *Information Services & Use*. 1995; 15: 373-384. ISSN: 0167-5265.

R232

ROSS, SEAMUS; HIGGS, EDWARD, eds. 1993. *Electronic Information Resources and Historians: European Perspectives*. St. Katharinen [Göttingen, DE]: Max-Planck- Institut für Geschichte in Kommission bei Scripta Mercaturae Verlag; 1993. 327p. (Halbgraue Reihe zur historischen Fackinformatik. Serie A: Historische Quellenkunden, Band 20). ISBN: 3-928134-95-7. (Also published as British Library Report, 6122).

R233
ROSS, SEAMUS; MOFFETT, JONATHAN; HENDERSON, JULIAN, eds. 1991. *Computing for Archeologists*. Oxford, UK: Oxford University Press; 1991. 205p. (Oxford University Committee for Archeology, no. 18). ISBN: 0947816186.

R234
ROSSER MATTHEWS, J. 1995. *Quantification and the Quest for Medical Certainty*. Princeton, NJ: Princeton University; 1995. 195p. ISBN: 0691037949.

R235
ROSZAK, THEODORE. 1969. *The Making of a Counter Culture: Reflections on the Technocratic Society and its Youthful Opposition*. Garden City, NY: Doubleday; 1969. 303p. LCCN: 69-15215; OCLC: 23039.

R236
ROTH, MICHAEL S. 1955. Introduction. In: Cohen, R. & Roth, M. S., eds. *History and Histories within the Human Sciences* (pp. 1-25). Charlottesville, VA: University of Virginia Press; 1955.

R237
ROTH, MICHAEL S. 1987. *Psycho-Analysis as History: Negation and Freedom in Freud*. Ithaca, NY: Cornell University Press; 1987. 196p. ISBN: 0801419573.

R238
ROTH, MICHAEL S. 1988. *Knowing and History: Appropriations of Hegel in Twentieth- century France*. Ithaca, NY: Cornell University Press; 1988. 264p. ISBN: 0801421365.

R239
ROTH, MICHAEL S. 1994. Performing History: Modernist Contextualism in Carl Schorske's *Fin-de-Siecle Vienna*. *American Historical Review*. 1994; 99(3): 729-745. ISSN: 0002-8762.

R240
ROTH, MICHAEL S. 1995. *The Ironist's Cage: Memory, Trauma and the Construction of History*. New York, NY; 1995. 240p. ISBN: 0231102443 (hbk.); 02231102453 (pbk.).

R241
ROTH, MICHAEL S., ed. 1994. *Rediscovering History: Culture, Politics, and the Psyche*. Stanford, CA: Stanford University Press; 1994. 535p. ISBN: 00804723095 (hbk.); 0804723133 (pbk.).

R242
ROTH, MICHAEL S.; ROSS, GLENN, eds. 1990. *Doubting: Contemporary Perspectives on Skepticism*. Dordrecht, NL: Kluwer Academic Publishers; 1990. 217p.(Philosophical Studies series, v. 48). ISBN: 0792305760.

R243
ROTH, PAUL A. 1981. Foucault's History of the Present. *History and Theory*. 1981; 20: 32-46. ISSN: 0018-2656.

R244
ROTH, PAUL A. 1988. Narrative Explanations: The Case of History. *History and Theory*. 1988; 27(1): 1-13. ISSN: 0018-2656.

R245
ROTH, PAUL A; RYCKMAN, THOMAS A. 1995. Chaos, Clio and Scientistic Illusions of Understanding. *History and Theory*. 1995 February; 34(1): 30-45. ISSN: 0018- 2656.

R246
ROTH, RANDOLPH. 1992. Is History a Process? *Social Science History*. 1992; 16: 197-243. ISSN: 0145-5532.

R247
ROTHENBERG, JEFF. 1995. Ensuring the Longevity of Digital Documents. *Scientific American*. 1995 January; 272: 40-48. ISSN:0036-8733.

R248
ROTHENBERG, JEFF. 1996. *Metadata to Support Data Quality and Longevity* [Electronic file]. 1996 March. Accessible at http://www.computer.org/conferen/meta96/rothenberg_paper/ iee.data-quality.html.

R249
ROTHENBURG, MARC. 1982; 1993. *The History of Science and Technology in the United States: A Critical and Selective Bibliography*. New York, NY: Garland Pub.; 1982; 1993. 2 vols. (Bibliographies of the History of Science and Technology, vols. 2, 17). ISBN: 0824092783 (vol. 1); 0824083490 (vol. 2); LCCN: 81043355.

R250
ROTHSTEIN, M. 1970. Quantification and American History: An Assessment. In: Bass, H. J., ed. *The State of American History* (pp. 298-329). Chicago, IL: Quadrangle Books; 1970. 426p. LCCN: 77-101068; OCLC: 89623.

R251
ROTHSTEIN, PAUL F. 1975; 1978-. *Federal Rules of Evidence: Rules of Evidence for the U.S. Courts and Magistrates.* Annotated. Washington, DC: Bureau of National Affairs; [1975]. 92p. ISBN: 0871792184; LCCN: 75-10794. Cont'd.; updated. Deerfield, IL: Clark Boardman Callaghan; 1978-. Loose-leaf service. ISBN: 0876320084; LCCN: 78-9296.

R252
ROTHSTEIN, PAUL F. 1986. *Evidence: Cases, Materials, and Problems.* New York, NY: N. Bender; 1986. 1589p. LCCN: 85-72836.

R253
ROTBERG, ROBERT I.; RABB, THEODORE K., eds. 1988/1991. *Art and History: Images and Their Meaning.* Brown, Jonathan, contributer. Cambridge, UK / New York, NY; c. 1986. (Studies in Interdisciplinary History). ISBN: 0521340187 (hbk.); 0521335698 (pbk.); LCCN: 87035474.

R254
ROUET, JEAN-FRANCOIS; BRITT, M. ANNE; MASON, ROBERT A.; PERFETTI, CHARLES A. 1996. Using Multiple Sources of Evidence to Reason about History. *Journal of Educational Psychology.* 1996 September; 88 (30): 478-492. ISSN: 0022- 0663.

R255
ROUGER, ERIC. 1994. Image Numerique et Archeologie [Numerical Images and Archeology]. See reference: BECK, P., ed. 1994. 7-11.

R256
ROUSE, WILLIAM B. 1991. *Design for Success: A Human-centered Approach to Designing Successful Products and Systems.* New York, NY: Wiley; 1991. 287p. ISBN: 0471524832.

R257
ROUSE, WILLIAM B. 1992. *Strategies for Innovation: Creating Successful Products, Systems, and Organizations.* New York, NY: John Wiley; 1992. 249p. ISBN: 0471559040.

R258
ROUSE, WILLIAM B. 1993. *Catalyst for Change: Concepts and Principles for Enabling Innovation.* New York, NY: John Wiley; 1993. 249p. (Wiley series in systems engineering). ISBN: 0471591963.

R259
ROUSE, WILLIAM B. 1998. Computer Support of Collaborative Planning: An Applications Report. See reference: MCNEESE, M. D., ed. 1998. 832-839.

R260
ROWE, JUDITH. 1982. Primary Data for Historical Research: New Machine-readable Resources. *RQ: Reference Quarterly.* 1982 Summer; 21(4): 351-56. ISSN: 0033-7072.

R261
ROWLAND, ROBERT. 1992. Full Text/Images DBMSs. See reference: THALLER, M., ed. 1992a. 155-158.

R262
ROWLINSON, MICHAEL; HASSARD, JOHN. 1993. The Invention of Corporate Culture: A History of the Histories of Cadbury. *Human Relations.* 1993 March; 46(3): 299-326. ISSN: 0018-7267.

R263
ROWNEY, DON K., ed. 1983/1984. *Soviet Quantitative History.* Berkeley, CA: University of California; 1983. 2nd ed. in *New Approaches to Social Science History*, 4. Beverly Hills, CA: Sage Publications with the Social Science History Association; 1984. 216p. ISBN: 080320822; LCCN: 83-19196; OCLC: 9945868.

R264
ROZENZWEIG, ROY. 1995. "So, What's Next for Clio?" CD-ROM and Historians. *Journal of American History.* 1995 March; 81(4): 1621-1641. ISSN: 0021-8723.

R265
RUBENFELD, DANIEL L. 1994. Reference Guide on Multiple Regression. See reference: FEDERAL JUDICIAL CENTER. 1994. 415-470.

R266
RUCK, PETER. 1991. *Pergament: Geschichte, Stucktur, Restaurierung* [Parchment: Its History, Structure, and Restoration]. Sigmaringen, DEU: J. Thorbecke; 1991. 480p. ISBN: 3799542027; LCCN: 92-250865.

R267
RUCK, PETER, ed. 1993. *Methoden des Schriftbeschreibung. Historische Hilfswissenschaften* [Methods of Describing Handwriting: Historical Auxiliary Science]. Sigmaringen, DEU: Jan Thorbecke Verlag; 1993.

R268
RUELLE, DAVID. 1991/1992. *Hasard et chaos*. Paris, 1991. Translated as*: Chance and Chaos*. Princeton, NJ: Princeton University Press; 1992. 195p. ISBN: 00691085749.

R269
RUGGLES, C. N. L.; RAHTZ, S. P. Q., eds. 1988. *Computing and Quantitative Methods in Archeology*. The 1987 Computer Applications in Archaeology (CAA) conference, University of Leicester. Oxford, UK: BAR; 1988. 299p.(BAR International Series, 393). ISBN: 0860545075; LCCN: 88-198636; OCLC: 17717158.

R270
RUGGLES, STEVEN. 1987. *Prolonged Connections: The Rise of the Extended Family in Nineteenth-Century England and America*. Madison, WI: University of Wisconsin Press; 1987. 282p.(Social Demography series). ISBN: 0299110303 (hbk.); 02991102346 (pbk.).

R271
RUGGLES, STEVEN. 1994. The Transformation of American Family Structures. *American Historical Review*. 1994; 99: 103-128. ISSN: 0002-8762.

R272
RUGGLES, STEVEN. 1994/1995. *Public Use Microdata Samples. User's Guide and Technical Documentation. 1880 United State Census of Population*. 1994. *1850 United States Census of Population*. Minneapolis, MN: Social History Research Laboratory, University of Minnesota; 1995.

R273
RUGGLES, STEVEN; SOBEK, M.; KELLY HALL, P.; RONNANDER, C. 1995. *Integrated Public Use Microdata Series Version 1.0*, volume 1. *Users Guide*. Minneapolis, MN: Social History Research Laboratory, University of Minnesota; 1995.

R274
RULLER, THOMAS J. 1993. A Review of Information Science and Computer Science Literature to Support Archival Work with Electronic Records. See reference: HEDSTROM, M.; WALCH, W., eds. 1993. 546-559.

R275
RUMELHART, D.; HINTON, G.; WILLIAMS, R. 1986. Learning Internal Representations by Error Propagation. In: Rumelhart, D.; McClelland, J., eds. *Parallel Distributed Processing: Explorations in the Microstructure of Cognition* (vol. 1, pp. 318-363). London, UK: Bradford Books; 1986. Cambridge, MA: MIT Press; 1986. 2 vols., 516p. ISBN: 0262181207 (vol. 1); 0262132184 (vol. 2); LCCN: 85-24073; OCLC: 12837549.

R276
RUNDELL, WALTER. 1970. *In Pursuit of American History: Research and Training in the United States*. Norman, OK: University of Oklahoma Press; 1970. 445p. ISBN: 0806108681; LCCN: 69-16725; OCLC: 67560.

R277
RUNDELL, WALTER; DOUGHTERY, JAMES J.; RITCHIE, DONALD. 1976. *AHA Bibliographical Study*. Washington, D.C.: American Historical Association; 1976. Available from the AHA. Summarized in the *AHA Newsletter*. 1976 May-June: 2-3. ISSN: 0001-138X.

R278
RUNDLE, JOHN; KLEIN, WILLIAM; TURCOTTE, DON, eds. 1996. *Reduction and Predictability of Natural Disasters*. Santa Fe Institute Studies in the Science of Complexity. Santa Fe, NM: Santa Fe Institute (SFI); 1996. ISBN: 0-201-87048-7 (hbk.); 0-201-87049-5 (pbk.).

R279
RUNYAN, LINDA. 1991. 40 Years of the Frontier. *Datamation*. 1991 March 15; 37(6): 34- 47. ISSN: 0011-6963. History of computing 1951-1991 and specific computers from UNIVAC I through the DEC VAX.

R280
RUNYON, RICHARD P. 1977. *Wining with Statistics: A Painless First Look at Numbers, Ratios, Percentages, Means, and Inference*. Reading, MA: Addison-Wesley Pub.; 1977. 210p. ISBN: 0201066548; LCCN: 76-17720.

R281
RUNYON, RICHARD P. 1981. *How Numbers Lie: A Consumer's Guide to the Fine Art of Numerical Description*. Lexington, MA: Lewns Pub.; 1981. 182p. ISBN: 0866160000 (hbk.); 0866160019 (pbk.); LCCN: 80-29415.

R282
RUNYON, RICHARD P. 1996. *Fundamentals of Behavioral Statistics*. Rev. 8th ed. New York, NY: McGraw-Hill; 1996. 721p. ISBN: 6070549850; ILC: 95-38509.

R283
RUNYON, RICHARD P.; ELIFSON, KIRK W.; HABER, AUDREY. [1998]. *Fundamentals of Social Statistics*. 3rd ed. Boston, MA: Irwin McGraw; [1998]. ISBN: 0070715790; LCCN: 97-25763.

R284
RUSEN, JOHN. 1987. Historical Narration: Foundation, Types, Reason. *History and Theory*. 1987; 26: 87-97. ISSN: 0018-2656.

R285
RUSEN, JOHN. 1996. Some Theoretical Approaches to Intercultural Comparative Historiography. *History and Theory*. 1996 December; 35(4): 5-23. ISSN: 0018- 2656.

R286
RUSH, JAMES E. 1988. The Library Automation Market: Why do Vendors Fail? A History of Vendors and their Characteristics. *Library Hi-Tech*. 1988; 6(3): 7-33. ISSN: 0737- 8831.

R287
RUSS, JOHN C. 1995. *The Image Processing Handbook*. 2nd ed. Boca Raton, FL: CRC Press; 1995. 688p. ISBN: 0-8493-2516-1.

R288
RUSSELL, DEBORAH; GANGEMI, G. T. 1992. *Computer Security Basics*. Sebastopol, CA: O'Reilly & Associates; 1992. 448p. ISBN: 0937175714.

R289
RUSSELL, MATTIE U. 1983. The Influence of Historians on the Archival Profession of the United States. *The American Archivist*. 1983; 46(3): 277-285. ISSN: 0360-9081.

R290
RUSSELL, PETER A. 1991. The Manx Peril: Archival Theory in Light of Recent American Historiography. *Archivaria* (CAN). 1991 Summer; 32: 1124-1137. ISSN: 0318-6954.

R291
RUSSIAN HISTORICAL DATA ARCHIVE. [1994]. *Catalogue*. Moscow, RU: Moscow State University Historical Informatics Laboratory; [1994].

R292
RUSSO, DAVID J. 1988. *Keepers of Our Past: Local Historical Writing in the United States, 1820s-1930s*. New York, NY: Greenwood Press; 1988. 281p. (Contributions to American History, 129). ISBN: 03132622365.

R293
RUSSO, DAVID J. 1996. *Clio Confused: Troubling Aspects of Historical Study from the Perspective of U.S. History*. Westport, CT: Greenwood Press; 1996. 158p. ISBN: 0313296820; LCCN: 95007909.

R294
RUTH, JANICE. 1997 [1998]. EAD in LC's Prints and Photographs Division. See reference: DOOLEY, J., ed. 1997 [1998].

R295
RUTIMANN, HANS; LYNN, M. STUART. 1992. *Computerization Project of the Archivo General de Indias, Seville, Spain*. Washington, D.C.; The Commission on Preservation and Access; 1992 March. 17p. (Commission report). LC call no.: Z701.R88.

R296
RUUSALEPP, RAIVO. 1995. Computer in the Communication with the Past. See reference: JARTIZ, G. *ET AL*., eds. 1995. 31-33.

R297
RUUSALEPP, RAIVO. 1996 [199-]. Nominal Record Linkage revisited: Towards more Interactive Linking of Records. See reference: BORODKIN, L., ed. 1996: English abstract of presentation, 88-99; paper in Russian [199- forthcoming].

R298
RYAN, N. 1985. *GTREE*: A System for Interactive Display and Manipulation of Genealogical Data. *Bulletin of Information on Computing in Anthropology*. 1985; 3: 6-20.

-S-

S1
SACKETT, R. P.; LARSON, J. R., Jr. 1990. Research Strategies and Tactics in Industrial and Organizational Psychology. See reference: DUNNETTE, M. D.; HOUGH, L. M., eds. 1990.

S2
SACKMANN, SONJA A. 1991. *Cultural Knowledge in Organizations: Exploring the Collective Mind*. Newbury Park, CA: Sage; 1991. 221p. ISBN: 08039429231 (hbk.); 0803942931 (pbk.).

S3
SACKMANN, SONJA A. 1992. Culture and Subcultures: An Analysis of Organizational Knowledge. *Administrative Science Quarterly.* 1992 March; 37(1): 140-161. ISSN: 0001-8392.

S4
SACKMANN, SONJA A. 1997. *Cultural Complexity in Organizations: Inherent Contrasts and Contradictions.* Thousand Oaks, CA: Sage Publications; 1997. 402p. ISBN: 076190574X (hbk.); 0761905758 (pbk.).

S5
SAFFADY, WILLIAM. 1988/[1995]. *Optical Disk Systems for Records Management.* Prairie Village, KS: Association of Records Managers and Administrators (ARMA), Int.; 1988. 2nd ed. Oxon Hall, MD: NISO Press; 1995. 48p. ISBN: 0-933887-54-X.

S6
SAFFADY, WILLIAM. 1992. *Managing Electronic Records.* Prairie Village, KS: Association of Records Managers and Administrators (ARMA) International; 1992. 184p. ISBN: 0933887418.

S7
SAFFADY, WILLIAM. [1995]. Digital Library Concepts and Technologies for the Management of Library Collections: An Analysis of Methods and Costs. *Library Technology Reports.* 1995 June: 31(3): 166p. (Entire issue on this topic). ISSN: 0024-2586. Available from: Oxon Hall, MD: NISO Press.

S8
SAFFADY, WILLIAM. 1996a. *Computer Storage Technologies: A Guide for Electronic Recordkeeping.* Praire Village, KS: ARMA International; 1996. 108p. ISBN: 0- 933887-60-4.

S9
SAFFADY, WILLIAM. 1996b. *Electronic Document Imaging: A State of the Art Report.* Prairie Village, KS: ARMA; 1996. 198p. ISBN: 0-933887-59-0.

S10
SAFFADY, WILLIAM. 1997. *Document Life Cycle: A White Paper.* Silver Spring, MD: AIIM; 1997. [15p.] Available through the Association for Information and Image Management (AIIM), Silver Spring, MD.

S11
SAGREDO FERNANDEZ, FELIX; GARCIA MORENO, ANTONIA. 1997. History of Information Science in Spain: A Selected Bibliography. See reference: BUCKLAND, M.; BELLARDO HAHN, eds. 1997. 369-372.

S12
SAHLI, NANCY A. 1985. *MARC for Archives and Manuscripts: The AMC Format.* Chicago, IL: Society of American Archivists; 1985. 261p. ISBN: 0-931828-65-1.

S13
SAINT CLAIR, GUY. [1997]. *Corporate Memory. Information Management in the Electronic Age.* New Providence, RI: Bowker-Saur; [1997 May]. [200 p.] ISBN: 1- 85739-158-6.

S14
SALE, KIRPATRICK. 1990. *The Conquest of Paradise: Christopher Columbus and the Columbian Legacy.* New York, NY: Alfred A. Knopf; 1990. 453p. ISBN: 039457429X; LCCN: 90-53069; OCLC: 22276966.

S15
SALEM, ANDRE; LEBART, LUDOVIC. 1994. *Statistique Textuelle* [Textual Statistiques]. Paris, FR: Dunod; 1994. 342p. (In French). ISBN: 2100022393; OCLC: 30614707.

S16
SALL, JOHN; LEHMAN, ANN. 1996. *JMP Start Statistics. A Guide to Statistics and Data Analysis using JMP and JMP IN Software.* Belmont, CA: Duxbury Press of ITP for the SAS Institute; 1996. 521p. ISBN: 0-534-26565-0. See software reference: SAS INSTITUTE INC. 1996.

S17
SALMINEN, AIRI; KAUPPINEN, KATRI; LEHTOVARRA, MERJA. 1997. Towards a Methodology for Document Analysis. See reference: LOGAN, E.; POLLARD, M. 1997b. 644-655.

S18
SALMON, WESLEY C. 1997. *Causality and Explanation.* New York, NY: Oxford University Press; c1997. ISBN: 0195108639 (hbk.); 0195108647 (pbk.); LCCN: 960488651.

S19
SALOMON, GAVRIEL. 1979. *Interaction of Media, Cognition, and Learning.* San Francisco, CA: Jossey-Bass; 1979. 282p. ISBN: 0875894038.

S20
SALOMON, JEAN-JACQUES, ed. 1972. *The Research System*. Paris, FR: OECD; 1972. 2 vols.

S21
SALOMON, JEAN-JACQUES; LEBEAU, ANDRE. 1988. *L'Écrivain Publique et l'Ordinateur: Merager du Developement* [Public Writing and Computing: Overview of Developments]. Paris, FR: Hachette; 1988. 269p. ISBN: 2010136020; LCCN: 89-154840.

S22
SALOMON, JEAN-JACQUES; SAGASTI, FRANCISCO R.; SACKS-JEANTET, CELINE, eds. 1994. *The Uncertain Quest: Science, Technology, and Development*. New York, NY /Tokyo, JA: United Nations University Press; 1994. 532p. ISBN: 928008354; LCCN: 96-138477.

S23
SALTON, GERARD. 1970. Automatic Text Analysis. *Science*. 1970; 168: 335-343. ISSN: 0036-8075. Overview of work on *The SMART Retrieval System*.

S24
SALTON, GERARD. 1971. *The SMART Retrieval System; Experiments in Automatic Document Processing*. Englewood Cliffs, NJ: Prentice-Hall; [1971]. 556p. (Prentice-Hall series in automatic computation). LCCN: 70-159122.

S25
SALTON, GERARD. 1975. *A Theory of Indexing*. Outgrowth of the Regional Conference on Automatic Information Organization and Retrieval, University of Missouri, Columbia, MO, July 1973. Philadelphia, PA: Society for Industrial and Applied Mathematics / Bristol, UK: Arrowsmith, Ltd.; 1975. 56p. (Philosophical Society for Industrial and Applied Mathematics, Conference series, 18). LCCN: 75-321414.

S26
SALTON, GERARD. 1976. Computers and Information Science. In: *Information Science in America. Bulletin of the American Society for Information Science*. 1976 March; 2(8): 19-21. (Entire issue on title topic). ISSN: 0095-4403.

S27
SALTON, GERARD. 1988. The Past Thirty Years in Information Retrieval. *Journal of the Society for Information Science*. 1988 September; 38(5): 375-380. ISSN: 0002-8231.

S28
SALTON, GERARD. 1989. *Automatic Text Processing: The Transformation, Analysis, and Retrieval of Information by Computer*. Reading, MA: Addison-Wesley Publishing Co.; 1989. 530p. (Computer Science series). ISBN: 0-201-12227-8; LCCN: 88-000467.

S29
SALTON, GERARD; BUCKLEY, C. 1990. Improving Retrieval Performance by Relevance Feedback. *Journal of the American Society for Information Science*. 1990; 41: 288- 297. ISSN: 0002-8231.

S30
SALTON, GERARD.; LESK, MICHAEL E. 1971. *The Smart Retrieval System—Experiments in Automatic Document Processing*. Englewood Cliffs, NJ: Prentice-Hall; 1971.

S31
SALTON, GERARD.; MCGILL, MICHAEL J. 1983. *Introduction to Modern Information Retrieval*. New York, NY: McGraw-Hill; 1983. 448p. ISBN: 0070544840.

S32
SAMARAN, CHARLES, ed. 1961. *L'histoire et ses méthodes* [History and Its Methods]. Paris, FR: Gallimard-Pleiade; 1961. OCLC: 61-44760; OCLC: 19750211.

S33
SAMBURTHY, V.; POOLE, MARSHALL SCOTT. 1992. The Effects of Variations in Capabilities of CDSS [Group Decision Support Systems] Designs on Management of Cognitive Conflict in Groups. *Information Systems Research*. 1992 September; 3(3): 224-252. ISSN: 1047-7074.

S34
SAMMET, JEAN E. 1991. Some Approaches to and Illustrations of Programming Language History. *Annals of the History of Computing*. 1991; 13(1): 33-50. ISSN: 0164-1239.

S35
SAMUEL, RAPHAEL. 1994. *Past and Present in Contemporary Culture*. In his: *Theatres of Memory*, vol. I. London, UK: Verso; 1994. 479p. ISBN: 0860912094.

S36
SAMUEL, RAPHAEL, ed. 1991. *History Workshop: A Collectanea, 1967-1991; Documents, Memoirs, Critique, and Cumulative Index to the History Workshop Journal.* Cumulative proceedings from workshops of Ruskin College's Centre for Social History. Oxford, UK: History Workshop; 1991. 213p. ISBN: 095186090.

S37
SAMUEL, RAPHAEL; THOMPSON, PAUL RICHARD. 1990. *The Myths We Live By.* Sixth International Oral History Conference, "Myth and History," at St. John's College, Oxford, September 11-13, 1987. London, UK / New York, NY: Routledge; 1990. 262p. ISBN: 0415024906 (hbk.); 0415036097 (pbk.).

S38
SAMUELS, HELEN W. 1986. Who Controls the Past? *American Archivist.* 1986 Spring; 49: 109-124. ISSN: 0360-9081.

S39
SAMUELS, HELEN W. 1991-1992. Improving our Disposition: Documentation Strategy. *Archivaria* (CAN). 35 Winter; 33: 124-140. ISSN: 0318-6954.

S40
SAMUELS, HELEN W. 1992. *Varsity Letters: Documenting Modern Colleges and Universities.* Society of American Archivists series. Metuchen, NJ: Scarecrow Press and SAA; 1992. 281p. ISBN: 0-8108-2596-1. Available from the Society of American Archivists, T. Brinati, Managing Editor, 600 S. Federal, Suite 504, Chicago, IL 60605.

S41
SANCHEZ, ELIE; ZADEH, LOFTI A. 1987. *Approximate Reasoning in Intelligent Systems, Decision, and Control.* Oxford, UK: Pergamon Press; 1987. 195p. ISBN: 008034335X.

S42
SANDERSON, STEPHEN K. 1995a. *Civilizations and World Systems: Studying World- Historical Change.* Walnut Creek, CA: Altamira Press; 1995. 324p. ISBN: 0761991042 (hbk.); 0761991050 (pbk.).

S43
SANDERSON, STEPHEN K. 1995b. *Social Transformations: A General Theory of Historical Development.* Cambridge MA: Blackwell; 1995. 452p. ISBN: 1557864039 (hbk.); 1557864047 (pbk.).

S44
SANGREN, P. STEVEN. 1988. Rhetoric and the Authority of Ethnography: "Postmodernism" and the Social Reproduction of Texts. *Current Anthropology.* 1988 June; 29: 405-424. ISSN: 0011-3204.

S45
SANTA FE INSTITUTE (SFI). 1989-. *Lectures in Complex Systems.* Santa Fe, NM: Santa Fe Institute (SFI); 1989. Jen, Erica ed. 1989. ISBN: 0-201-50936-9 (hbk.). Nadel, Lynn; Stein, Daniel L., eds., 1990-1993. ISBN: 0-201-52757-5 (1990, hbk.); 0-201-57834-4 (1991, hbk.); 0-201-62498-2 (1993, hbk.); 0-201-48368-8 (1995, hbk.).

S46
SANTA FE INSTITUTE (SFI). 1996. *Bulletin* [electronic file]. Santa Fe, NM: SFI; 1996-. Accessible at http://www.santafe.edu/sfi/search.html.

S47
SAPERSTEIN, ALVIN. 1984. Chaos: A Model for the Outbreak of War. *Nature* (UK). 1984 May 24; 309: 303-305. ISSN: 0028-0836.

S48
SAPERSTEIN, ALVIN. 1995. War and Chaos. *American Scientist.* 1995 November-December; 83(6): 548-558. ISSN 0003-0996.

S49
SAPIN, CHRISTIAN. 1994. L'Archéologie face aux Images de Synthèse [Archeology confronts Visions of Synthesis]. See reference: BECK, P., ed. 1994. 53-57.

S50
SARACENI, JESSICA E. 1997. What's On Line? Digging into the World Wide Web. *Archaeology.* 1997 March-April; 50(2): 71-75.

S51
SARACEVIC, TEFKO. 1975. Relevance: A Review of and a Framework for Thinking on the Notion in Information Science. *Journal of the American Society for Information Science.* 1975; 26: 321-343. ISSN: 0002-8231.

S52
SARACEVIC, TEFKO. 1992. Information Science: Origin, Evolution and Relations. See reference: VAKKARI, P.; CRONIN, B., eds. 1992. 5-27.

S53
SARACEVIC, TEFKO. 1999. Information Science. See reference: BATES, M., ed. 1999. Pt. 2: 1051-1063.

S54
SARACEVIC, TEFKO; KANTOR, PAUL B. 1997. Studying the Value of Library and Information Services. Part I. Establishing a Theoretical Framework. Part 2. Methodology and Taxonomy. *Jounral of the American Society for Information Science.* 1997 January; 48(6): 4527-542, 543-563. ISSN: 0002-8231.

S55
SARACEVIC, TEFKO; KANTOR, PAUL B.; CHAMIS, A. Y.; TRIVISON, D. 1988. A Study of Information Seeking and Retrieving. Background and Methodology. *Journal of the American Society for Information Science.* 1988; 39: 161-176. ISSN: 0002- 8231.

S56
SARKAR, SAHOTRA., ed. 1996. *Logical Empiricism at its Peak: Schlick, Carnap, and Neurath.* New York, NY: Garland Publishing Co.; 1996. 404p. (Science and Philosophy in the Twentieth Century, v. 2). ISBN: 0815322631; LCCN: 95026649.

S57
SARTORI, GIOVANNI. 1970. Concept Misformation in Comparative Politics. *American Political Science Review.* 1970; 64(4): 1033-1056. ISSN: 0003-0554.

S58
SAS INSTITUTE INC. 1996. *JMP Start Statistics. Statistical Discovery for Windows* (software). Version 3.2.1. Belmont, CA: Duxbury Press of ITP for the SAS Institute; 1996. 4 diskettes. ISBN: 0- 534-34031-9; 0-534-26564-2 (JMP IN 3 Windows version); 0=534-26562-6 (JMP IN 3 Macintosh version). See guide reference, SALL, J.; LEHMAN, A. 1996.

S59
SASSOON, JOSEPH. 1990. Colors, Artifacts, and Ideologies. See reference: GAGLIARDI, P., ed. 1992. 169-184.

S60
SASSOON, ROSEMARY; GAUR, ALBERTINE. 1997. *Signs, Symbols, and Icons: Pre-History to the Computer Age.* Exeter, UK: Intellect; 1997. 191p. ISBN: 1871516730.

S61
SATIJA, MOHINDER P. 1987. History of Book Numbers. *International Classification.* 1987; 14(2): 70-76. ISSN: 0340-0050.

S62
SATIJA, MOHINDER P. 1990. Book Number and Call Number. See reference: KENT, A., ed.; 1990; 45: 18-45.

S63
SAUNDERS, D.; HAMBER, A. 1989. IMAGE. An International Meeting on Museums and Art Galleries Image Databases, London, 18-20 May, 1989. *Computers and the History of Art.* 1989; 11: 5-10. ISSN: 7081-239.

S64
SAUNDERS, LAVERNA M., ed. 1996. *The Evolving Virtual Library: Visions and Case Studies.* Medford, NJ: Information Today; 1996. 153p. ISBN: 1573870137.

S65
SAUSSURE, FERDINAND DE. 1966. *Cours de linguistique générale.* Baskin, W., trans. *Course in General Linguistics* C. Balley, A. Sechehaye, & A. Riedlinger, eds. New York, NY: McGraw-Hill Book Co.; 1966. 240p. ISBN: 0070165246; OCLC: 295045.

S66
SAXBY, STEPHEN. 1990. *The Age of Information: The Past Development and Future Significance of Computing and Communications.* New York, NY: New York University Press; 1990. 322p. ISBN: 0-8147-7922-0.

S67
SCALERA, NICHOLAS. 1995. Public-Key Encryption and the Clipper-Chip: Implications for the Archival Administration of Electronic Records. See reference: GILLILAND-SWETLAND, ANNE, ed. 1995. 65-78.

S68
SCHAMA, SIMON. 1991. Clio has a Problem: History's Muse has been Muffled, a Historian Argues, Her Poetic Voices Stilled. *The New York Times Magazine.* 1991 September 8; 140: 30 (col. 1). ISSN: 0028-7822.

S69
SCHAMA, SIMON. 1992. *Dead Certainties (Unwarranted Speculations).* New York, NY: Alfred Knopf; 1991. 322p. ISBN: 0679402136; LCCN: 90-52902; OCLC: 22488508.

S70
SCHAMA, SIMON. 1995. *Landscape and Memory*. Toronto, CAN: Random House; 1995. 652p. ISBN: 0679402551.

S71
SCHAMBER, L. 1994. Relevance and Information Behavior. In: M. Williams, ed. *Annual Review of Information Science and Technology*. Medford, NJ: Learned Information, Inc.; 1994; 29: 3-48. ISBN: 1-57387-019-6; ISSN: 0066-4200; CODEN: ARISBC; LCCN: 66-25096

S72
SCHAMBER, L.; EISENBERG, M. B.; NILAN, M. S. 1990. A Re-examination of Relevance: Toward a Dynamic, Situational Definition. *Information Processing & Management*. 1990; 26: 755-776. ISSN: 0306-4573. S59

S73
SCHATZ, BRUCE R.; CAPLINGER, M. A. 1989. Searching in a Hyperlibrary. In: *Proceedings of the Fifth International Conference on Data Engineering*. Washington, D.C.; IEEE Computer Society Press; 1989. 188-197.

S74
SCHATZ, BRUCE R.; CHEN, HSINCHUN, eds. 1996. Building Large-Scale Digital Libraries. In: *Computer. Innovative Technology for Computer Professionals* (pp. 22- 26) 1996 May: 29 (5): 22-76. (Entire issue on title topic). ISSN: 0018-9162.

S75
SCHEIN, EDGAR H. [1965]. *Organizational Psychology*. Englewood Cliffs, NJ: Prentice- Hall; [1965]. 114p.

S76
SCHEIN, EDGAR H. 1984. Coming to a New Awareness of Organizational Culture. *Sloan Management Review*. 1984; 25(4): 3-16. ISSN: 0019-848X.

S77
SCHEIN, EDGAR H. 1987. *The Clinical Perspective in Fieldwork*. Beverly Hills, CA: Sage; 1987. 72p. ISBN: 08039297871 (hbk.); 0803929765 (pbk.).

S78
SCHEIN, EDGAR H. 1992. *Organizational Culure and Leadership*. 2nd ed. San Francisco, CA: Jossey-Bass Publishers; 1992. 418p. ISBN: 155542872.

S79
SCHEIN, EDGAR H. 1993a. How can Organizations Learn Faster? The Challenge of Entering the Green Room. *Sloan Management Review*. 1993 Winter; 34(2): 85-92. ISSN: 0019- 848X; OCLC: 14120806; LCCN: 73-612734.

S80
SCHEIN, EDGAR H. 1993b. On Dialogue, Culture, and Organizational Learning. *Organizational Dynamics*. 1993 Autumn; 22(2): 40-51. ISSN: 0090-2616.

S81
SCHEINES, RICHARD P. 1987. *Causal Models in Social Science: Determining the Causal Structure of a Social System in a Non-experimental Setting*. Pittsburgh, PA: University of Pittsburgh; 1987. 221p. (Ph.D. dissertation; *DAI*, vol. 49/05-A: 1170). Available from: University Microfilms, Ann Arbor, MI (Order no. AAD88-10076).

S82
SCHELLENBERG, THEODORE R. 1956. *Modern Archives: Principles and Techniques*. Chicago, IL: University of Chicago Press; 1956. Midway Reprint, 1975. ISBN: 0-226-73684-9.

S83
SCHELLENBERG, THEODORE R. 1965/1988. *The Management of Archives*. New York, NY: Columbia University Press; 1965. 383p. Reprint. Washington, D.C.: NARA [1988]. ISBN: 091133272X; LCCN: 88-600028.

S84
SCHELLENBERG, THEODORE R. 1969. Archival Training in Library Schools. *The American Archivist*. 1969; 31: 155-165. ISSN: 0002-8231.

S85
SCHEMENT, JORGE R. 1987. *Competing Visions: Complex Realities. Social Aspects of the Information Society*. Norwood, NJ: Ablex Pub. Co.; 1987. 167p. ISBN: 0893914029; LCCN: 87-14318.

S86
SCHEMENT, JORGE R. 1989. The Origins of the Information Society in the United States: Competing Visions. In: Salvaggio, Jerry L., ed. *The Information Society: Economic, Social, and Structural Issues* (pp. 29-50). Hillsdale, NJ: Lawrence Erlbaum Associates; 1989; 29-50. ISBN: 0-08058-0103-0.

S87

SCHEMENT, JORGE R. 1990. Porat, Bell, and the Information Society Reconsidered: The Growth of Information Work in the Early Twentieth Century. *Information Processing & Management.* 1990; 26(6): 449-465. ISSN: 0306-4573.

S88

SCHEMENT, JORGE R.; CURTIS, TERRY. 1995. *Tendencies and Tensions of the Information Age: The Production and Distribution of Information in the United States.* New Brunswick, NJ: Transaction Publications; 1995. 285p. ISBN: 1560001666; LCCN: 94-4440.

S89

SCHEMENT, JORGE R.; SHERIF, CAROLYN W. 1965/1981. *Attitudes and Attitude Change: The Social Judgement-Awareness Approach.* Westport, CT: Greenwood; 1981 reprint. 264p. ISBN: 0313232601; LCCN: 81-13265.

S90

SCHICK, JAMES B. M. 1990. *Teaching History with a Computer. A Complete Guide.* Chicago, IL: Lyceum Books, Inc.; 1990. 251p. ISBN: 0925065323; LCCN: 89-13883; OCLC: 20930401.

S91

SCHIJVENAARS, TOINE. 1995. Concepts of Data Modeling. See reference: BOONSTRA, O., *ET AL.*, eds. 1995. 165-177.

S92

SCHLATTERER, HELEN M. FELL. 1989. *Educational Documentation to accompany the Great American History Machine.* Pittsburgh, PA: Carnegie-Mellon University; 1989. 279p. (D.A. dissertation; *DAI*, vol. 50/06-A: 1783). Available from: University Microfilms, Ann Arbor, MI (Order no. AAD89-200610).

S93

SCHLEGEL, JOHN H. 1995. *American Legal Realism and Empirical Social Science.* Chapel Hill, NC: University of North Carolina Press; 1995. 418p. ISBN: 0807821799.

S94

SCHLESINGER, ARTHUR, Jr. 1961. The Humanist Looks at Empirical Social Research. *American Sociological Review.* 1961; 26: 770-80. ISSN: 0003-1224.

S95

SCHMAUCH, CHARLES. 1995. *ISO 9000 Software Developers.* Rev. ed. Los Alamitos, CA: IEEE; 1995. 168p. ISBN: 0-87389-4.

S96

SCHMIDT, DAVID P. 1992. Integrating Ethics into Organizational Networks. *Journal of Management Development.* 1992; 11 (4): 34-43. ISSN: 0262-1711; OCLC: 8735092; LCCN: 82-646056.

S97

SCHMIDT, WOLFGANG; THOMAS, GRAHAM. 1996. A Virtual Studio for Live Broadcasting: The Mona Lisa Project. *IEEE Multmedia.* 1996 Summer; 3(2):18-29. ISSN: 1070-986X.

S98

SCHMITT, MARILYN, ed. 1988. *Object, Image, Inquiry, the Art Historian at Work.* Santa Monica, CA: Getty AHIP; 1988.

S99

SCHMITZ, M. D.; SCHAEFER, D. F. 1986. Using Manuscript Census Samples to Interpret Antebellum Southern Agriculture. *Journal of Interdisciplinary History.* 1986; 17: 399- 414. ISSN: 0022-1953.

S100

SCHNEIDER, BENJAMIN; GUNNARSON, SARAH K.; NILES-JOLLY, KATHRYN. 1994. Creating the Climate and Culture of Success. *Organizational Dynamics.* 1994 Summer; 23(1): 17-29. ISSN: 0090-2616; OCLC: 1784891; LCCN: 73-640917.

S101

SCHNEIDER, JANE; RAPP, RAYNA, eds. 1994. *Articulating Hidden Histories: Exploring the Influence of Eric R. Wolf.* Berkeley, CA: University of California Press; 1994. 400p. ISBN: 0520085817 (hbk.); 0520085825 (pbk.).

S102

SCHNEIDER, SUSAN C.; ANGELMAR, REINHARD. 1993. Cognition in Organizational Analysis: Who's Minding the Store? *Organization Studies.* 1993. 14(3): 347-374. ISSN: 0170-8406.

S103

SCHNEIDERMAN, BEN. 1987/1992. *Designing the User Interface: Strategies for Effective Human-Computer Interaction.* Reading, MA: Addison-Wesley; 1987. 2nd ed., 1992. 573p. ISBN: 0201165058 (hbk.); 02151572869 (pbk.).

S104
SCHNEIER, BRUCE. 1995a/1996. *Applied Cryptography. Protocols, Algorithms, and Source Code in C.* 2nd ed. Somerset, NJ: J. Wiley & Sons, Inc.; 1995; 2nd printing, 1996. 758p. ISBN: 0471128457 (hbk.); 0471117099 (pbk.).

S105
SCHNEIER, BRUCE. 1995. *E-Mail Security: How to Keep your Electronic Messages Private.* New York, NY: John Wiley & Sons; 1995. 365p. ISBN: 047105318X.

S106
SCHOFIELD, ROGER S. 1972. Sampling in Historical Research. See reference: WRIGLEY, E. A., ed. 1972: 146-190.

S107
SCHOLZ, CHRISTIAN. 1990. The Symbolic Value of Computerized Information Systems. See reference: GAGLIARDI, P., ed. 1990b. 233-254.

S108
SCHOLZ, GUNTER. 1989. Des Historismus problem und die Geisteswissenschaften im 20. Jahrhundert [The Historismus Problem and the Arts]. *Archiv für Kulturgeshichte* (DEU). 1989; 71: 463-486. (In German). ISSN: 0003-9233.

S109
SCHOLZ, ROLAND W. 1987. *Cognitive Strategies in Stochastic Thinking.* Dordrecht, NL: D. Reidel; 1987. 218p. ISBN: 9027724547. Distributed by Kluwer Academic Publishers.

S110
SCHOLZ, ROLAND W., ed. 1983. *Decision Making under Uncertainty: Cognitive Decision Research, Social Interaction, Development and Epistemology.* New York, NY: Elsevier Science Publishers/North Holland; 1983. 445p. ISBN: 0444867384.

S111
SCHOMAKER, LAMBERT R. B. 1991. *Simulation and Recognition of Handwriting Movements.* Nijmegen University; 1991. (Doctoral Dissertation, no. RD-91-03). Available from NICI, Nijmegen University, NL.

S112
SCHOMAKER, LAMBERT R. B.; TEULINGS, H. L. 1990. A Handwriting Recognition System based on the Properties and Architectures of [the] Human Motor System. In: Suen, Ching Y., ed. *First International Conference on Frontiers on Handwriting Recognition.* Held at Montreal, April 2-3, 1990. Montreal, CAN: Concordia University CENPARMI; 1990. 211p. ISBN: 1895193001; LCCN: 90-10068; OCLC: 22386722.

S113
SCHORZMAN, TERRI A., ed. 1993. *A Practical Introduction to Videohistory: The Smithsonian Institution and Alfred P. Sloan Foundation Experiment.* Malabar, FL: Krieger; 1993. 243p. (Public History series). ISBN: 0894647253.

S114
SCHRADER, A. M. 1984. In Search of a Name: Information Science and Its Conceptual Antecedents. *Library and Information Science Research.* 1984; 6: 227-271.

S115
SCHRAGE, MICHAEL. 1990. *Shared Minds: The New Technologies of Collaboration.* New York, NY: Random House; 1990. 227p. ISBN: 0394565878; LCCN: 89-43430.

S116
SCHULLER, DIETRICH. 1991. The Ethics of Preservation, Restoration, and Re-Issues of Historical Sound Recordings. *Journal of the Audio Engineering Society.* 1991 December; 39: 1014-1017. ISSN: 0004-754.

S117
SCHULTE, T. J. 1989. Artificial Intelligence Techniques for Historians: Expert Systems, Knowledge Representation, and High-Level Programming. See reference: DENLEY, P. *ET AL.*, eds. 1989. 90-96.

S118
SCHULTZ, MAJKEN. 1992. Postmodern Pictures of Culture: A Postmodern Reflection on the "Modern Notion" of Corporate Culture. *International Studies of Management & Organization.* 1992 Summer; 22(2): 15-35. ISSN: 0020-8825.

S119
SCHULTZ, ALFRED. 1967. *The Phenomenology of the Social World.* Evanston, IL: Northwestern University Press; 1967. 255p. ISBN: 0810103907.

S120
SCHULTZ, ALFRED 1970. *Reflection on the Problem of Relevance.* New Haven, CT: Yale University Press; 1970. 186p. ISBN: 0300012217.

S121
SCHUMAN, HOWARD; BELLI, ROBERT F.; BISCHOPING, KATHERINE. 1997. The Generational Basis of Historical Knowledge. See reference: PENNEBAKER, J. W., *ET AL.*, eds. 1997.

S122
SCHURER, KEVIN. 1985. Historical Research in the Age of the Computer: An Assessment of the Present Situation. *Historische Sozialforschungen /Historical Social Research* (DEU). 1985; 36: 43-54. ISSN: 0172-6404.

S123
SCHURER, KEVIN. 1990a. Artificial Intelligence and the Historian—Prospects and Possibilities. See reference: ENNALS, R.; GARDIN, J. C., eds. 1990. 169-195.

S124
SCHURER, KEVIN. 1990b. The Historical Researcher and Codes: Master and Slave or Slave and Master? See reference: MAWDSLEY, E., *ET AL.*, eds. 1990. 74-82.

S125
SCHURER, KEVIN; ANDERSON, SHIELA. J., comps. 1992. *A Guide to Historical Datafiles held in Machine-readable Form.* J. A. Duncan, asst. London: Association for History and Computing; 1992. 339p. ISBN: 0951535218; OCLC: 26039261.

S126
SCHURER, KEVIN; DIEDERIKS, HERMAN, eds. 1993. *The Use of Occupations in Historical Analysis.* St. Katharinen [Gottingen]: Max-Planck-Institut fur Geschichte in Kommission bei Scripta Mercaturae Verlag; 1993. 162p. (Halbgraue Reihe zur historischen Fackinformatik. Serie A: Historische Quellenkunden, Band 19). ISBN: 3- 928134-96-5. (See their introduction, "Occupations and the computer in history," pp. 1-4).

S127
SCHURER, KEVIN; WALL, R. 1986. Computing the History of the Family: A Question of Standards. See reference: THALLER, M., ed. 1986. 159-174.

S128
SCHUSTER, H. G. 1984/1988. *Deterministic Chaos: An Introduction.* Weinman, DEU: VCH Verlagsgesellschaft mbH; 1988. 220p. ISBN: 3876641012 (hbk.); 0895732238. 2nd ed. 270p. ISBN: 089573611X

S129
SCHUTTE, JERALD G. [1997]. Virtual Teaching in Higher Education. The New Intellectual Superhighway or Just Another Traffic Jam? San Fernando, CA: California State University, Northridge, Department of Sociology. [1997]: 5 pp. Computer file Accessible at http://csun.edu/sociology/virexp/htm. Cf., the popularization on several listservs and *Chronicle of Higher Education*, Feb. 21, 1997, p. A23; and the critical review by NEAL, ED.

S130
SCHWANDT, THOMAS A. 1997. *Qualitative Inquiry: A Dictionary of Terms.* Thousand Oaks, CA: Sage Publ.; 1997. 192p. ISBN: 0761902538 (hbk.); 0761902546 (pbk.).

S131
SCHWARTZ, CANDY; HERNON, PETER. 1993. *Records Management and the Library: Issues and Practices.* Norwood, NJ: Ablex Pub. Corp.; c1993. 313p. ISBN: 0893919640 (hbk.); 0893919985 (pbk.); LCCN: 92041735.

S132
SCHWARTZ, CHARLES A. 1997. The Rise and Fall of Uncitedness. *College & Research Libraries.* 1997 January; 59(1): 19-29. ISSN: 0010-0870.

S133
SCHWARTZ, HILLEL. 1995/1996. *The Culture of the Copy: Striking Likeness and Unreasonable Facsimiles.* New York, NY: Knopf; 1995. Reprint. New York, NY: Zane Books; 1996. 565p. ISBN: 0942299352; LCCN: 96-10162.

S134
SCHWOB, ANTON; KRANICH-HOFBAUER, KARIN; SUNTINGER, DIETHARD, eds. 1989. *Historische Edition und Computer. Mögligkeiten und Probleme Interdisziplinarer Textverarbeitung und Textbearbeitung* [Historical Editing and Computing. Possibilities and Problems in Textual Editing and Analysis]. Graz, AT: Carl Franz Josef Universität; 1989. ISBN:3701172099; LCCN: 89-172091; OCLC: 20319748.

S135
SCOTT, D. W. 1988. Museum Data Bank Research Report: The Yogi and the Registrar. *Library Trends.* 1988; 37(2): 130-141. ISSN: 0024-2594.

S136
SCOTT, JOAN W. 1991. The Evidence of Experience. *Critical Inquiry.* 1991; 17: 773-793. ISSN: 0093-1896.

S137
SCOTT, PETER J. 1966. The Record Group Concept: A Case for abandonment. *American Archivist*. 1966 October: 29(4): 493-504. ISSN: 0360-9081.

S138
SCOTT, PETER J. 1974. Facing the reality of administrative change—Some further remarks on the Record Group concept. *Journal of the Society of Archivists*. 1974: 5(2): [90-100].ISSN: 0037-9816.

S139
SCOTT, PETER J.; FINLAY, GAIL. 1978-1979. Archives and Administrative Change: Some Methods and Approaches (pts. 1-2). *Archives and Manuscripts*. Pt. 1: 1978 August; 7: 115-127. Pt. 2: 1979 April; 7: 151-165. ISSN: 0157-6895.

S140
SCUDDER, NORMAL I. 1988. *The History of the Inventions leading to the Development of Computers and the Related Effects on Educational Instruction and Society*. 185p. Stillwater, OK: Oklahoma State University; 1988. (Ed.D. dissertation; *DAI*, vol. 49/10-A: 3002. Available from: University Microfilms, Ann Arbor, MI (Order no. AAD89-00434).

S141
SEAMAN, DAVID. 1997 [1998]. A Multi-Dimensional Implementation of EAD: the American Heritage Project. See reference: DOOLEY, J., ed. 1997 [1998].

S142
SEBEOK, THOMAS A., ed. 1960. *Style in Language*. Conference on Style at Indiana University, 1958. Cambridge, MA: Massachusetts Institute of Technology Press; 1960. 470p.LCCN: 60-11729; OCLC: 328373.

S143
SEBEOK, THOMAS A., ed. 1994. *Encyclopedic Dictionary of Semiotics*. 2nd ed. Berlin, DEU: Mouton de Gruyter; 1994. 3 vols. ISBN: 3110142295.

S144
SEED, PATRICIA. 1998. Teaching with the Web.: Two Approaches. See reference: AHA. 1998. 9-14.

S145
SEGAL, HOWARD P. 1985. *Technological Utopianism in American Culture*. Chicago, IL: University of Chicago Press; 1985. 301p. ISBN: 0226744361 (hbk.); 0226744388 (pbk.).

S146
SEGAL, HOWARD P. 1994. *Future Imperfect: The Mixed Blessings of Technology in America*. Amherst, MA: University of Massachusetts Press; 1994. 245p. ISBN: 0870238817 (hbk.); 0870238825 (pbk.).

S147
SEIDELMAN, RAYMOND; HARPHAM, EDWARD J. 1985. *Disenchanted Realists: Political Science and the American Crisis, 1884-1984*. Albany, NY: State University of New York Press; 1985. 295p. ISBN: 0873959949 (hbk.); 0873959957 (pbk.).

S148
SEIFERT, C. M.; HUTCHINS, E. L. 1992. *Error as Opportunity: Learning in a Situated Task*. Ann Arbor, MI: University of Michigan Press; San Diego, CA: University of California; 1992.

S149
SEITZ, JAY A. 1998. Nonverbal Metaphor: A Review of Theories and Evidence. *Genetic, Social, and General Psychology*. 1998 Feb.; 1124 (1): 95-120.

S150
SELINGO, JEFFREY. 1998. A New Archive and Internet Search Engine may Change the Nature of On-Line Research. Information Technology Section. *The Chronicle of Higher Education*. 1998 March 6: A27-A28. (About Bewster Kahle's *Alexa* software and Internet Archives). ISSN: 0009-5982; OCLC: 1554535.

S151
SELLEN, MARY K.. 1993. *Bibliometrics: An Annotated Bibliography, 1970-1990*. New York, NY: G. K. Hall; 1993. 169p. ISBN: 0816119546; LCCN: 93016426.

S152
SELMAN, ALAN L., ed. 1990. *Complexity Theory Retrospective: In Honor of Juris Hartmanis on the Occasion of his Sixtieth Birthday, July 5, 1988*. Proceedings: Conference on the Structure in Complexity Theory. New York, NY: Springer-Verlag; 1990. 234p. ISBN: 0387973508.

S153
SELOUNSKAYA, NATALIA. 1996a. Ot Kvantifikatsii k Istoricheskoj—Ot Istoricheskoj k Virtualnoj Realnosti? [From Quantification to Historical Informatics—From Historical to Virtual Reality?]. See reference: BORODKIN, L. I., ed. 1996. 92-100. (In Russian).

S154

SELOUNSKAYA, NATALIA. 1996b[199-]. Toward a Theory of Historical Computing [Commentary in Russian, IACH 1996]. See reference: BORODKIN, L., ed. [199-, forthcoming]. (In Russian?).

S155

SELZ, MARION. 1987a. Geneaologies et systemes experts [Geneaology and Expert Systems]. *Informatique et science humanines* (FR). 1987; 74. (In French).

S156

SELZ, MARION. 1987b. Parente et informatique [Computing Parentage]. *Mathematiques et sciences humaines*. 1987: 97: 57-66. (In French]. ISSN: 0025-5815.

S157

SELZ, MARION. 1989. Outils et demarches: Procedures d'aide à la reconstitution de généalogies [Tools and Measures: Procedures to assist in the reconstruction of genealogies]. *Histoire et Mesure*. 1989; 4(1-2): 3-19. (In French). ISSN: 0982-1782.

S158

SELZ, MARION. 1993. Informatique et sciences humaines. Formalisation et demarche d'exlication [Humanities Computing: Formalization and Means of Explication]. *Gradhiva*. 1993; (14). (In French). ISSN: 0764-8928.

S159

SELZ, MARION. 1994. Traitement informatique de données généalogiques: Le Logiciel GEN-PAR [Computing Treatments of Genealogical Data]. *L'Homme* (FR). 1994; 34 (130): 129-136. (In French). ISSB: 0439-4216/0046-7790.

S160

SELZ, MARION. 1997a. Informatique, généalogies, parente [Computing, Genealogy, and Parentage]. (In French). See reference: BOURIN, M.; CHAREILLE, P., eds. 1997. 16-19.

S161

SELZ, MARION. 1997b. Interpretation des resultats du traitement informatique de données généalogiques [Interpretation of the results from computer processing of genealogical data]. See reference: BARTHLEMEY, T.; PINGAUD, M-C., eds. 1997.

S162

SELZ, MARION; LAMAISON, PIERRE. 1985. Genealogies, alliances, et informatique [Genealogy, Alliances, and Computing]. *Terrain* (FR). 1985; 4: 3-4. (In French).

S163

SELZ-LAURIERE, MARION; FLAVIGNY, PIERRE-OLIVIER; JANE, PIERRE. 1989. Genealogical Data Acquisition and Request. *Historische Sozialforschungen/Historical Social Research*. 1989; 14: 30-34. ISSN: 0172-6404.

S164

SEMIN, C. R.; GERGEN, KENNETH J., eds. 1990. *Everyday Understanding: Social and Scientific Implications*. London, UK; Newbury Park, CA: Sage; 1990. 248p. ISBN: 0803982364 (hbk.); 0803982372 (pbk.).

S165

SEMOCHE, JOHN. 1987. Computer Simulations, the Teaching of History, and the Goals of a Liberal Education. *Academic Computing*. 1987 September; 2: 20-23, 46-50. ISSN: 0892-4694.

S166

SEMOCHE, JOHN. 1989. Making History Come Alive: Designing and Using Computer Simulations in U.S. History Survey Courses. *History Microcomputer Review*. 1989 Spring; 5: 5-12. ISSN: 0887-1078.

S167

SENGE, PETER M. 1990/1994. *The Fifth Discipline: The Art and Practice of the Learning Organization*. New York, NY: Doubleday/Currency; 1990. ISBN: 0-385-26094-6. New York, NY: Doubleday; 1994. 593p. ISBN: 0385472560.

S168

SENGUPTA, ARJIT; DILLON, ANDREW. 1997. Extending SGML to Accommodate Database Functions: A Methodological Overview. See reference: LOGAN, E.; POLLARD, M. 1997b. 629-637.

S169

SENGUPTA, JATI KUMAR. 1985. *Optimal Decisions under Uncertainty: Methods, Models, and Management*. Berlin, DEU: Springer-Verlag; 1985. 286p. ISBN: 0387150323.

S170

SENGUPTA, JATI KUMAR. 1993. *Econometrics of Information and Efficiency*. Dordrecht, NL: Kluwer Academic Publishers; 1993. 256p. ISBN: 079232353X; LCCN: 93-4584.

S171

SENIOR, ANDREW. 1992. *Off-line Handwriting Recognition: A Review and Experiments*. (Electronic file). Cambridge, UK: Cambridge University Department of Engineering; 1992. (Technical report TR105). Accessible via anonymous FTP from: svr- ftp.eng.cam.ac.uk.

S172

SENIOR, ANDREW. 1993. A Recurrent Network Approach to the Automatic Reading of Handwriting. See reference: DOORN, P. *ET AL.*, eds. 1993. 59-66.

S173

SENNER, WAYNE M., ed. *The Origins of Writing*. Lincoln, NE: University of Nebraska Press; 1989. 245p. ISBN: 0803242026.

S174

SERIALS INDUSTRY ADVISORY COMMITTEE (SISAC). PUBLISHERS TECHNICAL ADVISORY SUBCOM-MITTEE. 1992. *Serial Item Identification: Bar code Symbol Implementation Guidelines*. [New York, NY]: Book Industry Study Group; c1992. 1 vol. ISBN: 0940016362; LCCN: 91048127.

S175

SERRES, MICHEL. 1990/1995. *La Contrat Naturel*. Paris, FR: Francois Bourin; 1990. E. MacArthur; W. Paulson, trans. *The Natural Contract*. Ann Arbor, MI: University of Michigan Press; 1995. 1124p. ISBN: 04720954998 (hbk.); 0472065491 (pbk.); LCCN: 95002685.

S176

SERRES, MICHEL; LATOUR, BRUNO. 1992/1995. *Éclaircissements: Entretiens avec Bruno Latour*. Bourin, F., trans. *Conversations on Science, Culture, and Time*. Ann Arbor, MI: University of Michigan Press; 1995. 204p. ISBN: 047209548X; LCCN: 95002706.

S177

SESSIONS, VIVIAN S., ed. [1974]. *Directory to Data Bases in the Social and Behavioral Sciences*. New York, NY: Science Associates, in cooperation with the City University of New York; [1974]. 300p. ISBN: 0878370048; LCCN: 72-86759; OCLC: 749458.

S178

SETHI, AMARJIT SINGH. 1987. *Strategic Management of Technostress in an Information Society*. Lewistown, NY: Hofgrefe; 1987. 399p. ISBN: 0889370125.

S179

SEVER, H. 1995. *Knowledge Structuring for Database Mining and Text Retrieval using Past Optimal Queries*. Ph.D. dissertation in Computer Science. University of Louisiana at Lafayette, LA; 1995. Available form University Microfilms, Ann Arbor, MI.

S180

SHACHTER, R. D.; HECKERMAN, D. 1987. Thinking Backwards for Knowledge Acquisition. *AI Magazine*. 1987 Fall; 8: 55-61. ISSN: 0738-4602.

S181

SHADE, W. G. 1981. "New Political History": Some Statistical Questions Raised. *Social Science History*. 1981; 5: 171-196. ISSN: 0145-5532.

S182

SHAFER, GLENN. 1976. *A Mathematical Theory of Evidence*. Princeton, NJ: Princeton University Press; c1976. 297p. ISBN: 0691081751 (hbk.); 069110042 (pbk.); LCCN: 75030208.

S183

SHAFER, GLENN. 1996a. *The Art of Causal Conjecture*. Cambridge, MA: MIT Press; c1996. 511p. (Artificial Intelligence series). ISBN: 026219368X; LCCN: 06012572.

S184

SHAFER, GLENN. 1996b. *Probabilistic Expert Systems*. Philadelphia, PA: Society for Industrial and Applied Mathematics; c1996. 80p. (CBMS-NSF Series in Applied Mathematics, 67). ISBN: 08987113730 (pbk); LCCN: 96018757.

S185

SHAFER, GLENN; PEARL, JUDEA eds. 1990. *Readings in Uncertain Reasoning*. San Mateo, CA: Morgan Kaufmann; c1990. 768p. ISBN: 1558601252; LCCN: 90033564.

S186

SHAH, ARVIND; MILSTEIN, BARNEY M. [1996]. *Data Warehousing: Practical Tips for Successful Implementation* (Electronic file). 13p. Accessible at http://www.sw- expo.com./data-warehousing.html.

S187
SHAMIR, ILANAH. 1996. *Hantsahah ve-zikaron: Darkah shel ha-hevrah ha-Yisre'elit be- \Itsuv ha-zikaron*. [War Memorials: Places of Commemoration in the Making of Israeli Self-Identity]. Tel Aviv, IS: Am\oved; 1996. 234p. (In Hebrew). ISBN: 96511311363.

S188
SHANNON, CLAUDE E. 1948. A Mathematical Theory of Communication. *Bell Technical Journal*. 1948; 27: 379-423, 623-656. ISBN: 0882-1143

S189
SHANNON, CLAUDE E.; WEAVER, WARREN. 1949. *The Mathematical Theory of Communication*. Urbana, IL: University of Illinois Press; 1949. 117p. LCCN: 49-11922; OCLC: 1561841.

S190
SHAPIRO, FRED R. 1987. *The Most Cited Law Review Articles*. Buffalo, NJ: W./ Hein Co.; 1987. 1146p. ISBN: 0899415784; LCCN: 87-81962.

S191
SHAPIRO, FRED R. 1992. Origins of Bibliometrics, Citation Indexing, and Citation Analysis: The Neglected Legal Literature. *Journal of the American Society for Information Science*. 1992 June; 43(5): 337-339. ISSN: 0002-8231.

S192
SHAPIRO, FRED R. 1995. Coinage of the term Information Science. *Journal of the American Society for Information Science*. 1995: 46: 384-385. ISSN: 0002-8231.

S193
SHAPIRO, FRED R., ed. 1996. *Symposium on Trends in Legal Citations and Scholarship*. New York, NY; 1996.

S194
SHAPIRO, JEFFREY ALAN. 1995. *Collaborative Computing. Multimedia Across the Network*. San Diego, CA: Academic Press; 1995. 268p. ISBN: 0-12-63867-7.

S195
SHAPIRO, SAMUEL S. 1981. *Statistical Modeling Techniques*. New York, NY: M. Dekker; 1981. 367p. ISBN: 082471387.

S196
SHAPIRO, SHELLY. 1996. *Truth Prevails; Demolishing Holocaust Denial: End of the the Leuchter Report*. New York, NY: B. Klarsfeld Foundation; 1996. 135p. ISBN: 1879437007.

S197
SHAPIRO, STUART. 1997. Splitting the Difference: The Historical Necessity of Synthesis in Software Engineering. *Annals of the History of Computing*. 1997; 19(1): 20-54. ISSN: 1058-6180.

S198
SHAPIRO, STUART; ECKROTH, DAVID, eds. 1992. *The Encyclopedia of Artificial Intelligence*. 2nd ed. New York, NY: Wiley; 1992. 2 vols., 1219p. ISBN: 0471807486.

S199
SHATFORD LAYNE, SARA. 1986. Analyzing the Subject of a Picture: A Theoretical Approach. *Cataloging and Classification Quarterly*. 1986; 6(3): 39-62. ISSN: 0163- 9374.

S200
SHATFORD LAYNE, SARA. 1991. MARC Format for Medieval Manuscript Images. *Rare Books & Manuscripts Librarianship*. 1991; 6(1): 39-52. ISSN: 0884-450X.

S201
SHAW, MARY; GARLAN, DAVID. 1996. *Software Architecture. Perspectives on an Emerging Discipline*. Los Alamitos, CA: IEEE; 1996. 270p. ISBN: 0-13-18297-2.

S202
SHELDRAKE, RUPERT. 1981. *A New Science of Life: The Hypothesis of Formative Causation Formation*. London, UK: Blond & Briggs / Los Angeles, CA: Jeremy Tarcher; 1981. 229p. ISBN: 0856341150; LCCN: 81-148699.

S203
SHENK, DAVID. 1997. *Data Smog: Surviving the Information Glut*. San Francisco, CA: Harper Collins Publ; 1997. 250p. ISBN: 0-06-018701-8; LCCN: 96-39496.

S204
SHENOI, S.; MELTON, A; FAN, L. T. 1992. Functional Dependencies and Normal Norms in the Fuzzy Relational Database Model. *Information Sciences*. 1992; 60: 1-28.

S205
SHERA, JESSE H. 1953. *Historians, Books, and Libraries: A Survey of Historical Scholarship in Relation to Library Resources, Organization, and Services*. Cleveland, OH: Case-Western Reserve University Press; 1953. 126p. LCCN: 53-12240; OCLC: 697817.

S206
SHERIF, MUZAFER; SHERIF, CAROLYN, eds. 1969. *Interdisciplinary Relationships in the Social Sciences*. Chicago, IL: Aldine; 1969. 360p. LCCN: 68008161.

S207
SHERMAN, DANIEL J. 1989. *Worthy Monuments: Art Museums and the Politics of Culture in Nineteenth-century France*. Cambridge, MA: Harvard University Press; 1989. 337p. ISBN: 0674962303.

S208
SHERMAN, DANIEL J.; ROGOFF, IRIT, eds. 1994. *Museum Culture: Histories, Discourses, Spectacles*. Minneapolis, MN: University of Minnesota Press; 1994. 301p. ISBN: 0816619514 (hbk.); 0816619530 (pbk.).

S209
SHERMER, MICHAEL. 1993. The Chaos of History: On a Chaotic Model that represents the Role of Contingency and Necessity in Historical Sequences. *Nonlinear Science Today*. 1993; 2: 1-13. ISSN: 0938-9008.

S210
SHERMER, MICHAEL. 1995. Exorcising Laplace's Demon: Chaos and Antichaos, History and Metahistory. *History and Theory*. 1995 Feb.; 34 (1): 59-84. ISSN: 0018-2656.

S211
SHERWIN, C. W.; ISENSON, R. S. 1967. Project Hindsight. *Science*. 1967; 156: 1571- 1577. ISSN: 0036-8075.

S212
SHERWOOD, LYN E. 1997. Moving from Experiment to Reality: Choices for Cultural Heritage Institutions and their Governments. See reference: JONES-GARMIL, K., ed. 1997. 129-152.

S213
SHETH, A.; LARSON, J. 1990. Federated Database Systems for Managing Distributed Heterogeneous, and Autonomous Databses. *ACM Computing Surveys*. New York, NY: ACM Press; 1990. 1990 Sept.; 22 (3): 183-236. ISSN: 360-0300.

S214
SHIELDS, MARK A., ed. 1995. *Work and Technology in Higher Education: The Social Construction of Academic Computing*. Hillsdale, NJ: Lawrence Erlbaum Associates; 1995. 198p. ISBN: 005803564.

S215
SHIFLETT, LEE. Clio's Claim: The Role of Historical Research in Library and Information Science. *Library Trends*. 1984 Spring; 32: 385-406. ISSN: 0024-2594.

S216
SHILLINGSBURG, P. 1986. *Scholarly Editing in the Computer Age: Theory and Practice*. Athens, GA / London, UK: University of Georgia Press; 1986. ISBN: 0837125588.

S217
SHILS, E. 1981. *Tradition*. Chicago, IL: University of Chicago Press; 1981.

S218
SHIRK, HENRIETTA NICKELS; SMITH, HOWARD T. Some Issues influencing Computer Icon Design. *Technical Communication*. 1994 Nov.; 41(4): 680-. ISSN: 0049-3155.

S219
SHIVELY, W. P. 1969. Ecological Inference: The Use of Aggregate Data to Study Individuals. *American Political Science Review*. 1969; 63: 1183-1196. ISSN: 0003- 0054.

S220
SHORTER, EDWARD. 1971. *The Historian and the Computer*. Englewood Cliffs, NJ: Prentice-Hall; 1971. 149p. ISBN: 0133892131; LCCN: 79-123083; OCLC: 109917.

S221
SHROCK, S. 1991. A Brief History of Instructional Development. See reference: ANGLIN, G. J. 1991. 1-20.

S222
SHU, NAN S. 1988. *Visual Programming*. New York, NY: Van Nostrand Reinhold; 1988. 315p. ISBN: 0442280149.

S223
SIBLEY, J. 1972. Clio and Computers: Moving into Phase II. *Computers and the Humanities.* 1972; 7: 67-81. ISSN: 0010-4817.

S224
SICHEL, H. S. 1975. On a Distribution Law for Word Frequencies. *Journal of the American Statistical Association.* 1975; 70: 542-547.

S225
SIEBER, JOAN E., ed. 1991. *Sharing Social Science Data: Advantages and Challenges.* Newbury Park, CA: Sage Publications; 1991. 168p. ISBN: 0803940823 (hbk.); 0803940831 (pbk.).

S226
SIEGFRIED, SUSAN L.; BATES, MARCIA J.; WILDE, DEBORAH N. 1993a. An Analysis of Search Terminology Used by Humanities Scholars: The Getty Online Searching Project Report Number 1. *Library Trends.* 1993 January; 63: 1-39. ISSN: 0024-2594.

S227
SIEGFRIED, SUSAN L.; BATES, MARCIA J.; WILDE, DEBORAH N. 1993b. A Profile of End-User Searching Behavior by Humanities Scholars: The Getty Online Searching Project Report 2. *Journal of the American Society for Information Science.* 1993; 44(5): 273-291. ISSN: 0002-8231.

S228
SIEGFRIED, SUSAN L.; WILDE, DEBORAH N. 1990. Scholars Go Online. *Art Documentation.* 1990 fall; 10: 139-141. ISSN: 0730-7187.

S229
SIEHL, C.; MARTIN, J. 1989. Measuring Organizational Culture: Mixing Qualitative and Quantitative Methods. *Inside Organizations* (pp. 79-103). M. O. Jones; M. D. Moore; R. C. Snyder, eds. Beverly Hills, CA: Sage; 1989. 384p. ISBN: 0803919801 (hbk.); 0803931999 (pbk.).

S230
SIGELMAN, LEE; MARTINDALE, COLIN; MCKENZIE, DEAN. 1996/1997. The Common Style of *Common Sense.* See reference: IGARTUA, J. E., ed. 1996/1997. 373-3379.

S231
SIGFRIED, STEFAN. 1996. *Understanding Object-Oriented Software Engineering.* Los Alamitos, CA: IEEE; 1996. 478p. ISBN: 0-7803-1095-0.

S232
SIGNORE, O.; BARTOLI, R. 1989. Managing Art History Fuzzy Dates: An Application in Historico-Geographical Authority. *Historische Sozialforschung / Historical Social Research* (DEU). 1989; 14(3): 98-105. ISSN: 0172-6404.

S233
SIMMONS, R. O.; THURGOOD, D. H. 1996. *Humanities Doctorates in the United States.* Washington, D.C.: National Academy Press; 1996. Part of series: Humanities Doctorates in the United States. 1986-. Biennial. (Supported by the National Research Council). ISSN: 90016168; LCCN: 97643508; OCLC: 17238293.

S234
SIMMONS, ROBERT H. 1990. *Wheeling and the Hinterland: An Egalitarian Society?* Morgantown, WVA: University of West Virginia; 1990. 343p. (Ph.D. dissertation; *DAI*, vol. 51/06-A: 2139). Available from: University Microfilms, Ann Arbor, MI (Order no. AAD90-29366).

S235
SIMON, HERBERT A. [1944]. *Decision-making and Administrative Organization.* N.p.; [1944]. 30p. LCCN: 44004706.

S236
SIMON, HERBERT A. 1957. *Models of Man: Social and Rational. Mathematical Essays on Rational Human Behavior in a Social Setting.* New York, NY: J. Wiley & Sons; 1957. 287p. LCCN: 57005933.

S237
SIMON, HERBERT A. 1973. The Structure of Ill Structured Problems. *Artificial Intelligence.* 1973; 4: 181-201. ISSN: 000-3702.

S238
SIMON, HERBERT A. 1979 [1989]. *Models of Thought.* New Haven, CT: Yale University Press; 1979 [1989]. Vols. 1-2. ISBN: 03000023472; LCCN: 78031744.

S239
SIMON, HERBERT A. 1982. *Models of Bounded Rationality.* Vol. 1: *Economic Analysis and Public Policy.* Vol. 2: *Behavioral Economics and Business Organization.* Cambridge, MA: MIT Press; 1982. 2 vols. ISBN: 0262192055(vol. 1); -063 (vol. 2).

S240
SIMON, HERBERT A. 1991. Bounded Rationality and Organizational Learning. *Organizational Science* (JP). 1991: 2(1): 125-134. ISSN: 0286-3702.

S241
SIMON, HERBERT A. 1996. *The Sciences of the Artificial*. 3rd ed. Cambridge, MA: MIT Press; 1996. 231p. ISBN: 0-262-69191-4 (pbk.); 0-262-19374-4 (hbk.). Note: first ed.; 1969; LCCN: 69011312. 2nd ed.; 1981. ISBN: 0262191938; LCCN: 80028273.

S242
SIMON, HERBERT A.; SIKLOSSY, LAURENT, comps. [1972]. *Representation and Meaning: Experiments with Information Processing Systems*. Englewood Cliffs, NJ: Prentice-Hall; [1972]. 440p. ISBN: 0137735499.

S243
SIMONTON, DEAN K. 1984. *Genius, Creativity, and Leadership: Historiometric Inquiries*. Cambridge, MA: Harvard University Press; 1984. 231p. ISBN: 0674346807.

S244
SIMONTON, DEAN K. 1988. *Scientific Genius: A Psychology of Science*. New York, NY: Cambridge University Press; 1988. 229p. ISBN: 0521352878.

S245
SIMONTON, DEAN K. 1990. *Psychology, Science, and History: An Introduction to Historiometry*. New Haven, CT: Yale University Press; 1990. 291p. ISBN: 0300047711.

S246
SIMONTON, DEAN K. 1994. *Greatness: Who Makes History and Why*. New York, NY: Guilford; 1994. 502p. ISBN: 0898623707.

S247
SIMONTON, DEAN K. 1997. *Genius and Creativity: Selected Papers*. Greenwich, CT: Ablex Pub. Col; 1997. 318p. ISBN: 1567502563 (hbk.); 1567502571 (pbk.).

S248
SIMOUDIS, E. 1996. Reality Check for Data Mining. *IEEE Expert*. 1996; 10: 26-33. ISSN: 0665-9000.

S249
SIMPSON, LORENZO C. 1995. *Technology, Time, and the Conversations of Modernity*. New York, NY: Routledge; 1995. 232p. ISBN: 0415907713 (hbk.); 0415907721 (pbk.).

S250
SINCLAIR, AMANDA. 1993. Approaches to Organizational Culture and Ethics. *Journal of Business Ethics*. 1993 January; 12(1): 63-73. ISSN: 0167-4544.

S251
SINGER, DOROTHY, ed. 1991/1997. *A Piaget Primer: How a Child Thinks*. New York, NY: Plume; 1996. LCCN: 96-1932. Reprint. Madison, CT: International University Press; 1997. 146p. LCCN: 97-6225.

S252
SINGER, MILTON. 1968. Culture. *International Encyclopedia of the Social Sciences* (vol. 3, pp. 527-543). David A. Sills, ed. New York, NY: Macmillan; [1968]; 3: 527-543. 17 vols.

S253
SINGHAI, S. K. 1994. Using a Position-History-Based Protocol for Distributed Object Visualization. In: *Designing Real-Time Graphics for Entertainment*. New York, NY: ACM Press; 1994.

S254
SKEMER, DON C. 1989. Diplomatics and Archives. *The American Archivist*. 1989; 52(3): 376-82. ISSN: 0360-9081.

S255
SKINNER, QUENTIN. 1969. Meaning and Understanding in the History of Ideas. *History and Theory*. 1969; 8: 3-53. ISSN: 0018-2656. Also in TULLY, ed. 1988.

S256
SKINNER, QUENTIN. 1985. *The Return of Grand Theory in the Human Sciences*. Cambridge, UK: Cambridge University Press; 1985. ISBN: 0521266920 (hbk.); 0521318084 (pbk.).

S257
SKLAR, E. S. 1976. The Possessive Apostrophe: The Development and Decline of a Crooked Mark. *College English*. 1976; 38: 175-183.

S258

SKOCPOL. THEDA, ed. 1984. *Vision and Method in Historical Sociology.* Conference on Methods of Historical Social Analysis, Cambridge, MA, October 1979. Cambridge, UK: Cambridge University Press; 1984. 410p. ISBN: 0521229286 (hbk.); 0521297249.

S259

SKOWRON, A.; GRYMALA-BUSSE, J. 1994. From Rough Set Theory to the Evidence Theory. See reference: YAGER, R.; FEDRIZZI, M.; KROSPRYK, J., eds. 1994. 193-236.

S260

SKRÄMM, YNGVE. 1995. Hypertext: Historical Structure or Research Tool? See reference: BOONSTRA, O., *ET AL.*, eds. 1995. 265-272.

S261

SKUPSKY, DONALD S. 1988/1995. *Recordkeeping Requirements: The First Practical Guide to Help You Control your Records—What You Need to Keep and What you Can Safely Destroy.* Denver, CO: Information Requirements Clearinghouse; 1988. 2nd ed. 1995. 246p. USBN: 0929316185; LC: 88-013335.

S262

SKUPSKY, DONALD S. 1991/1996. *Legal Requirements for Microfilm, Computer and Optical Disk Records: Evidence, Regulation, Government and International Requirements.* Denver, CO: Information Requirements Clearinghouse; 1991. 370p. 2nd ed., 1994. Supplement, 1996. ISBN: 0929316045.

S263

SKYRMS, BRIAN; HARPER, WILLIAM L., eds. 1988. *Causation, Chance, and Credence.* Irvine Conference on Probability and Causation, 1. Boston, MA: Kluwer Academic Press; c1988. 284p. ISBN: 9027726337; LCCN: 87028857. 284p. ISBN: 9027726227; LCCN: 87028857.

S264

SLAVIN, TIMOTHY A., ed. [1997]. *Model Guidelines for Electronic Records* [electronic file]. Dover, DE: Delaware Public Archives; [1997]. 13p. Accessible at http://www.lib.de.us/ archives/.

S265

SLOWINSKI, ROMAN, ed. 1992. *Intelligent Decision Support: Handbook of Applications and Advances of the Rough Sets Theory.* Dordrecht, NL / Boston, MA: Kluwer Academic Publishers; 1992. 471p. (Theory and Decision library series d., vol. 11). ISBN: 0792319230.

S266

SLY, MARGERY. 1994. *Provenance*: Regional Journal as Training Ground. See reference: COX, R., ed. 1994. 300-303.

S267

SMALL, HENRY G. 1981. The Relationship of Information Science to the Social Sciences: A Co-citation Analysis. *Information Processing and Management.* 1981; 17: 39-50. ISSN: 0306-4573.

S268

SMALL, HENRY G.; GARFIELD, EUGENE. 1985. The Geography of Science Disciplinary and National Mappings. *Journal of Information Science* (UK). 1985; 35: 268-278. ISSN: 0165-5515.

S269

SMALL, JOCELYN PENNY. 1997. *Wax Tablets of the Mind: Cognitive Studies of Memory and Literacy in Classical Antiquity.* New York, NY: Routledge; 1997. ISBN: 0415149835; LCCN: 960037725.

S270

SMALL, MELVIN; LAUREN, PAUL G. 1979. The Quantification of Diplomatic History. In: Lauren, Paul G., ed. *Diplomacy: New Approaches in History, Theory, and Policy.* New York, NY: Free Press; 1979; 69-96. ISBN: 0029180708.

S271

SMEATON, ALAN. 1991. Prospects for Intelligent, Language-based Information Retrieval. *Online Review.* 1991 Dec.: 15(6): 373-382. ISSN: 0309-314.

S272

SMETS, JOSEF, ed. 1992. *Histoire et Informatique* [History and Informatics]. Ve Congrés International "Association for History and Computing" / Montpellier Computing Conference, 4-7 Septembre 1990: Volume des Actes. Montpellier, FR: University of Montpellier; 1992. 600p.

S273

SMIRAGLIA, RICHARD P. [199?]. *The Nature of "The Work": Reflections on the Creative Task and Implications for Knowledge Organization of Bibliographic Works.* Dordrecht, NL: Kluwer; [1999 forthcoming].

S274
SMIRAGLIA, RICHARD P.; LEAZER, G. H. 1999. Derivative Bibliographic Relationships: The Work Relationship in a Global Bibliographic Database. *Journal of the American Society for Information Science.* 1999; 50: 493-505. ISSN: 0002-8231.

S275
SMIRCICH, L. 1983. Concepts of Culture and Organizational Analysis. *Administrative Science Quarterly.* 1983; 28 (3): 339-358. ISSN: 0001-8392.

S276
SMIRCICH, L.; MORGAN, G. 1982. Leadership: The Management of Meaning. *The Journal of Applied Behavioral Science.* 1982; 18 (3): 257-273. ISSN: 0021-8863.

S277
SMITH, BONNIE. 1984. Women's Contributions to Modern Historiography in Great Britain, France, and the United States, 1750-1940. *American Historical Review.* 1984 June; 89: 709-732. ISSN: 0002-8762.

S278
SMITH, BONNIE. 1995. Gender and the Practices of Scientific History: The Seminar and Archival Research in the Nineteenth Century. *American Historical Review.* 1995 October; 100(4): 1150-1176. ISSN: 0002-8762.

S279
SMITH, CARL. 1998. Can You do Serious History on the Web? See reference: AHA. 1998. 5- 8.

S280
SMITH, CLIVE D. 1997. Implementation of Imaging Technology for Recordkeeping at the World Bank. See reference: TRAVIS, I., ed. 1997. 25-29.

S281
SMITH, COLIN. 1986. A Case for Abandonment of 'Respect'. *Archives and Manuscripts.* 1986 November: 14(2): [150-160]. ISSN: 0003-5991.

S282
SMITH, D. S. 1984. A Mean and Random Past: The Implications of Variance in History. *Historical Methods.* 1984; 17: 141-148. ISSN: 0161-5440.

S283
SMITH, ELDRED R. 1990. *The Librarian, the Scholar, and the Future of the Research Library.* New York, NY: Greenwood Press; 1990. 119p. ISBN: 0313272107; LCCN: 9-25665; OCLC: 20671859.

S284
SMITH, GEORGE DAVID; STEADMAN, LAURENCE E. 1993. Present Value of Corporate History. See reference: JONES, A. A.; CANTELON, P. L., eds. 1993.

S285
SMITH, HEDRICK. 1995. *Rethinking America.* New York, NY: Random House; 1995. 474p. ISBN: 0679435514.

S286
SMITH, JAY M. 1997. No More Language Games: Words, Beliefs, and the Political Culture of Early Modern France. *American Historical Review.* 1997 Dec.; 102 (5): 1413-1440. ISSN: 0002-8762.

S287
SMITH, LAWRENCE D. 1986. *Behavioralism and Logical Positivism.* Palo Alto, CA: Stanford University Press; 1986.

S288
SMITH, LINDA C. 1981. Citation Analysis. *Library Trends.* 1981; 30: 83-106. ISSN: 0024-2594.

S289
SMITH, LINDA C. 1991. Memex as an Image of Potentiality Revisited. See reference: NYCE, J.; KAHN, P., eds; 1991. 261-286. ISBN: 0-12-523270-5.

S290
SMITH, LINDA C. 1992. Interdisciplinarity: Approaches to Understanding Library and Information Science as an Interdisciplinary Field. In: VAKKARI, P.; CRONIN, B., eds. 1992; 253-267.

S291
SMITH, LINDA B.; SAMUELSON, LARISSA K. 1997. Perceiving and Remembering: Category Stability, Variability, and Development. See reference: LAMBERT, K.; SHANKS, D., eds. 1997.

S292

SMITH, MARK C. 1994. *Social Science in the Crucible: The American Debate over Objectivity and Purpose, 1918-1941.* Durham, NC: Duke University Press; 1994. 353p. ISBN: 0822314975 (hbk.); 0822314843 (pbk.); LCCN: 94-7823.

S293

SMITH, R. E. 1989. A Historical Overview of Computer Architecture. *Annals of the History of Computing.* 1989; 10(4): 227-303. ISSN: 1058-6180.

S294

SMITH, TERENCE R. 1996. A Digital Library for Geographically Referenced Materials. See reference: SCHATZ, B.; CHEN, H., eds. 1996. 46-52.

S295

SMURR, JOHN W. 1990. *Toynbee at Home.* Hanover, MA: Christopher Pub. House; c1990. 383p. ISBN: 0815804512; LCCN: 88071449.

S296

SMYTH, ALFRED. 1996. Whose Past is it Anyway? *Times Educational Supplement* (UK). 1996 April 19; 4164: 1. (Concerns revisionism in British History). ISSN: 0040-7887.

S297

SNYDER, DAVID PEARCE. 1997. *Roller Coaster 2000: New Dynamics, New Environments, New Strategies* (Video). Workshop conducted for the fall 1996 World Congress of the International Development Research Council. Bethesda, MD: Synder Family Enterprise; 1997. Available via e-mail: SnyderFam1@AOL.com.

S298

SNYDER, JOEL. 1989. Inventing Photography. In: Greenough, Sarah, ed. *On the Art of Fixing a Shadow: One Hundred and Fifty Years of Photography.* Washington, D.C.: National Gallery of Art; 1989. 3-38.

S299

SNYDER, TERRI L. *1992. "Rich Widows are the Best Commodity this Country Affords": Gender Relations and the Rehabilitation of Patriarchy in Virginia, 1660-1700.* Iowa City: University of Iowa; 336p. (Ph.D. dissertation; DAI, 53/11-A: 3960). Available from: University Microfilms, Ann Arbor MI (Order no. AAD93-08124).

S300

SOBEL, ROBERT. 1981. *IBM: Colossus in Transition.* New York, NY: Times Books; 1981. 360p. ISBN: 0812910001.

S301

SOBEL, ROBERT. 1991. Big Blues: The Unmaking of IBM. *Electronic News.* 1994, January 10; 40 (1996): 9. ISSN: 1061-6624.

S302

SOCIAL SCIENCE COMPUTER REVIEW (SSCORE). 1982-. Durham, NC: Duke University Press; 1982. Qtly. ISSN: 0894-4393. Continuation of *Social Science Microcomputer Review.* Raleigh, NC: North Carolina State University Social Science Research and Instructional Computing Laboratory; 1982. ISSN: 0885-0011.

S303

SOCIAL SCIENCE HISTORY ASSOCIATION. 1976-. *Social Science History.* Beverley Hills, CA: Sage Publications for the Social Science History Association; 1976-. Qtly. ISSN: 0145-5532; LCCN: 77-640161; OCLC: 2761258. Note related monographic series: *New Approaches to Social Science History,* 1981-: see references to TILLY, 1981; BOGUE, 1983; MOCH, 1983; ROWNEY, 1984.

S304

SOCIAL SCIENCE RESEARCH COUNCIL. 1946. *Theory and Practice in Historical Study.* New York, NY: SSRC; 1946. 177p.(Report of the Committee on Historiography. Bulletin 54). LCCN: 46-3597; OCLC: 395002.

S305

SOCIAL SCIENCE RESEARCH COUNCIL. 1954. *The Social Sciences in Historical Study.* New York, NY: SSRC; 1954. 181p. (Bulletin 64). LCCN: 54-9680; OCLC: 342862.

S306

SOCIAL SCIENCE RESEARCH COUNCIL (SSRC-UK). 1974. *Computing and the Social Sciences.* A Report to the SSRC. London, UK: SSRC; 1974. 26f. ISBN: 0900296143; LCCN: 75-318852; OCLC: 1551817.

S307

SOCIETY FOR HISTORY EDUCATION. 1967-. *The History Teacher.* Long Beach, CA: California State University at Long Beach Dept. of History; 1967-. Quarterly. Formerly published for the History Teacher's Association by the University of Notre Dame, IN (1967-1974). ISSN: 0018-2745; LCCN: 74-3356; OCLC: 1794874.

S308
SOCIETY FOR THE HISTORY OF TECHNOLOGY. 1959-. *Technology and Culture*. Chicago, IL: University of Chicago Press; c1961. Qtly. ISSN: 0040-165X.

S309
SOCIETY OF AMERICAN ARCHIVISTS (SAA). 1937-. *The American Archivist*. Chicago, IL: SAA; 1937-. ISSN: 0360-9081.

S310
SOCIETY OF AMERICAN ARCHIVISTS (SAA). 1990. *Preservation*. Kenney, Anne R., ed. *The American Archivist*. 1990 Spring; 53(2): 181-369. (Entire issue on title topic). ISSN: 0360-9081.

S311
SOCIETY OF AMERICAN ARCHIVISTS (SAA). COMMITTEE ON ARCHIVAL INFORMATION EXCHANGE (CAIE). [1997]. *Standard Generalized Mark-up Language / Encoded Archival Description Document Type Definition* (SGML/EAD DTD). Chicago, IL: SAA; [1997].

S312
SOCIETY OF AMERICAN ARCHIVISTS (SAA). COMMITTEE ON AUTOMATED RECORDS AND TECH-NIQUES (CART). 1993. Curriculum Development Project. In: *The American Archivist*. 1993; 56(3): 400-559. (Entire issue on title topic). ISSN: 0360-9081.

S313
SOCIETY OF AMERICAN ARCHIVISTS (SAA). COMMITTEE ON GOALS AND PRIORITIES (CGAP). 1986. *Planning for the Archival Profession: A Report to the SAA Task Force on Goals and Priorities*. Chicago, IL: SAA; 1986. Available from: SAA, 600 Federal Suite 504, Chicago, IL 606605.

S314
SOCIETY OF AMERICAN ARCHIVISTS (SAA). WORKING GROUP ON STANDARDS FOR ARCHIVAL DESCRIPTION (WGSAD). 1989. *Standards for Archival Description*. Dowler, Lawrence, chair. *The American Archivist*. 1989; 52(4): 427-537. (Entire issue on title topic). ISSN: 0360-9081.

S315
SOCIETY OF AMERICAN ARCHIVISTS (SAA). WORKING GROUP ON STANDARDS FOR ARCHIVAL DESCRIPTION (WGSAD). 1994. *Standards for Archival Descriptions: A Handbook*. Irons Walch, V., comp.; Matters, M., contributor. Chicago, IL: SAA; 1994. 320p. ISBN: 0-931828-96-1.

S316
SOCIETY OF ARCHIVISTS. 1955-. *Journal of the Society of Archivists* (UK). London, UK: Society of Archivists; 1955-. Semiannual. ISSN: 0037-9816; LCCN: 64-53272; OCLC: 1586854.

S317
SOCIETY OF PHOTO-OPTICAL INSTRUMENTATION ENGINEERS (SPIE). 1993-1995. *Storage and Retrieval for Image and Video Databases*. Bellingham, WA: International Society for Optical Engineering SPIE; 1993-95. 3 vols. ISSN: 1084-2926.

S318
SOCIETY OF PHOTO-OPTICAL INSTRUMENTATION ENGINEERS (SPIE). 1996-. *Storage and Retrieval for Still Image and Video Databases*. Bellingham, WA: International Society for Optical Engineering SPIE; 1996-. ISSN: 1084-2926; OCLC: 32652959.

S319
SOERGEL, DAGOBERT. 1971. *Dokumentation und Organisation des Wissens: Versuch einer methodischen und the-oretischen Grundlegung am Beispeil der Sozialwissenschaften* [Documentation and Organization of Knowledge: Toward a Methodological and Theoretical Foundation for the Social Sciences]. Berlin, DEU: Dunker & Humbolt; 1971. 380p. ISBN: 3428024419.

S320
SOERGEL, DAGOBERT. 1974. *Indexing Languages and Thesauri: Construction and Maintenance*. Los Angeles, CA: Melville Pub. Co.; 1974. 632p. ISBN: 0471810479.

S321
SOERGEL, DAGOBERT. 1985. *Organizing Information: Principles of Data Base and Retrieval Systems*. Orlando, FL: Academic Press; 1985. 450p. ISBN: 0126542600.

S322
SOERGEL, DAGOBERT. 1994. Information Structure Management: A Unified Framework for Indexing and Searching in Database, Expert, Information-Retrieval and Hypermedia Systems. See reference: FIDEL, R., *ET AL.*, eds. 1994. 111-156.

S323
SOERGEL, DAGOBERT. 1999. The Rise of Ontologies or the Re-invention of Classification. See reference: BATES, MARCIA, ed. 1999. 1119-1120.

S324
SOFFER, GAIL. 1996. Heidegger, Humanism, and the Destruction of History. *The Review of Metaphysics.* 1996 March; 49 (3): 547-577. ISSN: 0034-6632.

S325
SOKOLOV, ANDREY K. 1996. [Historical Informatics: Commentary]. See reference: BORODKIN, L. I., ed. 1996. 111-117. (In Russian)

S326
SOKOLOV, ANDREY K.; BONIUSHKINA, LIUDMILA; MIAKUSHEV, SERGEY. 1996 [1999-]. The Database as a Means of Historical Synthesis. See reference: BORODKIN, L., ed. 1996. English abstract of presentation, 63-64; paper in Russian [199-, forthcoming].

S327
SOLOMON, JON, ed. 1993. *Accessing Antiquity: The Computerization of Classical Studies.* Tucson, AZ: University of Arizona; 1993. 186p. ISBN: 0816513902; LCCN: 93-25963; OCLC: 28420789.

S328
SOLOMON, PAUL R., ed. 1989. *Memory: Interdisciplinary Approaches.* Proceedings, Congress on Social Memory. New York, NY: Springer-Verlag; 1989. 300p. ISBN: 0387967249; LCCN: 88004923..

S329
SOLSO, ROBERT L. 1995. *Cognitive Psychology.* 4th ed. Boston, MA; 1995. 575p. ISBN: 0205158315.

S330
SOLTOW, JAMES H. 1978. Recent Literature in American Economic History. *American Studies International.* 1978; 16: 5-33. ISSN: 0883-105X.

S331
SOMERS, MARGARET. 1984. Beyond the Economistic Fallacy: The Holistic Social Science of Karl Polanyi. See reference: SKOCPOL, T., ed. 1984. 47-84.

S332
SOMMERVILLE, C. JOHN. 1996. *News Revolution in England: Cultural Dynamics of Daily Information.* New York, NY: Oxford University Press; 1996. 197p. ISBN: 0- 19-510667-9.

S333
SONKA, MILAN; HLAVAC, VACLAV; BOYLE, ROGER. 1993. *Image Processing, Analysis, and Machine Vision.* London, UK: Chapman & Hall; 1993. 555p. ISBN: 0412455706.

S334
SORKOW, JANICE. 1997. Pricing and Licensing for Museum Digital Content. See reference: TRANT, J., ed. 1997. 165-179.

S335
SOUTHGATE, BEVERLEY. 1996. History and Metahistory: Marwick versus White. *Journal of Contemporary History.* 1996 January; 31(1): 209-215. ISSN: 0022-0094.

S336
SOWA, JOHN F.; BORGIDA, ALEXANDER, eds. 1991. *Principles of Semantic Networks.* San Mateo, CA: Morgan Kaufmann Publishers, Inc.; 1991. 582p. ISBN: 1558600884.

S337
SOWIZRAL, HENRY A. 1985. Expert Systems. In: Williams, M., ed. *Annual Review of Information Science and Technology.* Medford, NJ: Information Today; 1985; 20: 179-199. ISBN: 1-57387-019-6; ISSN: 0066-4200; CODEN: ARISBC; LC no. 66-25096

S338
SPAETH, DONALD A. 1996. Computer Assisted Teaching and Learning in History. In: Booth, A.; Hyland, P., eds. *Teaching History in Higher Education: New Directions in Teaching and Learning.* Oxford, UK: Blackwells; 1996. 155-177.

S339
SPAETH, DONALD A., comp. 1991. *A Guide to Software for Historians.* Glasgow, Scotland: University of Glasgow, Computers in Teaching Initiative, Centre for History; 1991. 98p. ISBN: 0-9517514-0-9; LCCN: 91-58342; OCLC: 24796567.

S340
SPAETH, DONALD A., ed. 1992. *Towards an International Curriculum for History and Computing.* A Workshop of the International Association for History and Computing, University of Glasgow, 15-17 May 1992. St. Katharinen [Gottingen, DE]: Scripta Mercaturae Verlag for the Max-Planck-Institut fur Geschichte; 1992. (Halbgraue Reihe zur historischen Fackinformatik. Serie B: Historische Quellenkunden).

S341
SPENCE RICHARDS, PAMELA. 1992. Education and Training for Information Science in the Soviet Union. In: Williams, Martha, ed. *Annual Review of Information Science and Technology:* vol. 27. Medford, NJ: Information Today; 1992. 267-290. ISSN: 0066-4200; ISBN: 0-938734-66-0.

S342
SPENCE RICHARDS, PAMELA. 1994a. Scientific Information for Stalin's Scientists: The NKVD and Postwar Documentation in the USSR, 1946-1953. Paper in: *pre-conference seminar on the History of Information Science,* at the American Society for Information Science Conference, October 17-20, 1994, Alexandria, VA.

S343
SPENCE RICHARDS, PAMELA. 1994b. *Scientific Information in Wartime. The Allied-German Rivalry, 1939-1945.* Westport, C: Greenwood Press; 1994. 177p. ISBN: 0313290628.

S344
SPENDOLINI, MICHAEL J. 1992. *The Benchmarking Book.* New York, NY: American Management Assn.; 1992. ISBN: 0-8144-5077-6.

S345
SPERBERG MCQUEEN, C. MICHAEL; BURNARD, LOU D., eds. 1990. *Guidelines for the Encoding and Interchange of Machine-Readable Texts.* Edition TEI P2. Chicago, IL and Oxford, UK: Oxford University Press for ACH, ACL, ALLC; 1990. 290p. Revised: *Guidelines for Electronic Text Encoding and Interchange (TEI P3).* Chicago, IL/Oxford, UK: ACH-ACL-ALLC Text Encoding Initiative; 1994. Updated revisions available from TEI, Computer Center 135, University of Illinois at Chicago Circle, Box 6998, Chicago IL 60680.

S346
SPERBERG-MCQUEEN, C. MICHAEL; BURNARD, LOU, eds. 1994/ [1995]. *TEI Guidelines (Text Encoding Initiative): Hardcopy and CD-ROM.* Oxon Hall, MD: NISO Press, [1995]. 2 vols., 1,200p. (Corrected version of 1994 ed.). Available from NISO Press at 1-800- 282-NISO; Fax 301-567-9553.

S347
SPICER, R. D. 1988. Computer Graphics and the Perception of Archeological Information: Lies, Damned Lies, Statistics, and.. Graphics! See reference: RUGGLES, C. N. L.; RAHTZ, S. P. Q., eds. 1988. 187-200.

S348
SPIEGEL, GABRIELLE M. 1990. History, Historicism, and the Social Logic of the Text in the Middle Ages. *Speculum.* 1990; 69: 64-78. ISSN: 0038-7134.

S349
SPIEGEL, GABRIELLE M. 1992. History and Post-Modernism IV. *Past and Present.* 1992; 135: 194-208. ISSN: 0031-2746. See references: JOYCE, P.; KELLY, C.; and STONE, L. 1992-1992.

S350
SPIEGEL, GABRIELLE M. 1993. *Romancing the Past: The Rise of Vernacular Prose Historiography in Thirteenth Century France.* Berkeley, CA: University of California Press; 1993. 422p. ISBN: 0520077105.

S351
SPIEGEL, GABRIELLE M. 1997. *The Past as Text. The Theory and Practice of Medieval Historiography.* Baltimore, MD: The Johns Hopkins University Press; 1997. 329p. ISBN: 0-8018-5555-1.

S352
SPILLNER, BERND. 1974. *Linguistik und Literaturwissenschaft: Stilforschung, Rhetorick, Textlinguistik* [Linguistics and Literary Criticism: Research Methods, Rhetoric, and Textual Linguistics]. Stuttgart, DEU: W. Kohlhammer; 1974. 147p. ISBN: 3170017349; LCCN: 75-556412; OCLC: 1405582.

S353
SPINK, AMANDA; ROBINS, DAVID; SCHAMBER, LINDA. 1998. Use of Scholarly Book Reviews: Implications for Electronic Publishing and Scholarly Communication. *Journal of the American Society for Information Science.* 1998; 49(4): 364-374. ISSN: 0002- 8231.

S354
SPIRTES, PETER; GLYMOUR, CLARK; SCHEINES, RICHARD. 1993. *Causation, Prediction, and Search.* New York, NY: Springer-Verlag; 1993. 526p. ISBN: 0387979794.

S355
SPIVAK, STEVEN M.; WINSELL, KEITH ANDEW. 1991. *A Sourcebook on Standards Information: Education, Access, and Development.* Boston, MA: G. K. Hall; 1991. 451p. ISBN: 0816119481 (hbk.); 081611949X (pbk.).

S356
SPOEHR, KATHRYN T.; LEHMKUHLE, STEPHEN W. 1982. *Visual Information Processing.* San Francisco, CA: W. H. Freeman; 1982. 298p. ISBN: 071671371X (hbk.); 0716713748 (pbk.).

S357
SPOHER, JAMES H. 1992. French Studies in the Automation Age: *ARTFL*, a Full-text French Database. *Collection Management.* 1992; 15(3/4): 417-24. ISSN: 0146-2679.

S358
SPRAGUE, D. N. 1978. A Quantitative Assessment of the Quantitative Revolution. *Journal of Canadian History* (CAN). 1978; 13: 177-192.

S359
SPRAGUE, RALPH H.; CARLSON, E. D. 1982. *Building Effective Decision Support Systems.* Engelwood Cliffs, NJ: Prentice-Hall, Inc.; 1982. 329p. ISBN: 0130862150.

S360
SPROUL, LEE.; KIESLER, SARA B. 1991. *Connections: New Ways of Working in the Networked Organization.* Cambridge, MA: MIT Press; c1991. 212p. ISBN: 026219306X.

S361
SPURR, DAVID. 1993. *The Rhetoric of Empire: Colonial Discourse in Journalism, Travel Writing, and Imperial Administration.* Durham, N.C.: Duke University Press; 1993. 212p. ISBN: 0822313030; LCCN: 92-23232; OCLC: 26256638.

S362
SRIHARI, M. 1995. Automatic Indexing and Content-based Retrieval of Captioned Images. *IEEE Computer.* 1995; 28 (9): 49-56. ISSN: 0180-9162.

S363
SRIHARI, S. N.; BOZINOVIC, R. M. 1987. A Multi-level Perception Approach to Reading Cursive Script. *Artificial Intelligence.* 1987; 33: 217-255. ISSN: 0004-3702 / 0374- 2539. (See update under BOZINOVIC & SRIHARI, 1989).

S364
STAFFORD, BARBARA M. 1994. *Artful Science: Enlightenment Entertainment and the Eclipse of Visual Education.* Cambridge, MA: MIT Press; 1994. 350p. ISBN: 026219426; LCCN: 93-20984.

S365
STAFFORD, BARBARA M. 1996. *Good Looking: Essays on the Virtue of Images.* Cambridge, MA: MIT Press; 1996. ISBN: 0262193698; LCCN: 96-7079.

S366
STALLINGS, WILLIAM. 1995. *Protect your Privacy: The PGP User's Guide.* Englewood Cliffs, NJ: Prentice-Hall PTR; 1995. 302p. ISBN: 0131855964 (pbk.); LCCN: 94-041526.

S367
STAM, DIERDRE C. 1984. *The Information-seeking Practices of Art Historians in Museums and Colleges in the United States, 1982-83.* New York, NY: Columbia University; 1984. (Doctoral Dissertation. *DAI:* AA8427477). Available from University Microfilms, Ann Arbor, MI.

S368
STAM, DIERDRE C. 1989. The Quest for a Code, or a Brief History of the Computerization of Art Objects. *Art Documentation.* 1989 Spring; 8(1): 7-15. ISSN: 0730-7187.

S369
STAM, DIERDRE C. 1991. What about the Mona Lisa? Making Bibliographic Databases More Useful to Art Historians by Classifying Documents According to the Aspect of Art Object(s) Under Consideration. *Art Documentation.* 1991 Fall; 10: 127-130. ISSN: 0730-7187.

S370
STAM, DIERDRE C.; PALMQUIST, RUTH. 1989. *SUART: A MARC-based Information Structure and Data Dictionary for the Syracuse University Art Collection.* Syracuse, NY: Museum Computer Network; 1989. 223p. (Grant support by the Council on Library Resources). LC call no.: Z699.5.A75.

S371
STANDARDS ASSOCIATION OF AUSTRALIA. COMMITTEE IT/21 ON RECORDS MANAGEMENT SYSTEMS. 1996. *Records Management.* Pt. 3: *Strategies.* Homebusch, NSW AU: Standards Assn. of Australia; 1996.

S372
STANLEY, BARBARA; SIEBER, JOAN E.; NELTON, GARY B. 1996. *Research Ethics: A Psychological Approach.* Lincoln, NE: University of Nebraska; 1996. 273p. ISBN: 0803241887.

S373
STANNARD, DAVID E. 1992. *American Holocaust: Columbus and the Conquest of the New World.* New York and Oxford: Oxford University Press; 1992. 358p. ISBN: 0195075811; LCCN: 92-6922; OCLC: 25316563.

S374
STARRE, J. V. D. 1992. Een Weeld aan Plaatjes: enkele voorbeelden van Beelddocumentatiesystemen [A World of Images: some examples of Image Retrieval Systems]. *Open* (NL). September 1992; 24(9): 299-300. (In Dutch). ISSN: 0030-3372.

S375
STAUDENMAIER, JOHN M. 1985/1989. *Technology's Storytellers: Reweaving the Human Fabric.* Cambridge, MA: MIT Press; 1985. 1989 reprint. 282p. ISBN: 0262192373.

S376
STEARNS, PETER N. 1976. Coming of Age. *Journal of Social history.* 1976; 10(2): 246-55. ISSN: 0022-4529.

S377
STEARNS, PETER N. 1980. Toward a Wider Vision: Trends in Social History. See reference: KAMMEN, M., ed. 1980. 226-29.

S378
STEARNS, PETER N. 1993. *Meaning over Memory: Recasting the Teaching of Culture and History.* Chapel Hill, NC: University of North Carolina Press; 1993. 254p. ISBN: 008078209031 (hbk.); 0807844160(pbk.).

S379
STEARNS, PETER N., ed. 1994. *Encyclopedia of Social History..* New York, NY: Garland; 1994. 856p. (Garland Reference Library of Social Science, v. 780). ISBN: 0815303424.

S380
STEDMANN JONES, GARETH. 1976. From historical sociology to theoretical history. *British Journal of Sociology.* 1976; 27: 295-305. ISSN: 007-1315.

S381
STEELE, G. 1984. *COMMON LISP: The Language.* Bedford, MA: Digital Press; 1984.

S382
STEELE, MARTHA. [199-]. The Photograph Collection of Illuminated Manuscripts at the Getty Center for the History of Art. See reference: HAMESSE, J., ed. [199-, forthcoming].

S383
STEELS, L. 1990. Components of Expertise. *AI Magazine.* 1990 Summer; s.n.: 29-49. ISSN: 0738-4602.

S384
STEENBLOCK, VOLKER. 1991. *Transformationem des Historismus* [The Transformation of Historical Science]. Munich, DEU: Fink; c1991. 205p. (Historiography; in German). ISBN: 3770526945; LCCN: 91224662.

S385
STEFIK, MARK, ed. 1996. *Internet Dreams: Archetypes, Myths, and Metaphors for Inventing the Net.* Cambridge, MA: MIT Press; 1996. 406p. ISBN: 0-262-19373-6.

S386
STEHR, NICO. 1992. *Practical Knowledge: Applying the Social Sciences.* London, UK: Sage; 1992. 188p. ISBN: 080398998.

S387
STEINKE, CYNTHIA, ed. 1994. *History of Science and Technology: A Sampler of Centers and Collections of Distinction.* Binghamton, NY: Haworth Press; 1994. 124p. Also published In: *Science & Technology Libraries.* 1994; 14(4). (Entire issue on topic). ISSN: 0194-262X.

S388
STEINMETZ ARCHIVE. 1986. *Catalogue and Guide.* 3rd rev. ed. Amsterdam, NL: North Holland; 1974. 167p. (In Dutch). ISBN: 072048295X; LCCN: 75-503906; OCLC: 1365663. Enlarged ed. Amsterdam, NL: Steinmetz Archive; 1986. (Updated by its newsletter, *Bulletin van het Steinmetzarchief*).

S389
STELLA, E. 1986. *Working Space.* Cambridge, MA: Harvard University Press; 1986. 177p. ISBN: 0674959604; LCCN: 85046053.

S390
STENVERT, RONALD. 1991. The Use of Computer-Aided Design in Art- and Architectural History. See reference: BEST, H. *ET AL.*, eds. 1991. 68-74.

S391
STEPHAN, PAULA E.; LEVIN, SHARON G. 1992. *Striking the Mother Lode in Science: The Importance of Age, Place, and Time.* New York, NY: Oxford University Press; 1992. 194p. ISBN: 0195064054.

S392
STEPHENS, KAREN L. 1991. *Temporal Reasoning in Real-Time Experts.* University of New Brunswick; 1991. 182p. (M.C.S. Thesis; *DAI* file 35, Masters Abstracts, vol. 30/04: 1389. Available from: University Microfilms, Ann Arbor, MI (Order no. AADMM-66131).

S393
STEPHENSON, MARY SUE. 1992. *The American Archivist*, 1971-1990: A Demographic Analysis of the Articles. *The American Archivist.* 1992 Fall; 55: 538-561. ISSN: 0360-9081.

S394
STEPPI, H. 1989. *Computer Based Training: Plannung, Design, und Entwicklung interaktiver Lernprogramme* [CBT: Planning, Design and Development of Interactive Instructional Programs]. Stuttgart, DEU; 1989

S395
STERLING, CHRISTOPHER H.; HEAD, SYDNEY W. 1995. *Broadcasting in America: A Survey of Electronic Media.* Boston, MA: Houghton-Mifflin; 1995. 381p. LCCN: 95-776949.

S396
STERLING, CHRISTOPHER H.; KITTROSS, JOHN M. 1990. *Stay Tuned: A Concise History of American Broadcasting.* 2nd ed. Belmont, CA: Wadsworth; 1990. 562p. ISBN: 0534119042; LCCN: 89-16675.

S397
STERLING, PEON; SHAPIRO, EHUD. 1994. *The Art of Prolog; Advanced Programming* Techniques. Cambridge, MA: MIT Press; c1994. 5009p. ISBN: 0262193388; LCCN: 933049494.

S398
STERN, FRITZ, ed. 1956; repr. 1973. *The Varieties of History from Voltaire to the Present.* New York, NY: Vintage Books; 1973. 528p. ISBN: 039471962X; LCCN: 73-6547; OCLC: 1178887.

S399
STERN, NANCY B.; STERN, ROBERT A. 1978. *Computing in the Information Age.* New York, NY: 1978. ISBN: 0534005144.

S400
STERN, PAUL C.; KALOF, LINDA. 1996. *Evaluating Social Science Research.* 2nd ed. New York, NY: Oxford University Press; 1996. 279p. ISBN: 0195079698 (hbk.); 0195079701 (pbk.).

S401
STEVEN, GUNTER. 1995. Europe's Way toward the Information Society in the Electronic Age. Paper delivered before the joint FID/ASIS session, ASIS Annual Conference, October 11, 1995. Slide series 1-34 and 1A-8A supplied by the author, European Commission, DG XIII/E, Luxembourg.

S402
STEVEN P.; ROESCHEISEN, MARTIN; WINOGRAD, TERRY. 1996. Using Distributed Objects for Digital Library Interoperability. See reference: SCHATZ, B.; CHEN, H., eds. 1996. 61-66.

S403
STEVENS, NORMAN D. 1986. *The History of Information.* Advances in Librarianship, 14. San Diego, CA: Academic Press; 1986. ISBN: 0120246147.

S404
STEVENS, WESLEY M., ed. 1991/1992. *Bibliographic Access to Medieval and Renaissance Manuscripts: A Survey of Computerized Data Bases and Information Services.* Binghamton, NY: Haworth Press; c.1992. 196p. ISBN: 1-56024-224-8. Co-published in: *Primary Sources and Original Works.* 1991/1992; 1(3/4). ISSN: 1042-8216.

S405
STEVENSON, CHARLES. 1976. Approaches to Social Science History: Quantification in the Classroom. *Journal of Methods.* 1976; 1(2): 54-60. ISSN: 0024-8509.

S406
STEWART, DAVID W.; KAMINS, MICHAEL A. 1993. *Secondary Research: Information Sources and Methods.* 2nd ed. Thousand Oaks, CA: Sage Publications; 1993. 158p. (Applied Social Research Methods series, no. 4). ISBN: 0803950365; 0803950373 (pbk.); LCCN: 92-35501; OCLC: 26763286.

S407
STEWART, IAN. 1989. *Does God Play Dice? The Mathematics of Chaos.* London, UK: B. Blackwell; 1989. 317p. ISBN: 0631168478.

S408
STIEG, MARGARET F. 1980. The Nineteenth-century Information Revolution. *Journal of Library History.* 1980 Winter; 15: 22-52. ISSN: 0022-2259.

S409
STIEG, MARGARET F. 1981. The Information Needs of Historians. *College & Research Libraries.* 1981 November; 42(6): 549-560. ISSN: 0010-0870.

S410
STIEG, MARGARET F. 1983. Refereeing and the Editorial Process: The *AHR* and Webb. *Scholarly Publishing.* 1983 February; 14(2): 99-122. ISSN: 0036-634X.

S411
STIEG, MARGARET F. 1986. *The Origin and Development of Scholarly Historical Periodicals.* Tuscaloosa, AL: University of Alabama Press; 1986. 261p. ISBN: 0-8173- 0273-5.

S412
STIEG, MARGARET F. 1990. Information Science and the Humanities: The Odd Couple. See reference: PEMBER-TON, J. M.; PRENTICE, A. E., eds. 1990. 60-69.

S413
STIEG, MARGARET F. 1992. *Change and Challenge in Library and Information Science.* Chicago, Il: American Library Association; 1992. 206p. ISBN: 0838905765.

S414
STIEG, MARGARET F. 1993. The Dangers of Ahistoricism [History in Library and Information Science education]. *Journal of Education for Library and Information Science.* 1993 Fall; 34: 275-278. ISSN: 0748-5786.

S415
STIEG DALTON, MARGARET F. 1995. Refereeing of Scholarly Works for Primary Publishing. In: Williams, Martha E., ed. *Annual Review of Information Science and Technology* (30: 213-250). Medford, NJ: Information Today, Inc. for ASIS; 1995; 30: 213-250. ISBN: 1-57387-019-6; ISSN: 0066-4200; CODEN: ARISBC; LC no. 66-25096.

S416
STIELOW, FREDERICK J. 1985. Continuing Education and Information Management: Or, the Monk's Dilemma. *Provenance.* 1985 Spring; 3: 13-22. ISSN: 0739-4241 / 0095- 6201.

S417
STIELOW, FREDERICK J. 1986. *The Management of Oral History and Sound Archives.* Westport, CT: Greenwood Press; 1986. 158p. ISBN: 0-313-24442-1.

S418
STIELOW, FREDERICK J. 1991. Archival Theory Redux and Redeemed; Definition and Content toward a General Theory. *The American Archivist.* 1991 Winter; 54(1): 14-26. ISSN: 0360-9081.

S419
STIELOW, FREDERICK J. 1993. The Impact on Information Technology on Archival Theory: A Discourse on an Automation Pedagogy. *Journal of Education for Library and Information Science.* 1993; 34: 48-65. ISSN: 0748-5786.

S420
STIELOW, FREDERICK J. 1994. Library and Information Science Research. See reference: WIEGAND, W.; DAVIS, D., eds. 1994. 338-342.

S421
STIER, WINFRIED. 1991. Basic Concepts and New Methods of Time Series Analysis in Historical Social Research. See reference: BEST, H.; MOCHMAN, E.; THALLER, M., eds. 1991. 263-268.

S422
STILES, H. E. 1961. The Association Factor in Information Retrieval. *Journal of the Association of Computing Machinery.* 1961; 8(2): 271-279.

S423
STILL, JULIE. 1992. ABC-CLIO's History Databases on CD-ROM (Historical Abstracts and America: History and Life). *CD-ROM Professional.* 1992 May; 5(3): 83-87. ISSN: 1049-0833.

S424
STINCHCOMBE, CHARLES. 1997. *Roads from Past to Future: Charles Tilly—A Review Essay.* Lanham, MD: Rowan & Littlefield; 1997. ISBN: 0847684091 (hbk.); 0847084105 (pbk.); LCCN: 97-21729.

S425
STINSON, DOUGLAS R. 1995. *Cryptography. Theory and Practice.* In: Discrete Mathematics and its Applications series. Rosen, K. H., ed. Boca Raton, FL: CRC Press; 1995. 448p. ISBN: 0-8493-8521-0.

S426
STITES, JANET. Complexity. *Omni.* 1994 May; 16(8): 42-50. ISSN: 0149-8711.

S427
STOAN, STEPHEN K. 1984. Research and Library Skills: An Analysis and Interpretation. *College and Research Libraries.* 1984 March; 45(2): 99-109. ISSN: 0010-0870. See his: Historians and Librarians: A Response. *College & Research Libraries News.* 1986 September; 47: 503. ISSN: 0099-0086.

S428
STOAN, STEPHEN K. 1991. Research and Information Retrieval among Academic Researchers: Implications for Library Instruction. *Library Trends.* 1991 Winter; 39: 238-258. ISSN: 0024-2594.

S429
STOCK, BRIAN. 1983. *The Implications of Literacy. Written Language and Models of Interpretation in the Eleventh and Twelfth Centuries.* Princeton, NJ: Princeton University Press; 1983. 604p. ISBN: 0691053685; LCCN: 82-47616; OCLC: 8554299.

S430
STOCK, BRIAN. 1997. *Listening for the Text. On the Uses of the Past.* Philadelphia, PA: University of Pennsylvania Press; 1997. 208p. ISBN: 1612-1. B149

S431
STOCK, OLIVIERO, ed. 1997. *Spatial and Temporal Reasoning.* Boston, MA: Kluwer Academic Publishers; c1997. ISBN: 0792346440 (pbk.); LCCN: 97029914.

S432
STOCKING, GEORGE W., Jr., ed. 1984. *Functionalism Historicized: Essays on British Social Anthropology.* Madison, WI: University of Wisconsin Press; 1984. 244p. ISBN: 0299099008.

S433
STOCKING, GEORGE W., Jr., ed. 1985. *Objects and Others. Essays on Museums and Material Culture.* In: *History of Anthropology,* vol. 3. Madison, WI: University of Wisconsin Press; 1985. 255p. ISBN: 029910320X.

S434
STOLKE, VERENA. 1995. Talking Culture: New Boundaries, New Rhetoric of Exclusion in Europe. *Current Anthropology.* 1995 February; 36(1): 1-24. ISSN: 0011-3204.

S435
STONE, ALLUCQUERE ROSANNE. 1995. *The War of Desire and Technology at the Close of the Mechanical Age.* Cambridge, MA: MIT Press; 1995. 212p. ISBN: 0-262-19362-0.

S436
STONE, GAYNELL. 1987. *Spatial and Material Aspects of Culture: Ethnicity and Ideology in Long Island Gravestones, 1670-1820.* Stony Brook, NY: SUNY at Stony Brook; 1987. 417p. (Ph.D. dissertation; DAI, vol. 49/06-A: 1500). Available from: University Microfilms, Ann Arbor, MI (Order no. AAD88-13513).

S437
STONE, GERALD; SYLVAIN, PHILIP. 1990. *ArchiVISTA:* A New Horizon in Providing Access to Visual Records of the National Archives of Canada. *Library Trends.* 1990 Spring; 39: 737-750. ISSN: 0024-2594.

S438
STONE, LAWRENCE. 1979. The Revival of Narrative: Reflections of a New Old History. *Past and Present.* 1979; 85: 3-24. ISSN: 0031-2746.

S439
STONE, LAWRENCE. 1981. *The Past and Present.* London, UK: Routledge and Kegan Paul; 1981. 274p. ISBN: 0710006284; LCCN: 80-41657; OCLC: 7339264.

S440
STONE, LAWRENCE. 1991-1992. History and Post-Modernism. *Past and Present.* 1991; 131: 217-1218. See rejoinder by P. JOYCE and commentary by C. KELLY, to which Stone responded: History and Post-Modernism III. *Past and Present.* 1992; 135: 189- 194. ISSN: 0031-2746. See also a fourth contribution to this debate by G. SPIEGEL, 1992.

S441
STONE, LAWRENCE. 1993. The Future of History. See reference: BARROS, C., ed. 1995: 177-190.

S442
STONE, SUE. 1980. CRUS Humanities Research Programme. In: *Humanities Information Research: Proceedings of a Seminar*. Shefield, UK: University of Sheffield Centre for Research in User Studies; 1980. 15-16. (CRUS Occasional paper, 4) British Library Research and Development Department, report no. 5588.

S443
STONE, SUE. 1982. Humanities Scholars: Information Needs and Uses. *Journal of Documentation*. 1982 December; 38(4): 293-313. ISSN: 0022-0418.

S444
STORMORKEN, BJORN. 1985. *HURIDOCS: Human Rights Information and Documentation System*. A. McMorris, Asst. Dordrecht, NL; Lancaster, UK; Boston, MA: Martinus Nijhoff Publishers; 1985. 175p. ISBN: 90-247-3187-9.

S445
STOVER, MARK, ed. 1992. Electronic Information for the Humanities. In: *Library Trends*. 1992 Spring; 40: 575-830. (Entire issue of title topic). ISSN: 0024-2594.

S446
STOYAN, DIETRICH; STOYAN, HELGA. 1994. *Fraktale-Formen-Puntfelder*. Trans. *Fractals, Random Shapes, and Point Fields: Methods of Geometrical Statistics*. Chichester UK; New York, NY: Wiley; 1994. 389p. ISBN: 0471937576.

S447
STRANGELOVE, M.; KOVAS, D., eds. 1991-. *Directory of Electronic Journals, Newsletters and Academic Discussion Lists*. Washington, D.C.: Association of Research Libraries, Office of Scientific and Academic Publishing; 1991-. ISSN: 1057-1337. Available from: ARL, 1527 New Hampshire Ave. NW, Washington, DC 20036.

S448
STRASSMAN, PAUL A. 1985. *Information Payoff: The Transformation of Work in the Electronic Age*. New York, NY: Free Press; 1985. 298p. ISBN: 2029317207; LCCN: 84-26737.

S449
STRASSMAN, PAUL A. 1990. *The Business Value of Computers. An Executive's Guide*. New Canaan, CT: Information Economics Press; 1990. 530p. ISBN: 0-9620413-2-7; LCCN: 88-80753.

S450
STRASSMAN, PAUL A. 1995. *The Politics of Information Management: Policy Guidelines*. New Canaan, CT: Information Economics Press; 1995. ISBN: 0962041343; LCCN: 93-80110.

S451
STRATHERN, MARILYN, ed. 1995. *Shifting Contexts: Transformations in Anthropological Knowledge*. Conference on "The Uses of Knowledge," proceedings of the Association of Social Anthropologists of the Commonwealth, in Oxford, 1993. London, UK / New York, NY: Routledge; 1995. 193p. ISBN: 0415107946 (hbk.); 0415107954 (pbk.).

S452
STRAUB, DETMAR W. 1989. Validating Instruments in MIS Research. *MIS Quarterly*. 1989; 14: 147-170. ISSN: 0276-7783.

S453
STRAUSS, ANSELM L. 1982. Social Worlds and Legitimization Processes. *Studies in Symbolic Interaction*. 1982; 4: 171-190.

S454
STRAUSS, ANSELM L.; CORBIN, JULIET M. 1990. *Basics of Qualitative Research: Grounded Theory Procedures and Techniques*. Newbury Park, CA: Sage Publications; 1990. 220p. ISBN: 00803932502 (hbk.); 0803932510 (hbk.).

S455
STROETMANN, KARL A. 1991. Management and Economic Issues of Library and Information Services: A Review of the German Literature. *Journal of Information Science Principles & Practice*. 1991; 17(3): 161-173. ISSN: 0165-5515.

S456
STROGATZ, STEVEN. 1994. *Nonlinear Dynamics and Chaos*. Studies in Nonlinearity series. Reading, MA: Addison, Wesley, Longman; 1994. ISBN: 0-201-54344-3 (hbk.).

S457
STRUEVER, NANCY S. 1970. *The Language of History in the Renaissance: Rhetoric and Historical Consciousness in Florentine Humanism*. Princeton, NJ: Princeton University Press; 1970. 212p. ISBN: 0691061807; LCCN: 69-18072; OCLC: 96091.

S458
STRUEVER, NANCY S. 1974. The Study of Language and the Study of History. *Journal of Interdisciplinary History.* 1974; 4:401-415. ISSN: 0022-1953.

S459
STRUEVER, NANCY S. 1979. Historiography and Linguistics. See reference: IGGERS, G.; PARKER, eds. 1979. 127-150.

S460
STRUEVER, NANCY S. 1985. Historical Discourse. See reference: VAN DIJK, T. A., ed., 1985. 249-271.

S461
STUBBS, MICHAEL. 1983. *Discourse Analysis: The Socio-Linguistic Analysis of Natural Language.* Oxford, UK: B. Blackwell; 1983. 272p. (Language in Society series, 4). ISBN: 0631103813 (hbk.); 0631127631 (pbk.).

S462
STUDDERT-KENNEDY, GERALD. 1975. *Evidence and Explanation in Social Science: An Interdisciplinary Approach.* London, UK: Routledge and K. Paul; 1975. 246p. ISBN: 071008157X.

S463
STUNKEL, KENNETH R. 1998. The Lecture: A Powerful Tool for Intellectual Liberation. *The Chronicle of Higher Education.* 1998, April 26; 44(42): A52. ISSN: 0009-5982.

S464
SUBRAHMANIAN, V. S.; JAJODIA, SUSHIL, eds. 1996. *Multimedia Database Systems: Issues and Research Directions.* Berlin, DEU / New York, NY: Springer Verlag; 1996. 274p. ISBN: 3540587101.

S465
SUBRAHMANIAN, V. S.; MARCUS, SHERRY. 1996. Towards a Theory of Multimedia Database Systems. See reference: SUBRAHMANIAN, V. S.; JAJODIA, S., eds. 1996. 1-20.

S466
SUCHER, DAVID. 1995. *City Comforts: How to Build an Urban Village.* City Comfort Press; 1995. 176p. ISBN: 0964268000.

S467
SULLIVAN, WILLIAM M. 1995. *Work and Integrity: The Crisis and Promise of Professionalism in America.* New York, NY: Harper Business; c1995. 268p. ISBN: 0887307272; LCCN: 94037870.

S468
SUMMERS, RON; OPPENHEIM, CHARLES; MEADOWS, JACK; MCKNIGHT, CLIFF; KINNEL, MARGARET. 1999. Information Science in 2010: A Loughborough University View. See reference: BATES, M., ed. 1999. Pt. 2: 1153-1162.

S469
SUNDERLAND, J. 1989. The Catalog as Database: The Indexing of Information in Visual Archives. See reference: HAMBER, A.; MILES, J; VAUGHAN, W., eds. 1989. 130-143.

S470
SUNDSTROM, ERIC D; SUNDSTROM, MARY G. 1986. *Work Places: The Psychology of the Physical Environment in Offices and Factories.* New York, NY: Cambridge University Press; 1986. 461p. ISBN: 0521265452 (hbk.); 0521319471 (pbk.); LCCN: 85-457.

S471
SUSMAN, WARREN. 1984. *Culture as History: The Transformation of American Society in the Twentieth Century.* New York, NY: Pantheon Books; 1984. 321p. ISBN: 039453364X (hbk.); 0394721616 (pbk.).

S472
SVENONIUS, ELAINE. 1990. Design of Controlled Vocabularies. See reference: KENT, A., ed. 1990. 45. 82-109.

S473
SVENONIUS, ELAINE, ed. 1989. *The Conceptual Foundations of Descriptive Cataloging.* Conference proceedings, UCLA, Feb. 14-15, 1987, sponsored by the Council of Library Resources. San Diego, CA: Academic Press; 1989. 241p. ISBN: 0126782105.

S474
SWADE, DORON D. 1991. Napoleon's Waistcoat Button: Modern Artifacts and Museum Culture. In: *Museum Collecting Policies in Modern Science and Technology.* Proceedings of a Seminar held at the Science Museum, London, 3 November 1988. London, UK: Science Museum; 1991. 52p. ISBN: 0901805378. LCCN: 92-35562; OCLC: 27817558.

S475
SWADE, DORON D. 1993. Collecting Software: Preserving Information in an Object-Centered Culture. See reference: ROSS, S.; HIGGS, E., eds.; 1993. 93-103. Illustrated and expanded from shorter version in *History and Computing*. 1992; 4(3). ISSN: 0957-0144.

S476
SWAIN, M. J. 1993-95. Interactive Indexing into Image Databases. In: *Storage and Retrieval for Image and Video Databases* (pp. 95-103). Proceedings of SPIE conference, February 1993. Bellingham, WA: SPIE; 1993-95. ISSN: 1084-2926.

S477
SWAIN, M. J.; BALLARD, D. H. 1991. Color Indexing. *International Journal of Computer Vision*. 1991; 7(1): 11-32. ISSN: 0920-5691.

S478
SWANSON, DON R. 1986. Undiscovered public knowledge. *Library Quarterly*. 1986; 56: 103-118. ISSN: 0024-2519.

S479
SWANSON, DON R. 1988. Information Retrieval and the Future of an Illusion. *Journal of the American Society for Information Science*. 1988 March; 39(2): 92-98. ISSN: 0002-8231.

S480
SWANSON, DON R. 1993. Intervening in the Life Cycles of Scientific Knowledge. *Library Trends*. 1993; 41: 505-631. ISSN: 0024-2594.

S481
SWARTZBERG, SUSAN G., ed. 1983. *Conservation in the Library: A Handbook of Use and Care of Traditional and non-Traditional Materials*. Westport, CT: Greenwood Press; 1983.

S482
SWEDISH SOCIAL SCIENCE DATA ARCHIVE (SSD). 1990. *SSD Data Collections*. Goteberg, SE: SSD; 1990. (Updated by the SSD newsletter, *SSDkontkat*) .

S483
SWEETLAND, JAMES H. 1983. *America: History and Life*—A Wide Ranging Database. *Database*. 1983; 6(4): 15-29.ISSN: 0162-4105.

S484
SWEIG, RONALD W. 1992. Virtual Records and Real History. *History and Computing*. 1992; 4: 174-182. ISSN: 0957-0144.

S485
SWEIG, RONALD W. 1993. Beyond Content: Electronic Fingerprints and the Use of Documents. See reference: ROSS, S.; HIGGS, E., eds., 1993. 251-259.

S486
SWIDLER, ANN. 1996. Geertz's Ambiguous Legacy. *Contemporary Sociology*. 1996 May; 25(3): 299-304. ISSN: 0094-3061.

S487
SWIERENGA, ROBERT P. 1970a. *Quantification in American History: Theory and Research*. Athenaeum, 161. New York, NY: Athenaeum; 1970. 417p. LCCN: 76-108827; OCLC: 162427.

S488
SWIERENGA, ROBERT P. 1970b. Clio and Computers: A Survey of Computerized Research in History. *Computers and the Humanities*. 1970; 5: 1-21. ISSN: 0010-4817.

S489
SWIERENGA, ROBERT P. 1974a. Computers and American History: The Impact of the "New" Generation. *Journal of American History*. 1974; 60(4): 1045-70. ISSN: 0021-8723.

S490
SWIERENGA, ROBERT P. 1974b. Computers and Comparative History. *Journal of Interdisciplinary History*. 1974; 5(2): 267-86. ISSN: 0022-1953.

S491
SWIERENGA, ROBERT P. 1984. Bibliographic Instruction in Historical Methods Courses: Kent State University. *The History Teacher*. 1984 May; 17(3): 391-397. ISSN: 0018-2745.

S492
SYKES, LISA. 1997. History of the Future. *Geographical Magazine*. 1997 Feb.; 69(2): 28-30. Note: Virtual Heritage Exhibits, i.e., Virtual Stonehenge Project.

S493

SZRAJBERT, T. 1990. CDMS: The Computerization of the British Museum Collections. *Computers and the History of Art.* 1990; 1(1): 9-19. ISBN: 3-7186-5103-3.

S494

SZRAJBERT, T. 1992. European Museum Documentation Strategies and Standards Conference, Eliot College, University of Kent, Canterbury, September 2-6, 1991. *Computers and the History of Art.* 1992; 3(1): 75-83. ISBN: 3-7186-5363-X; ISSN: 1048-6798.

-T-

T1

TABAH, A. N.; SABER, A. J. 1990. Chaotic Structures in Informetrics. See reference: EGGHE, L; ROUSSEAU, R., eds. 1990. 281-289.

T2

TABER, CHARLES S. 1991. *The Policy Arguer: A Computational Model of United States Foreign Policy Belief Systems, 1949-1960.* Champaign-Urbana, IL: University of Illinois; 1991. (Ph.D. dissertation; *DAI*, vol. 53/03-A: 1070). Available from: University Microfilms, Ann arbor, MI (Order no. AAD91-24496).

T3

TAGG, JOHN. 1988. *The Burden of Representation. Essays on Photographies and Histories.* Amherst, MA: University of Massachusetts Press; 1988. 242p. ISBN: 087023625 (hbk.); 0870236261 (pbk.).

T4

TAGUE[-SUTCLIFFE], JEAN. 1981. The Success-Breeds-Success Phenomenon and Bibliometric Processes. *Journal of the American Society for Information Science.* 1981; 32: 280-286. ISSN: 0002-8231; CODEN: AISJB6.

T5

TAGUE-SUTCLIFFE, JEAN. 1994. Quantitative Methods in Documentation. See reference: VICKERY, B. C., ed. 1994. 147-188.

T6

TAGUE-SUTCLIFFE, JEAN. 1995. *Measuring Information. An Information Services Perspective.* San Diego, CA: Academic Press; 1995. 206p. ISBN: 0-12-682660-9.

T7

TAINTER, JOSEPH A.; BAGLEY, BONNIE TAINTER, eds. 1996. *Evolving Complexity and Environmental Risk in the Prehistoric Southwest.* Santa Fe, NM: Santa Fe Institute (SFI); 1996. (Santa Fe Institute Studies in the Science of Complexity). ISBN: 0-201-52763-4 (hbk.); 0-201-52766-9 (pbk.). See also reference: GUMERMAN, G. J.; GELL-MANN, M., eds. 1994.

T8

TANNENBAUM, ROBERT S. 1988. *Computing in the Humanities and Social Sciences.* Rockville, MD: Computer Science Press; 1988. 2 vols. ISBN: 088175174X; LCCN: 87-33848; OCLC: 17202901.

T9

TANNER, MARTIN A. 1993/1996. *Tools for Statistical Inference: Methods for the Exploration of Posterior Distributions and Likelihood Functions.* 2nd ed. New York, NY: Springer-Verlag; 1993. 156p. ISBN: 0387940316. 3rd ed.; 1996. ISBN: 0387946888.

T10

TANSELLE, G. THOMAS. 1991. *Textual Criticism and Scholarly Editing.* Charlottesville, VA: University of Virginia Press; 1991. 353p. ISBN: 0813913039.

T11

TANUR, JUDITH M., ed. 1992. *Questions about Questions: Inquiries into the Cognitive Bases of Surveys.* New York, NY: Russel Sage Foundation; 1992. 306p. ISBN: 0871548429.

T12

TANUR, JUDITH M.; LEHMAN, E. L., eds. 1972/1978. *Statistics: A Guide to the Unknown.* San Francisco CA: Holden Day; 1972. 430p. ISBN: 0816286042 (hbk.); 08162865942 (pbk.). 2nd ed; 1978. 496p. ISBN: 0816286051.

T13

TARROW, SIDNEY. 1995. Bridging the Quantitative-Qualitative Divide in Political Science—*Designing Social Inquiry: Scientific Inference in Qualitative Research* [Review essay]. The *American Political Science Review.* 1995 June; 89(2): 471-478. ISSN: 0003-0554.

T14
TATEM, JILL; ROLLISON, JEFF. 1986. *Thesaurus of University Terms.* Chicago, IL: Society of American Archivists; 1986. 46p. (Based on Case-Western Reserve University's archives).

T15
TAYEB, MONIR. 1994. Organizations and National Culture: Methodology Considered. *Organizational Studies.* 1994; 15 (3): 429-446. ISSN: 0170-8406.

T16
TAYLOR, HUGH A. 1972. Clio in the Raw: Archival Materials and the Teaching of History. *The American Archivist.* 1972; 35: 317-330. ISSN: 0360-9081.

T17
TAYLOR, HUGH A. 1977. The Discipline of History and the Education of an Archivist. *The American Archivist.* 1977; 40: 395-402. ISSN: 0360-9081.

T18
TAYLOR, HUGH A. 1987-1988. Transformation in the Archives: Technological Adjustment of Paradigm Shift? *Archivaria.* 1987-1988 Winter; 25: 12-28. ISSN: 0318-6954.

T19
TAYLOR, HUGH A. 1988. "My Very Act and Deed": Some Reflections on the Role of Textual Records in the Conduct of Affairs. *The American Archivist.* 1988; 51(4): 456-485. ISSN: 0360-9081.

T20
TAYLOR, HUGH A. 1993. Recycling the Past: The Archivist in the Age of Ecology. *Archivaria.* 1993 Spring; 35: 201-213. ISSN: 0318-6954.

T21
TAYLOR, K. W,; CHAPPELL, N. L. 1980. Multivariate Analysis of Qualitative Data. *Canadian Review of Sociology and Anthropology.* 1980; 17: 93-108. ISSN: 0008-4948.

T22
TAYLOR, LORETTA M. 1990. *Fabric in Women's Costumes from 1860 to 1880: A Comparison of Fashion Periodicals and Selected Canadian Museum Collections.* Edmonton, AA: University of Alberta; 1990. 202p. (MSC. thesis; *DAI,* file 35, Masters Abstracts, vol. 30/04: 1066). Available from: University Microfilms, Ann Arbor, MI (Order no. AADMM-65052).

T23
TAYLOR, M. F. 1988. Standards for the Documentation and Description of Machine-Readable Files: Some UK Initiatives. See reference: GENET, J.-P., ed. 1988. 103-118.

T24
TAYLOR, ROBERT S. 1986. *Value-added Processes in Information Systems.* Norwood, NJ: Ablex; 1986. 257p. ISBN: 0893912735.

T25
TAYLOR, ROBERT S. 1991. Information Use Environments. In: Dervin, Brenda., ed. *Progress in Communication Sciences.* Norwood, NJ: Ablex Publication Corporation; 1991; 10: 218-255.

T26
TEDD, LUCY A. 1987. Computer-Based Library Systems: A Review of the Last Twenty-One Years. *Journal of Documentaiton* (UK). 1987 June; 43 (2): 145-165. ISSN: 0022-0418.

T27
TEMIN, PETER. 1991. *Inside the Business Enterprise: Historical Perspectives on the Use of Information.* Chicago, IL / London, UK: University of Chicago Press; 1991. 260p. ISBN: 0226792021; 0226792048 (pbk.); LCCN: 91-27377; OCLC: 24174331.

T28
TENENBAUM, GERALD. 1995. *Introduction à la théorie analytique et probabiliste des nombres.* Trans.: *Introduction to Analytic and Probabilistic Number Theory.* Cambridge, UK/ New York, NY: Cambridge University Press; 1995. 448p. (Cambridge Studies in Advanced Mathematics, 46). ISBN: 0521412617; LCCN: 94046436.

T29
TENNER, EDWARD. 1992a. From Slip to Chip: How Evolving Techniques of Information Gathering, Storage, and Retrieval Have Shaped the Way We Do Mental Work. *Microform Review.* 1992 Summer; 21 (3): 123-127. ISSN: 0002-6530.

T30
TENNER, EDWARD. 1992b. "Information Age" at the National Museum of American History. 1992; 33 (4): 780-87. (Exhibition review). ISSN: 0040-165X. See reference: LUBAR, S. 1993.

T31
TENOPIR, CAROL. 1985. Full-text Database Retrieval Performance. *Online Review*. 1985 April; 9(2): 149-64. ISSN: 0309-314X.

T32
TENOPIR, CAROL. 1988. Users and Uses of Full-text Databases. In: *Online Information 88. Proceedings of the 12th International Online Information meeting, London, 6-9 December 1988*. Oxford, UK: Learned Information (Europe); 1988; 263-270. 2 vols. ISBN: 0904933687.

T33
TENOPIR, CAROL; RO, JUNG S. 1990. *Full Text Databases*. New York, NY: Greenwood Press; 1990. 251p. ISBN: 0313263035.

T34
TER MEULEN, ALICE G. B. 1995. *Representing Time in natural Language. The Dynamic Interpretation of Tense and Aspect*. Cambridge, MA: Bradford Book; 1995. 160p. ISBN: 0-262-20099-6. Distributed by MIT Press.

T35
TERDIMAN, RICHARD. 1993. *Present Past: Modernity and the Memory Crisis*. Ithaca, NY: Cornell University Press; 1993. 389p. ISBN: 0801428971 (hbk.); 0801481325 (pbk.).

T36
TESSIER, GEORGES. 1952. *La Diplomatique* [Diplomatics]. Paris, FR: Presses Universitaires de France; 1952. 125p. LCCN: 53024649.

T37
TEUHOLA, JUKKA. 1996. Path Signatures: A Way to Speed Up Recursion in Relational Databases. *IEEE Transactions on Knowledge and Data Engineering*. 1996; 8 no. 3: 446-454. ISSN: 1041-4347.

T38
TEXT ENCODING INITIATIVE (TEI). 1988. *Text Encoding Initiative: Initiative for Text Encoding and a Common Interchange Format for Literary and Linguistic Data*. Document TEI J 3. Sperberg-McQueen, C.M.; Burnard, L., eds. Chicago, IL; Oxford, UK: TEI. 1988 September 4. 2p. (Irregular document series). Available from: TEI, University of Illinois, Chicago Circle, Chicago, IL; or TEI, Computing Center, Oxford University, Oxford, UK.

T39
THALLER, MANFRED. 1976. Descriptor. Probleme der Entwicklung eines Programmsystems zum computerunterstutzen Auswertung mittelalterlicher Bildquellen [Descriptor. Problem of the Development of a Systems Program for Computing Evidence from Medieval Image Collections]. In: *Die Funktion der schriftlichen Quellen in der Sachkulturforschung*. Vienna, AT: Institut für mittelalterliche Realienkunde Osterreichs; 1976. 167-195. (Ver öffentlichungen des Instituts für mittelalterliche Realienkunde Osterreichs, 1). (In German). ISBN: 3700101457; LCCN: 81-451380; OCLC: 7280565.

T40
THALLER, MANFRED. 1980. Automation on Parnassus. *CLIO*—A Databank Oriented System for Historians. *Historische Sozialforschung / Historical Social Research* (DEU). 1980; 15: 40-65. ISSN: 0172-6404.

T41
THALLER, MANFRED. 1983. Ein Neues Eingabegeraet: Die Kurzweil Data Entry Machine (KDEM) [A New Advance: KDEM]. *Nachrichten fur Dokumentation* (DEU). December 1983; 34(6): 283-87. (In German). ISSN: 0027-7436.

T42
THALLER, MANFRED, ed. 1986a. *Datenbanken und Datenverwaltungssysteme als Werkzeuge Historische Forschung. Historisch-Sozialwissenschafte Studien* [Data Bases and Data Management Systems as Tools for Historical Science: Historical Social Science Studies]. St. Katharinen [Göttingen, DEU]: Max Planck Institut für Geschichte; 1986. (Halbgraue Reihe zur historischen Fackinformatik. Historisch-Sozialwissenschaftliche Forschungen, Band 20). (In German). ISBN: 3-922661-30-0.

T43
THALLER, MANFRED. 1986c. A Draft Proposal for the Coding of Machine Readable Sources. *Historische Sozialforschung / Historical Social Research* (DEU). 1986 October; 40: 3-46. ISSN: 0172-6404.

T44
THALLER, MANFRED. 1987. The Daily Life in the Middle Ages: Editions of Sources and Data Processing. *Medium Aevum Quotidianum Newsletter* (DEU). 1987; 10: 6-28. OCLC: 30949256.

T45
THALLER, MANFRED. 1988a. A Draft Proposal for a Format Exchange Program. See reference: GENET, J.-P., ed. 1988. 329-375.

T46

THALLER, MANFRED, ed. 1988b. *Database Oriented Source Editions*. Papers from Two Sessions at the 23rd International Congress on Medieval Studies, Kalamazoo, MI, 5-8 May, 1988. Kalamazoo, MI: Western Michigan University / Göttingen, DE: Max Planck Institut für Geschichte; 1988. 54p. Available from the Max-Planck-Institut fur Geschichte, Hermann-Foge Weg 11, D-2400 Göttingen, DE.

T47

THALLER, MANFRED. 1988c. Data Bases vs. Critical Editions. See reference: THALLER, M., ed. 1988a. 1-8.

T48

THALLER, MANFRED. 1989. The Need for a Theory of Historical Computing. See reference: DENLEY, P., *ET AL.*, eds. 1988. 2-11.

T49

THALLER, MANFRED. 1990. The Historical Workstation Project. In: Metz, R.; Van Cauwenbergh, E.; Van der Voort, R., eds. *Proceedings of the 10th International Economic History Congress* [Leuven, August 1990]. Leuven, BE: Leuven University Press; 1990. 118p. (Historical Information Systems, vol. B12b). ISBN: 9061863880; OCLC: 30885116.

T50

THALLER, MANFRED. 1991a. The Historical Workstation Project. *Computers and the Humanities* (NL). 1991; 25(2-3): 149-162. ISSN: 0010-4817.

T51

THALLER, MANFRED. 1991b. The Need for Standards: Data Modelling and Exchange. See reference: GREEN-STEIN, D. I., ed. 1991. 1-18.

T52

THALLER, MANFRED. 1991c. *Klieu 3.1.1. Ein Datenbanksystem*.(Electronic shareware). St. Katharinen [Göttingen, DEU]: Scripta Mercaturae Verlag for the Max-Planck-Institut für Geschichte; 1991. (Halbgraue Reihe zur historischen Fackinformatik. Serie B: Historische Quellenkunden, Band B1). (Diskette).

T53

THALLER, MANFRED. 1991/1992. The Historical Workstation Project. In: *Historische Sozialforschung / Historical Social Research* (DEU). 1991/1992; 16: 51-61. ISSN: 0172-6404.

T54

THALLER, MANFRED. 1992a. The Historical Workstation Project. SMETS, J., ed., 1992. 251-250. (Still another version was distributed by the author at the 1992 AHC Conference, Graz. 20p.).

T55

THALLER, MANFRED, ed. 1992b. *Images and Manuscripts in Historical Computing*. St. Katharinen [Göttingen]: Scripta Mercaturae Verlag for the Max-Planck-Institut für Geschichte; 1992. (Halbgraue Reihe zur historischen Fackinformatik. Serie A: Historische Quellenkunden, Band 14). ISBN: 3-928134-53-1.

T56

THALLER, MANFRED. 1992c. The Need for Standards: Data Modeling and Exchange. See reference: GREEN-STEIN, D., ed. 1992. 1-18.

T57

THALLER, MANFRED. 1992d. The Processing of Manuscripts. See reference: THALLER, M.,ed. 1992a. 97-121.

T58

THALLER, MANFRED. 1993a. Levels of "Computing in History" Curricula. See reference: DAVIS, V. *ET AL.*, eds. 1993. 5-9.

T59

THALLER, MANFRED. 1993b. The Archive[s] on the Top of your Desk? On Self-Documenting Image Files. See reference: FIKFAK, J.; JARITZ, G., eds. 1993. 21-44.

T60

THALLER, MANFRED. 1994. What is "Source Oriented Data Processing"; what is a "Historical Computer Science"? See reference: OLDERVOLL, J., ed. 1994. 30-43.

T61

THALLER, MANFRED. [199-]. "Virtual Reality?" The Mind of the Historian and the Conflict between "Data" and "Reality". See reference: BOONSTRA, O. *ET AL.*, eds. [199-, forthcoming].

T62

THALLER, MANFRED. 1996 [199-]. Towards a Theory of Historical Computing [commentary]. See reference: BORODKIN, L., ed. 1996: English abstract, 18. Commentary in Russian.1996; 86-91.

T63

THALLER, MANFRED, ed. 1986. *Datenbanken und datenverwaltungssysteme als werkzeuge historische forschung. Historisch-sozialwissenschafte studien* [Data bases and data management systems as tools for historical science: Historical Social Science Studies]. Halbgraue reihe zur historischen Fackinformatik. (Historisch-sozialwissenschaftliche forschungen, Band 20). St. Katharinen [Göttingen, DEU]: Max-Planck Institut für Geschichte; 1986.

T64

THALLER, MANFRED; MULLER, ALBERT, eds. 1989. *Computer in den Geisteswissenschaften: Konzepte und Berichte* [Computers in Historical Science: Concepts and Report] Frankfurt am Main, DEU: Campus Verlag; 1989. 336p. (Studien zur Historischen Sozialwissenschaft, Band 7). ISBN: 3593338815; LCCN: 90-203665; OCLC: 22908843.

T65

THAYER, RICHARD H., ed. 1988. *Software Engineering Project Management.* Los Alamitos, CA: IEEE; 1988. 512p. ISBN: 0-8186-0751-3.

T66

THAYER, RICHARD H.; DORFMAN, MERLIN, eds. 1997. *Software Requirements Engineering.* 2nd ed. Los Alamitos, CA: IEEE; 1997. 540p. ISBN: 0-8186-7738-4.

T67

THELLEN, DAVID P., ed. 1989. Introduction. Memory and American History. In: *Journal of American History.* 1989; 75(4): 1117-29. (Entire issue on title topic). ISSN: 0021-8723. Republished as *Memory and American History.* Bloomington, IN: Indiana University Press; 1990. 156p. ISBN: 0253359406 (hbk.); 0253205700 (pbl.); LCCN: 89-024667.

T68

THERNSTROM, STEPHAN T. 1964. *Poverty and Progress: Social Mobility in a Nineteenth-century City.* New York, NY: Athenaeum/Cambridge, MA: Harvard University Press; 1964. 286 p.

T69

THERNSTROM, STEPHAN T. 1971. Reflections on the New Urban History. *Daedalus.* 1971 Spring; 16: 359-376. ISSN: 0011-5266.

T70

THERNSTROM, STEPHAN T.; DELZELL, CHARLES F. 1977. The New Urban History. In: Delzell, Charles F., ed. *The Future of History: Essays in the Vanderbilt University Centennial Symposium* (pp. 43-51). Centennial Symposium on the Future of History. Nashville, TN: Vanderbilt University Press; 1977. 263p. ISBN: 0826512054; LCCN: 76-48199.

T71

THERNSTROM, STEPHAN T.; SENNETT, RICHARD, eds. 1969. *Nineteenth-century Cities: Essays in the New Urban History.* Yale [University] Conference on the Nineteenth-century Industrial City; 1968. New Haven, CT: Yale University Press; 1969. 430p. ISBN: 0300011512 (pbk.).

T72

THESAURUS ARTIS UNIVERSALIS; COMITÉ INTERNATIONAL D'HISTOIRE DE L'ART. 1989. *A Methodological Approach to Producing a Historical / Geographical Databank.* Papaldo, S.; Signore, O., eds. Rome, IT: Multigrafica Editrice; 1989.

T73

THESAURUS ARTIS UNIVERSALIS; COMITÉ INTERNATIONAL D'HISTOIRE DE L'ART. 1992. *International Database of Artists Biographical Data.* Thuiller, J.; Clergeau, M.-F., eds. Goodmna, J.; Baca, M., trans. Los Angeles, CA: J. Paul Getty Trust; 1992.

T74

THIBAULT, PAUL J. 1997. *Re-reading Saussure: The Dynamics of Signs in Social Life.* London, UK: Routledge; 1997. 360p. ISBN: 0415104106 (hbk.); 0415104114 (pbk.).

T75

THIBIDEAU, KENNETH. 1991. To Be or Not to Be: Archives for Electronic Records. See reference: BEARMAN, D., ed. 1991. 1-13.

T76

THIEL, THOMAS J. 1991. Document Indexing for Image-based Optical Information Systems. *Document Image Automation.* 1991; 11(2): 82-88. ISSN: 1054-9692.

T77

THOMAS, DAVID H. 1994. Business Functions: Toward a Methodology. See reference: UNIVERSITY OF PITTSBURGH. 1994. (Paper no. 7: 1-25).

T78
THOMAS, DAVID HAYWARD. 1992. *Archival Information Processing for Sound Recordings: The Design of a Database for the Rodgers & Hammerstein Archives of Recorded Sound.* Canton, MA: Music Library Association; 1992. 132p. ISBN: 0914954458.

T79
THOMAS, DAVID HURST. [1974]. *Predicting the Past: An Introduction to Anthropological Archeaology.* New York, NY: Holt, Rinehart, and Winston; [1974]. 84p. ISBN: 0030911540.

T80
THOMAS, DAVID HURST. 1976. *Figuring Anthropology: First Principles of Probability and Statistics.* New York, NY: Holt, Rinehart, and Winston; 1976. 532p. ISBN: 0030028566; LCCN: 75-42101.

T81
THOMAS, MICHAEL. 1985. In Search of Culture: Holy Grail or Gravy Train? *Personnel Management.* 1985 September: 17(9): 24-27. ISSN: 0031-5761.

T82
THOMAS, S.; MINTZ, A., eds. 1998. *The Virtual and the Real: Media in the Museum.* Washington, D.C.: The American Association of Museums; 1998.

T83
THOMPSON, EDWARD P. 1963/1966/1986. *The Making of the English Working Class.* London, UK: Gollaway; 1963. 848p. Reprint. New York, NY: Vintage; 1966. Rev. ed. London, UK: Penguin; 1968. 958p. LCCN: 75-397165.

T84
THOMPSON, EDWARD P. 1972. Anthropology and the Discipline of Historical Context. *Midland History* (UK). 1971; 1: 40-53. ISSN: 0047-729X.

T85
THOMPSON, EDWARD P. 1978. *The Poverty of Theory and Other Essays.* New York, NY: Merlin Press; 1978. 406p. ISBN: 0850362318; 0850362326 (pbk.); OCLC: 4829990.

T86
THOMPSON, JAMES B. 1990. *Design Evolution Management: A Design Methodology for Representing and Utilizing Design Rationale.* Urbana-Champaign, IL: University of Illinois; 1990. 195p. (Ph.D. dissertation; *DAI*, vol. 51/12-B: 5069). Available from: University Microfilms, Ann Arbor, MI (Order no. AAD91-14440).

T87
THOMPSON, JEREMY, ed. 1993. *Virtual Reality: An International Directory of Research Projects.* Westport, CT: Meckler; c1993. 235p. ISBN: 088736862X; LCCN: 93015445.

T88
THOMPSON, JOSEPH B. 1979. *Analyzing Psychological Data.* New York, NY: Scribner; 1979. 310p. ISBN: 0684159813.

T89
THORNDYKE, P. W. 1977. Cognitive Structures in Comprehension and Memory of Narrative Discourse. *Cognitive Psychology.* 1977; 7: 77-110. ISSN: 0010-0285.

T90
THORNDYKE, P. W.; HAYES-ROTH, B. 1979. The Use of Schemata in the Acquisition and Transfer of Knowledge. *Cognitive Psychology.* 1979; 11: 82-106. ISSN: 0010-0285.

T91
THORNTON, GLENDA A. 1993. *An Examination of the Relationship between Published Book Reviews and the Circulation of Books at an Academic Library.* Denton, TX: University of North Texas; December 1993; 87p. (Ph.D. Dissertation in Higher Education). (Copy sent courtesy of the author). Available from University Microfilms, Ann Arbor, MI.

T92
THORVALDSEN, GUNNAR; RIISE, ROGER. 1995. Using a Text-to-Speech Converter to Proofread Historical Source Material. See reference: JARTIZ, G. *ET AL.*, eds. 1995. 264-270.

T93
TIBBO, HELEN R. 1989. *Abstracts, Online Searching and the Humanities: An Analysis of the Structure and Content of Abstracts of Historical Discourse.* College Park, MD: University of Maryland College of Library and Information Services; 1989. 3 vols.; 879p. (Ph.D. dissertation. *DAI*, 50/09-A: 2687). Available from University Microfilms, Ann Arbor, MI (Order no. AAD89-24240).

T94
TIBBO, HELEN R. 1991. Information Systems, Services, and Technology for the Humanities. In: Williams, Martha E., ed. *Annual Review of Information Science and Technology*: volume 26. Medford, NJ: Information Today, Inc. for ASIS; 1991. 287-346. ISBN: 1-57387-019-6; ISSN: 0066-4200; CODEN: ARISBC; LC no. 66-25096

T95
TIBBO, HELEN R. 1992. Abstracting across the Disciplines. A Content analysis of Abstracts from the National Sciences, the Social Sciences, and the Humanities with Implications for Abstracting Standards and Online Information Retrieval. *Library & Information Science Research*. 1992; 14: 31-56. ISSN: 0740-8188.

T96
TIBBO, HELEN R. 1993. *Abstracting, Information Retrieval, and the Humanities: Providing Access to Historical Literature*. Chicago, IL: American Library Association; 1993. 263p. (ACRL Publications in Librarianship, 48). ISBN: 0-8389-3430-7.

T97
TIBBO, HELEN R. [199- forthcoming]. Indexing for the Humanities. *Journal of the American Society for Information Science*. [199-]; ms. 31p. (Pre-publication ms. courtesy of the author).

T98
TIBBO, HELEN R. 1994. The Epic Struggle: Subject Retrieval from Large Bibliographic Databases. *The American Archivist*. 1994 Spring [1995]; 57(2): 310-326. ISSN: 0360-9081.

T99
TIBBO, HELEN R. 1995. Interviewing Techniques for Remote Reference: Electronic Versus Traditional Environments. *American Archivist*. 1995 Summer; 58: 294-310. ISSN: 0360-9081.

T100
TICHY, PAVEL. 1974. On Popper's Definitions of Verisimilitude. *The British Journal of the Philosophy of Science*. 1974; 25: 155-160. ISSN: 0031-8248.

T101
TICHY, PAVEL. 1978. Verisimilitude Redefined. *Synthese*. 1978; 38: 175-198.

T102
TIKHONOV, A. N.; DOLGOV, O. A.; LUK'IANOV, A. V.; TSUKANOV, N. A. 1990. Integrator Luk'ianova v istorii Vychislitel'noi Tekhniki [V. S. Luk'ianov's Integrator in the History of Computational Technology]. *Voprosy Istorii Estestvoznanija i Tekhniki* (Moscow, RU). 1990; 1: 49-57. (In Russian; English summaries). ISSN:0507-3367/0205-9606; LCCN: 81-643157; OCLC: 7695384.

T103
TILLY, CHARLES. 1981. *As Sociology Meets History*. New York, NY: Academic Press; 1981. 237p. ISBN: 0126912807.

T104
TILLY, CHARLES. 1984. *Big Structures, Large Processes, Huge Comparisons*. New York, NY: Russell Sage Foundation; 1984. 176p. ISBN: 0871548798.

T105
TILLY, CHARLES. 1987. Formalization and Quantification in Historical Analysis. See reference: JARAUSCH, K. H.; SCHRADER, W. H., eds. 1987. 19-29.

T106
TILLY, CHARLES. 1994. Remapping History [Commentary]. See reference: BOYARIN, J. 1994.

T107
TILLY, CHARLES. 1995. *Popular Contention in Great Britain, 1758-1834*. Cambridge, MA: Harvard University Press; 1995. 476p. ISBN: 06774689801; LCCN: 94-41325. See review of Tilly's work by STINCHCOMBE, C.

T108
TILLY, CHARLES, ed. [1995]. *Citizenship, Identity and Social History*. In: *International Review of Social History*, supplement 3. Cambridge, UK: Cambridge University Press; [1995]. 236p. ISBN: 052155814X (pbk.).

T109
TILLY, LOUISE A.; COHEN, M. 1982. Does the Family Have a History? A Review of Theory and Practice in Family History. *Social Science History*. 1982; 6: 131-180. ISSN: 0145-5532.

T110
TILLY, LOUISE A.; TILLY, CHARLES, eds. 1981. *Class Conflict and Collective Action*. Beverly Hills, CA: Sage Publications for Social Science History Assn.; 1981. 260p. (New Approaches to Social Science History, 1). ISBN: 080391587X (hbk.); 0803915888 (pbk.).

T111
TIMES. 1994. Peace Move over History Changes. *Times Educational Supplement* (UK). 1994 September 16; 4081: 4. ISSN: 0040-7887.

T112
TIRADO, THOMAS C., comp. 1992-. *Index to the Computerized Information Retrieval System on Columbus and the Age of Discovery* [Electronic file]. Millersville, PA: Columbian Quincentenary Project, Millersville State University; 1992-.

T113
TOBIN, YISHAI, ed. 1989. *From Sign to Text: A Semiotic View of Communication* Amsterdam, NL / Philadelphia, PA: J. Benjamin; 1989. 545p. (Foundations of Semiotics, vol. 20). ISBN: 902723292X.

T114
TOCK, BENOIT-MICHEL. 1997a. Les mutations du vocabulaire latin des chartes au Xe siècle. [Mutations of Latin Vocabulary in 10th-century charters]. *Bibliotheque de l'École des Chartres* (FR). 1997; 155: 119-148. (In French). LC call no. D111.B5.

T115
TOCK, BENOIT-MICHEL. 1997b. L'utilité des bases de données diplomatiques pout l'étude des généalogies [The Utility of Diplomatics Databases for the Study of Geneaologies]. (In French). See reference: BOURIN, M.; CHAREILLE, P., eds. 1997. 11-15.

T116
TODOROV, TZVETAN. 1967. *Litterateur et Signification* (Literature and Signification [Semiotics]). Paris, FR: Larouse; 1967. 120p. LCCN: 68-82639; OCLC: 254640.

T117
TODOROV, TZVETAN. 1975. *Introducion à la littérateur fantastique*. Howard, R., trans. *The Fantastic: A Structural Approach to a Literary Genre*. Ithaca, NY: Cornell University Press; 1975. 180p. ISBN: 0801491460; LCCN: 74-10407; OCLC: 1383490.

T118
TODOROV, TZVETAN. 1978/1990. *Les Genres du Discours*. 2nd ed. Paris, FR: Editions du Seuil; 1978. 309p. ISBN: 2020050005. Trans. as: *Genres in Discourse*. Cambridge, UK: Cambridge Univeristy Press; 1990. 136p. ISBN: 052134249X (hbk.); 05221349990 (pbk.).

T119
TODOROV, TZVETAN. 1984. *La conquête de l'Amérique: La Question de l'autre*. Howard, R., trans. *The Conquest of America: The Question of the Other*. New York, NY: Harper and Row; 1984. 274p. ISBN: 0060151803; LCCN: 83-47545; OCLC: 9441416.

T120
TODOROV, TZVETAN. 1995. *Les Morales de l'histoire*. Trans. *The Morals of History*. Minneapolis, MN: University of Minnesota Press; 1995. 228p. ISBN: 0816622973 (hbk.); 0816622981 (pbk.).

T121
TOEWS, JOHN E. 1987. Intellectual History after the Linguistic Turn: The Autonomy of Meaning and the Irreductibility of Experience. *American Historical Review*. 1987; 92: 879-907. ISSN: 0002-8762.

T122
TOFFLER, ALVIN. [1974]. *Learning for Tomorrow: The Role of the Future in Education*. New York, NY: Random House; [1974]. 421p. ISBN: 0394483138.

T123
TOFFLER, ALVIN. 1981. *The Third Wave*. New York, NY: Bantam Books; 1981. 537p. ISBN: 0553144315 (hbk.); 05532336355 (pbk.).

T124
TOFFLER, ALVIN; TOFFLER, HEIDE. 1994. *Creating a New Civilization: The Politics of the Third Wave*. Washington, DC: Progress & Freedom Foundation; c1994. 98p. LCCN: 94241499.

T125
TOMBEUR, PAUL. 1981. *La constitution d'un Thésaurus pour les pères de l'église latine* [Thesaurus Construction for the Fathers of the Latin Church]. Actes du Congrés International Informatique et Sicences Humaines, Liège, 18-21 Novembre 1981. Liège, BE: LASLA; 1981. 875p.

T126
TOMITA, TETSUO; HATTORI, KAZUTOSHI. 1975. Some Considerations of Quasi-Quantitative Analysis of the History of Science in Japan by Key-words: Trial of Quantitative History. *Japanese Studies in the History of Science*. 1975; 14: 13-38. ISSN: 0090-0176.

T127

TOMLINS, CHRISTOPHER L. 1998. Don't Mourn, Organize! A Rumination on Printed Scholarly Journals at the Edge of the Internet. See reference: AHA. 1998. 21-27.

T128

TOPOLSKI, JERZY. 1979. The Role of Theory and Measurement in Economic History. See reference: IGGERS, G.; PARKER, eds., 1979. 43-54.

T129

TOSH, JOHN. 1984. *The Pursuit of History. Aims, Methods and New Directions in the Study of Modern History.* London and New York: Longman; 1984. 205p. ISBN 0-582- 49218-1.

T130

TOURAINE, ALAINE. 1988. Sociology without Society. *Current Sociology.* 1988; 46(2): 119-144. ISSN: 0011-3921.

T131

TOURAINE, ALAINE. 1998. Social Transformations of the Twentieth Century. *International Social Science Journal.* 1998 June; 50(2): 165-172.

T132

TOWERY, MARGIE, ed. [1998]. *Indexing Specialties: History.* Medford, NJ: Information Today, Inc. for the American Society of Indexers; [1998]. [60] p. ISBN: 1-57387-055-2 (pbk.).

T133

TOWNSEND, ROBERT. 1996a. History Salaries Show Continued Improvement—for Some. *AHA Perspectives.* 1996 March; 34(3): 7-9. ISSN: 0743-7021.

T134

TOWNSEND, ROBERT. 1996b. Survey Finds More Ph.D.'s, Less Success in Job Market. *AHA Perspectives.* 1996 April; 34 (4): 11-15. ISSN: 0743-7021. AHA survey data and charts are accessible at http://web.gmu.edu/chnm/aha.

T135

TOWNSEND, ROBERT B. 1997a. AHA Surveys Indicate Bleak Outlook in History Job Market. *AHA Perspectives.* 1997 April; 35(4): 7-13. ISSN: 0743-7021.

T136

TOWNSEND, ROBERT B. 1997b. Studies Report Mixed News for History Job Seekers. *AHA Perspectives.* 1997 March; 35(3): 7-10. ISSN: 0743-7021.

T137

TOWNSEND, ROBERT B. 1997c. Mixed News for History in Latest Academic Salary Surveys: History falls below Salary Average, but Hiring is Up. *AHA Perspectives.* 1997 September; 35(6): 3, 17-18. ISSN: 0743-7021.

T138

TOYNBEE, ARNOLD. 1933-1954. *A Study of History.* London, UK: Oxford University Press.
12 vols. Reprint, 1961-63. Abridgement by D. C. Somerville. New York, NY: Oxford University Press; 1957.

T139

TOYNBEE, ARNOLD. 1961. *Reconsiderations.* In his: *A Study of History,* vol. 12. New York, NY: Galaxy Books of Oxford University Press; 1961. 739p. Abridgement, 1987. LCCN: 87-12291.

T140

TOYNBEE, ARNOLD. 1966/1968. *Change and Habit: The Challenge of Our Time.* Oxford, UK: Oxford University Press; 1966. 2nd printing, 1967; 3rd, 1968. 240p. LCCN: 66-25824.

T141

TRABASSO, T.; SPERRY, L. 1985. Causal Relatedness and Importance of Story Events. *Journal of Memory and Language.* 1985; 24: 595-611. ISSN: 8749-596x.

T142

TRAINOR, RICHARD. 1988. Implementing Computer-based Teaching and Research: The Need for a Collaborative Approach. *Computers and Education.* 1988; 12: 37-41. ISSN: 0360-1315.

T143

TRAINOR, RICHARD. 1989. History, Computing and Higher Education. See reference: DENLEY, P., *ET AL.*, eds. 1989. 35-42.

T144

TRAINOR, RICHARD. 1990. Using Computers in Historical Teaching and Research: The British Experience. *Tijdschrift voor Geschiedenis* (NL). 1990; 103: 373-380. ISSN: 0040-7518.

T145
TRAINOR, RICHARD. 1991. The Interaction of Teaching and Research in Computer-Based History. See reference: BEST, H. *ET AL.*, eds. 1991. 484-490.

T146
TRANT, JENNIFER. 1993. "On Speaking terms": Towards Virtual Integration of Art Information. *Knowledge Organization*. 1993; 20: 8-11. ISSN: 0943-7444.

T147
TRANT, JENNIFER, ed. 1997. Museums and the Web. In: *Archives and Museum Informatics: Cultural Heritage Informatics Quarterly*. 1997; 11 (2): 73-195. (Entire issue on title topic). ISSN: 1042-1467; CODEN: AMUIEA.

T148
TRAVIS, BRIAN; WALDT, DALE. 1995. *The SGML Implementation Guide: A Blueprint for SGML Migration*. New York, NY: Springer-Verlag; 1995. 582p. ISBN: 3540577300.

T149
TRAVIS, IRENE, ed. 1997. Electronic Systems and Records Management in the Information Age. In: *Bulletin of the American Society for Information Science*. 1997 June/July; 23(5): 1-29. (Entire issue of title topic). ISSN: 0095-4403; CODEN: BASICR.

T150
TREMBLE, STANLEY; COOKE, RONALD U. 1991. Historical Sources for Geomorphological Research in the United States. *Professional Geographer*. 1991; 43(2): 212-228. ISSN: 0033-0124.

T151
TREPANIER, PIERRE. 1981. Plaidoyer pour d'histoire comme Genre Littéraire [A Plea for History as a Literary Genre]. *Action national* (FR). 1981; 70(10): 811-21. (In French). ISSN: 0001-7469.

T152
TRICE, HARRISON. 1993. *Occupational Subcultures in the Workplace*. Ithaca, NY: IRL Press; 1993. 286p. ISBN: 075463929 (hbk.); 0875463037 (pbk.).

T153
TRICE, HARRISON M.; BEYER, JANICE M. 1984. Studying Organizational Cultures through Rites and Ceremonials. *Academy of Management Review*. 1984; 9(4): 653-669. ISBN: 0363-7425.

T154
TRICE, HARRISON M.; BEYER, JANICE M. 1993. *The Cultures of Work Organizations*. Englewood Cliffs, NJ: Prentice Hall; 1993. 510p. ISBN: 0131914383.

T155
TRIFAN, DANIEL D. 1997. Active Learning: A Critical Examination. *AHA Perspectives*. 1997 March; 35(3): 1, 23-28. Rejoinders and commentaries by R. Marchand and J. W. Oberly, pp. 27-30. ISSN: 0743-7021.

T156
TRIGG, ROBERT H.; WEISER, M. 1986. *TEXTNBET*: A Network-based Approach to Text Handling. *ACM Transactions on Office Information Systems*. 1986; 4: 1-23. ISSN: 0734-2097.

T157
TRINKLE, DENNIS A. 1997. *The History Highway: A Guide to Internet Resources*. Armonk, NY: M. E. Sharpe; 1997. 249p. ISBN: 076560012 (pbk.); 0765600110 (hbk.).

T158
TRYBULA, WALTER J. 1997. Data Mining and Knowledge Discovery. In: Williams, Martha, ed. *Annual Review of Information Science and Technology* (vol. 32). Medford, NJ: Information Today, Inc.; 1997. ISBN: 1-57387-047-1.

T159
TYRON, ROBERT. C.; BAILEY, DANIEL E. 1970. *Cluster Analysis*. New York, NY: McGraw-Hill; 1970. 387p.

T160
TRYON, ROBERT C. 1939. *Cluster Analysis*. Ann Arbor, MI: Edwards Brothers, Inc.; 1939. 122p. LCCN: 39-025023. Applied in: *Identification of Social Areas by Cluster Analysis: A General Method with an Application to the San Francisco Bay Area*. Berkeley, CA: University of California Press; 1955. 99p. (Publications in Psychology, 8 [1]).

T161
TUCKER, WILLIAM. 1996. Complex Questions: The New Science of Spontaneous Order [Complexity theory]. *Reason*. 1996 Jan.; 27(8): 34-. ISSN: 0048-6906.

T162

TUFILLARO, NICHOLAS B.; ABBOT, TYLER; REILLY, JEREMIAH. 1992. *An Experimental Approach to Nonlinear Dynamics and Chaos.* Studies in Nonlinearity series. Reading, MA: Addison, Wesley, Longman; 1992. Guide with Macintosh disc. ISBN: 0-201-55441-0 (hbk.).

T163

TUFTE, EDWARD R. [1970]. *The Quantitative Analysis of Social Problems.* Reading, MA: Addison-Wesley Pub. Co.; [1970]. 449p. LCCN: 70-100889.

T164

TUFTE, EDWARD R. 1974 *Data Analysis for Politics and Policy.* Dahl, Robert A., ed. Foundations of Modern Political Science series. Englewood Cliffs, NJ: Prentice-Hall, Inc.; 1974. 179p. ISBN: 0-13-197541-2; 0-13-197525-0 (pbk.).

T165

TUFTE, EDWARD R. 1983. *The Visual Display of Quantitative Information.* Cheshire, CT: Graphics Press; 1983. 197p. LCCN: 83-156861; OCLC: 9480885.

T166

TUFTE, EDWARD R. 1990/1992. *Envisioning Information.* Cheshire, CT: Graphics Press; 1990. 126p. 3rd printing; 1992. ISBN: 0-961-3921-8.

T167

TUFTE, EDWARD R. 1997. *Visual Explanation: Images and Quantities, Evidence and Narration.* Cheshire, CT: Graphics Press; 1997. 156p. ISBN: 0-961-3921-2-6.

T168

TUFTE, VIRGINIA; MYERHOFF, BARBARA G. 1979. *Changing Images of the Family.* New Haven, CT: Yale University Press; 1979. 403p.

T169

TULLY, JAMES, ed. 1988. *Meaning and Context: Quentin Skinner and His Critics.* Cambridge, UK: Polity Press; 1988. 353p. ISBN: 0745601243.

T170

TURK, CHRISTOPHER, ed. 1991. *Humanities Research Using Computers.* London, UK: Chapman & Hall; 1991. 184p. ISBN: 0442313500; LCCN: 94-152942; OCLC: 27815768.

T171

TURKLE, SHERRY. 1984. *The Second Self: Computers and the Human Spirit.* New York, NY: Simon & Schuster; 1984. 362p. ISBN: 0671468480.

T172

TURKLE, SHERRY. 1995. *Life on the Screen: Identity in the Age of the Internet.* New York, NY: Simon & Schuster; 1995. 347p. ISBN: 0684803534.

T173

TURNER, E. 1995. *An Overview of the Z39.50 Information Retrieval Standard.* UDT Occasional Paper, 3. Accessible at http://www.nlc-bnc.ca/ifla.VI/5/op/udtop3.htm.

T174

TURNER, RAYMOND. 1991. *Truth and Modality for Knowledge Representation.* Cambridge, MA: Pitman Pub.; 1990. 119p. ISBN: 0262200805; LCCN: 90019128.

T175

TURNER, STEPHEN P. 1994. *The Social Theory of Practices: Tradition, Tacit Knowledge, and Presuppositions.* Chicago, IL: University of Chicago Press; 1994. 145p. ISBN: 0226817377 (hbk.); 0226817385; LCCN: 93-44989.

T176

TURNER, STEPHEN P.; TURNER, JONATHAN H. 1990. *The Impossible Science: An Institutional Analysis of American Sociology.* Newbury Park, CA: Sage; 1990. 222p. (Sage Library of Social Research, 181). ISBN: 0803938381 (hbk.); 080393839X (hbk.).

T177

TURNER, THOMAS E. 1991. Integrated Imaging: A Strategic Information Systems Weapon. *International Journal of Micrographics & Optical Technology.* 1991; 9(1): 1-5. ISSN: 0958-9961.

T178

TVERSKY, AMOS. 1977. Features of Similarity. *Psychological Review.* 1977; 84: 327- 352. ISSN: 0033-295X.

T179
TVERSKY, AMOS; GATI, I. 1978. Studies in Similarity. In: Rosch, Eleanor B.; Lloyd, Barbara B., eds. *Cognition and Categorization*. Hillsdale, NJ: L. Ehrbaum; 1978. 328p. ISBN: 0470263776.

T180
TVERSKY, AMOS; KAHNEMAN, DAVID. 1974. Judgement under Uncertainty: Heuristics and Biases. *Science*. 1974; 185: 1124-1131. ISSN: 0036-8075.

T181
TVERSKY, AMOS; KAHNEMAN, DAVID; SLOVIC, PUAL , eds. 1982. *Judgement under Uncertainty*. New York, NY: Cambridge University Press; 1982. 555p. ISBN: 0521240646 (hbk.); 052128284117 (hbk.).

T182
TYRE, MARCIE; ORLIKOWSI, WANDA. 1994. Windows of Opportunity: Temporal Patterns of Technological Adaptation in Organizations. *Organization Science*. 1994; 5: 98-118. ISSN: 1047-7039.

-U-

U1
ÜBE, GOTZ; HIBER, GEORG; FISHER, JOACHIM, eds. 1985. *Maco-economic Models: An International Bibliography*. Brookfield, VT: Gower Pub. Co.; 1985. 149p., 20 microfiche. ISBN: 05660007886.

U2
ULLRICH, WILLIAM; HAYES, IAN. 1997. *The Year 2000 Software Crisis. Challenge of the Century*. Los Alamitos, CA: IEEE; 1997. 340p. ISBN: 0-13-655664-7.

U3
UMAR, AMJAD. 1993. *Distributed Computing and Client-Server Systems*. Engleside Cliff, NJ: Prentice-Hall; 1993. 736p. ISBN: 0-13-036252-2.

U4
UMBAUGH, ROBERT E., ed. *Handbook of IS Management*. 4th ed. Boston, MA / New York, NY: Auerbach Publications; 1995. 702p. ISBN: 0-7913-2159-2. Updated by: *IS Management 1996-97 Yearbook*. New York, NY: Auerbach Publications; 1996. 362p. ISBN: 0-7913-2634-9.

U5
UNDERWOOD, WILLIAM E. 1997. Records Management Research Sponsored by the US Army and the Department of Defense. See reference: BEARMAN, D.; TRANT, J., eds. 1997. 261-267.

U6
UNDERWOOD, WILLIAM E. 1997a. *The Language of Records Classification, AIAI TR 97- 02, CSTD*. Atlanta, GA: Georgia Institute of Technology; 1997.

U7
UNDERWOOD, WILLIAM E.; LAIB, S. 1995. *The Language of Records Disposition, AIAI TR 95-01, ARL, CSTD*. Atlanta, GA: Georgia Institute of Technology; 1995.

U8
UNICODE CONSORTIUM. 1996. *The Unicode Standard, version 2.0*. Reading, MA: Addison-Wesley; 1996.

U9
UNITED NATIONS. ADVISORY COMMITTEE FOR COORDINATION OF INFORMATION SYSTEMS (ACCIS). 1990. *Management of Electronic Records: Issues and Guidelines*. Barry, Richard, E., ed. Report of the Advisory Committee for the Co-ordination of Information Systems. New York, NY: United Nations; 1990. 189p. ISBN: 92-1-100348-2; OCLC: 21396209. UN Sales no. GV.E.89.0.15.

U10
UNITED NATIONS EDUCATIONAL, SCIENTIFIC AND CULTURAL ORGANIZATION (UNESCO) 1979. UNESCO *Journal of Information Science, Librarianship, and Archives Administration*. [Paris, FR]: UNESCO; 1979-. Qtly. ISSN: 0379-122X.

U11
UNITED STATES. ADVISORY COUNCIL ON THE NATIONAL INFORMATION INFRASTRUCTURE. 1996. *A Nation of Opportunity: Realizing the Promise of the Information Superhighway*. Washington, D.C.: West Publishing for the Council; 1996.

U12

UNITED STATES. CONGRESS. HOUSE OF REPRESENTATIVES. COMMITTEE ON GOVERNMENT OPERA-
TIONS. 1990. *Taking a Byte Out of History: The Archival Preservation of Federal Computer Records.* Washington,
D.C.: U.S. Government Printing Office; 1990. (House Report no. 101-987).

U13

UNITED STATES. CONGRESS. HOUSE OF REPRESENTATIVES. COMMITTEE ON THE JUDICIARY. 1973-.
Federal Rules of Evidence. Washington, D.C.: GPO; 1973-. Annual. Gov. Doc. Y4.J89/1.

U14

UNITED STATES. CONGRESS. OFFICE OF TECHNOLOGY ASSESSMENT (OTA). 1988. *Informing the Nation:
Federal Information Dissemination in an Electronic Age.* Washington, D.C.: OTA; 1988. 333p. (OTA-CIT-396).
LCCN: 88-600567.

U15

UNITED STATES CONGRESS. OFFICE OF TECHNOLOGY ASSESSMENT (OTA). 1995. Federal Technology
Transfer and the Human Genome Project. Washington, D.C.: GPO; 1995 September. 118p. Report no. OTA-BP-
EHR-162. ISBN: 0160482917.

U16

UNITED STATES. DEPARTMENT OF COMMERCE. 1995. *Federal Information Processing Standards (FIPS).*
Washington, D.C.: Dept. of Commerce Technology Administration and the National Institute of Standards and
Technology (NISO); 1995 March 13. (Publication 194).

U17

UNITED STATES. DEPARTMENT OF COMMERCE. NATIONAL INSTITUTE OF STANDARDS AND TECH-
NOLOGY. 1983-. *Federal Information Processing Standards (FIPS).* Washington, D.C.: GPO for NIST Computer
Systems Laboratory; 1983-. (NIST Pub. 58). Gov. Doc.: C 13.37:58.

U18

UNITED STATES. DEPARTMENT OF INTERIOR. 1969-. *The National Register of Historic Places.* Washington,
D.C.: GPO for the National park Service; 1969-. *Index.* Washington, D.C.: Buckmaster Publishing; 1989. GOV.
DOC.: I29.76:976.

U19

UNITED STATES. NATIONAL BUREAU OF STANDARDS. 1986-. *Federal Information Processing Standards
(FIPS).* Washington, D.C.: GPO; 1986-. ISSN: 0083-1816; Gov. Doc.: C 13.52.

U20

UNITED STATES. NATIONAL COMMISSION ON LIBRARIES AND INFORMATION SCIENCE (NCLIS). 1996.
The 1996 National Survey of Public Libraries and the Internet: Progress and Issues. Bertot, J. C.; McClure, C. R.;
Zweizig, D. L., investigators. Washington, D.C.: NCLIS; 1996. Accessible at http://www.nclis.gov/info/
gpo1.html.

U21

UNITED STATES. NATIONAL COMMISSION ON LIBRARIES AND INFORMATION SCIENCE (NCLIS). 1997.
*Assessment of Formats and Standards for the Creation, Dissemination, and Permanent Accessibility of Electronic
Government Information Products* (draft, electronic file). Blumenthal, Marjory S; Inouye, Alan S., investigators of
the National Research Council Computer Science and Telecommunications Board. Washington, D.C.: NCLIS;
1997. 12p., 9p. bibliography. Accessible at http://www.nclis.gov/info/gpo1.html.://www.imagedir.com

U22

UNITED STATES. OFFICE OF MANAGEMENT AND BUDGET (OMB). 1996. *Management of Federal
Information Resources.* Revised. Washington, D.C.: OMB; 1996. (Circular A-130).

U23

UNITED STATES GEOGRAPHIC SURVEY. FEDERAL GEOGRAPHIC DATA COMMITTEE. 1994. *Content
Standard for Digital Geospatial Metadata.* Washington, D.C.: USGS; 1994 June 8. Available from: USGS, 590
National Center, Reston, VA 22092; or via anonymous FTP at ftp://er.usgs.gov.

U24

UNIVERSITÉ DE MONTREAL. 1973-. *Computers and Medieval Data Processing/ Informatique et etudes medievales.*
Montreal, CA: Universite de Montreal Institut d'Etudes Medievales; 1973-. Biennial. ISSN: 0384-5060. U22

U25

UNIVERSITY OF BRITISH COLUMBIA MASS RESEARCH TEAM; U.S. DEPARTMENT OF DEFENSE
RECORDS MANAGEMENT PROGRAM MANAGEMENT OFFICE. [1997a]. *Genesis and Preservation of an
Agencies Archival Funds: Glossary* [electronic file]. Vancouver, BC: UBC Archival Studies Program; [1997]. 21p.
Accessible at http://www.slais.ubc.ca/users/duranti/gloss.htm#A. See also: DURANTI, L.

U26
UNIVERSITY OF BRITISH COLUMBIA MAS RESEARCH TEAM; U.S. DEPARTMENT OF DEFENSE RECORDS MANAGEMENT PROGRAM MANAGEMENT OFFICE. [1997b]. Templates (1-7) (electronic file). Vancouver, BC: UBC Archival Studies Program; [1997]. 7 templates; activity models, node tree. Accessible at http://www.slais.ubc.ca/ users/duranti/tem1.htm.

U27
UNIVERSITY OF CALIFORNIA, SANTA BARBARA. ALEXANDRIA PROJECT. 1996. *Principles for Selection for Digitization* (Electronic file). Santa Barbara, CA: UCSB Map Library; June 20, 1996. Accessible at http://alexandria.ucsb.edu.

U28
UNIVERSITY OF LEEDS. INTERNATIONAL MEDIEVAL INSTITUTE. 1995-. *International Medieval Bibliography* (CD-ROM). Leeds, UK and Turnhout, BE: Brépols Publishers; 1995-. ISSN: 0020-7950. (Coverage began in 1967).

U29
UNIVERSITY OF NORTH CAROLINA. INSTITUTE FOR RESEARCH IN SOCIAL SCIENCE (IRSS). 1989-. *IRSS Catalog of Data Holdings* [Computer file]. 3rd ed. Chapel Hill, NC: IRSS. Online database access: uirdss@uncvm1.bitnet.

U30
UNIVERSITY OF PENNSYLVANIA. ANNENBERG SCHOOL OF COMMUNICATIONS. *1994. The Future of Fact*. The Annenberg Scholars Program for 1995-96 (Announcement). Elihu Katz, director. Available from: Annenberg Scholars Program, Annenberg School for Communication, University of Pennsylvania, 3620 Walnut Street, Philadelphia, PA 19104-6220.

U31
UNIVERSITY OF PITTSBURGH. DEPARTMENT OF HISTORY. 1967-1977. *Historical Methods Newsletter*. Pittsburgh, PA: University Center for International Studies and the Dept. of History. 1967-77; 1-10. ISSN: 0018-2494.

U32
UNIVERSITY OF PITTSBURGH. SCHOOL OF LIBRARY AND INFORMATION SCIENCE. 1991. *Archival Administration in the Electronic Information Age: An Advanced Institute for Government Archivists*. [Pittsburgh, PA]: University of Pittsburgh SLIS; 1991. 74p. OCLC: 257751153.

U33
UPWARD, FRANK. 1993. Institutionalizing the Archival Document: Some Theoretical Perspectives on Terry Eastwood's Challenge. See reference: MCKEMMISH, S.; UPWARD, F., eds. 1993. 41-54.

U34
URBACH, PAUL. 1983. Limitations of Similarity: The Shaky Basis of Verisimilitude. *The British Journal of the Philosophy of Science*. 1983; 34: 266-275. ISSN: 0031-8248.

U35
URBAN, GREG. 1991. *A Discourse-centered Approach to Culture: Native South American Myths and Rituals*. Austin, TX: University of Texas Press; 1991. 215p.(Texas Linguistic series). ISBN: 0292715625.

U36
USSELMANN, STEVEN W. 1993. IBM and Its Imitators: Organizational Capabilities and the Emergence of the International Computer Industry. *Business and Economic History*. 1993; 22(2): 1-35. ISSN: 0894-6825.

U37
USSELMANN, STEVEN W. 1996. Fostering a Capacity for Compromise: Business, Government, and the Stages of Innovation in American Computing. See reference: WILLIAMS, MICHAEL, ed. 1996. 30-39.

-V-

V1
VAILLANCOURT ROSENAU, PAULINE. 1992. *Post Modernism and the Social Sciences: Insights, Inroads, and Intrusions*. Princeton, NJ: Princeton University Press; 1992. 229p. ISBN: 069086192 (hbk.); 0691023476 (hbk.); LCCN: 91019258..

V2
VAKKARI, PERTTI. 1994a. From Library Science to Information Studies. In: Verwer, Renzo; Nijboer, Jelke; Bruyns, Ruud, eds. *The Future of Librarianship: Proceedings of the 2nd International Budapest Symposium, January 1994*. Amsterdam, NL: Higeschool van Amsterdam, Faculteit Economie en Informatie; 1994. OCLC: 30617207.

V3

VAKKARI, PERTTI. 1994b. Library and Information Science: Its Content and Scope. In: Godden Irene, P., ed. *Advances in librarianship*. San Diego, CA: Academic Press; 1994. 18: 1-55. ISSN: 0065-2830; ISBN: 0-12-024618-X.

V4

VAKKARI, PERTTI; CRONIN, BLAISE, eds. 1992. *Conceptions of Library and Information Science: Historical, Empirical and Theoretical Perspectives*: Proceedings of the International Conference Held for the Celebration of the 20th Anniversary of the Department of Information Studies, University of Tampere; 1991 August 26-28, Tampere, FI. London, UK: Taylor Graham; 1992. 314p. ISBN: 0-947568-52-2.

V5

VAKKARI, PERTTI; SAVOLAINEN, REIJO; DERVIN, BRENDA, eds. 1997. *Information Seeking in Context*. Selected papers form a conference at the University of Tampere, FI. London: Taylor Graham; 1997. 467p. ISBN: 0-947568-71-9.

V6

VALACICH, JOSEPH D.; DENNIS, ALAN R.; NUNAMAKER, JAY F. 1991. Electronic Meeting Support: The Systems Concept. International Journal of Man-Machine Studies. 1991 February; 34(2): 261-282. ISSN: 0020-7373.

V7

VALIANT, L. G. 1984. A Theory of the Learnable. *Communications of ACM* (Assn. of Computing Machinery). 1984; 27: 1134-1142. ISSN: 0001-0782.

V8

VAN BOGART, JOHN W. C. [1995]. *Magnetic Tape Storage and Handling: A Guide for Libraries and Archives*. St. Paul, MN: National Media Lab for the Commission on Preservation and Access; [1995]. 34p. ISBN: 1887334408.

V9

VAN BOGART, JOHN W. C. 1996. *Media Stability Studies*. St. Paul, MN: National Media Lab; 1996.

V10

VAN BOGART, JOHN W. C. [1998]. *Storage Life Expectancies: Digital Archives Direction* (DAD) [Electronic file]. Accessible at http://ssdoo.gsfc.nasa.gov/nost/isoas/dads/ws/htm.

V11

VAN DER VOORT, R. C. W. 1990. The Growth of Historical Information Systems in Historical Sciences. See reference: METZ, R., ed. 1990. 3-9.

V12

VAN ENGEN, JOHN, ed. 1994. *The Past and Future of Medieval Studies*. South Bend, IN: University of Notre Dame Press; 1994. 431p. (Notre Dame Conference of Medieval Studies, 4). ISBN: 0268038007.

V13

VAN GYSEGHEM, NANCY; DE CALUWE, RITA. 1998. Imprecision and Uncertainty in the UFO [Uncertainty and Fuzziness in an Object-oriented] Database Model. *Journal of the American Society for Information Science*. 1998; 49 (3); 236-252. ISSN: 0002-8231.

V14

VAN HALL, NINETTE S. 1989. Towards a Standard for the Description of Historical Datasets. *Historisch Sozialforschung/ Historical Social Research* (DEU). 1989; 14(1): 89-125. ISSN: 0172-6404. (English; German abstract).

V15

VAN HALL, NINETTE S. 1991. Towards a Standard for the Description of Historical Datasets. See reference: BEST, H., *ET AL.*, eds. 1991. 496-501.

V16

VAN HERWIJNEN, ERIC. [1995]. *Practical SGML*. 2nd ed. Oxon Hall, MD: NISO Press; [1995]. 350p. Oxon Hill, MD: NISO Press; 1997. 2 vols., 1200p.; or CD-ROM. SGML (ISO 8879) compliant DTDs. ISBN: 0-7923-9434-8. Available from NISO Press at 1-800-282-NISO; Fax 301-567-9553.

V17

VAN HORIK, M. P. M. 1990. Development of a New Standard: The Historical Dataset Descriptive Scheme. In: Doorn, P.; Van Horik, M. P.; Touwen, L. J., eds. *Nederlands Historische Data Archief I: Einverslag van een pilot-project*. Amsterdam, NL: Netherlands Historical Data Archives; 1990. 39-58.

V18

VAN HORIK, RENE. 1992a. Optical Character Recognition and Historical Documents: Some Programs Reviewed. *History and Computing*. 1992; 3: 211-220. ISSN: 0957- 0144.

V19
VAN HORIK, RENE. 1992b. *Van beeldpunt tot betekenis. Scanning en optische tekenherkenning van gedrukt histor-ish bronnenmateriaal* [From Start to Finish: Optical Scanning for the Conversion of Historical Primary Materials]. Amsterdam, NL: Amsterdam University Press; 1992. (In Dutch).

V20
VAN HORIK, RENE. 1993. Pattern Recognition of Gothic Fonts. See reference: DOORN, P., *ET AL.*, eds. 1993. 155-165.

V21
VAN HORIK, RENE. 1996 [1999-]. Conversion of Latin Fonts: The Possibilities of Optical Character Recognition. See reference: BORODKIN, L., ed. 1996: English abstract of presentation, 54-55; paper in Russian [199- forthcoming].

V22
VAN MAANEN, J. 1979. Qualitative Methods Reclaimed. *Administrative Science Quarterly.* 1979: 24(4): 511-526. ISSN: 0001-8392.

V23
VAN PEER, W. 1989. Quantitative Studies of Literature: A Critique and an Outlook. *Computers and the Humanities* (NL). 1989 August-October; 23(4-5): 301-307. ISSN: 0010-4817.

V24
VAN RIJSBERGEN, C. 1979. *Information Retrieval.* 2nd ed. London, UK: Butterworths; 1979.

V25
VAN TASSEL, DAVID. D. 1960. *Recording America's Past: An Interpretation of the Development of Historical Studies in America.* Chicago, IL: University of Chicago Press; 1960. 222p. LCCN: 60-14404; OCLC: 1598910.

V26
VANDERBILT UNIVERSITY. COGNITION AND TECHNOLOGY GROUP. 1997. *The Jasper Project. Lessons in Curriculum, Instruction, Assessment, and Professional Development.* Mahwah, NJ: Lawrence Earlbaum Associates, Inc.; 1997. 200p. and CD-ROM. ISBN: 0-8058-2592-4 (hbk.); 0-8058-2593-2 (pbk.).

V27
VANDERMEER, PHILIP R. 1979. The New Political History: Progress and Prospects. See reference: IGGERS & PARKER, eds. 1979. 87-108.

V28
VANN, RICHARD T. 1979. The New Demographic History. See reference: IGGERS, G.; PARKER, eds.; 1979. 29-42.

V29
VARENNE, HERVE; HILL, CLIFFORD; BYERS, PAUL. 1992. *Ambiguous Harmony: Family Talk in America.* Norwood, NJ: Ablex Publishing Corp.; 1992. 256p. (Advances in Discourse Analysis, 44). ISBN: 089391763X; LCCN: 91-30864; OCLC: 24319516.

V30
VASILEVA, G. G. 1982. [Thesauri of historicisms, archaisms, literary and rarely used terms]. *Naucho-Technicheskaya Informatsiya* [Scientific and Technical Information Processing] (USSR). Seriia 2. 1982; 5: 227-234. (In Russian; English translation). ISSN: 0028-1131.

V31
VAUGHAN, SALLY. 1995. Charles H. Haskins. See reference: D'AMICO, H.; ZAVADIL, B., eds. 1995. 168-181.

V32
VAUGHAN, WILLIAM. 1987. The Automated Connoisseur: Image Analysis and Art History. See DENLEY, P; HOP-KINS, P., eds. 1987. 215-221.

V33
VAUGHAN, WILLIAM. 1989. Painting by Number: Art History and the Digital Image. See reference: HAMBER, A.; MYLES, J.; VAUGHAN, W., eds. 1989. 74-97.

V34
VEENSTRA, JAN R. 1995. The New Historicsm of Stephen Greenblatt: On Poetics of Culture and the Interpretation of Shakespeare. *History and Theory.* 1995; 34: 174-198. ISSN: 0018-2656.

V35
VEESER, H. ARAM, ed. 1989. *The New Historicism.* New York, NY: Routledge; 1989. 317p. ISBN: 0415900697; 0415900700 (pbk.); LCCN: 88-20935; OCLC: 18165521.

V36
VEITH, RICHARD H. 1988. *Visual Information Systems: The Power of Graphics and Video.* Boston, MA: G. K. Hall & Co; 1988. 321p. ISBN: 0816118612 (hbk.); 0816118817 (pbk.).

V37
VELLUCCI, SHERRY L. 1998. Metadata. In: Williams, Martha E., ed. *Annual Review of Information Science and Technology (ARIST)*: vol. 33. Medford, NJ: Information Today, Inc.; 1998. ISBN: 1-57387-065-X.

V38
VENARDE, BRUCE LANIER. 1992. *Women, Monasticism, and Social Change: the Foundation of Nunneries in Western Europe, c. 890-c. 1215.* Cambridge, MA: Harvard University; 1992. 409p. (Ph.D. dissertation; *DAI*, 53/11-A: 4044). Available from: University Microfilms, Ann Arbor, MI (Order no. AAD93-07616).

V39
VERBRUGGE, R. R. 1977. Resemblance in Language and Perception. In: Shaw, R.; Bransford, J., eds. *Perceiving, Acting, and Knowing. Toward an Ecological Psychology* (pp. 365-389). University of Minnesota Center for Research in Learning conference, July 23-August 17, 1973. Hilllsdale, NY: Lawrence Erlbaum; 1977. 492p. ISBN: 0470990147.

V40
VERGO, PETER, ed. 1989/1991. *The New Museology.* 1989. 2nd ed. London, UK: Reaction Books; 1991. 230p. ISBN: 0948464043 (hbk.); 0968462035 (pbk.).

V41
VERNON, E. 1973. Linguistique et Sociologie [Linguistics and Sociology]. *Communications.* 1973; 20: 246-296. (In French). ISSN: 0010-356X.

V42
VERVLIET, HENDRIK D. L., ed. 1969-. *Annual Bibliography of the History of the Printed Book and Libraries.* The Hague, NL / Boston, MA / London, UK: Martinus Nijhoff for the Committee on Rare and Precious Books and Documents of the International Federation of Library Associations (IFLA); 1969-. Annual. ISBN: 90-247-2062-1.

V43
VEYNE, PAUL. 1971/1984. *Comment en écrit l'histoire.* Paris, FR: Seuil; 1971. Moore- Rinvolucri, M., trans. *Writing History: Essays on Epistemology.* Middleton, CT: Wesleyan University Press; 1984. 342p. ISBN: 0819550671; 0819560766 (pbk.); LCCN: 4-7281; OCLC: 10727296.

V44
VICKERY, BRIAN C. 1987. *Information Science in Theory and Practice.* London, UK: Butterworths; 1987. 384p. ISBN: 0408106840.

V45
VICKERY, BRIAN C., ed. 1994. *Fifty Years of Information Progress: A Journal of Documentation Review.* London, UK: Aslib; 1994. 243p. ISSN: 0-85142-327-2; LCCN: 95158244.

V46
VICKERY, BRIAN C; VICKERY, ALINA. 1992. *Information Science in Theory and Practice.* Revised edition. London, UK / New York, NY: Bowker-Saur; 1992. 387p. ISBN: 0-408-10684-0.

V47
VIDAL-NAQUET, PIERRE. 1987/1992. *Les Assassins de la mémoire: Un Eichmann de papier et autres essais sur le revisionisme.* Paris, FR: Editions la Decouverté; 1987. 231p. ISBN: 2707117048. Trans. *The Assassins of Memory: Essays on the Denial of the Holocaust.* New York, NY: Columbia University Press; 1992. 205p. ISBN: 0231074581.

V48
VIDAL-NAQUET, PIERRE. 1996. *Juifs, la mémoire et le present.* Curtis, David Ames, ed., trans. *The Jews: History, Memory, and the Present.* New York, NY; 1996. 337p. ISBN: 0231102089 (hbk.); 023110209 (pbk.).

V49
VILAR, PIERRE. 1962. *La Catalogne dans l'Espagne moderne: Recherches sur les fondements économiques des structures nationales* [Catalonia in Modern Spain: Research concerning the economic fundamentals of natioanl structures]. Paris, FR: SEVPEN; 1962. 3 vols. (Bibliotheque générale de l'Ecole pratique des hautes études, 6). (In French). LCCN: FR 79-368734; OCLC: 2076136.

V50
VILHAUER, JÉRRY. 1991. *Introduction to Micrographics.* Silver Spring, MD: AIIIM; 1991; 38p. AIM Catalog C101. ISBN: 0892582197.

V51
VINCENT, GEORGE E. 1916. *The Social Memory.* St. Paul, MN: [Minnesota Historical Society]; 259p. LCCN: 17027324. Note: About historical societies.

V52
VINCENTI, WALTER G. 1990/1993. *What Engineers Know and How They Know It: Analytical Studies from Aeronautical History.* Baltimore, MD: The Johns Hopkins University Press; 1990; reprint, 1993. 336p. ISBN: 0801839742; LCCN: 89-49003.

V53
VINCENTI, WALTER G.; ROSENBERG, NATHAN. 1978. *The Brittania Bridge: The Generation and Diffusion of Technical Knowledge.* Cambridge, MA: MIT Press; 1978. 107p. (Society for the History of Technology series, 10). ISBN: 0262180871; LCCN: 78-4831.

V54
VINDEN, ROBIN J. 1990. *Data Dictionaries for Database Administrators.* Blue Ridge Summit, PA: McGraw-Hill TAB Books; 1990. 176p. ISBN: 0830675159 (hbk.); 0830635157 (pbk.).

V55
VINKLER, P. 1988. An Attempt of Surveying and Classifying [*sic*] Bibliometric Indicators for Scientometric Purposes. *Scientometrics* (NL). 1988; 13(5-6): 239-250. ISSN: 0138- 9130.

V56
VIREL, ANDRE. 1965. Du chronique au chronologique. In his: *Histoire de notre image: dessins a la plume* (pp. 109-141). Geneva, CH: Ed. du Mont-Blanc; 1965. 326p. LCCN: 67-78087; OCLC: 5372566.

V57
VLADIMIROV, VLADIMIR. 1996a [199-]. Spatial Aspects of Altai History: The Impact of Computer Mapping. See reference: BORODKIN, L., ed. 1996: English abstract of presentation, 98; paper in Russian [199- forthcoming].

V58
VLADIMIROV, VLADIMIR. 1996b. Staraja Opera o Glavnom [Old Opera about Core Principals]. See reference: BORODKIN, L.I., ed. 1996. 117-121.

V59
VOGT, W. PAUL. 1993. *Dictionary of Statistics and Methodology. A Nontechnical Guide for the Social Sciences.* Thousand Oaks, CA: Sage Publications; 1993. 253p. ISBN: 0-8039-5276-7 (hbk.); 0-8039-5277-5 (pbk.).

V60
VOLLMER, JÜRGEN H. 1989. Investigation into the Reusability of Machine-Readable Dictionaries for Machine Translation Purposes. See reference: MCCRANK, L., ed. 1989. 653-658.

V61
VON DRAN, RAYMOND F. 1976. *The Effect of Method of Research on the Information Seeking Behavior of Academic Historians.* Ph.D. Dissertation. Madison, WI: University of Wisconsin; 1976.

V62
VON HIPPEL, ERIC. 1994. "Sticky Information" and the Locus of Problem Solving: Implications for Innovation. *Management Science.* 1994; 40: 429-439. ISSN: 0025-1909.

V63
VON HIPPEL, ERIC; TYRE, MARCIE. 1995. The Mechanics of Learning by Doing: Problem Discovery during Process Machine Use. *Technology and Culture.* 1995; 37(2): 312-329. ISSN: 0040-165X. 1360.

V64
VON NEUMANN, JOHN. 1959. *The Computer and the Brain.* New Haven, CT: Yale University Press; 1959.

V65
VOORBIJ, J. B. 1995. Information technology and the Humanities: On Dreamers and Acrobats. *Le Medieviste et l'Ordinateur.* 1995 Printemps-Automne; 31-32: 36-41. ISSN: 0223-3843.

V66
VOSNIADOV, STELLA, ed. 1996. *International Perspectives on the Design of Technology Supported Learning Environments.* Mahwah, NJ: Lawrence Erlbaum Associates; 1996. 396p. ISBN: 0805818545 (hbk.); 0805818537 (pbk.); LCCN: 95-47474.

V67
VOVELLE, MICHEL. 1990. *Idéologies et mentalites.* Trans. as: *Ideologies and Mentalities.* Cambridge, UK: Polity, in association with Basil Blackwell; 1990. 263p. ISBN: 0745603440.

V68
VYGOTSKII, LEV S. 1926/1997. *Pedagogicheskaia psikhologiia: kratkii kurs.* Silverman, R., trans.; Davydov, V. V., ed. *Educational Psychology.* Boca Raton, FL: St. Lucie Press; c1997. 374p. ISBN: 1878205153; LCCN: 91070614.

V69

VYGOTSKII, LEV S. 1932/1967/1986. *Myshelenie i rech*. Kozulin, Alex, ed. and trans. *Thought and Language*. Cambridge, MA: MIT Press; 1967 reprint. 1986. 287p. ISBN: 0262220296 (hbk.); 0262720108 (pbk.); LCCN: 85-24-40.

V70

VYGOTSKII, LEV S. 1978. *Mind in Society: The Development of Higher Psychological Processes*. Cole, M.; John-Steiner, S.; Scribner, S.; Souberman, E., eds. Cambridge, MA: Harvard University Press; 1978.

V71

VYGOTSKII, LEV S. 1987. *Sobranie sochinenii*. Rieber, Robert W.; Carton, Aaron, eds.; Hall, M. J.; Veer, Rene van der; Minick, N., trans. *The Collected Works of L. S. Vigotsky*. New York, NY: Plenum Press; c1987. 5 vols. ISBN: 030642441X; LCCN: 887007219.

V72

VYGOTSKII, LEV S. 1993. *Etiudy po istorii povedeniia*. Golod, Victor; Knox, Jane E., eds., trans. *Studies on the History of Behavior: Ape, Primitive, and Child*. Hillsdale, NJ: Lawrence Earlbaum Associates; 1993. 246p. ISBN: 0805810145; LCCN: 920223404.

V73

VYGOTSKII, LEV S. 1994. *The Vygotsky Reader*. Veer, Rene van der; Valsiner, Jaan, eds. Rout, Theresa, trans. Oxford, UK / Cambridge, MA; 1994. 378p. ISBN:0631188967 (hbk.); 063118897775 (pbk.); LCCN: 93037353.

-W-

W1

WACTLAR, HOWARD; KANADE, TAKEO; SMITH, MICHAEL A.; STEVENS, SCOTT M. 1996. Intelligent Access to Digital Video: Informedia Project. See reference: SCHATZ, B.; CHEN, H., eds. 1996. 46-52.

W2

WAGERS, ROBERT. 1983. Effective Searching in Database Abstracts. *Online*. 1983 September; 7(5): 60-63, 66-77. ISSN: 0146-5422.

W3

WAGNER, P.; WITTOCK, B.; WHITLEY, R., eds. 1991. *Discourses on Society: The Shaping of the Social Science Disciplines*. London, UK: Kluwer; c1991. 385p. (Sociology of the Sciences, 15). ISBN: 0792310012; LCCN: 91192805.

W4

WAGNER, RICHARD A. 1989. The Rise of Computing in Anthropology: Hammers and Nails. *Social Science Computer Review*. 1989 Winter; 7: 418-429. ISSN: 0894-4393.

W5

WAHL, BERNT. 1995. *Exploring Fractals on the Macintosh*. Reading, MA: Addison- Wesley Pub. Co.; 1995. 340p. and 3.5 disk. ISBN: 02101626306.

W6

WALCH, VICTORIA IRONS. 1990. The Role of Standards in the Archival Management of Electronic Records. *The American Archivist*. 1990 Winter; 53: 30-43. ISSN: 0360- 9081.

W7

WALCH, VICTORIA IRONS. 1993. *Recognizing Leadership and Partnership: A Report on the Condition of Historical Records in the States and Efforts to Ensure Their Preservation and Use, with a Focus on State Historical Records Advisory Boards and State Archives and Records Management Programs*. Iowa City, IA: The Printing House; 1993. 365p. in 2 vols. (NHPRC funded Report for the Council of State Historical Records Coordinators).

W8

WALCH, VICTORIA IRONS. 1994. *Standards for Archival Description: A Handbook*. Chicago, IL: SAA; 1994. 325p. ISBN: 0-931828-96-1. Available from NISO Press at 1-800-282-NISO; Fax 301-567-9553.

W9

WALDEN, IAN. 1993. Electronic Documentation and the Law. See reference: ROSS, S.; HIGGS, E., eds., 1993. 119-133.

W10

WALDROP, M. MITCHAEL. 1992. *Complexity: The Emerging Science at the Edge of Order*. New York, NY: Simon & Schuster; 1992. 380p. ISBN: 0671767895.

W11
WALKER, ADRIAN. 1990. *Knowledge Systems and Prolog: Developing Expert, Database, and Natural Language Systems*. Reading, MA: Addison-Wesley; 1990. 538p. ISBN: 0201524244; LCCN: 89018658.

W12
WALKER, LARRY L. 1984. I consulenti del futuro i computer [Consultations of the Future and the Computer]. *Informatica e Documentazione* (IT). 1984 October-December; 11(4): 258-64. ISSN: 0390-2439.

W13
WALKER, ROBERT. 1796. *Analysis of Researches into the Origin and Progress of Historical Time*. London, UK: T. Cadell and W. Davies; 1796. LCCN: 07006050.

W14
WALKER, TERRI C. 1990. *Geographic Information Systems: An Assessment of Technology, Applications, and Products*. Madison, GA: SEAI Technical Publications; 1990. 3 vols., 588p. ISBN: 0896711102; LCCN: 90-139117.

W15
WALKER, TERRI C.; MILLER, RICHARD K. 1990. *Expert Systems Handbook: An Assessment of Technology, Applications, and Products*. Liburn, GA: Fairmount Press; 1990. Paperback ed. Englewood Cliffs, NJ: Prentice Hall; 1990. 772p. ISBN: 0881731013 (hbk.); 0132965429 (pbk.); LCCN: 89-37668.

W16
WALKER, TERRI C.; MILLER, RICHARD K. 1991. *Electronic Imaging and Image Processing: An Assessment of Technology, Applications, and Products*. Norcross, CA: SEAI Technical Publications; 1991. 3 vols.

W17
WALKER, THOMAS D. 1997. *Journal of Documentary Reproduction*, 1938-1942: Domain as Reflected in Characteristics of Authorship and Citation. See reference: BUCKLAND, M.; BELLARDO HAHN, eds. 1997. 361-368.

W18
WALKER, THOMAS D., ed. 1996. *L'Aparition du Computer: Epistemology and the Impact of Networked Computers on Society*. 4th International ISKO Conference, Washington, D.C., Berlin, DEU: Indeks Verlag; 1996. ISBN: 3886720241. (In English).

W19
WALKOWITZ, JUDITH R. 1992. *City of Dreadful Delight: Narratives of Sexual Danger in Late-Victorian London*. Chicago, IL: University of Chicago Press; 1992. 353p. ISBN: 0226871452 (hbk.); 0226871460 (pbk.); LCCN: 91048153.

W20
WALLACE, DAVID. 1993. Metadata and the Archival Management of Electronic Records: A Review. *Archivaria* (CAN). 1993 Spring; 36: 87-110. ISSN: 0318-6954.

W21
WALLACE, DAVID. 1994a. The Internet: Basic Navigation and Resources. *Archives and Museum Informatics: Cultural Heritage Informatics Quarterly*. 1994 Summer; 8(1): 110-20. ISSN: 0091-5971.

W22
WALLACE, DAVID. 1994b. Listservs. *Archives and Museum Informatics: Cultural Heritage Informatics Quarterly*. 1994 Summer; 8(2): 116-123. Reprinted in *Archival Outlook*. 1995 January; s.n.: 6. ISSN: 0091-5971.

W23
WALLERSTEIN, IMMANUEL M. 1974. *The Modern World-System*. San Diego, CA: Academic Press. 2nd ed. New York, NY: 1976. 2 vols. (Studies in Discontinuity series).

W24
WALLERSTEIN, IMMANUEL M. 1991. *Unthinking Social Science: The Limits of Nineteenth-century Paradigms*. [Cambridge, MA]: Polity Press with B. Blackwell; 1991. 286p. ISBN: 074608760 (hbk.); 0745609112 (pbk.); LCCN: 91007177.

W25
WALLERSTEIN, IMMANUEL M. 1996. *The Structures of Knowledge, or, How Many Ways May We Know?* Binghamton, NY: SUNY at Binghamton, Fernand Braudel Center for the Study of Economics, Historical Systems, and Civilizations; 1996.

W26
WALLERSTEIN, IMMANUEL M. 1997. *The Time of Space and the Space of Time: The Future of Social Science*. Binghamton, NY: SUNY at Binghamton, Fernand Braudel Center for the Study of Economics, Historical Systems, and Civilizations; 1997.

W27

WALLERSTEIN, IMMANUEL M. [1999]. *The End of the World as We Know It: Social Sciences for the Twenty-first Century*. Minneapolis, MN: University of Minnesota Press; [1999]. ISBN: 0816633975 (hbk.); 0816633983 (pbk.); LCCN: 99026087.

W28

WALNE, PETER; EVANS, FRANK; HIMLY, FRANCOIS J., ed. 1984/1988. *Dictionary of Archival Terminology / Dictionnaire de Terminologie Archivistique*. Munchen, DEU/New York, NY: K. G. Saur; 1984. Reprint, 1988. 212p. (Multi-lingual lexicon). ISBN: 3598202792.

W29

WALNUT CREEK, INC. 1994. *Project Gutenberg* [CD-ROM]. Walnut Creek, Inc.; 1994. Cf., e-text archives at: www.gutenberg.net.

W30

WALSH, KEVIN: 1992. *The Representation of the Past. Museums and Heritage in the Post-Modern World*. London, UK: Routledge; 1992. 204p. ISBN: 041505026X (hbk.); 0415079446 (pbk.); LCCN: 91-30400.

W31

WALSH, W. H. 1974. Colligatory Concepts of History. See reference: GARDINER, P., ed. 1974. 127-144.

W32

WALSHAM, GEOFF. 1993. *Interpreting Information Systems in Organizations*. Chichester, UK: John Wiley; 1993.

W33

WALTERS, RONALD G. 1980. Signs of the Times; Clifford Geertz and Historians. *Social Research*. 1980; 47(3): 537-56. ISSN: 0037-783X.

W34

WALTERS, RONALD G., ed. 1997. *Scientific Authority and Twentieth-century America*. Baltimore, MD: The Johns Hopkins Press; 1997. 280p. ISBN: 0-8018-5389-3.

W35

WALTERS, TYLER O. 1991. Possible Educations for Archivists: Integrating Graduate Archival Education with Public History Education Programs. *The American Archivist*. 1991; 54(4): 484-492. ISSN: 0360-9081.

W36

WALTERS, TYLER O. 1995. Thinking about Archival Preservation in the '90s and Beyond: Some Recent Publications and their Implications for Archivists. *The American Archivist*. 1995 Fall; 58(4): 476-493. ISSN: 0360-9081.

W37

WANG, Y.-C.; VANDENDORPE, J.; EVENS, M. 1985. Relational Thesauri in Information Retrieval. *Journal of the American Society for Information Science*. 1985; 36: ISSN: 0002-8231.

W38

WARNER, AMY J. 1987. Natural Language Processing. In: Williams, M. ed. *Annual Review of Information Science and Technology:* vol. 22. Medford, NJ: Information Today for ASIS; 1987. 79-108. ISBN: 1-57387-019-6; ISSN: 0066-4200; CODEN: ARISBC; LC no. 66-25096

W39

WARNER AMY J. 1991. Quantitative and Qualitative Assessments of the Impact of Linguistic Theory on Information Science. *Journal of the American Society for Information Science*. 1991; 42: 64-71. ISSN: 0002-8231.

W40

WARNER, JULIAN. 1990. Semiotics, Information Science, Documents, and Computers. *Journal of Documentation* (UK). 1990; 46: 16-32. ISSN: 0022-0418.

W41

WARNER, JULIAN. 1999. An Information View of History. See reference: BATES, M., ed. 1999. Pt. 2: 1125-1126.

W42

WARNER, MALCOLM. 1994. Organizational Behavior Revisited. *Human Relations*. 1994 October; 47(10): 1151-1166. ISSN: 0018-7267.

W43

WARNER, ROBERT M. 1995. *Diary of a Dream. A History of the National Archives Independence Movement, 1980-1985*. Lanham, MD: Scarecrow Press for SAA; 1995. 241 p. ISBN: 0-8108-2956-8.

W44

WASKO, JANET. 1994/1995. *Hollywood in the Information Age: Beyond the Silver Screen*. Oxford, UK: Oxford University Press; 1994. Austin, TX: University of Texas Press; 1995. 308p. ISBN: 0745603181 (hbk.); 074560319X (pbk.).

W45
WASKO, JANET; MOSCO, VINCENT. 1992. *Democratic Communications in the Information Age*. Toronto, CAN: Garamond Press; 1992. ISBN: 092005983X.

W46
WASSERMAN, PAUL. 1972. *The New Librarianship: A Challenge for Change*. New York, NY: Bowker; 1972. 287p. ISBN: 0835206041; LCCN: 72-8621; OCLC: 417026.

W47
WATSON, ANDREW B. 1993. *Digital Images and Human Vision*. Cambridge, MA: Bradford Book; 1993. 234p. ISBN: 0-262-23171-9. Distributed by MIT Press.

W48
WATSON, HUGH J.; RAINER, R. KELLY; HOUDESHEL, GEORGE. 1997. *Executive Information Systems: Emerging Developments*. New York, NY: Wiley; 1997. 357p. ISBN: 0471555541.

W49
WATSON, PATTY J. 1995. Archeology, Anthropology, and the Culture Concept. *American Anthropologist*. 1995 December; 97(4): 683-695. ISSN: 0002-7294.

W50
WATSON, PATTY J.; LEBLANC, STEVEN A.; REDMAN, CHARLES L. 1971/1984. *Explanation in Archeology: An Explicitly Scientific Approach*. New York, NY: Columbia University Press; 1971. 191p. Rev.ed. *Archeological Explanation: the Scientific Method in Archeology*. New York, NY: Columbia University Press; 1984. 309p. ISBN: 0231060289.

W51
WATTEL, EVERT; VAN REENEN, PIETER. 1995. Visualization of Extrapolated Social-Geographical Data. See reference: BOONSTRA, O., *ET AL.*, eds.; 1995. 253-264.

W52
WEBB, KEITH. 1995. *An Introduction to the Problems in the Philosophy of Social Science*. London, UK: Cassell; 1995. 256p. ISBN: 1-85567-291-X.

W53
WEBER, LISA, ed. 1984. *Documenting America: Assessing the Condition of Historical Records in the United States*. NHPRC Conference Report, Atlanta, June 24-25, 1983. Albany, NY: NAGARA; 1984. 71p. Includes a summary of about half of the state historical records assessment projects undertaken in the 1980s.

W54
WEBER, ROBERT P. 1985/1990. *Basic Content Analysis*. Beverley Hills, CA: Sage Publications; 1985. 236p. 2nd ed., 1990. ISBN: 0803924488 (pbk.); LCCN: 85- 50051; OCLC: 12279797.

W55
WEDGEWORTH, ROBERT, ed. 1980; 1993. *World of Library and Information Services*. Chicago, IL: American Library Association; 1980. 601 p. ISBN: 0838903053; LCCN: 80010912. Rev. ed. Chicago, IL: ALA; 1993. 905p. ISBN: 0838906905; LCCN: 93025159.

W56
WEGNER, PEER; DOYLE, JON. 1996. Strategic Directions in Computing Research. *ACM Computing Surveys*. 1996 December; 28(4): 565-575. ISSN: 0360-0300.

W57
WEICK, KARL E. [1969]. *The Social Psychology of Organizing*. Reading, MA: Addison- Wesley Pub. CO.; [1969]. 121p. LCCN: 74-083466.

W58
WEICK, KARL E. 1985. Cosmos v. Chaos: Sense and Nonsense in Electronic Contexts. *Organizational Dynamics*. 1985; 13 (2): 51-64. ISSN: 0319-0161.

W59
WEICK, KARL E.; MEADER, DAVID K. 1993. Sense-making and Group Support Systems. See reference: JESSUP, L. M.; VALACICH, J., eds.; 1993. 230-252.

W60
WEIGAND, ANDREAS S.; GERSHENFELD, NEIL A., eds. 1994. *Time Series Prediction. Forecasting the Future and Understanding the Past*. Santa Fe, NM: Santa Fe Institute (SFI); 1994. (Santa Fe Institute Studies in the Science of Complexity). ISBN: 0-201- 62602-0 (pbk.).

W61
WEIGAND, WAYNE A. 1997. MisReading LIS Education. *Library Journal*. 1997 June 15; 122(11): 36-38. ISSN: 0363-0277.

W62
WEIGAND, WAYNE A.; DAVIS, DONALD G., Jr., eds. 1994. *Encyclopedia of Library History*. New York, NY/ London, UK: Garland Publishing, Inc.; 1994. 707p. ISBN: 0-8240-5787-2.

W63
WEIGEL, FRIEDEMANN. 1996. EDI in the Library Market: How Close are We? See reference: BLUH, P., ed. 1996. 141-150.

W64
WEIL, S., ed. 1996. *Museums for the New Millennium: A Symposium for the Museum Community*. Washington, D.C.: American Association of Museums; 1996.

W65
WEINBERG, BELLA HASS. 1995. In-Depth Book Review: *Art & Architecture Thesaurus* (2nd *Guide to Indexing and Cataloging With the Art & Architecture Thesaurus,* edited by Toni Petersen and Patricia J. Barnett . *Journal of the American Society for Information Science*). 1995 March; 46(2): 152-159. ISSN: 0002-8231.

W66
WEINGARTNER, RUDOLPH H. 1961. The Quarrel about Historical Explanation. *The Journal of Philosophy*. 1961; 58: 29-45. ISSN: 0160-9335.

W67
WEINSHALL, THEODORE D., ed. 1993. *Societal Culture and Management*. Berlin, DGR/New York, NY: W. De Gruyter; 1993. 587p. ISBN: 3110127111 (hbk.); 0899256147 (hbk.); LCCN: 92-37993.

W68
WEINTRAUB, KARL J. 1980. The Humanistic Scholar and the Library. *Library Quarterly*. 1980 January; 50(1): 22-39. ISSN: 0024-2519.

W69
WEIR, ROBERT E.; LAWRENCE, SUSAN C.; FALES, EVAN, eds. 1994. *Genes and Human Self-Knowledge: Historical and Philosophical Reflections on Modern Genetics*. Iowa City: University of Iowa Press; 1994. 248p. ISBN: 0877454558 (hbk); 0877454566 (pbk.).

W70
WEISBORD, MARVIN; JANOFF, SANDRA. 1995. *Future Search: An Action Guide to Finding Common Ground in Organizations and Communities*. San Francisco, CA: Berret-Koehler Publishers; 1995. 219p. ISBN: 1881052125.

W71
WEISELMAN, IRVING L.; TOMASH, ERWIN. 1991. Marks on Paper: pts. 1-2. A Historical Survey of Computer Output Printing. *Annals of the History of Computing.* 1991; 13(1): 63-79; 13(2): 203-222. ISSN: 0164-1239.

W72
WEISGERBER, DAVID W. 1997. Chemical Abstracts Service Chemical Registry System: History, Scope, and Impact. See reference: BUCKLAND, M.; BELLARDO HAHN, eds. 1997. 349-360.

W73
WEISS, ERIC. 1996. Konrad Zuse Obituary. See reference: WILLIAMS, MICHAEL R., ed. 1996. 3-5.

W74
WEISSMAN, RONALD E. F. 1988. Strategic Directions in Computing and the Historian's Craft. *American History: A Bibliographic Review*. 1988; 4: 23-36. ISSN: 0748-6731.

W75
WEISSMAN, RONALD E. F. 1990. Virtual Documents on an Electronic Desktop: Hypermedia, Emerging Computer Environments and the Future of Information Management. See reference: DURANCE, C., ed. 1990.

W76
WEITZMAN, EBEN A.; MILES, MATTHEW B. 1995. *Computer Programs for Qualitative Data Analysis: A Software Sourcebook*. Thousand Oaks, CA: Sage Publications; c1995. 371p. ISBN: 0802955367 (hbk.); 0803955375 (pbk.); LCCN: 94040647.

W77
WELFORD, RICHARD, ed. 1990. *Information Technology for Social Scientists*. Shipley, UK: European Research Press; 1990. 192p. ISBN: 1872677002 (pbk.); LC- 90-18624; OCLC: 21232070.

W78
WELLER, ANN C. 1996. The Human Genome Project. See reference: CRAWFORD, S.; J. HURD; A. C. WELLER, eds. 1996.

W79
WELLING, GEORGE. 1993a. The Programme for Historical and Cultural Informatics at the University of Groningen-Netherlands. See reference: DAVIS, D., *ET AL.*, eds. 1993. 85-90.

W80
WELLING, GEORGE. 1993b. A Strategy for Intelligent Input Programs for Structured Data. *History and Computing* (UK). 1993; 5: 35-41. ISSN: 0957-0144.

W81
WELLING, GEORGE. 1996. How to Lie with Graphics: Having fun with a New Scanner (electronic file). Groningen, NL: Department of History; 1996 March 8. 6 p. Accessible at http://odur.let.rug.nl/~welling/bergen/forum.html.

W82
WELLISCH, HANS. 1972. From Information Science to Informatics: A Terminological Investigation. *Journal of Librarianship* (UK). 1972; 4(3): 157-187. ISSN: 0022-2232.

W83
WELLS, HERBERT. G. 1938. *World Brain.* Garden City, NY: Doubleday, Doran & Co. / London, UK: Methuen; 1938. 194p.

W84
WENGER, ETIENNE. 1998. *Communities of Practice: Learning, Meaning, and Identity.* Cambridge, UK / New York, NY: Cambridge University Press; 1998. 318p. ISBN: 0521430178; LCCN: 98202423.

W85
WENTWORTH, WILLIAM. M. 1980. *Context and Understanding: An Inquiry into Socialization Theory.* New York, NY: Elservier; c1980. 183p. ISBN: 0444990739; LCCN: 80011424.

W86
WERNER, KARL FERDINAND. 1977. *Liéns de parente et noms de personne. Un problème historique et méthodologique.* In: *Familles et parentes dans l'Occident médiéval* [Parental lineage and Personal Names: A Problem in Historical Methodology. Families and Parentage in the Medieval West]. Actes du colloque international de Rome, École française de Rome, 1974. In: *Collection de l'École française de Rome.* Rome, IT: École française; 1977. (In French).

W87
WERNER, THOMAS. [1993]. Transforming Machine Readable Sources. In: Thaller, M., comp. *The Historical Workstation Project.* Der Arbeitsplatzrechner für den Historiker. Distributed at the Graz AHC Conference, 1993. 10p. Available from the Historical Workstation Project group, Max-Planck-Institut für Geschichte, Göttingen, DEU .

W88
WERSIG, G. 1971. *Information—Kommunikation—Dokumentation.* Munich, DEU: Verlag Dokumentation; 1971.

W89
WERSIG, G. 1993. Information Science: The Study of Postmodern Knowledge Usage. *Information Processing & Management.* 1993: 29(2): 229-239. ISSN: 0306-4573.

W90
WERTSCH, J. 1992. *Voices of the Mind: A Socio-cultural Approach to Mediated Action.* Cambridge, MA: Harvard University Press; 1992. 169p. ISBN: 06749430031; LCCN: 90047211. Note: Activity Theory.

W91
WESLING, D. 1997. Michel Serres, Bruno Latour, and the edges of historical periods. *Clio.* 1997 Winter; 26: 189-204. ISSN: 0884-2043.

W92
WEST, BRUCE J.; DEERING, WILLIAM D. 1995. *The Lure of Modern Science: Fractal Thinking* River Edge, NJ: World Scientific Pub.; c1995. 421p. (Studies in Nonlinear Phenomena in Life Sciences, 3). ISBN: 9810221915; LCCN: 95018257.

W93
WEST, BRUCE J., ed. 1980. *Mathematical Models as a Tool for Social Sciences.* New York, NY: Gordon and Breach; c1980. 120p. LCCN: 79023974.

W94
WEST, MARTHA W. 1983. *Research and Information Science: What Where We've Been Says about Where We Are.* Halifax, CA: Dalhousie University School of Library Service; 1983. 65p. (Occassional Paper, 32). ISSN: 0318-7403; ISBN: 0-7703-0175- 4.

W95
WEST, THOMAS G. 1991. *In the Mind's Eye: Visual Thinkers, Gifted People and Learning Difficulties, Computer Images, and the Ironies of Creativity.* Buffalo, NY: Prometheus Books; 1991. 359p. ISBN: 79756462.

W96
WETHERELL, CHARLES. 1987. Managing Cultural Resource Information: The California Experience. *The Public Historian.* 1987; 9(1): 31-45. ISSN: 0272-3433.

W97
WEXELBLAT, RICHARD L., ed. 1981. *History of Programming Languages.* New York, NY: Academic Press; 1981. 758p. (ACM Monograph Series). ISBN: 0127450408.

W98
WHALEY, JOHN H. 1994. Digitizing History. *American Archivist.* 1994 Fall; 57(4): 660-672. ISSN: 0360-9081.

W99
WHEATLEY, MARGARET. 1992. *Leadership and the New Science: Learning about Organizations from an Orderly Universe.* San Francisco, CA: Berrett-Koehler; 1992. Video based on this book released under same title. Carlsbad, CA: CRM Films; 1993. Videocassette; guide, 42p.; workbook, 16p.

W100
WHEATLEY, MARGARET; KELLNER-ROGERS, MYRON. 1996. *The Simpler Way.* San Francisco, CA: Berret-Koehler; 1996. 135p. ISBN: 1881052958; LCCN: 96-015999.

W101
WHEATON, BRUCE R. 1982. A Computer Database System to Store and Display Archival Data on Correspondence of Historical Significance. *The American Archivist.* 1982 Fall; 45(4): 455-66. ISSN: 0360-9081.

W102
WHEELER, MARY BRAY, ed. 1990-. *Directory of Historical Organizations in the United States and Canada.* 14th ed. Nashville, TN: American Association for State and Local History Press; 1990-. ISSN: 1045-456X; DLC: 8665731; OCLC: 13726814.

W103
WHICKER, MARCIA LYNN; SIGELMAN, LEE. 1991. *Computer Simulation Applications: An Introduction.* Thousand Oaks, CA: Sage Publications; 1991. 152p. ISBN: 0803932456; 0803932464 (pbk.); LCCN: 90-25980.

W104
WHISTON, THOMAS G.; GEIGER, ROGER L., eds. 1992. *Research and Higher Education: The United Kingdom and the United States.* Buckingham, UK; Bristol, PA: Society for Research into Higher Education & Open University Press; 1992. 205p. ISBN; 03351564X.

W105
WHITBECK, GEORGE W. 1990. Recent Developments in Library and Information Science Education in the United Kingdom. *Journal of Education for Library and Information Science.* 1990; 30(3): 238-241. ISSN: 0748-5786.

W106
WHITBECK, GEORGE W. 1991. Doctoral Programs in Library and Information Science. *Journal of Education for Library and Information Science.* 1991; 32(3/4): 178-187. ISSN: 0748-5786.

W107
WHITE, CAROL. 1994. Benchmark Guidance is the Priority Now. *Times Educational Supplement* (UK). 1994 December 2; 4092: R2-3. About the British School Curriculum and Assessment Authority.

W108
WHITE, CLYDE A., prod. 1992. *Map of Life: Science, Society and the Human Genome Project* (Video). Burlington, NC: Carolina Audiovisuals, Inc.; 1992. (VHS cassette 1/2"; 46 min.).

W109
WHITE, DOUGLAS R.; TRUEX, GREGORY F. 1988. Anthropology and Computing: The Challenges of the 1990s. *Social Science Computer Review.* 1988 Winter; 6: 481-497. ISSN: -894-4393.

W110
WHITE, HAYDEN V. [1973]. *Metahistory: The Historical Imagination in Nineteenth-century Europe.* Baltimore, MD: The Johns Hopkins University Press; [1973]. 441p. ISBN: 0801814693; LCCN: 73-008110.

W111
WHITE, HAYDEN V. 1978a. *The Content of the Form: Narrative Discourse and Historical Representation.* Baltimore, MD: Johns Hopkins University Press; 1978. 244p. ISBN: 001829372; LCCN: 86-21404.

W112
WHITE, HAYDEN. 1978b. The Historical Text as Literary Artifact. See reference: CANARY, R. F.; KOZICKI, H., eds. 1978. 41-62.

W113
WHITE, HAYDEN V. 1978c. *Tropics of Discourse: Essays in Cultural Criticism.* Baltimore, MD: The Johns Hopkins Press; 1978. 244p. ISBN: 0801829372; LCCN: 86-21404; OCLC: 14412413.

W114
WHITE, HAYDEN V. 1984. The Question of Narrative in Contemporary Historical Theory. *History and Theory.* 1984; 23(1): 1-33. ISSN: 0018-2656.

W115
WHITE, HAYDEN V. 1987a *The Content of Form: Narrative Discourse and Historical Representation.* Baltimore: Johns Hopkins University Press; 1987. 244p. ISBN: 0801829372; LCCN: 86-21404; OCLC: 14412413.

W116
WHITE, HAYDEN V. 1987b. Foucault's Discourse: The Rhetoric of Anti-Humanism. See reference: WHITE, HAYDEN V. 1987a.

W117
WHITE, HAYDN. 1992. Historical Emplotment and the Problem of Truth. See reference: FRIEDLANDER, SAUL, ed. 1992. 35-52.

W118
WHITE, HOWARD D.; MCCAIN, KATHERINE W. 1989. Bibliometrics. In: Williams, M., ed. *Annual Review of Information Science and Technology:* vol.24. Medford, NJ: Learned Information for ASIS; 1989. 119-186. ISBN: 1-57387-019-6; ISSN: 0066-4200; CODEN: ARISBC; LCCN: 66-25096.

W119
WHITE, HOWARD D.; MCCAIN, KATHERINE W. 1997. Visualization of Literatures. In: Williams, Martha, ed. *Annual Review of Information Science and Technology:* vol. 32. Medford, NJ: Information Today, Inc.; 1997. ISBN: 1-57387-047-1; ISSN: 0066-4200; CODEN: ARISBC; LCCN: 66-25096.

W120
WHITE, HOWARD D.; MCCAIN, KATHERINE W. 1998. Visualizing a Discipline: An Author Co-citation Analysis of Information Science, 1972-1995. *Journal of the American Society for Information Science.* 1998; 49 (4): 327-355. ISSN: 0002-8231.

W121
WHITE, MORTON G. 1969. *The Foundations of Historical Knowledge.* New York, NY: Harper and Row; c1965. 299p. LCCN: 70004667.

W122
WHITE, WILLIAM. 1992. *The Microdot: History and Application.* Williamstown, NJ: Phillips Publications; 1992. 158p. ISBN: 0-932572-20-0.

W123
WHITEFIELD, ANDY; ESGATE, A; DENLEY, IAN.; BYERLEY, P. 1993. On Distinguishing Work Tasks and Enabling Tasks. *Interacting with Computers.* 1993; 5(3): 333-348. ISSN: 0953-5438. Accessible also at http://peak.umdl.umich.edu/cgi-bin/peak/listjournal. (Study cont'd. below).

W124
WHITEFIELD, ANDY; HILL, B. 1994. A Comparative Analysis of Task Analysis Products. *Interacting with Computers.* 1994; 6 (3): 289-309. ISSN: 0953-5438. Accessible also at http://peak.umdl.umich.edu/cgi-bin/peak/listjournal.

W125
WHITEHEAD, ALFRED H. 1968/1979. *Models of Thought.* New York, NY: Free Press; 1968. 179p. New Haven, CT: Yale University Press; 1979. 2 vols. ISBN: 0300023472; LCCN: 78-031744.

W126
WHITTEMORE, N. J.; YOTIS, M. C. 1973. A Generalized Conceptual Development for the Analysis and Flow of Information. *Journal of the Society for Information Science.* 1973; 24(30): 221-231. ISSN: 0002-8231.

W127
WIBERLEY, STEPHEN E., Jr. 1983. Subject Access in the Humanities and the Precision of the Humanist's Vocabulary. *Library Quarterly.* 1983 October; 53 (4): 420-433. ISSN: 0024-2519.

W128
WIBERLEY, STEPHEN E., Jr. 1988. Names in Space and Time: The Indexing Vocabulary in the Humanities. *Library Quarterly.* 1988 January; 58 (1): 1-28. ISSN: 0024-2519.

W129
WIBERLEY, STEPHEN E., Jr. 1991. Habits of Humanists: Scholarly Behavior and New Information Technologies. *Library Hi-Tech.* 1991; 9 (1): 17-21. ISSN: 0737-8831.

W130
WIBERLEY, STEPHEN E., Jr.; DAUGHERTY, R. A.; DANOWSKI, J. A. 1990. User Persistence in Scanning Postings of a Computer-driven Information System. *Library and Information Science Research*. 1990; 12: 341-353. ISSN: 0740-8188.

W131
WIBERLEY, STEPHEN E., Jr.; JONES, WILLIAM G. 1989. Patterns of Information Seeking in the Humanities. *College & Research Libraries*. 1989 November; 50 (6): 638-645. ISSN: 0010-0870.

W132
WIBERLEY, STEPHEN E., Jr.; JONES, WILLIAM G. 1994. Humanists Revisited: A Longitudinal Look at the Adoption of Information Technology. *College & Research Libraries*. 1994 November; 55 (6): 499-510. ISSN: 0010-0870.

W133
WIERERHOLD, G. 1992. Mediators in the Architecture of Future Information Systems. *Computer*. 1992 March; 25 (3): 38-49. ISSN: 0018-9162.

W134
WIESELMAN, IRVING; TOMASH, ERWIN. 1991. Marks on paper: A Historical Survey of Computer Output Printing. *Annals of the History of Computing*. Pt. I; 13 (1): 63- 79. Pt. II: 1991; 13 (2): 203-222. ISSN: 0164-1239.

W135
WILBUR, W. J. 1996. Human Subjectivity and Performance Limits in Document Retrieval. *Information Processing & Management*. 1994; 32: 515-527. ISSN: 0306-4573.

W136
WILBUR, W. J.; COFFEE, L. 1994. The Effectiveness of Document Neighboring in Search Enhancement. *Information Processing & Management*. 1994; 30: 253-266. ISSN: 0306-4573.

W137
WILD, MARTIN. 1988. 1066 and all that! *Times Educational Supplement* (UK). 1988 November 18; 3777: 65. ISSN: 0040-7887.

W138
WILDEMUTH, B. M. 1993. Post-postive Research: Two Examples of Methodological Plurality. *Library Quarterly*. 1993; 63(4): 450-468. ISSN: 0024-2519.

W139
WILENSKY, HAROLD L. 1967. *Organizational Intelligence: Knowledge and Policy in Government and Industry*. New York, NY: Basic Books; 1967. 226p. LCCN: 67- 017540.

W140
WILENSKY, ROBERT. 1996. Toward Work-Centered Digital Information Services. See reference: SCHATZ, B.; CHEN, H., eds. 1996. 37-44.

W141
WILKES, MAURICE V.; SPATZ, BRUCE, eds. 1995. *Computing Perspectives*. San Francisco, CA: Morgan Kaufmann Publishers; 1995. 207p. 18 essays. ISBN: 15586033174.

W142
WILKIE, TOM. 1993/1994. *Perilous Knowledge. The Human Genome Project and Its Implications.* Berkeley, CA: University of California Press; 1993. ISBN: 0520085531. London, UK: Faber; 1993. Pbk. Ed., 1994. 195p. ISBN: 0-571-17051-X.

W143
WILKINS, A. L. 1983. The Culture Audit: A Tool for Understanding Organizations. *Organizational Dynamics*. 1983; 12(2): 24-38. ISSN: 0090-2616.

W144
WILKS, YORICK A.; SLATOR, BRIAN M.; GUTHRIE, LOUISE M. 1996. *Electric Words. Dictionaries, Computers, and Meanings.* Cambridge, MA: Bradford Book; 1996. 288p. ISBN: 0-262-23182-4. Distributed by MIT Press.

W145
WILL, GEORGE F. 1996. Intellectual Segregation. *Newsweek*. 1996 February 19; 2: 87. ISSN: 0028-9604.

W146
WILLIAMS, FREDERICK. 1986. *Reasoning with Statistics: How to Read Quantitative Research*. New York, NY: Holt, Rinehard, and Winston; 1986. 214p. ISBN: 00370718473.

W147
WILLIAMS, JAMES G. 1997a. Information Science: A Proposed Model for Curriculum Development. See reference: WILLIAMS, J. G.; CARBO, T., eds. 1997.

W148
WILLIAMS, JAMES G. 1997b. Information Science: Definition and Scope. See reference: WILLIAMS, J. G.; CARBO, T., eds. 1997.

W149
WILLIAMS, JAMES G.; CARBO, TONI, eds. 1997. *Information Science: Still an Emerging Discipline*. Studies honoring Allen Kent. Pittsburgh, PA: Cathedral Publishing; 1997. 231p. ISBN: 1-887969-03-9.

W150
WILLIAMS, JAMES G.; SOCHATS, KENNETH M.; MORSE, EMILE. 1995. Visualization. In: Williams, Martha E., ed. *Annual Review of Information Science and Technology:* volume 30. Medford, NJ: Information Today, Inc. for ASIS; 1995. 161-208. ISBN: 1- 57387-019-6; ISSN: 0066-4200; CODEN: ARISBC; LCCN: 66-25096.

W151
WILLIAMS, MARTHA. 1977. Databases—a History of Development and Trends from 1966 through 1975. *Journal of the American Society for Information Science*. 1977; 28: 71- 78. ISSN: 0002-8231.

W152
WILLIAMS, MARTHA. 1994. State of Databases Today: 1994. In: Maraccio, Kathleen Young *et. al.*, eds. *Directory of Databases*. 3rd ed. Detroit, MI: Gale Research, Inc.; 1994. xix-xxx. ISBN: 0-8103-5747-X

W153
WILLIAMS, MARTHA, ed. 1965-. *Annual Review of Information Science and Technology (ARIST)*. White Plains, NY: Knowledge Industry Publications, Inc.; Medford, NJ: Learned Information, Inc., for ASIS; 1965-. (35 vols. to date). ISBN: 1-57387-019-6; ISSN: 0066-4200; CODEN: ARISBC; LCCN: 66-25096.

W154
WILLIAMS, MARTHA; SUTTON, ELLEN; SUTTON, BRETT. 1994. New Database Products: Social Sciences, Humanities, News and General. *Online and CD-ROM Review: International Journal of Online, Optical, and Networked Information*.1994; 18 (2): 95-105. ISSN: 0309-314X.

W155
WILLIAMS, MICHAEL R. 1985/1996/1997. *A History of Computing Technology*. Englewood Cliffs, NJ: Prentice-Hall; 1985. 432 pp. ISBN: 0133899179; LCCN: 85-6357; OCLC: 11865896. Rev. ed. Los Alamitos, CA: IEEE Press; 1996. 530p. 2nd ed. Los Alamitos, CA: IEEE; 1997. 530p. ISBN: 0-8186-7739-2.

W156
WILLIAMS, MICHAEL R., ed. 1996. 50 Years of Computing. Special Issue of *IEEE Annals of the History of Computing*. 1996 Summer; 18(2): 1-80. (Observation of the IEEE Computer Society, 50 Years of Service, 1946-1996). ISSN: 1058-6180.

W157
WILLIAMS, PETER W. 1979/1982. The Varieties of American Medievalism. *Studies in Medievalism*. 1879. 1982; 1 (2): 1-15.

W158
WILLIAMS, ROBERT F. 1987-. *Legality of Optical Storage: Admissibility of Optically Stored Records*. 1 vol., loose-leaf service. Chicago, IL: Cohasset Associates; 1987-. LCCN: 87-24288.

W159
WILLIAMS, ROBERT F., ed. 1980-. *Legality of Microfilms: Admissibility of Evidence from Microfilm Records*. Updated from 1971; loose-leaf service. Chicago, IL: Cohasset Associates for Nixon, Hargrave, Devan and Doyle, Inc.; 1980-. LCCN: 80-80848.

W160
WILLIAMS, ROBERT F. [1996-]. Legality of Optical Storage: New Perspectives—Referenced Laws [electronic file]. Chicago, IL: Cohasset, Inc.; [1996]. Updated 7/30/97. Accessible at http://www.cohasset.com/.

W161
WILLIAMS, ROBERT V. 1994. *A Directory of Archival Resources for the History of Information Science: Brief Report on a new ASIS funded project*. Paper in: pre-conference seminar on the History of Information Science, at the American Society for Information Science Conference, October 17-20, 1994, Alexandria, VA.

W162
WILLIAMS, ROBERT V. 1997. The Documentation and Special Libraries Movements in the United States, 1910-1960. See reference: BELLARDO HAHN, T.; BUCKLAND, M., eds. 1997. Pt. 2: 775-781.

W163
WILLIAMS, ROBERT V.; WHITMIRE, LAIRD; BRADLEY, COLLEEN. 1997. Bibliography of the History of Information Science in North America, 1900-1995. See reference: BUCKLAND, M.; BELLARDO HAHN, eds., 1997. 373-379.

W164
WILLIAMS, W. H. 1978. How bad can "good" data really be? *The American Statistician*. 1978; 32: 61-65. ISSN: 0003-1305.

W165
WILLIAMSON, JUDITH. 1985. *Decoding Advertisements: Ideology and Meaning in Advertizing*. 4th ed. London, UK: Marion Boyars; 1985. 180p. ISBN: 01745261421 (hbk.); 0714526150 (hbk.). LCCN: 79-307415.

W166
WILLIGAN, J. DENNIS; LYNCH, KATHERINE A. 1982. *Sources and Methods of Historical Demography*. New York, NY: Academic Press; 1982. 505p. ISBN: 0127570225 (hbk.); 0127570209 (pbk.); LCCN: 82-8819.

W167
WILLIS, DONALD. 1992. *A Hybrid Systems Approach to Preservation of Printed Materials*. Washington, D.C.: NARA Commission on Preservation and Access; 1992 November. 44p. Available from: NARA, Washington, D.C.

W168
WILLS, MARGARET F. 1992. *A Computer-Assisted Content Analysis of the Treatment of Religion during the Colonial Period of American History in College Level United States History Textbooks*. Lafayette, AK: University of Arkansas; 1992. 224p. (Ed.D. dissertation; *DAI*, 53/08-A: 2712). Available from: University Microfilms, Ann Arbor, MI (Order no. AAD92-37334).

W169
WILSON, DAVID. 1996. The Next Wave of Computer Modeling. *The Chronicle of Higher Education*. 1996 April 12; 42(31): A25, A28. ISSN: 0009-5982.

W170
WILSON, EDWARD O. 1998. *The Unity of Knowledge*. New York, NY: Alfred A. Knopf; 1998. 332p. ISBN: 0679450777; LCCN: 97-002816. Distributed by Random House.

W171
WILSON, FIONA. 1992. Language, Technology, Gender and Power. *Human Relations*. 1992 September; 45(9): 883-904. ISSN: 0018-7267.

W172
WILSON, IAN E. 1990-1991. Towards a Vision of Archival Service. *Archivaria* (CAN). 1990-91 Winter; 31: 91-100. ISSN: 0318-6954.

W173
WILSON, IAN E. 1995. Reflections on *Archival Strategies*. *The American Archivist*. 1995 Fall; 58(4): 414-238. ISSN: 0360-9081. Commentary on work of David Bearman.

W174
WILSON, JANE B. 1991. *The Very Quiet Baltimoreans: A Guide to the Historic Cemeteries and Burial Sites of Baltimore*. Baltimore, MD: White Mane Publishing Co., Inc.; 1991. 130p. ISBN: 0-942597-40-0.

W175
WILSON, MARY G. 1992. *Analysis of Expert and Learner Interactions during Looking at and Talking about Art Activities*. Bloomington, IN: Indiana University; 1992. (Ph.D. dissertation; *DAI*, vol. 53/07-A: 2213). Available from: University Microfilms, Ann Arbor, MI (Order no. AAD92-31636).

W176
WILSON, PATRICK G. 1968. *Two Kinds of Power: An Essay on Bibliographical Control*. University of California Publications in Librarianship, 5. Berkeley, CA: University of California Press; 1968. 155p. LCCN: 68-5961; OCLC: 433797.

W177
WILSON, PATRICK G. 1980. Limits to the Growth of Knowledge: The Case of the Social and Behavioral Sciences. *Journal of Documentation*. 1980; 50(1): 4-21. ISSN: 0022-0418.

W178
WILSON, PATRICK G. 1993. Communication Efficiency in Research and Development. *Journal of the American Society for Information Science*. 1993; 44: 376-382. ISSN: 0002-8231.

W179
WILSON, PATRICK G. 1995. Unused Relevant Information in Research and Development. *Journal of the American Society for Information Science*. 1995; 46(1): 45-51. ISSN: 0002-8231.

W180
WILSON, PATRICK G. 1996. The Future of Research in our Field. See reference: OLAISEN, J.; MUNCH-PETERSEN, E.; WILSON, P., eds. 1996. 319-323.

W181
WILSON, PAULINE. 1978. Impending Change in Library Education: Implications for Planning. *Journal of Education for Librarianship.* 1978; 18: 159-174. ISSN: 0022-0604.

W182
WILSON, THOMAS D. 1981. On User Studies and Information Needs. *Journal of Documentation* (UK). 1981; 37: 3-15. ISSN: 0022-0418.

W183
WILSON, THOMAS D. 1989. Towards an Information Management Curriculum. *Journal of Information Science.* 1989; 15: 203-209. ISSN: 0165-5515.

W184
WILSON, THOMAS D. 1994. Information Needs and Uses: Fifty Years of Progress? See reference: VICKERY, B. C., ed; 1994. 15-51.

W185
WILSON, THOMAS D. 1998. EQUIP: A European Survey of Quality Criteria for the Evaluation of Databases. *Journal of Information Science.* 1998; 24(5): 345-357. ISSN: 0165-5515.

W186
WILSTED, THOMAS; NOLTE, WILLIAM. 1991. *Managing Archival and Manuscript Repositories.* Chicago, IL: Society of American Archivists; 1991. 105p. ISBN: 0931828783.

W187
WINCHESTER, IAN. 1970. The Linkage of Historical Records by Man and Computer: Techniques and Problems. *Journal of Interdisciplinary History.* 1970; 1: 107-124. ISSN: 0022-1953.

W188
WINCHESTER, IAN. 1980. Priorities for Record Linkage: A Theoretical and Practical Checklist. In: Clubb, Jerome M. and Scheuch, Erwin K., eds. *Records Linkage.* In: *Historical Social Research* (DEU). Stuttgart, DEU: QUANTUM; 1980. 414-30.(*Historisch-Sozialwissenschaftliche Forschungen*, 6). (Entire issue on title topic). ISSN: 0173-2145.

W189
WINCHESTER, IAN. 1984. History, Scientific History, and Physics. *Historical Methods.* 1984 Summer; 17(3). ISSN: 0161-5440.

W190
WINCHESTER, IAN. 1985. Record Linking in the Microcomputer Era: A Survey. *Demographic Database Newsletters.* 1985; 3: 3.

W191
WINCHESTER, IAN. 1992. What Every Historian Needs to Know about Record Linkage in the Microcomputer Era. *Historical Methods.* 1992; 25(4): 149-165. ISSN: 0161-5440.

W192
WINEBURG, SAMUEL S. 1991. Historical Problem Solving: A Study of the Cognitive Processes Used in the Evaluation of Documentary and Pictorial Evidence. *Journal of Educational Psychology.* 1991 (March); 83: 73-87. ISSN: 0022-0663.

W193
WINER, B. J. 1962/1991. *Statistical Principles in Experimental Design.* New York, NY: McGraw-Hill; 1962. 672p. LCCN: 61-013174. 2nd ed. [1971]. 907p. ISBN: 0070709815; LCCN: 79-133392. Revised and expanded by BROWN, DONALD R.; MICHELS, KENNETH M. Mew York, NY: McGraw-Hill; 1991. 3rd ed. 1057p. ISBN: 0070709823; LCCN: 90-027253.

W194
WINKLER, KAREN. 1987. Interdisciplinary Research: How Big a Challenge to Traditional Fields? *Chronicle of Higher Education.* 1987 October 7; 34(1): A-1, A-14. ISSN: 0009-5982.

W195
WINKLER, KAREN J. 1995. History in Hollywood: the Way Films present the Past. *The Chronicle of Higher Education.* 1995 December 15; 42(16): A10-13. ISSN: 0009-5982.

W196
WINKLER, R. L. 1967. The Quantification of Judgement: Some Methodological Suggestions. *SIAM Journal of Computing.* 1967; 105-120.

W197
WINOGRAD, EUGENE; NEISSER, ULRIC, eds. 1995. *Affect and Accuracy in Recall: Studies of "Flashbulb" Memories.* Papers from the Emory Cognition Project Conference, Feb. 2-3, 1990. New York, NY & Cambridge, UK: Cambridge University Press; 1992. 315p. ISBN: 05214001887. See also reference: NEISSER, U.; WINOGRD, E., eds. 1988.

W198
WINOGRAD, TERRY. [1989?]. *Computerized Understanding of Language* (VHS Videocassette). Stanford University Computer Science Video Journal: Artificial Intelligence Research Lectures. San Mateo, CA: Morgan Kaufmann Publishers; [1989?]. ISBN: 0934613850.

W199
WINOGRAD, TERRY; FLORES, CARLOS F. 1987. *Understanding Computers and Cognition: A New Foundation for Design.* Reading, MA: Addison-Wesley Publishing Co.; 1987. 207p. ISBN: 0893910503.

W200
WINSTON, PATRICK H. 1975. Learning Structural Descriptions from Examples. In: Winston, P. H.; Horn, B., eds. *The Psychology of Computer Vision.* New York, NY: McGraw-Hill; 1975. 282p. ISBN: 0070710481.

W201
WINTERS, MARILYN B. 1984. *The Course of Study in American Education: Past, Present and Future.* Los Angeles, CA: Claremont Graduate School; 1984. 242p. (Ph.D. dissertation; *DAI*, vol. 44/08-A: 2387). Available from: University Microfilms, Ann Arbor, MI (Order no. AAD83-28283).

W202
WISBEY, ROY A., ed. 1990-. *Altdeutsche Predigen, I-III. Altdeutsche Predigen und Gebete* [Old German Sermons and Prayers] (Electronic files). St. Katharinen [Göttingen]: Max-Planck-Institut für Geschichte in Kommission bei Scripta Mercaturae Verlag; 1990-. (Halbgraue Reihe zur historischen Fackinformatik Serie C: Datenbasen als Editionem, Bande 4-7). ISBN: 3-928134-07-8; 3-928134-09-4; 3-928134-11-6; 3- 928134-12-4. (Sample of machine-readable encoded medieval texts from ongoing series, 20 vols. to date; in Old German). Available from the Institut or the Dansk Data Arkiv, Odense, DK.

W203
WISE, GENE. 1980. *American Historical Explanations: A Strategy for Grounded Inquiry.* 2nd rev. ed. Minneapolis, MN: University of Minnesota Press; 1980. 381p. ISBN: 0816609543 (hbk.); 08816609578 (pbk.); LCCN: 80-17697; OCLC: 6422938.

W204
WISE, M. NORTON, ed. 1995. *The Values of Precision.* Princeton, NJ: Princeton University Press; 1995. 372p. ISBN: 0691037590.

W205
WISSENBURG, ASTRID M.; SPAETH, DONALD A. 1995. In Search of a Metaphor for Hypermedia: The Enriched Lecture. See reference: BOONSTRA, O. *ET AL.*, eds., 1995. 306-310.

W206
WITTEN, IAN H.; MOFFAT, ALISTAIR; BELL, TRIMOTHY C. 1994. *Managing Gigabytes: Compressing and Indexing Documents and Images.* New York, NY: Van Nostrand Reinhold; 1994. 429p. ISBN: 0442018630; LCCN: 93-049066.

W207
WITTGENSTEIN, LUDWIG. 1953/1958, 1977/1980. *Philosophische Untersuchungen: Ausw. Aus d. Nachlass.* Wright, G. H. von; Nyman, H., eds. Frankfurt am Main, DEU: Suhrkamp; 1977. 169p. (Bibliothek Suhrkamp, Bd. 535). ISBN: 3518015354. 2nd rev. ed. Oxford, UK: B. Blackwell; 1980. (In German and English parallel texts). ISBN: 0631127526. Trans. also as: *Philosophical Investigations.* Anscombe, G. E. M., trans. Oxford, UK: Blackwell; 1953. 2nd ed., 1958. 232p. (In German with English parallel texts).

W208
WITTGENSTEIN, LUDWIG. 1969/1970. *Über Gewissenheit.* Anscombe, G.E. M; Von Wright, G. H., eds. D. Paul & G. E. M. Anscombe, trans. *On Certainty.* Oxford, UK: Basil Blackwell; 1969. New York, NY: Harper; 1970. 90p. LCCN: 70-82552; OCLC: 177990.

W209
WITTGENSTEIN, LUDWIG. 1980. *Vermischte Bemerkungen.* Trans. as: *Culture and Value.* Wright, Georg H. von, trans. Rev. 2nd ed. Oxford, UK: B. Blackwell; 1980. 94p. (Parallel German and English texts). ISBN: 0631127526.

W210
WOLCOT, PETER. 1993. *Soviet Advanced Technology: The Case of High-Performance Computing.* Tucson, AZ: University of Arizona; 1993. 569p. (Ph.D. dissertation; *DAI*, 54/07-A: 2713. Available from University Microfilms, Ann Arbor, MI.

W211
WOLEDGE, G. 1983. "Bibliography" and "Documentation": Words and Ideas. *Journal of Documentation* (UK). 1983; 39: 266-279. ISSN: 0022-0418.

W212
WOLF, ERIC R. 1982. *Europe and the People without History.* Berkeley, CA: University of California Press; 1982. 503p. ISBN: 0520044592 (hbk.); 0520048989 (pbk.).

W213
WOLF, ERIC R. 1994. Perilous Ideas: Race, Culture, People. Sidney W. Mintz Lecture for 1992. *Current Anthropology.* 1994 February; 35(1): 1-12. ISSN: 0011-3204.

W214
WOLF, KEN. 1994. Teaching History the Old-Fashioned Way—Through Biography. *AHA Perspectives.* 1994 May/June; 32(5): 3-6. ISSN: 0743-7021.

W215
WOLKENHAUER, OLAF. 1997. *Possibility Theory with Applications to Data Analysis.* Taunton Sommerset, UK: Research Studies Press; New York, NY: J. Wiley; 1997. ISBN: 086380229X (hbk.); 0471981613 (pbk.).

W216
WOLPERT, DAVID H. 1995. *The Mathematics of Generalization.* Santa Fe, NM: Santa Fe Institute (SFI); 1995. (Santa Fe Institute Studies in the Science of Complexity). ISBN: 0-201-40985-2 (hbk.); 0-201-40983-6 (pbk.).

W217
WOOD, DENIS. 1992. *The Power of Maps.* Fells, John, collaborator. New York, NY: The Guilford Press; 1992. 248p. ISBN: 0898624924 (hbk.); 0898624932 (pbk.).

W218
WOOD, MICHAEL R.; ZURCHER, LOUIS A., Jr. 1988. *The Development of a Post- Modern Self: A Computer- Assisted Comparative Analysis of Personal Documents.* New York, NY: Greenwood Press; 1988. 179p. ISBN: 0313254583; LCCN: 87-23666; OCLC: 16579488.

W219
WOOD, NANCY. 1994. Memory's Remains: *Les lieux de memoire* (Review essay). *History and Memory.* 1994 Spring/Summer; 6: 123-149.

W220
WOODCOCK, ALEXANDER E.; POSTON, T. 1974. *A Geometrical Study of the Elementary Catastrophes.* Berlin, DEU / New York, NY: Springer Velrag; 1974. 257p. ISBN: 0387066810.

W221
WOODS, LARRY, ed. 1999. *Knowledge: Creation, Organization and Use.* ASIS '99 Proceedings of the 62nd ASIS Annual Meeting, Oct. 31-Nov. 4, 1999, Washington, D.C. Medford, NJ: Information Today, Inc. for ASIS; 1999. 868p. ISBN: 1-57387-091-9; ISSN: 004-7870; CODEN: PAISDQ.

W222
WOODS, THOMAS A. 1995. Museums and the Public: Doing History Together. *Journal of American History.* 1995 December; 82(3): 1111-1116. ISSN: 0021-8723.

W223
WOOLLARD, MATTHEW; DENLEY, PETER. 1992. *Source-Oriented Data Processing for Historians: A Tutorial for KLIEU.* (Electronic Diskette). London, UK: University of London, Queen Mary & Westfield College, KLIEU Support Team of the Humanities Computing Center; 1992. (Part of the *KLIEU* 5.1.1 package).

W224
WORKMAN, LESLIE J., ed. 1994. *Medievalism in Europe* [I]. Cambridge, UK: D. S. Brewer; 1997. 241p. ISBN: 0859914003 (hbk.). Available also in *Studies in Medievalism*, v. 58. (Entire issue on title topic). ISSN: 0738-7164.

W225
WORKMAN, LESLIE J.; VERDUIN, KATHLEEN, eds. 1997. *Medievalism in Europe,* II. Cambridge, UK: D. S. Brewer; 1997. 243p. ISBN: 0859914321 (hbk.). Co-published in: *Studies in Medievalism*, v. 8. (Entire issue on title topic). ISSN: 0738-7164.

W226
WORLD WIDE WEB CONSORTIUM. 1994. *Historical Style Sheet Proposals* (Electronic file). Accessible at http://www/w3.org/pub/WWW/Style/.

W227
WORLD WIDE WEB CONSORTIUM. 1997. XML: Extensible Markup Language. Bray, Tim; Sperberg-McQueen, C. M., eds. 1997 March. Accessible at http://www/w3.org/pub/ WWW/TR/.

W228

WORSLEY, PETER. 1997. *Knowledges: Culture, Counterculture, Subculture*. New York, NY; 1997. 407p. ISBN: 1565843835.

W229

WOUDE, A. M. VAN DER; HAYAMI, AKIRA; DE VRIES, JAN, eds. 1990. *Urbanization in History: A Process of Dynamic Interactions*. Oxford, UK: Clarendon Press/ New York, NY: Oxford Universitiy Press; 1990. 371p. ISBN: 0198286791; LCCN: 89070901

W230

WRIGHT, BENJAMIN. 1991. *The Law of Electronic Commerce: EDI, FAX, and E-Mail—Technology, Proof, and Liability*. Boston, MA: Little, Brown; 1991. 432p. ISBN: 0316956325.

W231

WRIGHT, H. CURTIS. 1985. [Jesse H.] Shera as a Bridge between Librarianship and Information Science. *The Journal of Library History, Philosophy & Comparative Librarianship*. 1985 Spring; 20: 137-156. ISSN: 0275-3650.

W232

WRIGHT, H. CURTIS. 1988. *Jesse Shera, Librarianship and Information Science*. Provo, UT: Brigham Young University School of Library and Information Sciences; 1988. 103p. (Occasional Papers, 5). ISSN: 0148-2068.

W233

WRIGHT, PATRICK M.; MCMAHAN, GARY C. 1992. Theoretical Perspectives for Strategic Human Resource Management. *Journal of Management*. 1992 June: 18 (2): 295-320. ISSN: 0149-2063.

W234

WRIGLEY, EDWARD A. [1969]. *Population and History*. New York, NY: McGraw-Hill; [1969]. 256p.

W235

WRIGLEY, EDWARD A. 1973. *Identifying People in the Past*. London, UK: Edward Arnold; 1973. 159p. ISBN: 0713156945; LCCN: 74-180608; OCLC: 1057487.

W236

WRIGLEY, EDWARD A. 1985. *The Local and the General in Population History*. Exeter, UK: University of Exeter Press; 1985. 19p. (The 16th Hart Lecture, 1983). ISBN: 085982379.

W237

WRIGLEY, EDWARD A., ed. *Nineteenth-century Society: Essays in the Use of Quantitative Methods for the Study of Social Data*. Cambridge Group for the History of Population and Social Structure. Cambridge, UK: Cambridge University Press; 1972. 448p. ISBN: 0521084121.

W238

WRIGLEY, EDWARD A.; SCHOFIELD, ROGER S. 1973. Nominal Record Linkage by Computer and the Logic of Family Reconstitution. See reference: WRIGLEY, E. A., ed. 1973. 64-101.

W239

WRIGHT, ROGER. 1982. *Late Latin and Early Romance in Spain and Carolingian France*. Liverpool, UK: F. Cairns; 1982. 322p. ISBN: 090520512X; LCCN: 82197587.

W240

WRIGHT, ROGER. 1991. *Latin and the Romance Languages in the Early Middle Ages*. London, UK / New York, NY: Routledge; 1991. 262p. ISBN: 0415056063; LCCN: 90008308.

W241

WU, XINDONG. 1995. *Knowledge Acquisition from Databases*. Norwood, NJ: Ablex Publishing Corp.; 1995. 211p. ISBN: 1567502067 (hbk.); 1567502059 (hbk.).

W242

WURL, JOEL. 1994. *Archival Issues*: Past, Present, and Future. See reference: COX, ed. 1994d. 304-308.

W243

WURMAN, RICHARD S. 1989. *Information Anxiety*. New York, NY: Doubleday; 1989. 356p. ISBN: 0385243944.

W244

WYATT, DAVID H. 1984. *Computer Assisted Language Instruction*. Oxford, UK: Oxford University Press; 1984. 89p. ISBN: 0080303277.

W245

WYER, ROBERT S.; SRULL, THOMAS K. 1989. *Memory and Cognition in its Social Context*. Hillsdale, NJ: E. Erlbaum Associates; 1989. 491p. ISBN: 0805805990; LCCN: 89036227.

W246
WYER, ROBERT S.; SRULL, THOMAS K., eds. 1984. *Handbook of Social Cognition.* Hillsdale, NJ: E. Erlbaum Associates; 1984. 3 vols. ISBN: 0898593379 (set).

W247
WYSZECKI, GUNTER.; STILES, WALTER S. 1967/1982. *Color Science: Concepts and Methods: Quantitative Data and Formulae.* New York, NY: John Wiley; 1967. 628p. 2nd ed.; c1982. 950p. (Wiley series in Pure and Applied Optics). ISBN: 0471021067.

-X-Y-

Y1
YAGER, RONALD R.; FEDRIZZI, MARIO; KOSPRYK, JANUSZ, eds. 1994. *Advances in the Dempster-Shafer Theory of Evidence: Advances in Evidential Reasoning.* New York, NY: J. Wiley; 1994. 5997p. ISBN: 0471552488.

Y2
YAGER, RONALD R.; ZADEH, LOFTI A. 1992. *An Introduction to Fuzzy Logic Applications in Intelligent Systems.* Boston, MA: Kluwer Academic; 1992. 356p. ISBN: 0792391918.

Y3
YAKEL, ELIZABETH. 1996. The Way Things Work: Procedures, Processes and Institutional Records. See reference: BLOUIN, F.; DELMAS, B., eds. 1996. 454-464.

Y4
YATES, FRANCES A. 1966. *The Art of Memory.* Chicago, IL: University of Chicago Press; 1966. 400p. (Mnemonics). LCCN: 66022770; OCLC: 2669718. Reprinted in: *Selected Works,* vol. 3. London, UK / New York, NY: Routledge; 1999. ISBN: 0415220432 (set).

Y5
YATES, JOANNE. 1989; 1993. *Control through Communication: The Rise of the System in American Management.* Baltimore, MD: The Johns Hopkins University Press; 1989. 339p. (Studies in Industry and Society series). ISBN: 0-8018-3757-X. 1993 ed. 368p. ISBN: 0-81018-4613-7.

Y6
YATES, JOANNE. 1991. Investing in Information: Supply and Demand Forces in the Use of Information in American Firms, 1850-1920. In: Temin, Peter, ed. *Inside the Business Enterprise: Historical Perspectives on the Use of Information.* Chicago, IL: University of Chicago Press; 1991. 117-154. ISBN: 0-226-79202-1.

Y7
YATES, JOANNE. 1993. Co-Evolution of Information Processing Technology and Use: Interaction between the Life Insurance and Tabulating Industries. *Business Historical Review.* 1993 Spring; 67(1): 1-51. ISSN: 0007-6805.

Y8
YATES, JOANNE; ORLIKOWSKI, WANDA J. 1992. Genres of Organizational Communication: A Structurational Approach to Studying Communication and Media. *Academy of Management Review.* 1992 April; 17(2); 299-326. ISSN: 0363-7425.

Y9
YEAGER, ELIZABETH ANNE; MORRIS, JAMES W. 1995. History and Computers: The Views from Selected Social Studies Journals. *The Social Studies.* 1995 Nov.-Dec.; 86(6): 27-293. ISSN: 0037-7996.

Y10
YEE, MARTHA. 1988. *Moving Image Materials: Genre Terms.* Washington, D.C.: Library of Congress Cataloging Division; 1988. 108p. Compiled for the National Center for Film and Video Preservation at the American Film Institute. LCC: 87004004.

Y11
YEE, MARTHA. 1993. *Moving Image Works and Manifestations.* Los Angeles, CA: University of California; 1993. 230p. (Ph.D. dissertation). Available from University Microfilms International, Ann Arbor, MI.

Y12
YELICH, HOPE, comp. 1993. *Desperately Seeking Sources: Library Use and the Historian. A Selective Bibliography* (Brochure). Prepared for the RASD History Section, Bibliography and Indexes Committee, for the American Library Association Conference, New Orleans, LA; 1993. 4p.

Y13
YELSEY, MICHAEL S. [1992]. *ELSI Bibliography: Ethical, Legal, and Social Implications of the Human Genome Project.* Washington, DC: US Dept. of Energy, Energy Research Office; [1992] May. 145p. (Report no.: DOE/ER-0543T).

Y14
YIN, ROBERT K. 1984/1989. *Case Study Research: Design and Methods*. Newbury Park, CA: Sage; 1984. Rev. ed., 1989. (Applied Social Science Research Methods, 5). ISBN: 0803920571 (hbk.); 080392058X (pbk.).

Y15
YIN, ROBERT K. 1993. *Applications of Case Study Research*. Newbury Park, CA: Sage Publ.; 1993. 131p. ISBN: 0803951183 (hbk.); 0803951191 (hbk.).

Y16
YORKE, STEPHEN, ed. 1995. *Playing for Keeps: The Proceedings of an Electronic Records Management Conference hosted by Australian Archives*. Canberra, Australia 8-10 November 1994. Canberra, AS: Australian Archives Assn.; 1995. 356p.

Y17
YOUNG, ARTHUR P. 1988. *American Library History: A Bibliography of Dissertations and* Theses. 3rd rev. ed. Metuchen, NJ: Scarecrow Press, Inc.; 1988. 469p. ISBN: 0-8108-2138-9.

Y18
YOUNG, JAMES E. 1997. Toward a Received History of the Holocaust. *History and Theory*. 1997 Dec.; 36(4): 21-43. ISSN: 0018-2656.

Y19
YOUNG, JEFFREY R. 1996. Spies Like Us. *Forbes ASAP*. 1996 June; 158: 70-92. ISSN: 0015-6914.

Y20
YOUNG, JEFFREY R. 1997. New Metaphors for Organizing Data Could Change the Nature of Computers. *Chronicle of Higher Education*. 1997 April 4; A19-20. (Note: About Eric Freeman's *Lifestreams* software). ISSN: 0009-5982.

Y21
YOURDON, EDWARD. 1979. *Classics in Software Engineering*. New York, NY: Yourdon Press; 1979. 424p. ISBN: 091702146.

Y22
YOURDON, EDWARD. 1986. *Managing the Structured Techniques: Strategies for Software Development in the 1990s*. 3rd ed. New York, NY: Yourdon Press; 1986. 279p. ISBN: 091702561 (pbk.).

Y23
YOURDON, EDWARD. 1992. *Decline and Fall of the American Programmer*. Englewood Cliffs, NJ: Yourdon Press; 1992. 312p. ISBN: 0132036703.

Y24
YOURDON, EDWARD; YOURDON, JENNIFER. 1998. *Time Bomb 2000: What the Year 2000 Computer Crisis Means to You*! Upper Saddle Mountain, NJ: Prentice Hall PTR; 1998. 416p. ISBN: 01309522842.

Y25
YUEXIAO, Z. 1988. Definitions and Sciences of Information. *Information Processing & Management*. 1988; 24: 479-491. ISSN: 0306-4573.

Y26
YUSHIN, I. F. 1996. Nominalisty i Realisty Istoricheskoy Informatiki [Nominalists and Realists in Historical Informatics]. See reference: BORODKIN, L. I., ed. 1996. 147- 152. (In Russian).

-Z-

Z1
ZADEH, LOFTI A. 1965. Fuzzy Sets. *Information and Control*. 1965; 8: 338-353.

Z2
ZADEH, LOFTI A. 1987. *Fuzzy Sets and Applications: Selected Papers*. Yager, Ronald R., ed. New York, NY: John Wiley; 1987. 684p. ISBN: 0471857106. See also reference: YAGER, R.; ZADEH, L. 1992.

Z3
ZADEH, LOFTI A. 1988. Fuzzy Logic. *IEEE Computer*. 1988; 21: 83-93. ISSN: 0018-9162.

Z4
ZADEH, LOFTI A.; KACPRZYK, JANUSZ. 1992. *Fuzzy Logic for the Management of Uncertainty*. New York, NY: John Wiley; 1992. 676p. ISBN: 0471547999.

Z5
ZADORA-RIO, ELISABETH. 1994. Le Systéme de Gestion des Données de Fouilles de Rigny [A System for Generating Data from the Rigny Accounts]. See reference: BECK, P., ed., 1994. 31-34.

Z6
ZAGORIN, PEREZ. 1990. *Ways of Lying: Dissimulation, Persecution, and Conformity in Early Modern Europe.* Cambridge, MA: Harvard University Press; 1990. 337p. ISBN: 067948343.

Z7
ZAGORIN, PEREZ. 1996. The Historical Significance of Lying and Dissimulation. *Social Research.* 1996 Fall; 63(3): 863-889. ISSN: 0037-783X

Z8
ZARRI, GIAN P. 1977. Organisation générale. In: *Projet RESEDA: Rapport sur les recherches* effectuées du 1er oct. 1975 au 1er avril 1976 [The RESDA Project: Research Report]. Rapport/CNRS/ERHF/1976/DGRST-1. In: *Informatica e dirino* (IT). 1977; 3:148-167. (In French). Cf., related reports by Monique Ornato and A. Zwiebel, *Étude de Metalanguage*; Lucia Zarri-Baldi, *Programmation*; and C. Bozzolo *Données bibliographiques* (CNRS-UPR 52).

Z9
ZEISEL, HANS. 1947/1985. *Say It with Figures.* New York, NY: Columbia University, Bureau of Applied Social Research; 1947. 6th ed. New York, NY: Harper & Row; 1985. 272p. ISBN: 0061819824 (hbk.); 0061319945 (pbk.).

Z10
ZEMANKOVA-LEECH, MARIA; KANDEL, ABRAHAM. 1984. *Fuzzy Relational Databases—A Key to Expert Systems.* Cologne, DEU: TUV Theinland; 1984. 180p. ISBN: 388581881 (pbk.); LCCN: 84-231696.

Z11
ZEMSKY, ROBERT M. 1969. Numbers and History: The Dilemma of Measurement. *Computers and the Humanities* (NL). 1969; 4(1): 31-39. ISSN: 0010-4817.

Z12
ZENTRALARCHIV FÜR EMPIRISCHE SOZIALFORSCHUNG (ZA). 1983/1986. *Umfragen aus der Empirischen Sozialforschung, 1945-1982: Datenbestandskatalog des Zentralarchive für Empirische Sozialforschung* [Inquiry about Empirical Social Science, 1945-1982: Database Catalog of the Central Archives for Empirical Social Research]. F. Bauske, comp. Frankfurt, DEU / New York, NY: Campus Verlag; 1983. 532p. ISBN: 3593332167; OCLC: 9729889. (In German). Updated by the newsletter *ZA- Information* and journal *Zeitschrift für Soziologie.*

Z13
ZENTRUM FÜR HISTORISCHE SOZIALFORSCHUNG. 1979-. *Historische Sozialforschung / Historical Social Research* (DEU). Cologne, DEU: Zentrum für Historische Sozialforschung and the Informationszentrum Sozialwissenschaften, Bonn, DEU; 1979-. Co-sponsored by Quantum. Annual. ISSN: 0173-2145.

Z14
ZERUBAVEL, EVIATAR. 1997. *Social Mindscapes: An Invitation to Cognitive Psychology.* Cambridge, MA: Harvard University Press; 1997. 164p. ISBN: 06781391X

Z15
ZERUBAVEL, YAEL. 1995. *Recovered Roots: Collective Memory and the Making of Israeli National Tradition.* Chicago, IL: University of Chicago Press; 1995. 340p. ISBN: 0226981576; LCCN: 94009441.

Z16
ZHANG, JIAJIE. 1998. A Distributed Representation Approach to Group Problem Solving. See reference: MCNEESE, M. D., ed. 1998. 801-816.

Z17
ZHANG, YUEMEI. 1991. *Knowledge-based Discourse Generation for an Intelligent Tutoring System.* Illinois Institute of Technology; 1991. 150p. (Ph.D. dissertation; *DAI*, vol. 53/03-B: 1478). Available from: University Microfilms, Ann Arbor, MI (Order no. AAD92-22196).

Z18
ZIARKO, WOJCIECH, ed. 1994. *Rough Sets, Fuzzy Sets and Knowledge Discovery.* Proceedings of the International Conference on Rough Sets and Knowledge Discovery (RSKD'93), Banff, Alberta, Canada, 12-15 October 1993. New York, NY: Springer-Verlag; 1994. 476p. ISBN: 03540198857.

Z19
ZILVERSMIT, ARTHUR. 1988. Another Report Card, Another "F". *Reviews in American History.* 1988; 16(2): 314-20. ISSN: 0048-7511.

Z20
ZIMMERMAN, ANN. 1995. Partnership and Opportunities: The Archival Management of Geographic Information Systems. See reference: GILLILAND-SWETLAND, ANNE, ed. 1995: 23-38.

Z21
ZIMMERMANN, PHILLIP R. 1995. *The Official PGP User's Guide*. Cambridge, MA: MIT Press; 1995. 127p. ISBN: 0262740176 (pbk.)

Z22
ZINK, STEVEN D. 1986. Clio's Blind Spot: Historians' Underutilization of United States Government Publications in Historical Research. *Government Publications Review*. 1991; 13 January/February: 67-78. ISSN: 0093-061X.

Z23
ZINKHAN, GEORGE M.; JOHNSON, MADELINE. 1994. The Use of Parody in Advertising. *Journal of Advertising*. 1994 September; 23(3): iii-viii. ISSN: 0091-3367.

Z24
ZINKHAM, HELENA; BETZ PARKER, ELIZABETH. 1986. *Descriptive Terms for Graphic Materials: Genre and Physical Characteristic Headings*. Washington, DC: Library of Congress; 1986. 135p. LCCN: 86-20017; OCLC: 14099492.

Z25
ZIPF, GEORGE K. 1935. *The Psycho-Biology of Language: An Introduction to Dynamic Philology*. Boston, MA: Houghton-Mifflin Co.; 1935. 336p. LCCN: 35-009154.

Z26
ZIPF, GEORGE K. 1949/1965. *Human Behavior and the Principle of Least Effort*. Cambridge, MA: Addison-Wesley Pub.; 1949. Reprinted. New York, NY: Hafner Pub. Co.; 1965. 573p. LCCN: 65-020086.

Z27
ZORICH, DIANE M. 1997. Beyond Bitslag: Integrating Museum Resources on the Internet. See reference: JONES-GARMIL, K., ed. 1997. 171-202.

Z28
ZUBOFF, SHOSHAMA. 1984. *In the Age of the Smart Machine*. New York, NY: Basic Books; 1984. 468p. ISBN: 0465032125; LCCN: 87-4777; OCLC: 17480009.

Z29
ZVIGLIANICH, VLADIMIR A. 1993. *Nauchnoe poznanie kakkk kul'turno istoricheskii protsese*. Trans. as: *Scientific Knowledge as a Cultural and Historical Process; the Cultural Prospects of Science*. Lewiston, NY: E. Mellen Press; 1993. ISBN: 0773498656.

Z30
ZWEIG, RONALD W. 1993a. Electronically Generated Records and Twentieth-century History. *Computers and Humanities*. 1993; 27(2): 73-84. ISSN: 0010-4817.

Z31
ZWEIG, RONALD W. 1993b. Beyond Content: Electronic Fingerprints and the Use of Documents. See reference: ROSS, S.; HIGGS, E., eds., 1993. 251-260.

Z32
ZYTKOW, JAN M.; ZEMBOWICZ, R. 1993. Database Exploration in Search of Regularities. *Journal of Intelligent Information Systems*. 1993; 2: 39-81. ISSN: 0925-9902.

ABOUT THE AUTHOR

Lawrence J. McCrank, Ph.D., is Professor of Library and Information Science and Dean of Library and Information Services at Chicago State University, with a purview over the university library, archives, and Learning Resource Center for instructional technology. He is currently involved in reorganization, automation, and networking; curricular development; the building of a state-of-the-art 140,000 square-foot library; and the remodeling of a 192,000 square-foot facility into a media union. He has worked previously in business information services as the Executive Director of Libraries for the Davenport University system in Michigan and in technical education and information services for ITT Inc.'s Educational Services. He has served also  as a dean and university librarian at Ferris State University in Michigan (1988–96), where he initiated a major renovation and building program, and at Auburn University at Montgomery (1984–88). At Indiana State University he served as department head (1982–84) for Rare Books and Special Collections as well as University Archives, working in lexicology, U.S. labor history, the history of American education, and state and regional studies.

It is this interdisciplinary fusion of historical and information studies, with special expertise in documentation, diplomatics, codicology and analytical bibliography, archives, manuscripts, etc.—interests represented in this book—that was the focus of Professor McCrank's work at the University of Maryland (1976–1982) in forging one of the first double Masters Degrees in the U.S. (MA and MLS) in History and Information Science with the primary specialization in Archival Science. He mentored over two hundred graduate students into the profession for careers in archives, museums, public history, library special collections, and government services. He taught History at the University of Virginia and at Whitman College, has held visiting professorships in History at the universities of Oregon, California (Berkeley), and Western Michigan, where as a University Scholar he also consulted on its nascent doctoral program; and in library, archives, and information sciences at the universities of Western Ontario and Alabama. In 1995 he became a Fellow of the Society of American Archivists (SAA), the society's highest honor.

Professor McCrank was trained as a medievalist and early modern European historian after completing his undergraduate education at Moorhead State University, MN, with his MA in History with Honors at the University of Kansas working under Professor Lynn Nelson in socio-economic and monastic history. He became a student of Professor Charles J. Bishko to earn his Ph.D. (1974) at the University of Virginia, focusing on medieval frontier history and European expansionism in the Iberian peninsula and beyond to Africa and the New World. Having gained paraprofessional experience in librarianship at the University of Kansas Spencer Library and U.VA's Alderman Library, he returned to graduate school after doctoral studies to earn an MLS at the University of Oregon in academic library and archives administration. He subsequently continued his education at leadership and advanced administration institutes at the University of Maryland, Miami University, and Harvard University in conjunction with the Assn. of College and University Libraries (ACRL).

Studies have identified Professor McCrank as one of a dozen most published academic librarians in North America, having authored and edited some twenty monographs, collected studies, and research reports; over seventy articles in History and the Information fields; and two dozen reviews, as well as public media presentations, interviews, and distance education courses. His subjects in the latter range from library history, archives, preservation, descriptive cataloging, rare book librarianship, graduate education programming, and information resource management. He served on several editorial boards, including *Computing and the Humanities* and *The American Archivist*, and was recently a senior editor for Haworth Press, having produced eight volumes in the series *Primary Sources & Original Works*. He has been active in ASIST, IASSIST, ALA, ACRL, SAA, and MAC, and was a promoter of the early conference series on *Data Bases in the Humanities and Social Sciences* (having hosted and edited the 1987 international conference). His early ventures into natural language computing, indexing, and thesaurus or terminological research resulted in one of the first fully computer-generated books published in the U.S. with experimental rotational string indexing for improved access to rare manuscript, incunabula, and early printed books and manuscripts from the twelfth century onward cataloged at Mt. Angel Abbey, OR.

In History his research has focused on monastic and ecclesiastical institutions during the Reconquista, in the tenth-twelfth century Christian vs. Muslim frontier, centering around Tarragona, Spain. A collection of his studies on *Medieval Frontier History in New Catalonia* was reprinted by Variorum Press (1996), leading to an invitation to keynote the 1999 annual congress of the Real Societat Arqueologic de Tarraconensis in Tarragona and subsequently speak on this city's twelfth-century urban history at the History of the Corona d'Arago Conference in Barcelona. A revision of his dissertation on the reconquest and restoration of Tarragona is being published by RSAT in an illustrated Spanish version to celebrate this city's designation by UNESCO as an international historic site for all mankind. A follow-up *Digital Frontiers* international collaborative project is envisioned for a computer GIS simulation and electronic archives. Other projects include another book about nineteenth-century visualization, imagery, and instructional media for cross-cultural communication, *Conversions: Information and Transformation of the Catholic Mission to Oregon*; a computer-assisted analysis of medieval Cistercian cartularies; and a projected textbook on documentation, diplomatics, and forensics.

Subject Index

The following subject index refers to both the text and the bibliography: the former by page references (number only, to specific pages or inclusive sections); and the latter by citation (alpha-numeric references beginning with the first letter of the author entry by which the citation is alphabetized, followed by sequential numbers for each citation within the alpha-class). The bibliographic references are arranged by main and lead author and corporate author entries. Collaborators (joint authors, translators, editors, etc.) are not indexed separately. Citations which serve only to acknowledge references in the text are indexed by a single entry. Citations recommended as resources are indexed more fully for multiple access points. In the latter case subject strings are permutated, so that the entry can be either from the most general subject headings or more specific descriptors. This index was prepared with Master Index software. In all, approximately 5600 citations are so indexed. This is a faceted string index. Alpha-numeric references are to bibliographic citations; numbers are page references to the text. See also the Author Name Index beginning on p. 1169.

-B-

-C-

-D-

-E-

E-commerce. See Electronic Commerce.
E-D Catia software—Imaging, 491
E-mail. See Electronic Mail.
EAD. See Encoded Archival Description. See also Archives
     Description.
Early American Fiction project—Literature (US)—
     Electronic library—Virginia, University of, 440
Early Modern Europe:
     European expansion, L157
     Historical bibliography, E39
     Historiography, H210
     Mediterranean history, B483
     Museum collecting, I24
     Nation state—Elites, 12-18th c., G76
     Persecution, Z6
     Revisionism, H210
Earth Sciences—Fractals, B77
Ease of access. See Access / Accessibility.
EC / EEC. See European Economic Community.
Eckert, J. Presper, 173
Eco, Umberto—Semiotics, 416
École d'Chartes—Archival Science (FR)—Documents, 43
École de Hautes Études, Paris, FR—Manuscripts—
     Codices, 466
École des Hautes Études en Sciences Sociales—
     Research institutes (FR), R105
Écological regression—Regression analysis, K183
Ecology:
     Elections, J67
     Environmental history, L47
     Documentation, T20
     Psychology, B551
Ecology of mind, B95
Econometrics (Economic metrics), 334, 378
     See also Economic history; Economics.
     Economic History, M322
     Handbooks, manuals, etc., M23
     History, F122
     Information economics—Efficiency, S170
     Theory, G153
Economics/Economic:
Economic and Social History. See Socio-economic history.
Economic and Social Research Council (ESRC)(UK):
     Data archives—Essex, University of, 263, Q3
          Guide, E15
Economic data bases, M322
Economic development—Information, I46
Economic History:
     Cities, T68-71
     Cliometrics, F77
     Company profiling—Business intelligence, 169
     Data analysis, D202
     Data processing—Computer industry—
          History and development, F87
     Econometrics, M322
     Historical information systems, M300
     Historical methods—Measurement, B222, T128
     History computing, M320-321
     Labor force—Work, R136
     Management Information Systems (MIS), M300
     Models—Archives administration, B126
     Polanyi brothers, H221
     Quantification, C423, C426
          Research methods, M144
     Research methods, A117
     Rigny accounts, Z5
     Russia (RU)—Historiography, M354
     Slavery, F126
     Spreadsheets, K155, M322
     Sources—VISA credit cards—Banking transactions—
          Data processing, 265-266
     Technology—History and development, B186

United States—American History, E68
     Bibliographic review, S330
     Historiography, F123, F126
     Union Pacific Railroad, F121
Economics. See also Macro- / Micro economics.
     Bibliography, U1
     Business ethics, 229
     Chaos theory, B101
     Complexity theory, A180
     Data analysis theory, D202
     Empiricism, H261
     Forecasting, C186
     Historical methods, 32, M320-321
     Historical systems, 22, F51
     History and development, B222
     Imperfect data, P132
     Information economics:
          Capital investment—Human resources, M11
          Value, M179, R92
     Information structures, N90 See also Data structures.
     International—Globalization—World economics, N4
     Measurement, B222, B222
     Production-distribution paradigm, 47
     Prosperity—Business, D47
     Quantification, A117, C186
     Rhetoric, M174, M179
          Influence, K137
     Statistics, G153
     Sublanguages, M174-177
     Technology interdependence, R208
     Trends—Forecasting, 30-31, N4
          Social issues, E24-26
     Uncertainty, H238
Economistic fallacy—Polanyi, Karl—Criticism, interpretation,
     etc., S331
EDI. See Electronic Data Interchange.
Edification—History, 134
Edinburgh, University of—Institute for Advanced Studies in the
     Humanities—Symposium (1972), A29
Editing/Editions.
     See also Types of editing, e.g., image, sound, text, etc.
     Analytical Bibliography—Text criticism, 246
     Computing—Data processing, S216
     Documentary editing—Handbooks, manuals, etc., K143
     Documents, A189
     Medieval studies—Text bases—Electronic editions, R101
     Models—Text bases, L156
     Text analysis, B411
     Text criticism, S134, T10
Edition control—Alert systems, 308
Editions—States, 246-248
EDLIBE. See Electronic Data Interchange for
     Libraries and Booksellers in Europe.
EDMS. See Electronic Document Management Systems.
EDP (Electronic Data Processing). See Data processing.
Education. See also Higher education; Learning; Teaching.
     Activity theory—Theory, E70
     Archival Science, A115, M184-184
          Education standards—SAA, B347
          Archivist training—History programs, 271
     Assessment, V26
     Benchmarking, W107
     Chaos theory, I3
     Civics, A94
     Culture, transmission of, B554
     Democracy—Civics—History, G17
     Electronic records—Archivist training, 267
     Entertainment industry, 353
     Ethics, M164
     Future of education—Forecasting, T122
     Historical literacy, G18
     History—Archival Science, M185, M192
     History and development—Computing, S141
     History awareness, W138
          Software engineering—Computer science, C177

-F-

-G-

-H-

H-Net, 78-80, 142, 615, H1
Electronic reviews—Bibliographic services, 96-99
Website, 607-608
Resource enhancement—Hyperlinks, 285
H-Teach syllabi—History teaching, 80
Habermas, Jurgen—Social scientist, H8-9
HABET. See History Advisory Board for Educational
Technology.
Habit:
Change, T140
Quantification—Research methods—Technique, 594-595
Tradition, T174
Habitat project—Lukas Films, 470
Habitus:
Concept—Bourdieu, Pierre, 196
Environment—Locale, E51
Halbwachs, Maurice—Sociologist, 187, H23-26
Halgraue Reihe zur historischen Fachinformatik (series)
Max Planck Institut für Geschichte, Gottingen, DEU,114,
T42, T46, T52, T55
Hallmark Cards—NCR Data Warehouse—Data warehouse
application, 327
Handbooks, manuals, etc.:
Archival Science, D69, B223, L175, L183
Archives:
Administration, B475, J39, W186
Electronic archives, I43
Arrangement—Description, N447
Automation, H211
Description, C297
Standards, W8
Manuscripts, O12
Practice, H328, (FR) F28
Research (USSR)—Russian History, R77
Bureau of Canadian Archivists, B281
Cataloging, O50
AACR2 (Anglo American Cataloging Rules, 2nd ed.),
D174
Cognitive Psychology, S338
Combinatorics—Statistics, G208
Communication research—History and development, D95
Complexity, N113
Computer security—Privacy, R288
Conservation—Collection management, M189, S481
Content analysis, W54
Court procedure—Legal guides, 272
Cryptography, M286
Data analysis:
Methodology, M337
Modeling, R78
Qualitative research—Software, W76
Data warehouses, I20-21, K121
Decision Support systems—Rough set theory, B163, S265
Digital imaging, K77
Diplomatics, G136,T36
Discourse analysis, D162b
Distributed data bases—Data management, R204
Documentary editing—Relations of the Southwest project,
P171
Econometrics, M23
Editing—Documentary editing, K143
Education—Teaching methods, E76
Electronic records—Records Management, N27, S6
Evidence, U13
Expert systems, W15
Federal Judicial Center—Reference Manual on Scientific
Evidence—Research methods, 343
Scientific research—Evidence, 272
Film archives, B453
Fuzzy data—Data bases, P123
Fuzzy mathematics, K17
Gaming, H144

Geographic Information Systems, M30-31
Historical demography, H182
Historical methods, H208-210
History computing, J23-24, M145-145, S220
History, International, I19
Humanities computing, C420, H253-254, P46
Hytime software, D118
ICONCLASS Research and Development Group, I4
Image processing, R288
Information retrieval, V24
Information services—Policies and procedures, J36
Information Systems Management (ISM), U4
Executive systems, B272
Integrated Public Use Microdata Series—
Data archives—Social data sources, R273-274
Intellectual property law, 272
ISO 9000 standard, P52, H304
Klieu software, 538
Libraries—Information services, W55
Linguistics, B141, S65
LISP programming, J73
COMMON LISP language, S381
Manuscripts—Conservation, R154, R157
Descriptive cataloging, H184
MARC, Archives and Manuscript format (AMC), E88, S12
Micrographics, V50
Modeling, M445
Mathematics, G135
Modern Language Association (MLA), H78
Multiple regression—Regression analysis, R265
Narratology, O46, P216
Optical Character Recognition, O22
Oral History, R150
Oxford Concordance Program (OCP), H255
Paiget, Jean—Child psychology, P136, S251
Photographic archives—Archives administration, R155
Privacy— Computer security, S366, Z21
Probability theory, L185
Project management, L143
Qualitative research—Research methods, D115
Records Management, P86
Research design—Data analysis—Research methods, K87
Research methods, B3, B5
Rules of evidence—Presentation, 272
Serials Industry Advisory Committee (SISAC)—
Bar codes—Identification technology, S174
SGML, H201, K122, P152, V16
Text encoding, G158-159, G162
Simulation, W103
Social cognition—Recognition, W246
Social Sciences—Research methods, B252, V59
Social data analysis, F111-112
Software design, L246
Engineering, 533
Testing, 531
Spatial statistics—Measurement—Distance, R142
Standards, S355
Statistics, 345, F179, K53, M409, M452, M457, R280
Historical methods, 32, D187
Strategic management, N152
Structuralism, L37
Style, citations, L126-127
TEI guidelines, S345-346
Telecommunications, F194
Uncertainty—Decision making—Quantitative risk, 414
Vancouver Island History Project—Data base management
Code book, G11
Virtual Reality, H266
Witness examination, 272
WWW, F118
Z39.50 standard—Networking, M309, M384
Handwriting. See also Manuscripts.
Cybernetics, E17
Longhand, 515
Notarial hands, 515

-I-

-J-

-K-

-L-

London, University of—Wartburg Institute (UK), 463
Long Island, NY—Gravestones, S436
Long-term data utility—Time-variant searching, 310
Long-term history—Data structures, O26
Long-term use—Probability—Risk management—
     Information need, 284
Longevity—Electronic records—Preservation, R248-249
Longhand—Handwriting, 515
Longitudinal analysis, 36. See also History.
     Data series, A119, H308
     Event data:
          Cohort analysis, 354
          Social Science History, 36, A54
     Induction—Probabilities, E30
  Time-event analysis, A119, H308
Los Angeles (CA):
     Information System for Los Angeles (ISLA), 262, 472
     Local History— Cultural Memory, K140
Los Angeles Historical Society—Local history—
     Data base design, C203-204
Lotka's law, 332, L208
     Data processing, C165
     Empiricism—Experimentation— Information Science,
          P30-31
Lotus 1-4 Software, 312, 586
     Lotus Notes software—Zeta Software, Inc. 276
Louis XIV's court—Simulation, L211
Low Countries Assn. For History and Computing /
     Verniging voor Geschiedenis en Informatica (VGI), 143
Lower Manhattan Project—Computer-assisted Instruction, C427
Lucas, George—Film maker, 470-471
     Lucas Films—Habitat project, 470
Lucent Technologies—Bell Laboratories, 504
Luminance—Color characteristics—Hues—Tones, 351
Lying:
     Disinformation, B344
     Dissimulation, Z6-7
     Falsification, K246
     Misrepresentation, 341
     Sociology, 429, B44
Lyon, FR—Archaeology, A160-162
Lyotard, Jean-François—Philosopher, 418, L240-242

-M-

Machine Age—Human intelligence, N137
Machine processing. See Computing. See also Data processing.
Machine learning (ML), thinking, etc. See Artificial
     Intelligence. See also Decision and expert systems; Neural
     networks.
Machine translation, 145
     Document reconstruction, 517
     History and development, 168
     Termight software, D4
     Viterbi decoder—Uncertain reasoning—
          Word inference, 519
MAchine-Readable Cataloging (MARC).
     See MARC formats. See also Cataloging standards.
Machine-readable data. See also Data archives; Electronic
     archives; Electronic records.
Machine-Readable Data Files (MDRF). See also Data bases;
     Electronic records.
     Cataloging—Computer files—MARC formats, 525
     Descriptive cataloging, O54, O56, T23
     Machine-readability— Census records, 178
Machine-readable texts. See Text bases. See also Text archives.
Machlup. Fritz—Information scientist, M7-13
     Classification—Organization of knowledge, M331
Macro-appraisal. See Appraisal.
Macro-economics— Bibliography, U1. See also Economics.
     Dynamic systems—Modeling, G217
Macro-history 40, 60
     Biography, G30

Macro-Sociology, C195
Magic Information systems, L38
     Virtual realism—Reality, K62
Magnetic recording:
     History and development, 178
          Technology History (US), M447
     Magnetic tape—Life expectancy—
          Preservation, 283, V8-10
Magnification—Fractals—Sizing—Scales, 385
Make believe—Historical fiction—Simulation—Virtuality,
     568-569
Making history—Socio-cultural models—Ideal types, 409
     Invention, 66, 73
Making of America (MOA) project—Michigan, University—
     Cornell University—Mellon Foundation, 442, 561
Male dominance in Scientific History—
     Gender bias, 421-422
Man-computer interaction. See Human-Computer interaction.
Man-Machine interface. See Human-computer interaction. See
     also Graphic User Interface (GUI).
Man-made objects. See Artifacts. See also Material culture.
Management:
     Accountability, 213
     Administration Science—Cultural studies, 182-183
     Archives administration, S83
     Cause maps, E19
     Coaching—Counseling—Guidance, 223
     Collaboration— Coordination, K115
     Collaborative Hypertext in Research Organizations
          (CHIRO)—Hypertext—Research projects, M258
     Communication, P162
     Conflict resolution, F145
     Consensus development, W70
     Corporate culture, H214, K119
     Corporate memory, 85
     Culture:
          Humanities—Professional studies, 85
          Social behavior, W67
     Definition and concept, 213
     Description—Sense making, B168
     Functions —Responsibilities, B16
     History and development, Y5
     Information systems management (ISM), A60
     Information Technology, M62
     Leadership, B536, D230-235, W99-100
     Non-profit business, L236
     Organizational change, F45
     Organizational culture—Corporate culture, C151
     Organizational design, K118
          Organization structures, P210
     Paradigms—Information Age, D178
     Quantification, F149
     Rate of change—Acceleration, 397-398, C275
     Systems management—Policies and procedures, 304
Management by objective (MBO)—
     Decision support systems, A28
Management Information Systems (MIS), 308. See also
     Electronic Document Management Systems.
     Decision making, M449
     Economic history, M300
     Electronic archives, M224-228
          Business records, L31
     Executive Information systems, R179
          Software selection, R194
     Expert systems, K57
     Museums, L146
     Records Management—Electronic records, M288, T149
     Research methods, S452
     Trends and development, L216
Management literature:
     Bibliotherapy, 227
     Sayings, clichés, etc., L42
Management Science:
     Accounting, R92
     Action theory, A155-157

-N-

Identification, B382
Names. See also Nomenclatures, terminologies,
    anthroponomies, etc. See also Nominal data, linkage, etc.
    See also Types of names: national, personal, place, etc.
    Anthroponomies—Catalonia, B350
    History, synonyms for—Terminology, R22
    Identification—Nominal information, B544, F90
        Identities—Credibility, 364
    Normalization—Orthography—Punctuation, 365
Names, historical—Identification of individuals—
    Onomastics, B521
    Names, medieval—Surnames— Nominal linkage, W86,
        Medieval people, G77, G96
Names, personal:
    Formalism, R207
    Idiosyncracies—Used names— Official names, 365
    Prosopography—Anthroponomies, B435
    Surnames—Baptismal names—Confirmation names, 365
Naming:
    Belief— Identification, F90
    Believing—Identity, 364
    Conventions—Attributes—Syntax, 364-365, B544
        Hungarian Naming convention—Tagging, 320
        Leszynski/Reddick nomenclature—
            Nemonic commands, 320
    Identification—Onomastics, L72
    Information Science— Definition and concept, S114
    Nominal linkage, 367
    Objects, B544, C247
    Onomastics, C36, K212, M17
    Perception, M427
    Psychology—Reference, C58
    Sublanguages, 133
    Term ambiguity—Language problem, 365
NAPA. See National Academy of Public Administration.
NARA. See National Archives and Records Administration.
NARCISSE. See Network of Art Research Computer
    Image Systems.
Narration/Narrative. See also Storytelling; History teaching.
    Causality, B282
    Community, H229
    Construction—Serial records, B246
    Description—Explanation—History, R244
    Discourse—Cognition—Reception, 20, T89
    Explanation—Visual aids, T167
    History—Style, C53-56
    Identity, H229
    Misrepresentation, K66
    Political process—Rites and rituals, J11
    Rhetoric, 404, K134
    Semiotics, J11
    Social control, M465
    Time expression, C77
    Time-event analysis, C77
    Trauma—Memory, C63-64
    Visualization, 407-476
Narration, historical. See Narrative History.
Narrative history:
    Chaos theory—Historiography, R84
    Classification, R287
    Criticism, interpretation, etc.—Historiography, R164
        Debate, controversy, etc., K185
        Narrative vs. Quantitative history—Description vs.
            Counting—Hard vs. Soft Sciences—
            False dichotomies, 52
    Descriptors, 133
    Discourse analysis—Representation
        Form criticism, W111, W114
    Explanation—Series analysis, A6
    Film making, R215
    Gender influence, 421
    Historiography, L210, K185, M155, S438
    Language studies, M174-175
    Linearity—Storyline—Plots, 399
    Logic, A127-130

New Historicism, F70
Plots—Grand themes, 337
Qualitative research, K165
Quantification, 378, C153
Realism—Surrealism—Subjectivity, 409
Reasoning, R284
Reconstruction, B246
Revival, K185
Scientific historicism, 134
Static views vs. Linear action—Storylines, 404-405
Stone, Lawrence, 63-64
Storytelling, 423
    Stories, moral, T120
Teaching history, R212, R214, R217
Time-dependence—Temporal reasoning—
    Contextual meaning, R131
Women historians—Subjectivity, 422
Narrative literary technique, analysis, etc. See Narratology.
Narrative mastery. See Master Narrative. See also Narration.
Narratives. See also Stories, storytelling.
    Anecdotes, F70
    Computer analysis, B400
    Constructs and structure, L117
    Control mechanisms—Synthesis—Integration, 404
    Fragmentation—Episodic history, 29, 381
    French literature, H65
    Grand Themes—Human Sciences—Philosophy of History,
        S256
    History as Synthesis, G294
    Meta-narratives, 418
    Mythology—Classics—Event-centered history, 381
    Organizational culture, H229, M465
    Paradigm, B624
    Plots, W117
    Post-modernism, K139
    Post-Structuralism—History narration, K66, P194
    Social action, J11
Narrativity—History, K65
Narratology:
    Criticism and debate, C5
    Criticism, interpretation, etc., M178, W114
    Cultural history, M155
    Dictionaries and encyclopedia, P217
    Form criticism, P216-218
    Handbooks, manuals, etc., O46, P216
    Literary genre—History literature, 408
    Literature, H65
    Social constructs—Reconstruction, 220
    Terminology, P217
NASA. See National Aeronautics and Space Administration.
Nash, Gary B.—Historian, 546-547
Nation Standards controversy, N12-13, N33, N26-37
Nation at Risk report—Criticism and debate, etc., B191, G22
Nation state—Elites, 12-18th c.—Early-modern History, G76
National Academy of Public Administration (NAPA)—
    Preservation—Research reports for NARA, 289-291,
    N17-19
National Academy Press—National Research Council (US)-
    Research reports (NCR), N60-64
National Aeronautics and Space Administration (NASA):
    Astronomy—Chronology—Historical methods, P175
    Digital Library Initiative (US), 441
    DOE, 141
    Satellite surveillance—Landsat, 385
    Space exploration—Electronic records—Preservation
        failure, 385, 503
National Alliance (US)—National Endowment for the
    Humanities, 141
National Archives and Records Administration (NARA;
    US), N21-29
    Archives Institute, 257
    Center for Electronic Records (NARA)—
        History and development, 259-260
    Electronic archives, 259, P184
        Electronic records program, E11-12

-O-

-P-

-Q-

-R-

-S-

Search engines, 324:
Browsers, L142
Vendors:
Angoss—Knowledge Seeker, 328
Brio—Query, 324
Prism—Directory Manager, 324
SAS—ACCESS, IBM—Dataguide, 324
Software AG—Esperant, 324
Trinzic—Forest and Trees, 324
Search keys. See also Online searching.
Information retrieval, F57
Search strategies, 128
Term matching—Word searching, 133
Search strategies:
Information retrieval,, B91-92, C122
Online searching, 107, 158, B283
Search keys, 128
Terminology, S226-228
Search warrants—Electronic records—Discovery action, legal, 301
Secondary education:
American Historical Assn. (AHA)
Teaching Division—Social studies, 574
Delphi study—Data base usage, N96
Teaching history, B310
Debate and controversy, 547-548
Secondary sources. See Bibliography. See also History literature.
Secrecy—Bush, Vannevar, B593
Secretaries—Correspondence—Letters, C141-143
Secure Analysis Tool for Auditing Networks (SATAN), 428
Security:
Cryptography, N64
Encryption, 296, 508-509
Information systems, I36
Log analysis, 510
Read-only media, 510
SATAN software, 428
Tripwire software, 428
Trust—Transactions, 304-305
Seeing. See Vision. See also Cognition; Visual perception.
Segmentation:
Programs— Classifiers, 519
Static scenes—Image analysis, R146
Segregation—Disciplinarity—Academe, W145
Seidell, Atherton—Photo-duplication—Reprography, H240
Selection—Knowable past, concept, 163
Selection bias:
Bias, L226
History standards—Revisionism, 547
Self-actualization—Exceptionalism—Identities, 204-205
Self-awareness. See also Self-identity; History Awareness.
Autobiography—Identity, C281-288
Social behavior, J11
Self-correction—Ordering processes, 395
Self-determinism, 213
Self-documentation. See also Autobiography.
Selection bias—History writing, future, 437
Self-documenting files—Files management—Records creation—Electronic archives, 279-281
Self-identity:
Historical awareness, C154
Personal papers, W218
Personality—Psychology, C430
Self-interest—Learning organization, 304
Self-management—Cultures, R165
Self-organization. See also Chaos Theory; Organizational Science; Psychology; Sociology.
Actualization—Emergence, 385
Associative memory, K170-171
Communications, L230
Complexity theory, K50
Laws of assembly, 395
Mapping, K170
Psychology, B78

Semantics:
Ambiguity—Specification, D82. See also Disambiguation.
Computerization, effects of, B202
Historical time—Temporal reasoning—
Historical reasoning, K179
Indexing—Knowledge discovery—Literature, G185
Linguistics, F175
Probability—Axiomatic study, D205
Semantic analysis:
History literature, A127-130
Semantic maps—GUIs, L151-153
Semantic networks—Linguistics—Natural Language processing, S336
Semantic standards—DSSL (Document Style and Specification Language), I59
Semi-colon—Punctuation, 365
Seminar method:
Archives—Historical methods, S278
History and development, C210
Research methods—History, 338
Teaching history, B444
Semiology. See Semiotics.
Semiotics. See also Signification, signs, symbols, etc.
Advertisements—Image analysis, W165
Architectural design, A34-36
Archives—Symbolism, O13
Art, G180
Cognition, H112
Communications, T113
Computer icons, S60
Conference proceedings, semiotics, Berkeley, CA, 1994, R34
Criticism, interpretation, etc., J33
Dictionaries and encyclopedia, S142
Dress, B45
Eco, Umberto, 416
Geographic orientation—Tradition, 375
History, G147
Iconography, M294-294
Icons, computer—Graphic design, S218
Information design, E6
Information Science, W40
Interior design, H116
Language studies—Signifiers, 416
Linguistics, G282
Narratology—Reading history, 434
Literature and Art, K215
Management science, A61
Meaning, G250
Meaning, embedded—Anthroplogical linguistics, H4
Medieval studies, J26-29
Metaphor analysis—Language use, 215
Narration, J11
Organizational culture, D10, F44, G15
Ritual space, 222
Sebeok, Thomas, S142-143
Self-identify—Society, L76
Signs, B301
Social History, T74
Structures, G248
Symbols:
Culture—Diversity, R34
Nationality, L166
Symbol production, C14
Symbolic management, L40
Texts as images—Symbolism, 411
Theory, B70-73, E14
Weaponry—Computers, G211
Sensation—Information—Perception, N143
Sense making. See also Meaning.
Collaboration—Information management, 276
Cognition—Language, A224
Conceptualization—Context building
Interpretation, 37
Context—Electronic records, W58-59

-T-

-U-

-V-

-W-

-X-

-Y-

-Z-

Author Name Index

This index includes names of authors cited in the text. See also the Subject Index beginning on p. 979.

-C-

-D-

-G-

-H-

-I-

-J-

-K-

-L-

-M-

-N-

-O-

-P-

-Q-

-R-

-S-

-T-

-X-

-Y-

More Great Books from Information Today, Inc.

ARIST 35: Annual Review of Information Science and Technology

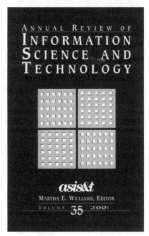

Edited by Martha E. Williams

Contents of Volume 35 include:

♦ *The Concept of Situation in Information Science*, by Colleen Cool

♦ *Conceptual Frameworks in Information Behavior*, by Karen E. Pettigrew, Raya Fidel, and Harry Bruce

♦ *Distributed Information Management*, by William M. Pottenger, Miranda R. Callahan, and Michael A. Padgett

♦ *Digital Privacy: Toward a New Politics and Discursive Practice*, by Philip Doty

♦ *Subject Access Points in Electronic Retrieval*, by Birger Hjorland and Lykke Kyllesbech Nielsen

♦ *Methods of Generating and Evaluating Hypertext*, by James Blustein and Mark S. Staveley

♦ *Digital Preservation*, by Elizabeth Yakel

♦ *Knowledge Management*, by Noreen Mac Morrow

♦ *Library and Information Science Education in the Nineties*, by Elisabeth Logan and Ingrid Hseieh-Yee

2001/600 pp/hardbound/ISBN 1-57387-115-X
ASIST Members $79.95 • Non-Members $99.95

Evaluating Networked Information Services
Techniques, Policy, and Issues

Edited by Charles R. McClure and John Carlo Bertot

As information services and resources are made available in the global networked environment, there is a critical need to evaluate their usefulness, impact, cost, and effectiveness. This new book brings together an introduction and overview of evaluation techniques and methods, information policy issues and initiatives, and other critical issues related to the evaluation of networked information services.

2001/300 pp/hardbound/ISBN 1-57387-118-4
ASIST Members $35.60 • Non-Members $44.50

ARIST 36: Annual Review of Information Science and Technology

Edited by Blaise Cronin

Contents of Volume 36:
- ◆ *Scholarly Communication and Bibliometrics*, by Christine Borgman and Jonathan Furner
- ◆ *Collaboratories*, by Thomas A. Finholt
- ◆ *Computer Mediated Communication on the Internet*, by Susan C. Herring
- ◆ *Organizational Knowledge and Communities of Practice*, by E. Davenport and H. Hall
- ◆ *Discovering Information in Context*, by Paul Solomon
- ◆ *Data Mining*, by Gerald Benoît
- ◆ *Intelligence, Information Technology, and Information Warfare*, by Philip H. J. Davies
- ◆ *Competitive Intelligence*, by Pierrette Bergeron and Christine A. Hiller
- ◆ *Theorizing Information for Information Science*, by Ian Cornelius
- ◆ *Social Informatics* by Steve Sawyer and Kristin Eschenfelder
- ◆ *Intellectual Capital*, by Herbert W. Snyder and Jennifer Buerk Pierce
- ◆ *Digital Libraries*, by Edward A. Fox and Shalini R. Urs
- ◆ *Health Informatics*, by Marie Russell and J. Michael Brittain

2001/650 pp/hardbound/ISBN 1-57387-131-1
ASIST Members $79.95 • Non-Members $99.95

Historical Studies in Information Science

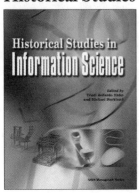

Edited by Trudi Bellardo Hahn and Michael Buckland

The field of information science has a broad history spanning nearly a century. *Historical Studies in Information Science* focuses on the progression of this dynamic and evolving industry by looking at some of its pioneers. This informative volume concentrates on the following areas: Historiography of Information Science; Paul Otlet and His Successors; Techniques, Tools, and Systems; People and Organizations; Theoretical Topics; and Literature.

1998/317 pp/softbound/ISBN 1-57387-062-5
ASIST Members $31.60 • Non-Members $39.50

Editorial Peer Review
Its Strengths and Weaknesses

By Ann C. Weller

This important book is the first to provide an in-depth analysis of the peer review process in scholarly publishing. Author Weller (Associate Professor and Deputy Director at the Library of the Health Sciences, University of Illinois at Chicago) offers a carefully researched, systematic review of published studies of editorial peer review in the following broad categories: general studies of rejection rates, studies of editors, studies of authors, and studies of reviewers. The book concludes with an examination of new models of editorial peer review intended to enhance the scientific communication process as it moves from a print to an electronic environment. *Editorial Peer Review* is an essential monograph for editors, reviewers, publishers, professionals from learned societies, writers, scholars, and librarians who purchase and disseminate scholarly material.

2001/360 pp/hardbound/ISBN 1-57387-100-1
ASIST Members $35.60 • Non-Members $44.50

Statistical Methods for the Information Professional

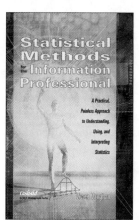

By Liwen Vaughan

For most of us, "painless" is not the word that comes to mind when we think of statistics, but author and educator Liwen Vaughan wants to change that. In this unique and useful book, Vaughan clearly explains the statistical methods used in information science research, focusing on basic logic rather than mathematical intricacies. Her emphasis is on the meaning of statistics, when and how to apply them, and how to interpret the results of statistical analysis. Through the use of real-world examples, she shows how statistics can be used to improve services, make better decisions, and conduct more effective research.

Whether you are doing statistical analysis or simply need to better understand the statistics you encounter in professional literature and the media, this book will be a valuable addition to your personal toolkit. Includes more than 80 helpful figures and tables, 7 appendices, bibliography, and index.

2001/240 pp/hardbound/ISBN 1-57387-110-9
ASIST Members $31.60 • Non-Members $39.50

The Web of Knowledge

A Festschrift in Honor of Eugene Garfield

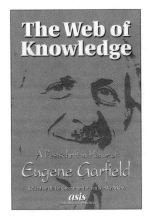

Edited by Blaise Cronin and Helen Barsky Atkins

Dr. Eugene Garfield, the founder of the Institute for Scientific Information (ISI), has devoted his life to the creation and development of the multidisciplinary Science Citation Index. The index, a unique resource for scientists, scholars, and researchers in virtually every field of intellectual endeavor, has been the foundation for a multidisciplinary research community. This ASIS monograph is the first to comprehensively address the history, theory, and practical applications of the Science Citation Index and to examine its impact on scholarly and scientific research 40 years after its inception. In bringing together the analyses, insights, and reflections of more than 35 leading lights, editors Cronin and Atkins have produced both a comprehensive survey of citation indexing and analysis and a beautifully realized tribute to Eugene Garfield and his vision.

2000/544 pp/hardbound/ISBN 1-57387-099-4
ASIST Members $39.60 • Non-Members $49.50

Intelligent Technologies in Library and Information Service Applications

By F.W. Lancaster and Amy Warner

Librarians and library school faculty have been experimenting with artificial intelligence (AI) and expert systems for 30 years, but there has been no comprehensive survey of the results available until now. In this carefully researched monograph, authors Lancaster and Warner report on the applications of AI technologies in library and information services, assessing their effectiveness, reviewing the relevant literature, and offering a clear-eyed forecast of future use and impact. Includes almost 500 bibliographic references.

2001/214 pp/hardbound/ISBN 1-57387-103-6
ASIST Members $31.60 • Non-Members $39.50

Information Management for the Intelligent Organization, 3rd Edition

By Chun Wei Choo

The intelligent organization is one that is skilled at marshalling its information resources and capabilities, transforming information into knowledge, and using this knowledge to sustain and enhance its performance in a restless environment. The objective of this newly updated and expanded book is to develop an understanding of how an organization may manage its information processes more effectively in order to achieve these goals. The third edition features new sections on information culture, information overload, and organizational learning; a new chapter on Knowledge Management (KM) and the role of information professionals; and numerous extended case studies of environmental scanning by organizations in Asia, Europe, and North America. This book is a must-read for senior managers and administrators, information managers, information specialists and practitioners, information technologists, and anyone whose work in an organization involves acquiring, creating, organizing, or using knowledge.

2001/352 pp/hardbound/ISBN 1-57387-125-7
ASIST Members $31.60 • Non-Members $39.50

Introductory Concepts in Information Science

By Melanie J. Norton

Melanie J. Norton presents a unique introduction to the practical and theoretical concepts of information science while examining the impact of the Information Age on society. Drawing on recent research into the field, as well as from scholarly and trade publications, the monograph provides a brief history of information science and coverage of key topics, including communications and cognition, information retrieval, bibliometrics, modeling, economics, information policies, and the impact of information technology on modern management. This is an essential volume for graduate students, practitioners, and any professional who needs a solid grounding in the field of information science.

2000/127 pp/hardbound/ISBN 1-57387-087-0
ASIST Members $31.60 • Non-Members $39.50

Knowledge Management for the Information Professional

Edited by T. Kanti Srikantaiah and Michael Koenig

Written from the perspective of the information community, this book examines the business community's recent enthusiasm for Knowledge Management (KM). With contributions from 26 leading KM practitioners, academicians, and information professionals, editors Srikantaiah and Koenig bridge the gap between two distinct perspectives, equipping information professionals with the tools to make a broader and more effective contribution in developing KM systems and creating a Knowledge Management culture within their organizations.

2000/608 pp/hardbound/ISBN 1-57387-079-X
ASIST Members $35.60 • Non-Members $44.50

Knowledge Management: The Bibliography

Compiled by Paul Burden

Knowledge Management (KM) is a holistic process by which an organization may effectively gather, evaluate, share, analyze, integrate, and use information from both internal and external sources. *Knowledge Management: The Bibliography* is the first comprehensive reference to the literature available for the individual interested in KM, and features citations to over 1500 published articles, 150+ Web sites, and more than 400 books. Organized by topic area (i.e., "KM and Intranets," "KM and Training," "KM and eCommerce"), this work is a natural companion volume to the ASIS monograph *Knowledge Management for the Information Professional* and an important new tool for anyone charged with contributing to or managing an organization's intellectual assets.

2000/160 pp/softbound/ISBN: 1-57387-101-X
ASIS Members $18.00 • Non-Members $22.50